THE
COMPLETE WORKS OF

WILLIAM
SHAKESPEARE

THE
COMPLETE WORKS OF

WILLIAM
SHAKESPEARE

The Cambridge text established by
JOHN DOVER WILSON
for the
CAMBRIDGE UNIVERSITY PRESS

This edition first published in Great Britain in 1982 by

Octopus Books Limited
59 Grosvenor Street
London W1

for

Marks and Spencer p.l.c.
Baker Street, London, England

Revised edition 1983

Copyright © The Cambridge text of the Complete Works of
William Shakespeare Cambridge University Press
1921, 1922, 1923, 1924, 1926, 1928, 1929, 1930,
1931, 1934, 1936, 1939, 1946, 1947, 1949, 1950,
1952, 1954, 1955, 1956, 1957, 1960, 1962, 1966
Copyright © 1982 arrangement Hennerwood Publications Limited

Case illustration: *Miniature of a Young Man* by Nicholas Hilliard
Victoria and Albert Museum, Crown copyright

ISBN 086273 105 4

Printed and bound in Great Britain
by Collins, Glasgow

1361/2304

Contents

Not marble, nor the gilded monuments
Of princes shall outlive this powerful rhyme.

Sonnet 55

The Tempest

The scene, an uninhabited island

CHARACTERS IN THE PLAY

ALONSO, *King of Naples*
SEBASTIAN, *his brother*
PROSPERO, *the right Duke of Milan*
ANTONIO, *his brother, the usurping Duke of Milan*
FERDINAND, *son to the King of Naples*
GONZALO, *an honest old Councillor*
ADRIAN *and* FRANCISCO, *Lords*
CALIBAN, *a savage and deformed slave*
TRINCULO, *a Jester*
STEPHANO, *a drunken Butler*

SHIP-MASTER
BOATSWAIN
Mariners
MIRANDA, *daughter to Prospero*
ARIEL, *an airy Spirit*
IRIS
CERES
JUNO } *Spirits*
Nymphs
Reapers

The Tempest

ACT 1

Scene 1: *A tempestuous noise of thunder and lightning heard. A ship is seen*

A Ship-master and a Boatswain

MASTER. Bos'n!

BOATSWAIN. Here, master: what cheer?

MASTER. Good: speak to th'mariners: fall to't—yarely—or we run ourselves aground. Bestir, bestir.

He goes

Enter mariners

BOATSWAIN. Heigh my hearts! cheerly, cheerly my hearts ... yare, yare ... take in the topsail ... tend to th' master's whistle ... Blow till thou burst thy wind—if room enough!

Alonso, Sebastian, Antonio, Ferdinand, Gonzalo, and others come on deck

ALONSO. Good bos'n, have care, Where's the master? Play the men.   10

BOATSWAIN. I pray now, keep below.

ANTONIO. Where is the master, bos'n?

BOATSWAIN. Do you not hear him? You mar our labour. Keep your cabins: you do assist the storm.

GONZALO. Nay, good, be patient.

BOATSWAIN.   When the sea is ... Hence! What care these roarers for the name of king? To cabin ... silence ... trouble us not!

GONZALO. Good, yet remember whom thou hast aboard.

BOATSWAIN. None that I more love than myself ... 20 You are a Councillor—if you can command these elements to silence, and work the peace of the present, we will not hand a rope more. Use your authority ... If you cannot, give thanks you have lived so long, and make yourself ready in your cabin for the mischance of the hour, if it so hap ... Cheerly, good hearts ... Out of our way, I say.

He goes

GONZALO. I have great comfort from this fellow ... Methinks he hath no drowning mark upon him, his complexion is perfect gallows ... Stand fast, good 30 Fate, to his hanging, make the rope of his destiny our cable, for our own doth little advantage ... If he be born to be hanged, our case is miserable.

They go below

Boatswain returns

BOATSWAIN. Down with the topmast ... yare, lower, lower! bring her to try with main-course.... [*A cry is heard below*] A plague upon this howling ... they are louder than the weather, or our office ...

Sebastian, Antonio, and Gonzalo return

Yet again? What do you here? Shall we give o'er and drown? Have you a mind to sink?

SEBASTIAN. A pox o' your throat, you bawling, blas- 40 phemous, incharitable dog!

BOATSWAIN. Work you, then.

ANTONIO. Hang, cur; hang, you whoreson, insolent noise-maker! we are less afraid to be drowned than thou art.

GONZALO. I'll warrant him for drowning, though the ship were no stronger than a nutshell, and as leaky as an unstaunched wench.

BOATSWAIN. Lay her a-hold, a-hold! Set her two courses. Off to sea again! lay her off!   50

Enter mariners wet

MARINERS. All lost! to prayers, to prayers! all lost!

BOATSWAIN. What, must our mouths be cold?

GONZALO. The king and prince at prayers. Let's assist them, For our case is as theirs.

SEBASTIAN.   I am out of patience.

ANTONIO. We are merely cheated of our lives by drunkards— This wide-chopped rascal—would thou mightst lie drowning The washing of ten tides!'

GONZALO.   He'll be hanged yet, Though every drop of water swear against it, And gape at wid'st to glut him. [*A confused noise below*]   Mercy on us!— We split, we split!—Farewell, my wife and children!—   60 Farewell, brother!—We split, we split, we split!

ANTONIO. Let's all sink wi' th' king.

SEBASTIAN.   Let's take leave of him.

They go below

GONZALO. Now would I give a thousand furlongs of sea—for an acre of barren ground ... long heath, brown furze, any thing ... The wills above be done, but I would fain die a dry death!

Scene 2: *The Island. The entrance of a cave*

Enter Miranda and Prospero

MIRANDA. If by your art—my dearest father—you have Put the wild waters in this roar—allay them: The sky, it seems, would pour down stinking pitch, But that the sea, mounting to th' welkin's cheek, Dashes the fire out.... O! I have suffered With those that I saw suffer: A brave vessel, (Who had no doubt some noble creature in her!) Dashed all to pieces: O the cry did knock Against my very heart ... poor souls, they perished.... Had I been any god of power, I would   10 Have sunk the sea within the earth, or o'er It should the good ship so have swallowed, and The fraughting souls within her.

PROSPERO.   Be collected, No more amazement: Tell your piteous heart There's no harm done.

MIRANDA.   O woe the day!

PROSPERO.   No harm:
  I have done nothing, but in care of thee
  (Of thee, my dear one; thee, my daughter) who
  Art ignorant of what thou art ... nought knowing
  Of whence I am ... nor that I am more better
  Than Prospero, master of a full poor cell,   20
  And thy no greater father.
MIRANDA.   More to know
  Did never meddle with my thoughts.
PROSPERO.   'Tis time
  I should inform thee farther: Lend thy hand
  And pluck my magic garment from me ... So,
                He lays aside his mantle
  Lie there my art: Wipe thou thine eyes, have
    comfort,
  The direful spectacle of the wreck, which touched
  The very virtue of compassion in thee ...
  I have with such provision in mine art
  So safely ordered, that there is no soil,
  No, not so much perdition as an hair,   30
  Betid to any creature in the vessel
  Which thou heard'st cry, which thou saw'st sink:
    Sit down,
  For thou must now know farther.
MIRANDA.   You have often
  Begun to tell me what I am, but stopped,
  And left me to a bootless inquisition,
  Concluding, 'Stay: not yet.'
PROSPERO.   The hour's now come,
  The very minute bids thee ope thine ear,
  Obey, and be attentive.... Canst thou remember
  A time before we came unto this cell?
  I do not think thou canst, for then thou wast not 40
  Out three years old.
MIRANDA.   Certainly sir, I can.
PROSPERO. By what? by any other house, or person?
  Of any thing the image, tell me, that
  Hath kept with thy remembrance.
MIRANDA.   'Tis far off ...
  And rather like a dream, than an assurance
  That my remembrance warrants ... Had I not
  Four—or five—women once, that tended me?
PROSPERO. Thou hadst; and more, Miranda: But how
    is it,
  That this lives in thy mind? What seest thou else
  In the dark backward and abysm of time?   50
  If thou rememb'rest aught ere thou cam'st here,
  How thou cam'st here thou mayst.
MIRANDA.   But that I do not.
PROSPERO. Twelve year since—Miranda—twelve
    year since,
  Thy father was the Duke of Milan and
  A prince of power ...
MIRANDA.   Sir, are not you my father?
PROSPERO. Thy mother was a piece of virtue, and
  She said thou wast my daughter; and thy father
  Was Duke of Milan, and his only heir—
  A princess; no worse issued.
MIRANDA.   O the heavens,
  What foul play had we, that we came from thence? 60
  Or blessèd was't we did?
PROSPERO.   Both, both, my girl....
  By foul play—as thou sayst—were we heaved
    thence,
  But blessedly holp hither.
MIRANDA.   O my heart bleeds

To think o'th' teen that I have turned you to,
  Which is from my remembrance. Please you,
  farther ...
PROSPERO. My brother, and thy uncle, called
  Antonio ...
  I pray thee mark me, that a brother should
  Be so perfidious ... he, whom next thyself
  Of all the world I loved, and to him put
  The manage of my state, as at that time   70
  Through all the signories it was the first,
  And Prospero, the prime duke, being so reputed
  In dignity—and for the liberal arts,
  Without a parallel; those being all my study,
  The government I cast upon my brother,
  And to my state grew stranger, being transported
  And rapt in secret studies. Thy false uncle—
  Dost thou attend me?
MIRANDA.   Sir, most heedfully.
PROSPERO. Being once perfected how to grant suits,
  How to deny them: who t'advance, and who   80
  To trash for over-topping; new created
  The creatures that were mine, I say, or changed 'em,
  Or else new formed 'em; having both the key
  Of officer and office, set all hearts i'th' state
  To what tune pleased his ear, that now he was
  The ivy which had hid my princely trunk,
  And sucked my verdure out on't: Thou attend'st
  not!
MIRANDA. O good sir, I do.
PROSPERO.   I pray thee mark me ...
  I thus neglecting worldly ends, all dedicated
  To closeness, and the bettering of my mind   90
  With that which, but by being so retired,
  O'er-prized all popular rate, in my false brother
  Awaked an evil nature; and my trust,
  Like a good parent, did beget of him
  A falsehood in its contrary, as great
  As my trust was, which had indeed no limit,
  A confidence sans bound.... He, being thus lorded,
  Not only with what my revénue yielded,
  But what my power might else exact.... like one,
  Who having minted truth by telling of it,   100
  Made such a sinner of his memory,
  To credit his own lie, he did believe
  He was indeed the duke, out o'th' substitution
  And executing th'outward face of royalty
  With all prerogative: Hence his ambition
    growing ...
  Dost thou hear?
MIRANDA.   Your tale, sir, would cure deafness.
PROSPERO. To have no screen between this part he
    played
  And him he played it for, he needs will be
  Absolute Milan—me (poor man) my library
  Was dukedom large enough: of temporal royalties 110
  He thinks me now incapable.... confederates
  (So dry he was for sway) wi' th' King of Naples
  To give him annual tribute, do him homage,
  Subject his 'coronet' to his 'crown,' and bend
  The dukedom yet unbowed (alas, poor Milan!)
  To most ignoble stooping.
MIRANDA.   O the heavens!
PROSPERO. Mark his condition, and th'event, then tell
  me,
  If this might be a brother.
MIRANDA.   I should sin

To think but nobly of my grandmother,
Good wombs have borne bad sons.
PROSPERO.   Now the condition.... 120
This King of Naples, being an enemy
To me inveterate, hearkens my brother's suit,
Which was, that he in lieu o'th' premises
Of homage, and I know not how much tribute,
Should presently extirpate me and mine
Out of the dukedom, and confer fair Milan,
With all the honours, on my brother: Whereon,
A treacherous army levied, one midnight,
Fated to th' purpose, did Antonio open
The gates of Milan, and i'th' dead of darkness   130
The ministers for th' purpose hurried thence
Me—and thy crying self.
MIRANDA.   Alack, for pity:
I not remembering how I cried out then
Will cry it o'er again: it is a hint
That wrings mine eyes to't.
PROSPERO.   Hear a little further
And then I'll bring thee to the present business
Which now's upon's: without the which, this story
Were most impertinent.
MIRANDA.   Wherefore did they not
That hour destroy us?
PROSPERO.   Well demanded, wench:
My tale provokes that question. Dear, they durst
not,   140
So dear the love my people bore me: nor set
A mark so bloody on the business; but
With colours fairer painted their foul ends....
In few, they hurried us aboard a bark,
Bore us some leagues to sea; where they prepared
A rotten carcass of a butt, not rigged,
Nor tackle, sail, nor mast, the very rats
Instinctively have quit it: There they hoist us
To cry to th' sea, that roared to us; to sigh
To th' winds, whose pity sighing back again   150
Did us but loving wrong.
MIRANDA.   Alack, what trouble
Was I then to you!
PROSPERO.   O, a cherubin
Thou wast that did preserve me; thou didst smile,
Infuséd with a fortitude from heaven—
When I have decked the sea with drops full salt,
Under my burden groaned—which raised in me
An undergoing stomach, to bear up
Against what should ensue.
MIRANDA.   How came we ashore?
PROSPERO. By Providence divine....
Some food we had, and some fresh water, that   160
A noble Neapolitan, Gonzalo,
Out of his charity, who being then appointed
Master of this design, did give us, with
Rich garments, linens, stuffs, and necessaries,
Which since have steaded much. So of his
  gentleness,
Knowing I love my books, he furnished me
From mine own library with volumes that
I prize above my dukedom.
MIRANDA.   Would I might
But ever see that man.
PROSPERO.   Now I arise,
Sit still and hear the last of our sea-sorrow ...   170
                              He resumes his mantle
Here in this island we arrived, and here

Have I, thy schoolmaster, made thee more profit
Than other princess' can, that have more time
For vainer hours—and tutors not so careful.
MIRANDA. Heaven thank you for't.... And now I
  pray you sir—
For still 'tis beating in my mind—your reason
For raising this sea-storm?
PROSPERO.   Know thus far forth.
By accident most strange, bountiful Fortune—
Now my dear lady—hath mine enemies
Brought to this shore: and by my prescience   180
I find my zenith doth depend upon
A most auspicious star, whose influence
If now I court not, but omit, my fortunes
Will ever after droop: Here cease more questions.
Thou art inclined to sleep ... 'tis a good dulness,
And give it way ... I know thou canst not choose...
                                   She sleeps
Come away, servant, come; I am ready now,
Approach my Ariel.... Come!

Ariel appears

ARIEL. All hail, great master, grave sir, hail: I come
To answer thy best pleasure; be't to fly,   190
To swim, to dive into the fire ... to ride
On the curled clouds, to thy strong bidding task
Ariel, and all his quality.
PROSPERO.   Hast thou, spirit,
Performed to point the tempest that I bade thee?
ARIEL. To every article....
I boarded the king's ship: now on the beak,
Now in the waist, the deck, in every cabin,
I flamed amazement. Sometime I'ld divide
And burn in many places; on the topmast,
The yards and bowsprit, would I flame distinctly,   200
Then meet, and join; Jove's lightning, the precursors
O'th' dreadful thunder-claps, more momentary
And sight-outrunning were not; the fire and cracks
Of sulphurous roaring the most mighty Neptune
Seem to besiege, and make his bold waves tremble,
Yea, his dread trident shake.
PROSPERO.   My brave spirit!
Who was so firm, so constant that this coil
Would not infect his reason?
ARIEL.   Not a soul
But felt a fever of the mad, and played
Some tricks of desperation; all but mariners   210
Plunged in the foaming brine, and quit the vessel;
Then all afire with me the king's son Ferdinand,
With hair up-staring—then like reeds, not hair—
Was the first man that leaped; cried, 'Hell is empty,
And all the devils are here.'
PROSPERO.   Why, that's my spirit:
But was not this nigh shore?
ARIEL.   Close by, my master.
PROSPERO. But are they, Ariel, safe?
ARIEL.   Not a hair perished:
On their sustaining garments not a blemish,
But fresher than before: and, as thou bad'st me,
In troops I have dispersed them 'bout the isle: 220
The king's son have I landed by himself,
Whom I left cooling of the air with sighs,
In an odd angle of the isle, and sitting,
His arms in this sad knot.
PROSPERO.   Of the king's ship,
The mariners, say, how thou hast disposed,

And all the rest o'th' fleet?
ARIEL.   Safely in harbour
Is the king's ship; in the deep nook, where once
Thou call'dst me up at midnight to fetch dew
From the still-vexed Bermoothes, there she's hid;
The mariners all under hatches stowed,   230
Who, with a charm joined to their suff'red labour,
I have left asleep: and for the rest o'th' fleet,
Which I dispersed, they all have met again,
And are upon the Mediterranean flote
Bound sadly home for Naples,
Supposing that they saw the king's ship wrecked,
And his great person perish.
PROSPERO.   Ariel, thy charge
Exactly is performed; but there's more work:
What is the time o'th' day?
ARIEL.   Past the mid season.
PROSPERO. At least two glasses ... The time 'twixt six
      and now,   240
Must by us both be spent most preciously.
ARIEL. Is there more toil? Since thou dost give me
      pains,
Let me remember thee what thou hast promised,
Which is not yet performed me.
PROSPERO.   How now? moody?
What is't thou canst demand?
ARIEL.   My liberty.
PROSPERO. Before the time be out? no more ...
ARIEL.   I prithee,
Remember I have done thee worthy service,
Told thee no lies, made no mistakings, served
Without or grudge or grumblings; thou didst
      promise
To bate me a full year.
PROSPERO.   Dost thou forget   250
From what a torment I did free thee?
ARIEL.   No.
PROSPERO. Thou dost: and think'st it much to tread
      the ooze
Of the salt deep,
To run upon the sharp wind of the north,
To do me business in the veins o'th'earth
When it is baked with frost.
ARIEL.   I do not, sir.
PROSPERO. Thou liest, malignant thing: hast thou
      forgot
The foul witch Sycorax, who with age and envy
Was grown into a hoop? hast thou forgot her?
ARIEL. No, sir.
PROSPERO.   Thou hast, Where was she born? speak:
      tell me ...   260
ARIEL. Sir, in Argier.
PROSPERO.   O, was she so? I must
Once in a month recount what thou hast been,
Which thou forget'st.... This damned witch,
      Sycorax,
For mischiefs manifold, and sorceries terrible
To enter human hearing, from Argier
Thou know'st was banished: for one thing she did
They would not take her life ... Is not this true?
ARIEL. Ay, sir.
PROSPERO. This blue-eyed hag was hither brought
      with child,
And here was left by th' sailors; thou, my slave,   270
As thou report'st thyself, was then her servant,
And for thou wast a spirit too delicate

To act her earthy and abhorred commands,
Refusing her grand hests, she did confine thee,
By help of her more potent ministers,
And in her most unmitigable rage,
Into a cloven pine—within which rift
Imprisoned, thou didst painfully remain
A dozen years: within which space she died,
And left thee there: where thou didst vent thy
      groans,   280
As fast as mill-wheels strike: Then was this island,
(Save for the son that she did litter here,
A freckled whelp, hag-born) not honoured with
A human shape.
ARIEL.   Yes: Caliban her son.
PROSPERO. Dull thing, I say so: he, that Caliban
Who now I keep in service. Thou best know'st
What torment I did find thee in; thy groans
Did make wolves howl, and penetrate the breasts
Of ever-angry bears; it was a torment
To lay upon the damned, which Sycorax   290
Could not again undo: it was mine art,
When I arrived, and heard thee, that made gape
The pine, and let thee out.
ARIEL.   I thank thee master.
PROSPERO. If thou more murmur'st, I will rend an oak,
And peg thee in his knotty entrails, till
Thou hast howled away twelve winters.
ARIEL.   Pardon, master.
I will be correspondent to command,
And do my spriting gently.
PROSPERO.   Do so: and after two days
I will discharge thee.
ARIEL.   That's my noble master!
What shall I do? say what? what shall I do?   300
PROSPERO. Go make thyself like a nymph o'th' sea,
      be subject
To no sight but thine and mine; invisible
To every eye-ball else: go take this shape,
And hither come in't ... go ... hence
With diligence.   Ariel vanishes
Awake, dear heart, awake, thou hast slept well,
Awake.
MIRANDA. The strangeness of your story put
Heaviness in me.
PROSPERO.   Shake it off ... Come on,
We'll visit Caliban, my slave, who never
Yields us kind answer.   They approach a hole
MIRANDA.   'Tis a villain, sir,   310
I do not love to look on.
PROSPERO.   But, as 'tis,
We cannot miss him: he does make our fire,
Fetch in our wood, and serves in offices
That profit us ... What ho! slave! Caliban!
Thou earth, thou! speak.
CALIBAN [from the hole]. There's wood enough within.
PROSPERO. Come forth, I say, there's other business
      for thee:
Come, thou tortoise, when?

Ariel reappears, like a water-nymph

Fine apparition: my quaint Ariel,
Hark in thine ear.
ARIEL.   My lord, it shall be done.
                                 Vanishes
PROSPERO. Thou poisonous slave, got by the devil
      himself   320

Upon thy wickeḋ dam; come forth.

Caliban comes from the hole

CALIBAN. As wicked dew as e'er my mother brushed
With raven's feather from unwholesome fen
Drop on you both: a south-west blow on ye,
And blister you all o'er!

PROSPERO. For this, be sure, to-night thou shalt have
cramps,
Side-stitches that shall pen thy breath up—urchins
Shall, for that vast of night that they may work,
All exercise on thee: thou shalt be pinched
As thick as honeycomb, each pinch more stinging 330
Than bees had made 'em.

CALIBAN.   I must eat my dinner ...
This island's mine, by Sycorax my mother,
Which thou tak'st from me: when thou cam'st first,
Thou strok'st me, and made much of me ... wouldst
give me
Water with berries in't; and teach me how
To name the bigger light, and how the less,
That burn by day and night: and then I loved thee,
And showed thee all the qualities o'th'isle,
The fresh springs, brine-pits, barren place and
fertile.
Curst be I that did so! All the charms   340
Of Sycorax: toads, bettles, bats, light on you!
For I am all the subjects that you have,
Which first was mine own king: and here you sty
me
In this hard rock, whiles you do keep from me
The rest o'th'island.

PROSPERO.   Thou most lying slave,
Whom stripes may move, not kindness: I have used
thee—
Filth as thou art!—with human care, and lodged
thee
In mine own cell, till thou didst seek to violate
The honour of my child.

CALIBAN. O ho, O ho! would't had been done!   350
Thou didst prevent me—I had peopled else
This isle with Calibans.

MIRANDA.   Abhorréd slave,
Which any print of goodness will not take,
Being capable of all ill: I pitied thee,
Took pains to make thee speak, taught thee each
hour
One thing or other: when thou didst not—
savage!—
Know thine own meaning, but wouldst gabble like
A thing most brutish, I endowed thy purposes
With words that made them known. But thy vile
race,
Though thou didst learn, had that in't which good
natures   360
Could not abide to be with; therefore wast thou
Deservedly confined into this rock,
Who hadst deserved more than a prison.

CALIBAN. You taught me language, and my profit on't
Is, I know how to curse: the red-plague rid you,
For learning me your language.

PROSPERO.   Hag-seed, hence ...
Fetch us in fuel, and be quick thou'rt best
To answer other business: Shrug'st thou, malice?
If thou neglect'st, or dost unwillingly
What I command, I'll rack thee with old cramps, 370

Fill all thy bones with achës, make thee roar,
That beasts shall tremble at thy din.

CALIBAN.   No, pray thee....
[*aside*] I must obey—his art is of such power,
It would control my dam's god Setebos,
And make a vassal of him.

PROSPERO.   So, slave, hence!

Caliban goes

Enter Ferdinand, and Ariel invisible, playing and singing

                    Ariel's SONG.
      Come unto these yellow sands,
         And then take hands:
      Curtsied when you have, and kissed
         The wild waves whist:
      Foot it featly here and there,   380
      And sweet sprites bear
         The burthen ... Hark!
            Hark!
BURTHEN [*dispersedly*]. Bow-wow!
ARIEL. The watch-dogs bark:
BURTHEN. Bow-wow!
ARIEL. Hark, hark, I hear
      The strain of strutting chanticleer
      Cry—
BURTHEN. Cockadiddle-dow!   390

FERDINAND. Where should this music be? i'th'air, or
th'earth?
It sounds no more: and sure it waits upon
Some god o'th'island. Sitting on a bank,
Weeping again the king my father's wreck....
This music crept by me upon the waters,
Allaying both their fury and my passion
With its sweet air: thence I have followed it—
Or it hath drawn me rather. But 'tis gone....
No, it begins again.

                    Ariel's SONG.
      Full fathom five thy father lies,   400
         Of his bones are coral made:
      Those are pearls that were his eyes.
         Nothing of him that doth fade,
      But doth suffer a sea-change
      Into something rich and strange ...
      Sea-nymphs hourly ring his knell.
BURTHEN. Ding-dong.
ARIEL. Hark! now I hear them—
            Ding-dong bell.

FERDINAND. The ditty does remember my drowned
father.   410
This is no mortal business, nor no sound
That the earth owes: I hear it now above me.

PROSPERO. The fringéd curtains of thine eye advance,
And say what thou seest yond.

MIRANDA.   What is't? a spirit?
Lord, how it looks about ... Believe me, sir,
It carries a brave form.... But 'tis a spirit.

PROSPERO. No wench, it eats and sleeps and hath such
senses
As we have—such.... This gallant which thou seest
Was in the wreck: and but he's something stained
With grief—that's beauty's canker—thou mightst
call him   420
A goodly person: he hath lost his fellows,
And strays about to find 'em.

MIRANDA.   I might call him
A thing divine—for nothing natural
I ever saw so noble.
PROSPERO [*holding back*]. It goes on I see,
As my soul prompts it ... Spirit, fine spirit, I'll
  free thee
Within two days for this.
FERDINAND.   Most sure, the goddess
On whom these airs attend ... Vouchsafe my prayer
May know if you remain upon this island,
And that you will some good instruction give
How I may bear me here ... My prime request,   430
Which I do last pronounce, is—O you wonder!—
If you be maid, or no?
MIRANDA.   No wonder, sir,
But certainly a maid.
FERDINAND.   My language? heavens ...
I am the best of them that speak this speech,
Were I but where 'tis spoken.
PROSPERO.   How? the best?
What wert thou if the King of Naples heard thee?
FERDINAND. A single thing, as I am now, that wonders
To hear thee speak of Naples ... He does hear me,
And that he does, I weep: myself am Naples,
Who with mine eyes—never since at ebb—beheld 440
The king my father wrecked.
MIRANDA.   Alack, for mercy!
FERDINAND. Yes, faith, and all his lords—the Duke of
  Milan
And his brave son being twain.
PROSPERO [*to himself*].   The Duke of Milan
And his more braver daughter could control thee,
If now 'twere fit to do't ... At the first sight
They have changed eyes ... Delicate Ariel,
I'll set thee free for this.... A word, good sir.
I fear you have done yourself some wrong: a word.
MIRANDA. Why speaks my father so ungently? This
Is the third man that e'er I saw ... the first,   450
That e'er I sighed for: pity move my father
To be inclined my way.
FERDINAND.   O, if a virgin,
And your affection not gone forth, I'll make you
The queen of Naples.
PROSPERO.   Soft, sir, one word more....
They are both in either's powers: but this swift
  business
I must uneasy make, lest too light winning
Make the prize light.... One word more: I charge
  thee
That thou attend me: thou dost here usurp
The name thou ow'st not—and hast put thyself
Upon this island, as a spy, to win it   460
From me, the lord on't.
FERDINAND.   No, as I am a man.
MIRANDA. There's nothing ill can dwell in such a
  temple.
If the ill spirit have so fair a house,
Good things will strive to dwell with't.
PROSPERO.   Follow me ...
Speak not you for him: he's a traitor ... Come,
I'll manacle thy neck and feet together:
Sea-water shalt thou drink: thy food shall be
The fresh-brook mussels, withered roots, and husks
Wherein the acorn cradled.... Follow.
FERDINAND.   No,
I will resist such entertainment, till   470

Mine enemy has more power.
                    He draws and is charmed from moving
MIRANDA.   O dear father,
Make not too rash a trial of him, for
He's gentle, and not fearful.
PROSPERO.   What, I say,
My foot my tutor! Put thy sword up traitor,
Who mak'st a show, but dar'st not strike, thy
  conscience
Is so possessed with guilt: come, from thy ward,
For I can here disarm thee with this stick,
And make thy weapon drop.
MIRANDA.   Beseech you father.
PROSPERO. Hence: hang not on my garments.
MIRANDA.   Sir have pity,
I'll be his surety.
PROSPERO.   Silence: one word more   480
Shall make me chide thee, if not hate thee: what,
An advocate for an impostor! Hush:
Thou think'st there is no more such shapes as he,
Having seen but him and Caliban ... Foolish wench,
To th' most of men, this is a Caliban,
And they to him are angels.
MIRANDA.   My affections
Are then most humble: I have no ambition
To see a goodlier man.
PROSPERO.   Come on, obey:
Thy nerves are in their infancy again,
And have no vigour in them.
FERDINAND.   So they are: 490
My spirits, as in a dream, are all bound up ...
My father's loss, the weakness which I feel,
The wreck of all my friends, nor this man's threats,
To whom I am subdued, are but light to me,
Might I but through my prison once a day
Behold this maid: all corners else o'th' earth
Let liberty make use of ... space enough
Have I in such a prison.
PROSPERO.   It works ... [*to Ferdinand*] Come on....
[*to Ariel*] Thou hast done well, fine Ariel ...
[*to Ferdinand*] Follow me.
[*to Ariel*] Hark what thou else shalt do me.
MIRANDA.   Be of comfort, 500
My father's of a better nature, sir,
Than he appears by speech: this is unwonted
Which now came from him.
PROSPERO.   Thou shalt be as free
As mountain winds; but then exactly do
All points of my command.
ARIEL.   To th' syllable.
PROSPERO [*to Ferdinand*]. Come, follow:
[*to Miranda*] speak not for him.

ACT 2

Scene 1: *Another part of the Island*

*King Alonso, Gonzalo, Adrian, Francisco, Sebastian,
Antonio and others*

GONZALO. Beseech you, sir, be merry; you have cause,
So have we all, of joy; for our escape
Is much beyond our loss; our hint of woe
Is common—every day some sailor's wife,
The masters of some merchant, and the merchant,
Have just our theme of woe: But for the miracle—
I mean our preservation—few in millions
Can speak like us: then wisely, good sir, weigh

Our sorrow with our comfort.
ALONSO.   Prithee, peace.   10
SEBASTIAN. He receives comfort like cold porridge.
ANTONIO. The visitor will not give him o'er so.
SEBASTIAN. Look, he's winding up the watch of his
    wit—by and by it will strike.
GONZALO. Sir—
SEBASTIAN. One . . . tell.
GONZALO. When every grief is entertained that's
    offered,
Comes to the entertainer—
SEBASTIAN.   A dollar.
GONZALO. Dolour comes to him, indeed. You have
    spoken truer than you purposed.   20
SEBASTIAN. You have taken it wiselier than I meant
    you should.
GONZALO. Therefore, my lord,—
ANTONIO. Fie, what a spendthrift is he of his tongue.
ALONSO. I prithee, spare.
GONZALO. Well, I have done: But yet—
SEBASTIAN. He will be talking.
ANTONIO. Which, of he or Adrian, for a good wager,
    first begins to crow?
SEBASTIAN. The old cock.   30
ANTONIO. The cockerel.
SEBASTIAN. Done: the wager?
ANTONIO. A laughter.
SEBASTIAN. A match!
ADRIAN. Though this island seem to be desert,—
ANTONIO. Ha, ha, ha!
SEBASTIAN. So! you're paid.
ADRIAN. —uninhabitable, and almost inaccessible,—
SEBASTIAN. Yet—
ADRIAN. —yet—   40
ANTONIO. He could not miss't.
ADRIAN. —it must needs be of subtle, tender and
    delicate temperance.
ANTONIO. 'Temperance' was a delicate wench.
SEBASTIAN. Ay, and a subtle, as he most learnedly
    delivered.
ADRIAN. The air breathes upon us here most sweetly.
SEBASTIAN. As if it had lungs, and rotten ones.
ANTONIO. Or, as 'twere perfumed by a fen.
GONZALO. Here is every thing advantageous to life. 50
ANTONIO. True, save means to live.
SEBASTIAN. Of that there's none, or little.
GONZALO. How lush and lusty the grass looks! how
    green!
ANTONIO. The ground, indeed, is tawny.
SEBASTIAN. With an eye of green in't.
ANTONIO. He misses not much.
SEBASTIAN. No: he doth but mistake the truth totally.
GONZALO. But the rarity of it is, which is indeed
    almost beyond credit,—   60
SEBASTIAN. As many vouched rarities are.
GONZALO. —that our garments, being, as they were,
    drenched in the sea, hold notwithstanding their
    freshness and glosses, being rather new dyed than
    stained with salt water.
ANTONIO. If but one of his pockets could speak, would
    it not say he lies?
SEBASTIAN. Ay, or very falsely pocket up his report.
GONZALO. Methinks our garments are now as fresh as
    when we put them on first in Afric, at the marriage 70
    of the king's fair daughter Claribel to the King of
    Tunis.

SEBASTIAN. 'Twas a sweet marriage, and we prosper
    well in our return.
ADRIAN. Tunis was never graced before with such a
    paragon to their queen.
GONZALO. Not since widow Dido's time.
ANTONIO. Widow? a pox o'that: How came that
    widow in? Widow Dido!
SEBASTIAN. What if he had said 'widower Æneas' too? 80
    Good Lord, how you take it!
ADRIAN. Widow Dido, said you? you make me study
    of that: She was of Carthage, not of Tunis.
GONZALO. This Tunis, sir, was Carthage.
ADRIAN. Carthage?
GONZALO. I assure you, Carthage.
ANTONIO. His word is more than the miraculous harp.
SEBASTIAN. He hath raised the wall, and houses too.
ANTONIO. What impossible matter will he make easy
    next?   90
SEBASTIAN. I think he will carry this island home in
    his pocket, and give it his son for an apple.
ANTONIO. And, sowing the kernels of it in the sea,
    bring forth more islands.
GONZALO. Ay.
ANTONIO. Why, in good time.
GONZALO. Sir, we were talking, that our garments
    seem now as fresh as when we were at Tunis at the
    marriage of your daughter, who is now queen.
ANTONIO. And the rarest that e'er came there.   100
SEBASTIAN. Bate, I beseech you, widow Dido.
ANTONIO. O, widow Dido! ay, widow Dido.
GONZALO. Is not, sir, my doublet as fresh as the first
    day I wore it? I mean, in a sort.
ANTONIO. That sort was well fished for.
GONZALO. When I wore it at your daughter's mar-
    riage?
ALONSO. You cram these words into mine ears, against
    The stomach of my sense . . . Would I had never
    Married my daughter there: for, coming thence,   110
    My son is lost, and, in my rate, she too,
    Who is so far from Italy removed,
    I ne'er again shall see her . . . O thou mine heir
    Of Naples and of Milan, what strange fish
    Hath made his meal on thee?
FRANCISCO.   Sir, he may live.
    I saw him beat the surges under him,
    And ride upon their backs; he trod the water,
    Whose enmity he flung aside, and breasted
    The surge most swoln that met him: his bold head
    'Bove the contentious waves he kept, and oared   120
    Himself with his good arms in lusty stroke
    To th' shore, that o'er his wave-worn basis bowed,
    As stooping to relieve him: I not doubt
    He came alive to land.
ALONSO.   No, no, he's gone.
SEBASTIAN. Sir, you may thank yourself for this great
    loss,
    That would not bless our Europe with your
        daughter,
    But rather loose her to an African,
    Where she, at least, is banished from your eye,
    Who hath cause to wet the grief on't.
ALONSO.   Prithee, peace.
SEBASTIAN. You were kneeled to, and importuned
        otherwise   130
    By all of us: and the fair soul herself
    Weighed between loathness and obedience, at

Which end o'th' beam sh'ould bow ... We have
   lost your son,
I fear, for ever: Milan and Naples have
Moe widows in them of this business' making,
Than we bring men to comfort them:
The fault's your own.
ALONSO.   So is the dear'st o'th' loss.
GONZALO. My lord Sebastian,
   The truth you speak doth lack some gentleness,
   And time to speak it in: you rub the sore,   140
   When you should bring the plaster.
SEBASTIAN.   Very well.
ANTONIO. And most chirurgeonly.
GONZALO. It is foul weather in us all, good sir,
   When you are cloudy.
SEBASTIAN.   Foul weather?
ANTONIO.   Very foul.
GONZALO. Had I plantation of this isle, my lord,—
ANTONIO. He'd sow't with nettle-seed.
SEBASTIAN.   Or docks, or mallows.
GONZALO. And were the king on't, what would I do?
SEBASTIAN. 'Scape being drunk, for want of wine.
GONZALO. I'th' commonwealth I would by contraries
   Execute all things: for no kind of traffic   150
   Would I admit: no name of magistrate:
   Letters should not be known: riches, poverty,
   And use of service—none: contract, succession,
   Bourn, bound of land, tilth, vineyard—none:
   No use of metal, corn, or wine, or oil:
   No occupation, all men idle, all:
   And women too, but innocent and pure:
   No sovereignty—
SEBASTIAN.   Yet he would be king on't.
ANTONIO. The latter end of his commonwealth forgets
   the beginning.   160
GONZALO. All things in common nature should
   produce
   Without sweat or endeavour: treason, felony,
   Sword, pike, knife, gun, or need of any engine,
   Would I not have: but nature should bring forth,
   Of its own kind, all foison, all abundance,
   To feed my innocent people.
SEBASTIAN. No marrying 'mong his subjects?
ANTONIO. None, man, all idle; whores and knaves ...
GONZALO. I would with such perfection govern, sir,
   T'excel the golden age, and—
SEBASTIAN.   'Save his majesty!   170
ANTONIO. Long live Gonzalo!
GONZALO.   Do you mark me, sir?
ALONSO. Prithee, no more: thou dost talk nothing to
   me.
GONZALO. I do well believe your highness, and did it
   to minister occasion to these gentlemen, who are of
   such sensible and nimble lungs, that they always use
   to laugh at nothing.
ANTONIO. 'Twas you we laughed at.
GONZALO. Who, in this kind of merry fooling, am
   nothing to you: so you may continue, and laugh at 180
   nothing still.
ANTONIO. What a blow was there given!
SEBASTIAN. An it had not fallen flat-long.
GONZALO. You are gentlemen of brave mettle: you
   would lift the moon out of her sphere—if she would
   continue in it five weeks without changing!

Ariel appears aloft, playing solemn music

SEBASTIAN. We would so, and then go a bat-fowling.
ANTONIO. Nay, good my lord, be not angry.
GONZALO. No, I warrant you. I will not adventure my
   discretion so weakly ... Will you laugh me asleep, 190
   for I am very heavy?
ANTONIO. Go sleep, and hear us.
         All sleep but Alonso, Sebastian and Antonio
ALONSO. What, all so soon asleep? I wish mine eyes
   Would, with themselves, shut up my thoughts. I
   find,
   They are inclined to do so.
SEBASTIAN.   Please you, sir,
   Do not omit the heavy offer of it:
   It seldom visits sorrow; when it doth,
   It is a comforter.
ANTONIO.   We two, my lord,
   Will guard your person, while you take your rest,
   And watch your safety.
ALONSO.   Thank you ... wondrous heavy. 200
                Alonso sleeps. Ariel vanishes
SEBASTIAN. What a strange drowsiness possesses them!
ANTONIO. It is the quality o'th' climate.
SEBASTIAN.   Why
   Doth it not then our eyelids sink? I find not
   Myself disposed to sleep.
ANTONIO.   Nor I. My spirits are nimble:
   They fell together all, as by consent;
   They dropped—as by a thunder-stroke ... What
   might,
   Worthy Sebastian? O, what might? No more ...
   And yet, methinks, I see it in thy face,
   What thou shouldst be: th'occasion speaks thee, and
   My strong imagination sees a crown   210
   Dropping upon thy head.
SEBASTIAN.   What! art thou waking?
ANTONIO. Do you not hear me speak?
SEBASTIAN.   I do, and surely
   It is a sleepy language; and thou speak'st
   Out of thy sleep: What is it thou didst say?
   This is a strange repose, to be asleep
   With eyes wide open; standing, speaking,
   moving ...
   And yet so fast asleep.
ANTONIO.   Noble Sebastian,
   Thou let'st thy fortune sleep ... die rather ...
   wink'st
   Whiles thou art waking.
SEBASTIAN.   Thou dost snore distinctly,
   There's meaning in thy snores.   220
ANTONIO. I am more serious than my custom: you
   Must be so too, if heed me: which to do,
   Trebles thee o'er.
SEBASTIAN.   Well: I am standing water.
ANTONIO. I'll teach you how to flow.
SEBASTIAN.   Do so: to ebb
   Hereditary sloth instructs me.
ANTONIO.   O!
   If you but knew how you the purpose cherish
   Whiles thus you mock it: how, in stripping it,
   You more invest it: ebbing men, indeed,—
   Most often—do so near the bottom run
   By their own fear, or sloth.
SEBASTIAN.   Prithee, say on.   230
   The setting of thine eye and cheek proclaim
   A matter from thee; and a birth, indeed,
   Which throes thee much to yield.

ANTONIO.   Thus, sir:
Although this lord of weak remembrance; this,
Who shall be of as little memory
When he is earthed, hath here almost persuaded—
For he's a spirit of persuasion, only
Professes to persuade—the king his son's alive,
'Tis as impossible that he's undrowned,
As he that sleeps here swims.
SEBASTIAN.   I have no hope   240
That he's undrowned.
ANTONIO.   O, out of that 'no hope'
What great hope have you! no hope, that way, is
Another way so high an hope, that even
Ambition cannot pierce a wink beyond,
But doubt discovery there. Will you grant with me
That Ferdinand is drowned?
SEBASTIAN.   He's gone.
ANTONIO.   Then, tell me,
Who's the next heir of Naples?
SEBASTIAN.   Claribel.
ANTONIO. She that is queen of Tunis: she that dwells
Ten leagues beyond man's life: she that from Naples
Can have no note—unless the sun were post: 250
The man i'th' moon's too slow—till new-born chins
Be rough and razorable: she that ... from whom
We were all sea-swallowed, though some cast again,
And that by destiny—to perform an act,
Whereof what's past is prologue; what to come,
In yours and my discharge.
SEBASTIAN.   What stuff is this? How say you?
'Tis true, my brother's daughter's queen of Tunis,
So is she heir of Naples—'twixt which regions
There is some space.
ANTONIO.   A space whose every cubit
Seems to cry out, 'How shall that Claribel   260
Measure us back to Naples? Keep in Tunis,
And let Sebastian wake' ... Say, this were death
That now hath seized them—why, they were no
worse
Than now they are: There be that can rule Naples,
As well as he that sleeps: lords, that can prate
As amply and unnecessarily
As this Gonzalo: I myself could make
A chough of as deep chat: O, that you bore
The mind that I do; what a sleep were this
For your advancement! Do you understand me?   270
SEBASTIAN. Methinks I do.
ANTONIO.   And how does your content
Tender your own good fortune?
SEBASTIAN.   I remember
You did supplant your brother Prospero.
ANTONIO.   True:
And look how well my garments sit upon me,
Much feater than before: my brother's servants
Were then my fellows, now they are my men.
SEBASTIAN. But, for your conscience?
ANTONIO. Ay, sir: where lies that? if 'twere a kibe,
'Twould put me to my slipper: but I feel not
This deity in my bosom ... Twenty consciences,   280
That stand 'twixt me and Milan, candied be they,
And melt ere they molest ... Here lies your brother,
No better than the earth he lies upon.
If he were that which now he's like—that's dead—
Whom I with this obedient steel—three inches of
it—
Can lay to bed for ever ... whiles you, doing thus,

To the perpetual wink for aye might put
This ancient morsel ... this Şir Prudence, who
Should not upbraid our course ... For all the rest,
They'll take suggestion, as a cat laps milk—   290
They'll tell the clock to any business that
We say befits the hour.
SEBASTIAN.   Thy case, dear friend,
Shall be my precedent: as thou got'st Milan,
I'll come by Naples ... Draw thy sword. One stroke
Shall free thee from the tribute which thou payest,
And I the king shall love thee.
ANTONIO.   Draw together:
And when I rear my hand, do you the like
To fall it on Gonzalo.
SEBASTIAN.   O, but one word.
                                            They talk apart

Music. Ariel appears again, unseen by them

ARIEL. My master through his art foresees the danger,
That you—his friend—are in, and sends me forth,   300
(For else his project dies) to keep them living.
                                  Sings in Gonzalo's ear
        While you here do snoring lie,
        Open-eyed conspiracy
              His time doth take:
        If of life you keep a care,
        Shake of slumber, and beware....
              Awake! Awake!
ANTONIO. Then let us both be sudden.
GONZALO [*waking*]. Now, good angels preserve the
        king!
Why, how now? Ho! awake!
                            Shaking Alonso, who wakes.
ALONSO.   Why are you drawn?   310
Wherefore this ghastly looking? What's the matter?
SEBASTIAN. Whiles we stood here securing your
        repose,
Even now, we heard a hollow burst of bellowing
Like bulls, or rather lions—did't not wake you?
It struck mine ear most terribly.
ALONSO.   I heard nothing.
ANTONIO. O, 'twas a din to fright a monster's ear;
To make an earthquake! sure, it was the roar
Of a whole herd of lions.
ALONSO.   Heard you this, Gonzalo?
GONZALO. Upon mine honour, sir, I heard a
        humming—
And that a strange one too—which did awake
me ...   320
I shaked you, sir, and cried: as mine eyes opened,
I saw their weapons drawn ... there was a noise,
That's verity. 'Tis best we stand upon our guard;
Or that we quit this place: let's draw our weapons.
ALONSO. Lead off this ground, and let's make further
        search
For my poor son.
GONZALO.   Heavens keep him from these beasts ...
For he is, sure, i'th'island.
ALONSO.   Lead away.
ARIEL. Prospero my lord shall know what I have
        done....
So, king, go safely on to seek thy son.   *Vanishes*

Scene 2 ✳

Enter Caliban, with a burden of wood. A noise of thunder heard

CALIBAN. All the infections that the sun sucks up
From bogs, fens, flats, on Prosper fall, and make him
By inch-meal a disease: His spirits hear me,
And yet I needs must curse.... But they'll nor
    pinch,
Fright me with urchin-shows, pitch me i'th' mire,
Nor lead me, like a firebrand, in the dark
Out of my way, unless he bid 'em; but
For every trifle are they set upon me—
Sometime like apes, that mow and chatter at me,
And after bite me: then like hedgehogs which   10
Lie tumbling in my barefoot way, and mount
Their pricks at my footfall: sometime am I
All wound with adders, who with cloven tongues
Do hiss me into madness ...

Enter Trinculo

                        Lo, now, lo!
Here comes a spirit of his—and to torment me,
For bringing wood in slowly: I'll fall flat—
Perchance he will not mind me.
TRINCULO. Here's neither bush nor shrub, to bear off
any weather at all ... and another storm brew-
ing, I hear it sing i'th' wind: yond same black 20
cloud, yond huge one, looks like a foul bombard that would shed his liquor: if it should
thunder, as it did before, I know not where to hide
my head: yond same cloud cannot choose but fall
by pailfuls.... What have we here? a man or a fish?
dead or alive? A fish, he smells like a fish ... a very
ancient and fish-like smell ... a kind of not-of-the-
newest poor-john: a strange fish ... Were I in
England now, as once I was, and had but this fish
painted,—not a holiday fool there but would give a 30
piece of silver: there would this monster make a
man: any strange beast there makes a man: when
they will not give a doit to relieve a lame beggar,
they will lay out ten to see a dead Indian ...
Legged like a man; and his fins like arms ... Warm,
o' my troth! I do now let loose my opinion; hold
it no longer; this is no fish, but an islander, that
hath lately suffered by a thunderbolt: [*more thunder*]
Alas! the storm is come again: my best way is to
creep under his gaberdine: there is no other shelter 40
hereabout: misery acquaints a man with strange
bed-fellows: I will here shroud till the dregs of the
storm be past.

Enter Stephano, singing; a bottle in his hand

STEPHANO. I shall no more to sea, to sea,
          Here shall I die ashore,—
This is a very scurvy tune to sing at a man's funeral:
Well, here's my comfort.   *Drinks*
[*sings*] The master, the swabber, the bos'n, and I,
      The gunner, and his mate,
Loved Mall, Meg, and Marian, and Margery,   50
      But none of us cared for Kate....
      For she had a tongue with a tang,
      Would cry to a sailor, 'Go hang':
She loved not the savour of tar nor of pitch,
Yet a tailor might scratch her where'er she did
      itch....

Then to sea, boys, and let her go hang.
This is a scurvy tune too: but here's my comfort.
                              Drinks
CALIBAN. Do not torment me ... O!
STEPHANO. What's the matter? Have we devils here?
Do you put tricks upon's with savages and men 60
of Ind, ha? I have not 'scaped drowning, to be
afeard now of your four legs: for it hath been said;
As proper a man as ever went on four legs cannot
make him give ground: and it shall be said so again,
while Stephano breathes at' nostrils.
CALIBAN. The spirit torments me ... O!
STEPHANO. This is some monster of the isle, with four
legs; who hath got, as I take it, an ague ... Where
the devil should he learn our language? I will give
him some relief, if it be but for that ... If I can 70
recover him, and keep him tame, and get to Naples
with him, he's a present for any emperor that ever
trod on neat's-leather.
CALIBAN. Do not torment me, prithee: I'll bring my
wood home faster.
STEPHANO. He's in his fit now; and does not talk after
the wisest; he shall taste of my bottle: if he have
never drink wine afore, it will go near to remove
his fit: if I can recover him, and keep him tame, I
will not take too much for him; he shall pay for 80
him that hath him, and that soundly.
CALIBAN. Thou dost me yet but little hurt;
Thou wilt anon, I know it by thy trembling:
Now Prosper works upon thee.
STEPHANO. Come on your ways: open your mouth:
here is that which will give language to you, cat;
open your mouth; this will shake your shaking, I
can tell you, and that soundly ... you cannot tell
who's your friend; open your chaps again.
                              Caliban drinks
TRINCULO. I should know that voice: It should be— 90
but he is drowned; and these are devils; O, defend
me!
STEPHANO. Four legs and two voices; a most delicate
monster ... His forward voice now is to speak well
of his friend; his backward voice is to utter foul
speeches, and to detract: If all the wine in my bottle
will recover him, I will help his ague: Come ...
[*Caliban drinks again*] Amen, I will pour some in thy
other mouth.
TRINCULO. Stephano,—   100
STEPHANO. Doth thy other mouth call me? Mercy,
mercy! This is a devil, and no monster: I will leave
him—I have no long spoon.
TRINCULO. Stephano ... if thou beest Stephano, touch
me, and speak to me: for I am Trinculo; be not
afeard—thy good friend Trinculo.
STEPHANO. If thou beest Trinculo ... [*returns*] come
forth: I'll pull thee by the lesser legs: if any be
Trinculo's legs, these are they: Thou art very
Trinculo, indeed: How cam'st thou to be the siege 110
of this moon-calf? Can he vent Trinculos?
TRINCULO. I took him to be killed with a thunder-
stroke ... But art thou not drowned, Stephano? I
hope now, thou art not drowned: Is the storm
overblown? I hid me under the dead moon-calf's
gaberdine, for fear of the storm: And art thou living,
Stephano? O Stephano, two Neapolitans 'scaped!
STEPHANO. Prithee do not turn me about, my stomach
is not constant.

CALIBAN. These be fine things, an if they be not
    sprites: 120
    That's a brave god, and bears celestial liquor:
    I will kneel to him.
STEPHANO. How didst thou 'scape? How cam'st thou
    hither? Swear by this bottle, how thou cam'st hither
    ... I escaped upon a butt of sack, which the sailors
    heaved o'er-board—by this bottle! which I made of
    the bark of a tree, with mine own hands, since I
    was cast ashore.
CALIBAN. I'll swear upon that bottle, to be thy true
    subject, for the liquor is not earthly.   130
STEPHANO. Here: swear then how thou escapedst.
TRINCULO. Swam ashore, man, like a duck ... I can
    swim like a duck, I'll be sworn.
STEPHANO. Here, kiss the book.... [Trinculo drinks]
    Though thou canst swim like a duck, thou art made
    like a goose
TRINCULO. O Stephano, hast any more of this?
STEPHANO. The whole butt, man. My cellar is in a rock
    by th' sea-side, where my wine is hid ... How now,
    moon-calf? how does thine ague?   140
CALIBAN. Hast thou not dropped from heaven?
STEPHANO. Out o'th' moon, I do assure thee.... I was
    the man i'th' moon, when time was.
CALIBAN. I have seen thee in her: and I do adore
    thee:
    My mistress showed me thee, and thy dog, and thy
    bush.
STEPHANO. Come, swear to that: kiss the book ... I
    will furnish it anon with new 'contents'. Swear.
TRINCULO. By this good light, this is a very shallow
    monster: I afeard of him? a very weak monster ...
    The man i'th' moon! a most poor credulous mon-   150
    ster ... Well drawn, monster, in good sooth.
CALIBAN. I'll show thee every fertile inch of the island:
    And I will kiss thy foot: I prithee be my god.
TRINCULO. By this light, a most perfidious and
    drunken monster. When's god's asleep, he'll rob his
    bottle.
CALIBAN. I'll kiss thy foot, I'll swear myself thy
    subject.
STEPHANO. Come on then: down, and swear.
TRINCULO. I shall laugh myself to death at this puppy- 160
    headed monster: a most scurvy monster: I could
    find in my heart to beat him—
STEPHANO. Come, kiss.
TRINCULO. —but that the poor monster's in drink ...
    An abominable monster!
CALIBAN. I'll show thee the best springs: I'll pluck thee
    berries:
    I'll fish for thee, and get thee wood enough....
    A plague upon the tyrant that I serve;
    I'll bear him no more sticks, but follow thee,
    Thou wondrous man.   170
TRINCULO. A most ridiculous monster, to make a
    wonder of a poor drunkard!
CALIBAN. I prithee, let me bring thee where crabs
    grow;
    And I with my long nails will dig thee pig-nuts;
    Show thee a jay's nest, and instruct thee how
    To snare the nimble marmozet: I'll bring thee
    To clustring filberts, and sometimes I'll get thee
    Young scamels from the rock: Wilt thou go with
    me?
STEPHANO. I prithee now, lead the way, without any

more talking.... Trinculo, the king and all our   180
    company else being drowned, we will inherit here:
    Here; bear my bottle: Fellow Trinculo; we'll fill
    him by and by again.
CALIBAN. [sings drunkenly]. Farewell master; farewell,
    farewell.
TRINCULO. A howling monster: a drunken monster.
CALIBAN.   No more dams I'll make for fish,
        Nor fetch in firing
        At requiring,
        Nor scrape trenchering, nor wash dish,
        'Ban 'Ban, Ca-Caliban   190
        Has a new master—get a new man.
    Freedom, high-day! high-day, freedom! freedom,
    high-day, freedom!
STEPHANO. O brave monster; lead the way.   *They go*

ACT 3
Scene 1: *Before Prospero's cell*

Enter Ferdinand, bearing a log

FERDINAND. There be some sports are painful; and
    their labour
    Delight in them sets off: some kinds of baseness
    Are nobly undergone; and most poor matters
    Point to rich ends ... This my mean task
    Would be as heavy to me as odious, but
    The mistress which I serve quickens what's dead,
    And makes my labours—pleasures ... O, she is
    Ten times more gentle than her father's crabbed;
    And he's composed of harshness ... I must remove
    Some thousands of these logs, and pile them up,   10
    Upon a sore injunction; my sweet mistress
    Weeps, when she sees me work, and says, such
    baseness
    Had never like executor ... I forget ...
    But these sweet thoughts do even refresh my
    labours—
    Most busie lest, when I doe it.

Enter Miranda and Prospero, behind her, unseen

MIRANDA.   Alas, now pray you,
    Work not so hard: I would the lightning had
    Burnt up those logs that you are enjoined to pile:
    Pray, set it down, and rest you: when this burns,
    'Twill weep for having wearied you ... My father
    Is hard at study; pray now, rest yourself—   20
    He's safe for these three hours.
FERDINAND.   O most dear mistress,
    The sun will set before I shall discharge
    What I must strive to do.
MIRANDA.   If you'll sit down,
    I'll bear your logs the while: pray give me that,
    I'll carry it to the pile.
FERDINAND.   No, precious creature,—
    I had rather crack my sinews, break my back,
    Than you should such dishonour undergo,
    While I sit lazy by.
MIRANDA.   It would become me
    As well as it does you; and I should do it
    With much more ease: for my good will is to it,   30
    And yours it is against.
PROSPERO.   Poor worm thou art infected,
    This visitation shows it.

MIRANDA. You look wearily.

FERDINAND. No, noble mistress, 'tis fresh morning
  with me
  When you are by at night: I do beseech you—
  Chiefly that I might set it in my prayers—
  What is your name?

MIRANDA. Miranda,—O my father,
  I have broke your hest to say so!

FERDINAND. Admired Miranda!
  Indeed the top of admiration, worth
  What's dearest to the world! Full many a lady
  I have eyed with best regard, and many a time   40
  Th'harmony of their tongues hath into bondage
  Brought my too diligent ear: for several virtues
  Have I liked several women—never any
  With so full soul, but some defect in her
  Did quarrel with the noblest grace she owed,
  And put it to the foil.... But you, O you,
  So perfect, and so peerless, are created
  Of every creature's best.

MIRANDA. I do not know
  One of my sex; no woman's face remember,
  Save, from my glass, mine own: nor have I seen   50
  More that I may call men than you, good friend,
  And my dear father: how features are abroad,
  I am skilless of; but, by my modesty—
  The jewel in my dower—I would not wish
  Any companion in the world but you;
  Nor can imagination form a shape,
  Besides yourself, to like of ... But I prattle
  Something too wildly, and my father's precepts
  I therein do forget.

FERDINAND. I am, in my condition,
  A prince, Miranda—I do think, a king,   60
  (I would not so!) and would no more endure
  This wooden slavery, than to suffer
  The flesh-fly blow my mouth ... Hear my soul
  speak....
  The very instant that I saw you, did
  My heart fly to your service, there resides
  To make me slave to it, and for your sake
  Am I this patient log-man.

MIRANDA. Do you love me?

FERDINAND. O heaven, O earth, bear witness to this
  sound,
  And crown what I profess with kind event
  If I speak true ... if hollowly, invert   70
  What best is boded me to mischief ... I,
  Beyond all limit of what else i'th' world,
  Do love, prize, honour you.

MIRANDA. I am a fool
  To weep at what I am glad of.

PROSPERO. Fair encounter
  Of two most rare affections: heavens rain grace
  On that which breeds between 'em!

FERDINAND. Wherefore weep you?

MIRANDA. At mine unworthiness, that dare not offer
  What I desire to give; and much less take
  What I shall die to want ... But this is trifling—
  And all the more it seeks to hide itself,   80
  The bigger bulk it shows ... Hence bashful
  cunning,
  And prompt me plain and holy innocence....
  I am your wife, if you will marry me;
  If not, I'll die your maid: to be your fellow
  You may deny me, but I'll be your servant,
  Whether you will or no.

FERDINAND. My mistress,—dearest!
  And I thus humble ever.

MIRANDA. My husband then?

FERDINAND. Ay, with a heart as willing
  As bondage e'er of freedom: here's my hand.

MIRANDA. And mine, with my heart in't; and now
  farewell.   90
  Till half an hour hence.

FERDINAND. A thousand! thousand!

  *Miranda and Ferdinand
  go their separate ways*

PROSPERO. So glad of this as they I cannot be,
  Who are surprised with all; but my rejoicing
  At nothing can be more. I'll to my book,
  For yet, ere supper time, must I perform
  Much business appertaining.

Scene 2

Stephano, Trinculo and Caliban

STEPHANO. Tell not me—when the butt is out we will
  drink water, not a drop before; therefore bear up,
  and board 'em. Servant-monster, drink to me.

TRINCULO. Servant-monster! The Sophy of this island!
  They say there's but five upon this isle; we are three
  of them—if th'other two be brained like us, the
  state totters.

STEPHANO. Drink servant-monster when I bid thee.
  Thy eyes are almost set in thy head.

TRINCULO. Where should they be set else? he were a   10
  brave monster indeed, if they were set in his tail.

STEPHANO. My man-monster hath drowned his
  tongue in sack: for my part, the sea cannot drown
  me—I swam, ere I could recover the shore, five-
  and-thirty leagues, off and on. By this light thou
  shalt be my lieutenant, monster, or my standard.

TRINCULO. Your lieutenant if you list—he's no standard.

STEPHANO. We'll not run, Monsieur Monster.

TRINCULO. Nor go neither: but you'll lie, like dogs,   20
  and yet say nothing neither.

STEPHANO. Moon-calf, speak once in thy life, if thou
  beest a good moon-calf.

CALIBAN. How does thy honour? Let me lick thy shoe:
  I'll not serve him, he is not valiant.

TRINCULO. Thou liest, most ignorant monster, I am in
  case to justle a constable: Why, thou debauched
  fish thou, was there ever a man a coward, that
  hath drunk so much sack as I to-day? Wilt thou
  tell a monstrous lie, being but half a fish, and   30
  half a monster?

CALIBAN. Lo how he mocks me! wilt thou let him, my
  lord?

TRINCULO. 'Lord,' quoth he! that a monster should
  be such a natural!

CALIBAN. Lo, lo, again! bite him to death, I prithee.

STEPHANO. Trinculo, keep a good tongue in your
  head: if you prove a mutineer,—the next tree! The
  poor monster's my subject, and he shall not suffer
  indignity.   40

CALIBAN. I thank my noble lord.... Wilt thou be
  pleased
  To hearken once again to the suit I made to thee?

STEPHANO. Marry will I: kneel and repeat it. I will
  stand, and so shall Trinculo.

Enter Ariel, invisible

CALIBAN. As I told thee before, I am subject to a
　　tyrant—
　　A sorcerer, that by his cunning hath
　　Cheated me of the island.
ARIEL.　　　　　　　　　　Thou liest.
CALIBAN. Thou liest, thou jesting monkey, thou:
　　I would, my valiant master would destroy thee....
　　I do not lie.　　　　　　　　　　　　　　　　50
STEPHANO. Trinculo, if you trouble him any more in's
　　tale, by this hand, I will supplant some of your teeth.
TRINCULO. Why, I said nothing.
STEPHANO. Mum then, and no more: Proceed.
CALIBAN. I say, by sorcery, he got this isle—
　　From me he got it. If thy greatness will
　　Revenge it on him—for I know thou dar'st,
　　But this thing dare not—
STEPHANO.　　　　　　　That's most certain.
CALIBAN. Thou shalt be lord of it, and I will serve thee.
STEPHANO. How now shall this be compassed? Canst　60
　　thou bring me to the party?
CALIBAN. Yea, yea, my lord, I'll yield him thee asleep,
　　Where thou mayst knock a nail into his head.
ARIEL. Thou liest, thou canst not.
CALIBAN. What a pied ninny's this! Thou scurvy patch!
　　I do beseech thy greatness, give him blows,
　　And take his bottle from him: when that's gone,
　　He shall drink nought but brine, for I'll not show
　　　him
　　Where the quick freshes are.
STEPHANO. Trinculo, run into no further danger: in-　70
　　terrupt the monster one word further, and, by this
　　hand, I'll turn my mercy out of doors, and make a
　　stock-fish of thee.
TRINCULO. Why, what did I? I did nothing: I'll go
　　further off.
STEPHANO. Didst thou not say he lied?
ARIEL. Thou liest.
STEPHANO. Do I so? take thou that [*strikes him*]. As you
　　like this, give me the lie another time.
TRINCULO. I did not give the lie: Out of your wits,
　　and hearing too?　　　　　　　　　　　　　80
　　A pox o' your bottle! this can sack, and drinking do:
　　a murrain on your monster, and the devil take your
　　fingers!
CALIBAN. Ha, ha, ha!
STEPHANO. Now, forward with your tale ...
　　Prithee stand further off.
CALIBAN. Beat him enough: after a little time,
　　I'll beat him too.
STEPHANO.　　　　　Stand further: Come, proceed.
CALIBAN. Why, as I told thee, 'tis a custom with him
　　I'th'afternoon to sleep: there thou mayst brain him,　90
　　Having first seized his books: or with a log
　　Batter his skull, or paunch him with a stake,
　　Or cut his wezand with thy knife.... Remember,
　　First to possess his books; for without them
　　He's but a sot, as I am; nor hath not
　　One spirit to command: they all do hate him,
　　As rootedly as I. Burn but his books.
　　He has brave utensils—for so he calls them—
　　Which, when he has a house, he'll deck withal.
　　And that most deeply to consider, is　　　　　100
　　The beauty of his daughter.... he himself
　　Calls her a nonpareil: I never saw a woman,

But only Sycorax my dam and she;
　　But she as far surpasseth Sycorax,
　　As great'st does least.
STEPHANO.　　　　　　　Is it so brave a lass?
CALIBAN. Ay lord, she will become thy bed, I warrant,
　　And bring thee forth brave brood.
STEPHANO. Monster, I will kill this man: his daughter
　　and I will be king and queen—save our graces!—
　　and Trinculo and thyself shall be viceroys ...　　110
　　Does thou like the plot, Trinculo?
TRINCULO. Excellent.
STEPHANO. Give me thy hand—I am sorry I beat thee:
　　but, while thou liv'st, keep a good tongue in thy
　　head.
CALIBAN. Within this half hour will he be asleep.
　　Wilt thou destroy him then?
STEPHANO.　　　　　　　Ay, on mine honour.
ARIEL. This will I tell my master.
CALIBAN. Thou mak'st me merry: I am full of pleasure,
　　Let us be jocund.... Will you troll the catch　　120
　　You taught me but while-ere?
STEPHANO. At thy request, monster, I will do reason,
　　any reason: Come on, Trinculo, let us sing.　*Sings*
　　Flout'em, and cout'em: and scout'em,
　　　and flout'em,
　　Thought is free.
CALIBAN. That's not the tune.

Ariel plays the tune on a tabor and pipe

STEPHANO. What is this same?
TRINCULO. This is the tune of our catch, played by
　　the picture of Nobody.
STEPHANO. If thou beest a man, show thyself in thy　130
　　likeness: if thou beest a devil, take't as thou list.
TRINCULO. O forgive me my sins!
STEPHANO. He that dies, pays all debts: I defy thee;
　　Mercy upon us!
CALIBAN. Art thou afeard?
STEPHANO. No, monster, not I.
CALIBAN. Be not afeard—the isle is full of noises,
　　Sounds and sweet airs, that give delight and hurt
　　　not:
　　Sometimes a thousand twangling instruments
　　Will hum about mine ears; and sometimes voices,　140
　　That, if I then had waked after long sleep,
　　Will make me sleep again—and then, in dreaming,
　　The clouds methought would open, and show riches
　　Ready to drop upon me, that when I waked
　　I cried to dream again.
STEPHANO. This will prove a brave kingdom to me,
　　where I shall have my music for nothing.
CALIBAN. When Prospero is destroyed.
STEPHANO. That shall be by and by: I remember the
　　story.　　　　　　　　　　　　　　　　　150
TRINCULO. The sound is going away. Let's follow it,
　　and after do our work.
STEPHANO. Lead monster, we'll follow: I would I
　　could see this taborer—he lays it on.
TRINCULO. Wilt come? I'll follow, Stephano.
　　　　　　　　　　　　　　　They follow Ariel

Scene 3

Enter Alonso, his train, and Gonzalo

GONZALO. By'r lakin, I can go no further, sir.
　　My old bones ache: here's a maze trod, indeed,

Through forth-rights and meanders: by your
  patience,
I needs must rest me.

ALONSO.   Old lord, I cannot blame thee,
Who am myself attached with weariness,
To th' dulling of my spirits: sit down, and rest ...
Even here I will put off my hope, and keep it
No longer for my flatterer: he is drowned
Whom thus we stray to find, and the sea mocks
Our frustrate search on land ... well, let him go. 10

ANTONIO [*standing, with Sebastian, apart from the rest*].
I am right glad that he's so out of hope:
Do not, for one repulse, forego the purpose
That you resolved t'effect.

SEBASTIAN.   The next advantage
Will we take throughly.

ANTONIO.   Let it be to-night,
For, now they are oppressed with travel, they
Will not, nor cannot, use such vigilance
As when they are fresh.

SEBASTIAN.   I say, to-night: no more.

Solemn and strange music and Prospero on the top, invisible

ALONSO. What harmony is this? my good friends,
  hark!

GONZALO. Marvellous sweet music!

*Enter several strange shapes, bringing in a banquet; and
dance about it with gentle actions of salutation; and, inviting the king, & c. to eat, they depart*

ALONSO. Give us kind keepers, heavens: what were
  these?   20

SEBASTIAN. A living drollery: now I will believe
That there are unicorns: that in Arabia
There is one tree, the phœnix' throne, one phœnix
At this hour reigning there.

ANTONIO.   I'll believe both:
And what does else want credit, come to me,
And I'll be sworn 'tis true: travellers ne'er did lie,
Though fools at home condemn 'em.

GONZALO.   If in Naples
I should report this now, would they believe me?
If I should say, I saw such islanders,—
For, certes, these are people of the island,   30
Who, though they are of monstrous shape, yet note
Their manners are more gentle-kind, than of
Our human generation you shall find
Many, nay, almost any.

PROSPERO.   Honest lord,
Thou hast said well: for some of you there
  present ...
Are worse than devils.

ALONSO.   I cannot too much muse
Such shapes, such gesture, and such sound,
  expressing—
Although they want the use of tongue—a kind
Of excellent dumb discourse.

PROSPERO.   Praise in departing.

FRANCISCO. They vanished strangely.

SEBASTIAN.   No matter, since 40
They have left their viands behind; for we have
  stomachs. ...
Will't please you taste of what is here?

ALONSO.   Not I.

GONZALO. Faith, sir, you need not fear. When we
  were boys,

Who would believe that there were mountaineers,
Dew-lapped like bulls, whose throats had hanging
  at 'em
Wallets of flesh? or that there were such men
Whose heads stood in their breasts? which now we
  find
Each putter-out of five for one that will bring us
Good warrant of.

ALONSO.   I will stand to, and feed,
Although my last—no matter, since I feel   50
The best is past ... Brother: my lord the duke,
Stand to and do as we.

*Thunder and lightning. Enter Ariel like a harpy; claps
his wings upon the table, and, with a quaint device, the
banquet vanishes*

ARIEL. You are three men of sin, whom destiny,
That hath to instrument this lower world
And what is in't, the never-surfeited sea
Hath caused to belch up you; and on this island,
Where man doth not inhabit, you 'mongst men
Being most unfit to live. I have made you mad;
And even with such-like valour men hang and
  drown
Their proper selves: [*they make to attack, but are
  charmed from moving*] You fools! I and my fellows 60
Are ministers of fate. The elements,
Of whom your swords are tempered, may as well
Wound the loud winds, or with bemocked-at stabs
Kill the still-closing waters, as diminish
One dowle that's in my plume: my fellow-
  ministers
Are like invulnerable. If you could hurt,
Your swords are now too massy for your strengths,
And will not be uplifted ... But, remember
(For that's my business to you!) that you three
From Milan did supplant good Prospero;   70
Exposed unto the sea—which hath requit it!—
Him, and his innocent child: for which foul deed
The powers, delaying, not forgetting, have
Incensed the seas and shores—yea, all the creatures,
Against your peace ... Thee of thy son, Alonso,
They have bereft; and do pronounce by me,
Ling'ring perdition (worse than any death
Can be at once!) shall step by step attend
You, and your ways; whose wraths to guard you
  from—
Which here, in this most desolate isle, else falls 80
Upon your heads—is nothing but heart's sorrow,
And a clear life ensuing.

*He vanishes in thunder: then, to soft music, enter the
shapes again, and dance, with mocks and mows, and carrying
out the table*

PROSPERO. Bravely the figure of this harpy hast thou
Performed, my Ariel,—a grace it had, devouring:
Of my instruction hast thou nothing bated
In what thou hadst to say: so, with good life
And observation strange, my meaner ministers
Their several kinds have done: my high charms
  work,
And these, mine enemies, are all knit up
In their distractions: they now are in my power; 90
And in these fits I leave them, whilst I visit
Young Ferdinand—whom they suppose is
  drowned—

And mine and his loved darling.   *He departs*

GONZALO. I'th' name of something holy, sir, why
  stand you
In this strange stare?

ALONSO.   O, it is monstrous, monstrous!
Methought the billows spoke, and told me of it,
The winds did sing it to me; and the thunder,
That deep and dreadful organ-pipe, pronounced
The name of Prosper: it did bass my trespass.
Therefore my son i'th'ooze is bedded; and   100
I'll seek him deeper than e'er plummet sounded,
And with him there lie mudded.   *He goes*

SEBASTIAN.   But one fiend at a time,
I'll fight their legions o'er.

ANTONIO.   I'll be thy second.
                    They leave

GONZALO. All three of them are desperate: their great
  guilt,
Like poison given to work a great time after,
Now 'gins to bite the spirit: I do beseech you,
That are of suppler joints, follow them swiftly,
And hinder them from what this ecstasy
May now provoke them to.

ADRIAN.   Follow, I pray you.

ACT 4

Scene 1: *Before Prospero's cell*

Prospero with Ferdinand and Miranda

PROSPERO. If I have too austerely punished you,
Your compensation makes amends, for I
Have given you here a third of mine own life,
Or that for which I live: who once again
I tender to thy hand ... All thy vexations
Were but my trials of thy love, and thou
Hast strangely stood the test: here, afore Heaven,
I ratify this my rich gift: O Ferdinand,
Do not smile at me that I boast hereof,
For thou shalt find she will outstrip all praise   10
And make it halt behind her.

FERDINAND.   I do believe it
Against an oracle.

PROSPERO. Then, as my gift, and thine own acquisition
Worthily purchased, take my daughter: but
If thou dost break her virgin-knot before
All sanctimonious ceremonies may
With full and holy rite be minist'red,
No sweet aspersion shall the heavens let fall
To make this contract grow; but barren hate,
Sour-eyed disdain and discord shall bestrew   20
The union of your bed with weeds so loathly
That you shall hate it both: therefore take heed,
As Hymen's lamp shall light you.

FERDINAND.   As I hope
For quiet days, fair issue, and long life,
With such love as 'tis now, the murkiest den,
The most opportune place, the strong'st suggestion
Our worser genius can, shall never melt
Mine honour into lust, to take away
The edge of that day's celebration,
When I shall think, or Phœbus' steeds are foundered,   30
Or Night kept chained below.

PROSPERO.   Fairly spoke;
Sit then, and talk with her, she is thine own ...
What, Ariel; my industrious servant Ariel!

Ariel appears

ARIEL. What would my potent master? here I am.

PROSPERO. Thou and thy meaner fellows your last
  service
Did worthily perform: and I must use you
In such another trick: go, bring the rabble,
(O'er whom I give thee power) here, to this place:
Incite them to quick motion, for I must
Bestow upon the eyes of this young couple   40
Some vanity of mine art: it is my promise,
And they expect it from me.

ARIEL.   Presently?

PROSPERO. Ay: with a twink.

ARIEL. Before you can say 'come' and 'go,'
And breathe twice; and cry 'so, so,'
Each one, tripping on his toe,
Will be here with mop and mow....
Do you love me, master? no?

PROSPERO. Dearly, my delicate Ariel ... Do not
  approach,
Till thou dost hear me call.

ARIEL.   Well: I conceive.   *Vanishes*   50

PROSPERO. Look thou be true: do not give dalliance
Too much the rein: the strongest oaths are straw
To th' fire i'th' blood: be more abstemious,
Or else good night your vow.

FERDINAND.   I warrant you, sir,
The white cold virgin snow upon my heart
Abates the ardour of my liver.

PROSPERO.   Well....
Now come my Ariel. Bring a corollary,
Rather than want a spirit; appear, and pertly!
No tongue ... all eyes ... be silent.   *Soft music*

THE MASQUE

Iris appears

IRIS. Ceres, most bounteous lady, thy rich leas   60
Of wheat, rye, barley, vetches, oats, and pease;
Thy turfy mountains, where live nibbling sheep,
And flat meads thatched with stover, them to keep:
Thy banks with pionèd and twillèd brims,
Which spongy April at thy hest betrims—
To make cold nymphs chaste crowns; and thy
  broom-groves,
Whose shadow the dismissèd bachelor loves,
Being lass-lorn; thy poll-clipt vinèyard;
And thy sea-marge, sterile and rocky-hard,
Where thou thyself dost air—the queen o'th' sky,   70
Whose watry arch and messenger am I,
Bids thee leave these, and with her sovereign grace,
Here on this grass-plot, in this very place,
To come and sport: her peacocks fly amain:
       Juno's car appears in the sky
Approach, rich Ceres, her to entertain.

Enter Ceres

CERES. Hail, many-coloured messenger, that ne'er
Dost disobey the wife of Jupiter:
Who, with thy saffron wings, upon my flowers
Diffusest honey-drops, refreshing showers,
And with each end of thy blue bow dost crown   80
My bosky acres, and my unshrubbed down,
Rich scarf to my proud earth ... why hath thy
  queen

Summoned me hither, to this short-grassed green?
IRIS. A contract of true love to celebrate,
And some donation freely to estate
On the blessed lovers.
CERES.   Tell me, heavenly bow,
If Venus or her son, as thou dost know,
Do now attend the queen? since they did plot
The means that dusky Dis my daughter got,
Her and her blind boy's scandalled company   90
I have forsworn.
IRIS.   Of her society
Be not afraid: I met her deity
Cutting the clouds towards Paphos; and her son
Dove-drawn with her: here thought they to have
      done
Some wanton charm upon this man and maid,
Whose vows are, that no bed-rite shall be paid
Till Hymen's torch be lighted: but in vain
Mars's hot minion is returned again
Her waspish-headed son has broke his arrows,
Swears he will shoot no more, but play with
      sparrows   100
And be a boy right out.

Juno alights from her car

CERES.   Highest queen of state,
Great Juno comes; I know her by her gait.
JUNO. How does my bounteous sister? Go with me
To bless this twain, that they may prosperous be,
And honoured in their issue.   *They sing*
JUNO. Honour, riches, marriage-blessing,
Long continuance, and increasing,
Hourly joys be still upon you!
Juno sings her blessings on you.
CERES. Earth's increase, foison plenty,   110
Barns and garners never empty,
Vines with clustring bunches growing,
Plants with goodly burden bowing;
Spring come to you, at the farthest,
In the very end of harvest!
Scarcity and want shall shun you;
Ceres' blessing so is on you.
FERDINAND. This is a most majestic vision, and
Harmonious charmingly: may I be bold
To think these spirits?
PROSPERO.   Spirits, which by mine art 120
I have from their confines called to enact
My present fancies.
FERDINAND.   Let me live here ever—
So rare a wond'red father and a wise
Makes this place Paradise.

Juno and Ceres whisper, and send Iris on employment

PROSPERO.   Sweet, now silence:
Juno and Ceres whisper seriously.
There's something else to do: hush, and be mute.
Or else our spell is marred.
IRIS. You nymphs, called Naiads, of the wand'ring
      brooks,
With your sedged crowns and ever harmless looks,
Leave your crisp channels, and on this green land 130
Answer your summons; Juno does command....
Come, temperate nymphs, and help to celebrate
A contract of true love: be not too late.

Enter certain Nymphs

You sunburnt sicklemen, of August weary,
Come hither from the furrow, and be merry.
Make holiday: your rye-straw hats put on,
And these fresh nymphs encounter every one
In country footing.

*Enter certain Reapers, properly habited: they join with the
Nymphs in a graceful dance; towards the end whereof
Prospero starts suddenly, and speaks; after which, to a
strange, hollow, and confused noise, they heavily vanish*

PROSPERO [to himself]. I had forgot that foul conspiracy
Of the beast Caliban and his confederates   140
Against my life: the minute of their plot
Is almost come: [to the spirits] Well done! avoid:
      no more.
FERDINAND. This is strange: your father's in some
      passion,
That works him strongly.
MIRANDA.   Never till this day,
Saw I him touched with anger so distempered.
PROSPERO. You do look, my son, in a moved sort,
As if you were dismayed: be cheerful, sir.
Our revels now are ended ... These our actors,
As I foretold you, were all spirits, and
Are melted into air, into thin air,   150
And, like the baseless fabric of this vision,
The cloud-capped towers, the gorgeous palaces,
The solemn temples, the great globe itself,
Yea, all which it inherit, shall dissolve,
And, like this insubstantial pageant faded,
Leave not a rack behind: we are such stuff
As dreams are made on; and our little life
Is rounded with a sleep ... Sir, I am vexed.
Bear with my weakness, my old brain is troubled:
Be not disturbed with my infirmity.   160
If you be pleased, retire into my cell,
And there repose. A turn or two I'll walk,
To still my beating mind.
FERDINAND, MIRANDA [retiring]. We wish your peace.
PROSPERO. Come with a thought; I thank thee.
      Ariel: come.

Ariel appears

ARIEL. Thy thoughts I cleave to. What's thy pleasure?
PROSPERO.   Spirit,
We must prepare to meet with Caliban.
ARIEL. Ay, my commander; when I presented Ceres,
I thought to have told thee of it, but I feared
Lest I might anger thee.
PROSPERO. Say again, where didst thou leave these
      varlets?   170
ARIEL. I told you, sir, they were red-hot with
      drinking—
So full of valour, that they smote the air
For breathing in their faces: beat the ground
For kissing of their feet; yet always bending
Towards their project: Then I beat my tabor,
At which like unbacked colts they pricked their ears,
Advanced their eyelids, lifted up their noses,
As they smelt music. So I charmed their ears
That calf-like they my lowing followed, through
Toothed briers, sharp furzes, pricking gorse, and
      thorns,   180
Which ent'red their frail shins: at last I left them

I'th' filthy mantled pool beyond your cell,
There dancing up to th' chins, that the foul lake
O'er-stunk their sweat.
PROSPERO.   This was well done, my bird.
Thy shape invisible retain thou still:
The trumpery in my house, go, bring it hither,
For stale to catch these thieves.
ARIEL.   I go, I go.
PROSPERO. A devil, a born devil, on whose nature
Nurture can never stick: on whom my pains,
Humanely taken, all, all lost, quite lost—   190
And as with age his body uglier grows,
So his mind cankers. I will plague them all,
Even to roaring.

Ariel returns loaden with glistering apparel, etc.

                    Come, hang them on this line.

*Prospero and Ariel remain invisible. Enter Caliban,
Stephano, and Trinculo, all wet*

CALIBAN. Pray you, tread softly, that the blind mole
   may
   Not hear a foot fall: we now are near his cell.
STEPHANO. Monster, your fairy, which you say is a
   harmless fairy, has done little better than played the
   Jack with us.
TRINCULO. Monster, I do smell all horse-piss, at which
   my nose is in great indignation.   200
STEPHANO. So is mine. Do you hear, monster? If I
   should take a displeasure against you: look you.
TRINCULO. Thou wert but a lost monster.
CALIBAN. Good my lord, give me thy favour still.
   Be patient, for the prize I'll bring thee to
   Shall hoodwink this mischance: therefore, speak
   softly—
   All's hushed as midnight yet.
TRINCULO. Ay, but to lose our bottles in the pool,—
STEPHANO. There is not only disgrace and dishonour in
   that, monster, but an infinite loss.   210
TRINCULO. That's more to me than my wetting: yet
   this is your harmless fairy, monster.
STEPHANO. I will fetch off my bottle, though I be o'er
   ears for my labour.
CALIBAN. Prithee, my king, be quiet.... Seest thou
   here,
   This is the mouth o'th' cell... no noise, and enter...
   Do that good mischief which may make this island
   Thine own for ever, and I, thy Caliban,
   For aye thy foot-licker.   220
STEPHANO. Give me thy hand. I do begin to have
   bloody thoughts.
TRINCULO. O King Stephano, O peer! O worthy
   Stephano, look what a wardrobe here is for thee!
CALIBAN. Let it alone, thou fool—it is but trash.
TRINCULO. O, ho, monster: we know what belongs to
   a frippery. O King Stephano!
STEPHANO. Put off that gown, Trinculo. By this hand,
   I'll have that gown.
TRINCULO. Thy grace shall have it.
CALIBAN. The dropsy drown this fool! what do you
   mean,   230
   To dote thus on such luggage? Let't alone!
   And do the murder first: if he awake,
   From toe to crown he'll fill our skins with pinches—
   Make us strange stuff.
STEPHANO. Be you quiet, monster. Mistress line, is not

this my jerkin? Now is the jerkin under the line:
now jerkin you are like to lose your hair, and
prove a bald jerkin.
TRINCULO. Do, do! We steal by line and level, an't like
   your grace.   240
STEPHANO. I thank thee for that jest; here's a garment
   for't: wit shall not go unrewarded while I am king
   of this country: 'steal by line and level' is an excellent
   pass of pate; there's another garment for't.
TRINCULO. Monster, come, put some lime upon your
   fingers, and away with the rest.
CALIBAN. I will have none on't: we shall lose our time,
   And all be turned to barnacles, or to apes
   With foreheads villainous low.
STEPHANO. Monster, lay-to your fingers: help to bear 250
   this away where my hogshead of wine is, or I'll
   turn you out of my kingdom: go to, carry this.
TRINCULO. And this.
STEPHANO. Ay, and this.

*A noise of hunters heard. Enter divers spirits, in shape of
dogs and hounds, hunting them about; Prospero and Ariel
setting them on*

PROSPERO. Hey, Mountain, hey!
ARIEL. Silver ... there it goes, Silver!
PROSPERO. Fury, Fury ... there, Tyrant, there ... hark,
   hark!
                            *Caliban, Stephano and
                            Trinculo are driven out*
   Go, charge my goblins, that they grind their joints
   With dry convulsions, shorten up their sinews
   With agèd cramps, and more pinch-spotted make
   them   260
   Than pard or cat o' mountain.
ARIEL.   Hark, they roar.
PROSPERO. Let them be hunted soundly ... At this
   hour
   Lies at my mercy all mine enemies:
   Shortly shall all my labours end, and thou
   Shalt have the air at freedom: for a little
   Follow, and do me service.   *They go*

                    ACT 5
                    Scene 1

Prospero in his magic robes and Ariel

PROSPERO. Now does my project gather to a head:
   My charms crack not: my spirits obey, and Time
   Goes upright with his carriage ... How's the day?
ARIEL. On the sixth hour, at which time, my lord,
   You said our work should cease.
PROSPERO.   I did say so,
   When first I raised the tempest. Say, my spirit,
   How fares the king and's followers?
ARIEL.   Confined together
   In the same fashion as you gave in charge,
   Just as you left them—all prisoners, sir,
   In the line-grove which weather-fends your cell.   10
   They cannot budge till your release: The king,
   His brother, and yours, abide all three distracted;
   And the remainder mourning over them,
   Brimful of sorrow and dismay: but chiefly
   Him you termed, sir, 'The good old lord, Gonzalo.'
   His tears run down his beard, like winter's drops
   From eaves of reeds ... Your charm so strongly
   works 'em,

That if you now beheld them, your affections
Would become tender.

PROSPERO.   Dost thou think so, spirit?

ARIEL. Mine would, sir, were I human.

PROSPERO.   And mine shall.... 20
Hast thou—which art but air—a touch, a feeling
Of their afflictions, and shall not myself,
One of their kind, that relish all as sharply,
Passion as they, be kindlier moved than thou art?
Though with their high wrongs I am struck to th'
    quick,
Yet, with my nobler reason, 'gainst my fury
Do I take part: the rarer action is
In virtue than in vengeance: they being penitent,
The sole drift of my purpose doth extend
Not a frown further. Go, release them, Ariel. 30
My charms I'll break, their senses I'll restore,
And they shall be themselves.

ARIEL.   I'll fetch them, sir. *Vanishes*

PROSPERO [*traces a magic circle with his staff*]. Ye elves
    of hills, brooks, standing lakes and groves,
And ye, that on the sands with printless foot
Do chase the ebbing Neptune, and do fly him
When he comes back; you demi-puppets that
By moonshine do the green-sour ringlets make,
Whereof the ewe not bites: and you, whose pastime
Is to make midnight mushrooms, that rejoice
To hear the solemn curfew,—by whose aid, 40
Weak ministers though ye be, I have bedimmed
The noontide sun, called forth the mutinous winds,
And 'twixt the green sea and the azured vault
Set roaring war: to the dread rattling thunder
Have I given fire, and rifted Jove's stout oak
With his own bolt: the strong-based promontory
Have I made shake, and by the spurs plucked up
The pine and cedar: graves at my command
Have waked their sleepers, oped, and let 'em forth
By my so potent art. But this rough magic 50
I here abjure: and, when I have required
Some heavenly music—which even now I do—
To work mine end upon their senses, that
This airy charm is for, I'll break my staff,
Bury it certain fathoms in the earth,
And deeper than did ever plummet sound
I'll drown my book.   *Solemn music*

*Here enters Ariel before: then Alonso, with a frantic
gesture, attended by Gonzalo; Sebastian and Antonio in
like manner, attended by Adrian and Francisco: they all
enter the circle which Prospero had made, and there stand
charmed; which Prospero observing, speaks*

A solemn air, and the best comforter   *To Alonso*
To an unsettled fancy, cure thy brains,
Now useless boil within thy skull. There stand, 60
For you are spell-stopped....
Holy Gonzalo, honourable man,
Mine eyes, ev'n sociable to the show of thine,
Fall fellowly drops ... The charm dissolves apace,
And as the morning steals upon the night,
Melting the darkness, so their rising senses
Begin to chase the ignorant fumes that mantle
Their clearer reason.... O good Gonzalo,
My true preserver, and a loyal sir
To him thou follow'st; I will pay thy graces 70
Home, both in word and deed ... Most cruelly
Didst thou, Alonso, use me and my daughter:

Thy brother was a furtherer in the act—
Thou art pinched for't now, Sebastian. Flesh and
    blood,
You, brother mine, that entertained ambition,
Expelled remorse and nature—who, with Sebastian,
(Whose inward pinches therefore are most strong)
Would here have killed your king—I do forgive
    thee,
Unnatural though thou art ... Their understanding
Begins to swell, and the approaching tide 80
Will shortly fill the reasonable shores
That now lies foul and muddy. Not one of them
That yet looks on me, or would know me. Ariel,
Fetch me the hat and rapier in my cell.
                            Ariel goes to the cave
I will discase me, and myself present
As I was sometime Milan: quickly spirit,
Thou shalt ere long be free.

Returning Ariel sings, and helps to attire him

ARIEL. Where the bee sucks, there suck I.
        In a cowslip's bell I lie.
        There I couch, when owls do cry. 90
        On the bat's back I do fly
        After summer merrily....
    Merrily, merrily, shall I live now,
    Under the blossom that hangs on the bough.

PROSPERO. Why, that's my dainty Ariel: I shall miss
    thee,
But yet thou shalt have freedom: so, so, so....
To the king's ship, invisible as thou art—
There shalt thou find the mariners asleep
Under the hatches: the master and the boatswain
Being awake, enforce them to this place; 100
And presently, I prithee.

ARIEL. I drink the air before me, and return
Or ere your pulse twice beat.   *Vanishes*

GONZALO. All torment, trouble, wonder, and
    amazement
Inhabits here: some heavenly power guide us
Out of this fearful country.

PROSPERO.   Behold, sir king,
The wrongèd Duke of Milan, Prospero:
For more assurance that a living prince
Does now speak to thee, I embrace thy body,
And to thee and thy company I bid 110
A hearty welcome.

ALONSO.   Whe'er thou be'st he or no,
Or some enchanted trifle to abuse me,
As late I have been, I not know: thy pulse
Beats, as of flesh and blood: and, since I saw thee,
Th'affliction of my mind amends, with which
I fear a madness held me: this must crave—
An if this be at all—a most strange story.
Thy dukedom I resign, and do entreat
Thou pardon me my wrongs ... But how should
    Prospero
Be living, and be here?

PROSPERO [*to Gonzalo*]. First, noble friend, 120
Let me embrace thine age, whose honour cannot
Be measured or confined.

GONZALO.   Whether this be
Or be not, I'll not swear.

PROSPERO.   You do yet taste
Some subtilties o'th'isle, that will not let you
Believe things certain: Welcome, my friends all!

[*aside to Sebastian and Antonio*] But you, my brace of
      lords, were I so minded,
I here could pluck his highness' frown upon you,
And justify you traitors: at this time
I will tell no tales.
SEBASTIAN [*aside to Antonio*]. The devil speaks in
      him ...
PROSPERO. No ...   130
For you—most wicked sir—whom to call brother
Would even infect my mouth, I do forgive
Thy rankest fault—all of them; and require
My dukedom of thee, which, perforce, I know,
Thou must restore.
ALONSO.   If thou beest Prospero,
Give us particulars of thy preservation,
How thou hast met us here, who three hours since
Were wrecked upon this shore; where I have lost—
How sharp the point of this remembrance is!—
My dear son Ferdinand.
PROSPERO.   I am woe for't, sir.   140
ALONSO. Irreparable is the loss, and patience
Says it is past her cure.
PROSPERO.   I rather think
You have not sought her help, of whose soft grace
For the like loss I have her sovereign aid,
And rest myself content.
ALONSO.   You the like loss?
PROSPERO. As great to me as late, and súpportable
To make the dear loss, have I means much weaker
Than you may call to comfort you; for I
Have lost my daughter.
ALONSO.   A daughter?
O heavens, that they were living both in Naples, 150
The king and queen there! that they were, I wish
Myself were mudded in that oozy bed
Where my son lies ... When did you lose your
      daughter?
PROSPERO. In this last tempest.... I perceive these lords
At this encounter do so much admire
That they devour their reason, and scarce think
Their eyes do offices of truth, their words
Are natural breath: but, howsoe'er you have
Been justled from your senses, know for certain,
That I am Prospero, and that very duke   160
Which was thrust forth of Milan, who most
      strangely
Upon this shore, where you were wrecked, was
      landed,
To be the lord on't: No more yet of this,
For 'tis a chronicle of day by day,
Not a relation for a breakfast, nor
Befitting this first meeting: Welcome, sir;
This cell's my court: here have I few attendants,
And subjects none abroad: pray you, look in:
My dukedom since you have given me again,
I will requite you with as good a thing—   170
At least, bring forth a wonder, to content ye
As much as me my dukedom.

*Here Prospero discovers Ferdinand and Miranda, playing
at chess*

MIRANDA. Sweet lord, you play me false.
FERDINAND.   My dearest love,
I would not for the world.
MIRANDA. Yet, for a score of kingdoms you should
      wrangle,

And I would call it fair play.
ALONSO.   If this prove
A vision of the island, one dear son
Shall I twice lose.
SEBASTIAN.   A most high miracle!
FERDINAND. Though the seas threaten, they are
      merciful—
I have cursed them without cause.   *He kneels*
ALONSO.   Now all the blessings 180
Of a glad father compass thee about:
Arise, and say how thou cam'st here.
MIRANDA.   O, wonder!
How many goodly creatures are there here!
How beauteous mankind is! O brave new world,
That has such people in't!
PROSPERO.   'Tis new to thee.
ALONSO. What is this maid, with whom thou wast at
      play?
Your eld'st acquaintance cannot be three hours:
Is she the goddess that hath severed us,
And brought us thus together?
FERDINAND.   Sir, she is mortal;
But, by immortal Providence, she's mine;   190
I chose her when I could not ask my father
For his advice, nor thought I had one: She
Is daughter to this famous Duke of Milan,
Of whom so often I have heard renown,
But never saw before: of whom I have
Received a second life; and second father
This lady makes him to me.
ALONSO.   I am hers;
But O, how oddly will it sound, that I
Must ask my child forgiveness!
PROSPERO.   There, sir, stop.
Let us not burden our remembrance with   200
A heaviness that's gone.
GONZALO.   I have inly wept,
Or should have spoke ere this ... Look down, you
      gods,
And on this couple drop a blessèd crown;
For it is you that have chalked forth the way
Which brought us hither.
ALONSO.   I say 'Amen,' Gonzalo.
GONZALO. Was Milan thrust from Milan, that his issue
Should become kings of Naples? O, rejoice
Beyond a common joy, and set it down
With gold on lasting pillars: 'In one voyage
Did Claribel her husband find at Tunis,   210
And Ferdinand, her brother, found a wife,
Where he himself was lost, Prospero his dukedom
In a poor isle, and all of us ourselves,
When no man was his own.'
ALONSO [*to Ferdinand and Miranda*]. Give me your
      hands:
Let grief and sorrow still embrace his heart
That doth not wish you joy.
GONZALO.   Be it so, Amen.

*Enter Ariel with the Master and Boatswain amazedly
following*

O look sir, look sir, here is more of us ...
I prophesied, if a gallows were on land,
This fellow could not drown. Now, blasphemy,
That swear'st grace o'er-board, not an oath on
      shore?   220
Hast thou no mouth by land?

What is the news?
BOATSWAIN. The best news is, that we have safely
  found
  Our king and company: the next, our ship,
  Which, but three glasses since, we gave out split,
  Is tight and yare and bravely rigged as when
  We first put out to sea.
ARIEL [*at Prospero's ear*]. Sir, all this service
  Have I done since I went.
PROSPERO.   My tricksy spirit!
ALONSO. These are not natural events—they
  strengthen
  From strange to stranger: say, how came you hither? 230
BOATSWAIN. If I did think, sir, I were well awake,
  I'ld strive to tell you ... We were dead of sleep,
  And—how we know not—all clapped under
  hatches,
  Where, but even now, with strange and several
  noises
  Of roaring, shrieking, howling, jingling chains,
  And moe diversity of sounds, all horrible,
  We were awaked ... straightway, at liberty;
  Where we, in all her trim, freshly beheld
  Our royal, good, and gallant ship: our master
  Cap'ring to eye her ... On a trice, so please you, 240
  Even in a dream, were we divided from them,
  And were brought moping hither.
ARIEL [*at Prospero's ear*].   Was't well done?
PROSPERO. Bravely, my diligence,—thou shalt be free.
ALONSO. This is as strange a maze as e'er men trod.
  And there is in this business more than nature
  Was ever conduct of: some oracle
  Must rectify our knowledge.
PROSPERO.   Sir, my liege,
  Do not infest your mind with beating on
  The strangeness of this business. At picked leisure,
  Which shall be shortly single, I'll resolve you— 250
  Which to you shall seem probable—of every
  These happened accidents: till when, be cheerful
  And think of each thing well.... [*to Ariel*] Come
  hither, spirit.
  Set Caliban and his companions free:
  Untie the spell ... [*Ariel goes*] How fares my
  gracious sir?
  There are yet missing of your company
  Some few odd lads, that you remember not.

Enter Ariel, driving in Caliban, Stephano, and Trinculo,
in their stolen apparel

STEPHANO. Every man shift for all the rest, and let no
  man take care for himself; for all is but fortune:
  coragio, bully-monster, coragio! 260
TRINCULO. If these be true spies which I wear in my
  head, here's a goodly sight.
CALIBAN. O Setebos, these be brave spirits, indeed!
  How fine my master is! I am afraid
  He will chastise me.
SEBASTIAN.   Ha, ha!
  What things are these, my lord Antonio?
  Will money buy 'em?
ANTONIO.   Very like: one of them
  Is a plain fish, and no doubt marketable.
PROSPERO. Mark but the badges of these men, my
  lords,
  Then say if they be true. This mis-shaped knave— 270
  His mother was a witch, and one so strong

That could control the moon, make flows and ebbs,
  And deal in her command without her power.
  These three have robbed me, and this demi-devil—
  For he's a bastard one—had plotted with them
  To take my life. Two of these fellows you
  Must know and own, this thing of darkness I
  Acknowledge mine.
CALIBAN.   I shall be pinched to death.
ALONSO. Is not this Stephano, my drunken butler?
SEBASTIAN. He is drunk now; where had he wine? 280
ALONSO. And Trinculo is reeling ripe: where should
  they
  Find this grand liquor that hath gilded 'em?
  How cam'st thou in this pickle?
TRINCULO. I have been in such a pickle since I saw you
  last that, I fear me, will never out of my bones:
  I shall not fear fly-blowing.
SEBASTIAN. Why, how now, Stephano?
STEPHANO. O, touch me not—I am not Stephano, but
  a cramp.
PROSPERO. You'ld be king o'th'isle, sirrah? 290
STEPHANO. I should have been a sore one then.
ALONSO. This is as strange a thing as e'er I looked on.
                              Pointing at Caliban
PROSPERO. He is as disproportioned in his manners
  As in his shape. Go, sirrah, to my cell;
  Take with you your companions; as you look
  To have my pardon, trim it handsomely.
CALIBAN. Ay, that I will: and I'll be wise hereafter,
  And seek for grace. What a thrice-double ass
  Was I, to take this drunkard for a god!
  And worship this dull fool!
PROSPERO.   Go to, away. 300
ALONSO. Hence—and bestow your luggage where
  you found it.
SEBASTIAN. Or stole it rather.
                Caliban, Stephano and Trinculo depart
PROSPERO. Sir, I invite your Highness and your train
  To my poor cell: where you shall take your rest
  For this one night, which—part of it—I'll waste
  With such discourse as, I not doubt, shall make it
  Go quick away ... the story of my life,
  And the particular accidents gone by
  Since I came to this isle: and in the morn
  I'll bring you to your ship, and so to Naples, 310
  Where I have hope to see the nuptial
  Of these our dear-beloved solémnizéd—
  And thence retire me to my Milan, where
  Every third thought shall be my grave.
ALONSO.   I long
  To hear the story of your life; which must
  Take the ear strangely.
PROSPERO.   I'll deliver all—
  And promise you calm seas, auspicious gales,
  And sail so expeditious, that shall catch
  Your royal fleet far off ... My Ariel—chick,
  That is thy charge: then to the elements 320
  Be free, and fare thou well ... Please you draw near.
                              They all go

EPILOGUE

SPOKEN BY PROSPERO

Now my charms are all o'erthrown,
And what strength I have's mine own,

Which is most faint: now, 'tis true,
I must be here confined by you,
Or sent to Naples. Let me not,
Since I have my dukedom got,
And pardoned the deceiver, dwell
In this bare island, by your spell.
But release me from my bands,
With the help of your good hands:
Gentle breath of yours my sails 10
Must fill, or else my project fails,
Which was to please: Now I want
Spirits to enforce ... art to enchant—
And my ending is despair,
Unless I be reliev'd by prayer,
Which pierces so, that it assaults
Mercy itself, and frees all faults....
    As you from crimes would pardoned be,
    Let your indulgence set me free. 20

The Two Gentlemen of Verona

The scene: Verona, Milan and a forest near Milan

CHARACTERS IN THE PLAY

DUKE OF MILAN, *father to Silvia*
VALENTINE ⎱ *the two gentlemen*
PROTEUS ⎰
ANTONIO, *father to Proteus*
THURIO, *a foolish rival to Valentine*
EGLAMOUR, *agent for Silvia in her escape*
SPEED, *a clownish servant to Valentine*
LAUNCE, *the like to Proteus*

PANTHINO, *servant to Antonio*
HOST, *where Julia lodges*
OUTLAWS, *with Valentine*
JULIA, *beloved of Proteus*
SILVIA, *beloved of Valentine*
LUCETTA, *waiting-woman to Julia*
Servants, musicians

The Two Gentlemen of Verona

ACT 1
Scene 1: *Verona: a street near Julia's house*

Valentine and Proteus

VALENTINE. Cease to persuade, my loving Proteus;
Home-keeping youth have ever homely wits.
Were't not affection chains thy tender days
To the sweet glances of thy honoured love,
I rather would entreat thy company
To see the wonders of the world abroad,
Than, living dully sluggardized at home,
Wear out thy youth with shapeless idleness....
But, since thou lov'st; love still and thrive therein,
Even as I would when I to love begin. 10
PROTEUS. Wilt thou be gone? Sweet Valentine, adieu.
Think on thy Proteus, when thou—haply—seest
Some rare note-worthy object in thy travel....
Wish me partaker in thy happiness,
When thou dost meet good hap; and in thy
danger—
If ever danger do environ thee—
Commend thy grievance to my holy prayers,
For I will be thy beadsman, Valentine.
VALENTINE. And on a love-book pray for my success!
PROTEUS. Upon some book I love I'll pray for thee. 20
VALENTINE. That's on some shallow story of deep love,
How young Leander crossed the Hellespont.
PROTEUS. That's a deep story of a deeper love,
For he was more than over-shoes in love.
VALENTINE. 'Tis true; for you are over-boots in love,
And yet you never swam the Hellespont.
PROTEUS. Over the boots? nay, give me not the boots.
VALENTINE. No, I will not; for it boots thee not.
PROTEUS.   What?
VALENTINE. To be in love; where scorn is bought
with groans:
Coy looks, with heart-sore sighs: one fading
moment's mirth, 30
With twenty watchful, weary, tedious nights;
If haply won, perhaps a hapless gain;
If lost, why then a grievous labour won;
How ever ... but a folly bought with wit,
Or else a wit by folly vanquishéd.
PROTEUS. So, by your circumstance, you call me fool.
VALENTINE. So, by your circumstance, I fear, you'll
prove.
PROTEUS. 'Tis Love you cavil at. I am not Love.
VALENTINE. Love is your master, for he masters you;
And he that is so yokéd by a fool, 40
Methinks should not be chronicled for wise.
PROTEUS. Yet writers say; As in the sweetest bud
The eating canker dwells, so eating love
Inhabits in the finest wits of all.
VALENTINE. And writers say; As the most forward bud
Is eaten by the canker ere it blow,
Even so by love the young and tender wit
Is turned to folly—blasting in the bud,
Losing his verdure even in the prime,
And all the fair effects of future hopes.... 50
But wherefore waste I time to counsel thee

That art a votary to fond desire?
Once more adieu: my father at the road
Expects my coming, there to see me shipped.
PROTEUS. And thither will I bring thee, Valentine.
VALENTINE. Sweet Proteus, no: now let us take our
leave;
To Milan let me hear from thee by letters
Of thy success in love; and what news else
Betideth here in absence of thy friend:
And I likewise will visit thee with mine. 60
PROTEUS. All happiness bechance to thee in Milan.
VALENTINE. As much to you at home: and so, farewell.
Valentine goes
PROTEUS. He after honour hunts, I after love;
He leaves his friends, to dignify them more;
I leave myself, my friends, and all for love ...
Thou, Julia, thou hast metamorphosed me:
Made me neglect my studies, loose my time;
War with good counsel; set the world at nought;
Made wit with musing, weak; heart sick with
thought.

Speed runs up

SPEED. Sir Proteus ... 'save you ... saw you my
master? 70
PROTEUS. But now he parted hence to embark for
Milan.
SPEED. Twenty to one then he is shipped already,
And I have played the sheep in losing him.
PROTEUS. Indeed a sheep doth very often stray,
An if the shepherd be awhile away.
SPEED. You conclude that my master is a shepherd
then, and I a sheep?
PROTEUS. I do.
SPEED. Why then my horns are his horns, whether
I wake or sleep.
PROTEUS. A silly answer, and fitting well a sheep.
SPEED. This proves me still a sheep. 80
PROTEUS. True: and thy master a shepherd.
SPEED. Nay, that I can deny by a circumstance.
PROTEUS. It shall go hard but I'll prove it by another.
SPEED. The shepherd seeks the sheep, and not the sheep
the shepherd; but I seek my master, and my master
seeks not me: therefore I am no sheep.
PROTEUS. The sheep for fodder follow the shepherd,
the shepherd for food follows not the sheep: thou for
wages followest thy master, thy master for wages
follows not thee: therefore thou art a sheep. 90
SPEED. Such another proof will make me cry 'baa.'
PROTEUS. But dost thou hear? gav'st thou my letter to
Julia?
SPEED. Ay, sir: I, a lost mutton, gave your letter to
her, a laced mutton, and she, a laced mutton, gave
me, a lost mutton, nothing for my labour.
PROTEUS. Here's too small a pasture for such store of
muttons.
SPEED. If the ground be overcharged, you were best
stick her. 100
PROTEUS. Nay, in that you are a-stray ... 'twere best
pound you.

SPEED. Nay sir, less than a pound shall serve me for carrying your letter.

PROTEUS. You mistake; I mean the pound, a pinfold.

SPEED. From a pound to a pin—fold it over and over, 'Tis threefold too little for carrying a letter to your lover.

PROTEUS. But what said she? [*Speed nods*] Nod?

SPEED. Ay.

PROTEUS. Nod-ay, why that's noddy.   110

SPEED. You mistook, sir: I say she did nod; and you ask me if she did nod, and I say, 'Ay.'

PROTEUS. And that set together, is 'noddy.'

SPEED. Now you have taken the pains to set it together, take it for your pains.

PROTEUS. No, no, you shall have it for bearing the letter.

SPEED. Well, I perceive I must be fain to bear with you.

PROTEUS. Why, sir, how do you bear with me?

SPEED. Marry sir, the letter very orderly—having 120 nothing but the word 'noddy' for my pains.

PROTEUS. Beshrew me, but you have a quick wit.

SPEED. And yet it cannot overtake your slow purse.

PROTEUS. Come, come, open the matter in brief; what said she?

SPEED. Open your purse, that the money and the matter may be both at once delivered.

PROTEUS. Well, sir: here is for your pains . . . What said she?

SPEED. Truly sir, I think you'll hardly win her.   130

PROTEUS. Why! couldst thou perceive so much from her?

SPEED. Sir, I could perceive nothing at all from her;
No, not so much as a ducat for delivering
   your letter:
And being so hard to me that brought your
   mind;
I fear she'll prove as hard to you in telling your
   mind. . . .
Give her no token but stones, for she's as hard as
   steel.

PROTEUS. What, said she—nothing?

SPEED. No, not so much as 'Take this for thy pains' . . .
To testify your bounty, I thank you, you have 140
testerned me; in requital whereof, henceforth carry
your letters yourself; and so, sir, I'll commend you
to my master.   *He goes off*

PROTEUS. Go, go, be gone, to save your ship from
   wrack,
Which cannot perish having thee aboard,
Being destined to a drier death on shore . . .
I must go send some better messenger.
I fear my Julia would not deign my lines,
Receiving them from such a worthless post.
                                    He goes

Scene 2

Enter Julia and Lucetta

JULIA. But say, Lucetta—now we are alone—
Wouldst thou then counsel me to fall in love?

LUCETTA. Ay madam, so you stumble not unheedfully.

JULIA. Of all the fair resort of gentlemen
That every day with parle encounter me,
In thy opinion which is worthiest love?

LUCETTA. Please you repeat their names, I'll show my mind
According to my shallow simple skill.

JULIA. What think'st thou of the fair Sir Eglamour? 10

LUCETTA. As of a knight, well-spoken, neat, and fine;
But, were I you, he never should be mine.

JULIA. What think'st thou of the rich Mercatio?

LUCETTA. Well of his wealth; but of himself, so, so.

JULIA. What think'st thou of the gentle Proteus?

LUCETTA. Lord, lord . . . to see what folly reigns in us!

JULIA. How now! what means this passion at his name?

LUCETTA. Pardon, dear madam—'tis a passing shame,
That I (unworthy body as I am!)
Should censure thus on lovely gentlemen.   20

JULIA. Why not on Proteus, as of all the rest?

LUCETTA. Then thus . . . of many good I think him best.

JULIA. Your reason?

LUCETTA. I have no other but a woman's reason:
I think him so, because I think him so.

JULIA. And wouldst thou have me cast my love on him?

LUCETTA. Ay . . . if you thought your love not cast away.

JULIA. Why, he, of all the rest, hath never moved me.

LUCETTA. Yet he, of all the rest, I think best loves ye.

JULIA. His little speaking shows his love but small. 30

LUCETTA. Fire, that's closest kept, burns most of all.

JULIA. They do not love, that do not show their love.

LUCETTA. O they love least, that let me know their love.

JULIA. I would, I knew his mind.

LUCETTA. Peruse this paper, madam.

JULIA. 'To Julia' . . . Say, from whom?

LUCETTA. That the contents will show.

JULIA. Say, say . . . who gave it thee?

LUCETTA. Sir Valentine's page: and sent,
I think, from Proteus;   40
He would have given it you, but I, being in
   the way,
Did in your name receive it: pardon the fault, I pray.

JULIA. Now—by my modesty!—a goodly broker . . .
Dare you presume to harbour wanton lines?
To whisper, and conspire against my youth?
Now trust me, 'tis an office of great worth,
And you an officer fit for the place . . .
There . . . take the paper . . . see it be returned,
Or else return no more into my sight.

LUCETTA. To plead for love deserves more fee
   than hate.   50

JULIA. Will you be gone?

LUCETTA [*going within*]. That you may ruminate.

JULIA. And yet I would I had o'erlooked the letter;
It were a shame to call her back again,
And pray her to a fault for which I chid her. . . .
What 'fool is she, that knows I am a maid,
And would not force the letter to my view?
Since maids, in modesty, say 'no' to that
Which they would have the profferer construe
   'ay'. . . .
Fie, fie! how wayward is this foolish love;
That, like a testy babe, will scratch the nurse, 60
And presently, all humbled, kiss the rod!
How churlishly I chid Lucetta hence,
When willingly I would have had her here!
How angerly I taught my brow to frown,

When inward joy enforced my heart to smile!
My penance is, to call Lucetta back
And ask remission for my folly past....
What ho! Lucetta!

Lucetta returns

LUCETTA.   What would your ladyship?
JULIA. Is it near dinner-time?
LUCETTA.   I would it were—
That you might kill your stomach on your meat, 70
And not upon your maid.
JULIA.   What is't that you
Took up so gingerly?
LUCETTA.   Nothing.
JULIA.   Why didst thou stoop then?
LUCETTA. To take a paper up, that I let fall.
JULIA.   And is that paper nothing?
LUCETTA.   Nothing concerning me.
JULIA. Then let it lie, for those that it concerns.
LUCETTA. Madam, it will not lie where it concerns,
Unless it have a false interpreter.
JULIA. Some love of yours hath writ to you in rhyme.
LUCETTA. That I might sing it, madam, to a
tune ...   80
Give me a note—your ladyship can set.
JULIA. As little by such toys as may be possible:
Best sing it to the tune of 'Light o' love.'
LUCETTA. It is too heavy for so light a tune.
JULIA. Heavy? belike it hath some burden then.
LUCETTA. Ay ... and melodious were it, would you
sing it.
JULIA. And why not you?
LUCETTA.   I cannot reach so high.
JULIA. Let's see your song ...

She snatches at the letter

                    How now, minion!
LUCETTA. Keep tune there still; so you will sing it
out ...
And yet, methinks, I do not like this tune.   90
JULIA. You do not?
LUCETTA.   No, madam, 'tis too sharp.
JULIA. You—minion—are too saucy.
LUCETTA.   Nay, now you are too flat;
And mar the concord, with too harsh a descant:
There wanteth but a 'mean' to fill your song.
JULIA. The mean is drowned with your unruly bass.
LUCETTA. Indeed, I 'bid the base' for Proteus.
JULIA. This babble shall not henceforth trouble me;
                    She tears the letter
Here is a coil with protestation ...
Go, get you gone ... and let the papers
lie ...
You would be fingring them, to anger me.   100
LUCETTA. She makes it strange, but she would be
best pleased
To be so angred with another letter.
                    She goes within
JULIA. Nay, would I were so angred with the
same ...
O hateful hands, to tear such loving words;
Injurious wasps, to feed on such sweet honey,
And kill the bees that yield it with your stings;
I'll kiss each several paper, for amends ...
Look, here is writ 'kind Julia' ... unkind Julia,
As in revenge of thy ingratitude,

I throw thy name against the bruising stones,   110
Trampling contemptuously on thy disdain....
And here is writ 'love-wounded Proteus'....
Poor wounded name: my bosom, as a bed,
Shall lodge thee till thy wound be throughly
healed;
And thus I search it with a sovereign kiss....
But twice, or thrice, was 'Proteus' written
down ...
Be calm, good wind, blow not a word away,
Till I have found each letter in the letter,
Except mine own name: that, some whirlwind
bear
Unto a ragged, fearful-hanging rock,   120
And throw it thence into the raging sea....
Lo, here in one line is his name twice writ:
'Poor forlorn Proteus, passionate Proteus:
To the sweet Julia' ... that I'll tear away ...
And yet I will not, sith so prettily
He couples it to his complaining names;
Thus will I fold them, one upon another;
Now kiss, embrace, contend, do what you will.

Lucetta returns

LUCETTA. Madam ...
Dinner is ready ... and your father stays.   130
JULIA. Well, let us go.
LUCETTA. What, shall these papers lie like tell-tales
here?
JULIA. If you respect them, best to take them up.
LUCETTA. Nay, I was taken up for laying them
down....
Yet here they shall not lie, for catching cold.
JULIA. I see you have a month's mind to them.
LUCETTA. Ay, madam, you may say what sights
you see;
I see things too, although you judge I wink.
JULIA. Come, come, will't please you go?   *They go*

Scene 3: *Verona: Antonio's house*

Antonio enters with Panthino, his man

ANTONIO. Tell me, Panthino, what sad talk was
that,
Wherewith my brother held you in the cloister?
PANTHINO. 'Twas of his nephew Proteus, your son.
ANTONIO. Why? what of him?
PANTHINO.   He wondred that your lordship
Would suffer him to spend his youth at home,
While other men, of slender reputation,
Put forth their sons to seek preferment out:
Some to the wars, to try their fortune there;
Some, to discover islands far away;
Some, to the studious universities.   10
For any or for all these exercises
He said that Proteus, your son, was meet;
And did request me to importune you
To let him spend his time no more at home;
Which would be great impeachment to his age,
In having known no travel in his youth.
ANTONIO. Nor need'st thou much importune me to
that
Whereon this month I have been hammering....
I have considered well his loss of time,
And how he cannot be a perfect man,   20

Not being tried and tutored in the world:
Experience is by industry achieved,
And perfected by the swift course of time:
Then, tell me, whither were I best to send him?
PANTHINO. I think your lordship is not ignorant,
How his companion, youthful Valentine,
Attends the emperor in his royal court.
ANTONIO. I know it well.
PANTHINO. 'Twere good, I think, your lordship sent
him thither.
There shall he practise tilts and tournaments,   30
Hear sweet discourse, converse with noblemen,
And· be in eye of every exercise
Worthy his youth and nobleness of birth.
ANTONIO. I like thy counsel ... well hast thou
advised ...
And that thou mayst perceive how well I like it,
The execution of it shall make known;
Even with the speediest expedition
I will despatch him to the emperor's court.
PANTHINO. To-morrow, may it please you, Don
Alphonso,
With other gentlemen of good esteem,   40
Are journeying to salute the emperor,
And to commend their service to his will.
ANTONIO. Good company: with them shall Proteus
go ...

Proteus enters

And in good time ... now will we break with him.
PROTEUS. Sweet love, sweet lines, sweet life—
Here is her hand, the agent of her heart;
Here is her oath for love, her honour's pawn:
O, that our fathers would applaud our loves,
To seal our happiness with their consents....
O heavenly Julia....   50
ANTONIO. How now! what letter are you reading
there?
PROTEUS. May't please your lordship, 'tis a word or
two
Of commendations sent from Valentine;
Delivered by a friend that came from him.
ANTONIO. Lend me the letter: let me see what news.
PROTEUS. There is no news, my lord, but that he
writes
How happily he lives, how well beloved,
And daily gracéd by the emperor;
Wishing me with him, partner of his fortune.
ANTONIO. And how stand you affected to his wish?   60
PROTEUS. As one relying on your lordship's will,
And not depending on his friendly wish.
ANTONIO. My will is something sorted with his wish:
Muse not that I thus suddenly proceed;
For what I will, I will, and there an end ...
I am resolved that thou shalt spend some time
With Valentinus in the emperor's court:
What maintenance he from his friends receives,
Like exhibition thou shalt have from me.
To-morrow be in readiness to go—   70
Excuse it not ... for I am péremptory.
PROTEUS. My lord, I cannot be so soon provided,
Please you deliberate a day or two.
ANTONIO. Look, what thou want'st shall be sent
after thee:
No more of stay; to-morrow thou must go:
Come on, Panthino; you shall be employed
To hasten on his expedition.
                    Antonio goes out, followed by Panthino
PROTEUS. Thus have I shunned the fire, for fear of
burning,
And drenched me in the sea, where I am
drowned....
I feared to show my father Julia's letter,   80
Lest he should take exceptions to my love,
And with the vantage of mine own excuse
Hath he excepted most against my love....
O, how this spring of love resembleth
The uncertain glory of an April day,
Which now shows all the beauty of the sun,
And by and by a cloud takes all away.

Panthino returns

PANTHINO. Sir Proteus, your father calls for you—
He is in haste,, therefore I pray you go.
PROTEUS. Why, this it is: my heart accords thereto,   90
And yet a thousand times it answers 'no.'
                                He goes out

ACT 2
Scene 1: *A street in Milan*

Enter Valentine with Speed following

SPEED. Sir, your glove.
VALENTINE. Not mine: my gloves are on.
SPEED. Why then this may be yours, for this is but one.
VALENTINE. Ha! let me see ... ay, give it me, it's
mine ...
Sweet ornament that decks a thing divine—
Ah Silvia, Silvia.
SPEED [*calls*]. Madam Silvia! Madam Silvia!
VALENTINE. How now, sirrah!
SPEED. She is not within hearing, sir.
VALENTINE. Why, sir, who bade you call her?   10
SPEED. Your worship, sir, or else I mistook.
VALENTINE. Well: you'll still be too forward.
SPEED. And yet I was last chidden for being too slow.
VALENTINE. Go to, sir, tell me: do you know Madam
Silvia?
SPEED. She that your worship loves?
VALENTINE. Why, how know you that I am in love?
SPEED. Marry, by these special marks: first, you have
learned—like Sir Proteus—to wreath your arms
like a malcontent; to relish a love-song, like a robin-   20
redbreast; to walk alone, like one that had the
pestilence; to sigh, like a school-boy that had lost
his A B C; to weep, like a young wench that
had buried her grandam; to fast, like one that takes
diet; to watch, like one that fears robbing; to speak
puling, like a beggar at Hallowmas ... You were
wont, when you laughed, to crow like a cock;
when you walked, to walk like one of the lions;
when you fasted, it was presently after dinner; when
you looked sadly, it was for want of money: and   30
now you are metamorphosed with a mistress, that,
when I look on you, I can hardly think you my
master.
VALENTINE. Are all these things perceived in me?
SPEED. They are all perceived without ye.
VALENTINE. Without me? they cannot.
SPEED. Without you? nay, that's certain; for, without
you were so simple, none else would: but you are so

without these follies, that these follies are within
you, and shine through you like the water in an 40
urinal: that not an eye that sees you, but is a physician
to comment on your malady.
VALENTINE. But tell me: dost thou know my Lady
Silvia?
SPEED. She that you gaze on so, as she sits at supper?
VALENTINE. Hast thou observed that? even she I mean.
SPEED. Why sir, I know her not.
VALENTINE. Dost thou know her by my gazing on her,
and yet know'st her not?
SPEED. Is she not hard-favoured, sir?   50
VALENTINE. Not so fair, boy, as well-favoured.
SPEED. Sir, I know that well enough.
VALENTINE. What dost thou know?
SPEED. That she is not so fair, as (of you) well-
favoured.
VALENTINE. I mean that her beauty is exquisite, but her
favour infinite.
SPEED. That's because the one is painted, and the other
out of all count.
VALENTINE. How painted? and how out of count?   60
SPEED. Marry, sir, so painted, to make her fair, that no
man counts of her beauty.
VALENTINE. How esteem'st thou me? I account of her
beauty.
SPEED. You never saw her since she was deformed.
VALENTINE. How long hath she been deformed?
SPEED. Ever since you loved her.
VALENTINE. I have loved her ever since I saw her, and
still I see her beautiful.
SPEED. If you love her, you cannot see her.   70
VALENTINE. Why?
SPEED. Because love is blind ... O, that you had mine
eyes, or your own eyes had the lights they were
wont to have, when you chid at Sir Proteus for
going ungartered.
VALENTINE. What should I see then?
SPEED. Your own present folly, and her passing de-
formity: for he, being in love, could not see to garter
his hose; and you, being in love, cannot see to put on
your hose.   80
VALENTINE. Belike, boy, then you are in love—for last
morning you could not see to wipe my shoes.
SPEED. True, sir: I was in love with my bed. I thank
you, you swinged me for my love, which makes me
the bolder to chide you for yours.
VALENTINE. In conclusion, I stand affected to her.
SPEED. I would you were set, so your affection would
cease.
VALENTINE. Last night she enjoined me to write some
lines to one she loves.   90
SPEED. And have you?
VALENTINE. I have.
SPEED. Are they not lamely writ?
VALENTINE. No, boy, but as well as I can do them ...
Peace, here she comes.

Silvia approaches

SPEED. O excellent motion ... O exceeding puppet ...
now will he interpret to her.
VALENTINE. Madam and mistress, a thousand good-
morrows.
SPEED. O, 'give-ye-good-e'en ... here's a million of 10c
manners!

SILVIA. Sir Valentine and servant, to you two thou-
sand.
SPEED. He should give her interest: and she gives it
him.
VALENTINE. As you enjoined me; I have writ your
letter
Unto the secret nameless friend of yours ...
Which I was much unwilling to proceed in,
But for my duty to your ladyship.
SILVIA. I thank you, gentle servant—'tis very clerkly
done.   110
VALENTINE. Now trust me, madam, it came hardly off:
For, being ignorant to whom it goes,
I writ at random, very doubtfully.
SILVIA. Perchance you think too much of so much
pains?
VALENTINE. No, madam, so it stead you, I will
write—
Please you command—a thousand times as much ...
And yet—
SILVIA. A pretty period ... well ... I guess the sequel;
'And yet I will not name it': 'and yet I care not'....
And yet take this again: and yet I thank you: 120
Meaning henceforth to trouble you no more.
SPEED. And yet you will: and yet another 'yet.'
VALENTINE [*flushing*]. What means your ladyship? Do
you not like it?
SILVIA. Yes, yes: the lines are very quaintly writ,
But—since unwillingly—take them again....
Nay, take them.
VALENTINE.   Madam, they are for you.
SILVIA. Ay, ay: you writ them, sir, at my request,
But I will none of them: they are for you:
I would have had them writ more movingly ...
VALENTINE. Please you, I'll write your ladyship
another.   130
SILVIA. And when it's writ ... for my sake read it
over,
And, if it please you, so ... if not ... why, so ...
VALENTINE. If it please me, madam, what then?
SILVIA. Why, if it please you, take it for your labour;
And so good-morrow, servant.   *She passes on*
SPEED. O jest unseen ... inscrutable ... invisible,
As a nose on a man's face, or a weathercock on a
steeple ...
My master sues to her: and she hath taught her
suitor,
He being her pupil, to become her tutor....
O excellent device! was there ever heard a better? 140
That my master, being scribe, to himself should
write the letter?
VALENTINE. How now, sir! what are you reasoning
with yourself?
SPEED. Nay ... I was rhyming ... 'tis you that have the
reason.
VALENTINE. To do what?
SPEED. To be a spokesman from Madam Silvia.
VALENTINE. To whom?
SPEED. To yourself ... why, she wooes you by a figure.
VALENTINE. What figure?   150
SPEED. By a letter, I should say.
VALENTINE. Why, she hath not writ to me?
SPEED. What need she, when she hath made you write
to yourself? Why, do you not perceive the jest?
VALENTINE. No, believe me.
SPEED. No believing you indeed, sir:

But did you perceive her earnest?
VALENTINE. She gave me none, except an angry word.
SPEED. Why, she hath given you a letter.
VALENTINE. That's the letter I writ to her friend.   160
SPEED. And that letter hath she delivered, and there an end.
VALENTINE. I would it were no worse.
SPEED. I'll warrant you, 'tis as well:
For often you have writ to her: and she, in modesty,
Or else for want of idle time, could not again reply—
Or fearing else some messenger, that might her mind discover,
Herself hath taught her love himself to write unto her lover!
All this I speak in print, for in print I found it....
Why muse you, sir? 'tis dinner-time.   170
VALENTINE. I have dined.
SPEED. Ay, but hearken, sir: though the chameleon Love can feed on the air, I am one that am nourished by my victuals; and would fain have meat: O, be not like your mistress—be moved, be moved.

They move on

Scene 2: *Verona: the street near Julia's house*

Enter Proteus and Julia

PROTEUS. Have patience, gentle Julia ...
JULIA. I must, where is no remedy.
PROTEUS. When possibly I can, I will return.
JULIA. If you turn not ... you will return the sooner:
Keep this remembrance for thy Julia's sake.

She gives him a ring

PROTEUS. Why then we'll make exchange; here, take you this.
JULIA. And seal the bargain with a holy kiss.
PROTEUS. Here is my hand for my true constancy ...
And when that hour o'er-slips me in the day,
Wherein I sigh not, Julia, for thy sake,   10
The next ensuing hour home foul mischance
Torment me for my love's forgetfulness ...
My father stays my coming ... answer not ...
The tide is now; nay, not thy tide of tears—
That tide will stay me longer than I should....
Julia, farewell ...   *She goes within*
What! gone without a word?
Ay, so true love should do: it cannot speak—
For truth hath better deeds than words to grace it.

Panthino appears

PANTHINO. Sir Proteus! you are stayed for.
PROTEUS.   Go ... I come, I come ...
Alas, this parting strikes poor lovers dumb.   20

He goes

Scene 3

Launce approaches, leading a dog

LAUNCE. Nay, 'twill be this hour ere I have done weeping: all the kind of the Launces have this very fault ... I have received my proportion, like the Prodigious Son, and am going with Sir Proteus to the Imperial's court ... I think Crab, my dog, be the sourest-natured dog that lives: my mother weeping; my father wailing; my sister crying; our maid howling; our cat wringing her hands; and all our house

in a great perplexity—yet did not this cruel-hearted cur shed one tear: he is a stone, a very pebble-stone,   10 and has no more pity in him than a dog: a Jew would have wept to have seen our parting: why, my grandam having no eyes, look you, wept herself blind at my parting: nay, I'll show you the manner of it.... This shoe is my father ... no, this left shoe is my father; no, no, this left shoe is my mother ... nay, that cannot be so neither ... yes; it is so, it is so: it hath the worser sole ... this shoe, with the hole in it, is my mother, and this my father ... a vengeance on't! there 'tis.... Now, sir, this   20 staff is my sister; for, look you, she is as white as a lily, and as small as a wand: this hat is Nan, our maid: I am the dog ... no, the dog is himself, and I am the dog ... O, the dog is me, and I am myself: ay; so, so ... Now come I to my father; 'Father, your blessing': now should not the shoe speak a word for weeping: now should I kiss my father; well, he weeps on ... Now come I to my mother: O, that she could speak now, like a wood woman: well, I kiss her: why there 'tis; here's my mother's breath up and   30 down ... Now come I to my sister; mark the moan she makes ... now the dog all this while sheds not a tear; nor speaks a word: but see how I lay the dust with my tears.

Panthino returns

PANTHINO. Launce, away, away ... aboard ... thy master is shipped, and thou art to post after with oars ... What's the matter? why weep'st thou, man? Away ass, you'll lose the tide, if you tarry any longer.
LAUNCE. It is no matter if the tied were lost, for it is   40 the unkindest tied that ever any man tied.
PANTHINO. What's the unkindest tide?
LAUNCE. Why, he that's tied here, Crab, my dog.
PANTHINO. Tut, man: I mean thou'lt lose the flood, and in losing the flood lose thy voyage, and in losing thy voyage lose thy master, and in losing thy master lose thy service, and in losing thy service—why dost thou stop my mouth?
LAUNCE. For fear thou shouldst lose thy tongue.   50
PANTHINO. Where should I lose my tongue?
LAUNCE. In thy tale.
PANTHINO. In my tail!
LAUNCE. Lose the tide, and the voyage, and the master, and the service—and the tied ... Why, man, if the river were dry, I am able to fill it with my tears; if the wind were down, I could drive the boat with my sighs.
PANTHINO. Come: come away, man—I was sent to call thee.
LAUNCE. Sir ... call me what thou dar'st!   60
PANTHINO. Wilt thou go?
LAUNCE. Well, I will go.   *They depart*

Scene 4: *Milan: the Duke's palace*

Enter Valentine, Silvia, Speed and Sir Thurio

SILVIA. Servant.
VALENTINE. Mistress!
SPEED. Master, Sir Thurio frowns on you.
VALENTINE. Ay, boy, it's for love.
SPEED. Not of you.
VALENTINE. Of my mistress then.

SPEED. 'Twere good you knocked him.   *He goes out*
SILVIA. Servant, you are sad.
VALENTINE. Indeed, madam, I seem so.
THURIO. Seem you that you are not?   10
VALENTINE. Haply I do.
THURIO. So do counterfeits.
VALENTINE. So do you.
THURIO. What seem I that I am not?
VALENTINE. Wise.
THURIO. What instance of the contrary?
VALENTINE. Your folly.
THURIO. And how quote you my folly?
VALENTINE. I quote it in your jerkin.
THURIO. My jerkin is a doublet.   20
VALENTINE. Well, then, I'll double your folly.
THURIO. How!
SILVIA. What, angry, Sir Thurio? do you change
  colour?
VALENTINE. Give him leave, madam— he is a kind of
  chameleon.
THURIO. That hath more mind to feed on your blood,
  than live in your air.
VALENTINE. You have said, sir.
THURIO. Ay, sir, and done too, for this time.   30
VALENTINE. I know it well, sir, you always end ere you
  begin.
SILVIA. A fine volley of words, gentlemen, and quickly
  shot off.
VALENTINE. 'Tis indeed, madam—we thank the giver.
SILVIA. Who is that, servant?
VALENTINE. Yourself, sweet lady, for you gave the fire.
  Sir Thurio borrows his wit from your ladyship's
  looks, and spends what he borrows, kindly in your
  company.   40
THURIO. Sir, if you spend word for word with me, I
  shall make your wit bankrupt.
VALENTINE. I know it well, sir: you have an exchequer
  of words, and, I think, no other treasure to give your
  followers: for it appears by their bare liveries, that
  they live by your bare words.
SILVIA. No more, gentlemen, no more . . . Here comes
  my father.

The Duke enters

DUKE. Now, daughter Silvia, you are hard beset. . . .
  Sir Valentine, your father is in good health—   50
  What say you to a letter from your friends
  Of much good news?
VALENTINE.   My lord, I will be thankful
  To any happy messenger from thence.
DUKE. Know you Don Antonio, your countryman?
VALENTINE. Ay, my good lord, I know the gentleman
  To be of worth, and worthy estimation,
  And not without desert so well reputed.
DUKE. Hath he not a son?
VALENTINE. Ay, my good lord—a son that well
  deserves
  The honour and regard of such a father.   60
DUKE. You know him well?
VALENTINE. I know him as myself: for from our
  infancy
  We have conversed, and spent our hours together,
  And though myself have been an idle truant,
  Omitting the sweet benefit of time
  To clothe mine age with angel-like perfection . . .
  Yet hath Sir Proteus, for that's his name,

Made use and fair advantage of his days:
His years but young, but his experience old:
His head unmellowed, but his judgement ripe: 70
And, in a word, (for far behind his worth
Come all the praises that I now bestow)
He is complete in feature and in mind,
With all good grace, to grace a gentleman.
DUKE. Beshrew me, sir, but if he make this good,
He is as worthy for an empress' love,
As meet to be an emperor's counsellor . . .
Well, sir: this gentleman is come to me
With commendation from great potentates,
And here he means to spend his time awhile.   80
I think 'tis no unwelcome news to you.
VALENTINE. Should I have wished a thing, it had
  been he.
DUKE. Welcome him then according to his worth:
Silvia, I speak to you, and you, Sir Thurio—
For Valentine, I need not cite him to it.
I will send him hither to you presently.
                                        He goes out
VALENTINE. This is the gentleman I told your ladyship
Had come along with me, but that his mistress
Did hold his eyes locked in her crystal looks.
SILVIA. Belike that now she hath enfranchised them   90
Upon some other pawn for fealty.
VALENTINE. Nay, sure, I think she holds them prisoners
  still.
SILVIA. Nay, then he should be blind—and, being
  blind,
How could he see his way to seek out you?
VALENTINE. Why, lady, love hath twenty pair of eyes.
THURIO. They say that Love hath not an eye at all.
VALENTINE. To see such lovers, Thurio, as
  yourself—
Upon a homely object love can wink.
SILVIA. Have done, have done: here comes the
  gentleman.   *Thurio goes out*

Proteus enters

VALENTINE. Welcome, dear Proteus . . . Mistress, I
  beseech you,   100
Confirm his welcome with some special favour.
SILVIA. His worth is warrant for his welcome hither,
If this be he you oft have wished to hear from.
VALENTINE. Mistress, it is . . . Sweet lady, entertain him
To be my fellow-servant to your ladyship.
SILVIA [*bowing*]. Too low a mistress for so high a
  servant.
PROTEUS. Not so, sweet lady, but too mean a servant
To have a look of such a worthy mistress.
VALENTINE. Leave off discourse of disability . . .
Sweet lady, entertain him for your servant.   110
PROTEUS. My duty will I boast of, nothing else.
SILVIA. And duty never yet did want his meed. . . .
Servant, you are welcome to a worthless mistress.
PROTEUS. I'll die on him that says so, but yourself.
SILVIA. That you are welcome?
PROTEUS.   That you are worthless.

Thurio returns

THURIO. Madam, my lord your father would speak
  with you.
SILVIA. I wait upon his pleasure . . . Come, Sir Thurio,
Go with me . . . Once more, new servant, welcome;
I'll leave you to confer of home-affairs.

When you have done, we look to hear from you. 120
PROTEUS. We'll both attend upon your ladyship.
                              Silvia goes out, with Thurio
VALENTINE. Now tell me: how do all from whence
  you came?
PROTEUS. Your friends are well, and have them much
  commended.
VALENTINE. And how do yours?
PROTEUS.   I left them all in health.
VALENTINE. How does your lady? and how thrives
  your love?
PROTEUS. My tales of love were wont to weary you,
  I know you joy not in a love-discourse.
VALENTINE. Ay, Proteus, but that life is altered now.
  I have done penance for contemning Love,
  Whose high imperious thoughts have punished me 130
  With bitter fasts, with penitential groans,
  With nightly tears, and daily heart-sore sighs,
  For, in revenge of my contempt of love,
  Love hath chased sleep from my enthrallèd eyes,
  And made them watchers of mine own heart's
    sorrow....
  O, gentle Proteus, Love's a mighty lord,
  And hath so humbled me, as I confess
  There is no woe to his correction,
  Nor to his service no such joy on earth:
  Now, no discourse, except it be of love: 140
  Now can I break my fast, dine, sup, and sleep,
  Upon the very naked name of love.
PROTEUS. Enough! I read your fortune in your eye:
  Was this the idol that you worship so?
VALENTINE. Even she; and is she not a heavenly saint?
PROTEUS. No; but she is an earthly paragon.
VALENTINE. Call her divine.
PROTEUS.   I will not flatter her.
VALENTINE. O, flatter me; for love delights in praises.
PROTEUS. When I was sick, you gave me bitter pills,
  And I must minister the like to you. 150
VALENTINE. Then speak the truth by her; if not divine,
  Yet let her be a principality,
  Sovereign to all the creatures on the earth.
PROTEUS. Except my mistress.
VALENTINE.   Sweet: except not any,
  Except thou wilt except against my love.
PROTEUS. Have I not reason to prefer mine own?
VALENTINE. And I will help thee to prefer her too:
  She shall be dignified with this high honour—
  To bear my lady's train, lest the base earth
  Should from her vesture chance to steal a kiss, 160
  And, of so great a favour growing proud,
  Disdain to root the summer-swelling flower,
  And make rough winter everlastingly.
PROTEUS. Why, Valentine, what braggardism is this?
VALENTINE. Pardon me, Proteus, all I can is nothing
  To her, whose worth makes other worthies nothing;
  She is alone.
PROTEUS.   Then let her alone.
VALENTINE. Not for the world: why man, she is mine
    own,
  And I as rich in having such a jewel
  As twenty seas, if all their sand were pearl, 170
  The water nectar, and the rocks pure gold....
  Forgive me that I do not dream on thee,
  Because thou seest me dote upon my love:
  My foolish rival, that her father likes—
  Only for his possessions are so huge—

Is gone with her along, and I must after,
  For love, thou know'st, is full of jealousy.
PROTEUS. But she loves you?
VALENTINE. Ay, and we are betrothed: nay more, our
    marriage hour,
  With all the cunning manner of our flight, 180
  Determined of: how I must climb her window—
  The ladder made of cords—and all the means
  Plotted and 'greed on for my happiness....
  Good Proteus, go with me to my chamber,
  In these affairs to aid me with thy counsel.
PROTEUS. Go on before: I shall enquire you forth:
  I must unto the road, to disembark
  Some necessaries that I needs must use,
  And then I'll presently attend you.
VALENTINE. Will you make haste? 190
PROTEUS. I will....   *Valentine departs*
  Even as one heat another heat expels,
  Or as one nail by strength drives out another,
  So the remembrance of my former love
  Is by a newer object quite forgotten.
  It is mine.... or Valentine's praise,
  Her true perfection, or my false transgression,
  That makes me, reasonless, to reason thus?
  She is fair; and so is Julia that I love—
  That I did love, for now my love is thawed, 200
  Which, like a waxen image 'gainst a fire,
  Bears no impression of the thing it was....
  Methinks my zeal to Valentine is cold,
  And that I love him not as I was wont:
  O, but I love his lady too-too much,
  And that's the reason I love him so little....
  How shall I dote on her with more advice,
  That thus without advice begin to love her?
  'Tis but her picture I have yet beheld,
  And that hath dazzlèd my reason's light: 210
  But when I look on her perfections,
  There is no reason but I shall be blind....
  If I can check my erring love, I will—
  If not, to compass her I'll use my skill.
                                          He goes out

Scene 5: *Milan: a street*

Speed meeting Launce

SPEED. Launce! by mine honesty, welcome to Padua.
LAUNCE. Forswear not thyself, sweet youth, for I am
  not welcome.... I reckon this always—that a man is
  never undone till he be hanged, nor never welcome
  to a place till some certain shot be paid and the
  hostess say 'welcome.'
SPEED. Come on, you madcap: I'll to the alehouse with
  you presently; where, for one shot of five pence,
  thou shalt have five thousand welcomes ... But,
  sirrah, how did thy master part with Madam Julia? 10
LAUNCE. Marry, after they closed in earnest, they
  parted very fairly in jest.
SPEED. But shall she marry him?
LAUNCE. No.
SPEED. How then? Shall he marry her?
LAUNCE. No, neither.
SPEED. What, are they broken?
LAUNCE. No; they are both as whole as a fish.
SPEED. Why then, how stands the matter with them?
LAUNCE. Marry, thus—when it stands well with him, 20
  it stands well with her.

SPEED. What an ass art thou! I understand thee not.

LAUNCE. What a block art thou, that thou canst not!
My staff understands me!

SPEED. What thou sayst?

LAUNCE. Ay, and what I do too: look thee, I'll but lean,
and my staff understands me.

SPEED. It stands under thee, indeed.

LAUNCE. Why, stand under ... and understand is all
one.   30

SPEED. But tell me true, will't be a match?

LAUNCE. Ask my dog—if he say 'ay,' it will: if he say
'no,' it will: if he shake his tail and say nothing, it
will.

SPEED. The conclusion is then, that it will.

LAUNCE. Thou shalt never get such a secret from me,
but by a parable.

SPEED. 'Tis well that I get it so ... But Launce, how
sayst thou, that my master is become a notable
lover?   40

LAUNCE. I never knew him otherwise.

SPEED. Than how?

LAUNCE. A notable lubber: as thou reportest him to be.

SPEED. Why, thou whoreson ass, thou mistak'st me.

LAUNCE. Why, fool, I meant not thee, I meant thy
master.

SPEED. I tell thee, my master is become a hot lover.

LAUNCE. Why, I tell thee, I care not though he burn
himself in love.... If thou wilt, go with me to the
alehouse; if not, thou art an Hebrew, a Jew, and not   50
worth the name of a Christian.

SPEED. Why?

LAUNCE. Because thou hast not so much charity in
thee, as to 'go to the ale' with a Christian ... Wilt
thou go?

SPEED. At thy service.   *They go*

Scene 6

Enter Proteus

PROTEUS. To leave my Julia ... shall I be forsworn?
To love fair Silvia ... shall I be forsworn?
To wrong my friend, I shall be much forsworn....
And e'en that power, which gave me first my oath,
Provokes me to this threefold perjury....
Love bade me swear, and love bids me forswear;
O sweet-suggesting Love, if thou has sinned,
Teach me—thy tempted subject—to excuse it....
At first I did adore a twinkling star,
But now I worship a celestial sun: 10
Unheedful vows may heedfully be broken,
And he wants wit that wants resolvéd will
To learn his wit t'exchange the bad for better;
Fie, fie, unreverend tongue, to call her bad,
Whose sovereignty so oft thou hast preferred
With twenty thousand soul-confirming oaths....
I cannot leave to love; and yet I do:
But there I leave to love where I should love....
Julia I lose, and Valentine I lose—
If I keep them, I needs must lose myself: 20
If I lose them, thus find I by their loss—
For Valentine, myself: for Julia, Silvia....
I to myself am dearer than a friend,
For love is still more precious in itself:
And Silvia—witness Heaven, that made her fair!—
Shews Julia but a swarthy Ethiop....
I will forget that Julia is alive,

Remembering that my love to her is dead....
And Valentine I'll hold an enemy,
Aiming at Silvia as a sweeter friend....   30
I cannot now prove constant to myself,
Without some treachery used to Valentine....
This night he meaneth with a corded ladder
To climb celestial Silvia's chamber-window,
Myself in counsel his competitor....
Now presently I'll give her father notice
Of their disguising and pretended flight:
Who, all enraged, will banish Valentine:
For Thurio he intends shall wed his daughter.
But, Valentine being gone, I'll quickly cross   40
By some sly trick blunt Thurio's dull proceeding....
Love, lend me wings to make my purpose swift,
As thou hast lent me wit to plot this drift!
                 He continues his way

Scene 7: *Verona: Julia's house*

Enter Julia and Lucetta

JULIA. Counsel, Lucetta, gentle girl assist me.
And, e'en in kind love, I do cónjure thee,
Who art the table wherein all my thoughts
Are visibly charáctered and engraved,
To lesson me, and tell me some good mean,
How, with my honour, I may undertake
A journey to my loving Proteus.

LUCETTA. Alas, the way is wearisome and long.

JULIA. A true-devoted pilgrim is not weary
To measure kingdoms with his feeble steps—   10
Much less shall she that hath Love's wings to fly,
And when the flight is made to one so dear,
Of such divine perfection, as Sir Proteus.

LUCETTA. Better forbear till Proteus make return.

JULIA. O, know'st thou not his looks are my soul's
food?
Pity the dearth that I have pinéd in,
By longing for that food so long a time....
Didst thou but know the inly touch of love,
Thou wouldst as soon go kindle fire with snow,
As seek to quench the fire of love with words.   20

LUCETTA. I do not seek to quench your love's hot fire,
But qualify the fire's éxtreme rage,
Lest it should burn above the bounds of reason.

JULIA. The more thou damm'st it up, the more it
burns:
The current that with gentle murmur glides,
Thou know'st, being stopped, impatiently doth
rage:
But when his fair course is not hinderéd
He makes sweet music with th'enamelled stones,
Giving a gentle kiss to every sedge
He overtaketh in his pilgrimage;   30
And so by many winding nooks he strays,
With willing sport, to the wild ocean....
Then let me go, and hinder not my course:
I'll be as patient as a gentle stream,
And make a pastime of each weary step,
Till the last step have brought me to my love—
And there I'll rest, as after much turmoil
A blesséd soul doth in Elysium.

LUCETTA. But in what habit will you go along?

JULIA. Not like a woman, for I would prevent   40
The loose encounters of lascivious men:
Gentle Lucetta, fit me with such weeds

As may beseem some well-reputed page.

LUCETTA. Why then your ladyship must cut your hair.

JULIA. No, girl, I'll knit it up in silken strings,
With twenty odd-conceited true-love knots:
To be fantastic may become a youth
Of greater time than I shall show to be.

LUCETTA. What fashion—madam—shall I make your breeches?

JULIA. That fits as well as 'Tell me, good my lord, 50
What compass will you wear your farthingale?'
Why, e'en what fashion thou best likes, Lucetta.

LUCETTA. You must needs have them with a cod-piece, madam.

JULIA. Out, out, Lucetta! that will be ill-favoured.

LUCETTA. A round hose, madam, now's not worth a pin,
Unless you have a cod-piece to stick pins on.

JULIA. Lucetta, as thou lov'st me, let me have
What thou think'st meet, and is most mannerly....
But tell me, wench, how will the world repute me
For undertaking so unstaid a journey? 60
I fear me, it will make me scandalized.

LUCETTA. If you think so, then stay at home and go not.

JULIA. Nay, that I will not.

LUCETTA. Then never dream on infamy, but go:
If Proteus like your journey when you come,
No matter who's displeased when you are gone:
I fear me, he will scarce be pleased with all.

JULIA. That is the least, Lucetta, of my fear:
A thousand oaths, an ocean of his tears,
And instances of infinite of love, 70
Warrant me welcome to my Proteus.

LUCETTA. All these are servants to deceitful men.

JULIA. Base men, that use them to so base effect;
But truer stars did govern Proteus' birth—
His words are bonds, his oaths are oracles,
His love sincere, his thoughts immaculate,
His tears pure messengers sent from his heart,
His heart as far from fraud as heaven from earth.

LUCETTA. Pray heaven he prove so, when you come to him.

JULIA. Now, as thou lov'st me, do him not that wrong 80
To bear a hard opinion of his truth:
Only deserve my love by loving him,
And presently go with me to my chamber,
To take a note of what I stand in need of
To furnish me upon my longing journey:
All that is mine I leave at thy dispose,
My goods, my lands, my reputation,
Only, in lieu thereof, dispatch me hence:
Come; answer not: but to it presently—
I am impatient of my tarriance.   *They go out*

ACT 3

Scene 1: *Milan: the Duke's palace*

Enter the Duke, Thurio, and Proteus

DUKE. Sir Thurio, give us leave, I pray, awhile—
We have some secrets to confer about....
                                  Thurio departs
Now, tell me, Proteus, what's your will with me?

PROTEUS. My gracious lord, that which I would discover

The law of friendship bids me to conceal,
But when I call to mind your gracious favours
Done to me—undeserving as I am—
My duty pricks me on to utter that
Which else no worldly good should draw from me:
Know, worthy prince, Sir Valentine, my friend, 10
This night intends to steal away your daughter:
Myself am one made privy to the plot....
I know you have determined to bestow her
On Thurio, whom your gentle daughter hates,
And should she thus be stol'n away from you,
It would be much vexation to your age....
Thus—for my duty's sake—I rather chose
To cross my friend in his intended drift,
Than, by concealing it, heap on your head
A pack of sorrows which would press you down, 20
Being unprevented, to your timeless grave.

DUKE. Proteus, I thank thee for thine honest care,
Which to requite, command me while I live....
This love of theirs myself have often seen,
Haply when they have judged me fast asleep,
And oftentimes have purposed to forbid
Sir Valentine her company and my court:
But, fearing lest my jealous aim might err,
And so, unworthily, disgrace the man—
A rashness that I ever yet have shunned— 30
I gave him gentle looks, thereby to find
That which thyself hast now disclosed to me....
And, that thou mayst perceive my fear of this,
Knowing that tender youth is soon suggested,
I nightly lodge her in an upper tower,
The key whereof myself have ever kept:
And thence she cannot be conveyed away.

PROTEUS. Know, noble lord, they have devised a mean
How he her chamber-window will ascend,
And with a corded ladder fetch her down: 40
For which the youthful lover now is gone,
And this way comes he with it presently;
Where, if it please you, you may intercept him....
But, good my lord, do it so cunningly,
That my discovery be not aimèd at:
For love of you, not hate unto my friend,
Hath made me publisher of this pretence.

DUKE. Upon mine honour, he shall never know
That I had any light from thee of this.

PROTEUS. Adieu, my lord, Sir Valentine is coming. 50
                                  He retires

Valentine passes

DUKE. Sir Valentine, whither away so fast?

VALENTINE. Please it your grace, there is a messenger
That stays to bear my letters to my friends,
And I am going to deliver them.

DUKE. Be they of much import?

VALENTINE. The tenour of them doth but signify
My health and happy being at your court.

DUKE. Nay then, no matter: stay with me awhile—
I am to break with thee of some affairs
That touch me near: wherein thou must be secret.... 60
'Tis not unknown to thee, that I have sought
To match my friend Sir Thurio to my daughter.

VALENTINE. I know it well, my lord—and, sure, the match
Were rich and honourable: besides, the gentleman

Is full of virtue, bounty, worth, and qualities
Beseeming such a wife as your fair daughter:
Cannot your grace win her to fancy him?
DUKE. No, trust me, she is peevish, sullen, froward,
Proud, disobedient, stubborn, lacking duty,
Neither regarding that she is my child,   70
Nor fearing me as if I were her father:
And, may I say to thee, this pride of hers—
Upon advice—hath drawn my love from her,
And where I thought the remnant of mine age
Should have been cherished by her child-like duty,
I now am full resolved to take a wife,
And turn her out to who will take her in:
Then let her beauty be her wedding-dower:
For me, and my possessions, she esteems not.
VALENTINE. What would your grace have me to do in
this?   80
DUKE. There is a lady in Verona here
Whom I affect: but she is nice and coy,
And nought esteems my agéd eloquence....
Now, therefore, would I have thee to my tutor—
For long agone I have forgot to court,
Besides, the fashion of the time is changed—
How and which way I may bestow myself
To be regarded in her sun-bright eye.
VALENTINE. Win her with gifts, if she respect not
words.
Dumb jewels often, in their silent kind,   90
More than quick words do move a woman's mind.
DUKE. But she did scorn a present that I sent her.
VALENTINE. A woman sometime scorns what best
contents her....
Send her another: never give her o'er—
For scorn at first makes after-love the more:
If she do frown, 'tis not in hate of you,
But rather to beget more love in you:
If she do chide, 'tis not to have you gone,
For why, the fools are mad, if left alone:
Take no repulse, whatever she doth say—   100
For 'get you gone' she doth not mean 'away':
Flatter and praise, commend, extol their graces:
Though ne'er so black, say they have angels' faces.
That man that hath a tongue, I say, is no man,
If with his tongue he cannot win a woman.
DUKE. But she I mean is promised by her friends
Unto a youthful gentleman of worth,
And kept severely from resort of men,
That no man hath access by day to her.
VALENTINE. Why, then, I would resort to her by night.   110
DUKE. Ay, but the doors be locked and keys kept safe,
That no man hath recourse to her by night.
VALENTINE. What lets but one may enter at her
window?
DUKE. Her chamber is aloft, far from the ground,
And built so shelving, that one cannot climb it
Without apparent hazard of his life.
VALENTINE. Why, then, a ladder quaintly made of
cords,
To cast up, with a pair of anchoring hooks,
Would serve to scale another Hero's tower,
So bold Leander would adventure it.   120
DUKE. Now, as thou art a gentleman of blood,
Advise me where I may have such a ladder.
VALENTINE. When would you use it? pray sir, tell me
that.
DUKE. This very night; for Love is like a child,

That longs for every thing that he can come by.
VALENTINE. By seven o'clock I'll get you such a
ladder.
DUKE. But, hark thee: I will go to her alone—
How shall I best convey the ladder thither?
VALENTINE. It will be light, my lord, that you may bear
it
Under a cloak that is of any length.   130
DUKE. A cloak as long as thine will serve the turn?
VALENTINE. Ay, my good lord.
DUKE.   Then let me see thy cloak—
I'll get me one of such another length.
VALENTINE. Why, any cloak will serve the turn, my
lord.
DUKE. How shall I fashion me to wear a cloak?
I pray thee, let me feel thy cloak upon me....
What letter is this same? What's here?—'To Silvia'?
And here an engine fit for my proceeding!
I'll be so bold to break the seal for once.
                                            He reads
'My thoughts do harbour with my Silvia nightly,   140
'And slaves they are to me, that send them flying.
'O, could their master come, and go as lightly,
'Himself would lodge, where—senseless—they
are lying.
'My herald thoughts in thy pure bosom rest them,
'Why I, their king, that thither them importune,
'Do curse the grace that with such grace hath
blessed them,
'Because myself do want my servants' fortune.
'I curse myself, for they are sent by me,
'That they should harbour where their lord
should be.'
What's here?   150
'Silvia, this night I will enfranchise thee'....
'Tis so: and here's the ladder for the purpose....
Why, Phaethon—for thou art Merops' son!—
Wilt thou aspire to guide the heavenly car,
And with thy daring folly burn the world?
Wilt thou reach stars, because they shine on thee?
Go base intruder, over-weening slave,
Bestow thy fawning smiles on equal mates,
And think my patience, more than thy desert,
Is privilege for thy departure hence....   160
Thank me for this more than for all the favours,
Which—all too much!—I have bestowed on
thee....
But if thou linger in my territories
Longer than swiftest expedition
Will give thee time to leave our royal court,
By heaven, my wrath shall far exceed the love
I ever bore my daughter, or thyself....
Be gone, I will not hear thy vain excuse,
But, as thou lov'st thy life, make speed from hence.
                                            He goes
VALENTINE. And why not death, rather than living
torment?   170
To die, is to be banished from myself,
And Silvia is myself: banished from her,
Is self from self.... Ah! deadly banishment:
What light is light, if Silvia be not seen?
What joy is joy, if Silvia be not by?
Unless it be to think that she is by,
And feed upon the shadow of perfection....
Except I be by Silvia in the night,
There is no music in the nightingale....

Unless I look on Silvia in the day,
There is no day for me to look upon....
She is my essence—and I leave to be,
If I be not by her fair influence
Fostered, illumined, cherished, kept alive....
I fly not death, to fly his deadly doom—
Tarry I here, I but attend on death—
But, fly I hence, I fly away from life.

Enter Proteus and Launce

PROTEUS. Run, boy, run, run, and seek him out.
LAUNCE. So-ho! so-ho!
PROTEUS. What seest thou?   190
LAUNCE. Him we go to find.
    There's not a hair on's head but 'tis a valentine.
PROTEUS. Valentine!
VALENTINE. No.
PROTEUS. Who then? his spirit?
VALENTINE. Neither.
PROTEUS. What then?
VALENTINE. Nothing.
LAUNCE. Can nothing speak? Master, shall I strike?
PROTEUS. Who wouldst thou strike?   200
LAUNCE. Nothing.
PROTEUS. Villain, forbear.
LAUNCE. Why, sir, I'll strike nothing: I pray you—
PROTEUS. Sirrah, I say, forbear ... Friend Valentine,
    a word.
VALENTINE. My ears are stopped, and cannot hear
    good news,
So much of bad already hath possessed them.
PROTEUS. Then in dumb silence will I bury mine,
    For they are harsh, untuneable and bad.
VALENTINE. Is Silvia dead?
PROTEUS. No, Valentine.   210
VALENTINE. No Valentine, indeed, for sacred Silvia.
    Hath she forsworn me?
PROTEUS. No, Valentine.
VALENTINE. No valentine, if Silvia have forsworn
    me—
What is your news?
LAUNCE. Sir, there is a proclamation that you are
    vanished.
PROTEUS. That thou art banishéd ... O, that's the
    news—
From hence, from Silvia, and from me thy friend.
VALENTINE. O, I have fed upon this woe already,
    And now excess of it will make me surfeit....   220
Doth Silvia know that I am banishéd?
PROTEUS. Ay, ay: and she hath offered to the doom—
Which, unreversed, stands in effectual force—
A sea of melting pearl, which some call tears,
Those at her father's churlish feet she tendered,
With them, upon her knees, her humble self,
Wringing her hands, whose whiteness so became
    them,
As if but now they waxéd pale for woe:
But neither bended knees, pure hands held up,
Sad sighs, deep groans, nor silver-shedding tears,   230
Could penetrate her uncompassionate sire;
But Valentine, if he be ta'en, must die....
Besides, her intercession chafed him so,
When she for thy repeal was suppliant,
That to close prison he commanded her,
With many bitter threats of biding there.

VALENTINE. No more ... unless the next word that   180
    thou speak'st
Have some malignant power upon my life:
If so ... I pray thee breathe it in mine ear,
As ending anthem of my endless dolour.   240
PROTEUS. Cease to lament for that thou canst not help,
And study help for that which thou lament'st.
Time is the nurse and breeder of all good;
Here if thou stay, thou canst not see thy love:
Besides, thy staying will abridge thy life:
Hope is a lover's staff—walk hence with that,
And manage it against despairing thoughts:
Thy letters may be here, though thou art hence,
Which, being writ to me, shall be delivered
Even in the milk-white bosom of thy love....   250
The time now serves not to expostulate—
Come, I'll convey thee through the city-gate....
And, ere I part with thee, confer at large
Of all that may concern thy love-affairs:
As thou lov'st Silvia, though not for thyself,
Regard thy danger, and along with me.
VALENTINE. I pray thee, Launce, an if thou seest my
    boy,
Bid him make haste and meet me at the North-gate.
PROTEUS. Go, sirrah, find him out.... Come,
    Valentine.
VALENTINE. O my dear Silvia; hapless Valentine.   260
                                                They go
LAUNCE. I am but a fool, look you, and yet I have the
    wit to think my master is a kind of a knave: but that's
    all one, if he be but one knave ... He lives not now
    that knows me to be in love—yet I am in love—but
    a team of horse shall not pluck that from me: nor
    who 'tis I love: and yet 'tis a woman; but what
    woman, I will not tell myself: and yet 'tis a milk-
    maid: yet 'tis not a maid: for she hath had gossips:
    yet 'tis a maid, for she is her master's maid, and
    serves for wages.... She hath more qualities than a   270
    water-spaniel—which is much in a bare Chris-
    tian.... [*pulls out a paper*] Here is the catalogue of
    her condition. '*Inprimis*, She can fetch and carry' ...
    Why, a horse can do no more; nay, a horse cannot
    fetch, but only carry; therefore is she better than a
    jade. '*Item*, She can milk'—look you, a sweet virtue
    in a maid with clean hands.

Speed comes up

SPEED. How now, Signior Launce! what news with
    your mastership?
LAUNCE. With my master's ship? why, it is at sea.   280
SPEED. Well, your old vice still: mistake the word ...
    What news, then, in your paper?
LAUNCE. The black'st news that ever thou heard'st.
SPEED. Why, man, how black?
LAUNCE. Why, as black as ink.
SPEED. Let me read them.
LAUNCE. Fie on thee jolthead, thou canst not read.
SPEED. Thou liest ... I can.
LAUNCE. I will try thee: tell me this: who begot thee?
SPEED. Marry, the son of my grandfather.   290
LAUNCE. O illiterate loiterer; it was the son of thy
    grandmother ... This proves that thou canst not
    read.
SPEED. Come, fool, come: try me in thy paper.
LAUNCE. There ... and Saint Nicholas be thy speed!

SPEED. 'Inprimis, She can milk.'

LAUNCE. Ay, that she can.

SPEED. 'Item, She brews good ale.'

LAUNCE. And thereof comes the proverb: 'Blessing of your heart, you brew good ale.'   300

SPEED. 'Item, She can sew.'

LAUNCE. That's as much as to say, 'Can she so?'

SPEED. 'Item, She can knit.'

LAUNCE. What need a man care for a stock with a wench, when she can knit him a stock.

SPEED. 'Item, She can wash and scour.'

LAUNCE. A special virtue: for then she need not be washed and scoured.

SPEED. 'Item, She can spin.'

LAUNCE. Then may I set the world on wheels, when   310 she can spin for her living.

SPEED. 'Item, She hath many nameless virtues.'

LAUNCE. That's as much as to say, bastard virtues: that, indeed, know not their fathers; and therefore have no names.

SPEED. 'Here follow her vices.'

LAUNCE. Close at the heels of her virtues.

SPEED. 'Item, She is not to be—fasting, in respect of her breath.'

LAUNCE. Well ... that may be mended with a break-   320 fast ... Read on.

SPEED. 'Item, She hath a sweet mouth.'

LAUNCE. That makes amends for her sour breath.

SPEED. 'Item, She doth talk in her sleep.'

LAUNCE. It's no matter for that; so she slip not in her talk.

SPEED. 'Item, She is slow in words.'

LAUNCE. O villain, that set this down among her vices! To be slow in words is a woman's only virtue: I pray thee, out with't, and place it for her chief virtue.   330

SPEED. 'Item, She is proud.'

LAUNCE. Out with that too ... It was Eve's legacy, and cannot be ta'en from her.

SPEED. 'Item, She hath no teeth.'

LAUNCE. I care not for that neither ... because I love crusts.

SPEED. 'Item, She is curst.'

LAUNCE. Well ... the best is, she hath no teeth to bite.

SPEED. 'Item, She will often praise her liquor.'

LAUNCE. If her liquor be good, she shall: if she will not,   340 will; for good things should be praised.

SPEED. 'Item, She is too liberal.'

LAUNCE. Of her tongue she cannot; for that's writ down she is slow of: of her purse she shall not, for that I'll keep shut: now, of another thing she may, and that cannot I help.... Well, proceed.

SPEED. 'Item, She hath more hair than wit, and more faults than hairs, and more wealth than faults.'

LAUNCE. Stop there ... I'll have her ... she was mine, and not mine, twice or thrice in that last article: 350 rehearse that once more.

SPEED. 'Item, She hath more hair than wit'—

LAUNCE. More hair than wit: it may be I'll prove it ... The cover of the salt hides the salt, and therefore it is more than the salt; the hair that covers the wit is more than the wit; for the greater hides the less ... What's next?

SPEED. —'And more faults than hairs'—

LAUNCE. That's monstrous: O, that that were out!

SPEED. —'And more wealth than faults.'   360

LAUNCE. Why, that word makes the faults gracious ...

Well, I'll have her: and if it be a match, as nothing is impossible—

SPEED. What then?

LAUNCE. Why, then will I tell thee—that thy master stays for thee at the North-gate.

SPEED. For me!

LAUNCE. For thee? ay, who art thou? he hath stayed for a better man than thee.

SPEED. And must I go to him?   370

LAUNCE. Thou must run to him; for thou hast stayed so long, that going will scarce serve the turn.

SPEED. Why didst not tell me sooner? 'pox of your love-letters!   *He runs off*

LAUNCE. Now will he be swinged for reading my letter ...

An unmannerly slave, that will thrust himself into secrets ...

I'll after, to rejoice in the boy's correction.

He follows

Scene 2

Enter the Duke and Thurio

DUKE. Sir Thurio, fear not but that she will love you,
  Now Valentine is banished from her sight.

THURIO. Since his exile she hath despised me most,
  Forsworn my company and railed at me,
  That I am desperate of obtaining her.

DUKE. This weak impress of love is as a figure
  Trenchéd in ice, which with an hour's heat
  Dissolves to water and doth lose his form....
  A little time will melt her frozen thoughts,
  And worthless Valentine shall be forgot....   10

Proteus enters

  How now, Sir Proteus! Is your countryman,
  According to our proclamation, gone?

PROTEUS. Gone, my good lord.

DUKE. My daughter takes his going grievously!

PROTEUS. A little time, my lord, will kill that grief.

DUKE. So I believe: but Thurio thinks not so ...
  Proteus, the good conceit I hold of thee—
  For thou hast shown some sign of good desert—
  Makes me the better to confer with thee.

PROTEUS. Longer than I prove loyal to your grace   20
  Let me not live to look upon your grace.

DUKE. Thou know'st how willingly I would effect
  The match between Sir Thurio and my daughter?

PROTEUS. I do, my lord.

DUKE. And also, I think, thou art not ignorant
  How she opposes her against my will?

PROTEUS. She did, my lord, when Valentine was here.

DUKE. Ay, and perversely she persévers so ...
  What might we do to make the girl forget
  The love of Valentine, and love Sir Thurio?   30

PROTEUS. The best way is to slander Valentine
  With falsehood, cowardice, and poor descent:
  Three things that women highly hold in hate.

DUKE. Ay, but she'll think that it is spoke in hate.

PROTEUS. Ay, if his enemy deliver it....
  Therefore it must with circumstance be spoken
  By one whom she esteemeth as his friend.

DUKE. Then you must undertake to slander him.

PROTEUS. And that, my lord, I shall be loath to do ...
  'Tis an ill office for a gentleman,   40

Especially against his very friend.

DUKE. Where your good word cannot advantage him,
Your slander never can endamage him;
Therefore the office is indifferent,
Being entreated to it by your friend.

PROTEUS. You have prevailed, my lord. If I can do it,
By aught that I can speak in his dispraise,
She shall not long continue love to him:
But say this weed her love from Valentine,
It follows not that she will love Sir Thurio.   50

THURIO. Therefore, as you unwind her love from
  him—
Lest it should ravel and be good to none—
You must provide to bottom it on me:
Which must be done, by praising me as much
As you in worth dispraise Sir Valentine.

DUKE. And, Proteus, we dare trust you in this kind
Because we know, on Valentine's report,
You are already Love's firm votary,
And cannot soon revolt and change your mind...
Upon this warrant, shall you have access   60
Where you with Silvia may confer at large....
For she is lumpish, heavy, melancholy,
And—for your friend's sake—will be glad of you;
Where you may temper her, by your persuasion,
To hate young Valentine and love my friend.

PROTEUS. As much as I can do, I will effect ...
But you, Sir Thurio, are not sharp enough:
You must lay lime to tangle her desires
By wailful sonnets, whose composéd rhymes
Should be full-fraught with serviceable vows.   70

DUKE. Ay,
Much is the force of heaven-bred poesy.

PROTEUS. Say that upon the altar of her beauty
You sacrifice your tears, your sighs, your heart:
Write till your ink be dry: and with your tears
Moist it again: and frame some feeling line
That may discover such integrity ...
For Orpheus' lute was strung with poets' sinews—
Whose golden touch could soften steel and stones;
Make tigers tame and huge leviathans   80
Forsake unsounded deeps to dance on sands....
After your dire-lamenting elegies,
Visit by night your lady's chamber-window
With some sweet consort; to their instruments
Tune a deploring dump: the night's dead silence
Will well become such sweet-complaining
  grievance ...
This, or else nothing, will inherit her.

DUKE. This discipline shows thou hast been in love.

THURIO. And thy advice, this night, I'll put in
  practice:
Therefore, sweet Proteus, my direction-giver,   90
Let us into the city presently
To sort some gentlemen well skilled in music....
I have a sonnet that will serve the turn
To give the onset to thy good advice.

DUKE. About it, gentlemen.

PROTEUS. We'll wait upon your grace till after supper,
And afterward determine our proceedings.

DUKE. Even now about it. I will pardon you.

                                    They go

ACT 4

Scene 1: *A forest*

Enter three outlaws, Valentine and Speed

1 OUTLAW. Fellows, stand fast ... I see a passenger.

2 OUTLAW. If there be ten, shrink not, but down with
  'em.

3 OUTLAW. Stand, sir, and throw us that you have
  about ye....
If not ... we'll make you sit, and rifle you.

SPEED. Sir, we are undone; these are the villains
That all the travellers do fear so much.

VALENTINE. My friends—

1 OUTLAW. That's not so, sir: we are your enemies.

2 OUTLAW. Peace ... we'll hear him.

3 OUTLAW. Ay, by my beard, will we: for he's a
  proper man.   10

VALENTINE. Then know, that I have little wealth to
  lose;
A man I am crossed with adversity:
My riches are these poor habiliments,
Of which if you should here disfurnish me,
You take the sum and substance that I have.

2 OUTLAW. Whither travel you?

VALENTINE. To Verona.

1 OUTLAW. Whence came you?

VALENTINE. From Milan.

3 OUTLAW. Have you long sojourned there?   20

VALENTINE. Some sixteen months, and longer might
  have stayed,
If crooked fortune had not thwarted me.

1 OUTLAW. What, were you banished thence?

VALENTINE. I was.

2 OUTLAW. For what offence?

VALENTINE. For that which now torments me to
  rehearse;
I killed a man, whose death I much repent.
But yet I slew him manfully in fight,
Without false vantage, or base treachery.

1 OUTLAW. Why, ne'er repent it, if it were done so;   30
But were you banished for so small a fault?

VALENTINE. I was, and held me glad of such a doom.

2 OUTLAW. Have you the tongues?

VALENTINE. My youthful travel therein made me
  happy;
Or else I often had been miserable.

3 OUTLAW. By the bare scalp of Robin Hood's fat friar,
This fellow were a king for our wild faction.

1 OUTLAW. We'll have him ... Sirs, a word.

SPEED. Master, be one of them:
It's an honourable kind of thievery.   40

VALENTINE. Peace, villain.

2 OUTLAW. Tell us this: have you any thing to take to?

VALENTINE. Nothing but my fortune.

3 OUTLAW. Know then, that some of us are
  gentlemen,
Such as the fury of ungoverned youth
Thrust from the company of awful men....
Myself was from Verona banished,
For practising to steal away a lady,
An heir, and near allied unto the duke.

2 OUTLAW. And I from Mantua, for a gentleman   50
Whom, in my mood, I stabbed unto the heart.

1 OUTLAW. And I, for such like petty crimes as
  these....
But to the purpose: for we cite our faults,

That they may hold excused our lawless lives;
And partly, seeing you are beautified
With goodly shape, and by your own report
A linguist, and a man of such perfection
As we do in our quality much want—
2 OUTLAW. Indeed, because you are a banished man,
Therefore, above the rest, we parley to you: 60
Are you content to be our general?
To make a virtue of necessity,
And live as we do in this wilderness?
3 OUTLAW. What sayst thou? wilt thou be of our
consórt?
Say 'ay,' and be the captain of us all:
We'll do thee homage and be ruled by thee,
Love thee as our commander and our king.
1 OUTLAW. But if thou scorn our courtesy, thou diest.
2 OUTLAW. Thou shalt not live to brag what we have
offered.
VALENTINE. I take your offer, and will live with you, 70
Provided that you do no outrages
On silly women or poor passengers.
3 OUTLAW. No, we detest such vile base practices....
Come, go with us, we'll bring thee to our crew,
And show thee all the treasure we have got;
Which, with ourselves, all rest at thy dispose.
They go

Scene 2: *Behind the Duke's palace*

Enter Proteus

PROTEUS. Already have I been false to Valentine,
And now I must be as unjust to Thurio.
Under the colour of commending him,
I have access my own love to prefer....
But Silvia is too fair, too true, too holy,
To be corrupted with my worthless gifts;
When I protest true loyalty to her,
She twits me with my falsehood to my friend;
When to her beauty I commend my vows,
She bids me think how I have been forsworn   10
In breaking faith with Julia whom I loved;
And notwithstanding all her sudden quips,
The least whereof would quell a lover's hope ...
Yet, spaniel-like, the more she spurns my love,
The more it grows, and fawneth on her still;

Enter Thurio and musicians

But here comes Thurio; now must we to her
window,
And give some evening music to her ear.
THURIO. How now, Sir Proteus, are you crept before
us?
PROTEUS. Ay, gentle Thurio, for you know that love
Will creep in service where it cannot go.   20
THURIO. Ay, but I hope, sir, that you love not here.
PROTEUS. Sir, but I do: or else I would be hence.
THURIO. Who? Silvia?
PROTEUS.   Ay, Silvia—for your sake.
THURIO. I thank you for your own ... Now,
gentlemen,
Let's tune, and to it lustily awhile.

Enter an old Host and Julia, disguised as a boy

HOST. Now, my young guest; methinks you're allicholy; I pray you, why is it?
JULIA. Marry, mine host, because I cannot be merry.

HOST. Come, we'll have you merry: I'll bring you
where you shall hear music, and see the gentleman 30
that you asked for.
JULIA. But shall I hear him speak?
HOST. Ay, that you shall.
JULIA. That will be music.   *The musicians strike up*
HOST. Hark! hark!
JULIA. Is he among these?
HOST. Ay: but peace, let's hear 'em.

SONG.

Who is Silvia? what is she,
That all our swains commend her?
Holy, fair, and wise is she.   40
The heaven such grace did lend her,
That she might admiréd be.

Is she kind as she is fair?
For beauty lives with kindness:
Love doth to her eyes repair,
To help him of his blindness:
And, being helped, inhabits there.

Then to Silvia let us sing,
That Silvia is excelling;
She excels each mortal thing,   50
Upon the dull earth dwelling.
To her let us garlands bring.

HOST. How now! are you sadder than you were
before? How do you, man? the music likes you not.
JULIA. You mistake: the musician likes me not.
HOST. Why, my pretty youth?
JULIA. He plays false, father.
HOST. How? out of tune on the strings?
JULIA. Not so: but yet so false, that he grieves my very
heart-strings.   60
HOST. You have a quick ear.
JULIA. Ay, I would I were deaf ... it makes me have a
slow heart.
HOST. I perceive you delight not in music.
JULIA. Not a whit, when it jars so.
HOST. Hark, what fine change is in the music!
JULIA. Ay: that change is the spite.
HOST. You would have them always play but one
thing.
JULIA. I would always have one play but one thing.... 70
But, host, doth this Sir Proteus that we talk on
Often resort unto this gentlewoman?
HOST. I tell you what Launce, his man, told me—he
loved her out of all nick.
JULIA. Where is Launce?
HOST. Gone to seek his dog, which to-morrow, by his
master's command, he must carry for a present to his
lady.
JULIA. Peace, stand aside, the company parts.
PROTEUS. Sir Thurio, fear not you. I will so plead,   80
That you shall say my cunning drift excels.
THURIO. Where meet we?
PROTEUS.   At Saint Gregory's well.
THURIO.   Farewell.
Thurio and the musicians go

Silvia appears on balcony above

PROTEUS. Madam: good even to your ladyship.
SILVIA. I thank you for your music, gentlemen.
Who is that that spake?
PROTEUS. One, lady, if you knew his pure heart's truth,
You would quickly learn to know him by his voice.

SILVIA. Sir Proteus, as I take it.
PROTEUS. Sir Proteus, gentle lady, and your servant.
SILVIA. What is your will?
PROTEUS.　　　　　　　That I may compass yours. 90
SILVIA. You have your wish: my will is even this—
　　That presently you hie you home to bed ...
　　Thou subtle, perjured, false, disloyal man!
　　Think'st thou I am so shallow, so conceitless,
　　To be seducéd by thy flattery,
　　That hast deceived so many with thy vows?
　　Return, return, and make thy love amends:
　　For me—by this pale queen of night I swear!
　　I am so far from granting thy request,
　　That I despise thee for thy wrongful suit; 100
　　And by and by intend to chide myself
　　Even for this time I spend in talking to thee.
PROTEUS. I grant, sweet love, that I did love a lady—
　　But she is dead:
JULIA.　　　　　　　'Twere false, if I should speak it;
　　For I am sure she is not buriéd.
SILVIA. Say that she be: yet Valentine thy friend
　　Survives; to whom—thyself art witness—
　　I am betrothed; and art thou not ashamed
　　To wrong him with thy importúnacy?
PROTEUS. I likewise hear that Valentine is dead. 110
SILVIA. And so suppose am I; for in his grave
　　Assure thyself my love is buriéd.
PROTEUS. Sweet lady, let me rake it from the earth.
SILVIA. Go to thy lady's grave and call her's thence
　　Or, at the least, in her's sepúlchre thine.
JULIA. He heard not that.
PROTEUS. Madam ... if your heart be so obdurate ...
　　Vouchsafe me yet your picture for my love,
　　The picture that is hanging in your chamber:
　　To that I'll speak, to that I'll sigh and weep; 120
　　For since the substance of your perfect self
　　Is else devoted, I am but a shadow;
　　And to your shadow—will I make true love.
JULIA. If 'twere a substance, you would, sure, deceive
　　it,
　　And make it but a shadow, as I am.
SILVIA. I am very loath to be your idol, sir;
　　But, since your falsehood shall become you well
　　To worship shadows and adore false shapes,
　　Send to me in the morning, and I'll send it:
　　And so, good rest.　　　　　　　*She shuts her window*
PROTEUS.　　　　　　　As wretches have o'ernight 130
　　That wait for execution in the morn.　　*He goes*
JULIA. Host, will you go?
HOST. By my halidom, I was fast asleep.
JULIA. Pray you, where lies Sir Proteus?
HOST. Marry, at my house ... Trust me, I think 'tis
　　almost day.
JULIA. Not so: but it hath been the longest night,
　　That e'er I watched, and the most heaviest.
　　　　　　　　　　　　　　　　　　　They go

Scene 3

Enter Eglamour

EGLAMOUR. This is the hour that Madam Silvia
　　Entreated me to call and know her mind:
　　There's some great matter she'ld employ me in....
　　Madam, madam!

The window opens and Silvia appears

SILVIA.　　　　　　　Who calls?
EGLAMOUR.　　　　　　Your servant, and your friend;
　　One that attends your ladyship's command.
SILVIA. Sir Eglamour, a thousand times good morrow.
EGLAMOUR. As many, worthy lady, to yourself ...
　　According to your ladyship's impose,
　　I am thus early come to know what service
　　It is your pleasure to command me in. 10
SILVIA. O Eglamour, thou art a gentleman—
　　Think not I flatter, for I swear I do not—
　　Valiant, wise, remorseful, well-accomplished.
　　Thou art not ignorant what dear good will
　　I bear unto the banished Valentine ...
　　Nor how my father would enforce me marry
　　Vain Thurio—whom my very soul abhors....
　　Thyself hast loved, and I have heard thee say
　　No grief did ever come so near my heart,
　　As when thy lady and thy true love died, 20
　　Upon whose grave thou vow'dst pure chastity ...
　　Sir Eglamour ... I would to Valentine,
　　To Mantua, where I hear he makes abode;
　　And, for the ways are dangerous to pass,
　　I do desire thy worthy company,
　　Upon whose faith and honour I repose....
　　Urge not my father's anger, Eglamour,
　　But think upon my grief—a lady's grief—
　　And on the justice of my flying hence,
　　To keep me from a most unholy match, 30
　　Which heaven and fortune still rewards with
　　　　plagues....
　　I do desire thee, even from a heart
　　As full of sorrows as the sea of sands,
　　To bear me company, and go with me:
　　If not, to hide what I have said to thee,
　　That I may venture to depart alone.
EGLAMOUR. Madam, I pity much your grievances,
　　Which since I know they virtuously are placed,
　　I give consent to go along with you,
　　Recking as little what betideth me, 40
　　As much I wish all good befortune you....
　　When will you go?
SILVIA.　　　　　　　This evening coming.
EGLAMOUR. Where shall I meet you?
SILVIA.　　　　　　　At Friar Patrick's cell,
　　Where I intend holy confession.
EGLAMOUR. I will not fail your ladyship: good
　　morrow, gentle lady.　　　　　　　*He goes*
SILVIA. Good morrow, kind Sir Eglamour.
　　　　　　　　　　　　　　　She closes her window

Scene 4

Enter Launce, with his dog

LAUNCE. When a man's servant shall play the cur with
　　him—look you—it goes hard: one that I brought
　　up of a puppy: one that I saved from drowning,
　　when three or four of his blind brothers and sisters
　　went to it: I have taught him—even as one would
　　say precisely, 'Thus I would teach a dog.' I was sent
　　to deliver him, as a present to Mistress Silvia from
　　my master; and I came no sooner into the dining-
　　chamber, but he steps me to her trencher, and steals
　　her capon's leg ... O, 'tis a foul thing, when a cur 10
　　cannot keep himself in all companies: I would have
　　—as one should say—one that takes upon him to be
　　a dog indeed, to be, as it were, a dog at all things....

If I had not had more wit than he, to take a fault upon me that he did, I think verily he had been hanged for't: sure as I live, he had suffered for't: you shall judge ... He thrusts me himself into the company of three or four gentlemen-like dogs, under the duke's table: he had not been there (bless the mark!) a pissing-while, but all the chamber smelt him ... 'Out with the dog,' says one—'What cur is that?' says another—'Whip him out,' says the third—'Hang him up,' says the duke.... I, having been acquainted with the smell before, knew it was Crab; and goes me to the fellow that whips the dogs: 'Friend,' quoth I, 'you mean to whip the dog?' 'Ay, marry, do I,' quoth he. 'You do him the more wrong,' quoth I, ''twas I did the thing you wot of': he makes me no more ado, but whips me out of the chamber ... How many masters would do this for his servant? Nay, I'll be sworn, I have sat in the stocks for puddings he hath stol'n, otherwise he had been executed: I have stood on the pillory for geese he hath killed, otherwise he had suffered for't ... Thou think'st not of this now ... Nay, I remember the trick you served me, when I took my leave of Madam Silvia: did not I bid thee still mark me, and do as I do? when didst thou see me heave up my leg, and make water against a gentlewoman's farthingale? didst thou ever see me do such a trick?

Proteus and Julia (disguised as a boy) pass by

PROTEUS. Sebastian is thy name: I like thee well, And will employ thee in some service presently.
JULIA. In what you please. I will do what I can.
PROTEUS. I hope thou wilt ... *[he spies Launce]* How now, you whoreson peasant!
Where have you been these two days loitering?
LAUNCE. Marry, sir, I carried Mistress Silvia the dog you bade me.
PROTEUS. And what says she to my little Jewel?
LAUNCE. Marry, she says your dog was a cur, and tells you currish thanks is good enough for such a present.
PROTEUS. But she received my dog?
LAUNCE. No, indeed, did she not: here have I brought him back again.
PROTEUS. What! didst thou offer her this from me?
LAUNCE. Ay sir, the other squirrel was stol'n from me by the hangman boys in the market-place, and then I offered her mine own, who is a dog as big as ten of yours, and therefore the gift the greater.
PROTEUS. Go, get thee hence, and find my dog again, Or ne'er return again into my sight....
Away, I say ... stayest thou to vex me here? A slave, that still an-end turns me to shame ...
Launce goes
Sebastian, I have entertainéd thee, Partly that I have need of such a youth, That can with some discretion do my business ... For 'tis no trusting to yond foolish lout ... But chiefly for thy face and thy behaviour, Which, if my augury deceive me not, Witness good bringing up, fortune, and truth: Therefore know thou, for this I entertain thee.... Go presently, and take this ring with thee, Deliver it to Madam Silvia ...
She loved me well delivered it to me.
JULIA. It seems you loved not her, nor love her token ...

She is dead, belike?
PROTEUS.   Not so ... I think she lives.
JULIA. Alas!
PROTEUS. Why dost thou cry 'alas'?
JULIA. I cannot choose but pity her.
PROTEUS. Wherefore shouldst thou pity her?
JULIA. Because, methinks, that she loved you as well As you do love your lady Silvia ...
She dreams on him that has forgot her love— You dote on her that cares not for your love....
'Tis pity love should be so contrary:
And thinking on it makes me cry, 'alas!'
PROTEUS. Well ... give her that ring, and therewithal This letter ... That's her chamber ... Tell my lady I claim the promise for her heavenly picture:
Your message done, hie home unto my chamber, Where thou shalt find me sad—and solitary.
He goes
JULIA. How many women would do such a message? Alas, poor Proteus, thou hast entertained A fox to be the shepherd of thy lambs;
Alas, poor fool, why do I pity him That with his very heart despiseth me?
Because he loves her, he despiseth me— Because I love him, I must pity him....
This ring I gave him, when he parted from me, To bind him to remember my good will:
And now am I—unhappy messenger!— To plead for that, which I would not obtain;
To carry that, which I would have refused;
To praise his faith, which I would have dispraised....
I am my master's true confirméd love, But cannot be true servant to my master, Unless I prove false traitor to myself....
Yet will I woo for him, but yet so coldly, As, heaven it knows, I would not have him speed....

Silvia comes in

Gentlewoman, good day: I pray you be my mean To bring me where to speak with Madam Silvia.
SILVIA. What would you with her, if that I be she?
JULIA. If you be she, I do entreat your patience To hear me speak the message I am sent on.
SILVIA. From whom?
JULIA. From my master, Sir Proteus, madam.
SILVIA. O ... he sends you for a picture?
JULIA. Ay, madam.
SILVIA *[calling]*. Ursula, bring my picture there.
The maid brings the picture
Go give your master this: tell him from me, One Julia, that his changing thoughts forget, Would better fit his chamber than this shadow.
JULIA. Madam, please you peruse this letter ...
Pardon me, madam, I have unadvised Delivered you a paper that I should not ...
This is the letter to your ladyship.
SILVIA. I pray thee, let me look on that again.
JULIA. It may not be: good madam, pardon me.
SILVIA. There, hold ...
I will not look upon your master's lines:
I know they are stuffed with protestations, And full of new-found oaths, which he will break As easily as I do tear his paper.
JULIA. Madam, he sends your ladyship this ring.
SILVIA. The more shame for him, that he sends it me;

For I have heard him say a thousand times
His Julia gave it him at his departure:
Though his false finger have profaned the ring,
Mine shall not do his Julia so much wrong.
JULIA. She thanks you.   140
SILVIA. What sayst thou?
JULIA. I thank you, madam, that you tender her:
Poor gentlewoman, my master wrongs her much.
SILVIA. Dost thou know her?
JULIA. Almost as well as I do know myself....
To think upon her woes, I do protest
That I have wept a hundred several times.
SILVIA. Belike she thinks that Proteus hath forsook
her?
JULIA. I think she doth: and that's her cause of sorrow.
SILVIA. Is she not passing fair?   150
JULIA. She hath been fairer, madam, than she is;
When she did think my master loved her well,
She, in my judgement, was as fair as you....
But since she did neglect her looking-glass,
And threw her sun-expelling mask away,
The air hath starved the roses in her cheeks,
And pinched the lily-tincture of her face,
That now she is become as black as I.
SILVIA. How tall was she?
JULIA. About my stature: for, at Pentecost,   160
When all our pageants of delight were played,
Our youth got me to play the woman's part,
And I was trimmed in Madam Julia's gown,
Which served me as fit, by all men's judgement,
As if the garment had been made for me:
Therefore, I know she is about my height.
And at that time I made her weep agood,
For I did play a lamentable part....
Madam, 'twas Ariadne, passioning
For Theseus' perjury and unjust flight;   170
Which I so lively acted with my tears ...
That my poor mistress, movéd therewithal,
Wept bitterly ... and, would I might be dead,
If I in thought felt not her very sorrow.
SILVIA. She is beholding to thee, gentle youth.
Alas, poor lady! desolate and left;
I weep myself to think upon thy words ...
Here, youth: there is my purse; I give thee this
For thy sweet mistress' sake, because thou lov'st her.
Farewell.   180
JULIA. And she shall thank you for't, if e'er you
know her....   *Silvia goes*
A virtuous gentlewoman, mild, and beautiful....
I hope my master's suit will be but cold,
Since she respects my mistress' love so much....
Alas, how love can trifle with itself:
Here is her picture ... Let me see. I think
If I had such a tire, this face of mine
Were full as lovely as is this of hers;
And yet the painter flattered her a little,
Unless I flatter with myself too much....   190
Her hair is auburn, mine is perfect yellow;
If that be all the difference in his love,
I'll get me such a coloured periwig:
Her eyes are grey as glass, and so are mine:
Ay, but her forehead's low, and mine's as high:
What should it be that he respects in her,
But I can make respective in myself,
If this fond Love were not a blinded god?
Come, shadow, come, and take this shadow up,
For 'tis thy rival: O thou senseless form,   200

Thou shalt be worshipped, kissed, loved, and
adored;
And, were there sense in his idolatry,
My substance should be statue in thy stead....
I'll use thee kindly, for thy mistress' sake
That used me so .... or else, by Jove I vow,
I should have scratched out your unseeing eyes,
To make my master out of love with thee.
                        She bears away the picture

ACT 5
Scene 1: *An abbey near Milan*

Eglamour

EGLAMOUR. The sun begins to gild the western sky,
And now it is about the very hour
That Silvia, at Friar Patrick's cell, should meet me.
She will not fail; for lovers break not hours,
Unless it be to come before their time—
So much they spur their expedition....

Silvia approaches

See, where she comes ... Lady, a happy evening!
SILVIA. Amen, amen ... go on, good Eglamour,
Out at the postern by the abbey-wall;
I fear I am attended by some spies.   10
EGLAMOUR. Fear not: the forest is not three leagues off.
If we recover that, we are sure enough.
                                              They depart

Scene 2: *Milan: the Duke's palace*

Enter Thurio, Proteus and Julia (as Sebastian)

THURIO. Sir Proteus, what says Silvia to my suit?
PROTEUS. O sir, I find her milder than she was,
And yet she takes exceptions at your person.
THURIO. What?—that my leg is too long?
PROTEUS. No, that it is too little.
THURIO. I'll wear a boot, to make it somewhat
rounder.
JULIA. But love will not be spurred to what it loathes.
THURIO. What says she to my face?
PROTEUS. She says it is a fair one.
THURIO. Nay then the wanton lies: my face is black. 10
PROTEUS. But pearls are fair; and the old saying is,
Black men are pearls in beauteous ladies' eyes.
JULIA. 'Tis true, such pearls as put out ladies' eyes,
For I had rather wink than look on them.
THURIO. How likes she my discourse?
PROTEUS. Ill, when you talk of war.
THURIO. But well, when I discourse of love and peace.
JULIA. But better, indeed, when you hold your peace.
THURIO. What says she to my valour?
PROTEUS. O sir, she makes no doubt of that.   20
JULIA. She needs not, when she knows it cowardice.
THURIO. What says she to my birth?
PROTEUS. That you are well derived.
JULIA. True: from a gentleman to a fool.
THURIO. Considers she my possessions?
PROTEUS. O, ay: and pities them.
THURIO. Wherefore?
JULIA. That such an ass should owe them.
PROTEUS. That they are out by lease.
JULIA. Here comes the duke.   30

The Duke enters

DUKE. How now, Sir Proteus! how now, Thurio!
  Which of you saw Sir Eglamour of late?
THURIO. Not I.
PROTEUS.   Nor I.
DUKE.   Saw you my daughter?
PROTEUS.   Neither.
DUKE. Why then,
  She's fled unto that peasant Valentine;
  And Eglamour is in her company:
  Tis true ... for Friar Laurence met them both,
  As he in penance wandered through the forest:
  Him he knew well: and guessed that it was she,
  But, being masked, he was not sure of it.... 40
  Besides, she did intend confession
  At Patrick's cell this even—and there she was
    not....
  These likelihoods confirm her flight from hence;
  Therefore, I pray you, stand not to discourse,
  But mount you presently, and meet with me
  Upon the rising of the mountain-foot
  That leads towards Mantua, whither they are fled:
  Dispatch—sweet gentlemen!—and follow me.
                                    He goes out
THURIO. Why, this it is to be a peevish girl,
  That flies her fortune when it follows her: 50
  I'll after; more to be revenged on Eglamour
  Than for the love of reckless Silvia.   *He follows*
PROTEUS. And I will follow, more for Silvia's love
  Than hate of Eglamour that goes with her.
                                    He follows
JULIA. And I will follow, more to cross that love
  Than hate for Silvia that is gone for love.
                                    She follows

              Scene 3: *The forest*

Enter Silvia and the Outlaws

1 OUTLAW. Come, come, be patient: we must bring
  you to our captain.
SILVIA. A thousand more mischances than this one
  Have learned me how to brook this patiently.
2 OUTLAW. Come, bring her away.
1 OUTLAW. Where is the gentleman that was with her?
3 OUTLAW. Being nimble-footed, he hath outrun
  us....
  But Moses and Valerius follow him:
  Go thou with her to the west end of the wood,
  There is our captain: we'll follow him that's fled—
  The thicket is beset, he cannot 'scape.   10
1 OUTLAW. Come, I must bring you to our
  captain's cave....
  Fear not: he bears an honourable mind,
  And will not use a woman lawlessly.
SILVIA. O Valentine ... this I endure for thee.
                                    They go

              Scene 4

VALENTINE. How use doth breed a habit in a man!
  This shadowy desert, unfrequented woods,
  I better brook than flourishing peopled towns:
  Here can I sit alone, unseen of any,
  And to the nightingale's complaining notes
  Tune my distresses and record my woes....
  O thou that dost inhabit in my breast,
  Leave not the mansion so long tenantless,
  Lest, growing ruinous, the building fall,

And leave no memory of what it was.   10
Repair me with thy presence, Silvia:
Thou gentle nymph, cherish thy forlorn swain....

Cries and the sound of blows are heard

  What halloing and what stir is this to-day?
  These are my mates, that make their wills their law,
  Have some unhappy passenger in chase;
  They love me well: yet I have much to do,
  To keep them from uncivil outrages....
  Withdraw thee, Valentine; who's this comes here?

*He withdraws; Silvia comes in, Proteus and Julia (as
Sebastian) following*

PROTEUS. Madam, this service I have done for you—
  Though you respect not aught your servant doth— 20
  To hazard life and rescue you from him
  That would have forced your honour and your love.
  Vouchsafe me, for my meed, but one fair look:
  A smaller boon than this I cannot beg,
  And less than this, I am sure, you cannot give.
VALENTINE [*aside*]. How like a dream is this! I see—and
  hear ...
  Love, lend me patience to forbear awhile.
SILVIA. O miserable, unhappy that I am!
PROTEUS. Unhappy were you, madam, ere I came:
  But, by my coming, I have made you happy.   30
SILVIA. By thy approach thou mak'st me most
  unhappy.
JULIA [*aside*]. And me, when he approacheth to your
  presence.
SILVIA. Had I been seizéd by a hungry lion,
  I would have been a breakfast to the beast,
  Rather than have false Proteus rescue me:
  O, heaven be judge, how I love Valentine,
  Whose life's as tender to me as my soul—
  And full as much (for more there cannot be!)
  I do detest false perjured Proteus ...
  Therefore be gone, solicit me no more.   40
PROTEUS. What dangerous action, stood it next to
  death,
  Would I not undergo for one calm look?
  O, 'tis the curse in love, and still approved,
  When women cannot love where they're beloved.
SILVIA. When Proteus cannot love where he's
  beloved ...
  Read over Julia's heart—thy first best love—
  For whose dear sake thou didst then rend thy faith
  Into a thousand oaths; and, all those oaths
  Descended into perjury—to love me.
  Thou hast no faith left now, unless thou'dst
    two,   50
  And that's far worse than none: better have none
  Than plural faith, which is too much by one ...
  Thou counterfeit, to thy true friend!
PROTEUS.   In love,
  Who respects friend?
SILVIA.   All men but Proteus.
PROTEUS. Nay, if the gentle spirit of moving words
  Can no way change you to a milder form ...
  I'll woo you like a soldier, at arms' end,
  And love you 'gainst the nature of love ... force ye.
SILVIA. O heaven!
PROTEUS.   I'll force thee yield to my desire.
VALENTINE. Ruffian! [*leaping out upon him*] let go that
  rude uncivil touch,   60
  Thou friend of an ill fashion!

PROTEUS. Valentine!

VALENTINE. Thou common friend, that's without
faith or love—
For such is a friend now: treacherous man,
Thou hast beguiled my hopes; nought but mine eye
Could have persuaded me: now I dare not say
I have one friend alive; thou wouldst disprove
me ...
Who should be trusted, when one's own right hand
Is perjured to the bosom? Proteus,
I am sorry I must never trust thee more,
But count the world a stranger for thy sake: 70
The private wound is deepest: O time, most
accurst ...
'Mongst all foes that a friend should be the worst!

PROTEUS. My shame and guilt confounds me ...
Forgive me, Valentine ... if hearty sorrow
Be a sufficient ransom for offence,
I tender't here; I do as truly suffer,
As e'er I did commit.

VALENTINE. Then I am paid:
And once again I do receive thee honest;
Who by repentance is not satisfied,
Is nor of heaven nor earth; for these are pleased: 80
By penitence th'Eternal's wrath's appeased ...
And that my love may appear plain and free,
All that was mine in Silvia I give thee.

JULIA. O me, unhappy!   *She swoons*

PROTEUS. Look to the boy.

VALENTINE. Why, boy!
Why wag! how now? what's the matter? Look up:
speak.

JULIA. O good sir, my master charged me to deliver a
ring to Madam Silvia ... which, out of my neglect,   90
was never done.

PROTEUS. Where is that ring, boy?

JULIA. Here 'tis.... this is it.

PROTEUS. How! let me see....   *Taking it*
Why this is the ring I gave to Julia.

JULIA. O, cry you mercy, sir, I have mistook:
This is the ring you sent to Silvia.
                    She proffers another ring

PROTEUS. But how cam'st thou by this ring? at my
depart
I gave this unto Julia.

JULIA. And Julia herself did give it me—   100
And Julia herself hath brought it hither.

PROTEUS. How! Julia!

JULIA. Behold her that gave aim to all thy oaths,
And entertained 'em deeply in her heart....
How oft hast thou with perjury cleft the root!
O Proteus, let this habit make thee blush....
Be thou ashamed that I have took upon me
Such an immodest raiment; if shame live
In a disguise of love!
It is the lesser blot, modesty finds,   110
Women to change their shapes than men their
minds.

PROTEUS. Than men their minds? 'tis true ... O
heaven, were man
But constant, he were perfect; that one error
Fills him with faults ... makes him run through
all th'sins;
Inconstancy falls off ere it begins:
What is in Silvia's face, but I may spy
More fresh in Julia's with a constant eye?

VALENTINE. Come, come: a hand from either:

Let me be blest to make this happy close:
'Twere pity two such friends should be long foes.   120

PROTEUS. Bear witness, heaven, I have my wish for
ever.

JULIA. And I mine.

Outlaws appear with the Duke and Thurio

OUTLAW. A prize ... a prize ... a prize!

VALENTINE. Forbear, forbear, I say: it is my lord the
duke....
Your grace is welcome to a man disgraced,
Banishéd Valentine.

DUKE. Sir Valentine!

THURIO. Yonder is Silvia: and Silvia's mine.

VALENTINE. Thurio give back; or else embrace thy
death:
Come not within the measure of my wrath: 130
Do not name Silvia thine: if once again,
Verona shall not hold thee ... Here she stands,
Take but possession of her—with a touch ...
I dare thee but to breathe upon my love!

THURIO. Sir Valentine, I care not for her, I:
I hold him but a fool that will endanger
His body for a girl that loves him not:
I claim her not, and therefore she is thine.

DUKE. The more degenerate and base art thou,
To make such means for her as thou hast done,   140
And leave her on such slight conditions....
Now, by the honour of my ancestry,
I do applaud thy spirit, Valentine,
And think thee worthy of an empress' love:
Know then, I here forget all former griefs,
Cancel all grudge, repeal thee home again,
Plead a new state in thy unrivalled merit,
To which I thus subscribe: Sir Valentine,
Thou art a gentleman, and well derived.
Take thou thy Silvia, for thou hast deserved her.   150

VALENTINE. I thank your grace; the gift hath
made me happy:
I now beseech you—for your daughter's sake—
To grant one boon that I shall ask of you.

DUKE. I grant it—for thine own—whate'er it be.

VALENTINE. These banished men, that I have kept
withal,
Are men endued with worthy qualities:
Forgive them what they have committed here,
And let them be recalled from their exile:
They are reforméd, civil, full of good,
And fit for great employment, worthy lord.   160

DUKE. Thou hast prevailed, I pardon them and thee:
Dispose of them, as thou know'st their deserts....
Come, let us go. We will include all jars
With triumphs, mirth, and rare solemnity.

VALENTINE. And, as we walk along, I dare be bold
With our discourse to make your grace to smile....
What think you of this page, my lord?

DUKE. I think the boy hath grace in him—he blushes.

VALENTINE. I warrant you, my lord, more grace than
boy.

DUKE. What mean you by that saying?   170

VALENTINE. Please you, I'll tell you as we pass along,
That you will wonder what hath fortunéd:
Come Proteus, 'tis your penance but to hear
The story of your loves discovered....
That done, our day of marriage shall be yours—
One feast, one house, one mutual happiness.
                            They go

The
Merry Wives
of Windsor

The scene: Windsor

CHARACTERS IN THE PLAY

SIR JOHN FALSTAFF
FENTON, *a young gentleman*
ROBERT SHALLOW, *a country justice*
ABRAHAM SLENDER, *his wise cousin*
FRANK FORD } *two citizens of Windsor*
GEORGE PAGE
WILLIAM PAGE, *a boy, son to Master Page*
SIR HUGH EVANS, *a Welsh parson*
DOCTOR CAIUS, *a French physician*
The Host of the Garter Inn
BARDOLPH
PISTOL } *irregular humorists, followers of Falstaff*
NYM

ROBIN, *page to Falstaff*
SIMPLE, *servant to Slender*
JOHN RUGBY, *servant to Doctor Caius*
JOHN } *servants to Master Ford*
ROBERT
MISTRESS FORD } *the merry wives*
MISTRESS PAGE
ANNE PAGE, *her daughter, beloved of Fenton*
MISTRESS QUICKLY, *servant to Doctor Caius*

The Merry Wives of Windsor

ACT 1

Scene 1: *Windsor, before the house of Master Page*

Justice Shallow, Slender, and Sir Hugh Evans approach

SHALLOW. Sir Hugh, persuade me not: I will make a Star-chamber matter of it. If he were twenty Sir John Falstaffs, he shall not abuse Robert Shallow, esquire.

SLENDER. In the county of Gloucester, justice of peace and 'Coram.'

SHALLOW. Ay, cousin Slender, and 'Custalorum.'

SLENDER. Ay, and 'Ratolorum' too; and a gentleman born, master parson, who writes himself 'Armigero,' in any bill, warrant, quittance, or obligation 10 —'Armigero.'

SHALLOW. Ay, that I do, and have done any time these three hundred years.

SLENDER. All his successors—gone before him—have done't: and all his ancestors—that come after him—may ... They may give the dozen white luces in their coat.

SHALLOW. It is an old coat.

EVANS. The dozen white louses do become an old coat well: it agrees well, passant: it is a familiar beast to 20 man, and signifies love.

SHALLOW. The luce is the fresh fish—the salt fish is an old cod.

SLENDER. I may quarter, coz.

SHALLOW. You may—by marrying.

EVANS. It is marring indeed, if he quarter it.

SHALLOW. Not a whit.

EVANS. Yes, py'rlady: if he has a quarter of your coat, there is but three skirts for yourself, in my simple conjectures; but that is all one ... If Sir John Falstaff 30 have committed disparagements unto you, I am of the Church, and will be glad to do my benevolence, to make atonements and compromises between you.

SHALLOW. The Council shall hear it! it is a riot.

EVANS. It is not meet the council hear a riot: there is no fear of Got in a riot: the council, look you, shall desire to hear the fear of Got, and not to hear a riot: take your vizaments in that.

SHALLOW. Ha ... o'my life, if I were young again, the sword should end it. 40

EVANS. It is petter that friends is the swort, and end it: and there is also another device in my prain, which peradventure prings goot discretions with it.... There is Anne Page, which is daughter to Master Thomas Page, which is pretty virginity.

SLENDER. Mistress Anne Page? She has brown hair, and speaks small like a woman.

EVANS. It is that fery person for all the 'orld, as just as you will desire, and seven hundred pounds of moneys, and gold, and silver, is her grandsire, upon 50 his death's-bed—Got deliver to a joyful resurrections!—give, when she is able to overtake seventeen years old.... It were a goot motion if we leave our pribbles and prabbles, and desire a marriage between Master Abraham and Mistress Anne Page.

SHALLOW. Did her grandsire leave her seven hundred pound?

EVANS. Ay, and her father is make her a petter penny. 60

SHALLOW. I know the young gentlewoman. She has good gifts.

EVANS. Seven hundred pounds, and possibilities, is goot gifts.

SHALLOW. Well, let us see honest Master Page ... Is Falstaff there?

EVANS. Shall I tell you a lie? I do despise a liar as I do despise one that is false, or as I despise one that is not true: the knight, Sir John, is there, and I beseech you be ruled by your well-willers: I will peat the door for 70 Master Page.... [*knocks*] What, ho! Got-pless your house here!

PAGE [*within*]. Who's there?

EVANS. Here is Got's plessing, and your friend, and Justice Shallow, and here young Master Slender ... that peradventures shall tell you another tale, if matters grow to your likings.

PAGE [*opens the door and comes out*]. I am glad to see your worships well ... I thank you for my venison, Master Shallow. 80

SHALLOW. Master Page, I am glad to see you: much good do it your good heart: I wished your venison better—it was ill killed ... How doth good Mistress Page?—and I thank you always with my heart, la! with my heart.

PAGE. Sir, I thank you.

SHALLOW. Sir, I thank you: by yea and no, I do.

PAGE. I am glad to see you, good Master Slender.

SLENDER. How does your fallow greyhound, sir? I heard say he was outrun on Cotsall. 90

PAGE. It could not be judged, sir.

SLENDER. You'll not confess ... you'll not confess.

SHALLOW. That he will not. 'Tis your fault, 'tis your fault: 'tis a good dog.

PAGE. A cur, sir.

SHALLOW. Sir: he's a good dog, and a fair dog—can there be more said? he is 'good and fair'.... Is Sir John Falstaff here?

PAGE. Sir, he is within: and I would I could do a good office between you. 100

EVANS. It is spoke as a Christians ought to speak.

SHALLOW. He hath wronged me, Master Page.

PAGE. Sir, he doth in some sort confess it.

SHALLOW. If it be confessed, it is not redressed; is not that so, Master Page? He hath wronged me, indeed he hath, at a word he hath: believe me—Robert Shallow, esquire, saith he is wronged.

PAGE. Here comes Sir John.

Enter Sir John Falstaff, Bardolph, Nym, and Pistol

FALSTAFF. Now, Master Shallow, you'll complain of me to the king? 110

SHALLOW. Knight, you have beaten my men, killed my deer, and broke open my lodge.

FALSTAFF. But not kissed your keeper's daughter!

SHALLOW. Tut, a pin! this shall be answered.

FALSTAFF. I will answer it straight. I have done all this ... That is now answered.

SHALLOW. The Council shall know this.

FALSTAFF. 'Twere better for you, if it were known in counsel: you'll be laughed at.

EVANS. Pauca verba; Sir John—goot worts.   120

FALSTAFF. Good worts! good cabbage ... Slender, I broke your head: what matter have you against me?

SLENDER. Marry, sir, I have matter in my head against you, and against your cony-catching rascals, Bardolph, Nym, and Pistol. [They carried me to the tavern, and made me drunk, and afterward picked my pocket.]

BARDOLPH. You Banbury cheese!

SLENDER. Ay, it is no matter.

PISTOL. How now, Mephostophilus!

SLENDER. Ay, it is no matter.   130

NYM. Slice, I say; pauca, pauca: slice! that's my humour.

SLENDER. Where's Simple, my man? can you tell, cousin?

EVANS. Peace, I pray you ... Now let us understand ... There is three umpires in this matter, as I understand; that is, Master Page (fidelicet Master Page) and there is myself (fidelicet myself) and the three party is (lastly and finally) mine host of the Garter.   140

PAGE. We three, to hear it and end it between them.

EVANS. Fery goot. I will make a prief of it in my note-book, and we will afterwards 'ork upon the cause, with as great discreetly as we can.

FALSTAFF. Pistol.

PISTOL. He hears with ears.

EVANS. The tevil and his tam! what phrase is this, 'He hears with ear'? why, it is affectations.

FALSTAFF. Pistol, did you pick Master Slender's purse?

SLENDER. Ay, by these gloves, did he—or I would I   150
might never come in mine own great chamber again else—of seven groats in mill-sixpences, and two Edward shovel-boards, that cost me two shilling and two pence a-piece of Yed Miller ... by these gloves!

FALSTAFF. Is this true, Pistol?

EVANS. No, it is false, if it is a pick-purse.

PISTOL. Ha, thou mountain-foreigner! Sir John, and master mine,

I combat challenge of this latten bilbo:
Word of denial in thy labras here;   160
Word of denial; froth and scum, thou liest!

SLENDER. By these gloves, then 'twas he.

NYM. Be advised, sir, and pass good humours: I will say 'marry trap' with you, if you run the nuthook's humour on me—that is the very note of it.

SLENDER. By this hat, then he in the red face had it: for though I cannot remember what I did when you made me drunk, yet I am not altogether an ass.

FALSTAFF. What say you, Scarlet and John?

BARDOLPH. Why, sir, for my part, I say the gentleman   170
had drunk himself out of his five sentences.

EVANS. It is his five senses: fie, what the ignorance is!

BARDOLPH. And being fap, sir, was, as they say, cashiered ... and so conclusions passed the careers.

SLENDER. Ay, you spake in Latin then too: but 'tis no matter; I'll ne'er be drunk whilst I live again, but in honest, civil, godly company, for this trick: if I be drunk, I'll be drunk with those that have the fear of God, and not with drunken knaves.

EVANS. So Got-'udge me, that is a virtuous mind.   180

FALSTAFF. You hear all these matters denied, gentle-men; you hear it.

Enter Anne Page, bearing wine, with Mistress Page and Mistress Ford

PAGE. Nay daughter, carry the wine in—we'll drink within.   *She goes*

SLENDER. O heaven ... this is Mistress Anne Page!

PAGE. How now, Mistress Ford!

FALSTAFF. Mistress Ford, by my troth, you are very well met: by your leave, good mistress.

Kisses her

PAGE. Wife, bid these gentlemen welcome ... Come, we have a hot venison pasty to dinner; come, gentle-men, I hope we shall drink down all unkindness.   190

All but Slender go

SLENDER. I had rather than forty shillings I had my Book of Songs and Sonnets here ...

Enter Simple

How now Simple, where have you been? I must wait on myself, must I? You have not the Book of Riddles about you, have you?

SIMPLE. Book of Riddles? why, did you not lend it to Alice Shortcake upon Allhallowmas last, a fortnight afore Michaelmas?

Shallow and Evans return to look for Slender

SHALLOW. Come coz, come coz, we stay for you ...   200
A word with you, coz ... marry, this, coz ... there is as 'twere a tender, a kind of tender, made afar off by Sir Hugh here ... Do you understand me?

SLENDER. Ay, sir, you shall find me reasonable; if it be so, I shall do that that is reason.

SHALLOW. Nay, but understand me.

SLENDER. So I do, sir.

EVANS. Give ear to his motions; Master Slender, I will description the matter to you, if you be capacity of it.   210

SLENDER. Nay, I will do as my cousin Shallow says: I pray you pardon me—he's a justice of peace in his country, simple though I stand here.

EVANS. But that is not the question: the question is concerning your marriage.

SHALLOW. Ay, there's the point, sir.

EVANS. Marry, is it: the very point of it—to Mistress Anne Page.

SLENDER. Why, if it be so ... I will marry her upon any reasonable demands.   220

EVANS. But can you affection the 'oman? Let us command to know that of your mouth, or of your lips: for divers philosophers hold that the lips is parcel of the mouth: therefore, precisely, can you carry your good will to the maid?

SHALLOW. Cousin Abraham Slender, can you love her?

SLENDER. I hope, sir, I will do as it shall become one that would do reason.

EVANS. Nay, Got's lords and his ladies! you must speak   230
possitable, if you can carry-her your desires towards her.

SHALLOW. That you must ... Will you—upon good dowry—marry her?

SLENDER. I will do a greater thing than that, upon your request, cousin, in any reason.

SHALLOW. Nay, conceive me, conceive me, sweet coz:

what I do is to pleasure you, coz: can you love the
maid?

SLENDER. I will marry her, sir, at your request; but if 240
there be no great love in the beginning, yet heaven
may decrease it upon better acquaintance, when we
are married and have more occasion to know one
another: I hope upon familiarity will grow more
contempt: but if you say, 'marry her,' I will marry
her—that I am freely dissolved, and dissolutely.

EVANS. It is a fery discretion-answer; save the fall is in
the 'ort 'dissolutely': the 'ort is, according to our
meaning, 'resolutely': his meaning is goot.

SHALLOW. Ay ... I think my cousin meant well.   250

SLENDER. Ay, or else I would I might be hanged, la!

Anne Page returns

SHALLOW. Here comes fair Mistress Anne; Would I
were young for your sake, Mistress Anne!

ANNE. The dinner is on the table. My father desires
your worships' company.

SHALLOW. I will wait on him, fair Mistress Anne.

EVANS. Od's plessed-will ... I will not be absence at the
grace.   *Evans and Shallow leave*

ANNE. Will't please your worship to come in, sir?

SLENDER. No—I thank you forsooth—heartily; I am   260
very well.

ANNE. The dinner attends you, sir.

SLENDER. I am not a-hungry, I thank you, forsooth ...
Go, sirrah, for all you are my man, go wait upon
my cousin Shallow ... [*Simple goes*] A justice of
peace sometime may be beholding to his friend, for
a man; I keep but three men and a boy yet, till my
mother be dead: but what though? yet I live like a
poor gentleman born.

ANNE. I may not go in without your worship: they   270
will not sit till you come.

SLENDER. I'faith, I'll eat nothing: I thank you as much
as though I did.

ANNE. I pray you sir walk in.

SLENDER. I had rather walk here—I thank you. I
bruised my shin th'other day with playing at sword
and dagger with a master of fence—three veneys for
a dish of stewed prunes—[and I with my ward
defending my head, he hot my shin,] and, by my
troth, I cannot abide the smell of hot meat since.... 280
Why do your dogs bark so? be there bears i'th'
town?

ANNE. I think there are, sir. I heard them talked of.

SLENDER. I love the sport well, but I shall as soon
quarrel at it as any man in England ... You are
afraid, if you see the bear loose, are you not?

ANNE. Ay, indeed, sir.

SLENDER. That's meat and drink to me, now: I have
seen Sackerson loose—twenty times, and have taken
him by the chain: but, I warrant you, the women   290
have so cried and shrieked at it, that it passed ...
But women, indeed, cannot abide 'em—they are
very ill-favoured rough things.

Enter Page

PAGE. Come, gentle Master Slender, come; we stay for
you.

SLENDER. I'll eat nothing, I thank you, sir.

PAGE. By cock and pie, you shall not choose, sir: come,
come!

SLENDER. Nay, pray you lead the way.

PAGE. Come on, sir.   300

SLENDER. Mistress Anne ... yourself shall go first.

ANNE. Not I, sir! pray you keep on.

SLENDER. Truly, I will not go first: truly, la! I will not
do you that wrong.

ANNE. I pray you, sir.

SLENDER. I'll rather be unmannerly than troublesome:
you do yourself wrong, indeed, la!

They go

Scene 2

Sir Hugh Evans and Simple enter

EVANS. Go your ways, and ask of Doctor Caius' house
which is the way; and there dwells one Mistress
Quickly; which is in the manner of his nurse—or his
dry nurse—or his cook—or his laundry—his washer
and his wringer.

SIMPLE. Well, sir.

EVANS. Nay, it is petter yet ....Give her this letter; for
it is a 'oman, that altogether's acquaintance with
Mistress Anne Page; and the letter is to desire and
require her to solicit your master's desires to Mistress 10
Anne Page: I pray you, be gone ... I will make an
end of my dinner; there's pippins and seese to come.

They go

Scene 3: *A room in the Garter Inn*

Falstaff, Host, Pistol, Nym, Bardolph and Robin

FALSTAFF. Mine host of the Garter!

HOST. What says my bully-rook? speak scholarly and
wisely.

FALSTAFF. Truly, mine host; I must turn away some of
my followers.

HOST. Discard, bully Hercules, cashier; let them wag;
trot, trot.

FALSTAFF. I sit at ten pounds a week.

HOST. Thou'rt an emperor—Cæsar, Keisar, and Pheazar. I will entertain Bardolph: he shall draw; he shall 10
tap; said I well, bully Hector?

FALSTAFF. Do so, good mine host.

HOST. I have spoke: let him follow ... [*to Bardolph*] Let
me see thee froth and lime: I am at a word: follow.

He goes out

FALSTAFF. Bardolph, follow him: a tapster is a good
trade: an old cloak makes a new jerkin: a withered
serving-man a fresh tapster ... Go, adieu.

BARDOLPH. It is a life that I have desired: I will thrive.

PISTOL. O base Hungarian wight: wilt thou the spigot
wield?   *Bardolph follows Host* 20

NYM. He was gotten in drink. [His mind is not heroic,
and there's the humour of it] ... Is not the humour
conceited?

FALSTAFF. I am glad I am so acquit of this tinderbox:
his thefts were too open: his filching was like an
unskilful singer, he kept not time.

NYM. The good humour is to steal at a minim-rest.

PISTOL. 'Convey,' the wise it call ... 'Steal!' foh! a fico
for the phrase.

FALSTAFF. Well, sirs, I am almost out at heels.   30

PISTOL. Why, then, let kibes ensue.

FALSTAFF. There is no remedy: I must cony-catch, I
must shift.

PISTOL. Young ravens must have food.

FALSTAFF. Which of you know Ford of this town?

PISTOL. I ken the wight: he is of substance good.

FALSTAFF. My honest lads, I will tell you what I am about.

PISTOL. Two yards, and more.

FALSTAFF. No quips now, Pistol . . . Indeed, I am in the 40 waist two yards about: but I am now about no waste: I am about thrift—Briefly: I do mean to make love to Ford's wife: I spy entertainment in her: she discourses: she carves: she gives the leer of invitation . . . I can construe the action of her familiar style, and the hardest voice of her behaviour—to be Englished rightly—is, 'I am Sir John Falstaff's.'

PISTOL. He hath studied her well, and translated her will . . . out of honesty into English.

NYM. The anchor is deep: will that humour pass? 50

FALSTAFF. Now, the report goes she has all the rule of her husband's purse: he hath a legion of angels.

PISTOL. As many devils entertain! and 'To her, Boy,' say I.

NYM. The humour rises: it is good: humour me the angels.

FALSTAFF. I have writ me here a letter to her: and here another to Page's wife; who even now gave me good eyes too; examined my parts with most judicious œillades: sometimes the beam of her view 60 gilded my foot . . . sometimes my portly belly.

PISTOL. Then did the sun on dunghill shine.

NYM. I thank thee for that humour.

FALSTAFF. O, she did so course o'er my exteriors with such a greedy intention, that the appetite of her eye did seem to scorch me up like a burning-glass . . . Here's another letter to her: she bears the purse too: she is a region in Guiana: all gold and bounty . . . I will be cheaters to them both, and they shall be exchequers to me: they shall be my East and West 70 Indies, and I will trade to them both . . . Go, bear thou this letter to Mistress Page; and thou this to Mistress Ford: we will thrive, lads, we will thrive.

PISTOL. Shall I Sir Pandarus of Troy become— And by my side wear steel! then, Lucifer take all!

NYM. I will run no base humour: here, take the humour-letter; I will keep the haviour of reputation.

FALSTAFF [to Robin]. Hold, sirrah, bear you these letters tightly, Sail like my pinnace to these golden shores. . . . Rogues, hence, avaunt, vanish like hail-stones; go! 80 Trudge; plod away i'th' hoof; seek shelter, pack . . . Falstaff will learn the humour of this age, French thrift, you rogues—myself and skirted page! *He goes out, with Robin following*

PISTOL. Let vultures gripe thy guts: for gourd and fullam holds, And high and low beguiles the rich and poor: Tester I'll have in pouch when thou shalt lack, Base Phrygian Turk!

NYM. I have operations [in my head] which be humours of revenge.

PISTOL. Wilt thou revenge?

NYM. By welkin and her star! 90

PISTOL. With wit or steel?

NYM. With both the humours, I: I will discuss the humour of this love to Page.

PISTOL. And I to Ford shall eke unfold, How Falstaff, varlet vile, His dove will prove, his gold will hold, And his soft couch defile.

NYM. My humour shall not cool: I will incense Page to deal with poison: I will possess him with' yellows, for the revolt of mind is dangerous: that is my true humour. 100

PISTOL. Thou art the Mars of malcontents: I second thee: troop on. *They go*

Scene 4: *A room in Doctor Caius' house*

Enter Mistress Quickly and Simple

QUICKLY [*calling*]. What, John Rugby!

Rugby enters

I pray thee, go to the casement, and see if you can see my master, Master Doctor Caius, coming: if he do, i'faith, and find any body in the house . . . here will be an old abusing of God's patience and the king's English.

RUGBY. I'll go watch.

QUICKLY. Go, and we'll have a posset for't soon at night, in faith at the latter end of a sea-coal fire . . . [*Rugby goes to the window*] An honest, willing, kind 10 fellow, as ever servant shall come in house withal: and, I warrant you, no tell-tale nor no breed-bate: his worst fault is, that he is given to prayer; he is something peevish that way: but nobody but has his fault: but let that pass. . . . Peter Simple, you say your name is?

SIMPLE. Ay . . . for fault of a better.

QUICKLY. And Master Slender's your master?

SIMPLE. Ay, forsooth.

QUICKLY. Does he not wear a great round beard, like a 20 glover's paring-knife?

SIMPLE. No, forsooth: he hath but a little whey-face; with a little yellow beard . . . a cane-coloured beard.

QUICKLY. A softly-sprighted man, is he not?

SIMPLE. Ay, forsooth: but he is as tall a man of his hands as any is between this and his head: he hath fought with a warrener!

QUICKLY. How say you?—O, I should remember him: does he not hold up his head, as it were, and strut in his gait? 30

SIMPLE. Yes, indeed, does he.

QUICKLY. Well, heaven send Anne Page no worse fortune . . . Tell Master Parson Evans I will do what I can for your master: Anne is a good girl, and I wish—

RUGBY [*calls from the window*]. Out, alas! here comes my master.

QUICKLY. We shall all be shent . . . Run in here, good young man: go into this closet . . . [*she shuts Simple in the closet*] He will not stay long . . . What, John 40 Rugby! John! what, John, I say!

Caius enters

Go, John, go enquire for my master. I doubt he be not well, that he comes not home . . . *She sings* And down, down, adown-a, &c.

CAIUS. Vat is you sing? I do not like des toys: pray you, go and vetch me in my closet un boitier vert; a box, a green-a box . . . Do intend vat I speak? a green-a box.

QUICKLY. Ay, forsooth, I'll fetch it you . . . [*to Rugby*] I am glad he went not in himself: if he had found the 50 young man, he would have been horn-mad.

CAIUS. Fe, fe, fe, fe! ma foi, il fait fort chaud. Je m'en vais à la cour—la grande affaire.

QUICKLY. Is it this, sir?

CAIUS. Oui, mette le au mon pocket, dépêche Quickly ... Vere is dat knave Rugby?

QUICKLY. What, John Rugby! John!

RUGBY [comes forward]. Here, sir.

CAIUS. You are John Rugby, and you are Jack Rugby ... Come, tak-a your rapier, and come after my heel to de court. 60

RUGBY. 'Tis ready, sir, here in the porch.

CAIUS. By my trot: I tarry too long ... Od's me ... Qu'ai-j'oublié! dere is some simples in my closet, dat I vill not for the varld I shall leave behind.

QUICKLY. Ay me, he'll find the young man there, and be mad.

CAIUS [discovers Simple]. O diable, diable! vat is in my closet? Villainy! laroon! [pulling him out] Rugby, my rapier. 70

QUICKLY. Good master, be content.

CAIUS. Verefore shall I be content-a?

QUICKLY. The young man is an honest man.

CAIUS. Vat shall de honest man do in my closet? dere is no honest man dat shall come in my closet.

QUICKLY. I beseech you, be not so phlegmatic: hear the truth of it.... He came of an errand to me from Parson Hugh.

CAIUS. Vell.

SIMPLE. Ay, forsooth ... to desire her to— 80

QUICKLY. Peace, I pray you.

CAIUS. Peac-a your tongue ... Speak-a your tale.

SIMPLE. To desire this honest gentlewoman, your maid, to speak a good word to Mistress Anne Page —for my master in the way of marriage.

QUICKLY. This is all, indeed, la! but I'll ne'er put my finger in the fire, and need not.

CAIUS. Sir Hugh send-a you! Rugby, baillez me some paper ... tarry you a littl-a while. He writes

QUICKLY [draws Simple aside]. I am glad he is so quiet: 90 if he had been throughly moved, you should have heard him so loud, and so melancholy ... But notwithstanding, man, I'll do your master what good I can: and the very yea and the no is, the French doctor, my master—I may call him my master, look you, for I keep his house; and I wash, wring, brew, bake, scour, dress meat and drink, make the beds, and do all myself—

SIMPLE. 'Tis a great charge to come under one body's hand. 100

QUICKLY. Are you avised o'that? you shall find it a great charge: and to be up early, and down late ... but notwithstanding (to tell you in your ear, I would have no words of it) my master himself is in love with Mistress Anne Page: but notwithstanding that I know Anne's mind, that's neither here nor there.

CAIUS. You, jack'nape! giv-a this letter to Sir Hugh. By gar, it is a shallenge: I vill cut his troat in de Park, and I vill teach a scurvy jack-a-nape priest to meddle or make!—You may be gone: it is not good you 110 tarry here ... [Simple goes] By gar, I vill cut all his two stones: by gar, he shall not have a stone to trow at his dog.

QUICKLY. Alas: he speaks but for his friend.

CAIUS. It is no matter-a ver dat: do not you tell-a me dat I shall have Anne Page for myself? By gar, I vill kill de Jack-priest ... and I have appointed mine host

of de Jarteer to measure our weapon ... by gar, I vill myself have Anne Page.

QUICKLY. Sir, the maid loves you, and all shall be well: 120 We must give folks leave to prate ... What the good-jer!

CAIUS. Rugby, come to the court vit me ... By gar, if I have not Anne Page, I shall turn your head out of my door ... Follow my heels, Rugby.

He goes out, followed by Rugby

QUICKLY. You shall have An fool's-head of your own ... No, I know Anne's mind for that: never a woman in Windsor knows more of Anne's mind than I do, nor can do more than I do with her, I thank heaven. 130

FENTON [from outside]. Who's within there, ho!

QUICKLY. Who's there, I trow? Come near the house, I pray you.

Fenton enters

FENTON. How now, good woman, how dost thou?

QUICKLY. The better that it pleases your good worship to ask.

FENTON. What news? how does pretty Mistress Anne?

QUICKLY. In truth, sir, and she is pretty, and honest, and gentle, and one that is your friend, I can tell you that by the way, I praise heaven for it. 140

FENTON. Shall I do any good, think'st thou? Shall I not lose my suit?

QUICKLY. Troth, sir, all is in his hands above: but notwithstanding, Master Fenton, I'll be sworn on a book she loves you ... Have not your worship a wart above your eye?

FENTON. Yes marry have I, what of that?

QUICKLY. Well, thereby hangs a tale ... good faith, it is such another Nan; but—I detest—an honest maid as ever broke bread ... We had an hour's talk of that 150 wart; I shall never laugh but in that maid's company ... but, indeed, she is given too much to allicholy and musing ... But for you—well—go to—

FENTON. Well ... I shall see her to-day: hold, there's money for thee ... Let me have thy voice in my behalf: if thou seest her before me, commend me—

QUICKLY. Will I? i'faith, that we will: and I will tell your worship more of the wart the next time we have confidence, and of other wooers.

FENTON. Well, farewell. I am in great haste now. 160

He goes out

QUICKLY. Farewell to your worship ... Truly, an honest gentleman: but Anne loves him not: for I know Anne's mind as well as another does ... Out upon't! what have I forgot? She hurries away

ACT 2

Scene 1: Before the house of Master Page

Mistress Page, with a letter

MISTRESS PAGE. What, have I 'scaped love-letters in the holiday time of my beauty, and am I now a subject for them? Let me see! She reads 'Ask me no reason why I love you, for though Love use Reason for his precisian, he admits him not for his councillor ... You are not young, no more am I: go to then, there's sympathy ... you are merry, so am I: ha! ha! then there's more sympathy ... you love sack, and so do I: would you desire better

sympathy? Let it suffice thee, Mistress Page, at the 10
least if the love of a soldier can suffice, that I love
thee: I will not say, pity me—'tis not a soldier-like
phrase; but I say, love me ...
By me, thine own true knight, by day or night:
> Or any kind of light, with all his might,
> For thee to fight.

JOHN FALSTAFF.'

What a Herod of Jewry is this! O wicked, wicked
world! One that is well-nigh worn to pieces with
age to show himself a young gallant! What an 20
unweighed behaviour hath this Flemish drunkard
picked (with the devil's name!) out of my conversation, that he dares in this manner assay me? Why, he
hath not been thrice in my company: what should I
say to him? I was then frugal of my mirth ... Heaven
forgive me! Why, I'll exhibit a bill in the parliament
for the putting down of men ... How shall I be
revenged on him? for revenged I will be!—as sure
as his guts are made of puddings.

Mistress Ford appears

MISTRESS FORD. Mistress Page! trust me, I was going 30
to your house.
MISTRESS PAGE. And, trust me, I was coming to you ...
You look very ill.
MISTRESS FORD. Nay, I'll ne'er believe that; I have to
show to the contrary.
MISTRESS PAGE. Faith, but you do, in my mind.
MISTRESS FORD. Well: I do then: yet, I say, I could show
you to the contrary ... O Mistress Page, give me
some counsel!
MISTRESS PAGE. What's the matter, woman? 40
MISTRESS FORD. O woman ... if it were not for one
trifling respect, I could come to such honour.
MISTRESS PAGE. Hang the trifle, woman, take the
honour: what is it? Dispense with trifles: what is it?
MISTRESS FORD. If I would but go to hell for an eternal
moment or so ... I could be knighted!
MISTRESS PAGE. What? thou liest! Sir Alice Ford! These
knights will hack, and so thou shouldst not alter the
article of thy gentry.
MISTRESS FORD. We burn day-light ... Here, read, 50
read: perceive how I might be knighted. I shall think
the worse of fat men, as long as I have an eye to
make difference of men's liking: and yet he would
not swear; praised women's modesty; and gave such
orderly and well-behaved reproof to all uncomeli-
ness, that I would have sworn his disposition would
have gone to the truth of his words: but they do
no more adhere and keep place together than the
Hundredth Psalm to the tune of 'Green-sleeves' ...
What tempest, I trow, threw this whale, with so 60
many tuns of oil in his belly, ashore at Windsor?
How shall I be revenged on him? I think the
best way were to entertain him with hope, till
the wicked fire of lust have melted him in his own
grease ... Did you ever hear the like?
MISTRESS PAGE. Letter for letter; but that the name of
Page and Ford differs ... To thy great comfort in
this mystery of ill opinions, here's the twin-brother
of thy letter: but let thine inherit first, for I protest
mine never shall: I warrant he hath a thousand of 70
these letters, writ with blank space for different names
—sure more!—and these are of the second edition:
he will print them out of doubt; for he cares not

what he puts into the press, when he would put us
two ... I had rather be a giantess, and lie under
Mount Pelion ... Well; I will find you twenty
lascivious turtles ere one chaste man.
MISTRESS FORD. Why, this is the very same ... the very
hand ... the very words! What doth he think of us?
MISTRESS PAGE. Nay, I know not: it makes me almost 80
ready to wrangle with mine own honesty: I'll entertain myself like one that I am not acquainted withal;
for, sure, unless he know some strain in me, that I
know not myself, he would never have boarded me
in this fury.
MISTRESS FORD. 'Boarding,' call you it? I'll be sure to
keep him above deck.
MISTRESS PAGE. So will I: if he come under my hatches,
I'll never to sea again ... Let's be revenged on him:
let's appoint him a meeting; give him a show of 90
comfort in his suit, and lead him on with a fine-
baited delay, till he hath pawned his horses to mine
host of the Garter.
MISTRESS FORD. Nay, I will consent to act any villainy
against him, that may not sully the chariness of our
honesty ... O, that my husband saw this letter: it
would give eternal food to his jealousy.
MISTRESS PAGE. Why, look where he comes; and my
good man too: he's as far from jealousy, as I am
from giving him cause—and that, I hope, is an 100
unmeasurable distance.
MISTRESS FORD. You are the happier woman.
MISTRESS PAGE. Let's consult together against this
greasy knight ... Come hither.

They seat themselves unseen, within earshot: Ford and
Pistol, Page and Nym come up in pairs

FORD. Well ... I hope it be not so.
PISTOL. Hope is a curtal-dog in some affairs:
> Sir John affects thy wife.
FORD. Why, sir, my wife is not young.
PISTOL. He wooes both high and low, both rich and
> poor,
> Both young and old, one with another, Ford. 110
> He loves the gallimaufry—Ford, perpend.
FORD. Love my wife!
PISTOL. With liver burning hot: prevent ... or go
> thou,
> Like Sir Actæon be, with Ringwood at thy heels ...
> O, odious is the name!
FORD. What name, sir?
PISTOL. The horn, I say ... Farewell ...
> Take heed, have open eye, for thieves do foot by
> night....
> Take heed, ere summer comes or cuckoo-birds do
> sing....
> Away, Sir Corporal Nym ... [*to Page*] Believe it, he
> speaks sense. *Pistol goes off* 120
FORD. I will be patient ... I will find out this.
NYM [*to Page*]. And this is true: I like not the humour
of lying: he hath wronged me in some humours: I
should have borne the humoured letter to her: but I
have a sword: and it shall bite upon my necessity:
he loves your wife; there's the short and the long ...
> My name is Coporal Nym: I speak, and I avouch;
> 'Tis true: my name is Nym: and Falstaff loves
> your wife
... Adieu. I love not the humour of bread and
cheese, [and there's the humour of it] ... Adieu. 130

He follows Pistol

PAGE. 'The humour of it,' quoth 'a! here's a fellow frights English out of his wits.

FORD. I will seek out Falstaff.

PAGE. I never heard such a drawling, affecting rogue.

FORD. If I do find it ... well.

PAGE. I will not believe such a Cataian, though the priest o'th' town commended him for a true man.

FORD. 'Twas a good sensible fellow ... well.

Mistress Page and Mistress Ford come forward

PAGE. How now, Meg!

MISTRESS PAGE. Whither go you, George? Hark you. 140

MISTRESS FORD. How now, sweet Frank! why art thou melancholy?

FORD. I melancholy? I am not melancholy ... Get you home: go.

MISTRESS FORD. Faith, thou hast some crotchets in thy head now ... Will you go, Mistress Page?

MISTRESS PAGE. Have with you.... You'll come to dinner, George? [*in Mistress Ford's ear*] Look, who comes yonder: she shall be our messenger to this paltry knight. 150

MISTRESS FORD. Trust me, I thought on her: she'll fit it.

Mistress Quickly comes up

MISTRESS PAGE. You are come to see my daughter Anne?

QUICKLY. Ay, forsooth: and, I pray, how does good Mistress Anne?

MISTRESS PAGE. Go in with us and see: we have an hour's talk with you.   *They go within*

PAGE. How now, Master Ford!

FORD. You heard what this knave told me, did you not? 160

PAGE. Yes, and you heard what the other told me?

FORD. Do you think there is truth in them?

PAGE. Hang 'em, slaves: I do not think the knight would offer it: but these that accuse him in his intent towards our wives are a yoke of his discarded men ... very rogues, now they be out of service.

FORD. Were they his men?

PAGE. Marry, were they.

FORD. I like it never the better for that. Does he lie at the Garter? 170

PAGE. Ay, marry, does he ... If he should intend this voyage towards my wife, I would turn her loose to him; and what he gets more of her than sharp words, let it lie on my head.

FORD. I do not misdoubt my wife ... but I would be loath to turn them together ... a man may be too confident ... I would have nothing lie on my head ... I cannot be thus satisfied.

Host approaches with Shallow following

PAGE. Look where my ranting host of the Garter comes: there is either liquor in his pate, or money in his purse, when he looks so merrily ... How now, mine host! 180

HOST. How now, bully-rook! thou'rt a gentleman. Cavaliero-justice, I say!

SHALLOW. I follow, mine host, I follow.... Good even and twenty, good Master Page! Master Page, will you go with us? we have sport in hand.

HOST. Tell him, cavaliero-justice: tell him, bully-rook.

SHALLOW. Sir, there is a fray to be fought, between Sir Hugh the Welsh priest and Caius the French doctor. 190

FORD. Good mine host o'th' Garter ... a word with you.

HOST. What sayst thou, my bully-rook?

They talk together apart

SHALLOW [*to Page*]. Will you go with us to behold it? My merry host hath had the measuring of their weapons; and, I think, hath appointed them contrary places: for, believe me, I hear the parson is no jester: hark, I will tell you what our sport shall be.

They talk together apart

HOST. Hast thou no suit against my knight, my guest-cavalier? 200

FORD. None, I protest: but I'll give you a pottle of burnt sack to give me recourse to him, and tell him my name is Brook ... only for a jest.

HOST. My hand, bully: thou shalt have egress and regress—said I well?—and thy name shall be Brook.... It is a merry knight: Will you go, Ameers?   *Going*

SHALLOW. Have with you, mine host.

PAGE. I have heard the Frenchman hath good skill in his rapier. 210

SHALLOW. Tut, sir! I could have told you more: in these times you stand on distance ... your passes, stoccadoes, and I know not what ... 'tis the heart, Master Page—'tis here, 'tis here: I have seen the time, with my long sword I would have made you four tall fellows skip like rats.

HOST. Here, boys, here, here! shall we wag?

PAGE. Have with you ... I had rather hear them scold than fight.   *Shallow and Page follow Host*

FORD. Though Page be a secure fool, and stands so 220 firmly on his wife's frailty—yet I cannot put off my opinion so easily: she was in his company at Page's house ... and, what they made there, I know not.... Well, I will look further into't, and I have a disguise to sound Falstaff ... If I find her honest, I lose not my labour: if she be otherwise, 'tis labour well bestowed.   *He goes*

Scene 2: *The room in the Garter Inn*

Enter Falstaff and Pistol

[PISTOL. I will retort the sum in equipage.]

FALSTAFF. I will not lend thee a penny.

PISTOL. Why, then the world's mine oyster, Which I with sword will open.

FALSTAFF. Not a penny: I have been content, sir, you should lay my countenance to pawn: I have grated upon my good friends for three reprieves for you and your coach-fellow, Nym; or else you had looked through the grate, like a geminy of baboons: I am damned in hell for swearing to gentlemen my 10 friends, you were good soldiers and tall fellows.... and when Mistress Bridget lost the handle of her fan, I took't upon mine honour thou hadst it not.

PISTOL. Didst thou not share? hadst thou not fifteen pence?

FALSTAFF. Reason, you rogue, reason: think'st thou I'll endanger my soul gratis? At a word, hang no more about me, I am no gibbet for you ... Go—a short knife and a throng—to your manor of Pickt-hatch ... Go. You'll not bear a letter for me, you rogue! you stand upon your honour!.why, thou unconfin- 20

able baseness, it is as much as I can do, to keep the
terms of my honour precise ... Ay, ay, I myself
sometimes, leaving the fear of God on the left hand,
and hiding mine honour in my necessity, am fain to
shuffle, to hedge, and to lurch—and yet you, rogue,
will ensconce your rags, your cat-a-mountain looks,
your red-lattice phrases, and your bold-beating
oaths, under the shelter of your honour! You will
not do it? you!

PISTOL. I do relent: what wouldst thou more of man? 30

Robin enters

ROBIN. Sir, here's a woman would speak with you.
FALSTAFF. Let her approach.

Mistress Quickly enters

QUICKLY. Give your worship good-morrow.
FALSTAFF. Good-morrow, good wife.
QUICKLY. Not so, an't please your worship.
FALSTAFF. Good maid, then.
QUICKLY. I'll be sworn,
As my mother was, the first hour I was born.
FALSTAFF. I do believe the swearer; what with me?
QUICKLY. Shall I vouchsafe your worship a word or 40
two?
FALSTAFF. Two thousand—fair woman—and I'll
vouch-safe thee the hearing.
QUICKLY. There is one Mistress Ford—Sir, I pray,
come a little nearer this ways ... I myself dwell with
Master Doctor Caius ...
FALSTAFF. Well, on; Mistress Ford, you say—
QUICKLY. Your worship says very true: I pray your
worship, come a little nearer this ways.
FALSTAFF. I warrant thee, nobody hears: mine own 50
people, mine own people.
QUICKLY. Are they so? God bless them, and make
them his servants!
FALSTAFF. Well; Mistress Ford, what of her?
QUICKLY. Why, sir; she's a good creature; Lord, Lord!
your worship's a wanton ... well ... God forgive
you, and all of us, I pray—
FALSTAFF. Mistress Ford ... come, Mistress Ford.
QUICKLY. Marry, this is the short and the long of it:
you have brought her into such a canaries, as 'tis 60
wonderful: the best courtier of them all (when the
court lay at Windsor) could never have brought her
to such a canary: yet there has been knights, and
lords, and gentlemen, with their coaches; I warrant
you, coach after coach, letter after letter, gift after
gift; smelling so sweetly, all musk, and so rushling,
I warrant you, in silk and gold, and in such alligant
terms, and in such wine and sugar of the best, and
the fairest, that would have won any woman's heart:
and, I warrant you, they could never get an eye- 70
wink of her: I had myself twenty angels given me
this morning, but I defy all angels—in any such
sort, as they say—but in the way of honesty: and, I
warrant you, they could never get her so much as sip
on a cup with the proudest of them all, and yet there
has been earls ... nay, which is more, pensioners—
but, I warrant you, all is one with her.
FALSTAFF. But what say, she to me? be brief, my good
she-Mercury.
QUICKLY. Marry, she hath received your letter: for the 80
which she thanks you a thousand times; and she

gives you to notify that her husband will be absence
from his house between ten and eleven.
FALSTAFF. Ten and eleven.
QUICKLY. Ay, forsooth: and then you may come and
see the picture, she says, that you wot of: Master
Ford, her husband, will be from home: alas! the
sweet woman leads an ill life with him: he's a very
jealousy man; she leads a very frampold life with
him—good heart!   90
FALSTAFF. Ten and eleven.... Woman, commend me
to her. I will not fail her.
QUICKLY. Why, you say well ... But I have another
messenger to your worship: Mistress Page hath her
hearty commendations to you, too: and let me tell
you in your ear, she's as fartuous a civil modest wife,
and one, I tell you, that will not miss you morning
nor evening prayer, as any is in Windsor, whoe'er be
the other: and she bade me tell your worship that
her husband is seldom from home, but she hopes 100
there will come a time.... I never knew a woman
so dote upon a man; surely, I think you have charms,
la ... yes, in truth.
FALSTAFF. Not I, I assure thee; setting the attraction of
my good parts aside, I have no other charms.
QUICKLY. Blessing on your heart for't!
FALSTAFF. But I pray thee tell me this: has Ford's
wife, and Page's wife, acquainted each other how
they love me?
QUICKLY. That were a jest, indeed! they have not so 110
little grace, I hope—that were a trick, indeed! But
Mistress Page would desire you to send her your
little page, of all loves: her husband has a marvellous
infection to the little page: and, truly, Master Page
is an honest man: never a wife in Windsor leads a
better life than she does: do what she will, say what
she will, take all, pay all, go to bed when she list, rise
when she list, all is as she will: and, truly, she deserves
it; for if there be a kind woman in Windsor, she is
one: you must send her your page—no remedy.   120
FALSTAFF. Why, I will.
QUICKLY. Nay, but do so then—and, look you, he
may come and go between you both: and, in any
case, have a nay-word, that you may know one
another's mind, and the boy never need to understand any thing; for 'tis not good that children
should know any wickedness: old folks, you know,
have discretion, as they say, and know the world.
FALSTAFF. Fare thee well. Commend me to them both:
there's my purse—I am yet thy debtor ... Boy, go 130
along with this woman. [*Quickly and Robin go out*]
This news distracts me....
PISTOL. This pink is one of Cupid's carriers—
Clap on more sails, pursue: up with your fights:
Give fire: she is my prize, or ocean whelm them all!
                                        He pursues them
FALSTAFF. Sayst thou so, old Jack? go thy ways? I'll
make more of thy old body than I have done: will
they yet look after thee? wilt thou, after the expense
of so much money, be now a gainer? Good body,
I thank thee: let them say 'tis grossly done—so it be 140
fairly done, no matter.

Bardolph enters

BARDOLPH. Sir John, there's one Master Brook below
would fain speak with you, and be acquainted with

you; and hath sent your worship a morning's draught of sack.

FALSTAFF. Brook is his name?

BARDOLPH. Ay, sir.

FALSTAFF. Call him in ... [*Bardolph goes out*] Such Brooks are welcome to me, that o'erflow such liquor ... Ah, ha! Mistress Ford and Mistress Page, have I encompassed you? go to, via! 150

Bardolph returns, with Ford disguised

FORD. Bless you, sir.

FALSTAFF. And you, sir: would you speak with me?

FORD. I make bold, to press with so little preparation upon you.

FALSTAFF. You're welcome. What's your will? Give us leave, drawer.   *Bardolph leaves them*

FORD. Sir, I am a gentleman that have spent much. My name is Brook.

FALSTAFF. Good Master Brook, I desire more acquaint- 160 ance of you.

FORD. Good Sir John, I sue for yours: not to charge you, for I must let you understand I think myself in better plight for a lender than you are: the which hath something emboldened me to this unseasoned intrusion: for they say, if money go before, all ways do lie open.

FALSTAFF. Money is a good soldier, sir, and will on.

FORD. Troth, and I have a bag of money here troubles me: if you will help me to bear it, Sir John, take all, 170 or half, for easing me of the carriage.

FALSTAFF. Sir, I know not how I may deserve to be your porter.

FORD. I will tell you, sir, if you will give me the hearing.

FALSTAFF. Speak, good Master Brook. I shall be glad to be your servant.

FORD. Sir, I hear you are a scholar—I will be brief with you—and you have been a man long known to me, though I had never so good means, as desire, to 180 make myself acquainted with you.... I shall discover a thing to you, wherein I must very much lay open mine own imperfection: but, good Sir John, as you have one eye upon my follies, as you hear them unfolded, turn another into the register of your own, that I may pass with a reproof the easier, sith you yourself know how easy it is to be such an offender.

FALSTAFF. Very well, sir. Proceed.

FORD. There is a gentlewoman in this town—her 190 husband's name is Ford.

FALSTAFF. Well, sir.

FORD. I have long loved her, and, I protest to you, bestowed much on her: followed her with a doting observance; engrossed opportunities to meet her; fee'd every slight occasion that could but niggardly give me sight of her; not only bought many presents to give her, but have given largely to many to know what she would have given: briefly, I have pursued her, as love hath pursued me, which hath been on 200 the wing of all occasions ... but whatsoever I have merited—either in my mind or in my means—meed, I am sure, I have received none, unless experience be a jewel. That I have purchased at an infinite rate, and that hath taught me to say this—

"Love like a shadow flies when substance love pursues,

"Pursuing that that flies, and flying what pursues."

FALSTAFF. Have you received no promise of satisfaction at her hands?

FORD. Never.   210

FALSTAFF. Have you importuned her to such a purpose?

FORD. Never.

FALSTAFF. Of what quality was your love, then?

FORD. Like a fair house built upon another man's ground—so that I have lost my edifice by mistaking the place where I erected it.

FALSTAFF. To what purpose have you unfolded this to me?

FORD. When I have told you that, I have told you all ... Some say, that though she appear honest to 220 me, yet in other places she enlargeth her mirth so far that there is shrewd construction made of her.... Now, Sir John, here is the heart of my purpose: you are a gentleman of excellent breeding, admirable discourse, of great admittance, authentic in your place and person, generally allowed for your many warlike, court-like, and learned preparations.

FALSTAFF. O, sir!

FORD. Believe it, for you know it ... There is money. Spend it, spend it, spend more; spend all I have, only 230 give me so much of your time in exchange of it, as to lay an amiable siege to the honesty of this Ford's wife: use your art of wooing; win her to consent to you: if any man may, you may as soon as any.

FALSTAFF. Would it apply well to the vehemency of your affection, that I should win what you would enjoy? Methinks you prescribe to yourself very preposterously.

FORD. O, understand my drift: she dwells so securely on the excellency of her honour, that the folly of my 240 soul dares not present itself; she is too bright to be looked against.... Now, could I come to her with any detection in my hand ... my desires had instance and argument to commend themselves. I could drive her then from the ward of her purity, her reputation, her marriage-vow, and a thousand other her defences, which now are too-too strongly embattled against me: what say you to't, Sir John?

FALSTAFF. Master Brook, I will first make bold with your money; next, give me your hand; and last, as 250 I am a gentleman, you shall, if you will, enjoy Ford's wife.

FORD. O good sir!

FALSTAFF. I say you shall.

FORD. Want no money, Sir John, you shall want none.

FALSTAFF. Want no Mistress Ford, Master Brook, you shall want none: I shall be with her—I may tell you—by her own appointment. Even as you came in to me, her assistant, or go-between, parted from me: I say I shall be with her between ten and 260 eleven; for at that time the jealous rascally knave, her husband, will be forth ... Come you to me at night, you shall know how I speed.

FORD. I am blest in your acquaintance ... Do you know Ford, sir?

FALSTAFF. Hang him, poor cuckoldly knave! I know him not: yet I wrong him to call him poor: they say the jealous wittolly knave hath masses of money, for the which his wife seems to me wellfavoured: I will use her as the key of the cuckoldly 270 rogue's coffer—and there's my harvest-home.

FORD. I would you knew Ford, sir, that you might avoid him, if you saw him.

FALSTAFF. Hang him, mechanical salt-butter rogue! I will stare him out of his wits: I will awe him with my cudgel: it shall hang like a meteor o'er the cuckold's horns ... Master Brook, thou shalt know, I will predominate over the peasant, and thou shalt lie with his wife.... Come to me soon at night: Ford's a knave, and I will aggravate his style: thou, Master 280 Brook, shalt know him for knave—and cuckold.... Come to me soon at night.   *He goes*

FORD. What a damned Epicurean rascal is this! My heart is ready to crack with impatience ... Who says this is improvident jealousy? my wife hath sent to him, the hour is fixed, the match is made ... Would any man have thought this? See the hell of having a false woman: my bed shall be abused, my coffers ransacked, my reputation gnawn at, and I shall not only receive this villainous wrong, but stand under 290 the adoption of abominable terms, and by him that does me this wrong ... Terms, names! Amaimon sounds well; Lucifer, well; Barbason, well; yet they are devils' additions, the names of fiends: but Cuckold! Wittol!—Cuckold! the devil himself hath not such a name.... Page is an ass, a secure ass; he will trust his wife, he will not be jealous: I will rather trust a Fleming with my butter, Parson Hugh the Welshman with my cheese, an Irishman with my aqua-vitæ bottle, or a thief to walk my ambling 300 gelding, than my wife with herself.... Then she plots, then she ruminates, then she devises: and what they think in their hearts they may effect, they will break their hearts but they will effect.... God be praised for my jealousy ... Eleven o'clock the hour. I will prevent this, detect my wife, be revenged on Falstaff, and laugh at Page.... I will about it—better three hours too soon, than a minute too late.... Fie, fie, fie! cuckold! cuckold! cuckold!   *He goes*

Scene 3: *A field near Windsor*

Enter Caius and Rugby

CAIUS. Jack Rugby!

RUGBY. Sir.

CAIUS. Vat is de clock, Jack?

RUGBY. 'Tis past the hour, sir, that Sir Hugh promised to meet.

CAIUS. By gar, he has save his soul, dat he is no-come: he has pray his Pible well, dat he is no-come: by gar, Jack Rugby, he is dead already, if he be come.

RUGBY. He is wise, sir: he knew your worship would 10 kill him if he came.

CAIUS. By gar, de herring is no dead, so as I vill kill him ... Take your rapier, Jack! I vill tell you how I vill kill him.

RUGBY. Alas, sir, I cannot fence.

CAIUS. Villainy, take your rapier.

RUGBY. Forbear ... here's company.

Host, Shallow, Slender, and Page come up

HOST. Bless thee, bully doctor.

SHALLOW. Save you, Master Doctor Caius.

PAGE. Now, good master doctor!

SLENDER. Give you good-morrow, sir.   20

CAIUS. Vat be all you, one, two, tree, four, come for?

HOST. To see thee fight, to see thee foin, to see thee traverse, to see thee here, to see thee there, to see thee pass thy punto, thy stock, thy reverse, thy distance, thy montánt ... Is he dead, my Ethiopian? is he dead, my Francisco? ha, bully! What says my Æsculapius? my Galen? my heart of elder? Ha! is he dead, bully-stale? is he dead?

CAIUS. By gar, he is de Coward-Jack-Priest of de vorld: he is not show his face.   30

HOST. Thou art a Castillian-King-Urinal! Hector of Greece, my boy!

CAIUS. I pray you, bear vitness that me have stay six or seven, two, tree hours for him, and he is no-come.

SHALLOW. He is the wiser man, master doctor! he is a curer of souls, and you a curer of bodies: if you should fight, you go against the hair of your professions: is it not true, Master Page?

PAGE. Master Shallow ... you have yourself been a great fighter, though now a man of peace.   40

SHALLOW. Bodykins, Master Page, though I now be old, and of the peace ... if I see a sword out, my finger itches to make one ... Though we are justices, and doctors, and churchmen, Master Page, we have some salt of our youth in us—we are the sons of women, Master Page.

PAGE. 'Tis true, Master Shallow.

SHALLOW. It will be found so, Master Page ... Master Doctor Caius, I am come to fetch you home ... I am sworn of the peace: you have showed yourself a wise 50 physician, and Sir Hugh hath shown himself a wise and patient churchman ... You must go with me, master doctor.

HOST. Pardon, guest-justice ... a [word,] Mounseur Mock-water.

CAIUS. Mock-vater? vat is dat?

HOST. Mock-water, in our English tongue, is valour, bully.

CAIUS. By gar, then I have as much mock-vater as de Englishman ... scurvy jack-dog priest! by gar, me 60 vill cut his ears.

HOST. He will clapper-claw thee tightly, bully.

CAIUS. Clapper-de-claw! vat is dat?

HOST. That is, he will make thee amends.

CAIUS. By gar, me do look he shall clapper-de-claw me—for, by gar, me vill have it.

HOST. And I will provoke him to't, or let him wag.

CAIUS. Me tank you for dat.

HOST. And moreover, bully,—[*aside*] But first, master guest, and Master Page, and eke Cavaliero Slender, 70 go you through the town to Frogmore.

PAGE. Sir Hugh is there, is he?

HOST. He is there. See what humour he is in; and I will bring the doctor about by the fields: will it do well?

SHALLOW. We will do it.

PAGE, SHALLOW, SLENDER. Adieu, good master doctor.
                                        They depart

CAIUS. By gar, me vill kill de priest, for he speak for a jack-an-ape to Anne Page.

HOST. Let him die: [but, first,] sheathe thy impatience; throw cold water on thy choler: go about the fields 80 with me through Frogmore. I will bring thee where Mistress Anne Page is, at a farm-house a-feasting; and thou shalt woo her ... Cried-game, said I well?

CAIUS. By gar, me dank you vor dat: by gar, I love you; and I shall procur-a you de good guest: de earl, de knight, de lords, de gentlemen, my patients.

HOST. For the which, I will be thy adversary toward
Anne Page: said I well?

CAIUS. By gar, 'tis good: vell said.

HOST. Let us wag then.   90

CAIUS. Come at my heels, Jack Rugby.

They go off

ACT 3

Scene 1: *A meadow near Frogmore*

Sir Hugh Evans, Simple

EVANS. I pray you now, good Master Slender's
serving-man, and friend Simple by your name,
which way have you looked for Master Caius, that
calls himself doctor of physic?

SIMPLE. Marry, sir, the pittie-ward, the park-ward,
every way: old Windsor way, and every way but the
town way.

EVANS. I most fehemently desire you, you will also
look that way.

SIMPLE. I will, sir.   10

EVANS. Pless my soul! how full of cholers I am, and
trempling of mind ... I shall be glad, if he have
deceived me ... how melancholies I am!—I will
knog his urinals about his knave's costard, when I
have goot opportunities for the 'ork ... Pless my
soul!   *He sings*
   To shallow rivers, to whose falls:
   Melodious birds sing madrigals:
   There will we make our peds of roses:
   And a thousand fragrant posies....   20
   To shallow—
Mercy on me! I have a great dispositions to cry....
                                                   He sings again
   Melodious birds sing madrigals—
   When as I sat in Pabylon—
   And a thousand vagram posies....
   To shallow, etc.—

SIMPLE. Yonder he is coming, this way, Sir Hugh.

EVANS. He's welcome ... [*sings*] To shallow rivers, to
whose falls ... Heaven prosper the right ... What
weapons is he?   30

SIMPLE. No weapons, sir ... There comes my master,
Master Shallow, and another gentleman; from
Frogmore, over the stile, this way.

EVANS. Pray you, give me my gown—or else keep it
in your arms.

Page and Shallow come in, with Slender following

SHALLOW. How now, master parson! Good-morrow,
good Sir Hugh ... Keep a gamester from the dice,
and a good student from his book, and it is wonderful.

SLENDER [*sighs*]. Ah, sweet Anne Page.   40

PAGE. Save you, good Sir Hugh.

EVANS. Got-pless you from his mercy sake, all of you.

SHALLOW. What! the Sword and the Word! do you
study them both, master parson?

PAGE. And youthful still, in your doublet and hose, this
raw rheumatic day?

EVANS. There is reasons and causes for it.

PAGE. We are come to you, to do a good office, master
parson.

EVANS. Fery well: what is it?   50

PAGE. Yonder is a most reverend gentleman; who
belike, having received wrong by some person, is at
most odds with his own gravity and patience that
ever you saw.

SHALLOW. I have lived fourscore years and upward:
I never heard a man of his place, gravity, and
learning, so wide of his own respect.

EVANS. What is he?   *Host, Caius and Rugby approach*

PAGE. I think you know him ... Master Doctor Caius,
the renowned French physician!   60

EVANS. Got's will, and his passion of my heart! I had as
lief you would tell me of a mess of porridge.

PAGE. Why?

EVANS. He has no more knowledge in Hibocrates and
Galen—and he is a knave besides: a cowardly
knave as you would desires to be acquainted withal.

PAGE. I warrant you, he's the man should fight with
him.

SLENDER [*sighs*]. O, sweet Anne Page!

SHALLOW. It appears so, by his weapons ... Keep   70
them asunder ... Here comes Doctor Caius!

PAGE. Nay, good master parson, keep in your weapon.

SHALLOW. So do you, good master doctor.

HOST. Disarm them, and let them question: let them
keep their limbs whole, and hack our English.

CAIUS. I pray you, let-a me speak a word with your
ear; Verefore vill you not meet-a me?

EVANS. Pray you, use your patience in good time.

CAIUS. By gar, you are de coward ... de Jack-dog ...
John ape.   80

EVANS [*aside*]. Pray you, let us not be laughing-stogs to
other men's humours: I desire you in friendship, and
I will one way or other make you amends ...
[*aloud*] I will knog your urinals about your knave's
cogscomb, [for missing your meetings and appointments!]

CAIUS. Diable ... Jack Rugby ... mine host de
Jarteer ... have I not stay for him, to kill him? have
I not, at de place I did appoint?

EVANS. As I am a Christians-soul, now look you: this   90
is the place appointed—I'll be judgement by mine
host of the Garter.

HOST. Peace, I say, Gallia and Gaul, French and
Welsh, soul-curer and body-curer.

CAIUS. Ay, dat is very good! excellent!

HOST. Peace, I say, I say; hear mine host of the Garter. Am I
politic? am I subtle? am I a Machiavel? Shall I lose
my doctor? no—he gives me the potions and the
motions.... Shall I lose my parson? my priest? my
Sir Hugh? no—he gives me the proverbs and the   100
no-verbs.... [Give me thy hand, terrestrial; so ...]
Give me thy hand, celestial; so ... Boys of art, I have
deceived you both: I have directed you to wrong
places: your hearts are mighty, your skins are whole,
and let burnt sack be the issue ... Come, lay their
swords to pawn ... Follow me, lads of peace—
follow, follow, follow.   *He goes*

SHALLOW. Trust me, a mad host ... Follow, gentlemen, follow.

SLENDER [*sighs*]. O, sweet Anne Page!   110

Shallow, Page and Slender follow Host

CAIUS. Ha! do I perceive dat? have you mak-a de sot
of us? ha, ha!

EVANS. This is well! he has made us his vlouting-stog
... I desire you that we may be friends: and let us
knog our prains together to be revenge on this same

scall, scurvy, cogging companion, the host of the
Garter.

CAIUS. By gar, with all my heart: he promise to bring
me where is Anne Page: by gar, he deceive me too.

EVANS. Well, I will smite his noddles ... Pray you, 120
follow.   *They go*

Scene 2: *A street in Windsor*

Mistress Page approaches with Robin

MISTRESS PAGE. Nay, keep your way, little gallant; you
were wont to be a follower, but now you are a
leader ... Whether had you rather, lead mine eyes
or eye your master's heels?

ROBIN. I had rather, forsooth, go before you like a man
than follow him like a dwarf.

MISTRESS PAGE. O you are a flattering boy. Now, I see,
you'll be a courtier.

Ford comes up

FORD. Well met, Mistress Page. ... Whither go you?

MISTRESS PAGE. Truly, sir, to see your wife. Is she at 10
home?

FORD. Ay—and as idle as she may hang together, for
want of company: I think, if your husbands were
dead, you two would marry.

MISTRESS PAGE. Be sure of that—two other husbands.

FORD. Where had you this pretty weathercock?

MISTRESS PAGE. I cannot tell what the dickens his name
is my husband had him of. What do you call your
knight's name, sirrah?

ROBIN. Sir John Falstaff.   20

FORD. Sir John Falstaff!

MISTRESS PAGE. He, he—I can never hit on's name;
there is such a league between my good man and
he! Is your wife at home, indeed?

FORD. Indeed she is.

MISTRESS PAGE. By your leave, sir. I am sick, till I see
her.   *She leaves with Robin*

FORD. Has Page any brains? hath he any eyes? hath he
any thinking? Sure, they sleep—he hath no use of
them ... Why, this boy will carry a letter twenty 30
mile as easy—as a cannon will shoot point blank
twelve score! He pieces out his wife's inclination;
he gives her folly motion and advantage: and now
she's going to my wife, and Falstaff's boy with her
... A man may hear this shower sing in the wind
... and Falstaff's boy with her ... good plots, they
are laid, and our revolted wives share damnation
together ... Well, I will take him, then torture my
wife, pluck the borrowed veil of modesty from the
so-seeming Mistress Page, divulge Page himself for a 40
secure and wilful Actæon—and to these violent
proceedings all my neighbours shall cry aim....
[the town-clock strikes] The clock gives me my cue,
and my assurance bids me search—there I shall find
Falstaff ... I shall be rather praised for this than
mocked; for it is as positive as the earth is firm that
Falstaff is there ... I will go.

*Page, Shallow, Slender, Host, Sir Hugh Evans, Caius,
and Rugby come up*

ALL. Well met, Master Ford.

FORD. Trust me, a good knot; I have good cheer at
home, and I pray you all go with me.   50

SHALLOW. I must excuse myself, Master Ford.

SLENDER. And so must I, sir. We have appointed to
dine with Mistress Anne, and I would not break
with her for more money than I'll speak of.

SHALLOW. We have lingered about a match between
Anne Page and my cousin Slender, and this day we
shall have our answer.

SLENDER. I hope I have your good will, father Page.

PAGE. You have, Master Slender. I stand wholly for
you—but my wife, master doctor, is for you 60
altogether.

CAIUS. Ay, be-gar, and de maid is lov-a me: my
nursh-a Quickly tell me so mush.

HOST. What say you to young Master Fenton? he
capers, he dances, he has eyes of youth ... he writes
verses, he speaks holiday, he smells April and May.
He will carry't, he will carry't—'tis in his buttons—
he will carry't.

PAGE. Not by my consent, I promise you.... The
gentleman is of no having—he kept company with 70
the wild Prince and Poins: he is of too high a region,
he knows too much ... No, he shall not knit a knot
in his fortunes with the finger of my substance: if
he take her, let him take her simply: the wealth I
have waits on my consent, and my consent goes not
that way.

FORD. I beseech you, heartily, some of you go home
with me to dinner: besides your cheer, you shall have
sport—I will show you a monster! Master doctor,
you shall go—so shall you, Master Page—and you, 80
Sir Hugh.

SHALLOW. Well, fare you well: we shall have the freer
wooing at Master Page's.

                        He goes off with Slender

CAIUS. Go home, John Rugby. I come anon.

                                    Rugby goes

HOST. Farewell, my hearts. I will to my honest knight
Falstaff, and drink canary with him.

                            He follows Rugby

FORD *[aside]*. I think I shall drink in pipe-wine first
with him—I'll make him dance!
[aloud] Will you go, gentles?

PAGE, CAIUS, EVANS. Have with you, to see this 90
monster.   *They go with Ford*

Scene 3: *The hall of Master Ford's house*

Enter Mistress Ford and Mistress Page

MISTRESS FORD. What, John! what, Robert!

MISTRESS PAGE. Quickly, quickly ... is the buck-
basket—

MISTRESS FORD. I warrant.... What, Robin, I say!

Two servants enter carrying a large basket

MISTRESS PAGE. Come, come, come!

MISTRESS FORD. Here, set it down.

MISTRESS PAGE. Give your men the charge. We must
be brief.

MISTRESS FORD. Marry, as I told you before, John and
Robert, be ready here hard by in the brew-house, 10
and when I suddenly call you, come forth, and—
without any pause or staggering—take this basket
on your shoulders: that done, trudge with it in all
haste, and carry it among the whitsters in Datchet-
mead, and there empty it in the muddy ditch, close
by the Thames side.

MISTRESS PAGE. You will do it?

MISTRESS FORD. I ha' told them over and over. They lack no direction.... Be gone, and come when you are called.   *The servants go out; Robin enters* 20

MISTRESS PAGE. Here comes little Robin.

MISTRESS FORD. How now, my eyas-musket! what news with you?

ROBIN. My master, Sir John, is come in at your back-door, Mistress Ford, and requests your company.

MISTRESS PAGE. You little Jack-a-lent, have you been true to us?

ROBIN. Ay, I'll be sworn ... My master knows not of your being here: and hath threatened to put me into everlasting liberty, if I tell you of it; for he swears 30 he'll turn me away.

MISTRESS PAGE. Thou'rt a good boy: this secrecy of thine shall be a tailor to thee, and shall make thee a new doublet and hose.... I'll go hide me.

MISTRESS FORD. Do so ... Go tell thy master, I am alone ... [*he goes*] Mistress Page, remember you your cue.

MISTRESS PAGE. I warrant thee. If I do not act it, hiss me.

MISTRESS FORD. Go to then: we'll use this unwhole- 40 some humidity, this gross watery pumpion; we'll teach him to know turtles from jays.

Mistress Page goes; Falstaff enters

FALSTAFF. 'Have I caught my heavenly jewel?' Why, now let me die, for I have lived long enough ... This is the period of my ambition ... O this blessed hour!

MISTRESS FORD. O sweet Sir John!

FALSTAFF. Mistress Ford, I cannot cog, I cannot prate, Mistress Ford. Now shall I sin in my wish; I would thy husband were dead. I'll speak it before the best 50 lord, I would make thee my lady.

MISTRESS FORD. I your lady, Sir John! alas, I should be a pitiful lady.

FALSTAFF. Let the court of France show me such another: I see how thine eye would emulate the diamond: thou hast the right arched beauty of the brow that becomes the ship-tire, the tire-valiant, or any tire of Venetian admittance.

MISTRESS FORD. A plain kerchief, Sir John: my brows become nothing else—nor that well, neither. 60

FALSTAFF. Thou art a tyrant to say so: thou wouldst make an absolute courtier, and the firm fixture of thy foot would give an excellent motion to thy gait, in a semi-circled farthingale.... I see what thou wert, if fortune thy foe were not, nature thy friend ... Come, thou canst not hide it.

MISTRESS FORD. Believe me, there's no such thing in me.

FALSTAFF. What made me love thee? let that persuade thee there's something extraordinary in thee ... 70 Come, I cannot cog and say thou art this and that, like a many of these lisping hawthorn-buds, that come like women in men's apparel, and smell like Bucklersbury in simple-time: I cannot—but I love thee; none but thee; and thou deserv'st it.

MISTRESS FORD. Do not betray me, sir. I fear you love Mistress Page.

FALSTAFF. Thou mightst as well say, I love to walk by the Counter-gate, which is as hateful to me as the reek of a lime-kiln. 80

MISTRESS FORD. Well, heaven knows how I love you—and you shall one day find it.

FALSTAFF. Keep in that mind. I'll deserve it.

MISTRESS FORD. Nay, I must tell you, so you do; or else   3.3 I could not be in that mind.

Robin enters

ROBIN. Mistress Ford, Mistress Ford! here's Mistress Page at the door, sweating, and blowing, and looking wildly, and would needs speak with you presently.

FALSTAFF. She shall not see me. I will ensconce me 90 behind the arras.

MISTRESS FORD. Pray you, do so—she's a very tattling woman....   *Falstaff stands behind the arras*

Mistress Page enters

What's the matter? how now!

MISTRESS PAGE. O Mistress Ford, what have you done? You're shamed, you're overthrown, you're undone for ever!

MISTRESS FORD. What's the matter, good Mistress Page?

MISTRESS PAGE. O well-a-day, Mistress Ford! having an 100 honest man to your husband, to give him such cause of suspicion!

MISTRESS FORD. What cause of suspicion?

MISTRESS PAGE. What cause of suspicion! Out upon you! how am I mistook in you!

MISTRESS FORD. Why, alas, what's the matter?

MISTRESS PAGE. Your husband's coming hither, woman, with all the officers in Windsor, to search for a gentleman that he says is here now in the house —by your consent—to take an ill advantage of his 110 absence ... You are undone.

MISTRESS FORD. 'Tis not so, I hope.

MISTRESS PAGE. Pray heaven it be not so, that you have such a man here: but 'tis most certain your husband's coming, with half Windsor at his heels, to search for such a one. I come before to tell you ... If you know yourself clear, why I am glad of it: but if you have a friend here, convey, convey him out.... Be not amazed, call all your senses to you, defend your reputation, or bid farewell to your good life for 120 ever.

MISTRESS FORD. What shall I do? There is a gentleman, my dear friend: and I fear not mine own shame so much—as his peril.... I had rather than a thousand pound, he were out of the house.

MISTRESS PAGE. For shame, never stand 'you had rather,' and 'you had rather': your husband's here at hand! Bethink you of some conveyance: in the house you cannot hide him.... O, how have you deceived me! Look, here is a basket, if he be of any reason- 130 able stature, he may creep in here—and throw foul linen upon him, as if it were going to bucking: or—it is whiting-time—send him by your two men to Datchet-mead.

MISTRESS FORD. He's too big to go in there: what shall I do?

Falstaff thrusting the arras aside, rushes towards the basket

FALSTAFF. Let me see't, let me see't, O let me see't ... I'll in, I'll in ... follow your friend's counsel—I'll in.

MISTRESS PAGE. What! Sir John Falstaff! [*in his ear*] 140 Are these your letters, knight?
FALSTAFF [*climbing into the basket*]. I love thee, help me away ... let me creep in here ... I'll never—

He crouches; they cover him with foul linen

MISTRESS PAGE. Help to cover your master, boy! Call your men, Mistress Ford.... You dissembling knight!
MISTRESS FORD. What, John, Robert, John!

Robin goes; servants enter

Go take up these clothes here, quickly ... Where's the cowl-staff? look, how you drumble ... Carry them to the laundress in Datchet-mead ... quickly, 150 come!

Ford, Page, Caius, and Sir Hugh Evans enter

FORD. Pray you, come near: if I suspect without cause, why then make sport at me, then let me be your jest—I deserve it ... How now! [*who goes here?*] whither bear you this?
SERVANTS. To the laundress, forsooth.
MISTRESS FORD. Why, what have you to do whither they bear it? You were best meddle with buck-washing.
FORD. Buck? I would I could wash myself of the buck! 160 Buck, buck, buck! Ay, buck: I warrant you, buck—and of the season too it shall appear.... [*the servants bear away the basket*] Gentlemen, I have dreamed to-night. I'll tell you my dream ... Here, here, here be my keys. Ascend my chambers, search, seek, find out: I'll warrant we'll unkennel the fox.... [*goes to the door*] Let me stop this way first ... [*locks it*] So, now untapis!—
PAGE. Good Master Ford, be contented: you wrong yourself too much.   170
FORD. True, Master Page. Up, gentlemen—you shall see sport anon ... Follow me, gentlemen.
                                                        He goes
EVANS. This is fery fantastical humours and jealousies.
CAIUS. By gar, 'tis no the fashion of France: it is not jealous in France.
PAGE. Nay, follow him, gentlemen. See the issue of his search.   *They go after Ford*
MISTRESS PAGE. Is there not a double excellency in this?
MISTRESS FORD. I know not which pleases me better, that my husband is deceived, or Sir John.   180
MISTRESS PAGE. What a taking was he in, when your husband asked who was in the basket!
MISTRESS FORD. I am half afraid he will have need of washing: so throwing him into the water will do him a benefit.
MISTRESS PAGE. Hang him, dishonest rascal ... I would all of the same strain were in the same distress.
MISTRESS FORD. I think my husband hath some special suspicion of Falstaff's being here; for I never saw him so gross in his jealousy till now.   190
MISTRESS PAGE. I will lay a plot to try that—and we will yet have more tricks with Falstaff: his dissolute disease will scarce obey this medicine.
MISTRESS FORD. Shall we send that foolish carrion, Mistress Quickly, to him, and excuse this throwing into the water, and give him another hope, to betray him to another punishment?

MISTRESS PAGE. We will do it: let him be sent for to-morrow, eight o'clock, to have amends.

The seekers return

FORD. I cannot find him: may be the knave bragged 200 of that he could not compass.
MISTRESS PAGE. Heard you that?
MISTRESS FORD. You use me well, Master Ford, do you?
FORD. Ay, I do so.
MISTRESS FORD. Heaven make you better than your thoughts.
FORD. Amen.
MISTRESS PAGE. You do yourself mighty wrong, Master Ford.   210
FORD. Ay, ay: I must bear it.
EVANS. If there be any pody in the house, and in the chambers, and in the coffers, and in the presses ... heaven forgive my sins at the day of judgement!
CAIUS. By gar, nor I too: there is no bodies.
PAGE. Fie, fie, Master Ford! are you not ashamed? What spirit, what devil suggests this imagination? I would not ha' your distemper in this kind, for the wealth of Windsor Castle.
FORD. 'Tis my fault, Master Page—I suffer for it.   220
EVANS. You suffer for a pad conscience: your wife is as honest a 'omans, as I will desires among five thousand, and five hundred too.
CAIUS. By gar, I see 'tis an honest woman.
FORD. Well, I promised you a dinner ... Come, come, walk in the Park. I pray you, pardon me: I will here-after make known to you why I have done this.... Come, wife; come, Mistress Page—I pray you pardon me.... Pray heartily, pardon me.
                        Mistress Ford and Mistress Page go
PAGE. Let's go in, gentlemen—but, trust me, we'll 230 mock him ... I do invite you to-morrow morning to my house to breakfast: after, we'll a-birding together—I have a fine hawk for the bush.... Shall it be so?
FORD. Any thing.
EVANS. If there is one, I shall make two in the com-pany.
CAIUS. If there be one or two, I shall mak-a the turd.
FORD. Pray you go, Master Page.
                                        Ford and Page go
EVANS. I pray you now, remembrance to-morrow on 240 the lousy knave, mine host.
CAIUS. Dat is good, by gar—vit all my heart.
EVANS. A lousy knave, to have his gibes and his mockeries.
                        They follow Ford and Page

Scene 4: Before the house of Master Page

Enter Fenton and Anne

FENTON. I see I cannot get thy father's love,
    Therefore no more turn me to him, sweet Nan.
ANNE. Alas, how then?
FENTON.   Why, thou must be thyself....
    He doth object I am too great of birth,
    And that, my state being galled with my expense,
    I seek to heal it only by his wealth....
    Besides these, other bars he lays before me—
    My riots past, my wild societies—
    And tells me 'tis a thing impossible

I should love thee but as a property ...   10

ANNE. May be he tells you true.

FENTON. No, heaven so speed me in my time to come!
Albeit I will confess thy father's wealth
Was the first motive that I wooed thee, Anne:
Yet, wooing thee, I found thee of more value
Than stamps in gold or sums in sealéd bags:
And 'tis the very riches of thyself
That now I aim at.

ANNE.   Gentle Master Fenton,
Yet seek my father's love—still seek it, sir.
If opportunity and humblest suit   20
Cannot attain it, why then hark you hither!

Shallow and Slender come forth with Mistress Quickly

SHALLOW. Break their talk, Mistress Quickly. My
kinsman shall speak for himself.

SLENDER. I'll make a shaft or a bolt on't. 'Slid, 'tis but
venturing.

SHALLOW. Be not dismayed.

SLENDER. No, she shall not dismay me: I care not for
that—but that I am afeard.

QUICKLY. Hark ye, Master Slender would speak a
word with you.   30

ANNE. I come to him.... [*to Fenton*] This is my father's
choice:
O, what a world of vile ill-favoured faults
Looks handsome in three hundred pounds a-year!

QUICKLY. And how does good Master Fenton? Pray
you, a word with you.

SHALLOW. She's coming; to her, coz ... O boy, thou
hadst a father!

SLENDER. I had a father, Mistress Anne. My uncle can
tell you good jests of him: pray you, uncle, tell
Mistress Anne the jest, how my father stole two   40
geese out of a pen, good uncle.

SHALLOW. Mistress Anne, my cousin loves you.

SLENDER. Ay, that I do—as well as I love any woman
in Gloucestershire.

SHALLOW. He will maintain you like a gentlewoman.

SLENDER. Ay, that I will, come cut and long-tail—
under the degree of a squire.

SHALLOW. He will makc you a hundred and fifty
pounds jointure.

ANNE. Good Master Shallow, let him woo for himself.   50

SHALLOW. Marry, I thank you for it: I thank you for
that good comfort ... She calls you, coz. I'll leave
you.

ANNE. Now, Master Slender.

SLENDER. Now, good Mistress Anne.

ANNE. What is your will?

SLENDER. My will! od's heartlings, that's a pretty jest,
indeed. I ne'er made my will yet, I thank heaven! I
am not such a sickly creature, I give heaven praise.

ANNE. I mean, Master Slender, what would you with   60
me?

SLENDER. Truly, for mine own part, I would little or
nothing with you ... Your father and my uncle hath
made motions: if it be my luck, so; if not, happy
man be his dole! They can tell you how things go,
better than I can: you may ask your father; here he
comes.

Page and Mistress Page come up

PAGE. Now, Master Slender; love him, daughter
Anne....

Why, how now! what does Master Fenton here?
You wrong me, sir, thus still to haunt my house....   70
I told you, sir, my daughter is disposed of.

FENTON. Nay, Master Page, be not impatient.

MISTRESS PAGE. Good Master Fenton, come not to
my child.

PAGE. She is no match for you.

FENTON. Sir, will you hear me?

PAGE.   No, good Master Fenton....
Come, Master Shallow; come, son Slender, in ...
Knowing my mind, you wrong me, Master
Fenton.   *Page, Shallow and Slender go*

QUICKLY. Speak to Mistress Page.

FENTON. Good Mistress Page, for that I love your
daughter
In such a righteous fashion as I do,   80
Perforce, against all checks, rebukes and manners,
I must advance the colours of my love,
And not retire.... Let me have your good will.

ANNE. Good mother, do not marry me to yond fool.

MISTRESS PAGE. I mean it not. I seek you a better
husband.

QUICKLY. That's my master, master doctor.

ANNE. Alas, I had rather be set quick i'th'earth,
And bowled to death with turnips.

MISTRESS PAGE. Come, trouble not yourself good
Master Fenton,
I will not be your friend nor enemy: 90
My daughter will I question how she loves you,
And as I find her, so am I affected:
Till then, farewell, sir. She must needs go in—
Her father will be angry.

Mistress Page goes, Anne follows

FENTON. Farewell, gentle mistress: farewell, Nan.

QUICKLY. This is my doing now: 'Nay,' said I, 'will
you cast away your child on a fool, and a physician?
Look on Master Fenton.' This is my doing.

FENTON. I thank thee; and I pray thee, once to-night
Give my sweet Nan this ring ... There's for thy   100
pains.   *He departs*

QUICKLY. Now heaven send thee good fortune! A kind
heart he hath: a woman would run through fire and
water for such a kind heart.... But yet, I would my
master had Mistress Anne; or I would Master
Slender had her; or, in sooth, I would Master Fenton
had her: I will do what I can for them all three— for
so I have promised, and I'll be as good as my word,
but speciously for Master Fenton.... Well, I must
of another errand to Sir John Falstaff from my two   110
mistresses: what a beast am I to slack it!

                         She goes away

Scene 5: *The room in the Garter Inn*

Falstaff enters

FALSTAFF. Bardolph, I say!

BARDOLPH [*runs in*]. Here, sir.

FALSTAFF. Go fetch me a quart of sack—put a toast
in't.... [*Bardolph goes*] Have I lived to be carried in
a basket, like a barrow of butcher's offal, and to be
thrown in the Thames? Well, if I be served such
another trick, I'll have my brains ta'en out, and
buttered, and give them to a dog for a new-year's
gift.... The rogues slighted me into the river with as
little remorse as they would have drowned a blind   10

bitch's puppies, fifteen i'th' litter: and you may
know by my size, that I have a kind of alacrity in
sinking; if the bottom were as deep as hell, I should
down.... I had been drowned, but that the shore
was shelvy and shallow ... a death that I abhor; for
the water swells a man; and what a thing should I
have been, when I had been swelled! I should have
been a mountain of mummy.

Bardolph returns with sack

BARDOLPH. Here's Mistress Quickly, sir, to speak with
you.   20
FALSTAFF. Come, let me pour in some sack to the
Thames water; for my belly's as cold as if I had
swallowed snowballs for pills to cool the reins....
Call her in.
BARDOLPH. Come in, woman.

Mistress Quickly enters

QUICKLY. By your leave ... I cry you mercy! Give
your worship good-morrow.
FALSTAFF. Take away these chalices ... Go brew me a
pottle of sack finely.
BARDOLPH. With eggs, sir?   30
FALSTAFF. Simple of itself; I'll no pullet-sperm in my
brewage.... [*Bardolph leaves*] How now!
QUICKLY. Marry, sir, I come to your worship from
Mistress Ford.
FALSTAFF. Mistress Ford! I have had ford enough: I was
thrown into the ford; I have my belly full of ford.
QUICKLY. Alas the day! good heart, that was not her
fault: she does so take on with her men; they mistook
their erection.
FALSTAFF. So did I mine, to build upon a foolish   40
woman's promise.
QUICKLY. Well, she laments, sir, for it, that it would
yearn your heart to see it ... Her husband goes this
morning a-birding; she desires you once more to
come to her, between eight and nine: I must carry
her word quickly. She'll make you amends, I
warrant you.
FALSTAFF. Well, I will visit her. Tell her so; and bid her
think what a man is: let her consider his frailty, and
then judge of my merit.   50
QUICKLY. I will tell her.
FALSTAFF. Do so.... Between nine and ten, sayst thou?
QUICKLY. Eight and nine, sir.
FALSTAFF. Well, be gone: I will not miss her.
QUICKLY. Peace be with you, sir!   *She goes*
FALSTAFF. I marvel I hear not of Master Brook; he
sent me word to stay within: I like his money
well.... O, here he comes.

Ford enters, disguised as Brook

FORD. Bless you, sir!
FALSTAFF. Now, Master Brook—you come to know   60
what hath passed between me and Ford's wife?
FORD. That, indeed, Sir John, is my business.
FALSTAFF. Master Brook, I will not lie to you. I was at
her house the hour she appointed me—
FORD. And sped you, sir?
FALSTAFF. Very ill-favouredly, Master Brook.
FORD. How so, sir? Did she change her determination?
FALSTAFF. No, Master Brook—but the peaking
cornuto her husband, Master Brook, dwelling in a
continual 'larum of jealousy, comes me in the instant 70

of our encounter, after we had embraced, kissed,
protested, and, as it were, spoke the prologue of our
comedy; and at his heels a rabble of his companions,
thither provoked and instigated by his distemper,
and, forsooth, to search his house for his wife's
love.
FORD. What! while you were there?
FALSTAFF. While I was there.
FORD. And did he search for you, and could not find
you?   80
FALSTAFF. You shall hear.... As good luck would have
it, comes in one Mistress Page, gives intelligence of
Ford's approach .... and, in her invention and
Ford's wife's distraction, they conveyed me into a
buck-basket.
FORD. A buck-basket!
FALSTAFF. [By the Lord,] a buck-basket: rammed me
in with foul shirts and smocks, socks, foul stockings,
greasy napkins—that, Master Brook, there was the
rankest compound of villainous smell, that ever   90
offended nostril.
FORD. And how long lay you there?
FALSTAFF. Nay, you shall hear, Master Brook, what I
have suffered to bring this woman to evil for your
good ... Being thus crammed in the basket, a couple
of Ford's knaves, his hinds, were called forth by their
mistress, to carry me in the name of foul clothes to
Datchet-lane: they took me on their shoulders; met
the jealous knave their master in the door; who
asked them once or twice what they had in their   100
basket! I quaked for fear, lest the lunatic knave
would have searched it; but fate, ordaining he
should be a cuckold, held his hand ... Well, on went
he for a search, and away went I for foul clothes:
but mark the sequel, Master Brook. I suffered the
pangs of three several deaths: first, an intolerable
fright, to be detected with a jealous rotten bell-
wether; next, to be compassed, like a good bilbo, in
the circumference of a peck, hilt to point, heel to
head.... and then, to be stopped in, like a strong   110
distillation, with stinking clothes that fretted in their
own grease ... think of that—a man of my kidney;
think of that—that am as subject to heat, as butter; a
man of continual dissolution and thaw; it was a
miracle to 'scape suffocation.... And in the height
of this bath, when I was more than half stewed in
grease, like a Dutch dish, to be thrown into the
Thames, and cooled, glowing-hot (in that surge!)
like a horse-shoe; think of that—hissing hot; think
of that, Master Brook!   120
FORD. In good sadness, sir, I am sorry that for my sake
you have suffered all this.... My suit then is
desperate: you'll undertake her no more?
FALSTAFF. Master Brook ... I will be thrown into Etna,
as I have been into Thames, ere I will leave her thus
... Her husband is this morning gone a-birding: I
have received from her another embassy of meeting:
'twixt eight and nine is the hour, Master Brook.
FORD. 'Tis past eight already, sir.
FALSTAFF. Is it? I will then address me to my appoint- 130
ment ... Come to me at your convenient leisure,
and you shall know how I speed: and the conclusion
shall be crowned with your enjoying her ... Adieu
... You shall have her, Master Brook. Master
Brook, you shall cuckold Ford.   *He goes out*
FORD. Hum ... ha! is this a vision? is this a dream? do

I sleep? Master Ford awake, awake Master Ford! there's a hole made in your best coat, Master Ford ... This 'tis to be married; this 'tis to have linen and buck-baskets ... Well, I will proclaim myself what I am: I will now take the lecher: he is at my house: he cannot 'scape me: 'tis impossible he should: he cannot creep into a halfpenny purse, nor into a pepper-box ... but, lest the devil that guides him should aid him, I will search impossible places ... Though what I am I cannot avoid, yet to be what I would not shall not make me tame: if I have horns to make one mad, let the proverb go with me—I'll be horn-mad. *He goes out*

ACT 4

Scene 1: *The street before the house of Master Page*

Mistress Page, with Mistress Quickly and William

MISTRESS PAGE. Is he at Master Ford's already, think'st thou?

QUICKLY. Sure, he is by this; or will be presently; but truly he is very courageous mad, about his throwing into the water.... Mistress Ford desires you to come suddenly.

MISTRESS PAGE. I'll be with her by and by: I'll but bring my young man here to school ... Look where his master comes; 'tis a playing-day, I see ...

Sir Hugh Evans approaches

How now, Sir Hugh! no school to-day?

EVANS. No: Master Slender is let the boys leave to play.

QUICKLY. Blessing of his heart!

MISTRESS PAGE. Sir Hugh, my husband says my son profits nothing in the world at his book: I pray you, ask him some questions in his accidence.

EVANS. Come hither, William; hold up your head; come.

MISTRESS PAGE. Come on, sirrah; hold up your head; answer your master, be not afraid.

EVANS. William, how many numbers is in nouns?

WILLIAM. Two.

QUICKLY. Truly, I thought there had been one number more; because they say, 'Od's nouns.'

EVANS. Peace your tattlings! What is 'fair,' William?

WILLIAM. Pulcher.

QUICKLY. Polecats! there are fairer things than polecats, sure.

EVANS. You are a very simplicity 'oman: I pray you, peace.... What is 'lapis,' William?

WILLIAM. A stone.

EVANS. And what is 'a stone,' William?

WILLIAM. A pebble.

EVANS. No; it is 'lapis': I pray you remember in your prain.

WILLIAM. Lapis.

EVANS. That is a good William ... What is he, William, that does lend articles?

WILLIAM. Articles are borrowed of the pronoun; and be thus declined, Singulariter, nominativo, hic, hæc, hoc.

EVANS. Nominativo, hig, hag, hog: pray you, mark: genitivo, hujus ... Well: what is your accusative case?

WILLIAM. Accusativo, hinc.

EVANS. I pray you, have your remembrance, child— accusativo, hung, hang, hog.

QUICKLY. 'Hang-hog' is Latin for bacon, I warrant you.

EVANS. Leave your prabbles, 'oman.... What is the focative case, William?

WILLIAM. O! vocativo—O.

EVANS. Remember, William—focative is caret.

QUICKLY. And that's a good root.

EVANS. 'Oman, forbear.

MISTRESS PAGE. Peace.

EVANS. What is your genitive case plural, William?

WILLIAM. Genitive case?

EVANS. Ay.

WILLIAM. Genitive—horum, harum, horum.

QUICKLY. Vengeance of Jenny's case! fie on her! never name her, child, if she be a whore.

EVANS. For shame, 'oman.

QUICKLY. You do ill to teach the child such words: he teaches him to hick and to hack—which they'll do fast enough of themselves, and to call 'horum'; fie upon you!

EVANS. 'Oman, art thou lunatics? hast thou no understandings for thy cases, and the numbers of the genders? Thou art as foolish Christian creatures as I would desires.

MISTRESS PAGE. Prithee hold thy peace.

EVANS. Show me now, William, some declensions of your pronouns.

WILLIAM. Forsooth, I have forgot.

EVANS. It is qui quæ, quod; if you forget your qui's, your quæ's, and your quod's, you must be preeches ... Go your ways and play, go.

MISTRESS PAGE. He is a better scholar than I thought he was.

EVANS. He is a good sprag memory ... Farewell, Mistress Page. *He goes*

MISTRESS PAGE. Adieu, good Sir Hugh ... Get you home, boy. Come, we stay too long.

She goes off with Mistress Quickly

Scene 2: *The hall in Master Ford's house*

Enter Falstaff and Mistress Ford

FALSTAFF. Mistress Ford, your sorrow hath eaten up my sufferance; I see you are obsequious in your love, and I profess requital to a hair's breadth, not only, Mistress Ford, in the simple office of love, but in all the accoutrement, complement, and ceremony of it ... But are you sure of your husband now?

MISTRESS FORD. He's a-birding, sweet Sir John.

MISTRESS PAGE [*calling without*]. What ho, gossip Ford! what ho!

MISTRESS FORD. Step into th' chamber, Sir John.

Falstaff goes

Mistress Page enters

MISTRESS PAGE. How now, sweetheart! who's at home besides yourself?

MISTRESS FORD. Why, none but mine own people.

MISTRESS PAGE. Indeed?

MISTRESS FORD. No, certainly ... [*whispers*] Speak louder.

MISTRESS PAGE. Truly, I am so glad you have nobody here.

MISTRESS FORD. Why?

MISTRESS PAGE. Why, woman, your husband is in his old lunes again: he so takes on yonder with my husband; so rails against all married mankind; so curses all Eve's daughters, of what complexion soever; and so buffets himself on the forehead, crying, 'Peer out, peer out!' that any madness I ever yet beheld seemed but tameness, civility, and patience, to this his distemper he is in now ... I am glad the fat knight is not here.

MISTRESS FORD. Why, does he talk of him?

MISTRESS PAGE. Of none but him—and swears he was 30 carried out the last time he searched for him in a basket; protests to my husband he is now here; and hath drawn him and the rest of their company from their sport, to make another experiment of his suspicion ... But I am glad the knight is not here; now he shall see his own foolery.

MISTRESS FORD. How near is he, Mistress Page?

MISTRESS PAGE. Hard by, at street end; he will be here anon.

MISTRESS FORD. I am undone!—the knight is here.   40

MISTRESS PAGE. Why, then you are utterly shamed, and he's but a dead man... What a woman are you! Away with him, away with him: better shame than murder!

MISTRESS FORD. Which way should he go? how should I bestow him? Shall I put him into the basket again?

FALSTAFF [rushes forward]. No, I'll come no more i'th' basket ... May I not go out, ere he come?

MISTRESS PAGE. Alas: three of Master Ford's brothers watch the door with pistols, that none shall issue 50 out: otherwise you might slip away ere he came ... But what make you here?

FALSTAFF. What shall I do?—I'll creep up into the chimney.

MISTRESS PAGE. There they always use to discharge their birding-pieces ... Creep into the kiln-hole.

FALSTAFF. Where is it?

MISTRESS FORD. He will seek there on my word ... Neither press, coffer, chest, trunk, well, vault, but he hath an abstract for the remembrance of such places, 60 and goes to them by his note ... There is no hiding you in the house.

FALSTAFF. I'll go out then.

MISTRESS PAGE. If you go out in your own semblance, You die, Sir John—unless you go out disguised.

MISTRESS FORD. How might we disguise him?

MISTRESS PAGE. Alas the day, I know not. There is no woman's gown big enough for him; otherwise, he might put on a hat, a muffler, and a kerchief, and so escape.   70

FALSTAFF. Good hearts, devise something: any extremity, rather than a mischief.

MISTRESS FORD. My maid's aunt, the fat woman of Brainford, has a gown above.

MISTRESS PAGE. On my word, it will serve him; she's as big as he is: and there's her thrummed hat, and her muffler too ... Run up, Sir John.

MISTRESS FORD. Go, go, sweet Sir John ... Mistress Page and I will look some linen for your head.

MISTRESS PAGE. Quick, quick! we'll come dress you 80 straight: put on the gown the while.

Falstaff goes

MISTRESS FORD. I would my husband would meet him in this shape: he cannot abide the old woman of Brainford; he swears she's a witch, forbade her my house, and hath threatened to beat her.

MISTRESS PAGE. Heaven guide him to thy husband's

cudgel: and the devil guide his cudgel afterwards!

MISTRESS FORD. But is my husband coming?

MISTRESS PAGE. Ay, in good sadness, is he—and talks of the basket too, howsoever he hath had intelligence.   90

MISTRESS FORD. We'll try that; for I'll appoint my men to carry the basket again, to meet him at the door with it, as they did last time.

MISTRESS PAGE. Nay, but he'll be here presently: let's go dress him like the witch of Brainford.

MISTRESS FORD. I'll first direct my men what they shall do with the basket ... Go up, I'll bring linen for him straight.   *She goes*

MISTRESS PAGE. Hang him, dishonest varlet! we cannot misuse him enough ...   100
    We'll leave a proof, by that which we will do,
    Wives may be merry, and yet honest too:
    We do not act that often jest and laugh—
    'Tis old but true, 'Still swine eats all the draff.'
                                                She goes

Mistress Ford returns with the two servants

MISTRESS FORD. Go, sirs, take the basket again on your shoulders: your master is hard at door: if he bid you set it down, obey him ... quickly, dispatch.
                                                She goes

FIRST SERVANT. Come, come, take it up.

SECOND SERVANT. Pray heaven it be not full of knight again.   110

FIRST SERVANT. I hope not. I had as lief bear so much lead.

Ford, Page, Shallow, Caius, and Sir Hugh Evans enter

FORD. Ay, but if it prove true, Master Page, have you any way then to unfool me again? ... Set down the basket, villain ... Somebody call my wife ... Youth in a basket ... O, you pandarly rascals! there's a knot ... a ging, a pack, a conspiracy against me ... Now shall the devil be shamed.... What! wife, I say ... Come, come forth ... Behold what honest clothes you send forth to bleaching!   120

PAGE. Why, this passes, Master Ford! you are not to go loose any longer—you must be pinioned.

EVANS. Why, this is lunatics! this is mad, as a mad dog!

SHALLOW. Indeed, Master Ford, this is not well, indeed.

FORD. So say I too, sir. [*Mistress Ford appears*] Come hither, Mistress Ford! Mistress Ford, the honest woman, the modest wife, the virtuous creature, that hath the jealous fool to her husband ... I suspect without cause, mistress, do I?   130

MISTRESS FORD. Heaven be my witness you do, if you suspect me in any dishonesty.

FORD. Well said, brazen-face, hold it out ... Come forth, sirrah.   *Plucking out the clothes*

PAGE. This passes!

MISTRESS FORD. Are you not ashamed? let the clothes alone.

FORD. I shall find you anon.

EVANS. 'Tis unreasonable! Will you take up your wife's clothes? Come, away!   140

FORD. Empty the basket, I say.

MISTRESS FORD. Why, man, why?

FORD. Master Page, as I am a man, there was one conveyed out of my house yesterday in this basket: why may not he be there again? In my house I am sure he is: my intelligence is true, my jealousy is reasonable, pluck me out all the linen!

MISTRESS FORD. If you find a man there, he shall die a flea's death.

PAGE. Here's no man.   150

SHALLOW. By my fidelity, this is not well, Master Ford: this wrongs you.

EVANS. Master Ford, you must pray, and not follow the imaginations of your own heart: this is jealousies.

FORD. Well, he's not here I seek for.

PAGE. No, nor nowhere else but in your brain.

FORD. Help to search my house this one time: if I find not what I seek, show no colour for my extremity ... let me for ever be your table-sport ... let them say of me, 'As jealous as Ford, that searched a hollow   160 walnut for his wife's leman'.... Satisfy me once more, once more search with me.

MISTRESS FORD. What ho, Mistress Page! come you and the old woman down: my husband will come into the chamber.

FORD. Old woman! What old woman's that?

MISTRESS FORD. Why, it is my maid's aunt of Brainford.

FORD. A witch, a quean, an old cozening quean! Have I not forbid her my house? She comes of errands,   170 does she? We are simple men, we do not know what's brought to pass under the profession of fortune-telling.... She works by charms, by spells, by th' figure, and such daubery as this is, beyond our element: we know nothing.... Come down, you witch, you hag you, come down, I say.

MISTRESS FORD. Nay, good, sweet husband—good gentlemen, let him not strike the old woman.

Enter Falstaff, in women's clothes, and Mistress Page

MISTRESS PAGE. Come, Mother Prat, come, give me your hand.   180

FORD. I'll prat her ... [*Falstaff runs; Ford cudgels*] Out of my door, you witch, you rag, you baggage, you polecat, you ronyon! out! out! I'll conjure you, I'll fortune-tell you.   *Falstaff goes*

MISTRESS PAGE. Are you not ashamed? I think, you have killed the poor woman.

MISTRESS FORD. Nay, he will do it. 'Tis a goodly credit for you.

FORD. Hang her, witch!

EVANS. By yea and no, I think the 'oman is a witch   190 indeed: I like not when a 'oman has a great peard; I spy a great peard under his muffler.

FORD. Will you follow, gentlemen? I beseech you, follow: see but the issue of my jealousy: if I cry out thus upon no trail, never trust me when I open again.

PAGE. Let's obey his humour a little further ... Come, gentlemen.   *They follow him out*

MISTRESS PAGE. Trust me, he beat him most pitifully.

MISTRESS PAGE. Nay, by th' mass, that he did not: 200 he beat him most unpitifully methought.

MISTRESS PAGE. I'll have the cudgel hallowed and hung o'er the altar—it hath done meritorious service.

MISTRESS FORD. What think you? May we, with the warrant of womanhood and the witness of a good conscience, pursue him with any further revenge?

MISTRESS PAGE. The spirit of wantonness is, sure, scared out of him. If the devil have him not in fee-simple,

with fine and recovery, he will never, I think, in the way of waste, attempt us again.   210

MISTRESS FORD. Shall we tell our husbands how we have served him?

MISTRESS PAGE. Yes, by all means; if it be but to scrape the figures out of your husband's brains ... If they can find in their hearts the poor unvirtuous fat knight shall be any further afflicted, we two will still be the ministers.

MISTRESS FORD. I'll warrant they'll have him publicly shamed—and methinks there would be no period to the jest, should he not be publicly shamed.   220

MISTRESS PAGE. Come, to the forge with it! then shape it: I would not have things cool.   *They go*

Scene 3: *The room in the Garter Inn*

Host and Bardolph enter

BARDOLPH. Sir, the Germans desire to have three of your horses: the duke himself will be to-morrow at court, and they are going to meet him.

HOST. What duke should that be comes so secretly? I hear not of him in the court ... Let me speak with the gentlemen—they speak English?

BARDOLPH. Ay, sir; I'll call them to you.

HOST. They shall have my horses, but I'll make them pay: I'll sauce them. They have had my house a week at command; I have turned away my other guests.   10 They must come off. I'll sauce them, come.

They go out

Scene 4: *The hall in Master Ford's house*

Enter Page, Ford, Mistress Page, Mistress Ford, and Sir Hugh Evans

EVANS. 'Tis one of the pest discretions of a 'oman as ever I did look upon.

PAGE. And did he send you both these letters at an instant?

MISTRESS PAGE. Within a quarter of an hour.

FORD. Pardon me, wife. Henceforth do what thou wilt:

I rather will suspect the sun with cold
Than thee with wantonness: now doth thy honour stand,
In him that was of late an heretic,
As firm as faith.

PAGE.   'Tis well, 'tis well—no more: 10
Be not as éxtreme in submission,
As in offence.
But let our plot go forward: let our wives
Yet once again, to make us public sport,
Appoint a meeting with this old fat fellow,
Where we may take him, and disgrace him for it.

FORD. There is no better way than that they spoke of.

PAGE. How? to send him word they'll meet him in the Park at midnight? fie, fie! he'll never come.

EVANS. You say he has been thrown in the rivers,   20 and has been grievously peaten, as an old 'oman: methinks there should be terrors in him, that he should not come: methinks his flesh is punished, he shall have no desires.

PAGE. So think I too.

MISTRESS FORD. Devise but how you'll use him, when he comes,
And let us two devise to bring him thither.

MISTRESS PAGE. There is an old tale goes, that Herne
    the hunter,
Sometime a keeper here in Windsor forest,
Doth all the winter-time, at still midnight,   30
Walk round about an oak, with great ragg'd
    horns—
And there he blasts the tree, and takes the cattle,
And makes milch-kine yield blood, and shakes a
    chain
In a most hideous and dreadful manner....
You have heard of such a spirit, and well you know
The superstitious idle-headed eld
Received, and did deliver to our age,
This tale of Herne the hunter for a truth.
PAGE. Why, yet there want not many that do fear
In deep of night to walk by this Herne's oak: 40
But what of this?
MISTRESS FORD.   Marry, this is our device—
That Falstaff at that oak shall meet with us,
[Disguised like Herne, with huge horns on his head.]
PAGE. Well, let it not be doubted but he'll come,
And in this shape. When you have brought him
    thither,
What shall be done with him? what is your plot?
MISTRESS PAGE. That likewise have we thought
    upon, and thus:
Nan Page my daughter and my little son
And three or four more of their growth we'll dress
Like urchins, ouphs, and fairies, green and white,   50
With rounds of waxen tapers on their heads,
And rattles in their hands; upon a sudden,
As Falstaff, she, and I are newly met,
Let them from forth a saw-pit rush at once
With some diffuséd song: upon their sight,
We two in great amazedness will fly:
Then let them all encircle him about,
And, fairy-like, to pinch the unclean knight;
And ask him why, that hour of fairy revel,
In their so sacred paths he dares to tread   60
In shape profane.
MISTRESS FORD.   And till he tell the truth,
Let the supposéd fairies pinch him sound,
And burn him with their tapers.
MISTRESS PAGE.   The truth being known,
We'll all present ourselves; dis-horn the spirit,
And mock him home to Windsor.
FORD.   The children must
Be practised well to this, or they'll ne'er do't.
EVANS. I will teach the children their behaviours: and
I will be like a jack-an-apes also, to burn the knight
with my taber.
FORD. That will be excellent. I'll go buy them   70
vizards.
MISTRESS PAGE. My Nan shall be the queen of all the
    fairies,
Finely attiréd in a robe of white.
PAGE. That silk will I go buy—[aside] and in that time
Shall Master Slender steal my Nan away,
And marry her at Eton ... Go, send to Falstaff
straight.
FORD. Nay, I'll to him again in name of Brook:
He'll tell me all his purpose: sure, he'll come.
MISTRESS PAGE. Fear not you that ... Go, get us
    properties,
And tricking for our fairies.   80
EVANS. Let us about it: it is admirable pleasures and

fery honest knaveries.
                    Page, Ford, and Evans depart
MISTRESS PAGE. Go, Mistress Ford,
Send Quickly to Sir John, to know his mind ...
                    Mistress Ford goes
I'll to the doctor—he hath my good will,
And none but he, to marry with Nan Page ...
That Slender, though well landed, is an idiot;
And he my husband best of all affects:
The doctor is well moneyed, and his friends
Potent at court: he, none but he, shall have her,   90
Though twenty thousand worthier come to crave
    her.   She goes

Scene 5

Simple stands waiting; Host enters

HOST. What wouldst thou have, boor? what, thick-
skin? speak, breathe, discuss; brief, short, quick,
snap.
SIMPLE. Marry, sir, I come to speak with Sir John
Falstaff from Master Slender.
HOST. There's his chamber, his house, his castle, his
standing-bed, and truckle-bed; 'tis painted about
with the story of the Prodigal, fresh and new: go,
knock and call: he'll speak like an Anthropophaginian unto thee: knock, I say.   10
SIMPLE. There's an old woman, a fat woman, gone up
into his chamber: I'll be so bold as stay, sir, till she
come down: I come to speak with her, indeed.
HOST. Ha! a fat woman! the knight may be robbed:
I'll call.... Bully knight! bully Sir John! speak from
thy lungs military: art thou there? it is thine host,
thine Ephesian, calls.
FALSTAFF [above]. How now, mine host?
HOST. Here's a Bohemian-Tartar tarries the coming
down of thy fat woman ... Let her descend, bully,   20
let her descend: my chambers are honourable: fie!
privacy? fie!

Falstaff enters

FALSTAFF. There was, mine host, an old fat woman
even now with me—but she's gone.
SIMPLE. Pray you, sir, was't not the wise woman of
Brainford?
FALSTAFF. Ay, marry, was it, mussel-shell—what
would you with her?
SIMPLE. My master, sir, Master Slender, sent to her,
seeing her go thorough the streets, to know, sir,   30
whether one Nym, sir, that beguiled him of a chain,
had the chain, or no.
FALSTAFF. I spake with the old woman about it.
SIMPLE. And what says she, I pray, sir?
FALSTAFF. Marry, she says that the very same man that
beguiled Master Slender of his chain cozened him of
it.
SIMPLE. I would I could have spoken with the woman
herself. I had other things to have spoken with her
too, from him.   40
FALSTAFF. What are they? let us know.
HOST. Ay ... come ... quick!
SIMPLE. I may not conceal them, sir.
HOST. Conceal them, or thou diest.
SIMPLE. Why, sir, they were nothing but about
Mistress Anne Page—to know if it were my master's
fortune to have her, or no.

FALSTAFF. 'Tis, 'tis his fortune.

SIMPLE. What, sir?

FALSTAFF. To have her, or no ... Go; say the woman 50
told me so.

SIMPLE. May I be so bold to say so, sir?

FALSTAFF. Ay, Sir Tyke; who more bold?

SIMPLE. I thank your worship: I shall make my master
glad with these tidings.   *He goes out*

HOST. Thou art clerkly! thou art clerkly, Sir John. Was
there a wise woman with thee?

FALSTAFF. Ay, that there was, mine host—one that
hath taught me more wit than ever I learned before
in my life: and I paid nothing for it neither, but was 60
paid for my learning.

Bardolph enters

BARDOLPH. Out, alas, sir! cozenage ... mere cozenage!

HOST. Where be my horses? speak well of them,
varletto.

BARDOLPH. Run away with the cozeners ... for so
soon as I came beyond Eton, they threw me off,
from behind one of them, in a slough of mire ...
and set spurs, and away ... like three German devils
... three Doctor Faustuses.

HOST. They are gone but to meet the duke, villain. 70
Do not say, they be fled; Germans are honest men.

Sir Hugh Evans enters

EVANS. Where is mine host?

HOST. What is the matter, sir?

EVANS. Have a care of your entertainments: there is a
friend of mine come to town, tells me there is three
cozen-germans that has cozened all the hosts of
Readins, of Maidenhead, of Colebrook, of horses
and money ... I tell you for good will, look you!
you are wise, and full of gibes and vlouting-stogs
... and 'tis not convenient you should be cozened! 80
Fare you well.   *He goes*

Doctor Caius enters

CAIUS. Vere is mine host de Jarteer?

HOST. Here, master doctor, in perplexity and doubtful
dilemma.

CAIUS. I cannot tell vat is dat: but it is tell-a me dat
you make grand preparation for a duke de Jarmany:
by my trot, dere is no duke, dat de court is know to
come: I tell you for good vill: adieu.   *He goes*

HOST. Hue and cry, villain! go ... Assist me, knight.
I am undone ... Fly, run ... hue and cry, villain! 90
I am undone!   *He goes with Bardolph after*

FALSTAFF. I would all the world might be cozened, for
I have been cozened and beaten too ... If it should
come to the ear of the court, how I have been
transformed ... and how my transformation hath
been washed and cudgelled, they would melt me out
of my fat, drop by drop, and liquor fishermen's
boots with me: I warrant they would whip me with
their fine wits till I were as crest-fallen as a dried pear
... I never prospered since I forswore myself at 100
primero: well, if my wind were but long enough
[to say my prayers], I would repent ...

Mistress Quickly enters

Now! whence come you?

QUICKLY. From the two parties, forsooth.

FALSTAFF. The devil take one party, and his dam the
other! and so they shall be both bestowed ... I have
suffered more for their sakes—more than the
villainous inconstancy of man's disposition is able to
bear.

QUICKLY. And have not they suffered? Yes, I warrant; 110
speciously one of them; Mistress Ford, good heart!
is beaten black and blue, that you cannot see a white
spot about her.

FALSTAFF. What, tell'st thou me of black and blue! I
was beaten myself into all the colours of the
rainbow: and I was like to be apprehended for the
witch of Brainford. But that my admirable
dexterity of wit, my counterfeiting the action of an
old woman, delivered me, the knave constable had
set me i'th' common stocks, for a witch.   120

QUICKLY. Sir: let me speak with you in your chamber,
you shall hear how things go, and I warrant to your
content ... Here is a letter will say somewhat ...
Good hearts, what ado here is to bring you together!
Sure, one of you does not serve heaven well, that
you are so crossed.

FALSTAFF. Come up into my chamber.   *They go*

Scene 6

Host returns, with Fenton

HOST. Master Fenton, talk not to me,
My mind is heavy: I will give over all.

FENTON. Yet hear me speak: assist me in my purpose,
And, as I am a gentleman, I'll give thee
A hundred pound in gold more than your loss.

HOST. I will hear you, Master Fenton; and I will at the
least keep your counsel.

FENTON. From time to time I have acquainted you
With the dear love I bear to fair Anne Page,
Who mutually hath answered my affection,   10
So far forth as herself might be her chooser,
Even to my wish; I have a letter from her
Of such contents as you will wonder at;
The mirth whereof so larded with my matter,
That neither, singly, can be manifested,
Without the show of both: fat Falstaff
Hath a great scene; the image of the jest
I'll show you here at large. Hark, good mine
host ...
To-night at Herne's oak, just 'twixt twelve and one,
Must my sweet Nan present the Fairy-Queen ...   20
The purpose why, is here ... in which disguise,
While other jests are something rank on foot,
Her father hath commanded her to slip
Away with Slender, and with him at Eton
Immediately to marry: she hath consented ...
Now, sir,
Her mother, ever strong against that match
And firm for Doctor Caius, hath appointed
That he shall likewise shuffle her away,
While other sports are tasking of their minds,   30
And at the deanery, where a priest attends,
Straight marry her: to this her mother's plot
She seemingly obedient likewise hath
Made promise to the doctor ... Now, thus it rests—
Her father means she shall be all in white;
And in that habit, when Slender sees his time
To take her by the hand and bid her go,
She shall go with him: her mother hath intended—
The better to denote her to the doctor,

For they must all be masked and vizarded—   40
That quaint in green she shall be loose enrobed,
With ribands pendent, flaring 'bout her head;
And when the doctor spies his vantage ripe,
To pinch her by the hand, and, on that token,
The maid hath given consent to go with him.
HOST. Which means she to deceive? father or mother?
FENTON. Both, my good host, to go along with me:
And here it rests—that you'll procure the vicar
To stay for me at church, 'twixt twelve and one,
And, in the lawful name of marrying,   50
To give our hearts united ceremony.
HOST. Well, husband your device; I'll to the vicar.
Bring you the maid, you shall not lack a priest.
FENTON. So shall I evermore be bound to thee;
Besides, I'll make a present recompence.
They go out

ACT 5
Scene 1

Falstaff and Mistress Quickly come in

FALSTAFF. Prithee, no more prattling: go. I'll hold.
This is the third time: I hope good luck lies in odd
numbers ... Away, go. They say there is divinity in
odd numbers, either in nativity, chance, or death ...
Away!
QUICKLY. I'll provide you a chain, and I'll do what I
can to get you a pair of horns.
FALSTAFF. Away, I say—time wears—hold up your
head, and mince....
                    Mistress Quickly goes out; Ford enters
How now, Master Brook! Master Brook, the matter   10
will be known to-night, or never.... Be you in the
Park about midnight, at Herne's oak, and you shall
see wonders.
FORD. Went you not to her yesterday, sir, as you told
me you had appointed?
FALSTAFF. I went to her, Master Brook, as you see, like
a poor old man, but I came from her, Master Brook,
like a poor old woman ... That same knave
Ford, her husband, hath the finest mad devil of
jealousy in him, Master Brook, that ever governed   20
frenzy.... I will tell you he beat me grievously, in
the shape of a woman: for in the shape of man,
Master Brook, I fear not Goliath with a weaver's
beam, because I know also life is a shuttle. I am
in haste—go along with me—I'll tell you all, Master
Brook ... Since I plucked geese, played truant, and
whipped top, I knew not what it was to be beaten,
till lately.... Follow me. I'll tell you strange things
of this knave Ford, on whom to-night I will be
revenged, and I will deliver his wife into your   30
hand.... [*goes out*] Follow. Strange things in hand,
Master Brook! follow.   *Ford follows*

Scene 2: *The outskirts of Windsor Park*

Page, Shallow, and Slender appear

PAGE. Come, come; we'll couch i'th' castle-ditch till
we see the light of our fairies.... Remember, son
Slender, my daughter.
SLENDER. Ay, forsooth—I have spoke with her, and
we have a nay-word how to know one another.... I
come to her in white, and cry 'mum'; she cries

'budget,' and by that we know one another.
SHALLOW. That's good too: but what needs either your
'mum' or her 'budget'? the white will decipher her
well enough.... It hath struck ten o'clock.   10
PAGE. The night is dark—light and spirits will become
it well ... Heaven prosper our sport! No man means
evil but the devil, and we shall know him by his
horns.... Let's away; follow me.   *They depart*

Scene 3

Mistress Page, Mistress Ford, and Doctor Caius come up

MISTRESS PAGE. Master doctor, my daughter is in
green. When you see your time, take her by the
hand, away with her to the deanery, and dispatch it
quickly ... Go before into the Park: we two must
go together.
CAIUS. I know vat I have to do. Adieu.   *He goes*
MISTRESS PAGE. Fare you well, sir.... My husband will
not rejoice so much at the abuse of Falstaff as he will
chafe at the doctor's marrying my daughter: but 'tis
no matter; better a little chiding than a great deal of   10
heart-break.
MISTRESS FORD. Where is Nan now, and her troop of
fairies, and the Welsh devil-hern?
MISTRESS PAGE. They are all couched in a pit hard by
Herne's oak, with obscured lights; which at the very
instant of Falstaff's and our meeting, they will at
once display to the night.
MISTRESS FORD. That cannot choose but amaze him.
MISTRESS PAGE. If he be not amazed, he will be mocked;
if he be amazed, he will every way be mocked.   20
MISTRESS FORD. We'll betray him finely.
MISTRESS PAGE. Against such lewdsters and their
lechery
Those that betray them do no treachery.
MISTRESS FORD. The hour draws on ... To the oak, to
the oak!   *They depart*

Scene 4

*Enter Sir Hugh Evans, disguised as a Satyr, Pistol,
Quickly, Anne Page, William, and many other boys,
disguised as Fairies*

EVANS. Trib, trib, fairies; come; and remember your
parts: be pold, I pray you; follow me into the pit;
and when I give the watch-'ords, do as I pid you
... Come, come—trib, trib.   *They go*

Scene 5: *In Windsor Park*

*Enter Falstaff disguised as Herne the hunter, with a buck's
head upon him*

FALSTAFF. The Windsor bell hath struck twelve: the
minute draws on ... Now, the hot-blooded gods
assist me! Remember, Jove, thou wast a bull for thy
Europa—love set on thy horns.... O powerful love,
that, in some respects, makes a beast a man; in some
other, a man a beast.... You were also, Jupiter, a
swan, for the love of Leda ... O omnipotent love,
how near the god drew to the complexion of a
goose: a fault done first in the form of a beast—O
Jove, a beastly fault!—and then another fault in the   10
semblance of a fowl—think on't, Jove, a foul fault!
When gods have hot backs, what shall poor men do?
For me, I am here a Windsor stag, and the fattest, I

think, i'th' forest.... Send me a cool rut-time, Jove,
or who can blame me to piss my tallow? Who comes
here? my doe?

Mistress Ford comes in, Mistress Page following

MISTRESS FORD. Sir John? art thou there—my deer? my
male deer?

FALSTAFF. My doe with the black scut! Let the sky rain
potatoes; let it thunder to the tune of 'Green- 20
sleeves,' hail kissing-comfits, and snow eringoes; let
there come a tempest of provocation, I will shelter
me here.   *He embraces her*

MISTRESS FORD. Mistress Page is come with me, sweet-
heart.

FALSTAFF. Divide me like a bribed-buck, each a
haunch: I will keep my sides to myself, my shoulders
for the fellow of this walk—and my horns I
bequeath your husbands! Am I a woodman, ha?
Speak I like Herne the hunter? Why, now is Cupid a 30
child of conscience—he makes restitution.... As I
am a true spirit, welcome!

There is a noise of horns

MISTRESS PAGE. Alas! what noise?

MISTRESS FORD. Heaven forgive our sins!

FALSTAFF. What should this be?

MISTRESS FORD, MISTRESS PAGE. Away, away!

The two women run away

FALSTAFF. I think the devil will not have me damned,
Lest the oil that's in me should set hell on fire;
—he would never else cross me thus.

*The Fairies appear, led by a Satyr holding a taper; they
dance towards Falstaff, singing*

FAIRY-QUEEN. Fairies, black, grey, green, and white, 40
You moonshine revellers, and shades of night,
You orphan heirs of fixéd destiny,
Attend your office, and your quality....
Crier Hobgoblin, make the fairy oyes.

PUCK. Elves, list your names: silence, you airy toys....
Crickét, to Windsor chimneys shalt thou leap;
Where fires thou find'st unraked and hearths
unswept,
There pinch the maids as blue as bilberry.
Our radiant queen hates sluts and sluttery.

FALSTAFF. They are fairies! he that speaks to them shall
die   50
I'll wink and couch: no man their works must eye.

He lies upon his face

SATYR. Where's Bead? Go you, and where you find
a maid
That, ere she sleep, has thrice her prayers said,
Raise up the organs of her fantasy,
Sleep she as sound as careless infancy.
But those as sleep and think not on their sins,
Pinch them, arms, legs, backs, shoulders, sides, and
shins.

FAIRY-QUEEN. About, about ...
Search Windsor Castle, elves, within and out....
Strew good luck, ouphs, on every sacred room, 60
That it may stand till the perpetual doom,
In state as wholesome as in state 'tis fit,
Worthy the owner, and the owner it....
The several chairs of order look you scour
With juice of balm, and every precious flower:
Each fair instalment, coat, and several crest,
With loyal blazon, evermore be blest!

And nightly, meadow-fairies, look you sing,
Like to the Garter's compass, in a ring.
Th'expressure that it bears, green let it be, 70
More fertile-fresh than all the field to see;
And, 'Honi soit qui mal y pense' write,
In emerald tufts, flowers purple, blue, and white—
Like sapphire, pearl, and rich embroidery,
Buckled below fair knighthood's bending knee:
Fairies use flowers for their charáctery....
Away, disperse! but till 'tis one o'clock,
Our dance of custom round about the oak
Of Herne the hunter, let us not forget.

SATYR. Pray you, lock hand in hand; yourselves in
order set ...   80
And twenty glow-worms shall our lanterns be,
To guide our measure round about the tree....
But stay—I smell a man of middle earth.

FALSTAFF. Heavens defend me from that Welsh fairy,
Lest he transform me to a piece of cheese!

PUCK. Vile worm, thou wast o'er-looked even in thy
birth.

FAIRY-QUEEN. With trial-fire touch me his finger-end:
If he be chaste, the flame will back descend,
And turn him to no pain; but if he start,
It is the flesh of a corrupted heart.   90

PUCK. A trial, come!

SATYR. Come: will this wood take fire?

*They put the tapers to his fingers,
and he starts*

FALSTAFF. Oh, oh, oh!

FAIRY-QUEEN. Corrupt, corrupt, and tainted in desire!
About him, fairies, sing a scornful rhyme—
And, as you trip, still pinch him to your time.

The Fairies sing

Fie on sinful fantasy: fie on lust and luxury:
Lust is but a bloody fire, kindled with unchaste
desire,
Fed in heart, whose flames aspire,
As thoughts do blow them, higher and higher. 100
Pinch him, fairies, mutually: pinch him for his
villainy.
Pinch him, and burn him, and turn him about,
Till candles, and star-light, and moon-shine be
out.

*As they sing, they pinch Falstaff. Doctor Caius comes one
way, and steals away a fairy in green; Slender another way,
and takes off a fairy in white; and Fenton comes, and steals
away Mistress Anne Page. A noise of hunting is heard; and
all the Fairies run away. Falstaff rises up, pulls off his buck's
head, and would escape, but Page, Ford, Mistress Page, and
Mistress Ford confront him.*

PAGE. Nay, do not fly! I think we have watched you
now ...
Will none but Herne the hunter serve your turn?

MISTRESS PAGE. I pray you, come, hold up the jest no
higher....
Now, good Sir John, how like you Windsor wives?
See you these, husband? do not these fair yokes
Become the forest better than the town?

FORD. Now, sir, who's a cuckold now?—Master 110
Brook, Falstaff's a knave, a cuckoldly knave—here
are his horns, Master Brook ... And, Master Brook,
he hath enjoyed nothing of Ford's but his buck-
basket, his cudgel, and twenty pounds of money,

which must be paid to Master Brook—his horses are arrested for it, Master Brook.

MISTRESS FORD. Sir John, we have had ill luck; we could never mate ... I will never take you for my love again but I will always count you my deer.

FALSTAFF. I do begin to perceive that I am made an ass. 120

FORD. Ay, and an ox too: both the proofs are extant.

FALSTAFF. And these are not fairies! I was three or four times in the thought they were not fairies—and yet the guiltiness of my mind, the sudden surprise of my powers, drove the grossness of the foppery into a received belief, in despite of the teeth of all rhyme and reason, that they were fairies. ... See now, how wit may be made a Jack-a-lent, when 'tis upon ill employment!

EVANS [returns]. Sir John Falstaff, serve Got, and leave 130 your desires, and fairies will not pinse you.

FORD. Well said, fairy Hugh.

EVANS. And leave you your jealousies too, I pray you.

FORD. I will never mistrust my wife again, till thou art able to woo her in good English.

FALSTAFF. Have I laid my brain in the sun, and dried it, that it wants matter to prevent so gross o'er-reaching as this? Am I ridden with a Welsh goat too? shall I have a coxcomb of frieze? 'tis time I were choked with a piece of toasted cheese. 140

EVANS. Seese is not good to give putter; your pelly is all putter.

FALSTAFF. 'Seese' and 'putter'! Have I lived to stand at the taunt of one that makes fritters of English? This is enough to be the decay of lust and late-walking through the realm.

MISTRESS PAGE. Why, Sir John, do you think, though we would have thrust virtue out of our hearts by the head and shoulders, and have given ourselves without scruple to hell, that ever the devil could 150 have made you our delight?

FORD. What, a hodge-pudding? a bag of flax?

MISTRESS PAGE. A puffed man?

PAGE. Old, cold, withered, and of intolerable entrails?

FORD. And one that is as slanderous as Satan?

PAGE. And as poor as Job?

FORD. And as wicked as his wife?

EVANS. And given to fornications, and to taverns, and sack, and wine, and metheglins, and to drinkings, and swearings and starings, pribbles and prabbles? 160

FALSTAFF. Well, I am your theme ... you have the start of me, I am dejected ... I am not able to answer the Welsh flannel. Ignorance itself is a plummet o'er me. Use me as you will.

FORD. Marry, sir, we'll bring you to Windsor, to one Master Brook, that you have cozened of money, to whom you should have been a pandar: over and above that you have suffered, I think to repay that money will be a biting affliction.

PAGE. Yet be cheerful, knight: thou shalt eat a posset 170 to-night at my house, where I will desire thee to laugh at my wife, that now laughs at thee ... Tell her Master Slender hath married her daughter.

MISTRESS PAGE. Doctors doubt that ... [aside] If Anne Page be my daughter, she is, by this, Doctor Caius' wife.

Slender enters

SLENDER. Whoa, ho, ho! father Page!

PAGE. Son, how now! how now, son! have you dispatched?

SLENDER. Dispatched! I'll make the best in Gloucester- 180 shire know on't; would I were hanged, la, else.

PAGE. Of what, son?

SLENDER. I came yonder at Eton to marry Mistress Anne Page, and she's a great lubberly boy.... If it had not been i'th' church, I would have swinged him, or he should have swinged me.... If I did not think it had been Anne Page, would I might never stir—and 'tis a postmaster's boy!

PAGE. Upon my life, then, you took the wrong.

SLENDER. What need you tell me that? I think so, when 190 I took a boy for a girl ... If I had been married to him, for all he was in woman's apparel, I would not have had him.

PAGE. Why, this is your own folly. Did not I tell you, how you should know my daughter—by her garments?

SLENDER. I went to her in white, and cried 'mum,' and she cried 'budget,' as Anne and I had appointed, and yet it was not Anne, but a postmaster's boy.

MISTRESS PAGE. Good George, be not angry. I knew of 200 your purpose ... turned my daughter into green— and, indeed, she is now with the doctor at the deanery, and there married.

Caius enters

CAIUS. Vere is Mistress Page? By gar, I am cozened! I ha' married un garçon, a boy; un paysan, by gar.... a boy! it is not Anne Page—by gar, I am cozened!

MISTRESS PAGE. Why! did you take her in green?

CAIUS. Ay, by gar, and 'tis a boy: by gar, I'll raise all Windsor! *He goes away*

FORD. This is strange ... Who hath got the right Anne? 210

PAGE. My heart misgives me—here comes Master Fenton....

Fenton and Anne Page appear

How now, Master Fenton!

ANNE. Pardon, good father! good my mother, pardon!

PAGE. Now, Mistress! how chance you went not with Master Slender?

MISTRESS PAGE. Why went you not with master doctor, maid?

FENTON. You do amaze her ... Hear the truth of it.
You would have married her most shamefully,
Where there was no proportion held in love ...
The truth is, she and I—long since contracted— 220
Are now so sure that nothing can dissolve us ...
Th'offence is holy that she hath committed,
And this deceit loses the name of craft,
Of disobedience or unduteous title,
Since therein she doth evitate and shun
A thousand irreligious cursèd hours,
Which forcèd marriage would have brought upon her.

FORD. Stand not amazed. Here is no remedy:
In love, the heavens themselves do guide the state—
Money buys lands, and wives are sold by fate. 230

FALSTAFF. I am glad, though you have ta'en a special stand to strike at me, that your arrow hath glanced.

PAGE. Well, what remedy? Fenton, heaven give thee joy!
What cannot be eschewed, must be embraced.

FALSTAFF. When night-dogs run, all sorts of deer are
  chased.

MISTRESS PAGE. Well, I will muse no further ...
  Master Fenton,
  Heaven give you many, many merry days!
  Good husband, let us every one go home,

And laugh this sport o'er by a country fire—
Sir John and all.

FORD.   Let it be so. Sir John,   240
To Master Brook you yet shall hold your word,
For he to-night shall lie with Mistress Ford.

They go

Measure
for Measure

The scene: Vienna

CHARACTERS IN THE PLAY

VINCENTIO, *the Duke*
ANGELO, *the Deputy*
ESCALUS, *an ancient Lord*
CLAUDIO, *a young gentleman*
LUCIO, *a fantastic*
Two other like gentlemen
VARRIUS
A Provost
THOMAS
PETER } *two friars*
A Justice

ELBOW, *a simple constable*
FROTH, *a foolish gentleman*
POMPEY, *a clown, servant to Mistress Overdone*
ABHORSON, *an executioner*
BARNARDINE, *a dissolute prisoner*
ISABELLA, *sister to Claudio*
MARIANA, *betrothed to Angelo*
JULIET, *beloved of Claudio*
FRANCISCA, *a nun*
MISTRESS OVERDONE, *a bawd*
Lords, officers, citizens, boy, and attendants

Measure for Measure

ACT 1

Scene 1: *The Duke's palace*

Escalus, councillors, the Duke and attendants

DUKE. Escalus.

ESCALUS. My lord.

DUKE. Of government the properties to unfold
Would seem in me t'affect speech and discourse,
Since I am put to know that your own science
Exceeds, in that, the lists of all advice
My strength can give you: then no more remains
But that to your sufficiency, as your worth is able,
And let them work ... The nature of our people,
Our city's institutions, and the terms   10
For common justice, y'are as pregnant in
As art and practice hath enrichéd any
That we remember ... There is our commission,
From which we would not have you warp ...
    Call hither,
I say, bid come before us Angelo ...
                                    An attendant goes
What figure of us think you he will bear?
For you must know, we have with special soul
Elected him our absence to supply;
Lent him our terror, dressed him with our love,
And given his deputation all the organs   20
Of our own power: what think you of it?

ESCALUS. If any in Vienna be of worth
To undergo such ample grace and honour,
It is Lord Angelo.

DUKE.   Look where he comes.

Angelo enters

ANGELO. Always obedient to your grace's will,
I come to know your pleasure.

DUKE.   Angelo ...
There is a kind of character in thy life,
That to th'observer doth thy history
Fully unfold: thyself and thy belongings
Are not thine own so proper, as to waste   30
Thyself upon thy virtues, they on thee.
Heaven doth with us as we with torches do,
Not light them for themselves: for if our virtues
Did not go forth of us, 'twere all alike
As if we had them not: spirits are not finely
    touched
But to fine issues: nor Nature never lends
The smallest scruple of her excellence,
But, like a thrifty goddess, she determines
Herself the glory of a creditor,
Both thanks and use ... But I do bend my speech 40
To one that can my part in him advértise;
Hold therefore, Angelo ...
In our remove, be thou at full ourself:
Mortality and mercy in Vienna
Live in thy tongue, and heart ... Old Escalus,
Though first in question, is thy secondary....
Take thy commission.

ANGELO.   Now, good my lord,
Let there be some more test made of my mettle,

Before so noble and so great a figure
Be stamped upon it.

DUKE.   No more evasion: 50
We have with a leavened and preparéd choice
Proceeded to you; therefore take your honours ...
Our haste from thence is of so quick condition,
That it prefers itself, and leaves unquestioned
Matters of needful value ... We shall write to you,
As time and our concernings shall impórtune,
How it goes with us—and do look to know
What doth befall you here.... So, fare you well:
To th'hopeful execution do I leave you
Of your commissions.

ANGELO.   Yet give leave, my lord,   60
That we may bring you something on the way.

DUKE. My haste may not admit it,
Nor need you, on mine honour, have to do
With any scruple: your scope is as mine own,
So to enforce or qualify the laws,
As to your soul seems good ... Give me your hand.
I'll privily away: I love the people,
But do not like to stage me to their eyes:
Though it do well, I do not relish well
Their loud applause and 'aves' vehement: 70
Nor do I think the man of safe discretion
That does affect it.... Once more, fare you well.

ANGELO. The heavens give safety to your purposes.

ESCALUS. Lead forth and bring you back in happiness.

DUKE. I thank you. Fare you well.   *He departs*

ESCALUS. I shall desire you, sir, to give me leave
To have free speech with you; and it concerns me
To look into the bottom of my place:
A power I have—but of what strength and nature
I am not yet instructed.   80

ANGELO. 'Tis so with me ... Let us withdraw together,
And we may soon our satisfaction have
Touching that point.

ESCALUS.   I'll wait upon your honour.
                                    They go

Scene 2: *A street*

Lucio and two gentlemen enter

LUCIO. If the duke, with the other dukes, come not to
composition with the King of Hungary, why then
all the dukes fall upon the king.

FIRST GENTLEMAN. Heaven grant us its peace, but not
the King of Hungary's!

SECOND GENTLEMAN. Amen.

LUCIO. Thou conclud'st like the sanctimonious pirate,
that went to sea with the Ten Commandments, but
scraped one out of the table.

SECOND GENTLEMAN. 'Thou shalt not steal'?   10

LUCIO. Ay, that he razed.

FIRST GENTLEMAN. Why, 'twas a commandment to
command the captain and all the rest from their
functions: they put forth to steal ... There's not a
soldier of us all, that, in the thanksgiving before
meat, do relish the petition well that prays for peace.

SECOND GENTLEMAN. I never heard any soldier dislike it.

LUCIO. I believe thee: for I think thou never wast where grace was said. 20

SECOND GENTLEMAN. No? a dozen times at least.

FIRST GENTLEMAN. What? in metre?

LUCIO. In any proportion or in any language.

FIRST GENTLEMAN. I think, or in any religion.

LUCIO. Ay, why not? Grace is grace, despite of all controversy: as for example; thou thyself art a wicked villain, despite of all grace.

FIRST GENTLEMAN. Well: there went but a pair of shears between us.

LUCIO. I grant: as there may between the lists and the 30 velvet.... Thou art the list.

FIRST GENTLEMAN. And thou the velvet; thou art good velvet; thou'rt a three-piled piece, I warrant thee ... I had as lief be a list of an English kersey, as be piled, as thou art piled, for a French velvet.... Do I speak feelingly now?

LUCIO. I think thou dost: and, indeed, with most painful feeling of thy speech: I will, out of thine own confession, learn to begin thy health; but, whilst I live, forget to drink after thee. 40

FIRST GENTLEMAN. I think I have done myself wrong, have I not?

SECOND GENTLEMAN. Yes, that thou hast; whether thou art tainted or free.

Enter Mistress Overdone the bawd

LUCIO. Behold, behold, where Madam Mitigation comes! I have purchased as many diseases under her roof, as come to—

SECOND GENTLEMAN. To what, I pray?

LUCIO. Judge.

SECOND GENTLEMAN. To three thousand dolours a 50 year.

FIRST GENTLEMAN. Ay, and more.

LUCIO. A French crown more.

FIRST GENTLEMAN. Thou art always figuring diseases in me; but thou art full of error—I am sound.

LUCIO. Nay, not as one would say, healthy: but so sound as things that are hollow; thy bones are hollow; impiety has made a feast of thee.

FIRST GENTLEMAN. How now! Which of your hips has the most profound sciatica? 60

OVERDONE. Well, well: there's one yonder arrested and carried to prison was worth five thousand of you all.

SECOND GENTLEMAN. Who's that, I pray thee?

OVERDONE. Marry, sir, that's Claudio, Signior Claudio.

FIRST GENTLEMAN. Claudio to prison! 'tis not so.

OVERDONE. Nay, but I know 'tis so: I saw him arrested ... saw him carried away ... and, which is more, within these three days his head to be chopped 70 off.

LUCIO. But, after all this fooling, I would not have it so ... Art thou sure of this?

OVERDONE. I am too sure of it: and it is for getting Madam Julietta with child.

LUCIO. Believe me, this may be: he promised to meet me two hours since; and he was ever precise in promise-keeping.

SECOND GENTLEMAN. Besides, you know, it draws

something near to the speech we had to such a 80 purpose.

FIRST GENTLEMAN. But most of all agreeing with the proclamation.

LUCIO. Away: let's go learn the truth of it.

Lucio and the gentlemen go

OVERDONE. Thus, what with the war, what with the sweat, what with the gallows, and what with poverty, I am custom-shrunk.

Pompey approaches

How now! what's the news with you?

POMPEY. Yonder man is carried to prison.

OVERDONE. Well: what has he done? 90

POMPEY. A woman.

OVERDONE. But what's his offence?

POMPEY. Groping for trouts in a peculiar river.

OVERDONE. What, is there a maid with child by him?

POMPEY. No: but there's a woman with maid by him ... You have not heard of the proclamation, have you?

OVERDONE. What proclamation, man?

POMPEY. All houses in the suburbs of Vienna must be plucked down. 100

OVERDONE. And what shall become of those in the city?

POMPEY. They shall stand for seed: they had gone down too, but that a wise burgher put in for them.

OVERDONE. But shall all our houses of resort in the suburbs be pulled down?

POMPEY. To the ground, mistress.

OVERDONE. Why, here's a change indeed in the commonwealth ... What shall become of me?

POMPEY. Come: fear not you: good counsellors lack no 110 clients: though you change your place, you need not change your trade: I'll be your tapster still ... Courage, there will be pity taken on you; you, that have worn your eyes almost out in the service, you will be considered.

OVERDONE. What's to do here, Thomas Tapster? Let's withdraw.

POMPEY. Here comes Signior Claudio, led by the provost to prison: and there's Madam Juliet.

They go

Enter the Provost, officers, Claudio and Juliet; Lucio and the two gentlemen following

CLAUDIO. Fellow, why dost thou show me thus to th' world? 120
　Bear me to prison, where I am committed.

PROVOST. I do it not in evil disposition,
　But from Lord Angelo by special charge.

CLAUDIO. Thus can the demi-god, Authority,
　Make us pay down for our offence by weight—
　The words of heaven; on whom it will, it will—
　On whom it will not, so. Yet still 'tis just.

LUCIO. Why, how now, Claudio! whence comes this restraint?

CLAUDIO. From too much liberty, my Lucio, liberty: 130
　As surfeit is the father of much fast,
　So every scope by the immoderate use
　Turns to restraint: Our natures do pursue,
　Like rats that ravin down their proper bane,
　A thirsty evil—and, when we drink, we die.

LUCIO. If I could speak so wisely under an arrest, I would send for certain of my creditors: and yet, to

say the truth, I had as lief have the foppery of
freedom as the morality of imprisonment ... What's
thy offence, Claudio?   140
CLAUDIO. What (but to speak of) would offend again.
LUCIO. What is't? murder?
CLAUDIO. No.
LUCIO. Lechery?
CLAUDIO. Call it so.
PROVOST. Away, sir! you must go.
CLAUDIO. One word, good friend ... Lucio, a word
with you.
LUCIO. A hundred, if they'll do you any good ...
Is lechery so looked after?   150
CLAUDIO. Thus stands it with me: upon a true contract
I got possession of Julietta's bed.
You know the lady—she is fast my wife,
Save that we do the denunciation lack
Of outward order.... This we came not to,
Only for propagation of a dower
Remaining in the coffer of her friends,
From whom we thought it meet to hide our love
Till time had made them for us.... But it chances
The stealth of our most mutual entertainment   160
With character too gross is writ on Juliet.
LUCIO. With child, perhaps?
CLAUDIO.   Unhappily, even so.
And the new deputy, now for the duke,—
Whether it be the fault and glimpse of newness,
Or whether that the body public be
A horse whereon the governor doth ride,
Who, newly in the seat, that it may know
He can command, lets it straight feel the spur:
Whether the tyranny be in his place,
Or in his eminence that fills it up,   170
I stagger in ... But this new governor
Awakes me all the enrollèd penalties,
Which have, like unscoured armour, hung by th'
wall
So long, that nineteen zodiacs have gone round,
And none of them been worn; and, for a name,
Now puts the drowsy and neglected act
Freshly on me ... 'tis surely for a name.
LUCIO. I warrant, it is: and thy head stands so tickle
on thy shoulders, that a milk-maid, if she be in love,
may sigh it off ... Send after the duke, and appeal   180
to him.
CLAUDIO. I have done so, but he's not to be found....
I prithee, Lucio, do me this kind service:
This day my sister should the cloister enter,
And there receive her approbation....
Acquaint her with the danger of my state,
Implore her, in my voice, that she make friends
To the strict deputy: bid herself assay him—
I have great hope in that: for in her youth
There is a prone and speechless dialect,   190
Such as move men: beside, she hath prosperous art
When she will play with reason and discourse,
And well she can persuade.
LUCIO.   I pray she may;
as well for the encouragement of the like, which
else would stand under grievous imposition, as for
the enjoying of thy life, who I would be sorry
should be thus foolishly lost at a game of tick-
tack ...
I'll to her.
CLAUDIO.   I thank you, good friend Lucio.

LUCIO. Within two hours.
CLAUDIO.   Come, officer, away.   *They go* 200

Scene 3: *A friar's cell*

Enter Duke and Friar Thomas

DUKE. No ... holy father, throw away that thought.
Believe not that the dribbling dart of love
Can pierce a cómplęte bosom: why I desire thee
To give me secret harbour, hath a purpose
More grave and wrinkled than the aims and ends
Of burning youth.
FRIAR.   May your grace speak of it?
DUKE. My holy sir, none better knows than you
How I have ever loved the life removed,
And held in idle price to haunt assemblies,
Where youth and cost a witless bravery keeps.... 10
I have delivered to Lord Angelo,
A man of stricture and firm abstinence,
My absolute power and place here in Vienna,
And he supposes me travellèd to Poland—
For so I have strewed it in the common ear,
And so it is received ... Now, pious sir,
You will demand of me why I do this?
FRIAR. Gladly, my lord.
DUKE. We have strict statutes and most biting laws,
The needful bits and curbs for headstrong steeds,   20
Which for these fourteen years we have let slip,
Even like an o'ergrown lion in a cave,
That goes not out to prey ... Now, as fond fathers,
Having bound up the threat'ning twigs of birch,
Only to stick it in their children's sight,
For terror, not to use ... in time the rod
Becomes more mocked than feared ... so our
decrees,
Dead to infliction, to themselves are dead,
And liberty plucks justice by the nose;
The baby beats the nurse, and quite athwart   30
Goes all decorum.
FRIAR.   It rested in your grace
To unloose this tied-up justice when you pleased:
And it in you more dreadful would have seemed
Than in Lord Angelo.
DUKE.   I do fear ... too dreadful:
Sith 'twas my fault to give the people scope,
'Twould be my tyranny to strike and gall them
For what I bid them do: for we bid this be done,
When evil deeds have their permissive pass,
And not the punishment ... Therefore, indeed, my
father,
I have on Angelo imposed the office,   40
Who may, in th'ambush of my name, strike home,
And yet my nature never in the fight,
To do it slander ... And to behold his sway,
I will, as 'twere a brother of your order,
Visit both prince and people: Therefore, I prithee,
Supply me with the habit, and instruct
How I may formally in person bear me
Like a true friar ... Moe reasons for this action
At our more leisure shall I render you;
Only, this one: Lord Angelo is precise;   50
Stands at a guard with envy; scarce confesses
That his blood flows; or that his appetite
Is more to bread than stone: hence shall we see,
If power change purpose ... what our seemers be.
                                                       They go

Scene 4: *A nunnery*

Enter Isabella and Francisca, a nun

ISABELLA. And have you nuns no farther privileges?

NUN. Are not these large enough?

ISABELLA. Yes, truly; I speak not as desiring more,
But rather wishing a more strict restraint
Upon the sisterhood, the votarists of Saint Clare.

A VOICE WITHOUT. Ho! Peace be in this place!

ISABELLA.   Who's that which calls?

NUN. It is a man's voice: gentle Isabella,
Turn you the key, and know his business of him;
You may; I may not: you are yet unsworn:
When you have vowed, you must not speak with
    men   10
But in the presence of the prioress;
Then, if you speak, you must not show your face;
Or, if you show your face, you must not speak....
He calls again: I pray you, answer him.

ISABELLA. Peace and prosperity! Who is't that calls?

Lucio enters

LUCIO. Hail, virgin, if you be, as those cheek-roses
Proclaim you are no less ... Can you so stead me
As bring me to the sight of Isabella,
A novice of this place, and the fair sister
To her unhappy brother Claudio?   20

ISABELLA. Why 'her unhappy brother'? Let me ask,
The rather for I now must make you know
I am that Isabella and his sister.

LUCIO. Gentle and fair ... your brother kindly greets
    you;
Not to be weary with you—he's in prison.

ISABELLA. Woe me; for what?

LUCIO. For that which, if myself might be his judge,
He should receive his punishment in thanks:
He hath got his friend with child.

ISABELLA. Sir, make me not your story.

LUCIO.   It is true;   30
I would not—though 'tis my familiar sin
With maids to seem the lapwing, and to jest,
Tongue far from heart—play with all virgins so:
I hold you as a thing enskied and sainted,
By your renouncement—an immortal spirit,
And to be talked with in sincerity,
As with a saint.

ISABELLA. You do blaspheme the good, in mocking
    me.

LUCIO. Do not believe it ... Fewness and truth, 'tis
    thus—
Your brother and his lover have embraced;   40
As those that feed grow full ... as blossoming
    time,
That from the seedness the bare fallow brings
To teeming foison ... even so her plenteous womb
Expresseth his full tilth and husbandry.

ISABELLA. Some one with child by him? My cousin
    Juliet?

LUCIO. Is she your cousin?

ISABELLA. Adoptedly—as school-maids change their
    names,
By vain though apt affection.

LUCIO.   She it is.

ISABELLA. O, let him marry her.

LUCIO.   This is the point....
The duke is very strangely gone from hence;   50

Bore many gentlemen, myself being one,
In hand on hope of action: but we do learn
By those that know the very nerves of state,
His givings-out were of an infinite distance
From his true-meant design ... Upon his place,
And with full line of his authority,
Governs Lord Angelo; a man whose blood
Is very snow-broth; one who never feels
The wanton stings and motions of the sense;
But doth rebate and blunt his natural edge   60
With profits of the mind, study and fast.
He—to give fear to use and liberty,
Which have for long run by the hideous law,
As mice by lions—hath picked out an act,
Under whose heavy sense your brother's life
Falls into forfeit: he arrests him on it,
And follows close the rigour of the statute,
To make him an example ... All hope is gone,
Unless you have the grace by your fair prayer
To soften Angelo: and that's my pith of business   70
'Twixt you and your poor brother.

ISABELLA. Doth he so seek his life?

LUCIO.   Has censured him
Already—and, as I hear, the provost hath
A warrant for his execution.

ISABELLA. Alas ... what poor ability's in me
To do him good?

LUCIO.   Assay the power you have.

ISABELLA. My power! alas, I doubt—

LUCIO.   Our doubts are traitors,
And make us lose the good we oft might win,
By fearing to attempt ... Go to Lord Angelo,
And let him learn to know, when maidens sue,   80
Men give like gods: but when they weep and kneel,
All their petitions are as freely theirs
As they themselves would owe them.

ISABELLA. I'll see what I can do.

LUCIO.   But speedily.

ISABELLA. I will about it straight;
No longer staying but to give the Mother
Notice of my affair ... I humbly thank you:
Commend me to my brother: soon at night
I'll send him certain word of my success.

LUCIO. I take my leave of you.   90

ISABELLA. Good sir, adieu.   *They go*

ACT 2

Scene 1: *A Court of Justice*

*Enter Angelo, Escalus, a Justice, the Provost, officers and
other attendants*

ANGELO. We must not make a scarecrow of the law,
Setting it up to fear the birds of prey,
And let it keep one shape, till custom make it
Their perch and not their terror.

ESCALUS.   Ay, but yet
Let us be keen and rather cut a little,
Than fall, and bruise to death ... Alas, this
    gentleman,
Whom I would save, had a most noble father.
Let but your honour know,
Whom I believe to be most strait in virtue,
That, in the working of your own affections,   10
Had time cohered with place or place with wishing,
Or that the resolute acting of your blood

Could have attained th'effect of your own purpose,
Whether you had not sometime in your life
Erred in this point which now you censure him,
And pulled the law upon you.
ANGELO. 'Tis one thing to be tempted, Escalus,
Another thing to fall ... I not deny,
The jury, passing on the prisoner's life,
May in the sworn twelve have a thief or two   20
Guiltier than him they try ... What's open made
   to justice,
That justice seizes. What knows the laws
That thieves do pass on thieves? 'Tis very pregnant,
The jewel that we find, we stoop and take't,
Because we see it; but what we do not see
We tread upon, and never think of it....
You may not so extenuate his offence,
For I have had such faults; but rather tell me,
When I, that censure him, do so offend,
Let mine own judgement pattern out my death,   30
And nothing come in partial.... Sir, he must die.
ESCALUS. Be it as your wisdom will.
ANGELO.   Where is the provost?
PROVOST. Here, if it like your honour.
ANGELO.   See that Claudio
Be executed by nine to-morrow morning.
Bring him his confessor, let him be prepared—
For that's the utmost of his pilgrimage.
                The Provost goes out
ESCALUS. Well ... heaven forgive him; and forgive
   us all ...
Some rise by sin, and some by virtue fall:
Some run from breaks of ice, and answer none;
And some condemnéd for a fault alone.   40

Enter Elbow, officers, Pompey and Froth

ELBOW. Come, bring them away: if these be good
people in a commonweal, that do nothing but use
their abuses in common houses, I know no law:
bring them away.
ANGELO. How now, sir! What's your name? and
   what's the matter?
ELBOW. If it please your honour, I am the poor
duke's constable, and my name is Elbow; I do lean
upon justice, sir, and do bring in here before your
good honour two notorious benefactors.
ANGELO. Benefactors! Well: what benefactors are   50
they? are they not malefactors?
ELBOW. If it please your honour, I know not well what
they are: but precise villains they are, that I am sure
of: and void of all profanation in the world that
good Christians ought to have.
ESCALUS. This comes off well: here's a wise officer.
ANGELO. Go to: what quality are they of? Elbow is
your name? why dost thou not speak, Elbow?
POMPEY. He cannot, sir: he's out at elbow.
ANGELO. What are you, sir?   60
ELBOW. He sir? a tapster, sir: parcel-bawd: one that
serves a bad woman: whose house, sir, was, as they
say, plucked down in the suburbs: and now she professes a hot-house; which, I think, is a very ill house
too.
ESCALUS. How know you that?
ELBOW. My wife, sir, whom I detest before heaven
and your honour—
ESCALUS. How! thy wife?

ELBOW. Ay, sir: whom, I thank heaven, is an honest   70
woman—
ESCALUS. Dost thou detest her therefore?
ELBOW. I say, sir, I will detest myself also, as well as
she, that this house, if it be not a bawd's house, it
is pity of her life, for it is a naughty house.
ESCALUS. How dost thou know that, constable?
ELBOW. Marry, sir, by my wife: who, if she had been
a woman cardinally given, might have been accused
in fornication, adultery, and all uncleanliness there.
ESCALUS. By the woman's means?   80
ELBOW. Ay, sir, by Mistress Overdone's means: but,
as she spit in his face, so she defied him.
POMPEY. Sir, if it please your honour, this is not so.
ELBOW. Prove it before these varlets here, thou
honourable man, prove it.
ESCALUS [*to Angelo*]. Do you hear how he misplaces?
POMPEY. Sir, she came in great with child: and longing
—saving your honour's reverence!—for stewed
prunes; sir, we had but two in the house, which at
that very distant time stood, as it were, in a fruit-   90
dish, a dish of some threepence; your honours have
seen such dishes—they are not China-dishes, but
very good dishes.
ESCALUS. Go to: go to: no matter for the dish, sir.
POMPEY. No, indeed, sir, not of a pin; you are therein
in the right: but, to the point ... As I say, this
Mistress Elbow, being, as I say, with child, and
being great-bellied, and longing, as I said, for
prunes: and having but two in the dish, as I said,
Master Froth here, this very man, having eaten the   100
rest, as I said, and, as I say, paying for them very
honestly: for, as you know, Master Froth, I could
not give you threepence again.
FROTH. No, indeed.
POMPEY. Very well: you being then, if you be remembred, cracking the stones of the foresaid prunes—
FROTH. Ay, so I did, indeed.
POMPEY. Why, very well: I telling you then, if you be
remembred, that such a one and such a one were
past cure of the thing you wot of, unless they kept   110
very good diet, as I told you—
FROTH. All this is true.
POMPEY. Why, very well then—
ESCALUS. Come; you are a tedious fool: to the purpose
... What was done to Elbow's wife, that he hath
cause to complain of? Come me to what was done
to her.
POMPEY. Sir, your honour cannot come to that yet.
ESCALUS. No, sir, nor I mean it not.
POMPEY. Sir, but you shall come to it, by your   120
honour's leave ... And, I beseech you, look into
Master Froth here, sir—a man of fourscore pound
a year; whose father died at Hallowmas ... was't
not at Hallowmas, Master Froth?
FROTH. All-hallond eve.
POMPEY. Why, very well: I hope here be truths ...
He, sir, sitting, as I say, in a lower chair, sir—'twas
in the Bunch of Grapes, where, indeed, you have a
delight to sit, have you not?
FROTH. I have so, because it is an open room, and   130
good for winter.
POMPEY. Why, very well then: I hope here be truths—
ANGELO. This will last out a night in Russia,
When nights are longest there: I'll take my leave,
And leave you to the hearing of the cause;

Hoping you'll find good cause to whip them all.
ESCALUS. I think no less: good morrow to your lord-
ship ...   *Angelo goes out*
Now, sir, come on: what was done to Elbow's wife,
once more?
POMPEY. Once, sir? there was nothing done to her   140
once.
ELBOW. I beseech you, sir, ask him what this man did
to my wife.
POMPEY. I beseech your honour, ask me.
ESCALUS. Well, sir, what did this gentleman to her?
POMPEY. I beseech you, sir, look in this gentleman's
face ... Good Master Froth, look upon his honour;
'tis for a good purpose ... Doth your honour mark
his face?
ESCALUS. Ay, sir, very well.   150
POMPEY. Nay, I beseech you, mark it well.
ESCALUS. Well, I do so.
POMPEY. Doth your honour see any harm in his face?
ESCALUS. Why, no.
POMPEY. I'll be supposed upon a book, his face is the
worst thing about him ... Good then: if his face be
the worst thing about him, how could Master Froth
do the constable's wife any harm? I would know
that of your honour.
ESCALUS. He's in the right. Constable, what say you 160
to it?
ELBOW. First, an it like you, the house is a respected
house; next, this is a respected fellow; and his
mistress is a respected woman.
POMPEY. By this hand, sir, his wife is a more respected
person than any of us all.
ELBOW. Varlet, thou liest; thou liest, wicked varlet:
the time is yet to come that she was ever respected
with man, woman, or child.
POMPEY. Sir, she was respected with him, before he   170
married with her.
ESCALUS. Which is the wiser here? Justice or Iniquity?
Is this true?
ELBOW. O thou caitiff ... O thou varlet ... O thou
wicked Hannibal ... I respected with her, before I
was married to her! If ever I was respected with
her, or she with me, let not your worship think me
the poor duke's officer ... Prove this, thou wicked
Hannibal, or I'll have mine action of batt'ry on thee.
ESCALUS. If he took you a box o'th'ear, you might   180
have your action of slander too.
ELBOW. Marry, I thank your good worship for it:
what is't your worship's pleasure I shall do with this
wicked caitiff?
ESCALUS. Truly, officer, because he hath some offences
in him that thou wouldst discover if thou couldst,
let him continue in his courses till thou know'st
what they are.
ELBOW. Marry, I thank your worship for it ... Thou
seest, thou wicked varlet now, what's come upon   190
thee! Thou art to continue now, thou varlet, thou
art to continue.
ESCALUS. Where you were born, friend?
FROTH. Here in Vienna, sir.
ESCALUS. Are you of fourscore pounds a year?
FROTH. Yes, an't please you, sir.
ESCALUS. So ... [*to Pompey*] What trade are you of, sir?
POMPEY. A tapster—a poor widow's tapster.
ESCALUS. Your mistress' name?
POMPEY. Mistress Overdone.   200

ESCALUS. Hath she had any more than one husband?
POMPEY. Nine, sir: Overdone by the last.
ESCALUS. Nine! Come hither to me, Master Froth ...
Master Froth, I would not have you acquainted
with tapsters; they will draw you, Master Froth,
and you will hang them ... Get you gone, and let
me hear no more of you.
FROTH. I thank your worship ... For mine own part,
I never come into any room in a taphouse, but
I am drawn in.   210
ESCALUS. Well: no more of it, Master Froth: farewell
... [*Froth goes*] Come you hither to me, Master
Tapster: what's your name, Master Tapster?
POMPEY. Pompey.
ESCALUS. What else?
POMPEY. Bum, sir.
ESCALUS. Troth, and your bum is the greatest thing
about you, so that, in the beastliest sense, you are
Pompey the Great ... Pompey, you are partly a
bawd, Pompey—howsoever you colour it in being 220
a tapster—are you not? Come, tell me true. It shall
be the better for you.
POMPEY. Truly, sir, I am a poor fellow that would
live.
ESCALUS. How would you live, Pompey? by being a
bawd? What do you think of the trade, Pompey?
is it a lawful trade?
POMPEY. If the law would allow it, sir.
ESCALUS. But the law will not allow it, Pompey; nor
it shall not be allowed in Vienna.   230
POMPEY. Does your worship mean to geld and splay
all the youth of the city?
ESCALUS. No, Pompey.
POMPEY. Truly, sir, in my poor opinion, they will to't
then ... If your worship will take order for the
drabs and the knaves, you need not to fear the
bawds.
ESCALUS. There is pretty orders beginning, I can tell
you: it is but heading and hanging.
POMPEY. If you head and hang all that offend that way 240
but for ten year together, you'll be glad to give out
a commission for more heads ... If this law hold in
Vienna ten year, I'll rent the fairest house in it after
threepence a bay: if you live to see this come to pass,
say Pompey told you so.
ESCALUS. Thank you, good Pompey: and, in requital
of your prophecy, hark you: I advise you let me not
find you before me again upon any complaint
whatsoever; no, not for dwelling where you do: if
I do, Pompey, I shall beat you to your tent, and   250
prove a shrewd Cæsar to you: in plain dealing,
Pompey, I shall have you whipt; so, for this time,
Pompey, fare you well.
POMPEY. I thank your worship for your good counsel;
[*aside*] but I shall follow it as the flesh and fortune
shall better determine ...
Whip me? No, no, let carman whip his jade;
The valiant heart's not whipt out of his trade.
                                            He goes
ESCALUS. Come hither to me, Master Elbow: come
hither, master constable ... How long have you   260
been in this place of constable?
ELBOW. Seven year and a half, sir.
ESCALUS. I thought, by the readiness in the office, you
had continued in it some time ... You say, seven
years together?

ELBOW. And a half, sir.

ESCALUS. Alas, it hath been great pains to you: they do you wrong to put you so oft upon't.... Are there not men in your ward sufficient to serve it?

ELBOW. Faith, sir, few of any wit in such matters: as 270 they are chosen, they are glad to choose me for them; I do it for some piece of money, and go through with all.

ESCALUS. Look you bring me in the names of some six or seven, the most sufficient of your parish.

ELBOW. To your worship's house, sir?

ESCALUS. To my house: fare you well ... *Elbow goes* What's o'clock, think you?

JUSTICE. Eleven, sir.

ESCALUS. I pray you home to dinner with me.   280

JUSTICE. I humbly thank you.

ESCALUS. It grieves me for the death of Claudio— But there's no remedy.

JUSTICE. Lord Angelo is severe.

ESCALUS.   It is but needful....
Mercy is not itself, that oft looks so,
Pardon is still the nurse of second woe ...
But yet, poor Claudio! There is no remedy....
Come, sir.   *They depart*

    Scene 2: *The Provost enters with a servant*

SERVANT. He's hearing of a cause; he will come straight.
I'll tell him of you.   *He goes*

PROVOST.   Pray you, do ... I'll know
His pleasure—may be he will relent ... Alas,
He hath but as offended in a dream.
All sects, all ages smack of this vice—and he
To die for't!

Angelo enters

ANGELO.   Now, what's the matter, provost?

PROVOST. Is it your will Claudio shall die to-morrow?

ANGELO. Did I not tell thee yea? hadst thou not order?
Why dost thou ask again?

PROVOST.   Lest I might be too rash:
Under your good correction, I have seen,   10
When, after execution, Judgement hath
Repented o'er his doom.

ANGELO.   Go to; let that be mine.
Do you your office, or give up your place,
And you shall well be spared.

PROVOST.   I crave your honour's pardon ...
What shall be done, sir, with the groaning Juliet?
She's very near her hour.

ANGELO.   Dispose of her
To some more fitter place; and that with speed.

The servant comes to the door

SERVANT. Here is the sister of the man condemned
Desires access to you.

ANGELO.   Hath he a sister?

PROVOST. Ay, my good lord—a very virtuous maid, 20
And to be shortly of a sisterhood,
If not already.

ANGELO.   Well: let her be admitted.
                        The servant departs
See you, the fornicatress be removed.
Let her have needful, but not lavish, means.
There shall be order for't.

Enter Isabella and Lucio

PROVOST.   Save your honour!

ANGELO. Stay a little while ... [*to Isabella*] Y'are welcome: what's your will?

ISABELLA. I am a woeful suitor to your honour,
Please but your honour hear me.

ANGELO.   Well: what's your suit?

ISABELLA. There is a vice that most I do abhor,
And most desire should meet the blow of justice; 30
For which I would not plead, but that I must—
For which I must not plead, but that I am
At war 'twixt will and will not.

ANGELO.   Well: the matter?

ISABELLA. I have a brother is condemned to die,
I do beseech you, let it be his fault,
And not my brother.

PROVOST.   Heaven give thee moving graces!

ANGELO. Condemn the fault, and not the actor of it?
Why, every fault's condemned ere it be done:
Mine were the very cipher of a function,
To fine the faults whose fine stands in record,   40
And let go by the actor.

ISABELLA.   O just, but severe law ...
I had a brother then; heaven keep your honour.

LUCIO. Give't not o'er so: to him again, entreat him,
Kneel down before him, hang upon his gown.
You are too cold: if you should need a pin,
You could not with more tame a tongue desire it:
To him, I say.

ISABELLA. Must he needs die?

ANGELO.   Maiden, no remedy.

ISABELLA. Yes: I do think that you might pardon him,
And neither heaven nor man grieve at the mercy.   50

ANGELO. I will not do't.

ISABELLA.   But can you, if you would?

ANGELO. Look what I will not, that I cannot do.

ISABELLA. But might you do't, and do the world
no wrong,
If so your heart were touched with that remorse
As mine is to him!

ANGELO.   He's sentenced—'tis too late.

LUCIO. You are too cold.

ISABELLA. Too late? why, no: I, that do speak a word,
May call it in again ... Well, believe this,
No ceremony that to great ones 'longs,
Not the king's crown ... nor the deputed sword, 60
The marshal's truncheon, nor the judge's robe,
Become them with one half so good a grace
As mercy does ...
If he had been as you, and you as he,
You would have slipped like him—but he, like you,
Would not have been so stern.

ANGELO.   Pray you, be gone.

ISABELLA. I would to heaven I had your potency,
And you were Isabel ... should it then be thus?
No: I would tell what 'twere to be a judge,
And what a prisoner.

LUCIO.   Ay, touch him: there's the vein. 70

ANGELO. Your brother is a forfeit of the law,
And you but waste your words.

ISABELLA.   Alas, alas,
Why, all the souls that were were forfeit once,
And He that might the vantage best have took
Found out the remedy: how would you be,
If He, which is the top of judgement, should

But judge you, as you are? O, think on that,
And mercy then will breathe within your lips,
Like man new made.
ANGELO.   Be you content—fair maid.
  It is the law, not I, condemns your brother.   80
  Were he my kinsman, brother, or my son,
  It should be thus with him: he must die to-morrow.
ISABELLA. To-morrow? O, that's sudden.
  Spare him, spare him ...
  He's not prepared for death ... even for our
    kitchens
  We kill the fowl of season ... shall we serve heaven
  With less respect than we do minister
  To our gross selves? Good, good my lord, bethink
    you;
  Who is it that hath died for this offence?
  There's many have committed it.
LUCIO.   Ay, well said.   90
ANGELO. The law hath not been dead, though it
    hath slept.
  Those many had not dared to do that evil,
  If that the first that did th'edict infringe
  Had answered for his deed.... Now 'tis awake,
  Takes note of what is done, and, like a prophet,
  Looks in a glass that shows what future evils—
  Either new or by remissness new-conceived,
  And so in progress to be hatched and born—
  Are now to have no successive degrees,
  But, ere they live, to end.
ISABELLA.   Yet show some pity.   100
ANGELO. I show it most of all when I show justice;
  For then I pity those I do not know,
  Which a dismissed offence would after gall,
  And do him right that, answering one foul wrong,
  Lives not to act another.... Be satisfied;
  Your brother dies to-morrow; be content.
ISABELLA. So you must be the first that gives this
    sentence,
  And he, that suffers ... O, it is excellent
  To have a giant's strength: but it is tyrannous
  To use it like a giant.   110
LUCIO. That's well said.
ISABELLA.   Could great men thunder
  As Jove himself does, Jove would ne'er be quiet,
  For every pelting, petty officer
  Would use his heaven for thunder;
  Nothing but thunder ... Merciful heaven,
  Thou rather with thy sharp and sulphurous bolt
  Splits the unwedgeable and gnarléd oak
  Than the soft myrtle: but man, proud man,
  Dressed in a little brief authority,
  Most ignorant of what he's most assured—   120
  His glassy essence—like an angry ape,
  Plays such fantastic tricks before high heaven
  As make the angels weep; who, with our spleens,
  Would all themselves laugh mortal.
LUCIO. O, to him, to him, wench: he will relent.
  He's coming: I perceive't.
PROVOST.   Pray heaven, she win him.
ISABELLA. We cannot weigh our brother with ourself.
  Great men may jest with saints: 'tis wit in them,
  But in the less foul profanation.
LUCIO. Thou'rt i'th' right, girl—more o'that.   130
ISABELLA. That in the captain's but a choleric word,
  Which in the soldier is flat blasphemy.

LUCIO. Art avised o'that? more on't.
ANGELO. Why do you put these sayings upon me?
ISABELLA. Because authority, though it err like others,
  Hath yet a kind of medicine in itself,
  That skins the vice o'th' top; go to your bosom,
  Knock there, and ask your heart what it doth know
  That's like my brother's fault: if it confess
  A natural guiltiness such as is his,   140
  Let it not sound a thought upon your tongue
  Against my brother's life.
ANGELO.   She speaks, and 'tis such sense,
  That my sense breeds with it ... [aloud] Fare you
    well.
ISABELLA. Gentle my lord, turn back.
ANGELO. I will bethink me: come again to-morrow.
ISABELLA. Hark how I'll bribe you: good my lord,
    turn back.
ANGELO. How! bribe me!
ISABELLA. Ay, with such gifts that heaven shall share
    with you.
LUCIO. You had marred all else.
ISABELLA. Not with fond sicles of the tested gold,   150
  Or stones whose rates are either rich or poor
  As fancy values them: but with true prayers,
  That shall be up at heaven and enter there
  Ere sun-rise: prayers from preservéd souls,
  From fasting maids whose minds are dedicate
  To nothing temporal.
ANGELO.   Well: come to me to-morrow.
LUCIO. Go to; 'tis well; away.
ISABELLA. Heaven keep your honour safe!
ANGELO.   Amen....
  For I am that way going to temptation,
  Where prayers cross.
ISABELLA.   At what hour to-morrow   160
  Shall I attend your lordship?
ANGELO.   At any time 'fore-noon.
ISABELLA. 'Save your honour!
                    She goes out followed by
                    Lucio and the Provost
ANGELO.   From thee ... even from thy virtue....
  What's this? what's this? is this her fault, or mine?
  The tempter, or the tempted, who sins most?
  Ha! not she ... nor doth she tempt ... but it is I
  That, lying by the violet in the sun,
  Do as the carrion does, not as the flower,
  Corrupt with virtuous season ... Can it be,
  That modesty may more betray our sense
  Than woman's lightness? Having waste ground
    enough,   170
  Shall we desire to raze the sanctuary,
  And pitch our evils there? O, fie, fie, fie ...
  What dost thou? or what art thou, Angelo?
  Dost thou desire her foully for those things
  That make her good? O, let her brother live:
  Thieves for their robbery have authority,
  When judges steal themselves ... What, do I love
    her,
  That I desire to hear her speak again?
  And feast upon her eyes? What is't I dream on?
  O cunning enemy, that, to catch a saint,   180
  With saints dost bait thy hook: most dangerous
  Is that temptation that doth goad us on
  To sin, in loving virtue: never could the strumpet,
  With all her double vigour, art, and nature,

Once stir my temper: but this virtuous maid
Subdues me quite ... Ever till now,
When men were fond, I smiled, and wond'red how.
                                        He goes

Scene 3: *Prison*

Enter the Duke, disguised as a friar and the Provost

DUKE. Hail to you, provost—so, I think you are.
PROVOST. I am the provost ... What's your will,
  good friar?
DUKE. Bound by my charity and my blest order,
  I come to visit the afflicted spirits
  Here in the prison: do me the common right
  To let me see them ... and to make me know
  The nature of their crimes, that I may minister
  To them accordingly.
PROVOST. I would do more than that, if more
  were needful.

Enter Juliet

Look, here comes one: a gentlewoman of mine,   10
Who, falling in the flaws of her own youth,
Hath blistered her report ... She is with child,
And he that got it, sentenced: a young man
More fit to do another such offence,
Than die for this.
DUKE. When must he die?
PROVOST.   As I do think, to-morrow....
  I have provided for you—stay awhile,   *To Juliet*
  And you shall be conducted.
DUKE. Repent you, fair one, of the sin you carry?
JULIET. I do; and bear the shame most patiently.   20
DUKE. I'll teach you how you shall arraign your
    conscience,
  And try your penitence, if it be sound,
  Or hollowly put on.
JULIET.   I'll gladly learn.
DUKE. Love you the man that wronged you?
JULIET. Yes, as I love the woman that wronged him.
DUKE. So then it seems your most offenceful act
  Was mutually committed?
JULIET.   Mutually
DUKE. Then was your sin of heavier kind than his.
JULIET. I do confess it, and repent it, father.
DUKE. 'Tis meet so, daughter—but lest you do repent,   30
  As that the sin hath brought you to this shame,
  Which sorrow is always toward ourselves, not
    heaven;
  Showing, we would not spare heaven as we love it,
  But as we stand in fear—
JULIET. I do repent me, as it is an evil;
  And take the shame with joy.
DUKE.   There rest ...
  Your partner, as I hear, must die to-morrow,
  And I am going with instruction to him ...
  Grace go with you. Benedicite!   *He goes*
JULIET. Must die to-morrow! O, injurious law,   40
  That respites me a life, whose very comfort
  Is still a dying horror.
PROVOST.   'Tis pity of him.
                                    They leave

Scene 4: *A room in the house of Lord Angelo*

Enter Angelo

ANGELO. When I would pray and think, I think and
    pray
  To several subjects: heaven hath my empty words,
  Whilst my invention, hearing not my tongue,
  Anchors on Isabel: heaven in my mouth,
  As if I did but only chew his name,
  And in my heart the strong and swelling evil
  Of my conception ... The state whereon I studied
  Is like a good thing, being often read,
  Grown sere and tedious: yea, my gravity,
  Wherein (let no man hear me) I take pride,   10
  Could I, with boot, change for an idle plume,
  Which the air beats for vain ... O place, O form,
  How often dost thou with thy case, thy habit,
  Wrench awe from fools, and tie the wiser souls
  To thy false seeming! Blood, thou art blood—
  Let's write 'good Angel' on the devil's horn,
  'Tis not the devil's crest.

A servant enters

                    How now, who's there?
SERVANT. One Isabel, a sister, desires access to you.
ANGELO. Teach her the way ... [*the servant goes*]
    O heavens,
  Why does my blood thus muster to my heart,   20
  Making both it unable for itself,
  And dispossessing all my other parts
  Of necessary fitness?
  So play the foolish throngs with one that swoons—
  Come all to help him, and so stop the air
  By which he should revive: and even so
  The general, subject to a well-wished king,
  Quit their own part, and in obsequious fondness
  Crowd to his presence, where their untaught love
  Must needs appear offence.

Isabella enters

                    How now, fair maid?   30
ISABELLA. I am come to know your pleasure.
ANGELO. That you might know it, would much better
    please me,
  Than to demand what 'tis ... Your brother cannot
    live.
ISABELLA. Even so ... Heaven keep your honour.
ANGELO. Yet may he live awhile: and, it may be,
  As long as you or I ... Yet he must die.
ISABELLA. Under your sentence?
ANGELO. Yea.
ISABELLA. When, I beseech you? that in his reprieve,
  Longer or shorter, he may be so fitted   40
  That his soul sicken not.
ANGELO. Ha! fie, these filthy vices: it were as good
  To pardon him, that hath from nature stol'n
  A man already made, as to remit
  Their saucy sweetness, that do coin heaven's image,
  In stamps that are forbid: 'tis all as easy
  Falsely to take away a life true made,
  As to put mettle in restrainéd mints,
  To make a false one.
ISABELLA. 'Tis set down so in heaven, but not in earth.   50
ANGELO. Say you so? then I shall pose you quickly....
  Which had you rather—that the most just law
  Now took your brother's life, or to redeem him
  Give up your body to such sweet uncleanness
  As she that he hath stained?

ISABELLA.   Sir, believe this,
I had rather give my body than my soul.
ANGELO. I talk not of your soul: our compelled sins
Stand more for number than accompt.
ISABELLA.   How say you?
ANGELO. Nay, I'll not warrant that: for I can speak
Against the thing I say ... Answer to this—   60
I (now the voice of the recorded law)
Pronounce a sentence on your brother's life:
Might there not be a charity in sin,
To save this brother's life?
ISABELLA.   Please you to do't,
I'll take it as a peril to my soul,
It is no sin at all, but charity.
ANGELO. Pleased you to do't at peril of your soul,
Were equal poise of sin and charity.
ISABELLA. That I do beg his life, if it be sin,
Heaven let me bear it! You granting of my suit,   70
If that be sin, I'll make it my morn-prayer
To have it added to the faults of mine,
And nothing of your answer.
ANGELO.   Nay, but hear me.
Your sense pursues not mine: either you are
    ignorant,
Or seem so, craftily; and that's not good.
ISABELLA. Let me be ignorant, and in nothing good,
But graciously to know I am no better.
ANGELO. Thus wisdom wishes to appear most bright,
When it doth tax itself: as these black masques
Proclaim an enshield beauty ten times louder   80
Than beauty could displayed ... But mark me—
To be received plain. I'll speak more gross:
Your brother is to die.
ISABELLA. So.
ANGELO. And his offence is so, as it appears,
Accountant to the law upon that pain.
ISABELLA. True.
ANGELO. Admit no other way to save his life—
As I subscribe not that, nor any other,
But in the loose of question—that you, his sister,   90
Finding yourself desired of such a person,
Whose credit with the judge, or own great place,
Could fetch your brother from the manacles
Of the all-binding law: and that there were
No earthly mean to save him, but that either
You must lay down the treasures of your body
To this supposed, or else to let him suffer ...
What would you do?
ISABELLA. As much for my poor brother, as myself ...
That is: were I under the terms of death,   100
Th'impression of keen whips I'ld wear as rubies,
And strip myself to death, as to a bed
That long I have been sick for, ere I'ld yield
My body up to shame.
ANGELO.   Then must your brother die.
ISABELLA. And 'twere the cheaper way:
Better it were, a brother died at once,
Than that a sister, by redeeming him,
Should die for ever.
ANGELO. Were not you then as cruel as the sentence
That you have slandered so?   110
ISABELLA. Ignomy in ransom and free pardon
Are of two houses: lawful mercy
Is nothing kin to foul redemption.
ANGELO. You seemed of late to make the law a tyrant,
And rather proved the sliding of your brother

A merriment than a vice.
ISABELLA. O, pardon me, my lord, it oft falls out,
To have what we would have, we speak not what
    we mean:
I something do excuse the thing I hate,
For his advantage that I dearly love.   120
ANGELO. We are all frail.
ISABELLA.   Else let my brother die,
If not a fedary, but only he,
Owe and succeed thy weakness.
ANGELO. Nay, women are frail too.
ISABELLA. Ay, as the glasses where they view
    themselves,
Which are as easy broke as they make forms:
Women! help heaven; men their creation mar
In profiting by them ... Nay, call us ten times frail,
For we are soft as our complexions are,
And credulous to false prints.
ANGELO.   I think it well: 130
And from this testimony of your own sex—
Since I suppose we are made to be no stronger
Than faults may shake our frames—let me be bold;
I do arrest your words.... Be that you are,
That is, a woman; if you be more, you're none....
If you be one (as you are well expressed
By all external warrants) show it now,
By putting on the destined livery.
ISABELLA. I have no tongue but one; gentle my lord,
Let me entreat you speak the former language.   140
ANGELO. Plainly conceive, I love you.
ISABELLA. My brother did love Juliet,
And you tell me that he shall die for't.
ANGELO. He shall not, Isabel, if you give me love.
ISABELLA. I know your virtue hath a licence in't,
Which seems a little fouler than it is,
To pluck on others.
ANGELO.   Believe me, on mine honour,
My words express my purpose.
ISABELLA. Ha! little honour to be much believed,
And most pernicious purpose ... Seeming,
    seeming....   150
I will proclaim thee, Angelo—look for't!
Sign me a present pardon for my brother,
Or with an outstretched throat I'll tell the world
    aloud
What man thou art.
ANGELO.   Who will believe thee, Isabel?
My unsoiled name, th'austereness of my life,
My vouch against you, and my place i'th' state,
Will so your accusation overweigh,
That you shall stifle in your own report,
And smell of calumny.... I have begun,
And now I give my sensual race the rein.   160
Fit thy consent to my sharp appetite,
Lay by all nicety and prolixious blushes
That banish what they sue for ... redeem thy
    brother
By yielding up thy body to my will,
Or else he must not only die the death,
But thy unkindness shall his death draw out
To ling'ring sufferance ... Answer me to-morrow.
Or, by the affection that now guides me most,
I'll prove a tyrant to him.... As for you,
Say what you can; my false o'erweighs your true.   170
                                    He leaves her
ISABELLA. To whom should I complain? Did I tell this,

Who would believe me? O perilous mouths,
That bear in them one and the self-same tongue,
Either of condemnation or approof,
Bidding the law make curtsy to their will,
Hooking both right and wrong to th'appetite,
To follow as it draws.... I'll to my brother.
Though he hath fall'n by prompture of the blood,
Yet hath he in him such a mind of honour,
That had he twenty heads to tender down   180
On twenty bloody blocks, he'ld yield them up,
Before his sister should her body stoop
To such abhorred pollution....
Then Isabel live chaste, and brother die;
'More than our brother is our chastity....'
I'll tell him yet of Angelo's request,
And fit his mind to death, for his soul's rest.

                                      She departs

ACT 3
Scene 1: *The prison*

The disguised Duke, Claudio, and the Provost

DUKE. So then you hope of pardon from Lord Angelo?
CLAUDIO. The miserable have no other medicine
   But only hope:
   I 'have hope to live, and am prepared to die.
DUKE. Be absolute for death: either death or life
   Shall thereby be the sweeter.... Reason thus with
      life:
   If I do lose thee, I do lose a thing
   That none but fools would keep: a breath thou art,
   Servile to all the skyey influences,
   That dost this habitation where thou keep'st   10
   Hourly afflict: merely, thou art death's fool,
   For him thou labour'st by thy flight to shun,
   And yet runn'st toward him still.... Thou art not
      noble,
   For all th'accommodations that thou bear'st,
   Are nursed by baseness ... Thou'rt by no means
      valiant,
   For thou dost fear the soft and tender fork
   Of a poor worm: thy best of rest is sleep,
   And that thou oft provok'st, yet grossly fear'st
   Thy death, which is no more.... Thou art not
      thyself,
   For thou exists on many a thousand grains   20
   That issue out of dust.... Happy thou art not,
   For what thou hast not, still thou striv'st to get,
   And what thou hast, forget'st.... Thou art not
      certain,
   For thy complexion shifts to strange effects,
   After the moon ... If thou art rich, thou'rt poor,
   For like an ass whose back with ingots bows,
   Thou bear'st thy heavy riches but a journey,
   And death unloads thee ... Friend hast thou none,
   For thine own bowels, which do call thee sire,
   The mere effusion of thy proper loins,
   Do curse the gout, serpigo, and the rheum,   30
   For ending thee no sooner.... Thou hast nor youth
      nor age,
   But as it were an after-dinner's sleep,
   Dreaming on both—for all thy blessèd youth
   Becomes as agèd, and doth beg the alms
   Of palsied eld: and when thou art old and rich,
   Thou hast neither heat, affection, limb, nor beauty,

To make thy riches pleasant ... What's yet in this,
That bears the name of life? Yet in this life
Lie hid moe thousand deaths; yet death we fear,   40
That makes these odds all even.
CLAUDIO.   I humbly thank you....
   To sue to live, I find I seek to die—
   And, seeking death, find life: let it come on.
A VOICE WITHOUT. What, ho! Peace here; grace and
   good company.
PROVOST. Who's there? come in, the wish deserves a
   welcome.

Isabella enters

DUKE. Dear sir, ere long I'll visit you again.
CLAUDIO. Most holy sir, I thank you.
ISABELLA. My business is a word or two with Claudio.
PROVOST. And very welcome ... Look, signior, here's
   your sister.
DUKE. Provost a word with you.   50
PROVOST. As many as you please.
DUKE. Bring me to hear them speak, where I may be
   concealed.   *The Duke and Provost withdraw*
CLAUDIO. Now, sister, what's the comfort?
ISABELLA. Why,
   As all comforts are: most good, most good indeed.
   Lord Angelo, having affairs to heaven,
   Intends you for his swift ambassador,
   Where you shall be an everlasting leiger;
   Therefore your best appointment make with
      speed—
   To-morrow you set on.
CLAUDIO.   Is there no remedy?   60
ISABELLA. None, but such remedy as, to save a head,
   To cleave a heart in twain ...
CLAUDIO. But is there any?
ISABELLA.   Yes, brother, you may live;
   There is a devilish mercy in the judge,
   If you'll implore it, that will free your life,
   But fetter you till death.
CLAUDIO.   Perpetual durance?
ISABELLA. Ay, just—perpetual durance, a restraint,
   Though all the world's vastidity you had,
   To a determined scope.
CLAUDIO.   But in what nature?
ISABELLA. In such a one as, you consenting to't,   70
   Would bark your honour from that trunk you bear,
   And leave you naked.
CLAUDIO.   Let me know the point.
ISABELLA. O, I do fear thee Claudio, and I quake,
   Lest thou a feverous life shouldst entertain,
   And six or seven winters more respect
   Than a perpetual honour.... Dar'st thou die?
   The sense of death is most in apprehension,
   And the poor beetle that we tread upon
   In corporal sufferance finds a pang as great
   As when a giant dies.
CLAUDIO.   Why give you me this shame? 80
   Think you I can a resolution fetch
   From flowery tenderness? If I must die,
   I will encounter darkness as a bride,
   And hug it in mine arms.
ISABELLA. There spake my brother: there my
      father's grave
   Did utter forth a voice.... Yes, thou must die:
   Thou art too noble to conserve a life
   In base appliances.... This outward-sainted deputy,

Whose settled visage and deliberate word
Nips youth i'th' head, and follies doth enew,   90
As falcon doth the fowl, is yet a devil:
His filth within being cast, he would appear
A pond as deep as hell.
CLAUDIO.   The prenzie Angelo!
ISABELLA. O, 'tis the cunning livery of hell,
The damned'st body to invest and cover
In prenzie guards ... Dost thou think, Claudio—
If I would yield him my virginity,
Thou mightst be freed!
CLAUDIO.   O, heavens! it cannot be.
ISABELLA. Yes, he would give't thee; from this
    rank offence
So to offend him still.... This night's the time   100
That I should do what I abhor to name,
Or else thou diest to-morrow.
CLAUDIO.   Thou shalt not do't.
ISABELLA. O, were it but my life,
I'd throw it down for your deliverance
As frankly as a pin.
CLAUDIO.   Thanks, dear Isabel.
ISABELLA. Be ready, Claudio, for your death
    to-morrow.
CLAUDIO. Yes.... Has he affections in him,
That thus can make him bite the law by th' nose,
When he would force it? Sure it is no sin—
Or of the deadly seven it is the least.   110
ISABELLA. Which is the least?
CLAUDIO. If it were damnable, he being so wise,
Why would he for the momentary trick
Be perdurably fined? O Isabel!
ISABELLA. What says my brother?
CLAUDIO.   Death is a fearful thing.
ISABELLA. And shamèd life a hateful.
CLAUDIO. Ay, but to die, and go we know not where,
To lie in cold obstruction, and to rot,
This sensible warm motion—to become
A kneaded clod; and the delighted spirit   120
To bathe in fiery floods, or to reside
In thrilling region of thick-ribbèd ice,
To be imprisoned in the viewless winds
And blown with restless violence round about
The pendent world ... or to be worse than worst
Of those that lawless and incertain thoughts
Imagine howling—'tis too horrible....
The weariest and most loathèd worldly life
That age, ache, penury, and imprisonment
Can lay on nature—is a paradise   130
To what we fear of death.
ISABELLA.   Alas! alas!
CLAUDIO. Sweet sister, let me live....
What sin you do, to save a brother's life,
Nature dispenses with the deed so far,
That it becomes a virtue.
ISABELLA.   O, you beast,
O, faithless coward, O, dishonest wretch,
Wilt thou be made a man out of my vice?
Is't not a kind of incest, to take life
From thine own sister's shame? What should I think?,
Heaven shield my mother played my father fair ... 140
For such a warpèd slip of wilderness
Ne'er issued from his blood.... Take my defiance,
Die, perish ... Might but my bending down
Reprieve thee from thy fate, it should proceed....
I'll pray a thousand prayers for thy death,

No word to save thee.
CLAUDIO.   Nay, hear me, Isabel.
ISABELLA. O, fie, fie, fie ...
Thy sin's not accidental, but a trade;
Mercy to thee would prove itself a bawd.
'Tis best that thou diest quickly.
CLAUDIO.   O hear me, Isabella. 150

The Duke comes forward

DUKE. Vouchsafe a word, young sister, but one word.
ISABELLA. What is your will?
DUKE. Might you dispense with your leisure, I would
by and by have some speech with you: the satisfaction I would require is likewise your own benefit.
ISABELLA. I have no superfluous leisure. My stay must
be stolen out of other affairs: but I will attend you
a while.
DUKE [*takes Claudio aside*]. Son, I have overheard what
hath passed between you and your sister.... Angelo   160
had never the purpose to corrupt her; only he hath
made an assay of her virtue, to practise his judgement with the disposition of natures.... She, having
the truth of honour in her, hath made him that
gracious denial which he is most glad to receive: I
am confessor to Angelo, and I know this to be true.
Therefore prepare yourself to death: do not satisfy
your resolution with hopes that are fallible. To-
morrow you must die—go to your knees, and make
ready.   170
CLAUDIO. Let me ask my sister pardon. I am so out of
love with life, that I will sue to be rid of it.
DUKE. Hold you there: farewell ...
            Claudio goes; the Provost enters
Provost, a word with you.
PROVOST. What's your will, father?
DUKE. That now you are come, you will be gone:
leave me awhile with the maid. My mind promises
with my habit, no loss shall touch her by my
company.
PROVOST. In good time.   *He goes* 180
DUKE [*turns to Isabella*]. The hand that hath made you
fair hath made you good: the goodness that is cheap
in beauty makes beauty brief in goodness; but grace,
being the soul of your complexion, shall keep the
body of it ever fair ... The assault that Angelo
hath made to you, fortune hath conveyed to my
understanding; and, but that frailty hath examples
for his falling, I should wonder at Angelo ... How
will you do to content this substitute, and to save
your brother?   190
ISABELLA. I am now going to resolve him: I had rather
my brother die by the law than my son should be
unlawfully born.... But, O, how much is the good
duke deceived in Angelo: if ever he return, and I
can speak to him, I will open my lips in vain, or
discover his government.
DUKE. That shall not be much amiss: yet, as the matter
now stands, he will avoid your accusation: he made
trial of you only.... Therefore fasten your ear on
my advisings. To the love I have in doing good a   200
remedy presents itself.... I do make myself believe
that you may most uprightously do a poor
wronged lady a merited benefit; redeem your
brother from the angry law; do no stain to your own
gracious person; and much please the absent duke,

if peradventure he shall ever return to have hearing
of this business.

ISABELLA. Let me hear you speak farther; I have spirit
to do any thing that appears not foul in the truth of
my spirit.　　　　　　　　　　　　　　　　　210

DUKE. Virtue is bold, and goodness never fearful ...
Have you not heard speak of Mariana, the sister of
Frederick, the great soldier who miscarried at sea?

ISABELLA. I have heard of the lady, and good words
went with her name.

DUKE. She should this Angelo have married: was
affianced to her by oath, and the nuptial appointed:
between which time of the contract and limit of the
solemnity, her brother Frederick was wrecked at
sea, having in that perished vessel the dowry of his　220
sister ... But mark how heavily this befell to the
poor gentlewoman. There she lost a noble and
renowned brother, in his love toward her ever most
kind and natural: with him the portion and sinew of
her fortune, her marriage-dowry: with both, her
combinate-husband, this well-seeming Angelo.

ISABELLA. Can this be so? Did Angelo so leave her?

DUKE. Left her in her tears, and dried not one of them
with his comfort: swallowed his vows whole, pretending in her discoveries of dishonour: in few,　　230
bestowed her on her own lamentation, which she
yet wears for his sake: and he, a marble to her tears,
is washed with them, but relents not.

ISABELLA. What a merit were it in death to take this
poor maid from the world! What corruption in this
life, that it will let this man live! But how out of
this can she avail?

DUKE. It is a rupture that you may easily heal: and the
cure of it not only saves your brother, but keeps you
from dishonour in doing it.　　　　　　　　240

ISABELLA. Show me how, good father.

DUKE. This forenamed maid hath yet in her the continuance of her first affection: his unjust unkindness,
that in all reason should have quenched her love,
hath, like an impediment in the current, made it
more violent and unruly ... Go you to Angelo,
answer his requiring with a plausible obedience,
agree with his demands to the point: only refer
yourself to this advantage; first, that your stay with
him may not be long; that the time may have all　250
shadow and silence in it; and the place answer to
convenience ... This being granted in course, and
now follows all: we shall advise this wronged maid
to stead up your appointment, go in your place:
if the encounter acknowledge itself hereafter, it may
compel him to her recompense; and here, by this,
is your brother saved, your honour untainted, the
poor Mariana advantaged, and the corrupt deputy
scaled.... The maid will I frame and make fit for
his attempt.... If you think well to carry this as you　260
may, the doubleness of the benefit defends the
deceit from reproof.... What think you of it?

ISABELLA. The image of it gives me content already,
and I trust it will grow to a most prosperous
perfection.

DUKE. It lies much in your holding up ... Haste you
speedily to Angelo—if for this night he entreat you
to his bed, give him promise of satisfaction ... I
will presently to Saint Luke's; there, at the moated
grange, resides this dejected Mariana; at that place　270
call upon me—and dispatch with Angelo, that it

may be quickly.

ISABELLA. I thank you for this comfort: fare you well,
good father.　　　　　　　　　　　　　*She goes out*

Scene 2

Elbow enters with officers and Pompey

ELBOW. Nay, if there be no remedy for it, but that
you will needs buy and sell men and women like
beasts, we shall have all the world drink brown and
white bastard.

DUKE. O, heavens, what stuff is here?

POMPEY. 'Twas never merry world since, of two
usuries, the merriest was put down, and the worser
allowed by order of law a furred gown to keep
him warm; and furred with fox on lamb-skins too,
to signify that craft, being richer than innocency,　10
stands for the facing.

ELBOW. Come your way, sir ... Bless you, good father
friar.

DUKE. And you, good brother father ... What offence
Hath this man made you, sir?

ELBOW. Marry, sir, he hath offended the law; and, sir,
we take him to be a thief too, sir ... for we have
found upon him, sir, a strange picklock, which we
have sent to the deputy.

DUKE. Fie, sirrah, a bawd, a wicked bawd!　　　20
The evil that thou causest to be done,
That is thy means to live.... Do thou but think
What 'tis to cram a maw or clothe a back
From such a filthy vice: say to thyself,
'From their abominable and beastly touches
I drink, I eat, array myself, and live' ...
Canst thou believe thy living is a life,
So stinkingly depending? Go mend, go mend.

POMPEY. Indeed, it does stink in some sort, sir; but yet,
sir, I would prove—　　　　　　　　　　30

DUKE. Nay, if the devil have given thee proofs for sin,
Thou wilt prove his.... Take him to prison, officer:
Correction and instruction must both work,
Ere this rude beast will profit.

ELBOW. He must before the deputy, sir—he has given
him warning: the deputy cannot abide a whore-
master: if he be a whoremonger, and comes before
him, he were as good go a mile on his errand.

DUKE. That we were all, as some would seem to be,
Free from our faults, as faults from seeming free!　40

Lucio enters

ELBOW. His neck will come to your waist—a cord, sir.

POMPEY. I spy comfort, I cry, bail ... Here's a gentleman and a friend of mine.

LUCIO. How now, noble Pompey? What, at the
wheels of Cæsar? Art thou led in triumph? What, is
there none of Pygmalion's images, newly made
woman, to be had now, for putting the hand in the
pocket and extracting it clutched? What reply, ha?
What say'st thou to this tune, matter, and method?
Is't not drowned i'th' last rain, ha? What say'st　50
thou, trot? Is the world as it was, man? Which is
the way? Is it sad, and few words? Or how? The
trick of it?

DUKE. Still thus, and thus: still worse!

LUCIO. How doth my dear morsel, thy mistress? Procures she still, ha?

POMPEY. Troth, sir, she hath eaten up all her beef, and she is herself in the tub.

LUCIO. Why, 'tis good: it is the right of it: it must be so.... Ever your fresh whore, and your powdered 60 bawd—an unshunned consequence, it must be so.... Are going to prison, Pompey?

POMPEY. Yes, faith, sir.

LUCIO. Why, 'tis not amiss, Pompey: farewell: go, say I sent thee thither ... For debt, Pompey, or how?

ELBOW. For being a bawd, for being a bawd.

LUCIO. Well, then imprison him: if imprisonment be the due of a bawd, why, 'tis his right.... Bawd is he, doubtless, and of antiquity too: bawd-born.... Farewell, good Pompey: commend me to the 70 prison, Pompey. You will turn good husband now, Pompey—you will keep the house.

POMPEY. I hope, sir, your good worship will be my bail?

LUCIO. No, indeed, will I not, Pompey—it is not the wear ... I will pray, Pompey, to increase your bondage: if you take it not patiently—why, your mettle is the more ... Adieu, trusty Pompey.... Bless you, friar.

DUKE. And you.   80

LUCIO. Does Bridget paint still, Pompey, ha?

ELBOW. Come your ways, sir—come.

POMPEY. You will not bail me then, sir?

LUCIO. Then, Pompey, nor now ... What news abroad, friar? what news?

ELBOW. Come your ways, sir—come.

LUCIO. Go to kennel, Pompey, go ...

Elbow, officers and Pompey go

What news, friar, of the duke?

DUKE. I know none: can you tell me of any?

LUCIO. Some say he is with the Emperor of Russia: 90 other some, he is in Rome: but where is he, think you?

DUKE. I know not where: but wheresoever, I wish him well.

LUCIO. It was a mad fantastical trick of him to steal from the state, and usurp the beggary he was never born to ... Lord Angelo dukes it well in his absence: he puts transgression to't.

DUKE. He does well in't.

LUCIO. A little more lenity to lechery would do no 100 harm in him: something too crabbed that way, friar.

DUKE. It is too general a vice, and severity must cure it.

LUCIO. Yes, in good sooth, the vice is of a great kindred; it is well allied—but it is impossible to extirp it quite, friar, till eating and drinking be put down. They say this Angelo was not made by man and woman, after the downright way of creation: is it true, think you?

DUKE. How should he be made then?

LUCIO. Some report a sea-maid spawned him.... 110 some, that he was begot between two stock-fishes.... But it is certain, that when he makes water, his urine is congealed ice—that I know to be true: and he is a motion generative—that's infallible.

DUKE. You are pleasant, sir, and speak apace.

LUCIO. Why, what a ruthless thing is this in him, for the rebellion of a codpiece to take away the life of a man? Would the duke that is absent have done this? Ere he would have hanged a man for the getting a hundred bastards, he would have paid for the nurs- 120 ing a thousand.... He had some feeling of the sport

—he knew the service, and that instructed him to mercy.

DUKE. I never heard the absent duke much detected for women—he was not inclined that way.

LUCIO. O, sir, you are deceived.

DUKE. 'Tis not possible.

LUCIO. Who? not the duke? Yes, your beggar of fifty ... and his use was to put a ducat in her clack- dish; the duke had crotchets in him.... He would 130 be drunk too—that let me inform you.

DUKE. You do him wrong, surely.

LUCIO. Sir, I was an inward of his ... A shy fellow was the duke—and I believe I know the cause of his withdrawing.

DUKE. What, I prithee, might be the cause?

LUCIO. No, pardon: 'tis a secret must be locked within the teeth and the lips: but this I can let you under- stand, the greater file of the subject held the duke to be wise.   140

DUKE. Wise! why, no question but he was.

LUCIO. A very superficial, ignorant, unweighing fel- low.

DUKE. Either this is envy in you, folly, or mistaking: the very stream of his life and the business he hath helmed must, upon a warranted need, give him a better proclamation.... Let him be but testimonied in his own bringings-forth, and he shall appear to the envious a scholar, a statesman and a soldier ... Therefore you speak unskilfully: or, if your know- 150 ledge be more, it is much darkened in your malice.

LUCIO. Sir, I know him, and I love him.

DUKE. Love talks with better knowledge, and know- ledge with dearer love.

LUCIO. Come, sir, I know what I know.

DUKE. I can hardly believe that, since you know not what you speak.... But, if ever the duke return, as our prayers are he may, let me desire you to make your answer before him: if it be honest you have spoke, you have courage to maintain it; I am bound 160 to call upon you, and I pray you your name?

LUCIO. Sir, my name is Lucio, well known to the duke.

DUKE. He shall know you better, sir, if I may live to report you.

LUCIO. I fear you not.

DUKE. O, you hope the duke will return no more: or you imagine me too unhurtful an opposite ... But, indeed, I can do you little harm: you'll forswear this again!

LUCIO. I'll be hanged first: thou art deceived in me, 170 friar.... But no more of this: canst thou tell if Claudio die to-morrow or no?

DUKE. Why should he die, sir?

LUCIO. Why? for filling a bottle with a tun-dish ... I would the duke we talk of were returned again: this ungenitured agent will unpeople the province with continency... Sparrows must not build in his house- eaves, because they are lecherous ... The duke yet would have dark deeds darkly answered—he would never bring them to light: would he were re- 180 turned..... Marry, this Claudio is condemned for untrussing.... Farewell, good friar. I prithee, pray for me ... The duke, I say to thee again, would eat mutton on Fridays ... He's now past it, yet (and I say to thee now), he would mouth with a beggar, though she smelt brown bread and garlic: say that I said so ... Farewell.   _He goes_

DUKE. No might nor greatness in mortality
  Can censure 'scape: back-wounding calumny
  The whitest virtue strikes.... What king so strong 190
  Can tie the gall up in the slanderous tongue?
  But who comes here?

*Enter Escalus and the Provost, with officers guarding
Mistress Overdone*

ESCALUS. Go, away with her to prison.

OVERDONE. Good my lord, be good to me—your
  honour is accounted a merciful man ... good my
  lord.

ESCALUS. Double and treble admonition, and still forfeit in the same kind? This would make mercy
  swear and play the tyrant.

PROVOST. A bawd of eleven years' continuance, may it 200
  please your honour.

OVERDONE. My lord, this is one Lucio's information
  against me. Mistress Kate Keepdown was with child
  by him in the duke's time—he promised her marriage: his child is a year and a quarter old, come
  Philip and Jacob: I have kept it myself; and see how
  he goes about to abuse me.

ESCALUS. That fellow is a fellow of much license: let
  him be called before us.... Away with her to prison:
  go to, no more words.... [*the officers take her away*] 210
  Provost, my brother Angelo will not be altered,
  Claudio must die to-morrow: let him be furnished
  with divines, and have all charitable preparation....
  If my brother wrought by my pity, it should not
  be so with him.

PROVOST. So please you, this friar hath been with him,
  and advised him for th'entertainment of death.

ESCALUS. Good even, good father.

DUKE. Bliss and goodness on you!

ESCALUS. Of whence are you? 220

DUKE. Not of this country, though my chance is now
  To use it for my time: I am a brother
  Of gracious order, late come from the See,
  In special business from his Holiness.

ESCALUS. What news abroad i'th' world?

DUKE. None; but that there is so great a fever on
  goodness, that the dissolution of it must cure it.
  Novelty is only in request, and it is as dangerous
  to be aged in any kind of course, as it is virtuous
  to be inconstant in any undertaking.... There is 230
  scarce truth enough alive to make societies secure,
  but security enough to make fellowships accursed:
  much upon this riddle runs the wisdom of the world
  ... This news is old enough, yet it is every day's
  news.... I pray you, sir, of what disposition was
  the duke?

ESCALUS. One, that, above all other strifes, contended
  especially to know himself.

DUKE. What pleasure was he given to?

ESCALUS. Rather rejoicing to see another merry, than 240
  merry at any thing which professed to make him
  rejoice: a gentleman of all temperance.... But leave
  we him to his events, with a prayer they may prove
  prosperous, and let me desire to know how you find
  Claudio prepared. I am made to understand that you
  have lent him visitation.

DUKE. He professes to have received no sinister measure from his judge, but most willingly humbles
  himself to the determination of justice: yet had he
  framed to himself, by the instruction of his frailty, 250

many deceiving promises of life, which I, by my
  good leisure, have discredited to him, and now is he
  resolved to die.

ESCALUS. You have paid the heavens your function,
  and the prisoner the very debt of your calling....
  I have laboured for the poor gentleman to the
  extremest shore of my modesty—but my brother-
  justice have I found so severe, that he hath forced
  me to tell him he is indeed Justice.

DUKE. If his own life answer the straitness of his pro- 260
  ceeding, it shall become him well: wherein if he
  chance to fail, he hath sentenced himself.

ESCALUS. I am going to visit the prisoner. Fare you
  well.

DUKE. Peace be with you....

Escalus and the Provost go

  He, who the sword of heaven will bear,
  Should be as holy as severe:
  Pattern in himself to know,
  Grace to stand, an virtue go:
  More nor less to others paying, 270
  Than by self-offences weighing....
  Shame to him whose cruel striking
  Kills for faults of his own liking:
  Twice treble shame on Angelo,
  To weed my vice and let his grow....
  O, what may man within him hide,
  Though angel on the outward side!
  How may likeness, made in crimes,
  Making practice on the times,
  To draw with idle spiders' strings 280
  Most ponderous and substantial things!
  Craft against vice I must apply....
  With Angelo to-night shall lie
  His old betrothéd, but despiséd:
  So disguise shall, by th' disguiséd,
  Pay with falsehood false exacting,
  And perform an old contracting.   *He goes*

ACT 4
Scene 1: *The moated grange*

Mariana and a page

                    The boy sings
  Take, oh take those lips away,
    That so sweetly were forsworn,
  And those eyes ... the break of day,
    Lights that do mislead the morn;
  But my kisses bring again, bring again,
  Seals of love, but sealed in vain, sealed in vain.

The disguised Duke enters

MARIANA. Break off thy song, and haste thee
  quick away.
  Here comes a man of comfort, whose advice
  Hath often stilled my brawling discontent....
                        The boy goes
  I cry you mercy, sir, and well could wish 10
  You had not found me here so musical....
  Let me excuse me, and believe me so,
  My mirth it much displeased, but pleased my woe.

DUKE. 'Tis good; though music oft hath such a charm
  To make a bad good, and good provoke to harm....
  I pray you tell me, hath any body inquired for me

here to-day? much upon this time have I promised
here to meet.
MARIANA. You have not been inquired after: I have
sat here all day.   20

Isabella approaches

DUKE. I do constantly believe you ... The time is
come, even now.... I shall crave your forbearance
a little—may be I will call upon you anon, for some
advantage to yourself.
MARIANA. I am always bound to you.   *Mariana goes*
DUKE. Very well met, and well come ...
What is the news from this good deputy?
ISABELLA. He hath a garden circummured with brick,
Whose western side is with a vineyard backed;
And to that vineyard is a planchéd gate,   30
That makes his opening with this bigger key:
This other doth command a little door,
Which from the vineyard to the garden leads—
There have I made my promise
Upon the heavy middle of the night
To call upon him.
DUKE. But shall you on your knowledge find this way?
ISABELLA. I have ta'en a due and wary note upon't.
With whispering and most guilty diligence,
In action all of precept he did show me   40
The way twice o'er.
DUKE.   Are there no other tokens
Between you 'greed concerning her observance?
ISABELLA. No: none, but only a repair i'th' dark,
And that I have possessed him my most stay
Can be but brief: for I have made him know
I have a servant comes with me along,
That stays upon me; whose persuasion is
I come about my brother.
DUKE.   'Tis well borne up....
I have not yet made known to Mariana
A word of this ... What ho, within! come forth! 50

Mariana returns

I pray you, be acquainted with this maid—
She comes to do you good.
ISABELLA.   I do desire the like.
DUKE. Do you persuade yourself that I respect you?
MARIANA. Good friar, I know you do, and have found
it.
DUKE. Take then this your companion by the hand,
Who hath a story ready for your ear:
I shall attend your leisure, but make haste—
The vaporous night approaches.
MARIANA.   Will't please you walk aside?
                                      They withdraw
DUKE. O place and greatness ... millions of false eyes 60
Are stuck upon thee: volumes of report
Run with these false and most contrarious quests
Upon thy doings: thousand escapes of wit
Make thee the father of their idle dream,
And rack thee in their fancies....

Mariana and Isabella return

                         Welcome, how agreed?
ISABELLA. She'll take the enterprise upon her, father,
If you advise it.
DUKE.   It is not my consent,
But my entreaty too.
ISABELLA.   Little have you to say

When you depart from him, but, soft and low,
'Remember now my brother.'
MARIANA.   Fear me not.·   70
DUKE. Nor, gentle daughter, fear you not at all:
He is your husband on a pre-contráct:
To bring you thus together 'tis no sin,
Sith that the justice of your title to him
Doth flourish the deceit.... Come, let us go;
Our corn's to reap, for yet our tilth's to sow.
                                      They depart

Scene 2: *The prison*

The Provost enters followed by Pompey

PROVOST. Come hither, sirrah; can you cut off a
man's head?
POMPEY. If the man be a bachelor, sir, I can: but if he
be a married man, he's his wife's head, and I can
never cut off a woman's head.
PROVOST. Come, sir, leave me your snatches, and yield
me a direct answer.... To-morrow morning are to
die Claudio and Barnardine: here is in our prison a
common executioner, who in his office lacks a
helper. If you will take it on you to assist him, it 10
shall redeem you from your gyves: if not, you shall
have your full time of imprisonment, and your
deliverance with an unpitied whipping; for you
have been a notorious bawd.
POMPEY. Sir, I have been an unlawful bawd, time out
of mind, but yet I will be content to be a lawful
hangman ... I would be glad to receive some
instruction from my fellow partner.
PROVOST. What ho! Abhorson ... Where's Abhorson,
there?   20

Abhorson comes in

ABHORSON. Do you call, sir?
PROVOST. Sirrah, here's a fellow will help you to-
morrow in your execution: if you think it meet,
compound with him by the year, and let him abide
here with you—if not, use him for the present,
and dismiss him. He cannot plead his estimation
with you: he hath been a bawd.
ABHORSON. A bawd, sir? Fie upon him, he will discredit our mystery.
PROVOST. Go to, sir, you weigh equally: a feather 30
will turn the scale.   *He goes out*
POMPEY. Pray, sir, by your good favour ... for surely,
sir, a good favour you have, but that you have a
hanging look ... do you call, sir, your occupation a
mystery?
ABHORSON. Ay sir, a mystery.
POMPEY. Painting, sir, I have heard say, is a mystery;
and your whores, sir, being members of my occupation, using painting, do prove my occupation a
mystery: but what mystery there should be in hang- 40
ing, if I should be hanged, I cannot imagine.
ABHORSON. Sir, it is a mystery.
POMPEY. Proof?
ABHORSON. Every true man's apparel fits your thief:
if it be too little for your thief, your true man
thinks it big enough; if it be too big for your thief,
your thief thinks it little enough: so every true man's
apparel fits your thief.

The Provost returns

PROVOST. Are you agreed?

POMPEY. Sir, I will serve him: for I do find your hang- 50
man is a more penitent trade than your bawd: he
doth oftener ask forgiveness.

PROVOST. You, sirrah, provide your block and your
axe to-morrow, four o'clock.

ABHORSON. Come on, bawd, I will instruct thee in my
trade: follow.

POMPEY. I do desire to learn, sir: and, I hope, if you
have occasion to use me for your own turn, you
shall find me yare.... for, truly sir, for your kindness, I owe you a good turn. 60

PROVOST. Call hither Barnardine and Claudio ...
Pompey and Abhorson go out
Th'one has my pity; not a jot the other,
Being a murderer, though he were my brother.

Claudio enters

Look, here's the warrant, Claudio, for thy death.
'Tis now dead midnight, and by eight to-morrow
Thou must be made immortal.... Where's
Barnardine?

CLAUDIO. As fast locked up in sleep, as guiltless labour,
When it lies starkly in the traveller's bones.
He will not wake.

PROVOST.   Who can do good on him?
Well, go, prepare yourself.... *Knocking without*
But hark, what noise? 70
Heaven give your spirits comfort ... *Claudio goes*
By and by!
I hope it is some pardon, or reprieve,
For the most gentle Claudio....

The disguised Duke enters

     Welcome, father
DUKE. The best and wholesom'st spirits of the night
Envelop you, good provost ... Who called here of
late?

PROVOST. None, since the curfew rung.

DUKE. Not Isabel?

PROVOST.   No.

DUKE.   They will then, ere't be long.

PROVOST. What comfort is for Claudio?

DUKE. There's some in hope.

PROVOST.   It is a bitter deputy.

DUKE. Not so, not so: his life is paralleled 80
Even with the stroke and line of his great justice:
He doth with holy abstinence subdue
That in himself which he spurs on his power
To qualify in others: were he mealed with that
Which he corrects, then were he tyrannous—
But this being so, he's just.... Now are they
come....

More knocking; the Provost goes within

This is a gentle provost. Seldom, when
The steeléd gaoler is the friend of men ...
The knocking grows louder
How now! What noise? That spirit's possessed
with haste,
That wounds the resisting postern with these
strokes.   *The Provost returns* 90

PROVOST. There he must stay until the officer
Arise to let him in: he is called up.

DUKE. Have you no countermand for Claudio yet,
But he must die to-morrow?

PROVOST.   None, sir, none.

DUKE. As near the dawning, provost, as it is,
You shall hear more ere morning.

PROVOST.   Happily
You something know: yet I believe there comes
No countermand: no such example have we ...
Besides, upon the very siege of justice,
Lord Angelo hath to the public ear 100
Professed the contrary.

A messenger enters

     This is his lordship's man.

DUKE. And here comes Claudio's pardon.

MESSENGER [*delivers a letter*]. My lord hath sent you
this note, and by me this further charge; that you
swerve not from the smallest article of it, neither
in time, matter, or any other circumstance.... Good
morrow: for, as I take it, it is almost day.
He goes

PROVOST. I shall obey him.

DUKE. This is his pardon, purchased by such sin
For which the pardoner himself is in: 110
Hence that offence his quick celerity,
When it is borne in high authority....
When vice makes mercy, mercy's so extended,
That for the fault's love is th'offender friended....
Now, sir, what news?

PROVOST. I told you ... Lord Angelo, belike thinking
me remiss in mine office, awakens me with this
unwonted putting on—methinks, strangely ... for
he hath not used it before.

DUKE. Pray you, let's hear. 120

PROVOST [*reads*]. 'Whatsoever you may hear to the
contrary, let Claudio be executed by four of the
clock, and in the afternoon Barnardine: for my
better satisfaction, let me have Claudio's head sent
me by five.... Let this be duly performed, with
a thought that more depends on it than we must yet
deliver.... Thus fail not to do your office, as you
will answer it at your peril.'
What say you to this, sir?

DUKE. What is that Barnardine, who is to be executed 130
in th'afternoon?

PROVOST. A Bohemian born: but here nursed up and
bred—
One that is a prisoner nine years old.

DUKE. How came it that the absent duke had not
either delivered him to his liberty or executed him?
I have heard it was ever his manner to do so.

PROVOST. His friends still wrought reprieves for him:
and, indeed, his fact, till now in the government
of Lord Angelo, came not to an undoubtful proof.

DUKE. It is now apparent? 140

PROVOST. Most manifest, and not denied by himself.

DUKE. Hath he borne himself penitently in prison?
How seems he to be touched?

PROVOST. A man that apprehends death no more
dreadfully but as a drunken sleep—careless, reckless,
and fearless of what's past, present, or to come:
insensible of mortality, and desperately mortal.

DUKE. He wants advice.

PROVOST. He will hear none: he hath evermore had the
liberty of the prison: give him leave to escape hence, 150
he would not.... Drunk many times a day, if not
many days entirely drunk.... We have very oft
awaked him, as if to carry him to execution, and

showed him a seeming warrant for it—it hath not
moved him at all.

DUKE. More of him anon ... There is written in your
brow, provost, honesty and constancy; if I read it
not truly, my ancient skill beguiles me: but in the
boldness of my cunning, I will lay myself in
hazard ... Claudio, whom here you have warrant to 160
execute, is no greater forfeit to the law than Angelo
who hath sentenced him.... To make you understand this in a manifested effect, I crave but four
days' respite: for the which you are to do me both
a present, and a dangerous, courtesy.

PROVOST. Pray, sir, in what?

DUKE.   In the delaying death.

PROVOST. Alack, how may I do it, having the hour
limited, and an express command, under penalty,
to deliver his head in the view of Angelo? I may
make my case as Claudio's, to cross this in the 170
smallest.

DUKE. By the vow of mine order, I warrant you.
If my instructions may be your guide,
Let this Barnardine be this morning executed,
And his head borne to Angelo.

PROVOST. Angelo hath seen them both, and will discover the favour.

DUKE. O, death's a great disguiser, and you may add
to it ... Shave the head, and tie the beard, and say
it was the desire of the penitent to be so bared 180
before his death: you know the course is common.... If any thing fall to you upon this more
than thanks and good fortune, by the saint whom I
profess, I will plead against it with my life.

PROVOST. Pardon me, good father—it is against my
oath.

DUKE. Were you sworn to the duke, or to the deputy?

PROVOST. To him, and to his substitutes.

DUKE. You will think you have made no offence, if the
duke avouch the justice of your dealing?   190

PROVOST. But what likelihood is in that?

DUKE. Not a resemblance, but a certainty; yet since
I see you fearful, that neither my coat, integrity, nor
persuasion can with ease attempt you, I will go
further than I meant, to pluck all fears out of you....
Look you, sir, here is the hand and seal of the duke:
you know the character, I doubt not, and the signet
is not strange to you.

PROVOST. I know them both.

DUKE. The contents of this is the return of the duke; 200
you shall anon over-read it at your pleasure: where
you shall find within these two days he will be
here.... This is a thing that Angelo knows not, for
he this very day receives letters of strange tenour—
perchance of the duke's death, perchance entering
into some monastery, but by chance nothing of
what is writ.... Look, th'unfolding star calls up the
shepherd ... Put not yourself into amazement how
these things should be; all difficulties are but easy
when they are known.... Call your executioner, 210
and off with Barnardine's head: I will give him a
present shrift, and advise him for a better place....
Yet you are amazed, but this shall absolutely resolve
you ... Come away, it is almost clear dawn.

They go out

Scene 3

Pompey enters

POMPEY. I am as well acquainted here as I was in our
house of profession: one would think it were Mistress Overdone's own house, for here be many of
her old customers.... First, here's young Master
Rash; he's in for a commodity of brown paper and
old ginger—ninescore and seventeen pounds, of
which he made five marks, ready money: marry
then ginger was not much in request, for the old
women were all dead.... Then is there here one
Master Caper, at the suit of Master Three-pile the 10
mercer, for some four suits of peach-coloured satin,
which now peaches him a beggar.... Then have we
here young Dizy, and young Master Deepvow, and
Master Copperspur, and Master Starvelackey the
rapier and dagger man, and young Dropheir that
killed lusty Pudding, and Master Forthright the
tilter, and brave Master Shoetie the great traveller,
and wild Halfcan that stabbed Pots, and, I think,
forty more—all great doers in our trade, and are
now 'for the Lord's sake.'   20

Abhorson comes in

ABHORSON. Sirrah, bring Barnardine hither.

POMPEY. Master Barnardine! you must rise and be
hanged, Master Barnardine!

ABHORSON. What, ho, Barnardine!

BARNARDINE [*from within*]. A pox o' your throats!
Who makes that noise there? What are you?

POMPEY. Your friends, sir—the hangman ... You
must be so good, sir, to rise and be put to death.

BARNARDINE. Away, you rogue, away. I am sleepy.

ABHORSON. Tell him, he must awake, and that quickly 30
too.

POMPEY. Pray, Master Barnardine, awake till you are
executed, and sleep afterwards.

ABHORSON. Go in to him, and fetch him out.

POMPEY. He is coming, sir, he is coming ... I hear
his straw rustle.

Barnardine enters

ABHORSON. Is the axe upon the block, sirrah?

POMPEY. Very ready, sir.

BARNARDINE. How now, Abhorson! what's the news
with you?   40

ABHORSON. Truly, sir, I would desire you to clap into
your prayers: for, look you, the warrant's come.

BARNARDINE. You rogue, I have been drinking all
night, I am not fitted for't.

POMPEY. O, the better, sir: for he that drinks all night,
and is hanged betimes in the morning, may sleep
the sounder all the next day.

The disguised Duke enters

ABHORSON. Look you, sir, here comes your ghostly
father: do we jest now, think you?

DUKE. Sir, induced by my charity, and hearing how 50
hastily you are to depart, I am come to advise you,
comfort you, and pray with you.

BARNARDINE. Friar, not I: I have been drinking hard
all night, and I will have more time to prepare me,
or they shall beat out my brains with billets ... I
will not consent to die this day, that's certain.

DUKE. O, sir, you must: and therefore I beseech you

Look forward on the journey you shall go.
BARNARDINE. I swear I will not die to-day for any
man's persuasion.   60
DUKE. But hear you ...
BARNARDINE. Not a word: if you have any thing to say
to me, come to my ward: for thence will not I
to-day.   *He goes*

The Provost enters

DUKE. Unfit to live or die ... O, gravel heart!
After him, fellows, bring him to the block.
                 Abhorson and Pompey go
PROVOST. Now, sir, how do you find the prisoner?
DUKE. A creature unprepared, unmeet for death;
And to transport him in the mind he is
Were damnable.
PROVOST.   Here in the prison, father,   70
There died this morning of a cruel fever
One Ragozine, a most notorious pirate,
A man of Claudio's years: his beard and head
Just of his colour.... What if we do omit
This reprobate, till he were well inclined,
And satisfy the deputy with the visage
Of Ragozine, more like to Claudio?
DUKE. O, 'tis an accident that heaven provides ...
Dispatch it presently, the hour draws on
Prefixed by Angelo ... See this be done,   80
And sent according to command, whiles I
Persuade this rude wretch willingly to die.
PROVOST. This shall be done, good father, presently:
But Barnardine must die this afternoon—
And how shall we continue Claudio,
To save me from the danger that might come,
If he were known alive?
DUKE.   Let this be done—
Put them in secret holds, both Barnardine
And Claudio.
Ere twice the sun hath made his journal greeting   90
To th'under generation, you shall find
Your safety manifested.
PROVOST. I am your free dependant.
DUKE. Quick, dispatch, and send the head to Angelo.

The Provost goes out

Now will I write letters to Angelo—
The provost, he shall bear them—whose contents
Shall witness to him I am near at home:
And that, by great injunctions, I am bound
To enter publicly: him I'll desire
To meet me at the consecrated fount,   100
A league below the city; and from thence,
By cold gradation and well-balanced form,
We shall proceed with Angelo.

The Provost returns

PROVOST. Here is the head—I'll carry it myself.
DUKE. Convenient is it ... Make a swift return,
For I would commune with you of such things
That want no ear but yours.
PROVOST.   I'll make all speed.   *He goes*
A VOICE WITHOUT. Peace, ho, be here!
DUKE. The tongue of Isabel.... She's come to know
If yet her brother's pardon be come hither: 110
But I will keep her ignorant of her good,
To make her heavenly comforts of despair,
When it is least expected.

Isabella enters

ISABELLA.   Ho, by your leave!
DUKE. Good morning to you, fair and gracious
daughter.
ISABELLA. The better, given me by so holy a man.
Hath yet the deputy sent my brother's pardon?
DUKE. He hath released him, Isabel, from the
world.
His head is off and sent to Angelo.
ISABELLA. Nay, but it is not so.
DUKE. It is no other. Show your wisdom, daughter,   120
In your close patience.
ISABELLA. O, I will to him, and pluck out his eyes.
DUKE. You shall not be admitted to his sight.
ISABELLA. Unhappy Claudio, wretched Isabel,
Injurious world, most damnèd Angelo!
DUKE. This nor hurts him, nor profits you a jot.
Forbear it therefore, give your cause to heaven.
Mark what I say, which you shall find
By every syllable a faithful verity....
The duke comes home to-morrow: nay, dry your
eyes—   130
One of our covent, and his confessor,
Gives me this instance: already he hath carried
Notice to Escalus and Angelo,
Who do prepare to meet him at the gates,
There to give up their power ... If you can, pace
your wisdom
In that good path that I would wish it go,
And you shall have your bosom on this wretch,
Grace of the duke, revenges to your heart,
And general honour.
ISABELLA.   I am directed by you.
DUKE. This letter then to Friar Peter give—   140
'Tis he that sent me of the duke's return:
Say, by this token, I desire his company
As Mariana's house to-night.... Her cause and
yours
I'll perfect him withal, and he shall bring you
Before the duke; and to the head of Angelo
Accuse him home and home.... For my poor self,
I am combinèd by a sacred vow,
And shall be absent.... Wend you with this letter:
Command these fretting waters from your eyes
With a light heart; trust not my holy order,   150
If I pervert your course ... Who's here?

Lucio enters

LUCIO. Good even ... Friar, where's the provost?
DUKE. Not within, sir.
LUCIO. O, pretty Isabella, I am pale at mine heart to
see thine eyes so red: thou must be patient; I am
fain to dine and sup with water and bran: I dare not
for my head fill my belly.... one fruitful meal
would set me to't ... but they say the duke will
be here to-morrow.... By my troth, Isabel, I loved
thy brother. If the old fantastical duke of dark   160
corners had been at home, he had lived.
                 Isabella goes
DUKE. Sir, the duke is marvellous little beholding to
your reports—but the best is, he lives not in them.
LUCIO. Friar, thou knowest not the duke so well as I
do: he's a better woodman than thou tak'st him for.
DUKE. Well: you'll answer this one day.... Fare ye
well.

LUCIO. Nay, tarry—I'll go along with thee—I can tell thee pretty tales of the duke.

DUKE. You have told me too many of him already, 170 sir, if they be true: if not true, none were enough.

LUCIO. I was once before him for getting a wench with child.

DUKE. Did you such a thing?

LUCIO. Yes, marry did I; but I was fain to forswear it—they would else have married me to the rotten ·medlar.

DUKE. Sir, your company is fairer than honest—Rest you well.

LUCIO. By my troth, I'll go with thee to the lane's 180 end. If bawdy talk offend you, we'll have very little of it ... Nay, friar, I am a kind of burr, I shall stick.

He follows the Duke out

Scene 4: *A room in the house of Lord Angelo*

Enter Angelo and Escalus

ESCALUS. Every letter he hath writ hath disvouched other.

ANGELO. In most uneven and distracted manner. His actions show much like to madness—pray heaven his wisdom be not tainted: and why meet him at the gates, and redeliver our authorities there?

ESCALUS. I guess not.

ANGELO. And why should we proclaim it an hour before his entring, that if any crave redress of injustice, they should exhibit their petitions in the street? 10

ESCALUS. He shows his reason for that: to have a dispatch of complaints, and to deliver us from devices hereafter, which shall then have no power to stand against us.

ANGELO. Well: I beseech you, let it be proclaimed. Betimes i'th' morn, I'll call you at your house: Give notice to such men of sort and suit As are to meet him.

ESCALUS.   I shall, sir: fare you well.

ANGELO. Good night.... *Escalus departs*
This deed unshapes me quite, makes me unpregnant 20
And dull to all proceedings.... A deflowered maid,
And by an eminent body that enforced
The law against it! But that her tender shame
Will not proclaim against her maiden loss,
How might she tongue me! Yet reason dares her no,
For my authority bears a credent bulk,
That no particular scandal once can touch,
But it confounds the breather.... He should have lived,
Save that his riotous youth, with dangerous sense,
Might in the times to come have ta'en revenge, 30
By so receiving a dishonoured life
With ransom of such shame ... Would yet he had lived!
Alack, when once our grace we have forgot,
Nothing goes right—we would, and we would not.

He goes out

Scene 5: *Outside*

Enter the Duke in his own habit, and Friar Peter

DUKE [*giving him papers*]. These letters at fit time deliver me....
The provost knows our purpose, and our plot.

The matter being afoot, keep your instruction,
And hold you ever to our special drift,
Though sometimes you do blench from this to that,
As cause doth minister ... Go, call at Flavius' house,
And tell him where I stay: give the like notice
To Valentinus, Rowland, and to Crassus,
And bid them bring the trumpets to the gate:
But send me Flavius first.

FRIAR PETER.   It shall be speeded well. 10

He goes

Varrius comes up

DUKE. I thank thee, Varrius. Thou hast made good haste.
Come, we will walk ... There's other of our friends
Will greet us here anon, my gentle Varrius.

They go

Scene 6: *A street near the city-gate*

Enter Isabella and Mariana

ISABELLA. To speak so indirectly I am loath.
I would say the truth—but to accuse him so,
That is your part. Yet I am advised to do it,
He says, to veil full purpose.

MARIANA.   Be ruled by him.

ISABELLA. Besides, he tells me that, if peradventure
He speak against me on the adverse side,
I should not think it strange, for 'tis a physic
That's bitter to sweet end.

MARIANA. I would Friar Peter—

ISABELLA.   O, peace, the friar is come.

Friar Peter comes up

FRIAR PETER. Come, I have found you out a stand most fit, 10
Where you may have such vantage on the duke,
He shall not pass you ... Twice have the trumpets sounded;
The generous and gravest citizens
Have hent the gates, and very near upon
The duke is ent'ring ... therefore hence, away.

They hasten away

ACT 5

Scene 1: *A public place without the city-gates: a crowd of citizens*

Angelo, Escalus, with the Provost and officers; Lucio, Isabella, Mariana veiled, and Friar Peter at their post. The Duke approaches with Varrius and other Lords

DUKE. My very worthy cousin, fairly met!
Our old and faithful friend, we are glad to see you.

ANGELO AND ESCALUS. Happy return be to your royal grace!

DUKE. Many and hearty thankings to you both:
We have made inquiry of you, and we hear
Such goodness of your justice, that our soul
Cannot but yield you forth to public thanks,
Forerunning more requital.

ANGELO.   You make my bonds still greater.

DUKE. O, your desert speaks loud, and I should wrong it,
To lock it in the wards of covert bosom, 10
When it deserves with characters of brass
A forted residence 'gainst the tooth of time

And razure of oblivion ... Give me your hand—
And let the subject see, to make them know
That outward courtesies would fain proclaim
Favours that keep within ... Come, Escalus,
You must walk by us on our other hand:
And good supporters are you.

Friar Peter and Isabella come forward

FRIAR PETER. Now is your time—speak loud, and kneel
  before him.
ISABELLA. Justice, O royal duke! Vail your regard   20
  Upon a wronged—I would fain have said a maid.
  O worthy prince, dishonour not your eye
  By throwing it on any other object,
  Till you have heard me, in my true complaint,
  And given me justice, justice, justice, justice!
DUKE. Relate your wrongs; in what? by whom?
  be brief:
  Here is Lord Angelo shall give you justice—
  Reveal yourself to him.
ISABELLA.   O worthy duke,
  You bid me seek redemption of the devil!
  Hear me yourself: for that which I must speak   30
  Must either punish me, not being believed,
  Or wring redress from you ... Hear me, O, hear
  me, here.
ANGELO. My lord, her wits I fear me are not firm:
  She hath been a suitor to me for her brother,
  Cut off by course of justice—
ISABELLA.   By course of justice!
ANGELO. And she will speak most bitterly and strange.
ISABELLA. Most strange ... but yet most truly will
  I speak.
  That Angelo's forsworn, is it not strange?
  That Angelo's a murderer, is't not strange?
  That Angelo is an adulterous thief,   40
  An hypocrite, a virgin-violator—
  Is it not strange and strange?
DUKE.   Nay, it is ten times strange!
ISABELLA. It is not truer he is Angelo
  Than this is all as true as it is strange;
  Nay, it is ten times true, for truth is truth
  To th'end of reck'ning.
DUKE.   Away with her ... Poor soul,
  She speaks this in th'infirmity of sense.
ISABELLA. O prince, I cónjure thee, as thou believ'st
  There is another comfort than this world,
  That thou neglect me not, with that opinion   50
  That I am touched with madness: make not
    impossible
  That which but seems unlike. 'Tis not impossible
  But one, the wicked'st caitiff on the ground,
  May seem as shy, as grave, as just, as absolute ...
  As Angelo! even so may Angelo,
  In all his dressings, caracts, titles, forms,
  Be an arch-villain ... Believe it, royal prince,
  If he be less, he's nothing, but he's more,
  Had I more name for badness.
DUKE.   By mine honesty,
  If she be mad—as I believe no other—   60
  Her madness hath the oddest frame of sense,
  Such a dependency of thing on thing,
  As e'er I heard in madness.
ISABELLA.   O, gracious duke,
  Harp not on that; nor do not banish reason
  For inequality, but let your reason serve

To make the truth appear where it seems hid,
And hide the false seems true.
DUKE.   Many that are not mad,
  Have, sure, more lack of reason ... What would
    you say?
ISABELLA. I am the sister of one Claudio,
  Condemned upon the act of fornication   70
  To lose his head, condemned by Angelo.
  I, in probation of a sisterhood,
  Was sent to by my brother; one Lucio
  As then the messenger—
LUCIO.   That's I, an't like your grace:
  I came to her from Claudio, and desired her
  To try her gracious fortune with Lord Angelo,
  For her poor brother's pardon.
ISABELLA.   That's he, indeed.
DUKE. You were not bid to speak.
LUCIO.   No, my good lord—
  Nor wished to hold my peace.
DUKE.   I wish you now then.
  Pray you, take note of it: and when you have   80
  A business for yourself ... pray heaven you then
  Be perfect.
LUCIO.   I warrant your honour.
DUKE. The warrant's for yourself: take heed to't.
ISABELLA. This gentleman told somewhat of my tale.
LUCIO. Right.
DUKE.   It may be right, but you are i'the wrong
  To speak before your time.... Proceed.
ISABELLA.   I went
  To this pernicious caitiff deputy.
DUKE. That's somewhat madly spoken.
ISABELLA.   Pardon it,
  The phrase is to the matter.
DUKE. Mended again ... The matter: proceed.   90
ISABELLA. In brief, to set the needless process by ...
  How I persuaded, how I prayed, and kneeled,
  How he refelled me, and how I replied—
  For this was of much length—the vile conclusion
  I now begin with grief and shame to utter....
  He would not, but by gift of my chaste body
  To his concupiscible intemperate lust,
  Release my brother; and, after much debatement,
  My sisterly remorse confutes mine honour,
  And I did yield to him ... But the next morn
    betimes,   100
  His purpose surfeiting, he sends a warrant
  For my poor brother's head.
DUKE.   This is most likely!
ISABELLA. O, that it were as like, as it is true!
DUKE. By heaven, fond wretch! thou know'st not
    what thou speak'st,
  Or else thou art suborned against his honour
  In hateful practice ... First, his integrity
  Stands without blemish: next, it imports no reason,
  That with such vehemency he should pursue
  Faults proper to himself: if he had so offended,
  He would have weighed thy brother by himself,   110
  And not have cut him off ... Some one hath set
    you on:
  Confess the truth, and say by whose advice
  Thou cam'st here to complain.
ISABELLA.   And is this all?
  Then, O you blessèd ministers above,
  Keep me in patience, and, with ripened time
  Unfold the evil, which is here wrapt up

In countenance ... Heaven shield your grace from
  woe,
As I, thus wrongèd, hence unbelievéd go.
DUKE. I know you'ld fain be gone ... An officer!
  To prison with her ... Shall we thus permit   120
  A blasting and a scandalous breath to fall
  On him so near us? This needs must be a practice;
  Who knew of your intent, and coming hither?
ISABELLA. One that I would were here, Friar
  Lodowick.
DUKE. A ghostly father, belike ... Who knows
  that Lodowick?
LUCIO. My lord, I know him, 'tis a meddling friar.
  I do not like the man: had he been lay, my lord,
  For certain words he spake against your grace
  In your retirement, I had swinged him soundly.
DUKE. Words against me! This' a good friar, belike!   130
  And to set on this wretched woman here
  Against our substitute ... Let this friar be found.
LUCIO. But, yesternight, my lord, she and that friar,
  I saw them at the prison: a saucy friar,
  A very scurvy fellow.
FRIAR PETER.   Blessèd be your royal grace!
  I have stood by, my lord, and I have heard
  Your royal ear abused ... First hath this woman
  Most wrongfully accused your substitute,
  Who is as free from touch or soil with her,
  As she from one ungot.
DUKE.   We did believe no less....   140
  Know you that Friar Lodowick that she speaks of?
FRIAR PETER. I know him for a man divine and holy—
  Not scurvy, nor a temporary meddler,
  As he's reported by this gentleman:
  And, on my trust, a man that never yet
  Did, as he vouches, misreport your grace.
LUCIO. My lord, most villainously—believe it.
FRIAR PETER. Well: he in time may come to
  clear himself;
  But at this instant he is sick, my lord,
  Of a strange fever ... Upon his mere request—   150
  Being come to knowledge that there was complaint
  Intended 'gainst Lord Angelo—came I hither
  To speak, as from his mouth, what he doth know
  Is true and false: and what he with his oath
  And all probation will make up full clear,
  Whensoever he's convented ... First, for this
  woman—
  To justify this worthy nobleman,
  So vulgarly and personally accused—
  Her shall you hear disprovéd to her eyes,
  Till she herself confess it.
DUKE.   Good friar, let's hear it ...   160
  Do you not smile at this, Lord Angelo?
  O heaven! the vanity of wretched fools....
  Give us some seats—Come, cousin Angelo,
  In this I'll be impartial: be you judge
  Of your own cause....

Mariana and Friar Peter come forward

                Is this the witness, friar?
  First, let her show her face, and after speak.
MARIANA. Pardon, my lord, I will not show my face
  Until my husband bid me.
DUKE.   What, are you married?
MARIANA. No, my lord.

DUKE. Are you a maid?   170
MARIANA. No, my lord.
DUKE. A widow then?
MARIANA. Neither, my lord.
DUKE. Why, you are nothing then: neither maid,
  widow, nor wife?
LUCIO. My lord, she may be a punk: for many of them
  are neither maid, widow, nor wife.
DUKE. Silence that fellow: I would, he had
  some cause
  To prattle for himself.
LUCIO. Well, my lord.   180
MARIANA. My lord, I do confess I ne'er was married,
  And I confess besides I am no maid.
  I have known my husband, yet my husband knows
  not
  That ever he knew me.
LUCIO. He was drunk then, my lord—it can be no
  better.
DUKE. For the benefit of silence, would thou wert so
  too.
LUCIO. Well, my lord.
DUKE. This is no witness for Lord Angelo.   190
MARIANA. Now I come to't, my lord....
  She that accuses him of fornication,
  In self-same manner doth accuse my husband,
  And charges him, my lord, with such a time
  When I'll depose I had him in mine arms,
  With all th'effects of love.
ANGELO. Charges she moe than me?
MARIANA.   Not that I know.
DUKE. No? you say your husband.
MARIANA. Why, just, my lord, and that is Angelo,
  Who thinks he knows that he ne'er knew my body,   200
  But knows, he thinks, that he knows Isabel's.
ANGELO. This is a strange abuse ... Let's see thy face.
MARIANA. My husband bids me—now I will
  unmask....   *She puts off her veil*
  This is that face, thou cruel Angelo,
  Which once thou swor'st was worth the looking on:
  This is the hand which, with a vowèd contráct,
  Was fast belockèd in thine: this is the body
  That took away the match from Isabel,
  And did supply thee at thy garden-house
  In her imagined person.
DUKE.   Know you this woman?   210
LUCIO. Carnally, she says.
DUKE.   Sirrah, no more!
LUCIO. Enough, my lord.
ANGELO. My lord, I must confess, I know this
  woman—
  And five years since there was some speech of
  marriage
  Betwixt myself and her: which was broke off,
  Partly for that her promisèd proportions
  Came short of composition: but in chief,
  For that her reputation was disvalued
  In levity: since which time of five years
  I never spake with her, saw her, nor heard from her,   220
  Upon my faith and honour.
MARIANA.   Noble prince,
  As there comes light from heaven, and words
  from breath,
  As there is sense in truth, and truth in virtue,
  I am affianced this man's wife, as strongly
  As words could make up vows: and, my good lord,

But Tuesday night last gone, in's garden-house,
He knew me as a wife.... As this is true,
Let me in safety raise me from my knees,
Or else for ever be confixéd here
A marble monument.

ANGELO.   I did but smile till now.   230
Now, good my lord, give me the scope of justice—
My patience here is touched: I do perceive
These poor informal women are no more
But instruments of some more mightier member
That sets them on.... Let me have way, my lord,
To find this practice out.

DUKE.   Ay, with my heart—
And punish them to your height of pleasure....
Thou foolish friar, and thou pernicious woman,
Compact with her that's gone ... think'st thou thy
    oaths,
Though they would swear down each particular
    saint,   240
Were testimonies against his worth and credit,
That's sealed in approbation? You, Lord Escalus,
Sit with my cousin, lend him your kind pains
To find out this abuse, whence 'tis derived....
There is another friar that set them on—
Let him be sent for.

FRIAR PETER. Would he were here, my lord, for
    he indeed
Hath set the women on to this complaint;
Your provost knows the place where he abides,
And he may fetch him.

DUKE.   Go, do it instantly ...   250
                    The Provost goes
And you, my noble and well-warranted cousin,
Whom it concerns to hear this matter forth,
Do with your injuries as seems you best,
In any chastisement; I for a while will leave you;
But stir not you, till you have well determined
Upon these slanderers.

ESCALUS.   My lord, we'll do it throughly ...
                    The Duke goes
Signior Lucio, did not you say you knew that Friar
Lodowick to be a dishonest person?

LUCIO. 'Cucullus non facit monachum'—honest in
nothing but in his clothes, and one that hath spoke   260
most villainous speeches of the duke.

ESCALUS. We shall entreat you to abide here till he
come and enforce them against him: we shall find
this friar a notable fellow.

LUCIO. As any in Vienna, on my word.

ESCALUS. Call that same Isabel here once again, I
would speak with her ... Pray you, my lord, give
me leave to question. You shall see how I'll handle
her.

LUCIO. Not better than he, by her own report.   270

ESCALUS. Say you?

LUCIO. Marry, sir, I think if you handled her privately,
she would sooner confess—perchance, publicly,
she'll be ashamed.

Isabella draws near, in custody of the officer

ESCALUS. I will go darkly to work with her.

LUCIO. That's the way: for women are light at midnight.

ESCALUS. Come on, mistress. Here's a gentlewoman
denies all that you have said.

The Provost approaches, with the Duke in his friar's habit

LUCIO. My lord, here comes the rascal I spoke of—   280
Here with the provost.

ESCALUS.   In very good time:
Speak not you to him, till we call upon you.

LUCIO. Mum.

ESCALUS. Come, sir! did you set these women on to
slander Lord Angelo? they have confessed you did.

DUKE. 'Tis false.

ESCALUS. How! know you where you are?

DUKE. Respect to your great place! and let the devil
Be sometime honoured for his burning throne....
Where is the duke? 'tis he should hear me speak.   290

ESCALUS. The duke's in us: and we will hear
    you speak.
Look you speak justly.

DUKE.   Boldly, at least.... But, O, poor souls,
Come you to seek the lamb here of the fox?
Good night to your redress ... Is the duke gone?
Then is your cause gone too ... The duke's unjust,
Thus to retort your manifest appeal,
And put your trial in the villain's mouth
Which here you come to accuse.

LUCIO. This is the rascal: this is he I spoke of.

ESCALUS. Why, thou unreverend and unhallowed
    friar: 300
Is't not enough thou hast suborned these women
To accuse this worthy man, but, in foul mouth,
And in the witness of his proper ear,
To call him villain?
And then to glance from him to th' duke himself,
To tax him with injustice? Take him hence;
To th' rack with him ... We'll touse you joint by
    joint,
But we will know his purpose ... What, 'unjust'!

DUKE. Be not so hot: the duke
Dare no more stretch this finger of mine than he   310
Dare rack his own: his subject am I not,
Not here provincial ... My business in this state
Made me a looker-on here in Vienna,
Where I have seen corruption boil and bubble,
Till it o'er-run the stew: laws for all faults,
But faults so countenanced, that the strong statutes
Stand like the forfeits in a barber's shop,
As much in mock as mark.

ESCALUS. Slander to th' state! Away with him
    to prison.

ANGELO. What can you vouch against him,
    Signior Lucio?   320
Is this the man, that you did tell us of?

LUCIO. 'Tis he, my lord ... Come hither, goodman
    bald-pate,
Do you know me?

DUKE. I remember you, sir, by the sound of your
voice. I met you at the prison, in the absence of
the duke.

LUCIO. O, did you so? and do you remember what
you said of the duke?

DUKE. Most notedly, sir.

LUCIO. Do you so, sir? And was the duke a flesh-   330
monger, a fool, and a coward, as you then reported
him to be?

DUKE. You must, sir, change persons with me, ere you
make that my report: you, indeed, spoke so of him
—and much more, much worse.

LUCIO. O thou damnable fellow! Did not I pluck thee
    by the nose, for thy speeches?
DUKE. I protest I love the duke, as I love myself.
ANGELO. Hark how the villain would close now, after
    his treasonable abuses!   340
ESCALUS. Such a fellow is not to be talked withal ...
    Away with him to prison ... Where is the provost?
    Away with him to prison: lay bolts enough upon
    him: let him speak no more ... Away with those
    giglots too, and with the other confederate com-
    panion!
            The Provost lays hands on the Duke
DUKE. Stay sir, stay awhile.
ANGELO. What, resists he? Help him, Lucio.
LUCIO. Come sir, come sir, come sir: foh sir, why you
    bald-pated lying rascal ... you must be hooded,   350
    must you? Show your knave's visage, with a pox
    to you ... show your sheep-biting face, and be
    hanged an hour ... Will't not off?

He plucks off the friar's hood and discovers the Duke:

DUKE. Thou art the first knave that e'er mad'st
    a duke....
    First, provost, let me bail these gentle three ...
    [*to Lucio*] Sneak not away, sir, for the friar and you
    Must have a word anon: lay hold on him.
LUCIO. This may prove worse than hanging.
DUKE [*to Escalus*]. What you have spoke, I pardon:
    sit you down,
    We'll borrow place of him; sir, by your leave ... 360

He sits in Angelo's place

    Hast thou or word, or wit, or impudence,
    That yet can do thee office? If thou hast
    Rely upon it, till my tale be heard,
    And hold no longer out.
ANGELO.   O, my dread lord,
    I should be guiltier than my guiltiness,
    To think I can be undiscernible,
    When I perceive your grace, like power divine,
    Hath looked upon my passes.... Then, good prince,
    No longer session hold upon my shame,
    But let my trial be mine own confession: 370
    Immediate sentence then, and sequent death,
    Is all the grace I beg.
DUKE.   Come hither, Mariana.
    Say: wast thou e'er contracted to this woman?
ANGELO. I was, my lord.
DUKE. Go take her hence, and marry her instantly....
    Do you the office, friar—which consummate,
    Return him here again ... Go with him, provost.
    Angelo, Mariana, Friar Peter, and the Provost depart
ESCALUS. My lord, I am more amazed at this
        dishonour,
    Than at the strangeness of it.
DUKE.   Come hither, Isabel—
    Your friar is now your prince: as I was then   380
    Advertising, and holy to your business—
    Not changing heart with habit—I am still
    Attorneyed at your service.
ISABELLA.   O give me pardon
    That I, your vassal, have employed and pained
    Your unknown sovereignty.
DUKE.   You are pardoned, Isabel:
    And now, dear maid, be you as free to us....
    Your brother's death, I know, sits at your heart:

And you may marvel why I obscured myself,
Labouring to save his life: and would not rather
Make rash remonstrance of my hidden power,   390
Than let him so be lost ... O, most kind maid,
It was the swift celerity of his death,
Which I did think with slower foot came on,
That brained my purpose: but, peace be with him!
That life is better life, past fearing death,
Than that which lives to fear: make it your comfort,
So happy is your brother.
ISABELLA.   I do, my lord.

Angelo, Mariana, Friar Peter, ·and the Provost return

DUKE. For this new-married man, approaching here,
    Whose salt imagination yet hath wronged
    Your well-defended honour ... you must pardon   400
    For Mariana's sake: but as he adjudged your
        brother—
    Being criminal, in double violation
    Of sacred chastity, and of promise-breach,
    Thereon dependent, for your brother's life—
    The very mercy of the law cries out
    Most audible, even from his proper tongue,
    'An Angelo for Claudio, death for death' ...
    Haste still pays haste, and leisure answers leisure;
    Like doth quit like, and Measure still for
        Measure ...
    Then, Angelo, thy fault's thus manifested;   410
    Which, though thou wouldst deny, denies
        thee vantage....
    We do condemn thee to the very block
    Where Claudio stooped to death, and with like
        haste....
    Away with him!
MARIANA.   O my most gracious lord,
    I hope you will not mock me with a husband!
DUKE. It is your husband mocked you with a
        husband.
    Consenting to the safeguard of your honour,
    I thought your marriage fit: else imputation,
    For that he knew you, might reproach your life,
    And choke your good to come: for his possessions, 420
    Although by confiscation they are ours,
    We do instate and widow you withal,
    To buy you a better husband.
MARIANA.   O my dear lord,
    I crave no other, nor no better man.
DUKE. Never crave him—we are definitive.
MARIANA. Gentle my liege—   *She kneels*
DUKE.   You do but lose your labour....
    Away with him to death ... [*to Lucio*] Now, sir,
    to you.
MARIANA. O my good lord! Sweet Isabel, take
    my part,
    Lend me your knees, and all my life to come
    I'll lend you all my life to do you service.   430
DUKE. Against all sense you do importune her.
    Should she kneel down, in mercy of this fact,
    Her brother's ghost his pavèd bed would break,
    And take her hence in horror.
MARIANA.   Isabel ...
    Sweet Isabel, do yet but kneel by me,
    Hold up your hands, say nothing: I'll speak all....
    They say, best men are moulded out of faults,
    And, for the most, become much more the better
    For being a little bad: so may my husband....

O, Isabel ... will you not lend a knee?
DUKE. He dies for Claudio's death.
ISABELLA [*kneels*]. Most bounteous sir,
Look, if it please you, on this man condemned,
As if my brother lived: I partly think
A due sincerity governéd his deeds,
Till he did look on me: since it is so,
Let him not die ... My brother had but justice,
In that he did the thing for which he died....
For Angelo,
His act did o'ertake his bad intent, 450
And must be buried but as an intent
That perished by the way ... Thoughts are no
subjects,
Intents but merely thoughts.
MARIANA. Merely, my lord.
DUKE. Your suit's unprofitable: stand up, I say ...
I have bethought me of another fault....
Provost, how came it Claudio was beheaded
At an unusual hour?
PROVOST. It was commanded so.
DUKE. Had you a special warrant for the deed?
PROVOST. No, my good lord: it was by private
message.
DUKE. For which I do discharge you of your office. 460
Give up your keys.
PROVOST. Pardon me, noble lord,
I thought it was a fault, but knew it not—
You did repent me, after more advice,
For testimony whereof, one in the prison,
That should by private order else have died,
I have reserved alive.
DUKE. What's he?
PROVOST. His name is Barnardine.
DUKE. I would thou hadst done so by Claudio ...
Go, fetch him hither—let me look upon him.
The Provost goes
ESCALUS. I am sorry, one so learned and so wise
As you, Lord Angelo, have still appeared, 470
Should slip so grossly, both in the heat of blood,
And lack of tempered judgement afterward.
ANGELO. I am sorry that such sorrow I procure—
And so deep sticks it in my penitent heart,
That I crave death more willingly than mercy.
'Tis my deserving, and I do entreat it.

*The Provost returns, with Barnardine, Claudio muffled,
and Juliet*

DUKE. Which is that Barnardine?
PROVOST. This, my lord.
DUKE. There was a friar told me of this man....
Sirrah, thou art said to have a stubborn soul,
That apprehends no further than this world, 480
And squar'st thy life according ... Thou'rt
condemned—
But, for those earthly faults, I quit them all,
And pray thee take this mercy to provide
For better times to come ... Friar, advise him,
I leave him to your hand.... What muffled
fellow's that?

PROVOST. This is another prisoner that I saved, 440
Who should have died when Claudio lost his
head—
As like almost to Claudio as himself.
He unmuffles Claudio
DUKE [*to Isabella*]. If he be like your brother, for
his sake
Is he pardoned—and, for your lovely sake, 490
Give me your hand, and say you will be mine,
He is my brother too: but fitter time for that ...
By this Lord Angelo perceives he's safe—
Methinks I see a quick'ning in his eye:
Well, Angelo, your evil quits you well....
Look that you love your wife; her worth, worth
yours.
I find an apt remission in myself:
And yet here's one in place I cannot pardon—
[*to Lucio*] You, sirrah, that knew me for a fool,
a coward,
One all of luxury, an ass, a madman ... 500
Wherein have I deserved so of you,
That you extol me thus?
LUCIO. Faith, my lord, I spoke it but according to the
trick: if you will hang me for it, you may: but I
had rather it would please you I might be whipped.
DUKE. Whipped first, sir, and hanged after.
Proclaim it, provost, round about the city,
If any woman's wronged by this lewd fellow—
As I have heard him swear himself there's one
Whom he begot with child—let her appear, 510
And he shall marry her: the nuptial finished,
Let him be whipped and hanged.
LUCIO. I beseech your highness, do not marry me to a
whore ... Your highness said even now I made you
a duke—good my lord, do not recompense me in
making me a cuckold.
DUKE. Upon mine honour, thou shalt marry her. Thy
slanders I forgive, and therewithal
Remit thy other forfeits ... Take him to prison:
And see our pleasure herein executed.
LUCIO. Marrying a punk, my lord, is pressing to death, 520
Whipping, and hanging.
DUKE. Slandering a prince deserves it ...
She, Claudio, that you wronged, look you
restore....
Joy to you, Mariana—love her, Angelo:
I have confessed her, and I know her virtue....
Thanks, good friend Escalus, for thy much
goodness,
There's more behind that is more gratulate....
Thanks, provost, for thy care and secrecy,
We shall employ thee in a worthier place....
Forgive him, Angelo, that brought you home
The head of Ragozine for Claudio's— 530
Th'offence pardons itself.... Dear Isabel,
I have a motion much imports your good,
Whereto if you'll a willing ear incline ...
What's mine is yours, and what is yours is mine.
So, bring us to our palace, where we'll show
What's yet behind, that's meet you all should know.
They pass through the gates

The Comedy of Errors

The scene: Ephesus

CHARACTERS IN THE PLAY

SÖLINUS, *Duke of Ephesus*
ÆGEON, *a merchant of Syracuse*
ANTIPHOLUS *of Ephesus* } *twin brothers, and sons*
ANTIPHOLUS *of Syracuse* } *to Ægeon and Æmilia*
DROMIO *of Ephesus* } *twin brothers, and bondmen*
DROMIO *of Syracuse* } *to the two Antipholuses*
BALTHAZAR
ANGELO, *a goldsmith*
A Merchant, friend to Antipholus of Syracuse

Another Merchant, to whom Angelo is in debt
DOCTOR PINCH, *a schoolmaster*
ÆMILIA, *an abbess at Ephesus, wife to Ægeon*
ADRIANA, *wife to Antipholus of Ephesus*
LUCIANA, *her sister*
LUCE, *or* NELL, *kitchen-maid to Adriana*
A Courtesan
Gaoler, officers, and other attendants

The Comedy of Errors

ACT 1

Scene 1: *Ephesus*

The Duke of Ephesus, attendants, a gaoler, Ægeon, officers and a crowd of citizens

ÆGEON. Proceed, Solinus, to procure my fall,
And by the doom of death end woes and all.
DUKE. Merchant of Syracusa, plead no more;
I am not partial to infringe our laws.
The enmity and discord which of late
Sprung from the rancorous outrage of your duke
To merchants, our well-dealing countrymen,
Who, wanting guilders to redeem their lives,
Have sealed his rigorous statutes with their bloods,
Excludes all pity from our threat'ning looks. 10
For, since the mortal and intestine jars
'Twixt thy seditious countrymen and us,
It hath in solemn synods been decreed,
Both by the Syracusians and ourselves,
To admit no traffic to our adverse towns:
Nay, more—if any born at Ephesus
Be seen at Syracusian marts and fairs;
Again, if any Syracusian born
Come to the bay of Ephesus—he dies;
His goods confiscate to the duke's dispose, 20
Unless a thousand marks be levièd,
To quit the penalty and to ransom him.
Thy substance, valued at the highest rate,
Cannot amount unto a hundred marks—
Therefore by law thou art condemned to die.
ÆGEON. Yet this my comfort: when your words are done,
My woes end likewise with the evening sun.
DUKE. Well, Syracusian, say, in brief, the cause
Why thou departed'st from thy native home,
And for what cause thou cam'st to Ephesus. 30
ÆGEON. A heavier task could not have been imposed
Than I to speak my griefs unspeakable:
Yet, that the world may witness that my end
Was wrought by nature, not by vile offence,
I'll utter what my sorrow gives me leave.
In Syracusa was I born, and wed
Unto a woman, happy but for me,
And by me too—had not our hap been bad:
With her I lived in joy; our wealth increased
By prosperous voyages I often made 40
To Epidamnum; till my factor's death
And the great care of goods at random left
Drew me from kind embracements of my spouse;
From whom my absence was not six months old,
Before herself—almost at fainting under
The pleasing punishment that women bear—
Had made provision for her following me,
And soon, and safe, arrivèd where I was.
There had she not been long but she became
A joyful mother of two goodly sons: 50
And, which was strange, the one so like the other,
As could not be distinguished but by names.
That very hour, and in the self-same inn,
A meaner woman was deliverèd

Of such a burden male, twins both alike.
Those, for their parents were exceeding poor,
I bought, and brought up to attend my sons.
My wife, not meanly proud of two such boys,
Made daily motions for our home return:
Unwilling I agreed. Alas, too soon 60
We came aboard.
A league from Epidamnum had we sailed
Before the always-wind-obeying deep
Gave any tragic instance of our harm:
But longer did we not retain much hope;
For what obscurèd light the heavens did grant
Did but convey unto our fearful minds
A doubtful warrant of immediate death,
Which, though myself would gladly have embraced,
Yet the incessant weepings of my wife, 70
Weeping before for what she saw must come,
And piteous plainings of the pretty babes,
That mourned for fashion, ignorant what to fear,
Forced me to seek delays for them and me.
And this it was—for other means was none:
The sailors sought for safety by our boat,
And left the ship, then sinking-ripe, to us:
My wife, more careful for the latter-born,
Had fast'ned him unto a small spare mast,
Such as seafaring men provide for storms: 80
To him one of the other twins was bound,
Whilst I had been like heedful of the other.
The children thus disposed, my wife and I,
Fixing our eyes on whom our care was fixed,
Fast'ned ourselves at either end the mast;
And floating straight, obedient to the stream,
Were carried towards Corinth, as we thought.
At length the sun, gazing upon the earth,
Dispersed those vapours that offended us,
And, by the benefit of his wishèd light, 90
The seas waxed calm, and we discoverèd
Two ships from far making amain to us:
Of Corinth that, of Epidaurus this.
But ere they came—O, let me say no more!—
Gather the sequel by that went before.
DUKE. Nay, forward, old man—do not break off so,
For we may pity, though not pardon thee.
ÆGEON. O, had the gods done so, I had not now
Worthily termed them merciless to us.
For, ere the ships could meet by twice five leagues, 100
We were encount'red by a mighty rock,
Which being violently borne upon,
Our helpful ship was splitted in the midst;
So that, in this unjust divorce of us,
Fortune had left to both of us alike
What to delight in, what to sorrow for.
Her part, poor soul, seeming as burdenèd
With lesser weight, but not with lesser woe,
Was carried with more speed before the wind,
And in our sight they three were taken up 110
By fishermen of Corinth, as we thought.
At length, another ship had seized on us;
And, knowing whom it was their hap to save,

Gave healthful welcome to their shipwrecked
  guests—
And would have reft the fishers of their prey,
Had not their bark been very slow of sail;
And therefore homeward did they bend their
  course.
Thus have you heard me severed from my bliss,
That by misfortunes was my life prolonged
To tell sad stories of my own mishaps. 120
DUKE. And, for the sake of them thou sorrowest for,
Do me the favour to dilate at full
What hath befall'n of them and thee till now.
ÆGEON. My youngest boy, and yet my eldest care,
At eighteen years became inquisitive
After his brother; and importuned me,
That his attendant—for his case was like,
Reft of his brother, but retained his name—
Might bear him company in the quest of him;
Whom whilst I laboured of a love to see, 130
I hazarded the loss of whom I loved.
Five summers have I spent in farthest Greece,
Roaming clean through the bounds of Asia,
And, coasting homeward, came to Ephesus;
Hopeless to find, yet loath to leave unsought
Or that, or any place that harbours men.
But here must end the story of my life—
And happy were I in my timely death,
Could all my travels warrant me they live.
DUKE. Hapless Ægeon, whom the fates have marked 140
To bear the extremity of dire mishap.
Now, trust me, were it not against our laws,
Against my crown, my oath, my dignity,
Which princes, would they, may not disannul,
My soul should sue as advocate for thee:
But, though thou art adjudgéd to the death,
And passéd sentence may not be recalled
But to our honour's great disparagement.
Yet will I favour thee in what I can;
Therefore, merchant, I'll limit thee this day 150
To seek thy help by beneficial hap.
Try all the friends thou hast in Ephesus—
Beg thou, or borrow, to make up the sum,
And live: if no, then thou art doomed to die.
Gaoler, take him to thy custody.
GAOLER. I will, my lord.
ÆGEON. Hopeless, and helpless, doth Ægeon wend,
But to procrastinate his lifeless end. *They depart*

Scene 2: The Mart

*Antipholus of Syracuse, his man Dromio and a merchant
enter*

MERCHANT. Therefore, give out you are of
  Epidamnum,
Lest that your goods too soon be confiscate:
This very day, a Syracusian merchant
Is apprehended for arrival here,
And, not being able to buy out his life,
According to the statute of the town,
Dies ere the weary sun set in the west.
There is your money that I had to keep.
S. ANTIPHOLUS. Go bear it to the Centaur, where we
  host,
And stay there, Dromio, till I come to thee; 10
Within this hour it will be dinner-time;
Till that, I'll view the manners of the town,
Peruse the traders, gaze upon the buildings,

And then return and sleep within mine inn;
For with long travel I am stiff and weary.
Get thee away.
S. DROMIO. Many a man would take you at your word,
And go indeed, having so good a mean. *He goes*
S. ANTIPHOLUS. A trusty villain, sir, that very oft,
When I am dull with care and melancholy, 20
Lightens my humour with his merry jests.
What, will you walk with me about the town,
And then go to my inn, and dine with me?
MERCHANT. I am invited, sir, to certain merchants,
Of whom I hope to make much benefit:
I crave your pardon. Soon at five o'clock,
Please you, I'll meet with you upon the mart,
And afterward consort you till bed-time:
My present business calls me from you now.
S. ANTIPHOLUS. Farewell till then: I will go lose myself, 30
And wander up and down to view the city.
MERCHANT. Sir, I commend you to your own content.
  He departs
S. ANTIPHOLUS. He, that commends me to mine own
  content,
Commends me to the thing I cannot get.
I to the world am like a drop of water
That in the ocean seeks another drop,
Who, falling there to find his fellow forth,
Unseen, inquisitive, confounds himself.
So I, to find a mother and a brother,
In quest of them, unhappier, lose myself. 40

Dromio of Ephesus enters

Here comes the almanac of my true date:
What now! How chance thou art returned so soon?
E. DROMIO. Returned so soon! rather approached too
  late.
The capon burns, the pig falls from the spit;
The clock hath strucken twelve upon the bell;
My mistress made it one upon my cheek:
She is so hot, because the meat is cold:
The meat is cold, because you come not home:
You come not home, because you have no stomach:
You have no stomach, having broke your fast: 50
But we, that know what 'tis to fast and pray,
Are penitent for your default to-day.
S. ANTIPHOLUS. Stop in your wind, sir—tell me this,
  I pray!
Where have you left the money that I gave you?
E. DROMIO. O—sixpence, that I had o'Wednesday
  last,
To pay the saddler for my mistress' crupper?
The saddler had it, sir, I kept it not.
S. ANTIPHOLUS. I am not in a sportive humour now:
Tell me, and dally not, where is the money?
We being strangers here, how dar'st thou trust 60
So great a charge from thine own custody?
E. DROMIO. I pray you, jest, sir, as you sit at dinner:
I from my mistress come to you in post:
If I return, I shall be post indeed,
For she will score your fault upon my pate.
Methinks your maw, like mine, should be your
  clock,
And strike you home without a messenger.
S. ANTIPHOLUS. Come Dromio, come, these jests are
  out of season:
Reserve them till a merrier hour than this.
Where is the gold I gave in charge to thee? 70

E. DROMIO. To me sir? why you gave no gold to me.

S. ANTIPHOLUS. Come on, sir knave, have done your foolishness,
And tell me how thou hast disposed thy charge.

E. DROMIO. My charge was but to fetch you from the mart
Home to your house, the Phœnix, sir, to dinner.
My mistress and her sister stay for you.

S. ANTIPHOLUS. Now, as I am a Christian, answer me,
In what safe place you have bestowed my money;
Or I shall break that merry sconce of yours
That stands on tricks when I am undisposed: 80
Where is the thousand marks thou hadst of me?

E. DROMIO. I have some marks of yours upon my pate:
Some of my mistress' marks upon my shoulders:
But not a thousand marks between you both.
If I should pay your worship those again,
Perchance you will not bear them patiently.

S. ANTIPHOLUS. Thy mistress' marks! what mistress, slave, hast thou?

E. DROMIO. Your worship's wife, my mistress at the Phœnix;
She that doth fast till you come home to dinner,
And prays that you will hie you home to dinner.   90

S. ANTIPHOLUS. What, wilt thou flout me thus unto my face,
Being forbid? There, take you that, sir knave.
                                          He beats him

E. DROMIO. What mean you, sir? for God's sake hold your hands!
Nay, an you will not, sir, I'll take my heels.
                                          He takes flight

S. ANTIPHOLUS. Upon my life, by some device or other,
The villain is o'er-raught of all my money.
They say this town is full of cozenage:
As, nimble jugglers that deceive the eye,
Dark-working sorcerers that change the mind,
Soul-killing witches that deform the body,   100
Disguisèd cheaters, prating mountebanks,
And many such-like liberties of sin:
If it prove so, I will be gone the sooner.
I'll to the Centaur, to go seek this slave.
I greatly fear my money is not safe.
                                          He follows Dromio

ACT 2

Scene 1: *The house of Antipholus*

Adriana and Luciana enter

ADRIANA. Neither my husband nor the slave returned,
That in such haste I sent to seek his master!
Sure, Luciana, it is two o'clock.

LUCIANA. Perhaps some merchant hath invited him,
And from the mart he's somewhere gone to dinner.
Good sister, let us dine, and never fret;
A man is master of his liberty:
Time is their master, and when they see time,
They'll go or come; if so, be patient, sister.

ADRIANA. Why should their liberty than ours be more?   10

LUCIANA. Because their business still lies out o' door.

ADRIANA. Look when I serve him so, he takes it ill.

LUCIANA. O, know he is the bridle of your will.

ADRIANA. There's none but asses will be bridled so.

LUCIANA. Why, headstrong liberty is lashed with woe:
There's nothing situate under heaven's eye
But hath his bound, in earth, in sea, in sky:
The beasts, the fishes, and the wingèd fowls
Are their males' subjects and at their controls:
Men, more divine, the masters of all these,   20
Lords of the wide world and wild watry seas,
Indued with intellectual sense and souls,
Of more pre-eminence than fish and fowls,
Are masters to their females, and their lords:
Then let your will attend on their accords.

ADRIANA. This servitude makes you to keep unwed.

LUCIANA. Not this, but troubles of the marriage-bed.

ADRIANA. But, were you wedded, you would bear some sway.

LUCIANA. Ere I learn love, I'll practise to obey.

ADRIANA. How if your husband start some other where?   30

LUCIANA. Till he come home again, I would forbear—

ADRIANA. Patience unmoved! no marvel though she pause—
They can be meek that have no other cause:
A wretched soul, bruised with adversity,
We bid be quiet when we hear it cry;
But were we burd'ned with like weight of pain,
As much, or more, we should ourselves complain:
So thou, that hast no unkind mate to grieve thee,
With urging helpless patience wouldst relieve me;
But, if thou live to see like right bereft,   40
This fool-begged patience in thee will be left.

LUCIANA. Well, I will marry one day, but to try.
Here comes your man, now is your husband nigh.

Dromio of Ephesus enters

ADRIANA. Say, is your tardy master now at hand?

E. DROMIO. Nay, he's at two hands with me, and that my two ears can witness.

ADRIANA. Say, didst thou speak with him? know'st thou his mind?

E. DROMIO. Ay, ay, he told his mind upon mine ear—
Beshrew his hand, I scarce could understand it.

LUCIANA. Spake he so doubtfully, thou couldst not feel his meaning?   50

E. DROMIO. Nay, he struck so plainly, I could too well feel his blows; and withal so doubtfully, that I could scarce understand them.

ADRIANA. But say, I prithee, is he coming home?
It seems he hath great care to please his wife.

E. DROMIO. Why, mistress, sure my master is horn-mad.

ADRIANA. Horn-mad, thou villain!

E. DROMIO.   I mean not cuckold-mad—
But, sure, he is stark mad:
When I desired him to come home to dinner,   60
He asked me for a thousand marks in gold:
''Tis dinner-time,' quoth I: 'My gold!' quoth he:
'Your meat doth burn,' quoth I: 'My gold!' quoth he:
'Will you come home?' quoth I: 'My gold!' quoth he:
'Where is the thousand marks I gave thee, villain?'
'The pig,' quoth I, 'is burned': 'My gold!' quoth he:
'My mistress, sir—' quoth I: 'Hang up thy mistress!
I know not thy mistress, out on thy mistress!'

LUCIANA. Quoth who?

E. DROMIO. Quoth my master.   70
'I know,' quoth he, 'no house, no wife, no mistress.'

So that my errand, due unto my tongue,
I thank him, I bare home upon my shoulders;
For, in conclusion, he did beat me there.
ADRIANA. Go back again, thou slave, and fetch him
    home.
E. DROMIO. Go back again, and be new beaten home?
For God's sake send some other messenger.
ADRIANA. Back, slave, or I will break thy pate across.
E. DROMIO. And he will bless that cross with other
    beating:
Between you, I shall have a holy head.   80
ADRIANA. Hence, prating peasant; fetch thy master
    home.
E. DROMIO. Am I so round with you, as you with me,
That like a football you do spurn me thus?
You spurn me hence, and he will spurn me hither.
If I last in this service, you must case me in leather.
                                        He goes
LUCIANA. Fie, how impatience loureth in your face!
ADRIANA. His company must do his minions grace,
Whilst I at home starve for a merry look:
Hath homely age th'alluring beauty took
From my poor cheek? then he hath wasted it.   90
Are my discourses dull? barren my wit?
If voluble and sharp discourse be marred,
Unkindness blunts it more than marble hard.
Do their gay vestments his affections bait?
That's not my fault, he's master of my state.
What ruins are in me that can be found,
By him not ruined? then is he the ground
Of my defeatures. My decayéd fair
A sunny look of his would soon repair.
But, too unruly deer, he breaks the pale,   100
And feeds from home; poor I am but his stale.
LUCIANA. Self-harming jealousy! fie, beat it hence.
ADRIANA. Unfeeling fools can with such wrongs
    dispense.
I know his eye doth homage otherwhere,
Or else what lets it but he would be here?
Sister, you know he promised me a chain—
Would that alone o' love he would detain,
So he would keep fair quarter with his bed!
I see the jewel best enamelléd
Will lose his beauty; and though gold bides still 110
That others touch, yet often touching will
Wear gold, and no man that hath a name
But falsehood and corruption doth it shame.
Since that my beauty cannot please his eye,
I'll weep what's left away and weeping die.
LUCIANA. How many fond fools serve mad jealousy!
                                        They go

Scene 2: *The Mart*

Antipholus of Syracuse enters

S. ANTIPHOLUS. The gold I gave to Dromio is laid up
Safe at the Centaur, and the heedful slave
Is wand'red forth, in care to seek me out,
By computation and mine host's report,
I could not speak with Dromio since at first
I sent him from the mart! See, here he comes.

Dromio of Syracuse approaches

How now, sir! is your merry humour altered?
As you love strokes, so jest with me again.
You know no Centaur? you received no gold?

Your mistress sent to have me home to dinner?   10
My house was at the Phœnix? Wast thou mad,
That thus so madly thou didst answer me?
S. DROMIO. What answer, sir? when spake I such a
    word?
S. ANTIPHOLUS. Even now, even here, not half an hour
    since.
S. DROMIO. I did not see you since you sent me hence,
Home to the Centaur, with the gold you gave me.
S. ANTIPHOLUS. Villain, thou didst deny the gold's
    receipt,
And told'st me of a mistress, and a dinner—
For which, I hope, thou felt'st I was displeased.
S. DROMIO. I am glad to see you in this merry vein. 20
What means this jest? I pray you, master, tell me.
S. ANTIPHOLUS. Yea, dost thou jeer, and flout me in the
    teeth?
Think'st thou, I jest? Hold, take thou that, and that.
                                        Beats Dromio
S. DROMIO. Hold, sir, for God's sake! now your jest
    is earnest.
Upon what bargain do you give it me?
S. ANTIPHOLUS. Because that I familiarly sometimes
Do use you for my fool and chat with you,
Your sauciness will jest upon my love,
And make a common of my serious hours.
When the sun shines, let foolish gnats make sport, 30
But creep in crannies, when he hides his beams.
If you will jest with me, know my aspéct,
And fashion your demeanour to my looks,
Or I will beat this method in your sconce.
S. DROMIO. Sconce, call you it? so you would leave
battering, I had rather have it a head. An you use
these blows long, I must get a sconce for my head,
and ensconce it too, or else I shall seek my wit in
my shoulders. But, I pray, sir, why am I beaten?
S. ANTIPHOLUS. Dost thou not know?   40
S. DROMIO. Nothing, sir, but that I am beaten.
S. ANTIPHOLUS. Shall I tell you why?
S. DROMIO. Ay, sir, and wherefore; for they say every
why hath a wherefore.
S. ANTIPHOLUS. Why, first for flouting me, and then
    wherefore,
For urging it the second time to me.
S. DROMIO. Was there ever any man thus beaten out
    of season,
When in the why and the wherefore is neither
    rhyme nor reason?
Well, sir, I thank you.
S. ANTIPHOLUS.   Thank me, sir, for what?
S. DROMIO. Marry, sir, for this something that you   50
gave me for nothing.
S. ANTIPHOLUS. I'll make you amends next, to give you
nothing for something. But say, sir, is it dinner-time?
S. DROMIO. No, sir. I think the meat wants that I have.
S. ANTIPHOLUS. In good time, sir: what's that?
S. DROMIO. Basting.
S. ANTIPHOLUS. Well, sir, then 'twill be dry.
S. DROMIO. If it be, sir, I pray you eat none of it.
S. ANTIPHOLUS. Your reason?
S. DROMIO. Lest it make you choleric and purchase me 60
another dry basting.
S. ANTIPHOLUS. Well, sir, learn to jest in good time—
there's a time for all things.
S. DROMIO. I durst have denied that, before you were
so choleric.

s. ANTIPHOLUS. By what rule, sir?

s. DROMIO. Marry, sir, by a rule as plain as the plain bald pate of Father Time himself.

s. ANTIPHOLUS. Let's hear it.

s. DROMIO. There's no time for a man to recover his 70 hair that grows bald by nature.

s. ANTIPHOLUS. May he not do it by fine and recovery?

s. DROMIO. Yes, to pay a fine for a periwig and recover the lost hair of another man.

s. ANTIPHOLUS. Why is Time such a niggard of hair, being, as it is, so plentiful an excrement?

s. DROMIO. Because it is a blessing that he bestows on beasts: and what he hath scanted men in hair, he hath given them in wit.

s. ANTIPHOLUS. Why, but there's many a man hath 80 more hair than wit.

s. DROMIO. Not a man of those but he hath the wit to lose his hair.

s. ANTIPHOLUS. Why, thou didst conclude hairy men plain dealers without wit.

s. DROMIO. The plainer dealer, the sooner lost; yet he loseth it in a kind of jollity.

s. ANTIPHOLUS. For what reason?

s. DROMIO. For two—and sound ones too.

s. ANTIPHOLUS. Nay, not sound, I pray you. 90

s. DROMIO. Sure ones then.

s. ANTIPHOLUS. Nay, not sure, in a thing falsing.

s. DROMIO. Certain ones then.

s. ANTIPHOLUS. Name them.

s. DROMIO. The one, to save the money that he spends in tiring; the other, that at dinner they should not drop in his porridge.

s. ANTIPHOLUS. You would all this time have proved there is no time for all things.

s. DROMIO. Marry, and did, sir: namely, e'en no time 100 to recover hair lost by nature.

s. ANTIPHOLUS. But your reason was not substantial why there is no time to recover.

s. DROMIO. Thus I mend it: Time himself is bald, and therefore, to the world's end, will have bald followers.

s. ANTIPHOLUS. I knew 'twould be a bald conclusion. But soft, who wafts us yonder?

Adriana enters with Luciana

ADRIANA. Ay, ay, Antipholus, look strange and frown,
Some other mistress hath thy sweet aspécts: 110
I am not Adriana, nor thy wife.
The time was once, when thou unurged wouldst vow
That never words were music to thine ear,
That never object pleasing in thine eye,
That never touch well welcome to thy hand,
That never meat sweet-savoured in thy taste,
Unless I spake, or looked, or touched, or carved to thee.
How comes it now, my husband, O, how comes it,
That thou art then estrangéd from thyself?
Thy self I call it, being strange to me, 120
That, undividable, incorporate,
Am better than thy dear self's better part.
Ah, do not tear away thyself from me;
For know, my love, as easy mayst thou fall
A drop of water in the breaking gulf,
And take unmingled thence that drop again,

Without addition or diminishing,
As take from me thyself, and not me too.
How dearly would it touch thee to the quick,
Shouldst thou but hear I were licentious! 130
And that this body, consecrate to thee,
By ruffian lust should be contaminate!
Wouldst thou not spit at me, and spurn at me,
And hurl the name of husband in my face,
And tear the stained skin off my harlot-brow,
And from my false hand cut the wedding-ring,
And break it with a deep-divorcing vow?
I know thou canst—and therefore, see thou do it.
I am possessed with an adulterate blot,
My blood is mingled with the grime of lust: 140
For, if we two be one, and thou play false,
I do digest the poison of thy flesh,
Being strumpeted by thy contagion.
Keep then fair league and truce with thy true bed,
I live unstained, thou undishonouréd.

s. ANTIPHOLUS. Plead you to me, fair dame? I know you not:
In Ephesus I am but two hours old,
As strange unto your town as to your talk—
Who, every word by all my wit being scanned,
Want wit in all one word to understand. 150

LUCIANA. Fie, brother! how the world is changed with you:
When were you wont to use my sister thus?
She sent for you by Dromio home to dinner.

s. ANTIPHOLUS. By Dromio?

s. DROMIO. By me?

ADRIANA. By thee, and this thou didst return from him—
That he did buffet thee, and in his blows
Denied my house for his, me for his wife.

s. ANTIPHOLUS. Did you converse, sir, with this gentlewoman?
What is the course and drift of your compáct? 160

s. DROMIO. I, sir? I never saw her till this time.

s. ANTIPHOLUS. Villain, thou liest; for even her very words
Didst thou deliver to me on the mart.

s. DROMIO. I never spake with her in all my life.

s. ANTIPHOLUS. How can she thus then call us by our names?
Unless it be by inspiration.

ADRIANA. How ill agrees it with your gravity
To counterfeit thus grossly with your slave,
Abetting him to thwart me in my mood!
Be it my wrong you are from me exempt, 170
But wrong not that wrong with a more contempt.
Come, I will fasten on this sleeve of thine:
Thou art an elm, my husband, I a vine,
Whose weakness, married to thy stronger state,
Makes me with thy strength to communicate:
If aught possess thee from me, it is dross,
Usurping ivy, briar, or idle moss,
Who, all for want of pruning, with intrusion
Infect thy sap and live on thy confusion.

s. ANTIPHOLUS. To me she speaks, she moves me for her theme; 180
What, was I married to her in my dream?
Or sleep I now, and think I hear all this?
What error drives our eyes and ears amiss?
Until I know this sure uncertainty,
I'll entertain the offered fallacy.

LUCIANA. Dromio, go bid the servants spread for
dinner.
S. DROMIO. O, for my beads! I cross me for a sinner.
This is the fairy land—O, spite of spites!—
We talk with goblins, owls, and sprites;
If we obey them not, this will ensue: 190
They'll suck our breath, or pinch us black and blue.
LUCIANA. Why prat'st thou to thyself and answer'st
not?
Dromio, thou drone, thou snail, thou slug, thou sot.
S. DROMIO. I am transforméd, master am not I?
S. ANTIPHOLUS. I think thou art in mind, and so am I.
S. DROMIO. Nay, master, both in mind and in my
shape.
S. ANTIPHOLUS. Thou hast thine own form.
S. DROMIO.   No, I am an ape.
LUCIANA. If thou art changed to aught, 'tis to an ass.
S. DROMIO. 'Tis true, she rides me and I long for grass.
'Tis so, I am an ass—else it could never be   200
But I should know her as well as she knows me.
ADRIANA. Come, come, no longer will I be a fool,
To put the finger in the eye and weep,
Whilst man and master laugh my woes to scorn.
Come, sir, to dinner. Dromio, keep the gate:
Husband, I'll dine above with you to-day,
And shrive you of a thousand idle pranks:
Sirrah, if any ask you for your master,
Say he dines forth, and let no creature enter.
Come, sister, Dromio, play the porter well.   210
S. ANTIPHOLUS. Am I in earth, in heaven, or in hell?
Sleeping or waking? mad or well-advised?
Known unto these, and to myself disguised!
I'll say as they say, and perséver so ...
And in this mist at all adventures go.
S. DROMIO. Master, shall I be porter at the gate?
ADRIANA. Ay, and let none enter, lest I break your
pate.
LUCIANA. Come, come, Antipholus, we dine too late.
                                                They go

ACT 3
Scene 1: *Before the house of Antipholus*

*Antipholus of Ephesus, his man Dromio, Angelo and
Balthazar enter*

E. ANTIPHOLUS. Good Signior Angelo, you must
excuse us all—
My wife is shrewish when I keep not hours;
Say that I lingered with you at your shop
To see the making of her carcanet,
And that to-morrow you will bring it home.
But here's a villain that would face me down
He met me on the mart, and that I beat him,
And charged him with a thousand marks in gold,
And that I did deny my wife and house;
Thou drunkard, thou, what didst thou mean by this?   10
E. DROMIO. Say what you will, sir, but I know what
I know—
That you beat me at the mart, I have your hand to
show;
If the skin were parchment and the blows you gave
were ink,
Your own handwriting would tell you what I think.
E. ANTIPHOLUS. I think thou art an ass.
E. DROMIO.   Marry, so it doth appear

By the wrongs I suffer and the blows I bear.
I should kick, being kicked, and being at that pass,
You would keep from my heels and beware of
an ass.
E. ANTIPHOLUS. You're sad, Signior Balthazar—pray
God, our cheer
May answer my good will and your good welcome
here.   20
BALTHAZAR. I hold your dainties cheap, sir, and your
welcome dear.
E. ANTIPHOLUS. O, Signior Balthazar, either at flesh or
fish,
A table-full of welcome makes scarce one dainty
dish.
BALTHAZAR. Good meat, sir, is common; that every
churl affords.
E. ANTIPHOLUS. And welcome more common, for
that's nothing but words.
BALTHAZAR. Small cheer and great welcome makes a
merry feast.
E. ANTIPHOLUS. Ay, to a niggardly host and more
sparing guest.
But though my cates be mean, take them in good
part.
Better cheer may you have, but not with better
heart.
But soft, my door is locked; go, bid them let us in.   30
E. DROMIO. Maud, Bridget, Marian, Cicely, Gillian,
Ginn!
S. DROMIO [*from within*]. Mome, malt-horse, capon,
coxcomb, idiot, patch!
Either get thee from the door or sit down at the
hatch.
Dost thou conjure for wenches, that thou call'st for
such store,
When one is one too many? Go, get thee from the
door.
E. DROMIO. What patch is made our porter? My master
stays in the street.
S. DROMIO. Let him walk from whence he came, lest
he catch cold on's feet.
E. ANTIPHOLUS. Who talks within there? ho, open the
door!
S. DROMIO. Right sir, I'll tell you when, an you'll tell
me wherefore.
E. ANTIPHOLUS. Wherefore? for my dinner: I have not
dined to-day.   40
S. DROMIO. Nor to-day here you must not; come again
when you may.
E. ANTIPHOLUS. What art thou that keep'st me out
from the house I owe?
S. DROMIO. The porter for this time, sir, and my name
is Dromio.
E. DROMIO. O villain, thou hast stol'n both mine office
and my name.
The one ne'er got me credit, the other mickle
blame ...
If thou hadst been Dromio to-day in my place,
Thou wouldst have changed thy face for an aim, or
thy name for an ass.

Enter Luce, the kitchen-maid, within

LUCE. What a coil is there, Dromio? who are those at
the gate?
E. DROMIO. Let my master in, Luce.
LUCE.   Faith no, he comes too late.

And so tell your master.

E. DROMIO.   .   O lord, I must laugh!   50
Have at you with a proverb—Shall I set in my staff?

LUCE. Have at you with another, that's—When? can
you tell?

S. DROMIO. If thy name be called Luce—Luce, thou
hast answered him well.

E. ANTIPHOLUS. Do you hear, you minion? you'll let us
in, I hope?

LUCE. I thought to have asked you.

S. DROMIO.   And you said, no.

E. DROMIO. So, come, help—well struck—there was
blow for blow.

E. ANTIPHOLUS. Thou baggage, let me in.

LUCE.   Can you tell for whose sake?

E. DROMIO. Master, knock the door hard.

LUCE.   Let him knock till it ache.

E. ANTIPHOLUS. You'll cry for this, minion, if I beat
the door down.

LUCE. What needs all that, and a pair of stocks in the
town?   60

Enter Adriana, within

ADRIANA. Who is that at the door that keeps all this
noise?

S. DROMIO. By my troth, your town is troubled with
unruly boys.

E. ANTIPHOLUS. Are you there, wife? you might have
come before.

ADRIANA. Your wife, sir knave! go, get you from the
door.

E. DROMIO. If you went in pain, master, this 'knave'
would go sore.

ANGELO. Here is neither cheer, sir, nor welcome! We
would fain have either.

BALTHAZAR. In debating which was best, we shall part
with neither.

E DROMIO. They stand at the door, master. Bid them
welcome hither.

E. ANTIPHOLUS. There is something in the wind, that
we cannot get in.

E. DROMIO. You would say so, master, if your
garments were thin.   70
Your cake here is warm within: you stand here in
the cold.
It would make a man mad as a buck to be so bought
and sold.

E. ANTIPHOLUS. Go, fetch me something—I'll break
ope the gate.

S. DROMIO. Break any breaking here, and I'll break
your knave's pate.

E. DROMIO. A man may break a word with you, sir,
and words are but wind:
Ay, and break it in your face, so he break it not
behind.

S. DROMIO. It seems thou want'st breaking. Out upon
thee, hind!

E. DROMIO. Here's too much 'out upon thee'! I pray
thee, let me in.

S. DROMIO. Ay, when fowls have no feathers, and fish
have no fin.

E. ANTIPHOLUS. Well, I'll break in. Go borrow me a
crow.   80

E. DROMIO. A crow without feather? master, mean
you so?

For a fish without a fin, there's a fowl without a
feather.
If a crow help us in, sirrah, we'll pluck a crow
together.

E. ANTIPHOLUS. Go, get thee gone, fetch me an iron
crow.

BALTHAZAR. Have patience, sir—O, let it not be so!
Herein you war against your reputation,
And draw within the compass of suspect
Th'unviolated honour of your wife.
Once this—your long experience of her wisdom,
Her sober virtue, years, and modesty,   90
Plead on her part some cause to you unknown;
And doubt not, sir, but she will well excuse
Why at this time the doors are made against you.
Be ruled by me, depart in patience,
And let us to the Tiger all to dinner.
And, about evening, come yourself alone,
To know the reason of this strange restraint.
If by strong hand you offer to break in,
Now in the stirring passage of the day,
A vulgar comment will be made of it;   100
And that supposèd by the common rout
Against your yet ungallèd estimation,
That may with foul intrusion enter in
And dwell upon your grave when you are dead;
For slander lives upon succession;
For ever housed where it gets possession.

E. ANTIPHOLUS. You have prevailed. I will depart in
quiet,
And, in despite of mirth, mean to be merry.
I know a wench of excellent discourse,
Pretty and witty; wild and yet, too, gentle;   110
There will we dine: this woman that I mean,
My wife—but, I protest, without desert—
Hath oftentimes upbraided me withal:
To her will we to dinner. [*to Angelo*] Get you home,
And fetch the chain—by this, I know, 'tis made—
Bring it, I pray you, to the Porpentine,
For there's the house. That chain will I bestow—
Be it for nothing but to spite my wife—
Upon mine hostess there. Good sir, make haste.
Since mine own doors refuse to entertain me,   120
I'll knock elsewhere, to see if they'll disdain me.

ANGELO. I'll meet you at that place some hour hence.

E. ANTIPHOLUS. Do so. This jest shall cost me some
expense.   *They go*

Scene 2

Enter Luciana and Antipholus of Syracuse

LUCIANA. And may it be that you have quite forgot
A husband's office? Shall, Antipholus, hate
Even in the spring of love thy love-springs rot?
Shall love, in building, grow so ruinate?
If you did wed my sister for her wealth,
Then for her wealth's sake use her with more
kindness:
Or, if you like elsewhere, do it by stealth,
Muffle your false love with some show of blindness:
Let not my sister read it in your eye:
Be not thy tongue thy own shame's orator: 10
Look sweet, speak fair, become disloyalty:
Apparel vice like virtue's harbinger:
Bear a fair presence, though your heart be tainted,
Teach sin the carriage of a holy saint,

Be secret-false: what need she be acquainted?
What simple thief brags of his own attaint?
'Tis double wrong, to truant with your bed
And let her read it in thy looks at board:
Shame hath a bastard fame, well managéd;
Ill deed is doubled with an evil word.   20
Alas, poor women! make us but believe,
Being compact of credit, that you love us—
Though others have the arm, show us the sleeve:
We in your motion turn, and you may move us.
Then, gentle brother, get you in again;
Comfort my sister, cheer her, call her wife;
'Tis holy sport, to be a little vain,
When the sweet breath of flattery conquers strife.

S. ANTIPHOLUS. Sweet mistress—what your name is
    else, I know not;
Nor by what wonder you do hit of mine—   30
Less in your knowledge and your grace you show not
Than our earth's wonder, more than earth divine.
Teach me, dear creature, how to think and speak:
Lay open to my earthy-gross conceit,
Smoth'red in errors, feeble, shallow, weak,
The folded meaning of your words' deceit.
Against my soul's pure truth why labour you
To make it wander in an unknown field?
Are you a god? would you create me new?
Transform me, then, and to your power I'll yield. 40
But if that I am I, then well I know
Your weeping sister is no wife of mine,
Nor to her bed no homage do I owe:
Far more, far more, to you do I decline.
O, train me not, sweet mermaid, with thy note,
To drown me in thy sister's flood of tears:
Sing, siren, for thyself, and I will dote:
Spread o'er the silver waves thy golden hairs;
And as a bed I'll take them, and there lie:
And, in that glorious supposition, think   50
He gains by death that hath such means to die:
Let Love, being light, be drownéd if she sink!

LUCIANA. What, are you mad, that you do reason so?
S. ANTIPHOLUS. Not mad, but mated—how, I do not
    know.
LUCIANA. It is a fault that springeth from your eye.
S. ANTIPHOLUS. For gazing on your beams, fair sun,
    being by.
LUCIANA. Gaze where you should, and that will clear
    your sight.
S. ANTIPHOLUS. As good to wink, sweet love, as look
    on night.
LUCIANA. Why call you me love? call my sister so.
S. ANTIPHOLUS. Thy sister's sister.
LUCIANA.   That's my sister.
S. ANTIPHOLUS.   No: 60
It is thyself, mine own self's better part:
Mine eye's clear eye, my dear heart's dearer heart;
My food, my fortune, and my sweet hope's aim;
My sole earth's heaven, and my heaven's claim.
LUCIANA. All this my sister is, or else should be.
S. ANTIPHOLUS. Call thyself sister, sweet, for I am thee:
Thee will I love, and with thee lead my life;
Thou hast no husband yet, nor I no wife:
Give me thy hand.
LUCIANA.   O, soft, sir, hold you still.
I'll fetch my sister, to get her good will. *She goes* 70

Dromio of Syracuse enters

S. ANTIPHOLUS. Why, how now, Dromio! where
    run'st thou so fast?
S. DROMIO. Do you know me, sir? am I Dromio? am
    I your man? am I myself?
S. ANTIPHOLUS. Thou art Dromio, thou art my man,
    thou art thyself.
S. DROMIO. I am an ass, I am a woman's man, and
    besides myself.
S. ANTIPHOLUS. What woman's man? and how besides
    thyself?   80
S. DROMIO. Marry, sir, besides myself, I am due to a
    woman; one that claims me, one that haunts me,
    one that will have me.
S. ANTIPHOLUS. What claim lays she to thee?
S. DROMIO. Marry, sir, such claim as you would lay
    to your horse; and she would have me as a beast—
    not that, I being a beast, she would have me, but that
    she, being a very beastly creature, lays claim to me.
S. ANTIPHOLUS. What is she?
S. DROMIO. A very reverend body: ay, such a one as   90
    a man may not speak of without he say 'Sir-
    reverence.' I have but lean luck in the match, and
    yet is she a wondrous fat marriage.
S. ANTIPHOLUS. How dost thou mean a fat marriage?
S. DROMIO. Marry, sir, she's the kitchen-wench, and
    all grease—and I know not what use to put her to,
    but to make a lamp of her, and run from her by
    her own light. I warrant her rags and the tallow in
    them will burn a Poland winter: if she lives till
    doomsday, she'll burn a week longer than the whole 100
    world.
S. ANTIPHOLUS. What complexion is she of?
S. DROMIO. Swart, like my shoe, but her face nothing
    like so clean kept: for why? she sweats, a man may
    go over shoes in the grime of it.
S. ANTIPHOLUS. That's a fault that water will mend.
S. DROMIO. No, sir, 'tis in grain—Noah's flood could
    not do it.
S. ANTIPHOLUS. What's her name?
S. DROMIO. Nell, sir: but her name and three quarters, 110
    that's an ell and three quarters, will not measure her
    from hip to hip.
S. ANTIPHOLUS. Then she bears some breadth?
S. DROMIO. No longer from head to foot than from
    hip to hip: she is spherical, like a globe: I could find
    out countries in her.
S. ANTIPHOLUS. In what part of her body stands
    Ireland?
S. DROMIO. Marry, sir, in her buttocks—I found it out
    by the bogs.   120
S. ANTIPHOLUS. Where Scotland?
S. DROMIO. I found it by the barren-nesses, hard in the
    palm of the hand.
S. ANTIPHOLUS. Where France?
S. DROMIO. In her forehead—armed and reverted,
    making war against her heir.
S. ANTIPHOLUS. Where England?
S. DROMIO. I looked for the chalky cliffs, but I could
    find no whiteness in them. But I guess, it stood in
    her chin, by the salt rheum that ran between France 130
    and it.
S. ANTIPHOLUS. Where Spain?
S. DROMIO. Faith, I saw it not: but I felt it hot in her
    breath.
S. ANTIPHOLUS. Where America, the Indies?
S. DROMIO. O, sir, upon her nose, all o'er embellished

with rubies, carbuncles, sapphires, declining their
rich aspect to the hot breath of Spain, who sent
whole armadoes of carracks to be ballast at her nose.

S. ANTIPHOLUS. Where stood Belgia, the Netherlands? 140

S. DROMIO. O, sir, I did not look so low. To conclude, this drudge, or diviner, laid claim to me—
called me Dromio, swore I was assured to her, told
me what privy marks I had about me, as the mark
of my shoulder, the mole in my neck, the great wart
on my left arm, that I, amazed, ran from her as a
witch.

And, I think, if my breast had not been made
of faith, and my heart of steel,
She had transformed me to a curtal-dog, and made
me turn i'th' wheel.

S. ANTIPHOLUS. Go, hie thee presently post to the road, 150
An if the wind blow any way from shore,
I will not harbour in this town to-night.
If any bark put forth, come to the mart,
Where I will walk till thou return to me.
If every one know us, and we know none,
'Tis time, I think, to trudge, pack, and be gone.

S. DROMIO. As from a bear a man would run for life,
So fly I from her that would be my wife. *He goes*

S. ANTIPHOLUS. There's none but witches do inhabit
here,
And therefore 'tis high time that I were hence. 160
She that doth call me husband, even my soul
Doth for a wife abhor. But her fair sister,
Possessed with such a gentle sovereign grace,
Of such enchanting presence and discourse,
Hath almost made me traitor to myself:
But, lest myself be guilty to self-wrong,
I'll stop mine ears against the mermaid's song.

Enter Angelo with the chain

ANGELO. Master Antipholus—

S. ANTIPHOLUS.   Ay, that's my name.

ANGELO. I know it well, sir. Lo, here is the chain.
I thought to have ta'en you at the Porpentine. 170
The chain unfinished made me stay thus long.

S. ANTIPHOLUS. What is your will that I shall do with
this?

ANGELO. What please yourself, sir: I have made it for
you.

S. ANTIPHOLUS. Made it for me, sir! I bespoke it not.

ANGELO. Not once, nor twice, but twenty times you
have:
Go home with it and please your wife withal,
And soon at supper-time I'll visit you,
And then receive my money for the chain.

S. ANTIPHOLUS. I pray you, sir, receive the money now,
For fear you ne'er see chain nor money more. 180

ANGELO. You are a merry man, sir. Fare you well.
He goes

S. ANTIPHOLUS. What I should think of this, I cannot
tell:
But this I think, there's no man is so vain
That would refuse so fair an offered chain.
I see a man here needs not live by shifts,
When in the streets he meets such golden gifts:
I'll to the mart, and there for Dromio stay—
If any ship put out, then straight away.

He departs

ACT 4
Scene 1: *The Mart*

Angelo, a merchant and an officer

MERCHANT. You know since Pentecost the sum is due,
And since I have not much importuned you,
Nor now I had not, but that I am bound
To Persia, and want guilders for my voyage:
Therefore make present satisfaction,
Or I'll attach you by this officer.

ANGELO. Even just the sum that I do owe to you
Is growing to me by Antipholus,
And in the instant that I met with you
He had of me a chain. At five o'clock, 10
I shall receive the money for the same:
Pleaseth you walk with me down to his house,
I will discharge my bond, and thank you too.

*Antipholus of Ephesus, and Dromio of Ephesus
come from the courtesan's*

OFFICER. That labour may you save: see where he
comes.

E. ANTIPHOLUS. While I go to the goldsmith's house,
go thou
And buy a rope's end—that will I bestow
Among my wife and her confederates,
For locking me out of my doors by day.
But soft, I see the goldsmith; get thee gone,
Buy thou a rope, and bring it home to me. 20

E. DROMIO. I buy a thousand pound a year! I buy a
rope! *He goes*

E. ANTIPHOLUS. A man is well holp up that trusts to
you!
I promised your presence and the chain,
But neither chain nor goldsmith came to me:
Belike you thought our love would last too long,
If it were chained together; and therefore came not.

ANGELO. Saving your merry humour, here's the note,
How much your chain weighs to the utmost carat,
The fineness of the gold, and chargeful fashion—
Which doth amount to three odd ducats more 30
Than I stand debted to this gentleman.
I pray you, see him presently discharged,
For he is bound to sea, and stays but for it.

E. ANTIPHOLUS. I am not furnished with the present
money:
Besides, I have some business in the town.
Good signior, take the stranger to my house,
And with you take the chain, and bid my wife
Disburse the sum on the receipt thereof.
Perchance I will be there as soon as you.

ANGELO. Then you will bring the chain to her
yourself? 40

E. ANTIPHOLUS. No, bear it with you, lest I come not
time enough.

ANGELO. Well, sir, I will. Have you the chain about
you?

E. ANTIPHOLUS. An if I have not, sir, I hope you have:
Or else you may return without your money.

ANGELO. Nay, come, I pray you, sir, give me the chain:
Both wind and tide stays for this gentleman,
And I, to blame, have held him here too long.

E. ANTIPHOLUS. Good Lord! you use this dalliance to
excuse
Your breach of promise to the Porpentine.
I should have chid you for not bringing it, 50

But, like a shrew, you first begin to brawl.

MERCHANT. The hour steals on—I pray you, sir,
  dispatch.

ANGELO. You hear how he impórtunes me—the chain!

E. ANTIPHOLUS. Why, give it to my wife, and fetch
  your money.

ANGELO. Come, come, you know, I gave it you even
  now;
  Either send the chain or send by me some token.

E. ANTIPHOLUS. Fie! now you run this humour out of
  breath.
  Come, where's the chain? I pray you, let me see it.

MERCHANT. My business cannot brook this dalliance.
  Good sir, say whe'er you'll answer me or no: 60
  If not, I'll leave him to the officer.

E. ANTIPHOLUS. I answer you! What should I answer
  you?

ANGELO. The money that you owe me for the chain.

ANTIPHOLUS. I owe you none till I receive the chain.

ANGELO. You know I gave it you half an hour since.

E. ANTIPHOLUS. You gave me none, you wrong me
  much to say so.

ANGELO. You wrong me more, sir, in denying it.
  Consider how it stands upon my credit.

MERCHANT. Well, officer, arrest him at my suit.

OFFICER. I do,   70
  And charge you in the duke's name to obey me.

ANGELO. This touches me in reputation.
  Either consent to pay this sum for me,
  Or I attach you by this officer.

E. ANTIPHOLUS. Consent to pay thee that I never had!
  Arrest me, foolish fellow, if thou dar'st.

ANGELO. Here is thy fee, arrest him officer.
  I would not spare my brother in this case,
  If he should scorn me so apparently.

OFFICER. I do arrest you, sir. You hear the suit.   80

E. ANTIPHOLUS. I do obey thee, till I give thee bail.
  But, sirrah, you shall buy this sport as dear
  As all the metal in your shop will answer.

ANGELO. Sir, sir, I shall have law in Ephesus,
  To your notorious shame, I doubt it not.

Dromio of Syracuse returns from the Bay

S. DROMIO. Master, there's a bark of Epidamnum,
  That stays but till her owner comes aboard,
  And then she bears away....Our fraughtage, sir,
  I have conveyed aboard, and I have bought
  The oil, the balsamum, and aqua-vitæ.   90
  The ship is in her trim, the merry wind
  Blows fair from land: they stay for nought at all
  But for their owner, master, and yourself.

E. ANTIPHOLUS. How now! a madman? Why, thou
  peevish sheep,
  What ship of Epidamnum stays for me?

S. DROMIO. A ship you sent me to, to hire waftage.

E. ANTIPHOLUS. Thou drunken slave, I sent thee for
  a rope,
  And told thee to what purpose and what end.

S. DROMIO. You sent me for a rope's-end, sir, as soon.
  You sent me to the Bay, sir, for a bark.   100

E. ANTIPHOLUS. I will debate this matter at more
  leisure,
  And teach your ears to list me with more heed.
  To Adriana, villain, hie thee straight:
  Give her this key, and tell her, in the desk
  That's covered o'er with Turkish tapestry

There is a purse of ducats—let her send it:
Tell her I am arrested in the street,
And that shall bail me: hie thee, slave—be gone.
On, officer, to prison till it come.

     He departs with the officer; Angelo and
              the merchant following

S. DROMIO. To Adriana! that is where we dined,   110
Where Dowsabel did claim me for her husband.
She is too big, I hope, for me to compass.
Thither I must, although against my will;
For servants must their masters' minds fulfil.

                    He goes

Scene 2: *The house of Antipholus*

Enter Adriana and Luciana

ADRIANA. Ah, Luciana, did he tempt thee so?
  Mightst thou perceive a surety in his eye,
  That he did plead in earnest? yea or no?
  Looked he or red or pale, or sad or merrily?
  What observation mad'st thou in this case,
  Of his heart's meteors tilting in his face?

LUCIANA. First, he denied you had in him no right.

ADRIANA. He meant he did me none: the more my
  spite.

LUCIANA. Then swore he that he was a stranger here.

ADRIANA. And true he swore, though yet forsworn he
  were.   10

LUCIANA. Then pleaded I for you.

ADRIANA.   And what said he?

LUCIANA. That love I begged for you, he begged
  of me.

ADRIANA. With what persuasion did he tempt thy
  love?

LUCIANA. With words that in an honest suit might
  move.
  First, he did praise my beauty, then my speech.

ADRIANA. Didst speak him fair?

LUCIANA.   Have patience, I beseech.

ADRIANA. I cannot, nor I will not, hold me still.
  My tongue, though not my heart, shall have his will.
  He is deforméd, crookéd, old and sere,
  Ill-faced, worse bodied, shapeless every where: 20
  Vicious, ungentle, foolish, blunt, unkind,
  Stigmatical in making, worse in mind.

LUCIANA. Who would be jealous then of such a one?
  No evil lost is wailed when it is gone.

ADRIANA. Ah, but I think him better than I say;
  And yet would herein others' eyes were worse.
  Far from her nest the lapwing cries away;
  My heart prays for him, though my tongue do curse.

Dromio of Syracuse enters

S. DROMIO. Here, go—the desk, the purse! sweet now,
  make haste.

LUCIANA. How hast thou lost thy breath?

S. DROMIO.   By running fast. 30

ADRIANA. Where is thy master, Dromio? is he well?

S. DROMIO. No, he's in Tartar limbo, worse than hell:
  A devil in an everlasting garment hath him;
  One whose hard heart is buttoned up with steel:
  A fiend, a fury, pitiless and rough:
  A wolf, nay worse, a fellow all in buff:
  A back-friend, a shoulder-clapper, one that
  countermands
  The passages of alleys, creeks, and narrow lands;

A hound that runs counter, and yet draws dry-foot
well;
One that, before the Judgement, carries poor souls
to 'hell.'   40
ADRIANA. Why, man, what is the matter?
S. DROMIO. I do not know the matter, he is 'rested on
the case.
ADRIANA. What, is he arrested? tell me, at whose suit.
S. DROMIO. I know not at whose suit he is arrested
well;
But he's in a suit of buff which 'rested him, that
can I tell.
Will you send him, mistress redemption, the money
in his desk?
ADRIANA. Go fetch it, sister. This I wonder at,
                                            Luciana goes
That he, unknown to me, should be in debt.
Tell me, was he arrested on a band?
S. DROMIO. Not on a band, but on a stronger thing: 50
A chain, a chain! Do you not hear it ring?
ADRIANA. What, the chain?
S. DROMIO.   No, no, the bell, 'tis time that
I were gone!
It was two ere I left him, and now the clock strikes
one.
ADRIANA. The hours come back! that did I never hear.
S. DROMIO. O yes. If any hour meet a sergeant, a'
turns back for very fear.
ADRIANA. As if Time were in debt! how fondly dost
thou reason!
S. DROMIO. Time is a very bankrupt, and owes more
than he's worth to season.
Nay, he's a thief too: have you not heard men say,
That Time comes stealing on by night and day?
If a' be in debt and theft, and a sergeant in the way, 60
Hath he not reason to turn back an hour in a day?

Luciana returns with a purse

ADRIANA. Go, Dromio. There's the money, bear it
straight,
And bring thy master home immediately.
Come, sister. I am pressed down with conceit:
Conceit, my comfort and my injury   *They go within*

Scene 3: *The Mart*

Enter Antipholus of Syracuse

S. ANTIPHOLUS. There's not a man I meet but doth
salute me
As if I were their well-acquainted friend,
And every one doth call me by my name:
Some tender money to me, some invite me;
Some other give me thanks for kindnesses;
Some offer me commodities to buy.
Even now a tailor called me in his shop,
And showed me silks that he had bought for me,
And, therewithal, took measure of my body.
Sure, these are but imaginary wiles,   10
And Lapland sorcerers inhabit here.

Dromio of Syracuse enters

S. DROMIO. Master, here's the gold you sent me for.
Where have you got the picture of old Adam new-
apparelled?

S. ANTIPHOLUS. What gold is this? What Adam dost
thou mean?
S. DROMIO. Not that Adam that kept the Paradise, but
that Adam that keeps the prison; he that goes in
the calf's skin that was killed for the Prodigal; he that
came behind you, sir, like an evil angel, and bid you
forsake your liberty.   20
S. ANTIPHOLUS. I understand thee not.
S. DROMIO. No? why, 'tis a plain case: he that went,
like a bass-viol, in a case of leather; the man, sir, that
when gentlemen are tired gives them a sob, and
'rests them; he, sir, that takes pity on decayed men,
and gives them suits of durance; he that sets up his
rest to do more exploits with his mace than a morris-
pike.
S. ANTIPHOLUS. What, thou mean'st an officer?
S. DROMIO. Ay, sir, the sergeant of the band: he that 30
brings any man to answer it that breaks his band:
one that thinks a man always going to bed, and says,
'God give you good rest!'
S. ANTIPHOLUS. Well, sir, there rest in your foolery.
Is there any ship puts forth to-night? may we be
gone?
S. DROMIO. Why, sir, I brought you word an hour
since that the bark 'Expedition' put forth to-night,
and then were you hindered by the sergeant to tarry
for the hoy 'Delay'. Here are the angels that you 40
sent for to deliver you.
S. ANTIPHOLUS. The fellow is distract, and so am I,
And here we wander in illusions:
Some blessèd power deliver us from hence!

The Courtesan enters

COURTESAN. Well met, well met, Master Antipholus.
I see, sir, you have found the goldsmith now:
Is that the chain you promised me to-day?
S. ANTIPHOLUS. Satan, avoid! I charge thee tempt me
not!
S. DROMIO. Master, is this Mistress Satan?
S. ANTIPHOLUS. It is the devil.   50
S. DROMIO. Nay, she is worse, she is the devil's dam;
and here she comes in the habit of a light wench,
and thereof comes that the wenches say 'God damn
me,' that's as much to say 'God make me a light
wench.' It is written, they appear to men like angels
of light. Light is an effect of fire, and fire will burn:
ergo, light wenches will burn. Come not near her.
COURTESAN. Your man and you are marvellous merry,
sir.
Will you go with me? We'll mend our dinner here.
S. DROMIO. Master, if you do, expect spoon-meat, or 60
bespeak a long spoon.
S. ANTIPHOLUS. Why, Dromio?
S. DROMIO. Marry, he must have a long spoon that
must eat with the devil.
S. ANTIPHOLUS. Avoid, thou fiend! what tell'st thou
me of supping?
Thou art, as you are all, a sorceress:
I conjure thee to leave me and be gone.
COURTESAN. Give me the ring of mine you had at
dinner,
Or, for my diamond, the chain you promised,
And I'll be gone, sir, and not trouble you.   70
S. DROMIO. Some devils ask but the parings of one's
nail,
A rush, a hair, a drop of blood, a pin,

A nut, a cherry-stone;
But she, more covetous, would have a chain.
Master, be wise—an if you give it her,
The devil will shake her chain, and fright us with it.

COURTESAN. I pray you, sir, my ring, or else the chain.
I hope you do not mean to cheat me so!

S. ANTIPHOLUS. Avaunt, thou witch! Come, Dromio,
   let us go.   *He departs*

S. DROMIO. 'Fly pride,' says the peacock—Mistress,
   that you know.   *He follows* 80

COURTESAN. Now, out of doubt, Antipholus is mad,
Else would he never so demean himself.
A ring he hath of mine worth forty ducats,
And for the same he promised me a chain—
Both one and other he denies me now.
The reason that I gather he is mad,
Besides this present instance of his rage,
Is a mad tale he told to-day at dinner,
Of his own doors being shut against his entrance.
Belike his wife, acquainted with his fits,   90
On purpose shut the doors against his way.
My way is now to hie home to his house,
And tell his wife that, being lunatic,
He rushed into my house and took perforce
My ring away. This course I fittest choose,
For forty ducats is too much to lose.   *She goes*

Scene 4

Antipholus of Ephesus enters with the officer

E. ANTIPHOLUS. Fear me not, man, I will not break
   away.
I'll give thee, ere I leave thee, so much money,
To warrant thee, as I am 'rested for.
My wife is in a wayward mood to-day,
And will not lightly trust the messenger.
That I should be attached in Ephesus,
I tell you, 'twill sound harshly in her ears.

Enter Dromio of Ephesus, with a rope's end

Here comes my man, I think he brings the money.
How now, sir! have you that I sent you for?

E. DROMIO. Here's that, I warrant you, will pay
   them all.   10

E. ANTIPHOLUS. But where's the money?

E. DROMIO. Why, sir, I gave the money for the rope.

E. ANTIPHOLUS. Five hundred ducats, villain, for a
   rope?

E. DROMIO. I'll serve you, sir, five hundred at the
   rate.

E. ANTIPHOLUS. To what end did I bid thee hie thee
   home?

E. DROMIO. To a rope's-end, sir, and to that end am
   I returned.

E. ANTIPHOLUS. And to that end, sir, I will welcome
   you.   *He beats him*

OFFICER. Good sir, be patient.

E. DROMIO. Nay, 'tis for me to be patient. I am in
   adversity.   20

OFFICER. Good now, hold thy tongue.

E. DROMIO. Nay, rather persuade him to hold his
   hands.

E. ANTIPHOLUS. Thou whoreson, senseless villain!

E. DROMIO. I would I were senseless, sir, that I might
   not feel your blows.

E. ANTIPHOLUS. Thou art sensible in nothing but

blows, and so is an ass.

E. DROMIO. I am an ass, indeed—you may prove it by
   my long 'ears. I have served him from the hour of   30
   my nativity to this instant, and have nothing at his
   hands for my service but blows. When I am cold,
   he heats me with beating: when I am warm, he cools
   me with beating: I am waked with it when I sleep,
   raised with it when I sit, driven out of doors with it
   when I go from home, welcomed home with it
   when I return; nay, I bear it on my shoulders, as a
   beggar wont her brat: and, I think, when he hath
   lamed me, I shall beg with it from door to door.

*Enter Adriana, Luciana, the Courtesan and a schoolmaster
called Pinch*

E. ANTIPHOLUS. Come, go along—my wife is coming
   yonder.   40

E. DROMIO. Mistress, 'respice finem,' respect your end,
   or rather, to prophesy like the parrot, 'beware the
   rope's-end.'

E. ANTIPHOLUS. Wilt thou still talk?   *He beats him*

COURTESAN. How say you now? is not your husband
   mad?

ADRIANA. His incivility confirms no less.
Good Doctor Pinch, you are a conjurer—
Establish him in his true sense again,
And I will please you what you will demand.

LUCIANA. Alas, how fiery and how sharp he looks!   50

COURTESAN. Mark how he trembles in his ecstasy!

PINCH. Give me your hand, and let me feel your pulse.
                              Antipholus strikes him

E. ANTIPHOLUS. There is my hand, and let it feel your
   ear.

PINCH. I charge thee, Satan, housed within this man,
To yield possession to my holy prayers,
And to thy state of darkness hie thee straight.
I conjure thee by all the saints in heaven.

E. ANTIPHOLUS. Peace, doting wizard, peace; I am
   not mad.

ADRIANA. O, that thou wert not, poor distressèd soul!

E. ANTIPHOLUS. You minion, you, are these your
   customers?   60
Did this companion with the saffron face
Revel and feast it at my house to-day,
Whilst upon me the guilty doors were shut,
And I denied to enter in my house?

ADRIANA. O, husband, God doth know you dined at
   home,
Where would you had remained until this time,
Free from these slanders and this open shame.

E. ANTIPHOLUS. Dined at home! Thou villain, what
   sayest thou?

E. DROMIO. Sir, sooth to say, you did not dine at home.

E. ANTIPHOLUS. Were not my doors locked up, and I
   shut out?   70

E. DROMIO. Perdie, your doors were locked, and you
   shut out.

E. ANTIPHOLUS. And did not she herself revile me
   there?

E. DROMIO. Sans fable, she herself reviled you there.

E. ANTIPHOLUS. Did not her kitchen-maid rail, taunt,
   and scorn me?

E. DROMIO. Certes, she did—the kitchen-vestal
   scorned you.

E. ANTIPHOLUS. And did not I in rage depart from
   thence?

E. DROMIO. In verity, you did—my bones bear
   witness,
That since have felt the vigour of his rage.
ADRIANA. Is't good to soothe him in these contraries?
PINCH. It is no shame. The fellow finds his vein,   80
And yielding to him humours well his frenzy.
E. ANTIPHOLUS. Thou hast suborned the goldsmith to
   arrest me.
ADRIANA. Alas, I sent you money to redeem you,
By Dromio here, who came in haste for it.
E. DROMIO. Money by me? heart and good-will you
   might,
But, surely, master, not a rag of money.
E. ANTIPHOLUS. Went'st not thou to her for a purse
   of ducats?
ADRIANA. He came to me, and I delivered it.
LUCIANA. And I am witness with her that she did.
E. DROMIO. God and the rope-maker bear me
   witness   90
That I was sent for nothing but a rope.
PINCH. Mistress, both man and master is possessed—
I know it by their pale and deadly looks.
They must be bound, and laid in some dark room.
E. ANTIPHOLUS. Say, wherefore didst thou lock me
   forth to-day,
And why dost thou deny the bag of gold?
ADRIANA. I did not, gentle husband, lock thee forth.
E. DROMIO. And, gentle master, I received no gold:
But I confess sir, that we were locked out.
ADRIANA. Dissembling villain, thou speak'st false in
   both.   100
E. ANTIPHOLUS. Dissembling harlot, thou art false in
   all,
And art confederate with a damnéd pack,
To make a loathsome abject scorn of me:
But with these nails I'll pluck out these false eyes
That would behold in me this shameful sport.

Enter three or four, and offer to bind him: he strives

ADRIANA. O, bind him, bind him, let him not come
   near me.
PINCH. More company! The fiend is strong within
   him!
LUCIANA. Ay me! poor man, how pale and wan he
   looks.
E. ANTIPHOLUS. What, will you murder me? Thou
   gaoler, thou,
I am thy prisoner; wilt thou suffer them   110
To make a rescue?
OFFICER.   Masters, let him go:
He is my prisoner, and you shall not have him.
PINCH. Go, bind this man, for he is frantic too.
                    They bind Dromio of Ephesus
ADRIANA. What wilt thou do, thou peevish officer?
Hast thou delight to see a wretched man
Do outrage and displeasure to himself?
OFFICER. He is my prisoner—if I let him go,
The debt he owes will be required of me.
ADRIANA. I will discharge thee ere I go from thee.
Bear me forthwith unto his creditor,   120
And, knowing how the debt grows, I will pay it.
Good master doctor, see him safe conveyed
Home to my house. O most unhappy day!
E. ANTIPHOLUS. O most unhappy strumpet!
E. DROMIO. Master, I am here entred in bond for you.

E. ANTIPHOLUS. Out on thee, villain! wherefore dost
   thou mad me?
E. DROMIO. Will you be bound for nothing? be mad,
   good master—
Cry, 'The devil!'
LUCIANA. God help, poor souls, how idly do they talk.
ADRIANA. Go bear him hence. Sister, go you with me.   130

*Pinch and his assistants carry off Antipholus of Ephesus and
Dromio of Ephesus*

Say now, whose suit is he arrested at?
OFFICER. One Angelo a goldsmith, do you know him?
ADRIANA. I know the man: what is the sum he owes?
OFFICER. Two hundred ducats.
ADRIANA.   Say, how grows it due?
OFFICER. Due for a chain your husband had of him.
ADRIANA. He did bespeak a chain for me, but had it
   not.
COURTESAN. When as your husband, all in rage, to-day
Came to my house, and took away my ring—
The ring I saw upon his finger now—
Straight after did I meet him with a chain.   140
ADRIANA. It may be so, but I did never see it.
Come, gaoler, bring me where the goldsmith is,
I long to know the truth hereof at large.

*Enter Antipholus of Syracuse, with his rapier drawn, and
Dromio of Syracuse*

LUCIANA. God, for thy mercy! they are loose again.
ADRIANA. And come with naked swords—let's call
   more help
To have them bound again.
OFFICER.   Away, they'll kill us.
      They run all out, as fast as may be, frighted
S. ANTIPHOLUS. I see these witches are afraid of swords.
S. DROMIO. She that would be your wife now ran
   from you.
S. ANTIPHOLUS. Come to the Centaur, fetch our stuff
   from hence:
I long that we were safe and sound aboard.   150
S. DROMIO. Faith, stay here this night, they will surely
do us no harm: you see they speak us fair, give us
gold: methinks they are such a gentle nation, that
but for the mountain of mad flesh that claims
marriage of me, I could find in my heart to stay
here still, and turn witch.
S. ANTIPHOLUS. I will not stay to-night for all the
   town—
Therefore away, to get our stuff aboard.   *They go*

ACT 5
Scene 1: *Before a Priory*

Angelo and the merchant

ANGELO. I am sorry, sir, that I have hind'red you,
But I protest he had the chain of me.
Though most dishonestly he doth deny it.
MERCHANT. How is the man esteemed here in the city?
ANGELO. Of very reverend reputation, sir,
Of credit infinite, highly beloved,
Second to none that lives here in the city:
His word might bear my wealth at any time.
MERCHANT. Speak softly—yonder, as I think, he
   walks.

Antipholus and Dromio of Syracuse approach

ANGELO. 'Tis so; and that self chain about his neck,   10
  Which he forswore most monstrously to have.
  Good sir, draw near with me, I'll speak to him.
  Signior Antipholus, I wonder much
  That you would put me to this shame and trouble,
  And not without some scandal to yourself,
  With circumstance and oaths so to deny
  This chain which now you wear so openly.
  Beside the charge, the shame, imprisonment,
  You have done wrong to this my honest friend,
  Who, but for staying on our controversy,   20
  Had hoisted sail and put to sea to-day:
  This chain you had of me, can you deny it?
S. ANTIPHOLUS. I think I had. I never did deny it.
MERCHANT. Yes, that you did, sir, and forswore it too.
S. ANTIPHOLUS. Who heard me to deny it or forswear
  it?
MERCHANT. These ears of mine, thou know'st, did hear
  thee.
  Fie on thee, wretch! 'tis pity that thou liv'st
  To walk where any honest men resort.
S. ANTIPHOLUS. Thou art a villain to impeach me thus.
  I'll prove mine honour and mine honesty   30
  Against thee presently, if thou dar'st stand.
MERCHANT. I dare, and do defy thee for a villain.
                                        They draw

Adriana, Luciana, the Courtesan, and others enter

ADRIANA. Hold, hurt him not for God's sake! he is
  mad.
  Some get within him, take his sword away:
  Bind Dromio too, and bear them to my house.
S. DROMIO. Run, master, run—for God's sake take a
  house—
  This is some priory—in—or we are spoiled.

S. Dromio and S. Antipholus go into the Priory
The Lady Abbess enters

ABBESS. Be quiet, people. Wherefore throng you
  hither?
ADRIANA. To fetch my poor distracted husband hence.
  Let us come in, that we may bind him fast,   40
  And bear him home for his recovery.
ANGELO. I knew he was not in his perfect wits.
MERCHANT. I am sorry now that I did draw on him.
ABBESS. How long hath this possession held the man?
ADRIANA. This week he hath been heavy, sour, sad,
  And much much different from the man he was:
  But till this afternoon his passion
  Ne'er brake into extremity of rage.
ABBESS. Hath he not lost much wealth by wreck of
  sea?
  Buried some dear friend? Hath not else his eye   50
  Strayed his affection in unlawful love?
  A sin prevailing much in youthful men,
  Who give their eyes the liberty of gazing.
  Which of these sorrows is he subject to?
ADRIANA. To none of these, except it be the last,
  Namely, some love that drew him oft from home.
ABBESS. You should for that have reprehended him.
ADRIANA. Why, so I did.
ABBESS.   Ay, but not rough enough.
ADRIANA. As roughly as my modesty would let me.
ABBESS. Haply, in private.

ADRIANA.   And in assemblies too.   60
ABBESS. Ay, but not enough.
ADRIANA. It was the copy of our conference.
  In bed, he slept not for my urging it:
  At board, he fed not for my urging it:
  Alone, it was the subject of my theme:
  In company I often glancéd it:
  Still did I tell him it was vile and bad.
ABBESS. And thereof came it that the man was mad.
  The venom clamours of a jealous woman
  Poison more deadly than a mad dog's tooth.   70
  It seems his sleeps were hind'red by thy railing,
  And thereof comes it that his head is light.
  Thou say'st his meat was sauced with thy
    upbraidings,
  Unquiet meals make ill digestions,
  Thereof the raging fire of fever bred—
  And what's a fever but a fit of madness?
  Thou say'st his sports were hind'red by thy brawls:
  Sweet recreation barred, what doth ensue
  But moody and dull melancholy,
  Kinsman to grim and comfortless despair,   80
  And at her heels a huge infectious troop
  Of pale distemperatures and foes to life?
  In food, in sport, and life preserving rest
  To be disturbed, would mad or man or beast:
  The consequence is, then, thy jealous fits
  Hath scared thy husband from the use of wits.
LUCIANA. She never reprehended him but mildly,
  When he demeaned himself rough, rude, and
    wildly.
  Why bear you these rebukes and answer not?
ADRIANA. She did betray me to my own reproof.   90
  Good people, enter and lay hold on him.
ABBESS. No, not a creature enters in my house.
ADRIANA. Then, let your servants bring my husband
  forth.
ABBESS. Neither. He took this place for sanctuary,
  And it shall privilege him from your hands
  Till I have brought him to his wits again,
  Or lose my labour in assaying it.
ADRIANA. I will attend my husband, be his nurse,
  Diet his sickness, for it is my office,
  And will have no attorney but myself,   100
  And therefore let me have him home with me.
ABBESS. Be patient, for I will not let him stir
  Till I have used the approvéd means I have,
  With wholesome syrups, drugs, and holy prayers,
  To make of him a formal man again:
  It is a branch and parcel of mine oath,
  A charitable duty of my order,
  Therefore depart, and leave him here with me.
ADRIANA. I will not hence, and leave my husband
  here:
  And ill it doth beseem your holiness   110
  To separate the husband and the wife.
ABBESS. Be quiet and depart, thou shalt not have him.
                                        She goes
LUCIANA. Complain unto the duke of this indignity.
ADRIANA. Come, go, I will fall prostrate at his feet,
  And never rise until my tears and prayers
  Have won his grace to come in person hither,
  And take perforce my husband from the abbess.
MERCHANT. By this, I think, the dial points at five:
  Anon, I'm sure, the duke himself in person
  Comes this way to the melancholy vale;   120

The place of death and sorry execution,
Behind the ditches of the abbey here.
ANGELO. Upon what cause?
MERCHANT. To see a reverend Syracusian merchant,
Who put unluckily into this Bay
Against the laws and statutes of this town,
Beheaded publicly for his offence.
ANGELO. See, where they come, we will behold his
death.
LUCIANA. Kneel to the duke before he pass the abbey.

Enter the Duke of Ephesus, Ægeon the merchant of Syracuse, bareheaded, with the headsman and other officers

DUKE. Yet once again proclaim it publicly, 130
If any friend will pay the sum for him,
He shall not die—so much we tender him.
ADRIANA. Justice, most sacred duke, against the abbess!
DUKE. She is a virtuous and a reverend lady.
It cannot be that she hath done thee wrong.
ADRIANA. May it please your grace, Antipholus, my
husband—
Who I made lord of me and all I had,
At your important letters—this ill day
A most outrageous fit of madness took him:
That desp'rately he hurried through the street— 140
With him his bondman all as mad as he—
Doing displeasure to the citizens
By rushing in their houses—bearing thence
Rings, jewels, anything his rage did like.
Once did I get him bound, and sent him home,
Whilst to take order for the wrongs I went,
That here and there his fury had committed.
Anon, I wot not by what strong escape,
He broke from those that had the guard of him,
And with his mad attendant and himself, 150
Each one with ireful passion, with drawn swords,
Met us again and, madly bent on us,
Chased us away: till, raising of more aid,
We came again to bind them. Then they fled
Into this abbey, whither we pursued them;
And here the abbess shuts the gates on us,
And will not suffer us to fetch him out,
Nor send him forth that we may bear him hence.
Therefore, most gracious duke, with thy command,
Let him be brought forth and borne hence for help. 160
DUKE. Long since thy husband served me in my wars;
And I to thee engaged a prince's word,
When thou didst make him master of thy bed,
To do him all the grace and good I could.
Go, some of you, knock at the abbey-gate,
And bid the lady abbess come to me:
I will determine this before I stir.

A servant enters

SERVANT. O mistress, mistress! shift and save yourself.
My master and his man are both broke loose,
Beaten the maids a-row, and bound the doctor, 170
Whose beard they have singed off with brands of
fire,
And ever as it blazed, they threw on him
Great pails of puddled mire to quench the hair;
My master preaches patience to him, and the while
His man with scissors nicks him like a fool:
And, sure, unless you send some present help,
Between them they will kill the conjurer.
ADRIANA. Peace, fool, thy master and his man are here,

And that is false thou dost report to us.
SERVANT. Mistress, upon my life, I tell you true, 180
I have not breathed almost since I did see it.
He cries for you and vows, if he can take you,
To scorch your face, and to disfigure you.

Cries heard from the house

Hark, Hark, I hear him, mistress: fly, be gone.
DUKE. Come, stand by me, fear nothing. Guard with
halberds!

Antipholus and Dromio of Ephesus enter

ADRIANA. Ay me, it is my husband! Witness you,
That he is borne about invisible!
Even now we housed him in the abbey here;
And now he's there, past thought of human reason.
E. ANTIPHOLUS. Justice, most gracious duke! O, grant
me justice, 190
Even for the service that long since I did thee,
When I bestrid thee in the wars, and took
Deep scars to save thy life; even for the blood
That then I lost for thee, now grant me justice.
ÆGEON. Unless the fear of death doth make me dote,
I see my son Antipholus, and Dromio.
E. ANTIPHOLUS. Justice, sweet prince, against that
woman there!
She whom thou gav'st to me to be my wife;
That hath abused and dishonoured me,
Even in the strength and height of injury: 200
Beyond imagination is the wrong
That she this day hath shameless thrown on me.
DUKE. Discover how, and thou shalt find me just.
E. ANTIPHOLUS. This day, great duke, she shut the
doors upon me,
While she with harlots feasted in my house.
DUKE. A grievous fault. Say, woman, didst thou so?
ADRIANA. No, my good lord. Myself, he, and my sister
To-day did dine together: so befall my soul
As this is false he burdens me withal.
LUCIANA. Ne'er may I look on day, nor sleep on night, 210
But she tells to your highness simple truth.
ANGELO. O perjured woman! They are both forsworn.
In this the madman justly chargeth them.
E. ANTIPHOLUS. My liege, I am advisèd what I say—
Neither disturbed with the effect of wine,
Nor heady-rash, provoked with raging ire,
Albeit my wrongs might make one wiser mad.
This woman locked me out this day from dinner;
That goldsmith there, were he not packed with her,
Could witness it—for he was with me then, 220
Who parted with me to go fetch a chain,
Promising to bring it to the Porpentine,
Where Balthazar and I did dine together.
Our dinner done, and he not coming thither,
I went to seek him. In the street I met him,
And in his company that gentleman.
There did this perjured goldsmith swear me down
That I this day of him received the chain,
Which, God he knows, I saw not; for the which,
He did arrest me with an officer. 230
I did obey, and sent my peasant home
For certain ducats: he with none returned.
Then fairly I bespoke the officer
To go in person with me to my house.
By th' way we met
My wife, her sister, and a rabble more

Of vile confederates. Along with them
They brought one Pinch, a hungry lean-faced
   villain;
A mere anatomy, a mountebank,
A threadbare juggler, and a fortune-teller,   240
A needy, hollow-eyed, sharp-looking wretch;
A living-dead man. This pernicious slave,
Forsooth, took on him as a conjurer;
And, gazing in mine eyes, feeling my pulse,
And with no face, as 'twere, out-facing me,
Cries out, I was possessed. Then all together
They fell upon me, bound me, bore me thence,
And in a dark and dankish vault at home
There left me and my man, both bound together—
Till gnawing with my teeth my bonds in sunder,   250
I gained my freedom; and immediately
Ran hither to your grace, whom I beseech
To give me ample satisfaction
For these deep shames and great indignities.

ANGELO. My lord, in truth, thus far I witness with him;
   That he dined not at home, but was locked out.

DUKE. But had he such a chain of thee, or no?

ANGELO. He had, my lord, and when he ran in here,
   These people saw the chain about his neck.

MERCHANT. Besides, I will be sworn these ears of mine   260
   Heard you confess you had the chain of him,
   After you first forswore it on the mart,
   And, thereupon, I drew my sword on you:
   And then you fled into this abbey here,
   From whence, I think, you are come by miracle.

E. ANTIPHOLUS. I never came within these abbey-walls,
   Nor ever didst thou draw thy sword on me:
   I never saw the chain, so help me Heaven:
   And this is false you burden me withal.

DUKE. Why, what an intricate impeach is this!   270
   I think you all have drunk of Circe's cup:
   If here you housed him, here he would have been;
   If he were mad, he would not plead so coldly:
   You say he dined at home, the goldsmith here
   Denies that saying. Sirrah, what say you?

E. DROMIO. Sir, he dined with her there at the
   Porpentine.

COURTESAN. He did, and from my finger snatched that
   ring.

E. ANTIPHOLUS. 'Tis true, my liege, this ring I had of
   her.

DUKE. Saw'st thou him enter at the abbey here?

COURTESAN. As sure, my liege, as I do see your grace.   280

DUKE. Why, this is strange. Go call the abbess hither.
   I think you are all mated, or stark mad.

An attendant enters the abbey-gate

ÆGEON. Most mighty duke, vouchsafe me speak a
   word:
   Haply I see a friend will save my life,
   And pay the sum that may deliver me.

DUKE. Speak freely, Syracusian, what thou wilt.

ÆGEON. Is not your name, sir, called Antipholus?
   And is not that your bondman Dromio?

E. DROMIO. Within this hour I was his bondman, sir,
   But he, I thank him, gnawed in two my cords.   290
   Now am I Dromio, and his man, unbound.

ÆGEON. I am sure you both of you remember me.

E. DROMIO. Ourselves we do remember, sir, by you:
   For lately we were bound, as you are now.
   You are not Pinch's patient, are you, sir?

ÆGEON. Why look you strange on me? you know me
   well.

E. ANTIPHOLUS. I never saw you in my life till now.

ÆGEON. O, grief hath changed me since you saw me
   last,
   And careful hours with Time's deformèd hand
   Have written strange defeatures in my face: 300
   But tell me yet, dost thou not know my voice?

E. ANTIPHOLUS. Neither.

ÆGEON. Dromio, nor thou?

E. DROMIO.   No, trust me, sir, nor I.

ÆGEON. I am sure thou dost!

E. DROMIO. Ay, sir, but I am sure I do not—and whatsoever a man denies, you are now bound to believe
   him.

ÆGEON. Not know my voice! O, time's extremity,
   Hast thou so cracked and splitted my poor tongue
   In seven short years, that here my only son   310
   Knows not my feeble key of untuned cares?
   Though now this grainèd face of mine be hid
   In sap-consuming winter's drizzled snow,
   And all the conduits of my blood froze up,
   Yet hath my night of life some memory:
   My wasting lamps some fading glimmer left:
   My dull deaf ears a little use to hear:
   All these old witnesses—I cannot err—
   Tell me thou art my son Antipholus.

E. ANTIPHOLUS. I never saw my father in my life.   320

ÆGEON. But seven years since, in Syracusa, boy,
   Thou know'st we parted. But, perhaps, my son,
   Thou sham'st to acknowledge me in misery.

E. ANTIPHOLUS. The duke and all that know me in the
   city
   Can witness with me that it is not so.
   I ne'er saw Syracusa in my life.

DUKE. I tell thee, Syracusian, twenty years
   Have I been patron to Antipholus,
   During which time he ne'er saw Syracusa:
   I see thy age and dangers make thee dote.   330

*Enter the Abbess, Antipholus of Syracuse and Dromio of
Syracuse*

ABBESS. Most mighty duke, behold a man much
   wronged.   *All gather to see them*

ADRIANA. I see two husbands, or mine eyes deceive me.

DUKE. One of these men is Genius to the other:
   And so of these, which is the natural man,
   And which the spirit? Who deciphers them?

S. DROMIO. I, sir, am Dromio—command him away.

E. DROMIO. I, sir, am Dromio—pray let me stay.

S. ANTIPHOLUS. Ægeon art thou not? or else his ghost?

S. DROMIO. O, my old master! who hath bound him
   here?

ABBESS. Whoever bound him, I will loose his bonds,   340
   And gain a husband by his liberty.
   Speak, old Ægeon, if thou beest the man
   That hadst a wife once called Æmilia,
   That bore thee at a burden two fair sons!
   O, if thou beest the same Ægeon, speak;
   And speak unto the same Æmilia.

DUKE. Why, here begins his morning story right:
   These two Antipholuses, these two so like,
   And these two Dromios, one in semblance—
   Besides her urging of her wreck at sea—   350
   These are the parents to these children,
   Which accidentally are met together.

ÆGEON. If I dream not, thou art Æmilia.
If thou art she, tell me where is that son
That floated with thee on the fatal raft?

ABBESS. By men of Epidamnum, he and I
And the twin Dromio, all were taken up;
But by and by rude fishermen of Corinth
By force took Dromio and my son from them,
And me they left with those of Epidamnum.   360
What then became of them, I cannot tell;
I to this fortune that you see me in.

DUKE [to S. Antipholus]. Antipholus, thou cam'st from
Corinth first.

S. ANTIPHOLUS. No, sir, not I. I came from Syracuse.

DUKE. Stay, stand apart—I know not which is which.

E. ANTIPHOLUS. I came from Corinth, my most
gracious lord.

E. DROMIO. And I with him.

E. ANTIPHOLUS. Brought to this town by that most
famous warrior,
Duke Menaphon, your most renownéd uncle.

ADRIANA. Which of you two did dine with me to-day? 370

S. ANTIPHOLUS. I, gentle mistress.

ADRIANA.   And are not you my husband?

E. ANTIPHOLUS. No, I say nay to that.

S. ANTIPHOLUS. And so do I, yet did she call me so:
And this fair gentlewoman, her sister here,
Did call me brother. What I told you then,
I hope I shall have leisure to make good,
If this be not a dream I see and hear.

ANGELO. That is the chain, sir, which you had of me.

S. ANTIPHOLUS. I think it be, sir. I deny it not.

E. ANTIPHOLUS. And you, sir, for this chain arrested
me.   380

ANGELO. I think I did, sir. I deny it not.

ADRIANA. I sent you money, sir, to be your bail,
By Dromio—but I think he brought it not.

E. DROMIO. No, none by me.

S. ANTIPHOLUS. This purse of ducats I received from
you,
And Dromio my man did bring them me:
I see we still did meet each other's man,
And I was ta'en for him, and he for me,
And thereupon these errors are arose.

E. ANTIPHOLUS. These ducats pawn I for my father
here.   390

DUKE. It shall not need, thy father hath his life.

COURTESAN. Sir, I must have that diamond from you.

E. ANTIPHOLUS. There, take it, and much thanks for my
good cheer.

ABBESS. Renownéd duke, vouchsafe to take the pains
To go with us into the abbey here,
And hear at large discourséd all our fortunes:
And all that are assembled in this place,
That by this sympathizéd one day's error
Have suffered wrong, go, keep us company,   400
And we shall make full satisfaction.
Thirty-three years have I but gone in travail
Of you, my sons—and till this present hour
My heavy burden ne'er deliveréd.
The duke, my husband, and my children both,
And you the calendars of their nativity,
Go to a gossips' feast, and joy with me
After so long grief such Nativity!

DUKE. With all my heart I'll gossip at this feast.
                All go except the four brothers

S. DROMIO. Master, shall I fetch your stuff from
shipboard?

E. ANTIPHOLUS. Dromio, what stuff of mine hast thou
embarked?   410

S. DROMIO. Your goods that lay at host, sir, in the
Centaur.

S. ANTIPHOLUS. He speaks to me. I am your master,
Dromio.
Come, go with us, we'll look to that anon.
Embrace thy brother there, rejoice with him.
                Antipholus of Syracuse and
                Antipholus of Ephesus go

S. DROMIO. There is a fat friend at your master's house,
That kitchened me for you to-day at dinner:
She now shall be my sister, not my wife.

E. DROMIO. Methinks you are my glass, and not my
brother:
I see by you I am a sweet-faced youth.
Will you walk in to see their gossiping?   420

S. DROMIO. Not I, sir, you are my elder.

E. DROMIO. That's a question—how shall we try it?

S. DROMIO. We'll draw cuts for the senior—till then,
lead thou first.

E. DROMIO. Nay, then thus:
We came into the world like brother and brother:
And now let's go hand in hand, not one before
another.
                             They go

Much Ado About Nothing

The scene: Messina

CHARACTERS IN THE PLAY

DON PEDRO, *Prince of Arragon*
DON JOHN, *his bastard brother*
CLAUDIO, *a young lord of Florence*
BENEDICK, *a young lord of Padua*
LEONATO, *governor of Messina*
ANTONIO, *an old man, his brother*
BALTHAZAR, *a singer in the service of Don Pedro*
BORACHIO }
CONRADE } *followers of Don John*
A Messenger
FRIAR FRANCIS
DOGBERRY, *a constable*

VERGES, *a headborough*
First Watchman
Second Watchman
A Sexton
A Boy
A Lord
HERO, *daughter to Leonato*
BEATRICE, *niece to Leonato*
MARGARET }
URSULA } *waiting-gentlewomen to Hero*
Antonio's son, musicians, watchmen, attendants, etc.

Much Ado About Nothing

ACT 1

Scene 1: *Before the house of Leonato*

*Leonato, governor of Messina, Hero, his daughter, and
Beatrice, his niece, with a messenger*

LEONATO. I learn in this letter that Don Pedro of
Arragon comes this night to Messina.

MESSENGER. He is very near by this. He was not three
leagues off when I left him.

LEONATO. How many gentlemen have you lost in this
action?

MESSENGER. But few of any sort, and none of name.

LEONATO. A victory is twice itself when the achiever
brings home full numbers. I find here that Don 10
Pedro hath bestowed much honour on a young
Florentine called Claudio.

MESSENGER. Much deserved on his part, and equally
remembered by Don Pedro. He hath borne himself
beyond the promise of his age, doing in the figure
of a lamb the feats of a lion. He hath indeed better
bettered expectation than you must expect of me to
tell you how.

LEONATO. He hath an uncle here in Messina will be
very much glad of it.

MESSENGER. I have already delivered him letters, and 20
there appears much joy in him—even so much, that
joy could not show itself modest enough without a
badge of bitterness.

LEONATO. Did he break out into tears?

MESSENGER. In great measure.

LEONATO. A kind overflow of kindness. There are no
faces truer than those that are so washed. How much
better is it to weep at joy than to joy at weeping!

BEATRICE. I pray you, is Signior Mountanto returned
from the wars or no? 30

MESSENGER. I know none of that name, lady. There
was none such in the army of any sort.

LEONATO. What is he that you ask for, niece?

HERO. My cousin means Signior Benedick of Padua.

MESSENGER. O, he's returned, and as pleasant as ever
he was.

BEATRICE. He set up his bills here in Messina and
challenged Cupid at the flight, and my uncle's fool
reading the challenge subscribed for Cupid, and
challenged him at the birdbolt. I pray you, how 40
many hath he killed and eaten in these wars? But
how many hath he killed? for indeed I promised to
eat all of his killing.

LEONATO. Faith, niece, you tax Signior Benedick too
much—but he'll be meet with you, I doubt it not.

MESSENGER. He hath done good service, lady, in these
wars.

BEATRICE. You had musty victual, and he hath holp
to eat it. He is a very valiant trencher-man, he hath
an excellent stomach. 50

MESSENGER. And a good soldier too, lady.

BEATRICE. And a good soldier to a lady, but what is
he to a lord?

MESSENGER. A lord to a lord, a man to a man—stuffed
with all honourable virtues.

BEATRICE. It is so, indeed. He is no less than a stuffed
man, but for the stuffing—well, we are all mortal.

LEONATO. You must not, sir, mistake my niece. There
is a kind of merry war betwixt Signior Benedick
and her. They never meet but there's a skirmish of 60
wit between them.

BEATRICE. Alas, he gets nothing by that. In our last
conflict, four of his five wits went halting off, and
now is the whole man governed with one—so that
if he have wit enough to keep himself warm, let him
bear it for a difference between himself and his
horse, for it is all the wealth that he hath left to be
known a reasonable creature. Who is his companion
now? he hath every month a new sworn brother.

MESSENGER. Is't possible? 70

BEATRICE. Very easily possible. He wears his faith but
as the fashion of his hat, it ever changes with the
next block.

MESSENGER. I see, lady, the gentleman is not in your
books.

BEATRICE. No, an he were, I would burn my study.
But I pray you who is his companion? Is there no
young squarer now that will make a voyage with
him to the devil?

MESSENGER. He is most in the company of the right 80
noble Claudio.

BEATRICE. O Lord, he will hang upon him like a disease
—he is sooner caught than the pestilence, and the
taker runs presently mad. God help the noble
Claudio. If he have caught the Benedict, it will cost
him a thousand pound ere a' be cured.

MESSENGER. I will hold friends with you, lady.

BEATRICE. Do, good friend.

LEONATO. You will never run mad, niece.

BEATRICE. No, not till a hot January. 90

MESSENGER. Don Pedro is approached.

*Enter Don Pedro, Claudio, Benedick, Balthazar and John
the Bastard*

DON PEDRO. Good Signior Leonato, are you come to
meet your trouble? the fashion of the world is to
avoid cost, and you encounter it.

LEONATO. Never came trouble to my house in the
likeness of your grace. For trouble being gone, comfort should remain: but when you depart from me,
sorrow abides and happiness takes his leave.

DON PEDRO. You embrace your charge too willingly.
I think this is your daughter. 100

LEONATO. Her mother hath many times told me so.

BENEDICK. Were you in doubt, sir, that you asked her?

LEONATO. Signior Benedick, no—for then were you a
child.

DON PEDRO. You have it full, Benedick—we may
guess by this what you are, being a man. Truly the
lady fathers herself. Be happy, lady, for you are like
an honourable father.

BENEDICK. If Signior Leonato be her father, she would
not have his head on her shoulders for all Messina, 110
as like him as she is.

BEATRICE. I wonder that you will still be talking, Signior Benedick—nobody marks you.

BENEDICK. What, my dear Lady Disdain! are you yet living?

BEATRICE. Is it possible Disdain should die, while she hath such meet food to feed it as Signior Benedick? Courtesy itself must convert to disdain, if you come in her presence.

BENEDICK. Then is courtesy a turn-coat. But it is certain I am loved of all ladies, only you excepted: and I would I could find in my heart that I had not a hard heart, for truly I love none.

BEATRICE. A dear happiness to women—they would else have been troubled with a pernicious suitor. I thank God and my cold blood, I am of your humour for that. I had rather hear my dog bark at a crow than a man swear he loves me.

BENEDICK. God keep your ladyship still in that mind, so some gentleman or other shall 'scape a predestinate scratched face.

BEATRICE. Scratching could not make it worse, an 'twere such a face as yours were.

BENEDICK. Well, you are a rare parrot-teacher.

BEATRICE. A bird of my tongue is better than a beast of yours.

BENEDICK. I would my horse had the speed of your tongue, and so good a continuer. But keep your way a God's name—I have done.

BEATRICE. You always end with a jade's trick. I know you of old.

DON PEDRO. That is the sum of all, Leonato. Signior Claudio and Signior Benedick, my dear friend Leonato hath invited you all. I tell him we shall stay here at the least a month, and he heartily prays some occasion may detain us longer. I dare swear he is no hypocrite, but prays from his heart.

LEONATO. If you swear, my lord, you shall not be forsworn. [to Don John] Let me bid you welcome, my lord—being reconciled to the prince your brother. I owe you all duty.

DON JOHN. I thank you. I am not of many words, but I thank you.

LEONATO. Please it your grace lead on?

DON PEDRO. Your hand, Leonato—we will go together. *All depart save Benedick and Claudio*

CLAUDIO. Benedick, didst thou note the daughter of Signior Leonato?

BENEDICK. I noted her not, but I looked on her.

CLAUDIO. Is she not a modest young lady?

BENEDICK. Do you question me as an honest man should do, for my simple true judgement? or would you have me speak after my custom, as being a professed tyrant to their sex?

CLAUDIO. No, I pray thee speak in sober judgement.

BENEDICK. Why, i'faith, methinks she's too low for a high praise, too brown for a fair praise, and too little for a great praise—only this commendation I can afford her, that were she other than she is, she were unhandsome, and being no other but as she is, I do not like her.

CLAUDIO. Thou thinkest I am in sport. I pray thee tell me truly how thou lik'st her.

BENEDICK. Would you buy her, that you inquire after her?

CLAUDIO. Can the world buy such a jewel?

BENEDICK. Yea, and a case to put it into. But speak you this with a sad brow? or do you play the flouting Jack, to tell us Cupid is a good hare-finder, and Vulcan a rare carpenter? Come, in what key shall a man take you to go in the song?

CLAUDIO. In mine eye, she is the sweetest lady that ever I looked on.

BENEDICK. I can see yet without spectacles, and I see no such matter: there's her cousin, an she were not possessed with a fury, exceeds her as much in beauty as the first of May doth the last of December. But I hope you have no intent to turn husband, have you?

CLAUDIO. I would scarce trust myself, though I had sworn the contrary, if Hero would be my wife.

BENEDICK. Is't come to this? In faith hath not the world one man but he will wear his cap with suspicion? Shall I never see a bachelor of threescore again? Go to i'faith, an thou wilt needs thrust thy neck into a yoke, wear the print of it, and sigh away Sundays.

Don Pedro returns

Look, Don Pedro is returned to seek you.

DON PEDRO. What secret hath held you here, that you followed not to Leonato's?

BENEDICK. I would your grace would constrain me to tell.

DON PEDRO. I charge thee on thy allegiance.

BENEDICK. You hear, Count Claudio. I can be secret as a dumb man, I would have you think so—but on my allegiance, mark you this, on my allegiance! He is in love—with who? now that is your grace's part. Mark, how short his answer is—with Hero, Leonato's short daughter.

CLAUDIO. If this were so, so were it uttered.

BENEDICK. Like the old tale, my lord—'it is not so, nor 'twas not so: but indeed, God forbid it should be so.'

CLAUDIO. If my passion change not shortly, God forbid it should be otherwise.

DON PEDRO. Amen, if you love her—for the lady is very well worthy.

CLAUDIO. You speak this to fetch me in, my lord.

DON PEDRO. By my troth, I speak my thought.

CLAUDIO. And in faith, my lord, I spoke mine.

BENEDICK. And by my two faiths and troths, my lord, I spoke mine.

CLAUDIO. That I love her, I feel.

DON PEDRO. That she is worthy, I know.

BENEDICK. That I neither feel how she should be loved, nor know how she should be worthy, is the opinion that fire cannot melt out of me—I will die in it at the stake.

DON PEDRO. Thou wast ever an obstinate heretic in the despite of beauty.

CLAUDIO. And never could maintain his part but in the force of his will.

BENEDICK. That a woman conceived me, I thank her: that she brought me up, I likewise give her most humble thanks: but that I will have a recheat winded in my forehead, or hang my bugle in an invisible baldric, all women shall pardon me. Because I will not do them the wrong to mistrust any, I will do myself the right to trust none: and the fine is—for the which I may go the finer—I will live a bachelor.

DON PEDRO. I shall see thee, ere I die, look pale with love.

BENEDICK. With anger, with sickness, or with hunger,

my lord—not with love: prove that ever I lose more blood with love than I will get again with drinking, pick out mine eyes with a ballad-maker's pen, and hang me up at the door of a brothel-house for the sign of blind Cupid.

DON PEDRO. Well, if ever thou dost fall from this faith, thou wilt prove a notable argument.

BENEDICK. If I do, hang me in a bottle like a cat and shoot at me, and he that hits me, let him be clapped on the shoulder and called Adam. 250

DON PEDRO. Well, as time shall try:
'In time the savage bull doth bear the yoke.'

BENEDICK. The savage bull may—but if ever the sensible Benedick bear it, pluck off the bull's horns and set them in my forehead. And let me be vilely painted—and in such great letters as they write, 'Here is good horse to hire,' let them signify under my sign, 'Here you may see Benedick the married man.' 260

CLAUDIO. If this should ever happen, thou wouldst be horn-mad.

DON PEDRO. Nay, if Cupid have not spent all his quiver in Venice, thou wilt quake for this shortly.

BENEDICK. I look for an earthquake too then.

DON PEDRO. Well, you will temporize with the hours. In the meantime, good Signior Benedick, repair to Leonato's, commend me to him, and tell him I will not fail him at supper—for indeed he hath made great preparation. 270

BENEDICK. I have almost matter enough in me for such an embassage, and so I commit you—

CLAUDIO. To the tuition of God: from my house if I had it—

DON PEDRO. The sixth of July: your loving friend, Benedick.

BENEDICK. Nay, mock not, mock not. The body of your discourse is sometime guarded with fragments, and the guards are but slightly basted on neither. Ere you flout old ends any further, examine your conscience—and so I leave you. *He goes* 280

CLAUDIO. My liege, your highness now may do me good.

DON PEDRO. My love is thine to teach. Teach it but how,
And thou shalt see how apt it is to learn
Any hard lesson that may do thee good.

CLAUDIO. Hath Leonato any son, my lord?

DON PEDRO. No child but Hero, she's his only heir:
Dost thou affect her, Claudio?

CLAUDIO.   O my lord,
When you went onward on this ended action, 290
I looked upon her with a soldier's eye,
That liked, but had a rougher task in hand
Than to drive liking to the name of love:
But now I am returned, and that war-thoughts
Have left their places vacant, in their rooms
Come thronging soft and delicate desires,
All prompting me how fair young Hero is,
Saying I liked her ere I went to wars.

DON PEDRO. Thou wilt be like a lover presently,
And tire the hearer with a book of words.
If thou dost love fair Hero, cherish it, 300
And I will break with her, and with her father,
And thou shalt have her. Was't not to this end
That thou began'st to twist so fine a story?

CLAUDIO. How sweetly you do minister to love,

That know love's grief by his complexion!
But lest my liking might too sudden seem,
I would have salved it with a longer treatise.

DON PEDRO. What need the bridge much broader than the flood?
The fairest grant is the necessity:
Look, what will serve is fit: 'tis once, thou lovest, 310
And I will fit thee with the remedy.
I know we shall have revelling to-night—
I will assume thy part in some disguise,
And tell fair Hero I am Claudio,
And in her bosom I'll unclasp my heart,
And take her hearing prisoner with the force
And strong encounter of my amorous tale:
Then after to her father will I break—
And the conclusion is, she shall be thine.
In practice let us put it presently. *They leave* 320

Scene 2: *The hall of Leonato's house*

Enter Leonato and Antonio

LEONATO. How now brother, where is my cousin your son? Hath he provided this music?

ANTONIO. He is very busy about it. But brother, I can tell you strange news that you yet dreamt not of.

LEONATO. Are they good?

ANTONIO. As the event stamps them, but they have a good cover: they show well outward. The prince and Count Claudio, walking in a thick-pleached alley in mine orchard, were thus much overheard by a man of mine: the prince discovered to Claudio 10 that he loved my niece your daughter, and meant to acknowledge it this night in a dance—and if he found her accordant, he meant to take the present time by the top and instantly break with you of it.

LEONATO. Hath the fellow any wit that told you this?

ANTONIO. A good sharp fellow. I will send for him, and question him yourself.

LEONATO. No, no, we will hold it as a dream till it appear itself: but I will acquaint my daughter withal, that she may be the better prepared for an answer, 20 if peradventure this be true. Go you and tell her of it. [*Antonio goes out at one door; his son enters at another, followed by a musician*] Cousin, you know what you have to do—O, I cry you mercy friend, go you with me and I will use your skill. Good cousin have a care this busy time. *They go*

Scene 3

Enter Don John and Conrade

CONRADE. What the good-year, my lord! why are you thus out of measure sad?

DON JOHN. There is no measure in the occasion that breeds, therefore the sadness is without limit.

CONRADE. You should hear reason.

DON JOHN. And when I have heard it, what blessing brings it?

CONRADE. If not a present remedy, at least a patient sufferance.

DON JOHN. I wonder that thou—being as thou say'st 10 thou art born under Saturn—goest about to apply a moral medicine to a mortifying mischief. I cannot hide what I am: I must be sad when I have cause, and smile at no man's jests; eat when I have stomach, and wait for no man's leisure; sleep when I am drowsy, and tend on no man's business; laugh when I am merry, and claw no man in his humour.

CONRADE. Yea, but you must not make the full show of this till you may do it without controlment. You have of late stood out against your brother, and he 20 hath ta'en you newly into his grace, where it is impossible you should take true root but by the fair weather that you make yourself. It is needful that you frame the season for your own harvest.

DON JOHN. I had rather be a canker in a hedge than a rose in his grace, and it better fits my blood to be disdained of all than to fashion a carriage to rob love from any: in this, though I cannot be said to be a flattering honest man, it must not be denied but I am a plain-dealing villain. I am trusted with a 30 muzzle and enfranchised with a clog—therefore I have decreed not to sing in my cage. If I had my mouth, I would bite: if I had my liberty, I would do my liking: in the meantime, let me be that I am, and seek not to alter me.

CONRADE. Can you make no use of your discontent?

DON JOHN. I make all use of it, for I use it only. Who comes here?

Borachio enters

What news, Borachio?

BORACHIO. I came yonder from a great supper. The 40 prince your brother is royally entertained by Leonato, and I can give you intelligence of an intended marriage.

DON JOHN. Will it serve for any model to build mischief on? What is he for a fool that betroths himself to unquietness?

BORACHIO. Marry, it is your brother's right hand.

DON JOHN. Who, the most exquisite Claudio?

BORACHIO. Even he.

DON JOHN. A proper squire! and who, and who, which 50 way looks he?

BORACHIO. Marry, on Hero the daughter and heir of Leonato.

DON JOHN. A very forward March-chick! How came you to this?

BORACHIO. Being entertained for a perfumer, as I was smoking a musty room, comes me the prince and Claudio, hand in hand in sad conference: I whipt me behind the arras, and there heard it agreed upon that the prince should woo Hero for himself, and having 60 obtained her, give her to Count Claudio.

DON JOHN. Come, come, let us thither—this may prove food to my displeasure. That young start-up hath all the glory of my overthrow: if I can cross him any way, I bless myself every way. You are both sure, and will you assist me?

CONRADE. To the death, my lord.

DON JOHN. Let us to the great supper—their cheer is the greater that I am subdued. Would the cook were o' my mind. Shall we go prove what's to be 70 done?

BORACHIO. We'll wait upon your lordship.

They leave

ACT 2
Scene 1

Leonato, Antonio, Hero, Beatrice, Margaret, Ursula, and others of Leonato's household

LEONATO. Was not Count John here at supper?

ANTONIO. I saw him not.

BEATRICE. How tartly that gentleman looks. I never can see him but I am heart-burned an hour after.

HERO. He is of a very melancholy disposition.

BEATRICE. He were an excellent man that were made just in the mid-way between him and Benedick. The one is too like an image and says nothing, and the other too like my lady's eldest son, evermore tattling. 10

LEONATO. Then half Signior Benedick's tongue in Count John's mouth, and half Count John's melancholy in Signior Benedick's face—

BEATRICE. With a good leg and a good foot, uncle, and money enough in his purse, such a man would win any woman in the world if a' could get her good will.

LEONATO. By my troth, niece, thou wilt never get thee a husband, if thou be so shrewd of thy tongue.

ANTONIO. In faith, she's too curst. 20

BEATRICE. Too curst is more than curst. I shall lessen God's sending that way, for it is said, 'God sends a curst cow short horns'—but to a cow too curst he sends none.

LEONATO. So, by being too curst, God will send you no horns?

BEATRICE. Just, if he send me no husband—for the which blessing I am at him upon my knees every morning and evening. Lord! I could not endure a husband with a beard on his face—I had rather lie 30 in the woollen!

LEONATO. You may light on a husband that hath no beard.

BEATRICE. What should I do with him? dress him in my apparel and make him my waiting-gentlewoman? He that hath a beard is more than a youth; and he that hath no beard is less than a man: and he that is more than a youth is not for me, and he that is less than a man I am not for him. Therefore I will even take sixpence in earnest of the bear'ard 40 and lead his apes into hell.

LEONATO. Well then, go you into hell?

BEATRICE. No—but to the gate, and there will the devil meet me like an old cuckold with horns on his head, and say, 'Get you to heaven, Beatrice, get you to heaven—here's no place for you maids.' So deliver I up my apes, and away to Saint Peter: for the heavens, he shows me where the bachelors sit, and there live we as merry as the day is long. 50

ANTONIO [*to Hero*]. Well niece, I trust you will be ruled by your father.

BEATRICE. Yes faith, it is my cousin's duty to make curtsy, and say, 'Father, as it please you'. But yet for all that, cousin, let him be a handsome fellow, or else make another curtsy, and say, 'Father, as it please me.'

LEONATO. Well, niece, I hope to see you one day fitted with a husband.

BEATRICE. Not till God make men of some other 60 mettle than earth. Would it not grieve a woman to be over-mastered with a piece of valiant dust? to make an account of her life to a clod of wayward marl? No, uncle, I'll none: Adam's sons are my brethren, and truly I hold it a sin to match in my kindred.

LEONATO. Daughter, remember what I told you. If the

prince do solicit you in that kind, you know your answer.

BEATRICE. The fault will be in the music, cousin, if 70 you be not wooed in good time: if the prince be too important, tell him there is measure in every thing, and so dance out the answer. For hear me, Hero—wooing, wedding, and repenting, is as a Scotch jig, a measure, and a cinque-pace: the first suit is hot and hasty like a Scotch jig, and full as fantastical; the wedding mannerly-modest, as a measure, full of state and ancientry; and then comes Repentance, and with his bad legs falls into the cinque-pace faster and faster, till he sink into his 80 grave.

LEONATO. Cousin, you apprehend passing shrewdly.

BEATRICE. I have a good eye, uncle—I can see a church by daylight.

LEONATO. The revellers are ent'ring, brother. Make good room.   *They put on their masks*

Enter Don Pedro, Claudio, Benedick, Don John, Borachio and others of Don Pedro's party also masked

DON PEDRO. Lady, will you walk a bout with your friend?

HERO. So you walk softly and look sweetly and say nothing, I am yours for the walk—and especially 90 when I walk away.

DON PEDRO. With me in your company?

HERO. I may say so when I please.

DON PEDRO. And when please you to say so?

HERO. When I like your favour, for God defend the lute should be like the case!

DON PEDRO. My visor is Philemon's roof—within the house is Jove.

HERO. Why, then your visor should be thatched.

DON PEDRO.   Speak low if you speak love.
            They pass on round the room

BORACHIO. Well, I would you did like me.   100

MARGARET. So would not I for your own sake, for I have many ill qualities.

BORACHIO. Which is one?

MARGARET. I say my prayers aloud.

BORACHIO. I love you the better, the hearers may cry Amen.

MARGARET. God match me with a good dancer.

BORACHIO. Amen.

MARGARET. And God keep him out of my sight when the dance is done: answer, clerk.   110

BORACHIO. No more words—the clerk is answered.
            They pass on round the room

URSULA. I know you well enough—you are Signior Antonio.

ANTONIO. At a word, I am not.

URSULA. I know you by the waggling of your head.

ANTONIO. To tell you true, I counterfeit him.

URSULA. You could never do him so ill-well, unless you were the very man: here's his dry hand up and down—you are he, you are he.

ANTONIO. At a word, I am not.   120

URSULA. Come, come, do you think I do not know you by your excellent wit? Can virtue hide itself? Go to, mum, you are he. Graces will appear, and there's an end.   *They pass on round the room*

BEATRICE. Will you not tell me who told you so?

BENEDICK. No, you shall pardon me.

BEATRICE. Nor will you not tell me who you are?

BENEDICK. Not now.

BEATRICE. That I was disdainful, and that I had my good wit out of the 'Hundred Merry Tales'. Well, 130 this was Signior Benedick that said so.

BENEDICK. What's he?

BEATRICE. I am sure you know him well enough.

BENEDICK. Not I, believe me.

BEATRICE. Did he never make you laugh?

BENEDICK. I pray you, what is he?

BEATRICE. Why, he is the prince's jester, a very dull fool—only his gift is in devising impossible slanders. None but libertines delight in him, and the commendation is not in his wit but in his villainy, for 140 he both pleases men and angers them, and then they laugh at him and beat him. I am sure he is in the fleet—I would he had boarded me.

BENEDICK. When I know the gentleman, I'll tell him what you say.

BEATRICE. Do, do. He'll but break a comparison or two on me, which peradventure, not marked or not laughed at, strikes him into melancholy—and then there's a partridge wing saved, for the fool will eat no supper that night. We must follow the leaders. 150

BENEDICK. In every good thing.

BEATRICE. Nay, if they lead to any ill, I will leave them at the next turning.

*The musicians strike up,
and the couples dance;
at the end all go except for
Don John, Borachio and Claudio*

DON JOHN. Sure my brother is amorous on Hero, and hath withdrawn her father to break with him about it ... The ladies follow her, and but one visor remains.

BORACHIO. And that is Claudio. I know him by his bearing.

DON JOHN. Are not you Signior Benedick?

CLAUDIO. You know me well—I am he.   160

DON JOHN. Signior, you are very near my brother in his love. He is enamoured on Hero. I pray you, dissuade him from her, she is no equal for his birth. You may do the part of an honest man in it.

CLAUDIO. How know you he loves her?

DON JOHN. I heard him swear his affection.

BORACHIO. So did I too, and he swore he would marry her to-night.

DON JOHN. Come, let us to the banquet.
            He and Borachio go

CLAUDIO. Thus answer I in name of Benedick,   170
But hear these ill news with the ears of Claudio ...
'Tis certain so—the prince wooes for himself.
Friendship is constant in all other things
Save in the office and affairs of love:
Therefore all hearts in love use their own
     tongues....
Let every eye negotiate for itself,
And trust no agent: for beauty is a witch
Against whose charms faith melteth into blood:
This is an accident of hourly proof,
Which I mistrusted not ... Farewell, therefore,
Hero.   180

Benedick returns

BENEDICK. Count Claudio?

CLAUDIO. Yea, the same.

BENEDICK. Come, will you go with me?

CLAUDIO. Whither?

BENEDICK. Even to the next willow, about your own business, county. What fashion will you wear the garland of? about your neck, like an usurer's chain? or under your arm, like a lieutenant's scarf? You must wear it one way, for the prince hath got your Hero.   190

CLAUDIO. I wish him joy of her.

BENEDICK. Why, that's spoken like an honest drover—so they sell bullocks: but did you think the prince would have served you thus?

CLAUDIO. I pray you, leave me.

BENEDICK. Ho, now you strike like the blind man. 'Twas the boy that stole your meat, and you'll beat the post.

CLAUDIO. If it will not be, I'll leave you.   *He goes*

BENEDICK. Alas, poor hurt fowl—now will he creep   200
into sedges. But, that my Lady Beatrice should know me, and not know me. The prince's fool! ha, it may be I go under that title because I am merry: yea, but so I am apt to do myself wrong: I am not so reputed—it is the base, the bitter disposition of Beatrice that puts the world into her person, and so gives me out. Well, I'll be revenged as I may.

Don Pedro returns with Leonato and Hero; Leonato and Hero talk apart

DON PEDRO. Now, signior, where's the count? Did you see him?

BENEDICK. Troth, my lord, I have played the part of   210
Lady Fame. I found him here as melancholy as a lodge in a warren. I told him, and I think I told him true, that your grace had got the good will of this young lady—and I off'red him my company to a willow tree, either to make him a garland, as being forsaken, or to bind him up a rod, as being worthy to be whipped.

DON PEDRO. To be whipped! What's his fault?

BENEDICK. The flat transgression of a school-boy, who, being overjoyed with finding a bird's-nest,   220
shows it his companion, and he steals it.

DON PEDRO. Wilt thou make a trust a transgression? The transgression is in the stealer.

BENEDICK. Yet it had not been amiss the rod had been made, and the garland too—for the garland he might have worn himself, and the rod he might have bestowed on you, who, as I take it, have stolen his bird's-nest.

DON PEDRO. I will but teach them to sing, and restore them to the owner.   230

BENEDICK. If their singing answer your saying, by my faith you say honestly.

DON PEDRO. The Lady Beatrice hath a quarrel to you. The gentleman that danced with her told her she is much wronged by you.

BENEDICK. O, she misused me past the endurance of a block: an oak but with one green leaf on it would have answered her: my very visor began to assume life and scold with her. She told me, not thinking I had been myself, that I was the prince's jester, that   240
I was duller than a great thaw—huddling jest upon jest with such impossible conveyance upon me, that I stood like a man at a mark, with a whole army shooting at me. She speaks poniards, and every word stabs: if her breath were as terrible as her terminations, there were no living near her, she would infect to the north star. I would not marry her, though she were endowed with all that Adam had left him before he transgressed. She would have made Hercules have turned spit, yea, and have cleft   250
his club to make the fire too. Come, talk not of her. You shall find her the infernal Ate in good apparel—I would to God some scholar would conjure her, for certainly, while she is here, a man may live as quiet in hell as in a sanctuary—and people sin upon purpose because they would go thither, so indeed all disquiet, horror, and perturbation follow her.

Claudio and Beatrice enter

DON PEDRO. Look, here she comes.

BENEDICK. Will your grace command me any service to the world's end? I will go on the slightest errand   260
now to the Antipodes that you can devise to send me on: I will fetch you a tooth-picker now from the furthest inch of Asia: bring you the length of Prester John's foot: fetch you a hair off the great Cham's beard: do you any embassage to the Pigmies—rather than hold three words' conference with this harpy. You have no employment for me?

DON PEDRO. None, but to desire your good company.

BENEDICK. O God, sir, here's a dish I love not—I cannot endure my Lady Tongue.   *He goes*   270

DON PEDRO. Come, lady, come, you have lost the heart of Signior Benedick.

BEATRICE. Indeed my lord, he lent it me awhile, and I gave him use for it—a double heart for his single one. Marry, once before he won it of me with false dice, therefore your grace may well say I have lost it.

DON PEDRO. You have put him down, lady, you have put him down.

BEATRICE. So I would not he should do me, my lord, lest I should prove the mother of fools. I have   280
brought Count Claudio, whom you sent me to seek.

DON PEDRO. Why, how now count, wherefore are you sad?

CLAUDIO. Not sad, my lord.

DON PEDRO. How then? Sick?

CLAUDIO. Neither, my lord.

BEATRICE. The count is neither sad, nor sick, nor merry, nor well: but civil count—civil as an orange, and something of that jealous complexion.

DON PEDRO. I'faith lady, I think your blazon to be   290
true, though I'll be sworn, if he be so, his conceit is false ... Here, Claudio, I have wooed in thy name and fair Hero is won, I have broke with her father and his good will obtained. Name the day of marriage, and God give thee joy.

LEONATO. Count, take of me my daughter, and with her my fortunes: his grace hath made the match, and all grace say Amen to it.

BEATRICE. Speak, count, 'tis your cue.

CLAUDIO. Silence is the perfectest herald of joy—I   300
were but little happy, if I could say how much! Lady, as you are mine, I am yours. I give away myself for you and dote upon the exchange.

BEATRICE. Speak cousin, or, if you cannot, stop his mouth with a kiss, and let not him speak neither.

DON PEDRO. In faith, lady, you have a merry heart.

BEATRICE. Yea, my lord, I thank it—poor fool, it keeps on the windy side of care. My cousin tells him in his ear that he is in her heart.

CLAUDIO. And so she doth, cousin.   310

BEATRICE. Good Lord, for alliance! Thus goes every

one to the world but I, and I am sun-burnt. I may sit
in a corner and cry 'heigh-ho for a husband.'
DON PEDRO. Lady Beatrice, I will get you one.
BEATRICE. I would rather have one of your father's
getting: hath your grace ne'er a brother like you?
Your father got excellent husbands if a maid could
come by them.
DON PEDRO. Will you have me, lady?
BEATRICE. No, my lord, unless I might have another 320
for working-days—your grace is too costly to wear
every day. But I beseech your grace pardon me, I
was born to speak all mirth and no matter.
DON PEDRO. Your silence most offends me, and to be
merry best becomes you, for out o' question you
were born in a merry hour.
BEATRICE. No, sure, my lord, my mother cried—but
then there was a star danced, and under that was I
born. Cousins, God give you joy!
LEONATO. Niece, will you look to those things I told 330
you of?
BEATRICE. I cry you mercy, uncle. By your grace's
pardon.   *She goes*
DON PEDRO. By my troth, a pleasant-spirited lady.
LEONATO. There's little of the melancholy element in
her, my lord. She is never sad but when she sleeps,
and not ever sad then: for I have heard my daughter
say, she hath often dreamt of unhappiness and
waked herself with laughing.
DON PEDRO. She cannot endure to hear tell of a 340
husband.
LEONATO. O, by no means—she mocks all her wooers
out of suit.
DON PEDRO. She were an excellent wife for Benedick.
LEONATO. O Lord, my lord, if they were but a week
married, they would talk themselves mad.
DON PEDRO. County Claudio, when mean you to go
to church?
CLAUDIO. To-morrow, my lord. Time goes on
crutches till love have all his rites.   350
LEONATO. Not till Monday, my dear son, which is
hence a just seven-night—and a time too brief too,
to have all things answer my mind.
DON PEDRO. Come, you shake the head at so long
a breathing—but I warrant thee, Claudio, the time
shall not go dully by us. I will in the interim
undertake one of Hercules' labours, which is, to
bring Signior Benedick and the Lady Beatrice into
a mountain of affection th'one with th'other. I
would fain have it a match—and I doubt not but 360
to fashion it, if you three will but minister such
assistance as I shall give you direction.
LEONATO. My lord, I am for you, though it cost me
ten nights' watchings.
CLAUDIO. And I, my lord.
DON PEDRO. And you too, gentle Hero?
HERO. I will do any modest office, my lord, to help
my cousin to a good husband.
DON PEDRO. And Benedick is not the unhopefullest
husband that I know: thus far can I praise him— 370
he is of a noble strain, of approved valour, and confirmed honesty. I will teach you how to humour
your cousin, that she shall fall in love with Benedick.
And I, with your two helps, will so practise on
Benedick that, in despite of his quick wit and his
queasy stomach, he shall fall in love with Beatrice.
If we can do this, Cupid is no longer an archer,

his glory shall be ours—for we are the only love-
gods. Go in with me, and I will tell you my drift.
                                          They go

Scene 2

Enter Don John and Borachio

DON JOHN. It is so—the Count Claudio shall marry the
daughter of Leonato.
BORACHIO. Yea my lord, but I can cross it.
DON JOHN. And bar, any cross, any impediment will
be medicinable to me. I am sick in displeasure to
him, and whatsoever comes athwart his affection
ranges evenly with mine. How canst thou cross this
marriage?
BORACHIO. Not honestly, my lord—but so covertly
that no dishonesty shall appear in me.   10
DON JOHN. Show me briefly how.
BORACHIO. I think I told your lordship, a year since,
how much I am in the favour of Margaret, the
waiting-gentlewoman to Hero.
DON JOHN. I remember.
BORACHIO. I can, at any unseasonable instant of the
night, appoint her to look out at her lady's chamber-
window.
DON JOHN. What life is in that to be the death of this
marriage?   20
BORACHIO. The poison of that lies in you to temper.
Go you to the prince your brother, spare not to tell
him that he hath wronged his honour in marrying
the renowned Claudio—whose estimation do you
mightily hold up—to a contaminated stale, such a
one as Hero.
DON JOHN. What proof shall I make of that?
BORACHIO. Proof enough to misuse the prince, to vex
Claudio, to undo Hero, and kill Leonato. Look you
for any other issue?   30
DON JOHN. Only to despite them, I will endeavour
any thing.
BORACHIO. Go then, find me a meet hour to draw Don
Pedro and the Count Claudio alone, tell them that
you know that Hero loves me, intend a kind of
zeal both to the prince and Claudio, as in love of
your brother's honour, who hath made this match,
and his friend's reputation, who is thus like to be
cozened with the semblance of a maid. That you
have discovered this they will scarcely believe with- 40
out trial: offer them instances, which shall bear no less
likelihood than to see me at her chamber-window,
hear me call Margaret Hero, hear Margaret term
me Claudio—and bring them to see this the very
night before the intended wedding. For in the meantime I will so fashion the matter that Hero shall
be absent, and there shall appear such seeming truth
of Hero's disloyalty, that jealousy shall be called
assurance, and all the preparation overthrown.
DON JOHN. Grow this to what adverse issue it can, I 50
will put it in practice. Be cunning in the working
this, and thy fee is a thousand ducats.
BORACHIO. Be you constant in the accusation, and my
cunning shall not shame me.
DON JOHN. I will presently go learn their day of
marriage.   *They go*

Scene 3: *Leonato's orchard*

Benedick enters

BENEDICK. Boy!   *A boy runs up*
BOY. Signior.
BENEDICK. In my chamber-window lies a book, bring
it hither to me in the orchard.
BOY. I am here already, sir.
BENEDICK. I know that—but I would have thee hence,
and here again. [*the boy departs*] I do much wonder,
that one man seeing how much another man is a
fool when he dedicates his behaviours to love, will
after he hath laughed at such shallow follies in   10
others, become the argument of his own scorn by
falling in love. And such a man is Claudio. I have
known when there was no music with him but the
drum and the fife, and now had he rather hear the
tabor and the pipe: I have known when he would
have walked ten mile afoot, to see a good armour,
and now will he lie ten nights awake carving the
fashion of a new doublet: he was wont to speak
plain, and to the purpose (like an honest man and a
soldier) and now is he turned orthography—his   20
words are a very fantastical banquet, just so many
strange dishes. May I be so converted, and see with
these eyes? I cannot tell—I think not: I will not be
sworn but love may transform me to an oyster, but
I'll take my oath on it, till he have made an oyster
of me, he shall never make me such a fool. One
woman is fair, yet I am well: another is wise, yet I
am well: another virtuous, yet I am well: but till all
graces be in one woman, one woman shall not come
in my grace. Rich she shall be, that's certain: wise,   30
or I'll none: virtuous, or I'll never cheapen her: fair,
or I'll never look on her: mild, or come not near
me: noble, or not I for an angel: of good discourse,
an excellent musician, and her hair shall be of what
colour it please God. Ha! the prince and Monsieur
Love! I will hide me in the arbour.   *He does so*

*Enter Don Pedro, Leonato, Claudio and Balthazar with
a lute*

DON PEDRO. Come, shall we hear this music?
CLAUDIO. Yea, my good lord. How still the evening is,
As hushed on purpose to grace harmony!
DON PEDRO. See you where Benedick hath hid
himself?   40
CLAUDIO. O very well, my lord: the music ended,
We'll fit the hid-fox with a pennyworth.
DON PEDRO. Come Balthazar, we'll hear that song
again.
BALTHAZAR. O good my lord, tax not so bad a voice
To slander music any more than once.
DON PEDRO. It is the witness still of excellency,
To put a strange face on his own perfection.
I pray thee sing, and let me woo no more.
BALTHAZAR. Because you talk of wooing, I will sing,
Since many a wooer doth commence his suit   50
To her he thinks not worthy, yet he wooes,
Yet will he swear he loves.
DON PEDRO.   Nay, pray thee come,
Or if thou wilt hold longer argument,
Do it in notes.
BALTHAZAR.   Note this before my notes—
There's not a note of mine that's worth the noting.

DON PEDRO. Why these are very crotchets that he
speaks—
Note notes, forsooth, and nothing!
                            Balthazar begins to play
BENEDICK. Now, divine air! now is his soul ravished.
Is it not strange that sheeps' guts should hale souls
out of men's bodies? Well, a horn for my money,   60
when all's done.

BALTHAZAR [*sings*].
    Sigh no more, ladies, sigh no more,
        Men were deceivers ever,
    One foot in sea, and one on shore,
        To one thing constant never.
            Then sigh not so, but let them go,
                And be you blithe and bonny,
            Converting all your sounds of woe
                Into Hey nonny, nonny.

    Sing no more ditties, sing no mo   70
        Of dumps so dull and heavy,
    The fraud of men was ever so,
        Since summer first was leavy.
            Then sigh not so, but let them go,
                And be you blithe and bonny,
            Converting all your sounds of woe
                Into Hey nonny, nonny.

DON PEDRO. By my troth, a good song.
BALTHAZAR. And an ill singer, my lord.
DON PEDRO. Ha, no; no, faith; thou sing'st well enough   80
for a shift.
BENEDICK. An he had been a dog that should have
howled thus, they would have hanged him. And I
pray God his bad voice bode no mischief—I had as
lief have heard the night-raven, come what plague
could have come after it.
DON PEDRO. Yea, marry. Dost thou hear, Balthazar?
I pray thee get us some excellent music: for to-
morrow night we would have it at the Lady Hero's
chamber-window.   90
BALTHAZAR. The best I can, my lord.
DON PEDRO. Do so, farewell.   *Balthazar goes*
Come hither, Leonato. What was it you told me of
today? that your niece Beatrice was in love with
Signior Benedick?
CLAUDIO. O ay, stalk on, stalk on—the fowl sits.
[*aloud*] I did never think that lady would have loved
any man.
LEONATO. No, nor I neither—but most wonderful that
she should so dote on Signior Benedick, whom she   100
hath in all outward behaviours seemed ever to abhor.
BENEDICK. Is't possible? Sits the wind in that corner?
LEONATO. By my troth, my lord, I cannot tell what
to think of it, but that she loves him with an
enraged affection—it is past the infinite of thought.
DON PEDRO. May be she doth but counterfeit.
CLAUDIO. Faith, like enough.
LEONATO. O God! counterfeit? There was never
counterfeit of passion came so near the life of passion
as she discovers it.   110
DON PEDRO. Why, what effects of passion shows she?
CLAUDIO. Bait the hook well—this fish will bite.
LEONATO. What effects, my lord! She will sit you—
You heard my daughter tell you how.
CLAUDIO. She did, indeed.
DON PEDRO. How, how, I pray you! You amaze me.

I would have thought her spirit had been invincible against all assaults of affection.

LEONATO. I would have sworn it had, my lord— especially against Benedick.

BENEDICK. I should think this a gull, but that the white-bearded fellow speaks it: knavery cannot, sure, hide himself in such reverence.

CLAUDIO. He hath ta'en th'infection—hold it up.

DON PEDRO. Hath she made her affection known to Benedick?

LEONATO. No, and swears she never will. That's her torment.

CLAUDIO. 'Tis true indeed, so your daughter says: 'Shall I,' says she, 'that have so oft encountered him 130 with scorn, write to him that I love him?'

LEONATO. This says she now when she is beginning to write to him, for she'll be up twenty times a night, and there will she sit in her smock till she have writ a sheet of paper: my daughter tells us all.

CLAUDIO. Now you talk of a sheet of paper, I remember a pretty jest your daughter told us of.

LEONATO. O, when she had writ it, and was reading it over, she found 'Benedick' and 'Beatrice' between the sheet? 140

CLAUDIO. That.

LEONATO. O, she tore the letter into a thousand half-pence, railed at herself that she should be so immodest to write to one that she knew would flout her. 'I measure him,' says she, 'by my own spirit, for I should flout him if he writ to me—yea, though I love him, I should.'

CLAUDIO. Then down upon her knees she falls, weeps, sobs, beats her heart, tears her hair, prays, curses— 'O sweet Benedick! God give me patience!' 150

LEONATO. She doth indeed—my daughter says so. And the ecstasy hath so much overborne her, that my daughter is sometime afeard she will do a desperate outrage to herself. It is very true.

DON PEDRO. It were good that Benedick knew of it by some other, if she will not discover it.

CLAUDIO. To what end? he would make but a sport of it, and torment the poor lady worse.

DON PEDRO. An he should, it were an alms to hang him. She's an excellent sweet lady, and—out of all 160 suspicion—she is virtuous.

CLAUDIO. And she is exceeding wise.

DON PEDRO. In every thing but in loving Benedick.

LEONATO. O my lord, wisdom and blood combating in so tender a body, we have ten proofs to one that blood hath the victory. I am sorry for her, as I have just cause, being her uncle and her guardian.

DON PEDRO. I would she had bestowed this dotage on me. I would have daffed all other respects, and made her half myself. I pray you tell Benedick of it, and 170 hear what a' will say.

LEONATO. Were it good, think you?

CLAUDIO. Hero thinks surely she will die—for she says she will die if he love her not, and she will die ere she make her love known, and she will die if he woo her rather than she will bate one breath of her accustomed crossness.

DON PEDRO. She doth well. If she should make tender of her love, 'tis very possible he'll scorn it—for the man, as you know all, hath a contemptible 180 spirit.

CLAUDIO. He is a very proper man.

DON PEDRO. He hath indeed a good outward happiness.

CLAUDIO. Before God, and in my mind, very wise.

DON PEDRO. He doth indeed show some sparks that 120 are like wit.

CLAUDIO. And I take him to be valiant.

DON PEDRO. As Hector, I assure you. And in the managing of quarrels you may say he is wise, for 190 either he avoids them with great discretion, or undertakes them with a most Christian-like fear.

LEONATO. If he do fear God, a' must necessarily keep peace. If he break the peace, he ought to enter into a quarrel with fear and trembling.

DON PEDRO. And so will he do—for the man doth fear God, howsoever it seems not in him by some large jests he will make. Well, I am sorry for your niece. Shall we go seek Benedick, and tell him of her love?

CLAUDIO. Never tell him, my lord. Let her wear it out 200 with good counsel.

LEONATO. Nay, that's impossible—she may wear her heart out first.

DON PEDRO. Well, we will hear further of it by your daughter. Let it cool the while. I love Benedick well, and I could wish he would modestly examine himself, to see how much he is unworthy so good a lady.

LEONATO. My lord, will you walk? dinner is ready.

CLAUDIO. If he do not dote on her upon this, I will never trust my expectation. 210

DON PEDRO. Let there be the same net spread for her— and that must your daughter and her gentle-women carry. The sport will be, when they hold one an opinion of another's dotage, and no such matter. That's the scene that I would see, which will be merely a dumb-show. Let us send her to call him in to dinner.   *They depart*

Benedick returns

BENEDICK. This can be no trick. The conference was sadly borne. They have the truth of this from Hero. They seem to pity the lady. It seems her affections 220 have their full bent. Love me! why, it must be requited. I hear how I am censured—they say I will bear myself proudly, if I perceive the love come from her: they say too that she will rather die than give any sign of affection. I did never think to marry. I must not seem proud. Happy are they that hear their detractions, and can put them to mending. They say the lady is fair—'tis a truth, I can bear them witness: and virtuous—'tis so, I cannot reprove it: and wise, but for loving me—by my troth, it is no 230 addition to her wit, nor no great argument of her folly, for I will be horribly in love with her. I may chance have some odd quirks and remnants of wit broken on me, because I have railed so long against marriage: but doth not the appetite alter? a man loves the meat in his youth that he cannot endure in his age. Shall quips and sentences and these paper bullets of the brain awe a man from the career of his humour? No—the world must be peopled. When I said I would die a bachelor, I did not think I should 240 live till I were married.

Beatrice approaches

Here comes Beatrice. By this day, she's a fair lady. I do spy some marks of love in her.

BEATRICE. Against my will I am sent to bid you come
   in to dinner.
BENEDICK. Fair Beatrice, I thank you for your pains.
BEATRICE. I took no more pains for those thanks than
   you take pains to thank me. If it had been painful,
   I would not have come.
BENEDICK. You take pleasure then in the message.   250
BEATRICE. Yea, just so much as you may take upon a
   knife's point, and choke a daw withal. You have no
   stomach, signior—fare you well.   *She goes*
BENEDICK. Ha! 'Against my will I am sent to bid you
   come in to dinner': there's a double meaning in that.
   'I took no more pains for those thanks than you took
   pains to thank me'—that's as much as to say, Any
   pains that I take for you is as easy as thanks. If I do
   not take pity of her, I am a villain. If I do not love
   her, I am a Jew. I will go get her picture.   260
                              He departs

                    ACT 3
            Scene 1: *The orchard*

Hero, Margaret, and Ursula

HERO. Good Margaret, run thee to the parlour,
   There shalt thou find my cousin Beatrice
   Proposing with the prince and Claudio.
   Whisper her ear, and tell her I and Ursley
   Walk in the orchard, and our whole discourse
   Is all of her. Say that thou overheard'st us,
   And bid her steal into the pleachéd bower,
   Where honeysuckles, ripened by the sun,
   Forbid the sun to enter. Like favourites,
   Made proud by princes, that advance their pride   10
   Against that power that bred it. There will she hide
      her,
   To listen our propose. This is thy office—
   Bear thee well in it and leave us alone.
MARGARET. I'll make her come, I warrant you,
   presently.   *She leaves them*
HERO. Now, Ursula, when Beatrice doth come,
   As we do trace this alley up and down,
   Our talk must only be of Benedick.
   When I do name him, let it be thy part
   To praise him more than ever man did merit.
   My talk to thee must be how Benedick   20
   Is sick in love with Beatrice: of this matter
   Is little Cupid's crafty arrow made,
   That only wounds by hearsay.

Beatrice approaches, and enters the arbour

                         Now begin,
   For look where Beatrice like a lapwing runs
   Close by the ground, to hear our conference.
URSULA. The pleasant'st angling is to see the fish
   Cut with her golden oars the silver stream,
   And greedily devour the treacherous bait:
   So angle we for Beatrice, who even now
   Is couchéd in the woodbine coverture.   30
   Fear you not my part of the dialogue.
HERO. Then go we near her, that her ear lose nothing
   Of the false sweet bait that we lay for it.
                    They approach the arbour
   No, truly, Ursula, she is too disdainful—
   I know her spirits are as coy and wild

   As haggards of the rock.
URSULA.   But are you sure
   That Benedick loves Beatrice so entirely?
HERO. So says the prince, and my new-trothéd lord.
URSULA. And did they bid you tell her of it, madam?
HERO. They did entreat me to acquaint her of it.   40
   But I persuaded them, if they loved Benedick,
   To wish him wrestle with affection,
   And never to let Beatrice know of it.
URSULA. Why did you so? Doth not the gentleman
   Deserve at full as fortunate a bed
   As ever Beatrice shall couch upon?
HERO. O god of love! I know he doth deserve
   As much as may be yielded to a man:
   But nature never framed a woman's heart
   Of prouder stuff than that of Beatrice: 50
   Disdain and scorn ride sparkling in her eyes,
   Misprizing what they look on, and her wit
   Values itself so highly, that to her
   All matter else seems weak: she cannot love,
   Nor take no shape nor project of affection,
   She is so self-endeared.
URSULA.   Sure, I think so.
   And therefore certainly it were not good
   She knew his love, lest she'll make sport at it.
HERO. Why, you speak truth. I never yet saw man,
   How wise, how noble, young, how rarely featured,   60
   But she would spell him backward: if fair-faced,
   She would swear the gentleman should be her sister;
   If black, why nature, drawing of an antic,
   Made a foul blot: if tall, a lance ill-headed;
   If low, an agate very vilely cut:
   If speaking, why a vane blown with all winds;
   If silent, why a block movéd with none.
   So turns she every man the wrong side out,
   And never gives to truth and virtue that
   Which simpleness and merit purchaseth.   70
URSULA. Sure, sure, such carping is not commendable.
HERO. No, nor to be so odd and from all fashions,
   As Beatrice is, cannot be commendable.
   But who dare tell her so? If I should speak,
   She would mock me into air—O, she would laugh
      me
   Out of myself, press me to death with wit.
   Therefore let Benedick, like covered fire,
   Consume away in sighs, waste inwardly:
   It were a better death than die with mocks,
   Which is as bad as die with tickling.   80
URSULA. Yet tell her of it, hear what she will say.
HERO. No, rather I will go to Benedick,
   And counsel him to fight against his passion.
   And, truly, I'll devise some honest slanders
   To stain my cousin with. One doth not know,
   How much an ill word may empoison liking.
URSULA. O, do not do your cousin such a wrong.
   She cannot be so much without true judgement—
   Having so swift and excellent a wit,
   As she is prized to have—as to refuse   90
   So rare a gentleman as Signior Benedick.
HERO. He is the only man of Italy,
   Always excepted my dear Claudio.
URSULA. I pray you be not angry with me, madam,
   Speaking my fancy: Signior Benedick,
   For shape, for bearing, argument, and valour,
   Goes foremost in report through Italy.
HERO. Indeed, he hath an excellent good name.

URSULA. His excellence did earn it, ere he had it.
When are you married, madam?   100
HERO. Why, every day to-morrow! Come, go in.
I'll show thee some attires, and have thy counsel
Which is the best to furnish me to-morrow.
URSULA. She's limed I warrant you—we have caught
her, madam.
HERO. If it prove so, then loving goes by haps,
Some Cupid kills with arrows, some with traps.
                                        They go

Beatrice comes from the arbour

BEATRICE. What fire is in mine ears? Can this be true?
Stand I condemned for pride and scorn so much?
Contempt, farewell! and maiden pride, adieu!
No glory lives behind the back of such.   110
And, Benedick, love on, I will requite thee,
Taming my wild heart to thy loving hand:
If thou dost love, my kindness shall incite thee
To bind our loves up in a holy band:
For others say thou dost deserve, and I
Believe it better than reportingly.   *She goes*

Scene 2: *The parlour in Leonato's house*

Enter Don Pedro, Claudio, Benedick and Leonato

DON PEDRO. I do but stay till your marriage be consummate, and then go I toward Arragon.
CLAUDIO. I'll bring you thither, my lord, if you'll
vouchsafe me.
DON PEDRO. Nay, that would be as great a soil in the
new gloss of your marriage, as to show a child his
new coat and forbid him to wear it. I will only be
bold with Benedick for his company—for, from the
crown of his head to the sole of his foot, he is all
mirth. He hath twice or thrice cut Cupid's bow- 10
string, and the little hangman dare not shoot at him.
He hath a heart as sound as a bell, and his tongue is
the clapper—for what his heart thinks his tongue
speaks.
BENEDICK. Gallants, I am not as I have been.
LEONATO. So say I. Methinks you are sadder.
CLAUDIO. I hope he be in love.
DON PEDRO. Hang him, truant! there's no true drop of
blood in him to be truly touched with love. If he be
sad, he wants money.   20
BENEDICK. I have the toothache.
DON PEDRO. Draw it.
BENEDICK. Hang it!
CLAUDIO. You must hang it first, and draw it after-
wards.
DON PEDRO. What! sigh for the toothache?
LEONATO. Where is but a humour or a worm?
BENEDICK. Well, every one can master a grief but he
that has it.
CLAUDIO. Yet say I, he is in love.   30
DON PEDRO. There is no appearance of fancy in him,
unless it be a fancy that he hath to strange disguises—
as, to be a Dutchman to-day, a Frenchman to-
morrow, or in the shape of two countries at once,
as a German from the waist downward, all slops,
and a Spaniard from the hip upward, no doublet.
Unless he have a fancy to this foolery, as it appears
he hath, he is no fool for fancy, as you would have
it appear he is.
CLAUDIO. If he be not in love with some woman, there 40

is no believing old signs. A' brushes his hat a morn-
ings—what should that bode?
DON PEDRO. Hath any man seen him at the barber's?
CLAUDIO. No, but the barber's man hath been seen
with him, and the old ornament of his cheek hath
already stuffed tennis-balls.
LEONATO. Indeed, he looks younger than he did, by
the loss of a beard.
DON PEDRO. Nay, a' rubs himself with civet—can you
smell him out by that?   50
CLAUDIO. That's as much as to say the sweet youth's
in love.
DON PEDRO. The greatest note of it is his melancholy.
CLAUDIO. And when was he wont to wash his face?
DON PEDRO. Yea, or to paint himself? for the which,
I hear what they say of him.
CLAUDIO. Nay, but his jesting spirit, which is new-
crept into a lute-string and now governed by stops.
DON PEDRO. Indeed, that tells a heavy tale for him;
conclude, conclude, he is in love.   60
CLAUDIO. Nay, but I know who loves him.
DON PEDRO. That would I know too. I warrant, one
that knows him not.
CLAUDIO. Yes, and his ill conditions—and in despite of
all, dies for him.
DON PEDRO. She shall be buried with her face upwards.
BENEDICK. Yet is this no charm for the toothache. Old
signior, walk aside with me. I have studied eight or
nine wise words to speak to you, which these
hobby-horses must not hear.   70
                        Benedick and Leonato go out
DON PEDRO. For my life, to break with him about
Beatrice.
CLAUDIO. 'Tis even so. Hero and Margaret have by
this played their parts with Beatrice, and then the
two bears will not bite one another when they
meet.

Don John enters

DON JOHN. My lord and brother, God save you.
DON PEDRO. Good-den, brother.
DON JOHN. If your leisure served, I would speak with
you.   80
DON PEDRO. In private?
DON JOHN. If it please you—yet Count Claudio may
hear, for what I would speak of concerns him.
CLAUDIO. What's the matter?
DON JOHN. Means your lordship to be married to-
morrow?
DON PEDRO. You know he does.
DON JOHN. I know not that, when he knows what I
know.
CLAUDIO. If there be any impediment, I pray you dis- 90
cover it.
DON JOHN. You may think I love you not—let that
appear hereafter, and aim better at me by that I now
will manifest. For my brother, I think he holds you
well, and in dearness of heart hath holp to effect
your ensuing marriage: surely, suit ill spent, and
labour ill bestowed.
DON PEDRO. Why, what's the matter?
DON JOHN. I came hither to tell you, and, circumstances shortened—for she has been too long a talk- 100
ing of—the lady is disloyal.
CLAUDIO. Who, Hero?

DON JOHN. Even she—Leonato's Hero, your Hero, every man's Hero.

CLAUDIO. Disloyal?

DON JOHN. The word is too good to paint out her wickedness. I could say she were worse. Think you of a worse title, and I will fit her to it. Wonder not till further warrant: go but with me to-night, you shall see her chamber-window entered, even the night before her wedding-day. If you love her then, to-morrow wed her, but it would better fit your honour to change your mind.

CLAUDIO. May this be so?

DON PEDRO. I will not think it.

DON JOHN. If you dare not trust that you see, confess not that you know: if you will follow me, I will show you enough, and when you have seen more and heard more, proceed accordingly.

CLAUDIO. If I see any thing to-night why I should not marry her to-morrow, in the congregation, where I should wed, there will I shame her.

DON PEDRO. And as I wooed for thee to obtain her, I will join with thee to disgrace her.

DON JOHN. I will disparage her no farther till you are my witnesses. Bear it coldly but till midnight, and let the issue show itself.

DON PEDRO. O day untowardly turned!

CLAUDIO. O mischief strangely thwarting!

DON JOHN. O plague right well prevented! So will you say, when you have seen the sequel.

They go

Scene 3: *A street*

Master Constable Dogberry, Verges, and the Watch

DOGBERRY. Are you good men and true?

VERGES. Yea, or else it were pity but they should suffer salvation, body and soul.

DOGBERRY. Nay, that were a punishment too good for them, if they should have any allegiance in them, being chosen for the prince's watch.

VERGES. Well, give them their charge, neighbour Dogberry.

DOGBERRY. First, who think you the most desertless man to be constable?

1 WATCHMAN. Hugh Oatcake, sir, or George Seacoal, for they can write and read.

DOGBERRY. Come hither, neighbour Seacoal. God hath blessed you with a good name: to be a well-favoured man is the gift of fortune, but to write and read comes by nature.

2 WATCHMAN. Both which, Master Constable—

DOGBERRY. You have: I knew it would be your answer. Well, for your favour, sir, why give God thanks, and make no boast of it—and for your writing and reading, let that appear when there is no need of such vanity. You are thought here to be the most senseless and fit man for the constable of the watch: therefore bear you the lantern. This is your charge—you shall comprehend all vagrom men, you are to bid any man stand, in the prince's name.

2 WATCHMAN. How if a' will not stand?

DOGBERRY. Why then take no note of him, but let him go, and presently call the rest of the watch together, and thank God you are rid of a knave.

VERGES. If he will not stand when he is bidden, he is none of the prince's subjects.

DOGBERRY. True, and they are to meddle with none but the prince's subjects. You shall also make no noise in the streets: for, for the watch to babble and to talk, is most tolerable and not to be endured.

2 WATCHMAN. We will rather sleep than talk—we know what belongs to a watch.

DOGBERRY. Why, you speak like an ancient and most quiet watchman, for I cannot see how sleeping should offend: only have a care that your bills be not stolen. Well, you are to call at all the ale-houses, and bid those that are drunk get them to bed.

2 WATCHMAN. How if they will not?

DOGBERRY. Why then, let them alone till they are sober. If they make you not then the better answer, you may say they are not the men you took them for.

2 WATCHMAN. Well, sir.

DOGBERRY. If you meet a thief, you may suspect him, by virtue of your office, to be no true man: and, for such kind of men, the less you meddle or make with them, why the more is for your honesty.

2 WATCHMAN. If we know him to be a thief, shall we not lay hands on him?

DOGBERRY. Truly by your office you may, but I think they that touch pitch will be defiled: the most peaceable way for you, if you do take a thief, is to let him show himself what he is, and steal out of your company.

VERGES. You have been always called a merciful man, partner.

DOGBERRY. Truly, I would not hang a dog by my will, much more a man who hath any honesty in him.

VERGES. If you hear a child cry in the night, you must call to the nurse and bid her still it.

2 WATCHMAN. How if the nurse be asleep and will not hear us?

DOGBERRY. Why then, depart in peace, and let the child wake her with crying—for the ewe that will not hear her lamb when it baes, will never answer a calf when he bleats.

VERGES. 'Tis very true.

DOGBERRY. This is the end of the charge: you, constable, are to present the prince's own person—if you meet the prince in the night, you may stay him.

VERGES. Nay, by'r lady, that I think a' cannot.

DOGBERRY. Five shillings to one on't with any man that knows the statutes, he may stay him—marry, not without the prince be willing, for indeed the watch ought to offend no man, and it is an offence to stay a man against his will.

VERGES. By'r lady, I think it be so.

DOGBERRY. Ha, ah, ha! Well, masters, good night. An there be any matter of weight chances, call up me. Keep your fellows' counsels and your own, and good night. Come, neighbour.

2 WATCHMAN. Well, masters, we hear our charge. Let us go sit here upon the church-bench till two, and then all to bed.

DOGBERRY. One word more, honest neighbours. I pray you, watch about Signior Leonato's door, for the wedding being there to-morrow, there is a great coil to-night. Adieu, be vigitant, I beseech you.

Dogberry and Verges go

Borachio and Conrade enter

BORACHIO. What, Conrade!

2 WATCHMAN [aside]. Peace, stir not.

BORACHIO. Conrade, I say!

CONRADE. Here, man, I am at thy elbow.

BORACHIO. Mass, and my elbow itched—I thought there would a scab follow. 100

CONRADE. I will owe thee an answer for that, and now forward with thy tale.

BORACHIO. Stand thee close then under this penthouse, for it drizzles rain, and I will, like a true drunkard, utter all to thee.

2 WATCHMAN [aside]. Some treason, masters—yet stand close.

BORACHIO. Therefore know, I have earned of Don John a thousand ducats. 110

CONRADE. Is it possible that any villainy should be so dear?

BORACHIO. Thou shouldst rather ask if it were possible any villainy should be so rich, for when rich villains have need of poor ones, poor ones may make what price they will.

CONRADE. I wonder at it.

BORACHIO. That shows thou art unconfirmed. Thou knowest that the fashion of a doublet, or a hat, or a cloak, is nothing to a man. 120

CONRADE. Yes, it is apparel.

BORACHIO. I mean the fashion.

CONRADE. Yes, the fashion is the fashion.

BORACHIO. Tush, I may as well say the fool's the fool. But seest thou not what a deformed thief this fashion is?

2 WATCHMAN [aside]. I know that Deformed, a' has been a vile thief this seven year, a' goes up and down like a gentleman: I remember his name.

BORACHIO. Didst thou not hear somebody? 130

CONRADE. No, 'twas the vane on the house.

BORACHIO. Seest thou not, I say, what a deformed thief this fashion is? how giddily a' turns about all the hot-bloods between fourteen and five-and-thirty? sometimes fashioning them like Pharaoh's soldiers in the reechy painting, sometime like god Bel's priests in the old church window, sometime like the shaven Hercules in the smirched worm-eaten tapestry, where his cod-piece seems as massy as his club? 140

CONRADE. All this I see, and I see that the fashion wears out more apparel than the man.... But art not thou thyself giddy with the fashion too, that thou hast shifted out of thy tale into telling me of the fashion?

BORACHIO. Not so neither. But know that I have tonight wooed Margaret, the Lady Hero's gentlewoman, by the name of Hero. She leans me out at her mistress' chamber-window, bids me a thousand times good night. I tell this tale vilely—I should first tell thee how the prince, Claudio, and my 150 master, planted and placed and possessed by my master Don John, saw afar off in the orchard this amiable encounter.

CONRADE. And thought they Margaret was Hero?

BORACHIO. Two of them did, the prince and Claudio. But the devil, my master, knew she was Margaret—and partly by his oaths, which first possessed them, partly by the dark night, which did deceive them, but chiefly by my villainy, which did confirm any slander that Don John had made, away went 160 Claudio enraged, swore he would meet her as he was

appointed next morning at the temple, and there, before the whole congregation, shame her with what he saw o'er-night, and send her home again without a husband.

2 WATCHMAN. We charge you in the prince's name, stand.

1 WATCHMAN. Call up the right Master Constable. We have here recovered the most dangerous piece of lechery that ever was known in the commonwealth. 170

2 WATCHMAN. And one Deformed is one of them—I know him, a' wears a lock.

CONRADE. Masters, masters.

2 WATCHMAN. You'll be made bring Deformed forth, I warrant you.

CONRADE. Masters—

1 WATCHMAN. Never speak, we charge you. Let us obey you to go with us.

BORACHIO. We are like to prove a goodly commodity, being taken up of these men's bills. 180

CONRADE. A commodity in question, I warrant you. Come, we'll obey you.   *They go*

Scene 4: *Hero's apartment*

Enter Hero, Margaret, and Ursula

HERO. Good Ursula, wake my cousin Beatrice, and desire her to rise.

URSULA. I will, lady.

HERO. And bid her come hither.

URSULA. Well.   *She goes out*

MARGARET. Troth, I think your other rebato were better.

HERO. No, pray thee good Meg, I'll wear this.

MARGARET. By my troth's not so good, and I warrant your cousin will say so. 10

HERO. My cousin's a fool, and thou art another. I'll wear none but this.

MARGARET. I like the new tire within excellently, if the hair were a thought browner: and your gown's a most rare fashion i'faith. I saw the Duchess of Milan's gown that they praise so—

HERO. O, that exceeds, they say.

MARGARET. By my troth's but a night-gown in respect of yours—cloth o' gold and cuts, and laced with silver, set with pearls down sleeves, side-sleeves, and 20 skirts, round underborne with a bluish tinsel—but for a fine quaint graceful and excellent fashion, yours is worth ten on't.

HERO. God give me joy to wear it, for my heart is exceeding heavy.

MARGARET. 'Twill be heavier soon by the weight of a man.

HERO. Fie upon thee, art not ashamed?

MARGARET. Of what, lady? of speaking honourably? is not marriage honourable in a beggar? is not your 30 lord honourable without marriage? I think you would have me say, 'saving your reverence, a husband': an bad thinking do not wrest true speaking—I'll offend nobody—is there any harm in 'the heavier for a husband'? none I think, an it be the right husband, and the right wife, otherwise 'tis light and not heavy—ask my Lady Beatrice else, here she comes.

Beatrice enters

HERO. Good morrow, coz.

BEATRICE. Good morrow, sweet Hero. 40
HERO. Why how now? do you speak in the sick tune?
BEATRICE. I am out of all other tune, methinks.
MARGARET. Clap's into 'Light o' love'—that goes without a burden—do you sing it, and I'll dance it.
BEATRICE. Yea, light o' love with your heels—then if your husband have stables enough you'll see he shall lack no barns.
MARGARET. O illegitimate construction! I scorn that with my heels.
BEATRICE. 'Tis almost five o'clock cousin, 'tis time 50 you were ready. By my troth I am exceeding ill. Heigh-ho!
MARGARET. For a hawk, a horse, or a husband?
BEATRICE. For the letter than begins them all, H.
MARGARET. Well, an you be not turned Turk, there's no more sailing by the star.
BEATRICE. What means the fool, trow?
MARGARET. Nothing I—but God send every one their heart's desire.
HERO. These gloves the count sent me, they are an 60 excellent perfume.
BEATRICE. I am stuffed, cousin, I cannot smell.
MARGARET. A maid and stuffed! there's goodly catching of cold.
BEATRICE. O, God help me, God help me, how long have you professed apprehension?
MARGARET. Ever since you left it. Doth not my wit become me rarely?
BEATRICE. It is not seen enough, you should wear it in your cap. By my troth I am sick. 70
MARGARET. Get you some of this distilled Carduus Benedictus, and lay it to your heart—it is the only thing for a qualm.
HERO. There thou prick'st her with a thistle.
BEATRICE. Benedictus, why Benedictus? you have some moral in this Benedictus.
MARGARET. Moral? no, by my troth, I have no moral meaning—I meant plain holy-thistle. You may think perchance that I think you are in love—nay by'r lady I am not such a fool to think what I list, 80 nor I list not to think what I can, nor indeed I cannot think, if I would think my heart out of thinking, that you are in love, or that you will be in love, or that you can be in love: yet Benedick was such another and now is he become a man, he swore he would never marry, and yet now in despite of his heart he eats his meat without grudging—and how you may be converted I know not, but methinks you look with your eyes as other women do.
BEATRICE. What pace is this that thy tongue keeps? 90
MARGARET. Not a false gallop.

Ursula returns

URSULA. Madam, withdraw. The prince, the count, Signior Benedick, Don John, and all the gallants of the town are come to fetch you to church.
HERO. Help to dress me, good coz, good Meg, good Ursula. *They go*

Scene 5: The hall in Leonato's house

Enter Leonato, Dogberry and Verges

LEONATO. What would you with me, honest neighbour?

DOGBERRY. Marry, sir, I would have some confidence with you, that decerns you nearly.
LEONATO. Brief I pray you, for you see it is a busy time with me.
DOGBERRY. Marry, this it is, sir.
VERGES. Yes, in truth it is, sir.
LEONATO. What is it, my good friends?
DOGBERRY. Goodman Verges, sir, speaks a little off the 10 matter—an old man, sir, and his wits are not so blunt, as God help I would desire they were, but in faith honest, as the skin between his brows.
VERGES. Yes, I thank God, I am as honest as any man living, that is an old man, and no honester than I.
DOGBERRY. Comparisons are odorous—palabras, neighbour Verges.
LEONATO. Neighbours, you are tedious.
DOGBERRY. It pleases your worship to say so, but we are the poor duke's officers. But truly for mine own 20 part if I were as tedious as a king I could find in my heart to bestow it all of your worship.
LEONATO. All thy tediousness on me, ah?
DOGBERRY. Yea, an 'twere a thousand pound more than 'tis, for I hear as good exclamation on your worship as of any man in the city, and though I be but a poor man, I am glad to hear it.
VERGES. And so am I.
LEONATO. I would fain know what you have to say.
VERGES. Marry, sir, our watch to-night, excepting 30 your worship's presence, ha' ta'en a couple of as arrant knaves as any in Messina.
DOGBERRY. A good old man, sir, he will be talking—as they say, 'when the age is in, the wit is out.' God help us, it is a world to see. Well said, i'faith, neighbour Verges. Well, God's a good man—an two men ride of a horse, one must ride behind. An honest soul i'faith, sir, by my troth he is, as ever broke bread, but—God is to be worshipped—all men are not alike, alas, good neighbour. 40
LEONATO. Indeed, neighbour, he comes too short of you.
DOGBERRY. Gifts that God gives.
LEONATO. I must leave you.
DOGBERRY. One word, sir—our watch, sir, have indeed comprehended two aspicious persons, and we would have them this morning examined before your worship.
LEONATO. Take their examination yourself, and bring it me, I am now in great haste, as it may appear 50 unto you.
DOGBERRY. It shall be suffigance.
LEONATO. Drink some wine ere you go: fare you well.
A messenger enters
MESSENGER. My lord, they stay for you to give your daughter to her husband.
LEONATO. I'll wait upon them—I am ready.
Leonato and the messenger go
DOGBERRY. Go good partner, go get you to Francis Seacoal, bid him bring his pen and inkhorn to the gaol: we are now to examination these men.
VERGES. And we must do it wisely. 60
DOGBERRY. We will spare for no wit, I warrant you: here's that shall drive some of them to a 'non-come.' Only get the learned writer to set down our excommunication, and meet me at the gaol.
They depart

ACT 4
Scene 1: *A church*

Don Pedro, Don John, Leonato, Friar Francis, Claudio,
Benedick, Hero, Beatrice, etc.

LEONATO. Come Friar Francis, be brief—only to the
plain form of marriage, and you shall recount their
particular duties afterwards.

FRIAR. You come hither, my lord, to marry this lady?

CLAUDIO. No.

LEONATO. To be married to her: friar, you come to
marry her.

FRIAR. Lady, you come hither to be married to this
count?

HERO. I do.   10

FRIAR. If either of you know any inward impediment
why you should not be conjoined, I charge you on
your souls to utter it.

CLAUDIO. Know you any, Hero?

HERO. None my lord.

FRIAR. Know you any, count?

LEONATO. I dare make his answer, 'none.'

CLAUDIO. O, what men dare do! what men may do!
what men daily do, not knowing what they do!

BENEDICK. How now! interjections? Why then, some 20
be of laughing, as 'ah! ha! he!'

CLAUDIO. Stand thee by, friar. Father, by your leave—
Will you with free and unconstrainèd soul
Give me this maid your daughter?

LEONATO. As freely, son, as God did give her me.

CLAUDIO. And what have I to give you back whose
worth
May counterpoise this rich and precious gift?

DON PEDRO. Nothing, unless you render her again.

CLAUDIO. Sweet prince, you learn me noble
thankfulness.
There Leonato, take her back again,   30
Give not this rotten orange to your friend,
She's but the sign and semblance of her honour.
Behold how like a maid she blushes here!
O, what authority and show of truth
Can cunning sin cover itself withal!
Comes not that blood, as modest evidence,
To witness simple virtue? would you not swear,
All you that see her, that she were a maid,
By these exterior shows? But she is none:
She knows the heat of a luxurious bed: 40
Her blush is guiltiness, not modesty.

LEONATO. What do you mean my lord?

CLAUDIO.   Not to be married,
Not to knot my soul to an approvèd wanton.

LEONATO. Dear my lord, if you in your own proof,
Have vanquished the resistance of her youth,
And made defeat of her virginity—

CLAUDIO. I know what you would say: if I have
known her,
You will say she did embrace me as a husband,
And so extenuate the 'forehand sin.
No Leonato,   50
I never tempted her with word too large,
But as a brother to his sister showed
Bashful sincerity, and comely love.

LEONATO. And seemed I ever otherwise to you?

CLAUDIO. Out on the seeming, I will write against it.
You seem to me as Dian in her orb,
As chaste as is the bud ere it be blown:

But you are more intemperate in your blood
Than Venus, or those pamp'red animals
That rage in savage sensuality.   60

HERO. Is my lord well that he doth speak so wide?

LEONATO. Sweet prince, why speak not you?

DON PEDRO.   What should I speak?
I stand dishonoured that have gone about
To link my dear friend to a common stale.

LEONATO. Are these things spoken, or do I but dream?

DON JOHN. Sir, they are spoken, and these things are
true.

BENEDICK. This looks not like a nuptial.

HERO. 'True,' O God!

CLAUDIO.   Leonato, stand I here?
Is this the prince? is this the prince's brother?
Is this face Hero's? are our eyes our own?   70

LEONATO. All this is so, but what of this my lord?

CLAUDIO. Let me but move one question to your
daughter,
And by that fatherly and kindly power
That you have in her, bid her answer truly.

LEONATO. I charge thee do so, as thou art my child.

HERO. O God defend me how am I beset!
What kind of catechizing call you this?

CLAUDIO. To make you answer truly to your name.

HERO. Is it not Hero? who can blot that name
With any just reproach?

CLAUDIO.   Marry, that can Hero— 80
Hero itself can blot out Hero's virtue.
What man was he talked with you yesternight,
Out at your window betwixt twelve and one?
Now if you are a maid, answer to this.

HERO. I talked with no man at that hour my lord.

DON PEDRO. Why then are you no maiden. Leonato,
I am sorry you must hear: upon mine honour,
Myself, my brother, and this grievèd count,
Did see her, hear her, at that hour last night,
Talk with a ruffian at her chamber-window—   90
Who hath indeed, most like a liberal villain,
Confessed the vile encounters they have had
A thousand times in secret.

DON PEDRO. Fie, fie! they are not to be named, my
lord,
Not to be spoke of.
There is not chastity enough in language,
Without offence, to utter them. Thus, pretty lady,
I am sorry for thy much misgovernment.

CLAUDIO. O Hero! what a Hero hadst thou been,
If half thy outward graces had been placed   100
About the thoughts and counsels of thy heart!
But, fare thee well, most foul, most fair—farewell,
Thou pure impiety, and impious purity,
For thee I'll lock up all the gates of love,
And on my eyelids shall conjecture hang,
To turn all beauty into thoughts of harm,
And never shall it more be gracious.

LEONATO. Hath no man's dagger here a point for me?
                                        Hero swoons

BEATRICE. Why, how now cousin, wherefore sink you
down?

DON JOHN. Come let us go: these things, come thus
to light,   110
Smother her spirits up.
                          Don Pedro, Don John,
                          and Claudio leave the church

BENEDICK. How doth the lady?

BEATRICE.   Dead I think—help uncle—
Hero—why Hero—uncle—Signior Benedick—
    Friar!
LEONATO. O Fate! take not away thy heavy hand.
    Death is the fairest cover for her shame
    That may be wished for.
BEATRICE. How now cousin Hero?
FRIAR.   Have comfort lady.
LEONATO. Dost thou look up?
FRIAR.   Yea, wherefore should she not?
LEONATO. Wherefore? why, doth not every earthly
        thing
    Cry shame upon her? could she here deny   120
    The story that is printed in her blood?
    Do not live Hero, do not ope thine eyes:
    For did I think thou wouldst not quickly die,
    Thought I thy spirits were stronger than thy shames,
    Myself would on the rearward of reproaches
    Strike at thy life.... Grieved I, I had but one?
    Chid I for that frugal nature's frame?
    O, one too much by thee. Why had I one?
    Why ever wast thou lovely in my eyes?
    Why had I not with charitable hand   130
    Took up a beggar's issue at my gates,
    Who smirchéd thus, and mired with infamy,
    I might have said, 'No part of it is mine,
    This shame derives itself from unknown loins'?
    But mine, and mine I loved, and mine I praised,
    And mine that I was proud on, mine so much
    That I myself was to myself not mine,
    Valuing of her—why she, O she is fall'n
    Into a pit of ink, that the wide sea
    Hath drops too few to wash her clean again, 140
    And salt too little which may season give
    To her foul tainted flesh.
BENEDICK. Sir, sir, be patient. For my part, I am so
    attired in wonder, I know not what to say.
BEATRICE. O, on my soul, my cousin is belied!
BENEDICK. Lady, were you her bedfellow last night?
BEATRICE. No, truly, not—although, until last night,
    I have this twelvemonth been her bedfellow.
LEONATO. Confirmed, confirmed—O, that is stronger
        made,
    Which was before barred up with ribs of iron. 150
    Would the two princes lie? and Claudio lie,
    Who loved her so, that, speaking of her foulness,
    Washed it with tears! Hence from her, let her die.
FRIAR. Hear me a little—
    [For I have only been silent so long,
    And given way unto this course of fortune,]
    By noting of the lady, I have marked
    A thousand blushing apparitions
    To start into her face, a thousand innocent shames
    In angel whiteness beat away those blushes,   160
    And in her eye there hath appeared a fire,
    To burn the errors that these princes hold
    Against her maiden truth. Call me a fool,
    Trust not my reading, nor my observations,
    Which with experimental seal doth warrant
    The tenour of my book: trust not my age,
    My reverence, calling, nor divinity,
    If this sweet lady lie not guiltless here
    Under some biting error.
LEONATO.   Friar, it cannot be.
    Thou seest that all the grace that she hath left 170
    Is that she will not add to her damnation

A sin of perjury—she not denies it:
    Why seek'st thou then to cover with excuse
    That which appears in proper nakedness?
FRIAR. Lady, what man is he you are accused of?
HERO. They know that do accuse me, I know none.
    If I know more of any man alive
    Than that which maiden modesty doth warrant,
    Let all my sins lack mercy. O my father,
    Prove you that any man with me conversed   180
    At hours unmeet, or that I yesternight
    Maintain the change of words with any
        creature—
    Refuse me, hate me, torture me to death.
FRIAR. There is some strange misprision in the princes.
BENEDICK. Two of them have the very bent of honour,
    And if their wisdoms be misled in this,
    The practice of it lives in John the bastard,
    Whose spirits toil in frame of villainies.
LEONATO. I know not. If they speak but truth of her,
    These hands shall tear her—if they wrong her
        honour,   190
    The proudest of them shall well hear of it.
    Time hath not yet so dried this blood of mine,
    Nor age so eat up my invention,
    Nor fortune made such havoc of my means,
    Nor my bad life reft me so much of friends,
    But they shall find, awaked in such a kind,
    Both strength of limb, and policy of mind,
    Ability in means, and choice of friends,
    To quit me of them throughly.
FRIAR.   Pause awhile,
    And let my counsel sway you in this case.   200
    Your daughter here the princes left for dead,
    Let her awhile be secretly kept in,
    And publish it that she is dead indeed,
    Maintain a mourning ostentation,
    And on your family's old monument
    Hang mournful epitaphs, and do all rites
    That appertain unto a burial.
LEONATO. What shall become of this? what will this
        do?
FRIAR. Marry, this well carried, shall on her behalf
    Change slander to remorse—that is some good. 210
    But not for that dream I on this strange course,
    But on this travail look for greater birth:
    She dying, as it must be so maintained,
    Upon the instant that she was accused,
    Shall be lamented, pitied, and excused
    Of every hearer: for it so falls out
    That every hearer: for it so falls out
    That what we have we prize not to the worth,
    Whiles we enjoy it, but being lacked and lost,
    Why then we rack the value, then we find   220
    The virtue that possession would not show us
    Whiles it was ours—so will it fare with Claudio:
    When he shall hear she died upon his words,
    Th'idea of her life shall sweetly creep
    Into his study of imagination,
    And every lovely organ of her life
    Shall come apparelled in more precious habit,
    More moving-delicate and full of life,
    Into the eye and prospect of his soul,
    Than when she lived indeed: then shall he mourn— 230
    If ever love had interest in his liver—
    And wish he had not so accuséd her:
    No, though he thought his accusation true.

Let this be so, and doubt not but success
Will fashion the event in better shape
Than I can lay it down in likelihood.
But if all aim but this be levelled false,
The supposition of the lady's death
Will quench the wonder of her infamy.
And if it sort not well, you may conceal her— 240
As best befits her wounded reputation—
In some reclusive and religious life,
Out of all eyes, tongues, minds, and injuries.

BENEDICK. Signior Lenato, let the friar advise you,
And though you know my inwardness and love
Is very much unto the prince and Claudio,
Yet, by mine honour, I will deal in this
As secretly and justly as your soul
Should with your body.

LEONATO.   Being that I flow in grief,
The smallest twine may lead me. 250

FRIAR. 'Tis well consented—presently away—
For to strange sores strangely they strain the cure.
Come lady, die to live—this wedding day
Perhaps is but prolonged—have patience and
endure.   *All go except Benedick and Beatrice*

BENEDICK. Lady Beatrice, have you wept all this
while?

BEATRICE. Yea, and I will weep a while longer.

BENEDICK. I will not desire that.

BEATRICE. You have no reason, I do it freely.

BENEDICK. Surely I do believe your fair cousin is 260
wronged.

BEATRICE. Ah, how much might the man deserve of
me that would right her!

BENEDICK. Is there any way to show such friendship?

BEATRICE. A very even way, but no such friend.

BENEDICK. May a man do it?

BEATRICE. It is a man's office, but not yours.

BENEDICK. I do love nothing in the world so well as
you—is not that strange?

BEATRICE. As strange as the thing I know not. It were 270
as possible for me to say I loved nothing so well as
you—but believe me not—and yet I lie not—I confess nothing, nor I deny nothing—I am sorry for my
cousin.

BENEDICK. By my sword Beatrice, thou lovest me.

BEATRICE. Do not swear and eat it.

BENEDICK. I will swear by it that you love me, and I
will make him eat it that says I love not you.

BEATRICE. Will you not eat your word?

BENEDICK. With no sauce that can be devised to it—I 280
protest I love thee.

BEATRICE. Why then God forgive me—

BENEDICK. What offence sweet Beatrice?

BEATRICE. You have stayed me in a happy hour, I was
about to protest I loved you.

BENEDICK. And do it with all thy heart.

BEATRICE. I love you with so much of my heart, that
none is left to protest.

BENEDICK. Come bid me do any thing for thee.

BEATRICE. Kill Claudio. 290

BENEDICK. Ha! not for the wide world.

BEATRICE. You kill me to deny it—farewell.

BENEDICK. Tarry sweet Beatrice.

BEATRICE. I am gone, though I am here—there is no
love in you—nay I pray you let me go.

BENEDICK. Beatrice—

BEATRICE. In faith I will go.

BENEDICK. We'll be friends first.

BEATRICE. You dare easier be friends with me than
fight with mine enemy. 300

BENEDICK. Is Claudio thine enemy?

BEATRICE. Is a' not approved in the height a villain,
that hath slandered, scorned, dishonoured my kinswoman? O that I were a man! What, bear her in
hand until they come to take hands, and then with
public accusation, uncovered slander, unmitigated
rancour—O God that I were a man! I would eat
his heart in the market-place.

BENEDICK. Hear me Beatrice,—

BEATRICE. Talk with a man out at a window—a proper 310
saying!

BENEDICK. Nay but Beatrice,—

BEATRICE. Sweet Hero, she is wronged, she is slandred,
she is undone.

BENEDICK. Beat—

BEATRICE. Princes and counties! Surely a princely
testimony, a goodly count, Count Comfect—a
sweet gallant surely. O that I were a man for his
sake! or that I had any friend that would be a man
for my sake! But manhood is melted into curtsies, 320
valour into complément, and men are only turned
into tongue, and trim ones too: he is now as valiant
as Hercules, that only tells a lie and swears it ... I
cannot be a man with wishing, therefore I will die
a woman with grieving.

BENEDICK. Tarry good Beatrice—by this hand I love
thee.

BEATRICE. Use it for my love some other way than
swearing by it.

BENEDICK. Think you in your soul the Count Claudio 330
hath wronged Hero?

BEATRICE. Yea, as sure as I have a thought or a soul.

BENEDICK. Enough, I am engaged, I will challenge
him. I will kiss your hand, and so I leave you ...
By this hand, Claudio shall render me a dear account
... As you hear of me, so think of me ... Go
comfort your cousin. I must say she is dead—and so
farewell.   *They go*

Scene 2: *A gaol*

*Enter Dogberry and Verges in their robes of office, the
Sexton in his clerk's gown, and the Watch guarding Conrade and Borachio*

DOGBERRY. Is our whole dissembly appeared?

VERGES. O, a stool and a cushion for the sexton!

SEXTON. Which be the malefactors?

DOGBERRY. Marry, that am I, and my partner.

VERGES. Nay, that's certain. We have the exhibition to
examine.

SEXTON. But which are the offenders that are to be
examined? let them come before Master Constable.

DOGBERRY. Yea marry, let them come before me.
What is your name, friend? 10

BORACHIO. Borachio.

DOGBERRY. Pray write down 'Borachio'.... Yours,
sirrah?

CONRADE. I am a gentleman, sir, and my name is
Conrade.

DOGBERRY. Write down 'Master Gentleman Conrade'
... Masters, do you serve God?

CONRADE, BORACHIO. Yea, sir, we hope.

DOGBERRY. Write down that they hope they serve

God: and write 'God' first, for God defend but God 20
should go before such villains ... Masters, it is
proved already that you are little better than false
knaves, and it will go near to be thought so shortly.
How answer you for yourselves?

CONRADE. Marry, sir, we say we are none.

DOGBERRY. A marvellous witty fellow, I assure you—
but I will go about with him ... Come you hither
sirrah—a word in your ear. Sir, I say to you, it is
thought you are false knaves.

BORACHIO. Say, I say to you, we are none.   30

DOGBERRY. Well, stand aside. 'Fore God, they are
both in a tale. Have you writ down, that they are
none?

SEXTON. Master Constable, you go not the way to
examine. You must call forth the watch that are
their accusers.

DOGBERRY. Yea marry, that's the eftest way, let the
watch come forth. Masters, I charge you in the
prince's name accuse these men.

1 WATCHMAN. This man said, sir, that Don John the 40
prince's brother was a villain.

DOGBERRY. Write down 'Prince John a villain' ...
Why this is flat perjury, to call a prince's brother
villain.

BORACHIO. Master Constable—

DOGBERRY. Pray thee fellow peace. I do not like thy
look, I promise thee.

SEXTON. What heard you him say else?

2 WATCHMAN. Marry, that he had received a thousand
ducats of Don John, for accusing the Lady Hero 50
wrongfully.

DOGBERRY. Flat burglary as ever was committed.

VERGES. Yea by mass that it is.

SEXTON. What else fellow?

1 WATCHMAN. And that Count Claudio did mean,
upon his words, to disgrace Hero before the whole
assembly, and not marry her.

DOGBERRY. O villain! thou wilt be condemned into
everlasting redemption for this.

SEXTON. What else?   60

WATCHMEN. This is all.

SEXTON. And this is more, masters, than you can deny.
Prince John is this morning secretly stolen away:
Hero was in this manner accused, in this very
manner refused, and upon the grief of this suddenly
died. Master Constable, let these men be bound, and
brought to Leonato's. I will go before and show him
their examination.   *He goes*

DOGBERRY. Come, let them be opinioned.

VERGES. Let them be—in the hands.   70

CONRADE. Off, coxcomb!

DOGBERRY. God's my life, where's the sexton? let him
write down the prince's officer 'coxcomb' ...
Come, bind them. Thou naughty varlet!

CONRADE. Away! you are an ass, you are an ass.

DOGBERRY. Dost thou not suspect my place? Dost thou
not suspect my years? O that he were here to write
me down an ass! but, masters, remember that I am
an ass—though it be not written down, yet forget
not that I am an ass. No, thou villain, thou art full 80
of piety, as shall be proved upon thee by good
witness. I am a wise fellow, and which is more—
an officer, and which is more—a householder, and
which is more—as pretty a piece of flesh as any is
in Messina, and one that knows the law, go to, and

a rich fellow enough, go to, and a fellow that hath
had losses, and one that hath two gowns and everything handsome about him. Bring him away. O that
I had been writ down an ass!   *They go*

ACT 5

Scene 1: *Before the house of Leonato*

Leonato and Antonio

ANTONIO. If you go on thus, you will kill yourself,
And 'tis not wisdom thus to second grief
Against yourself.

LEONATO.   I pray thee cease thy counsel,
Which falls into mine ears as profitless
As water in a sieve: give not me counsel,
Nor let no comforter delight mine ear,
But such a one whose wrongs do suit with mine.
Bring me a father that so loved his child,
Whose joy of her is overwhelmed like mine,
And bid him speak of patience,   10
Measure his woe the length and breadth of mine,
And let it answer every strain for strain,
As thus for thus, and such a grief for such,
In every lineament, branch, shape, and form:
If such a one will smile and stroke his beard,
And—sorry wag—cry 'hem' when he should
groan,
Patch grief with proverbs, make misfortune drunk
With candle-wasters—bring him yet to me,
And I of him will gather patience.
But there is no such man—for, brother, men   20
Can counsel and speak comfort to that grief
Which they themselves not feel, but tasting it,
Their counsel turns to passion, which before
Would give preceptial medicine to rage,
Fetter strong madness in a silken thread,
Charm ache with air, and agony with words.
No, no—'tis all men's office to speak patience
To those that wring under the load of sorrow,
But no man's virtue nor sufficiency
To be so moral when he shall endure   30
The like himself. Therefore give me no counsel.
My griefs cry louder than advertisement.

ANTONIO. Therein do men from children nothing
differ.

LEONATO. I pray thee peace. I will be flesh and blood—
For there was never yet philosopher
That could endure the toothache patiently,
However they have writ the style of gods,
And made a 'push' at chance and sufferance.

ANTONIO. Yet bend not all the harm upon yourself,
Make those that do offend you suffer too.   40

LEONATO. There thou speak'st reason, nay I will do so.
My soul doth tell me Hero is belied—
And that shall Claudio know, so shall the prince,
And all of them that thus dishonour her.

Don Pedro and Claudio approach

ANTONIO. Here comes the prince and Claudio hastily.

DON PEDRO. Good-den, good-den.

CLAUDIO.   Good day to both of you.

LEONATO. Hear you, my lords,—

DON PEDRO.   We have some haste, Leonato.

LEONATO. Some haste, my lord! well, fare you well
my lord.

Are you so hasty now? well, all is one.
DON PEDRO Nay, do not quarrel with us, good old
man.   50
ANTONIO. If he could right himself with quarrelling,
Some of us would lie low.
CLAUDIO.   Who wrongs him?
LEONATO. Marry, thou dost wrong me, thou
dissembler, thou.
Nay, never lay thy hand upon thy sword,
I fear thee not.
CLAUDIO.   Marry, beshrew my hand,
If it should give your age such cause of fear.
In faith my hand meant nothing to my sword.
LEONATO. Tush, tush, man, never fleer and jest at me.
I speak not like a dotard nor a fool,
As under privilege of age to brag   60
What I have done being young, or what would do
Were I not old. Know, Claudio, to thy head,
Thou hast so wronged mine innocent child and me,
That I am forced to lay my reverence by,
And with grey hairs and bruise of many days,
Do challenge thee to trial of a man.
I say thou hast belied mine innocent child,
Thy slander hath gone through and through her
heart,
And she lies buried with her ancestors:
O in a tomb where never scandal slept,   70
Save this of hers, framed by thy villainy.
CLAUDIO. My villainy!
LEONATO.   Thine Claudio, thine I say.
DON PEDRO. You say not right, old man.
LEONATO.   My lord, my lord,
I'll prove it on his body if he dare—
Despite his nice fence and his active practice,
His May of Youth and bloom of lustihood.
CLAUDIO. Away, I will not have to do with you.
LEONATO. Canst thou so daff me? Thou hast killed my
child—
If thou kill'st me, boy, thou shalt kill a man.
ANTONIO. He shall kill two of us, and men indeed—   80
But that's no matter, let him kill one first ...
Win me and wear me! Let him answer me.
Come follow me boy, come sir boy, come follow
me.
Sir boy, I'll whip you from your foining fence—
Nay, as I am a gentleman, I will.
LEONATO. Brother—
ANTONIO. Content yourself, God knows I loved my
niece,
And she is dead, slandered to death by villains,
That dare as well answer a man indeed
As I dare take a serpent by the tongue.   90
Boys, apes, braggarts, Jacks, milksops!
LEONATO.   Brother Antony—
ANTONIO. Hold you content. What, man! I know
them, yea,
And what they weigh, even to the utmost scruple—
Scambling, out-facing, fashion-monging boys,
That lie, and cog, and flout, deprave, and slander,
Go anticly, and show outward hideousness,
And speak off half a dozen dang'rous words,
How they might hurt their enemies, if they durst,
And this is all.
LEONATO. But brother Antony—
ANTONIO.   Come, 'tis no matter—   100
Do not you meddle, let me deal in this.

DON PEDRO. Gentlemen both, we will not wake your
patience.
My heart is sorry for your daughter's death:
But on my honour she was charged with nothing
But what was true, and very full of proof.
LEONATO. My lord, my lord,—
DON PEDRO.   I will not hear you.
LEONATO.   No?
Come brother, away. [I will be heard.
ANTONIO. And shall, or some of us will smart for it.]
              Leonato and Antonio enter the house

Benedick comes up

DON PEDRO. See, see, here comes the man we went to
seek.   110
CLAUDIO. Now signior, what news?
BENEDICK. Good day, my lord.
DON PEDRO. Welcome, signior, you are almost come
to part almost a fray.
CLAUDIO. We had liked to have had our two noses
snapped off with two old men without teeth.
DON PEDRO. Leonato and his brother. What think'st
thou? Had we fought I doubt we should have been
too young for them.
BENEDICK. In a false quarrel there is no true valour. I   120
came to seek you both.
CLAUDIO. We have been up and down to seek thee, for
we are high-proof melancholy, and would fain have
it beaten away. Wilt thou use thy wit?
BENEDICK. It is in my scabbard—shall I draw it?
DON PEDRO. Dost thou wear thy wit by thy side?
CLAUDIO. Never any did so, though very many have
been beside their wit. I will bid thee draw, as we
do the minstrels—draw to pleasure us.
DON PEDRO. As I am an honest man he looks pale.   130
Art thou sick, or angry?
CLAUDIO. What, courage, man: what though care
killed a cat, thou hast mettle enough in thee to kill
care.
BENEDICK. Sir, I shall meet your wit in the career, an
you charge it against me. I pray you choose another
subject.
CLAUDIO. Nay then, give him another staff—this last
was broke cross.
DON PEDRO. By this light, he changes more and more.   140
I think he be angry indeed.
CLAUDIO. If he be, he knows how to turn his girdle.
BENEDICK. Shall I speak a word in your ear?
CLAUDIO. God bless me from a challenge!
BENEDICK. You are a villain—I jest not—I will make
it good how you dare, with what you dare, and
when you dare: do me right, or I will protest your
cowardice: you have killed a sweet lady, and her
death shall fall heavy on you. [*aloud*] Let me hear
from you.   150
CLAUDIO. Well, I will meet you, so I may have good
cheer.
DON PEDRO. What, a feast, a feast?
CLAUDIO. I'faith, I thank him, he hath bid me to a
calf's-head and a capon, the which if I do not carve
most curiously, say my knife's naught. Shall I not
find a woodcock too?
BENEDICK. Sir, your wit ambles well—it goes easily.
DON PEDRO. I'll tell thee how Beatrice praised thy wit
the other day. I said, thou hadst a fine wit. 'True,'   160
said she, 'a fine little one': 'No,' said I, 'a great wit':

'Right,' says she, 'a great gross one': 'Nay,' said I,
'a good wit': 'Just,' said she, 'it hurts nobody': 'Nay,'
said I, 'the gentleman is wise': 'Certain,' said she, 'a
wise gentleman': 'Nay,' said I, 'he hath the tongues':
'That I believe,' said she, 'for he swore a thing to me
on Monday night, which he forswore on Tuesday
morning—there's a double tongue, there's two
tongues.' Thus did she an hour together trans-shape
thy particular virtues—yet at last she concluded 170
with a sigh, thou wast the proper'st man in Italy.
CLAUDIO. For the which she wept heartily and said
she cared not.
DON PEDRO. Yea, that she did—but yet, for all that,
an if she did not hate him deadly, she would love
him dearly. The old man's daughter told us all.
CLAUDIO. All, all—and moreover, God saw him when
he was hid in the garden.
DON PEDRO. But when shall we set the savage bull's
horns on the sensible Benedick's head?   180
CLAUDIO. Yea, and text underneath, 'Here dwells
Benedick the married man'?
BENEDICK. Fare you well, boy—you know my mind.
I will leave you now to your gossip-like humour.
You break jests as braggarts do their blades, which
God be thanked hurt not. My lord, for your many
courtesies I thank you. I must discontinue your
company—your brother the bastard is fled from
Messina: you have among you killed a sweet and
innocent lady: for my Lord Lack-beard, there, he 190
and I shall meet, and till then peace be with him.
                                        He goes
DON PEDRO. He is in earnest.
CLAUDIO. In most profound earnest, and I'll warrant
you, for the love of Beatrice.
DON PEDRO. And hath challenged thee?
CLAUDIO. Most sincerely.
DON PEDRO. What a pretty thing man is, when he goes
in his doublet and hose and leaves off his wit!
CLAUDIO. He is then a giant to an ape, but then is an
ape a doctor to such a man.   200
DON PEDRO. But soft you, let me be—pluck up, my
heart, and be sad—did he not say my brother was
fled?

*Enter Dogberry, Verges, and the Watch with Conrade and
Borachio*

DOGBERRY. Come you sir, if justice cannot tame you,
she shall ne'er weigh more reasons in her balance.
Nay, an you be a cursing hypocrite once, you must
be looked to.
DON PEDRO. How now, two of my brother's men
bound? Borachio, one?
CLAUDIO. Hearken after their offence, my lord.   210
DON PEDRO. Officers, what offence have these men
done?
DOGBERRY. Marry sir, they have committed false
report—moreover, they have spoken untruths—
secondarily, they are slanders—sixth and lastly, they
have belied a lady—thirdly, they have verified
unjust things—and to conclude, they are lying
knaves.
DON PEDRO. First, I ask thee what they have done—
thirdly, I ask thee what's their offence—sixth and 220
lastly, why they are committed—and to conclude,
what you lay to their charge.
CLAUDIO. Rightly reasoned, and in his own division—

and by my troth there's one meaning well suited.
DON PEDRO. Who have you offended, masters, that
you are thus bound to your answer? this learned
constable is too cunning to be understood. What's
your offence?
BORACHIO. Sweet prince, let me go no farther to mine
answer: do you hear me, and let this count kill me. 230
I have deceived even your very eyes: what your
wisdoms could not discover, these shallow fools
have brought to light—who in the night overheard
me confessing to this man how Don John your
brother incensed me to slander the Lady Hero, how
you were brought into the orchard and saw me
court Margaret in Hero's garments, how you
disgraced her when you should marry her. My
villainy they have upon record, which I had rather
seal with my death than repeat over to my shame. 240
The lady is dead upon mine and my master's false
accusation: and briefly, I desire nothing but the
reward of a villain.
DON PEDRO. Runs not this speech like iron through
your blood?
CLAUDIO. I have drunk poison whiles he uttered it.
DON PEDRO. But did my brother set thee on to this?
BORACHIO. Yea, and paid me richly for the practice
of it.
DON PEDRO. He is composed and framed of treachery,
And fled he is upon this villainy.
CLAUDIO. Sweet Hero, now thy image doth appear 250
In the rare semblance that I loved it first.
DOGBERRY. Come, bring away the plaintiffs. By this
time our sexton hath reformed Signior Leonato of
the matter . . . And masters, do not forget to specify,
when time and place shall serve, that I am an ass.
VERGES. Here, here comes Master Signior Leonato,
and the sexton too.

Leonato and Antonio come from the house, with the Sexton

LEONATO. Which is the villain? Let me see his eyes,
That when I note another man like him,
I may avoid him: which of these is he?   260
BORACHIO. If you would know your wronger, look on
me.
LEONATO. Art thou the slave that with thy breath hast
killed
Mine innocent child?
BORACHIO.   Yea, even I alone.
LEONATO. No, not so villain, thou beliest thyself,
Here stand a pair of honourable men,
A third is fled that had a hand in it.
I thank you, princes, for my daughter's death,
Record it with your high and worthy deeds,
'Twas bravely done, if you bethink you of it.
CLAUDIO. I know not how to pray your patience,   270
Yet I must speak. Chose your revenge yourself,
Impose me to what penance your invention
Can lay upon my sin—yet sinned I not,
But in mistaking.
DON PEDRO.   By my soul nor I,
And yet to satisfy this good old man,
I would bend under any heavy weight
That he'll enjoin me to.
LEONATO. I cannot bid you bid my daughter live—
That were impossible—but I pray you both,
Possess the people in Messina here   280
How innocent she died, and if your love

Can labour aught in sad invention,
Hang her an epitaph upon her tomb,
And sing it to her bones—sing it to-night:
To-morrow morning come you to my house,
And since you could not be my son-in-law,
Be yet my nephew: my brother hath a daughter,
Almost the copy of my child that's dead,
And she alone is heir to both of us—
Give her the right you should have giv'n her cousin,   290
And so dies my revenge.
CLAUDIO.   O noble sir!
Your over-kindness doth wring tears from me.
I do embrace your offer, and dispose
For henceforth of poor Claudio.
LEONATO. To-morrow then I will expect your
    coming,
To-night I take my leave. This naughty man
Shall face to face be brought to Margaret,
Who I believe was packed in all this wrong,
Hired to it by your brother.
BORACHIO.   No, by my soul she was not,
Nor knew not what she did when she spoke to me,   300
But always hath been just and virtuous
In anything that I do know by her.
DOGBERRY. Moreover, sir—which indeed is not under
white and black—this plaintiff here, the offender,
did call me ass. I beseech you let it be remembered
in his punishment. And also the watch heard them
talk of one Deformed—they say he wears a key in
his ear and a lock hanging by it, and borrows money
in God's name, the which he hath used so long and
never paid, that now men grow hard-hearted and   310
will lend nothing for God's sake. Pray you examine
him upon that point.
LEONATO. I thank thee for thy care and honest pains.
DOGBERRY. Your worship speaks like a most thankful
and reverend youth, and I praise God for you.
LEONATO. There's for thy pains.
DOGBERRY. God save the foundation!
LEONATO. Go, I discharge thee of thy prisoner, and I
thank thee.
DOGBERRY. I leave an arrant knave with your worship,   320
which I beseech your worship to correct yourself,
for the example of others. God keep your worship,
I wish your worship well, God restore you to health,
I humbly give you leave to depart—and if a merry
meeting may be wished, God prohibit it. Come
neighbour.   *Dogberry and Verges depart*
LEONATO. Until to-morrow morning, lords, farewell.
ANTONIO. Farewell my lords, we look for you
    to-morrow.
DON PEDRO. We will not fail.
CLAUDIO.   To-night I'll mourn with Hero.
                        Don Pedro and Claudio leave
LEONATO. Bring you these fellows on. We'll talk with
    Margaret,   330
How her acquaintance grew with this lewd fellow.
                        *Leonato and Antonio go within,
                        followed by the Sexton,
                        the Watch and the prisoners*

                        Scene 2
Enter Benedick and Margaret
BENEDICK. Pray thee sweet Mistress Margaret, deserve
well at my hands, by helping me to the speech of
Beatrice.

MARGARET. Will you then write me a sonnet in praise
of my beauty?
BENEDICK. In so high a style, Margaret, that no man
living shall come over it, for in most comely truth
thou deservest it.
MARGARET. To have no man come over me? why, shall   10
I always keep below stairs?
BENEDICK. Thy wit is as quick as the greyhound's
mouth, it catches.
MARGARET. And yours—as blunt as the fencer's foils,
which hit, but hurt not.
BENEDICK. A most manly wit Margaret, it will not
hurt a woman ... and so I pray thee call Beatrice—
I give thee the bucklers.
MARGARET. Give us the swords, we have bucklers of
our own.
BENEDICK. If you use them, Margaret, you must put   20
in the pikes with a vice—and they are dangerous
weapons for maids.
MARGARET. Well, I will call Beatrice to you, who I
think hath legs.   *Margaret enters the house*
BENEDICK. And therefore will come.
[*sings*]   The god of love,
                    That sits above,
            And knows me, and knows me,
                    How pitiful I deserve.
I mean in singing. But in loving—Leander the good   30
swimmer, Troilus the first employer of pandars, and
a whole bookful of these quondam carpet-mongers,
whose names yet run smoothly in the even road of a
blank verse, why, they were never so truly turned
over and over as my poor self, in love. Marry, I
cannot show it in rhyme—I have tried. I can find out
no rhyme to 'lady' but 'baby,' an innocent rhyme:
for 'scorn,' 'horn,' a hard rhyme: for 'school,' 'fool,'
a babbling rhyme ... very ominous endings. No,
I was not born under a rhyming planet, nor I cannot   40
woo in festival terms ...

Beatrice enters

Sweet Beatrice, wouldst thou come when I called
thee?
BEATRICE. Yea signior, and depart when you bid me.
BENEDICK. O stay but till then.
BEATRICE. 'Then' is spoken: fare you well now—and
yet, ere I go, let me go with that I came for, which
is, with knowing what hath passed between you and
Claudio.
BENEDICK. Only foul words—and thereupon I will   50
kiss thee.
BEATRICE. Foul words is but foul wind, and foul wind
is but foul breath, and foul breath in noisome—
therefore I will depart unkissed.
BENEDICK. Thou hast frighted the word out of his right
sense, so forcible is thy wit. But I must tell thee
plainly, Claudio undergoes my challenge, and either
I must shortly hear from him, or I will subscribe
him a coward. And I pray thee now tell me, for
which of my bad parts didst thou first fall in love   60
with me?
BEATRICE. For them all together, which maintain so
politic a state of evil that they will not admit any
good part to intermingle with them. But for which
of my good parts did you first suffer love for me?
BENEDICK. 'Suffer love!' a good epithet. I do suffer
love indeed, for I love thee against my will.

BEATRICE. In spite of your heart, I think. Alas, poor
heart, if you spite it for my sake, I will spite it for
yours, for I will never love that which my friend 70
hates.

BENEDICK. Thou and I are too wise to woo peaceably.

BEATRICE. It appears not in this confession—there's not
one wise man among twenty that will praise
himself.

BENEDICK. An old, an old instance, Beatrice, that lived
in the time of good neighbours. If a man do not erect
in this age his own tomb ere he dies, he shall live no
longer in monument than the bell rings and the
widow weeps.   80

BEATRICE. And how long is that, think you?

BENEDICK. Question! Why, an hour in clamour and a
quarter in rheum. Therefore is it most expedient for
the wise—if Don Worm, his conscience, find no
impediment to the contrary—to be the trumpet of
his own virtues, as I am to myself. So much for
praising myself, who, I myself will bear witness, is
praiseworthy. And now tell me, how doth your
cousin?

BEATRICE. Very ill.   90

BENEDICK. And how do you?

BEATRICE. Very ill too.

BENEDICK. Serve God, love me, and mend. There will
I leave you too, for here comes one in haste.

Ursula enters

URSULA. Madam, you must come to your uncle—
yonder's old coil at home. It is proved my Lady
Hero hath been falsely accused, the prince and
Claudio mightily abused, and Don John is the
author of all, who is fled and gone. Will you come
presently?   100

BEATRICE. Will you go hear this news, signior?

BENEDICK. I will live in thy heart, die in thy lap, and
be buried in thy eyes: and moreover, I will go with
thee to thy uncle's.   *They go within*

Scene 3: *A church-yard*

*Don Pedro, Claudio and other lords approach with tapers,
followed by Balthazar and musicians*

CLAUDIO. Is this the monument of Leonato?

A LORD. It is, my lord.

CLAUDIO. [*reads from a scroll*].
        Done to death by slanderous tongues
        Was the Hero that here lies:
        Death, in guerdon of her wrongs,
        Gives her fame which never dies:
        So the life that died with shame,
        Lives in death with glorious fame.
            Hang thou there upon the tomb,
                                    Affixing it
        Praising her when I am dumb.   10
    Now, music, sound, and sing your solemn hymn.

BALTHAZAR [*sings*].
        Pardon, goddess of the night,
        Those that slew thy virgin knight,
        For the which, with songs of woe,
        Round about her tomb they go:
        Midnight, assist our moan,
        Help us to sigh and groan,
            Heavily, heavily.
        Graves, yawn and yield your dead,

        Till death be utteréd,   20
            Heavily, heavily.

CLAUDIO. Now, unto thy bones good night.
        Yearly will I do this rite.

DON PEDRO. Good morrow masters, put your torches
out.
        The wolves have preyed, and look, the gentle day,
        Before the wheels of Phœbus, round about
        Dapples the drowsy east with spots of grey:
        Thanks to you all, and leave us. Fare you well.

CLAUDIO. Good morrow masters—each his several
way.

DON PEDRO. Come let us hence, and put on other
weeds,   30
        And then to Leonato's we will go.

CLAUDIO. And Hymen now with luckier issue speeds,
        Than this for whom we rendred up this woe!
                                            They go

Scene 4: *The hall in Leonato's house*

*Leonato, Antonio, Benedick and Friar Francis enter,
followed by Hero, Beatrice, Margaret and Ursula, who
talk apart*

FRIAR. Did I not tell you she was innocent?

LEONATO. So are the prince and Claudio, who accused
        her
        Upon the error that you heard debated:
        But Margaret was in some fault for this,
        Although against her will, as it appears
        In the true course of all the question.

ANTONIO. Well, I am glad that all things sort so well.

BENEDICK. And so am I, being else by faith enforced
        To call young Claudio to a reckoning for it.

LEONATO. Well daughter, and you gentlewomen all, 10
        Withdraw into a chamber by yourselves,
        And when I send for you come hither masked.
                                        The ladies go
        The prince and Claudio promised by this hour
        To visit me. You know your office, brother—
        You must be father to your brother's daughter,
        And give her to young Claudio.

ANTONIO. Which I will do with confirmed countenance.

BENEDICK. Friar, I must entreat your pains, I think.

FRIAR. To do what, signior?

BENEDICK. To bind me, or undo me—one of them: 20
        Signior Leonato, truth it is, good signior,
        Your niece regards me with an eye of favour.

LEONATO. That eye my daughter lent her. 'Tis most
        true.

BENEDICK. And I do with an eye of love requite her.

LEONATO. The sight whereof I think you had from me,
        From Claudio, and the prince. But what's your will?

BENEDICK. Your answer, sir, is enigmatical:
        But for my will, my will is your good will
        May stand with ours, this day to be conjoined
        In the state of honourable marriage—   30
        In which, good friar, I shall desire your help.

LEONATO. My heart is with your liking.

FRIAR.   And my help.
        Here comes the prince and Claudio.

Don Pedro and Claudio enter with two or three other lords

DON PEDRO. Good morrow to this fair assembly.

LEONATO. Good morrow prince, good morrow
        Claudio:

We here attend you. Are you yet determined
To-day to marry with my brother's daughter?
CLAUDIO. I'll hold my mind, were she an Ethiope.
LEONATO. Call her forth, brother. Here's the friar
ready.   *Antonio goes*
DON PEDRO. Good morrow Benedick. Why, what's   40
the matter,
That you have such a February face,
So full of frost, of storm, and cloudiness?
CLAUDIO. I think he thinks upon the savage bull:
Tush, fear not, man, we'll tip thy horns with gold,
And all Europa shall rejoice at thee,
As once Europa did at lusty Jove,
When he would play the noble beast in love.
BENEDICK. Bull Jove, sir, had an amiable low—
And some such strange bull leaped your father's
cow,
And got a calf in that same noble feat,   50
Much like to you, for you have just his bleat.

Antonio returns, with the ladies masked

CLAUDIO. For this I owe you: here comes
other reck'nings.
Which is the lady I must seize upon?
ANTONIO. This same is she, and I do give you her.
CLAUDIO. Why, then she's mine. Sweet, let me see
your face.
LEONATO. No, that you shall not, till you take her hand
Before this friar, and swear to marry her.
CLAUDIO. Give me your hand before this holy friar—
I am your husband if you like of me.
HERO. And when I lived I was your other wife—   60
                                        She unmasks
And when you loved, you were my other husband.
CLAUDIO. Another Hero!
HERO.   Nothing certainer.
One Hero died defiled, but I do live,
And surely as I live, I am a maid.
DON PEDRO. The former Hero! Hero that is dead!
LEONATO. She died, my lord, but whiles her slander
lived.
FRIAR. All this amazement can I qualify.
When after that the holy rites are ended,
I'll tell you largely of fair Hero's death,
Meantime let wonder seem familiar,   70
And to the chapel let us presently.
BENEDICK. Soft and fair, friar. Which is Beatrice?
BEATRICE. I answer to that name. *[unmasks]* What is
your will?
BENEDICK. Do not you love me?
BEATRICE.   Why no, no more than reason.
BENEDICK. Why then your uncle, and the prince, and
Claudio,
Have been deceivéd, for they swore you did.
BEATRICE. Do not you love me?
BENEDICK.   Troth no, no more than reason.
BEATRICE. Why then my cousin, Margaret, and Ursula,
Are much deceived, for they did swear you did.
BENEDICK. They swore that you were almost sick for
me.   80

BEATRICE. They swore that you were well-nigh dead
for me.
BENEDICK. 'Tis no such matter. Then, you do not love
me?
BEATRICE. No, truly, but in friendly recompense.
LEONATO. Come cousin, I am sure you love the
gentleman.
CLAUDIO. And I'll be sworn upon't, that he loves her,
For here's a paper written in his hand,
A halting sonnet of his own pure brain,
Fashioned to Beatrice.
HERO.   And here's another,
Writ in my cousin's hand, stol'n from her pocket,
Containing her affection unto Benedick.   90
BENEDICK. A miracle! here's our own hands against
our hearts. Come, I will have thee—but by this light
I take thee for pity.
BEATRICE. I would not deny you—but by this good
day I yield upon great persuasion, and partly to save
your life, for I was told you were in a consumption.
BENEDICK. Peace, I will stop your mouth.
                                        He kisses her
DON PEDRO. How dost thou, Benedick the married
man?
BENEDICK. I'll tell thee what, prince: a college of wit- 100
crackers cannot flout me out of my humour. Dost
thou think I care for a satire or an epigram? no, if
a man will be beaten with brains, a' shall wear
nothing handsome about him. In brief, since I do
purpose to marry, I will think nothing to any
purpose that the world can say against it—and
therefore never flout at me for what I have said
against it: for man is a giddy thing, and this is my
conclusion. For thy part, Claudio, I did think to
have beaten thee, but in that thou art like to be my 110
kinsman, live unbruised, and love my cousin.
CLAUDIO. I had well hoped thou wouldst have denied
Beatrice, that I might have cudgelled thee out of thy
single life, to make thee a double-dealer—which out
of question thou wilt be, if my cousin do not look
exceeding narrowly to thee.
BENEDICK. Come, come, we are friends. Let's have a
dance ere we are married, that we may lighten our
own hearts, and our wives' heels.
LEONATO. We'll have dancing afterward.   120
BENEDICK. First, of my word—therefore play music.
Prince, thou art sad—get thee a wife, get thee a wife.
There is no staff more reverend than one tipped with
horn.

A messenger enters

MESSENGER. My lord, your brother John is ta'en in
flight,
And brought with armed men back to Messina.
BENEDICK. Think not on him till to-morrow. I'll
devise thee brave punishments for him … Strike up,
pipers!

Music and dance

Love's Labour's Lost

The scene: the royal park in Navarre

CHARACTERS IN THE PLAY

FERDINAND, *King of Navarre*
BEROWNE
LONGAVILLE } *young lords, attending on the King*
DUMAINE
BOYET, *an elderly lord, attending on the Princess of France*
MERCADÉ, *a messenger*
DON ADRIANO DE ARMADO, *a fantastical Spaniard*
SIR NATHANIEL, *a curate*
HOLOFERNES, *a schoolmaster*
DULL, *a constable*

COSTARD, *a clown*
MOTH, *page to Armado*
A Forester
THE PRINCESS OF FRANCE
ROSALINE
KATHARINE } *ladies, attending on the Princess*
MARIA
JAQUENETTA, *a country wench*
Officers and others, attendant on the King and the Princess

Love's Labour's Lost

ACT 1

Scene 1: *The Park of Ferdinand, King of Navarre*

The King, Berowne, Longaville, and Dumaine

KING. Let fame, that all hunt after in their lives,
　Live regist'red upon our brazen tombs,
　And then grace us, in the disgrace of death;
　When, spite of cormorant devouring Time,
　Th'endeavour of this present breath may buy
　That honour which shall bate his scythe's keen edge,
　And make us heirs of all eternity.
　Therefore, brave conquerors—for so you are
　That war against your own affections
　And the huge army of the world's desires—　　10
　Our late edict shall strongly stand in force:
　Navarre shall be the wonder of the world,
　Our court shall be a little academe,
　Still and contemplative in living art.
　You three, Berowne, Dumaine, and Longaville,
　Have sworn for three years' term to live with me,
　My fellow-scholars, and to keep those statutes
　That are recorded in this schedule here.
　Your oaths are passed; and now subscribe your
　　names,
　That his own hand may strike his honour down　　20
　That violates the smallest branch herein.
　If you are armed to do, as sworn to do,
　Subscribe to your deep oaths, and keep it too.
LONGAVILLE. I am resolved—'tis but a three years' fast:
　The mind shall banquet, though the body pine.
　Fat paunches have lean pates; and dainty bits
　Make rich the ribs, but bankrupt quite the wits.
DUMAINE. My loving lord, Dumaine is mortified.
　The grosser manner of these world's delights
　He throws upon the gross world's baser slaves.　　30
　To love, to wealth, to pomp, I pine and die—
　With all these living in philosophy.
BEROWNE. I can but say their protestation over—
　So much, dear liege, I have already sworn,
　That is, to live and study here three years.
　But there are other strict observances:
　As not to see a woman in that term,
　Which I hope well is not enrollèd there—
　And one day in a week to touch no food,
　And but one meal on every day beside,　　40
　The which I hope is not enrollèd there—
　And then to sleep but three hours in the night
　And not be seen to wink of all the day,
　When I was wont to think no harm all night,
　And make a dark night too of half the day,
　Which I hope well is not enrollèd there.
　O, these are barren tasks, too hard to keep,
　Not to see ladies, study, fast, not sleep.
KING. Your oath is passed to pass away from these.
BEROWNE. Let me say no, my liege, an if you please.　　50
　I only swore to study with your grace,
　And stay here in your court for three years' space.
LONGAVILLE. You swore to that, Berowne, and to
　the rest.
BEROWNE. By yea and nay, sir, then I swore in jest.

What is the end of study? let me know.
KING. Why, that to know which else we should
　not know.
BEROWNE. Things hid and barred, you mean, from
　common sense?
KING. Ay, that is study's god-like recompense.
BEROWNE. Com' on then—I will swear to study so,
　To know the thing I am forbid to know:　　60
　As thus—to study where I well may dine
　When I to feast expressly am forbid,
　Or study where to meet some mistress fine
　When mistresses from common senses are hid,
　Or, having sworn too hard-a-keeping oath,
　Study to break it and not break my troth.
　If study's gain be thus, and this be so,
　Study knows that which yet it doth not know.
　Swear me to this, and I will ne'er say no.
KING. These be the stops that hinder study quite,　　70
　And train our intellects to vain delight.
BEROWNE. Why, all delights are vain, but that most
　vain
　Which, with pain purchased, doth inherit pain—
　As painfully to pore upon a book
　To seek the light of truth, while truth the while
　Doth falsely blind the eyesight of his look:
　Light, seeking light, doth light of light beguile:
　So, ere you find where light in darkness lies,
　Your light grows dark by losing of your eyes.
　Study me how to please the eye indeed,　　80
　By fixing it upon a fairer eye,
　Who dazzling so, that eye shall be his heed,
　And give him light that it was blinded by.
　Study is like the heaven's glorious sun,
　That will not be deep-searched with saucy looks:
　Small have continual plodders ever won,
　Save base authority from others' books.
　These earthly godfathers of heaven's lights
　That give a name to every fixèd star
　Have no more profit of their shining nights,　　90
　Than those that walk and wot not what they are.
　Too much to know is to know nought but fame;
　And every godfather can give a name.
KING. How well he's read, to reason against reading.
DUMAINE. Proceeded well, to stop all good
　proceeding.
LONGAVILLE. He weeds the corn and still lets grow
　the weeding.
BEROWNE. The spring is near when green geese
　are a-breeding.
DUMAINE. How follows that?
BEROWNE. 　　　　　　　　　Fit in his place and time.
DUMAINE. In reason nothing.
BEROWNE. 　　　　　　　　Something then in rhyme.
KING. Berowne is like an envious sneaping frost　　100
　That bites the first-born infants of the spring.
BEROWNE. Well, say I am—why should proud
　summer boast,
　Before the birds have any cause to sing?
　Why should I joy in an abortive birth?
　At Christmas I no more desire a rose

Than wish a snow in May's new-fangled shows;
But like of each thing that in season grows.
So you to study now it is too late,
Climb o'er the house to unlock the little gate.
KING. Well, sit you out: go home Berowne: adieu!   110
BEROWNE. No my good lord, I have sworn to stay
     with you.
And though I have for barbarism spoke more
Than for that angel knowledge you can say,
Yet confident I'll keep what I have swore,
And bide the penance of each three years' day.
Give me the paper, let me read the same,
And to the strictest decrees I'll write my name.
KING. How well this yielding rescues thee
     from shame.
BEROWNE [reads]. 'Item, That no woman shall come
within a mile of my court....' Hath this been pro-   120
claimed?
LONGAVILLE. Four days ago.
BEROWNE. Let's see the penalty. [reads] '... on pain of
losing her tongue.' Who devised this penalty?
LONGAVILLE. Marry, that did I.
BEROWNE. Sweet lord, and why?
LONGAVILLE. To fright them hence with that
     dread penalty.
BEROWNE. A dangerous law against gentility....
     [reads] 'Item, if any man be seen to talk with a
     woman within the term of three years, he shall   130
     endure such public shame as the rest of the court
     can possible devise,'
This article, my liege, yourself must break,
For well you know here comes in embassy
The French king's daughter with yourself to
     speak—
A maid of grace and cómplete majesty—
About surrender up of Aquitaine
To her decrepit, sick, and bedrid father.
Therefore this article is made in vain,
Or vainly comes th'admiréd princess hither.   140
KING. What say you lords? why, this was quite forgot.
BEROWNE. So study evermore is overshot.
While it doth study to have what it would,
It doth forget to do the thing it should:
And when it hath the thing it hunteth most,
'Tis won, as towns with fire—so won, so lost.
KING. We must of force dispense with this decree.
She must lie here on mere necessity.
BEROWNE. Necessity will make us all forsworn
Three thousand times within this three years' space: 150
For every man with his affects is born,
Not by might mast'red, but by special grace.
If I break faith, this word shall speak for me,
I am forsworn 'on mere necessity.'
So to the laws at large I write my name,
And he that breaks them in the least degree
Stands in attainder of eternal shame.
Suggestions are to other as to me:
But I believe, although I seem so loath,
I am the last that will last keep his oath....   160
                              He subscribes
But is there no quick recreation granted?
KING. Ay that there is, our court you know
     is haunted
With a refinéd traveller of Spain—
A man in all the world's new fashion planted,
That hath a mint of phrases in his brain:

One who the music of his own vain tongue
Doth ravish like enchanting harmony:
A man of complements, whom right and wrong
Have chose as umpire of their mutiny.
This child of fancy, that Armado hight,   170
For interim to our studies shall relate
In high-born words the worth of many a knight
From tawny Spain lost in the world's debate.
How you delight, my lords, I know not I,
But I protest I love to hear him lie,
And I will use him for my minstrelsy.
BEROWNE. Armado is a most illustrious wight.
A man of fire-new words, fashion's own knight.
LONGAVILLE. Costard the swain and he shall be
     our sport,
And so to study three years is but short.   180

Dull, the constable, and Costard approach

DULL. Which is the duke's own person?
BEROWNE. This, fellow. What wouldst?
DULL. I myself reprehend his own person, for I am
     his grace's farborough. But I would see his own
     person in flesh and blood.
BEROWNE. This is he.
DULL. Signior Arm—Arm—commends you.... [*he
     presents a letter*] There's villainy abroad. This letter
     will tell you more.
COSTARD. Sir, the contempts thereof are as touching   190
     me.
KING. A letter from the magnificent Armado.
BEROWNE. How low soever the matter, I hope in God
     for high words.
LONGAVILLE. A high hope for a low heaven. God grant
     us patience.
BEROWNE. To hear, or forbear hearing?
LONGAVILLE. To hear meekly sir, and to laugh moder-
     ately—or to forbear both.
BEROWNE. Well sir, be it as the style shall give us   200
     cause to climb in the merriness.
COSTARD. The matter is to me, sir, as concerning
     Jaquenetta:
The manner of it is, I was taken with the manner.
BEROWNE. In what manner?
COSTARD. In manner and form following, sir—all
     those three: I was seen with her in the manor-house,
     sitting with her upon the form, and taken following
     her into the park: which put together, is in manner
     and form following. Now sir for the manner—it is   210
     the manner of a man to speak to a woman. For the
     form—in some form.
BEROWNE. For the following, sir?
COSTARD. As it shall follow in my correction—and
     God defend the right.
KING. Will you hear this letter with attention?
BEROWNE. As we would hear an oracle.
COSTARD. Such is the simplicity of man to hearken
     after the flesh.
KING [reads]. 'Great Deputy, the welkin's Vice-
     regent, and sole dominator of Navarre, my soul's   220
     earth's God, and body's fost'ring patron:'
COSTARD. Not a word of Costard yet.
KING [reads]. 'So it is,'
COSTARD. It may be so: but if he say it is so, he is,
     in telling true—but so.
KING. Peace!

COSTARD. —be to me, and every man that dares not fight.

KING. No words.

COSTARD. —of other men's secrets I beseech you.

KING [reads]. 'So it is, besieged with sable-coloured melancholy, I did commend the black-oppressing humour to the most wholesome physic of thy health-giving air: And, as I am a gentleman, betook myself to walk: the time When? about the sixth hour, When Beasts most graze, Birds best peck, and Men sit down to that nourishment which is called Supper: So much for the time When. Now for the ground Which? which I mean I walked upon, it is ycleped Thy Park. Then for the place Where? where I mean I did encounter that obscene and most prepostrous event, that draweth from my snow-white pen the ebon-coloured Ink, which here thou viewest, beholdest, surveyest, or seest. But to the place Where? It standeth North North-east and by East from the West corner of thy curious-knotted garden. There did I see that low-spirited Swain, that base Minion of thy mirth,'

COSTARD. Me?

KING. 'that unlettered small-knowing soul,'

COSTARD. Me?

KING. 'that shallow vassal,'

COSTARD. Still me?

KING. 'which, as I remember, hight Costard,'

COSTARD. O me!

KING. 'sorted and consorted, contrary to thy established proclaimed Edict and continent Canon, with, with, O with, but with this I passion to say where-with:'

COSTARD. With a wench.

KING. 'with a child of our Grandmother Eve, a female; or for thy more sweet understanding a Woman: him, I (as my ever-esteemed duty pricks me on) have sent to thee, to receive the meed of punishment, by thy sweet Grace's Officer, Antony Dull, a man of good repute, carriage, bearing, and estimation.'

DULL. Me, an't shall please you! I am Antony Dull.

KING. 'For Jaquenetta (so is the weaker vessel called) which I apprehended with the aforesaid Swain, I keep here as a vessel of thy Law's fury, and shall at the least of thy sweet notice, bring her to trial. Thine, in all complements of devoted and heart-burning heat of duty,

　　　　　　　DON ADRIANO DE ARMADO.'

BEROWNE. This is not so well as I looked for, but the best that ever I heard.

KING. Ay, the best for the worst.... But sirrah, what say you to this?

COSTARD. Sir I confess the wench.

KING. Did you hear the proclamation?

COSTARD. I do confess much of the hearing of it, but little of the marking of it.

KING. It was proclaimed a year's imprisonment to be taken with a wench.

COSTARD. I was taken with none sir, I was taken with a damsel.

KING. Well, it was proclaimed 'damsel.'

COSTARD. This was no damsel neither sir, she was a virgin.

KING. It is so varied too, for it was proclaimed 'virgin.'

COSTARD. If it were, I deny her virginity: I was taken with a maid.

KING. This 'maid' will not serve your turn, sir.

COSTARD. This maid will serve my turn, sir.

KING. Sir I will pronounce your sentence: you shall fast a week with bran and water.

COSTARD. I had rather pray a month with mutton and porridge.

KING. And Don Armado shall be your keeper. My Lord Berowne see him delivered o'er— And go we lords to put in practice that Which each to other hath so strongly sworn.

　　　　　　　The King, Longaville and Dumaine go

BEROWNE. I'll lay my head to any goodman's hat, These oaths and laws will prove an idle scorn— Sirrah, come on.

COSTARD. I suffer for the truth, sir: for true it is, I was taken with Jaquenetta, and Jaquenetta is a true girl, and therefore welcome the sour cup of prosperity. Affliction may one day smile again, and till then sit thee down, sorrow.　　　　　　　They go

Scene 2

Enter Armado and Moth

ARMADO. Boy, what sign is it when a man of great spirit grows melancholy?

MOTH. A great sign sir that he will look sad.

ARMADO. Why, sadness is one and the self-same thing, dear imp.

MOTH. No no, O Lord sir, no.

ARMADO. How canst thou part sadness and melancholy, my tender juvenal?

MOTH. By a familiar demonstration of the working, my tough signior.

ARMADO. Why tough signior? why tough signior?

MOTH. Why tender juvenal? why tender juvenal?

ARMADO. I spoke it, tender juvenal, as a congruent epitheton, appertaining to thy young days, which we may nominate tender.

MOTH. And I, tough signior, as an appertinent title to your old time, which we may name tough.

ARMADO. Pretty and apt.

MOTH. How mean you sir, I pretty, and my saying apt? or I apt, and my saying pretty?

ARMADO. Thou pretty, because little.

MOTH. Little pretty, because little: wherefore apt?

ARMADO. And therefore apt, because quick.

MOTH. Speak you this in my praise, master?

ARMADO. In thy condign praise.

MOTH. I will praise an eel with the same praise.

ARMADO. What, that an eel is ingenious?

MOTH. That an eel is quick.

ARMADO. I do say thou art quick in answers. Thou heat'st my blood.

MOTH. I am answered, sir.

ARMADO. I love not to be crossed.

MOTH [aside]. He speaks the mere contrary, crosses love not him.

ARMADO. I have promised to study three years with the duke.

MOTH. You may do it in an hour, sir.

ARMADO. Impossible.

MOTH. How many is one thrice told?

ARMADO. I am ill at reck'ning, it fitteth the spirit of a tapster.

MOTH. You are a gentleman and a gamester, sir.

ARMADO. I confess both—they are both the varnish of a complete man.

MOTH. Then I am sure you know how much the gross sum of deuce-ace amounts to.

ARMADO. It doth amount to one more than two.

MOTH. Which the base vulgar do call three.

ARMADO. True.

MOTH. Why sir, is this such a piece of study? Now 50 here is three studied ere ye'll thrice wink: and how easy it is to put 'years' to the word 'three,' and study 'three years' in two words, the dancing horse will tell you.

ARMADO. A most fine figure!

MOTH [aside]. To prove you a cipher.

ARMADO. I will hereupon confess I am in love: and as it is base for a soldier to love, so am I in love with a base wench. If drawing my sword against the humour of affection would deliver me from the 60 reprobate thought of it, I would take Desire prisoner, and ransom him to any French courtier for a new-devised curtsy. I think scorn to sigh—methinks I should outswear Cupid.... Comfort me, boy. What great men have been in love?

MOTH. Hercules, master.

ARMADO. Most sweet Hercules! More authority, dear boy, name more; and, sweet my child, let them be men of good repute and carriage.

MOTH. Samson, master—he was a man of good car- 70 riage, great carriage: for he carried the town-gates on his back like a porter: and he was in love.

ARMADO. O well-knit Samson! strong-jointed Samson! I do excel thee in my rapier as much as thou didst me in carrying gates. I am in love too. Who was Samson's, my dear Moth?

MOTH. A woman, master.

ARMADO. Of what complexion?

MOTH. Of all the four, or the three, or the two, or one of the four.

ARMADO. Tell me precisely of what complexion? 80

MOTH. Of the sea-water green, sir.

ARMADO. Is that one of the four complexions?

MOTH. As I have read sir, and the best of them too.

ARMADO. Green indeed is the colour of lovers: but to have a love of that colour, methinks Samson had small reason for it. He surely affected her for her wit.

MOTH. It was so sir—for she had a green wit.

ARMADO. My love is most immaculate white and red.

MOTH. Most maculate thoughts, master, are masked 90 under such colours.

ARMADO. Define, define, well-educated infant.

MOTH. My father's wit, and my mother's tongue assist me!

ARMADO. Sweet invocation of a child, most pretty and pathetical.

MOTH. If she be made of white and red,
        Her faults will ne'er be known;
     For blushing cheeks by faults are bred,
        And fears by pale white shown: 100
     Then if she fear, or be to blame,
        By this you shall not know,
     For still her cheeks possess the same,
        Which native she doth owe.
A dangerous rhyme, master, against the reason of white and red.

ARMADO. Is there not a ballad, boy, of the King and the Beggar?

MOTH. The world was very guilty of such a ballad some three ages since, but I think now 'tis not to be 110 found: or if it were, it would neither serve for the writing nor the tune.

ARMADO. I will have that subject newly writ o'er, that I may example my digression by some mighty precedent. Boy, I do love—that country girl that I took in the park with the rational hind Costard: she deserves well.

MOTH [aside]. To be whipped: and yet a better love than my master.

ARMADO. Sing, boy. My spirit grows heavy in love. 120

MOTH. And that's great marvel, loving a light wench.

ARMADO. I say, sing.

MOTH. Forbear till this company be past.

Dull, Costard, and Jaquenetta enter

DULL. Sir, the duke's pleasure is that you keep Costard safe—and you must suffer him to take no delight, nor no penance, but a' must fast three days a week. For this damsel, I must keep her at the park—she is allowed for the dey-woman. Fare you well.

ARMADO. I do betray myself with blushing. Maid!

JAQUENETTA. Man. 130

ARMADO. I will visit thee at the lodge.

JAQUENETTA. That's hereby.

ARMADO. I know where it is situate.

JAQUENETTA. Lord, how wise you are!

ARMADO. I will tell thee wonders.

JAQUENETTA. With that face?

ARMADO. I love thee.

JAQUENETTA. So I heard you say.

ARMADO. And so farewell.

JAQUENETTA. Fair weather after you! 140

DULL. Come Jaquenetta, away.

                              Dull and Jaquenetta go

ARMADO. Villain, thou shalt fast for thy offences ere thou be pardoned.

COSTARD. Well sir, I hope when I do it, I shall do it on a full stomach.

ARMADO. Thou shalt be heavily punished.

COSTARD. I am more bound to you than your fellows, for they are but lightly rewarded.

ARMADO. Take away this villain, shut him up.

MOTH. Come you transgressing slave, away. 150

COSTARD. Let me not be pent up sir, I will fast being loose.

MOTH. No sir, that were fast and loose: thou shalt to prison.

COSTARD. Well, if ever I do see the merry days of desolation that I have seen, some shall see—

MOTH. What shall some see?

COSTARD. Nay nothing, Master Moth, but what they look upon. It is not for prisoners to be too silent in their words, and therefore I will say nothing: I 160 thank God I have as little patience as another man, and therefore I can be quiet.

                              Moth and Costard depart

ARMADO. I do affect the very ground (which is base) where her shoe (which is baser) guided by her foot (which is basest) doth tread. I shall be forsworn (which is a great argument of falsehood) if I love. And how can that be true love, which is falsely at-

tempted? Love is a familiar; love is a devil. There is
no evil angel but love. Yet was Samson so tempted,
and he had an excellent strength: yet was Solomon   170
so seduced, and he had a very good wit. Cupid's
butt-shaft is too hard for Hercules' club, and therefore too much odds for a Spaniard's rapier. The
first and second cause will not serve my turn: the
passado he respects not, the duello he regards not;
his disgrace is to be called boy, but his glory is
to subdue men. Adieu valour, rust rapier, be still
drum! for your manager is in love; yea he loveth.
Assist me some extemporal god of rhyme, for I am
sure I shall turn sonnet. Devise wit, write pen,   180
for I am for whole volumes in folio.   *He goes*

ACT 2
Scene 1

The Princess of France, Rosaline, Maria, Katharine,
Boyet, lords and other attendants

BOYET. Now, madam, summon up your
        dearest spirits,
    Consider who the king your father sends.
    To whom he sends, and what's his embassy.
    Yourself, held precious in the world's esteem,
    To parley with the sole inheritor
    Of all perfections that a man may owe,
    Matchless Navarre; the plea of no less weight
    Than Aquitaine, a dowry for a queen.
    Be now as prodigal of all dear grace,
    As nature was in making graces dear,   10
    When she did starve the general world beside,
    And prodigally gave them all to you.
PRINCESS. Good Lord Boyet, my beauty, though
        but mean,
    Needs not the painted flourish of your praise:
    Beauty is bought by judgement of the eye,
    Not utt'red by base sale of chapmen's tongues.
    I am less proud to hear you tell my worth
    Than you much willing to be counted wise
    In spending your wit in the praise of mine.
    But now to task the tasker—good Boyet,   20
    You are not ignorant all-telling fame
    Doth noise abroad Navarre hath made a vow,
    Till painful study shall outwear three years,
    No woman may approach his silent court:
    Therefore to's seemeth it a needful course,
    Before we enter his forbidden gates,
    To know his pleasure; and in that behalf,
    Bold of your worthiness, we single you,
    As our best-moving fair solicitor.
    Tell him, the daughter of the King of France,   30
    On serious business craving quick dispatch,
    Importunes personal conference with his grace.
    Haste, signify so much, while we attend,
    Like humble-visaged suitors, his high will.
BOYET. Proud of employment, willingly I go.
PRINCESS. All pride is willing pride, and yours is so.
                                        He goes
    Who are the votaries, my loving lords,
    That are vow-fellows with this virtuous duke?
A LORD. Lord Longaville is one.
PRINCESS.   Know you the man?
MARIA. I know him, madam: at a marriage-feast,   40

Between Lord Perigort and the beauteous heir
Of Jaquës Falconbridge, solemnizéd
In Normandy, saw I this Longaville.
A man of sovereign parts he is esteemed;
Well fitted in arts, glorious in arms:
Nothing becomes him ill that he would well.
The only soil of his fair virtue's gloss—
If virtue's gloss will stain with any soil—
Is a sharp wit matched with too blunt a will;
Whose edge hath power to cut, whose will still wills 50
It should none spare that come within his power.
PRINCESS. Some merry mocking lord belike, is't so?
MARIA. They say so most that most his humours know.
PRINCESS. Such short-lived wits do wither as they
        grow.
    Who are the rest?
KATHARINE. The young Dumaine, a well-
        accomplished youth,
    Of all that virtue love for virtue loved:
    Most power to do most harm, least knowing ill;
    For he hath wit to make an ill shape good,
    And shape to win grace though he had no wit.   60
    I saw him at the Duke Alanson's once,
    And much too little of that good I saw
    Is my report to his great worthiness.
ROSALINE. Another of these students at that time
    Was there with him, if I have heard a truth—
    Berowne they call him—but a merrier man,
    Within the limit of becoming mirth,
    I never spent an hour's talk withal.
    His eye begets occasion for his wit,
    For every object that the one doth catch   70
    The other turns to a mirth-moving jest,
    Which his fair tongue—conceit's expositor—
    Delivers in such apt and gracious words,
    That aged ears play truant at his tales,
    And younger hearings are quite ravishéd,
    So sweet and voluble is his discourse.
PRINCESS. God bless my ladies! are they all in love,
    That every one her own hath garnishéd
    With such bedecking ornaments of praise?

Boyet returns

A LORD. Here comes Boyet.
PRINCESS.   Now, what admittance, lord?   80
BOYET. Navarre had notice of your fair approach,
    And he and his competitors in oath
    Were all addressed to meet you, gentle lady,
    Before I came. Marry, thus much I have learnt:
    He rather means to lodge you in the field,
    Like one that comes here to besiege his court,
    Than seek a dispensation for his oath,
    To let you enter his unpeopled house.
    Here comes Navarre.

The King, Longaville, Dumaine, Berowne and attendants
enter. [The ladies mask]

KING. Fair princess, welcome to the court of Navarre.   90
PRINCESS. 'Fair' I give you back again, and 'welcome'
    I have not yet: the roof of this court is too high to
    be yours, and welcome to the wide fields too base
    to be mine.
KING. You shall be welcome, madam, to my court.
PRINCESS. I will be welcome then—conduct me
    thither.

KING. Hear me dear lady, I have sworn an oath.
PRINCESS. Our Lady help my lord! he'll be forsworn.
KING. Not for the world fair madam, by my will.
PRINCESS. Why, will shall break it; will, and
    nothing else.   100
KING. Your ladyship is ignorant what it is.
PRINCESS. Were my lord so, his ignorance were wise.
    Where now his knowledge must prove ignorance.
    I hear your grace hath sworn out house-keeping:
    'Tis deadly sin to keep that oath, my lord,
    And sin to break it.
    But pardon me, I am too sudden-bold—
    To teach a teacher ill beseemeth me.
    Vouchsafe to read the purpose of my coming,
    And suddenly resolve me in my suit.   110
                She gives a paper
KING. Madam I will, if suddenly I may.
PRINCESS. You will the sooner that I were away,
    For you'll prove perjured if you make me stay.
⌈BEROWNE. Did not I dance with you in Brabant
    once?
KATHARINE. Did not I dance with you in Brabant
    once?
BEROWNE. I know you did.
KATHARINE.   How needless was it then
    To ask the question!
BEROWNE.   You must not be so quick.
KATHARINE. 'Tis 'long of you that spur me with
    such questions.
BEROWNE. Your wit's too hot, it speeds too fast,
    'twill tire.
KATHARINE. Not till it leave the rider in the mire.   120
BEROWNE. What time o'day?
KATHARINE.   The hour that fools should ask.
BEROWNE. Now fair befall your mask!
KATHARINE. Fair fall the face it covers!
BEROWNE. And send you many lovers!
KATHARINE. Amen, so you be none.
BEROWNE. Nay then will I be gone.⌋
KING. Madam, your father here doth intimate
    The payment of a hundred thousand crowns,
    Being but the one half of an entire sum
    Disbursèd by my father in his wars.   130
    But say that he, or we—as neither have—
    Received that sum, yet there remains unpaid
    A hundred thousand more, in surety of the which
    One part of Aquitaine is bound to us,
    Although not valued to the money's worth.
    If then the king your father will restore
    But that one half which is unsatisfied,
    We will give up our right in Aquitaine,
    And hold fair friendship with his majesty.
    But that, it seems, he little purposeth,   140
    For here he doth demand to have repaid
    A hundred thousand crowns, and not demands,
    On payment of a hundred thousand crowns,
    To have his title live in Aquitaine;
    Which we much rather had depart withal,
    And have the money by our father lent,
    Than Aquitaine, so gelded as it is.
    Dear princess, were not his requests so far
    From reason's yielding, your fair self should make
    A yielding 'gainst some reason in my breast,   150
    And go well satisfied to France again.
PRINCESS. You do the king my father too much
    wrong,

And wrong the reputation of your name,
In so unseeming to confess receipt
Of that which hath so faithfully been paid.
KING. I do protest I never heard of it:
    And if you prove it, I'll repay it back
    Or yield up Aquitaine.
PRINCESS.   We arrest your word.
    Boyet, you can produce acquittances
    For such a sum from special officers   160
    Of Charles his father.
KING.   Satisfy me so.
BOYET. So please your grace, the packet is not come
    Where that and other specialties are bound:
    To-morrow you shall have a sight of them.
KING. It shall suffice me; at which interview
    All liberal reason I will yield unto.
    Meantime, receive such welcome at my hand
    As honour—without breach of honour—may
    Make tender of to thy true worthiness.
    You may not come, fair princess, within my gates,   170
    But here without you shall be so received,
    As you shall deem yourself lodged in my heart,
    Though so denied fair harbour in my house.
    Your own good thoughts excuse me, and farewell—
    To-morrow shall we visit you again.
PRINCESS. Sweet health and fair desires consort
    your grace!
KING. Thy own wish wish I thee in every place!
                The King and his train go
⌈BEROWNE. Lady, I will commend you to mine own
    heart.
ROSALINE. Pray you, do my commendations—I   180
    would be glad to see it.
BEROWNE. I would you heard it groan.
ROSALINE. Is the fool sick?
BEROWNE. Sick at the heart.
ROSALINE. Alack, let it blood.
BEROWNE. Would that do it good?
ROSALINE. My physic says, 'ay.'
BEROWNE. Will you prick't with your eye?
ROSALINE. No point, with my knife.
BEROWNE. Now God save thy life!   190
ROSALINE. And yours from long living!
BEROWNE. I cannot stay thanksgiving.⌋

Dumaine returns

DUMAINE. Sir, I pray you a word. What lady is
    that same?
BOYET. The heir of Alanson, Katharine her name.
DUMAINE. A gallant lady. Monsieur, fare you well.
                He goes

Longaville returns

LONGAVILLE. I beseech you a word. What is she in
    the white?
BOYET. A woman sometimes, an you saw her in
    the light.
LONGAVILLE. Perchance light in the light. I desire
    her name.
BOYET. She hath but one for herself—to desire that
    were a shame.
LONGAVILLE. Pray you sir, whose daughter?   200
BOYET. Her mother's, I have heard.
LONGAVILLE. God's blessing on your beard!
BOYET. Good sir be not offended.
    She is an heir of Falconbridge.

LONGAVILLE. Nay, my choler is ended.
She is a most sweet lady.
BOYET. Not unlike, sir, that may be.   *Longaville goes*

Berowne returns

BEROWNE. What's her name in the cap?
BOYET. Rosaline by good hap.
BEROWNE. Is she wedded or no?   210
BOYET. To her will sir, or so.
BEROWNE. You are welcome sir, adieu.
BOYET. Farewell to me sir, and welcome to you.
                                          Berowne goes
MARIA. That last is Berowne, the merry mad-cap
lord—
Not a word with him but a jest.
BOYET.   And every jest but a word.
PRINCESS. It was well done of you to take him at
his word.
BOYET. I was as willing to grapple as he was to board.
KATHARINE. Two hot sheeps, marry!
BOYET.   And wherefore not ships?
No sheep, sweet lamb, unless we feed on your lips.
KATHARINE. You sheep, and I pasture: shall that finish
the jest?   220
BOYET. So you grant pasture for me.
                                  He offers to kiss her
KATHARINE.   Not so, gentle beast—
My lips are no common, though several they be.
BOYET. Belonging to whom?
KATHARINE.   To my fortunes and me.
PRINCESS. Good wits will be jangling, but gentles
agree.
This civil war of wits were much better used
On Navarre and his book-men, for here 'tis abused.
BOYET. If my observation—which very seldom lies—
By the heart's still rhetoric disclosèd with eyes,
Deceive me not now, Navarre is infected.
PRINCESS. With what?   230
BOYET. With that which we lovers entitle 'affected.'
PRINCESS. Your reason?
BOYET. Why, all his behaviours did make their retire
To the court of his eye, peeping thorough desire.
His heart like an agate with your print impressed,
Proud with his form, in his eye pride expressed.
His tongue all impatient to speak and not see,
Did stumble with haste in his eyesight to be.
All senses to that sense did make their repair,
To feel only looking on fairest of fair: 240
Methought all his senses were locked in his eye,
As jewels in crystal for some prince to buy,
Who, tend'ring their own worth from where they
were glassed,
Did point you to buy them, along as you passed.
His face's own margent did quote such amazes,
That all eyes saw his eyes enchanted with gazes.
I'll give you Aquitaine, and all that is his,
An you give him for my sake but one loving kiss.
PRINCESS. Come, to our pavilion! Boyet is disposed.
BOYET. But to speak that in words which his eye
hath disclosed.   250
I only have made a mouth of his eye,
By adding a tongue which I know will not lie.
ROSALINE. Thou art an old love-monger, and
speakest skilfully.
MARIA. He is Cupid's grandfather, and learns news
of him.

KATHARINE. Then was Venus like her mother, for
her father is but grim.
BOYET. Do you hear, my mad wenches?
MARIA.   No.
BOYET.   What then, do you see?
ROSALINE. Ay, our way to be gone.
BOYET.   You are too hard for me.
                                          They go

ACT 3
Scene 1
Armado and Moth

ARMADO. Warble, child, make passionate my sense
of hearing.
MOTH [*singing*]. Concolinel.
ARMADO. Sweet air! Go, tenderness of years, take this
key, give enlargement to the swain, bring him
festinately hither. I must employ him in a letter to
my love.
MOTH. Master, will you win your love with a French
brawl?
ARMADO. How meanest thou? brawling in French?   10
MOTH. No, my complete master—but to jig off a tune
at the tongue's end, canary to it with your feet,
humour it with turning up your eyelids, sigh a note
and sing a note, sometime through the throat as if
you swallowed love with singing love, sometime
through the nose as if you snuffed up love by
smelling love, with your hat penthouse-like o'er the
shop of your eyes, with your arms crossed on your
thin-belly doublet like a rabbit on a spit, or your
hands in your pocket like a man after the old paint-   20
ing—and keep not too long in one tune, but a snip
and away. These are complements, these are
humours, these betray nice wenches that would be
betrayed without these, and make them men of
note—do you note me?—that most are affected to
these.
ARMADO. How hast thou purchased this experience?
MOTH. By my penny of observation.
ARMADO. But O—but O—
MOTH. —'the hobby-horse is forgot.'   30
ARMADO. Call'st thou my love 'hobby-horse'?
MOTH. No master, the hobby-horse is but a colt—
[*aside*] and your love, perhaps, a hackney....
But have you forgot your love?
ARMADO. Almost I had.
MOTH. Negligent student! learn her by heart.
ARMADO. By heart, and in heart, boy.
MOTH. And out of heart, master: all those three I will
prove.
ARMADO. What wilt thou prove?   40
MOTH. A man, if I live—and this 'by, in, and
without,' upon the instant. By heart you love her,
because your heart cannot come by her: in heart you
love her, because your heart is in love with her:
and out of heart you love her, being out of heart
that you cannot enjoy her.
ARMADO. I am all these three.
MOTH. And three times as much more—[*aside*] and yet
nothing at all.
ARMADO. Fetch hither the swain. He must carry me   50
a letter.
MOTH. A message well sympathized—a horse to be
ambassador for an ass!

ARMADO. Ha? ha? what sayest thou?

MOTH. Marry sir, you must send the ass upon the horse, for he is very slow-gaited. But I go.

ARMADO. The way is but short—away.

MOTH. As swift as lead, sir.

ARMADO. The meaning, pretty ingenious? Is not lead a metal heavy, dull, and slow?   60

MOTH. Minime, honest master, or rather master, no.

ARMADO. I say lead is slow.

MOTH.   You are too swift, sir, to say so. Is that lead slow which is fired from a gun?

ARMADO. Sweet smoke of rhetoric! He reputes me a cannon—and the bullet, that's he: I shoot thee at the swain.

MOTH.   Thump then, and I flee.   *He goes*

ARMADO. A most acute juvenal, volable and free of grace! By thy favour, sweet welkin, I must sigh in thy face: Most rude melancholy, valour gives thee place. My herald is returned.   70

Moth returns with Costard

MOTH. A wonder, master! here's a costard broken in a shin.

ARMADO. Some enigma, some riddle—come, thy l'envoy—begin.

COSTARD. No egma, no riddle, no l'envoy, no salve in the mail, sir. O sir, plantain, a plain plantain! no l'envoy, no l'envoy, no salve sir, but a plantain!

ARMADO. By virtue, thou enforcest laughter—thy silly thought, my spleen. The heaving of my lungs provokes me to ridiculous smiling: O, pardon me my stars! Doth the inconsiderate take 'salve' for 'l'envoy,' and the word l'envoy for a salve?   80

MOTH. Do the wise think them other? is not l'envoy a salve?

ARMADO. No page, it is an epilogue or discourse to make plain Some obscure precedence that hath tofore been sain. I will example it: The Fox, the Ape, and the Humble-bee, Were still at odds, being but three. There's the moral: now the l'envoy.

MOTH. I will add the l'envoy. Say the moral again.

ARMADO. The Fox, the Ape, and the Humble-bee,   90 Were still at odds, being but three.

MOTH.   Until the Goose came out of door, And stayed the odds by adding four. Now will I begin your moral, and do you follow with my l'envoy. The Fox, the Ape, and the Humble-bee, Were still at odds, being but three.

ARMADO. Until the Goose came out of door, Staying the odds by adding four.

MOTH. A good l'envoy, ending in the goose: would   100 you desire more?

COSTARD. The boy hath sold him a bargain, a goose, that's flat. Sir, your pennyworth is good, an your goose be fat. To sell a bargain well is as cunning as fast and loose: Let me see, a fat l'envoy—ay, that's a fat goose.

ARMADO. Come hither, come hither. How did this argument begin?

MOTH. By saying that a costard was broken in a shin— Then called you for the l'envoy.

COSTARD. True, and I for a plantain—thus came your argument in— Then the boy's fat l'envoy, the goose that you bought—   110 And he ended the market.

ARMADO. But tell me. How was there a costard broken in a shin?

MOTH. I will tell you sensibly.

COSTARD. Thou hast no feeling of it, Moth—I will speak that l'envoy. I, Costard, running out, that was safely within, Fell over the threshold and broke my shin.

ARMADO. We will talk no more of this matter.

COSTARD. Till there be more matter in the shin.   120

ARMADO. Sirrah Costard, I will enfranchise thee.

COSTARD. O, marry me to one Frances! I smell some l'envoy, some goose, in this.

ARMADO. By my sweet soul, I mean setting thee at liberty, enfreedoming thy person: thou wert immured, restrained, captivated, bound.

COSTARD. True, true—and now you will be my purgation, and let me loose.

ARMADO. I give thee thy liberty, set thee from durance, and in lieu thereof impose on thee nothing but this!   130 [*he proffers a letter*] Bear this significant to the country maid Jaquenetta . . . There is remuneration—for the best ward of mine honour is rewarding my dependents. Moth, follow.   *He departs*

MOTH. Like the sequel, I. Signior Costard, adieu. *He follows Armado*

COSTARD. My sweet ounce of man's flesh! my incony Jew! Now will I look to his remuneration. Remuneration! O, that's the Latin word for three-farthings: three-farthings—remuneration. 'What's the price of this inkle?' 'One penny.' 'No, I'll give you a   140 remuneration': why, it carries it. Remuneration! why, it is a fairer name than French crown. I will never buy and sell out of this word.

Berowne approaches

BEROWNE. My good knave Costard, exceedingly well met.

COSTARD. Pray you sir, how much carnation ribbon may a man buy for a remuneration?

BEROWNE. What is a remuneration?

COSTARD. Marry sir, halfpenny farthing.

BEROWNE. Why then, three-farthing worth of silk.   150

COSTARD. I thank your worship. God be wi' you.

BEROWNE. Stay slave, I must employ thee. As thou wilt win my favour, good my knave, Do one thing for me that I shall entreat.

COSTARD. When would you have it done, sir?

BEROWNE. This afternoon.

COSTARD. Well, I will do it, sir: fare you well.

BEROWNE. Thou knowest not what it is.

COSTARD. I shall know, sir, when I have done it.

BEROWNE. Why, villain, thou must know first.   160

COSTARD. I will come to your worship to-morrow morning.

BEROWNE. It must be done this afternoon. Hark, slave, it is but this: The princess comes to hunt here in the park,

And in her train there is a gentle lady:
When tongues spake sweetly, then they name her
    name,
And Rosaline they call her. Ask for her;
And to her white hand see thou do commend
This sealed-up counsel.
              There's thy guerdon: go
              He gives him a shilling
COSTARD. Gardon, O sweet gardon! better than re-   170
muneration, eleven-pence farthing better: most
sweet gardon. I will do it, sir, in print! Gardon—
remuneration—   *He goes*
BEROWNE. And I—
    Forsooth in love, I that have been love's whip!
A very beadle to a humorous sigh,
A critic, nay, a night-watch constable,
A domineering pedant o'er the boy,
Than whom no mortal so magnificent—
This wimpled, whining, purblind, wayward boy,   180
This Signior Junior, giant-dwarf, Dan Cupid,
Regent of love-rhymes, lord of folded arms,
Th'anointed sovereign of sighs and groans,
Liege of all loiterers and malcontents,
Dread Prince of Plackets, King of Codpieces,
Sole imperator and great general
Of trotting paritors—O my little heart!
And I to be a corporal of his field,
And wear his colours like a tumbler's hoop!
What I! I love! I sue! I seek a wife!   190
A woman, that is like a German clock,
Still a-repairing, ever out frame,
And never going aright, being a watch,
But being watched that it may still go right.
Nay, to be perjured, which is worst of all;
And among three to love the worst of all—
A whitely wanton with a velvet brow,
With two pitch-balls stuck in her face for eyes,
Ay and, by heaven, one that will do the deed,
Though Argus were her eunuch and her guard!   200
And I to sigh for her, to watch for her,
To pray for her, go to: it is a plague
That Cupid will impose for my neglect
Of his almighty dreadful little might.
Well, I will love, write, sigh, pray, sue, and groan—
Some men must love my lady, and some Joan.
              He goes

ACT 4
Scene 1

The Princess, Rosaline, Maria, Katharine, Boyet, lords, attendants, and a Forester draw near

PRINCESS. Was that the king that spurred his horse
    so hard
Against the steep-up rising of the hill?
BOYET. I know not, but I think it was not he.
PRINCESS. Whoe'er a' was, a' showed a mounting
    mind.
Well lords, to-day we shall have our dispatch,
On Saturday we will return to France.
Then, forester, my friend, where is the bush
That we must stand and play the murderer in?
FORESTER. Hereby upon the edge of yonder coppice—
A stand where you may make the fairest shoot.   10
PRINCESS. I thank my beauty, I am fair that shoot,

And thereupon thou speak'st the fairest shoot.
FORESTER. Pardon me madam, for I meant not so.
PRINCESS. What, what! first praise me, and again say
    no?
O short-lived pride. Not fair? alack for woe!
FORESTER. Yes madam, fair.
PRINCESS.   Nay, never paint me now.
Where fair is not, praise cannot mend the brow.
Here—good my glass!—take this for telling true:
              She gives him money
Fair payment for foul words is more than due.
FORESTER. Nothing but fair is that which you inherit.
PRINCESS. See, see, my beauty will be saved by merit!   20
O heresy in fair, fit for these days!
A giving hand, though foul, shall have fair praise.
But come, the bow: now mercy goes to kill,
And shooting well is then accounted ill.
Thus will I save my credit in the shoot:
Not wounding, pity would not let me do't;
If wounding, then it was to show my skill,
That more for praise than purpose meant to kill.
And, out of question, so it is sometimes: 30
Glory grows guilty of detested crimes,
When, for fame's sake, for praise, an outward part,
We bend to that the working of the heart:
As I for praise alone now seek to spill
The poor deer's blood, that my heart means no ill.
BOYET. Do not curst wives hold that self sovereignty
Only for praise sake, when they strive to be
Lords o'er their lords?
PRINCESS. Only for praise—and praise we may afford
To any lady that subdues a lord.   40

Costard enters

PRINCESS. Here comes a member of the common-
    wealth.
COSTARD. God dig-you-den all, pray you which is the
head lady?
PRINCESS. Thou shalt know her, fellow, by the rest
that have no heads.
COSTARD. Which is the greatest lady, the highest?
PRINCESS. The thickest, and the tallest.
COSTARD. The thickest and the tallest! It is so—truth
is truth.
    An your waist, mistress, were as slender as my wit,   50
    One o' these maids' girdles for your waist should
    be fit.
    Are not you the chief woman? you are the
    thickest here.
PRINCESS. What's your will, sir? what's your will?
COSTARD. I have a letter from Monsieur Berowne, to
one Lady Rosaline.
PRINCESS. O, thy letter, thy letter: he's a good friend
of mine.
Stand aside, good bearer. Boyet, you can carve.
Break up this capon.
BOYET.   I am bound to serve.
This letter is mistook: it importeth none here.
It is writ to Jaquenetta.
PRINCESS.   We will read it, I swear.
Break the neck of the wax, and every one give ear.   60

Boyet reads

'By heaven, that thou art fair is most infallible;
true that thou art beauteous; truth itself that thou
art lovely. More fairer than fair, beautiful than

beauteous, truer than truth itself, have commiseration on thy heroical vassal. The magnanimous and most illustrate King Cophetua set eye upon the penurious and indubitate beggar Zenelophon: and he it was that might rightly say 'veni, vidi, vici': which to anatomize in the vulgar—O base and obscure vulgar!—videlicet, he came, saw, and overcame: he 70 came, one; saw, two; overcame, three. Who came? the king. Why did he come? to see. Why did he see? to overcome. To whom came he? to the beggar. What saw he? the beggar. Who overcame he? the beggar. The conclusion is victory: on whose side? the king's: the captive is enriched—on whose side? the beggar's. The catastrophe is a nuptial—on whose side? the king's: no, on both in one, or one in both. I am the king, for so stands the comparison—thou the beggar, for so witnesseth thy lowliness. Shall I 80 command thy love? I may. Shall I enforce thy love? I could. Should I entreat thy love? I will. What shalt thou exchange for rags?—robes. For tittles?—titles. For thyself?—me! Thus expecting thy reply, I profane my lips on thy foot, my eyes on thy picture, and my heart on thy every part.
Thine in the dearest design of industry,
DON ADRIANO DE ARMADO.
Thus dost thou hear the Nemean lion roar
'Gainst thee, thou lamb, that standest as his prey: 90
Submissive fall his princely feet before,
And he from forage will incline to play.
But if thou strive, poor soul, what art thou then?
Food for his rage, repasture for his den.'
PRINCESS. What plume of feathers is he that indited this letter?
What vane? what weathercock? did you ever hear better?
BOYET. I am much deceived but I remember the style.
PRINCESS. Else your memory is bad, going o'er it erewhile.
BOYET. This Armado is a Spaniard that keeps here in court,
A phantasime, a Monarcho, and one that makes sport
To the prince and his book-mates. 100
PRINCESS [beckons him aside]. Thou, fellow, a word. Who gave thee this letter?
COSTARD.   I told you—my lord.
PRINCESS. To whom shouldst thou give it?
COSTARD.   From my lord to my lady.
PRINCESS. From which lord, to which lady?
COSTARD. From my Lord Berowne, a good master of mine,
To a lady of France, that he called Rosaline.
PRINCESS. Thou hast mistaken his letter. Come lords, away.   To Rosaline
Here, sweet, put up this—'twill be thine another day.

All depart save Boyet,
Rosaline, Maria and Costard
BOYET. Who is the suitor? who is the suitor?
ROSALINE.   Shall I teach you to know?
BOYET. Ay, my continent of beauty.
ROSALINE.   Why, she that bears the bow. 110
Finely put off!
BOYET. My lady goes to kill horns—but if thou marry,

Hang me by the neck, if horns that year miscarry. Finely put on!
ROSALINE. Well then, I am the shooter.
BOYET.   And who is your deer?
ROSALINE. If we choose by the horns, yourself come not near.
Finely put on, indeed!
MARIA. You still wrangle with her, Boyet, and she strikes at the brow.
BOYET. But she herself is hit lower: have I hit her now?
ROSALINE. Shall I come upon thee with an old saying, 120 there was a man when King Pepin of France was a little boy, as touching the hit it?
BOYET. So I may answer thee with one as old, that was a woman when Queen Guinever of Britain was a little wench, as touching the hit it.

Rosaline and Boyet dance together and sing

ROSALINE.   Thou canst not hit it, hit it, hit it:
             Thou canst not hit it, my good man.
BOYET.   An I cannot, cannot, cannot:
             An I cannot, another can.   *Rosaline goes*
COSTARD. By my troth, most pleasant! how both did fit it! 130
MARIA. A mark marvellous well shot, for they both did hit it.
BOYET. A mark! O mark but that mark: 'A mark,' says my lady!
Let the mark have a prick in't, to mete at if it may be.
MARIA. Wide o' the bow hand! I'faith, your hand is out.
COSTARD. Indeed a' must shoot nearer, or he'll ne'er hit the clout.
BOYET. An if my hand be out, then belike your hand is in.
COSTARD. Then will she get the upshoot by cleaving the pin.
MARIA. Come come, you talk greasily, your lips grow foul.
COSTARD. She's too hard for you at pricks, sir—challenge her to bowl.
BOYET. I fear too much rubbing. Good night, my good owl.   *Boyet and Maria go* 140
COSTARD. By my soul, a swain, a most simple clown! Lord, lord, how the ladies and I have put him down! O' my troth, most sweet jests, most incony vulgar wit,
When it comes so smoothly off, so obscenely as it were, so fit.
Armado to th'one side, O, a most dainty man.
To see him walk before a lady, and to bear her fan.
To see him kiss his hand, and how most sweetly a' will swear!
And his page o' t'other side, that handful of wit!
Ah, heavens, it is a most pathetical nit!

A shout is heard

Sola, sola!   *He runs off* 150

Scene 2

Enter Holofernes, Sir Nathaniel, and Dull

SIR NATHANIEL. Very reverend sport truly, and done in the testimony of a good conscience.

HOLOFERNES. The deer was, as you know, in sanguis, blood—ripe as the pomewater who now hangeth like a jewel in the ear of caelum, the sky, the welkin, the heaven, and anon falleth like a crab on the face of terra, the soil, the land, the earth.

SIR NATHANIEL. Truly, Master Holofernes, the epithets are sweetly varied, like a scholar at the least: but sir, I assure ye it was a buck of the first head. 10

HOLOFERNES. Sir Nathaniel, haud credo.

DULL. 'Twas not a haud credo, 'twas a pricket.

HOLOFERNES. Most barbarous intimation! yet a kind of insinuation, as it were in via, in way, of explication; facere as it were replication, or rather ostentare, to show as it were his inclination—after his undressed, unpolished, uneducated, unpruned, untrained, or rather unlettered, or ratherest, unconfirmed fashion —to insert again my haud credo for a deer.

DULL. I said the deer was not a haud credo, 'twas a 20 pricket.

HOLOFERNES. Twice sod simplicity, bis coctus!
  O thou monster Ignorance, how deformed dost
    thou look!

SIR NATHANIEL. Sir, he hath never fed of the dainties
    that are bred in a book.
  He hath not eat paper, as it were; he hath not
    drunk ink:
  His intellect is not replenished, he is only an animal,
    only sensible in the duller parts:
  And such barren plants are set before us, that we
    thankful should be,
  Which we of taste and feeling are, for those parts
    that do fructify in us more than he.
  For as it would ill become me to be vain, indiscreet,
    or a fool, 30
  So were there a patch set on learning, to see him
    in a school:
  But omne bene say I, being of an old father's
    mind,
  Many can brook the weather that love not the
    wind.

DULL. You two are book-men—can you tell me by
    your wit,
  What was a month old at Cain's birth, that's not five
    weeks old as yet?

HOLOFERNES. Dictynna, goodman Dull—Dictynna,
    goodman Dull.

DULL. What is Dictynna?

SIR NATHANIEL. A title to Phœbe, to Luna, to the
    moon.

HOLOFERNES. The moon was a month old when Adam
    was no more, 40
  And raught not to five weeks when he came to
    five-score.
  Th'allusion holds in the exchange.

DULL. 'Tis true indeed—the collusion holds in the
    exchange.

HOLOFERNES. God comfort thy capacity! I say, th'allu-
    sion holds in the exchange.

DULL. And I say, the pollution holds in the exchange;
    for the moon is never but a month old. And I say
    beside that 'twas a pricket that the princess killed.

HOLOFERNES. Sir Nathaniel, will you hear an extem- 50
    poral epitaph on the death of the deer? and, to
    humour the ignorant, I call the deer the princess
    killed, a pricket.

SIR NATHANIEL. Perge, good Master Holofernes, perge,

so it shall please you to abrogate scurrility.

HOLOFERNES. I will something affect the letter, for it
    argues facility.
  The preyful princess pierced and pricked
  A pretty pleasing pricket—
  Some say a sore, but not a sore,
  Till now made sore with shooting.
  The dogs did yell—put 'ell to sore, 60
  Then sorel jumps from thicket;
  Or pricket sore—or else sore'll
  The people fall a-hooting.
  If sore be sore, then L to sore
  Make fifty sores o'sorel:
  Of one sore I an hundred make,
  By adding but one more L.

SIR NATHANIEL. A rare talent! 70

DULL. If a talent be a claw, look how he claws him
    with a talent.

HOLOFERNES. This is a gift that I have, simple, simple;
    a foolish extravagant spirit, full of forms, figures,
    shapes, objects, ideas, apprehensions, motions,
    revolutions. These are begot in the ventricle of
    memory, nourished in the womb of pia mater, and
    delivered upon the mellowing of occasion. But the
    gift is good in those in whom it is acute, and I
    am thankful for it. 80

SIR NATHANIEL. Sir, I praise the Lord for you, and so
    may my parishioners, for their sons are well tutored
    by you, and their daughters profit very greatly
    under you: you are a good member of the common-
    wealth.

HOLOFERNES. Mehercle! if their sons be ingenious, they
    shall want no instruction: if their daughters be
    capable, I will put it to them. But, vir sapit qui
    pauca loquitur—a soul feminine saluteth us.

Jaquenetta and Costard enter

JAQUENETTA. God give you good morrow, Master 90
    Person.

HOLOFERNES. Master Person—quasi pierce-one? And
    if one should be pierced, which is the one?

COSTARD. Marry, master schoolmaster, he that is like-
    liest to a hogshead.

HOLOFERNES. Piercing a hogshead! a good lustre of
    conceit in a turf of earth, fire enough for a flint,
    pearl enough for a swine: 'tis pretty, it is well.

JAQUENETTA. Good Master Person, be so good as read
    me this letter. It was given me by Costard, and 100
    sent me from Don Armado: I beseech you, read it.

HOLOFERNES.
  'Fauste precor gelida quando pecus omne sub umbra
  Ruminat,' and so forth. Ah, good old Mantuan!
  I may speak of thee as the traveller doth of Venice:
      Venetia, Venetia,
      Chi non ti vede, non ti pretia.
  Old Mantuan! old Mantuan! Who understandeth
  thee not, loves thee not. Ut, re, sol, la, mi, fa. Under
  pardon, sir, what are the contents? or, rather, as
  Horace says in his—What, my soul, verses? 110

SIR NATHANIEL. Ay sir, and very learned.

HOLOFERNES. Let me hear a staff, a stanze, a verse.
  Lege, domine.

SIR NATHANIEL [*reads*]. 'If love make me forsworn,
    how shall I swear to love?
  Ah, never faith could hold, if not to beauty vowed!

Though to myself forsworn, to thee I'll faithful
    prove.
Those thoughts to me were oaks, to thee like
    osiers bowed.
Study his bias leaves, and makes his book thine eyes,
Where all those pleasures live that art
    would comprehend:
If knowledge be the mark, to know thee shall
    suffice.   120
Well learnéd is that tongue, that well can
    thee commend,
All ignorant that soul, that sees thee without
    wonder—
Which is to me some praise that I thy parts admire.
Thy eye Jove's lightning bears, thy voice
    his dreadful thunder,
Which, not to anger bent, is music and
    sweet fire.
Celestial as thou art, O pardon love this wrong,
That singës heaven's praise with such an earthly
    tongue!'
HOLOFERNES. You find not the apostrophus, and so
miss the accent. Let me supervise the canzonet. [*he
takes the letter*] Here are the only numbers ratified, 130
but for the elegancy, facility, and golden cadence
of poesy, caret: Ovidius Naso was the man. And
why, indeed, 'Naso,' but for smelling out the odoriferous flowers of fancy, the jerks of invention?
Imitari is nothing: so doth the hound his master,
the ape his keeper, the tired horse his rider ... But,
damosella virgin, was this directed to you?
JAQUENETTA. Ay sir, from one Monsieur Berowne,
one of the strange queen's lords.
HOLOFERNES. I will overglance the superscript: 'To the 140
snow-white hand of the most beauteous Lady
Rosaline'.
    I will look again on the intellect of the letter, for
the nomination of the party writing to the person
written unto:
'Your Ladyship's in all desired employment,
                                    BEROWNE.'
Sir Nathaniel, this Berowne is one of the votaries
with the king, and here he hath framed a letter to
a sequent of the stranger queen's: which acci- 150
dentally, or by the way of progression, hath miscarried. Trip and go, my sweet, deliver this paper
into the royal hand of the king—it may concern
much: stay not thy complement, I forgive thy duty
—adieu.
JAQUENETTA. Good Costard go with me ... Sir, God
save your life!
COSTARD. Have with thee, my girl.   *They go together*
SIR NATHANIEL. Sir, you have done this in the fear of
God, very religiously: and, as a certain father saith— 160
HOLOFERNES. Sir, tell not me of the father, I do fear
colourable colours.... But to return to the verses—
did they please you, Sir Nathaniel?
SIR NATHANIEL. Marvellous well for the pen.
HOLOFERNES. I do dine to-day at the father's of a certain
pupil of mine, where if—before repast—it shall
please you to gratify the table with a grace, I will,
on my privilege I have with the parents of the
foresaid child or pupil, undertake your ben venuto;
where I will prove those verses to be very unlearned, 170
neither savouring of poetry, wit, nor invention. I
beseech your society.

SIR NATHANIEL. And thank you too: for society—saith
the text—is the happiness of life.
HOLOFERNES. And, certes, the text most infallibly concludes it. [*to Dull*] Sir, I do invite you too, you
shall not say me nay: pauca verba. Away, the
gentles are at their game, and we will to our
recreation.   *They depart*

Scene 3

Enter Berowne, with a paper in his hand, alone

BEROWNE [*reads*]. 'The king he is hunting the deer' ...
I am coursing myself....'
They have pitched a toil, I am toiling in a pitch—
pitch that defiles; defile! a foul word. Well, set thee
down, sorrow; for so they say the fool said, and so
say I, and I the fool: well proved, wit! By the Lord,
this love is as mad as Ajax, it kills sheep, it kills me,
I a sheep—well proved again o' my side! I will not
love; if I do, hang me: i'faith I will not. O, but
her eye! by this light, but for her eye, I would not 10
love her; yes, for her two eyes. Well, I do nothing
in the world but lie, and lie in my throat. By heaven,
I do love, and it hath taught me to rhyme, and to
be melancholy: and here is part of my rhyme, and
here my melancholy. Well, she hath one o' my
sonnets already. The clown bore it, the fool sent it,
and the lady hath it: sweet clown, sweeter fool,
sweetest lady! By the world, I would not care a pin
if the other three were in. Here comes one with
a paper—God give him grace to groan!   20
                             He climbs into a tree

The King approaches with a paper in his hand

KING. Ay me!
BEROWNE [*aside*]. Shot, by heaven! Proceed, sweet
Cupid. Thou hast thumped him with thy birdbolt
under the left pap. In faith secrets!
KING [*reads*]. 'So sweet a kiss the golden sun gives not
To those fresh morning drops upon the rose,
As thy eye-beams, when their fresh rays have smote
The night of dew that on my cheeks down flows:
Nor shines the silver moon one half so bright
Through the transparent bosom of the deep,   30
As doth thy face through tears of mine give light:
Thou shin'st in every tear that I do weep,
No drop but as a coach doth carry thee:
So ridest thou triumphing in my woe.
Do but behold the tears that swell in me,
And they thy glory through my grief
    will show:
But do not love thyself—then thou wilt keep
My tears for glasses, and still make me weep.
O queen of queens, how far dost thou excel
No thought can think, nor tongue of mortal tell.' 40
How shall she know my griefs? I'll drop the paper.
Sweet leaves, shade folly. Who is he comes here?
                                   He hides

Longaville enters, with a paper

What, Longaville! and reading! listen ear.
BEROWNE. Now, in thy likeness, one more fool appear!
LONGAVILLE. Ay me! I am forsworn.
BEROWNE. Why, he comes in like a perjure, wearing
papers.
KING. In love I hope—sweet fellowship in shame!

BEROWNE. One drunkard loves another of the name.
LONGAVILLE. Am I the first that have been perjured so? 50
BEROWNE. I could put thee in comfort—not by two
    that I know.
    Thou makest the triumviry, the corner-cap of
      society,
    The shape of Love's Tyburn, that hangs up
      Simplicity.
LONGAVILLE. I fear these stubborn lines lack power
    to move....
    [reads] 'O sweet Maria, empress of my love!'
    These numbers will I tear, and write in prose.
BEROWNE. O, rhymes are guards on wanton
    Cupid's hose—
    Disfigure not his shop.
LONGAVILLE.   This same shall go.

He reads the sonnet

    'Did not the heavenly rhetoric of thine eye,
    'Gainst whom the world cannot hold argument, 60
    Persuade my heart to this false perjury?
    Vows for thee broke deserve not punishment.
    A woman I forswore, but I will prove,
    Thou being a goddess, I forswore not thee.
    My vow was earthly, thou a heavenly love.
    Thy grace being gained cures all disgrace in me.
    Vows are but breath, and breath a vapour is.
    Then thou, fair sun, which on my earth dost shine,
    Exhal'st this vapour-vow—in thee it is:
    If broken then, it is no fault of mine: 70
    If by me broke, what fool is not so wise
    To loose an oath to win a paradise?
BEROWNE. This is the liver vein, which makes flesh
    a deity,
    A green goose a goddess—pure, pure idolatry.
    God amend us, God amend, we are much out
    o'th'way.
LONGAVILLE. By whom shall I send this?—

Dumaine approaches, with a paper

                  Company! stay.   *He steps aside*
BEROWNE. All hid, all hid! an old infant play—
    Like a demigod here sit I in the sky,
    And wretched fools' secrets heedfully o'er-eye.
    More sacks to the mill! O heavens, I have my wish— 80
    Dumaine transformed, four woodcocks in a dish!
DUMAINE. O most divine Kate!
BEROWNE. O most profane coxcomb!
DUMAINE. By heaven, the wonder in a mortal eye!
BEROWNE. By earth, she is not, corporal, there
    you lie.
DUMAINE. Her amber hair for foul hath amber quoted.
BEROWNE. An amber-coloured raven was well noted.
DUMAINE. As upright as the cedar,
BEROWNE.   Stoop, I say!
    Her shoulder is with child.
DUMAINE.   As fair as day!
BEROWNE. Ay, as some days, but then no sun
    must shine. 90
DUMAINE. O that I had my wish!
LONGAVILLE.   And I had mine!
KING. And I mine too, good Lord!
BEROWNE. Amen, so I had mine. Is not that a
    good word?
DUMAINE. I would forget her, but a fever she

Reigns in my blood, and will rememb'red be.
BEROWNE. A fever in your blood! why then incision,
    Would let her out in saucers—sweet misprision!
DUMAINE. Once more I'll read the ode that I have
    writ.
BEROWNE. Once more I'll mark how love can vary
    wit.

Dumaine reads his sonnet

DUMAINE. 'On a day, alack the day!   100
    Love, whose month is ever May,
    Spied a blossom passing fair
    Playing in the wanton air:
    Through the velvet leaves the wind,
    All unseen, can passage find;
    That the lover, sick to death,
    Wished himself the heaven's breath.
    Air, quoth he, thy cheeks may blow—
    Air, would I might triumph so.
    But alack, my hand is sworn,   110
    Ne'er to pluck thee from thy thorn:
    Vow, alack, for youth unmeet,
    Youth so apt to pluck a sweet.
    Do not call it sin in me,
    That I am forsworn for thee;
    Thou for whom e'en Jove would swear
    Juno but an Ethiope were,
    And deny himself for Jove,
    Turning mortal for thy love.'
    This will I send, and something else more plain. 120
    That shall express my true-love's fasting pain.
    O, would the King, Berowne, and Longaville,
    Were lovers too! Ill, to example ill,
    Would from my forehead wipe a perjured note;
    For none offend, where all alike do dote.
LONGAVILLE [*advances*]. Dumaine, thy love is far
    from charity,
    That in love's grief desir'st society:
    You may look pale, but I should blush, I know,
    To be o'erheard and taken napping so.
KING [*advances*]. Come sir, you blush; as his your
    case is such;   130
    You chide at him, offending twice as much.
    You do not love Maria? Longaville
    Did never sonnet for her sake compile,
    Nor never lay his wreathéd arms athwart
    His loving bosom to keep down his heart.
    I have been closely shrouded in this bush,
    And marked you both, and for you both did
      blush.
    I heard your guilty rhymes, observed your fashion,
    Saw sighs reek from you, noted well your passion.
    'Ay me,' says one! 'O Jove,' the other cries!   140
    One, her hairs were gold, crystal the other's eyes.
    [*to Longaville*] You would for paradise break faith
    and troth—
    [*to Dumaine*] and Jove, for your love, would
    infringe an oath.
    What will Berowne say, when that he shall hear
    Faith so infringéd, with such zeal did swear?
    How will he scorn! how will he spend his wit!
    How will he triumph, leap, and laugh at it!
    For all the wealth that ever I did see,
    I would not have him know so much by me.
BEROWNE. Now step I forth to whip hypocrisy.... 150
                      He descends from the tree

Ah, good my liege, I pray thee, pardon me:
Good heart! what grace hast thou, thus to reprove
These worms for loving, that art most in love?
Your eyes do make no coaches; in your tears
There is no certain princess that appears;
You'll not be perjured, 'tis a hateful thing;
Tush, none but minstrels like of sonneting.
But are you not ashamed? nay, are you not,
All three of you, to be thus much o'er-shot?
You found his mote; the king your mote did see; 160
But I a beam do find in each of three.
O, what a scene of fool'ry have I seen,
Of sighs, of groans, of sorrow, and of teen:
O me, with that strict patience have I sat,
To see a king transforméd to a gnat!
To see great Hercules whipping a gig,
And profound Solomon to tune a jig,
And Nestor play a push-pin with the boys,
And critic Timon laugh at idle toys!
Where lies thy grief, O tell me, good Dumaine? 170
And, gentle Longaville, where lies thy pain?
And where my liege's? all about the breast.
A caudle, ho!
KING.   Too bitter is thy jest.
Are we betrayed thus to thy over-view?
BEROWNE. Not you to me, but I betrayed by you.
I that am honest, I that hold it sin
To break the vow that I am engagéd in,
I am betrayed by keeping company
With moon-like men, men of inconstancy.
When shall you see me write a thing in rhyme? 180
Or groan for Joan? or spend a minute's time
In pruning me? When shall you hear that I
Will praise a hand, a foot, a face, an eye,
A gait, a state, a brow, a breast, a waist,
A leg, a limb?—
KING.   Soft! Whither away so fast?
A true man or a thief that gallops so?
BEROWNE. I post from love, good lover let me go.

Costard and Jaquenetta approach

JAQUENETTA. God bless the king!
KING.   What present hast thou there?
COSTARD. Some certain treason.
KING.   What makes treason here?
COSTARD. Nay, it makes nothing, sir.
KING.   If it mar nothing neither, 190
The treason and you go in peace away together.
JAQUENETTA. I beseech your grace, let this letter be
read.
Our Person misdoubts it; 'twas treason, he said.
KING. Berowne, read it over.   *He reads the letter*
                    Where hadst thou it?
JAQUENETTA. Of Costard.
KING. Where hadst thou it?
COSTARD. Of Dun Adramadio, Dun Adramadio.
                    Berowne tears the letter
KING. How now, what is in you? why dost thou
tear it?
BEROWNE. A toy my liege, a toy; your grace needs not
fear it.
LONGAVILLE. It did move him to passion, and therefore
let's hear it.   200
DUMAINE [*picks up the pieces*]. It is Berowne's writing,
and here is his name.
BEROWNE [*to Costard*]. Ah, you whoreson loggerhead,

you were born to do me shame!
Guilty, my lord, guilty! I confess, I confess.
KING. What?
BEROWNE. That you three fools lacked me fool to
make up the mess.
He, he, and you, and you my liege, and I,
Are pick-purses in love, and we deserve to die.
O, dismiss this audience, and I shall tell you more.
DUMAINE. Now the number is even.
BEROWNE.   True, true, we are four.
Will these turtles be gone?
KING.   Hence, sirs, away.   210
COSTARD. Walk aside the true folk, and let the
traitors stay.
                    Costard and Jaquenetta depart
BEROWNE. Sweet lords, sweet lovers, O let us embrace!
As true we are as flesh and blood can be—
The sea will ebb and flow, heaven show his face;
Young blood doth not obey an old decree:
We cannot cross the cause why we were born;
Therefore of all hands must we be forsworn.
KING. What, did these rent lines show some love
of thine?
BEROWNE. 'Did they,' quoth you? Who sees the
heavenly Rosaline,
That, like a rude and savage man of Inde,   220
At the first op'ning of the gorgeous east,
Bows not his vassal head, and strucken blind,
Kisses the base ground with obedient breast?
What péremptory eagle-sighted eye
Dares look upon the heaven of her brow,
That is not blinded by her majesty?
KING. What zeal, what fury hath inspired
thee now?
My love, her mistress, is a gracious moon,
She, an attending star, scarce seen a light.
BEROWNE. My eyes are then no eyes, nor I Berowne. 230
O, but for my love, day would turn to night!
Of all complexions the culled sovereignty
Do meet as at a fair in her fair cheek,
Where several worthies make one dignity,
Where nothing wants that want itself doth seek.
Lend me the flourish of all gentle tongues—
Fie, painted rhetoric, O she needs it not,
To things of sale a seller's praise belongs:
She passes praise—then praise too short doth blot.
A withered hermit, five-score winters worn,   240
Might shake off fifty, looking in her eye:
Beauty doth varnish age, as if new-born,
And gives the crutch the cradle's infancy.
O, 'tis the sun that maketh all things shine!
KING. By heaven, thy love is black as ebony.
BEROWNE. Is ebony like her? O wood divine!
A wife of such wood were felicity.
O, who can give an oath? where is a book?
That I may swear beauty doth beauty lack,
If that she learn not of her eye to look: 250
No face is fair that is not full so black.
KING. O paradox! Black is the badge of hell,
The hue of dungeons and the School of Night—
A beauty's crest becomes the heavens well!
BEROWNE. Devils soonest tempt, resembling spirits
of light.
O, if in black my lady's brows be decked,
It mourns that painting and usurping hair
Should ravish doters with a false aspéct;

And therefore is she born to make black fair.
Her favour turns the fashion of the days, 260
For native blood is counted painting now;
And therefore red, that would avoid dispraise,
Paints itself black, to imitate her brow.
DUMAINE. To look like her are chimney-
  sweepers black.
LONGAVILLE. And since her time are colliers
  counted bright.
KING. And Ethiopes their sweet complexion crack.
DUMAINE. Dark needs no candles now, for dark
  is light.
BEROWNE. Your mistresses dare never come in rain,
For fear their colours should be washed away.
KING. 'Twere good, yours did; for sir, to tell you plain, 270
I'll find a fairer face not washed to-day.
BEROWNE. I'll prove her fair, or talk till doomsday
  here.
KING. No devil will fright thee then so much as she.
DUMAINE. I never knew man hold vile stuff so dear.
LONGAVILLE [thrusts out his boot]. Look, here's thy love
  —my foot and her face see.
BEROWNE. O, if the streets were pavéd with thine eyes,
Her feet were much too dainty for such tread.
DUMAINE. O vile! then as she goes what upward lies
The street should see as she walked overhead.
KING. But what of this, are we not all in love? 280
BEROWNE. Nothing so sure, and thereby all forsworn.
KING. Then leave this chat, and good Berowne
  now prove
Our loving lawful, and our faith not torn.
DUMAINE. Ay marry, there—some flattery for this
  evil.
LONGAVILLE. O, some authority how to proceed—
Some tricks, some quillets, how to cheat the devil.
DUMAINE. Some salve for perjury.
BEROWNE.   'Tis more than need.
Have at you then affection's men at arms!
Consider what you first did swear unto:
To fast, to study, and to see no woman; 290
Flat treason 'gainst the kingly state of youth.
Say, can you fast? your stomachs are too young;
And abstinence engenders maladies.
⌈And where that you have vowed to study, lords,
In that each of you have forsworn this book,
Can you still dream and pore and thereon look?
For when would you my lord, or you, or you,
Have found the ground of study's excellence
Without the beauty of a woman's face?
From women's eyes, this doctrine I derive— 300
They are the ground, the books, the academes,
From whence doth spring the true Promethean fire.
Why, universal plodding prisons up
The nimble spirits in the arteries,
As motion and long-during action tires
The sinewy vigour of the traveller.
Now, for not looking on a woman's face,
You have in that forsworn the use of eyes;
And study too, the causer of your vow.
For where is any author in the world, 310
Teaches such beauty as a woman's eye?
Learning is but an adjunct to ourself,
And where we are our learning likewise is.
Then, when ourselves we see in ladies' eyes,
.........with ourselves
Do we not likewise see our learning there?⌋

O! we have made a vow to study, lords,
And in that vow we have forsworn our books;
For when would you, my liege, or you, or you,
In leaden contemplation have found out
Such fiery numbers as the prompting eyes 320
Of beauty's tutors have enriched you with?
Other slow arts entirely keep the brain;
And therefore, finding barren practisers,
Scarce show a harvest of their heavy toil.
But love, first learnéd in a lady's eyes,
Lives not alone immuréd in the brain;
But with the motion of all elements,
Courses as swift as thought in every power,
And gives to every power a double power,
Above their functions and their offices. 330
It adds a precious seeing to the eye;
A lover's eyes will gaze an eagle blind;
A lover's ear will hear the lowest sound,
When the suspicious heed of theft is stopped;
Love's feeling is more soft and sensible
Than are the tender horns of cockled snails;
Love's tongue proves dainty Bacchus gross in taste.
For valour, is not Love a Hercules,
Still climbing trees in the Hesperides?
Subtle as Sphinx, as sweet and musical 340
As bright Apollo's lute, strung with his hair;
And, when Love speaks, the voice of all the gods
Make heaven drowsy with the harmony.
Never durst poet touch a pen to write,
Until his ink were temp'red with Love's sighs;
O, then his lines would ravish savage ears,
And plant in tyrants mild humility.
From women's eyes this doctrine I derive:
They sparkle still the right Promethean fire—
They are the books, the arts, the academes, 350
That show, contain, and nourish all the world;
Else none at all in aught proves excellent.
Then fools you were these women to forswear;
Or, keeping what is sworn, you will prove fools.
For wisdom's sake, a word, that all men love;
Or for love's sake, a word that loves all men;
Or for men's sake, the authors of these women;
Or women's sake, by whom we men are men;
Let us once loose our oaths, to find ourselves,
Or else we lose ourselves to keep our oaths. 360
It is religion to be thus forsworn:
For charity itself fulfils the law;
And who can sever love from charity?
KING. Saint Cupid then! and soldiers to the field!
BEROWNE. Advance your standards, and upon
  them, lords!
Pell-mell, down with them! but be first advised,
In conflict that you get the sun of them.
LONGAVILLE. Now to plain-dealing; lay these
  glozes by.
Shall we resolve to woo these girls of France?
KING. And win them too. Therefore let us devise 370
Some entertainment for them in their tents.
BEROWNE. First from the park let us conduct
  them thither,
Then homeward every man attach the hand
Of his fair mistress. In the afternoon
We will with some strange pastimes solace them:
Such as the shortness of the time can shape—
For revels, dances, masks, and merry hours,
Forerun fair Love, strewing her way with flowers.

KING. Away, away! no time shall be omitted,
That will betime, and may by us be fitted.   380
BEROWNE. Allons! Allons! Sowed cockle reaped
    no corn,
And justice always whirls in equal measure:
Light wenches may prove plagues to men
    forsworn—
If so, our copper buys no better treasure.

                                    They go

                    ACT 5
                    Scene 1

Holofernes, Sir Nathaniel, and Dull return

HOLOFERNES. Satis quod sufficit.
SIR NATHANIEL. I praise God for you, sir. Your reasons
    at dinner have been sharp and sententious; pleasant
    without scurrility, witty without affection, auda-
    cious without impudency, learned without opinion,
    and strange without heresy. I did converse this
    quondam day with a companion of the king's, who
    is entitled, nominated, or called, Don Adriano de
    Armado.
HOLOFERNES. Nove hominem tanquam te. His   10
    humour is lofty, his discourse peremptory: his
    tongue filed, his eye ambitious, his gait majestical,
    and his general behaviour vain, ridiculous, and
    thrasonical. He is too picked, too spruce, too
    affected, too odd as it were, too peregrinate as I may
    call it.
SIR NATHANIEL. A most singular and choice epithet.
                        Draws out his table-book
HOLOFERNES. He draweth out the thread of his ver-
    bosity finer than the staple of his argument. I abhor
    such fanatical phantasimes, such insociable and   20
    point-devise companions, such rackers of ortho-
    graphy, as to speak 'dout' sine b, when he should
    say 'doubt'; 'det,' when he should pronounce 'debt';
    d, e, b, t, not d, e, t: he clepeth a calf 'cauf'; half,
    'hauf'; neighbour vocatur 'nebour'; neigh ab-
    breviated 'ne'. This is abhominable—which he
    would call abbominable. It insinuateth me of in-
    sania: intelligis ne domine? to make frantic, lunatic.
SIR NATHANIEL. Laus Deo, bone, intelligo.
HOLOFERNES. Bone?—'bone' for 'bene'—Priscian a   30
    little scratched—'twill serve.

Armado, Moth and Costard come up

SIR NATHANIEL. Videsne quis venit?
HOLOFERNES. Video, et gaudeo.
ARMADO. Chirrah!
HOLOFERNES. Quare 'chirrah' not 'sirrah'?
ARMADO. Men of peace, well encountered.
HOLOFERNES. Most military sir, salutation.
MOTH [*aside*]. They have been at a great feast of lan-
    guages, and stolen the scraps.
COSTARD. O, they have lived long on the alms-basket   40
    of words! I marvel thy master hath not eaten thee
    for a word, for thou art not so long by the head
    as 'honorificabilitudinitatibus': thou art easier swal-
    lowed than a flap-dragon.
MOTH. Peace! the peal begins.
ARMADO [*to Holofernes*]. Monsieur, are you not let-
    tered?

MOTH. Yes yes, he teaches boys the horn-book.
    What is a, b, spelt backward with the horn on his
    head?   50
HOLOFERNES. Ba, pueritia, with a horn added.
MOTH. Ba! most silly sheep with a horn. You hear his
    learning.
HOLOFERNES. Quis, quis, thou consonant?
MOTH. The last of the five vowels if 'you' repeat
    them, or the fifth if 'I'.
HOLOFERNES. I will repeat them, a, e, i—
MOTH. The sheep! the other two concludes it—o, u!
ARMADO. Now by the salt wave of the Mediter-
    raneum, a sweet touch, a quick venew of wit—snip,   60
    snap, quick and home. It rejoiceth my intellect—
    true wit.
MOTH. Offered by a child to an old man; which is
    wit-old.
HOLOFERNES. What is the figure? what is the figure?
MOTH. Horns!
HOLOFERNES. Thou disputes like an infant: go whip
    thy gig.
MOTH. Lend me your horn to make one, and I will
    whip about your infamy, manu cita—a gig of a   70
    cuckold's horn!
COSTARD. An I had but one penny in the world, thou
    shouldst have it to buy gingerbread ... Hold, there
    is the very remuneration I had of thy master, thou
    halfpenny purse of wit, thou pigeon-egg of dis-
    cretion. O, an the heavens were so pleased that
    thou wert but my bastard, what a joyful father
    wouldst thou make me! Go to, thou hast it ad dung-
    hill, at the fingers' ends, as they say.
HOLOFERNES. O, I smell false Latin—'dunghill' for   80
    'unguem'.
ARMADO. Arts-man, preambulate. We will be singled
    from the barbarous. ... Do you not educate youth
    at the charge-house on the top of the mountain?
HOLOFERNES. Or mons, the hill.
ARMADO. At your sweet pleasure, for the mountain.
HOLOFERNES. I do, sans question.
ARMADO. Sir, it is the king's most sweet pleasure and
    affection to congratulate the princess at her pavilion
    in the posteriors of this day, which the rude multi-   90
    tude call the afternoon.
HOLOFERNES. The posterior of the day, most generous
    sir, is liable, congruent, and measurable for the after-
    noon: the word is well culled, choice, sweet, and
    apt, I do assure you sir, I do assure.
ARMADO. Sir, the king is a noble gentleman, and my
    familiar, I do assure ye, very good friend. For what
    is inward between us, let it pass, I do beseech thee
    remember thy courtesy; I beseech thee apparel thy
    head—. And among other importunate and most   100
    serious designs, and of great import indeed, too. ...
    But let that pass—for I must tell thee, it will please
    his grace (by the world) sometime to lean upon my
    poor shoulder, and with his royal finger, thus dally
    with my excrement, with my mustachio: but sweet
    heart, let that pass. By the world, I recount no
    fable—some certain special honours it pleaseth his
    greatness to impart to Armado, a soldier, a man of
    travel, that hath seen the world: but let that pass.
    The very all of all is—but, sweet heart, I do implore   110
    secrecy—that the king would have me present the
    princess (sweet chuck!) with some delightful osten-
    tation, or show, or pageant, or antic, or firework.

Now, understanding that the curate and your sweet
self are good at such eruptions and sudden breaking out of mirth, as it were, I have acquainted you
withal, to the end to crave your assistance.

HOLOFERNES. Sir, you shall present before her the Nine
Worthies.... Sir Nathaniel, as concerning some
entertainment of time, some show in the posterior   120
of this day, to be rend'red by our assistance,
the king's command, and this most gallant, illustrate, and learned gentleman, before the princess. I
say none so fit as to present the Nine Worthies.

SIR NATHANIEL. Where will you find men worthy
enough to present them?

HOLOFERNES. Joshua yourself, [myself, and] this gallant
gentleman, Judas Maccabæus; this swain, because of
his great limb or joint, shall pass Pompey the great—
the page, Hercules.   130

ARMADO. Pardon, sir—error: he is not quantity
enough for that worthy's thumb. He is not so big
as the end of his club.

HOLOFERNES. Shall I have audience? he shall present
Hercules in minority: his 'enter' and 'exit' shall be
strangling a snake; and I will have an apology for
that purpose.

MOTH. An excellent device! So, if any of the audience
hiss, you may cry, 'Well done, Hercules, now thou
crushest the snake.' That is the way to make an   140
offence gracious, though few have the grace to do it.

ARMADO. For the rest of the worthies?

HOLOFERNES. I will play three myself.

MOTH. Thrice-worthy gentleman!

ARMADO. Shall I tell you a thing?

HOLOFERNES. We attend.

ARMADO. We will have, if this fadge not, an antic.
I beseech you, follow.

HOLOFERNES. Via, goodman Dull! thou hast spoken no
word all this while.   150

DULL. Nor understood none neither, sir.

HOLOFERNES. Allons! we will employ thee.

DULL. I'll make one in a dance, or so; or I will play
On the tabor to the worthies, and let them dance
the hay.

HOLOFERNES. Most dull, honest Dull! to our sport:
away!   *They all go*

Scene 2

Enter the Princess, Katharine, Rosaline, and Maria

PRINCESS. Sweet hearts, we shall be rich ere we depart,
If fairings come thus plentifully in.
A lady walled about with diamonds!
Look you, what I have from the loving king.

ROSALINE. Madam, came nothing else along with
that?

PRINCESS. Nothing but this! Yes, as much love in
rhyme
As would be crammed up in a sheet of paper
Writ o' both sides the leaf, margent and all—
That he was fain to seal on Cupid's name.

ROSALINE. That was the way to make his godhead
wax;   10
For he hath been five thousand years a boy.

KATHARINE. Ay, and a shrewd unhappy gallows too.

ROSALINE. You'll ne'er be friends with him, a' killed
your sister.

KATHARINE. He made her melancholy, sad, and
heavy—

And so she died: had she been light, like you,
Of such a merry, nimble, stirring spirit,
She might ha' been a grandam ere she died.
And so may you; for a light heart lives long.

ROSALINE. What's your dark meaning, mouse, of this
light word?

KATHARINE. A light condition in a beauty dark.   20

ROSALINE. We need more light to find your meaning
out.

KATHARINE. You'll mar the light by taking it in snuff;
Therefore, I'll darkly end the argument.

ROSALINE. Look, what you do, you do it still i'th' dark.

KATHARINE. So do not you, for you are a light
wench.

ROSALINE. Indeed I weigh not you, and therefore light.

KATHARINE. You weigh me not? O, that's you care
not for me.

ROSALINE. Great reason; for, 'past cure is still past care.'

PRINCESS. Well bandied both—a set of wit well
played.
But Rosaline, you have a favour too!   30
Who sent it? and what is it?

ROSALINE.   I would you knew.
An if my face were but as fair as yours,
My favour were as great—be witness this.
Nay, I have verses too, I thank Berowne—
The numbers true, and were the numb'ring too,
I were the fairest goddess on the ground.
I am compared to twenty thousand fairs.
O, he hath drawn my picture in his letter!

PRINCESS. Anything like?

ROSALINE. Much in the letters, nothing in the praise.   40

PRINCESS. Beauteous as ink: a good conclusion.

KATHARINE. Fair as a text B in a copy-book.

ROSALINE. 'Ware pencils, ho! Let me not die your
debtor,
My red dominical, my golden letter.
O, that your face were not so full of O's!

KATHARINE. A pox of that jest! and I beshrow all
shrows!

PRINCESS. But what was sent to you from fair
Dumaine?

KATHARINE. Madam, this glove.

PRINCESS.   Did he not sent you twain?

KATHARINE. Yes madam; and, moreover,
Some thousand verses of a faithful lover—   50
A huge translation of hypocrisy,
Vilely compiled, profound simplicity.

MARIA. This, and these pearls, to me sent Longaville;
The letter is too long by half a mile.

PRINCESS. I think no less. Dost thou not wish in heart
The chain were longer and the letter short?

MARIA. Ay, or I would these hands might
never part.

PRINCESS. We are wise girls to mock our lovers so.

ROSALINE. They are worse fools to purchase mocking
so.
That same Berowne I'll torture ere I go.   60
O, that I knew he were but in by th' week,
How I would make him fawn, and beg, and seek,
And wait the season, and observe the times,
And spend his prodigal wits in bootless rhymes,
And shape his service wholly to my hests,
And make him proud to make me proud, that
jests!
So planet-like would I o'ersway his state

That he should be my fool, and I his fate.
PRINCESS. None are so surely caught, when they
    are catched,
  As wit turned fool. Folly, in wisdom hatched,   70
  Hath wisdom's warrant, and the help of school,
  And wit's own grace to grace a learnéd fool.
ROSALINE. The blood of youth burns not with
    such excess,
  As gravity's revolt to wantonness.
MARIA. Folly in fools bears not so strong a note
  As fool'ry in the wise, when wit doth dote:
  Since all the power thereof it doth apply,
  To prove, by wit, worth in simplicity.

Boyet approaches

PRINCESS. Here comes Boyet, and mirth is in his face.
BOYET. O, I am stabbed with laughter! Where's
  her grace?   80
PRINCESS. Thy news, Boyet?
BOYET.   Prepare, madam, prepare!
  Arm, wenches, arm! encounters mounted are
  Against your peace. Love doth approach disguised,
  Arméd in arguments. You'll be surprised.
  Muster your wits, stand in your own defence,
  Or hide your heads like cowards and fly hence.
PRINCESS. Saint Denis to Saint Cupid! What are they,
  That charge their breath against us? say, scout, say.
BOYETT. Under the cool shade of a sycamore,
  I thought to close mine eyes some half an hour: 90
  When lo, to interrupt my purposed rest,
  Towards that shade I might behold address
  The king and his companions: warily
  I stole into a neighbour thicket by,
  And overheard what you shall overhear—
  That, by and by, disguised they will be here.
  Their herald is a pretty knavish page,
  That well by heart hath conned his embassage.
  Action and accent did they teach him there—
  'Thus must thou speak', and 'thus thy body bear';   100
  And ever and anon they made a doubt
  Presence majestical would put him out:
  'For,' quoth the king, 'an angel shalt thou see;
  Yet fear not thou, but speak audaciously.'
  The boy replied, 'An angel is not evil;
  I should have feared her had she been a devil.'
  With that all laughed, and clapped him on the
    shoulder,
  Making the bold wag by their praises bolder.
  One rubbed his elbow thus, and fleered, and swore
  A better speech was never spoke before.   110
  Another with his finger and his thumb
  Cried 'Via! we will do't, come what will come.'
  The third he capered and cried, 'All goes well.'
  The fourth turned on the toe, and down he fell.
  With that they all did tumble on the ground,
  With such a zealous laughter so profound,
  That in this spleen ridiculous appears,
  To check their folly, passion's solemn tears.
PRINCESS. But what, but what? come they to visit us?
BOYET. They do, they do; and are apparelled thus,   120
  Like Muscovites or Russians, as I guess.
  Their purpose is to parley, court, and dance—
  And every one his love-suit will advance
  Unto his several mistress; which they'll know
  By favours several which they did bestow.

PRINCESS. And will they so? the gallants shall be
    tasked:
  For, ladies, we will every one be masked,
  And not a man of them shall have the grace,
  Despite of suit, to see a lady's face.
  Hold Rosaline, this favour thou shalt wear,   130
  And then the king will court thee for his dear;
  Hold, take thou this my sweet, and give me thine,
  So shall Berowne take me for Rosaline.
  And change you favours too, so shall your loves
  Woo contrary, deceived by these removes.
ROSALINE. Come on then, wear the favours most
    in sight.
KATHARINE. But in this changing what is your intent?
PRINCESS. The effect of my intent is to cross theirs:
  They do it but in mockery-merriment,
  And mock for mock is only my intent.   140
  Their several counsels they unbosom shall
  To loves mistook, and so be mocked withal
  Upon the next occasion that we meet,
  With visages displayed, to talk and greet.
ROSALINE. But shall we dance, if they desire us to't?
PRINCESS. No, to the death, we will not move a foot—
  Nor to their penned speech render we no grace;
  But while 'tis spoke each turn away her face.
BOYET. Why, that contempt will kill the speaker's
    heart,
  And quite divorce his memory from his part.   150
PRINCESS. Therefore I do it, and I make no doubt
  The rest will e'er come in, if he be out.
  There's no such sport as sport by sport o'erthrown,
  To make theirs ours and ours none but our own:
  So shall we stay, mocking intended game,
  And they, well mocked, depart away with shame.
                                          A trumpet
BOYET. The trumpet sounds! be masked, the
    maskers come.   *The ladies mask*

*Enter Blackamoors with music, the Boy (Moth) with a
speech, and the rest of the Lords disguised and masked as
Russians*

MOTH. 'All hail, the richest beauties on the earth'—
BOYET. Beauties no richer than rich tafetta.
MOTH. 'A holy parcel of the fairest dames,   160

The ladies turn their backs to him

  That ever turned their backs to mortal views!'
BEROWNE. 'Their eyes,' villain, 'their eyes.'
MOTH. 'That ever turned their eyes to mortal views.
  Out—'
BOYET. True, 'out' indeed.
MOTH. 'Out of your favours, heavenly spirits,
    vouchsafe
  Not to behold—'
BEROWNE. 'Once to behold,' rogue.
MOTH. 'Once to behold with your sun-beaméd eyes,
    —with your sun-beaméd eyes—'   170
BOYET. They will not answer to that epithet—
  You were best call it 'daughter-beaméd eyes.'
MOTH. They do not mark me, and that brings me out.
BEROWNE. Is this your perfectness? be gone you rogue.
                                          Moth goes
ROSALINE. What would these strangers? Know their
    minds, Boyet.
  If they do speak our language, 'tis our will
  That some plain man recount their purposes.

Know what they would.
BOYET.   What would you with the princess?
BEROWNE. Nothing but peace and gentle visitation.
ROSALINE. What would they, say they?   180
BOYET. Nothing but peace and gentle visitation.
ROSALINE. Why, that they have—and bid them so
   be gone.
BOYET. She says you have it, and you may be gone.
KING. Say to her we have measured many miles
   To tread a measure with her on this grass.
BOYET. They say that they have measured many a
   mile,
   To tread a measure with you on this grass.
ROSALINE. It is not so! Ask them how many inches
   Is in one mile. If they have measured many,
   The measure then of one is eas'ly told.   190
BOYET. If to come hither you have measured miles,
   And many miles, the princess bids you tell
   How many inches doth fill up one mile.
BEROWNE. Tell her we measure them by weary steps.
BOYET. She hears herself.
ROSALINE.   How many weary steps,
   Of many weary miles you have o'ergone,
   Are numb'red in the travel of one mile?
BEROWNE. We number nothing that we spend for
   you—
   Our duty is so rich, so infinite,
   That we may do it still without account.   200
   Vouchsafe to show the sunshine of your face,
   That we—like savages—may worship it.
ROSALINE. My face is but a moon, and clouded too.
KING. Blessèd are clouds, to do as such clouds do.
   Vouchsafe bright moon, and these thy stars to
   shine—
   These clouds removed—upon our watery eyne.
ROSALINE. O vain petitioner, beg a greater matter—
   Thou now requests but moonshine in the water.
KING. Then, in our measure, do but vouchsafe
   one change.
   Thou bid'st me beg—this begging is not strange.   210
ROSALINE. Play music then! nay, you must do it soon!
   Not yet?—no dance! Thus change I like the moon.
KING. Will you not dance? How come you
   thus estranged?
ROSALINE. You took the moon at full, but now
   she's changed!   *The musicians strike up*
KING. Yet still she is the Moon, and I the Man.
   The music plays—vouchsafe some motion to it.
ROSALINE. Our ears vouchsafe it.
KING.   But your legs should do it.
ROSALINE. Since you are strangers, and come here
   by chance,
   We'll not be nice—take hands—We will not dance.
KING. Why take we hands then?
ROSALINE.   Only to part friends.   220
   Curtsy sweethearts, and so the measure ends.
KING. More measure of this measure—be not nice.
ROSALINE. We can afford no more at such a price.
KING. Price you yourselves. What buys
   your company?
ROSALINE. Your absence only.
KING.   That can never be.
ROSALINE. Then cannot we be bought: and so adieu—
   Twice to your visor, and half once to you!
KING. If you deny to dance, let's hold more chat.
ROSALINE. In private then.

KING.   I am best pleased with that.
                        They talk apart
BEROWNE. White-handed mistress, one sweet word
   with thee.   230
PRINCESS. Honey, and milk, and sugar; there is three.
BEROWNE. Nay then, two treys—an if you grow so
   nice—
   Metheglin, wort, and malmsey; well run, dice!
   There's half-a-dozen sweets.
PRINCESS.   Seventh sweet, adieu?
   Since you can cog, I'll play no more with you.
BEROWNE. One word in secret.
PRINCESS.   Let it not be sweet.
BEROWNE. Thou grievest my gall.
PRINCESS.   Gall? bitter.
BEROWNE.   Therefore meet.
                        They talk apart
DUMAINE. Will you vouchsafe with me to change
   a word?
MARIA. Name it.
DUMAINE.   Fair lady,—
MARIA.   Say you so? Fair lord,—
   Take that for your fair lady.
DUMAINE.   Please it you,   240
   As much in private, and I'll bid adieu.
                        They talk apart
KATHARINE. What, was your vizard made without
   a tongue?
LONGAVILLE. I know the reason, lady, why you ask.
KATHARINE. O, for your reason! quickly, sir—I long.
LONGAVILLE. You have a double tongue within
   your mask,
   And would afford my speechless vizard half.
KATHARINE. 'Veal' quoth the Dutchman. Is not 'veal'
   a calf?
LONGAVILLE. A calf, fair lady?
KATHARINE.   No, a fair lord calf.
LONGAVILLE. Let's part the word.
KATHARINE.   No, I'll not be your half:
   Take all and wean it—it may prove an ox.   250
LONGAVILLE. Look how you butt yourself in these
   sharp mocks.
   Will you give horns, chaste lady? do not so.
KATHARINE. Then die a calf, before your horns do
   grow.
LONGAVILLE. One word in private with you ere I die.
KATHARINE. Bleat softly then, the butcher hears
   you cry.   *They talk apart*
BOYET. The tongues of mocking wenches are
   as keen
   As is the razor's edge invisible,
   Cutting a smaller hair than may be seen:
   Above the sense of sense: so sensible
   Seemeth their conference, their conceits have wings,   260
   Fleeter than arrows, bullets, wind, thought,
   swifter things.
ROSALINE. Not one word more my maids,
   break off, break off.
BEROWNE. By heaven, all dry-beaten with pure scoff!
KING. Farewell mad wenches, you have simple wits.
PRINCESS. Twenty adieus, my frozen Muscovits.

The King departs with his train

   Are these the breed of wits so wondered at?
BOYET. Tapers they are with your sweet breaths
   puffed out.

ROSALINE. Well-liking wits they have—gross gross,
    fat fat
PRINCESS. O poverty in wit, kingly-poor flout!
    Will they not, think you, hang themselves to-night? 270
    Or ever but in vizards show their faces?
    This pert Berowne was out of count'nance quite.
ROSALINE. O, they were all in lamentable cases!
    The king was weeping-ripe for a good word.
PRINCESS. Berowne did swear himself out of all suit.
MARIA. Dumaine was at my service, and his sword.
    'No point,' quoth I—my servant straight was mute.
KATHARINE. Lord Longaville said I came o'er his heart:
    And trow you what he called me?
PRINCESS.   Qualm, perhaps.
KATHARINE. Yes, in good faith.
PRINCESS.   Go, sickness as thou art. 280
ROSALINE. Well, better wits have worn plain
    statute-caps.
    But will you hear? the king is my love sworn.
PRINCESS. And quick Berowne hath plighted faith
    to me.
KATHARINE. And Longaville was for my service born.
MARIA. Dumaine is mine as sure as bark on tree.
BOYET. Madam, and pretty mistresses, give ear.
    Immediately they will again be here
    In their own shapes; for it can never be
    They will digest this harsh indignity.
PRINCESS. Will they return?
BOYET.   They will, they will, God knows; 290
    And leap for joy, though they are lame with blows:
    Therefore change favours, and when they repair,
    Blow like sweet roses in this summer air.
PRINCESS. How blow? how blow? speak to
    be understood.
BOYET. Fair ladies, masked, are roses in their bud:
    Dismasked, their damask sweet commixture shown,
    Are angels vailing clouds, or roses blown.
PRINCESS. Avaunt, perplexity! What shall we do
    If they return in their own shapes to woo?
ROSALINE. Good madam, if by me you'll be advised, 300
    Let's mock them still as well known as disguised:
    Let us complain to them what fools were here,
    Disguised like Muscovites, in shapeless gear;
    And wonder what they were, and to what end
    Their shallow shows and prologue vilely penned,
    And their rough carriage so ridiculous,
    Should be presented at our tent to us.
BOYET. Ladies, withdraw; the gallants are at hand.
PRINCESS. Whip to our tents as roes run o'er the land.
                                        The ladies go

The King, Berowne, Longaville, and Dumaine return in
their proper habits

KING. Fair sir, God save you! where's the princess? 310
BOYET. Gone to her tent. Please it your majesty,
    Command me any service to her thither?
KING. That she vouchsafe me audience for one word.
BOYET. I will, and so will she, I know, my lord.
                                        He goes
BEROWNE. This fellow pecks up wit, as pigeons pease,
    And utters it again when God doth please.
    He is Wit's pedler, and retails his wares
    At wakes and wassails, meetings, markets, fairs:
    And we that sell by gross, the Lord doth know,
    Have not the grace to grace it with such show. 320
    This gallant pins the wenches on his sleeve.

Had he been Adam, he had tempted Eve.
A' can carve too, and lisp: why, this is he
That kissed his hand away in courtesy.
This is the ape of form, monsieur the nice,
That when he plays at tables chides the dice
In honourable terms; nay, he can sing
A mean most meanly, and, in ushering,
Mend him who can. The ladies call him sweet.
The stairs as he treads on them kiss his feet.   330
This is the flower that smiles on every one,
To show his teeth as white as whalës-bone.
And consciences that will not die in debt
Pay him the due of honey-tongued Boyet.
BOYET. A blister on his sweet tongue, with my heart,
    That pur Armado's page out of his part.

The ladies return, Boyet ushering the Princess

BEROWNE. See where it comes! Behaviour, what
    wert thou
    Till this man showed thee? and what art thou now?
KING. All hail sweet madam, and fair time of day!
PRINCESS. 'Fair' in 'all hail' is foul, as I conceive.   340
KING. Construe my speeches better, if you may.
PRINCESS. Then wish me better, I will give
    you leave.
KING. We came to visit you, and purpose now
    To lead you to our court—vouchsafe it then.
PRINCESS. This field shall hold me, and so hold
    your vow:
    Nor God nor I delights in perjured men.
KING. Rebuke me not for that which you provoke:
    The virtue of your eye must break my oath.
PRINCESS. You nickname virtue—'vice' you should
    have spoke;
    For virtue's office never breaks men's troth.   350
    Now by my maiden honour, yet as pure
    As the unsullied lily, I protest,
    A world of torments though I should endure,
    I would not yield to be your house's guest:
    So much I hate a breaking cause to be
    Of heavenly oaths vowed with integrity.
KING. O, you have lived in desolation here,
    Unseen, unvisited, much to our shame.
PRINCESS. Not so my lord, it is not so, I swear.
    We have had pastimes here and pleasant game.   360
    A mess of Russians left us but of late.
KING. How madam? Russians?
PRINCESS.   Ay, in truth my lord;
    Trim gallants, full of courtship and of state.
ROSALINE. Madam speak true. It is not so my lord.
    My lady, to the manner of the days,
    In courtesy gives undeserving praise.
    We four indeed confronted were with four
    In Russian habit: here they stayed an hour,
    And talked apace; and in that hour, my lord,
    They did not bless us with one happy word.   370
    I dare not call them fools; but this I think,
    When they are thirsty, fools would fain have drink.
BEROWNE. This jest is dry to me. My gentle sweet,
    Your wit makes wise things foolish: when we greet,
    With eyes best seeing, heaven's fiery eye,
    By light we lose light; your capacity
    Is of that nature that to your huge store
    Wise things seem foolish and rich things but poor.
ROSALINE. This proves you wise and rich; for in
    my eye—

BEROWNE. I am a fool, and full of poverty.
ROSALINE. But that you take what doth to you belong,
It were a fault to snatch words from my tongue.
BEROWNE. O, I am yours, and all that I possess.
ROSALINE. All the fool mine?
BEROWNE.   I cannot give you less.
ROSALINE. Which of the vizards was it that you wore?
BEROWNE. Where, when, what vizard? why demand
you this?
ROSALINE. There, then, that vizard—that super-
fluous case
That hid the worse and showed the better face.
KING. We were descried, they'll mock us
now downright.
DUMAINE. Let us confess, and turn it to a jest.
PRINCESS. Amazed, my lord? Why looks your
highness sad?
ROSALINE. Help, hold his brows! he'll swoon! Why
look you pale?
Sea-sick, I think, coming from Muscovy.
BEROWNE. Thus pour the stars down plagues
for perjury.
Can any face of brass hold longer out?
Here stand I, lady—dart thy skill at me,
Bruise me with scorn, confound me with a flout,
Thrust thy sharp wit quite through my ignorance,
Cut me to pieces with thy keen conceit,
And I will wish thee never more to dance,
Nor never more in Russian habit wait.
O, never will I trust to speeches penned,
Nor to the motion of a schoolboy's tongue,
Nor never come in vizard to my friend,
Nor woo in rhyme, like a blind harper's song.
Taffeta phrases, silken terms precise,
Three-piled hyperboles, spruce affectation,
Figures pedantical—these summer-flies
Have blown me full of maggot ostentation.
I do forswear them, and I here protest,
By this white glove (how white the hand,
God knows!)
Henceforth my wooing mind shall be expressed
In russet yeas and honest kersey noes.
And, to begin, wench—so God help me, la!—
My love to thee is sound, sans crack or flaw.
ROSALINE. Sans 'sans,' I pray you.
BEROWNE.   Yet I have a trick
Of the old rage; bear with me, I am sick—
I'll leave it by degrees. Soft, let us see;
Write 'Lord have mercy on us' on those three.
They are infected, in their hearts it lies;
They have the plague, and caught it of your eyes.
These lords are visited; you are not free,
For the Lord's tokens on you do I see.
PRINCESS. No, they are free that gave these tokens
to us.
BEROWNE. Our states are forfeit, seek not to undo us.
ROSALINE. It is not so. For how can this be true,
That you stand forfeit, being those that sue?
BEROWNE. Peace! for I will not have to do with you.
ROSALINE. Nor shall not, if I do as I intend.
BEROWNE. Speak for yourselves, my wit is at an end.
KING. Teach us, sweet madam, for our
rude transgression
Some fair excuse.
PRINCESS.   The fairest is confession.
Were you not here but even now, disguised?

380 KING. Madam, I was.
PRINCESS.   And were you well advised?
KING. I was, fair madam.
PRINCESS.   When you then were here,
What did you whisper in your lady's ear?
KING. That more than all the world I did respect her.
PRINCESS. When she shall challenge this, you will
reject her.
KING. Upon mine honour, no.
PRINCESS.   Peace, peace, forbear;
Your oath once broke, you force not to forswear. 440
KING. Despise me when I break this oath of mine.
PRINCESS. I will, and therefore keep it.... Rosaline,
What did the Russian whisper in your ear?
390 ROSALINE. Madam, he swore that he did hold me dear
As precious eyesight, and did value me
Above this world: adding thereto, moreover,
That he would wed me, or else die my lover.
PRINCESS. God give thee joy of him! the noble lord
Most honourably doth uphold his word.
KING. What mean you, madam? by my life, my troth, 450
I never swore this lady such an oath.
ROSALINE. By heaven you did; and to confirm it plain,
You gave me this.... but take it, sir, again.
KING. My faith and this the princess I did give,
I knew her by this jewel on her sleeve.
PRINCESS. Pardon me sir, this jewel did she wear,
And Lord Berowne (I thank him!) is my dear.
What, will you have me, or your pearl again?
BEROWNE. Neither of either: I remit both twain.
I see the trick on't: here was a consent— 460
Knowing aforehand of our merriment—
To dash it like a Christmas comedy:
Some carry-tale, some please-man, some slight
zany,
Some mumble-news, some trencher-knight, some
Dick,
400 That smiles his cheek in years, and knows the trick
To make my lady laugh, when she's disposed,
Told our intents before; which once disclosed,
The ladies did change favours; and then we,
Following the signs, wooed but the sign of she.
Now to our perjury to add more terror, 470
We are again forsworn, in will and error.
Much upon this 'tis! [to Boyet] And might
not you
Forestall our sport, to make us thus untrue?
Do not you know my lady's foot by th' square,
410 And laugh upon the apple of her eye?
And stand between her back, sir, and the fire,
Holding a trencher, jesting merrily?
You put our page out: go, you are allowed!
Die when you will, a smock shall be your shroud.
You leer upon me, do you? there's an eye 480
Wounds like a leaden sword.
BOYET.   Full merrily
Hath this brave manage, this career, been run.
BEROWNE. Lo, he is tilting straight. Peace, I have done.

420 *Costard enters*

Welcome, pure wit! thou partest a fair fray.
COSTARD. O Lord, sir, they would know
Whether the three Worthies shall come in or no.
BEROWNE. What, are there but three?
COSTARD.   No sir, but it is vara fine,
For every one pursents three.

BEROWNE.   And three times thrice is nine.
COSTARD. Not so, sir—under correction, sir—I hope
it is not so.
You cannot beg us, sir, I can assure you, sir; we
know what we know:
I hope, sir, three times thrice, sir—   490
BEROWNE. Is not nine.
COSTARD. Under correction, sir, we know whereuntil
it doth amount.
BEROWNE. By Jove, I always took three threes for nine.
COSTARD. O Lord, sir, it were a pity you should get
your living by reck'ning, sir.
BEROWNE. How much is it?
COSTARD. O Lord, sir, the parties themselves, the
actors, sir, will show whereuntil it doth amount: for 500
mine own part, I am, as they say, but to parfect
one man in one poor man—Pompion the Great, sir.
BEROWNE. Art thou one of the Worthies?
COSTARD. It pleased them to think me worthy of
Pompey the Great: for mine own part I know not
the degree of the Worthy, but I am to stand for
him.
BEROWNE. God bid them prepare.
COSTARD. We will turn it finely off sir, we will take
some care.   *He goes*
KING. Berowne, they will shame us: let them   510
not approach.
BEROWNE. We are shame-proof, my lord: and 'tis
some policy
To have one show worse than the King's and
his company.
KING. I say they shall not come.
PRINCESS. Nay, my good lord, let me o'errule you
now,
That sport best pleases that doth lease know how:
Where zeal strives to content, and the contents
Dies in the zeal of that which it presents:
There form confounded makes most form in mirth,
When great things labouring perish in their birth.
BEROWNE. A right description of our sport, my lord. 520

Armado appears

ARMADO. Anointed, I implore so much expense of thy
royal sweet breath as will utter a brace of words.
    He talks apart with the King,
    and delivers him a paper
PRINCESS. Doth this man serve God?
BEROWNE. Why ask you?
PRINCESS. A' speaks not like a man of God his making.
ARMADO. That is all one, my fair, sweet honey mon-
arch: for, I protest, the schoolmaster is exceeding
fantastical—too-too vain, too-too vain: but we will
put it, as they say, to fortuna de la guerra. I wish
you the peace of mind, most royal couplement!   530
    He departs
KING. Here is like to be a good presence of Worthies.
He presents Hector of Troy, the swain Pompey the
Great, the parish curate Alexander, Armado's page
Hercules, the pedant Judas Maccabæus.   *He reads*
'And if these four worthies in their first show thrive,
These four will change habits, and present the
other five.'
BEROWNE. There is five in the first show.
KING. You are deceived, 'tis not so.
BEROWNE. The pedant, the braggart, the hedge-priest,
the fool, and the boy—   540

Abate throw at novum, and the whole world again
Cannot pick out five such, take each one in
his vein.
KING. The ship is under sail, and here she
comes amain.

Enter Costard, for Pompey

COSTARD. 'I Pompey am'—
BEROWNE.   You lie, you are not he.
COSTARD. 'I Pompey am'—
BOYET.   With libbard's head on knee.
BEROWNE. Well said old mocker, I must needs be
friends with thee.
COSTARD. 'I Pompey am, Pompey surnamed the
Big'—
DUMAINE. The Great.
COSTARD. It is 'great,' sir.—'Pompey surnamed
the Great,
That oft in field with targe and shield did make my
foe to sweat,   550
And travelling along this coast I here am come by
chance,
And lay my arms before the legs of this sweet lass
of France.'
If your ladyship would say, 'Thanks Pompey,' I
had done.
PRINCESS. Great thanks, Great Pompey.
COSTARD. 'Tis not so much worth; but I hope I was
perfect. I made a little fault in 'Great'.
BEROWNE. My hat to a halfpenny, Pompey proves the
best Worthy.

Enter Sir Nathaniel armed, for Alexander

SIR NATHANIEL. 'When in the world I lived, I was
the world's commander:
By east, west, north, and south, I spread my
conquering might: 560
My scutcheon plain declares that I am Alisander.'
BOYET. Your nose says, no, you are not; for it stands
too right.
BEROWNE. Your nose smells 'no' in this, most tender-
smelling knight.
PRINCESS. The conqueror is dismayed. Proceed,
good Alexander.
SIR NATHANIEL. 'When in the world I lived, I was the
world's commander,'—
BOYET. Most true, 'tis right; you were so, Alisander.
BEROWNE. Pompey the Great,—
COSTARD. Your servant, and Costard.
BEROWNE. Take away the conqueror, take away
Alisander.   570
COSTARD [*to Sir Nathaniel*]. O, sir, you have overthrown Alisander the conqueror! You will be
scraped out of the painted cloth for this. Your
lion, that holds his poll-axe sitting on a close-stool,
will be given to Ajax—he will be the ninth Worthy.
A conqueror, and afeard to speak! run away for
shame, Alisander. [*Sir Nathaniel departs*] There, an't
shall please you, a foolish mild man—an honest
man, look you, and soon dashed. He is a marvellous good neighbour, faith, and a very good bowler: 580
but for Alisander, alas you see how 'tis—a little
o'erparted. But there are Worthies a-coming will
speak their mind in some other sort.
PRINCESS. Stand aside, good Pompey.
    Costard departs

Enter Holofernes, for Judas, and Moth, for Hercules

HOLOFERNES. 'Great Hercules is presented by this imp,
Whose club killed Cerberus, that three-
headed Canis,
And when he was a babe, a child, a shrimp,
Thus did he strangle serpents in his manus.
Quoniam he seemeth in minority,
Ergo I come with this apology'.   590
Keep some state in thy exit, and vanish.
                                              Moth departs
'Judas I am,'—
DUMAINE. A Judas!
HOLOFERNES. Not Iscariot, sir.
'Judas I am, yclipéd Maccabæus.'
DUMAINE. Judas Maccabæus clipt in plain Judas.
BEROWNE. A kissing traitor. How, art thou proved
Judas?
HOLOFERNES. 'Judas I am,'—
DUMAINE. The more shame for you, Judas.   600
HOLOFERNES. What mean you, sir?
BOYET. To make Judas hang himself.
HOLOFERNES. Begin sir, you are my elder.
BEROWNE. Well followed. Judas was hanged on an
elder.
HOLOFERNES. I will not be put out of countenance.
BEROWNE. Because thou hast no face.
HOLOFERNES. What is this?
BOYET. A cittern-head.
DUMAINE. The head of a bodkin.   610
BEROWNE. A death's face in a ring.
LONGAVILLE. The face of an old Roman coin, scarce
seen.
BOYET. The pummel of Cæsar's falchion.
DUMAINE. The carved-bone face on flask.
BEROWNE. St George's half-cheek in a brooch.
DUMAINE. Ay, and in a brooch of lead.
BEROWNE. Ay, and worn in the cap of a tooth-drawer.
And now forward, for we have put thee in coun-
tenance.   620
HOLOFERNES. You have put me out of countenance.
BEROWNE. False—we have given thee faces.
HOLOFERNES. But you have out-faced them all.
BEROWNE. As thou wert a lion, we would do so.
BOYET. Therefore, as he is an ass, let him go.
And so adieu, sweet Jude! Nay, why dost
thou stay?
DUMAINE. For the latter end of his name.
BEROWNE. For the ass to the Jude: give it him—
Jud-as, away.
HOLOFERNES. This is not generous, not gentle,
not humble.
BOYET. A light for Monsieur Judas! it grows dark, he
may stumble.   *Holofernes retires* 630
PRINCESS. Alas, poor Maccabæus, how hath he
been baited!

Enter Armado armed, for Hector

BEROWNE. Hide thy head, Achilles—here comes Hec-
tor in arms.
DUMAINE. Though my mocks come home by me, I
will now be merry.
KING. Hector was but a Troyan in respect of this.
BOYET. But is this Hector?
KING. I think Hector was not so clean-timbered.
LONGAVILLE. His leg is too big for Hector's.
DUMAINE. More calf, certain.   640

BOYET. No, he is best indued in the small.
BEROWNE. This cannot be Hector.
DUMAINE. He's a god or a painter; for he makes
faces.
ARMADO. 'The armipotent Mars, of lances
the almighty,
Gave Hector a gift,'—
DUMAINE. A gilt nutmeg.
BEROWNE. A lemon.
LONGAVILLE. Stuck with cloves.
DUMAINE. No, cloven.   650
ARMADO. Peace!
'The armipotent Mars, of lances the almighty,
Gave Hector a gift, the heir of Ilion,
A man so breathed, that certain he would fight ye,
From morn till night, out of his pavilion.
I am that flower,'—
DUMAINE.   That mint.
LONGAVILLE.   That columbine.
ARMADO. Sweet Lord Longaville, rein thy tongue.
LONGAVILLE. I must rather give it the rein; for it runs
against Hector.
DUMAINE. Ay, and Hector's a greyhound.   660
ARMADO. The sweet war-man is dead and rotten—
sweet chucks, beat not the bones of the buried: when
he breathed, he was a man. But I will forward with
my device. [*to the Princess*] Sweet royalty, bestow on
me the sense of hearing.   *Berowne steps forth*
PRINCESS. Speak brave Hector, we are much delighted.
ARMADO. I do adore thy sweet grace's slipper.
BOYET. Loves her by the foot.
DUMAINE. He may not by the yard.
ARMADO. 'This Hector far surmounted Hannibal.   670
The party is gone' ...

Costard returns, with Berowne following

COSTARD. Fellow Hector, she is gone; she is two
months on her way.
ARMADO. What meanest thou?
COSTARD. Faith, unless you play the honest Troyan,
the poor wench is cast away: she's quick—the child
brags in her belly already: 'tis yours.
ARMADO. Dost thou infamonize me among poten-
tates? thou shalt die.
COSTARD. Then shall Hector be whipped for Jaquen-   680
etta that is quick by him, and hanged for Pompey
that is dead by him.
DUMAINE. Most rare Pompey!
BOYET. Renowned Pompey!
BEROWNE. Greater than great, great, great, great Pom-
pey! Pompey the Huge!
DUMAINE. Hector trembles.
BEROWNE. Pompey is moved. More Ates, more Ates!
stir them on! stir them on!
DUMAINE. Hector will challenge him.   690
BEROWNE. Ay, if a' have no more man's blood in's
belly than will sup a flea.
ARMADO. By the north pole, I do challenge thee.
COSTARD. I will not fight with a pole like a northern
man; I'll slash, I'll do it by the sword. I bepray
you let me borrow my arms again.
DUMAINE. Room for the incensed Worthies.
COSTARD. I'll do it in my shirt.
DUMAINE. Most resolute Pompey!
MOTH. Master, let me take you a button-hole lower. 700
Do you not see Pompey is uncasing for the combat?

What mean you? you will lose your reputation.

ARMADO. Gentlemen, and soldiers, pardon me, I will
not combat in my shirt.

DUMAINE. You may not deny it, Pompey hath made
the challenge.

ARMADO. Sweet bloods, I both may and will.

BEROWNE. What reason have you for't?

ARMADO. The naked truth of it is, I have no shirt. I
go woolward for penance.   710

MOTH. True, and it was enjoined him in Rome for
want of linen: since when, I'll be sworn, he wore
none but a dish-clout of Jaquenetta's, and that a'
wears next his heart for a favour.

Monsieur Mercadé, a messenger, enters

MERCADÉ. God save you, madam!

PRINCESS.   Welcome, Mercadé,
But that thou interrupt'st our merriment.

MERCADÉ. I am sorry, madam—for the news I bring,
Is heavy in my tongue. The king your father—

PRINCESS. Dead, for my life!

MERCADÉ.   Even so; my tale is told.

BEROWNE. Worthies, away! the scene begins to cloud.   720

ARMADO. For mine own part, I breathe free breath:
I have seen the day of wrong through the little hole
of discretion, and I will right myself like a soldier.
                                        The Worthies depart

KING. How fares your majesty?

PRINCESS. Boyet, prepare—I will away to-night.

KING. Madam, not so—I do beseech you stay.

PRINCESS. Prepare, I say, I thank you,
        gracious lords,
For all your fair endeavours, and entreat,
Out of a new-sad soul, that you vouchsafe
Is your rich wisdom to excuse, or hide,   730
The liberal opposition of our spirits,
If over-boldly we have borne ourselves
In the converse of breath—your gentleness
Was guilty of it. Farewell, worthy lord:
A heavy heart bears not a nimble tongue.
Excuse me so, coming too short of thanks
For my great suit so easily obtained.

KING. The extreme parts of time extremely forms
All causes to the purpose of his speed;
And often, at his very loose, decides   740
That which long process could not arbitrate.
And though the mourning brow of progeny
Forbid the smiling courtesy of love
The holy suit which fain it would convince,
Yet since love's argument was first on foot,
Let not the cloud of sorrow justle it
From what it purposed—since to wail friends lost
Is not by much so wholesome-profitable
As to rejoice at friends but newly found.

PRINCESS. I understand you not—my griefs
        are double.   750

BEROWNE. Honest plain words best pierce the ear
        of grief—
And by these bodges understand the king.
For your fair sakes have we neglected time,
Played foul-play with our oaths. Your beauty,
        ladies,
Hath much deformed us, fashioning our humours
Even to the opposéd end of our intents:
And what in us hath seemed ridiculous—
As love is full of unbefitting strains,

All wanton as a child, skipping and vain,
Formed by the eye, and therefore, like the eye   760
Full of straying shapes, of habits and of forms,
Varying in subjects as the eye doth roll
To every varied object in his glance:
Which parti-coated presence of loose love
Put on by us, if, in your heavenly eyes,
Have misbecomed our oaths and gravities,
Those heavenly eyes, that look into these faults,
Suggested us to make. Therefore, ladies,
Our love being yours, the error that love makes
Is likewise yours: we to ourselves prove false,   770
By being once false for ever to be true
To those that make us both—fair ladies, you.
And even that falsehood, in itself a sin,
Thus purifies itself and turns to grace.

PRINCESS. We have received your letters, full of love;
Your favours, the ambassadors of love;
And in our maiden council rated them
At courtship, pleasant jest, and courtesy,
As bombast and as lining to the time:
But more devout than this in our respects   780
Have we not been, and therefore met your loves
In their own fashion, like a merriment.

DUMAINE. Our letters, madam, showed much more
        than jest.

LONGAVILLE. So did our looks.

ROSALINE.   We did not quote them so.

KING. Now, at the latest minute of the hour,
Grant us your loves.

PRINCESS.   A time methinks too short.
To make a world-without-end bargain in:
No no, my lord, your grace is perjured much,
Full of dear guiltiness; and therefore this—
If for my love (as there is no such cause)   790
You will do aught, this shall you do for me:
Your oath I will not trust, but go with speed
To some forlorn and naked hermitage,
Remote from all the pleasures of the world;
There stay until the twelve celestial signs
Have brought about the annual reckoning.
If this austere insociable life
Change not your offer made in heat of blood,
If frosts and fasts, hard lodging and thin weeds,
Nip not the gaudy blossoms of your love,   800
But that it bear this trial and last love:
Then, at the expiration of the year,
Come challenge me, challenge by these deserts,
And by this virgin palm now kissing thine,
I will be thine; and till that instant shut
My woeful self up in a mourning house,
Raining the tears of lamentation
For the remembrance of my father's death.
If this thou do deny, let our hands part,
Neither entitled in the other's heart.   810

KING. If this, or more than this, I would deny,
To flatter up these powers of mine with rest,
The sudden hand of death close up mine eye!
Hence hermit, then—my heart is in thy breast.
                                        They talk apart

⌜BEROWNE. And what to me, my love? and what
        to me?

ROSALINE. You must be purgéd too; your sins are rank.
You are attaint with faults and perjury;
Therefore if you my favour mean to get,
A twelvemonth shall you spend, and never rest,

But seek the weary beds of people sick.⌋   820
DUMAINE. But what to me, my love? but what to me?
    A wife?
KATHARINE. A beard, fair health, and honesty—
    With three-fold love I wish you all these three.
DUMAINE. O, shall I say, I thank you gentle wife?
KATHARINE. Not so my lord, a twelvemonth and a day
    I'll mark no words that smooth-faced wooers say.
    Come when the king doth to my lady come;
    Then if I have much love, I'll give you some.
DUMAINE. I'll serve thee true and faithfully till then.   830
KATHARINE. Yet swear not, lest ye be forsworn again.
                              They talk apart
LONGAVILLE. What says Maria?
MARIA.   At the twelvemonth's end,
    I'll change my black gown for a faithful friend.
LONGAVILLE. I'll stay with patience; but the time is
    long.
MARIA. The liker you—few taller are so young.
                              They talk apart
BEROWNE. Studies my lady? mistress look on me,
    Behold the window of my heart, mine eye,
    What humble suit attends thy answer there:
    Impose some service on me for thy love.
ROSALINE. Oft have I heard of you, my Lord
    Berowne,   840
    Before I saw you: and the world's large tongue
    Proclaims you for a man replete with mocks,
    Full of comparisons and wounding flouts,
    Which you on all estates will execute
    That lie within the mercy of your wit.
    To weed this wormwood from your fructful brain,
    And therewithal to win me, if you please—
    Without the which I am not to be won—
    Yet shall this twelvemonth term from day to day
    Visit the speechless sick, and still converse   850
    With groaning wretches; and your task shall be,
    With all the fierce endeavour of your wit,
    To enforce the painéd impotent to smile.
BEROWNE. To move wild laughter in the throat
    of death?
    It cannot be, it is impossible.
    Mirth cannot move a soul in agony.
ROSALINE. Why, that's the way to choke a gibing
    spirit,
    Whose influence is begot of that loose grace,
    Which shallow laughing hearers give to fools.
    A jest's prosperity lies in the ear   860
    Of him that hears it, never in the tongue
    Of him that makes it: then if sickly ears,
    Deafed with the clamours of their own dear groans,
    Will hear your idle scorns, continue then,
    And I will have you, and that fault withal.
    But if they will not, throw away that spirit,
    And I shall find you empty of that fault,
    Right joyful of your reformation.
BEROWNE. A twelvemonth? well; befall what
    will befall,
    I'll jest a twelvemonth in an hospital.   870
                The King and the Princess come forward
PRINCESS. Ay, sweet my lord—and so I take my leave.
KING. No madam, we will bring you on your way.
BEROWNE. Our wooing doth not end like an old play:
    Jack hath not Jill: these ladies' courtesy
    Might well have made our sport a comedy.

KING. Come, sir, it wants a twelvemonth an' a day,   820
    And then 'twill end.
BEROWNE.   That's too long for a play.
Armado returns
ARMADO. Sweet majesty, vouchsafe me,—
PRINCESS. Was not that Hector?
DUMAINE. The worthy knight of Troy.   880
ARMADO. I will kiss thy royal finger, and take leave.
    I am a votary; I have vowed to Jaquenetta
    To hold the plough for her sweet love three year.
    But, most esteemed greatness, will you hear the
    dialogue that the two learned men have compiled,
    in praise of the owl and the cuckoo? it should have
    followed in the end of our show.
KING. Call them forth quickly, we will do so.
ARMADO. Holla! approach.
Enter all
    This side is Hiems, winter; this Ver, the spring—the 890
    one maintained by the Owl, th'other by the
    Cuckoo. Ver begin.

                The Cuckoo sings
    When daisies pied and violets blue
        And lady-smocks all silver-white
    And cuckoo-buds of yellow hue
        Do paint the meadows with delight,
    The cuckoo then on every tree,
    Mocks married men; for thus sings he,
            Cuckoo....
    Cuckoo, cuckoo: O word of fear,   900
    Unpleasing to a married ear!

    When shepherds pipe on oaten straws,
        And merry larks are ploughmen's clocks,
    When turtles tread, and rooks, and daws,
        And maidens bleach their summer smocks,
    The cuckoo then, on every tree,
    Mocks married men; for thus sings he,
            Cuckoo....
    Cuckoo, cuckoo: O word of fear,
    Unpleasing to a married ear!   910

                The Owl sings
    When icicles hang by the wall,
        And Dick the shepherd blows his nail,
    And Tom bears logs into the hall,
        And milk comes frozen home in pail,
    When blood is nipped, and ways be foul,
    Then nightly sings the staring owl,
            'Tu-who....
    Tu-whit to-who'—a merry note,
    While greasy Joan doth keel the pot.

    When all aloud the wind doth blow,   920
        And coughing drowns the parson's saw,
    And birds sit brooding in the snow,
        And Marian's nose looks red and raw,
    When roasted crabs hiss in the bowl,
    Then nightly sings the staring owl,
            'Tu-who....
    Tu-whit to-who'—a merry note,
    While greasy Joan doth keel the pot.

    The words of Mercury are harsh after the songs
    of Apollo.

A Midsummer-Night's Dream

Scene: Athens, and a wood hard by

CHARACTERS IN THE PLAY

THESEUS, *Duke of Athens*

HIPPOLYTA, *Queen of the Amazons, betrothed to Theseus*

EGEUS, *an old man, father to Hermia*

LYSANDER
DEMETRIUS } *young gentlemen, in love with Hermia*

PHILOSTRATE, *master of the revels to Theseus*

HERMIA (*short and dark*), *daughter to Egeus, in love with Lysander*

HELENA (*tall and fair*), *in love with Demetrius*

PETER QUINCE, *a carpenter*

NICK BOTTOM, *a weaver*

FRANCIS FLUTE, *a bellows-mender*

TOM SNOUT, *a tinker*

ROBIN STARVELING, *a tailor*

SNUG, *a joiner*

OBERON, *King of the Fairies*

TITANIA, *Queen of the Fairies*

ROBIN GOODFELLOW, THE PUCK

PEASEBLOSSOM
COBWEB
MOTH } *fairies*
MUSTARDSEED

Other fairies attending their King and Queen

Attendants on Theseus and Hippolyta

A Midsummer-Night's Dream

ACT 1

Scene 1: *The palace of Duke Theseus*

Theseus and Hippolyta enter and take their seats, followed by Philostrate and attendants

THESEUS. Now, fair Hippolyta, our nuptial hour
  Draws on apace: four happy days bring in
  Another moon: but O, methinks how slow
  This old moon wanes! she lingers my desires,
  Like to a step-dame, or a dowager,
  Long withering out a young man's revenue.
HIPPOLYTA. Four days will quickly steep themselves
    in night:
  Four nights will quickly dream away the time:
  And then the moon, like to a silver bow
  New-bent in heaven, shall behold the night   10
  Of our solemnities.
THESEUS.   Go, Philostrate,
  Stir up the Athenian youth to merriments,
  Awake the pert and nimble spirit of mirth,
  Turn melancholy forth to funerals:
  The pale companion is not for our pomp.
                          Philostrate departs
  Hippolyta, I wooed thee with my sword,
  And won thy love doing thee injuries:
  But I will wed thee in another key,
  With pomp, with triumph, and with revelling.

Egeus enters, with his daughter Hermia, followed by Lysander and Demetrius

EGEUS. Happy be Theseus, our renownéd duke.   20
THESEUS. Thanks, good Egeus. What's the news
    with thee?
EGEUS. Full of vexation come I, with complaint
  Against my child, my daughter Hermia.
  Stand forth, Demetrius. My noble lord,
  This man hath my consent to marry her.
  Stand forth, Lysander. And, my gracious duke,
  This man hath witched the bosom of my child.
  Thou, thou, Lysander, thou hast given her rhymes,
  And interchanged love-tokens with my child:
  Thou hast by moonlight at her window sung,   30
  With feigning voice, verses of feigning love:
  And stol'n the impression of her fantasy
  With bracelets of thy hair, rings, gauds, conceits,
  Knacks, trifles, nosegays, sweetmeats—messengers
  Of strong prevailment in unhardened youth.
  With cunning hast thou filched my daughter's heart,
  Turned her obedience, which is due to me,
  To stubborn harshness. And, my gracious duke,
  Be it so she will not here before your grace
  Consent to marry with Demetrius,   40
  I beg the ancient privilege of Athens:
  As she is mine, I may dispose of her:
  Which shall be either to this gentleman,
  Or to her death; according to our law
  Immediately provided in that case.
THESEUS. What say you, Hermia? be advised, fair
    maid.
  To you your father should be as a god;
  One that composed your beauties; yea and one
  To whom you are but as a form in wax
  By him imprinted, and within his power   50
  To leave the figure or disfigure it.
  Demetrius is a worthy gentleman.
HERMIA. So is Lysander.
THESEUS.   In himself he is:
  But in this kind, wanting your father's voice,
  The other must be held the worthier.
HERMIA. I would my father looked but with my eyes.
THESEUS. Rather your eyes must with his judgement
    look.
HERMIA. I do entreat your grace to pardon me.
  I know not by what power I am made bold;
  Nor how it may concern my modesty   60
  In such a presence here to plead my thoughts:
  But I beseech your grace that I may know
  The worst that may befall me in this case
  If I refuse to wed Demetrius.
THESEUS. Either to die the death, or to abjure
  For ever the society of men.
  Therefore, fair Hermia, question your desires,
  Know of your youth, examine well your blood,
  Whether, if you yield not to your father's choice,
  You can endure the livery of a nun,   70
  For aye to be in shady cloister mewed,
  To live a barren sister all your life,
  Chanting faint hymns to the cold fruitless moon.
  Thrice blessèd they that master so their blood,
  To undergo such maiden pilgrimage:
  But earthlier happy is the rose distilled,
  Than that which withering on the virgin thorn
  Grows, lives and dies in single blessedness.
HERMIA. So will I grow, so live, so die, my lord,
  Ere I will yield my virgin patent up   80
  Unto his lordship, whose unwishèd yoke
  My soul consents not to give sovereignty.
THESEUS. Take time to pause, and by the next new
    moon—
  The sealing-day betwixt my love and me
  For everlasting bond of fellowship—
  Upon that day either prepare to die
  For disobedience to your father's will,
  Or else to wed Demetrius as he would,
  Or on Diana's altar to protest
  For aye austerity and single life.   90
DEMETRIUS. Relent, sweet Hermia—and, Lysander,
    yield
  Thy crazèd title to my certain right.
LYSANDER. You have her father's love, Demetrius;
  Let me have Hermia's: do you marry him.
EGEUS. Scornful Lysander! true, he hath my love;
  And what is mine my love shall render him.
  And she is mine, and all my right of her
  I do estate unto Demetrius.
LYSANDER. I am, my lord, as well derived as he,
  As well possessed: my love is more than his: 100
  My fortunes every way as fairly ranked—
  If not with vantage—as Demetrius':
  And, which is more than all these boasts can be,

I am beloved of beauteous Hermia.
Why should not I then prosecute my right?
Demetrius, I'll avouch it to his head,
Made love to Nedar's daughter, Helena,
And won her soul; and she, sweet lady, dotes,
Devoutly dotes, dotes in idolatry,
Upon this spotted and inconstant man.   110
THESEUS. I must confess that I have heard so much:
And with Demetrius thought to have spoke thereof;
But, being over-full of self-affairs,
My mind did lose it. But Demetrius come,
And come Egeus, you shall go with me:
I have some private schooling for you both.
For you, fair Hermia, look you arm yourself
To fit your fancies to your father's will;
Or else the law of Athens yields you up
(Which by no means we may extenuate)   120
To death, or to a vow of single life.
Come, my Hippolyta: what cheer, my love?
Demetrius and Egeus, go along:
I must employ you in some business
Against our nuptial, and confer with you
Of something nearly that concerns yourselves.
EGEUS. With duty and desire we follow you.

All depart save Hermia and Lysander

LYSANDER. How now, my love? Why is your cheek
   so pale?
How chance the roses there do fade so fast?
HERMIA. Belike for want of rain, which I could well   130
Beteem them from the tempest of my eyes.
LYSANDER. Ay me! for aught that I could ever read,
Could ever hear by tale or history
The course of true love never did run smooth;
But, either it was different in blood—
HERMIA. O cross! too high to be enthralled to low.
LYSANDER. Or else misgraffèd in respect of years—
HERMIA. O spite! too old to be engaged to young.
LYSANDER. Or else it stood upon the choice of
   friends—
HERMIA. O hell! to choose love by another's eyes!   140
LYSANDER. Or, if there were a sympathy in choice,
War, death, or sickness did lay siege to it—
Making it momentary as a sound,
Swift as a shadow, short as any dream,
Brief as the lightning in the collied night
That, in a spleen, unfolds both heaven and earth;
And ere a man hath power to say 'Behold!'
The jaws of darkness do devour it up:
So quick bright things come to confusion.
HERMIA. If then true lovers have been ever crossed,   150
It stands as an edict in destiny:
Then let us teach our trial patience,
Because it is a customary cross,
As due to love as thoughts and dreams and sighs,
Wishes and tears; poor Fancy's followers.
LYSANDER. A good persuasion: therefore hear me,
   Hermia:
I have a widow aunt, a dowager
Of great revénue, and she hath no child:
From Athens is her house remote seven leagues:
And she respects me as her only son ...   160
There, gentle Hermia, may I marry thee:
And to that place the sharp Athenian law
Cannot pursue us. If thou lovest me then,
Steal forth thy father's house to-morrow night;
And in the wood, a league without the town,

Where I did meet thee once with Helena,
To do observance to a morn of May,
There will I stay for thee.
HERMIA.   My good Lysander,
I swear to thee by Cupid's strongest bow,
By his best arrow with the golden head,   170
By the simplicity of Venus' doves,
By that which knitteth souls and prospers loves,
And by that fire which burned the Carthage queen,
When the false Troyan under sail was seen,
By all the vows that ever men have broke—
In number more than ever women spoke—
In that same place thou hast appointed me,
To-morrow truly will I meet with thee.
LYSANDER. Keep promise, love ... Look, here comes
   Helena.

Helena enters

HERMIA. God speed, fair Helena: whither away?   180
HELENA. Call you me fair? that 'fair' again unsay.
Demetrius loves your fair: O happy fair!
Your eyes are lode-stars, and your tongue's sweet air
More tuneable than lark to shepherd's ear,
When wheat is green, when hawthorn buds appear.
Sickness is catching: O, were favour so,
Yours would I catch, fair Hermia, ere I go!
My ear should catch your voice, my eye your eye,
My tongue should catch your tongue's sweet
   melody.
Were the world mine, Demetrius being bated,   190
The rest I'ld give to be to you translated.
O, teach me how you look, and with what art
You sway the motion of Demetrius' heart.
HERMIA. I frown upon him; yet he loves me still.
HELENA. O that your frowns would teach my smiles
   such skill.
HERMIA. I give him curses; yet he gives me love.
HELENA. O that my prayers could such affection move.
HERMIA. The more I hate, the more he follows me.
HELENA. The more I love, the more he hateth me.
HERMIA. His folly, Helena, is no fault of mine.   200
HELENA. None, but your beauty; would that fault
   were mine.
HERMIA. Take comfort: he no more shall see my face:
Lysander and myself will fly this place.
Before the time I did Lysander see,
Seemed Athens as a paradise to me:
O then, what graces in my love do dwell,
That he hath turned a heaven unto a hell!
LYSANDER. Helen, to you our minds we will unfold:
To-morrow night, when Phœbe doth behold
Her silver visage in the wat'ry glass,   210
Decking with liquid pearl the bladed grass—
A time that lovers' flights doth still conceal—
Through Athens' gates have we devised to steal.
HERMIA. And in the wood, where often you and I
Upon faint primrose beds were wont to lie,
Emptying our bosoms of their counsel sweet,
There my Lysander and myself shall meet,
And thence from Athens turn away our eyes,
To seek new friends and stranger companies.
Farewell, sweet playfellow: pray thou for us!   220
And good luck grant thee thy Demetrius!
Keep word, Lysander: we must starve our sight
From lovers' food till morrow deep midnight.

She goes

LYSANDER. I will, my Hermia. Helena, adieu:
As you on him, Demetrius dote on you!

He goes

HELENA. How happy some o'er other some can be!
Through Athens I am thought as fair as she,
But what of that? Demetrius thinks not so:
He will not know what all but he do know.
And as he errs, doting on Hermia's eyes,   230
So I, admiring of his qualities.
Things base and vile, holding no quantity,
Love can transpose to form and dignity.
Love looks not with the eyes, but with the mind:
And therefore is winged Cupid painted blind.
Nor hath Love's mind of any judgement taste:
Wings and no eyes figure unheedy haste.
And therefore is Love said to be a child:
Because in choice he is so oft beguiled.
As waggish boys in game themselves forswear: 240
So the boy Love is perjured every where.
For ere Demetrius looked on Hermia's eyne,
He hailed down oaths that he was only mine.
And when this hail some heat from Hermia felt,
So he dissolved, and show'rs of oaths did melt.
I will go tell him of fair Hermia's flight:
Then to the wood will he to-morrow night
Pursue her: and for this intelligence
If I have thanks, it is a dear expense:
But herein mean I to enrich my pain,   250
To have his sight thither and back again.

She goes

Scene 2: *The cottage of Peter Quince*

Enter Quince, Bottom, Snug, Flute, Snout, and Starveling

QUINCE. Is all our company here?

BOTTOM. You were best to call them generally, man by man, according to the scrip.

QUINCE. Here is the scroll of every man's name, which is thought fit, through all Athens, to play in our interlude before the duke and the duchess, on his wedding-day at night.

BOTTOM. First, good Peter Quince, say what the play treats on: then read the names of the actors: and so grow to a point.   10

QUINCE. Marry, our play is 'The most lamentable comedy, and most cruel death of Pyramus and Thisby.'

BOTTOM. A very good piece of work, I assure you, and a merry. Now, good Peter Quince, call forth your actors by the scroll. Masters, spread yourselves.

QUINCE. Answer, as I call you. Nick Bottom, the weaver.

BOTTOM. Ready: name what part I am for, and proceed.   20

QUINCE. You, Nick Bottom, are set down for Pyramus.

BOTTOM. What is Pyramus? a lover, or a tyrant?

QUINCE. A lover that kills himself, most gallant for love.

BOTTOM. That will ask some tears in the true performing of it. If I do it, let the audience look to their eyes: I will move storms: I will condole in some measure. To the rest—yet my chief humour is for a tyrant. I could play Ercles rarely, or a part to tear a cat in,   30 to make all split.

'The raging rocks
And shivering shocks
Shall break the locks
Of prison-gates,
And Phibbus' car
Shall shine from far
And make and mar
The foolish Fates.'

This was lofty. Now name the rest of the players.   40 This is Ercles' vein, a tyrant's vein: a lover is more condoling.

QUINCE. Francis Flute, the bellows-mender.

FLUTE. Here, Peter Quince.

QUINCE. Flute, you must take Thisby on you.

FLUTE. What is Thisby? a wand'ring knight?

QUINCE. It is the lady that Pyramus must love.

FLUTE. Nay, faith: let not me play a woman: I have a beard coming.

QUINCE. That's all one: you shall play it in a mask: and   50 you may speak as small as you will.

BOTTOM. An I may hide my face, let me play Thisby too: I'll speak in a monstrous little voice. 'Thisne, Thisne'—'Ah, Pyramus, my lover dear, thy Thisby dear, and lady dear.'

QUINCE. No, no, you must play Pyramus: and Flute, you Thisby.

BOTTOM. Well, proceed.

QUINCE. Robin Starveling, the tailor.

STARVELING. Here, Peter Quince.   60

QUINCE. Robin Starveling, you must play Thisby's mother. Tom Snout, the tinker.

SNOUT. Here, Peter Quince.

QUINCE. You, Pyramus' father, myself, Thisby's father; Snug, the joiner, you the lion's part: and I hope here is a play fitted.

SNUG. Have you the lion's part written? pray you, if it be, give it me: for I am slow of study.

QUINCE. You may do it extempore: for it is nothing but roaring.   70

BOTTOM. Let me play the lion too. I will roar that I will do any man's heart good to hear me. I will roar that I will make the duke say, 'Let him roar again: let him roar again.'

QUINCE. An you should do it too terribly, you would fright the duchess and the ladies, that they would shriek: and that were enough to hang us all.

ALL. That would hang us, every mother's son.

BOTTOM. I grant you, friends if you should fright the ladies out of their wits, they would have no more   80 discretion but to hang us: but I will aggravate my voice so, that I will roar you as gently as any sucking dove: I will roar you an 'twere any nightingale

QUINCE. You can play no part but Pyramus: for Pyramus is a sweet-faced man; a proper man as one shall see in a summer's day; a most lovely, gentleman-like man: therefore you must needs play Pyramus.

BOTTOM. Well, I will undertake it. What beard were I best to play it in?   90

QUINCE. Why, what you will.

BOTTOM. I will discharge it in either your straw-colour beard, your orange-tawny beard, your purple-in-grain beard, or your French-crown-colour beard, your perfect yellow.

QUINCE. Some of your French crowns have no hair at all; and then you will play barefaced.... But,

masters, here are your parts, and I am to entreat you,
request you, and desire you, to con them by to-
morrow night: and meet me in the palace wood, 100
a mile without the town, by moonlight; there will
we rehearse: for if we meet in the city, we shall be
dogged with company, and our devices known. In
the meantime, I will draw a bill of properties, such as
our play wants. I pray you, fail me not.

BOTTOM. We will meet, and there we may rehearse
most obscenely and courageously. Take pains, be
perfect: adieu.

QUINCE. At the duke's oak we meet.

BOTTOM. Enough: hold, or cut bow-strings. 110

They go

ACT 2
Scene 1: *The palace wood, Athens*

Puck and a Fairy, meeting

PUCK. How now, spirit! whither wander you?
FAIRY. Over hill, over dale,
    Thorough bush, thorough briar,
  Over park, over pale,
    Thorough flood, thorough fire,
  I do wander every where,
  Swifter than the moonës sphere:
  And I serve the Fairy Queen,
  To dew her orbs upon the green.
  The cowslips tall her pensioners be, 10
  In their gold coats spots you see:
  Those be rubies, fairy favours:
  In those freckles live their savours:
  I must go seek some dewdrops here,
  And hang a pearl in every cowslip's ear.
  Farewell, thou lob of spirits: I'll be gone—
  Our queen and all her elves come here anon.
PUCK. The king doth keep his revels here to-night.
  Take heed the queen come not within his sight.
  For Oberon is passing fell and wrath, 20
  Because that she as her attendant hath
  A lovely boy, stol'n from an Indian king:
  She never had so sweet a changeling.
  And jealous Oberon would have the child
  Knight of his train, to trace the forests wild.
  But she, perforce, withholds the lovèd boy,
  Crowns him with flowers, and makes him all her
    joy.
  And now they never meet in grove, or green,
  By fountain clear, or spangled starlight sheen,
  But they do square—that all their elves, for fear, 30
  Creep into acorn cups and hide them there.
FAIRY. Either I mistake your shape and making quite
  Or else you are that shrewd and knavish sprite
  Called Robin Goodfellow. Are not you he
  That frights the maidens of the villagery,
  Skim milk, and sometimes labour in the quern,
  And bootless make the breathless housewife churn,
  And sometime make the drink to bear no barm,
  Mislead night-wanderers, laughing at their harm?
  Those that Hobgoblin call you and sweet Puck, 40
  You do their work, and they shall have good luck.
  Are not you he?
PUCK. Thou speak'st aright;
  I am that merry wanderer of the night.
  I jest to Oberon, and make him smile

When I a fat and bean-fed horse beguile,
Neighing in likeness of a filly foal;
And sometime lurk I in a gossip's bowl,
In very likeness of a roasted crab,
And, when she drinks, against her lips I bob,
And on her withered dewlap pour the ale. 50
The wisest aunt, telling the saddest tale,
Sometime for three-foot stool mistaketh me:
Then slip I from her bum, down topples she,
And 'tailor' cries, and falls into a cough:
And then the whole choir hold their hips and
  laugh,
And waxen in their mirth, and neeze, and swear
A merrier hour was never wasted there.
But room, faëry: here comes Oberon.
FAIRY. And here my mistress. Would that he were
  gone.

Enter fairies: Oberon and Titania confront each other

OBERON. Ill met by moonlight, proud Titania. 60
TITANIA. What, jealous Oberon! Fairies, skip
  hence—
I have forsworn his bed and company.
OBERON. Tarry, rash wanton. Am not I thy lord?
TITANIA. Then I must be thy lady: but I know
  When thou hast stol'n away from fairy land,
  And in the shape of Corin sat all day,
  Playing on pipes of corn, and versing love,
  To amorous Phillida. Why art thou here,
  Come from the farthest steep of India?
  But that, forsooth, the bouncing Amazon, 70
  Your buskined mistress and your warrior love,
  To Theseus must be wedded; and you come
  To give their bed joy and prosperity.
OBERON. How canst thou thus for shame, Titania,
  Glance at my credit with Hippolyta,
  Knowing I know thy love to Theseus?
  Didst thou not lead him through the glimmering
    night
  From Perigouna, whom he ravishéd?
  And make him with fair Ægles break his faith,
  With Ariadne, and Antiopa? 80
TITANIA. These are the forgeries of jealousy:
  And never, since the middle summer's spring,
  Met we on hill, in dale, forest, or mead,
  By pavèd fountain, or by rushy brook,
  Or in the beachèd margent of the sea,
  To dance our ringlets to the whistling wind,
  But with thy brawls thou hast disturbed our sport.
  Therefore the winds, piping to us in vain,
  As in revenge, have sucked up from the sea
  Contagious fogs: which falling in the land, 90
  Hath every pelting river made so proud
  That they have overborne their continents.
  The ox hath therefore stretched his yoke in vain,
  The ploughman lost his sweat, and the green corn
  Hath rotted ere his youth attained a beard;
  The fold stands empty in the drownèd field,
  And crows are fatted with the murrion flock;
  The nine men's morris is filled up with mud,
  And the quaint mazes in the wanton green
  For lack of tread are indistinguishable. 100
  The human mortals want their winter cheer;
  No night is now with hymn or carol blest;
  Therefore the moon, the governess of floods,
  Pale in her anger, washes all the air,

That rheumatic diseases do abound.
And thorough this distemperature we see
The seasons alter: hoary-headed frosts
Fall in the fresh lap of the crimson rose,
And on old Hiems' thin and icy crown
An odorous chaplet of sweet summer buds   110
Is, as in mockery, set. The spring, the summer,
The childing autumn, angry winter, change
Their wonted liveries; and the mazéd world,
By their increase, now knows not which is which.
And this same progeny of evils comes
From our debate, from our dissension:
We are their parents and original.
OBERON. Do you amend it then: it lies in you.
Why should Titania cross her Oberon?
I do but beg a little changeling boy,   120
To be my henchman.
TITANIA.   Set your heart at rest,
The fairy land buys not the child of me.
His mother was a vot'ress of my order;
And in the spicéd Indian air, by night,
Full often hath she gossiped by my side;
And sat with me on Neptune's yellow sands,
Marking th'embarkéd traders on the flood;
When we have laughed to see the sails conceive
And grow big-bellied with the wanton wind;
Which she, with pretty and with swimming gait   130
Following—her womb then rich with my young
    squire—
Would imitate, and sail upon the land,
To fetch me trifles, and return again,
As from a voyage, rich with merchandise.
But she, being mortal, of that boy did die;
And for her sake do I rear up her boy;
And for her sake I will not part with him.
OBERON. How long within this wood intend you stay?
TITANIA. Perchance till after Theseus' wedding-day.
If you will patiently dance in our round,   140
And see our moonlight revels, go with us:
If not, shun me, and I will spare your haunts.
OBERON. Give me that boy, and I will go with thee.
TITANIA. Not for thy fairy kingdom.... Fairies, away!
We shall chide downright, if I longer stay.
               Titania departs with her train
OBERON. Well: go thy way. Thou shalt not from
    this grove,
Till I torment thee for this injury.
My gentle Puck, come hither. Thou rememb'rest
Since once I sat upon a promontory,
And heard a mermaid, on a dolphin's back,   150
Uttering such dulcet and harmonious breath
That the rude sea grew civil at her song,
And certain stars shot madly from their spheres
To hear the sea-maid's music.
PUCK.   I remember.
OBERON. That very time I saw—but thou couldst
    not—
Flying between the cold moon and the earth,
Cupid all armed: a certain aim he took
At a fair Vestal, thronéd by the west,
And loosed his love-shaft smartly from his bow,
As it should pierce a hundred thousand hearts: 160
But I might see young Cupid's fiery shaft
Quenched in the chaste beams of the wat'ry moon:
And the imperial Vot'ress passéd on,
In maiden meditation, fancy-free.

Yet marked I where the bolt of Cupid fell.
It fell upon a little western flower;
Before, milk-white; now purple with love's
    wound—
And maidens call it Love-in-idleness.
Fetch me that flower, the herb I showed thee once.
The juice of it, on sleeping eyelids laid,   170
Will make or man or woman madly dote
Upon the next live creature that it sees.
Fetch me this herb, and be thou here again
Ere the leviathan can swim a league.
PUCK. I'll put a girdle round about the earth
In forty minutes.   *He goes*
OBERON.   Having once this juice,
I'll watch Titania when she is asleep,
And drop the liquor of it in her eyes:
The next thing then she waking looks upon—
Be it on lion, bear, or wolf, or bull,   180
On meddling monkey, or on busy ape—
She shall pursue it with the soul of love.
And ere I take this charm from off her sight—
As I can take it with another herb—
I'll make her render up her page to me.
But who comes here? I am invisible,
And I will overhear their conference.

Demetrius enters, Helena following him

DEMETRIUS. I love thee not ... therefore pursue me
    not.
Where is Lysander and fair Hermia?
The one I'll slay ... the other slayeth me.   190
Thou told'st me they were stol'n unto this wood:
And here am I, and wood within this wood,
Because I cannot meet my Hermia:
Hence, get thee gone, and follow me no more.
HELENA. You draw me, you hard-hearted adamant;
But yet you draw not iron, for my heart
Is true as steel. Leave you your power to draw,
And I shall have no power to follow you.
DEMETRIUS. Do I entice you? Do I speak you fair
Or rather do I not in plainest truth   200
Tell you I do not nor I cannot love you?
HELENA. And even for that do I love you the more:
I am your spaniel; and, Demetrius,
The more you beat me, I will fawn on you.
Use me but as your spaniel: spurn me, strike me,
Neglect me, lose me: only give me leave,
Unworthy as I am, to follow you.
What worser place can I beg in your love—
And yet a place of high respect with me—
Than to be uséd as you use your dog?   210
DEMETRIUS. Tempt not too much the hatred of my
    spirit,
For I am sick when I do look on thee.
HELENA. And I am sick when I look not on you.
DEMETRIUS. You do impeach your modesty too much
To leave the city and commit yourself
Into the hands of one that loves you not,
To trust the opportunity of night
And the ill counsel of a desert place
With the rich worth of your virginity.
HELENA. Your virtue is my privilege for that: 220
It is not night when I do see your face,
Therefore I think I am not in the night—
Nor doth this wood lack worlds of company,
For you in my respect are all the world.

Then how can it be said I am alone
When all the world is here to look on me?
DEMETRIUS. I'll run from thee and hide me in the
   brakes,
And leave thee to the mercy of wild beasts.
HELENA. The wildest hath not such a heart as you.
Run when you will; the story shall be changed: 230
Apollo flies, and Daphne holds the chase;
The dove pursues the griffin; the mild hind
Makes speed to catch the tiger . . . . bootless speed,
When cowardice pursues and valour flies.
DEMETRIUS. I will not stay thy questions—let me go:
Or, if thou follow me, do not believe
But I shall do thee mischief in the wood.
HELENA. Ay, in the temple, in the town, the field,
You do me mischief. Fie, Demetrius!
Your wrongs do set a scandal on my sex: 240
We cannot fight for love, as men may do;
We should be wooed and were not made to woo.
                              He goes
I'll follow thee and make a heaven of hell,
To die upon the hand I love so well.
                         She follows after
OBERON. Fare thee well, nymph. Ere he do leave this
   grove,
Thou shalt fly him, and he shall seek thy love.

Puck reappears

Welcome, wanderer. Hast thou the flower there?
PUCK. Ay, there it is.
OBERON.   I pray thee, give it me.
I know a bank where the wild thyme blows,
Where oxlips and the nodding violet grows,   250
Quite over-canopied with luscious woodbine,
With sweet musk-roses, and with eglantine:
There sleeps Titania sometime of the night,
Lulled in these flowers with dances and delight;
And there the snake throws her enamelled skin,
Weed wide enough to wrap a fairy in.
And with the juice of this I'll streak her eyes,
And make her full of hateful fantasies.
Take thou some of it, and seek through this grove:
A sweet Athenian lady is in love   260
With a disdainful youth; anoint his eyes—
But do it when the next thing he espies
May be the lady. Thou shalt know the man
By the Athenian garments he hath on.
Effect it with some care, that he may prove
More fond on her than she upon her love.
And look thou meet me ere the first cock crow.
PUCK. Fear not, my lord: your servant shall do so.
                              They depart

Scene 2: *Another part of the wood*

Enter Titania; her fairies attending her

TITANIA. Come now, a roundel and a fairy song:
Then, for the third part of a minute, hence—
Some to kill cankers in the musk-rose buds,
Some war with rere-mice for their leathern wings,
To make my small elves coats, and some keep back
The clamorous owl that nightly hoots and wonders
At out quaint spirits. Sing me now asleep;
Then to your offices, and let me rest.

Fairies sing

You spotted snakes, with double tongue,
   Thorny hedgehogs, be not seen;   10
Newts and blind-worms do no wrong,
   Come not near our Fairy Queen.
Philomele, with melody,
   Sing in our sweet lullaby,
      Lulla, lulla, lullaby,
      Lulla, lulla, lullaby,
   Never harm,
   Nor spell, nor charm,
Come our lovely lady nigh.
So good night, with lullaby.   20
1 FAIRY. Weaving spiders come not here:
   Hence you long-legged spinners, hence:
Beetles black approach not near:
   Worm nor snail do no offence.
Philomele, with melody,
   Sing in our sweet lullaby,
      Lulla, lulla, lullaby,
      Lulla, lulla, lullaby,
   Never harm,
   Nor spell, nor charm,   30
Come our lovely lady nigh.
So good night, with lullaby.
                         Titania sleeps
2 FAIRY. Hence, away: now all is well:
   One aloof stand sentinel.
                     The fairies steal away

*Oberon appears and anoints the eyes of Titania with the
juice of the flower*

OBERON. What thou see'st when thou dost wake,
Do it for thy true-love take;
Love and languish for his sake.
Be it ounce, or cat, or bear,
Pard, or boar with bristled hair,
In thy eye that shall appear   40
When thou wak'st, it is thy dear:
Wake when some vile thing is near.
                              He goes

Lysander and Hermia enter

LYSANDER. Fair love, you faint with wandr'ing in the
   wood;
And to speak troth I have forgot our way.
We'll rest us, Hermia, if you think it good,
And tarry for the comfort of the day.
HERMIA. Be't so, Lysander: find you out a bed:
For I upon this bank will rest my head.
LYSANDER. One turf shall serve as pillow for us both,
One heart, one bed, two bosoms, and one troth.   50
HERMIA. Nay, good Lysander: for my sake, my dear,
Lie further off yet; do not lie so near.
LYSANDER. O take the sense, sweet, of my innocence!
Love takes the meaning in love's conference.
I mean that my heart unto yours is knit,
So that but one heart we can make of it:
Two bosoms interchainèd with an oath,
So then two bosoms and a single troth.
Then by your side no bed-room me deny,
For lying so, Hermia, I do not lie.   60
HERMIA. Lysander riddles very prettily.
Now much beshrew my manners and my pride,
If Hermia meant to say Lysander lied.
But, gentle friend, for love and courtesy
Lie further off—in human modesty:

Such separation as may well be said
Becomes a virtuous bachelor and a maid,
So far be distant—and good night, sweet friend:
Thy love ne'er alter till thy sweet life end!

LYSANDER. Amen, amen, to that fair prayer, say I— 70
And then end life when I end loyalty!
Here is my bed: sleep give thee all his rest.

HERMIA. With half that wish the wisher's eyes be
pressed.   *They sleep*

Puck appears

PUCK. Through the forest have I gone,
But Athenian found I none
On whose eyes I might approve
This flower's force in stirring love.
Night and silence—who is here?
Weeds of Athens he doth wear:
This is he, my master said,   80
Despisèd the Athenian maid:
And here the maiden, sleeping sound,
On the dank and dirty ground.
Pretty soul, she durst not lie
Near this lack-love, this kill-courtesy.
Churl, upon thy eyes I throw
All the power this charm doth owe:
When thou wak'st, let love forbid
Sleep his seat on thy eyelid.
So awake when I am gone;   90
For I must now to Oberon.   *He goes*

Enter Demetrius and Helena, running

HELENA. Stay; though thou kill me, sweet Demetrius.
DEMETRIUS. I charge thee, hence, and do not haunt
me thus.
HELENA. O, wilt thou darkling leave me? do not so.
DEMETRIUS. Stay, on thy peril; I alone will go.
                                          He goes
HELENA. O, I am out of breath in this fond chase!
The more my prayer, the lesser is my grace.
Happy is Hermia, wheresoe'er she lies;
For she hath blessèd and attractive eyes.
How came her eyes so bright? Not with salt tears— 100
If so, my eyes are oft'ner washed than hers.
No, no: I am as ugly as a bear,
For beasts that meet me run away for fear.
Therefore no marvel though Demetrius
Do, as a monster, fly my presence thus.
What wicked and dissembling glass of mine
Made me compare with Hermia's sphery eyne?
But who is here? Lysander! on the ground!
Dead? or asleep? I see no blood, no wound.
Lysander, if you live, good sir, awake.   110
LYSANDER [*leaps up*]. And run through fire I will, for
thy sweet sake.
Transparent Helena! Nature shows her art,
That through thy bosom makes me see thy heart.
Where is Demetrius? O, how fit a word
Is that vile name to perish on my sword!
HELENA. Do not say so, Lysander, say not so.
What though he love your Hermia? Lord! what
though?
Yet Hermia still loves you: then be content.
LYSANDER. Content with Hermia? No: I do repent
The tedious minutes I with her have spent.   120
Not Hermia, but Helena I love—
Who will not change a raven for a dove?

The will of man is by his reason swayed;
And reason says you are the worthier maid.
Things growing are not ripe until their season:
So I, being young, till now ripe not to reason—
And touching now the point of human skill,
Reason becomes the marshal to my will,
And leads me to your eyes; where I o'erlook
Love's stories, written in Love's richest book.   130
HELENA. Wherefore was I to this keen mockery born?
When at your hands did I deserve this scorn?
Is't not enough, is't not enough, young man,
That I did never, no, nor never can,
Deserve a sweet look from Demetrius' eye,
But you must flout my insufficiency?
Good troth, you do me wrong, good sooth, you do,
In such disdainful manner me to woo.
But fare you well: perforce I must confess
I thought you lord of more true gentleness.   140
O, that a lady, of one man refused,
Should of another therefore be abused!   *She goes*
LYSANDER. She sees not Hermia. Hermia, sleep thou
there,
And never mayst thou come Lysander near.
For, as a surfeit of the sweetest things
The deepest loathing to the stomach brings,
Or as the heresies that men do leave
Are hated most of those they did deceive,
So thou, my surfeit and my heresy,
Of all be hated, but the most of me!   150
And all my powers, address your love and might
To honour Helen, and to be her knight.
                                   He follows Helena
HERMIA [*awaking*]. Help me, Lysander, help me; do
thy best
To pluck this crawling serpent from my breast.
Ay me, for pity! what a dream was here?
Lysander, look how I do quake with fear.
Methought a serpent eat my heart away,
And you sat smiling at his cruel prey....
Lysander! what, removed?—Lysander! lord!
What, out of hearing gone? no sound, no word?   160
Alack, where are you? speak, an if you hear;
Speak, of all loves! I swoon again with fear.
No? then I will perceive you are not nigh.
Either death or you I'll find immediately.
                                          She goes

ACT 3
Scene 1

Enter Quince, Snug, Bottom, Flute, Snout, and Starveling

BOTTOM. Are we all met?
QUINCE. Pat, pat: and here's a marvellous convenient
place for our rehearsal. This green plot shall be our
stage, this hawthorn-brake our tiring-house—and
we will do it in action as we will do it before the
duke.
BOTTOM. Peter Quince!
QUINCE. What say'st thou, bully Bottom?
BOTTOM. There are things in this comedy of Pyramus
and Thisby that will never please. First, Pyramus   10
must draw a sword to kill himself; which the ladies
cannot abide. How answer you that?
SNOUT. By'r lakin, a parlous fear.
STARVELING. I believe we must leave the killing out,
when all is done.

BOTTOM. Not a whit: I have a device to make all well. Write me a prologue, and let the prologue seem to say we will do no harm with our swords, and that Pyramus is not killed indeed: and, for the more better assurance, tell them that I, Pyramus, am not 20 Pyramus but Bottom the weaver: this will put them out of fear.

QUINCE. Well, we will have such a prologue, and it shall be written in eight and six.

BOTTOM. No, make it two more: let it be written in eight and eight.

SNOUT. Will not the ladies be afeard of the lion?

STARVELING. I fear it, I promise you.

BOTTOM. Masters, you ought to consider with your-selves—to bring in (God shield us!) a lion among 30 ladies is a most dreadful thing. For there is not a more fearful wild-fowl than your lion living; and we ought to look to't.

SNOUT. Therefore, another prologue must tell he is not a lion.

BOTTOM. Nay, you must name his name, and half his face must be seen through the lion's neck, and he himself must speak through, saying thus, or to the same defect: 'Ladies,' or 'Fair ladies—I would wish you,' or 'I would request you,' or 'I would entreat 40 you, not to fear, not to tremble: my life for yours. If you think I come hither as a lion, it were pity of my life. No: I am no such thing: I am a man as other men are'. And there indeed let him name his name, and tell them plainly he is Snug the joiner.

QUINCE. Well, it shall be so. But there is two hard things: that is, to bring the moonlight into a chamber: for you know, Pyramus and Thisby meet by moonlight.

SNOUT. Doth the moon shine that night we play our 50 play?

BOTTOM. A calendar, a calendar! Look in the almanac; find out moonshine, find out moonshine.

QUINCE. Yes, it doth shine that night.

BOTTOM. Why, then may you leave a casement of the great chamber window, where we play, open; and the moon may shine in at the casement.

QUINCE. Ay, or else one must come in with a bush of thorns and a lantern, and say he comes to disfigure or to present the person of Moonshine. Then, there 60 is another thing: we must have a wall in the great chamber; for Pyramus and Thisby, says the story, did talk through the chink of a wall.

SNOUT. You can never bring in a wall. What say you, Bottom?

BOTTOM. Some man or other must present wall; and let him have some plaster, or some loam, or some rough-cast about him, to signify wall; and let him hold his fingers thus ... and through that cranny shall Pyramus and Thisby whisper. 70

QUINCE. If that may be, then all is well... Come, sit down, every mother's son, and rehearse your parts. Pyramus, you begin: when you have spoken your speech, enter into that brake—and so every one according to his cue.

Puck appears, behind

PUCK. What hempen home-spuns have we swagg'ring here,
So near the cradle of the Fairy Queen?
What, a play toward? I'll be an auditor,

An actor too perhaps, if I see cause.

QUINCE. Speak, Pyramus, Thisby, stand forth. 80

BOTTOM. 'Thisby, the flowers ha' odious savours sweet,'—

QUINCE. 'Odious'?—odorous!

BOTTOM. —'odours savours sweet,
So hath thy breath, my dearest Thisby dear.
But hark, a voice! stay thou but here awhile,
And by and by I will to thee appear.'
He goes

PUCK. A stranger Pyramus than e'er played here!
He follows Bottom

FLUTE. Must I speak now?

QUINCE. Ay, marry, must you. For you must under-stand he goes but to see a noise that he heard, and is 90 to come again.

FLUTE. 'Most radiant Pyramus, most lily-white of hue,
Of colour like the red rose on triumphant briar,
Most brisky juvenal, and eke most lovely Jew,
As true as truest horse that yet would never tire,
I'll meet thee, Pyramus, at Ninny's tomb.'

QUINCE. 'Ninus' tomb,' man! Why, you must not speak that yet! That you answer to Pyramus. You speak all your part at once, cues and all. Pyramus enter; your cue is past; it is, 'never tire.' 100

FLUTE. O,—'As true as truest horse that yet would never tire.'

Enter Bottom with an ass's head; Puck following

BOTTOM. 'If I were fair, Thisby, I were only thine.'

QUINCE. O monstrous! O strange! We are haunted. Pray, masters! fly, masters! help!
They all go

PUCK. I'll follow you: I'll lead you about a round,
Through bog, through bush, through brake, through briar;
Sometime a horse I'll be, sometime a hound,
A hog, a headless bear, sometime a fire,
And neigh, and bark, and grunt, and roar, and burn,
Like horse, hound, hog, bear, fire, at every turn. 110
He pursues them

BOTTOM. Why do they run away? This is a knavery of them to make me afeard.

Snout returns

SNOUT. O Bottom, thou art changed! What do I see on thee?

BOTTOM. What do you see? you see an ass-head of your own, do you? *Snout goes*

Quince returns

QUINCE. Bless thee Bottom, bless thee! thou art translated. *He goes*

BOTTOM. I see their knavery. This is to make an ass of me, to fright me if they could: but I will not stir 120 from this place, do what they can. I will walk up and down here, and will sing that they shall hear I am not afraid.... *He sings*
The ousel cock, so black of hue,
With orange-tawny bill,
The throstle with his note so true,
The wren with little quill....

TITANIA [*comes from the bower*]. What angel wakes me from my flow'ry bed?

BOTTOM. The finch, the sparrow, and the lark,
The plain-song cuckoo gray: 130

Whose note full many a man doth mark,
   And dares not answer, nay....
for indeed, who would set his wit to so foolish a
bird? who would give a bird the lie, though he cry
'cuckoo' never so?

TITANIA. I pray thee, gentle mortal, sing again!
   Mine ear is much enamoured of thy note;
   So is mine eye enthrallèd to thy shape,
   And thy fair virtue's force—perforce—doth move
      me,
   On the first view, to say, to swear, I love thee. 140

BOTTOM. Methinks, mistress, you should have little
   reason for that. And yet, to say the truth, reason and
   love keep little company together now-a-days. The
   more the pity, that some honest neighbours will not
   make them friends. Nay, I can gleek upon occasion.

TITANIA. Thou art as wise as thou art beautiful.

BOTTOM. Not so, neither: but if I had wit enough to
   get out of this wood, I have enough to serve mine
   own turn.

TITANIA. Out of this wood do not desire to go: 150
   Thou shalt remain here, whether thou wilt or no.
   I am a spirit of no common rate:
   The summer still doth tend upon my state,
   And I do love thee: therefore go with me.
   I'll give thee fairies to attend on thee:
   And they shall fetch thee jewels from the deep,
   And sing, while thou on pressèd flowers dost sleep:
   And I will purge thy mortal grossness so,
   That thou shalt like an airy spirit go.
   Peaseblossom, Cobweb, Moth, and Mustardseed! 160

PEASEBLOSSOM. Ready!

COBWEB.   And I—

MOTH.   And I—

MUSTARDSEED.   And I—

ALL [bowing].   Where shall we go?

TITANIA. Be kind and courteous to this gentleman;
   Hop in his walks and gambol in his eyes;
   Feed him with apricocks and dewberries,
   With purple grapes, green figs, and mulberries;
   The honey-bags steal from the humble-bees,
   And for night-tapers crop their waxen thighs,
   And light them at the fiery glow-worm's eyes,
   To have my love to bed and to arise;
   And pluck the wings from painted butterflies, 170
   To fan the moonbeams from his sleeping eyes.
   Nod to him, elves, and do him courtesies.

PEASEBLOSSOM. Hail, mortal!

COBWEB. Hail!

MOTH. Hail!

MUSTARDSEED. Hail!

BOTTOM. I cry your worships mercy, heartily. I
   beseech your worship's name.

COBWEB. Cobweb.

BOTTOM. I shall desire you of more acquaintance, good 180
   Master Cobweb: if I cut my finger, I shall make bold
   with you. Your name, honest gentleman?

PEASEBLOSSOM. Peaseblossom.

BOTTOM. I pray you, commend me to Mistress Squash,
   your mother, and to Master Peascod, your father.
   Good Master Peaseblossom, I shall desire you of
   more acquaintance too. Your name, I beseech you
   sir?

MUSTARDSEED. Mustardseed.

BOTTOM. Good Master Mustardseed, I know your 190
   patience well. That same cowardly, giant-like, Ox-

beef hath devoured many a gentleman of your
house. I promise you your kindred hath made my
eyes water ere now. I desire you of more acquaintance, good Master Mustardseed.

TITANIA. Come, wait upon him; lead him to my
   bower.
   The moon, methinks, looks with a wat'ry eye:
   And when she weeps, weeps every little flower,
   Lamenting some enforcèd chastity.
   Tie up my love's tongue, bring him silently. 200
                                          They go

Scene 2: A clearing in the wood

Oberon appears

OBERON. I wonder if Titania be awaked;
   Then, what it was that next came in her eye,
   Which she must dote on in extremity.

Puck enters

Here comes my messenger. How now, mad spirit?
   What night-rule now about this haunted grove?

PUCK. My mistress with a monster is in love.
   Near to her close and consecrated bower,
   While she was in her dull and sleeping hour,
   A crew of patches, rude mechanicals,
   That work for bread upon Athenian stalls, 10
   Were met together to rehearse a play
   Intended for great Theseus' nuptial-day.
   The shallowest thick-skin of that barren sort,
   Who Pyramus presented, in their sport
   Forsook his scene and ent'red in a brake;
   When I did him at this advantage take,
   An ass's noll I fixèd on his head.
   Anon his Thisbe must be answerèd,
   And forth my mimic comes. When they him spy,
   As wild geese that the creeping fowler eye, 20
   Or russet-pated choughs, many in sort,
   Rising and cawing at the gun's report,
   Sever themselves and madly sweep the sky,
   So, at his sight, away his fellows fly;
   And at a stump here o'er and o'er one falls—
   He 'murder' cries, and help from Athens calls.
   Their sense thus weak, lost with their fears thus
      strong,
   Made senseless things begin to do them wrong.
   For briars and thorns at their apparel snatch:
   Some sleeves, some hats; from yielders all things
      catch. 30
   I led them on in this distracted fear,
   And left sweet Pyramus translated there:
   When in that moment (so it came to pass)
   Titania waked and straightway loved an ass.

OBERON. This falls out better than I could devise.
   But hast thou yet latched the Athenian's eyes
   With the love-juice, as I did bid thee do?

PUCK. I took him sleeping—that is finished too—
   And the Athenian woman by his side;
   That, when he waked, of force she must be eyed. 40

Demetrius and Hermia approach

OBERON. Stand close; this is the same Athenian.

PUCK. This is the woman: but not this the man.

DEMETRIUS. O, why rebuke you him that loves you so?
   Lay breath so bitter on your bitter foe.

HERMIA. Now I but chide: but I should use thee worse,

For thou, I fear, hast given me cause to curse ...
If thou hast slain Lysander in his sleep,
Being o'er-shoes in blood, plunge in the deep,
And kill me too.
The sun was not so true unto the day   50
As he to me. Would he have stolen away
From sleeping Hermia? I'll believe as soon
This whole earth may be bored, and that the moon
May through the centre creep and so displease
Her brother's noontide with th'Antipodes.
It cannot be but thou hast murd'red him—
So should a murderer look; so dead, so grim.
DEMETRIUS. So should the murdered look, and so
    should I,
Pierced through the heart with your stern cruelty.
Yet you, the murderer, look as bright, as clear,   60
As yonder Venus in her glimmering sphere.
HERMIA. What's this to my Lysander? Where is he?
Ah, good Demetrius, wilt thou give him me?
DEMETRIUS. I had rather give his carcase to my hounds.
HERMIA. Out, dog! out, cur! thou driv'st me past
    the bounds
Of maiden's patience. Hast thou slain him then?
Henceforth be never numb'red among men!
O, once true! tell true, even for my sake:
Durst thou have looked upon him being awake?
And hast thou killed him, sleeping? O brave touch! 70
Could not a worm, an adder, do so much?
An adder did it; for with doubler tongue
Than thine, thou serpent, never adder stung.
DEMETRIUS. You spend your passion on a misprized
    mood:
I am not guilty of Lysander's blood;
Nor is he dead, for aught that I can tell.
HERMIA. I pray thee, tell me then that he is well.
DEMETRIUS. An if I could, what should I get therefore?
HERMIA. A privilege never to see me more,
And from thy hated presence part I so: 80
See me no more, whether he be dead or no.
                                   She goes
DEMETRIUS. There is no following her in this fierce
    vein.
Here therefore for a while I will remain.
So sorrow's heaviness doth heavier grow
For debt that bankrupt sleep doth sorrow owe;
Which now in some slight measure it will pay,
If for his tender here I make some stay.
                                 He lies down
OBERON. What hast thou done? thou hast mistaken
    quite,
And laid the love-juice on some true-love's sight.
Of thy misprision must perforce ensue   90
Some true love turned, and not a false turned true.
PUCK. Then fate o'er-rules, that, one man holding
    troth,
A million fail, confounding oath on oath.
OBERON. About the wood go swifter than the wind,
And Helena of Athens look thou find.
All fancy-sick she is, and pale of cheer
With sighs of love that costs the fresh blood
    dear.
By some illusion see thou bring her here:
I'll charm his eyes against she do appear.
PUCK. I go, I go—look how I go—   100
Swifter than arrow from the Tartar's bow.
                                  He goes

OBERON. Flower of this purple dye,
Hit with Cupid's archery,
Sink in apple of his eye.
When his love he doth espy,
Let her shine as gloriously
As the Venus of the sky.
When thou wak'st, if she be by,
Beg of her for remedy.

Puck reappears

PUCK. Captain of our fairy band,   110
Helena is here at hand,
And the youth, mistook by me,
Pleading for a lover's fee.
Shall we their fond pageant see?
Lord, what fools these mortals be!
OBERON. Stand aside. The noise they make
Will cause Demetrius to awake.
PUCK. Then will two at once woo one;
That must needs be sport alone.
And those things do best please me   120
That befall prepost'rously.
                          They stand aside

Helena comes up, followed by Lysander

LYSANDER. Why should you think that I should woo
    in scorn?
Scorn and derision never come in tears.
Look when I vow, I weep; and vows so born
In their nativity all truth appears.
How can these things in me seem scorn to you,
Bearing the badge of faith to prove them true?
HELENA. You do advance your cunning more and
    more.
When truth kills truth, O devilish-holy fray!
These vows are Hermia's—will you give her o'er? 130
Weigh oath with oath, and you will nothing weigh:
Your vows, to her and me, put in two scales,
Will even weigh; and both as light as tales.
LYSANDER. I had no judgement when to her I swore.
HELENA. Nor none, in my mind, now you give her
    o'er.
LYSANDER. Demetrius loves her: and he loves not you.
DEMETRIUS [*awaking*]. O Helen, goddess, nymph,
    perfect, divine!
To what, my love, shall I compare thine eyne?
Crystal is muddy. O, how ripe in show
Thy lips, those kissing cherries, tempting grow! 140
That pure congealéd white, high Taurus' snow,
Fanned with the eastern wind, turns to a crow,
When thou hold'st up thy hand. O let me kiss
This princess of pure white, this seal of bliss!
HELENA. O spite! O hell! I see you all are bent
To set against me for your merriment.
If you were civil and knew courtesy,
You would not do me thus much injury.
Can you not hate me, as I know you do,
But you must join in souls to mock me too?   150
If you were men, as men you are in show,
You would not use a gentle lady so:
To vow, and swear, and superpraise my parts,
When I am sure you hate me with your hearts.
You both are rivals, and love Hermia;
And now both rivals, to mock Helena.
A trim exploit, a manly enterprise,
To conjure tears up in a poor maid's eyes

With your derision! none of noble sort
Would so offend a virgin, and extort 160
A poor soul's patience, all to make you sport.
LYSANDER. You are unkind, Demetrius; be not so—
For you love Hermia; this you know I know;
And here, with all good will, with all my heart,
In Hermia's love I yield you up my part:
And yours of Helena to me bequeath,
Whom I do love, and will do till my death.
HELENA. Never did mockers waste more idle breath.
DEMETRIUS. Lysander, keep thy Hermia: I will none.
If e'er I loved her, all that love is gone. 170
My heart to her but as guest-wise sojourned,
And now to Helen is it home returned,
There to remain.
LYSANDER. Helen, it is not so.
DEMETRIUS. Disparage not the faith thou dost not
    know,
Lest to thy peril thou aby it dear....
Look where thy love comes: yonder is thy dear.

Hermia enters

HERMIA. Dark night, that from the eye his function
    takes,
The ear more quick of apprehension makes.
Wherein it doth impair the seeing sense,
It pays the hearing double recompense. 180
Thou art not by mine eye, Lysander, found;
Mine ear, I thank it, brought me to thy sound.
But why unkindly didst thou leave me so?
LYSANDER. Why should he stay whom love doth
    press to go?
HERMIA. What love could press Lysander from my
    side?
LYSANDER. Lysander's love, that would not let him
    bide—
Fair Helena! who more engilds the night
Than all yon fiery oes and eyes of light.
Why seek'st thou me? could not this make thee
    know
The hate I bear thee made me leave thee so? 190
HERMIA. You speak not as you think: it cannot be.
HELENA. Lo! she is one of this confederacy.
Now I perceive they have conjoined all three
To fashion this false sport in spite of me.
Injurious Hermia, most ungrateful maid,
Have you conspired, have you with these contrived,
To bait me with this foul derision?
Is all the counsel that we two have shared,
The sisters' vows, the hours that we have spent,
When we have chid the hasty-footed time 200
For parting us—O! is all forgot?
All school-days' friendship, childhood innocence?
We, Hermia, like two artificial gods, ˙
Have with our needles created both one flower,
Both on one sampler, sitting on one cushion,
Both warbling of one song, both in one key;
As if our hands, our sides, voices, and minds,
Had been incorporate. So we grew together,
Like to a double cherry, seeming parted,
But yet an union in partition, 210
Two lovely berries moulded on one stem:
So, with two seeming bodies, but one heart,
Two of the first, like coats in heraldry,
Due but to one, and crownéd with one crest.
And will you rend our ancient love asunder,

To join with men in scorning your poor friend?
It is not friendly, 'tis not maidenly—
Our sex, as well as I, may chide you for it;
Though I alone do feel the injury.
HERMIA. Helen, I am amazéd at your words. 220
I scorn you not—it seems that you scorn me.
HELENA. Have you not set Lysander, as in scorn,
To follow me and praise my eyes and face?
And made your other love, Demetrius
(Who even but now did spurn me with his foot!)
To call me goddess, nymph, divine and rare,
Precious, celestial? Wherefore speaks he this
To her he hates? and wherefore doth Lysander
Deny your love (so rich within his soul)
And tender me (forsooth!) affection, 230
But by your setting on, by your consent?
What though I be not so in grace as you,
So hung upon with love, so fortunate,
But miserable most, to love unloved?
This you should pity rather than despise.
HERMIA. I understand not what you mean by this.
HELENA. Ay, do! perséver, counterfeit sad looks,
Make mouths upon me when I turn my back,
Wink at each other, hold the sweet jest up.
This sport, well carried, shall be chronicled. 240
If you have any pity, grace, or manners,
You would not make me such an argument.
But, fare ye well: 'tis partly my own fault:
Which death or absence soon shall remedy.
LYSANDER. Stay, gentle Helena; hear my excuse,
My love, my life, my soul, fair Helena!
HELENA. O excellent!
HERMIA.   Sweet, do not scorn her so.
DEMETRIUS. If she cannot entreat, I can compel.
LYSANDER. Thou canst compel no more than she
    entreat.
Thy threats have no more strength than her weak
    prayers. 250
Helen, I love thee—by my life I do;
I swear by that which I will lose for thee,
To prove him false that says I love thee not.
DEMETRIUS. I say I love thee more than he can do.
LYSANDER. If thou say so, withdraw, and prove it too.
DEMETRIUS. Quick, come,—
HERMIA.   Lysander, whereto tends all this?
LYSANDER. Away, you Ethiop!
HERMIA. No, no!
DEMETRIUS. Ye'll
Seem to break loose! take on as you would follow! 260
But yet come not. You are a tame man, go!
LYSANDER. Hang off, thou cat, thou burr! vile thing,
    let loose;
Or I will shake thee from me like a serpent.
HERMIA. Why are you grown so rude? what change
    is this,
Sweet love?
LYSANDER.   Thy love! out, tawny Tartar, out!
Out, loathéd med'cine! O, hated potion, hence!
HERMIA. Do you not jest?
HELENA.   Yes, sooth: and so do you.
LYSANDER. Demetrius, I will keep my word with thee.
DEMETRIUS. I would I had your bond, for I perceive
A weak bond holds you. I'll not trust you word. 270
LYSANDER. What? should I hurt her, strike her, kill
    her dead?
Although I hate her, I'll not harm her so.

HERMIA. What? can you do me greater harm than
  hate?
  Hate me! wherefore? O me, what news, my love!
  Am not I Hermia? are not you Lysander?
  I am as fair now as I was erewhile.
  Since night you loved me; yet since night you left
  me.
  Why then, you left me—O, the gods forbid!—
  In earnest, shall I say?
LYSANDER.   Ay, by my life!
  And never did desire to see thee more.   280
  Therefore be out of hope, of question or doubt:
  Be certain: nothing truer: 'tis no jest
  That I do hate thee and love Helena.
HERMIA [to Helena]. O me, you juggler, you
  canker-blossom.
  You thief of love! What! have you come by night
  And stol'n my love's heart from him?
HELENA.   Fine, i'faith!
  Have you no modesty, no maiden shame,
  No touch of bashfulness? What! will you tear
  Impatient answers from my gentle tongue?
  Fie, fie, you counterfeit, you puppet you!   290
HERMIA. 'Puppet?' Why, so,—ay, that way goes
  the game!
  Now I perceive that she hath made compare
  Between our statures; she hath urged her height;
  And with her personage, her tall personage,
  Her height, forsooth, she hath prevailed with him.
  And are you grown so high in his esteem
  Because I am so dwarfish and so low?
  How low am I, thou painted maypole? speak;
  How low am I? I am not yet so low,
  But that my nails can reach unto thine eyes.   300
HELENA. I pray you, though you mock me, gentlemen,
  Let her not hurt me. I was never curst:
  I have no gift at all in shrewishness:
  I am a right maid for my cowardice:
  Let her not strike me. You perhaps may think,
  Because she is something lower than myself,
  That I can match her.
HERMIA.   Lower! hark, again.
HELENA. Good Hermia, do not be so bitter with me.
  I evermore did love you, Hermia,
  Did ever keep your counsels, never wronged you;   310
  Save that, in love unto Demetrius,
  I told him of your stealth unto this wood.
  He followed you; for love I followed him.
  But he hath chid me hence, and threat'ned me
  To strike me, spurn me; nay, to kill me too.
  And now, so you will let me quiet go,
  To Athens will I bear my folly back,
  And follow you no further. Let me go.
  You see how simple and how fond I am.
HERMIA. Why, get you gone. Who is't that hinders
  you?   320
HELENA. A foolish heart that I leave here behind.
HERMIA. What! with Lysander?
HELENA.   With Demetrius.
LYSANDER. Be not afraid: she shall not harm thee,
  Helena.
DEMETRIUS. No, sir; she shall not, though you take
  her part.
HELENA. When she is angry, she is keen and shrewd.
  She was a vixen when she went to school;
  And though she be but little, she is fierce.

HERMIA. 'Little' again? nothing but 'low' and 'little'!
  Why will you suffer her to flout me thus?
  Let me come to her.
LYSANDER.   Get you gone, you dwarf;   330
  You minimus, of hind'ring knot-grass made;
  You bead, you acorn.
DEMETRIUS.   You are too officious
  In her behalf that scorns your services.
  Let her alone; speak not of Helena;
  Take not her part; for if thou dost intend
  Never so little show of love to her,
  Thou shalt aby it.
LYSANDER.   Now she holds me not;
  Now follow, if thou dar'st, to try whose right,
  Of thine or mine, is most in Helena.
                                        He goes
DEMETRIUS. Follow! nay, I'll go with thee, cheek by
  jowl.   He follows after 340
HERMIA. You, mistress, all this coil is 'long of you:
  Nay: go not back.
HELENA.   I will not trust you, I,
  Nor longer stay in your curst company.
  Your hands than mine are quicker for a fray;
  My legs are longer though to run away.
                                        She goes
HERMIA. I am amazed, and know not what to say.
                                        She follows
OBERON. This is thy negligence. Still thou mistak'st,
  Or else committ'st thy knaveries wilfully.
PUCK. Believe me, king of shadows, I mistook.
  Did not you tell me I should know the man   350
  By the Athenian garments he had on?
  And so far blameless proves my enterprise
  That I have 'nointed an Athenian's eyes:
  And so far am I glad it so did sort,
  As this their jangling I esteem a sport.
OBERON. Thou see'st these lovers seek a place to fight:
  Hie therefore, Robin, overcast the night,
  The starry welkin cover thou anon
  With drooping fog as black as Acheron,
  And lead these testy rivals so astray,   360
  As one come not within another's way.
  Like to Lysander sometime frame thy tongue;
  Then stir Demetrius up with bitter wrong;
  And sometime rail thou like Demetrius;
  And from each other look thou lead them thus;
  Till o'er their brows death-counterfeiting sleep
  With leaden legs and batty wings doth creep.
  Then crush this herb into Lysander's eye;
  Whose liquor hath this virtuous property,
  To take from thence all error with his might,   370
  And make his eyeballs roll with wonted sight.
  When they next wake, all this derision
  Shall seem a dream and fruitless vision,
  And back to Athens shall the lovers wend
  With league whose date till death shall never end.
  Whiles I in this affair do thee employ,
  I'll to my queen and beg her Indian boy;
  And then I will her charmèd eye release
  From monster's view, and all things shall be peace.
PUCK. My fairy lord, this must be done with haste,   380
  For night's swift dragons cut the clouds full fast;
  And yonder shines Aurora's harbinger,
  At whose approach ghosts wand'ring here and
  there,
  Troop home to churchyards. Damnèd spirits all,

That in crossways and floods have burial,
Already to their wormy beds are gone;
For fear lest day should look their shames upon,
They wilfully themselves exile from light,
And must for aye consort with black-browed night.

OBERON. But we are spirits of another sort. 390
I with the morning's love have oft made sport,
And like a forester the groves may tread,
Even till the eastern gate, all fiery-red,
Opening on Neptune with fair blessèd beams,
Turns into yellow gold his salt green streams.
But, notwithstanding, haste—make no delay:
We may effect this business yet ere day.
He goes

PUCK. Up and down, up and down,
I will lead them up and down.
I am feared in field and town. 400
Goblin, lead them up and down....
He vanishes
Here comes one.

Lysander returns

LYSANDER. Where art thou, proud Demetrius? speak
thou now.
PUCK AS DEMETRIUS. Here, villain! drawn and ready.
Where art thou?
LYSANDER. I will be with thee straight.
Follow me then
To plainer ground. *Lysander follows the voice*

Demetrius approaches

DEMETRIUS. Lysander! speak again.
Thou runaway, thou coward, art thou fled?
Speak! In some bush? Where dost thou hide thy
head?
PUCK AS LYSANDER. Thou coward, art thou bragging
to the stars,
Telling the bushes that thou look'st for wars, 410
And wilt not come? Come recreant, come thou
child,
I'll whip thee with a rod. He is defiled
That draws a sword on thee.
DEMETRIUS. Yea, art thou there?
THE VOICE RECEDING. Follow my voice: we'll try no
manhood here. *Demetrius follows the voice*

Lysander returns

LYSANDER. He goes before me and still dares me on:
When I come where he calls, then he is gone.
The villain is much lighter-heeled than I:
I followed fast; but faster he did fly;
That fallen am I in dark uneven way,
And here will rest me.... *He lies down*
Come, thou gentle day, 420
For if but once thou show me thy grey light,
I'll find Demetrius and revenge this spite.
He sleeps

Demetrius returns

PUCK AS LYSANDER. Ho, ho, ho! Coward, why com'st
thou not?
DEMETRIUS. Abide me if thou dar'st, for well
I wot
Thou runn'st before me, shifting every place,
And dar'st not stand, nor look me in the face.
Where art thou now?

PUCK AS LYSANDER. Come hither; I am here.
DEMETRIUS. Nay, then thou mock'st me. Thou shalt
buy this dear,
If ever I thy face by daylight see.
Now, go thy way. Faintness constraineth me 430
To measure out my length on this cold bed.
By day's approach look to be visited.
He lies down and sleeps

Helena enters

HELENA. O weary night, O long and tedious night,
Abate thy hours! Shine comforts from the east,
That I may back to Athens by daylight,
From these that my poor company detest.
And sleep, that sometimes shuts up sorrow's eye,
Steal me awhile from mine own company.
She lies down and falls asleep

Puck reappears

PUCK. Yet but three? Come one more.
Two of both kinds makes up four. 440
Here she comes, curst and sad.
Cupid is a knavish lad,
Thus to make poor females mad.

Hermia returns

HERMIA. Never so weary, never so in woe;
Bedabbled with the dew and torn with briars;
I can no further crawl, no further go;
My legs can keep no pace with my desires.
Here will I rest me till the break of day.
Heavens shield Lysander, if they mean a fray!
She lies down and falls asleep
PUCK. On the ground 450
Sleep sound:
I'll apply
To your eye,
Gentle lover, remedy.
He anoints Lysander's eyes with the love-juice
When thou wak'st,
Thou tak'st
True delight
In the sight
Of thy former lady's eye:
And the country proverb known, 460
That every man should take his own,
In your waking shall be shown.
Jack shall have Jill;
Nought shall go ill;
The man shall have his mare again, and all shall be
well.
He goes

ACT 4
Scene 1

*Titania approaches with Bottom, his ass's head garlanded
with flowers; fairies follow in their train, Oberon behind
all, unseen*

TITANIA. Come, sit thee down upon this flow'ry bed;
While I thy amiable cheeks do coy,
And stick musk-roses in thy sleek smooth head,
And kiss thy fair large ears, my gentle joy.
BOTTOM. Where's Peaseblossom?
PEASEBLOSSOM. Ready.

BOTTOM. Scratch my head, Peaseblossom. Where's
Monsieur Cobweb?

COBWEB. Ready.

BOTTOM. Monsieur Cobweb, good monsieur, get you 10
your weapons in your hand and kill me a red-hipped
humble-bee on the top of a thistle; and, good
monsieur, bring me the honey-bag. Do not fret
yourself too much in the action, monsieur; and,
good monsieur, have a care the honey-bag break
not—I would be loath to have you overflown with
a honey-bag, signior. Where's Monsieur Mustardseed?

MUSTARDSEED. Ready.

BOTTOM. Give me your neaf, Monsieur Mustardseed. 20
Pray you, leave your curtsy, good monsieur.

MUSTARDSEED. What's your will?

BOTTOM. Nothing, good monsieur, but to help
Cavalery Cobweb to scratch. I must to the barber's,
monsieur; for methinks I am marvellous hairy about
the face—and I am such a tender ass, if my hair
do but tickle me I must scratch.

TITANIA. What, wilt thou hear some music, my
sweet love?

BOTTOM. I have a reasonable good ear in music. Let's
have the tongs and the bones. 30

TITANIA. Or say, sweet love, what thou desir'st to eat.

BOTTOM. Truly, a peck of provender. I could munch
your good dry oats. Methinks I have a great desire
to a bottle of hay. Good hay, sweet hay, hath no
fellow.

TITANIA. I have a venturous fairy, that shall seek
The squirrel's hoard, and fetch thee thence new nuts.

BOTTOM. I had rather have a handful or two of dried
peas. But, I pray you, let none of your people stir
me; I have an exposition of sleep come upon me. 40

TITANIA. Sleep thou, and I will wind thee in my arms.
Fairies, be gone, and be all ways away.
The fairies go
So doth the woodbine the sweet honeysuckle
Gently entwist: the female ivy so
Enrings the barky fingers of the elm.
O, how I love thee! how I dote on thee!
They sleep

Oberon advances and Puck appears

OBERON. Welcome, good Robin. See'st thou this
sweet sight?
Her dotage now I do begin to pity.
For meeting her of late behind the wood,
Seeking sweet favours for this hateful fool, 50
I did upbraid her and fall out with her.
For she his hairy temples then had rounded
With coronet of fresh and fragrant flowers;
And that same dew which sometime on the buds
Was wont to swell like round and orient pearls
Stood now within the pretty flowerets' eyes
Like tears that did their own disgrace bewail.
When I had at my pleasure taunted her,
And she in mild terms begged my patience,
I then did ask of her her changeling child; 60
Which straight she gave me, and her fairy sent
To bear him to my bower in Fairyland.
And now I have the boy, I will undo
This hateful imperfection of her eyes.
And, gentle Puck, take this transformèd scalp
From off the head of this Athenian swain;

That he, awaking when the other do,
May all to Athens back again repair,
And think no more of this night's accidents
But as the fierce vexation of a dream. 70
But first I will release the Fairy Queen....
He anoints her eyes
Be as thou wast wont to be:
See, as thou wast wont to see.
Dian's bud o'er Cupid's flower
Hath such force and blessèd power.
Now, my Titania! wake you, my sweet queen.

TITANIA. My Oberon! what visions have I seen!
Methought I was enamoured of an ass.

OBERON. There lies your love.

TITANIA.   How came these things to pass?
O, how mine eyes do loathe his visage now! 80

OBERON. Silence, awhile. Robin, take off this head.
Titania, music call; and strike more dead
Than common sleep of all these five the sense.

TITANIA. Music, ho! music! such as charmeth sleep.
Soft music

PUCK. Now, when thou wak'st, with thine own fool's
eyes peep.

OBERON. Sound, music. [louder music] Come, my
queen, take hands with me,
And rock the ground whereon these sleepers be.
Now thou and I are new in amity.
And will to-morrow midnight solemnly
Dance in Duke Theseus' house triumphantly, 90
And bless it to all fair prosperity.
There shall the pairs of faithful lovers be
Wedded, with Theseus, all in jollity.

PUCK.   Fairy King, attend, and mark:
I do hear the morning lark.

OBERON. Then, my queen, in silence sad,
Trip we after the night's shade:
We the globe can compass soon,
Swifter than the wand'ring moon.

TITANIA. Come my lord, and in our flight, 100
Tell me how it came this night
That I sleeping here was found
With these mortals on the ground.
They go

*There is a sound of horns; Theseus, Hippolyta, Egeus
and others approach*

THESEUS. Go, one of you, find out the forester;
For now our observation is performed,
And since we have the vaward of the day,
My love shall hear the music of my hounds.
Uncouple in the western valley, let them go:
Dispatch, I say, and find the forester.
A servant departs
We will, fair queen, up to the mountain's top, 110
And mark the musical confusion
Of hounds and echo in conjunction.

HIPPOLYTA. I was with Hercules and Cadmus once,
When in a wood of Crete they bayed the bear
With hounds of Sparta: never did I hear
Such gallant chiding; for, besides the groves,
The skies, the fountains, every region near
Seemed all one mutual cry. I never heard
So musical a discord, such sweet thunder.

THESEUS. My hounds are bred out of the Spartan kind: 120
So flewed, so sanded; and their heads are hung
With ears that sweep away the morning dew—

Crook-kneed, and dewlapped like Thessalian bulls;
Slow in pursuit; but matched in mouth like bells,
Each under each. A cry more tuneable
Was never holloed to, nor cheered with horn,
In Crete, in Sparta, nor in Thessaly.
Judge when you hear. But, soft, what nymphs are
these?

EGEUS. My lord, this is my daughter here asleep—   130
And this Lysander—this Demetrius is—
This Helena, old Nedar's Helena.
I wonder of their being here together.

THESEUS. No doubt they rose up early to observe
The rite of May; and, hearing our intent,
Came here in grace of our solemnity....
But, speak, Egeus; is not this the day
That Hermia should give answer of her choice?

EGEUS. It is, my lord.

THESEUS. Go, bid the huntsmen wake them with their
horns.

*Horns, and a shout; the lovers
awake and start up*

Good morrow, friends. Saint Valentine is past;   140
Begin these wood-birds but to couple now?

LYSANDER. Pardon, my lord.   *They kneel to Theseus*

THESEUS.   I pray you all, stand up.
I know you two are rival enemies:
How comes this gentle concord in the world,
That hatred is so far from jealousy
To sleep by hate, and fear no enmity?

LYSANDER. My lord, I shall reply amazedly,
Half sleep, half waking.... but as yet, I swear,
I cannot truly say how I came here....
But, as I think—for truly would I speak,   150
And now I do bethink me, so it is—
I came with Hermia hither. Our intent
Was to be gone from Athens ... where we might,
Without the peril of the Athenian law—

EGEUS. Enough, enough, my lord; you have enough.
I beg the law, the law, upon his head.
They would have stol'n away, they would,
    Demetrius,
Thereby to have defeated you and me:
You of your wife, and me of my consent—
Of my consent that she should be your wife.   160

DEMETRIUS. My lord, fair Helen told me of their stealth
Of this their purpose hither to this wood,
And I in fury hither followed them;
Fair Helena in fancy following me.
But, my good lord, I wot not by what power—
But by some power it is—my love to Hermia,
Melted as melts the snow, seems to me now
As the remembrance of an idle gaud
Which in my childhood I did dote upon:
And all the faith, the virtue of my heart,   170
The object and the pleasure of mine eye,
Is only Helena. To her, my lord,
Was I betrothed ere I saw Hermia;
But, like in sickness, did I loathe this food,
So, as in health, come to my natural taste,
Now I do wish it, love it, long for it,
And will for evermore be true to it.

THESEUS. Fair lovers, you are fortunately met.
Of this discourse we more will hear anon.
Egeus, I will overbear your will;   180
For in the temple, by and by, with us,
These couples shall eternally be knit.

And, for the morning now is something worn,
Our purposed hunting shall be set aside.
Away with us, to Athens! Three and three,
We'll hold a feast in great solemnity.
Come, Hippolyta.

*Theseus, Hippolyta, Egeus
and their train depart*

DEMETRIUS. These things seem small and
    undistinguishable,
Like far-off mountains turnéd into clouds.

HERMIA. Methinks I see these things with parted eye,   190
When everything seems double.

HELENA.   So methinks:
And I have found Demetrius like a jewel,
Mine own, and not mine own.

DEMETRIUS.   Are you sure
That we are well awake? It seems to me,
That yet we sleep, we dream. Do not you think
The duke was here, and bid us follow him?

HERMIA. Yea, and my father.

HELENA.   And Hippolyta.

LYSANDER. And he did bid us follow to the
temple.

DEMETRIUS. Why then, we are awake; let's follow him;
And by the way let us recount our dreams.   200

They follow Theseus

BOTTOM [*awaking*]. When my cue comes, call me, and
I will answer. My next is, 'Most fair Pyramus.'
Heigh-ho! Peter Quince! Flute, the bellows-
mender! Snout, the tinker! Starveling! God's my
life! stol'n hence, and left me asleep! I have had a
most rare vision. I have had a dream—past the wit of
man to say what dream it was. Man is but an ass,
if he go about to expound this dream. Methought
I was—there is no man can tell what.... Methought
I was, and methought I had .... but man is but a   210
patched fool, if he will offer to say what methought
I had. The eye of man hath not heard, the ear of man
hath not seen, man's hand is not able to taste, his
tongue to conceive, nor his heart to report, what my
dream was. I will get Peter Quince to write a ballad
of this dream: it shall be called Bottom's Dream;
because it hath no bottom: and I will sing it in the
latter end of our play, before the duke. Peradventure, to make it the more gracious, I shall sing
it at her death.   *He goes*   220

Scene 2: *Peter Quince's cottage*

Enter Quince, Flute, Snout, and Starveling

QUINCE. Have you sent to Bottom's house? is he come
home yet?

STARVELING. He cannot be heard of. Out of doubt he
is transported.

FLUTE. If he come not, then the play is marred. It goes
not forward, doth it?

QUINCE. It is not possible. You have not a man in all
Athens able to discharge Pyramus but he.

FLUTE. No, he hath simply the best wit of any handi-
craft man in Athens.   10

QUINCE. Yea, and the best person too—and he is a
very paramour for a sweet voice.

FLUTE. You must say 'paragon'. A paramour is, God
bless us! a thing of naught.

Snug enters

SNUG. Masters, the duke is coming from the temple, and there is two or three lords and ladies more married—if our sport had gone forward, we had all been made men.

FLUTE. O sweet bully Bottom! Thus hath he lost six- 20 pence a day during his life: he could not have 'scaped sixpence a day. An the duke had not given him six- pence a day for playing Pyramus, I'll be hanged. He would have deserved it: sixpence a day in Pyramus, or nothing.

Bottom enters

BOTTOM. Where are these lads? where are these hearts?

QUINCE. Bottom! O most courageous day! O most happy hour!

BOTTOM. Masters, I am to discourse wonders: but ask me not what; for if I tell you, I am not true Athenian. I will tell you every thing, right as it fell out. 30

QUINCE. Let us hear, sweet Bottom.

BOTTOM. Not a word of me. All that I will tell you is, that the duke hath dined. Get your apparel to- gether—good strings to your beards, new ribbons to your pumps—meet presently at the palace, every man look o'er his part; for the short and the long is, our play is preferred. In any case, let Thisby have clean linen; and let not him that plays the lion pare his nails; for they shall hang out for the lion's claws.... And, most dear actors, eat no onions nor 40 garlic; for we are to utter sweet breath; and I do not doubt but to hear them say, it is a sweet comedy. No more words .... away, go away!

They go

ACT 5
Scene 1: *The palace of Duke Theseus*

Theseus and Hippolyta enter, followed by Philostrate, lords and attendants

HIPPOLYTA. 'Tis strange, my Theseus, that these lovers speak of.

THESEUS. More strange than true. I never may believe These antic fables, nor these fairy toys.
Lovers and madmen have such seething brains,
Such shaping fantasies, that apprehend
More than cool reason ever comprehends.
The lunatic, the lover, and the poet,
Are of imagination all compact.
One sees more devils than vast hell can hold;
That is, the madman. The lover, all as frantic, 10
Sees Helen's beauty in a brow of Egypt.
The poet's eye, in a fine frenzy rolling,
Doth glance from heaven to earth, from earth to heaven;
And as imagination bodies forth
The forms of things unknown, the poet's pen
Turns them to shapes, and gives to airy nothing
A local habitation and a name.
Such tricks hath strong imagination
That, if it would but apprehend some joy,
It comprehends some bringer of that joy; 20
Or in the night, imagining some fear,
How easy is a bush supposed a bear!

HIPPOLYTA. But all the story of the night told over,
And all their minds transfigured so together,
More witnesseth than fancy's images,
And grows to something of great constancy—
But howsoever strange and admirable.

THESEUS. Here come the lovers, full of joy and mirth.

Lysander and Hermia, Demetrius and Helena enter

Joy, gentle friends! joy and fresh days of love
Accompany your hearts!

LYSANDER.   More than to us 30
Wait in your royal walks, your board, your bed!

THESEUS. Come now; what masques, what dances shall we have,
To wear away this long age of three hours
Between our after-supper and bed-time?
Where is our usual manager of mirth?
What revels are in hand? Is there no play
To ease the anguish of a torturing hour?
Call Philostrate.

PHILOSTRATE.   Here, mighty Theseus.

THESEUS. Say, what abridgment have you for this evening?
What masque? what music? How shall we beguile 40
The lazy time, if not with some delight?

PHILOSTRATE. There is a brief how many sports are ripe;
Make choice of which your highness will see first.

He presents a paper

THESEUS. 'The battle with the Centaurs, to be sung,
By an Athenian eunuch to the harp.'
We'll none of that: that have I told my love,
In glory of my kinsman Hercules.
'The riot of the tipsy Bacchanals,
Tearing the Thracian singer in their rage'
That is an old device; and it was played 50
When I from Thebes came last a conqueror.
'The thrice three Muses mourning for the death
Of Learning, late deceased in beggary.'
That is some satire, keen and critical,
Not sorting with a nuptial ceremony.
'A tedious brief scene of young Pyramus
And his love Thisby; very tragical mirth.'
Merry and tragical! tedious and brief!
That is hot ice and wondrous strange snow.
How shall we find the concord of this discord? 60

PHILOSTRATE. A play there is, my lord, some ten words long;
Which is as brief as I have known a play;
But by ten words, my lord, it is too long;
Which makes it tedious: for in all the play
There is not one word apt, one player fitted.
And tragical, my noble lord, it is;
For Pyramus therein doth kill himself.
Which when I saw rehearsed, I must confess,
Made mine eyes water; but more merry tears
The passion of loud laughter never shed. 70

THESEUS. What are they that do play it?

PHILOSTRATE. Hard-handed men that work in Athens here,
Which never laboured in their minds till now;
And now have toiled their unbreathed memories
With this same play against your nuptial.

THESEUS. And we will hear it.

PHILOSTRATE.   No, my noble lord,
It is not for you: I have heard it over,
And it is nothing, nothing in the world;
Unless you can find sport in their intents,
Extremely stretched and conned with cruel pain, 80
To do you service.

THESEUS.   I will hear that play:

For never anything can be amiss,
When simpleness and duty tender it.
Go bring them in; and take your places, ladies.
Philostrate departs
HIPPOLYTA. I love not to see wretchedness
o'ercharged,
And duty in his service perishing.
THESEUS. Why, gentle sweet, you shall see no such
thing.
HIPPOLYTA. He says they can do nothing in this kind.
THESEUS. The kinder we, to give them thanks for
nothing.
Our sport shall be to take what they mistake: 90
And what poor duty cannot do, noble respect
Takes it in might not merit.
Where I have come, great clerks have purposéd
To greet me with premeditated welcomes;
Where I have seen them shiver and look pale,
Make periods in the midst of sentences,
Throttle their practised accent in their fears,
And in conclusion dumbly have broke off,
Not paying me a welcome. Trust me, sweet,
Out of this silence yet I picked a welcome;   100
And in the modesty of fearful duty
I read as much as from the rattling tongue
Of saucy and audacious eloquence.
Love, therefore, and tongue-tied simplicity
In least speak most, to my capacity.

Philostrate returns

PHILOSTRATE. So please your grace, the Prologue is
addressed.
THESEUS. Let him approach.

Enter Quince for the Prologue

QUINCE. 'If we offend, it is with our good will.
That you should think, we come not to offend,
But with good will. To show our simple skill,   110
That is the true beginning of our end.
Consider then, we come but in despite.
We do not come, as minding to content you,
Our true intent is. All for your delight
We are not here. That you should here repent you,
The actors are at hand: and, by their show,
You shall know all, that you are like to know,'
THESEUS. This fellow doth not stand upon points.
LYSANDER. He hath rid his prologue like a rough colt:
he knows not the stop. A good moral, my lord—it   120
is not enough to speak; but to speak true.
HIPPOLYTA. Indeed he hath played on his prologue like
a child on a recorder—a sound, but not in govern-
ment.
THESEUS. His speech was like a tangled chain; nothing
impaired, but all disordered. Who is next?

*Enter Pyramus and Thisby, Wall, Moonshine, and Lion,
as in dumb-show, with Quince for the Presenter*

QUINCE. 'Gentles, perchance you wonder at this show,
But wonder on, till truth make all things plain.
This man is Pyramus, if you would know:
This beauteous lady Thisby is certain.   130
This man, with lime and rough-cast, doth present
Wall, that vile Wall which did these lovers sunder:
And through Wall's chink, poor souls, they are
content
To whisper. At the which let no man wonder.

This man, with lantern, dog, and bush of thorn,
Presenteth Moonshine. For, if you will know,
By moonshine did these lovers think no scorn
To meet at Ninus' tomb, there, there to woo:
This grisly beast (which Lion hight by name)
The trusty Thisby, coming first by night,   140
Did scare away, or rather did affright:
And, as she fled, her mantle she did fall:
Which Lion vile with bloody mouth did stain.
Anon comes Pyramus, sweet youth, and tall,
And finds his trusty Thisby's mantle slain:
Whereat, with blade, with bloody blameful blade,
He bravely broached his boiling bloody breast.
And Thisby, tarrying in mulberry shade,
His dagger drew, and died. For all the rest,
Let Lion, Moonshine, Wall, and lovers twain,   150
At large discourse, while here they do remain.'
THESEUS. I wonder if the lion be to speak.
DEMETRIUS. No wonder, my lord: one lion may, when
many asses do.   *Exeunt all save Wall and Pyramus*

Wall steps forward

WALL. 'In this same interlude it doth befall
That I, one Snout by name, present a wall:
And such a wall, as I would have you think,
That had in it a crannied hole or chink,
Through which the lovers, Pyramus and Thisby,
Did whisper often very secretly....   160
This loam, this rough-cast, and this stone, doth show
That I am that same wall; the truth is so.
And this the cranny is, right and sinister,
Through which the fearful lovers are to whisper.'
THESEUS. Would you desire lime and hair to speak
better?
DEMETRIUS. It is the wittiest partition that ever I heard
discourse, my lord.

Pyramus steps forward

THESEUS. Pyramus draws near the wall: silence!
PYRAMUS. 'O grim-looked night! O night with hue
so black!   170
O night, which ever art when day is not:
O night, O night, alack, alack, alack,
I fear my Thisby's promise is forgot!
And thou, O wall! O sweet, O lovely wall!
That stand'st between her father's ground and mine,
Thou wall, O wall! O sweet and lovely wall!
Show me thy chink to blink through with mine
eyne.   *Wall obeys*
Thanks, courteous wall. Jove shield thee well for
this!
But what see I? No Thisby do I see.
O wicked wall, through whom I see no bliss,   180
Cursed be thy stones for thus deceiving me!'
THESEUS. The wall, methinks, being sensible, should
curse again.
PYRAMUS. No, in truth, sir, he should not. 'Deceiving
me' is Thisby's cue: she is to enter now, and I am to
spy her through the wall. You shall see, it will fall
pat as I told you. Yonder she comes.

Enter Thisby

THISBY. 'O wall! full often hast thou heard my moans,
For parting my fair Pyramus and me.
My cherry lips have often kissed thy stones;   190
Thy stones with lime and hair knit up in thee.'

PYRAMUS. 'I see a voice: now will I to the chink,
To spy an I can hear my Thisby's face.
Thisby!'
THISBY.   'My love thou art my love, I think.'
PYRAMUS. 'Think what thou wilt, I am thy lover's
grace;
And, like Limander, am I trusty still.'
THISBY. 'And I like Helen, till the Fates me kill.'
PYRAMUS. 'Not Shafalus to Procrus was so true.'
THISBY. 'As Shafalus to Procrus, I to you.'
PYRAMUS. 'O! kiss me through the hole of this vile
wall.'   200
THISBY. 'I kiss the wall's hole, not your lips at all.'
PYRAMUS. 'Wilt thou at Ninny's tomb meet me
straightway?'
THISBY. ' 'Tide life, 'tide death, I come without delay.'·
                        Exeunt Pyramus and Thisby
WALL. 'Thus have I, Wall, my part dischargéd so;
And being done, thus Wall away doth go.'
                                        Exit Wall
THESEUS. Now is the moon used between the two
neighbours.
DEMETRIUS. No remedy, my lord, when walls are so
wilful to hear without warning.
HIPPOLYTA. This is the silliest stuff that ever I heard. 210
THESEUS. The best in this kind are but shadows: and
the worst are no worse, if imagination amend them.
HIPPOLYTA. It must be your imagination then; and not
theirs.
THESEUS. If we imagine no worse of them than they of
themselves, they may pass for excellent men. Here
come two noble beasts, in a moon and a lion.

Enter Lion and Moonshine

LION. 'You ladies, you, whose gentle hearts do fear
The smallest monstrous mouse that creeps on floor,
May now perchance both quake and tremble here,   220
When lion rough in wildest rage doth roar.
Then know that I, as Snug the joiner am
A lion fell, nor else no lion's dam.
For if I should as lion come in strife
Into this place, 'twere pity on my life.'
THESEUS. A very gentle beast, and of a good con-
science.
DEMETRIUS. The very best at a beast, my lord, that e'er
I saw.
LYSANDER. This lion is a very fox for his valour.   230
THESEUS. True: and a goose for his discretion.
DEMETRIUS. Not so, my lord, for his· valour cannot
carry his discretion; and the fox carries the goose.
THESEUS. His discretion, I am sure, cannot carry his
valour, for the goose carries not the fox. It is well:
leave it to his discretion, and let us listen to the
moon.
MOONSHINE. 'This lanthorn doth the hornéd moon
present'—
DEMETRIUS. He should have worn the horns on his
head.   240
THESEUS. He is no crescent, and his horns are invisible
within the circumference.
MOONSHINE. 'This lanthorn doth the hornéd moon
present,
Myself the man i'th' moon do seem to be.'
THESEUS. This is the greatest error of all the rest: the
man should be put into the lantern. How is it else the
man i'th' moon?

DEMETRIUS. He dares not come there for the candle—
for, you see, it is already in snuff.
HIPPOLYTA. I am aweary of this moon. Would he   250
would change!
THESEUS. It appears, by his small light of discretion,
that he is in the wane: but yet, in courtesy, in all
reason, we must stay the time.
LYSANDER. Proceed, Moon.
MOONSHINE. All that I have to say, is to tell you that
the lanthorn is the moon, I the man i'th' moon,
this thorn-bush my thorn-bush, and this dog my
dog.
DEMETRIUS. Why, all these should be in the lantern; 260
for all these are in the moon. But, silence; here
comes Thisby.

Enter Thisby

THISBY. 'This is old Ninny's tomb. Where is my love?'
LION [*roars*]. 'Oh'—   *Thisby runs away*
DEMETRIUS. Well roared, Lion.
THESEUS. Well run, Thisby.
HIPPOLYTA. Well shone, Moon. Truly, the moon
shines with a good grace.
                        Lion paws Thisby's mantle
THESEUS. Well moused, Lion.
DEMETRIUS. And then came Pyramus.   270

Enter Pyramus; exit Lion

LYSANDER. And so the lion vanished.
PYRAMUS. 'Sweet moon, I thank thee for thy sunny
beams.
I thank thee, moon, for shining now so bright.
For, by thy gracious, golden, glittering gleams,
I trust to take of truest Thisby sight.
      But stay ... O spite!
      But mark, poor knight,
      What dreadful dole is here!
          Eyes, do you see?
          How can it be?   280
      O dainty duck, O dear!
          Thy mantle good,
          What, stained with blood?
      Approach, ye Furies fell!
          O Fates, come, come,
          Cut thread and thrum,
      Quail, crush, conclude, and quell!'
THESEUS. This passion—and the death of a dear
friend—would go near to make a man look sad.
HIPPOLYTA. Beshrew my heart, but I pity the man.   290
PYRAMUS. 'O wherefore, Nature, didst thou lions
frame?
Since lion. vile hath here deflowered my dear.
Which is—no, no—which was the fairest dame
That lived, that loved, that liked, that looked
with cheer.
          Come, tears, confound;
          Out, sword, and wound
      The pap of Pyramus:
          Ay, that left pap,
          Where heart doth hop....
                        He stabs himself
      Thus die I, thus, thus, thus....   300
          Now am I dead,
          Now am I fled,
      My soul is in the sky.

Tongue, lose thy light!
Moon, take thy flight!

Exit Moonshine

Now die, die, die, die, die.'   *He dies*

DEMETRIUS. No die, but an ace, for him—for he is but one.

LYSANDER. Less than an ace, man—for he is dead, he is nothing.   310

THESEUS. With the help of a surgeon, he might yet recover, and prove an ass.

HIPPOLYTA. How chance Moonshine is gone before Thisby comes back and finds her lover?

THESEUS. She will find him by starlight. Here she comes, and her passion ends the play.

Enter Thisby

HIPPOLYTA. Methinks she should not use a long one for such a Pyramus: I hope she will be brief.

DEMETRIUS. A mote will turn the balance, which Pyramus, which Thisby, is the better: he for a man, 320 God warr'nt us; she for a woman, God bless us.

LYSANDER. She hath spied him already with those sweet eyes.

DEMETRIUS. And thus she means, videlicet:—

THISBY. 'Asleep, my love?
          What, dead, my dove?
     O Pyramus, arise,
          Speak, speak. Quite dumb?
          Dead, dead? A tomb
     Must cover thy sweet eyes.   330
          These lily lips,
          This cherry nose,
     These yellow cowslip cheeks,
          Are gone, are gone:
          Lovers, make moan:
     His eyes were green as leeks.
          O Sisters Three,
          Come, come, to me,
     With hands as pale as milk;
          Lay them in gore,   340
          Since you have shore
     With shears his thread of silk.
          Tongue, not a word:
          Come, trusty sword,
     Come, blade, my breast imbrue ...

She stabs herself

          And farewell, friends:
          Thus Thisby ends:
     Adieu, adieu, adieu.'

She dies

THESEUS. Moonshine and Lion are left to bury the dead.   350

DEMETRIUS. Ay, and Wall too.

LION. No, I assure you, the wall is down that parted their fathers. Will it please you to see the Epilogue, or to hear a Bergomask dance between two of our company?

THESEUS. No Epilogue, I pray you—for your play needs no excuse. Never excuse; for when the players are all dead, there need none to be blamed. Marry, if he that writ it had played Pyramus and hanged himself in Thisby's garter, it would have been a fine 360 tragedy: and so it is truly, and very notably discharged.... But come, your Bergomask: let your Epilogue alone.

Moonshine and Wall dance the Bergomask and go out;
Theseus rises

The iron tongue of midnight hath told twelve!
Lovers, to bed—'tis almost fairy time.
I fear we shall out-sleep the coming morn,
As much as we this night have overwatched.
This palpable-gross play hath well beguiled
The heavy gait of night. Sweet friends, to bed.
A fortnight hold we this solemnity,   370
In nightly revels, and new jollity.

The Duke leads Hippolyta out,
followed by the lovers,
and the rest of the court

Puck appears

PUCK.   Now the hungry lion roars,
             And the wolf behowls the moon;
        Whilst the heavy ploughman snores,
             All with weary task fordone.
        Now the wasted brands do glow,
             Whilst the screech-owl, screeching loud,
        Puts the wretch that lies in woe
             In remembrance of a shroud.
        Now it is the time of night,   380
             That the graves, all gaping wide,
        Every one lets forth his sprite,
             In the church-way paths to glide.
        And we fairies, that do run
             By the triple Hecate's team
        From the presence of the sun,
             Following darkness like a dream,
        Now are frolic. Not a mouse
        Shall disturb this hallowed house....
        I am sent with broom before,   390
        To sweep the dust behind the door.

Oberon, Titania and the fairy-host enter

OBERON. Through the house give glimmering light,
             By the dead and drowsy fire;
         Every elf and fairy sprite
             Hop as light as bird from briar;
         And this ditty after me
         Sing, and dance it trippingly.

TITANIA. First rehearse your song by rote,
         To each word a warbling note;
         Hand in hand, with fairy grace,   400
         Will we sing and bless this place.

All the Fairies sing and dance

The Song

        Now, until the break of day,
        Through this house each fairy stray.
        To the best bride-bed will we:
        Which by us shall blessèd be:
        And the issue, there create
        Ever shall be fortunate:
        So shall all the couples three
        Ever true in loving be:
        And the blots of Nature's hand   410
        Shall not in their issue stand.
        Never mole, hare-lip, nor scar,
        Nor mark prodigious, such as are
        Despisèd in nativity,
        Shall upon their children be.
        With this field-dew consecrate,

Every fairy take his gait,
And each several chamber bless,
Through this palace, with sweet peace;
And the owner of it blest
Ever shall in safety rest.
    Trip away:
    Make no stay: 420
Meet me all by break of day.

They go

EPILOGUE

Spoken by Puck

If we shadows have offended,
Think but this, and all is mended,

That you have but slumb'red here
While these visions did appear.
And this weak and idle theme,
No more yielding but a dream,
Gentles, do not reprehend.
If you pardon, we will mend.
And, as I am an honest Puck,
If we have unearnéd luck   10
Now to 'scape the serpent's tongue,
We will make amends ere long:
Else the Puck a liar call.
So, good night unto you all.
Give me your hands, if we be friends:
And Robin shall restore amends.

He goes

The Merchant of Venice

The scene: Venice, and Portia's house at Belmont

CHARACTERS IN THE PLAY

The Duke of Venice
The Prince of Morocco ⎤
The Prince of Arragon ⎦ suitors to Portia
ANTONIO, a Merchant of Venice
BASSANIO, his friend, suitor to Portia
GRATIANO ⎤
SOLANIO ⎬ friends to Antonio and Bassanio
SALERIO ⎦
LORENZO, in love with Jessica
SHYLOCK, a Jew
TUBAL, another Jew, friend to Shylock

LANCELOT GOBBO, a clown, servant to Shylock
OLD GOBBO, father to Lancelot
LEONARDO, servant to Bassanio
BALTHAZAR ⎤ servants to Portia
STEPHANO ⎦
PORTIA, a lady of Belmont
NERISSA, her waiting-maid
JESSICA, daughter to Shylock
Magnificoes of Venice, officers of the Court of Justice,
     a gaoler, servants, and other attendants

The Merchant of Venice

ACT 1

Scene 1: *A quay in Venice*

Antonio, Salerio, and Solanio approach

ANTONIO. In sooth I know not why I am so sad,
  It wearies me, you say it wearies you;
  But how I caught it, found it, or came by it,
  What stuff'tis made of, whereof it is born,
  I am to learn:
  And such a want-wit sadness makes of me,
  That I have much ado to know myself.
SALERIO. Your mind is tossing on the ocean,
  There, where your argosies with portly sail—
  Like signiors and rich burghers on the flood,   10
  Or as it were the pageants of the sea—
  Do overpeer the petty traffickers,
  That curtsy to them, do them reverence,
  As they fly by them with their woven wings.
SOLANIO. Believe me, sir, had I such venture forth,
  The better part of my affections would
  Be with my hopes abroad. I should be still
  Plucking the grass to know where sits the wind,
  Piring in maps for ports and piers and roads:
  And every object that might make me fear   20
  Misfortune to my ventures, out of doubt,
  Would make me sad.
SALERIO.   My wind, cooling my broth,
  Would blow me to an ague when I thought
  What harm a wind too great might do at sea.
  I should not see the sandy hour-glass run
  But I should think of shallows and of flats,
  And see my wealthy Andrew docked in sand,
  Vailing her high-top lower than her ribs
  To kiss her burial ... Should I go to church
  And see the holy edifice of stone,   30
  And not bethink me straight of dangerous rocks,
  Which touching but my gentle vessel's side
  Would scatter all her spices on the stream,
  Enrobe the roaring waters with my silks,
  And, in a word, but even now worth this,
  And now worth nothing? Shall I have the thought
  To think on this, and shall I lack the thought
  That such a thing bechanced would make me sad?
  But tell not me—I know Antonio
  Is sad to think upon his merchandise.   40
ANTONIO. Believe me, no—I thank my fortune for
  it—
  My ventures are not in one bottom trusted,
  Nor to one place; nor is my whole estate
  Upon the fortune of this present year:
  Therefore my merchandise makes me not sad.
SOLANIO. Why then you are in love.
ANTONIO.   Fie, fie!
SOLANIO. Not in love neither? then let us say you are
  sad
  Because you are not merry; and 'twere as easy
  For you to laugh and leap, and say you are merry,
  Because you are not sad. Now, by two-headed
  Janus,   50
  Nature hath framed strange fellows in her time:
Some that will evermore peep through their eyes,
  And laugh like parrots at a bag-piper;
  And other of such vinegar aspect,
  That they'll not show their teeth in way of smile,
  Though Nestor swear the jest be laughable ...

Bassanio, Lorenzo, and Gratiano approach

  Here comes Bassanio, your most noble kinsman,
  Gratiano, and Lorenzo ... Fare ye well,
  We leave you now with better company.
SALERIO. I would have stayed till I had made you
  merry,   60
  If worthier friends had not prevented me.
ANTONIO. Your worth is very dear in my regard.
  I take it your own business calls on you,
  And you embrace th'occasion to depart.
SALERIO. Good morrow, my good lords.
BASSANIO. Good signiors both, when shall we laugh?
  say when?
  You grow exceeding strange: must it be so?
SALERIO. We'll make our leisures to attend on yours.
                          Salerio and Solanio depart
LORENZO. My Lord Bassanio, since you have found
  Antonio,
  We two will leave you, but at dinner-time   70
  I pray you have in mind where we must meet.
BASSANIO. I will not fail you.
GRATIANO. You look not well, Signior Antonio,
  You have too much respect upon the world:
  They lose it that do buy it with much care,
  Believe me you are marvellously changed.
ANTONIO. I hold the world but as the world,
  Gratiano—
  A stage, where every man must play a part,
  And mine a sad one.
GRATIANO.   Let me play the fool,
  With mirth and laughter let old wrinkles come,   80
  And let my liver rather heat with wine,
  Than my heart cool with mortifying groans.
  Why should a man, whose blood is warm within,
  Sit like his grandsire cut in alabaster?
  Sleep when he wakes? and creep into the jaundice
  By being peevish? I tell thee what, Antonio—
  I love thee, and it is my love that speaks—
  There are a sort of men whose visages
  Do cream and mantle like a standing pond,
  And do a wilful stillness entertain,   90
  With purpose to be dressed in an opinion
  Of wisdom, gravity, profound conceit,
  As who should say, 'I am Sir Oracle,
  And when I ope my lips let no dog bark'....
  O, my Antonio, I do know of these
  That therefore only are reputed wise
  For saying nothing ... when, I am very sure,
  If they should speak, would almost damn those ears
  Which, hearing them, would call their brothers
  fools.
  I'll tell thee more of this another time.   100
  But fish not with this melancholy bait
  For this fool gudgeon, this opinion ...

Come, good Lorenzo. Fare ye well awhile,
I'll end my exhortation after dinner.
LORENZO. Well, we will leave you then till dinner-
time.
I must be one of these same dumb wise men,
For Gratiano never lets me speak.
GRATIANO. Well, keep me company but two years mo,
Thou shalt not know the sound of thine own
tongue.
ANTONIO. Fare you well. I'll grow a talker for this
gear.   110
GRATIANO. Thanks, i'faith—for silence is only
commendable
In a neat's tongue dried, and a maid not vendible.
                                    Gratiano and Lorenzo go
ANTONIO. Is that any thing now?
BASSANIO. Gratiano speaks an infinite deal of nothing,
more than any man in all Venice. His reasons are as
two grains of wheat hid in two bushels of chaff: you
shall seek all day ere you find them, and when you
have them they are not worth the search.
ANTONIO. Well, tell me now what lady is the same
To whom you swore a secret pilgrimage,   120
That you to-day promised to tell me of?
BASSANIO. 'Tis not unknown to you, Antonio,
How much I have disabled mine estate,
By something showing a more swelling port
Than my faint means would grant continuance:
Nor do I now make moan to be abridged
From such a noble rate, but my chief care
Is to come fairly off from the great debts
Wherein my time, something too prodigal,
Hath left me gaged. To you, Antonio,   130
I owe the most in money and in love,
And from your love I have a warranty
To unburthen all my plots and purposes
How to get clear of all the debts I owe.
ANTONIO. I pray you, good Bassanio, let me know it,
And if it stand, as you yourself still do,
Within the eye of honour, be assured,
My purse, my person, my extremest means,
Lie all unlocked to your occasions.
BASSANIO. In my school-days, when I had lost one
shaft,   140
I shot his fellow of the self-same flight
The self-same way, with more advisèd watch,
To find the other forth, and by adventuring both,
I oft found both: I urge this childhood proof,
Because what follows is pure innocence....
I owe you much, and, like a wilful youth,
That which I owe is lost—but if you please
To shoot another arrow that self way
Which you did shoot the first, I do not doubt,
As I will watch the aim, or to find both,   150
Or bring your latter hazard back again,
And thankfully rest debtor for the first.
ANTONIO. You know me well, and herein spend but
time
To wind about my love with circumstance,
And out of doubt you do me now more wrong
In making question of my uttermost
Than if you had made waste of all I have:
Then do but say to me what I should do
That in your knowledge may by me be done,
And I am prest unto it: therefore, speak.   160
BASSANIO. In Belmont is a lady richly left,

And she is fair, and, fairer than that word,
Of wondrous virtues—sometimes from her eyes
I did receive fair speechless messages.
Her name is Portia, nothing undervalued
To Cato's daughter, Brutus' Portia;
Nor is the wide world ignorant of her worth,
For the four winds blow in from every coast
Renownèd suitors, and her sunny locks
Hang on her temples like a golden fleece,   170
Which makes her seat of Belmont Colchos' strand,
And many Jasons come in quest of her.
O my Antonio, had I but the means
To hold a rival place with one of them,
I have a mind presages me such thrift,
That I should questionless be fortunate.
ANTONIO. Thou know'st that all my fortunes are at sea,
Neither have I money nor commodity
To raise a present sum, therefore go forth,
Try what my credit can in Venice do—   180
That shall be racked, even to the uttermost,
To furnish thee to Belmont, to fair Portia.
Go, presently inquire, and so will I,
Where money is, and I no question make
To have it of my trust or for my sake.   *They go*

Scene 2: *The hall of Portia's house at Belmont*

Enter Portia and her waiting-woman Nerissa

PORTIA. By my troth, Nerissa, my little body is aweary
of this great world.
NERISSA. You would be, sweet madam, if your
miseries were in the same abundance as your good
fortunes are: and yet for aught I see, they are as sick
that surfeit with too much as they that starve with
nothing; it is no mean happiness therefore to be
seated in the mean—superfluity comes sooner by
white hairs, but competency lives longer.
PORTIA. Good sentences, and well pronounced.   10
NERISSA. They would be better if well followed.
PORTIA. If to do were as easy as to know what were
good to do, chapels had been churches, and poor
men's cottages princes' palaces. It is a good divine
that follows his own instructions. I can easier teach
twenty what were good to be done, than be one of
the twenty to follow mine own teaching ... The
brain may devise laws for the blood, but a hot
temper leaps o'er a cold decree—such a hare is
madness the youth, to skip o'er the meshes of good   20
counsel the cripple ... But this reasoning is not in
the fashion to choose me a husband. O me, the word
'choose'! I may neither choose whom I would nor
refuse whom I dislike—so is the will of a living
daughter curbed by the will of a dead father ... Is
it not hard, Nerissa, that I cannot choose one, nor
refuse none?
NERISSA. Your father was ever virtuous, and holy men
at their death have good inspirations, therefore the
lottery that he hath devised in these three chests of 30
gold, silver and lead, whereof who chooses his
meaning chooses you, will no doubt never be chosen
by any rightly, but one whom you shall rightly love.
But what warmth is there in your affection towards
any of these princely suitors that are already come?
PORTIA. I pray thee over-name them, and as thou
namest them, I will describe them, and according to
my description level at my affection.

NERISSA. First there is the Neapolitan prince.

PORTIA. Ay, that's a colt indeed, for he doth nothing 40 but talk of his horse, and he makes it a great appropriation to his own good parts that he can shoe him himself: I am much afeard my lady his mother played false with a smith.

NERISSA. Then is there the County Palatine.

PORTIA. He doth nothing but frown, as who should say, 'An you will not have me, choose!' He hears merry tales, and smiles not. I fear he will prove the weeping philosopher when he grows old, being so full of unmannerly sadness in his youth. I had rather 50 be married to a death's-head with a bone in his mouth than to either of these: God defend me from these two!

NERISSA. How say you by the French lord, Monsieur Le Bon?

PORTIA. God made him, and therefore let him pass for a man—In truth, I know it is a sin to be a mocker, but he! why, he hath a horse better than the Neapolitan's, a better bad habit of frowning than the Count Palatine—he is every man in no man—if a 60 throstle sing, he falls straight a cap'ring—he will fence with his own shadow. If I should marry him, I should marry twenty husbands. If he would despise me I would forgive him, for if he love me to madness, I shall never requite him.

NERISSA. What say you then to Falconbridge, the young baron of England?

PORTIA. You know I say nothing to him, for he understands not me, nor I him: he hath neither Latin, French, nor Italian, and you will come into the court 70 and swear that I have a poor pennyworth in the English. He is a proper man's picture, but, alas! who can converse with a dumb-show? How oddly is he suited! I think he bought his doublet in Italy, his round hose in France, his bonnet in Germany, and his behaviour every where.

NERISSA. What think you of the Scottish lord, his neighbour?

PORTIA. That he hath a neighbourly charity in him, for he borrowed a box of the ear of the English- 80 man, and swore he would pay him again when he was able: I think the Frenchman became his surety, and sealed under for another.

NERISSA. How like you the young German, the Duke of Saxony's nephew?

PORTIA. Very vilely in the morning when he is sober, and most vilely in the afternoon when he is drunk: when he is best, he is a little worse than a man, and when he is worst, he is little better than a beast. An the worst fall that ever fell, I hope I shall make 90 shift to go without him.

NERISSA. If he should offer to choose, and choose the right casket, you should refuse to perform your father's will, if you should refuse to accept him.

PORTIA. Therefore, for fear of the worst, I pray thee set a deep glass of rhenish wine on the contrary casket, for if the devil be within, and that temptation without, I know he will choose it. I will do any thing, Nerissa, ere I will be married to a sponge.

NERISSA. You need not fear, lady, the having any of 100 these lords—they have acquainted me with their determinations, which is indeed to return to their home, and to trouble you with no more suit, unless you may be won by some other sort than your father's imposition depending on the caskets.

PORTIA. If I live to be as old as Sibylla, I will die as chaste as Diana, unless I be obtained by the manner of my father's will. I am glad this parcel of wooers are so reasonable, for there is not one among them but I dote on his very absence: and I pray God 110 grant them a fair departure.

NERISSA. Do you not remember, lady, in your father's time, a Venetian, a scholar and a soldier, that came hither in company of the Marquis of Montferrat?

PORTIA. Yes, yes, it was Bassanio, as I think so was he called.

NERISSA. True, madam, he, of all the men that ever my foolish eyes looked upon, was the best deserving a fair lady.

PORTIA. I remember him well, and I remember him 120 worthy of thy praise.

A servant enters

How now! what news?

SERVANT. The four strangers seek for you, madam, to take their leave: and there is a forerunner come from a fifth, the Prince of Morocco, who brings word the prince his master will be here to-night.

PORTIA. If I could bid the fifth welcome with so good heart as I can bid the other four farewell, I should be glad of his approach: if he have the condition of a saint, and the complexion of a devil, I had 130 rather he should shrive me than wive me.
Come, Nerissa. Sirrah, go before:
Whiles we shut the gate upon one wooer, another knocks at the door.   *They go*

Scene 3: *A street in Venice*

Bassanio and Shylock

SHYLOCK. Three thousand ducats—well.

BASSANIO. Ay, sir, for three months.

SHYLOCK. For three months—well.

BASSANIO. For the which, as I told you, Antonio shall be bound.

SHYLOCK. Antonio shall become bound—well.

BASSANIO. May you stead me? Will you pleasure me? Shall I know your answer?

SHYLOCK. Three thousand ducats for three months— and Antonio bound.   10

BASSANIO. Your answer to that.

SHYLOCK. Antonio is a good man.

BASSANIO. Have you heard any imputation to the contrary?

SHYLOCK. Ho no, no, no, no . . . my meaning in saying he is a good man, is to have you understand me that he is sufficient. Yet his means are in supposition: he hath an argosy bound to Tripolis, another to the Indies; I understand moreover upon the Rialto, he hath a third at Mexico, a fourth for England, and 20 other ventures he hath squandered abroad. But ships are but boards, sailors but men—there be land-rats and water-rats, land-thieves and water-thieves—I mean pirates—and then there is the peril of waters, winds, and rocks. The man is, notwithstanding, sufficient. Three thousand ducats—I think I may take his bond.

BASSANIO. Be assured you may.

SHYLOCK. I will be assured I may: and, that I may be

assured, I will bethink me—may I speak with 30
Antonio?
BASSANIO. If it please you to dine with us.
SHYLOCK. Yes, to smell pork, to eat of the habitation
which your prophet the Nazarite conjured the devil
into! I will buy with you, sell with you, talk with
you, walk with you, and so following: but I will
not eat with you, drink with you, nor pray with
you ... What news on the Rialto? Who is he comes
here?

Antonio approaches

BASSANIO. This is Signior Antonio. 40
He draws Antonio aside
SHYLOCK [*aside*]. How like a fawning publican he looks!
I hate him for he is a Christian:
But more for that in low simplicity
He lends out money gratis, and brings down
The rate of usance here with us in Venice.
If I can catch him once upon the hip,
I will feed fat the ancient grudge I bear him.
He hates our sacred nation, and he rails,
Even there where merchants most do congregate,
On me, my bargains, and my well-won thrift, 50
Which he calls interest. Cursèd be my tribe,
If I forgive him!
BASSANIO. Shylock, do you hear?
SHYLOCK. I am debating of my present store,
And by the near guess of my memory
I cannot instantly raise up the gross
Of full three thousand ducats: what of that?
Tubal a wealthy Hebrew of my tribe
Will furnish me; but soft—how many months
Do you desire? [*to Antonio*] Rest you fair, good
signior,
Your worship was the last man in our mouths. 60
ANTONIO. Shylock, albeit I neither lend nor borrow
By taking nor giving of excess,
Yet to supply the ripe wants of my friend
I'll break a custom ... [*to Bassanio*] Is he yet possessed
How much ye would?
SHYLOCK. Ay, ay, three thousand ducats.
ANTONIO. And for three months.
SHYLOCK. I had forgot—three months—you told me
so.
Well then, your bond: and let me see—but hear you,
Methoughts you said you neither lend nor borrow
Upon advantage.
ANTONIO. I do never use it. 70
SHYLOCK. When Jacob grazed his uncle Laban's sheep,
This Jacob from our holy Abram was
(As his wise mother wrought in his behalf)
The third possessor; ay, he was the third—
ANTONIO. And what of him? did he take interest?
SHYLOCK. No, not take interest—not as you would say
Directly interest. Mark what Jacob did.
When Laban and himself were compromised
That all the eanlings which were streaked and pied
Should fall as Jacob's hire, the ewes, being rank 80
In end of autumn, turnèd to the rams,
And when the work of generation was
Between these woolly breeders in the act,
The skilful shepherd pilled me certain wands,
And, in the doing of the deed of kind,
He stuck them up before the fulsome ewes,

Who, then conceiving, did in eaning time
Fall parti-coloured lambs, and those were Jacob's.
This was a way to thrive, and he was blest:
And thrift is blessing if men steal it not. 90
ANTONIO. This was a venture, sir, that Jacob served
for—
A thing not in his power to bring to pass,
But swayed and fashioned by the hand of heaven.
Was this inserted to make interest good?
Or is your gold and silver ewes and rams?
SHYLOCK. I cannot tell, I make it breed as fast!
But note me, signior.
ANTONIO. Mark you this, Bassanio,
The devil can cite Scripture for his purpose.
An evil soul, producing holy witness,
Is like a villain with a smiling cheek, 100
A goodly apple rotten at the heart.
O, what a goodly outside falsehood hath!
SHYLOCK. Three thousand ducats—'tis a good
round sum.
Three months from twelve, then let me see the
rate.
ANTONIO. Well, Shylock, shall we be beholding to
you?
SHYLOCK. Signior Antonio, many a time and oft
In the Rialto you have rated me
About my moneys and my usances:
Still have I borne it with a patient shrug,
For suff'rance is the badge of all our tribe. 110
You call me misbeliever, cut-throat dog,
And spit upon my Jewish gaberdine,
And all for use of that which is mine own.
Well then, it now appears you need my help:
Go to then, you come to me, and you say,
'Shylock, we would have moneys'—you say so!
You that did void your rheum upon my beard,
And foot me as you spurn a stranger cur
Over your threshold. Moneys is your suit.
What should I say to you? Should I not say 120
'Hath a dog money? is it possible
A cur can lend three thousand ducats?' or
Shall I bend low, and in a bondman's key,
With bated breath, and whisp'ring humbleness,
Say this:
'Fair sir, you spit on me on Wednesday last—
You spurned me such a day—another time
You called me dog: and for these courtesies
I'll lend you thus much moneys'?
ANTONIO. I am as like to call thee so again, 130
To spit on thee again, to spurn thee too.
If thou wilt lend this money, lend it not
As to thy friends—for when did friendship take
A breed for barren metal of his friend?—
But lend it rather to thine enemy,
Who if he break, thou mayst with better face
Exact the penalty.
SHYLOCK. Why, look you, how you storm!
I would be friends with you, and have your love,
Forget the shames that you have stained me with,
Supply your present wants, and take no doit 140
Of usance for my moneys, and you'll not hear me:
This is kind I offer.
ANTONIO. This were kindness!
SHYLOCK. This kindness will I show.
Go with me to a notary, seal me there
Your single bond, and, in a merry sport,

If you repay me not on such a day,
In such a place, such sum or sums as are
Expressed in the condition, let the forfeit
Be nominated for an equal pound
Of your fair flesh, to be cut off and taken   150
In what part of your body pleaseth me.
ANTONIO. Content, in faith—I'll seal to such a bond,
And say there is much kindness in the Jew.
BASSANIO. You shall not seal to such a bond for me,
I'll rather dwell in my necessity.
ANTONIO. Why, fear not man, I will not forfeit it.
Within these two months, that's a month before
This bond expires, I do expect return
Of thrice three times the value of this bond.
SHYLOCK. O father Abram! what these Christians
are,   160
Whose own hard dealing teaches them suspect
The thoughts of others. Pray you, tell me this—
If he should break his day, what should I gain
By the exaction of the forfeiture?
A pound of man's flesh, taken from a man,
Is not so estimable, profitable neither,
As flesh of muttons, beefs, or goats. I say,
To buy his favour, I extend this friendship.
If he will take it, so—if not, adieu,
And, for my love, I pray you wrong me not.   170
ANTONIO. Yes, Shylock, I will seal unto this bond.
SHYLOCK. Then meet me forthwith at the notary's,
Give him direction for this merry bond,
And I will go and purse the ducats straight,
See to my house left in the fearful guard
Of an unthrifty knave; and presently
I will be with you.
ANTONIO.   Hie thee, gentle Jew....
                                          Shylock goes
The Hebrew will turn Christian—he grows kind.
BASSANIO. I like not fair terms and a villain's mind.
ANTONIO. Come on—in this there can be no dismay,   180
My ships come home a month before the day.
                                              They go

ACT 2
Scene 1: *Portia's house at Belmont*

*Enter the Prince of Morocco, a tawny Moor all in white,
and three or four followers accordingly, with Portia, Nerissa,
and their train*

MOROCCO. Mislike me not for my complexion,
The shadowed livery of the burnished sun,
To whom I am a neighbour and near bred.
Bring me the fairest creature northward born,
Where Phœbus' fire scarce thaws the icicles,
And let us make incision for your love,
To prove whose blood is reddest, his or mine.
I tell thee, lady, this aspéct of mine
Hath feared the valiant. By my love, I swear
The best-regarded virgins of our clime   10
Have loved it too. I would not change this hue,
Except to steal your thoughts, my gentle queen.
PORTIA. In terms of choice I am not solely led
By nice direction of a maiden's eyes:
Besides, the lott'ry of my destiny
Bars me the right of voluntary choosing:
But if my father had not scanted me
And hedged me by his wit, to yield myself
His wife who wins me by that means I told you,

Yourself, renownéd prince, then stood as fair   20
As any comer I have looked on yet
For my affection.
MOROCCO.   Even for that I thank you.
Therefore, I pray you, lead me to the caskets
To try my fortune. By this scimitar—
That slew the Sophy and a Persian prince
That won three fields of Sultan Solyman—
I would o'erstare the sternest eyes that look:
Outbrave the heart most daring on the earth:
Pluck the young sucking cubs from the she-bear,
Yea, mock the lion when a' roars for prey,   30
To win thee, lady. But alas the while!
If Hercules and Lichas play at dice
Which is the better man, the greater throw
May turn by fortune from the weaker hand:
So is Alcides, beaten by his page,
And so may I, blind fortune leading me,
Miss that which one unworthier may attain,
And die with grieving.
PORTIA.   You must take your chance—
And either not attempt to choose at all,
Or swear, before you choose, if you choose wrong,   40
Never to speak to lady afterward
In way of marriage. Therefore be advised.
MOROCCO. Nor will not. Come, bring me unto my
chance.
PORTIA. First, forward to the temple. After dinner
Your hazard shall be made.
MOROCCO.   Good fortune then!
To make me blest or cursed'st among men.
                                              They go

Scene 2: *A street in Venice*

Enter Lancelot Gobbo

LANCELOT. Certainly my conscience will serve me to
run from this Jew my master. The fiend is at mine
elbow, and tempts me, saying to me, 'Gobbo,
Lancelot Gobbo, good Lancelot,' or 'good Gobbo,'
or 'good Lancelot Gobbo, use your legs, take the
start, run away.' My conscience says, 'No; take heed
honest Lancelot, take heed honest Gobbo,' or as
aforesaid, 'honest Lancelot Gobbo, do not run, scorn
running with thy heels'. Well, the most courageous
fiend bids me pack. 'Fia!' says the fiend, 'away!' says 10
the fiend, 'for the heavens, rouse up a brave mind,'
says the fiend, 'and run'. Well, my conscience, hanging about the neck of my heart, says very wisely
to me: 'My honest friend, Lancelot, being an honest
man's son,'—or rather an honest woman's son—for
indeed my father did something smack, something
grow to; he had a kind of taste; well, my conscience
says, 'Lancelot, budge not.' 'Budge,' says the fiend.
'Budge not,' says my conscience. 'Conscience,' say
I, 'you counsel well.' 'Fiend,' say I, 'you counsel   20
well.' To be ruled by my conscience, I should stay
with the Jew my master, who (God bless the mark!)
is a kind of devil; and to run away from the Jew,
I should be ruled by the fiend, who, saving your
reverence, is the devil himself. Certainly, the Jew is
the very devil incarnation—and, in my conscience,
my conscience is but a kind of hard conscience, to
offer to counsel me to stay with the Jew. The fiend
gives the more friendly counsel. I will run, fiend,
My heels are at your commandment, I will run.   30

Old Gobbo enters with a basket

OLD GOBBO. Master young-man, you I pray you, which is the way to Master Jew's?

LANCELOT. [*aside*]. O heavens, this is my true-begotten father, who being more than sand-blind, high gravel-blind, knows me not. I will try confusions with him.

OLD GOBBO. Master, young gentleman, I pray you which is the way to Master Jew's?

LANCELOT. Turn up on your right hand at the next turning, but at the next turning of all on your left; 40 marry at the very next turning turn of no hand, but turn down indirectly to the Jew's house.

OLD GOBBO. Be God's sonties, 'twill be a hard way to hit. Can you tell me whether one Lancelot that dwells with him, dwell with him or no?

LANCELOT. Talk you of young Master Lancelot?— [*aside*] Mark me now, now will I raise the waters! Talk you of young Master Lancelot?

OLD GOBBO. No 'master,' sir, but a poor man's son. His father, though I say't, is an honest exceeding 50 poor man, and God be thanked well to live.

LANCELOT. Well, let his father be what a' will, we talk of young Master Lancelot.

OLD GOBBO. Your worship's friend and Lancelot, sir.

LANCELOT. But I pray you ergo old man, ergo I beseech you, talk you of young Master Lancelot.

OLD GOBBO. Of Lancelot, an't please your mastership.

LANCELOT. Ergo—Master Lancelot! Talk not of Master Lancelot, father, for the young gentleman— according to fates and destinies, and such odd say- 60 ings, the sisters three, and such branches of learning —is indeed deceased, or as you would say in plain terms, gone to heaven.

OLD GOBBO. Marry, God forbid! the boy was the very staff of my age, my very prop.

LANCELOT. Do I look like a cudgel or a hovel-post, a staff or a prop?
Do you know me, father?

OLD GOBBO. Alack the day, I know you not, young gentleman, but I pray you tell me, is my boy—God 70 rest his soul!—alive or dead?

LANCELOT. Do you not know me, father?

OLD GOBBO. Alack, sir, I am sand-blind, I know you not.

LANCELOT. Nay, indeed, if you had your eyes, you might fail of the knowing me: it is a wise father that knows his own child. Well, old man, I will tell you news of your son. Give me your blessing. Truth will come to light, murder cannot be hid long, a man's son may, but in the end truth will out. 80

OLD GOBBO. Pray you, sir, stand up. I am sure you are not Lancelot, my boy.

LANCELOT. Pray you let's have no more fooling about it, but give me your blessing: I am Lancelot, your boy that was, your son that is, your child that shall be.

OLD GOBBO. I cannot think you are my son.

LANCELOT. I know not what I shall think of that: but I am Lancelot, the Jew's man, and I am sure Margery, your wife, is my mother. 90

OLD GOBBO. Her name is Margery, indeed. I'll be sworn, if thou be Lancelot, thou art mine own flesh and blood ... Lord worshipped might he be! what a beard hast thou got! thou hast got more hair on thy chin than Dobbin my fill-horse has on his tail.

LANCELOT. It should seem then that Dobbin's tail grows backward. I am sure he had more hair of his tail than I have of my face, when I last saw him.

OLD GOBBO. Lord, how art thou changed! How dost thou and thy master agree? I have brought him a 100 present. How 'gree you now?

LANCELOT. Well, well—but, for mine own part, as I have set up my rest to run away, so I will not rest till I have run some ground. My master's a very Jew—give him a present! give him a halter—I am famished in his service: you may tell every finger I have with my ribs. Father, I am glad you are come. Give me your present to one Master Bassanio, who indeed gives rare new liveries. If I serve not him, I will run as far as God has any ground. O rare 110 fortune! here comes the man—to him, father, for I am a Jew if I serve the Jew any longer.

Bassanio approaches with Leonardo and other followers

BASSANIO [*to a servant*]. You may do so, but let it be so hasted that supper be ready at the farthest by five of the clock. See these letters delivered, put the liveries to making, and desire Gratiano to come anon to my lodging.   *The servant goes*

LANCELOT. To him, father.

OLD GOBBO. God bless your worship!

BASSANIO. Gramercy, wouldst thou aught with me? 120

OLD GOBBO. Here's my son, sir, a poor boy—

LANCELOT. Not a poor boy, sir, but the rich Jew's man that would, sir, as my father shall specify—

OLD GOBBO. He hath a great infection, sir, as one would say to serve—

LANCELOT. Indeed the short and the long is, I serve the Jew, and have a desire as my father shall specify—

OLD GOBBO. His master and he (saving your worship's reverence) are scarce cater-cousins—   130

LANCELOT. To be brief, the very truth is, that the Jew having done me wrong, doth cause me as my father being I hope an old man shall frutify unto you—

OLD GOBBO. I have here a dish of doves that I would bestow upon your worship, and my suit is—

LANCELOT. In very brief, the suit is impertinent to myself, as your worship shall know by this honest old man, and though I say it, though old man, yet poor man, my father.

BASSANIO. One speak for both. What would you? 140

LANCELOT. Serve you, sir.

OLD GOBBO. That is the very defect of the matter, sir.

BASSANIO. I know thee well, thou hast obtained thy suit.
Shylock, thy master, spoke with me this day,
And hath preferred thee, if it be preferment
To leave a rich Jew's service, to become
The follower of so poor a gentleman.

LANCELOT. The old proverb is very well parted between my master Shylock and you, sir—you have 'the grace of God,' sir, and he hath 'enough.'   150

BASSANIO. Thou speak'st it well; go, father, with thy son.
Take leave of thy old master, and inquire
My lodging out. Give him a livery
More guarded than his fellows': see it done.

LANCELOT. Father, in. I cannot get a service, no! I have ne'er a tongue in my head! Well ... [*looking*

on his palm] if any man in Italy have a fairer table
which doth offer to swear upon a book I shall have
good fortune. Go to, here's a simple line of life,
here's a small trifle of wives—alas, fifteen wives is 160
nothing, eleven widows, and nine maids, is a simple
coming-in for one man—and then to scape drowning thrice, and to be in peril of my life with the
edge of a feather-bed. Here are simple scapes. Well,
if Fortune be a woman, she's a good wench for this
gear. Father, come. I'll take my leave of the Jew in
the twinkling.   *Lancelot and Old Gobbo go*
BASSANIO. I pray thee, good Leonardo, think on this.
These things being bought and orderly bestowed,
Return in haste, for I do feast to-night   170
My best-esteemed acquaintance. Hie thee, go.
LEONARDO. My best endeavours shall be done herein.

Gratiano enters

GRATIANO. Where's your master?
LEONARDO.   Yonder, sir, he walks.
                              Leonardo departs
GRATIANO. Signior Bassanio!
BASSANIO.   Gratiano!
GRATIANO. I have a suit to you.
BASSANIO.   You have obtained it.
GRATIANO. You must not deny me—I must go with
you to Belmont.
BASSANIO. Why, then you must. But hear thee
Gratiano,
Thou art too wild, too rude, and bold of voice—
Parts that become thee happily enough,   180
And in such eyes as ours appear not faults;
But where thou art not known, why, there they
show
Something too liberal. Pray thee, take pain
To allay with some cold drops of modesty
Thy skipping spirit, lest through thy wild behaviour
I be miscónstrued in the place I go to,
And lose my hopes.
GRATIANO.   Signior Bassanio, hear me—
If I do not put on a sober habit,
Talk with respect, and swear but now and then,
Wear prayer-books in my pocket, look demurely, 190
Nay more, while grace is saying, hood mine eyes
Thus with my hat, and sigh, and say 'amen';
Use all the observance of civility,
Like one well studied in a sad ostent
To please his grandam, never trust me more.
BASSANIO. Well, we shall see your bearing.
GRATIANO. Nay, but I bar to-night, you shall not
gauge me
By what we do to-night.
BASSANIO.   No, that were pity,
I would entreat you rather to put on
Your boldest suit of mirth, for we have friends 200
That purpose merriment. But fare you well,
I have some business.
GRATIANO. And I must to Lorenzo, and the rest.
But we will visit you at supper-time.   *They go*

Scene 3: *Shylock's house*

Enter Jessica and Lancelot

JESSICA. I am sorry thou wilt leave my father so—
Our house is hell, and thou, a merry devil,
Didst rob it of some taste of tediousness.

But fare thee well, there is a ducat for thee.
And, Lancelot, soon at supper shalt thou see
Lorenzo, who is thy new master's guest,
Give him this letter, do it secretly,
And so farewell: I would not have my father
See me in talk with thee.
LANCELOT. Adieu! tears exhibit my tongue. Most 10
beautiful pagan, most sweet Jew! if a Christian do
not play the knave and get thee, I am much
deceived. But adieu, these foolish drops do some-
thing drown my manly spirit; adieu!
                              He goes
JESSICA. Farewell, good Lancelot.
Alack, what heinous sin is it in me
To be ashamed to be my father's child!
But though I am a daughter to his blood,
I am not to his manners. O Lorenzo,
If thou keep promise, I shall end this strife,   20
Become a Christian, and thy loving wife.
                              She goes

Scene 4: *A street in Venice*

Enter Gratiano, Lorenzo, Salerio and Solanio

LORENZO. Nay, we will slink away in supper-time,
Disguise us at my lodging, and return
All in an hour.
GRATIANO. We have not made good preparation.
SALERIO. We have not spoke as yet of torch-bearers.
SOLANIO. 'Tis vile, unless it may be quaintly ordered,
And better in my mind not undertook.
LORENZO. 'Tis now but four o'clock—we have two
hours
To furnish us.

Lancelot comes up with a letter

                    Friend Lancelot, what's the news?
LANCELOT. An it shall please you to break up this, it 10
shall seem to signify.
LORENZO. I know the hand. In faith 'tis a fair hand,
And whiter than the paper it writ on,
Is the fair hand that writ.
GRATIANO.   Love-news, in faith.
LANCELOT. By your leave, sir.
LORENZO. Whither goest thou?
LANCELOT. Marry, sir, to bid my old master the Jew
to sup to-night with my new master the Christian.
LORENZO. Hold here, take this. Tell gentle Jessica
I will not fail her—speak it privately.   20
                              Lancelot goes
Go, gentlemen,
Will you prepare you for this masque to-night?
I am provided of a torch-bearer.
SALERIO. Ay, marry, I'll be gone about it straight.
SOLANIO. And so will I.
LORENZO.   Meet me and Gratiano
At Gratiano's lodging some hour hence.
SALERIO. 'Tis good we do so.
                              Salerio and Solanio leave
GRATIANO. Was not that letter from fair Jessica?
LORENZO. I must needs tell thee all. She hath directed
How I shall take her from her father's house,   30
What gold and jewels she is furnished with,
What page's suit she hath in readiness.
If e'er the Jew her father come to heaven
It will be for his gentle daughter's sake,

And never dare misfortune cross her foot
Unless she do it under this excuse—
That she is issue to a faithless Jew.
Come, go with me. Peruse this, as thou goest.
Fair Jessica shall be my torch-bearer.   *They go*

Scene 5: *The street before Shylock's house*

Enter Shylock and Lancelot

SHYLOCK. Well, thou shalt see, thy eyes shall be thy
    judge,
The difference of old Shylock and Bassanio—
What, Jessica!—Thou shalt not gormandise,
As thou hast done with me—What, Jessica!—
And sleep and snore, and rend apparel out—
Why, Jessica, I say!
LANCELOT.   Why, Jessica!
SHYLOCK. Who bids thee call? I do not bid thee call.
LANCELOT. Your worship was wont to tell me I could
    do nothing without bidding.

Jessica appears at the door

JESSICA. Call you? What is your will?   10
SHYLOCK. I am bid forth to supper, Jessica.
    There are my keys ... But wherefore should I go?
    I am not bid for love—they flatter me.
    But yet I'll go in hate, to feed upon
    The prodigal Christian. Jessica, my girl,
    Look to my house. I am right loath to go:
    There is some ill a-brewing towards my rest,
    For I did dream of money-bags to-night.
LANCELOT. I beseech you, sir, go. My young master
    doth expect your reproach.   20
SHYLOCK. So do I his.
LANCELOT. And they have conspired together—I will
    not say you shall see a masque, but if you do, then it
    was not for nothing that my nose fell a-bleeding on
    Black-Monday last, at six o'clock i'th' morning, fall-
    ing out that year on Ash-Wednesday was four year,
    in th'afternoon.
SHYLOCK. What, are there masques? Hear you me,
    Jessica—
    Lock up my doors, and when you hear the drum
    And the vile squealing of the wry-necked fife,   30
    Clamber not you up to the casements then,
    Nor thrust your head into the public street
    To gaze on Christian fools with varnished faces:
    But stop my house's ears, I mean my casements,
    Let not the sound of shallow fopp'ry enter
    My sober house. By Jacob's staff I swear
    I have no mind of feasting forth to-night:
    But I will go. Go you before me, sirrah—
    Say I will come.
LANCELOT.   I will go before sir....
    Mistress, look out at window, for all this—   40
         There will come a Christian by,
         Will be worth a Jewess' eye.   *He goes*
SHYLOCK. What says that fool of Hagar's offspring, ha?
JESSICA. His words were, 'Farewell, mistress'—
    nothing else.
SHYLOCK. The patch is kind enough, but a huge feeder,
    Snail-slow in profit, and he sleeps by day
    More than the wild-cat: drones hive not with me.
    Therefore I part with him, and part with him
    To one that I would have him help to waste
    His borrowed purse. Well, Jessica, go in.   50

Perhaps I will return immediately.
Do as I bid you, shut doors after you.
Fast bind, fast find,
A proverb never stale in thrifty mind.   *He goes*
JESSICA. Farewell—and if my fortune be not crost,
    I have a father, you a daughter, lost.
                                 She goes within

Scene 6
Enter Gratiano and Salerio, in masquing attire

GRATIANO. This is the pent-house, under which
    Lorenzo
    Desired us to make stand.
SALERIO.   His hour is almost past.
GRATIANO. And it is marvel he out-dwells his hour,
    For lovers ever run before the clock.
SALERIO. O, ten times faster Venus' pigeons fly
    To seal love's bonds new-made, than they are wont
    To keep obligéd faith unforfeited!
GRATIANO. That ever holds: who riseth from a feast
    With that keen appetite that he sits down?
    Where is the horse that doth untread again   10
    His tedious measures with the unbated fire
    That he did pace them first? All things that are,
    Are with more spirit chaséd than enjoyed.
    How like a younger or a prodigal
    The scarféd bark puts from her native bay,
    Hugged and embracéd by the strumpet wind!
    How like the prodigal doth she return,
    With over-weathered ribs and ragged sails,
    Lean, rent and beggared by the strumpet wind!

Lorenzo approaches

SALERIO. Here comes Lorenzo—more of this here-
    after.   20
LORENZO. Sweet friends, your patience for my long
    abode.
    Not I, but my affairs, have made you wait:
    When you shall please to play the thieves for wives
    I'll watch as long for you then. Approach.
    Here dwells my father Jew. Ho! who's within?

A window opens above and Jessica leans out, clad as a boy

JESSICA. Who are you? Tell me, for more certainty,
    Albeit I'll swear that I do know your tongue.
LORENZO. Lorenzo, and thy love.
JESSICA. Lorenzo, certain, and my love indeed,
    For who love I so much? And now who knows   30
    But you, Lorenzo, whether I am yours?
LORENZO. Heaven and thy thoughts are witness that
    thou art.
JESSICA. Here, catch this casket, it is worth the pains.
    I am glad 'tis night, you do not look on me,
    For I am much ashamed of my exchange:
    But love is blind, and lovers cannot see
    The pretty follies that themselves commit,
    For if they could, Cupid himself would blush
    To see me thus transforméd to a boy.
LORENZO. Descend, for you must be my torch-bearer. 40
JESSICA. What, must I hold a candle to my shames?
    They in themselves, good sooth, are too too light.
    Why, 'tis an office of discovery, love,
    And I should be obscured.
LORENZO.   So are you, sweet,
    Even in the lovely garnish of a boy.
    But come at once,

For the close night doth play the runaway,
And we are stayed for at Bassanio's feast.
JESSICA. I will make fast the doors, and gild myself
  With some moe ducats, and be with you straight. 50
                              She closes the window
GRATIANO. Now, by my hood, a gentle and no Jew.
LORENZO. Beshrew me but I love her heartily,
  For she is wise, if I can judge of her,
  And fair she is, if that mine eyes be true,
  And true she is, as she hath proved herself:
  And therefore, like herself, wise, fair, and true,
  Shall she be placéd in my constant soul.

Jessica comes from the house

  What, art thou come? On, gentlemen, away—
  Our masquing mates by this time for us stay.
                    He departs with Jessica and Salerio

Enter Antonio

ANTONIO. Who's there?   60
GRATIANO. Signior Antonio?
ANTONIO. Fie, fie, Gratiano! where are all the rest?
  'Tis nine o'clock—our friends all stay for you.
  No masque to-night, the wind is come about,
  Bassanio presently will go aboard.
  I have sent twenty out to seek for you.
GRATIANO. I am glad on't. I desire no more delight
  Than to be under sail and gone to-night. *They go*

Scene 7: *Portia's house at Belmont*

Portia enters, with the Prince of Morocco, and their trains

PORTIA. Go, draw aside the curtains, and discover
  The several caskets to this noble prince.
  Now make your choice.
MOROCCO. The first, of gold, who this inscription
    bears:
  'Who chooseth me shall gain what many men
    desire'.
  The second, silver, which this promise carries:
  'Who chooseth me shall get as much as he deserves'.
  This third, dull lead, with warning all as blunt:
  'Who chooseth me must give and hazard all he
    hath'.
  How shall I know if I do choose the right?   10
PORTIA. The one of them contains my picture, prince.
  If you choose that, then I am yours withal.
MOROCCO. Some god direct my judgement! Let
    me see,
  I will survey th'inscriptions back again.
  What says this leaden casket?
  'Who chooseth me must give and hazard all he
    hath.'
  Must give—for what? for lead? hazard for lead?
  This casket threatens. Men that hazard all
  Do it in hope of fair advantages:
  A golden mind stoops not to shows of dross.   20
  I'll then nor give nor hazard aught for lead.
  What says the silver with her virgin hue?
  'Who chooseth me shall get as much as he deserves.'
  As much as he deserves! Pause there, Morocco,
  And weigh thy value with an even hand.
  If thou be'st rated by thy estimation,
  Thou dost deserve enough—and yet enough
  May not extend so far as to the lady:
  And yet to be afeard of my deserving

Were but a weak disabling of myself.   30
As much as I deserve! Why, that's the lady.
I do in birth deserve her, and in fortunes,
In graces, and in qualities of breeding:
But more than these, in love I do deserve.
What if I strayed no further, but chose here?
Let's see once more this saying graved in gold:
'Who chooseth me shall gain what many men
  desire'.
Why, that's the lady—all the world desires her.
From the four corners of the earth they come,
To kiss this shrine, this mortal-breathing saint. 40
The Hyrcanian deserts and the vasty wilds
Of wide Arabia are as throughfares now
For princes to come view fair Portia.
The watery kingdom, whose ambitious head
Spets in the face of heaven, is no bar
To stop the foreign spirits, but they come,
As o'er a brook, to see fair Portia.
One of these three contains her heavenly picture.
Is't like that lead contains her? 'Twere damnation
To think so base a thought—it were too gross   50
To rib her cerecloth in the obscure grave.
Or shall I think in silver she's immured,
Being ten times undervalued to tried gold?
O sinful thought! Never so rich a gem
Was set in worse than gold. They have in England
A coin that bears the figure of an angel
Stampéd in gold, but that's insculped upon;
But here an angel in a golden bed
Lies all within.... Deliver me the key:
Here do I choose, and thrive I as I may!   60
PORTIA. There, take it, prince, and if my form lie
    there,
  Then I am yours.   *He unlocks the golden casket*
MOROCCO.   O hell! what have we here?
  A carrion Death, within whose empty eye
  There is a written scroll! I'll read the writing.
    'All that glisters is not gold,
    Often have you heard that told.
    Many a man his life hath sold,
    But my outside to behold.
    Gilded tombs do worms infold.
    Had you been as wise as bold,   70
    Young in limbs, in judgement old,
    Your answer had not been inscrolled—
    Fare you well, your suit is cold.'
  Cold, indeed, and labour lost.
  Then, farewell heat, and welcome frost.
  Portia, adieu! I have too grieved a heart
  To take a tedious leave: thus losers part.
                          He departs with his retinue
PORTIA. A gentle riddance. Draw the curtains, go.
  Let all of his complexion choose me so. *They go*

Scene 8: *A street in Venice*

Enter Salerio and Solanio

SALERIO. Why man, I saw Bassanio under sail,
  With him is Gratiano gone along;
  And in their ship I am sure Lorenzo is not.
SOLANIO. The villain Jew with outcries raised the
    duke,
  Who went with him to search Bassanio's ship.
SALERIO. He came too late, the ship was under sail,
  But there the duke was given to understand

That in a gondola were seen together
Lorenzo and his amorous Jessica.
Besides, Antonio certified the duke   10
They were not with Bassanio in his ship.
SOLANIO. I never heard a passion so confused,
So strange, outrageous, and so variable,
As the dog Jew did utter in the streets.
'My daughter! O my ducats! O my daughter!
Fled with a Christian! O my Christian ducats!
Justice! the law! my ducats, and my daughter!
A sealéd bag, two sealéd bags of ducats,
Of double ducats, stol'n from me by my daughter!
And jewels—two stones, two rich and precious
    stones,   20
Stol'n by my daughter! Justice! find the girl!
She hath the stones upon her, and the ducats!'
SALERIO. Why, all the boys in Venice follow him,
Crying, his stones, his daughter, and his ducats.
SOLANIO. Let good Antonio look he keep his day,
Or he shall pay for this.
SALERIO.   Marry, well remembered:
I reasoned with a Frenchman yesterday,
Who told me, in the narrow seas that part
The French and English, there miscarriéd
A vessel of our country richly fraught: 30
I thought upon Antonio when he told me,
And wished in silence that it were not his.
SOLANIO. You were best to tell Antonio what you
    hear—
Yet do not suddenly, for it may grieve him.
SALERIO. A kinder gentleman treads not the earth.
I saw Bassanio and Antonio part.
Bassanio told him he would make some speed
Of his return: he answered, 'Do not so.
Slubber not business for my sake, Bassanio,
But stay the very riping of the time.   40
And for the Jew's bond which he hath of me,
Let it not enter in your mind of love:
Be merry, and employ your chiefest thoughts
To courtship, and such fair ostents of love
As shall conveniently become you there.'
And even there, his eye being big with tears,
Turning his face, he put his hand behind him,
And with affection wondrous sensible
He wrung Bassanio's hand, and so they parted.
SOLANIO. I think he only loves the world for him.   50
I pray thee, let us go and find him out,
And quicken his embracéd heaviness
With some delight or other.
SALERIO.   Do we so. *They go*

Scene 9: *Portia's house at Belmont*

Enter Nerissa and a servitor

NERISSA. Quick, quick, I pray thee—draw the curtain
    straight.
The Prince of Arragon hath ta'en his oath,
And comes to his election presently.

Portia enters with the Prince of Arragon, and their trains

PORTIA. Behold, there stand the caskets, noble prince.
If you choose that wherein I am contained,
Straight shall our nuptial rites be solemnized:
But if you fail, without more speech, my lord,
You must be gone from hence immediately.

ARRAGON. I am enjoined by oath to observe three
    things—
First, never to unfold to any one   10
Which casket 'twas I chose; next, if I fail
Of the right casket, never in my life
To woo a maid in way of marriage;
Lastly,
If I do fail in fortune of my choice,
Immediately to leave you and be gone.
PORTIA. To these injunctions every one doth swear,
That comes to hazard for my worthless self.
ARRAGON. And so have I addressed me. Fortune now
To my heart's hope! Gold, silver, and base lead.   20
'Who chooseth me must give and hazard all he hath'
You shall look fairer, ere I give or hazard.
What says the golden chest? ha! let me see:
'Who chooseth me shall gain what many men
    desire.'
What many men desire! that 'many' may be meant
By the fool multitude, that choose by show,
Not learning more than the fond eye doth teach;
Which pries not to th'interior, but like the
    martlet,
Builds in the weather on the outward wall,
Even in the force and road of casualty.   30
I will not choose what many men desire,
Because I will not jump with common spirits,
And rank me with the barbarous multitudes.
Why, then to thee, thou silver treasure-house!
Tell me once more what title thou dost bear:
'Who chooseth me shall get as much as he deserves.'
And well said too; for who shall go about
To cozen fortune and be honourable
Without the stamp of merit. Let none presume
To wear an undeservéd dignity.   40
O, that estates, degrees and offices,
Were not derived corruptly, and that clear honour
Were purchased by the merit of the wearer—
How many then should cover that stand bare!
How many be commanded that command!
How much low peasantry would then be gleaned
From the true seed of honour! and how much
    honour
Picked from the chaff and ruin of the times,
To be new varnished! Well, but to my choice.
'Who chooseth me shall get as much as he deserves.'   50
I will assume desert. Give me a key for this—
And instantly unlock my fortunes here.
                        He opens the silver casket
PORTIA. Too long a pause for that which you find
    there.
ARRAGON. What's here? the portrait of a blinking
    idiot,
Presenting me a schedule! I will read it.
How much unlike art thou to Portia!
How much unlike my hopes and my deservings!
'Who chooseth me shall have as much as he
    deserves.'
Did I deserve no more than a fool's head?
Is that my prize? are my deserts no better?   60
PORTIA. To offend and judge are distinct offices,
And of opposéd natures.
ARRAGON [*unfolds the paper*]. What is here?
    'The fire seven times tried this—
        Seven times tried that judgement is,
        That did never choose amiss.

Some there be that shadows kiss,
Such have but a shadow's bliss:
There be fools alive, I wis,
Silvered o'er—and so was this.
Take what wife you will to bed,   70
I will ever be your head:
So be gone, you are sped.'

Still more fool I shall appear
By the time I linger here.
With one fool's head I came to woo,
But I go away with two.
Sweet, adieu! I'll keep my oath,
Patiently to bear my roth.
                         He departs with his train
PORTIA. Thus hath the candle singed the moth:
O, these deliberate fools! when they do choose,   80
They have the wisdom by their wit to lose.
NERISSA. The ancient saying is no heresy,
Hanging and wiving goes by destiny.
PORTIA. Come, draw the curtain, Nerissa.

A servant enters

SERVANT. Where is my lady?
PORTIA.   Here—what would my lord?
SERVANT. Madam, there is alighted at your gate
A young Venetian, one that comes before
To signify th'approaching of his lord,
From whom he bringeth sensible regreets:
To wit, besides commends and courteous breath,   90
Gifts of rich value ... Yet I have not seen
So likely an ambassador of love.
A day in April never came so sweet,
To show how costly summer was at hand,
As this fore-spurrer comes before his lord.
PORTIA. No more, I pray thee. I am half afeard,
Thou wilt say anon he is some kin to thee,
Thou spend'st such high-day wit in praising him.
Come, come, Nerissa, for I long to see
Quick Cupid's post that comes so mannerly.   100
NERISSA. Bassanio—Lord Love, if thy will it be!
                                        They go

ACT 3
Scene 1: *The street before Shylock's house*

Solanio and Solerio

SOLANIO. Now, what news on the Rialto?
SALERIO. Why, yet it lives there unchecked that
Antonio hath a ship of rich lading wracked on the
narrow seas; the Goodwins, I think they call the
place—a very dangerous flat and fatal, where the
carcases of many a tall ship lie buried, as they say,
if my gossip Report be an honest woman of her
word.
SOLANIO. I would she were as lying a gossip in that,
as ever knapped ginger, or made her neighbours   10
believe she wept for the death of a third husband.
But it is true, without any slips of prolixity or
crossing the plain highway of talk, that the good
Antonio, the honest Antonio—O, that I had a title
good enough to keep his name company—
SALERIO. Come, the full stop.
SOLANIO. Ha! what sayest thou? Why, the end is, he
hath lost a ship.
SALERIO. I would it might prove the end of his losses.

SOLANIO. Let me say 'amen' betimes, lest the devil   20
cross my prayer, for here he comes in the likeness of
a Jew....

Shylock comes from his house

How now, Shylock! what news among the mer-
chants?
SHYLOCK. You knew, none so well, none so well as
you, of my daughter's flight.
SALERIO. That's certain! I, for my part, knew the tailor
that made the wings she flew withal.
SOLANIO. And Shylock, for his own part, knew the
bird was fledge, and then it is the complexion of   30
them all to leave the dam.
SHYLOCK. She is damned for it.
SALERIO. That's certain, if the devil may be her judge.
SHYLOCK. My own flesh and blood to rebel!
SOLANIO. Out upon it, old carrion, rebels it at these
years?
SHYLOCK. I say, my daughter is my flesh and blood.
SALERIO. There is more difference between thy flesh
and hers than between jet and ivory, more between
your bloods than there is between red wine and   40
rhenish. But tell us, do you hear whether Antonio
have had any loss at sea or no?
SHYLOCK. There I have another bad match—a bankrupt, a prodigal, who dare scarce show his head on
the Rialto, a beggar that was used to come so smug
upon the mart. Let him look to his bond! he was
wont to call me usurer, let him look to his bond!
he was wont to lend money for a Christian curtsy,
let him look to his bond!
SALERIO. Why, I am sure, if he forfeit, thou wilt not   50
take his flesh—what's that good for?
SHYLOCK. To bait fish withal! if it will feed nothing
else, it will feed my revenge. He hath disgraced me
and hindred me half a million, laughed at my losses,
mocked at my gains, scorned my nation, thwarted
my bargains, cooled my friends, heated mine
enemies—and what's his reason? I am a Jew. Hath
not a Jew eyes? hath not a Jew hands, organs,
dimensions, senses, affections, passions? fed with the
same food, hurt with the same weapons, subject to   60
the same diseases, healed by the same means,
warmed and cooled by the same winter and
summer, as a Christian is? If you prick us, do we
not bleed? if you tickle us, do we not laugh? if you
poison us, do we not die? and if you wrong us, shall
we not revenge? if we are like you in the rest, we
will resemble you in that. If a Jew wrong a Christian,
what is his humility? Revenge. If a Christian wrong
a Jew, what should his sufferance be by Christian
example? Why, revenge. The villainy you teach me   70
I will execute, and it shall go hard but I will better
the instruction.

A servant accosts Solanio and Salerio

SERVANT. Gentlemen, my master Antonio is at his
house, and desires to speak with you both.
SALERIO. We have been up and down to seek him.

Tubal appears

SOLANIO. Here comes another of the tribe—a third
cannot be matched, unless the devil himself turn
Jew.
                         Solanio and Salerio depart,
                           followed by the servant

SHYLOCK. How now, Tubal! what news from Genoa?
hast thou found my daughter? 80

TUBAL. I often came where I did hear of her, but
cannot find her.

SHYLOCK. Why there, there, there, there—a diamond
gone, cost me two thousand ducats in Frankfort—
the curse never fell upon our nation till now, I never
felt it till now—two thousand ducats in that, and
other precious, precious jewels. I would my
daughter were dead at my foot, and the jewels in
her ear! would she were hearsed at my foot, and the
ducats in her coffin! No news of them? Why, so— 90
and I know not what's spent in the search: why,
thou loss upon loss! the thief gone with so much and
so much to find the thief, and no satisfaction, no
revenge, nor no ill luck stirring but what lights o'
my shoulders, no sighs but o' my breathing, no tears
but o' my shedding. *He weeps*

TUBAL. Yes, other men have ill luck too. Antonio, as
I heard in Genoa—

SHYLOCK. What, what, what? ill luck, ill luck?

TUBAL. —hath an argosy cast away, coming from 100
Tripolis.

SHYLOCK. I thank God, I thank God! Is it true? is it
true?

TUBAL. I spoke with some of the sailors that escaped
the wrack.

SHYLOCK. I thank thee good Tubal, good news, good
news: ha, ha! Heard in Genoa?

TUBAL. Your daughter spent in Genoa, as I heard,
one night, fourscore ducats.

SHYLOCK. Thou stick'st a dagger in me. I shall never 110
see my gold again—fourscore ducats at a sitting!
fourscore ducats!

TUBAL. There came divers of Antonio's creditors in
my company to Venice, that swear he cannot choose
but break.

SHYLOCK. I am very glad of it, I'll plague him, I'll
torture him, I am glad of it.

TUBAL. One of them showed me a ring that he had
of your daughter for a monkey.

SHYLOCK. Out upon her! thou torturest me, Tubal—it 120
was my turquoise—I had it of Leah when I was a
bachelor: I would not have given it for a wilderness
of monkeys.

TUBAL. But Antonio is certainly undone.

SHYLOCK. Nay, that's true, that's very true, go Tubal,
fee me an officer, bespeak him a fortnight before.
I will have the heart of him if he forfeit, for were
he out of Venice I can make what merchandise I
will. Go, Tubal, and meet me at our synagogue—
go, good Tubal—at our synagogue, Tubal. 130

Tubal departs and Shylock goes within

Scene 2: *Portia's house at Belmont.*

*Enter Bassanio with Portia, Gratiano with Nerissa; the
servitor and other attendants*

PORTIA. I pray you tarry, pause a day or two
Before you hazard, for in choosing wrong
I lose your company; therefore, forbear awhile.
There's something tells me (but it is not love)
I would not lose you, and you know yourself,
Hate counsels not in such a quality;
But lest you should not understand me well—
And yet a maiden hath no tongue but thought—

I would detain you here some month or two
Before you venture for me. I could teach you 10
How to choose right, but then I am forsworn,
So will I never be, so may you miss me;
But if you do, you'll make me wish a sin,
That I had been forsworn. Beshrew your eyes,
They have o'er-looked me and divided me,
One half of me is yours, the other half yours—
Mine own I would say: but if mine then yours,
And so all yours. O, these naughty times
Put bars between the owners and their rights,
And so though yours, not yours. Prove it so— 20
Let Fortune go to hell for it, not I.
I speak too long, but 'tis to peise the time,
To eche it and to draw it out in length,
To stay you from election.

BASSANIO.   Let me choose,
For as I am, I live upon the rack.

PORTIA. Upon the rack, Bassanio? then confess
What treason there is mingled with your love.

BASSANIO. None but that ugly treason of mistrust,
Which makes me fear th'enjoying of my love.
There may as well be amity and life 30
'Tween snow and fire, as treason and my love.

PORTIA. Ay, but I fear you speak upon the rack,
Where men enforcéd do speak any thing.

BASSANIO. Promise me life, and I'll confess the truth.

PORTIA. Well then, confess and live.

BASSANIO.   'Confess' and 'love'
Had been the very sum of my confession:
O happy torment, when my torturer
Doth teach me answers for deliverance.
But let me to my fortune and the caskets.

PORTIA. Away then! I am locked in one of them— 40
If you do love me, you will find me out.
Nerissa and the rest, stand all aloof.
Let music sound while he doth make his choice—
Then if he lose, he makes a swan-like end,
Fading in music. That the comparison
May stand more proper, my eye shall be the stream,
And wat'ry death-bed for him. He may win,
And what is music then? then music is
Even as the flourish when true subjects bow
To a new-crownéd monarch: such it is, 50
As are those dulcet sounds in break of day
That creep into the dreaming bridegroom's ear,
And summon him to marriage. Now he goes,
With no less presence, but with much more love,
Than young Alcides, when he did redeem
The virgin tribute paid by howling Troy
To the sea-monster. I stand for sacrifice:
The rest aloof are the Dardanian wives,
With bleared visages, come forth to view
The issue of th'exploit. Go, Hercules! 60
Live thou, I live. With much much more dismay
I view the fight than thou that mak'st the fray.

*A song, the whilst Bassanio comments on the caskets to
himself*

Tell me where is Fancy bred,
Or in the heart, or in the head?
How begot, how nourishéd?

ALL. Reply, reply.
It is engendred in the eyes,
With gazing fed, and Fancy dies
In the cradle where it lies.

Let us all ring Fancy's knell: 70
I'll begin it—Ding, dong, bell.
ALL.   Ding, dong, bell.
BASSANIO. So may the outward shows be least them-
      selves—
The world is still deceived with ornament.
In law, what plea so tainted and corrupt,
But, being seasoned with a gracious voice,
Obscures the show of evil? In religion,
What damnèd error, but some sober brow
Will bless it, and approve it with a text,
Hiding the grossness with fair ornament?   80
There is no vice so simple, but assumes
Some mark of virtue on his outward parts.
How many cowards, whose hearts are all as false
As stairs of sand, wear yet upon their chins
The beards of Hercules and frowning Mars;
Who, inward searched, have livers white as milk?
And these assume but valour's excrement
To render them redoubted. Look on beauty,
And you shall see 'tis purchased by the weight,
Which therein works a miracle in nature,   90
Making them lightest that wear most of it:
So are those crispèd snaky golden locks
Which make such wanton gambols with the wind,
Upon supposèd fairness, often known
To be the dowry of a second head,
The skull that bred them in the sepulchre.
Thus ornament is but the guilèd shore
To a most dangerous sea; the beauteous scarf
Veiling an Indian beauty; in a word,
The seeming truth which cunning times put on   100
To entrap the wisest. Therefore, thou gaudy gold,
Hard food for Midas, I will none of thee—
Nor none of thee, thou pale and common drudge
'Tween man and man: but thou, thou meagre lead,
Which rather threaten'st than dost promise aught,
Thy plainness moves me more than eloquence,
And here choose I—joy be the consequence!
PORTIA [aside]. How all the other passions fleet to air,
As doubtful thoughts, and rash-embraced despair,
And shudd'ring fear and green-eyed jealousy!   110
O love, be moderate, allay thy ecstasy,
In measure rain thy joy, scant this excess—
I feel too much thy blessing, make it less,
For fear I surfeit!
BASSANIO. [opens the leaden casket]. What find I
      here?
Fair Portia's counterfeit! What demi-god
Hath come so near creation? Move these eyes?
Or whether, riding on the balls of mine,
Seem they in motion? Here are severed lips,
Parted with sugar breath—so sweet a bar   120
Should sunder such sweet friends. Here in her hairs
The painter plays the spider, and hath woven
A golden mesh t'entrap the hearts of men,
Faster than gnats in cobwebs—But her eyes!
How could he see to do them? having made one,
Methinks it should have power to steal both his,
And leave itself unfurnished: yet look, how far
The substance of my praise doth wrong this shadow
In underprizing it, so far this shadow
Doth limp behind the substance. Here's the scroll, 130
The continent and summary of my fortune.
      'You that choose not by the view
      Chance as fair and choose as true:

Since this fortune falls to you,
Be content, and seek no new.
If you be well pleased with this,
And hold your fortune for your bliss,
Turn you where your lady is,
And claim her with a loving kiss.'
A gentle scroll . . . Fair lady, by your leave,   140
I come by note, to give and to receive.
Like one of two contending in a prize,
That thinks he hath done well in people's eyes,
Hearing applause and universal shout,
Giddy in spirit, still gazing in a doubt
Whether those peals of praise be his or no,
So thrice-fair lady stand I, even so,
As doubtful whether what I see be true,
Until confirmed, signed, ratified by you.
PORTIA. You see me, Lord Bassanio, where I stand, 150
Such as I am. Though for myself alone
I would not be ambitious in my wish
To wish myself much better, yet for you
I would be trebled twenty times myself—
A thousand times more fair, ten thousand times
More rich.
That only to stand high in your account,
I might in virtues, beauties, livings, friends,
Exceed account. But the full sum of me
Is some of something which, to term in gross,   160
Is an unlessoned girl, unschooled, unpractised,
Happy in this, she is not yet so old
But she may learn; happier than this,
She is not bred so dull but she can learn;
Happiest of all is that her gentle spirit
Commits itself to yours to be directed,
As from her lord, her governor, her king. . . .
Myself and what is mine to you and yours
Is now converted. But now I was the lord
Of this fair mansion, master of my servants,   170
Queen o'er myself; and even now, but now,
This house, these servants, and this same myself,
Are yours—my lord's!—I give them with this ring,
Which when you part from, lose, or give away,
Let it presage the ruin of your love,
And be my vantage to exclaim on you.
BASSANIO. Madam, you have bereft me of all words,
Only my blood speaks to you in my veins,
And there is such confusion in my powers,
As, after some oration fairly spoke   180
By a belovèd prince there doth appear
Among the buzzing pleasèd multitude,
Where every something, being blent together,
Turns to a wild of nothing, save of joy,
Expressed and not expressed. But when this ring
Parts from this finger, then parts life from hence!
O, then be bold to say Bassanio's dead.
NERISSA. My lord and lady, it is now our time,
That have stood by and seen our wishes prosper,
To cry 'good joy.' Good joy, my lord, and lady!   190
GRATIANO. My Lord Bassanio, and my gentle lady,
I wish you all the joy that you can wish;
For I am sure you can wish none from me:
And, when your honours mean to solemnize
The bargain of your faith, I do beseech you,
Even at that time I may be married too.
BASSANIO. With all my heart, so thou canst get a wife.
GRATIANO. I thank your lordship, you have got me
      one.

My eyes, my lord, can look as swift as yours:
You saw the mistress, I beheld the maid;   200
You loved, I loved—for intermission
No more pertains to me, my lord, than you;
Your fortune stood upon the caskets there,
And so did mine too, as the matter falls:
For wooing here until I sweat again,
And swearing till my very roof was dry
With oaths of love, at last—if promise last—
I got a promise of this fair one here,
To have her love, provided that your fortune
Achieved her mistress.
PORTIA.   Is this true, Nerissa?   210
NERISSA. Madam, it is, so you stand pleased withal.
BASSANIO. And do you, Gratiano, mean good faith?
GRATIANO. Yes, faith, my lord.
BASSANIO. Our feast shall be much honoured in your
    marriage.
GRATIANO. We'll play with them the first boy for a
    thousand ducats.
NERISSA. What! and stake down?
GRATIANO. No, we shall ne'er win at that sport, and
    stake down.

Lorenzo, Jessica, and Salerio enter

But who comes here? Lorenzo and his infidel?   220
What, and my old Venetian friend, Salerio?
BASSANIO. Lorenzo and Salerio, welcome hither,
If that the youth of my new interest here
Have power to bid you welcome ... By your leave,
I bid my very friends and countrymen,
Sweet Portia, welcome.
PORTIA.   So do I, my lord.
They are entirely welcome.
LORENZO. I thank your honour. For my part, my lord,
My purpose was not to have seen you here,
But meeting with Salerio by the way,   230
He did entreat me, past all saying nay,
To come with him along.
SALERIO.   I did, my lord,
And I have reason for it. Signior Antonio
Commends him to you.   *He gives Bassanio a letter*
BASSANIO.   Ere I ope his letter,
I pray you, tell me how my good friend doth.
SALERIO. Not sick, my lord, unless it be in mind—
Nor well, unless in mind: his letter there
Will show you his estate.   *Bassanio opens the letter*
GRATIANO. Nerissa, cheer yon stranger, bid her
    welcome....
Your hand, Salerio. What's the news from Venice? 240
How doth that royal merchant, good Antonio?
I know he will be glad of our success,
We are the Jasons, we have won the fleece!
SALERIO. I would you had won the fleece that he hath
    lost.   *They talk apart*
PORTIA. There are some shrewd contents in yon same
    paper,
That steals the colour from Bassanio's cheek—
Some dear friend dead, else nothing in the world
Could turn so much the constitution
Of any constant man. What, worse and worse!
With leave, Bassanio—I am half yourself,   250
And I must freely have the half of anything
That this same paper brings you.
BASSANIO.   O sweet Portia,
Here are a few of the unpleasant'st words,

That ever blotted paper. Gentle lady,
When I did first impart my love to you,
I freely told you all the wealth I had
Ran in my veins—I was a gentleman—
And then I told you true: and yet, dear lady,
Rating myself at nothing, you shall see
How much I was a braggart. When I told you   260
My state was nothing, I should then have told you
That I was worse than nothing; for, indeed,
I have engaged myself to a dear friend,
Engaged my friend to his mere enemy,
To feed my means.... Here is a letter, lady,
The paper as the body of my friend,
And every word in it a gaping wound,
Issuing life-blood. But is it true, Salerio?
Here all his ventures failed? What, not one hit?
From Tripolis, from Mexico, and England,   270
From Lisbon, Barbary, and India?
And not one vessel scape the dreadful touch
Of merchant-marring rocks?
SALERIO.   Not one, my lord.
Besides, it should appear, that if he had
The present money to discharge the Jew,
He would not take it: never did I know
A creature that did bear the shape of man
So keen and greedy to confound a man.
He plies the duke at morning and at night,
And doth impeach the freedom of the state,   280
If they deny him justice. Twenty merchants,
The duke himself, and the magnificoes
Of greatest port, have all persuaded with him,
But none can drive him from the envious plea
Of forfeiture, of justice, and his bond.
JESSICA. When I was with him, I have heard him
    swear
To Tubal and to Chus, his countrymen,
That he would rather have Antonio's flesh
Than twenty times the value of the sum
That he did owe him: and I know, my lord,   290
If law, authority, and power deny not,
It will go hard with poor Antonio.
PORTIA. Is it your dear friend that is thus in trouble?
BASSANIO. The dearest friend to me, the kindest man,
The best-conditioned and unwearied spirit
In doing courtesies: and one in whom
The ancient Roman honour more appears
Than any that draws breath in Italy.
PORTIA. What sum owes he the Jew?
BASSANIO. For me, three thousand ducats.
PORTIA.   What, no more? 300
Pay him six thousand, and deface the bond;
Double six thousand, and then treble that,
Before a friend of this description
Shall lose a hair through Bassanio's fault.
First, go with me to church, and call me wife,
And then away to Venice to your friend;
For never shall you lie by Portia's side
With an unquiet soul! You shall have gold
To pay the petty debt twenty times over.
When it is paid, bring your true friend along.   310
My maid Nerissa and myself meantime
Will live as maids and widows ... Come, away!
For you shall hence upon your wedding-day:
Bid your friends welcome, show a merry cheer,
Since you are dear bought, I will love you dear.
But let me hear the letter of your friend.

BASSANIO [*reads*]. 'Sweet Bassanio, my ships have all miscarried, my creditors grow cruel, my estate is very low, my bond to the Jew is forfeit, and since, in paying it, it is impossible I should live, all debts 320 are cleared between you and I, if I might but see you at my death: notwithstanding, use your pleasure —if your love do not persuade you to come, let not my letter.'

PORTIA. O love, dispatch all business and be gone!

BASSANIO. Since I have your good leave to go away, I will make haste; but, till I come again, No bed shall e'er be guilty of my stay, No rest be interposer 'twixt us twain.   *They go*

Scene 3: *The street before Shylock's house*

Enter Shylock, Solanio, Antonio, and a Gaoler

SHYLOCK. Gaoler, look to him—tell not me of mercy— This is the fool that lent out money gratis. Gaoler, look to him.

ANTONIO.   Hear me yet, good Shylock.

SHYLOCK. I'll have my bond, speak not against my bond, I have sworn an oath that I will have my bond: Thou call'dst me dog before thou hadst a cause, But since I am a dog beware my fangs. The duke shall grant me justice. I do wonder, Thou naughty gaoler, that thou art so fond To come abroad with him at his request.   10

ANTONIO. I pray thee, hear me speak.

SHYLOCK. I'll have my bond—I will not hear thee speak. I'll have my bond, and therefore speak no more. I'll not be made a soft and dull-eyed fool, To shake the head, relent, and sigh, and yield To Christian intercessors. Follow not— I'll have no speaking, I will have my bond.
        He goes within, slamming the door behind him

SOLANIO. It is the most impenetrable cur, That ever kept with men.

ANTONIO.   Let him alone, I'll follow him no more with bootless prayers.   20 He seeks my life—his reason well I know; I oft delivered from his forfeitures Many that have at times made moan to me. Therefore he hates me.

SOLANIO.   I am sure, the duke Will never grant this forfeiture to hold.

ANTONIO. The duke cannot deny the course of law: For the commodity that strangers have With us in Venice, if it be denied, Will much impeach the justice of the state, Since that the trade and profit of the city   30 Consisteth of all nations. Therefore, go. These griefs and losses have so bated me, That I shall hardly spare a pound of flesh To-morrow to my bloody creditor. Well, gaoler, on. Pray God, Bassanio come To see me pay his debt, and then I care not!
                                        They go

Scene 4: *Portia's house at Belmont*

Enter Portia, Nerissa, Lorenzo, Jessica, and a man of Portia's, called Balthazar

LORENZO. Madam, although I speak it in your presence, You have a noble and a true conceit Of god-like amity, which appears most strongly In bearing thus the absence of your lord. But if you knew to whom you show this honour, How true a gentleman you send relief, How dear a lover of my lord your husband, I know you would be prouder of the work, Than customary bounty can enforce you.

PORTIA. I never did repent for doing good,   10 Nor shall not now: for in companions That do converse and waste the time together, Whose souls do bear an egall yoke of love, There must be needs a like proportion Of lineaments, of manners, and of spirit; Which makes me think that this Antonio, Being the bosom lover of my lord, Must needs be like my lord. If it be so, How little is the cost I have bestowed In purchasing the semblance of my soul   20 From out the state of hellish cruelty? This comes too near the praising of myself, Therefore no more of it: hear other things. Lorenzo, I commit into your hands The husbandry and manage of my house, Until my lord's return: for mine own part, I have toward heaven breathed a secret vow To live in prayer and contemplation, Only attended by Nerissa here, Until her husband and my lord's return.   30 There is a monastery two miles off, And there we will abide. I do desire you Not to deny this imposition, The which my love and some necessity Now lays upon you.

LORENZO.   Madam, with all my heart I shall obey you in all fair commands.

PORTIA. My people do already know my mind, And will acknowledge you and Jessica In place of Lord Bassanio and myself. So fare you well till we shall meet again.   40

LORENZO. Fair thoughts and happy hours attend on you!

JESSICA. I wish your ladyship all heart's content.

PORTIA. I thank you for your wish, and am well pleased To wish it back on you: fare you well, Jessica....
                          Jessica and Lorenzo go
Now, Balthazar, As I have ever found thee honest-true, So let me find thee still. Take this same letter, And use thou all th'endeavour of a man In speed to Padua; see thou render this Into my cousin's hand, Doctor Bellario,   50 And look what notes and garments he doth give thee, Bring them, I pray thee, with imagined speed Unto the tranect, to the common ferry Which trades to Venice. Waste no time in words, But get thee gone. I shall be there before thee.

BALTHAZAR. Madam, I go with all convenient speed.
                                        He departs

PORTIA. Come on, Nerissa—I have work in hand That you yet know not of; we'll see our husbands Before they think of us!

NERISSA.   Shall they see us?

PORTIA. They shall, Nerissa; but in such a habit,   60
That they shall think we are accomplishéd
With that we lack. I'll hold thee any wager,
When we are both accoutred like young men,
I'll prove the prettier fellow of the two,
And wear my dagger with the braver grace,
And speak between the change of man and boy
With a reed-voice, and turn two mincing steps
Into a manly stride; and speak of frays
Like a fine bragging youth; and tell quaint lies,
How honourable ladies sought my love,   70
Which I denying, they fell sick and died—
I could not do withal! Then I'll repent,
And wish, for all that, that I had not killed them.
And twenty of these puny lies I'll tell,
That men shall swear I have discontinued school
Above a twelvemonth. I have within my mind
A thousand raw tricks of these bragging Jacks,
Which I will practise.

NERISSA.   Why, shall we turn to men?

PORTIA. Fie, what a question's that,
If thou wert near a lewd interpreter!   80
But come, I'll tell thee all my whole device,
When I am in my coach, which stays for us
At the park-gate; and therefore haste away,
For we must measure twenty miles to-day.

They go

Scene 5: *Portia's garden*

Enter Lancelot and Jessica

LANCELOT. Yes truly, for look you, the sins of the
father are to be laid upon the children—therefore,
I promise you, I fear you. I was always plain with
you, and so now I speak my agitation of the matter:
therefore, be o' good cheer, for truly I think you
are damned. There is but one hope in it that can do
you any good, and that is but a kind of bastard hope
neither.

JESSICA. And what hope is that, I pray thee?

LANCELOT. Marry, you may partly hope that your   10
father got you not, that you are not the Jew's
daughter.

JESSICA. That were a kind of bastard hope, indeed!
So the sins of my mother should be visited upon me.

LANCELOT. Truly then I fear you are damned both by
father and mother: thus when I shun Scylla, your
father, I fall into Charybdis, your mother: well, you
are gone both ways.

JESSICA. I shall be saved by my husband—he hath
made me a Christian.   20

LANCELOT. Truly, the more to blame he. We were
Christians enow before, e'en as many as could well
live, one by another. This making of Christians will
raise the price of hogs—if we grow all to be pork-
eaters, we shall not shortly have a rasher on the coals
for money.

Lorenzo enters

JESSICA. I'll tell my husband, Lancelot, what you say—
here he comes.

LORENZO. I shall grow jealous of you shortly, Lancelot,
if you thus get my wife into corners.   30

JESSICA. Nay, you need not fear us, Lorenzo. Lancelot
and I are out. He tells me flatly there's no mercy
for me in heaven, because I am a Jew's daughter:

and he says you are no good member of the
commonwealth, for, in converting Jews to
Christians, you raise the price of pork.

LORENZO. I shall answer that better to the commonwealth than you can the getting up of the negro's
belly: the Moor is with child by you, Lancelot.

LANCELOT. It is much that the Moor should be more   40
than reason: but if she be less than an honest woman,
she is indeed more than I took her for.

LORENZO. How every fool can play upon the word!
I think the best grace of wit will shortly turn into
silence, and discourse grow commendable in none
only but parrots. Go in, sirrah—bid them prepare
for dinner.

LANCELOT. That is done, sir—they have all stomachs.

LORENZO. Goodly Lord, what a wit-snapper are you!
then bid them prepare dinner.   50

LANCELOT. That is done too, sir—only 'cover' is the
word.

LORENZO. Will you cover then, sir?

LANCELOT. Not so, sir, neither—I know my duty.

LORENZO. Yet more quarrelling with occasion! Wilt
thou show the whole wealth of thy wit in an instant?
I pray thee, understand a plain man in his plain
meaning: go to thy fellows, bid them cover the
table, serve in the meat, and we will come in
to dinner.   60

LANCELOT. For the table, sir, it shall be served in—
for the meat, sir, it shall be covered—for your
coming in to dinner, sir, why, let it be as humours
and conceits shall govern.   *He goes*

LORENZO. O dear discretion, how his words are suited!
The fool hath planted in his memory
An army of good words, and I do know
A many fools that stand in better place
Garnished like him, that for a tricksy word
Defy the matter. How cheer'st thou, Jessica?   70
And now, good sweet, say thy opinion,
How dost thou like the Lord Bassanio's wife?

JESSICA. Past all expressing. It is very meet,
The Lord Bassanio live an upright life,
For having such a blessing in his lady
He finds the joys of heaven here on earth,
And if on earth he do not merit it,
In reason he should never come to heaven!
Why, if two gods should play some heavenly match,
And on the wager lay two earthly women,   80
And Portia one, there must be something else
Pawned with the other, for the poor rude world
Hath not her fellow.

LORENZO.   Even such a husband
Hast thou of me, as she is for a wife.

JESSICA. Nay, but ask my opinion too of that.

LORENZO. I will anon—first, let us go to dinner.

JESSICA. Nay, let me praise you while I have a stomach.

LORENZO. No, pray thee, let it serve for table-talk—
Then, howsome'er thou speak'st, 'mong other things
I shall digest it.

JESSICA.   Well, I'll set you forth.   *They go* 90

ACT 4

Scene 1: *A Court of Justice*

*Enter Antonio, Bassanio, Gratiano, Solanio, the Duke, the
Magnificoes, officers, clerks, attendants, and others*

DUKE. What, is Antonio here?

ANTONIO. Ready, so please your grace.

DUKE. I am sorry for thee—thou art come to answer
  A stony adversary, an inhuman wretch
  Uncapable of pity, void and empty
  From any dram of mercy.

ANTONIO.   I have heard,
  Your grace hath ta'en great pains to qualify
  His rigorous course; but since he stands obdúrate,
  And that no lawful means can carry me
  Out of his envy's reach, I do oppose   10
  My patience to his fury, and am armed
  To suffer with a quietness of spirit
  The very tyranny and rage of his.

DUKE. Go one, and call the Jew into the court.

SOLANIO. He is ready at the door, he comes, my lord.

DUKE. Make room, and let him stand before our face.

Shylock enters

  Shylock, the world thinks, and I think so too,
  That thou but leadest this fashion of thy malice
  To the last hour of act, and then 'tis thought
  Thou'lt show thy mercy and remorse more strange 20
  Than is thy strange apparent cruelty;
  And where thou now exacts the penalty,
  Which is a pound of this poor merchant's flesh,
  Thou wilt not only loose the forfeiture,
  But touched with human gentleness and love,
  Forgive a moiety of the principal;
  Glancing an eye of pity on his losses,
  That have of late so huddled on his back;
  Enow to press a royal merchant down,
  And pluck commiseration of his state   30
  From brassy bosoms and rough hearts of flint,
  From stubborn Turks and Tartars, never trained
  To offices of tender courtesy.
  We all expect a gentle answer, Jew.

SHYLOCK. I have possessed your grace of what I
    purpose,
  And by our holy Sabbath have I sworn
  To have the due and forfeit of my bond.
  If you deny it, let the danger light
  Upon your charter and your city's freedom!
  You'll ask me why I rather choose to have   40
  A weight of carrion flesh than to receive
  Three thousand ducats: I'll not answer that!
  But say it is my humour, is it answered?
  What if my house be troubled with a rat,
  And I be pleased to give ten thousand ducats
  To have it baned? what, are you answered yet?
  Some men there are love not a gaping pig,
  Some that are mad if they behold a cat,
  And others when the bag-pipe sings i'th' nose
  Cannot contain their urine: for affection,   50
  Mistress of passion, sways it to the mood
  Of what it likes or loathes. Now, for your answer:
  As there is no firm reason to be rendred,
  Why he cannot abide a gaping pig;
  Why he, a harmless necessary cat;
  Why he, a woollen bag-pipe; but of force
  Must yield to such inevitable shame,
  As to offend, himself being offended;
  So can I give no reason, nor I will not,
  More than a lodged hate and a certain loathing 60
  I bear Antonio, that I follow thus
  A losing suit against him! Are you answered?

BASSANIO. This is no answer, thou unfeeling man,

  To excuse the current of thy cruelty!

SHYLOCK. I am not bound to please thee with my
  answers!

BASSANIO. Do all men kill the things they do not love?

SHYLOCK. Hates any man the thing he would not kill?

BASSANIO. Every offence is not a hate at first!

SHYLOCK. What, wouldst thou have a serpent sting
  thee twice?

ANTONIO. I pray you, think you question with the Jew 70
  You may as well go stand upon the beach
  And bid the main flood bate his usual height;
  You may as well use question with the wolf
  Why he hath made the ewe bleat for the lamb;
  You may as well forbid the mountain pines
  To way their high tops and to make no noise
  When they are fretten with the gusts of heaven;
  You may as well do any thing most hard,
  As seek to soften that—than which what's harder?—
  His Jewish heart. Therefore, I do beseech you, 80
  Make no moe offers, use no farther means,
  But with all brief and plain conveniency
  Let me have judgement and the Jew his will!

BASSANIO. For thy three thousand ducats here is six.

SHYLOCK. If every ducat in six thousand ducats
  Were in six parts and every part a ducat,
  I would not draw them, I would have my bond!

DUKE. How shalt thou hope for mercy, rendring
  none?

SHYLOCK. What judgement shall I dread, doing no
  wrong?
  You have among you many a purchased slave, 90
  Which, like your asses and your dogs and mules,
  You use in abject and in slavish parts,
  Because you bought them—shall I say to you,
  'Let them be free, marry them to your heirs?
  Why sweat they under burthens? let their beds
  Be made as soft as yours, and let their palates
  Be seasoned with such viands?' You will answer,
  'The slaves are ours.' So do I answer you:
  The pound of flesh, which I demand of him
  Is dearly bought, 'tis mine, and I will have it: 100
  If you deny me, fie upon your law!
  There is no force in the decrees of Venice!
  I stand for judgement. Answer—shall I have it?

DUKE. Upon my power, I may dismiss this court,
  Unless Bellario, a learned doctor,
  Whom I have sent for to determine this,
  Come here to-day.

SOLANIO.   My lord, here stays without
  A messenger with letters from the doctor,
  New come from Padua.

DUKE. Bring us the letters; call the messenger. 110

BASSANIO. Good cheer, Antonio! what man, courage
  yet!
  The Jew shall have my flesh, blood, bones, and all,
  Ere thou shalt lose for me one drop of blood.

ANTONIO. I am a tainted wether of the flock,
  Meetest for death. The weakest kind of fruit
  Drops earliest to the ground, and so let me;
  You cannot better be employed, Bassanio,
  Than to live still, and write mine epitaph.

Nerissa enters, dressed as a lawyer's clerk

DUKE. Came you from Padua, from Bellario?

NERISSA. From both, my lord. Bellario greets your
  grace.   *She presents a letter* 120

BASSANIO. Why dost thou whet thy knife so earnestly?

SHYLOCK. To cut the forfeiture from that bankrupt there.

GRATIANO. Not on thy sole, but on thy soul, harsh Jew,
Thou mak'st thy knife keen: but no metal can,
No, not the hangman's axe, bear half the keenness
Of thy sharp envy: can no prayers pierce thee?

SHYLOCK. No, none that thou hast wit enough to make.

GRATIANO. O, be thou damned, inexorable dog,
And for thy life let justice be accused!
Thou almost mak'st me waver in my faith,   130
To hold opinion with Pythagoras
That souls of animals infuse themselves
Into the trunks of men: thy currish spirit
Governed a Wolf, who hanged for human
   slaughter,
Even from the gallows did his fell soul fleet,
And whilst thou layest in thy unhallowed dam,
Infused itself in thee; for thy desires
Are wolvish, bloody, starved, and ravenous.

SHYLOCK. Till thou canst rail the seal from off my
   bond,
Thou but offend'st thy lungs to speak so loud: 140
Repair thy wit, good youth, or it will fall
To cureless ruin. I stand here for law.

DUKE. This letter from Bellario doth commend
A young and learned doctor to our court:
Where is he?

NERISSA.   He attendeth here hard by
To know your answer, whether you'll admit him.

DUKE. With all my heart: some three or four of you,
Go give him courteous conduct to this place.
Meanwhile, the court shall hear Bellario's letter....

He reads out the letter

'Your grace shall understand that at the receipt of   150
your letter I am very sick, but in the instant that
your messenger came, in loving visitation was with
me a young doctor of Rome, his name is Balthazar.
I acquainted him with the cause in controversy
between the Jew and Antonio the merchant; we
turned oe'r many books together; he is furnished
with my opinion, which bettered with his own
learning, the greatness whereof I cannot enough
commend, comes with him at my importunity to
fill up your grace's request in my stead. I beseech   160
you, let his lack of years be no impediment to let
him lack a reverend estimation, for I never knew so
young a body with so old a head. I leave him to
your gracious acceptance, whose trial shall better
publish his commendation.'
You hear the learned Bellario, what he writes.

Portia enters, dressed as a doctor of civil law

And here, I take it, is the doctor come.
Give me your hand. Come you from old Bellario?

PORTIA. I did, my lord.

DUKE.   You are welcome. Take your place ...
Are you acquainted with the difference   170
That holds this present question in the court?

PORTIA. I am informéd throughly of the cause.
Which is the merchant here, and which the Jew?

DUKE. Antonio and old Shylock, both stand forth.

PORTIA. Is your name Shylock?

SHYLOCK.   Shylock is my name.

PORTIA. Of a strange nature is the suit you follow,
Yet in such rule that the Venetian law
Cannot impugn you as you do proceed.
You stand within his danger, do you not?

ANTONIO. Ay, so he says.

PORTIA.   Do you confess the bond?   180

ANTONIO. I do.

PORTIA.   Then must the Jew be merciful.

SHYLOCK. On what compulsion must I? tell me that.

PORTIA. The quality of mercy is not strained,
It droppeth as the gentle rain from heaven
Upon the place beneath. It is twice blessed:
It blesseth him that gives, and him that takes,
'Tis mightiest in the mightiest, it becomes
The thronéd monarch better than his crown:
His sceptre shows the force of temporal power,
The attribute to awe and majesty,   190
Wherein doth sit the dread and fear of kings:
But mercy is above this sceptred sway,
It is enthronéd in the hearts of kings,
It is an attribute to God himself;
And earthly power doth then show likest God's,
When mercy seasons justice. Therefore, Jew,
Though justice be thy plea, consider this,
That in the course of justice none of us
Should see salvation: we do pray for mercy,
And that same prayer doth teach us all to render   200
The deeds of mercy. I have spoke thus much,
To mitigate the justice of thy plea,
Which if thou follow, this strict court of Venice
Must needs give sentence 'gainst the merchant there.

SHYLOCK. My deeds upon my head! I crave the law,
The penalty and forfeit of my bond.

PORTIA. Is he not able to discharge the money?

BASSANIO. Yes, here I tender it for him in the court,
Yea, twice the sum. If that will not suffice,
I will be bound to pay it ten times o'er,   210
On forfeit of my hands, my head, my heart.
If this will not suffice, it must appear
That malice bears down truth. And I beseech you,
Wrest once the law to your authority—
To do a great right, do a little wrong,
And curb this cruel devil of his will.

PORTIA. It must not be, there is no power in Venice
Can alter a decree estáblishéd:
'Twill be recorded for a precedent,
And many an error by the same example   220
Will rush into the state. It cannot be.

SHYLOCK. A Daniel come to judgement: yea, a Daniel!
O wise young judge, how I do honour thee!

PORTIA. I pray you, let me look upon the bond.

SHYLOCK. Here 'tis, most reverend doctor, here it is.

PORTIA. Shylock, there's thrice thy money offered
thee.

SHYLOCK. An oath, an oath, I have an oath in heaven.
Shall I lay perjury upon my soul?
No, not for Venice.

PORTIA.   Why, this bond is forfeit,
And lawfully by this the Jew may claim   230
A pound of flesh, to be by him cut off
Nearest the merchant's heart. Be merciful,
Take thrice thy money, bid me tear the bond.

SHYLOCK. When it is paid according to the tenour.
It doth appear you are a worthy judge,
You know the law, your exposition
Hath been most sound: I charge you by the law,

Whereof you are a well-deserving pillar,
Proceed to judgement: by my soul I swear,
There is no power in the tongue of man   240
To alter me. I stay here on my bond.
ANTONIO. Most heartily I do beseech the court
To give the judgement.
PORTIA.   Why then, thus it is.
You must prepare your bosom for his knife.
SHYLOCK. O noble judge! O excellent young man!
PORTIA. For the intent and purpose of the law
Hath full relation to the penalty,
Which here appeareth due upon the bond.
SHYLOCK. 'Tis very true: O wise and upright judge!
How much more elder art thou than thy looks!   250
PORTIA. Therefore, lay bare your bosom.
SHYLOCK.   Ay, his breast,
So says the bond, doth it not, noble judge?
'Nearest his heart,' those are the very words.
PORTIA. It is so. Are there balance here, to weigh
The flesh?
SHYLOCK.   I have them ready.
PORTIA. Have by some surgeon, Shylock, on your
charge,
To stop his wounds, lest he do bleed to death.
SHYLOCK. Is it so nominated in the bond?
PORTIA. It is not so expressed, but what of that?
'Twere good you do so much for charity   260
SHYLOCK. I cannot find it, 'tis not in the bond.
PORTIA. You merchant, have you any thing to say?
ANTONIO. But little; I am armed and well prepared.
Give me your hand, Bassanio, fare you well!
Grieve not that I am fall'n to this for you;
For herein Fortune shows herself more kind
Than is her custom: it is still her use,
To let the wretched man outlive his wealth,
To view with hollow eye and wrinkled brow
An age of poverty; from which ling'ring penance 270
Of such misery doth she cut me off.
Commend me to your honourable wife,
Tell her the process of Antonio's end,
Say how I loved you, speak me fair in death;
And when the tale is told, bid her be judge
Whether Bassanio had not once a love.
Repent but you that you shall lose your friend,
And he repents not, that he pays your debt.
For if the Jew do cut but deep enough,
I'll pay it instantly with all my heart.   280
BASSANIO. Antonio, I am married to a wife
Which is as dear to me as life itself,
But life itself, my wife, and all the world,
Are not with me esteemed above thy life.
I would lose all, ay, sacrifice them all
Here to this devil, to deliver you.
PORTIA. Your wife would give you little thanks for
that,
If she were by, to hear you make the offer.
GRATIANO. I have a wife, whom, I protest, I love—
I would she were in heaven, so she could   290
Entreat some power to change this currish Jew.
NERISSA. 'Tis well you offer it behind her back,
The wish would make else an unquiet house.
SHYLOCK. [aside]. These be the Christian husbands! I
have a daughter—
Would any of the stock of Bárrabas
Had been her husband, rather than a Christian....
[aloud] We trifle time, I pray thee pursue sentence.

PORTIA. A pound of that same merchant's flesh is thine,
The court awards it, and the law doth give it.
SHYLOCK. Most rightful judge!   300
PORTIA. And you must cut this flesh from off his
breast,
The law allows it, and the court awards it.
SHYLOCK. Most learnéd judge—a sentence—come,
prepare.
PORTIA. Tarry a little, there is something else.
This bond doth give thee here no jot of blood—
The words expressly are 'a pound of flesh':
Take then thy bond, take thou thy pound of flesh,
But, in the cutting it, if thou dost shed
One drop of Christian blood, thy lands and goods
Are by the laws of Venice confiscate   310
Unto the state of Venice.
GRATIANO. O upright judge!—mark, Jew—O learnéd
judge!
SHYLOCK. Is that the law?
PORTIA. Thyself shalt see the act:
For, as thou urgest justice, be assured
Thou shalt have justice more than thou desir'st.
GRATIANO. O learnéd judge!—mark, Jew—a learnéd
judge!
SHYLOCK. I take this offer then—pay the bond thrice,
And let the Christian go.
BASSANIO.   Here is the money.
PORTIA.   Soft!
The Jew shall have all justice—soft, no haste—   320
He shall have nothing but the penalty.
GRATIANO. O Jew! an upright judge, a learnéd judge!
PORTIA. Therefore, prepare thee to cut off the flesh.
Shed thou no blood, nor cut thou less nor more
But just a pound of flesh: if thou tak'st more
Or less than a just pound, be it but so much
As makes it light or heavy in the substance,
Or the division of the twentieth part
Of one poor scruple, nay, if the scale do turn
But in the estimation of a hair,   330
Thou diest and all thy goods are confiscate.
GRATIANO. A second Daniel, a Daniel, Jew!
Now, infidel, I have you on the hip.
PORTIA. Why doth the Jew pause? take thy forfeiture.
SHYLOCK. Give me my principal, and let me go.
BASSANIO. I have it ready for thee, here it is.
PORTIA. He hath refused it in the open court,
He shall have merely justice and his bond.
GRATIANO. A Daniel, still say I, a second Daniel!
I thank thee, Jew, for teaching me that word.   340
SHYLOCK. Shall I not have barely my principal?
PORTIA. Thou shalt have nothing but the forfeiture
To be so taken at thy peril, Jew.
SHYLOCK. Why then the devil give him good of it!
I'll stay no longer question.
PORTIA.   Tarry, Jew.
The law hath yet another hold on you....
It is enacted in the laws of Venice,
If it be proved against an alien,
That by direct or indirect attempts
He seek the life of any citizen,   350
The party 'gainst the which he doth contrive
Shall seize one half his goods, the other half
Comes to the privy coffer of the state,
And the offender's life lies in the mercy
Of the duke only, 'gainst all other voice.
In which predicament, I say, thou stand'st:

For it appears by manifest proceeding,
That indirectly and directly too
Thou hast contrived against the very life
Of the defendant; and thou hast incurred 360
The danger formerly by me rehearsed.
Down, therefore, and beg mercy of the duke.
GRATIANO. Beg that thou mayst have leave to hang
thyself,
And yet thy wealth being forfeit to the state,
Thou hast not left the value of a cord,
Therefore thou must be hanged at the state's charge.
DUKE. That thou shalt see the difference of our spirit,
I pardon thee thy life before thou ask it:
For half thy wealth, it is Antonio's—
The other half comes to the general state, 370
Which humbleness may drive unto a fine.
PORTIA. Ay, for the state, not for Antonio.
SHYLOCK. Nay, take my life and all, pardon not that.
You take my house, when you do take the prop
That doth sustain my house; you take my life,
When you do take the means whereby I live.
PORTIA. What mercy can you render him, Antonio?
GRATIANO. A halter gratis—nothing else, for God's
sake.
ANTONIO. So please my lord the duke and all the
court
To quit the fine for one half of his goods, 380
I am content; so he will let me have
The other half in use, to render it
Upon his death unto the gentleman
That lately stole his daughter;
Two things provided more, that, for this favour,
He presently become a Christian;
The other, that he do record a gift,
Here in the court, of all he dies possessed,
Unto his son Lorenzo and his daughter.
DUKE. He shall do this, or else I do recant 390
The pardon that I late pronouncéd here.
PORTIA. Art thou contented, Jew? what dost thou say?
SHYLOCK. I am content.
PORTIA.   Clerk, draw a deed of gift.
SHYLOCK. I pray you give me leave to go from hence,
I am not well, send the deed after me,
And I will sign it.
DUKE.   Get thee gone, but do it.
GRATIANO. In christ'ning thou shalt have two
godfathers—
Had I been judge, thou shouldst have had ten more,
To bring thee to the gallows, not the font.
                                         Shylock goes
DUKE. Sir, I entreat you home with me to dinner. 400
PORTIA. I humbly do desire your grace of pardon,
I must away this night toward Padua,
And it is meet I presently set forth.
DUKE. I am sorry that your leisure serves you not.
Antonio, gratify this gentleman,
For in my mind you are much bound to him.
    The Duke, the Magnificoes and their train depart;
                              the crowd disperses
BASSANIO. Most worthy gentleman, I and my friend
Have by your wisdom been this day acquitted
Of grievous penalties, in lieu whereof,
Three thousand ducats, due unto the Jew, 410
We freely cope your courteous pains withal.
ANTONIO. And stand indebted, over and above,
In love and service to you evermore.

PORTIA. He is well paid that is well satisfied,
And I, delivering you, am satisfied,
And therein do account myself well paid.
My mind was never yet more mercenary.
I pray you, know me when we meet again.
I wish you well, and so I take my leave.
BASSANIO. Dear sir, of force I must attempt you
further.   420
Take some remembrance of us, as a tribute,
Not as a fee: grant me two things, I pray you,
Not to deny me, and to pardon me.
PORTIA. You press me far, and therefore I will yield.
Give me your gloves, I'll wear them for your sake.
And, for your love, I'll take this ring from you—
Do not draw back your hand—I'll take no more,
And you in love shall not deny me this?
BASSANIO. This ring, good sir—alas, it is a trifle—
I will not shame myself to give you this. 430
PORTIA. I will have nothing else but only this;
And now, methinks, I have a mind to it.
BASSANIO. There's more depends on this than on the
value.
The dearest ring in Venice will I give you,
And find it out by proclamation,
Only for this, I pray you, pardon me.
PORTIA. I see, sir, you are liberal in offers.
You taught me first to beg, and now, methinks,
You teach me how a beggar should be answered.
BASSANIO. Good sir, this ring was given me by my
wife,   440
And when she put it on, she made me vow
That I should neither sell nor give nor lose it.
PORTIA. That 'scuse serves many men to save their
gifts.
And if your wife be not a mad-woman,
And know how well I have deserved this ring,
She would not hold out enemy for ever,
For giving it to me ... Well, peace be with you!
                         She goes, Nerissa following
ANTONIO. My Lord Bassanio, let him have the ring.
Let his deservings and my love withal
Be valued 'gainst your wife's commandment. 450
BASSANIO. Go, Gratiano, run and overtake him,
Give him the ring, and bring him if thou canst
Unto Antonio's house—away, make haste.
                                         Gratiano goes
Come, you and I will thither presently,
And in the morning early will we both
Fly toward Belmont. Come, Antonio. *They go*

Scene 2: *A street in Venice*

Enter Portia and Nerissa

PORTIA. Inquire the Jew's house out, give him this
deed,
And let him sign it. We'll away to-night,
And be a day before our husbands home:
This deed will be well welcome to Lorenzo.

Gratiano enters

GRATIANO. Fair sir, you are well o'erta'en.
My Lord Bassanio, upon more advice,
Hath sent you here this ring, and doth entreat
Your company at dinner.
PORTIA.   That cannot be:
His ring I do accept most thankfully,

And so I pray you tell him: furthermore,   10
I pray you, show my youth old Shylock's house.
GRATIANO. That will I do.
NERISSA.   Sir, I would speak with you ...
                              Takes Portia aside
I'll see if I can get my husband's ring,
Which I did make him swear to keep for ever.
PORTIA. Thou mayst, I warrant. We shall have old
    swearing
That they did give the rings away to men;
But we'll outface them, and outswear them too.
Away, make haste, thou know'st where I will tarry.
NERISSA. Come, good sir, will you show me to this
    house?   *They go*

ACT 5

Scene 1: *The avenue before Portia's house at Belmont*

Lorenzo and Jessica

LORENZO. The moon shines bright. In such a night as
    this,
When the sweet wind did gently kiss the trees,
And they did make no noise, in such a night
Troilus methinks mounted the Troyan walls,
And sighed his soul toward the Grecian tents,
Where Cressid lay that night.
JESSICA.   In such a night
Did Thisbe fearfully o'ertrip the dew,
And saw the lion's shadow ere himself,
And ran dismayed away.
LORENZO.   In such a night
Stood Dido with a willow in her hand   10
Upon the wild sea banks, and waft her love
To come again to Carthage.
JESSICA.   In such a night
Medea gathered the enchanted herbs
That did renew old Æson.
LORENZO.   In such a night
Did Jessica steal from the wealthy Jew,
And with an unthrift love did run from Venice
As far as Belmont.
JESSICA.   In such a night
Did young Lorenzo swear he loved her well,
Stealing her soul with many vows of faith,
And ne'er a true one.
LORENZO.   In such a night   20
Did pretty Jessica (like a little shrew!)
Slander her love, and he forgave it her.
JESSICA. I would out-night you, did no body come:
But, hark, I hear the footing of a man.

Stephano approaches

LORENZO. Who comes so fast in silence of the night?
STEPHANO. A friend.
LORENZO. A friend! what friend? your name, I pray
    you, friend?
STEPHANO. Stephano is my name, and I bring word
My mistress will before the break of day
Be here at Belmont—she doth stray about   30
By holy crosses, where she kneels and prays
For happy wedlock hours.
LORENZO.   Who comes with her?
STEPHANO. None, but a holy hermit and her maid.
I pray you, is my master yet returned?
LORENZO. He is not, nor we have not heard from him.

But go we in, I pray thee, Jessica,
And ceremoniously let us prepare
Some welcome for the mistress of the house.

Lancelot enters

LANCELOT. Sola, sola! wo, ha, ho, sola, sola!
LORENZO. Who calls?   40
LANCELOT. Sola! did you see Master Lorenzo? Master
    Lorenzo? sola, sola!
LORENZO. Leave hollaing, man—here!
LANCELOT. Sola! where? where?
LORENZO. Here!
LANCELOT. Tell him, there's a post come from my
    master, with his horn full of good news. My master
    will be here ere morning.   *He goes*
LORENZO. Sweet soul, let's in, and there expect their
    coming.
And yet no matter: why should we go in?   50
My friend Stephano, signify, I pray you,
Within the house, your mistress is at hand,
And bring your music forth into the air.
                              Stephano goes
How sweet the moonlight sleeps upon this bank!
Here will we sit and let the sounds of music
Creep in our ears—soft stillness and the night
Become the touches of sweet harmony.
Sit, Jessica. Look how the floor of heaven
Is thick inlaid with patens of bright gold.
There's not the smallest orb which thou behold'st   60
But in his motion like an angel sings,
Still choiring to the young-eyed cherubins;
Such harmony is in immortal souls!
But whilst this muddy vesture of decay
Doth grossly close it in, we cannot hear it.

Enter musicians

Come, ho, and wake Diana with a hymn!
With sweetest touches pierce your mistress' ear,
And draw her home with music.   *Music*
JESSICA. I am never merry when I hear sweet music.
LORENZO. The reason is, your spirits are attentive: 70
For do but note a wild and wanton herd,
Or race of youthful and unhandled colts,
Fetching mad bounds, bellowing and neighing
    loud—
Which is the hot condition of their blood—
If they but hear perchance a trumpet sound,
Or any air of music touch their ears,
You shall perceive them make a mutual stand,
Their savage eyes turned to a modest gaze
By the sweet power of music: therefore, the poet
Did feign that Orpheus drew trees, stones, and
    floods,   80
Since nought so stockish, hard, and full of rage,
But music for the time doth change his nature.
The man that hath no music in himself,
Nor is not moved with concord of sweet sounds,
Is fit for treasons, stratagems, and spoils,
The motions of his spirit are dull as night,
And his affections dark as Erebus:
Let no such man be trusted. Mark the music.

Portia and Nerissa enter

PORTIA. That light we see is burning in my hall.
How far that little candle throws his beams!   90
So shines a good deed in a naughty world.

NERISSA. When the moon shone, we did not see the candle.
PORTIA. So doth the greater glory dim the less—
A substitute shines brightly as a king,
Until a king be by, and then his state
Empties itself, as doth an inland brook
Into the main of waters. Music! hark!
NERISSA. It is your music, madam, of the house.
PORTIA. Nothing is good, I see, without respect—
Methinks it sounds much sweeter than by day.   100
NERISSA. Silence bestows that virtue on it, madam.
PORTIA. The crow doth sing as sweetly as the lark
When neither is attended: and I think
The nightingale, if she should sing by day
When every goose is cackling, would be thought
No better a musician than the wren.
How many things by season seasoned are
To their right praise and true perfection.
Peace, ho! the moon sleeps with Endymion,
And would not be awaked.   *The music ceases*
LORENZO.   That is the voice,   110
Or I am much deceived, of Portia.
PORTIA. He knows me, as the blind man knows the cuckoo,
By the bad voice.
LORENZO.   Dear lady, welcome home.
PORTIA. We have been praying for our husbands'
welfare,
Which speed we hope the better for our words.
Are they returned?
LORENZO.   Madam, they are not yet;
But there is come a messenger before,
To signify their coming.
PORTIA.   Go in, Nerissa,
Give order to my servants that they take
No note at all of our being absent hence—   120
Nor you, Lorenzo—Jessica, nor you.
                              A tucket sounds
LORENZO. Your husband is at hand, I hear his trumpet.
We are no tell-tales, madam—fear you not.
PORTIA. This night methinks is but the daylight sick,
It looks a little paler—'tis a day,
Such as the day is when the sun is hid.

Bassanio, Antonio, Gratiano, and their followers come up

BASSANIO. We should hold day with the Antipodes,
If you would walk in absence of the sun.
PORTIA. Let me give light, but let me not be light,
For a light wife doth make a heavy husband,   130
And never be Bassanio so for me.
But God sort all. You are welcome home, my lord.
                    Gratiano and Nerissa talk apart
BASSANIO. I thank you, madam. Give welcome to my
friend—
This is the man, this is Antonio,
To whom I am so infinitely bound.
PORTIA. You should in all sense be much bound to
him,
For, as I hear, he was much bound for you.
ANTONIO. No more than I am well acquitted of.
PORTIA. Sir, you are very welcome to our house:
It must appear in other ways than words,   140
Therefore I scant this breathing courtesy.
GRATIANO. By yonder moon I swear you do me
wrong,
In faith I gave it to the judge's clerk.

Would he were gelt that had it for my part,
Since you do take it, love, so much at heart.
PORTIA. A quarrel, ho, already! what's the matter?
GRATIANO. About a hoop of gold, a paltry ring
That she did give to me, whose posy was
For all the world like cutler's poetry
Upon a knife, 'Love me, and leave me not.'   150
NERISSA. What talk you of the posy or the value?
You swore to me when I did give it you
That you would wear it till your hour of death,
And that it should lie with you in your grave.
Though not for me, yet for your vehement oaths,
You should have been respective and have kept it.
Gave it a judge's clerk! no, God's my judge,
The clerk will ne'er wear hair on's face that had it.
GRATIANO. He will, an if he live to be a man.
NERISSA. Ay, if a woman live to be a man.   160
GRATIANO. Now, by this hand, I gave it to a youth,
A kind of boy, a little scrubbéd boy,
No higher than thyself, the judge's clerk,
A prating boy, that begged it as a fee—
I could not for my heart deny it him.
PORTIA. You were to blame, I must be plain with you,
To part so slightly with your wife's first gift,
A thing stuck on with oaths upon your finger,
And riveted with faith unto your flesh.
I gave my love a ring, and made him swear   170
Never to part with it, and here he stands;
I dare be sworn for him he would not leave it,
Nor pluck it from his finger, for the wealth
That the world masters. Now, in faith, Gratiano,
You give your wife too unkind cause of grief.
An 'twere to me, I should be mad at it.
BASSANIO. Why, I were best to cut my left hand
off,
And swear I lost the ring defending it.
GRATIANO. My Lord Bassanio gave his ring away
Unto the judge that begged it, and indeed   180
Deserved it too; and then the boy, his clerk,
That took some pains in writing, he begged mine,
And neither man nor master would take aught
But the two rings.
PORTIA.   What ring gave you, my lord?
Not that, I hope, which you received of me.
BASSANIO. If I could add a lie unto a fault,
I would deny it; but you see my finger
Hath not the ring upon it, it is gone.
PORTIA. Even so void is your false heart of truth!
By heaven, I will ne'er come in your bed   190
Until I see the ring.
NERISSA.   Nor I in yours,
Till I again see mine.
BASSANIO.   Sweet Portia,
If you did know to whom I gave the ring,
If you did know for whom I gave the ring,
And would conceive for what I gave the ring,
And how unwillingly I left the ring,
When naught would be accepted but the ring,
You would abate the strength of your displeasure.
PORTIA. If you had known the virtue of the ring,
Or half her worthiness that gave the ring,   200
Or your own honour to contain the ring,
You would not then have parted with the ring . . .
What man is there so much unreasonable,
If you had pleased to have defended it
With any terms of zeal, wanted the modesty

To urge the thing held as a ceremony?
Nerissa teaches me what to believe—
I'll die for't but some woman had the ring.
BASSANIO. No, by my honour, madam, by my soul,
  No woman had it, but a civil doctor,   210
  Which had refuse three thousand ducats of me,
  And begged the ring, the which I did deny him,
  And suffered him to go displeased away,
  Even he that had held up the very life
  Of my dear friend.... What should I say, sweet
    lady?
  I was enforced to send it after him,
  I was beset with shame and courtesy,
  My honour would not let ingratitude
  So much besmear it ... Pardon me, good lady,
  For by these blessèd candles of the night,   220
  Had you been there, I think you would have begged
  The ring of me to give the worthy doctor.
PORTIA. Let not that doctor e'er come near my house.
  Since he hath got the jewel that I loved,
  And that which you did swear to keep for me,
  I will become as liberal as you,
  I'll not deny him any thing I have,
  No, not my body, nor my husband's bed:
  Know him I shall, I am well sure of it.
  Lie not a night from home. Watch me, like Argus.   230
  If you do not, if I be left alone,
  Now, by mine honour, which is yet mine own,
  I'll have that doctor for my bedfellow.
NERISSA. And I his clerk; therefore be well advised
  How you do leave me to mine own protection.
GRATIANO. Well, do you so: let not me take him then,
  For if I do, I'll mar the young clerk's pen.
ANTONIO. I am th'unhappy subject of these quarrels.
PORTIA. Sir, grieve not you—you are welcome
    notwithstanding.
BASSANIO. Portia, forgive me this enforcèd wrong,   240
  And in the hearing of these many friends
  I swear to thee, even by thine own fair eyes
  Wherein I see myself—
PORTIA.   Mark you but that!
  In both my eyes he doubly sees himself:
  In each eye, one. Swear by your double self,
  And there's an oath of credit.
BASSANIO.   Nay, but hear me....
  Pardon this fault, and by my soul I swear,
  I never more will break an oath with thee.
ANTONIO. I once did lend my body for his wealth,
  Which but for him that had your husband's ring   250
  Had quite miscarried. I dare be bound again,
  My soul upon the forfeit, that your lord
  Will never more break faith advisedly.
PORTIA. Then you shall be his surety.... Give him this,
  And bid him keep it better than the other.
ANTONIO. Here, Lord Bassanio, swear to keep this
  ring.

BASSANIO. By heaven, it is the same I gave the doctor!
PORTIA. I had it of him: pardon me, Bassanio,
  For by this ring the doctor lay with me.
NERISSA. And pardon me, my gentle Gratiano,   260
  For that same scrubbèd boy, the doctor's clerk,
  In lieu of this last night did lie with me.
GRATIANO. Why, this is like the mending of highways
  In summer, where the ways are fair enough.
  What! are we cuckolds ere we have deserved it?
PORTIA. Speak not so grossly. You are all amazed:
  Here is a letter, read it at your leisure—
  It comes from Padua, from Bellario.
  There you shall find that Portia was the doctor,
  Nerissa there, her clerk. Lorenzo here   270
  Shall witness I set forth as soon as you,
  And even but now returned; I have not yet
  Entered my house. Antonio, you are welcome,
  And I have better news in store for you
  Than you expect: unseal this letter soon,
  There you shall find three of your argosies
  Are richly come to harbour suddenly.
  You shall not know by what strange accident
  I chancèd on this letter.
ANTONIO.   I am dumb!
BASSANIO. Were you the doctor, and I knew you not?   280
GRATIANO. Were you the clerk that is to make me
  cuckold?
NERISSA. Ay, but the clerk that never means to do it,
  Unless he live until he be a man.
BASSANIO. Sweet doctor, you shall be my bedfellow—
  When I am absent, then lie with my wife.
ANTONIO. Sweet lady, you have given me life and
    living;
  For here I read for certain that my ships
  Are safely come to road.
PORTIA.   How now, Lorenzo?
  My clerk hath some good comforts too for you.
NERISSA. Ay, and I'll give them him without a fee.   290
  There do I give to you and Jessica,
  From the rich Jew, a special deed of gift,
  After his death, of all he dies possessed of.
LORENZO. Fair ladies, you drop manna in the way
  Of starvèd people.
PORTIA.   It is almost morning,
  And yet I am sure you are not satisfied
  Of these events at full. Let us go in,
  And charge us there upon inter'gatories,
  And we will answer all things faithfully.
GRATIANO. Let it be so. The first inter'gatory   300
  That my Nerissa shall be sworn on is,
  Whether till the next night she had rather stay,
  Or go to bed now, being two hours to-day:
  But were the day come, I should wish it dark,
  Till I were couching with the doctor's clerk.
  Well, while I live I'll fear no other thing
  So sore as keeping safe Nerissa's ring. *They all go*

As You Like It

The scene: Oliver's house, Duke Frederick's court,
and the Forest of Arden

CHARACTERS IN THE PLAY

A banished DUKE
FREDERICK, his brother, and usurper of his dominions
AMIENS } lords attending on the banished Duke
JAQUES }
LE BEAU, a courtier attending upon Frederick
CHARLES, wrestler to Frederick
OLIVER
JAQUES } sons of Sir Rowland de Boys
ORLANDO
ADAM } servants to Oliver
DENNIS

TOUCHSTONE, a clown
SIR OLIVER MARTEXT, a vicar
CORIN } shepherds
SILVIUS }
WILLIAM, a country fellow, in love with Audrey
A person representing Hymen
ROSALIND, daughter to the banished Duke
CELIA, daughter to Frederick
PHEBE, a shepherdess
AUDREY, a country wench
Lords, pages, foresters, and attendants

As You Like It

ACT 1
Scene 1: *An orchard, near Oliver's house*

Orlando and Adam

ORLANDO. As I remember, Adam, it was upon this fashion: a' bequeathed me by will but poor thousand crowns and, as thou say'st, charged my brother on his blessing to breed me well: and there begins my sadness... My brother Jaques he keeps at school, and report speaks goldenly of his profit: for my part, he keeps me rustically at home, or, to speak more properly, stays me here at home unkept: for call you that 'keeping' for a gentleman of my birth, that differs not from the stalling of an ox? His horses are 10 bred better—for, besides that they are fair with their feeding, they are taught their manage, and to that end riders dearly hired: but I, his brother, gain nothing under him but growth, for the which his animals on his dunghills are as much bound to him as I ... Besides this nothing that he so plentifully gives me, the something that nature gave me his countenance seems to take from me: he lets me feed with his hinds, bars me the place of a brother, and, as much as in him lies, mines my gentility with my 20 education.... This is it, Adam, that grieves me—and the spirit of my father, which I think is within me, begins to mutiny against this servitude.... I will no longer endure it, though yet I know no wise remedy how to avoid it.

Oliver enters

ADAM. Yonder comes my master, your brother.
ORLANDO. Go apart, Adam, and thou shalt hear how he will shake me up.
OLIVER. Now, sir! what make you here?
ORLANDO. Nothing: I am not taught to make any 30 thing.
OLIVER. What mar you then, sir?
ORLANDO. Marry, sir, I am helping you to mar that which God made, a poor unworthy brother of yours, with idleness.
OLIVER. Marry, sir, be better employed, and be naught awhile.
ORLANDO. Shall I keep your hogs and eat husks with them? What prodigal portion have I spent, that I should come to such penury? 40
OLIVER. Know you where you are, sir?
ORLANDO. O, sir, very well: here in your orchard.
OLIVER. Know you before whom, sir?
ORLANDO. Ay, better than him I am before knows me ... I know you are my eldest brother, and in the gentle condition of blood you should so know me ... The courtesy of nations allows you my better, in that you are the first-born, but the same tradition takes not away my blood, were there twenty brothers betwixt us: I have as much of my father in 50 me as you, albeit I confess your coming before me is nearer to his reverence.
OLIVER. What, boy! *He strikes him*
ORLANDO. Come, come, elder brother, you are too young in this. *He takes him by the throat*
OLIVER. Wilt thou lay hands on me, villain?
ORLANDO. I am no villain: I am the youngest son of Sir Rowland de Boys, he was my father, and he is thrice a villain that says such a father begot villains ... Wert thou not my brother, I would not take this 60 hand from thy throat, till this other had pulled out thy tongue for saying so—thou hast railed on thyself.
ADAM. Sweet masters, be patient. For your father's remembrance, be at accord.
OLIVER. Let me go, I say.
ORLANDO. I will not till I please: you shall hear me ... My father charged you in his will to give me good education: you have trained me like a peasant, obscuring and hiding from me all gentleman-like 70 qualities ... The spirit of my father grows strong in me, and I will no longer endure it: therefore allow me such exercises as may become a gentleman, or give me the poor allottery my father left me by testament—with that I will go buy my fortunes.
OLIVER. And what wilt thou do? beg when that is spent? Well, sir, get you in: I will not long be troubled with you: you shall have some part of your 'will.' I pray you, leave me.
ORLANDO. I will no further offend you than becomes 80 me for my good. *He turns to go*
OLIVER. Get you with him, you old dog.
ADAM. Is 'old dog' my reward? Most true, I have lost my teeth in your service ... God be with my old master! he would not have spoke such a word.
Orlando and Adam depart
OLIVER. Is it even so? begin you to grow upon me? I will physic your rankness, and yet give no thous-and crowns neither ... Holla, Dennis!

Dennis enters

DENNIS. Calls your worship?
OLIVER. Was not Charles, the duke's wrestler, here to 90 speak with me?
DENNIS. So please you, he is here at the door, and importunes access to you.
OLIVER. Call him in ... [*Dennis goes*] 'Twill be a good way ... and to-morrow the wrestling is.

Charles enters

CHARLES. Good morrow to your worship.
OLIVER. Good Monsieur Charles ... What's the new news at the new court?
CHARLES. There's no news at the court, sir, but the old news: that is, the old duke is banished by his younger 100 brother the new duke, and three or four loving lords have put themselves into voluntary exile with him, whose lands and revenues enrich the new duke, therefore he gives them good leave to wander.
OLIVER. Can you tell if Rosalind, the duke's daughter, be banished with her father?
CHARLES. O, no; for the duke's daughter, her cousin, so loves her—being ever from their cradles bred together—that she would have followed her exile,

or have died to stay behind her . . . She is at the court, 110
and no less beloved of her uncle than his own
daughter—and never two ladies loved as they do.

OLIVER. Where will the old duke live?

CHARLES. They say he is already in the forest of Arden,
and a many merry men with him; and there they live
like the old Robin Hood of England: they say many
young gentlemen flock to him every day, and fleet
the time carelessly as they did in the golden world.

OLIVER. What, you wrestle to-morrow before the new
duke? 120

CHARLES. Marry, do I, sir: and I came to acquaint you
with a matter . . . I am given, sir, secretly to understand that your younger brother, Orlando, hath a
disposition to come in disguised against me to try a
fall: to-morrow, sir, I wrestle for my credit, and he
that escapes me without some broken limb shall
acquit him well: your brother is but young and
tender, and for your love I would be loath to foil
him, as I must for my own honour if he come in:
therefore, out of my love to you, I came hither 130
to acquaint you withal, that either you might stay
him from his intendment, or brook such disgrace
well as he shall run into, in that it is a thing of his
own search, and altogether against my will.

OLIVER. Charles, I thank thee for thy love to me, which
thou shalt find I will most kindly requite . . . I had
myself notice of my brother's purpose herein, and
have by underhand means laboured to dissuade him
from it; but he is resolute. . . . I'll tell thee, Charles—
it is the stubbornest young fellow of France, full of 140
ambition, an envious emulator of every man's good
parts, a secret and villanous contriver against me his
natural brother: therefore use thy discretion, I had as
lief thou didst break his neck as his finger. . . . And
thou wert best look to't; for if thou dost him any
slight disgrace, or if he do not mightily grace himself
on thee, he will practise against thee by poison,
entrap thee by some treacherous device, and never
leave thee till he hath ta'en thy life by some indirect
means or other: for, I assure thee (and almost with 150
tears I speak it), there is not one so young, and so
villanous this day living. . . . I speak but brotherly of
him, but should I anatomize him to thee as he is,
I must blush and weep, and thou must look pale and
wonder.

CHARLES. I am heartily glad I came hither to you . . .
If he come to-morrow, I'll give him his payment:
if ever he go alone again, I'll never wrestle for prize
more: and so, God keep your worship!

OLIVER. Farewell, good Charles. . . . [Charles goes] 160
Now will I stir this gamester: I hope I shall see
an end of him; for my soul (yet I know not why)
hates nothing more than he . . . Yet he's gentle, never
schooled and yet learned, full of noble device, of all
sorts enchantingly beloved, and indeed so much in
the heart of the world, and especially of my own
people, who best know him, that I am altogether
misprized: but it shall not be so long— this wrestler
shall clear all . . . Nothing remains but that I kindle
the boy thither, which now I'll go about. 170

He goes

Scene 2: *A lawn near the palace of Duke Frederick*
Enter Rosalind and Celia

CELIA. I pray thee, Rosalind, sweet my coz, be merry.

ROSALIND. Dear Celia, I show more mirth than I am
mistress of, and would you yet I were merrier?
Unless you could teach me to forget a banished
father, you must not learn me how to remember any
extraordinary pleasure.

CELIA. Herein, I see, thou lov'st me not with the full
weight that I love thee; if my uncle, thy banished
father, had banished thy uncle, the duke my father,
so thou hadst been still with me, I could have taught 10
my love to take thy father for mine; so wouldst
thou, if the truth of thy love to me were so
righteously tempered as mine is to thee.

ROSALIND. Well, I will forget the condition of my
estate, to rejoice in yours.

CELIA. You know my father hath no child but I, nor
none is like to have; and truly when he dies, thou
shalt be his heir: for what he hath taken away from
thy father perforce, I will render thee again in
affection . . . by mine honour I will, and when I 20
break that oath, let me turn monster: therefore, my
sweet Rose, my dear Rose, be merry.

ROSALIND. From henceforth I will, coz, and devise
sports . . . Let me see—what think you of falling
in love?

CELIA. Marry, I prithee, do, to make sport withal: but
love no man in good earnest, nor no further in sport
neither, than with safety of a pure blush thou mayst
in honour come off again.

ROSALIND. What shall be our sport then? 30

CELIA. Let us sit and mock the good housewife Fortune
from her wheel, that her gifts may henceforth be
bestowed equally.

ROSALIND. I would we could do so; for her benefits
are mightily misplaced, and the bountiful blind
woman doth most mistake in her gifts to women.

CELIA. 'Tis true, for those that she makes fair she scarce
makes honest, and those that she makes honest she
makes very ill-favouredly.

ROSALIND. Nay, now thou goest from Fortune's office 40
to Nature's: Fortune reigns in gifts of the world, not
in the lineaments of Nature.

Touchstone approaches

CELIA. No? When Nature hath made a fair creature,
may she not by Fortune fall into the fire? Though
Nature hath given us wit to flout at Fortune, hath
not Fortune sent in this fool to cut off the argument?

ROSALIND. Indeed, there is Fortune too hard for
Nature, when Fortune makes Nature's natural the
cutter-off of Nature's wit.

CELIA. Peradventure this is not Fortune's work 50
neither, but Nature's, who perceiveth our natural
wits too dull to reason of such goddesses and hath
sent this natural for our whetstone: for always the
dulness of the fool is the whetstone of the wits. . . .
How now, wit! whither wander you?

TOUCHSTONE. Mistress, you must come away to your
father.

CELIA. Were you made the messenger?

TOUCHSTONE. No, by mine honour, but I was bid to
come for you. 60

ROSALIND. Where learned you that oath, fool?

TOUCHSTONE. Of a certain knight, that swore by his
honour they were good pancakes, and swore by his
honour the mustard was naught: now I'll stand to it,

the pancakes were naught and the mustard was good, and yet was not the knight forsworn.

CELIA. How prove you that, in the great heap of your knowledge?

ROSALIND. Ay, marry, now unmuzzle your wisdom.

TOUCHSTONE. Stand you both forth now: stroke your 70 chins, and swear by your beards that I am a knave.

CELIA. By our beards (if we had them) thou art.

TOUCHSTONE. By my knavery (if I had it) then I were: but if you swear by that that is not, you are not forsworn: no more was this knight, swearing by his honour, for he never had any; or if he had, he had sworn it away, before ever he saw those pancakes or that mustard.

CELIA. Prithee, who is't that thou mean'st?

TOUCHSTONE [to Rosalind]. One that old Frederick, 80 your father, loves.

ROSALIND. My father's love is enough to honour him. Enough! speak no more of him—you'll be whipped for taxation one of these days.

TOUCHSTONE. The more pity, that fools may not speak wisely what wise men do foolishly.

CELIA. By my troth, thou sayest true: for since the little wit that fools have was silenced, the little foolery that wise men have makes a great show ... Here comes Monsieur Le Beau.   90

Le Beau enters

ROSALIND. With his mouth full of news.

CELIA. Which he will put on us, as pigeons feed their young.

ROSALIND. Then shall we be news-crammed.

CELIA. All the better: we shall be the more marketable. Bon jour, Monsieur Le Beau! what's the news?

LE BEAU. Fair princess, you have lost much good sport.

CELIA. Sport? Of what colour?

LE BEAU. What colour, madam? How shall I answer you?   100

ROSALIND. As wit and fortune will.

TOUCHSTONE. Or as the Destinies decree.

CELIA. Well said, that was laid on with a trowel.

TOUCHSTONE. Nay, if I keep not my rank—

ROSALIND. Thou losest thy old smell.

LE BEAU. You amaze me, ladies: I would have told you of good wrestling, which you have lost the sight of.

ROSALIND. Yet tell us the manner of the wrestling.

LE BEAU. I will tell you the beginning, and, if it please your ladyships, you may see the end—for the best 110 is yet to do, and here, where you are, they are coming to perform it.

CELIA. Well, the beginning, that is dead and buried?

LE BEAU. There comes an old man and his three sons—

CELIA. I could match this beginning with an old tale.

LE BEAU. Three proper young men, of excellent growth and presence.

ROSALIND. With bills on their necks: 'Be it known unto all men by these presents.'

LE BEAU. The eldest of the three wrestled with Charles, 120 the duke's wrestler, which Charles in a moment threw him and broke three of his ribs, that there is little hope of life in him: so he served the second, and so the third ... Yonder they lie, the poor old man their father making such pitiful dole over them that all the beholders take his part with weeping.

ROSALIND. Alas!

TOUCHSTONE. But what is the sport, monsieur, that the ladies have lost?

LE BEAU. Why, this that I speak of.   130

TOUCHSTONE. Thus men may grow wiser every day. It is the first time that ever I heard breaking of ribs was sport for ladies.

CELIA. Or I, I promise thee.

ROSALIND. But is there any else longs to see this broken music in his sides? is there yet another dotes upon rib-breaking? Shall we see this wrestling, cousin?

LE BEAU. You must if you stay here, for here is the place appointed for the wrestling, and they are ready to perform it.   140

CELIA. Yonder, sure, they are coming.... Let us now stay and see it.

A flourish of trumpets. Enter Duke Frederick with his lords, Orlando, Charles, and attendants

DUKE FREDERICK. Come on. Since the youth will not be entreated, his own peril on his forwardness.

ROSALIND. Is yonder the man?

LE BEAU. Even he, madam.

CELIA. Alas, he is too young: yet he looks successfully.

DUKE FREDERICK. How now, daughter and cousin! are you crept hither to see the wrestling?

ROSALIND. Ay, my liege, so please you give us leave. 150

DUKE FREDERICK. You will take little delight in it, I can tell you, there is such odds in the man ... In pity of the challenger's youth I would fain dissuade him, but he will not be entreated.... Speak to him, ladies —see if you can move him.

CELIA. Call him hither, good Monsieur Le Beau.

DUKE FREDERICK. Do so: I'll not be by.

LE BEAU. Monsieur the challenger, the princess calls for you.

ORLANDO. I attend them with all respect and duty.   160

ROSALIND. Young man, have you challenged Charles the wrestler?

ORLANDO. No, fair princess: he is the general challenger. I come but in, as others do, to try with him the strength of my youth.

CELIA. Young gentleman, your spirits are too bold for your years ... You have seen cruel proof of this man's strength. If you saw yourself with your eyes, or knew yourself with your judgement, the fear of your adventure would counsel you to a more equal 170 enterprise.... We pray you, for your own sake, to embrace your own safety, and give over this attempt.

ROSALIND. Do, young sir, your reputation shall not therefore be misprized: we will make it our suit to the duke that the wrestling might not go forward.

ORLANDO. I beseech you, punish me not with your hard thoughts, wherein I confess me much guilty to deny so fair and excellent ladies any thing. But let your fair eyes and gentle wishes go with me to my 180 trial: wherein if I be foiled, there is but one shamed that was never gracious; if killed, but one dead that is willing to be so: I shall do my friends no wrong, for I have none to lament me; the world no injury, for in it I have nothing: only in the world I fill up a place, which may be better supplied when I have made it empty.

ROSALIND. The little strength that I have, I would it were with you.

CELIA. And mine, to eke out hers.   190

ROSALIND. Fare you well ... Pray heaven, I be deceived in you!

CELIA. Your heart's desires be with you!

CHARLES. Come, where is this young gallant that is so desirous to lie with his mother earth?

ORLANDO. Ready, sir, but his will hath in it a more modest working.

DUKE FREDERICK. You shall try but one fall.

CHARLES. No, I warrant your grace, you shall not entreat him to a second, that have so mightily   200
persuaded him from a first.

ORLANDO. An you mean to mock me after, you should not have mocked me before: but come your ways.

ROSALIND. Now, Hercules be thy speed, young man!

CELIA. I would I were invisible, to catch the strong fellow by the leg.   *The wrestling begins*

ROSALIND. O excellent young man!

CELIA. If I had a thunderbolt in mine eye, I can tell who should down.
                  Charles is thrown; a great shout

DUKE FREDERICK. No more, no more.   210

ORLANDO. Yes, I beseech your grace—I am not yet well breathed.

DUKE FREDERICK. How dost thou, Charles?

LE BEAU.   He cannot speak, my lord.

DUKE FREDERICK. Bear him away ...
            They take up Charles and carry him out
                  What is thy name, young man?

ORLANDO. Orlando, my liege; the youngest son of Sir Rowland de Boys.

DUKE FREDERICK. I would thou hadst been son to some man else.
The world esteemed thy father honourable,
But I did find him still mine enemy:
Thou shouldst have better pleased me with this deed,   220
Hadst thou descended from another house:
But fare thee well, thou art a gallant youth.
I would thou hadst told me of another father.
      Duke Frederick, Le Beau and the other lords depart

CELIA. Were I my father, coz, would I do this?

ORLANDO. I am more proud to be Sir Rowland's son,
His youngest son, and would not change that calling,
To be adopted heir to Frederick.

ROSALIND. My father loved Sir Rowland as his soul,
And all the world was of my father's mind.
Had I before known this young man his son,   230
I should have given him tears unto entreaties,
Ere he should thus have ventured.

CELIA.   Gentle cousin,
Let us go thank him, and encourage him:
My father's rough and envious disposition
Sticks me at heart ... Sir, you have well deserved.
If you do keep your promises in love
But justly as you have exceeded promise,
Your mistress shall be happy.

ROSALIND [*takes a chain from her neck*]. Gentleman,
Wear this for me ... one out of suits with fortune,
That could give more, but that her hand lacks means....   240
Shall we go, coz?

CELIA.   Ay: fare you well, fair gentleman.

ORLANDO. Can I not say, 'I thank you'? My better parts
Are all thrown down, and that which here stands up

Is but a quintain, a mere lifeless block.

ROSALIND. He calls us back: my pride fell with my fortunes—
I'll ask him what he would ... Did you call, sir?
Sir, you have wrestled well and overthrown
More than your enemies.

CELIA.   Will you go, coz?

ROSALIND. Have with you ... Fare you well.
                  She goes, Celia following

ORLANDO. What passion hangs these weights upon my tongue?   250
I cannot speak to her, yet she urged conference.

Le Beau returns

O poor Orlando, thou art overthrown!
Or Charles, or something weaker, masters thee.

LE BEAU. Good sir, I do in friendship counsel you
To leave this place ... Albeit you have deserved
High commendation, true applause, and love,
Yet such is now the duke's condition,
That he misconstrues all that you have done ...
The duke is humorous—what he is, indeed,
More suits you to conceive than I to speak of.   260

ORLANDO. I thank you, sir: and, pray you, tell me this,
Which of the two was daughter of the duke,
That here was at the wrestling?

LE BEAU. Neither his daughter, if we judge by manners,
But yet, indeed, the smaller is his daughter.
The other is daughter to the banished duke,
And here detained by her usurping uncle,
To keep his daughter company—whose loves
Are dearer than the natural bond of sisters ...
But I can tell you that of late this duke   270
Hath ta'en displeasure 'gainst his gentle niece,
Grounded upon no other argument
But that the people praise her for her virtues,
And pity her for her good father's sake;
And, on my life, his malice 'gainst the lady
Will suddenly break forth ... Sir, fare you well.
Hereafter, in a better world than this,
I shall desire more love and knowledge of you.

ORLANDO. I rest much bounden to you: fare you well....   *Le Beau goes*
Thus must I from the smoke into the smother,   280
From tyrant duke unto a tyrant brother....
But heavenly Rosalind!   *He departs*

Scene 3: *A room in the palace of Duke Frederick*

Enter Rosalind and Celia

CELIA. Why cousin, why Rosalind ... Cupid have mercy! Not a word?

ROSALIND. Not one to throw at a dog.

CELIA. No, thy words are too precious to be cast away upon curs, throw some of them at me; come, lame me with reasons.

ROSALIND. Then there were two cousins laid up, when the one should be lamed with reasons, and the other mad without any.

CELIA. But is all this for your father?   10

ROSALIND. No, some of it is for my child's father ...
O, how full of briars is this working-day world!

CELIA. They are but burs, cousin, thrown upon thee

in holiday foolery. If we walk not in the trodden
paths, our very petticoats will catch them.
ROSALIND. I could shake them off my coat—these burs
are in my heart.
CELIA. Hem them away.
ROSALIND. I would try, if I could cry 'hem' and have
him.   20
CELIA. Come, come, wrestle with thy affections.
ROSALIND. O, they take the part of a better wrestler
than myself.
CELIA. O, a good wish upon you! you will try in time,
in despite of a fall. . . . But turning these jests out of
service, let us talk in good earnest: is it possible, on
such a sudden, you should fall into so strong a liking
with old Sir Rowland's youngest son?
ROSALIND. The duke my father loved his father dearly.
CELIA. Doth it therefore ensue that you should love   30
his son dearly? By this kind of chase, I should hate
him, for my father hated his father dearly; yet I hate
not Orlando.
ROSALIND. No, faith, hate him not, for my sake.
CELIA. Why should I not? doth he not deserve well?
ROSALIND. Let me love him for that, and do you love
him because I do. . . . [Duke Frederick enters, preceded
by attendants and the lords of his council] Look, here
comes the duke.
CELIA. With his eyes full of anger.   40
DUKE FREDERICK. Mistress, dispatch you with your
safest haste
And get you from our court.
ROSALIND.   Me, uncle?
DUKE FREDERICK.   You, cousin.
Within these ten days if that thou be'st found
So near our public court as twenty miles,
Thou diest for it.
ROSALIND.   I do beseech your grace,
Let me the knowledge of my fault bear with me:
If with myself I hold intelligence
Or have acquaintance with mine own desires,
If that I do not dream or be not frantic—
As I do trust I am not—then, dear uncle,   50
Never so much as in a thought unborn
Did I offend your highness.
DUKE FREDERICK.   Thus do all traitors!
If their purgation did consist in words,
They are as innocent as grace itself:
Let it suffice thee that I trust thee not.
ROSALIND. Yet your mistrust cannot make me a
traitor:
Tell me whereon the likelihood depends.
DUKE FREDERICK. Thou art thy father's daughter,
there's enough.
ROSALIND. So was I when your highness took his
dukedom,
So was I when your highness banished him;   60
Treason is not inherited, my lord,
Or, if we did derive it from our friends,
What's that to me? my father was no traitor,
Then, good my liege, mistake me not so much
To think my poverty is treacherous.
CELIA. Dear sovereign, hear me speak.
DUKE FREDERICK. Ay, Celia, we stayed her for your
sake,
Else had she with her father ranged along.
CELIA. I did not then entreat to have her stay,
It was your pleasure and your own remorse.   70

I was too young that time to value her,
But now I know her: if she be a traitor,
Why so am I: we still have slept together,
Rose at an instant, learned, played, eat together,
And wheresoe'er we went, like Juno's swans,
Still we went coupled and inseparable.
DUKE FREDERICK. She is too subtle for thee, and her
smoothness,
Her very silence and her patience
Speak to the people, and they pity her . . .
Thou art a fool—she robs thee of thy name,   80
And thou wilt show more bright and seem more
virtuous
When she is gone: then open not thy lips.
Firm and irrevocable is my doom
Which I have passed upon her—she is banished.
CELIA. Pronounce that sentence then on me, my liege,
I cannot live out of her company.
DUKE FREDERICK. You are a fool . . . You, niece,
provide yourself.
If you outstay the time, upon mine honour,
And in the greatness of my word, you die.
                         He leaves, his lords following him
CELIA. O my poor Rosalind, whither wilt thou go?   90
Wilt thou change fathers? I will give thee mine . . .
I charge thee, be not thou more grieved than I am.
ROSALIND. I have more cause.
CELIA.   Thou hast not, cousin.
Prithee, be cheerful; know'st thou not, the duke
Hath banished me his daughter?
ROSALIND.   That he hath not.
CELIA. No, hath not? Rosalind lacks then the love
Which teacheth thee that thou and I am one.
Shall we be sundred? shall we part, sweet girl?
No, let my father seek another heir . . .
Therefore devise with me how we may fly,   100
Whither to go and what to bear with us,
And do not seek to take your change upon you,
To bear your griefs yourself and leave me out;
For, by this heaven, now at our sorrows pale,
Say what thou canst, I'll go along with thee.
ROSALIND. Why, whither shall we go?
CELIA. To seek my uncle in the forest of Arden.
ROSALIND. Alas, what danger will it be to us,
Maids as we are, to travel forth so far!
Beauty provoketh thieves sooner than gold.   110
CELIA. I'll put myself in poor and mean attire,
And with a kind of umber smirch my face,
The like do you, so shall we pass along
And never stir assailants.
ROSALIND.   Were it not better,
Because that I am more than common tall,
That I did suit me all points like a man?
A gallant curtle-axe upon my thigh,
A boar-spear in my hand, and in my heart
Lie there what hidden woman's fear there will,
We'll have a swashing and a martial outside,   120
As many other mannish cowards have
That do outface it with their semblances.
CELIA. What shall I call thee when thou art a man?
ROSALIND. I'll have no worse a name than Jove's
own page,
And therefore look you call me Ganymede.
But what will you be called?
CELIA. Something that hath a reference to my state;
No longer Celia, but Aliena.

ROSALIND. But, cousin, what if we assayed to steal
The clownish fool out of your father's court? 130
Would he not be a comfort to our travel?
CELIA. He'll go along o'er the wide world with me,
Leave me alone to woo him ... Let's away,
And get our jewels and our wealth together,
Devise the fittest time and safest way
To hide us from pursuit that will be made
After my flight ... Now go we in content
To liberty, and not to banishment. *They go*

ACT 2
Scene 1: *The forest of Arden*

Enter the exiled Duke, Amiens, and two or three Lords like foresters

DUKE. Now, my co-mates and brothers in exile,
Hath not old custom made this life more sweet
Than that of painted pomp? Are not these woods
More free from peril than the envious court?
Here feel we not the penalty of Adam,
The seasons' difference?—as the icy fang
And churlish chiding of the winter's wind,
Which, when it bites and blows upon my body,
Even till I shrink with cold, I smile and say
'This is no flattery: these are counsellors 10
That feelingly persuade me what I am' ...
Sweet are the uses of adversity,
Which like the toad, ugly and venomous,
Wears yet a precious jewel in his head:
And this our life, exempt from public haunt,
Finds tongues in trees, books in the running brooks,
Sermons in stones, and good in every thing.
I would not change it.
AMIENS. Happy is your grace,
That can translate the stubbornness of fortune
Into so quiet and so sweet a style. 20
DUKE. Come, shall we go and kill us venison?
And yet it irks me the poor dappled fools,
Being native burghers of this desert city,
Should in their own confines with forkéd heads
Have their round haunches gored.
FIRST LORD. Indeed, my lord,
The melancholy Jaques grieves at that,
And, in that kind, swears you do more usurp
Than doth your brother that hath banished you:
To-day my Lord of Amiens and myself
Did steal behind him as he lay along 30
Under an oak, whose antique root peeps out
Upon the brook that brawls along this wood,
To the which place a poor sequestred stag,
That from the hunter's aim had ta'en a hurt,
Did come to languish; and, indeed, my lord,
The wretched animal heaved forth such groans,
That their discharge did stretch his leathern coat
Almost to bursting, and the big round tears
Coursed one another down his innocent nose
In piteous chase: and thus the hairy fool, 40
Much markéd of the melancholy Jaques,
Stood on th'extremest verge of the swift brook,
Augmenting it with tears.
DUKE. But what said Jaques?
Did he not moralize this spectacle?
FIRST LORD. O, yes, into a thousand similes.
First, for his weeping in the needless stream;

'Poor deer,' quoth he, 'thou mak'st a testament
As worldlings do, giving thy sum of more
To that which had too much': then, being there
alone,
Left and abandoned of his velvet friends; 50
''Tis right,' quoth he, 'thus misery doth part
The flux of company': anon a careless herd,
Full of the pasture, jumps along by him
And never stays to greet him; 'Ay,' quoth Jaques,
'Sweep on, you fat and greasy citizens!
'Tis just the fashion; wherefore do you look
Upon that poor and broken bankrupt there?'
Thus most invectively he pierceth through
The body of the country, city, court,
Yea, and of this our life, swearing that we 60
Are mere usurpers, tyrants and what's worse,
To fright the animals and to kill them up
In their assigned and native dwelling-place.
DUKE. And did you leave him in this contemplation?
SECOND LORD. We did, my lord, weeping and
commenting
Upon the sobbing deer.
DUKE. Show me the place,
I love to cope him in these sullen fits,
For then he's full of matter.
FIRST LORD. I'll bring you to him straight.
They go

Scene 2: *A room in the palace of Duke Frederick*

Enter Duke Frederick, lords, and attendants

DUKE FREDERICK. Can it be possible that no man
saw them?
It cannot be. Some villains of my court
Are of consent and sufferance in this.
FIRST LORD. I cannot hear of any that did see her.
The ladies, her attendants of her chamber,
Saw her abed, and in the morning early
They found the bed untreasured of their mistress.
SECOND LORD. My lord, the roynish clown, at whom
so oft
Your grace was wont to laugh, is also missing.
Hisperia, the princess' gentlewoman, 10
Confesses that she secretly o'erheard
Your daughter and her cousin much commend
The parts and graces of the wrestler
That did but lately foil the sinewy Charles,
And she believes wherever they are gone
That youth is surely in their company.
DUKE FREDERICK. Send to his brother, fetch that
gallant hither.
If he be absent, bring his brother to me—
I'll make him find him: do this suddenly;
And let not search and inquisition quail 20
To bring again these foolish runaways.
They go

Scene 3: *The orchard near Oliver's house*

Enter Orlando and Adam, meeting

ORLANDO. Who's there?
ADAM. What! my young master? O my gentle master,
O my sweet master, O you memory
Of old Sir Rowland ... why, what make you here?
Why are you virtuous? Why do people love you?
And wherefore are you gentle, strong, and valiant?

Why would you be so fond to overcome
The bonny prizer of the humorous duke?
Your praise is come too swiftly home before you.
Know you not, master, to some kind of men   10
Their graces serve them but as enemies?
No more do yours; your virtues, gentle master,
And sanctified and holy traitors to you …
O, what a world is this, when what is comely
Envenoms him that bears it!

ORLANDO. Why, what's the matter?

ADAM.   O unhappy youth,
Come not within these doors; within this roof
The enemy of all your graces lives …
Your brother—no, no brother—yet the son
(Yet not the son, I will not call him son)   20
Of him I was about to call his father—
Hath heard your praises, and this night he means
To burn the lodging where you use to lie,
And you within it: if he fail of that,
He will have other means to cut you off:
I overheard him … and his practices …
This is no place, this house is but a butchery;
Abhor it, fear it, do not enter it.

ORLANDO. Why, whither, Adam, wouldst thou have
  me go?

ADAM. No matter whither, so you come not here.   30

ORLANDO. What, wouldst thou have me go and beg
  my food?
Or with a base and boisterous sword enforce
A thievish living on the common road?
This I must do, or know not what to do:
Yet this I will not do, do how I can—
I rather will subject me to the malice
Of a diverted blood and bloody brother.

ADAM. But do not so: I have five hundred crowns,
The thrifty hire I saved under your father,
Which I did store to be my foster-nurse   40
When service should in my old limbs lie lame,
And unregarded age in corners thrown.
Take that, and He that doth the ravens feed,
Yea providently caters for the sparrow,
Be comfort to my age … Here is the gold;
All this I give you. Let me be your servant.
Though I look old, yet I am strong and lusty;
For in my youth I never did apply
Hot and rebellious liquors in my blood,
Nor did not with unbashful forehead woo   50
The means of weakness and debility.
Therefore my age is as a lusty winter,
Frosty, but kindly: let me go with you,
I'll do the service of a younger man
In all your business and necessities.

ORLANDO. O good old man, how well in thee appears
The constant service of the antique world,
When service sweat for duty, not for meed!
Thou art not for the fashion of these times,
Where none will sweat but for promotion,   60
And having that do choke their service up
Even with the having—it is not so with thee …
But, poor old man, thou prun'st a rotten tree,
That cannot so much as a blossom yield,
In lieu of all thy pains and husbandry.
But come thy ways, we'll go along together,
And ere we have thy youthful wages spent,
We'll light upon some settled low content.

ADAM. Master, go on, and I will follow thee

To the last gasp with truth and loyalty.   70
From seventeen years till now almost fourscore
Here lived I, but now live here no more.
At seventeen years many their fortunes seek,
But at fourscore it is too late a week.
Yet fortune cannot recompense me better
Than to die well, and not my master's debtor.
                                        They leave

Scene 4: *The forest*

*Enter Rosalind (as Ganymede) in forester's dress, and Celia
(as Aliena) clad as a shepherdess, with Touchstone*

ROSALIND. O Jupiter! how weary are my spirits!

TOUCHSTONE. I care not for my spirits, if my legs were
  not weary.

ROSALIND. I could find in my heart to disgrace my
  man's apparel, and to cry like a woman: but I must
  comfort the weaker vessel, as doublet-and-hose
  ought to show itself courageous to petticoat: therefore courage, good Aliena!

CELIA. I pray you, bear with me, I cannot go no   10
  further.

TOUCHSTONE. For my part, I had rather bear with you
  than bear you: yet I should bear no cross if I did
  bear you, for I think you have no money in your
  purse.

ROSALIND. Well, this is the forest of Arden!

TOUCHSTONE. Ay, now am I in Arden, the more fool I.
  When I was at home I was in a better place, but
  travellers must be content.

ROSALIND.   Ay,
Be so, good Touchstone …

Corin and Silvius enter

                          Look you, who comes here—
A young man and an old in solemn talk.   20

CORIN. That is the way to make her scorn you still.

SILVIUS. O Corin, that thou knew'st how I do love
  her!

CORIN. I partly guess: for I have loved ere now.

SILVIUS. No, Corin, being old, thou canst not guess,
Though in thy youth thou wast as true a lover
As ever sighed upon a midnight pillow:
But if thy love were ever like to mine—
As sure I think did never man love so—
How many actions most ridiculous
Hast thou been drawn to by thy fantasy?   30

CORIN. Into a thousand that I have forgotten.

SILVIUS. O, thou didst then ne'er love so heartily.
If thou remembrest not the slightest folly
That ever love did make thee run into,
Thou hast not loved….
Or if thou hast not sat as I do now,
Wearing thy hearer in thy mistress' praise,
Thou hast not loved….
Or if thou hast not broke from company
Abruptly, as my passion now makes me,   40
Thou hast not loved….
O Phebe, Phebe, Phebe!   *He goes*

ROSALIND. Alas, poor shepherd! searching of thy
  wound, I have by hard adventure found mine own.

TOUCHSTONE. And I mine: I remember, when I was
  in love I broke my sword upon a stone, and bid him
  take that for coming a-night to Jane Smile, and I
  remember the kissing of her batler and the cow's

dugs that her pretty chopt hands had milked; and I
remember the wooing of a peascod instead of her, 50
from whom I took two cods, and giving her them
again, said with weeping tears, 'Wear these for my
sake' ... We that are true lovers run into strange
capers; but as all is mortal in nature, so is all nature in
love mortal in folly.
ROSALIND. Thou speak'st wiser than thou art ware of.
TOUCHSTONE. Nay, I shall ne'er be ware of mine own
    wit till I break my shins against it.
ROSALIND. Jove, Jove! this shepherd's passion
            Is much upon my fashion.   60
TOUCHSTONE. And mine—but it grows something
    stale with me.
CELIA. I pray you, one of you question yond man
    If he for gold will give us any food,
    I faint almost to death.
TOUCHSTONE.   Holla; you, clown!
ROSALIND. Peace, fool, he's not thy kinsman.
CORIN.   Who calls?
TOUCHSTONE. Your betters, sir.
CORIN.   Else are they very wretched.
ROSALIND. Peace, I say ... Good even to you, friend.
CORIN. And to you, gentle sir, and to you all.
ROSALIND. I prithee, shepherd, if that love or gold
    Can in this desert place buy entertainment,   70
    Bring us where we may rest ourselves and feed:
    Here's a young maid with travel much oppressed,
    And faints for succour.
CORIN.   Fair sir, I pity her,
    And wish, for her sake more than for mine own,
    My fortunes were more able to relieve her:
    But I am shepherd to another man,
    And do not shear the fleeces that I graze:
    My master is of churlish disposition,
    And little recks to find the way to heaven   80
    By doing deeds of hospitality:
    Besides, his cote, his flocks and bounds of feed
    Are now on sale, and at our sheepcote now
    By reason of his absence there is nothing
    That you will feed on; but what is, come see,
    And in my voice most welcome shall you be.
ROSALIND. What is he that shall buy his flock and
    pasture?
CORIN. That young swain that you saw here but
    erewhile,
    That little cares for buying any thing.
ROSALIND. I pray thee, if it stand with honesty,
    Buy thou the cottage, pasture, and the flock,   90
    And thou shalt have to pay for it of us.
CELIA. And we will mend thy wages: I like this place,
    And willingly could waste my time in it.
CORIN. Assuredly, the thing is to be sold ...
    Go with me. If you like upon report
    The soil, the profit, and this kind of life,
    I will your very faithful feeder be,
    And buy it with your gold right suddenly.
                      He goes; they follow him

                Scene 5: The forest

Enter Amiens, Jaques, and others

AMIENS [sings].
            Under the greenwood tree,
            Who loves to lie with me,
            And turn his merry note

            Unto the sweet bird's throat ...
            Come hither, come hither, come hither:
                Here shall he see
                No enemy,
            But winter and rough weather.
JAQUES. More, more, I prithee, more.
AMIENS. It will make you melancholy, Monsieur 10
    Jaques.
JAQUES. I thank it ... More, I prithee, more. I can
    suck melancholy out of a song, as a weasel sucks eggs
    ... More, I prithee, more.
AMIENS. My voice is ragged, I know I cannot please
    you.
JAQUES. I do not desire you to please me, I do desire
    you to sing ... Come, more, another stanzo: call
    you 'em stanzos?
AMIENS. What you will, Monsieur Jaques.   20
JAQUES. Nay, I care not for their names, they owe me
    nothing ... Will you sing?
AMIENS. More at your request than to please myself.
JAQUES. Well then, if ever I thank any man, I'll thank
    you: but that they call compliment is like
    th'encounter of two dog-apes; and when a man
    thanks me heartily, methinks I have given him a
    penny and he renders me the beggarly thanks....
    Come, sing; and you that will not, hold your
    tongues.   30
AMIENS. Well, I'll end the song.... Sirs, cover the
    while—the duke will drink under this tree ... He
    hath been all this day to look you.
JAQUES. And I have been all this day to avoid him ...
    He is too disputable for my company ... I think of as
    many matters as he, but I give heaven thanks, and
    make no boast of them.... Come, warble, come.

They sing altogether here
            Who doth ambition shun,
            And loves to live i'th' sun ...
            Seeking the food he eats,
            And pleased with what he gets ...   40
        Come hither, come hither, come hither:
                Here shall he see
                No enemy,
            But winter and rough weather.
JAQUES. I'll give you a verse to this note, that I made
    yesterday in despite of my invention.
AMIENS. And I'll sing it.
JAQUES. Thus it goes: Gives a paper to Amiens
AMIENS.   If it do come to pass,   50
            That any man turn ass ...
            Leaving his wealth and ease,
            A stubborn will to please,
        Ducdame, ducdame, ducdame:
                Here shall he see,
                Gross fools as he,
            An if he will come to me.
    What's that 'ducdame'?
JAQUES. 'Tis a Greek invocation, to call fools into a
    circle.... I'll go sleep, if I can: if I cannot, I'll rail 60
    against all the first-born of Egypt.
AMIENS. And I'll go seek the duke; his banquet is
    prepared.   They depart in different directions

                Scene 6: The forest

Orlando and Adam approach

ADAM. Dear master, I can go no further: O, I die for

food.... Here lie I down, and measure out my
grave.... Farewell, kind master.
ORLANDO. Why, how now, Adam! no greater heart in
thee? Live a little, comfort a little, cheer thyself a
little. If this uncouth forest yield any thing savage,
I will either be food for it or bring it for food to thee
... Thy conceit is nearer death than thy powers....
For my sake be comfortable—hold death awhile at
the arm's end: I will here be with thee presently, and   10
if I bring thee not something to eat, I will give thee
leave to die: but if thou diest before I come, thou art
a mocker of my labour.... Well said! thou look'st
cheerly, and I'll be with thee quickly ... Yet thou
liest in the bleak air.... Come, I will bear thee
to some shelter—and thou shalt not die for lack of a
dinner, if there live any thing in this desert....
Cheerly, good Adam!   *He carries him away*

Scene 7: *The forest*

Enter the Duke and some of his lords

DUKE. I think he be transformed into a beast,
   For I can no where find him like a man.
FIRST LORD. My lord, he is but even now gone hence,
   Here was he merry, hearing of a song.
DUKE. If he, compact of jars, grow musical,
   We shall have shortly discord in the spheres:
   Go, seek him, tell him I would speak with him.

Jaques enters, and shortly behind him Amiens

FIRST LORD. He saves my labour by his own approach.
DUKE. Why, how now, monsieur! what a life is this,
   That your poor friends must woo your company?   10
   What, you look merrily!
JAQUES. A fool, a fool! I met a fool i'th' forest,
   A motley fool—a miserable world!—
   As I do live by food, I met a fool,
   Who laid him down and basked him in the sun,
   And railed on Lady Fortune in good terms,
   In good set terms, and yet a motley fool....
   'Good morrow, fool,' quoth I: 'No, sir,' quoth he,
   'Call me not fool till heaven hath sent me fortune.'
   And then he drew a dial from his poke,   20
   And looking on it with lack-lustre eye,
   Says very wisely, 'It is ten o'clock:
   Thus we may see,' quoth he, 'how the world wags:
   'Tis but an hour ago since it was nine,
   And after one hour more 'twill be eleven,
   And so from hour to hour, we ripe, and ripe,
   And then from hour to hour, we rot, and rot—
   And thereby hangs a tale.' ... When I did hear
   The motley fool thus moral on the time,
   My lungs began to crow like chanticleer,   30
   That fools should be so deep-contemplative;
   And I did laugh, sans intermission,
   An hour by his dial.... O noble fool!
   O worthy fool! Motley's the only wear.
DUKE. What fool is this?
JAQUES. A worthy fool ... one that hath been a
      courtier,
   And says, if ladies be but young and fair,
   They have the gift to know it: and in his brain,
   Which is as dry as the remainder biscuit
   After a voyage, he hath strange places crammed   40
   With observation, the which he vents
   In mangled forms.... O, that I were a fool!

I am ambitious for a motley coat.
DUKE. Thou shalt have one.
JAQUES.   It is my only suit—
   Provided that you weed your better judgements
   Of all opinion that grows rank in them
   That I am wise.... I must have liberty
   Withal, as large a charter as the wind,
   To blow on whom I please, for so fools have:
   And they that are most galléd with my folly,   50
   They most must laugh: and why, sir, must they so?
   The 'why' is plain as way to parish church:
   He that a fool doth very wisely hit
   Doth very foolishly, although he smart,
   Not to seem senseless of the bob: if not,
   The wise man's folly is anatomized
   Even by the squand'ring glances of the fool....
   Invest me in my motley; give me leave
   To speak my mind, and I will through and through
   Cleanse the foul body of th'infected world,   60
   If they will patiently receive my medicine.
DUKE. Fie on thee! I can tell what thou wouldst do.
JAQUES. What, for a counter, would I do but good?
DUKE. Most mischievous foul sin, in chiding sin:
   For thou thyself hast been a libertine,
   As sensual as the brutish sting itself,
   And all th'embosséd sores and headed evils,
   That thou with licence of free foot hast caught,
   Wouldst thou disgorge into the general world.
JAQUES. Why, who cries out on pride,   70
   That can therein tax any private party?
   Doth it not flow as hugely as the sea,
   Till that the weary very means do ebb?
   What woman in the city do I name,
   When that I say the city-woman bears
   The cost of princes on unworthy shoulders?
   Who can come in and say that I mean her,
   When such a one as she such is her neighbour?
   Or what is he of basest function,
   That says his bravery is not on my cost,   80
   Thinking that I mean him, but therein suits
   His folly to the mettle of my speech?
   There then!—how then? what then? Let me see
      wherein
   My tongue hath wronged him: if it do him right,
   Then he hath wronged himself; if he be free,
   Why then my taxing like a wild-goose flies,
   Unclaimed of any man.... But who comes here?

Orlando appears before them, with his sword drawn

ORLANDO. Forbear, and eat no more.
JAQUES.   Why, I have eat none yet.
ORLANDO. Nor shalt not, till necessity be served.
JAQUES. Of what kind should this cock come of?   90
DUKE. Art thou thus boldened, man, by thy distress?
   Or else a rude despiser of good manners,
   That in civility thou seem'st so empty?
ORLANDO. You touched my vein at first. The thorny
      point
   Of bare distress hath ta'en from me the show
   Of smooth civility: yet am I inland bred,
   And know some nurture ... But forbear, I say,
   He dies that touches any of this fruit
   Till I and my affairs are answeréd.
JAQUES. An you will, not be answered with reason,   100
   I must die.

DUKE. What would you have? Your gentleness shall force,
More than your force move us to gentleness.
ORLANDO. I almost die for food, and let me have it.
DUKE. Sit down and feed, and welcome to our table.
ORLANDO. Speak you so gently? Pardon me, I pray you—
I though that all things had been savage here,
And therefore put I on the countenance
Of stern commandment. But whate'er you are
That in this desert inaccessible,   110
Under the shade of melancholy boughs,
Lose and neglect the creeping hours of time;
If ever you have looked on better days;
If ever been where bells have knolled to church;
If ever sat at any good man's feast;
If ever from your eyelids wiped a tear,
And know what 'tis to pity and be pitied,
Let gentleness my strong enforcement be:
In the which hope I blush, and hide my sword.
DUKE. True is it that we have seen better days,   120
And have with holy bell been knolled to church,
And sat at good men's feasts, and wiped our eyes
Of drops that sacred pity hath engendred:
And therefore sit you down in gentleness,
And take upon command what help we have
That to your wanting may be ministred.
ORLANDO. Then but forbear your food a little while,
Whiles, like a doe, I go to find my fawn,
And give it food.... There is an old poor man,
Who after me hath many a weary step   130
Limped in pure love: till he be first sufficed,
Oppressed with two weak evils, age and hunger,
I will not touch a bit.
DUKE.   Go find him out,
And we will nothing waste till you return.
ORLANDO. I thank ye, and be blessed for your good comfort!   He goes
DUKE. Thou seest we are not all alone unhappy:
This wide and universal theatre
Presents more woeful pageants than the scene
Wherein we play in.
JAQUES.   All the world's a stage,
And all the men and women merely players;   140
They have their exits and their entrances,
And one man in his time plays many parts,
His acts being seven ages.... At first the infant,
Mewling and puking in the nurse's arms:
Then the whining school-boy, with his satchel
And shining morning face, creeping like snail
Unwillingly to school: and then the lover,
Sighing like furnace, with a woeful ballad
Made to his mistress' eyebrow: then a soldier,
Full of strange oaths and bearded like the pard,   150
Jealous in honour, sudden and quick in quarrel,
Seeking the bubble reputation
Even in the cannon's mouth: and then the justice,
In fair round belly with good capon lined,
With eyes severe and beard of formal cut,
Full of wise saws and modern instances,
And so he plays his part.... The sixth age shifts
Into the lean and slippered pantaloon,
With spectacles on nose and pouch on side,
His youthful hose, well saved, a world too wide   160
For his shrunk shank, and his big manly voice,
Turning again toward childish treble, pipes

And whistles in his sound.... Last scene of all,
That ends this strange eventful history,
Is second childishness, and mere oblivion,
Sans teeth, sans eyes, sans taste, sans every thing.

Orlando returns with Adam

DUKE. Welcome ... Set down your venerable burden,
And let him feed.
ORLANDO. I thank you most for him.
ADAM.   So had you need,
I scarce can speak to thank you for myself.   170
DUKE. Welcome, fall to: I will not trouble you
As yet to question you about your fortunes:
Give us some music, and good cousin, sing.
AMIENS [*sings*].
      Blow, blow, thou winter wind,
      Thou art not so unkind
          As man's ingratitude;
      Thy tooth is not so keen,
      Because thou art not seen,
          Although thy breath be rude....
Hey-ho, sing hey-ho, unto the green holly,   180
Most friendship is feigning; most loving mere folly:
      Then hey-ho, the holly,
      This life is most jolly.

      Freeze, freeze, thou bitter sky,
      That dost not bite so nigh
          As benefits forgot:
      Though thou the waters warp,
      Thy sting is not so sharp
          As friend remembred not....
Hey-ho, sing hey-ho, unto the green holly,   190
Most friendship is feigning; most loving mere folly:
      Then hey-ho, the holly,
      This life is most jolly.

DUKE. If that you were the good Sir Rowland's son,

As you have whispered faithfully you were,
And as mine eye doth his effigies witness
Most truly limned and living in your face,
Be truly welcome hither: I am the duke
That loved your father. The residue of your fortune,
Go to my cave and tell me.... Good old man,   200
Thou art right welcome as thy master is:
Support him by the arm.... Give me your hand,
And let me all your fortunes understand.
                                        They go

ACT 3
Scene 1: *A room in the palace of Duke Frederick*

Enter Duke Frederick, lords, and Oliver

DUKE FREDERICK. Not see him since? Sir, sir, that cannot be:
But were I not the better part made mercy,
I should not seek an absent argument
Of my revenge, thou present: but look to it,
Find out thy brother wheresoe'er he is—
Seek him with candle; bring him dead or living
Within this twelvemonth, or turn thou no more
To seek a living in our territory....
Thy lands and all things that thou dost call thine
Worth seizure do we seize into our hands,   10
Till thou canst quit thee by thy brother's mouth
Of what we think against thee.

OLIVER. O, that your highness knew my heart in this! I never loved my brother in my life.

DUKE FREDERICK. More villain thou.... Well, push him out of doors,
And let my officers of such a nature
Make an extent upon his house and lands:
Do this expediently and turn him going.

They go

Scene 2: *The forest, near the sheepcote*

Orlando with a paper

ORLANDO. Hang there, my verse, in witness of my love,
And thou, thrice-crownéd queen of night, survey
With thy chaste eye, from thy pale sphere above,
Thy huntress' name that my full life doth sway....
O Rosalind! these trees shall be my books,
And in their barks my thoughts I'll character,
That every eye which in this forest looks
Shall see thy virtue witnessed every where....
Run, run, Orlando, carve on every tree
The fair, the chaste and unexpressive she. 10

He goes

Corin and Touchstone come up

CORIN. And how like you this shepherd's life, Master Touchstone?

TOUCHSTONE. Truly, shepherd, in respect of itself, it is a good life; but in respect that it is a shepherd's life, it is naught. In respect that it is solitary, I like it very well; but in respect that it is private, it is a very vile life. Now in respect it is in the fields, it pleaseth me well; but in respect it is not in the court, it is tedious. As it is a spare life, look you, it fits my humour well; but as there is no more plenty in it, it goes much 20 against my stomach. Hast any philosophy in thee, shepherd?

CORIN. No more, but that I know the more one sickens, the worse at ease he is; and that he that wants money, means and content is without three good friends; that the property of rain is to wet and fire to burn; that good pasture makes fat sheep; and that a great cause of the night, is lack of the sun; that he that hath learned no wit by nature nor art may complain of good breeding or comes of a very dull 30 kindred.

TOUCHSTONE. Such a one is a natural philosopher ... Wast ever in court, shepherd?

CORIN. No, truly.

TOUCHSTONE. Then thou art damned.

CORIN. Nay, I hope.

TOUCHSTONE. Truly thou art damned, like an ill-roasted egg all on one side.

CORIN. For not being at court? Your reason.

TOUCHSTONE. Why, if thou never wast at court, thou 40 never saw'st good manners; if thou never saw'st good manners, then thy manners must be wicked, and wickedness is sin, and sin is damnation ... Thou art in a parlous state, shepherd.

CORIN. Not a whit, Touchstone. Those that are good manners at the court are as ridiculous in the country, as the behaviour of the country is most mockable at the court. You told me you salute not at the court, but you kiss your hands; that courtesy would be uncleanly, if courtiers were shepherds. 50

TOUCHSTONE. Instance, briefly; come, instance.

CORIN. Why, we are still handling our ewes, and their fells you know are greasy.

TOUCHSTONE. Why, do not your courtier's hands sweat? and is not the grease of a mutton as wholesome as the sweat of a man?
Shallow, shallow: a better instance, I say: come.

CORIN. Besides, our hands are hard.

TOUCHSTONE. Your lips will feel them the sooner.
Shallow, again: a more sounder instance, come. 60

CORIN. And they are often tarred over with the surgery of our sheep; and would you have us kiss tar? The courtier's hands are perfumed with civet.

TOUCHSTONE. Most shallow man! thou worms-meat, in respect of a good piece of flesh indeed! Learn of the wise, and perpend: civet is of a baser birth than tar, the very uncleanly flux of a cat. Mend the instance, shepherd.

CORIN. You have too courtly a wit for me, I'll rest.

TOUCHSTONE. Wilt thou rest damned? God help thee, 70 shallow man! God make incision in thee! thou art raw.

CORIN. Sir, I am a true labourer. I earn that I eat, get that I wear, owe no man hate, envy no man's happiness, glad of other men's good, content with my harm; and the greatest of my pride is to see my ewes graze and my lambs suck.

TOUCHSTONE. That is another simple sin in you, to bring the ewes and the rams together, and to offer to get your living by the copulation of cattle—to be 80 bawd to a bell-wether, and to betray a she-lamb of a twelvemonth to a crooked-pated, old, cuckoldy ram, out of all reasonable match. If thou beest not damned for this, the devil himself will have no shepherds—I cannot see else how thou shouldst 'scape.

CORIN. Here comes young Master Ganymede, my new mistress's brother.

Enter Rosalind, reading

ROSALIND. 'From the east to western Ind,
No jewel is like Rosalind.
Her worth, being mounted on the wind, 90
Through all the world bears Rosalind.
All the pictures fairest lined
Are but black to Rosalind....
Let no face be kept in mind
But the fair of Rosalind.'

TOUCHSTONE. I'll rhyme you so eight years together, dinners, and suppers, and sleeping-hours excepted: it is the right butter-women's rank to market.

ROSALIND. Out, fool!

TOUCHSTONE. For a taste.... 100
If a hart do lack a hind,
Let him seek out Rosalind:
If the cat will after kind,
So be sure will Rosalind:
Wintered garments must be lined,
So must slender Rosalind.
They that reap must sheaf and bind,
Then to cart with Rosalind.
Sweetest nut hath sourest rind,
Such a nut is Rosalind. 110
He that sweetest rose will find,
Must find love's prick and Rosalind.
This is the very false gallop of verses. Why do you infect yourself with them?

ROSALIND. Peace, you dull fool! I found them on a tree.

TOUCHSTONE. Truly, the tree yields bad fruit.

ROSALIND. I'll graff it with you, and then I shall graff it with a medlar: then it will be the earliest fruit i'th' country: for you'll be rotten ere you be half ripe, and that's the right virtue of the medlar. 120

TOUCHSTONE. You have said: but whether wisely or no, let the forest judge.

Celia enter, reading a paper

ROSALIND. Peace!
Here comes my sister, reading. Stand aside.

CELIA. 'Why should this a desert be?
    For it is unpeopled? No;
Tongues I'll hang on every tree,
    That shall civil sayings show.
Some, how brief the life of man
    Runs his erring pilgrimage, 130
That the stretching of a span
    Buckles in his sum of age;
Some, of violated vows
    'Twixt the souls of friend and friend:
But upon the fairest boughs,
    Or at every sentence end,
Will I Rosalinda write,
    Teaching all that read to know
The quintessence of every sprite
    Heaven would in little show. 140
Therefore Heaven Nature charged,
    That one body should be filled
With all graces wide-enlarged:
    Nature presently distilled
Helen's cheek, but not her heart,
    Cleopatra's majesty,
Atalanta's better part,
    Sad Lucretia's modesty....
Thus Rosalind of many parts
    By heavenly synod was devised, 150
Of many faces, eyes, and hearts,
    To have the touches dearest prized....
Heaven would that she these gifts should have,
And I to live and die her slave.'

ROSALIND. O most gentle pulpiter, what tedious homily of love have you wearied your parishioners withal, and never cried, 'Have patience, good people!'

CELIA. How now, back-friends! Shepherd, go off a little.... Go with him, sirrah. 160

TOUCHSTONE. Come, shepherd, let us make an honourable retreat—though not with bag and baggage, yet with scrip and scrippage.
                        Touchstone departs with Corin

CELIA. Didst thou hear these verses?

ROSALIND. O, yes, I heard them all, and more too, for some of them had in them more feet than the verses would bear.

CELIA. That's no matter: the feet might bear the verses.

ROSALIND. Ay, but the feet were lame, and could not bear themselves without the verse, and therefore 170 stood lamely in the verse.

CELIA. But didst thou hear without wondering how thy name should be hanged and carved upon these trees?

ROSALIND. I was seven of the nine days out of the wonder before you came; for look here what I found

on a palm-tree ... I was never so be-rhymed since Pythagoras' time, that I was an Irish rat, which I can hardly remember.

CELIA. Trow you who hath done this? 180

ROSALIND. Is it a man?

CELIA. And a chain that you once wore about his neck! Change you colour?

ROSALIND. I prithee, who?

CELIA. O Lord, Lord! it is a hard matter for friends to meet; but mountains may be removed with earthquakes and so encounter.

ROSALIND. Nay, but who is it?

CELIA. Is it possible?

ROSALIND. Nay, I prithee now with most petitionary 190 vehemence, tell me who it is.

CELIA. O wonderful, wonderful, and most wonderful wonderful! and yet again wonderful, and after that out of all whooping!

ROSALIND. Good my complexion! dost thou think, though I am caparisoned like a man, I have a doublet-and-hose in my disposition? One inch of delay more is a South-sea of discovery.... I prithee, tell me who is it quickly, and speak apace: I would thou couldst stammer, that thou mightst pour this 200 concealed man out of thy mouth, as wine comes out of a narrow-mouthed bottle; either too much at once, or none at all. I prithee take the cork out of thy mouth that I may drink thy tidings.

CELIA. So you may put a man in your belly.

ROSALIND. Is he of God's making? What manner of man? Is his head worth a hat? or his chin worth a beard?

CELIA. Nay, he hath but a little beard.

ROSALIND. Why, God will send more, if the man will 210 be thankful: let me stay the growth of his beard, if thou delay me not the knowledge of his chin.

CELIA. It is young Orlando, that tripped up the wrestler's heels, and your heart, both in an instant.

ROSALIND. Nay, but the devil take mocking; speak sad brow and true maid.

CELIA. I'faith, coz, 'tis he.

ROSALIND. Orlando?

CELIA. Orlando.

ROSALIND. Alas the day, what shall I do with my 220 doublet and hose? What did he when thou saw'st him? What said he? How looked he? Wherein went he? What makes he here? Did he ask for me? Where remains he? How parted he with thee? and when shalt thou see him again? Answer me in one word.

CELIA. You must borrow me Gargantua's mouth first: 'tis a word too great for any mouth of this age's size. To say ay and no to these particulars is more than to answer in a catechism.

ROSALIND. But doth he know that I am in this forest 230 and in man's apparel? Looks he as freshly as he did the day he wrestled?

CELIA. It is as easy to count atomies as to resolve the propositions of a lover: but take a taste of my finding him, and relish it with a good observance. I found him under a tree, like a dropped acorn.

ROSALIND. It may well be called Jove's tree, when it drops forth such fruit.

CELIA. Give me audience, good madam.

ROSALIND. Proceed. 240

CELIA. There lay he, stretched along, like a wounded knight.

ROSALIND. Though it be pity to see such a sight, it well becomes the ground.

CELIA. Cry 'holla' to thy tongue, I prithee; it curvets unseasonably.... He was furnished like a hunter.

ROSALIND. O ominous! he comes to kill my heart.

CELIA. I would sing my song without a burden—thou bring'st me out of tune.

ROSALIND. Do you not know I am a woman? when I think, I must speak ... Sweet, say on. 250

Orlando and Jaques enter

CELIA. You bring me out.... Soft! comes he not here?

ROSALIND. 'Tis he—slink by, and note him.

JAQUES. I thank you for your company—but, good faith,
I had as lief have been myself alone.

ORLANDO. And so had I: but yet, for fashion sake, I thank you too for your society.

JAQUES. God buy you, let's meet as little as we can.

ORLANDO. I do desire we may be better strangers.

JAQUES. I pray you, mar no more trees with writing love-songs in their barks. 260

ORLANDO. I pray you, mar no moe of my verses with reading them ill-favouredly.

JAQUES. Rosalind is your love's name?

ORLANDO. Yes, just.

JAQUES. I do not like her name.

ORLANDO. There was no thought of pleasing you when she was christened.

JAQUES. What stature is she of?

ORLANDO. Just as high as my heart. 270

JAQUES. You are full of pretty answers: have you not been acquainted with goldsmiths' wives, and conned them out of rings?

ORLANDO. Not so; but I answer you right painted cloth, from whence you have studied your questions.

JAQUES. You have a nimble wit; I think 'twas made of Atalanta's heels.... Will you sit down with me? and we two will rail against our mistress the world, and all our misery. 280

ORLANDO. I will chide no breather in the world but myself, against whom I know most faults.

JAQUES. The worst fault you have is to be in love.

ORLANDO. 'Tis a fault I will not change for your best virtue ... I am weary of you.

JAQUES. By my troth, I was seeking for a fool when I found you.

ORLANDO. He is drowned in the brook—look but in, and you shall see him.

JAQUES. There I shall see mine own figure. 290

ORLANDO. Which I take to be either a fool or a cipher.

JAQUES. I'll tarry no longer with you. Farewell, good Signior Love.

ORLANDO. I am glad of your departure: adieu, good Monsieur Melancholy. *Jaques departs*

ROSALIND [*aside to Celia*]. I will speak to him like a saucy lackey, and under that habit play the knave with him.
[*calls*] Do you hear forester? 300

ORLANDO [*turns*]. Very well. What would you?

ROSALIND. I pray you, what is't o'clock?

ORLANDO. You should ask me what time o'day: there's no clock in the forest.

ROSALIND. Then there is no true lover in the forest, else

sighing every minute and groaning every hour would detect the lazy foot of Time as well as a clock.

ORLANDO. And why not the swift foot of Time? had not that been as proper?

ROSALIND. By no means, sir: Time travels in divers 310 paces with divers persons ... I'll tell you who Time ambles withal, who Time trots withal, who Time gallops withal, and who he stands still withal.

ORLANDO. I prithee, who doth he trot withal?

ROSALIND. Marry, he trots hard with a young maid between the contract of her marriage and the day it is solemnized: if the interim be but a se'nnight, Time's pace is so hard that it seems the length of seven year.

ORLANDO. Who ambles Time withal? 320

ROSALIND. With a priest that lacks Latin, and a rich man that hath not the gout: for the one sleeps easily because he cannot study, and the other lives merrily because he feels no pain: the one lacking the burden of lean and wasteful learning; the other knowing no burden of heavy tedious penury.... These Time ambles withal.

ORLANDO. Who doth he gallop withal?

ROSALIND. With a thief to the gallows: for though he go as softly as foot can fall, he thinks himself too 330 soon there.

ORLANDO. Who stays it still withal?

ROSALIND. With lawyers in the vacation: for they sleep between term and term, and then they perceive not how Time moves.

ORLANDO. Where dwell you, pretty youth?

ROSALIND. With this shepherdess, my sister; here in the skirts of the forest, like fringe upon a petticoat.

ORLANDO. Are you native of this place?

ROSALIND. As the cony that you see dwell where she is 340 kindled.

ORLANDO. Your accent is something finer than you could purchase in so removed a dwelling.

ROSALIND. I have been told so of many: but indeed an old religious uncle of mine taught me to speak, who was in his youth an inland man—one that knew courtship too well, for there he fell in love.... I have heard him read many lectures against it, and I thank God I am not a woman, to be touched with so many giddy offences as he hath generally taxed their 350 whole sex withal.

ORLANDO. Can you remember any of the principal evils that he laid to the charge of women?

ROSALIND. There were none principal, they were all like one another as half-pence are, every one fault seeming monstrous till his fellow-fault came to match it.

ORLANDO. I prithee, recount some of them.

ROSALIND. No: I will not cast away my physic but on those that are sick.... There is a man haunts the 360 forest, that abuses our young plants with carving 'Rosalind' on their barks; hangs odes upon hawthorns and elegies on brambles; all, forsooth, deifying the name of Rosalind: if I could meet that fancy-monger, I would give him some good counsel, for he seems to have the quotidian of love upon him.

ORLANDO. I am he that is so love-shaked. I pray you, tell me your remedy.

ROSALIND. There is none of my uncle's marks upon 370 you: he taught me how to know a man in love;

in which cage of rushes I am sure you are not prisoner.

ORLANDO. What were his marks?

ROSALIND. A lean cheek, which you have not: a blue eye and sunken, which you have not: an unquestionable spirit, which you have not: a beard neglected, which you have not ... but I pardon you for that, for simply your having in beard is a younger brother's revenue. Then your hose should be ungartered, your bonnet unbanded, your sleeve unbuttoned, your shoe untied, and every thing about you demonstrating a careless desolation: but you are no such man; you are rather point-device in your accoutrements, as loving yourself than seeming the lover of any other. 380

ORLANDO. Fair youth, I would I could make thee believe I love.

ROSALIND. Me believe it! you may as soon make her that you love believe it, which I warrant she is apter to do than to confess she does: that is one of the points in the which women still give the lie to their consciences.... But, in good sooth, are you he that hangs the verses on the trees, wherein Rosalind is so admired? 390

ORLANDO. I swear to thee, youth, by the white hand of Rosalind, I am that he, that unfortunate he.

ROSALIND. But are you so much in love as your rhymes speak?

ORLANDO. Neither rhyme nor reason can express how much. 400

ROSALIND. Love is merely a madness, and I tell you deserves as well a dark house and a whip as madmen do: and the reason why they are not so punished and cured is, that the lunacy is so ordinary that the whippers are in love too ... Yet I profess curing it by counsel.

ORLANDO. Did you ever cure any so?

ROSALIND. Yes, one, and in this manner. He was to imagine me his love, his mistress; and I set him every day to woo me: at which time would I, being but a moonish youth, grieve, be effeminate, changeable, longing and liking, proud, fantastical, apish, shallow, inconstant, full of tears, full of smiles; for every passion something, and for no passion truly any thing, as boys and women are for the most part cattle of this colour: would now like him, now loath him; then entertain him, then forswear him; now weep for him, then spit at him; that I drave my suitor from his mad humour of love to a living humour of madness—which was, to forswear the full stream of the world and to live in a nook merely monastic ... And thus I cured him, and this way will I take upon me to wash your liver as clean as a sound sheep's heart, that there shall not be one spot of love in't. 410

420

ORLANDO. I would not be cured, youth.

ROSALIND. I would cure you, if you would but call me Rosalind, and come every day to my cote, and woo me.

ORLANDO. Now, by the faith of my love, I will ... Tell me where it is. 430

ROSALIND. Go with me to it, and I'll show it you: and by the way you shall tell me where in the forest you live ... Will you go?

ORLANDO. With all my heart, good youth.

ROSALIND. Nay, you must call me Rosalind ... Come, sister, will you go?   *They go*

Scene 3: *The clearing near the sheepcote* (*as before*)

Enter Touchstone and Audrey; Jaques following at a little distance

TOUCHSTONE. Come apace, good Audrey. I will fetch up your goats, Audrey ... And how, Audrey? am I the man yet? Doth my simple feature content you?

AUDREY. Your features, Lord warrant us! what features?

TOUCHSTONE. I am here with thee and thy goats, as the most capricious poet, honest Ovid, was among the Goths.

JAQUES. O knowledge ill-inhabited! worse than Jove in a thatched house! 10

TOUCHSTONE. When a man's verses cannot be understood, nor a man's good wit seconded with the forward child, understanding, it strikes a man more dead than a great reckoning in a little room.... Truly, I would the gods had made thee poetical.

AUDREY. I do not know what 'poetical' is: is it honest in deed and word? is it a true thing?

TOUCHSTONE. No, truly; for the truest poetry is the most feigning; and lovers are given to poetry; and what they swear in poetry it may be said as lovers they do feign. 20

AUDREY. Do you wish then that the gods had made me poetical?

TOUCHSTONE. I do, truly: for thou swear'st to me thou art honest; now, if thou wert a poet, I might have some hope thou didst feign.

AUDREY. Would you not have me honest?

TOUCHSTONE. No, truly, unless thou wert hardfavoured: for honesty coupled to beauty is to have honey a sauce to sugar. 30

JAQUES. A material fool!

AUDREY. Well, I am not fair, and therefore I pray the gods make me honest.

TOUCHSTONE. Truly, and to cast away honesty upon a foul slut were to put good meat into an unclean dish.

AUDREY. I am not a slut, though I thank the gods I am foul.

TOUCHSTONE. Well, praised be the gods for thy foulness! sluttishness may come hereafter.... But be it as it may be, I will marry thee: and to that end, I have been with Sir Oliver Martext the vicar of the next village, who hath promised to meet me in this place of the forest and to couple us. 40

JAQUES. I would fain see this meeting.

AUDREY. Well, the gods give us joy!

TOUCHSTONE. Amen.... A man may, if he were of a fearful heart, stagger in this attempt; for here we have no temple but the wood, no assembly but horn-beasts. But what though? Courage! As horns are odious, they are necessary. It is said, 'many a man knows no end of his goods': right; many a man has good horns, and knows no end of them. Well, that is the dowry of his wife; 'tis none of his own getting ... Horns? Even so. Poor men alone? No, no, the noblest deer hath them as huge as the rascal ... Is the single man therefore blessed? No, as a walled town is more worthier than a village, so is the forehead of a married man more honourable than the bare brow of a bachelor: and by how much defence is better than no skill, by so much is a horn more precious than to want.... 50

60

Sir Oliver Martext enters

Here comes Sir Oliver ... Sir Oliver Martext, you
are well met. Will you dispatch us here under this
tree, or shall we go with you to your chapel?

SIR OLIVER MARTEXT. Is there none here to give the
woman?

TOUCHSTONE. I will not take her on gift of any man.

SIR OLIVER MARTEXT. Truly, she must be given, or the
marriage is not lawful.

JAQUES [comes forward]. Proceed, proceed; I'll give her. 70

TOUCHSTONE. Good even, good Master What-ye-
call't: how do you, sir? You are very well met:
God'ild you for your last company—I am very glad
to see you—even a toy in hand here, sir ... Nay,
pray be covered.

JAQUES. Will you be married, motley?

TOUCHSTONE. As the ox hath his bow, sir, the horse his
curb, and the falcon her bells, so man hath his
desires; and as pigeons bill, so wedlock would be
nibbling.   80

JAQUES. And will you, being a man of your breeding,
be married under a bush like a beggar? Get you to
church, and have a good priest that can tell you what
marriage is—this fellow will but join you together
as they join wainscot, then one of you will prove a
shrunk panel, and like green timber warp, warp.

TOUCHSTONE. I am not in the mind but I were better
to be married of him than of another, for he is not
like to marry me well ... and not being well
married, it will be a good excuse for me hereafter to 90
leave my wife.

JAQUES. Go thou with me, and let me counsel thee.

TOUCHSTONE. Come, sweet Audrey,
We must be married, or we must live in bawdry ...
Farewell, good Master Oliver: not—
                                              Sings and dances

        O sweet Oliver,
        O brave Oliver,
        Leave me not behind thee:
but—
        Wind away,   100
        Begone, I say,
        I will not to wedding with thee.

              He goes, Jaques and Audrey following
SIR OLIVER MARTEXT. 'Tis no matter; ne'er a fantastical
knave of them all shall flout me out of my calling.
                                              He goes

              Scene 4: *The forest*

Enter Rosalind and Celia

ROSALIND. Never talk to me, I will weep.

CELIA. Do, I prithee—but yet have the grace to consider that tears do not become a man.

ROSALIND. But have I not cause to weep?

CELIA. As good cause as one would desire, therefore
weep.

ROSALIND. His very hair is of the dissembling colour.

CELIA. Something browner than Judas's: marry, his
kisses are Judas's own children.

ROSALIND. I'faith, his hair is of a good colour.   10

CELIA. An excellent colour: your chestnut was ever
the only colour.

ROSALIND. And his kissing is as full of sanctity as the
touch of holy bread.

CELIA. He hath bought a pair of cast lips of Diana:
a nun of winter's sisterhood kisses not more
religiously, the very ice of chastity is in them.

ROSALIND. But why did he swear he would come this
morning, and comes not?

CELIA. Nay, certainly, there is no truth in him.   20

ROSALIND. Do you think so?

CELIA. Yes, I think he is not a pick-purse nor a horse-
stealer, but for his verity in love I do think him as
concave as a covered goblet or a worm-eaten nut.

ROSALIND. Not true in love?

CELIA. Yes, when he is in—but I think he is not in.

ROSALIND. You have heard him swear downright he
was.

CELIA. 'Was' is not 'is': besides, the oath of a lover
is no stronger than the word of a tapster, they are 30
both the confirmer of false reckonings. He attends
here in the forest on the duke your father.

ROSALIND. I met the duke yesterday and had much
question with him: he asked me of what parentage
I was; I told him, of as good as he—so he laughed
and let me go.... But what talk we of fathers,
when there is such a man as Orlando?

CELIA. O, that's a brave man! he writes brave verses,
speaks brave words, swears brave oaths and breaks
them bravely, quite traverse, athwart the heart of his 40
lover—as a puny tilter, that spurs his horse but on
one side, breaks his staff like a noble goose; but all's
brave that youth mounts and folly guides.... Who
comes here?

Corin enters

CORIN. Mistress and master, you have oft inquired
After the shepherd that complained of love,
Who you saw sitting by me on the turf,
Praising the proud disdainful shepherdess
That was his mistress.

CELIA.   Well: and what of him?

CORIN. If you will see a pageant truly played,   50
Between the pale complexion of true love
And the red glow of scorn and proud disdain,
Go hence a little and I shall conduct you,
If you will mark it.

ROSALIND.   O, come, let us remove.
The sight of lovers feedeth those in love:
Bring us to this sight, and you shall say
I'll prove a busy actor in their play.   *They go*

              Scene 5: *Another part of the forest*

Enter Phebe, followed by Silvius

SILVIUS. Sweet Phebe, do not scorn me, do not,
    Phebe:
Say that you love me not, but say not so
In bitterness ... The common executioner,
Whose heart th'accustomed sight of death makes
    hard,
Falls not the axe upon the humbled neck
But first begs pardon: will you sterner be
Than he that dies and lives by bloody drops?

Rosalind, Celia, and Corin come up behind, unseen

PHEBE. I would not be thy executioner.
I fly thee, for I would not injure thee ...
Thou tell'st me there is murder in mine eye—   10
'Tis pretty, sure, and very probable,

That eyes, that are the frail'st and softest things,
Who shut their coward gates on atomies,
Should be called tyrants, butchers, murderers!
Now I do frown on thee with all my heart,
And if mine eyes can wound, now let them kill thee;
Now counterfeit to swoon, why now fall down,
Or if thou canst not, O for shame, for shame,
Lie not, to say mine eyes are murderers!
Now show the wound mine eye hath made in thee. 20
Scratch thee but with a pin, and there remains
Some scar of it: lean upon a rush,
The cicatrice and capable impressure
Thy palm some moment keeps: but now mine eyes,
Which I have darted at thee, hurt thee not,
Nor, I am sure, there is no force in eyes
That can do hurt.
SILVIUS.   O dear Phebe,
If ever—as that ever may be near—
You meet in some fresh cheek the power of fancy,
Than shall you know the wounds invisible   30
That love's keen arrows make.
PHEBE.   But till that time
Come not thou near me: and when that time comes,
Afflict me with thy mocks, pity me not,
As till that time I shall not pity thee.
ROSALIND [advancing]. And why, I pray you? Who
    might be your mother,
That you insult, exult, and all at once,
Over the wretched? What though you have no
    beauty—
As, by my faith, I see no more in you
Than without candle may go dark to bed—
Must you be therefore proud and pitiless?   40
Why, what means this? Why do you look on me?
I see no more in you than in the ordinary
Of nature's sale-work! 'Od's my little life,
I think she means to tangle my eyes too:
No, faith, proud mistress, hope not after it.
'Tis not your inky brows, your black silk hair,
Your bugle eyeballs, nor your cheek of cream,
That can entame my spirits to your worship ...
You foolish shepherd, wherefore do you follow her,
Like foggy south, puffing with wind and rain?   50
You are a thousand times a properer man
Than she a woman: 'tis such fools as you
That makes the world full of ill-favoured children:
'Tis not her glass, but you, that flatters her,
And out of you she sees herself more proper
Than any of her lineaments can show her ...
But, mistress, know yourself—down on your knees,
And thank heaven, fasting, for a good man's love;
For I must tell you friendly in your ear,
Sell when you can—you are not for all markets: 60
Cry the man mercy, love him, take his offer.
Foul is most foul, being foul to be a scoffer....
So take her to thee, shepherd—fare you well.
PHEBE. Sweet youth, I pray you chide a year together.
I had rather hear you chide than this man woo.
ROSALIND. He's fallen in love with your foulness, and
she'll fall in love with my anger. If it be so, as fast
as she answers thee with frowning looks, I'll sauce
her with bitter words ... Why look you so upon
me?   70
PHEBE. For no ill will I bear you.
ROSALIND. I pray you, do not fall in love with me,
For I am falser than vows made in wine:

Besides, I like you not ... If you will know my
    house,
'Tis at the tuft of olives here hard by ...
Will you go, sister? Shepherd, ply her hard ...
Come, sister ... Shepherdess, look on him better,
And be not proud—though all the world could see,
None could be so abused in sight as he....
Come, to our flock.   80
        She goes, followed by Celia and Corin
PHEBE. Dead Shepherd, now I find thy saw of might,
'Who ever loved that loved not at first sight?'
SILVIUS. Sweet Phebe—
PHEBE.   Ha! what say'st thou, Silvius?
SILVIUS. Sweet Phebe, pity me.
PHEBE. Why, I am sorry for thee, gentle Silvius.
SILVIUS. Wherever sorrow is, relief would be:
If you do sorrow at my grief in love,
By giving love your sorrow and my grief
Were both extermined.
PHEBE. Thou hast my love—is not that neighbourly? 90
SILVIUS. I would have you.
PHEBE.   Why, that were covetousness ...
Silvius, the time was that I hated thee,
And yet it is not that I bear thee love;
But since that thou canst talk of love so well,
Thy company, which erst was irksome to me,
I will endure; and I'll employ thee too:
But do not look for further recompense
Than thine own gladness that thou art employed.
SILVIUS. So holy and so perfect is my love,
And I in such a poverty of grace,   100
That I shall think it a most plenteous crop
To glean the broken ears after the man
That the main harvest reaps: loose now and then
A scattered smile, and that I'll live upon.
PHEBE. Know'st thou the youth that spoke to me
    erewhile?
SILVIUS. Not very well, but I have met him oft,
And he hath bought the cottage and the bounds
That the old carlot once was master of.
PHEBE. Think not I love him, though I ask for him.
'Tis but a peevish boy—yet he talks well—   110
But what care I for words?—yet words do well,
When he, that speaks them pleases those that hear:
It is a pretty youth—not very pretty—
But, sure, he's proud—and yet his pride becomes
    him:
He'll make a proper man: the best thing in him
Is his complexion; and faster than his tongue
Did make offence, his eye did heal it up:
He is not very tall—yet for his years he's tall:
His leg is but so so—and yet 'tis well:
There was a pretty redness in his lip,   120
A little riper and more lusty red
Than that mixed in his cheek; 'twas just the
    difference
Betwixt the constant red and mingled damask....
There be some women, Silvius, had they marked
    him
In parcels as I did, would have gone near
To fall in love with him: but, for my part,
I love him not, nor hate him not; and yet
I have more cause to hate him than to love him,
For what had he to do to chide at me?
He said mine eyes were black and my hair black,   130
And, now I am remembered, scorn'd at me:

I marvel why I answered not again:
But that's all one; omittance is no quittance:
I'll write to him a very taunting letter,
And thou shalt bear it—wilt thou, Silvius?
SILVIUS. Phebe, with all my heart.
PHEBE.   I'll write it straight;
The matter's in my head and in my heart.
I will be bitter with him and passing short:
Go with me, Silvius.   *They go*

ACT 4

Scene 1: *The clearing near the sheepcote*

Enter Rosalind, Celia, and Jaques

JAQUES. I prithee, pretty youth, let me be better
acquainted with thee.
ROSALIND. They say you are a melancholy fellow.
JAQUES. I am so: I do love it better than laughing.
ROSALIND. Those that are in extremity of either are
abominable fellows, and betray themselves to every
modern censure worse than drunkards.
JAQUES. Why, 'tis good to be sad and say nothing.
ROSALIND. Why then, 'tis good to be a post.
JAQUES. I have neither the scholar's melancholy, 10
which is emulation; nor the musician's, which is
fantastical; nor the courtier's, which is proud; nor
the soldier's, which is ambitious; nor the lawyer's,
which is politic; nor the lady's, which is nice; nor the
lover's, which is all these: but it is a melancholy of
mine own, compounded of many simples, extracted
from many objects, and indeed the sundry contemplation of my travels, in which my often rumin-
ation wraps me in a most humorous sadness.
ROSALIND. A traveller! By my faith, you have great 20
reason to be sad: I fear you have sold your own
lands to see other men's; then, to have seen much,
and to have nothing, is to have rich eyes and poor
hands.
JAQUES. Yes, I have gained my experience.

Orlando enters

ROSALIND. And your experience makes you sad: I had
rather have a fool to make me merry than experience to make me sad—and to travel for it too!
ORLANDO. Good day, and happiness, dear Rosalind!
JAQUES. Nay then, God buy you, an you talk in blank 30
verse.
ROSALIND. Farewell, Monsieur Traveller: look you
lisp and wear strange suits; disable all the benefits of
your own country; be out of love with your
nativity, and almost chide God for making you that
countenance you are; or I will scarce think you have
swam in a gondola.... [*Jaques goes*] Why, how now,
Orlando! where have you been all this while? You a
lover! An you serve me such another trick, never
come in my sight more.   40
ORLANDO. My fair Rosalind, I come within an hour of
my promise.
ROSALIND. Break an hour's promise in love? He that
will divide a minute into a thousand parts, and break
but a part of the thousandth part of a minute in the
affairs of love, it may be said of him that Cupid hath
clapped him o'th' shoulder, but I'll warrant him
heartwhole.
ORLANDO. Pardon me, dear Rosalind.

ROSALIND. Nay, an you be so tardy come no more in 50
my sight, I had as lief be wooed of a snail.
ORLANDO. Of a snail?
ROSALIND. Ay, of a snail; for though he comes slowly,
he carries his house on his head; a better jointure, I
think, than you make a woman: besides, he brings
his destiny with him.
ORLANDO. What's that?
ROSALIND. Why, horns; which such as you are fain to
be beholding to your wives for: but he comes armed
in his fortune, and prevents the slander of his wife. 60
ORLANDO. Virtue is no horn-maker ... and my
Rosalind is virtuous.
ROSALIND. And I am your Rosalind.
CELIA. It pleases him to call you so; but he hath a
Rosalind of a better leer than you.
ROSALIND. Come, woo me, woo me; for now I am in
a holiday humour, and like enough to consent ...
What would you say to me now, an I were your
very very Rosalind?
ORLANDO. I would kiss before I spoke.   70
ROSALIND. Nay, you were better speak first, and when
you were gravelled for lack of matter, you might
take occasion to kiss: very good orators, when they
are out, they will spit, and for lovers, lacking (God
warr'nt us!) matter, the cleanliest shift is to kiss.
ORLANDO. How if the kiss be denied?
ROSALIND. Then she puts you to entreaty and there
begins new matter.
ORLANDO. Who could be out, being before his beloved
mistress?   80
ROSALIND. Marry, that should you if I were your mistress, or I should think my honesty ranker than my
wit.
ORLANDO. What, of my suit?
ROSALIND. Not out of your apparel, and yet out of
your suit ... Am not I your Rosalind?
ORLANDO. I take some joy to say you are, because I
would be talking of her.
ROSALIND. Well, in her person, I say I will not have
you.   90
ORLANDO. Then in mine own person, I die.
ROSALIND. No, faith, die by attorney: the poor world
is almost six thousand years old, and in all this time
there was not any man died in his own person, videlicet, in a love-cause: Troilus had his brains dashed
out with a Grecian club, yet he did what he could
to die before, and he is one of the patterns of love:
Leander, he would have lived many a fair year,
though Hero had turned nun, if it had not been for
a hot midsummer night; for, good youth, he went 100
but forth to wash him in the Hellespont and being
taken with the cramp was drowned, and the foolish
chroniclers of that age found it was 'Hero of Sestos.'
... But these are all lies. Men have died from time to
time, and worms have eaten them, but not for love.
ORLANDO. I would not have my right Rosalind of this
mind, for I protest her frown might kill me.
ROSALIND. By this hand, it will not kill a fly ... But
come, now I will be your Rosalind in a more
coming-on disposition; and ask me what you will, 110
I will grant it.
ORLANDO. Then love me, Rosalind.
ROSALIND. Yes, faith will I, Fridays and Saturdays and
all.
ORLANDO. And wilt thou have me?

ROSALIND. Ay, and twenty such.

ORLANDO. What sayest thou?

ROSALIND. Are you not good?

ORLANDO. I hope so.

ROSALIND. Why then, can one desire too much of a 120 good thing? Come, sister, you shall be the priest and marry us.... Give me your hand, Orlando ... What do you say, sister?

ORLANDO. Pray thee, marry us.

CELIA. I cannot say the words.

ROSALIND. You must begin, 'Will you, Orlando'—

CELIA. Go to ... Will you, Orlando, have to wife this Rosalind?

ORLANDO. I will.

ROSALIND. Ay, but when? 130

ORLANDO. Why now, as fast as she can marry us.

ROSALIND. Then you must say, 'I take thee, Rosalind, for wife.'

ORLANDO. I take thee, Rosalind, for wife.

ROSALIND. I might ask you for your commission, but I do take thee, Orlando, for my husband ... There's a girl goes before the priest, and certainly a woman's thought runs before her actions.

ORLANDO. So do all thoughts, they are winged.

ROSALIND. Now tell me how long you would have her 140 after you have possessed her.

ORLANDO. For ever and a day.

ROSALIND. Say 'a day' without the 'ever' ... No, no, Orlando, men are April when they woo, December when they wed; maids are May when they are maids, but the sky changes when they are wives ... I will be more jealous of thee than a Barbary cock-pigeon over his hen, more clamorous than a parrot against rain, more new-fangled than an ape, more giddy in my desires than a monkey: I will weep for 150 nothing, like Diana in the fountain, and I will do that when you are disposed to be merry; I will laugh like a hyen, and that when thou art inclined to sleep.

ORLANDO. But will my Rosalind do so?

ROSALIND. By my life, she will do as I do.

ORLANDO. O, but she is wise.

ROSALIND. Or else she could not have the wit to do this: the wiser, the waywarder: make the doors upon a woman's wit, and it will out at the casement; shut that, and 'twill out at the key-hole; stop that, 160 'twill fly with the smoke out at the chimney.

ORLANDO. A man that had a wife with such a wit, he might say 'Wit, whither wilt?'

ROSALIND. Nay, you might keep that check for it, till you met your wife's wit going to your neighbour's bed.

ORLANDO. And what wit could wit have to excuse that?

ROSALIND. Marry, to say she came to seek you there ... You shall never take her without her answer, 170 unless you take her without her tongue: O, that woman that cannot make her fault her husband's occasion, let her never nurse her child herself, for she will breed it like a fool.

ORLANDO. For these two hours, Rosalind, I will leave thee.

ROSALIND. Alas, dear love, I cannot lack thee two hours!

ORLANDO. I must attend the duke at dinner. By two o'clock I will be with thee again. 180

ROSALIND. Ay, go your ways, go your ways; I knew

what you would prove, my friends told me as much, and I thought no less: that flattering tongue of yours won me: 'tis but one cast away, and so, come death.... Two o'clock is your hour?

ORLANDO. Ay, sweet Rosalind.

ROSALIND. By my troth, and in good earnest, and so God mend me, and by all pretty oaths that are not dangerous, if you break one jot of your promise, or come one minute behind your hour, I will think you 190 the most pathetical break-promise, and the most hollow lover, and the most unworthy of her you call Rosalind, that may be chosen out of the gross band of the unfaithful: therefore beware my censure, and keep your promise.

ORLANDO. With no less religion than if thou wert indeed my Rosalind: so adieu.

ROSALIND. Well, Time is the old justice that examines all such offenders, and let Time try: adieu!

He goes

CELIA. You have simply misused our sex in your love- 200 prate: we must have your doublet and hose plucked over your head, and show the world what the bird hath done to her own nest.

ROSALIND. O coz, coz, coz ... my pretty little coz, that thou didst know how many fathom deep I am in love! But it cannot be sounded; my affection hath an unknown bottom, like the bay of Portugal.

CELIA. Or rather, bottomless—that as fast as you pour affection in, it runs out.

ROSALIND. No, that same wicked bastard of Venus, 210 that was begot of thought, conceived of spleen, and born of madness—that blind rascally boy that abuses every one's eyes because his own are out—let him be judge how deep I am in love ... I'll tell thee, Aliena, I cannot be out of the sight of Orlando: I'll go find a shadow and sigh till he come.

CELIA. And I'll sleep. *They go*

Scene 2: *The forest*

Enter Amiens and other lords, dressed as foresters, with Jaques

JAQUES. Which is he that killed the deer?

A LORD. Sir, it was I.

JAQUES. Let's present him to the duke, like a Roman conqueror. And it would do well to set the deer's horns upon his head, for a branch of victory ... Have you no song, forester, for this purpose?

AMIENS. Yes, sir.

JAQUES. Sing it: 'tis no matter how it be in tune, so it make noise enough.

The company sing, Amiens leading and the rest joining in chorus

THE SONG

What shall he have that killed the deer? 10
His leather skin and horns to wear:
Then sing him home—the rest shall bear
      This burden ...
      Take thou no scorn to wear the horn,
      It was a crest ere thou wast born,
      Thy father's father wore it,
      And thy father bore it,
The horn, the horn, the lusty horn,
Is not a thing to laugh to scorn.
                                          They go

Scene 3: *The clearing near the sheepcote*

Enter Rosalind and Celia

ROSALIND. How say you now? Is it not past two
o'clock? and here much Orlando!

CELIA. I warrant you, with pure love and troubled
brain, he hath ta'en his bow and arrows, and is gone
forth to sleep ... Look, who comes here.

Silvius approaches

SILVIUS. My errand is to you, fair youth—
My gentle Phebe bid me give you this:
                        He gives Rosalind a letter
I know not the contents, but as I guess
By the stern brow and waspish action
Which she did use as she was writing of it,   10
It bears an angry tenour: pardon me,
I am but as a guiltless messenger.

ROSALIND. Patience herself would startle at this letter,
And play the swaggerer—bear this, bear all:
She says I am not fair, that I lack manners,
She calls me proud, and that she could not love me
Were man as rare as phœnix: 'od's my will!
Her love is not the hare that I do hunt.
Why writes she so to me? Well, shepherd, well,
This is a letter of your own device.   20

SILVIUS. No, I protest, I know not the contents—
Phebe did write it.

ROSALIND.   Come, come, you are a fool,
And turned into the extremity of love.
I saw her hand—she has a leathern hand,
A freestone-coloured hand: I verily did think
That her old gloves were on, but 'twas her hands:
She has a huswife's hand—but that's no matter:
I say she never did invent this letter,
This is a man's invention, and his hand.

SILVIUS. Sure, it is hers.   30

ROSALIND. Why, 'tis a boisterous and a cruel style,
A style for challengers; why, she defies me,
Like Turk to Christian; women's gentle brain
Could not drop forth such giant-rude invention,
Such Ethiop words, blacker in their effect
Than in their countenance ... Will you hear the
letter?

SILVIUS. So please you, for I never heard it yet;
Yet heard too much of Phebe's cruelty.

ROSALIND. She Phebes me: mark how the tyrant
writes.

[*reads*] 'Art thou god to shepherd turned,   40
          That a maiden's heart hath burned?'
Can a woman rail thus?

SILVIUS. Call you this railing?

ROSALIND.
      'Why, thy godhead laid apart,
      Warr'st thou with a woman's heart?'
Did you ever hear such railing?
      'Whiles the eye of man did woo me,
      That could do no vengeance to me.'
Meaning me a beast.
      'If the scorn of your bright eyne   50
      Have power to raise such love in mine,
      Alack, in me what strange effect
      Would they work in mild aspéct?
Whiles you chid me I did love.
How then might your prayers move?
      He that brings this love to thee
      Little knows this love in me:

And by him seal up thy mind,
      Whether that thy youth and kind
      Will the faithful offer take   60
      Of me and all that I can make,
      Or else by him my love deny,
      And then I'll study how to die.'

SILVIUS. Call you this chiding?

CELIA. Alas, poor shepherd!

ROSALIND. Do you pity him? no, he deserves no pity
... Wilt thou love such a woman? What, to make
thee an instrument and play false strains upon thee!
not to be endured! Well, go your way to her (for I
see love hath made thee a tame snake) and say   70
this to her: that if she love me, I charge her to love
thee: if she will not, I will never have her, unless thou
entreat for her.... If you be a true lover, hence, and
not a word; for here comes more company.
                                              He goes

Oliver enters

OLIVER. Good morrow, fair ones: pray you, if you
know,
      Where in the purlieus of this forest stands
      A sheepcote fenced about with olive-trees?

CELIA. West of this place, down in the neighbour
bottom—
      The rank of osiers by the murmuring stream
      Left on your right hand brings you to the place   80
      But at this hour the house doth keep itself,
      There's none within.

OLIVER. If that an eye may profit by a tongue,
      Then should I know you by description—
      Such garments and such years: 'The boy is fair,
      Of female favour, and bestows himself
      Like a ripe forester: the woman low,
      And browner than her brother.' ... Are not you
      The owner of the house I did inquire for?

CELIA. It is no boast, being asked, to say we are.   90

OLIVER. Orlando doth commend him to you both,
      And to that youth he calls his Rosalind
      He sends this bloody napkin; are you he?

ROSALIND. I am: what must we understand by this?

OLIVER. Some of my shame, if you will know of me
      What man I am, and how, and why, and where
      This handkercher was stained.

CELIA.   I pray you, tell it.

OLIVER. When last the young Orlando parted from
you
      He left a promise to return again
      Within an hour, and pacing through the forest, 100
      Chewing the food of sweet and bitter fancy,
      Lo, what befel! he threw his eye aside,
      And mark what object did present itself!
      Under an oak, whose boughs were mossed with age
      And high top bald with dry antiquity,
      A wretched ragged man, o'ergrown with hair,
      Lay sleeping on his back: about his neck
      A green and gilded snake had wreathed itself,
      Who with her head nimble in threats approached
      The opening of his mouth; but suddenly   110
      Seeing Orlando, it unlinked itself,
      And with indented glides did slip away
      Into a bush: under which bush's shade
      A lioness, with udders all drawn dry,
      Lay couching, head on ground, with catlike watch,
      When that the sleeping man should stir; for 'tis

The royal disposition of that beast
To prey on nothing that doth seem as dead:
This seen, Orlando did approach the man,
And found it was his brother, his elder brother.   120

CELIA. O, I have heard him speak of that same brother,
And he did render him the most unnatural
That lived 'mongst men.

OLIVER.   And well he might so do,
For well I know he was unnatural.

ROSALIND. But, to Orlando: did he leave him there,
Food to the sucked and hungry lioness?

OLIVER. Twice did he turn his back and purposed so:
but kindness, nobler ever than revenge,
And nature, stronger than his just occasion,
Made him give battle to the lioness,   130
Who quickly fell before him: in which hurtling
From miserable slumber I awaked.

CELIA. Are you his brother?

ROSALIND.   Was't you he rescued?

CELIA. Was't you that did so oft contrive to kill him?

OLIVER. 'Twas I; but 'tis not I: I do not shame
To tell you what I was, since my conversion
So sweetly tastes, being the thing I am.

ROSALIND. But, for the bloody napkin?—

OLIVER.   By and by ...
When from the first to last betwixt us two
Tears our recountments had most kindly bathed,   140
As how I came into that desert place....
In brief, he led me to the gentle duke,
Who gave me fresh array and entertainment,
Committing me unto my brother's love,
Who led me instantly unto his cave,
There stripped himself, and here upon his arm
The lioness had torn some flesh away,
Which all this while had bled; and now he fainted,
And cried, in fainting, upon Rosalind....
Brief, I recovered him, bound up his wound,   150
And after some small space being strong at heart,
He sent me hither, stranger as I am,
To tell this story, that you might excuse
His broken promise, and to give this napkin,
Dyed in his blood, unto the shepherd youth
That he in sport doth call his Rosalind.

                              Rosalind faints

CELIA. Why, how now, Ganymede! sweet Ganymede!

OLIVER. Many will swoon when they do look on
blood.

CELIA. There is more in it ... Cousin, Ganymede!

OLIVER. Look, he recovers.

ROSALIND.   I would I were at home.   160

CELIA. We'll lead you thither ...
I pray you, will you take him by the arm?

OLIVER. Be of good cheer, youth: you a man!
You lack a man's heart.

ROSALIND.   I do so, I confess it ...
Ah, sirrah, a body would think this was well
counterfeited. I pray you, tell your brother how
well I counterfeited.... Heigh-ho!

OLIVER. This was not counterfeit, there is too great
testimony in your complexion that it was a passion
of earnest.   170

ROSALIND. Counterfeit, I assure you.

OLIVER. Well then, take a good heart, and counterfeit
to be a man.

ROSALIND. So I do: but, i'faith, I should have been a
woman by right.

CELIA. Come, you look paler and paler; pray you,
draw homewards ... Good sir, go with us.

OLIVER. That will I: for I must bear answer back.
How you excuse my brother, Rosalind.

ROSALIND. I shall devise something: but, I pray you   180
commend my counterfeiting to him ... Will you
go?

                                        They go

ACT 5
Scene 1

Enter Touchstone and Audrey

TOUCHSTONE. We shall find a time, Audrey—
patience, gentle Audrey.

AUDREY. Faith, the priest was good enough, for all the
old gentleman's saying.

TOUCHSTONE. A most wicked Sir Oliver, Audrey, a
most vile Martext.... But, Audrey, there is a youth
here in the forest lays claim to you.

AUDREY. Ay, I know who 'tis; he hath no interest in
me in the world: here comes the man you mean.

William enters

TOUCHSTONE. It is meat and drink to me to see a   10
clown. By my troth, we that have good wits have
much to answer for; we shall be flouting; we cannot
hold.

WILLIAM. Good ev'n, Audrey.

AUDREY. God ye good ev'n, William.

WILLIAM. And good ev'n to you, sir.

TOUCHSTONE. Good ev'n, gentle friend. Cover thy
head, cover thy head; nay, prithee, be covered....
How old are you, friend?

WILLIAM. Five-and-twenty, sir.   20

TOUCHSTONE. A ripe age ... Is thy name, William?

WILLIAM. William, sir.

TOUCHSTONE. A fair name ... Wast born i'th' forest
here?

WILLIAM. Ay sir, I thank God.

TOUCHSTONE. 'Thank God'; a good answer ... Art
rich?

WILLIAM. Faith sir, so so.

TOUCHSTONE. 'So so' is good, very good, very excellent good: and yet it is not, it is but so so ... Art   30
thou wise?

WILLIAM. Ay sir, I have a pretty wit.

TOUCHSTONE. Why, thou say'st well.... I do now remember a saying: 'The fool doth think he is wise,
but the wise man knows himself to be a fool' ...
The heathen philosopher, when he had a desire to eat
a grape, would open his lips when he put it into his
mouth, meaning thereby that grapes were made to
eat and lips to open.... You do love this maid?

WILLIAM. I do, sir.   40

TOUCHSTONE. Give me your hand ... Art thou
learned?

WILLIAM. No, sir.

TOUCHSTONE. Then learn this of me—to have, is to
have; for it is a figure in rhetoric that drink, being
poured out of a cup into a glass, by filling the one
doth empty the other; for all your writers do consent
that ipse is he: now, you are not ipse, for I am he.

WILLIAM. Which he, sir?

TOUCHSTONE. He, sir, that must marry this woman ...   50
Therefore, you clown, abandon (which is in the

vulgar 'leave') the society (which in the boorish is 'company') of this female (which in the common is 'woman'); which together is, 'abandon the society of this female,' or, clown, thou perishest; or, to thy better understanding, diest? or, to wit, I kill thee, make thee away, translate thy life into death, thy liberty into bondage: I will deal in poison with thee, or in bastinado, or in steel; I will bandy with thee in faction; I will o'er-run thee with policy; I will kill 60 thee a hundred and fifty ways—therefore tremble and depart.

AUDREY. Do, good William.

WILLIAM. God rest you merry, sir.   *He goes*

Corin enters

CORIN. Our master and mistress seek you: come, away, away.

TOUCHSTONE. Trip, Audrey, trip, Audrey—I attend, I attend.   *They go*

Scene 2

Enter Oliver and Orlando

ORLANDO. Is't possible that on so little acquaintance you should like her? that but seeing you should love her? and loving woo? and, wooing, she should grant? and will you persever to enjoy her?

OLIVER. Neither call the giddiness of it in question, the poverty of her, the small acquaintance, my sudden wooing, nor her sudden consenting; but say with me, I love Aliena; say with her that she loves me; consent with both that we may enjoy each other: it shall be to your good; for my father's house and all 10 the revenue that was old Sir Rowland's will I estate upon you, and here live and die a shepherd.

Rosalind enters

ORLANDO. You have my consent.... Let your wedding be to-morrow: thither will I invite the duke and all's contented followers ... Go you and prepare Aliena; for look you, here comes my Rosalind.

ROSALIND. God save you, brother.

OLIVER. And you, fair sister.   *He goes*

ROSALIND. O, my dear Orlando, how it grieves me to see thee wear thy heart in a scarf.   20

ORLANDO. It is my arm.

ROSALIND. I thought thy heart had been wounded with the claws of a lion.

ORLANDO. Wounded it is, but with the eyes of a lady.

ROSALIND. Did your brother tell you how I counterfeited to swoon, when he showed me your handkercher?

ORLANDO. Ay, and greater wonders than that.

ROSALIND. O, I know where you are: nay, 'tis true: there was never any thing so sudden but the fight of 30 two rams, and Cæsar's thrasonical brag of 'I came, saw, and overcame': for your brother and my sister no sooner met but they looked; no sooner looked but they loved; no sooner loved but they sighed; no sooner sighed but they asked one another the reason; no sooner knew the reason but they sought the remedy: and in these degrees have they made a pair of stairs to marriage, which they will climb incontinent, or else be incontinent before marriage: they are in the very wrath of love, and they will 40 together; clubs cannot part them.

ORLANDO. They shall be married to-morrow; and I will bid the duke to the nuptial.... But, O, how bitter a thing it is to look into happiness through another man's eyes! By so much the more shall I to-morrow be at the height of heart-heaviness, by how much I shall think my brother happy in having what he wishes for.

ROSALIND. Why then, to-morrow I cannot serve your turn for Rosalind?   50

ORLANDO. I can live no longer by thinking.

ROSALIND. I will weary you then no longer with idle talking.... Know of me then, for now I speak to some purpose, that I know you are a gentleman of good conceit: I speak not this that you should bear a good opinion of my knowledge, insomuch I say I know you are; neither do I labour for a greater esteem than may in some little measure draw a belief from you, to do yourself good and not to grace me.... Believe then, if you please, that I can do 60 strange things: I have, since I was three year old, conversed with a magician, most profound in his art, and yet not damnable.... If you do love Rosalind so near the heart as your gesture cries it out, when your brother marries Aliena, shall you marry her. I know into what straits of fortune she is driven, and it is not impossible to me, if it appear not inconvenient to you, to set her before your eyes to-morrow, human as she is, and without any danger.   70

ORLANDO. Speak'st thou in sober meanings?

ROSALIND. By my life I do, which I tender dearly, though I say I am a magician ... Therefore, put you in your best array, bid your friends; for if you will be married to-morrow, you shall; and to Rosalind, if you will.

Silvius and Phebe enter

Look, here comes a lover of mine and a lover of hers.

PHEBE. Youth, you have done me much ungentleness, To show the letter that I writ to you.   80

ROSALIND. I care not if I have: it is my study To seem despiteful and ungentle to you: You are there followed by a faithful shepherd— Look upon him, love him; he worships you.

PHEBE. Good shepherd, tell this youth what 'tis to love.

SILVIUS. It is to be all made of sighs and tears, And so am I for Phebe.

PHEBE. And I for Ganymede.

ORLANDO. And I for Rosalind.

ROSALIND. And I for no woman.   90

SILVIUS. It is to be all made of faith and service, And so am I for Phebe.

PHEBE. And I for Ganymede.

ORLANDO. And I for Rosalind.

ROSALIND. And I for no woman.

SILVIUS. It is to be all made of fantasy, All made of passion, and all made of wishes, All adoration, duty, and observance, All humbleness, all patience, and impatience, All purity, all trial, all obedience;   100 And so am I for Phebe.

PHEBE. And so am I for Ganymede.

ORLANDO. And so am I for Rosalind.

ROSALIND. And so am I for no woman.

PHEBE [*to Rosalind*]. If this be so, why blame you me to love you?

SILVIUS [*to Phebe*]. If this be so, why blame you me to love you?

ORLANDO. If this be so, why blame you me to love you?

ROSALIND. Who do you speak to, 'Why blame you me to love you?'

ORLANDO. To her that is not here, nor doth not hear.

ROSALIND. Pray you no more of this, 'tis like the 110 howling of Irish wolves against the Moon ... [*to Silvius*] I will help you, if I can ... [*to Phebe*] I would love you, if I could ... To-morrow meet me all together ... [*to Phebe*] I will marry you, if ever I marry woman, and I'll be married to-morrow ... [*to Orlando*] I will satisfy you, if ever I satisfied man, and you shall be married to-morrow ... [*to Silvius*] I will content you, if what pleases you contents you, and you shall be married to-morrow ... [*to Orlando*] As you love Rosalind, meet. [*to Silvius*] As you love 120 Phebe, meet. And as I love no woman, I'll meet.... So, fare you well; I have left you commands.

SILVIUS. I'll not fail, if I live.

PHEBE. Nor I.

ORLANDO. Nor I. *They go*

Scene 3

Touchstone and Audrey enter

TOUCHSTONE. To-morrow is the joyful day, Audrey. To-morrow will we be married.

AUDREY. I do desire it with all my heart: and I hope it is no dishonest desire to desire to be a woman of the world. Here come two of the banished duke's pages.

Two pages enter

FIRST PAGE. Well met, honest gentleman.

TOUCHSTONE. By my troth, well met ... Come, sit, sit, and a song.

SECOND PAGE. We are for you: sit i' th' middle. 10

FIRST PAGE. Shall we clap into't roundly, without hawking or spitting or saying we are hoarse, which are the only prologues to a bad voice?

SECOND PAGE. I'faith i'faith; and both in a tune, like two gipsies on a horse.

SONG

It was a lover and his lass,
  With a hey, and a ho, and a hey nonino:
That o'er the green corn-field did pass,
  In spring time, the only pretty ring time,
When birds do sing, hey ding a ding, ding, 20
Sweet lovers love the spring.

Between the acres of the rye,
  With a hey, and a ho, and a hey nonino:
These pretty country folks would lie,
  In spring time, the only pretty ring time,
When birds do sing, hey ding a ding, ding,
Sweet lovers love the spring.

This carol they began that hour,
  With a hey, and a ho, and a hey nonino:
How that life was but a flower,
  In spring time, the only pretty ring time, 30
When birds do sing, hey ding a ding, ding,
Sweet lovers love the spring.

And therefore take the present time,
  With a hey, and a ho, and a hey nonino:
For love is crownéd with the prime,
  In spring time, the only pretty ring time,
When birds do sing, hey ding a ding, ding,
Sweet lovers love the spring.

TOUCHSTONE. Truly, young gentlemen, though there 40 was no great matter in the ditty, yet the note was very untuneable.

FIRST PAGE. You are deceived, sir—we kept time, we lost not our time.

TOUCHSTONE. By my troth, yes; I count it but time lost to hear such a foolish song.... God buy you, and God mend your voices! Come, Audrey. *They go*

Scene 4: *The clearing near the sheepcote (as before)*

Enter the exiled Duke, Amiens, Jaques, Orlando, Oliver, and Celia

DUKE. Dost thou believe, Orlando, that the boy Can do all this that he hath promiséd?

ORLANDO. I sometimes do believe, and sometimes do not,
  As those that fear they hope, and know they fear.

Rosalind, Silvius, and Phebe enter

ROSALIND. Patience once more, whiles our compáct is urged:
  You say, if I bring in your Rosalind,
  You will bestow her on Orlando here?

DUKE. That would I, had I kingdoms to give with her.

ROSALIND. And you say you will have her, when I bring her?

ORLANDO. That would I, were I of all kingdoms king. 10

ROSALIND. You say you'll marry me, if I be willing?

PHEBE. That will I, should I die the hour after.

ROSALIND. But if you do refuse to marry me,
  You'll give yourself to this most faithful shepherd?

PHEBE. So is the bargain.

ROSALIND. You say that you'll have Phebe, if she will?

SILVIUS. Though to have her and death were both one thing.

ROSALIND. I have promised to make all this matter even ...
  Keep you your word, O duke, to give your daughter—
  You yours, Orlando, to receive his daughter: 20
  Keep your word, Phebe, that you'll marry me,
  Or else refusing me, to wed this shepherd:
  Keep your word, Silvius, that you'll marry her,
  If she refuse me—and from hence I go,
  To make these doubts all even.
                  Rosalind and Celia depart

DUKE. I do remember in this shepherd-boy Some lively touches of my daughter's favour.

ORLANDO. My lord, the first time that I ever saw him,
  Methought he was a brother to your daughter:
  But, my good lord, this boy is forest-born, 30
  And hath been tutored in the rudiments
  Of many desperate studies by his uncle,
  Whom he reports to be a great magician,
  Obscuréd in the circle of this forest.

Touchstone and Audrey enter

JAQUES. There is, sure, another flood toward, and these couples are coming to the ark. Here comes a pair of very strange beasts, which in all tongues are called fools.

TOUCHSTONE. Salutation and greeting to you all!

JAQUES. Good my lord, bid him welcome: this is the 40 motley-minded gentleman that I have so often met in the forest: he hath been a courtier, he swears.

TOUCHSTONE. If any man doubt that, let him put me to my purgation. I have trod a measure—I have flattered a lady—I have been politic with my friend, smooth with mine enemy—I have undone three tailors—I have had four quarrels, and like to have fought one.

JAQUES. And how was that ta'en up?

TOUCHSTONE. Faith, we met, and found the quarrel 50 was upon the seventh cause.

JAQUES. How seventh cause? Good my lord, like this fellow.

DUKE. I like him very well.

TOUCHSTONE. God'ild you, sir, I desire you of the like ... I press in here, sir, amongst the rest of the country copulatives, to swear and to forswear, according as marriage binds and blood breaks ... A poor virgin, sir, an ill-favoured thing, sir, but mine own—a poor humour of mine, sir, to take 60 that that no man else will: rich honesty dwells like a miser, sir, in a poor house, as your pearl in your foul oyster.

DUKE. By my faith, he is very swift and sententious.

TOUCHSTONE. According to the fool's bolt, sir, and such dulcet diseases.

JAQUES. But, for the seventh cause. How did you find the quarrel on the seventh cause?

TOUCHSTONE. Upon a lie seven times removed ... bear your body more seeming, Audrey ... as thus, sir: I 70 did dislike the cut of a certain courtier's beard: he sent me word, if I said his beard was not cut well, he was in the mind it was: this is called the Retort Courteous. If I sent him word again 'it was not well cut,' he would send me word, he cut it to please himself: this is called the Quip Modest. If again 'it was not well cut,' he disabled my judgement: this is called the Reply Churlish. If again 'it was not well cut,' he would answer, I spake not true: this is called the Reproof Valiant. If again 'it was not well cut,' he 80 would say, I lie: this is called the Countercheck Quarrelsome: and so to the Lie Circumstantial and the Lie Direct.

JAQUES. And how oft did you say his beard was not well cut?

TOUCHSTONE. I durst go no further than the Lie Circumstantial: nor he durst not give me the Lie Direct: and so we measured swords and parted.

JAQUES. Can you nominate in order now the degrees of the lie? 90

TOUCHSTONE. O sir, we quarrel in print—by the book: as you have books for good manners ... I will name you the degrees. The first, the Retort Courteous; the second, the Quip Modest; the third, the Reply Churlish; the fourth, the Reproof Valiant; the fifth, the Countercheck Quarrelsome; the sixth, the Lie with Circumstance; the seventh, the Lie Direct ... All these you may avoid, but the Lie Direct; and you may avoid that too, with an If. I knew when seven justices could not take up a quarrel, but when the 100

parties were met themselves, one of them thought but of an If; as, 'If you said so, then I said so': and they shook hands and swore brothers. Your If is the only peace-maker; much virtue in If.

JAQUES. Is not this a rare fellow, my lord? he's as good at any thing, and yet a fool!

DUKE. He uses his folly like a stalking-horse, and under the presentation of that he shoots his wit.

Enter, as in a masque, persons representing Hymen and his train, together with Rosalind and Celia in their proper habits. Still music

HYMEN [*sings*].
    Then is there mirth in heaven,
    When earthly things made even   110
        Atone together.
    Good duke, receive thy daughter,
    Hymen from heaven brought her,
        Yea, brought her hither,
    That thou mightst join her hand with his
    Whose heart within her bosom is.

ROSALIND [*to the Duke*]. To you I give myself, for I am yours.
    [*to Orlando*] To you I give myself, for I am yours.

DUKE. If there be truth in sight, you are my daughter.

ORLANDO. If there be truth in sight, you are my Rosalind. 120

PHEBE. If sight and shape be true,
Why then, my love adieu!

ROSALIND. I'll have no father, if you be not he:
I'll have no husband, if you be not he:
Nor ne'er wed woman, if you be not she.

HYMEN. Peace, ho! I bar confusion.
    'Tis I must make conclusion
      Of these most strange events:
    Here's eight that must take hands,
    To join in Hymen's bands,   130
      If truth holds true contents.
    You and you no cross shall part:
    You and you are heart in heart:
    You to his love must accord,
    Or have a woman to your lord.
    You and you are sure together,
    As the winter to foul weather.
    Whiles a wedlock-hymn we sing,
    Feed yourselves with questioning;
    That reason wonder may diminish,   140
    How thus we met, and these things finish.

CHORIC SONG

    Wedding is great Juno's crown,
      O blesséd bond of board and bed:
    'Tis Hymen peoples every town,
      High wedlock then be honouréd:
    Honour, high honour and renown,
    To Hymen, god of every town!

DUKE. O my dear niece, welcome thou art to me,
Even daughter, welcome, in no less degree.

PHEBE. I will not eat my word, now thou art mine, 150
Thy faith my fancy to thee doth combine.

Enter Jaques de Boys

JAQUES DE BOYS. Let me have audience for a word or two:
I am the second son of old Sir Rowland,

That bring these tidings to this fair assembly.
Duke Frederick, hearing how that every day
Men of great worth resorted to this forest,
Addressed a mighty power, which were on foot,
In his own conduct, purposely to take
His brother here and put him to the sword:
And to the skirts of this wild wood he came;   160
Where, meeting with an old religious man,
After some question with him, was converted
Both from his enterprise and from the world:
His crown bequeathing to his banished brother,
And all their lands restored to them again
That were with him exiled ... This to be true,
I do engage my life.
DUKE.   Welcome, young man;
Thou offer'st fairly to thy brothers' wedding:
To one his lands withheld, and to the other
A land itself at large, a potent dukedom.   170
First, in this forest, let us do those ends
That here were well begun and well begot:
And after, every of this happy number,
That have endured shrewd days and nights with us,
Shall share the good of our returnéd fortune,
According to the measure of their states.
Meantime, forget this new-fall'n dignity,
And fall into our rustic revelry ...
Play, music! and you brides and bridegrooms all,
With measure heaped in joy, to th' measures fall.   180
JAQUES. Sir, by your patience ...
                          If I heard you rightly,
The duke hath put on a religious life,
And thrown into neglect the pompous court?
JAQUES DE BOYS. He hath.
JAQUES. To him will I: out of these convertites
There is much matter to be heard and learned....
[to the Duke] You to your former honour I
  bequeath,
Your patience and your virtue well deserves it:
[to Orlando] You to a love, that your true faith doth
  merit:
[to Oliver] You to your land, and love, and great
  allies: 190

[to Silvius] You to a long and well-deservéd bed:
[to Touchstone] And you to wrangling, for thy
  loving voyage
Is but for two months victualled ... So to your
  pleasures,
I am for other than for dancing measures.
DUKE. Stay, Jaques, stay.   160
JAQUES. To see no pastime, I: what you would have
  I'll stay to know at your abandoned cave.
                                              He goes
DUKE. Proceed, proceed: we will begin these rites,
  As we do trust they'll end in true delights.

Music and dance

EPILOGUE

Spoken by Rosalind

It is not the fashion to see the lady the epilogue:
but it is no more unhandsome than to see the lord
the prologue. If it be true that good wine needs no
bush, 'tis true that a good play needs no epilogue:
yet to good wine they do use good bushes; and good
plays prove the better by the help of good epilogues
... What a case am I in then, that am neither a good
epilogue nor cannot insinuate with you in the behalf
of a good play! I am not furnished like a beggar,
therefore to beg will not become me: my way is to   10
conjure you, and I'll begin with the women. I charge
you, O women, for the love you bear to men, to like
as much of this play as please you: and I charge you,
O men, for the love you bear to women—as I
perceive by your simpering, none of you hates them
—that between you and the women the play may
please. If I were a woman, I would kiss as many of
you as had beards that pleased me, complexions that
liked me, and breaths that I defied not: and, I am
sure, as many as have good beards, or good faces, or 20
sweet breaths, will, for my kind offer, when I make
curtsy, bid me farewell.

The Taming of the Shrew

Scene: Padua, and Petruchio's house in the country

CHARACTERS IN THE PLAY

(a) The Induction

A LORD
CHRISTOPHER SLY, *a drunken tinker*
A HOSTESS
Page, Players, Huntsmen, and Servants attending on the Lord

(b) *The Taming of the Shrew*

BAPTISTA, *a rich gentleman of Padua*
VINCENTIO, *an old gentleman of Pisa*
LUCENTIO, *son to Vincentio, in love with Bianca*
PETRUCHIO, *a gentleman of Verona, suitor to Katharina*
GREMIO ⎱ *suitors to Bianca*
HORTENSIO ⎰
TRANIO ⎱ *servants to Lucentio*
BIONDELLO, *a boy* ⎰

GRUMIO, *a man of small stature, Petruchio's lackey*
CURTIS, *an aged serving-man, in charge of Petruchio's house in the country*
NATHANIEL ⎫
PHILIP ⎪
JOSEPH ⎬ *other servants to Petruchio*
NICHOLAS ⎪
PETER ⎭
A Pedant of Mantua
KATHARINA, *the Shrew* ⎱ *daughters to Baptista*
BIANCA ⎰
A Widow
Tailor, Haberdasher, and Servants attending on Baptista and Petruchio

The Taming of the Shrew

THE INDUCTION
Scene I: *Before an alehouse on a heath*

Sly and the Hostess

SLY. I'll feeze you, in faith.

HOSTESS. A pair of stocks, you rogue!

SLY. Y'are a baggage, the Slys are no rogues.... Look
in the chronicles, we came in with Richard Conqueror ... Therefore paucas pallabris, let the world
slide: sessa!

HOSTESS. You will not pay for the glasses you have
burst?

SLY. No, not a denier ... Go by, S. Jeronimy—go to
thy cold bed, and warm thee.   10

HOSTESS. I know my remedy, I must go fetch the
third-borough.   *She goes*

SLY. Third, or fourth, or fifth borough, I'll answer
him by law. I'll not budge an inch, boy: let him
come, and kindly.   *Falls asleep*

*There is a sound of horns. A lord and his train enter as
from hunting*

LORD. Huntsman, I charge thee, tender well
my hounds.
Broach Merriman—the poor cur is embossed,
And couple Clowder with the deep-mouthed brach.
Saw'st thou not, boy, how Silver made it good
At the hedge corner, in the coldest fault?   20
I would not lose the dog for twenty pound.

1 HUNTSMAN. Why, Belman is as good as he, my
lord—
He cried upon it at the merest loss,
And twice to-day picked out the dullest scent.
Trust me, I take him for the better dog.

LORD. Thou art a fool. If Echo were as fleet,
I would esteem him worth a dozen such.
But sup them well, and look unto them all.
To-morrow I intend to hunt again.

1 HUNTSMAN. I will, my lord.   30

LORD. What's here? one dead, or drunk? See, doth
he breathe?

2 HUNTSMAN. He breathes, my lord, Were he not
warmed with ale,
This were a bed but cold to sleep so soundly.

LORD. O monstrous beast! how like a swine he lies!
Grim death, how foul and loathsome is thine image.
Sirs, I will practise on this drunken man.
What think you, if he were conveyed to bed,
Wrapped in sweet clothes, rings put upon his
fingers,
A most delicious banquet by his bed,
And brave attendants near him when he wakes,   40
Would not the beggar then forget himself?

1 HUNTSMAN. Believe me, lord, I think he
cannot choose.

2 HUNTSMAN. It would seem strange unto him when
he waked.

LORD. Even as a flatt'ring dream or worthless fancy.
Then take him up, and manage well the jest:
Carry him gently to my fairest chamber,
And hang it round with all my wanton pictures:
Balm his foul head with warm distilléd waters,
And burn sweet wood to make the lodging sweet:
Procure me music ready when he wakes,   50
To make a dulcet and a heavenly sound;
And if he chance to speak, be ready straight
And with a low submissive reverence
Say 'What is it your honour will command?'
Let one attend him with a silver basin
Full of rose-water and bestrewed with flowers,
Another bear the ewer, the third a diaper,
And say 'Will't please your lordship cool your
hands?'
Some one be ready with a costly suit,
And ask him what apparel he will wear;   60
Another tell him of his hounds and horse,
And that his lady mourns at his disease:
Persuade him that he hath been lunatic;
And when he says he is Sly, say that he dreams,
For he is nothing but a mighty lord.
This do, and do it kindly, gentle sirs—
It will be pastime passing excellent,
If it be husbanded with modesty.

1 HUNTSMAN. My lord, I warrant you we will play
our part,
As he shall think by our true diligence   70
He is no less than what we say he is.

LORD. Take him up gently and to bed with him,
And each one to his office when he wakes....
                    They bear Sly away. A trumpet sounds
Sirrah, go see what trumpet 'tis that sounds—
                              A serving-man goes
Belike some noble gentleman that means,
Travelling some journey, to repose him here.

The serving-man returns

How now? who is it?

SERVING-MAN.   An't please your honour, players
That offer service to your lordship.

LORD. Bid them come near.

The players approach

                    Now, fellows, you are welcome.

PLAYERS. We thank your honour.   80

LORD. Do you intend to stay with me to-night?

A PLAYER. So please your lordship to accept our duty.

LORD. With all my heart. This fellow I remember,
Since once he played a farmer's eldest son—
'Twas where you wooed the gentlewoman so well:
I have forgot your name; but, sure, that part
Was aptly fitted and naturally performed.

A PLAYER. I think 'twas Soto that your honour means.

LORD. 'Tis very true—thou didst it excellent.
Well, you are come to me in happy time,   90
The rather for I have some sport in hand,
Wherein your cunning can assist me much.
There is a lord will hear you play to-night;
But I am doubtful of your modesties,
Lest over-eyeing of his odd behaviour—
For yet his honour never heard a play—

You break into some merry passion,
And so offend him: for I tell you, sirs,
If you should smile, he grows impatient.
A PLAYER. Fear not, my lord, we can contain ourselves,   100
Were he the veriest antic in the world.
LORD. Go, sirrah, take them to the buttery,
And give them friendly welcome every one—
Let them want nothing that my house affords.
    A servant leads the players away
Sirrah, go you to Barthol'mew my page,
And see him dressed in all suits like a lady:
That done, conduct him to the drunkard's
    chamber,
And call him 'madam,' do him obeisance:
Tell him from me, as he will win my love,
He bear himself with honourable action,   110
Such as he hath observed in noble ladies
Unto their lords, by them accomplishéd:
Such duty to the drunkard let him do,
With soft low tongue and lowly courtesy,
And say :'What is't your honour will command,
Wherein your lady and your humble wife
May show her duty and make known her love?'
And then with kind embracements, tempting kisses,
And with declining head into his bosom,
Bid him shed tears, as being overjoyed   120
To see her noble lord restored to health,
Who for this seven years hath esteemed him
No better than a poor and loathsome beggar:
And if the boy have not a woman's gift
To rain a shower of commanded tears,
An onion will do well for such a shift,
Which in a napkin being close conveyed,
Shall in despite enforce a watery eye.
See this dispatched with all the haste thou canst—
Anon I'll give thee more instructions.   130
    A servant departs
I know the boy will well usurp the grace,
Voice, gait, and action of a gentlewoman:
I long to hear him call the drunkard husband,
And how my men will stay themselves from
    laughter
When they do homage to this simple peasant.
I'll in to counsel them: haply my presence
May well abate the over-merry spleen,
Which otherwise would grow into extremes.
    He goes, the huntsmen following

Scene 2: *A bedroom in the Lord's house*

*Enter Sly with attendants at hand; some with apparel, others
with basin and ewer and other appurtenances, and Lord*

SLY. For God's sake, a pot of small ale.
1 SERVANT. Will't please your lordship drink a cup
    of sack?
2 SERVANT. Will't please your honour taste of these
    conserves?
3 SERVANT. What raiment will your honour wear
    to-day?
SLY. I am Christophero Sly, call not me 'honour' nor
'lordship': I ne'er drank sack in my life: and if you
give me any conserves, give me conserves of beef:
ne'er ask me what raiment I'll wear, for I have no
more doublets than backs, no more stockings than
legs, nor no more shoes than feet, nay, sometime   10

more feet than shoes, or such shoes as my toes look
through the over-leather.
LORD. Heaven cease this idle humour in your honour!
O, that a mighty man, of such descent,
Of such possessions and so high esteem,
Should be infuséd with so foul a spirit!
SLY. What, would you make me mad? Am not I
Christopher Sly, old Sly's son of Burton-heath, by
birth a pedlar, by education a card-maker, by trans-
mutation a bear-herd, and now by present profes-   20
sion a tinker? Ask Marian Hacket, the fat ale-wife
of Wincot, if she know me not: if she say I am not
xiiii. d. on the score for sheer ale, score me up for
the lyingest knave in Christendom. What! I am not
bestraught: here's—
3 SERVANT. O, this it is that makes your lady mourn.
2 SERVANT. O, this it is that makes your servants droop.
LORD. Hence comes it that your kindred shuns
    your house,
As beaten hence by your strange lunacy.
O, noble lord, bethink thee of thy birth,   30
Call home thy ancient thoughts from banishment,
And banish thence these abject lowly dreams:
Look, how thy servants do attend on thee.
Each in his office ready at thy beck.
Wilt thou have music? Hark! Apollo plays,   *Music*
And twenty cagéd nightingales do sing.
Or wilt thou sleep? we'll have thee to a couch,
Softer and sweeter than the lustful bed
On purpose trimmed up for Semiramis.
Say thou wilt walk; we will bestrow the ground: 40
Or wilt thou ride? thy horses shall be trapped,
Their harness studded all with gold and pearl.
Does thou love hawking? thou hast hawks will soar
Above the morning lark. Or wilt thou hunt?
Thy hounds shall make the welkin answer them,
And fetch shrill echoes from the hollow earth.
1 SERVANT. Say thou wilt course—thy greyhounds are
    as swift
As breathéd stags: ay, fleeter than the roe.
2 SERVANT. Dost thou love pictures? we will fetch
    thee straight
Adonis painted by a running brook,   50
And Cytherea all in sedges hid,
Which seem to move and wanton with her breath,
Even as the waving sedges play with wind.
LORD. We'll show thee Io as she was a maid,
And how she was beguiléd and surprised,
As lively painted as the deed was done.
3 SERVANT. Or Daphne roaming through a thorny
    wood,
Scratching her legs that one shall swear she bleeds,
And at that sight shall sad Apollo weep,
So workmanly the blood and tears are drawn.   60
LORD. Thou art a lord, and nothing but a lord:
Thou hast a lady far more beautiful
Than any woman in this waning age.
1 SERVANT. And till the tears that she hath shed
    for thee
Like envious floods o'er-run her lovely face,
She was the fairest creature in the world—
And yet she is inferior to none.
SLY. Am I a lord? and have I such a lady?
Or do I dream? or have I dreamed till now?
I do not sleep: I see, I hear, I speak;   70
I smell sweet savours and I feel soft things:

Upon my life, I am a lord indeed,
And not a tinker nor Christophero Sly.
Well, bring our lady hither to our sight—
And once again a pot o'th' smallest ale.
2 SERVANT. Will't please your mightiness to wash
    your hands?
O, how we joy to see your wit restored!
O, that once more you knew but what you are!
These fifteen years you have been in a dream,
Or when you waked, so waked as if you slept.   80
SLY. These fifteen years! by my fay, a goodly nap.
But did I never speak of all that time?
1 SERVANT. O, yes, my lord, but very idle words,
For though you lay here in this goodly chamber,
Yet would you say ye were beaten out of door,
And rail upon the hostess of the house,
And say you would present her at the leet,
Because she brought stone jugs and no sealed quarts:
Sometimes, you would call out for Cicely Hacket.
SLY. Ay, the woman's maid of the house.   90
3 SERVANT. Why, sir, you know no house, nor no
    such maid,
Nor no such men as you have reckoned up,
As Stephen Sly, and old John Naps of Greece,
And Peter Turph, and Henry Pimpernell;
And twenty more such names and men as these,
Which never were nor no man ever saw.
SLY. Now, Lord be thankéd for my good amends!
ALL. Amen.
SLY. I thank thee, thou shalt not lose by it.

The page enters as a lady with attendants

PAGE. How fares my noble lord?   100
SLY. Marry, I fare well—for here is cheer enough.
Where is my wife?
PAGE. Here, noble lord, what is thy will with her?
SLY. Are you my wife and will not call me husband?
My men should call me 'lord,' I am your goodman.
PAGE. My husband and my lord, my lord and
    husband,
I am your wife in all obedience.
SLY. I know it well. What must I call her?
LORD. Madam.
SLY. Al'ce madam, or Joan madam?   110
LORD. 'Madam' and nothing else, so lords call ladies.
SLY. Madam wife, they say that I have dreamed
And slept above some fifteen year or more.
PAGE. Ay, and the time seems thirty unto me,
Being all this time abandoned from your bed.
SLY. 'Tis much! Servants, leave me and her alone.
                        The servants withdraw
Madam, undress you and come now to bed.
PAGE. Thrice-noble lord, let me entreat of you
To pardon me yet for a night or two;
Or, if not so, until the sun be set: 120
For your physicians have expressly charged,
In peril to incur your former malady,
That I should yet absent me from your bed:
I hope this reason stands for my excuse.
SLY. Ay, it stands so that I may hardly tarry so long.
But I would be loath to fall into my dreams again:
I will therefore tarry in despite of the flesh and the
    blood.

1 Servant re-enters

1 SERVANT. Your honour's players, hearing your
    amendment,
Are come to play a pleasant comedy,   130
For so your doctors hold it very meet,
Seeing too much sadness hath congealed your
    blood,
And melancholy is the nurse of frenzy.
Therefore they thought it good you hear a play
And frame your mind to mirth and merriment,
Which bars a thousand harms and lengthens life.
SLY. Marry, I will; let them play it. Is not a com-
modity a Christmas gambold or a tumbling-trick?
PAGE. No, my good lord, it is more pleasing stuff.
SLY. What, household stuff?   140
PAGE. It is a kind of history.
SLY. Well, we'll see't. Come, madam wife, sit by
my side and let the world slip, we shall ne'er be
younger.   *The page sits beside him*

A flourish of trumpets

ACT 1

Scene 1: *Padua. The houses of Baptista, Hortensio and
        others opening upon a public square*

Lucentio and his man Tranio enter the square

LUCENTIO. Tranio, since for the great desire I had
To see fair Padua, nursery of arts,
I am arrived for fruitful Lombardy,
The pleasant garden of great Italy,
And by my father's love and leave am armed
With his good will and thy good company,
My trusty servant, well approved in all,
Here let us breathe and haply institute
A course of learning and ingenious studies.
Pisa renownéd for grave citizens   10
Gave me my being and my father first,
A merchant of great traffic through the world,
Vincentio, come of the Bentivolii:
Vincentio's son, brought up in Florence,
It shall become to serve all hopes conceived.
To deck his fortune with his virtuous deeds:
And therefore, Tranio, for the time I study
Virtue, and that part of philosophy
Will I apply that treats of happiness
By virtue specially to be achieved.   20
Tell me thy mind, for I have Pisa left
And am to Padua come, as he that leaves
A shallow plash to plunge him in the deep,
And with satiety seeks to quench his thirst.
TRANIO. Mi perdonato, gentle master mine:
I am in all affected as yourself,
Glad that you thus continue your resolve,
To suck the sweets of sweet philosophy.
Only, good master, while we do admire
This virtue and this moral discipline,   30
Let's be no stoics nor no stocks I pray,
Or so devote to Aristotle's checks,
As Ovid be an outcast quite abjured:
Balk logic with acquaintance that you have,
And practise rhetoric in your common talk,
Music and poesy use to quicken you,
The mathematics and the metaphysics
Fall to them as you find your stomach serves you:
No profit grows where is no pleasure ta'en ...

In brief, sir, study what you most affect.   40
LUCENTIO. Gramercies, Tranio, well dost thou advise.
If, Biondello, thou wert come ashore,
We could at once put us in readiness,
And take a lodging fit to entertain
Such friends as time in Padua shall beget.
But stay awhile, what company is this?
TRANIO. Master, some show to welcome us to town.

*Enter Baptista, with his two daughters Katharina and
Bianca, followed by Gremio, a pantaloon, and Hortensio,
suitor to Bianca. Lucentio and Tranio stand by*

BAPTISTA. Gentlemen, importune me no farther,
For how I firmly am resolved you know;
That is, not to bestow my youngest daughter,   50
Before I have a husband for the elder:
If either of you both love Katharina,
Because I know you well, and love you well,
Leave shall you have to court her at your pleasure.
GREMIO. To cart her rather: she's too rough for me.
There, there, Hortensio, will you any wife?
KATHARINA. I pray you, sir, is it your will
To make a stale of me amongst these mates?
HORTENSIO. Mates, maid! how mean you that? no
mates for you,
Unless you were of gentler, milder mould.   60
KATHARINA. I'faith, sir, you shall never need
to fear.
Iwis it is not half way to her heart:
But if it were, doubt not her care should be
To comb your noddle with a three-legged stool,
And paint your face, and use you like a fool.
HORTENSIO. From all such devils, good Lord deliver
us!
GREMIO. And me too, good Lord!
TRANIO. Husht, master! here's some good
pastime toward;
That wench is stark mad or wonderful froward.
LUCENTIO. But in the other's silence do I see   70
Maid's mild behaviour and sobriety.
Peace, Tranio.
TRANIO. Well said, master—mum! and gaze
your fill.
BAPTISTA. Gentlemen, that I may soon make good
What I have said, Bianca, get you in.
And let it not displease thee, good Bianca,
For I will love thee ne'er the less, my girl.
KATHARINA. A pretty peat! it is best
Put finger in the eye, an she knew why.
BIANCA. Sister, content you in my discontent.   80
Sir, to your pleasure humbly I subscribe:
My books and instruments shall be my company,
On them to look and practise by myself.
LUCENTIO. Hark, Tranio! thou mayst hear
Minerva speak.
HORTENSIO. Signior Baptista, will you be so strange?
Sorry am I that our good will effects
Bianca's grief.
GREMIO.   Why will you mew her up,
Signior Baptista, for this fiend of hell,
And make her bear the penance of her tongue?
BAPTISTA. Gentlemen, content ye; I am resolved: 90
Go in, Bianca....   *Bianca goes*
And for I know she taketh most delight
In music, instruments and poetry,
Schoolmasters will I keep within my house,

Fit to instruct her youth. If you, Hortensio,
Or Signior Gremio, you, know any such,
Prefer them hither; for to cunning men
I will be very kind, and liberal
To mine own children in good bringing-up.
And so farewell ... Katharina you may stay,   100
For I have more to commune with Bianca.   *He goes*
KATHARINA. Why, and I trust I may go too, may I not?
What, shall I be appointed hours, as though, belike,
I knew not what to take, and what to leave? Ha!
GREMIO. You may go to the devil's dam: your gifts
are so good, here's none will hold you. [*she goes*]
There! love is not so great, Hortensio, but we may
blow our nails together, and fast it fairly out: our
cake's dough on both sides. Farewell: yet, for the
love I bear my sweet Bianca, if I can by any means   110
light on a fit man to teach her that wherein she
delights, I will wish him to her father.
HORTENSIO. So will I, Signior Gremio: but a word, I
pray. Though the nature of our quarrel yet never
brooked parle, know now, upon advice, it toucheth
us both—that we may yet again have access to our
fair mistress and be happy rivals in Bianca's love
—to labour and effect one thing specially.
GREMIO. What's that, I pray?
HORTENSIO. Marry, sir, to get a husband for her sister. 120
GREMIO. A husband! a devil.
HORTENSIO. I say, a husband.
GREMIO. I say, a devil. Think'st thou, Hortensio,
though her father be very rich, any man is so very
a fool to be married to hell?
HORTENSIO. Tush, Gremio: though it pass your
patience and mine to endure her loud alarums, why,
man, there be good fellows in the world, an a man
could light on them, would take her with all faults,
and money enough.   130
GREMIO. I cannot tell: but I had as lief take her dowry
with this condition—to be whipped at the high-
cross every morning.
HORTENSIO. Faith, as you say, there's small choice in
rotten apples. But come, since this bar in law makes
us friends, it shall be so far forth friendly maintained
till by helping Baptista's eldest daughter to a husband we set his youngest free for a husband, and
then have to't afresh. Sweet Bianca! Happy man be
his dole! He that runs fastest gets the ring. How   140
say you, Signior Gremio?
GREMIO. I am agreed, and would I had given him the
best horse in Padua to begin his wooing that would
thoroughly woo her, wed her and bed her and rid
the house of her! Come on.   *They go together*
TRANIO. I pray, sir, tell me, is it possible
That love should of a sudden take such hold?
LUCENTIO. O Tranio, till I found it to be true,
I never thought it possible or likely;
But see, while idly I stood looking on,   150
I found the effect of love in idleness,
And now in plainness do confess to thee—
That art to me as secret and as dear
As Anna to the Queen of Carthage was—
Tranio, I burn, I pine, I perish, Tranio,
If I achieve not this young modest girl.
Counsel me, Tranio, for I know thou canst:
Assist me, Tranio, for I know thou wilt.
TRANIO. Master, it is no time to chide you now;
Affection is not rated from the heart: 160

If love have touched you, nought remains but so—
'Redime te captum quam queas minimo.'
LUCENTIO. Gramercies, lad. Go forward, this contents.
The rest will comfort, for thy counsel's sound.
TRANIO. Master, you looked so longly on the maid,
Perhaps you marked not what's the pith of all.
LUCENTIO. O yes, I saw sweet beauty in her face,
Such as the daughter of Agenor had,
That made great Jove to humble him to her hand,
When with his knees he kissed the Cretan strand.   170
TRANIO. Saw you no more? marked you not how
her sister
Began to scold and raise up such a storm
That mortal ears might hardly endure the din?
LUCENTIO. Tranio, I saw her coral lips to move,
And with her breath she did perfume the air.
Sacred and sweet was all I saw in her.
TRANIO. Nay, then 'tis time to stir him from his trance.
I pray, awake, sir: if you love the maid,
Bend thoughts and wits to achieve her. Thus it
stands:
Her elder sister is so curst and shrewd   180
That till the father rid his hands of her,
Master, your love must live a maid at home,
And therefore has he closely mewed her up,
Because he will not be annoyed with suitors.
LUCENTIO. Ah, Tranio, what a cruel father's he!
But art thou not advised, he took some care
To get her cunning schoolmasters to instruct her?
TRANIO. Ay, marry, am I, sir—and now 'tis plotted.
LUCENTIO. I have it, Tranio.
TRANIO.   Master, for my hand,
Both our inventions meet and jump in one!   190
LUCENTIO. Tell me thine first.
TRANIO.   You will be schoolmaster,
And undertake the teaching of the maid:
That's your device.
LUCENTIO.   It is: may it be done?
TRANIO. Not possible; for who shall bear your part,
And be in Padua here Vincentio's son,
Keep house and ply his book, welcome his friends,
Visit his countrymen and banquet them?
LUCENTIO. Basta, content thee; for I have it full.
We have not yet been seen in any house,
Nor can we be distinguished by our faces   200
For man or master: then it follows thus;
Thou shalt be master, Tranio, in my stead,
Keep house and port and servants, as I should:
I will some other be—some Florentine,
Some Neapolitan, or mean man of Pisa.
'Tis hatched, and shall be so: Tranio, at once
Uncase thee; take my coloured hat and cloak:
When Biondello comes, he waits on thee,
But I will charm him first to keep his tongue.
TRANIO. So had you need.   210
In brief, sir, sith it your pleasure is,
And I am tied to be obedient—
For so your father charged me at our parting;
'Be serviceable to my son,' quoth he,
Although I think 'twas in another sense—
I am content to be obedient,
Because so well I love Lucentio.
LUCENTIO. Tranio, be so, because Lucentio loves,
And let me be a slave, t'achieve that maid
Whose sudden sight hath thralled my wounded eye.   220
Biondello approaches

Here comes the rogue. Sirrah, where have you been?
BIONDELLO. Where have I been! Nay, how now!
where are you?
Master, has my fellow Tranio stol'n your clothes?
Or you stol'n his? or both? pray, what's the news?
LUCENTIO. Sirrah, come hither. 'Tis no time to jest,
And therefore frame your manners to the time.
Your fellow Tranio here, to save my life,
Puts my apparel and my count'nance on,
And I for my escape have put on his;
For in a quarrel since I came ashore   230
I killed a man and fear I was descried:
Wait you on him, I charge you, as becomes,
While I make way from hence to save my life:
You understand me?
BIONDELLO.   Ay, sir, ne'er a whit.
LUCENTIO. And not a jot of Tranio in your mouth.
Tranio is changed into Lucentio.
BIONDELLO. The better for him, would I were so too!
TRANIO. So could I, faith, boy, to have the next
wish after,
That Lucentio indeed had Baptista's youngest
daughter.
But, sirrah, not for my sake, but your master's, I
advise   240
You use your manners discreetly in all kind
of companies:
When I am alone, why, then I am Tranio;
But in all places else, your master Lucentio.
LUCENTIO. Tranio, let's go:
One thing more rests, that thyself execute,
To make one among these wooers: if thou ask
me why,
Sufficeth my reasons are both good and weighty.
They go

The presenters above speak

1 SERVANT. My lord, you nod, you do not mind the
play.
SLY [*awakes*]. Yes, by Saint Anne, do I. A good matter,
surely: comes there any more of it?   250
PAGE. My lord, 'tis but begun.
SLY. 'Tis a very excellent piece of work, madam lady:
would 'twere done!   *They sit and mark*

Scene 2: *Padua; the square, as before*

Enter Petruchio and his man Grumio

PETRUCHIO. Verona, for a while I take my leave,
To see my friends in Padua, but of all
My best belovéd and approvéd friend,
Hortensio; and I trow this is his house ...
Here, sirrah Grumio, knock, I say.
GRUMIO. Knock, sir! whom should I knock? is there
any man has rebused your worship?
PETRUCHIO. Villain, I say, knock me here soundly.
GRUMIO. Knock you here, sir? why, sir, what am I,
sir, that I should knock you here, sir?   10
PETRUCHIO. Villain, I say, knock me at this gate,
And rap me well, or I'll knock your knave's pate.
GRUMIO. My master is grown quarrelsome: I should
knock you first,
And then I know after who comes by the worst.
PETRUCHIO. Will it not be?
Faith, sirrah, an you'll not knock, I'll ring it!
I'll try how you can 'sol, fa,' and sing it.

He wrings him by the ears

GRUMIO. Help, masters, help! my master is mad.
PETRUCHIO. Now, knock when I bid you:
   sirrah! villain!

Hortensio opens

HORTENSIO. How now! what's the matter? My old 20
   friend Grumio! and my good friend Petruchio!
   How do you all at Verona?
PETRUCHIO. Signior Hortensio, come you to part
   the fray?
   'Con tutto il cuore, ben trovato,' may I say.
HORTENSIO. 'Alla nostra casa ben venuto, molto
   honorato signor mio Petruchio.'
   Rise, Grumio, rise, we will compound this quarrel.
GRUMIO. Nay, 'tis no matter, sir, what he 'leges in
   Latin. If this be not a lawful cause for me to leave
   his service, look you, sir. He bid me knock him and 30
   rap him soundly, sir: well, was it fit for a servant to
   use his master so, being perhaps (for aught I see)
   two and thirty, a pip out?
   Whom would to God I had well knocked at first,
   Then had not Grumio come by the worst.
PETRUCHIO. A senseless villain! Good Hortensio,
   I bade the rascal knock upon your gate,
   And could not get him for my heart to do it.
GRUMIO. Knock at the gate! O heavens! Spake you
   not these words plain, 'Sirrah, knock me here: rap 40
   me here: knock me well, and knock me soundly'?
   And come you now with 'knocking at the gate'?
PETRUCHIO. Sirrah, be gone, or talk not, I advise you.
HORTENSIO. Petruchio, patience, I am Grumio's
   pledge:
   Why, this' a heavy chance 'twixt him and you,
   Your ancient, trusty, pleasant servant Grumio.
   And tell me now, sweet friend, what happy gale
   Blows you to Padua here from old Verona?
PETRUCHIO. Such wind as scatters young men through
   the world,
   To seek their fortunes farther than at home, 50
   Where small experience grows but in a few.
   Signior Hortensio, thus it stands with me—
   Antonio, my father, is deceased,
   And I have thrust myself into this maze,
   Haply to wive and thrive as best I may:
   Crowns in my purse I have, and goods at home,
   And so am come abroad to see the world.
HORTENSIO. Petruchio, shall I then come roundly to
   thee,
   And wish thee to a shrewd ill-favoured wife?
   Thou'dst thank me but a little for my counsel: 60
   And yet I'll promise thee she shall be rich,
   And very rich: but th'art too much my friend,
   And I'll not wish thee to her.
PETRUCHIO. Signior Hortensio, 'twixt such friends
   as we,
   Few words suffice: and therefore, if thou know
   One rich enough to be Petruchio's wife—
   As wealth is burden of my wooing dance—
   Be she as foul as was Florentius' love,
   As old as Sibyl, and as curst and shrewd
   As Socrates' Xanthippe, or a worse, 70
   She moves me not, or not removes, at least,
   Affection's edge in me, were she as rough
   As are the swelling Adriatic seas.

I come to wive it wealthily in Padua;
If wealthily, then happily in Padua.
GRUMIO. Nay, look you, sir, he tells you flatly what
   his mind is: why, give him gold enough, and marry
   him to a puppet or an aglet-baby, or an old trot
   with ne'er a tooth in her head, though she have as
   many diseases as two and fifty horses: why, nothing 80
   comes amiss, so money comes withal.
HORTENSIO. Petruchio, since we are stepped thus
   far in,
   I will continue that I broached in jest.
   I can, Petruchio, help thee to a wife
   With wealth enough, and young and beauteous,
   Brought up as best becomes a gentlewoman.
   Her only fault, and that is faults enough,
   Is that she is intolerable curst
   And shrewd and froward, so beyond all measure,
   That, were my state far worser than it is, 90
   I would not wed her for a mine of gold.
PETRUCHIO. Hortensio, peace; thou know'st not
   gold's effect.
   Tell me her father's name and 'tis enough;
   For I will board her, though she chide as loud
   As thunder when the clouds in autumn crack.
HORTENSIO. Her father is Baptista Minola,
   An affable and courteous gentleman,
   Her name is Katharina Minola,
   Renowned in Padua for her scolding tongue.
PETRUCHIO. I know her father, though I know not her, 100
   And he knew my deceasèd father well:
   I will not sleep, Hortensio, till I see her,
   And therefore let me be thus bold with you,
   To give you over at this first encounter,
   Unless you will accompany me thither.
GRUMIO. I pray you, sir, let him go while the humour
   lasts. O' my word, an she knew him as well as I do,
   she would think scolding would do little good upon
   him. She may perhaps call him half a score knaves
   or so: why, that's nothing; an he begin once, he'll 110
   rail in his rope-tricks. I'll tell you what, sir, an she
   stand him but a little, he will throw a figure in her
   face, and so disfigure her with it, that she shall have
   no more eyes to see withal than a cat. You know him
   not, sir.
HORTENSIO. Tarry, Petruchio, I must go with thee,
   For in Baptista's keep my treasure is:
   He hath the jewel of my life in hold,
   His youngest daughter, beautiful Bianca,
   And her withholds from me and other more, 120
   Suitors to her and rivals in my love;
   Supposing it a thing impossible,
   For those defects I have before rehearsed,
   That ever Katharina will be wooed:
   Therefore this order hath Baptista ta'en,
   That none shall have access unto Bianca,
   Till Katharine the curst have got a husband.
GRUMIO. Katharine the curst!
   A title for a maid of all titles the worst.
HORTENSIO. Now shall my friend Petruchio do
   me grace, 130
   And offer me disguised in sober robes
   To old Baptista as a schoolmaster
   Well seen in music, to instruct Bianca,
   That so I may by this device at least
   Have leave and leisure to make love to her,
   And unsuspected court her by herself.

GRUMIO. Here's no knavery! See, to beguile the old
folks, how the young folks lay their heads together!

*Gremio enters the square, with Lucentio disguised as
Cambio, a schoolmaster*

Master, master, look about you: who goes there? ha!
HORTENSIO. Peace, Grumio! it is the rival of my love. 140
Petruchio, stand by a while.
GRUMIO. A proper stripling and an amorous!

They stand by

GREMIO. O, very well—I have perused the note.
Hark you, sir, I'll have them very fairly bound—
All books of love, see that at any hand—
And see you read no other lectures to her:
You understand me. Over and beside
Signior Baptista's liberality,
I'll mend it with a largess. Take your paper too.
And let me have them very well perfumed;   150
For she is sweeter than perfume itself,
To whom they go. What will you read to her?
LUCENTIO. Whate'er I read to her, I'll plead for you
As for my patron, stand you so assured,
As firmly as yourself were still in place,
Yea, and perhaps with more successful words
Than you, unless you were a scholar, sir.
GREMIO. O this learning, what a thing it is!
GRUMIO. O this woodcock, what an ass it is!
PETRUCHIO. Peace, sirrah.   160
HORTENSIO. Grumio, mum!
[*comes forward*] God save you, Signior Gremio!
GREMIO. And you are well met, Signior Hortensio.
Trow you whither I am going? To Baptista Minola.
I promised to inquire carefully
About a schoolmaster for the fair Bianca,
And by good fortune I have lighted well
On this young man; for learning and behaviour
Fit for her turn, well read in poetry
And other books—good ones, I warrant ye.   170
HORTENSIO. 'Tis well: and I have met a gentleman
Hath promised me to help to another,
A fine musician to instruct our mistress,
So shall I no whit be behind in duty
To fair Bianca, so beloved of me.
GREMIO. Beloved of me, and that my deeds shall
prove.
GRUMIO. And that his bags shall prove.
HORTENSIO. Gremio, 'tis now no time to vent our love.
Listen to me, and if you speak me fair,   180
I'll tell you news indifferent good for either.
Here is a gentleman whom by chance I met,
Upon agreement from us to his liking,
Will undertake to woo curst Katharine,
Yea, and to marry her, if her dowry please.
GREMIO. So said, so done, is well.
Hortensio, have you told him all her faults?
PETRUCHIO. I know she is an irksome brawling scold:
If that be all, masters, I hear no harm.
GREMIO. No, say'st me so, friend? What countryman?
PETRUCHIO. Born in Verona, old Antonio's son: 190
My father dead, my fortune lives for me,
And I do hope good days and long to see.
GREMIO. Sir, such a life, with such a wife,
were strange!
But, if you have a stomach, to't a God's name—
You shall have me assisting you in all.
But will you woo this wild-cat?

PETRUCHIO.   Will I live?
GRUMIO. Will he woo her? ay, or I'll hang her.
PETRUCHIO. Why came I hither but to that intent?
Think you a little din can daunt mine ears?
Have I not in my time heard lions roar?   200
Have I not heard the sea puffed up with winds
Rage like an angry boar chaféd with sweat?
Have I not heard great ordnance in the field,
And heaven's artillery thunder in the skies?
Have I not in a pitchéd battle heard
Loud 'larums, neighing steeds, and trumpets' clang?
And do you tell me of a woman's tongue,
That gives not half so great a blow to hear,
As will a chestnut in a farmer's fire?
Tush! tush! fear boys with bugs.

GRUMIO.   For he fears none. 210
GREMIO. Hortensio, hark:
This gentleman is happily arrived,
My mind presumes, for his own good and ours.
HORTENSIO. I promised we would be contributors
And bear his charge of wooing, whatsoe'er.
GREMIO. And so we will, provided that he win her.
GRUMIO. I would I were as sure of a good dinner.

*Tranio, bravely apparelled as Lucentio, enters with Bion-
dello*

TRANIO. Gentlemen, God save you! If I may be bold,
Tell me, I beseech you, which is the readiest way
To the house of Signior Baptista Minola?   220
BIONDELLO. He that has the two fair daughters: is't he
you mean?
TRANIO. Even he, Biondello.
GREMIO. Hark you, sir! You mean not her too?
TRANIO. Perhaps, him and her, sir. What have you
to do?
PETRUCHIO. Not her that chides, sir, at any hand, I
pray.
TRANIO. I love no chiders, sir: Biondello, let's away.
LUCENTIO. Well begun, Tranio.
HORTENSIO.   Sir, a word ere you go:
Are you a suitor to the maid you talk of, yea or no?
TRANIO. And if I be, sir, is it any offence?
GREMIO. No; if without more words you will get
you hence.   230
TRANIO. Why, sir, I pray, are not the streets as free
For me as for you?
GREMIO.   But so is not she.
TRANIO. For what reason, I beseech you?
GREMIO.   For this reason, if you'll know,
That she's the choice love of Signior Gremio.
HORTENSIO. That she's the chosen of Signior Hor-
tensio.
TRANIO. Softly, my masters! if you be gentlemen,
Do me this right; hear me with patience.
Baptista is a noble gentleman,
To whom my father is not all unknown,
And were his daughter fairer than she is,   240
She may more suitors have and me for one.
Fair Leda's daughter had a thousand wooers,
Then well one more may fair Bianca have:
And so she shall; Lucentio shall make one,
Though Paris came in hope to speed alone.
GREMIO. What, this gentleman will out-talk us all!
LUCENTIO. Sir, give him head, I know he'll prove a
jade.

PETRUCHIO. Hortensio, to what end are all these words?

HORTENSIO. Sir, let me be so bold as ask you,
Did you yet ever see Baptista's daughter? 250

TRANIO. No, sir, but hear I do that he hath two:
The one as famous for a scolding tongue,
As is the other for beauteous modesty.

PETRUCHIO. Sir, sir, the first's for me, let her go by.

GREMIO. Yea, leave that labour to great Hercules,
And let it be more than Alcides' twelve.

PETRUCHIO. Sir, understand you this of me in sooth,
The youngest daughter whom you hearken for
Her father keeps from all access of suitors,
And will not promise her to any man, 260
Until the elder sister first be wed.
The younger then is free, and not before.

TRANIO. If it be so, sir, that you are the man
Must stead us all and me amongst the rest;
And if you break the ice and do this feat,
Achieve the elder, set the younger free
For our access—whose hap shall be to have her
Will not so graceless be to be ingrate.

HORTENSIO. Sir, you say well, and well you do conceive,
And since you do profess to be a suitor, 270
You must, as we do, gratify this gentleman,
To whom we all rest generally beholding.

TRANIO. Sir, I shall not be slack, in sign whereof,
Please ye we may contrive this afternoon,
And quaff carouses to our mistress' health,
And do as adversaries do in law,
Strive mightily, but eat and drink as friends.

GRUMIO, BIONDELLO. O excellent motion! Fellows, let's be gone.

HORTENSIO. The motion's good indeed, and be it so,
Petruchio, I shall be your ben venuto.   They go 280

ACT 2

Scene 1: *The house of Baptista*

Katharina and Bianca

BIANCA. Good sister, wrong me not, nor wrong yourself,
To make a bondmaid and a slave of me.
That I disdain: but for these other gauds,
Unbind my hands, I'll pull them off myself,
Yea, all my raiment, to my petticoat,
Or what you will command me will I do,
So well I know my duty to my elders.

KATHARINA. Of all thy suitors, here I charge thee, tell
Whom thou lov'st best: see thou dissemble not.

BIANCA. Believe me, sister, of all the men alive 10
I never yet beheld that special face
Which I could fancy more than any other.

KATHARINA. Minion, thou liest: is't not Hortensio?

BIANCA. If you affect him, sister, here I swear
I'll plead for you myself, but you shall have him.

KATHARINA. O then, belike, you fancy riches more—
You will have Gremio to keep you fair.

BIANCA. Is it for him you do envy me so?
Nay then you jest, and now I well perceive
You have but jested with me all this while: 20
I prithee, sister Kate, untie my hands.

KATHARINA [*strikes her*]. If that be jest, then all the rest was so.

Baptista enters

BAPTISTA. Why, how now, dame! whence grows this insolence?
Bianca, stand aside. Poor girl! she weeps.
Go ply thy needle, meddle not with her.
For shame, thou hilding of a devilish spirit,
Why dost thou wrong her that did ne'er wrong thee?
When did she cross thee with a bitter word?

KATHARINA. Her silence flouts me, and I'll be revenged.   *Flies after Bianca*

BAPTISTA. What, in my sight? Bianca, get thee in. 30
                                    Bianca departs

KATHARINA. What, will you not suffer me? Nay, now I see
She is your treasure, she must have a husband,
I must dance bare-foot on her wedding-day
And for your love to her lead apes in hell.
Talk not to me, I will go sit and weep
Till I can find occasion of revenge.   *She goes*

BAPTISTA. Was ever gentleman thus grieved as I?
But who comes here?

Gremio enters, with Lucentio as Cambio the schoolmaster, Petruchio, with Hortensio as Licio the musician, and Tranio as Lucentio, with his boy bearing a lute and books

GREMIO. Good morrow, neighbour Baptista.

BAPTISTA. Good morrow, neighbour Gremio. God 40
save you, gentlemen!

PETRUCHIO. And you, good sir: pray, have you not a daughter
Called Katharina, fair and virtuous?

BAPTISTA. I have a daughter, sir, called Katharina.

GREMIO. You are too blunt, go to it orderly.

PETRUCHIO. You wrong me, Signior Gremio, give me leave.
I am a gentleman of Verona, sir.
That, hearing of her beauty and her wit,
Her affability and bashful modesty,
Her wondrous qualities, and mild behaviour, 50
Am bold to show myself a forward guest
Within your house, to make mine eye the witness
Of that report which I so oft have heard.
And, for an entrance to my entertainment,
I do present you with a man of mine,
                            Presenting Hortensio
Cunning in music and the mathematics,
To instruct her fully in those sciences,
Whereof I know she is not ignorant.
Accept of him, or else you do me wrong.
His name is Licio, born in Mantua. 60

BAPTISTA. You're welcome, sir, and he for your good sake.
But for my daughter Katharine, this I know,
She is not for your turn, the more my grief.

PETRUCHIO. I see you do not mean to part with her,
Or else you like not of my company.

BAPTISTA. Mistake me not, I speak but as I find.
Whence are you, sir? what may I call your name?

PETRUCHIO. Petruchio is my name, Antonio's son,
A man well known throughout all Italy.

BAPTISTA. I know him well: you are welcome for his sake. 70

GREMIO. Saving your tale, Petruchio, I pray,
Let us, that are poor petitioners, speak too!
Backare! you are marvellous forward.

PETRUCHIO. O, pardon me, Signior Gremio, I would
fain be doing.

GREMIO. I doubt it not, sir; but you will curse
your wooing.

[to Baptista] Neighbour, this is a gift very grateful,
I am sure of it. To express the like kindness, myself,
that have been more kindly beholding to you than
any, freely give unto you this young scholar, [pre-
senting Lucentio] that hath been long studying at 80
Rheims, as cunning in Greek, Latin, and other
languages, as the other in music and mathematics.
His name is Cambio; pray accept his service.

BAPTISTA. A thousand thanks, Signior Gremio: welcome, good Cambio. [to Tranio] But, gentle sir,
methinks you walk like a stranger. May I be so
bold to know the cause of your coming?

TRANIO. Pardon me, sir, the boldness is mine own,
That, being a stranger in this city here,
Do make myself a suitor to your daughter, 90
Unto Bianca, fair, and virtuous:
Nor is your firm resolve unknown to me,
In the preferment of the eldest sister.
This liberty is all that I request,
That, upon knowledge of my parentage,
I may have welcome 'mongst the rest that woo,
And free access and favour as the rest.
And toward the education of your daughters
· I here bestow a simple instrument,
And this small packet of Greek and Latin books. 100
If you accept them, then their worth is great.

BAPTISTA. Lucentio is your name—of whence, I pray?

TRANIO. Of Pisa, sir, son to Vincentio.

BAPTISTA. A mighty man of Pisa—by report
I know him well: you are very welcome, sir.
Take you the lute, and you the set of books,
You shall go see your pupils presently.
Holla, within!

A servant enters

                    Sirrah, lead these gentlemen
To my daughters, and tell them both,
These are their tutors, bid them use them well. 110
                    Hortensio and Lucentio depart
We will go walk a little in the orchard,
And then to dinner. You are passing welcome,
And so I pray you all to think yourselves.

PETRUCHIO. Signior Baptista, my business asketh
haste,
And every day I cannot come to woo.
You knew my father well, and in him me,
Left solely heir to all his lands and goods,
Which I have bettered rather than decreased,
Then tell me—if I get your daughter's love,
What dowry shall I have with her to wife? 120

BAPTISTA. After my death, the one half of my lands,
And in possession twenty thousand crowns.

PETRUCHIO. And, for that dowry, I'll assure her of
Her widowhood—be it that she survive me—
In all my lands and leases whatsoever.
Let specialties be therefore drawn between us,
That covenants may be kept on either hand.

BAPTISTA. Ay, when the special thing is well obtained,
This is, her love; for that is all in all.

PETRUCHIO. Why, that is nothing; for I tell you, father, 130
I am as peremptory as the proud-minded;
And where two raging fires meet together,

They do consume the thing that feeds their fury.
Though little fire grows great with little wind,
Yet extreme gusts will blow out fire and all:
So I to her, and so she yields to me.
For I am rough and woo not like a babe.

BAPTISTA. Well mayst thou woo, and happy be
thy speed!
But be thou armed for some unhappy words.

PETRUCHIO. Ay, to the proof—as mountains are for
winds, 140
That shake not, though they blow perpetually.

Enters Hortensio with his head broke

BAPTISTA. How now, my friend! why dost thou look
so pale?

HORTENSIO. For fear, I promise you, if I look pale.

BAPTISTA. What, will my daughter prove a
good musician?

HORTENSIO. I think she'll sooner prove a soldier—
Iron may hold with her, but never lutes.

BAPTISTA. Why, then thou canst not break her to
the lute?

HORTENSIO. Why no, for she hath broke the lute
to me.
I did but tell her she mistook her frets,
And bowed her hand to teach her fingering, 150
When, with a most impatient devilish spirit,
'Frets, call you these?' quoth she, 'I'll fume with
them':
And, with that word, she struck me on the head,
And through the instrument my pate made way,
And there I stood amazéd for a while,
As on a pillory, looking through the lute.
While she did call me rascal fiddler,
And twangling Jack, with twenty such vile terms,
As had she studied to misuse me so.

PETRUCHIO. Now, by the world, it is a lusty wench. 160
I love her ten times more than e'er I did,
O, how I long to have some chat with her!

BAPTISTA. Well, go with me, and be not so discomfited
Proceed in practice with my younger daughter,
She's apt to learn and thankful for good turns.
Signior Petruchio, will you go with us,
Or shall I send my daughter Kate to you?

PETRUCHIO. I pray you do. I will attend her here,
                    All depart save Petruchio
And woo her with some spirit when she comes.
Say that she rail, why then I'll tell her plain 170
She sings as sweetly as a nightingale:
Say that she frown, I'll say she looks as clear
As morning roses newly washed with dew:
Say she be mute and will not speak a word,
Then I'll commend her volubility,
And say she uttereth piercing eloquence:
If she do bid me pack, I'll give her thanks,
As though she bid me stay by her a week:
If she deny to wed, I'll crave the day
When I shall ask the banns, and when be married. 180
But here she comes, and now, Petruchio, speak.

Katharina enters

Good morrow, Kate—for that's your name, I hear.

KATHARINA. Well have you heard, but something
hard of hearing;

They call me Katharine that do talk of me.
PETRUCHIO. You lie, in faith, for you are called
    plain Kate,
And bonny Kate, and sometimes Kate the curst:
But Kate, the prettiest Kate in Christendom,
Kate of Kate Hall, my super-dainty Kate,
For dainties are all cates, and therefore, Kate,
Take this of me, Kate of my consolation—
Hearing thy mildness praised in every town,
Thy virtues spoke of, and thy beauty sounded,
Yet not so deeply as to thee belongs,
Myself am moved to woo thee for my wife.
KATHARINA. Moved! in good time! let him that
    moved you hither,
Remove you hence: I knew you at the first
You were a moveable.
PETRUCHIO.   Why, what's a moveable?
KATHARINA. A joint-stool.
PETRUCHIO.   Thou hast hit it: come, sit on me.
KATHARINA. Asses are made to bear, and so are you.
PETRUCHIO. Women are made to bear, and so are you. 200
KATHARINA. No such a jade as you, if me you mean.
PETRUCHIO. Alas, good Kate! I will not burden thee,
For knowing thee to be but young and light,—
KATHARINA. Too light for such a swain as you to catch,
And yet as heavy as my weight should be.
PETRUCHIO. Should be! should—buzz!
KATHARINA.   Well ta'en, and like a buzzard.
PETRUCHIO. O, slow-winged turtle! shall a buzzard
    take thee?
KATHARINA. Ay, for a turtle, as he takes a buzzard.
PETRUCHIO. Come, come, you wasp, i'faith, you are
    too angry.
KATHARINA. If I be waspish, best beware my sting. 210
PETRUCHIO. My remedy is then, to pluck it out.
KATHARINA. Ay, if the fool could find it where it lies.
PETRUCHIO. Who knows not where a wasp doth wear
    his sting?
In his tail.
KATHARINA. In his tongue.
PETRUCHIO.   Whose tongue?
KATHARINA. Yours, if you talk of tales, and so farewell.
PETRUCHIO. What, with my tongue in your tail? nay,
    come again.
Good Kate, I am a gentleman—
KATHARINA.   That I'll try.
                                    She strikes him
PETRUCHIO. I swear I'll cuff you, if you strike again.
KATHARINA. So may you loose your arms!
If you strike me, you are no gentleman,   220
And if no gentleman, why then no arms.
PETRUCHIO. A herald, Kate? O, put me in thy books!
KATHARINA. What is your crest? a coxcomb?
PETRUCHIO. A combless cock, so Kate will be my hen.
KATHARINA. No cock of mine, you crow too like
    a craven.
PETRUCHIO. Nay, come, Kate, come; you must not
    look so sour.
KATHARINA. It is my fashion, when I see a crab.
PETRUCHIO. Why, here's no crab, and therefore look
    not sour.
KATHARINA. There is, there is.
PETRUCHIO. Then show it me.
KATHARINA.   Had I a glass, I would. 230
PETRUCHIO. What, you mean my face?
KATHARINA.   Well aimed of such a young one.

PETRUCHIO. Now, by S. George, I am too young
    for you.
KATHARINA. Yet you are withered.
PETRUCHIO.   'Tis with cares.
KATHARINA.   I care not!
PETRUCHIO. Nay, hear you, Kate. In sooth, you scape
    not so.
KATHARINA. I chafe you, if I tarry. Let me go!   190
PETRUCHIO. No, not a whit—I find you passing gentle:
'Twas told me you were rough and coy and sullen,
And now I find report a very liar;
For thou art pleasant, gamesome, passing courteous,
But slow in speech; yet sweet as spring-time flowers. 240
Thou canst not frown, thou canst not look askance,
Nor bite the lip, as angry wenches will,
Nor hast thou pleasure to be cross in talk;
But thou with mildness entertain'st thy wooers,
With gentle conference, soft and affable. . . .
Why does the world report that Kate doth limp?
O sland'rous world! Kate like the hazel-twig
Is straight and slender, and as brown in hue
As hazel-nuts and sweeter than the kernels . . .
O, let me see thee walk: thou dost not halt.   250
KATHARINA. Go, fool, and whom thou keep'st
    command.
PETRUCHIO. Did ever Dian so become a grove
As Kate this chamber with her princely gait?
O, be thou Dian and let her be Kate,
And then let Kate be chaste and Dian sportful!
KATHARINA. Where did you study all this goodly
    speech?
PETRUCHIO. It is extempore, from my mother-wit.
KATHARINA. A witty mother! witless else her son.
PETRUCHIO. Am I not wise?
KATHARINA.   Yes, keep you warm.
PETRUCHIO. Marry, so I mean, sweet Katharine, in
    thy bed: 260
And therefore, setting all this chat aside,
Thus in plain terms: your father hath consented
That you shall be my wife; your dowry 'greed on;
And, will you, nill you, I will marry you.
Now, Kate, I am a husband for your turn,
For by this light whereby I see thy beauty,
Thy beauty that doth make me like thee well,
Thou must be married to no man but me.
For I am he am born to tame you, Kate,
And bring you from a wild Kate to a Kate   270
Conformable as other household Kates.

Baptista, Gremio, and Tranio re-enter

Here comes your father—never make denial—
I must and will have Katharine to my wife.
BAPTISTA. Now, Signior Petruchio, how speed you
    with my daughter?
PETRUCHIO. How but well, sir? how but well?
It were impossible I should speed amiss.
BAPTISTA. Why, how now, daughter Katharine! in
    your dumps?
KATHARINA. Call you me daughter? now, I promise
    you
You have showed a tender fatherly regard,
To wish me wed to one half lunatic,   280
A mad-cap ruffian and a swearing Jack,
That thinks with oaths to face the matter out.
PETRUCHIO. Father, 'tis thus—yourself and all the
    world,

That talked of her, have talked amiss of her:
If she be curst, it is for policy:
For she's not froward, but modest as the dove;
She is not hot, but temperate as the morn;
For patience she will prove a second Grissel,
A Roman Lucrece for her chastity.
And to conclude, we have 'greed so well together, 290
That upon Sunday is the wedding-day.
KATHARINA. I'll see thee hanged on Sunday first.
GREMIO. Hark, Petruchio, she says she'll see thee
hanged first.
TRANIO. Is this your speeding? nay, then, good night
our part!
PETRUCHIO. Be patient, gentlemen, I choose her
for myself—
If she and I be pleased, what's that to you?
'Tis bargained 'twixt us twain, being alone,
That she shall still be curst in company.
I tell you, 'tis incredible to believe
How much she loves me: O, the kindest Kate! 300
She hung about my neck, and kiss on kiss
She vied so fast, protesting oath on oath,
That in a twink she won me to her love.
O, you are novices! 'tis a world to see,
How tame, when men and women are alone,
A meacock wretch can make the curstest shrew.
Give me thy hand, Kate, I will unto Venice,
To buy apparel 'gainst the wedding-day ...
Provide the feast, father, and bid the guests,
I will be sure my Katharine shall be fine. 310
BAPTISTA. I know not what to say—but give me
your hands.
God send you joy, Petruchio! 'tis a match.
GREMIO, TRANIO. Amen, say we. We will be witnesses.
PETRUCHIO. Father, and wife, and gentlemen, adieu,
I will to Venice—Sunday comes apace—
We will have rings, and things, and fine array,
And kiss me, Kate, we will be married o' Sunday.
She leaves; he departs by another door
GREMIO. Was ever match clapped up so suddenly?
BAPTISTA. Faith, gentlemen, now I play a
merchant's part,
And venture madly on a desperate mart. 320
TRANIO. 'Twas a commodity lay fretting by you,
'Twill bring you gain, or perish on the seas.
BAPTISTA. The gain I seek is quiet in the match.
GREMIO. No doubt but he hath got a quiet catch.
But now, Baptista, to your younger daughter—
Now is the day we long have lookéd for.
I am your neighbour, and was suitor first.
TRANIO. And I am one, that love Bianca more
Than words can witness, or your thoughts can guess.
GREMIO. Youngling! thou canst not love so dear as I. 330
TRANIO. Greybeard! thy love doth freeze.
GREMIO.   But thine doth fry,
Skipper, stand back—'tis age that nourisheth.
TRANIO. But youth in ladies' eyes that flourisheth.
BAPTISTA. Content you, gentlemen, I will compound
this strife.
'Tis deeds must win the prize, and he, of both,
That can assure my daughter greatest dower,
Shall have Bianca's love.
Say, Signior Gremio, what can you assure her?
GREMIO. First, as you know, my house within the city
Is richly furnishéd with plate and gold, 340
Basins and ewers to lave her dainty hands;

My hangings all of Tyrian tapestry;
In ivory coffers I have stuffed my crowns;
In cypress chests my arras counterpoints,
Costly apparel, tents, and canopies,
Fine linen, Turkey cushions bossed with pearl,
Valance of Venice gold in needlework,
Pewter and brass, and all things that belong
To house or housekeeping. Then, at my farm
I have a hundred milch-kine to the pail, 350
Sixscore fat oxen standing in my stalls,
And all things answerable to this portion.
Myself am struck in years, I must confess,
And if I die to-morrow this is hers,
If whilst I live she will be only mine.
TRANIO. That 'only' came well in. Sir, list to me,
I am my father's heir and only son.
If I may have your daughter to my wife,
I'll leave her houses three or four as good,
Within rich Pisa walls, as any one 360
Old Signior Gremio has in Padua,
Besides two thousand ducats by the year
Of fruitful land, all which shall be her jointure.
What, have I pinched you, Signior Gremio?
GREMIO. Two thousand ducats by the year, of land!
[aside] My land amounts not to so much in all.
That she shall have—besides an argosy
That now is lying in Marseilles' road.
What, have I choked you with an argosy?
TRANIO. Gremio, 'tis known my father hath no less 370
Than three great argosies, besides two galliasses,
And twelve tight galleys. These I will assure her,
And twice as much, whate'er thou offer'st next.
GREMIO. Nay, I have offered all, I have no more,
And she can have no more than all I have.
If you like me, she shall have me and mine.
TRANIO. Why, then the maid is mine from all
the world,
By your firm promise—Gremio is out-vied.
BAPTISTA. I must confess your offer is the best,
And, let your father make her the assurance, 380
She is your own—else, you must pardon me,
If you should die before him, where's her dower?
TRANIO. That's but a cavil; he is old, I young.
GREMIO. And may not young men die, as well as old?
BAPTISTA. Well, gentlemen,
I am thus resolved—On Sunday next you know
My daughter Katharine is to be married:
Now, on the Sunday following, shall Bianca
Be bride to you, if you make this assurance;
If not, to Signior Gremio: 390
And so I take my leave, and thank you both.
He departs
GREMIO. Adieu, good neighbour. Now I fear thee not;
Sirrah, young gamester, your father were a fool
To give thee all, and in his waning age
Set foot under thy table: tut, a toy!
An old Italian fox is not so kind, my boy. *He goes*
TRANIO. A vengeance on your crafty withered hide!
Yet I have faced it with a card of ten.
'Tis in my head to do my master good:
I see no reason but supposed Lucentio 400
Must get a father, called—supposed Vincentio.
And that's a wonder: fathers commonly
Do get their children; but, in this case of wooing,
A child shall get a sire, if I fail not of my cunning.
He goes

ACT 3

Scene 1: *The house of Baptista*

Bianca, Hortensio, disguised as Licio, and Lucentio, disguised as Cambio

LUCENTIO. Fiddler, forbear, you grow too forward, sir!
Have you so soon forgot the entertainment
Her sister Katharine welcomed you withal?

HORTENSIO. But, wrangling pedant, this is
The patroness of heavenly harmony:
Then give me leave to have prerogative,
And when in music we have spent an hour,
Your lecture shall have leisure for as much.

LUCENTIO. Preposterous ass, that never read so far
To know the cause why music was ordained!   10
Was it not to refresh the mind of man
After his studies or his usual pain?
Then give me leave to read philosophy,
And while I pause, serve in your harmony.

HORTENSIO. Sirrah, I will not bear these braves of thine.

BIANCA. Why, gentlemen, you do me double wrong,
To strive for that which resteth in my choice:
I am no breeching scholar in the schools,
I'll not be tied to hours nor 'pointed times,
But learn my lessons as I please myself.   20
And, to cut off all strife, here sit we down:
Take you your instrument, play you the whiles—
His lecture will be done ere you have tuned.

HORTENSIO. You'll leave his lecture when I am in tune?

LUCENTIO. That will be never! Tune your instrument.

BIANCA. Where left we last?

LUCENTIO. Here, madam:
'Hic ibat Simois, hic est Sigeia tellus,
Hic steterat Priami regia celsa senis.'

BIANCA. Construe them.   30

LUCENTIO. 'Hic ibat,' as I told you before—'Simois,'
I am Lucentio—'hic est,' son unto Vincentio of
Pisa—'Sigeia tellus,' disguised thus to get your love
—'Hic steterat,' and that Lucentio that comes
a-wooing—'Priami,' is my man Tranio—'regia,'
bearing my port—'celsa senis,' that we might
beguile the old pantaloon.

HORTENSIO. Madam, my instrument's in tune.

BIANCA. Let's hear—O fie! the treble jars.

LUCENTIO. Spit in the hole, man, and tune again.   40

BIANCA. Now let me see if I can construe it. 'Hic
ibat Simois,' I know you not—'hic est Sigeia tellus,'
I trust you not—'Hic steterat Priami,' take heed he
hear us not—'regia,' presume not—'celsa senis,'
despair not.

HORTENSIO. Madam, 'tis now in tune.

LUCENTIO.   All but the base.

HORTENSIO. The base is right, 'tis the base knave,
that jars.
[*aside*] How fiery and forward our pedant is!
Now, for my life, the knave doth court my love.
Pedascule, I'll watch you better yet.   50

BIANCA. In time I may believe, yet I mistrust.

LUCENTIO. Mistrust it not—for, sure, Æacides
Was Ajax, called so from his grandfather.

BIANCA. I must believe my master, else, I promise you,
I should be arguing still upon that doubt—
But let it rest. Now, Licio, to you.

Good master, take it not unkindly, pray,
That I have been thus pleasant with you both.

HORTENSIO. You may go walk, and give me leave awhile—
My lessons make no music in three parts.   60

LUCENTIO. Are you so formal, sir? well, I must wait—
[*aside*] And watch withal, for, but I be deceived,
Our fine musician groweth amorous.

HORTENSIO. Madam, before you touch the instrument,
To learn the order of my fingering,
I must begin with rudiments of art,
To teach you gamut in a briefer sort,
More pleasant, pithy, and effectual,
Than hath been taught by any of my trade:
And there it is in writing, fairly drawn.   70

BIANCA. Why, I am past my gamut long ago.

HORTENSIO. Yet read the gamut of Hortensio.

BIANCA [*reads*]. '"Gamut" I am, the ground of all accord;
"A re," to plead Hortensio's passion;
"B mi," Bianca, take him for thy lord,
"Ca fa ut," that loves with all affection:
"D sol re," one clef, two notes have I,
"E la mi," show pity, or I die.'
Call you this gamut? tut! I like it not.
Old fashions please me best—I am not so nice   80
To change true rules for odd inventions.

A servant enters

SERVANT. Mistress, your father prays you leave your books,
And help to dress your sister's chamber up.
You know to-morrow is the wedding-day.

BIANCA. Farewell sweet masters both, I must be gone.
                                        She departs

LUCENTIO. Faith, mistress, then I have no cause to stay.
                                        He goes

HORTENSIO. But I have cause to pry into this pedant,
Methinks he looks as though he were in love:
Yet if thy thoughts, Bianca, be so humble,
To cast thy wandring eyes on every stale,   90
Seize thee that list—if once I find thee ranging,
Hortensio will be quit with thee by changing.
                                        He goes

Scene 2: *The public square*

Enter Baptista, Gremio, Tranio (as Lucentio), Lucentio (as Cambio), Katharina (in bridal array), Bianca, attendants and a concourse of people

BAPTISTA [*to Tranio*]. Signior Lucentio, this is the 'pointed day,
That Katharine and Petruchio should be married,
And yet we hear not of our son-in-law:
What will be said? what mockery will it be,
To want the bridegroom when the priest attends
To speak the ceremonial rites of marriage?
What says Lucentio to this shame of ours?

KATHARINA. No shame but mine. I must forsooth be forced
To give my hand opposed against my heart
Unto a mad-brain rudesby, full of spleen,   10
Who wooed in haste, and means to wed at leisure ...
I told you, I, he was a frantic fool,
Hiding his bitter jests in blunt behaviour:
And to be noted for a merry man,

He'll woo a thousand, 'point the day of marriage,
Make feasts, invite friends, and proclaim the banns,
Yet never means to wed where he hath wooed.
Now must the world point at poor Katharine,
And say, 'Lo, there is mad Petruchio's wife,
If it would please him come and marry her.'   20
TRANIO. Patience, good Katharine, and Baptista too.
Upon my life, Petruchio means but well,
Whatever fortune stays him from his word.
Though he be blunt, I know him passing wise,
Though he be merry, yet withal he's honest.
KATHARINA. Would Katharine had never seen
    him though!

> *She goes weeping, followed by Bianca*
> *and the rest of the bridal train*

BAPTISTA. Go, girl, I cannot blame thee now to weep,
For such an injury would vex a saint,
Much more a shrew of thy impatient humour.

Biondello enters

BIONDELLO. Master, master! news, and such old news   30
    as you never heard of!
BAPTISTA. Is it new and old too? how may that be?
BIONDELLO. Why, is it not news, to hear of Petruchio's
    coming?
BAPTISTA. Is he come?
BIONDELLO. Why, no, sir.
BAPTISTA. What then?
BIONDELLO. He is coming.
BAPTISTA. When will he be here?
BIONDELLO. When he stands where I am and sees you   40
    there.
TRANIO. But say, what to thine old news?
BIONDELLO. Why, Petruchio is coming, in a new hat
    and an old jerkin; a pair of old breeches thrice
    turned; a pair of boots that have been candle-cases,
    one buckled, another laced; an old rusty sword ta'en
    out of the town-armoury, with a broken hilt, and
    chapeless; with two broken points: with an old
    mothy saddle and stirrups of no kindred: his horse
    hipped besides, possessed with the glanders and like   50
    to mose in the chine, troubled with the lampass,
    infected with the fashions, full of windgalls, sped
    with spavins, rayed with the yellows, past cure of
    the fives, stark spoiled with the staggers, begnawn
    with the bots, swayed in the back, and shoulder-
    shotten, near-legged before, and with a half-checked
    bit, and a head-stall of sheep's leather, which, being
    restrained to keep him from stumbling, hath been
    often burst and new-repaired with knots: one girth
    six times pieced, and a woman's crupper of velure,   60
    which hath two letters for her name, fairly set down
    in studs, and here and there pieced with pack-thread.
BAPTISTA. Who comes with him?
BIONDELLO. O, sir, his lackey, for all the world capa-
    risoned like the horse: with a linen stock on one leg,
    and a kersey boot-hose on the other, gartered with
    a red and blue list; an old hat, and the humour of
    forty fancies pricked in't for a feather; a monster, a
    very monster in apparel, and not like a Christian
    footboy or a gentleman's lackey.   70
TRANIO. 'Tis some odd humour pricks him to
    this fashion.
Yet oftentimes he goes but mean-apparelled.
BAPTISTA. I am glad he's come, howsoe'er he comes.
BIONDELLO. Why, sir, he comes not.

BAPTISTA. Didst thou not say he comes?
BIONDELLO. Who? that Petruchio came?
BAPTISTA. Ay, that Petruchio came.
BIONDELLO. No, sir, I say his horse comes, with him on
    his back.
BAPTISTA.   Why, that's all one.   80
BIONDELLO.   Nay, by S. Jamy,
            I hold you a penny,
            A horse and a man
            Is more than one,
            And yet not many.

Petruchio and Grumio enter

PETRUCHIO. Come, where be these gallants? who's
    at home?
BAPTISTA. You are welcome, sir.
PETRUCHIO.   And yet I come not well?
BAPTISTA. And yet you halt not.
TRANIO.   Not so well apparelled
As I wish you were.
PETRUCHIO. Were it not better I should rush in thus?   90
But where is Kate? where is my lovely bride?
How does my father? Gentles, methinks you frown
And wherefore gaze this goodly company,
As if they saw some wondrous monument,
Some comet, or unusual prodigy?
BAPTISTA. Why, sir, you know, this is your
    wedding-day:
First were we sad, fearing you would not come,
Now sadder, that you come so unprovided.
Fie! doff this habit, shame to your estate,
An eyesore to our solemn festival.   100
TRANIO. And tell us what occasion of import
Hath all so long detained you from your wife,
And sent you hither so unlike yourself?
PETRUCHIO. Tedious it were to tell, and harsh to
    hear—
Sufficeth I am come to keep my word,
Though in some part enforcéd to digress,
Which at more leisure I will so excuse
As you shall well be satisfied withal.
But where is Kate? I stay too long from her,
The morning wears, 'tis time we were at church.   110
TRANIO. See not your bride in these unreverent robes,
Go to my chamber, put on clothes of mine.
PETRUCHIO. Not I, believe me—thus I'll visit her.
BAPTISTA. But thus, I trust, you will not marry her.
PETRUCHIO. Good sooth, even thus: therefore ha' done
    with words,
To me she's married, not unto my clothes:
Could I repair what she will wear in me,
As I can change these poor accoutrements,
'Twere well for Kate, and better for myself.
But what a fool am I to chat with you,   120
When I should bid good morrow to my bride,
And seal the title with a lovely kiss.

> *He goes with Grumio behind him*

TRANIO. He hath some meaning in his mad attire.
We will persuade him, be it possible,
To put on better ere he go to church.
BAPTISTA. I'll after him, and see the event of this.

> *He follows Petruchio; Gremio and others also depart*

TRANIO. But to her love concerneth us to add
Her father's liking, which to bring to pass,
As I before imparted to your worship,
I am to get a man—whate'er he be,   130

It skills not much, we'll fit him to our turn—
And he shall be Vincentio of Pisa,
And made assurance here in Padua
Of greater sums than I have promiséd.
So shall you quietly enjoy your hope,
And marry sweet Bianca with consent.
LUCENTIO. Were it not that my fellow-schoolmaster
Doth watch Bianca's steps so narrowly,
'Twere good methinks to steal our marriage,
Which once performed, let all the world say no, 140
I'll keep mine own despite of all the world.
TRANIO. That by degrees we mean to look into,
And watch our vantage in this business.
We'll over-reach the greybeard, Gremio,
The narrow-prying father, Minola,
The quaint musician, amorous Licio—
All for my master's sake, Lucentio.

Gremio returns

Signior Gremio, came you from the church?
GREMIO. As willingly as e'er I came from school.
TRANIO. And is the bride and bridegroom
      coming home?   150
GREMIO. A bridegroom, say you? 'tis a groom, indeed,
A grumbling groom, and that the girl shall find.
TRANIO. Curster than she? why, 'tis impossible.
GREMIO. Why, he's a devil, a devil, a very fiend.
TRANIO. Why, she's a devil, a devil, the devil's dam.
GREMIO. Tut! she's a lamb, a dove, a fool to him …
I'll tell you, Sir Lucentio: when the priest
Should ask if Katharine should be his wife,
'Ay, by gogs-wouns,' quoth he, and swore so loud,
That all-amazed the priest let fall the book,   160
And as he stooped again to take it up,
This mad-brained bridegroom took him such a cuff,
That down fell priest and book, and book and priest.
'Now take them up,' quoth he, 'if any list.'
TRANIO. What said the wench, when he arose again?
GREMIO. Trembled and shook; for why, he stamped
      and swore,
As if the vicar meant to cozen him.
But after many ceremonies done,
He calls for wine—'A health,' quoth he, as if
He had been aboard, carousing to his mates   170
After a storm—quaffed off the muscadel,
And threw the sops all in the sexton's face;
Having no other reason
But that his beard grew thin and hungerly,
And seemed to ask him sops as he was drinking.
This done, he took the bride about the neck,
And kissed her lips with such a clamorous smack,
That at the parting all the church did echo:
And I seeing this came thence for very shame,
And after me, I know, the rout is coming.   180
Such a mad marriage never was before:
Hark, hark! I hear the minstrels play.

*The minstrels with the marriage procession enter the square,
Petruchio and Katharina leading, followed by Bianca,
Baptista, Hortensio, Grumio, and the rest of their train*

PETRUCHIO. Gentlemen and friends, I thank you for
      your pains,
I know you think to dine with me to-day,
And have prepared great store of wedding cheer,
But so it is, my haste doth call me hence,
And therefore here I mean to take my leave.

BAPTISTA. Is't possible you will away to-night?
PETRUCHIO. I must away to-day before night come.
Make it no wonder; if you knew my business,   190
You would entreat me rather go than stay.
And, honest company, I thank you all,
That have beheld me give away myself
To this most patient, sweet, and virtuous wife.
Dine with my father, drink a health to me,
For I must hence, and farewell to you all.
TRANIO. Let us entreat you stay till after dinner.
PETRUCHIO. It may not be.
GREMIO.   Let me entreat you.
PETRUCHIO. It cannot be.
KATHARINA.   Let me entreat you.
PETRUCHIO. I am content.
KATHARINA.   Are you content to stay? 200
PETRUCHIO. I am content you shall entreat me stay—
But yet not stay, entreat me how you can.
KATHARINA. Now, if you love me, stay.
PETRUCHIO.   Grumio, my horse.
GRUMIO. Ay, sir, they be ready—the oats have eaten
the horses.
KATHARINA. Nay, then,
Do what thou canst, I will not go to-day,
No, nor to-morrow, till I please myself.
The door is open, sir, there lies your way,
You may be jogging whiles your boots are green;   210
For me, I'll not be gone, till I please myself.
'Tis like you'll prove a jolly, surly groom,
That take it on you at the first so roundly.
PETRUCHIO. O, Kate, content thee, prithee, be not
      angry.
KATHARINA. I will be angry—what hast thou to do?
Father, be quiet—he shall stay my leisure.
GREMIO. Ay, marry, sir, now it begins to work.
KATHARINA. Gentlemen, forward to the bridal dinner.
I see a woman may be made a fool,
If she had not a spirit to resist.   220
PETRUCHIO. They shall go forward, Kate, at thy
      command.
Obey the bride, you that attend on her!
Go to the feast, revel and domineer,
Carouse full measure to her maidenhead,
Be mad and merry, or go hang yourselves;
But for my bonny Kate, she must with me.
Nay, look not big, nor stamp, nor stare, nor fret,
I will be master of what is mine own.
She is my goods, my chattels; she is my house,
My household stuff, my field, my barn,   230
My horse, my ox, my ass, my any thing—
And here she stands, touch her whoever dare!
I'll bring mine action on the proudest he
That stops my way in Padua. Grumio,
Draw forth thy weapon, we are beset with thieves,
Rescue thy mistress, if thou be a man.
Fear not, sweet wench, they shall not touch thee,
      Kate!
I'll buckler thee against a million.
      He carries her from the square, Grumio follows
BAPTISTA. Nay, let them go, a couple of quiet ones.
GREMIO. Went they not quickly, I should die
      with laughing.   240
TRANIO. Of all mad matches never was the like!
LUCENTIO. Mistress, what's your opinion of your
      sister?
BIANCA. That, being mad herself, she's madly mated.

GREMIO. I warrant him, Petruchio is Kated.

BAPTISTA. Neighbours and friends, though bride and
bridegroom wants
For to supply the places at the table,
You know, there wants no junkets at the feast.
Lucentio, you shall supply the bridegroom's place,
And let Bianca take her sister's room.

TRANIO. Shall sweet Bianca practise how to bride it? 250

BAPTISTA. She shall, Lucentio. Come, gentlemen,
let's go.   *They go*

ACT 4

Scene 1: *Petruchio's house in the country*

Grumio enters

GRUMIO. Fie, fie, on all tired jades, on all mad masters,
and all foul ways! Was ever man so beaten? was
ever man so rayed? was ever man so weary? I am
sent before to make a fire, and they are coming after
to warm them. Now, were not I a little pot, and
soon hot, my very lips might freeze to my teeth,
my tongue to the roof of my mouth, my heart in
my belly, ere I should come by a fire to thaw me.
But I, with blowing the fire, shall warm myself; for,
considering the weather, a taller man than I will take 10
cold. Holla, ho! Curtis!

Curtis enters

CURTIS. Who is that calls so coldly?

GRUMIO. A piece of ice: if thou doubt it, thou mayst
slide from my shoulder to my heel with no greater
a run but my head and my neck. A fire, good Curtis.

CURTIS. Is my master and his wife coming, Grumio?

GRUMIO. O, ay, Curtis, ay—and therefore fire, fire;
cast on no water.

CURTIS. Is she so hot a shrew as she's reported?

GRUMIO. She was, good Curtis, before this frost: but 20
thou know'st winter tames man, woman, and beast;
for it hath tamed my old master, and my new
mistress, and myself, fellow Curtis.

CURTIS. Away, you three-inch fool! I am no beast.

GRUMIO. Am I but three inches? why, thy horn is a
foot, and so long am I at the least. But wilt thou
make a fire, or shall I complain on thee to our
mistress, whose hand (she being now at hand) thou
shalt soon feel, to thy cold comfort, for being slow
in thy hot office?   30

CURTIS. I prithee, good Grumio, tell me, how goes the
world?

GRUMIO. A cold world, Curtis, in every office but
thine—and therefore fire. Do thy duty, and have thy
duty, for my master and mistress are almost frozen
to death.

CURTIS. There's fire ready, and therefore, good
Grumio, the news?

GRUMIO. Why, 'Jack boy! ho boy!' and as much news
as thou wilt.   40

CURTIS. Come, you are so full of cony-catching.

GRUMIO. Why therefore fire, for I have caught extreme cold. Where's the cook? is supper ready, the
house trimmed, rushes strewed, cobwebs swept, the
serving-men in their new fustian, their white stockings, and every officer his wedding-garment on? Be
the jacks fair within, the jills fair without, the carpets
laid, and every thing in order?

CURTIS. All ready: and therefore, I pray thee, news.

GRUMIO. First, know, my horse is tired, my master 50
and mistress fallen out—

CURTIS. How?

GRUMMIO. Out of their saddles into the dirt, and
thereby hangs a tale.

CURTIS. Let's ha't, good Grumio.

GRUMIO. Lend thine ear.

CURTIS. Here.

GRUMIO. There.   *He strikes him*

CURTIS. This is to feel a tale, not to hear a tale.

GRUMIO. And therefore 'tis called, a sensible tale: and 60
this cuff was but to knock at your ear and beseech
listening: now I begin—Imprimis, we came down
a foul hill, my master riding behind my mistress—

CURTIS. Both of one horse?

GRUMIO. What's that to thee?

CURTIS. Why, a horse.

GRUMIO. Tell thou the tale: but hadst thou not crossed
me, thou shouldst have heard how her horse fell,
and she under her horse; thou shouldst have heard
in how miry a place, how she was bemoiled, how 70
he left her with the horse upon her, how he beat
me because her horse stumbled, how she waded
through the dirt to pluck him off me; how he swore,
how she prayed that never prayed before; how I
cried, how the horses ran away, how her bridle was
burst; how I lost my crupper—with many things
of worthy memory, which now shall die in oblivion, and thou return unexperienced to thy grave.

CURTIS. By this reck'ning he is more shrew than she.

GRUMIO. Ay, and that thou and the proudest of you all 80
shall find when he comes home. But what talk I of
this? Call forth Nathaniel, Joseph, Nicholas, Philip,
Walter Sugarsop, and the rest; let their heads be
sleekly combed, their blue coats brushed, and their
garters of an indifferent knit; let them curtsy with
their left legs, and not presume to touch a hair of
my master's horse-tail, till they kiss their hands.
Are they all ready?

CURTIS. They are.

GRUMIO. Call them forth.   90

CURTIS [*calls*]. Do you hear, ho? you must meet my
master to countenance my mistress.

GRUMIO. Why, she hath a face of her own.

CURTIS. Who knows not that?

GRUMIO. Thou, it seems, that calls for company to
countenance her.

CURTIS. I call them forth to credit her.

GRUMIO. Why, she comes to borrow nothing of them.

Enter four of five serving-men

NATHANIEL. Welcome home, Grumio.

PHILIP. How now, Grumio!   100

JOSEPH. What, Grumio!

NICHOLAS. Fellow Grumio!

NATHANIEL. How now, old lad?

GRUMIO. Welcome, you!—how now, you!—what,
you!—fellow, you!—and thus much for greeting.
Now, my spruce companions, is all ready, and all
things neat?

NATHANIEL. All things is ready. How near is our
master?

GRUMIO. E'en at hand, alighted by this; and therefore 110
be not—Cock's passion, silence! I hear my master.

Petruchio enters with Katharina

PETRUCHIO. Where be these knaves? What, no man at
    the door,
To hold my stirrup, nor to take my horse!
Where is Nathaniel, Gregory, Philip?—
SERVANTS. Here, here, sir—here, sir.
PETRUCHIO. Here, sir! here, sir! here, sir! here, sir!—
You logger-headed and unpolished grooms!
What, no attendance? no regard? no duty?—
Where is the foolish knave I sent before?
GRUMIO. Here, sir, as foolish as I was before.   120
PETRUCHIO. You peasant swain! you whoreson malt-
    horse drudge!
Did I not bid thee meet me in the park,
And bring along these rascal knaves with thee?
GRUMIO. Nathaniel's coat, sir, was not fully made,
And Gabriel's pumps were all unpinked i'th' heel;
There was no link to colour Peter's hat,
And Walter's dagger was not come from sheathing:
There were none fine but Adam, Rafe, and
    Gregory—
The rest were ragged, old, and beggarly.
Yet, as they are, here are they come to meet you.   130
PETRUCHIO. Go, rascals, go, and fetch my supper in.
                                              They go
[he sings] 'Where is the life that late I led'—
              Where are those—
Sit down, Kate, and welcome. Food, food, food,
    food.

Enter servants with supper

Why, when, I say? Nay, good sweet Kate, be merry.
Off with my boots, you rogues! you villains, when?
[he sings] 'It was the friar of orders grey,
              As he forth walkéd on his way'—
Out, you rogue! you pluck my foot awry.   140
                                    He strikes him
Take that, and mend the plucking off the other.
Be merry, Kate. Some water, here: what, ho!

Enter one with water

Where's my spaniel Troilus? Sirrah, get you hence,
And bid my cousin Ferdinand come hither.
One, Kate, that you must kiss, and be acquainted
    with.
Where are my slippers? Shall I have some water?
Come, Kate, and wash, and welcome heartily.
You whoreson villain! will you let it fall?
                                    He strikes him
KATHARINA. Patience, I pray you, 'twas a fault
    unwilling.
PETRUCHIO. A whoreson, beetle-headed, flap-
    eared knave!   150
Come, Kate, sit down, I know you have a stomach.
Will you give thanks, sweet Kate, or else shall I?—
What's this? mutton?
1 SERVANT.   Ay.
PETRUCHIO.   Who brought it?
PETER.   I.
PETRUCHIO. 'Tis burnt, and so is all the meat:
What dogs are these! Where is the rascal cook?
How durst you, villains, bring it from the dresser,
And serve it thus to me that love it not?
There, take it to you, trenchers, cups and all:
              He throws the meal at the servants' heads
You heedless joltheads, and unmannered slaves!

What, do you grumble? I'll be with you straight.   160
                                    They all go
KATHARINA. I pray you, husband, be not so disquiet,
The meat was well, if you were so contented.
PETRUCHIO. I tell thee, Kate, 'twas burnt and dried
    away,
And I expressly am forbid to touch it:
For it engenders choler, planteth anger,
And better 'twere that both of us did fast—
Since, of ourselves, ourselves are choleric—
Than feed it with such over-roasted flesh.
Be patient, to-morrow't shall be mended,
And, for this night, we'll fast for company.   170
Come, I will bring thee to thy bridal chamber.
                      They go; the servants return severally
NATHANIEL. Peter, didst ever see the like?
PETER. He kills her in her own humour.

Curtis enters

GRUMIO. Where is he?
CURTIS. In her chamber, making a sermon of con-
    tinency to her,
And rails and swears and rates, that she, poor soul,
Knows not which way to stand, to look, to speak,
And sits as one new-risen from a dream.
Away, away! for he is coming hither.
                                              They go

Petruchio enters

PETRUCHIO. Thus have I politicly begun my reign,   180
And 'tis my hope to end successfully:
My falcon now is sharp and passing empty,
And till she stoop, she must not be full-gorged,
For then she never looks upon her lure.
Another way I have to man my haggard,
To make her come and know her keeper's call:
That is, to watch her, as we watch these kites
That bate and beat and will not be obedient.
She eat no meat to-day, nor none shall eat;
Last night she slept not, nor to-night she shall not; 190
As with the meat, some undeservéd fault
I'll find about the making of the bed,
And here I'll fling the pillow, there the bolster,
This way the coverlet, another way the sheets:
Ay, and amid this hurly I intend
That all is done in reverend care of her.
And, in conclusion, she shall watch all night,
And, if she chance to nod, I'll rail and brawl,
And with the clamour keep her still awake.
This is a way to kill a wife with kindness;   200
And thus I'll curb her mad and headstrong humour.
He that knows better how to tame a shrew,
Now let him speak—'tis charity to show.
                                              He goes

              Scene 2: *The public square in Padua*

*Lucentio (as Cambio), Bianca, Tranio (as Lucentio) and
Hortensio*

TRANIO. Is't possible, friend Licio, that Mistress Bianca
Doth fancy any other but Lucentio?
I tell you, sir, she bears me fair in hand.
HORTENSIO. Sir, to satisfy you in what I have said,
Stand by, and mark the manner of his teaching.
                                    They stand aside

LUCENTIO. Now, mistress, profit you in what you
    read?
BIANCA. What, master, read you? first resolve me that.
LUCENTIO. I read that I profess, the Art to Love.
BIANCA. And may you prove, sir, master of your art!
LUCENTIO. While you, sweet dear, prove mistress of
    my heart.   10
HORTENSIO. Quick proceeders, marry! Now, tell me,
    I pray,
    You that durst swear that your mistress Bianca
    Loved none in the world so well as Lucentio.
TRANIO. O despiteful love! unconstant womankind!
    I tell thee, Licio, this is wonderful.
HORTENSIO. Mistake no more, I am not Licio,
    Nor a musician, as I seem to be,
    But one that scorn to live in this disguise,
    For such a one as leaves a gentleman,
    And makes a god of such a cullion: 20
    Know, sir, that I am called Hortensio.
TRANIO. Signior Hortensio, I have often heard
    Of your entire affection to Bianca,
    And since mine eyes are witness of her lightness,
    I will with you, if you be so contented,
    Forswear Bianca and her love for ever.
HORTENSIO. See, how they kiss and court!
    Signior Lucentio,
    Here is my hand, and here I firmly vow
    Never to woo her more, but do forswear her,
    As one unworthy all the former favours   30
    That I have fondly flattered her withal.
TRANIO. And here I take the like unfeignéd oath,
    Never to marry with her, though she would entreat.
    Fie on her! see, how beastly she doth court him.
HORTENSIO. Would all the world but he had
    quite forsworn!
    For me, that I may surely keep mine oath,
    I will be married to a wealthy widow,
    Ere three days pass, which hath as long loved me
    As I have loved this proud disdainful haggard.
    And so farewell, Signior Lucentio.   40
    Kindness in women, not their beauteous looks,
    Shall win my love—and so I take my leave,
    In resolution as I swore before.
                                            He goes
TRANIO. Mistress Bianca, bless you with such grace
    As 'longeth to a lover's blesséd case!
    Nay, I have ta'en you napping, gentle love,
    And have forsworn you, with Hortensio.
BIANCA. Tranio, you jest—but have you both
    forsworn me?
TRANIO. Mistress, we have.
LUCENTIO.   Then we are rid of Licio.
TRANIO. I'faith, he'll have a lusty widow now,   50
    That shall be wooed and wedded in a day.
BIANCA. God give him joy!
TRANIO. Ay, and he'll tame her.
BIANCA.   He says so, Tranio.
TRANIO. Faith, he is gone unto the taming-school.
BIANCA. The taming-school! what, is there such a
    place?
TRANIO. Ay, mistress, and Petruchio is the master,
    That teacheth tricks eleven and twenty long,
    To tame a shrew and charm her chattering tongue.

Biondello enters

BIONDELLO. O master, master, I have watched so long

That I am dog-weary, but at last I spied   60
    An ancient angel coming down the hill,
    Will serve the turn.
TRANIO.   What is he, Biondello?
BIONDELLO. Master, a mercatantè, or a pedant,
    I know not what—but formal in apparel,
    In gait and countenance surely like a father.
LUCENTIO. And what of him, Tranio?
TRANIO. If he be credulous, and trust my tale,
    I'll make him glad to seem Vincentio,
    And give assurance to Baptista Minola,
    As if he were the right Vincentio.   70
    Take in your love, and then let me alone.
                                    Lucentio and Bianca go

The Pedant enters

PEDANT. God save you, sir!
TRANIO.   And you, sir! you are welcome.
    Travel you far on, or are you at the farthest?
PEDANT. Sir, at the farthest for a week or two,
    But then up farther, and as far as Rome,
    And so to Tripoli, if God lend me life.
TRANIO. What countryman, I pray?
PEDANT.   Of Mantua.
TRANIO. Of Mantua, sir? marry, God forbid!
    And come to Padua, careless of your life?
PEDANT. My life, sir! how, I pray? for that goes hard. 80
TRANIO. 'Tis death for any one in Mantua
    To come to Padua. Know you not the cause?
    Your ships are stayed at Venice, and the duke—
    For private quarrel 'twixt your duke and him—
    Hath published and proclaimed it openly:
    'Tis marvel, but that you are newly come,
    You might have heard it else proclaimed about.
PEDANT. Alas, sir, it is worse for me than so!
    For I have bills for money by exchange
    From Florence, and must here deliver them.   90
TRANIO. Well, sir, to do you courtesy,
    This will I do, and this I will advise you—
    First, tell me, have you ever been at Pisa?
PEDANT. Ay, sir, in Pisa have I often been,
    Pisa renownéd for grave citizens.
TRANIO. Among them know you one Vincentio?
PEDANT. I know him not, but I have heard of him;
    A merchant of incomparable wealth.
TRANIO. He is my father, sir, and sooth to say,
    In count'nance somewhat doth resemble you.   100
BIONDELLO [*aside*]. As much as an apple doth an oyster,
    and all one.
TRANIO. To save your life in this extremity,
    This favour will I do you for his sake—
    And think it not the worst of all your fortunes
    That you are like to Sir Vincentio—
    His name and credit shall you undertake,
    And in my house you shall be friendly lodged.
    Look that you take upon you as you should,
    You understand me, sir: so shall you stay   110
    Till you have done your business in the city:
    If this be court'sy, sir, accept of it.
PEDANT. O, sir, I do, and will repute you ever
    The patron of my life and liberty.
TRANIO. Then go with me to make the matter good.
    This, by the way, I let you understand—
    My father is here looked for every day,
    To pass assurance of a dower in marriage
    'Twixt me and one Baptista's daughter here:

In all these circumstances I'll instruct you.
Go with me, sir, to clothe you as becomes you.   120

They go

Scene 3: *Petruchio's house in the country*

Enter Katharina and Grumio

GRUMIO. No, no, forsooth, I dare not for my life.
KATHARINA. The more my wrong, the more his
    spite appears.
What, did he marry me to famish me?
Beggars that come unto my father's door,
Upon entreaty have a present alms,
If not, elsewhere they meet with charity:
But I, who never knew how to entreat,
Nor never needed that I should entreat,
Am starved for meat, giddy for lack of sleep,
With oaths kept waking, and with brawling fed: 10
And that which spites me more than all these wants,
He does it under name of perfect love;
As who should say—if I should sleep or eat,
'Twere deadly sickness or else present death.
I prithee go, and get me some repast,
I care not what, so it be wholesome food.
GRUMIO. What say you to a neat's foot?
KATHARINA. 'Tis passing good, I prithee let me have it.
GRUMIO. I fear it is too choleric a meat.
How say you to a fat tripe finely broiled?   20
KATHARINA. I like it well. Good Grumio, fetch it me.
GRUMIO. I cannot tell, I fear 'tis choleric.
What say you to a piece of beef and mustard?
KATHARINA. A dish that I do love to feed upon.
GRUMIO. Ay, but the mustard is too hot a little.
KATHARINA. Why then, the beef, and let the
    mustard rest.
GRUMIO. Nay then, I will not, you shall have
    the mustard,
Or else you get no beef of Grumio.
KATHARINA. Then both or one, or any thing thou wilt.
GRUMIO. Why then, the mustard without the beef.   30
KATHARINA. Go, get thee gone, thou false
    deluding slave,   *She beats him*
That feed'st me with the very name of meat.
Sorrow on thee and all the pack of you
That triumph thus upon my misery:
Go, get thee gone, I say.

Enter Petruchio and Hortensio with meat

PETRUCHIO. How fares my Kate? What, sweeting,
    all-amort?
HORTENSIO. Mistress, what cheer?
KATHARINA.   Faith, as cold as can be.
PETRUCHIO. Pluck up thy spirits, look cheerfully
    upon me.
Here, love, thou seest how diligent I am,
To dress thy meat myself, and bring it thee.   40
I am sure, sweet Kate, this kindness merits thanks.
What, not a word? Nay then, thou lov'st it not;
And all my pains is sorted to no proof.
Here, take away this dish.
KATHARINA.   I pray you, let it stand.
PETRUCHIO. The poorest service is repaid with thanks,
And so shall mine before you touch the meat.
KATHARINA. I thank you, sir.
HORTENSIO. Signior Petruchio, fie! you are to blame:
Come, Mistress Kate, I'll bear you company.

PETRUCHIO [*aside*]. Eat it up all, Hortensio, if thou
    lovest me: 50
Much good do it unto thy gentle heart.
[*aloud*] Kate, eat apace; and now, my honey love,
Will we return unto thy father's house,
And revel it as bravely as the best,
With silken coats and caps and golden rings,
With ruffs and cuffs and fardingales, and things;
With scarfs and fans and double change of brav'ry,
With amber bracelets, beads, and all this knav'ry.
What, hast thou dined? The tailor stays thy leisure,
To deck thy body with his ruffling treasure.   60

A tailor enters

Come, tailor, let us see these ornaments.
Lay forth the gown.

A haberdasher enters

                    What news with you, sir?
HABERDASHER. Here is the cap your worship did
    bespeak.
PETRUCHIO. Why, this was moulded on a porringer—
A velvet dish: fie, fie! 'tis lewd and filthy:
Why, 'tis a cockle or a walnut-shell,
A knack, a toy, a trick, a baby's cap:
Away with it! come, let me have a bigger.
KATHARINA. I'll have no bigger, this doth fit the time,
And gentlewomen wear such caps as these.   70
PETRUCHIO. When you are gentle, you shall have
    one too,
And not till then.
HORTENSIO [*aside*].   That will not be in haste.
KATHARINA. Why, sir, I trust, I may have leave to
    speak,
And speak I will! I am no child, no babe—
Your betters have endured me say my mind,
And if you cannot, best you stop your ears.
My tongue will tell the anger of my heart,
Or else my heart concealing it will break,
And rather than it shall, I will be free,
Even to the uttermost, as I please, in words.   80
PETRUCHIO. Why, thou say'st true—it is a paltry cap,
A custard-coffin, a bauble, a silken pie!
I love thee well, in that thou lik'st it not.
KATHARINA. Love me or love me not, I like the cap,
And it I will have, or I will have none.
PETRUCHIO. Thy gown? why, ay: come, tailor, let
    us see't.
                    The haberdasher goes
O mercy, God! what masquing-stuff is here?
What's this? a sleeve? 'tis like a demi-cannon.
What! up and down carved like an apple-tart?
Here's snip and nip and cut and slish and slash,   90
Like to a censer in a barber's shop:
Why, what a devil's name, tailor, call'st thou this?
HORTENSIO [*aside*]. I see she's like to have neither cap
    nor gown.
TAILOR. You bid me make it orderly and well,
According to the fashion and the time.
PETRUCHIO. Marry, and did; but if you be remembred,
I did not bid you mar it to the time.
Go, hop me over every kennel home,
For you shall hop without my custom, sir:
I'll none of it; hence, make your best of it.   100
KATHARINA. I never saw a better-fashioned gown,

More quaint, more pleasing, nor more
commendable:
Belike you mean to make a puppet of me.
PETRUCHIO. Why, true, he means to make a puppet
of thee.
TAILOR. She says your worship means to make a
puppet of her.
PETRUCHIO. O monstrous arrogance! Thou liest, thou
thread, thou thimble,
Thou yard, three-quarters, half-yard, quarter, nail!
Thou flea, thou nit, thou winter-cricket thou!
Braved in mine own house with a skein of thread? 110
Away, thou rag, thou quantity, thou remnant,
Or I shall so be-mete thee with thy yard,
As thou shalt think on prating whilst thou livest!
I tell thee, I, that thou hast marred her gown.
TAILOR. Your worship is deceived—the gown is made
Just as my master had direction:
Grumio gave order how it should be done.
GRUMIO. I gave him no order, I gave him the stuff.
TAILOR. But how did you desire it should be made?
GRUMIO. Marry, sir, with needle and thread. 120
TAILOR. But did you not request to have it cut?
GRUMIO. Thou hast faced many things.
TAILOR. I have.
GRUMIO. Face not me: thou hast braved many men,
brave not me; I will neither be faced nor braved. I
say unto thee, I bid thy master cut out the gown,
but I did not bid him cut it to pieces: ergo, thou
liest.
TAILOR. Why, here is the note of the fashion to testify.
PETRUCHIO. Read it. 130
GRUMIO. The note lies in's throat, if he say I said so.
TAILOR [reads]. 'Imprimis, a loose-bodied gown.'
GRUMIO. Master, if ever I said loose-bodied gown,
sew me in the skirts of it, and beat me to death
with a bottom of brown thread: I said a gown.
PETRUCHIO. Proceed.
TAILOR. 'With a small compassed cape.'
GRUMIO. I confess the cape.
TAILOR. 'With a trunk sleeve.'
GRUMIO. I confess two sleeves. 140
TAILOR. 'The sleeves curiously cut.'
PETRUCHIO. Ay, there's the villainy.
GRUMIO. Error i'th' bill, sir, error i'th' bill! I com-
manded the sleeves should be cut out, and sewed up
again, and that I'll prove upon thee, though thy little
finger be armed in a thimble.
TAILOR. This is true that I say, an I had thee in place
where, thou shouldst know it.
GRUMIO. I am for thee straight: take thou the bill, give
me thy mete-yard, and spare not me. 150
HORTENSIO. God-a-mercy, Grumio! then he shall have
no odds.
PETRUCHIO. Well, sir, in brief, the gown is not for me.
GRUMIO. You are i'th' right, sir, 'tis for my mistress.
PETRUCHIO. Go, take it up unto thy master's use.
GRUMIO. Villain, not for thy life: take up my mistress'
gown for thy master's use!
PETRUCHIO. Why, sir, what's your conceit in that?
GRUMIO. O, sir, the conceit is deeper than you think
for:
Take up my mistress' gown to his master's use! 160
O, fie, fie, fie!
PETRUCHIO [aside]. Hortensio, say thou wilt see the
tailor paid.

[aloud] Go take it hence, be gone, and say no more.
HORTENSIO. Tailor, I'll pay thee for thy gown
to-morrow.
Take no unkindness of his hasty words:
Away, I say. Commend me to thy master.
                                        The tailor goes
PETRUCHIO. Well, come my Kate, we will unto
your father's,
Even in these honest mean habiliments:
Our purses shall be proud, our garments poor:
For 'tis the mind that makes the body rich, 170
And as the sun breaks through the darkest clouds,
So honour peereth in the meanest habit.
What, is the jay more precious than the lark,
Because his feathers are more beautiful?
Or is the adder better than the eel,
Because his painted skin contents the eye?
O, no, good Kate; neither art thou the worse
For this poor furniture, and mean array.
If thou account'st it shame, lay it on me.
And therefore frolic, we will hence forthwith, 180
To feast and sport us at thy father's house.
Go, call my men, and let us straight to him,
And bring our horses unto Long-lane end,
There will we mount, and thither walk on foot.
Let's see, I think 'tis now some seven o'clock,
And well we may come there by dinner-time.
KATHARINA. I dare assure you, sir, 'tis almost two,
And 'twill be supper-time ere you come there.
PETRUCHIO. It shall be seven ere I go to horse:
Look, what I speak, or do, or think to do, 190
You are still crossing it. Sirs, let't alone,
I will not go to-day, and ere I do,
It shall be what o'clock I say it is.
HORTENSIO. Why, so this gallant will command the
sun.   They go

Scene 4: The square in Padua

Enter Tranio (as Lucentio) with the Pedant, dressed like
Vincentio, and booted

TRANIO. Sir, this is the house—please it you that I call?
PEDANT. Ay, what else? and but I be deceived
Signior Baptista may remember me,
Near twenty years ago, in Genoa,
Where we were lodgers at the Pegasus.
TRANIO. 'Tis well, and hold your own, in any case
With such austerity as 'longeth to a father.
PEDANT. I warrant you.

Biondello approaches

                              But, sir, here comes your boy.
'Twere good he were schooled.
TRANIO. Fear you not him. Sirrah Biondello, 10
Now do your duty throughly, I advise you;
Imagine 'twere the right Vincentio.
BIONDELLO. Tut, fear not me.
TRANIO. But hast thou done thy errand to Baptista?
BIONDELLO. I told him, that your father was at Venice,
And that you looked for him this day in Padua.
TRANIO. Th'art a tall fellow; hold thee that to drink.

Baptista enters followed by Lucentio, as Cambio

Here comes Baptista: set your countenance, sir.
Signior Baptista, you are happily met:

[*to the Pedant*] Sir, this is the gentleman I told
    you of.   20
I pray you, stand good father to me now,
Give me Bianca for my patrimony.
PEDANT. Soft, son!
    Sir, by your leave, having come to Padua
    To gather in some debts, my son Lucentio
    Made me acquainted with a weighty cause
    Of love between your daughter and himself:
    And for the good report I hear of you,
    And for the love he beareth to your daughter,
    And she to him, to stay him not too long,   30
    I am content, in a good father's care,
    To have him matched: and, if you please to like
    No worse than I, upon some agreement
    Me shall you find ready and willing
    With one consent to have her so bestowed:
    For curious I cannot be with you,
    Signior Baptista of whom I hear so well.
BAPTISTA. Sir, pardon me in what I have to say—
    Your plainness and your shortness please me well:
    Right true it is, your son Lucentio here   40
    Doth love my daughter, and she loveth him,
    Or both dissemble deeply their affections:
    And therefore, if you say no more than this,
    That like a father you will deal with him,
    And pass my daughter a sufficient dower,
    The match is made, and all is done—
    Your son shall have my daughter with consent.
TRANIO. I thank you, sir. Where then do you
        know best
    We be affied and such assurance ta'en
    As shall with either part's agreement 'stand?   50
BAPTISTA. Not in my house, Lucentio, for you know
    Pitchers have ears and I have many servants,
    Besides, old Gremio is heark'ning still,
    And happily we might be interrupted.
TRANIO. Then at my lodging, an it like you.
    There doth my father lie; and there this night
    We'll pass the business privately and well:
    Send for your daughter by your servant here,
    My boy shall fetch the scrivener presently.
    The worst is this, that, at so slender warning,   60
    You are like to have a thin and slender pittance.
BAPTISTA. It likes me well: Cambio, hie you home,
    And bid Bianca make her ready straight:
    And, if you will, tell what hath happenéd—
    Lucentio's father is arrived in Padua,
    And how she's like to be Lucentio's wife.
                                        Lucentio goes
BIONDELLO. I pray the gods she may, with all my heart!
TRANIO. Dally not with the gods, but get thee gone.
                                        Biondello goes
    Signior Baptista, shall I lead the way?
    Welcome! one mess is like to be your cheer.   70
    Come sir, we will better it in Pisa.
BAPTISTA. I follow you.
                        Tranio, Baptista and the Pedant go,

Lucentio and Biondello enter

BIONDELLO. Cambio.
LUCENTIO.   Why say'st thou, Biondello?
BIONDELLO. You saw my master wink and laugh
    upon you?
LUCENTIO. Biondello, what of that?
BIONDELLO. Faith nothing; but has left me here behind,

to expound the meaning or moral of his signs and
tokens.
LUCENTIO. I pray thee, moralize them.
BIONDELLO. Then thus … Baptista is safe, talking with   80
    the deceiving father of a deceitful son.
LUCENTIO. And what of him?
BIONDELLO. His daughter is to be brought by you to
    the supper.
LUCENTIO. And then?
BIONDELLO. The old priest at Saint Luke's church is
    at your command at all hours.
LUCENTIO. And what of all this?
BIONDELLO. I cannot tell—except they are busied
    about a counterfeit assurance: take you assurance of   90
    her, 'cum privilegio ad imprimendum solum.' To
    th' church! take the priest, clerk, and some sufficient
    honest witnesses.
    If this be not that you look for, I have no more
        to say,
    But bid Bianca farewell for ever and a day.
LUCENTIO. Hear'st thou, Biondello?
BIONDELLO. I cannot tarry: I knew a wench married
    in an afternoon as she went to the garden for parsley
    to stuff a rabbit—and so may you, sir; and so adieu,
    sir. My master hath appointed me to go to Saint   100
    Luke's, to bid the priest be ready to come against
    you come with your appendix.   *He goes*
LUCENTIO. I may and will, if she be so contented:
    She will be pleased, then wherefore should I doubt?
    Hap what hap may, I'll roundly go about her;
    It shall go hard, if Cambio go without her.
                                        He goes

Scene 5: *The highway leading to Padua*

Enter Petruchio, Katharina, Hortensio and servants

PETRUCHIO. Come on, a God's name! once more
        toward our father's.
    Good Lord, how bright and goodly shines the
        moon!
KATHARINA. The moon! the sun: it is not moon-
        light now.
PETRUCHIO. I say it is the moon that shines so bright.
KATHARINA. I know it is the sun that shines so bright.
PETRUCHIO. Now by my mother's son, and that's
        myself,
    It shall be moon, or star, or what I list,
    Or ere I journey to your father's house …
    Go on, and fetch our horses back again—
    Evermore crossed and crossed, nothing but crossed!   10
HORTENSIO. Say as he says, or we shall never go.
KATHARINA. Forward, I pray, since we have come so
        far,
    And be it moon, or sun, or what you please:
    And if you please to call it a rush-candle,
    Henceforth I vow it shall be so for me.
PETRUCHIO. I say it is the moon.
KATHARINA.   I know it is the moon.
PETRUCHIO. Nay, then you lie: it is the blesséd sun.
KATHARINA. Then, God be blessed, it is the blesséd
        sun—
    But sun it is not, when you say it is not,
    And the moon changes even as your mind: 20
    What you will have it named, even that it is,
    And so it shall be still, for Katharine.
HORTENSIO. Petruchio, go thy ways, the field is won.

PETRUCHIO. Well, forward, forward! thus the bowl
    should run,
And not unluckily against the bias.
But soft, what company is coming here?

Vincentio enters

[*to Vincentio*] Good morrow, gentle mistress,
    where away?
Tell me, sweet Kate, and tell me truly too,
Hast thou beheld a fresher gentlewoman?
Such war of white and red within her cheeks!   30
What stars do spangle heaven with such beauty,
As those two eyes become that heavenly face?
Fair lovely maid, once more good day to thee:
Sweet Kate, embrace her for her beauty's sake.
HORTENSIO. A' will make the man mad, to make a
    woman of him.
KATHARINA. Young budding virgin, fair and fresh
    and sweet,
Whither away, or where is thy abode?
Happy the parents of so fair a child;
Happier the man, whom favourable stars   40
Allot thee for his lovely bed-fellow!
PETRUCHIO. Why, how now, Kate! I hope thou art
    not mad.
This is a man, old, wrinkled, faded, withered,
And not a maiden, as thou say'st he is.
KATHARINA. Pardon, old father, my mistaking eyes,
That have been so bedazzled with the sun,
That every thing I look on seemeth green:
Now I perceive thou art a reverend father;
Pardon, I pray thee, for my mad mistaking.
PETRUCHIO. Do, good old grandsire, and withal
    make known   50
Which way thou travellest—if along with us,
We shall be joyful of thy company.
VINCENTIO. Fair sir, and you my merry mistress,
That with your strange encounter much
    amazed me,
My name is called Vincentio, my dwelling Pisa,
And bound I am to Padua, there to visit
A son of mine, which long I have not seen.
PETRUCHIO. What is his name?
VINCENTIO.   Lucentio, gentle sir.
PETRUCHIO. Happily met—the happier for thy son.
And now by law, as well as reverend age,   60
I may entitle thee my loving father.
The sister to my wife, this gentlewoman,
Thy son by this hath married. Wonder not,
Nor be not grieved—she is of good esteem,
Her dowry wealthy, and of worthy birth;
Beside, so qualified as may beseem
The spouse of any noble gentleman.
Let me embrace with old Vincentio,
And wander we to see thy honest son,
Who will of thy arrival be full joyous.   70
VINCENTIO. But is this true? or is it else your pleasure,
Like pleasant travellers, to break a jest
Upon the company you overtake?
HORTENSIO. I do assure thee, father, so it is.
PETRUCHIO. Come, go along, and see the truth hereof,
For our first merriment hath made thee jealous.
                        All depart save Hortensio
HORTENSIO. Well, Petruchio, this hath put me in heart.
Have to my widow! and if she be froward,

Then hast thou taught Hortensio to be untoward.
                                        He follows

ACT 5
Scene 1: *The square in Padua*

*Gremio seated; Biondello, Lucentio (in his proper habit)
and Bianca (muffled) enter*

BIONDELLO. Softly and swiftly, sir, for the priest is
    ready.
LUCENTIO. I fly, Biondello: but they may chance to   30
    need thee at home, therefore leave us.
                                    He and Bianca go
BIONDELLO [*follows*]. Nay, faith, I'll see the church
    o'your back, and then come back to my master's
    as soon as I can.
GREMIO. I marvel Cambio comes not all this while.

*Petruchio, Katharina, Vincentio, and Grumio with atten-
dants enter*

PETRUCHIO. Sir, here's the door, this is Lucentio's
    house.
My father's bears more toward the market-place,   10
Thither must I, and here I leave you, sir.
VINCENTIO. You shall not choose but drink before
    you go;
I think I shall command your welcome here,
And by all likelihood some cheer is toward.
                                        He knocks
GREMIO. They're busy within, you were best knock
    louder.

The Pedant looks out of the window

PEDANT. What's he that knocks as he would beat down   50
    the gate?
VINCENTIO. Is Signior Lucentio within, sir?
PEDANT. He's within, sir, but not to be spoken withal.   20
VINCENTIO. What if a man bring him a hundred pound
    or two, to make merry withal?
PEDANT. Keep your hundred pounds to yourself, he
    shall need none, so long as I live.
PETRUCHIO. Nay, I told you your son was well beloved
    in Padua ... Do you hear, sir?—to leave frivolous
    circumstances, I pray you tell Signior Lucentio that
    his father is come from Pisa, and is here at the door
    to speak with him.
PEDANT. Thou liest, his father is come from Mantua,   30
    and is here looking out at the window.
VINCENTIO. Art thou his father?
PEDANT. Ay, sir, so his mother says, if I may believe
    her.
PETRUCHIO [*to Vincentio*]. Why, how now, gentleman!
    why, this is flat knavery, to take upon you another
    man's name.
PEDANT. Lay hands on the villain! I believe, a' means
    to cozen somebody in this city under my coun-
    tenance.   40

Biondello returns

BIONDELLO. I have seen them in the church together,
    God send 'em good shipping. But who is here? mine
    old master Vincentio! now we are undone, and
    brought to nothing.
VINCENTIO [*sees Biondello*]. Come hither, crack-hemp.
BIONDELLO. I hope I may choose, sir.

VINCENTIO. Come hither, you rogue.
  What, have you forgot me?
BIONDELLO. Forgot you? no, sir: I could not forget
  you, for I never saw you before in all my life.   50
VINCENTIO. What, you notorious villain, didst thou
  never see thy master's father, Vincentio?
BIONDELLO. What, my old, worshipful old master?
  yes, marry, sir—see where he looks out of the
  window.
VINCENTIO. Is't so, indeed?   *He beats Biondello*
BIONDELLO. Help, help, help! here's a madman will
  murder me.   *He goes*
PEDANT. Help, son! help, Signior Baptista!
                                He shuts the window
PETRUCHIO. Prithee, Kate, let's stand aside, and see the   60
  end of this controversy.   *They retire*

*The Pedant with servants, Baptista and Tranio come from
the house*

TRANIO. Sir, what are you, that offer to beat my
  servant?
VINCENTIO. What am I, sir! nay, what are you, sir?
  O immortal gods! O fine villain! A silken doublet,
  a velvet hose, a scarlet cloak, and a copatain hat!
  O, I am undone, I am undone! while I play the
  good husband at home, my son and my servant
  spend all at the university.
TRANIO. How now! what's the matter?   70
BAPTISTA. What, is the man lunatic?
TRANIO. Sir, you seem a sober ancient gentleman by
  your habit: but your words show you a madman.
  Why, sir, what 'cerns it you, if I wear pearl and
  gold? I thank my good father, I am able to maintain it.
VINCENTIO. Thy father! O, villain, he is a sail-maker
  in Bergamo.
BAPTISTA. You mistake, sir—you mistake, sir—pray,
  what do you think is his name?   80
VINCENTIO. His name! as if I knew not his name: I
  have brought him up ever since he was three years
  old, and his name is Tranio.
PEDANT. Away, away, mad ass! his name is Lucentio,
  and he is mine only son, and heir to the lands of
  me, Signior Vincentio.
VINCENTIO. Lucentio! O, he hath murdered his master!
  Lay hold on him, I charge you, in the duke's name.
  O, my son, my son . . . Tell me, thou villain, where
  is my son Lucentio?   90
TRANIO. Call forth an officer.

An officer comes up

  Carry this mad knave to the gaol. Father Baptista,
  I charge you see that he be forthcoming.
VINCENTIO. Carry me to the gaol!
GREMIO. Stay, officer. He shall not go to prison.
BAPTISTA. Talk not, Signior Gremio; I say he shall go
  to prison.
GREMIO. Take heed, Signior Baptista, lest you be
  cony-catched in this business; I dare swear this is the
  right Vincentio.   100
PEDANT. Swear, if thou darest.
GREMIO. Nay, I dare not swear it.
TRANIO. Then thou wert best say that I am not
  Lucentio.
GREMIO. Yes, I know thee to be Signior Lucentio.

BAPTISTA. Away with the dotard, to the gaol with
  him!
VINCENTIO. Thus strangers may be haléd and abused.
  O monstrous villain!

Biondello returns with Lucentio and Bianca

BIONDELLO. O, we are spoiled, and—yonder he is!   110
  Deny him, forswear him, or else we are all undone.
LUCENTIO [*kneels*]. Pardon, sweet father.
VINCENTIO.   Lives my sweet son?

Biondello, Tranio, and Pedant run as fast as may be

BIANCA [*kneels*]. Pardon, dear father.
BAPTISTA.   How hast thou offended?
  Where is Lucentio?
LUCENTIO.   Here's Lucentio,
  Right son to the right Vincentio,
  That have by marriage made thy daughter mine,
  While counterfeit supposes bleared thine eyne.
GREMIO. Here's packing, with a witness, to deceive
  us all!
VINCENTIO. Where is that damnéd villain, Tranio,   120
  That faced and braved me in this matter so?
BAPTISTA. Why, tell me, is not this my Cambio?
BIANCA. Cambio is changed into Lucentio.
LUCENTIO. Love wrought these miracles. Bianca's
  love
  Made me exchange my state with Tranio,
  While he did bear my countenance in the town,
  And happily I have arrived at last
  Unto the wishéd haven of my bliss.
  What Tranio did, myself enforced him to;
  Then pardon him, sweet father, for my sake.   130
VINCENTIO. I'll slit the villain's nose, that would have
  sent me to the gaol.
BAPTISTA. But do you hear, sir? have you married
  my daughter without asking my good will?
VINCENTIO. Fear not, Baptista—we will content you,
  go to: but I will in, to be revenged for this
  villainy.
                                He goes
BAPTISTA. And I, to sound the depth of this knavery.
                                He goes
LUCENTIO. Look not pale, Bianca; thy father will
  not frown.   *They follow Baptista*
GREMIO. My cake is dough, but I'll in among the rest,   140
  Out of hope of all but my share of the feast.
                                He follows likewise
KATHARINA. Husband, let's follow, to see the end of
  this ado.
PETRUCHIO. First kiss me, Kate, and we will.
KATHARINA. What, in the midst of the street?
PETRUCHIO. What, art thou ashamed of me?
KATHARINA. No, sir, God forbid—but ashamed to kiss.
PETRUCHIO. Why, then let's home again. Come,
  sirrah, let's away.
KATHARINA. Nay, I will give thee a kiss. Now pray
  thee, love, stay.
PETRUCHIO. Is not this well? Come, my sweet Kate.
  Better once than never, for never too late.   150
                                They go

Scene 2: *Lucentio's house*

*Enter Baptista and Vincentio, Gremio and the Pedant,
Lucentio and Bianca, Petruchio and Katharina, Hortensio*

and the Widow; the serving-men with Tranio bringing in a banquet.

LUCENTIO. At last, though long, our jarring notes agree,
And time it is, when raging war is done,
To smile at scapes and perils overblown.
My fair Bianca, bid my father welcome,
Which I with self-same kindness welcome thine:
Brother Petruchio, sister Katharina,
And thou, Hortensio, with thy loving widow,
Feast with the best, and welcome to my house.
My banquet is to close our stomachs up,
After our great good cheer. Pray you, sit down, 10
For now we sit to chat, as well as eat.
PETRUCHIO. Nothing but sit and sit, and eat and eat!
BAPTISTA. Padua affords this kindness, son Petruchio.
PETRUCHIO. Padua affords nothing but what is kind.
HORTENSIO. For both our sakes, I would that word were true.
PETRUCHIO. Now, for my life, Hortensio fears his widow.
WIDOW. Then never trust me if I be afeard.
PETRUCHIO. You are very sensible, and yet you miss my sense:
I mean, Hortensio is afeard of you.
WIDOW. He that is giddy thinks the world turns round. 20
PETRUCHIO. Roundly replied.
KATHARINA. Mistress, how mean you that?
WIDOW. Thus I conceive by him.
PETRUCHIO. Conceives by me! How likes Hortensio that?
HORTENSIO. My widow says, thus she conceives her tale.
PETRUCHIO. Very well mended: kiss him for that, good widow.
KATHARINA. 'He that is giddy thinks the world turns round'—
I pray you, tell me what you meant by that.
WIDOW. Your husband, being troubled with a shrew,
Measures my husband's sorrow by his woe:
And now you know my meaning. 30
KATHARINA. A very mean meaning.
WIDOW. Right, I mean you.
KATHARINA. And I am mean, indeed, respecting you.
PETRUCHIO. To her, Kate!
HORTENSIO. To her, widow.
PETRUCHIO. A hundred marks, my Kate does put her down.
HORTENSIO. That's my office.
PETRUCHIO. Spoke like an officer: ha' to thee, lad!
He drinks to Hortensio
BAPTISTA. How likes Gremio these quick-witted folks?
GREMIO. Believe me, they butt heads together well.
BIANCA. Head and butt! an hasty-witted body 40
Would say your head and butt were head and horn.
VINCENTIO. Ay, mistress bride, hath that awakened you?
BIANCA. Ay, but not frighted me, therefore I'll sleep again.
PETRUCHIO. Nay, that you shall not: since you have begun,
Have at you for a bitter jest or two.
BIANCA. Am I your bird? I mean to shift my bush,
And then pursue me as you draw your bow.

You are welcome all.
She leaves, followed by Katharina and the Widow
PETRUCHIO. She hath prevented me. Here, Signior Tranio,
This bird you aimed at, though you hit her not— 50
Therefore, a health to all shot and missed.
TRANIO. O, sir, Lucentio slipped me like his greyhound,
Which runs himself, and catches for his master.
PETRUCHIO. A good swift simile, but something currish.
TRANIO. 'Tis well, sir, that you hunted for yourself:
'Tis thought, your deer does hold you at a bay.
BAPTISTA. O ho, Petruchio! Tranio hits you now.
LUCENTIO. I thank thee for that gird, good Tranio.
HORTENSIO. Confess, confess, hath he not hit you here?
PETRUCHIO. A' has a little galled me, I confess; 60
And as the jest did glance away from me,
'Tis ten to one it maimed you two outright.
BAPTISTA. Now, in good sadness, son Petruchio,
I think thou hast the veriest shrew of all.
PETRUCHIO. Well, I say no: and therefore for assurance
Let's each one send unto his wife,
And he whose wife is most obedient,
To come at first when he doth send for her,
Shall win the wager which we will propose.
HORTENSIO. Content. What is the wager?
LUCENTIO. Twenty crowns. 70
PETRUCHIO. Twenty crowns!
I'll venture so much of my hawk or hound,
But twenty times so much upon my wife.
LUCENTIO. A hundred then.
HORTENSIO. Content.
PETRUCHIO. A match! 'tis done.
HORTENSIO. Who shall begin?
LUCENTIO. That will I.
Go, Biondello, bid your mistress come to me.
BIONDELLO. I go. *He goes*
BAPTISTA. Son, I will be your half, Bianca comes.
LUCENTIO. I'll have no halves; I'll bear it all myself.

Biondello returns

How now! what news?
BIONDELLO. Sir, my mistress sends you word 80
That she is busy, and she cannot come.
PETRUCHIO. How! she is busy, and she cannot come!
Is that an answer!
GREMIO. Ay, and a kind one too:
Pray God, sir, your wife send you not a worse.
PETRUCHIO. I hope better.
HORTENSIO. Sirrah Biondello, go and entreat my wife
To come to me forthwith. *Exit Biondello*
PETRUCHIO. O, ho! entreat her!
Nay, then she must needs come.
HORTENSIO. I am afraid, sir,
Do what you can, yours will not be entreated ...

Biondello returns

Now, where's my wife? 90
BIONDELLO. She says you have some goodly jest in hand.
She will not come; she bids you come to her.
PETRUCHIO. Worse and worse, she will not come!
O vile,
Intolerable, not to be endured!
Sirrah, Grumio, go to your mistress;

Say, I command her come to me.   *Grumio goes*
HORTENSIO. I know her answer.
PETRUCHIO.   What?
HORTENSIO.   She will not.
PETRUCHIO. The fouler fortune mine, and there an
   end.

Katharina enters

BAPTISTA. Now, by my holidame, here comes
   Katharina!
KATHARINA. What is your will, sir, that you send
   for me?   100
PETRUCHIO. Where is your sister, and Hortensio's
   wife?
KATHARINA. They sit conferring by the parlour fire.
PETRUCHIO. Go, fetch them hither. If they deny
   to come,
Swinge me them soundly forth unto their husbands.
Away, I say, and bring them hither straight.
                                        She goes
LUCENTIO. Here is a wonder, if you talk of wonders.
HORTENSIO. And so it is; I wonder what it bodes.
PETRUCHIO. Marry, peace it bodes, and love, and
   quiet life,
An awful rule, and right supremacy;
And, to be short, what not, that's sweet and happy?   110
BAPTISTA. Now fair befal thee, good Petruchio!
The wager thou hast won, and I will add
Unto their losses twenty thousand crowns—
Another dowry to another daughter,
For she is changed, as she had never been.
PETRUCHIO. Nay, I will win my wager better yet,
And show more sign of her obedience,
Her new-built virtue and obedience.

Katharina returns with Bianca and the Widow

See, where she comes, and brings your froward
   wives
As prisoners to her womanly persuasion.   120
Katharine, that cap of yours becomes you not,
Off with that bauble, throw it under-foot.
                                        She obeys
WIDOW. Lord, let me never have a cause to sigh,
Till I be brought to such a silly pass!
BIANCA. Fie! what a foolish duty call you this?
LUCENTIO. I would your duty were as foolish too:
The wisdom of your duty, fair Bianca,
Hath cost one hundred crowns since supper-time.
BIANCA. The more fool you, for laying on my duty.
PETRUCHIO. Katharine, I charge thee, tell these
   headstrong women   130
What duty they do owe their lords and husbands.
WIDOW. Come, come, you're mocking; we will have
   no telling.
PETRUCHIO. Come on, I say, and first begin with her.
WIDOW. She shall not.
PETRUCHIO. I say, she shall—and first begin with her.
KATHARINA. Fie, fie! unknit that threatening
   unkind brow,
And dart not scornful glances from those eyes,

To wound thy lord, thy king, thy governor:
It blots thy beauty as frosts do bite the meads,
Confounds thy fame as whirlwinds shake fair buds,   140
And in no sense is meet or amiable.
A women moved is like a fountain troubled,
Muddy, ill-seeming, thick, bereft of beauty,
And while it is so, none so dry or thirsty
Will deign to sip or touch one drop of it.
Thy husband is thy lord, thy life, thy keeper,
Thy head, thy sovereign; one that cares for thee,
And for thy maintenance commits his body
To painful labour, both by sea and land;
To watch the night in storms, the day in cold,   150
Whilst thou liest warm at home, secure and safe,
And craves no other tribute at thy hands,
But love, fair looks, and true obedience;
Too little payment for so great a debt.
Such duty as the subject owes the prince,
Even such a woman oweth to her husband:
And when she is froward, peevish, sullen, sour,
And not obedient to his honest will,
What is she but a foul contending rebel,
And graceless traitor to her loving lord?   160
I am ashamed that women are so simple
To offer war where they should kneel for peace;
Or seek for rule, supremacy, and sway,
When they are bound to serve, love, and obey.
Why are our bodies soft, and weak, and smooth,
Unapt to toil and trouble in the world,
But that our soft conditions and our hearts
Should well agree with our external parts?
Come, come, you froward and unable worms!
My mind hath been as big as one of yours,   170
My heart as great, my reason haply more,
To bandy word for word, and frown for frown;
But now I see our lances are but straws,
Our strength as weak, our weakness past compare,
That seeming to be most which we indeed least are.
Then vail your stomachs, for it is no boot,
And place your hands below your husband's foot:
In token of which duty, if he please,
My hand is ready, may it do him ease.
PETRUCHIO. Why, there's a wench! Come on, and kiss
   me, Kate.   180
LUCENTIO. Well, go thy ways, old lad, for thou
   shalt ha't.
VINCENTIO. 'Tis a good hearing, when children
   are toward.
LUCENTIO. But a harsh hearing when women
   are froward.
PETRUCHIO. Come Kate, we'll to bed.
We three are married, but you two are sped.
'Twas I won the wager, though you hit the white,
                                        To Lucentio
And, being a winner, God give you good night!
                            Petruchio and Katharina depart
HORTENSIO. Now go thy ways, thou hast tamed a
   curst shrow.
LUCENTIO. 'Tis a wonder, by your leave, she will be
   taméd so.   *They all go*

All's Well that Ends Well

The scene: Rousillon, Paris, Florence, Marseilles

CHARACTERS IN THE PLAY

KING OF FRANCE

DUKE OF FLORENCE

BERTRAM, *the young Count of Rousillon*

LAFEU, *an old lord*

PAROLLES, *a follower of Bertram*

RINALDO, *Steward to the Countess of Rousillon*

LAVACHE, *Clown to the Countess*

Two French gentlemen at Court named DUMAIN,
later captains in the Florentine army

A soldier, pretending to be an interpreter

A gentleman, astringer to the French king

A Page

COUNTESS OF ROUSILLON, *mother to Bertram*

HELENA, *a waiting-gentlewoman to the Countess*

A Widow of Florence

DIANA, *daughter to the widow*

MARIANA, *neighbour to the widow*

Lords, officers, soldiers, etc., French and Florentine

All's Well that Ends Well

ACT 1
Scene 1: *The palace of Rousillon*

Enter Bertram the young Count of Rousillon, his mother the Countess, Helena, and Lord Lafeu, all in black

COUNTESS. In delivering my son from me I bury a second husband.

BERTRAM. And I in going, madam, weep o'er my father's death anew: but I must attend his majesty's command, to whom I am now in ward, evermore in subjection.

LAFEU. You shall find of the king a husband, madam—you, sir, a father. He that so generally is at all times good, must of necessity hold his virtue to you, whose worthiness would stir it up where it wanted 10 rather than lack it where there is such abundance.

COUNTESS. What hope is there of his majesty's amendment?

LAFEU. He hath abandoned his physicians, madam, under whose practices he hath persecuted time with hope, and finds no other advantage in the process but only the losing of hope by time.

COUNTESS. This young gentlewoman had a father—O, that 'had,' how sad a passage 'tis—whose skill was almost as great as his honesty; had it stretched 20 so far, would have made nature immortal, and death should have play for lack of work. Would, for the king's sake, he were living. I think it would be the death of the king's disease.

LAFEU. How called you the man you speak of, madam?

COUNTESS. He was famous, sir, in his profession, and it was his great right to be so: Gerard de Narbon.

LAFEU. He was excellent, indeed, madam. The king very lately spoke of him admiringly and mourn- 30 ingly: he was skilful enough to have lived still, if knowledge could be set up against mortality.

BERTRAM. What is it, my good lord, the king languishes of?

LAFEU. A fistula, my lord.

BERTRAM. I heard not of it before.

LAFEU. I would it were not notorious.... Was this gentlewoman the daughter of Gerard de Narbon?

COUNTESS. His sole child, my lord, and bequeathed to my overlooking. I have those hopes of her good that 40 her education promises: her dispositions she inherits, which make fair gifts fairer; for where an unclean mind carries virtuous qualities, there commendations go with pity, they are virtues and traitors too; in her they are the better for their simpleness; she derives her honesty and achieves her goodness.

LAFEU. Your commendations, madam, get from her tears.

COUNTESS. 'Tis the best brine a maiden can season her praise in. The remembrance of her father never 50 approaches her heart but the tyranny of her sorrows takes all livelihood from her cheek.... No more of this, Helena, go to, no more, lest it be rather thought you affect a sorrow than to have—

HELENA. I do affect a sorrow indeed, but I have it too.

LAFEU. How understand we that? Moderate lamentation is the right of the dead, excessive grief the enemy to the living.

COUNTESS. If the living be enemy to the grief, the excess makes it soon mortal. 60

BERTRAM. Madam, I desire your holy wishes.

COUNTESS. Be thou blest, Bertram, and succeed thy father
In manners as in shape: thy blood and virtue
Contend for empire in thee, and thy goodness
Share with thy birthright. Love all, trust a few,
Do wrong to none: be able for thine enemy
Rather in power than use; and keep thy friend
Under thy own life's key: be checked for silence,
But never taxed for speech.... What heaven more will,
That thee may furnish, and my prayers pluck down, 70
Fall on thy head.... Farewell, my lord,
'Tis an unseasoned courtier. Good my lord,
Advise him.

LAFEU.   He cannot want the best
That shall attend his lord.

COUNTESS. Heaven bless him! Farewell, Bertram.
                                                    She departs

BERTRAM. The best wishes that can be forged in your thoughts be servants to you! [*to Helena*] Be comfortable to my mother, your mistress, and make much of her.

LAFEU. Farewell, pretty lady, you must hold the credit 80 of your father.   *Bertram and Lafeu go*

HELENA. O, were that all! I think not on my father,
And these great tears grace his remembrance more
Than those I shed for him. What was he like?
I have forgot him: my imagination
Carries no favour in't but Bertram's....
I am undone, there is no living, none,
If Bertram be away.... 'Twere all one
That I should love a bright particular star,
And think to wed it, he is so above me: 90
In his bright radiance and collateral light
Must I be comforted, not in his sphere....
Th'ambition in my love thus plagues itself:
The hind that would be mated by the lion
Must die for love. 'Twas pretty, though a plague,
To see him every hour, to sit and draw
His archéd brows, his hawking eye, his curls,
In our heart's table; heart too capable
Of every line and trick of his sweet favour....
But now he's gone, and my idolatrous fancy 100
Must sanctify his relics. Who comes here?

Parolles enters

One that goes with him: I love him for his sake,
And yet I know him a notorious liar,
Think him a great way fool, solely a coward,
Yet these fixed evils sit so fit in him,
That they take place, when virtue's steely bones
Look bleak i'th' cold wind: withal, full oft we see
Cold wisdom waiting on superfluous folly.

PAROLLES. Save you, fair queen.

HELENA. And you, monarch.

PAROLLES. No.

HELENA. And no.

PAROLLES. Are you meditating on virginity?

HELENA. Ay ... You have some stain of soldier in you; let me ask you a question. Man is enemy to virginity, how may we barricado it against him?

PAROLLES. Keep him out.

HELENA. But he assails, and our virginity, though valiant in the defence, yet is weak: unfold to us some warlike resistance. 120

PAROLLES. There is none: man, setting down before you, will undermine you and blow you up.

HELENA. Bless our poor virginity from underminers and blowers up! Is there no military policy, how virgins might blow up men?

PAROLLES. Virginity being blown down, man will quicklier be blown up: marry, in blowing him down again, with the breach yourselves made, you lose your city. It is not politic in the commonwealth of nature to preserve virginity. Loss of 130 virginity is rational increase, and there was never virgin got till virginity was first lost. That you were made of is mettle to make virgins. Virginity by being once lost may be ten times found: by being ever kept, it is ever lost: 'tis too cold a companion: away with't!

HELENA. I will stand for't a little, though therefore I die a virgin.

PAROLLES. There's little can be said in't—'tis against the rule of nature. To speak on the part of virginity, 140 is to accuse your mothers; which is most infallible disobedience. He that hangs himself is a virgin: virginity murders itself, and should be buried in highways out of all sanctified limit, as a desperate offendress against nature. Virginity breeds mites— much like a cheese—consumes itself to the very paring, and so dies with feeding his own stomach. Besides, virginity is peevish, proud, idle, made of self-love, which is the most inhibited sin in the canon. Keep it not—you cannot choose but lose 150 by't. Out with't: within ten year it will make itself ten, which is a goodly increase—and the principal itself not much the worse. Away with't.

HELENA. How might one do, sir, to lose it to her own liking?

PAROLLES. Let me see. Marry, ill, to like him that ne'er it likes. 'Tis a commodity will lose the gloss with lying; the longer kept, the less worth: off with't while 'tis vendible; answer the time of request. Virginity, like an old courtier, wears her cap out of 160 fashion, richly suited, but unsuitable, just like the brooch and the toothpick, which wear not now ... Your date is better in your pie and your porridge than in your cheek: and your virginity, your old virginity, is like one of our French withered pears, it looks ill, it eats drily, marry 'tis a withered pear; it was formerly better, marry yet 'tis a withered pear: will you any thing with it?

HELENA. Not my virginity yet ...
There shall your master have a thousand loves, 170
A mother, and a mistress, and a friend,
A phœnix, captain, and an enemy,
A guide, a goddess, and a sovereign,
A counsellor, a traitress, and a dear;
His humble ambition, proud humility:

His jarring concord, and his discord dulcet:
His faith, his sweet distaster; with a world
Of pretty, fond, adoptious christendoms,
That blinking Cupid gossips. Now shall he ...
I know not what he shall. God send him well! 180
The court's a learning place, and he is one—

PAROLLES. What one, i' faith?

HELENA. That I wish well. 'Tis pity—

PAROLLES. What's pity?

HELENA. That wishing well had not a body in't,
Which might be felt, that we the poorer born,
Whose baser stars do shut us up in wishes,
Might with effects of them follow our friends,
And show what we alone must think, which never
Returns us thanks. 190

A page enters

PAGE. Monsieur Parolles, my lord calls for you.
He goes

PAROLLES. Little Helen, farewell. If I can remember thee, I will think of thee at court.

HELENA. Monsieur Parolles, you were born under a charitable star.

PAROLLES. Under Mars, I.

HELENA. I especially think, under Mars.

PAROLLES. Why under Mars?

HELENA. The wars have so kept you under, that you must needs be born under Mars. 200

PAROLLES. When he was predominant.

HELENA. When he was retrograde, I think, rather.

PAROLLES. Why think you so?

HELENA. You go so much backward when you fight.

PAROLLES. That's for advantage.

HELENA. So is running away, when fear proposes the safety: but the composition that your valour and fear makes in you is a virtue of a good wing, and I like the wear well.

PAROLLES. I am so full of businesses, I cannot answer 210 thee acutely: I will return perfect courtier, in the which my instruction shall serve to naturalize thee, so thou wilt be capable of a courtier's counsel, and understand what advice shall thrust upon thee—else thou diest in thine unthankfulness, and thine ignorance makes thee away. Farewell: when thou hast leisure, say thy prayers; when thou hast money, remember thy friends: get thee a good husband, and use him as he uses thee: so farewell. *He goes*

HELENA. Our remedies oft in ourselves do lie, 220
Which we ascribe to heaven: the fated sky
Gives us free scope; only doth backward pull
Our slow designs when we ourselves are dull.
What power is it which mounts my love so high?
That makes me see, and cannot feed mine eye?
The mightiest space in fortune nature brings
To join like likes, and kiss like native things.
Impossible be strange attempts to those
That weigh their pains in sense, and do suppose
What hath been cannot be: who ever strove 230
To show her merit that did miss her love?
The king's disease—my project may deceive me,
But my intents are fixed, and will not leave me.
She goes

Scene 2: *The King's palace at Paris*

A flourish of cornets: the King of France enters with attendants, lords, and councillors; letters are placed before him

KING. The Florentines and Senoys are by th'ears,
Have fought with equal fortune, and continue
A braving war.
1 LORD.   So 'tis reported, sir.
KING. Nay, 'tis most credible. We here receive it
A certainty, vouched from our cousin Austria,
With caution, that the Florentine will move us
For speedy aid; wherein our dearest friend
Prejudicates the business, and would seem
To have us make denial.
1 LORD.   His love and wisdom,
Approved so to your majesty, may plead   10
For amplest credence.
KING.   He hath armed our answer,
And Florence is denied before he comes:
Yet, for our gentlemen that mean to see
The Tuscan service, freely have they leave
To stand on either part.
2 LORD.   It well may serve
A nursery to our gentry, who are sick
For breathing and exploit.

Bertram, Lafeu, and Parolles enter

KING.   What's he comes here?
1 LORD. It is the Count Rousillon, my good lord,
Young Bertram.
KING.   Youth, thou bear'st thy father's face.
Frank nature, rather curious than in haste,   20
Hath well composed thee: thy father's moral parts
Mayst thou inherit too! Welcome to Paris.
BERTRAM. My thanks and duty are your majesty's.
KING. I would I had that corporal soundness now,
As when thy father and myself in friendship
First tried our soldiership! He did look far
Into the service of the time, and was
Discipled of the bravest: he lasted long,
But on us both did haggish age steal on,
And wore us out of act ... It much repairs me   30
To talk of your good father ... In his youth
He had the wit, which I can well observe
To-day in our young lords; but they may jest
Till their own scorn return to them unnoted
Ere they can hide their levity in honour:
So like a courtier, contempt nor bitterness
Were in his pride or sharpness; if they were,
His equal had awaked them, and his honour,
Clock to itself, knew the true minute when
Exception bid him speak, and at this time   40
His tongue obeyed his hand. Who were below him
He used as creatures of another place,
And bowed his eminent top to their low ranks,
Making them proud of his humility,
In their poor praise he humble ... Such a man
Might be a copy to these younger times;
Which, followed well, would demonstrate them
    now
But goers backward.
BERTRAM.   His good remembrance, sir,
Lies richer in your thoughts than on his tomb;
So in approof lives not his epitaph   50
As in your royal speech.

KING. Would I were with him! He would
    always say—
Methinks I hear him now; his plausive words
He scattered not in ears, but grafted them,
To grow there, and to bear—'Let me not live,'—
Thus his good melancholy oft began,
On the catastrophe and heel of pastime,
When it was out—'Let me not live,' quoth he,
'After my flame lacks oil, to be the snuff
Of younger spirits, whose apprehensive senses   60
All but new things disdain; whose judgements are
Mere fathers of their garments; whose constancies
Expire before their fashions' ... This he wished:
I after him do after him wish too,
Since I nor wax nor honey can bring home,
I quickly were dissolvèd from my hive,
To give some labourers room.
2 LORD.   You are loved, sir,
They that least lend it you shall lack you first.
KING. I fill a place, I know't.... How long is't, count,
Since the physician at your father's died?   70
He was much famed.
BERTRAM.   Some six months since, my lord.
KING. If he were living, I would try him yet.
Lend me an arm ... the rest have worn me out
With several applications: nature and sickness
Debate it at their leisure. Welcome, count,
My son's no dearer.
BERTRAM.   Thank your majesty.

*The King departs with a flourish
of trumpets; the court follows*

Scene 3: *The palace of Rousillon*

The Countess enters with Rinaldo her Steward; Lavache the Clown follows behind

COUNTESS. I will now hear. What say you of this
gentlewoman?
STEWARD. Madam, the care I have had to even your
content, I wish might be found in the calendar of
my past endeavours, for then we wound our
modesty, and make foul the clearness of our
deservings, when of ourselves we publish them.
COUNTESS. What does this knave here? Get you gone,
sirrah: the complaints I have heard of you if I do not
all believe, 'tis my slowness that I do not: for I   10
know you lack not folly to commit them, and have
ability enough to make such knaveries yours.
CLOWN. 'Tis not unknown to you, madam, I am a
poor fellow.
COUNTESS. Well, sir.
CLOWN. No, madam, 'tis not so well that I am poor,
though many of the rich are damned, but, if I may
have your ladyship's good will to go to the world,
Isbel the woman and I will do as we may.
COUNTESS. Wilt thou needs be a beggar?   20
CLOWN. I do beg your good will in this case.
COUNTESS. In what case?
CLOWN. In Isbel's case and mine own ... Service is no
heritage, and I think I shall never have the blessing
of God till I have issue o' my body: for they say
barnes are blessings.
COUNTESS. Tell me thy reason why thou wilt marry.
CLOWN. My poor body, madam, requires it. I am
driven on by the flesh, and he must needs go that
the devil drives.   30

COUNTESS. Is this all your worship's reason?

CLOWN. Faith, madam, I have other holy reasons, such as they are.

COUNTESS. May the world know them?

CLOWN. I have been, madam, a wicked creature, as you and all flesh and blood are, and indeed I do marry that I may repent.

COUNTESS. Thy marriage, sooner than thy wickedness.

CLOWN. I am out o' friends, madam, and I hope to have friends for my wife's sake. 40

COUNTESS. Such friends are thine enemies, knave.

CLOWN. Y'are shallow, madam, in great friends, for the knaves come to do that for me, which I am aweary of ... He that ears my land spares my team, and gives me leave to inn the crop: if I be his cuckold, he's my drudge; he that comforts my wife is the cherisher of my flesh and blood; he that cherishes my flesh and blood loves my flesh and blood; he that loves my flesh and blood is my friend: ergo, he that kisses my wife is my friend ... If men 50 could be contented to be what they are, there were no fear in marriage; for young Chairbonne the puritan and old Poisson the papist, howsome'er their hearts are severed in religion, their heads are both one—they may jowl horns together like any deer i'th' herd.

COUNTESS. Wilt thou ever be a foul-mouthed and calumnious knave?

CLOWN. A prophet I, madam, and I speak the truth the next way— 60

> For I the ballad will repeat,
> Which men full true shall find,
> Your marriage comes by destiny,
> Your cuckoo sings by kind.

COUNTESS. Get you gone, sir. I'll talk with you more anon.

STEWARD. May it please you, madam, that he bid Helen come to you. Of her I am to speak.

COUNTESS. Sirrah, tell my gentlewoman I would speak with her—Helen I mean. 70

CLOWN [sings].

> Was this fair face the cause, quoth she,
> Why the Grecians sackéd Troy?
> Fond done, done fond,
> Was this King Priam's joy?
> With that she sighéd as she stood,
> With that she sighéd as she stood,
> And gave this sentence then—
> Among nine bad if one be good,
> Among nine bad if one be good,
> There's yet one good in ten. 80

COUNTESS. What, one good in ten? you corrupt the song, sirrah.

CLOWN. One good woman in ten, madam, which is a purifying o'th' song: would God would serve the world so all the year! we'd find no fault with the tithe-woman, if I were the parson. One in ten, quoth a'! an we might have a good woman born but or every blazing star, or at an earthquake, 'twould mend the lottery well—a man may draw his heart out, ere a' pluck one. 90

COUNTESS. You'll be gone, sir knave, and do as I command you!

CLOWN. That man should be at woman's command, and yet no hurt done! Though honesty be no puritan, yet it will do no hurt; it will wear the sur-

plice of humility over the black gown of a big heart.... [the Countess stamps her foot] I am going, forsooth. The business is for Helen to come hither.

He goes

COUNTESS. Well, now.

STEWARD. I know, madam, you love your gentle- 100 woman entirely.

COUNTESS. Faith, I do: her father bequeathed her to me, and she herself, without other advantage, may lawfully make title to as much love as she finds. There is more owing her than is paid, and more shall be paid her than she'll demand.

STEWARD. Madam, I was very late more near her than I think she wished me. Alone she was, and did communicate to herself her own words to her own ears. She thought, I dare vow for her, they touched 110 not any stranger sense. Her matter was, she loved your son: Fortune, she said, was no goddess, that had put such difference betwixt their two estates; Love no god, that would not extend his might, only where qualities were level; Diana no queen of virgins, that would suffer her poor knight surprised, without rescue in the first assault, or ransom afterward ... This she delivered in the most bitter touch of sorrow that e'er I heard virgin exclaim in, which I held my duty speedily to acquaint you withal, 120 sithence in the loss that may happen it concerns you something to know it.

COUNTESS. You have discharged this honestly, keep it to yourself. Many likelihoods informed me of this before, which hung so tott'ring in the balance, that I could neither believe nor misdoubt ... Pray you, leave me. Stall this in your bosom, and I thank you for your honest care: I will speak with you further anon. *He goes*

Helena enters

[aside] Even so it was with me, when I was young ... 130
If ever we are nature's, these are ours. This thorn
Doth to our rose of youth rightly belong.
Our blood to us, this to our blood is born.
It is the show and seal of nature's truth,
Where love's strong passion is impressed in youth.
By our remembrances of days foregone,
Such were our faults, or then we thought them none.
Her eye is sick on't—I observe her now.

HELENA. What is your pleasure, madam?

COUNTESS.   You know, Helen,
I am a mother to you. 140

HELENA. Mine honourable mistress.

COUNTESS.   Nay, a mother.
Why not a mother? When I said 'a mother'
Methought you saw a serpent. What's in 'mother,'
That you start at it? I say, I am your mother,
And put you in the catalogue of those
That were enwombéd mine. 'Tis often seen
Adoption strives with nature, and choice breeds
A native slip to us from foreign seeds:
You ne'er oppressed me with a mother's groan,
Yet I express to you a mother's care— 150
God's mercy, maiden! does it curd thy blood
To say I am thy mother? What's the matter,
That this distempered messenger of wet,
The many-coloured Iris, rounds thine eye?
Why? that you are my daughter?

HELENA.   That I am not.
COUNTESS. I say, I am your mother.
HELENA.   Pardon, madam;
  The Count Rousillon cannot be my brother:
  I am from humble, he from honoured name;
  No note upon my parents, his all noble.
  My master, my dear lord he is, and I   160
  His servant live, and will his vassal die:
  He must not be my brother.
COUNTESS.   Nor I your mother?
HELENA. You are my mother, madam. Would you
    were—
  So that my lord, your son, were not my brother—
  Indeed my mother! or were you both our mothers.
  I care no more for than I do for heaven,
  So I were not his sister. Can't no other,
  But I your daughter, he must be my brother?
COUNTESS. Yes, Helen, you might be my
    daughter-in-law—
  God shield you mean it not, 'daughter' and 'mother' 170
  So strive upon your pulse! What, pale again?
  My fear hath catched your fondness! Now I see
  The mystery of your loneliness, and find
  Your salt tears' head. Now to all sense 'tis gross ...
  You love my son! invention is ashamed,
  Against the proclamation of thy passion,
  To say thou dost not: therefore tell me true—
  But tell me then, 'tis so—for look, thy cheeks
  Confess it, th'one to th'other, and thine eyes
  See it so grossly shown in thy behaviours,   180
  That in their kind they speak it—only sin
  And hellish obstinacy tie thy tongue,
  That truth should be suspected. Speak, is't so?
  If it be so, you have wound a goodly clew;
  If it be not, forswear't: howe'er, I charge thee,
  As heaven shall work in me for thine avail,
  To tell me truly.
HELENA.   Good madam, pardon me!
COUNTESS. Do you love my son?
HELENA.   Your pardon, noble mistress!
COUNTESS. Love you my son?
HELENA.   Do not you love him, madam?
COUNTESS. Go not about; my love hath in't a bond 190
  Whereof the world takes note: come, come, disclose
  The state of your affection, for your passions
  Have to the full appeached.
HELENA.   Then, I confess,
  Here on my knee, before high heaven and you,
  That before you, and next unto high heaven,
  I love your son ...
  My friends were poor but honest, so's my love:
  Be not offended, for it hurts not him
  That he is loved of me: I follow him not
  By any token of presumptuous suit,   200
  Nor would I have him till I do deserve him,
  Yet never know how that desert should be ...
  I know I love in vain, strive against hope;
  Yet, in this captious and inteemable sieve,
  I still pour in the waters of my love,
  And lack not to lose still: thus, Indian-like,
  Religious in mine error, I adore
  The sun, that looks upon his worshipper,
  But knows of him no more.... My dearest madam,
  Let not your hate encounter with my love   210
  For loving where you do: but if yourself,
  Whose aged honour cites a virtuous youth,

  Did ever in so true a flame of liking
  Love chastely, and wish dearly that your Dian
  Was both herself and Love, O, then give pity
  To her, whose state is such, that cannot choose
  But lend and give where she is sure to lose;
  That seeks not to find that her search implies,
  But, riddle-like, lives sweetly where she dies.
COUNTESS. Had you not lately an intent, speak truly, 220
  To go to Paris?
HELENA.   Madam, I had.
COUNTESS.   Wherefore? tell true.
HELENA. I will tell truth, by grace itself, I swear ...
  You know my father left me some prescriptions
  Of rare and proved effects, such as his reading
  And manifest experience had collected
  For general sovereignty; and that he willed me
  In heedfull'st reservation to bestow them,
  As notes, whose faculties inclusive were,
  More than they were in note: amongst the rest,
  There is a remedy, approved, set down,   230
  To cure the desperate languishings whereof
  The king is rendered lost.
COUNTESS.   This was your motive
  For Paris, was it? speak.
HELENA. My lord your son made me to think of this;
  Else Paris, and the medicine, and the king,
  Had from the conversation of my thoughts
  Haply been absent then.
COUNTESS.   But think you, Helen,
  If you should tender your supposèd aid,
  He would receive it? He and his physicians
  Are of a mind—he, that they cannot help him;   240
  They, that they cannot help. How shall they credit
  A poor unlearnèd virgin, when the schools,
  Embowelled of their doctrine, have left off
  The danger to itself?
HELENA.   There's something hints,
  More than my father's skill, which was the great'st
  Of his profession, that his good receipt
  Shall for my legacy be sanctified
  By th' luckiest stars in heaven, and would your
    honour
  But give me leave to try success, I'd venture
  The well-lost life of mine on his grace's cure   250
  By such a day and hour.
COUNTESS.   Dost thou believe't?
HELENA. Ay, madam, knowingly.
COUNTESS. Why, Helen, thou shalt have my leave and
    love,
  Means and attendants, and my loving greetings
  To those of mine in court. I'll stay at home
  And pray God's blessing into thy attempt:
  Be gone to-morrow, and be sure of this,
  What I can help thee to, thou shalt not miss.
                                      They go

ACT 2
Scene 1: *The King's palace at Paris*

A flourish of cornets. Enter the King with attendants and
with divers young lords taking leave for the Florentine war;
among them Bertram and Parolles

KING. Farewell, young lords! these warlike principles 210
  Do not throw from you—and you, my lords
    farewell!

Share the advice betwixt you. If both gain all,
The gift doth stretch itself as 'tis received,
And is enough for both.
1 LORD.   'Tis our hope, sir,
After, well-entered soldiers to return
And find your grace in health.
KING. No, no, it cannot be; and yet my heart
Will not confess he owes the malady
That doth my life besiege . . . Farewell, young lords! 10
Whether I live or die, be you the sons
Of worthy Frenchmen: let higher Italy
(Those bated that inherit but the fall
Of the last monarchy) see that you come
Not to woo honour, but to wed it. When
The bravest questant shrinks, find what you seek,
That fame may cry you loud . . . I say, farewell.
2 LORD. Health, at your bidding, serve your majesty!
KING. Those girls of Italy, take heed of them.
They say, our French lack language to deny,   20
If they demand: beware of being captives,
Before you serve.
BOTH.   Our hearts receive your warnings.
KING. Farewell. Come hither to me.
                                   He retires, attended
1 LORD. O my sweet lord, that you will stay behind
us!
PAROLLES. 'Tis not his fault, the spark.
2 LORD.   O, 'tis brave wars!
PAROLLES. Most admirable! I have seen those wars.
BERTRAM. I am commanded here, and kept a coil
with
'Too young,' and 'the next year,' and ''tis too early.'
PAROLLES. An thy mind stand to't, boy, steal away
bravely.
BERTRAM. I shall stay here the forehorse to a smock, 30
Creaking my shoes on the plain masonry,
Till honour be bought up, and no sword worn
But one to dance with! By heaven, I'll steal away.
1 LORD. There's honour in the theft.
PAROLLES.   Commit it, count.
2 LORD. I am your accessary, and so farewell.
BERTRAM. I grow to you, and our parting is a tortured
body.
1 LORD. Farewell, captain.
2 LORD. Sweet Monsieur Parolles!
PAROLLES. Noble heroes, my sword and yours are kin. 40
Good sparks and lustrous, a word, good metals: you
shall find in the regiment of the Spinii one Captain
Spurio, with an emblem of war, his cicatrice, here
on his sinister cheek; it was this very sword en-
trenched it: say to him, I live, and observe his reports
for me.
1 LORD. We shall, noble captain.
PAROLLES. Mars dote on you for his novices! [the lords
go] What will ye do?

The King comes forward

BERTRAM. Stay: the king!   50
PAROLLES. Use a more spacious ceremony to the noble
lords, you have restrained yourself within the list of
too cold an adieu: be more expressive to them; for
they wear themselves in the cap of the time, there
do muster true gait, eat, speak, and move under the
influence of the most received star, and though the
devil lead the measure, such are to be followed; after
them, and take a more dilated farewell.

BERTRAM. And I will do so.
PAROLLES. Worthy fellows; and like to prove most 60
sinewy sword-men.   Bertram and Parolles go

Lafeu enters

LAFEU [kneels]. Pardon, my lord, for me and for my
tidings.
KING. I'll fee thee to stand up.
LAFEU [rises]. Then here's a man stands that has
brought his pardon.
I would you had kneeled, my lord, to ask me mercy,
And that at my bidding you could so stand up.
KING. I would I had, so I had broke thy pate
And asked thee mercy for't.
LAFEU.   Good faith, across!
But, my good lord, 'tis thus—will you be cured
Of your infirmity?
KING.   No.
LAFEU.   O, will you eat   70
No grapes, my royal fox? yes, but you will
My noble grapes, an if my royal fox
Could reach them: I have seen a medicine
That's able to breathe life into a stone,
Quicken a rock, and make you dance canary
With spritely fire and motion, whose simple touch
Is powerful to araise King Pepin, nay,
To give great Charlemain a pen in's hand,
And write to her a love-line.
KING.   What 'her' is this?
LAFEU. Why, Doctor She: my lord, there's one
arrived,   80
If you will see her: now, by my faith and honour,
If seriously I may convey my thoughts
In this my light deliverance, I have spoke
With one that, in her sex, her years, profession,
Wisdom and constancy, hath amazed me more
Than I dare blame my weakness: will you see her,
For that is her demand, and know her business?
That done, laugh well at me.
KING.   Now, good Lafeu,
Bring in the admiration, that we with thee
May spend our wonder too, or take off thine   90
By wond'ring how thou took'st it.
LAFEU.   Nay, I'll fit you,
And not be all day neither.   Lafeu goes
KING. Thus he his special nothing ever prologues.

Lafeu returns, holding open the door

LAFEU. Nay, come your ways.

Helena enters

KING.   This haste hath wings indeed.
LAFEU. Nay, come your ways!
This is his majesty, say your mind to him.
A traitor you do look like, but such traitors
His majesty seldom fears. I am Cressid's uncle,
That dare leave two together. Fare you well.
                                          He goes
KING. Now, fair one, does your business follow us? 100
HELENA. Ay, my good lord.
Gerard de Narbon was my father;
In what he did profess, well-found.
KING.   I knew him.
HELENA. The rather will I spare my praises towards
him—
Knowing him is enough . . . On's bed of death

Many receipts he gave me, chiefly one,
Which as the dearest issue of his practice
And of his old experience th'only darling,
He bad me store up, as a triple eye,
Safer than mine own two, more dear; I have so: 110
And, hearing your high majesty is touched
With that malignant cause wherein the honour
Of my dear father's gift stands chief in power,
I come to tender it, and my appliance,
With all bound humbleness.
KING.   We thank you, maiden,
But may not be so credulous of cure,
When our most learnéd doctors leave us, and
The congregated College have concluded
That labouring art can never ransom nature
From her inaidible estate: I say we must not   120
So stain our judgement, or corrupt our hope,
To prostitute our past-cure malady
To empirics, or to dissever so
Our great self and our credit, to esteem
A senseless help, when help past sense we deem.
HELENA. My duty then shall pay me for my pains:
I will no more enforce mine office on you;
Humbly entreating from your royal thoughts
A modest one, to bear me back again.
KING. I cannot give thee less, to be called grateful ...   130
Thou thought'st to help me, and such thanks I give
As one near death to those that wish him live:
But what at full I know, thou know'st no part,
I knowing all my peril, thou no art.
HELENA. What I can do can do no hurt to try,
Since you set up your rest 'gainst remedy:
He that of greatest works is finisher,
Oft does them by the weakest minister:
So holy writ in babes hath judgement shown,
When judges have been babes; great floods have
flown   140
From simple sources; and great seas have dried
When miracles have by the greatest been denied.
Oft expectation fails, and most oft there
Where most it promises; and oft it hits,
Where hope is coldest, and despair most fits.
KING. I must not hear thee, fare thee well,
kind maid.
Thy pains not used must by thyself be paid.
Proffers not took reap thanks for their reward.
HELENA. Inspiréd merit so by breath is barred.
It is not so with Him that all things knows,   150
As 'tis with us that square our guess by shows:
But most it is presumption in us, when
The help of heaven we count the act of men.
Dear sir, to my endeavours give consent,
Of heaven, not me, make an experiment.
I am not an impostor, that proclaim
Myself against the level of mine aim,
But know I think, and think I know most sure,
My art is not past power, nor you past cure.
KING. Art thou so confident? Within what space   160
Hop'st thou my cure?
HELENA.   The great'st grace lending grace,
Ere twice the horses of the sun shall bring
Their fiery torcher his diurnal ring,
Ere twice in murk and occidental damp
Moist Hesperus hath quenched her sleepy lamp;
Or four and twenty times the pilot's glass
Hath told the thievish minutes how they pass;

What is infirm from your sound parts shall fly,
Health shall live free, and sickness freely die.
KING. Upon thy certainty and confidence,   170
What dar'st thou venture?
HELENA.   Tax of impudence,
A strumpet's boldness, a divulgéd shame,
Traduced by odious ballads; my maiden's name
Seared; otherwise—ne worse of worst—extended
With vilest torture let my life be ended.
KING. Methinks in thee some blesséd spirit doth speak
His powerful sound within an organ weak:
And what impossibility would slay
In common sense, sense saves another way ...
Thy live is dear, for all that life can rate   180
Worth name of life in thee hath estimate;
Youth, beauty, wisdom, courage, all
That happiness and prime can happy call:
Thou this to hazard needs must intimate
Skill infinite or monstrous desperate.
Sweet practiser, thy physic I will try,
That ministers thine own death if I die.
HELENA. If I break time, or flinch in property
Of what I spoke, unpitied let me die,
And well deserved: not helping, death's my fee,   190
But if I help what do you promise me?
KING. Make thy demand.
HELENA.   But will you make it even?
KING. Ay, by my sceptre and my hopes of heaven.
HELENA. Then shalt thou give me with thy kingly
hand
What husband in thy power I will command:
Exempted be from me the arrogance
To choose from forth the royal blood of France,
My low and humble name to propagate
With any branch or image of thy state:
But such a one, thy vassal, whom I know   200
Is free for me to ask, thee to bestow.
KING. Here is my hand—the premises observed,
Thy will by my performance shall be served:
So make the choice of thy own time, for I,
Thy resolved patient, on thee still rely ...
More should I question thee, and more I must,
Though more to know could not be more to trust;
From whence thou cam'st, how tended on—but rest
Unquestioned welcome, and undoubted blest.
Give me some help here, ho! If thou proceed   210
As high as word, my deed shall match thy deed.
        A flourish of trumpets; they all depart

Scene 2: *The palace of Rousillon*

Enter Countess and Clown

COUNTESS. Come on, sir. I shall now put you to the
height of your breeding.
CLOWN. I will show myself highly fed and lowly
taught. I know my business is but to the court.
COUNTESS. To the court! why, what place make you
special, when you put off that with such contempt?
'But to the court!'
CLOWN. Truly, madam, if God have lent a man any
manners, he may easily put it off at court: he that
cannot make a leg, put off's cap, kiss his hand, and   10
say nothing, has neither leg, hands, lip, nor cap; and,
indeed, such a fellow, to say precisely, were not for
the court. But for me, I have an answer will serve all
men.

COUNTESS. Marry, that's a bountiful answer that fits all questions.

CLOWN. It is like a barber's chair that fits all buttocks—the pin-buttock, the quatch-buttock, the brawn-buttock, or any buttock.

COUNTESS. Will your answer serve fit to all questions? 20

CLOWN. As fit as ten groats is for the hand of an attorney, as your French crown for your taffety punk, as Tib's rush for Tom's forefinger, as a pancake for Shrove Tuesday, a morris for May-day, as the nail to his hole, the cuckold to his horn, as a scolding quean to a wrangling knave, as the nun's lip to the friar's mouth, nay, as the pudding to his skin.

COUNTESS. Have you, I say, an answer of such fitness for all questions?

CLOWN. From below your duke to beneath your 30 constable, it will fit any question.

COUNTESS. It must be an answer of most monstrous size that must fit all demands.

CLOWN. But a trifle neither, in good faith, if the learned should speak truth of it: here it is, and all that belongs to 't. Ask me if I am a courtier, it shall do you no harm to learn.

COUNTESS. To be young again, if we could ... I will be a fool in question, hoping to be the wiser by your answer. I pray you, sir, are you a courtier? 40

CLOWN. O Lord, sir!—There's a simple putting off: more, more, a hundred of them.

COUNTESS. Sir, I am a poor friend of yours, that loves you.

CLOWN. O Lord, sir!—Thick! thick! spare not me.

COUNTESS. I think, sir, you can eat none of this homely meat.

CLOWN. O Lord, sir!—Nay, put me to 't, I warrant you.

COUNTESS. You were lately whipped, sir, as I think. 50

CLOWN. O Lord, sir!—Spare not me.

COUNTESS. Do you cry, 'O Lord, sir!' at your whipping, and 'spare not me'? Indeed, your 'O Lord, sir!' is very sequent to your whipping; you would answer very well to a whipping, if you were but bound to 't.

CLOWN. I ne'er had worse luck in my life in my 'O Lord, sir!' I see things may serve long, but not serve ever.

COUNTESS. I play the noble housewife with the time, 60 To entertain it so merrily with a fool.

CLOWN. O Lord, sir!—Why, there 't serves well again.

COUNTESS. An end, sir, to your business: give Helen this,
And urge her to a present answer back.
Commend me to my kinsmen and my son.
This is not much.

CLOWN. Not much commendation to them?

COUNTESS. Not much employment for you. You understand me?

CLOWN. Most fruitfully. I am there before my legs. 70

COUNTESS. Haste you again.   *They go*

Scene 3: *The King's palace at Paris*

Enter Bertram, Lafeu, and Parolles

LAFEU. They say miracles are past, and we have our philosophical persons, to make modern and familiar, things supernatural and causeless. Hence is it that we make trifles of terrors, ensconcing ourselves into seeming knowledge, when we should submit ourselves to an unknown fear.

PAROLLES. Why, 'tis the rarest argument of wonder that hath shot out in our latter times.

BERTRAM. And so 'tis.

LAFEU. To be relinquished of the artists— 10

PAROLLES. So I say.

LAFEU. Both of Galen and Paracelsus.

PAROLLES. So I say.

LAFEU. Of all the learned and authentic fellows—

PAROLLES. Right, so I say.

LAFEU. That gave him out incurable—

PAROLLES. Why, there 'tis, so say I too.

LAFEU. Not to be helped—

PAROLLES. Right, as 'twere a man assured of a—

LAFEU. Uncertain life, and sure death. 20

PAROLLES. Just, you say well: so would I have said.

LAFEU. I may truly say, it is a novelty to the world.

PAROLLES. It is, indeed: if you will have it in showing, you shall read it in what-do-ye-call 't there?

LAFEU [*takes a ballad from his belt*]. 'A showing of a heavenly effect in an earthly actor.'

PAROLLES. That's it, I would have said the very same.

LAFEU. Why, your dolphin is not lustier: 'fore me I speak in respect—

PAROLLES. Nay, 'tis strange, 'tis very strange, that is the 30 brief and the tedious of it, and he's of a most facinorous spirit that will not acknowledge it to be the—

LAFEU. Very hand of heaven.

PAROLLES. Ay, so I say.

LAFEU. In a most weak—

PAROLLES. And debile minister, great power, great transcendence, which should, indeed, give us a further use to be made than alone the recovery of the king, as to be— 40

LAFEU. Generally thankful.

The King enters with Helena and attendants

PAROLLES. I would have said it. You say well ... Here comes the king.

LAFEU. Lustick! as the Dutchman says: I'll like a maid the better, whilst I have a tooth in my head: why, he's able to lead her a coranto.

PAROLLES. Mort du vinaigre! Is not this Helen?

LAFEU. 'Fore God, I think so.

KING. Go, call before me all the lords in court.
Sit, my preserver, by thy patient's side, 50
And with this healthful hand, whose banished sense
Thou hast repealed, a second time receive
The confirmation of my promised gift,
Which but attends thy naming....   *They sit*

Enter three or four lords

Fair maid, send forth thine eye—this youthful parcel
Of noble bachelors stand at my bestowing,
O'er whom both sovereign power and father's voice
I have to use: thy frank election make,
Thou hast power to choose, and they none to forsake.

HELENA. To each of you one fair and virtuous mistress 60
Fall, when Love please! marry, to each but one!

LAFEU. I'd give bay Curtal and his furniture,
My mouth no more were broken than these boys',
And writ as little beard.

KING.   Peruse them well:

Not one of those but had a noble father.

HELENA [*rises*]. Gentlemen,
Heaven hath, through me, restored the king to
    health.

ALL. We understand it, and thank heaven for you.

HELENA. I am a simple maid, and therein wealthiest
That I protest I simply am a maid ...   70
Please it your majesty, I have done already:
The blushes in my cheeks thus whisper me,
'We blush that thou shouldst choose; but, be
    refused ...
Let the white death sit on thy cheek for ever,
We'll ne'er come there again.'

KING.   Make choice and see,
Who shuns thy love shuns all his love in me.

HELENA. Now, Dian, from thy altar do I fly,
And to imperial Love, that god most high,
Do my sighs stream ... [*she addresses her to a lord*]
Sir, will you hear my suit?

1 LORD. And grant it.

HELENA.   Thanks, sir—all the rest is mute.   80

LAFEU. I had rather be in this choice, than throw ames-
ace for my life.

HELENA [*to another lord*]. The honour, sir, that flames
in your fair eyes,
Before I speak, too threat'ningly replies:
Love make your fortunes twenty times above
Her that so wishes and her humble love!

2 LORD. No better, if you please.

HELENA.   My wish receive,
Which great Love grant! and so, I take my leave.

LAFEU. Do all they deny her? An they were sons
of mine, I'd have them whipped, or I would send   90
them to th' Turk to make eunuchs of.

HELENA [*to the third lord*]. Be not afraid that I your
hand should take,
I'll never do you wrong for your own sake:
Blessing upon your vows! and in your bed
Find fairer fortune, if you ever wed!

LAFEU. These boys are boys of ice, they'll none have
her: sure, they are bastards to the English, the French
ne'er got 'em.

HELENA [*to the fourth lord*]. You are too young, too
happy, and too good,
To make yourself a son out of my blood.   100

4 LORD. Fair one, I think not so.

LAFEU. There's one grape yet—I am sure thy father
drunk wine—but if thou be'st not an ass, I am a
youth of fourteen; I have known thee already.

HELENA [*to Bertram*]. I dare not say I take you, but I give
Me and my service, ever whilst I live,
Into your guiding power ... This is the man.

KING. Why then, young Bertram, take her, she's thy
    wife.

BERTRAM. My wife, my liege? I shall beseech your
    highness,
In such a business give me leave to use   110
The help of mine own eyes.

KING.   Know'st thou not, Bertram,
What she has done for me?

BERTRAM.   Yes, my good lord;
But never hope to know why I should marry her.

KING. Thou know'st she has raised me from my sickly
    bed.

BERTRAM. But follows it, my lord, to bring me down
Must answer for your raising? I know her well;

She had her breeding at my father's charge:
A poor physician's daughter my wife! Disdain
Rather corrupt me ever!

KING. 'Tis only title thou disdain'st in her, the
which   120
I can build up ... Strange is it, that our bloods,
Of colour, weight, and heat, poured all together,
Would quite confound distinction, yet stand off
In differences so mighty.... If she be
All that is virtuous (save what thou dislik'st,
A poor physician's daughter) thou dislik'st
Of virtue for a name; but do not so:
From lowest place when virtuous things proceed,
The place is dignified by th'doer's deed:
Where great additions swell's, and virtue none,   130
It is a dropsied honour: good alone
Is good, without a name; vileness is so:
The property by what it is should go,
Not by the title.... She is young, wise, fair;
In these to nature she's immediate heir;
And these breed honour: that is honour's scorn,
Which challenges itself as honour's born,
And is not like the sire: honours thrive,
When rather from our acts we them derive
Than our foregoers: the mere word's a slave,   140
Deboshed on every tomb, on every grave
A lying trophy, and as oft is dumb
Where dust and damned oblivion is the tomb
Of honoured bones indeed. What should be said?
If thou canst like this creature as a maid,
I can create the rest: virtue and she
Is her own dower; honour and wealth, from me.

BERTRAM. I cannot love her, nor will strive to do't.

KING. Thou wrong'st thyself, if thou shouldst strive to
    choose.

HELENA. That you are well restored, my lord, I'm glad; 150
Let the rest go.

KING. My honour's at the stake, which to defeat,
I must produce my power. Here, take her hand,
Proud scornful boy, unworthy this good gift,
That dost in vile misprision shackle up
My love and her desert; that canst not dream,
We, poising us in her defective scale,
Shall weigh thee to the beam: that wilt not know,
It is in us to plant thine honour where
We please to have it grow. Check thy contempt: 160
Obey our will, which travails in thy good:
Believe not thy disdain, but presently
Do thine own fortunes that obedient right
Which both thy duty owes and our power claims,
Or I will throw thee from my care for ever
Into the staggers and the careless lapse
Of youth and ignorance; both my revenge and hate,
Loosing upon thee in the name of justice,
Without all terms of pity. Speak, thine answer!

BERTRAM. Pardon, my gracious lord; for I submit   170
My fancy to your eyes. When I consider
What great creation and what dole of honour
Flies where you bid it, I find that she which late
Was in my nobler thoughts most base, is now
The praiséd of the king—who, so ennobled,
Is as 'twere born so.

KING.   Take her by the hand,
And tell her she is thine: to whom I promise
A counterpoise; if not to thy estate,
A balance more replete.

BERTRAM.   I take her hand.

KING. Good fortune and the favour of the king   180
Smile upon this contract; whose ceremony
Shall seem expedient on the now-born brief,
And be performed to-night: the solemn feast
Shall more attend upon the coming space,
Expecting absent friends. As thou lov'st her,
Thy love's to me religious; else, does err.

*All depart save Lafeu and
Parolles who stay behind,
commenting of this wedding*

LAFEU. Do you hear, monsieur? a word with you.

PAROLLES. Your pleasure, sir?

LAFEU. Your lord and master did well to make his
recantation.   190

PAROLLES. Recantation! My lord! my master!

LAFEU. Ay; is it not a language I speak?

PAROLLES. A most harsh one, and not to be understood
without bloody succeeding. My master!

LAFEU. Are you companion to the Count Rousillon?

PAROLLES. To any count, to all counts: to what is man!

LAFEU. To what is count's man: count's master is of
another style.

PAROLLES. You are too old, sir; let it satisfy you, you
are too old.   200

LAFEU. I must tell thee, sirrah, I write man; to which
title age cannot bring thee.

PAROLLES. What I dare too well do, I dare not do.

LAFEU. I did think thee, for two ordinaries, to be a
pretty wise fellow; thou didst make tolerable vent of
thy travel—it might pass: yet the scarfs and the
bannerets about thee did manifoldly dissuade me
from believing thee a vessel of too great a burden.
I have now found thee—when I lose thee again, I
care not: yet art thou good for nothing but taking   210
up, and that thou'rt scarce worth.

PAROLLES. Hadst thou not the privilege of antiquity
upon thee,—

LAFEU. Do not plunge thyself too far in anger, lest thou
hasten thy trial; which if—Lord have mercy on thee
for a hen! So, my good window of lattice, fare thee
well, thy casement I need not open, for I look
through thee. . . . Give me thy hand.

PAROLLES. My lord, you give me most egregious
indignity.   220

LAFEU. Ay, with all my heart, and thou art worthy of
it.

PAROLLES. I have not, my lord, deserved it.

LAFEU. Yes, good faith, every dram of it, and I will
not bate thee a scruple.

PAROLLES. Well, I shall be wiser.

LAFEU. E'en as soon as thou canst, for thou hast to pull
at a smack o'th' contrary. If ever thou be'st bound in
thy scarf and beaten, thou shalt find what it is to be
proud of thy bondage. I have a desire to hold my   230
acquaintance with thee, or rather my knowledge,
that I may say, in the default, he is a man I know.

PAROLLES. My lord, you do me most insupportable
vexation.

LAFEU. I would it were hell-pains for thy sake, and
my poor doing eternal: for doing I am past, as I will
by thee, in what motion age will give me leave.

He goes

PAROLLES. Well, thou hast a son shall take this disgrace
off me; scurvy, old, filthy, scurvy lord! Well, I must
be patient, there is no fettering of authority. I'll beat   240

him, by my life, if I can meet him with any convenience, an he were double and double a lord. I'll
have no more pity of his age than I would have of
—I'll beat him, an if I could but meet him again.

Lafeu returns

LAFEU. Sirrah, your lord and master's married, there's
news for you; you have a new mistress.

PAROLLES. I most unfeignedly beseech your lordship
to make some reservation of your wrongs. He is my
good lord—whom I serve above, is my master.

LAFEU. Who? God?   250

PAROLLES. Ay, sir.

LAFEU. The devil it is that's thy master. Why dost thou
garter up thy arms o' this fashion? dost make hose of
thy sleeves? do other servants so? Thou wert best set
thy lower part where thy nose stands. By mine
honour, if I were but two hours younger, I'd beat
thee: methink'st thou art a general offence, and
every man should beat thee: I think thou wast
created for men to breathe themselves upon thee.

PAROLLES. This is hard and undeserved measure, my   260
lord.

LAFEU. Go to, sir, you were beaten in Italy for picking
a kernel out of a pomegranate, you are a vagabond
and no true traveller; you are more saucy with lords
and honourable personages than the commission of
your birth and virtue gives you heraldry. You are
not worth another word else I'd call you knave. I
leave you.   *He goes*

PAROLLES. Good, very good, it is so then: good, very
good, let it be concealed awhile.   270

Bertram enters

BERTRAM. Undone, and forfeited to cares for ever!

PAROLLES. What's the matter, sweet-heart?

BERTRAM. Although before the solemn priest I
have sworn,
I will not bed her.

PAROLLES. What, what, sweet-heart?

BERTRAM. O my Parolles, they have married me:
I'll to the Tuscan wars, and never bed her.

PAROLLES. France is a dog-hole, and it no more merits
The tread of a man's foot: to th' wars!

BERTRAM. There's letters from my mother: what
th'import is,   280
I know not yet.

PAROLLES. Ay, that would be known . . . To th' wars,
my boy, to th' wars!
He wears his honour in a box unseen,
That hugs his kicky-wicky here at home,
Spending his manly marrow in her arms,
Which should sustain the bound and high curvet
Of Mars's fiery steed . . . To other regions!
France is a stable, we that dwell in't jades,
Therefore to th' war!

BERTRAM. It shall be so. I'll send her to my house,   290
Acquaint my mother with my hate to her,
And wherefore I am fled; write to the king
That which I durst not speak: his present gift
Shall furnish me to those Italian fields,
Where noble fellows strike: war is no strife
To the dark house and the detested wife.

PAROLLES. Will this capriccio hold in thee, art sure?

BERTRAM. Go with me to my chamber, and advise me.
I'll send her straight away: to-morrow
I'll to the wars, she to her single sorrow.   300

PAROLLES. Why, these balls bound, there's noise in it.
  'Tis hard;
A young man married is a man that's marred:
Therefore away, and leave her bravely; go.
The king has done you wrong; but, hush, 'tis so.
                                        They go

Scene 4: *The King's palace*

Enter Helena and Clown

HELENA. My mother greets me kindly. Is she well?
CLOWN. She is not well, but yet she has her health,
  she's very merry, but yet she is not well: but thanks
  be given, she's very well and wants nothing i'th'
  world; but yet she is not well.
HELENA. If she be very well, what does she ail, that
  she's not very well?
CLOWN. Truly, she's very well indeed, but for two
  things.
HELENA. What two things?   10
CLOWN. One, that she's not in heaven, whither God
  send her quickly: the other, that she's in earth, from
  whence God send her quickly.

Parolles comes in

PAROLLES. Bless you, my fortunate lady!
HELENA. I hope, sir, I have your good will to have
  mine own good fortunes.
PAROLLES. You had my prayers to lead them on, and
  to keep them on have them still. O, my knave, how
  does my old lady?
CLOWN. So that you had her wrinkles, and I her   20
  money, I would she did as you say.
PAROLLES. Why, I say nothing.
CLOWN. Marry, you are the wiser man; for many a
  man's tongue shakes out his master's undoing: to say
  nothing, to do nothing, to know nothing, and to
  have nothing, is to be a great part of your title—
  which is within a very little of nothing.
PAROLLES. Away, th'art a knave.
CLOWN. You should have said, sir, 'before a knave
  th'art a knave,' that's, before me th'art a knave: this 30
  had been truth, sir.
PAROLLES. Go to, thou art a witty fool, I have found
  thee.
CLOWN. Did you find me in yourself, sir? or were you
  taught to find me?
PAROLLES. In myself.
CLOWN. The search, sir, was profitable; and much fool
  may you find in you, even to the world's pleasure
  and the increase of laughter.
PAROLLES. A good knave, i' faith, and well fed.   40
  Madam, my lord will go away to-night,
A very serious business calls on him:
The great prerogative and rite of love,
Which as your due time claims, he does
  acknowledge,
But puts it off to a compelled restraint;
Whose want, and whose delay, is strewed with
  sweets,
Which they distil now in the curbéd time,
To make the coming hour o'erflow with joy,
And pleasure drown the brim.
HELENA.   What's his will else?
PAROLLES. That you will take your instant leave o'th'
  king,   50

And make this haste as your own good proceeding,
Strengthened with what apology you think
May make it probable need.
HELENA.   What more commands he?
PAROLLES. That, having this obtained, you presently
Attend his further pleasure.
HELENA. In every thing I wait upon his will.
PAROLLES. I shall report it so.   *Goes*
HELENA.   I pray you.—Come, sirrah.
                                        They go

Scene 5: *Another room in the same*

Enter Lafeu and Bertram

LAFEU. But I hope your lordship thinks not him a
  soldier.
BERTRAM. Yes, my lord, and of very valiant approof.
LAFEU. You have it from his own deliverance.
BERTRAM. And by other warranted testimony.
LAFEU. Then my dial goes not true, I took this lark for
  a bunting.
BERTRAM. I do assure you, my lord, he is very great in
  knowledge, and accordingly valiant.
LAFEU. I have then sinned against his experience and 10
  transgressed against his valour, and my state that
  way is dangerous, since I cannot yet find in my heart
  to repent . . .

Enter Parolles

Here he comes, I pray you make us friends, I will
  pursue the amity.
PAROLLES [*to Bertram*]. These things shall be done, sir.
LAFEU. Pray you, sir, who's his tailor?
PAROLLES. Sir?
LAFEU. O, I know him well. Ay sir, he, sir, 's a good
  workman, a very good tailor.   20
BERTRAM. Is she gone to the king?
PAROLLES. She is.
BERTRAM. Will she away to-night?
PAROLLES. As you'll have her.
BERTRAM. I have writ my letters, casketed my treasure,
Given order for our horses—and to-night,
When I should take possession of the bride,
End ere I do begin.
LAFEU. A good traveller is something at the latter end
  of a dinner, but one that lies three thirds and uses   30
  a known truth to pass a thousand nothings with,
  should be once heard and thrice beaten. . . . God save
  you, captain.
BERTRAM. Is there any unkindness between my lord
  and you, monsieur?
PAROLLES. I know not how I have deserved to run into
  my lord's displeasure.
LAFEU. You have made shift to run into't, boots and
  spurs and all, like him that leaped into the custard;
  and of it you'll run again, rather than suffer question 40
  for your residence.
BERTRAM. It may be you have mistaken him, my lord.
LAFEU. And shall do so ever, though I took him at's
  prayers. Fare you well, my lord, and believe this of
  me, there can be no kernel in this light nut; the soul
  of this man is his clothes: trust him not in matter of
  heavy consequence; I have kept of them tame and
  know their natures. . . . Farewell, monsieur, I have
  spoken better of you than you have or will to

deserve at my hand, but we must do good against   50
evil.   *He goes*
PAROLLES. An idle lord, I swear.
BERTRAM. I think so.
PAROLLES. Why, do you not know him?
BERTRAM. Yes, I do know him well, and common
   speech
Gives him a worthy pass.…

Helena enters

                 Here comes my clog.
HELENA. I have, sir, as I was commanded from you,
Spoke with the king, and have procured his leave
For present parting—only he desires
Some private speech with you.
BERTRAM.   I shall obey his will.   60
You must not marvel, Helen, at my course,
Which holds not colour with the time, nor does
The ministration and required office
On my particular. Prepared I was not
For such a business, therefore am I found
So much unsettled … This drives me to entreat you
That presently you take your way for home,
And rather muse than ask why I entreat you,
For my respects are better than they seem,
And my appointments have in them a need   70
Greater than shows itself at the first view
To you that know them not.… [*gives a letter*] This
   to my mother.
'Twill be two days ere I shall see you, so
I leave you to your wisdom.
HELENA.   Sir, I can nothing say,
But that I am your most obedient servant.
BERTRAM. Come, come, no more of that.
HELENA.   And ever shall
With true observance seek to eke out that
Wherein toward me my homely stars have failed
To equal my great fortune.
BERTRAM.   Let that go:
My haste is very great. Farewell; hie home.
HELENA. Pray, sir, your pardon.
BERTRAM.   Well, what would you say?
HELENA. I am not worthy of the wealth I owe,
Nor dare I say 'tis mine … and yet it is—
But like a timorous thief most fain would steal
What law does vouch mine own.
BERTRAM.   What would you have?
HELENA. Something, and scarce so much:
   nothing, indeed.
I would not tell you what I would, my lord …
Faith, yes—
Strangers and foes do sunder, and not kiss.
BERTRAM. I pray you stay not, but in haste to horse.   90
HELENA. I shall not break your bidding, good my
   lord …
BERTRAM. Where are my other men, monsieur?—
Farewell.   *Helena departs*
Go thou toward home, where I will never come,
Whilst I can shake my sword, or hear the drum …
Away, and for our flight.
PAROLLES.   Bravely, coragio!
                        They go

ACT 3

Scene 1: *Florence. Before the Duke's palace*

*Flourish. Enter the Duke of Florence, the two Frenchmen
with a troop of soldiers*

DUKE. So that from point to point now have you
   heard
The fundamental reasons of this war;
Whose great decision hath much blood let forth,
And more thirsts after.
1 LORD.   Holy seems the quarrel
Upon your grace's part; black and fearful
On the opposer.
DUKE. Therefore we marvel much our cousin France
Would in so just a business shut his bosom
Against our borrowing prayers.
2 LORD.   Good my lord,
The reasons of our state I cannot yield,   10
But like a common and an outward man,
That the great figure of a council frames
By self-unable motion—therefore dare not
Say what I think of it, since I have found
Myself in my incertain grounds to fail
As often as I guessed.
DUKE.   Be it his pleasure.
1 LORD. But I am sure the younger of our nature,
That surfeit on their ease, will day by day
Come here for physic.
DUKE.   Welcome shall they be:
And all the honours that can fly from us   20
Shall on them settle … You know your places well;
When better fall, for your avails they fell:
To-morrow to th' field!   *A flourish; they go*

Scene 2: *The palace of Rousillon*

Enter the Countess and the Clown

COUNTESS. It hath happened all as I would have had
it, save that he comes not along with her.
CLOWN. By my troth, I take my young lord to be a
very melancholy man.
COUNTESS. By what observance, I pray you?
CLOWN. Why, he will look upon his boot and sing,
mend the ruff and sing, ask questions and sing, pick
his teeth and sing: I know a man that had this trick
of melancholy sold a goodly manor for a song.
COUNTESS. Let me see what he writes, and when he   10
means to come.   *She opens a letter*
CLOWN. I have no mind to Isbel, since I was at court.
Our old ling and our Isbels o'the country are
nothing like your old ling and your Isbels o'the
court: the brains of my Cupid's knocked out, and I
begin to love, as an old man loves money, with no
stomach.
COUNTESS. What have we here?
CLOWN. E'en that you have there.   *He goes*
COUNTESS [*reads*]. 'I have sent you a daughter-in-law.   20
She hath recovered the king, and undone me: I have
wedded her, not bedded her, and sworn to make the
'not' eternal. You shall hear I am run away, know it
before the report come. If there be breadth enough
in the world, I will hold a long distance. My duty to
you.

            Your unfortunate son,
                BERTRAM.'
This is not well, rash and unbridled boy,

To fly the favours of so good a king,   30
To pluck his indignation on thy head,
By the misprising of a maid too virtuous
For the contempt of empire.

The Clown returns

CLOWN. O madam, yonder is heavy news within
between two soldiers and my young lady.
COUNTESS. What is the matter?
CLOWN. Nay, there is some comfort in the news, some
comfort—your son will not be killed so soon as I
thought he would.
COUNTESS. Why should he be killed?   40
CLOWN. So say I, madam, if he run away, as I hear
he does. The danger is in standing to't, that's the loss
of men, though it be the getting of children. Here
they come will tell you more. For my part, I only
hear your son was run away.

Helena enters with two gentlemen

1 GENTLEMAN. Save you, good madam.
HELENA. Madam, my lord is gone, for ever gone.
2 GENTLEMAN. Do not say so.
COUNTESS [*takes her in her arms*]. Think upon patience.
Pray you, gentlemen,
I have felt so many quirks of joy and grief,   50
That the first face of neither, on the start,
Can woman me unto't ... Where is my son, I pray
you?
2 GENTLEMAN. Madam, he's gone to serve the Duke
of Florence.
We met him thitherward, for thence we came:
And after some dispatch in hand at court
Thither we bend again.
HELENA. Look on his letter, madam, here's my
passport.
[*reads*] 'When thou canst get the ring upon my
finger, which never shall come off, and show me a
child begotten of thy body that I am father to, then   60
call me husband: but in such a 'then' I write a
'never'.'
This is a dreadful sentence.
COUNTESS. Brought you this letter, gentlemen?
1 GENTLEMAN.   Ay, madam,
And for the contents' sake are sorry for our pains.
COUNTESS. I prithee lady have a better cheer,
If thou engrossest all the griefs are thine,
Thou robb'st me of a moiety ... He was my son,
But I do wash his name out of my blood,
And thou art all my child.... Towards Florence is
he?   70
2 GENTLEMAN. Ay, madam.
COUNTESS.   And to be a soldier?
2 GENTLEMAN. Such is his noble purpose,
and, believe't,
The duke will lay upon him all the honour
That good convenience claims.
COUNTESS.   Return you thither?
1 GENTLEMAN. Ay, madam, with the swiftest wing
of speed.
HELENA [*reads*]. 'Till I have no wife, I have nothing
in France.'
'Tis bitter.
COUNTESS.   Find you that there?
HELENA.   Ay, madam.
1 GENTLEMAN. 'Tis but the boldness of his hand,

haply, which his heart was not consenting to.
COUNTESS. Nothing in France, until he have no wife!   80
There's nothing here that is too good for him
But only she, and she deserves a lord
That twenty such rude boys might tend upon
And call her hourly mistress. Who was with him?
1 GENTLEMAN. A servant only, and a gentleman
Which I have sometime known.
COUNTESS.   Parolles, was it not?
1 GENTLEMAN. Ay, my good lady, he.
COUNTESS. A very tainted fellow, and full of
wickedness.
My son corrupts a well-derivèd nature
With his inducement.
1 GENTLEMAN.   Indeed, good lady,   90
The fellow has a deal of that too much,
Which holds him much to have.
COUNTESS. Y'are welcome, gentlemen.
I will entreat you, when you see my son,
To tell him that his sword can never win
The honour that he loses: more I'll entreat you
Written to bear along.
2 GENTLEMAN.   We serve you, madam,
In that and all your worthiest affairs.
COUNTESS. Not so, but as we change our courtesies.
Will you draw near?   100
          *The Countess goes out with the gentlemen;
                              the Clown follows*
HELENA. 'Till I have no wife, I have nothing in
France.'
Nothing in France, until he has no wife!
Thou shalt have none, Rousillon, none in France,
Then hast thou all again.... Poor lord! is't I
That chase thee from thy country and expose
Those tender limbs of thine to the event
Of the none-sparing war? and is it I
That drive thee from the sportive court, where thou
Wast shot at with fair eyes, to be the mark
Of smoky muskets? O you leaden messengers,   110
That ride upon the violent speed of fire,
Fly with false aim, move the still-piecing air
That sings with piercing, do not touch my lord!
Whoever shoots at him, I set him there.
Whoever charges on his forward breast,
I am the caitiff that do hold him to't.
And, though I kill him not, I am the cause
His death was so effected: better 'twere
I met the ravin lion when he roared
With sharp constraint of hunger: better 'twere   120
That all the miseries which nature owes
Were mine at once. No, come thou home,
Rousillon,
Whence honour but of danger wins a scar,
As oft it loses all.... I will be gone:
My being here it is that holds thee hence—
Shall I stay here to do't? no, no, although
The air of paradise did fan the house,
And angels officed all: I will be gone,
That pitiful rumour may report my flight,
To consolate thine ear. Come night! end day!   130
For with the dark, poor thief, I'll steal away.
                                              She goes

Scene 3: *Florence. Before the Duke's palace*

*Flourish. Enter the Duke of Florence, Bertram, Parolles,
officers, soldiers, drum and trumpets*

DUKE. The general of our horse thou art, and we,
  Great in our hope, lay our best love and credence
  Upon thy promising fortune.
BERTRAM.   Sir, it is
  A charge too heavy for my strength, but yet
  We'll strive to bear it for your worthy sake
  To th'extreme edge of hazard.
DUKE.   Then go thou forth,
  And fortune play upon thy prosperous helm,
  As thy auspicious mistress!
BERTRAM.   This very day,
  Great Mars, I put myself into thy file!
  Make me but like my thoughts, and I shall prove 10
  A lover of thy drum, hater of love.   *They go*

Scene 4: *The palace of Rousillon*

Enter Countess and Steward

COUNTESS. Alas! and would you take the letter of her?
  Might you not know she would do as she has done,
  By sending me a letter? Read it again.
STEWARD [*reads*]. 'I am S. Jaques' pilgrim, thither gone:
  Ambitious love hath so in me offended,
  That barefoot plod I the cold ground upon,
  With sainted vow my faults to have amended.
  Write, write, that from the bloody course of war
  My dearest master, your dear son, may hie:
  Bless him at home in peace, whilst I from far   10
  His name with zealous fervour sanctify:
  His taken labours bid him me forgive;
  I, his despiteful Juno, sent him forth
  From courtly friends with camping foes to live,
  Where death and danger dogs the heels of worth.
  He is too good and fair for death and me,
  Whom I myself embrace to set him free.'
COUNTESS. Ah, what sharp stings are in her mildest
      words!
  Rinaldo, you did never lack advice so much,
  As letting her pass so: had I spoke with her,   20
  I could have well diverted her intents,
  Which thus she hath prevented.
STEWARD.   Pardon me, madam.
  If I had given you this at over-night,
  She might have been o'erta'en: and yet she writes,
  Pursuit would be but vain.
COUNTESS.   What angel shall
  Bless this unworthy husband? he cannot thrive,
  Unless her prayers, whom heaven delights to hear
  And loves to grant, reprieve him from the wrath
  Of greatest justice.... Write, write, Rinaldo,
  To this unworthy husband of his wife,   30
  Let every word weigh heavy of her worth
  That he does weigh too light: my greatest grief,
  Though little he do feel it, set down sharply. .
  Dispatch the most convenient messenger.
  When haply he shall hear that she is gone,
  He will return, and hope I may that she,
  Hearing so much, will speed her foot again,
  Led hither by pure love: which of them both
  Is dearest to me, I have no skill in sense
  To make distinction ... Provide this messenger ... 40
  My heart is heavy and mine age is weak,
  Grief would have tears, and sorrow bids me speak.
                                           They go

Scene 5: *Without the walls of Florence*

*Enter an old Widow of Florence, her daughter Diana, and
Mariana, with other citizens; a tucket afar off*

WIDOW. Nay come, for if they do approach the city,
  we shall lose all the sight.
DIANA. They say the French count has done most
  honourable service.
WIDOW. It is reported that he has taken their great'st
  commander, and that with his own hand he slew the
  duke's brother ... [*tucket*] We have lost our labour,
  they are gone a contrary way—hark! you may
  know by their trumpets.
MARIANA. Come, let's return again, and suffice our- 10
  selves with the report of it.... Well, Diana, take
  heed of this French earl. The honour of a maid is
  her name, and no legacy is so rich as honesty.
WIDOW. I have told my neighbour how you have
  been solicited by a gentleman his companion.
MARIANA. I know that knave, hang him! one Parolles,
  a filthy officer he is in those suggestions for the
  young earl. Beware of them, Diana: their promises,
  enticements, oaths, tokens, and all these engines of
  lust, are not the things they go under: many a maid 20
  hath been seduced by them. And the misery is,
  example, that so terrible shows in the wrack of
  maidenhood, cannot for all that dissuade succession,
  but that they are limed with the twigs that threaten
  them. I hope I need not to advise you further, but
  I hope your own grace will keep you where you are,
  though there were no further danger known but the
  modesty which is so lost.
DIANA. You shall not need to fear me.

Helena approaches disguised as a pilgrim

WIDOW. I hope so ... Look, here comes a pilgrim, I   30
  know she will lie at my house, thither they send one
  another. I'll question her.
  God save you, pilgrim! whither are you bound?
HELENA. To S. Jaques le Grand.
  Where do the palmers lodge, I do beseech you?
WIDOW. At the S. Francis here, beside the port.
HELENA. Is this the way?
WIDOW. Ay, marry, is't.... [*a march afar*] Hark you!
  they come this way.
  If you will tarry, holy pilgrim,
  But till the troops come by,   40
  I will conduct you where you shall be lodged,
  The rather for I think I know your hostess?
  As ample as myself.
HELENA.   Is it yourself?
WIDOW. If you shall please so, pilgrim.
HELENA. I thank you, and will stay upon your leisure.
WIDOW. You came, I think, from France?
HELENA.   I did so.
WIDOW. Here you shall see a countryman of yours,
  That has done worthy service.
HELENA.   His name, I pray you.
DIANA. The Count Rousillon: know you such a one?
HELENA. But by the ear, that hears most nobly of him: 50
  His face I know not.
DIANA.   Whatsome'er he is,
  He's bravely taken here. He stole from France,
  As 'tis reported, for the king had married him
  Against his liking. Think you it is so?
HELENA. Ay, surely, the mere truth. I know his lady.

DIANA. There is a gentleman that serves the count
Reports but coarsely of her.
HELENA.   What's his name?
DIANA. Monsieur Parolles.
HELENA.   O, I believe with him,
In argument of praise, or to the worth
Of the great count himself, she is too mean   60
To have her name repeated—all her deserving
Is a reservéd honesty, and that
I have not heard examined.
DIANA.   Alas, poor lady!
'Tis a hard bondage to become the wife
Of a detesting lord.
WIDOW. I warrant, good creature, wheresoe'er she is,
Her heart weighs sadly: this young maid might do
     her
A shrewd turn, if she pleased.
HELENA.   How do you mean?
May be the amorous count solicits her
In the unlawful purpose.
WIDOW.   He does indeed,   70
And brokes with all that can in such a suit
Corrupt the tender honour of a maid:
But she is armed for him, and keeps her guard
In honestest defence.
MARIANA. The gods forbid else!
WIDOW.   So, now they come . . .

The Florentine army draws near with colours flying and
drums beating; Bertram and Parolles in the foremost ranks

That is Antonio, the dukè's eldest son,
That, Escalus.
HELENA.   Which is the Frenchman?
DIANA.   He—
That with the plume—'tis a most gallant fellow.
I would he loved his wife: if he were honester
He were much goodlier. Is't not a handsome
     gentleman?   80
HELENA. I like him well.
DIANA. 'Tis pity he is not honest: yond's that same
     knave
That leads him to these places: were I his lady,
I would poison that vile rascal.
HELENA.   Which is he?
DIANA. That jack-an-apes with scarfs. Why is he
melancholy?
HELENA. Perchance he's hurt i'th' battle.
PAROLLES. Lose our drum! well.
MARIANA. He's shrewdly vexed at something. Look,
he has spied us.
WIDOW. Marry, hang you!   90
MARIANA. And your curtsy, for a ring-carrier!
     The soldiers go
WIDOW. The troop is past . . . Come, pilgrim, I will
bring you
Where you shall host: of enjoined penitents
There's four or five, to great S. Jaques bound,
Already at my house.
HELENA.   I humbly thank you:
Please it this matron and this gentle maid
To eat with us to-night, the charge and thanking
Shall be for me; and, to requite you further,
I will bestow some precepts of this virgin
Worthy the note.
BOTH.   We'll take your offer kindly.   100
     They go

Scene 6: *The camp before Florence*

Bertram and the two French Lords approach

2 LORD. Nay, good my lord, put him to't; let him have
his way.
1 LORD. If your lordship find him not a hilding, hold
me no more in your respect.
2 LORD. On my life, my lord, a bubble.
BERTRAM. Do you think I am so far deceived in him?
2 LORD. Believe it, my lord, in mine own direct knowledge, without any malice, but to speak of him as
my kinsman, he's a most notable coward, an infinite
and endless liar, an hourly promise-breaker, the   10
owner of no one good quality worthy your lordship's entertainment.
1 LORD. It were fit you knew him, lest reposing too
far in his virtue which he hath not, he might at some
great and trusty business in a main danger fail you.
BERTRAM. I would I knew in what particular action
to try him.
1 LORD. None better than to let him fetch off his drum,
which you hear him so confidently undertake to do.
2 LORD. I, with a troop of Florentines, will suddenly   20
surprise him; such I will have, whom I am sure he
knows not from the enemy: we will bind and hoodwink him so, that he shall suppose no other but that
he is carried into the leaguer of the adversaries, when
we bring him to our own tents . . . Be but your lordship present at his examination—if he do not, for the
promise of his life and in the highest compulsion of
base fear, offer to betray you and deliver all the
intelligence in his power against you, and that with
the divine forfeit of his soul upon oath, never trust   30
my judgement in any thing.
1 LORD. O, for the love of laughter, let him fetch his
drum. He says he has a stratagem for't: when your
lordship sees the bottom of his success in't, and to
what metal this counterfeit lump of ore will be
melted, if you give him not John Drum's entertainment, your inclining cannot be removed. Here he
comes.

Parolles enters

2 LORD. O, for the love of laughter, hinder not the
honour of his design, let him fetch off his drum in   40
any hand.
BERTRAM. How now, monsieur! this drum sticks
sorely in your disposition.
1 LORD. A pox on't, let it go, 'tis but a drum.
PAROLLES. 'But a drum!' is't 'but a drum'? A drum
so lost! There was excellent command—to charge in
with our horse upon our own wings, and to rend
our own soldiers!
1 LORD. That was not to be blamed in the command
of the service: it was a disaster of war that Cæsar   50
himself could not have prevented, if he had been
there to command.
BERTRAM. Well, we cannot greatly condemn our success: some dishonour we had in the loss of that drum:
but it is not to be recovered.
PAROLLES. It might have been recovered.
BERTRAM. It might, but it is not now.
PAROLLES. It is to be recovered. But that the merit of
service is seldom attributed to the true and exact per-
former, I would have that drum or another, or 'hic   60
jacet.'

BERTRAM. Why, if you have a stomach, to't monsieur: if you think your mystery in stratagem can bring this instrument of honour again into his native quarter, be magnanimous in the enterprise, and go on—I will grace the attempt for a worthy exploit: if you speed well in it, the duke shall both speak of it, and extend to you what further becomes his greatness, even to the utmost syllable of your worthiness. 70

PAROLLES. By the hand of a soldier, I will undertake it.

BERTRAM. But you must not now slumber in it.

PAROLLES. I'll about it this evening, and I will presently pen down my dilemmas, encourage myself in my certainty, put myself into my mortal preparation; and by midnight look to hear further from me.

BERTRAM. May I be bold to acquaint his grace you are gone about it?

PAROLLES. I know not what the success will be, my lord, but the attempt I vow. 80

BERTRAM. I know, th'art valiant—and, to the possibility of thy soldiership, will subscribe for thee ... Farewell.

PAROLLES. I love not many words. *He goes*

2 LORD. No more than a fish loves water.... Is not this a strange fellow, my lord, that so confidently seems to undertake this business—which he knows is not to be done—damns himself to do, and dares better be damned than to do't.

1 LORD. You do not know him, my lord, as we do. 90 Certain it is, that he will steal himself into a man's favour and for a week escape a great deal of discoveries, but when you find him out you have him ever after.

BERTRAM. Why, do you think he will make no deed at all of this that so seriously he does address himself unto?

2 LORD. None in the world, but return with an invention, and clap upon you two or three probable lies: but we have almost embossed him, you shall see 100 his fall to-night; for indeed he is not for your lordship's respect.

1 LORD. We'll make you some sport with the fox ere we case him. He was first smoked by the old lord Lafeu. When his disguise and he is parted, tell me what a sprat you shall find him, which you shall see this very night.

2 LORD. I must go look my twigs, he shall be caught.

BERTRAM. Your brother, he shall go along with me.

2 LORD. As't please your lordship: I'll leave you. 110
He goes

BERTRAM. Now will I lead you to the house, and show you The lass I spoke of.

1 LORD. But you say she's honest.

BERTRAM. That's all the fault: I spoke with her but once, And found her wondrous cold, but I sent to her, By this same coxcomb that we have i'th' wind, Tokens and letters which she did re-send, And this is all I have done ... She's a fair creature, Will you go see her?

1 LORD. With all my heart, my lord.
They go

Scene 7: *The Widow's house at Florence*

Enter Helena and Widow

HELENA. If you misdoubt me that I am not she, I know not how I shall assure you further, But I shall lose the grounds I work upon.

WIDOW. Though my estate be fall'n, I was well born, Nothing acquainted with these businesses, And would not put my reputation now In any staining act.

HELENA. Nor would I wish you. First give me trust the count he is my husband, And what to your sworn counsel I have spoken Is so from word to word; and then you cannot, 10 By the good aid that I of you shall borrow, Err in bestowing it.

WIDOW. I should believe you, For you have showed me that which well approves Y'are great in fortune.

HELENA. Take this purse of gold, And let me buy your friendly help thus far, Which I will over-pay and pay again When I have found it.... The count he wooes your daughter, Lays down his wanton siege before her beauty, Resolved to carry her: let her in fine consent, As we'll direct her how 'tis best to bear it: 20 Now his important blood will nought deny That she'll demand: a ring the county wears, That downward hath succeeded in his house From son to son, some four or five descents Since the first father wore it: this ring he holds In most rich choice; yet in his idle fire, To buy his will, it would not seem too dear, Howe'er repented after.

WIDOW. Now I see The bottom of your purpose.

HELENA. You see it lawful then. It is no more 30 But that your daughter, ere she seems as won, Desires this ring; appoints him an encounter; In fine, delivers me to fill the time, Herself most chastely absent: after this, To marry her, I'll add three thousand crowns To what is past already.

WIDOW. I have yielded: Instruct my daughter how she shall persever, That time and place with this deceit so lawful May prove coherent. Every night he comes With musics of all sorts and songs composed 40 To her unworthiness: it nothing steads us To chide him from our eaves, for he persists As if his life lay on't.

HELENA. Why then to-night Let us assay our plot, which if it speed, Is wicked meaning in a lawful deed, And lawful meaning in a lawful act, Where both not sin, and yet a sinful fact: But let's about it. *They go*

ACT 4

Scene 1: *A field near the Florentine camp*

The second French Lord, with five or six other soldiers in ambush

2 LORD. He can come no other way but by this hedgecorner ... When you sally upon him, speak what terrible language you will: though you understand it not yourselves, no matter: for we must not seem to understand him, unless some one among us whom

we must produce for an interpreter.

1 SOLDIER. Good captain, let me be th'interpreter.

2 LORD. Art not acquainted with him? knows he not thy voice?

1 SOLDIER. No, sir, I warrant you.   10

2 LORD. But what linsey-woolsey hast thou to speak to us again?

1 SOLDIER. E'en such as you speak to me.

2 LORD. He must think us some band of strangers i'the adversary's entertainment. Now he hath a smack of all neighbouring languages; therefore we must every one be a man of his own fancy; not to know what we speak one to another, so we seem to know, is to know straight our purpose: choughs' language, gabble enough, and good enough. As for you, inter- 20 preter, you must seem very politic. But couch, ho! here he comes—to beguile two hours in a sleep, and then to return and swear the lies he forges.

Parolles enters

PAROLLES. Ten o'clock: within these three hours 'twill be time enough to go home. What shall I say I have done? It must be a very plausive invention that carries it. They begin to smoke me, and disgraces have of late knocked too often at my door ... I find my tongue is too foolhardy, but my heart hath the fear of Mars before it and of his creatures, not daring 30 the reports of my tongue.

2 LORD [*aside*]. This is the first truth that e'er thine own tongue was guilty of.

PAROLLES. What the devil should move me to under- take the recovery of this drum, being not ignorant of the impossibility, and knowing I had no such pur- pose? I must give myself some hurts, and say I got them in exploit ... Yet slight ones will not carry it. They will say, 'Came you off with so little?' And great ones I dare not give. Wherefore, what's the 40 instance? Tongue, I must put you into a butter- woman's mouth, and buy myself another of Bajazet's mate, if you prattle me into these perils.

2 LORD [*aside*]. Is it possible he should know what he is, and be that he is?

PAROLLES. I would the cutting of my garments would serve the turn, or the breaking of my Spanish sword.

2 LORD [*aside*]. We cannot afford you so.

PAROLLES. Or the baring of my beard, and to say it was in stratagem.   50

2 LORD [*aside*]. 'Twould not do.

PAROLLES. Or to drown my clothes, and say I was stripped.

2 LORD [*aside*]. Hardly serve.

PAROLLES. Though I swore I leaped from the window of the citadel—

2 LORD [*aside*]. How deep?

PAROLLES. Thirty fathom.

2 LORD [*aside*]. Three great oaths would scarce make that be believed.   60

PAROLLES. I would I had any drum of the enemy's, I would swear I recovered it.

2 LORD [*aside*]. You shall hear one anon.

PAROLLES. A drum now of the enemy's—

2 LORD. Throca movousus, cargo, cargo, cargo.

ALL. Cargo, cargo, cargo, villianda par corbo, cargo.

PAROLLES. O! ransom, ransom! Do not hide mine eyes.

They bind him and blindfold
his eyes in his scarf

1 SOLDIER. Boskos thromuldo boskos.

PAROLLES. I know you are the Muskos' regiment. And I shall lose my life for want of language.   70 If there be here German, or Dane, low Dutch, Italian, or French, let him speak to me, I will discover that which shall undo The Florentine.

1 SOLDIER.   Boskos vauvado—
I understand thee, and can speak thy tongue:
Kerelybonto, sir,
Betake thee to thy faith, for seventeen poniards
Are at thy bosom.

PAROLLES.   O!

1 SOLDIER.   O, pray, pray, pray!
Manka revania dulche.

2 LORD. Oscorbidulchos volivorco.   80

1 SOLDIER. The general is content to spare thee yet, And, hoodwinked as thou art, will lead thee on To gather from thee. Haply thou mayst inform Something to save thy life.

PAROLLES.   O, let me live!
And all the secrets of our camp I'll show,
Their force, their purposes: nay, I'll speak that
Which you will wonder at.

1 SOLDIER.   But wilt thou faithfully?

PAROLLES. If I do not, damn me.

1 SOLDIER.   Acordo linta.
Come on, thou art granted space.

The interpreter and
other soldiers carry off Parolles

2 LORD. Go, tell the Count Rousillon, and my brother,   90
We have caught the woodcock, and will keep him muffled
Till we do hear from them.

2 SOLDIER.   Captain, I will.

2 LORD. A' will betray us all unto ourselves—
Inform 'em that.

2 SOLDIER.   So I will, sir.

2 LORD. Till then, I'll keep him dark, and safely locked.

They go

Scene 2: *The Widow's house at Florence*

Enter Bertram and Diana

BERTRAM. They told me that your name was Fontibell.

DIANA. No, my good lord, Diana.

BERTRAM.   Titled goddess!
And worth it, with addition ... But, fair soul,
In your fine frame hath love no quality?
If the quick fire of youth light not your mind,
You are no maiden but a monument.
When you are dead, you should be such a one
As you are now, for you are cold and stern;
And now you should be as your mother was
When your sweet self was got.   10

DIANA. She then was honest.

BERTRAM.   So should you be.

DIANA.   No:
My mother did but duty—such, my lord,
As you owe to your wife.

BERTRAM.   No more o' that:
I prithee, do not strive against my vows:
I was compelled to her, but I love thee
By love's own sweet constraint, and will for ever
Do thee all rights of service.

DIANA.   Ay, so you serve us

Till we serve you: but when you have our roses,
You barely leave our thorns to prick ourselves,
And mock us with our bareness.
BERTRAM.   How have I sworn! 20
DIANA. 'Tis not the many oaths that makes the truth,
But the plain single vow that is vowed true:
What is not holy, that we swear not by,
But take the High'st to witness: then, pray you, tell
    me,
If I should swear by Jove's great attributes
I loved you dearly, would you believe my oaths
When I did love you ill? This has no holding,
To swear by Him whom I protest to love,
That I will work against Him. Therefore your oaths
Are words and poor, conditions but unsealed,   30
At least in my opinion.
BERTRAM.   Change it, change it;
Be not so holy-cruel: love is holy,
And my integrity ne'er knew the crafts
That you do charge men with . . . Stand no more off,
But give thyself unto my sick desires,
Who then recover. Say thou art mine, and ever
My love as it begins shall so persever.
DIANA. I see that men make rope's in such a scarre,
That we'll forsake ourselves. Give me that ring.
BERTRAM. I'll lend it thee, my dear; but have no
    power   40
To give it from me.
DIANA.   Will you not, my lord?
BERTRAM. It is an honour 'longing to our house,
Bequeathéd down from many ancestors,
Which were the greatest obloquy i'th' world
In me to lose.
DIANA.   Mine honour's such a ring,
My chastity's the jewel of our house,
Bequeathéd down from many ancestors,
Which were the greatest obloquy i'th' world
In me to lose. Thus your own proper wisdom
Brings in the champion Honour on my part,   50
Against your vain assault.
BERTRAM.   Here, take my ring.
My house, mine honour, yea, my life be thine,
And I'll be bid by thee.
DIANA. When midnight comes, knock at my chamber
    window:
I'll order take my mother shall not hear.
Now will I charge you in the band of truth,
When you have conquered my yet maiden bed,
Remain there but an hour, nor speak to me:
My reasons are most strong, and you shall know
    them
When back again this ring shall be delivered: 60
And on your finger in the night I'll put
Another ring, that what in time proceeds
May token to the future our past deeds.
Adieu till then, then fail not: you have won
A wife of me, though there my hope be done.
BERTRAM. A heaven on earth I have won by
    wooing thee.
DIANA. For which live long to thank both heaven
    and me!   *He goes*
You may so in the end.
My mother told me just how he would woo,
As if she sat in's heart. She says all men   70
Have the like oaths: he had sworn to marry me
When his wife's dead; therefore I'll lie with him

When I am buried. Since Frenchmen are so braid,
Marry that will, I live and die a maid:
Only in this disguise I think't no sin
To cozen him that would unjustly win.   *She goes*

Scene 3: *The Florentine camp*

Enter the two French Lords, and two or three soldiers

2 LORD. You have not given him his mother's letter?
1 LORD. I have delivered it an hour since. There is
something in't that stings his nature; for on the
reading it he changed almost into another man.
2 LORD. He has much worthy blame laid upon him
for shaking off so good a wife and so sweet a lady.
1 LORD. Especially he hath incurred the everlasting
displeasure of the king, who had even tuned his
bounty to sing happiness to him. I will tell you a
thing, but you shall let it dwell darkly with you. 10
2 LORD. When you have spoken it, 'tis dead, and I am
the grave of it.
1 LORD. He hath perverted a young gentlewoman here
in Florence, of a most chaste renown, and this night
he fleshes his will in the spoil of her honour: he hath
given her his monumental ring, and thinks himself
made in the unchaste composition.
2 LORD. Now, God lay our rebellion! as we are ourselves, what things are we!
1 LORD. Merely our own traitors. And as in the   20
common course of all treasons, we still see them
reveal themselves, till they attain to their abhorred
ends; so he that in this action contrives against his
own nobility in his proper stream o'erflows himself.
2 LORD. Is it not meant damnable in us, to be
trumpeters of our unlawful intents? We shall not
then have his company to-night?
1 LORD. Not till after midnight; for he is dieted to his
hour.
2 LORD. That approaches apace: I would gladly have 30
him see his company anatomized, that he might take
a measure of his own judgement, wherein so
curiously he had set this counterfeit.
1 LORD. We will not meddle with him till he come;
for his presence must be the whip of the other.
2 LORD. In the mean time, what hear you of these
wars?
1 LORD. I hear there is an overture of peace.
2 LORD. Nay, I assure you, a peace concluded.
1 LORD. What will Count Rousillon do then? will he 40
travel higher, or return again into France?
2 LORD. I perceive, by this demand, you are not
altogether of his council.
1 LORD. Let it be forbid, sir, so should I be a great
deal of his act.
2 LORD. Sir, his wife some two months since fled from
his house: her pretence is a pilgrimage to S. Jaques
le Grand; which holy undertaking with most austere
sanctimony she accomplished: and, there residing,
the tenderness of her nature became as a prey to her 50
grief; in fine, made a groan of her last breath, and
now she sings in heaven.
1 LORD. How is this justified?
2 LORD. The stronger part of it by her own letters,
which makes her story true, even to the point of her
death: her death itself, which could not be her office
to say is come, was faithfully confirmed by the
rector of the place.

1 LORD. Hath the count all this intelligence?

2 LORD. Ay, and the particular confirmations, point 60 from point, to the full arming of the verity.

1 LORD. I am heartily sorry that he'll be glad of this.

2 LORD. How mightily sometimes we make us comforts of our losses!

1 LORD. And how mightily some other times we drown our gain in tears! The great dignity that his valour hath here acquired for him shall at home be encountered with a shame as ample.

2 LORD. The web of our life is of a mingled yarn, good and ill together: our virtues would be proud, if our 70 faults whipped them not, and our crimes would despair, if they were not cherished by our virtues.

A servant comes in

How now! where's your master?

SERVANT. He met the duke in the street, sir, of whom he hath taken a solemn leave; his lordship will next morning for France. The Duke hath offered him letters of commendations to the king.

2 LORD. They shall be no more than needful there, if they were more than they can commend.

1 LORD. They cannot be too sweet for the king's 80 tartness.

Bertram enters

Here's his lordship now. How now, my lord, is't not after midnight?

BERTRAM. I have to-night dispatched sixteen businesses, a month's length a-piece, by an abstract of success: I have congied with the duke, done my adieu with his nearest, buried a wife, mourned for her, writ to my lady mother I am returning, entertained my convoy, and between these main parcels of dispatch, effected many nicer needs: the last was 90 the greatest, but that I have not ended yet.

2 LORD. If the business be of any difficulty, and this morning your departure hence, it requires haste of your lordship.

BERTRAM. I mean, the business is not ended, as fearing to hear of it hereafter ... But shall we have this dialogue between the Fool and the Soldier? Come, bring forth this counterfeit module, has deceived me like a double-meaning prophesier.

2 LORD. Bring him forth. [*a soldier goes out*] Has sat 100 i'th' stocks all night, poor gallant knave.

BERTRAM. No matter, his heels have deserved it, in usurping his spurs so long. How does he carry himself?

2 LORD. I have told your lordship already; the stocks carry him. But to answer you as you would be understood, he weeps like a wench that had shed her milk. He hath confessed himself to Morgan, whom he supposes to be a friar, from the time of his remembrance to this very instant disaster of his 110 setting i'th' stocks: and what think you he hath confessed?

BERTRAM. Nothing of me, has a'?

2 LORD. His confession is taken, and it shall be read to his face. If your lordship be in't, as I believe you are, you must have the patience to hear it.

Soldiers bring in Parolles, with his Interpreter

BERTRAM. A plague upon him! muffled! he can say nothing of me.

1 LORD. Hush! hush! Hoodman comes! Portotar- 120 tarossa.

INTERPRETER. He calls for the tortures. What will you say without 'em?

PAROLLES. I will confess what I know without constraint. If ye pinch me like a pasty, I can say no more.

INTERPRETER. Bosko chimurcho.

1 LORD. Boblibindo chicurmurco.

INTERPRETER. You are a merciful general ... Our general bids you answer to what I shall ask you out of a note.

PAROLLES. And truly, as I hope to live. 130

INTERPRETER. 'First demand of him how many horse the duke is strong.' What say you to that?

PAROLLES. Five or six thousand, but very weak and unserviceable: the troops are all scattered, and the commanders very poor rogues, upon my reputation and credit, and as I hope to live.

INTERPRETER. Shall I set down your answer so?

PAROLLES. Do, I'll take the sacrament on't, how and which way you will.

BERTRAM. All's one to him. What a past-saving slave 140 is this!

1 LORD. Y'are deceived, my lord, this is Monsieur Parolles, the gallant militarist—that was his own phrase—that had the whole theoric of war in the knot of his scarf, and the practice in the chape of his dagger.

2 LORD. I will never trust a man again for keeping his sword clean, nor believe he can have every thing in him by wearing his apparel neatly.

INTERPRETER. Well, that's set down. 150

PAROLLES. Five or six thousand horse, I said—I will say true—or thereabouts, set down, for I'll speak truth.

1 LORD. He's very near the truth in this.

BERTRAM. But I con him no thanks for't, in the nature he delivers it.

PAROLLES. Poor rogues, I pray you, say.

INTERPRETER. Well, that's set down.

PAROLLES. I humbly thank you, sir—a truth's a truth—the rogues are marvellous poor.

INTERPRETER. 'Demand of him, of what strength they 160 are a-foot.' What say you to that?

PAROLLES. By my troth, sir, if I were to leave this present hour, I will tell true. Let me see—Spurio a hundred and fifty, Sebastian so many, Corambus so many, Jaques so many; Guiltian, Cosmo, Lodowick, and Gratii, two hundred and fifty each: mine own company, Chitopher, Vaumond, Bentii, two hundred and fifty each: so that the muster-file, rotten and sound, upon my life, amounts not to fifteen thousand poll, half of the which dare not shake the 170 snow from off their cassocks, lest they shake themselves to pieces.

BERTRAM. What shall be done to him?

1 LORD. Nothing, but let him have thanks. Demand of him my condition, and what credit I have with the duke.

INTERPRETER. Well, that's set down. 'You shall demand of him, whether one Captain Dumain be i'th' camp, a Frenchman: what his reputation is with the duke, what his valour, honesty, 180 and expertness in wars; or whether he thinks it were not possible, with well-weighing sums of gold, to corrupt him to a revolt.' What say you to this? what do you know of it?

PAROLLES. I beseech you, let me answer to the particular of the inter'gatories. Demand them singly.

INTERPRETER. Do you know this Captain Dumain?

PAROLLES. I know him, a' was a botcher's prentice in Paris, from whence he was whipped for getting the shrieve's fool with child—a dumb innocent, that could not say him nay.

BERTRAM. Nay, by your leave, hold your hands, though I know his brains are forfeit to the next tile that falls.

INTERPRETER. Well, is this captain in the Duke of Florence's camp?

PAROLLES. Upon my knowledge he is, and lousy.

1 LORD. Nay, look not so upon me; we shall hear of your lordship anon.

INTERPRETER. What is his reputation with the duke?

PAROLLES. The duke knows him for no other but a poor officer of mine, and writ to me this other day to turn him out o'th' band. I think I have his letter in my pocket.

INTERPRETER. Marry, we'll search.

PAROLLES. In good sadness, I do not know—either it is there, or it is upon a file with the duke's other letters in my tent.

INTERPRETER. Here 'tis, here's a paper, shall I read it to you?

PAROLLES. I do not know if it be it or no.

BERTRAM. Our interpreter does it well.

1 LORD. Excellently.

INTERPRETER [reads the paper]. 'Dian, the count's a fool, and full of gold'—

PAROLLES. That is not the duke's letter, sir; that is an advertisement to a proper maid in Florence, one Diana, to take heed of the allurement of one Count Rousillon, a foolish idle boy: but for all that very ruttish. I pray you, sir, put it up again.

INTERPRETER. Nay, I'll read it first, by your favour.

PAROLLES. My meaning in't, I protest, was very honest in the behalf of the maid: for I knew the young count to be a dangerous and lascivious boy, who is a whale to virginity, and devours up all the fry it finds.

BERTRAM. Damnable both-sides rogue!

INTERPRETER [reads]. 'When he swears oaths, bid him drop gold, and take it;
After he scores, he never pays the score:
Half won is match well made, match and well make it,
He ne'er pays after-debts, take it before.
And say a soldier, Dian, told thee this:
Men are to mell with, boys are but to kiss:
For count of this, the count's a fool, I know it,
Who pays before, but not when he does owe it.
Thine, as he vowed to thee in thine ear,
                        PAROLLES.'

BERTRAM. He shall be whipped through the army with this rhyme in's forehead.

2 LORD. This is your devoted friend, sir, the manifold linguist, and the armipotent soldier.

BERTRAM. I could endure any thing before but a cat, and now he's a cat to me.

INTERPRETER. I perceive, sir, by the general's looks, we shall be fain to hang you.

PAROLLES. My life, sir, in any case! not that I am afraid to die, but that my offences being many I would repent out the remainder of nature. Let me live, sir,

in a dungeon, i'th' stocks, or any where, so I may live.

INTERPRETER. We'll see what may be done, so you confess freely; therefore, once more to this Captain Dumain: you have answered to his reputation with the duke and to his valour: what is his honesty?

PAROLLES. He will steal, sir, an egg out of a cloister: for rapes and ravishments he parallels Nessus. He professes not keeping of oaths, in breaking 'em he is stronger than Hercules. He will lie, sir, with such volubility, that you would think truth were a fool: drunkenness is his best virtue, for he will be swine-drunk, and in his sleep he does little harm, save to his bed-clothes about him; but they know his conditions and lay him in straw. I have but little more to say, sir, of his honesty—he has every thing that an honest man should not have; what an honest man should have, he has nothing.

1 LORD. I begin to love him for this.

BERTRAM. For this description of thine honesty? A pox upon him! For me, he's more and more a cat.

INTERPRETER. What say you to his expertness in war?

PAROLLES. Faith, sir, has led the drum before the English tragedians; to belie him, I will not, and more of his soldiership I know not, except in that country he had the honour to be the officer at a place there called Mile-end, to instruct for the doubling of files. I would do the man what honour I can, but of this I am not certain.

1 LORD. He hath out-villained villainy so far, that the rarity redeems him.

BERTRAM. A pox on him, he's a cat still.

INTERPRETER. His qualities being at this poor price, I need not to ask you, if gold will corrupt him to revolt.

PAROLLES. Sir, for a cardecue he will sell the fee-simple of his salvation, the inheritance of it; and cut th'entail from all remainders, and a perpetual succession for it perpetually.

INTERPRETER. What's his brother, the other Captain Dumain?

2 LORD. Why does he ask him of me?

INTERPRETER. What's he?

PAROLLES. E'en a crow o'th' same nest; not altogether so great as the first in goodness, but greater a great deal in evil. He excels his brother for a coward, yet his brother is reputed one of the best that is. In a retreat he outruns any lackey; marry, in coming on he has the cramp.

INTERPRETER. If your life be saved, will you undertake to betray the Florentine?

PAROLLES. Ay, and the captain of his horse, Count Rousillon.

INTERPRETER. I'll whisper with the general, and know his pleasure.

PAROLLES [aside]. I'll no more drumming, a plague of all drums. Only to seem to deserve well, and to beguile the supposition of that lascivious young boy, the count, have I run into this danger: yet, who would have suspected an ambush where I was taken?

INTERPRETER. There is no remedy, sir, but you must die: the general says, you that have so traitorously discovered the secrets of your army and made such pestiferous reports of men very nobly held, can serve the world for no honest use; therefore you must die. Come, headsman, off with his head.

PAROLLES. O Lord, sir, let me live, or let me see my death!

INTERPRETER. That shall you, and take your leave of all your friends ...   *He takes the scarf from his eyes* So, look about you. Know you any here?

BERTRAM. Good morrow, noble captain.

2 LORD. God bless you, Captain Parolles.   320

1 LORD. God save you, noble captain.

2 LORD. Captain, what greeting will you to my Lord Lafeu? I am for France.

1 LORD. Good captain, will you give me a copy of the sonnet you writ to Diana in behalf of the Count Rousillon? an I were not a very coward, I'd compel it of you, but fare you well.

Bertram and the Lords go

INTERPRETER. You are undone, captain, all but your scarf—that has a knot on't yet.

PAROLLES. Who cannot be crushed with a plot?   330

INTERPRETER. If you could find out a country where but women were that had received so much shame, you might begin an impudent nation. Fare ye well, sir, I am for France too, we shall speak of you there.

He goes

PAROLLES. Yet am I thankful: if my heart were great, 'Twould burst at this ... Captain I'll be no more, But I will eat and drink, and sleep as soft As captain shall: simply the thing I am Shall make me live. Who knows himself a braggart, Let him fear this; for it will come to pass   340 That every braggart shall be found an ass. Rust, sword! cool, blushes! and, Parolles, live Safest in shame! being fooled, by foolery thrive! There's place and means for every man alive. I'll after them.   *He goes*

Scene 4: *The Widow's house at Florence*

Enter Helena, Widow, and Diana

HELENA. That you may well perceive I have not wronged you,
One of the greatest in the Christian world
Shall be my surety: 'fore whose throne 'tis needful,
Ere I can perfect mine intents, to kneel.
Time was, I did him a desiréd office,
Dear almost as his life, which gratitude
Through flinty Tartar's bosom would peep forth,
And answer, thanks. I duly am informed
His grace is at Marseillës, to which place
We have convenient convoy ... You must know,   10
I am supposéd dead: the army breaking,
My husband hies him home, where, heaven aiding,
And by the leave of my good lord the king,
We'll be before our welcome.

WIDOW.   Gentle madam,
You never had a servant to whose trust
Your business was more welcome.

HELENA.   Nor you, mistress,
Ever a friend whose thoughts more truly labour
To recompense your love: doubt not but heaven
Hath brought me up to be your daughter's dower,
As it hath fated her to be my motive   20
And helper to a husband. But, O strange men,
That can such sweet use make of what they hate,
When saucy trusting of the cozened thoughts
Defiles the pitchy night! so lust doth play
With what it loathes, for that which is away.

But more of this hereafter ... You, Diana,
Under my poor instructions yet must suffer
Something in my behalf.

DIANA.   Let death and honesty
Go with your impositions, I am yours
Upon your will to suffer.

HELENA.   Yet, I pray you ...   30
But with the word, that time will bring on summer,
When briars shall have leaves as well as thorns,
And be as sweet as sharp ... We must away,
Our waggon is prepared, and time revives us.
'All's well that ends well,' still the fine's the crown;
Whate'er the course, the end is the renown.

They go

Scene 5: *The palace of Rousillon*

Enter Countess, Lafeu, and Clown

LAFEU. No, no, no, your son was misled with a snipt-taffeta fellow there, whose villainous saffron would have made all the unbaked and doughy youth of a nation in his colour: your daughter-in-law had been alive at this hour, and your son here at home, more advanced by the king than by that red-tailed humble-bee I speak of.

COUNTESS. I would I had not known him—it was the death of the most virtuous gentlewoman that ever nature had praise for creating. If she had partaken of   10 my flesh, and cost me the dearest groans of a mother, I could not have owed her a more rooted love.

LAFEU. 'Twas a good lady, 'twas a good lady. We may pick a thousand salads ere we light on such another herb.

CLOWN. Indeed, sir, she was the sweet-marjoram of the salad, or rather, the herb of grace.

LAFEU. They are knot-herbs, you knave, they are nose-herbs.

CLOWN. I am no great Nebuchadnezzar, sir, I have   20 not much skill in grass.

LAFEU. Whether dost thou profess thyself, a knave or a fool?

CLOWN. A fool, sir, at a woman's service, and a knave at a man's.

LAFEU. Your distinction?

CLOWN. I would cozen the man of his wife, and do his service.

LAFEU. So you were a knave at his service, indeed.

CLOWN. And I would give his wife my bauble, sir,   30 to do her service.

LAFEU. I will subscribe for thee, thou art both knave and fool.

CLOWN. At your service.

LAFEU. No, no, no.

CLOWN. Why, sir, if I cannot serve you, I can serve as great a prince as you are.

LAFEU. Who's that? a Frenchman?

CLOWN. Faith, sir, a' has an English name, but his fisnamy is more hotter in France than there.   40

LAFEU. What prince is that?

CLOWN. The Black Prince, sir, alias the prince of darkness, alias the devil.

LAFEU. Hold thee, there's my purse. I give thee not this to suggest thee from thy master thou talk'st of—serve him still.

CLOWN. I am a woodland fellow, sir, that always loved a great fire, and the master I speak of ever keeps a good fire. But, sure, he is the prince of the world, let his nobility remain in's court. I am for the house 50 with the narrow gate, which I take to be too little for pomp to enter: some that humble themselves may, but the many will be too chill and tender, and they'll be for the flowery way that leads to the broad gate and the great fire.

LAFEU. Go thy ways, I begin to aweary of thee, and I tell thee so before, because I would not fall out with thee. Go thy ways, let my horses be well looked to, without any tricks.

CLOWN. If I put any tricks upon 'em, sir, they shall 60 be jades' tricks, which are their own right by the law of nature.   *He goes*

LAFEU. A shrewd knave and an unhappy.

COUNTESS. So a' is. My lord that's gone made himself much sport out of him: by his authority he remains here, which he thinks is a patent for his sauciness, and indeed he has no pace, but runs where he will.

LAFEU. I like him well, 'tis not amiss ... And I was about to tell you, since I heard of the good lady's death and that my lord your son was upon his return 70 home, I moved the king my master to speak in the behalf of my daughter—which, in the minority of them both, his majesty out of a self-gracious remembrance did first propose. His highness hath promised me to do it—and, to stop up the displeasure he hath conceived against your son, there is no fitter matter. How does your ladyship like it?

COUNTESS. With very much content, my lord, and I wish it happily effected.

LAFEU. His highness comes post from Marseilles, of 80 as able body as when he numbered thirty—a' will be here to-morrow, or I am deceived by him that in such intelligence hath seldom failed.

COUNTESS. It rejoices me, that I hope I shall see him ere I die. I have letters that my son will be here to-night: I shall beseech your lordship to remain with me till they meet together.

LAFEU. Madam, I was thinking with what manners I might safely be admitted.

COUNTESS. You need but plead your honourable 90 privilege.

LAFEU. Lady, of that I have made a bold charter, but I thank my God it holds yet.

Clown returns

CLOWN. O madam, yonder's my lord your son with a patch of velvet on's face—whether there be a scar under't or no, the velvet knows, but 'tis a goodly patch of velvet—his left cheek is a cheek of two pile and a half, but his right cheek is worn bare.

LAFEU. A scar nobly got, or a noble scar, is a good livery of honour—so belike is that.   100

CLOWN. But it is your carbonadoed face.

LAFEU. Let us go see your son, I pray you. I long to talk with the young noble soldier.

CLOWN. Faith, there's a dozen of 'em, with delicate fine hats and most courteous feathers, which bow the head, and nod at every man.   *They go*

ACT 5

Scene 1: *A street in Marseilles*

Helena, Widow, and Diana, with two attendants

HELENA. But this exceeding posting day and night Must wear your spirits low—we cannot help it: But since you have made the days and nights as one, 50 To wear your gentle limbs in my affairs, Be hold you do so grow in my requital As nothing can unroot you.

Enter a gentle astringer

                              In happy time—
This man may help me to his majesty's ear, If he would spend his power. God save you, sir.

GENTLEMAN. And you.

HELENA. Sir, I have seen you in the court of France.   10

GENTLEMAN. I have been sometimes there.

HELENA. I do presume, sir, that you are not fall'n From the report that goes upon your goodness, And therefore, goaded with most sharp occasions, Which lay nice manners by, I put you to The uśe of your own virtues, for the which I shall continue thankful.

GENTLEMAN.   What's your will?

HELENA. That it will please you To give this poor petition to the king, And aid me with that store of power you have   20 To come into his presence.

GENTLEMAN. The king's not here.

HELENA.   Not here, sir!

GENTLEMAN.   Not indeed, He hence removed last night, and with more haste Than is his use.

WIDOW.   Lord, how we lose our pains!

HELENA. 'All's well that ends well' yet, Though time seem so adverse and means unfit.... I do beseech you, whither is he gone?

GENTLEMAN. Marry, as I take it, to Rousillon, Whither I am going.

HELENA.   I do beseech you, sir, Since you are like to see the king before me,   30 Commend the paper to his gracious hand, Which I presume shall render you no blame But rather make you thank your pains for it. I will come after you with what good speed Our means will make us means.

GENTLEMAN.   This I'll do for you.

HELENA. And you shall find yourself to be well thanked, Whate'er falls more. We must to horse again. Go, go, provide.   *They go*

Scene 2: *In the park near the palace of Rousillon*

Clown and Parolles

PAROLLES. Good Master Lavache, give my Lord Lafeu this letter. I have ere now, sir, been better known to you, when I have held familiarity with fresher clothes; but I am now, sir, muddied in fortune's mood, and smell somewhat strong of her strong displeasure.

CLOWN. Truly, fortune's displeasure is but sluttish, if it smell so strongly as thou speak'st of: I will henceforth eat no fish of fortune's butt'ring. Prithee, allow the wind.   10

PAROLLES. Nay, you need not to stop your nose, sir; I spake but by a metaphor.

CLOWN. Indeed, sir, if your metaphor stink, I will stop my nose, or against any man's metaphor. Prithee, get thee further.

PAROLLES. Pray you, sir, deliver me this paper.
CLOWN. Foh! prithee, stand away: a paper from
fortune's close-stool to give to a nobleman! Look,
here he comes himself.

Lafeu approaches

Here is a pur of fortune's, sir, or of fortune's cat— 20
but not a musk-cat—that has fallen into the unclean
fishpond of her displeasure, and, as he says, is
muddied withal: pray you, sir, use the carp as you
may, for he looks like a poor, decayed, ingenerous,
foolish, rascally knave. I do pity his distress in my
similes of comfort, and leave him to your lordship.
                                            He goes
PAROLLES. My lord, I am a man whom fortune hath
cruelly scratched.
LAFEU. And what would you have me to do? 'tis too
late to pare her nails now. Wherein have you played 30
the knave with fortune, that she should scratch you,
who of herself is a good lady and would not have
knaves thrive long under her? There's a cardecue for
you: let the justices make you and fortune friends;
I am for other business.
PAROLLES. I beseech your honour to hear me one single
word.
LAFEU. You beg a single penny more: come, you shall
ha't—save your word.
PAROLLES. My name, my good lord, is Parolles.   40
LAFEU. You beg more than one word then. Cox my
passion! give me your hand ... How does your
drum?
PAROLLES. O my good lord, you were the first that
found me.
LAFEU. Was I, in sooth? and I was the first that lost
thee.
PAROLLES. It lies in you, my lord, to bring me in some
grace, for you did bring me out.
LAFEU. Out upon thee, knave! dost thou put upon me 50
at once both the office of God and the devil? one
brings thee in grace and the other brings thee out.
[*trumpets sound*] The king's coming, I know by his
trumpets. Sirrah, inquire further after me. I had talk
of you last night—though you are a fool and a
knave, you shall eat. Go to, follow.   *He goes*
PAROLLES. I praise God for you.   *He follows*

Scene 3: *The palace of Rousillon*

*Flourish. Enter King, Countess, Lafeu, lords, gentlemen,
guards, etc.*

KING. We lost a jewel of her, and our esteem
Was made much poorer by it: but your son,
As mad in folly, lacked the sense to know
Her estimation home.
COUNTESS.   'Tis past, my liege,
And I beseech your majesty to make it
Natural rebellion, done i'th' blaze of youth,
When oil and fire, too strong for reason's force,
O'erbears it and burns on.
KING.   My honoured lady,
I have forgiven and forgotten all,'
Though my revenges were high bent upon him,   10
And watched the time to shoot.
LAFEU.   This I must say—
But first I beg my pardon—the young lord
Did to his majesty, his mother and his lady

Offence of mighty note; but to himself
The greatest wrong of all. He lost a wife
Whose beauty did astonish the survey
Of richest eyes, whose words all ears took captive,
Whose dear perfection hearts that scorned to serve
Humbly called mistress.
KING.   Praising what is lost
Makes the remembrance dear. Well, call him
hither—   20
We are reconciled, and the first view shall kill
All repetition: let him not ask our pardon,
The nature of his great offence is dead,
And deeper than oblivion we do bury
Th'incensing relics of it. Let him approach,
A stranger, no offender; and inform him
So 'tis our will he should.
GENTLEMAN.   I shall, my liege.
                                            He goes
KING. What says he to your daughter? have you spoke?
LAFEU. All that he is hath reference to your highness.
KING. Then shall we have a match. I have letters sent
me,   30
That sets him high in fame.

Bertram enters

LAFEU.   He looks well on't.
KING. I am not a day of season,
For thou mayst see a sunshine and a hail
In me at once: but to the brightest beams
Distracted clouds give way—so stand thou forth,
The time is fair again.
BERTRAM.   My high-repented blames,
Dear sovereign pardon to me.
KING.   All is whole,
Not one word more of the consuméd time.
Let's take the instant by the forward top:
For we are old, and on our quick'st decrees   40
Th'inaudible and noiseless foot of Time
Steals ere we can effect them. You remember
The daughter of this lord?
BERTRAM. Admiringly, my liege. At first
I stuck my choice upon her, ere my heart
Durst make too bold a herald of my tongue:
Where the impression of mine eye infixing,
Contempt his scornful perspective did lend me,
Which warped the line of every other favour,
Scorned a fair colour or expressed it stol'n,   50
Extended or contracted all proportions
To a most hideous object. Thence it came
That she whom all men praised and whom myself,
Since I have lost, have loved, was in mine eye
The dust that did offend.
KING.   Well excused:
That thou didst love her, strikes some scores away
From the great compt: but love that comes too late,
Like a remorseful pardon slowly carried,
To the great sender turns a sour offence,
Crying 'That's good that's gone' ... Our rash faults 60
Make trivial price of serious things we have,
Not knowing them, until we know their grave.
Oft our displeasures, to ourselves unjust,
Destroy our friends and after weep their dust:
Our own love waking cries to see what's done,
While shameful hate sleeps out the afternoon.
Be this sweet Helen's knell, and now forget her.
Send forth your amorous token for fair Maudlin.

The main consents are had, and here we'll stay
To see our widower's second marriage-day.   70
COUNTESS. Which better than the first, O dear heaven,
  bless!
Or, ere they meet, in me, O nature, cesse!
LAFEU. Come on, my son, in whom my house's name
  Must be digested, give a favour from you,
  To sparkle in the spirits of my daughter,
  That she may quickly come.... [*Bertram gives a ring*]
    By my old beard,
  And every hair that's on't, Helen that's dead
  Was a sweet creature: such a ring as this,
  The last that e'er I took her leave at court,
  I saw upon her finger.
BERTRAM.   Hers it was not.   80
KING. Now pray you, let me see it; for mine eye,
  While I was speaking, oft was fastened to't ...
  This ring was mine, and when I gave it Helen
  I bade her, if her fortunes ever stood
  Necessitied to help, that by this token
  I would relieve her. Had you that craft, to reave her
  Of what should stead her most?
BERTRAM.   My gracious sovereign,
  Howe'er it pleases you to take it so,
  The ring was never hers.
COUNTESS.   Son, on my life,
  I have seen her wear it, and she reckoned it   90
  At her life's rate.
LAFEU.   I am sure I saw her wear it.
BERTRAM. You are deceived, my lord, she never saw it:
  In Florence was it from a casement thrown me,
  Wrapped in a paper, which contained the name
  Of her that threw it: noble she was, and thought
  I stood ungaged: but when I had subscribed
  To mine own fortune and informed her fully
  I could not answer in that course of honour
  As she had made the overture, she ceased
  In heavy satisfaction and would never   100
  Receive the ring again.
KING.   Plutus himself,
  That knows the tinct and multiplying med'cine,
  Hath not in nature's mystery more science
  Than I have in this ring. 'Twas mine, 'twas Helen's,
  Whoever gave it you: then, if you know
  That you are well acquainted with yourself,
  Confess 'twas hers, and by what rough enforcement
  You got it from her. She called the saints to surety,
  That she would never put it from her finger,
  Unless she gave it to yourself in bed—   110
  Where you have never come—or sent it us
  Upon her great disaster.
BERTRAM.   She never saw it.
KING. Thou speak'st it falsely, as I love mine
  honour;
  And mak'st conjectural fears to come into me,
  Which I would fain shut out. If it should prove
  That thou art so inhuman—'twill not prove so ...
  And yet I know not—thou didst hate her deadly,
  And she is dead, which nothing but to close
  Her eyes myself could win me to believe,
  More than to see this ring. Take him away.   120
                     Guards seize Bertram
  My fore-past proofs, howe'er the matter fall,
  Shall tax my fears of little vanity,
  Having vainly feared too little. Away with him,
  We'll sift this matter further.

BERTRAM.   If you shall prove
  This ring was ever hers, you shall as easy
  Prove that I husbanded her bed in Florence,
  Where yet she never was.
                  The guards lead him away
KING. I am wrapped in dismal thinkings.

A gentleman enters

GENTLEMAN.   Gracious sovereign,
  Whether I have been to blame or no, I know not,
  Here's a petition from a Florentine,   130
  Who hath for four or five removes come short
  To tender it herself. I undertook it,
  Vanquished thereto by the fair grace and speech
  Of the poor suppliant, who by this I know
  Is here attending: her business looks in her
  With an importing visage, and she told me,
  In a sweet verbal brief, it did concern
  Your highness with herself.
KING [*reads*]. 'Upon his many protestations to marry
  me when his wife was dead, I blush to say it, he won 140
  me. Now is the Count Rousillon a widower, his
  vows are forfeited to me, and my honour's paid to
  him. He stole from Florence, taking no leave, and I
  follow him to his country for justice: grant it me,
  O king! in you it best lies, otherwise a seducer
  flourishes and a poor maid is undone.
                         DIANA CAPULET.'
LAFEU. I will buy me a son-in-law in a fair, and toll
  for this. I'll none of him.
KING. The heavens have thought well on thee, Lafeu, 150
  To bring forth this discov'ry. Seek these suitors ...
                     The gentleman goes
  Go, speedily and bring again the count.
                          Attendants go
  I am afeard the life of Helen, lady,
  Was foully snatched.
COUNTESS.   Now, justice on the doers!

The guards return with Bertram

KING. I wonder, sir, sith wives are monsters to you,
  And that you fly them as you swear them lordship,
  Yet you desire to marry.

The gentleman returns with Widow and Diana

                   What woman's that?
DIANA. I am, my lord, a wretched Florentine,
  Derivéd from the ancient Capulet.
  My suit, as I do understand, you know,   160
  And therefore know how far I may be pitied.
WIDOW. I am her mother, sir, whose age and honour
  Both suffer under this complaint we bring,
  And both shall cease, without your remedy.
KING. Come hither, count—do you know these
  women?
BERTRAM. My lord, I neither can nor will deny
  But that I know them. Do they charge me further?
DIANA. Why do you look so strange upon your wife?
BERTRAM. She's none of mine, my lord.
DIANA.   If you shall marry,
  You give away this hand, and that is mine;   170
  You give away heaven's vows, and those are mine;
  You give away myself, which is known mine;
  For I by vow am so embodied yours,
  That she which marries you must marry me,
  Either both or none.

LAFEU. Your reputation comes too short for my
daughter, you are no husband for her.

BERTRAM. My lord, this is a fond and desp'rate
creature,
Whom sometime I have laughed with: let your
highness
Lay a more noble thought upon mine honour,   180
Than for to think that I would sink it here.

KING. Sir, for my thoughts, you have them ill to
friend
Till your deeds gain them: fairer prove your honour
Than in my thought it lies.

DIANA.   Good my lord,
Ask him upon his oath, if he does think
He had not my virginity.

KING. What say'st thou to her?

BERTRAM.   She's impudent, my lord,
And was a common gamester to the camp.

DIANA. He does me wrong, my lord; if I were so,
He might have bought me at a common price.   190
Do not believe him. O, behold this ring,
Whose high respect and rich validity
Did lack a parallel; yet for all that
He gave it to a commoner o'th' camp,
If I be one.

COUNTESS.   He blushes, and 'tis it!
Of six preceding ancestors, that gem,
Conferred by testament to th' sequent issue,
Hath it been owed and worn. This is his wife,
That ring's a thousand proofs.

KING.   Methought you said
You saw one here in court could witness it.   200

DIANA. I did, my lord, but loath am to produce
So bad an instrument. His name's Parolles.

LAFEU. I saw the man to-day, if man he be.

KING. Find him, and bring him hither.

                     Lafeu goes out

BERTRAM.   What of him?
He's quoted for a most perfidious slave,
With all the spots o'th' world taxed and deboshed;
Whose nature sickens but to speak a truth.
Am I or that or this for what he'll utter,
That will speak any thing?

KING.   She hath that ring of yours.

BERTRAM. I think she has: certain it is I liked her,   210
And boarded her i'th' wanton way of youth:
She knew her distance, and did angle for me,
Madding my eagerness with her restraint—
As all impediments in fancy's course
Are motives of more fancy—and in fine
Her infinite cunning with her modern grace
Subdued me to her rate. She got the ring,
And I had that which any inferior might
At market-price have bought.

DIANA.   I must be patient:
You that turned off a first so noble wife,   220
May justly diet me. I pray you yet—
Since you lack virtue I will lose a husband—
Send for your ring, I will return it home,
And give me mine again.

BERTRAM.   I have it not.

KING. What ring was yours, I pray you?

DIANA.   Sir, much like
The same upon your finger.

KING. Know you this ring? this ring was his of late.

DIANA. And this was it I gave him, being abed.

KING. The story then goes false, you threw it him
Out of a casement?

DIANA.   I have spoke the truth.   230

Lafeu returns with Parolles

BERTRAM. My lord, I do confess, the ring was hers.

KING. You boggle shrewdly, every feather starts
you ...
Is this the man you speak of?

DIANA.   Ay, my lord.

KING. Tell me, sirrah, but tell me true, I charge you,
Not fearing the displeasure of your master—
Which on your just proceeding I'll keep off—
By him and by this woman here what know you?

PAROLLES. So please your majesty, my master hath
been an honourable gentleman: tricks he hath had in
him, which gentlemen have.   240

KING. Come, come, to th' purpose: did he love this
woman?

PAROLLES. Faith, sir, he did love her, but how?

KING. How, I pray you?

PAROLLES. He did love her, sir, as a gentleman loves
a woman.

KING. How is that?

PAROLLES. He loved her, sir, and loved her not.

KING. As thou art a knave, and no knave. What an
equivocal companion is this!   250

PAROLLES. I am a poor man, and at your majesty's
command.

LAFEU. He's a good drum, my lord, but a naughty
orator.

DIANA. Do you know he promised me marriage?

PAROLLES. Faith, I know more than I'll speak.

KING. But wilt thou not speak all thou know'st?

PAROLLES. Yes, so please your majesty ... I did go
between them as I said—but more than that, he
loved her, for indeed he was mad for her, and talked   260
of Satan, and of Limbo, and of Furies, and I know
not what: yet I was in that credit with them at that
time, that I knew of their going to bed, and of other
motions, as promising her marriage, and things
which would derive me ill will to speak of—therefore I will not speak what I know.

KING. Thou hast spoken all already, unless thou canst
say they are married. But thou art too fine in thy
evidence, therefore stand aside....
This ring, you say, was yours?

DIANA.   Ay, my good lord.   270

KING. Where did you buy it? or who gave it you?

DIANA. It was not given me, nor I did not buy it.

KING. Who lent it you?

DIANA.   It was not lent me neither.

KING. Where did you find it then?

DIANA.   I found it not.

KING. If it were yours by none of all these ways,
How could you give it him?

DIANA.   I never gave it him.

LAFEU. This woman's an easy glove, my lord, she goes
off and on at pleasure.

KING. This ring was mine, I gave it his first wife.

DIANA. It might be yours or hers, for aught I know.   280

KING. Take her away, I do not like her now,
To prison with her: and away with him.
Unless thou tell'st me where thou hadst this ring,
Thou diest within this hour.

DIANA.   I'll never tell you.
KING. Take her away.
DIANA.   I'll put in bail, my liege.
KING. I think thee now some common customer.
DIANA [to Lafeu]. By Jove, if ever I knew man, 'twas
  you.
KING. Wherefore hast thou accused him all this while?
DIANA. Because he's guilty, and he is not guilty:
  He knows I am no maid, and he'll swear to't: 290
  I'll swear I am a maid, and he knows not.
  Great king, I am no strumpet, by my life,
  I am either maid, or else this old man's wife.
KING. She does abuse our ears—to prison with her!
DIANA. Good mother, fetch my bail.... [Widow goes]
  Stay, royal sir,
  The jeweller that owes the ring is sent for,
  And he shall surety me. But for this lord,
  Who hath abused me, as he knows himself,
  Though yet he never harmed me, here I quit him.
  He knows himself my bed he hath defiled,   300
  And at that time he got his wife with child:
  Dead though she be, she feels her young one kick:
  So there's my riddle—One that's dead is quick.
  And now behold the meaning.

Widow returns with Helena

KING.   Is there no exorcist
  Beguiles the truer office of mine eyes?
  Is't real that I see?
HELENA.   No, my good lord,
  'Tis but the shadow of a wife you see,
  The name and not the thing.
BERTRAM [kneels].   Both, both. O, pardon!
HELENA. O, my good lord, when I was like this maid,
  I found you wondrous kind. There is your ring,   310
  And, look you, here's your letter: this it says,

'When from my finger you can get this ring,
And are by me with child,' &c. This is done.
Will you be mine, now you are doubly won?
BERTRAM. If she, my liege, can make me know this
  clearly,
  I'll love her dearly, ever, ever dearly.
HELENA. If it appear not plain and prove untrue,
  Deadly divorce step between me and you!
  O, my dear mother, do I see you living?
LAFEU. Mine eyes smell onions, I shall weep anon: 320
  [to Parolles] Good Tom Drum, lend me a handker-
  cher: so, I thank thee. Wait on me home, I'll make
  sport with thee: let thy curtsies alone, they are scurvy
  ones.
KING. Let us from point to point this story know,
  To make the even truth in pleasure flow ...
  [to Diana] If thou be'st yet a fresh uncroppéd flower,
  Choose thou thy husband, and I'll pay thy dower,
  For I can guess that by thy honest aid
  Thou kept'st a wife herself, thyself a maid.   330
  Of that and all the progress, more and less,
  Resolvedly more leisure shall express:
  All yet seems well, and if it end so meet,
  The bitter past, more welcome is the sweet.

A flourish. The King advances to speak the Epilogue

EPILOGUE

The king's a beggar now the play is done.
All is well ended, if this suit be won,
That you express content; which we will pay,
With strife to please you, day exceeding day:
Ours be your patience then, and yours our parts,
Your gentle hands lend us, and take our hearts.
                            They go

Twelfth Night, or What You Will

The scene: Illyria

CHARACTERS IN THE PLAY

ORSINO, *Duke of Illyria*
SEBASTIAN, *brother to Viola*
ANTONIO, *a sea-captain, friend to Sebastian*
Another sea-captain, friend to Viola
VALENTINE } *gentlemen attending on the Duke*
CURIO
SIR TOBY BELCH, *kinsman to Olivia*
SIR ANDREW AGUECHEEK

MALVOLIO, *steward to Olivia*
FABIAN, *a gentleman in the service of Olivia*
FESTE, *fool to Olivia*
OLIVIA, *a rich countess*
VIOLA, *in love with the Duke*
MARIA, *Olivia's gentlewoman (small of stature)*
Lords, priests, sailors, officers, musicians, and other attendants

Twelfth Night, or What You Will

ACT 1
Scene 1: *The Duke's palace*

The Duke Orsino, Curio and Lords; musicians attending

DUKE. If music be the food of love, play on,
Give me excess of it; that, surfeiting,
The appetite may sicken, and so die....
That strain again! it had a dying fall:
O, it came o'er my ear like the sweet south
That breathes upon a bank of violets;
Stealing and giving odour.... Enough, no more!
'Tis not so sweet now as it was before.
O spirit of love, how quick and fresh art thou,
That, notwithstanding thy capacity   10
Receiveth as the sea, nought enters there,
Of what validity and pitch soe'er,
But falls into abatement and low price,
Even in a minute ... So full of shapes is fancy,
That it alone is high fantastical.
CURIO. Will you go hunt, my lord?
DUKE.   What, Curio?
CURIO.   The hart.
DUKE. Why, so I do, the noblest that I have:
O, when mine eyes did see Olivia first,
Methought she purged the air of pestilence;
That instant was I turned into a hart,   20
And my desires, like fell and cruel hounds,
E'er since pursue me....

Valentine enters

                How now? what news from her?
VALENTINE. So please my lord, I might not be
    admitted,
But from her handmaid do return this answer:
The element itself, till seven years hence,
Shall not behold her face at ample view;
But like a cloistress she will veiled walk,
And water once a day her chamber round
With eye-offending brine: all this to season
A brother's dead love, which she would keep fresh   30
And lasting, in her sad remembrance.
DUKE. O, she that hath a heart of that fine frame
To pay this debt of love but to a brother,
How will she love, when the rich golden shaft
Hath killed the flock of all affections else
That live in her; when liver, brain and heart,
These sovereign thrones, are all supplied and filled,
Her sweet perfections, with one self king!
Away before me to sweet beds of flowers—
Love-thoughts lie rich when canopied with bowers. 40
                                    They go

Scene 2: *Near the sea-coast*

Enter Viola, Captain, and sailors

VIOLA. What country, friends, is this?
CAPTAIN. This is Illyria, lady.
VIOLA. And what should I do in Illyria?
My brother he is in Elysium.

Perchance he is not drowned: what think you,
    sailors?
CAPTAIN. It is perchance that you yourself were saved.
VIOLA. O my poor brother! and so perchance may he
    be.
CAPTAIN. True, madam, and to comfort you with
    chance,
Assure yourself, after our ship did split,
When you and those poor number saved with you   10
Hung on our driving boat ... I saw your brother,
Most provident in peril, bind himself—
Courage and hope both teaching him the practice—
To a strong mast that lived upon the sea;
Where, like Arion on the dolphin's back,
I saw him hold acquaintance with the waves
So long as I could see.
VIOLA.   For saying so, there's gold:
Mine own escape unfoldeth to my hope,
Whereto thy speech serves for authority,
The like of him. Know'st thou this country?   20
CAPTAIN. Ay, madam, well, for I was bred and born
Not three hours' travel from this very place.
VIOLA. Who governs here?
CAPTAIN. A noble duke, in nature as in name.
VIOLA. What is his name?
CAPTAIN. Orsino.
VIOLA. Orsino: I have heard my father name him.
He was a bachelor then.
CAPTAIN. And so is now, or was so very late:
For but a month ago I went from hence,   30
And then 'twas fresh in murmur—as, you know,
What great ones do the less will prattle of—
That he did seek the love of fair Olivia.
VIOLA. What's she?
CAPTAIN. A virtuous maid, the daughter of a count
That died some twelvemonth since—then leaving
    her
In the protection of his son, her brother,
Who shortly also died: for whose dear love,
They say, she hath abjured the company
And sight of men.
VIOLA.   O, that I served that lady,   40
And might not be delivered to the world,
Till I had made mine own occasion mellow,
What my estate is.
CAPTAIN.   That were hard to compass,
Because she will admit no kind of suit,
No, not the duke's.
VIOLA. There is a fair behaviour in thee, captain,
And though that nature with a beauteous wall
Doth oft close in pollution, yet of thee
I will believe thou hast a mind that suits
With this thy fair and outward character.   50
I prithee, and I'll pay thee bounteously,
Conceal me what I am, and be my aid
For such disguise as haply shall become
The form of my intent. I'll serve this duke,
Thou shalt present me as an eunuch to him,
It may be worth thy pains: for I can sing,
And speak to him in many sorts of music,

That will allow me very worth his service.
What else may hap to time I will commit,
Only shape thou thy silence to my wit. 60
CAPTAIN. Be you his eunuch, and your mute I'll be,
When my tongue blabs, then let mine eyes not see!
VIOLA. I thank thee: lead me on. *They go*

Scene 3: *Olivia's house*

Enter Sir Toby Belch and Maria

SIR TOBY. What a plague means my niece, to take the death of her brother thus? I am sure care's an enemy to life.
MARIA. By my troth, Sir Toby, you must come in earlier o' nights: your cousin, my lady, takes great exceptions to your ill hours.
SIR TOBY. Why, let her except before excepted.
MARIA. Ay, but you must confine yourself within the modest limits of order.
SIR TOBY. Confine? I'll confine myself no finer than I 10 am: these clothes are good enough to drink in, and so be these boots too: an they be not, let them hang themselves in their own straps.
MARIA. That quaffing and drinking will undo you: I heard my lady talk of it yesterday: and of a foolish knight, that you brought in one night here, to be her wooer.
SIR TOBY. Who? Sir Andrew Aguecheek?
MARIA. Ay, he.
SIR TOBY. He's as tall a man as any's in Illyria. 20
MARIA. What's that to th' purpose?
SIR TOBY. Why, he has three thousand ducats a year.
MARIA. Ay, but he'll have but a year in all these ducats; he's a very fool and a prodigal.
SIR TOBY. Fie, that you'll say so! he plays o'th' viol-de-gamboys, and speaks three or four languages word for word without book, and hath all the good gifts of nature.
MARIA. He hath, indeed, almost natural: for, besides that he's a fool, he's a great quarreller: and but that 30 he hath the gift of a coward to allay the gust he hath in quarrelling, 'tis thought among the prudent he would quickly have the gift of a grave.
SIR TOBY. By this hand, they are scoundrels and sub-stractors that say so of him. Who are they?
MARIA. They that add, moreover, he's drunk nightly in your company.
SIR TOBY. With drinking healths to my niece: I'll drink to her as long as there is a passage in my throat and drink in Illyria: he's a coward and a coystrill that will 40 not drink to my niece, till his brains turn o'th' toe like a parish-top.... [*he seizes her about the waist and they dance a turn*] What, wench! Castiliano vulgo; for here comes Sir Andrew Agueface.

Sir Andrew Aguecheek enters

SIR ANDREW. Sir Toby Belch! how now, Sir Toby Belch?
SIR TOBY. Sweet Sir Andrew!
SIR ANDREW. Bless you, fair shrew.
MARIA And you too, sir!
SIR TOBY. Accost, Sir Andrew, accost. 50
SIR ANDREW. What's that?
SIR TOBY. My niece's chambermaid.
SIR ANDREW. Good Mistress Accost, I desire better acquaintance.

MARIA. My name is Mary, sir.
SIR ANDREW. Good Mistress Mary Accost,—
SIR TOBY. You mistake, knight: 'accost' is front her, board her, woo her, assail her.
SIR ANDREW. By my troth, I would not undertake her in this company. Is that the meaning of 'accost'? 60
MARIA. Fare you well, gentlemen.
SIR TOBY. An thou let part so, Sir Andrew, would thou mightst never draw sword again.
SIR ANDREW. An you part so, mistress, I would I might never draw sword again ... Fair lady, do you think you have fools in hand?
MARIA. Sir, I have not you by th'hand.
SIR ANDREW. Marry, but you shall have—and here's my hand.
MARIA. Now, sir, 'thought is free' ... I pray you, bring 70 your hand to th' buttery-bar, and let it drink.
SIR ANDREW. Wherefore, sweet-heart? what's your metaphor?
MARIA. It's dry, sir.
SIR ANDREW. Why, I think so; I am not such an ass, but I can keep my hand dry. But what's your jest?
MARIA. A dry jest, sir.
SIR ANDREW. Are you full of them?
MARIA. Ay, sir; I have them at my fingers' ends: marry, now I let go your hand, I am barren. 80
She goes
SIR TOBY. O knight, thou lack'st a cup of canary: when did I see thee so put down?
SIR ANDREW. Never in your life, I think, unless you see canary put me down ... Methinks sometimes I have no more wit than a Christian or an ordinary man has: but I am a great eater of beef and I believe that does harm to my wit.
SIR TOBY. No question.
SIR ANDREW. An I thought that, I'd forswear it. I'll ride home to-morrow, Sir Toby. 90
SIR TOBY. Pourquoi, my dear knight?
SIR ANDREW. What is 'pourquoi'? do or not do? I would I had bestowed that time in the tongues, that I have in fencing, dancing and bear-baiting: O, had I but followed the arts!
SIR TOBY. Then hadst thou had an excellent head of hair.
SIR ANDREW. Why, would that have mended my hair?
SIR TOBY. Past question, for thou seest it will not curl by nature. 100
SIR ANDREW. But it becomes me well enough, does't not?
SIR TOBY. Excellent! it hangs like flax on a distaff; and I hope to see a housewife take thee between her legs and spin it off.
SIR ANDREW. Faith, I'll home to-morrow, Sir Toby. Your niece will not be seen, or if she be it's four to one she'll none of me: the count himself here hard by woos her.
SIR TOBY. She'll none o'th' count—she'll not match 110 above her degree, neither in estate, years, nor wit; I have heard her swear't. Tut, there's life in't, man.
SIR ANDREW. I'll stay a month longer.... I am a fellow o'th' strangest mind i'th' world: I delight in masques and revels sometimes altogether.
SIR TOBY. Art thou good at these kickshawses, knight?
SIR ANDREW. As any man in Illyria, whatsoever he be, under the degree of my betters, and yet I will not compare with an old man.

SIR TOBY. What is thy excellence in a galliard, knight? 120
SIR ANDREW. Faith, I can cut a caper.
SIR TOBY. And I can cut the mutton to't.
SIR ANDREW. And I think I have the back-trick simply as strong as any man in Illyria.
SIR TOBY. Wherefore are these things hid? wherefore have these gifts a curtain before 'em? are they like to take dust, like Mistress Mall's picture? why dost thou not go to church in a galliard and come home in a coranto? My very walk should be a jig; I would not so much as make water but in a sink-a-pace. 130 What dost thou mean? Is it a world to hide virtues in? I did think, by the excellent constitution of thy leg, it was formed under the star of a galliard.
SIR ANDREW. Ay, 'tis strong, and it does indifferent well in a dun-coloured stock. Shall we set about some revels?
SIR TOBY. What shall we do else? were we not born under Taurus?
SIR ANDREW. Taurus! That's sides and heart.
SIR TOBY. No, sir, it is legs and thighs ... Let me see 140 thee caper.... Ha! higher: ha, ha! excellent!

They go

Scene 4: *The Duke's palace*

Enter Valentine, and Viola in man's attire

VALENTINE. If the duke continue these favours towards you, Cesario, you are like to be much advanced. He hath known you but three days, and already you are no stranger.
VIOLA. You either fear his humour or my negligence, that you call in question the continuance of his love. Is he inconstant, sir, in his favours?
VALENTINE. No, believe me.
VIOLA. I thank you. Here comes the count.

Enter Duke, Curio and attendants

DUKE. Who saw Cesario, ho! 10
VIOLA. On your attendance, my lord, here.
DUKE. Stand you awhile aloof.... Cesario,
Thou know'st no less but all: I have unclasped
To thee the book even of my secret soul.
Therefore, good youth, address thy gait unto her,
Be not denied access, stand at her doors,
And tell them, there thy fixèd foot shall grow
Till thou have audience.
VIOLA.   Sure, my noble lord,
If she be so abandoned to her sorrow
As it is spoke, she never will admit me. 20
DUKE. Be clamorous and leap all civil bounds
Rather than make unprofited return.
VIOLA. Say I do speak with her, my lord, what then?
DUKE. O, then unfold the passion of my love,
Surprise her with discourse of my dear faith:
It shall become thee well to act my woes;
She will attend it better in thy youth
Than in a nuncio's of more grave aspect.
VIOLA. I think not so, my lord.
DUKE.   Dear lad, believe it;
For they shall yet belie thy happy years, 30
That say thou art a man: Diana's lip
Is not more smooth and rubious; thy small pipe
Is as the maiden's organ, shrill and sound—
And all is semblative a woman's part.
I know thy constellation is right apt

For this affair ... Some four or five attend him,
All if you will; for I myself am best
When least in company ... Prosper well in this,
And thou shalt live as freely as thy lord,
To call his fortunes thine.
VIOLA.   I'll do my best, 40
To woo your lady ... [*aside*] Yet, a barful strife!
Whoe'er I woo, myself would be his wife.

They go

Scene 5: *Olivia's house*

Enter Maria and Clown

MARIA. Nay, either tell me where thou hast been, or I will not open my lips so wide as a bristle may enter in way of thy excuse: my lady will hang thee for thy absence.
CLOWN. Let her hang me: he that is well hanged in this world needs to fear no colours.
MARIA. Make that good.
CLOWN. He shall see none to fear.
MARIA. A good lenten answer: I can tell thee where that saying was born, of 'I fear no colours.' 10
CLOWN. Where, good Mistress Mary?
MARIA. In the wars—and that may you be bold to say in your foolery.
CLOWN. Well, God give them wisdom that have it; and those that are fools, let them use their talents.
MARIA. Yet you will be hanged for being so long absent; or to be turned away, is not that as good as a hanging to you?
CLOWN. Many a good hanging prevents a bad marriage; and, for turning away, let summer bear it out. 20
MARIA. You are resolute, then?
CLOWN. Not so neither, but I am resolved on two points—
MARIA. That if one break, the other will hold; or if both break, your gaskins fall.
CLOWN. Apt in good faith, very apt ... [*she turns to go*] Well, go thy way—if Sir Toby would leave drinking, thou wert as witty a piece of Eve's flesh as any in Illyria.
MARIA. Peace, you rogue, no more o'that: here comes 30 my lady: make your excuse wisely, you were best.

She goes

The Lady Olivia enters, Malvolio and attendants following

CLOWN. Wit, an't be thy will, put me into good fooling! Those wits that think they have thee, do very oft prove fools; and I, that am sure I lack thee, may pass for a wise man. For what says Quinapalus? 'Better a witty fool than a foolish wit.' God bless thee, lady!
OLIVIA. Take the fool away.
CLOWN. Do you not hear, fellows? Take away the lady. 40
OLIVIA. Go to, y'are a dry fool: I'll no more of you: besides, you grow dishonest.
CLOWN. Two faults, madonna, that drink and good counsel will amend: for give the dry fool drink, then is the fool not dry: bid the dishonest man mend himself; if he mend, he is no longer dishonest; if he cannot, let the botcher mend him: any thing that's mended is but patched: virtue that transgresses, is but patched with sin, and sin that amends is but patched with virtue.... If that this simple syllogism 50

will serve, so: if it will not, what remedy? As there
is no true cuckold but calamity, so beauty's a flower:
the lady bade take away the fool, therefore I say
again, take her away.

OLIVIA. Sir, I bade them take away you.

CLOWN. Misprision in the highest degree! Lady,
'Cucullus non facit monachum'; that's as much to
say as I wear not motley in my brain ... Good
madonna, give me leave to prove you a fool.

OLIVIA. Can you do it?   60

CLOWN. Dexteriously, good madonna.

OLIVIA. Make your proof.

CLOWN. I must catechize you for it, madonna. Good
my mouse of virtue, answer me.

OLIVIA. Well, sir, for want of other idleness, I'll bide
your proof.

CLOWN. Good madonna, why mourn'st thou?

OLIVIA. Good fool, for my brother's death.

CLOWN. I think his soul is in hell, madonna.

OLIVIA. I know his soul is in heaven, fool.   70

CLOWN. The more fool, madonna, to mourn for your
brother's soul, being in heaven.... Take away the
fool, gentlemen.

OLIVIA. What think you of this fool, Malvolio? doth
he not mend?

MALVOLIO. Yes, and shall do, till the pangs of death
shake him: infirmity, that decays the wise, doth ever
make the better fool.

CLOWN. God send you, sir, a speedy infirmity, for the
better increasing your folly! Sir Toby will be sworn 80
that I am no fox, but he will not pass his word for
two pence that you are no fool.

OLIVIA. How say you to that, Malvolio?

MALVOLIO. I marvel you ladyship takes delight in such
a barren rascal: I saw him put down the other day
with an ordinary fool that has no more brain than a
stone. Look you now, he's out of his guard already;
unless you laugh and minister occasion to him, he is
gagged. I protest, I take these wise men, that crow
so at these set kind of fools, no better than the fools' 90
zanies.

OLIVIA. O, you are sick of self-love, Malvolio, and
taste with a distempered appetite. To be generous,
guiltless, and of free disposition, is to take those
things for bird-bolts that you deem cannon-bullets:
there is no slander in an allowed fool, though he do
nothing but rail; nor no railing in a known discreet
man, though he do nothing but reprove.

CLOWN. Now Mercury endue thee with leasing, for
thou speakest well of fools!   100

Maria returns

MARIA. Madam, there is at the gate a young gentleman
much desires to speak with you.

OLIVIA. From the Count Orsino, is it?

MARIA. I know not, madam—'tis a fair young man,
and well attended.

OLIVIA. Who of my people hold him in delay?

MARIA. Sir Toby, madam, your kinsman.

OLIVIA. Fetch him off, I pray you! he speaks nothing
but madman: fie on him.... [*Maria goes*] Go you,
Malvolio: if it be a suit from the count, I am sick, 110
or not at home ... what you will, to dismiss it.
[*Malvolio goes*] Now you see, sir, how your fooling
grows old, and people dislike it.

CLOWN. Thou hast spoke for us, madonna, as if thy

eldest son should be a fool: whose skull Jove cram
with brains! for—here he comes—one of thy kin,
has a most weak pia mater.

Sir Toby Belch enters

OLIVIA. By mine honour, half drunk.... What is he at
the gate, cousin?

SIR TOBY. A gentleman.   120

OLIVIA. A gentleman? What gentleman?

SIR TOBY. 'Tis a gentleman here ... A plague o'these
pickle-herring.... How now, sot!

CLOWN. Good Sir Toby—

OLIVIA. Cousin, cousin, how have you come so early
by this lethargy?

SIR TOBY. Lechery! I defy lechery ... There's one at
the gate.

OLIVIA. Ay, marry, what is he?

SIR TOBY. Let him be the devil, an he will, I care not: 130
give me 'faith,' say I.... Well, it's all one.

                                                 He goes

OLIVIA. What's a drunken man like, fool?

CLOWN. Like a drowned man, a fool, and a mad man:
one draught above heat makes him a fool, the second
mads him, and a third drowns him.

OLIVIA. Go thou and seek the crowner, and let him
sit o' my coz; for he's in the third degree of drink:
he's drowned: go look after him.

CLOWN. He is but mad yet, madonna, and the fool
shall look to the madman.   *He follows Sir Toby* 140

Malvolio returns

MALVOLIO. Madam, yon young fellow swears he will
speak with you. I told him you were sick, he takes
on him to understand so much, and therefore comes
to speak with you. I told him you were asleep, he
seems to have a foreknowledge of that too, and
therefore comes to speak with you. What is to be
said to him, lady? he's fortified against any denial.

OLIVIA. Tell him he shall not speak with me.

MALVOLIO. Has been told so; and he says he'll stand at
your door like a sheriff's post, and be the supporter 150
to a bench, but he'll speak with you.

OLIVIA. What kind o' man is he?

MALVOLIO. Why, of mankind.

OLIVIA. What manner of man?

MALVOLIO. Of very ill manner; he'll speak with you,
will you, or no.

OLIVIA. Of what personage and years is he?

MALVOLIO. Not yet old enough for a man, nor young
enough for a boy; as a squash is before 'tis a peascod,
or a codling when 'tis almost an apple: 'tis with him 160
in standing water between boy and man. He is very
well-favoured and he speaks very shrewishly; one
would think his mother's milk were scarce out of
him.

OLIVIA. Let him approach ... Call in my gentlewoman.

MALVOLIO. Gentlewoman, my lady calls.

                                             He departs

Maria returns

OLIVIA. Give me my veil: come, throw it o'er my
face—
We'll once more hear Orsino's embassy.

Viola (as Cesario) enters

VIOLA. The honourable lady of the house, which is 170
she?

OLIVIA. Speak to me, I shall answer for her: your will?

VIOLA. Most radiant, exquisite, and unmatchable
beauty!—I pray you, tell me if this be the lady of
the house, for I never saw her. I would be loath to
cast away my speech; for besides that it is excellently
well penned, I have taken great pains to con it.
Good beauties, let me sustain no scorn; I am very
comptible, even to the least sinister usage.

OLIVIA. Whence came you, sir?   180

VIOLA. I can say little more than I have studied, and
that question's out of my part. Good gentle one,
give me modest assurance if you be the lady of the
house, that I may proceed in my speech.

OLIVIA. Are you a comedian?

VIOLA. No, my profound heart: and yet, by the very
fangs of malice I swear, I am not that I play. Are
you the lady of the house?

OLIVIA. If I do not usurp myself, I am.

VIOLA. Most certain, if you are she, you do usurp your- 190
self; for what is yours to bestow, is not yours to
reserve. But this is from my commission: I will on
with my speech in your praise, and then show you
the heart of my message.

OLIVIA. Come to what is important in't: I forgive you
the praise.

VIOLA. Alas, I took great pains to study it, and 'tis
poetical.

OLIVIA. It is the more like to be feigned, I pray you
keep it in. I heard you were saucy at my gates, and 200
allowed your approach rather to wonder at you than
to hear you. If you be not mad, be gone; if you
have reason, be brief: 'tis not that time of moon with
me to make one in so skipping a dialogue.

MARIA. Will you hoist sail, sir? here lies your way.

VIOLA. No, good swabber; I am to hull here a little
longer.... Some mollification for your giant, sweet
lady!

OLIVIA. Tell me your mind.

VIOLA. I am a messenger.   210

OLIVIA. Sure, you have some hideous matter to deliver, when the courtesy of it is so fearful. Speak
your office.

VIOLA. It alone concerns your ear. I bring no overture
of war, no taxation of homage; I hold the olive in
my hand: my words are as full of peace as matter.

OLIVIA. Yet you began rudely. What are you? what
would you?

VIOLA. The rudeness that hath appeared in me have I
learned from my entertainment. What I am, and 220
what I would, are as secret as maidenhead: to your
ears, divinity; to any other's, profanation.

OLIVIA. Give us the place alone: we will hear this
divinity.... [Maria and attendants withdraw] Now,
sir, what is your text?

VIOLA. Most sweet lady,—

OLIVIA. A comfortable doctrine, and much may be
said of it. Where lies your text?

VIOLA. In Orsino's bosom.

OLIVIA. In his bosom! In what chapter of his bosom? 230

VIOLA. To answer by the method, in the first of his
heart.

OLIVIA. O, I have read it; it is heresy. Have you no
more to say?

VIOLA. Good madam, let me see your face.

OLIVIA. Have you any commission from your lord to
negotiate with my face? you are now out of your
text: but we will draw the curtain, and show you
the picture.... [she unveils] Look you, sir, such a one
I was—this present! Is't not well done?   240

VIOLA. Excellently done, if God did all.

OLIVIA. 'Tis in grain, sir, 'twill endure wind and
weather.

VIOLA. 'Tis beauty truly blent, whose red and white
Nature's own sweet and cunning hand laid on:
Lady, you are the cruell'st she alive,
If you will lead these graces to the grave,
And leave the world no copy.

OLIVIA. O, sir, I will not be so hard-hearted; I will
give out divers schedules of my beauty: it shall be 250
inventoried, and every particle and utensil labelled
to my will: as, Item, Two lips indifferent red; Item,
Two grey eyes with lids to them; Item, One neck,
one chin, and so forth. Were you sent hither to praise
me?

VIOLA. I see you what you are, you are too proud;
But, if you were the devil, you are fair . . .
My lord and master loves you; O, such love
Could be but recompensed, though you were
crowned
The nonpareil of beauty!

OLIVIA.   How does he love me?   260

VIOLA. With adorations, fertile tears,
With groans that thunder love, with sighs of fire.

OLIVIA. Your lord does know my mind, I cannot love
him:
Yet I suppose him virtuous, know him noble,
Of great estate, of fresh and stainless youth;
In voices well divulged, free, learned and valiant,
And in dimension and the shape of nature
A gracious person: but yet I cannot love him;
He might have took his answer long ago.

VIOLA. If I did love you in my master's flame,   270
With such a suff'ring, such a deadly life,
In your denial I would find no sense,
I would not understand it.

OLIVIA.   Why, what would you?

VIOLA. Make me a willow cabin at your gate,
And call upon my soul within the house,
Write loyal cantons of contemnèd love,
And sing them loud even in the dead of night;
Holla your name to the reverberate hills,
And make the babbling gossip of the air
Cry out 'Olivia!' O, you should not rest   280
Between the elements of air and earth,
But you should pity me.

OLIVIA.   You might do much:
What is your parentage?

VIOLA. Above my fortunes, yet my state is well:
I am a gentleman.

OLIVIA.   Get you to your lord;
I cannot love him: let him send no more,
Unless—perchance—you come to me again,
To tell me how he takes it . . . Fare you well:
I thank you for your pains: spend this for me.

VIOLA. I am no fee'd post, lady; keep your purse.   290
My master, not myself, lacks recompense.
Love make his heart of flint that you shall love,
And let your fervour like my master's be
Placed in contempt! Farewell, fair cruelty.

                                          She goes

OLIVIA. 'What is your parentage?'
'Above my fortunes, yet my state is well:
I am a gentleman'.... I'll be sworn thou art!
Thy tongue, thy face, thy limbs, actions, and spirit,
Do give thee five-fold blazon ... Not too fast: soft!
    soft!
Unless the master were the man ... How now!   300
Even so quickly may one catch the plague?
Methinks I feel this youth's perfections
With an invisible and subtle stealth
To creep in at mine eyes.... Well, let it be....
What, ho, Malvolio!

Malvolio returns

MALVOLIO.   Here, madam, at your service.
OLIVIA. Run after that same peevish messenger,
The county's man: he left this ring behind him,
Would I or not; tell him I'll none of it.
Desire him not to flatter with his lord,
Nor hold him up with hopes—I am not for him: 310
If that the youth will come this way to-morrow,
I'll give him reasons for't ... Hie thee, Malvolio.
MALVOLIO. Madam, I will.   *He goes*
OLIVIA. I do I know not what, and fear to find
Mine eye too great a flatterer for my mind ...
Fate, show thy force—ourselves we do not owe—
What is decreed, must be; and be this so!
                                        She goes

ACT 2
Scene 1: *Antonio's house*

Antonio and Sebastian

ANTONIO. Will you stay no longer? nor will you not
that I go with you?
SEBASTIAN. By your patience, no: my stars shine darkly
over me; the malignancy of my fate might perhaps
distemper yours; therefore I shall crave of you your
leave that I may bear my evils alone: it were a bad
recompense for your love, to lay any of them on
you.
ANTONIO. Let me yet know of you whither you are
bound.   10
SEBASTIAN. No, sooth, sir: my determinate voyage is
mere extravagancy. But I perceive in you so excellent a touch of modesty, that you will not extort
from me what I am willing to keep in; therefore it
charges me in manners the rather to express myself
... You must know of me then, Antonio, my name
is Sebastian, which I called Roderigo. My father was
that Sebastian of Messaline, whom I know you have
heard of. He left behind him myself and a sister,
both born in an hour: if the heavens had been   20
pleased, would we had so ended! But you, sir,
altered that, for some hour before you took me
from the breach of the sea was my sister drowned.
ANTONIO. Alas, the day!
SEBASTIAN. A lady, sir, though it was said she much
resembled me, was yet of many accounted beautiful:
but, though I could not with such estimable wonder
overfar believe that, yet thus far I will boldly publish
her—she bore a mind that envy could not but call
fair ... She is drowned already, sir, with salt water,   30
though I seem to drown her remembrance again
with more.

ANTONIO. Pardon me, sir, your bad entertainment.
SEBASTIAN. O, good Antonio, forgive me your
trouble.
ANTONIO. If you will not murder me for my love, let
me be your servant.
SEBASTIAN. If you will not undo what you have done,
that is, kill him whom you have recovered, desire it
not. Fare ye well at once. My bosom is full of kind-   40
ness, and I am yet so near the manners of my
mother, that upon the least occasion more mine eyes
will tell tales of me ... I am bound to the Count
Orsino's court—farewell!   *He goes*
ANTONIO. The gentleness of all the gods go with thee!
I have many enemies in Orsino's court,
Else would I very shortly see thee there:
But, come what may, I do adore thee so,
That danger shall seem sport, and I will go.

Scene 2: *A street near Olivia's house*

Viola approaches, Malvolio following after

MALVOLIO. Were not you e'en now with the Countess
Olivia?
VIOLA. Even now, sir. On a moderate pace I have
since arrived but hither.
MALVOLIO. She returns this ring to you, sir; you might
have saved me my pains, to have taken it away yourself. She adds moreover, that you should put your
lord into a desperate assurance she will none of him:
and one thing more, that you be never so hardy to
come again in his affairs, unless it be to report your   10
lord's taking of this ... Receive it so.
VIOLA. She took the ring of me ... I'll none of it.
MALVOLIO. Come, sir, you peevishly threw it to her;
and her will is, it should be so returned: if it be
worth stooping for, there it lies in your eye; if not,
be it his that finds it.   *He goes*
VIOLA. I left no ring with her: what means this lady?
Fortune forbid my outside have not charmed her!
She made good view of me, indeed so much,
That as methought her eyes had lost her tongue,   20
For she did speak in starts distractedly....
She loves me, sure—the cunning of her passion
Invites me in this churlish messenger ...
None of my lord's ring! why, he sent her none ...
I am the man—if it be so, as 'tis,
Poor lady, she were better love a dream ...
Disguise, I see thou art a wickedness,
Wherein the pregnant enemy does much.
How easy is it for the proper-false
In women's waxen hearts to set their forms!   30
Alas, our frailty is the cause, not we,
For such as we are made of, such we be ...
How will this fadge? My master loves her dearly,
And I (poor monster!) fond as much on him:
And she, mistaken, seems to dote on me:
What will become of this? As I am man,
My state is desperate for my master's love;
As I am woman—now alas the day!—
What thriftless sighs shall poor Olivia breathe?
O time, thou must untangle this, not I,   40
It is too hard a knot for me t'untie.   *She goes*

Scene 3: *Olivia's house*

Enter Sir Toby Belch and Sir Andrew Aguecheek

SIR TOBY. Approach, Sir Andrew: not to be a-bed after

midnight is to be up betimes; and 'diluculo surgere,' thou know'st,—

SIR ANDREW. Nay, by my troth, I know not: but I know, to be up late is to be up late.

SIR TOBY. A false conclusion: I hate it as an unfilled can. To be up after midnight and to go to bed then, is early; so that to go to bed after midnight is to go to bed betimes. Does not our life consist of the four elements? 10

SIR ANDREW. Faith, so they say—but I think it rather consists of eating and drinking.

SIR TOBY. Th'art a scholar; let us therefore eat and drink. Marian, I say! a stoup of wine!

The Clown comes in

SIR ANDREW. Here comes the fool, i'faith.

CLOWN. How now, my hearts! Did you never see the picture of 'we three'?

SIR TOBY. Welcome, ass. Now let's have a catch.

SIR ANDREW. By my troth, the fool has an excellent breast. I had rather than forty shillings I had such a 20 leg, and so sweet a breath to sing, as the fool has. In sooth, thou wast in very gracious fooling last night, when thou spok'st of Pigrogromitus, of the Vapians passing the equinoctial of Queubus; 'twas very good, i'faith ... I sent thee sixpence for thy leman—hadst it?

CLOWN. I did impetticoat thy gratillity: for Malvolio's nose is no whipstock: my lady has a white hand, and the Myrmidons are no bottle-ale houses.

SIR ANDREW. Excellent! why, this is the best fooling, 30 when all is done. Now, a song.

SIR TOBY. Come on, there is sixpence for you. Let's have a song.

SIR ANDREW. There's a testril of me too: if one knight give a—

CLOWN. Would you have a love-song, or a song of good life?

SIR TOBY. A love-song, a love-song.

SIR ANDREW. Ay, ay. I care not for good life.

CLOWN [*sings*].
　　O mistress mine, where are you roaming? 40
　　O, stay and hear, your true love's coming,
　　　　That can sing both high and low.
　　Trip no further pretty sweeting:
　　Journeys end in lovers meeting,
　　　　Every wise man's son doth know.

SIR ANDREW. Excellent good, i'faith!

SIR TOBY. Good, good.

CLOWN [*sings*].
　　What is love, 'tis not hereafter,
　　Present mirth hath present laughter:
　　　　What's to come is still unsure. 50
　　In delay there lies no plenty,
　　Then come kiss me, sweet and twenty:
　　　　Youth's a stuff will not endure.

SIR ANDREW. A mellifluous voice, as I am true knight.

SIR TOBY. A contagious breath.

SIR ANDREW. Very sweet and contagious, i'faith.

SIR TOBY. To hear by the nose, it is dulcet in contagion.... But shall we make the welkin dance indeed? Shall we rouse the night-owl in a catch, that will draw three souls out of one weaver? shall we 60 do that?

SIR ANDREW. An you love me, let's do't: I am dog at a catch.

CLOWN. By'r lady, sir, and some dogs will catch well.

SIR ANDREW. Most certain ... Let our catch be, 'Thou knave.'

CLOWN. 'Hold thy peace, thou knave,' knight? I shall be constrained in't to call thee knave, knight.

SIR ANDREW. 'Tis not the first time I have constrained one to call me knave. Begin, fool; it begins, 'Hold 70 thy peace.'

CLOWN. I shall never begin if I hold my peace.

SIR ANDREW. Good, i'faith! Come, begin.

They sing the catch

Maria enters

MARIA. What a caterwauling do you keep here! If my lady have not called up her steward Malvolio and bid him turn you out of doors, never trust me.

SIR TOBY. 'My lady''s a Cataian, we are politicians, Malvolio's a Peg-a-Ramsey, and

[*sings*]　'Three merry men be we.'

Am not I consanguineous? am I not of her blood? 80 Tillyvally! 'lady'!

[*sings*]　'There dwelt a man in Babylon,
　　　　　　Lady, lady!'

CLOWN. Beshrew me, the knight's in admirable fooling.

SIR ANDREW. Ay, he does well enough, if he be disposed, and so do I too; he does it with a better grace, but I do it more natural.

SIR TOBY [*sings*]. 'O' the twelfth day of December,'—

MARIA. For the love o' God, peace. 90

Malvolio enters

MALVOLIO. My masters, are you mad? or what are you? Have you no wit, manners, nor honesty, but to gabble like tinkers at this time of night? Do ye make an ale-house of my lady's house, that ye squeak out your coziers' catches without any mitigation or remorse of voice? Is there no respect of place, persons, nor time in you?

SIR TOBY. We did keep time, sir, in our catches. Sneck up!

MALVOLIO. Sir Toby, I must be round with you. My 100 lady bade me tell you, that, though she harbours you as her kinsman, she's nothing allied to your disorders. If you can separate yourself and your misdemeanours, you are welcome to the house; if not, an it would please you to take leave of her, she is very willing to bid you farewell.

SIR TOBY [*sings*]. Farewell, dear heart, since I must needs be gone.'

MARIA. Nay, good Sir Toby.

CLOWN [*sings*]. 'His eyes do show his days are almost 110 done.'

MALVOLIO. Is't even so?

SIR TOBY [*sings*]. 'But I will never die.'

CLOWN [*sings*]. Sir Toby, there you lie.

MALVOLIO. This is much credit to you.

SIR TOBY [*sings*]. 'Shall I bid him go?'

CLOWN [*sings*]. 'What an if you do?'

SIR TOBY [*sings*]. 'Shall I bid him go, and spare not?'

CLOWN [*sings*]. 'O no, no, no, no, you dare not.'

SIR TOBY [*to Clown*]. Out o' tune, sir! ye lie ... [*to* 120 *Malvolio*] Art any more than a steward? Dost thou think because thou art virtuous, there shall be no more cakes and ale?

CLOWN. Yes, by Saint Anne, and ginger shall be hot i'th' mouth too.

SIR TOBY. Th'art i'th' right.... Go, sir, rub your chain with crumbs.... A stoup of wine, Maria!

MALVOLIO. Mistress Mary, if you prized my lady's favour at any thing more than contempt, you would not give means for this uncivil rule; she shall know 130 of it, by this hand. *He departs*

MARIA. Go shake your ears.

SIR ANDREW. 'Twere as good a deed as to drink when a man's a-hungry, to challenge him the field, and then to break promise with him and make a fool of him.

SIR TOBY. Do't, knight. I'll write thee a challenge; or I'll deliver thy indignation to him by word of mouth.

MARIA. Sweet Sir Toby, be patient for to-night: since 140 the youth of the count's was to-day with my lady, she is much out of quiet. For Monsieur Malvolio, let me alone with him: if I do not gull him into a nayword, and make him a common recreation, do not think I have wit enough to lie straight in my bed: I know I can do it.

SIR TOBY. Possess us, possess us, tell us something of him.

MARIA. Marry, sir, sometimes he is a kind of puritan.

SIR ANDREW. O, if I thought that, I'd beat him like a 150 dog.

SIR TOBY. What, for being a puritan? thy exquisite reason, dear knight?

SIR ANDREW. I have no exquisite reason for't, but I have reason good enough.

MARIA. The devil a puritan that he is, or any thing constantly but a time-pleaser, an affectioned ass, that cons state without book and utters it by great swarths: the best persuaded of himself, so crammed, as he thinks, with excellencies, that it is his ground 160 of faith that all that look on him love him; and on that vice in him will my revenge find notable cause to work.

SIR TOBY. What wilt thou do?

MARIA. I will drop in his way some obscure epistles of love, wherein by the colour of his beard, the shape of his leg, the manner of his gait, the expressure of his eye, forehead, and complexion, he shall find himself most feelingly personated. I can write very like my lady your niece, on a forgotten matter we 170 can hardly make distinction of our hands.

SIR TOBY. Excellent! I smell a device.

SIR ANDREW. I have't in my nose too.

SIR TOBY. He shall think by the letters that thou wilt drop that they come from my niece, and that she's in love with him.

MARIA. My purpose is, indeed, a horse of that colour.

SIR ANDREW. And your horse now would make him an ass.

MARIA. Ass, I doubt not. 180

SIR ANDREW. O, 'twill be admirable.

MARIA. Sport royal, I warrant you: I know my physic will work with him. I will plant you two, and let the fool make a third, where he shall find the letter: observe his construction of it ... For this night, to bed, and dream on the event ... Farewell. *She goes*

SIR TOBY. Good night, Penthesilea.

SIR ANDREW. Before me, she's a good wench.

SIR TOBY. She's a beagle, true-bred, and one that adores me ... what o' that? 190

SIR ANDREW. I was adored once too.

SIR TOBY. Let's to bed, knight.... Thou hadst need send for more money.

SIR ANDREW. If I cannot recover your niece, I am a foul way out.

SIR TOBY. Send for money knight, if thou hast her not i'th'end, call me cut.

SIR ANDREW. If I do not, never trust me, take it how you will.

SIR TOBY. Come, come, I'll go burn some sack, 'tis too 200 late to go to bed now: come knight; come knight. *They go*

Scene 4: *The Duke's palace*

Enter Duke, Viola, Curio and others

DUKE. Give me some music ... Now—good morrow, friends. ...
Now, good Cesario, but that piece of song,
That old and antic song we heard last night:
Methought it did relieve my passion much,
More than light airs and recollected terms
Of these most brisk and giddy-pacéd times.
Come, but one verse.

CURIO. He is not here, so please your lordship, that should sing it.

DUKE. Who was it? 10

CURIO. Feste, the jester, my lord, a fool that the Lady Olivia's father took much delight in. He is about the house.

DUKE. Seek him out, and play the tune the while.
Curio goes; music plays
Come hither, boy—if ever thou shalt love,
In the sweet pangs of it remember me:
For, such as I am all true lovers are,
Unstaid and skittish in all motions else,
Save in the constant image of the creature
That is beloved.... How dost thou like this tune? 20

VIOLA. It gives a very echo to the seat
Where Love is throned.

DUKE. Thou dost speak masterly.
My life upon't, young though thou art, thine eye
Hath stayed upon some favour that it loves:
Hath it not, boy?

VIOLA. A little, by your favour.

DUKE. What kind of woman is't?

VIOLA. Of your complexion.

DUKE. She is not worth thee then. What years, i'faith?

VIOLA. About your years, my lord.

DUKE. Too old, by heaven: let still the woman take
An elder than herself; so wears she to him, 30
So sways she level in her husband's heart:
For, boy, however we do praise ourselves,
Our fancies are more giddy and unfirm,
More longing, wavering, sooner lost and won,
Than women's are.

VIOLA. I think it well, my lord.

DUKE. Then let thy love be younger than thyself,
Or thy affection cannot hold the bent:
For women are as roses, whose fair flower
Being once displayed doth fall that very hour.

VIOLA. And so they are: alas, that they are so; 40
To die, even when they to perfection grow!

Curio re-enters with Clown

DUKE. O fellow, come, the song we had last night ...
Mark it, Cesario, it is old and plain:
The spinsters and the knitters in the sun,
And the free maids that weave their thread with
bones
Do use to chant it; it is silly sooth,
And dallies with the innocence of love,
Like the old age.
CLOWN. Are you ready, sir?
DUKE. Ay, prithee, sing.   *Music* 50
CLOWN [*sings*].
Come away, come away death,
And in sad cypress let me be laid:
    Fly away, fly away breath,
I am slain by a fair cruel maid:
My shroud of white, stuck all with yew,
    O, prepare it!
My part of death no one so true
    Did share it.
Not a flower, not a flower sweet
On my black coffin let there be strown: 60
    Not a friend, not a friend greet
My poor corpse, where my bones shall be
    thrown:
A thousand thousand sighs to save,
    Lay me O where
Sad true lover never find my grave,
    To weep there.
DUKE. There's for thy pains.
CLOWN. No pains, sir, I take pleasure in singing, sir.
DUKE. I'll pay thy pleasure then.
CLOWN. Truly, sir, and pleasure will be paid, one time 70
or another.
DUKE. Give me now leave to leave thee.
CLOWN. Now, the melancholy god protect thee, and
the tailor make thy doublet of changeable taffeta,
for thy mind is a very opal. I would have men of
such constancy put to sea, that their business might
be every thing and their intent every where, for
that's it that always makes a good voyage of
nothing.... Farewell.   *He goes*
DUKE. Let all the rest give place ...
                    Curio and attendants depart
        Once more, Cesario,   80
Get thee to yon same sovereign cruelty:
Tell her, my love, more noble than the world,
Prizes not quantity of dirty lands;
The parts that fortune hath bestowed upon her,
Tell her, I hold as giddily as fortune;
But 'tis that miracle and queen of gems
That nature pranks her in attracts my soul.
VIOLA. But if she cannot love you, sir?
DUKE. I cannot be so answered.
VIOLA.   Sooth, but you must.
Say that some lady, as perhaps there is,   90
Hath for your love as great a pang of heart
As you have for Olivia: you cannot love her;
You tell her so; must she not then be answered?
DUKE. There is no woman's sides
Can bide the beating of so strong a passion
As love doth give my heart: no woman's heart
So big, to hold so much, they lack retention.
Alas, their love may be called appetite—
No motion of the liver, but the palate—

That suffers surfeit, cloyment and revolt;   100
But mine is all as hungry as the sea,
And can digest as much. Make no compare
Between that love a woman can bear me
And that I owe Olivia.
VIOLA.   Ay, but I know—
DUKE. What dost thou know?
VIOLA. Too well what love women to men may owe:
In faith they are as true of heart as we.
My father had a daughter loved a man,
As it might be, perhaps, were I a woman,
I should your lordship.
DUKE.   And what's her history?   110
VIOLA. A blank, my lord: she never told her love,
But let concealment like a worm i'th' bud
Feed on her damask cheek: she pined in thought,
And with a green and yellow melancholy
She sat like Patience on a monument,
Smiling at grief. Was not this love, indeed?
We men may say more, swear more—but indeed
Our shows are more than will; for still we prove
Much in our vows, but little in our love.
DUKE. But died thy sister of her love, my boy?   120
VIOLA. I am all the daughters of my father's house,
And all the brothers too ... and yet I know not....
Sir, shall I to this lady?
DUKE.   Ay, that's the theme.
To her in haste; give her this jewel; say,
My love can give no place, bide no denay.
                            They go

Scene 5: A garden adjoining the house of Olivia

Enter Sir Toby Belch with Sir Andrew Aguecheek

SIR TOBY. Come thy ways, Signior Fabian.
FABIAN. Nay, I'll come: if I lose a scruple of this sport,
let me be boiled to death with melancholy.
SIR TOBY. Wouldst thou not be glad to have the
niggardly rascally sheep-biter come by some notable
shame?
FABIAN. I would exult, man: you know, he brought
me out o'favour with my lady about a bear-baiting
here.
SIR TOBY. To anger him, we'll have the bear again, 10
and we will fool him black and blue—shall we not,
Sir Andrew?
SIR ANDREW. An we do not, it is pity of our lives.

Maria appears

SIR TOBY. Here comes the little villain ... How now,
my metal of India?
MARIA. Get ye all three into the box-tree: Malvolio's
coming down this walk, he has been yonder i'the
sun practising behaviour to his own shadow this half
hour: observe him, for the love of mockery; for I
know this letter will make a contemplative idiot of 20
him. Close, in the name of jesting! [*the men hide in
a box-tree*] Lie thou there [*throws down a letter*] ...
for here comes the trout that must be caught with
tickling.   *She goes within*

Malvolio enters

MALVOLIO. 'Tis but fortune, all is fortune.... Maria
once told me she did affect me, and I have heard
herself come thus near, that should she fancy it
should be one of my complexion.... Besides, she

uses me with a more exalted respect than any one else that follows her.... What should I think on't? 30

SIR TOBY. Here's an overweening rogue!

FABIAN. O, peace! Contemplation makes a rare turkey-cock of him. How he jets under his advanced plumes!

SIR ANDREW. 'Slight, I could so beat the rogue!

FABIAN. Peace, I say.

MALVOLIO. To be Count Malvolio!

SIR TOBY. Ah, rogue!

SIR ANDREW. Pistol him, pistol him.

FABIAN. Peace, peace! 40

MALVOLIO. There is example for't; the lady of the Strachy married the yeoman of the wardrobe.

SIR ANDREW. Fie on him, Jezebel!

FABIAN. O, peace! now he's deeply in: look, how imagination blows him.

MALVOLIO. Having been three months married to her, sitting in my state—

SIR TOBY. O, for a stone-bow, to hit him in the eye!

MALVOLIO. Calling my officers about me, in my branched velvet gown; having come from a day- 50 bed, where I have left Olivia sleeping—

SIR TOBY. Fire and brimstone!

FABIAN. O, peace, peace!

MALVOLIO. And then to have the humour of state: and after a demure travel of regard, telling them I know my place as I would they should do theirs, to ask for my kinsman Toby—

SIR TOBY. Bolts and shackles!

FABIAN. O, peace, peace, peace! now, now.

MALVOLIO. Seven of my people, with an obedient 60 start, make out for him: I frown the while, and perchance wind up my watch, or play with my— some rich jewel ... Toby approaches; curtsies there to me—

SIR TOBY. Shall this fellow live?

FABIAN. Though our silence be drawn from us with cars, yet peace.

MALVOLIO. I extend my hand to him thus; quenching my familiar smile with an austere regard of con- trol— 70

SIR TOBY. And does not 'Toby' take you a blow o'the lips then?

MALVOLIO. Saying, 'Cousin Toby, my fortunes hav- ing cast me on your niece give me this prerogative of speech'—

SIR TOBY. What, what?

MALVOLIO. 'You must amend your drunkenness.'

SIR TOBY. Out, scab!

FABIAN. Nay, patience, or we break the sinews of our plot. 80

MALVOLIO. 'Besides, you waste the treasure of your time with a foolish knight'—

SIR ANDREW. That's me, I warrant you.

MALVOLIO. 'One Sir Andrew'—

SIR ANDREW. I knew 'twas I, for many do call me fool.

MALVOLIO [takes up the letter]. What employment have we here?

FABIAN. Now is the woodcock near the gin.

SIR TOBY. O, peace! and the spirit of humours intimate reading aloud to him! 90

MALVOLIO. By my life, this is my lady's hand: these be her very c's, her u's, and her t's, and thus makes she her great P's. It is, in contempt of question, her hand.

SIR ANDREW. Her c's, her u's, and her t's: why that?

MALVOLIO [reads]. 'To the unknown beloved, this, and my good wishes' ... her very phrases! By your leave, wax. Soft!—and the impressure her Lucrece, with which she uses to seal: 'tis my lady ... To whom should this be? 100

FABIAN. This wins him, liver and all.

MALVOLIO [reads]. 'Jove knows I love:
But who?
Lips, do not move!
No man must know.'
'No man must know'.... What follows? the num- bers altered ... 'No man must know'—if this should be thee, Malvolio!

SIR TOBY. Marry, hang thee, brock!

MALVOLIO [reads].
'I may command where I adore: 110
But silence, like a Lucrece knife,
With bloodless stroke my heart doth gore:
M, O, A, I, doth sway my life.'

FABIAN. A fustian riddle!

SIR TOBY. Excellent wench, say I.

MALVOLIO. 'M, O, A, I, doth sway my life.'—Nay, but first, let me see, let me see, let me see.

FABIAN. What dish o' poison has she dressed him!

SIR TOBY. And with what wing the stallion checks at it! 120

MALVOLIO. 'I may command where I adore' ... Why, she may command me; I serve her, she is my lady.... Why, this is evident to any formal capacity. There is no obstruction in this. And the end: what should that alphabetical position portend? If I could make that resemble something in me! Softly! 'M, O, A, I,'—

SIR TOBY. O, ay, make up that—he is now at a cold scent.

FABIAN. Sowter will cry upon't for all this, though it 130 be as rank as a fox.

MALVOLIO. 'M,'—Malvolio—'M,'—why, that begins my name.

FABIAN. Did not I say he would work it out? the cur is excellent at faults.

MALVOLIO. 'M'—but then there is no consonancy in the sequel that suffers under probation: 'A' should follow, but 'O' does.

FABIAN. And O shall end, I hope.

SIR TOBY. Ay, or I'll cudgel him, and make him cry 140 'O!'

MALVOLIO. And then 'I' comes behind.

FABIAN. Ay, an you had any eye behind you, you might see more detraction at your heels, than for- tunes before you.

MALVOLIO. 'M, O, A, I.' ... This simulation is not as the former: and yet, to crush this a little, it would bow to me, for every one of these letters are in my name. Soft! here follows prose....
[reads] 'If this fall into thy hand, revolve. In my stars 150 I am above thee, but be not afraid of greatness: some are born great, some achieve greatness, and some have greatness thrust upon 'em. Thy Fates open their hands, let thy blood and spirit embrace them; and to inure thyself to what thou art like to be, cast thy humble slough, and appear fresh. Be opposite with a kinsman, surly with servants; let thy tongue tang arguments of state; put thyself into the trick of singularity. She thus advises thee that sighs for thee.

Remember who commended thy yellow stockings, 160
and wished to see thee ever cross-gartered: I say,
remember. Go to, thou art made, if thou desir'st to
be so; if not, let me see thee a steward still, the fellow
of servants, and not worthy to touch Fortune's
fingers. Farewell. She, that would alter services with
thee,   THE FORTUNATE-UNHAPPY.'

Daylight and champian discovers not more: this is
open. I will be proud, I will read politic authors,
I will baffle Sir Toby, I will wash off gross acquaintance, I will be point-devise the very man. I do not 170
now fool myself, to let imagination jade me; for
every reason excites to this, that my lady loves me.
She did commend my yellow stockings of late, she
did praise my leg being cross-gartered, and in this
she manifests herself to my love, and with a kind of
injunction drives me to these habits of her liking. I
thank my stars, I am happy ... I will be strange,
stout, in yellow stockings, and cross-gartered, even
with the swiftness of putting on. Jove, and my stars
be praised! Here is yet a postscript.   180
[reads] 'Thou canst not choose but know who I am.
If thou entertain'st my love, let it appear in thy
smiling, thy smiles become thee well. Therefore in
my presence still smile, dear, O my sweet, I prithee.'
Jove, I thank thee! I will smile, I will do everything
that thou wilt have me.   *He goes within*
FABIAN. I will not give my part of this sport for a
pension of thousands to be paid from the Sophy.
SIR TOBY. I could marry this wench for this device—
SIR ANDREW. So could I too.   190
SIR TOBY. And ask no other dowry with her but such
another jest.
SIR ANDREW. Nor I neither.

Maria comes from the house

FABIAN. Here comes my noble gull-catcher.
SIR TOBY. Wilt thou set thy foot o' my neck?
SIR ANDREW. Or o' mine either?
SIR TOBY. Shall I play my freedom at trey-trip, and
become thy bond-slave?
SIR ANDREW. I'faith or I either?
SIR TOBY. Why, thou hast put him in such a dream, 200
that when the image of it leaves him he must run
mad.
MARIA. Nay, but say true, does it work upon him?
SIR TOBY. Like aqua-vitæ with a midwife.
MARIA. If you will then see the fruits of the sport,
mark his first approach before my lady: he will come
to her in yellow stockings, and 'tis a colour she
abhors, and cross-gartered, a fashion she detests; and
he will smile upon her, which will now be so unsuitable to her disposition, being addicted to a 210
melancholy as she is, that it cannot but turn him
into a notable contempt: if you will see it, follow
me.
SIR TOBY. To the gates of Tartar, thou most excellent
devil of wit!
SIR ANDREW. I'll make one too.   *They enter the house*

ACT 3
Scene 1

Enter Viola and the Clown, with his tabor

VIOLA. Save thee, friend, and thy music: dost thou live
by thy tabor?

CLOWN. No, sir, I live by the church.
VIOLA. Art thou a churchman?
CLOWN. No such matter, sir, I do live by the church:
for I do live at my house, and my house doth stand
by the church.
VIOLA. So thou mayst say the king lies by a beggar, if
a beggar dwell near him: or the church stands by
thy tabor, if thy tabor stand by the church.   10
CLOWN. You have said, sir ... To see this age! A sentence is but a cheveril glove to a good wit—how
quickly the wrong side may be turned outward!
VIOLA. Nay, that's certain; they that dally nicely with
words may quickly make them wanton.
CLOWN. I would therefore my sister had had no name,
sir.
VIOLA. Why, man?
CLOWN. Why, sir, her name's a word, and to dally
with that word might make my sister want-one ... 20
But indeed words are very rascals since bonds dis-
graced them.
VIOLA. Thy reason, man?
CLOWN. Troth, sir, I can yield you none without
words, and words are grown so false I am loath to
prove reason with them.
VIOLA. I warrant thou art a merry fellow and car'st
for nothing.
CLOWN. Not so, sir, I do care for something: but in
my conscience, sir, I do not care for you: if that be 30
to care for nothing, sir, I would it would make you
invisible.
VIOLA. Art not thou the Lady Olivia's fool?
CLOWN. No indeed sir, the Lady Olivia has no folly.
She will keep no fool, sir, till she be married, and
fools are as like husbands as pilchards are to herrings
—the husband's the bigger. I am, indeed, not her
fool, but her corrupter of words.
VIOLA. I saw thee late at the Count Orsino's.
CLOWN. Foolery, sir, does walk about the orb like the 40
sun, it shines every where. I would be sorry, sir, but
the fool should be as oft with your master as with
my mistress: I think I saw your wisdom there.
VIOLA. Nay, an thou pass upon me, I'll no more with
thee. Hold, there's expenses for thee.
CLOWN. Now Jove, in his next commodity of hair,
send thee a beard!
VIOLA. By my troth I'll tell thee, I am almost sick for
one—[aside] though I would not have it grow on
my chin. Is thy lady within?   50
CLOWN. Would not a pair of these have bred, sir?
VIOLA. Yes, being kept together and put to use.
CLOWN. I would play Lord Pandarus of Phrygia, sir,
to bring a Cressida to this Troilus.
VIOLA. I understand you, sir, 'tis well begged.
CLOWN. The matter, I hope, is not great, sir; begging
but a beggar: Cressida was a beggar. My lady is
within, sir. I will conster to them whence you come,
who you are and what you would are out of my
welkin—I might say 'element,' but the word is 60
over-worn.   *He goes within*
VIOLA. This fellow is wise enough to play the fool,
And to do that well craves a kind of wit:
He must observe their mood on whom he jests,
The quality of persons, and the time;
And, like the haggard, check at every feather
That comes before his eye. This is a practice,
As full of labour as a wise man's art:

For folly that he wisely shows is fit;
But wise men, folly-fall'n, quite taint their wit.   70

Sir Toby Belch and Sir Andrew Aguecheek enter

SIR TOBY. Save you, gentleman.
VIOLA. And you, sir.
SIR ANDREW. Dieu vous garde, monsieur.
VIOLA. Et vous aussi; votre serviteur.
SIR ANDREW. I hope, sir, you are—and I am yours.
SIR TOBY. Will you encounter the house? my niece is
   desirous you should enter, if your trade be to her.
VIOLA. I am bound to your niece, sir. I mean, she is
   the list of my voyage.
SIR TOBY. Taste your legs, sir, put them to motion.   80
VIOLA. My legs do better under-stand me, sir, than I
   understand what you mean by bidding me taste my
   legs.
SIR TOBY. I mean, to go, sir, to enter.
VIOLA. I will answer you with gate and entrance—but
   we are prevented.

Olivia comes from the house with Maria

   Most excellent accomplished lady, the heavens rain
   odours on you!
SIR ANDREW. That youth's a rare courtier—'Rain
   odours'—well!   90
VIOLA. My matter hath no voice, lady, but to your
   own most pregnant and vouchsafed ear.
SIR ANDREW. 'Odours,' 'pregnant,' and 'vouchsafed':
   I'll get 'em all three all ready.
OLIVIA. Let the garden door be shut, and leave me to
   my hearing. . . .
                Sir Toby, Sir Andrew and Maria depart
   Give me your hand, sir.
VIOLA. My duty, madam, and most humble service.
OLIVIA. What is your name?
VIOLA. Cesario is your servant's name, fair princess. 100
OLIVIA. My servant, sir! 'Twas never merry world,
   Since lowly feigning was called compliment:
   Y'are servant to the Count Orsino, youth.
VIOLA. And he is yours, and his must needs be yours;
   Your servant's servant is your servant, madam.
OLIVIA. For him, I think not on him: for his thoughts,
   Would they were blanks, rather than filled with me!
VIOLA. Madam, I come to whet your gentle thoughts
   On his behalf.
OLIVIA.   O, by your leave, I pray you;
   I bade you never speak again of him: 110
   But, would you undertake another suit,
   I had rather hear you to solicit that
   Than music from the spheres.
VIOLA.   Dear lady,—
OLIVIA. Give me leave, beseech you: I did send,
   After the last enchantment you did here,
   A ring in chase of you; so did I abuse
   Myself, my servant and, I fear me, you:
   Under your hard construction must I sit,
   To force that on you in a shameful cunning
   Which you knew none of yours: what might you
      think?   120
   Have you not set mine honour at the stake,
   And baited it with all th'unmuzzled thoughts
   That tyrannous heart can think?
   To one of your receiving enough is shown,
   A cypress, not a bosom, hides my heart:
   So let me hear you speak.

VIOLA.   I pity you.
OLIVIA. That's a degree to love.
VIOLA.   No, not a grise;
   For 'tis a vulgar proof,
   That very oft we pity enemies.
OLIVIA. Why then methinks 'tis time to smile again: 130
   O world, how apt the poor are to be proud!
   If one should be a prey, how much the better
   To fall before the lion than the wolf?
                                          Clock strikes
   The clock upbraids me with the waste of time . . .
   Be not afraid, good youth, I will not have you:
   And yet, when wit and youth is come to harvest,
   Your wife is like to reap a proper man:
   There lies your way, due west.
VIOLA.   Then westward-ho!
   Grace and good disposition attend your ladyship!
   You'll nothing, madam, to my lord by me?   140
OLIVIA. Stay:
   I prithee, tell me what thou think'st of me.
VIOLA. That you do think you are not what you are.
OLIVIA. If I think so, I think the same of you.
VIOLA. Then think you right; I am not what I am.
OLIVIA. I would you were as I would have you be!
VIOLA. Would it be better, madam, than I am,
   I wish it might, for now I am your fool.
OLIVIA. O, what a deal of scorn looks beautiful
   In the contempt and anger of his lip!   150
   A murd'rous guilt shows not itself more soon
   Than love that would seem hid: love's night is
      noon.
   Cesario, by the roses of the spring,
   By maidhood, honour, truth, and every thing,
   I love thee so, that, maugre all thy pride,
   Nor wit nor reason can my passion hide.
   Do not extort thy reasons from this clause,
   For that I woo, thou therefore hast no cause:
   But rather reason thus with reason fetter,
   Love sought is good . . . but given unsought is
      better.   160
VIOLA. By innocence I swear, and by my youth,
   I have one heart, one bosom, and one truth,
   And that no woman has, nor never none
   Shall mistress be of it, save I alone.
   And so adieu, good madam! never more
   Will I my master's tears to you deplore.
OLIVIA. Yet come again: for thou perhaps mayst move
   That heart, which now abhors, to like his love.
                                              They go

Scene 2: *Olivia's house*

Enter Sir Toby Belch, Sir Andrew Aguecheek, and Fabian

SIR ANDREW. No, faith, I'll not stay a jot longer.
SIR TOBY. Thy reason, dear venom, give thy reason.
FABIAN. You must needs yield your reason, Sir
   Andrew.
SIR ANDREW. Marry, I saw your niece do more favours
   to the count's serving-man than ever she bestowed
   upon me; I saw't i'th'orchard.
SIR TOBY. Did she see thee the while, old boy? tell me
   that.
SIR ANDREW. As plain as I see you now.   10
FABIAN. This was a great argument of love in her
   toward you.
SIR ANDREW. 'Slight! will you make an ass o' me?

FABIAN. I will prove it legitimate, sir, upon the oaths of judgement and reason.

SIR TOBY. And they have been grand-jurymen since before Noah was a sailor.

FABIAN. She did show favour to the youth in your sight, only to exasperate you, to awake your dormouse valour, to put fire in your heart, and brimstone in your liver: you should then have accosted her, and with some excellent jests, fire-new from the mint, you should have banged the youth into dumbness: this was looked for at your hand, and this was balked: the double gilt of this opportunity you let time wash off, and you are now sailed into the north of my lady's opinion, where you will hang like an icicle on a Dutchman's beard, unless you do redeem it by some laudable attempt, either of valour or policy. 30

SIR ANDREW. An't be any way, it must be with valour, for policy I hate: I had as lief be a Brownist, as a politician.

SIR TOBY. Why then, build me thy fortunes upon the basis of valour. Challenge me the count's youth to fight with him, hurt him in eleven places—my niece shall take note of it, and assure thyself there is no love-broker in the world can more prevail in man's commendation with woman than report of valour.

FABIAN. There is no way but this, Sir Andrew. 40

SIR ANDREW. Will either of you bear me a challenge to him?

SIR TOBY. Go, write it in a martial hand, be curst and brief; it is no matter how witty, so it be eloquent and full of invention: taunt him with the license of ink: if thou 'thou'st' him some thrice, it shall not be amiss; and as many lies as will lie in thy sheet of paper, although the sheet were big enough for the bed of Ware in England, set'em down—go, about it. Let there be gall enough in thy ink, though thou 50 write with a goose-pen, no matter: about it.

SIR ANDREW. Where shall I find you?

SIR TOBY. We'll call thee at thy cubicle: go.

Sir Andrew goes

FABIAN. This is a dear manakin to you, Sir Toby.

SIR TOBY. I have been dear to him, lad—some two thousand strong, or so.

FABIAN. We shall have a rare letter from him ... but you'll not deliver't?

SIR TOBY. Never trust me then; and by all means stir on the youth to an answer. I think oxen and wain- 60 ropes cannot hale them together. For Andrew, if he were opened and you find so much blood in his liver as will clog the foot of a flea, I'll eat the rest of th'anatomy.

FABIAN. And his opposite, the youth, bears in his visage no great presage of cruelty.

Maria comes in

SIR TOBY. Look, where the youngest wren of nine comes.

MARIA. If you desire the spleen, and will laugh yourselves into stitches, follow me ... Yon gull Malvolio 70 is turned heathen, a very renegado; for there is no Christian, that means to be saved by believing rightly, can ever believe such impossible passages of grossness.... He's in yellow stockings!

SIR TOBY. And cross-gartered?

MARIA. Most villainously; like a pedant that keeps a

school i'th' church ... I have dogged him like his murderer. He does obey every point of the letter that I dropped to betray him: he does smile his face into more lines than is in the new map, with the 80 augmentation of the Indies: you have not seen such a thing as 'tis ... I can hardly forbear hurling things at him, I know my lady will strike him: if she do, he'll smile and take't for a great favour.

SIR TOBY. Come, bring us, bring us where he is.

They go

Scene 3: *A street*

Antonio and Sebastian approach

SEBASTIAN. I would not by my will have troubled you,
  But since you make your pleasure of your pains,
  I will no further chide you.

ANTONIO. I could not stay behind you: my desire,
  More sharp than filéd steel, did spur me forth;
  And not all love to see you, though so much
  As might have drawn one to a longer voyage,
  But jealousy what might befall your travel,
  Being skilless in these parts; which to a stranger,
  Unguided and unfriended, often prove 10
  Rough and unhospitable: my willing love,
  The rather by these arguments of fear,
  Set forth in your pursuit.

SEBASTIAN.   My kind Antonio,
  I can no other answer make but thanks,
  And thanks, and ever thanks; and oft good turns
  Are shuffled off with such uncurrent pay:
  But, were my worth as is my conscience firm,
  You should find better dealing ... What's to do?
  Shall we go see the relics of this town?

ANTONIO. To-morrow sir—best first go see your
  lodging. 20

SEBASTIAN. I am not weary, and 'tis long to night:
  I pray you, let us satisfy our eyes
  With the memorials and the things of fame
  That do renown this city.

ANTONIO.   Would you'ld pardon me;
  I do not without danger walk these streets.
  Once in a sea-fight 'gainst the count his galleys
  I did some service, of such note indeed
  That were I ta'en here it would scarce be answered.

SEBASTIAN. Belike you slew great number of his
  people.

ANTONIO. Th'offence is not of such a bloody nature, 30
  Albeit the quality of the time and quarrel
  Might well have given us bloody argument:
  It might have since been answered in repaying
  What we took from them, which for traffic's sake
  Most of our city did: only myself stood out,
  For which, if I be lapséd in this place,
  I shall pay dear.

SEBASTIAN.   Do not then walk too open.

ANTONIO. It doth not fit me ... Hold, sir, here's my
  purse.
  In the south suburbs, at the Elephant,
  Is best to lodge: I will bespeak our diet, 40
  Whiles you beguile the time and feed your
  knowledge
  With viewing of the town; there shall you have me.

SEBASTIAN. Why I your purse?

ANTONIO. Haply your eye shall light upon some toy

You have desire to purchase; and your store,
I think, is not for idle markets, sir.
SEBASTIAN. I'll be your purse-bearer, and leave you for
an hour.
ANTONIO. To th'Elephant.
SEBASTIAN. I do remember.   50

They go off in different directions

Scene 4: *Olivia's garden*

Olivia enters followed by Maria

OLIVIA [*aside*]. I have sent after him, he says he'll come;
How shall I feast him? what bestow of him?
For youth is bought more oft than begged or
   borrowed.
I speak too loud ...
[*to Maria*] Where's Malvolio? he is sad and civil,
And suits well for a servant with my fortunes—
Where is Malvolio?
MARIA. He's coming, madam; but in very strange
manner. He is, sure, possessed, madam.
OLIVIA. Why, what's the matter? does he rave?   10
MARIA. No, madam, he does nothing but smile: your
ladyship were best to have some guard about you,
if he come, for sure the man is tainted in's wits.
OLIVIA. Go, call him hither. . . .

Malvolio enters

                              I am as mad as he,
If sad and merry madness equal be.
How now, Malvolio?
MALVOLIO. Sweet lady, ho, ho.
OLIVIA. Smil'st thou?
I sent for thee upon a sad occasion.
MALVOLIO. Sad, lady? I could be sad: this does make 20
some obstruction in the blood, this cross-gartering
—but what of that? if it please the eye of one, it is
with me as the very true sonnet is: 'Please one and
please all.'
OLIVIA. Why, how dost thou, man? what is the matter
with thee?
MALVOLIO. Not black in my mind, though yellow in
my legs ... It did come to his hands, and commands
shall be executed. I think we do know the sweet
Roman hand.   30
OLIVIA. Wilt thou go to bed, Malvolio?
MALVOLIO. To bed! ay, sweet-heart, and I'll come to
thee.
OLIVIA. God comfort thee! Why dost thou smile so,
and kiss thy hand so oft?
MARIA. How do you, Malvolio?
MALVOLIO. At your request! yes, nightingales answer
daws.
MARIA. Why appear you with this ridiculous boldness
before my lady?   40
MALVOLIO. 'Be not afraid of greatness': 'twas well
writ.
OLIVIA. What mean'st thou by that, Malvolio?
MALVOLIO. 'Some are born great,'—
OLIVIA. Ha?
MALVOLIO. 'Some achieve greatness,'—
OLIVIA. What say'st thou?
MALVOLIO. 'And some have greatness thrust upon
them.'
OLIVIA. Heaven restore thee!   50

MALVOLIO. 'Remember, who commended thy yellow
stockings'—
OLIVIA. Thy yellow stockings!
MALVOLIO. 'And wished to see thee cross-gartered.'
OLIVIA. Cross-gartered?
MALVOLIO. 'Go to, thou art made, if thou desir'st to
be so'—
OLIVIA. Am I made?
MALVOLIO. 'If not, let me see thee a servant still.'
OLIVIA. Why, this is very midsummer madness.   60

A servant comes from the house

SERVANT. Madam, the young gentleman of the Count
Orsino's is returned—I could hardly entreat him
back: he attends your ladyship's pleasure.
OLIVIA. I'll come to him. [*the servant goes*] Good Maria,
let this fellow be looked to. Where's my cousin
Toby? let some of my people have a special care of
him, I would not have him miscarry for the half of
my dowry.

She enters the house followed by Maria

MALVOLIO. O, ho! do you come near me now? no
worse man than Sir Toby to look to me! This con- 70
curs directly with the letter—she sends him on purpose, that I may appear stubborn to him; for she
incites me to that in the letter. 'Cast thy humble
slough,' says she; 'be opposite with a kinsman, surly
with servants, let thy tongue tang with arguments
of state, put thyself into the trick of singularity'; and
consequently sets down the manner how; as, a sad
face, a reverend carriage, a slow tongue, in the habit
of some sir of note, and so forth. I have limed her,
but it is Jove's doing, and Jove make me thankful! 80
And when she went away now, 'Let this fellow be
looked to': fellow! not Malvolio, nor after my
degree, but 'fellow.' Why, every thing adheres
together, that no dram of a scruple, no scruple of
a scruple, no obstacle, no incredulous or unsafe
circumstance—what can be said?—nothing that can
be, can come between me and the full prospect of
my hopes. Well, Jove, not I, is the doer of this, and
he is to be thanked.

Maria returns with Sir Toby Belch and Fabian

SIR TOBY. Which way is he, in the name of sanctity? 90
If all the devils of hell be drawn in little, and
Legion himself possessed him, yet I'll speak to him.
FABIAN. Here he is, here he is ... How is't with you,
sir?
SIR TOBY. How is't with you, man?
MALVOLIO. Go off, I discard you; let me enjoy my
private: go off.
MARIA. Lo, how hollow the fiend speaks within him!
did not I tell you? Sir Toby, my lady prays you to
have a care of him.   100
MALVOLIO. Ah, ha! does she so!
SIR TOBY. Go to, go to: peace, peace, we must deal
gently with him: let me alone. How do you, Mal-
volio? how is't with you? What, man! defy the devil:
consider, he's an enemy to mankind.
MALVOLIO. Do you know what you say?
MARIA. La you! an you speak ill of the devil, how he
takes it at heart! Pray God, he be not bewitched!
FABIAN. Carry his water to th'wise woman.
MARIA. Marry, and it shall be done to-morrow morn- 110

ing, if I live. My lady would not lose him for more than I'll say.

MALVOLIO. How now, mistress!

MARIA. O Lord!

SIR TOBY. Prithee, hold thy peace, this is not the way: do you not see you move him? let me alone with him.

FABIAN. No way but gentleness, gently, gently: the fiend is rough, and will not be roughly used.

SIR TOBY. Why, how now, my bawcock! how dost 120 thou, chuck?

MALVOLIO. Sir!

SIR TOBY. Ay, Biddy, come with me. What, man! 'tis not for gravity to play at cherry-pit with Satan. Hang him, foul collier!

MARIA. Get him to say his prayers, good Sir Toby, get him to pray.

MALVOLIO. My prayers, minx!

MARIA. No, I warrant you, he will not hear of god-liness. 130

MALVOLIO. Go, hang yourselves all! you are idle shallow things—I am not of your element—you shall know more hereafter. *He goes*

SIR TOBY. Is't possible?

FABIAN. If this were played upon a stage now, I could condemn it as an improbable fiction.

SIR TOBY. His very genius hath taken the infection of the device, man.

MARIA. Nay, pursue him now, lest the device take air and taint. 140

FABIAN. Why, we shall make him mad indeed.

MARIA. The house will be the quieter.

SIR TOBY. Come, we'll have him in a dark room and bound. My niece is already in the belief that he's mad; we may carry it thus, for our pleasure and his penance, till our very pastime, tired out of breath, prompt us to have mercy on him: at which time we will bring the device to the bar and crown thee for a finder of madmen ... But see, but see.

Sir Andrew Aguecheek enters

FABIAN. More matter for a May morning! 150

SIR ANDREW. Here's the challenge, read it: I warrant there's vinegar and pepper in't.

FABIAN. Is't so saucy?

SIR ANDREW. Ay, is't! I warrant him: do but read.

SIR TOBY. Give me. [*he reads*] 'Youth, whatsoever thou art, thou art but a scurvy fellow.'

FABIAN. Good, and valiant.

SIR TOBY. 'Wonder not, nor admire not in thy mind, why I do call thee so, for I will show thee no reason for't.' 160

FABIAN. A good note, that keeps you from the blow of the law.

SIR TOBY. 'Thou com'st to the Lady Olivia, and in my sight she uses thee kindly: but thou liest in thy throat, that is not the matter I challenge thee for.'

FABIAN. Very brief, and to exceeding good sense—less.

SIR TOBY. 'I will waylay thee going home, where if it be thy chance to kill me,'—

FABIAN. Good.

SIR TOBY. 'Thou kill'st me like a rogue and a villain.' 170

FABIAN. Still you keep o'th' windy side of the law: good.

SIR TOBY. 'Fare thee well, and God have mercy upon one of our souls! He may have mercy upon mine,

but my hope is better, and so look to thyself. Thy friend, as thou usest him, and thy sworn enemy,
ANDREW AGUECHEEK.'
If this letter move him not, his legs cannot: I'll give't him.

MARIA. You may have very fit occasion for't: he is now in some commerce with my lady, and will by 180 and by depart.

SIR TOBY. Go, Sir Andrew; scout me for him at the corner of the orchard like a bum-baily: so soon as ever thou seest him, draw, and as thou draw'st, swear horrible; for it comes to pass oft that a terrible oath, with a swaggering accent sharply twanged off, gives manhood more approbation than ever proof itself would have earned him. Away!

SIR ANDREW. Nay, let me alone for swearing.
He goes

SIR TOBY. Now will not I deliver his letter: for the 190 behaviour of the young gentleman gives him out to be of good capacity and breeding; his employment between his lord and my niece confirms no less; therefore this letter, being so excellently ignorant, will breed no terror in the youth: he will find it comes from a clodpole. But, sir, I will deliver his challenge by word of mouth; set upon Aguecheek a notable report of valour; and drive the gentleman, as I know his youth will aptly receive it, into a most hideous opinion of his rage, skill, fury and 200 impetuosity. This will so fright them both, that they will kill one another by the look, like cockatrices.

Olivia and Viola come from the house

FABIAN. Here he comes with your niece—give them way till he take leave, and presently after him.

SIR TOBY. I will meditate the while upon some horrid message for a challenge.
Sir Toby, Fabian and Maria go

OLIVIA. I have said too much unto a heart of stone,
And laid mine honour too unchary out:
There's something in me that reproves my fault;
But such a headstrong potent fault it is, 210
That it but mocks reproof.

VIOLA. With the same 'haviour that your passion bears
Goes on my master's grief.

OLIVIA. Here, wear this jewel for me, 'tis my picture;
Refuse it not, it hath no tongue to vex you:
And I beseech you come again to-morrow.
What shall you ask of me, that I'll deny,
That honour saved may upon asking give?

VIOLA. Nothing but this—your true love for my master.

OLIVIA. How with mine honour may I give him that 220
Which I have given to you?

VIOLA. I will acquit you.

OLIVIA. Well, come again to-morrow: fare thee well.
A fiend, like thee, might bear my soul to hell.
She goes within

Sir Toby Belch and Fabian return

SIR TOBY. Gentleman, God save thee.

VIOLA. And you, sir.

SIR TOBY. That defence thou hast, betake thee to't: of what nature the wrongs are thou hast done him, I know not; but thy intercepter, full of despite, bloody as the hunter, attends thee at the orchard-

end: dismount thy tuck, be yare in thy preparation, 230
for thy assailant is quick, skilful and deadly.

VIOLA. You mistake, sir. I am sure no man hath any
quarrel to me; my remembrance is very free and
clear from any image of offence done to any man.

SIR TOBY. You'll find it otherwise, I assure you: therefore, if you hold your life at any price, betake you
to your guard; for your opposite hath in him what
youth, strength, skill and wrath can furnish man
withal.

VIOLA. I pray you, sir, what is he?   240

SIR TOBY. He is knight, dubbed with unhatched rapier
and on carpet consideration, but he is a devil in
private brawl: souls and bodies hath he divorced
three, and his incensement at this moment is so
implacable, that satisfaction can be none but by
pangs of death and sepulchre ... Hob, nob, is his
word; give't or take't.

VIOLA. I will return again into the house and desire
some conduct of the lady. I am no fighter. I have
heard of some kind of men that put quarrels pur-   250
posely on others, to taste their valour: belike this is
a man of that quirk.

SIR TOBY. Sir, no; his indignation derives itself out of
a very competent injury, therefore get you on and
give him his desire. Back you shall not to the house,
unless you undertake that with me which with as
much safety you might answer him: therefore on, or
strip your sword stark naked; for meddle you must,
that's certain, or forswear to wear iron about you.

VIOLA. This is as uncivil as strange. I beseech you, do 260
me this courteous office, as to know of the knight
what my offence to him is; it is something of my
negligence, nothing of my purpose.

SIR TOBY. I will do so. Signior Fabian, stay you by this
gentleman till my return.   *He goes*

VIOLA. Pray you, sir, do you know of this matter?

FABIAN. I know the knight is incensed against you,
even to a mortal arbitrement, but nothing of the
circumstance more.

VIOLA. I beseech you, what manner of man is he?   270

FABIAN. Nothing of that wonderful promise, to read
him by his form, as you are like to find him in the
proof of his valour. He is indeed, sir, the most skilful,
bloody and fatal opposite that you could possibly
have found in any part of Illyria ... Will you walk
towards him? I will make your peace with him if I
can.

VIOLA. I shall be much bound to you for't: I am one,
that had rather go with sir priest than sir knight: I
care not who knows so much of my mettle.   280
                                        They go

Sir Toby and Sir Andrew enter

SIR TOBY. Why, man, he's a very devil, I have not seen
such a firago ... I had a pass with him, rapier,
scabbard and all, and he gives me the stuck in with
such a mortal motion that it is inevitable; and on the
answer, he pays you as surely as your feet hit the
ground they step on. They say he has been fencer to
the Sophy.

SIR ANDREW. Pox on't, I'll not meddle with him.

SIR TOBY. Ay, but he will not now be pacified: Fabian
can scarce hold him yonder.   290

SIR ANDREW. Plague on't, an I thought he had been
valiant and so cunning in fence, I'd have seen him

damned ere I'd have challenged him. Let him let the
matter slip, and I'll give him my horse, grey Capilet.

SIR TOBY. I'll make the motion: stand here, make a
good show on't—this shall end without the perdition of souls. [*aside*] Marry, I'll ride your horse as
well as I ride you.

Fabian and Viola enter. Sir Toby beckons Fabian aside

I have his horse to take up the quarrel; I have
persuaded him the youth's a devil.   300

FABIAN. He is as horribly conceited of him; and pants
and looks pale, as if a bear were at his heels.

SIR TOBY [*to Viola*]. There's no remedy, sir, he will
fight with you for's oath sake: marry, he hath better
bethought him of his quarrel, and he finds that now
scarce to be worth talking of: therefore draw for the
supportance of his vow, he protests he will not hurt
you.

VIOLA [*aside*]. Pray God defend me! A little thing
would make me tell them how much I lack of a 310
man.

FABIAN. Give ground, if you see him furious.

SIR TOBY. Come, Sir Andrew, there's no remedy, the
gentleman will for his honour's sake have one bout
with you: he cannot by the duello avoid it: but he
has promised me, as he is a gentleman and a soldier,
he will not hurt you. Come on, to't!

SIR ANDREW. Pray God, he keep his oath!

VIOLA. I do assure you, 'tis against my will.

They make ready to fight; Antonio enters

ANTONIO [*to Sir Andrew*]. Put up your sword: if this
young gentleman   320
Have done offence, I take the fault on me;
If you offend him, I for him defy you.

SIR TOBY. You, sir! why, what are you?

ANTONIO. One, sir, that for his love dares yet do more
Than you have heard him brag to you he will.

SIR TOBY. Nay, if you be an undertaker, I am for you.
                                        They draw

Two officers approach

FABIAN. O good Sir Toby, hold; here come the
officers.

SIR TOBY [*to Antonio*]. I'll be with you anon.
            He hides from the officers behind a tree

VIOLA. Pray, sir, put your sword up, if you please.

SIR ANDREW. Marry, will I, sir; and, for that I promised 330
you, I'll be as good as my word. He will bear you
easily, and reins well.

1 OFFICER. This is the man, do thy office.

2 OFFICER. Antonio, I arrest thee at the suit
Of Count Orsino.

ANTONIO.   You do mistake me, sir.

1 OFFICER. No, sir, no jot; I know your favour well:
Though now you have no sea-cap on your head ...
Take him away, he knows I know him well.

ANTONIO. I must obey. [*to Viola*] This comes with
seeking you;
But there's no remedy, I shall answer it ...   340
What will you do, now my necessity
Makes me to ask you for my purse? it grieves me
Much more for what I cannot do for you
Than what befalls myself ... You stand amazed,
But be of comfort.

2 OFFICER. Come, sir, away.

ANTONIO. I must entreat of you some of that money.
VIOLA. What money, sir?
  For the fair kindness you have showed me here,
  And part being prompted by your present trouble, 350
  Out of my lean and low ability
  I'll lend you something ... My having is not much,
  I'll make division of my present with you:
  Hold, there's half my coffer.
ANTONIO.   Will you deny me now?
  Is't possible that my deserts to you
  Can lack persuasion? Do not tempt my misery,
  Lest that it make me so unsound a man
  As to upbraid you with those kindnesses
  That I have done for you.
VIOLA.   I know of none,
  Nor know I you by voice or any feature: 360
  I hate ingratitude more in a man,
  Than lying vainness, babbling drunkenness,
  Or any taint of vice whose strong corruption
  Inhabits our frail blood.
ANTONIO.   O heavens themselves!
2 OFFICER. Come, sir, I pray you, go.
ANTONIO.   Let me speak a little.
  This youth that you see here
  I snatched one half out of the jaws of death,
  Relieved him with such sanctity of love,
  And to his image, which methought did promise
  Most venerable worth, did I devotion.   370
1 OFFICER. What's that to us? The time goes by: away!
ANTONIO. But, O, how vile an idol proves this god!
  Thou hast, Sebastian, done good feature shame.
  In nature there's no blemish but the mind;
  None can be called deformed but the unkind:
  Virtue is beauty, but the beauteous evil
  Are empty trunks o'erflourished by the devil.
1 OFFICER. The man grows mad, away with him!
  Come, come, sir.
ANTONIO. Lead me on.   They carry him off 380
VIOLA. Methinks his words do from such passion fly,
  That he believes himself—so do not I?
  Prove true, imagination, O prove true,
  That I, dear brother, be now ta'en for you!
SIR TOBY. Come hither, knight—come hither, Fabian;
  we'll whisper o'er a couplet or two of most sage
  saws.
VIOLA. He named Sebastian; I my brother know
  Yet living in my glass; even such and so
  In favour was my brother, and he went   390
  Still in this fashion, colour, ornament,
  For him I imitate: O, if it prove,
  Tempests are kind and salt waves fresh in love!
                              She goes
SIR TOBY. A very dishonest paltry boy, and more a
  coward than a hare. His dishonesty appears in leav-
  ing his friend here in necessity and denying him; and
  for his cowardship, ask Fabian.
FABIAN. A coward, a most devout coward, religious
  in it.
SIR ANDREW. 'Slid, I'll after him again and beat him. 400
SIR TOBY. Do, cuff him soundly, but never draw thy
  sword.
SIR ANDREW. An I do not,—   He goes
FABIAN. Come, let's see the event.
SIR TOBY. I dare lay any money, 'twill be nothing yet.
                              They follow

ACT 4

Scene 1: *Before Olivia's house*

Sebastian and Clown

CLOWN. Will you make me believe that I am not sent
  for you?
SEBASTIAN. Go to, go to, thou art a foolish fellow;
  Let me be clear of thee.
CLOWN. Well held out, i'faith! No, I do not know you,
  nor I am not sent to you by my lady to bid you
  come speak with her, nor your name is not Master
  Cesario, nor this is not my nose neither: nothing that
  is so, is so.
SEBASTIAN. I prithee, vent thy folly somewhere else, 10
  Thou know'st not me.
CLOWN. Vent my folly! He has heard that word of
  some great man and now applies it to a fool. Vent
  my folly! I am afraid this great lubber, the world,
  will prove a cockney ... I prithee now, ungird thy
  strangeness and tell me what I shall vent to my lady:
  shall I vent to her that thou art coming?
SEBASTIAN. I prithee, foolish Greek, depart from me.
  There's money for thee if you tarry longer
  I shall give worse payment.   20
CLOWN. By my troth, thou hast an open hand ...
  These wise men that give fools money get themselves a good report—after fourteen years' purchase.

Sir Andrew enters, Sir Toby and Fabian following

SIR ANDREW. Now, sir, have I met you again? there's
  for you.   *He strikes wide*
SEBASTIAN [*replies with his fists*]. Why, there's for thee,
  and there, and there!   *He knocks him down*
  Are all the people mad?   *His hand upon his dagger*
SIR TOBY [*seizes him from behind*]. Hold, sir, or I'll
  throw your dagger o'er the house.
CLOWN. This will I tell my lady straight: I would not 30
  be in some of your coats for two pence.   *He goes*
SIR TOBY. Come on, sir! hold!
SIR ANDREW. Nay, let him alone, I'll go another way
  to work with him: I'll have an action of battery
  against him, if there be any law in Illyria: though I
  struck him first, yet it's no matter for that.
SEBASTIAN. Let go thy hand!
SIR TOBY. Come, sir, I will not let you go. Come, my
  young soldier, put up your iron: you are well
  fleshed ... Come on.   40
SEBASTIAN. I will be free from thee.... [*he throws him
  off*] What wouldst thou now?   *He draws*
  If thou dar'st tempt me further, draw thy sword.
SIR TOBY. What, what? [*he also draws*] Nay, then I
  must have an ounce or two of this malapert blood
  from you.

Olivia enters

OLIVIA. Hold, Toby! on thy life, I charge thee, hold!
SIR TOBY. Madam!
OLIVIA. Will it be ever thus? Ungracious wretch,
  Fit for the mountains and the barbarous caves,
  Where manners ne'er were preached! out of my
    sight!   50
  Be not offended, dear Cesario ...
  Rudesby, be gone!
        Sir Toby, Sir Andrew and Fabian go
                    I prithee, gentle friend,
  Let thy fair wisdom, not thy passion, sway

In this uncivil and unjust extent
Against thy peace. Go with me to my house,
And hear thou there how many fruitless pranks
This ruffian hath botched up, that thou thereby
Mayst smile at this ... Thou shalt not choose but go;
Do not deny. Beshrew his soul for me,
He started one poor heart of mine in thee.   60
SEBASTIAN. What relish is in this? how runs the stream?
Or I am mad, or else this is a dream:
Let fancy still my sense in Lethe steep—
If it be thus to dream, still let me sleep!
OLIVIA. Nay, come, I prithee: would thou'dst be ruled
    by me!
SEBASTIAN. Madam, I will.
OLIVIA.   O, say so, and so be!
                                        They go

Scene 2: *Olivia's house*

Enter Clown and Maria

MARIA. Nay, I prithee, put on this gown and this
beard, make him believe thou art Sir Topas the
curate, do it quickly. I'll call Sir Toby the whilst.
                                    She goes out
CLOWN. Well, I'll put it on, and I will dissemble myself
in't, and I would I were the first that ever dissembled
in such a gown. I am not tall enough to become the
function well, nor lean enough to be thought a good
student: but to be said an honest man and a good
housekeeper goes as fairly as to say a careful man
and a great scholar. The competitors enter.   10

Maria returns with Sir Toby

SIR TOBY. Jove bless thee, Master Parson!
CLOWN [*in feigned voice*]. Bonos dies, Sir Toby: for as
the old hermit of Prague, that never saw pen and
ink, very wittily said to a niece of King Gorboduc,
'That that is, is': so I, being Master Parson, am
Master Parson; for what is 'that' but that? and 'is'
but is?
SIR TOBY. To him, Sir Topas.
CLOWN. What, ho, I say! peace in this prison!
SIR TOBY. The knave counterfeits well; a good knave.   20
MALVOLIO [*within*]. Who calls there?
CLOWN. Sir Topas the curate, who comes to visit
Malvolio the lunatic.
MALVOLIO. Sir Topas, Sir Topas, good sir Topas, go
to my lady.
CLOWN. Out, hyperbolical fiend! how vexest thou this
man? talkest thou nothing but of ladies?
SIR TOBY. Well said, Master Parson.
MALVOLIO. Sir Topas, never was man thus wronged—
good sir Topas, do not think I am mad; they have   30
laid me here in hideous darkness.
CLOWN. Fie, thou dishonest Satan! I call thee by the
most modest terms, for I am one of those gentle ones
that will use the devil himself with courtesy: say'st
thou that house is dark?
MALVOLIO. As hell, Sir Topas.
CLOWN. Why, it hath bay windows transparent as
barricadoes, and the clerestories toward the south-
north are as lustrous as ebony; and yet complainest
thou of obstruction?   40
MALVOLIO. I am not mad, Sir Topas. I say to you, this
house is dark.

CLOWN. Madman, thou errest: I say, there is no darkness but ignorance, in which thou art more puzzled
than the Egyptians in their fog.
MALVOLIO. I say, this house is as dark as ignorance,
though ignorance were as dark as hell; and I say,
there was never man thus abused. I am no more mad
than you are—make the trial of it in any constant
question.   50
CLOWN. What is the opinion of Pythagoras concerning wild fowl?
MALVOLIO. That the soul of our grandam might haply
inhabit a bird.
CLOWN. What think'st thou of his opinion?
MALVOLIO. I think nobly of the soul, and no way
approve his opinion.
CLOWN. Fare thee well: remain thou still in darkness.
Thou shalt hold th'opinion of Pythagoras ere I will
allow of thy wits, and fear to kill a woodcock, lest   60
thou dispossess the soul of thy grandam. Fare thee
well.
MALVOLIO. Sir Topas, Sir Topas!
SIR TOBY. My most exquisite Sir Topas!
CLOWN. Nay, I am for all waters.
MARIA. Thou mightst have done this without thy
beard and gown, he sees thee not.
SIR TOBY. To him in thine own voice, and bring me
word how thou find'st him ... I would we were
well rid of this knavery. If he may be conveniently   70
delivered, I would he were, for I am now so far in
offence with my niece, that I cannot pursue with
any safety this sport to the upshot. Come by and by
to my chamber.   *Sir Toby and Maria go*
CLOWN [*sings*]. 'Hey Robin, jolly Robin,
                    Tell me how thy lady does.'
MALVOLIO. Fool,—
CLOWN [*sings*]. 'My lady is unkind, perdy.'
MALVOLIO. Fool,—
CLOWN [*sings*]. 'Alas, why is she so?'   80
MALVOLIO. Fool, I say,—
CLOWN [*sings*]. 'She loves another'—Who calls, ha?
MALVOLIO. Good fool, as ever thou wilt deserve well
at my hand, help me to a candle, and pen, ink and
paper; as I am a gentleman, I will live to be thankful
to thee for't.
CLOWN. Master Malvolio!
MALVOLIO. Ay, good fool.
CLOWN. Alas, sir, how fell you besides your five wits?
MALVOLIO. Fool, there was never man so notoriously 90
abused: I am as well in my wits, fool, as thou art.
CLOWN. But as well? then you are mad indeed, if you
be no better in your wits than a fool.
MALVOLIO. They have here propertied me; keep me in
darkness, send ministers to me, asses, and do all they
can to face me out of my wits.
CLOWN. Advise you what you say; the minister is
here. ... Malvolio, Malvolio, thy wits the heavens
restore! endeavour thyself to sleep, and leave thy
vain bibble babble.   100
MALVOLIO. Sir Topas,—
CLOWN. Maintain no words with him, good fellow.—
Who, I, sir? not I, sir. God buy you, good Sir
Topas.—Marry, amen.—I will, sir, I will.
MALVOLIO. Fool, fool, fool, I say,—
CLOWN. Alas, sir, be patient. What say you, sir? I am
shent for speaking to you.
MALVOLIO. Good fool, help me to some light and some

paper. I tell thee, I am as well in my wits, as any man
in Illyria.   110
CLOWN. Well-a-day that you were, sir!
MALVOLIO. By this hand, I am ... Good fool, some
ink, paper and light: and convey what I will set
down to my lady; it shall advantage thee more than
ever the bearing of letter did.
CLOWN. I will help you to't. But tell me true, are you
not mad indeed? or do you but counterfeit?
MALVOLIO. Believe me, I am not—I tell thee true.
CLOWN. Nay, I'll ne'er believe a madman till I see his
brains. I will fetch you light and paper and ink.   120
MALVOLIO. Fool, I'll requite it in the highest degree:
I prithee, be gone.
CLOWN [sings].
　　I am gone, sir, and anon, sir,
　　I'll be with you again:
　　　In a trice, like to the old Vice,
　　　Your need to sustain.
　　Who with dagger of lath,
　　In his rage and his wrath,
　　　Cries ah ha, to the devil:
　　Like a mad lad,   130
　　Pare thy nails dad,
　　　Adieu goodman devil.   He goes

Scene 3: Olivia's garden

Sebastian comes from the house

SEBASTIAN. This is the air, that is the glorious sun,
This pearl she gave me, I do feel't and see't,
And though 'tis wonder that enwraps me thus,
Yet 'tis not madness. Where's Antonio then?
I could not find him at the Elephant,
Yet there he was, and there I found this credit,
That he did range the town to seek me out.
His counsel now might do me golden service,
For though my soul disputes well with my sense,
That this may be some error, but no madness,   10
Yet doth this accident and flood of fortune
So far exceed all instance, all discourse,
That I am ready to distrust mine eyes
And wrangle with my reason, that persuades me
To any other trust but that I am mad,
Or else the lady's mad; yet, if 'twere so,
She could not sway her house, command her
　followers,
Take and give back affairs and their dispatch,
With such a smooth, discreet, and stable bearing
As I perceive she does: there's something in't   20
That is deceivable. But here the lady comes.

Olivia comes forth with a priest

OLIVIA. Blame not this haste of mine ... If you mean
well,
Now go with me and with this holy man
Into the chantry by: there, before him,
And underneath that consecrated roof,
Plight me the full assurance of your faith,
That my most jealous and too doubtful soul
May live at peace. He shall conceal it,
Whiles you are willing it shall come to note,
What time we will our celebration keep   30
According to my birth. What do you say?
SEBASTIAN. I'll follow this good man and go with you,
And having sworn truth, ever will be true.

OLIVIA. Then lead the way, good father, and heavens
so shine,
That they may fairly note this act of mine!
　　　　　　　　　　　　　　　　　They go

ACT 5
Scene 1: *Before Olivia's house*

Clown and Fabian

FABIAN. Now, as thou lov'st me, let me see his letter.
CLOWN. Good Master Fabian, grant me another re-
quest.
FABIAN. Any thing.
CLOWN. Do not desire to see this letter.
FABIAN. This is, to give a dog, and in recompense
desire my dog again.

The Duke and Viola (as Cesario) enter with attendants

DUKE. Belong you to the Lady Olivia, friends?
CLOWN. Ay, sir, we are some of her trappings.
DUKE. I know thee well: how dost thou, my good   10
fellow?
CLOWN. Truly, sir, the better for my foes and the
worse for my friends.
DUKE. Just the contrary; the better for thy friends.
CLOWN. No, sir, the worse.
DUKE. How can that be?
CLOWN. Marry, sir, they praise me and make an ass of
me; now my foes tell me plainly I am an ass: so that
by my foes, sir, I profit in the knowledge of myself,
and by my friends I am abused: so that, conclusions 20
to be as kisses, if your four negatives make your two
affirmatives, why then—the worse for my friends
and the better for my foes.
DUKE. Why, this is excellent.
CLOWN. By my troth, sir, no; though it please you to
be one of my friends.
DUKE. Thou shalt not be the worse for me—there's
gold.
CLOWN. But that it would be double-dealing, sir, I
would you could make it another.   30
DUKE. O, you give me ill counsel.
CLOWN. Put your grace in your pocket, sir, for this
once, and let your flesh and blood obey it.
DUKE. Well, I will be so much a sinner, to be a double-
dealer; there's another.
CLOWN. Primo, secundo, tertio, is a good play, and the
old saying is, the third pays for all: the triplex, sir,
is a good tripping measure, or the bells of St Bennet,
sir, may put you in mind—one, two, three!
DUKE. You can fool no more money out of me at this   40
throw: if you will let your lady know I am here to
speak with her, and bring her along with you, it
may awake my bounty further.
CLOWN. Marry, sir, lullaby to your bounty till I come
again. I go, sir, but I would not have you to think
that my desire of having is the sin of covetousness:
but, as you say, sir, let your bounty take a nap, I will
awake it anon.   He goes

Officers approach with Antonio

VIOLA. Here comes the man, sir, that did rescue me.
DUKE. That face of his I do remember well,   50
Yet when I saw it last it was besmeared
As black as Vulcan in the smoke of war:

A baubling vessel was he captain of,
For shallow draught and bulk unprizable,
With which such scathful grapple did he make
With the most noble bottom of our fleet,
That very envy and the tongue of loss
Cried fame and honour on him. What's the matter?
1 OFFICER. Orsino, this is that Antonio
That took the Phœnix and her fraught from Candy, 60
And this is he that did the Tiger board,
When your young nephew Titus lost his leg:
Here in the streets, desperate of shame and state,
In private brabble did we apprehend him.
VIOLA. He did me kindness, sir, drew on my side,
But in conclusion put strange speech upon me,
I know not what 'twas but distraction.
DUKE. Notable pirate! thou salt-water thief!
What foolish boldness brought thee to their mercies,
Whom thou, in terms so bloody and so dear, 70
Hast made thine enemies?
ANTONIO.   Orsino, noble sir,
Be pleased that I shake off these names you give me;
Antonio never yet was thief or pirate,
Though I confess, on base and ground enough,
Orsino's enemy. A witchcraft drew me hither:
That most ingrateful boy there by your side,
From the rude sea's enraged and foamy mouth
Did I redeem; a wrack past hope he was:
His life I gave him and did thereto add
My love, without retention or restraint, 80
All his in dedication. For his sake
Did I expose myself—pure for his love!—
Into the danger of this adverse town,
Drew to defend him when he was beset:
Where being apprehended, his false cunning,
Not meaning to partake with me in danger,
Taught him to face me out of his acquaintance,
And grew a twenty years removéd thing
While one would wink; denied me mine own
purse,
Which I had recommended to his use 90
Not half an hour before.
VIOLA.   How can this be?
DUKE. When came he to this town?
ANTONIO. To-day, my lord; and for three months
before,
No interim, not a minute's vacancy,
Both day and night did we keep company.

Olivia comes from her house, attended

DUKE. Here comes the countess! now heaven walks
on earth ...
But for thee, fellow—fellow, thy words are
madness,
Three months this youth hath tended upon me.
But more of that anon.... Take him aside.
OLIVIA. What would my lord, but that he may not
have, 100
Wherein Olivia may seem serviceable?
Cesario, you do not keep promise with me.
VIOLA. Madam?
DUKE. Gracious Olivia,—
OLIVIA. What do you say, Cesario?—Good my
lord,—
VIOLA. My lord would speak, my duty hushes me.
OLIVIA. If it be aught to the old tune, my lord,
It is as fat and fulsome to mine ear

As howling after music.
DUKE.   Still so cruel?
OLIVIA. Still so constant, lord. 110
DUKE. What, to perverseness? you uncivil lady,
To whose ingrate and unauspicious altars
My soul the faithfull'st off'rings hath breathed out,
That e'er devotion tendered! What shall I do?
OLIVIA. Even what it please my lord, that shall
become him.
DUKE. Why should I not, had I the heart to do it,
Like to th'Egyptian thief, at point of death,
Kill what I love?—a savage jealousy
That sometime savours nobly. But hear me this:
Since you to non-regardance cast my faith, 120
And that I partly know the instrument
That screws me from my true place in your favour,
Live you, the marble-breasted tyrant, still;
But this your minion, whom I know you love,
And whom, by heaven I swear, I tender dearly,
Him will I tear out of that cruel eye,
Where he sits crownéd in his master's spite....
Come boy with me. My thoughts are ripe in
mischief:
I'll sacrifice the lamb that I do love,
To spite a raven's heart within a dove. 130
VIOLA. And I, most jocund, apt and willingly,
To do you rest, a thousand deaths would die.
OLIVIA. Where goes Cesario?
VIOLA.   After him I love
More than I love these eyes, more than my life,
More, by all mores, than e'er I shall love wife.
If I do feign, you witnesses above
Punish my life for tainting of my love!
OLIVIA. Ay me, detested! how am I beguiled!
VIOLA. Who does beguile you? who does do you
wrong?
OLIVIA. Hast thou forgot thyself? is it so long? 140
Call forth the holy father.
DUKE.   Come, away!
OLIVIA. Whither, my lord? Cesario, husband, stay.
DUKE. Husband?
OLIVIA.   Ay, husband. Can he that deny?
DUKE. Her husband, sirrah?
VIOLA.   No, my lord, not I.
OLIVIA. Alas, it is the baseness of thy fear,
That makes thee strangle thy propriety:
Fear not, Cesario, take thy fortunes up,
Be that thou know'st thou art, and then thou art
As great as that thou fear'st.

The priest comes forth

                         O, welcome, father!
Father, I charge thee, by thy reverence, 150
Here to unfold—though lately we intended
To keep in darkness, what occasion now
Reveals before 'tis ripe—what thou dost know
Hath newly passed between this youth and me.
PRIEST. A contract of eternal bond of love,
Confirmed by mutual joinder of your hands,
Attested by the holy close of lips,
Strength'ned by interchangement of your rings,
And all the ceremony of this compact
Sealed in my function, by my testimony: 160
Since when, my watch hath told me, toward my
grave,
I have travelled but two hours.

DUKE. O, thou dissembling cub! what wilt thou be
When time hath sowed a grizzle on thy case?
Or will not else thy craft so quickly grow,
That thine own trip shall be thine overthrow?
Farewell, and take her, but direct thy feet
Where thou and I henceforth may never meet.
VIOLA. My lord, I do protest—
OLIVIA.   O, do not swear!
Hold little faith, though thou hast too much fear. 170

Sir Andrew Aguecheek enters

SIR ANDREW. For the love of God, a surgeon! Send one
presently to Sir Toby.
OLIVIA. What's the matter?
SIR ANDREW. H'as broke my head across and has given
Sir Toby a bloody coxcomb too: for the love of
God, your help! I had rather than forty pound I were
at home.
OLIVIA. Who has done this, Sir Andrew?
SIR ANDREW. The count's gentleman, one Cesario: we
took him for a coward, but he's the very devil 180
incardinate.
DUKE. My gentleman, Cesario?
SIR ANDREW. 'Od's lifelings, here he is! You broke my
head for nothing, and that that I did, I was set on to
do't by Sir Toby.
VIOLA. Why do you speak to me? I never hurt you:
You drew your sword upon me without cause,
But I bespake you fair, and hurt you not.
SIR ANDREW. If a bloody coxcomb be a hurt, you have
hurt me; I think you set nothing by a bloody cox- 190
comb.

Sir Toby approaches with the Clown

Here comes Sir Toby halting, you shall hear more:
but if he had not been in drink, he would have
tickled you othergates than he did.
DUKE. How now, gentleman! how is't with you?
SIR TOBY. That's all one—has hurt me, and there's
th'end on't ... Sot, didst see Dick surgeon, sot?
CLOWN. O he's drunk, Sir Toby, an hour agone; his
eyes were set at eight i'th' morning.
SIR TOBY. Then he's a rogue, and a passy-measures 200
pavin: I hate a drunken rogue.
OLIVIA. Away with him! Who hath made this havoc
with them?
SIR ANDREW. I'll help you, Sir Toby, because we'll be
dressed together.
SIR TOBY. Will you help? an ass-head, and a coxcomb,
and a knave! a thin-faced knave, a gull!
OLIVIA. Get him to bed, and let his hurt be looked to.
                    Clown, Sir Toby, and Sir Andrew go

Sebastian enters

SEBASTIAN. I am sorry, madam, I have hurt your
kinsman;
But, had it been the brother of my blood,   210
I must have done no less with wit and safety.
You throw a strange regard upon me, and by that
I do perceive it hath offended you;
Pardon me, sweet one, even for the vows
We made each other but so late ago.
DUKE. One face, one voice, one habit, and two
persons,
A natural perspective, that is and is not.
SEBASTIAN. Antonio! O my dear Antonio!

How have the hours racked and tortured me,
Since I have lost thee!   220
ANTONIO. Sebastian are you?
SEBASTIAN.   Fear'st thou that, Antonio?
ANTONIO. How have you made division of yourself?
An apple, cleft in two, is not more twin
Than these two creatures. Which is Sebastian?
OLIVIA. Most wonderful!
SEBASTIAN. Do I stand there? I never had a brother:
Nor can there be that deity in my nature,
Of here and every where. I had a sister,
Whom the blind waves and surges have
devoured ...
Of charity, what kin are you to me?   230
What countryman? what name? what parentage?
VIOLA. Of Messaline: Sebastian was my father—
Such a Sebastian was my brother too:
So went he suited to his watery tomb:
If spirits can assume both form and suit,
You come to fright us.
SEBASTIAN.   A spirit I am indeed,
But am in that dimension grossly clad,
Which from the womb I did participate.
Were you a woman, as the rest goes even,
I should my tears let fall upon your cheek,   240
And say 'Thrice-welcome, drownèd Viola!'
VIOLA. My father had a mole upon his brow.
SEBASTIAN. And so had mine.
VIOLA. And died that day when Viola from her birth
Had numb'red thirteen years.
SEBASTIAN. O, that record is lively in my soul!
He finishèd indeed his mortal act,
That day that made my sister thirteen years.
VIOLA. If nothing lets to make us happy both,
But this my masculine usurped attire,   250
Do not embrace me till each circumstance
Of place, time, fortune, do cohere and jump
That I am Viola—which to confirm,
I'll bring you to a captain in this town,
Where lie my maiden weeds; by whose gentle help
I was preserved to serve this noble count ...
All the occurrence of my fortune since
Hath been between this lady and this lord.
SEBASTIAN [*to Olivia*]. So comes it, lady, you have
been mistook;
But nature to her bias drew in that.   260
You would have been contracted to a maid,
Nor are you therein, by my life, deceived,
You are betrothed both to a maid and man.
DUKE. Be not amazed—right noble is his blood ...
If this be so, as yet the glass seems true,
I shall have share in this most happy wrack.
[*to Viola*] Boy, thou hast said to me a thousand times
Thou never shouldst love woman like to me.
VIOLA. And all those sayings will I over-swear,
And all those swearings keep as true in soul,   270
As doth that orbèd continent the fire
That severs day from night.
DUKE.   Give me thy hand,
And let me see thee in thy woman's weeds.
VIOLA. The captain that did bring me first on shore,
Hath my maid's garments: he upon some action
Is now in durance, at Malvolio's suit,
A gentleman and follower of my lady's.
OLIVIA. He shall enlarge him ... Fetch Malvolio
hither—

And yet, alas, now I remember me,
They say, poor gentleman, he's much distract.   280

*The Clown returns with a letter in his hand, Fabian
following*

A most extracting frenzy of mine own
From my remembrance clearly banished his.
How does he, sirrah?
CLOWN. Truly, madam, he holds Belzebub at the
stave's end as well as a man in his case may do: has
here writ a letter to you, I should have given't you
to-day morning: but as a madman's epistles are no
gospels, so it skills not much when they are delivered.
OLIVIA. Open't, and read it.   290
CLOWN. Look then to be well edified, when the fool
delivers the madman. [*he shrieks*] 'By the Lord,
madam,'—
OLIVIA. How now! art thou mad?
CLOWN. No, madam, I do but read madness: an your
ladyship will have it as it ought to be, you must
allow Vox.
OLIVIA. Prithee, read i'thy right wits.
CLOWN. So I do, madonna; but to read his right wits,
is to read thus: therefore perpend, my princess, and 300
give ear.
OLIVIA [*to Fabian*]. Read it you, sirrah.
FABIAN [*reads*]. 'By the Lord, madam, you wrong me,
and the world shall know it: though you have put
me into darkness, and given your drunken cousin
rule over me, yet have I the benefit of my senses as
well as your ladyship. I have your own letter that
induced me to the semblance I put on; with the
which I doubt not but to do myself much right, or
you much shame. Think of me as you please. I   310
leave my duty a little unthought of, and speak out
of my injury.
                          THE MADLY-USED MALVOLIO.'
OLIVIA. Did he write this?
CLOWN. Ay, madam.
DUKE. This savours not much of distraction.
OLIVIA. See him delivered, Fabian, bring him
hither ...   *Fabian goes*
My lord, so please you, these things further thought
on,
To think me as well a sister as a wife,
One day shall crown th'alliance on't, so please you, 320
Here at my house and at my proper cost.
DUKE. Madam, I am most apt t'embrace your offer ...
[*to Viola*] Your master quits you; and for your
service done him,
So much against the mettle of your sex,
So far beneath your soft and tender breeding,
And since you called me master for so long,
Here is my hand—you shall from this time be
Your master's mistress.
OLIVIA.   A sister! you are she.

Fabian returns with Malvolio

DUKE. Is this the madman?
OLIVIA.   Ay, my lord, this same:
How now, Malvolio?
MALVOLIO.   Madam, you have done me wrong, 330
Notorious wrong.
OLIVIA.   Have I, Malvolio? no!

MALVOLIO. Lady, you have. Pray you, peruse that
letter. ...
You must not now deny it is your hand,
Write from it, if you can, in hand or phrase,
Or say 'tis not your seal, not your invention:
You can say none of this. Well, grant it then,
And tell me, in the modesty of honour,
Why you have given me such clear lights of favour,
Bade me come smiling and cross-gartered to you,
To put on yellow stockings and to frown   340
Upon Sir Toby and the lighter people:
And, acting this in an obedient hope,
Why have you suffered me to be imprisoned,
Kept in a dark house, visited by the priest,
And made the most notorious geck and gull
That e'er invention played on? tell me why.
OLIVIA. Alas, Malvolio, this is not my writing,
Though, I confess, much like the character:
But, out of question, 'tis Maria's hand.
And now I do bethink me, it was she   350
First told me thou wast mad; then cam'st in smiling,
And in such forms which here were presupposed
Upon thee in the letter ... Prithee, be content—
This practice hath most shrewdly passed upon thee;
But, when we know the grounds and authors of it,
Thou shalt be both the plaintiff and the judge
Of thine own cause.
FABIAN.   Good madam, hear me speak;
And let no quarrel nor no brawl to come
Taint the condition of this present hour,
Which I have wond'red at. In hope it shall not,   360
Most freely I confess, myself and Toby
Set this device against Malvolio here,
Upon some stubborn and uncourteous parts
We had conceived in him: Maria writ
The letter at Sir Toby's great importance,
In recompense whereof he hath married her ...
How with a sportful malice it was followed,
May rather pluck on laughter than revenge,
If that the injuries be justly weighed
That have on both sides passed.   370
OLIVIA. Alas, poor fool! how have they baffled thee!
CLOWN. Why, 'Some are born great, some achieve
greatness, and some have greatness thrown upon
them.' I was one, sir, in this interlude, one Sir
Topas, sir—but that's all one ... 'By the Lord, fool,
I am not mad!' But do you remember? 'Madam,
why laugh you at such a barren rascal? an you smile
not, he's gagged' ... And thus the whirligig of time
brings in his revenges.
MALVOLIO. I'll be revenged on the whole pack of you. 380
                                            He goes
OLIVIA. He hath been most notoriously abused.
DUKE. Pursue him, and entreat him to a peace:
He hath not told us of the captain yet.
When that is known, and golden time convents,
A solemn combination shall be made
Of our dear souls ... Meantime, sweet sister,
We will not part from hence. Cesario, come!
For so you shall be, while you are a man;
But, when in other habits you are seen,
Orsino's mistress and his fancy's queen.   390
                              All save the Clown go
CLOWN [*sings*].
When that I was and a little tiny boy,
    With hey, ho, the wind and the rain:

A foolish thing was but a toy,
  For the rain it raineth every day.

But when I came to man's estate,
  With hey, ho, the wind and the rain:
'Gainst knaves and thieves men shut their gate,
  For the rain it raineth every day.

But when I came alas to wive,
  With hey, ho, the wind and the rain: 400
By swaggering could I never thrive,
  For the rain it raineth every day.

But when I came unto my beds,
  With hey, ho, the wind and the rain:
With toss-pots still had drunken heads,
  For the rain it raineth every day.

A great while ago the world begun,
  With hey, ho, the wind and the rain:
But that's all one, our play is done,
  And we'll strive to please you every day.   410

He goes

The Winter's Tale

The scene: now in Sicilia, now in Bohemia

CHARACTERS IN THE PLAY

LEONTES, *King of Sicilia*
MAMILLIUS, *young Prince of Sicilia*
CAMILLO
ANTIGONUS } *four Lords of Sicilia*
CLEOMENES
DION
POLIXENES, *King of Bohemia*
FLORIZEL, *Prince of Bohemia*
ARCHIDAMUS, *a Lord of Bohemia*
OLD SHEPHERD, *reputed father of Perdita*
CLOWN, *his son*
AUTOLYCUS, *a rogue*

A Mariner
A gaoler
HERMIONE, *Queen to Leontes*
PERDITA, *daughter to Leontes and Hermione*
PAULINA, *wife to Antigonus*
EMILIA, *a Lady*
MOPSA } *shepherdesses*
DORCAS
Other Lords and Gentlemen, Ladies, Officers and Servants,
    Shepherds and Shepherdesses
TIME, *as Chorus*

The Winter's Tale

ACT 1

Scene 1: *Sicilia. The Palace of Leontes*

Enter Camillo and Archidamus

ARCHIDAMUS. If you shall chance, Camillo, to visit
Bohemia, on the like occasion whereon my services
are now on foot, you shall see, as I have said, great
difference betwixt our Bohemia and your Sicilia.

CAMILLO. I think, this coming summer, the King of
Sicilia means to pay Bohemia the visitation which
he justly owes him.

ARCHIDAMUS. Wherein our entertainment shall shame
us: we will be justified in our loves: for, indeed ...

CAMILLO. Beseech you ...   10

ARCHIDAMUS. Verily I speak it in the freedom of my
knowledge: we cannot with such magnificence ...
in so rare ... I know not what to say ... We will
give you sleepy drinks, that your senses (un-
intelligent of our insufficience) may, though they
cannot praise us, as little accuse us.

CAMILLO. You pay a great deal too dear for what's
given freely.

ARCHIDAMUS. Believe me, I speak as my understanding instructs me, and as mine honesty puts it to   20
utterance.

CAMILLO. Sicilia cannot show himself over-kind to
Bohemia ... They were trained together in their
childhoods; and there rooted betwixt them then
such an affection, which cannot choose but branch
now. Since their more mature dignities and royal
necessities made separation of their society, their
encounters (though not personal) have been royally
attorneyed with interchange of gifts, letters, loving
embassies—that they have seemed to be together,   30
though absent; shook hands, as over a vast; and
embraced as it were from the ends of opposed winds.
The heavens continue their loves.

ARCHIDAMUS. I think there is not in the world, either
malice or matter, to alter it.... You have an unspeakable comfort of your young prince Mamillius:
it is a gentleman of the greatest promise that ever
came into my note.

CAMILLO. I very well agree with you in the hopes of
him: it is a gallant child; one that, indeed, physics 40
the subject, makes old hearts fresh: they that went
on crutches ere he was born desire yet their life to
see him a man.

ARCHIDAMUS. Would they else be content to die?

CAMILLO. Yes; if there were no other excuse why they
should desire to live.

ARCHIDAMUS. If the king had no son, they would
desire to live on crutches till he had one. *They go*

Scene 2

*Enter Leontes, Hermione, Mamillius, Polixenes, and
attendants*

POLIXENES. Nine changes of the wat'ry star hath been
The shepherd's note, since we have left our throne
Without a burthen: time as long again
Would be filled up, my brother, with our thanks,
And yet we should, for perpetuity,
Go hence in debt: and therefore, like a cipher
(Yet standing in rich place), I multiply,
With one 'We thank you,' many thousands moe
That go before it.

LEONTES.   Stay your thanks a while,
And pay them when you part.

POLIXENES.   Sir, that's to-morrow ...   10
I am questioned by my fears, of what may chance
Or breed upon our absence, that may blow
No sneaping winds at home, to make us say
'This is put forth too truly' ... Besides, I have stayed
To tire your royalty.

LEONTES.   We are tougher, brother,
Than you can put us to't.

POLIXENES.   No longer stay.

LEONTES. One se'nnight longer.

POLIXENES.   Very sooth, to-morrow.

LEONTES. We'll part the time between's then: and in
that
I'll no gainsaying.

POLIXENES.   Press me not, beseech you, so:
There is no tongue that moves ... none, none i'th'
world,   20
So soon as yours, could win me: so it should now,
Were there necessity in your request, although
'Twere needful I denied it. My affairs
Do even drag me homeward: which to hinder
Were (in your love) a whip to me; my stay,
To you a charge and trouble: to save both,
Farewell, our brother.

LEONTES.   Tongue-tied, our queen? speak you.

HERMIONE. I had thought, sir, to have held my peace,
until
You had drawn oaths from him not to stay: you, sir,
Charge him too coldly. Tell him, you are sure   30
All in Bohemia's well: this satisfaction
The by-gone day proclaimed—say this to him,
He's beat from his best ward.

LEONTES.   Well said, Hermione.

HERMIONE. To tell, he longs to see his son, were strong:
But let him say so then, and let him go;
But let him swear so, and he shall not stay,
We'll thwack him hence with distaffs....
Yet of your royal presence I'll adventure
The borrow of a week. When at Bohemia
You take my lord, I'll give him my commission 40
To let him there a month behind the gest
Prefixed for's parting: yet, good deed, Leontes,
I love thee not a jar o'th' clock behind
What Lady She her lord.... You'll stay?

POLIXENES.   No, madam.

HERMIONE. Nay, but you will?

POLIXENES.   I may not, verily.

HERMIONE. 'Verily!'
You put me off with limber vows: but I,
Though you would seek t'unsphere the stars with
oaths,
Should yet say, 'Sir, no going' ... Verily
You shall not go; a lady's Verily 'is   50

As potent as a lord's. Will you go yet?
Force me to keep you as a prisoner,
Not like a guest; so you shall pay your fees
When you depart, and save your thanks. How say
  you?
My prisoner? or my guest? by your dread Verily,
One of them you shall be.
POLIXENES.   Your guest then, madam:
To be your prisoner should import offending;
Which is for me less easy to commit
Than you to punish.
HERMIONE.   Not your gaoler then,
But your kind hostess.... Come, I'll question you 60
Of my lord's tricks and yours, when you were boys:
You were pretty lordings then?
POLIXENES.   We were, fair queen,
Two lads, that thought there was no more behind,
But such a day to-morrow, as to-day,
And to be boy eternal.
HERMIONE.   Was not my lord
The verier wag o'th' two?
POLIXENES. We were as twinned lambs, that did frisk
  i'th' sun,
And bleat the one at th'other: what we changed
Was innocence for innocence; we knew not
The doctrine of ill-doing, nor dreamed   70
That any did ... Had we pursued that life,
And our weak spirits ne'er been higher reared
With stronger blood, we should have answered
  heaven
Boldly 'not guilty'; the imposition cleared,
Hereditary ours.
HERMIONE.   By this we gather
You have tripped since.
POLIXENES.   O my most sacred lady,
Temptations have since then been born to's: for
In those unfledged days was my wife a girl;
Your precious self had then not crossed the eyes
Of my young play-fellow.
HERMIONE.   Grace to boot!   80
Of this make no conclusion, lest you say
Your queen and I are devils: yet, go on,
Th'offences we have made you do we'll answer,
If you first sinned with us; and that with us
You did continue fault; and that you slipped not
With any, but with us.
LEONTES.   Is he won yet?
HERMIONE. He'll stay, my lord.
LEONTES.   At my request he would not ...
Hermione, my dearest, thou never spok'st
To better purpose.
HERMIONE.   Never?
LEONTES.   Never, but once.
HERMIONE. What? have I twice said well? when was't
  before?   90
I prithee tell me: cram's with praise, and make's
As fat as tame things: one good deed, dying
  tongueless,
Slaughters a thousand waiting upon that.
Our praises are our wages: you may ride's
With one soft kiss a thousand furlongs ere
With spur we heat an acre. But to th' goal:
My last good deed was to entreat his stay;
What was my first? it has an elder sister,
Or I mistake you: O, would her name were Grace!
But once before I spoke to th' purpose? When?   100

Nay, let me have't: I long.
LEONTES.   Why, that was when
Three crabbéd months had soured themselves to
  death,
Ere I could make thee open thy white hand,
And clap thyself my love; then didst thou utter
'I am yours for ever.'
HERMIONE.   'Tis Grace, indeed....
Why, lo you now, I have spoke to th' purpose twice:
The one, for ever earned a royal husband;
Th'other, for some while a friend.
          She gives her hand to Polixenes; they talk apart
LEONTES.   Too hot, too hot:
To mingle friendship far, is mingling bloods.
I have *tremor cordis* on me: my heart dances,   110
But not for joy; not joy.... This entertainment
May a free face put on; derive a liberty
From heartiness, from bounty, fertile bosom,
And well become the agent: 't may; I grant:
But to be paddling palms and pinching fingers,
As now they are, and making practised smiles
As in a looking-glass; and then to sigh, as 'twere
The mort o'th' deer; O, that is entertainment
My bosom likes not, nor my brows.... Mamillius,
Art thou my boy?
MAMILLIUS.   Ay, my good lord.
LEONTES.   I'fecks!   120
Why, that's my bawcock.... What! hast smutched
  thy nose?
They say it is a copy out of mine.... Come, captain,
We must be neat; not neat, but cleanly, captain:
And yet the steer, the heifer, and the calf,
Are all called 'neat'.... Still virginalling
Upon his palm.... How now, you wanton calf?
Art thou my calf?
MAMILLIUS.   Yes, if you will, my lord.
LEONTES. Thou want'st a rough pash and the shoots
  that I have,
To be full like me: yet they say we are
Almost as like as eggs; women say so   130
(That will say any thing!) but were they false
As o'er-dyed blacks, as wind, as waters; false
As dice are to be wished, by one that fixes
No bourn 'twixt his and mine; yet were it true
To say this boy were like me.... Come, sir page,
Look on me with your welkin eye: sweet villain!
Most dear'st! my collop! Can thy dam?—may't be?
Affection! thy intention stabs the centre:
Thou dost make possible things not so held,
Communicat'st with dreams—how can this be?—   140
With what's unreal thou coactive art,
And fellow'st nothing: then 'tis very credent
Thou mayst co-join with something, and thou dost
(And that beyond commission) and I find it,
(And that to the infection of my brains,
And hard'ning of my brows.)
POLIXENES.   What means Sicilia?
HERMIONE. He something seems unsettled.
POLIXENES.   How, my lord!
LEONTES. What cheer? how is't with you, best brother?
HERMIONE.   You look
As if you held a brow of much distraction:
Are you moved, my lord?
LEONTES.   No, in good earnest.   150
How sometimes nature will betray its folly!
Its tenderness! and make itself a pastime

To harder bosoms! Looking on the lines
Of my boy's face, methoughts I did recoil
Twenty-three years, and saw myself unbreeched,
In my green velvet coat; my dagger muzzled
Lest it should bite its master, and so prove
(As ornaments oft do) too dangerous ...
How like, methought, I then was to this kernel,
This squash, this gentleman. Mine honest friend, 160
Will you take eggs for money?
MAMILLIUS. No, my lord, I'll fight.
LEONTES. You will? why, happy man be's dole! My
          brother,
Are you so fond of your young prince, as we
Do seem to be of ours?
POLIXENES.   If at home, sir,
He's all my exercise, my mirth, my matter:
Now my sworn friend, and then mine enemy;
My parasite, my soldier, statesman, all:
He makes a July's day short as December;
And with his varying childness cures in me 170
Thoughts that would thick my blood.
LEONTES.   So stands this squire
Officed with me: we two will walk, my lord,
And leave you to your graver steps.... Hermione,
How thou lov'st us, show in our brother's welcome;
Let what is dear in Sicily be cheap:
Next to thyself and my young rover, he's
Apparent to my heart.
HERMIONE.   If you would seek us,
We are yours i'th' garden: shall's attend you there?
LEONTES. To your own bents dispose you: you'll be
          found,
Be you beneath the sky ... [aside] I am angling now, 180
Though you perceive me not how I give line.
Go to, go to!
How she holds up the neb! the bill to him!
And arms her with the boldness of a wife
To her allowing husband! [they go out] Gone already,
Inch-thick, knee-deep! O'er head and ears a forked
one....
Go, play, boy, play: thy mother plays, and I
Play too; but so disgraced a part, whose issue
Will hiss me to my grave: contempt and clamour
Will be my knell.... Go, play, boy, play. There
          have been 190
(Or I am much deceived) cuckolds ere now,
And many a man there is (even at this present,
Now, while I speak this) holds his wife by th'arm,
That little thinks she has been sluiced in's absence,
And his pond fished by his next neighbour (by
Sir Smile, his neighbour): nay, there's comfort in't,
Whiles other men have gates, and those gates opened,
As mine, against their will. Should all despair
That have revolted wives, the tenth of mankind
Would hang themselves. Physic for't there's none: 200
It is a bawdy planet, that will strike
Where 'tis predominant; and 'tis powerful ... think
it ...
From east, west, north, and south! be it concluded,
No barricado for a belly ... know't,
It will let in and out the enemy,
With bag and baggage ... many thousand on's
Have the disease, and feel't not.... How now, boy?
MAMILLUIS. I am like you, they say.
LEONTES.   Why, that's some comfort.
What! Camillo there?

CAMILLO. Ay, my good lord.   210
LEONTES. Go play, Mamillius. Thou'rt an honest
          man ...   The boy goes
Camillo, this great sir will yet stay longer.
CAMILLO. You had much ado to make his anchor hold,
When you cast out, it still came home.
LEONTES.   Didst note it?
CAMILLO. He would not stay at your petitions, made
His business more material.
LEONTES.   Didst perceive it?
[aside] They're here with me already; whisp'ring,
          rounding:
'Sicilia is a—so-forth': 'tis far gone,
When I shall gust it last.... How came't, Camillo,
That he did stay?
CAMILLO.   At the good queen's entreaty. 220
LEONTES. At the queen's be't: 'good,' should be
          pertinent,
But so it is, it is not. Was this taken
By any understanding pate but thine?
For thy conceit is soaking, will draw in
More than the common blocks ... not noted, is't,
But of the finer natures? by some severals
Of head-piece extraordinary? lower messes
Perchance are to this business purblind? say.
CAMILLO. Business, my lord? I think most understand
Bohemia stays here longer.
LEONTES.   Ha!
CAMILLO.   Stays here longer. 230
LEONTES. Ay, but why?
CAMILLO. To satisfy your highness, and the entreaties
Of our most gracious mistress.
LEONTES.   Satisfy?
Th'entreaties of your mistress? satisfy?
Let that suffice.... I have trusted thee, Camillo,
With all the nearest things to my heart, as well
My chamber-counsels, wherein, priest-like, thou
Hast cleansed my bosom; ay, from thee departed
Thy penitent reformed: but we have been
Deceived in thy integrity, deceived 240
In that which seems so.
CAMILLO.   Be it forbid, my lord!
LEONTES. To bide upon't: thou art not honest: or,
If thou inclin'st that way, thou art a coward,
Which hoxes honesty behind, restraining
From course required: or else thou must be counted
A servant, grafted in my serious trust,
And therein negligent; or else a fool,
That seest a game played home, the rich stake
          drawn,
And tak'st it all for jest.
CAMILLO.   My gracious lord,
I may be negligent, foolish, and fearful— 250
In every one of these no man is free,
But that his negligence, his folly, fear,
Among the infinite doings of the world,
Sometime puts forth. In your affairs, my lord,
If ever I were wilful-negligent,
It was my folly; if industriously
I played the fool, it was my negligence,
Not weighing well the end; if ever fearful
To do a thing, where I the issue doubted,
Whereof the execution did cry out 260
Against the non-performance, 'twas a fear
Which oft infects the wisest: these, my lord,
Are such allowed infirmities, that honesty

Is never free of. But, beseech your grace,
Be plainer with me, let me know my trespass
By its own visage: if I then deny it,
'Tis none of mine.
LEONTES.   Ha' not you seen, Camillo
(But that's past doubt: you have, or your eye-glass
Is thicker than a cuckold's horn), or heard
(For to a vision so apparent rumour   270
Cannot be mute) or thought (for cogitation
Resides not in that man that does not think)
My wife is slippery? If thou wilt confess,
Or else be impudently negative,
To have nor eyes, nor ears, nor thought, then say
My wife's a hobby-horse, deserves a name
As rank as any flax-wench that puts to
Before her troth-plight: say't, and justify't.
CAMILLO. I would not be a stander-by, to hear
My sovereign mistress clouded so, without   280
My present vengeance taken: 'shrew my heart,
You never spoke what did become you less
Than this; which to reiterate, were sin
As deep as that, though true.
LEONTES.   Is whispering nothing?
Is leaning cheek to cheek? is meeting noses?
Kissing with inside lip? stopping the career
Of laughter with a sigh (a note infallible
Of breaking honesty)? horsing foot on foot?
Skulking in corners? wishing clocks more swift?
Hours, minutes? noon, midnight? and all eyes   290
Blind with the pin and web but theirs; theirs only,
That would unseen be wicked? Is this nothing?
Why then the world, and all that's in't, is nothing,
The covering sky is nothing, Bohemia nothing,
My wife is nothing, nor nothing have these
    nothings,
If this be nothing.
CAMILLO.   Good my lord, be cured
Of this diseased opinion, and betimes,
For 'tis most dangerous.
LEONTES.   Say it be, 'tis true.
CAMILLO. No, no, my lord.
LEONTES.   It is; you lie, you lie:
I say thou liest, Camillo, and I hate thee,   300
Pronounce thee a gross lout, a mindless slave,
Or else a hovering temporizer, that
Canst with thine eyes at once see good and evil,
Inclining to them both: were my wife's liver
Infected as her life, she would not live
The running of one glass.
CAMILLO.   Who does infect her?
LEONTES. Why, he that wears her like her medal,
    hanging
About his neck—Bohemia! who, if I
Had servants true about me, that bare eyes
To see alike mine honour, as their profits   310
(Their own particular thrifts) they would do that
Which should undo more doing: ay, and thou
His cupbearer, whom I from meaner form
Have benched and reared to worship, who mayst see
Plainly as heaven sees earth and earth sees heaven,
How I am galled, mightst bespice a cup,
To give mine enemy a lasting wink;
Which draught to me, were cordial.
CAMILLO.   Sir, my lord,
I could do this, and that with no rash potion,
But with a ling'ring dram, that should not work   320

Maliciously like poison: but I cannot
Believe this crack to be in my dread mistress
(So sovereignly being honourable!)
I have loved the—
LEONTES.   Make that thy question, and go rot!
Dost think I am so muddy, so unsettled,
To appoint myself in this vexation, sully
The purity and whiteness of my sheets
(Which to preserve is sleep, which being spotted
Is goads, thorns, nettles, tails of wasps),
Give scandal to the blood o'th' prince my son   330
(Who I do think is mine, and love as mine),
Without ripe moving to't? Would I do this?
Could man so blench?
CAMILLO.   I must believe you, sir,
I do, and will fetch off Bohemia for't:
Provided, that when he's removed, your highness
Will take again your queen, as yours at first,
Even for your son's sake, and thereby forestalling
The injury of tongues in courts and kingdoms
Known and allied to yours.
LEONTES.   Thou dost advise me,
Even so as I mine own course have set down: 340
I'll give no blemish to her honour, none.
CAMILLO. My lord,
Go then; and with a countenance as clear
As friendship wears at feasts, keep with Bohemia,
And with your queen ... I am his cupbearer,
If from me he have wholesome beverage,
Account me not your servant.
LEONTES.   This is all:
Do't, and thou hast the one half of my heart;
Do't not, thou spilt'st thine own.
CAMILLO.   I'll do't, my lord.
LEONTES. I will seem friendly, as thou hast advised me. 350
                                        He goes
CAMILLO. O miserable lady.... But, for me,
What case stand I in? I must be the poisoner
Of good Polixenes, and my ground to do't
Is the obedience to a master; one,
Who in rebellion with himself, will have
All that are his, so too.... To do this deed,
Promotion follows ... If I could find example
Of thousands that had struck anointed kings
And flourished after, I'ld not do't: but since
Nor brass, nor stone, nor parchment, bears not one, 360
Let villainy itself forswear't.... I must
Forsake the court: to do't, or no, is certain
To me a break-neck.... Happy star reign now!
Here comes Bohemia.

Polixenes enters

POLIXENES.   This is strange: methinks
My favour here begins to warp. Not speak!
Good day, Camillo.
CAMILLO.   Hail, most royal sir!
POLIXENES. What is the news i'th' court?
CAMILLO.   None rare, my lord.
POLIXENES. The king hath on him such a countenance
As he had lost some province, and a region
Loved as he loves himself: even now I met him   370
With customary compliment, when he,
Wafting his eyes to th' contrary, and falling
A lip of much contempt, speeds from me, and
So leaves me, to consider what is breeding
That changes thus his manners.

CAMILLO. I dare not know, my lord.

POLIXENES. How! dare not? do not. Do you know, and
    dare not?
  Be intelligent to me—'tis thereabouts:
  For, to yourself, what you do know, you must,
  And cannot say you dare not.... Good Camillo, 380
  Your changed complexions are to me a mirror,
  Which shows me mine changed too: for I must be
  A party in this alteration, finding
  Myself thus altered with't.

CAMILLO.   There is a sickness
  Which puts some of us in distemper, but
  I cannot name the disease, and it is caught
  Of you, that yet are well.

POLIXENES.   How! caught of me?
  Make me not sighted like the basilisk:
  I have looked on thousands, who have sped the
    better
  By my regard, but killed none so ... Camillo— 390
  As you are certainly a gentleman, thereto
  Clerk-like experienced, which no less adorns
  Our gentry than our parents' noble names,
  In whose success we are gentle—I beseech you,
  If you know aught which does behove my
    knowledge
  Thereof to be informed, imprison't not
  In ignorant concealment.

CAMILLO.   I may not answer.

POLIXENES. A sickness caught of me, and yet I well!
  I must be answered.... Dost thou hear, Camillo,
  I conjure thee, by all the parts of man 400
  Which honour does acknowledge, whereof the least
  Is not this suit of mine, that thou declare
  What incidency thou dost guess of harm
  Is creeping toward me; how far off, how near;
  Which way to be prevented, if to be;
  If not, how best to bear it.

CAMILLO.   Sir, I will tell you,
  Since I am charged in honour and by him
  That I think honourable: therefore mark my
    counsel,
  Which must be even as swiftly followed, as
  I mean to utter it; or both yourself and me 410
  Cry 'lost,' and so good night!

POLIXENES.   On, good Camillo.

CAMILLO. I am appointed him to murder you.

POLIXENES. By whom, Camillo?

CAMILLO.   By the king.

POLIXENES.   For what!

CAMILLO. He thinks, nay with all confidence he
    swears,
  As he had seen't, or been an instrument
  To vice you to't, that you have touched his queen
  Forbiddenly.

POLIXENES.   O, then my best blood turn
  To an infected jelly, and my name
  Be yoked with his that did betray the Best!
  Turn then my freshest reputation to 420
  A savour that may strike the dullest nostril
  Where I arrive, and my approach be shunned,
  Nay hated too, worse than the great'st infection
  That e'er was heard or read!

CAMILLO.   Swear his thought over
  By each particular star in heaven and
  By all their influences! you may as well
  Forbid the sea for to obey the moon,

As or by oath remove or counsel shake
The fabric of his folly, whose foundation
Is piled upon his faith, and will continue 430
The standing of his body.

POLIXENES.   How should this grow?

CAMILLO. I know not: but I am sure 'tis safer to
  Avoid what's grown than question how 'tis born.
  If therefore you dare trust my honesty,
  That lies enclosèd in this trunk which you
  Shall bear along impawned, away to-night!
  Your followers I will whisper to the business,
  And will by twos and threes, at several posterns,
  Clear them o'th' city: for myself, I'll put
  My fortunes to your service, which are here 440
  By this discovery lost.... Be not uncertain,
  For by the honour of my parents I
  Have uttered truth: which if you seek to prove,
  I dare not stand by; nor shall you be safer
  Than one condemned by the king's own mouth:
  Thereon his execution sworn.

POLIXENES.   I do believe thee:
  I saw his heart in's face.... Give me thy hand,
  Be pilot to me, and thy places shall
  Still neighbour mine. My ships are ready, and
  My people did expect my hence departure 450
  Two days ago.... This jealousy
  Is for a precious creature: as she's rare,
  Must it be great; and, as his person's mighty,
  Must it be violent; and as he does conceive
  He is dishonoured by a man which ever
  Professed to him, why, his revenges must
  In that be made more bitter. Fear o'ershades me:
  Good expedition be my friend, and comfort
  The gracious queen, part of his theme, but nothing
  Of his ill-ta'en suspicion! Come, Camillo, 460
  I will respect thee as a father, if
  Thou bear'st my life off. Hence: let us avoid.

CAMILLO. It is in mine authority to command
  The keys of all the posterns: please your highness
  To take the urgent hour.... Come, sir, away.

                      They go

ACT 2
Scene 1

Hermione enters with her ladies and Mamillius

HERMIONE. Take the boy to you: he so troubles me,
  'Tis past enduring.

1 LADY.   Come, my gracious lord,
  Shall I be your playfellow?

MAMILLIUS.   No, I'll none of you.

1 LADY. Why, my sweet lord?

MAMILLIUS. You'll kiss me hard, and speak to me as if
  I were a baby still.... I love you better.

2 LADY. And why so, my lord?

MAMILLIUS.   Not for because
  Your brows are blacker; yet black brows, they say,
  Become some women best, so that there be not
  Too much hair there, but in a semicircle, 10
  Or a half-moon made with a pen.

2 LADY.   Who taught' this?

MAMILLIUS. I learned it out of women's faces.... Pray
  now
  What colour are your eyebrows?

1 LADY.   Blue, my lord.

MAMILLIUS. Nay, that's a mock: I have seen a lady's
    nose
That has been blue, but not her eyebrows.
1 LADY.   Hark ye,
The queen your mother rounds apace: we shall
Present our services to a fine new prince
One of these days, and then you'ld wanton with us,
If we would have you.
2 LADY.   She is spread of late
Into a goodly bulk (good time encounter her!)   20
HERMIONE. What wisdom stirs amongst you? Come,
    sir, now
I am for you again: pray you, sit by us,
And tell's a tale.
MAMILLIUS.   Merry, or sad, shall't be?
HERMIONE. As merry as you will.
MAMILLIUS. A sad tale's best for winter: I have one
Of sprites and goblins.
HERMIONE.   Let's have that, good sir.
Come on, sit down, come on, and do your best
To fright me with your sprites: you're powerful
    at it.
MAMILLIUS. There was a man—
HERMIONE.   Nay, come, sit down; then on.
MAMILLIUS. Dwelt by a churchyard ... I will tell it
    softly,   30
Yon crickets shall not hear it.
HERMIONE.   Come on then,
And give't me in mine ear.

Leontes enters, with Antigonus, lords and a guard

LEONTES. Was he met there? his train? Camillo with
    him?
1 LORD. Behind the tuft of pines I met them, never
Saw I men scour so on their way: I eyed them
Even to their ships.
LEONTES.   How blest am I
In my just censure! in my true opinion!
Alack, for lesser knowledge! how accursed,
In being so blest! There may be in the cup
A spider steeped, and one may drink, depart,   40
And yet partake no venom (for his knowledge
Is not infected): but if one present
Th'abhorred ingredient to his eye, make known
How he hath drunk, he cracks his gorge, his sides,
With violent hefts: I have drunk, and seen the
    spider. . . .
Camillo was his help in this, his pandar:
There is a plot against my life, my crown;
All's true that is mistrusted: that false villain
Whom I employed was pre-employed by him:
He has discovered my design, and I   50
Remain a pinched thing; yea, a very trick
For them to play at will ... How came the posterns
So easily open?
1 LORD.   By his great authority,
Which often hath no less prevailed than so
On your command.
LEONTES.   I know't too well. . . .
Give me the boy, I am glad you did not nurse him:
Though he does bear some signs of me, yet you
Have too much blood in him.
HERMIONE.   What is this? sport?
LEONTES. Bear the boy hence, he shall not come about
    her,
Away with him! and let her sport herself   60

With that she's big with—for 'tis Polixenes
Has made thee swell thus.
HERMIONE.   But I'ld say he had not,
And I'll be sworn you would believe my saying,
Howe'er you lean to th' nayward.
                     They carry the boy away
LEONTES.   You, my lords,
Look on her, mark her well; be but about
To say 'she is a goodly lady,' and
The justice of your hearts will thereto add
' 'Tis pity she's not honest ... honourable':
Praise her but for this her without-door form
(Which on my faith deserves high speech) and
    straight   70
The shrug, the hum or ha!—these petty brands
That calumny doth use; O, I am out,
That mercy does, for calumny will sear
Virtue itself—these shrugs, these hums, and ha's,
When you have said 'she's goodly,' come between
Ere you can say 'she's honest': but be't known,
(From him that has most cause to grieve it should
    be)
She's an adultress.
HERMIONE.   Should a villain say so
(The most replenished villain in the world),
He were as much more villain ... You, my lord,   80
Do but mistake.
LEONTES.   You have mistook, my lady,
Polixenes for Leontes: O thou thing!
Which I'll not call a creature of thy place,
Lest barbarism, making me the precedent,
Should a like language use to all degrees,
And mannerly distinguishment leave out
Betwixt the prince and beggar: I have said
She's an adultress, I have said with whom:
More; she's a traitor, and Camillo is
A fedary with her, and one that knows   90
What she should shame to know herself
But with her most vile principal ... that she's
A bed-swerver, even as bad as those
That vulgars give bold'st titles; ay, and privy
To this their late escape.
HERMIONE.   No, by my life,
Privy to none of this ... How will this grieve you,
When you shall come to clearer knowledge, that
You thus have published me? Gentle my lord,
You scarce can right me throughly then, to say
You did mistake.
LEONTES.   No: if I mistake   100
In those foundations which I build upon,
The Centre is not big enough to bear
A school-boy's top. . . . Away with her to prison:
He who shall speak for her is afar off guilty,
But that he speaks.
HERMIONE.   There's some ill planet reigns:
I must be patient, till the heavens look
With an aspect more favourable. . . . Good my lords,
I am not prone to weeping, as our sex
Commonly are, the want of which vain dew
Perchance shall dry your pities: but I have   110
That honourable grief lodged here, which burns
Worse than tears drown: beseech you all, my lords,
With thoughts so qualified as your charities
Shall best instruct you, measure me; and so
The king's will be performed!
LEONTES.   Shall I be heard?

HERMIONE. Who is't that goes with me? Beseech your
    highness,
My women may be with me, for you see
My plight requires it. Do not weep, good fools,
There is no cause: when you shall know your
    mistress
Has deserved prison, then abound in tears   120
As I come out: this action I now go on
Is for my better grace.... Adieu, my lord!
I never wished to see you sorry, now
I trust I shall.... My women come, you have leave.
LEONTES. Go, do our bidding; hence.
            They lead the Queen away; her ladies follow
I LORD. Beseech your highness, call the queen again.
ANTIGONUS. Be certain what you do, sir, lest your
    justice
Prove violence, in the which three great ones suffer,
Yourself, your queen, your son.
I LORD.   For her, my lord,
I dare my life lay down and will do't, sir,   130
Please you t'accept it, that the queen is spotless
I'th'eyes of heaven, and to you—I mean
In this which you accuse her.
ANTIGONUS.   If it prove
She's otherwise, I'll keep my stables where
I lodge my wife, I'll go in couples with her;
Than when I feel and see her no farther trust her;
For every inch of woman in the world,
Ay, every dram of woman's flesh is false,
If she be.
LEONTES.   Hold your peaces.
I LORD.   Good my lord—
ANTIGONUS. It is for you we speak, not for ourselves: 140
You are abused, and by some putter-on
That will be damned for't; would I knew the villain,
I would lam-damn him ... Be she honour-flawed,
I have three daughters; the eldest is eleven;
The second and the third, nine and some five;
If this prove true, they'll pay for't: by mine honour,
I'll geld 'em all; fourteen they shall not see,
To bring false generations: they are co-heirs,
And I had rather glib myself, than they
Should not produce fair issue.
LEONTES.   Cease, no more!   150
You smell this business with a sense as cold
As is a dead man's nose: but I do see't and feel't,
As you feel doing thus ... and see withal
The instruments that feel.
ANTIGONUS.   If it be so,
We need no grave to bury honesty,
There's not a grain of it the face to sweeten
Of the whole dungy earth.
LEONTES.   What! lack I credit?
I LORD. I had rather you did lack than I, my lord,
Upon this ground: and more it would content me
To have her honour true than your suspicion,   160
Be blamed for't how you might.
LEONTES.   Why, what need we
Commune with you of this, but rather follow
Our forceful instigation? Our prerogative
Calls not your counsels, but our natural goodness
Imparts this: which if you, or stupefied,
Or seeming so in skill, cannot or will not
Relish a truth like us ... inform yourselves
We need no more of your advice: the matter,
The loss, the gain, the ord'ring on't, is all

Properly ours.
ANTIGONUS.   And I wish, my liege,   170
You had only in your silent judgement tried it,
Without more overture.
LEONTES.   How could that be?
Either thou art most ignorant by age,
Or thou wert born a fool ... Camillo's flight,
Added to their familiarity
(Which was as gross as ever touched conjecture,
That lacked sight only, nought for approbation
But only seeing, all other circumstances
Made up to th' deed) doth push on this proceeding:
Yet, for a greater confirmation   180
(For in an act of this importance, 'twere
Most piteous to be wild), I have dispatched in post
To sacred Delphos, to Apollo's temple,
Cleomenes and Dion, whom you know
Of stuffed sufficiency: now from the oracle
They will bring all—whose spiritual counsel had,
Shall stop or spur me.... Have I done well?
I LORD. Well done, my lord.
LEONTES. Though I am satisfied, and need no more
Than what I know, yet shall the oracle   190
Give rest to th' minds of others; such as he,
                        Points at Antigonus
Whose ignorant credulity will not
Come up to th' truth.... So have we thought it
    good,
From our free person she should be confined,
Lest that the treachery of the two fled hence
Be left her to perform. Come, follow us,
We are to speak in public; for this business
Will raise us all.
ANTIGONUS.   To laughter, as I take it,
If the good truth were known.   *They go*

Scene 2: *A prison in Sicilia*

Paulina, a gentleman, and attendants enter

PAULINA. The keeper of the prison, call to him;
Let him have knowledge who I am....
                        The gentleman goes
                                Good lady,
No court in Europe is too good for thee,
What dost thou then in prison?

The gentleman returns with the Gaoler.

                                Now, good sir,
You know me, do you not?
GAOLER.   For a worthy lady,
And one whom much I honour.
PAULINA.   Pray you then,
Conduct me to the queen.
GAOLER.   I may not, madam.
To the contrary I have express commandment.
PAULINA. Here's ado,
To lock up honesty and honour from   10
Th'access of gentle visitors! Is't lawful, pray you,
To see her women? any of them? Emilia?
GAOLER. So please you, madam,
To put apart these your attendants, I
Shall bring Emilia forth.
PAULINA.   I pray now, call her ...
Withdraw yourselves.   *The attendants depart*
GAOLER.   And, madam,
I must be present at your conference.

PAULINA. Well: be't so: prithee.   *The Gaoler goes*
  Here's such ado to make no stain a stain,
  As passes colouring....

The Gaoler returns with Emilia

                            Dear gentlewoman,   20
  How fares our gracious lady?
EMILIA. As well as one so great and so forlorn
  May hold together: on her frights and griefs
  (Which never tender lady hath borne greater)
  She is, something before her time, delivered.
PAULINA. A boy?
EMILIA.   A daughter—and a goodly babe,
  Lusty and like to live: the Queen receives
  Much comfort in't: says, 'My poor prisoner,
  I am innocent as you.'
PAULINA.   I dare be sworn ...
  These dangerous unsafe lunes i'th' king, beshrew
    them!   30
  He must be told on't, and he shall: the office
  Becomes a woman best; I'll take't upon me,
  If I prove honey-mouthed, let my tongue blister,
  And never to my red-looked anger be
  The trumpet any more ... Pray you, Emilia,
  Commend my best obedience to the queen,
  If she dares trust me with her little babe,
  I'll show't the king and undertake to be
  Her advocate to th' loud'st.... We do not know
  How he may soften at the sight o'th' child: 40
  The silence often of pure innocence
  Persuades when speaking fails.
EMILIA.   Most worthy madam,
  Your honour and your goodness is so evident,
  That your free undertaking cannot miss
  A thriving issue: there is no lady living
  So meet for this great errand.... Please your
    ladyship
  To visit the next room, I'll presently
  Acquaint the queen of your most noble offer,
  Who, but to-day, hammered of this design,
  But durst not tempt a minister of honour,   50
  Lest she should be denied.
PAULINA.   Tell her, Emilia,
  I'll use that tongue I have: if wit flow from't
  As boldness from my bosom, let't not be doubted
  I shall do good.
EMILIA.   Now be you blest for it!
  I'll to the queen: please you, come something
    nearer.   *She goes*
GAOLER. Madam, if't please the queen to send the
    babe,
  I know not what I shall incur to pass it,
  Having no warrant.
PAULINA.   You need not fear it, sir:
  This child was prisoner to the womb, and is
  By law and process of great nature thence   60
  Freed and enfranchised—not a party to
  The anger of the king, nor guilty of
  (If any be) the trespass of the queen.
GAOLER. I do believe it.
PAULINA. Do not you fear: upon mine honour, I
  Will stand betwixt you and danger.
                            They follow Emilia

          Scene 3: *The Palace (as before)*

Enter Leontes

LEONTES. Nor night, nor day, no rest: it is but
    weakness
  To bear the matter thus; mere weakness. If
  The cause were not in being ... part o'th' cause,
  She, th'adultress ... for the harlot king
  Is quite beyond mine arm, out of the blank
  And level of my brain: plot-proof: but she
  I can hook to me: say that she were gone,
  Given to the fire, a moiety of my rest
  Might come to me again ...Who's there?

A servant enters

SERVANT.   My lord!
LEONTES. How does the boy?
SERVANT.   He took good rest to-night;   10
  'Tis hoped his sickness is discharged.
LEONTES. To see his nobleness!
  Conceiving the dishonour of his mother,
  He straight declined, drooped, took it deeply,
  Fastened and fixed the shame on't in himself;
  Threw off his spirit, his appetite, his sleep,
  And downright languished.... Leave me solely: go,
  See how he fares ... [*the servant goes*] Fie, fie! no
    thought of him—
  The very thought of my revenges that way
  Recoil upon me: in himself too mighty,   20
  And in his parties, his alliance; let him be,
  Until a time may serve. For present vengeance,
  Take it on her ... Camillo and Polixenes
  Laugh at me; make their pastime at my sorrow:
  They should not laugh if I could reach them, nor
  Shall she, within my power.

*Paulina, with a baby, enters, followed by her husband
Antigonus, lords, and the servant, who try to prevent her*

1 LORD.   You must not enter.
PAULINA. Nay, rather, good my lords, be second
    to me:
  Fear you his tyrannous passion more, alas,
  Than the queen's life? a gracious innocent soul,
  More free than he is jealous.
ANTIGONUS.   That's enough.   30
2 SERVANT. Madam; he hath not slept to-night,
    commanded
  None should come at him.
PAULINA.   Not so hot, good sir,
  I come to bring him sleep.... 'Tis such as you,
  That creep like shadows by him, and do sigh
  At each his needless heavings ... such as you
  Nourish the cause of his awaking. I
  Do come with words as medicinal as true,
  Honest, as either; to purge him of that humour,
  That presses him from sleep.
LEONTES.   What noise there, ho?
PAULINA. No noise, my lord, but needful conference, 40
  About some gossips for your highness.
LEONTES.   How!
  Away with that audacious lady. Antigonus,
  I charged thee that she should not come about me,
  I knew she would.
ANTIGONUS.   I told her so, my lord,
  On your displeasure's peril, and on mine,
  She should not visit you.
LEONTES.   What! canst not rule her?
PAULINA. From all dishonesty he can: in this—
  Unless he take the course that you have done,

Commit me for committing honour—trust it,
He shall not rule me.
ANTIGONUS.   La you now! you hear!   50
When she will take the rein I let her run,
[aside] But she'll not stumble.
PAULINA.   Good my liege, I come ...
And I beseech you hear me, who profess
Myself your loyal servant, your physician,
Your most obedient counsellor; yet that dare
Less appear so, in comforting your evils,
Than such as most seem yours.... I say, I come
From your good queen.
LEONTES. Good queen!
PAULINA. Good queen, my lord, good queen, I say
   good queen,   60
And would by combat make her good, so were I
A man, the worst about you.
LEONTES.   Force her hence.
PAULINA. Let him that makes but trifles of his eyes
First hand me; on mine own accord, I'll off,
But first I'll do my errand. The good queen
(For she is good) hath brought you forth a
   daughter—
Here 'tis ... [she lays the child before him] commends
it to your blessing.
LEONTES.   Out!
A mankind witch! Hence with her, out o' door:
A most intelligencing bawd!
PAULINA.   Not so:
I am as ignorant in that, as you   70
In so entitling me: and no less honest
Than you are mad; which is enough, I'll warrant,
As this world goes, to pass for honest.
LEONTES.   Traitors!
Will you not push her out? [to Antigonus] Give her
   the bastard,
Thou dotard—thou art woman-tired, unroosted
By thy Dame Partlet here ... Take up the bastard,
Take't up, I say; give't to thy crone.
PAULINA.   For ever
Unvenerable be thy hands, if thou
Tak'st up the princess, by that forcéd baseness
Which he has put upon't!
LEONTES.   He dreads his wife.   80
PAULINA. So I would you did; then 'twere past all
   doubt,
You'ld call your children yours.
LEONTES.   A nest of traitors!
ANTIGONUS. I am none, by this good light.
PAULINA.   Nor I; nor any
But one that's here; and that's himself: for he
The sacred honour of himself, his queen's,
His hopeful son's, his babe's, betrays to slander,
Whose sting is sharper than the sword's; and will not
(For, as the case now stands, it is a curse
He cannot be compelled to't) once remove
The root of his opinion, which is rotten,   90
As ever oak or stone was sound.
LEONTES.   A callet
Of boundless tongue, who late hath beat her
   husband,
And now baits me! This brat is none of mine,
It is the issue of Polixenes....
Hence with it, and together with the dam
Commit them to the fire!
PAULINA.   It is yours;

And, might we lay th'old proverb to your charge,
So like you, 'tis the worse. Behold, my lords,
Although the print be little, the whole matter
And copy of the father: eye, nose, lip,   100
The trick of's frown, his forehead, nay, the valley,
The pretty dimples of his chin and cheek; his smiles;
The very mould and frame of hand, nail, finger:
And, thou, good goddess Nature, which hast
   made it
So like to him that got it, if thou hast
The ordering of the mind too, 'mongst all colours
No yellow in't, lest she suspect, as he does,
Her children not her husband's!
LEONTES.   A gross hag!
And, lozel, thou art worthy to be hanged,
That wilt not stay her tongue.
ANTIGONUS.   Hang all the husbands   110
That cannot do that feat, you'll leave yourself
Hardly one subject.
LEONTES.   Once more, take her hence.
PAULINA. A most unworthy and unnatural lord
Can do no more.
LEONTES.   I'll ha' thee burnt.
PAULINA.   I care not:
It is an heretic that makes the fire,
Not she which burns in't. I'll not call you tyrant;
But this most cruel usage of your queen
(Not able to produce more accusation
Than your own weak-hinged fancy) something
   savours
Of tyranny, and will ignoble make you,   120
Yea, scandalous to the world.
LEONTES.   On your allegiance,
Out of the chamber with her! Were I a tyrant,
Where were her life? she durst not call me so,
If she did know me one. Away with her!
PAULINA. I pray you, do not push me, I'll be gone.
Look to your babe, my lord, 'tis yours: Jove send her
A better guiding spirit! What needs these hands?
You, that are thus so tender o'er his follies,
Will never do him good, not one of you.
So, so: farewell, we are gone.   She goes   130
LEONTES. Thou, traitor, hast set on thy wife to this.
My child! away with't! Even thou, that hast
A heart so tender o'er it, take it hence,
And see it instantly consumed with fire;
Even thou and none but thou. Take it up straight:
Within this hour bring me word 'tis done,
And by good testimony, or I'll seize thy life,
With what thou else call'st thine ... If thou refuse,
And will encounter with my wrath, say so;
The bastard brains with these my proper hands   140
Shall I dash out. Go, take it to the fire,
For thou set'st on thy wife.
ANTIGONUS.   I did not, sir:
These lords, my noble fellows, if they please,
Can clear me in't.
LORDS.   We can; my royal liege,
He is not guilty of her coming hither.
LEONTES. You're liars all.
1 LORD. Beseech your highness, give us better credit:
We have always truly served you, and beseech'
So to esteem of us: and on our knees we beg
(As recompense of our dear services,   150
Past, and to come) that you do change this purpose,
Which being so horrible, so bloody, must

Lead on to some foul issue ... We all kneel.
LEONTES. I am a feather for each wind that blows:
    Shall I live on, to see this bastard kneel
    And call me father? better burn it now
    Than curse it then.... But be it: let it live....
    It shall not neither.... [to Antigonus] You, sir, come
        you hither;
    You, that have been so tenderly officious
    With Lady Margery, your midwife there,   160
    To save this bastard's life; for 'tis a bastard,
    So sure as this beard's grey.... What will you
        adventure
    To save this brat's life?
ANTIGONUS.   Any thing, my lord,
    That my ability may undergo,
    And nobleness impose: at least, thus much;
    I'll pawn the little blood which I have left
    To save the innocent: any thing possible.
LEONTES. It shall be possible ... Swear by this sword
    Thou wilt perform my bidding.
ANTIGONUS.   I will, my lord.
LEONTES. Mark and perform it: seest thou? for the fail 170
    Of any point in't shall not only be
    Death to thyself, but to thy lewd-tongued wife
    (Whom for this time we pardon). We enjoin thee,
    As thou art liege-man to us, that thou carry
    This female bastard hence, and that thou bear it
    To some remote and desert place, quite out
    Of our dominions; and that there thou leave it
    (Without more mercy) to it own protection
    And favour of the climate: as by strange fortune
    It came to us, I do in justice charge thee,   180
    On thy soul's peril and thy body's torture,
    That thou commend it strangely to some place
    Where chance may nurse or end it: take it up.
ANTIGONUS. I swear to do this; though a present death
    Had been more merciful.... Come on, poor babe!
    Some powerful spirit instruct the kites and ravens
    To be thy nurses! Wolves and bears, they say,
    Casting their savageness aside, have done
    Like offices of pity.... Sir, be prosperous
    In more than this deed does require; and blessing,   190
    Against this cruelty, fight on thy side,
    Poor thing, condemned to loss!
                              He bears away the child
LEONTES.   No! I'll not rear
    Another's issue.

A servant enters

SERVANT.   Please your highness, posts
    From those you sent to th'oracle are come
    An hour since: Cleomenes and Dion,
    Being well arrived from Delphos, are both landed,
    Hasting to th' court.
1 LORD.   So please you, sir, their speed
    Hath been beyond accompt.
LEONTES.   Twenty three days
    They have been absent: 'tis good speed; foretells
    The great Apollo suddenly will have   200
    The truth of this appear ... Prepare you, lords,
    Summon a session, that we may arraign
    Our most disloyal lady: for as she hath
    Been publicly accused, so shall she have
    A just and open trial.... While she lives,
    My heart will be a burthen to me.... Leave me,
    And think upon my bidding.   *They go*

ACT 3
Scene 1: *A high road in Sicilia*

Cleomenes and Dion

CLEOMENES. The climate's delicate, the air most sweet,
    Fertile the isle, the temple much surpassing
    The common praise it bears.
DION.   I shall report,
    For most it caught me, the celestial habits
    (Methinks I so should term them) and the reverence
    Of the grave wearers. O, the sacrifice!
    How ceremonious, solemn, and unearthly
    It was i'th' off'ring!
CLEOMENES.   But of all, the burst
    And the ear-deaf'ning voice o'th'oracle,
    Kin to Jove's thunder, so surprised my sense,   10
    That I was nothing.
DION.   If th'event o'th' journey
    Prove as successful to the queen (O be't so!)
    As it hath been to us, rare, pleasant, speedy,
    The time is worth the use on't.
CLEOMENES.   Great Apollo,
    Turn all to th' best! These proclamations,
    So forcing faults upon Hermione,
    I little like.
DION.   The violent carriage of it
    Will clear or end the business; when the oracle
    (Thus by Apollo's great divine sealed up)
    Shall the contents discover, something rare   20
    Even then will rush to knowledge.... Go: fresh
        horses!
    And gracious be the issue!   *They go*

Scene 2: *A Court of Justice*

*Enter Leontes, his lords and officers about him. A great
concourse of people*

LEONTES. This sessions (to our great grief we
        pronounce)
    Even pushes 'gainst our heart: the party tried,
    The daughter of a king, our wife, and one
    Of us too much beloved.... Let us be cleared
    Of being tyrannous, since we so openly
    Proceed in justice, which shall have due course,
    Even to the guilt or the purgation ...
    Produce the prisoner.
OFFICER. It is his highness' pleasure, that the queen
    Appear in person, here in court.   10

*Hermione is brought in guarded, Paulina and
ladies attending.*

OFFICER. Silence!
LEONTES. Read the indictment.
OFFICER [*reads*]. 'Hermione, queen to the worthy
    Leonites, King of Sicilia, thou art here accused and
    arraigned of high treason, in committing adultery
    with Polixenes, King of Bohemia, and conspiring
    with Camillo to take away the life of our sovereign
    lord the king, thy royal husband: the pretence
    whereof being by circumstances partly laid open,
    thou, Hermione, contrary to the faith and allegiance 20
    of a true subject, didst counsel and aid them, for their
    better safety, to fly away by night.'

HERMIONE. Since what I am to say must be but that
Which contradicts my accusation, and
The testimony on my part no other
But what comes from myself, it shall scarce boot me
To say 'not guilty': mine integrity,
Being counted falsehood, shall, as I express it,
Be so received.... But thus, if powers divine
Behold our human actions (as they do), 30
I doubt not then but innocence shall make
False accusation blush, and tyranny
Tremble at patience.... You, my lord, best know
(Who least will seem to do so) my past life
Hath been as continent, as chaste, as true,
As I am now unhappy; which is more
Than history can pattern, though devised
And played to take spectators. For behold me,
A fellow of the royal bed, which owe
A moiety of the throne ... a great king's daughter, 40
The mother to a hopeful prince, here standing
To prate and talk for life and honour, 'fore
Who please to come and hear. For life, I prize it
As I weigh grief (which I would spare): for honour,
'Tis a derivative from me to mine,
And only that I stand for.... I appeal
To your own conscience, sir, before Polixenes
Came to your court, how I was in your grace,
How merited to be so; since he came,
With what encounter so uncurrent I 50
Have strained t'appear thus: if one jot beyond
The bound of honour, or in act or will
That way inclining, hard'ned be the hearts
Of all that hear me, and my near'st of kin
Cry fie upon my grave!
LEONTES.   I ne'er heard yet,
That any of these bolder vices wanted
Less impudence to gainsay what they did,
Than to perform it first.
HERMIONE.   That's true enough,
Though 'tis a saying, sir, not due to me.
LEONTES. You will not own it.
HERMIONE.   More than mistress of 60
Which comes to me in name of fault, I must not
At all acknowledge.... For Polixenes
(With whom I am accused) I do confess
I loved him, as in honour he required;
With such a kind of love as might become
A lady like me; with a love, even such,
So, and no other, as yourself commanded:
Which not to have done, I think had been in me
Both disobedience and ingratitude
To you, and toward your friend, whose love had
      spoke, 70
Even since it could speak, from an infant, freely,
That it was yours. Now, for conspiracy,
I know not how it tastes, though it be dished
For me to try how: all I know of it,
Is, that Camillo was an honest man;
And why he left your court, the gods themselves
(Wotting no more than I) are ignorant.
LEONTES. You knew of his departure, as you know
What you have underta'en to do in's absence.
HERMIONE. Sir, 80
You speak a language that I understand not:
My life stands in the level of your dreams,
Which I'll lay down.
LEONTES.   Your actions are my dreams.

You had a bastard by Polixenes,
And I but dreamed it! As you were past all shame
(Those of your fact are so), so past all truth;
Which to deny, concerns more than avails: for as
Thy brat hath been cast out, like to itself,
No father owning it (which is indeed
More criminal in thee than it) so thou 90
Shalt feel our justice; in whose easiest passage
Look for no less than death.
HERMIONE.   Sir, spare your threats:
The bug which you would fright me with I seek:
To me can life be no commodity:
The crown and comfort of my life (your favour)
I do give lost, for I do feel it gone,
But know not how it went. My second joy,
And first-fruits of my body, from his presence
I am barred, like one infectious. My third comfort
(Starred most unluckily!) is from my breast, 100
The innocent milk in it most innocent mouth,
Haled out to murder. Myself on every post
Proclaimed a strumpet: with immodest hatred
The child-bed privilege denied, which 'longs
To women of all fashion. Lastly, hurried
Here, to this place, i'th' open air, before
I have got strength of limit. Now, my liege,
Tell me what blessings I have here alive,
That I should fear to die? Therefore, proceed ...
But yet hear this: mistake me not: no life!— 110
I prize it not a straw—but for mine honour,
Which I would free ... If I shall be condemned
Upon surmises (all proofs sleeping else
But what your jealousies awake) I tell you,
'Tis rigour and not law.... Your honours all,
I do refer me to the oracle;
Apollo be my judge.
I LORD.   This your request
Is altogether just: therefore bring forth,
And in Apollo's name, his oracle. *Officers depart*
HERMIONE. The Emperor of Russia was my father: 120
O that he were alive, and here beholding
His daughter's trial! that he did but see
The flatness of my misery; yet with eyes
Of pity, not revenge!

Officers return with Cleomenes and Dion

OFFICERS. You here shall swear upon this sword of
      justice,
That you, Cleomenes and Dion, have
Been both at Delphos, and from thence have
      brought
This sealed-up oracle, by the hand delivered
Of great Apollo's priest; and that since then
You have not dared to break the holy seal, 130
Nor read the secrets in't.
CLEOMENES, DION.   All this we swear.
LEONTES. Break up the seals and read.
OFFICER [*reads*]. 'Hermione is chaste, Polixenes blame-
less, Camillo a true subject, Leontes a jealous tyrant,
his innocent babe truly begotten, and the king shall
live without an heir, if that which is lost be not
found.'
LORDS. Now blessed be the great Apollo!
HERMIONE.   Praised!
LEONTES. Hast thou read truth?
OFFICER.   Ay, my lord, even so
As it is here set down. 140

LEONTES. There is no truth at all i'th'oracle:
The sessions shall proceed; this is mere falsehood.

A servant enters

SERVANT. My lord the king ... the king!
LEONTES.   What is the business?
SERVANT. O sir, I shall be hated to report it!
The prince your son, with mere conceit and fear
Of the queen's speed, is gone.
LEONTES.   How! gone!
SERVANT.   Is dead.
LEONTES. Apollo's angry, and the heavens themselves
Do strike at my injustice. [*Hermione faints*] How
now there!
PAULINA. This news is mortal to the queen: look down
And see what death is doing.
LEONTES.   Take her hence: 150
Her heart is but o'ercharged: she will recover....
I have too much believed mine own suspicion:
Beseech you, tenderly apply to her
Some remedies for life....
            Paulina and ladies carry Hermione away
                            Apollo, pardon
My great profaneness 'gainst thine oracle!
I'll reconcile me to Polixenes,
New woo my queen, recall the good Camillo,
Whom I proclaim a man of truth, of mercy ...
For being transported by my jealousies
To bloody thoughts and to revenge, I chose   160
Camillo for the minister to poison
My friend Polixenes: which had been done,
But that the good mind of Camillo tardied
My swift command; though I with death, and with
Reward, did threaten and encourage him,
Not doing it, and being done; he (most humane,
And filled with honour) to my kingly guest
Unclasped my practice, quit his fortunes here
(Which you knew great) and to the certain hazard
Of all incertainties himself commended,   170
No richer than his honour ... How he glisters
Thorough my rust! and how his piety
Does my deeds make the blacker!

Paulina returns

PAULINA.   Woe the while!
O, cut my lace, lest my heart, cracking it,
Break too!
I LORD.   What fit is this, good lady?
PAULINA. What studied torments, tyrant, hast for me?
What wheels? racks? fires? what flaying? boiling,
In leads or oils? what old or newer torture
Must I receive, whose every word deserves
To taste of thy most worst? Thy tyranny   180
(Together working with thy jealousies,
Fancies too weak for boys, too green and idle
For girls of nine) O, think what they have done,
And then run mad indeed: stark mad! for all
Thy by-gone fooleries were but spices of it.
That thou betray'dst Polixenes, 'twas nothing—
That did but show thee, of a fool, inconstant,
And damnable ingrateful: nor was't much,
Thou wouldst have poisoned good Camillo's
honour,
To have him kill a king; poor trespasses,   190
More monstrous standing by: whereof I reckon
The casting forth to crows thy baby-daughter,

To be or none or little; though a devil
Would have shed water out of fire, ere done't:
Nor is't directly laid to thee, the death
Of the young prince, whose honourable thoughts
(Thoughts high for one so tender) cleft the heart
That could conceive a gross and foolish sire
Blemished his gracious dam: this is not, no,
Laid to thy answer: but the last ... O lords,   200
When I have said, cry 'woe!' The queen, the queen,
The sweet'st, dear'st creature's dead! and vengeance
for't
Not dropped down yet.
I LORD.   The higher powers forbid!
PAULINA. I say she's dead: I'll swear't. If word nor
oath
Prevail not, go and see: if you can bring
Tincture or lustre in her lip, her eye,
Heat outwardly, or breath within, I'll serve you
As I would do the gods.... But, O thou tyrant!
Do not repent these things, for they are heavier
Than all thy woes can stir: therefore betake thee   210
To nothing but despair.... A thousand knees
Ten thousand years together, naked, fasting,
Upon a barren mountain, and still winter
In storm perpetual, could not move the gods
To look that way thou wert.
LEONTES.   Go on, go on:
Thou canst not speak too much, I have deserved
All tongues to talk their bitt'rest.
I LORD.   Say no more;
Howe'er the business goes, you have made fault
I'th' boldness of your speech.
PAULINA.   I am sorry for't;
All faults I make, when I shall come to know them,   220
I do repent: alas, I have showed too much
The rashness of a woman: he is touched
To th' noble heart.... What's gone, and what's past
help,
Should be past grief: do not receive affliction
At my petition; I beseech you, rather
Let me be punished, that have minded you
Of what you should forget. Now (good my liege!)
Sir, royal sir, forgive a foolish woman:
The love I bore your queen—lo, fool again!
I'll speak of her no more, nor of your children;   230
I'll not remember you of my own lord,
(Who is lost too) ... Take your patience to you,
And I'll say nothing.
LEONTES.   Thou didst speak but well,
When most the truth; which I receive much better
Than to be pitied of thee. Prithee, bring me
To the dead bodies of my queen and son.
One grave shall be for both; upon them shall
The causes of their death appear (unto
Our shame perpetual). Once a day I'll visit
The chapel where they lie, and tears shed there   240
Shall be my recreation. So long as nature
Will bear up with this exercise, so long
I daily vow to use it. Come, and lead me
To these sorrows.   *They go*

                Scene 3: Bohemia. Near the sea

Enter Antigonus carrying the babe, with a mariner

ANTIGONUS. Thou art perfect then, our ship hath
touched upon

The deserts of Bohemia?
MARINER.   Ay, my lord, and fear
We have landed in ill time; the skies look grimly,
And threaten present blusters. In my conscience,
The heavens with that we have in hand are angry,
And frown upon's.
ANTIGONUS. Their sacred wills be done! Go, get
    aboard,
Look to thy bark, I'll not be long before
I call upon thee.
MARINER. Make your best haste, and go not   10
Too far i'th' land: 'tis like to be loud weather;
Besides, this place is famous for the creatures
Of prey that keep upon't.
ANTIGONUS.   Go thou away,
I'll follow instantly.
MARINER.   I am glad at heart
To be so rid o'th' business.   *He goes*
ANTIGONUS.   Come, poor babe ...
I have heard (but not believed) the spirits o'th' dead
May walk again: if such thing be, thy mother
Appeared to me last night; for ne'er was dream
So like a waking. To me comes a creature,
Sometimes her head on one side, some another—   20
I never saw a vessel of like sorrow,
So filled, and so becoming: in pure white robes,
Like very sanctity, she did approach
My cabin where I lay: thrice bowed before me,
And (gasping to begin some speech) her eyes
Became two spouts; the fury spent, anon
Did this break from her. 'Good Antigonus,
Since fate (against thy better disposition)
Hath made thy person for the thrower-out
Of my poor babe according to thine oath,   30
Places remote enough are in Bohemia,
There weep and leave it crying; and for the babe
Is counted lost for ever, Perdita
I prithee call't ... For this ungentle business,
Put on thee by my lord, thou ne'er shalt see
Thy wife Paulina more' ... and so, with shrieks
She melted into air. Affrighted much,
I did in time collect myself, and thought
This was so, and no slumber ... Dreams are toys,
Yet for this once, yea superstitiously,   40
I will be squared by this. I do believe,
Hermione hath suffered death, and that
Apollo would (this being indeed the issue
Of King Polixenes) it should here be laid
(Either for life or death) upon the earth
Of its right father.... [*he lays down the child*]
    Blossom, speed thee well!
There lie, and there thy character: there these,
                        He sets a box and papers beside it
Which may, if fortune please, both breed thee,
    pretty,
And still rest thine.... [*thunder heard*] The storm
    begins! Poor wretch,
That for thy mother's fault art thus exposed   50
To loss, and what may follow! Weep I cannot,
But my heart bleeds: and most accursed am I,
To be by oath enjoined to this. Farewell!
The day frowns more and more; thou'rt like to have
A lullaby too rough: I never saw
The heavens so dim by day. A savage clamour!
Well may I get aboard! This is the chase—
I am gone for ever!   *Exit pursued by a bear*

An old Shepherd enters

SHEPHERD. I would there were no age between ten and
three-and-twenty, or that youth would sleep out the 60
rest; for there is nothing in the between but getting
wenches with child, wronging the ancientry, stealing, fighting. Hark you now! Would any but these
boiled-brains of nineteen and two-and-twenty hunt
this weather? They have scared away two of my
best sheep, which I fear the wolf will sooner find
than the master: if any where I have them, 'tis by
the seaside, browsing of ivy.... Good-luck (an't be
thy will) what have we here? Mercy on's, a barne?
a very pretty barne! A boy or a child, I wonder?— 70
a pretty one, a very pretty one! Sure, some scape:
though I am not bookish, yet I can read waiting-
gentlewoman in the scape: this has been some stair-
work, some trunk-work, some behind-door-work:
they were warmer that got this than the poor thing
is here. I'll take it up for pity—yet I'll tarry till my
son come; he hollaed but even now.... Whoa, ho
hoa!

Clown enters

CLOWN. Hilloa, loa!
SHEPHERD. What, art so near? If thou'lt see a thing 80
to talk on when thou art dead and rotten, come
hither ... What ailest thou, man?
CLOWN. I have seen two such sights, by sea and by
land! but I am not to say it is a sea, for it is now
the sky— betwixt the firmament and it you cannot
thrust a bodkin's point.
SHEPHERD. Why, boy, how is it?
CLOWN. I would you did but see how it chafes, how it
rages, how it takes up the shore! but that's not to
the point ... O, the most piteous cry of the poor   90
souls! sometimes to see 'em, and not to see 'em: now
the ship boring the moon with her main-mast, and
anon swallowed with yeast and froth, as you'ld
thrust a cork into a hogshead.... And then for the
land-service! to see how the bear tore out his shoulder-
bone, how he cried to me for help, and said his name
was Antigonus, a nobleman ... But to make an end
of the ship—to see how the sea flap-dragoned it:
but first, how the poor souls roared, and the sea
mocked them: and how the poor gentleman roared, 100
and the bear mocked him, both roaring louder than
the sea or weather.
SHEPHERD. Name of mercy, when was this, boy?
CLOWN. Now, now: I have not winked since I saw
these sights: the men are not yet cold under water,
nor the bear half dined on the gentleman: he's at it
now.
SHEPHERD. Would I had been by, to have helped the
old man!
CLOWN. I would you had been by the ship side, to   110
have helped her; there your charity would have
lacked footing.
SHEPHERD. Heavy matters, heavy matters ... but look
thee here, boy. Now bless thyself; thou met'st with
things dying, I with things new-born. Here's a sight
for thee; look thee, a bearing-cloth for a squire's
child! look thee here, take up, take up, boy;
open't ... So, let's see, it was told me I should be
rich by the fairies. This is some changeling ... Open't:
what's within, boy?   120

CLOWN. You're a made old man; if the sins of your youth are forgiven you, you're well to live. Gold! all gold!

SHEPHERD. This is fairy gold, boy, and 'twill prove so: up with't, keep it close; home, home, the next way. We are lucky, boy, and to be so still requires nothing but secrecy. Let my sheep go: come, good boy, the next way home.

CLOWN. Go you the next way with your findings. I'll go see if the bear be gone from the gentleman, and how much he hath eaten: they are never curst but when they are hungry: if there be any of him left, I'll bury it.   130

SHEPHERD. That's a good deed: if thou mayest discern by that which is left of him, what he is, fetch me to th' sight of him.

CLOWN. Marry, will I; and you shall help to put him i'th' ground.

SHEPHERD. 'Tis a lucky day, boy, and we'll do good deeds on't.   *They go* 140

ACT 4
Scene 1

Enter Time, the Chorus

TIME. I that please some, try all: both joy and terror
Of good and bad, that makes and unfolds error,
Now take upon me, in the name of Time,
To use my wings ... Impute it not a crime
To me, or my swift passage, that I slide
O'er sixteen years, and leave the growth untried
Of that wide gap, since it is in my power
To o'erthrow law and in one self-born hour
To plant and o'erwhelm custom. Let me pass—
The same I am, ere ancient'st order was,   10
Or what is now received: I witness to
The times that brought them in, so shall I do
To th' freshest things now reigning, and make stale
The glistering of this present, as my tale
Now seems to it ... Your patience this allowing,
I turn my glass, and give my scene such growing,
As you had slept between: Leontes leaving—
Th'effects of his fond jealousies so grieving
That he shuts up himself—imagine me,
Gentle spectators, that I now may be   20
In fair Bohemia, and remember well
I mentioned a son o'th' king's, which Florizel
I now name to you; and with speed so pace
To speak of Perdita, now grown in grace
Equal with wond'ring: what of her ensues,
I list not prophesy; but let Time's news
Be known when 'tis brought forth. A shepherd's daughter,
And what to her adheres, which follows after,
Is th'argument of Time: of this allow,
If ever you have spent time worse ere now;   30
If never, yet that Time himself doth say
He wishes earnestly you never may.   *Exit*

Scene 2: *Bohemia. The palace of Polixenes*

Enter Polixenes and Camillo

POLIXENES. I pray thee, good Camillo, be no more importunate: 'tis a sickness denying thee any thing; a death to grant this.

CAMILLO. It is fifteen years since I saw my country:

though I have, for the most part, been aired abroad, I desire to lay my bones there. Besides, the penitent kings, my master, hath sent for me, to whose feeling sorrows I might be some allay (or I o'erween to think so) which is another spur to my departure.

POLIXENES. As thou lov'st me, Camillo, wipe not out 10
the rest of thy services by leaving me now: the need I have of thee, thine own goodness hath made; better not to have had thee than thus to want thee: thou, having made me businesses, which none without thee can sufficiently manage, must either stay to execute them thyself, or take away with thee the very services thou hast done: which if I have not enough considered (as too much I cannot), to be more thankful to thee shall be my study, and my profit therein the heaping friendships. Of that fatal 20 country Sicilia prithee speak no more, whose very naming punishes me with the remembrance of that penitent, as thou call'st him, and reconciled king, my brother, whose loss of his most precious queen and children are even now to be afresh lamented. Say to me, when saw'st thou the Prince Florizel my son? Kings are no less unhappy, their issue not being gracious, than they are in losing them when they have approved their virtues.

CAMILLO. Sir, it is three days since I saw the prince: 30 what his happier affairs may be, are to me unknown: but I have (missingly) noted he is of late much retired from court, and is less frequent to his princely exercises then formerly he hath appeared.

POLIXENES. I have considered so much, Camillo, and with some care—so far that I have eyes under my service which look upon his removedness: from whom I have this intelligence, that he is seldom from the house of a most homely shepherd; a man, they say, that from very nothing, and beyond the 40 imagination of his neighbours, is grown into an unspeakable estate.

CAMILLO. I have heard, sir, of such a man, who hath a daughter of most rare note: the report of her is extended more than can be thought to begin from such a cottage.

POLIXENES. That's likewise part of my intelligence: but, I fear, the angle that plucks our son thither. Thou shalt accompany us to the place, where we will (not appearing what we are) have some 50 question with the shepherd; from whose simplicity I think it not uneasy to get the cause of my son's resort thither. Prithee, be my present partner in this business, and lay aside the thoughts of Sicila.

CAMILLO. I willingly obey your command.

POLIXENES. My best Camillo! We must disguise ourselves.   *They go*

Scene 3: *Bohemia. A field-path hard by the Shepherd's cottage*

Enter Autolycus singing

When daffodils begin to peer,
   With, heigh! the doxy over the dale,
Why then comes in the sweet o'the year,
   For the red blood reigns in the winter's pale.

The white sheet bleaching on the hedge,
   With hey! the sweet birds, O how they sing:
Doth set my pugging tooth on edge,
   For a quart of ale is a dish for a king.

The lark, that tirra-lyra chants,
   With heigh! with hey! the thrush and the jay: 10
Are summer songs for me and my aunts,
   While we lie tumbling in the hay.

I have served Prince Florizel, and in my time wore
three-pile, but now I am out of service.

But shall I go mourn for that, my dear?
   The pale moon shines by night:
And when I wander here and there,
   I then do most go right.

If tinkers may have leave to live,
   And bear the sow-skin budget, 20
Then my account I well may give,
   And in the stocks avouch it.

My traffic is sheets: when the kite builds, look to
lesser linen. My father named me Autolycus, who
being, as I am, littered under Mercury, was likewise
a snapper-up of unconsidered trifles ... With die
and drab I purchased this caparison, and my revenue
is the silly cheat. Gallows and knock are too powerful on the highway: beating and hanging are terrors
to me: for the life to come, I sleep out the thought 30
of it. A prize! a prize!

Clown enters

CLOWN. Let me see—every 'leven wether tods, every
   tod yields pound and odd shilling: fifteen hundred
   shorn—what comes the wool to?
ANTOLYCUS [*aside*]. If the springe hold, the cock's mine.
CLOWN. I cannot do't without counters. ... Let me see,
   what am I to buy for our sheep-shearing feast? Three
   pound of sugar, five pound of currants, rice ... what
   will this sister of mine do with rice? but my father
   hath made her Mistress of the Feast, and she lays it 40
   on. She hath made me four and twenty nosegays for
   the shearers—three-man song-men all, and very
   good ones; but they are most of them means and
   bases; but one puritan amongst them, and he sings
   psalms to hornpipes. ... I must have saffron to
   colour the warden pies: mace: dates, none; that's out
   of my note: nutmegs, seven; a race or two of ginger
   —but that I may beg: four pound of prunes, and as
   many of raisins o'th' sun.
AUTOLYCUS [*staggers forward and falls upon the ground*].
   O, that ever I was born! 50
CLOWN. I'th' name of me!
AUTOLYCUS. O, help me, help me! pluck but off these
   rags; and then, death, death!
CLOWN. Alack, poor soul! thou hast need of more rags
   to lay on thee, rather than have these off.
AUTOLYCUS. O, sir, the loathsomeness of them offends
   me more than the stripes I have received, which are
   mighty ones and millions.
CLOWN. Alas, poor man! a million of beating may
   come to a great matter. 60
AUTOLYCUS. I am robbed, sir, and beaten; my money
   and apparel ta'en from me, and these detestable
   things put upon me.
CLOWN. What, by a horseman or a footman?
AUTOLYCUS. A footman, sweet sir, a footman.
CLOWN. Indeed, he should be a footman, by the garments he has left with thee; if this be a horseman's
   coat, it hath seen very hot service. Lend me thy
   hand, I'll help thee: come, lend me thy hand.
AUTOLYCUS. O, good sir, tenderly, O! 70

CLOWN. Alas, poor soul.
AUTOLYCUS. O, good sir, softly, good sir: I fear, sir,
   my shoulder-blade is out.
CLOWN. How now? canst stand?
AUTOLYCUS. Softly, dear sir ... [*picking his pocket*]
   good sir, softly ... you ha' done me a charitable
   office.
CLOWN. Dost lack any money? I have a little money
   for thee.
AUTOLYCUS. No, good sweet sir; no, I beseech you, 80
   sir: I have a kinsman not past three quarters of a
   mile hence, unto whom I was going; I shall there
   have money, or any thing I want ... Offer me no
   money, I pray you—that kills my heart.
CLOWN. What manner of fellow was he that robbed
   you?
AUTOLYCUS. A fellow, sir, that I have known to go
   about with troll-my-dames: I knew him once a
   servant of the prince; I cannot tell, good sir, for
   which of his virtues it was, but he was certainly 90
   whipped out of the court.
CLOWN. His vices, you would say; there's no virtue
   whipped out of the court: they cherish it to make
   it stay there; and yet it will no more but abide.
AUTOLYCUS. Vices I would say, sir. I know this man
   well, he hath been since an ape-bearer, then a
   process-server, a bailiff, then he compassed a motion
   of the Prodigal Son, and married a tinker's wife
   within a mile where my land and living lies; and
   having flown over many knavish professions, he 100
   settled only in rogue: some call him Autolycus.
CLOWN. Out upon him! prig, for my life, prig: he
   haunts wakes, fairs, and bear-baitings.
AUTOLYCUS. Very true, sir; he, sir, he; that's the rogue
   that put me into this apparel.
CLOWN. Not a more cowardly rogue in all Bohemia;
   if you had but looked big, and spit at him, he'ld
   have run.
AUTOLYCUS. I must confess to you, sir, I am no fighter:
   I am false of heart that way, and that he knew, I 110
   warrant him.
CLOWN. How do you now?
AUTOLYCUS. Sweet sir, much better than I was; I can
   stand, and walk: I will even take my leave of you,
   and pace softly towards my kinsman's.
CLOWN. Shall I bring thee on the way?
AUTOLYCUS. No, good-faced sir, no, sweet sir.
CLOWN. Then fare thee well, I must go buy spices for
   our sheep-shearing.
AUTOLYCUS. Prosper you, sweet sir! [*the Clown goes*] 120
   Your purse is not hot enough to purchase your spice:
   I'll be with you at your sheep-shearing too: if I make
   not this cheat bring out another, and the shearers
   prove sheep, let me be unrolled, and my name put
   in the book of virtue!
[*sings*] Jog on, jog on, the foot-path way,
      And merrily hent the stile-a:
      A merry heart goes all the day,
      Your sad tires in a mile-a.

He goes

Scene 4: *The Shepherd's cottage*

Florizel and Perdita

FLORIZEL. These your unusual weeds to each part of
   you

Do give a life: no shepherdess, but Flora
Peering in April's front. This your sheep-shearing
Is as a meeting of the petty gods,
And you the queen on't.
PERDITA.   Sir ... my gracious lord,
To chide at your extremes, it not becomes me:
(O, pardon, that I name them!) Your high self,
The gracious mark o'th' land, you have obscured
With a swain's wearing; and me (poor lowly maid)
Most goddess-like pranked up ... But that our feasts   10
In every mess have folly and feeders
Digest it with a custom, I should blush
To see you so attired; swoon, I think,
To show myself a glass.
FLORIZEL.   I bless the time
When my good falcon made her flight across
Thy father's ground.
PERDITA.   Now Jove afford you cause!
To me the difference forges dread (your greatness
Hath not been used to fear): even now I tremble
To think your father, by some accident,
Should pass this way, as you did: O the Fates!   20
How would he look, to see his work, so noble,
Vilely bound up? What would he say? Or how
Should I (in these my borrowed flaunts) behold
The sternness of his presence?
FLORIZEL.   Apprehend
Nothing but jollity: the gods themselves
(Humbling their deities to love) have taken
The shapes of beasts upon them: Jupiter
Became a bull, and bellowed; the green Neptune
A ram, and bleated; and the fire-robed god,
Golden Apollo, a poor humble swain,   30
As I seem now.... Their transformations
Were never for a piece of beauty rarer,
Nor in a way so chaste: since my desires
Run not before mine honour; nor my lusts
Burn hotter than my faith.
PERDITA.   O but, sir,
Your resolution cannot hold, when 'tis
Opposed (as it must be) by th' power of the king:
One of these two must be necessities,
Which then will speak, that you must change this
      purpose,
Or I my life.
FLORIZEL.   Thou dearest Perdita,   40
With these forced thoughts, I prithee, darken not
The mirth o'th' feast: or I'll be thine, my fair,
Or not my father's: for I cannot be
Mine own, nor any thing to any, if
I be not thine: to this I am most constant,
Though destiny say no. Be merry, gentle,
Strangle such thoughts as these with any thing
That you behold the while.... Your guests are
      coming:
Lift up your countenance, as it were the day
Of celebration of that nuptial which   50
We two have sworn shall come.
PERDITA.   O lady Fortune,
Stand you auspicious!

The Shepherd, Clown, Mopsa, Dorcas and others enter,
with Polixenes and Camillo, disguised

FLORIZEL.   See, your guests approach,
Address yourself to entertain them sprightly,
And let's be red with mirth.

SHEPHERD. Fie, daughter! when my old wife lived,
      upon
This day she was both pantler, butler, cook,
Both dame and servant: welcomed all, served all:
Would sing her song and dance her turn: now here,
At upper end o'th' table; now i'th' middle:
On his shoulder, and his: her face o'fire   60
With labour, and the thing she took to quench it
She would to each one sip.... You are retired,
As if you were a feasted one, and not
The hostess of the meeting: pray you, bid
These unknown friends to's welcome, for it is
A way to make us better friends, more known:
Come, quench your blushes, and present yourself
That which you are, Mistress o'th' Feast. Come on,
And bid us welcome to your sheep-shearing,
As your good flock shall prosper.
PERDITA [*to Polixenes*].   Sir, welcome: 70
It is my father's will, I should take on me
The hostess-ship o'th' day ... [*to Camillo*] You're
      welcome, sir!
Give me those flowers there, Dorcas.... Reverend
      sirs,
For you there's rosemary and rue—these keep
Seeming and savour all the winter long:
Grace and remembrance be to you both,
And welcome to our shearing!
POLIXENES.   Shepherdess,
(A fair one are you!) well you fit our ages
With flowers of winter.
PERDITA.   Sir, the year growing ancient—
Not yet on summer's death nor on the birth   80
Of trembling winter—the fairest flowers o'th'
      season
Are our carnations and streaked gillyvors,
Which some call nature's bastards. Of that kind
Our rustic garden's barren, and I care not
To get slips of them.
POLIXENES.   Wherefore, gentle maiden,
Do you neglect them?
PERDITA.   For I have heard it said
There is an art which in their piedness shares
With great creating Nature.
POLIXENES.   Say, there be;
Yet nature is made better by no mean,
But nature makes that mean: so, over that art   90
Which you say adds to nature, is an art
That nature makes ... You see, sweet maid, we
      marry
A gentler scion to the wildest stock,
And make conceive a bark of baser kind
By bud of nobler race. This is an art
Which does mend nature ... change it rather, but
The art itself, is nature.
PERDITA.   So it is.
POLIXENES. Then make your garden rich in gillyvors,
And do not call them bastards.
PERDITA.   I'll not put   100
The dibble in earth to set one slip of them:
No more than, were I painted, I would wish
This youth should say 'twere well; and only
      therefore
Desire to breed by me.... Here's flowers for you;
Hot lavender, mints, savory, marjoram,
The marigold, that goes to bed with' sun,
And with him rises, weeping; these are flowers

Of middle summer, and I think they are given
To men of middle age ... Y'are very welcome.
CAMILLO. I should leave grazing, were I of your flock,
And only live by gazing.
PERDITA. Out, alas! 110
You'ld be so lean, that blasts of January
Would blow you through and through.... Now,
my fair'st friend,
I would I had some flowers o'th' spring that might
Become your time of day; and yours and yours,
That wear upon your virgin branches yet
Your maidenheads growing: O Proserpina,
For the flowers now, that frighted thou let'st fall
From Dis's waggon! daffodils,
That come before the swallow dares, and take
The winds of March with beauty; violets (dim, 120
But sweeter than the lids of Juno's eyes
Or Cytherea's breath); pale primroses,
That die unmarried, ere they can behold
Bright Phœbus in his strength (a malady
Most incident to maids); bold oxlips and
The crown imperial; lilies of all kinds,
The flower-de-luce being one! O, these I lack,
To make you garlands of—and my sweet friend,
To strew him o'er and o'er.
FLORIZEL. What, like a corse?
PERDITA. No, like a bank, for love to lie and play on; 130
Not like a corse: or if ... not to be buried,
But quick, and in mine arms. Come, take your
flowers,
Methinks I play as I have seen them do
In Whitsun-pastorals: sure this robe of mine
Does change my disposition.
FLORIZEL. What you do
Still betters what is done. When you speak, sweet,
I'ld have you do it ever: when you sing,
I'ld have you buy and sell so; so give alms,
Pray so; and for the ord'ring your affairs,
To sing them too: when you do dance, I wish you 140
A wave o'th' sea, that you might ever do
Nothing but that; move still, still so;
And own no other function. Each your doing
(So singular in each particular)
Crowns what you are doing in the present deeds,
That all your acts are queens.
PERDITA. O Doricles,
Your praises are too large: but that your youth,
And the true blood which peepeth fairly through't,
Do plainly give you out an unstained shepherd,
With wisdom I might fear, my Doricles, 150
You wooed me the false way.
FLORIZEL. I think you have
As little skill to fear, as I have purpose
To put you to't.... But, come, our dance I pray,
Your hand, my Perdita! so turtles pair,
That never mean to part.
PERDITA. I'll swear for 'em.
POLIXENES. This is the prettiest low-born lass that ever
Ran on the green-sward: nothing she does or seems
But smacks of something greater than herself,
Too noble for this place.
CAMILLO. He tells her something
That makes her blood look out: good sooth she is 160
The queen of curds and cream.
CLOWN. Come on: strike up!
DORCAS. Mopsa must be your mistress: marry, garlic,

To mend her kissing with!
MOPSA. Now, in good time!
CLOWN. Not a word, a word, we stand upon our
manners.
Come, strike up. Music

Here a dance of shepherds and shepherdesses

POLIXENES. Pray, good shepherd, what fair swain is
this,
Which dances with your daughter?
SHEPHERD. They call him Doricles, and boasts himself
To have a worthy feeding: but I have it
Upon his own report, and I believe it; 170
He looks like sooth ... He says he loves my
daughter,
I think so too; for never gazed the moon
Upon the water, as he'll stand and read
As 'twere my daughter's eyes: and to be plain,
I think there is not half a kiss to choose,
Who loves another best.
POLIXENES. She dances featly.
SHEPHERD. So she does any thing, though I report it,
That should be silent: if young Doricles
Do light upon her, she·shall bring him that
Which he not dreams of. 180

A servant enters

SERVANT. O master! if you did but hear the pedlar at
the door, you would never dance again after a tabor
and pipe; no, the bagpipe could not move you: he
sings several tunes, faster than you'll tell money: he
utters them as he had eaten ballads, and all men's
ears grew to his tunes.
CLOWN. He could never come better: he shall come in:
I love a ballad but even too well, if it be doleful
matter merrily set down, or a very pleasant thing
indeed and sung lamentally. 190
SERVANT. He hath songs for man, or woman, of all
sizes; no milliner can so fit his customers with gloves:
he has the prettiest love-songs for maids, so without
bawdry (which is strange), with such delicate
burthens of dildos and fadings, 'jump her and thump
her'; and where some stretch-mouthed rascal would,
as it were, mean mischief, and break a foul gap into
the matter, he makes the maid to answer, 'Whoop,
do me no harm, good man'; puts him off, slights
him, with 'Whoop, do me no harm, good man.' 200
POLIXENES. This is a brave fellow.
CLOWN. Believe me, thou talkest of an admirable conceited fellow. Has he any unbraided wares?
SERVANT. He hath ribbons of all the colours i'th' rainbow; points, more than all the lawyers in Bohemia
can learnedly handle, though they come to him by
th' gross; inkles, caddisses, cambrics, lawns: why, he
sings 'em over, as they were gods or goddesses; you
would think a smock were a she-angel, he so chants
to the sleeve-hand, and the work about the square 210
on't.
CLOWN. Prithee, bring him in, and let him approach
singing.
PERDITA. Forewarn him that he use no scurrilous
words in's tunes.
CLOWN. You have of these pedlars, that have more
in them than you'ld think, sister.
PERDITA. Ay, good brother, or go about to think.

Enter Autolycus, singing

    Lawn as white as driven snow,
    Cypress black as e'er was crow,   220
    Gloves as sweet as damask roses,
    Masks for faces and for noses:
    Bugle-bracelet, necklace amber,
    Perfume for a lady's chamber:
    Golden quoifs and stomachers
    For my lads to give their dears:
    Pins and poking-sticks of steel,
    What maids lack from head to heel:
      Come buy of me, come: come buy, come buy,
      Buy lads, or else your lasses cry: 230
    Come, buy!

CLOWN. If I were not in love with Mopsa, thou shouldst take no money of me, but being enthralled as I am, it will also be the bondage of certain ribbons and gloves.

MOPSA. I was promised them against the feast, but they come not too late now.

DORCAS. He hath promised you more than that, or there be liars.

MOPSA. He hath paid you all he promised you: may be he has paid you more, which will shame you to give him again.

CLOWN. Is there no manners left among maids? will they wear their plackets where they should bear their faces? Is there not milking-time? when you are going to bed? or kill-hole? to whistle off these secrets, but you must be tittle-tattling before all our guests? 'tis well they are whisp'ring: clammer your tongues, and not a word more.

MOPSA. I have done ... Come, you promised me a tawdry-lace and a pair of sweet gloves.

CLOWN. Have I not told thee how I was cozened by the way and lost all my money?

AUTOLYCUS. And, indeed, sir, there are cozeners abroad, therefore it behoves men to be wary.

CLOWN. Fear not thou, man, thou shalt lose nothing here.

AUTOLYCUS. I hope so, sir, for I have about me many parcels of charge.

CLOWN. What hast here? ballads?

MOPSA. Pray now, buy some: I love a ballad in print o' life, for then we are sure they are true.

AUTOLYCUS. Here's one, to a very doleful tune, How a usurer's wife was brought to bed of twenty money-bags at a burthen, and how she longed to eat adders' heads and toads carbonadoed.

MOPSA. Is it true, think you?

AUTOLYCUS. Very true, and but a month old.

DORCAS. Bless me from marrying a usurer!

AUTOLYCUS. Here's the midwife's name to't, one Mistress Tale-porter, and five or six honest wives that were present. Why should I carry lies abroad?

MOPSA. Pray you now, buy it.

CLOWN. Come on, lay it by: and let's first see moe ballads; we'll buy the other things anon.

AUTOLYCUS. Here's another ballad of a fish, that appeared upon the coast, on Wednesday the fourscore of April, forty thousand fathom above water, and sung this ballad against the hard hearts of maids: it was thought she was a woman, and was turned into a cold fish, for she would not exchange flesh with one that loved her: the ballad is very pitiful, and as true.

DORCAS. Is it true too, think you?

AUTOLYCUS. Five justices' hands at it, and witnesses more than my pack will hold.

CLOWN. Lay it by too: another.

AUTOLYCUS. This is a merry ballad, but a very pretty one.

MOPSA. Let's have some merry ones.

AUTOLYCUS. Why, this is a passing merry one, and goes to the tune of 'Two maids wooing a man': there's scarce a maid westward but she sings it; 'tis in request, I can tell you.

MOPSA. We can both sing it; if thou'lt bear a part, thou shalt hear—'tis in three parts.

DORCAS. We had the tune on't a month ago.

AUTOLYCUS. I can bear my part—you must know 'tis my occupation: have at it with you.

SONG

AUTOLYCUS.   Get you hence, for I must go   300
       Where it fits not you to know.
DORCAS.   Whither?
MOPSA.   O, whither?
DORCAS.   Whither?
MOPSA.   It becomes thy oath full well,
       Thou to me thy secrets tell.
DORCAS.   Me too: let me go thither.
MOPSA.   Or thou goest to th' grange or mill.
DORCAS.   If to either, thou dost ill.
AUTOLYCUS. Neither.   310
DORCAS.   What, neither?
AUTOLYCUS. Neither.
DORCAS.   Thou hast sworn my love to be.
MOPSA.   Thou hast sworn it more to me.
       Then, whither goest? say, whither?

CLOWN. We'll have this song out anon by ourselves: my father and the gentlemen are in sad talk, and we'll not trouble them ... Come, bring away thy pack after me. Wenches, I'll buy for you both: pedlar, let's have the first choice: follow me, girls.

                          They go

AUTOLYCUS. And you shall pay well for 'em.

            He goes out after them, singing
    Will you buy any tape, or lace for your cape,
      My dainty duck, my dear-a?
    Any silk, any thread, any toys for your head,
      Of the new'st, and fin'st, fin'st wear-a?
    Come to the pedlar, money's a meddler,
    That doth utter all men's ware-a.

The servant enters again

SERVANT. Master, there is three carters, three shepherds, three neat-herds, three swine-herds, that have made themselves all men of hair, they call themselves Saltiers, and they have a dance which the wenches say is a gallimaufry of gambols, because they are not in't: but they themselves are o'th' mind (if it be not too rough for some that know little but bowling) it will please plentifully.

SHEPHERD. Away! we'll none on't; here has been too much homely foolery already.... I know, sir, we weary you.

POLIXENES. You weary those that refresh us: pray, let's see these four threes of herdsmen.

SERVANT. One three of them, by their own report, sir, hath danced before the king; and not the worst of the three but jumps twelve foot and a half by th' squier.

SHEPHERD. Leave your prating—since these good men
   are pleased, let them come in; but quickly now.
SERVANT. Why, they stay at door, sir.
                              He lets the herdsmen in

Here a dance of twelve Satyrs

POLIXENES. O, father, you'll know more of that here-
   after ...
   [*to Camillo*] Is it not too far gone? 'Tis time to part
   them—
   He's simple, and tells much.... [*to Florizel*] How
   now, fair shepherd!   350
   Your heart is full of something that does take
   Your mind from feasting. Sooth, when I was young
   And handed love as you do, I was wont
   To load my She with knacks: I would have ran-
   sacked
   The pedlar's silken treasury, and have poured it
   To her acceptance; you have let him go,
   And nothing marted with him. If your lass
   Interpretation should abuse, and call this
   Your lack of love or bounty, you were straited
   For a reply, at least if you make a care   360
   Of happy holding her.
FLORIZEL.   Old sir, I know
   She prizes not such trifles as these are:
   The gifts she looks from me are packed and locked
   Up in my heart, which I have given already,
   But not delivered.... O, hear me breathe my life
   Before this ancient sir, who, it should seem,
   Hath sometime loved: I take thy hand, this hand,
   As soft as dove's down and as white as it,
   Or Ethiopian's tooth, or the fanned snow that's
   bolted
   By th' northern blasts twice o'er.
POLIXENES.   What follows this? 370
   How prettily th' young swain seems to wash
   The hand was fair before! I have put you out—
   But to your protestation; let me hear
   What you profess.
FLORIZEL.   Do, and be witness to't.
POLIXENES. And this my neighbour too?
FLORIZEL.   And he, and more
   Than he, and men, the earth, the heavens, and all ...
   That, were I crowned the most imperial monarch,
   Thereof most worthy; were I the fairest youth
   That ever made eye swerve, had force and know-
   ledge
   More than was ever man's—I would not prize them,   380
   Without her love: for her, employ them all,
   Commend them and condemn them to her service
   Or to their own perdition.
POLIXENES.   Fairly offered.
CAMILLO. This shows a sound affection.
SHEPHERD.   But, my daughter,
   Say you the like to him?
PERDITA.   I cannot speak
   So well (nothing so well), no, nor mean better:
   By th' pattern of mine own thoughts I cut out
   The purity of his.
SHEPHERD.   Take hands, a bargain ...
   And, friends unknown, you shall bear witness to't:
   I give my daughter to him, and will make   390
   Her portion equal his.
FLORIZEL.   O, that must be
   I'th' virtue of your daughter; one being dead,

I shall have more than you can dream of yet,
   Enough then for your wonder ... But, come on,
   Contract us 'fore these witnesses.
SHEPHERD.   Come, your hand;
   And, daughter, yours.
POLIXENES.   Soft, swain, awhile, beseech you—
   Have you a father?
FLORIZEL.   I have: but what of him?
POLIXENES. Knows he of this?
FLORIZEL.   He neither does nor shall.
POLIXENES. Methinks, a father
   Is at the nuptial of his son a guest   400
   That best becomes the table ... Pray you once more,
   Is not your father grown incapable
   Of reasonable affairs? is he not stupid
   With age and alt'ring rheums? can he speak? hear?
   Know man from man? dispute his own estate?
   Lies he not bed-rid? and again does nothing,
   But what he did being childish?
FLORIZEL.   No, good sir;
   He has his health, and ampler strength indeed
   Than most have of his age.
POLIXENES.   By my white beard,
   You offer him, if this be so, a wrong   410
   Something unfilial: reason my son
   Should choose himself a wife, but as good reason
   The father (all whose joy is nothing else
   But fair posterity) should hold some counsel
   In such a business.
FLORIZEL.   I yield all this;
   But for some other reasons, my grave sir,
   Which 'tis not fit you know, I not acquaint
   My father of this business.
POLIXENES.   Let him know't.
FLORIZEL. He shall not.
POLIXENES.   Prithee, let him.
FLORIZEL.   No, he must not.
SHEPHERD. Let him, my son, he shall not need to grieve 420
   At knowing of thy choice.
FLORIZEL.   Come, come he must not:
   Mark our contract.
POLIXENES [*discovers himself*]. Mark your divorce,
      young sir,
   Whom son I dare not call; thou art too base
   To be acknowledged.... Thou a sceptre's heir,
   That thus affects a sheep-hook! Thou, old traitor,
   I am sorry, that by hanging thee, I can
   But shorten thy life one week.... And thou, fresh
   piece
   Of excellent witchcraft, who, of force, must know
   The royal fool thou cop'st with—
SHEPHERD.   O, my heart!
POLIXENES. I'll have thy beauty scratched with briars,
      and made   430
   More homely than thy state.... For thee, fond boy,
   If I may ever know thou dost but sigh
   That thou no more shalt see this knack (as never
   I mean thou shalt) we'll bar thee from succession,
   Not hold thee of our blood, no not our kin,
   Farre than Deucalion off: mark thou my words!
   Follow us to the court.... Thou churl, for this time
   (Though full of our displeasure) yet we free thee
   From the dead blow of it.... And you, enchant-
      ment—
   Worthy enough a herdsman; yea, him too,   440
   That makes himself (but for our honour therein)

Unworthy thee—if ever henceforth thou
These rural latches to his entrance open,
Or hoop his body more with thy embraces,
I will devise a death as cruel for thee,
As thou art tender to't.   *He goes*
PERDITA.   Even here, undone,
I was not much afeard: for once or twice
I was about to speak and tell him plainly,
The selfsame sun that shines upon his court
Hides not his visage from our cottage, but   450
Looks on alike.... Will't please you, sir, be gone?
I told you what would come of this: beseech you,
Of your own state take care: this dream of mine—
Being now awake, I'll queen it no inch farther,
But milk my ewes, and weep.
CAMILLO.   Why, how now, father!
Speak ere thou diest.
SHEPHERD.   I cannot speak, nor think,
Nor dare to know that which I know.... [*to
Florizel*] O, sir.
You have undone a man of fourscore three,
That thought to fill his grave in quiet; yea,
To die upon the bed my father died,   460
To lie close by his honest bones: but now
Some hangman must put on my shroud, and lay me
Where no priest shovels-in dust.... [*to Perdita*] O
curséd wretch!
That knew'st this was the prince, and wouldst
adventure
To mingle faith with him.... Undone! undone!
If I might die within this hour, I have lived
To die when I desire.
FLORIZEL.   Why look you so upon me?
I am but sorry, not afeard; delayed,
But nothing alt'red: what I was, I am:
More straining on for plucking back; not following 470
My leash unwillingly.
CAMILLO.   Gracious my lord,
You know your father's temper: at this time
He will allow no speech ... which, I do guess,
You do not purpose to him ... and as hardly
Will he endure your sight as yet, I fear:
Then, till the fury of his highness settle,
Come not before him.
FLORIZEL.   I not purpose it ...
I think, Camillo?
CAMILLO.   Even he, my lord.
PERDITA. How often have I told you 'twould be thus?
How often said, my dignity would last   480
But till 'twere known?
FLORIZEL.   It cannot fail but by
The violation of my faith, and then
Let nature crush the sides o'th'earth together,
And mar the seeds within! Lift up thy looks:
From my succession wipe me, father, I
Am heir to my affection.
CAMILLO.   Be advised.
FLORIZEL. I am; and by my fancy: if my reason
Will thereto be obedient, I have reason;
If not, my senses, better pleased with madness,
Do bid it welcome.
CAMILLO.   This is desperate, sir.   490
FLORIZEL. So call it: but it does fulfil my vow;
I needs must think it honesty.... Camillo,
Not for Bohemia, nor the pomp that may
Be thereat gleaned; for all the sun sees, or

The close earth wombs, or the profound seas hides
In unknown fathoms, will I break my oath
To this my fair beloved: therefore, I pray you,
As you have ever been my father's honoured friend,
When he shall miss me (as, in faith, I mean not
To see him any more) cast your good counsels   500
Upon his passion; let myself and Fortune
Tug for the time to come.... This you may know
And so deliver, I am put to sea
With her whom here I cannot hold on shore;
And most opportune to our need I have
A vessel rides fast by, but not prepared
For this design.... What course I mean to hold
Shall nothing benefit your knowledge, nor
Concern me the reporting.
CAMILLO.   O my lord,
I would your spirit were easier for advice,   510
Or stronger for your need.
FLORIZEL.   Hark, Perdita!   *He draws her aside*
[*to Camillo*] I'll hear you by and by.
CAMILLO.   He's irremoveable,
Resolved for flight ... Now were I happy, if
His going I could frame to serve my turn,
Save him from danger, do him love and honour,
Purchase the sight again of dear Sicilia,
And that unhappy king, my master, whom
I so much thirst to see.
FLORIZEL.   Now, good Camillo,
I am so fraught with curious business, that
I leave out ceremony.
CAMILLO.   Sir, I think   520
You have heard of my poor services i'th' love
That I have borne your father?
FLORIZEL.   Very nobly
Have you deserved: it is my father's music
To speak your deeds; not little of his care
To have them recompensed as thought on.
CAMILLO.   Well, my lord,
If you may please to think I love the king,
And through him what is nearest to him, which is
Your gracious self, embrace but my direction,
If your more ponderous and settled project
May suffer alteration. On mine honour   530
I'll point you where you shall have such receiving
As shall become your highness, where you may
Enjoy your mistress; from the whom, I see,
There's no disjunction to be made, but by
(As heavens forfend!) your ruin; marry her;
And—with my best endeavours in your absence—
Your discontenting father strive to qualify,
And bring him up to liking.
FLORIZEL.   How, Camillo,
May this (almost a miracle) be done?
That I may call thee something more than man,   540
And after that trust to thee.
CAMILLO.   Have you thought on
A place whereto you'll go?
FLORIZEL.   Not any yet:
But as th'unthought-on accident is guilty
To what we wildly do, so we profess
Ourselves to be the slaves of chance, and flies
Of every wind that blows.
CAMILLO.   Then list to me:
This follows, if you will not change your purpose,
But undergo this flight; make for Sicilia,
And there present yourself and your fair princess,

(For so I see she must be) 'fore Leontes: 550
She shall be habited, as it becomes
The partner of your bed.... Methinks I see
Leontes opening his free arms and weeping
His welcomes forth: asks thee, the son, forgiveness,
As 'twere i'th' father's person: kisses the hands
Of your fresh princess: o'er and o'er divides him
'Twixt his unkindness and his kindness; th'one
He chides to hell and bids the other grow
Faster than thought or time.

FLORIZEL.   Worthy Camillo,
What colour for my visitation shall I 560
Hold up before him?

CAMILLO.   Sent by the king your father
To greet him, and to give him comforts. Sir,
The manner of your bearing towards him, with
What you (as from your father) shall deliver,
Things known betwixt us three, I'll write you
  down,
The which shall point you forth at every sitting
What you must say; that he shall not perceive,
But that you have your father's bosom there,
And speak his very heart.

FLORIZEL.   I am bound to you:
There is some sap in this.

CAMILLO.   A course more promising 570
Than a wild dedication of yourselves
To unpathed waters, undreamed shores; most
  certain,
To miseries enough: no hope to help you,
But as you shake off one to take another:
Nothing so certain as your anchors, who
Do their best office, if they can but stay you
Where you'll be loath to be: besides you know
Prosperity's the very bond of love,
Whose fresh complexion and whose heart together
Affliction alters.

PERDITA.   One of these is true. 580
I think affliction may subdue the cheek,
But not take in the mind.

CAMILLO.   Yea? say you so?
There shall not at your father's house these seven
  years
Be born another such.

FLORIZEL.   My good Camillo,
She is as forward of her breeding as
She is i'th' rear 'our birth.

CAMILLO.   I cannot say 'tis pity
She lacks instructions, for she seems a mistress
To most that teach.

PERDITA.   Your pardon, sir. For this
I'll blush you'thanks.

FLORIZEL.   My prettiest Perdita....
But, O, the thorns we stand upon! Camillo— 590
Preserver of my father, now of me,
The medicine of our house ... how shall we do?
We are not furnished like Bohemia's son,
Nor shall appear in Sicilia.

CAMILLO.   My lord,
Fear none of this: I think you know my fortunes
Do all lie there: it shall be so my care
To have you royally appointed, as if
The scene you play, were mine. For instance, sir,
That you may know you shall not want ... one
  word.   *They draw apart*

Autolycus enters

AUTOLYCUS. Ha, ha! what a fool Honesty is! and Trust, 600
his sworn brother, a very simple gentleman! I have
sold all my trumpery: not a counterfeit stone, not a
ribbon, glass, pomander, brooch, table-book,
ballad, knife, tape, glove, shoe-tie, bracelet, horn-
ring, to keep my pack from fasting: they throng
who should buy first, as if my trinkets had been
hallowed, and brought a benediction to the buyer:
by which means I saw whose purse was best in
picture; and, what I saw, to my good use I remembered. My clown (who wants but something 610
to be a reasonable man) grew so in love with the
wenches' song, that he would not stir his pettitoes
till he had both tune and words, which so drew the
rest of the herd to me, that all their other senses
stuck in ears: you might have pinched a placket, it
was senseless; 'twas nothing to geld a codpiece of a
purse; I would have filed keys off that hung in
chains: no hearing, no feeling, but my sir's song, and
admiring the nothing of it. So that, in this time of
lethargy, I picked and cut most of their festival 620
purses: and had not the old man come in with a
hubbub against his daughter and the king's son, and
scared my choughs from the chaff, I had not left
a purse alive in the whole army.

          Camillo, Florizel, and Perdita come forward

CAMILLO. Nay, but my letters, by this means being
  there
So soon as you arrive, shall clear that doubt.

FLORIZEL. And those that you'll procure from King
  Leontes?

CAMILLO. Shall satisfy your father.

PERDITA.   Happy be you!
·All that you speak shows fair.

CAMILLO [*seeing Autolycus*].   Who have we here?
We'll make an instrument of this; omit 630
Nothing may give us aid.

AUTOLYCUS. If they have overheard me now ... why,
hanging!

CAMILLO. How now, good fellow! Why shak'st thou
so? Fear not, man—here's no harm intended to thee.

AUTOLYCUS. I am a poor fellow, sir.

CAMILLO. Why, be so still; here's nobody will steal that
from thee: yet for the outside of thy poverty, we
must make an exchange; therefore discase thee
instantly (thou must think there's a necessity in't) 640
and change garments with this gentleman: though
the pennyworth, on his side, be the worst, yet hold
thee, there's some boot.   *Gives him money*

AUTOLYCUS. I am a poor fellow, sir ... [*aside*] I know
ye well enough.

CAMILLO. Nay, prithee, dispatch: the gentleman is half
flayed already.

AUTOLYCUS. Are you in earnest, sir? [*aside*] I smell the
trick on't.

FLORIZEL. Dispatch, I prithee. 650

AUTOLYCUS. Indeed, I have had earnest, but I cannot
with conscience take it.

CAMILLO. Unbuckle, unbuckle!

          Autolycus exchanges Florizel garments
Fortunate mistress (let my prophecy
Come home to ye!) you must retire yourself
Into some covert: take your sweetheart's hat
And pluck it o'er your brows, muffle your face,
Dismantle you, and (as you can) disliken
The truth of your own seeming, that you may

(For I do fear eyes over) to shipboard   660
Get undescried.
PERDITA.   I see the play so lies
That I must bear a part.
CAMILLO.   No remedy....
Have you done there?
FLORIZEL.   Should I now meet my father,
He would not call me son.   *Takes his hat*
CAMILLO [*snatches it and gives it to Perdita*]. Nay, you
    shall have no hat....
Come, lady, come ... Farewell, my friend.
AUTOLYCUS.   Adieu, sir.
FLORIZEL. O Perdita! what have we twain forgot?
Pray you, a word.   *They talk apart*
CAMILLO [*aside*]. What I do next, shall be to tell the
    king
Of this escape and whither they are bound;   670
Wherein, my hope is, I shall so prevail,
To force him after: in whose company
I shall review Sicilia; for whose sight
I have a woman's longing.
FLORIZEL.   Fortune speed us!
Thus we set on, Camillo, to th' sea-side.
CAMILLO. The swifter speed, the better.
             Florizel, Perdita, and Camillo go out
AUTOLYCUS. I understand the business, I hear it: to
have an open ear, a quick eye, and a nimble hand,
is necessary for a cut-purse; a good nose is requisite
also, to smell out work for th'other senses. I see this 680
is the time that the unjust man doth thrive. What
an exchange had this been, without boot! What a
boot is here, with this exchange! Sure, the gods
do this year connive at us, and we may do any thing
extempore. The prince himself is about a piece of
iniquity, stealing away from his father, with his clog
at his heels: if I thought it were a piece of honesty
to acquaint the king withal, I would not do't: I hold
it the more knavery to conceal it; and therein am
I constant to my profession.   690

The Clown and Shepherd enter

Aside, aside! here is more matter for a hot brain:
every lane's end, every shop, church, session, hanging, yields a careful man work.
CLOWN. See, see; what a man you are now! there is
no other way but to tell the king she's a changeling
and none of your flesh and blood.
SHEPHERD. Nay, but hear me.
CLOWN. Nay, but hear me.
SHEPHERD. Go to then.
CLOWN. She being none of your flesh and blood, your 700
flesh and blood has not offended the king, and so
your flesh and blood is not to be punished by him.
Show those things you found about her—those
secret things, all but what she has with her: this being
done, let the law go whistle; I warrant you.
SHEPHERD. I will tell the king all, every word, yea,
and his son's pranks too; who, I may say, is no honest
man, neither to his father nor to me, to go about to
make me the king's brother-in-law.
CLOWN. Indeed, brother-in-law was the farthest off 710
you could have been to him, and then your blood
had been the dearer by I know not how much an
ounce.
AUTOLYCUS [*aside*]. Very wisely—puppies!
SHEPHERD. Well; let us to the king ... [*takes a bundle*

from the press] There is that in this fardel will make
him scratch his beard.
AUTOLYCUS [*aside*]. I know not what impediment this
complaint may be to the flight of my master.
CLOWN. Pray heartily he be at' palace.   720
AUTOLYCUS [*aside*]. Though I am not naturally honest,
I am so sometimes by chance: let me pocket up my
pedlar's excrement.... [*takes off his false beard and
steps forth*] How now, rustics? whither are you
bound?
SHEPHERD. To th' palace, an it like your worship.
AUTOLYCUS. Your affairs there? what? with whom?
the condition of that fardel, the place of your
dwelling, your names, your ages, of what having,
breeding, and any thing that is fitting to be known, 730
discover.
CLOWN. We are but plain fellows, sir.
AUTOLYCUS. A lie; you are rough and hairy: let me
have no lying; it becomes none but tradesmen, and
they often give us soldiers the lie, but we pay them
for it with stamped coin, not stabbing steel, therefore they do not give us the lie.
CLOWN. Your worship had like to have given us one,
if you had not taken yourself with the manner.
SHEPHERD. Are you a courtier, an't like you, sir?   740
AUTOLYCUS. Whether it like me or no, I am a courtier.
Seest thou not the air of the court in these en-
foldings? hath not my gait in it the measure of the
court? receives not thy nose court-odour from me?
reflect I not on thy baseness court-contempt?
Think'st thou, for that I insinuate to toaze from thee
thy business, I am therefore no courtier? I am courtier
cap-a-pe; and one that will either push on or pluck
back thy business there: whereupon I command thee
to open thy affair.   750
SHEPHERD. My business, sir, is to the king.
AUTOLYCUS. What advocate hast thou to him?
SHEPHERD. I know not, an't like you.
CLOWN. Advocate's the court-word for a pheasant;
say you have none.
SHEPHERD. None, sir; I have no pheasant, cock nor hen.
AUTOLYCUS. How blessed are we that are not simple
men! Yet nature might have made me as these are,
Therefore I will not disdain.
CLOWN. This cannot but be a great courtier!   760
SHEPHERD. His garments are rich, but he wears them
not handsomely.
CLOWN. He seems to be the more noble in being
fantastical: a great man, I'll warrant; I know by the
picking on's teeth.
AUTOLYCUS. The fardel there? what's i'th' fardel?
Wherefore that box?
SHEPHERD. Sir, there lies such secrets in this fardel and
box, which none must know but the king, and
which he shall know within this hour, if I may come 770
to th' speech of him.
AUTOLYCUS. Age, thou hast lost thy labour.
SHEPHERD. Why, sir?
AUTOLYCUS. The king is not at the palace, he is gone
aboard a new ship to purge melancholy and air himself: for, if thou beest capable of things serious, thou
must know the king is full of grief.
SHEPHERD. So 'tis said, sir; about his son, that should
have married a shepherd's daughter.
AUTOLYCUS. If that shepherd be not in hand-fast, let 780
him fly; the curses he shall have, the tortures he shall

feel, will break the back of man, the heart of monster.

CLOWN. Think you so, sir?

AUTOLYCUS. Not he alone shall suffer what wit can make heavy and vengeance bitter; but those that are germane to him, though removed fifty times, shall all come under the hangman: which though it be great pity, yet it is necessary. An old sheep-whistling rogue, a ram-tender, to offer to have his daughter come into grace! Some say he shall be stoned; but that death is too soft for him, say I: draw our throne into a sheep-cote! all deaths are too few, the sharpest too easy.

CLOWN. Has the old man e'er a son, sir, do you hear, an't like you, sir?

AUTOLYCUS. He has a son ... who shall be flayed alive, then 'nointed over with honey, set on the head of a wasp's nest, then stand till he be three quarters and a dram dead; then recovered again with aqua-vitæ or some other hot infusion; then, raw as he is, and in the hottest day prognostication proclaims, shall he be set against a brick-wall, the sun looking with a southward eye upon him; where he is to behold him with flies blown to death. But what talk we of these traitorly rascals, whose miseries are to be smiled at, their offences being so capital? Tell me (for you seem to be honest plain men) what you have to the king: being something gently considered, I'll bring you where he is aboard, tender your persons to his presence, whisper him in your behalfs; and, if it be in man, besides the king, to effect your suits, here is man shall do it.

CLOWN. He seems to be of great authority: close with him, give him gold; and though authority be a stubborn bear, yet he is oft led by the nose with gold: show the inside of your purse to the outside of his hand, and no more ado. Remember 'stoned,' and 'flayed alive!'

SHEPHERD. An't please you, sir, to undertake the business for us, here is that gold I have: I'll make it as much more, and leave this young man in pawn, till I bring it you.

AUTOLYCUS. After I have done what I promised?

SHEPHERD. Ay, sir.

AUTOLYCUS. Well, give me the moiety ... Are you a party in this business?

CLOWN. In some sort, sir: but though my case be a pitiful one, I hope I shall not be flayed out of it.

AUTOLYCUS. O, that's the case of the shepherd's son: hand him, he'll be made an example.

CLOWN. Comfort, good comfort! We must to the king, and show our strange sights: he must know 'tis none of your daughter nor my sister; we are gone else.... [to Autolycus] Sir, I will give you as much as this old man does, when the business is performed, and remain, as he says, your pawn till it be brought you.

AUTOLYCUS. I will trust you. Walk before toward the sea-side, go on the right hand, I will but look upon the hedge and follow you.

CLOWN. We are blest in this man, as I may say, even blest.

SHEPHERD. Let's before, as he bids us: he was pro-vided to do us good.   *Shepherd and Clown go*

AUTOLYCUS. If I had a mind to be honest, I see Fortune would not suffer me; she drops booties in my mouth. I am courted now with a double occasion: gold and a means to do the prince my master good; which who knows how that may turn back to my advancement? I will bring these two moles, these blind ones, aboard him: if he think it fit to shore them again, and that the complaint they have to the king concerns him nothing, let him call me rogue for being so far officious, for I am proof against that title and what shame else belongs to't ... To him will I present them, there may be matter in it.

He goes

ACT 5
Scene 1: *Sicilia. The palace of Leontes*

Leontes, Cleomenes, Dion, Paulina, and others

CLEOMENES. Sir, you have done enough, and have per-formed
A saint-like sorrow: no fault could you make,
Which you have not redeemed; indeed, paid down
More penitence than done trespass: at the last,
Do as the heavens have done, forget your evil;
With them forgive yourself.

LEONTES.   Whilst I remember
Her and her virtues, I cannot forget
My blemishes in them, and so still think of
The wrong I did myself: which was so much,
That heirless it hath made my kingdom, and
Destroyed the sweet'st companion that e'er man
Bred his hopes out of.

PAULINA.   True, too true, my lord:
If, one by one, you wedded all the world,
Or from the all that are took something good
To make a perfect woman ... she you killed
Would be unparalleled.

LEONTES.   I think so.... Killed!
She I killed! I did so: but thou strik'st me
Sorely, to say I did; it is as bitter
Upon thy tongue, as in my thought.... Now, good now,
Say so but seldom.

CLEOMENES.   Not at all, good lady:
You might have spoken a thousand things that would
Have done the time more benefit and graced
Your kindness better.

PAULINA.   You are one of those
Would have him wed again.

DION.   If you would not so,
You pity not the state, nor the remembrance
Of his most sovereign name; consider little
What dangers, by his highness' fail of issue,
May drop upon his kingdom, and devour
Incertain lookers on. What were more holy
Than to rejoice the former queen is well?
What holier than, for royalty's repair,
For present comfort and for future good,
To bless the bed of majesty again
With a sweet fellow to't?

PAULINA.   There is none worthy,
Respecting her that's gone ... Besides, the gods
Will have fulfilled their secret purposes:
For has not the divine Apollo said,
Is't not the tenour of his oracle,
That King Leontes shall not have an heir

Till his lost child be found? which, that it shall,   40
Is all as monstrous to our human reason,
As my Antigonus to break his grave,
Did perish with the infant. 'Tis your counsel
My lord should to the heavens be contrary,
Oppose against their wills.... [to Leontes] Care not
    for issue—
The crown will find an heir: great Alexander
Left his to th' worthiest; so his successor
Was like to be the best.
LEONTES.   Good Paulina,
Who hast the memory of Hermione
I know in honour ... O, that ever I   50
Had squared me to thy counsel! then, even now,
I might have looked upon my queen's full eyes,
Have taken treasure from her lips—
PAULINA.   And left them
More rich for what they yielded.
LEONTES.   Thou speak'st truth:
No more such wives, therefore no wife: one worse,
And better used, would make her sainted spirit
Again possess her corpse, and on this stage,
Where we offenders move, appear soul-vexed,
And begin, 'Why to me?'
PAULINA.   Had she such power,
She had just cause.
LEONTES.   She had, and would incense me   60
To murder her I married.
PAULINA.   I should so:
Were I the ghost that walked, I'ld bid you mark
Her eye, and tell me for what dull part in't
You chose her: then I'ld shriek, that even your ears
Should rift to hear me, and the words that followed
Should be, 'Remember mine!'
LEONTES.   Stars, stars,
And all eyes else dead coals! Fear thou no wife;
I'll have no wife, Paulina.
PAULINA.   Will you swear
Never to marry, but by my free leave?
LEONTES. Never, Paulina, so be blest my spirit!   70
PAULINA. Then, good my lords, bear witness to his
    oath.
CLEOMENES. You tempt him over-much.
PAULINA.   Unless another,
As like Hermione as is her picture,
Affront his eye.
CLEOMENES.   Good madam,—
PAULINA.   I have done.
Yet, if my lord will marry ... if you will, sir ...
No remedy, but you will ... give me the office
To choose you a queen: she shall not be so young
As was your former, but she shall be such
As, walked your first queen's ghost, it should take
    joy
To see her in your arms.
LEONTES.   My true Paulina,   80
We shall not marry, till thou bid'st us.
PAULINA.   That
Shall be when your first queen's again in breath;
Never till then.

A gentleman enters

GENTLEMAN. One that gives out himself Prince
    Florizel,
Son of Polixenes, with his princess (she

The fairest I have yet beheld) desires access
To your high presence.
LEONTES.   What with him? he comes not
Like to his father's greatness: his approach
(So out of circumstance and sudden) tells us
'Tis not a visitation framed, but forced   90
By need and accident. What train?
GENTLEMAN.   But few,
And those but mean.
LEONTES.   His princess, say you, with him?
GENTLEMAN. Ay; the most peerless piece of earth, I
    think,
That e'er the sun shone bright on.
PAULINA.   O Hermione,
As every present time doth boast itself
Above a better gone, so must thy grave
Give way to what's seen now! Sir, you yourself
Have said and writ so; but your writing now
Is colder than that theme: 'She had not been,
Nor was not to be equalled'—thus your verse   100
Flowed with her beauty once; 'tis shrewdly ebbed,
To say you have seen a better.
GENTLEMAN.   Pardon, madam:
The one I have almost forgot—your pardon—
The other, when she has obtained your eye,
Will have your tongue too. This is a creature,
Would she begin a sect, might quench the zeal
Of all professors else; make proselytes
Of who she but bid follow.
PAULINA.   How! not women?
GENTLEMAN. Women will love her, that she is a
    woman
More worth than any man; men, that she is   110
The rarest of all women.
LEONTES.   Go, Cleomenes,
Yourself, assisted with your honoured friends,
Bring them to our embracement....
                    Cleomenes and others go
                    Still, 'tis strange,
He thus should steal upon us.
PAULINA.   Had our prince
(Jewel of children) seen this hour, he had paired
Well with this lord; there was not full a month
Between their births.
LEONTES. Prithee, no more; cease; thou know'st,
He dies to me again when talked of: sure,
When I shall see this gentleman, thy speeches   120
Will bring me to consider that which may
Unfurnish me of reason. They are come.

Cleomenes returns with Florizel, Perdita, and attendants

Your mother was most true to wedlock, prince,
For she did print your royal father off,
Conceiving you: were I but twenty-one,
Your father's image is so hit in you
(His very air!) that I should call you brother,
As I did him, and speak of something wildly
By us performed before. Most dearly welcome!
And your fair princess—goddess! O! ... Alas,   130
I lost a couple, that 'twixt heaven and earth
Might thus have stood begetting wonder, as
You, gracious couple, do: and then I lost
(All mine own folly) the society,
Amity too, of your brave father, whom
(Though bearing misery) I desire my life
Once more to look on him.

FLORIZEL.   By his command
    Have I here touched Sicilia, and from him
    Give you all greetings, that a king, at friend,
    Can send his brother: and, but infirmity,   140
    Which waits upon worn times, hath something
        seized
    His wished ability, he had himself
    The lands and waters 'twixt your throne and his
    Measured to look upon you; whom he loves
    (He bade me say so) more than all the sceptres,
    And those that bear them, living.
LEONTES.   O my brother
    (Good gentleman!) the wrongs I have done thee stir
    Afresh within me; and these thy offices,
    So rarely kind, are as interpreters
    Of my behind-hand slackness.... Welcome hither,   150
    As is the spring to th'earth. And hath he too
    Exposed this paragon to th' fearful usage
    (At least ungentle) of the dreadful Neptune,
    To greet a man not worth her pains, much less
    Th'adventure of her person?
FLORIZEL.   Good my lord,
    She came from Libya.
LEONTES.   Where the warlike Smalus,
    That noble honoured lord, is feared and loved?
FLORIZEL. Most royal sir, from thence; from him,
        whose daughter
    His tears proclaimed his, parting with her: thence
    (A prosperous south-wind friendly) we have
        crossed,   160
    To execute the charge my father gave me,
    For visiting your highness: my best train
    I have from your Sicilian shores dismissed;
    Who for Bohemia bend, to signify
    Not only my success in Libya, sir,
    But my arrival, and my wife's, in safety
    Here, where we are.
LEONTES.   The blessed gods
    Purge all infection from our air, whilst you
    Do climate here! You have a holy father,
    A graceful gentleman, against whose person   170
    (So sacred as it is) I have done sin,
    For which the heavens, taking angry note,
    Have left me issueless; and your father's blessed
    (As he from heaven merits it) with you,
    Worthy his goodness.... What might I have been,
    Might I a son and daughter now have looked on,
    Such goodly things as you?

A lord enters

LORD.   Most noble sir,
    That which I shall report will bear no credit,
    Were not the proof so nigh. Please you, great sir,
    Bohemia greets you from himself, by me: 180
    Desires you to attach his son, who has
    (His dignity and duty both cast off)
    Fled from his father, from his hopes, and with
    A shepherd's daughter.
LEONTES.   Where's Bohemia? speak!
LORD. Here in your city; I now came from him.
    I speak amazedly, and it becomes
    My marvel and my message. To your court
    Whiles he was hast'ning (in the chase, it seems,
    Of this fair couple) meets he on the way
    The father of this seeming lady, and   190

Her brother, having both their country quitted
    With this young prince.
FLORIZEL.   Camillo has betrayed me;
    Whose honour and whose honesty till now
    Endured all weathers.
LORD.   Lay't so to his charge:
    He's with the king your father.
LEONTES.   Who? Camillo?
LORD. Camillo, sir; I spake with him; who now
    Has these poor men in question. Never saw I
    Wretches so quake: they kneel, they kiss the earth;
    Forswear themselves as often as they speak:
    Bohemia stops his ears, and threatens them   200
    With divers deaths in death.
PERDITA.   O, my poor father!
    The heaven sets spies upon us, will not have
    Our contract celebrated.
LEONTES.   You are married?
FLORIZEL. We are not, sir, nor are we like to be;
    The stars, I see, will kiss the valleys first:
    The odds for high and low's alike.
LEONTES.   My lord,
    Is this the daughter of a king?
FLORIZEL.   She is,
    When once she is my wife.
LEONTES. That 'once,' I see, by your good father's
        speed,
    Will come on very slowly. I am sorry   210
    (Most sorry) you have broken from his liking,
    Where you were tied in duty: and as sorry,
    Your choice is not so rich in worth as beauty,
    That you might well enjoy her.
FLORIZEL.   Dear, look up:
    Though Fortune, visible an enemy,
    Should chase us with my father; power no jot
    Hath she to change our loves.... Beseech you, sir,
    Remember since you owed no more to time
    Than I do now: with thought of such affections,
    Step forth mine advocate; at your request,   220
    My father will grant precious things as trifles.
LEONTES. Would he do so, I'ld beg your precious
        mistress,
    Which he counts but a trifle.
PAULINA.   Sir, my liege,
    Your eye hath too much youth in't: not a month
    'Fore your queen died, she was more worth such
        gazes
    Than what you look on now.
LEONTES.   I thought of her.
    Even in these looks I made.... *[to Florizel]* But your
        petition
    Is yet unanswered: I will to your father:
    Your honour not o'erthrown by your desires,
    I am friend to them and you: upon which errand   230
    I now go toward him; therefore follow me,
    And mark what way I make; come, good my lord.
                                            They go

Scene 2: *Before the palace of Leontes*

Enter Autolycus and a gentleman

AUTOLYCUS. Beseech you, sir, were you present at this
    relation?
1 GENTLEMAN. I was by at the opening of the fardel,
    heard the old shepherd deliver the manner how he
    found it: whereupon, after a little amazedness, we

were all commanded out of the chamber; only this
methought I heard the shepherd say, he found the
child.

AUTOLYCUS. I would most gladly know the issue of
it.   10

1 GENTLEMAN. I make a broken delivery of the business: but the changes I perceived in the king and
Camillo were very notes of admiration: they seemed
almost, with staring on one another, to tear the cases
of their eyes; there was speech in their dumbness,
language in their very gesture; they looked as they
had heard of a world ransomed, or one destroyed:
a notable passion of wonder appeared in them: but
the wisest beholder, that knew no more but seeing,
could not say if th'importance were joy or sorrow;   20
but in the extremity of the one, it must needs be.

Another gentleman comes up

Here comes a gentleman, that haply knows more:
the news, Rogero?

2 GENTLEMAN. Nothing but bonfires: the oracle is fulfilled; the king's daughter is found: such a deal of
wonder is broken out within this hour, that ballad-
makers cannot be able to express it.

A third gentleman approaches

Here comes the Lady Paulina's steward, he can
deliver you more. How goes it now, sir? this news
which is called true is so like an old tale, that the   30
verity of it is in strong suspicion: has the king found
his heir?

3 GENTLEMAN. Most true, if ever Truth were pregnant
by Circumstance: that which you hear you'll swear
you see, there is such unity in the proofs. The mantle
of Queen Hermione's: her jewel about the neck of it:
the letters of Antigonus found with it, which they
know to be his character: the majesty of the creature,
in resemblance of the mother: the affection of nobleness, which nature shows above her breeding—and   40
many other evidences, proclaim her, with all
certainty, to be the king's daughter. Did you see the
meeting of the two kings?

2 GENTLEMAN. No.

3 GENTLEMAN. Then have you lost a sight, which was
to be seen, cannot be spoken of. There might you
have beheld one joy crown another, so and in such
manner, that it seemed sorrow wept to take leave
of them; for their joy waded in tears. There was
casting up of eyes, holding up of hands, with counte-   50
nance of such distraction, that they were to be
known by garment, not by favour. Our king being
ready to leap out of himself for joy of his found
daughter; as if that joy were now become a loss,
cries, 'O, thy mother, thy mother!' then asks
Bohemia forgiveness, then embraces his son-in-law;
then again worries he his daughter, with clipping
her; now he thanks the old shepherd, which stands
by, like a weather-bitten conduit of many kings'
reigns. I never heard of such another encounter,   60
which lames report to follow it, and undoes description to do it.

2 GENTLEMAN. What, pray you, became of Antigonus,
that carried hence the child?

3 GENTLEMAN. Like an old tale still, which will have
matter to rehearse, though credit be asleep and not
an ear open; he was torn to pieces with a bear:

this avouches the shepherd's son; who has not only
his innocence (which seems much) to justify him,
but a handkerchief and rings of his that Paulina   70
knows.

1 GENTLEMAN. What became of his bark and his
followers?

3 GENTLEMAN. Wracked the same instant of their
master's death, and in the view of the shepherd: so
that all the instruments which aided to expose the
child were even then lost, when it was found. But,
O, the noble combat that 'twixt joy and sorrow was
fought in Paulina! She had one eye declined for the
loss of her husband, another elevated that the oracle   80
was fulfilled: she lifted the princess from the earth,
and so locks her in embracing, as if she would pin
her to her heart, that she might no more be in
danger of losing.

1 GENTLEMAN. The dignity of this act was worth the
audience of kings and princes, for by such was it
acted.

3 GENTLEMAN. One of the prettiest touches of all, and
that which angled for mine eyes (caught the water,
though not the fish) was, when at the relation of the 90
queen's death (with the manner how she came to't,
bravely confessed and lamented by the king) how
attentiveness wounded his daughter, till, from one
sign of dolour to another, she did, with an 'Alas,'
I would fain say, bleed tears; for, I am sure, my heart
wept blood. Who was most marble, there changed
colour; some swooned, all sorrowed: if all the world
could have seen't, the woe had been universal.

1 GENTLEMAN. Are they returned to the court?

3 GENTLEMAN. No: the princess hearing of her   100
mother's statue, which is in the keeping of Paulina—
a piece many years in doing, and now newly performed, by that rare Italian master, Julio Romano,
who, had he himself eternity and could put breath
into his work, would beguile nature of her custom,
so perfectly he is her ape: he so near to Hermione
hath done Hermione, that they say one would speak
to her and stand in hope of answer. Thither with
all greediness of affection are they gone, and there
they intend to sup.   110

2 GENTLEMAN. I thought she had some great matter
there in hand, for she hath privately twice or thrice
a day, ever since the death of Hermione, visited that
removed house. Shall we thither, and with our
company piece the rejoicing?

1 GENTLEMAN. Who would be thence that has the
benefit of access? Every wink of an eye, some new
grace will be born: our absence makes us unthrifty
to our knowledge. Let's along.

                                The three gentlemen go

AUTOLYCUS. Now, had I not the dash of my former   120
life in me, would preferment drop on my head. I
brought the old man and his son aboard the prince;
told him I heard them talk of a fardel and I know not
what: but he at that time, over-fond of the
shepherd's daughter (so he then took her to be) who
began to be much sea-sick, and himself little better,
extremity of weather continuing, this mystery remained undiscovered. But 'tis all one to me: for had
I been the finder out of this secret, it would not
have relished among my other discredits.   130

The Shepherd and Clown approach

Here come those I have done good to against my
will, and already appearing in the blossoms of their
fortune.

SHEPHERD. Come, boy; I am past moe children; but
thy sons and daughters will be all gentlemen born.

CLOWN. You are well met, sir. You denied to fight
with me this other day, because I was no gentleman
born. See you these clothes? Say you see them not
and think me still no gentleman born: you were best
say these robes are not gentleman born. Give me the 140
lie; do; and try whether I am not now a gentleman
born.

AUTOLYCUS. I know, you are now, sir, a gentleman
born.

CLOWN. Ay, and have been so any time these four
hours.

SHEPHERD. And so have I, boy.

CLOWN. So you have: but I was a gentleman born
before my father: for the king's son took me by
the hand, and called me brother; and then the two 150
kings called my father brother; and then the prince,
my brother, and the princess, my sister, called my
father father; and so we wept: and there was the
first gentleman-like tears that ever we shed.

SHEPHERD. We may live, son, to shed many more.

CLOWN. Ay; or else 'twere hard luck, being in so
preposterous estate as we are.

AUTOLYCUS. I humbly beseech you, sir, to pardon me
all the faults I have committed to your worship, and
to give me your good report to the prince my 160
master.

SHEPHERD. Prithee, son, do; for we must be gentle,
now we are gentlemen.

CLOWN. Thou wilt amend thy life?

AUTOLYCUS. Ay, an it like your good worship.

CLOWN. Give me thy hand: I will swear to the prince
thou art as honest a true fellow as any is in Bohemia.

SHEPHERD. You may say it, but not swear it.

CLOWN. Not swear it, now I am a gentleman? Let
boors and franklins say it, I'll swear it. 170

SHEPHERD. How if it be false, son?

CLOWN. If it be ne'er so false, a true gentleman may
swear it, in the behalf of his friend: and I'll swear
to the prince thou art a tall fellow of thy hands, and
that thou wilt not be drunk; but I know thou art
no tall fellow of thy hands and that thou wilt be
drunk; but I'll swear it, and I would thou wouldst
be a tall fellow of thy hands.

AUTOLYCUS. I will prove so, sir, to my power.

CLOWN. Ay, by any means prove a tall fellow: if I do 180
not wonder how thou darest venture to be drunk,
not being a tall fellow, trust me not. Hark! the kings
and the princes, our kindred, are going to see the
queen's picture. Come, follow us: we'll be thy good
masters.   *They go*

Scene 3: *Paulina's house*

Leontes, Polixenes, Florizel, Perdita, Camillo, and
Paulina enter with lords and attendants

LEONTES. O grave and good Paulina, the great comfort
That I have had of thee!

PAULINA.   What, sovereign sir,
I did not well, I meant well; all my services
You have paid home: but that you have vouchsafed,
With your crowned brother and these contracted

Heirs of your kingdoms, my poor house to visit,
It is a surplus of your grace, which never
My life may last to answer.

LEONTES.   O Paulina,
We honour you with trouble: but we came
To see the statue of our queen: your gallery 10
Have we passed through, not without much content
In many singularities; but we saw not
That which my daughter came to look upon,
The statue of her mother.

PAULINA.   As she lived peerless,
So her dead likeness, I do well believe,
Excels whatever yet you looked upon,
Or hand of man hath done; therefore I keep it
Lonely, apart. But here it is: prepare
To see the life as lively mocked, as ever
Still sleep mocked death: behold, and say 'tis well.... 20
    Paulina draws the curtain, and discovers the figure
I like your silence, it the more shows off
Your wonder: but yet speak—first, you, my liege—
Comes it not something near?

LEONTES.   Her natural posture!
Chide me, dear stone, that I may say indeed
Thou art Hermione; or rather, thou art she
In thy not chiding; for she was as tender
As infancy and grace. But yet, Paulina,
Hermione was not so much wrinkled, nothing
So agéd as this seems.

POLIXENES.   O, not by much.

PAULINA. So much the more our carver's excellence, 30
Which lets go by some sixteen years, and makes her
As she lived now.

LEONTES.   As now she might have done,
So much to my good comfort, as it is
Now piercing to my soul. O, thus she stood,
Even with such life of majesty (warm life,
As now it coldly stands) when first I wooed her!
I am ashamed: does not the stone rebuke me,
For being more stone than it? O royal piece!
There's magic in thy majesty, which has
My evils conjured to remembrance, and 40
From thy admiring daughter took the spirits,
Standing like stone with thee!

PERDITA.   And give me leave,
And do not say 'tis superstition, that
I kneel and then implore her blessing.... Lady,
Dear queen, that ended when I but began,
Give me that hand of yours to kiss.

PAULINA [*prevents her*].   O, patience;
The statue is but newly fixed; the colour's
Not dry.

CAMILLO. My lord, your sorrow was too sore laid on,
Which sixteen winters cannot blow away, 50
So many summers dry: scarce any joy
Did ever so long live; no sorrow,
But killed itself much sooner.

POLIXENES.   Dear my brother,
Let him that was the cause of this have power
To take off so much grief from you, as he
Will piece up in himself.

PAULINA.   Indeed, my lord,
If I had thought the sight of my poor image
Would thus have wrought you (for the stone is
mine)
I'ld not have showed it.

LEONTES.   Do not draw the curtain.

PAULINA. No longer shall you gaze on't, lest your
    fancy   60
  May think anon it moves.
LEONTES.   Let be, let be!
  Would I were dead, but that, methinks, already!—
  What was he that did make it?—See, my lord,
  Would you not deem it breathed? and that those
    veins
  Did verily bear blood?
POLIXENES.   Masterly done:
  The very life seems warm upon her lip.
LEONTES. The fixure of her eye has motion in't,
  As we are mocked with art.
PAULINA.   I'll draw the curtain:
  My lord's almost so far transported that
  He'll think anon it lives.
LEONTES.   O sweet Paulina,   70
  Make me to think so twenty years together;
  No settled senses of the world can match
  The pleasure of that madness. Let't alone.
PAULINA. I am sorry, sir, I have thus far stirred you:
  but
  I could afflict you farther.
LEONTES.   Do, Paulina;
  For this affliction has a taste as sweet
  As any cordial comfort. Still methinks
  There is an air comes from her. What fine chisel
  Could ever yet cut breath? Let no man mock me,
  For I will kiss her.
PAULINA.   Good my lord, forbear: 80
  The ruddiness upon her lip is wet;
  You'll mar it, if you kiss it; stain your own
  With oily painting ... Shall I draw the curtain?
LEONTES. No! not these twenty years.
PERDITA.   So long could I
  Stand by, a looker on.
PAULINA.   Either forbear,
  Quit presently the chapel, or resolve you
  For more amazement: if you can behold it,
  I'll make the statue move indeed; descend,
  And take you by the hand: but then you'll think
  (Which I protest against) I am assisted   90
  By wicked powers.
LEONTES.   What you can make her do,
  I am content to look on: what to speak,
  I am content to hear; for 'tis as easy
  To make her speak, as move.
PAULINA.   It is required
  You do awake your faith: then all stand still;
  Or those that think it is unlawful business
  I am about, let them depart.
LEONTES.   Proceed:
  No foot shall stir.
PAULINA.   Music; awake her: strike!
                                 Music
  'Tis time; descend; be stone no more; approach;
  Strike all that look upon with marvel; come;   100
  I'll fill your grave up; stir; nay, come away;
  Bequeath to death your numbness, for from him
  Dear life redeems you! You perceive, she stirs:
      Hermione comes down from the pedestal
  Start not: her actions shall be holy, as

  You hear my spell is lawful: do not shun her
  Until you see her die again; for then
  You kill her double: nay, present your hand:
  When she was young, you wooed her; now, in age,
  Is she become the suitor?
LEONTES.   O, she's warm!
  If this be magic, let it be an art   110
  Lawful as eating.
POLIXENES.   She embraces him!
CAMILLO. She hangs about his neck—
  If she pertain to life, let her speak too.
POLIXENES. Ay, and make it manifest where she has
    lived,
  Or how stol'n from the dead.
PAULINA.   That she is living,
  Were it but told you, should be hooted at
  Like an old tale; but it appears she lives,
  Though yet she speak not. Mark a little while ...
  Please you to interpose, fair madam, kneel
  And pray your mother's blessing.... Turn, good
    lady,   120
  Our Perdita is found.
HERMIONE.   You gods look down,
  And from your sacred vials pour your graces
  Upon my daughter's head! Tell me (mine own)
  Where hast thou been preserved? where lived? how
    found
  Thy father's court? for thou shalt hear that I,
  Knowing by Paulina that the oracle
  Gave hope thou wast in being, have preserved
  Myself to see the issue.
PAULINA.   There's time enough for that,
  Lest they desire (upon this push) to trouble
  Your joys with like relation.... Go together,   130
  You precious winners all; your exultation
  Partake to every one: I (an old turtle)
  Will wing me to some withered bough, and there
  My mate (that's never to be found again)
  Lament, till I am lost.
LEONTES.   O peace, Paulina!
  Thou shouldst a husband take by my consent,
  As I by thine a wife: this is a match,
  And made between's by vows. Thou hast found
    mine,
  But how, is to be questioned: for I saw her,
  As I thought, dead; and have, in vain, said many   140
  A prayer upon her grave: I'll not seek far
  (For him, I partly know his mind) to find thee
  An honourable husband—come, Camillo,
  And take her by the hand—whose worth and
    honesty
  Is richly noted; and here justified
  By us, a pair of kings.... Let's from this place....
  What? look upon my brother: both your pardons,
  That e'er I put between your holy looks
  My ill suspicion.... This' your son-in-law,
  And son unto the king, whom heavens directing,   150
  Is troth-plight to your daughter. Good Paulina,
  Lead us from hence, where we may leisurely
  Each one demand and answer to his part
  Performed in this wide gap of time, since first
  We were dissevered: hastily lead away.   *They go*

King John

The scene: now in England, now in France

CHARACTERS IN THE PLAY

KING JOHN
PRINCE HENRY, *son to the king*
ARTHUR, *Duke of Britain, nephew to the king*
The Earl of Pembroke
The Earl of Essex
The Earl of Salisbury
The Lord BIGOT
HUBERT DE BURGH
ROBERT FAULCONBRIDGE, *son of Sir Robert Faulconbridge*
PHILIP THE BASTARD, *his half-brother*
JAMES GURNEY
PETER *of Pomfret, a prophet*
PHILIP, *King of France*

LEWIS, *the Dauphin*
LYMOGES, *Duke of Austria*
CARDINAL PANDULPH, *the Pope's legate*
MELUN, *a French Lord*
CHATILLION, *ambassador from France to King John*
A Citizen of Angiers
QUEEN ELINOR, *mother to King John*
CONSTANCE, *mother to Arthur*
BLANCH, *of Spain, niece to King John*
LADY FAULCONBRIDGE
*Lords, Ladies, Citizens of Angiers, Sheriff, Heralds,
Officers, Soldiers, Messengers, and other Attendants*

King John

ACT 1

Scene 1: *England. The palace of King John*

Enter King John, Queen Elinor, Pembroke, Essex, Salisbury, with the Chatillion of France, Attendants

K. JOHN. Now, say, Chatillion, what would France
  with us?
CHATILLION. Thus, after greeting, speaks the King of
  France
In my behaviour to the majesty,
The borrowed majesty, of England here.
ELINOR. A strange beginning: 'borrowed majesty'!
K. JOHN. Silence, good mother, hear the embassy.
CHATILLION. Philip of France, in right and true behalf
Of thy deceaséd brother Geffrey's son,
Arthur Plantagenet, lays most lawful claim
To this fair island and the territories,   10
To Ireland, Poictiers, Anjou, Touraine, Maine,
Desiring thee to lay aside the sword
Which sways usurpingly these several titles,
And put the same into young Arthur's hand,
Thy nephew and right royal sovereign.
K. JOHN. What follows if we disallow of this?
CHATILLION. The proud control of fierce and bloody
  war,
To enforce these rights so forcibly withheld.
K. JOHN. Here have we war for war and blood for
  blood,
Controlment for control: so answer France.   20
CHATILLION. Then take my king's defiance from my
  mouth,
The farthest limit of my embassy.
K. JOHN. Bear mine to him, and so depart in peace:
Be thou as lightning in the eyes of France;
For ere thou canst report I will be there,
The thunder of my cannon shall be heard.
So hence! Be thou the trumpet of our wrath,
And sullen presage of your own decay:
An honourable conduct let him have,
Pembroke, look to't: farewell, Chatillion.   30
              Chatillion and Pembroke depart
ELINOR. What now, my son? have I not ever said
How that ambitious Constance would not cease
Till she had kindled France and all the world,
Upon the right and party of her son?
This might have been prevented and made whole
With very easy arguments of love,
Which now the manage of two kingdoms must
With fearful-bloody issue arbitrate.
K. JOHN. Our strong possession and our right for us.
ELINOR. Your strong possession much more than your
  right,   40
Or else it must go wrong with you and me—
So much my conscience whispers in your ear,
Which none but heaven, and you, and I, shall hear.

Enter a Sheriff and speaks aside with Essex

ESSEX. My liege, here is the strangest controversy,
Come from the country to be judged by you,
That e'er I heard: shall I produce the men?

K. JOHN. Let them approach ...
Our abbeys and our priories shall pay
This expedition's charge ...

Robert Faulconbridge, and Philip his bastard brother enter

            What men are you?
BASTARD. Your faithful subject I, a gentleman,   50
Born in Northamptonshire, and eldest son,
As I suppose, to Robert Faulconbridge,
A soldier, by honour-giving hand
Of Cordelion knighted in the field.
K. JOHN. What art thou?
ROBERT. The son and heir to that same Faulconbridge.
K. JOHN. Is that the elder, and art thou the heir?
You came not of one mother then, it seems.
BASTARD. Most certain of one mother, mighty king—
That is well known—and as I think one father: 60
But for the certain knowledge of that truth
I put you o'er to heaven and to my mother;
Of that I doubt, as all men's children may.
ELINOR. Out on thee, rude man! thou dost shame thy
  mother,
And wound her honour with this diffidence.
BASTARD. I, madam? no, I have no reason for it,
That is my brother's plea and none of mine,
The which if he can prove, a' pops me out
At least from fair five hundred pound a year:
Heaven guard my mother's honour, and my land!   70
K. JOHN. A good blunt fellow ... Why, being
  younger born,
Doth he lay claim to thine inheritance?
BASTARD. I know not why, except to get the land:
But once he slandered me with bastardy:
Now whe'r I be as true begot or no,
That still I lay upon my mother's head,
But that I am as well begot, my liege,
(Fair fall the bones that took the pains for me!)
Compare our faces and be judge yourself.
If old Sir Robert did beget us both,   80
And were our father, and this son like him,
O old Sir Robert, father, on my knee
I give heaven thanks I was not like to thee!
K. JOHN. Why, what a madcap hath heaven lent us
  here!
ELINOR. He hath a trick of Cordelion's face,
The accent of his tongue affecteth him:
Do you not read some tokens of my son
In the large composition of this man?
K. JOHN. Mine eye hath well examinéd his parts,
And finds them perfect Richard ... Sirrah, speak,   90
What doth move you to claim your brother's land?
BASTARD. Because he hath a half-face like my father!
With half that face would he have all my land—
A half-faced groat five hundred pound a year!
ROBERT. My gracious liege, when that my father lived,
Your brother did employ my father much—
BASTARD. Well, sir, by this you cannot get my land,
Your tale must be how he employed my mother.
ROBERT. And once dispatched him in an embassy
To Germany, there with the emperor   100

To treat of high affairs touching that time:
Th' advantage of his absence took the king,
And in the mean time sojourned at my father's;
Where how he did prevail I shame to speak,
But truth is truth: large lengths of seas and shores
Between my father and my mother lay,
As I have heard my father speak himself,
When this same lusty gentleman was got:
Upon his death-bed he by will bequeathed
His lands to me, and took it on his death   110
That this my mother's son was none of his;
And if he were, he came into the world
Full fourteen weeks before the course of time:
Then, good my liege, let me have what is mine,
My father's land, as was my father's will.

K. JOHN. Sirrah, your brother is legitimate,
Your father's wife did after wedlock bear him:
And if she did play false, the fault was hers,
Which fault lies on the hazards of all husbands
That marry wives: tell me, how if my brother,   120
Who as you say took pains to get this son,
Had of your father claimed this son for his?
In sooth, good friend, your father might have kept
This calf, bred from his cow, from all the world:
In sooth, he might: then, if he were my brother's,
My brother might not claim him, nor your father
Being none of his refuse him: this concludes—
My mother's son did get your father's heir,
Your father's heir must have your father's land.

ROBERT. Shall then my father's will be of no force   130
To dispossess that child which is not his?

BASTARD. Of no more force to dispossess me, sir,
Than was his will to get me, as I think.

ELINOR. Whether hadst thou rather be a
    Faulconbridge,
And like thy brother, to enjoy thy land,
Or the reputed son of Cordelion,
Lord of thy presence and no land beside?

BASTARD. Madam, an if my brother had my shape,
And I had his, Sir Robert's his, like him,
And if my legs were two such riding-rods,   140
My arms such eel-skins stuffed, my face so thin
That in mine ear I durst not stick a rose
Lest men should say 'Look, where three-farthings
    goes!'
And, to his shape, were heir to all this land,
Would I might never stir from off this place,
I would give it every foot to have this face;
I would not be Sir Nob in any case.

ELINOR. I like thee well: wilt thou forsake thy fortune,
Bequeath thy land to him, and follow me?
I am a soldier, and now bound to France.   150

BASTARD. Brother, take you my land, I'll take my
    chance;
Your face hath got five hundred pound a year,
Yet sell your face for five pence and 'tis dear:
Madam, I'll follow you unto the death.

ELINOR. Nay, I would have you go before me thither.

BASTARD. Our country manners give our betters way.

K. JOHN. What is thy name?

BASTARD. Philip, my liege, so is my name begun,
Philip, good old Sir Robert's wife's eldest son.

K. JOHN. From henceforth bear his name whose
    form thou bearest: 160
Kneel thou down Philip, but rise more great—
Arise Sir Richard, and Plantagenet.

BASTARD. Brother, by th'mother's side, give me your
    hand.
My father gave me honour, yours gave land ...
Now blessèd be the hour, by night or day,
When I was got, Sir Robert was away.

ELINOR. The very spirit of Plantagenet!
I am thy grandam, Richard, call me so.

BASTARD. Madam, by chance but not by truth,
    what though?
Something about, a little from the right,   170
In at the window, or else o'er the hatch:
Who dares not stir by day must walk by night,
And have is have, however men do catch:
Near or far off, well won is still well shot,
And I am I, howe'er I was begot.

K. JOHN. Go, Faulconbridge, now hast thou thy
    desire,
A landless knight makes thee a landed squire:
Come, madam, and come, Richard, we must speed
For France, for France, for it is more than need.

BASTARD. Brother, adieu, good fortune come to
    thee!   180
For thou was got i'th' way of honesty....

                         Exeunt all but Bastard

A foot of honour better than I was,
But many a many foot of land the worse....
Well, now can I make any Joan a lady.
'Good den, Sir Richard!'—'God-a-mercy,
    fellow'—
And if his name be George, I'll call him Peter;
For new-made honour doth forget men's names;
'Tis too respective and too sociable
For your conversion. Now your traveller,
He and his toothpick at my worship's mess,   190
And when my knightly stomach is sufficed,
Why then I suck my teeth, and catechize
My pickèd man of countries: 'My dear sir',
Thus leaning on mine elbow I begin,
'I shall beseech you'—that is question now;
And then comes answer like an Absey book:
'O sir,' says answer, 'at your best command,
At your employment, at your service, sir:'
'No, sir,' says question, 'I, sweet sir, at yours.'
And so, ere answer knows what question would,   200
Saving in dialogue of compliment,
And talking of the Alps and Apennines,
The Pyrenean and the river Po,
It draws toward supper in conclusion so....
But this is worshipful society,
And fits the mounting spirit like myself;
For he is but a bastard to the time
That doth not smack of observation.
And so am I, whether I smack or no:
And not alone in habit and device,   210
Exterior form, outward accoutrement;
But from the inward motion to deliver
Sweet, sweet, sweet poison for the age's tooth—
Which, though I will not practise to deceive,
Yet, to avoid deceit, I mean to learn;
For it shall strew the footsteps of my rising ...
But who comes in such haste in riding-robes?
What woman-post is this? hath she no husband
That will take pains to blow a horn before her?

Enter Lady Faulconbridge and James Gurney

O me! it is my mother: how now, good lady?   220

What brings you here to court so hastily?
LADY FAULCONBRIDGE. Where is that slave, thy
brother? where is he,
That holds in chase mine honour up and down?
BASTARD. My brother Robert? old Sir Robert's
son?
Colbrand the giant, that same mighty man?
Is it Sir Robert's son that you seek so?
LADY FAULCONBRIDGE. Sir Robert's son! Ay, thou
unreverend boy,
Sir Robert's son: why scorn'st thou at Sir Robert?
He is Sir Robert's son, and so art thou.
BASTARD. James Gurney, wilt thou give us leave
awhile?   230
GURNEY. Good leave, good Philip.
BASTARD.   Philip Sparrow, James!
There's toys abroad, anon I'll tell thee more....
                                                             Gurney goes
Madam, I was not old Sir Robert's son,
Sir Robert might have eat his part in me
Upon Good-Friday and ne'er broke his fast:
Sir Robert could do well—marry, to confess—
Could he get me. Sir Robert could not do it;
We know his handiwork. Therefore, good mother,
To whom am I beholding for these limbs?
Sir Robert never holp to make this leg.   240
LADY FAULCONBRIDGE. Hast thou conspiréd with thy
brother too,
That for thine own gain shouldst defend mine
honour?
What means this scorn, thou most untoward knave?
BASTARD. Knight, knight, good mother,
Basilisco-like:
What! I am dubbed, I have it on my shoulder:
But, mother, I am not Sir Robert's son,
I have disclaimed Sir Robert and my land,
Legitimation, name, and all is gone:
Then, good my mother, let me know my father,
Some proper man I hope, who was it, mother?   250
LADY FAULCONBRIDGE. Hast thou denied thyself a
Faulconbridge?
BASTARD. As faithfully as I deny the devil.
LADY FAULCONBRIDGE. King Richard Cordelion was
thy father.
By long and vehement suit I was seduced
To make room for him in my husband's bed:
Heaven lay not my transgression to thy charge,
That art the issue of my dear offence,
Which was so strongly urged past my defence.
BASTARD. Now, by this light, were I to get again,
Madam, I would not wish a better father: 260
Some sins do bear their privilege on earth,
And so doth yours; your fault was not your folly.
Needs must you lay your heart at his dispose,
Subjected tribute to commanding love,
Against whose fury and unmatchéd force
The aweless lion could not wage the fight,
Nor keep his princely heart from Richard's hand:
He that perforce robs lions of their hearts
May easily win a woman's.... Ay, my mother,
With all my heart I thank thee for my father!   270
Who lives and dares but say thou didst not well
When I was got, I'll send his soul to hell....
Come, lady, I will show thee to my kin,
And they shall say, when Richard me begot,
If thou hadst said him nay, it had been sin:

Who says it was, he lies; I say 'twas not.
                                                       They go

ACT 2

Scene 1: *France. Before Angiers*

Enter King Philip of France, Lewis the Dauphin, Constance and Arthur, meeting the Duke of Austria and his forces

K. PHILIP. Before Angiers well met, brave Austria.
Arthur, that great forerunner of thy blood,
Richard, that robbed the lion of his heart
And fought the holy wars in Palestine,
By this brave duke came early to his grave:
And for amends to his posterity,
At out importance hither is he come,
To spread his colours, boy, in thy behalf,
And to rebuke the usurpation
Of thy unnatural uncle, English John.   10
Embrace him, love him, give him welcome hither.
ARTHUR. God shall forgive you Cordelion's death
The rather that you give his offspring life,
Shadowing their right under your wings of war:
I give you welcome with a powerless hand,
But with a heart full of unstainéd love.
Welcome before the gates of Angiers, duke.
K. PHILIP. A noble boy! Who would not do thee
right?
AUSTRIA. Upon thy cheek lay I this zealous kiss,
As seal to this indenture of my love: 20
That to my home I will no more return,
Till Angiers and the right thou hast in France,
Together with that pale, that white-faced shore,
Whose foot spurns back the ocean's roaring tides
And coops from other lands her islanders,
Even till that England, hedged in with the main,
That water-walléd bulwark, still secure
And confident from foreign purposes,
Even till that utmost corner of the west
Salute thee for her king—till then, fair boy,   30
Will I not think of home, but follow arms.
CONSTANCE. O, take his mother's thanks, a widow's
thanks,
Till your strong hand shall help to give him
strength,
To make a more requital to your love.
AUSTRIA. The peace of heaven is theirs that lift their
swords
In such a just and charitable war.
K. PHILIP. Well then, to work; our cannon shall be
bent
Against the brows of this resisting town.
Call for our chiefest men of discipline,
To cull the plots of best advantages: 40
We'll lay before this town our royal bones,
Wade to the market-place in Frenchmen's blood,
But we will make it subject to this boy.
CONSTANCE. Stay for an answer to your embassy,
Lest unadvised you stain your swords with blood.
My Lord Chatillion may from England bring
That right in peace which here we urge in war,
And then we shall repent each drop of blood
That hot rash haste so indirectly shed.

Enter Chatillion

K. PHILIP. A wonder, lady! lo, upon thy wish,   50
  Our messenger Chatillion is arrived.
  What England says, say briefly, gentle lord,
  We coldly pause for thee, Chatillion, speak.
CHATILLION. Then turn your forces from this paltry
    siege,
  And stir them up against a mightier task:
  England, impatient of your just demands,
  Hath put himself in arms. The adverse winds,
  Whose leisure I have stayed, have given him time
  To land his legions all as soon as I:
  His marches are expedient to this town,   60
  His forces strong, his soldiers confident:
  With him along is come the mother-queen,
  An Até stirring him to blood and strife,
  With her her niece, the Lady Blanch of Spain,
  With them a bastard of the king's deceased,
  And all th'unsettled humours of the land,
  Rash, inconsiderate, fiery voluntaries,
  With ladies' faces and fierce dragons' spleens,
  Have sold their fortunes at their native homes,
  Bearing their birthrights proudly on their backs,   70
  To make a hazard of new fortunes here:
  In brief, a braver choice of dauntless spirits
  Than now the English bottoms have waft o'er
  Did never float upon the swelling tide,
  To do offence and scath in Christendom:
                       Drum beats
  The interruption of their churlish drums
  Cuts off more circumstance. They are at hand,
  To parley or to fight, therefore prepare.
K. PHILIP. How much unlooked for is this expedition!
AUSTRIA. By how much unexpected, by so much   80
  We must awake endeavour for defence,
  For courage mounteth with occasion.
  Let them be welcome then, we are prepared.

*Enter King John, Elinor, Blanch, the Bastard, Pembroke,
and forces*

K. JOHN. Peace be to France: if France in peace permit
  Our just and lineal entrance to our own;
  If not, bleed France, and peace ascend to heaven,
  Whiles we, God's wrathful agent, do correct
  Their proud contempt that beats his peace to
    heaven.
K. PHILIP. Peace be to England, if that war return
  From France to England, there to live in peace: 90
  England we love, and for that England's sake
  With burden of our armour here we sweat:
  This toil of ours should be a work of thine;
  But thou from loving England art so far,
  That thou hast under-wrought his lawful king,
  Cut off the sequence of posterity,
  Out-faced infant state, and done a rape
  Upon the maiden virtue of the crown:
  Look here upon thy brother Geffrey's face—
  These eyes, these brows, were moulded out of his;   100
  This little abstract doth contain that large
  Which died in Geffrey; and the hand of time
  Shall draw this brief into as huge a volume:
  That Geffrey was thy elder brother born,
  And this his son: England was Geffrey's right,
  And this is Geffrey's in the name of God:
  How comes it then that thou art called a king,
  When living blood doth in these temples beat,

Which owe the crown that thou o'ermasterest?
K. JOHN. From whom hast thou this great commission,
  France,   110
  To draw my answer from thy articles?
K. PHILIP. From that supernal judge, that stirs good
    thoughts
  In any breast of strong authority,
  To look into the blots and stains of right.
  That judge hath made me guardian to this boy,
  Under whose warrant I impeach thy wrong,
  And by whose help I mean to chastise it.
K. JOHN. Alack, thou dost usurp authority.
K. PHILIP. Excuse it is, to beat usurping down.
ELINOR. Who is it thou dost call usurper, France?   120
CONSTANCE. Let me make answer: thy usurping son.
ELINOR. Out, insolent! thy bastard shall be king,
  That thou mayst be a queen, and check the world!
CONSTANCE. My bed was ever to thy son as true,
  As thine was to thy husband, and this boy
  Liker in feature to his father Geffrey
  Than thou and John in manners; being as like
  As rain to water, or devil to his dam ...
  My boy a bastard! By my soul, I think
  His father never was so true begot—   130
  It cannot be an if thou wert his mother.
ELINOR. There's a good mother, boy, that blots thy
    father.
CONSTANCE. There's a good grandam, boy, that
    would blot thee.
AUSTRIA. Peace!
BASTARD.   Hear the crier.
AUSTRIA.   What the devil art thou?
BASTARD. One that will play the devil, sir, with you,
  An a' may catch your hide and you alone:
  You are the hare of whom the proverb goes,
  Whose valour plucks dead lions by the beard;
  I'll smoke your skin-coat an I catch you right.
  Sirrah, look to't, i'faith I will, i'faith.   140
BLANCH. O, well did he become that lion's robe
  That did disrobe the lion of that robe!
BASTARD. It lies as sightly on the back of him,
  As great Alcides' shows upon an ass:
  But, ass, I'll take that burden from your back,
  Or lay on that shall make your shoulders crack.
AUSTRIA. What cracker is this same that deafs our ears
  With this abundance of superfluous breath?
  King Philip, determine what we shall do straight.
K. PHILIP. Women and fools, break off your
    conference....   150
  King John, this is the very sum of all:
  England and Ireland, Anjou, Touraine, Maine,
  In right of Arthur do I claim of thee:
  Wilt thou resign them and lay down thy arms?
K. JOHN. My life as soon: I do defy thee, France.
  Arthur of Britain, yield thee to my hand,
  And out of my dear love I'll give thee more
  Than e'er the coward hand of France can win:
  Submit thee, boy.
ELINOR.   Come to thy grandam, child.
CONSTANCE. Do, child, go to it grandam, child,   160
  Give grandam kingdom, and it grandam will
  Give it a plum, a cherry, and a fig.
  There's a good grandam.
ARTHUR.   Good my mother, peace!
  I would that I were low laid in my grave,
  I am not worth this coil that's made for me.

ELINOR. His mother shames him so, poor boy, he
   weeps.
CONSTANCE. Now shame upon you, whe'r she does or
   no!
   His grandam's wrongs, and not his mother's shames,
   Draw those heaven-moving pearls from his poor
      eyes,
   Which heaven shall take in nature of a fee: 170
   Ay, with these crystal beads heaven shall be bribed
   To do him justice and revenge on you.
ELINOR. Thou monstrous slanderer of heaven and
   earth!
CONSTANCE. Thou monstrous injurer of heaven and
   earth!
   Call not me slanderer; thou and thine usurp
   The dominations, royalties and rights
   Of this oppressèd boy: this is thy eldest son's son,
   Infortunate in nothing but in thee:
   Thy sins are visited in this poor child,
   The canon of the law is laid on him,   180
   Being but the second generation
   Removèd from thy sin-conceiving womb.
K. JOHN. Bedlam, have done.
CONSTANCE.   I have but this to say,
   That he's not only plagued for her sin,
   But God hath made her sin and her the plague
   On this removèd issue, plagued for her
   And with her plague, her sin; his injury
   Her injury, the beadle to her sin—
   All punished in the person of this child,
   And all for her—a plague upon her!   190
ELINOR. Thou unadvisèd scold, I can produce
   A will that bars the title of thy son.
CONSTANCE. Ay, who doubts that? a will! a wicked
   will,
   A woman's will, a cank'red grandam's will!
K. PHILIP. Peace, lady! pause, or be more temperate.
   It ill beseems this presence to cry aim
   To these ill-tunèd repetitions:
   Some trumpet summon hither to the walls
   These men of Angiers—let us hear them speak
   Whose title they admit, Arthur's or John's.   200

Trumpet sounds. Enter a Citizen upon the walls

CITIZEN. Who is it that hath warned us to the walls?
K. PHILIP. 'Tis France, for England.
K. JOHN.   England, for itself:
   You men of Angiers, and my loving subjects—
K. PHILIP. You loving men of Angiers, Arthur's
   subjects,
   Our trumpet called you to this gentle parle.
K. JOHN. For our advantage—therefore, hear us first:
   These flags of France, that are advancèd here
   Before the eye and prospect of your town,
   Have hither marched to your endamagement:
   The cannons have their bowels full of wrath,   210
   And ready mounted are they to spit forth
   Their iron indignation 'gainst your walls:
   All preparation for a bloody siege
   And merciless proceeding by these French
   Confronts your city's eyes, your winking gates;
   And but for our approach those sleeping stones,
   That as a waist doth girdle you about,
   By the compulsion of their ordinance
   By this time from their fixèd beds of lime
   Had been dishabited, and wide havoc made   220

For bloody power to rush upon your peace.
But on the sight of us your lawful king,
Who painfully with much expedient march
Have brought a countercheck before your gates,
To save unscratched your city's threat'ned cheeks,
Behold, the French amazed vouchsafe a parle:
And now, instead of bullets wrapped in fire,
To make a shaking fever in your walls,
They shoot but calm words folded up in smoke,
To make a faithless error in your ears: 230
Which trust accordingly, kind citizens,
And let us in, your king, whose laboured spirits,
Forwearied in this action of swift speed,
Crave harbourage within your city walls.
K. PHILIP. When I have said, make answer to us both.
Lo, in this right hand, whose protection
Is most divinely vowed upon the right
Of him it holds, stands young Plantagenet,
Son to the elder brother of this man,
And king o'er him and all that he enjoys: 240
For this down-trodden equity, we tread
In warlike march these greens before your town,
Being no further enemy to you
Than the constraint of hospitable zeal
In the relief of this oppressèd child
Religiously provokes. Be pleasèd then
To pay that duty which you truly owe
To him that owes it, namely this young prince,
And then our arms, like to a muzzled bear,
Save in aspect, hath all offence sealed up: 250
Our cannons' malice vainly shall be spent
Against th'invulnerable clouds of heaven,
And with a blessèd and unvexed retire,
With unhacked swords and helmets all unbruised,
We will bear home that lusty blood again
Which here we came to spout against your town,
And leave your children, wives, and you in
   peace....
But if you fondly pass our proffered offer,
'Tis not the roundure of your old-faced walls
Can hide you from our messengers of war,   260
Though all these English and their discipline
Were harboured in their rude circumference:
Then tell us, shall your city call us lord,
In that behalf which we have challenged it?
Or shall we give the signal to our rage
And stalk in blood to our possession?
CITIZEN. In brief, we are the King of England's
   subjects:
For him, and in his right, we hold this town.
K. JOHN. Acknowledge then the king, and let me in.
CITIZEN. That can we not: but he that proves the king, 270
   To him will we prove loyal. Till that time
   Have we rammed up our gates against the world.
K. JOHN. Doth not the crown of England prove
   the king?
   And, if not that, I bring you witnesses,
   Twice fifteen thousand hearts of England's breed—
BASTARD. Bastards and else.
K. JOHN. To verify our title with their lives.
K. PHILIP. As many and as well-born bloods as those—
BASTARD. Some bastards too.
K. PHILIP. Stand in his face to contradict his claim. 280
CITIZEN. Till you compound whose right is worthiest,
   We for the worthiest hold the right from both.
K. JOHN. Then God forgive the sin of all those souls

That to their everlasting residence,
Before the dew of evening fall, shall fleet,
In dreadful trial of our kingdom's king!
K. PHILIP. Amen, amen! Mount, chevaliers! to arms!
BASTARD. Saint George, that swinged the dragon, and
  e'er since
Sits on his horse back at mine hostess' door,
Teach us some fence! [to Austria] Sirrah, were I at
  home,   290
At your den, sirrah, with your lioness,
I would set an ox-head to your lion's hide,
And make a monster of you.
AUSTRIA.   Peace, no more.
BASTARD. O, tremble! for you hear the lion roar.
K. JOHN. Up higher to the plain, where we'll set forth
In best appointment all our regiments.
BASTARD. Speed then to take advantage of the field.
K. PHILIP. It shall be so, and at the other hill
Command the rest to stand, God, and our right!
                                              They go

*Here, after excursions, enter the Herald of France with
Trumpets to the gates*

FRENCH HERALD. You men of Angiers, open wide
  your gates,   300
And let young Arthur, Duke of Britain, in,
Who by the hand of France this day hath made
Much work for tears in many an English mother,
Whose sons lie scattered on the bleeding ground:
Many a widow's husband grovelling lies,
Coldly embracing the discoloured earth,
And victory with little loss doth play
Upon the dancing banners of the French,
Who are at hand, triumphantly displayed,
To enter conquerors, and to proclaim   310
Arthur of Britain England's king and yours.

Enter English Herald with Trumpet

ENGLISH HERALD. Rejoice, you men of Angiers, ring
  your bells,
King John, your king and England's, doth approach,
Commander of this hot malicious day!
Their armours, that marched hence so silver-bright,
Hither return all gilt with Frenchmen's blood:
There stuck no plume in any English crest,
That is removéd by a staff of France:
Our colours do return in those same hands
That did display them when we first marched forth;   320
And like a jolly troop of huntsmen come
Our lusty English, all with purpled hands,
Dyed in the dying slaughter of their foes.
Open your gates and give the victors way.
CITIZEN. Heralds, from off our towers we might
  behold,
From first to last, the onset and retire
Of both your armies, whose equality
By our best eyes cannot be censuréd:
Blood hath bought blood, and blows have answered
  blows;
Strength matched with strength, and power
  confronted power.   330
Both are alike, and both alike we like:
One must prove greatest: while they weigh so even,
We hold our town for neither; yet for both.

Enter the two Kings with their powers severally

K. JOHN. France, hast thou yet more blood to cast
  away?
Say, shall the current of our right run on?
Whose passage, vexed with thy impediment,
Shall leave his native channel, and o'erswell
With course disturbed even thy confining shores,
Unless thou let his silver water keep
A peaceful progress to the ocean.   340
K. PHILIP. England, thou hast not saved one drop of
  blood
In this hot trial more than we of France,
Rather lost more. And by this hand I swear,
That sways the earth this climate overlooks,
Before we will lay down our just-borne arms,
We'll put thee down, 'gainst whom these arms we
  bear,
Or add a royal number to the dead,
Gracing the scroll that tells of this war's loss
With slaughter coupled to the name of kings.
BASTARD. Ha, majesty! how high thy glory towers,   350
When the rich blood of kings is set on fire!
O, now doth death line his dead chaps with steel,
The swords of soldiers are his teeth, his fangs,
And now he feasts, mousing the flesh of men,
In undetermined differences of kings....
Why stand these royal fronts amazéd thus?
Cry 'havoc!' kings, back to the stainéd field,
You equal potents, fiery-kindled spirits!
Then let confusion of one part cônfirm
The other's peace; till then, blows, blood, and death!   360
K. JOHN. Whose party do the townsmen yet admit?
K. PHILIP. Speak, citizens, for England; who's your
  king?
CITIZEN. The King of England, when we know the
  king.
K. PHILIP. Know him in us, that here hold up his
  right.
K. JOHN. In us, that are our own great deputy,
And bear possession of our person here,
Lord of our presence, Angiers, and of you.
CITIZEN. A greater power than we denies all this,
And till it be undoubted, we do lock
Our former scruple in our strong-barred gates: 370
Kinged of our fears, until our fears, resolved,
Be by some certain king purged and deposed.
BASTARD. By heaven, these scroyles of Angiers flout
  you, kings,
And stand securely on their battlements,
As in a theatre, whence they gape and point
At your industrious scenes and acts of death.
Your royal presences be ruled by me,
Do like the mutines of Jerusalem
Be friends awhile and both conjointly bend
Your sharpest deeds of malice on this town: 380
By east and west let France and England mount
Their battering cannon chargéd to the mouths,
Till their soul-fearing clamours have brawled down
The flinty ribs of this contemptuous city.
I'd play incessantly upon these jades,
Even till unfencéd desolation
Leave them as naked as the vulgar air:
That done, dissever your united strengths,
And part your mingled colours once again,
Turn face to face, and bloody point to point: 390
Then in a moment Fortune shall cull forth
Out of one side her happy minion,

To whom in favour she shall give the day,
And kiss him with a glorious victory ...
How like you this wild counsel, mighty states?
Smacks it not something of the policy?
K. JOHN. Now, by the sky that hangs above our heads,
I like it well. France, shall we knit our powers
And lay this Angiers even with the ground,
Then after fight who shall be king of it?   400
BASTARD. An if thou hast the mettle of a king,
Being wronged as we are by this peevish town,
Turn thou the mouth of thy artillery,
As we will ours, against these saucy walls,
And when that we have dashed them to the ground,
Why then defy each other, and pell-mell
Make work upon ourselves, for heaven or hell.
K. PHILIP. Let it be so: say, where will you assault?
K. JOHN. We from the west will send destruction
Into this city's bosom.   410
AUSTRIA. I from the north.
K. PHILIP.   Our thunder from the south,
Shall rain their drift of bullets on this town.
BASTARD [aside]. O prudent discipline! From north to
south:
Austria and France shoot in each other's mouth.
I'll stir them to it ... [shouts] Come, away, away!
CITIZEN. Hear us, great kings, vouchsafe awhile to
stay
And I shall show you peace and fair-faced league:
Win you this city without stroke or wound,
Rescue those breathing lives to die in beds,
That here comes sacrifices for the field: 420
Persever not, but hear me, mighty kings.
K. JOHN. Speak on with favour, we are bent to hear.
CITIZEN. That daughter there of Spain, the Lady
Blanch,
Is niece to England. Look upon the years
Of Lewis the Dauphin and that lovely maid:
If lusty love should go in quest of beauty,
Where should he find it fairer than in Blanch?
If zealous love should go in search of virtue,
Where should he find it purer than in Blanch?
If love ambitious sought a match of birth,
Whose veins bound richer blood than Lady Blanch?
Such as she is, in beauty, virtue, birth,   430
Is the young Dauphin every way complete:
If not complete of, say he is not she,
And she again wants nothing, to name want,
If want it be not that she is not he:
He is the half part of a blessèd man,
Left to be finishèd by such a she;
And she a fair divided excellence,
Whose fulness of perfection lies in him.   440
O, two such silver currents when they join
Do glorify the banks that bound them in:
And two such shores to two such streams made one,
Two such controlling bounds shall you be, kings,
To these two princes, if you marry them:
This union shall do more than battery can
To our fast-closèd gates; for at this match,
With swifter spleen than powder can enforce,
The mouth of passage shall we fling wide ope,
And give you entrance; but, without this match,   450
The sea enragèd is not half so deaf,
Lions more confident, mountains and rocks
More free from motion, no, not Death himself
In mortal fury half so peremptory,

As we to keep this city.
BASTARD.   Here's a stay
That shakes the rotten carcass of old Death
Out of his rags! Here's a large mouth, indeed,
That spits forth death and mountains, rocks and seas,
Talks as familiarly of roaring lions
As maids of thirteen do of puppy-dogs!   460
What cannoneer begot this lusty blood?
He speaks plain cannon fire, and smoke and bounce,
He gives the bastinado with his tongue:
Our ears are cudgelled—not a word of his
But buffets better than a fist of France:
Zounds! I was never so bethumped with words
Since I first called my brother's father 'dad'.
ELINOR. Son, list to this conjunction, make this match;
Give with our niece a dowry large enough,
For by this knot thou shalt so surely tie   470
Thy now unsured assurance to the crown,
That yon green boy shall have no sun to ripe
The bloom that promiseth a mighty fruit.
I see a yielding in the looks of France:
Mark how they whisper, urge them while their souls
Are capable of this ambition,
Lest zeal, now melted by the windy breath
Of soft petitions, pity and remorse,
Cool and congeal again to what it was.
CITIZEN. Why answer not the double majesties   480
This friendly treaty of our threat'ned town?
K. PHILIP. Speak England first, that hath been forward
first
To speak unto this city: what say you?
K. JOHN. If that the Dauphin there, thy princely son,
Can in this book of beauty read 'I love',
Her dowry shall weigh equal with a queen:
For Anjou, and fair Touraine, Maine, Poictiers,
And all that we upon this side the sea
(Except this city now by us besieged)
Find liable to our crown and dignity,   490
Shall gild her bridal bed, and make her rich
In titles, honours and promotions,
As she in beauty, education, blood,
Holds hand with any princess of the world.
K. PHILIP. What say'st thou, boy? look in the
lady's face.
LEWIS. I do, my lord, and in her eye I find
A wonder, or a wondrous miracle,
The shadow of myself formed in her eye,
Which, being but the shadow of your son,
Becomes a sun, and makes your son a shadow: 500
I do protest, I never loved myself,
Till now infixèd I beheld myself,
Drawn in the flattering table of her eye.
                              Whispers with Blanch
BASTARD [aside]. Drawn in the flattering table of her
eye,
Hanged in the frowning wrinkle of her brow,
And quartered in her heart, he doth espy
Himself love's traitor. This is pity now:
That hanged, and drawn, and quartered, there
should be
In such a love so vile a lout as he.
BLANCH. My uncle's will in this respect is mine.   510
If he see aught in you that makes him like,
That anything he sees, which moves his liking,
I can with ease translate it to my will:
Or if you will, to speak more properly,

I will enforce it easily to my love.
Further I will not flatter you, my lord,
That all I see in you is worthy love,
Than this—that nothing do I see in you,
Though churlish thoughts themselves should be
  your judge,
That I can find should merit any hate.   520
K. JOHN. What say these young ones? What say you,
  my niece?
BLANCH. That she is bound in honour still to do
What you in wisdom still vouchsafe to say.
K. JOHN. Speak then, Prince Dauphin, can you love
  this lady?
LEWIS. Nay, ask me if I can refrain from love,
For I do love her most unfeignedly.
K. JOHN. Then do I give Volquessen, Touraine, Maine,
Poictiers and Anjou, these five provinces,
With her to thee, and this addition more,
Full thirty thousand marks of English coin: 530
Philip of France, if thou be pleased withal,
Command thy son and daughter to join hands.
K. PHILIP. It likes us well; young princes, close your
  hands.
AUSTRIA. And your lips too, for I am well assured
That I did so when I was first assured.
K. PHILIP. Now, citizens of Angiers, ope your gates,
Let in that amity which you have made,
For at Saint Mary's chapel presently
The rites of marriage shall be solemnized.   540
Is not the Lady Constance in this troop?
I know she is not, for this match made up
Her presence would have interrupted much:
Where is she and her son? tell me, who knows.
LEWIS. She is sad and passionate at your highness' tent.
K. PHILIP. And, by my faith, this league that we have
  made
Will give her sadness very little cure:
Brother of England, how may we content
This widow lady? In her right we came,
Which we, God knows, have turned another way,
To our own vantage.
K. JOHN.   We will heal up all,   550
For we'll create young Arthur Duke of Britain
And Earl of Richmond, and this rich fair town
We make him lord of.... Call the Lady Constance.
Some speedy messenger bid her repair
To our solemnity: I trust we shall,
If not fill up the measure of her will,
Yet in some measure satisfy her so
That we shall stop her exclamation.
Go we, as well as haste will suffer us,
To this unlooked for, unprepared pomp.   560
                    They all go, except the Bastard
BASTARD. Mad world! mad kings! mad composition!
John, to stop Arthur's title in the whole,
Hath willingly departed with a part,
And France—whose armour conscience buckled on,
Whom zeal and charity brought to the field
As God's own soldier—rounded in the ear
With that same purpose-changer, that sly devil,
That broker that still breaks the pate of faith,
That daily break-vow, he that wins of all,
Of kings, of beggars, old men, young men, maids,   570
Who, having no external thing to lose
But the word 'maid', cheats the poor maid of that,
That smooth-faced gentleman, tickling Commodity,

Commodity, the bias of the world,
The world, who of itself is peised well,
Made to run even upon even ground,
Till this advantage, this vile-drawing bias,
This sway of motion, this Commodity,
Makes it take head from all indifferency,
From all direction, purpose, course, intent: 580
And this same bias, this Commodity,
This bawd, this broker, this all-changing word,
Clapped on the outward eye of fickle France,
Hath drawn him from his own determined aid,
From a resolved and honourable war,
To a most base and vile-concluded peace....
And why rail I on this Commodity?
But for because he hath not wooed me yet:
Not that I have the power to clutch my hand,
When his fair angels would salute my palm,   590
But for my hand, as unattempted yet,
Like a poor beggar, raileth on the rich:
Well, whiles I am a beggar, I will rail,
And say there is no sin but to be rich;
And being rich, my virtue then shall be
To say there is no vice but beggary:
Since kings break faith upon commodity,
Gain, be my lord, for I will worship thee.
                                        He goes

ACT 3

Scene 1: *The French King's tent*

Enter Constance, Arthur, and Salisbury

CONSTANCE. Gone to be married! gone to swear a
  peace!
False blood to false blood joined! gone to be friends!
Shall Lewis have Blanch, and Blanch those
  provinces?
It is not so, thou hast misspoke, misheard,
Be well advised, tell o'er thy tale again.
It cannot be, thou dost but say 'tis so.
I trust I may not trust thee, for thy word
Is but the vain breath of a common man:
Believe me, I do not believe thee, man,
I have a king's oath to the contrary.   10
Thou shalt be punished for thus frighting me,
For I am sick and capable of fears,
Oppressed with wrongs, and therefore full of fears,
A widow, husbandless, subject to fears,
A woman naturally born to fears;
And though thou now confess thou didst but jest,
With my vexed spirits I cannot take a truce,
But they will quake and tremble all this day....
What dost thou mean by shaking of thy head?
Why dost thou look so sadly on my son?   20
What means that hand upon that breast of thine?
Why holds thine eye that lamentable rheum,
Like a proud river peering o'er his bounds?
Be these sad signs confirmers of thy words?
Then speak again, not all thy former tale,
But this one word, whether thy tale be true.
SALISBURY. As true as I believe you think them false
That give you cause to prove my saying true.
CONSTANCE. O, if thou teach me to believe this
  sorrow,
Teach thou this sorrow how to make me die,   30
And let belief and life encounter so

As doth the fury of two desperate men
Which in the very meeting fall and die....
Lewis marry Blanch! O boy, then where art thou?
France friend with England, what becomes of me?
Fellow, be gone: I cannot brook thy sight—
This news hath made thee a most ugly man.
SALISBURY. What other harm have I, good lady, done,
But spoke the harm that is by others done?
CONSTANCE. Which harm within itself so heinous is   40
As it makes harmful all that speak of it.
ARTHUR. I do beseech you, madam, be content.
CONSTANCE. If thou, that bid'st me be content, wert
    grim,
Ugly and sland'rous to thy mother's womb,
Full of unpleasing blots and sightless stains,
Lame, foolish, crooked, swart, prodigious,
Patched with foul moles and eye-offending marks,
I would not care, I then would be content,
For then I should not love thee; no, nor thou
Become thy great birth nor deserve a crown.   50
But thou art fair, and at thy birth, dear boy,
Nature and Fortune joined to make thee great.
Of Nature's gifts thou mayst with lilies boast
And with the half-blown rose. But Fortune, O,
She is corrupted, changed and won from thee;
Sh'adulterates hourly with thine uncle John,
And with her golden hand hath plucked on France
To tread down fair respect of sovereignty,
And made his majesty the bawd to theirs.
France is a bawd to Fortune and King John,   60
That strumpet Fortune, that usurping John:
Tell me, thou fellow, is not France forsworn?
Envenom him with words, or get thee gone,
And leave those woes alone which I alone
Am bound to under-bear.
SALISBURY.   Pardon me, madam,
I may not go without you to the kings.
CONSTANCE. Thou mayst, thou shalt, I will not go
    with thee.
I will instruct my sorrows to be proud,
For grief is proud and makes his owner stoop.
To me and to the state of my great grief   70
Let kings assemble; for my grief's so great
That no supporter but the huge firm earth
Can hold it up: here I and sorrows sit,
Here is my throne, bid kings come bow to it.
                        She seats herself on the ground

Enter King John, King Philip, Lewis, Blanch, Elinor, the
Bastard, Austria, and attendants

K. PHILIP. 'Tis true, fair daughter, and this blessed day
Ever in France shall be kept festival:
To solemnize this day, the glorious sun
Stays in his course and plays the alchemist,
Turning with splendour of his precious eye
The meagre cloddy earth to glittering gold: 80
The yearly course that brings this day about
Shall never see it but a holiday.
CONSTANCE [*rising*]. A wicked day, and not a holy day!
What hath this day deserved? what hath it done,
That it in golden letters should be set
Among the high tides in the calendar?
Nay, rather turn this day out of the week,
This day of shame, oppression, perjury.
Or, if it must stand still, let wives with child
Pray that their burdens may not fall this day,   90

Lest that their hopes prodigiously be crossed:
But on this day let seamen fear no wrack,
No bargains break that are not this day made:
This day, all things begun come to ill end;
Yea, faith itself to hollow falsehood change!
K. PHILIP. By heaven, lady, you shall have no cause
To curse the fair proceedings of this day:
Have I not pawned to you my majesty?
CONSTANCE. You have beguiled me with a counterfeit
Resembling majesty, which being touched and tried   100
Proves valueless: you are forsworn, forsworn!
You came in arms to spill mine enemies' blood,
But now in arms you strengthen it with yours.
The grappling vigour and rough frown of war
Is cold in amity and painted peace,
And our oppression hath made up this league ...
Arm, arm, you heavens, against these perjured
    kings!
A widow cries; be husband to me, heavens!
Let not the hours of this ungodly day
Wear out the day in peace; but, ere sun set,   110
Set arméd discord 'twixt these perjured kings!
Hear me, O, hear me!
AUSTRIA.   Lady Constance, peace.
CONSTANCE. War! war! no peace! peace is to me a war:
O Lymoges! O Austria! thou dost shame
That bloody spoil: thou slave, thou wretch, thou
    coward,
Thou little valiant, great in villany!
Thou ever strong upon the stronger side!
Thou Fortune's champion, that dost never fight
But when her humorous ladyship is by
To teach thee safety! thou art perjured too,   120
And sooth'st up greatness. What a fool art thou,
A ramping fool, to brag and stamp and swear
Upon my party! Thou cold-blooded slave,
Hast thou not spoke like thunder on my side,
Been sworn my soldier, bidding me depend
Upon thy stars, thy fortune and thy strength,
And dost thou now fall over to my foes?
Thou wear a lion's hide! doff it for shame,
And hang a calf's-skin on those recreant limbs.
AUSTRIA. O, that a man should speak those words to
    me!   130
BASTARD. And hang a calf's-skin on those recreant
limbs.
AUSTRIA. Thou dar'st not say so, villain, for thy life.
BASTARD. And hang a calf's-skin on those recreant
limbs.
K. JOHN. We like not this, thou dost forget thyself.

Enter Pandulph

K. PHILIP. Here comes the holy legate of the Pope.
PANDULPH. Hail, you anointed deputies of heaven!
To thee, King John, my holy errand is:
I Pandulph, of fair Milan cardinal,
And from Pope Innocent the legate here,
Do in his name religiously demand   140
Why thou against the church, our holy mother,
So wilfully dost spurn; and force perforce
Keep Stephen Langton, chosen archbishop
Of Canterbury, from that holy see:
This, in our foresaid holy father's name,
Pope Innocent, I do demand of thee.
K. JOHN. What earthly name to interrogatories
Can task the free breath of a sacred king?

Thou canst not, cardinal, devise a name
So slight, unworthy and ridiculous, 150
To charge me to an answer, as the Pope:
Tell him this tale, and from the mouth of England
Add thus much more, that no Italian priest
Shall tithe or toll in our dominions;
But as we, under heaven, are supreme head,
So under Him that great supremacy,
Where we do reign, we will alone uphold,
Without th' assistance of a mortal hand:
So tell the Pope, all reverence set apart
To him and his usurped authority. 160
K. PHILIP. Brother of England, you blaspheme in this.
K. JOHN. Though you and all the kings of
  Christendom
Are led so grossly by this meddling priest,
Dreading the curse that money may buy out,
And by the merit of vile gold, dross, dust,
Purchase corrupted pardon of a man,
Who in that sale sells pardon from himself;
Though you and all the rest so grossly led
This juggling witchcraft with revenue cherish,
Yet I alone, alone do me oppose 170
Against the Pope and count his friends my foes.
PANDULPH. Then, by the lawful power that I have,
Thou shalt stand cursed and excommunicate,
And blessèd shall he be that doth revolt
From his allegiance to an heretic,
And meritorious shall that hand be called,
Canónizèd and worshipped as a saint,
That takes away by any secret course
Thy hateful life.
CONSTANCE.   O, lawful let it be
That I have room with Rome to curse awhile! 180
Good father cardinal, cry thou amen
To my keen curses; for without my wrong
There is no tongue hath power to curse him right.
PANDULPH. There's law and warrant, lady, for my
  curse.
CONSTANCE. And for mine too. When law can do no
  right,
Let it be lawful that law bar no wrong:
Law cannot give my child his kingdom here;
For he that holds his kingdom holds the law:
Therefore, since law itself is perfect wrong,
How can the law forbid my tongue to curse? 190
PANDULPH. Philip of France, on peril of a curse,
Let go the hand of that arch-heretic,
And raise the power of France upon his head,
Unless he do submit himself to Rome.
ELINOR. Look'st thou pale, France? do not let go thy
  hand.
CONSTANCE. Look to that, devil, lest that France
  repent,
And by disjoining hands, hell lose a soul.
AUSTRIA. King Philip, listen to the cardinal.
BASTARD. And hang a calf's-skin on his recreant limbs.
AUSTRIA. Well, ruffian, I must pocket up these
  wrongs, 200
Because—
BASTARD. Your breeches best may carry them.
K. JOHN. Philip, what say'st thou to the cardinal?
CONSTANCE. What should he say, but as the cardinal?
LEWIS. Bethink you, father, for the difference
Is purchase of a heavy curse from Rome,
Or the light loss of England for a friend:

Forgo the easier.
BLANCH.   That's the curse of Rome.
CONSTANCE. O Lewis, stand fast, the devil tempts thee
  here
In likeness of a new untrimmèd bride. 210
BLANCH. The Lady Constance speaks not from her
  faith,
But from her need.
CONSTANCE.   O, if thou grant my need,
Which only lives but by the death of faith,
That need must needs infer this principle,
That faith would live again by death of need:
O then, tread down my need, and faith mounts up,
Keep my need up, and faith is trodden down.
K. JOHN. The king is moved, and answers not to this.
CONSTANCE. O, be removed from him, and answer
  well.
AUSTRIA. Do so, King Philip, hang no more in doubt. 220
BASTARD. Hang nothing but a calf's-skin, most sweet
  lout.
K. PHILIP. I am perplexed, and know not what to say.
PANDULPH. What canst thou say but will perplex
  thee more,
If thou stand excommunicate and cursed?
K. PHILIP. Good reverend father, make my person
  yours,
And tell me how you would bestow yourself.
This royal hand and mine are newly knit,
And the conjunction of our inward souls
Married in league, coupled and linked together
With all religious strength of sacred vows: 230
The latest breath that gave the sound of words
Was deep-sworn faith, peace, amity, true love
Between our kingdoms and our royal selves,
And even before this truce, but new before,
No longer than we well could wash our hands
To clap this royal bargain up of peace,
Heaven knows, they were besmeared and
  overstained
With slaughter's pencil, where revenge did paint
The fearful difference of incensèd kings:
And shall these hands, so lately purged of blood, 240
So newly joined in love, so strong in both,
Unyoke this seizure and this kind regreet?
Play fast and loose with faith? so jest with heaven,
Mak such unconstant children of ourselves,
As now again to snatch our palm from palm,
Unswear faith sworn, and on the marriage-bed
Of smiling peace to march a bloody host,
And make a riot on the gentle brow
Of true sincerity? O holy sir,
My reverend father, let it not be so: 250
Out of your grace, devise, ordain, impose
Some gentle order, and then we shall be blest
To do your pleasure and continue friends.
PANDULPH. All form is formless, order orderless,
Save what is opposite to England's love.
Therefore, to arms! be champion of our church,
Or let the church, our mother, breathe her curse,
A mother's curse, on her revolting son:
France, thou mayst hold a serpent by the tongue,
A chafèd lion by the mortal paw, 260
A fasting tiger safer by the tooth,
Than keep in peace that hand which thou dost hold.
K. PHILIP. I may disjoin my hand, but not my faith.
PANDULPH. So mak'st thou faith an enemy to faith,

And like a civil war set'st oath to oath,
Thy tongue against thy tongue. O, let thy vow
First made to heaven, first be to heaven performed,
That is, to be the champion of our church.
What since thou swor'st is sworn against thyself
And may not be performéd by thyself,   270
For that which thou hast sworn to do amiss
Is not amiss when it is truly done;
And being not done, where doing tends to ill,
The truth is then most done not doing it:
The better act of purposes mistook
Is to mistake again; though indirect,
Yet indirection thereby grows direct,
And falsehood falsehood cures, as fire cools fire
Within the scorchéd veins of one new-burned:
It is religion that doth make vows kept,   280
But thou hast sworn against religion,
By what thou swear'st against the thing thou
swear'st,
And mak'st an oath the surety for thy truth
Against an oath: the truth thou art unsure
To swear, swears only not to be forsworn;
Else what a mockery should it be to swear!
But thou dost swear only to be forsworn,
And most forsworn to keep what thou dost swear.
Therefore thy later vows against thy first
Is in thyself rebellion to thyself: 290
And better conquest never canst thou make
Than arm thy constant and thy nobler parts
Against these giddy loose suggestions:
Upon which better part our prayers come in,
If thou vouchsafe them: but if not, then know
The peril of our curses light on thee
So heavy as thou shalt not shake them off,
But in despair die under their black weight.
AUSTRIA. Rebellion, flat rebellion!
BASTARD.   Will't not be?
Will not a calf's-skin stop that mouth of thine?   300
LEWIS. Father, to arms!
BLANCH.   Upon thy wedding-day?
Against the blood that thou hast married?
What, shall our feast be kept with slaughtered
men?
Shall braying trumpets and loud churlish drums,
Clamours of hell, be measures to our pomp?
O husband, hear me! ay, alack, how new
Is husband in my mouth! even for that name,
Which till this time my tongue did ne'er pronounce,
Upon my knee I beg, go not to arms
Against mine uncle.
CONSTANCE.   O, upon my knee,   310
Made hard with kneeling, I do pray to thee,
Thou virtuous Dauphin, alter not the doom
Forethought by heaven.
BLANCH. Now shall I see thy love. What motive may
Be stronger with thee than the name of wife?
CONSTANCE. That which upholdeth him that thee
upholds,
His honour. O, thine honour, Lewis, thine honour!
LEWIS. I muse your majesty doth seem so cold,
When such profound respects do pull you on.
PANDULPH. I will denounce a curse upon his head.   320
K. PHILIP. Thou shalt not need. England, I will fall
from thee.
CONSTANCE. O fair return of banished majesty!
ELINOR. O foul revolt of French inconstancy!

K. JOHN. France, thou shalt rue this hour within this
hour.
BASTARD. Old Time the clock-setter, that bald sexton
Time,
Is it as he will? well then, France shall rue.
BLANCH. The sun's o'ercast with blood: fair day, adieu!   270
Which is the side that I must go withal?
I am with both. Each army hath a hand,
And in their rage, I having hold of both,   330
They whirl asunder and dismember me.
Husband, I cannot pray that thou mayst win;
Uncle, I needs must pray that thou mayst lose;
Father, I may not wish the fortune thine;
Grandam, I will not wish thy wishes thrive:
Whoever wins, on that side shall I lose;
Assuréd loss before the match be played.
LEWIS. Lady, with me, with me thy fortune lies.
BLANCH. There where my fortune lives, there my life
dies.
K. JOHN. Cousin, go draw our puissance together.   340
                              The Bastard goes
France, I am burned up with inflaming wrath,
A rage whose heat hath this condition,
That nothing can allay, nothing but blood,
The blood, and dearest-valued blood, of France.
K. PHILIP. Thy rage shall burn thee up, and thou shalt
turn.
To ashes, ere our blood shall quench that fire:
Look to thyself, thou art in jeopardy.
K. JOHN. No more than he that threats. To arms
let's hie!   *They go*

Scene 2: Before Angiers

Alarums, excursions: enter the Bastard, with Austria's head

BASTARD. Now, by my life, this day grows wondrous
hot,
Some airy devil hovers in the sky,
And pours down mischief. Austria's head lie there,
While Philip breathes.

Enter King John, Arthur, and Hubert

K. JOHN. Hubert, keep this boy . . . Philip, make up.
My mother is assailéd in our tent,
And ta'en, I fear.
BASTARD.   My lord, I rescued her,
Her highness is in safety, fear you not:
But on, my liege, for very little pains
Will bring this labour to an happy end.   10
                                        They go

Scene 3

*After further alarums and excursions a retreat is sounded,
and King John enters with Elinor, Arthur, the Bastard,
Hubert, and Lords*

K. JOHN [*to Elinor*]. So shall it be; your grace shall
stay behind,
More strongly guarded . . . [*to Arthur*] Cousin, look
not sad.
Thy grandam loves thee, and thy uncle will
As dear be to thee as thy father was.
ARTHUR. O, this will make my mother die with grief.
K. JOHN [*to the Bastard*]. Cousin, away for England!
haste before,

And ere our coming see thou shake the bags
Of hoarding abbots; imprisoned angels
Set at liberty: the fat ribs of peace
Must by the hungry now be fed upon: 10
Use our commission in his utmost force.
BASTARD. Bell, book, and candle shall not drive
    me back,
When gold and silver becks me to come on.
I leave your highness: Grandam, I will pray
(If ever I remember to be holy)
For your fair safety; so I kiss your hand.
ELINOR. Farewell, gentle cousin.
K. JOHN.   Coz, farewell.   *The Bastard goes*
ELINOR. Come hither, little kinsman; hark, a word.
K. JOHN. Come hither, Hubert. O my gentle Hubert,
We owe thee much; within this wall of flesh   20
There is a soul counts thee her creditor,
And with advantage means to pay thy love:
And, my good friend, thy voluntary oath
Lives in this bosom, dearly cherishéd....
Give me thy hand. I had a thing to say,
But I will fit it with some better time....
By heaven, Hubert, I am almost ashamed
To say what good respect I have of thee.
HUBERT. I am much bounden to your majesty.
K. JOHN. Good friend, thou hast no cause to say
    so yet,   30
But thou shalt have; and creep time ne'er so slow,
Yet it shall come for me to do thee good....
I had a thing to say, but let it go:
The sun is in the heaven, and the proud day,
Attended with the pleasures of the world,
Is all too wanton and too full of gawds
To give me audience: if the midnight bell
Did, with his iron tongue and brazen mouth,
Sound on into the drowsy ear of night;
If this same were a churchyard where we stand,   40
And thou possessèd with a thousand wrongs;
Or if that surly spirit, melancholy,
Had baked thy blood and made it heavy-thick,
Which else runs tickling up and down the veins,
Making that idiot, laughter, keep men's eyes
And strain their cheeks to idle merriment,
A passion hateful to my purposes;
Or if that thou couldst see me without eyes,
Hear me without thine ears, and make reply
Without a tongue, using conceit alone,   50
Without eyes, ears and harmful sound of words;
Then, in despite of broad-eyed watchful day,
I would into thy bosom pour my thoughts:
But, ah, I will not! yet I love thee well,
And, by my troth, I think, thou lov'st me well.
HUBERT. So well, that what you bid me undertake,
Though that my death were adjunct to my act,
By heaven, I would do it.
K. JOHN.   Do not I know thou wouldst?
Good Hubert, Hubert, Hubert, throw thine eye
On yon young boy: I'll tell thee what, my friend,   60
He is a very serpent in my way,
And wheresoe'er this foot of mine doth tread,
He lies before me: dost thou understand me?
Thou art his keeper.
HUBERT.   And I'll keep him so,
That he shall not offend your majesty.
K. JOHN.   Death.
HUBERT. My lord?

K. JOHN.   A grave.
HUBERT.   He shall not live.
K. JOHN.   Enough....
I could be merry now. Hubert, I love thee.
Well, I'll not say what I intend for thee:
Remember ... Madam, fare you well,
I'll send those powers o'er to your majesty.   70
ELINOR. My blessings go with thee!
K. JOHN.   For England, cousin, go.
Hubert shall be your man, attend on you
With all true duty ... On toward Calais, ho!
                          They go

Scene 4: *Before the French King's tent*

Enter King Philip, Lewis, Pandulph, and attendants

K. PHILIP. So, by a roaring tempest on the flood,
A whole armado of convicted sail
Is scattered and disjoined from fellowship.
PANDULPH. Courage and comfort! all shall yet go well.
K. PHILIP. What can go well, when we have run so ill?
Are we not beaten? Is not Angiers lost?
Arthur ta'en prisoner? divers dear friends slain?
And bloody England into England gone,
O'erbearing interruption, spite of France?
LEWIS. What he hath won, that hath he fortified: 10
So hot a speed with such advice disposed,
Such temperate order in so fierce a cause,
Doth want example: who hath read or heard
Of any kindred action like to this?
K. PHILIP. Well could I bear that England had this
    praise,
So we could find some pattern of our shame.

Constance enters

Look, who comes here! a grave unto a soul,
Holding th'eternal spirit, against her will,
In the vile prison of afflicted breath ...
I prithee, lady, go away with me.   20
CONSTANCE. Lo, now! now see the issue of your peace!
K. PHILIP. Patience, good lady! comfort, gentle
    Constance!
CONSTANCE. No, I defy all counsel, all redress,
But that which ends all counsel, true redress ...
Death, death. O amiable lovely death!
Thou odoriferous stench! sound rottenness!
Arise forth from the couch of lasting night,
Thou hate and terror to prosperity,
And I will kiss thy detestable bones,
And put my eyeballs in thy vaulty brows,   30
And ring these fingers with thy household worms,
And stop this gap of breath with fulsome dust,
And be a carrion monster like thyself:
Come, grin on me, and I will think thou smil'st,
And buss thee as thy wife! Misery's love,
O, come to me!
K. PHILIP.   O fair affliction, peace.
CONSTANCE. No, no, I will not, having breath to cry:
O, that my tongue were in the thunder's mouth!
Then with a passion would I shake the world,
And rouse from sleep that fell anatomy,   40
Which cannot hear a lady's feeble voice,
Which scorns a modern invocation.
PANDULPH. Lady, you utter madness, and not sorrow.
CONSTANCE. Thou art not holy to belie me so.
I am not mad: this hair I tear is mine,

My name is Constance, I was Geffrey's wife,
Young Arthur is my son, and he is lost:
I am not mad, I would to heaven I were,
For then 'tis like I should forget myself:
O, if I could, what grief should I forget!   50
Preach some philosophy to make me mad,
And thou shalt be canónized, cardinal;
For, being not mad but sensible of grief,
My reasonable part produces reason
How I may be delivered of these woes,
And teaches me to kill or hang myself:
If I were mad, I should forget my son,
Or madly think a babe of clouts were he:
I am not mad; too well, too well I feel
The different plague of each calamity.   60
K. PHILIP. Bind up those tresses ... O, what love I note
In the fair multitude of those her hairs!
Where but by chance a silver drop hath fallen,
Even to that drop ten thousand wiry friends
Do glue themselves in sociable grief,
Like true, inseparable, faithful loves,
Sticking together in calamity.
CONSTANCE. To England, if you will.
K. PHILIP.   Bind up your hairs.
CONSTANCE. Yes, that I will; and wherefore will I do
  it?
I tore them from their bonds and cried aloud,   70
'O that these hands could so redeem my son,
As they have given these hairs their liberty!'
But now I envy at their liberty,
And will again commit them to their bonds,
Because my poor child is a prisoner....
And, father cardinal, I have heard you say
That we shall see and know our friends in heaven:
If that be true, I shall see my boy again;
For, since the birth of Cain, the first male child,
To him that did but yesterday suspire,   80
There was not such a gracious creature born:
But now will canker-sorrow eat my bud
And chase the native beauty from his cheek,
And he will look as hollow as a ghost,
As dim and meagre as an ague's fit,
And so he'll die; and, rising so again,
When I shall meet him in the court of heaven
I shall not know him: therefore never, never
Must I behold my pretty Arthur more.
PANDULPH. You hold too heinous a respect of grief.   90
CONSTANCE. He talks to me that never had a son.
K. PHILIP. You are as fond of grief as of your child.
CONSTANCE. Grief fills the room up of my absent child:
Lies in his bed, walks up and down with me,
Puts on his pretty looks, repeats his words,
Remembers me of all his gracious parts,
Stuffs out his vacant garments with his form;
Then have I reason to be fond of grief?
Fare you well: had you such a loss as I,
I could give better comfort than you do.   100
I will not keep this form upon my head,
When there is such disorder in my wit ...
                                    She tears her hair
O Lord! my boy, my Arthur, my fair son!
My life, my joy, my food, my all the world!
My widow-comfort, and my sorrows' cure!
                                    She goes
K. PHILIP. I fear some outrage, and I'll follow her.
                                    He goes

LEWIS. There's nothing in this world can make me joy:
Life is as tedious as a twice-told tale
Vexing the dull ear of a drowsy man;
And bitter shame hath spoiled the sweet world's
  taste,   110
That it yields nought but shame and bitterness.
PANDULPH. Before the curing of a strong disease,
Even in the instant of repair and health,
The fit is strongest; evils that take leave,
On their departure most of all show evil:
What have you lost by losing of this day?
LEWIS. All days of glory, joy and happiness.
PANDULPH. If you had won it, certainly you had.
No, no: when Fortune means to men most good,
She looks upon them with a threat'ning eye: 120
'Tis strange to think how much King John hath lost
In this which he accounts so clearly won:
Are not you grieved that Arthur is his prisoner?
LEWIS. As heartily as he is glad he hath him.
PANDULPH. Your mind is all as youthful as your blood.
Now hear me speak with a prophetic spirit;
For even the breath of what I mean to speak
Shall blow each dust, each straw, each little rub,
Out of the path which shall directly lead
Thy foot to England's throne: and therefore mark.   130
John hath seized Arthur, and it cannot be
That, whiles warm life plays in that infant's veins,
The misplaced John should entertain an hour,
One minute, nay, one quiet breath of rest.
A sceptre snatched with an unruly hand
Must be as boisterously maintained as gained;
And he that stands upon a slippery place
Makes nice of no vile hold to stay him up:
That John may stand, then Arthur needs must fall,
So be it, for it cannot be but so.   140
LEWIS. But what shall I gain by young Arthur's fall?
PANDULPH. You, in the right of Lady Blanch your
  wife,
May then make all the claim that Arthur did.
LEWIS. And lose it, life and all, as Arthur did.
PANDULPH. How green you are, and fresh in this old
  world!
John lays you plots; the times conspire with you;
For he that steeps his safety in true blood
Shall find but bloody safety and untrue.
This act so evilly borne shall cool the hearts
Of all his people and freeze up their zeal,   150
That none so small advantage shall step forth
To check his reign, but they will cherish it;
No natural exhalation in the sky,
No scope of nature, no distempered day,
No common wind, no customéd event,
But they will pluck away his natural cause,
And call them meteors, prodigies and signs,
Abortives, presages and tongues of heaven,
Plainly denouncing vengeance upon John.
LEWIS. May be he will not touch young Arthur's life,   160
But hold himself safe in his prisonment.
PANDULPH. O, sir, when he shall hear of your
  approach,
If that young Arthur be not gone already,
Even at that news he dies; and then the hearts
Of all his people shall revolt from him,
And kiss the lips of unacquainted change,
And pick strong matter of revolt and wrath
Out of the bloody fingers' ends of John....

Methinks I see this hurly all on foot;
And, O, what better matter breeds for you   170
Than I have named! The bastard Faulconbridge
Is now in England, ransacking the church,
Offending charity: if but a dozen French
Were there in arms, they would be as a call
To train ten thousand English to their side;
Or as a little snow, tumbled about,
Anon becomes a mountain.... O noble Dauphin,
Go with me to the king. 'Tis wonderful
What may be wrought out of their discontent,
Now that their souls are topfull of offence.   180
For England go! I will whet on the king.
LEWIS. Strong reasons make strong actions: let us go.
If you say ay, the king will not say no.   *They go*

ACT 4
Scene 1: *England. A room in a castle*

Enter Hubert and Executioners

HUBERT. Heat me these irons hot, and look thou stand
Within the arras: when I strike my foot
Upon the bosom of the ground, rush forth,
And bind the boy which you shall find with me
Fast to the chair: be heedful: hence, and watch.
1 EXECUTIONER. I hope your warrant will bear out the
deed.
HUBERT. Uncleanly scruples! fear not you: look
to't....   *The Executioners go*
Young lad, come forth; I have to say with you.

Arthur enters

ARTHUR. Good morrow, Hubert.
HUBERT.   Good morrow, little prince.
ARTHUR. As little prince, having so great a title   10
To be more prince, as may be ... You are sad.
HUBERT. Indeed, I have been merrier.
ARTHUR.   Mercy on me!
Methinks no body should be sad but I:
Yet I remember, when I was in France,
Young gentlemen would be as sad as night,
Only for wantonness: by my christendom,
So I were out of prison and kept sheep,
I should be as merry as the day is long;
And so I would be here, but that I doubt
My uncle practises more harm to me: 20
He is afraid of me and I of him:
Is it my fault that I was Geffrey's son?
No, indeed is't not; and I would to heaven
I were your son, so you would love me, Hubert.
HUBERT [*aside*]. If I talk to him, with his innocent prate
He will awake my mercy which lies dead:
Therefore I will be sudden and dispatch.
ARTHUR. Are you sick, Hubert? you look pale to-day.
In sooth, I would you were a little sick,
That I might sit all night and watch with you.   30
I warrant I love you more than you do me.
HUBERT [*aside*]. His words do take possession of my
bosom....
[*he shows a paper*] Read here, young Arthur....
            [*aside*] How now, foolish rheum!
Turning dispiteous torture out of door!
I must be brief, lest resolution drop
Out at mine eyes in tender womanish tears....
Can you not read it? is it not fair writ?

ARTHUR. Too fairly, Hubert, for so foul effect.
Must you, with hot irons, burn out both mine eyes?
HUBERT. Young boy, I must.
ARTHUR.   And will you?
HUBERT.   And I will.   40
ARTHUR. Have you the heart? When your head did
but ache,
I knit my handkercher about your brows,
(The best I had, a princess wrought it me)
And I did never ask it you again:
And with my hand at midnight held your head;
And like the watchful minutes to the hour,
Still and anon cheered up the heavy time;
Saying, 'What lack you?' and 'Where lies your
grief?'
Or 'What good love may I perform for you?'
Many a poor man's son would have lien still,   50
And ne'er have spoke a loving word to you;
But you at your sick service had a prince:
Nay, you may think my love was crafty love,
And call it cunning: do, an if you will:
If heaven be pleased that you must use me ill,
Why then you must.... Will you put out mine eyes?
These eyes that never did nor never shall
So much as frown on you?
HUBERT.   I have sworn to do it;
And with hot irons must I burn them out.
ARTHUR. Ah, none but in this iron age would do it!   60
The iron of itself, though heat red-hot,
Approaching near these eyes, would drink my tears,
And quench his fiery indignation,
Even in the matter of mine innocence:
Nay, after that, consume away in rust,
But for containing fire to harm mine eye:
Are you more stubborn-hard than hammered iron?
An if an angel should have come to me,
And told me Hubert should put out mine eyes,
I would not have believed him ... no tongue but
Hubert's!   70
HUBERT [*stamps*]. Come forth.

The Executioners enter with cord, irons, etc.

Do as I bid you do.
ARTHUR. O, save me, Hubert, save me! my eyes are
out,
Even with the fierce looks of these bloody men.
HUBERT. Give me the iron, I say, and bind him here.
ARTHUR. Alas, what need you be so boist'rous-rough?
I will not struggle, I will stand stone-still:
For heaven sake, Hubert, let me not be bound!
Nay, hear me, Hubert, drive these men away,
And I will sit as quiet as a lamb;   80
I will not stir, not wince, nor speak a word,
Nor look upon the iron angerly:
Thrust but these men away, and I'll forgive you,
Whatever torment you do put to me.
HUBERT. Go, stand within: let me alone with him.
1 EXECUTIONER. I am best pleased to be from such
a deed.   *The Executioners go*
ARTHUR. Alas! I then have chid away my friend!
He hath a stern look, but a gentle heart:
Let him come back, that his compassion may
Give life to yours.
HUBERT.   Come, boy, prepare yourself.   90
ARTHUR. Is there no remedy?
HUBERT.   None, but to lose your eyes.

ARTHUR. O heaven! that there were but a mote in
        yours,
    A grain, a dust, a gnat, a wandering hair,
    Any annoyance in that precious sense!
    Then, feeling what small things are boisterous there,
    Your vile intent must needs seem horrible.
HUBERT. Is this your promise? go to, hold your
        tongue.
ARTHUR. Hubert, the utterance of a brace of tongues
    Must needs want pleading for a pair of eyes:
    Let me not hold my tongue; let me not, Hubert!   100
    Or, Hubert, if you will, cut out my tongue,
    So I may keep mine eyes.... O, spare mine eyes,
    Though to no use, but still to look on you!
    Lo, by my troth, the instrument is cold,
    And would not harm me.
HUBERT.   I can heat it, boy.
ARTHUR. No, in good sooth; the fire is dead with grief,
    Being create for comfort, to be used
    In undeserved extremes: see else yourself,
    There is no malice in this burning coal,
    The breath of heaven hath blown his spirit out,   110
    And strewed repentant ashes on his head.
HUBERT. But with my breath I can revive it, boy.
ARTHUR. An if you do, you will but make it blush,
    And glow with shame of your proceedings, Hubert:
    Nay, it perchance will sparkle in your eyes;
    And like a dog that is compelled to fight,
    Snatch at his master that doth tarre him on.
    All things that you should use to do me wrong
    Deny their office: only you do lack
    That mercy which fierce fire and iron extend,   120
    Creatures of note for mercy-lacking uses.
HUBERT. Well, see to live; I will not touch thine eyes
    For all the treasure that thine uncle owes.
    Yet am I sworn, and I did purpose, boy,
    With this same very iron to burn them out.
ARTHUR. O, now you look like Hubert! all this while
    You were disguiséd.
HUBERT.   Peace: no more. Adieu.
    Your uncle must not know but you are dead.
    I'll fill these doggéd spies with false reports:
    And, pretty child, sleep doubtless and secure,   130
    That Hubert, for the wealth of all the world,
    Will not offend thee.
ARTHUR.   O heaven! I thank you, Hubert
HUBERT. Silence, no more: go closely in with me.
    Much danger do I undergo for thee.   *They go*

Scene 2: *King John's palace*

Enter King John, Pembroke, Salisbury and other lords

K. JOHN. Here once again we sit; once again crowned,
    And looked upon, I hope, with cheerful eyes.
PEMBROKE. This 'once again' (but that your highness
        pleased)
    Was once superfluous: you were crowned before,
    And that high royalty was ne'er plucked off;
    The faiths of men ne'er stainéd with revolt;
    Fresh expectation troubled not the land,
    With any longed-for change or better state.
SALISBURY. Therefore, to be possessed with double
        pomp,
    To guard a title that was rich before,   10
    To gild refinéd gold, to paint the lily,
    To throw a perfume on the violet,

To smooth the ice, or add another hue
Unto the rainbow, or with taper-light
To seek the beauteous eye of heaven to garnish,
Is wasteful and ridiculous excess.
PEMBROKE. But that your royal pleasure must be done,
    This act is as an ancient tale new told,
    And in the last repeating troublesome,
    Being urgéd at a time unseasonable.   20
SALISBURY. In this the antique and well noted face
    Of plain old form is much disfiguréd,
    And like a shifted wind unto a sail,
    It makes the course of thoughts to fetch about,
    Startles and frights consideration,
    Makes sound opinion sick and truth suspected,
    For putting on so new a fashioned robe.
PEMBROKE. When workmen strive to do better than
        well,
    They do confound their skill in covetousness,
    And oftentimes excusing of a fault   30
    Doth make the fault the worse by the excuse;
    As patches set upon a little breach
    Discredit more in hiding of the fault
    Than did the fault before it was so patched.
SALISBURY. To this effect, before you were new
        crowned,
    We breathed our counsel: but it pleased your
        highness
    To overbear it, and we are all well pleased,
    Since all and every part of what we would
    Doth make a stand at what your highness will.
K. JOHN. Some reasons of this double coronation   40
    I have possessed you with and think them strong;
    And more, more strong when lesser is my fear,
    I shall indue you with: meantime but ask
    What you would have reformed that is not well,
    And well shall you perceive how willingly
    I will both hear and grant you your requests.
PEMBROKE. Then I, as one that am the tongue of these,
    To sound the purposes of all their hearts,
    Both for myself and them ... but, chief of all,
    Your safety ... for the which myself and they   50
    Bend their best studies, heartily request
    Th'enfranchisement of Arthur, whose restraint
    Doth move the murmuring lips of discontent
    To break into this dangerous argument,—
    If what in rest you have in right you hold,
    Why then your fears, which as they say attend
    The steps of wrong, should move you to mew up
    Your tender kinsman, and to choke his days
    With barbarous ignorance, and deny his youth
    The rich advantage of good exercise.   60
    That the time's enemies may not have this
    To grace occasions, let it be our suit
    That you have bid us ask his liberty,
    Which for our goods we do no further ask
    Than whereupon our weal, on you depending,
    Counts it your weal he have this liberty.

Hubert enters

K. JOHN. Let it be so: I do commit his youth
    To your direction.... Hubert, what news with you?
                                    They talk apart
PEMBROKE. This is the man should do the bloody deed;
    He showed his warrant to a friend of mine.   70
    The image of a wicked heinous fault
    Lives in his eye; that close aspect of his

Doth show the mood of a much troubled breast,
And I do fearfully believe 'tis done,
What we so feared he had a charge to do.
SALISBURY. The colour of the king doth come and go
Between his purpose and his conscience,
Like heralds 'twixt two dreadful battles set:
His passion is so ripe, it needs must break.
PEMBROKE. And when it breaks, I fear will issue thence 80
The foul corruption of a sweet child's death.
K. JOHN. We cannot hold mortality's strong hand ...
Good lords, although my will to give is living,
The suit which you demand is gone and dead.
He tells us Arthur is deceased to-night.
SALISBURY. Indeed we feared his sickness was past cure.
PEMBROKE. Indeed we heard how near his death he
was,
Before the child himself felt he was sick:
This must be answered either here or hence.
K. JOHN. Why do you bend such solemn brows on
me? 90
Think you I bear the shears of destiny?
Have I commandment on the pulse of life?
SALISBURY. It is apparent foul-play, and 'tis shame
That greatness should so grossly offer it:
So thrive it in your game! and so farewell.
PEMBROKE. Stay yet, Lord Salisbury, I'll go with thee,
And find th'inheritance of this poor child,
His little kingdom of a forcéd grave.
That blood which owed the breadth of all this isle,
Three foot of it doth hold: bad world the while! 100
This must not be thus borne: this will break out
To all our sorrows, and ere long I doubt.
The Lords depart
K. JOHN. They burn in indignation ... I repent ...
There is no sure foundation set on blood ...
No certain life achieved by others' death ...

A Messenger enters

A fearful eye thou hast. Where is that blood
That I have seen inhabit in those cheeks?
So foul a sky clears not without a storm.
Pour down thy weather: how goes all in France?
MESSENGER. From France to England. Never such a
power 110
For any foreign preparation
Was levied in the body of a land!
The copy of your speed is learned by them;
For when you should be told they do prepare,
The tidings comes that they are all arrived.
K. JOHN. O, where hath our intelligence been drunk?
Where hath it slept? Where is my mother's care,
That such an army could be drawn in France,
And she not hear of it?
MESSENGER.   My liege, her ear
Is stopped with dust: the first of April died 120
Your noble mother; and as I hear, my lord,
The Lady Constance in a frenzy died
Three days before: but this from rumour's tongue
I idly heard; if true or false I know not.
K. JOHN. Withhold thy speed, dreadful occasion!
O, make a league with me, till I have pleased
My discontented peers! What! mother dead!
How wildly then walks my estate in France!
Under whose conduct came those powers of France
That thou for truth giv'st out are landed here? 130
MESSENGER. Under the Dauphin.

K. JOHN.   Thou hast made me giddy
With these ill tidings ...

The Bastard enters with Peter of Pomfret

          Now, what says the world
To your proceedings? do not seek to stuff
My head with more ill news, for it is full.
BASTARD. But if you be afeard to hear the worst,
Then let the worst unheard fall on your head.
K. JOHN. Bear with me, cousin, for I was amazed
Under the tide; but now I breathe again
Aloft the flood, and can give audience
To any tongue, speak it of what it will. 140
BASTARD. How I have sped among the clergymen,
The sums I have collected shall express:
But as I travelled hither through the land,
I find the people strangely fantasied,
Possessed with rumours, full of idle dreams,
Not knowing what they fear, but full of fear.
And here's a prophet, that I brought with me
From forth the streets of Pomfret, whom I found
With many hundreds treading on his heels;
To whom he sung, in rude harsh-sounding rhymes, 150
That, ere the next Ascension-day at noon,
Your highness should deliver up your crown.
K. JOHN. Thou idle dreamer, wherefore didst thou so?
PETER. Foreknowing that the truth will fall out so.
K. JOHN. Hubert, away with him! imprison him,
And on that day at noon, whereon he says
I shall yield up my crown, let him be hanged.
Deliver him to safety, and return,
For I must use thee....   *Hubert takes Peter away*
          O, my gentle cousin,
Hear'st thou the news abroad, who are arrived? 160
BASTARD. The French, my lord. Men's mouths are
full of it:
Besides, I met Lord Bigot and Lord Salisbury,
With eyes as red as new-enkindled fire,
And others more, going to seek the grave
Of Arthur, whom they say is killed to-night
On your suggestion.
K. JOHN.   Gentle kinsman, go,
And thrust thyself into their companies.
I have a way to win their loves again;
Bring them before me.
BASTARD.   I will seek them out.
K. JOHN. Nay, but make haste; the better foot before. 170
O, let me have no subject enemies,
When adverse foreigners affright my towns
With dreadful pomp of stout invasion!
Be Mercury, set feathers to thy heels,
And fly—like thought—from them to me again.
BASTARD. The spirit of the time shall teach me speed.
          He goes
K. JOHN. Spoke like a sprightful noble gentleman....
Go after him; for he perhaps shall need
Some messenger betwixt me and the peers,
And be thou he.
MESSENGER.   With all my heart, my liege. 180
          He goes
K. JOHN. My mother dead!

Hubert returns

HUBERT. My lord, they say five moons were seen
tonight:
Four fixéd, and the fifth did whirl about

The other four in wondrous motion.
K. JOHN. Five moons!
HUBERT.   Old men and beldams in the streets
Do prophesy upon it dangerously:
Young Arthur's death is common in their mouths,
And when they talk of him, they shake their heads
And whisper one another in the ear;
And he that speaks doth gripe the hearer's wrist,   190
Whilst he that hears makes fearful action,
With wrinkled brows, with nods, with rolling eyes.
I saw a smith stand with his hammer, thus,
The whilst his iron did on the anvil cool,
With open mouth swallowing a tailor's news,
Who with his shears and measure in his hand,
Standing on slippers, which his nimble haste
Had falsely thrust upon contrary feet,
Told of a many thousand warlike French
That were embattléd and ranked in Kent: 200
Another lean unwashed artificer
Cuts off his tale and talks of Arthur's death.
K. JOHN. Why seek'st thou to possess me with these
        fears?
Why urgest thou so oft young Arthur's death?
Thy hand hath murdered him: I had a mighty cause
To wish him dead, but thou hadst none to kill him.
HUBERT. No had, my lord? why, did you not provoke
        me?
K. JOHN. It is the curse of kings to be attended
By slaves that take their humours for a warrant
To break within the bloody house of life,   210
And on the winking of authority
To understand a law; to know the meaning
Of dangerous majesty, when perchance it frowns
More upon humour than advised respect.
HUBERT. Here is your hand and seal for what I did.
K. JOHN. O, when the last account 'twixt heaven
        and earth
Is to be made, then shall this hand and seal
Witness against us to damnation!
How oft the sight of means to do ill deeds
Make deeds ill done! Hadst not thou been by,   220
A fellow by the hand of nature marked,
Quoted and signed to do a deed of shame,
This murder had not come into my mind:
But taking note of thy abhorred aspect,
Finding thee fit for bloody villany,
Apt, liable to be employed in danger,
I faintly broke with thee of Arthur's death;
And thou, to be endearéd to a king,
Made it no conscience to destroy a prince.
HUBERT. My lord—   230
K. JOHN. Hadst thou but shook thy head or made a
        pause
When I spake darkly what I purposéd,
Or turned an eye of doubt upon my face,
As bid me tell my tale in express words,
Deep shame had struck me dumb, made me break
        off,
And those thy fears might have wrought fears in me:
But thou didst understand me by my signs
And didst in signs again parley with sin;
Yea, without stop, didst let thy heart consent,
And consequently thy rude hand to act   240
The deed, which both our tongues held vile to
        name. . . .
Out of my sight, and never see me more!

My nobles leave me, and my state is braved,
Even at my gates, with ranks of foreign powers:
Nay, in the body of this fleshly land,
This kingdom, this confine of blood and breath,
Hostility and civil tumult reigns
Between my conscience and my cousin's death.
HUBERT. Arm you against your other enemies,
I'll make a peace between your soul and you.   250
Young Arthur is alive: this hand of mine
Is yet a maiden and an innocent hand,
Not painted with the crimson spots of blood.
Within this bosom never entered yet
The dreadful motion of a murderous thought,
And you have slandered nature in my form,
Which, howsoever rude exteriorly,
Is yet the cover of a fairer mind
Than to be butcher of an innocent child.
K. JOHN. Doth Arthur live? O, haste thee to the
        peers,   260
Throw this report on their incenséd rage,
And make them tame to their obedience!
Forgive the comment that my passion made
Upon thy feature, for my rage was blind,
And foul imaginary eyes of blood
Presented thee more hideous than thou art.
O, answer not; but to my closet bring
The angry lords, with all expedient haste.
I conjure thee but slowly; run more fast.
                                    They go

Scene 3: *Before the castle*

Arthur appears on the walls

ARTHUR. The wall is high, and yet will I leap down.
Good ground, be pitiful and hurt me not!
There's few or none do know me—if they did,
This ship-boy's semblance hath disguised me
        quite. . . .
I am afraid, and yet I'll venture it. . . .
If I get down, and do not break my limbs,
I'll find a thousand shifts to get away:
As good to die and go, as die and stay. . . .
                                    He leaps
O me! my uncle's spirit is in these stones.
Heaven take my soul, and England keep my bones!   10
                                    He dies

Pembroke, Salisbury, and Bigot enter

SALISBURY. Lords, I will meet him at Saint
        Edmundsbury.
It is our safety, and we must embrace
This gentle offer of the perilous time.
PEMBROKE. Who brought that letter from the cardinal?
SALISBURY. The Count Melun, a noble lord of France;
Whose private with me of the Dauphin's love
Is much more general than these lines import.
BIGOT. To-morrow morning let us meet him then.
SALISBURY. Or rather then set forward, for 'twill be
Two long days' journey, lords, or ere we meet.   20

The Bastard approaches

BASTARD. Once more to-day well met, distempered
        lords!
The king by me requests your presence straight.
SALISBURY. The king hath dispossessed himself of us.
We will not line his thin bestainéd cloak

With our pure honours, not attend the foot
That leaves the print of blood where'er it walks.
Return and tell him so: we know the worst.
BASTARD. Whate'er you think, good words, I think,
　were best.
SALISBURY. Our griefs, and not our manners, reason
　now.
BASTARD. But there is little reason in your grief,　30
Therefore 'twere reason you had manners now.
PEMBROKE. Sir, sir, impatience hath his privilege.
BASTARD. 'Tis true, to hurt his master, no man else.
SALISBURY. This is the prison ... [sees Arthur] What is
　he lies here?
PEMBROKE. O death, made proud with pure and
　princely beauty!
The earth had not a hole to hide this deed.
SALISBURY. Murder, as hating what himself hath done,
Doth lay it open to urge on revenge.
BIGOT. Or, when he doomed this beauty to a grave,
Found it too precious-princely for a grave.　40
SALISBURY. Sir Richard, what think you? have you
　beheld,
Or have you read or heard? or could you think?
Or do you almost think, although you see,
That you do see? could thought, without this object,
Form such another? This is the very top,
The height, the crest, or crest unto the crest,
Of murder's arms: this is the bloodiest shame,
The wildest savagery, the vilest stroke,
That ever wall-eyed wrath or staring rage
Presented to the tears of soft remorse.　50
PEMBROKE. All murders past do stand excused in this:
And this, so sole and so unmatchable,
Shall give a holiness, a purity,
To the yet unbegotten sin of times;
And prove a deadly bloodshed but a jest,
Exampled by this heinous spectacle.
BASTARD. It is a damnéd and a bloody work,
The graceless action of a heavy hand,
If that it be the work of any hand.
SALISBURY. If that it be the work of any hand!　60
We had a kind of light what would ensue:
It is the shameful work of Hubert's hand,
The practice and the purpose of the king:
From whose obedience I forbid my soul,
Kneeling before this ruin of sweet life,
And breathing to his breathless excellence
The incense of a vow, a holy vow,
Never to taste the pleasures of the world,
Never to be infected with delight,
Nor conversant with ease and idleness,　70
Till I have set a glory to this hand,
By giving it the worship of revenge.
PEMBROKE. BIGOT. Our souls religiously confirm thy
　words.

Hubert enters

HUBERT. Lords, I am hot with haste in seeking you,
Arthur doth live, the king hath sent for you.
SALISBURY. O, he is bold, and blushes not at death.
Avaunt, thou hateful villain, get thee gone!
HUBERT. I am no villain.
SALISBURY [draws his sword]. Must I rob the law?
BASTARD. Your sword is bright, sir, put it up again.　80
SALISBURY. Not till I sheathe it in a murderer's skin.
HUBERT. Stand back, Lord Salisbury, stand back, I say;

By heaven, I think my sword's as sharp as yours.
I would not have you, lord, forget yourself,
Nor tempt the danger of my true defence;
Lest I, by marking of your rage, forget
Your worth, your greatness, and nobility.
BIGOT. Out, dunghill! dar'st thou brave a nobleman?
HUBERT. Not for my life: but yet I dare defend
My innocent life against an emperor.　90
SALISBURY. Thou art a murderer.
HUBERT.　　　　　　　Do not prove me so;
Yet I am none. Whose tongue soe'er speaks false,
Not truly speaks; who speaks not truly, lies.
PEMBROKE. Cut him to pieces.
BASTARD.　　　　　　Keep the peace, I say.
SALISBURY. Stand by, or I shall gall you,
　Faulconbridge.
BASTARD. Thou wert better gall the devil, Salisbury.
If thou but frown on me, or stir thy foot,
Or teach thy hasty spleen to do me shame,
I'll strike thee dead. Put up thy sword betime,
Or I'll so maul you and your toasting-iron,　100
That you shall think the devil is come from hell.
BIGOT. What wilt thou do, renownéd Faulconbridge?
Second a villain and a murderer?
HUBERT. Lord Bigot, I am none.
BIGOT.　　　　　　Who killed this prince?
HUBERT. 'Tis not an hour since I left him well:
I honoured him, I loved him, and will weep
My date of life out for his sweet life's loss.
SALISBURY. Trust not those cunning waters of his eyes,
For villany is not without such rheum,
And he, long traded in it, makes it seem　110
Like rivers of remorse and innocency.
Away, with me, all you whose souls abhor
Th'uncleanly savours of a slaughter-house,
For I am stifled with this smell of sin.
BIGOT. Away toward Bury, to the Dauphin there!
PEMBROKE. There, tell the king, he may inquire us out.
　　　　　　　　　　　　The Lords depart
BASTARD. Here's a good world! Knew you of this
　fair work?
Beyond the infinite and boundless reach
Of mercy (if thou didst this deed of death)
Art thou damned, Hubert.
HUBERT.　　　　　　Do but hear me, sir.　120
BASTARD. Ha! I'll tell thee what;
Thou'rt damned as black—nay, nothing is so black.
Thou art more deep damned than Prince Lucifer:
There is not yet so ugly a fiend of hell
As thou shalt be, if thou didst kill this child.
HUBERT. Upon my soul—
BASTARD.　　　　　If thou didst but consent
To this most cruel act, do but despair,
And if thou want'st a cord, the smallest thread
That ever spider twisted from her womb
Will serve to strangle thee; a rush will be a beam　130
To hang thee on; or, wouldst thou drown thyself,
Put but a little water in a spoon,
And it shall be as all the ocean,
Enough to stifle such a villain up.
I do suspect thee very grievously.
HUBERT. If I in act, consent, or sin of thought,
Be guilty of the stealing that sweet breath
Which was embounded in this beauteous clay,
Let hell want pains enough to torture me ...
I left him well.

BASTARD.   Go, bear him in thine arms: 140
I am amazed, methinks, and lose my way
Among the thorns and dangers of this world.
How easy dost thou take all England up
From forth this morsel of dead royalty,
The life, the right and truth of all this realm
Is fled to heaven; and England now is left
To tug and scamble, and to part by th'teeth
The unowed interest of proud-swelling state:
Now, for the bare-picked bone of majesty,
Doth doggéd war bristle his angry crest,   150
And snarleth in the gentle eyes of peace:
Now powers from home and discontents at home
Meet in one line; and vast confusion waits,
As doth a raven on a sick-fall'n beast,
The imminent decay of wrested pomp.
Now happy he whose cloak and centure can
Hold out this tempest. Bear away that child,
And follow me with speed; I'll to the king:
A thousand businesses are brief in hand,
And heaven itself doth frown upon the land.   160

They go

ACT 5

Scene 1: *King John's palace*

Pandulph, King John, Lords, and others in attendance

K. JOHN. Thus have I yielded up into your hand
The circle of my glory.
PANDULPH [*places the crown upon John's head*].
                Take again
From this my hand, as holding of the Pope,
Your sovereign greatness and authority.
K. JOHN. Now keep your holy word, go meet the
French,
And from his holiness use all your power
To stop their marches 'fore we are inflamed:
Our discontented counties do revolt;
Our people quarrel with obedience,
Swearing allegiance and the love of soul   10
To stranger blood, to foreign royalty:
This inundation of mistempered humour
Rests by you only to be qualified.
Then pause not; for the present time's so sick,
That present medicine must be ministered,
Or overthrow incurable ensues.
PANDULPH. It was my breath that blew this tempest up,
Upon your stubborn usage of the Pope;
But since you are a gentle convertite,
My tongue shall hush again this storm of war,   20
And make fair weather in your blust'ring land ...
On this Ascension-day, remember well,
Upon your oath of service to the Pope,
Go I to make the French lay down their arms.
                                He departs
K. JOHN. Is this Ascension-day? Did not the prophet
Say that before Ascension-day at noon
My crown I should give off? Even so I have:
I did suppose it should be on constraint,
But, heaven be thanked, it is but voluntary.

The Bastard enters

BASTARD. All Kent hath yielded; nothing there holds
out   30
But Dover castle: London hath received,

Like a kind host, the Dauphin and his powers:
Your nobles will not hear you, but are gone
To offer service to your enemy;
And wild amazement hurries up and down
The little number of your doubtful friends.
K. JOHN. Would not my lords return to me again,
After they heard young Arthur was alive?
BASTARD. They found him dead and cast into the
streets,
An empty casket, where the jewel of life   40
By some damned hand was robbed and ta'en away.
K. JOHN. That villain Hubert told me he did live.
BASTARD. So, on my soul, he did, for aught he
knew. . . .
But wherefore do you droop? why look you sad?
Be great in act, as you have been in thought;
Let not the world see fear and sad distrust
Govern the motion of a kingly eye:
Be stirring as the time, be fire with fire,
Threaten the threat'ner, and outface the brow
Of bragging horror: so shall inferior eyes,   50
That borrow their behaviours from the great,
Grow great by your example and put on
The dauntless spirit of resolution. . . .
Away, and glister like the god of war;
When he intendeth to become the field:
Show boldness and aspiring confidence:
What, shall they seek the lion in his den?
And fright him there? and make him tremble there?
O, let it not be said: forage, and run
To meet displeasure farther from the doors,   60
And grapple with him, ere he come so nigh.
K. JOHN. The legate of the Pope hath been with me,
And I have made a happy peace with him,
And he hath promised to dismiss the powers
Led by the Dauphin.
BASTARD.   O inglorious league!
Shall we, upon the footing of our land,
Send fair-play orders and make compromise,
Insinuation, parley and base truce
To arms invasive? shall a beardless boy,
A cock'red silken wanton, brave our fields,   70
And flesh his spirit in a warlike soil,
Mocking the air with colours idly spread,
And find no check? Let us, my liege, to arms:
Perchance the cardinal cannot make your peace;
Or if he do, let it at least be said
They saw we had a purpose of defence.
K. JOHN. Have thou the ordering of this present time.
BASTARD. Away then, with good courage! yet, I
know,
Our party may well meet a prouder foe.

They go

Scene 2: *The Dauphin's camp near St Edmundsbury*

*Enter, in arms, Lewis, Salisbury, Melun, Pembroke, Bigot,
Soldiers*

LEWIS. My Lord Melun, let this be copied out,
And keep it safe for our remembrance:
Return the precedent to these lords again,
That, having our fair order written down,
Both they and we, perusing o'er these notes,
May know wherefore we took the sacrament
And keep our faiths firm and inviolable.
SALISBURY. Upon our sides it never shall be broken.

And, noble Dauphin, albeit we swear
A voluntary zeal and an unurgéd faith   10
To your proceedings; yet believe me, prince,
I am not glad that such a sore of time
Should seek a plaster by contemnèd revolt,
And heal the inveterate canker of one wound
By making many: O, it grieves my soul,
That I must draw this metal from my side
To be a widow-maker! O, and there
Where honourable rescue and defence
Cries out upon the name of Salisbury!
But such is the infection of the time,   20
That, for the health and physic of our right,
We cannot deal but with the very hand
Of stern injustice and confusèd wrong:
And is't not pity, O my grievéd friends,
That we, the sons and children of this isle,
Were born to see so sad an hour as this,
Wherein we step after a stranger, march
Upon her gentle bosom, and fill up
Her enemies' ranks—I must withdraw and weep
Upon the spot of this enforcèd cause—   30
To grace the gentry of a land remote,
And follow unacquainted colours here?
What, here? O nation, that thou could'st remove!
That Neptune's arms, who clippeth thee about,
Would bear thee from the knowledge of thyself,
And grapple thee unto a pagan shore,
Where these two Christian armies might combine
The blood of malice in a vein of league,
And not to spend it so unneighbourly!
LEWIS. A noble temper dost thou show in this;   40
And great affections wrastling in thy bosom
Doth make an earthquake of nobility:
O, what a noble combat hast thou fought,
Between compulsion and a brave respect!
Let me wipe off this honourable dew,
That silverly doth progress on thy cheeks:
My heart hath melted at a lady's tears,
Being an ordinary inundation;
But this effusion of such manly drops,
This shower, blown up by tempest of the soul,   50
Startles mine eyes, and makes me more amazed
Than had I seen the vaulty top of heaven
Figured quite o'er with burning meteors.
Lift up thy brow, renownèd Salisbury,
And with a great heart heave away this storm:
Commend these waters to those baby eyes
That never saw the giant world enragèd,
Nor met with fortune other than at feasts,
Full of warm blood, of mirth, of gossiping:
Come, come; for thou shalt thrust thy hand as deep   60
Into the purse of rich prosperity
As Lewis himself: so, nobles, shall you all,
That knit your sinews to the strength of mine. . . .
And even there, methinks, an angel spake.

Pandulph approaches

Look, where the holy legate comes apace,
To given us warrant from the hand of heaven,
And on our actions set the name of right
With holy breath.
PANDULPH.   Hail, noble prince of France!
The next is this: King John hath reconciled
Himself to Rome, his spirit is come in,   70
That so stood out against the holy church,

The great metropolis and see of Rome:
Therefore thy threat'ning colours now wind up,
And tame the savage spirit of wild war,
That, like a lion fostered up at hand,
It may lie gently at the foot of peace,
And be no further harmful than in show.
LEWIS. Your grace shall pardon me, I will not back:
I am too high-born to be propertied,
To be a secondary at control,   80
Or useful serving-man and instrument
To any sovereign state throughout the world.
Your breath first kindled the dead coal of wars
Between this chastisèd kingdom and myself,
And brought in matter that should feed this fire;
And now 'tis far too huge to be blown out
With that same weak wind which enkindled it:
You taught me how to know the face of right,
Acquainted me with interest to this land,
Yea, thrust this enterprise into my heart,   90
And come ye now to tell me John hath made
His peace with Rome? What is that peace to me?
I, by the honour of my marriage-bed,
After young Arthur, claim this land for mine,
And now it is half-conquered must I back,
Because that John hath made his peace with Rome?
Am I Rome's slave? What penny hath Rome borne,
What men provided, what munition sent,
To underprop this action? Is't not I
That undergo this charge? who else but I,   100
And such as to my claim are liable,
Sweat in this business and maintain this war?
Have I not heard these islanders shout out,
'Vive le roy!' as I have banked their towns?
Have I not here the best cards for the game,
To win this easy match played for a crown?
And shall I now give o'er the yielded set?
No, no, on my soul, it never shall be said.
PANDULPH. You look but on the outside of this work.
LEWIS. Outside or inside, I will not return   110
Till my attempt so much be glorified
As to my ample hope was promisèd
Before I drew this gallant head of war,
And culled these fiery spirits from the world,
To outlook conquest and to win renown
Even in the jaws of danger and of death . . .
                A trumpet sounds
What lusty trumpet thus doth summon us?

The Bastard enters, attended by officers

BASTARD. According to the fair-play of the world,
Let me have audience; I am sent to speak:
My holy lord of Milan, from the king   120
I come, to learn how you have dealt for him;
And, as you answer, I do know the scope
And warrant limited unto my tongue.
PANDULPH. The Dauphin is too wilful-opposite,
And will not temporize with my entreaties;
He flatly says he'll not lay down his arms.
BASTARD. By all the blood that ever fury breathed,
The youth says well. . . . Now hear our English king
For thus his royalty doth speak in me:
He is prepared, and reason too he should.   130
This apish and unmannerly approach,
This harnessed masque and unadvisèd revel,
This unhaired sauciness and boyish troops,
The king doth smile at, and is well prepared

To whip this dwarfish war, these pigmy arms,
From out the circle of his territories,
That hand which had the strength, even at your
    door,
To cudgel you and make you take the hatch,
To dive like buckets in concealéd wells,
To crouch in litter of your stable planks,   140
To lie like pawns locked up in chests and trunks,
To hug with swine, to seek sweet safety out
In vaults and prisons, and to thrill and shake
Even at the crying of your nation's crow,
Thinking his voice an arméd Englishman;
Shall that victorious hand be feebled here,
That in your chambers gave you chastisement?
No: know, the gallant monarch is in arms,
And like an eagle o'er his aery towers,
To souse annoyance that comes near his nest ...   150
And you degenerate, you ingrate revolts,
You bloody Neroes, ripping up the womb
Of your dear mother England, blush for shame:
For your own ladies and pale-visaged maids
Like Amazons come tripping after drums,
Their thimbles into arméd gauntlets change,
Their needles to lances, and their gentle hearts
To fierce and bloody inclination.
LEWIS. There end thy brave, and turn thy face in peace.
We grant thou canst outscold us: fare thee well.   160
We hold our time too precious to be spent
With such a brabbler.
PANDULPH.   Give me leave to speak.
BASTARD. No, I will speak.
LEWIS.   We will attend to neither ...
Strike up the drums, and let the tongue of war
Plead for our interest and our being here.
BASTARD. Indeed, your drums, being beaten, will cry
    out;
And so shall you, being beaten: do but start
An echo with the clamour of thy drum,
And even at hand a drum is ready braced
That shall reverberate all as loud as thine;   170
Sound but another, and another shall
(As loud as thine) rattle the welkin's ear,
And mock the deep-mouthed thunder: for at hand
(Not trusting to this halting legate here,
Whom he hath used rather for sport than need)
Is warlike John; and in his forehead sits
A bare-ribbed death, whose office is this day
To feast upon whole thousands of the French.
LEWIS. Strike up our drums, to find this danger out.
BASTARD. And thou shalt find it, Dauphin, do not
    doubt.   *They go* 180

Scene 3: *The field of battle*

Alarums. Enter King John and Hubert

K. JOHN. How goes the day with us? O, tell me,
    Hubert.
HUBERT. Badly, I fear: how fares your majesty?
K. JOHN. This fever, that hath troubled me so long,
Lies heavy on me; O, my heart is sick!

A Messenger enters

MESSENGER. My lord, your valiant kinsman,
    Faulconbridge,
Desires your majesty to leave the field,
And send him word by me which way you go.

K. JOHN. Tell him, toward Swinstead, to the abbey
    there.
MESSENGER. Be of good comfort; for the great supply
That were expected by the Dauphin here,   10
Are wracked three nights ago on Goodwin Sands.
This news was brought to Richard but even now.
The French fight coldly, and retire themselves.
K. JOHN. Ay me! this tyrant fever burns me up,
And will not let me welcome this good news.
Set on toward Swinstead: to my litter straight,
Weakness possesseth me, and I am faint.
                              They go

Scene 4

Enter Salisbury, Pembroke, and Bigot

SALISBURY. I did not think the king so stored with
    friends.
PEMBROKE. Up once again: put spirit in the French.
If they miscarry, we miscarry too.
SALISBURY. That misbegotten devil, Faulconbridge,
In spite of spite, alone upholds the day.
PEMBROKE. They say King John sore sick hath left
    the field.

Enter Melun, wounded

MELUN. Lead me to the revolts of England here.
SALISBURY. When we were happy we had other
    names.
PEMBROKE. It is the Count Melun.
SALISBURY.   Wounded to death.
MELUN. Fly, noble English, you are bought and sold, 10
Unthread the rude eye of rebellion,
And welcome home again discarded faith.
Seek out King John and fall before his feet;
For if the French be lord of this loud day,
He means to recompense the pains you take
By cutting off your heads: thus hath he sworn,
And I with him, and many moe with me,
Upon the altar at Saint Edmundsbury,
Even on that altar where we swore to you
Dear amity and everlasting love.   20
SALISBURY. May this be possible? may this be true?
MELUN. Have I not hideous death within my view,
Retaining but a quantity of life,
Which bleeds away, even as a form of wax
Resolveth from his figure 'gainst the fire?
What in the world should make me now deceive,
Since I must lose the use of all deceit?
Why should I then be false, since it is true
That I must die here and live hence by Truth?
I say again, if Lewis do win the day,   30
He is forsworn, if e'er those eyes of yours
Behold another day break in the east:
But even this night, whose black contagious breath
Already smokes about the burning crest
Of the old, feeble and day-wearied sun,
Even this ill night, your breathing shall expire,
Paying the fine of rated treachery,
Even with a treacherous fine of all your lives,
If Lewis by your assistance win the day....
Commend me to one Hubert, with your king;   40
The love of him, and this respect besides,
For that my grandsire was an Englishman,
Awakes my conscience to confess all this....
In lieu whereof, I pray you, bear me hence

From forth the noise and rumour of the field,
Where I may think the remnant of my thoughts
In peace, and part this body and my soul
With contemplation and devout desires.
SALISBURY. We do believe thee—and beshrew my
    soul
But I do love the favour and the form   50
Of this most fair occasion, by the which
We will untread the steps of damnéd flight,
And like a bated and retired flood,
Leaving our rankness and irregular course,
Stoop low within those bounds we have o'erlooked,
And calmly run on in obedience,
Even to our ocean, to our great King John....
My arm shall give thee help to bear thee hence,
For I do see the cruel pangs of death
Right in thine eye.... Away, my friends! New
    flight!   60
And happy newness, that intends old right.

      They go, bearing Melun in their arms

Scene 5: *The Dauphin's camp*

Enter Lewis and his train return after the battle

LEWIS. The sun of heaven methought was loath to
    set,
But stayed, and made the western welkin blush,
When English measured backward their own
    ground
In faint retire: O, bravely came we off,
When with a volley of our needless shot,
After such bloody toil, we bid good night,
And wound our tattering colours clearly up,
Last in the field, and almost lords of it!

A Messenger enters

MESSENGER. Where is my prince, the Dauphin?
LEWIS.   Here: what news?
MESSENGER. The Count Melun is slain; the English
    lords   10
By his persuasion are again fall'n off,
And your supply, which you have wished so long,
Are cast away and sunk on Goodwin Sands.
LEWIS. Ah, foul shrewd news! beshrew thy very heart!
I did not think to be so sad to-night
As this hath made me.... Who was he that said
King John did fly an hour or two before
The stumbling night did part our weary powers?
MESSENGER. Whoever spoke it, it is true, my lord.
LEWIS. Well; keep good quarter and good care
    to-night.   20
The day shall not be up so soon as I,
To try the fair adventure of to-morrow.

      They go

Scene 6: *Near Swineshead Abbey*

Enter the Bastard and Hubert, meeting

BASTARD. Who's there? speak, ho! speak quickly, or I
    shoot.
HUBERT. A friend.... What art thou?
BASTARD.   Of the part of England.
HUBERT. Whither dost thou go?
BASTARD. What's that to thee?
HUBERT.   Why may not I demand
Of thine affairs, as well as thou of mine?

BASTARD. Hubert, I think.
HUBERT.   Thou hast a perfect thought:
I will upon all hazards well believe
Thou art my friend, that know'st my tongue so
    well:
Who art thou?
BASTARD.   Who thou wilt: and if thou please,
Thou mayst befriend me so much as to think   10
I come one way of the Plantagenets.
HUBERT. Unkind remembrance! thou and eyeless
    night
Have done me shame: brave soldier, pardon me,
That any accent breaking from thy tongue
Should 'scape the true acquaintance of mine ear.
BASTARD. Come, come; sans compliment, what
    news abroad?
HUBERT. Why, here walk I in the black brow of night
To find you out.
BASTARD.   Brief, then; and what's the news?
HUBERT. O, my sweet sir, news fitting to the night,
Black, fearful, comfortless, and horrible.   20
BASTARD. Show me the very wound of this ill
    news—
I am no woman, I'll not swoon at it.
HUBERT. The king, I fear, is poisoned by a monk.
I left him almost speechless, and broke out
To acquaint you with this evil, that you might
The better arm you to the sudden time,
Than if you had at leisure known of this.
BASTARD. How did he take it? who did taste to him?
HUBERT. A monk, I tell you, a resolvéd villain,
Whose bowels suddenly burst out: the king   30
Yet speaks and peradventure may recover.
BASTARD. Who didst thou leave to tend his majesty?
HUBERT. Why, know you not? the lords are all
    come back,
And brought Prince Henry in their company,
At whose request the king hath pardoned them,
And they are all about his majesty.
BASTARD. Withhold thine indignation, mighty
    heaven,
And tempt us not to bear above our power!
I'll tell thee, Hubert, half my power this night,
Passing these flats, are taken by the tide,
These Lincoln Washes have devouréd them.   40
Myself, well mounted, hardly have escaped....
Away before: conduct me to the king.
I doubt he will be dead or ere I come.

      They go

Scene 7: *The orchard of Swinestead Abbey*

Enter Prince Henry, Salisbury and Bigot

P. HENRY. It is too late! the life of all his blood
Is touched corruptibly: and his pure brain
(Which some suppose the soul's frail
    dwelling-house)
Doth by the idle comments that it makes
Foretell the ending of mortality.

Pembroke enters

PEMBROKE. His highness yet doth speak, and holds
    belief
That, being brought into the open air,
It would allay the burning quality
Of that fell poison which assaileth him.

P. HENRY. Let him be brought into the orchard here ... 10
Doth he still rage?   *Bigot goes*
PEMBROKE.   He is more patient
Than when you left him; even now he sung.
P. HENRY. O vanity of sickness! fierce extremes
In their continuance will not feel themselves.
Death, having preyed upon the outward parts,
Leaves them invisible, and his siege is now
Against the mind, the which he pricks and wounds
With many legions of strange fantasies,
Which, in their throng and press to that last hold,
Confound themselves.... 'Tis strange, that death
should sing: 20
I am the cygnet to this pale faint swan,
Who chants a doleful hymn to his own death,
And from the organ-pipe of frailty sings
His soul and body to their lasting rest.
SALISBURY. Be of good comfort, prince, for you are
born
To set a form upon that indigest
Which he hath left so shapeless and so rude.

Bigot returns with attendants carrying King John in a chair

K. JOHN. Ay, marry, now my soul hath elbow-room.
It would not out at windows nor at doors.
There is so hot a summer in my bosom,   30
That all my bowels crumble up to dust:
I am a scribbled form drawn with a pen
Upon a parchment, and against this fire
Do I shrink up.
P. HENRY.   How fares your majesty?
K. JOHN. Poisoned—ill fare: dead, forsook, cast off,
And none of you will bid the winter come
To thrust his icy fingers in my maw;
Nor let my kingdom's rivers take their course
Through my burned bosom; nor entreat the north
To make his bleak winds kiss my parchéd lips   40
And comfort me with cold.... I do not ask you
much,
I beg cold comfort; and you are so strait
And so ingrateful, you deny me that.
P. HENRY. O, that there were some virtue in my
tears,
That might relieve you!
K. JOHN.   The salt in them is hot....
Within me is a hell, and there the poison
Is, as a fiend, confined to tyrannize
On unreprievable condemnéd blood.

The Bastard enters

BASTARD. O, I am scalded with my violent motion,
And spleen of speed to see your majesty!   50
K. JOHN. O cousin, thou art come to set mine eye:
The tackle of my heart is cracked and burnt,
And all the shrouds wherewith my life should sail
Are turnéd to one thread, one little hair:
My heart hath one poor string to stay it by,
Which holds but till thy news be utteréd,
And then all this thou see'st is but a clod
And module of confounded royalty.
BASTARD. The Dauphin is preparing hitherward,
Where heaven He knows how we shall answer him: 60
For in a night the best part of my power,

As I upon advantage did remove,
Were in the Washes all unwarily
Devouréd by the unexpected flood. *The King dies*
SALISBURY. You breathe these dead news in as dead an
ear.
My liege! my lord! but now a king, now thus.
P. HENRY. Even so must I run on, and even so stop!
What surety of the world, what hope, what stay,
When this was now a king, and now is clay!
BASTARD. Art thou gone so? I do but stay behind   70
To do the office for thee of revenge,
And then my soul shall wait on thee to heaven,
As it on earth hath been thy servant still....
Now, now, you stars, that move in your right
spheres,
Where be your powers? show now your mended
faiths,
And instantly return with me again,
To push destruction and perpetual shame
Out of the weak door of our fainting land:
Straight let us seek, or straight we shall be sought—
The Dauphin rages at our very heels.   80
SALISBURY. It seems you know not, then, so much
as we.
The Cardinal Pandulph is within at rest,
Who half an hour since came from the Dauphin,
And brings from him such offers of our peace
As we with honour and respect may take,
With purpose presently to leave this war.
BASTARD. He will the rather do it, when he sees
Ourselves well sinewéd to our defence.
SALISBURY. Nay, it is in a manner done already,
For many carriages he hath dispatched   90
To the sea-side, and put his cause and quarrel
To the disposing of the cardinal:
With whom yourself, myself and other lords,
If you think meet, this afternoon will post
To consummate this business happily.
BASTARD. Let it be so. And you, my noble prince,
With other princes that may best be spared,
Shall wait upon your father's funeral.
P. HENRY. At Worcester must his body be interred,
For so he willed it.
BASTARD.   Thither shall it then.   100
And happily may your sweet self put on
The lineal state and glory of the land!
To whom, with all submission, on my knee
I do bequeath my faithful services
And true subjection everlastingly.
SALISBURY. And the like tender of our love we make,
To rest without a spot for evermore.
P. HENRY. I have a kind soul that would give you
thanks,
And knows not how to do it but with tears.
BASTARD. O, let us pay the time but needful woe,   110
Since it hath been beforehand with our griefs....
This England never did, nor never shall,
Lie at the proud foot of a conqueror,
But when it first did help to wound itself....
Now these her princes are come home again,
Come the three corners of the world in arms,
And we shall shock them: nought shall make us rue,
If England to itself do rest but true.   *They go*

King Richard II

The scene: England and Wales

CHARACTERS IN THE PLAY

KING RICHARD THE SECOND
JOHN OF GAUNT, *Duke of Lancaster* ⎱ *uncles to the king*
EDMUND, *Duke of York* ⎰
HENRY BOLINGBROKE, *Duke of Hereford, son to John of Gaunt; afterwards King* HENRY IV
DUKE OF AUMERLE, *son to the Duke of York*
THOMAS MOWBRAY, *Duke of Norfolk*
DUKE OF SURREY
EARL OF SALISBURY
LORD BERKELEY
BUSHY ⎱
BAGOT ⎰ *servants to King Richard*
GREEN
EARL OF NORTHUMBERLAND
HENRY PERCY, *his son*

LORD ROSS
LORD WILLOUGHBY
LORD FITZWATER
BISHOP OF CARLISLE
ABBOT OF WESTMINSTER
SIR STEPHEN SCROOP
SIR PIERCE OF EXTON
Lord Marshal
Captain of a band of Welshmen
QUEEN *to King Richard*
DUCHESS OF YORK
DUCHESS OF GLOUCESTER
Lady attending on the Queen
Lords, Heralds, Officers, Soldiers, two Gardeners, Keeper, Messenger, Groom, and other Attendants

King Richard II

ACT 1
Scene 1: *The castle at Windsor*

*Enter King Richard, John of Gaunt, with the Duke of
Surrey, other nobles and attendants*

K. RICHARD. Old John of Gaunt, time-honoured
  Lancaster,
  Hast thou according to thy oath and band
  Brought hither Henry Hereford thy bold son,
  Here to make good the boist'rous late appeal,
  Which then our leisure would not let us hear,
  Against the Duke of Norfolk, Thomas Mowbray?
GAUNT. I have, my liege.
K. RICHARD. Tell me, moreover, hast thou sounded
  him,
  If he appeal the duke on ancient malice,
  Or worthily as a good subject should 10
  On some known ground of treachery in him?
GAUNT. As near as I could sift him on that argument,
  On some apparent danger seen in him
  Aimed at your highness, no inveterate malice.
K. RICHARD. Then call them to our presence—face
  to face,
  And frowning brow to brow, ourselves will hear
  The accuser and the accused freely speak:
  High-stomached are they both and full of ire,
  In rage, deaf as the sea, hasty as fire.

Enter Bolingbroke and Mowbray

BOLINGBROKE. Many years of happy days befal 20
  My gracious sovereign, my most loving liege!
MOWBRAY. Each day still better other's happiness,
  Until the heavens, envying earth's good hap,
  Add an immortal title to your crown!
K. RICHARD. We thank you both, yet one but
  flatters us,
  As well appeareth by the cause you come,
  Namely, to appeal each other of high treason:
  Cousin of Hereford, what dost thou object
  Against the Duke of Norfolk, Thomas Mowbray?
BOLINGBROKE. First—heaven be the record to
  my speech 30
  In the devotion of a subject's love,
  Tend'ring the precious safety of my prince,
  And free from other misbegotten hate,
  Come I appellant to this princely presence....
  Now Thomas Mowbray do I turn to thee,
  And mark my greeting well: for what I speak
  My body shall make good upon this earth,
  Or my divine soul answer it in heaven:
  Thou art a traitor and a miscreant,
  Too good to be so, and too bad to live, 40
  Since the more fair and crystal is the sky,
  The uglier seem the clouds that in it fly:
  Once more, the more to aggravate the note,
  With a foul traitor's name stuff I thy throat,
  And wish (so please my sovereign) ere I move,
  What my tongue speaks my right drawn sword
  may prove.

MOWBRAY. Let not my cold words here accuse
  my zeal,
  'Tis not the trial of a woman's war,
  The bitter clamour of two eager tongues,
  Can arbitrate this cause betwixt us twain. 50
  The blood is hot that must be cooled for this.
  Yet can I not of such tame patience boast
  As to be hushed and nought at all to say....
  First the fair reverence of your highness curbs me
  From giving reins and spurs to my free speech,
  Which else would post until it had returned
  These terms of treason doubled down his throat:
  Setting aside his high blood's royalty,
  And let him be no kinsman to my liege,
  I do defy him, and I spit at him, 60
  Call him a slanderous coward, and a villain,
  Which to maintain I would allow him odds,
  And meet him were I tied to run afoot,
  Even to the frozen ridges of the Alps,
  Or any other ground inhabitable,
  Where ever Englishman durst set his foot.
  Mean time, let this defend my loyalty—
  By all my hopes most falsely doth he lie.
BOLINGBROKE. Pale trembling coward there I
  throw my gage,
  Disclaiming here the kindred of the king, 70
  And lay aside my high blood's royalty,
  Which fear, not reverence, makes thee to
  except....
  If guilty dread have left thee so much strength,
  As to take up mine honour's pawn, then stoop.
  By that, and all the rites of knighthood else,
  Will I make good against thee, arm to arm,
  What I have spoke, or thou canst worse devise.
MOWBRAY. I take it up, and by that sword I swear.
  Which gently laid my knighthood on my
  shoulder,
  I'll answer thee in any fair degree, 80
  Or chivalrous design of knightly trial:
  And when I mount, alive may I not light,
  If I be traitor or unjustly fight!
K. RICHARD. What doth our cousin lay to
  Mowbray's charge?
  It must be great that can inherit us
  So much as of a thought of ill in him.
BOLINGBROKE. Look what I speak, my life shall
  prove it true,
  That Mowbray hath received eight thousand
  nobles
  In name of 'lendings' for your highness' soldiers,
  The which he hath detained for lewd
  employments, 90
  Like a false traitor, and injurious villain:
  Besides I say, and will in battle prove,
  Or here, or elsewhere to the furthest verge
  That ever was surveyed by English eye,
  That all the treasons for these eighteen years,
  Complotted and contrived in this land ...
  Fetch from false Mowbray their first head
  and spring!

Further I say, and further will maintain
Upon his bad life to make all this good,
That he did plot the Duke of Gloucester's death,   100
Suggest his soon-believing adversaries,
And consequently like a traitor coward,
Sluiced out his innocent soul through streams
    of blood,
Which blood, like sacrificing Abel's, cries,
Even from the tongueless caverns of the earth,
To me for justice and rough chastisement:
And by the glorious worth of my descent,
This arm shall do it, or this life be spent.
K. RICHARD. How high a pitch his resolution soars!
Thomas of Norfolk, what say'st thou to this?   110
MOWBRAY. O, let my sovereign turn away his face,
And bid his ears a little while be deaf,
Till I have told this slander of his blood,
How God and good men hate so foul a liar.
K. RICHARD. Mowbray, impartial are our eyes
    and ears,
Were he my brother, nay, my kingdom's heir,
As he is but my father's brother's son,
Now by my sceptre's awe I make a vow,
Such neighbour nearness to our sacred blood
Should nothing privilege him nor partialize   120
The unstooping firmness of my upright soul.
He is our subject, Mowbray, so art thou,
Free speech and fearless I to thee allow.
MOWBRAY. Then Bolingbroke as low as to thy
    heart
Through the false passage of thy throat thou liest!
Three parts of that receipt I had for Calais
Disbursed I duly to his highness' soldiers,
The other part reserved I by consent,
For that my sovereign liege was in my debt,
Upon remainder of a dear account,   130
Since last I went to France to fetch his queen:
Now swallow down that lie.... For Gloucester's
    death,
I slew him not, but to my own disgrace
Neglected my sworn duty in that case:
For you, my noble lord of Lancaster,
The honourable father to my foe,
Once did I lay an ambush for your life,
A trespass that doth vex my grievéd soul:
But ere I last received the sacrament,
I did confess it, and exactly begged   140
Your grace's pardon, and I hope I had it....
This is my fault—as for the rest appealed
It issues from the rancour of a villain,
A recreant and most degenerate traitor,
Which in myself I boldly will defend,
And interchangeably hurl down my gage
Upon this overweening traitor's foot,
To prove myself a loyal gentleman,
Even in the best blood chambered in his bosom,
In haste whereof most heartily I pray   150
Your highness to assign our trial day.
K. RICHARD. Wrath-kindled gentlemen, be ruled
    by me,
Let's purge this choler without letting blood.
This we prescribe, though no physician—
Deep malice makes too deep incision—
Forget, forgive, conclude and be agreed.
Our doctors say this is no month to bleed ...
Good uncle, let this end where it begun,

We'll calm the Duke of Norfolk, your son.
GAUNT. To be a make-peace shall become my age.   160
Throw down, my son, the Duke of Norfolk's
    gage.
K. RICHARD. And, Norfolk, throw down his.
GAUNT.   When, Harry? when?
Obedience bids I should not bid again.
K. RICHARD. Norfolk, throw down we bid, there
    is no boot.
MOWBRAY. Myself I throw, dread sovereign, at
    thy foot,
My life thou shalt command, but not my shame,
The one my duty owes, but my fair name,
Despite of death that lives upon my grave,
To dark dishonour's use thou shalt not have:
I am disgraced, impeached, and baffled here,   170
Pierced to the soul with slander's venomed spear,
The which no calm can cure but his heart-blood
Which breathed this poison.
K. RICHARD.   Rage must be withstood.
Give me his gage; lions make leopards tame.
MOWBRAY. Yea, but not change his spots: take but
    my shame,
And I resign my gage. My dear dear lord,
The purest treasure mortal times afford,
Is spotless reputation—that away
Men are but gilded loam, or painted clay.
A jewel in a ten-times-barred-up chest   180
Is a bold spirit in a loyal breast:
Mine honour is my life, both grow in one,
Take honour from me, and my life is done:
Then, dear my liege, mine honour let me try—
In that I live, and for that will I die.
K. RICHARD. Cousin, throw up your gage, do
    you begin.
BOLINGBROKE. O God defend my soul from such
    deep sin!
Shall I seem crest-fallen in my father's sight?
Or with pale beggar-fear impeach my height
Before this out-dared dastard? ere my tongue   190
Shall wound my honour with such feeble wrong,
Or sound so base a parle, my teeth shall tear
The slavish motive of recanting fear,
And spit it bleeding in his high disgrace,
Where shame doth harbour, even in Mowbray's
    face.
K. RICHARD. We were not born to sue, but to
    command.
Which since we cannot do, to make you friends,
Be ready, as your lives shall answer it,
At Coventry upon Saint Lambert's day.
There shall your swords and lances arbitrate   200
The swelling difference of your settled hate.
Since we not atone you, we shall see
Justice design the victor's chivalry.
Lord marshal, command our officers at arms
Be ready to direct these home alarms.   *They go*

Scene 2: *The Duke of Lancaster's house*

Enter John of Gaunt with the Duchess of Gloucester

GAUNT. Alas, the part I had in Woodstock's blood
Doth more solicit me than your exclaims
To stir against the butchers of his life,
But since correction lieth in those hands,
Which made the fault that we cannot correct ...

Put we our quarrel to the will of heaven,
Who, when they see the hours ripe on earth,
Will rain hot vengeance on offenders' heads.
DUCHESS. Finds brotherhood in thee no sharper spur?
Hath love in thy old blood no living fire?   10
Edward's seven sons, whereof thyself art one,
Were as seven vials of his sacred blood,
Or seven fair branches springing from one root:
Some of those seven are dried by nature's course,
Some of those branches by the Destinies cut:
But Thomas, my dear lord, my life, my
    Gloucester,
One vial full of Edward's sacred blood,
One flourishing branch of his most royal root,
Is cracked, and all the precious liquor spilt,
Is hacked down, and his summer leaves all faded,   20
By envy's hand, and murder's bloody axe....
Ah, Gaunt, his blood was thine! that bed,
    that womb,
That mettle, that self mould, that fashioned thee
Made him a man; and though thou livest
    and breathest,
Yet art thou slain in him. Thou dost consent
In some large measure to thy father's death,
In that thou seest thy wretched brother die,
Who was the model of thy father's life ...
Call it not patience, Gaunt, it is despair.
In suff'ring thus thy brother to be slaught'red,   30
Thou showest the naked pathway to thy life,
Teaching stern murder how to butcher thee:
That which in mean men we intitle patience,
Is pale cold cowardice in noble breasts....
What shall I say? to safeguard thine own life,
The best way is to venge my Gloucester's death.
GAUNT. God's is the quarrel—for God's substitute,
His deputy anointed in His sight,
Hath caused his death, the which if wrongfully,
Let heaven revenge, for I may never lift   40
An angry arm against His minister.
DUCHESS. Where then, alas, may I complain myself?
GAUNT. To God, the widow's champion and defence.
DUCHESS. Why then, I will ... Farewell, old Gaunt.
Thou goest to Coventry, there to behold
Our cousin Hereford and fell Mowbray fight.
O, sit my husband's wrongs on Hereford's spear,
That it may enter butcher Mowbray's breast!
Or if misfortune miss the first career,
Be Mowbray's sins so heavy in his bosom,   50
That they may break his foaming courser's back,
And throw the rider headlong in the lists,
A caitiff recreant to my cousin Hereford!
Farewell old Gaunt, thy sometimes brother's wife
With her companion Grief must end her life.
GAUNT. Sister farewell, I must to Coventry,
As much good stay with thee, as go with me!
DUCHESS. Yet one word more—Grief boundeth
    where it falls,
Not with the empty hollowness, but weight:
I take my leave before I have begun,   60
For sorrow ends not when it seemeth done:
Commend me to thy brother, Edmund York.
Lo, this is all ... nay, yet depart not so,
Though this be all, do not so quickly go ...
I shall remember more ... Bid him—ah, what?—
With all good speed at Plashy visit me.
Alack and what shall good old York there see

But empty lodgings and unfurnished walls,
Unpeopled offices, untrodden stones?
And what hear there for welcome but my groans?   70
Therefore commend me, let him not come there,
To seek out sorrow that dwells every where.
Desolate, desolate, will I hence and die:
The last leave of thee takes my weeping eye.
                                    They go

Scene 3: *The lists at Coventry*

Enter the Lord Marshall and the Duke Aumerle

MARSHAL. My Lord Aumerle, is Harry Hereford
    armed?
AUMERLE. Yea, at all points, and longs to enter in.
MARSHAL. The Duke of Norfolk, sprightfully and
    bold,
Stays but the summons of the appellant's trumpet.
AUMERLE. Why then, the champions are prepared
    and stay
For nothing but his majesty's approach.

*The trumpets sound and the King enters with his nobles
(Gaunt among them): when they are set, enter the Duke of
Norfolk in arms defendant*

K. RICHARD. Marshal, demand of yonder champion
The cause of his arrival here in arms,
Ask him his name, and orderly proceed
To swear him in the justice of his cause.   10
MARSHAL. In God's name and the king's way who
    thou art,
And why thou comest thus knightly clad in arms,
Against what man thou com'st, and what thy
    quarrel.
Speak truly, on thy knighthood, and thy oath,
And so defend thee heaven and thy valour!
MOWBRAY. My name is Thomas Mowbray, Duke
    of Norfolk,
Who hither come engagéd by my oath
(Which God defend a knight should violate!)
Both to defend my loyalty and truth,
To God, my king, and my succeeding issue,   20
Against the Duke of Hereford that appeals me,
And by the grace of God, and this mine arm,
To prove him, in defending of myself,
A traitor to my God, my king, and me—
And as I truly fight, defend me heaven!

*The trumpets sound. Enter the Duke of Hereford appellant
in armour*

K. RICHARD. Marshal, ask yonder knight in arms,
Both who he is, and why he cometh hither,
Thus plated in habiliments of war,
And formally, according to our law,
Depose him in the justice of his cause.   30
MARSHAL. What is thy name? and wherefore
    com'st thou hither,
Before King Richard in his royal lists?
Against whom comest thou? and what's thy
    quarrel?
Speak like a true knight, so defend thee heaven!
BOLINGBROKE. Harry of Hereford, Lancaster
    and Derby
Am I, who ready here do stand in arms
To prove by God's grace, and my body's valour
In lists, on Thomas Mowbray Duke of Norfolk,

That he is a traitor foul and dangerous,
To God of heaven, King Richard and to me: 40
And as I truly fight, defend me heaven!
MARSHAL. On pain of death, no person be so bold,
Or daring-hardy, as to touch the lists,
Except the marshal and such officers
Appointed to direct these fair designs.
BOLINGBROKE. Lord marshal, let me kiss my
    sovereign's hand,
And bow my knee before his majesty,
For Mowbray and myself are like two men
That vow a long and weary pilgrimage,
Then let us take a ceremonious leave, 50
And loving farewell of our several friends.
MARSHAL. The appellant in all duty greets your
    highness,
And craves to kiss your hand, and take his leave.
K. RICHARD. We will descend and fold him in
    our arms.
Cousin of Hereford, as thy cause is right,
So be thy fortune in this royal fight . . .
Farewell, my blood, which if to-day thou shed,
Lament we may, but not revenge thee dead.
BOLINGBROKE. O, let no noble eye profane a tear
For me, if I be gored with Mowbray's spear: 60
As confident as is the falcon's flight
Against a bird, do I with Mowbray fight. . . .
My loving lord, I take my leave of you:
Of you, my noble cousin, Lord Aumerle—
Not sick, although I have to do with death,
But lusty, young, and cheerly drawing breath:
Lo, as at English feasts, so I regreet
The daintiest last, to make the end most sweet. . . .
O thou, the earthly author of my blood,
Whose youthful spirit in me regenerate 70
Doth with a twofold vigour lift me up
To reach at victory above my head . . .
Add proof unto mine armour with thy prayers,
And with thy blessings steel my lance's point,
That it may enter Mowbray's waxen coat,
And furbish new the name of John a Gaunt,
Even in the lusty haviour of his son.
GAUNT. God in thy good cause make thee
    prosperous,
Be swift like lightning in the execution,
And let thy blows, doubly redoubled, 80
Fall like amazing thunder on the casque
Of thy adverse pernicious enemy!
Rouse up thy youthful blood, be valiant and
    live.
BOLINGBROKE. —Mine innocency and Saint George
    to thrive!
MOWBRAY. However God or fortune cast my lot,
There lives or dies true to King Richard's throne.
A loyal, just, and upright gentleman:
Never did captive with a freer heart
Cast off his chains of bondage, and embrace
His golden uncontrolled enfranchisement,
More than my dancing soul doth celebrate 90
This feast of battle with mine adversary.
Most mighty liege, and my companion peers,
Take from my mouth the wish of happy years:
As gentle and as jocund as to jest
Go I to fight—truth hath a quiet breast.
K. RICHARD. Farewell, my lord, securely I espy
Virtue with valour couchèd in thine eye.

Order the trial, marshal, and begin.
MARSHAL. Harry of Hereford, Lancaster and Derby, 100
Receive thy lance, and God defend the right!
BOLINGBROKE. Strong as a tower in hope I cry
'amen'.
MARSHAL [to a knight]. Go bear this lance to Thomas,
Duke of Norfolk.
1 HERALD. Harry of Hereford, Lancaster, and Derby,
Stands here, for God, his sovereign, and himself,
On pain to be found false and recreant,
To prove the Duke of Norfolk, Thomas
    Mowbray,
A traitor to his God, his king, and him,
And dares him to set forward to the fight.
2 HERALD. Here standeth Thomas Mowbray, Duke
of Norfolk, 110
On pain to be found false and recreant,
Both to defend himself, and to approve
Henry of Hereford, Lancaster, and Derby,
To God, his sovereign, and to him disloyal,
Courageously, and with a free desire,
Attending but the signal to begin.
MARSHAL. Sound, trumpets, and set forward,
    combatants . . .

A charge sounded.

Stay, the king hath thrown his warder down.
K. RICHARD. Let them lay by their helmets and
    their spears,
And both return back to their chairs again. 120
Withdraw with us, and let the trumpets sound,
While we return these dukes what we decree. . . .

The trumpets sound a long flourish

Draw near
And list what with our council we have done . . .
For that our kingdom's earth should not be soiled
With that dear blood which it hath fosterèd;
And for our eyes do hate the dire aspect
Of civil wounds ploughed up with neighbours'
    sword,
And for we think the eagle-wingèd pride
Of sky-aspiring and ambitious thoughts, 130
With rival-hating envy, set on you
To wake our peace, which in our country's cradle
Draws the sweet infant breath of gentle sleep;
Which so roused up with boist'rous untuned drums,
With harsh-resounding trumpets' dreadful bray,
And grating shock of wrathful iron arms,
Might from our quiet confines fright fair peace,
And make us wade even in our kindred's blood;
Therefore we banish you our territories:
You, cousin Hereford, upon pain of life, 140
Till twice five summers have enriched our fields,
Shall not regreet our fair dominions,
But tread the stranger paths of banishment.
BOLINGBROKE. Your will be done; this must my
    comfort be,
That sun that warms you here, shall shine on me,
And those his golden beams to you here lent,
Shall point on me, and gild my banishment.
K. RICHARD. Norfolk, for thee remains a heavier
    doom,
Which I with some unwillingness pronounce.
The sly slow hours shall not determinate 150

The dateless limit of thy dear exile.
The hopeless word of 'never to return'
Breathe I against thee, upon pain of life.
MOWBRAY. A heavy sentence, my most sovereign
    liege,
And all unlooked for from your highness' mouth.
A dearer merit, not so deep a maim
As to be cast forth in the common air,
Have I deservéd at your highness' hands ...
The language I have learnt these forty years,
My native English, now I must forego,   160
And now my tongue's use is to me no more
Than an unstringéd viol or a harp,
Or like a cunning instrument cased up—
Or being open, put into his hands
That knows no touch to tune the harmony:
Within my mouth you have engaoled my tongue,
Doubly portcullised with my teeth and lips,
And dull unfeeling barren ignorance
Is made my gaoler to attend on me:
I am too old to fawn upon a nurse,   170
Too far in years to be a pupil now,
What is thy sentence then but speechless death,
Which robs my tongue from breathing native
    breath?
K. RICHARD. It boots thee not to be compassionate,
After our sentence plaining comes too late.
MOWBRAY. Then thus I turn me from my country's
    light,
To dwell in solemn shades of endless night.
K. RICHARD. Return again, and take an oath with thee.
Lay on our royal sword your banished hands,
Swear by the duty that you owe to God   180
(Our part therein we banish with yourselves,)
To keep the oath that we administer:
You never shall, so help you truth and God,
Embrace each other's love in banishment,
Nor never look upon each other's face,
Nor never write, regreet, nor reconcile
This louring tempest of your home-bred hate,
Nor never by adv`séd purpose meet,
To plot, contrive, or complot any ill,
'Gainst us, our state, our subjects, or our land.   190
BOLINGBROKE. I swear.
MOWBRAY. And I, to keep all this.
BILINGBROKE. Norfolk, so fare as to mine enemy ...
By this time, had the king permitted us,
One of our souls had wand'red in the air,
Banished this frail sepulchre of our flesh,
As now our flesh is banished from this land.
Confess thy treasons ere thou fly the realm—
Since thou hast far to go, bear not along
The clogging burthen of a guilty soul.   200
MOWBRAY. No, Bolingbroke, if ever I were traitor,
My name be blotted from the book of life,
And I from heaven banished as from hence:
But what thou art, God, thou, and I do know,
And all too soon, I fear, the king shall rue:
Farewell, my liege. Now no way can I stray—
Save back to England all the world's my way.
                                          He goes
K. RICHARD. Uncle, even in the glasses of thine eyes
I see thy grievéd heart: thy sad aspect
Hath from the number of his banished years   210
Plucked four away. [*to Bolingbroke*] Six frozen
    winters spent,

Return with welcome home from banishment.
BOLINGBROKE. How long a time lies in one little word!
Four lagging winters and four wanton springs
End in a word—such is the breath of kings.
GAUNT. I thank my liege that, in regard of me,
He shortens four years of my son's exile,
But little vantage shall I reap thereby:
For, ere the six years that he hath to spend
Can change their moons, and bring their times
    about,   220
My oil-dried lamp and time-bewasted light
Shall be extinct with age and endless night,
My inch of taper will be burnt and done,
And blindfold Death not let me see my son.
K. RICHARD. Why, uncle, thou hast many years to live.
GAUNT. But not a minute, king, that thou canst give,
Shorten my days thou canst with sullen sorrow,
And pluck nights from me, but not lend a morrow:
Thou canst help time to furrow me with age,
But stop no wrinkle in his pilgrimage: 230
Thy word is current with him for my death,
But dead, thy kingdom cannot buy my breath.
K. RICHARD. Thy son is banished upon good advice,
Whereto thy tongue a party-verdict gave,
Why at our justice seem'st thou then to lour?
GAUNT. Things sweet to taste, prove in
    digestion sour....
You urged me as a judge, but I had rather,
You would have bid me argue like a father:
O, had it been a stranger, not my child,
To smooth his fault I should have been more mild: 240
A partial slander sought I to avoid,
And in the sentence my own life destroyed:
Alas, I looked when some of you should say,
I was too strict to make mine own away:
But you gave leave to my unwilling tongue,
Against my will to do myself this wrong.
K. RICHARD. Cousin, farewell—and uncle, bid him so,
Six years we banish him and he shall go.
          Flourish. K. Richard departs with his train
AUMERLE. Cousin, farewell, what presence must
    not know,
From where you do remain let paper show.   250
MARSHAL. My lord, no leave take I, for I will ride
As far as land will let me by your side.
GAUNT. O, to what purpose dost thou hoard thy
    words,
That thou returnest no greeting to thy friends?
BOLINGBROKE. I have too few to take my leave of you,
When the tongue's office should be prodigal
To breathe the abundant dolour of the heart.
GAUNT. Thy grief is but thy absence for a time.
BOLINGBROKE. Joy absent, grief is present for that time.
GAUNT. What is six winters? they are quickly gone— 260
BOLINGBROKE. To men in joy, but grief makes one
    hour ten.
GAUNT. Call it a travel that thou tak'st for pleasure.
BOLINGBROKE. My heart will sigh when I miscall it so,
Which finds it an inforcéd pilgrimage.
GAUNT. The sullen passage of thy weary steps
Esteem as foil wherein thou art to set
The precious jewel of thy home return.
BOLINGBROKE. Nay, rather, every tedious stride I make
Will but remember me what a deal of world
I wander from the jewels that I love....   270
Must I not serve a long apprenticehood

To foreign passages, and in the end,
Having my freedom, boast of nothing else,
But that I was a journeyman to grief?

GAUNT. All places that the eye of heaven visits
Are to a wise man ports and happy havens:
Teach thy necessity to reason thus—
There is no virtue like necessity.
Think not the king did banish thee,
But thou the king.... Woe doth the heavier sit,   280
Where it perceives it is but faintly borne:
Go, say I sent thee forth to purchase honour,
And not the king exiled thee; or suppose
Devouring pestilence hangs in our air,
And thou art flying to a fresher clime:
Look, what thy soul holds dear, imagine it
To lie that way thou goest, not whence thou com'st:
Suppose the singing birds musicians,
The grass whereon thou tread'st the presence
    strewed,
The flowers fair ladies, and thy steps no more   290
Than a delightful measure or a dance,
For gnarling sorrow hath less power to bite
The man that mocks at it and sets it light.

BOLINGBROKE. O, who can hold a fire in his hand
By thinking on the frosty Caucasus?
Or cloy the hungry edge of appetite
By bare imagination of a feast?
Or wallow naked in December snow
By thinking on fantastic summer's heat?
O no, the apprehension of the good   300
Gives but the greater feeling to the worse:
Fell sorrow's tooth doth never rankle more
Than when he bites, but lanceth not the sore.

GAUNT. Come, come, my son, I'll bring thee on
    thy way,
Had I thy youth and cause, I would not stay.

BOLINGBROKE. Then England's ground farewell, sweet
    soil adieu,
My mother and my nurse that bears me yet!
Where'er I wander boast of this I can,
Though banished, yet a trueborn Englishman.
                        They go

Scene 4: *The court*

*Enter the King with Bagot and Green at one door, and the
Lord Aumerle at another*

K. RICHARD. We did observe.... Cousin Aumerle,
How far brought you high Hereford on his way?

AUMERLE. I brought high Hereford, if you call
    him so,
But to the next highway, and there I left him.

K. RICHARD. And say, what store of parting tears
    were shed?

AUMERLE. Faith, none for me, except the north-east
    wind
Which then blew bitterly against our faces,
Awaked the sleeping rheum, and so by chance
Did grace our hollow parting with a tear.

K. RICHARD. What said our cousin when you parted
    with him?   10

AUMERLE. 'Farewell'—
And for my heart disdainéd that my tongue
Should so profane the word, that taught me craft
To counterfeit oppression of such grief
That words seemed buried in my sorrow's grave:

Marry, would the word 'farewell' have length'ned
    hours,
And added years to his short banishment,
He should have had a volume of farewells:
But since it would not, he had none of me.

K. RICHARD. He is our cousin's cousin, but 'tis doubt,   20
When time shall call him home from banishment,
Whether our kinsman come to see his friends....
Ourself and Bushy
Observed his courtship to the common people,
How he did seem to dive into their hearts,
With humble and familiar courtesy,
What reverence he did throw away on slaves,
Wooing poor craftsmen with the craft of smiles
And patient underbearing of his fortune,
As 'twere to banish their affects with him.   30
Off goes his bonnet to an oyster-wench,
A brace of draymen bid God speed him well,
And had the tribute of his supple knee,
With 'Thanks, my countrymen, my loving
    friends'—
As were our England in reversion his,
And he our subjects' next degree in hope.

GREEN. Well, he is gone; and with him go
    these thoughts.
Now for the rebels which stand out in Ireland,
Expedient manage must be made, my liege,
Ere further leisure yield them further means   40
For their advantage and your highness' loss.

K. RICHARD. We will ourself in person to this war,
And for our coffers with too great a court
And liberal largess are grown somewhat light,
We are inforced to farm our royal realm,
The revenue whereof shall furnish us
For our affairs in hand—if that come short,
Our substitutes at home shall have blank charters,
Whereto, when they shall know what men are rich,
They shall subscribe them for large sums of gold,   50
And send them after to supply our wants,
For we will make for Ireland presently....

Bushy enters

What news?

BUSHY. Old John of Gaunt is grievous sick, my lord,
Suddenly taken, and hath sent post haste
To entreat your majesty to visit him.

K. RICHARD. Where lies he?

BUSHY. At Ely House.

K. RICHARD. Now put it, God, in the physician's
    mind,
To help him to his grave immediately!   60
The lining of his coffers shall make coats
To deck our soldiers for these Irish wars....
Come, gentlemen, let's all go visit him,
Pray God we may make haste and come too late!

ALL. Amen.   *They go*

ACT 2
Scene 1: *Ely House*

*Enter John of Gaunt sick borne in a chair, with the Duke
of York, etc.*

GAUNT. Will the king come that I may breathe my last
In wholesome counsel to his unstaid youth?

YORK. Vex not yourself, nor strive not with your
    breath,

For all in vain comes counsel to his ear.
GAUNT. O, but they say the tongues of dying men
Enforce attention like deep harmony:
Where words are scarce they are seldom spent in
vain,
For they breathe truth that breathe their words in
pain:
He that no more must say is listened more
Than they whom youth and ease have taught to
glose,   10
More are men's ends marked than their lives before:
The setting sun, and music at the close,
As the last taste of sweets, is sweetest last,
Writ in remembrance more than things lost past.
Though Richard my life's counsel would not hear,
My death's sad tale may yet undeaf his ear.
YORK. No, it is stopped with other flattering sounds,
As praises, of whose taste the wise are fond,
Lascivious metres, to whose venom sound
The open ear of youth doth always listen,   20
Report of fashions in proud Italy,
Whose manners still our tardy apish nation
Limps after in base imitation:
Where doth the world thrust forth a vanity—
So it be new, there's no respect how vile—
That is not quickly buzzed into his ears?
Then all too late comes counsel to be heard,
Where will doth mutiny with wit's regard:
Direct not him whose way himself will choose,
'Tis breath thou lack'st, and that breath wilt thou
lose.   30
GAUNT. Methinks I am a prophet new inspired—
And thus expiring do foretell of him—
His rash fierce blaze of riot cannot last;
For violent fires soon burn out themselves,
Small showers last long, but sudden storms are short:
He tires betimes that spurs too fast betimes:
With eager feeding food doth choke the feeder:
Light vanity, insatiate cormorant,
Consuming means, soon preys upon itself:
This royal throne of kings, this sceptred isle,   40
This earth of majesty, this seat of Mars,
This other Eden, demi-paradise,
This fortress built by nature for herself
Against infection and the hand of war,
This happy breed of men, this little world,
This precious stone set in the silver sea,
Which serves it in the office of a wall,
Or as a moat defensive to a house,
Against the envy of less happier lands. . . .
This blessed plot, this earth, this realm, this England, 50
This nurse, this teeming womb of royal kings,
Feared by their breed, and famous by their birth,
Renownèd for their deeds as far from home,
For Christian service and true chivalry,
As is the sepulchre in stubborn Jewry
Of the world's ransom, blessèd Mary's Son:
This land of such dear souls, this dear dear land,
Dear for her reputation through the world,
Is now leased out—I die pronouncing it—
Like to a tenement or pelting farm. . . .   60
England, bound in with the triumphant sea,
Whose rocky shore beats back the envious siege
Of wat'ry Neptune, is now bound in with shame,
With inky blots, and rotten parchment bonds:
That England, that was wont to conquer others,

Hath made a shameful conquest of itself:
Ah, would the scandal vanish with my life,
How happy then were my ensuing death!

*Enter King, Queen, Aumerle, Bushy, Green, Bagot, Ross,
and Willoughby*

YORK. The king is come, deal mildly with his youth,
For young hot colts, being ragged, do rage the
more.   70
QUEEN. How fares our noble uncle, Lancaster?
K. RICHARD. What comfort, man? how is't with
aged Gaunt?
GAUNT. O, how that name befits my composition!
Old Gaunt indeed, and gaunt in being old:
Within me grief hath kept a tedious fast,
And who abstains from meat that is not gaunt?
For sleeping England long time have I watched,
Watching breeds leanness, leanness is all gaunt:
The pleasure that some fathers feed upon
Is my strict fast; I mean my children's looks,   80
And therein fasting hast thou made me gaunt:
Gaunt am I for the grave, gaunt as a grave,
Whose hollow womb inherits nought but bones.
K. RICHARD. Can sick men play so nicely with
their names?
GAUNT. No, misery makes sport to mock itself—
Since thou dost seek to kill my name in me,
I mock my name, great king, to flatter thee.
K. RICHARD. Should dying men flatter with those
that live?
GAUNT. No, no, men living flatter those that die.
K. RICHARD. Thou now a-dying sayest thou
flatterest me.   90
GAUNT. Oh no, thou diest, though I the sicker be.
K. RICHARD. I am in health, I breathe, and see thee ill.
GAUNT. Now He that made me knows I see thee ill,
Ill in myself to see, and in thee, seeing ill.
Thy death-bed is no lesser than thy land,
Wherein thou liest in reputation sick,
And thou too careless patient as thou art
Commit'st thy anointed body to the cure
Of those physicians that first wounded thee.
A thousand flatterers sit within thy crown,   100
Whose compass is no bigger than thy head,
And yet incagèd in so small a verge,
The waste is no whit lesser than thy land:
O, had thy grandsire with a prophet's eye
Seen how his son's son should destroy his sons,
From forth thy reach he would have laid thy
shame,
Deposing thee before thou wert possessed,
Which art possessed now to depose thyself:
Why, cousin, wert thou regent of the world,
It were a shame to let this land by lease: 110
But for thy world enjoying but this land,
Is it not more than shame to shame it so?
Landlord of England art thou now, not king,
Thy state of law is bondslave to the law,
And thou—
K. RICHARD.   A lunatic lean-witted fool,
Presuming on an ague's privilege,
Darest with thy frozen admonition
Make pale our cheek, chasing the royal blood
With fury from his native residence. . . .
Now by my seat's right royal majesty,   120
Wert thou not brother to great Edward's son,

This tongue that runs so roundly in thy head
Should run thy head from thy unreverent shoulders.
GAUNT. O, spare me not, my brother Edward's son,
For that I was his father Edward's son,
That blood already, like the pelican,
Hast thou tapped out and drunkenly caroused.
My brother Gloucester, plain well-meaning soul,
Whom fair befal in heaven 'mongst happy souls,
May be a precedent and witness good ...   130
That thou respect'st not spilling Edward's blood!
Join with the present sickness that I have,
And thy unkindness be like crooked age,
To crop at once a too long withered flower.
Live in thy shame, but die not shame with thee!
These words hereafter thy tormentors be!
Convey me to my bed, then to my grave—
Love they to live that love and honour have.
          He is borne out by attendants
K. RICHARD. And let them die that age and sullens have,
For both hast thou, and both become the grave.   140
YORK. I do beseech your majesty, impute his words
To wayward sickliness and age in him.
He loves you, on my life, and holds you dear
As Harry Duke of Hereford, were he here.
K. RICHARD. Right, you say true—as Hereford's love,
    so his,
As theirs, so mine, and all be as it is.

Northumberland enters

NORTHUMBERLAND. My liege, old Gaunt commends
    him to your majesty.
K. RICHARD. What says he?
NORTHUMBERLAND.   Nay nothing, all is said:
His tongue is now a stringless instrument,
Words, life, and all, old Lancaster hath spent.   150
YORK. Be York the next that must be bankrupt so!
Though death be poor, it ends a mortal woe.
K. RICHARD. The ripest fruit first falls, and so doth he,
His time is spent, our pilgrimage must be;
So much for that.... Now for our Irish wars—
We must supplant those rough rug-headed kerns,
Which live like venom, where no venom else
But only they have privilege to live.
And for these great affairs do ask some charge,
Towards our assistance we do seize to us ...   160
The plate, coin, revenues, and moveables,
Whereof our uncle Gaunt did stand possessed.
YORK. How long shall I be patient? ah, how long
Shall tender duty make me suffer wrong?
Not Gloucester's death, nor Hereford's banishment,
Not Gaunt's rebukes, nor England's private wrongs,
Nor the prevention of poor Bolingbroke
About his marriage, nor my own disgrace,
Have ever made me sour my patient cheek,
Or bend one wrinkle on my sovereign's face: 170
I am the last of noble Edward's sons,
Of whom thy father, Prince of Wales, was first.
In war was never lion raged more fierce,
In peace was never gentle lamb more mild,
Than was that young and princely gentleman:
His face thou hast, for even so looked he,
Accomplished with the number of thy hours;
But when he frowned it was against the French,
And not against his friends; his noble hand
Did win what he did spend, and spent not that   180

Which his triumphant father's hand had won:
His hands were guilty of no kindred blood,
But bloody with the enemies of his kin:
O, Richard ... York is too far gone with grief,
Or else he never would compare between....
K. RICHARD. Why, uncle, what's the matter?
YORK.   O, my liege,
Pardon me, if you please—if not, I pleased
Not to be pardoned, am content withal.
Seek you to seize and gripe into your hands
The royalties and rights of banished Hereford?   190
Is not Gaunt dead? and doth not Hereford live?
Was not Gaunt just? and is not Harry true?
Did not the one deserve to have an heir?
Is not his heir a well-deserving son?
Take Hereford's rights away, and take from Time
His charters and his customary rights;
Let not to-morrow then ensue to-day;
Be not thyself.... for how art thou a king
But by fair sequence and succession?
Now, afore God—God forbid I say true!—   200
If you do wrongfully seize Hereford's rights,
Call in the letters-patents that he hath
By his attorneys-general to sue
His livery, and deny his off'red homage,
You pluck a thousand dangers on your head,
You lose a thousand well-disposed hearts,
And prick my tender patience to those thoughts
Which honour and allegiance cannot think.
K. RICHARD. Think what you will, we seize into
    our hands
His plate, his goods, his money and his lands.   210
YORK. I'll not be by the while—my liege, farewell—
What will ensue hereof there's none can tell:
But by bad courses may be understood,
That their events can never fall out good.   *He goes*
K. RICHARD. Go, Bushy, to the Earl of Wiltshire
    straight,
Bid him repair to us to Ely House,
To see this business: to-morrow next
We will for Ireland, and 'tis time, I trow.
And we create, in absence of ourself,
Our uncle York lord governor of England;   220
For he is just, and always loved us well ...
Come on, our queen, to-morrow must we part,
Be merry, for our time of stay is short.
              He leads out the Queen, followed
              by Bushy, Aumerle, Green, and Bagot
NORTHUMBERLAND. Well, lords, the Duke of Lancaster
    is dead.
ROSS. And living too, for now his son is duke.
WILLOUGHBY. Barely in title, not in revenues.
NORTHUMBERLAND. Richly in both, if justice had
    her right.
ROSS. My heart is great, but it must break with silence,
    Ere't be disburdened with a liberal tongue.
NORTHUMBERLAND. Nay, speak thy mind, and let him
    ne'er speak more   230
That speaks thy words again to do thee harm.
WILLOUGHBY. Tends that thou wouldst speak to the
    Duke of Hereford?
If it be so, out with it boldly, man.
Quick is mine ear to hear of good towards him.
ROSS. No good at all that I can do for him,
    Unless you call it good to pity him,
    Bereft, and gelded of his patrimony.

NORTHUMBERLAND. Now afore God 'tis shame such
  wrongs are borne
In him, a royal prince, and many moe
Of noble blood in this declining land.   240
The king is not himself, but basely led
By flatterers, and what they will inform,
Merely in hate, 'gainst any of us all,
That will the king severely prosecute
'Gainst us, our lives, our children, and our heirs.
ROSS. The commons hath he pilled with grievous
  taxes,
And quite lost their hearts. The nobles hath he fined
For ancient quarrels, and quite lost their hearts.
WILLOUGHBY. And daily new exactions are devised,
As blanks, benevolences, and I wot not what: 250
But what a God's name doth become of this?
NORTHUMBERLAND. Wars hath not wasted it, for
  warred he hath not,
But basely yielded upon compromise
That which his noble ancestors achieved with blows.
More hath he spent in peace than they in wars.
ROSS. The Earl of Wiltshire hath the realm in farm.
WILLOUGHBY. The king's grown bankrupt like a
  broken man.
NORTHUMBERLAND. Reproach and dissolution
hangeth over him.
ROSS. He hath not money for these Irish wars,
His burthenous taxations notwithstanding,   260
But by the robbing of the banished duke.
NORTHUMBERLAND. His noble kinsman—most
  degenerate king!
But, lords, we hear this fearful tempest sing,
Yet seek no shelter to avoid the storm:
We see the wind sit sore upon our sails,
And yet we strike not, but securely perish.
ROSS. We see the very wrack that we must suffer,
And unavoided is the danger now,
For suffering so the causes of our wrack.
NORTHUMBERLAND. Not so, even through the hollow
  eyes of death   270
I spy life peering, but I dare not say
How near the tidings of our comfort is.
WILLOUGHBY. Nay, let us share thy thoughts as thou
dost ours.
ROSS. Be confident to speak, Northumberland,
We three are but thyself, and speaking so
Thy words are but as thoughts, therefore be bold.
NORTHUMBERLAND. Then thus—I have from le
  Port Blanc,
A bay in Britain, received intelligence
That Harry Duke of Hereford, Rainold Lord
  Cobham,
[The son of Richard Earl of Arundel,]   280
That late broke from the Duke of Exeter,
His brother, Archbishop late of Canterbury,
Sir Thomas Erpingham, Sir John Ramston,
Sir John Norbery, Sir Robert Waterton and
  Francis Coint;
All these, well furnished by the Duke of Britain,
With eight tall ships, three thousand men of war,
Are making hither with all due expedience,
And shortly mean to touch our northern shore:
Perhaps they had ere this, but that they stay
The first departing of the king for Ireland....   290
If then we shall shake off our slavish yoke,
Imp out our drooping country's broken wing,

Redeem from broking pawn the blemished crown,
Wipe off the dust that hides our sceptre's gilt,
And make high majesty look like itself,
Away with me in post to Ravenspurgh: 240
But if you faint, as fearing to do so,
Stay, and be secret, and myself will go.
ROSS. To horse, to horse! urge doubts to them
  that fear.
WILLOUGHBY. Hold out my horse, and I will first
  be there.   *They go* 300

Scene 2: *Windsor Castle*

Enter the Queen, Bushy, Bagot

BUSHY. Madam, your majesty is too much sad.
You promised, when you parted with the king,
To lay aside life-harming heaviness,
And entertain a cheerful disposition.
QUEEN. To please the king I did—to please myself
I cannot do it; yet I know no cause
Why I should welcome such a guest as grief,
Save bidding farewell to so sweet a guest
As my sweet Richard: yet again methinks
Some unborn sorrow ripe in Fortune's womb   10
Is coming towards me, and my inward soul
With nothing trembles, yet at something grieves,
More than with parting from my lord the king.
BUSHY. Each substance of a grief hath twenty shadows, 260
Which shows like grief itself, but is not so:
For Sorrow's eye glazéd with blinding tears,
Divides one thing entire to many objects,
Like perspectives, which rightly gazed upon
Show nothing but confusion; eyed awry
Distinguish form: so your sweet majesty,   20
Looking awry upon your lord's departure,
Find shapes of grief more than himself to wail,
Which looked on as it is, is nought but shadows
Of what it is not; then, thrice-gracious queen,
More than your lord's departure weep not—more
  is not seen,
Or if it be, 'tis with false Sorrow's eye,
Which, for things true, weeps things imaginary.
QUEEN. It may be so; but yet my inward soul
Persuades me it is otherwise: howe'er it be,
I cannot but be sad; so heavy sad,   30
As, though on thinking on no thought I think,
Makes me with heavy nothing faint and shrink.
BUSHY. 'Tis nothing but conceit, my gracious lady.
QUEEN. 'Tis nothing less: conceit is still derived
From some forefather grief. Mine is not so,
For nothing hath begot my something grief,
Or something hath the nothing that I grieve—
'Tis in reversion that I do possess—
But what it is that is not yet known, what
I cannot name, 'tis nameless woe I wot.   40

Green enters

GREEN. God save your majesty! and well
  met, gentlemen.
I hope the king is not yet shipped for Ireland.
QUEEN. Why hopest thou so? 'tis better hope he is,
For his designs crave haste, his haste good hope:
Then wherefore dost thou hope he is not shipped?
GREEN. That he, our hope, might have retired   290
  his power,
And driven into despair an enemy's hope,

Who strongly hath set footing in this land.
The banished Bolingbroke repeals himself,
And with uplifted arms is safe arrived 50
At Ravenspurgh.
QUEEN.   Now God in heaven forbid!
GREEN. Ah madam, 'tis too true, and that is worse ...
The Lord Northumberland, his son young Henry
Percy,
The Lords of Ross, Beaumond, and Willoughby,
With all their powerful friends are fled to him.
BUSHY. Why have you not proclaimed
Northumberland
And all the rest revolted faction traitors?
GREEN. We have, whereupon the Earl of Worcester
Hath broken his staff, resigned his stewardship,
And all the household servants fled with him 60
To Bolingbroke.
QUEEN. So, Green, thou art the midwife to my woe,
And Bolingbroke my sorrow's dismal heir.
Now hath my soul brought forth her prodigy,
And I, a gasping new-delivered mother,
Have woe to woe, sorrow to sorrow joined.
BUSHY. Despair, not, madam.
QUEEN.   Who shall hinder me?
I will despair, and be at enmity
With cozening Hope—he is a flatterer,
A parasite, a keeper back of Death, 70
Who gently would dissolve the bands of life,
Which false Hope lingers in extremity.

York enters

GREEN. Here comes the Duke of York.
QUEEN. With signs of war about his aged neck.
O, full of careful business are his looks!
Uncle, for God's sake, speak comfortable words.
YORK. Should I do so, I should belie my thoughts.
Comfort's in heaven, and we are on the earth,
Where nothing lives but crosses, cares, and grief:
Your husband he is gone to save far off, 80
Whilst others come to make him lose at home:
Here am I left to underprop his land,
Who weak with age cannot support myself.
Now comes the sick hour that his surfeit made,
Now shall he try his friends that flattered him.

A servingman enters

SERVINGMAN. My lord, your son was gone before
I came.
YORK. He was? Why, so! go all which way it will!
The nobles they are fled, the commons cold,
And will, I fear, revolt on Hereford's side....
Sirrah, 90
Get thee to Plashy, to my sister Gloucester,
Bid her send me presently a thousand pound.
Hold, take my ring.
SERVINGMAN. My lord, I had forgot to tell
your lordship:
To-day as I came by I callèd there—
But I shall grieve you to report the rest.
YORK. What is't, knave?
SERVINGMAN. An hour before I came the duchess died.
YORK. God for his mercy, what a tide of woes
Comes rushing on this woeful land at once! 100
I know not what to do: I would to God
(So my untruth had not provoked him to it)
The king had cut off my head with my brother's....

What, are there no posts dispatched for Ireland?
How shall we do for money for these wars?
Come, sister—cousin, I would say, pray pardon me:
Go, fellow, get thee home, provide some carts,
And bring away the armour that is there....
                    The servingman goes
Gentlemen, will you go muster men?
If I know 110
How or which way to order these affairs,
Thus thrust disorderly into my hands,
Never believe me ... Both are my kinsmen—
Th'one is my sovereign, whom both my oath
And duty bids defend; th'other again
Is my kinsman, whom the king hath wronged,
Whom conscience and my kindred bids to right....
Well, somewhat we must do.... Come, cousin, I'll
Dispose of you:
Gentlemen, go, muster up your men, 120
And meet me presently at Berkeley:
I should to Plashy too,
But time will not permit: all is uneven,
And every thing is left at six and seven.
                    He leads the Queen out
BUSHY. The wind sits fair for news to go to Ireland,
But none returns. For us to levy power
Proportionable to the enemy
Is all unpossible.
GREEN. Besides, our nearness to the king in love
Is near the hate of those love not the king. 130
BAGOT. And that is the wavering commons, for
their love
Lies in their purses, and whoso empties them,
By so much fills their hearts with deadly hate.
BUSHY. Wherein the king stands generally
condemned.
BAGOT. If judgement lie in them, then so do we,
Because we ever have been near the king.
GREEN. Well, I will for refuge straight to Bristol
Castle—
The Earl of Wiltshire is already there.
BUSHY. Thither will I with you, for little office 140
The hateful commons will perform for us,
Except like curs to tear us all to pieces:
Will you go along with us?
BAGOT. No, I will to Ireland to his majesty.
Farewell—if heart's presages be not vain,
We three here part that ne'er shall meet again.
BUSHY. That's as York thrives to beat back
Bolingbroke.
GREEN. Alas, poor duke! the task he undertakes
Is numb'ring sands, and drinking oceans dry—
Where one on his side fights, thousands will fly:
Farewell at once, for once, for all, and ever. 150
BUSHY. Well, we may meet again.
BAGOT.   I fear me, never.
                    They go

Scene 3: Near Berkeley Castle

Enter Bolingbroke and Northumberland with forces

BOLINGBROKE. How far is it, my lord, to Berkeley
now?
NORTHUMBERLAND. Believe me, noble lord,
I am a stranger here in Gloucestershire.
These high wild hills and rough uneven ways
Draws out our miles and makes them wearisome,

And yet your fair discourse hath been as sugar,
Making the hard way sweet and delectable.
But I bethink me what a weary way
From Ravenspurgh to Cotswold will be found
In Ross and Willoughby, wanting your company, 10
Which I protest hath very much beguiled
The tediousness and process of my travel:
But theirs is sweet'ned with the hope to have
The present benefit which I possess,
And hope to joy is little less in joy
Than hope enjoyed: by this the weary lords
Shall make their way seem short, as mine hath done
By sight of what I have, your noble company.
BOLINGBROKE. Of much less value is my company
Than your good words.... But who comes here? 20

Harry Percy enters

NORTHUMBERLAND. It is my son, young Harry Percy,
Sent from my brother Worcester,
whencesoever....
Harry, how fares your uncle?
PERCY. I had thought, my lord, to have learned his
health of you.
NORTHUMBERLAND. Why, is he not with the queen?
PERCY. No, my good lord, he hath forsook the court,
Broken his staff of office, and dispersed
The household of the king.
NORTHUMBERLAND.   What was his reason?
He was not so resolved, when last we spake together.
PERCY. Because your lordship was proclaiméd traitor. 30
But he, my lord is gone to Ravenspurgh,
To offer service to the Duke of Hereford,
And sent me over by Berkeley to discover
What power the Duke of York has levied there,
Then with directions to repair to Ravenspurgh.
NORTHUMBERLAND. Have you forgot the Duke of
Hereford, boy?
PERCY. No, my good lord, for that is not forgot
Which ne'er I did remember—to my knowledge
I never in my life did look on him.
NORTHUMBERLAND. Then learn to know him now.
This is the duke.   40
PERCY. My gracious lord, I tender you my service,
Such as it is, being tender, raw, and young,
Which elder days shall ripen and confirm
To more approvéd service and desert.
BOLINGBROKE. I thank thee, gentle Percy, and be sure
I count myself in nothing else so happy
As in a soul rememb'ring my good friends,
And as my fortune ripens with thy love,
It shall be still thy true love's recompense.
My heart this covenant makes, my hand thus seals it. 50
NORTHUMBERLAND. How far is it to Berkeley? And
what stir
Keep good old York there with his men of war?
PERCY. There stands the castle, by yon tuft of trees,
Manned with three hundred men, as I have heard,
And in it are the Lords of York, Berkeley, and
Seymour—
None else of name and noble estimate.

Ross and Willoughby enter

NORTHUMBERLAND. Here come the Lords of Ross
and Willoughby,
Bloody with spurring, fiery-red with haste.

BOLINGBROKE. Welcome, my lords. I wot your
love pursues
A banished traitor: all my treasury   60
Is yet but unfelt thanks, which more enriched
Shall be your love and labour's recompense.
ROSS. Your presence makes us rich, most noble lord.
WILLOUGHBY. And far surmounts our labour to
attain it.
BOLINGBROKE. Evermore thank's the exchequer of
the poor,
Which till my infant fortune comes to years,
Stands for my bounty: but who comes here?

Berkeley approaches

NORTHUMBERLAND. It is my Lord of Berkeley, as
I guess.
BERKELEY. My Lord of Hereford, my message is
to you.
BOLINGBROKE. My lord, my answer is to 'Lancaster,' 70
And I am come to seek that name in England,
And I must find that title in your tongue,
Before I make reply to aught you say.
BERKELEY. Mistake me not, my lord, 'tis not
my meaning
To raze one title of your honour out:
To you, my lord, I come, what lord you will,
From the most gracious regent of this land,
The Duke of York; to know what pricks you on
To take advantage of the absent time,
And fright our native peace with self-borne arms. 80

York enters, with a retinue

BOLINGBROKE. I shall not need transport my words
by you,
Here comes his grace in person.
                      My noble uncle!   *He kneels*
YORK. Show me thy humble heart, and not thy knee,
Whose duty is deceivable and false.
BOLINGBROKE. My gracious uncle!
YORK. Tut, tut!
Grace me no grace, nor uncle me no uncle,
I am no traitor's uncle, and that word 'grace'
In an ungracious mouth is but profane:
Why have those banished and forbidden legs   90
Dared once to touch a dust of England's ground?
But then more 'why?' why have they dared to
march
So many miles upon her peaceful bosom,
Frighting her pale-faced villages with war,
And ostentation of despiséd arms?
Com'st thou because the anointed king is hence?
Why, foolish boy, the king is left behind,
And in my loyal bosom lies his power.
Were I but now the lord of such hot youth,
As when brave Gaunt, thy father, and myself, 100
Rescued the Black Prince, that young Mars of men,
From forth the ranks of many thousand French,
O, then how quickly should this arm of mine,
Now prisoner to the palsy, chastise thee,
And minister correction to thy fault!
BOLINGBROKE. My gracious uncle, let me know
my fault,
On what condition stands it and wherein?
YORK. Even in condition of the worst degree—
In gross rebellion and detested treason.

Thou art a banished man, and here art come,   110
Before the expiration of thy time,
In braving arms against thy sovereign.
BOLINGBROKE. As I was banished, I was
   banished Hereford,
But as I come, I come for Lancaster....
And, noble uncle, I beseech your grace
Look on my wrongs with an indifferent eye:
You are my father, for methinks in you
I see old Gaunt alive.... O then my father,
Will you permit that I shall stand condemned
A wandering vagabond, my rights and royalties   120
Plucked from my arms perforce . . . and given away
To upstart unthrifts? Wherefore was I born?
If that my cousin king be king in England,
It must be granted I am Duke of Lancaster:
You have a son, Aumerle, my noble cousin,
Had you first died, and he been thus trod down,
He should have found his uncle Gaunt a father,
To rouse his wrongs and chase them to the bay...
I am denied to sue my livery here,
And yet my letters-patent give me leave....   130
My father's goods are all distrained and sold,
And these and all are all amiss employed....
What would you have me do? I am a subject;
And I challenge law. Attorneys are denied me,
And therefore personally I lay my claim
To my inheritance of free descent.
NORTHUMBERLAND. The noble duke hath been too
   much abused.
ROSS. It stands your grace upon to do him right.
WILLOUGHBY. Base men by his endowments are
   made great.
YORK. My lords of England, let me tell you this: 140
I have had feeling of my cousin's wrongs,
And laboured all I could to do him right:
But in this kind to come, in braving arms,
Be his own carver and cut out his way,
To find out right with wrong, it may not be:
And you that do abet him in this kind
Cherish rebellion, and are rebels all.
NORTHUMBERLAND. The noble duke hath sworn his
   coming is
But for his own; and for the right of that
We all have strongly sworn to give him aid: 150
And let him never see joy that breaks that oath.
YORK. Well, well, I see the issue of these arms.
I cannot mend it, I must needs confess,
Because my power is weak and all ill left:
But if I could, by Him that gave me life,
I would attach you all, and make you stoop
Unto the sovereign mercy of the king;
But, since I cannot, be it known unto you,
I do remain as neuter. So, fare you well,
Unless you please to enter in the castle,   160
And there repose you for this night.
BOLINGBROKE. An offer, uncle, that we will accept.
But we must win your grace to go with us
To Bristow castle, which, they say, is held
By Bushy, Bagot, and their complices,
The caterpillars of the commonwealth,
Which I have sworn to weed and pluck away.
YORK. It may be I will go with you—but yet
   I'll pause,
For I am loath to break our country's laws.
Nor friends nor foes, to me welcome you are: 170

Things past redress are now with me past care.
                     They go

Scene 4: *A camp in Wales*

Enter Salisbury, and a Welsh Captain

CAPTAIN. My Lord of Salisbury, we have stayed
   ten days,
And hardly kept our countrymen together,
And yet we hear no tidings from the king,
Therefore we will disperse ourselves. Farewell.
SALISBURY. Stay yet another day, thou trusty
   Welshman.
The king reposeth all his confidence in thee.
CAPTAIN. 'Tis thought the king is dead; we will
   not stay.
The bay-trees in our country are all withered,
And meteors fright the fixéd stars of heaven,
The pale-faced moon looks bloody on the earth,   10
And lean-looked prophets whisper fearful change,
Rich men look sad, and ruffians dance and leap—
The one in fear to lose what they enjoy,
The other to enjoy by rage and war:
These signs forerun the death or fall of kings....
Farewell. Our countrymen are gone and fled,
As well assured Richard their king is dead.   *He goes*
SALISBURY. Ah, Richard! with the eyes of heavy mind
I see thy glory like a shooting star
Fall to the base earth from the firmament.   20
Thy sun sets weeping in the lowly west,
Witnessing storms to come, woe, and unrest.
Thy friends are fled to wait upon thy foes,
And crossly to thy good all fortune goes.   *He goes*

ACT 3
Scene 1: *Bristol. Before the castle*

Enter Bolingbroke, York, Northumberland, with Bushy and Green, prisoners

BOLINGBROKE. Bring forth these men....
Bushy and Green, I will not vex your souls,
Since presently your souls must part your bodies,
With too much urging your pernicious lives,
For 'twere no charity; yet to wash your blood
From off my hands, here in the view of men,
I will unfold some causes of your deaths:
You have misled a prince, a royal king,
A happy gentleman in blood and lineaments,
By you unhappied and disfigured clean.   10
You have in manner with your sinful hours
Made a divorce betwixt his queen and him,
Broke the possession of a royal bed,
And stained the beauty of a fair queen's cheeks
With tears, drawn from her eyes by your
   foul wrongs.
Myself, a prince by fortune of my birth,
Near to the king in blood, and near in love,
Till you did make him misinterpret me,
Have stooped my neck under your injuries,
And sighed my English breath in foreign clouds,   20
Eating the bitter bread of banishment,
Whilst you have fed upon my signories,
Disparked my parks, and felled my forest woods;
From my own windows torn my household coat,
Razed out my imprese, leaving me no sign,

Save men's opinions and my living blood,
To show the world I am a gentleman. . . .
This and much more, much more than twice all this,
Condemns you to the death . . . See them delivered
over
To execution and the hand of death.   30

BUSHY. More welcome is the stroke of death to me
Than Bolingbroke to England. Lords, farewell.

GREEN. My comfort is, that heaven will take our
souls,
And plague injustice with the pains of hell.

BOLINGBROKE. My Lord Northumberland, see
them dispatched . . .

*Northumberland and others
depart with the prisoners*

Uncle, you say, the queen is at your house,
For God's sake fairly let her be entreated,
Tell her I send to her my kind commends;
Take special care my greetings be delivered.

YORK. A gentleman of mine I have dispatched   40
With letters of your love to her at large.

BOLINGBROKE. Thanks, gentle uncle . . . Come,
lords, away,
To fight with Glendower and his complices.
Awhile to work, and after holiday.   *They go*

Scene 2: *Near the coast of Wales*

*Enter King Richard, the Bishop of Carlisle, Aumerle, and
Soldiers*

K. RICHARD. Barkloughly castle call they this at hand?

AUMERLE. Yea, my lord. How brooks your grace
the air,
After your late tossing on the breaking seas?

K. RICHARD. Needs must I like it well. I weep for joy
To stand upon my kingdom once again:
Dear earth, I do salute thee with my hand,
Though rebels wound thee with their horses' hoofs:
As a long-parted mother with her child
Plays fondly with her tears and smiles in meeting;
So, weeping, smiling, greet I thee, my earth,   10
And do thee favours with my royal hands;
Feed not thy sovereign's foe, my gentle earth,
Nor with thy sweets comfort his ravenous sense,
But let thy spiders that suck up thy venom
And heavy-gaited toads lie in their way,
Doing annoyance to the treacherous feet,
Which with usurping steps do trample thee.
Yield stinging nettles to mine enemies:
And when they from thy bosom pluck a flower,
Guard it, I pray thee, with a lurking adder,   20
Whose double tongue may with a mortal touch
Throw death upon thy sovereign's enemies. . . .
Mock not my senseless conjuration, lords,
This earth shall have a feeling, and these stones
Prove arméd soldiers, ere her native king
Shall falter under foul rebellion's arms.

CARLISLE. Fear not, my lord. That Power that made
you king,
Hath power to keep you king in spite of all.
The means that heaven yields must be embraced,
And not neglected; else, if heaven would,   30
And we will not, heaven's offer we refuse,
The proffered means of succour and redress.

AUMERLE. He means, my lord, that we are too remiss,
Whilst Bolingbroke, through our security,

Grows strong and great in substance and in power.

K. RICHARD. Discomfortable cousin! know'st thou not
That when the searching eye of heaven is hid,
Behind the globe, that lights the lower world,
Then thieves and robbers range abroad unseen,
In murders and in outrage, boldly here,   40
But when from under this terrestrial ball
He fires the proud tops of the eastern pines,
And darts his light through every guilty hole,
Then murders, treasons, and detested sins,
The cloak of night being plucked from off their
backs,
Stand bare and naked, trembling at themselves?
So when this thief, this traitor, Bolingbroke,
Who all this while hath revelled in the night,
Whilst we were wand'ring with the antipodes,
Shall see us rising in our throne the east,   50
His treasons will sit blushing in his face,
Not able to endure the sight of day,
But self-affrighted tremble at his sin.
Not all the water in the rough rude sea
Can wash the balm off from an anointed king.
The breath of worldly men cannot depose
The deputy elected by the Lord,
For every man that Bolingbroke hath pressed
To lift shrewd steel against our golden crown,
God for his Richard hath in heavenly pay   60
A glorious angel; then, if angels fight,
Weak men must fall, for heaven still guards the
right.

Salisbury enters

Welcome, my lord: how far off lies your power?

SALISBURY. Nor near nor farther off, my gracious lord,
Than this weak arm; discomfort guides my tongue,
And bids me speak of nothing but despair.
One day too late, I fear me, noble lord,
Hath clouded all thy happy days on earth:
O, call back yesterday, bid time return,
And thou shalt have twelve thousand fighting men!   70
To-day, to-day, unhappy day too late,
O'erthrows thy joys, friends, fortune and thy state,
For all the Welshmen, hearing thou wert dead,
Are gone to Bolingbroke, dispersed and fled.

AUMERLE. Comfort, my liege, why looks your
grace so pale?

K. RICHARD. But now the blood of twenty
thousand men
Did triumph in my face, and they are fled:
And till so much blood thither come again,
Have I not reason to look pale and dead?
All souls that will be safe, fly from my side,   80
For time hath set a blot upon my pride.

AUMERLE. Comfort, my liege, remember who
you are.

K. RICHARD. I had forgot myself, am I not king?
Awake thou coward majesty! thou sleepest.
Is not the king's name twenty thousand names?
Arm, arm, my name! a puny subject strikes
At thy great glory. Look not to the ground,
Ye favourites of a king, are we not high?
High be our thoughts. I know my uncle York
Hath power enough to serve our turn: but who
comes here?   90

Scroop enters

SCROOP. More health and happiness betide my liege
  Than can my care-tuned tongue deliver him.
K. RICHARD. Mine ear is open, and my heart prepared,
  The worst is worldly loss thou canst unfold.
  Say, is my kingdom lost? why, 'twas my care,
  And what loss is it to be rid of care?
  Strives Bolingbroke to be as great as we?
  Greater he shall not be. If he serve God,
  We'll serve him too, and be his fellow so:
  Revolt our subjects? that we cannot mend,   100
  They break their faith to God as well as us:
  Cry, woe, destruction, ruin, and decay,
  The worst is death, and death will have his day.
SCROOP. Glad am I, that your highness is so armed
  To bear the tidings of calamity.
  Like an unseasonable stormy day,
  Which makes the silver rivers drown their shores,
  As if the world were all dissolved to tears;
  So high above his limits swells the rage
  Of Bolingbroke, covering your fearful land   110
  With hard bright steel, and hearts harder than steel.
  White-beards have armed their thin and hairless
    scalps
  Against thy majesty: boys, with women's voices,
  Strive to speak big and clap their female joints
  In stiff unwieldy arms against thy crown,
  Thy very beadsmen learn to bend their bows
  Of double-fatal yew against thy state,
  Yea, distaff-women manage rusty bills
  Against thy seat. Both young and old rebel,
  And all goes worse than I have power to tell.   120
K. RICHARD. Too well, too well thou tell'st a tale so ill.
  Where is the Earl of Wiltshire? where is Bagot?
  What is become of Bushy? where is Green?
  That they have let the dangerous enemy
  Measure our confines with such peaceful steps?
  If we prevail, their heads shall pay for it:
  I warrant they have made peace with Bolingbroke.
SCROOP. Peace have they made with him, indeed,
  my lord.
K. RICHARD. O villains, vipers, damned
  without redemption!
  Dogs, easily won to fawn on any man!   130
  Snakes, in my heart-blood warmed, that sting
  my heart!
  Three Judases, each one thrice worse than Judas!
  Would they make peace? terrible hell
  Make war upon their spotted souls for this!
SCROOP. Sweet love, I see, changing his property,
  Turns to the sourest and most deadly hate.
  Again uncurse their souls, their peace is made
  With heads and not with hands, those whom
  you curse
  Have felt the worst of death's destroying wound,
  And lie full low graved in the hollow ground.   140
AUMERLE. Is Bushy, Green, and the Earl of
  Wiltshire dead?
SCROOP. Ay, all of them at Bristow lost their heads.
AUMERLE. Where is the duke my father with his
  power?
K. RICHARD. No matter where, of comfort no
  man speak:
  Let's talk of graves, of worms, and epitaphs,
  Make dust our paper, and with rainy eyes
  Write sorrow on the bosom of the earth. . . .
  Let's choose executors and talk of wills:

And yet not so, for what can we bequeath,
Save our deposéd bodies to the ground?   150
Our lands, our lives, and all are Bolingbroke's,
And nothing can we call our own, but death;
And that small model of the barren earth,
Which serves as paste and cover to our bones.
For God's sake let us sit upon the ground,
And tell sad stories of the death of kings—
How some have been deposed, some slain in war,
Some haunted by the ghosts they have deposed,
Some poisoned by their wives, some sleeping killed;
All murdered—for within the hollow crown   160
That rounds the mortal temples of a king,
Keeps Death his court, and there the antic sits,
Scoffing his state and grinning at his pomp,
Allowing him a breath, a little scene,
To monarchize, be feared, and kill with looks,
Infusing him with self and vain conceit,
As if this flesh which walls about our life,
Were brass impregnable: and humoured thus,
Comes at the last, and with a little pin
Bores through his castle wall, and farewell king!   170
Cover your heads, and mock not flesh and blood
With solemn reverence, throw away respect,
Tradition, form, and ceremonious duty,
For you have but mistook me all this while:
I live with bread like you, feel want,
Taste grief, need friends—subjected thus,
How can you say to me, I am a king?
CARLISLE. My lord, wise men ne'er sit and wail
  their woes,
  But presently prevent the ways to wail.
  To fear the foe, since fear oppresseth strength,   180
  Gives in your weakness strength unto your foe,
  And so your follies fight against yourself:
  Fear and be slain, no worse can come to fight,
  And fight and die is death destroying death,
  Where fearing dying pays death servile breath.
AUMERLE. My father hath a power, inquire of him,
  And learn to make a body of a limb.
K. RICHARD. Thou chid'st me well—proud
  Bolingbroke, I come
  To change blows with thee for our day of doom:
  This ague fit of fear is over-blown.   190
  An easy task it is to win our own. . . .
  Say, Scroop, where lies our uncle with his power?
  Speak sweetly, man, although thy looks be sour.
SCROOP. Men judge by the complexion of the sky
  The state and inclination of the day;
  So may you by my dull and heavy eye,
  My tongue hath but a heavier tale to say.
  I play the torturer by small and small
  To lengthen out the worst that must be spoken:
  Your uncle York is joined with Bolingbroke,   200
  And all the northern castles yielded up,
  And all your southern gentlemen in arms
  Upon his party.
K. RICHARD.   Thou hast said enough:
                        To Aumerle
  Beshrew thee, cousin, which didst lead me forth
  Of that sweet way I was in to despair!
  What say you now? what comfort have we now?
  By heaven I'll hate him everlastingly
  That bids me be of comfort any more. . . .
  Go to Flint castle, there I'll pine away—
  A king, woe's slave, shall kingly woe obey: 210

That power I have, discharge, and let them go
To ear the land that hath some hope to grow,
For I have none. Let no man speak again,
To alter this, for counsel is but vain.
AUMERLE. My liege, one word.
K. RICHARD.   He does me double wrong,
That wounds me with the flatteries of his tongue. . . .
Discharge my followers, let them hence away,
From Richard's night, to Bolingbroke's fair day.
                                                        They go

Scene 3: *Wales. Before Flint Castle*

*Enter marching with drum and colours, Bolingbroke, York,
Northumberland, and their forces*

BOLINGBROKE. So that by this intelligence we learn
The Welshmen are dispersed, and Salisbury
Is gone to meet the king, who lately landed
With some few private friends upon this coast.
NORTHUMBERLAND. The news is very fair and good,
    my lord,
Richard, not far from hence, hath hid his head.
YORK. It would beseem the Lord Northumberland,
To say 'King Richard': alack the heavy day,
When such a sacred king should hide his head.
NORTHUMBERLAND. Your grace mistakes; only to
    be brief   10
Left I his title out.
YORK.   The time hath been,
Would you have been so brief with him, he would
Have been so brief with you, to shorten you,
For taking so the head, your whole head's length.
BOLINGBROKE. Mistake not, uncle, further than
    you should.
YORK. Take not, good cousin, further than you
    should,
Lest you mis-take: the heavens are o'er our heads.
BOLINGBROKE. I know it, uncle, and oppose not myself
Against their will. . . . But who comes here?

Enter Percy

Welcome, Harry; what, will not this castle yield? 20
PERCY. The castle royally is manned, my lord,
Against thy entrance.
BOLINGBROKE. Royally!
Why, it contains no king?
PERCY.   Yes, my good lord,
It doth contain a king. King Richard lies
Within the limits of yon lime and stone,
And with him are the Lord Aumerle, Lord
    Salisbury,
Sir Stephen Scroop, besides a clergyman
Of holy reverence, who I cannot learn.
NORTHUMBERLAND. O belike it is the Bishop of
    Carlisle.   30
BOLINGBROKE. Noble lord,   *To Northumberland*
Go to the rude ribs of that ancient castle,
Through brazen trumpet send the breath of parley
Into his ruined ears, and thus deliver. . . .
Henry Bolingbroke
On both his knees doth kiss King Richard's hand,
And sends allegiance and true faith of heart
To his most royal person: hither come
Even at his feet to lay my arms and power;
Provided that my banishment repealed   40
And lands restored again be freely granted;
If not, I'll use the advantage of my power,

And lay the summer's dust with showers of blood,
Rained from the wounds of slaughtered
    Englishmen,
The which, how far off from the mind of
    Bolingbroke
It is such crimson tempest should bedrench
The fresh green lap of fair King Richard's land,
My stooping duty tenderly shall show:
Go, signify as much, while here we march
Upon the grassy carpet of this plain . . .   50
    *Northumberland advances to the castle,
                                    with a trumpeter*
Let's march without the noise of threat'ning drum,
That from this castle's tattered battlements
Our fair appointments may be well perused. . . .
Methinks, King Richard and myself should meet
With no less terror than the elements
Of fire and water, when their thund'ring shock
At meeting tears the cloudy cheeks of heaven.
Be he the fire, I'll be the yielding water;
The rage be his, whilst on the earth I rain
My waters—on the earth, and not on him. . . .   60
March on, and mark King Richard how he looks.

*Northumberland sounds a parle without, and is answered
by another trumpet within: then a flourish. Enter on the
walls King Richard, the Bishop of Carlisle, Aumerle,
Scroop, and Salisbury*

See, see, King Richard doth himself appear,
As doth the blushing discontented sun
From out the fiery portal of the east,
When he perceives the envious clouds are bent
To dim his glory, and to stain the track
Of his bright passage to the occident.
YORK. Yet looks he like a king! behold his eye,
As bright as is the eagle's, lightens forth
Controlling majesty; alack, alack, for woe,   70
That any harm should stain so fair a show!
K. RICHARD [*to Northumberland*]. We are amazed, and
    thus long have we stood
To watch the fearful bending of thy knee,
Because we thought ourself thy lawful king:
And if we be, how dare thy joints forget
To pay their awful duty to our presence?
If we be not, show us the hand of God
That hath dismissed us from our stewardship,
For well we know no hand of blood and bone
Can gripe the sacred handle of our sceptre,   80
Unless he do profane, steal, or usurp.
And though you think that all, as you have done,
Have torn their souls, by turning them from us,
And we are barren and bereft of friends . . .
Yet know, my master, God omnipotent,
Is mustering in his clouds, on our behalf,
Armies of pestilence, and they shall strike
Your children yet unborn, and unbegot,
That lift your vassal hands against my head,
And threat the glory of my precious crown. . . . 90
Tell Bolingbroke—for yon methinks he stands—
That every stride he makes upon my land,
Is dangerous treason: he is come to open
The purple testament of bleeding war:
But ere the crown he looks for live in peace,
Ten thousand bloody crowns of mothers' sons
Shall ill become the flower of England's face,
Change the complexion of her maid-pale peace

To scarlet indignation and bedew
Her pasture's grass with faithful English blood. 100
NORTHUMBERLAND. The king of heaven forbid our
    lord the king
Should so with civil and uncivil arms
Be rushed upon! Thy thrice noble cousin,
Harry Bolingbroke, doth humbly kiss thy hand,
And by the honourable tomb he swears,
That stands upon your royal grandsire's bones,
And by the royalties of both your bloods,
Currents that spring from one most gracious head,
And by the buried hand of warlike Gaunt,
And by the worth and honour of himself, 110
Comprising all that may be sworn or said,
His coming hither hath no further scope
Than for his lineal royalties, and to beg
Enfranchisement immediate on his knees,
Which on thy royal party granted once,
His glittering arms he will commend to rust,
His barbéd steeds to stables, and his heart
To faithful service of your majesty....
This swears he, as he is a prince, is just;
And, as I am a gentleman, I credit him. 120
K. RICHARD. Northumberland, say thus the
    king returns—
His noble cousin is right welcome hither,
And all the number of his fair demands
Shall be accomplished without contradiction.
With all the gracious utterance thou hast,
Speak to his gentle hearing kind commends....
        Northumberland retires to Bolingbroke
[*to Aumerle*] We do debase ourselves, cousin, do
    we not,
To look so poorly, and to speak so fair?
Shall we call back Northumberland and send
Defiance to the traitor, and so die? 130
AUMERLE. No, good my lord; let's fight with
    gentle words,
Till time lend friends, and friends their helpful
    swords.
K. RICHARD. O God! O God! that e'er this tongue
    of mine,
That laid the sentence of dread banishment
On yon proud man, should take it off again
With words of sooth! O, that I were as great
As is my grief, or lesser than my name!
Or that I could forget what I have been!
Or not remember what I must be now!
Swell'st thou, proud heart? I'll give thee scope
    to beat, 140
Since foes have scope to beat both thee and me.
AUMERLE. Northumberland comes back
    from Bolingbroke.
K. RICHARD. What must the king do now? must
    he submit?
The king shall do it: must he be deposed?
The king shall be contented: must he lose
The name of king? a God's name let it go:
I'll give my jewels for a set of beads:
My gorgeous palace for a hermitage:
My gay apparel for an almsman's gown:
My figured goblets for a dish of wood:
My sceptre for a palmer's walking-staff:
My subjects for a pair of carvéd saints, 150
And my large kingdom for a little grave,
A little little grave, an obscure grave,

Or I'll be buried in the king's highway,
Some way of common trade, where subjects' feet
May hourly trample on their sovereign's head;
For on my heart they tread now whilst I live:
And buried once, why not upon my head?
Aumerle, thou weep'st (my tender-hearted cousin!), 160
We'll make foul weather with despiséd tears;
Our sighs and they shall lodge the summer corn,
And make a dearth in this revolting land:
Or shall we play the wantons with our woes,
And make some pretty match with shedding tears?
As thus to drop them still upon one place,
Till they have fretted us a pair of graves
Within the earth, and therein laid ... there lies
Two kinsmen digged their graves with weeping
    eyes!
Would not this ill do well? Well, well, I see 170
I talk but idly, and you laugh at me....
Most mighty prince, my Lord Northumberland,
What says King Bolingbroke? will his majesty
Give Richard leave to live till Richard die?
You make a leg, and Bolingbroke says 'ay'.
NORTHUMBERLAND. My lord, in the base court he
    doth attend,
To speak with you, may it please you to come
    down?
K. RICHARD. Down, down I come, like
    glist'ring Phaethon:
Wanting the manage of unruly jades....
In the base court? Base court, where kings
    grow base, 180
To come at traitors' calls, and do them grace.
In the base court? Come down? Down court!
    down king!
For night-owls shriek where mounting larks
    should sing.
                He goes from the battlements
BOLINGBROKE. What says his majesty?
NORTHUMBERLAND.   Sorrow and grief of heart
Makes him speak fondly like a frantic man,
Yet he is come.

Enter King Richard, the Duke of York and attendants

BOLINGBROKE. Stand all apart,
And show fair duty to his majesty ...
My gracious lord.   *He kneels down*
K. RICHARD. Fair cousin, you debase your
    princely knee, 190
To make the base earth proud with kissing it:
Me rather had my heart might feel your love,
Than my unpleased eye see your courtesy:
Up, cousin, up—your heart is up, I know,
Thus high [*touching his own head*] at least, although
    your knee be low.
BOLINGBROKE. My gracious lord, I come but for
    mine own.
K. RICHARD. Your own is yours, and I am yours
    and all.
BOLINGBROKE. So far be mine, my most redoubted
    lord,
As my true service shall deserve your love.
K. RICHARD. Well you deserve: they well deserve
    to have, 200
That know the strong'st and surest way to get.
Uncle, give me your hands, nay, dry your eyes,
Tears show their love, but want their remedies....

Cousin, I am too young to be your father,
Though you are old enough to be my heir.
What you will have, I'll give, and willing too,
For do we must, what force will have us do ...
Set on towards London, cousin, is it so?

BOLINGBROKE. Yea, my good lord.

K. RICHARD.   Then I must not say no.
They go

Scene 4: *The Duke of York's garden*

Enter the Queen and two Ladies

QUEEN. What sport shall we devise here in this garden,
To drive away the heavy thought of care?

LADY. Madam, we'll play at bowls.

QUEEN. 'Twill make me think the world is full
of rubs,
And that my fortune runs against the bias.

LADY. Madam, we'll dance.

QUEEN. My legs can keep no measure in delight,
When my poor heart no measure keeps in grief:
Therefore, no dancing, girl—some other sport.

LADY. Madam, we'll tell tales.   10

QUEEN. Of sorrow or of joy?

LADY.   Of either, madam.

QUEEN. Of neither, girl:
For if of joy, being altogether wanting,
It doth remember me the more of sorrow;
Or if of grief, being altogether had,
It adds more sorrow to my want of joy:
For what I have I need not to repeat,
And what I want it boots not to complain.

LADY. Madam, I'll sing.

QUEEN. 'Tis well that thou hast cause,   20
But thou shouldst please me better, wouldst
thou weep.

LADY. I could weep, madam, would it do you good.

QUEEN. And I could sing, would weeping do
me good,
And never borrow any tear of thee....

Enter Gardeners with spades etc.

But stay, here comes the gardeners.
Let's step into the shadow of these trees.
My wretchedness unto a row of pins,
They will talk of state, for every one doth so
Against a change: woe is forerun with woe.
Queen and her ladies retire

GARDENER. Go, bind thou up yon dangling apricocks,   30
Which like unruly children make their sire
Stoop with oppression of their prodigal weight,
Give some supportance to the bending twigs.
Go thou, and like an executioner
Cut off the heads of too fast growing sprays,
That look too lofty in our commonwealth—
All must be even in our government....
You thus employed, I will go root away
The noisome weeds which without profit suck
The soil's fertility from wholesome flowers.   40

MAN. Why should we, in the compass of a pale,
Keep law and form and due proportion,
Showing as in a model our firm estate,
When our sea-wallèd garden, the whole land,
Is full of weeds, her fairest flowers choked up,
Her fruit-trees all unpruned, her hedges ruined,

Her knots disordered, and her wholesome herbs
Swarming with caterpillars?

GARDENER.   Hold thy peace—
He that hath suffered this disordered spring
Hath now himself met with the fall of leaf: 50
The weeds which his broad-spreading leaves
did shelter,
That seemed in eating him to hold him up,
Are plucked up root and all by Bolingbroke—
I mean the Earl of Wiltshire, Bushy, Green.

MAN. What, are they dead?

GARDENER.   They are, and Bolingbroke
Hath seized the wasteful king. O! what pity is it
That he had not so trimmed and dressed his land,
As we this garden! We at time of year
Do wound the bark, the skin of our fruit-trees,
Lest being over-proud in sap and blood,   60
With too much riches it confound itself.
Had he done so to great and growing men,
They might have lived to bear, and he to taste,
Their fruits of duty: superfluous branches
We lop away, that bearing boughs may live:
Had he done so, himself had borne the crown,
Which waste of idle hours hath quite thrown down.

MAN. What, think you then the king shall be deposed?

GARDENER. Depressed he is already, and deposed
'Tis doubt he will be.... Letters came last night   70
To a dear friend of the good Duke of York's,
That tell black tidings.

QUEEN. O, I am pressed to death through want
of speaking!   *Comes forth*
Thou, old Adam's likeness, set to dress this garden,
How dares thy harsh rude tongue sound this
unpleasing news?
What Eve, what serpent, hath suggested thee
To make a second fall of cursèd man?
Why dost thou say King Richard is deposed?
Dar'st thou, thou little better thing than earth,
Divine his downfal? Say, where, when, and how,   80
Cam'st thou by these ill tidings? speak, thou wretch!

GARDENER. Pardon me, madam. Little joy have I
To breathe this news, yet what I say is true:
King Richard, he is in the mighty hold
Of Bolingbroke: their fortunes both are weighed:
In your lord's scale is nothing but himself,
And some few vanities that make him light;
But in the balance of great Bolingbroke,
Besides himself, are all the English peers,
And with that odds he weighs King Richard down;   90
Post you to London, and you will find it so,
I speak no more than every one doth know.

QUEEN. Nimble mischance, that art so light of foot,
Doth not thy embassage belong to me,
And am I last that knows it? O, thou thinkest
To serve me last, that I may longest keep
Thy sorrow in my breast ... Come, ladies, go,
To meet at London London's king in woe....
What, was I born to this, that my sad look
Should grace the triumph of great Bolingbroke?   100
Gardener, for telling me these news of woe,
Pray God the plants thou graft'st may never grow.
She leaves the garden with her ladies

GARDENER. Poor queen! so that thy state might be
no worse,
I would my skill were subject to thy curse:
Here did she fall a tear, here in this place

I'll set a bank of rue, sour herb of grace.
Rue, even for ruth, here shortly shall be seen,
In the remembrance of a weeping queen. *They go*

ACT 4
Scene 1: *Westminster Hall*

*Enter as to the Parliament Bolingbroke, Aumerle, Surrey,
Northumberland, Percy, Fitzwater, and other lords, the
Bishop of Carlisle, and the Abbot of Westminster. Herald
and Officers with Bagot*

BOLINGBROKE. Call forth Bagot....
                                He is brought forward
Now, Bagot, freely speak thy mind,
What thou dost know of noble Gloucester's death,
Who wrought it with the king, and who performed
The bloody office of his timeless end.
BAGOT. Then set before my face the Lord Aumerle.
BOLINGBROKE. Cousin, stand forth, and look upon
    that man.
BAGOT. My Lord Aumerle, I know your daring
    tongue
Scorns to unsay what once it hath delivered.
In that dead time when Gloucester's death was
    plotted,   10
I heard you say, 'Is not my arm of length,
That reacheth from the restful English court
As far as Calais, to my uncle's head?'
Amongst much other talk that very time
I heard you say that you had rather refuse
The offer of an hundred thousand crowns
Than Bolingbroke's return to England—
Adding withal, how blest this land would be,
In this your cousin's death.
AUMERLE.   Princes and noble lords,
What answer shall I make to this base man?   20
Shall I so much dishonour my fair stars,
On equal terms to give him chastisement?
Either I must, or have mine honour soiled
With the attainder of his slanderous lips.
There is my gage, the manual seal of death,
That marks thee out for hell! I say thou liest,
And will maintain what thou hast said is false
In thy heart-blood, though being all too base
To stain the temper of my knightly sword.
BOLINGBROKE. Bagot, forbear, thou shalt not take
    it up.   30
AUMERLE. Excepting one, I would he were the best
In all this presence that hath moved me so.
FITZWATER. If that thy valour stand on sympathy,
There is my gage, Aumerle, in gage to thine:
By that fair sun which shows me where thou
    stand'st,
I heard thee say, and vauntingly thou spak'st it,
That thou wert cause of noble Gloucester's death.
If thou deny'st it twenty times, thou liest,
And I will turn thy falsehood to thy heart,
Where it was forged, with my rapier's point.   40
AUMERLE. Thou dar'st not, coward, live to see
    that day.
FITZWATER. Now, by my soul, I would it were this
    hour.
AUMERLE. Fitzwater, thou art damned to hell for this.
PERCY. Aumerle, thou liest, his honour is as true
In this appeal as thou art all unjust,

And that thou art so, there I throw my gage,
To prove it on thee to the extremest point
Of mortal breathing—seize if thou dar'st.
AUMERLE. An if I do not, may my hands rot off,
And never brandish more revengeful steel   50
Over the glittering helmet of my foe!
ANOTHER LORD. I task the earth to the like,
    forsworn Aumerle,
And spur thee on with full as many lies
As may be holloaed in thy treacherous ear
From sun to sun: there is my honour's pawn—
Engage it to the trial if thou darest.
AUMERLE. Who sets me else? by heaven, I'll throw
    at all!
I have a thousand spirits in one breast,
To answer twenty thousand such as you.
SURREY. My Lord Fitzwater, I do remember well   60
The very time Aumerle and you did talk.
FITZWATER. 'Tis very true, you were in presence then,
And you can witness with me this is true.
SURREY. As false, by heaven, as heaven itself is true.
FITZWATER. Surrey, thou liest.
SURREY.   Dishonourable boy!
That lie shall lie so heavy on my sword,
That it shall render vengeance and revenge,
Till thou the lie-giver, and that lie, do lie
In earth as quiet as thy father's skull....
In proof whereof, there is my honour's pawn—   70
Engage it to the trial if thou dar'st.
FITZWATER. How fondly dost thou spur a
    forward horse!
If I dare eat, or drink, or breathe, or live,
I dare meet Surrey in a wilderness,
And spit upon him, whilst I say he lies,
And lies, and lies: there is my bond of faith,
To tie thee to my strong correction:
As I intend to thrive in this new world,
Aumerle is guilty of my true appeal:
Besides, I heard the banished Norfolk say,   80
That thou, Aumerle, didst send two of thy men
To execute the noble duke at Calais.
AUMERLE. Some honest Christian trust me with a gage,
That Norfolk lies—here do I throw down this,
If he may be repealed to try his honour.
BOLINGBROKE. These differences shall all rest
    under gage,
Till Norfolk be repealed. Repealed he shall be,
And, though mine enemy, restored again
To all his lands and signories: when he's returned,
Against Aumerle we will enforce his trial.   90
CARLISLE. That honourable day shall ne'er be seen.
Many a time hath banished Norfolk fought
For Jesu Christ in glorious Christian field,
Streaming the ensign of the Christian cross
Against black pagans, Turks, and Saracens,
And toiled with works of war, retired himself
To Italy, and there at Venice gave
His body to that pleasant country's earth,
And his pure soul unto his captain Christ
Under whose colours he had fought so long.   100
BOLINGBROKE. Why, bishop, is Norfolk dead?
CARLISLE. As surely as I live, my lord.
BOLINGBROKE. Sweet peace conduct his sweet soul to
    the bosom
Of good old Abraham! Lord appellants,
Your differences shall all rest under gage,

Till we assign you to your days of trial.

York enters

YORK. Great Duke of Lancaster, I come to thee
  From plume-plucked Richard, who with willing
    soul
  Adopts thee heir, and his high sceptre yields
  To the possession of thy royal hand: 110
  Ascend his throne, descending now from him,
  And long live Henry, of that name the fourth!
BOLINGBROKE. In God's name, I'll ascend the
    regal throne.
CARLISLE. Marry, God forbid!
  Worst in this royal presence may I speak,
  Yet best beseeming me to speak the truth.
  Would God that any in this noble presence
  Were enough noble to be upright judge
  Of noble Richard.... Then true noblesse would
  Learn him forbearance from so foul a wrong.   120
  What subject can give sentence on his king?
  And who sits here that is not Richard's subject?
  Thieves are not judged but they are by to hear,
  Although apparent guilt be seen in them,
  And shall the figure of God's majesty,
  His captain, steward, deputy-elect,
  Anointed, crowned, planted many years,
  Be judged by subject and inferior breath,
  And he himself not present? O, forfend it, God,
  That in a Christian climate souls refined   130
  Should show so heinous, black, obscene a deed!
  I speak to subjects, and a subject speaks,
  Stirred up by God thus boldly for his king.
  My Lord of Hereford here, whom you call king,
  Is a foul traitor to proud Hereford's king,
  And if you crown him, let me prophesy,
  The blood of English shall manure the ground,
  And future ages groan for this foul act,
  Peace shall go sleep with Turks and infidels,
  And, in this seat of peace, tumultous wars   140
  Shall kin with kin, and kind with kind confound;
  Disorder, horror, fear, and mutiny
  Shall here inhabit, and this land be called
  The field of Golgotha and dead men's skulls.
  O, if you raise this house against this house,
  It will the woefullest division prove
  That ever fell upon this cursèd earth:
  Prevent it, resist it, let it not be so,
  Lest child, child's children, cry against you 'woe!'
NORTHUMBERLAND. Well have you argued, sir, and,
    for your pains,   150
  Of capital treason we arrest you here:
  My Lord of Westminster, be it your charge
  To keep him safely till his day of trial....
  May it please you, lords, to grant the commons'
    suit?
BOLINGBROKE. Fetch hither Richard, that in
    common view
  He may surrender; so we shall proceed
  Without suspicion.
YORK.   I will be his conduct. *He goes*
BOLINGBROKE. Lords, you that here are under
    our arrest,
  Procure your sureties for your days of answer:
  Little are we beholding to your love,   160
  And little looked for at your helping hands.

*York returns with King Richard; Officers follow bearing
the Crown, etc.*

K. RICHARD. Alack, why am I sent for to a king,
  Before I have shook off the regal thoughts
  Wherewith I reigned? I hardly yet have learned
  To insinuate, flatter, bow, and bend my knee:
  Give sorrow leave awhile to tutor me
  To this submission.... Yet I well remember
  The favours of these men: were they not mine?
  Did they not sometime cry 'all hail!' to me?
  So Judas did to Christ: but he, in twelve,   170
  Found truth in all, but one; I, in twelve thousand,
    none....
  God save the king! Will no man say amen?
  Am I both priest and clerk? well then, amen.
  God save the king! although I be not he;
  And yet, amen, if heaven do think him me....
  To do what service am I sent for hither?
YORK. To do that office of thine own good will,
  Which tired majesty did make thee offer:
  The resignation of thy state and crown
  To Henry Bolingbroke.   180
K. RICHARD. Give me the crown.... Here, cousin,
    seize the crown:
  Here, cousin,
  On this side, my hand, and on that side, thine....
  Now is this golden crown like a deep well
  That owes two buckets, filling one another,
  The emptier ever dancing in the air,
  The other down, unseen, and full of water:
  That bucket down, and full of tears, am I,
  Drinking my griefs, whilst you mount up on high.
BOLINGBROKE. I thought you had been willing to
    resign.   190
K. RICHARD. My crown I am, but still my griefs
    are mine:
  You may my glories and my state depose,
  But not my griefs; still am I king of those.
BOLINGBROKE. Part of your cares you give me with
    your crown.
K. RICHARD. Your cares set up do not pluck my
    cares down.
  My care is loss of care, by old care done,
  Your care is gain of care, by new care won:
  The cares I give, I have, though given away,
  They tend the crown, yet still with me they stay.
BOLINGBROKE. Are you contented to resign the crown? 200
K. RICHARD. Ay, no; no, ay; for I must nothing be:
  Therefore no 'no,' for I resign to thee....
  Now mark me how I will undo myself:
  I give this heavy weight from off my head,
  And this unwieldy sceptre from my hand,
  The pride of kingly sway from out my heart;
  With mine own tears I wash away my balm,
  With mine own hands I give away my crown,
  With mine own tongue deny my sacred state,
  With mine own breath release all duteous oaths: 210
  All pomp and majesty I do forswear;
  My manors, rents, revenues, I forgo;
  My acts, decrees, and statutes, I deny:
  God pardon all oaths that are broke to me!
  God keep all vows unbroke are made to thee!
  Make me, that nothing have, with nothing grieved,
  And thou with all pleased, that hast all achieved!
  Long mayst thou live in Richard's seat to sit,

And soon lie Richard in an earthy pit....
God save King Henry, unkinged Richard says, 220
And send him many years of sunshine days....
What more remains?
NORTHUMBERLAND.   No more, but that you read
These accusations and these grievous crimes,
Committed by your person and your followers
Against the state and profit of this land;
That, by confessing them, the souls of men
May deem that you are worthily deposed.
K. RICHARD. Must I do so? and must I ravel out
My weaved-up follies? Gentle Northumberland,
If thy offences were upon record, 230
Would it not shame thee, in so fair a troop,
To read a lecture of them? If thou wouldst,
There shouldst thou find one heinous article,
Containing the deposing of a king,
And cracking the strong warrant of an oath,
Marked with a blot, damned in the book of
heaven....
Nay, all of you, that stand and look upon me,
Whilst that my wretchedness doth bait myself,
Though some of you, with Pilate, wash your hands,
Showing an outward pity; yet you Pilates 240
Have here delivered me to my sour cross,
And water cannot wash away your sin.
NORTHUMBERLAND. My lord, dispatch, read o'er
these articles.
K. RICHARD. Mine eyes are full of tears, I cannot see:
And yet salt water blinds them not so much,
But they can see a sort of traitors here.
Nay, if I turn mine eyes upon myself,
I find myself a traitor with the rest:
For I have given here my soul's consent
T' undeck the pompous body of a king; 250
Made glory base; and sovereignty, a slave;
Proud majesty, a subject; state, a peasant.
NORTHUMBERLAND. My lord—
K. RICHARD. No lord of thine, thou haught,
insulting man;
Nor no man's lord; I have no name, no title;
No, not that name was given me at the font,
But 'tis usurped: alack the heavy day,
That I have worn so many winters out,
And know not now what name to call myself!
O, that I were a mockery king of snow, 260
Standing before the sun of Bolingbroke,
To melt myself away in water-drops!
Good king, great king, and yet not greatly good,
An if my word be sterling yet in England,
Let it command a mirror hither straight,
That it may show me what a face I have,
Since it is bankrupt of his majesty.
BOLINGBROKE. Go some of you, and fetch a
looking-glass.   *An attendant goes out*
NORTHUMBERLAND. Read o'er this paper, while the
glass doth come.
K. RICHARD. Fiend, thou torments me ere I come
to hell. 270
BOLINGBROKE. Urge it no more, my Lord
Northumberland.
NORTHUMBERLAND. The commons will not then
be satisfied.
K. RICHARD. They shall be satisfied; I'll read enough,
When I do see the very book indeed
Where all my sins are writ, and that's myself.

The attendant returns with a glass

Give me that glass, and therein will I read....
No deeper wrinkles yet? hath sorrow struck
So many blows upon this face of mine,
And made no deeper wounds? O, flatt'ring glass,
Like to my followers in prosperity, 280
Thou dost beguile me! Was this face the face
That every day under his household roof
Did keep ten thousand men? Was this the face,
That, like the sun, did make beholders wink?
Was this the face, that faced so many follies,
And was at last out-faced by Bolingbroke?
A brittle glory shineth in this face,
As brittle as the glory is the face,
                    He dashes the glass to the ground
For there it is, cracked in a hundred shivers....
Mark, silent king, the moral of this sport, 290
How soon my sorrow hath destroyed my face.
BOLINGBROKE. The shadow of your sorrow
hath destroyed
The shadow of your face.
K. RICHARD.   Say that again.
The shadow of my sorrow ... ha! let's see—
'Tis very true, my grief lies all within,
And these external manners of lament
Are merely shadows to the unseen grief,
That swells with silence in the tortured soul....
There lies the substance: and I thank thee, king,
For thy great bounty, that not only giv'st 300
Me cause to wail, but teachest me the way
How to lament the cause.... I'll beg one boon,
And then be gone, and trouble you no more.
Shall I obtain it?
BOLINGBROKE.   Name it, fair cousin.
K. RICHARD. 'Fair cousin'? I am greater than a king:
For when I was a king, my flatterers
Were then but subjects; being now a subject,
I have a king here to my flatterer:
Being so great, I have no need to beg.
BOLINGBROKE. Yet ask. 310
K. RICHARD. And shall I have?
BOLINGBROKE. You shall.
K. RICHARD. Then give me leave to go.
BOLINGBROKE. Whither?
K. RICHARD. Whither you will, so I were from
your sights.
BOLINGBROKE. Go, some of you, convey him to the
Tower.
K. RICHARD. O, good! convey? conveyers are you all,
That rise thus nimbly by a true king's fall.
                    *Certain lords conduct Richard
                    guarded from the hall*
BOLINGBROKE. On Wednesday next we solemnly
set down
Our coronation: lords, prepare yourselves. 320

*Bolingbroke and the Lords depart: the Abbot of West-
minster, the Bishop of Carlisle and Aumerle remain behind*

ABBOT. A woeful pageant have we here beheld.
CARLISLE. The woe's to come—the children yet
unborn
Shall feel this day as sharp to them as thorn.
AUMERLE. You holy clergymen, is there no plot
To rid the realm of this pernicious blot?
ABBOT. My lord,

Before I freely speak with my mind herein,
You shall not only take the sacrament
To bury mine intents, but also to effect
Whatever I shall happen to devise: 330
I see your brows are full of discontent,
Your hearts of sorrow, and your eyes of tears:
Come home with me to supper; I will lay
A plot shall show us all a merry day.   *They go*

ACT 5

Scene 1: *London. A street leading to the Tower*

Enter the Queen with her attendants

QUEEN. This way the king will come, this is the way
To Julius Cæsar's ill-erected tower,
To whose flint bosom my condemnèd lord
Is doomed a prisoner by proud Bolingbroke....
Here let us rest, if this rebellious earth
Have any resting for her true king's queen.

Enter Richard with guards

But soft, but see, or rather do not see,
My fair rose wither—yet look up, behold,
That you in pity may dissolve to dew,
And wash him fresh again with true-love tears ...   10
Ah, thou, the model where old Troy did stand!
Thou map of honour, thou King Richard's tomb,
And not King Richard; thou most beauteous inn,
Why should hard-favoured grief be lodged in thee,
When triumph is become an alehouse guest?
RICHARD. Join not with grief, fair woman, do not so,
To make my end too sudden. Learn, good soul,
To think our former state a happy dream,
From which awaked, the truth of what we are
Shows us but this: I am sworn brother, sweet,   20
To grim Necessity, and he and I
Will keep a league till death.... Hie thee to France,
And cloister thee in some religious house.
Our holy lives must win a new world's crown,
Which our profane hours here have thrown down.
QUEEN. What, is my Richard both in shape and mind
Transformed and weak'ned? hath Bolingbroke
    deposed
Thine intellect? hath he been in thy heart?
The lion dying thrusteth forth his paw,
And wounds the earth, if nothing else, with rage   30
To be o'erpowered, and wilt thou pupil-like
Take the correction, mildly kiss the rod,
And fawn on rage with base humility,
Which art a lion and the king of beasts?
RICHARD. A king of beasts, indeed! if aught but beasts,
I had been still a happy king of men....
Good sometimes queen, prepare thee hence for
    France.
Think I am dead, and that even here thou takest
As from my death-bed thy last living leave;
In winter's tedious nights sit by the fire   40
With good old folks, and let them tell thee tales
Of woeful ages long ago betid;
And ere thou bid good night, to quit their griefs,
Tell thou the lamentable fall of me,
And send the hearers weeping to their beds:
For why, the senseless brands will sympathize
The heavy accent of thy moving tongue,
And in compassion weep the fire out,
And some will mourn in ashes, some coal-black,
For the deposing of a rightful king.   50

Northumberland comes up

NORTHUMBERLAND. My lord, the mind of
    Bolingbroke is changed,
You must to Pomfret, not unto the Tower....
And, madam, there is order ta'en for you,
With all swift speed you must away to France.
RICHARD. Northumberland, thou ladder wherewithal
The mounting Bolingbroke ascends my throne,
The time shall not be many hours of age
More than it is, ere foul sin gathering head
Shall break into corruption. Thou shalt think,
Though he divide the realm and give thee half,   60
It is too little, helping him to all....
And he shall think that thou, which knowest
    the way
To plant unrightful kings, wilt know again,
Being ne'er so little urged another way
To pluck him headlong from the usurped throne:
The love of wicked men converts to fear,
That fear to hate, and hate turns one or both
To worthy danger and deservèd death.
NORTHUMBERLAND. My guilt be on my head, and
    there an end:
Take leave and part, for you must part forthwith.   70
RICHARD. Doubly divorced! Bad men, you violate
A twofold marriage—'twixt my crown and me,
And then betwixt me and my married wife....
Let me unkiss the oath 'twixt thee and me;
And yet not so, for with a kiss 'twas made....
Part us, Northumberland—I towards the north,
Where shivering cold and sickness pines the clime;
My wife to France, from whence set forth in pomp
She came adornèd hither like sweet May,
Sent back like Hallowmas or short'st of day.   80
QUEEN. And must we be divided? must we part?
RICHARD. Ay, hand from hand, my love, and heart
    from heart.
QUEEN. Banish us both, and send the king with me.
NORTHUMBERLAND. That were some love, but
    little policy.
QUEEN. Then whither he goes, thither let me go.
RICHARD. So two, together weeping, make one woe.
Weep thou for me in France, I for thee here;
Better far off than near, be ne'er the near.
Go, count thy way with sighs, I mine with groans.
QUEEN. So longest way shall have the longest moans. 90
RICHARD. Twice for one step I'll groan, the way
    being short,
And piece the way out with a heavy heart....
Come, come, in wooing sorrow let's be brief,
Since, wedding it, there is such length in grief:
One kiss shall stop our mouths, and dumbly part—
Thus give I mine, and thus take I thy heart.
QUEEN. Give me mine own again, 'twere no good part
To take on me to keep and kill thy heart:
So, now I have mine own again, be gone,
That I may strive to kill it with a groan.   100
RICHARD. We make woe wanton with this fond delay,
Once more, adieu, the rest let sorrow say.   *They go*

Scene 2: *The Duke of York's palace*

Enter the Duke of York and the Duchess

DUCHESS. My lord, you told me you would tell
    the rest,

When weeping made you break the story off
Of our two cousins coming into London.
YORK. Where did I leave?
DUCHESS.   At that sad stop, my lord,
Where rude misgoverned hands, from windows'
    tops,
Threw dust and rubbish on King Richard's head.
YORK. Then, as I said, the duke, great Bolingbroke,
Mounted upon a hot and fiery steed,
Which his aspiring rider seemed to know,
With slow but stately pace kept on his course,   10
Whilst all tongues cried 'God save thee,
    Bolingbroke!'
You would have thought the very windows spake,
So many greedy looks of young and old
Through casements darted their desiring eyes
Upon his visage, and that all the walls
With painted imagery had said at once
'Jesu preserve thee! welcome, Bolingbroke!'
Whilst he from one side to the other turning
Bareheaded, lower than his proud steed's neck,
Bespake them thus: 'I thank you, countrymen':   20
And thus still doing, thus he passed along.
DUCHESS. Alack poor Richard! where rode he
    the whilst?
YORK. As in a theatre the eyes of men,
After a well-graced actor leaves the stage,
Are idly bent on him that enters next,
Thinking his prattle to be tedious;
Even so, or with much more contempt, men's eyes
Did scowl on Richard; no man cried, 'God
    save him!'
No joyful tongue gave him his welcome home,
But dust was thrown upon his sacred head;   30
Which with such gentle sorrow he shook off,
His face still combating with tears and smiles,
The badges of his grief and patience,
That had not God for some strong purpose steeled
The hearts of men, they must perforce have melted,
And barbarism itself have pitied him:
But heaven hath a hand in these events,
To whose high will we bound our calm
    contents....
To Bolingbroke are we sworn subjects now,
Whose state and honour I for aye allow.   40

Aumerle enters

DUCHESS. Here comes my son Aumerle.
YORK.   Aumerle that was,
But that is lost for being Richard's friend:
And, madam, you must call him Rutland now:
I am in parliament pledge for his truth
And lasting fealty to the new made king.
DUCHESS. Welcome, my son. Who are the violets
    now,
That strew the green lap of the new come spring?
AUMERLE. Madam, I know not, nor I greatly care not.
God knows I had as lief be none as one.
YORK. Well, bear you well in this new spring of time,   50
Lest you be cropped before you come to prime.
What news from Oxford? do these justs and
    triumphs hold?
AUMERLE. For aught I know, my lord, they do.
YORK. You will be there, I know.
AUMERLE. If God prevent not, I purpose so.

YORK. What seal is that, that hangs without thy
    bosom?
Yea, look'st thou pale? let me see the writing.
AUMERLE. My lord, 'tis nothing.
YORK.   No matter then who see it.
I will be satisfied, let me see the writing.
AUMERLE. I do beseech your grace to pardon me;   60
It is a matter of small consequence,
Which for some reasons I would not have seen.
YORK. Which for some reasons, sir, I mean to see....
I fear, I fear—
DUCHESS.   What should you fear?
'Tis nothing but some bond that he is ent'red into
For gay apparel 'gainst the triumph day.
YORK. Bound to himself! what doth he with a bond,
That he is bound to! Wife, thou art a fool....
Boy, let me see the writing.
AUMERLE. I do beseech you, pardon me, I may not
    show it.   70
YORK. I will be satisfied, let me see it, I say.
                *He plucks it out of his bosom
                              and reads it*
Treason! foul treason! villain! traitor! slave!
DUCHESS. What is the matter, my lord?
YORK. Ho! who is within there? saddle my horse.
God for his mercy! what treachery is here!
DUCHESS. Why, what is it, my lord?
YORK. Give me my boots I say, saddle my horse.
Now by mine honour, by my life, by my troth,
I will appeach the villain.
DUCHESS.   What is the matter?
YORK. Peace, foolish woman.   80
DUCHESS. I will not peace. What is the matter,
    Aumerle?
AUMERLE. Good mother, be content—it is no more
Than my poor life must answer.
DUCHESS.   Thy life answer!
YORK. Bring me my boots, I will unto the king.

His man enters with his boots

DUCHESS. Strike him, Aumerle. Poor boy, thou
    art amazed.
Hence, villain! never more come in my sight.
YORK. Give me my boots, I say.
                The man helps him into them
DUCHESS. Why, York, what wilt thou do?
Wilt thou not hide the trespass of thine own?
Have we more sons? or are we like to have?   90
Is not my teeming date drunk up with time?
And wilt thou pluck my fair son from mine age,
And rob me of a happy mother's name?
Is he not like thee? is he not thine own?
YORK. Thou fond mad woman,
Wilt thou conceal this dark conspiracy?
A dozen of them here have ta'en the sacrament,
And interchangeably set down their hands,
To kill the king at Oxford.
DUCHESS.   He shall be none.
We'll keep him here, then what is that to him?   100
YORK. Away, fond woman! were he twenty times
    my son,
I would appeach him.
DUCHESS.   Hadst thou groaned for him
As I have done, thou wouldst be more pitiful.
But now I know thy mind, thou dost suspect
That I have been disloyal to thy bed,

And that he is a bastard, not thy son:
Sweet York, sweet husband, be not of that mind,
He is as like thee as a man may be,
Not like to me, or any of my kin,
And yet I love him.
YORK.   Make way, unruly woman.   110
                                        He goes
DUCHESS. After, Aumerle; mount thee upon his horse,
Spur post, and get before him to the king,
And beg thy pardon ere he do accuse thee.
I'll not be long behind—though I be old,
I doubt not but to ride as fast as York,
And never will I rise up from the ground,
Till Bolingbroke have pardoned thee: away,
  be gone!   *They go*

Scene 3: *Windsor Castle*

Enter Bolingbroke, Percy and other nobles

BOLINGBROKE. Can no man tell me of my unthrifty
  son?
'Tis full three months since I did see him last,
If any plague hang over us, 'tis he:
I would to God, my lords, he might be found:
Inquire at London, 'mongst the taverns there,
For, they say, he daily doth frequent,
With unrestrainéd loose companions,
Even such, they say, as stand in narrow lanes,
And beat our watch, and rob our passengers,
While he, young wanton and effeminate boy,   10
Takes on the point of honour to support
So dissolute a crew.
PERCY. My lord, some two days since I saw the prince,
And told him of those triumphs held at Oxford.
BOLINGBROKE. And what said the gallant?
PERCY. His answer was, he would unto the stews,
And from the common'st creature pluck a glove,
And wear it as a favour, and with that
He would unhorse the lustiest challenger.
BOLINGBROKE. As dissolute as desperate—yet
  through both   20
I see some sparks of better hope, which elder years
May happily bring forth.... But who comes here?

Enter Aumerle amazed

AUMERLE. Where is the king?
BOLINGBROKE. What means our cousin, that he stares
  and looks
So wildly?
AUMERLE. God save your grace, I do beseech
  your majesty,
To have some conference with your grace alone.
BOLINGBROKE. Withdraw yourselves, and leave us
  here alone....   *Percy and the rest withdraw*
What is the matter with our cousin now?
AUMERLE [*kneels*]. For ever may my knees grow to
  the earth,   30
My tongue cleave to my roof within my mouth,
Unless a pardon ere I rise or speak.
BOLINGBROKE. Intended, or committed, was this fault?
If on the first, how heinous e'er it be,
To win thy after-love, I pardon thee.
AUMERLE. Then give me leave that I may turn the key,
That no man enter till my tale be done.
BOLINGBROKE. Have thy desire.   *The key is turned*

The Duke of York knocks at the door and crieth

YORK [*without*]. My liege, beware, look to thyself,
Thou hast a traitor in thy presence there.   40
BOLINGBROKE. Villain, I'll make thee safe.   *He draws*
AUMERLE. Stay thy revengeful hand, thou hast no
  cause to fear.
YORK [*without*]. Open the door, secure, foolhardy
  king,
Shall I for love speak treason to thy face?
Open the door, or I will break it open.

Bolingbroke opens, admits York and locks the door again

BOLINGBROKE. What is the matter, uncle? speak,
  recover breath,
Tell us how near is danger,
That we may arm us to encounter it.
YORK. Peruse this writing here, and thou shalt know
The treason that my haste forbids me show.   50
AUMERLE. Remember, as thou read'st, thy
  promise passed.
I do repent me, read not my name there,
My heart is not confederate with my hand.
YORK. It was, villain, ere thy hand did set it down....
I tore it from the traitor's bosom, king.
Fear, and not love, begets his penitence:
Forget to pity him, lest thy pity prove
A serpent that will sting thee to the heart.
BOLINGBROKE. O heinous, strong, and bold
  conspiracy!
O loyal father of a treacherous son!   60
Thou sheer, immaculate and silver fountain,
From whence this stream, through muddy passages,
Hath held his current, and defiled himself!
Thy overflow of good converts to bad;
And thy abundant goodness shall excuse
This deadly blot in thy digressing son.
YORK. So shall my virtue he his vice's bawd,
And he shall spend mine honour with his shame,
As thriftless sons their scraping fathers' gold:
Mine honour lives when his dishonour dies,   70
Or my shamed life in his dishonour lies.
Thou kill'st me in his life—giving him breath,
The traitor lives, the true man's put to death.
DUCHESS [*without*]. What ho, my liege! for God's sake,
  let me in.
BOLINGBROKE. What shrill-voiced suppliant makes this
  eager cry?
DUCHESS. A woman, and thy aunt, great king—'tis I
Speak with me, pity me, open the door,
A beggar begs that never begged before.
BOLINGBROKE. Our scene is altered from a serious
  thing,
And now changed to 'The Beggar and the King': 80
My dangerous cousin, let your mother in,
I know she is come to pray for your foul sin.
YORK. If thou do pardon, whosoever pray,
More sins for this forgiveness prosper may:
This fest'red joint cut off, the rest rest sound,
This let alone with all the rest confound.

Aumerle admits the Duchess

DUCHESS. O king, believe not this hard-hearted man!
Love loving not itself none other can.
YORK. Thou frantic woman, what dost thou
  make here?

Shall thy old dugs once more a traitor rear? 90
DUCHESS. Sweet York, be patient. Hear me,
  gentle liege.   *She kneels*
BOLINGBROKE. Rise up, good aunt.
DUCHESS.   Not yet, I thee beseech.
  For ever will I walk upon my knees,
  And never see day that the happy sees,
  Till thou give joy—until thou bid me joy,
  By pardoning Rutland, my transgressing boy.
AUMERLE. Unto my mother's prayers I bend my knee.
                      Kneels
YORK. Against them both my true joints bended be.
                      Kneels
  Ill mayst thou thrive, if thou grant any grace!
DUCHESS. Pleads he in earnest? look upon his face; 100
  His eyes do drop no tears, his prayers are in jest.
  His words come from his mouth, ours from our
    breast.
  He prays but faintly, and would be denied,
  We pray with heart and soul, and all beside.
  His weary joints would gladly rise, I know,
  Our knees shall kneel till to the ground they grow.
  His prayers are full of false hypocrisy,
  Ours of true zeal and deep integrity.
  Our prayers do out-pray his—then let them have
  That mercy which true prayer ought to have. 110
BOLINGBROKE. Good aunt, stand up.
DUCHESS.   Nay, do not say 'stand up';
  Say 'pardon' first, and afterwards 'stand up'.
  An if I were thy nurse, thy tongue to teach,
  'Pardon' should be the first word of thy speech:
  I never longed to hear a word till now,
  Say 'pardon,' king, let pity teach thee how.
  The word is short, but not so short as sweet,
  No words like 'pardon' for kings' mouths so meet.
YORK. Speak it in French, king, say 'pardonne moy'.
DUCHESS. Dost thou teach pardon pardon to destroy? 120
  Ah, my sour husband, my hard-hearted lord,
  That sets the word itself against the word!
  Speak 'pardon' as 'tis current in our land—
  The chopping French we do not understand.
  Thine eye begins to speak, set thy tongue there:
  Or in thy piteous heart plant thou thine ear,
  That hearing how our plaints and prayers do pierce,
  Pity may move thee 'pardon' to rehearse.
BOLINGBROKE. Good aunt, stand up.
DUCHESS.   I do not sue to stand.
  Pardon is all the suit I have in hand. 130
BOLINGBROKE. I pardon him, as God shall pardon me.
DUCHESS. O happy vantage of a kneeling knee!
  Yet am I sick for fear, speak it again,
  Twice saying 'pardon' doth not pardon twain,
  But makes one pardon strong.
BOLINGBROKE.   With all my heart
  I pardon him.
DUCHESS.   A god on earth thou art.
BOLINGBROKE. But for our trusty brother-in-law, and
  the abbot,
  With all the rest of that consorted crew,
  Destruction straight shall dog them at the heels.
  Good uncle, help to order several powers 140
  To Oxford, or where'er these traitors are.
  They shall not live within this world, I swear,
  But I will have them, if I once know where....
  Uncle, farewell, and cousin too, adieu—
  Your mother well hath prayed, and prove you true!

DUCHESS. Come, my old son—I pray God make
  thee new.   *They go*

Scene 4

Sir Pierce of Exton enters with his manservant

EXTON. Didst thou mark the king, what words
  he spake?
  'Have I no friend will rid me of this living fear?'
  Was it not so?
SERVANT.   These were his very words.
EXTON. 'Have I no friend?' quoth he—he spake
  it twice,
  And urged it twice together, did he not?
SERVANT. He did.
EXTON. And, speaking it, he wishtly looked on me,
  As who should say, 'I would thou wert the man
  That would divorce this terror from my heart,'
  Meaning the king at Pomfret.... Come, let's go, 10
  I am the king's friend, and will rid his foe.   *They go*

Scene 5: *Pomfret Castle*

Enter Richard alone

RICHARD. I have been studying how I may compare
  This prison where I live unto the world:
  And for because the world is populous,
  And here is not a creature but myself,
  I cannot do it; yet I'll hammer it out.
  My brain I'll prove the female to my soul,
  My soul the father, and these two beget
  A generation of still-breeding thoughts:
  And these same thoughts people this little world,
  In humours like the people of this world: 10
  For no thought is contented: the better sort,
  As thoughts of things divine, are intermixed
  With scruples, and do set the word itself
  Against the word,
  As thus: 'Come, little ones', and then again,
  'It is as hard to come, as for a camel
  To thread the postern of a small needle's eye' ...
  Thoughts tending to ambition, they do plot
  Unlikely wonders: how these vain weak nails
  May tear a passage through the flinty ribs 20
  Of this hard world, my ragged prison walls;
  And, for they cannot, die in their own pride.
  Thoughts tending to content flatter themselves
  That they are not the first of fortune's slaves,
  Nor shall not be the last—like silly beggars
  Who sitting in the stocks refuge their shame,
  That many have and others must sit there:
  And in this thought they find a kind of ease,
  Bearing their own misfortunes on the back
  Of such as have before endured the like.... 30
  Thus play I in one person many people,
  And none contented: sometimes am I king,
  Then treasons make me wish myself a beggar,
  And so I am: then crushing penury
  Persuades me I was better when a king;
  Then am I kinged again, and by and by
  Think that I am unkinged by Bolingbroke,
  And straight am nothing.... But whate'er I be,
  Nor I, nor any man that but man is,
  With nothing shall be pleased, till he be eased 40
  With being nothing.... Music do I hear?
                        Music plays

Ha, ha! keep time—how sour sweet music is,
When time is broke and no proportion kept!
So is it in the music of men's lives:
And here have I the daintiness of ear
To check time broke in a disordered string;
But for the concord of my state and time
Had not an ear to hear my true time broke.
I wasted time, and now doth time waste me:
For now hath time made me his numb'ring clock;   50
My thoughts are minutes, and with sighs they jar
Their watches on unto mine eyes, the outward
   watch,
Whereto my finger, like a dial's point,
Is pointing still, in cleansing them from tears.
Now, sir, the sound that tells what hour it is
Are clamorous groans which strike upon my heart,
Which is the bell—so sighs, and tears, and groans,
Show minutes, times, and hours: but my time
Runs posting on in Bolingbroke's proud joy,
While I stand fooling here, his Jack of the clock.... 60
This music mads me, let it sound no more,
For though it have holp madmen to their wits,
In me it seems it will make wise men mad:
Yet blessing on his heart that gives it me!
For 'tis a sign of love; and love to Richard
Is a strange brooch in this all-hating world.

Enter a Groom of the stable

GROOM. Hail, royal prince!
RICHARD.   Thanks, noble peer;
   The cheapest of us is ten groats too dear.
   What art thou? and how comest thou hither,
   Where no man ever comes, but that sad dog   70
   That brings me food to make misfortune live?
GROOM. I was a poor groom of thy stable, king,
   When thou wert king; who, travelling towards
      York,
   With much ado at length have gotten leave
   To look upon my sometimes royal master's face:
   O, how it erned my heart when I beheld,
   In London streets that coronation day,
   When Bolingbroke rode on roan Barbary!
   That horse that thou so often hast bestrid,
   That horse that I so carefully have dressed!   80
RICHARD. Rode he on Barbary? tell me, gentle friend,
   How went he under him?
GROOM. So proudly as if he disdained the ground.
RICHARD. So proud that Bolingbroke was on his
      back ...
   That jade hath eat bread from my royal hand,
   This hand hath made him proud with clapping him:
   Would he not stumble? would he not fall down,
   Since pride must have a fall, and break the neck
   Of that proud man that did usurp his back?
   Forgiveness, horse! why do I rail on thee,   90
   Since thou, created to be awed by man,
   Wast born to bear? I was not made a horse,
   And yet I bear a burthen like an ass,
   Spurred, galled, and tired by jauncing Bolingbroke.

Enter one to Richard with meat

KEEPER. Fellow, give place, here is no longer stay.
RICHARD. If thou love me' tis time thou wert away.
GROOM. What my tongue dares not, that my heart
   shall say.   *He goes*
KEEPER. My lord, will't please you to fall to?

RICHARD. Taste of it first, as thou art wont to do.
KEEPER. My lord, I dare not, Sir Pierce of Exton, who 100
   lately came from the king, commands the contrary.
RICHARD. The devil take Henry of Lancaster and thee!
   Patience is stale, and I am weary of it..
                                   He beats the Keeper
KEEPER. Help, help, help!

Exton and the other murderers rush in

RICHARD. How now! what means death in this
      rude assault?
   Villain, thy own hand yields thy death's
      instrument....
                              He snatches an axe from one
                                        and kills him
   Go thou, and fill another room in hell.
                              He kills another, but here
                                  Exton strikes him down
   That hand shall burn in never-quenching fire
   That staggers thus my person: Exton, thy fierce
      hand
   Hath with the king's blood stained the king's own
      land....   110
   Mount, mount, my soul! thy seat is up on high,
   Whilst my gross flesh sinks downward, here to die.
                                             He dies
EXTON. As full of valour as of royal blood:
   Both have I spilled. O, would the deed were good!
   For now the devil that told me I did well
   Says that this deed is chronicled in hell:
   This dead king to the living king I'll bear....
   Take hence the rest, and give them burial here.
                              They carry out the bodies

Scene 6: *Windsor Castle*

Enter Bolingbroke and the Duke of York

BOLINGBROKE. Kind uncle York, the latest news we
      hear,
   Is that the rebels have consumed with fire
   Our town of Cicester in Gloucestershire,
   But whether they be ta'en or slain we hear not.

Northumberland enters

   Welcome, my lord, what is the news?
NORTHUMBERLAND. First, to thy sacred state wish I
      all happiness.
   The next news is, I have to London sent
   The heads of Salisbury, Spencer, Blunt and Kent.
   The manner of their taking may appear
   At large discoursèd in this paper here.   10
BOLINGBROKE. We thank thee, gentle Percy, for
      thy pains,
   And to thy worth will add right worthy gains.

Fitzwater enters

FITZWATER. My lord, I have from Oxford sent
      to London
   The heads of Brocas and Sir Bennet Seely,
   Two of the dangerous consorted traitors,
   That sought at Oxford thy dire overthrow.
BOLINGBROKE. Thy pains, Fitzwater, shall not be
      forgot,
   Right noble is thy merit, well I wot.

Percy enters, with the Bishop of Carlisle guarded

PERCY. The grand conspirator, Abbot of Westminster,
  With clog of conscience and sour melancholy   20
  Hath yielded up his body to the grave.
  But here is Carlisle living, to abide
  Thy kingly doom and sentence of his pride.
BOLINGBROKE. Carlisle, this is your doom:
  Choose out some secret place, some reverend room,
  More than thou hast, and with it joy thy life;
  So as thou liv'st in peace, die free from strife,
  For though mine enemy thou hast ever been,
  High sparks of honour in thee have I seen.

Enter Exton, with persons bearing a coffin

EXTON. Great king, within this coffin I present   30
  Thy buried fear: herein all breathless lies
  The mightiest of thy greatest enemies,
  Richard of Bordeaux, by me hither brought.
BOLINGBROKE. Exton, I thank thee not, for thou
    hast wrought
  A deed of slander with thy fatal hand

Upon my head and all this famous land.
EXTON. From your own mouth, my lord, did I
  this deed.
BOLINGBROKE. They love not poison that do poison
  need,
  Nor do I thee; though I did wish him dead,
  I hate the murderer, love him murderéd: 40
  The guilt of conscience take thou for thy labour,
  But neither my good word, nor princely favour:
  With Cain go wander through the shades of night,
  And never show thy head by day nor light....
  Lords, I protest, my soul is full of woe,
  That blood should sprinkle me to make me grow:
  Come, mourn with me for what I do lament,
  And put on sullen black incontinent.
  I'll make a voyage to the Holy Land,
  To wash this blood off from my guilty hand: 50
  March sadly after, grace my mournings here,
  In weeping after this untimely bier.

              The coffin is borne slowly out, Bolingbroke
                        and the rest following

The First Part of the History of Henry IV

The scene: England

CHARACTERS IN THE PLAY

KING HENRY *the Fourth*

HENRY, *Prince of Wales*

LORD JOHN *of* LANCASTER } *sons to the king*

EARL *of* WESTMORELAND

SIR WALTER BLUNT

THOMAS PERCY, *Earl of Worcester*

HENRY PERCY, *Earl of Northumberland*

HENRY PERCY, *surnamed* HOTSPUR, *his son*

EDMUND MORTIMER, *Earl of March*

RICHARD SCROOP, *Archbishop of York*

ARCHIBALD, *Earl of Douglas*

OWEN GLENDOWER

SIR RICHARD VERNON

SIR MICHAEL, *of the household of the Archbishop of York*

EDWARD POINS, *gentleman-in-waiting to Prince Henry*

SIR JOHN FALSTAFF

GADSHILL

PETO

BARDOLPH

LADY PERCY, *wife to Hotspur, and sister to Mortimer*

LADY MORTIMER, *daughter to Glendower, and wife to Mortimer*

MISTRESS QUICKLY, *hostess of the Boar's Head tavern, Eastcheap*

Lords, Officers, Sheriff, Vintner, Chamberlain, Drawers, two Carriers, Travellers, and Attendants

The First Part of the History of Henry IV

King Henry with Sir Walter Blunt, meeting
Westmoreland and others

KING. So shaken as we are, so wan with care,
 Find we a time for frighted peace to pant,
 And breathe short-winded accents of new broils
 To be commenced in strands afar remote:
 No more the thirsty entrance of this soil
 Shall daub her lips with her own children's blood,
 No more shall trenching war channel her fields,
 Nor bruise her flowerets with the arméd hoofs
 Of hostile paces: those opposéd eyes,
 Which, like the meteors of a troubled heaven,   10
 All of one nature, of one substance bred,
 Did lately meet in the intestine shock
 And furious close of civil butchery,
 Shall now, in mutual well-beseeming ranks,
 March all one way, and be no more opposed
 Against acquaintance, kindred, and allies....
 The edge of war, like an ill-sheathéd knife,
 No more shall cut his master ... Therefore, friends,
 As far as to the sepulchre of Christ,
 Whose soldier now, under whose blesséd cross   20
 We are impressèd and engaged to fight,
 Forthwith a power of English shall we levy,
 Whose arms were moulded in their mothers' womb
 To chase these pagans in those holy fields
 Over whose acres walked those blessèd feet
 Which fourteen hundred years ago were nailed
 For our advantage on the bitter cross....
 But this our purpose now is twelve month old,
 And bootless 'tis to tell you we will go:
 Therefore we meet not now. Then let me hear   30
 Of you, my gentle cousin Westmoreland,
 What yesternight our council did decree
 In forwarding this dear expedience.
WESTMORELAND. My liege, this haste was hot in
   question,
 And many limits of the charge set down
 But yesternight, when all athwart there came
 A post from Wales, loaden with heavy news,
 Whose worst was that the noble Mortimer,
 Leading the men of Herefordshire to fight
 Against the irregular and wild Glendower,   40
 Was by the rude hands of that Welshman taken,
 A thousand of his people butcheréd,
 Upon whose dead corpse there was such misuse,
 Such beastly shameless transformation,
 By those Welshwomen done, as may not be
 Without much shame retold or spoken of.
KING. It seems then that the tidings of this broil
 Brake off our business for the Holy Land.
WESTMORELAND. This matched with other did, my
   gracious lord,
 For more uneven and unwelcome news   50
 Came from the north, and thus it did import:
 On Holy-rood day the gallant Hotspur there,

Young Harry Percy, and brave Archibald,
 That ever-valiant and approvéd Scot,
 At Holmedon met,
 Where they did spend a sad and bloody hour;
 As by discharge of their artillery,
 And shape of likelihood, the news was told;
 For he that brought them, in the very heat
 And pride of their contention did take horse,   60
 Uncertain of the issue any way.
KING. Here is a dear, a true industrious friend,
 Sir Walter Blunt, new lighted from his horse,
 Stained with the variation of each soil
 Betwixt that Holmedon and this seat of ours;
 And he hath brought us smooth and welcome
   news.
 The Earl of Douglas is discomfited,
 Ten thousand bold Scots, two and twenty knights,
 Balked in their own blood did Sir Walter see
 On Holmedon's plains. Of prisoners, Hotspur took   70
 Mordake Earl of Fife, and eldest son
 To beaten Douglas, and the Earl of Athol,
 Of Murray, Angus, and Menteith ...
 And is not this an honourable spoil?
 A gallant prize? ha, cousin, is it not?
WESTMORELAND. In faith,
 It is a conquest for a prince to boast of.
KING. Yea, there thou mak'st me sad, and mak'st me
   sin
 In envy, that my Lord Northumberland
 Should be the father to so blest a son ...   80
 A son who is the theme of honour's tongue,
 Amongst a grove the very straightest plant,
 Who is sweet Fortune's minion and her pride,
 Whilst I by looking on the praise of him
 See riot and dishonour stain the brow
 Of my young Harry.... O that it could be proved
 That some night-tripping fairy had exchanged
 In cradle-clothes our children where they lay,
 And called mine Percy, his Plantagenet,
 Then would I have his Harry, and he mine: 90
 But let him from my thoughts.... What think you,
   coz,
 Of this young Percy's pride? The prisoners,
 Which he in this adventure hath surprised,
 To his own use he keeps, and sends me word,
 I shall have none but Mordake Earl of Fife.
WESTMORELAND. This is his uncle's teaching, this is
   Worcester,
 Malevolent to you in all aspects,
 Which makes him prune himself, and bristle up
 The crest of youth against your dignity.
KING. But I have sent for him to answer this;   100
 And for this cause awhile we must neglect
 Our holy purpose to Jerusalem....
 Cousin, on Wednesday next our council we
 Will hold at Windsor, so inform the lords:
 But come yourself with speed to us again,
 For more is to be said and to be done
 Than out of anger can be utteréd.
WESTMORELAND. I will, my liege.   *Exeunt*

Scene 2: *London. The house of the Prince of Wales*

Enter Sir John Falstaff and the Prince of Wales

FALSTAFF. Now, Hal, what time of day is it, lad?

PRINCE. Thou art so fat-witted with drinking of old sack, and unbuttoning thee after supper, and sleeping upon benches after noon, that thou hast forgotten to demand that truly which thou wouldest truly know. What a devil hast thou to do with the time of the day? Unless hours were cups of sack, and minutes capons, and clocks the tongues of bawds, and dials the signs of leaping-houses, and the blessed sun himself a fair hot wench in flame-coloured taffeta, I see no reason why thou shouldst be so superfluous to demand the time of the day. 10

FALSTAFF. Indeed, you come near me now, Hal, for we that take purses go by the moon and the seven stars, and not by Phœbus, he, 'that wandering knight so fair'.... And, I prithee, sweet wag, when thou art king, as God save thy grace—majesty I should say, for grace thou wilt have none.

PRINCE. What, none?

FALSTAFF. No, by my troth, not so much as will serve 20 to be prologue to an egg and butter.

PRINCE. Well, how then? come, roundly, roundly.

FALSTAFF. Marry then, sweet wag, when thou art king let not us that are squires of the night's body be called thieves of the day's beauty; let us be Diana's foresters, gentlemen of the shade, minions of the moon, and let men say we be men of good government, being governed as the sea is by our noble and chaste mistress the moon, under whose countenance we steal. 30

PRINCE. Thou sayest well, and it holds well too, for the fortune of us that are the moon's men doth ebb and flow like the sea, being governed as the sea is by the moon—as for proof now, a purse of gold most resolutely snatched on Monday night and most dissolutely spent on Tuesday morning, got with swearing 'lay by' and spent with crying 'bring in'—now in as low an ebb as the foot of the ladder, and by and by in as high a flow as the ridge of the gallows. 40

FALSTAFF. By the Lord, thou sayst true, lad, and is not my hostess of the tavern a most sweet wench?

PRINCE. As the honey of Hybla, my old lad of the castle, and is not a buff jerkin a most sweet robe of durance?

FALSTAFF. How now, how now, mad wag? what, in thy quips and thy quiddities? what a plague have I to do with a buff jerkin?

PRINCE. Why, what a pox have I to do with my hostess of the tavern? 50

FALSTAFF. Well, thou hast called her to a reckoning many a time and oft.

PRINCE. Did I ever call for thee to pay thy part?

FALSTAFF. No, I'll give thee thy due, thou hast paid all there.

PRINCE. Yea, and elsewhere, so far as my coin would stretch, and where it would not, I have used my credit.

FALSTAFF. Yea, and so used it that, were it not here apparent that thou art heir apparent—But, I prithee, 60 sweet wag, shall there be gallows standing in England when thou art king? and resolution thus fubbed as it is with the rusty curb of old father

Antic the law? Do not thou, when thou art king, hang a thief.

PRINCE. No, thou shalt.

FALSTAFF. Shall I? O rare! By the Lord, I'll be a brave judge!

PRINCE. Thou judgest false already. I mean, thou shalt have the hanging of the thieves and so become a 70 rare hangman.

FALSTAFF. Well, Hal, well—and in some sort it jumps with my humour, as well as waiting in the court, I can tell you.

PRINCE. For obtaining of suits?

FALSTAFF. Yea, for obtaining of suits, whereof the hangman hath no lean wardrobe.... 'Sblood, I am as melancholy as a gib cat or a lugged bear.

PRINCE. Or an old lion, or a lover's lute.

FALSTAFF. Yea, or the drone of a Lincolnshire bagpipe. 80

PRINCE. What sayest thou to a hare, or the melancholy of Moor-ditch?

FALSTAFF. Thou hast the most unsavoury similes and art indeed the most comparative, rascalliest, sweet young prince.... But, Hal, I prithee, trouble me no more with vanity. I would to God thou and I knew where a commodity of good names were to be bought: an old lord of the council rated me the other day in the street about you, sir, but I marked him not, and yet he talked very wisely, but I regarded 90 him not, and yet he talked wisely and in the street too.

PRINCE. Thou didst well, for wisdom cries out in the streets, and no man regards it.

FALSTAFF. O, thou hast damnable iteration, and art indeed able to corrupt a saint: thou hast done much harm upon me, Hal—God forgive thee for it: before I knew thee, Hal, I knew nothing, and now am I, if a man should speak truly, little better than one of the wicked ... I must give over this life, and I will 100 give it over: by the Lord, an I do not, I am a villain. I'll be damned for never a king's son in Christendom.

PRINCE. Where shall we take a purse to-morrow, Jack?

FALSTAFF. 'Zounds, where thou wilt, lad, I'll make one, an I do not, call me villain and baffle me.

PRINCE. I see a good amendment of life in thee, from praying to purse-taking.

FALSTAFF. Why, Hal, 'tis my vocation, Hal, 'tis no sin for a man to labour in his vocation. 110

Poins enters

Poins! Now shall we know if Gadshill have set a match. [*points*] O, if men were to be saved by merit, what hole in hell were hot enough for him? This is the most omnipotent villain that ever cried 'Stand' to a true man.

PRINCE. Good morrow, Ned.

POINS. Good morrow, sweet Hal. What says Monsieur. Remorse? What says Sir John Sack and Sugar? Jack, how agrees the devil and thee about thy soul, that thou soldest him on Good Friday last, for a cup 120 of Madeira and a cold capon's leg?

PRINCE. Sir John stands to his word, the devil shall have his bargain, for he was never yet a breaker of proverbs: he will give the devil his due.

POINTS. Then art thou damned for keeping thy word with the devil.

PRINCE. Else he had been damned for cozening the devil.

POINS. But, my lads, my lads, to-morrow morning, by four o'clock, early at Gad's Hill, there are pilgrims 130 going to Canterbury with rich offerings, and traders riding to London with fat purses.... I have vizards for you all, you have horses for yourselves, Gadshill lies to-night in Rochester, I have bespoke supper to-morrow night in Eastcheap: we may do it as secure as sleep. If you will go, I will stuff your purses full of crowns; if you will not, tarry at home and be hanged.

FALSTAFF. Hear ye, Yedward, if I tarry at home and go not, I'll hang you for going. 140

POINS. You will, chops?

FALSTAFF. Hal, wilt thou make one?

PRINCE. Who, I? rob? I a thief? not I, by my faith.

FALSTAFF. There's neither honesty, manhood, nor good fellowship in thee, nor thou cam'st not of the blood royal, if thou darest not stand for ten shillings.

PRINCE. Well then, once in my days I'll be a madcap.

FALSTAFF. Why, that's well said.

PRINCE. Well, come what will, I'll tarry at home.

FALSTAFF. By the Lord, I'll be a traitor then, when thou 150 art king.

PRINCE. I care not.

POINS. Sir John, I prithee, leave the prince and me alone, I will lay him down such reasons for this adventure that he shall go.

FALSTAFF. Well, God give thee the spirit of persuasion, and him the ears of profiting, that what thou speakest may move, and what he hears may be believed, that the true prince may (for recreation sake) prove a false thief, for the poor abuses of the time want 160 countenance ... Farewell, you shall find me in Eastcheap.

PRINCE. Farewell, the latter spring! Farewell, All-hallown summer! *Falstaff goes*

POINS. Now, my good sweet honey lord, ride with us to-morrow. I have a jest to execute that I cannot manage alone. Falstaff, Bardolph, Peto and Gadshill shall rob those men that we have already waylaid— yourself and I will not be there: and when they have the booty, if you and I do not rob them, cut this 170 head off from my shoulders.

PRINCE. How shall we part with them in setting forth?

POINS. Why, we will set forth before or after them, and appoint them a place of meeting, wherein it is at our pleasure to fail; and then will they adventure upon the exploit themselves, which they shall have no sooner achieved but we'll set upon them.

PRINCE. Yea, but 'tis like that they will know us by our horses, by our habits, and by every other appointment, to be ourselves. 180

POINS. Tut! our horses they shall not see, I'll tie them in the wood; our vizards we will change after we leave them; and, sirrah, I have cases of buckram for the nonce, to immask our noted outward garments.

PRINCE. Yea, but I doubt they will be too hard for us.

POINS. Well, for two of them, I know them to be as true-bred cowards as ever turned back; and for the third, if he fight longer than he sees reason, I'll forswear arms. The virtue of this jest will be the incomprehensible lies that this same fat rogue will 190 tell us when we meet at supper, how thirty at least he fought with, what wards, what blows, what

extremities he endured, and in the reproof of this lives the jest.

PRINCE. Well, I'll go with thee. Provide us all things necessary, and meet me to-morrow night in East-cheap, there I'll sup ... Farewell.

POINS. Farewell, my lord. *Poins goes*

PRINCE. I know you all, and will awhile uphold
The unyoked humour of your idleness. 200
Yet herein will I imitate the sun,
Who doth permit the base contagious clouds
To smother up his beauty from the world,
That when he please again to be himself,
Being wanted he may be more wond'red at,
By breaking through the foul and ugly mists
Of vapours that did seem to strangle him.
If all the year were playing holidays,
To sport would be as tedious as to work;
But when they seldom come, they wished for come, 210
And nothing pleaseth but rare accidents:
So, when this loose behaviour I throw off,
And pay the debt I never promisèd,
By how much better than my word I am,
By so much shall I falsify men's hopes,
And like bright metal on a sullen ground,
My reformation, glitt'ring o'er my fault,
Shall show more goodly, and attract more eyes,
Than that which hath no foil to set it off.
I'll so offend, to make offence a skill, 220
Redeeming time when men think least I will.
He goes

Scene 3: *Windsor. The Council Chamber*

Enter the King, Northumberland, Worcester, Hotspur, Sir Walter Blunt, with others

KING. My blood hath been too cold and temperate,
Unapt to stir at these indignities,
And you have found me—for accordingly
You tread upon my patience. But be sure
I will from henceforth rather be myself,
Mighty and to be feared, than my condition,
Which hath been smooth as oil, soft as young down,
And therefore lost that title of respect
Which the proud soul ne'er pays but to the proud.

WORCESTER. Our house, my sovereign liege, little deserves 10
The scourge of greatness to be used on it,
And that same greatness too which our own hands
Have holp to make so portly.

NORTHUMBERLAND. My lord,—

KING. Worcester, get thee gone, for I do see
Danger and disobedience in thine eye:
O, sir, your presence is too bold and peremptory,
And majesty might never yet endure
The moody frontier of a servant brow.
You have good leave to leave us. When we need 20
Your use and counsel, we shall send for you....
Worcester goes
You were about to speak.

NORTHUMBERLAND. Yea, my good lord.
Those prisoners in your highness' name demanded,
Which Harry Percy here at Holmedon took,
Were, as he says, not with such strength denied
As is delivered to your majesty.
Either envy, therefore, or misprision
Is guilty of this fault, and not my son.

HOTSPUR. My liege, I did deny no prisoners,   30
  But I remember, when the fight was done,
  When I was dry with rage and extreme toil,
  Breathless and faint, leaning upon my sword,
  Came there a certain lord, neat and trimly dressed,
  Fresh as a bridegroom, and his chin new reaped
  Showed like a stubble-land at harvest-home.
  He was perfuméd like a milliner,
  And 'twixt his finger and his thumb he held
  A pouncet-box, which ever and anon
  He gave his nose and took't away again—   40
  Who therewith angry, when it next came there,
  Took it in snuff—and still he smiled and talked:
  And as the soldiers bore dead bodies by,
  He called them untaught knaves, unmannerly,
  To bring a slovenly unhandsome corse
  Betwixt the wind and his nobility:
  With many holiday and lady terms
  He questioned me, amongst the rest demanded
  My prisoners in your majesty's behalf.
  I then, all smarting with my wounds being cold,   50
  To be so pest'red with a popinjay,
  Out of my grief and my impatience,
  Answered neglectingly I know not what,
  He should, or he should not, for he made me mad
  To see him shine so brisk, and smell so sweet,
  And talk so like a waiting-gentlewoman
  Of guns, and drums, and wounds, God save the
    mark!
  And telling me the sovereignest thing on earth
  Was parmaceti for an inward bruise,
  And that it was great pity, so it was,   60
  This villainous salt-petre should be digged
  Out of the bowels of the harmless earth,
  Which many a good tall fellow had destroyed
  So cowardly, and but for these vile guns
  He would himself have been a soldier. . . .
  This bald unjointed chat of his, my lord,
  I answered indirectly, as I said,
  And I beseech you, let not his report
  Come current for an accusation
  Betwixt my love and your high majesty.   70
BLUNT. The circumstance considered, good my lord,
  Whate'er Lord Harry Percy then had said
  To such a person, and in such a place,
  At such a time, with all the rest retold,
  May reasonably die, and never rise
  To do him wrong, or any way impeach
  What then he said, so he unsay it now.
KING. Why, yet he doth deny his prisoners,
  But with proviso and exception,
  That we at our own charge shall ransom straight   80
  His brother-in-law, the foolish Mortimer,
  Who, on my soul, hath wilfully betrayed
  The lives of those that he did lead to fight
  Against the great magician, damned Glendower,
  Whose daughter, as we hear, that Earl of March
  Hath lately married . . . Shall our coffers then
  Be emptied to redeem a traitor home?
  Shall we buy treason? and indent with fears,
  When they have lost and forfeited themselves?
  No, on the barren mountains let him starve;   90
  For I shall never hold that man my friend,
  Whose tongue shall ask me for one penny cost
  To ransom home revolted Mortimer.
HOTSPUR. Revolted Mortimer!

He never did fall off, my sovereign liege,
  But by the chance of war. To prove that true
  Needs no more but one tongue for all those
    wounds,
  Those mouthéd wounds, which valiantly he took,
  When on the gentle Severn's sedgy bank,
  In single opposition, hand to hand,   100
  He did confound the best part of an hour
  In changing hardiment with great Glendower.
  Three times they breathed and three times did they
    drink,
  Upon agreement, of swift Severn's flood,
  Who then affrighted with their bloody looks,
  Ran fearfully among the trembling reeds,
  And hid his crisp head in the hollow bank
  Bloodstainéd with these valiant combatants.
  Never did bare and rotten policy
  Colour her working with such deadly wounds,   110
  Nor never could the noble Mortimer
  Receive so many, and all willingly.
  Then let him not be slandered with revolt.
KING. Thou dost belie him, Percy, thou dost belie him.
  He never did encounter with Glendower:
  I tell thee,
  He durst as well have met the devil alone,
  As Owen Glendower for an enemy.
  Art thou not ashamed? But, sirrah, henceforth
  Let me not hear you speak of Mortimer: 120
  Send me your prisoners with the speediest means,
  Or you shall hear in such a kind from me
  As will displease you. . . . My Lord
    Northumberland,
  We license your departure with your son.
  Send us your prisoners, or you'll hear of it.
        King Henry, Blunt and other nobles leave
HOTSPUR. And if the devil come and roar for them,
  I will not send them: I will after straight
  And tell him so, for I will ease my heart,
  Albeit I make a hazard of my head.
NORTHUMBERLAND. What, drunk with choler? stay
    and pause awhile,   130
  Here comes your uncle.

Worcester returns

HOTSPUR.   Speak of Mortimer!
  'Zounds, I will speak of him, and let my soul
  Want mercy if I do not join with him:
  Yea, on his part, I'll empty all these veins,
  And shed my dear blood drop by drop in the dust,
  But I will lift the down-trod Mortimer
  As high in the air as this unthankful king,
  As this ingrate and cank'red Bolingbroke.
NORTHUMBERLAND. Brother, the king hath made your
    nephew mad.
WORCESTER. Who struck this heat up after I was gone?   140
HOTSPUR. He will forsooth have all my prisoners,
  And when I urged the ransom once again
  Of my wife's brother, then his cheek looked pale,
  And on my face he turned an eye of death,
  Trembling even at the name of Mortimer.
WORCESTER. I cannot blame him, was not he
    proclaimed,
  By Richard that dead is, the next of blood?
NORTHUMBERLAND. He was, I heard the proclamation:
  And then it was when the unhappy king
  (Whose wrongs in us God pardon!) did set forth   150

Upon his Irish expedition;
From whence he intercepted did return
To be deposed and shortly murderéd.
WORCESTER. And for whose death we in the world's
　　wide mouth
Live scandalized and foully spoken of.
HOTSPUR. But soft, I pray you, did King Richard then
Proclaim my brother Edmund Mortimer
Heir to the crown?
NORTHUMBERLAND. 　　　 He did, myself did hear it.
HOTSPUR. Nay, then I cannot blame his cousin king,
That wished him on the barren mountains starve. 160
But shall it be that you, that set the crown
Upon the head of this forgetful man,
And for his sake wear the detested blot
Of murderous subornation, shall it be
That you a world of curses undergo,
Being the agents, or base second means,
The cords, the ladder, or the hangman rather?—
O, pardon me that I descend so low,
To show the line, and the predicament,
Wherein you range under this subtle king!— 170
Shall it for shame be spoken in these days,
Or fill up chronicles in time to come,
That men of your nobility and power
Did gage them both in an unjust behalf
(As both of you, God pardon it! have done)
To put down Richard, that sweet lovely rose,
And plant this thorn, this canker, Bolingbroke?
And shall it in more shame be further spoken,
That you are fooled, discarded, and shook off
By him for whom these shames ye underwent? 180
No, yet time serves wherein you may redeem
Your banished honours, and restore yourselves
Into the good thoughts of the world again:
Revenge the jeering and disdained contempt
Of this proud king, who studies day and night
To answer all the debt he owes to you,
Even with the bloody payment of your deaths:
Therefore, I say—
WORCESTER. 　　　 Peace, cousin, say no more.
And now I will unclasp a secret book,
And to your quick-conceiving discontents
I'll read you matter deep and dangerous, 190
As full of peril and adventurous spirit
As to o'er-walk a current roaring loud
On the unsteadfast footing of a spear.
HOTSPUR. If he fall in, good night! or sink or swim.
Send danger from the east unto the west,
So honour cross it from the north to south,
And let them grapple: O, the blood more stirs
To rouse a lion than to start a hare!
NORTHUMBERLAND. Imagination of some great exploit 200
Drives him beyond the bounds of patience.
HOTSPUR. By heaven, methinks it were an easy leap,
To pluck bright honour from the pale-faced moon,
Or dive into the bottom of the deep,
Where fathom-line could never touch the ground,
And pluck up drownéd honour by the locks,
So he that doth redeem her thence might wear
Without corrival all her dignities:
But out upon this half-faced fellowship!
WORCESTER. He apprehends a world of figures here, 210
But not the form of what he should attend.
Good cousin, give me audience for a while.
HOTSPUR. I cry you mercy.

WORCESTER. 　　　　　 Those same noble Scots
That are your prisoners,—
HOTSPUR. 　　　　　 I'll keep them all;
By God, he shall not have a Scot of them.
No, if a Scot would save his soul, he shall not.
I'll keep them, by this hand.
WORCESTER. 　　　　　 You start away,
And lend no ear unto my purposes . . .
Those prisoners you shall keep.
HOTSPUR. 　　　　 Nay, I will: that's flat:
He said he would not ransom Mortimer, 220
Forbad my tongue to speak of Mortimer,
But I will find him when he lies asleep,
And in his ear I'll holla 'Mortimer!'
Nay,
I'll have a starling shall be taught to speak
Nothing but 'Mortimer', and give it him
To keep his anger still in motion.
WORCESTER. Hear you, cousin, a word.
HOTSPUR. All studies here I solemnly defy,
Save how to gall and pinch this Bolingbroke. 230
And that same sword-and-buckler Prince of Wales,
But that I think his father loves him not
And would be glad he met with some mischance,
I would have him poisoned with a pot of ale.
WORCESTER. Farewell, kinsman! I'll talk to you
When you are better tempered to attend.
NORTHUMBERLAND. Why, what a wasp-stung and
　　impatient fool
Art thou, to break into this woman's mood,
Tying thine ear to no tongue but thine own!
HOTSPUR. Why, look you, I am whipped and
　　scourged with rods, 240
Nettled, and stung with pismires, when I hear
Of this vile politician, Bolingbroke.
In Richard's time—what de'ye call the place?—
A plague upon't, it is in Gloucestershire;
'Twas where the madcap duke his uncle kept,
His uncle York—where I first bowed my knee
Unto this king of smiles, this Bolingbroke—
'Sblood! When you and he came back from
　　Ravenspurgh—
NORTHUMBERLAND. At Berkeley castle.
HOTSPUR. You say true. 250
Why, what a candy deal of courtesy
This fawning greyhound then did proffer me!
'Look when his infant fortune came to age',
And, 'gentle Harry Percy', and 'kind cousin':
O, the devil take such cozeners! God forgive me!
Good uncle, tell your tale—I have done.
WORCESTER. Nay, if you have not, to it again,
We will stay your leisure.
HOTSPUR. 　　　　　 I have done, i'faith.
WORCESTER. Then once more to your Scottish
　　prisoners.
Deliver them up without their ransom straight, 260
And make the Douglas' son your only mean
For powers in Scotland, which, for divers reasons
Which I shall send you written, be assured
Will easily be granted. You, my lord,
　　　　　　　　　　　　 To Northumberland
Your son in Scotland being thus employed,
Shall secretly into the bosom creep
Of that same noble prelate, well beloved,
The archbishop.
HOTSPUR. 　　　　 Of York, is't not?

WORCESTER.   True; who bears hard
His brother's death at Bristow, the Lord Scroop.
I speak not this in estimation,
As what I think might be, but what I know
Is ruminated, plotted, and set down,
And only stays but to behold the face
Of that occasion that shall bring it on.
HOTSPUR. I smell it. Upon my life, it will do well.
NORTHUMBERLAND. Before the game's afoot thou still
    let'st slip.
HOTSPUR. Why, it cannot choose but be a noble plot.
And then the power of Scotland and of York,
To join with Mortimer, ha?
WORCESTER.   And so they shall.
HOTSPUR. In faith, it is exceedingly well aimed.   280
WORCESTER. And 'tis no little reason bids us speed,
To save our heads by raising of a head,
For, bear ourselves as even as we can,
The king will always think him in our debt,
And think we think ourselves unsatisfied,
Till he hath found a time to pay us home.
And see already how he doth begin
To make us strangers to his looks of love.
HOTSPUR. He does, he does, we'll be revenged on him.
WORCESTER. Cousin, farewell. No further go in this   290
Than I by letters shall direct your course.
When time is ripe, which will be suddenly,
I'll steal to Glendower and Lord Mortimer,
Where you and Douglas and our powers at once,
As I will fashion it, shall happily meet,
To bear our fortunes in our own strong arms,
Which now we hold at much uncertainty.
NORTHUMBERLAND. Farewell, good brother, we shall
    thrive, I trust.
HOTSPUR. Uncle, adieu: O, let the hours be short,
Till fields, and blows, and groans applaud our
    sport!   *They go*   300

ACT 2

Scene 1: *An inn yard at Rochester*

Enter a Carrier with a lantern in his hand

1 CARRIER. Heigh-ho! An't be not four by the day, I'll
be hanged. Charles' wain is over the new chimney,
and yet our horse not packed. What, ostler!
OSTLER [*within*]. Anon, anon.
1 CARRIER. I prithee, Tom, beat Cut's saddle, put a
few flocks in the point, poor jade is wrung in the
withers, out of all cess.

Enter another Carrier

2 CARRIER. Peas and beans are as dank here as a dog,
and that is the next way to give poor jades the bots:
this house is turned upside down since Robin Ostler   10
died.
1 CARRIER. Poor fellow never joyed since the price of
oats rose, it was the death of him.
2 CARRIER. I think this be the most villanous house in
all London road for fleas, I am stung like a tench.
1 CARRIER. Like a tench! by the mass, there is ne'er a
king christen could be better bit than I have been
since the first cock.
2 CARRIER. Why, they will allow us ne'er a jordan, and
then we leak in your chimney, and your chamber-   20
lye breeds fleas like a loach.

1 CARRIER. What, ostler! come away, and be hanged,
come away.
2 CARRIER. I have a gammon of bacon, and two razes   270
of ginger, to be delivered as far as Charing-cross.
1 CARRIER. God's body! the turkeys in my pannier are
quite starved.... What, ostler! a plague on thee! hast
thou never an eye in thy head? canst not hear? An
'twere not as good deed as drink, to break the pate
on thee, I am a very villain. Come, and be hanged!   30
hast no faith in thee?

Enter Gadshill

GADSHILL. Good morrow, carriers, what's o'clock?
1 CARRIER. I think it be two o'clock.
GADSHILL. I prithee, lend me thy lantern to see my
gelding in the stable.
1 CARRIER. Nay, by God, soft, I know a trick worth
two of that, ay, faith!
GADSHILL. I pray thee, lend me thine.
2 CARRIER. Ay, when? canst tell? Lend me thy lantern,
quoth-a? marry, I'll see thee hanged first.   40
GADSHILL. Sirrah carrier, what time do you mean to
come to London?
2 CARRIER. Time enough to go to bed with a candle,
I warrant thee. Come, neighbour Mugs, we'll call
up the gentlemen. They will along with company,
for they have great charge.   *The carriers go*
GADSHILL. What, ho! chamberlain!
VOICE FROM WITHIN. At hand, quoth pick-purse.
GADSHILL. That's even as fair as—at hand, quoth the
chamberlain: for thou variest no more from picking   50
of purses than giving direction doth from labouring;
thou layest the plot how.

A Chamberlain comes from the inn

CHAMBERLAIN. Good morrow, Master Gadshill. It
holds current that I told you yesternight. There's a
franklin in the wild of Kent, hath brought three
hundred marks with him in gold, I heard him tell it
to one of his company last night at supper, a kind
of auditor, one that hath abundance of charge too,
God knows what. They are up already, and call for
eggs and butter. They will away presently.   60
GADSHILL. Sirrah, if they meet not with Saint Nicholas' clerks, I'll give thee this neck.
CHAMBERLAIN. No, I'll none of it. I pray thee, keep that
for the hangman, for I know thou worshippest Saint
Nicholas, as truly as a man of falsehood may.
GADSHILL. What talkest thou to me of the hangman? if
I hang, I'll make a fat pair of gallows: for, if I hang,
old Sir John hangs with me, and thou knowest he's
no starveling. Tut! there are other Trojans that thou
dream'st not of, the which for sport sake are content   70
to do the profession some grace, that would, if
matters should be looked into, for their own credit
sake make all whole. I am joined with no foot-land-
rakers, no long-staff sixpenny strikers, none of these
mad mustachio purple-hued malt-worms, but with
nobility and tranquillity, burgomasters and great
onyers, such as can hold in, such as will strike sooner
than speak, and speak sooner than drink, and drink
sooner than pray. And yet, 'zounds, I lie, for they
pray continually to their saint, the commonwealth,   80
or rather not pray to her, but prey on her, for they
ride up and down on her, and make her their boots.

CHAMBERLAIN. What, the commonwealth their boots? will she hold out water in foul way?

GADSHILL. She will, she will—Justice hath liquored her: we steal as in a castle, cock-sure: we have the receipt of fern-seed, we walk invisible.

CHAMBERLAIN. Nay, by my faith, I think you are more beholding to the night than to fern-seed for your walking invisible. 90

GADSHILL. Give me thy hand, thou shalt have a share in our purchase, as I am a true man.

CHAMBERLAIN. Nay, rather let me have it, as you are a false thief.

GADSHILL. Go to, 'homo' is a common name to all men: bid the ostler bring my gelding out of the stable. Farewell, you muddy knave.   *They go*

Scene 2: A lane near Gad's Hill, some two miles from Rochester

Enter the Prince, Peto and Bardolph; Poins hurrying after

POINS. Come, shelter, shelter! I have removed Falstaff's horse, and he frets like a gummed velvet.

PRINCE. Stand close.   *Poins hides behind a bush*

Falstaff enters

FALSTAFF. Poins! Poins, and be hanged! Poins!

PRINCE. Peace, ye fat-kidneyed rascal! what a brawling dost thou keep!

FALSTAFF. Where's Poins, Hal?

PRINCE. He is walked up to the top of the hill, I'll go seek him.   *He joins Poins*

FALSTAFF. I am accursed to rob in that thief's company. 10 The rascal hath removed my horse, and tied him I know not where. If I travel but four foot by the squier further afoot, I shall break my wind. . . . Well, I doubt not but to die a fair death for all this, if I 'scape hanging for killing that rogue. I have forsworn his company hourly any time this two and twenty years, and yet I am bewitched with the rogue's company. If the rascal have not given me medicines to make me love him, I'll be hanged. It could not be else—I have drunk medicines. Poins! 20 Hal! a plague upon you both! Bardolph! Peto! I'll starve ere I'll rob a foot further. An 'twere not as good a deed as drink, to turn true man and to leave these rogues, I am the veriest varlet that ever chewed with a tooth . . . Eight yards of uneven ground is threescore and ten miles afoot with me, and the stony-hearted villains know it well enough. A plague upon't, when thieves cannot be true one to another! *[they whistle]* Whew! A plague upon you all! Give me my horse, you rogues, give me my 30 horse and be hanged.

PRINCE *[coming forward]*. Peace, ye fat-guts! lie down, lay thine ear close to the ground and list if thou canst hear the tread of travellers.

FALSTAFF. Have you any levers to lift me up again, being down? 'Sblood, I'll not bear mine own flesh so far afoot again for all the coin in thy father's exchequer. What a plague mean ye to colt me thus?

PRINCE. Thou liest, thou art not colted, thou art uncolted. 40

FALSTAFF. I prithee, good Prince Hal, help me to my horse, good king's son.

PRINCE. Out, ye rogue! shall I be your ostler?

FALSTAFF. Go hang thyself in thine own heir-apparent

garters! If I be ta'en, I'll peach for this . . . An I have not ballads made on you all and sung to filthy tunes, let a cup of sack be my poison—when a jest is so forward, and afoot too! I hate it.

Gadshill approaches

GADSHILL. Stand!

FALSTAFF. So I do, against my will. 50

Poins, Bardolph, and Peto come forward

POINS. O, 'tis our setter. I know his voice.

BARDOLPH. What news?

GADSHILL. Case ye, case ye, on with your vizards, there's money of the king's coming down the hill, 'tis going to the king's exchequer.

FALSTAFF. You lie, ye rogue, 'tis going to the king's tavern.

GADSHILL. There's enough to make us all.

FALSTAFF. —To be hanged.

PRINCE. Sirs, you four shall front them in the narrow 60 lane: Ned Poins and I will walk lower. If they 'scape from your encounter, then they light on us.

PETO. How many be there of them?

GADSHILL. Some eight, or ten.

FALSTAFF. 'Zounds, will they not rob us?

PRINCE. What, a coward, Sir John Paunch?

FALSTAFF. Indeed, I am not John of Gaunt, your grandfather, but yet no coward, Hal.

PRINCE. Well, we leave that to the proof.

POINS. Sirrah Jack, thy horse stands behind the hedge, 70 when thou need'st him, there thou shalt find him . . . Farewell, and stand fast.

FALSTAFF. Now cannot I strike him, if I should be hanged.

PRINCE. Ned, where are our disguises?

POINS. Here, hard by, stand close.
    The Prince and Poins go

FALSTAFF. Now, my masters, happy man be his dole! say I; every man to his business.

The Travellers enter

1 TRAVELLER. Come, neighbour, the boy shall lead our horses down the hill, we'll walk afoot awhile and 80 ease our legs.

THIEVES. Stand!

TRAVELLERS. Jesus bless us!

FALSTAFF. Strike, down with them, cut the villains' throats! Ah, whoreson caterpillars! bacon-fed knaves! they hate us youth. Down with them, fleece them.

1 TRAVELLER. O, we are undone, both we and ours for ever.

FALSTAFF. Hang ye, gorbellied knaves, are ye undone? 90 No, ye fat chuffs. I would your store were here! On, bacons, on! What, ye knaves? young men must live. You are grandjurors, are ye? We'll jure ye, faith.
    Here they rob them and bind them and
            then drive them down the hill

The Prince and Poins return, disguised in buckram

PRINCE. The thieves have bound the true men. Now could thou and I rob the thieves, and go merrily to London, it would be argument for a week, laughter for a month, and a good jest for ever.

POINS. Stand close, I hear them coming.

The Thieves return

FALSTAFF. Come, my masters, let us share, and then to
horse before day. An the Prince and Poins be not 100
two arrant cowards, there's no equity stirring.
There's no more valour in that Poins than in a
wild-duck.

As they are sharing, the Prince and
Poins set upon them

PRINCE. Your money!
POINS. Villains!

They all run away, leaving the booty behind them,
and Falstaff, after a blow or two, runs away too

PRINCE. Got with much ease. Now merrily to horse:
the thieves are all scattered, and possessed with fear
so strongly that they dare not meet each other. Each
takes his fellow for an officer. Away, good Ned.
Falstaff sweats to death, and lards the lean earth as 110
he walks along. Were't not for laughing, I should
pity him.
POINS. How the fat rogue roared!   *They go*

Scene 3: *Warkworth Castle*

Enter Hotspur, solus, reading a letter

HOTSPUR. 'But, for mine own part, my lord, I could
be well contented to be there, in respect of the love
I bear your house.'
He could be contented: why is he not then? In
respect of the love he bears our house: he shows in
this, he loves his own barn better than he loves our
house. Let me see some more.
'The purpose you undertake is dangerous.'
Why, that's certain. 'Tis dangerous to take a cold, to
sleep, to drink, but I tell you, my lord fool, out of 10
this nettle, danger, we pluck this flower, safety.
'The purpose you undertake is dangerous, the
friends you have named uncertain, the time itself
unsorted, and your whole plot too light for the
counterpoise of so great an opposition.'
Say you so, say you so? I say unto you again, you
are a shallow cowardly hind, and you lie ... What
a lack-brain is this! By the Lord, our plot is a good
plot as ever was laid, our friends true and constant: a
good plot, good friends, and full of expectation: an 20
excellent plot, very good friends ... What a frosty-
spirited rogue is this! Why, my lord of York commends the plot and the general course of the action.
'Zounds, an I were now by this rascal, I could brain
him with his lady's fan. Is there not my father, my
uncle, and myself? Lord Edmund Mortimer, my
lord of York, and Owen Glendower? is there not
besides the Douglas? have I not all their letters to
meet me in arms by the ninth of the next month?
and are they not some of them set forward already? 30
What a pagan rascal is this! an infidel! Ha! you shall
see now, in very sincerity of fear and cold heart, will
he to the king, and lay open all our proceedings! O,
I could divide myself and go to buffets, for moving
such a dish of skim milk with so honourable an
action! Hang him! let him tell the king, we are prepared: I will set forward to-night.

Enter his Lady

How now, Kate? I must leave you within these two
hours.
LADY PERCY. O my good lord, why are you thus
alone?   40

For what offence have I this fortnight been
A banished woman from my Harry's bed?
Tell me, sweet lord, what is't that takes from thee
Thy stomach, pleasure, and thy golden sleep?
Why dost thou bend thine eyes upon the earth,
And start so often when thou sit'st alone?
Why hast thou lost the fresh blood in thy cheeks,
And given my treasures and my rights of thee
To thick-eyed musing and curst melancholy?
In thy faint slumbers I by thee have watched,   50
And heard thee murmur tales of iron wars,
Speak terms of manage to thy bounding steed,
Cry 'Courage! to the field!' And thou hast talked
Of sallies and retires, of trenches, tents,
Of palisadoes, frontiers, parapets,
Of basilisks, of cannon, culverin,
Of prisoners' ransom, and of soldiers slain,
And all the currents of a heady fight.
Thy spirit within thee hath been so at war,
And thus hath so bestirred thee in thy sleep,   60
That beads of sweat have stood upon thy brow,
Like bubbles in a late-disturbéd stream,
And in thy face strange motions have appeared,
Such as we see when men restrain their breath
On some great sudden hest. O, what portents are
    these?
Some heavy business hath my lord in hand,
And I must know it, else he loves me not.
HOTSPUR. What, ho!

A servant enters

            Is Gilliams with the packet gone?
SERVANT. He is, my lord, an hour ago.
HOTSPUR Hath Butler brought those horses from the
    sheriff?   70
SERVANT. One horse, my lord, he brought even now.
HOTSPUR. What horse? a roan, a crop-ear, is it not?
SERVANT. It is, my lord.
HOTSPUR [*rapt*].   That roan shall be my throne.
Well, I will back him straight: O esperance!
Bid Butler lead him forth into the park.
                                    The servant goes
LADY PERCY. But hear you, my lord.
HOTSPUR. What say'st thou, my lady?
LADY PERCY. What is it carries you away?
HOTSPUR. Why, my horse, my love, my horse.
LADY PERCY. Out, you mad-headed ape!   80
A weasel hath not such a deal of spleen
As you are tossed with. In faith,
I'll know your business, Harry, that I will.
I fear my brother Mortimer doth stir
About his title, and hath sent for you
To line his enterprize. But if you go—
HOTSPUR. So far afoot, I shall be weary, love.
LADY PERCY. Come, come, you paraquito, answer me
Directly unto this question that I ask.
In faith, I'll break thy little finger, Harry,   90
An if thou wilt not tell me all things true.
HOTSPUR. Away,
Away, you trifler! Love! I love thee not,
I care not for thee, Kate. This is no world
To play with mammets and to tilt with lips.
We must have bloody noses and cracked crowns,
And pass them current too.... God's me, my
    horse!

What say'st thou, Kate? what wouldst thou have with me?

LADY PERCY. Do you not love me? do you not, indeed?
Well, do not then, for since you love me not 100
I will not love myself. Do you not love me?
Nay, tell me if you speak in jest or no.

HOTSPUR. Come, wilt thou see me ride?
And when I am a-horseback, I will swear
I love thee infinitely. But hark you, Kate,
I must not have you henceforth question me
Whither I go, nor reason whereabout.
Whither I must, I must. And, to conclude,
This evening must I leave you, gentle Kate.
I know you wise, but yet no farther wise 110
Than Harry Percy's wife; constant you are,
But yet a woman, and for secrecy,
No lady closer, for I well believe
Thou wilt not utter what thou dost not know.
And so far will I trust thee, gentle Kate!

LADY PERCY. How! so far?

HOTSPUR. Not an inch further. But hark you, Kate,
Whither I go, thither shall you go too:
To-day will I set forth, to-morrow you—
Will this content you, Kate?

LADY PERCY.   It must, of force. 120

They go

Scene 4: *The Boar's Head Tavern in Eastcheap*

The Prince enters

PRINCE. Ned, prithee, come out of that fat room, and lend me thy hand to laugh a little.

POINS. Where hast been, Hal?   *Comes forth*

PRINCE. With three or four loggerheads, amongst three or four score hogsheads. I have sounded the very base-string of humility. Sirrah, I am sworn brother to a leash of drawers, and can call them all by their christen names, as Tom, Dick, and Francis. They take it already upon their salvation, that though I be but Prince of Wales, yet I am the king 10 of Courtesy, and tell me flatly I am no proud Jack like Falstaff, but a Corinthian, a lad of mettle, a good boy (by the Lord, so they call me!) and when I am king of England, I shall command all the good lads in Eastcheap. They call drinking deep 'dyeing scarlet', and when you breathe in your watering, they cry 'hem!' and bid you 'play it off'. To conclude, I am so good a proficient in one quarter of an hour, that I can drink with any tinker in his own language during my life. I tell thee, Ned, thou hast lost much 20 honour, that thou wert not with me in this action . . . But, sweet Ned—to sweeten which name of Ned, I give thee this pennyworth of sugar, clapped even now into my hand by an underskinker, one that never spake other English in his life than 'Eight shillings and sixpence', and 'You are welcome', with this shrill addition, 'Anon, anon, sir! Score a pint of bastard in the Half-moon', or so. But, Ned, to drive away the time till Falstaff come, I prithee, do thou stand in some by-room, while I question my puny 30 drawer to what end he gave me the sugar, and do thou never leave calling 'Francis', that his tale to me may be nothing but 'Anon'. Step aside, and I'll show thee a precedent.

Poins returns to the room whence he came

POINS [*calls*]. Francis!

PRINCE. Thou art perfect.

POINS. Francis!

Francis enters

FRANCIS. Anon, anon, sir.
Look down into the Pomgarnet, Ralph.

PRINCE. Come hither, Francis. 40

FRANCIS. My lord?

PRINCE. How long hast thou to serve, Francis?

FRANCIS. Forsooth, five years, and as much as to—

POINS [*within*]. Francis!

FRANCIS. Anon, anon, sir.

PRINCE. Five year! by'r lady, a long lease for the clinking of pewter . . . But, Francis, darest thou be so valiant as to play the coward with thy indenture and show it a fair pair of heels and run from it?

FRANCIS. O Lord, sir! I'll be sworn upon all the books 50 in England, I could find in my heart—

POINS [*within*]. Francis!

FRANCIS. Anon, sir.

PRINCE. How old art thou, Francis?

FRANCIS. Let me see—about Michaelmas next I shall be—

POINS [*within*]. Francis!

FRANCIS. Anon, sir. Pray stay a little, my lord.

PRINCE. Nay, but hark you, Francis. For the sugar thou gavest me—'twas a pennyworth, was't not? 60

FRANCIS. O Lord, I would it had been two!

PRINCE. I will give thee for it a thousand pound. Ask me when thou wilt, and thou shalt have it—

POINS [*within*]. Francis!

FRANCIS. Anon, anon.

PRINCE. Anon, Francis? No, Francis, but to-morrow, Francis; or, Francis, a-Thursday; or, indeed, Francis, when thou wilt. But, Francis!

FRANCIS. My lord?

PRINCE. Wilt thou rob this leathern jerkin, crystal- 70 button, not-pated, agate-ring, puke-stocking, caddis-garter, smooth-tongue, Spanish-pouch,—

FRANCIS. O Lord, sir, who do you mean?

PRINCE. Why then, your brown bastard is your only drink! for, look you, Francis, your white canvas doublet will sully. In Barbary, sir, it cannot come to so much.

FRANCIS. What, sir?

POINS [*within*]. Francis!

PRINCE. Away, you rogue, dost thou not hear them 80 call?

Here they both call him; the drawer stands amazed, not knowing which way to go

The Vintner comes in

VINTNER. What! stand'st thou still, and hear'st such a calling? Look to the guests within. [*Francis goes*] My lord, old Sir John, with half-a-dozen more, are at the door. Shall I let them in?

PRINCE. Let them alone awhile, and then open the door. [*Vintner goes*] Poins!

POINS [*returning*]. Anon, anon, sir.

PRINCE. Sirrah, Falstaff and the rest of the thieves are at the door. Shall we be merry? 90

POINS. As merry as crickets, my lad. But hark ye, what cunning match have you made with this jest of the drawer? come, what's the issue?

PRINCE. I am now of all humours that have showed

themselves humours since the old days of goodman
Adam to the pupil age of this present twelve o'clock
at midnight. What's o'clock, Francis?

FRANCIS. Anon, anon, sir.   *He goes out*

PRINCE. That ever this fellow should have fewer words
than a parrot, and yet the son of a woman! His 100
industry is up-stairs and down-stairs, his eloquence
the parcel of a reckoning. . . . I am not yet of Percy's
mind, the Hotspur of the north, he that kills me
some six or seven dozen of Scots at a breakfast,
washes his hands, and says to his wife, 'Fie upon this
quiet life! I want work.' 'O my sweet Harry,' says
she, 'how many hast thou killed to-day?' 'Give my
roan horse a drench', says he, and answers, 'Some
fourteen', an hour after; 'a trifle, a trifle.' I prithee,
call in Falstaff. I'll play Percy, and that damned 110
brawn shall play Dame Mortimer his wife. 'Rivo!'
says the drunkard: call in Ribs, call in Tallow.

*Falstaff enters with Gadshill, Bardolph and Peto; Francis
follows with cups of sack*

POINS. Welcome, Jack. Where hast thou been?

FALSTAFF. A plague of all cowards, I say, and a vengeance too! marry, and amen! Give me a cup of
sack, boy. Ere I lead this life long, I'll sew nether-
stocks, and mend them, and foot them too. A plague
of all cowards! Give me a cup of sack, rogue. Is there
no virtue extant?   *He drinketh*

PRINCE. Didst thou never see Titan kiss a dish of butter 120
(pitiful-hearted Titan!) that melted at the sweet tale
of the sun's? If thou didst, then behold that compound.

FALSTAFF. You rogue, here's lime in this sack too . . .
There is nothing but roguery to be found in villainous man, yet a coward is worse than a cup of sack
with lime in it. A villainous coward! Go thy ways,
old Jack, die when thou wilt. If manhood, good
manhood, be not forgot upon the face of the earth,
then am I a shotten herring . . . There lives not three 130
good men unhanged in England, and one of them
is fat, and grows old. God help the while! a bad
world, I say. I would I were a weaver—I could sing
psalms or any thing. A plague of all cowards, I say
still.

PRINCE. How now, wool-sack! what mutter you?

FALSTAFF. A king's son! If I do not beat thee out of thy
kingdom with a dagger of lath, and drive all thy
subjects afore thee like a flock of wild-geese, I'll
never wear hair on my face more. You, Prince of 140
Wales!

PRINCE. Why, you whoreson round man! what's the
matter?

FALSTAFF. Are not you a coward? answer me to that—
and Poins there?

POINS. 'Zounds, ye fat paunch, an ye call me coward,
by the Lord I'll stab thee.

FALSTAFF. I call thee coward! I'll see thee damned ere
I call thee coward—but I would give a thousand
pound I could run as fast as thou canst. You are 150
straight enough in the shoulders, you care not who
sees your back: call you that backing of your friends?
A plague upon such backing! give me them that will
face me. Give me a cup of sack—I am a rogue, if
I drunk to-day.

PRINCE. O villain! thy lips are scarce wiped since thou
drunk'st last.

FALSTAFF. All's one for that. [*he drinketh*] A plague of
all cowards, still say I.

PRINCE. What's the matter?   160

FALSTAFF. What's the matter? there be four of us here
have ta'en a thousand pound this day morning.

PRINCE. Where is it, Jack? where is it?

FALSTAFF. Where is it? taken from us it is: a hundred
upon poor four of us.

PRINCE. What, a hundred, man?

FALSTAFF. I am a rogue, if I were not at half-sword
with a dozen of them two hours together. I have
'scaped by miracle. I am eight times thrust through
the doublet, four through the hose, my buckler cut 170
through and through, my sword hacked like a handsaw, *ecce signum!* I never dealt better since I was a
man: all would not do. A plague of all cowards! Let
them speak. If they speak more or less than truth,
they are villains and the sons of darkness.

PRINCE. Speak, sirs, how was it?

GADSHILL. We four set upon some dozen—

FALSTAFF. Sixteen at least, my lord.

GADSHILL. And bound them.

PETO. No, no, they were not bound.   180

FALSTAFF. You rogue, they were bound, every man of
them, or I am a Jew else, an Ebrew Jew.

GADSHILL. As we were sharing, some six or seven fresh
men set upon us—

FALSTAFF. And unbound the rest, and then come in the
other.

PRINCE. What, fought you with them all?

FALSTAFF. All! I know not what you call all, but if I
fought not with fifty of them I am a bunch of
radish: if there were not two or three and fifty upon 190
poor old Jack, then am I no two-legged creature.

PRINCE. Pray God you have not murdered some of
them.

FALSTAFF. Nay, that's past praying for. I have peppered
two of them. Two I am sure I have paid, two rogues
in buckram suits . . . I tell thee what, Hal, if I tell
thee a lie, spit in my face, call me horse. Thou
knowest my old ward: here I lay, and thus I bore
my point. Four rogues in buckram let drive at me—

PRINCE. What, four? thou said'st but two even now.   200

FALSTAFF. Four, Hal, I told thee four.

POINS. Ay, ay, he said four.

FALSTAFF. These four came all afront, and mainly
thrust at me. I made me no more ado, but took all
their seven points in my target, thus.

PRINCE. Seven? why, there were but four even now.

FALSTAFF. In buckram?

POINS. Ay, four, in buckram suits.

FALSTAFF. Seven, by these hilts, or I am a villain else.

PRINCE. Prithee, let him alone, we shall have more 210
anon.

FALSTAFF. Dost thou hear me, Hal?

PRINCE. Ay, and mark thee too, Jack.

FALSTAFF. Do so, for it is worth the listening to. These
nine in buckram that I told thee of—

PRINCE. So, two more already.

FALSTAFF. Their points being broken—

POINS. Down fell their hose.

FALSTAFF. Began to give me ground: but I followed me
close, came in foot and hand, and with a thought, 220
seven of the eleven I paid.

PRINCE. O monstrous! eleven buckram men grown
out of two!

FALSTAFF. But, as the devil would have it, three misbegotten knaves in Kendal green came at my back,
and let drive at me, for it was so dark, Hal, that thou
couldest not see thy hand.

PRINCE. These lies are like their father that begets
them, gross as a mountain, open, palpable. Why,
thou clay-brained guts, thou knotty-pated fool,   230
thou whoreson, obscene, greasy tallow-catch—

FALSTAFF. What, art thou mad? art thou mad? is not
the truth the truth?

PRINCE. Why, how couldst thou know these men in
Kendal green, when it was so dark thou couldst not
see thy hand? come tell us your reason. What sayest
thou to this?

POINS. Come, your reason, Jack, your reason.

FALSTAFF. What, upon compulsion? 'Zounds, an I
were at the strappado, or all the racks in the world,   240
I would not tell you on compulsion. Give you a
reason on compulsion! if reasons were as plentiful
as blackberries, I would give no man a reason upon
compulsion, I.

PRINCE. I'll be no longer guilty of this sin. This
sanguine coward, this bed-presser, this horseback-
breaker, this huge hill of flesh—

FALSTAFF. 'Sblood, you starveling, you eel-skin, you
dried neat's-tongue, you bull's-pizzle, you stock-
fish! O, for breath to utter what is like thee! you   250
tailor's-yard, you sheath, you bow-case, you vile
standing tuck—

PRINCE. Well, breathe awhile, and then to it again, and
when thou hast tired thyself in base comparisons,
hear me speak but this.

POINS. Mark, Jack.

PRINCE. We two saw you four set on four, and bound
them and were masters of their wealth: mark now,
how a plain tale shall put you down. Then did we
two set on you four, and with a word, out-faced   260
you from your prize, and have it, yea, and can show
it you here in the house: and, Falstaff, you carried
your guts away as nimbly, with as quick dexterity,
and roared for mercy, and still run and roared, as
ever I heard bull-calf. What a slave art thou, to hack
thy sword as thou hast done, and then say it was
in fight! What trick, what device, what starting-
hole, canst thou now find out, to hide thee from this
open and apparent shame?

POINS. Come, let's hear, Jack—what trick hast thou   270
now?

FALSTAFF. By the Lord, I knew ye as well as he that
made ye.... Why, hear you, my masters—was it for
me to kill the heir-apparent? should I turn upon the
true prince? why, thou knowest I am as valiant as
Hercules: but beware instinct—the lion will not
touch the true prince. Instinct is a great matter—I
was now a coward on instinct. I shall think the better
of myself and thee during my life; I for a valiant
lion, and thou for a true prince ... But, by the Lord,   280
lads, I am glad you have the money. Hostess, clap to
the doors. Watch to-night, pray to-morrow. Gallants, lads, boys, hearts of gold, all the titles of good
fellowship come to you! What, shall we be merry?
shall we have a play extempore?

PRINCE. Content—and the argument shall be thy running away.

FALSTAFF. Ah! no more of that, Hal, an thou lovest
me.

Hostess enters

HOSTESS. O Jesu, my lord the prince,—

PRINCE. How now, my lady the hostess! what say'st   290
thou to me?

HOSTESS. Marry, my lord, there is a nobleman of the
court at door would speak with you: he says he
comes from your father.

PRINCE. Give him as much as will make him a royal
man, and send him back again to my mother.

FALSTAFF. What manner of man is he?

HOSTESS. An old man.

FALSTAFF. What doth gravity out of his bed at midnight? Shall I give him his answer?   300

PRINCE. Prithee, do, Jack.

FALSTAFF. Faith, and I'll send him packing.

He goes out

PRINCE. Now, sirs! By'r lady, you fought fair, so did
you, Peto, so did you, Bardolph. You are lions too,
you ran away upon instinct, you will not touch the
true prince, no, fie!

BARDOLPH. Faith, I ran when I saw others run.

PRINCE. Faith, tell me now in earnest, how came
Falstaff's sword so hacked?

PETO. Why, he hacked it with his dagger, and said he   310
would swear truth out of England but he would
make you believe it was done in fight, and persuaded
us to do the like.

BARDOLPH. Yea, and to tickle our noses with spear-
grass to make them bleed, and then to beslubber our
garments with it, and swear it was the blood of true
men. I did that I did not this seven year before, I
blushed to hear his monstrous devices.

PRINCE. O villain, thou stolest a cup of sack eighteen
years ago, and wert taken with the manner, and ever   320
since thou hast blushed extempore. Thou hadst fire
and sword on thy side, and yet thou ran'st away.
What instinct hadst thou for it?

BARDOLPH [*thrusts forward his face*]. My lord, do you
see these meteors? do you behold these exhalations?

PRINCE. I do.

BARDOLPH. What think you they portend?

PRINCE. Hot livers, and cold purses.

BARDOLPH. Choler, my lord, if rightly taken.

PRINCE. No, if rightly taken, halter.   330

Falstaff returns

Here comes lean Jack, here comes bare-bone: how
now, my sweet creature of bombast? how long is't
ago, Jack, since thou sawest thine own knee?

FALSTAFF. My own knee! when I was about thy years,
Hal, I was not an eagle's talon in the waist, I could
have crept into any alderman's thumb-ring: a plague
of sighing and grief! it blows a man up like a bladder.
There's villanous news abroad. Here was Sir John
Bracy from your father: you must to the court in the
morning. That same mad fellow of the north, Percy,   340
and he of Wales, that gave Amaimon the bastinado,
and made Lucifer cuckold, and swore the devil his
true liegeman upon the cross of a Welsh hook ...
what a plague call you him?

POINS. Owen Glendower.

FALSTAFF. Owen, Owen, the same—and his son-in-
law, Mortimer, and old Northumberland, and that
sprightly Scot of Scots, Douglas, that runs a-horseback up a hill perpendicular—

PRINCE. He that rides at high speed, and with his pistol kills a sparrow flying.

FALSTAFF. You have hit it.

PRINCE. So did he never the sparrow.

FALSTAFF. Well, that rascal hath good mettle in him, he will not run.

PRINCE. Why, what a rascal art thou then, to praise him so for running.

FALSTAFF. A-horseback, ye cuckoo, but afoot he will not budge a foot.

PRINCE. Yes, Jack, upon instinct.   350

FALSTAFF. I grant ye, upon instinct ... Well, he is there too, and one Mordake, and a thousand blue-caps more. Worcester is stolen away to-night, thy father's beard is turned white with the news, you may buy land now as cheap as stinking mackerel.

PRINCE. Why then, it is like, if there come a hot June, and this civil buffeting hold, we shall buy maiden-heads as they buy hob-nails, by the hundreds.

FALSTAFF. By the mass, lad, thou sayest true, it is like we shall have good trading that way ... But, tell me,   360 Hal, art not thou horrible afeard? thou being heir-apparent, could the world pick thee out three such enemies again, as that fiend Douglas, that spirit Percy, and that devil Glendower? art thou not horribly afraid? doth not thy blood thrill at it?

PRINCE. Not a whit, i'faith, I lack some of thy instinct.

FALSTAFF. Well, thou wilt be horribly chid to-morrow when thou comest to thy father. If thou love me, practise an answer.

PRINCE. Do thou stand for my father, and examine me   370 upon the particulars of my life.

FALSTAFF. Shall I? content. This chair shall be my state, this dagger my sceptre, and this cushion my crown.

PRINCE. Thy state is taken for a joined-stool, thy golden sceptre for a leaden dagger, and thy precious rich crown for a pitiful bald crown!

FALSTAFF. Well, an the fire of grace be not quite out of thee, now shalt thou be moved. Give me a cup of sack to make my eyes look red, that it may be thought I have wept—for I must speak in passion,   380 and I will do it in King Cambyses' vein.

PRINCE. Well, here is my leg.

FALSTAFF. And here is my speech.... Stand aside, nobility.

HOSTESS. O Jesu, this is excellent sport, i'faith.

FALSTAFF. Weep not, sweet queen, for trickling tears are vain.

HOSTESS. O, the father, how he holds his countenance!

FALSTAFF. For God's sake, lords, convey my tristful queen,

For tears do stop the flood-gates of her eyes.

HOSTESS. O Jesu, he doth it as like one of these harlotry   390 players as ever I see!

FALSTAFF. Peace, good pint-pot, peace, good tickle-brain.

Harry, I do not only marvel where thou spendest thy time, but also how thou art accompanied: for though the camomile, the more it is trodden on the faster it grows, yet youth, the more it is wasted the sooner it wears ... That thou art my son, I have partly thy mother's word, partly my own opinion, but chiefly a villainous trick of thine eye, and a   400 foolish hanging of thy nether lip, that doth warrant me. If then thou be son to me, here lies the point—why, being son to me, art thou so pointed at? Shall

the blessed sun of heaven prove a micher and eat blackberries? a question not to be asked. Shall the son of England prove a thief and take purses? a question to be asked. There is a thing, Harry, which thou hast often heard of, and it is known to many in our land by the name of pitch: this pitch (as ancient writers do report) doth defile, so doth the   410 company thou keepest: for, Harry, now I do not speak to thee in drink, but in tears; not in pleasure, but in passion; not in words only, but in woes also: and yet there is a virtuous man whom I have often noted in thy company, but I know not his name.

PRINCE. What manner of man, an it like your majesty?

FALSTAFF. A goodly portly man, i'faith, and a corpu-lent, of a cheerful look, a pleasing eye, and a most noble carriage, and as I think his age some fifty, or by'r lady inclining to threescore. And now I remem-   420 ber me, his name is Falstaff. If that man should be lewdly given, he deceiveth me; for, Harry, I see virtue in his looks ... If then the tree may be known by the fruit, as the fruit by the tree, then, peremp-torily I speak it, there is virtue in that Falstaff—him keep with, the rest banish. And tell me now, thou naughty varlet, tell me, where hast thou been this month?

PRINCE. Dost thou speak like a king? Do thou stand for me, and I'll play my father.   430

FALSTAFF. Depose me? if thou dost if half so gravely, so majestically, both in word and matter, hang me up by the heels for a rabbit-sucker, or a poulter's hare.

PRINCE. Well, here I am set.

FALSTAFF. And here I stand—judge, my masters.

PRINCE. Now, Harry, whence come you?

FALSTAFF. My noble lord, from Eastcheap.

PRINCE. The complaints I hear of thee are grievous.

FALSTAFF. 'Sblood, my lord, they are false: nay, I'll   440 tickle ye for a young prince, i'faith.

PRINCE. Swearest thou, ungracious boy? henceforth ne'er look on me. Thou art violently carried away from grace, there is a devil haunts thee in the like-ness of an old fat man, a tun of man is thy com-panion: why dost thou converse with that trunk of humours, that bolting-hutch of beastliness, that swollen parcel of dropsies, that huge bombard of sack, that stuffed cloak-bag of guts, that roasted Manningtree ox with the pudding in his belly, that   450 reverend vice, that grey iniquity, that father ruffian, that vanity in years? Wherein is he good, but to taste sack and drink it? wherein neat and cleanly, but to carve a capon and eat it? wherein cunning, but in craft? wherein crafty, but in villainy? wherein villainous, but in all things? wherein worthy, but in nothing?

FALSTAFF. I would your grace would take me with you. Whom means your grace?

PRINCE. That villainous abominable misleader of   460 youth, Falstaff, that old white-bearded Satan.

FALSTAFF. My lord, the man I know.

PRINCE. I know thou dost.

FALSTAFF. But to say I know more harm in him than in myself, were to say more than I know: that he is old, the more the pity, his white hairs do witness it, but that he is, saving your reverence, a whore-master, that I utterly deny: if sack and sugar be a fault, God help the wicked! if to be old and merry

be a sin, then many an old host that I know is 470
damned: if to be fat be to be hated, then Pharaoh's
lean kine are to be loved. No, my good lord—banish
Peto, banish Bardolph, banish Poins, but for sweet
Jack Falstaff, kind Jack Falstaff, true Jack Falstaff,
valiant Jack Falstaff, and therefore more valiant
being as he is old Jack Falstaff, banish not him thy
Harry's company, banish not him thy Harry's company, banish plump Jack, and banish all the world.

PRINCE. I do, I will.

Enter Bardolph, running

BARDOLPH. O, my lord, my lord, the sheriff with a 480
most monstrous watch is at the door!

FALSTAFF. Out, ye rogue! play out the play. I have
much to say in the behalf of that Falstaff.

Enter the Hostess

HOSTESS. O Jesu, my lord, my lord!—

PRINCE. Heigh, heigh! the devil rides upon a fiddlestick. What's the matter?

HOSTESS. The sheriff and all the watch are at the door,
they are come to search the house, shall I let them in?

FALSTAFF. Dost thou hear, Hal? never call a true piece
of gold a counterfeit. Thou art essentially made, 490
without seeming so.

PRINCE. And thou a natural coward, without instinct.

FALSTAFF. I deny your major, if you will deny the
sheriff, so, if not, let him enter. If I become not a
cart as well as another man, a plague on my bringing
up! I hope I shall as soon be strangled with a halter
as another.

PRINCE. Go, hide thee behind the arras, the rest walk
up above. Now, my masters, for a true face and
good conscience.   500

FALSTAFF. Both which I have had, but their date is out,
and therefore I'll hide me.

*He does so; all but the Prince and Poins
go out*

PRINCE. Call in the sheriff.—

Enter Sheriff and the Carrier

Now, master sheriff, what is your will with me?

SHERIFF. First, pardon me, my lord. A hue and cry
Hath followed certain men unto this house.

PRINCE. What men?

SHERIFF. One of them is well known, my gracious
lord,
A gross fat man.

CARRIER. As fat as butter.   510

PRINCE. The man, I do assure you, is not here,
For I myself at this time have employed him:
And, sheriff, I will engage my word to thee
That I will by to-morrow dinner-time
Send him to answer thee, or any man,
For any thing he shall be charged withal.
And so let me entreat you leave the house.

SHERIFF. I will, my lord ... There are two gentlemen
Have in this robbery lost three hundred marks.

PRINCE. It may be so: if he have robbed these men, 520
He shall be answerable—and so, farewell.

SHERIFF. Good night, my noble lord.

PRINCE. I think it is good morrow, is it not?

SHERIFF. Indeed, my lord, I think it be two o'clock.

Sheriff and Carrier depart

PRINCE. This oily rascal is known as well as Paul's ...

Go, call him forth.

POINS. Falstaff! fast asleep behind the arras, and snorting like a horse.

PRINCE. Hark, how hard he fetches breath. Search his
pockets. [*He searcheth his pocket, and findeth certain* 530
papers] What hast thou found?

POINS. Nothing but papers, my lord.

PRINCE. Let's see what they be—read them.

POINS. Item, A capon . . . . . 2s. 2d.
Item, Sauce . . . . . 4d.
Item, Sack, two gallons . . . 5s. 8d.
Item, Anchovies and sack after supper . 2s. 6d.
Item, Bread . . . . . ob.

PRINCE. O monstrous! but one half-pennyworth of
bread to this intolerable deal of sack! What there is 540
else keep close, we'll read it at more advantage; there
let him sleep till day. I'll to the court in the morning. We must all to the wars, and thy place shall be
honourable. I'll procure this fat rogue a charge of
foot, and I know his death will be a march of twelve-
score. The money shall be paid back again with
advantage.... Be with me betimes in the morning,
and so good morrow, Poins.

POINS. Good morrow, good my lord.   *They go*

ACT 3
Scene 1: *Wales. Glendower's house*

*Enter Hotspur, Worcester, Lord Mortimer, and Owen
Glendower*

MORTIMER. These promises are fair, the parties sure,
And our induction full of prosperous hope.

HOTSPUR. Lord Mortimer, and cousin Glendower,
will you sit down? and uncle Worcester: a plague
upon it, I have forgot the map!

GLENDOWER. No, here it is ... Sit cousin Percy, sit
good cousin Hotspur, for by that name as oft as
Lancaster doth speak of you, his cheek looks pale,
and with a rising sigh he wisheth you in heaven.

HOTSPUR. And you in hell, as oft as he hears Owen 10
Glendower spoke of.

GLENDOWER. I cannot blame him: at my nativity
The front of heaven was full of fiery shapes,
Of burning cressets, and at my birth
The frame and huge foundation of the earth
Shaked like a coward.

HOTSPUR. Why, so it would have done at the same
season, if your mother's cat had but kittened,
though yourself had never been born.

GLENDOWER. I say the earth did shake, when I was 20
born.

HOTSPUR. And I say the earth was not of my mind,
If you suppose as fearing you it shook.

GLENDOWER. The heavens were all on fire, the earth
did tremble.

HOTSPUR. O, then the earth shook to see the heavens
on fire,
And not in fear of your nativity.
Diseaséd nature oftentimes breaks forth
In strange eruptions; oft the teeming earth
Is with a kind of colic pinched and vexed
By the imprisoning of unruly wind
Within her womb, which for enlargement striving 30
Shakes the old beldam earth, and topples down
Steeples and moss-grown towers. At your birth

Our grandam earth, having this distemperature,
In passion shook.
GLENDOWER.   Cousin, of many men
I do not bear these crossings. Give me leave
To tell you once again that at my birth
The front of heaven was full of fiery shapes,
The goats ran from the mountains, and the herds
Were strangely clamorous to the frighted fields.
These signs have marked me extraordinary,   40
And all the courses of my life do show
I am not in the roll of common men ...
Where is he living, clipped in with the sea
That chides the banks of England, Scotland, Wales,
Which calls me pupil or hath read to me?
And bring him out that is but woman's son
Can trace me in the tedious ways of art,
And hold me pace in deep experiments.
HOTSPUR. I think there's no man speaks better Welsh:
I'll to dinner.   50
MORTIMER. Peace, cousin Percy, you will make him
mad.
GLENDOWER. I can call spirits from the vasty deep.
HOTSPUR. Why, so can I, or so can any man,
But will they come when you do call for them?
GLENDOWER. Why, I can teach you, cousin, to
command the devil.
HOTSPUR. And I can teach thee, coz, to shame the
devil,
By telling truth. Tell truth and shame the devil ...   60
If thou have power to raise him, bring him hither,
And I'll be sworn I have power to shame him hence:
O, while you live, tell truth and shame the devil.
MORTIMER. Come, come, no more of this unprofitable
chat.
GLENDOWER. Three times hath Henry Bolingbroke
made head
Against my power—thrice from the banks of Wye
And sandy-bottomed Severn have I sent him
Bootless home and weather-beaten back.
HOTSPUR. Home without boots, and in foul weather
too!
How 'scapes he agues, in the devil's name?
GLENDOWER. Come, here's the map, shall we divide
our right,
According to our threefold order ta'en?
MORTIMER. The archdeacon hath divided it   70
Into three limits, very equally:
England, from Trent to Severn hitherto,
By south and east is to my part assigned:
All westward, Wales beyond the Severn shore,
And all the fertile land within that bound,
To Owen Glendower: and, dear coz, to you
The remnant northward, lying off from Trent.
And our indentures tripartite are drawn,
Which being sealéd interchangeably,
(A business that this night may execute)
To-morrow, cousin Percy, you and I   80
And my good Lord of Worcester will set forth
To meet your father and the Scottish power,
As is appointed us, at Shrewsbury.
My father Glendower is not ready yet,
Nor shall we need his help these fourteen days.
Within that space you may have drawn together
Your tenants, friends, and neighbouring gentlemen.
GLENDOWER. A shorter time shall send me to you,
lords,

And in my conduct shall your ladies come,   90
From whom you now must steal and take no leave,
For there will be a world of water shed
Upon the parting of your wives and you.
HOTSPUR. Methinks, my moiety, north from Burton
here,
In quantity equals not one of yours.
See how this river comes me cranking in,
And cuts me from the best of all my land
A huge half-moon, a monstrous cantle out.
I'll have the current in this place dammed up,
And here the smug and silver Trent shall run   100
In a new channel, fair and evenly.
It shall not wind with such a deep indent,
To rob me of so rich a bottom here.
GLENDOWER. Not wind? it shall, it must—you see, it
doth.
MORTIMER. Yea, but
Mark how he bears his course, and runs me up
With like advantage on the other side,
Gelding the opposéd continent as much
As on the other side it takes from you.
WORCESTER. Yea, but a little charge will trench him
here,   110
And on this north side win this cape of land,
And then he runs straight and even.
HOTSPUR. I'll have it so, a little charge will do it.
GLENDOWER. I'll not have it altered.
HOTSPUR.   Will not you?
GLENDOWER. No, nor you shall not.
HOTSPUR.   Who shall say me nay?
GLENDOWER. Why, that will I.
HOTSPUR. Let me not understand you then, speak it in
Welsh.
GLENDOWER. I can speak English, lord, as well as you,
For I was trained up in the English court,   120
Where being but young I framéd to the harp
Many an English ditty, lovely well,
And gave the tongue a helpful ornament,
A virtue that was never seen in you.
HOTSPUR. Marry,
And I am glad of it with all my heart!
I had rather be a kitten and cry mew
Than one of these same metre ballad-mongers—
I had rather hear a brazen canstick turned,
Or a dry wheel grate on the axle-tree,   130
And that would set my teeth nothing on edge,
Nothing so much as mincing poetry—
'Tis like the forced gait of a shuffling nag.
GLENDOWER. Come, you shall have Trent turned.
HOTSPUR. I do not care, I'll give thrice so much land
To any well-deserving friend:
But in the way of bargain, mark ye me,
I'll cavil on the ninth part of a hair.
Are the indentures drawn? shall we be gone?
GLENDOWER. The moon shines fair, you may away
by night: 140
I'll haste the writer, and withal
Break with your wives of your departure hence.
I am afraid my daughter will run mad,
So much she doteth on her Mortimer.   *He goes*
MORTIMER. Fie, cousin Percy! how you cross my
father!
HOTSPUR. I cannot choose. Sometime he angers me
With telling me of the moldwarp and the ant,
Of the dreamer Merlin and his prophecies,

And of a dragon and a finless fish,
A clip-winged griffin and a moulten raven,   150
A couching lion and a ramping cat,
And such a deal of skimble-skamble stuff
As puts me from my faith. I tell you what—
He held me last night at least nine hours
In reckoning up the several devils' names
That were his lackeys. I cried, 'hum', and 'well, go
  to',
But marked him not a word. O, he is as tedious
As a tired horse, a railing wife,
Worse than a smoky house—I had rather live
With cheese and garlic in a windmill, far,   160
Than feed on cates and have him talk to me
In any summer house in Christendom.

MORTIMER. In faith, he is a worthy gentleman,
Exceedingly well read, and profited
In strange concealments, valiant as a lion,
And wondrous affable, and as bountiful
As mines of India ... Shall I tell you, cousin?
He holds your temper in a high respect,
And curbs himself even of his natural scope,
When you come 'cross his humour, faith, he does.   170
I warrant you, that man is not alive
Might so have tempted him as you have done,
Without the taste of danger and reproof—
But do not use it oft, let me entreat you.

WORCESTER. In faith, my lord, you are too wilful
  blame,
And since your coming hither have done enough
To put him quite beside his patience.
You must needs learn, lord, to amend this fault.
Though sometimes it show greatness, courage,
  blood—
And that's the dearest grace it renders you—   180
Yet oftentimes it doth present harsh rage,
Defect of manners, want of government,
Pride, haughtiness, opinion, and disdain,
The least of which haunting a nobleman
Loseth men's hearts, and leaves behind a stain
Upon the beauty of all parts besides,
Beguiling them of commendation.

HOTSPUR. Well, I am schooled—good manners be
  your speed!
Here come our wives, and let us take our leave.

Enter Glendower with the Ladies

MORTIMER. This is the deadly spite that angers me—   190
My wife can speak no English, I no Welsh.

GLENDOWER. My daughter weeps, she'll not part with
  you,
She'll be a soldier too, she'll to the wars.

MORTIMER. Good father, tell her that she and my aunt
  Percy
Shall follow in your conduct speedily.
        Glendower speaks to her in Welsh, and she
                  answers him in the same

GLENDOWER. She is desperate here, a peevish self-
willed harlotry, one that no persuasion can do good
upon.
      She turns to Mortimer and speaks in Welsh

MORTIMER. I understand thy looks. That pretty Welsh
Which thou pourest down from these swelling
  heavens
I am too perfect in, and but for shame
In such a parley should I answer thee.   200

The lady speaks again in Welsh

I understand thy kisses and thou mine,
And that's a feeling disputation,
But I will never be a truant, love,
Till I have learned thy language, for thy tongue
Makes Welsh as sweet as ditties highly penned,
Sung by a fair queen in a summer's bower,
With ravishing division, to her lute.

GLENDOWER. Nay, if you melt, then will she run mad.   210
                  The lady speaks again in Welsh

MORTIMER. O, I am ignorance itself in this!

GLENDOWER. She bids you on the wanton rushes lay
  you down,
And rest your gentle head upon her lap,
And she will sing the song that pleaseth you,
And on your eyelids crown the god of sleep,
Charming your blood with pleasing heaviness,
Making such difference 'twixt wake and sleep
As is the difference betwixt day and night,
The hour before the heavenly-harnessed team
Begins his golden progress in the east.   220

MORTIMER. With all my heart I'll sit and hear her sing,
By that time will our book, I think, be drawn.

GLENDOWER. Do so,
And those musicians that shall play to you
Hang in the air a thousand leagues from hence,
And straight they shall be here. Sit and attend.

HOTSPUR. Come, Kate, thou art perfect in lying down.
Come, quick, quick, that I may lay my head in thy
  lap.

LADY PERCY. Go, ye giddy goose.
                       The music plays

HOTSPUR. Now I perceive the devil understands
  Welsh,   230
And 'tis no marvel, he is so humorous.
By'r lady, he is a good musician.

LADY PERCY. Then should you be nothing but musical,
for you are altogether governed by humours. Lie
still, ye thief, and hear the lady sing in Welsh.

HOTSPUR. I had rather hear Lady, my brach, howl in
Irish.

LADY PERCY. Wouldst thou have thy head broken?

HOTSPUR. No.

LADY PERCY. Then be still.   240

HOTSPUR. Neither—'tis a woman's fault.

LADY PERCY. Now God help thee!

HOTSPUR. To the Welsh lady's bed.

LADY PERCY. What's that?

HOTSPUR. Peace! she sings.
         Here the lady sings a Welsh song

HOTSPUR. Come, Kate, I'll have your song too.

LADY PERCY. Not mine, in good sooth.

HOTSPUR. Not yours, in good sooth! Heart! you swear
like a comfit-maker's wife—'not you, in good
sooth', and 'as true as I live', and 'as God shall   250
mend me', and 'as sure as day'—
And givest such sarcenet surety for thy oaths,
As if thou never walk'st further than Finsbury.
Swear me, Kate, like a lady as thou art,
A good mouth-filling oath, and leave 'in sooth',
And such protest of pepper-gingerbread,
To velvet-guards and Sunday citizens.
Come, sing.

LADY PERCY. I will not sing.

HOTSPUR. 'Tis the next way to turn tailor, or be red-   260
breast teacher. An the indentures be drawn, I'll away

within these two hours—and so come in when ye
will.   *He goes*
GLENDOWER. Come, come, Lord Mortimer, you are as
    slow
    As hot Lord Percy is on fire to go.
    By this our book is drawn. We'll but seal,
    And then to horse immediately.
MORTIMER.   With all my heart.
                                    They go

Scene 2: *London. The palace*

The King, Prince of Wales, and others

KING. Lords, give us leave. The Prince of Wales and I
    Must have some private conference. But be near at
    hand,
    For we shall presently have need of you. . . .
                                    Lords withdraw
    I know not whether God will have it so
    For some displeasing service I have done,
    That, in his secret doom, out of my blood
    He'll breed revengement and a scourge for me;
    But thou dost in thy passages of life
    Make me believe that thou art only marked
    For the hot vengeance and the rod of heaven,   10
    To punish my mistreadings. Tell me else,
    Could such inordinate and low desires,
    Such poor, such bare, such lewd, such mean
        attempts,
    Such barren pleasures, rude society,
    As thou art matched withal, and grafted to,
    Accompany the greatness of thy blood,
    And hold their level with thy princely heart?
PRINCE. So please your majesty, I would I could
    Quit all offences with as clear excuse
    As well as I am doubtless I can purge   20
    Myself of many I am charged withal.
    Yet such extenuation let me beg,
    As, in reproof of many tales devised,
    Which oft the ear of greatness needs must hear,
    By smiling pickthanks and base newsmongers,
    I may for some things true, wherein my youth
    Hath faulty wand'red and irregular,
    Find pardon on my true submission.
KING. God pardon thee! yet let me wonder, Harry,
    At thy affections, which do hold a wing   30
    Quite from the flight of all thy ancestors.
    Thy place in council thou hast rudely lost,
    Which by thy younger brother is supplied,
    And art almost an alien to the hearts
    Of all the court and princes of my blood.
    The hope and expectation of thy time
    Is ruined, and the soul of every man
    Prophetically do forethink thy fall . . .
    Had I so lavish of my presence been,
    So common-hackneyed in the eyes of men,   40
    So stale and cheap to vulgar company,
    Opinion, that did help me to the crown,
    Had still kept loyal to possession,
    And left me in reputeless banishment,
    A fellow of no mark nor likelihood.
    By being seldom seen, I could not stir
    But like a comet I was wond'red at;
    That men would tell their children 'This is he!'
    Others would say 'Where? which is Bolingbroke?'
    And then I stole all courtesy from heaven,   50

And dressed myself in such humility
That I did pluck allegiance from men's hearts,
Loud shouts and salutations from their mouths,
Even in the presence of the crownèd king. . . .
Thus did I keep my person fresh and new,
My presence like a robe pontifical,
Ne'er seen but wond'red at, and so my state,
Seldom but sumptuous, showèd like a feast,
And wan by rareness such solemnity. . . .
The skipping king, he ambled up and down   60
With shallow jesters and rash bavin wits,
Soon kindled and soon burnt, carded his state,
Mingled his royalty with cap'ring fools,
Had his great name profanèd with their scorns,
And gave his countenance, against his name,
To laugh at gibing boys, and stand the push
Of every beardless vain comparative,
Grew a companion to the common streets,
Enfeoffed himself to popularity,
That, being daily swallowed by men's eyes,   70
They surfeited with honey and began
To loathe the taste of sweetness, whereof a little
More than a little is by much too much.
So when he had occasion to be seen,
He was but as the cuckoo is in June,
Heard, not regarded; seen, but with such eyes
As, sick and blunted with community,
Afford no extraordinary gaze,
Such as is bent on sun-like majesty,
When it shines seldom in admiring eyes;   80
But rather drowzed and hung their eyelids down,
Slept in his face, and rend'red such aspect
As cloudy men use to their adversaries,
Being with his presence glutted, gorged, and full.
And in that very line, Harry, standest thou,
For thou hast lost thy princely privilege
With vile participation. Not an eye
But is a-weary of thy common sight,
Save mine, which hath desired to see thee more,
Which now doth that I would not have it do,   90
Make blind itself with foolish tenderness.
PRINCE. I shall hereafter, my thrice gracious lord,
    Be more myself.
KING.   For all the world
    As thou art to this hour was Richard then,
    When I from France set foot at Ravenspurgh,
    And even as I was then is Percy now.
    Now by my sceptre and my soul to boot,
    He hath more worthy interest to the state
    Than thou the shadow of succession.
    For of no right, nor colour like to right,   100
    He doth fill fields with harness in the realm,
    Turns head against the lion's armèd jaws,
    And, being no more in debt to years than thou,
    Leads ancient lords and reverend bishops on
    To bloody battles and to bruising arms.
    What never-dying honour hath he got
    Against renownèd Douglas! whose high deeds,
    Whose hot incursions and great name in arms
    Holds from all soldiers chief majority,
    And military title capital,   110
    Through all the kingdoms that acknowledge
        Christ.
    Thrice hath this Hotspur, Mars in swathling
        clothes,
    This infant warrior, in his enterprizes

Discomfited great Douglas, ta'en him once,
Enlargéd him and made a friend of him,
To fill the mouth of deep defiance up,
And shake the peace and safety of our throne.
And what say you to this? Percy, Northumberland,
The Archbishop's grace of York, Douglas,
    Mortimer,
Capitulate against us and are up....   120
But wherefore do I tell these news to thee?
Why, Harry, do I tell thee of my foes,
Which art my nearest and dearest enemy?
Thou that art like enough, through vassal fear,
Base inclination and the start of spleen,
To fight against me under Percy's pay,
To dog his heels and curtsy at his frowns,
To show how much thou art degenerate.

PRINCE. Do not think so, you shall not find it so;
And God forgive them that so much have swayed 130
Your majesty's good thoughts away from me!
I will redeem all this on Percy's head,
And in the closing of some glorious day
Be bold to tell you that I am your son,
When I will wear a garment all of blood,
And stain my favours in a bloody mask,
Which washed away shall scour my shame with it.
And that shall be the day, whene'er it lights,
That this same child of honour and renown,
This gallant Hotspur, this all-praiséd knight, 140
And your unthought-of Harry chance to meet.
For every honour sitting on his helm
Would they were multitudes, and on my head
My shames redoubled! for the time will come,
That I shall make this northern youth exchange
His glorious deeds for my indignities.
Percy is but my factor, good my lord,
To engross up glorious deeds on my behalf,
And I will call him to so strict account
That he shall render every glory up, 150
Yea, even the slightest worship of his time,
Or I will tear the reckoning from his heart....
This, in the name of God, I promise here,
The which if He be pleased I shall perform,
I do beseech your majesty may salve
The long-grown wounds of my intemperature:
If not, the end of life cancels all bands,
And I will die a hundred thousand deaths
Ere break the smallest parcel of this vow.

KING. A hundred thousand rebels die in this— 160
Thou shalt have charge and sovereign trust herein.

Enter Blunt

How now, good Blunt? thy looks are full of speed.

BLUNT. So hath the business that I come to speak of.
Lord Mortimer of Scotland hath sent word
That Douglas and the English rebels met
The eleventh of this month at Shrewsbury.
A mighty and a fearful head they are,
If promises be kept on every hand,
As ever off'red foul play in a state.

KING. The Earl of Westmoreland set forth to-day, 170
With him my son, Lord John of Lancaster,
For this advertisement is five days old.
On Wednesday next, Harry, you shall set forward,
On Thursday, we ourselves will march: our
    meeting
Is Bridgenorth, and, Harry, you shall march

Through Gloucestershire; by which account,
Our business valuéd, some twelve days hence
Our general forces at Bridgenorth shall meet.
Our hands are full of business, let's away,
Advantage feeds him fat while men delay. 180

They go

Scene 3: *The Boar's Head Tavern in Eastcheap*

Enter Falstaff and Bardolph

FALSTAFF. Bardolph, am I not fallen away vilely since
this last action? do I not bate? do I not dwindle?
Why, my skin hangs about me like an old lady's
loose gown, I am withered like an old apple-John.
Well, I'll repent, and that suddenly, while I am in
some liking. I shall be out of heart shortly, and then
I shall have no strength to repent. An I have not
forgotten what the inside of a church is made of, I
am a peppercorn, a brewer's horse. The inside of a
church! Company, villainous company, hath been 10
the spoil of me.

BARDOLPH. Sir John, you are so fretful you cannot live
long.

FALSTAFF. Why, there is it: come, sing me a bawdy
song, make me merry.... I was as virtuously given
as a gentleman need to be; virtuous enough, swore
little, diced not above seven times a week, went to
a bawdy-house not above once in a quarter of an
hour, paid money that I borrowed three or four
times, lived well, and in good compass: and now I 20
live out of all order, out of all compass.

BARDOLPH. Why, you are so fat, Sir John, that you
must needs be out of all compass; out of all reasonable compass, Sir John.

FALSTAFF. Do thou amend thy face, and I'll amend my
life: thou art our admiral, thou bearest the lantern
in the poop, but 'tis in the nose of thee: thou art the
Knight of the Burning Lamp.

BARDOLPH. Why, Sir John, my face does you no harm.

FALSTAFF. No, I'll be sworn—I make as good use of it 30
as many a man doth of a death's-head or a memento
mori. I never see thy face but I think upon hell-fire,
and Dives that lived in purple; for there he is in his
robes, burning, burning. If thou wert any way given
to virtue, I would swear by thy face; my oath should
be, 'by this fire, that's God's angel'. But thou art
altogether given over; and wert indeed, but for the
light in thy face, the son of utter darkness. When
thou ran'st up Gad's Hill in the night to catch my
horse, if I did not think thou hadst been an ignis 40
fatuus or a ball of wildfire, there's no purchase in
money. O, thou art a perpetual triumph, an everlasting bonfire-light! Thou hast saved me a thousand
marks in links and torches, walking with thee in the
night betwixt tavern and tavern: but sack that thou
hast drunk me would have bought me lights as good
cheap at the dearest chandler's in Europe. I have
maintained that salamander of yours with fire any
time this two and thirty years, God reward me for it!

BARDOLPH. 'Sblood, I would my face were in your 50
belly!

FALSTAFF. God-a-mercy! so should I be sure to be
heartburned.

Hostess enters

How now, Dame Partlet the hen! have you inquired yet who picked my pocket!

HOSTESS. Why, Sir John, what do you think, Sir John? do you think I keep thieves in my house? I have searched, I have inquired, so has my husband, man by man, boy by boy, servant by servant. The tithe of a hair was never lost in my house before.   60

FALSTAFF. Ye lie, hostess—Bardolph was shaved, and lost many a hair, and I'll be sworn my pocket was picked: go to, you are a woman, go.

HOSTESS. Who, I? no, I defy thee: God's light, I was never called so in mine own house before.

FALSTAFF. Go to, I know you well enough.

HOSTESS. No, Sir John, you do not know me, Sir John. I know you, Sir John. You owe me money, Sir John, and now you pick a quarrel to beguile me of it. I bought you a dozen of shirts to your back.   70

FALSTAFF. Dowlas, filthy dowlas. I have given them away to bakers' wives. They have made bolters of them.

HOSTESS. Now, as I am a true woman, holland of eight shillings an ell! You owe money here besides, Sir John, for your diet and by-drinkings, and money lent you, four and twenty pound.

FALSTAFF. He had his part of it, let him pay.

HOSTESS. He? alas, he is poor, he hath nothing.

FALSTAFF. How! poor? look upon his face. What call   80 you rich? let them coin his nose, let them coin his cheeks. I'll not pay a denier! What, will you make a younker of me? shall I not take mine ease in mine inn but I shall have my pocket picked? I have lost a seal-ring of my grandfather's worth forty mark.

HOSTESS. O Jesu! I have heard the prince tell him, I know not how oft, that that ring was copper.

FALSTAFF. How! the prince is a Jack, a sneak-up. 'Sblood, an he were here, I would cudgel him like a dog, if he would say so.   90

Enter the Prince and Poins, marching; Falstaff meets them playing upon his truncheon like a fife

FALSTAFF. How now, lad! is the wind in that door, i'faith? must we all march?

BARDOLPH. Yea, two and two, Newgate fashion.

HOSTESS. My lord, I pray you, hear me.

PRINCE. What say'st thou, Mistress Quickly? How doth thy husband? I love him well, he is an honest man.

HOSTESS. Good my lord, hear me.

FALSTAFF. Prithee, let her alone, and list to me.

PRINCE. What say'st thou, Jack?   100

FALSTAFF. The other night I fell asleep here, behind the arras, and had my pocket picked. This house is turned bawdy-house, they pick pockets.

PRINCE. What didst thou lose, Jack?

FALSTAFF. Wilt thou believe me, Hal? three or four bonds of forty pound a-piece, and a seal-ring of my grandfather's.

PRINCE. A trifle, some eight-penny matter.

HOSTESS. So I told him, my lord, and I said I heard your grace say so: and, my lord, he speaks most   110 vilely of you, like a foul-mouthed man as he is, and said he would cudgel you.

PRINCE. What! he did not?

HOSTESS. There's neither faith, truth, nor womanhood in me else.

FALSTAFF. There's no more faith in thee than in a stewed prune, nor no more truth in thee than in a drawn fox—and for womanhood, Maid Marian may be the deputy's wife of the ward to thee. Go, you thing, go.   120

HOSTESS. Say, what thing? what thing?

FALSTAFF. What thing? why, a thing to thank God on.

HOSTESS. I am nothing to thank God on, I would thou shouldst know it. I am an honest man's wife, and setting thy knighthood aside, thou art a knave to call me so.

FALSTAFF. Setting thy womanhood aside, thou art a beast to say otherwise.

HOSTESS. Say, what beast, thou knave, thou?

FALSTAFF. What beast? why, an otter.

PRINCE. An otter, Sir John! why an otter?   130

FALSTAFF. Why? she's neither fish nor flesh, a man knows not where to have her.

HOSTESS. Thou art an unjust man in saying so, thou or any man knows where to have me, thou knave, thou!

PRINCE. Thou say'st true, hostess, and he slanders thee most grossly.

HOSTESS. So he doth you, my lord, and said this other day you ought him a thousand pound.   140

PRINCE. Sirrah, do I owe you a thousand pound?

FALSTAFF. A thousand pound, Hal? a million. Thy love is worth a million, thou owest me thy love.

HOSTESS. Nay, my lord, he called you Jack, and said he would cudgel you.

FALSTAFF. Did I, Bardolph?

BARDOLPH. Indeed, Sir John, you said so.

FALSTAFF. Yea, if he said my ring was copper.

PRINCE. I say 'tis copper. Darest thou be as good as thy word now?   150

FALSTAFF. Why, Hal, thou knowest, as thou art but man I dare, but as thou art prince I fear thee as I fear the roaring of the lion's whelp.

PRINCE. And why not as the lion?

FALSTAFF. The king himself is to be feared as the lion. Dost thou think I'll fear thee as I fear thy father? nay, an I do, I pray God my girdle break.

PRINCE. O, if it should, how would thy guts fall about thy knees! But, sirrah, there's no room for faith, truth, nor honesty, in this bosom of thine—it is all   160 filled up with guts and midriff. Charge an honest woman with picking thy pocket! why, thou whore-son, impudent, embossed rascal, if there were any-thing in thy pocket but tavern-reckonings, memorandums of bawdy-houses, and one poor pennyworth of sugar-candy to make thee long-winded—if thy pocket were enriched with any other injuries but these, I am a villain. And yet you will stand to it, you will not pocket up wrong! Art thou not ashamed?   170

FALSTAFF. Dost thou hear, Hal? thou knowest in the state of innocency Adam fell, and what should poor Jack Falstaff do in the days of villainy? Thou seest I have more flesh than another man, and therefore more frailty ... You confess then, you picked my pocket?

PRINCE. It appears so by the story.

FALSTAFF. Hostess, I forgive thee. Go, make ready breakfast, love thy husband, look to thy servants, cherish thy guests. Thou shalt find me tractable to   180 any honest reason, thou seest I am pacified still. Nay, prithee, be gone. [*Hostess goes*] Now Hal, to the

news at court: for the robbery, lad, how is that
answered?

PRINCE. O, my sweet beef, I must still be good angel
to thee. The money is paid back again.

FALSTAFF. O, I do not like that paying back, 'tis a
double labour.

PRINCE. I am good friends with my father, and may
do any thing.   190

FALSTAFF. Rob me the exchequer the first thing thou
doest, and do it with unwashed hands too.

BARDOLPH. Do, my lord.

PRINCE. I have procured thee, Jack, a charge of foot.

FALSTAFF. I would it had been of horse. Where shall I
find one that can steal well? O for a fine thief, of
the age of two and twenty or thereabouts! I am
heinously unprovided. Well, God be thanked for
these rebels, they offend none but the virtuous; I
laud them, I praise them.   200

PRINCE. Bardolph—

BARDOLPH. My lord.

PRINCE. Go bear this letter to Lord John of Lancaster,
to my brother John, this to my Lord of Westmoreland.

Go, Poins, to horse, to horse, for thou and I
Have thirty miles to ride yet ere dinner time.
Jack, meet me to-morrow in the Temple hall
at two o'clock in the afternoon.
There shalt thou know thy charge, and there receive   210
Money and order for their furniture.
The land is burning, Percy stands on high,
And either we or they must lower lie.

                    He follows Bardolph and Poins

FALSTAFF. Rare words! brave world! Hostess, my
breakfast, come!
O, I could wish this tavern were my drum.

                              He goes

                    ACT 4
            Scene 1: *The rebel camp near Shrewsbury*

Hotspur, Worcester, and Douglas

HOTSPUR. Well said, my noble Scot! If speaking truth
In this fine age were not thought flattery,
Such attribution should the Douglas have,
As not a soldier of this season's stamp
Should go so general current through the world.
By God, I cannot flatter, I do defy
The tongues of soothers, but a braver place
In my heart's love hath no man than yourself.
Nay, task me to my word, approve me, lord.

DOUGLAS. Thou art the king of honour.   10
No man so potent breathes upon the ground
But I will beard him.

HOTSPUR.   Do so, and 'tis well.

Enter one with letters

What letters hast thou there?—I can but thank you.

MESSENGER. These letters come from your father—

HOTSPUR. Letters from him! why comes he not
himself?

MESSENGER. He cannot come, my lord, he is grievous
sick.

HOTSPUR. 'Zounds! how has he the leisure to be sick
In such a justling time? Who leads his power?
Under whose government come they along?

MESSENGER. His letters bear his mind, not I, my lord.   20

WORCESTER. I prithee, tell me, doth he keep his bed?

MESSENGER. He did, my lord, four days ere I set forth,
And at the time of my departure thence
He was much feared by his physicians.

WORCESTER. I would the state of time had first been
whole,
Ere he by sickness had been visited.
His health was never better worth than now.

HOTSPUR. Sick now! droop now! this sickness doth
infect
The very life-blood of our enterprise,
'Tis catching hither, even to our camp.   30
He writes me here that inward sickness—
And that his friends by deputation could not
So soon be drawn, nor did he think it meet
To lay so dangerous and dear a trust
On any soul removed but on his own.
Yet doth he give us bold advertisement
That with our small conjunction we should on,
To see how fortune is disposed to us.
For as he writes there is no quailing now,
Because the king is certainly possessed   40
Of all our purposes. What say you to it?

WORCESTER. Your father's sickness is a maim to us.

HOTSPUR. A perilous gash, a very limb lopped off—
And yet, in faith, it is not. His present want
Seems more than we shall find it: were it good
To set the exact wealth of all our states
All at one cast? to set so rich a main
On the nice hazard of one doubtful hour?
It were not good, for therein should we read
The very bottom and the soul of hope,   50
The very list, the very utmost bound
Of all our fortunes.

DOUGLAS.   Faith, and so we should.
Where now remains a sweet reversion,
We may boldly spend upon the hope of what
Is to come in.
A comfort of retirement lives in this.

HOTSPUR. A rendezvous, a home to fly unto,
If that the devil and mischance look big
Upon the maidenhead of our affairs.

WORCESTER. But yet I would your father had been
here ...   60
The quality and hair of our attempt
Brooks no division. It will be thought,
By some that know not why he is away,
That wisdom, loyalty, and mere dislike
Of our proceedings kept the earl from hence.
And think how such an apprehension
May turn the tide of fearful faction,
And breed a kind of question in our cause:
For well you know we of the off'ring side
Must keep aloof from strict arbitrement,   70
And stop all sight-holes, every loop from whence
The eye of reason may pry in upon us.
This absence of your father's draws a curtain
That shows the ignorant a kind of fear
Before not dreamt of.

HOTSPUR.   You strain too far.
I rather of his absence make this use—
It lends a lustre and more great opinion,
A larger dare to our great enterprise,
Than if the earl were here; for men must
think,

If we without his help can make a head 80
To push against a kingdom, with his help
We shall o'erturn it topsy-turvy down.
Yet all goes well, yet all our joints are whole.
DOUGLAS. As heart can think. There is not such a word
Spoke of in Scotland as this term of fear.

Sir Richard Vernon enters

HOTSPUR. My cousin Vernon! welcome, by my soul.
VERNON. Pray God, my news be worth a welcome,
lord.
The Earl of Westmoreland, seven thousand strong,
Is marching hitherwards, with him Prince John.
HOTSPUR. No harm—what more?
VERNON.   And further, I have learned, 90
The king himself in person is set forth,
Or hitherwards intended speedily,
With strong and mighty preparation.
HOTSPUR. He shall be welcome too: where is his son,
The nimble-footed madcap Prince of Wales,
And his comrades, that daffed the world aside,
And bid it pass?
VERNON.   All furnished, all in arms;
All plumed like estridges that wing the wind,
Baited like eagles having lately bathed,
Glittering in golden coats like images, 100
As full of spirit as the month of May,
And gorgeous as the sun at midsummer,
Wanton as youthful goats, wild as young bulls.
I saw young Harry with his beaver on,
His cushes on his thighs, gallantly armed,
Rise from the ground like feathered Mercury,
And vaulted with such ease into his seat,
As if an angel dropped down from the clouds,
To turn and wind a fiery Pegasus,
And witch the world with noble horsemanship. 110
HOTSPUR. No more, no more! worse than the sun in
March,
This praise doth nourish agues. Let them come,
They come like sacrifices in their trim,
And to the fire-eyed maid of smoky war
All hot and bleeding will we offer them.
The mailèd Mars shall on his altar sit,
Up to the ears in blood. I am on fire
To hear this rich reprisal is so nigh,
And yet not ours . . . Come, let me taste my horse,
Who is to bear me like a thunderbolt 120
Against the bosom of the Prince of Wales.
Harry to Harry shall, hot horse to horse,
Meet and ne'er part till one drop down a corse.
O, that Glendower were come!
VERNON.   There is more news.
I learned in Worcester, as I rode along,
He cannot draw his power this fourteen days.
DOUGLAS. That's the worst tidings that I hear of yet.
WORCESTER. Ay, by my faith, that bears a frosty sound.
HOTSPUR. What may the king's whole battle reach
unto?
VERNON. To thirty thousand.
HOTSPUR.   Forty let it be! 130
My father and Glendower being both away,
The powers of us may serve so great a day.
Come, let us take a muster speedily—
Doomsday is near—die all, die merrily.
DOUGLAS. Talk not of dying, I am out of fear

Of death or death's hand for this one half year.
                         They go

Scene 2: *A highway near Coventry*

Enter Falstaff with Bardolph

FALSTAFF. Bardolph, get thee before to Coventry, fill
me a bottle of sack, our soldiers shall march through.
We'll to Sutton Co'fil' to-night.
BARDOLPH. Will you give me money, captain?
FALSTAFF. Lay out, lay out.
BARDOLPH. This bottle makes an angel.
FALSTAFF. An if it do, take it for thy labour—and if it
make twenty, take them all, I'll answer the coinage.
Bid my lieutenant Peto meet me at town's end.
BARDOLPH. I will, captain. Farewell.   *He goes* 10
FALSTAFF. If I be not ashamed of my soldiers, I am a
soused gurnet. I have misused the king's press damn-
ably. I have got in exchange of a hundred and fifty
soldiers three hundred and odd pounds. I press me
none but good householders, yeomen's sons, inquire
me out contracted bachelors, such as had been asked
twice on the banns, such a commodity of warm
slaves, as had as lieve hear the devil as a drum, such
as fear the report of a caliver worse than a struck
fowl or a hurt wild-duck: I pressed me none but 20
such toasts-and-butter, with hearts in their bellies no
bigger than pins' heads, and they have bought out
their services, and now my whole charge consists of
ancients, corporals, lieutenants, gentlemen of companies—slaves as ragged as Lazarus in the painted
cloth, where the Glutton's dogs licked his sores, and
such as indeed were never soldiers, but discarded
unjust serving-men, younger sons to younger
brothers, revolted tapsters, and ostlers trade-fallen,
the cankers of a calm world and a long peace, ten 30
times more dishonourable ragged than an old feazed
ancient; and such have I to fill up the rooms of them
as have bought out their services, that you would
think that I had a hundred and fifty tattered prodi-
gals, lately come from swine-keeping, from eating
draff and husks. A mad fellow met me on the way,
and told me I had unloaded all the gibbets and
pressed the dead bodies. No eye hath seen such
scarecrows. I'll not march through Coventry with
them, that's flat: nay, and the villains march wide 40
betwixt the legs as if they had gyves on, for indeed
I had the most of them out of prison. There's not
a shirt and a half in all my company, and the half
shirt is two napkins tacked together and thrown
over the shoulders like a herald's coat without
sleeves, and the shirt, to say the truth, stolen from
my host at Saint Alban's or the red-nose innkeeper
of Daventry. But that's all one; they'll find linen
enough on every hedge.

Enter Prince Henry and Westmoreland

PRINCE. How now, blown Jack? how now, quilt? 50
FALSTAFF. What, Hal? how now, mad wag? what a
devil dost thou in Warwickshire?—My good Lord
of Westmoreland, I cry you mercy. I thought your
honour had already been at Shrewsbury.
WESTMORELAND. Faith, Sir John, 'tis more than time
that I were there, and you too; but my powers are
there already. The king, I can tell you, looks for us
all, we must away all night.

FALSTAFF. Tut, never fear me, I am as vigilant as a cat
to steal cream.   60
PRINCE. I think, to steal cream indeed, for thy theft
hath already made thee butter. But tell me, Jack,
whose fellows are these that come after?
FALSTAFF. Mine, Hal, mine.
PRINCE. I did never see such pitiful rascals.
FALSTAFF. Tut, tut, good enough to toss, food for
powder, food for powder—they'll fill a pit as well
as better; tush, man, mortal men, mortal men.
WESTMORELAND. Ay, but, Sir John, methinks they are
exceeding poor and bare, too beggarly.   70
FALSTAFF. Faith, for their poverty, I know not where
they had that, and for their bareness I am sure they
never learned that of me.
PRINCE. No, I'll be sworn, unless you call three fingers
in the ribs, bare. But, sirrah, make haste. Percy is
already in the field.   *He goes*
FALSTAFF. What, is the king encamped?
WESTMORELAND. He is, Sir John. I fear we shall stay
too long.   *He goes*
FALSTAFF. Well,   80
To the latter end of a fray and the beginning of a
feast
Fits a dull fighter and a keen guest.   *He follows*

Scene 3: *The rebel camp near Shrewsbury*

Enter Hotspur, Worcester, Douglas, and Vernon

HOTSPUR. We'll fight with him to-night.
WORCESTER.   It may not be.
DOUGLAS. You give him then advantage.
VERNON.   Not a whit.
HOTSPUR. Why say you so? looks he not for supply?
VERNON. So do we.
HOTSPUR.   His is certain, ours is doubtful.
WORCESTER. Good cousin, be advised, stir not
to-night.
VERNON. Do not, my lord.
DOUGLAS.   You do not counsel well;
You speak it out of fear and cold heart.
VERNON. Do me no slander, Douglas. By my life,
And I dare well maintain it with my life,
If well-respected honour bid me on,   10
I hold as little counsel with weak fear
As you, my lord, or any Scot that this day lives.
Let it be seen to-morrow in the battle,
Which of us fears.
DOUGLAS.   Yea, or to-night.
VERNON.   Content.
HOTSPUR. To-night, say I.
VERNON. Come, come, it may not be. I wonder much,
Being men of such great leading as you are,
That you foresee not what impediments
Drag back our expedition. Certain horse
Of my cousin Vernon's are not yet come up,   20
Your uncle Worcester's horse came but to-day,
And now their pride and mettle is asleep,
Their courage with hard labour tame and dull,
That not a horse is half the half himself.
HOTSPUR. So are the horses of the enemy
In general, journey-bated and brought low.
The better part of ours are full of rest.
WORCESTER. The number of the king exceedeth ours.
For God's sake, cousin, stay till all come in.
              The trumpet sounds a parley

Sir Walter Blunt comes up

BLUNT. I come with gracious offers from the king,   30
If you vouchsafe me hearing and respect.
HOTSPUR. Welcome, Sir Walter Blunt; and would to
God,
You were of our determination!
Some of us love you well, and even those some
Envy your great deservings and good name,
Because you are not of our quality,
But stand against us like an enemy.
BLUNT. And God defend but still I should stand so,
So long as out of limit and true rule
You stand against anointed majesty.   40
But to my charge. The king hath sent to know
The nature of your griefs, and whereupon,
You conjure from the breast of civil peace
Such bold hostility, teaching his duteous land
Audacious cruelty. If that the king
Have any way your good deserts forgot,
Which he confesseth to be manifold,
He bids you name your griefs, and with all speed
You shall have your desires with interest,
And pardon absolute for yourself and these   50
Herein misled by your suggestion.
HOTSPUR. The king is kind, and well we know the
king
Knows at what time to promise, when to pay:
My father and my uncle and myself
Did give him that same royalty he wears:
And when he was not six and twenty strong,
Sick in the world's regard, wretched and low,
A poor unminded outlaw sneaking home,
My father gave him welcome to the shore;
And when he heard him swear and vow to God   60
He came but to be Duke of Lancaster,
To sue his livery and beg his peace
With tears of innocency and terms of zeal,
My father, in kind heart and pity moved,
Swore him assistance and performed it too.
Now when the lords and barons of the realm
Perceived Northumberland did lean to him,
The more and less came in with cap and knee,
Met him in boroughs, cities, villages,
Attended him on bridges, stood in lanes,   70
Laid gifts before him, proffered him their oaths,
Gave him their heirs as pages, followed him
Even at the heels in golden multitudes.
He presently, as greatness knows itself,
Steps me a little higher than his vow
Made to my father while his blood was poor
Upon the naked shore at Ravenspurgh;
And now, forsooth, takes on him to reform
Some certain edicts and some strait decrees
That lie too heavy on the commonwealth,   80
Cries out upon abuses, seems to weep
Over his country's wrongs, and by this face,
This seeming brow of justice, did he win
The hearts of all that he did angle for;
Proceeded further—cut me off the heads
Of all the favourites that the absent king
In deputation left behind him here,
When he was personal in the Irish war.
BLUNT. Tut, I came not to hear this.
HOTSPUR.   Then to the point.
In short time after he deposed the king,   90

Soon after that deprived him of his life,
And in the neck of that tasked the whole state;
To make that worse, suffered his kinsman March
(Who is, if every owner were well placed,
Indeed his king) to be engaged in Wales,
There without ransom to lie forfeited;
Disgraced me in my happy victories,
Sought to entrap me by intelligence,
Rated mine uncle from the council-board,
In rage dismissed my father from the court,   100
Broke oath on oath, committed wrong on wrong,
And in conclusion drove us to seek out
This head of safety, and withal to pry
Into his title, the which we find
Too indirect for long continuance.
BLUNT. Shall I return this answer to the king?
HOTSPUR. Not so, Sir Walter. We'll withdraw awhile;
Go to the king, and let there be impawned
Some surety for a safe return again,
And in the morning early shall mine uncle   110
Bring him our purposes—and so farewell.
BLUNT. I would you would accept of grace and love.
HOTSPUR. And may be so we shall.
BLUNT.   Pray God you do.
                                              They go

Scene 4: *The Archbishop's palace*

Enter the Archbishop of York, and Sir Michael

ARCHBISHOP. Hie, good Sir Michael, bear this sealéd
      brief
With wingéd haste to the lord marshal,
This to my cousin Scroop, and all the rest
To whom they are directed. If you knew
How much they do import, you would make haste.
SIR MICHAEL. My good lord,
I guess their tenour.
ARCHBISHOP.   Like enough you do.
To-morrow, good Sir Michael, is a day
Wherein the fortune of ten thousand men
Must bide the touch; for, sir, at Shrewsbury,   10
As I am truly given to understand,
The king with mighty and quick-raiséd power
Meets with Lord Harry: and I fear, Sir Michael,
What with the sickness of Northumberland,
Whose power was in the first proportion,
And what with Owen Glendower's absence thence,
Who with them was a rated sinew too,
And comes not in, o'er-ruled by prophecies,
I fear the power of Percy is too weak
To wage an instant trial with the king.   20
SIR MICHAEL. Why, my good lord, you need not fear,
There is Douglas and Lord Mortimer.
ARCHBISHOP. No, Mortimer is not there.
SIR MICHAEL. But there is Mordake, Vernon, Lord
      Harry Percy,
And there is my Lord of Worcester, and a head
Of gallant warriors, noble gentlemen.
ARCHBISHOP. And so there is: but yet the king hath
      drawn
The special head of all the land together—
The Prince of Wales, Lord John of Lancaster,
The noble Westmoreland and warlike Blunt,   30
And many moe corrivals and dear men
Of estimation and command in arms.

SIR MICHAEL. Doubt not, my lord, they shall be well
      opposed.
ARCHBISHOP. I hope no less, yet needful 'tis to fear.
And, to prevent the worst, Sir Michael, speed:
For if Lord Percy thrive not, ere the king
Dismiss his power, he means to visit us,
For he hath heard of our confederacy,
And 'tis but wisdom to make strong against him.
Therefore, make haste. I must go write again   40
To other friends, and so farewell, Sir Michael.
                                              They go

ACT 5

Scene 1: *The King's camp near Shrewsbury*

*Enter the King, Prince Henry, Lord John of Lancaster,
Sir Walter Blunt, and Falstaff*

KING. How bloodily the sun begins to peer
Above yon busky hill! the day looks pale
At his distemp'rature.
PRINCE.   The southern wind
Doth play the trumpet to his purposes,
And by his hollow whistling in the leaves
Foretells a tempest and a blust'ring day.
KING. Then with the losers let it sympathize,
For nothing can seem foul to those that win.
                                              The trumpet sounds

Enter Worcester and Vernon

How now, my Lord of Worcester? 'tis not well
That you and I should meet upon such terms   10
As now we meet. You have deceived our trust,
And made us doff our easy robes of peace,
To crush our old limbs in ungentle steel.
This is not well, my lord, this is not well.
What say you to it? will you again unknit
This churlish knot of all-abhorréd war?
And move in that obedient orb again
Where you did give a fair and natural light,
And be no more an exhaled meteor,
A prodigy of fear, and a portent   20
Of broachéd mischief to the unborn times?
WORCESTER. Hear me, my liege:
For mine own part, I could be well content
To entertain the lag-end of my life
With quiet hours; for I do protest
I have not sought the day of this dislike.
KING. You have not sought it! how comes it then?
FALSTAFF. Rebellion lay in his way and he found it.
PRINCE. Peace, chewet, peace!
WORCESTER. It pleased your majesty to turn your looks   30
Of favour from myself and all our house,
And yet I must remember you, my lord,
We were the first and dearest of your friends.
For you my staff of office did I break
In Richard's time, and posted day and night
To meet you on the way, and kiss your hand,
When yet you were in place and in account
Nothing so strong and fortunate as I.
It was myself, my brother, and his son,
That brought you home, and boldly did outdare   40
The dangers of the time. You swore to us,
And you did swear that oath at Doncaster,
That you did nothing purpose 'gainst the state,
Nor claim no further than your new-fall'n right,

The seat of Gaunt, dukedom of Lancaster:
To this we swore our aid ... But in short space
It rained down fortune show'ring on your head,
And such a flood of greatness fell on you,
What with our help, what with the absent king,
What with the injuries of a wanton time, 50
The seeming sufferances that you had borne,
And the contrarious winds that held the king
So long in his unlucky Irish wars
That all in England did repute him dead:
And from this swarm of fair advantages
You took occasion to be quickly wooed
To gripe the general sway into your hand,
Forgot your oath to us at Doncaster,
And being fed by us you used us so
As that ungentle gull, the cuckoo's bird, 60
Useth the sparrow—did oppress our nest,
Grew by our feeding to so great a bulk
That even our love durst not come near your sight
For fear of swallowing; but with nimble wing
We were enforced for safety sake to fly
Out of your sight and raise this present head,
Whereby we stand opposéd by such means
As you yourself have forged against yourself,
By unkind usage, dangerous countenance,
And violation of all faith and troth 70
Sworn to us in your younger enterprise.
KING. These things indeed you have articulate,
Proclaimed at market-crosses, read in churches,
To face the garment of rebellion
With some fine colour that may please the eye
Of fickle changelings and poor discontents,
Which gape and rub the elbow at the news
Of hurlyburly innovation.
And never yet did insurrection want
Such water-colours to impaint his cause, 80
Nor moody beggars starving for a time
Of pellmell havoc and confusion.
PRINCE. In both our armies there is many a soul
Shall pay full dearly for this encounter,
If once they join in trial. Tell your nephew,
The Prince of Wales doth join with all the world
In praise of Henry Percy. By my hopes,
This present enterprise set off his head,
I do not think a braver gentleman,
More active-valiant or more valiant-young, 90
More daring or more bold, is now alive
To grace this latter age with noble deeds.
For my part, I may speak it to my shame,
I have a truant been to chivalry,
And so I hear he doth account me too;
Yet this before my father's majesty—
I am content that he shall take the odds
Of his great name and estimation,
And will, to save the blood on either side,
Try fortune with him in a single fight. 100
KING. And, Prince of Wales, so dare we venture thee,
Albeit considerations infinite
Do make against it ... No, good Worcester, no,
We love our people well—even those we love
That are misled upon your cousin's part—
And will they take the offer of our grace,
Both he, and they, and you, yea, every man
Shall be my friend again and I'll be his.
So tell your cousin, and bring me word
What he will do. But if he will not yield, 110

Rebuke and dread correction wait on us,
And they shall do their office. So, be gone;
We will not now be troubled with reply.
We offer fair, take it advisedly.
                              Worcester and Vernon go
PRINCE. It will not be accepted, on my life.
The Douglas and the Hotspur both together
Are confident against the world in arms.
KING. Hence, therefore, every leader to his charge,
For on their answer will we set on them,
And God befriend us, as our cause is just! 120
              They go; Falstaff and the Prince remain
FALSTAFF. Hal, if thou see me down in the battle and
bestride me, so, 'tis a point of friendship.
PRINCE. Nothing but a colossus can do thee that friend-
ship. Say thy prayers, and farewell.
FALSTAFF. I would 'twere bed-time, Hal, and all well.
PRINCE. Why, thou owest God a death.   *He goes*
FALSTAFF. 'Tis not due yet, I would be loath to pay him
before his day. What need I be so forward with
him that calls not on me? Well, 'tis no matter,
honour pricks me on. Yea, but how if honour prick 130
me off when I come on? how then? can honour set
to a leg? no—or an arm? no—or take away the
grief of a wound? no. Honour hath no skill in
surgery then? no. What is honour? a word. What is
in that word honour? what is that honour? air. A
trim reckoning! Who hath it? he that died a-
Wednesday. Doth he feel it? no. Doth he hear it?
no. 'Tis insensible then? yea, to the dead. But will
it not live with the living? no. Why? Detraction will
not suffer it. Therefore I'll none of it. Honour is a 140
mere scutcheon—and so ends my catechism.
                                            He goes

Scene 2: *A plain near the rebel camp*

Worcester and Vernon approach

WORCESTER. O, no, my nephew must not know, Sir
Richard,
The liberal and kind offer of the king.
VERNON. 'Twere best he did.
WORCESTER.   Then are we all undone.
It is not possible, it cannot be,
The king should keep his word in loving us.
He will suspect us still, and find a time
To punish this offence in other faults.
Supposition all our lives shall be stuck full
Of eyes,
For treason is but trusted like the fox, 10
Who, ne'er so tame, so cherished and locked up,
Will have a wild trick of his ancestors.
Look how we can, or sad or merrily,
Interpretation will misquote our looks,
And we shall feed like oxen at a stall,
The better cherished still the nearer death.
My nephew's trespass may be well forgot,
It hath the excuse of youth and heat of blood,
And an adopted name of privilege—
A hare-brained Hotspur, governed by a spleen. 20
All his offences live upon my head
And on his father's. We did train him on,
And his corruption being ta'en from us,
We as the spring of all shall pay for all ...
Therefore, good cousin, let not Harry know,
In any case, the offer of the king.

VERNON. Deliver what you will, I'll say 'tis so.
Here comes your cousin.

Hotspur and Douglas, with officers and soldiers come to
meet them

HOTSPUR. My uncle is returned.
Deliver up my Lord of Westmoreland.   30
Uncle, what news?
WORCESTER. The king will bid you battle presently.
DOUGLAS. Defy him by the Lord of Westmoreland.
HOTSPUR. Lord Douglas, go you and tell him so.
DOUGLAS. Marry, and shall, and very willingly.
                                              He goes
WORCESTER. There is no seeming mercy in the king.
HOTSPUR. Did you beg any? God forbid!
WORCESTER. I told him gently of our grievances,
Of his oath-breaking—which he mended thus,
By now forswearing that he is forsworn.   40
He calls us rebels, traitors, and will scourge
With haughty arms this hateful name in us.

Douglas returns

DOUGLAS. Arm, gentlemen, to arms! for I have
thrown
A brave defiance in King Henry's teeth,
And Westmoreland that was engaged did bear it,
Which cannot choose but bring him quickly on.
WORCESTER. The Prince of Wales stepped forth before
the king,
And, nephew, challenged you to single fight.
HOTSPUR. O, would the quarrel lay upon our heads,
And that no man might draw short breath to-day 50
But I and Harry Monmouth! Tell me, tell me,
How showed his tasking? seemed it in contempt?
VERNON. No, by my soul. I never in my life
Did hear a challenge urged more modestly,
Unless a brother should a brother dare
To gentle exercise and proof of arms.
He gave you all the duties of a man,
Trimmed up your praises with a princely tongue,
Spoke your deservings like a chronicle,
Making you ever better than his praise   60
By still dispraising praise valued with you,
And, which became him like a prince indeed,
He made a blushing cital of himself,
And chid his truant youth with such a grace,
As if he mast'red there a double spirit
Of teaching and of learning instantly.
There did he pause. But let me tell the world,
If he outlive the envy of this day,
England did never owe so sweet a hope,
So much misconstrued in his wantonness.   70
HOTSPUR. Cousin, I think thou art enamouréd
Upon his follies. Never did I hear
Of any prince so wild a liberty.
But be he as he will, yet once ere night
I will embrace him with a soldier's arm,
That he shall shrink under my courtesy.
Arm, arm, with speed—and, fellows, soldiers,
friends,
Better consider what you have to do
Than I, that have not well the gift of tongue,
Can lift your blood up with persuasion.   80

A messenger comes up

MESSENGER. My lord, here are letters for you.

HOTSPUR. I cannot read them now.
O gentlemen, the time of life is short!
To spend that shortness basely were too long,
If life did ride upon a dial's point,
Still ending at the arrival of an hour.
An if we live, we live to tread on kings,
If die, brave death, when princes die with us!
Now, for our consciences, the arms are fair,
When the intent of bearing them is just.   90

Another messenger enters

MESSENGER. My lord, prepare, the king comes on
apace.
HOTSPUR. I thank him that he cuts me from my tale,
For I profess not talking—only this,
Let each man do his best. And here draw I
A sword; whose temper I intend to stain
With the best blood that I can meet withal
In the adventure of this perilous day.
Now, Esperance! Percy! and set on.
Sound all the lofty instruments of war,
And by that music let us all embrace,   100
For, heaven to earth, some of us never shall
A second time do such a courtesy.
                        The trumpets sound. They embrace
                                        and depart

Scene 3

The king enters with his power and marches past.
Alarum to battle. Then enter Douglas and Sir Walter
Blunt (disguised as the king) fighting

BLUNT. What is thy name, that in the battle thus
Thou crossest me? what honour dost thou seek
Upon my head?
DOUGLAS.   Know then, my name is Douglas,
And I do haunt thee in the battle thus
Because some tell me that thou art a king.
BLUNT. They tell thee true.
DOUGLAS. The Lord of Stafford dear to-day hath
bought
Thy likeness, for instead of thee, King Harry,
This sword hath ended him. So shall it thee,
Unless thou yield thee as my prisoner.   10
BLUNT. I was not born a yielder, thou proud Scot,
And thou shalt find a king that will revenge
Lord Stafford's death.
                        They fight, Douglas kills Blunt

Hotspur comes up

HOTSPUR. O Douglas, hadst thou fought at
Holmedon thus,
I never had triumphed upon a Scot.
DOUGLAS. All's done, all's won! here breathless lies the
king.
HOTSPUR. Where?
DOUGLAS. Here.
HOTSPUR. This, Douglas? no, I know this face full
well.
A gallant knight he was, his name was Blunt,   20
Semblably furnished like the king himself.
DOUGLAS. A fool go with thy soul, whither it goes!
A borrowed title hast thou bought too dear.
Why didst thou tell me that thou wert a king?
HOTSPUR. The king hath many marching in his coats.
DOUGLAS. Now, by my sword, I will kill all his coats,

I'll murder all his wardrobe, piece by piece,
Until I meet the king.
HOTSPUR.   Up, and away!
Our soldiers stand full fairly for the day.
They go

Alarum. Enter Falstaff, solus

FALSTAFF. Though I could 'scape shot-free at London, 30
I fear the shot here, here's no scoring but upon the
pate. Soft! who are you? Sir Walter Blunt—there's
honour for you! here's no vanity! I am as hot as
molten lead, and as heavy too: God keep lead out
of me! I need no more weight than mine own
bowels. I have led my ragamuffins where they are
peppered, there's not three of my hundred and fifty
left alive, and they are for the town's end, to beg
during life ... But who comes here?

Prince Henry approaches

PRINCE. What, stand'st thou idle here? lend me thy
sword.   40
Many a nobleman lies stark and stiff
Under the hoofs of vaunting enemies,
whose deaths are yet unrevenged. I prithee, lend me
thy sword.
FALSTAFF. O Hal, I prithee, give me leave to breathe
awhile. Turk Gregory never did such deeds in arms
as I have done this day.
I have paid Percy, I have made him sure.
PRINCE. He is, indeed, and living to kill thee....
I prithee, lend me thy sword.   50
FALSTAFF. Nay, before God, Hal, if Percy be alive,
thou get'st not my sword, but take my pistol if thou
wilt.
PRINCE. Give it me. What, is it in the case?
FALSTAFF. Ay, Hal, 'tis hot, 'tis hot. There's that will
sack a city.
*The Prince draws it out and finds
it to be a bottle of sack*
PRINCE. What, is it a time to jest and dally now?
He throws the bottle at him, and goes
FALSTAFF. Well, if Percy be alive, I'll pierce him ...
[*aside*] If he do come in my way, so. If he do not, if
I come in his willingly, let him make a carbonado of 60
me. I like not such grinning honour as Sir Walter
hath. Give me life, which if I can save, so; if not,
honour comes unlooked for, and there's an end.
He goes

Scene 4

*Alarum, excursions. Enter the King, the Prince, wounded
in the cheek, Lord John of Lancaster, and Earl of
Westmoreland*

KING. I prithee,
Harry, withdraw thyself, thou bleedest too much.
Lord John of Lancaster, go you with him.
LANCASTER. Not I, my lord, unless I did bleed too.
PRINCE. I beseech your majesty, make up,
Lest your retirement do amaze your friends.
KING. I will do so. My Lord of Westmoreland, lead
him to his tent.
WESTMORELAND. Come, my lord, I'll lead you to your
tent.   10
PRINCE. Lead me, my lord? I do not need your help,
And God forbid a shallow scratch should drive

The Prince of Wales from such a field as this,
Where stained nobility lies trodden on,
And rebels' arms triumph in massacres!
LANCASTER. We breathe too long. Come, cousin
Westmoreland,
Our duty this way lies; for God's sake, come.
Lancaster and Westmoreland go
PRINCE. By God, thou hast deceived me, Lancaster,
I did not think thee lord of such a spirit.
Before, I loved thee as a brother, John,   20
But now, I do respect thee as my soul.
KING. I saw him hold Lord Percy at the point,
With lustier maintenance than I did look for
Of such an ungrown warrior.
PRINCE.   O, this boy
Lends mettle to us all!   *He follows*

Douglas appears

DOUGLAS. Another king! they grow like Hydra's
heads.
I am the Douglas, fatal to all those
That wear those colours on them. What art thou,
That counterfeit'st the person of a king?
KING. The king himself, who, Douglas, grieves at
heart   30
So many of his shadows thou hast met,
And not the very king. I have two boys
Seek Percy and thyself about the field,
But seeing thou fall'st on me so luckily
I will assay thee: so, defend thyself.
DOUGLAS. I fear thou art another counterfeit,
And yet in faith thou bear'st thee like a king,
But mine I am sure thou art, whoe'er thou be,
And thus I win thee.
*They fight. The King being in danger,
enter Prince of Wales*
PRINCE. Hold up thy head, vile Scot, or thou art like 40
Never to hold it up again! the spirits
Of valiant Shirley, Stafford, Blunt, are in my arms.
It is the Prince of Wales that threatens thee,
Who never promiseth but he means to pay....
They fight, Douglas flieth
Cheerly, my lord, how fares your grace?
Sir Nicholas Gawsey hath for succour sent,
And so hath Clifton—I'll to Clifton straight.
KING. Stay, and breathe awhile.
Thou hast redeemed thy lost opinion,
And showed thou mak'st some tender of my life,   50
In this fair rescue thou hast brought to me.
PRINCE. O God! they did me too much injury
That ever said I heark'ned for your death.
If it were so, I might have let alone
The insulting hand of Douglas over you,
Which would have been as speedy in your end
As all the poisonous potions in the world,
And saved the treacherous labour of your son.
KING. Make up to Clifton, I'll to Sir Nicholas Gawsey.
He goes

Hotspur enters

HOTSPUR. If I mistake not, thou art Harry Monmouth. 60
PRINCE. Thou speak'st as if I would deny my name.
HOTSPUR. My name is Harry Percy.
PRINCE.   Why, then I see
A very valiant rebel of the name.
I am the Prince of Wales, and think not, Percy,

To share with me in glory any more:
Two stars keep not their motion in one sphere,
Nor can one England brook a double reign,
Of Harry Percy and the Prince of Wales.
HOTSPUR. Nor shall it, Harry, for the hour is come
To end the one of us, and would to God   70
Thy name in arms were now as great as mine!
PRINCE. I'll make it greater ere I part from thee,
And all the budding honours on thy crest
I'll crop, to make a garland for my head.
HOTSPUR. I can no longer brook thy vanities.
They fight

Falstaff enters

FALSTAFF. Well said, Hal! to it, Hal! Nay, you shall
find no boy's play here, I can tell you.

*Douglas returns; he fighteth with Falstaff, who falls
down as if he were dead; he passes on. Hotspur is
wounded, and falls.*

HOTSPUR. O, Harry, thou hast robbed me of my
youth!
I better brook the loss of brittle life
Than those proud titles thou hast won of me.   80
They wound my thoughts worse than thy sword
my flesh.
But thought's the slave of life, and life time's fool,
And time that takes survey of all the world
Must have a stop. O, I could prophesy,
But that the earthy and cold hand of death
Lies on my tongue: no, Percy, thou art dust,
And food for—   *He dies*
PRINCE. For worms, brave Percy. Fare thee well,
great heart!
Ill-weaved ambition, how much art thou shrunk!
When that this body did contain a spirit,   90
A kingdom for it was too small a bound,
But now two paces of the vilest earth
Is room enough. This earth, that bears thee dead,
Bears not alive so stout a gentleman.
If thou wert sensible of courtesy,
I should not make so dear a show of zeal—
But let my favours hide thy mangled face!
And even in thy behalf I'll thank myself
For doing these fair rites of tenderness.
Adieu, and take thy praise with thee to heaven!   100
Thy ignominy sleep with thee in the grave,
But not remembered in thy epitaph!
He spieth Falstaff on the ground
What! old acquaintance! could not all this flesh
Keep in a little life? poor Jack, farewell!
I could have better spared a better man:
O, I should have a heavy miss of thee,
If I were much in love with vanity:
Death hath not struck so fat a deer to-day,
Though many dearer, in this bloody fray.
Embowelled will I see thee by and by,   110
Till then in blood by noble Percy lie.   *He goes*
FALSTAFF [*riseth up*]. Embowelled! if thou embowel
me to-day, I'll give you leave to powder me and eat
me too to-morrow. 'Sblood, 'twas time to counter-
feit, or that hot termagant Scot had paid me, scot
and lot too. Counterfeit? I lie, I am no counterfeit.
To die is to be a counterfeit, for he is but the
counterfeit of a man, who hath not the life of a man:
but to counterfeit dying, when a man thereby liveth,

is to be no counterfeit, but the true and perfect image   120
of life indeed. The better part of valour is discretion,
in the which better part I have saved my life.
'Zounds, I am afraid of this gunpowder Percy,
though he be dead. How, if he should counterfeit
too, and rise? by my faith, I am afraid he would
prove the better counterfeit. Therefore I'll make
him sure, yea, and I'll swear I killed him. Why may
not he rise as well as I? Nothing confutes me but
eyes, and nobody sees me: therefore, sirrah, [*stabs
him*] with a new wound in your thigh, come you   130
along with me.   *He takes up Hotspur on his back*

The Prince and Lord John of Lancaster return

PRINCE. Come, brother John, full bravely hast thou
fleshed
Thy maiden sword.
LANCASTER.   But, soft! whom have we here?
Did you not tell me this fat man was dead?
PRINCE. I did, I saw him dead,
Breathless and bleeding on the ground. Art thou
alive?
Or is it phantasy that plays upon our eyesight?
I prithee, speak. We will not trust our eyes,
Without our ears. Thou art not what thou seem'st.
FALSTAFF. No, that's certain, I am not a double-man: 140
but if I be not Jack Falstaff, then am I a Jack: there
is Percy! [*throws the body down*] If your father will
do me any honour, so; if not, let him kill the next
Percy himself ... I look to be either earl or duke, I
can assure you.
PRINCE. Why, Percy I killed myself, and saw thee
dead.
FALSTAFF. Didst thou? Lord, Lord, how this world is
given to lying! I grant you I was down and out of
breath, and so was he, but we rose both at an instant,   150
and fought a long hour by Shrewsbury clock. If I
may be believed, so: if not, let them that should
reward valour bear the sin upon their own heads.
I'll take it upon my death, I gave him this wound
in the thigh. If the man were alive, and would deny
it, 'zounds, I would make him eat a piece of my
sword.
LANCASTER. This is the strangest tale that ever I heard.
PRINCE. This is the strangest fellow, brother John.
Come, bring your luggage nobly on your back.   160
For my part, if a lie may do thee grace,
I'll gild it with the happiest terms I have.
A retreat is sounded
The trumpet sounds retreat, the day is ours.
Come, brother, let's to the highest of the field,
To see what friends are living, who are dead.
They go
FALSTAFF. I'll follow, as they say, for reward. He that
rewards me, God reward him! If I do grow great,
I'll grow less, for I'll purge, and leave sack, and live
cleanly as a nobleman should do.   *He follows*

Scene 5

*The Trumpets sound. Enter the King, Prince of Wales,
Lord John of Lancaster, Earl of Westmoreland, with
Worcester and Vernon prisoners*

KING. Thus ever did rebellion find rebuke.
Ill-spirited Worcester! did not we send grace,
Pardon and terms of love to all of you?

And wouldst thou turn our offers contrary?
Misuse the tenour of thy kinsman's trust?
Three knights upon our party slain to-day,
A noble earl and many a creature else,
Had been alive this hour,
If like a Christian thou hadst truly borne
Betwixt our armies true intelligence.   10
WORCESTER. What I have done my safety urged
    me to;
And I embrace this fortune patiently,
Since not to be avoided it falls on me.
KING. Bear Worcester to the death, and Vernon too:
Other offenders we will pause upon.
                    Worcester and Vernon are led away
How goes the field?
PRINCE. The noble Scot, Lord Douglas, when he saw
The fortune of the day quite turned from him,
The noble Percy slain, and all his men
Upon the foot of fear, fled with the rest,   20
And falling from a hill, he was so bruised
That the pursuers took him. At my tent
The Douglas is; and I beseech your grace
I may dispose of him.
KING.   With all my heart.

PRINCE. Then, brother John of Lancaster, to you
This honourable bounty shall belong.
Go to the Douglas, and deliver him
Up to his pleasure, ransomless and free.
His valours shown upon our crests to-day
Have taught us how to cherish such high deeds,   30
Even in the bosom of our adversaries.
LANCASTER. I thank your grace for this high courtesy,
Which I shall give away immediately.
KING. Then this remains, that we divide our power.
You, son John, and my cousin Westmoreland
Towards York shall bend, you with your dearest
    speed
To meet Northumberland and the prelate Scroop,
Who, as we hear, are busily in arms:
Myself and you, son Harry, will towards Wales,
To fight with Glendower and the Earl of March.   40
Rebellion in this land shall lose his sway,
Meeting the check of such another day,
And since this business so fair is done,
Let us not leave till all our own be won.
                    They go

The Second Part of the History of Henry IV

The scene: England

CHARACTERS IN THE PLAY

RUMOUR, *the Presenter*
KING HENRY *the Fourth*
PRINCE HENRY, *afterwards crowned*
  King Henry V
PRINCE JOHN OF LANCASTER
PRINCE HUMPHREY OF GLOUCESTER
PRINCE THOMAS OF CLARENCE
} *sons to King Henry the Fourth*

EARL *of* WARWICK
EARL *of* WESTMORELAND
EARL *of* SURREY (*mute*)
EARL *of* KENT (*mute*)
GOWER
HARCOURT
SIR JOHN BLUNT (*mute*)
LORD CHIEF JUSTICE
} *of the king's party*

A Servant to the Lord Chief Justice

EARL *of* NORTHUMBERLAND
SCROOP, *Archbishop of York*
LORD MOWBRAY
LORD HASTINGS
LORD BARDOLPH
SIR JOHN COLEVILLE
} *opposites against King Henry the Fourth*

TRAVERS *and* MORTON, *retainers to Northumberland*

EDWARD POINS, *gentleman-in-waiting to Prince Henry*
FALSTAFF
BARDOLPH
PISTOL
PETO
A Page
} *irregular humourists*

SHALLOW
SILENCE
} *country justices*

DAVY, *servant to Shallow*
FRANCIS *and another drawer*
FANG *and* SNARE, *a sergeant and his yeoman*
MOULDY
SHADOW
WART
FEEBLE
BULLCALF
} *country soldiers*

LADY NORTHUMBERLAND
LADY PERCY
HOSTESS QUICKLY
DOLL TEARSHEET
EPILOGUE
Lords and Attendants; a Porter, Beadles, three Strewers of rushes.

The Second Part of the History of Henry IV

INDUCTION

Warkworth. Before Northumberland's castle

Enter Rumour, painted full of tongues

RUMOUR. Open your ears; for which of you will stop
The vent of hearing when loud Rumour speaks?
I from the orient to the drooping west,
Making the wind my post-horse, still unfold
The acts commencéd on this ball of earth.
Upon my tongues continual slanders ride,
The which in every language I pronounce,
Stuffing the ears of men with false reports.
I speak of peace while covert enmity
Under the smile of safety wounds the world: 10
And who but Rumour, who but only I,
Make fearful musters and prepared defence,
Whiles the big year, swoln with some other grief,
Is thought with child by the stern tyrant war,
And no such matter? Rumour is a pipe
Blown by surmises, jealousies, conjectures,
And of so easy and so plain a stop
That the blunt monster with uncounted heads,
The still-discordant wav'ring multitude,
Can play upon it.... But what need I thus   20
My well-known body to anatomize
Among my household? Why is Rumour here?
I run before King Harry's victory,
Who in a bloody field by Shrewsbury
Hath beaten down young Hotspur and his troops,
Quenching the flame of bold rebellion,
Even with the rebels' blood. But what mean I
To speak so true at first? my office is
To noise abroad that Harry Monmouth fell
Under the wrath of noble Hotspur's sword,   30
And that the king before the Douglas' rage
Stooped his anointed head as low as death.
This have I rumoured through the peasant towns
Between that royal field of Shrewsbury
And this worm-eaten hold of ragged stone,
Where Hotspur's father, old Northumberland,
Lies crafty-sick. The posts coming tiring on,
And not a man of them brings other news
Than they have learned of me. From Rumour's
      tongues
They bring smooth comforts false, worse than
      true wrongs.   *He goes* 40

ACT 1
Scene I

Enter the Lord Bardolph

L. BARDOLPH. Who keeps the gate here, ho?
                              A Porter appears
                              Where is the earl?
PORTER. What shall I say you are?
L. BARDOLPH.   Tell thou the earl
That the Lord Bardolph doth attend him here.
PORTER. His lordship is walked forth into the orchard,
Please it your honour knock but at the gate,
And he himself will answer.

*Northumberland enters, hobbling upon a crutch and with
his head muffled*

L. BARDOLPH.   Here comes the earl.
NORTHUMBERLAND. What news, Lord Bardolph?
      every minute now
Should be the father of some stratagem.
The times are wild, contention like a horse,
Full of high feeding, madly hath broke loose,   10
And bears down all before him.
L. BARDOLPH.   Noble earl,
I bring you certain news from Shrewsbury.
NORTHUMBERLAND. Good, an God will!
L. BARDOLPH.   As good as heart can wish:
The king is almost wounded to the death,
And in the fortune of my lord your son
Prince Harry slain outright, and both the Blunts
Killed by the hand of Douglas, young Prince John
And Westmoreland and Stafford fled the field,
And Harry Monmouth's brawn, the hulk Sir
      John,
Is prisoner to your son: O, such a day,   20
So fought, so followed, and so fairly won,
Came not till now to dignify the times,
Since Cæsar's fortunes!
NORTHUMBERLAND.   How is this derived?
Saw you the field? came you from Shrewsbury?
L. BARDOLPH. I spake with one, my lord, that came
      from thence,
A gentleman well bred and of good name,
That freely rend'red me these news for true,

Travers approaches

NORTHUMBERLAND. Here comes my servant Travers,
      whom I sent
On Tuesday last to listen after news.
L. BARDOLPH. My lord, I over-rode him on the way,   30
And he is furnished with no certainties
More than he haply may retail from me.
NORTHUMBERLAND. Now, Travers, what good tidings
      comes with you?
TRAVERS. My lord, Sir John Umfrevile turned
      me back
With joyful tidings, and, being better horsed,
Out-rode me. After him came spurring hard
A gentleman, almost forspent with speed,
That stopped by me to breathe his bloodied horse.
He asked the way to Chester, and of him
I did demand what news from Shrewsbury.   40
He told me that rebellion had bad luck,
And that young Harry Percy's spur was cold:
With that he gave his able horse the head,
And bending forward struck his arméd heels
Against the panting sides of his poor jade
Up to the rowel-head, and starting so
He seemed in running to devour the way,
Staying no longer question.
NORTHUMBERLAND.   Ha? Again!
Said he young Harry Percy's spur was cold?

Of Hotspur Coldspur? that rebellion
Had met ill luck?
L. BARDOLPH.   My lord, I'll tell you what—
If my young lord your son have not the day,
Upon mine honour, for a silken point
I'll give my barony. Never talk of it.
NORTHUMBERLAND. Why should that gentleman that
  rode by Travers
Give then such instances of loss?
L. BARDOLPH.   Who, he?
He was some hilding fellow, that had stol'n
The horse he rode on, and upon my life
Spoke at a venture. Look, here comes more news.

Morton enters

NORTHUMBERLAND. Yea, this man's brow, like to
  a title-leaf,   60
Foretells the nature of a tragic volume.
So looks the strond whereon the imperious flood
Hath left a witnessed usurpation....
Say, Morton, didst thou come from Shrewsbury?
MORTON. I ran from Shrewsbury, my noble lord,
Where hateful death put on his ugliest mask
To fright our party.
NORTHUMBERLAND. How doth my son and brother?
Thou tremblest, and the whiteness in thy cheek
Is apter than thy tongue to tell thy errand.
Even such a man, so faint, so spiritless,   70
So dull, so dead in look, so woe-begone,
Drew Priam's curtain in the dead of night,
And would have told him half his Troy was burnt:
But Priam found the fire ere he his tongue,
And I my Percy's death ere thou report'st it.
This thou wouldst say, 'Your son did thus and thus,
Your brother thus; so fought the noble Douglas'—
Stopping my greedy ear with their bold deeds,
But in the end, to stop my ear indeed,
Thou hast a sigh to blow away this praise,   80
Ending with 'Brother, son, and all are dead.'
MORTON. Douglas is living, and your brother yet,
But for my lord your son ...
NORTHUMBERLAND.   Why, he is dead.
See what a ready tongue suspicion hath!
He that but fears the thing he would not know,
Hath by instinct knowledge from others' eyes
That what he feared is chancéd ... Yet speak,
  Morton.
Tell thou an earl his divination lies,
And I will take it as a sweet disgrace,
And make thee rich for doing me such wrong.   90
MORTON. You are too great to be by me gainsaid,
Your spirit is too true, your fears too certain.
NORTHUMBERLAND. Yet, for all this, say not that
  Percy's dead.
I see a strange confession in thine eye,
Thou shak'st thy head, and hold'st it fear or sin
To speak a truth: if he be slain, say so.
The tongue offends not that reports his death,
And he doth sin that doth belie the dead,
Not he which says the dead is not alive.
Yet the first bringer of unwelcome news   100
Hath but a losing office, and his tongue
Sounds ever after as a sullen bell,
Remembered tolling a departing friend.
L. BARDOLPH. I cannot think, my lord, your son
  is dead.

MORTON. I am sorry I should force you to believe   50
That which I would to God I had not seen,
But these mine eyes saw him in bloody state,
Rend'ring faint quittance, wearied and
  out-breathed,
To Harry Monmouth, whose swift wrath beat
  down
The never-daunted Percy to the earth,   110
From whence with life he never more sprung up.
In few, his death, whose spirit lent a fire
Even to the dullest peasant in his camp,
Being bruited once, took fire and heat away
From the best-tempered courage in his troops.
For from his mettle was his party steeled,
Which once in him abated, all the rest
Turned on themselves, like dull and heavy lead.
And as the thing that's heavy in itself,
Upon enforcement flies with greatest speed,   120
So did our men, heavy in Hotspur's loss,
Lend to this weight such lightness with their fear,
That arrows fled not swifter toward their aim
Than did our soldiers, aiming at their safety,
Fly from the field: then was that noble Worcester
Too soon ta'en prisoner, and that furious Scot,
The bloody Douglas, whose well-labouring sword
Had three times slain th' appearance of the king,
'Gan vail his stomach and did grace the shame
Of those that turned their backs, and in his flight, 130
Stumbling in fear, was took: the sum of all
Is that the king hath won, and hath sent out
A speedy power to encounter you, my lord,
Under the conduct of young Lancaster
And Westmoreland ... This is the news at full.
NORTHUMBERLAND. For this I shall have time enough
  to mourn.
In poison there is physic; and these news,
Having been well, that would have made me sick,
Being sick, have (in some measure) made me well:
And as the wretch whose fever-weak'ned joints,   140
Like strengthless hinges, buckle under life,
Impatient of his fit, breaks like a fire
Out of his keeper's arms; even so my limbs,
Weakened with grief, being now enraged with
  grief,
Are thrice themselves: hence therefore, thou nice
  crutch!
A scaly gauntlet now with joints of steel
Must glove this hand, and hence, thou sickly coif!
Thou art a guard too wanton for the head
Which princes, fleshed with conquest, aim to hit:
Now bind my brows with iron, and approach   150
The ragged'st hour that Time and Spite dare bring
To frown upon th'enragéd Northumberland!
Let heaven kiss earth! now let not Nature's hand
Keep the wild flood confined! let Order die!
And let this world no longer be a stage
To feed contention in a ling'ring act;
But let one spirit of the first-born Cain
Reign in all bosoms, that, each heart being set
On bloody courses, the rude scene may end,
And darkness be the burier of the dead!   160
L. BARDOLPH. This strainéd passion doth you wrong,
  my lord.
MORTON. Sweet earl, divorce not wisdom from your
  honour.
The lives of all your loving complices

Lean on your health, the which, if you give o'er
To stormy passion, must perforce decay.
You cast th'event of war, my noble lord,
And summed the account of chance, before you said
'Let us make head': it was your presurmise,
That, in the dole of blows, your son might drop:
You knew he walked o'er perils, on an edge,   170
More likely to fall in than to get o'er:
You were advised his flesh was capable
Of wounds and scars, and that his forward spirit
Would lift him where most trade of danger ranged.
Yet did you say 'Go forth'; and none of this,
Though strongly apprehended, could restrain
The stiff-borne action: what hath then befall'n,
Or what hath this bold enterprise brought forth,
More than that being which was like to be?

L. BARDOLPH. We all that are engaged to this loss   180
Knew that we ventured on such dangerous seas
That if we wrought out life 'twas ten to one,
And yet we ventured for the gain proposed,
Choked the respect of likely peril feared,
And, since we are o'erset, venture again . . .
Come, we will all put forth body and goods.

MORTON. 'Tis more than time: and, my most noble
     lord,
I hear for certain, and dare speak the truth,
The gentle Archbishop of York is up
With well-appointed powers; he is a man   190
Who with a double surety binds his followers.
My lord your son had only but the corpse,
But shadows and the shows of men, to fight:
For that same word, rebellion, did divide
The action of their bodies from their souls,
And they did fight with queasiness, constrained,
As men drink potions, that their weapons only
Seemed on our side; but, for their spirits and souls,
This word, rebellion, it had froze them up,
As fish are in a pond. But now the bishop   200
Turns insurrection to religion:
Supposed sincere and holy in his thoughts,
He's followed both with body and with mind;
And doth enlarge his rising with the blood
Of fair King Richard, scraped from Pomfret stones;
Derives from heaven his quarrel and his cause;
Tells them he doth bestride a bleeding land,
Gasping for life under great Bolingbroke;
And more and less do flock to follow him.

NORTHUMBERLAND. I knew of this before: but, to
     speak truth,   210
This present grief had wiped it from my mind.
Go in with me, and counsel every man
The aptest way for safety and revenge.
Get posts and letters, and make friends with speed;
Never so few, and never yet more need.   *They go*

Scene 2: *A street in London*

*Enter Sir John Falstaff; his Page, bearing his sword and
buckler, following*

FALSTAFF. Sirrah, you giant, what says the doctor to
my water?

PAGE. He said, sir, the water itself was a good healthy
water, but for the party that owed it, he might have
moe diseases than he knew for.

FALSTAFF. Men of all sorts take a pride to gird at me:
the brain of this foolish-compounded clay-man is
not able to invent any thing that intends to laughter,
more than I invent or is invented on me. I am not
only witty in myself, but the cause that wit is in   10
other men. I do here walk before thee like a sow
that hath overwhelmed all her litter but one. If the
prince put thee into my service for any other reason
than to set me off, why then I have no judgement.
Thou whoreson mandrake, thou art fitter to be
worn in my cap than to wait at my heels. I was
never manned with an agate till now: but I will
inset you neither in gold nor silver, but in vile
apparel, and send you back again to your master,
for a jewel—the juvenal, the prince your master,   20
whose chin is not yet fledge. I will sooner have a
beard grow in the palm of my hand than he shall
get one off his cheek; and yet he will not stick to say
his face is a face royal: God may finish it when he
will, 'tis not a hair amiss yet: he may keep it still
at a face-royal, for a barber shall never earn sixpence
out of it; and yet he'll be crowing as if he had writ
man ever since his father was a bachelor. He may
keep his own grace, but he's almost out of mine, I
can assure him . . . What said Master Dommelton   30
about the satin for my short cloak and my slops?

PAGE. He said, sir, you should procure him better
assurance than Bardolph, he would not take his band
and yours, he liked not the security.

FALSTAFF. Let him be damned like the Glutton! pray
God his tongue be hotter! A whoreson Achitophel!
a rascally yea-forsooth knave! to bear a gentleman
in hand, and then stand upon security! The whoreson smooth-pates do now wear nothing but high
shoes, and bunches of keys at their girdles, and if   40
a man is through with them in honest taking-up,
then they must stand upon security. I had as lief
they would put ratsbane in my mouth as offer to
stop it with security. I looked a' should have sent
me two and twenty yards of satin, as I am a true
knight, and he sends me 'security' . . . Well, he may
sleep in security, for he hath the horn of abundance,
and the lightness of his wife shines through it, and
yet cannot he see, though he have his own lanthorn
to light him. . . . Where's Bardolph?   50

PAGE. He's gone into Smithfield to buy your worship
a horse.

FALSTAFF. I bought him in Paul's, and he'll buy me a
horse in Smithfield; an I could get me but a wife in
the stews, I were manned, horsed, and wived.

The Lord Chief Justice approaches, with a servant

PAGE. Sir, here comes the nobleman that committed
the prince for striking him about Bardolph.

FALSTAFF. Wait close, I will not see him.

L. CHIEF JUSTICE. What's he that goes there?

SERVANT. Falstaff, an't please your lordship.   60

L. CHIEF JUSTICE. He that was in question for the
robbery?

SERVANT. He, my lord. But he hath since done good
service at Shrewsbury, and, as I hear, is now going
with some charge to the Lord John of Lancaster.

L. CHIEF JUSTICE. What, to York? Call him back again.

SERVANT. Sir John Falstaff!

FALSTAFF. Boy, tell him I am deaf.

PAGE. You must speak louder, my master is deaf.

L. CHIEF JUSTICE. I am sure he is, to the hearing of any 70 thing good. Go, pluck him by the elbow. I must speak with him.

SERVANT. Sir John!

FALSTAFF. What! a young knave, and begging! Is there not wars? is there not employment? doth not the king lack subjects? do not the rebels need soldiers? Though it be a shame to be on any side but one, it is worse shame to beg than to be on the worst side, were it worse than the name of rebellion can tell how to make it. 80

SERVANT. You mistake me, sir.

FALSTAFF. Why, sir, did I say you were an honest man? setting my knighthood and my soldiership aside, I had lied in my throat, if I had said so.

SERVANT. I pray you, sir, then set your knighthood and your soldiership aside, and give me leave to tell you, you lie in your throat, if you say I am any other than an honest man.

FALSTAFF. I give thee leave to tell me so! I lay aside that which grows to me! If thou get'st any leave of 90 me, hang me. If thou tak'st leave, thou wert better be hanged. You hunt counter, hence! avaunt!

SERVANT. Sir, my lord would speak with you.

L. CHIEF JUSTICE. Sir John Falstaff, a word with you.

FALSTAFF. My good lord! God give your lordship good time of day, I am glad to see your lordship abroad, I heard say your lordship was sick, I hope your lordship goes abroad by advice. Your lordship, though not clean past your youth, have yet some smack of age in you, some relish of the saltness of 100 time, and I most humbly beseech your lordship to have a reverend care of your health.

L. CHIEF JUSTICE. Sir John, I sent for you before your expedition to Shrewsbury.

FALSTAFF. An't please your lordship, I hear his majesty is returned with some discomfort from Wales.

L. CHIEF JUSTICE. I talk not of his majesty. You would not come when I sent for you.

FALSTAFF. And I hear, moreover, his highness is fallen into this same whoreson apoplexy. 110

L. CHIEF JUSTICE. Well, God mend him! I pray you, let me speak with you.

FALSTAFF. This apoplexy, as I take it, is a kind of lethargy, an't please your lordship, a kind of sleeping in the blood, a whoreson tingling.

L. CHIEF JUSTICE. What tell you me of it? be it as it is.

FALSTAFF. It hath it original from much grief, from study and perturbation of the brain. I have read the cause of his effects in Galen, it is a kind of deafness.

L. CHIEF JUSTICE. I think you are fallen into the disease, 120 for you hear not what I say to you.

FALSTAFF. Very well, my lord, very well—rather, an't please you, it is the disease of not listening, the malady of not marking, that I am troubled withal.

L. CHIEF JUSTICE. To punish you by the heels would amend the attention of your ears, and I care not if I do become your physician.

FALSTAFF. I am as poor as Job, my lord, but not so patient. Your lordship may minister the potion of imprisonment to me, in respect of poverty, but how 130 I should be your patient to follow your prescriptions, the wise may make some dram of a scruple, or indeed a scruple itself.

L. CHIEF JUSTICE. I sent for you, when there were

matters against you for your life, to come speak with me.

FALSTAFF. As I was then advised by my learned counsel in the laws of this land service, I did not come.

L. CHIEF JUSTICE. Well, the truth is, Sir John, you live in great infamy. 140

FALSTAFF. He that buckles himself in my belt cannot live in less.

L. CHIEF JUSTICE. Your means are very slender, and your waste is great.

FALSTAFF. I would it were otherwise, I would my means were greater and my waist slenderer.

L. CHIEF JUSTICE. You have misled the youthful prince.

FALSTAFF. The young prince hath misled me. I am the fellow with the great belly, and he my dog.

L. CHIEF JUSTICE. Well, I am loath to gall a new-healed 150 wound. Your day's service at Shrewsbury hath a little gilded over your night's exploit on Gad's Hill, you may thank th'unquiet time for your quiet o'erposting that action.

FALSTAFF. My lord!

L. CHIEF JUSTICE. But since all is well, keep it so, wake not a sleeping wolf.

FALSTAFF. To wake a wolf is as bad as smell a fox.

L. CHIEF JUSTICE. What, you are as a candle, the better part burnt out. 160

FALSTAFF. A wassail candle, my lord, all tallow—if I did say of wax, my growth would approve the truth.

L. CHIEF JUSTICE. There is not a white hair on your face, but should have his effect of gravity.

FALSTAFF. His effect of gravy, gravy, gravy.

L. CHIEF JUSTICE. You follow the young prince up and down, like his ill angel.

FALSTAFF. Not so, my lord, your ill angel is light, but I hope he that looks upon me will take me without 170 weighing, and yet in some respects I grant I cannot go.... I cannot tell. Virtue is of so little regard in these costermongers' times that true valour is turned bear'ard: pregnancy is made a tapster, and his quick wit wasted in giving reckonings: all the other gifts appertinent to man, as the malice of this age shapes them, are not worth a gooseberry. You that are old consider not the capacities of us that are young, you do measure the heat of our livers with the bitterness of your galls, and we that are in the 180 vaward of our youth, I must confess, are wags too.

L. CHIEF JUSTICE. Do you set down your name in the scroll of youth, that are written down old with all the characters of age? Have you not a moist eye? a dry hand? a yellow cheek? a white beard? a decreasing leg? an increasing belly? is not your voice broken? your wind short? your chin double? your wit single? and every part about you blasted with antiquity? and will you yet call yourself young? Fie, fie, fie, Sir John! 190

FALSTAFF. My lord, I was born about three of the clock in the afternoon, with a white head and something a round belly. For my voice, I have lost it with hallooing and singing of anthems.... To approve my youth further, I will not: the truth is, I am only old in judgement and understanding; and he that will caper with me for a thousand marks, let him lend me the money, and have at him. For the box of the ear that the prince gave you, he gave it like a rude prince, and you took it like a sensible lord: I have 200

checked him for it, and the young lion repents—
[*aside*] marry, not in ashes and sackcloth, but in new
silk and old sack.
L. CHIEF JUSTICE. Well, God send the prince a better
companion!
FALSTAFF. God send the companion a better prince!
I cannot rid my hands of him.
L. CHIEF JUSTICE. Well, the king hath severed you: I
hear you are going with Lord John of Lancaster
against the Archbishop and the Earl of Northum-   210
berland.
FALSTAFF. Yea, I thank your pretty sweet wit for it . . .
But look you, pray, all you that kiss my lady
Peace at home, that our armies join not in a hot
day! for, by the Lord, I take but two shirts out
with me, and I mean not to sweat extraordinarily:
if it be a hot day, and I brandish any thing but a
bottle, I would I might never spit white again . . .
There is not a dangerous action can peep out his head
but I am thrust upon it. Well, I cannot last ever,   220
but it was always yet the trick of our English
nation, if they have a good thing, to make it too
common. If ye will needs say I am an old man, you
should give me rest: I would to God my name were
not so terrible to the enemy as it is. I were better to
be eaten to death with a rust than to be scoured to
nothing with perpetual motion.
L. CHIEF JUSTICE. Well, be honest, be honest, and God
bless your expedition!
FALSTAFF. Will your lordship lend me a thousand   230
pound to furnish me forth?
L. CHIEF JUSTICE. Not a penny, not a penny, you are
too impatient to bear crosses: fare you well: commend me to my cousin Westmoreland.
He goes, the servant following
FALSTAFF. If I do, fillip me with a three-man beetle . . .
A man can no more separate age and covetousness
than a' can part young limbs and lechery: but the
gout galls the one, and the pox pinches the other;
and so both the degrees prevent my curses. Boy!
PAGE. Sir?   240
FALSTAFF. What money is in my purse?
PAGE. Seven groats and two pence.
FALSTAFF. I can get no remedy against this consumption of the purse, borrowing only lingers and lingers
it out, but the disease is incurable. . . . Go bear this
letter to my Lord of Lancaster, this to the prince,
this to the Earl of Westmoreland, and this to old
Mistress Ursula, whom I have weekly sworn to
marry since I perceived the first white hair of my
chin: about it, you know where to find me. [*Page*   250
goes] A pox of this gout! or, a gout of this pox! for
the one or the other plays the rogue with my great
toe. 'Tis no matter if I do halt, I have the wars
for my colour, and my pension shall seem the more
reasonable: a good wit will make use of any thing;
I will turn diseases to commodity.   *He goes*

Scene 3: *The Palace of the Archbishop of York*

*Enter the Archbishop of York, Hastings, Mowbray, and
Lord Bardolph*

ARCHBISHOP. Thus have you heard our cause and
known our means,
And, my most noble friends, I pray you all,
Speak plainly your opinions of our hopes.

And first, lord marshal, what say you to it?
MOWBRAY. I well allow the occasion of our arms,
But gladly would be better satisfied
How in our means we should advance ourselves
To look with forehead bold and big enough
Upon the power and puissance of the king.
HASTINGS. Our present musters grow upon the file   10
To five and twenty thousand men of choice,
And our supplies live largely in the hope
Of great Northumberland, whose bosom burns
With an incensèd fire of injuries.
L. BARDOLPH. The question then, Lord Hastings,
standeth thus—
Whether our present five and twenty thousand
May hold up head without Northumberland.
HASTINGS. With him, we may.
L. BARDOLPH.   Yea, marry, there's the point.
But if without him we be thought too feeble,
My judgement is, we should not step too far   20
Till we had his assistance by the hand.
For in a theme so bloody-faced as this
Conjecture, expectation, and surmise
Of aids incertain should not be admitted.
ARCHBISHOP. 'Tis very true, Lord Bardolph, for
indeed
It was young Hotspur's cause at Shrewsbury.
L. BARDOLPH. It was, my lord; who lined himself
with hope,
Eating the air on promise of supply,
Flatt'ring himself in project of a power
Much smaller than the smallest of his thoughts,   30
And so, with great imagination
Proper to madmen, led his powers to death,
And, winking, leaped into destruction.
HASTINGS. But, by your leave, it never yet did hurt
To lay down likelihoods and forms of hope.
L. BARDOLPH. Yes, if this present quality of war—
Indeed the instant action, a cause on foot—
Lives so in hope, as in an early spring
We see th'appearing buds; which to prove fruit
Hope gives not so much warrant as despair   40
That frosts will bite them. When we mean to build,
We first survey the plot, then draw the model,
And when we see the figure of the house,
Then must we rate the cost of the erection,
Which if we find outweighs ability,
What do we then, but draw anew the model
In fewer offices, or at least desist
To build at all? Much more, in this great work
(Which is almost to pluck a kingdom down
And set another up) should we survey   50
The plot of situation and the model,
Consent upon a sure foundation,
Question surveyors, know our own estate,
How able such a work to undergo,
To weigh against his opposite; or else
We fortify in paper and in figures,
Using the names of men instead of men:
Like one that draws the model of an house
Beyond his power to build it; who, half through,
Gives o'er, and leaves his part-created cost   60
A naked subject to the weeping clouds,
And waste for churlish winter's tyranny.
HASTINGS. Grant that our hopes (yet likely of
fair birth)
Should be still-born, and that we now possessed

The utmost man of expectation,
I think we are a body strong enough,
Even as we are, to equal with the king.
L. BARDOLPH. What, is the king but five and
    twenty thousand?
HASTINGS. To us no more, nay, not so much,
    Lord Bardolph.
For his divisions, as the times do brawl,   70
Are in three heads, one power against the French,
And one against Glendower; perforce a third
Must take up us: so is the unfirm king
In three divided, and his coffers sound
With hollow poverty and emptiness.
ARCHBISHOP. That he should draw his several
    strengths together
And come against us in full puissance,
Need not be dreaded.
HASTINGS.   If he should do so,
He leaves his back unarmed, the French and Welsh
Baying him at the heels: never fear that.   80
L. BARDOLPH. Who is it like should lead his forces
    hither?
HASTINGS. The Duke of Lancaster and Westmoreland:
Against the Welsh, himself and Harry Monmouth:
But who is substituted 'gainst the French,
I have no certain notice.
ARCHBISHOP.   Let us on;
And publish the occasion of our arms.
The commonwealth is sick of their own choice,
Their over-greedy love hath surfeited:
An habitation giddy and unsure
Hath he that buildeth on the vulgar heart.   90
O thou fond many, with what loud applause
Didst thou beat heaven with blessing Bolingbroke,
Before he was what thou wouldst have him be!
And being now trimmed in thine own desires,
Thou, beastly feeder, art so full of him,
That thou provok'st thyself to cast him up.
So, so, the common dog, didst thou disgorge
Thy glutton bosom of the royal Richard,
And now thou wouldst eat thy dead vomit up,
And howl'st to find it. What trust is in these times?   100
They that, when Richard lived, would have
    him die,
Are now become enamoured on his grave:
Thou, that threw'st dust upon his goodly head,
When through proud London he came sighing on
After th' admiréd heels of Bolingbroke,
Criest now 'O earth, yield us that king again,
And take thou this!' O thoughts of men accursed!
Past and to come seems best; things present, worst.
MOWBRAY. Shall we go draw our numbers, and set on?
HASTINGS. We are time's subjects, and time bids
    be gone.   *They go* 110

ACT 2
Scene I: *Eastcheap. Near the Boar's Head Tavern*

Enter Hostess, with Sergeant Fang

HOSTESS. Master Fang, have you entered the action?
FANG. It is entered.
HOSTESS. Where's your yeoman? Is't a lusty yeoman?
    will a' stand to't?
FANG. Sirrah! Where's Snare?
HOSTESS. O Lord, ay! good Master Snare.

Yeoman Snare enters

SNARE. Here, here.
FANG. Snare, we must arrest Sir John Falstaff!
HOSTESS. Yea, good Master Snare, I have entered him
    and all.   10
SNARE. It may chance cost some of us our lives, for he
    will stab.
HOSTESS. Alas the day, take heed of him, he stabbed me
    in mine own house, most beastly in good faith. A'
    cares not what mischief he does, if his weapon be
    out. He will foin like any devil, he will spare neither
    man, woman, nor child.
FANG. If I can close with him, I care not for his thrust.
HOSTESS. No, nor I neither, I'll be at your elbow.
FANG. An I but fist him once, an a' come but within   20
    my vice—
HOSTESS. I am undone by his going. I warrant you, he's
    an infinitive thing upon my score. Good Master
    Fang, hold him sure; good Master Snare, let him
    not 'scape. A' comes continuantly to Pie-corner
    (saving your manhoods) to buy a saddle, and he is
    indited to dinner to the Lubber's head in Lumbert
    street, to Master Smooth's the silkman. I pray you,
    since my exion is entered, and my case so openly
    known to the world, let him be brought in to his   30
    answer. A hundred mark is a long one for a poor
    lone woman to bear, and I have borne, and borne,
    and borne, and have been fubbed off, and fubbed
    off, and fubbed off, from this day to that day, that
    it is a shame to be thought on. There is no honesty
    in such dealing, unless a woman should be made an
    ass, and a beast, to bear every knave's wrong....

Enter Sir John Falstaff, Page, and Bardolph

Yonder he comes, and that arrant malmsey-nose
knave Bardolph with him. Do your offices, do your
offices, Master Fang and Master Snare, do me, do   40
me, do me your offices.
FALSTAFF. How now? whose mare's dead? what's the
    matter?
FANG. Sir John, I arrest you at the suit of Mistress
    Quickly.
FALSTAFF. Away, varlets! Draw, Bardolph, cut me off
    the villain's head, throw the quean in the channel.
HOSTESS. Throw me in the channel? I'll throw thee
    in the channel. Wilt thou? wilt thou? thou bastardly
    rogue! Murder, murder! Ah, thou honey-suckle   50
    villain! wilt thou kill God's officers and the king's?
    Ah, thou honey-seed rogue! thou art a honey-seed,
    a man-queller, and a woman-queller.
FALSTAFF. Keep them off, Bardolph.
FANG. A rescue! a rescue!
HOSTESS. Good people, bring a rescue or two. [*the
    Page attacks her*] Thou wot, wot thou? thou wot,
    wot ta? do! do! thou rogue! do, thou hempseed!
PAGE. Away, you scullion! you rampallian! you fusti-
    larian! I'll tickle your catastrophe.   60

Enter the L. Chief Justice and his men

L. CHIEF JUSTICE. What is the matter? keep the peace
    here, ho!
HOSTESS. Good my lord, be good to me. I beseech you,
    stand to me!
L. CHIEF JUSTICE. How, now, Sir John? what are you
    brawling here?

Doth this become your place, your time and
　　business?
You should have been well on your way to York.
Stand from him, fellow, wherefore hang'st upon
　　him?

HOSTESS. O my most worshipful lord, an't please your
grace, I am a poor widow of Eastcheap, and he is 70
arrested at my suit.

L. CHIEF JUSTICE. For what sum?

HOSTESS. It is more than for some, my lord, it is for all,
all I have. He hath eaten me out of house and home,
he hath put all my substance into that fat belly of his.
But I will have some of it out again, or I will ride
thee a-nights like the mare.

FALSTAFF. I think I am as like to ride the mare, if I
have any vantage of ground to get up.

L. CHIEF JUSTICE. How comes this, Sir John? Fie! what 80
man of good temper would endure this tempest of
exclamation? Are you not ashamed to enforce a
poor widow to so rough a course to come by her
own?

FALSTAFF. What is the gross sum that I owe thee?

HOSTESS. Marry, if thou wert an honest man, thyself
and the money too: thou didst swear to me upon a
parcel-gilt goblet, sitting in my Dolphin chamber,
at the round table by a sea-coal fire, upon Wednesday in Wheeson week, when the prince broke thy 90
head for liking his father to a singing-man of Windsor, thou didst swear to me then, as I was washing
thy wound, to marry me, and make me my lady
thy wife. Canst thou deny it? did not goodwife
Keech, the butcher's wife, come in then and call
me gossip Quickly? coming in to borrow a mess of
vinegar, telling us she had a good dish of prawns,
whereby thou didst desire to eat some, whereby I
told thee they were ill for a green wound? and didst
thou not, when she was gone down stairs, desire 100
me to be no more so familiarity with such poor
people, saying that ere long they should call me
madam? and didst thou not kiss me, and bid me
fetch thee thirty shillings? I put thee now to thy
book-oath, deny it if thou canst.

FALSTAFF. My lord, this is a poor mad soul, and she
says up and down the town that her eldest son is
like you. She hath been in good case, and the truth
is, poverty hath distracted her. But for these foolish
officers, I beseech you I may have redress against 110
them.

L. CHIEF JUSTICE. Sir John, Sir John, I am well
acquainted with your manner of wrenching the true
cause the false way: it is not a confident brow, nor
the throng of words that come with such more than
impudent sauciness from you, can thrust me from a
level consideration: you have, as it appears to me,
practised upon the easy-yielding spirit of this
woman, and made her serve your uses both in purse
and in person. 120

HOSTESS. Yea, in truth, my lord.

L. CHIEF JUSTICE. Pray thee, peace. Pay her the debt
you owe her, and unpay the villainy you have done
with her. The one you may do with sterling money,
and the other with current repentance.

FALSTAFF. My lord, I will not undergo this sneap
without reply. You call honourable boldness impudent sauciness: if a man will make curtsy and
say nothing, he is virtuous. No, my lord, my

humble duty remembered, I will not be your suitor. 130
I say to you, I do desire deliverance from these
officers, being upon hasty employment in the king's
affairs.

L. CHIEF JUSTICE. You speak as having power to do
wrong. But answer in th'effect of your reputation,
and satisfy the poor woman.

FALSTAFF. Come hither, hostess.

Gower comes up with a letter

L. CHIEF JUSTICE. Now, Master Gower, what news?

GOWER. The king, my lord, and Harry Prince of Wales
Are near at hand—the rest the paper tells. 140

FALSTAFF. As I am a gentleman!

HOSTESS. Faith, you said so before.

FALSTAFF. As I am a gentleman. Come, no more words
of it.

HOSTESS. By this heavenly ground I tread on, I must be
fain to pawn both my plate and the tapestry of my
dining-chambers.

FALSTAFF. Glasses, glasses, is the only drinking—and
for thy walls, a pretty slight drollery or the story
of the Prodigal or the German hunting, in water- 150
work, is worth a thousand of these bed-hangers and
these fly-bitten tapestries. Let it be ten pound, if thou
canst ... Come, an 'twere not for thy humours,
there's not a better wench in England. Go, wash
thy face, and draw the action. Come, thou must not
be in this humour with me, dost not know me?
Come, come, I know thou wast set on to this.

HOSTESS. Pray thee, Sir John, let it be but twenty
nobles. I' faith, I am loath to pawn my plate, so
God save me, la. 160

FALSTAFF. Let it alone, I'll make other shift, you'll be
a fool still.

HOSTESS. Well, you shall have it, though I pawn my
gown. I hope you'll come to supper. You'll pay
me all together?

FALSTAFF. Will I live? [*aside to Bardolph*] Go, with her,
with her, hook on, hook on.

HOSTESS. Will you have Doll Tearsheet meet you at
supper?

FALSTAFF. No more words, let's have her. 170

The Hostess goes off with Bardolph,
Officers and Page following

L. CHIEF JUSTICE. I have heard better news.

FALSTAFF. What's the news, my lord?

L. CHIEF JUSTICE. Where lay the king to-night?

GOWER. At Basingstoke, my lord.

FALSTAFF. I hope, my lord, all's well. What is the news,
my lord?

L. CHIEF JUSTICE. Come all his forces back?

GOWER. No, fifteen hundred foot, five hundred horse,
Are marched up to my lord of Lancaster,
Against Northumberland and the Archbishop. 180

FALSTAFF. Comes the king back from Wales, my noble
lord?

L. CHIEF JUSTICE. You shall have letters of me
presently.
Come, go along with me, good Master Gower.

FALSTAFF. My lord!

L. CHIEF JUSTICE. What's the matter?

FALSTAFF. Master Gower, shall I entreat you with me
to dinner?

GOWER. I must wait upon my good lord here, I thank
you, good Sir John. 190

L. CHIEF JUSTICE. Sir John, you loiter here too long, being you are to take soldiers up in counties as you go.

FALSTAFF. Will you sup with me, Master Gower?

L. CHIEF JUSTICE. What foolish master taught you these manners, Sir John?

FALSTAFF. Master Gower, if they become me not, he was a fool that taught them me.... This is the right fencing grace, my lord, tap for tap, and so part fair.

L. CHIEF JUSTICE. Now the Lord lighten thee! thou art a great fool. *They go*   200

Scene 2: *London. The Prince's house*

Enter Prince Henry and Poins

PRINCE. Before God, I am exceeding weary.

POINS. Is't come to that? I had thought weariness durst not have attached one of so high blood.

PRINCE. Faith, it does me, though it discolours the complexion of my greatness to acknowledge it ... Doth it not show vilely in me to desire small beer?

POINS. Why, a prince should not be so loosely studied as to remember so weak a composition.

PRINCE. Belike then my appetite was not princely got, for, by my troth, I do now remember the poor 10 creature, small beer. But indeed these humble considerations make me out of love with my greatness. What a disgrace is it to me to remember thy name! or to know thy face to-morrow! or to take note how many pair of silk stockings thou hast, viz. these, and those that were thy peach-coloured ones! or to bear the inventory of thy shirts—as, one for superfluity, and another for use! but that the tennis-court-keeper knows better than I, for it is a low ebb of linen with thee when thou keepest not racket there, 20 as thou hast not done a great while, because the rest of thy low countries have made a shift to eat up thy holland: and God knows whether those that bawl out the ruins of thy linen shall inherit his kingdom: but the midwives say the children are not in the fault, whereupon the world increases and kindreds are mightily strengthened.

POINS. How ill it follows, after you have laboured so hard, you should talk so idly! Tell me, how many good young princes would do so, their fathers being 30 so sick as yours at this time is?

PRINCE. Shall I tell thee one thing, Poins?

POINS. Yes faith, and let it be an excellent good thing.

PRINCE. It shall serve among wits of no higher breeding than thine.

POINS. Go to, I stand the push of your one thing that you will tell.

PRINCE. Marry, I tell thee, it is not meet that I should be sad now my father is sick, albeit I could tell to thee, as to one it pleases me for fault of a better to 40 call my friend, I could be sad, and sad indeed too.

POINS. Very hardly, upon such a subject.

PRINCE. By this hand, thou thinkest me as far in the devil's book as thou and Falstaff for obduracy and persistency. Let the end try the man. But I tell thee, my heart bleeds inwardly that my father is so sick, and keeping such vile company as thou art hath in reason taken from me all ostentation of sorrow.

POINS. The reason?

PRINCE. What wouldst thou think of me if I should 50 weep?

POINS. I would think thee a most princely hypocrite.

PRINCE. It would be every man's thought, and thou art a blessed fellow to think as every man thinks; never a man's thought in the world keeps the roadway better than thine: every man would think me an hypocrite indeed. And what accites your most worshipful thought to think so?

POINS. Why, because you have been so lewd, and so much engraffed to Falstaff.   60

PRINCE. And to thee.

POINS. By this light, I am well spoke on, I can hear it with mine own ears. The worst that they can say of me is that I am a second brother, and that I am a proper fellow of my hands, and those two things I confess I cannot help ... By the mass, here comes Bardolph.

Enter Bardolph, and Page

PRINCE. And the boy that I gave Falstaff. A' had him from me Christian, and look if the fat villain have not transformed him ape.   70

BARDOLPH. God save your grace!

PRINCE. And yours, most noble Bardolph!

POINS. Come, you virtuous ass, you bashful fool, must you be blushing? wherefore blush you now? What a maidenly man-at-arms are you become? It's such a matter to get a pottle-pot's maidenhead?

PAGE. A' calls me e'en now, my lord, through a red lattice, and I could discern no part of his face from the window. At last I spied his eyes, and methought he had made two holes in the ale-wife's new petti- 80 coat and so peeped through.

PRINCE. Has not the boy profited?

BARDOLPH. Away, you whoreson upright rabbit, away!

PAGE. Away, you rascally Althæa's dream, away!

PRINCE. Instruct us, boy. What dream, boy?

PAGE. Marry, my lord, Althæa dreamt she was delivered of a fire-brand, and therefore I call him her dream.

PRINCE. A crown's worth of good interpretation. 90 There 'tis, boy.

POINS. O, that this blossom could be kept from cankers! Well, there is sixpence to preserve thee.

BARDOLPH. An you do not make him be hanged among you, the gallows shall have wrong.

PRINCE. And how doth thy master, Bardolph?

BARDOLPH. Well, my lord. He heard of your grace's coming to town. There's a letter for you.

POINS. Delivered with good respect. And how doth the martlemas, your master?   100

BARDOLPH. In bodily health, sir.

POINS. Marry, the immortal part needs a physician, but that moves not him—though that be sick, it dies not.

PRINCE. I do allow this wen to be as familiar with me as my dog, and he holds his place, for look you how he writes.   *He shows the superscription*

POINS. 'John Falstaff, knight'—
Every man must know that as oft as he has occasion to name himself: even like those that are kin 110 to the king, for they never prick their finger but they say, 'There's some of the king's blood spilt.' 'How comes that?' says he, that takes upon him not to conceive. The answer is as ready as a borrower's cap, 'I am the king's poor cousin, sir.'

PRINCE. Nay, they will be kin to us, or they will fetch it from Japhet. But the letter—

[reads] 'Sir John Falstaff, knight, to the son of the king, nearest his father, Harry Prince of Wales, greeting.'

POINS. Why, this is a certificate.

PRINCE. Peace!

[reads] 'I will imitate the honourable Romans in brevity.'

POINS. He sure means brevity in breath, short-winded.

PRINCE [reads]. 'I commend me to thee, I commend thee, and I leave thee. Be not too familiar with Poins; for he misuses thy favours so much that he swears thou art to marry his sister Nell. Repent at idle times as thou may'st, and so farewell. 130

    'Thine, by yea and no, which is as much as to say as thou usest him, JACK FALSTAFF with my familiars, JOHN with my brothers and sisters, and SIR JOHN with all Europe.'

POINS. My lord, I'll steep this letter in sack, and make him eat it.

PRINCE. That's to make him eat twenty of his words. But do you use me thus, Ned? must I marry your sister?

POINS. God send the wench no worse fortune! but I 140 never said so.

PRINCE. Well, thus we play the fools with the time, and the spirits of the wise sit in the clouds and mock us. Is your master here in London?

BARDOLPH. Yea, my lord.

PRINCE. Where sups he? doth the old boar feed in the old frank?

BARDOLPH. At the old place, my lord, in Eastcheap.

PRINCE. What company?

PAGE. Ephesians, my lord, of the old church. 150

PRINCE. Sup any women with him?

PAGE. None, my lord, but old Mistress Quickly and Mistress Doll Tearsheet.

PRINCE. What pagan may that be?

PAGE. A proper gentlewoman, sir, and a kinswoman of my master's.

PRINCE. Even such kin as the parish heifers are to the town bull. Shall we steal upon them, Ned, at supper?

POINS. I am your shadow, my lord, I'll follow you. 160

PRINCE. Sirrah, you boy, and Bardolph, no word to your master that I am yet come to town ... There's for your silence.

BARDOLPH. I have no tongue, sir.

PAGE. As for mine, sir, I will govern it.

PRINCE. Fare you well; go. *Bardolph and the Page go*
This Doll Tearsheet should be some road.

POINS. I warrant you, as common as the way between Saint Albans and London.

PRINCE. How might we see Falstaff bestow himself 170 to-night in his true colours, and not ourselves be seen?

POINS. Put on two leathern jerkins and aprons, and wait upon him at his table as drawers.

PRINCE. From a god to a bull? a heavy descension! it was Jove's case. From a prince to a prentice? a low transformation! that shall be mine. For in every thing the purpose must weigh with the folly. Follow me, Ned.   *They go*

Scene 3: Warkworth. Before the Castle

Enter Northumberland, Lady Northumberland, and Lady Percy

NORTHUMBERLAND. I pray thee, loving wife, and gentle daughter, 120

Give even way unto my rough affairs.

Put not you on the visage of the times,

And be like them to Percy troublesome.

LADY NORTHUMBERLAND. I have given over, I will speak no more.

Do what you will, your wisdom be your guide.

NORTHUMBERLAND. Alas, sweet wife, my honour is at pawn,

And, but my going, nothing can redeem it.

LADY PERCY. O, yet, for God's sake, go not to these wars!

The time was, father, that you broke your word, 10

When you were more endeared to it than now,

When your own Percy, when my heart's dear Harry,

Threw many a northward look to see his father

Bring up his powers—but he did long in vain.

Who then persuaded you to stay at home?

There were two honours lost, yours and your son's.

For yours, the God of heaven brighten it!

For his, it stuck upon him, as the sun

In the grey vault of heaven, and by his light

Did all the chivalry of England move 20

To do brave acts. He was indeed the glass

Wherein the noble youth did dress themselves.

He had no legs that practised not his gait;

And speaking thick, which nature made his blemish,

Became the accents of the valiant,

For those that could speak low and tardily

Would turn their own perfection to abuse,

To seem like him: so that in speech, in gait,

In diet, in affections of delight,

In military rules, humours of blood, 30

He was the mark and glass, copy and book,

That fashioned others. And him, O wondrous him!

O miracle of men! him did you leave,

Second to none, unseconded by you,

To look upon the hideous god of war

In disadvantage, to abide a field

Where nothing but the sound of Hotspur's name

Did seem defensible: so you left him.

Never, O never, do his ghost the wrong

To hold your honour more precise and nice 40

With others than with him! let them alone:

The marshal and the archbishop are strong:

Had my sweet Harry had but half their numbers,

To-day might I, hanging on Hotspur's neck,

Have talked of Monmouth's grave.

NORTHUMBERLAND.   Beshrew your heart,

Fair daughter, you do draw my spirits from me

With new lamenting ancient oversights.

But I must go and meet with danger there,

Or it will seek me in another place,

And find me worse provided.

LADY NORTHUMBERLAND.   O, fly to Scotland, 50

Till that the nobles and the arméd commons

Have of their puissance made a little taste.

LADY PERCY. If they get ground and vantage of the king,

Then join you with them, like a rib of steel,

To make strength stronger; but, for all our loves,
First let them try themselves. So did your son,
He was so suffered, so came I a widow,
And never shall have length of life enough
To rain upon remembrance with mine eyes,
That it may grow and sprout as high as heaven,   60
For recordation to my noble husband.
NORTHUMBERLAND. Come, come, go in with me.
   'Tis with my mind
As with the tide swelled up unto his height,
That makes a still-stand, running neither way.
Fain would I go to meet the archbishop,
But many thousand reasons hold me back.
I will resolve for Scotland! there am I,
Till time and vantage crave my company.   *They go*

Scene 4: *London. The Boar's Head Tavern in Eastcheap*

Enter Francis and another Drawer

FRANCIS. What the devil hast thou brought there?
apple-johns? thou knowest Sir John cannot endure
an apple-john.
2 DRAWER. Mass, thou say'st true. The prince once
set a dish of apple-johns before him, and told him
there were five more Sir Johns, and putting off his
hat, said, 'I will now take my leave of these six
dry, round, old, withered knights.' It angered him
to the heart. But he hath forgot that.
FRANCIS. Why then, cover and set them down, and   10
see if thou canst find out Sneak's noise. Mistress
Tearsheet would fain hear some music.
2 DRAWER. Dispatch. The room where they supped is
too hot, they'll come in straight.
FRANCIS. Sirrah, here will be the prince and Master
Poins anon, and they will put on two of our jerkins
and aprons, and Sir John must not know of it.
Bardolph hath brought word.
2 DRAWER. By the mass, here will be old utis. It will
be an excellent stratagem.   20
FRANCIS. I'll see if I can find out Sneak.   *He goes*

The Hostess and Doll Tearsheet enter

HOSTESS. I'faith, sweetheart, methinks now you are in
an excellent good temperality: your pulsidge beats
as extraordinarily as heart would desire, and your
colour, I warrant you, is as red as any rose, in good
truth, la! But, i'faith, you have drunk too much
canaries, and that's a marvellous searching wine, and
it perfumes the blood ere one can say 'What's this?'
How do you now?
DOLL. Better than I was: hem!   30
HOSTESS. Why, that's well said—a good heart's worth
gold ... Lo, here comes Sir John.

Falstaff enters, singing

FALSTAFF. 'When Arthur first in court'—[*aside*] Empty
the jordan—'and was a worthy king' ... [*2 Drawer
goes*] How now, Mistress Doll?
HOSTESS. Sick of a calm, yea, good faith.
FALSTAFF. So is all her sect. An they be once in a calm,
they are sick.
DOLL. A pox damn you, you muddy rascal, is that all
the comfort you give me?   40
FALSTAFF. You make fat rascals, Mistress Doll.
DOLL. I make them! gluttony and diseases make them,
I make them not.

FALSTAFF. If the cook help to make the gluttony, you
help to make the diseases, Doll. We catch of you,
Doll, we catch of you. Grant that, my poor virtue,
grant that.
DOLL. Yea, joy, our chains and our jewels.
FALSTAFF. 'Your brooches, pearls, and ouches.' For to
serve bravely is to come halting off, you know—to   50
come off the breach with his pike bent bravely, and
to surgery bravely, to venture upon the charged
chambers bravely—
DOLL. Hang yourself, you muddy conger, hang yourself!
HOSTESS. By my troth, this is the old fashion! you two
never meet but you fall to some discord. You are
both, i' good troth, as rheumatic as two dry toasts,
you cannot one bear with another's confirmities.
What the good-year! one must bear, and that must   60
be you—you are the weaker vessel, as they say, the
emptier vessel.
DOLL. Can a weak empty vessel bear such a huge full
hogshead? there's a whole merchant's venture of
Bourdeaux stuff in him, you have not seen a hulk
better stuffed in the hold.... Come, I'll be friends
with thee, Jack. Thou art going to the wars, and
whether I shall ever see thee again or no, there is
nobody cares.

Francis returns

FRANCIS. Sir, Ancient Pistol's below, and would speak   70
with you.
DOLL. Hang him, swaggering rascal! let him not come
hither. It is the foul-mouth'dst rogue in England.
HOSTESS. If he swagger, let him not come here. No, by
my faith, I must live among my neighbours. I'll no
swaggerers, I am in good name and fame with the
very best: shut the door, there comes no swaggerers
here, I have not lived all this while to have swaggering now—shut the door, I pray you.
FALSTAFF. Dost thou hear, hostess?   80
HOSTESS. Pray ye, pacify yourself, Sir John. There
comes no swaggerers here.
FALSTAFF. Dost thou hear? it is mine ancient.
HOSTESS. Tilly-fally, Sir John, ne'er tell me: an your
ancient swagger, a' comes not in my doors. I was
before Master Tisick, the debuty, t'other day, and
(as he said to me)—'twas no longer ago than Wednesday last—'I' good faith, neighbour Quickly,'
says he—Master Dumb, our minister, was by then
—'Neighbour Quickly (says he) receive those that   90
are civil, for (said he) you are in an ill name'; now
a' said so, I can tell whereupon: 'for (says he) you
are an honest woman, and well thought on, therefore take heed what guests you receive: receive
(says he) no swaggering companions' ... There
comes none here: you would bless you to hear what
he said: no, I'll no swaggerers.
FALSTAFF. He's no swaggerer, hostess—a tame cheater,
i'faith. You may stroke him as gently as a puppy
greyhound. He'll not swagger with a Barbary hen,   100
if her feathers turn back in any show of resistance.
Call him up, drawer.   *Francis goes out*
HOSTESS. Cheater, call you him? I will bar no honest
man my house, nor no cheater, but I do not love
swaggering, by my troth. I am the worse, when
one says swagger: feel, masters, how I shake, look
you, I warrant you.

DOLL. So you do, hostess.

HOSTESS. Do I? yea, in very truth, do I, an 'twere an aspen leaf. I cannot abide swaggerers. 110

Pistol, Bardolph, and Page enter

PISTOL. God save you, Sir John!

FALSTAFF. Welcome, Ancient Pistol. Here, Pistol, I charge you with a cup of sack. Do you discharge upon mine hostess.

PISTOL. I will discharge upon her, Sir John, with two bullets.

FALSTAFF. She is pistol-proof, sir; you shall not hardly offend her.

HOSTESS. Come, I'll drink no proofs, nor no bullets. I'll drink no more than will do me good, for no 120 man's pleasure, I.

PISTOL. Then to you, Mistress Dorothy, I will charge you.

DOLL. Charge me! I scorn you, scurvy companion. What! you poor, base, rascally, cheating, lack-linen mate! Away, you mouldy rogue, away! I am meat for your master.

PISTOL. I know you, Mistress Dorothy.

DOLL. Away, you cut-purse rascal! you filthy bung, away! by this wine, I'll thrust my knife in your 130 mouldy chaps, an you play the saucy cuttle with me. Away, you bottle-ale rascal! you basket-hilt stale juggler, you!.... Since when, I pray you, sir? God's light, with two points on your shoulder? much!

PISTOL. God let me not live, but I will murder your ruff for this.

FALSTAFF. No more, Pistol, I would not have you go off here. Discharge yourself of our company, Pistol.

HOSTESS. No, good Captain Pistol, not here, sweet 140 captain.

DOLL. Captain! thou abominable damned cheater, art thou not ashamed to be called captain? An captains were of my mind, they would truncheon you out, for taking their names upon you before you have earned them ... You a captain! you slave, for what? for tearing a poor whore's ruff in a bawdy-house ... He a captain! hang him, rogue! he lives upon mouldy stewed prunes and dried cakes ... A captain! God's light, these villains will make the 150 word as odious as the word 'occupy', which was an excellent good word before it was ill sorted: therefore captains had need look to't.

BARDOLPH. Pray thee, go down, good ancient.

FALSTAFF. Hark thee hither, Mistress Doll.

They go aside

PISTOL. Not I. I tell thee what, Corporal Bardolph, I could tear her. I'll be revenged of her.

PAGE. Pray thee, go down.

PISTOL. I'll see her damned first,—to Pluto's damnéd lake, by this hand, to th'infernal deep, with Erebus 160 and tortures vile also: hold hook and line, say I: down! down, dogs! down faitors! have we not Hiren here?

He draws his sword

HOSTESS. Good Captain Peesel, be quiet—'tis very late, i'faith—I beseek you now, aggravate your choler.

PISTOL. These be good humours, indeed!
Shall pack-horses
And hollow pampered jades of Asia,

Which cannot go but thirty mile a day, 170
Compare with Cæsars and with Cannibals
And Trojant Greeks? nay, rather damn them with
King Cerberus, and let the welkin roar.
Shall we fall foul for toys?

HOSTESS. By my troth, captain, these are very bitter words.

BARDOLPH. Be gone, good ancient: this will grow to a brawl anon.

PISTOL. Die men, like dogs! give crowns like pins! Have we not Hiren here? 180

HOSTESS. O' my word, captain, there's none such here. What the good-year! do you think, I would deny her? For God's sake, be quiet.

PISTOL. Then, feed, and be fat, my fair Calipolis. Come, give's some sack.
'Si fortune me tormente, sperato me contento.'
Fear we broadsides? no, let the fiend give fire.
Give me some sack—and, sweetheart, lie thou there.

Laying down his sword

Come we to full points here? and are etceteras nothings?

FALSTAFF. Pistol, I would be quiet. 190

PISTOL. Sweet knight, I kiss thy neaf. What! we have seen the seven stars.

DOLL. For God's sake, thrust him down stairs. I cannot endure such a fustian rascal.

PISTOL. Thrust him down stairs! know we not Galloway nags?

FALSTAFF. Quoit him down, Bardolph, like a shove-groat shilling. Nay, an a' do nothing but speak nothing, a' shall be nothing here.

BARDOLPH. Come, get you down stairs.

PISTOL. What! shall we have incision? shall we imbrue? 200

He snatches up his sword

Then death rock me asleep, abridge my doleful days!
Why then, let grievous, ghastly, gaping wounds
Untwind the Sisters Three! Come, Atropos, I say!

HOSTESS. Here's goodly stuff toward!

FALSTAFF. Give me my rapier, boy.

DOLL. I pray thee, Jack, I pray thee, do not draw.

FALSTAFF [*draws*]. Get you down stairs.

Bardolph seizes Pistol and forces him back;
Falstaff follows behind

HOSTESS. Here's a goodly tumult! I'll forswear keeping house, afore I'll be in these tirrits and frights.
[*Falstaff thrusts at Pistol*] So! murder, I warrant now. 210
Alas, alas! put up your naked weapons, put up your naked weapons. *Bardolph and Pistol go*

DOLL. I pray thee, Jack, be quiet, the rascal's gone. Ah, you whoreson little valiant villain, you.

HOSTESS. Are you not hurt i'the groin? methought a' made a shrewd thrust at your belly.

Bardolph returns

FALSTAFF. Have you turned him out-a-doors?

BARDOLPH. Yea, sir. The rascal's drunk, you have hurt him, sir, i'th shoulder.

FALSTAFF. A rascal! to brave me! 220

DOLL. Ah, you sweet little rogue, you! Alas, poor ape, how thou sweat'st! come, let me wipe thy face, come on, you whoreson chops: ah, rogue! i'faith, I love thee. Thou art as valorous as Hector of Troy, worth five of Agamemnon, and ten times better than the Nine Worthies. Ah, villain!

FALSTAFF. A rascally slave! I will toss the rogue in a blanket.

DOLL. Do, an thou darest for thy heart. An thou dost, I'll canvass thee between a pair of sheets.   230

Musicians enter

PAGE. The music is come, sir.

FALSTAFF. Let them play. Play, sirs. Sit on my knee, Doll. A rascal bragging slave! the rogue fled from me like quicksilver.

DOLL. I'faith, and thou follow'dst him like a church. Thou whoreson little tidy Bartholomew boar-pig, when wilt thou leave fighting a days and foining a nights, and begin to patch up thine old body for heaven?

Enter behind, the Prince and Poins, disguised like Drawers

FALSTAFF. Peace, good Doll! do not speak like a   240
death's-head, do not bid me remember mine end.

DOLL. Sirrah, what humour's the prince of?

FALSTAFF. A good shallow young fellow, a' would have made a good pantler, a' would ha' chipped bread well.

DOLL. They say, Poins has a good wit.

FALSTAFF. He a good wit? hang him, baboon! his wit's as thick as Tewkesbury mustard, there's no more conceit in him than is in a mallet.

DOLL. Why does the prince love him so, then?   250

FALSTAFF. Because their legs are both of a bigness, and a' plays at quoits well, and eats conger and fennel, and drinks off candles' ends for flap-dragons, and rides the wild mare with the boys, and jumps upon joined-stools, and swears with a good grace, and wears his boots very smooth like unto the Sign of the Leg, and breeds no bate with telling of discreet stories—and such other gambol faculties a' has that show a weak mind and an able body, for the which the prince admits him: for the prince   260
himself is such another, the weight of a hair will turn the scales between their avoirdupois.

PRINCE. Would not this nave of a wheel have his ears cut off?

POINS. Let's beat him before his whore.

PRINCE. Look, whether the withered elder hath not his poll clawed like a parrot.

POINS. Is it not strange that desire should so many years outlive performance?

FALSTAFF. Kiss me, Doll.   270

PRINCE. Saturn and Venus this year in conjunction! what says th' almanac to that?

POINS. And look whether the fiery Trigon, his man, be not lisping to his master's old tables, his note-book, his counsel-keeper.

FALSTAFF. Thou dost give me flattering busses.

DOLL. By my troth, I kiss thee with a most constant heart.

FALSTAFF. I am old, I am old.

DOLL. I love thee better than I love e'er a scurvy young   280
boy of them all.

FALSTAFF. What stuff wilt have a kirtle of? I shall receive money o' Thursday—shalt have a cap to-morrow. A merry song, come! a' grows late, we'll to bed. Thou't forget me when I am gone.

DOLL. By my troth, thou't set me aweeping, an thou say'st so. Prove that ever I dress myself handsome till thy return. Well, hearken a'th' end.

FALSTAFF. Some sack, Francis.

PRINCE. }
POINS.   } Anon, anon, sir.   *They hurry forward* 290

FALSTAFF. Ha! a bastard son of the king's? And art not thou Poins his brother?

PRINCE. Why, thou globe of sinful continents, what a life dost thou lead?

FALSTAFF. A better than thou—I am a gentleman, thou art a drawer.

PRINCE. Very true, sir, and I come to draw you out by the ears.

HOSTESS. O, the Lord preserve thy good grace! by my troth, welcome to London. Now the Lord bless that   300
sweet face of thine! O Jesu, are you come from Wales?

FALSTAFF. Thou whoreson mad compound of majesty, by this light flesh and corrupt blood, thou art welcome.

DOLL. How! you fat fool, I scorn you.

POINS. My lord, he will drive you out of your revenge, and turn all to a merriment, if you take not the heat.

PRINCE. You whoreson candle-mine, you, how vilely did you speak of me even now, before this honest,   310
virtuous, civil gentlewoman!

HOSTESS. God's blessing of your good heart! and so she is, by my troth.

FALSTAFF. Didst thou hear me?

PRINCE. Yea, and you knew me, as you did when you ran away by Gad's Hill. You knew I was at your back, and spoke it on purpose to try my patience.

FALSTAFF. No, no, no, not so, I did not think thou wast within hearing.

PRINCE. I shall drive you then to confess the wilful   320
abuse, and then I know how to handle you.

FALSTAFF. No abuse, Hal, o' mine honour, no abuse.

PRINCE. Not! to dispraise me, and call me pantler and bread-chipper and I know not what?

FALSTAFF. No abuse, Hal.

POINS. No abuse?

FALSTAFF. No abuse, Ned, i'th' world, honest Ned, none. I dispraised him before the wicked, that the wicked might not fall in love with thee: in which doing, I have done the part of a careful friend and   330
a true subject, and thy father is to give me thanks for it. No abuse, Hal—none, Ned, none—no, faith, boys, none.

PRINCE. See now, whether pure fear and entire cowardice doth not make thee wrong this virtuous gentlewoman, to close with us ... Is she of the wicked! is thine hostess here of the wicked? or is thy boy of the wicked? or honest Bardolph, whose zeal burns in his nose, of the wicked?

POINS. Answer, thou dead elm, answer.   340

FALSTAFF. The fiend hath pricked down Bardolph irre-coverable, and his face is Lucifer's privy-kitchen, where he doth nothing but roast malt-worms. For the boy, there is a good angel about him, but the devil blinds him too.

PRINCE. For the women?

FALSTAFF. For one of them, she's in hell already, and burns poor souls. For th' other, I owe her money, and whether she be damned for that I know not.

HOSTESS. No, I warrant you.   350

FALSTAFF. No, I think thou art not. I think thou art quit for that. Marry, there is another indictment upon thee, for suffering flesh to be eaten in thy

house, contrary to the law, for the which I think
thou wilt howl.

HOSTESS. All victuallers do so. What's a joint of
mutton or two in a whole Lent?

PRINCE. You, gentlewoman—

DOLL. What says your grace?

FALSTAFF. His grace says that which his flesh rebels 360
against.   *A knocking heard without*

HOSTESS. Who knocks so loud at door? look to th'
door there, Francis,

Peto enters

PRINCE. Peto, how now? what news?

PETO. The king your father is at Westminster,
And there are twenty weak and wearied posts
Come from the north, and as I came along
I met and overtook a dozen captains,
Bare-headed, sweating, knocking at the taverns,
And asking every one for Sir John Falstaff.   370

PRINCE. By heaven, Poins, I feel me much to blame,
So idly to profane the precious time,
When tempest of commotion, like the south
Borne with black vapour, doth begin to melt,
And drop upon our bare unarmèd heads.
Give me my sword and cloak ... Falstaff, good
night.
       Prince Henry, Poins, Peto, and Bardolph go

FALSTAFF. Now comes in the sweetest morsel of the
night, and we must hence and leave it unpicked ...
[*more knocking heard*] More knocking at the door.

Bardolph returns

How now? what's the matter?   380

BARDOLPH. You must away to court, sir, presently;
A dozen captains stay at door for you.

FALSTAFF [*to the Page*]. Pay the musicians, sirrah. Farewell hostess, farewell Doll. You see, my good
wenches, how men of merit are sought after. The
undeserver may sleep, when the man of action
is called on. Farewell, good wenches: if I be not sent
away post, I will see you again ere I go.

DOLL. I cannot speak. If my heart be not ready to
burst ... Well, sweet Jack, have a care of thyself. 390

FALSTAFF. Farewell, farewell.
              He goes out with Bardolph

HOSTESS. Well, fare thee well. I have known thee these
twenty-nine years, come peascod-time, but an
honester and truer-hearted man ... Well, fare thee
well.

BARDOLPH [*at the door*]. Mistress Tearsheet!

HOSTESS. What's the matter?

BARDOLPH. Bid Mistress Tearsheet come to my
master.

HOSTESS. O run, Doll, run, run, good Doll.   400

BARDOLPH. Come!

HOSTESS. She comes blubbered.

BARDOLPH [*enters*]. Yea, will you come, Doll?
        He leads her forth; the Hostess goes out

ACT 3
Scene 1: *The palace at Westminster*

Enter the King in his nightgown, with a Page

KING. Go, call the Earls of Surrey and of Warwick:
But, ere they come, bid them o'er-read these letters,
And well consider of them—make good speed.
                     The Page goes
How many thousand of my poorest subjects
Are at this hour asleep! O sleep, O gentle sleep,
Nature's soft nurse, how have I frighted thee,
That thou no more wilt weigh my eyelids down,
And steep my senses in forgetfulness?
Why rather, sleep, liest thou in smoky cribs,
Upon uneasy pallets stretching thee,   10
And hushed with buzzing night-flies to thy slumber,
Than in the perfumed chambers of the great,
Under the canopies of costly state,
And lulled with sound of sweetest melody?
O thou dull god, why li'st thou with the vile
In loathsome beds, and leav'st the kingly couch
A watch-case or a common 'larum-bell?
Wilt thou upon the high and giddy mast
Seal up the ship-boy's eyes and rock his brains
In cradle of the rude imperious surge,   20
And in the visitation of the winds,
Who take the ruffian billows by the top,
Curling their monstrous heads, and hanging them
With deafing clamour in the slippery clouds,
That, with the hurly, death itself awakes?
Canst thou, O partial sleep! give thy repose
To the wet sea-boy in an hour so rude,
And in the calmest and most stillest night,
With all appliances and means to boot,
Deny it to a king? Then, happy low, lie down!   30
Uneasy lies the head that wears a crown.

Enter Warwick, Surrey and Sir John Blunt

WARWICK. Many good morrows to your majesty!

KING. Is it good morrow, lords?

WARWICK. 'Tis one o'clock, and past.

KING. Why then, good morrow to you all, my lords.
Have you read o'er the letters that I sent you?

WARWICK. We have, my liege.

KING. Then you perceive the body of our kingdom,
How foul it is—what rank diseases grow,
And with what danger, near the heart of it.   40

WARWICK. It is but as a body yet distempered,
Which to his former strength may be restored
With good advice and little medicine.
My Lord Northumberland will soon be cooled.

KING. O God! that one might read the book of fate,
And see the revolution of the times
Make mountains level, and the continent,
Weary of solid firmness, melt itself
Into the sea! and, other times, to see
The beachy girdle of the ocean   50
Too wide for Neptune's hips; how chances mock
And changes fill the cup of alteration
With divers liquors! O, if this were seen,
The happiest youth, viewing his progress through,
What perils passed, what crosses to ensue,
Would shut the book, and sit him down and die.
'Tis not ten years gone
Since Richard and Northumberland, great friends,
Did feast together, and in two years after
Were they at wars: it is but eight years since   60
This Percy was the man nearest my soul;
Who like a brother toiled in my affairs,
And laid his love and life under my foot;
Yea, for my sake, even to the eyes of Richard
Gave him defiance.... But which of you was by—

You, cousin Nevil, as I may remember—
                                            To Warwick
When Richard, with his eye brimful of tears,
Then checked and rated by Northumberland,
Did speak these words, now proved a prophecy?
'Northumberland, thou ladder by the which   70
My cousin Bolingbroke ascends my throne'
(Though then, God knows, I had no such intent,
But that necessity so bowed the state,
That I and greatness were compelled to kiss)
'The time shall come,' thus did he follow it,
'The time will come, that foul sin, gathering head
Shall break into corruption': so went on,
Foretelling this same time's condition,
And the division of our amity.
WARWICK. There is a history in all men's lives,   80
Figuring the natures or the times deceased:
The which observed, a man may prophesy,
With a near aim, of the main chance of things
As yet not come to life, who in their seeds
And weak beginnings lie intreasuréd:
Such things become the hatch and brood of time;
And by the necessary form of this
King Richard might create a perfect guess
That great Northumberland, then false to him,
Would of that seed grow to a greater falseness,   90
Which should not find a ground to root upon,
Unless on you.
KING.   Are these things then necessities?
Then let us meet them like necessities—
And that same word even now cries out on us:
They say the bishop and Northumberland
Are fifty thousand strong.
WARWICK.   It cannot be, my lord.
Rumour doth double, like the voice and echo,
The numbers of the feared. Please it your grace
To go to bed: upon my soul, my lord,
The powers that you already have sent forth   100
Shall bring this prize in very easily:
To comfort you the more, I have received
A certain instance that Glendower is dead ...
Your majesty hath been this fortnight ill,
And these unseasoned hours perforce must add
Unto your sickness.
KING.   I will take your counsel.
And were these inward wars once out of hand,
We would, dear lords, unto the Holy Land.
                                            They go

Scene 2: *Before Justice Shallow's house in Gloucestershire*

*Enter Shallow and Silence, meeting; Mouldy, Shadow,
Wart, Feeble, Bullcalf and servants, behind*

SHALLOW. Come on, come on, come on, give me your
hand, sir, give me your hand, sir! an early stirrer, by
the rood ... And how doth my good cousin Silence?
SILENCE. Good morrow, good cousin Shallow.
SHALLOW. And how doth my cousin, your bedfellow?
and your fairest daughter and mine, my god-
daughter Ellen?
SILENCE. Alas, a black ousel, cousin Shallow.
SHALLOW. By yea and no, sir, I dare say my cousin
William is become a good scholar. He is at Oxford   10
still, is he not?
SILENCE. Indeed, sir, to my cost.
SHALLOW. A' must then to the inns o' court shortly:

I was once of Clement's Inn, where I think they will
talk of mad Shallow yet.
SILENCE. You were called 'lusty Shallow' then, cousin.
SHALLOW. By the mass, I was called any thing, and I
would have done any thing indeed too, and roundly
too ... There was I, and little John Doit of Staf-
fordshire, and black George Barnes, and Francis   20
Pickbone, and Will Squele a Cots'ole man—you
had not four such swinge-bucklers in all the inns o'
court again: and I may say to you, we knew where
the bonas-robas were, and had the best of them all
at commandment ... Then was Jack Falstaff (now
Sir John) a boy, and a page to Thomas Mowbray,
Duke of Norfolk.
SILENCE. This Sir John, cousin, that comes hither anon
about soldiers?
SHALLOW. The same Sir John, the very same. I see   30
him break Scoggin's head at the court-gate, when a'
was a crack, not thus high: and the very same day
did I fight with one Sampson Stockfish, a fruiterer,
behind Gray's Inn ... Jesu, Jesu, the mad days that
I have spent! and to see how many of my old
acquaintance are dead!
SILENCE. We shall all follow, cousin.
SHALLOW. Certain, 'tis certain, very sure, very sure.
Death, as the Psalmist saith, is certain to all, all shall
die. How a good yoke of bùllocks at Stamford fair?   40
SILENCE. By my troth, I was not there.
SHALLOW. Death is certain. Is old Double of your town
living yet?
SILENCE. Dead, sir.
SHALLOW. Jesu, Jesu, dead! a' drew a good bow—and
dead! a' shot a fine shoot: John a Gaunt loved him
well, and betted much money on his head. Dead! a'
would have clapped i'th' clout at twelve score, and
carried you a forehand shaft a fourteen and fourteen
and a half, that it would have done a man's heart   50
good to see. How a score of ewes now?
SILENCE. Thereafter as they be, a score of good ewes
may be worth ten pounds.
SHALLOW. And is old Double dead!

Enter Bardolph, and one with him

SILENCE. Here come two of Sir John Falstaff's men,
as I think.
SHALLOW. Good morrow, honest gentlemen.
BARDOLPH. I beseech you, which is Justice Shallow?
SHALLOW. I am Robert Shallow, sir, a poor esquire of
this county, and one of the king's justices of the   60
peace: what is your good pleasure with me?
BARDOLPH. My captain, sir, commends him to you,
my captain, Sir John Falstaff, a tall gentleman, by
heaven, and a most gallant leader.
SHALLOW. He greets me well, sir. I knew him a good
backsword man. How doth the good knight? may
I ask how my lady his wife doth?
BARDOLPH. Sir, pardon! a soldier is better accommodated than with a wife.
SHALLOW. It is well said in faith, sir, and it is well said   70
indeed too. Better accommodated! it is good, yea,
indeed, is it. Good phrases are surely, and ever were,
very commendable. Accommodated: it comes of
'accommodo,' very good, a good phrase.
BARDOLPH. Pardon sir, I have heard the word. Phrase
call you it? By this day, I know not the phrase, but
I will maintain the word with my sword to be a

soldier-like word, and a word of exceeding good command, by heaven ... Accommodated, that is, when a man is, as they say, accommodated, or when a man is being whereby a' may be thought to be accommodated—which is an excellent thing.

Enter Falstaff

SHALLOW. It is very just ... Look, here comes good Sir John. Give me your good hand, give me your worship's good hand. By my troth, you like well, and bear your years very well. Welcome, good Sir John.

FALSTAFF. I am glad to see you well, good Master Robert Shallow. Master Surecard, as I think?

SHALLOW. No, Sir John, it is my cousin Silence, in commission with me.

FALSTAFF. Good Master Silence, it well befits you should be of the Peace.

SILENCE. Your good worship is welcome.

FALSTAFF. Fie! this is hot weather, gentlemen. Have you provided me here half a dozen sufficient men?

SHALLOW. Marry, have we, sir. Will you sit?

FALSTAFF. Let me see them, I beseech you.

SHALLOW. Where's the roll? where's the roll? where's the roll? So, so, so, so, so, so. Yea, marry, sir—Rafe Mouldy! Let them appear as I call, let them do so, let them do so. Let me see, where is Mouldy?

MOULDY. Here, an't please you.

SHALLOW. What think you, Sir John? a good-limbed fellow, young, strong, and of good friends.

FALSTAFF. Is thy name Mouldy?

MOULDY. Yea, an't please you.

FALSTAFF. 'Tis the more time thou wert used.

SHALLOW. Ha, ha, ha! most excellent, i'faith! things that are mouldy lack use: very singular good! in faith, well said, Sir John, very well said.

FALSTAFF. Prick him.

MOULDY. I was pricked well enough before, and you could have let me alone. My old dame will be undone now, for one to do her husbandry and her drudgery. You need not to have pricked me, there are other men fitter to go out than I.

FALSTAFF. Go to. Peace, Mouldy, you shall go. Mouldy, it is time you were spent.

MOULDY. Spent!

SHALLOW. Peace, fellow, peace—stand aside. Know you where you are? For th' other, Sir John: let me see—Simon Shadow!

FALSTAFF. Yea, marry, let me have him to sit under. He's like to be a cold soldier.

SHALLOW. Where's Shadow?

SHADOW. Here, sir.

FALSTAFF. Shadow, whose son art thou?

SHADOW. My mother's son, sir.

FALSTAFF. Thy mother's son! like enough, and thy father's shadow—so the son of the female is the shadow of the male: it is often so, indeed, but much of the father's substance!

SHALLOW. Do you like him, Sir John?

FALSTAFF. Shadow will serve for summer. Prick him, [*aside*] for we have a number of shadows to fill up the muster-book.

SHALLOW. Thomas Wart!

FALSTAFF. Where's he?

WART. Here, sir.

FALSTAFF. Is thy name Wart?

WART. Yea, sir.

FALSTAFF. Thou are a very ragged wart.

SHALLOW. Shall I prick him, Sir John?

FALSTAFF. It were superfluous, for his apparel is built up on his back, and the whole frame stands upon pins: prick him no more.

SHALLOW. Ha, ha, ha! you can do it, sir, you can do it, I commend you well ... Francis Feeble!

FEEBLE. Here, sir.

SHALLOW. What trade art thou, Feeble?

FEEBLE. A woman's tailor, sir.

SHALLOW. Shall I prick him, sir?

FALSTAFF. You may—but if he had been a man's tailor, he'd ha' pricked you. Wilt thou make as many holes in an enemy's battle as thou hast done in a woman's petticoat?

FEEBLE. I will do my good will, sir, you can have no more.

FALSTAFF. Well said, good woman's tailor! well said, courageous Feeble! thou wilt be as valiant as the wrathful dove or most magnanimous mouse. Prick the woman's tailor: well, Master Shallow; deep, Master Shallow.

FEEBLE. I would Wart might have gone, sir.

FALSTAFF. I would thou wert a man's tailor, that thou mightst mend him and make him fit to go. I cannot put him to a private soldier, that is the leader of so many thousands. Let that suffice, most forcible Feeble.

FEEBLE. It shall suffice, sir.

FALSTAFF. I am bound to thee, reverend Feeble. Who is next?

SHALLOW. Peter Bullcalf o' th' green!

FALSTAFF. Yea, marry, let's see Bullcalf.

BULLCALF. Here, sir.

FALSTAFF. 'Fore God, a likely fellow! Come, prick me Bullcalf, till he roar again.

BULLCALF. O Lord! good my lord captain—

FALSTAFF. What, dost thou roar before thou art pricked?

BULLCALF. O Lord, sir! I am a diseased man.

FALSTAFF. What disease hast thou?

BULLCALF. A whoreson cold, sir, a cough, sir, which I caught with ringing in the king's affairs upon his coronation-day, sir.

FALSTAFF. Come, thou shalt go to the wars in a gown, we will have away thy cold, and I will take such order that thy friends shall ring for thee.... Is here all?

SHALLOW. Here is two more called than your number, you must have but four here, sir. And so, I pray you, go in with me to dinner.

FALSTAFF. Come, I will go drink with you, but I cannot tarry dinner. I am glad to see you, by my troth, Master Shallow.

SHALLOW. O, Sir John, do you remember since we lay all night in the windmill in Saint George's field?

FALSTAFF. No more of that, good Master Shallow, no more of that.

SHALLOW. Ha, 'twas a merry night. And is Jane Nightwork alive?

FALSTAFF. She lives, Master Shallow.

SHALLOW. She never could away with me.

FALSTAFF. Never, never, she would always say she could not abide Master Shallow.

SHALLOW. By the mass, I could anger her to th' heart.

She was then a bona-roba. Doth she hold her own
well?

FALSTAFF. Old, old, Master Shallow.   210

SHALLOW. Nay, she must be old, she cannot choose but
be old, certain she's old, and had Robin Nightwork
by old Nightwork before I came to Clement's Inn.

SILENCE. That's fifty five year ago.

SHALLOW. Ha, cousin Silence, that thou hadst seen that
that this knight and I have seen! Ha, Sir John, said
I well?

FALSTAFF. We have heard the chimes at midnight,
Master Shallow.

SHALLOW. That we have, that we have, that we have,   220
in faith, Sir John, we have—our watch-word was
'Hem, boys!' Come, let's to dinner, come, let's to
dinner. Jesus, the days that we have seen! Come,
come.   *He leads Falstaff in; Silence follows*

BULLCALF. Good Master Corporate Bardolph, stand
my friend, and here's four Harry ten shillings in
French crowns for you. In very truth, sir, I had as
lief be hanged, sir, as go. And yet for mine own
part, sir, I do not care, but rather because I am
unwilling, and for mine own part have a desire to   230
stay with my friends; else, sir, I did not care for mine
own part so much.

BARDOLPH. Go to, stand aside.

MOULDY. And, good master corporal captain, for my
old dame's sake, stand my friend. She has nobody
to do any thing about her when I am gone, and
she is old and cannot help herself. You shall have
forty, sir.

BARDOLPH. Go to, stand aside.

FEEBLE. By my troth I care not, a man can die but   240
once, we owe God a death, I'll ne'er bear a base
mind. An't be my dest'ny, so—an't be not, so. No
man's too good to serve's prince, and let it go which
way it will, he that dies this year is quit for the next.

BARDOLPH. Well said! th'art a good fellow.

FEEBLE. Faith, I'll bear no base mind.

Falstaff and the Justices return

FALSTAFF. Come, sir, which men shall I have?

SHALLOW. Four of which you please.

BARDOLPH. Sir, a word with you. [*aside*] I have three
pound to free Mouldy and Bullcalf.   250

FALSTAFF. Go to, well.

SHALLOW. Come, Sir John, which four will you have?

FALSTAFF. Do you choose for me.

SHALLOW. Marry then, Mouldy, Bullcalf, Feeble, and
Shadow.

FALSTAFF. Mouldy and Bullcalf! for you, Mouldy, stay
at home till you are past service: and for your part,
Bullcalf, grow till you come unto it: I will none of
you.

SHALLOW. Sir John, Sir John, do not yourself wrong, 260
they are your likeliest men, and I would have you
served with the best.

FALSTAFF. Will you tell me, Master Shallow, how to
choose a man? Care I for the limb, the thews, the
stature, bulk, and big assemblance of a man? give me
the spirit, Master Shallow ... Here's Wart, you see
what a ragged appearance it is, a' shall charge you
and discharge you with the motion of a pewterer's
hammer, come off and on swifter than he that
gibbets on the brewer's bucket. And this same half- 270
faced fellow, Shadow—give me this man. He pre-

sents no mark to the enemy, the foeman may with
as great aim level at the edge of a penknife. And
for a retreat, how swiftly will this Feeble, the
woman's tailor, run off! O, give me the spare men,
and spare me the great ones. Put me a caliver into
Wart's hand, Bardolph.

BARDOLPH. Hold, Wart, traverse! thus, thus, thus.

FALSTAFF. Come, manage me your caliver. So, very
well, go to, very good, exceeding good. O, give   280
me always a little, lean, old, chopt, bald shot. ...
Well said, i'faith, Wart, th'art a good scab. Hold,
there's a tester for thee.

SHALLOW. He is not his craft's master, he doth not do
it right. I remember at Mile-end Green, when I lay
at Clement's Inn—I was then Sir Dagonet in
Arthur's show—there was a little quiver fellow, and
a' would manage you his piece thus, and a' would
about and about, and come you in, and come you in:
'rah-tah-tah,' would a' say; 'bounde,' would a' say; 290
and away again would a' go, and again would a'
come: I shall ne'er see such a fellow.

FALSTAFF. These fellows will do well, Master Shallow.
God keep you, Master Silence, I will not use many
words with you. Fare you well, gentlemen both. I
thank you. I must a dozen mile to-night ...
Bardolph, give the soldiers coats.

SHALLOW. Sir John, the Lord bless you! God prosper
your affairs! God send us peace! At your return,
visit our house, let our old acquaintance be renewed. 300
Peradventure I will with ye to the court.

FALSTAFF. 'Fore God, would you would, Master
Shallow.

SHALLOW. Go to, I have spoke at a word. God keep
you.

FALSTAFF. Fare you well, gentle gentlemen. [*Shallow
and Silence go in*] On, Bardolph; lead the men away.
[*Bardolph does so*] As I return, I will fetch off these
justices. I do see the bottom of Justice Shallow. Lord,
Lord, how subject we old men are to this vice of   310
lying! This same starved justice hath done nothing
but prate to me of the wildness of his youth, and
the feats he hath done about Turnbull Street—and
every third word a lie, duer paid to the hearer than
the Turk's tribute. I do remember him at Clement's
Inn, like a man made after supper of a cheese-paring.
When a' was naked, he was for all the world like
a forked radish, with a head fantastically carved
upon it with a knife. A' was so forlorn, that his
dimensions to any thick sight were invisible. A' was 320
the very genius of famine, yet lecherous as a
monkey, and the whores called him mandrake. A'
came ever in the rearward of the fashion, and sung
those tunes to the overscutched huswives that he
heard the carmen whistle, and sware they were his
fancies or his good-nights. And now is this Vice's
dagger become a squire, and talks as familiarly of
John a Gaunt as if he had been sworn brother to
him, and I'll be sworn a' ne'er saw him but once
in the Tilt-yard, and then he burst his head for   330
crowding among the marshal's men. I saw it, and
told John a Gaunt he beat his own name, for you
might have trussed him and all his apparel into an
eel-skin—the case of a treble hautboy was a mansion
for him, a court. And now has he land and beefs!
Well, I'll be acquainted with him if I return, and 't
shall go hard but I'll make him a philosopher's two

stones to me. If the young dace be a bait for the old pike, I see no reason in the law of nature but I may snap at him ... Let time shape, and there an 240 end.   *He goes*

ACT 4

Scene 1: *Gaultree Forest, Yorkshire*

The Archbishop of York, Mowbray, Hastings, Lord Bardolph and others

ARCHBISHOP. What is this forest called?

HASTINGS. 'Tis Gaultree Forest, an't shall please your grace.

ARCHBISHOP. Here stand, my lords, and send discoverers forth
To know the numbers of our enemies.

HASTINGS. We have sent forth already.

ARCHBISHOP.   'Tis well done.
My friends and brethren in these great affairs,
I must acquaint you that I have received
New-dated letters from Northumberland,
Their cold intent, tenour and substance, thus:
Here doth he wish his person, with such powers 10
As might hold sortance with his quality,
The which he could not levy; whereupon
He is retired, to ripe his growing fortunes,
To Scotland, and concludes in hearty prayers
That your attempts may overlive the hazard
And fearful meeting of their opposite.

MOWBRAY. Thus do the hopes we have in him touch ground
And dash themselves to pieces.

A Messenger comes up

HASTINGS.   Now, what news?

MESSENGER. West of this forest, scarcely off a mile,
In goodly form comes on the enemy, 20
And by the ground they hide I judge their number
Upon or near the rate of thirty thousand.

MOWBRAY. The just proportion that we gave them out
Let us sway on and face them in the field.

Westmoreland enters, with attendant officers

ARCHBISHOP. What well-appointed leader fronts us here?

MOWBRAY. I think it is my Lord of Westmoreland.

WESTMORELAND. Health and fair greeting from our general,
The prince, Lord John and Duke of Lancaster.

ARCHBISHOP. Say on, my Lord of Westmoreland, in peace.
What doth concern your coming?

WESTMORELAND.   Then, my lord, 30
Unto your grace do I in chief address
The substance of my speech ... If that rebellion
Came like itself, in base and abject routs,
Led on by bloody youth, guarded with rags,
And countenanced by boys and beggary;
I say, if damned commotion so appeared
In his true, native and most proper shape,
You, reverend father, and these noble lords
Had not been here, to dress the ugly form
Of base and bloody insurrection 40
With your fair honours. You, lord Archbishop,
Whose see is by a civil peace maintained,

Whose beard the silver hand of peace hath touched,
Whose learning and good letters peace hath tutored,
Whose white investments figure innocence,
The dove and very blessed spirit of peace,
Wherefore do you so ill translate yourself
Out of the speech of peace that bears such grace,
Into the harsh and boist'rous tongue of war?
Turning your books to graves, your ink to blood, 50
Your pens to lances, and your tongue divine
To a loud trumpet and a point of war?

ARCHBISHOP. Wherefore do I this? so the question stands.
Briefly to this end: we are all diseased,
And with our surfeiting and wanton hours
Have brought ourselves into a burning fever,
And we must bleed for it: of which disease
Our late king, Richard, being infected, died.
But, my most noble Lord of Westmoreland,
I take not on me here as a physician, 60
Nor do I as an enemy to peace
Troop in the throngs of military men;
But rather show awhile like fearful war,
To diet rank minds, sick of happiness,
And purge the obstructions, which begin to stop
Our very veins of life ... Hear me more plainly.
I have in equal balance justly weighed
What wrongs our arms may do, what wrongs we suffer,
And find our griefs heavier than our offences.
We see which way the stream of time doth run, 70
And are enforced from our most quiet shore
By the rough torrent of occasion,
And have the summary of all our griefs,
When time shall serve, to show in articles;
Which long ere this we offered to the king,
And might by no suit gain our audience:
When we are wronged and would unfold our griefs,
We are denied access unto his person
Even by those men that most have done us wrong.
The dangers of the days but newly gone, 80
Whose memory is written on the earth
With yet appearing blood, and the examples
Of every minute's instance (present now)
Hath put us in these ill-beseeming arms—
Not to break peace or any branch of it,
But to establish here a peace indeed,
Concurring both in name and quality.

WESTMORELAND. When ever yet was your appeal denied?
Wherein have you been galléd by the king?
What peer hath been suborned to grate on you, 90
That you should seal this lawless bloody book
Of forged rebellion with a seal divine,
And consecrate commotion's bitter edge?

ARCHBISHOP. My brother general, the commonwealth,
To brother born an household cruelty
I make my quarrel in particular.

WESTMORELAND. There is no need of any such redress,
Or if there were, it not belongs to you.

MOWBRAY. Why not to him in part, and to us all
That feel the bruises of the days before, 100
And suffer the condition of these times
To lay a heavy and unequal hand
Upon our honours?

WESTMORELAND.   O my good Lord Mowbray,

Construe the times to their necessities,
And you shall say, indeed, it is the time,
And not the king, that doth you injuries.
Yet for your part, it not appears to me,
Either from the king, or in the present time,
That you should have an inch of any ground
To build a grief on: were you not restored   110
To all the Duke of Norfolk's signories,
Your noble and right well remembered father's?
MOWBRAY. What thing, in honour, had my father lost,
That need to be revived and breathed in me?
The king that loved him, as the state stood then,
Was force perforce compelled to banish him:
And then that Henry Bolingbroke and he,
Being mounted and both rousèd in their seats,
Their neighing coursers daring of the spur,
Their armèd staves in charge, their beavers down,   120
Their eyes of fire sparkling through sights of steel,
And the loud trumpet blowing them together;
Then, then, when there was nothing could have
    stayed
My father from the breast of Bolingbroke ...
O, when the king did throw his warder down,
(His own life hung upon the staff he threw!)
Then threw he down himself and all their lives
That by indictment and by dint of sword
Have since miscarried under Bolingbroke.
WESTMORELAND. You speak, Lord Mowbray, now   130
    you know not what.
The Earl of Hereford was reputed then
In England the most valiant gentleman.
Who knows on whom fortune would then have
    smiled?
But if your father had been victor there,
He ne'er had borne it out of Coventry:
For all the country in a general voice
Cried hate upon him; and all their prayers and love
Were set on Hereford, whom they doted on,
And blessed and graced indeed more than the
    king. ...
But this is mere digression from my purpose.
Here come I from our princely general   140
To know your griefs, to tell you from his grace
That he will give you audience, and wherein
It shall appear that your demands are just
You shall enjoy them, every thing set off
That might so much as think you enemies.
MOWBRAY. But he hath forced us to compel this
    offer,
And it proceeds from policy, not love.
WESTMORELAND. Mowbray, you overwéen to take
    it so:
This offer comes from mercy, not from fear: 150
For, lo! within a ken our army lies,
Upon mine honour, all too confident
To give admittance to a thought of fear:
Our battle is more full of names than yours,
Our men more perfect in the use of arms,
Our armour all as strong, our cause the best;
Then reason will our hearts should be as good:
Say you not then our offer is compelled.
MOWBRAY. Well, by my will, we shall admit no
    parley.
WESTMORELAND. That argues but the shame of
    your offence.   160
A rotten case abides no handling.

HASTINGS. Hath the Prince John a full commission,
In very ample virtue of his father,
To hear and absolutely to determine
Of what conditions we shall stand upon?
WESTMORELAND. That is intended in the general's
    name.
I muse you make so slight a question.   110
ARCHBISHOP. Then take, my Lord of Westmoreland,
    this schedule,
For this contains our general grievances.
Each several article herein redressed,   170
All members of our cause, both here and hence,
That are insinewed to this action,
Acquitted by a true substantial form,
And present execution of our wills
To us and to our purposes confined,
We come within our awful banks again,
And knit our powers to the arm of peace.
WESTMORELAND. This will I show the general. Please
    you, lords,
In sight of both our battles we may meet;
And either end in peace, which God so frame!   180
Or to the place of diff'rence call the swords
Which must decide it.
ARCHBISHOP.   My lord, we will do so.
        Westmoreland departs with his men
MOWBRAY. There is a thing within my bosom tells me
That no conditions of our peace can stand.
HASTINGS. Fear you not that: if we can make our peace
Upon such large terms and so absolute
As our conditions shall consist upon,
Our peace shall stand as firm as rocky mountains.
MOWBRAY. Yea, but our valuation shall be such,
That every slight and false-derivèd cause,   190
Yea, every idle, nice and wanton reason,
Shall to the king taste of this action;
That were our royal faiths martyrs in love,
We shall be winnowed with so rough a wind
That even our corn shall seem as light as chaff,
And good from bad find no partition.
ARCHBISHOP. No, no, my lord. Note this—the king
    is weary
Of dainty and such picking grievances,
For he hath found to end one doubt by death
Revives two greater in the heirs of life: 200
And therefore will he wipe his tables clean,
And keep no tell-tale to his memory
That may repeat and history his loss
To new remembrance; for full well he knows
He cannot so precisely weed this land
As his misdoubts present occasion:
His foes are so enrooted with his friends,
That plucking to unfix an enemy,
He doth unfasten so and shake a friend.
So that this land, like an offensive wife   210
That hath enraged him on to offer strokes,
As he is striking, holds his infant up,
And hangs resolved correction in the arm
That was upreared to execution.
HASTINGS. Besides, the king hath wasted all his rods
On late offenders, that he now doth lack
The very instruments of chastisement,
So that his power, like to a fangless lion,
May offer, but not hold.
ARCHBISHOP.   'Tis very true,
And therefore be assured, my good lord marshal,   220

If we do now make our atonement well,
Our peace will, like a broken limb united,
Grow stronger for the breaking.
MOWBRAY.   Be it so.
Here is returned my Lord of Westmoreland.

*Westmoreland comes back; Prince John and his army being
seen in the distance*

WESTMORELAND. The prince is here at hand. Pleaseth
    your lordship
To meet his grace just distance 'tween our armies?
MOWBRAY. Your grace of York, in God's name then
    set forward.
ARCHBISHOP. Before! and greet his grace. My lord,
    we come.

Scene 2

They go forward

PRINCE JOHN [*meeting them*]. You are well encountered
    here, my cousin Mowbray.
Good day to you, gentle lord archbishop,
And so to you, Lord Hastings, and to all.
My Lord of York, it better showed with you
When that your flock, assembled by the bell,
Encircled you to hear with reverence
Your exposition on the holy text,
Than now to see you here an iron man talking,
Cheering a rout of rebels with your drum,
Turning the word to sword, and life to death.   10
That man that sits within a monarch's heart,
And ripens in the sunshine of his favour,
Would he abuse the countenance of the king,
Alack, what mischiefs might he set abroach
In shadow of such greatness! With you, lord bishop,
It is even so. Who hath not heard it spoken
How deep you were within the books of God?
To us the speaker in his parliament,
To us th'imagined voice of God himself,
The very opener and intelligencer   20
Between the grace, the sanctities of heaven
And our dull workings? O, who shall believe
But you misuse the reverence of your place,
Employ the countenance and grace of heaven,
As a false favourite doth his prince's name,
In deeds dishonourable? You have ta'en up,
Under the counterfeited zeal of God,
The subjects of His substitute, my father,
And both against the peace of heaven and him,
Have here up-swarmed them.
ARCHBISHOP.   Good my Lord of Lancaster, 30
I am not here against your father's peace,
But as I told my Lord of Westmoreland,
The time misordered doth, in common sense,
Crowd us and crush us to this monstrous form,
To hold our safety up ... I sent your grace
The parcels and particulars of our grief,
The which hath been with scorn shoved from
    the court,
Whereon this Hydra son of war is born,
Whose dangerous eyes may well be charmed asleep
With grant of our most just and right desires;   40
And true obedience, of this madness cured,
Stoop tamely to the foot of majesty.
MOWBRAY. If not, we ready are to try our fortunes
To the last man.

HASTINGS.   And though we here fall down,
We have supplies to second our attempt:
If they miscarry, theirs shall second them,
And so success of mischief shall be born,
And heir from heir shall hold this quarrel up,
Whiles England shall have generation.
PRINCE JOHN. You are too shallow, Hastings, much
    too shallow,   50
To sound the bottom of the after-times.
WESTMORELAND. Pleaseth your grace to answer
    them directly
How far forth you do like their articles?
PRINCE JOHN. I like them all, and do allow them
    well,
And swear here, by the honour of my blood,
My father's purposes have been mistook,
And some about him have too lavishly
Wrested his meaning and authority.
My lord, these griefs shall be with speed redressed—
Upon my soul, they shall. If this may please you,   60
Discharge your powers unto their several counties,
As we will ours, and here between the armies
Let's drink together friendly and embrace,
That all their eyes may bear those tokens home
Of our restoréd love and amity.
ARCHBISHOP. I take your princely word for these
    redresses.
PRINCE JOHN. I give it you, and will maintain my
    word.
And thereupon I drink unto your grace.
HASTINGS. Go, captain, and deliver to the army
This news of peace. Let them have pay, and part.   70
I know it will well please them. Hie thee, captain!
                      An officer obeys
ARCHBISHOP. To you, my noble Lord of
    Westmoreland.
WESTMORELAND. I pledge your grace, and if you knew
    what pains
I have bestowed to breed this present peace,
You would drink freely: but my love to ye
Shall show itself more openly hereafter.
ARCHBISHOP. I do not doubt you.
WESTMORELAND.   I am glad of it.
Health to my lord and gentle cousin, Mowbray.
MOWBRAY. You wish me health in very happy season,
For I am on the sudden something ill.   80
ARCHBISHOP. Against ill chances men are ever merry,
But heaviness foreruns the good event.
WESTMORELAND. Therefore be merry, coz, since
    sudden sorrow
Serves to say thus, 'some good thing comes
    to-morrow.'
ARCHBISHOP. Believe me, I am passing light in spirit.
MOWBRAY. So much the worse, if your own rule
    be true.
                         Shouts heard
PRINCE JOHN. The word of peace is rendered. Hark,
    how they shout!
MOWBRAY. This had been cheerful after victory.
ARCHBISHOP. A peace is of the nature of a conquest,
For then both parties nobly are subdued,   90
And neither party loser.
PRINCE JOHN.   Go, my lord,
And let our army be dischargéd too.
                     Westmoreland goes
And, good my lord, so please you, let our trains

March by us, that we may peruse the men
We should have coped withal.
ARCHBISHOP.   Go, good Lord Hastings.
And, ere they be dismissed, let them march by.
Hastings goes
PRINCE JOHN. I trust, lords, we shall lie to-night
together.

Westmoreland returns

Now, cousin, wherefore stands our army still?
WESTMORELAND. The leaders, having charge from
you to stand,
Will not go off until they hear you speak.   100
PRINCE JOHN. They know their duties.

Hastings returns

HASTINGS. My lord, our army is dispersed already:
Like youthful steers unyoked, they take their
courses
East, west, north, south, or like a school broke up,
Each hurries toward his home and sporting-place.
WESTMORELAND. Good tidings, my Lord Hastings!
for the which
I do arrest thee, traitor, of high treason,
And you, lord archbishop, and you, Lord
Mowbray,
Of capital treason I attach you both.
MOWBRAY. Is this proceeding just and honourable?   110
WESTMORELAND. Is your assembly so?
ARCHBISHOP. Will you thus break your faith?
PRINCE JOHN.   I pawned thee none.
I promised you redress of these same grievances
Whereof you did complain, which by mine honour
I will perform with a most Christian care.
But, for you, rebels, look to taste the due
Meet for rebellion and such acts as yours.
Most shallowly did you these arms commence,
Fondly brought here and foolishly sent hence.
Strike up our drums, pursue the scattered stray;   120
God, and not we, hath safely fought to-day.
Some guard these traitors to the block of death,
Treason's true bed and yielder up of breath.
                                          They go

Scene 3

*Alarum. Excursions. Falstaff comes up and encounters one
Colevile*

FALSTAFF. What's your name, sir? of what condition
are you, and of what place?
COLEVILE. I am a knight, sir, and my name is Colevile
of the Dale.
FALSTAFF. Well then, Colevile is your name, a knight is
your degree, and your place the dale: Colevile shall
be still your name, a traitor your degree, and the
dungeon your place—a dale deep enough, so shall
you be still Colevile of the Dale.
COLEVILE. Are not you Sir John Falstaff?   10
FALSTAFF. As good a man as he, sir, whoe'er I am ...
Do ye yield, sir? or shall I sweat for you? If I do
sweat, they are the drops of thy lovers, and they
weep for thy death. Therefore rouse up fear and
trembling, and do observance to my mercy.
COLEVILE. I think you are Sir John Falstaff, and in that
thought yield me.
FALSTAFF. I have a whole school of tongues in this belly
of mine, and not a tongue of them all speaks any

other word but my name. An I had but a belly of   20
any indifferency, I were simply the most active
fellow in Europe: my womb, my womb, my womb
undoes me. Here comes our general.

*Prince John of Lancaster, Westmoreland, Blunt and others
return*

PRINCE JOHN. The heat is past, follow no further now,
Call in the powers, good cousin Westmoreland.
Westmoreland goes
Now, Falstaff, where have you been all this while?
When every thing is ended, then you come:
These tardy tricks of yours will, on my life,
One time or other break some gallows' back.
FALSTAFF. I would be sorry, my lord, but it should be 30
thus: I never knew yet but rebuke and check was the
reward of valour: do you think me a swallow, an
arrow, or a bullet? have I, in my poor and old
motion, the expedition of thought? I have speeded
hither with the very extremest inch of possibility.
I have foundered nine score and odd posts, and here,
travel-tainted as I am, have, in my pure and
immaculate valour, taken Sir John Colevile of the
Dale, a most furious knight and valorous enemy ...
But what of that? he saw me and yielded, that I may 40
justly say, with the hook-nosed fellow of Rome, 'I
came, saw and overcame.'
PRINCE JOHN. It was more of his courtesy than your
deserving.
FALSTAFF. I know not. Here he is, and here I yield him.
And I beseech your grace, let it be booked with the
rest of this day's deeds, or by the Lord, I will have
it in a particular ballad else, with mine own picture
on the top on't, Colevile kissing my foot: to the
which course if I be enforced, if you do not all show 50
like gilt two-pences to me, and I in the clear sky
of fame o'ershine you as much as the full moon doth
the cinders of the element, which show like pins'
heads to her, believe not the word of the noble:
therefore let me have right, and let desert mount.
PRINCE JOHN. Thine's too heavy to mount.
FALSTAFF. Let it shine then.
PRINCE JOHN. Thine's too thick to shine.
FALSTAFF. Let it do something, my good lord, that may
do me good, and call it what you will.   60
PRINCE JOHN. Is thy name Colevile?
COLEVILE.   It is, my lord.
PRINCE JOHN. A famous rebel art thou, Colevile.
FALSTAFF. And a famous true subject took him.
COLEVILE. I am, my lord, but as my betters are
That led me hither. Had they been ruled by me,
You should have won them dearer than you have.
FALSTAFF. I know not how they sold themselves, but
thou like a kind fellow gavest thyself away gratis,
and I thank thee for thee.

Westmoreland returns

PRINCE JOHN. Now, have you left pursuit?   70
WESTMORELAND. Retreat is made and execution
stayed.
PRINCE JOHN. Send Colevile with his confederates
To York, to present execution.
Blunt, lead him hence, and see you guard
him sure.   *They lead Colevile away*
And now dispatch we toward the court, my lords,
I hear the king my father is sore sick.

Our news shall go before us to his majesty,
Which, cousin, you shall bear to comfort him,
And we with sober speed will follow you.

FALSTAFF. My lord, I beseech you, give me leave to go 80
through Gloucestershire: and, when you come to
court, stand my good lord, pray, in your good
report.

PRINCE JOHN. Fare you well, Falstaff. I, in my
condition,
Shall better speak of you than you deserve. *He goes*

FALSTAFF. I would you had but the wit, 'twere better
than your dukedom. Good faith, this same young
sober-blooded boy doth not love me, nor a man
cannot make him laugh—but that's no marvel, he
drinks no wine. There's never none of these demure 90
boys come to any proof, for thin drink doth so
over-cool their blood, and making many fish-meals,
that they fall into a kind of male green-sickness,
and then when they marry they get wenches. They
are generally fools and cowards, which some of us
should be too, but for inflammation ... A good
sherris-sack hath a two-fold operation in it. It
ascends me into the brain, dries me there all the
foolish and dull and crudy vapours which environ it,
makes it apprehensive, quick, forgetive, full of 100
nimble, fiery, and delectable shapes, which delivered
o'er to the voice, the tongue, which is the birth,
becomes excellent wit. The second property of your
excellent sherris is the warming of the blood, which
before (cold and settled) left the liver white and
pale, which is the badge of pusillanimity and
cowardice; but the sherris warms it and makes it
course from the inwards to the parts extremes. It
illumineth the face, which as a beacon gives warning
to all the rest of this little kingdom, man, to arm. 110
And then the vital commoners, and inland petty
spirits, muster me all to their captain, the heart;
who, great and puffed up with this retinue, doth
any deed of courage; and this valour comes of
sherris. So that skill in the weapon is nothing without sack (for that sets it a-work), and learning a mere
hoard of gold kept by a devil, till sack commences
it and sets it in act and use.... Hereof comes it that
Prince Harry is valiant, for the cold blood he did
naturally inherit of his father he hath, like lean, 120
sterile and bare land, manured, husbanded and tilled
with excellent endeavour of drinking good and
good store of fertile sherris, that he is become very
hot and valiant.... If I had a thousand sons, the
first humane principle I would teach them should
be, to forswear thin potations, and to addict themselves to sack.

Bardolph enters

How now, Bardolph?

BARDOLPH. The army is dischargéd all and gone.

FALSTAFF. Let them go. I'll through Gloucestershire, 130
and there will I visit Master Robert Shallow,
esquire. I have him already tempering between my
finger and my thumb, and shortly will I seal with
him. Come away. *They go*

Scene 4: *Westminster. The Jerusalem chamber*

*The King in a chair of state; Prince Thomas of Clarence,
Prince Humphrey of Gloucester, the Earls of Warwick,
Kent and others*

KING. Now, lords, if God doth give successful end
To this debate that bleedeth at our doors,
We will our youth lead on to higher fields,
And draw no swords but what are sanctified:
Our navy is addressed, our power collected,
Our substitutes in absence well invested,
And every thing lies level to our wish—
Only we want a little personal strength;
And pause us till these rebels now afoot
Come underneath the yoke of government. 10

WARWICK. Both which we doubt not but your
majesty
Shall soon enjoy.

KING. Humphrey, my son of Gloucester,
Where is the prince your brother?

GLOUCESTER. I think he's gone to hunt, my lord,
at Windsor.

KING. And how accompanied?

GLOUCESTER. I do not know, my lord.

KING. Is not his brother, Thomas of Clarence,
with him?

GLOUCESTER. No, my good lord, he is in presence here.

CLARENCE. What would my lord and father?

KING. Nothing but well to thee, Thomas of Clarence.
How chance thou art not with the prince thy
brother? 20
He loves thee, and thou dost neglect him, Thomas.
Thou hast a better place in his affection
Than all thy brothers: cherish it, my boy,
And noble offices thou mayst effect
Of mediation after I am dead,
Between his greatness and thy other brethren:
Therefore, omit him not, blunt not his love,
Nor lose the good advantage of his grace
By seeming cold or careless of his will.
For he is gracious, if he be observed: 30
He hath a tear for pity, and a hand
Open as day for melting charity:
Yet notwithstanding, being incensed, he's flint,
As humorous as winter, and as sudden
As flaws congealéd in the spring of day:
His temper, therefore, must be well observed.
Chide him for faults, and do it reverently,
When you perceive his blood inclined to mirth:
But, being moody, give him line and scope,
Till that his passions, like a whale on ground, 40
Confound themselves with working. Learn this,
Thomas,
And thou shalt prove a shelter to thy friends,
A hoop of gold to bind thy brothers in,
That the united vessel of their blood,
Mingled with venom of suggestion,
(As, force perforce, the age will pour it in)
Shall never leak, though it do work as strong
As aconitum or rash gunpowder.

CLARENCE. I shall observe him with all care and love.

KING. Why art thou not at Windsor with him,
Thomas? 50

CLARENCE. He is not there to-day, he dines in London.

KING. And how accompanied? canst thou tell that?

CLARENCE. With Poins, and other his continual
followers.

KING. Most subject is the fattest soil to weeds,
And he, the noble image of my youth,
Is overspread with them! therefore my grief
Stretches itself beyond the hour of death:

The blood weeps from my heart when I do shape,
In forms imaginary, th'unguided days
And rotten times that you shall look upon,   60
When I am sleeping with my ancestors:
For when his headstrong riot hath no curb,
When rage and hot blood are his counsellors,
When means and lavish manners meet together,
O, with what wings shall his affections fly
Towards fronting peril and opposed decay!
WARWICK. My gracious lord, you look beyond
   him quite:
The prince but studies his companions
Like a strange tongue, wherein, to gain the
   language,
'Tis needful that the most immodest word   70
Be looked upon and learned—which once attained,
Your highness knows, comes to no further use
But to be known and hated ... So, like gross terms,
The prince will in the perfectness of time
Cast off his followers, and their memory
Shall as a pattern or a measure live,
By which his grace must mete the lives of other,
Turning past evils to advantages.
KING. 'Tis seldom when the bee doth leave her comb
In the dead carrion ...

Westmoreland enters

          Who's here? Westmoreland?   80
WESTMORELAND. Health to my sovereign, and
   new happiness
Added to that that I am to deliver!
Prince John your son doth kiss your grace's hand:
Mowbray, the Bishop Scroop, Hastings and all
Are brought to the correction of your law;
There is not now a rebel's sword unsheathed,
But Peace puts forth her olive every where.
The manner how this action hath been borne
Here at more leisure may your highness read,
With every course in his particular.   90
KING. O Westmoreland, thou art a summer bird,
Which ever in the haunch of winter sings
The lifting up of day. Look! here's more news.

Harcourt enters

HARCOURT. From enemies heaven keep your majesty,
And when they stand against you, may they fall
As those that I am come to tell you of!
The Earl Northumberland and the Lord Bardolph,
With a great power of English and of Scots,
Are by the shrieve of Yorkshire overthrown.
The manner and true order of the fight,   100
This packet, please it you, contains at large.
KING. And wherefore should these good news make
   me sick?
Will Fortune never come with both hands full,
But mete her fair words still in foulest terms?
She either gives a stomach and no food—
Such are the poor, in health; or else a feast
And takes away the stomach—sure she the rich,
That have abundance and enjoy it not ...
I should rejoice now at this happy news,
And now my sight fails, and my brain is giddy.   110
O me! come near me, now I am much ill.
GLOUCESTER. Comfort, your majesty!
CLARENCE.   O my royal father!

WESTMORELAND. My sovereign lord, cheer up
   yourself, look up!
WARWICK. Be patient, princes. You do know these fits
Are with his highness very ordinary.
Stand from him, give him air, he'll straight be well.
CLARENCE. No, no, he cannot long hold out these
   pangs,
Th'incessant care and labour of his mind
Hath wrought the mure, that should confine it in,
So thin that life looks through and will break out.   120
GLOUCESTER. The people fear me, for they do observe
Unfathered heirs and loathly births of nature.
The seasons change their manners, as the year
Had found some months asleep and leaped them
   over.
CLARENCE. The river hath thrice flowed, no ebb
   between,
And the old folk (time's doting chronicles)
Say it did so a little time before
That our great-grandsire, Edward, sicked and died.
WARWICK. Speak lower, princes, for the king recovers.
GLOUCESTER. This apoplexy will certain be his end.   130
KING. I pray you, take me up, and bear me hence
Into some other chamber: softly, pray.
         Warwick and Westmoreland carry him out,
                     the princes following

        Scene 5: Another chamber

*The King on a bed; Clarence, Gloucester, Warwick and
others in attendance*

KING. Let there be no noise made, my gentle friends,
Unless some dull and favourable hand
Will whisper music to my weary spirit.
WARWICK. Call for the music in the other room.
KING. Set me the crown upon my pillow here.
CLARENCE. His eye is hollow, and he changes much.

Prince Henry enters

WARWICK. Less noise, less noise!
PRINCE.   Who saw the Duke of Clarence?
CLARENCE. I am here, brother, full of heaviness.
PRINCE. How now! rain within doors, and none
   abroad!
How doth the king?   10
GLOUCESTER. Exceeding ill.
PRINCE.   Heard he the good news yet?
Tell it him.
GLOUCESTER. He altered much upon the hearing it.
PRINCE. If he be sick with joy, he'll recover without
   physic.
WARWICK. Not so much noise, my lords. Sweet
   prince, speak low;
The king your father is disposed to sleep.
CLARENCE. Let us withdraw into the other room.
WARWICK. Will't please your grace to go along with
   us?
PRINCE. No, I will sit and watch here by the king.
                              They go
Why doth the crown lie there upon his pillow,   20
Being so troublesome a bedfellow?
O polished perturbation! golden care!
That keep'st the ports of slumber open wide
To many a watchful night! sleep with it now?
Yet not so sound and half so deeply sweet
As he whose brow with homely biggen bound

Snores out the watch of night. O majesty!
When thou dost pinch thy bearer, thou dost sit
Like a rich armour worn in heat of day,
That scald'st with safety … By his gates of breath 30
There lies a downy feather which stirs not:
Did he suspire, that light and weightless down
Perforce must move. My gracious lord! my father!
This sleep is sound indeed, this is a sleep
That from this golden rigol hath divorced
So many English kings. Thy due from me
Is tears and heavy sorrows of the blood,
Which nature, love, and filial tenderness,
Shall (O dear father!) pay thee plenteously:
My due from thee is this imperial crown, 40
Which, as immediate from thy place and blood,
Derives itself to me … [*he sets it on his head*] Lo,
   where it sits,
Which God shall guard! and put the world's
   whole strength
Into one giant arm, it shall not force
This lineal honour from me: this from thee
Will I to mine leave, as 'tis left to thee.
                    He departs

KING. Warwick! Gloucester! Clarence!

Warwick and the young princes return

CLARENCE.   Doth the king call?
WARWICK. What would your majesty? How fares
   your grace?
KING. Why did you leave me here alone, my lords?
CLARENCE. We left the prince my brother here, my
   liege, 50
Who undertook to sit and watch by you.
KING. The Prince of Wales! Where is he? let me
   see him:
He is not here.
WARWICK. This door is open, he is gone this way.
GLOUCESTER. He came not through the chamber
   where we stayed.
KING. Where is the crown? who took it from
   my pillow?
WARWICK. When we withdrew, my liege, we left
   it here.
KING. The prince hath ta'en it hence: go, seek him out:
Is he so hasty that he doth suppose
My sleep my death? 60
Find him, my Lord of Warwick. Chide him hither.
                    Warwick departs
This part of his conjoins with my disease,
And helps to end me … See, sons, what things
   you are!
How quickly nature falls into revolt
When gold becomes her object!
For this the foolish over-careful fathers
Have broke their sleep with thoughts,
Their brains with care, their bones with industry;
For this they have engrossèd and piled up
The cank'red heaps of strange-achievèd gold; 70
For this they have been thoughtful to invest
Their sons with arts and martial exercises.
When, like the bee, culling from every flower
 The virtuous sweets,
'Our thighs with wax, our mouths with honey,
   packed,
We bring it to the hive; and, like the bees,
Are murdered for our pains. This bitter taste

Yields his engrossments to the ending father.

Warwick returns

Now, where is he that will not stay so long
Till his friend sickness have determined me? 80
WARWICK. My lord, I found the prince in the
   next room,
Washing with kindly tears his gentle cheeks,
With such a deep demeanour in great sorrow,
That tyranny, which never quaffed but blood,
Would, by beholding him, have washed his knife
With gentle eye-drops. He is coming hither.
KING. But wherefore did he take away the crown?

The Prince enters

Lo, where he comes. Come hither to me, Harry.
Depart the chamber, leave us here alone.
            Exeunt Warwick and the rest
PRINCE. I never thought to hear you speak again. 90
KING. Thy wish was father, Harry, to that thought.
I stay too long by thee, I weary thee.
Dost thou so hunger for mine empty chair
That thou wilt needs invest thee with my honours
Before thy hour be ripe? O foolish youth!
Thou seek'st the greatness that will overwhelm thee.
Stay but a little, for my cloud of dignity
Is held from falling with so weak a wind
That it will quickly drop: my day is dim.
Thou hast stol'n that which after some few hours 100
Were thine without offence—and at my death
Thou hast sealed up my expectation!
Thy life did manifest thou lov'dst me not,
And thou wilt have me die assured of it.
Thou hid'st a thousand daggers in thy thoughts,
Whom thou hast whetted on thy stony heart,
To stab at-half an hour of my life.
What! canst thou not forbear me half an hour?
Then get thee gone and dig my grave thyself,
And bid the merry bells ring to thine ear 110
That thou art crownèd, not that I am dead:
Let all the tears that should bedew my hearse
Be drops of balm to sanctify thy head.
Only compound me with forgotten dust,
Give that which gave thee life unto the worms,
Pluck down my officers, break my decrees,
For now a time is come to mock at form:
Harry the Fifth is crowned! up, vanity!
Down, royal state! all you sage counsellors, hence!
And to the English court assemble now 120
From every region apes of idleness!
Now, neighbour confines, purge you of your scum:
Have you a ruffian that will swear, drink, dance,
Revel the night, rob, murder and commit
The oldest sins the newest kind of ways?
Be happy, he will trouble you no more:
England shall double gild his treble guilt,
England shall give him office, honour, might:
For the fifth Harry from curbed licence plucks
The muzzle of restraint, and the wild dog 130
Shall flesh his tooth on every innocent.
O my poor kingdom! sick with civil blows
When that my care could not withhold thy riots,
What wilt thou do when riot is thy care?
O, thou wilt be a wilderness again,
Peopled with wolves, thy old inhabitants!
PRINCE. O, pardon me, my liege! but for my tears,

The moist impediments unto my speech,
I had forestalled this dear and deep rebuke,
Ere you with grief had spoke and I had heard   140
The course of it so far ... There is your crown;
And He that wears the crown immortally
Long guard it yours! If I affect it more
Than as your honour and as your renown,
Let me no more from this obedience rise,
Which my most inward true and duteous spirit
Teacheth this prostrate and exterior bending!
God witness with me, when I here came in,
And found no course of breath within your majesty,
How cold it struck my heart! if I do feign,   150
O, let me in my present wildness die,
And never live to show th'incredulous world
The noble change that I have purposéd.
Coming to look on you, thinking you dead—
And dead almost, my liege, to think you were—
I spake unto this crown as having sense,
And thus upbraided it: 'The care on thee depending
Hath fed upon the body of my father,
Therefore, thou best of gold art worst of gold.
Other, less fine in carat, is more precious,   160
Preserving life in med'cine potable;
But thou, most fine, most honoured, most
  renownéd,
Hast eat thy bearer up' ... Thus, my most royal
  liege,
Accusing it, I put it on my head,
To try with it, as with an enemy
That had before my face murdered my father,
The quarrel of a true inheritor.
But if it did infect my blood with joy,
Or swell my thoughts to any strain of pride,
If any rebel or vain spirit of mine   170
Did with the least affection of a welcome
Give entertainment to the might of it,
Let God for ever keep it from my head,
And make me as the poorest vassal is,
That doth with awe and terror kneel to it!
KING. O my son!
God put it in thy mind to take it hence,
That thou mightst win the more thy father's love,
Pleading so wisely in excuse of it ...
Come hither, Harry, sit thou by my bed,   180
And hear, I think, the very latest counsel
That ever I shall breathe. God knows, my son,
By what by-paths and indirect crookt ways
I met this crown, and I myself know well
How troublesome it sate upon my head:
To thee it shall descend with better quiet,
Better opinion, better confirmation;
For all the soil of the achievement goes
With me into the earth. It seemed in me
But as an honour snatched with boist'rous hand,   190
And I had many living to upbraid
My gain of it by their assistances,
Which daily grew to quarrel and to bloodshed,
Wounding supposéd peace: all these bold fears
Thou see'st with peril I have answeréd:
For all my reign hath been but as a scene
Acting that argument; and now my death
Changes the mood: for what in me was purchased,
Falls upon thee in a more fairer sort;
So thou the garland wear'st successively.   200
Yet, though thou stand'st more sure than I could do,

Thou art not firm enough, since griefs are green,
And all my friends, which thou must make thy
  friends,
Have but their stings and teeth newly ta'en out;
By whose fell working I was first advanced,
And by whose power I well might lodge a fear
To be again displaced: which to avoid,
I cut them off—and had a purpose now
To lead out many to the Holy Land,
Lest rest and lying still might make them look   210
Too near unto my state ... Therefore, my Harry,
Be it thy course to busy giddy minds
With foreign quarrels; that action hence borne out
May waste the memory of the former, days....
More would I, but my lungs are wasted so
That strength of speech is utterly denied me.
How I came by the crown, O God, forgive!
And grant it may with thee in true peace live!
PRINCE. My gracious liege,
You won it, wore it, kept it, gave it me,   220
Then plain and right must my possession be,
Which I with more than with a common pain
'Gainst all the world will rightfully maintain.

Enter Prince John of Lancaster, Warwick, and others

KING. Look, look, here comes my John of Lancaster.
PRINCE JOHN. Health, peace, and happiness to my
  royal father!
KING. Thou bring'st me happiness and peace, son John,
  But health, alack, with youthful wings is flown
  From this bare withered trunk: upon thy sight
  My worldly business makes a period....
  Where is my Lord of Warwick?
PRINCE.   My Lord of Warwick!   230
                          Warwick comes forward
KING. Doth any name particular belong
  Unto the lodging where I first did swoon?
WARWICK. 'Tis called Jerusalem, my noble lord.
KING. Laud be to God! even there my life must end.
  It hath been prophesied to me many years,
  I should not die but in Jerusalem;
  Which vainly I supposed the Holy Land:
  But bear me to that chamber, there I'll lie,
  In that Jerusalem shall Harry die.
                          They carry him forth

ACT 5

Scene 1: *Gloucestershire. Shallow's house*

*Shallow enters, bringing in Falstaff; Bardolph and page
follow*

SHALLOW. By cock and pie, sir, you shall not away
  to-night. What, Davy, I say!
FALSTAFF. You must excuse me, Master Robert Shallow.
SHALLOW. I will not excuse you, you shall not be
  excused, excuses shall not be admitted, there is no
  excuse shall serve, you shall not be excused....
  Why, Davy!

Davy enters

DAVY. Here, sir.
SHALLOW. Davy, Davy, Davy, Davy, let me see,   10
  Davy, let me see, Davy, let me see—yea, marry,
  William cook, bid him come hither. Sir John, you
  shall not be excused.

DAVY. Marry, sir, thus: those precepts cannot be served. And, again, sir, shall we sow the hade land with wheat?

SHALLOW. With red wheat, Davy. But for William cook, are there no young pigeons?

DAVY. Yes, sir. Here is now the smith's note for shoeing and plough-irons. 20

SHALLOW. Let it be cast and paid ... Sir John, you shall not be excused.

DAVY. Now, sir, a new link to the bucket must needs be had: and, sir, do you mean to stop any of William's wages, about the sack he lost the other day at Hinckley fair?

SHALLOW. A' shall answer it ... Some pigeons, Davy, a couple of short-legged hens, a joint of mutton, and any pretty little tine kickshaws, tell William cook.

DAVY. Doth the man of war stay all night, sir? 30

SHALLOW. Yes, Davy. I will use him well. A friend i' th' court is better than a penny in purse. Use his men well, Davy, for they are arrant knaves, and will backbite.

DAVY. No worse than they are backbitten, sir, for they have marvellous foul linen.

SHALLOW. Well conceited, Davy. About thy business, Davy.

DAVY. I beseech you, sir, to countenance William Visor of Woncot against Clement Perkes o'th' hill. 40

SHALLOW. There .s many complaints, Davy, against that Visor. That Visor is an arrant knave, on my knowledge.

DAVY. I grant your worship, that he is a knave, sir: but yet, God forbid, sir, but a knave should have some countenance at his friend's request. An honest man, sir, is able to speak for himself, when a knave is not. I have served your worship truly, sir, this eight years, and if I cannot once or twice in a quarter bear out a knave against an honest man, 50 I have but a very little credit with your worship. The knave is mine honest friend, sir—therefore, I beseech your worship, let him be countenanced.

SHALLOW. Go to, I say he shall have no wrong. Look about, Davy ... [Davy goes]. Where are you, Sir John? Come, come, come, off with your boots. Give me your hand, Master Bardolph.

BARDOLPH. I am glad to see your worship.

SHALLOW. I thank thee with all my heart, kind Master Bardolph—and [to the Page] welcome, my tall 60 fellow. Come, Sir John.   He goes

FALSTAFF. I'll follow you, good Master Robert Shal-low. Bardolph, look to our horses. [Bardolph goes out, with the Page] If I were sawed into quantities, I should make four dozen of such bearded hermits' staves as Master Shallow ... It is a wonderful thing to see the semblable coherence of his men's spirits and his. They, by observing of him, do bear them-selves like foolish justices; he, by conversing with them, is turned into a justice-like serving-man. 70 Their spirits are so married in conjunction, with the participation of society, that they flock together in consent, like so many wild-geese. If I had a suit to Master Shallow, I would humour his men with the imputation of being near their master: if to his men, I would curry with Master Shallow that no man could better command his servants. It is certain that either wise bearing or ignorant carriage is caught, as men take diseases, one of another: therefore, let

men take heed of their company. I will devise 80 matter enough out of this Shallow to keep Prince Harry in continual laughter the wearing out of six fashions—which is four terms, or two actions—and a' shall laugh without intervallums. O, it is much that a lie with a slight oath, and a jest with a sad brow, will do with a fellow that never had the ache in his shoulders! O, you shall see him laugh till his face be like a wet cloak ill laid up!

SHALLOW [within]. Sir John!

FALSTAFF. I come, Master Shallow. I come, Master 90 Shallow.   He goes

Scene 2: *Westminster. A Room in the Palace.*

Warwick and the Lord Chief Justice, meeting

WARWICK. How now, my lord chief justice? whither away?

L. CHIEF JUSTICE. How doth the king?

WARWICK. Exceeding well, his cares are now all ended.

L. CHIEF JUSTICE. I hope, not dead.

WARWICK.   He's walked the way of nature, And to our purposes he lives no more.

L. CHIEF JUSTICE. I would his majesty had called me with him: The service that I truly did his life Hath left me open to all injuries.

WARWICK. Indeed I think the young king loves you not.

L. CHIEF JUSTICE. I know he doth not, and do arm myself 10 To welcome the condition of the time, Which cannot look more hideously upon me Than I have drawn it in my fantasy.

Enter Prince John, Clarence, Gloucester, Westmoreland, and others

WARWICK. Here come the heavy issue of dead Harry. O, that the living Harry had the temper Of he, the worst of these three gentlemen! How many nobles then should hold their places, That must strike sail to spirits of vile sort!

L. CHIEF JUSTICE. O God, I fear all will be overturned!

PRINCE JOHN. Good morrow, cousin Warwick, good morrow. 20

GLOUCESTER. ⎫
CLARENCE. ⎭ Good morrow, cousin.

PRINCE JOHN. We meet like men that had forgot to speak.

WARWICK. We do remember, but our argument Is all too heavy to admit much talk.

PRINCE JOHN. Well, peace be with him that hath made us heavy!

L. CHIEF JUSTICE. Peace be with us, lest we be heavier!

GLOUCESTER. O, good my lord, you have lost a friend, indeed, And I dare swear you borrow not that face Of seeming sorrow, it is sure your own.

PRINCE JOHN. Though no man be assured what grace to find, 30 You stand in coldest expectation. I am the sorrier, would 'twere otherwise.

CLARENCE. Well, you must now speak Sir John Falstaff fair, Which swims against your stream of quality.

L. CHIEF JUSTICE. Sweet princes, what I did, I did
    in honour,
  Led by th'impartial conduct of my soul;
  And never shall you see that I will beg
  A ragged and forestaled remission.
  If truth and upright innocency fail me,
  I'll to the king my master that is dead,   40
  And tell him who hath sent me after him.
WARWICK. Here comes the prince.

Enter the Prince and Blunt

L. CHIEF JUSTICE. Good morrow, and God save
    your majesty!
PRINCE. This new and gorgeous garment, majesty,
  Sits not so easy on me as you think ...
  Brothers, you mix your sadness with some fear:
  This is the English, not the Turkish court,
  Not Amurath an Amurath succeeds,
  But Harry Harry! Yet be sad, good brothers,
  For by my faith, it very well becomes you;   50
  Sorrow so royally in you appears
  That I will deeply put the fashion on,
  And wear it in my heart: why then, be sad,
  But entertain no more of it, good brothers,
  Than a joint burden laid upon us all.
  For me, by heaven, I bid you be assured,
  I'll be your father and your brother too.
  Let me but bear your love, I'll bear your cares:
  Yet weep that Harry's dead, and so will I.
  But Harry lives that shall convert those tears   60
  By number into hours of happiness.
PRINCE JOHN, ETC. We hope no otherwise from
    your majesty.
PRINCE. You all look strangely on me—and you most.
  You are, I think, assured I love you not.
L. CHIEF JUSTICE. I am assured, if I be measured
    rightly,
  Your majesty hath no just cause to hate me.
PRINCE. No!
  How might a prince of my great hopes forget
  So great indignities you laid upon me?
  What! rate, rebuke, and roughly send to prison   70
  Th'immediate heir of England! Was this easy?
  May this be washed in Lethe, and forgotten?
L. CHIEF JUSTICE. I then did use the person of
    your father,
  The image of his power lay then in me,
  And, in th'administration of his law,
  Whiles I was busy for the commonwealth,
  Your highness pleaséd to forget my place,
  The majesty and power of law and justice,
  The image of the king whom I presented,
  And struck me in my very seat of judgement;   80
  Whereon, as an offender to your father,
  I gave bold way to my authority,
  And did commit you: if the deed were ill,
  Be you contented, wearing now the garland,
  To have a son set your decrees at nought?
  To pluck down Justice from your awful bench?
  To trip the course of law and blunt the sword
  That guards the peace and safety of your person?
  Nay more, to spurn at your most royal image,
  And mock your workings in a second body?   90
  Question your royal thoughts, make the case yours;
  Be now the father and propose a son,
  Hear your own dignity so much profaned,

See your most dreadful laws so loosely slighted,
Behold yourself so by a son disdained;
And then imagine me taking your part,
And in your power soft silencing your son:
After this cold considerance sentence me,
And as you are a king speak in your state
What I have done that misbecame my place,   100
My person, or my liege's sovereignty.
PRINCE. You are right Justice, and you weigh this
    well.
  Therefore still bear the balance and the sword.
  And I do wish your honours may increase,
  Till you do live to see a son of mine
  Offend you, and obey you, as I did:
  So shall I live to speak my father's words:
  'Happy am I, that have a man so bold,
  That dares do justice on my proper son;
  And not less happy, having such a son,   110
  That would deliver up his greatness so
  Into the hands of Justice.'—You did commit me:
  For which, I do commit into your hand
  Th'unstainéd sword that you have used to bear;
  With this remembrance, that you use the same
  With the like bold, just, and impartial spirit
  As you have done 'gainst me ... There is my hand.
  You shall be as a father to my youth,
  My voice shall sound as you do prompt mine ear,
  And I will stoop and humble my intents   120
  To your well-practised wise directions....
  And, princes all, believe me, I beseech you—
  My father is gone wild into his grave!
  For in his tomb lie my affections,
  And with his spirits sadly I survive,
  To mock the expectation of the world,
  To frustrate prophecies, and to raze out
  Rotten opinion, who hath writ me down
  After my seeming. The tide of blood in me
  Hath proudly flowed in vanity till now: 130
  Now doth it turn and ebb back to the sea,
  Where it shall mingle with the state of floods,
  And flow henceforth in formal majesty.
  Now call we our high court of parliament,
  And let us choose such limbs of noble counsel,
  That the great body of our state may go
  In equal rank with the best governed nation,
  That war, or peace, or both at once, may be
  As things acquainted and familiar to us—
  In which you, father, shall have foremost hand.... 140
  Our coronation done, we will accite,
  As I before remembered, all our state.
  And (God consigning to my good intents)
  No prince nor peer shall have just cause to say,
  God shorten Harry's happy life one day.   *They go*

Scene 3: *Gloucestershire. The orchard behind Justice
        Shallow's house*

*Enter Shallow and Falstaff, followed by Silence, Bardolph,
Page and Davy*

SHALLOW. Nay, you shall see my orchard, where, in an
  arbour, we will eat a last year's pippin of my own
  graffing, with a dish of caraways, and so forth—
  come, cousin Silence—and then to bed.
FALSTAFF. 'Fore God, you have here a goodly dwelling
  and a rich.
SHALLOW. Barren, barren, barren—beggars all, beg-

gars all, Sir John—marry, good air. Spread, Davy,
spread, Davy, well said, Davy.

FALSTAFF. This Davy serves you for good uses, he is 10
your serving-man and your husband.

SHALLOW. A good varlet, a good varlet, a very good
varlet, Sir John: by the mass, I have drunk too much
sack at supper: a good varlet. Now sit down, now
sit down—come, cousin.

SILENCE. Ah, sirrah! quoth-a, we shall—

[sings] Do nothing but eat, and make good cheer,
And praise God for the merry year,
When flesh is cheap and females dear,
And lusty lads roam here and there   20
So merrily,
And ever among so merrily.

FALSTAFF. There's a merry heart! Good Master Silence,
I'll give you a health for that anon.

SHALLOW. Give Master Bardolph some wine, Davy.

DAVY. Sweet sir, sit—I'll be with you anon—Most
sweet sir, sit; master page, good master page, sit.
Proface! what you want in meat, we'll have in drink:
but you must bear; the heart's all.   He goes

SHALLOW. Be merry, Master Bardolph, and my little 30
soldier there, be merry.

SILENCE [sings].
Be merry, be merry, my wife has all,
For women are shrews, both short and tall,
'Tis merry in hall when beards wag all,
And welcome merry Shrove-tide.
Be merry, be merry.

FALSTAFF. I did not think Master Silence had been a
man of this mettle.

SILENCE. Who, I? I have been merry twice and once
ere now.   40

Davy returns

DAVY. There's a dish of leather-coats for you.

SHALLOW. Davy!

DAVY. Your worship! I'll be with you straight.
A cup of wine, sir?

SILENCE [sings].
A cup of wine, that's brisk and fine,
And drink unto thee, leman mine,
And a merry heart lives long-a.

FALSTAFF. Well said! Master Silence.

SILENCE. An we shall be merry, now comes in the
sweet o' th' night.   50

FALSTAFF. Health and long life to you, Master Silence.

SILENCE [sings].
Fill the cup and let it come,
I'll pledge you a mile to the bottom.

SHALLOW. Honest Bardolph, welcome. If thou want'st
any thing, and wilt not call, beshrew thy heart.
Welcome, my little tine thief [to the Page], and
welcome indeed too. I'll drink to Master Bardolph,
and to all the caballeros about London.

DAVY. I hope to see London once ere I die.

BARDOLPH. An I might see you there, Davy,—   60

SHALLOW. By the mass, you'll crack a quart together,
ha? will you not, Master Bardolph?

BARDOLPH. Yea, sir, in a pottle-pot.

SHALLOW. By God's liggens, I thank thee. The knave
will stick by thee, I can assure thee that. A' will
not out, a'. 'Tis true bred!   One knocks at door

BARDOLPH. And I'll stick by him, sir.

SHALLOW. Why, there spoke a king. Lack nothing, be

merry. [knocking again] Look who's at door there.
Ho! who knocks?   Davy goes 70

Silence drinks a bumper to Falstaff

FALSTAFF. Why, now you have done me right.

SILENCE [sings].   Do me right,
And dub me knight,
Samingo.
Is't not so?

FALSTAFF. 'Tis so.

SILENCE. Is't so? Why then, say an old man can do
somewhat.

Davy returns, with Pistol following

DAVY. An't please your worship, there's one Pistol
come from the court with news.   80

FALSTAFF. From the court? let him come in. How now,
Pistol?

PISTOL. Sir John, God save you.

FALSTAFF. What wind blew you hither, Pistol?

PISTOL. Not the ill wind which blows no man to good
... Sweet knight, thou art now one of the greatest
men in this realm.

SILENCE. By'r lady, I think a' be—but goodman Puff
of Barson.

PISTOL. Puff!   90
Puff i'thy teeth, most recreant coward base!
Sir John, I am thy Pistol and thy friend,
And helter-skelter have I rode to thee,
And tidings do I bring and lucky joys
And golden times and happy news of price.

FALSTAFF. I pray thee now, deliver them like a man of
this world.

PISTOL. A foutre for the world and worldlings base!
I speak of Africa and golden joys.

FALSTAFF. O base Assyrian knight, what is thy news? 100
Let King Cophetua know the truth thereof.

SILENCE [sings]. And Robin Hood, Scarlet and John.

PISTOL. Shall dunghill curs confront the Helicons?
And shall good news be baffled?
Then, Pistol, lay thy head in Furies' lap.

SHALLOW. Honest gentleman, I know not your breeding.

PISTOL. Why then, lament therefore.

SHALLOW. Give me pardon, sir. If, sir, you come with
news from the court, I take it there's but two ways, 110
either to utter them or conceal them. I am, sir, under
the king, in some authority.

PISTOL. Under which king, Besonian? speak, or die.

SHALLOW. Under King Harry.

PISTOL.   Harry the fourth? or fifth?

SHALLOW. Harry the fourth.

PISTOL.   A foutre for thine office!
Sir John, thy tender lambkin now is king;
Harry the fifth's the man: I speak the truth:
When Pistol lies, do this; and fig me, like
The bragging Spaniard.

FALSTAFF. What! is the old king dead?   120

PISTOL. As nail in door! the things I speak are just.

FALSTAFF. Away, Bardolph, saddle my horse. Master
Robert Shallow, choose what office thou wilt in the
land, 'tis thine: Pistol, I will double-charge thee with
dignities.

BARDOLPH. O joyful day! I would not take a knighthood for my fortune.

PISTOL. What! I do bring good news?

FALSTAFF [*to Davy*]. Carry Master Silence to bed ...
Master Shallow, my Lord Shallow—be what thou 130
wilt, I am Fortune's steward—get on thy boots,
we'll ride all night: O, sweet Pistol. Away, Bardolph. [*Bardolph goes*] Come, Pistol, utter more to
me, and withal devise something to do thyself good.
Boot, boot, Master Shallow! I know the young king
is sick for me. Let us take any man's horses—the
laws of England are at my commandment. Blessed
are they that have been my friends, and woe to my
lord chief justice!

PISTOL. Let vultures vile seize on his lungs also!   140
'Where is the life that late I led' say they?
Why, here it is; welcome these pleasant days.
                                             They go

Scene 4: *A street in London*

Enter Beadles, with Hostess Quickly and Doll Tearsheet

HOSTESS. No, thou arrant knave! I would to God that
I might die, that I might have thee hanged. Thou
hast drawn my shoulder out of joint.

1 BEADLE. The constables have delivered her over to
me, and she shall have whipping-cheer enough, I
warrant her. There hath been a man or two lately
killed about her.

DOLL. Nut-hook, nut-hook, you lie. Come on, I'll tell
thee what, thou damned tripe-visaged rascal, an the
child I go with do miscarry, thou wert better thou 10
hadst struck thy mother, thou paper-faced villain.

HOSTESS. O the Lord, that Sir John were come! he
would make this a bloody day to somebody: but
I pray God the fruit of her womb miscarry!

1 BEADLE. If it do, you shall have a dozen of cushions
again—you have but eleven now ... Come, I charge
you both go with me, for the man is dead that
you and Pistol beat amongst you.

DOLL. I'll tell you what, you thin man in a censer, I
will have you as soundly swinged for this—you 20
blue-bottle rogue, you filthy famished correctioner,
if you be not swinged, I'll forswear half-kirtles.

1 BEADLE. Come, come, you she knight-errant, come.

HOSTESS. O God, that right should thus overcome
might! Well, of sufferance comes ease.

DOLL. Come, you rogue, come, bring me to a justice.

HOSTESS. Ay, come, you starved blood-hound.

DOLL. Goodman death! goodman bones!

HOSTESS. Thou atomy thou!

DOLL. Come, you thin thing; come, you rascal!   30

1 BEADLE. Very well!   *They go*

Scene 5: *A public place near Westminster Abbey*

Enter strewers of rushes

1 STREWER. More rushes, more rushes.

2 STREWER. The trumpets have sounded twice.

3 STREWER. 'Twill be two o'clock ere they come from
the coronation. Dispatch, dispatch.   *They go*

*Trumpets sound; the King and his train come up in
procession, and pass into the Abbey; after a while Falstaff,
Shallow, Pistol, Bardolph, and the Page enter*

FALSTAFF. Stand here by me, Master Robert Shallow,
I will make the king do you grace, I will leer upon
him as a' comes by, and do but mark the countenance that he will give me.

PISTOL. God bless thy lungs, good knight.

FALSTAFF. Come here, Pistol, stand behind me. [*to* 10
Shallow] O, if I had had time to have made new
liveries, I would have bestowed the thousand pound
I borrowed of you. But 'tis no matter, this poor
show doth better, this doth infer the zeal I had to
see him.

SHALLOW. It doth so.

FALSTAFF. It shows my earnestness of affection—

PISTOL. It doth so.

FALSTAFF. My devotion—

PISTOL. It doth, it doth, it doth.   20

FALSTAFF. As it were, to ride day and night, and not to
deliberate, not to remember, not to have patience
to shift me—

SHALLOW. It is best, certain.

FALSTAFF. But to stand stained with travel, and sweating with desire to see him, thinking of nothing else,
putting all affairs else in oblivion, as if there were
nothing else to be done but to see him.

PISTOL. 'Tis 'semper idem,' for 'obsque hoc nihil est.'
'Tis 'all in every part'.   30

SHALLOW. 'Tis so, indeed.

PISTOL. My knight, I will inflame thy noble liver,
And make thee rage.
Thy Doll, and Helen of thy noble thoughts,
Is in base durance and contagious prison,
Haled thither
By most mechanical and dirty hand:
Rouse up revenge from ebon den with fell Alecto's
snake,
For Doll is in: Pistol speaks nought but truth.

FALSTAFF. I will deliver her.   40
                       Trumpets heard, and a great shout

PISTOL. There roared the sea, and trumpet-
clangor sounds.

Enter the King and his train, with the Lord Chief Justice

FALSTAFF. God save thy grace, King Hal! my royal Hal!

PISTOL. The heavens thee guard and keep, most royal
imp of fame!

FALSTAFF. God save thee, my sweet boy!

KING. My lord chief justice, speak to that vain man.

L. CHIEF JUSTICE. Have you your wits? know you what
'tis you speak?

FALSTAFF. My king! my Jove! I speak to thee, my heart!

KING. I know thee not, old man. Fall to thy prayers.
How ill white hairs become a fool and jester!   50
I have long dreamed of such a kind of man,
So surfeit-swelled, so old, and so profane;
But, being awaked, I do despise my dream.
Make less thy body hence, and more thy grace,
Leave gormandizing, know the grave doth gape
For thee thrice wider than for other men.
Reply not to me with a fool-born jest,
Presume not that I am the thing I was,
For God doth know, so shall the world perceive,
That I have turned away my former self;   60
So will I those that kept me company.
When thou dost hear I am as I have been,
Approach me, and thou shalt be as thou wast,
The tutor and the feeder of my riots:
Till then, I banish thee, on pain of death,
As I have done the rest of my misleaders,
Not to come near our person by ten mile ...
For competence of life I will allow you,

That lack of means enforce you not to evils.
As we hear you do reform yourselves,   70
We will, according to your strengths and qualities,
Give you advancement. Be it your charge, my lord,
To see performed the tenour of my word. . . .
Set on.   *The procession passes on*

FALSTAFF.. Master Shallow, I owe you a thousand
pound.

SHALLOW. Yea, marry, Sir John, which I beseech you
to let me have home with me.

FALSTAFF. That can hardly be, Master Shallow . . . Do
not you grieve at this. I shall be sent for in private   80
to him; look you, he must seem thus to the world:
fear not your advancements—I will be the man yet
that shall make you great.

SHALLOW. I cannot perceive how, unless you give me
your doublet, and stuff me out with straw. I beseech
you, good Sir John, let me have five hundred of my
thousand.

FALSTAFF. Sir, I will be as good as my word. This that
you heard was but a colour.

SHALLOW. A colour that I fear you will die in, Sir John.   90

FALSTAFF. Fear no colours, go with me to dinner: come
Lieutenant Pistol, come, Bardolph—I shall be sent
for soon at night.

Prince John returns with the Lord Chief Justice and officers

L. CHIEF JUSTICE. Go, carry Sir John Falstaff to the
Fleet,
Take all his company along with him.
               They arrest Falstaff and his party

FALSTAFF. My lord, my lord—

L. CHIEF JUSTICE. I cannot now speak, I will hear
you soon.
Take them away.

PISTOL. 'Si fortuna me tormenta, spero me contenta.'
               The officers lead them off

PRINCE JOHN. I like this fair proceeding of the king's.   100
He hath intent his wonted followers
Shall all be very well provided for;
But all are banished till their conversations
Appear more wise and modest to the world.

L. CHIEF JUSTICE. And so they are.

PRINCE JOHN. The king hath called his parliament,
my lord.

L. CHIEF JUSTICE. He hath.

PRINCE JOHN. I will lay odds that, ere this year expire,
We bear our civil swords and native fire
As far as France. I heard a bird so sing,   110
Whose music, to my thinking, pleased the king . . .
Come, will you hence?   *They go*

EPILOGUE

First my fear, then my curtsy, last my speech.

My fear is your displeasure, my curtsy my duty,
and my speech to beg your pardons. If you look for
a good speech now, you undo me, for what I have
to say is of mine own making, and what indeed I
should say will, I doubt, prove mine own marring:
but to the purpose, and so to the venture. Be it
known to you, as it is very well, I was lately here
in the end of a displeasing play, to pray your
patience for it and to promise you a better. I   10
meant indeed to pay you with this; which, if like
an ill venture it come unluckily home, I break, and
you, my gentle creditors, lose. Here I promised you
I would be, and here I commit my body to your
mercies: bate me some, and I will pay you some,
and, as most debtors do, promise you infinitely: and
so I kneel down before you; but, indeed, to pray
for the Queen.

If my tongue cannot entreat you to acquit me,
will you command me to use my legs? and yet that   20
were but light payment, to dance out of your debt.
But a good conscience will make any possible
satisfaction, and so would I . . . All the gentlewomen
here have forgiven me; if the gentlemen will not,
then the gentlemen do not agree with the gentlewomen, which was never seen before in such an
assembly.

One word more, I beseech you. If you be not too
much cloyed with fat meat, our humble author will
continue the story, with Sir John in it, and make   30
you merry with fair Katharine of France; where
(for any thing I know) Falstaff shall die of a sweat,
unless already a' be killed with your hard opinions;
for Oldcastle died martyr, and this is not the man
. . . My tongue is weary, when my legs are too, I
will bid you good night.

King Henry V

The scene: first England, then France

CHARACTERS IN THE PLAY

Chorus
KING HENRY *the Fifth*
HUMPHREY, DUKE OF GLOUCESTER
JOHN OF LANCASTER, DUKE OF BEDFORD ⎫ *brothers to*
THOMAS OF LANCASTER, DUKE OF ⎬ *the king*
  CLARENCE ⎭
DUKE OF EXETER, *uncle to the king*
DUKE OF YORK, *cousin to the king, formerly Aumerle*
EARLS OF SALISBURY, WESTMORELAND, *and* WARWICK
ARCHBISHOP OF CANTERBURY
BISHOP OF ELY
EARL OF CAMBRIDGE
LORD SCROOP
SIR THOMAS GREY
SIR THOMAS ERPINGHAM, GOWER, FLUELLEN, MACMORRIS,
  JAMY, *officers in King Henry's army*
BATES, COURT, WILLIAMS, *soldiers in the same*

PISTOL, NYM, BARDOLPH
BOY. A Herald
CHARLES *the Sixth, King of France*
LEWIS, *the Dauphin*
DUKES *of* BURGUNDY, ORLEANS, BRITAINE *and* BOURBON
The Constable of France
RAMBURES, *and* GRANDPRÉ, *French Lords*
Governor of Harfleur
MONTJOY, *a French herald*
Ambassadors to the King of England
ISABEL, *Queen of France*
KATHARINE, *daughter to Charles and Isabel*
ALICE, *a lady attending upon her*
Hostess, formerly MRS QUICKLY, *now Pistol's wife*
Lords, Ladies, Officers, French and English Soldiers,
  Messengers, and Attendants

King Henry V

ACT 1
Prologue

Enter Chorus

CHORUS. O for a Muse of fire, that would ascend
  The brightest heaven of invention:
  A kingdom for a stage, princes to act,
  And monarchs to behold the swelling scene.
  Then should the warlike Harry, like himself,
  Assume the port of Mars, and at his heels,
  Leashed in like hounds, should Famine, Sword, and
    Fire
  Crouch for employment. But pardon, gentles all,
  The flat unraiséd spirits that hath dared
  On this unworthy scaffold to bring forth   10
  So great an object. Can this cockpit hold
  The vasty fields of France? or may we cram
  Within this wooden O the very casques
  That did affright the air at Agincourt?
  O, pardon! since a crooked figure may
  Attest in little place a million;
  And let us, ciphers to this great accompt,
  On your imaginary forces work....
  Suppose within the girdle of these walls
  Are now confined two mighty monarchies,   20
  Whose high upreáred and abutting fronts
  The perilous narrow ocean parts asunder.
  Piece out our imperfections with your thoughts:
  Into a thousand parts divide one man,
  And make imaginary puissance.
  Think, when we talk of horses, that you see them
  Printing their proud hoofs i'th'receiving earth:
  For 'tis your thoughts that now must deck our kings,
  Carry them here and there: jumping o'er times;
  Turning th'accomplishment of many years   30
  Into an hour-glass: for the which supply,
  Admit me Chorus to this history;
  Who prologue-like your humble patience pray,
  Gently to hear, kindly to judge, our play.   *Exit*

Scene I: *London. An antechamber in the King's palace*

Enter the Archbishop of Canterbury and the Bishop of Ely

CANTERBURY. My lord, I'll tell you—that self bill
    is urged,
  Which in th' eleventh year of the last king's reign
  Was like, and had indeed against us passed,
  But that the scambling and unquiet time
  Did push it out of farther question.
ELY. But how, my lord, shall we resist it now?
CANTERBURY. It must be thought on ... If it pass
    against us,
  We lose the better half of our possession:
  For all the temporal lands which men devout
  By testament have given to the Church   10
  Would they strip from us; being valued thus—
  As much as would maintain, to the king's honour,
  Full fifteen earls, and fifteen hundred knights,
  Six thousand and two hundred good esquires:

And, to relief of lazers and weak age,
  Of indigent faint souls past corporal toil,
  A hundred almshouses right well supplied:
  And to the coffers of the king beside,
  A thousand pounds by th'year: thus runs the bill.
ELY. This would drink deep.
CANTERBURY.   'Twould drink the cup and all. 20
ELY. But what prevention?
CANTERBURY. The king is full of grace and fair regard,
    and a true lover of the holy Church.
ELY. The courses of his youth promised it not.
CANTERBURY. The breath no sooner left his father's
    body,
  But that his wildness, mortified in him,
  Seemed to die too: yea, at that very moment,
  Consideration like an angel came,
  And whipped th' offending Adam out of him;
  Leaving his body as a Paradise,
  T'envelop and contain celestial spirits....   30
  Never was such a sudden scholar made:
  Never came reformation in a flood,
  With such a heady currance, scouring faults:
  Nor never Hydra-headed wilfulness
  So soon did lose his seat—and all at once—
  As in this king.
ELY.   We are blesséd in the change.
CANTERBURY. Hear him but reason in divinity;
  And, all-admiring, with an inward wish
  You would desire the king were made a prelate:
  Hear him debate of commonwealth affairs;   40
  You would say it hath been all in all his study:
  List his discourse of war; and you shall hear
  A fearful battle rendered you in music.
  Turn him to any cause of policy,
  The Gordian knot of it he will unloose,
  Familiar as his garter: that, when he speaks,
  The air, a chartered libertine, is still,
  And the mute wonder lurketh in men's ears,
  To steal his sweet and honeyed sentences:
  So that the art and practic part of life   50
  Must be the mistress to this theoric;
  Which is a wonder, how his grace should glean it,
  Since his addiction was to courses vain,
  His companies unlettered, rude, and shallow,
  His hours filled up with riots, banquets, sports;
  And never noted in him any study,
  Any retirement, any sequestration,
  From open haunts and popularity.
ELY. The strawberry grows underneath the nettle,
  And wholesome berries thrive and ripen best   60
  Neighboured by fruit of baser quality:
  And so the prince obscured his contemplation
  Under the veil of wildness, which, no doubt,
  Grew like the summer grass, fastest by night,
  Unseen, yet crescive in his faculty.
CANTERBURY. It must be so; for miracles are ceased:
  And therefore we must needs admit the means
  How things are perfected.
ELY.   But, my good lord,
  How now for mitigation of this bill

Urged by the commons? Doth his majesty   70
Incline to it, or no?
CANTERBURY.   He seems indifferent—
Or rather swaying more upon our part
Than cherishing th' exhibiters against us:
For I have made an offer to his majesty,
Upon our spiritual convocation,
And in regard of causes now in hand,
Which I have opened to his grace at large,
As touching France, to give a greater sum
Than ever at one time the clergy yet
Did to his predecessors part withal.   80
ELY. How did this offer seem received, my lord?
CANTERBURY. With good acceptance of his majesty:
Save that there was not time enough to hear,
As I perceived his grace would fain have done,
The severals and unhidden passages
Of his true titles to some certain dukedoms,
And generally to the crown and seat of France
Derived from Edward, his great-grandfather.
ELY. What was th' impediment that broke this off?
CANTERBURY. The French ambassador upon that
     instant   90
Craved audience; and the hour, I think, is come
To give him hearing: is it four o'clock?
ELY. It is.
CANTERBURY. Then go we in, to know his embassy:
Which I could with a ready guess declare,
Before the Frenchman speak a word of it.
ELY. I'll wait upon you, and I long to hear it.
                     They go

Scene 2: *The Presence-chamber in the palace*

*Enter King Henry, Gloucester, Bedford, Exeter, Warwick,
Westmoreland, and attendants*

KING HENRY. Where is my gracious Lord of
     Canterbury?
EXETER. Not here in presence.
KING HENRY.   Send for him, good uncle.
WESTMORELAND. Shall we call in th'ambassador, my
     liege?
KING HENRY. Not yet, my cousin: we would be
     resolved,
Before we hear him, of some things of weight
That task our thoughts, concerning us and France.

The Archbishop of Canterbury and the Bishop of Ely enter

CANTERBURY. God and his angels guard your sacred
     throne,
And make you long become it!
KING HENRY.   Sure, we thank you....
My learnéd lord, we pray you to proceed,
And justly and religiously unfold   10
Why the law Salic that they have in France
Or should or should not bar us in our claim:
And God forbid, my dear and faithful lord,
That you should fashion, wrest, or bow your
     reading,
Or nicely charge your understanding soul
With opening titles miscreate, whose right
Suits not in native colours with the truth:
For God doth know how many now in health
Shall drop their blood in approbation
Of what your reverence shall incite us to.   20
Therefore take heed how you impawn our person,

How you awake our sleeping sword of war;
We charge you in the name of God, take heed:
For never two such kingdoms did contend
Without much fall of blood, whose guiltless drops
Are every one a woe, a sore complaint
'Gainst him whose wrongs gives edge unto the
     swords
That makes such waste in brief mortality....
Under this conjuration, speak, my lord:
For we will hear, note, and believe in heart,   30
That what you speak is in your conscience washed
As pure as sin with baptism.
CANTERBURY. Then hear me, gracious sovereign, and
     you peers,
That owe yourselves, your lives, and services
To this imperial throne.... There is no bar
To make against your highness' claim to France,
But this which they produce from Pharamond:
"In terram Salicam mulieres ne succedant"—
"No woman shall succeed in Salic land":
Which Salic land the French unjustly gloze   40
To be the realm of France, and Pharamond
The founder of this law and female bar.
Yet their own authors faithfully affirm
That the land Salic is in Germany,
Between the floods of Sala and of Elbe:
Where Charles the Great, having subdued the
     Saxons,
There left behind and settled certain French:
Who holding in disdain the German women
For some dishonest manners of their life,
Established then this law—to wit, no female   50
Should be inheritrix in Salic land:
Which Salic, as I said, 'twixt Elbe and Sala,
Is at this day in Germany called Meisen.
Then doth it well appear the Salic law
Was not devised for the realm of France:
Nor did the French possess the Salic land
Until four hundred one and twenty years
After defunction of King Pharamond,
Idly supposed the founder of this law,
Who died within the year of our redemption   60
Four hundred twenty-six: and Charles the Great
Subdued the Saxons, and did seat the French
Beyond the river Sala, in the year
Eight hundred five.... Besides, their writers say,
King Pepin, which deposed Childeric,
Did, as heir general, being descended
Of Blithild, which was daughter to King Clothair,
Make claim and title to the crown of France.
Hugh Capet also, who usurped the crown
Of Charles the duke of Lorraine, sole heir male   70
Of the true line and stock of Charles the Great,
To find his title with some shows of truth,
Though in pure truth it was corrupt and naught,
Conveyed himself as th'heir to th'Lady Lingare,
Daughter to Charlemain, who was the son
To Lewis the emperor, and Lewis the son
Of Charles the Great: also King Lewis the tenth,
Who was sole heir to the usurper Capet,
Could not keep quiet in his conscience,
Wearing the crown of France, till satisfied   80
That fair Queen Isabel, his grandmother,
Was lineal of the Lady Ermengare,
Daughter to Charles the foresaid duke of Lorraine:
By the which marriage the line of Charles the Great

Was re-united to the crown of France.
So that, as clear as is the summer's sun,
King Pepin's title and Hugh Capet's claim,
King Lewis his satisfaction, all appear
To hold in right and title of the female:
So do the kings of France unto this day.   90
Howbeit they would hold up this Salic law
To bar your highness claiming from the female,
And rather choose to hide them in a net
Than amply to imbare their crooked titles,
Usurped from you and your progenitors.
KING HENRY. May I with right and conscience make
    this claim?
CANTERBURY. The sin upon my head, dread sovereign!
For in the book of Numbers is it writ,
When the man dies, let the inheritance
Descend unto the daughter.... Gracious lord.   100
Stand for your own, unwind your bloody flag,
Look back into your mighty ancestors:
Go, my dread lord, to your great-grandsire's tomb,
From whom you claim; invoke his warlike spirit,
And your great-uncle's, Edward the Black Prince,
Who on the French ground played a tragedy,
Making defeat on the full power of France,
Whiles his most mighty father on a hill
Stood smiling to behold his lion's whelp
Forage in blood of French nobility....   110
O noble English, that could entertain
With half their forces the full pride of France,
And let another half stand laughing by,
All out of work and cold for action!
ELY. Awake remembrance of these valiant dead,
And with your puissant arm renew their feats;
You are their heir, you sit upon their throne:
The blood and courage that renownèd them
Runs in your veins: and my thrice-puissant liege
Is in the very May-morn of his youth,   120
Ripe for exploits and mighty enterprises.
EXETER. Your brother kings and monarchs of the earth
Do all expect that you should rouse yourself,
As did the former lions of your blood.
WESTMORELAND. They know your grace hath cause,
    and means, and might;
So hath your highness: never king of England
Had nobles richer, and more loyal subjects,
Whose hearts have left their bodies here in England,
And lie pavilioned in the fields of France.
CANTERBURY. O let their bodies follow, my dear liege,   130
With blood and sword and fire, to win your right:
In aid whereof, we of the spirituality
Will raise your highness such a mighty sum
As never did the clergy at one time
Bring in to any of your ancestors.
KING HENRY. We must not only arm t'invade the
    French,
But lay down our proportions to defend
Against the Scot, who will make road upon us
With all advantages.
CANTERBURY. They of those marches, gracious
    sovereign,   140
Shall be a wall sufficient to defend
Our inland from the pilfering borderers.
KING HENRY. We do not mean the coursing snatchers
    only,
But fear the main intendment of the Scot,
Who hath been still a giddy neighbour to us:

For you shall read that my great-grandfather
Never went with his forces into France,
But that the Scot on his unfurnished kingdom
Came pouring like the tide into a breach,
With ample and brim fulness of his force,   150
Galling the gleanèd land with hot assays,
Girding with grievous siege castles and towns:
That England, being empty of defence,
Hath shook and trembled at th'ill neighbourhood.
CANTERBURY. She hath been then more feared than
    harmed, my liege:
For hear her but exampled by herself—
When all her chivalry hath been in France,
And she a mourning widow of her nobles,
She hath herself not only well defended,
But taken and impounded as a stray   160
The King of Scots: whom she did send to France,
To fill King Edward's fame with prisoner kings,
And make her chronicle as rich with praise
As is the ooze and bottom of the sea
With sunken wrack and sumless treasuries.
ELY. But there's a saying very old and true—
    "If that you will France win,
       Then with Scotland first begin:"
For once the eagle England being in prey,
To her unguarded nest the weasel Scot   170
Comes sneaking, and so sucks her princely eggs,
Playing the mouse in absence of the cat,
To 'tame and havoc more than she can eat.
EXETER. It follows then the cat must stay at home.
Yet that is but a crushed necessity,
Since we have locks to safeguard necessaries,
And pretty traps to catch the petty thieves.
While that the armèd hand doth fight abroad
Th'advisèd head defends itself at home:
For government, though high, and low, and lower,   180
Put into parts, doth keep in one consent,
Congreeing in a full and natural close,
Like music.
CANTERBURY. Therefore doth heaven divide
The state of man in divers functions,
Setting endeavour in continual motion:
To which is fixèd, as an aim or butt,
Obedience: for so work the honey-bees,
Creatures that by a rule in nature teach
The act of order to a peopled kingdom.
They have a king and officers of sorts: 190
Where some, like magistrates, correct at home,
Others, like merchants, venture trade abroad:
Others, like soldiers, armèd in their stings
Make boot upon the summer's velvet buds:
Which pillage they with merry march bring home
To the tent-royal of their emperor:
Who, busied in his majesty, surveys
The singing masons building roofs of gold,
The civil citizens kneading up the honey;
The poor mechanic porters crowding in   200
Their heavy burdens at his narrow gate:
The sad-eyed justice, with his surly hum,
Delivering o'er to executors pale
The lazy yawning drone ... I this infer,
That many things, having full reference
To one consent, may work contrariously—
As many arrows loosèd several ways
Come to one mark:
As many several ways meet in one town:

As many fresh streams meet in one salt sea: 210
As many lines close in the dial's centre:
So may a thousand actions, once afoot,
End in one purpose, and be all well borne
Without defeat.... Therefore to France, my liege—
Divide your happy England into four,
Whereof take you one quarter into France,
And you withal shall make all Gallia shake.
If we, with thrice such powers left at home,
Cannot defend our own doors from the dog,
Let us be worried, and our nation lose   220
The name of hardiness and policy.
KING HENRY. Call in the messengers sent from the
     Dauphin.   *Attendants go*
Now are we well resolved, and by God's help
And yours, the noble sinews of our power,
France being ours, we'll bend it to our awe,
Or break it all to peices. Or there we'll sit,
Ruling in large and ample empery
O'er France and all her almost kingly dukedoms,
Or lay these bones in an unworthy urn,
Tombless, with no remembrance over them: 230
Either our history shall with full mouth
Speak freely of our acts, or else our grave,
Like Turkish mute, shall have a tongueless mouth,
Not worshipped with a waxen epitaph....

Enter Ambassadors of France

Now are we well prepared to know the pleasure
Of our fair cousin Dauphin: for we hear
Your greeting is from him, not from the king.
AMBASSADOR. May't please your majesty to give us
     leave
Freely to render what we have in charge:
Or shall we sparingly show you far off   240
The Dauphin's meaning and our embassy?
KING HENRY. We are no tyrant, but a Christian king,
Unto whose grace our passion is as subject
As is our wretches fettered in our prisons;
Therefore with frank and with uncurbéd plainness
Tell us the Dauphin's mind.
AMBASSADOR.   Thus then, in few:
Your highness, lately sending into France,
Did claim some certain dukedoms, in the right
Of your great predecessor, King Edward the third.
In answer of which claim, the prince our master   250
Says that you savour too much of your youth,
And bids you be advised there's nought in France
That can be with a nimble galliard won:
You cannot revel into dukedoms there....
He therefore sends you, meeter for your spirit,
This tun of treasure; and, in lieu of this,
Desires you let the dukedoms that you claim
Hear no more of you.... This the Dauphin speaks.
KING HENRY. What treasure, uncle?
EXETER.   Tennis-balls, my liege.
KING HENRY. We are glad the Dauphin is so pleasant
     with us—   260
His present and your pains we thank you for:
When we have matched our rackets to these balls,
We will in France, by God's grace, play a set
Shall strike his father's crown into the hazard.
Tell him he hath made a match with such a wrangler
That all the courts of France will be disturbed
With chases.... And we understand him well,
How he comes o'er us with our wilder days,

Not measuring what use we made of them.
We never valued this poor seat of England,   270
And therefore, living hence, did give ourself
To barbarous licence: as 'tis ever common
That men are merriest when they are from home....
But tell the Dauphin I will keep my state,
Be like a king, and show my sail of greatness,
When I do rouse me in my throne of France.
For that I have laid by my majesty,
And plodded like a man for working-days:
But I will rise there with so full a glory
That I will dazzle all the eyes of France,   280
Yea, strike the Dauphin blind to look on us.
And tell the pleasant prince this mock of his
Hath turned his balls to gun-stones, and his soul
Shall stand sore chargéd for the wasteful vengeance
That shall fly with them: for many a thousand
     widows
Shall this his mock mock out of their dear husbands;
Mock mothers from their sons, mock castles down:
And some are yet ungotten and unborn
That shall have cause to curse the Dauphin's scorn.
But this lies all within the will of God,   290
To whom I do appeal, and in whose name,
Tell you the Dauphin, I am coming on,
To venge me as I may, and to put forth
My rightful hand in a well-hallowed cause.
So get you hence in peace ... And tell the Dauphin
His jest will savour but of shallow wit,
When thousands weep more than did laugh at it....
Convey them with safe conduct. Fare you well.
                                        Exeunt Ambassadors
EXETER. This was a merry message.
KING HENRY. We hope to make the sender blush at it: 300
Therefore, my lords, omit no happy hour
That may give furth'rance to our expedition:
For we have now no thought in us but France,
Save those to God, that run before our business.
Therefore let our proportions for these wars
Be soon collected, and all things thought upon
That may with reasonable swiftness add
More feathers to our wings: for, God before,
We'll chide this Dauphin at his father's door.
Therefore let every man now task his thought,   310
That this fair action may on foot be brought.
                                  He departs, the rest following

ACT 2
Prologue

Flourish. Enter Chorus

CHORUS. Now all the youth of England are on fire,
     And silken dalliance in the wardrobe lies:
     Now thrive the armourers, and honour's thought
     Reigns solely in the breast of every man.
     They sell the pasture now, to buy the horse;
     Following the mirror of all Christian kings,
     With wingéd heels, as English Mercuries.
     For now sits Expectation in the air,
     And hides a sword, from hilts unto the point,
     With crowns imperial, crowns and coronets,   10
     Promised to Harry and his followers.
     The French, advised by good intelligence
     Of this most dreadful preparation,
     Shake in their fear, and with pale policy
     Seek to divert the English purposes.

O England! model to thy inward greatness,
Like little body with a mighty heart:
What might'st thou do, that honour would thee do,
Were all thy children kind and natural!
But see, thy fault France hath in thee found out,   20
A nest of hollow bosoms, which he fills
With treacherous crowns: and three corrupted men,
One, Richard Earl of Cambridge, and the second,
Henry Lord Scroop of Masham, and the third,
Sir Thomas Grey, knight of Northumberland,
Have for the gilt of France (O guilt indeed!)
Confirmed conspiracy with fearful France,
And by their hands this grace of kings must die,
If hell and treason hold their promises,
Ere he take ship for France, and in Southampton....   30
Linger your patience on, and we'll digest
Th'abuse of distance; force a play:
The sum is paid, the traitors are agreed,
The king is set from London, and the scene
Is now transported, gentles, to Southampton,
There is the playhouse now, there must you sit,
And thence to France shall we convey you safe,
And bring you back: charming the narrow seas
To give you gentle pass: for if we may,
We'll not offend one stomach with our play....   40
But till the king come forth, and not till then,
Unto Southampton do we shift our scene.   *Exit*

Scene 1: *London. A street*

Nym and Bardolph meeting

BARDOLPH. Well met, Corporal Nym.
NYM. Good morrow, Lieutenant Bardolph.
BARDOLPH. What, are Ancient Pistol and you friends yet?
NYM. For my part, I care not: I say little: but when time shall serve, there shall be smiles—but that shall be as it may. I dare not fight, but I will wink and hold out mine iron: it is a simple one, but what though? It will toast cheese, and it will endure cold, as another man's sword will: and there's an end.   10
BARDOLPH. I will bestow a breakfast to make you friends, and we'll be all three sworn brothers to France: let't be so, good Corporal Nym.
NYM. Faith, I will live so long as I may, that's the certain of it: and when I cannot live any longer, I will do as I may: that is my rest, that is the rendezvous of it.
BARDOLPH. It is certain, corporal, that he is married to Nell Quickly, and certainly she did you wrong, for you were troth-plight to her.   20
NYM. I cannot tell—things must be as they may: men may sleep, and they may have their throats about them at that time, and some say knives have edges ... It must be as it may—though patience be a tired mare, yet she will plod—there must be conclusions—well, I cannot tell.

Pistol and the Hostess approach

BARDOLPH. Here comes Ancient Pistol and his wife: good corporal, be patient here.
NYM. How now, mine host Pistol!
PISTOL. Base tike, call'st thou me host?   30
Now by this hand I swear I scorn the term:
Nor shall my Nell keep lodgers.

HOSTESS. No, by my troth, not long: for we cannot lodge and board a dozen or fourteen gentlewomen that live honestly by the prick of their needles, but it will be thought we keep a bawdy-house straight. [*Nym and Pistol draw*] O well-a-day, Lady, if he be not hewn now, we shall see wilful adultery and murder committed.
BARDOLPH. Good lieutenant, good corporal, offer   40 nothing here.
NYM. Pish!
PISTOL. Pish for thee, Iceland dog! thou prick-eared cur of Iceland!
HOSTESS. Good Corporal Nym, show thy valour, and put up your sword.
NYM. Will you shog off? I would have you solus.
PISTOL. 'Solus', egregious dog? O viper vile!
The 'solus' in thy most marvellous face,
The 'solus' in thy teeth, and in thy throat,   50
And in thy hateful lungs, yea in thy maw, perdy—
And, which is worse, within thy nasty mouth!
I do retort the 'solus' in thy bowels,
For I can take, and Pistol's cock is up,
And flashing fire will follow.
NYM. I am not Barbason, you cannot conjure me: I have an humour to knock you indifferently well ... If you grow foul with me, Pistol, I will scour you with my rapier, as I may, in fair terms. If you would walk off, I would prick your guts a little in good   60 terms, as I may, and that's the humour of it.
PISTOL. O braggart vile, and damnéd furious wight,
The grave doth gape, and doting death is near,
Therefore exhale!
BARDOLPH [*also drawing*]. Hear me, hear me what I say: he that strikes the first stroke, I'll run him up to the hilts, as I am a soldier.
PISTOL. An oath of mickle might, and fury shall abate....
Give me thy fist, thy fore-foot to me give:
Thy spirits are most tall.   70
NYM. I will cut thy throat one time or other in fair terms, that is the humour of it.
PISTOL. 'Couple a gorge',
That is the word. I thee defy again.
O hound of Crete, think'st thou my spouse to get?
No, to the spital go,
And from the powdering-tub of infamy
Fetch forth the lazar kit of Cressid's kind,
Doll Tearsheet she by name, and her espouse.
I have, and I will hold, the quondam Quickly   80
For the only she: and—pauca, there's enough.
Go to.

Enter the Boy

BOY. Mine host Pistol, you must come to my master, and you, hostess: he is very sick, and would to bed. Good Bardolph, put thy face between his sheets, and do the office of a warming-pan: faith, he's very ill.
BARDOLPH. Away, you rogue.   *The Boy runs off*
HOSTESS. By my troth, he'll yield the crow a pudding one of these days ... The king has killed his heart. Good husband, come home presently.   90
        Hostess follows the Boy
BARDOLPH. Come, shall I make you two friends? We must to France together: why the devil should we keep knives to cut one another's throats?

PISTOL. Let floods o'erswell, and fiends for food howl
on!

NYM. You'll pay me the eight shillings I won of you
at betting?

PISTOL. Base is the slave that pays.

NYM. That now I will have: that's the humour of it.

PISTOL. As manhood shall compound: push home.
                                                    They draw

BARDOLPH. By this sword, he that makes the first
thrust, I'll kill him: by this sword, I will.   100

PISTOL. Sword is an oath, and oaths must have their
course.

BARDOLPH. Corporal Nym, an thou wilt be friends, be
friends, an thou wilt not, why then be enemies with
me too: prithee put up.

NYM. I shall have my eight shillings I won of you
at betting?

PISTOL. A noble shalt thou have, and present pay,
And liquor likewise will I give to thee,
And friendship shall combine, and brotherhood.   110
I'll live by Nym, and Nym shall live by me—
Is not this just? for I shall sutler be
Unto the camp, and profits will accrue.
Give me thy hand.

NYM. I shall have my noble?

PISTOL. In cash, most justly paid.

NYM. Well, then that's the humour of 't.

Hostess returns

HOSTESS. As ever you come of women, come in
quickly to Sir John. Ah, poor heart! he is so shaked
of a burning quotidian tertian, that it is most lament-   120
able to behold. Sweet men, come to him.

NYM. The king hath run bad humours on the knight,
that's the even of it.

PISTOL. Nym, thou hast spoke the right,
His heart is fracted and corroborate.

NYM. The king is a good king, but it must be as it
may: he passes some humours and careers.

PISTOL. Let us condole the knight, for, lambkins, we
will live.   *They go*

Scene 2: *Southampton. A council-chamber*

Enter Exeter, Bedford, and Westmoreland

BEDFORD. 'Fore God, his grace is bold to trust these
traitors.

EXETER. They shall be apprehended by and by.

WESTMORELAND. How smooth and even they do bear
themselves,
As if allegiance in their bosoms sat
Crownéd with faith, and constant loyalty.

BEDFORD. The king hath note of all that they intend,
By interception which they dream not of.

EXETER. Nay, but the man that was his bedfellow,
Whom he hath dulled and cloyed with gracious
favours—
That he should for a foreign purse so sell   10
His sovereign's life to death and treachery.

*Trumpets sound. Enter the King, Scroop, Cambridge, and
Grey, with attendants*

KING HENRY. Now sits the wind fair, and we will
aboard....
My Lord of Cambridge, and my kind Lord of
Masham,

And you, my gentle knight, give me your thoughts:
Think you not that the powers we bear with us
Will cut their passage through the force of France,
Doing the execution, and the act
For which we have in head assembled them?

SCROOP. No doubt, my liege, if each man do his best.

KING HENRY. I doubt not that, since we are well
persuaded   20
We carry not a heart with us from hence,
That grows not in a fair consent with ours:
Nor leave not one behind, that doth not wish
Success and conquest to attend on us.

CAMBRIDGE. Never was monarch better feared and
loved
Than is your majesty; there's not, I think, a subject
That sits in heart-grief and uneasiness
Under the sweet shade of your government.

GREY. True: those that were your father's enemies
Have steeped their galls in honey, and do serve you   30
With hearts create of duty and of zeal.

KING HENRY. We therefore have great cause of
thankfulness,
And shall forget the office of our hand
Sooner than quittance of desert and merit,
According to the weight and worthiness.

SCROOP. So service shall with steelèd sinews toil,
And labour shall refresh itself with hope
To do your grace incessant services.

KING HENRY. We judge no less.... Uncle of Exeter,
Enlarge the man committed yesterday,   40
That railed against our person: we consider
It was excess of wine that set him on,
And on his more advice we pardon him.

SCROOP. That's mercy, but too much security:
Let him be punished, sovereign, lest example
Breed, by his sufferance, more of such a kind.

KING HENRY. O let us yet be merciful.

CAMBRIDGE. So may your highness, and yet punish
too.

GREY. Sir,
You show great mercy if you give him life,   50
After the taste of much correction.

KING HENRY. Alas, your too much love and care of me
Are heavy orisons 'gainst this poor wretch ...
If little faults, proceeding on distemper,
Shall not be winked at, how shall we stretch our eye
When capital crimes, chewed, swallowed, and
digested,
Appear before us? We'll yet enlarge that man,
Though Cambridge, Scroop, and Grey, in their
dear care
And tender preservation of our person
Would have him punished.... And now to our
French causes,   60
Who are the late commissioners?

CAMBRIDGE. I one, my lord,
Your highness bade me ask for it to-day.

SCROOP. So did you me, my liege.

GREY. And I, my royal sovereign.

KING HENRY. Then, Richard, Earl of Cambridge, there
is yours:
There yours, Lord Scroop of Masham: and, sir
knight,
Grey of Northumberland, this same is yours:
Read them, and know I know your worthiness....
My Lord of Westmoreland, and uncle Exeter,   70

We will aboard to night.... Why, how now,
   gentlemen?
What see you in those papers, that you lose
So much complexion? Look ye how they change:
Their cheeks are paper. Why, what read you there,
That have so cowarded and chased your blood
Out of appearance?

CAMBRIDGE.   I do confess my fault,
   And do submit me to your highness' mercy.

GREY.   } To which we all appeal.
SCROOP.   }

KING HENRY. The mercy that was quick in us but late,
   By your own counsel is suppressed and killed: 80
   You must not dare, for shame, to talk of mercy,
   For your own reasons turn into your bosoms,
   As dogs upon their masters, worrying you ...
   See you, my princes, and my noble peers,
   These English monsters: my Lord of Cambridge
   here,
   You know how apt our love was to accord
   To furnish him with all appertinents
   Belonging to his honour; and this man
   Hath for a few light crowns lightly conspired
   And sworn unto the practices of France   90
   To kill us here in Hampton. To the which
   This knight, no less for bounty bound to us
   Than Cambridge is, hath likewise sworn.... But O,
   What shall I say to thee, Lord Scroop, thou cruel,
   Ingrateful, savage, and inhuman creature?
   Thou that didst bear the key of all my counsels,
   That knew'st the very bottom of my soul,
   That (almost) mightst have coined me into gold,
   Wouldst thou have practised on me, for thy use?
   May it be possible, that foreign hire   100
   Could out of thee extract one spark of evil
   That might annoy my finger? 'Tis so strange,
   That though the truth of it stands off as gross
   As black on white, my eye will scarcely see it.
   Treason and murder ever kept together,
   As two yoke-devils sworn to either's purpose,
   Working so grossly in a natural cause,
   That admiration did not hoop at them.
   But thou, 'gainst all proportion, didst bring in
   Wonder to wait on treason and on murder: 110
   And whatsoever cunning fiend it was
   That wrought upon thee so preposterously,
   Hath got the voice in hell for excellence:
   All other devils that suggest by treasons
   Do botch and bungle up damnation,
   With patches, colours, and with forms being fetched
   From glist'ring semblances of piety:
   But he that tempered thee, bade thee stand up,
   Gave thee no instance why thou shouldst do treason,
   Unless to dub thee with the name of traitor.   120
   If that same demon that hath gulled thee thus
   Should with his lion gait walk the whole world,
   He might return to vasty Tartar back,
   And tell the legions, "I can never win
   A soul so easy as that Englishman's."
   O, how hast thou with jealousy infected
   The sweetness of affiance? Show men dutiful?
   Why, so didst thou: seem they grave and learnéd?
   Why, so didst thou: come they of noble family?
   Why, so didst thou: seem they religious?   130
   Why, so didst thou. Or are they spare in diet,
   Free from gross passion, or of mirth, or anger,

Constant in spirit, not swerving with the blood,
Garnished and decked in modest complement,
Not working with the eye without the ear,
And but in purgéd judgement trusting neither?
Such and so finely bolted didst thou seem:
And thus thy fall hath left a kind of blot,
To mark the full-fraught man and best indued
With some suspicion. I will weep for thee.   140
For this revolt of thine, methinks, is like
Another fall of man.... Their faults are open,
Arrest them to the answer of the law,
And God acquit them of their practices.

EXETER. I arrest thee of high treason, by the name of
   Richard Earl of Cambridge.
   I arrest thee of high treason, by the name of Henry
   Lord Scroop of Masham.
   I arrest thee of high treason, by the name of Thomas
   Grey, knight of Northumberland.   150

SCROOP. Our purposes God justly hath discovered,
   And I repent my fault more than my death,
   Which I beseech your highness to forgive,
   Although my body pay the price of it.

CAMBRIDGE. For me, the gold of France did not seduce,
   Although I did admit it as a motive,
   The sooner to effect what I intended:
   But God be thankéd for prevention,
   Which I in sufferance heartily will rejoice,
   Beseeching God, and you, to pardon me.   160

GREY. Never did faithful subject more rejoice
   At the discovery of most dangerous treason,
   Than I do at this hour joy o'er myself,
   Prevented from a damnéd enterprise;
   My fault, but not my body, pardon, sovereign.

KING HENRY. God quit you in his mercy! Hear your
   sentence.
   You have conspired against our royal person,
   Joined with an enemy proclaimed, and from his
   coffers
   Received the golden earnest of our death:
   Wherein you would have sold your king to
   slaughter,   170
   His princes and his peers to servitude,
   His subjects to oppression and contempt,
   And his whole kingdom into desolation ...
   Touching our person, seek we no revenge,
   But we our kingdom's safety must so tender,
   Whose ruin you have sought, that to her laws
   We do deliver you. Get you therefore hence,
   Poor miserable wretches, to your death:
   The taste whereof God of his mercy give
   You patience to endure, and true repentance   180
   Of all your dear offences.... Bear them hence....
       Exeunt Cambridge, Scroop, and Grey, guarded
   Now, lords, for France: the enterprise whereof
   Shall be to you as us, like glorious.
   We doubt not of a fair and lucky war,
   Since God so graciously hath brought to light
   This dangerous treason lurking in our way
   To hinder our beginnings. We doubt not now
   But every rub is smoothed on our way....
   Then forth, dear countrymen: let us deliver
   Our puissance into the hand of God,   190
   Putting it traight in expedition....
   Cheerly to sea, the signs of war advance,
   No king of England, if not king of France.
                 Flourish; they go

Scene 3: *London. Before a tavern*

Enter Pistol, Hostess, Nym, Bardolph, and Boy

HOSTESS. Prithee, honey-sweet husband, let me bring
thee to Staines.

PISTOL. No: for my manly heart doth earn.
Bardolph, he blithe: Nym, rouse thy vaunting veins:
Boy, bristle thy courage up: for Falstaff he is dead,
And we must earn therefore.

BARDOLPH. Would I were with him, wheresome'er he
is, either in heaven or in hell!

HOSTESS. Nay sure, he's not in hell: he's in Arthur's
bosom, if ever man went to Arthur's bosom: a' 10
made a finer end, and went away an it had been any
christom child: a' parted e'en just between twelve
and one, e'en at the turning o'th'tide: for after I saw
him fumble with the sheets, and play with flowers,
and smile upon his finger's end, I knew there was
but one way: for his nose was as sharp as a pen,
and a' babbled of green fields. 'How now, Sir John?'
quoth I. 'What, man! be o' good cheer': so a' cried
out, 'God, God, God!' three or four times: now I,
to comfort him, bid him a' should not think of God; 20
I hoped there was no need to trouble himself with
any such thoughts yet: so a' bade me lay more
clothes on his feet: I put my hand into the bed, and
felt them, and they were as cold as any stone: then
I felt to his knees, and so up'ard and up'ard, and all
was as cold as any stone.

NYM. They say he cried out of sack.

HOSTESS. Ay, that a' did.

BARDOLPH. And of women.

HOSTESS. Nay, that a' did not.   30

BOY. Yes, that a' did, and said they were devils
incarnate.

HOSTESS. A' could never abide carnation—'twas a
colour he never liked.

BOY. A' said once, the devil would have him about
women.

HOSTESS. A' did in some sort, indeed, handle women:
but then he was rheumatic, and talked of the whore
of Babylon.

BOY. Do you not remember a' saw a flea stick upon 40
Bardolph's nose, and a' said it was a black soul
burning in hell?

BARDOLPH. Well, the fuel is gone that maintained that
fire: that's all the riches I got in his service.

NYM. Shall we shog? the king will be gone from
Southampton.

PISTOL. Come, let's away.... My love, give me thy
lips . . .
Look to my chattels and my movables:
Let senses rule: the word is 'Pitch and pay':
Trust none: 50
For oaths are straws, men's faiths are wafer-cakes,
And Hold-fast is the only dog, my duck:
Therefore, Caveto be thy counsellor....
Go, clear thy crystals.... Yoke-fellows in arms,
Let us to France, like horse-leeches, my boys,
To suck, to suck, the very blood to suck!

BOY. And that's but unwholesome food, they say.

PISTOL. Touch her soft mouth, and march.

BARDOLPH. Farewell, hostess.   *Kissing her*

NYM. I cannot kiss, that is the humour of it: but adieu. 60

PISTOL. Let housewifery appear: keep close, I thee
command.

HOSTESS. Farewell: adieu.   *They go*

Scene 4: *The French King's Palace*

*Flourish. Enter the French King, the Dauphin, the Dukes
of Berri and Britaine, the Constable, and others*

FRENCH KING. Thus comes the English with full power
upon us,
And more than carefully it us concerns
To answer royally in our defences.
Therefore the Dukes of Berri and of Britaine,
Of Brabant and of Orleans, shall make forth,
And you, Prince Dauphin, with all swift dispatch
To line and new repair our towns of war
With men of courage and with means defendant:
For England his approaches makes as fierce
As waters to the sucking of a gulf.   10
It fits us then to be as provident
As fear may teach us, out of late examples
Left by the fatal and neglected English
Upon our fields.

DAUPHIN.   My most redoubted father,
It is most meet we arm us 'gainst the foe:
For peace itself should not so dull a kingdom,
(Though war nor no known quarrel were in
question)
But that defences, musters, preparations,
Should be maintained, assembled, and collected,
As were a war in expectation.   20
Therefore I say 'tis meet we all go forth
To view the sick and feeble parts of France:
And let us do it with no show of fear,
No, with no more than if we heard that England
Were busied with a Whitsun morris-dance:
For, my good liege, she is so idly kinged,
Her sceptre so fantastically borne
By a vain, giddy, shallow, humorous youth,
That fear attends her not.

CONSTABLE.   O peace, Prince Dauphin!
You are too much mistaken in this king: 30
Question your grace the late ambassadors,
With what great state he heard their embassy,
How well supplied with noble counsellors,
How modest in exception; and, withal,
How terrible in constant resolution:
And you shall find his vanities forespent
Were but the outside of the Roman Brutus,
Covering discretion with a coat of folly;
As gardeners do with ordure hide those roots
That shall first spring, and be most delicate.   40

DAUPHIN. Well, 'tis not so, my lord high constable.
But though we think it so, it is no matter:
In cases of defence, 'tis best to weigh
The enemy more mighty than he seems,
So the proportions of defence are filled:
Which, of a weak and niggardly projection,
Doth like a miser spoil his coat with scanting
A little cloth.

FRENCH KING. Think we King Harry strong:
And, princes, look you strongly arm to meet him.
The kindred of him hath been fleshed upon us: 50
And he is bred out of that bloody strain,
That haunted us in our familiar paths:
Witness our too much memorable shame,
When Cressy battle fatally was struck,
And all our princes captived, by the hand

Of that black name, Edward, Black Prince of Wales:
Whiles that his mountain sire, on mountain standing
Up in the air, crowned with the golden sun,
Saw his heroical seed, and smiled to see him
Mangle the work of nature, and deface   60
The patterns that by God and by French fathers
Had twenty years been made.... This is a stem
Of that victorious stock: and let us fear
The native mightiness and fate of him.

Enter a Messenger

MESSENGER. Ambassadors from Harry King of
   England
Do crave admittance to your majesty.
FRENCH KING. We'll give them present audience. Go,
   and bring them.
     The Messenger departs, with certain lords
You see this chase is hotly followed, friends.
DAUPHIN. Turn head, and stop pursuit: for coward
   dogs
Most spend their mouths, when what they seem to
   threaten   70
Runs far before them. Good my sovereign,
Take up the English short, and let them know
Of what a monarchy you are the head:
Self-love, my liege, is not so vile a sin
As self-neglecting.

Re-enter Lords, with Exeter and his train

FRENCH KING.   From our brother of England?
EXETER. From him, and thus he greets your majesty:
He wills you, in the name of God Almighty,
That you divest yourself, and lay apart
The borrowed glories that by gift of heaven,
By law of nature, and of nations, 'longs   80
To him and to his heirs, namely, the crown,
And all wide-stretchéd honours, that pertain
By custom, and the ordinance of times,
Unto the crown of France: that you may know
'Tis no sinister, nor no awkward claim,
Picked from the worm-holes of long-vanished days,
Nor from the dust of old oblivion raked,
He sends you this most memorable line,
     Gives a paper
In every branch truly demonstrative;
Willing you overlook this pedigree: 90
And when you find him evenly derived
From his most famed of famous ancestors,
Edward the third, he bids you then resign
Your crown and kingdom, indirectly held
From him the native and true challenger.
FRENCH KING. Or else what follows?
EXETER. Bloody constraint: for if you hide the crown
Even in your hearts, there will he rake for it.
Therefore in fierce tempest is he coming,
In thunder and in earthquake, like a Jove: 100
That, if requiring fail, he will compel.
And bids you, in the bowels of the Lord,
Deliver up the crown, and to take mercy
On the poor souls, for whom this hungry war
Opens his vasty jaws: and on your head
Turning the widow's tears, the orphans' cries,
The dead men's blood, the pining maidens' groans
For husbands, fathers, and betrothéd lovers,
That shall be swallowed in this controversy.
This is his claim, his threatening, and my message: 110

Unless the Dauphin be in presence here;
To whom expressly I bring greeting too.
FRENCH KING. For us, we will consider of this further:
To-morrow shall you bear our full intent
Back to our brother of England.
DAUPHIN.   For the Dauphin,
I stand here for him: what to him from England?
EXETER. Scorn and defiance, slight regard, contempt,
And any thing that may not misbecome
The mighty sender, doth he prize you at.
Thus says my king: an if your father's highness   120
Do not, in grant of all demands at large,
Sweeten the bitter mock you sent his majesty,
He'll call you to so hot an answer of it,
That caves and womby vaultages of France
Shall chide your trespass, and return your mock
In second accent of his ordinance.
DAUPHIN. Say: if my father render fair return,
It is against my will; for I desire
Nothing but odds with England. To that end,
As matching to his youth and vanity,   130
I did present him with the Paris-balls.
EXETER. He'll make your Paris Louvre shake for it,
Were it the mistress-court of mighty Europe:
And, be assured, you'll find a difference,
As we his subjects have in wonder found,
Between the promise of his greener days,
And these he masters now: now he weighs time
Even to the utmost grain: that you shall read
In your own losses, if he stay in France.
FRENCH KING. To-morrow shall you know our mind
   at full.   *Flourish*   140
EXETER. Dispatch us with all speed, lest that our king
Come here himself to question our delay;
For he is footed in this land already.
FRENCH KING. You shall be soon dispatched, with fair
   conditions.
A night is but small breath, and little pause,
To answer matters of this consequence.
     The King and his Courtiers leave,
     Exeter with his train following

ACT 3
Prologue

Flourish. Enter Chorus

CHORUS. Thus with imagined wing our swift scene
   flies,
In motion of no less celerity
Than that of thought.... Suppose that you have
   seen
The well-appointed king at Hampton pier
Embark his royalty: and his brave fleet
With silken streamers the young Phœbus fanning;
Play with your fancies: and in them behold,
Upon the hempen tackle, ship-boys climbing;
Hear the shrill whistle, which doth order give
To sounds confused: behold the threaden sails,   10
Borne with th'invisible and creeping wind,
Draw the huge bottoms through the furrowed sea,
Breasting the lofty surge.... O, do but think
You stand upon the rivage, and behold
A city on th'inconstant billows dancing:
For so appears this fleet majestical,
Holding due course to Harfleur.... Follow, follow!

Grapple your minds to sternage of this navy,
And leave your England as dead midnight, still,
Guarded with grandsires, babies, and old women, 20
Either past or not arrived to pith and puissance ...
For who is he, whose chin is but enriched
With one appearing hair, that will not follow
These culled and choice-drawn cavaliers to France?
Work, work your thoughts, and therein see a siege:
Behold the ordinance on their carriages,
With fatal mouths gaping on girded Harfleur....
Suppose th'ambassador from the French comes
    back:
Tells Harry that the king doth offer him
Katharine his daughter, and with her, to dowry, 30
Some petty and unprofitable dukedoms.
The offer likes not: and the nimble gunner
With linstock now the devilish cannon touches,
               Alarum, and chambers go off
And down goes all before them.... Still be kind,
And eke out our performance with your mind.
                            Exit

Scene 1: *France. Before the gates at Harfleur*

*Alarum. Enter the King, Exeter, Bedford, and Gloucester,
followed by soldiers with scaling ladders*

KING HENRY. Once more unto the breach, dear friends,
    once more;
Or close the wall up with our English dead ...
In peace, there's nothing so becomes a man,
As modest stillness, and humility:
But when the blast of war blows in our ears,
Then imitate the action of the tiger:
Stiffen the sinews, conjure up the blood,
Disguise fair nature with hard-favoured rage:
Then lend the eye a terrible aspect:
Let it pry through the portage of the head, 10
Like the brass cannon: let the brow o'erwhelm it
As fearfully as doth a gallèd rock
O'erhang and jutty his confounded base,
Swilled with the wild and wasteful ocean.
Now set the teeth, and stretch the nostril wide,
Hold hard the breath, and bend up every spirit
To his full height! On, on, you noblest English,
Whose blood is fet from fathers of war-proof:
Fathers, that like so many Alexanders,
Have in these parts from morn till even fought, 20
And sheathed their swords for lack of argument.
Dishonour not your mothers: now attest
That those whom you called fathers did beget you!
Be copy now to men of grosser blood,
And teach them how to war! And you, good
    yeomen,
Whose limbs were made in England; show us here
The mettle of your pasture: let us swear,
That you are worth your breeding—which I doubt
    not:
For there is none of you so mean and base,
That hath not noble lustre in your eyes. 30
I see you stand like greyhounds in the slips,
Straining upon the start. The game's afoot:
Follow your spirit; and upon this charge,
Cry, 'God for Harry, England, and Saint George!'
                       They go
           Alarum, and chambers go off

Scene 2

Enter Nym, Bardolph, Pistol, and the Boy

BARDOLPH. On, on, on, on, on! to the breach, to the
breach!
NYM. Pray thee, corporal, stay, the knocks are too hot:
and for mine own part, I have not a case of lives:
the humour of it is too hot, that is the very plain-
song of it.
PISTOL. The plain-song is most just: for humours do
    abound:
    Knocks go and come: God's vassals drop and die:
        And sword and shield,
           In bloody field,   10
        Doth win immortal fame.
BOY. Would I were in an alehouse in London! I would
give all my fame for a pot of ale, and safety.
PISTOL. And I:
        If wishes would prevail with me,
        My purpose should not fail with me;
           But thither would I hie.
BOY. As duly,
        But not as truly,
           As bird doth sing on bough.   20

Fluellen enters

FLUELLEN. Up to the breach, you dogs; avaunt, you
cullions!
PISTOL. Be merciful, great duke, to men of mould:
    Abate thy rate, abate thy manly rage;
    Abate thy rage, great duke!
    Good bawcock, bate thy rage: use lenity, sweet
    chuck!
NYM. These be good humours ... Your honour wins
bad humours.   *Fluellen drives them forward*
BOY. As young as I am, I have observed these three
swashers: I am boy to them all three, but all they 30
three, though they would serve me, could not be
man to me; for indeed three such antics do not
amount to a man ... For Bardolph, he is white-
livered and red-faced; by the means whereof a' faces
it out, but fights not: for Pistol, he hath a killing
tongue, and a quiet sword; by the means whereof a'
breaks words, and keeps whole weapons: for Nym,
he hath heard that men of few words are the best
men, and therefore he scorns to say his prayers, lest
a' should be thought a coward: but his few bad 40
words are matched with as few good deeds; for a'
never broke any man's head but his own, and that
was against a post, when he was drunk. They will
steal any thing, and call it purchase. Bardolph stole
a lute-case, bore it twelve leagues, and sold it for
three half-pence. Nym and Bardolph are sworn
brothers in filching: and in Calais they stole a fire-
shovel. I knew by that piece of service, the men
would carry coals. They would have me as familiar
with men's pockets as their gloves or their hand- 50
kerchers: which makes much against my manhood,
if I should take from another's pocket, to put into
mine; for it is plain pocketing up of wrongs.... I
must leave them, and seek some better service: their
villany goes against my weak stomach, and therefore I must cast it up.   *He goes*

Fluellen returns with Gower

GOWER. Captain Fluellen, you must come presently to

the mines; the Duke of Gloucester would speak with
you.

FLUELLEN. To the mines? Tell you the duke, it is not 60
so good to come to the mines: for look you, the
mines is not according to the disciplines of the war;
the concavities of it is not sufficient: for look you,
th'athversary—you may discuss unto the duke—
look you, is digt himself four yard under the
counter-mines: by Cheshu, I think a' will plow up
all, if there is not better directions.

GOWER. The Duke of Gloucester, to whom the order
of the siege is given, is altogether directed by an
Irishman, a very valiant gentleman, i'faith.   70

FLUELLEN. It is Captain Macmorris, is it not?

GOWER. I think it be.

FLUELLEN. By Cheshu, he is an ass, as in the world,
I will verify as much in his beard: he has no more
directions in the true disciplines of the wars, look
you, of the Roman disciplines, than is a puppy-dog.

Enter Macmorris and Captain Jamy

GOWER. Here a' comes, and the Scots captain, Captain
Jamy, with him.

FLUELLEN. Captain Jamy is a marvellous falorous
gentleman, that is certain, and of great expedition 80
and knowledge in th'ancient wars, upon my
particular knowledge of his directions: by Cheshu,
he will maintain his argument as well as any military
man in the world, in the disciplines of the pristine
wars of the Romans.

JAMY. I say gud-day, Captain Fluellen.

FLUELLEN. God-den to your worship, good Captain
James.

GOWER. How now, Captain Macmorris, have you
quit the mines? have the pioners given o'er?   90

MACMORRIS. By Chrish, la! tish ill done: the work ish
give over, the trompet sound the retreat. By my
hand I swear, and my father's soul, the work ish
ill done: it ish give over: I would have blowed up
the town, so Chrish save me, la, in an hour. O tish
ill done, tish ill done: by my hand, tish ill done!

FLUELLEN. Captain Macmorris, I beseech you now,
will you voutsafe me, look you, a few disputations
with you, partly touching or concerning the
disciplines of the war, the Roman wars, in the way 100
of argument, look you, and friendly communication: partly to satisfy my opinion, and partly for the
satisfaction, look you, of my mind: as touching the
direction of the military discipline, that is the point.

JAMY. It sall be vary gud, gud feith, gud captains
bath, and I sall quit you with gud leve, as I may pick
occasion: that sall I, marry.

MACMORRIS. It is no time to discourse, so Chrish save
me: the day is hot, and the weather, and the wars,
and the king, and the dukes: it is no time to dis- 110
course, the town is beseeched: an the trumpet call
us to the breach, and we talk, and, be Chrish, do
nothing, 'tis shame for us all: so God sa' me, 'tis
shame to stand still, it is shame, by my hand: an
there is throats to be cut, and works to be done, and
there ish nothing done, so Chrish sa' me, la!

JAMY. By the mess, ere these eyes of mine take themselves to slomber, ay'll de gude service, or ay'll lig
i'th'grund for it; ay, or go to death: and ay'll pay't
as valorously as I may, that sal I suerly do, that is 120

the breff and the long . . . Mary, I wad full fain hear
some question 'tween you tway.

FLUELLEN. Captain Macmorris, I think, look you,
under your correction, there is not many of your
nation—

MACMORRIS. Of my nation! What ish my nation? Ish
a villain, and a bastard; and a knave, and a rascal—
What ish my nation? Who talks of my nation?

FLUELLEN. Look you, if you take the matter otherwise
than is meant, Captain Macmorris, peradventure I 130
shall think you do not use me with that affability
as in discretion you ought to use me, look you, being
as good a man as yourself, both in the disciplines of
war, and in the derivation of my birth, and in other
particularities.

MACMORRIS. I do not know you so good a man as
myself: so Chrish save me, I will cut off your head.

GOWER. Gentlemen both, you will mistake each other.

JAMY. Ah! that's a foul fault.

A parley sounded from the walls

GOWER. The town sounds a parley.   140

FLUELLEN. Captain Macmorris, when there is more
better opportunity to be required, look you, I will
be so bold as to tell you I know the disciplines of
war: and there is an end.   *They stand aside*

Scene 3

*The Governor and some Citizens appear upon the walls.
Enter the King and all his train before the gates*

KING. How yet resolves the governor of the town?
This is the latest parle we will admit:
Therefore to our best mercy give yourselves,
Or, like to men proud of destruction,
Defy us to our worst: for, as I am a soldier,
A name that in my thoughts becomes me best,
If I begin the battery once again,
I will not leave the half-achieved Harfleur
Till in her ashes she lie buried.
The gates of mercy shall be all shut up,   10
And the fleshed soldier, rough and hard of heart,
In liberty of bloody hand, shall range
With conscience wide as hell, mowing like grass
Your fresh fair virgins, and your flowering infants.
What is it then to me, if impious war,
Arrayed in flames like to the prince of fiends,
Do with his smirched complexion all fell feats
Enlinked to waste and desolation?
What is't to me, when you yourselves are cause,
If your pure maidens fall into the hand   20
Of hot and forcing violation?
What rein can hold licentious wickedness,
When down the hill he holds his fierce career?
We may as bootless spend our vain command
Upon th'enragéd soldiers in their spoil,
As send precépts to the leviathan
To come ashore. Therefore, you men of Harfleur,
Take pity of your town and of your people,
Whiles yet my soldiers are in my command,
Whiles yet the cool and temperate wind of grace 30
O'erblows the filthy and contagious clouds
Of heady murder, spoil, and villany.
If not—why, in a moment look to see
The blind and bloody soldier with foul hand
Defile the locks of your shrill-shrieking daughters:

Your fathers taken by the silver beards,
And their most reverend heads dashed to the walls:
Your naked infants spitted upon pikes,
Whiles the mad mothers with their howls confused
Do break the clouds; as did the wives of Jewry, 40
At Herod's bloody-hunting slaughtermen.
What say you? Will you yield, and this avoid?
Or, guilty in defence, be thus destroyed?
GOVERNOR. Our expectation hath this day an end:
The Dauphin, whom of succours we entreated,
Returns us that his powers are yet not ready
To raise so great a siege ... Therefore, great king,
We yield our town and lives to thy soft mercy:
Enter our gates, dispose of us and ours,
For we no longer are defensible. 50
KING. Open your gates ... Come, uncle Exeter,
Go you and enter Harfleur; there remain,
And fortify it strongly 'gainst the French:
Use mercy to them all. For us, dear uncle,
The winter coming on, and sickness growing
Upon our soldiers, we will retire to Calais.
To-night in Harfleur will we be your guest,
To-morrow for the march are we addrest.
Flourish. The King and his forces enter the town

Scene 4: *Rouen. The French King's palace*

*Enter the Princess Katharine and Alice, an old Gentle-
woman, and other ladies-in-waiting*

KATHARINE. Alice, tu as été en Angleterre, et tu bien
parles le langage.
ALICE. Un peu, madame.
KATHARINE. Je te prie, m'enseignez—il faut que j'ap-
prenne à parler ... Comment appelez-vous la main
en Anglais?
ALICE. La main? elle est appelée de hand.
KATHARINE. De hand. Et les doigts?
ALICE. Les doigts? ma foi, j'oublie les doigts; mais je
me souviendrai. Les doigts? je pense qu'ils sont 10
appelés de fingres: oui, de fingres.
KATHARINE. La main, de hand: les doigts, de fingres.
Je pense que je suis le bon écolier. J'ai gagné deux
mots d'Anglais vitement. Comment appelez-vous
les ongles?
ALICE. Les ongles? nous les appelons de nailès.
KATHARINE. De nailès. Ecoutez: dites moi si je parle
bien: de hand, de fingres, et de nailès.
ALICE. C'est bien dit, madame; il est fort bon Anglais.
KATHARINE. Dites moi l'Anglais pour le bras. 20
ALICE. De arm, madame.
KATHARINE. Et le coude.
ALICE. D' elbow.
KATHARINE. D' elbow. Je m'en fais la répétition de
tous les mots que vous m'avez appris dès à présent.
ALICE. Il est trop difficile, madame, comme je pense.
KATHARINE. Excusez-moi, Alice; écoutez: d' hand, de
fingre, de nailès, d' arma, de bilbow.
ALICE. D' elbow, madame.
KATHARINE. O Seigneur Dieu, je m'en oublie! d' 30
elbow. Comment appelez-vous le col?
ALICE. De nick, madame.
KATHARINE. De nick. Et le menton?
ALICE. De chin.
KATHARINE. De sin. Le col, de nick: le menton, de sin.
ALICE. Oui. Sauf votre honneur, en vérité, vous pro-

noncez les mots aussi droit que les natifs d'Angle-
terre.
KATHARINE. Je ne doute point d'apprendre, par la grace
de Dieu, et en peu de temps. 40
ALICE. N'avez vous pas déjà oublié ce que je vous ai
enseigné?
KATHARINE. Non, je réciterai à vous promptement: d'
hand, de fingre, de mailès,—
ALICE. De nailès, madame.
KATHARINE. De nailès, de arm, de ilbow.
ALICE. Sauf votre honneur, d' elbow.
KATHARINE. Ainsi dis-je: d' elbow, de nick, et de sin.
Comment appelez-vous le pied et la robe?
ALICE. Le foot, madame, et le count. 50
KATHARINE. Le foot, et le count? O Seignieur Dieu!
ils sont mots de son mauvais, corruptible, gros, et
impudique, et non pour les dames d'honneur d'user:
je ne voudrais prononcer ces mots devant les
seigneurs de France pour tout le monde. Foh! le
foot et le count. Néanmoins, je réciterai une autre
fois ma leçon ensemble: d' hand, de fingre, de nailès,
d' arm, d' elbow, de nick, de sin, de foot, le count.
ALICE. Excellent, madame!
KATHARINE. C'est assez pour une fois: allons-nous à 60
dîner. *They go*

Scene 5

*Enter the King of France, the Dauphin, the Duke of
Britaine, the Constable of France, and others*

FRENCH KING. 'Tis certain he hath passed the river
Somme.
CONSTABLE. And if he be not fought withal, my lord,
Let us not live in France: let us quit all,
And give our vineyards to a barbarous people.
DAUPHIN. O Dieu vivant! shall a few sprays of us,
The emptying of our fathers' luxury,
Our scions, put in wild and savage stock,
Spirt up so suddenly into the clouds,
And overlook their grafters?
BRITAINE. Normans, but bastard Normans, Norman
bastards! 10
Mort Dieu! ma vie! if they march along
Unfought withal, but I will sell my dukedom,
To buy a slobbery and a dirty farm
In that nook-shotten isle of Albion.
CONSTABLE. Dieu de batailles! where have they this
mettle?
Is not their climate foggy, raw, and dull?
On whom, as in despite, the sun looks pale,
Killing their fruit with frowns. Can sodden water,
A drench for sur-reined jades, their barley broth,
Decoct their cold blood to such valiant heat? 20
And shall our quick blood, spirited with wine,
Seem frosty? O, for honour of our land,
Let us not hang like roping icicles
Upon our houses' thatch, whiles a more frosty
people
Sweat drops of gallant youth in our rich fields ...
Poor we may call them in their native lords.
DAUPHIN. By faith and honour,
Our madams mock at us, and plainly say
Our mettle is bred out, and they will give
Their bodies to the lust of English youth, 30
To new-store France with bastard warriors.
BRITAINE. They bid us to the English dancing-schools,

And teach lavoltas high, and swift corantos,
Saying our grace is only in our heels,
And that we are most lofty runaways.
FRENCH KING. Where is Montjoy the herald? speed him
hence,
Let him greet England with our sharp defiance....
Up, princes, and, with spirit of honour edged
More sharper than your swords, hie to the field:
Charles Delabreth, high constable of France,   40
You Dukes of Orleans, Bourbon, and of Berri,
Alençon, Brabant, Bar, and Burgundy,
Jacques Chatillon, Rambures, Vaudemont,
Beaumont, Grandpré, Roussi, and Faulconbridge,
Foix, Lestrake, Bouciqualt, and Charolois,
High dukes, great princes, barons, lords, and
knights;
For your great seats now quit you of great
shames ...
Bar Harry England, that sweeps through our land
With pennons painted in the blood of Harfleur:
Rush on his host, as doth the melted snow   50
Upon the valleys, whose low vassal seat
The Alps doth spit and void his rheum upon....
Go down upon him—you have power enough—
And in a chariot, captive into Rouen
Bring him our prisoner.
CONSTABLE.   This becomes the great.
Sorry am I his numbers are so few,
His soldiers sick and famished in their march:
For I am sure, when he shall see our army,
He'll drop his heart into the sink of fear,
And for achievement offer us his ransom.   60
FRENCH KING. Therefore, lord constable, haste on
Montjoy,
And let him say to England, that we send
To know what willing ransom he will give....
Prince Dauphin, you shall stay with us in Rouen.
DAUPHIN. Not so, I do beseech your majesty.
FRENCH KING. Be patient, for you shall remain with
us....
Now forth, lord constable and princes all,
And quickly bring us word of England's fall.
They go

Scene 6: *Near a river in Picardy*

*Enter the English and Welsh captains, Gower and
Fluellen, meeting*

GOWER. How now, Captain Fluellen! come you from
the bridge?
FLUELLEN. I assure you, there is very excellent services
committed at the bridge.
GOWER. Is the Duke of Exeter safe?
FLUELLEN. The Duke of Exeter is as magnanimous as
Agamemnon, and a man that I love and honour
with my soul, and my heart, and my duty, and my
live, and my living, and my uttermost power. He is
not—God be praised and blessed!—any hurt in the   10
world, but keeps the bridge most valiantly, with
excellent discipline. There is an ancient lieutenant
there at the pridge, I think in my very conscience
he is as valiant a man as Mark Antony, and he is
a man of no estimation in the world, but I did see
him do as gallant service.
GOWER. What do you call him?
FLUELLEN. He is called Ancient Pistol.

GOWER. I know him not.

Pistol enters

FLUELLEN. Here is the man.   20
PISTOL. Captain, I thee beseech to do me favours:
The duke of Exeter doth love thee well.
FLUELLEN. Ay, I praise God, and I have merited some
love at his hands.
PISTOL. Bardolph, a soldier firm and sound of heart,
And of buxom valour, hath, by cruel fate,
And giddy Fortune's furious fickle wheel,
That goddess blind,
That stands upon the rolling restless stone—
FLUELLEN. By your patience, Ancient Pistol ... For-   30
tune is painted blind, with a muffler afore his eyes,
to signify to you that Fortune is blind; and she is
painted also with a wheel, to signify to you, which
is the moral of it, that she is turning and inconstant,
and mutability, and variation: and her foot, look
you, is fixed upon a spherical stone, which rolls, and
rolls, and rolls: in good truth, the poet makes a most
excellent description of it: Fortune is an excellent
moral.
PISTOL. Fortune is Bardolph's foe, and frowns on him: 40
For he hath stolen a pax, and hangéd must a' be
A damnéd death!
Let gallows gape for dog, let man go free,
And let not hemp his wind-pipe suffocate:
But Exeter hath given the doom of death,
For pax of little price.
Therefore go speak, the duke will hear thy voice;
And let not Bardolph's vital thread be cut
With edge of penny cord, and vile reproach.
Speak, captain, for his life, and I will thee require.   50
FLUELLEN. Ancient Pistol, I do partly understand your
meaning.
PISTOL. Why then rejoice therefore.
FLUELLEN. Certainly, ancient, it is not a thing to rejoice
at: for if, look you, he were my brother, I would
desire the duke to use his good pleasure, and put
him to execution; for discipline ought to be used.
PISTOL. Die and be damned! and figo for thy friend-
ship!
FLUELLEN. It is well.
PISTOL. The fig of Spain!
FLUELLEN. Very good.   60
GOWER. Why, this is an arrant counterfeit rascal, I
remember him now: a bawd, a cutpurse.
FLUELLEN. I'll assure you, a' uttered as prave words at
the pridge as you shall see in a summer's day: but it
is very well: what he has spoke to me, that is well,
I warrant you, when time is serve.
GOWER. Why, 'tis a gull, a fool, a rogue, that now and
then goes to the wars, to grace himself at his return
into London, under the form of a soldier ... And
such fellows are perfect in the great commanders'   70
names, and they will learn you by rote where
services were done; at such and such a sconce, at
such a breach, at such a convoy: who came off
bravely, who was shot, who disgraced, what terms
the enemy stood on; and this they con perfectly in
the phrase of war, which they trick up with new-
tuned oaths: and what a beard of the general's cut,
and a horrid suit of the camp, will do among foaming bottles, and ale-washed wits, is wonderful to be
thought on. But you must learn to know such   80

slanders of the age, or else you may be marvellously mistook.

FLUELLEN. I tell you what, Captain Gower: I do perceive he is not the man that he would gladly make show to the world he is: if I find a hole in his coat, I will tell him my mind ... [*Drum heard*] Hark you, the king is coming, and I must speak with him from the pridge.

Drum and colours. Enter King Henry, Gloucester, and his poor soldiers

FLUELLEN. God pless your majesty!

KING HENRY. How now, Fluellen, cam'st thou from 90 the bridge?

FLUELLEN. Ay, so please your majesty ... The Duke of Exeter has very gallantly maintained the pridge; the French is gone off, look you, and there is gallant and most prave passages: marry, th'athversary was have possession of the pridge, but he is enforced to retire, and the Duke of Exeter is master of the pridge ... I can tell your majesty, the duke is a prave man.

KING HENRY. What men have you lost, Fluellen?

FLUELLEN. The perdition of th'athversary hath been 100 very great, reasonable great: marry, for my part, I think the duke hath lost never a man, but one that is like to be executed for robbing a church, one Bardolph, if your majesty know the man: his face is all bubukles and whelks, and knobs, and flames afire, and his lips blows at his nose, and it is like a coal of fire, sometimes plue, and sometimes red, but his nose is executed, and his fire's out.

KING HENRY. We would have all such offenders so cut off: and we give express charge that in our marches 110 through the country there be nothing compelled from the villages; nothing taken but paid for; none of the French upbraided or abused in disdainful language; for when lenity and cruelty play for a kingdom, the gentler gamester is the soonest winner.

A tucket sounds. Montjoy approaches

MONTJOY. You know me by my habit.

KING HENRY. Well then, I know thee: what shall I know of thee?

MONTJOY. My master's mind. 120

KING HENRY. Unfold it.

MONTJOY. Thus says my king: Say thou to Harry of England, Though we seemed dead, we did but sleep: advantage is a better soldier than rashness.... Tell him, we could have rebuked him at Harfleur, but that we thought not good to bruise an injury till it were full ripe. Now we speak upon our cue, and our voice is imperial: England shall repent his folly, see his weakness, and admire our sufferance. Bid him therefore consider of his ransom, which must pro- 130 portion the losses we have borne, the subjects we have lost, the disgrace we have digested; which in weight to re-answer, his pettiness would bow under. For our losses, his exchequer is too poor; for th'effusion of our blood, the muster of his kingdom too faint a number; and for our disgrace, his own person kneeling at our feet, but a weak and worthless satisfaction.... To this add defiance: and tell him, for conclusion, he hath betrayed his followers, whose condemnation is pronounced ... So far my 140 king and master; so much my office.

KING HENRY. What is thy name? I know thy quality.

MONTJOY. Montjoy.

KING HENRY. Thou dost thy office fairly. Turn thee back,
And tell thy king I do not seek him now,
But could be willing to march on to Calais
Without impeachment: for, to say the sooth,
Though 'tis no wisdom to confess so much
Unto an enemy of craft and vantage,
My people are with sickness much enfeebled, 150
My numbers lessened: and those few I have,
Almost no better than so many French;
Who when they were in health, I tell thee, herald,
I thought upon one pair of English legs
Did march three Frenchmen.... Yet forgive me, God,
That I do brag thus! This your air of France
Hath blown that vice in me. I must repent ...
Go therefore, tell thy master here I am;
My ransom is this frail and worthless trunk;
My army, but a weak and sickly guard: 160
Yet, God before, tell him we will come on,
Though France himself, and such another neighbour,
Stand in our way.... There's for thy labour, Montjoy.
Go bid thy master well advise himself.
If we may pass, we will: if we be hindered,
We shall your tawny ground with your red blood
Discolour ... And so, Montjoy, fare you well.
The sum of all our answer is but this:
We would not seek a battle as we are,
Nor, as we are, we say we will not shun it: 170
So tell your master.

MONTJOY. I shall deliver so ... Thanks to your highness. *He departs*

GLOUCESTER. I hope they will not come upon us now.

KING HENRY. We are in God's hand, brother, not in theirs ...
March to the bridge—it now draws toward night—
Beyond the river we'll encamp ourselves,
And on to-morrow bid them march away.
They go

Scene 7: *The French camp, near Agincourt*

Enter the Constable of France, the Lord Rambures, Orleans, Dauphin, with others

CONSTABLE. Tut! I have the best armour of the world: would it were day!

ORLEANS. You have an excellent armour: but let my horse have his due.

CONSTABLE. It is the best horse of Europe.

ORLEANS. Will it never be morning?

DAUPHIN. My Lord of Orleans, and my lord high constable, you talk of horse and armour?

ORLEANS. You are as well provided of both as any prince in the world. 10

DAUPHIN. What a long night is this! I will not change my horse with any that treads but on four pasterns. Ça, ha! he bounds from the earth, as if his entrails were hairs: le cheval volant, the Pegasus, chez les narines de feu! When I bestride him, I soar, I am a hawk: he trots the air: the earth sings when he touches it: the basest horn of his hoof is more musical than the pipe of Hermes.

ORLEANS. He's of the colour of the nutmeg.

DAUPHIN. And of the heat of the ginger. It is a beast for Perseus: he is pure air and fire; and the dull elements of earth and water never appear in him, but only in patient stillness while his rider mounts him: he is indeed a horse, and all other jades you may call beasts.

CONSTABLE. Indeed, my lord, it is a most absolute and excellent horse.

DAUPHIN. It is the prince of palfreys—his neigh is like the bidding of a monarch, and his countenance enforces homage.

ORLEANS. No more, cousin.

DAUPHIN. Nay, the man hath no wit that cannot, from the rising of the lark to the lodging of the lamb, vary deserved praise on my palfrey: it is a theme as fluent as the sea: turn the sands into eloquent tongues, and my horse is argument for them all: 'tis a subject for a sovereign to reason on, and for a sovereign's sovereign to ride on: and for the world, familiar to us and unknown, to lay apart their particular functions and wonder at him—I once writ a sonnet in his praise, and began thus, "Wonder of nature"—

ORLEANS. I have heard a sonnet begin so to one's mistress.

DAUPHIN. Then did they imitate that which I composed to my courser, for my horse is my mistress.

ORLEANS. Your mistress bears well.

DAUPHIN. Me well, which is the prescript praise and perfection of a good and particular mistress.

CONSTABLE. Nay, for methought yesterday your mistress shrewdly shook your back.

DAUPHIN. So perhaps did yours.

CONSTABLE. Mine was not bridled.

DAUPHIN. O then belike she was old and gentle, and you rode like a kern of Ireland, your French hose off, and in your strait strossers.

CONSTABLE. You have good judgement in horsemanship.

DAUPHIN. Be warned by me then: they that ride so, and ride not warily, fall into foul bogs: I had rather have my horse to my mistress.

CONSTABLE. I had as lief have my mistress a jade.

DAUPHIN. I tell thee, constable, my mistress wears his own hair.

CONSTABLE. I could make as true a boast as that, if I had a sow to my mistress.

DAUPHIN. "Le chien est retourné à son propre vomissement, et la truie lavée au bourbier": thou mak'st use of any thing.

CONSTABLE. Yet do I not use my horse for my mistress, or any such proverb so little kin to the purpose.

RAMBURES. My lord constable, the armour that I saw in your tent to-night, are those stars or suns upon it?

CONSTABLE. Stars, my lord.

DAUPHIN. Some of them will fall to-morrow, I hope.

CONSTABLE. And yet my sky shall not want.

DAUPHIN. That may be, for you bear a many superfluously, and 'twere more honour some were away.

CONSTABLE. Ev'n as your horse bears your praises, who would trot as well, were some of your brags dismounted.

DAUPHIN. Would I were able to load him with his desert! Will it never be day? I will trot to-morrow a mile, and my way shall be paved with English faces.

CONSTABLE. I will not say so, for fear I should be faced out of my way: but I would it were morning, for I would fain be about the ears of the English.

RAMBURES. Who will go to hazard with me for twenty prisoners?

CONSTABLE. You must first go yourself to hazard, ere you have them.

DAUPHIN. 'Tis midnight, I'll go arm myself.

He leaves

ORLEANS. The Dauphin longs for morning.

RAMBURES. He longs to eat the English.

CONSTABLE. I think he will eat all he kills.

ORLEANS. By the white hand of my lady, he's a gallant prince.

CONSTABLE. Swear by her foot, that she may tread out the oath.

ORLEANS. He is simply the most active gentleman of France.

CONSTABLE. Doing is activity, and he will still be doing.

ORLEANS. He never did harm, that I heard of.

CONSTABLE. Nor will do none to-morrow: he will keep that good name still.

ORLEANS. I know him to be valiant.

CONSTABLE. I was told that, by one that knows him better than you.

ORLEANS. What's he?

CONSTABLE. Marry, he told me so himself, and he said he cared not who knew it.

ORLEANS. He needs not, it is no hidden virtue in him.

CONSTABLE. By my faith, sir, but it is: never any body saw it, but his lackey: 'tis a hooded valour, and when it appears, it will bate.

ORLEANS. Ill will never said well.

CONSTABLE. I will cap that proverb with "There is flattery in friendship."

ORLEANS. And I will take up that with "Give the devil his due."

CONSTABLE. Well placed: there stands your friend for the devil: have at the very eye of that proverb with "A pox of the devil."

ORLEANS. You are the better at proverbs, by how much "A fool's bolt is soon shot."

CONSTABLE. You have shot over.

ORLEANS. 'Tis not the first time you were overshot.

Enter a Messenger

MESSENGER. My lord high constable, the English lie within fifteen hundred paces of your tents.

CONSTABLE. Who hath measured the ground?

MESSENGER. The lord Grandpré.

CONSTABLE. A valiant and most expert gentleman.... Would it were day! Alas, poor Harry of England! he longs not for the dawning, as we do.

ORLEANS. What a wretched and peevish fellow is this King of England, to mope with his fat-brained followers so far out of his knowledge!

CONSTABLE. If the English had any apprehension, they would run away.

ORLEANS. That they lack: for if their heads had any intellectual armour, they could never wear such heavy head-pieces.

RAMBURES. That island of England breeds very valiant creatures; their mastiffs are of unmatchable courage.

ORLEANS. Foolish curs, that run winking into the mouth of a Russian bear, and have their heads crushed like rotten apples! You may as well say, that's a valiant flea that dare eat his breakfast on the lip of a lion. 150

CONSTABLE. Just, just: and the men do sympathize with the mastiffs in robustious and rough coming on, leaving their wits with their wives: and then give them great meals of beef, and iron and steel; they will eat like wolves, and fight like devils.

ORLEANS. Ay, but these English are shrewdly out of beef.

CONSTABLE. Then shall we find to-morrow they have only stomachs to eat, and none to fight.... Now is it time to arm: come, shall we about it? 160

ORLEANS. It is now two o'clock: but, let me see, by ten
We shall have each a hundred Englishmen.

They go

ACT 4
Prologue

Enter Chorus

CHORUS. Now entertain conjecture of a time
When creeping murmur and the poring dark
Fills the wide vessel of the universe.
From camp to camp, through the foul womb of night
The hum of either army stilly sounds;
That the fixed sentinels almost receive
The secret whispers of each other's watch.
Fire answers fire, and through their paly flames
Each battle sees the other's umbered face.
Steed threatens steed, in high and boastful neighs 10
Piercing the night's dull ear: and from the tents
The armourers, accomplishing the knights,
With busy hammers closing rivets up,
Give dreadful note of preparation.
The country cocks do crow, the clocks do toll,
And the third hour of drowsy morning name.
Proud of their numbers, and secure in soul,
The confident and over-lusty French
Do the low-rated English play at dice;
And chide the cripple tardy-gaited night, 20
Who like a foul and ugly witch doth limp
So tediously away. The poor condemnéd English,
Like sacrifices, by their watchful fires
Sit patiently, and inly ruminate
The morning's danger: and their gesture sad,
Investing lank-lean cheeks, and war-worn coats,
Presenteth them unto the gazing moon
So many horrid ghosts. O now, who will behold
The royal captain of this ruined band
Walking from watch to watch, from tent to tent, 30
Let him cry, "Praise and glory on his head!"
For forth he goes, and visits all his host,
Bids them good morrow with a modest smile,
And calls them brothers, friends, and countrymen.
Upon his royal face there is no note,
How dread an army hath enrounded him;
Nor doth he dedicate one jot of colour
Unto the weary and all-watchéd night:

But freshly looks, and over-bears attaint
With cheerful semblance, and sweet majesty: 40
That every wretch, pining and pale before,
Beholding him, plucks comfort from his looks.
A largess universal, like the sun,
His liberal eye doth give to every one,
Thawing cold fear, that mean and gentle all
Behold, as may unworthiness define,
A little touch of Harry in the night.
And so our scene must to the battle fly:
Where—O for pity!—we shall much disgrace,
With four or five most vile and ragged foils, 50
Right ill-disposed, in brawl ridiculous,
The name of Agincourt: yet sit and see,
Minding true things by what their mock'ries be.

Exit

Scene 1: *The English camp at Agincourt.*

King Henry, Bedford, and Gloucester

KING HENRY. Gloucester, 'tis true that we are in great danger,
The greater therefore should our courage be....
Good morrow, brother Bedford ... God Almighty!
There is some soul of goodness in things evil,
Would men observingly distil it out.
For our bad neighbour makes us early stirrers,
Which is both healthful, and good husbandry.
Besides, they are our outward consciences
And preachers to us all, admonishing
That we should dress us fairly for our end. 10
Thus may we gather honey from the weed,
And make a moral of the devil himself.

Erpingham enters

Good morrow, old Sir Thomas Erpingham:
A good soft pillow for that good white head
Were better than a churlish turf of France.

ERPINGHAM. Not so, my liege—this lodging likes me better,
Since I may say 'Now lie I like a king.'

KING HENRY. 'Tis good for men to love their present pains,
Upon example—so the spirit is eased:
And when the mind is quickened, out of doubt 20
The organs, though defunct and dead before,
Break up their drowsy grave, and newly move
With casted slough and fresh legerity....
Lend me thy cloak, Sir Thomas ... Brothers both,
Commend me to the princes in our camp;
Do my good morrow to them, and anon
Desire them all to my pavilion.

GLOUCESTER. We shall, my liege.

ERPINGHAM. Shall I attend your grace?

KING HENRY. No, my good knight:
Go with my brothers to my lords of England: 30
I and my bosom must debate awhile,
And then I would no other company.

ERPINGHAM. The Lord in heaven bless thee, noble Harry!

KING HENRY. God-a-mercy, old heart! thou speak'st cheerfully. *They take leave of the King*

Pistol enters

PISTOL. Qui va là?

KING HENRY. A friend.

PISTOL. Discuss unto me, art thou officer,
  Or art thou base, common, and popular?
KING HENRY. I am a gentleman of a company.
PISTOL. Trail'st thou the puissant pike? 40
KING HENRY. Even so: what are you?
PISTOL. As good a gentleman as the emperor.
KING HENRY. Then you are a better than the king.
PISTOL. The king's a bawcock, and a heart of gold,
  A lad of life, an imp of Fame,
  Of parents good, of fist most valiant:
  I kiss his dirty shoe, and from heart-string
  I love the lovely bully.... What is thy name?
KING HENRY. Harry le Roy.
PISTOL. Le Roy? a Cornish name: art thou of Cornish
  crew? 50
KING HENRY. No, I am a Welshman.
PISTOL. Know'st thou Fluellen?
KING HENRY. Yes.
PISTOL. Tell him I'll knock his leek about his pate
  Upon Saint Davy's day.
KING HENRY. Do not you wear your dagger in your
  cap that day, lest he knock that about yours.
PISTOL. Art thou his friend?
KING HENRY. And his kinsman too.
PISTOL. The figo for thee then! 60
KING HENRY. I thank you: God be with you!
PISTOL. My name is Pistol called. *He goes*
KING HENRY. It sorts well with your fierceness.

*The King withdraws a little; Fluellen and Gower enter,
meeting*

GOWER. Captain Fluellen!
FLUELLEN. So! in the name of Jesu Christ, speak fewer
  ... It is the greatest admiration in the universal
  world, when the true and ancient prerogatifes and
  laws of the wars is not kept: if you would take the
  pains but to examine the wars of Pompey the Great,
  you shall find, I warrant you, that there is no tiddle 70
  taddle nor pibble pabble in Pompey's camp: I
  warrant you, you shall find the ceremonies of the
  wars, and the cares of it, and the forms of it, and
  the sobriety of it, and the modesty of it, to be
  otherwise.
GOWER. Why, the enemy is loud, you hear him all
  night.
FLUELLEN. If the enemy is an ass and a fool, and a 80
  prating coxcomb, is it meet, think you, that we
  should also, look you, be an ass and a fool, and a
  prating coxcomb? in your own conscience now?
GOWER. I will speak lower.
FLUELLEN. I pray you, and beseech you, that you will.
  They depart severally
KING HENRY. Though it appear a little out of fashion,
  There is much care and valour in this Welshman.

*Three soldiers, John Bates, Alexander Court, and
Michael Williams, come up*

COURT. Brother John Bates, is not that the morning
  which breaks yonder?
BATES. I think it be: but we have no great cause to
  desire the approach of day.
WILLIAMS. We see yonder the beginning of the day, 90
  but I think we shall never see the end of it.... Who
  goes there?
KING HENRY. A friend.
WILLIAMS. Under what captain serve you?

KING HENRY. Under Sir Thomas Erpingham.
WILLIAMS. A good old commander, and a most kind
  gentleman: I pray you, what thinks he of our estate?
KING HENRY. Even as men wracked upon a sand, that
  look to be washed off the next tide.
BATES. He hath not told his thought to the king? 100
KING HENRY. No: nor it is not meet he should: for,
  though I speak it to you, I think the king is but a
  man, as I am: the violet smells to him as it doth to
  me; the element shows to him as it doth to me;
  all his senses have but human conditions: his ceremonies laid by, in his nakedness he appears but a
  man; and though his affections are higher mounted
  than ours, yet, when they stoop, they stoop with the
  like wing: therefore, when he sees reason of fears,
  as we do, his fears, out of doubt, be of the same 110
  relish as ours are: yet, in reason, no man should
  possess him with any appearance of fear, lest he, by
  showing it, should dishearten his army.
BATES. He may show what outward courage he will:
  but I believe, as cold a night as 'tis, he could wish
  himself in Thames up to the neck; and so I would he
  were, and I by him, at all adventures, so we were
  quit here.
KING HENRY. By my troth, I will speak my conscience
  of the king: I think he would not wish himself any 120
  where but where he is.
BATES. Then I would he were here alone; so should
  he be sure to be ransomed, and a many poor men's
  lives saved.
KING HENRY. I dare say you love him not so ill, to wish
  him here alone: howsoever you speak this to feel
  other men's minds. Methinks I could not die any
  where so contented as in the king's company; his
  cause being just, and his quarrel honourable.
WILLIAMS. That's more than we know. 130
BATES. Ay, or more than we should seek after; for we
  know enough, if we know we are the king's subjects: if his cause be wrong, our obedience to the
  king wipes the crime of it out of us.
WILLIAMS. But if the cause be not good, the king
  himself hath a heavy reckoning to make, when all
  those legs, and arms, and heads, chopped off in a
  battle, shall join together at the latter day, and cry
  all "We died at such a place"; some swearing, some
  crying for a surgeon; some upon their wives, left 140
  poor behind them; some upon the debts they owe;
  some upon their children rawly left ... I am afeard
  there are few die well, that die in a battle: for how
  can they charitably dispose of any thing, when
  blood is their argument? Now, if these men do not
  die well, it will be a black matter for the king, that
  led them to it; who to disobey were against all proportion of subjection.
KING HENRY. So, if a son that is by his father sent
  about merchandise do sinfully miscarry upon the 150
  sea, the imputation of his wickedness, by your rule,
  should be imposed upon his father that sent him:
  or if a servant, under his master's command, transporting a sum of money, be assailed by robbers, and
  die in many irreconciled iniquities, you may call the
  business of the master the author of the servant's
  damnation ... But this is not so: the king is not
  bound to answer the particular endings of his
  soldiers, the father of his son, nor the master of his
  servant; for they purpose not their death, when they 160

purpose their services. Besides, there is no king, be his cause never so spotless, if it come to the arbitrement of swords, can try it out with all unspotted soldiers: some, peradventure, have on them the guilt of premeditated and contrived murder; some, of beguiling virgins with the broken seals of perjury; some, making the wars their bulwark, that have before gored the gentle bosom of peace with pillage and robbery. Now, if these men have defeated the law, and outrun native punishment, though they 170 can outstrip men, they have no wings to fly from God. War is His beadle, war is His vengeance: so that here men are punished, for before breach of the king's laws, in now the king's quarrel: where they feared the death, they have borne life away; and where they would be safe, they perish. Then if they die unprovided, no more is the king guilty of their damnation than he was before guilty of those impieties for the which they are now visited. Every subject's duty is the king's, but every subject's soul 180 is his own. Therefore should every soldier in the wars do as every sick man in his bed, wash every mote out of his conscience: and dying so, death is to him advantage; or not dying, the time was blessedly lost, wherein such preparation was gained: and in him that escapes, it were not sin to think that, making God so free an offer, He let him outlive that day, to see His greatness, and to teach others how they should prepare.

WILLIAMS. 'Tis certain, every man that dies ill, the ill 190 upon his own head, the king is not to answer it.

BATES. I do not desire he should answer for me, and yet I determine to fight lustily for him.

KING HENRY. I myself heard the king say he would not be ransomed.

WILLIAMS. Ay, he said so, to make us fight cheerfully: but when our throats are cut, he may be ransomed, and we ne'er the wiser.

KING HENRY. If I live to see it, I will never trust his word after. 200

WILLIAMS. You pay him then! That's a perilous shot out of an elder-gun, that a poor and a private displeasure can do against a monarch! you may as well go about to turn the sun to ice, with fanning in his face with a peacock's feather ... You'll never trust his word after! come, 'tis a foolish saying.

KING HENRY. Your reproof is something too round— I should be angry with you, if the time were convenient.

WILLIAMS. Let it be a quarrel between us, if you live. 210

KING HENRY. I embrace it.

WILLIAMS. How shall I know thee again?

KING HENRY. Give me any gage of thine, and I will wear it in my bonnet: then, if ever thou dar'st acknowledge it, I will make it my quarrel.

WILLIAMS. Here's my glove: give me another of thine.

KING HENRY. There.

WILLIAMS. This will I also wear in my cap: if ever thou come to me and say, after to-morrow, "This is my glove", by this hand I will take thee a box 220 on the ear.

KING HENRY. If ever I live to see it, I will challenge it.

WILLIAMS. Thou dar'st as well be hanged.

KING HENRY. Well, I will do it, though I take thee in the king's company.

WILLIAMS. Keep thy word: fare thee well.

BATES. Be friends, you English fools, be friends; we have French quarrels enow, if you could tell how to reckon.

KING HENRY. Indeed, the French may lay twenty 230 French crowns to one, they will beat us, for they bear them on their shoulders: but it is no English treason to cut French crowns, and to-morrow the king himself will be a clipper.   *The soldiers go*
Upon the king! let us our lives, our souls,
Our debts, our careful wives,
Our children, and our sins, lay on the king!
We must bear all. O hard condition,
Twin-born with greatness, subject to the breath
Of every fool, whose sense no more can feel   240
But his own wringing! What infinite heart's ease
Must kings neglect that private men enjoy!
And what have kings, that privates have not too,
Save Ceremony, save general Ceremony?
And what art thou, thou idol Ceremony?
What kind of god art thou, that suffer'st more
Of mortal griefs than do thy worshippers?
What are thy rents? what are thy comings in?
O Ceremony, show me but thy worth!
What! Is thy soul of adoration?   250
Art thou aught else but place, degree, and form,
Creating awe and fear in other men?
Wherein thou art less happy, being feared,
Than they in fearing.
What drink'st thou oft, instead of homage sweet,
But poisoned flattery? O, be sick, great greatness,
And bid thy ceremony give thee cure!
Thinkst thou the fiery fever will go out
With titles blown from adulation?
Will it give place to flexure and low bending?   260
Canst thou, when thou command'st the beggar's knee,
Command the health of it? No, thou proud dream,
That play'st so subtly with a king's repose.
I am a king that find thee: and I know,
'Tis not the balm, the sceptre, and the ball,
The sword, the mace, the crown imperial,
The intertissued robe of gold and pearl,
The farced title running 'fore the king,
The throne he sits on: nor the tide of pomp
That beats upon the high shore of this world: 270
No, not all these, thrice-gorgeous ceremony,
Not all these, laid in bed majestical,
Can sleep so soundly as the wretched slave:
Who, with a body filled, and vacant mind,
Gets him to rest, crammed with distressful bread,
Never sees horrid night, the child of hell:
But, like a lackey, from the rise to set,
Sweats in the eye of Phœbus; and all night
Sleeps in Elysium: next day, after dawn,
Doth rise, and help Hyperion to his horse,   280
And follows so the ever-running year
With profitable labour to his grave:
And, but for ceremony, such a wretch,
Winding up days with toil, and nights with sleep,
Had the fore-hand and vantage of a king.
The slave, a member of the country's peace,
Enjoys it; but in gross brain little wots
What watch the king keeps to maintain the peace,
Whose hours the peasant best advantages.

Erpingham returns

ERPINGHAM. My lord, your nobles, jealous of your
absence,   290
  Seek through your camp to find you.
KING HENRY.   Good old knight,
  Collect them all together at my tent:
  I'll be before thee.
ERPINGHAM.   I shall do't, my lord.   *He goes*
KING HENRY. O God of battles, steel my soldiers'
hearts,
  Possess them not with fear: take from them now
  The sense of reck'ning, or th'opposéd numbers
  Pluck their hearts from them. Not to-day, O Lord,
  O not to-day, think not upon the fault
  My father made in compassing the crown!
  I Richard's body have interréd new,   300
  And on it have bestowed more contrite tears,
  Than from it issued forcéd drops of blood.
  Five hundred poor I have in yearly pay,
  Who twice a day their withered hands hold up
  Toward heaven, to pardon blood: and I have built
  Two chantries, where the sad and solemn priests
  Sing still for Richard's soul. More will I do:
  Though all that I can do is nothing worth;
  Since that my penitence comes after all,
  Imploring pardon.   310

Gloucester returns

GLOUCESTER. My liege!
KING HENRY. My brother Gloucester's voice?
Ay:
  I know thy errand, I will go with thee:
  The day, my friends, and all things stay for me.
                  They go together

Scene 2: *The French camp (as before)*

Enter the Dauphin, Orleans, Rambures, and others

ORLEANS. The sun doth gild our armour. Up, my
lords!
DAUPHIN. Montez à cheval! My horse! varlet! laquais!
ha!
ORLEANS. O brave spirit!
DAUPHIN. Via! les eaux et la terre!
ORLEANS. Rien puis? l'air et le feu?
DAUPHIN. Ciel! cousin Orleans.

Constable enters

           Now, my lord Constable?
CONSTABLE. Hark how our steeds for present service
neigh.
DAUPHIN. Mount them, and make incision in their
hides,
  That their hot blood may spin in English eyes,   10
  And dout them with superfluous courage, ha!
RAMBURES. What, will you have them weep our
horses' blood?
  How shall we then behold their natural tears?

Enter Messenger

MESSENGER. The English are embattled, you French
peers.
CONSTABLE. To horse, you gallant princes, straight to
horse!
  Do but behold yon poor and starvéd band,
  And your fair show shall suck away their souls,
  Leaving them but the shales and husks of men.

There is not work enough for all our hands,
  Scarce blood enough in all their sickly veins,   20
  To give each naked curtle-axe a stain,
  That our French gallants shall to-day draw out,
  And sheathe for lack of sport. Let us but blow on
them,
  The vapour of our valour will o'erturn them.
  'Tis positive 'gainst all exceptions, lords,
  That our superfluous lackeys and our peasants,
  Who in unnecessary action swarm
  About our squares of battle, were enow
  To purge this field of such a hilding foe;
  Though we upon this mountain's basis by   30
  Took stand for idle speculation:
  But that our honours must not. What's to say?
  A very little little let us do,
  And all is done ... Then let the trumpets sound
  The tucket sonance, and the note to mount:
  For our approach shall so much dare the field,
  That England shall couch down in fear, and yield.

Enter Grandpré

GRANDPRÉ. Why do you stay so long, my lords of
France?
  Yon island carrions, desperate of their bones,
  Ill-favouredly become the morning field: 40
  Their ragged curtains poorly are let loose,
  And our air shakes them passing scornfully.
  Big Mars seems bankrout in their beggared host,
  And faintly through a rusty beaver peeps.
  The horsemen sit like fixéd candlesticks,
  With torch-staves in their hand: and their poor jades
  Lob down their heads, dropping the hides and hips,
  The gum down-roping from their pale-dead eyes,
  And in their pale dull mouths the gimmaled bit
  Lies foul with chawed-grass, still and motionless.   50
  And their executors, the knavish crows,
  Fly o'er them all, impatient for their hour.
  Description cannot suit itself in words,
  To demonstrate the life of such a battle,
  In life so lifeless as it shows itself.
CONSTABLE. They have said their prayers, and they
stay for death.
DAUPHIN. Shall we go send them dinners, and fresh
suits,
  And give their fasting horses provender,
  And after fight with them?
CONSTABLE. I stay but for my guidon: to the field!   60
  I will the banner from a trumpet take,
  And use it for my haste.... Come, come away!
  The sun is high, and we outwear the day.   *They go*

Scene 3: *The English camp*

*Enter Gloucester, Bedford, Exeter, Erpingham with all his
host: Salisbury and Westmoreland, with others*

GLOUCESTER. Where is the king?
BEDFORD. The king himself is rode to view their battle.
WESTMORELAND. Of fighting men they have full three-
score thousand.
EXETER. There's five to one, besides they all are fresh.
SALISBURY. God's arm strike with us! 'tis a fearful
odds....
  God bye you, princes all; I'll to my charge:
  If we no more meet till we meet in heaven,
  They joyfully, my noble Lord of Bedford,

My dear Lord Gloucester, and my good Lord
  Exeter,
And my kind kinsman, warriors all, adieu!   10
BEDFORD. Farewell, good Salisbury, and good luck go
  with thee!
EXETER. Farewell, kind lord: fight valiantly to-day:
And yet I do thee wrong, to mind thee of it,
For thou art framed of the firm truth of valour.
                                        Salisbury goes
BEDFORD. He is as full of valour as of kindness,
  Princely in both.

The King approaches

WESTMORELAND.   O that we now had here
  But one ten thousand of those men in England,
  That do no work to-day!
KING HENRY.   What's he that wishes so?
  My cousin Westmoreland? No, my fair cousin:
  If we are marked to die, we are enow   20
  To do our country loss: and if to live,
  The fewer men, the greater share of honour.
  God's will, I pray thee wish not one man more.
  By Jove, I am not covetous for gold,
  Nor care I who doth feed upon my cost:
  It earns me not if men my garments wear;
  Such outward things dwell not in my desires.
  But if it be a sin to covet honour,
  I am the most offending soul alive.
  No, faith, my coz, wish not a man from England: 30
  God's peace, I would not lose so great an honour,
  As one man more, methinks, would share from me,
  For the best hope I have. O, do not wish one more:
  Rather proclaim it, Westmoreland, through my
    host,
  That he which hath no stomach to this fight,
  Let him depart, his passport shall be made,
  And crowns for convoy put into his purse:
  We would not die in that man's company
  That fears his fellowship, to die with us.
  This day is called the feast of Crispian: 40
  He that outlives this day, and comes safe home,
  Will stand a tip-toe when this day is named,
  And rouse him at the name of Crispian.
  He that shall see this day, and live old age,
  Will yearly on the vigil feast his neighbours,
  And say, "To-morrow is Saint Crispian."
  Then will he strip his sleeve, and show his scars,
  And say, "These wounds I had on Crispin's day."
  Old men forget; yet all shall be forgot,
  But he'll remember, with advantages,   50
  What feats he did that day. Then shall our names,
  Familiar in his mouth as household words,
  Harry the king, Bedford and Exeter,
  Warwick and Talbot, Salisbury and Gloucester,
  Be in their flowing cups freshly remembered.
  This story shall the good man teach his son:
  And Crispin Crispian shall ne'er go by,
  From this day to the ending of the world,
  But we in it shall be remembered;
  We few, we happy few, we band of brothers: 60
  For he to-day that sheds his blood with me
  Shall be my brother: be he ne'er so vile,
  This day shall gentle his condition.
  And gentlemen in England, now a-bed,
  Shall think themselves accursed they were not here;
  And hold their manhoods cheap, whiles any speaks

That fought with us upon Saint Crispin's day.

Salisbury returns

SALISBURY. My sovereign lord, bestow yourself with
  speed:
  The French are bravely in their battles set,
  And will with all expedience charge on us.   70
KING HENRY. All things are ready, if our minds be so.
WESTMORELAND. Perish the man whose mind is
  backward now!
KING HENRY. Thou dost not wish more help from
  England, coz?
WESTMORELAND. God's will, my liege, would you and
  I alone,
  Without more help, could fight this royal battle!
KING HENRY. Why, now thou hast unwished five
  thousand men:
  Which likes me better than to wish us one....
  You know your places: God be with you all!

A tucket sounds and Montjoy approaches

MONTJOY. Once more I come to know of thee, King
  Harry,
  If for thy ransom thou wilt now compound,   80
  Before thy most assuréd overthrow:
  For certainly thou art so near the gulf,
  Thou needs must be englutted. Besides, in mercy,
  The Constable desires thee thou wilt mind
  Thy followers of repentance; that their souls
  May make a peaceful and a sweet retire
  From off these fields: where, wretches, their poor
    bodies
  Must lie and fester.
KING HENRY.   Who hath sent thee now?
MONTJOY. The Constable of France.
KING HENRY. I pray thee bear my former answer back: 90
  Bid them achieve me, and then sell my bones.
  Good God! why should they mock poor fellows
    thus?
  The man that once did sell the lion's skin
  While the beast lived, was killed with hunting him.
  A many of our bodies shall no doubt
  Find native graves: upon the which, I trust,
  Shall witness live in brass of this day's work.
  And those that leave their valiant bones in France,
  Dying like men, though buried in your dunghills,
  They shall be famed: for there the sun shall greet
    them,   100
  And draw their honours reeking up to heaven,
  Leaving their earthly parts to choke your clime,
  The smell whereof shall breed a plague in France.
  Mark then abounding valour in our English:
  That being dead, like to the bullet's crasing,
  Break out into a second course of mischief,
  Killing in relapse of mortality....
  Let me speak proudly: tell the Constable
  We are but warriors for the working-day:
  Our gayness and our gilt are all besmirched   110
  With rainy marching in the painful field.
  There's not a piece of feather in our host—
  Good argument, I hope, we will not fly—
  And time hath worn us into slovenry.
  But, by the mass, our hearts are in the trim:
  And my poor soldiers tell me, yet ere night
  They'll be in fresher robes, or they will pluck
  The gay new coats o'er the French soldiers' heads,

And turn them out of service. If they do this—
As, if God please, they shall—my ransom then   120
Will soon be levied. Herald, save thou thy labour:
Come thou no more for ransom, gentle herald,
They shall have none, I swear, but these my joints:
Which if they have, as I will leave 'em them,
Shall yield them little, tell the Constable.
MONTJOY. I shall, King Harry. And so fare thee well:
Thou never shalt hear herald any more.   *He goes*
KING HENRY. I fear thou wilt once more come again
for a ransom.

The Duke of York enters

YORK. My lord, most humbly on my knee I beg   130
The leading of the vaward.
KING HENRY. Take it, brave York.... Now soldiers,
march away,
And how thou pleasest, God, dispose the day!
They go

Scene 4: *Near the field of battle*

Alarum. Excursions. Enter Pistol, French Soldier, and Boy

PISTOL. Yield, cur!
FRENCH SOLDIER. Je pense que vous êtes le gentil-
homme de bonne qualité.
PISTOL. Qualtitie! Calen o custure me! Art thou a
gentleman? what is thy name? discuss.
FRENCH SOLDIER. O Seigneur Dieu!
PISTOL. O, Signieur Dew should be a gentleman:
Perpend my words, O Signieur Dew, and mark:
O Signieur Dew, thou diest on point of fox,
Except, O signieur, thou do give to me   10
Egregious ransom.
FRENCH SOLDIER. O, prenez miséricorde! ayez pitié de
moi!
PISTOL. Moy shall not serve, I will have forty moys:
Or I will fetch thy rim out at thy throat,
In drops of crimson blood.
FRENCH SOLDIER. Est-il impossible d'échapper la force
de ton bras?
PISTOL. Brass, cur?
Thou damnéd and luxurious mountain goat,   20
Offer'st me brass?
FRENCH SOLDIER. O pardonnez moi!
PISTOL. Say'st thou me so? is that a ton of moys?
Come hither, boy, ask me this slave in French
What is his name.
BOY. Écoutez: comment êtes-vous appelé?
FRENCH SOLDIER. Monsieur le Fer.
BOY. He says his name is Master Fer.
PISTOL. Master Fer! I'll fer him, and firk him, and
ferret him: discuss the same in French unto him.   30
BOY. I do not know the French for fer, and
ferret, and firk.
PISTOL. Bid him prepare, for I will cut his throat.
FRENCH SOLDIER. Que dit-il, monsieur?
BOY. Il me commande à vous dire que vous faites
vous prêt, car ce soldat ici est disposé tout à cette
heure de couper votre gorge.
PISTOL. Owy, cuppele gorge, permafoy,
Peasant, unless thou give me crowns, brave crowns;
Or mangled shalt thou be by this my sword.   40
FRENCH SOLDIER. O, je vous supplie, pour l'amour de
Dieu, me pardonner! Je suis le gentilhomme de

bonne maison, gardez ma vie, et je vous donnerai
deux cents écus.
PISTOL. What are his words?
BOY. He prays you to save his life, he is a gentleman
of a good house, and for his ransom he will give you
two hundred crowns.
PISTOL. Tell him my fury shall abate, and I
The crowns will take.   50
FRENCH SOLDIER. Petit monsieur, que dit-il?
BOY. Encore qu'il est contre son jurement de
pardonner aucun prisonnier: néanmoins, pour les
écus que vous l'avez promis, il est content à vous
donner la liberté, le franchisement.
FRENCH SOLDIER. Sur mes genoux je vous donne mille
remercîments, et je m'estime heureux que je suis
tombé entre les mains d'un chevalier, je pense, le
plus brave, vaillant, et très distingué seigneur
d'Angleterre.   60
PISTOL. Expound unto me, boy.
BOY. He gives you upon his knees a thousand thanks,
and he esteems himself happy that he hath fallen
into the hands of one, as he thinks, the most brave,
valorous, and thrice-worthy signieur of England.
PISTOL. As I suck blood, I will some mercy show.
Follow me!   *Pistol goes*
BOY. Suivez-vous le grand capitaine!
The French soldier follows
I did never know so full a voice issue from so empty
a heart: but the saying is true, "The empty vessel   70
makes the greatest sound." Bardolph and Nym had
ten times more valour than this roaring devil i'th'old
play, that every one may pare his nails with a
wooden dagger, and they are both hanged, and so
would this be, if he durst steal any thing adventur-
ously.... I must stay with the lackeys with the
luggage of our camp; the French might have a good
prey of us, if he knew of it, for there is none to
guard it but boys.   *He goes*

Scene 5

*Enter Constable, Orleans, Bourbon, Dauphin, and
Rambures*

CONSTABLE. O diable!
ORLEANS. O Seigneur! le jour est perdu, tout est perdu!
DAUPHIN. Mort Dieu! ma vie! all is confounded, all!
Reproach and everlasting shame
Sits mocking in our plumes.   *A short alarum*
O méchante fortune! Do not run away.
CONSTABLE. Why, all our ranks are broke.
DAUPHIN. O perdurable shame! let's stab ourselves:
Be these the wretches that we played at dice for?
ORLEANS. Is this the king we sent to for his ransom?   10
BOURBON. Shame, and eternal shame, nothing but
shame!
Let us die in harness: once more back again,
And he that will not follow Bourbon now,
Let him go hence, and with his cap in hand
Like a base pandar hold the chamber-door,
Whilst by a slave, no gentler than my dog,
His fairest daughter is contaminated.
CONSTABLE. Disorder, that hath spoiled us, friend us
now!
Let us on heaps go offer up our lives.
ORLEANS. We are enow yet living in the field   20
To smother up the English in our throngs,

If any order might be thought upon.

BOURBON. The devil take order now! I'll to the throng;
Let life be short, else shame will be too long.

They go

Scene 6

*Alarum. Enter the King and his train, with prisoners,
Exeter and others*

KING HENRY. Well have we done, thrice-valiant
countrymen,
But all's not done—yet keep the French the field.

EXETER. The Duke of York commends him to your
majesty.

KING HENRY. Lives he, good uncle? thrice within this
hour
I saw him down; thrice up again, and fighting,
From helmet to the spur all blood he was.

EXETER. In which array, brave soldier, doth he lie,
Larding the plain: and by his bloody side,
Yoke-fellow to his honour-owing wounds,
The noble Earl of Suffolk also lies.   10
Suffolk first died, and York, all haggled over,
Comes to him, where in gore he lay insteeped,
And takes him by the beard, kisses the gashes
That bloodily did yawn upon his face,
And cries aloud, 'Tarry, my cousin Suffolk!
My soul shall thine keep company to heaven:
Tarry, sweet soul, for mine, then fly abreast:
As in this glorious and well-foughten field
We kept together in our chivalry.'
Upon these words I came, and cheered him up,   20
He smiled me in the face, raught me his hand,
And, with a feeble gripe, says, 'Dear my lord,
Commend my service to my sovereign.'
So did he turn, and over Suffolk's neck
He threw his wounded arm, and kissed his lips,
And so espoused to death, with blood he sealed
A testament of noble-ending love:
The pretty and sweet manner of it forced
Those waters from me which I would have stopped,
But I had not so much of man in me,   30
And all my mother came into mine eyes,
And gave me up to tears.

KING HENRY.   I blame you not,
For, hearing this, I must perforce compound
With mistful eyes, or they will issue too....

Alarum

But hark! what new alarum is this same?
The French have reinforced their scattered men:
Then every soldier kill his prisoners,
Give the word through.   *They go*

Scene 7

Enter Fluellen and Gower

FLUELLEN. Kill the poys and the luggage! 'tis expressly
against the law of arms, 'tis as arrant a piece of
knavery, mark you now, as can be offert. In your
conscience now, is it not?

GOWER. 'Tis certain there's not a boy left alive, and
the cowardly rascals that ran from the battle ha'
done this slaughter: besides, they have burned and
carried away all that was in the king's tent, wherefore the king most worthily hath caused every
soldier to cut his prisoner's throat. O, 'tis a gallant   10
king!

FLUELLEN. Ay, he was porn at Monmouth, Captain
Gower: what call you the town's name where
Alexander the pig was born?

GOWER. Alexander the Great.

FLUELLEN. Why, I pray you, is not pig great? The pig,
or the great, or the mighty, or the huge, or the magnanimous, are all one reckonings, save the phrase is a
little variations.

GOWER. I think Alexander the Great was born in   20
Macedon, his father was called Philip of Macedon,
as I take it.

FLUELLEN. I think it is in Macedon where Alexander
is porn: I tell you, captain, if you look in the maps
of the 'orld, I warrant you sall find, in the comparisons between Macedon and Monmouth, that the
situations, look you, is both alike. There is a river
in Macedon, and there is also moreover a river at
Monmouth, it is called Wye at Monmouth: but it
is out of my prains what is the name of the other   30
river: but 'tis all one, 'tis alike as my fingers is to
my fingers, and there is salmons in both. If you mark
Alexander's life well, Harry of Monmouth's life is
come after it indifferent well, for there is figures in
all things. Alexander, God knows, and you know,
in his rages, and his furies, and his wraths, and his
cholers, and his moods, and his displeasures, and his
indignations, and also being a little intoxicates in his
prains, did in his ales and his angers, look you, kill
his best friend Cleitus.   40

GOWER. Our king is not like him in that, he never
killed any of his friends.

FLUELLEN. It is not well done, mark you now, to take
the tales out of my mouth, ere it is made and
finished. I speak but in the figures and comparisons
of it: as Alexander killed his friend Cleitus, being in
his ales and his cups; so also Harry Monmouth, being
in his right wits and his good judgements, turned
away the fat knight with the great-belly doublet:
he was full of jests, and gipes, and knaveries, and   50
mocks, I have forgot his name.

GOWER. Sir John Falstaff.

FLUELLEN. That is he: I'll tell you, there is good men
porn at Monmouth.

GOWER. Here comes his majesty.

*Alarum. Enter King Harry and Bourbon with prisoners,
meeting Warwick, Gloucester, Exeter, heralds and soldiers,
Williams among them. Flourish*

KING HENRY. I was not angry since I came to France
Until this instant.... Take a trumpet, herald,
Ride thou unto the horsemen on yon hill:
If they will fight with us, bid them come down,
Or void the field: they do offend our sight.   60
If they'll do neither, we will come to them,
And make them skirr away, as swift as stones
Enforcèd from the old Assyrian slings:
Besides, we'll cut the throats of those we have,
And not a man of them that we shall take
Shall taste our mercy.... Go and tell them so.

An English herald obeys

Montjoy approaches

EXETER. Here comes the herald of the French, my
liege.

GLOUCESTER. His eyes are humbler than they used
to be.

KING HENRY. How now, what means this, herald?
Know'st thou not   70
That I have fined these bones of mine for ransom?
Com'st thou again for ransom?
MONTJOY.   No, great king:
I come to thee for charitable licence,
That we may wander o'er this bloody field,
To book our dead, and then to bury them,
To sort our nobles from our common men.
For many of our princes—woe the while!—
Lie drowned and soaked in mercenary blood:
So do our vulgar drench their peasant limbs
In blood of princes, and their wounded steeds   80
Fret fetlock deep in gore, and with wild rage
Yerk out their armèd heels at their dead masters,
Killing them twice.... O, give us leave, great king,
To view the field in safety, and dispose
Of their dead bodies.
KING HENRY.   I tell thee truly, herald,
I know not if the day be ours or no,
For yet a many of your horsemen peer,
And gallop o'er the field.
MONTJOY.   The day is yours.
KING HENRY. Praisèd be God, and not our strength,
for it!
What is this castle called that stands hard by?   90
MONTJOY. They call it Agincourt.
KING HENRY. Then call we this the field of Agincourt,
Fought on the day of Crispin Crispianus.
FLUELLEN. Your grandfather of famous memory, an't
please your majesty, and your great-uncle Edward
the Plack Prince of Wales, as I have read in the
chronicles, fought a most prave pattle here in
France.
KING HENRY. They did, Fluellen.
FLUELLEN. Your majesty says very true: if your   100
majesties is remembered of it, the Welshmen did
good service in a garden where leeks did grow,
wearing leeks in their Monmouth caps, which your
majesty know to this hour is an honourable badge
of the service: and I do believe your majesty takes
no scorn to wear the leek upon Saint Tavy's day.
KING HENRY. I wear it for a memorable honour:
For I am Welsh, you know, good countryman.
FLUELLEN. All the water in Wye cannot wash your
majesty's Welsh plood out of your pody, I can tell 110
you that: God pless it, and preserve it, as long as it
pleases his grace, and his majesty too!
KING HENRY. Thanks, good my countryman.
FLUELLEN. By Jeshu, I am your majesty's countryman,
I care not who know it: I will confess it to all the
'orld, I need not to be ashamed of your majesty,
praised be God, so long as your majesty is an
honest man.
KING HENRY. God keep me so! Our heralds go with
him,
Bring me just notice of the numbers dead   120
On both our parts.... *Heralds depart with Montjoy*
Call yonder fellow hither ...
EXETER. Soldier, you must come to the king.
KING HENRY. Soldier, why wear'st thou that glove in
thy cap?
WILLIAMS. An't please your majesty, 'tis the gage of
one that I should fight withal, if he be alive.
KING HENRY. An Englishman?
WILLIAMS. An't please your majesty, a rascal that

swaggered with me last night: who, if a' live and
ever dare to challenge this glove, I have sworn to   130
take him a box o'th'ear: or if I can see my glove
in his cap—which he swore, as he was a soldier, he
would wear if alive—I will strike it out soundly.
KING HENRY. What think you, Captain Fluellen, is it
fit this soldier keep his oath?
FLUELLEN. He is a craven and a villain else, an't please
your majesty, in my conscience.
KING HENRY. It may be his enemy is a gentleman of
great sort, quite from the answer of his degree.
FLUELLEN. Though he be as good a gentleman as the   140
devil is, as Lucifer and Belzebub himself, it is
necessary, look your grace, that he keep his vow and
his oath: if he be perjured, see you now, his reputation is as arrant a villain and a Jack-sauce as ever his
black shoe trod upon God's ground and his earth,
in my conscience, la!
KING HENRY. Then keep thy vow, sirrah, when thou
meet'st the fellow.
WILLIAMS. So I will, my liege, as I live.
KING HENRY. Who serv'st thou under?   150
WILLIAMS. Under Captain Gower, my liege.
FLUELLEN. Gower is a good captain, and is good knowledge and literatured in the wars.
KING HENRY. Call him hither to me, soldier.
WILLIAMS. I will, my liege.   *He goes*
KING HENRY. Here, Fluellen, wear thou this favour
for me, and stick it in thy cap: when Alençon and
myself were down together, I plucked this glove
from his helm: if any man challenge this, he is a
friend to Alençon, and an enemy to our person; if   160
thou encounter any such, apprehend him, an thou
dost me love.
FLUELLEN. Your grace does me as great honours as can
be desired in the hearts of his subjects: I would fain
see the man that has but two legs that shall find
himself aggriefed at this glove; that is all: but I would
fain see it once, an please God of his grace that I
might see.
KING HENRY. Know'st thou Gower?
FLUELLEN. He is my dear friend, an please you.   170
KING HENRY. Pray thee, go seek him, and bring him to
my tent.
FLUELLEN. I will fetch him.   *He goes*
KING HENRY. My Lord of Warwick, and my brother
Gloucester,
Follow Fluellen closely at the heels.
The glove which I have given him for a favour
May haply purchase him a box o'th'ear.
It is the soldier's: I by bargain should
Wear it myself. Follow, good cousin Warwick:
If that the soldier strike him, as I judge   180
By his blunt bearing he will keep his word,
Some sudden mischief may arise of it:
For I do know Fluellen valiant,
And, touched with choler, hot as gunpowder,
And quickly will return an injury.
Follow, and see there be no harm between them....
Go you with me, uncle of Exeter.
              Gloucester and Warwick go after Fluellen;
                the King, Exeter and the rest following

Scene 8: *Before King Henry's pavilion*

Enter Gower and Williams

WILLIAMS. I warrant it is to knight you, captain.

Fluellen approaches

FLUELLEN. God's will, and his pleasure, captain, I
  beseech you now, come apace to the king: there is
  more good toward you, peradventure, than is in
  your knowledge to dream of.
WILLIAMS. Sir, know you this glove?
FLUELLEN. Know the glove? I know the glove is a
  glove.
WILLIAMS. I know this, and thus I challenge it.
                                    Strikes him
FLUELLEN. 'Sblood, an arrant traitor as any's in the
  universal world, or in France, or in England.   10
GOWER. How now, sir? you villain!
WILLIAMS. Do you think I'll be forsworn?
FLUELLEN. Stand away, Captain Gower, I will give
  treason his payment into plows, I warrant you.
WILLIAMS. I am no traitor.
FLUELLEN. That's a lie in thy throat. I charge you in
  his majesty's name, apprehend him, he's a friend of
  the Duke Alençon's.

*Warwick and Gloucester enter, with the King and
Exeter following*

WARWICK. How now, how now, what's the matter?
FLUELLEN. My Lord of Warwick, here is, praised be 20
  God for it, a most contagious treason come to light,
  look you, as you shall desire in a summer's day. . . .
  Here is his majesty.
KING HENRY. Now now, what's the matter?
FLUELLEN. My liege, here is a villain and a traitor, that,
  look your grace, has struck the glove which your
  majesty is take out of the helmet of Alençon.
WILLIAMS. My liege, this was my glove, here is the
  fellow of it: and he that I gave it to in change
  promised to wear it in his cap: I promised to strike 30
  him, if he did: I met this man with my glove in his
  cap, and I have been as good as my word.
FLUELLEN. Your majesty, hear now, saving your
  majesty's manhood, what an arrant, rascally,
  beggarly, lousy knave it is: I hope your majesty is
  pear me testimony and witness, and will avouch-
  ment, that this is the glove of Alençon, that your
  majesty is give me, in your conscience now.
KING HENRY. Give me thy glove, soldier; look, here
  is the fellow of it: 40
  'Twas I indeed thou promised'st to strike,
  And thou hast given me most bitter terms.
FLUELLEN. An please your majesty, let his neck
  answer for it, if there is any martial law in the
  world.
KING HENRY. How canst thou make me satisfaction?
WILLIAMS. All offences, my lord, come from the heart:
  never came any from mine that might offend your
  majesty.
KING HENRY. It was ourself thou didst abuse.   50
WILLIAMS. Your majesty came not like yourself: you
  appeared to me but as a common man; witness
  the night, your garments, your lowliness: and what
  your highness suffered under that shape, I beseech
  you take it for your own fault, and not mine: for
  had you been as I took you for, I made no offence;
  therefore I beseech your highness pardon me.
KING HENRY. Here, uncle Exeter, fill this glove with
  crowns.

And give it to this fellow. Keep it, fellow,
And wear it for an honour in thy cap,   60
Till I do challenge it. Give him the crowns:
And, captain, you must needs be friends with him.
FLUELLEN. By this day and this light, the fellow has
  mettle enough in his belly . . . Hold, there is twelve-
  pence for you, and I pray you to serve God, and keep
  you out of prawls and prabbles, and quarrels and
  dissensions, and I warrant you it is the better for you.
WILLIAMS. I will none of your money.
FLUELLEN. It is with a good will: I can tell you it will
  serve you to mend your shoes: come, wherefore   70
  should you be so pashful? your shoes is not so good:
  'tis a good silling, I warrant you, or I will change it.

An English Herald enters

KING HENRY. Now, herald, are the dead numbered?
HERALD. Here is the number of the slaughtered
  French.   *He delivers a paper*
KING HENRY. What prisoners of good sort are taken,
  uncle?
EXETER. Charles Duke of Orleans, nephew to the king,
  John Duke of Bourbon, and Lord Bouciqualt:
  Of other lords and barons, knights and squires,
  Full fifteen hundred, besides common men.
KING HENRY. This note doth tell me of ten thousand
  French   80
  That in the field lie slain: of princes, in this number,
  And nobles bearing banners, there lie dead
  One hundred twenty-six: added to these,
  Of knights, esquires, and gallant gentlemen,
  Eight thousand and four hundred: of the which,
  Five hundred were but yesterday dubbed knights.
  So that, in these ten thousand they have lost,
  There are but sixteen hundred mercenaries:
  The rest are princes, barons, lords, knights, squires,
  And gentlemen of blood and quality.   90
  The names of those their nobles that lie dead:—
  Charles Delabreth, high constable of France,
  Jaques of Chatillon, admiral of France,
  The master of the cross-bows, Lord Rambures,
  Great Master of France, the brave Sir Guichard
    Dolphin,
  John Duke of Alençon, Anthony Duke of Brabant,
  The brother to the Duke of Burgundy,
  And Edward Duke of Bar: of lusty earls,
  Grandpré and Roussi, Faulconbridge and Foix,
  Beaumont and Marle, Vaudemont and Lestrake.   100
  Here was a royal fellowship of death!
  Where is the number of our English dead?
                      The herald presents another paper
  Edward the Duke of York, the Earl of Suffolk,
  Sir Richard Kikely, Davy Gam, esquire;
  None else of name: and, of all other men,
  But five and twenty. . . . O God, thy arm was here:
  And not to us, but to thy arm alone,
  Ascribe we all: when, without stratagem,
  But in plain shock, and even play of battle,
  Was ever known so great and little loss,   110
  On one part and on th'other? Take it, God,
  For it is none but thine!
EXETER.   'Tis wonderful!
KING HENRY. Come, go we in procession to the village:
  And be it death proclaiméd through our host
  To boast of this or take that praise from God
  Which is his only.

FLUELLEN. Is it not lawful, an please your majesty, to
tell how many is killed?
KING HENRY. Yes, captain: but with this acknowledge-
ment,
That God fought for us.   120
FLUELLEN. Yes, my conscience, he did us great good.
KING HENRY. Do we all holy rites:
Let there be sung 'Non nobis' and 'Te Deum',
The dead with charity enclosed in clay:
And then to Calais, and to England then,
Where ne'er from France arrived more happy men.
                                                            They go

ACT 5
Prologue

Enter Chorus

CHORUS. Vouchsafe to those that have not read the
  story,
That I may prompt them: and of such as have,
I humbly pray them to admit th'excuse
Of time, of numbers, and due course of things,
Which cannot in their huge and proper life
Be here presented.... Now we bear the king
Toward Calais: grant him there; there seen,
Heave him away upon your wingéd thoughts,
Athwart the sea: behold the English beach
Pales in the flood with men, with wives, and boys,   10
Whose shouts and claps out-voice the deep-
  mouthed sea,
Which like a mighty whiffler 'fore the king
Seems to prepare his way: so let him land,
And solemnly see him set on to London.
So swift a pace hath thought, that even now
You may imagine him upon Blackheath:
Where that his lords desire him to have borne
His bruiséd helmet, and his bended sword
Before him through the city: he forbids it,
Being free from vainness and self-glorious pride;   20
Giving full trophy, signal, and ostent,
Quite from himself, to God.... But now behold,
In the quick forge and working-house of thought,
How London doth pour out her citizens—
The mayor and all his brethren in best sort,
Like to the senators of th'antique Rome,
With the plebeians swarming at their heels,
Go forth and fetch their conqu'ring Cæsar in:
As, by a lower but loving likelihood,
Were now the general of our gracious empress,   30
As in good time he may, from Ireland coming,
Bringing rebellion broachéd on his sword,
How many would the peaceful city quit,
To welcome him! much more, and much more
  cause,
Did they this Harry.... Now in London place
  him—
As yet the lamentation of the French
Invites the King of England's stay at home:
The emperor's coming in behalf of France,
To order peace between them—and omit
All the occurrences, whatever chanced,   40
Till Harry's back-return again to Fránce:
There must we bring him; and myself have played
The interim, by rememb'ring you 'tis past.
Then brook abridgement, and your eyes advance,
After your thoughts, straight back again to France.
                                                            Exit

Scene 1: *France. The English camp*

Enter Gower and Fluellen

GOWER. Nay, that's right ... But why wear you your
leek to-day? Saint Davy's day is past.
FLUELLEN. There is occasions and causes why and
wherefore in all things: I will tell you, ass my friend,
Captain Gower; the rascally, scauld, beggarly,
lousy, pragging knave Pistol, which you and yourself, and all the world, know to be no petter than a
fellow, look you now, of no merits—he is come to
me, and prings me pread and salt yesterday, look   10
you, and bid me eat my leek: it was in a place
where I could not breed no contention with him;
but I will be so bold as to wear it in my cap till
I see him once again, and then I will tell him a
little piece of my desires.

Pistol enters

GOWER. Why, here he comes, swelling like a turkey-
cock.
FLUELLEN. 'Tis no matter for his swellings, nor his
turkey-cocks.... God pless you, Ancient Pistol! you
scurvy lousy knave, God pless you.
PISTOL. Ha! art thou bedlam? Dost thou thirst, base   20
Trojan,
To have me fold up Parca's fatal web?
Hence! I am qualmish at the smell of leek.
FLUELLEN. I peseech you heartily, scurvy lousy knave,
at my desires, and my requests, and my petitions,
to eat, look you, this leek; because, look you, you
do not love it, nor your affections, and your
appetites and your disgestions does not agree with it,
I would desire you to eat it.
PISTOL. Not for Cadwallader and all his goats.
FLUELLEN. There is one goat for you. [*strikes him*] Will   30
you be so good, scauld knave, as eat it?
PISTOL. Base Trojan, thou shalt die.
FLUELLEN. You say very true, scauld knave, when
God's will is: I will desire you to live in the mean
time, and eat your victuals: come, there is sauce for
it.... [*striking him again*] You called me yesterday
mountain-squire, but I will make you to-day 'a
squire of low degree'.... I pray you fall to—if you
can mock a leek, you can eat a leek.
GOWER. Enough, captain, you have astonished him.   40
FLUELLEN. I say, I will make him eat some part of my
leek, or I will peat his pate four days: bite, I pray
you, it is good for your green wound, and your
ploody coxcomb.
                        He thrusts the leek between his teeth
PISTOL. Must I bite?
FLUELLEN. Yes certainly, and out of doubt and out of
question too, and ambiguities.
PISTOL. By this leek, I will most horribly revenge I eat
and eat I swear.
FLUELLEN. Eat, I pray you, will you have some more   50
sauce to your leek? there is not enough leek to
swear by.
PISTOL. Quiet thy cudgel, thou dost see I eat.
FLUELLEN. Much good do you, scauld knave,
heartily.... Nay, pray you throw none away, the
skin is good for your broken coxcomb; when you
take occasions to see leeks hereafter, I pray you mock
at 'em, that is all.

PISTOL. Good.

FLUELLEN. Ay, leeks is good ... Hold you, there is a 60
groat to heal your pate.

PISTOL. Me a groat!

FLUELLEN. Yes verily, and in truth you shall take it,
or I have another leek in my pocket, which you
shall eat.

PISTOL. I take thy groat in earnest of revenge.

FLUELLEN. If I owe you any thing, I will pay you in
cudgels, you shall be a woodmonger, and buy
nothing of me but cudgels ... God bye you, and
keep you, and heal your pate. *He goes* 70

PISTOL. All hell shall stir for this.

GOWER. Go, go, you are a counterfeit cowardly
knave—will you mock at an ancient tradition,
began upon an honourable respect, and worn as a
memorable trophy of predeceased valour, and dare
not avouch in your deeds any of your words? I have
seen you gleeking and galling at this gentleman
twice or thrice. You thought, because he could not
speak English in the native garb, he could not therefore handle an English cudgel: you find it otherwise, 80
and henceforth let a Welsh correction teach you a
good English condition—fare ye well. *He goes*

PISTOL. Doth Fortune play the huswife with me now?
News have I that my Doll is dead i'th'spital
O' malady of France,
And there my rendezvous is quite cut off ...
Old I do wax, and from my weary limbs
Honour is cudgelled.... Well, bawd I'll turn,
And something lean to cutpurse of quick hand:
To England will I steal, and there I'll steal: 90
And patches will I get unto these cudgelled scars,
And swear I got them in the Gallia wars. *He goes*

Scene 2: *France. A royal palace*

*Enter, at one door, King Henry, Exeter, Bedford,
Warwick, Gloucester, Westmoreland, and other Lords; at
another, Queen Isabel, the French King, the Princess
Katharine, Alice, and other Ladies, the Duke of Burgundy,
and other French*

KING HENRY. Peace to this meeting, wherefore we
are met!
Unto our brother France, and to our sister,
Health and fair time of day: joy and good wishes
To our most fair and princely cousin Katharine:
And, as a branch and member of this royalty,
By whom this great assembly is contrived,
We do salute you, Duke of Burgundy;
And, princes French, and peers, health to you all!

FRENCH KING. Right joyous are we to behold your
face,
Most worthy brother England, fairly met— 10
So are you, princes English, every one.

QUEEN ISABEL. So happy be the issue, brother England,
Of this good day, and of this gracious meeting,
As we are now glad to behold your eyes,
Your eyes which hitherto have borne in them
Against the French, that met them in their bent,
The fatal balls of murdering basilisks.
The venom of such looks, we fairly hope,
Have lost their quality, and that this day
Shall change all griefs and quarrels into love. 20

KING HENRY. To cry amen to that, thus we appear.

QUEEN ISABEL. You English princes all, I do salute you.

BURGUNDY. My duty to you both, on equal love....
Great kings of France and England: that I have
laboured
With all my wits, my pains, and strong endeavours,
To bring your most imperial majesties
Unto this bar and royal interview,
Your mightiness on both parts best can witness....
Since then my office hath so far prevailed,
That face to face, and royal eye to eye, 30
You have congreeted: let it not disgrace me,
If I demand before this royal view,
What rub, or what impediment there is,
Why that the naked, poor, and mangled Peace,
Dear nurse of arts, plenties, and joyful births,
Should not in this best garden of the world,
Our fertile France, put up her lovely visage?
Alas, she hath from France too long been chased,
And all her husbandry doth lie on heaps,
Corrupting in it own fertility. 40
Her vine, the merry cheerer of the heart,
Unprunéd, dies: her hedges even-pleached,
Like prisoners wildly over-grown with hair,
Put forth disordered twigs: her fallow leas
The darnel, hemlock, and rank fumitory
Doth root upon; while that the coulter rusts,
That should deracinate such savagery:
The even mead, that erst brought sweetly forth
The freckled cowslip, burnet, and green clover,
Wanting the scythe, all uncorrected, rank, 50
Conceives by idleness, and nothing teems
But hateful docks, rough thistles, kecksies, burs,
Losing both beauty and utility;
And as our vineyards, fallows, meads, and hedges,
Defective in their natures, grow to wildness,
Even so our houses, and ourselves, and children,
Have lost, or do not learn, for want of time,
The sciences that should become our country;
But grow like savages, as soldiers will,
That nothing do but meditate on blood, 60
To swearing, and stern looks, diffused attire,
And every thing that seems unnatural.
Which to reduce into our former favour,
You are assembled: and my speech entreats,
That I may know the let, why gentle Peace
Should not expel these inconveniences,
And bless us with her former qualities.

KING HENRY. If, Duke of Burgundy, you would the
peace,
Whose want gives growth to th'imperfections
Which you have cited, you must buy that peace 70
With full accord to all our just demands,
Whose tenours and particular effects
You have, enscheduled briefly, in your hands.

BURGUNDY. The king hath heard them: to the which,
as yet,
There is no answer made.

KING HENRY. Well then: the peace, which you before
so urged,
Lies in his answer.

FRENCH KING. I have but with a cursitory eye
O'erglanced the article: pleaseth your grace
To appoint some of your council presently 80
To sit with us once more, with better heed
To re-survey them; we will suddenly
Pass our accept and peremptory answer.

KING HENRY. Brother, we shall.... Go, uncle Exeter,
And brother Clarence, and you, brother Gloucester,
Warwick, and Huntingdon, go with the king,
And take with you free power, to ratify,
Augment, or alter, as your wisdoms best
Shall see advantageable for our dignity,
Any thing in or out of our demands,   90
And we'll consign thereto .... Will you, fair sister,
Go with the princes, or stay here with us?

QUEEN ISABEL. Our gracious brother, I will go
  with them:
Haply a woman's voice may do some good,
When articles too nicely urged be stood on.

KING HENRY. Yet leave our cousin Katharine here
  with us,
She is our capital demand, comprised
Within the fore-rank of our articles.

QUEEN ISABEL. She hath good leave.
      All depart but King Henry, Katharine, and
                  her Gentlewoman

KING HENRY.   Fair Katharine, and most fair,
Will you vouchsafe to teach a soldier terms,   100
Such as will enter at a lady's ear,
And plead his love-suit to her gentle heart?

KATHARINE. Your majesty shall mock at me, I cannot
speak your England.

KING HENRY. O fair Katharine, if you will love me
soundly with your French heart, I will be glad to
hear you confess it brokenly with your English
tongue. Do you like me, Kate?

KATHARINE. Pardonnez moi, I cannot tell vat is 'like
me.'   110

KING HENRY. An angel is like you, Kate, and you are
like an angel.

KATHARINE. Que dit-il? que je suis semblable à les
anges?

ALICE. Oui, vraiment, sauf votre grace, ainsi dit-il.

KING HENRY. I said so, dear Katharine, and I must not
blush to affirm it.

KATHARINE. O bon Dieu! les langues des hommes sont
pleines de tromperies.

KING HENRY. What says she, fair one? that the tongues 120
of men are full of deceits?

ALICE. Oui, dat de tongues of de mans is be full of
deceits: dat is de princess.

KING HENRY. The princess is the better English-
woman ... I'faith, Kate, my wooing is fit for thy
understanding; I am glad thou canst speak no better
English, for, if thou couldst, thou wouldst find me
such a plain king, that thou wouldst think I had sold
my farm to buy my crown.... I know no ways to
mince it in love, but directly to say "I love you"; 130
then if you urge me farther than to say "Do you in
faith?" I wear out my suit ... Give me your answer,
i'faith do, and so clap hands, and a bargain: how say
you, lady?

KATHARINE. Sauf votre honneur, me understand vell.

KING HENRY. Marry, if you would put me to verses,
or to dance for your sake, Kate, why, you undid me:
for the one, I have neither words nor measure; and
for the other, I have no strength in measure, yet a
reasonable measure in strength. If I could win a lady 140
at leap-frog, or by vaulting into my saddle with my
armour on my back, under the correction of
bragging be it spoken, I should quickly leap into a
wife: or if I might buffet for my love, or bound my

horse for her favours, I could lay on like a butcher,
and sit like a jack-an-apes, never off. But before
God, Kate, I cannot look greenly, nor gasp out my
eloquence, nor I have no cunning in protestation;
only downright oaths, which I never use till urged,
nor never break for urging. If thou canst love a 150
fellow of this temper, Kate, whose face is not worth
sun-burning, that never looks in his glass for love
of any thing he sees there, let thine eye be thy cook.
I speak to thee plain soldier: if thou canst love me for
this, take me; if not, to say to thee that I shall die
is true; but for thy love, by the Lord, no: yet I love
thee too. And while thou liv'st, dear Kate, take a
fellow of plain and uncoined constancy, for he perforce must do thee right, because he hath not the
gift to woo in other places: for these fellows of 160
infinite tongue, that can rhyme themselves into
ladies' favours, they do always reason themselves
out again. What! a speaker is but a prater, a rhyme is
but a ballad; a good leg will fall, a straight back will
stoop, a black beard will turn white, a curled pate
will grow bald, a fair face will wither, a full eye will
wax hollow: but a good heart, Kate, is the sun and
the moon, or rather the sun and not the moon; for
it shines bright, and never changes, but keeps his
course truly. If thou would have such a one, take me! 170
And take me, take a soldier, take a king. And what
say'st thou then to my love? speak, my fair, and
fairly, I pray thee.

KATHARINE. Is it possible dat I sould love de enemy of
France?

KING HENRY. No, it is not possible you should love
the enemy of France, Kate; but, in loving me, you
should love the friend of France: for I love France
so well that I will not part with a village of it; I
will have it all mine: and, Kate, when France is mine, 180
and I am yours, then yours is France, and you are
mine.

KATHARINE. I cannot tell vat is dat.

KING HENRY. No, Kate? I will tell thee in French,
which I am sure will hang upon my tongue like a
new-married wife about her husband's neck, hardly
to be shook off ... Je quand sur le possession de
France, et quand vous avez le possession de moi,—
let me see, what then? Saint Dennis be my speed!
—donc votre est France, et vous êtes mienne. It is 190
as easy for me, Kate, to conquer the kingdom, as
to speak so much more French: I shall never move
thee in French, unless it be to laugh at me.

KATHARINE. Sauf votre honneur, le Français que vous
parlez, il est meilleur que l'Anglais lequel je parle.

KING HENRY. No, faith, is't not, Kate: but thy speaking
of my tongue, and I thine, most truly falsely, must
needs be granted to be much at one. But, Kate, dost
thou understand thus much English? Canst thou
love me?   200

KATHARINE. I cannot tell.

KING HENRY. Can any of your neighbours tell, Kate?
I'll ask them.... Come, I know thou lovest me: and
at night, when you come into your closet, you'll
question this gentlewoman about me; and I know,
Kate, you will to her dispraise those parts in me that
you love with your heart: but, good Kate, mock me
mercifully, the rather, gentle princess, because I love
thee cruelly. If ever thou beest mine, Kate, as I have
a saving faith within me tells me thou shalt, I get thee 210

with scambling, and thou must therefore needs prove a good soldier-breeder: shall not thou and I, between Saint Dennis and Saint George, compound a boy, half French half English, that shall go to Constantinople, and take the Turk by the beard? shall we not? what say'st thou, my fair flower-de-luce?

KATHARINE. I do not know dat.

KING HENRY. No: 'tis hereafter to know, but now to promise: do but now promise, Kate, you will en- 220 deavour for your French part of such a boy; and, for my English moiety, take the word of a king and a bachelor. How answer you, la plus belle Katharine du monde, mon très cher et devin déesse?

KATHARINE. Your majestee 'ave fause French enough to deceive de most sage demoiselle dat is en France.

KING HENRY. Now fie upon my false French! By mine honour, in true English, I love thee, Kate; by which honour, I dare not swear thou lovest me, yet my blood begins to flatter me that thou dost; notwith- 230 standing the poor and untempering effect of my visage. Now beshrew my father's ambition! he was thinking of civil wars when he got me, therefore was I created with a stubborn outside, with an aspect of iron, that when I come to woo ladies, I fright them: but in faith, Kate, the elder I wax, the better I shall appear. My comfort is, that old age, that ill layer up of beauty, can do no more spoil upon my face. Thou hast me, if thou hast me, at the worst; and thou shalt wear me, if thou wear me, better and 240 better: and therefore tell me, most fair Katharine, will you have me? Put off your maiden blushes, avouch the thoughts of your heart with the looks of an empress, take me by the hand, and say "Harry of England, I am thine": which word thou shalt no sooner bless mine ear withal, but I will tell thee aloud "England is thine, Ireland is thine, France is thine, and Henry Plantagenet is thine"; who, though I speak it before his face, if he be not fellow with the best king, thou shalt find the best king of good 250 fellows.... Come, your answer in broken music; for thy voice is music, and thy English broken: therefore, queen of all, Katharine, break thy mind to me in broken English; wilt thou have me?

KATHARINE. Dat is as it sall please de roi mon père.

KING HENRY. Nay, it will please him well, Kate; it shall please him, Kate.

KATHARINE. Den it sall also content me.

KING HENRY. Upon that I kiss your hand, and I call you my queen. 260

KATHARINE. Laissez, mon seigneur, laissez, laissez: ma foi, je ne veux point que vous abaissiez votre grandeur en baisant la main d'une de votre seig- neurie indigne serviteur; excusez-moi, je vous supplie, mon très puissant seigneur.

KING HENRY. Then I will kiss your lips, Kate.

KATHARINE. Les dames et demoiselles pour être baisées devant leur noces, il n'est pas la coutume de France.

KING HENRY. Madam my interpreter, what says she?

ALICE. Dat it is not be de fashon pour les ladies of 270 France,—I cannot tell vat is baiser en Anglish.

KING HENRY. To kiss.

ALICE. Your majestee entendre bettre que moi.

KING HENRY. It is not a fashion for the maids in France to kiss before they are married, would she say?

ALICE. Oui, vraiment.

KING HENRY. O, Kate, nice customs curtsy to great kings. Dear Kate, you and I cannot be confined within the weak list of a country's fashion: we are the makers of manners, Kate; and the liberty that 280 follows our places stops the mouth of all find-faults, as I will do yours, for upholding the nice fashion of your country, in denying me a kiss: therefore patiently, and yielding. [kissing her] You have witch- craft in your lips, Kate: there is more eloquence in a sugar touch of them than in the tongues of the French council; and they should sooner persuade Harry of England than a general petition of monarchs.... Here comes your father.

The French King and Queen return with Burgundy, Exeter, Westmoreland, and other French and English Lords; the ladies talk apart

BURGUNDY. God save your majesty! my royal cousin, 290 teach you our princess English?

KING HENRY. I would have her learn, my fair cousin, how perfectly I love her, and that is good English.

BURGUNDY. Is she not apt?

KING HENRY. Our tongue is rough, coz, and my con- dition is not smooth: so that, having neither the voice nor the heart of flattery about me, I cannot so conjure up the spirit of love in her, that he will appear in his true likeness.

BURGUNDY. Pardon the frankness of my mirth, if I 300 answer you for that. If you would conjure in her, you must make a circle: if conjure up love in her in his true likeness, he must appear naked, and blind. Can you blame her then, being a maid yet rosed over with the virgin crimson of modesty, if she deny the appearance of a naked blind boy in her naked seeing self? It were, my lord, a hard condition for a maid to consign to.

KING HENRY. Yet they do wink and yield, as love is blind and enforces. 310

BURGUNDY. They are then excused, my lord, when they see not what they do.

KING HENRY. Then, good my lord, teach your cousin to consent winking.

BURGUNDY. I will wink on her to consent, my lord, if you will teach her to know my meaning: for maids, well summered and warm kept, are like flies at Bartholomewtide, blind, though they have their eyes, and then they will endure handling, which before would not abide looking on. 320

KING HENRY. This moral ties me over to time, and a hot summer; and so I shall catch the fly, your cousin, in the latter end, and she must be blind too.

BURGUNDY. As love is, my lord, before it loves.

KING HENRY. It is so: and you may, some of you, thank love for my blindness, who cannot see many a fair French city for one fair French maid that stands in my way.

FRENCH KING. Yes, my lord, you see them per- spectively: the cities turned into a maid; for they are 330 all girdled with maiden walls, that war hath never entered.

KING HENRY. Shall Kate be my wife?

FRENCH KING. So please you.

KING HENRY. I am content, so the maiden cities you talk of may wait on her: so the maid that stood in the way for my wish shall show me the way to my will.

FRENCH KING. We have consented to all terms of
reason.   340
KING HENRY. Is't so, my lords of England?
WESTMORELAND. The king hath granted every article:
His daughter first; and then in sequel all,
According to their firm proposéd natures.
EXETER. Only he hath not yet subscribéd this:
Where your majesty demands that the King of
France, having any occasion to write for matter of
grant, shall name your highness in this form, and
with this addition, in French: Notre très-cher fils
Henri, Roi d'Angleterre, Héritier de France: and 350
thus in Latin; Præclarissimus filius noster Henricus,
Rex Angliæ, et hæres Franciæ.
FRENCH KING. Nor this I have not, brother, so denied,
But your request shall make me let it pass.
KING HENRY. I pray you then, in love and dear alliance,
Let that one article rank with the rest,
And thereupon give me your daughter.
FRENCH KING. Take her, fair son, and from her blood
raise up
Issue to me, that the contending kingdoms
Of France and England, whose very shores look pale 360
With envy of each other's happiness,
May cease their hatred; and this dear conjunction
Plant neighbourhood and Christian-like accord
In their sweet bosoms: that never war advance
His bleeding sword 'twixt England and fair France.
ALL. Amen!
KING HENRY. Now welcome, Kate: and bear me
witness all,
That here I kiss her as my sovereign queen.
Flourish
QUEEN ISABEL. God, the best maker of all marriages,
Combine your hearts in one, your realms in one! 370

As man and wife, being two, are one in love,
So be there 'twixt your kingdoms such a spousal,
That never may ill office, or fell jealousy,
Which troubles oft the bed of blessèd marriage,
Thrust in between the paction of these kingdoms,
To make divorce of their incorporate league:
That English may as French, French Englishmen,
Receive each other.... God speak this Amen!
ALL. Amen!
KING HENRY. Prepare we for our marriage: on which
day,   380
My Lord of Burgundy, we'll take your oath,
And all the peers', for surety of our leagues.
Then shall I swear to Kate, and you to me,
And may our oaths well kept and prosp'rous be!
*A trumpet sounds as King Henry leads Katharine
out, the rest following in procession*

EPILOGUE

Enter Chorus

CHORUS. Thus far, with rough and all-unable pen,
Our bending author hath pursued the story,
In little room confining mighty men,
Mangling by starts the full course of their glory.
Small time: but, in that small, most greatly lived
This star of England. Fortune made his sword;
By which the world's best garden he achieved:
And of it left his son imperial lord.
Henry the Sixth, in infant bands crowned King
Of France and England, did this king succeed: 10
Whose state so many had the managing,
That they lost France, and made his England bleed:
Which oft our stage hath shown; and, for their sake,
In your fair minds let this acceptance take. *Exit*

The First Part of King Henry VI

The scene: partly in England, and partly in France

CHARACTERS IN THE PLAY

KING HENRY *the Sixth*

HUMPHREY, DUKE OF GLOUCESTER, *uncle to the King, and Protector*

JOHN, DUKE OF BEDFORD, *uncle to the King, and Regent of France*

THOMAS BEAUFORT, DUKE OF EXETER, *great-uncle to the King*

HENRY BEAUFORT, BISHOP OF WINCHESTER, *and Cardinal, great-uncle to the King*

DUKE OF SOMERSET

RICHARD PLANTAGENET, *afterwards Duke of York, son of Richard late Earl of Cambridge*

EARL OF WARWICK

EARL OF SALISBURY

WILLIAM DE LA POLE, EARL OF SUFFOLK

LORD TALBOT, *afterwards Earl of Shrewsbury*

JOHN TALBOT, *his son*

EDMUND MORTIMER, *Earl of March*

SIR JOHN FALSTAFF

SIR WILLIAM LUCY

SIR WILLIAM GLANSDALE

SIR THOMAS GARGRAVE

Mayor of London

WOODVILLE, *Lieutenant of the Tower*

VERNON, *of the White-Rose or York faction*

BASSET, *of the Red-Rose or Lancaster faction*

A Lawyer. Mortimer's Gaolers

CHARLES, *Dauphin, afterwards King, of France*

REIGNIER, *Duke of Anjou, and titular King of Naples*

DUKE OF BURGUNDY

DUKE OF ALENÇON

BASTARD OF ORLEANS

Governor of Paris

Master-Gunner of Orleans, and his Son

General of the French forces in Bordeaux

A French Sergeant. A Porter

An old Shepherd, father to Joan la Pucelle

MARGARET, *daughter to Reignier, afterwards married to King Henry*

COUNTESS OF AUVERGNE

JOAN LA PUCELLE, *commonly called Joan of Arc*

Lords, Warders of the Tower, Heralds, Officers, Soldiers, Messengers, and Attendants

Fiends appearing to La Pucelle

The First Part of King Henry VI

ACT 1
Scene 1: *Westminster Abbey*

Dead March. Enter the Funeral of King Henry the Fifth,
attended on by the Duke of Bedford, Regent of France;
the Duke of Gloucester, Protector; the Duke of Exeter,
the Earl of Warwick, the Bishop of Winchester, and the
Duke of Somerset, with Heralds, etc.

BEDFORD. Hung be the heavens with black, yield day
　　to night!
　Comets, importing change of times and states,
　Brandish your crystal tresses in the sky,
　And with them scourge the bad revolting stars
　That have consented unto Henry's death!
　King Henry the Fifth, too famous to live long!
　England ne'er lost a king of so much worth.
GLOUCESTER. England ne'er had a king until his time.
　Virtue he had, deserving to command:
　His brandished sword did blind men with his beams: 10
　His arms spread wider than a dragon's wings;
　His sparkling eyes, replete with wrathful fire,
　More dazzled and drove back his enemies
　Than mid-day sun fierce bent against their faces.
　What should I say? his deeds exceed all speech:
　He ne'er lift up his hand but conquerèd.
EXETER. We mourn in black: why mourn we not in
　　blood?
　Henry is dead and never shall revive:
　Upon a wooden coffin we attend,
　And death's dishonourable victory　　　　　　20
　We with our stately presence glorify,
　Like captives bound to a triumphant car.
　What! shall we curse the planets of mishap
　That plotted thus our glory's overthrow?
　Or shall we think the subtle-witted French
　Conjurers and sorcerers, that afraid of him
　By magic verses have contrived his end?
WINCHESTER. He was a king blessed of the King of
　　kings.
　Unto the French the dreadful judgement-day
　So dreadful will not be as was his sight.　　　30
　The battles of the Lord of hosts he fought:
　The church's prayers made him so prosperous.
GLOUCESTER. The church! where is it? Had not
　　churchmen prayed,
　His thread of life had not so soon decayed:
　None do you like but an effeminate prince,
　Whom, like a school-boy, you may over-awe.
WINCHESTER. Gloucester, whate'er we like, thou art
　　Protector
　And lookest to command the prince and realm.
　Thy wife is proud; she holdeth thee in awe,
　More than God or religious churchmen may.　　40
GLOUCESTER. Name not religion, for thou lov'st the
　　flesh,
　And ne'er throughout the year to church thou go'st
　Except it be to pray against thy foes.
BEDFORD. Cease, cease these jars and rest your minds in
　　peace:
　Let's to the altar: heralds, wait on us:

Instead of gold, we'll offer up our arms;
Since arms avail not now that Henry's dead.
Posterity, await for wretched years,
When at their mothers' moist'ned eyes babes shall
　suck,
Our isle be made a nourish of salt tears,　　　50
And none but women left to wail the dead.
Henry the Fifth, thy ghost I invocate:
Prosper this realm, keep it from civil broils,
Combat with adverse planets in the heavens!
A far more glorious star thy soul will make
Than Julius Caesar or bright——

Enter a Messenger

MESSENGER. My honourable lords, health to you all!
　Sad tidings bring I to you out of France,
　Of loss, of slaughter and discomfiture:
　Guienne, Champagne, Rheims, Rouen, Orleans, 60
　Paris, Guysors, Poictiers, are all quite lost.
BEDFORD. What say'st thou, man, before dead
　　Henry's corse?
　Speak softly, or the loss of those great towns
　Will make him burst his lead and rise from death.
GLOUCESTER. Is Paris lost? is Rouen yielded up?
　If Henry were recalled to life again,
　These news would cause him once more yield the
　　ghost.
EXETER. How were they lost? what treachery was
　　used?
MESSENGER. No treachery; but want of men and
　　money.
　Amongst the soldiers this is mutterèd,　　　70
　That here you maintain several factions,
　And whilst a field should be dispatched and fought,
　You are disputing of your generals:
　One would have ling'ring wars with little cost;
　Another would fly swift, but wanteth wings;
　A third thinks, without expense at all,
　By guileful fair words peace may be obtained.
　Awake, awake, English nobility!
　Let not sloth dim your honours new-begot:
　Cropped are the flower-de-luces in your arms;　80
　Of England's coat one half is cut away.　　*He goes*
EXETER. Were our tears wanting to this funeral,
　These tidings would call forth her flowing tides.
BEDFORD. Me they concern; Regent I am of France.
　Give me my steelèd coat. I'll fight for France.
　Away with these disgraceful wailing robes!
　Wounds will I lend the French instead of eyes,
　To weep their intermissive miseries.

Enter to them another Messenger

MESSENGER. Lords, view these letters full of bad
　　mischance.
　France is revolted from the English quite,　　90
　Except some petty towns of no import.
　The Dauphin Charles is crownèd king in Rheims;
　The Bastard of Orleans with him is joined;
　Reignier, Duke of Anjou, doth take his part;
　The Duke of Alençon flieth to his side.　*He goes*

EXETER. The Dauphin crownéd king! all fly to him!
    O, whither shall we fly from this reproach?
GLOUCESTER. We will not fly, but to our enemies'
    throats.
    Bedford, if thou be slack, I'll fight it out.
BEDFORD. Gloucester, why doubt'st thou of my
    forwardness?   100
    An army have I mustered in my thoughts,
    Wherewith already France is overrun.

Enter another Messenger

MESSENGER. My gracious lords, to add to your laments,
    Wherewith you now bedew King Henry's hearse,
    I must inform you of a dismal fight
    Betwixt the stout Lord Talbot and the French.
WINCHESTER. What! wherein Talbot overcame?
    is't so?
MESSENGER. O, no; wherein Lord Talbot was
    o'erthrown:
    The circumstance I'll tell you more at large.
    The tenth of August last this dreadful lord,   110
    Retiring from the siege of Orleans,
    Having full scarce six thousand in his troop,
    By three and twenty thousand of the French
    Was round encompasséd and set upon.
    No leisure had he to enrank his men;
    He wanted pikes to set before his archers;
    Instead whereof sharp stakes plucked out of hedges
    They pitchéd in the ground confusedly,
    To keep the horsemen off from breaking in.
    More than three hours the fight continuéd;   120
    Where valiant Talbot above human thought
    Enacted wonders with his sword and lance:
    Hundreds he sent to hell, and none durst stand him;
    Here, there, and everywhere, enragéd he flew:
    The French exclaimed the devil was in arms;
    All the whole army stood agazed on him:
    His soldiers, spying his undaunted spirit,
    A Talbot! a Talbot! cried out amain,
    And rushed into the bowels of the battle.
    Here had the conquest fully been sealed up,   130
    If Sir John Falstaff had not played the coward:
    He, being in the vaward, placed behind
    With purpose to relieve and follow them,
    Cowardly fled, not having struck one stroke.
    Hence grew the general wrack and massacre;
    Enclosed were they with their enemies:
    A base Walloon, to win the Dauphin's grace,
    Thrust Talbot with a spear into the back,
    Whom all France with their chief assembled
    strength
    Durst not presume to look once in the face.   140
BEDFORD. Is Talbot slain? then I will slay myself,
    For living idly here in pomp and ease,
    Whilst such a worthy leader, wanting aid,
    Unto his dastard foemen is betrayed.
MESSENGER. O no, he lives, but is took prisoner,
    And Lord Scales with him and Lord Hungerford:
    Most of the rest slaughtered or took likewise.
BEDFORD. His ransom there is none but I shall pay:
    I'll hale the Dauphin headlong from his throne:
    His crown shall be the ransom of my friend;   150
    Four of their lords I'll change for one of ours.
    Farewell, my masters; to my task will I;
    Bonfires in France forthwith I am to make,
    To keep our great Saint George's feast withal.

Ten thousand soldiers with me I will take,
    Whose bloody deeds shall make all Europe quake.
MESSENGER. So you had need; for Orleans is besieged;
    The English army is grown weak and faint:
    The Earl of Salisbury craveth supply,
    And hardly keeps his men from mutiny,   160
    Since they, so few, watch such a multitude.   *Goes*
EXETER. Remember, lords, your oaths to Henry
    sworn:
    Either to quell the Dauphin utterly,
    Or bring him in obedience to your yoke.
BEDFORD. I do remember it; and here take my leave,
    To go about my preparation.   *Goes*
GLOUCESTER. I'll to the Tower with all the haste I can,
    To view th' artillery and munition;
    And then I will proclaim young Henry king.
                                        Goes
EXETER. To Eltham will I, where the young king is,   170
    Being ordained his special governor,
    And for his safety there I'll best devise.   *Goes*
WINCHESTER. Each hath his place and function to
    attend:
    I am left out; for me nothing remains.
    But long I will not be Jack out of office:
    The king from Eltham I intend to send
    And sit at chiefest stern of public weal.   *Goes*

Scene 2: *France. Before Orleans*

*Sound a Flourish. Enter Charles, Alençon, and Reignier,
marching with Drum and Soldiers*

CHARLES. Mars his true moving, even as in the heavens
    So in the earth, to this day is not known:
    Late did he shine upon the English side;
    Now we are victors; upon us he smiles.
    What towns of any moment but we have?
    At pleasure here we lie near Orleans;
    Otherwhiles the famished English, like pale ghosts,
    Faintly besiege us one hour in a month.
ALENÇON. They want their porridge and their fat
    bull-beeves:
    Either they must be dieted like mules   10
    And have their provender tied to their mouths,
    Or piteous they will look, like drownéd mice.
REIGNIER. Let's raise the siege: why live we idly here?
    Talbot is taken, whom we wont to fear:
    Remaineth none but mad-brained Salisbury;
    And he may well in fretting spend his gall,
    Nor men nor money hath he to make war.
CHARLES. Sound, sound alarum! we will rush on them.
    Now for the honour of the forlorn French!
    Him I forgive my death that killeth me   20
    When he sees me go back one foot or fly.
                                      They go

*Here alarum; they are beaten back by the English with great
loss. Re-enter Charles, Alençon, and Reignier*

CHARLES. Who ever saw the like? what men have I!
    Dogs! cowards! dastards! I would ne'er have fled,
    But that they left me 'midst my enemies.
REIGNIER. Salisbury is a desperate homicide;
    He fighteth as one weary of his life.
    The other lords, like lions wanting food,
    Do rush upon us as their hungry prey.
ALENÇON. Froissart, a countryman of ours, records,
    England all Olivers and Rowlands bred   30

During the time Edward the Third did reign.
More truly now may this be verified;
For none but Samsons and Goliases
It sendeth forth to skirmish. One to ten!
Lean raw-boned rascals! who would e'er suppose
They had such courage and audacity?
CHARLES. Let's leave this town; for they are
    hair-brained slaves,
And hunger will enforce them to be more eager:
Of old I know them; rather with their teeth
The walls they'll tear down than forsake the siege. 40
REIGNIER. I think, by some odd gimmors or device
Their arms are set like clocks, still to strike on;
Else ne'er could they hold out so as they do.
By my consent, we'll even let them alone.
ALENÇON. Be it so.

Enter the Bastard of Orleans

BASTARD. Where's the Prince Dauphin? I have news
    for him.
CHARLES. Bastard of Orleans, thrice welcome to us.
BASTARD. Methinks your looks are sad, your cheer
    appaled:
Hath the late overthrow wrought this offence?
Be not dismayed, for succour is at hand: 50
A holy maid hither with me I bring,
Which by a vision sent to her from heaven
Ordainéd is to raise this tedious siege
And drive the English forth the bounds of France.
The spirit of deep prophecy she hath,
Exceeding the nine sibyls of old Rome:
What's past and what's to come she can descry.
Speak, shall I call her in? Believe my words,
For they are certain and unfallible.
CHARLES. Go, call her in. [*Bastard goes out*] But first,
    to try her skill,   60
Reignier, stand thou as Dauphin in my place:
Question her proudly; let thy looks be stern:
By this means shall we sound what skill she hath.

Re-enter the Bastard of Orleans, with Joan La Pucelle

REIGNIER. Fair maid, is't thou wilt do these wondrous
    feats?
PUCELLE. Reignier, is't thou that thinkest to beguile
    me?
Where is the Dauphin? Come, come from behind;
I know thee well, though never seen before.
Be not amazed, there's nothing hid from me:
In private will I talk with thee apart.
Stand back, you lords, and give us leave awhile. 70
REIGNIER. She takes upon her bravely at first dash.
                The lords withdraw
PUCELLE. Dauphin, I am by birth a shepherd's
    daughter,
My wit untrained in any kind of art.
Heaven and our Lady gracious hath it pleased
To shine on my contemptible estate:
Lo, whilst I waited on my tender lambs,
And to sun's parching heat displayed my cheeks,
God's mother deignéd to appear to me
And in a vision full of majesty
Willed me to leave my base vocation   80
And free my country from calamity:
Her aid she promised and assured success:
In complete glory she revealed herself;
And, whereas I was black and swart before,
With those clear rays which she infused on me

That beauty am I blessed with which you may see.
Ask me what question thou canst possible,
And I will answer unpremeditated:
My courage try by combat, if thou dar'st,
And thou shalt find that I exceed my sex.   90
Resolve on this, thou shalt be fortunate
If thou receive me for thy warlike mate.
CHARLES. Thou hast astonished me with thy high
    terms:
Only this proof I'll of thy valour make,
In single combat thou shalt buckle with me,
And if thou vanquishest, thy words are true;
Otherwise I renounce all confidence.
PUCELLE. I am prepared: here is my keen-edged sword,
Decked with five flower-de-luces on each side;
The which at Touraine, in Saint Katharine's
    churchyard,   100
Out of a great deal of old iron I chose forth.
CHARLES. Then come, a God's name; I fear no woman.
PUCELLE. And while I live, I'll ne'er fly from a man.
       Here they fight, and Joan La Pucelle
                        overcomes
CHARLES. Stay, stay thy hands! thou art an Amazon,
And fightest with the sword of Deborah.
PUCELLE. Christ's mother helps me, else I were too
    weak.
CHARLES. Whoe'er helps thee, 'tis thou that must help
    me:
Impatiently I burn with thy desire;
My heart and hands thou hast at once subdued.
Excellent Pucelle, if thy name be so,
Let me thy servant and not sovereign be: 110
'Tis the French Dauphin sueth to thee thus.
PUCELLE. I must not yield to any rites of love,
For my profession's sacred from above:
When I have chaséd all thy foes from hence,
Then will I think upon a recompense.
CHARLES. Meantime look gracious on thy prostrate
    thrall.
REIGNIER. My lord, methinks, is very long in talk.
ALENÇON. Doubtless he shrives this woman to her
    smock;
Else ne'er could he so long protract his speech. 120
REIGNIER. Shall we disturb him, since he keeps no
    mean?
ALENÇON. He may mean more than we poor men
    do know:
These women are shrewd tempters with their
    tongues.   *They come forward*
REIGNIER. My lord, where are you? what devise you
    on?
Shall we give o'er Orleans, or no?
PUCELLE. Why, no, I say, distrustful recreants!
Fight till the last gasp; I'll be your guard.
CHARLES. What she says I'll confirm: we'll fight it out.
PUCELLE. Assigned am I to be the English scourge.
This night the siege assuredly I'll raise: 130
Expect Saint Martin's summer, halcyon days,
Since I have enteréd into these wars.
Glory is like a circle in the water,
Which never ceaseth to enlarge itself
Till by broad spreading it disperse to nought.
With Henry's death the English circle ends;
Disperséd are the glories it included.
Now am I like that proud insulting ship
Which Caesar and his fortune bare at once.

CHARLES. Was Mahomet inspiréd with a dove?   140
  Thou with an eagle art inspiréd then.
  Helen, the mother of great Constantine,
  Nor yet Saint Philip's daughters, were like thee.
  Bright star of Venus, fall'n down on the earth,
  How may I reverently worship thee enough?
ALENÇON. Leave off delays, and let us raise the siege.
REIGNIER. Woman, do what thou canst to save
    our honours;
  Drive them from Orleans and be immortalized.
CHARLES. Presently we'll try: come, let's away
    about it:
  No prophet will I trust, if she prove false.   150
                                    They go

        Scene 3: *London. Before the Tower*

*Enter the Duke of Gloucester, with his Serving-men in
blue coats*

GLOUCESTER. I am come to survey the Tower this day:
  Since Henry's death, I fear, there is conveyance.
  Where be these warders, that they wait not here?
  Open the gates; 'tis Gloucester that calls.
              Serving-men knock at the gates
I WARDER [*within*]. Who's there that knocks so
    imperiously?
I SERVING-MAN. It is the noble Duke of Gloucester.
2 WARDER [*within*]. Whoe'er he be, you may not be
    let in.
I SERVING-MAN. Villains, answer you so the lord
    protector?
I WARDER [*within*]. The Lord protect him! so we
    answer him:
  We do no otherwise than we are willed.   10
GLOUCESTER. Who willéd you? or whose will stands
    but mine?
  There's none protector of the realm but I.
  Break up the gates, I'll be your warrantize:
  Shall I be flouted thus by dunghill grooms?
              *Gloucester's men rush at the
              Tower Gates, and Woodville
              the Lieutenant speaks within*
WOODVILLE. What noise is this? what traitors have
    we here?
GLOUCESTER. Lieutenant, is it you whose voice I hear?
  Open the gates; here's Gloucester that would enter.
WOODVILLE. Have patience, noble duke; I may not
    open;
  The Cardinal of Winchester forbids:
  From him I have express commandment   20
  That thou nor none of thine shall be let in.
GLOUCESTER. Faint-hearted Woodville, prizest him
    'fore me?
  Arrogant Winchester, that haughty prelate,
  Whom Henry, our late sovereign, ne'er could
    brook?
  Thou art no friend to God or to the king:
  Open the gates, or I'll shut thee out shortly.
SERVING-MEN. Open the gates unto the lord protector,
  Or we'll burst them open, if that you come not
    quickly.

*Enter to the Protector at the Tower Gates Winchester and
his men in tawny coats*

WINCHESTER. How now, ambitious Humphrey! what
  means this?

GLOUCESTER. Peeled priest, dost thou command me to
    be shut out?   30
WINCHESTER. I do, thou most usurping proditor,
  And not protector, of the king or realm.
GLOUCESTER. Stand back, thou manifest conspirator,
  Thou that contriv'dst to murder our dead lord;
  Thou that giv'st whores indulgences to sin:
  I'll canvass thee in thy broad cardinal's hat,
  If thou proceed in this thy insolence.
WINCHESTER. Nay, stand thou back, I will not budge
    a foot:
  This be Damascus, be thou curséd Cain,
  To slay thy brother Abel, if thou wilt.   40
GLOUCESTER. I will not slay thee, but I'll drive thee
    back:
  Thy scarlet robes as a child's bearing-cloth
  I'll use to carry thee out of this place.
WINCHESTER. Do what thou dar'st, I beard thee to thy
    face.
GLOUCESTER. What! am I dared and bearded to my
    face?
  Draw, men, for all this privilegéd place,
  Blue coats to tawny coats. Priest, beware your
    beard,
  I mean to tug it, and to cuff you soundly.
  Under my feet I'll stamp thy cardinal's hat:
  In spite of pope or dignities of church,   50
  Here by the cheeks I'll drag thee up and down.
WINCHESTER. Gloucester, thou wilt answer this before
    the pope.
GLOUCESTER. Winchester goose, I cry, a rope! a rope!
  Now beat them hence, why do you let them stay?
  Thee I'll chase hence, thou wolf in sheep's array.
  Out, tawny coats! out, scarlet hypocrite!

*Here Gloucester's men beat out the Cardinal's men, and
enter in the hurly-burly the Mayor of London and his
Officers*

MAYOR. Fie, lords! that you, being supreme
    magistrates,
  Thus contumeliously should break the peace!
GLOUCESTER. Peace, mayor! thou know'st little of my
    wrongs:
  Here's Beaufort, that regards nor God nor king,   60
  Hath here distrained the Tower to his use.
WINCHESTER. Here's Gloucester, a foe to citizens,
  One that still motions war and never peace,
  O'ercharging your free purses with large fines,
  That seeks to overthrow religion,
  Because he is protector of the realm,
  And would have armour here out of the Tower,
  To crown himself king and suppress the prince.
GLOUCESTER. I will not answer thee with words, but
    blows.   *Here they skirmish again*
MAYOR. Nought rests for me in this tumultuous strife   70
  But to make open proclamation:
  Come, officer, as loud as e'er thou canst,
  Cry.
OFFICER. All manner of men assembled here in arms
  this day against God's peace and the king's, we
  charge and command you, in his highness' name, to
  repair to your several dwelling-places; and not to
  wear, handle, or use any sword, weapon, or dagger,
  henceforward, upon pain of death.
GLOUCESTER. Cardinal, I'll be no breaker of the law: 80
  But we shall meet, and break our minds at large.

WINCHESTER. Gloucester, we'll meet; to thy cost, be
 sure:
 Thy heart-blood I will have for this day's work.
MAYOR. I'll call for clubs, if you will not away.
 This cardinal's more haughty than the devil.
GLOUCESTER. Mayor, farewell: thou dost but what
 thou mayst.
WINCHESTER. Abominable Gloucester, guard thy
 head;
 For I intend to have it ere long.
     Gloucester and Winchester withdraw
        with their Serving-men
MAYOR. See the coast cleared, and then we will depart.
 Good God, these nobles should such stomachs bear! 90
 I myself fight not once in forty year. *They go*

Scene 4: *Orleans*

Enter the Master Gunner of Orleans and his Boy

MASTER GUNNER. Sirrah, thou know'st how Orleans
 is besieged,
 And how the English have the suburbs won.
BOY. Father, I know, and oft have shot at them,
 Howe'er unfortunate I missed my aim.
MASTER GUNNER. But now thou shalt not. Be thou
 ruled by me:
 Chief master-gunner am I of this town,
 Something I must do to procure me grace.
 The prince's espials have informéd me
 How the English, in the suburbs close intrenched,
 Wont through a secret grate of iron bars 10
 In yonder tower to overpeer the city
 And thence discover how with most advantage
 They may vex us with shot or with assault.
 To intercept this inconvenience,
 A piece of ordnance 'gainst it I have placed,
 And even these three days have I watched,
 If I could see them. Now do thou watch,
 For I can stay no longer.
 If thou spy'st any, run and bring me word;
 And thou shalt find me at the governor's. 20
        He goes one way
BOY. Father, I warrant you; take you no care;
 I'll never trouble you, if I may spy them.
        He goes another

Enter Salisbury and Talbot on the turrets, with Glansdale,
Gargrave, and others

SALISBURY. Talbot, my life, my joy, again returned!
 How wert thou handled being prisoner?
 Or by what means gots thou to be released?
 Discourse, I prithee, on this turret's top.
TALBOT. The Earl of Bedford had a prisoner
 Called the brave Lord Ponton de Santrailles;
 For him was I exchanged and ransoméd.
 But with a baser man of arms by far 30
 Once in contempt they would have bartered me:
 Which I disdaining scorned and cravéd death
 Rather than I would be so pilled-esteemed.
 In fine, redeemed I was as I desired.
 But, O! the treacherous Falstaff wounds my heart,
 Whom with my bare fists I would execute,
 If I now had him brought into my power.
SALISBURY. Yet tell'st thou not how thou wert
 entertained.

TALBOT. With scoffs and scorns and contumelious
 taunts,
 In open market-place produced they me, 40
 To be a public spectacle to all:
 Here, said they, is the terror of the French,
 The scarecrow that affrights our children so.
 Then broke I from the officers that led me,
 And with my nails digged stones out of the ground,
 To hurl at the beholders of my shame.
 My grisly countenance made others fly;
 None durst come near for fear of sudden death.
 In iron walls they deemed me not secure;
 So great fear of my name 'mongst them was spread 50
 That they supposed I could rend bars of steel
 And spurn in pieces posts of adamant:
 Wherefore a guard of chosen shot I had
 That walked about me every minute while;
 And if I did but stir out of my bed,
 Ready they were to shoot me to the heart.

Enter the Boy with a linstock

SALISBURY. I grieve to hear what torments you
 endured,
 But we will be revenged sufficiently.
 Now it is supper-time in Orleans:
 Here, through this grate, I count each one 60
 And view the Frenchmen how they fortify:
 Let us look in; the sight will much delight thee.
 Sir Thomas Gargrave, and Sir William Glansdale,
 Let me have your express opinions
 Where is best place to make our battery next.
GARGRAVE. I think at the north gate; for there stands
 lords.
GLANSDALE. And I, here, at the bulwark of the bridge.
TALBOT. For aught I see, this city must be famished,
 Or with light skirmishes enfeebléd.
   Here cannon heard; Salisbury and Gargrave fall
SALISBURY. O Lord, have mercy on us, wretched
 sinners! 70
GARGRAVE. O Lord, have mercy on me, woeful man!
TALBOT. What chance is this that suddenly hath
 crossed us?
 Speak, Salisbury; at least, if thou canst speak:
 How far'st thou, mirror of all martial men?
 One of thy eyes and thy cheek's side struck off!
 Acccurséd tower! accurséd fatal hand
 That hath contrived this woful tragedy!
 In thirteen battles Salisbury o'ercame;
 Henry the Fifth he first trained to the wars;
 Whilst any trump did sound, or drum struck up, 80
 His sword did ne'er leave striking in the field.
 Yet liv'st thou, Salisbury? though thy speech doth
 fail,
 One eye thou hast, to look to heaven for grace:
 The sun with one eye vieweth all the world.
 Heaven, be thou gracious to none alive,
 If Salisbury wants mercy at thy hands!
 Bear hence his body; I will help to bury it.
 Sir Thomas Gargrave, hast thou any life?
 Speak unto Talbot; nay, look up to him.
 Salisbury, cheer thy spirit with this comfort; 90
 Thou shalt not die whiles—
 He beckons with his hand and smiles on me,
 As who should say 'When I am dead and gone,
 Remember to avenge me on the French.'
 Plantagenet, I will; and like thee, [Nero,]

Play on the lute, beholding the towns burn:
Wretched shall France be only in my name.

*Here an alarum, and it thunders
and lightens*

What stir is this? what tumult's in the heavens?
Whence cometh this alarum, and the noise?

Enter a Messenger

MESSENGER. My lord, my lord, the French have
gathered head: 100
The Dauphin, with one Joan la Pucelle joined,
A holy prophetess new risen up,
Is come with a great power to raise the siege.

*Here Salisbury lifteth himself up
and groans*

TALBOT. Hear, hear how dying Salisbury doth groan!
It irks his heart he cannot be revenged.
Frenchmen, I'll be a Salisbury to you:
Pucelle or pussel, dolphin or dogfish,
Your hearts I'll stamp out with my horse's heels,
And make a quagmire of your mingled brains.
Convey me Salisbury into his tent,   110
And then we'll try what these dastard Frenchmen
dare.

*Alarum; they bear out Salisbury
and Gargrave*

Scene 5

*Here an alarum again: and Talbot pursueth the Dauphin,
and driveth him: then enter Joan La Pucelle, driving
Englishmen before her, and exit after them: then re-enter
Talbot*

TALBOT. Where is my strength, my valour, and my
force?
Our English troops retire, I cannot stay them;
A woman clad in armour chaseth them.

Re-enter La Pucelle

Here, here she comes. I'll have a bout with thee;
Devil or devil's dam, I'll conjure thee:
Blood will I draw on thee, thou art a witch,
And straightway give thy soul to him thou serv'st.
PUCELLE. Come, come, 'tis only I that must disgrace
thee.   *Here they fight*
TALBOT. Heavens, can you suffer hell so to prevail?
My breast I'll burst with straining of my courage   10
And from my shoulders crack my arms asunder,
But I will chastise this high-minded strumpet.
                                          They fight again
PUCELLE. Talbot, farewell; thy hour is not yet come:
I must go victual Orleans forthwith.

*A short alarum: then enter the town
with soldiers*

O'ertake me, if thou canst; I scorn thy strength.
Go, go, cheer up thy hungry-starvéd men;
Help Salisbury to make his testament:
This day is ours, as many more shall be.   *She goes*
TALBOT. My thoughts are whirléd like a potter's
wheel;
I know not where I am, nor what I do: 20
A witch, by fear, not force, like Hannibal,
Drives back our troops and conquers as she lists:
So bees with smoke and doves with noisome stench
Are from their hives and houses driv'n away.
They called us for our fierceness English dogs;
Now, like to whelps, we crying run away.

A short alarum

Hark, countrymen! either renew the fight,
Or tear the lions out of England's coat;
Renounce your soil, give sheep in lions' stead:
Sheep run not half so treacherous from the wolf,   30
Or horse or oxen from the leopard,
As you fly from your oft-subdued slaves.

Alarum; here another skirmish

It will not be! retire into your trenches:
You all consented unto Salisbury's death,
For none would strike a stroke in his revenge.
Pucelle is entered into Orleans,
In spite of us or aught that we could do.
O, would I were to die with Salisbury!
The shame hereof will make me hide my head.

He goes

Scene 6: *Alarum; retreat; flourish*

*Enter on the walls La Pucelle, Dauphin, Reignier, Alençon,
and Soldiers*

PUCELLE. Advance our waving colours on the walls;
Rescuéd is Orleans from the English:
Thus Joan la Pucelle hath performed her word.
CHARLES. Divinest creature, Astræa's daughter,
How shall I honour thee for this success?
Thy promises are like Adonis' gardens
That one day bloomed and fruitful were the next.
France, triumph in thy glorious prophetess!
Recovered is the town of Orleans:
More blesséd hap did ne'er befall our state.   10
REIGNIER. Why ring not out the bells aloud
throughout the town?
Dauphin, command the citizens make bonfires
And feast and banquet in the open streets,
To celebrate the joy that God hath given us.
ALENÇON. All France will be replete with mirth and
joy,
When they shall hear how we have played the men.
CHARLES. 'Tis Joan, not we, by whom the day is won;
For which I will divide my crown with her,
And all the priests and friars in my realm
Shall in procession sing her endless praise.   20
A statelier pyramis to her I'll rear
Than Rhodope's of Memphis ever was:
In memory of her when she is dead,
Her ashes, in an urn more precious
Than the rich-jewelled coffer of Darius,
Transported shall be at high festivals
Before the kings and queens of France.
No longer on Saint Denis will we cry,
But Joan la Pucelle shall be France's saint.
Come in, and let us banquet royally,   30
After this golden day of victory.   *Flourish; they go*

ACT 2
Scene 1: *The same*

*Enter a French Sergeant of a band, with two Sentinels,
to the gate*

SERGEANT. Sirs, take your places and be vigilant:
If any noise or soldier you perceive
Near to the walls, by some apparent sign
Let us have knowledge at the court of guard.
1 SENTINEL. Sergeant, you shall. [*Sergeant goes*] Thus
are poor servitors,
When others sleep upon their quiet beds,

Constrained to watch in darkness, rain, and cold.

Enter Talbot, Bedford, Burgundy, and forces, with scaling-ladders

TALBOT. Lord Regent, and redoubted Burgundy,
By whose approach the regions of Artois,
Wallon and Picardy are friends to us, 10
This happy night the Frenchmen are secure,
Having all day caroused and banqueted:
Embrace we then this opportunity
As fitting best to quittance their deceit
Contrived by art and baleful sorcery.
BEDFORD. Coward of France! how much he wrongs
his fame,
Despairing of his own arm's fortitude,
To join with witches and the help of hell!
BURGUNDY. Traitors have never other company.
But what's that Pucelle whom they term so pure? 20
TALBOT. A maid, they say.
BEDFORD.   A maid? and be so martial?
BURGUNDY. Pray God she prove not masculine ere
long,
If underneath the standard of the French
She carry armour as she hath begun.
TALBOT. Well, let them practise and converse with
spirits:
God is our fortress, in whose conquering name
Let us resolve to scale their flinty bulwarks.
BEDFORD. Ascend, brave Talbot; we will follow thee.
TALBOT. Not all together: better far, I guess,
That we do make our entrance several ways; 30
That, if it chance the one of us do fail,
The other yet may rise against their force.
BEDFORD. Agreed: I'll to yond corner.
BURGUNDY.   And I to this.
TALBOT. And here will Talbot mount, or make his
grave.
Now, Salisbury, for thee, and for the right
Of English Henry, shall this night appear
How much in duty I am bound to both.
                    *The English, scaling the walls,
                    cry St. George! a Talbot!*
SENTINEL. Arm! arm! the enemy doth make assault!

*The French leap over the walls in their shirts; among them
the Bastard of Orleans, Alençon, and Reignier, half ready,
and half unready*

ALENÇON. How now, my lords! what, all unready so?
BASTARD. Unready! ay, and glad we 'scaped so well. 40
REIGNIER. 'Twas time, I trow, to wake and leave our
beds,
Hearing alarums at our chamber-doors.
ALENÇON. Of all exploits since first I followed arms,
Ne'er heard I of a warlike enterprise
More venturous or desperate than this.
BASTARD. I think this Talbot be a fiend of hell.
REIGNIER. If not of hell, the heavens, sure, favour him.
ALENÇON. Here cometh Charles: I marvel how he
sped.
BASTARD. Tut, holy Joan was his defensive guard.

Enter Charles and La Pucelle

CHARLES. Is this thy cunning, thou deceitful dame? 50
Didst thou at first, to flatter us withal,
Make us partakers of a little gain,
That now our loss might be ten times so much?

PUCELLE. Wherefore is Charles impatient with his
friend?
At all times will you have my power alike?
Sleeping or waking must I still prevail,
Or will you blame and lay the fault on me?
Improvident soldiers! had your watch been good,
This sudden mischief never could have fall'n.
CHARLES. Duke of Alençon, this was your default, 60
That, being captain of the watch to-night,
Did look no better to that weighty charge.
ALENÇON. Had all your quarters been as safely kept
As that whereof I had the government,
We had not been thus shamefully surprised.
BASTARD. Mine was secure.
REIGNIER.   And so was mine, my lord.
CHARLES. And, for myself, most part of all this night,
Within her quarter and mine own precinct
I was employed in passing to and fro,
About relieving of the sentinels: 70
Then how or which way should they first break in?
PUCELLE. Question, my lords, no further of the case,
How or which way: 'tis sure they found some place
But weakly guarded, where the breach was made.
And now there rests no other shift but this;
To gather our soldiers, scattered and dispersed,
And lay new platforms to endamage them.

*Alarum. Enter an English Soldier, crying A Talbot! a
Talbot! They fly, leaving their clothes behind*

SOLDIER. I'll be so bold to take what they have left.
The cry of Talbot serves me for a sword;
For I have loaden me with many spoils, 80
Using no other weapon but his name.   *He goes*

Scene 2: *Orleans. Within the town*

Enter Talbot, Bedford, Burgundy, a Captain, and others

BEDFORD. The day begins to break, and night is fled,
Whose pitchy mantle over-veiled the earth.
Here sound retreat, and cease our hot pursuit.
                              Retreat sounded
TALBOT. Bring forth the body of old Salisbury,
And here advance it in the market-place,
The middle centre of this cursèd town.
Now have I paid my vow unto his soul;
For every drop of blood was drawn from him
There hath at least five Frenchmen died to-night.
And that hereafter ages may behold 10
What ruin happened in revenge of him,
Within their chiefest temple I'll erect
A tomb, wherein his corpse shall be interred:
Upon the which, that every one may read,
Shall be engraved the sack of Orleans,
The treacherous manner of his mournful death
And what a terror he had been to France.
But, lords, in all our bloody massacre,
I muse we met not with the Dauphin's grace,
His new-come champion, virtuous Joan of Arc, 20
Nor any of his false confederates.
BEDFORD. 'Tis thought, Lord Talbot, when the fight
began,
Roused on the sudden from their drowsy beds,
They did amongst the troops of armèd men
Leap o'er the walls for refuge in the field.
BURGUNDY. Myself, as far as I could well discern
For smoke and dusky vapours of the night,

Am sure I scared the Dauphin and his trull,
When arm in arm they both came swiftly running,
Like to a pair of loving turtle-doves   30
That could not live asunder day or night.
After that things are set in order here,
We'll follow them with all the power we have.

Enter a Messenger

MESSENGER. All hail, my lords! Which of this princely
    train
Call ye the warlike Talbot, for his acts
So much applauded through the realm of France?
TALBOT. Here is the Talbot: who would speak with
    him?
MESSENGER. The virtuous lady, Countess of Auvergne,
With modesty admiring thy renown,
By me entreats, great lord, thou wouldst vouchsafe   40
To visit her poor castle where she lies,
That she may boast she hath beheld the man
Whose glory fills the world with loud report.
BURGUNDY. Is it even so? Nay, then, I see our wars
Will turn unto a peaceful comic sport,
When ladies crave to be encountered with.
You may not, my lord, despise her gentle suit.
TALBOT. Ne'er trust me then; for when a world of men
Could not prevail with all their oratory,
Yet hath a woman's kindness over-ruled: 50
And therefore tell her I return great thanks,
And in submission will attend on her.
Will not your honours bear me company?
BEDFORD. No, truly; 'tis more than manners will:
And I have heard it said, unbidden guests
Are often welcomest when they are gone.
TALBOT. Well then, alone, since there's no remedy,
I mean to prove this lady's courtesy.
Come hither, captain. [*whispers*] You perceive my
    mind?
CAPTAIN. I do, my lord, and mean accordingly.   60
                                            They go

Scene 3: *Auvergne. The Countess's castle*

Enter the Countess and her Porter

COUNTESS. Porter, remember what I gave in charge;
And when you have done so, bring the keys to me.
PORTER. Madam, I will.   *He goes*
COUNTESS. The plot is laid: if all things fall out right,
I shall as famous be by this exploit
As Scythian Tomyris by Cyrus' death.
Great is the rumour of this dreadful knight,
And his achievements of no less account:
Fain would mine eyes be witness with mine ears,
To give their censure of these rare reports.   10

Enter Messenger and Talbot

MESSENGER. Madam,
According as your ladyship desired,
By message craved, so is Lord Talbot come.
COUNTESS. And he is welcome. What! is this the
    man?
MESSENGER. Madam, it is.
COUNTESS.   Is this the scourge of France?
Is this the Talbot, so much feared abroad
That with his name the mothers still their babes?
I see report is fabulous and false:
I thought I should have seen some Hercules,
A second Hector, for his grim aspect,   20

And large proportion of his strong-knit limbs.
Alas, this is a child, a silly dwarf!
It cannot be this weak and writhled shrimp
Should strike such terror to his enemies.
TALBOT. Madam, I have been bold to trouble you;
But since your ladyship is not at leisure,
I'll sort some other time to visit you.
COUNTESS. What means he now? Go ask him whither
    he goes.
MESSENGER. Stay, my Lord Talbot; for my lady craves
To know the cause of your abrupt departure.   30
TALBOT. Marry, for that she's in a wrong belief,
I go to certify her Talbot's here.

Re-enter Porter with keys

COUNTESS. If thou be he, then art thou prisoner.
TALBOT. Prisoner! to whom?
COUNTESS.   To me, blood-thirsty lord;
And for that cause I trained thee to my house.
Long time thy shadow hath been thrall to me,
For in my gallery thy picture hangs:
But now the substance shall endure the like,
And I will chain these legs and arms of thine,
That hast by tyranny these many years   40
Wasted our country, slain our citizens,
And sent our sons and husbands captivate.
TALBOT. Ha, ha, ha!
COUNTESS. Laughest thou, wretch? thy mirth shall
    turn to moan.
TALBOT. I laugh to see your ladyship so fond
To think that you have aught but Talbot's shadow
Whereon to practise your severity.
COUNTESS. Why, art not thou the man?
TALBOT.   I am indeed.
COUNTESS. Then have I substance too.
TALBOT. No, no, I am but shadow of myself: 50
You are deceived, my substance is not here;
For what you see is but the smallest part
And least proportion of humanity:
I tell you, madam, were the whole frame here,
It is of such a spacious lofty pitch,
Your roof were not sufficient to contain 't.
COUNTESS. This is a riddling merchant for the nonce;
He will be here, and yet he is not here:
How can these contrarieties agree?
TALBOT. That will I show you presently.   60
            *Winds his horn: drums strike up: a peal
                        of ordnance: enter soldiers*
How say you, madam? are you now persuaded
That Talbot is but shadow of himself?
These are his substance, sinews, arms and strength,
With which he yoketh your rebellious necks,
Razeth your cities and subverts your towns
And in a moment makes them desolate.
COUNTESS. Victorious Talbot! pardon my abuse:
I find thou art no less than fame hath bruited
And more than may be gathered by thy shape.
Let my presumption not provoke thy wrath;   70
For I am sorry that with reverence
I did not entertain thee as thou art.
TALBOT. Be not dismayed, fair lady; nor misconster
The mind of Talbot, as you did mistake
The outward composition of his body.
What you have done hath not offended me;
Nor other satisfaction do I crave,
But only, with your patience, that we may

Taste of your wine and see what cates you have;
For soldiers' stomachs always serve them well.   80
COUNTESS. With all my heart, and think me
honouréd
To feast so great a warrior in my house.   *They go*

Scene 4: *London. The Temple-garden*

*Enter the Earls of Somerset, Suffolk, and Warwick;
Richard Plantagenet, Vernon, and another Lawyer*

PLANTAGENET. Great lords and gentlemen, what means
this silence?
Dare no man answer in a case of truth?
SUFFOLK. Within the Temple-hall we were too loud;
The garden here is more convenient.
PLANTAGENET. Then say at once if I maintained the
truth;
Or else was wrangling Somerset in th'error?
SUFFOLK. Faith, I have been a truant in the law,
And never yet could frame my will to it;
And therefore frame the law unto my will.
SOMERSET. Judge you, my lord of Warwick, then,
between us.   10
WARWICK. Between two hawks, which flies the
higher pitch;
Between two dogs, which hath the deeper mouth;
Between two blades, which bears the better temper;
Between two horses, which doth bear him best;
Between two girls, which hath the merriest eye;
I have perhaps some shallow spirit of judgement:
But in these nice sharp quillets of the law,
Good faith, I am no wiser than a daw.
PLANTAGENET. Tut, tut, here is a mannerly
forbearance.
The truth appears so naked on my side   20
That any purblind eye may find it out.
SOMERSET. And on my side it is so well apparelled,
So clear, so shining and so evident,
That it will glimmer through a blind man's eye.
PLATAGENET. Since you are tongue-tied and so loath to
speak,
In dumb significants proclaim your thoughts:
Let him that is a true-born gentleman,
And stands upon the honour of his birth,
If he suppose that I have pleaded truth,
From off this brier pluck a white rose with me.   30
SOMERSET. Let him that is no coward nor no flatterer,
But dare maintain the party of the truth,
Pluck a red rose from off this thorn with me.
WARWICK. I love no colours; and without all colour
Of base insinuating flattery
I pluck this white rose with Plantagenet.
SUFFOLK. I pluck this red rose with young Somerset
And say withal I think he held the right.
VERNON. Stay, lords and gentlemen, and pluck no
more,
Till you conclude that he upon whose side   40
The fewest roses are cropped from the tree
Shall yield the other in the right opinion.
SOMERSET. Good master Vernon, it is well objected:
If I have fewest, I subscribe in silence.
PLANTAGENET. And I.
VERNON. Then for the truth and plainness of the case,
I pluck this pale and maiden blossom here,
Giving my verdict on the white rose side.
SOMERSET. Prick not your finger as you pluck it off,

Lest bleeding you do paint the white rose red   50
And fall on my side so, against your will.
VERNON. If I, my lord, for my opinion bleed,
Opinion shall be surgeon to my hurt
And keep me on the side where still I am.
SOMERSET. Well, well, come on, who else?
LAWYER. Unless my study and my books be false,
The argument you held was wrong in you;
To Somerset
In sign whereof I pluck a white rose too.
PLANTAGENET. Now, Somerset, where is your
argument?
SOMERSET. Here in my scabbard, meditating that   60
Shall dye your white rose in a bloody red.
PLANTAGENET. Meantime your cheeks do counterfeit
our roses;
For pale they look with fear, as witnessing
The truth on our side.
SOMERSET.   No, Plantagenet,
'Tis not for fear but anger—that thy cheeks
Blush for pure shame to counterfeit our roses,
And yet thy tongue will not confess thy error.
PLANTAGENET. Hath not thy rose a canker, Somerset?
SOMERSET. Hath not thy rose a thorn, Plantagenet?
PLANTAGENET. Ay, sharp and piercing, to maintain his
truth;   70
Whiles thy consuming canker eats his falsehood.
SOMERSET. Well, I'll find friends to wear my bleeding
roses,
That shall maintain what I have said is true,
Where false Plantagenet dare not be seen.
PLANTAGENET. Now, by this maiden blossom in my
hand,
I scorn thee and thy fashion, peevish boy.
SUFFOLK. Turn not thy scorns this way, Plantagenet.
PLANTAGENET. Proud Pole, I will, and scorn both him
and thee.
SUFFOLK. I'll turn my part thereof into thy throat.
SOMERSET. Away, away, good William de la Pole!   80
We grace the yeoman by conversing with him.
WARWICK. Now, by God's will, thou wrong'st him,
Somerset;
His grandfather was Lionel Duke of Clarence,
Third son to the third Edward King of England:
Spring crestless yeomen from so deep a root?
PLANTAGENET. He bears him on the place's privilege,
Or durst not, for his craven heart, say thus.
SOMERSET. By him that made me, I'll maintain my
words
On any plot of ground in Christendom.
Was not thy father, Richard Earl of Cambridge,   90
For treason executed in our late king's days?
And, by his treason, stand'st not thou attainted,
Corrupted, and exempt from ancient gentry?
His trespass yet lives guilty in thy blood;
And, till thou be restored, thou art a yeoman.
PLANTAGENET. My father was attachéd, not attainted,
Condemned to die for treason, but no traitor;
And that I'll prove on better men than Somerset,
Were growing time once ripened to my will.
For your partaker Pole and you yourself,   100
I'll note you in my book of memory,
To scourge you for this apprehension:
Look to it well and say you are well warned.
SOMERSET. Ah, thou shalt find us ready for thee still;
And know us by these colours for thy foes,

For these my friends in spite of thee shall wear.
PLANTAGENET. And, by my soul, this pale and angry
  rose,
  As cognizance of my blood-drinking hate,
  Will I for ever and my faction wear,
  Until it wither with me to my grave   110
  Or flourish to the height of my degree.
SUFFOLK. Go forward and be choked with thy
  ambition!
  And so farewell until I meet thee next.   *He goes*
SOMERSET. Have with thee, Pole. Farewell, ambitious
  Richard.   *He goes*
PLANTAGENET. How I am braved and must perforce
  endure it!
WARWICK. This blot that they object against your
  house
  Shall be wiped out in the next parliament
  Called for the truce of Winchester and Gloucester;
  And if thou be not then created York,
  I will not live to be accounted Warwick.   120
  Meantime, in signal of my love to thee,
  Against proud Somerset and William Pole,
  Will I upon thy party wear this rose:
  And here I prophesy: this brawl to-day,
  Grown to this faction in the Temple-garden,
  Shall send between the red rose and the white
  A thousand souls to death and deadly night.
PLANTAGENET. Good Master Vernon, I am bound to
  you,
  That you on my behalf would pluck a flower.
VERNON. In your behalf still will I wear the same.   130
LAWYER. And so will I.
PLANTAGENET. Thanks, gentle sir.
  Come, let us four to dinner: I dare say
  This quarrel will drink blood another day.
                                                   They go

Scene 5: *The Tower of London*

Enter Mortimer, brought in a chair, and Gaolers

MORTIMER. Kind keepers of my weak decaying age,
  Let dying Mortimer here rest himself.
  Even like a man new haléd from the rack,
  So fare my limbs with long imprisonment;
  And these grey locks, the pursuivants of death,
  Nestor-like agéd in an age of care,
  Argue the end of Edmund Mortimer.
  These eyes, like lamps whose wasting oil is spent,
  Wax dim, as drawing to their exigent;
  Weak shoulders, overborne with burth'ning grief,   10
  And pithless arms, like to a withered vine
  That droops his sapless branches to the ground:
  Yet are these feet, whose strengthless stay is numb,
  Unable to support this lump of clay,
  Swift-wingéd with desire to get a grave,
  As witting I no other comfort have.
  But tell me, keeper, will my nephew come?
1 GAOLER. Richard Plantagenet, my lord, will come:
  We sent unto the Temple, unto his chamber;
  And answer was returned that he will come.   20
MORTIMER. Enough: my soul shall then be satisfied.
  Poor gentleman! his wrong doth equal mine.
  Since Henry Monmouth first began to reign,
  Before whose glory I was great in arms,
  This loathsome sequestration have I had;
  And even since then hath Richard been obscured,

Deprived of honour and inheritance.
  But now the arbitrator of despairs,
  Just Death, kind umpire of men's miseries,
  With sweet enlargement doth dismiss me hence: 30
  I would his troubles likewise were expired,
  That so he might recover what was lost.

Enter Richard Plantagenet

1 GAOLER. My lord, your loving nephew now is come.
MORTIMER. Richard Plantagenet, my friend, is
  he come?
PLANTAGENET. Ay, noble uncle, thus ignobly used,
  Your nephew, late despiséd Richard, comes.
MORTIMER. Direct mine arms I may embrace his neck,
  And in his bosom spend my latter gasp:
  O, tell me when my lips do touch his cheeks,
  That I may kindly give one fainting kiss.   40
  And now declare, sweet stem from York's great
  stock,
  Why didst thou say, of late thou wert despised?
PLANTAGENET. First, lean thine agéd back against
  mine arm,
  And, in that ease, I'll tell thee my disease.
  This day, in argument upon a case,
  Some words there grew 'twixt Somerset and me:
  Among which terms he used his lavish tongue
  And did upbraid me with my father's death:
  Which obloquy set bars before my tongue,
  Else with the like I had requited him.   50
  Therefore, good uncle, for my father's sake,
  In honour of a true Plantagenet
  And for alliance sake, declare the cause
  My father, Earl of Cambridge, lost his head.
MORTIMER. That cause, fair nephew, that imprisoned
  me
  And hath detained me all my flow'ring youth
  Within a loathsome dungeon, there to pine,
  Was curséd instrument of his decease.
PLANTAGENET. Discover more at large what cause
  that was,
  For I am ignorant and cannot guess.   60
MORTIMER. I will, if that my fading breath permit
  And death approach not ere my tale be done.
  Henry the Fourth, grandfather to this king,
  Deposed his nephew Richard, Edward's son,
  The first-begotten and the lawful heir
  Of Edward king, the third of that descent:
  During whose reign the Percies of the north,
  Finding his usurpation most unjust,
  Endeavoured my advancement to the throne:
  The reason moved these warlike lords to this   70
  Was, for that—young King Richard thus removed,
  Leaving no heir begotten of his body—
  I was the next by birth and parentage;
  For by my mother I derivéd am
  From Lionel Duke of Clarence, third son
  To King Edward the Third; whereas he
  From John of Gaunt doth bring his pedigree,
  Being but fourth of that heroic line.
  But mark: as in this haughty great attempt
  They labouréd to plant the rightful heir,   80
  I lost my liberty and they their lives.
  Long after this, when Henry the Fifth,
  Succeeding his father Bolingbroke, did reign,
  Thy father, Earl of Cambridge, then derived
  From famous Edmund Langley, Duke of York,

Marrying my sister that thy mother was,
Again in pity of my hard distress
Levied an army, weening to redeem
And have installed me in the diadem:
But, as the rest, so fell that noble earl   90
And was beheaded. Thus the Mortimers,
In whom the title rested, were suppressed.
PLANTAGENET. Of which, my lord, your honour is
    the last.
MORTIMER. True; and thou seest that I no issue have
And that my fainting words do warrant death:
Thou art my heir; the rest I wish thee gather:
But yet be wary in thy studious care.
PLANTAGENET. Thy grave admonishments prevail
    with me:
But yet, methinks, my father's execution
Was nothing less than bloody tyranny.   100
MORTIMER. With silence, nephew, be thou politic:
Strong-fixéd is the house of Lancaster,
And like a mountain, not to be removed.
But now thy uncle is removing hence;
As princes do their courts, when they are cloyed
With long continuance in a settled place.
PLANTAGENET. O, uncle, would some part of my
    young years
Might but redeem the passage of your age!
MORTIMER. Thou dost then wrong me, as that
    slaughterer doth
Which giveth many wounds when one will kill.   110
Mourn not, except thou sorrow for my good;
Only give order for my funeral:
And so farewell, and fair be all thy hopes
And prosperous be thy life in peace and war!
                                              Dies
PLANTAGENET. And peace, no war, befall thy parting
    soul!
In prison hast thou spent a pilgrimage
And like a hermit overpassed thy days.
Well, I will lock his counsel in my breast,
And what I do imagine let that rest.
Keepers, convey him hence, and I myself   120
Will see his burial better than his life.
    The Gaolers bear away the body of Mortimer
Here dies the dusky torch of Mortimer,
Choked with ambition of the meaner sort.
And for those wrongs, those bitter injuries,
Which Somerset hath offered to my house,
I doubt not but with honour to redress;
And therefore haste I to the parliament,
Either to be restoréd to my blood,
Or make my ill th'advantage of my good.
                                            He goes

ACT 3

Scene 1: *London. The Parliament-house*

*Flourish. Enter King, Exeter, Gloucester, Winchester,
Warwick, Somerset, Suffolk, Richard Plantagenet. Gloucester offers to put up a bill; Winchester snatches it, tears it*

WINCHESTER. Com'st thou with deep premeditated
    lines,
With written pamphlets studiously devised,
Humphrey of Gloucester? If thou canst accuse,
Or aught intend'st to lay unto my charge,
Do it without invention, suddenly,

As I with sudden and extemporal speech
Purpose to answer what thou canst object.
GLOUCESTER. Presumptuous priest! this place
    commands my patience,
Or thou shouldst find thou hast dishonoured me.
Think not, although in writing I preferred   10
The manner of thy vile outrageous crimes,
That therefore I have forged, or am not able
Verbatim to rehearse the method of my pen:
No, prelate; such is thy audacious wickedness,
Thy lewd, pestiferous and dissentious pranks,
As very infants prattle of thy pride.
Thou art a most pernicious usurer,
Froward by nature, enemy to peace;
Lascivious, wanton, more than well beseems
A man of thy profession and degree;   20
And for thy treachery, what's more manifest?
In that thou laid'st a trap to take my life,
As well at London Bridge as at the Tower.
Beside, I fear me, if thy thoughts were sifted,
The king, thy sovereign, is not quite exempt
From envious malice of thy swelling heart.
WINCHESTER. Gloucester, I do defy thee. Lords,
    vouchsafe
To give me hearing what I shall reply.
If I were covetous, ambitious or perverse,
As he will have me, how am I so poor?   30
Or how haps it I seek not to advance
Or raise myself, but keep my wonted calling?
And for dissension, who preferreth peace
More than I do?—except I be provoked.
No, my good lords, it is not that offends;
It is not that that hath incensed the duke:
It is, because no one should sway but he;
No one but he should be about the king;
And that engenders thunder in his breast
And makes him roar these accusations forth.   40
But he shall know I am as good—
GLOUCESTER.   As good!
Thou bastard of my grandfather!
WINCHESTER. Ay, lordly sir; for what are you, I pray,
But one imperious in another's throne?
GLOUCESTER. Am I not Protector, saucy priest?
WINCHESTER. And am not I a prelate of the church?
GLOUCESTER. Yes, as an outlaw in a castle keeps
And useth it, to patronage his theft.
WINCHESTER. Unreverent Gloster!
GLOUCESTER.   Thou art reverent
Touching thy spiritual function, not thy life.   50
WINCHESTER. Rome shall remedy this.
WARWICK.   Roam thither, then.
SOMERSET. My lord, it were your duty to forbear.
WARWICK. Ay, see the bishop be not overborne.
SOMERSET. Methinks my lord should be religious
And know the office that belongs to such.
WARWICK. Methinks his lordship should be humbler;
It fitteth not a prelate so to plead.
SOMERSET. Yes, when his holy state is touched so near.
WARWICK. State holy or unhallowed, what of that?
Is not his grace Protector to the king?   60
PLANTAGENET [*aside*]. Plantagenet, I see, must hold his
    tongue,
Lest it be said 'Speak, sirrah, when you should;
Must your bold verdict entertalk with lords?'
Else would I have a fling at Winchester.
KING. Uncles of Gloucester and of Winchester,

The special watchmen of our English weal,
I would prevail, if prayers might prevail,
To join your hearts in love and amity.
O, what a scandal is it to our crown,
That two such noble peers as ye should jar!   70
Believe me, lords, my tender years can tell
Civil dissension is a viperous worm
That gnaws the bowels of the commonwealth.
        Shouts without 'Down with the tawny-coats!'
What tumult's this?
WARWICK.   An uproar, I dare warrant,
Begun through malice of the bishop's men.
                Shouts again 'Stones! stones!'

Enter Mayor

MAYOR. O, my good lords, and virtuous Henry,
Pity the city of London, pity us!
The bishop and the Duke of Gloucester's men,
Forbidden late to carry any weapon,
Have filled their pockets full of pebble stones;   80
And banding themselves in contrary parts
Do pelt so fast at one another's pate
That many have their giddy brains knocked out:
Our windows are broke down in every street,
And we for fear compelled to shut our shops.

*Enter retainers of Gloucester and Winchester in skirmish,
with bloody pates*

KING. We charge you, on allegiance to ourself,
To hold your slaught'ring hands and keep the peace.
Pray, uncle Gloucester, mitigate this strife.
1 SERVING-MAN. Nay, if we be forbidden stones, we'll
fall to it with our teeth.   90
2 SERVING-MAN. Do what ye dare, we are as resolute.
                                Skirmish again
GLOUCESTER. You of my household, leave this
    peevish broil
And set this unaccustomed fight aside.
3 SERVING-MAN. My lord, we know your grace to be
    a man
Just and upright; and, for your royal birth,
Inferior to none but to his majesty:
And ere that we will suffer such a prince,
So kind a father of the commonweal,
To be disgracéd by an inkhorn mate,
We and our wives and children all will fight   100
And have our bodies slaughtered by thy foes.
1 SERVING-MAN. Ay, and the very parings of our nails
Shall pitch a field when we are dead.
                                They begin again
GLOUCESTER.   Stay, stay, I say!
And if you love me, as you say you do,
Let me persuade you to forbear awhile.
KING. O, how this discord doth afflict my soul!
Can you, my Lord of Winchester, behold
My sighs and tears and will not once relent?
Who should be pitiful, if you be not?
Or who should study to prefer a peace,   110
If holy churchmen take delight in broils?
WARWICK. Yield, my Lord Protector; yield,
    Winchester;
Except you mean with obstinate repulse
To slay your sovereign and destroy the realm.
You see what mischief and what murder too
Hath been enacted through your enmity;
Then be at peace, except ye thirst for blood.

WINCHESTER. He shall submit, or I will never yield
GLOUCESTER. Compassion on the king commands me
    stoop;
Or I would see his heart out, ere the priest   120
Should ever get that privilege of me.
WARWICK. Behold, my Lord of Winchester, the duke
Hath banished moody discontented fury,
As by his smoothéd brows it doth appear:
Why look you still so stern and tragical?
GLOUCESTER. Here, Winchester, I offer thee my hand.
KING. Fie, uncle Beaufort! I have heard you preach
That malice was a great and grievous sin;
And will not you maintain the thing you teach,
But prove a chief offender in the same?   130
WARWICK. Sweet king! the bishop hath a kindly gird.
For shame, my Lord of Winchester, relent!
What, shall a child instruct you what to do?
WINCHESTER. Well, Duke of Gloucester, I will yield to
    thee;
Love for thy love and hand for hand I give.
GLOUCESTER [*aside*]. Ay, but, I fear me, with a hollow
    heart.
    [*Aloud*] See here, my friends and loving
        countrymen;
This token serveth for a flag of truce
Betwixt ourselves and all our followers:
So help me God, as I dissemble not!   140
WINCHESTER [*aside*]. So help me God, as I intend it not!
KING. O loving uncle, kind Duke of Gloucester,
How joyful am I made by this contract!
Away, my masters! trouble us no more;
But join in friendship, as your lords have done.
1 SERVING-MAN. Content: I'll to the surgeon's.
2 SERVING-MAN.   And so will I.
3 SERVING-MAN. And I will see what physic the tavern
    affords.   *The Mayor and the retainers depart*
WARWICK. Accept this scroll, most gracious sovereign,
Which in the right of Richard Plantagenet   150
We do exhibit to your majesty.
GLOUCESTER. Well urged, my Lord of Warwick: for,
    sweet prince,
An if your grace mark every circumstance,
You have great reason to do Richard right;
Especially for those occasions
At Eltham Place I told your majesty.
KING. And those occasions, uncle, were of force:
Therefore, my loving lords, our pleasure is
That Richard be restoréd to his blood.
WARWICK. Let Richard be restoréd to his blood;   160
So shall his father's wrongs be recompensed.
WINCHESTER. As will the rest, so willeth Winchester.
KING. If Richard will be true, not that alone
But all the whole inheritance I give
That doth belong unto the house of York,
From whence you spring by lineal descent.
PLANTAGENET. Thy humble servant vows obedience
And humble service till the point of death.
KING. Stoop then and set your knee against my foot;
And, in reguerdon of that duty done,   170
I girt thee with the valiant sword of York:
Rise, Richard, like a true Plantagenet,
And rise created princely Duke of York.
PLANTAGENET. And so thrive Richard as thy foes may
    fall!
And as my duty springs, so perish they
That grudge one thought against your majesty!

ALL. Welcome, high prince, the mighty Duke of
York!
SOMERSET [aside]. Perish, base prince, ignoble Duke of
York!
GLOUCESTER. Now will it best avail your majesty
To cross the seas and to be crowned in France: 180
The presence of a king engenders love
Amongst his subjects and his loyal friends,
As it disanimates his enemies.
KING. When Gloucester says the word, King Henry
goes;
For friendly counsel cuts off many foes.
GLOUCESTER. Your ships already are in readiness.
Sennet; flourish; all go but Exeter
EXETER. Ay, we may march in England or in France,
Not seeing what is likely to ensue.
This late dissension grown betwixt the peers
Burns under feigned ashes of forged love   190
And will at last break out into a flame:
As festered members rot but by degree,
Till bones and flesh and sinews fall away,
So will this base and envious discord breed.
And now I fear that fatal prophecy
Which in the time of Henry named the fifth
Was in the mouth of every sucking babe;
That Henry born at Monmouth should win all
And Henry born at Windsor lose all:
Which is so plain that Exeter doth wish   200
His days may finish ere that hapless time.
He goes

Scene 2: *France. Before Rouen*

*Enter La Pucelle disguised, with four Soldiers with sacks
upon their backs*

PUCELLE. These are the city gates, the gates of Rouen,
Through which our policy must make a breach.
Take heed, be wary how you place your words,
Talk like the vulgar sort of market men
That come to gather money for their corn.
If we have entrance, as I hope we shall,
And that we find the slothful watch but weak,
I'll by a sign give notice to our friends,
That Charles the Dauphin may encounter them.
1 SOLDIER. Our sacks shall be a mean to sack the city, 10
And we be lords and rulers over Rouen,
Therefore we'll knock.   *Knocks*
WATCHMAN [*within*]. Qui est là?
PUCELLE. Paysans, pauvres gens de France;
Poor market folks that come to sell their corn.
WATCHMAN [*opens the gate*]. Enter, go in, the market
bell is rung.
PUCELLE. Now, Rouen, I'll shake thy bulwarks to the
ground.   *They enter*

*Charles, the Bastard of Orleans, Alençon, Reignier, and
forces approach*

CHARLES. Saint Denis bless this happy stratagem!
And once again we'll sleep secure in Rouen.
BASTARD. Here entered Pucelle and her practisants. 20
Now she is there, how will she specify
Where is the best and safest passage in?
REIGNIER. By thrusting out a torch from yonder
tower,
Which, once discerned, shows that her meaning is—
No way to that, for weakness, which she entered.

Enter La Pucelle on the top, thrusting out a torch, burning

PUCELLE. Behold, this is the happy wedding torch
That joineth Rouen unto her countrymen,
But burning fatal to the Talbotines!
She withdraws
BASTARD. See, noble Charles, the beacon of our friend,
The burning torch in yonder turret stands.   30
CHARLES. Now shine it like a comet of revenge,
A prophet to the fall of all our foes!
REIGNIER. Defer no time, delays have dangerous ends,
Enter and cry 'The Dauphin!' presently,
And then do execution on the watch.
Alarum; they storm the gate

Enter Talbot in an excursion from within

TALBOT. France, thou shalt rue this treason with thy
tears,
If Talbot but survive thy treachery.
Pucelle, that witch, that damnéd sorceress,
Hath wrought this hellish mischief unawares,
That hardly we escaped the pride of France.   40
He goes back

*An alarum: excursions. Bedford, brought out sick in a chair,
followed by Talbot and Burgundy in retreat: within La
Pucelle, Charles, Bastard, Alençon, and Reignier appear
on the walls*

PUCELLE. Good morrow, gallants! want ye corn for
bread?
I think the Duke of Burgundy will fast
Before he'll buy again at such a rate:
'Twas full of darnel; do you like the taste?
BURGUNDY. Scoff on, vile fiend and shameless
courtezan!
I trust ere long to choke thee with thine own
And make thee curse the harvest of that corn.
CHARLES. Your grace may starve perhaps before that
time.
BEDFORD. O, let no words, but deeds, revenge this
treason!
PUCELLE. What will you do, good grey-beard? break
a lance,   50
And run a tilt at death within a chair?
TALBOT. Foul fiend of France, and hag of all despite,
Encompassed with thy lustful paramours!
Becomes it thee to taunt his valiant age,
And twit with cowardice a man half dead?
Damsel, I'll have a bout with you again,
Or else let Talbot perish with this shame.
PUCELLE. Are ye so hot, sir? yet, Pucelle, hold thy
peace;
If Talbot do but thunder, rain will follow.
The English whisper together in council
God speed the parliament! who shall be the Speaker? 60
TALBOT. Dare ye come forth and meet us in the field?
PUCELLE. Belike your lordship takes us then for fools,
To try if that our own be ours or no.
TALBOT. I speak not to that railing Hecate,
But unto thee, Alençon, and the rest;
Will ye, like soldiers, come and fight it out?
ALENÇON. Signior, no.
TALBOT. Signior, hang! base muleters of France!
Like peasant foot-boys do they keep the walls
And dare not take up arms like gentlemen.   70
PUCELLE. Away, captains! let's get us from the walls;
For Talbot means no goodness by his looks.

Good-bye, my lord! we came but to tell you
That we are here.
           The French go down from the walls
TALBOT. And there will we be too, ere it be long,
   Or else reproach be Talbot's greatest fame.
   Vow, Burgundy, by honour of thy house,
   Pricked on by public wrongs sustained in France,
   Either to get the town again or die:
   And I, as sure as English Henry lives   80
   And as his father here was conqueror,
   As sure as in this late-betrayéd town
   Great Cordelion's heart was buriéd,
   So sure I swear to get the town or die.
BURGUNDY. My vows are equal partners with thy
   vows.
TALBOT. But, ere we go, regard this dying prince,
   The valiant Duke of Bedford. Come, my lord,
   We will bestow you in some better place,
   Fitter for sickness and for crazy age.
BEDFORD. Lord Talbot, do not so dishonour me: 90
   Here will I sit before the walls of Rouen
   And will be partner of your weal or woe.
BURGUNDY. Courageous Bedford, let us now persuade
   you.
BEDFORD. Not to be gone from hence; for once I
   read
   That stout Pendragon in his litter sick
   Came to the field and vanquishéd his foes:
   Methinks I should revive the soldiers' hearts,
   Because I ever found them as myself.
TALBOT. Undaunted spirit in a dying breast!
   Then be it so: heavens keep old Bedford safe!   100
   And now no more ado, brave Burgundy,
   But gather we our forces out of hand
   And set upon our boasting enemy.
        All go but Bedford and his attendants

*An alarum: excursions. Enter Sir John Falstaff and a
Captain*

CAPTAIN. Whither away, Sir John Falstaff, in such
   haste?
FALSTAFF. Whither away! to save myself by flight:
   We are like to have the overthrow again.
CAPTAIN. What! will you fly, and leave Lord Talbot?
FALSTAFF.   Ay,
   All the Talbots in the world, to save my life.
                        He goes
CAPTAIN. Cowardly knight! ill fortune follow thee!
                        He goes

*A retreat sounded: excursions, after which La Pucelle,
Alençon, and Charles are seen in flight*

BEDFORD. Now, quiet soul, depart when heaven
   please,   110
   For I have seen our enemies' overthrow.
   What is the trust or strength of foolish man?
   They that of late were daring with their scoffs
   Are glad and fain by flight to save themselves.
       *Bedford dies and is carried in by
                  two in his chair*

*An alarum. Talbot, Burgundy, and the rest of their men
come from the town*

TALBOT. Lost, and recovered in a day again!
   This is a double honour, Burgundy:
   Yet heavens have glory for this victory!
BURGUNDY. Warlike and martial Talbot, Burgundy

Enshrines thee in his heart and there erects
Thy noble deeds as valour's monuments.   120
TALBOT. Thanks, gentle duke. But where is Pucelle
   now?
   I think her old familiar is asleep:
   Now where's the Bastard's braves, and Charles
   his gleeks?
   What, all amort? Rouen hangs her head for grief
   That such a valiant company are fled.
   Now will we take some order in the town,
   Placing therein some expert officers,
   And then depart to Paris to the king,
   For there young Henry with his nobles lie.
BURGUNDY. What wills Lord Talbot pleaseth
   Burgundy.   130
TALBOT. But yet, before we go, let's not forget
   The noble Duke of Bedford late deceased,
   But see his exequies fulfilled in Rouen.
   A braver soldier never couchéd lance,
   A gentler heart did never sway in court;
   But kings and mightiest potentates must die,
   For that's the end of human misery.   *They go*

Scene 3: *The plains near Rouen*

*Enter Charles, the Bastard of Orleans, Alençon, La Pucelle,
and forces*

PUCELLE. Dismay not, princes, at this accident,
   Nor grieve that Rouen is so recoveréd.
   Care is no cure, but rather corrosive,
   For things that are not to be remedied.
   Let frantic Talbot triumph for a while
   And like a peacock sweep along his tail;
   We'll pull his plumes and take away his train,
   If Dauphin and the rest will be but ruled.
CHARLES. We have been guided by thee hitherto,
   And of thy cunning had no diffidence: 10
   One sudden foil shall never breed distrust.
BASTARD. Search out thy wit for secret policies,
   And we will make thee famous through the world.
ALENÇON. We'll set thy statue in some holy place,
   And have thee reverenced like a blessed saint.
   Employ thee then, sweet virgin, for our good.
PUCELLE. Then thus it must be; this doth Joan devise:
   By fair persuasions mixed with sugared words
   We will entice the Duke of Burgundy
   To leave the Talbot and to follow us.   20
CHARLES. Ay, marry, sweeting, if we could do that,
   France were no place for Henry's warriors,
   Nor should that nation boast it so with us,
   But be extirpéd from our provinces.
ALENÇON. For ever should they be expulsed from
   France,
   And not have title of an earldom here.
PUCELLE. Your honours shall perceive how I will work
   To bring this matter to the wishéd end.
               Drum sounds afar off
   Hark! by the sound of drum you may perceive
   Their powers are marching unto Paris-ward.   30

        Here sound an English march

   There goes the Talbot, with his colours spread,
   And all the troops of English after him.

French march. Enter the Duke of Burgundy and forces

   Now in the rearward comes the duke and his:

Fortune in favour makes him lag behind.
Summon a parley, we will talk with him.
Trumpets sound a parley
CHARLES. A parley with the Duke of Burgundy!
BURGUNDY. Who craves a parley with the Burgundy?
PUCELLE. The princely Charles of France, thy
countryman.
BURGUNDY. What say'st thou, Charles? for I am
marching hence.
CHARLES. Speak, Pucelle, and enchant him with thy
words.　　　　　　　　　　　　　　　　　　　40
PUCELLE. Brave Burgundy, undoubted hope of
France!
Stay, let thy humble handmaid speak to thee.
BURGUNDY. Speak on; but be not over-tedious.
PUCELLE. Look on thy country, look on fertile France,
And see the cities and the towns defaced
By wasting ruin of the cruel foe,
As looks the mother on her lowly babe
When death doth close his tender-dying eyes.
See, see the pining malady of France;
Behold the wounds, the most unnatural wounds,　50
Which thou thyself hast given her woful breast.
O, turn thy edgéd sword another way;
Strike those that hurt, and hurt not those that help.
One drop of blood drawn from thy country's
bosom
Should grieve thee more than streams of foreign
gore.
Return thee therefore with a flood of tears,
And wash away thy country's stainéd spots.
BURGUNDY. Either she hath bewitched me with her
words,
Or nature makes me suddenly relent.
PUCELLE. Besides, all French and France exclaims on
thee,　　　　　　　　　　　　　　　　　　60
Doubting thy birth and lawful progeny.
Who join'st thou with, but with a lordly nation
That will not trust thee but for profit's sake?
When Talbot hath set footing once in France
And fashioned thee that instrument of ill,
Who then but English Henry will be lord
And thou be thrust out like a fugitive?
Call we to mind, and mark but this for proof:
Was not the Duke of Orleans thy foe?
And was he not in England prisoner?　　　　　70
But when they heard he was thine enemy,
They set him free without his ransom paid,
In spite of Burgundy and all his friends.
See then, thou fight'st against thy countrymen
And join'st with them will be thy slaughter-men.
Come, come, return; return, thou wandering lord;
Charles and the rest will take thee in their arms.
BURGUNDY. I am vanquishéd; these haughty words of
hers
Have battered me like roaring cannon-shot,
And made me almost yield upon my knees.　　80
Forgive me, country, and sweet countrymen,
And, lords, accept this hearty kind embrace.
My forces and my power of men are yours.
So farewell, Talbot, I'll no longer trust thee.
PUCELLE [*aside*]. Done like a Frenchman: turn, and turn
again!
CHARLES. Welcome, brave duke! thy friendship makes
us fresh.
BASTARD. And doth beget new courage in our breasts.

ALENÇON. Pucelle hath bravely played her part in this,
And doth deserve a coronet of gold.
CHARLES. Now let us on, my lords, and join our
powers,　　　　　　　　　　　　　　　　90
And seek how we may prejudice the foe.
They go

Scene 4: *Paris. The Palace*

*Enter the King, Gloucester, Bishop of Winchester, York,
Suffolk, Somerset, Warwick, Exeter: Vernon, Basset, and
others. To them, with his Soldiers, Talbot*

TALBOT. My gracious prince, and honourable peers,
Hearing of your arrival in this realm,
I have awhile giv'n truce unto my wars,
To do my duty to my sovereign.
In sign whereof, this arm, that hath reclaimed
To your obedience fifty fortresses,
Twelve cities and seven walléd towns of strength,
Beside five hundred prisoners of esteem,
Lets fall his sword before your highness' feet,
And with submissive loyalty of heart　　　　　10
Ascribes the glory of his conquest got
First to my God and next unto your grace.
Kneels
KING. Is this the Lord Talbot, uncle Gloucester,
That hath so long been resident in France?
GLOUCESTER. Yes, if it please your majesty, my liege.
KING. Welcome, brave captain and victorious lord!
When I was young (as yet I am not old)
I do remember how my father said
A stouter champion never handled sword.
Long since we were resolvéd of your truth,　　20
Your faithful service and your toil in war;
Yet never have you tasted our reward,
Or been reguerdoned with so much as thanks,
Because till now we never saw your face:
Therefore, stand up, and for these good deserts
We here create you Earl of Shrewsbury;
And in our coronation take your place.
Sennet; flourish; all depart save
Vernon and Basset
VERNON. Now, sir, to you, that were so hot at sea,
Disgracing of these colours that I wear
In honour of my noble Lord of York—　　　　30
Dar'st thou maintain the former words thou spak'st?
BASSET. Yes, sir, as well as you dare patronage
The envious barking of your saucy tongue
Against my lord the Duke of Somerset.
VERNON. Sirrah, thy lord I honour as he is.
BASSET. Why, what is he? as good a man as York.
VERNON. Hark ye; not so: in witness, take ye that.
Strikes him
BASSET. Villain, thou know'st the law of arms is such
That whoso draws a sword, 'tis present death,
Or else this blow should broach thy dearest blood. 40
But I'll unto his majesty, and crave
I may have liberty to venge this wrong;
When thou shalt see I'll meet thee to thy cost.
VERNON. Well, miscreant, I'll be there as soon as you;
And, after, meet you sooner than you would.
They go

ACT 4
Scene 1: *The same*

Enter the King, Gloucester, Bishop of Winchester, York, Suffolk, Somerset, Warwick, Talbot, Exeter, the Governor of Paris and others

GLOUCESTER. Lord bishop, set the crown upon his head.
WINCHESTER. God save King Henry, of that name the sixth!
GLOUCESTER. Now, governor of Paris, take your oath,
That you elect no other king but him;
                                    The Governor kneels
Esteem none friends but such as are his friends,
And none your foes but such as shall pretend
Malicious practices against his state:
This shall ye do, so help you righteous God!

Enter Sir John Falstaff

FALSTAFF. My gracious sovereign, as I rode from Calais,
To haste unto your coronation,   10
A letter was delivered to my hands,
Writ to your grace from th' Duke of Burgundy.
TALBOT. Shame to the Duke of Burgundy and thee!
I vowed, base knight, when I did meet thee next,
To tear the garter from thy craven's leg,
                                    Plucking it off
Which I have done, because unworthily
Thou wast installéd in that high degree.
Pardon me, princely Henry, and the rest:
This dastard, at the battle of Poictiers,
When but in all I was six thousand strong   20
And that the French were almost ten to one,
Before we met or that a stroke was given,
Like to a trusty squire did run away.
In which assault we lost twelve hundred men;
Myself and divers gentlemen beside
Were there surprised and taken prisoners.
Then judge, great lords, if I have done amiss;
Or whether that such cowards ought to wear
This ornament of knighthood, yea or no.
GLOUCESTER. To say the truth, this fact was infamous   30
And ill beseeming any common man,
Much more a knight, a captain and a leader.
TALBOT. When first this order was ordained, my lords,
Knights of the Garter were of noble birth,
Valiant and virtuous, full of haughty courage,
Such as were grown to credit by the wars;
Not fearing death, nor shrinking for distress,
But always resolute in most extremes.
He then that is not furnished in this sort
Doth but usurp the sacred name of knight,   40
Profaning this most honourable order,
And should (if I were worthy to be judge)
Be quite degraded, like a hedge-born swain
That doth presume to boast of gentle blood.
KING. Stain to thy countrymen, thou hear'st thy doom!
Be packing, therefore, thou that wast a knight;
Henceforth we banish thee on pain of death.
                                    Falstaff goes
And now, my Lord Protector, view the letter
Sent from our uncle Duke of Burgundy.
GLOUCESTER. What means his grace, that he hath changed his style?   50

No more but, plain and bluntly, 'To the king!'
Hath he forgot he is his sovereign?
Or doth this churlish superscription
Pretend some alteration in good will?
What's here? [*reads*] 'I have, upon especial cause,
Moved with compassion of my country's wrack,
Together with the pitiful complaints
Of such as your oppression feeds upon,
Forsaken your pernicious faction
And join'd with Charles, the rightful King of France.'   60
O monstrous traechery! can this be so,
That in alliance, amity, and oaths,
There should be found such false dissembling guile?
KING. What! doth my uncle Burgundy revolt?
GLOUCESTER. He doth, my lord, and is become your foe.
KING. Is that the worst this letter doth contain?
GLOUCESTER. It is the worst, and all, my lord, he writes.
KING. Why, then, Lord Talbot there shall talk with him
And give him chastisement for this abuse.
How say you, my lord? are you not content?   70
TALBOT. Content, my liege! yes, but that I am prevented,
I should have begged I might have been employed.
KING. Then gather strength, and march unto him straight:
Let him perceive how ill we brook his treason
And what offence it is to flout his friends.
TALBOT. I go, my lord, in heart desiring still
You may behold confusion of your foes.   *He goes*

Enter Vernon and Basset

VERNON. Grant me the combat, gracious sovereign.
BASSET. And me, my lord, grant me the combat too.
YORK. This is my servant: hear him, noble prince.   80
SOMERSET. And this is mine: sweet Henry, favour him.
KING HENRY. Be patient, lords; and give them leave to speak.
Say, gentlemen, what makes you thus exclaim?
And wherefore crave you combat? or with whom?
VERNON. With him, my lord, for he hath done me wrong.
BASSET. And I with him, for he hath done me wrong.
KING HENRY. What is that wrong whereof you both complain?
First let me know, and then I'll answer you.
BASSET. Crossing the sea from England into France,
This fellow here, with envious carping tongue,   90
Upbraided me about the rose I wear;
Saying, the sanguine colour of the leaves
Did represent my master's blushing cheeks,
When stubbornly he did repugn the truth
About a certain question in the law
Argued betwixt the Duke of York and him;
With other vile and ignominious terms:
In confutation of which rude reproach
And in defence of my lord's worthiness,
I crave the benefit of law of arms.   100
VERNON. And that is my petition, noble lord:
For though he seem with forgéd quaint conceit
To set a gloss upon his bold intent,
Yet know, my lord, I was provoked by him;
And he first took exceptions at this badge,

Pronouncing that the paleness of this flower
Bewrayed the faintness of my master's heart.

YORK. Will not this malice, Somerset, be left?

SOMERSET. Your private grudge, my Lord of York, will out,
Though ne'er so cunningly you smother it. 110

KING HENRY. Good Lord, what madness rules in brainsick men,
When for so slight and frivolous a cause
Such factious emulations shall arise!
Good cousins both, of York and Somerset,
Quiet yourselves, I pray, and be at peace.

YORK. Let this dissension first be tried by fight,
And then your highness shall command a peace.

SOMERSET. The quarrel toucheth none but us alone;
Betwixt ourselves let us decide it then.

YORK. There is my pledge; accept it, Somerset. 120

VERNON. Nay, let it rest where it began at first.

BASSET. Confirm it so, mine honourable lord.

GLOUCESTER. Confirm it so! Confounded be your strife!
And perish ye, with your audacious prate!
Presumptuous vassals, are you not ashamed
With this immodest clamorous outrage
To trouble and disturb the king and us?
And you, my lords, methinks you do not well
To bear with their perverse objections;
Much less to take occasion from their mouths 130
To raise a mutiny betwixt yourselves.
Let me persuade you take a better course.

EXETER. It grieves his highness. Good my lords, be friends.

KING HENRY. Come hither, you that would be combatants:
Henceforth I charge you, as you love our favour,
Quite to forget this quarrel and the cause.
And you, my lords, remember where we are—
In France, amongst a fickle wavering nation:
If they perceive dissension in our looks
And that within ourselves we disagree, 140
How will their grudging stomachs be provoked
To wilful disobedience, and rebel!
Beside, what infamy will there arise,
When foreign princes shall be certified
That for a toy, a thing of no regard,
King Henry's peers and chief nobility
Destroyed themselves, and lost the realm of France!
O, think upon the conquest of my father,
My tender years, and let us not forgo
That for a trifle that was bought with blood! 150
Let me be umpire in this doubtful strife.
I see no reason, if I wear this rose,

Putting on a red rose

That any one should therefore be suspicious
I more incline to Somerset than York:
Both are my kinsmen, and I love them both.
As well they may upbraid me with my crown,
Because, forsooth, the king of Scots is crowned,
But your discretions better can persuade
Than I am able to instruct or teach:
And therefore, as we hither came in peace, 160
So let us still continue peace and love.
Cousin of York, we institute your grace
To be our Regent in these parts of France:
And, good my Lord of Somerset, unite
Your troops of horsemen with his bands of foot;

And, like true subjects, sons of your progenitors,
Go cheerfully together and digest
Your angry choler on your enemies.
Ourself, my Lord Protector, and the rest
After some respite will return to Calais; 170
From thence to England; where I hope ere long
To be presented, by your victories,
With Charles, Alençon, and that traitorous rout.

Flourish; all depart save York,
Warwick, Exeter and Vernon

WARWICK. My Lord of York, I promise you, the king
Prettily, methought, did play the orator.

YORK. And so he did; but yet I like it not,
In that he wears the badge of Somerset.

WARWICK. Tush, that was but his fancy, blame him not;
I dare presume, sweet prince, he thought no harm.

YORK. An if iwis he did—but let it rest; 180
Other affairs must now be managéd.

They follow: Exeter remains

EXETER. Well didst thou, Richard, to suppress thy voice;
For, had the passions of thy heart burst out,
I fear we should have seen deciphered there
More rancorous spite, more furious raging broils,
Than yet can be imagined or supposed.
But howsoe'er, no simple man that sees
This jarring discord of nobility,
This should'ring of each other in the court,
This factious bandying of their favourites, 190
But that he doth presage some ill event.
'Tis much when sceptres are in children's hands;
But more when envy breeds unkind division;
There comes the ruin, there begins confusion.

He goes

Scene 2: *Before Bordeaux*

Enter Talbot, with trump and drum

TALBOT. Go to the gates of Bordeaux, trumpeter;
Summon their general unto the wall.

Trumpet sounds

Enter General aloft with others

English John Talbot, captains, calls you forth,
Servant in arms to Harry King of England;
And thus he would: Open your city-gates,
Be humble to us, call my sovereign yours
And do him homage as obedient subjects,
And I'll withdraw me and my bloody power.
But, if you frown upon this proffered peace, 10
You tempt the fury of my three attendants,
Lean Famine, quartering Steel, and climbing Fire;
Who in a moment even with the earth
Shall lay your stately and air-braving towers,
If you forsake the offer of their love.

GENERAL. Thou ominous and fearful owl of death,
Our nation's terror and their bloody scourge!
The period of thy tyranny approacheth.
On us thou canst not enter but by death;
For, I protest, we are well fortified
And strong enough to issue out and fight. 20
If thou retire, the Dauphin, well appointed,
Stands with the snares of war to tangle thee.
On either hand thee there are squadrons pitched,
To wall thee from the liberty of flight;

And no way canst thou turn thee for redress,
But death doth front thee with apparent spoil
And pale destruction meets thee in the face.
Ten thousand French have ta'en the sacrament
To rove their dangerous artillery
Upon no Christian soul but English Talbot.   30
Lo, there thou stand'st, a breathing valiant man,
Of an invincible unconquered spirit:
This is the latest glory of thy praise
That I, thy enemy, due thee withal;
For ere the glass, that now begins to run,
Finish the process of his sandy hour,
These eyes, that see thee now well coloured,
Shall see thee withered, bloody, pale and dead.
                                        Drum afar off
Hark! hark! the Dauphin's drum, a warning bell,
Sings heavy music to thy timorous soul;   40
And mine shall ring thy dire departure out.
                                        He goes
TALBOT. He fables not, I hear the enemy:
Out, some light horsemen, and peruse their wings.
O, negligent and heedless discipline!
How are we parked and bounded in a pale,
A little herd of England's timorous deer,
Mazed with a yelping kennel of French curs!
If we be English deer, be then in blood,
Not rascal-like to fall down with a pinch,
But rather, moody, mad, and desperate stags,   50
Turn on the bloody hounds with heads of steel
And make the cowards stand aloof at bay:
Sell every man his life as dear as mine,
And they shall find dear deer of us, my friends.
God and Saint George, Talbot and England's right,
Prosper our colours in this dangerous fight!
                                        They go

Scene 3: *Plains in Gascony*

*Enter a Messenger that meets York. Enter York with
trumpet and many Soldiers*

YORK. Are not the speedy scouts returned again,
That dogged the mighty army of the Dauphin?
MESSENGER. They are returned, my lord, and give it
    out
That he is marched to Bordeaux with his power,
To fight with Talbot: as he marched along,
By your espials were discovered
Two mightier troops than that the Dauphin led,
Which joined with him and made their march for
    Bordeaux.
YORK. A plague upon that villain Somerset,
That thus delays my promised supply   10
Of horsemen, that were levied for this siege!
Renownéd Talbot doth expect my aid,
And I am louted by a traitor villain
And cannot help the noble chevalier.
God comfort him in this necessity!
If he miscarry, farewell wars in France.

Enter Sir William Lucy

LUCY. Thou princely leader of our English strength.
Never so needful on the earth of France,
Spur to the rescue of the noble Talbot,
Who now is girdled with a waist of iron   20
And hemmed about with grim destruction.
To Bordeaux, warlike duke! to Bordeaux, York!

Else, farewell Talbot, France, and England's honour.
YORK. O God, that Somerset, who in proud heart
    Doth stop my cornets, were in Talbot's place!
So should we save a valiant gentleman
By forfeiting a traitor and a coward.
Mad ire and wrathful fury makes me weep,
That thus we die, while remiss traitors sleep.
LUCY. O, send some succour to the distressed lord!   30
YORK. He dies, we lose; I break my warlike word;
We mourn, France smiles; we lose, they daily get;
All long of this vile traitor Somerset.
LUCY. Then God take mercy on brave Talbot's soul,
And on his son young John, who two hours since
I met in travel toward his warlike father!
This seven years did not Talbot see his son,
And now they meet where both their lives are
    done.
YORK. Alas, what joy shall noble Talbot have
To bid his young son welcome to his grave?   40
Away! vexation almost stops my breath,
That sundered friends greet in the hour of death.
Lucy, farewell, no more my fortune can,
But curse the cause I cannot aid the man.
Maine, Blois, Poictiers, and Tours, are won away,
Long all of Somerset and his delay.
                                He goes, with his soldiers
LUCY. Thus, while the vulture of sedition
Feeds in the bosom of such great commanders,
Sleeping neglection doth betray to loss
The conquest of our scarce-cold conqueror,   50
That ever living man of memory,
Henry the Fifth. Whiles they each other cross,
Lives, honours, lands and all hurry to loss.

Scene 4

*Enter Somerset, with his army; a Captain of Talbot's with
him*

SOMERSET. It is too late, I cannot send them now:
This expedition was by York and Talbot
Too rashly plotted. All our general force
Might with a sally of the very town
Be buckled with: the over-daring Talbot
Hath sullied all his gloss of former honour
By this unheedful, desperate, wild adventure:
York set him on to fight and die in shame,
That, Talbot dead, great York might bear the name.
CAPTAIN. Here is Sir William Lucy, who with me   10
Set from our o'er-matched forces forth for aid.
SOMERSET. How now, Sir William! whither were
    you sent?
LUCY. Whither, my lord? from bought and sold
    Lord Talbot;
Who, ringed about with bold adversity,
Cries out for noble York and Somerset,
To beat assailing death from his weak legions;
And whiles the honourable captain there
Drops bloody sweat from his war-wearied limbs,
And in advantage-ling'ring looks for rescue,
You, his false hopes, the trust of England's honour,   20
Keep off aloof with worthless emulation.
Let not your private discord keep away
The levied succours that should lend him aid,
While he, renownéd noble gentleman,
Yield up his life unto a world of odds:
Orleans the Bastard, Charles, Burgundy,

Alençon, Reignier, compass him about,
And Talbot perisheth by your default.
SOMERSET. York set him on, York should have sent
  him aid.
LUCY. And York as fast upon your grace exclaims;   30
  Swearing that you withhold his levied host,
  Collected for this expedition.
SOMERSET. York lies; he might have sent and had the
  horse:
  I owe him little duty, and less love;
  And take foul scorn to fawn on him by sending.
LUCY. The fraud of England, not the force of France,
  Hath now entrapped the noble-minded Talbot:
  Never to England shall he bear his life,
  But dies betrayed to fortune by your strife.
SOMERSET. Come, go; I will dispatch the horsemen
  straight: 40
  Within six hours they will be at his aid.
LUCY. Too late comes rescue, he is ta'en or slain;
  For fly he could not, if he would have fled;
  And fly would Talbot never though he might.
SOMERSET. If he be dead, brave Talbot, then adieu!
LUCY. His fame lives in the world, his shame in you.
                        They go

Scene 5: *The English camp near Bordeaux*

Enter Talbot and his son

TALBOT. O young John Talbot! I did send for thee
  To tutor thee in stratagems of war,
  That Talbot's name might be in thee revived
  When sapless age and weak unable limbs
  Should bring thy father to his drooping chair.
  But, O malignant and ill-boding stars!
  Now thou art come unto a feast of death,
  A terrible and unavoided danger:
  Therefore, dear boy, mount on my swiftest horse,
  And I'll direct thee how thou shalt escape   10
  By sudden flight. Come, dally not, be gone.
JOHN. Is my name Talbot? and am I your son?
  And shall I fly? O, if you love my mother,
  Dishonour not her honourable name,
  To make a bastard and a slave of me.
  The world will say, he is not Talbot's blood,
  That basely fled when noble Talbot stood.
TALBOT. Fly, to revenge my death, if I be slain.
JOHN. He that flies so will ne'er return again.
TALBOT. If we both stay, we both are sure to die.   20
JOHN. Then let me stay, and, father, do you fly.
  Your loss is great, so your regard should be;
  My worth unknown, no loss is known in me.
  Upon my death the French can little boast;
  In yours they will, in you all hopes are lost.
  Flight cannot stain the honour you have won;
  But mine it will, that no exploit have done:
  You fled for vantage, every one will swear;
  But, if I bow, they'll say it was for fear.
  There is no hope that ever I will stay,   30
  If the first hour I shrink and run away.
  Here on my knee I beg mortality,
  Rather than live preserved with infamy.
TALBOT. Shall all thy mother's hopes lie in one tomb?
JOHN. Ay, rather than I'll shame my mother's womb.
TALBOT. Upon my blessing, I command thee go.
JOHN. To fight I will, but not to fly the foe.
TALBOT. Part of thy father may be saved in thee.

JOHN. No part of him but will be shame in me.
TALBOT. Thou never hadst renown, nor canst not lose
  it.   40
JOHN. Yes, your renownéd name: shall flight abuse it?
TALBOT. Thy father's charge shall clear thee from
  that stain.
JOHN. You cannot witness for me, being slain.
  If death be so apparent, then both fly.
TALBOT. And leave my followers here to fight and die?
  My age was never tainted with such shame.
JOHN. And shall my youth be guilty of such blame?
  No more can I be severed from your side,
  Than can yourself yourself in twain divide.
  Stay, go, do what you will, the like do I;   50
  For live I will not, if my father die.
TALBOT. Then here I take my leave of thee, fair son,
  Born to eclipse thy live this afternoon.
  Come, side by side together live and die;
  And soul with soul from France to heaven fly.
                        They go

⌈Scene 6

*Alarum: excursions, wherein Talbot's son is hemmed
about, and Talbot rescues him*

TALBOT. Saint George and victory! fight, soldiers,
  fight!
  The Regent hath with Talbot broke his word
  And left us to the rage of France his sword.
  Where is John Talbot? Pause, and take thy breath;
  I gave thee life and rescued thee from death.
JOHN. O, twice my father, twice am I thy son!
  The life thou gav'st me first was lost and done,
  Till with thy warlike sword, despite of fate,
  To my determined time thou gav'st new date.
TALBOT. When from the Dauphin's crest thy sword
  struck fire,   10
  It warmed thy father's heart with proud desire
  Of bold-faced victory. Then leaden age,
  Quickened with youthful spleen and warlike rage,
  Beat down Alençon, Orleans, Burgundy,
  And from the pride of Gallia rescued thee.
  The ireful bastard Orleans, that drew blood
  From thee, my boy, and had the maidenhood
  Of thy first fight, I soon encounteréd,
  And interchanging blows I quickly shed
  Some of his bastard blood; and in disgrace   20
  Bespoke him thus; 'Contaminated, base,
  And misbegotten blood I spill of thine,
  Mean and right poor, for that pure blood of mine
  Which thou didst force from Talbot, my brave
  boy':
  Here, purposing the Bastard to destroy,
  Came in strong rescue. Speak, thy father's care,
  Art thou not weary, John? how dost thou fare?
  Wilt thou yet leave the battle, boy, and fly,
  Now thou art sealed the son of chivalry?
  Fly, to revenge my death when I am dead: 30
  The help of one stands me in little stead.
  O, too much folly is it, well I wot,
  To hazard all our lives in one small boat!
  If I to-day die not with Frenchmen's rage,
  To-morrow I shall die with mickle age:
  By me they nothing gain an if I stay;
  'Tis but the short'ning of my life one day:
  In thee thy mother dies, our household's name,

My death's revenge, thy youth, and England's fame:
All these and more we hazard by thy stay;   40
All these are saved if thou wilt fly away.
JOHN. The sword of Orleans hath not made me smart;
  These words of yours draw life-blood from my
      heart:
  On that advantage, bought with such a shame,
  To save a paltry life and slay bright fame!
  Before young Talbot from old Talbot fly,
  The coward horse that bears me fall and die!
  And like me to the peasant boys of France,
  To be shame's scorn and subject of mischance!
  Surely, by all the glory you have won,   50
  An if I fly, I am not Talbot's son:
  Then talk no more of flight, it is no boot;
  If son to Talbot, die at Talbot's foot.
TALBOT. Then follow thou thy desperate sire of Crete,
  Thou Icarus; thy life to me is sweet:
  If thou wilt fight, fight by thy father's side;
  And, commendable proved, let's die in pride.
                                        Exeunt]

                    Scene 7

Alarum: excursions. Enter old Talbot led by a Servant

TALBOT. Where is my other life? mine own is gone;
  O, where's young Talbot? where is valiant John?
  Triumphant death, smeared with captivity,
  Young Talbot's valour makes me smile at thee:
  When he perceived me shrink and on my knee,
  His bloody sword he brandished over me,
  And like a hungry lion did commence
  Rough deeds of rage and stern impatience;
  But when my angry guardant stood alone,
  Tend'ring my ruin and assailed of none,   10
  Dizzy-eyed fury and great rage of heart
  Suddenly made him from my side to start
  Into the clust'ring battle of the French;
  And in that sea of blood my boy did drench
  His over-mounting spirit; and there died,
  My Icarus, my blossom, in his pride.
SERVANT. O my dear lord, lo, where your son is borne!

Enter Soldiers, with the body of young Talbot

TALBOT. Thou antic death, which laugh'st us here to
      scorn,
  Anon, from thy insulting tyranny,
  Coupled in bonds of perpetuity,   20
  Two Talbots, wingèd through the lither sky,
  In thy despite shall 'scape mortality.
  O thou, whose wounds become hard-favoured
      death,
  Speak to thy father ere thou yield thy breath!
  Brave Death by speaking, whether he will or no;
  Imagine him a Frenchman and thy foe.
  Poor boy! he smiles, methinks, as who should say,
  'Had Death been French, then Death had died
      to-day.'
  Come, come and lay him in his father's arms:
  My spirit can no longer bear these harms.   30
  Soldiers, adieu! I have what I would have,
  Now my old arms are young John Talbot's grave.
                                        Dies

*Enter Charles, Alençon, Burgundy, Bastard, La Pucelle,
and forces*

CHARLES. Had York and Somerset brought rescue in,
  We should have found a bloody day of this.
BASTARD. How the young whelp of Talbot's, raging
      wood,
  Did flesh his puny sword in Frenchmen's blood!
PUCELLE. Once I encountered him, and thus I said:
  'Thou maiden youth, be vanquished by a maid':
  But, with a proud majestical high scorn,
  He answered thus: 'Young Talbot was not born   40
  To be the pillage of a giglot wench':
  So, rushing in the bowels of the French,
  He left me proudly, as unworthy fight.
BURGUNDY. Doubtless he would have made a noble
      knight:
  See, where he lies inhearsèd in the arms
  Of the most bloody nurser of his harms!
BASTARD. Hew them to pieces, hack their bones
      asunder,
  Whose life was England's glory, Gallia's wonder.
CHARLES. O, no, forbear! for that which we have fled
  During the life, let us not wrong it dead.   50

*Enter Sir William Lucy, attended; Herald of the French
preceding*

LUCY. Herald, conduct me to the Dauphin's tent,
  To know who hath obtained the glory of the day.
CHARLES. On what submissive message art thou sent?
LUCY. Submission, Dauphin! 'tis a mere French word;
  We English warriors wot not what it means.
  I come to know what prisoners thou hast ta'en
  And to survey the bodies of the dead.
CHARLES. For prisoners ask'st thou? hell our prison is.
  But tell me whom thou seek'st:
LUCY. But where's the great Alcides of the field,   60
  Valiant Lord Talbot, Earl of Shrewsbury,
  Created, for his rare success in arms,
  Great Earl of Washford, Waterford and Valence;
  Lord Talbot of Goodrig and Urchinfield,
  Lord Strange of Blackmere, Lord Verdum of Alton,
  Lord Cromwell of Wingfield, Lord Furnival of
      Sheffield,
  The thrice-victorious Lord of Falconbridge,
  Knight of the noble order of Saint George,
  Worthy Saint Michael and the Golden Fleece,
  Great Marshal to Henry the Sixth   70
  Of all his wars within the realm of France?
PUCELLE. Here's a silly stately style indeed!
  The Turk, that two and fifty kingdoms hath,
  Writes not so tedious a style as this.
  Him that thou magnifi'st with all these titles
  Stinking and fly-blown lies here at our feet.
LUCY. Is Talbot slain, the Frenchmen's only scourge,
  Your kingdom's terror and black Nemesis?
  O, were mine eye-balls into bullets turned,
  That I in rage might shoot them at your faces!   80
  O, that I could but call these dead to life!
  It were enough to fright the realm of France:
  Were but his picture left amongst you here,
  It would amaze the proudest of you all.
  Give me their bodies, that I may bear them hence
  And give them burial as beseems their worth.
PUCELLE. I think this upstart is old Talbot's ghost,
  He speaks with such a proud commanding spirit.
  For God's sake, let him have 'em; to keep them here,
  They would but stink, and putrefy the air.   90
CHARLES. Go, take their bodies hence.

LUCY. I'll bear them hence; but from their ashes shall
    be reared
  A phoenix that shall make all France afeard.
CHARLES. So we be rid of them, do with 'em what
    thou wilt.
  And now to Paris, in this conquering vein.
  All will be ours, now bloody Talbot's slain.
                                        They go

ACT 5
Scene 1: London. The palace

Sennet. Enter King, Gloucester, and Exeter

KING. Have you perused the letters from the pope,
  The emperor and the Earl of Armagnac?
GLOUCESTER. I have, my lord, and their intent is this:
  They humbly sue unto your excellence
  To have a godly peace concluded of
  Between the realms of England and of France.
KING. How doth your grace affect their motion?
GLOUCESTER. Well, my good lord; and as the only
    means
  To stop effusion of our Christian blood
  And stablish quietness on every side.   10
KING. Ay, marry, uncle, for I always thought
  It was both impious and unnatural
  That such immanity and bloody strife
  Should reign among professors of one faith.
GLOUCESTER. Beside, my lord, the sooner to effect
  And surer bind this knot of amity,
  The Earl of Armagnac, near knit to Charles,
  A man of great authority in France,
  Proffers his only daughter to your grace
  In marriage, with a large and sumptuous dowry. 20
KING. Marriage, uncle! alas, my years are young;
  And fitter is my study and my books
  Than wanton dalliance with a paramour.
  Yet call th'ambassadors, and, as you please,
  So let them have their answers every one:
  I shall be well content with any choice
  Tends to God's glory and my country's weal.

*Enter Winchester in Cardinal's habit, a Legate and two
Ambassadors*

EXETER. What! is my Lord of Winchester installed,
  And called unto a cardinal's degree?
  Then I perceive that will be verified   30
  Henry the Fifth did sometime prophesy,
  'If once he come to be a cardinal,
  He'll make his cap co-equal with the crown.'
KING. My lords ambassadors, your several suits
  Have been considered and debated on.
  Your purpose is both good and reasonable;
  And therefore are we certainly resolved
  To draw conditions of a friendly peace;
  Which by my Lord of Winchester we mean
  Shall be transported presently to France.   40
GLOUCESTER. And for the proffer of my lord your
    master,
  I have informed his highness so at large
  As liking of the lady's virtuous gifts,
  Her beauty and the value of her dower,
  He doth intend she shall be England's queen.
KING. In argument and proof of which contract,
  Bear her this jewel, pledge of my affection.

And so, my Lord Protector, see them guarded
And safely brought to Dover, wherein shipped
Commit them to the fortune of the sea.   50
        *The King, Gloucester, and Exeter
        retire; as the ambassadors leave,
        Winchester takes the Legate aside*
WINCHESTER. Stay, my Lord Legate: you shall first
    receive
  The sum of money which I promiséd
  Should be delivered to his Holiness
  For clothing me in these grave ornaments.
LEGATE. I will attend upon your lordship's leisure.
                        He follows the others
WINCHESTER. Now Winchester will not submit,
    I trow,
  Or be inferior to the proudest peer.
  Humphrey of Gloucester, thou shalt well perceive
  That, neither in birth or for authority,
  The bishop will be overborne by thee: 60
  I'll either make thee stoop and bend thy knee,
  Or sack this country with a mutiny.   *He goes*

Scene 2: France. Before Reignier's castle in Anjou

*Enter Charles, Burgundy, Alençon, Bastard, Reignier, La
Pucelle, and forces*

CHARLES. These news, my lords, may cheer our
    drooping spirits:
  'Tis said the stout Parisians do revolt
  And turn again unto the warlike French.
ALENÇON. Then march to Paris, royal Charles of
    France,
  And keep not back your powers in dalliance.
PUCELLE. Peace be amongst them, if they turn to us;
  Else, ruin combat with their palaces!

Enter a Scout

SCOUT. Success unto our valiant general,
  And happiness to his accomplices!
CHARLES. What tidings send our scouts? I prithee,
    speak.   10
SCOUT. The English army, that divided was
  Into two parties, is now conjoined in one,
  And means to give you battle presently.
CHARLES. Somewhat too sudden, sirs, the warning is,
  But we will presently provide for them.
BURGUNDY. I trust the ghost of Talbot is not there:
  Now he is gone, my lord, you need not fear.
PUCELLE. Of all base passions, fear is most accursed.
  Command the conquest, Charles, it shall be thine,
  Let Henry fret and all the world repine.   20
CHARLES. Then on, my lords, and France be fortunate!
                                        They go

Scene 3

Alarum. Excursions. La Pucelle returns

PUCELLE. The Regent conquers, and the Frenchmen
    fly.
  Now help, ye charming spells and periapts,
  And ye choice spirits that admonish me
  And give me signs of future accidents. · *Thunder*
  You speedy helpers, that are substitutes
  Under the lordly monarch of the north,
  Appear and aid me in this enterprise.

Enter Fiends

This speedy and quick appearance argues proof
Of your accustomed diligence to me.
Now, ye familiar spirits, that are culled   10
Out of the powerful regions under earth,
Help me this once, that France may get the field.
                    They walk, and speak not
O, hold me not with silence over-long!
Where I was wont to feed you with my blood,
I'll lop a member off and give it you
In earnest of a further benefit,
So you do condescend to help me now.
                    They hang their heads
No hope to have redress? My body shall
Pay recompense, if you will grant my suit.
                    They shake their heads
Cannot my body nor blood-sacrifice   20
Entreat you to your wonted furtherance?
Then take my soul, my body, soul and all,
Before that England give the French the foil.
                    They depart
See, they forsake me! Now the time is come
That France must vail her lofty-pluméd crest
And let her head fall into England's lap.
My ancient incantations are too weak,
And hell too strong for me to buckle with:
Now, France, thy glory droopeth to the dust.
                    She goes

*Excursions. Burgundy and York fight hand to hand. The
French fly. York pursues and returns with La Pucelle captive*

YORK. Damsel of France, I think I have you fast: 30
    Unchain your spirits now with spelling charms
    And try if they can gain your liberty.
    A goodly prize, fit for the devil's grace!
    See, how the ugly witch doth bend her brows,
    As if with Circe she would change my shape!
PUCELLE. Changed to a worser shape thou canst not be.
YORK. O, Charles the Dauphin is a proper man,
    No shape but his can please your dainty eye.
PUCELLE. A plaguing mischief light on Charles and
    thee!
    And may ye both be suddenly surprised   40
    By bloody hands, in sleeping on your beds!
YORK. Fell banning hag, enchantress, hold thy tongue!
PUCELLE. I prithee, give me leave to curse awhile.
YORK. Curse, miscreant, when thou comest to the
    stake.   *He takes her away*

Alarum. Enter Suffolk, with Margaret in his hand

SUFFOLK. Be what thou wilt, thou art my prisoner.
                    Gazes on her
    O fairest beauty, do not fear nor fly!
    For I will touch thee but with reverent hands;
    I kiss these fingers for eternal peace,
    And lay them gently on thy tender side.
    Who art thou? say, that I may honour thee.   50
MARGARET. Margaret my name, and daughter to a
    king,
    The King of Naples, whosoe'er thou art.
SUFFOLK. An earl I am, and Suffolk am I called.
    Be not offended, nature's miracle,
    Thou art allotted to be ta'en by me:
    So doth the swan her downy cygnets save,
    Keeping them prisoner underneath her wings,
    Yet if this servile usage once offend,

Go and be free again as Suffolk's friend.
                    She is going
O, stay! [*aside*] I have no power to let her pass,   60
My hand would free her, but my heart says no.
As plays the sun upon the glassy streams,
Twinkling another counterfeited beam,
So seems this gorgeous beuty to mine eyes.
Fain would I woo her, yet I dare not speak:
I'll call for pen and ink, and write my mind.
Fie, de la Pole! disable not thyself;
Hast not a tongue? is she not here?
Wilt thou be daunted at a woman's sight?
Ay, beauty's princely majesty is such,   70
Confounds the tongue and makes the senses rough.
MARGARET. Say, Earl of Suffolk, if thy name be so,
    What ransom must I pay before I pass?
    For I perceive I am thy prisoner.
SUFFOLK [*aside*]. How canst thou tell she will deny thy
    suit,
    Before thou make a trial of her love?
MARGARET. Why speak'st thou not? what ransom must
    I pay?
SUFFOLK [*aside*]. She's beautiful and therefore to be
    wooed;
    She is a woman, therefore to be won.
MARGARET. Wilt thou accept of ransom? yea, or no.   80
SUFFOLK [*aside*]. Fond man, remember that thou hast a
    wife;
    Then how can Margaret be thy paramour?
MARGARET. I were best to leave him, for he will not
    hear.
SUFFOLK. There all is marred; there lies a cooling card.
MARGARET. He talks at random; sure, the man is mad.
SUFFOLK. And yet a dispensation may be had.
MARGARET. And yet I would that you would answer
    me.
SUFFOLK. I'll win this Lady Margaret. For whom?
    Why, for my king: tush, that's a wooden thing!
MARGARET. He talks of wood: it is some carpenter.   90
SUFFOLK [*aside*]. Yet so my fancy may be satisfied,
    And peace establishéd between these realms.
    But there remains a scruple in that too;
    For though her father be the King of Naples,
    Duke of Anjou and Maine, yet is he poor,
    And our nobility will scorn the match.
MARGARET. Hear ye, captain, are you not at leisure?
SUFFOLK [*aside*]. It shall be so, disdain they ne'er so
    much:
    Henry is youthful and will quickly yield.
    Madam, I have a secret to reveal.   100
MARGARET [*aside*]. What though I be enthralled? he
    seems a knight,
    And will not any way dishonour me.
SUFFOLK. Lady, vouchsafe to listen what I say.
MARGARET [*aside*]. Perhaps I shall be rescued by the
    French;
    And then I need not crave his courtesy.
SUFFOLK. Sweet madam, give me hearing in a cause.
MARGARET [*aside*]. Tush, women have been captivate
    ere now.
SUFFOLK. Lady, wherefore talk you so?
MARGARET. I cry you mercy, 'tis but Quid for Quo.
SUFFOLK. Say, gentle princess, would you not suppose   110
    Your bondage happy, to be made a queen?
MARGARET. To be a queen in bondage is more vile,
    Than is a slave in base servility;

For princes should be free.
SUFFOLK.　　　　　　　　　　　And so shall you,
　If happy England's royal king be free.
MARGARET. Why, what concerns his freedom unto
　me?
SUFFOLK. I'll undertake to make thee Henry's queen,
　To put a golden sceptre in thy hand
　And set a precious crown upon thy head,
　If thou wilt condescend to be my—
MARGARET.　　　　　　　　　　What? 120
SUFFOLK. His love.
MARGARET. I am unworthy to be Henry's wife.
SUFFOLK. No, gentle madam, I unworthy am
　To woo so fair a dame to be his wife
　[aside] And have no portion in the choice myself....
　How say you, madam, are ye so content?
MARGARET. An if my father please, I am content.
SUFFOLK. Then call our captains and our colours forth.
　And, madam, at your father's castle walls
　We'll crave a parley, to confer with him. 130

A parley sounded. Enter Reignier on the walls

　See, Reignier, see, thy daughter prisoner!
REIGNIER. To whom?
SUFFOLK.　　　　　　　　To me.
REIGNIER.　　　　　　　　　　Suffolk, what remedy?
　I am a soldier and unapt to weep
　Or to exclaim on fortune's fickleness.
SUFFOLK. Yes, there is remedy enough, my lord:
　Consent, and for thy honour give consent,
　Thy daughter shall be wedded to my king;
　Whom I with pain have wooed and won thereto;
　And this her easy-held imprisonment
　Hath gained thy daughter princely liberty. 140
REIGNIER. Speaks Suffolk as he thinks?
SUFFOLK.　　　　　　　　Fair Margaret knows
　That Suffolk doth not flatter, face, or feign.
REIGNIER. Upon thy princely warrant, I descend
　To give thee answer of thy just demand.
　　　　　　　　He goes down from the walls
SUFFOLK. And here I will expect thy coming.

Trumpets sound. Enter Reignier from the castle-gate

REIGNIER. Welcome, brave earl, into our territories:
　Command in Anjou what your honour pleases.
SUFFOLK. Thanks, Reignier, happy for so sweet a
　child,
　Fit to be made companion with a king:
　What answer makes your grace unto my suit? 150
REIGNIER. Since thou dost to woo her little worth
　To be the princely bride of such a lord;
　Upon condition I may quietly
　Enjoy mine own, the country Maine and Anjou,
　Free from oppression or the stroke of war,
　My daughter shall be Henry's, if he please.
SUFFOLK. That is her ransom; I deliver her;
　And those two counties I will undertake
　Your grace shall well and quietly enjoy.
REIGNIER. And I again, in Henry's royal name, 160
　As deputy unto that gracious king,
　Give thee her hand, for sign of plighted faith.
SUFFOLK. Reignier of France, I give thee kingly
　thanks,
　Because this is in traffic of a king.
　[Aside] And yet, methinks, I could be well content
　To be mine own attorney in this case.

[Aloud] I'll over then to England with this news,
　And make this marriage to be solemnized.
　So farewell, Reignier: set this diamond safe
　In golden palaces, as it becomes. 170
REIGNIER. I do embrace thee, as I would embrace
　The Christian prince, King Henry, were he here.
MARGARET. Farewell, my lord: good wishes, praise
　and prayers
　Shall Suffolk ever have of Margaret. She is going
SUFFOLK. Farewell, sweet madam: but hark you,
　Margaret;
　No princely commendations to my king?
MARGARET. Such commendations as becomes a maid,
　A virgin and his servant, say to him.
SUFFOLK. Words sweetly placed and modestly
　directed.
　But, madam, I must trouble you again; 180
　No loving token to his majesty?
MARGARET. Yes, my good lord, a pure unspotted heart,
　Never yet taint with love, I send the king.
SUFFOLK. And this withal.　　　　　Kisses her
MARGARET. That for thyself: I will not so presume
　To send such peevish tokens to a king.
　　　　　　　　Reignier and Margaret go
SUFFOLK. O, wert thou for myself! But, Suffolk, stay;
　Thou mayst not wander in that labyrinth;
　There Minotaurs and ugly treasons lurk.
　Solicit Henry with her wondrous praise: 190
　Bethink thee on her virtues that surmount,
　'Mid natural graces that extinguish art;
　Repeat their semblance often on the seas,
　That, when thou com'st to kneel at Henry's feet,
　Thou mayst bereave him of his wits with wonder.
　　　　　　　　　　　　　　He goes

Scene 4: Camp of the Duke of York in Anjou

Enter York, Warwick, and others

YORK. Bring forth that sorceress condemned to burn.

Enter La Pucelle, guarded, and a Shepherd

SHEPHERD. Ah, Joan, this kills thy father's heart
　outright!
　Have I sought every country far and near,
　And now it is my chance to find thee out,
　Must I behold thy timeless cruel death?
　Ah, Joan, sweet daughter Joan, I'll die with thee!
PUCELLE. Decrepit miser! base ignoble wretch!
　I am descended of a gentler blood.
　Thou art no father nor no friend of mine.
SHEPHERD. Out, out! My lords, an please you, 'tis not
　so; 10
　I did beget her, all the parish knows.
　Her mother liveth yet, can testify
　She was the first fruit of my bachelorship.
WARWICK. Graceless! wilt thou deny thy parentage?
YORK. This argues what her kind of life hath been,
　Wicked and vile, and so her death concludes.
SHEPHERD. Fie, Joan, that thou wilt be so obstacle!
　God knows thou art a collop of my flesh;
　And for thy sake have I shed many a tear:
　Deny me not, I prithee, gentle Joan. 20
PUCELLE. Peasant, avaunt! You have suborned this
　man,
　Of purpose to obscure my noble birth.

SHEPHERD. 'Tis true, I gave a noble to the priest
The morn that I was wedded to her mother.
Kneel down and take my blessing, good my girl
Wilt thou not stoop? Now curséd be the time
Of thy nativity! I would the milk
Thy mother gave thee when thou suck'dst her
  breast,
Had been a little ratsbane for thy sake!
Or else, when thou didst keep my lambs a-field,   30
I wish some ravenous wolf had eaten thee!
Dost thou deny thy father, curséd drab?
O, burn her, burn her! hanging is too good.
                                        He goes
YORK. Take her away, for she hath lived too long,
To fill the world with vicious qualities.
PUCELLE. First, let me tell you whom you have
  condemned:
Not me begotten of a shepherd swain,
But issued from the progeny of kings;
Virtuous and holy; chosen from above,
By inspiration of celestial grace,   40
To work exceeding miracles on earth.
I never had to do with wicked spirits:
But you, that are polluted with your lusts,
Stained with the guiltless blood of innocents,
Corrupt and tainted with a thousand vices,
Because you want the grace that others have,
You judge it straight a thing impossible
To compass wonders but by help of devils.
No, misconceivéd! Joan of Arc hath been
A virgin from her tender infancy,   50
Chaste and immaculate in very thought,
Whose maiden blood, thus rigorously effused,
Will cry for vengeance at the gates of heaven.
YORK. Ay, ay: away with her to execution!
WARWICK. And hark ye, sirs; because she is a maid,
Spare for no faggots, let there be enow:
Place barrels of pitch upon the fatal stake,
That so her torture may be shortenéd.
PUCELLE. Will nothing turn your unrelenting hearts?
Then, Joan, discover thine infirmity,   60
That warranteth by law to be thy privilege.
I am with child, ye bloody homicides:
Murder not then the fruit within my womb,
Although ye hale me to a violent death.
YORK. Now heaven forfend! the holy maid with child!
WARWICK. The greatest miracle that e'er ye wrought:
Is all your strict preciseness come to this?
YORK. She and the Dauphin have been juggling:
I did imagine what would be her refuge.
WARWICK. Well, go to; we'll have no bastards live;   70
Especially since Charles must father it.
PUCELLE. You are deceived, my child is none of his,
It was Alençon that enjoyed my love.
YORK. Alençon! that notorious Machiavel!
It dies, an if it had a thousand lives.
PUCELLE. O, give me leave, I have deluded you:
'Twas neither Charles nor yet the duke I named,
But Reignier, king of Naples, that prevailed.
WARWICK. A married man! that's most intolerable.
YORK. Why, here's a girl! I think she knows not well,   80
There were so many, whom she may accuse.
WARWICK. It's sign she hath been liberal and free.
YORK. And yet, forsooth, she is a virgin pure.
Strumpet, thy words condemn thy brat and thee.
Use no entreaty, for it is in vain.

PUCELLE. Then lead me hence; with whom I leave
  my curse:
May never glorious sun reflex his beams
Upon the country where you make abode;
But darkness and the gloomy shade of death
Environ you, till mischief and despair   90
Drive you to break your necks or hang yourselves!
                                She is led away
YORK. Break thou in pieces and consume to ashes,
Thou foul accurséd minister of hell!

Enter Cardinal Beaufort, Bishop of Winchester, attended

WINCHESTER. Lord Regent, I do greet your excellence
With letters of commission from the king.
For know, my lords, the states of Christendom,
Moved with remorse of these outrageous broils,
Have earnestly implored a general peace
Betwixt our nation and the aspiring French;
And here at hand the Dauphin and his train   100
Approacheth, to confer about some matter.
YORK. Is all our travail turned to this effect?
After the slaughter of so many peers,
So many captains, gentlemen and soldiers,
That in this quarrel have been overthrown
And sold their bodies for their country's benefit,
Shall we at last conclude effeminate peace?
Have we not lost most part of all the towns,
By treason, falsehood, and by treachery,
Our great progenitors had conqueréd?   110
O, Warwick, Warwick! I foresee with grief
The utter loss of all the realm of France.
WARWICK. Be patient, York: if we conclude a peace,
It shall be with such strict and severe covenants
As little shall the Frenchmen gain thereby.

Enter Charles, Alençon, Bastard, Reignier

CHARLES. Since, lords of England, it is thus agreed
That peaceful truce shall be proclaimed in France,
We come to be informéd by yourselves
What the conditions of that league must be.
YORK. Speak, Winchester; for boiling choler chokes 120
The hollow passage of my poisoned voice,
By sight of these our baleful enemies.
WINCHESTER. Charles, and the rest, it is enacted thus:
That, in regard King Henry gives consent,
Of mere compassion and of lenity,
To ease your country of distressful war,
And suffer you to breathe in fruitful peace,
You shall become true liegemen to his crown.
And, Charles, upon condition thou wilt swear
To pay him tribute, and submit thyself,   130
Thou shalt be placed as viceroy under him,
And still enjoy thy regal dignity.
ALENÇON. Must he be then as shadow of himself?
Adorn his temples with a coronet,
And yet, in substance and authority,
Retain but privilege of a private man?
This proffer is absurd and reasonless.
CHARLES. 'Tis known already that I am possessed
With more than half the Gallian territories,
And therein reverenced for their lawful king: 140
Shall I, for lucre of the rest unvanquished,
Detract so much from that prerogative,
As to be called but viceroy of the whole?
No, lord ambassador, I'll rather keep
That which I have than, coveting for more,

Be cast from possibility of all.
YORK. Insulting Charles! hast thou by secret means
  Used intercession to obtain a league,
  And, now the matter grows to compromise,
  Stand'st thou aloof upon comparison?   150
  Either accept the title thou usurp'st,
  Of benefit proceeding from our king
  And not of any challenge of desert,
  Or we will plague thee with incessant wars.
REIGNIER [aside]. My lord, you do not well in obstinacy
  To cavil in the course of this contract:
  If once it be neglected, ten to one
  We shall not find like opportunity.
ALENÇON [aside]. To say the truth, it is your policy
  To save your subjects from such massacre   160
  And ruthless slaughters as are daily seen
  By our proceeding in hostility;
  And therefore take this compact of a truce,
  Although you break it when your pleasure serves.
WARWICK. How say'st thou, Charles? shall our
    condition stand?
CHARLES. It shall;
  Only reserved, you claim no interest
  In any of our towns of garrison.
YORK [stretches forth the hilt of his sword]. Then swear
    allegiance to his majesty,
  As thou art knight, never to disobey   170
  Nor be rebellious to the crown of England,
  Thou, nor thy nobles, to the crown of England.
        Charles lays his hand upon the hilt
  So, now dismiss your army when ye please;
  Hang up your ensigns, let your drums be still,
  For here we entertain a solemn peace.   They go

Scene 5: London. The royal palace

Enter Suffolk in conference with the King, Gloucester and
Exeter

KING. Your wondrous rare description, noble earl,
  Of beauteous Margaret hath astonished me.
  Her virtues gracéd with external gifts
  Do breed love's settled passions in my heart,
  And like as rigour of tempestuous gusts
  Provokes the mightiest hulk against the tide,
  So am I driven by breath of her renown
  Either to suffer shipwreck or arrive
  Where I may have fruition of her love.
SUFFOLK. Tush, my good lord, this superficial tale   10
  Is but a preface of her worthy praise;
  The chief perfections of that lovely dame,
  Had I sufficient skill to utter them,
  Would make a volume of enticing lines,
  Able to ravish any dull conceit,
  And, which is more, she is not so divine,
  So full replete with choice of all delights,
  But with as humble lowliness of mind
  She is content to be at your command;
  Command, I mean, of virtuous chaste intents,   20
  To love and honour Henry as her lord.
KING. And otherwise will Henry ne'er presume.
  Therefore, my Lord Protector, give consent
  That Margaret may be England's royal queen.
GLOUCESTER. So should I give consent to flatter sin.
  You know, my lord, your highness is betrothed
  Unto another lady of esteem:
  How shall we then dispense with that contract,

And not deface your honour with reproach?
SUFFOLK. As doth a ruler with unlawful oaths;   30
  Or one that, at a triumph having vowed
  To try his strength, forsaketh yet the lists
  By reason of his adversary's odds:
  A poor earl's daughter is unequal odds,
  And therefore may be broke without offence.
GLOUCESTER. Why, what, I pray, is Margaret more
    than that?
  Her father is no better than an earl,
  Although in glorious titles he excel.
SUFFOLK. Yes, my lord, her father is a king,
  The King of Naples and Jerusalem,   40
  And of such great authority in France
  As his alliance will confirm our peace
  And keep the Frenchmen in allegiance.
GLOUCESTER. And so the Earl of Armagnac may do,
  Because he is near kinsman unto Charles.
EXETER. Beside, his wealth doth warrant a liberal
    dower,
  Where Reignier sooner will receive than give.
SUFFOLK. A dower, my lords! disgrace not so your
    king,
  That he should be so abject, base and poor,
  To choose for wealth and not for perfect love.   50
  Henry is able to enrich his queen,
  And not to seek a queen to make him rich:
  So worthless peasants bargain for their wives,
  As market men for oxen, sheep, or horse.
  Marriage is a matter of more worth
  Than to be dealt in by attorneyship;
  Not whom we will, but whom his grace affects,
  Must be companion of his nuptial bed:
  And therefore, lords, since he affects her most,
  Which most of all these reasons bindeth us,   60
  In our opinions she should be preferred.
  For what is wedlock forcéd but a hell,
  An age of discord and continual strife?
  Whereas the contrary bringeth bliss,
  And is a pattern of celestial peace.
  Whom should we match with Henry, being a king,
  But Margaret, that is daughter to a king?
  Her peerless feature, joinéd with her birth,
  Approves her fit for none but for a king:
  Her valiant courage and undaunted spirit,   70
  More than in women commonly is seen,
  Will answer our hope in issue of a king;
  For Henry, son unto a conqueror,
  Is likely to beget more conquerors,
  If with a lady of so high resolve
  As is fair Margaret he be linked in love.
  Then yield, my lords; and here conclude with me
  That Margaret shall be queen, and none but she.
KING. Whether it be through force of your report,
  My noble Lord of Suffolk, or for that   80
  My tender youth was never yet attaint
  With any passion of inflaming love,
  I cannot tell; but this I am assured,
  I feel such sharp dissension in my breast,
  Such fierce alarums both of hope and fear,
  As I am sick with working of my thoughts.
  Take, therefore, shipping; post, my lord, to France;
  Agree to any covenants, and procure
  That Lady Margaret do vouchsafe to come
  To cross the seas to England and be crowned   90
  King Henry's faithful and anointed queen:

For your expenses and sufficient charge,
Among the people gather up a tenth.
Be gone, I say; for, till you do return,
I rest perplexéd with a thousand cares.
And you, good uncle, banish all offence:
If you do censure me by what you were,
Not what you are, I know it will excuse
This sudden execution of my will.
And so, conduct me where, from company,   100
I may revolve and ruminate my grief.   *He goes*

GLOUCESTER. Ay, grief, I fear me, both at first and last.
                              Gloucester and Exeter follow
SUFFOLK. Thus Suffolk hath prevailed; and thus he
    goes,
As did the youthful Paris once to Greece,
With hope to find the like event in love,
But prosper better than the Trojan did.
Margaret shall now be queen, and rule the king;
But I will rule both her, the king and realm.
                                            He goes

The Second Part of King Henry VI

The scene: England

CHARACTERS IN THE PLAY

KING HENRY *the Sixth*
HUMPHREY, DUKE OF GLOUCESTER, *uncle to the King,*
  and Protector
CARDINAL BEAUFORT, BISHOP OF WINCHESTER,
  great-uncle to the King
RICHARD PLANTAGENET, DUKE OF YORK
EDWARD *and* RICHARD, *his sons*
DUKE OF SOMERSET
WILLIAM DE LA POLE, DUKE OF SUFFOLK
HUMPHREY, DUKE OF BUCKINGHAM
LORD CLIFFORD
Young CLIFFORD, *his son*
EARL OF SALISBURY
EARL OF WARWICK
LORD SCALES
LORD SAY
SIR HUMPHREY STAFFORD, *and* WILLIAM STAFFORD, *his*
  brother
SIR JOHN STANLEY
VAUX
SIR MATTHEW GOUGH

A Lieutenant, Master, and Master's-Mate, and
  WALTER WHITMORE
Two Gentlemen, prisoners with Suffolk
JOHN HUM *and* JOHN SOUTHWELL, *priests*
BOLINGBROKE, *a conjuror*
A Spirit
THOMAS HORNER, *an armourer.* PETER, *his man*
Clerk of Chatham. Mayor of Saint Albans
SIMPCOX, *an impostor*
ALEXANDER IDEN, *a Kentish gentleman*
JACK CADE, *a rebel*
GEORGE BEVIS, JOHN HOLLAND, DICK *the butcher,*
  SMITH *the weaver,* MICHAEL, *etc., followers of Cade*
Two Murderers
MARGARET, *Queen to King Henry*
ELEANOR, *Duchess of Gloucester*
MARGERY JOURDAIN, *a witch*
Wife to Simpcox
Lords, Ladies, and Attendants, Petitioners, Aldermen, a
  Herald, a Beadle, Sheriff, and Officers, Citizens,
  Prentices, Falconers, Guards, Soldiers, Messengers, etc.

The Second Part of King Henry VI

ACT 1
Scene 1: *London. The palace*

*Flourish of trumpets: then hoboys. Enter the King,
Humphrey, Duke of Gloucester, Salisbury, Warwick,
and Cardinal Beaufort, on the one side; the Queen,
Suffolk, York, Somerset, and Buckingham, on the other*

SUFFOLK. As by your high imperial majesty
I had in charge at my depart for France,
As procurator to your excellence,
To marry Princess Margaret for your grace,
So, in the famous ancient city Tours,
In presence of the Kings of France and Sicil,
The Dukes of Orleans, Calaber, Bretagne and
  Alençon,
Seven earls, twelve barons and twenty reverend
  bishops,
I have performed my task and was espoused,
And humbly now upon my bended knee,   10
In sight of England and her lordly peers,
Deliver up my title in the queen
To your most gracious hands, that are the substance
Of that great shadow I did represent;
The happiest gift that ever marquess gave,
The fairest queen that ever king received.
KING. Suffolk, arise. Welcome, Queen Margaret!
I can express no kinder sign of love
Than this kind kiss. O Lord, that lends me life,
Lend me a heart replete with thankfulness!   20
For Thou hast given me in this beauteous face
A world of earthly blessings to my soul,
If sympathy of love unite our thoughts.
QUEEN. Great King of England and my gracious lord,
The mutual conference that my mind hath had,
By day, by night, waking and in my dreams,
In courtly company or at my beads,
With you, mine alder-liefest sovereign,
Makes me the bolder to salute my king
With ruder terms, such as my wit affords
And over-joy of heart doth minister.   30
KING. Her sight did ravish, but her grace in speech,
Her words y-clad with wisdom's majesty,
Makes me from wond'ring fall to weeping joys,
Such is the fulness of my heart's content.
Lords, with one cheerful voice welcome my love.
ALL [*kneeling*]. Long live Queen Margaret, England's
  happiness!
QUEEN. We thank you all.   *Flourish*
SUFFOLK. My Lord Protector, so it please your grace,
Here are the articles of contracted peace   40
Between our sovereign and the French king
  Charles,
For eighteen months concluded by consent.
GLOUCESTER [*reads*]. 'Imprimis, It is agreed between
the French king Charles, and William de la Pole,
Marquess of Suffolk, ambassador for Henry King of
England, that the said Henry shall espouse the Lady
Margaret, daughter unto Reignier King of Naples,
Sicilia and Jerusalem, and crown her Queen of

England ere the thirtieth of May next ensuing....
Item, That the duchy of Anjou and the county of   50
Maine shall be released and delivered to the king
her father'—   *Lets the paper fall*
KING. Uncle, how now?
GLOUCESTER.   Pardon me, gracious lord;
Some sudden qualm hath struck me at the heart,
And dimmed mine eyes, that I can read no further.
KING. Uncle of Winchester, I pray, read on.
CARDINAL [*reads*]. 'Item, It is further agreed between
them, that the duchies of Anjou and Maine shall be
released and delivered over to the king her father,
and she sent over of the King of England's own   60
proper cost and charges, without having any
dowry.'
KING. They please us well. Lord marquess, kneel
  down:
We here create thee the first duke of Suffolk,
And girt thee with the sword. Cousin of York,
We here discharge your grace from being regent
I'th'parts of France, till term of eighteen months
Be full expired. Thanks, uncle Winchester,
Gloucester, York, Buckingham, Somerset,
Salisbury, and Warwick;   70
We thank you all for this great favour done,
In entertainment to my princely queen.
Come, let us in, and with all speed provide
To see her coronation be performed.
          *The King departs with the Queen and
                Suffolk; Gloucester stays the rest*
GLOUCESTER. Brave peers of England, pillars of the
  state,
To you Duke Humphrey must unload his grief—
Your grief, the common grief of all the land.
What! did my brother Henry spend his youth,
His valour, coin, and people, in the wars?
Did he so often lodge in open field,   80
In winter's cold and summer's parching heat,
To conquer France, his true inheritance?
And did my brother Bedford toil his wits,
To keep by policy what Henry got?
Have you yourselves, Somerset, Buckingham,
Brave York, Salisbury, and victorious Warwick,
Received deep scars in France and Normandy?
Or hath mine uncle Beaufort and myself,
With all the learnèd council of the realm,
Studied so long, sat in the council-house   90
Early and late, debating to and fro
How France and Frenchmen might be kept in awe,
And had his highness in his infancy
Crownèd in Paris in despite of foes?
And shall these labours and these honours die?
Shall Henry's conquest, Bedford's vigilance,
Your deeds of war and all our counsel die?
O peers of England, shameful is this league!
Fatal this marriage, cancelling your fame,
Blotting your names from books of memory,   100
Razing the characters of your renown,
Defacing monuments of conquered France,
Undoing all, as all had never been!

CARDINAL. Nephew, what means this passionate
  discourse,
  This peroration with such circumstance?
  For France, 'tis ours; and we will keep it, still.
GLOUCESTER. Ay, uncle, we will keep it, if we can;
  But now it is impossible we should:
  Suffolk, the new-made duke that rules the roast,
  Hath given the duchy of Anjou and Maine 110
  Unto the poor King Reignier, whose large style
  Agrees not with the leanness of his purse.
SALISBURY. Now, by the death of Him that died for
  all,
  These counties were the keys of Normandy.
  But wherefore weeps Warwick, my valiant son?
WARWICK. For grief that they are past recovery:
  For, were there hope to conquer them again,
  My sword should shed hot blood, mine eyes no
  tears.
  Anjou and Maine! myself did win them both;
  Those provinces these arms of mine did conquer: 120
  And are the cities, that I got with wounds,
  Delivered up again with peaceful words?
  Mort Dieu!
YORK. For Suffolk's duke, may he be suffocate,
  That dims the honour of this warlike isle!
  France should have torn and rent my very heart,
  Before I would have yielded to this league.
  I never read but England's kings have had
  Large sums of gold and dowries with their wives;
  And our King Henry gives away his own, 130
  To match with her that brings no vantages.
GLOUCESTER. A proper jest, and never heard before,
  That Suffolk should demand a whole fifteenth
  For costs and charges in transporting her!
  She should have stayed in France and starved in
  France,
  Before—
CARDINAL. My lord of Gloucester, now ye grow too
  hot,
  It was the pleasure of my lord the king.
GLOUCESTER. My lord of Winchester, I know your
  mind;
  'Tis not my speeches that you do mislike, 140
  But 'tis my presence that doth trouble ye.
  Rancour will out: proud prelate, in thy face
  I see thy fury: if I longer stay,
  We shall begin our ancient bickerings.
  Lordings, farewell, and say when I am gone,
  I prophesied France will be lost ere long. *Goes*
CARDINAL. So, there goes our Protector in a rage.
  'Tis known to you he is mine enemy,
  Nay, more, an enemy unto you all,
  And no great friend, I fear me, to the king. 150
  Consider, lords, he is the next of blood,
  And heir apparent to the English crown:
  Had Henry got an empire by his marriage,
  And all the wealthy kingdoms of the west,
  There's reason he should be displeased at it.
  Look to it, lords, let not his smoothing words
  Bewitch your hearts, be wise and circumspect.
  What though the common people favour him,
  Calling him 'Humphrey, the good Duke of
  Gloucester,'
  Clapping their hands, and crying with loud voice, 160
  'Jesu maintain your royal excellence!'
  With 'God preserve the good Duke Humphrey!'

I fear me, lords, for all this flattering gloss,
  He will be found a dangerous Protector.
BUCKINGHAM. Why should he, then, protect our
  sovereign,
  He being of age to govern of himself?
  Cousin of Somerset, join you with me,
  And all together, with the Duke of Suffolk,
  We'll quickly hoise duke Humphrey from his seat.
CARDINAL. This weighty business will not brook
  delay; 170
  I'll to the Duke of Suffolk presently. *Goes*
SOMERSET. Cousin of Buckingham, though
  Humphrey's pride
  And greatness of his place be grief to us,
  Yet let us watch the haughty cardinal.
  His insolence is more intolerable
  Than all the princes in the land beside.
  If Gloucester be displaced, he'll be Protector.
BUCKINGHAM. Or thou or I, Somerset, will be
  Protector,
  Despite Duke Humphrey or the cardinal.
               Buckingham and Somerset go
SALISBURY. Pride went before, Ambition follows him. 180
  While these do labour for their own preferment,
  Behoves it us to labour for the realm.
  I never saw but Humphrey Duke of Gloucester
  Did bear him like a noble gentleman.
  Oft have I seen the haughty cardinal,
  More like a soldier than a man o'th'church,
  As stout and proud as he were lord of all,
  Swear like a ruffian and demean himself
  Unlike the ruler of a commonweal.
  Warwick, my son, the comfort of my age, 190
  Thy deeds, thy plainness, and thy housekeeping,
  Hath won the greatest favour of the commons,
  Excepting none but good Duke Humphrey:
  And, brother York, thy acts in Ireland,
  In bringing them to civil discipline,
  Thy late exploits done in the heart of France,
  When thou wert regent for our sovereign,
  Have made thee feared and honoured of the people:
  Join we together, for the public good,
  In what we can, to bridle and suppress 200
  The pride of Suffolk and the cardinal,
  With Somerset's and Buckingham's ambition;
  And, as we may, cherish Duke Humphrey's deeds,
  While they do tend the profit of the land.
WARWICK. So God help Warwick, as he loves the
  land,
  And common profit of his country!
YORK [*aside*]. And so says York, for he hath greatest
  cause.
SALISBURY. Then let's make haste away, and look unto
  the main.
WARWICK. Unto the main! O father, Maine is lost,
  That Maine which by main force Warwick did win, 210
  And would have kept so long as breath did last!
  Main chance, father, you meant; but I meant
  Maine,
  Which I will win from France, or else be slain.
               Warwick and Salisbury go,
               leaving York alone
YORK. Anjou and Maine are given to the French;
  Paris is lost; the state of Normandy
  Stands on a tickle point now they are gone.
  Suffolk concluded on the articles,

The peers agreed, and Henry was well pleased
To change two dukedoms for a duke's fair
    daughter.
I cannot blame them all—what is't to them?   220
'Tis thine they give away, and not their own.
Pirates may make cheap penn'orths of their pillage,
And purchase friends and give to courtezans,
Still revelling like lords till all be gone;
While as the silly owner of the goods
Weeps over them and wrings his hapless hands
And shakes his head and trembling stands aloof,
While all is shared and all is borne away,
Ready to starve and dare not touch his own:
So York must sit, and fret, and bite his tongue,   230
While his own lands are bargained for and sold.
Methinks the realms of England, France and Ireland
Bear that proportion to my flesh and blood
As did the fatal brand Althaea burned
Unto the prince's heart of Calydon.
Anjou and Maine both given unto the French!
Cold news for me, for I had hope of France,
Even as I have of fertile England's soil.
A day will come when York shall claim his own;
And therefore I will take the Nevils' parts   240
And make a show of love to proud Duke
    Humphrey,
And, when I spy advantage, claim the crown,
For that's the golden mark I seek to hit:
Nor shall proud Lancaster usurp my right,
Nor hold the sceptre in his childish fist,
Nor wear the diadem upon his head,
Whose church-like humours fits not for a crown.
Then, York, be still awhile, till time do serve:
Watch thou and wake when others be asleep,
To pry into the secrets of the state;   250
Till Henry, surfeiting in joys of love,
With his new bride and England's dear-bought
    queen,
And Humphrey with the peers be fall'n at jars:
Then will I raise aloft the milk-white rose,
With whose sweet smell the air shall be perfumed;
And in my standard bear the arms of York,
To grapple with the house of Lancaster;
And, force perforce, I'll make him yield the crown,
Whose bookish rule hath pulled fair England down.
                                                   Goes

Scene 2: *The Duke of Gloucester's house*

Enter Duke Humphrey and his wife Eleanor

DUCHESS. Why droops my lord, like over-ripened
    corn,
    Hanging the head at Ceres' plenteous load?
    Why doth the great Duke Humphrey knit his
        brows,
    As frowning at the favours of the world?
    Why are thine eyes fixed to the sullen earth,
    Gazing on that which seems to dim thy sight?
    What seest thou there? King Henry's diadem,
    Enchased with all the honours of the world?
    If so, gaze on, and grovel on thy face,
    Until thy head be circléd with the same.   10
    Put forth thy hand, reach at the glorious gold.
    What! is't too short? I'll lengthen it with mine;
    And, having both together heaved it up,
    We'll both together lift our heads to heaven,
    And never more abase our sight so low

As to vouchsafe one glance unto the ground.
GLOUCESTER. O Nell, sweet Nell, if thou dost love thy
    lord,
    Banish the canker of ambitious thoughts:
    And may that thought, when I imagine ill
    Against my king and nephew, virtuous Henry,   20
    Be my last breathing in this mortal world!
    My troublous dreams this night doth make me
        sad.
DUCHESS. What dreamed my lord? tell me, and I'll
    requite it
    With sweet rehearsal of my morning's dream.
GLOUCESTER. Methought this staff, mine office-badge
    in court,
    Was broke in twain; by whom I have forgot,
    But, as I think, it was by th'cardinal;
    And on the pieces of the broken wand
    Were placed the heads of Edmund Duke of
        Somerset,
    And William de la Pole, first Duke of Suffolk.   30
    This was my dream: what it doth bode, God knows.
DUCHESS. Tut, this was nothing but an argument
    That he that breaks a stick of Gloucester's grove
    Shall lose his head for his presumption.
    But list to me, my Humphrey, my sweet duke:
    Methought I sat in seat of majesty
    In the cathedral church of Westminster,
    And in that chair where kings and queens were
        crowned;
    Where Henry and Dame Margaret kneeled to me
    And on my head did set the diadem.   40
GLOUCESTER. Nay, Eleanor, then must I chide
    outright:
    Presumptuous dame, ill-nurtured Eleanor,
    Art thou not second woman in the realm,
    And the Protector's wife, beloved of him?
    Hast thou not worldly pleasure at command,
    Above the reach or compass of thy thought?
    And wilt thou still be hammering treachery,
    To tumble down thy husband and thyself
    From top of honour to disgrace's feet?
    Away from me, and let me hear no more!   50
DUCHESS. What, what, my lord! are you so choleric
    With Eleanor, for telling but her dream?
    Next time I'll keep my dreams unto myself,
    And not be checked.
GLOUCESTER. Nay, be not angry; I am pleased again.

Enter a Messenger

MESSENGER. My Lord Protector, 'tis his highness'
    pleasure
    You do prepare to ride unto Saint Albans,
    Where as the king and queen do mean to hawk.
GLOUCESTER. I go. Come, Nell, thou wilt ride with us?
DUCHESS. Yes, my good lord, I'll follow presently.   60
                            Gloucester and Messenger go
    Follow I must; I cannot go before,
    While Gloucester bears this base and humble mind.
    Were I a man, a duke, and next of blood,
    I would remove these tedious stumbling-blocks
    And smooth my way upon their headless necks;
    And, being a woman, I will not be slack
    To play my part in Fortune's pageant.
    Where are you there? Sir John! nay, fear not, man,
    We are alone; here's none but thee and I.

Enter Hum

HUM. Jesus preserve your royal majesty!   70
DUCHESS. What say'st thou? majesty! I am but grace.
HUM. But, by the grace of God, and Hum's advice,
   Your grace's title shall be multiplied.
DUCHESS. What say'st thou, man? hast thou as yet
   conferred
   With Margery Jourdain, the cunning witch,
   With Roger Bolingbroke, the conjuror?
   And will they undertake to do me good?
HUM. This they have promiséd, to show your
   highness
   A spirit raised from depth of underground,
   That shall make answer to such questions   80
   As by your grace shall be propounded him.
DUCHESS. It is enough. I'll think upon the questions:
   When from Saint Albans we do make return,
   We'll see these things effected to the full.
   Here, Hum, take this reward; make merry, man,
   With thy confederates in this weighty cause.
                         Goes
HUM. Hum must make merry with the duchess' gold;
   Marry, and shall. But, how now, Sir John Hum!
   Seal up your lips, and give no words but mum:
   The business asketh silent secrecy.   90
   Dame Eleanor gives gold to bring the witch:
   Gold cannot come amiss, were she a devil.
   Yet have I gold flies from another coast;
   I dare not say, from the rich cardinal
   And from the great and new-made Duke of
   Suffolk,
   Yet I do find it so; for, to be plain,
   They, knowing Dame Eleanor's aspiring humour,
   Have hiréd me to undermine the duchess
   And buzz these conjurations in her brain.
   They say 'A crafty knave does need no broker';   100
   Yet am I Suffolk and the cardinal's broker.
   Hum, if you take not heed, you shall go near
   To call them both a pair of crafty knaves.
   Well, so it stands; and thus, I fear, at last
   Hum's knavery will be the duchess' wrack,
   And her attainture will be Humphrey's fall:
   Sort how it will, I shall have gold for all.   *Goes*

Scene 3: *The palace*

Enter three or four Petitioners; Peter, the Armourer's man, being one

1 PETITIONER. My masters, let's stand close: my Lord
   Protector will come this way by and by, and then
   we may deliver our supplications in the quill.
2 PETITIONER. Marry, the Lord protect him, for he's a
   good man! Jesu bless him!

Enter Suffolk and Queen

PETER. Here a' comes, methinks, and the queen with
   him. I'll be the first, sure.
2 PETITIONER. Come back, fool; this is the duke of
   Suffolk, and not my Lord Protector.
SUFFOLK. How now, fellow! wouldst any thing with
   me?   10
1 PETITIONER. I pray, my lord, pardon me; I took ye
   for my Lord Protector.
QUEEN [*reading*]. 'To my Lord Protector!' Are your
   supplications to his lordship? Let me see them: what
   is thine?
1 PETITIONER. Mine is, an't please your grace, against

John Goodman, my Lord Cardinal's man, for keep-
   ing my house, and lands, and wife and all, from me.
SUFFOLK. Thy wife too! that's some wrong, indeed.
   What's yours? What's here? [*reads*] 'Against the   20
   Duke of Suffolk, for enclosing the commons of
   Melford.' How now, sir knave!
2 PETITIONER. Alas, sir, I am but a poor petitioner of
   our whole township.
PETER [*giving his petition*]. Against my master, Thomas
   Horner, for saying that the Duke of York was right-
   ful heir to the crown.
QUEEN. What say'st thou? did the Duke of York say
   he was rightful heir to the crown?
PETER. That my master was? no, forsooth: my master   30
   said that he was, and that the king was an usurper.
SUFFOLK. Who is there? [*enter servant*] Take this fellow
   in, and send for his master with a pursuivant
   presently: we'll hear more of your matter before the
   king.   *Servant departs with Peter*
QUEEN. And as for you, that love to be protected
   Under the wings of our Protector's grace,
   Begin your suits anew, and sue to him.
                     Tears the supplications
   Away, base cullions! Suffolk, let them go.   90
ALL. Come, let's be gone.   *The Petitioners go*   40
QUEEN. My Lord of Suffolk, say, is this the guise.
   Is this the fashion in the court of England?
   Is this the government of Britain's isle,
   And this the royalty of Albion's king?
   What! shall King Henry be a pupil still
   Under the surly Gloucester's governance?
   Am I a queen in title and in style,
   And must be made a subject to a duke?
   I tell thee, Pole, when in the city Tours
   Thou ran'st a tilt in honour of my love   50
   And stol'st away the ladies' hearts of France,
   I thought King Henry had resembléd thee
   In courage, courtship, and proportion:
   But all his mind is bent to holiness,
   To number Ave-Maries on his beads;
   His champions are the prophets and apostles,
   His weapons holy saws of sacred writ,
   His study is his tilt-yard, and his loves
   Are brazen images of canonized saints.
   I would the college of the cardinals   60
   Would choose him pope and carry him to Rome,
   And set the triple crown upon his head:
   That were a state fit for his holiness.
SUFFOLK. Madam, be patient: as I was cause
   Your highness came to England, so will I
   In England work your grace's full content.
QUEEN. Beside the haughty Protector, have we
   Beaufort,
   The imperious churchman, Somerset, Buckingham,
   And grumbling York; and not the least of these
   But can do more in England than the king.   70
SUFFOLK. And he of these that can do most of all
   Cannot do more in England than the Nevils:
   Salisbury and Warwick are no simple peers.
QUEEN. Not all these lords do vex me half so much
   As that proud dame, the Lord Protector's wife.
   She sweeps it through the court with troops of
   ladies,
   More like an empress than Duke Humphrey's wife:
   Strangers in court do take her for the queen:
   She bears a duke's revenues on her back,

And in her heart she scorns our poverty: 80
Shall I not live to be avenged on her?
Contemptuous base-born callet as she is,
She vaunted 'mongst her minions t'other day,
The very train of her worst wearing gown
Was better worth than all my father's lands,
Till Suffolk gave two dukedoms for his daughter.
SUFFOLK. Madam, myself have limed a bush for her,
And placed a choir of such enticing birds,
That she will light to listen to the lays,
And never mount to trouble you again.   90
So, let her rest: and, madam, list to me;
For I am bold to counsel you in this.
Although we fancy not the cardinal,
Yet must we join with him and with the lords,
Till we have brought Duke Humphrey in disgrace.
As for the Duke of York, this late complaint
Will make but little for his benefit.
So, one by one, we'll weed them all at last,
And you yourself shall steer the happy helm.

*Sound a Sennet. Enter the King with York and Somerset;
after them enter Duke Humphrey of Gloucester, Cardinal
Beaufort, Buckingham, York, Somerset, Salisbury, Warwick, and the Duchess of Gloucester*

KING. For my part, noble lords, I care not which;   100
Or Somerset or York, all's one to me.
YORK. If York have ill demeaned himself in France,
Then let him be denayed the regentship.
SOMERSET. If Somerset be unworthy of the place,
Let York be regent; I will yield to him.
WARWICK. Whether your grace be worthy, yea or no,
Dispute not that: York is the worthier.
CARDINAL. Ambitious Warwick, let thy betters speak.
WARWICK. The cardinal's not my better in the field.
BUCKINGHAM. All in this presence are thy betters,
Warwick.   110
WARWICK. Warwick may live to be the best of all.
SALISBURY. Peace, son! and show some reason,
Buckingham,
Why Somerset should be preferred in this.
QUEEN. Because the king, forsooth, will have it so.
GLOUCESTER. Madam, the king is old enough himself
To give his censure: these are no women's matters.
QUEEN. If he be old enough, what needs your grace
To be Protector of his excellence?
GLOUCESTER. Madam, I am Protector of the realm,
And at his pleasure will resign my place.   120
SUFFOLK. Resign it then and leave thine insolence.
Since thou wert king—as who is king but thou?—
The commonwealth hath daily run to wrack,
The Dauphin hath prevailed beyond the seas,
And all the peers and nobles of the realm
Have been as bondmen to thy sovereignty.
CARDINAL. The commons hast thou racked; the
clergy's bags
Are lank and lean with thy extortions.
SOMERSET. Thy sumptuous buildings and thy wife's
attire
Have cost a mass of public treasury.   130
BUCKINGHAM. Thy cruelty in execution
Upon offenders hath exceeded law,
And left thee to the mercy of the law.
QUEEN. Thy sale of offices and towns in France,
If they were known, as the suspect is great,
Would make thee quickly hop without thy head.

Gloucester goes. The Queen drops her fan
Give me my fan: what, minion! can ye not?
She gives the Duchess a box on the ear
I cry you mercy, madam; was it you?
DUCHESS. Was't I! yea, I it was, proud
Frenchwoman:
Could I come near your beauty with my nails,   140
I'ld set my ten commandments in your face.
KING. Sweet aunt, be quiet; 'twas against her will.
DUCHESS. Against her will! good king, look to't in
time;
She'll hamper thee, and dandle thee like a baby:
Though in this place most master wear no breeches,
She shall not strike dame Eleanor unrevenged.
Goes
BUCKINGHAM. Lord Cardinal, I will follow Eleanor,
And listen after Humphrey, how he proceeds:
She's tickled now; her fury needs no spurs,
She'll gallop far enough to her destruction.   150
Follows

Re-enter Gloucester
GLOUCESTER. Now, lords, my choler being
over-blown
With walking once about the quadrangle,
I come to talk of commonwealth affairs.
As for your spiteful false objections,
Prove them, and I lie open to the law:
But God in mercy so deal with my soul,
As I in duty love my king and country!
But to the matter that we have in hand:
I say, my sovereign, York is meetest man
To be your regent in the realm of France.   160
SUFFOLK. Before we make election, give me leave
To show some reason, of no little force,
That York is most unmeet of any man.
YORK. I'll tell thee, Suffolk, why I am unmeet:
First, for I cannot flatter thee in pride;
Next, if I be appointed for the place,
My Lord of Somerset will keep me here,
Without discharge, money, or furniture,
Till France be won into the dauphin's hands:
Last time, I danced attendance on his will   170
Till Paris was besieged, famished, and lost.
WARWICK. That can I witness, and a fouler fact
Did never traitor in the land commit.
SUFFOLK. Peace, headstrong Warwick!
WARWICK. Image of pride, why should I hold my
peace?

Enter Horner, the Armourer, and his man Peter, guarded
SUFFOLK. Because here is a man accused of treason:
Pray God the Duke of York excuse himself!
YORK. Doth any one accuse York for a traitor?
KING. What mean'st thou, Suffolk? tell me, what are
these?
SUFFOLK. Please it your majesty, this is the man   180
That doth accuse his master of high treason:
His words were these: that Richard Duke of York
Was rightful heir unto the English crown
And that your majesty was an usurper.
KING. Say, man, were these thy words?
HORNER. An't shall please your majesty, I never said
nor thought any such matter: God is my witness,
I am falsely accused by the villain.
PETER. By these ten bones, my lords, he did speak
them to me in the garret one night, as we were   190
scouring my Lord of York's armour.

YORK. Base dunghill villain and mechanical,
I'll have thy head for this thy traitor's speech.
I do beseech your royal majesty,
Let him have all the rigour of the law.
HORNER. Alas, my lord, hang me, if ever I spake the
words. My accuser is my prentice; and when I did
correct him for his fault the other day, he did vow
upon his knees he would be even with me: I have
good witness of this; therefore I beseech your 200
majesty, do not cast away an honest man for a
villain's accusation.
KING. Uncle, what shall we say to this in law?
GLOUCESTER. This doom, my lord, if I may judge:
Let Somerset be regent o'er the French,
Because in York this breeds suspicion:
And let these have a day appointed them
For single combat in convenient place,
For he hath witness of his servant's malice:
This is the law, and this Duke Humphrey's doom. 210
SOMERSET. I humbly thank your royal majesty.
HORNER. And I accept the combat willingly.
PETER. Alas, my lord, I cannot fight: for God's sake,
pity my case. The spite of man prevaileth against
me. O Lord, have mercy upon me! I shall never be
able to fight a blow. O Lord, my heart!
GLOUCESTER. Sirrah, or you must fight, or else be
hanged.
KING. Away with them to prison; and the day of
combat shall be the last of the next month. Come,
Somerset, we'll see thee sent away. 220
Flourish; they go

Scene 4: *Gloucester's house*

*Enter the witch Margery Jourdain, and the two priests,
Hum and Southwell, with Bolingbroke*

HUM. Come, my masters; the duchess, I tell you,
expects performance of your promises.
BOLINGBROKE. Master Hum, we are therefore provided: will her ladyship behold and hear our
exorcisms?
HUM. Ay, what else? fear you not her courage.
BOLINGBROKE. I have heard her reported to be a
woman of an invincible spirit: but it shall be convenient, Master Hum, that you be by her aloft,
while we be busy below; and so, I pray you, go, in 10
God's name, and leave us. [*Hum goes*] Mother
Jourdain, be you prostrate and grovel on the earth;
John Southwell, read you; and let us to our work.

Enter Duchess aloft, Hum following

DUCHESS. Well said, my masters; and welcome all. To
this gear, the sooner the better.
BOLINGBROKE. Patience, good lady, wizards know
their times.
Deep night, dark night, the silence of the night,
The time of night when Troy was set on fire,
The time when screech-owls cry and ban-dogs howl
And spirits walk and ghosts break up their graves, 20
That time best fits the work we have in hand.
Madam, sit you and fear not: whom we raise,
We will make fast within a hallowed verge.
*Here they do the ceremonies belonging,
and make the circle; Southwell reads,
Conjuro te, etc. It thunders and lightens
terribly; then the spirit riseth*

SPIRIT. Adsum.
MARGERY JOURDAIN. Asmath,
By the eternal God, whose name and power
Thou tremblest at, answer that I shall ask;
For, till thou speak, thou shalt not pass from hence.
SPIRIT. Ask what thou wilt. That I had said and done!
BOLINGBROKE. 'First of the king: what shall of him
become?'   *Reading out of a paper* 30
SPIRIT. The duke yet lives that Henry shall depose;
But him outlive, and die a violent death.
*As the spirit speaks, Southwell
writes the answer*
BOLINGBROKE. 'What fates await the Duke of Suffolk?'
SPIRIT. By water shall he die, and take his end.
BOLINGBROKE. 'What shall befall the Duke of
Somerset?'
SPIRIT. Let him shun castles;
Safer shall he be upon the sandy plains
Than where castles mounted stand.
Have done, for more I hardly can endure.
BOLINGBROKE. Descend to darkness and the burning
lake!   40
False fiend, avoid!
Thunder and lightning; spirit descends

*The Duke of York and the Duke of Buckingham with
their guard break in*

YORK. Lay hands upon these traitors and their trash.
Beldam, I think we watched you at an inch.
What! madam, are you there? the king and
commonweal
Are deeply indebted for this piece of pains:
My Lord Protector will, I doubt it not,
See you well guerdoned for these good deserts.
DUCHESS. Not half so bad as thine to England's king,
Injurious duke, that threatest where's no cause.
BUCKINGHAM. True, madam, none at all: what call
you this?   50
Away with them! let them be clapped up close,
And kept asunder. You, madam, shall with us.
Stafford, take her to thee.
Duchess and Hum are led off, guarded
We'll see your trinkets here all forthcoming.
All, away!
*Jourdain, Southwell, etc., also led off,
guarded*
YORK. Lord Buckingham, methinks, you watched her
well:
A pretty plot, well chosen to build upon!
Now, pray, my lord, let's see the devil's writ.
What have we here?   *Reads*
'The duke yet lives that Henry shall depose; 60
But him outlive, and die a violent death.'
Why, this is just
'Aio te, Aeacida, Romanos vincere posse.'
Well, to the rest:
'Tell me what fate awaits the Duke of Suffolk?
By water shall he die, and take his end.'
What shall betide the Duke of Somerset?
'Let him shun castles;
Safer shall he be upon the sandy plains
Than where castles mounted stand.' 70
Come, come, my lords;
These oracles are hardly attained,
And hardly understood.

The king is now in progress towards Saint Albans,
With him the husband of this lovely lady:
Thither go these news, as fast as horse can carry
them:
A sorry breakfast for my Lord Protector.
BUCKINGHAM. Your grace shall give me leave, my
Lord of York,
To be the post, in hope of his reward.
YORK. At your pleasure, my good lord. Who's within
there, ho!   80

Enter a Servingman

Invite my Lords of Salisbury and Warwick
To sup with me to-morrow night. Away!
                                                    They go

ACT 2
Scene 1: *Saint Albans*

*Enter the King, Queen, Gloucester, Cardinal, and
Suffolk, with falconers halloing*

QUEEN. Believe me, lords, for flying at the brook,
I saw not better sport these seven years' day:
Yet, by your leave, the wind was very high;
And, ten to one, old Joan had not gone out.
KING. But what a point, my lord, your falcon made,
And what a pitch she flew above the rest!
To see how God in all his creatures works!
Yea, man and birds are fain of climbing high.
SUFFOLK. No marvel, an it like your majesty,
My Lord Protector's hawks do tower so well;   10
They know their master loves to be aloft
And bears his thoughts above his falcon's pitch.
GLOUCESTER. My lord, 'tis but a base ignoble mind
That mounts no higher than a bird can soar.
CARDINAL. I thought as much; he would be above the
clouds.
GLOUCESTER. Ay, my Lord Cardinal? how think you
by that?
Were it not good your grace could fly to heaven?
KIING. The treasury of everlasting joy.
CARDINAL. Thy heaven is on earth; thine eyes and
thoughts
Beat on a crown, the treasure of thy heart,   20
Pernicious Protector, dangerous peer,
That smooth'st it so with king and commonweal!
GLOUCESTER. What! Cardinal, is your priesthood
grown peremptory?
Tantaene animis coelestibus irae?
Churchmen so hot? good uncle, hide such malice;
With such holiness can you do it?
SUFFOLK. No malice, sir; no more than well becomes
So good a quarrel and so bad a peer.
GLOUCESTER. As who, my lord?
SUFFOLK.   Why, as you, my lord,
An't like your lordly Lord-Protectorship.   30
GLOUCESTER. Why, Suffolk, England knows thine
insolence.
QUEEN. And thy ambition, Gloucester.
KING. I prithee, peace, good queen,
And.whet not on these furious peers,
For blessèd are the peacemakers on earth.
CARDINAL. Let me be blessèd for the peace I make,
Against this proud Protector, with my sword!
GLOUCESTER [*aside*]. Faith, holy uncle, would 'twere
come to that!

CARDINAL [*aside*]. Marry, when thou dar'st.
GLOUCESTER [*aside*]. Make up no factious numbers for
the matter;   40
In thine own person answer thy abuse.
CARDINAL [*aside*]. Ay, where thou dar'st not peep: an
if thou dar'st,
This evening, on the east side of the grove.
KING. How now, my lords!
CARDINAL.   Believe me, cousin Gloucester,
Had not your man put up the fowl so suddenly,
We had had more sport. [*aside*] Come with thy
two-hand sword.
GLOUCESTER. True, uncle.
CARDINAL [*aside*]. Are ye advised? the east side of the
grove?
GLOUCESTER [*aside*]. Cardinal, I am with you.
KING. Why, how now, uncle Gloucester!
GLOUCESTER. Talking of hawking; nothing else, my
lord.   50
[*aside*] Now, by God's mother, priest, I'll shave your
crown for this.
Or all my fence shall fail.
CARDINAL [*aside*]. Medice, teipsum—
Protector, see to't well, protect yourself.
KING. The winds grow high, so do your stomachs,
lords.
How irksome is this music to my heart!
When such strings jar, what hope of harmony?
I pray, my lords, let me compound this strife.

Enter a Townsman of Saint Albans crying A miracle!

GLOUCESTER. What means this noise?
Fellow, what miracle dost thou proclaim?   60
TOWNSMAN. A miracle! a miracle!
SUFFOLK. Come to the king and tell him what miracle.
TOWNSMAN. Forsooth, a blind man at Saint Alban's
shrine,
Within this half-hour, hath received his sight;
A man that ne'er saw in his life before.
KING. Now, God be praised, that to believing souls
Gives light in darkness, comfort in despair!

*Enter the Mayor of Saint Albans and his brethren,
bearing Simpcox between two in a chair, Simpcox's
Wife following*

CARDINAL. Here comes the townsmen on procession,
To present your highness with the man.
KING. Great is his comfort in this earthly vale,   70
Although by sight his sin be multiplied.
GLOUCESTER. Stand by, my masters: bring him near
the king;
His highness' pleasure is to talk with him.
KING. Good fellow, tell us here the circumstance,
That we for thee may glorify the Lord.
What! hast thou been long blind and now restored?
SIMPCOX. Born blind, an't please your grace.
WIFE. Ay, indeed, was he.
SUFFOLK. What woman is this?
WIFE. His wife, an't like your worship.   80
GLOUCESTER. Hadst thou been his mother, thou
couldst have better told.
KING. Where wert thou born?
SIMPCOX. At Berwick in the north, an't like your
grace.
KING. Poor soul, God's goodness hath been great to
thee:

Let never day nor night unhallowéd pass,
But still remember what the Lord hath done.
QUEEN. Tell me, good fellow, cam'st thou here by
    chance,
Or of devotion, to this holy shrine?
SIMPCOX. God knows, of pure devotion; being called
    A hundred times and oftener, in my sleep,   90
    By good Saint Alban; who said, 'Simpcox, come,
    Come, offer at my shrine, and I will help thee.'
WIFE. Most true, forsooth; and many time and oft
    Myself have heard a voice to call him so.
CARDINAL. What, art thou lame?
SIMPCOX.   Ay, God Almighty help me!
SUFFOLK. How cam'st thou so?
SIMPCOX.   A fall off of a tree.
WIFE. A plum-tree, master.
GLOUCESTER.   How long has thou been blind?
SIMPCOX. O, born so, master.
GLOUCESTER.   What! and wouldst climb a tree?
SIMPCOX. But that in all my life, when I was a youth.
WIFE. Too true, and bought his climbing very dear.   100
GLOUCESTER. Mass, thou lov'dst plums well, that
    wouldst venture so.
SIMPCOX. Alas, good master, my wife desired some
    damsons,
And made me climb, with danger of my life.
GLOUCESTER. A subtle knave! but yet it shall not serve.
Let me see thine eyes: wink now: now open them:
In my opinion yet thou see'st not well.
SIMPCOX. Yes, master, clear as day, I thank God and
    Saint Alban.
GLOUCESTER. Say'st thou me so? What colour is this
    cloak of?
SIMPCOX. Red, master; red as blood.
GLOUCESTER. Why, that's well said. What colour is
    my gown of?   110
SIMPCOX. Black, forsooth: coal-black as jet.
KING. Why, then, thou know'st what colour jet is of?
SUFFOLK. And yet, I think, jet did he never see.
GLOUCESTER. But cloaks and gowns, before this day,
    a many.
WIFE. Never, before this day, in all his life.
GLOUCESTER. Tell me, sirrah, what's my name?
SIMPCOX. Alas, master, I know not.
GLOUCESTER. What's his name?
SIMPCOX. I know not.
GLOUCESTER. Nor his?   120
SIMPCOX. No, indeed, master.
GLOUCESTER. What's thine own name?
SIMPCOX. Saunder Simpcox, an if it please you,
    master.
GLOUCESTER. Then, Saunder, sit there, the lyingest
    knave in Christendom. If thou hadst been born
    blind, thou mightst as well have known all our
    names as thus to name the several colours we do
    wear. Sight may distinguish of colours, but sud-
    denly to nominate them all, it is impossible. My
    lords, Saint Alban here hath done a miracle; and   130
    would ye not think his cunning to be great, that
    could restore this cripple to his legs again?
SIMPCOX. O master, that you could!
GLOUCESTER. My masters of Saint Albans, have you
    not beadles in your town, and things called whips?
MAYOR. Yes, my lord, if it please your grace.
GLOUCESTER. Then send for one presently.
MAYOR. Sirrah, go fetch the beadle hither straight.

An attendant obeys
GLOUCESTER. Now fetch me a stool hither by and by.
    [*they bring one*] Now, sirrah, if you mean to save 140
    yourself from whipping, leap me over this stool and
    run away.
SIMPCOX. Alas, master, I am not able to stand alone:
    You go about to torture me in vain.

Enter a Beadle with whips

GLOUCESTER. Well, sir, we must have you find your
    legs. Sirrah beadle, whip him till he leap over that
    same stool.
BEADLE. I will, my lord. Come on, sirrah; off with
    your doublet quickly.
SIMPCOX. Alas, master, what shall I do? I am not able 150
    to stand.

*After the Beadle hath hit him once, he
    leaps over the stool and runs away;
    and they follow and cry, A miracle!*
KING. O God, seest Thou this, and bearest so long?
QUEEN. It made me laugh to see the villain run.
GLOUCESTER. Follow the knave, and take this drab
    away.
WIFE. Alas, sir, we did it for pure need.
GLOUCESTER. Let them be whipped through every
    market-town, till they come to Berwick, from
    whence they came.

*The Mayor etc. depart, followed by
    the Beadle with Simpcox's Wife*
CARDINAL. Duke Humphrey has done a miracle
    to-day.
SUFFOLK. True; made the lame to leap and fly away.   160
GLOUCESTER. But you have done more miracles than I;
    You made in a day, my lord, whole towns to fly.

Enter Buckingham

KING. What tidings with our cousin Buckingham?
BUCKINGHAM. Such as my heart doth tremble to
    unfold.
    A sort of naughty persons, lewdly bent,
    Under the countenance and confederacy
    Of Lady Eleanor, the Protector's wife,
    The ringleader and head of all this rout,
    Have practised dangerously against your state,
    Dealing with witches and with conjurors: 170
    Whom we have apprehended in the fact;
    Raising up wicked spirits from under ground,
    Demanding of King Henry's life and death,
    And other of your highness' Privy Council;
    As more at large your grace shall understand.
CARDINAL [*to Gloucester*]. And so, my Lord Protector,
    by this means
    Your lady is forthcoming yet at London.
    This news, I think, hath turned your weapon's edge;
    'Tis like, my lord, you will not keep your hour.
GLOUCESTER. Ambitious churchman, leave to afflict
    my heart: 180
    Sorrow and grief have vanquished all my powers;
    And, vanquished as I am, I yield to thee,
    Or to the meanest groom.
KING. O God, what mischiefs work the wicked ones,
    Heaping confusion on their own heads thereby!
QUEEN. Gloucester, see here the tainture of thy nest,
    And look thyself be faultless, thou wert best.
GLOUCESTER. Madam, for myself, to heaven I do
    appeal,

How I have loved my king and commonweal:
And, for my wife, I know not how it stands; 190
Sorry I am to hear what I have heard:
Noble she is, but if she have forgot
Honour and virtue and conversed with such
As, like to pitch, defile nobility,
I banish her my bed and company
And give her as a prey to law and shame,
That hath dishonouréd Gloucester's honest name.
KING. Well, for this night we will repose us here:
To-morrow toward London back again,
To look into this business thoroughly 200
And call these foul offenders to their answers,
And poise the cause in justice' equal scales,
Whose beam stands sure, whose rightful cause
   prevails. *Flourish; they go*

Scene 2: *London. The Duke of York's garden*

Enter York, Salisbury, and Warwick

YORK. Now, my good Lords of Salisbury and
   Warwick,
Our simple supper ended, give me leave
In this close walk to satisfy myself,
In craving your opinion of my title,
Which is infallible, to England's crown.
SALISBURY. My lord, I long to hear it at full.
WARWICK. Sweet York, begin: and if thy claim be
   good,
The Nevils are thy subjects to command.
YORK. Then thus:
Edward the Third, my lords, had seven sons: 10
The first, Edward the Black Prince, Prince of Wales;
The second, William of Hatfield; and the third,
Lionel Duke of Clarence; next to whom
Was John of Gaunt, the Duke of Lancaster;
The fifth was Edmund Langley, Duke of York;
The sixth was Thomas of Woodstock, Duke of
   Gloucester;
William of Windsor was the seventh and last.
Edward the Black Prince died before his father
And left behind him Richard, his only son,
Who after Edward the Third's death reigned as
   king; 20
Till Henry Bolingbroke, Duke of Lancaster,
The eldest son and heir of John of Gaunt,
Crowned by the name of Henry the Fourth,
Seized on the realm, deposed the rightful king,
Sent his poor queen to France, from whence she
   came,
And him to Pomfret; where, as all you know,
Harmless Richard was murderéd traitorously.
WARWICK. Father, the duke hath told the truth;
Thus got the house of Lancaster the crown.
YORK. Which now they hold by force and not by
   right; 30
For Richard, the first son's heir, being dead,
The issue of the next son should have reigned.
SALISBURY. But William of Hatfield died without an
   heir.
YORK. The third son, Duke of Clarence, from whose
   line
I claim the crown, had issue, Philippa, a daughter,
Who married Edmund Mortimer, Earl of March:
Edmund had issue, Roger Earl of March;
Roger had issue, Edmund, Anne and Eleanor.

SALISBURY. This Edmund, in the reign of
   Bolingbroke,
As I have read, laid claim unto the crown; 40
And, but for Owen Glendower, had been king,
Who kept him in captivity till he died.
But to the rest.
YORK.   His eldest sister, Anne,
My mother, being heir unto the crown,
Married Richard Earl of Cambridge; who was son
To Edmund Langley, Edward the Third's fifth son.
By her I claim the kingdom: she was heir
To Roger Earl of March, who was the son
Of Edmund Mortimer, who marriéd Philippa,
Sole daughter unto Lionel Duke of Clarence: 50
So, if the issue of the elder son
Succeed before the younger, I am king.
WARWICK. What plain proceeding is more plain
   than this?
Henry doth claim the crown from John of Gaunt,
The fourth son; York claims it from the third.
Till Lionel's issue fails, his should not reign:
It fails not yet, but flourishes in thee
And in thy sons, fair slips of such a stock.
Then, father Salisbury, kneel we together;
And in this private plot be we the first 60
That shall salute our rightful sovereign
With honour of his birthright to the crown.
BOTH. Long live our sovereign Richard, England's
   king!
YORK. We thank you, lords. But I am not your king
Till I be crowned and that my sword be stained
With heart-blood of the house of Lancaster;
And that's not suddenly to be performed,
But with advice and silent secrecy.
Do you as I do in these dangerous days:
Wink at the Duke of Suffolk's insolence, 70
At Beaufort's pride, at Somerset's ambition,
At Buckingham and all the crew of them,
Till they have snared the shepherd of the flock,
That virtuous prince, the good Duke Humphrey:
'Tis that they seek, and they in seeking that
Shall find their deaths, if York can prophesy.
SALISBURY. My lord, break we off; we know your
   mind at full.
WARWICK. My heart assures me that the Earl of
   Warwick
Shall one day make the Duke of York a king.
YORK. And, Nevil, this I do assure myself: 80
Richard shall live to make the Earl of Warwick
The greatest man in England but the king.
   They go

Scene 3: *A hall of justice*

*Sound trumpets. Enter the King, the Queen, Gloucester,
York, Suffolk, and Salisbury; the Duchess of Gloucester,
Margery Jourdain, Southwell, Hum, and Bolingbroke,
under guard*

KING. Stand forth, Dame Eleanor Cobham,
   Gloucester's wife:
In sight of God and us, your guilt is great:
Receive the sentence of the law for sins
Such as by God's book are adjudged to death.
You four, from hence to prison back again;
From thence unto the place of execution:
The witch in Smithfield shall be burnt to ashes,

And you three shall be strangléd on the gallows.
You, madam, for you are more nobly born,
Despoiléd of your honour in your life,   10
Shall, after three days' open penance done,
Live in your country here in banishment,
With Sir John Stanley, in the Isle of Man.
DUCHESS. Welcome is banishment, welcome were my
    death.
GLOUCESTER. Eleanor, the law thou seest hath judgéd
    thee:
I cannot justify whom the law condemns.
                    The Duchess and other prisoners are
                            led away, guarded
Mine eyes are full of tears, my heart of grief.
Ah, Humphrey, this dishonour in thine age
Will bring thy head with sorrow to the ground!
I beseech your majesty, give me leave to go;   20
Sorrow would solace and mine age would ease.
KING. Stay, Humphrey Duke of Gloucester: ere thou
    go,
Give up thy staff: Henry will to himself
Protector be; and God shall be my hope,
My stay, my guide and lantern to my feet:
And go in peace, Humphrey, no less beloved
Than when thou wert Protector to thy king.
QUEEN. I see no reason why a king of years
Should be to be protected like a child.
God and King Henry govern England's realm.   30
Give up your staff, sir, and the king his realm.
GLOUCESTER. My staff? here, noble Henry, is my staff:
As willingly do I the same resign
As e'er thy father Henry made it mine;
And even as willingly at thy feet I leave it
As others would ambitiously receive it.
Farewell, good king: when I am dead and gone,
May honourable peace attend thy throne!
                                        He goes
QUEEN. Why, now is Henry king, and Margaret
    queen;
And Humphrey Duke of Gloucester scarce himself,   40
That bears so shrewd a maim; two pulls at once:
His lady banished, and a limb lopped off—
This staff of honour raught. There let it stand
Where it best fits to be, in Henry's hand.
SUFFOLK. Thus droops this lofty pine and hangs his
    sprays;
Thus Eleanor's pride dies in her youngest days.
YORK. Lords, let him go. Please it your majesty,
This is the day appointed for the combat,
And ready are the appellant and defendant,
The armourer and his man, to enter the lists,
So please your highness to behold the fight.   50
QUEEN. Ay, good my lord; for purposely therefore
Left I the court, to see this quarrel tried.
KING. O'God's name, see the lists and all things fit:
Here let them end it; and God defend the right!
YORK. I never saw a fellow worse bested,
Or more afraid to fight, than is the appellant,
The servant of this armourer, my lords.

Enter at one door the Armourer, and his neighbours,
drinking to him so much that he is drunk; and he enters
with a drum before him and his staff with a sand-bag
fastened to it; and at the other door his man, with a drum
and sand-bag, and Prentices drinking to him

1 NEIGHBOUR. Here, neighbour Horner, I drink to you

in a cup of sack: and fear not, neighbour, you shall   60
do well enough.
2 NEIGHBOUR. And here, neighbour, here's a cup of
charneco.
3 NEIGHBOUR. And here's a pot of good double beer,
neighbour: drink, and fear not your man.
HORNER. Let it come, i'faith, and I'll pledge you all,
and a fig for Peter!
1 PRENTICE. Here, Peter, I drink to thee, and be not
afraid.
2 PRENTICE. Be merry, Peter, and fear not thy master: 70
fight for credit of the prentices.
PETER. I thank you all: drink, and pray for me, I pray
you; for I think I have taken my last draught in
this world. Here, Robin, an if I die, I give thee my
apron: and, Will, thou shalt have my hammer: and
here, Tom, take all the money that I have. O Lord
bless me! I pray God! for I am never able to deal
with my master, he hath learnt so much fence
already.
SALISBURY. Come, leave your drinking, and fall to   80
blows. Sirrah, what's thy name?
PETER. Peter, forsooth.
SALISBURY. Peter! what more?
PETER. Thump.
SALISBURY. Thump! then see thou thump thy master
well.
HORNER. Masters, I am come hither, as it were upon
my man's instigation, to prove him a knave and
myself an honest man: and touching the Duke of
York, I will take my death, I never meant him any   90
ill, nor the king, nor the queen: and therefore, Peter,
have at thee with a downright blow!
YORK. Dispatch: this knave's tongue begins to double.
Sound, trumpets, alarum to the combatants!
                    Alarum; they fight, and Peter strikes
                                    him down
HORNER. Hold, Peter, hold! I confess, I confess treason.
                                                Dies
YORK. Take away his weapon. Fellow, thank God, and
the good wine in thy master's way.
PETER. O God, have I overcome mine enemy in this
presence? O Peter, thou hast prevailed in right!
KING. Go, take hence that traitor from our sight;   100
For by his death we do perceive his guilt:
And God in justice hath revealed to us
The truth and innocence of this poor fellow,
Which he had thought to have murdered
    wrongfully.
Come, fellow, follow us for thy reward.
                            Sound a flourish; they go

                    Scene 4: *A street*

Enter Duke Humphrey and his men, in mourning cloaks

GLOUCESTER. Thus sometimes hath the brightest day a
    cloud;
And after summer evermore succeeds
Barren winter with his wrathful nipping cold:
So cares and joys abound, as seasons fleet.
Sirs, what's o'clock?
SERVANT.   Ten, my lord.
GLOUCESTER. Ten is the hour that was appointed me
To watch the coming of my punished duchess:
Uneath may she endure the flinty streets,
To tread them with her tender-feeling feet.

Sweet Nell, ill can thy noble mind abrook   10
The abject people gazing on thy face,
With envious looks, laughing at thy shame,
That erst did follow thy proud chariot-wheels
When thou didst ride in triumph through the
   streets.
But, soft! I think she comes, and I'll prepare
My tear-stained eyes to see her miseries.

*Enter the Duchess in a white sheet, and a taper burning
in her hand; with the Sheriff, and officers; thereafter, Sir
John Stanley and a guard with bills and halberds*

SERVANT. So please your grace, we'll take her from the
   sheriff.
GLOUCESTER. No, stir not for your lives, let her pass by.
DUCHESS. Come you, my lord, to see my open shame?
   Now thou dost penance too. Look how they gaze!   20
   See how the giddy multitude do point,
   And nod their heads, and throw their eyes on thee!
   Ah, Gloucester, hide thee from their hateful looks,
   And, in thy closet pent up, rue my shame,
   And ban thine enemies, both mine and thine!
GLOUCESTER. Be patient, gentle Nell; forget this grief.
DUCHESS. Ah, Gloucester, teach me to forget myself!
   For whilst I think I am thy married wife
   And thou a prince, Protector of this land,
   Methinks I should not thus be led along,   30
   Mailed up in shame, with papers on my back,
   And followed with a rabble that rejoice
   To see my tears and hear my deep-fet groans.
   The ruthless flint doth cut my tender feet,
   And when I start, the envious people laugh
   And bid me be advised how I tread.
   Ah, Humphrey, can I bear this shameful yoke?
   Trow'st thou that e'er I'll look upon the world
   Or count them happy that enjoy the sun?
   No; dark shall be my light and night my day;   40
   To think upon my pomp shall be my hell.
   Sometime I'll say, I am Duke Humphrey's wife,
   And he a prince and ruler of the land:
   Yet so he ruled and such a prince he was
   As he stood by whilst I, his forlorn duchess,
   Was made a wonder and a pointing-stock
   To every idle rascal follower.
   But be thou mild and blush not at my shame,
   Nor stir at nothing till the axe of death
   Hang over thee, as, sure, it shortly will;   50
   For Suffolk—he that can do all in all
   With her that hateth thee and hates us all—
   And York and impious Beaufort, that false priest,
   Have all limed bushes to betray thy wings,
   And, fly thou how thou canst, they'll tangle thee:
   But fear not thou, until thy foot be snared,
   Nor never seek prevention of thy foes.
GLOUCESTER. Ah, Nell, forbear! thou aimest all awry;
   I must offend before I be attainted;
   And had I twenty times so many foes,   60
   And each of them had twenty times their power,
   All these could not procure me any scathe,
   So long as I am loyal, true and crimeless.
   Wouldst thou have me rescue thee from this reproach?
   Why, yet thy scandal were not wiped away,
   But I in danger for the breach of law.
   Thy greatest help is quiet, gentle Nell:
   I pray thee, sort thy heart to patience;
   These few days' wonder will be quickly worn.

Enter a Herald

HERALD. I summon your grace to his majesty's
   parliament,   70
   Holden at Bury the first of this next month.
GLOUCESTER. And my consent ne'er asked herein
   before!
   This is close dealing. Well, I will be there.
                            Herald goes
   My Nell, I take my leave: and, master sheriff,
   Let not her penance exceed the king's commission.
SHERIFF. An't please your grace, here my commission
   stays,
   And Sir John Stanley is appointed now
   To take her with him to the Isle of Man.
GLOUCESTER. Must you, Sir John, protect my lady
   here?
STANLEY. So am I given in charge, may't please your
   grace.   80
GLOUCESTER. Entreat her not the worse in that I pray
   You use her well: the world may laugh again;
   And I may live to do you kindness if
   You do it her: and so, Sir John, farewell!
DUCHESS. What! gone, my lord, and bid me not
   farewell!
GLOUCESTER. Witness my tears, I cannot stay to speak.
           Gloucester and serving-men depart
DUCHESS. Art thou gone too? all comfort go with
   thee!
   For none abides with me: my joy is death—
   Death, at whose name I oft have been afeared,
   Because I wished this world's eternity.   90
   Stanley, I prithee, go, and take me hence;
   I care not whither, for I beg no favour;
   Only convey me where thou art commanded.
STANLEY. Why, madam, that is to the Isle of Man;
   There to be used according to your state.
DUCHESS. That's bad enough, for I am but reproach:
   And shall I then be used reproachfully?
STANLEY. Like to a duchess, and Duke Humphrey's
   lady;
   According to that state you shall be used.
DUCHESS. Sheriff, farewell, and better than I fare,   100
   Although thou hast been conduct of my shame.
SHERIFF. It is my office; and, madam, pardon me.
DUCHESS. Ay, ay, farewell; thy office is discharged.
   Come, Stanley, shall we go?
STANLEY. Madam, your penance done, throw off this
   sheet,
   And go we to attire you for our journey.
DUCHESS. My shame will not be shifted with my
   sheet:
   No, it will hang upon my richest robes,
   And show itself, attire me how I can.
   Go, lead the way; I long to see my prison.   110
                             They go

ACT 3

Scene 1: *The Abbey at Bury St Edmunds*

*Sound a Sennet. Enter King, Queen, Cardinal, Suffolk,
York, Buckingham, Salisbury and Warwick to the
Parliament*

KING. I muse my Lord of Gloucester is not come:
   'Tis not his wont to be the hindmost man,
   Whate'er occasion keeps him from us now.

QUEEN. Can you not see? or will ye not observe
  The strangeness of his altered countenance?
  With what a majesty he bears himself,
  How insolent of late he is become,
  How proud, how peremptory, and unlike himself?
  We know the time since he was mild and affable,
  And if we did but glance a far-off look,   10
  Immediately he was upon his knee,
  That all the court admired him for submission:
  But meet him now, and, be it in the morn,
  When every one will give the time of day,
  He knits his brow and shows an angry eye
  And passeth by with stiff unbowéd knee,
  Disdaining duty that to us belongs.
  Small curs are not regarded when they grin;
  But great men tremble when the lion roars;
  And Humphrey is no little man in England.   20
  First note that he is near you in descent,
  And should you fall, he is the next will mount.
  Me seemeth then it is no policy,
  Respecting what a rancorous mind he bears
  And his advantage following your decease,
  That he should come about your royal person
  Or be admitted to your highness' council.
  By flattery hath he won the commons' hearts,
  And when he please to make commotion,
  'Tis to be feared they all will follow him.   30
  Now 'tis the spring, and weeds are shallow-rooted;
  Suffer them now, and they'll o'ergrow the garden
  And choke the herbs for want of husbandry.
  The reverent care I bear unto my lord
  Made me collect these dangers in the duke.
  If it be fond, call it a woman's fear;
  Which fear if better reasons can supplant,
  I will subscribe and say I wrongèd the duke.
  My Lord of Suffolk, Buckingham, and York,
  Reprove my allegation, if you can;   40
  Or else conclude my words effectual.
SUFFOLK. Well hath your highness seen into this duke;
  And, had I first been put to speak my mind,
  I think I should have told your grace's tale.
  The duchess by his subornation,
  Upon my life, began her devilish practices:
  Or, if he were not privy to those faults,
  Yet, by reputing of his high descent,
  As next the king he was successive heir,
  And such high vaunts of his nobility,   50
  Did instigate the bedlam brain-sick duchess
  By wicked means to frame our sovereign's fall.
  Smooth runs the water where the brook is deep;
  And in his simple show he harbours treason.
  The fox barks not when he would steal the lamb.
  No, no, my sovereign; Gloucester is a man
  Unsounded yet and full of deep deceit.
CARDINAL. Did he not, contrary to form of law,
  Devise strange deaths for small offences done?
YORK. And did he not, in his protectorship,   60
  Levy great sums of money through the realm
  For soldiers' pay in France, and never sent it?
  By means whereof the towns each day revolted.
BUCKINGHAM. Tut, these are petty faults to faults
    unknown,
  Which time will bring to light in smooth Duke
    Humphrey.
KING. My lords, at once: the care you have of us,
  To mow down thorns that would annoy our foot,

Is worthy praise: but, shall I speak my conscience,
  Our kinsman Gloucester is as innocent
  From meaning treason to our royal person   70
  As is the sucking lamb or harmless dove:
  The duke is virtuous, mild, and too well given
  To dream on evil or to work my downfall.
QUEEN. Ah, what's more dangerous than this fond
    affiance!
  Seems he a dove? his feathers are but borrowed,
  For he's disposéd as the hateful raven:
  Is he a lamb? his skin is surely lent him,
  For he's inclined as is the ravenous wolf.
  Who cannot steal a shape that means deceit?
  Take heed, my lord; the welfare of us all   80
  Hangs on the cutting short that fraudful man.

Enter Somerset

SOMERSET. All health unto my gracious sovereign!
KING. Welcome, Lord Somerset. What news from
    France?
SOMERSET. That all your interest in those territories
  Is utterly bereft you; all is lost.
KING. Cold news, Lord Somerset: but God's will be
    done!
YORK [*aside*]. Cold news for me; for I had hope of
    France
  As firmly as I hope for fertile England.
  Thus are my blossoms blasted in the bud
  And caterpillars eat my leaves away;   90
  But I will remedy this gear ere long,
  Or sell my title for a glorious grave.

Enter Gloucester

GLOUCESTER. All happiness unto my lord the king!
  Pardon, my liege, that I have stayed so long.
SUFFOLK. Nay, Gloucester, know that thou art come
    too soon,
  Unless thou wert more loyal than thou art:
  I do arrest thee of high treason here.
GLOUCESTER. Well, Suffolk, thou shalt not see me
    blush
  Nor change my countenance for this arrest:
  A heart unspotted is not easily daunted.   100
  The purest spring is not so free from mud
  As I am clear from treason to my sovereign.
  Who can accuse me? wherein am I guilty?
YORK. 'Tis thought, my lord, that you took bribes of
    France,
  And, being Protector, stayed the soldiers' pay;
  By means whereof his highness hath lost France.
GLOUCESTER. Is it but thought so? what are they that
    think it?
  I never robbed the soldiers of their pay,
  Nor ever had one penny bribe from France.
  So help me God, as I have watched the night,   110
  Ay, night by night, in studying good for England!
  That doit that e'er I wrested from the king,
  Or any groat I hoarded to my use,
  Be brought against me at my trial-day!
  No; many a pound of mine own proper store,
  Because I would not tax the needy commons,
  Have I dispurséd to the garrisons,
  And never asked for restitution.
CARDINAL. It serves you well, my lord, to say so much.
GLOUCESTER. I say no more than truth, so help me
    God!   120

YORK. In your protectorship you did devise
Strange tortures for offenders never heard of,
That England was defamed by tyranny.
GLOUCESTER. Why, 'tis well known that, whiles I was
Protector,
Pity was all the fault that was in me;
For I should melt at an offender's tears,
And lowly words were ransom for their fault.
Unless it were a bloody murderer,
Or foul felonious thief that fleeced poor passengers,
I never gave them condign punishment: 130
Murder indeed, that bloody sin, I tortured
Above the felon or what trespass else.
SUFFOLK. My lord, these faults are easy, quickly
answered:
But mightier crimes are laid unto your charge,
Whereof you cannot easily purge yourself.
I do arrest you in his highness' name;
And here commit you to my Lord Cardinal
To keep, until your further time of trial.
KING. My lord of Gloucester, 'tis my special hope
That you will clear yourself from all suspense.   140
My conscience tells me you are innocent.
GLOUCESTER. Ah, gracious lord, these days are
dangerous:
Virtue is choked with foul ambition,
And charity chased hence by rancour's hand;
Foul subornation is predominant,
And equity exiled your highness' land.
I know their complot is to have my life,
And if my death might make this island happy,
And prove the period of their tyranny,
I would expend it with all willingness: 150
But mine is made the prologue to their play;
For thousands more, that yet suspect no peril,
Will not conclude their plotted tragedy.
Beaufort's red sparkling eyes blab his heart's malice
And Suffolk's cloudy brow his stormy hate;
Sharp Buckingham unburthens with his tongue
The envious load that lies upon his heart;
And doggéd York, that reaches at the moon,
Whose overweening arm I have plucked back,
By false accuse doth level at my life: 160
And you, my sovereign lady, with the rest,
Causeless have laid disgraces on my head
And with your best endeavour have stirred up
My liefest liege to be mine enemy:
Ay, all of you have laid your heads together—
Myself had notice of your conventicles—
And all to make away my guiltless life.
I shall not want false witness to condemn me,
Nor store of treasons to augment my guilt;
The ancient proverb will be well effected: 170
'A staff is quickly found to beat a dog.'
CARDINAL. My liege, his railing is intolerable.
If those that care to keep your royal person
From treason's secret knife and traitors' rage
Be thus upbraided, chid, and rated at,
And the offender granted scope of speech,
'Twill make them cool in zeal unto your grace.
SUFFOLK. Hath he not twit our sovereign lady
here
With ignominious words, though clerkly couched,
As if she had subornéd some to swear   180
False allegations to o'erthrow his state?
QUEEN. But I can give the loser leave to chide.

GLOUCESTER. Far truer spoke than meant: I lose,
indeed;
Beshrew the winners, for they played me false!
And well such losers may have leave to speak.
BUCKINGHAM. He'll wrest the sense and hold us here
all day:
Lord Cardinal, he is your prisoner.
CARDINAL. Sirs, take away the duke, and guard him
sure.
GLOUCESTER. Ah! thus King Henry throws away his
crutch
Before his legs be firm to bear his body.   190
Thus is the shepherd beaten from thy side
And wolves are gnarling who shall gnaw thee first.
Ah, that my fear were false! ah, that it were!
For, good King Henry, thy decay I fear.
He goes under guard
KING. My lords, what to your wisdoms seemeth best,
Do or undo, as if ourself were here.
QUEEN. What, will your highness leave the
parliament?
KING. Ay, Margaret; my heart is drowned with grief,
Whose flood begins to flow within mine eyes;
My body round engirt with misery: 200
For what's more miserable than discontent?
Ah, uncle Humphrey! in thy face I see
The map of honour, truth, and loyalty:
And yet, good Humphrey, is the hour to come
That e'er I proved thee false or feared thy faith.
What louring star now envies thy estate,
That these great lords and Margaret our queen
Do seek subversion of thy harmless life?
Thou never didst them wrong nor no man wrong;
And as the butcher takes away the calf   210
And binds the wretch and beats it when it strays,
Bearing it to the bloody slaughter-house,
Even so remorseless have they borne him hence;
And as the dam runs lowing up and down,
Looking for where her harmless young one went,
And can do nought but wail her darling's loss,
Even so myself bewails good Gloucester's case
With sad unhelpful tears, and with dimmed eyes
Look after him and cannot do him good,
So mighty are his vowéd enemies.   220
His fortunes I will weep and 'twixt each groan
Say 'Who's a traitor? Gloucester he is none.'
*He goes out and all follow but Queen,
Cardinal Beaufort, Suffolk, and York,
together with Somerset,
who remains apart*
QUEEN. Free lords, cold snow melts with the sun's hot
beams.
Henry my lord is cold in great affairs,
Too full of foolish pity; and Gloucester's show
Beguiles him as the mournful crocodile
With sorrow snares relenting passengers,
Or as the snake rolled in a flow'ring bank,
With shining checkered slough, doth sting a child
That for the beauty thinks it excellent.   230
Believe me, lords, were none more wise than I—
And yet herein I judge mine own wit good—
This Gloucester should be quickly rid the world,
To rid us from the fear we have of him.
CARDINAL. That he should die is worthy policy;   180
But yet we want a colour for his death:
'Tis meet he be condemned by course of law.

SUFFOLK. But, in my mind, that were no policy:
The king will labour still to save his life,
The commons haply rise, to save his life;   240
And yet we have but trivial argument,
More than mistrust, that shows him worthy death.
YORK. So that, by this, you would not have him die.
SUFFOLK. Ah, York, no man alive so fain as I!
YORK. 'Tis York that hath more reason for his death.
But, my Lord Cardinal, and you, my Lord of
Suffolk,
Say as you think, and speak it from your souls:
Were't not all one, an empty eagle were set
To guard the chicken from a hungry kite,
As place Duke Humphrey for the king's Protector?   250
QUEEN. So the poor chicken should be sure of death.
SUFFOLK. Madam, 'tis true; and were't not madness,
then,
To make the fox surveyor of the fold?
Who being accused a crafty murderer,
His guilt should be but idly posted over,
Because his purpose is not executed.
No; let him die, in that he is a fox,
By nature proved an enemy to the flock,
Before his chaps be stained with crimson blood,
As Humphrey's, proved by reasons, to my liege.   260
And do not stand on quillets how to slay him:
Be it by gins, by snares, by subtlety,
Sleeping or waking, 'tis no matter how,
So he be dead; for that is good deceit
Which mates him first that first intends deceit.
QUEEN. Thrice-noble Suffolk, 'tis resolutely spoke.
SUFFOLK. Not resolute, except so much were done;
For things are often spoke and seldom meant:
But that my heart accordeth with my tongue,
Seeing the deed is meritorious,   270
And to preserve my sovereign from his foe,
Say but the word, and I will be his priest.
CARDINAL. But I would have him dead, my Lord of
Suffolk,
Ere you can take due orders for a priest:
Say you consent and censure well the deed,
And I'll provide his executioner,
I tender so the safety of my liege.
SUFFOLK. Here is my hand, the deed is worthy doing.
QUEEN. And so say I.
YORK. And I: and now we three have spoke it,   280
It skills not greatly who impugns our doom.

Enter a Post

POST. Great lords, from Ireland am I come amain,
To signify that rebels there are up
And put the Englishmen unto the sword:
Send succours, lords, and stop the rage betime,
Before the wound do grow uncurable:
For, being green, there is great hope of help.
CARDINAL. A breach that craves a quick expedient
stop!
What counsel give you in this weighty cause?
YORK. That Somerset be sent as regent thither: 290
'Tis meet that lucky ruler be employed;
Witness the fortune he hath had in France.
SOMERSET. If York, with all his far-fet policy,
Had been the regent there instead of me,
He never would have stayed in France so long.
YORK. No, not to lose it all, as thou hast done:
I rather would have lost my life betimes
Than bring a burden of dishonour home

By staying there so long till all were lost.
Show me one scar charactered on thy skin: 300
Men's flesh preserved so whole do seldom win.
QUEEN. Nay, then, this spark will prove a raging fire,
If wind and fuel be brought to feed it with:
No more, good York; sweet Somerset, be still:
Thy fortune, York, hadst thou been regent there,
Might happily have proved far worse than his.
YORK. What! worse than nought? nay, then, a shame
take all!
SOMERSET. And, in the number, thee that wishest
shame!
CARDINAL. My Lord of York, try what your fortune is.
Th'uncivil kerns of Ireland are in arms   310
And temper clay with blood of Englishmen:
To Ireland will you lead a band of men,
Collected choicely, from each county some,
And try your hap against the Irishmen?
YORK. I will, my lord, so please his majesty.
SUFFOLK. Why, our authority is his consent,
And what we do establish he confirms:
Then, noble York, take thou this task in hand.
YORK. I am content: provide me soldiers, lords,
Whiles I take order for mine own affairs.   320
SUFFOLK. A charge, Lord York, that I will see
performed.
But now return we to the false Duke Humphrey.
CARDINAL. No more of him; for I will deal with him
That henceforth he shall trouble us no more.
And so break off; the day is almost spent:
Lord Suffolk, you and I must talk of that event.
YORK. My Lord of Suffolk, within fourteen days
At Bristow I expect my soldiers;
For there I'll ship them all for Ireland.
SUFFOLK. I'll see it truly done, my Lord of York.   330
                    They go, leaving York behind
YORK. Now, York, or never, steel thy fearful
thoughts,
And change misdoubt to resolution:
Be that thou hop'st to be, or what thou art
Resign to death; it is not worth th'enjoying:
Let pale-faced fear keep with the mean-born man,
And find no harbour in a royal heart.
Faster than spring-time showers comes thought on
thought,
And not a thought but thinks on dignity.
My brain more busy than the labouring spider
Weaves tedious snares to trap mine enemies.   340
Well, nobles, well, 'tis politicly done,
To send me packing with an host of men:
I fear me you but warm the starvéd snake,
Who, cherished in your breasts, will sting your
hearts.
'Twas men I lacked, and you will give them me:
I take it kindly; yet be well assured
You put sharp weapons in a madman's hands.
Whiles I in Ireland nourish a mighty band,
I will stir up in England some black storm
Shall blow ten thousand souls to heaven or hell;   350
And this fell tempest shall not cease to rage
Until the golden circuit on my head,
Like to the glorious sun's transparent beams,
Do calm the fury of this mad-bred flaw.
And, for a minister of my intent,
I have seduced a headstrong Kentishman,
John Cade of Ashford,

To make commotion, as full well he can,
Under the title of John Mortimer.
In Ireland have I seen this stubborn Cade
Oppose himself against a troop of kerns,
And fought so long, till that his thighs with darts
Were almost like a sharp-quilled porpentine;
And, in the end being rescuéd, I have seen
Him caper upright like a wild Morisco,
Shaking the bloody darts as he his bells.
Full often, like a shag-haired crafty kern,
Hath he converséd with the enemy,
And undiscovered come to me again
And given me notice of their villanies.   370
This devil here shall be my substitute;
For that John Mortimer, which now is dead,
In face, in gait, in speech, he doth resemble:
By this I shall perceive the commons' mind,
How they affect the house and claim of York.
Say he be taken, racked, and torturéd,
I know no pain they can inflict upon him
Will make him say I moved him to those arms.
Say that he thrive, as 'tis great like he will,
Why, then from Ireland come I with my strength   380
And reap the harvest which that rascal sowed.
For Humphrey being dead, as he shall be,
And Henry put apart, the next for me.   *He goes*

Scene 2: *Bury St Edmunds. A room of state, with curtains
at the back*

Enter certain Murderers, hastily, from behind the curtains

1 MURDERER. Run to my Lord of Suffolk; let him
    know
We have dispatched the duke, as he commanded.
2 MURDERER. O that it were to do! What have we
    done?
Didst ever hear a man so penitent?

Enter Suffolk

1 MURDERER. Here comes my lord.
SUFFOLK. Now, sirs, have you dispatched this thing?
1 MURDERER. Ay, my good lord, he's dead.
SUFFOLK. Why, that's well said. Go, get you to my
    house;
I will reward you for this venturous deed.
The king and all the peers are here at hand.   10
Have you laid fair the bed? Is all things well,
According as I gave directions?
1 MURDERER. 'Tis, my good lord.
SUFFOLK. Away! be gone.   *Murderers go*

*Sound trumpets. Enter the King, the Queen, Cardinal,
Somerset, with attendants*

KING. Go, call our uncle to our presence straight;
Say we intend to try his grace to-day,
If he be guilty, as 'tis publishéd.
SUFFOLK. I'll call him presently, my noble lord.
                                      Goes within
KING. Lords, take your places; and, I pray you all,
Proceed no straiter 'gainst our uncle Gloucester   20
Than from true evidence of good esteem
He be approved in practice culpable.
QUEEN. God forbid any malice should prevail,
That faultless may condemn a nobleman!
Pray God he may acquit him of suspicion!

KING. I thank thee, Nell; these words content me
    much.
Re-enter Suffolk
How now! why look'st thou pale? why tremblest
    thou?
Where is our uncle? what's the matter, Suffolk?
SUFFOLK. Dead in his bed, my lord; Gloucester is dead.
QUEEN. Marry, God forfend!   30
CARDINAL. God's secret judgement: I did dream
    to-night
The duke was dumb and could not speak a word.
                                  The King swoons
QUEEN. How fares my lord? Help, lords! the king is
    dead.
SOMERSET. Rear up his body; wring him by the nose.
QUEEN. Run, go, help, help! O Henry, ope thine eyes!
SUFFOLK. He doth revive again: madam, be patient.
KING. O heavenly God!
QUEEN.   How fares my gracious lord?
SUFFOLK. Comfort, my sovereign! gracious Henry,
    comfort!
KING. What! doth my Lord of Suffolk comfort me?
Came he right now to sing a raven's note,   40
Whose dismal tune bereft my vital powers;
And thinks he that the chirping of a wren,
By crying comfort from a hollow breast,
Can chase away the first-conceivéd sound?
Hide not thy poison with such sugared words;
Lay not thy hands on me; forbear, I say;
Their touch affrights me as a serpent's sting.
Thou baleful messenger, out of my sight!
Upon thy eye-balls murderous tyranny
Sits in grim majesty, to fright the world.   50
Look not upon me, for thine eyes are wounding:
Yet do not go away: come, basilisk,
And kill the innocent gazer with thy sight;
For in the shade of death I shall find joy;
In life but double death, now Gloucester's dead.
QUEEN. Why do you rate my Lord of Suffolk thus?
Although the duke was enemy to him,
Yet he most Christian-like laments his death:
And for myself, foe as he was to me,
Might liquid tears or heart-offending groans   60
Or blood-consuming sighs recall his life,
I would be blind with weeping, sick with groans,
Look pale as primrose with blood-drinking sighs,
And all to have the noble duke alive.
What know I how the world may deem of me?
For it is known we were but hollow friends:
It may be judged I made the duke away;
So shall my name with slander's tongue be
    wounded,
And princes' courts be filled with my reproach.
This get I by his death: ay me, unhappy!   70
To be a queen, and crowned with infamy!
KING. Ah, woe is me for Gloucester, wretched man!
QUEEN. Be woe for me, more wretched than he is.
What! dost thou turn away and hide thy face?
I am no loathsome leper; look on me.
What! art thou, like the adder, waxen deaf?
Be poisonous too and kill thy forlorn queen.
Is all thy comfort shut in Gloucester's tomb?
Why, then, Dame Eleanor was ne'er thy joy.
Erect his statua and worship it,   80
And make my image but an alehouse sign.

Was I for this nigh wrecked upon the sea
And twice by awkward wind from England's bank
Drove back again unto my native clime?
What boded this, but well forewarning wind
Did seem to say 'Seek not a scorpion's nest,
Nor set no footing on this unkind shore?'
What did I then, but cursed the gentle gusts
And he that loosed them forth their brazen caves;
And bid them blow towards England's bléssed
    shore,   90
Or turn our stern upon a dreadful rock?
Yet Aeolus would not be a murderer,
But left that hateful office unto thee:
The pretty vaulting sea refused to drown me,   .
Knowing that thou wouldst have me drowned on
    shore,
With tears as salt as sea, through thy unkindness:
The splitting rocks cowered in the sinking sands
And would not dash me with their ragged sides,
Because thy flinty heart, more hard than they,
Might in thy palace perish Eleanor.   100
As far as I could ken thy chalky cliffs,
When from thy shore the tempest beat us back,
I stood upon the hatches in the storm,
And when the dusky sky began to rob
My earnest-gaping sight of thy land's view,   110
I took a costly jewel from my neck—
A heart it was, bound in with diamonds—
And threw it towards thy land: the sea received it,
And so I wished thy body might my heart;
And even with this I lost fair England's view
And bid mine eyes be packing with my heart
And called them blind and dusky spectacles,
For losing ken of Albion's wishéd coast.
How often have I tempted Suffolk's tongue,
The agent of thy foul inconstancy,
To sit and witch me, as Ascanius did
When he to madding Dido would unfold
His father's acts commenced in burning Troy!
Am I not witched like her? or thou not false like
    him?
Ay me, I can no more! die, Eleanor!   120
For Henry weeps that thou dost live so long.

Noise without. Enter Warwick, Salisbury and many
Commons

WARWICK. It is reported, mighty sovereign,
    That good Duke Humphrey traitorously is
        murdered
    By Suffolk and the Cardinal Beaufort's means.
    The commons, like an angry hive of bees
    That want their leader, scatter up and down,
    And care not who they sting in his revenge.
    Myself have calmed their spleenful mutiny,
    Until they hear the order of his death.
KING. That he is dead, good Warwick, 'tis too true;   130
    But how he died God knows, not Henry:
    Enter his chamber, view his breathless corpse,
    And comment then upon his sudden death.
WARWICK. That shall I do, my liege. Stay, Salisbury,
    With the rude multitude till I return.
                                            He goes within
KING. O Thou that judgest all things, stay my
        thoughts,
    My thoughts, that labour to persuade my soul
    Some violent hands were laid on Humphrey's life!

If my suspect be false, forgive me, God,
For judgement only doth belong to Thee.   140
Fain would I go to chafe his paly lips
With twenty thousand kisses, and to drain
Upon his face an ocean of salt tears,
To tell my love unto his dumb deaf trunk,
And with my fingers feel his hand unfeeling:
But all in vain are these mean obsequies;
And to survey his dead and earthy image,
What were it but to make my sorrow greater?

Re-enter Warwick and draws aside he curtains, revealing
Gloucester's body on a bed

WARWICK. Come hither, gracious sovereign, view this
        body.
KING. That is to see how deep my grave is made;   150
    For with his soul fled all my worldly solace,
    For seeing him I see my life in death.
WARWICK. As surely as my soul intends to live
    With that dread King that took our state upon him
    To free us from his Father's wrathful curse,
    I do believe that violent hands were laid
    Upon the life of this thrice-faméd duke.
SUFFOLK. A dreadful oath, sworn with a solemn
        tongue!
    What instance gives Lord Warwick for his vow?
WARWICK. See how the blood is settled in his face.   160
    Oft have I seen a timely-parted ghost,
    Of ashy semblance, meagre, pale and bloodless,
    Being all descended to the labouring heart;
    Who, in the conflict that it holds with death,
    Attracts the same for aidance 'gainst the enemy;
    Which with the heart there cools and ne'er
        returneth
    To blush and beautify the cheek again.
    But see, his face is black and full of blood,
    His eye-balls further out than when he lived,
    Staring full ghastly like a strangléd man;   170
    His hair upreared, his nostrils stretched with
        struggling;
    His hands abroad displayed, as one that grasped
    And tugged for life and was by strength subdued:
    Look, on the sheets his hair, you see, is sticking;
    His well-proportioned beard made rough and
        rugged,
    Like to the summer's corn by tempest lodgéd.
    It cannot be but he was murderéd here;
    The least of all these signs were probable.
SUFFOLK. Why, Warwick, who should do the duke to
        death?
    Myself and Beaufort had him in protection;   180
    And we, I hope, sir, are no murderers.
WARWICK. But both of you were vowed Duke
        Humphrey's foes,
    And you, forsooth, had the good duke to keep:
    'Tis like you would not feast him like a friend;
    And 'tis well seen he found an enemy.
QUEEN. Then you, belike, suspect these noblemen
    As guilty of Duke Humphrey's timeless death.
WARWICK. Who finds the heifer dead and bleeding
        fresh
    And sees fast by a butcher with an axe,
    But will suspect 'twas he that made the slaughter?   190
    Who finds the partridge in the puttock's nest,
    But may imagine how the bird was dead,
    Although the kite soar with unbloodied beak?

Even so suspicious is this tragedy.
QUEEN. Are you the butcher, Suffolk? Where's your
    knife?
  Is Beaufort termed a kite? Where are his talons?
SUFFOLK. I wear no knife to slaughter sleeping men;
  But here's a vengeful sword, rusted with ease,
  That shall be scoured in his rancorous heart
  That slanders me with murder's crimson badge.   200
  Say, if thou dar'st, proud Lord of Warwickshire,
  That I am faulty in Duke Humphrey's death.
                              The Cardinal goes
WARWICK. What dares not Warwick, if false Suffolk
    dare him?
QUEEN. He dares not calm his contumelious spirit
  Nor cease to be an arrogant controller,
  Though Suffolk dare him twenty thousand times.
WARWICK. Madam, be still; with reverence may I say;
  For every word you speak in his behalf
  Is slander to your royal dignity.
SUFFOLK. Blunt-witted lord, ignoble in demeanour!   210
  If ever lady wronged her lord so much,
  Thy mother took into her blameful bed
  Some stern untutored churl, and noble stock
  Was graft with crab-tree slip, whose fruit thou art
  And never of the Nevils' noble race.
WARWICK. But that the guilt of murder bucklers thee
  And I should rob the deathsman of his fee,
  Quitting thee thereby of ten thousand shames,
  And that my sovereign's presence makes me mild,
  I would, false murd'rous coward, on thy knee   220
  Make thee beg pardon for thy passèd speech
  And say it was thy mother that thou meant'st,
  That thou thyself wast born in bastardy;
  And after all this fearful homage done,
  Give thee thy hire and send thy soul to hell,
  Pernicious blood-sucker of sleeping men!
SUFFOLK. Thou shalt be waking while I shed thy
    blood,
  If from this presence thou dar'st go with me.
WARWICK. Away even now, or I will drag thee hence:
  Unworthy though thou art, I'll cope with thee   230
  And do some service to Duke Humphrey's ghost.
          *Suffolk and Warwick go out followed
                by all but the King and Queen*
KING. What stronger breastplate than a heart
    untainted!
  Thrice is he armed that hath his quarrel just,
  And he but naked, though locked up in steel,
  Whose conscience with injustice is corrupted.
                              A noise without
QUEEN. What noise is this?
Re-enter Suffolk and Warwick, with their weapons drawn
KING. Why, how now, lords! your wrathful weapons
    drawn
  Here in our presence! dare you be so bold?
  Why, what tumultuous clamour have we here?
SUFFOLK. The traitorous Warwick with the men of
    Bury   240
  Set all upon me, mighty sovereign.
Enter Salisbury
SALISBURY [*at the door, to the Commons without*]. Sirs,
    stand apart; the king shall know your mind.
  Dread Lord, the commons send you word by me,
  Unless Lord Suffolk straight be done to death,
  Or banishèd fair England's territories,

They will by violence tear him from your palace
And torture him with grievous ling'ring death.
They say, by him the good Duke Humphrey died;
They say, in him they fear your highness' death;
And mere instinct of love and loyalty,   250
Free from a stubborn opposite intent,
As being thought to contradict your liking,
Makes them thus forward in his banishment.
They say, in care of your most royal person,
That if your highness should intend to sleep,
And charge that no man should disturb your rest
In pain of your dislike or pain of death,
Yet, notwithstanding such a strait edict,
Were there a serpent seen, with forkèd tongue,
That slyly glided towards your majesty,   260
It were but necessary you were waked,
Lest, being suffered in that harmful slumber,
The mortal worm might make the sleep eternal.
And therefore do they cry, though you forbid,
That they will guard you, whe'r you will or no,
From such fell serpents as false Suffolk is,
With whose envenomèd and fatal sting,
Your loving uncle, twenty times his worth,
They say, is shamefully bereft of life.
COMMONS [*without*]. An answer from the king, my
    Lord of Salisbury!   270
SUFFOLK. 'Tis like the commons, rude unpolished
    hinds,
  Could send such message to their sovereign:
  But you, my lord, were glad to be employed,
  To show how quaint an orator you are.
  But all the honour Salisbury hath won
  Is, that he was the lord ambassador
  Sent from a sort of tinkers to the king.
COMMONS [*without*]. An answer from the king, or we
    will all break in!
KING. Go, Salisbury, and tell them all from me,
  I thank them for their tender loving care;   280
  And had I not been cited so by them,
  Yet did I purpose as they do entreat;
  For, sure, my thoughts do hourly prophesy
  Mischance unto my state by Suffolk's means:
  And therefore, by His majesty I swear,
  Whose far unworthy deputy I am,
  He shall not breathe infection in this air
  But three days longer, on the pain of death.
                              Salisbury goes
QUEEN. O Henry, let me plead for gentle Suffolk!
KING. Ungentle queen, to call him gentle Suffolk!   290
  No more, I say: if thou dost plead for him,
  Thou wilt but add increase unto my wrath.
  Had I but said, I would have kept my word;
  But when I swear, it is irrevocable.
  If, after three days' space, thou here be'st found
  On any ground that I am ruler of,
  The world shall not be ransom for thy life.
  Come, Warwick, come, good Warwick, go with
    me;
  I have great matters to impart to thee.
              *They go, leaving the Queen and
                           Suffolk behind*
QUEEN. Mischance and sorrow go along with you!   300
  Heart's discontent and sour affliction
  Be playfellows to keep you company!
  There's two of you; the devil make a third!
  And threefold vengeance tend upon your steps!

SUFFOLK. Cease, gentle queen, these execrations,
And let thy Suffolk take his heavy leave.
QUEEN. Fie, coward woman and soft-hearted wretch!
Hast thou not spirit to curse thine enemy?
SUFFOLK. A plague upon them! wherefore should I
curse them?
Would curses kill, as doth the mandrake's groan,   310
I would invent as bitter-searching terms,
As curst, as harsh, and horrible to hear,
Delivered strongly through my fixéd teeth,
With full as many signs of deadly hate,
As lean-faced Envy in her loathsome cave:
My tongue should stumble in mine earnest words;
Mine eyes should sparkle like the beaten flint;
Mine hair be fixed an end, as one distract;
Ay, every joint should seem to curse and ban:
And even now my burdened heart would break,   320
Should I not curse them. Poison be their drink!
Gall, worse than gall, the daintiest that they taste!
Their sweetest shade a grove of cypress trees!
Their chiefest prospect murdering basilisks!
Their softest touch as smart as lizards' stings!
Their music frightful as the serpent's hiss,
And boding screech-owls make the consort full!
All the foul terrors in dark-seated hell—
QUEEN. Enough, sweet Suffolk; thou torment'st
thyself;
And these dread curses, like the sun 'gainst glass,   330
Or like an overchargéd gun, recoil,
And turn the force of them upon thyself.
SUFFOLK. You bade me ban, and will you bid me
leave?
Now, by the ground that I am banished from,
Well could I curse away a winter's night,
Though standing naked on a mountain top,
Where biting cold would never let grass grow,
And think it but a minute spent in sport.
QUEEN. O, let me entreat thee cease. Give me thy
hand,
That I may dew it with my mournful tears;   340
Nor let the rain of heaven wet this place,
To wash away my woeful monuments.
O, could this kiss be printed in thy hand,
That thou mightst think upon these by the seal,
Through whom a thousand sighs are breathed for
thee!
So, get thee gone, that I may know my grief;
'Tis but surmised whiles thou art standing by,
As one that surfeits thinking on a want.
I will repeal thee, or, be well assured,
Adventure to be banishéd myself: 350
And banishéd I am, if but from thee.
Go, speak not to me; even now be gone.
O, go not yet! Even thus two friends condemned
Embrace and kiss and take ten thousand leaves,
Loather a hundred times to part than die.
Yet now farewell, and farewell life with thee!
SUFFOLK. Thus is poor Suffolk ten times banishéd;
Once by the king, and three times thrice by thee.
'Tis not the land I care for, wert thou thence;
A wilderness is populous enough,   360
So Suffolk had thy heavenly company:
For where thou art, there is the world itself,
With every several pleasure in the world,
And where thou art not, desolation.
I can no more: live thou to joy thy life;

Myself no joy in nought but that thou liv'st.

Enter Vaux

QUEEN. Whither goes Vaux so fast? what news, I
prithee?
VAUX. To signify unto his majesty
That Cardinal Beaufort is at point of death;
For suddenly a grievous sickness took him,   370
That makes him gasp and stare and catch the air,
Blaspheming God and cursing men on earth.
Sometime he talks as if Duke Humphrey's ghost
Were by his side; sometime he calls the king
And whispers to his pillow as to him
The secrets of his overchargéd soul:
And I am sent to tell his majesty
That even now he cries aloud for him.
QUEEN. Go tell this heavy message to the king.
Vaux departs
Ay me! what is this world! what news are these!   380
But wherefore grieve I at an hour's poor loss,
Omitting Suffolk's exile, my soul's treasure?
Why only, Suffolk, mourn I not for thee,
And with the southern clouds contend in tears,
Theirs for the earth's increase, mine for my sorrows?
Now get thee hence: the king, thou know'st, is
coming;
If thou be found by me, thou art but dead.
SUFFOLK. If I depart from thee, I cannot live;
And in thy sight to die, what were it else
But like a pleasant slumber in thy lap?   390
Here could I breathe my soul into the air,
As mild and gentle as the cradle-babe
Dying with mother's dug between its lips:
Where, from thy sight, I should be raging mad
And cry out for thee to close up mine eyes,
To have thee with thy lips to stop my mouth;
So shouldst thou either turn my flying soul,
Or I should breathe it so into thy body,
And then it lived in sweet Elysium.
To die by thee were but to die in jest;   400
From thee to die were torture more than death:
O, let me stay, befall what may befall!
QUEEN. Away! though parting be a fretful corrosive,
It is appliéd to a deathful wound.
To France, sweet Suffolk: let me hear from thee;
For wheresoe'er thou art in this world's globe,
I'll have an Iris that shall find thee out.
SUFFOLK. I go.
QUEEN. And take my heart with thee.
She kisses him
SUFFOLK. A jewel, locked into the wofull'st cask   410
That ever did contain a thing of worth.
Even as a splitted bark, so sunder we:
This way fall I to death.
QUEEN.   This way for me.
They part

Scene 3: *A bedchamber*

*Enter the King, Salisbury, and Warwick, to the Cardinal
in bed*

KING. How fares my lord? speak, Beaufort, to thy
sovereign.
CARDINAL. If thou be'st Death, I'll give thee England's
treasure,
Enough to purchase such another island,

So thou wilt let me live, and feel no pain.
KING. Ah, what a sign it is of evil life,
Where death's approach is seen so terrible!
WARWICK. Beaufort, it is thy sovereign speaks to thee.
CARDINAL. Bring me unto my trial when you will.
Died he not in his bed? where should he die?
Can I make men live, whe'r they will or no?   10
O, torture me no more! I will confess.
Alive again? then show me where he is:
I'll give a thousand pound to look upon him.
He hath no eyes, the dust hath blinded them.
Comb down his hair; look, look! it stands upright,
Like lime-twigs set to catch my wingéd soul.
Give me some drink, and bid the apothecary
Bring the strong poison that I bought of him.
KING. O thou eternal Mover of the heavens,
Look with a gentle eye upon this wretch!   20
O, beat away the busy meddling fiend
That lays strong siege unto this wretch's soul
And from his bosom purge this black despair!
WARWICK. See, how the pangs of death do make him
grin!
SALISBURY. Disturb him not, let him pass peaceably.
KING. Peace to his soul, if God's good pleasure be!
Lord Cardinal, if thou think'st on heaven's bliss,
Hold up thy hand, make signal of thy hope.
He dies, and makes no sign. O God, forgive him!
WARWICK. So bad a death argues a monstrous life.   30
KING. Forbear to judge, for we are sinners all.
Close up his eyes and draw the curtain close;
And let us all to meditation.   *They go*

ACT 4

Scene 1: *The coast of Kent*

*Alarum. Fight at sea. Ordnance goes off. Enter a Lieutenant,
a Master, a Master's-Mate, Walter Whitmore and soldiers;
with them Suffolk disguised and other gentlemen prisoners*

LIEUTENANT. The gaudy, blabbling and remorseful
day
Is crept into the bosom of the sea;
And now loud-howling wolves arouse the jades
That drag the tragic melancholy night;
Who, with their drowsy, slow and flagging wings,
Clip dead men's graves and from their misty jaws
Breathe foul contagious darkness in the air.
Therefore bring forth the soldiers of our prize;
For, whilst our pinnace anchors in the Downs,
Here shall they make their ransom on the sand,   10
Or with their blood stain this discoloured shore.
Master, this prisoner freely give I thee;
And thou that art his mate, make boot of this;
The other, Walter Whitmore, is thy share.
1 GENTLEMAN. What is my ransom, master? let me
know.
MASTER. A thousand crowns, or else lay down your
head.
MATE. And so much shall you give, or off goes yours.
LIEUTENANT. What! think you much to pay two
thousand crowns,
And bear the name and port of gentlemen?
Cut both the villains' throats; for die you shall: 20
The lives of those which we have lost in fight
Be counterpoised with such a petty sum!

1 GENTLEMAN. I'll give it, sir; and therefore spare my
life.
2 GENTLEMAN. And so will I, and write home for it
straight.
WHITMORE [*to Suffolk*]. I lost mine eye in laying the
prize aboard,
And therefore to revenge it shalt thou die;
And so should these, if I might have my will.
LIEUTENANT. Be not so rash; take ransom, let him live.
SUFFOLK. Look on my George; I am a gentleman:
Rate me at what thou wilt, thou shalt be paid.   30
WHITMORE. And so am I; my name is Walter
Whitmore.
How now! why starts thou? what, doth death
affright?
SUFFOLK. Thy name affrights me, in whose sound is
death.
A cunning man did calculate my birth
And told me that by 'water' I should die:
Yet let not this make thee be bloody-minded;
Thy name is Gaultier, being rightly sounded.
WHITMORE. Gaultier or Walter, which it is I care not:
Never yet did base dishonour blur our name,
But with our sword we wiped away the blot;   40
Therefore, when merchant-like I sell revenge,
Broke be my sword, my arms torn and defaced,
And I proclaimed a coward through the world!
SUFFOLK. Stay, Whitmore, for thy prisoner is a prince,
The Duke of Suffolk, William de la Pole.
WHITMORE. The Duke of Suffolk, muffled up in rags!
SUFFOLK. Ay, but these rags are no part of the duke:
Jove sometime went disguised, and why not I?
LIEUTENANT. But Jove was never slain, as thou shalt be.
SUFFOLK. Obscure and lousy swain, King Henry's
blood,   50
The honourable blood of Lancaster,
Must not be shed by such a jaded groom.
Hast thou not kissed thy hand and held my stirrup?
Bare-headed plodded by my foot-cloth mule
And thought thee happy when I shook my head?
How often hast thou waited at my cup,
Fed from my trencher, kneeled down at the board,
When I have feasted with Queen Margaret?
Remember it and let it make thee crest-fall'n,
Ay, and allay this thy abortive pride;   60
How in our voiding lobby hast thou stood
And duly waited for my coming forth?
This hand of mine hath writ in thy behalf
And therefore shall it charm thy riotous tongue.
WHITMORE. Speak, captain, shall I stab the forlorn
swain?
LIEUTENANT. First let my words stab him, as he hath
me.
SUFFOLK. Base slave, thy words are blunt and so art
thou.
LIEUTENANT. Convey him hence and on our
long-boat's side
Strike off his head.
SUFFOLK.   Thou dar'st not, for thy own.
LIEUTENANT. Yes, poll!
SUFFOLK.   Pole!
LIEUTENANT.   Sir Pool! Lord Pool! 70
Ay, kennel, puddle, sink, whose filth and dirt
Troubles the silver spring where England drinks.
Now will I dam up this thy yawning mouth
For swallowing the treasure of the realm:

Thy lips that kissed the queen shall sweep the
     ground;
And thou that smil'dst at good Duke Humphrey's
     death
Against the senseless winds shalt grin in vain,
Who in contempt shall hiss at thee again:
And wedded be thou to the hags of hell,
For daring to affy a mighty lord   80
Unto the daughter of a worthless king,
Having neither subject, wealth, nor diadem.
By devilish policy art thou grown great
And, like ambitious Sylla, overgorged
With gobbets of thy mother's bleeding heart.
By thee Anjou and Maine were sold to France,
The false revolting Normans thorough thee
Disdain to call us lord, and Picardy
Hath slain their governors, surprised our forts
And sent the ragged soldiers wounded home.   90
The princely Warwick, and the Nevils all,
Whose dreadful swords were never drawn in vain,
As hating thee, are rising up in arms:
And now the house of York, thrust from the crown
By shameful murder of a guiltless king
And lofty proud encroaching tyranny,
Burns with revenging fire; whose hopeful colours
Advance our half-faced sun, striving to shine,
Under the which is writ 'Invitis nubibus.'
The commons here in Kent are up in arms: 100
And, to conclude, reproach and beggary
Is crept into the palace of our king,
And all by thee. Away! convey him hence.
SUFFOLK. O that I were a god, to shoot forth thunder
Upon these paltry, servile, abject drudges!
Small things make base men proud: this villain here,
Being captain of a pinnace, threatens more
Than Bargulus the strong Illyrian pirate.
Drones suck not eagles' blood but rob bee-hives:
It is impossible that I should die   110
By such a lowly vassal as thyself.
Thy words move rage and not remorse in me:
I go of message from the queen to France;
I charge thee waft me safely cross the Channel.
LIEUTENANT. Walter,—
WHITMORE. Come, Suffolk, I must waft thee to thy
     death.
SUFFOLK. Pro! Gelidus timor occupat artus: it is thee I
     fear.
WHITMORE. Thou shalt have cause to fear before I
     leave thee.
What! are ye daunted now? now will ye stoop?
1 GENTLEMAN. My gracious lord, entreat him, speak
     him fair.   120
SUFFOLK. Suffolk's imperial tongue is stern and rough,
Used to command, untaught to plead for favour.
Far be it we should honour such as these
With humble suit: no, rather let my head
Stoop to the block than these knees bow to any
Save to the God of heaven and to my king;
And sooner dance upon a bloody pole
Than stand uncovered to the vulgar groom.
True nobility is exempt from fear:
More can I bear than you dare execute.   130
LIEUTENANT. Hale him away, and let him talk no
     more.
SUFFOLK. Come, soldiers, show what cruelty ye can,
That this my death may never be forgot!

Great men oft die by vile besonians:
A Roman sworder and bandetto slave
Murdered sweet Tully; Brutus' bastard hand
Stabbed Julius Caesar; savage islanders
Pompey the Great; and Suffolk dies by pirates.
                         Whitmore and others take him away
LIEUTENANT. And as for these whose ransom we have
     set,
It is our pleasure one of them depart: 140
Therefore come you with us and let him go.
                                   All depart but 1 Gentleman

Re-enter Whitmore with Suffolk's body

WHITMORE. There let his head and lifeless body lie,
Until the queen his mistress bury it.   *He goes*
1 GENTLEMAN. O barbarous and bloody spectacle!
His body will I bear unto the king:
If he revenge it not, yet will his friends;
So will the queen, that living held him dear.
                                        He bears off the body

Scene 2: *Blackheath*

Enter Bevis and John Holland

BEVIS. Come, and get thee a sword, though made of
a lath: they have been up these two days.
HOLLAND. They have the more need to sleep now,
then.
BEVIS. I tell thee, Jack Cade the clothier means to dress
the commonwealth, and turn it, and set a new nap
upon it.
HOLLAND. So he had need, for 'tis threadbare. Well, I
say, it was never merry world in England since
gentlemen came up.   10
BEVIS. O miserable age! virtue is not regarded in
handicrafts-men.
HOLLAND. The nobility think scorn to go in leather
aprons.
BEVIS. Nay, more, the king's council are no good
workmen.
HOLLAND. True; and yet it is said, labour in thy vocation; which is as much to say as, let the magistrates
be labouring men; and therefore should we be
magistrates.   20
BEVIS. Thou hast hit it; for there's no better sign of a
brave mind than a hard hand.
HOLLAND. I see them! I see them! There's Best's son,
the tanner of Wingham,—
BEVIS. He shall have the skins of our enemies, to make
dog's-leather of.
HOLLAND. And Dick the butcher,—
BEVIS. Then is sin struck down like an ox, and
iniquity's throat cut like a calf.
HOLLAND. And Smith the weaver,—   30
BEVIS. Argo, their thread of life is spun.
HOLLAND. Come, come, let's fall in with them.

*Drum. Enter Cade, Dick the Butcher, Smith the Weaver,
and a Sawyer, with infinite numbers.*

CADE. We John Cade, so termed of our supposed
father,—
DICK [*aside*]. Or rather, of stealing a cade of herrings.
CADE. For our enemies shall fall before us, inspired
with the spirit of putting down kings and princes . . .
Command silence.
DICK. Silence!

CADE. My father was a Mortimer,— 40
DICK [aside]. He was an honest man, and a good brick-
layer.
CADE. My mother a Plantagenet,—
DICK [aside]. I knew her well; she was a midwife.
CADE. My wife descended of the Lacies,—
DICK [aside]. She was, indeed, a pedlar's daughter, and
sold many laces.
SMITH [aside]. But now of late, not able to travel with
her furred pack, she washes bucks here at home.
CADE. Therefore am I of an honourable house. 50
DICK [aside]. Ay, by my faith, the field is honourable;
and there was he born, under a hedge; for his father
had never a house but the cage.
CADE. Valiant I am.
SMITH [aside]. A' must needs, for beggary is valiant.
CADE. I am able to endure much.
DICK [aside]. No question of that; for I have seen him
whipped three market-days together.
CADE. I fear neither sword nor fire.
SMITH [aside]. He need not fear the sword, for his coat 60
is of proof.
DICK [aside]. But methinks he should stand in fear of
fire, being burnt i'th'hand for stealing of sheep.
CADE. Be brave, then; for your captain is brave, and
vows reformation. There shall be in England seven
halfpenny loaves sold for a penny: the three-hooped
pot shall have ten hoops; and I will make it felony
to drink small beer: all the realm shall be in common; and in Cheapside shall my palfry go to grass:
and when I am king, as king I will be,— 70
ALL. God save your majesty!
CADE. I thank you, good people,—there shall be no
money; all shall eat and drink on my score; and I will
apparel them all in one livery, that they may agree
like brothers, and worship me their lord.
DICK [shouts]. The first thing we do, let's kill all the
lawyers.
CADE. Nay, that I mean to do. Is not this a lamentable
thing, that of the skin of an innocent lamb should
be made parchment? that parchment, being scrib- 80
bled o'er, should undo a man? Some say the bee
stings: but I say, 'tis the bee's wax; for I did but
seal once to a thing, and I was never mine own man
since. How now! who's there?

Enter some, bringing forward the Clerk of Chatham

SMITH. The clerk of Chatham: he can write and read
and cast accompt.
CADE. O monstrous!
SMITH. We took him setting of boys' copies.
CADE. Here's a villain!
SMITH. Has a book in his pocket with red letters in't. 90
CADE. Nay, then, he is a conjuror.
DICK. Nay, he can make obligations, and write court-
hand.
CADE. I am sorry for't: the man is a proper man, of
mine honour; unless I find him guilty, he shall not
die. Come hither, sirrah, I must examine thee: what
is thy name?
CLERK. Emmanuel.
DICK. They use to write it on the top of letters: 'twill
go hard with you. 100
CADE. Let me alone. Dost thou use to write thy name?
or hast thou a mark to thyself, like an honest plain-
dealing man?

CLERK. Sir, I thank God, I have been so well brought
up that I can write my name.
ALL. He hath confessed: away with him! he's a villain
and a traitor.
CADE. Away with him, I say! hang him with his pen
and ink-horn about his neck.
                              The Clerk is led away to death

Enter Michael

MICHAEL. Where's our general? 110
CADE. Here I am, thou particular fellow.
MICHAEL. Fly, fly, fly! Sir Humphrey Stafford and his
brother are hard by, with the king's forces.
CADE. Stand, villain, stand, or I'll fell thee down. He
shall be encount'red with a man as good as himself:
he is but a knight, is a'?
MICHAEL. No.
CADE. To equal him, I will make myself a knight
presently. [kneels] Rise up Sir John Mortimer. [rises]
Now have at him! 120

*Enter Sir Humphrey Stafford and his Brother, with a
herald, drum and soldiers*

STAFFORD. Rebellious hinds, the filth and scum of
Kent,
Marked for the gallows, lay your weapons down;
Home to your cottages, forsake this groom:
The king is merciful, if you revolt.
BROTHER. But angry, wrathful, and inclined to blood,
If you go forward; therefore yield, or die.
CADE. As for these silken-coated slaves, I pass not:
It is to you, good people, that I speak,
Over whom, in time to come, I hope to reign;
For I am rightful heir unto the crown. 130
STAFFORD. Villain, thy father was a plasterer;
And thou thyself a shearman, art thou not?
CADE. And Adam was a gardener.
BROTHER. And what of that?
CADE. Marry, this: Edmund Mortimer, Earl of March,
Married the Duke of Clarence' daughter, did he
not?
STAFFORD. Ay, sir.
CADE. By her he had two children at one birth.
BROTHER. That's false.
CADE. Ay, there's the question; but I say, 'tis true: 140
The elder of them, being put to nurse,
Was by a beggar-woman stol'n away;
And, ignorant of his birth and parentage,
Became a bricklayer when he came to age:
His son am I; deny it, if you can.
DICK. Nay, 'tis too true; therefore he shall be king.
SMITH. Sir, he made a chimney in my father's house,
and the bricks are alive at this day to testify it;
therefore deny it not.
STAFFORD. And will you credit this base drudge's
words, 150
That speaks he knows not what?
ALL. Ay, marry, will we; therefore get ye gone.
BROTHER. Jack Cade, the Duke of York hath taught
you this.
CADE [aside]. He lies, for I invented it myself.
[aloud] Go to, sirrah, tell the king from me, that, for
his father's sake, Henry the fifth, in whose time boys
went to span-counter for French crowns, I am
content he shall reign; but I'll be Protector over him.

DICK. And furthermore, we'll have the Lord Say's
head for selling the dukedom of Maine.　160
CADE. And good reason; for thereby is England
mained, and fain to go with a staff, but that my
puissance holds it up. Fellow kings, I tell you that
that Lord Say hath gelded the commonwealth, and
made it an eunuch: and more than that, he can speak
French, and therefore he is a traitor.
STAFFORD. O gross and miserable ignorance!
CADE. Nay, answer, if you can: the Frenchmen are our
enemies; go to, then, I ask but this: can he that
speaks with the tongue of an enemy be a good　170
counsellor, or no?
ALL. No, no, and therefore we'll have his head.
BROTHER. Well, seeing gentle words will not prevail,
Assail them with the army of the king.
STAFFORD. Herald, away; and thoughout every town
Proclaim them traitors that are up with Cade;
That those which fly before the battle ends
May, even in their wives' and children's sight,
Be hanged up for example at their doors:
And you that be the king's friends, follow me.　180

The Staffords and their guard retire

CADE. And you that love the commons, follow me.
Now show yourselves men; 'tis for liberty.
We will not leave one lord, one gentleman:
Spare none but such as go in clouted shoon;
For they are thrifty honest men and such
As would, but that they dare not, take our parts.
DICK. They are all in order and march toward us.
CADE. But then are we in order when we are most out
of order. come, march forward.

Alarums to the fight wherein both the Staffords are slain

Scene 3

Enter Cade and the rest

CADE. Where's Dick, the butcher of Ashford?
DICK. Here, sir.
CADE. They fell before thee like sheep and oxen, and
thou behav'dst thyself as it thou hadst been in thine
own slaughter-house: therefore thus will I reward
thee, the Lent shall be as long again as it is; and thou
shalt have a license to kill for a hundred lacking one
a week.
DICK. I desire no more.
CADE. And, to speak truth, thou deserv'st no less. This　10
monument of the victory will I bear [*putting on Sir
Humphrey's coat of amil*]. And the bodies shall be
dragged at my horse heels till I do come to London,
where we will have the mayor's sword borne before
us.
DICK. If we mean to thrive and do good, break open
the gaols and let out the prisoners.
CADE. Fear not that, I warrant thee. Come, let's march
towards London.　*They go*

Scene 4: *London. The palace*

*Enter the King with a supplication, and the Queen with
Suffolk's head, the Duke of Buckingham and the Lord Say*

QUEEN. Oft have I heard that grief softens the mind
And makes it fearful and degenerate;
Think therefore on revenge and cease to weep.
But who can cease to weep and look on this?

Here may his head lie on my throbbing breast:
But where's the body that I should embrace?
BUCKINGHAM. What answer makes your grace to the
rebels' supplication?
KING. I'll send some holy bishop to entreat;
For God forbid so many simple souls　10
Should perish by the sword! And I myself,
Rather than bloody war shall cut them short,
Will parley with Jack Cade their general:
But stay, I'll read it over once again.
QUEEN. Ah, barbarous villains! hath this lovely face
Ruled, like a wandering planet, over me,
And could it not enforce them to relent,
That were unworthy to behold the same?
KING. Lord Say, Jack Cade hath sworn to have thy
head.
SAY. Ay, but I hope your highness shall have his.　20
KING. How now, madam!
Still lamenting and mourning for Suffolk's death?
I fear me, love, if that I had been dead,
Thou wouldest not have mourned so much for me.
QUEEN. No, my love, I should not mourn, but die for
thee.

Enter a Messenger

KING. How now! what news? why com'st thou in such
haste?
MESSENGER. The rebels are in Southwark; fly, my lord!
Jack Cade proclaims himself Lord Mortimer,
Descended from the Duke of Clarence' house,
And calls your grace usurper openly,　30
And vows to crown himself in Westminster.
His army is a ragged multitude
Of hinds and peasants, rude and merciless:
Sir Humphrey Stafford and his brother's death
Hath given them heart and courage to proceed:
All scholars, lawyers, courtiers, gentlemen,
They call false caterpillars and intend their death.
KING. O graceless men! they know not what they do.
BUCKINGHAM. My gracious lord, retire to
Killingworth,
Until a power be raised to put them down.　40
QUEEN. Ah, were the Duke of Suffolk now alive,
These Kentish rebels would be soon appeased!
KING. Lord Say, the traitors hateth thee;
Therefore away with us to Killingworth.
SAY. So might your grace's person be in danger.
The sight of me is odious in their eyes;
And therefore in this city will I stay
And live alone as secret as I may.

Enter another Messenger

2 MESSENGER. Jack Cade hath gotten London Bridge:
The citizens fly and forsake their houses:　50
The rascal people, thirsting after prey,
Join with the traitor, and they jointly swear
To spoil the city and your royal court.
BUCKINGHAM. Then linger not, my lord; away, take
horse.
KING. Come, Margaret; God, our hope, will succour
us.
QUEEN. My hope is gone, now Suffolk is deceased.
KING. Farewell, my lord: trust not the Kentish rebels.
BUCKINGHAM. Trust nobody, for fear you be betrayed.
SAY. The trust I have is in mine innocence,
And therefore am I bold and resolute.　*They go*　60

Scene 5: *London. The Tower*

Enter Lord Scales upon the Tower, walking. Then enter two or three Citizens below

SCALES. How now! is Jack Cade slain?

1 CITIZEN. No, my lord, nor likely to be slain; for they have won the bridge, killing all those that withstand them: the Lord Mayor craves aid of your honour from the Tower to defend the city from the rebels.

SCALES. Such aid as I can spare you shall command;
But I am troubléd here with them myself;
The rebels have assayed to win the Tower.
But get you to Smithfield and gather head,   10
And thither I will send you Matthew Gough;
Fight for your king, your country and your lives;
And so, farewell, for I must hence again.

He goes within; the Citizens depart

Scene 6: *London. Cannon Street*

Enter Jack Cade and the rest, and strikes his sword on London Stone

CADE. Now is Mortimer lord of this city. And here, sitting upon London Stone, I charge and command that, of the city's cost, the pissing-conduit run nothing but claret wine this first year of our reign. And now henceforward it shall be treason for any that calls me other than Lord Mortimer.

Enter a Soldier, running

SOLDIER. Jack Cade! Jack Cade!

CADE. Knock him down there.   *They kill him*

SMITH. If this fellow be wise, he'll never call ye Jack Cade more: I think he hath a very fair warning.   10

DICK. My lord, there's an army gathered together in Smithfield.

CADE. Come, then, let's go fight with them: but first, go and set London Bridge on fire; and, if you can, burn down the Tower too. Come, let's away.

They go

Alarums. Citizens, led by Sir Matthew Gough, give battle to the rebels; Matthew Gough is slain, and all the rest

Scene 7

Then enter Jack Cade, with his company

CADE. So, sirs: now go some and pull down the Savoy; others to th'Inns of Court; down with them all.

DICK. I have a suit unto your lordship.

CADE. Be it a lordship, thou shalt have it for that word.

DICK. Only that the laws of England may come out of your mouth.

HOLLAND [*aside*]. Mass, 'twill be sore law, then; for he was thrust in the mouth with a spear, and 'tis not whole yet.

SMITH [*aside*]. Nay, John, it will be stinking law; for his   10
breath stinks with eating toasted cheese.

CADE. I have thought upon it, it shall be so. Away, burn all the records of the realm: my mouth shall be the parliament of England.

HOLLAND [*aside*]. Then we are like to have biting statutes, unless his teeth be pulled out.

CADE. And henceforward all things shall be in common.

Enter a Messenger

MESSENGER. My lord, a prize, a prize! here's the Lord Say, which sold the towns in France; he that made   20
us pay one and twenty fifteens, and one shilling to the pound, the last subsidy.

Enter George, with the Lord Say

CADE. Well, he shall be beheaded for it ten times. Ah, thou say, thou serge, nay, thou buckram lord! now art thou within point-blank of our jurisdiction regal. What canst thou answer to my majesty for giving up of Normandy unto Mounsieur Basimecu, the Dauphin of France? Be it known unto thee by these presence, even the presence of Lord Mortimer, that I am the besom that must sweep the court clean of   30
such filth as thou art. Thou hast most traitorously corrupted the youth of the realm in erecting a grammar school: and whereas, before, our forefathers had no other books but the score and the tally, thou hast caused printing to be used, and, contrary to the king, his crown and dignity, thou hast built a paper-mill. It will be provéd to thy face that thou hast men about thee that usually talk of a noun and a verb, and such abominable words as no Christian ear can endure to hear. Thou hast   40
appointed justices of peace, to call poor men before them about matters they were not able to answer. Moreover, thou hast put them in prison, and because they could not read thou hast hanged them, when, indeed, only for that cause they have been most worthy to live. Thou dost ride on foot-cloth, dost thou not?

SAY. What of that?

CADE. Marry, thou ought'st not to let thy horse wear a cloak, when honester men than thou go in their   50
hose and doublets.

DICK. And work in their shirt too; as myself, for example, that am a butcher.

SAY. You men of Kent,—

DICK. What say you of Kent?

SAY. Nothing but this; 'tis 'bona terra, mala gens.'

CADE. Away with him, away with him! he speaks Latin.

SAY. Hear me but speak, and bear me where you will.
Kent, in the Commentaries Caesar writ,   60
Is termed the civil'st place of all this isle:
Sweet is the country, because full of riches;
The people liberal, valiant, active, wealthy;
Which makes me hope you are not void of pity.
I sold not Maine, I lost not Normandy,
Yet to recover them would lose my life.
Justice with favour have I always done;
Prayers and tears have moved me, gifts could never.
When have I aught exacted at your hands,
But to maintain the king, the realm and you?   70
Large gifts have I bestowed on learnéd clerks,
Because my book preferred me to the king,
And seeing ignorance is the curse of God,
Knowledge the wing wherewith we fly to heaven,
Unless you be possessed with devilish spirits,
You cannot but forbear to murder me:
This tongue hath parleyed unto foreign kings
For your behoof,—

CADE. Tut, when struck'st thou one blow in the field?

SAY. Great men have reaching hands: oft have I struck 80
Those that I never saw and struck them dead.

GEORGE. O monstrous coward! what, to come behind
folks?

SAY. These cheeks are pale for watching for your
good.

CADE. Give him a box o'th'ear and that will make 'em
red again.

SAY. Long sitting to determine poor men's causes
Hath made me full of sickness and diseases.

CADE. Ye shall have a hempen caudle then and the
help of hatchet.   90

DICK. Why dost thou quiver, man?

SAY. The palsy, and not fear, provokes me.

CADE. Nay, he nods at us, as who should say, I'll be
even with you: I'll see if his head will stand steadier
on a pole, or no. Take him away, and behead him.

SAY. Tell me: wherein have I offended most?
Have I affected wealth or honour? speak.
Are my chests filled up with extorted gold?
Is my apparel sumptuous to behold?
Whom have I injured, that ye seek my death?   100
These hands are free from guiltless blood-shedding,
This breast from harbouring foul deceitful thoughts.
O, let me live!

CADE [aside]. I feel remorse in myself with his words;
but I'll bridle it: he shall die, an it be but for pleading
so well for his life. [aloud] Away with him! he has a
familiar under his tongue; he speaks not o' God's
name. Go, take him away, I say, and strike off his
head presently; and then break into his son-in-law's
house, Sir James Cromer, and strike off his head, and 110
bring them both upon two poles hither.

ALL. It shall be done.

SAY. Ah, countrymen! if when you make your
prayers,
God should be so obdurate as yourselves,
How would it fare with your departed souls?
And therefore yet relent, and save my life.

CADE. Away with him! and do as I command ye.
                                        They lead him away
The proudest peer in the realm shall not wear a head
on his shoulders, unless he pay me tribute; there shall
not a maid be married, but she shall pay to me her 120
maidenhead ere they have it: men shall hold of me
in capite; and we charge and command that their
wives be as free as heart can wish or tongue can tell.

DICK. My lord, when shall we go to Cheapside and
take up commodities upon our bills?

CADE. Marry, presently.

ALL. O, brave!

Enter one with the heads

CADE. But is not this braver? Let them kiss one
another, for they loved well when they were alive.
Now part them again, lest they consult about the   130
giving up of some more towns in France. Soldiers,
defer the spoil of the city until night: for with these
borne before us, instead of maces, will we ride
through the streets; and at every corner have them
kiss. Away!   The rebels go

Alarum and retreat

Scene 8

Enter again Cade and all his rabblement

CADE. Up Fish Street! down Saint Magnus' Corner!
kill and knock down! throw them into Thames!
[sound a parley] What noise is this I hear? Dare any
be so bold to sound retreat or parley, when I
command them kill?

Enter Buckingham and old Clifford, attended

BUCKINGHAM. Ay, here they be that dare and will
disturb thee:
Know, Cade, we come ambassadors from the king
Unto the commons whom thou hast misled,
And here pronounce free pardon to them all
That will forsake thee and go home in peace.   10

CLIFFORD. What say ye, countrymen? will ye relent,
And yield to mercy whilst 'tis offered you;
Or let a rebel lead you to your deaths?
Who loves the king and will embrace his pardon,
Fling up his cap, and say 'God save his majesty!'
Who hateth him and honours not his father,
Henry the Fifth, that made all France to quake,
Shake he his weapon at us and pass by.

ALL. God save the king! God save the king!

CADE. What, Buckingham and Clifford, are ye so   20
brave? And you, base peasants, do ye believe him?
will you needs be hanged with your pardons about
your necks? Hath my sword therefore broke
through London gates, that you should leave me at
the White Hart in Southwark? I thought ye would
never have given out these arms till you had
recovered your ancient freedom: but you are all
recreants and dastards, and delight to live in slavery
to the nobility. Let them break your backs with
burdens, take your houses over your heads, ravish 30
your wives and daughters before your faces: for me,
I will make shift for one; and so, God's curse light
upon you all!

ALL. We'll follow Cade, we'll follow Cade!

CLIFFORD. Is Cade the son of Henry the Fifth,
That thus you do exclaim you'll go with him?
Will he conduct you through the heart of France,
And make the meanest of you earls and dukes?
Alas, he hath no home, no place to fly to;
Nor knows he how to live but by the spoil,   40
Unless by robbing of your friends and us.
Were't not a shame, that whilst you live at jar,
The fearful French, whom you late vanquishéd,
Should make a start o'er seas and vanquish you?
Methinks already in this civil broil
I see them lording it in London streets,
Crying 'Villiago!' unto all they meet.
Better ten thousand base-born Cades miscarry
Than you should stoop unto a Frenchman's mercy.
To France, to France, and get what you have lost; 50
Spare England, for it is your native coast:
Henry hath money, you are strong and manly;
God on our side, doubt not of victory.

ALL. A Clifford! a Clifford! we'll follow the king and
Clifford.

CADE. Was ever feather so lightly blown to and fro as
this multitude? The name of Henry the Fifth hales
them to an hundred mischiefs and makes them leave
me desolate. I see them lay their heads together to
surprise me. My sword make way for me, for here 60

is no staying. In despite of the devils and hell, have
through the very middest of you! and heavens and
honour be witness that no want of resolution in me,
but only my followers' base and ignominious
treasons, makes me betake me to my heels.

He clears a path with his sword,
and goes

BUCKINGHAM. What, is he fled? Go some, and follow
him;
And he that brings his head unto the king
Shall have a thousand crowns for his reward.

Some of them follow

Follow me, soldiers: we'll devise a mean
To reconcile you all unto the king.   *They go* 70

Scene 9: *Kenilworth Castle*

Sound trumpets. Enter King, Queen, and Somerset, on
the wall

KING. Was ever king that joyed an earthly throne,
And could command no more content than I?
No sooner was I crept out of my cradle
But I was made a king, at nine months old.
Was never subject longed to be a king
As I do long and wish to be a subject.

Enter Buckingham and old Clifford

BUCKINGHAM. Health and glad tidings to your
majesty!
KING. Why, Buckingham, is the traitor Cade
surprised?
Or is he but retired to make him strong?

Enter, below, multitudes, with halters about their necks

CLIFFORD. He is fled, my lord, and all his powers do
yield,   10
And humbly thus, with halters on their necks,
Expect your highness' doom, of life or death.
KING. Then, heaven, set ope thy everlasting gates,
To entertain my vows of thanks and praise!
Soldiers, this day have you redeemed your lives
And showed how well you love your prince and
country:
Continue still in this so good a mind,
And Henry, though he be infortunate,
Assure yourselves, will never be unkind:
And so, with thanks and pardon to you all,   20
I do dismiss you to your several countries.
ALL. God save the king! God save the king!

Enter a Messenger

MESSENGER. Please it your grace to be advertisèd
The Duke of York is newly come from Ireland,
And with a puissant and a mighty power
Of gallowglasses and stout kerns
Is marching hitherward in proud array,
And still proclaimeth, as he comes along,
His arms are only to remove from thee
The Duke of Somerset, whom he terms a traitor.   30
KING. Thus stands my state, 'twixt Cade and York
distressed,
Like to a ship that, having 'scaped a tempest
Is straightway calmed and boarded with a pirate.
But now is Cade driven back, his men dispersed;
And now is York in arms to second him.
I pray thee, Buckingham, go and meet him,

And ask him what's the reason of these arms.
Tell him I'll send Duke Edmund to the Tower
And, Somerset, we will commit thee thither,
Until his army be dismissed from him.   40
SOMERSET. My lord,
I'll yield myself to prison willingly,
Or unto death, to do my country good.
KING. In any case, be not too rough in terms;
For he is fierce and cannot brook hard language.
BUCKINGHAM. I will, my lord; and doubt not so to
deal
As all things shall redound unto your good.
KING. Come, wife, let's in, and learn to govern better;
For yet may England curse my wretched reign.

Flourish as they go

Scene 10: *Kent. Iden's garden*

Enter Cade

CADE. Fie on ambitions! fie on myself, that have a
sword, and yet am ready to famish! These five days
have I hid me in these woods and durst not peep
out, for all the country is laid for me; but now am
I so hungry that if I might have a lease of my life
for a thousand years I could stay no longer. Wherefore, on a brick wall have I climbed into this garden,
to see if I can eat grass, or pick a sallet another while,
which is not amiss to cool a man's stomach this hot
weather. And I think this word 'sallet' was born to   10
do me good: for many a time, but for a sallet, my
brainpan had been cleft with a brown bill; and many
a time, when I have been dry and bravely marching,
it hath served me instead of a quart pot to drink in;
and now the word 'sallet' must serve me to feed on.

Enter Iden

IDEN. Lord, who would live turmoilèd in the court,
And may enjoy such quiet walks as these?
This small inheritance my father left me
Contenteth me, and worth a monarchy.
I seek not to wax great by others' waning,   20
Or gather wealth, I care not with what envy:
Sufficeth that I have maintains my state
And sends the poor well pleasèd from my gate.
CADE. Here's the lord of the soil come to seize me for
a stray, for entering his fee-simple without leave.
Ah, villain, thou wilt betray me, and get a thousand
crowns of the king by carrying my head to him: but
I'll make thee eat iron like an ostrich, and swallow
my sword like a great pin, ere thou and I part.
IDEN. Why, rude companion, whatsoe'er thou be,   30
I know thee not; why then should I betray thee?
Is't not enough to break into my garden,
And, like a thief, to come to rob my grounds,
Climbing my walls in spite of me the owner,
But thou wilt brave me with these saucy terms?
CADE. Brave thee! ay, by the best blood that ever was
broached, and beard thee too. Look on me well: I
have eat no meat these five days; yet, come thou and
thy five men, and if I do not leave you all as dead
as a door-nail, I pray God I may never eat grass   40
more.
IDEN. Nay, it shall ne'er be said, while England
stands,
That Alexander Iden, an esquire of Kent,
Took odds to combat a poor famished man.
Oppose thy steadfast-gazing eyes to mine,

See if thou canst outface me with thy looks:
Set limb to limb, and thou art far the lesser;
Thy hand is but a finger to my fist,
Thy leg a stick compared with this truncheon;
My foot shall fight with all the strength thou hast; 50
And if mine arm be heavéd in the air,
Thy grave is digged already in the earth.
As for words, whose greatness answers words,
Let this my sword report what speech forbears.

CADE. By my valour, the most complete champion
that ever I heard! Steel, if thou turn the edge, or
cut not out the burly-boned clown in chines of beef
ere thou sleep in thy sheath, I beseech God on my
knees thou mayst be turned to hobnails.

Here they fight; Cade falls

O, I am slain! famine and no other hath slain me: 60
let thousand devils come against me, and give me
but the ten meals I have lost, and I'ld defy them all.
Wither, garden; and be henceforth a burying-place
to all that do dwell in this house, because the un-
conqueréd soul of Cade is fled.

IDEN. Is't Cade that I have slain, that monstrous
traitor?
Sword, I will hallow thee for this thy deed,
And hang thee o'er my tomb when I am dead:
Ne'er shall this blood be wipéd from thy point:
But thou shalt wear it as a herald's coat, 70
To emblaze the honour that thy master got.

CADE. Iden, farewell, and be proud of thy victory. Tell
Kent from me, she hath lost her best man, and
exhort all the world to be cowards; for I, that never
feared any, am vanquishéd by famine, not by
valour.   *Dies*

IDEN. How much thou wrong'st me, heaven be my
judge.
Die, damnéd wretch, the curse of her that bare thee;
And as I thrust thy body in with my sword,
So wish I, I might thrust thy soul to hell. 80
Hence will I drag thee headlong by the heels
Unto a dunghill which shall be thy grave,
And there cut off thy most ungracious head;
Which I will bear in triumph to the king,
Leaving thy trunk for crows to feed upon.

He drags the body away

ACT 5

Scene 1: *Open country on the road between London and
Saint Albans; an ale-house near by*

Enter York, and his army of Irish, with drum and colours

YORK. From Ireland thus comes York to claim his
right,
And pluck the crown from feeble Henry's head.
Ring, bells, aloud; burn, bonfires, clear and bright,
To entertain great England's lawful king.
Ah! sancta majestas, who would not buy thee dear?
Let them obey that know not how to rule;
This hand was made to handle nought but gold.
I cannot give due action to my words,
Except a sword or sceptre balance it:
A sceptre shall it have, have I a soul, 10
On which I'll toss the flower-de-luce of France.

Enter Buckingham

Whom have we here? Buckingham, to disturb me?

The king hath sent him, sure: I must dissemble.

BUCKINGHAM. York, if thou meanest well, I greet thee
well.

YORK. Humphrey of Buckingham, I accept thy
greeting.
Art thou a messenger, or come of pleasure?

BUCKINGHAM. A messenger from Henry, our dread
liege,
To know the reason of these arms in peace;
Or why thou, being a subject as I am,
Against thy oath and true allegiance sworn, 20
Should raise so great a power without his leave,
Or dare to bring thy force so near the court.

YORK [aside]. Scarce can I speak, my choler is so great.
O, I could hew up rocks and fight with flint,
I am so angry at these abject terms;
And now, like Ajax Telamonius,
On sheep or oxen could I spend my fury.
I am far better born than is the king,
More like a king, more kingly in my thoughts:
But I must make fair weather yet awhile, 30
Till Henry be more weak and I more strong....
[aloud] Buckingham, I prithee, pardon me,
That I have given no answer all this while;
My mind was troubled with deep melancholy.
The cause why I have brought this army hither
Is to remove proud Somerset from the king,
Seditious to his grace and to the state.

BUCKINGHAM. That is too much presumption on thy
part:
But if thy arms be to no other end,
The king hath yielded unto thy demand: 40
The Duke of Somerset is in the Tower.

YORK. Upon thine honour, is he prisoner?

BUCKINGHAM. Upon mine honour, he is prisoner.

YORK. Then, Buckingham, I do dismiss my powers.
Soldiers, I thank you all; disperse yourselves;
Meet me to-morrow in Saint George's Field,
You shall have pay and every thing you wish.
And let my sovereign, virtuous Henry,
Command my eldest son, nay, all my sons,
As pledges of my fealty and love; 50
I'll send them all as willing as I live:
Lands, goods, horse, armour, any thing I have,
Is his to use, so Somerset may die.

BUCKINGHAM. York, I commend this kind submission:
We twain will go into his highness' tent.

The King enters

KING. Buckingham, doth York intend no harm to us,
That thus he marcheth with thee arm in arm?

YORK. In all submission and humility
York doth present himself unto your highness.

KING. Then what intends these forces thou dost bring? 60

YORK. To heave the traitor Somerset from hence,
And fight against that monstrous rebel Cade,
Who since I heard to be discomfited.

Enter Iden, with Cade's head

IDEN. If one so rude and of so mean condition
May pass into the presence of a king,
Lo, I present your grace a traitor's head,
The head of Cade, whom I in combat slew.

KING. The head of Cade! Great God, how just art
Thou!
O, let me view his visage, being dead,

That living wrought me such exceeding trouble.   70
Tell me, my friend, art thou the man that slew him?
IDEN. I was, an't like your majesty.
KING. How art thou called? and what is thy degree?
IDEN. Alexander Iden, that's my name;
A poor esquire of Kent, that loves his king.
BUCKINGHAM. So please it you, my lord, 'twere not
amiss
He were created knight for his good service.
KING. Iden, kneel down. [he kneels] Rise up a knight.
We give thee for reward a thousand marks,
And will that thou henceforth attend on us.   80
IDEN. May Iden live to merit such a bounty,
And never live but true unto his liege!   *Rises*

Enter Queen and Somerset

KING. See, Buckingham, Somerset comes with the
queen: ·
Go, bid her hide him quickly from the duke.
QUEEN. For thousand Yorks he shall not hide his head,
But boldly stand and front him to his face.
YORK. How now! is Somerset at liberty?
Then, York, unloose thy long-imprisoned
thoughts,
And let thy tongue be equal with thy heart.
Shall I endure the sight of Somerset?   90
False king! why hast thou broken faith with me,
Knowing how hardly I can brook abuse?
King did I call thee? no, thou art not king,
Not fit to govern and rule multitudes,
Which dar'st not, no, nor canst not rule a traitor.
That head of thine doth not become a crown;
Thy hand is made to grasp a palmer's staff,
And not to grace an awful princely sceptre.
That gold must round engirt these brows of mine,
Whose smile and frown, like to Achilles' spear,   100
Is able with the change to kill and cure.
Here is a hand to hold a sceptre up
And with the same to act controlling laws.
Give place: by heaven, thou shalt rule no more
O'er him whom heaven created for thy ruler.
SOMERSET. O monstrous traitor! I arrest thee, York,
Of capital treason 'gainst the king and crown:
Obey, audacious traitor; kneel for grace.
YORK. Wouldst have me kneel? first let me ask of
these,
If they can brook I bow a knee to man.   110
Sirrah, call in my sons to be my bail:
    A Yorkist soldier goes
I know ere they will have me go to ward,
They'll pawn their swords for my enfranchisement.
QUEEN. Call hither Clifford; bid him come amain,
To say if that the bastard boys of York
Shall be the surety for their traitor father.
    A Lancastrian soldier goes
YORK. O blood-bespotted Neapolitan,
Outcast of Naples, England's bloody scourge!
The sons of York, thy betters in their birth,
Shall be their father's bail; and bane to those   120
That for my surety will refuse the boys!

Enter Edward and Richard

See where they come: I'll warrant they'll make it
good.

Enter old Clifford and his Son

QUEEN. And here comes Clifford to deny their bail.
CLIFFORD. Health and all happiness to my lord the
king!   *Kneels*
YORK. I thank thee, Clifford: say, what news with
thee?
Nay, do not fright us with an angry look:
We are thy sovereign, Clifford, kneel again;
For thy mistaking so, we pardon thee.
CLIFFORD. This is my king, York, I do not mistake;
But thou mistakes me much to think I do: 130
To Bedlam with him! is the man grown mad?
KING. Ay, Clifford; a bedlam and ambitious humour
Makes him oppose himself against his king.
CLIFFORD. He is a traitor; let him to the Tower,
And chop away that factious pate of his.
QUEEN. He is arrested, but will not obey;
His sons, he says, shall give their words for him.
YORK. Will you not, sons?
EDWARD. Ay, noble father, if our words will serve.
RICHARD. And if words will not, then our weapons
shall.   140
CLIFFORD. Why, what a brood of traitors have we
here!
YORK. Look in a glass, and call thy image so:
I am thy king, and thou a false-heart traitor.
Call hither to the stake my two brave bears,
That with the very shaking of their chains
They may astonish these fell-lurking curs:
Bid Salisbury and Warwick come to me.

Enter the Earls of Warwick and Salisbury

CLIFFORD. Are these thy bears? we'll bait thy bears to
death,
And manacle the bear'ard in their chains,
If thou dar'st bring them to the baiting place.   150
RICHARD. Oft have I seen a hot o'erweening cur
Run back and bite, because he was withheld;
Who, being suffered with the bear's fell paw,
Hath clapped his tail between his legs and cried:
And such a piece of service will you do,
If you oppose yourselves to match Lord Warwick.
CLIFFORD. Hence, heap of wrath, foul indigested lump,
As crookéd in thy manners as thy shape!
YORK. Nay, we shall heat you thoroughly anon.
CLIFFORD. Take heed, lest by your heat you burn
yourselves.   160
KING. Why, Warwick, hath thy knee forgot to bow?
Old Salisbury, shame to thy silver hair,
Thou mad misleader of thy brain-sick son!
What! wilt thou on thy death-bed play the ruffian,
And seek for sorrow with thy spectacles?
O, where is faith? O, where is loyalty?
If it be banished from the frosty head,
Where shall it find a harbour in the earth?
Wilt thou go dig a grave to find out war,
And shame thine honourable age with blood?   170
Why art thou old, and want'st experience?
Or wherefore dost abuse it, if thou hast it?
For shame! in duty bend thy knee to me
That bows unto the grave with mickle age.
SALISBURY. My lord, I have considered with myself
The title of this most renownéd duke;
And in my conscience do repute his grace
The rightful heir to England's royal seat.
KING. Hast thou not sworn allegiance unto me?
SALISBURY. I have.   180

KING. Canst thou dispense with heaven for such an oath?

SALISBURY. It is great sin to swear unto a sin,
But greater sin to keep a sinful oath.
Who can be bound by any solemn vow
To do a murderous deed, to rob a man,
To force a spotless virgin's chastity,
To reave the orphan of his patrimony,
To wring the widow from her customed right,
And have no other reason for this wrong
But that he was bound by a solemn oath? 190

QUEEN. A subtle traitor needs no sophister.

KING. Call Buckingham, and bid him arm himself.

YORK. Call Buckingham, and all the friends thou hast,
I am resolved for death or dignity.

CLIFFORD. The first I warrant thee, if dreams prove true.

WARWICK. You were best to go to bed and dream again,
To keep thee from the tempest of the field.

CLIFFORD. I am resolved to bear a greater storm
Than any thou canst conjure up to-day;
And that I'll write upon thy burgonet, 200
Might I but know thee by thy house's badge.

WARWICK. Now, by my father's badge, old Nevil's crest,
The rampant bear chained to the ragged staff,
This day I'll wear aloft my burgonet,
As on a mountain top the cedar shows
That keeps his leaves in spite of any storm,
Even to affright thee with the view thereof.

CLIFFORD. And from thy burgonet I'll rend thy bear
And tread it under foot with all contempt,
Despite the bear'ard that protects the bear. 210

YOUNG CLIFFORD. And so to arms, victorious father,
To quell the rebels and their complices.

RICHARD. Fie! charity, for shame! speak not in spite,
For you shall sup with Jesu Christ to-night.

YOUNG CLIFFORD. Foul stigmatic, that's more than thou canst tell.

RICHARD. If not in heaven, you'll surely sup in hell.
They go

Scene 2

Enter Warwick

WARWICK. Clifford of Cumberland, 'tis Warwick calls:
And if thou dost not hide thee from the bear,
Now, when the angry trumpet sounds alarum
And dead men's cries do fill the empty air,
Clifford, I say, come forth and fight with me:
Proud northern lord, Clifford of Cumberland,
Warwick is hoarse with calling thee to arms.

Enter York

How now, my noble lord! what, all a-foot?

YORK. The deadly-handed Clifford slew my steed,
But match to match I have encount'red him 10
And made a prey for carrion kites and crows
Even of the bonny beast he loved so well.

Enter Clifford

WARWICK. Of one or both of us the time is come.

YORK. Hold, Warwick, seek thee out some other chase,

For I myself must hunt this deer to death.

WARWICK. Then, nobly, York; 'tis for a crown thou fight'st:
As I intend, Clifford, to thrive to-day,
It grieves my soul to leave thee unassailed.
He leaves

CLIFFORD. What seest thou in me, York? why dost thou pause?

YORK. With thy brave bearing should I be in love, 20
But that thou art so fast mine enemy.

CLIFFORD. Nor should thy prowess want praise and esteem,
But that 'tis shown ignobly and in treason.

YORK. So let it help me now against thy sword
As I in justice and true right express it.

CLIFFORD. My soul and body on the action both!

YORK. A dreadful lay! Address thee instantly.
They fight, and Clifford falls

CLIFFORD. La fin couronne les œuvres. *Dies*

YORK. Thus war hath given thee peace, for thou art still.
Peace with his soul, heaven, if it be thy will! 30
He goes

Enter young Clifford

YOUNG CLIFFORD. Shame and confusion! all is on the rout;
Fear frames disorder, and disorder wounds
Where it should guard. O war, thou son of hell,
Whom angry heavens do make their minister,
Throw in the frozen bosoms of our part
Hot coals of vengeance! Let no soldier fly.
He that is truly dedicate to war
Hath no self-love, nor he that loves himself
Hath not essentially but by circumstance
The name of valour. [*sees his dead father*] O, let the vile world end, 40
And the premiséd flames of the Last Day
Knit earth and heaven together!
Now let the general trumpet blow his blast,
Particularities and petty sounds
To cease! Wast thou ordained, dear father,
To lose thy youth in peace, and to achieve
The silver livery of advised age,
And, in thy reverence and thy chair-days, thus
To die in ruffian battle? Even at this sight
My heart is turned to stone: and while 'tis mine, 50
It shall be stony. York not our old men spares;
No more will I their babes: tears virginal
Shall be to me even as the dew to fire,
And beauty that the tyrant oft reclaims
Shall to my flaming wrath be oil and flax.
Henceforth I will not have to do with pity:
Meet I an infant of the house of York,
Into as many gobbets will I cut it
As wild Medea young Absyrtus did:
In cruelty will I seek out my fame. 60
Come, thou new ruin of old Clifford's house:
As did Aeneas old Anchises bear,
So bear I thee upon my manly shoulders;
But then Aeneas bare a living load,
Nothing so heavy as these woes of mine.
He bears away the body

Enter Richard and Somerset to fight. Somerset is killed

RICHARD. So, lie thou there;

For underneath an alehouse' paltry sign,
'The Castle in Saint Albans', Somerset
Hath made the wizard famous in his death.
Sword, hold thy temper; heart, be wrathful still: 70
Priests pray for enemies, but princes kill.

He goes

Fight: excursions. Enter King, Queen, and others

QUEEN. Away, my lord! you are slow; for shame,
  away!
KING. Can we outrun the heavens? good Margaret,
  stay.
QUEEN. What are you made of? you'll nor fight nor
  fly:
Now is it manhood, wisdom, and defence,
To give the enemy way, and to secure us
By what we can, which can no more but fly.

Alarum afar off

If you be ta'en, we then should see the bottom
Of all our fortunes: but if we haply scape,
As well we may, if not through your neglect,   80
We shall to London get, where you are loved
And where this breach now in our fortunes made
May readily be stopped.

Re-enter young Clifford

YOUNG CLIFFORD. But that my heart's on future
  mischief set,
I would speak blasphemy ere bid you fly:
But fly you must; uncurable discomfit
Reigns in the hearts of all our present parts.
Away, for your relief! and we will live
To see their day and them our fortune give:
Away, my lord, away!   *They go* 90

Scene 3

*Alarum, Retreat. Enter York, Richard, Warwick, and
soldiers, with drum and colours*

YORK. Of Salisbury, who can report of him,
That winter lion, who in rage forgets
Agéd contusions and all brush of time,
And, like a gallant in the brow of youth,
Repairs him with occasion? This happy day
Is not itself, nor have we won one foot,
If Salisbury be lost.
RICHARD.   My noble father,
Three times to-day I holp him to his horse,
Three times bestrid him: thrice I led him off,
Persuaded him from any further act: 10
But still, where danger was, still there I met him;
And like rich hangings in a homely house,
So was his will in his old feeble body.
But, noble as he is, look where he comes.

Enter Salisbury

Now, by my sword, well hast thou fought to-day.
SALISBURY. By th'mass, so did we all. I thank you,
  Richard:
God knows how long it is I have to live;
And it hath pleased him that three times to-day
You have defended me from imminent death.
Well, lords, we have not got that which we have: 20
'Tis not enough our foes are this time fled,
Being opposites of such repairing nature.
YORK. I know our safety is to follow them;
For, as I hear, the king is fled to London,
To call a present court of parliament.
Let us pursue him ere the writs go forth.
What says Lord Warwick? shall we after them?
WARWICK. After them! nay, before them, if we can.
Now, by my hand, lords, 'twas a glorious day:
Saint Albans battle won by famous York   30
Shall be eternized in all age to come.
Sound drums and trumpets, and to London all:
And more such days as these to us befall!

They go

The Third Part of King Henry VI

The scene: England and (at 3.3. only) France

CHARACTERS IN THE PLAY

KING HENRY *the Sixth*
EDWARD, PRINCE OF WALES, *his son*
LEWIS XI, *King of France*
DUKE OF SOMERSET
DUKE OF EXETER
EARL OF OXFORD
EARL OF NORTHUMBERLAND
EARL OF WESTMORELAND
LORD CLIFFORD (*Young Clifford in Part 2*)
RICHARD PLANTAGENET, *Duke of York*
EDWARD, *Earl of March, afterwards*
  King Edward IV
EDMUND, *Earl of Rutland*
GEORGE, *afterwards Duke of Clarence*
RICHARD, *afterwards Duke of Gloucester*
DUKE OF NORFOLK
EARL OF WARWICK
MARQUESS OF MONTAGUE, *his brother*
EARL OF PEMBROKE
LORD HASTINGS

} *his sons*

LORD STAFFORD
SIR JOHN MORTIMER
SIR HUGH MORTIMER } *uncles to the Duke of York*
HENRY, *Earl of Richmond, a youth*
LORD RIVERS, *brother to Lady Grey*
SIR WILLIAM STANLEY
SIR JOHN MONTGOMERY
SOMERVILLE
Tutor to Rutland
Mayor of York
Lieutenant of the Tower
A Nobleman
Two Keepers
A Huntsman
A Son that has killed his father
A Father that has killed his son
QUEEN MARGARET
LADY ELIZABETH GREY, *afterwards Queen to Edward IV*
BONA, *sister to the French Queen*
Soldiers, Attendants, Messengers, Watchmen, etc.

The Third Part of King Henry VI

ACT 1

Scene 1: *London. The Parliament-house*

Alarum. Enter the Duke of York, Edward, Richard, Norfolk, Montague, Warwick, and Soldiers, with white roses in their hats

WARWICK. I wonder how the king escaped our hands.
YORK. While we pursued the horsemen of the
    north,
  He slily stole away and left his men:
  Whereat the great Lord of Northumberland,
  Whose warlike ears could never brook retreat,
  Cheered up the drooping army; and himself,
  Lord Clifford, and Lord Stafford, all a-breast,
  Charged our main battle's front, and breaking in
  Were by the swords of common soldiers slain.
EDWARD. Lord Stafford's father, Duke of
    Buckingham, 10
  Is either slain or wounded dangerous;
  I cleft his beaver with a downright blow:
  That this is true, father, behold his blood.
MONTAGUE. And, brother, here's the Earl of
    Wiltshire's blood,
  Whom I encountered as the battles joined.
RICHARD. Speak thou for me and tell them what I did.
            He throws down the Duke of
                 Somerset's head
YORK. Richard hath best deserved of all my sons.
  But is your grace dead, my Lord of Somerset?
NORFOLK. Such hope have all the line of John of Gaunt!
RICHARD. Thus do I hope to shake King Henry's head. 20
WARWICK. And so do I. Victorious Prince of York,
  Before I see thee seated in that throne
  Which now the house of Lancaster usurps,
  I vow by heaven these eyes shall never close.
  This is the palace of the fearful king,
  And this the regal seat: possess it, York;
  For this is thine and not King Henry's heirs'.
YORK. Assist me, then, sweet Warwick, and I will;
  For hither we have broken in by force.
NORFOLK. We'll all assist you; he that flies shall die. 30
YORK. Thanks, gentle Norfolk: stay by me, my lords;
  And, soldiers, stay and lodge by me this night.
                      They go up
WARWICK. And when the king comes, offer him no
    violence,
  Unless he seek to thrust you out perforce.
YORK. The queen this day here holds her parliament,
  But little thinks we shall be of her council.
  By words or blows here let us win our right.
RICHARD. Armed as we are, let's stay within this house.
WARWICK. The bloody parliament shall this be called,
  Unless Plantagenet, Duke of York, be king, 40
  And bashful Henry deposed, whose cowardice
  Hath made us by-words to our enemies.
YORK. Then leave me not; my lords, be resolute;
  I mean to take possession of my right.
WARWICK. Neither the king, nor he that loves him
    best,
  The proudest he that holds up Lancaster,
  Dares stir a wing, if Warwick shake his bells.
  I'll plant Plantagenet, root him up who dares:
  Resolve thee, Richard; claim the English crown.
              He leads him to the throne

Flourish. Enter King Henry, Clifford, Northumberland, Westmoreland, Exeter, and the rest, with red roses in their hats

KING HENRY. My lords, look where the sturdy rebel
    sits, 50
  Even in the chair of state: belike he means,
  Backed by the power of Warwick, that false peer,
  To aspire unto the crown and reign as king.
  Earl of Northumberland, he slew thy father,
  And thine, Lord Clifford; and you both have
    vowed revenge
  On him, his sons, his favourites and his friends.
NORTHUMBERLAND. If I be not, heavens be revenged
    on me!
CLIFFORD. The hope thereof makes Clifford mourn in
    steel.
WESTMORELAND. What! shall we suffer this? let's
    pluck him down:
  My heart for anger burns; I cannot brook it. 60
KING HENRY. Be patient, gentle Earl of Westmoreland.
CLIFFORD. Patience is for poltroons, such as he:
  He durst not sit there, had your father lived.
  My gracious lord, here in the parliament
  Let us assail the family of York.
NORTHUMBERLAND. Well hast thou spoken, cousin,
    be it so.
KING HENRY. Ah, know you not the city favours them,
  And they have troops of soldiers at their beck?
EXETER. But when the duke is slain, they'll quickly
    fly.
KING HENRY. Far be the thought of this from Henry's
    heart, 70
  To make a shambles of the parliament-house!
  Cousin of Exeter, frowns, words, and threats
  Shall be the war that Henry means to use.
  Thou factious Duke of York, descend my throne,
  And kneel for grace and mercy at my feet.
  I am thy sovereign.
YORK.   I am thine.
EXETER. For shame, come down: he made thee Duke
    of York.
YORK. It was my inheritance, as the earldom was.
EXETER. Thy father was a traitor to the crown. 80
WARWICK. Exeter, thou art a traitor to the crown
  In following this usurping Henry.
CLIFFORD. When should he follow but his natural
    king?
WARWICK. True, Clifford; and that's Richard Duke of
    York.
KING HENRY. And shall I stand, and thou sit in my
    throne?
YORK. It must and shall be so: content thyself.
WARWICK. Be Duke of Lancaster; let him be king.
WESTMORELAND. He is both king and Duke of
    Lancaster;
  And that the Lord of Westmoreland shall maintain.

WARWICK. And Warwick shall disprove it. You forget
That we are those which chased you from the field 90
And slew your fathers, and with colours spread
Marched through the city to the palace gates.
NORTHUMBERLAND. Yes, Warwick, I remember it to
my grief;
And, by his soul, thou and thy house shall rue it.
WESTMORELAND. Plantagenet, of thee and these thy
sons,
Thy kinsmen and thy friends, I'll have more lives
Than drops of blood were in my father's veins.
CLIFFORD. Urge it no more; lest that, instead of words,
I send thee, Warwick, such a messenger
As shall revenge his death before I stir. 100
WARWICK. Poor Clifford! how I scorn his worthless
threats!
YORK. Will you we show our title to the crown?
If not, our swords shall plead it in the field.
KING HENRY. What title hast thou, traitor, to the
crown?
Thy father was, as thou art, Duke of York;
Thy grandfather, Roger Mortimer, Earl of March:
I am the son of Henry the Fifth,
Who made the Dauphin and the French to stoop
And seized upon their towns and provinces.
WARWICK. Talk not of France, sith thou hast lost it all. 110
KING HENRY. The Lord Protector lost it, and not I:
When I was crowned I was but nine months old.
RICHARD. You are old enough now, and yet,
methinks, you lose.
Father, tear the crown from the usurper's head.
EDWARD. Sweet father, do so; set it on your head.
MONTAGUE. Good brother, as thou lov'st and
honourest arms,
Let's fight it out and not stand cavilling thus.
RICHARD. Sound drums and trumpets, and the king
will fly.
YORK. Sons, peace!
KING HENRY. Peace, thou! and give King Henry leave
to speak. 120
WARWICK. Plantagenet shall speak first: hear him,
lords;
And be you silent and attentive too,
For he that interrupts him shall not live.
KING HENRY. Think'st thou that I will leave my kingly
throne,
Wherein my grandsire and my father sat?
No: first shall war unpeople this my realm;
Ay, and their colours, often borne in France,
And now in England to our heart's great sorrow,
Shall be my winding-sheet. Why faint you, lords?
My title's good, and better far than his. 130
WARWICK. Prove it, Henry, and thou shalt be king.
KING HENRY. Henry the Fourth by conquest got the
crown.
YORK. 'Twas by rebellion against his king.
KING HENRY [aside]. I know not what to say; my
title's weak.
[aloud] Tell me, may not a king adopt an heir?
YORK. What then?
KING HENRY. An if he may, then am I lawful king;
For Richard, in the view of many lords,
Resigned the crown to Henry the Fourth,
Whose heir my father was, and I am his. 140
YORK. He rose against him, being his sovereign,
And made him to resign his crown perforce.
WARWICK. Suppose, my lords, he did it unconstrained,

Think you 'twere prejudicial to his crown?
EXETER. No; for he could not so resign his crown
But that the next heir should succeed and reign.
KING HENRY. Art thou against us, Duke of Exeter?
EXETER. His is the right, and therefore pardon me.
YORK. Why whisper you, my lords, and answer not?
EXETER. My conscience tells me he is lawful king. 150
KING HENRY [aside]. All will revolt from me, and turn
to him.
NORTHUMBERLAND. Plantagenet, for all the claim thou
lay'st,
Think not that Henry shall be so deposed.
WARWICK. Deposed he shall be, in despite of all.
NORTHUMBERLAND. Thou art deceived: 'tis not thy
southern power,
Of Essex, Norfolk, Suffolk, nor of Kent,
Which makes thee thus presumptuous and proud,
Can set the duke up in despite of me.
CLIFFORD. King Henry, be thy title right or wrong,
Lord Clifford vows to fight in thy defence: 160
May that ground gape and swallow me alive,
Where I shall kneel to him that slew my father!
KING HENRY. O Clifford, how thy words revive
my heart!
YORK. Henry of Lancaster, resign thy crown.
What mutter you, or what conspire you, lords?
WARWICK. Do right unto this princely Duke of York,
Or I will fill the house with arméd men,
And o'er the chair of state, where now he sits,
Write up his title with usurping blood.

He stamps with his foot, and
the soldiers show themselves

KING HENRY. My Lord of Warwick, hear but one
word: 170
Let me for this my life-time reign as king.
YORK. Confirm the crown to me and to mine heirs,
And thou shalt reign in quiet while thou liv'st.
KING HENRY. I am content: Richard Plantagenet,
Enjoy the kingdom after my decease.
CLIFFORD. What wrong is this unto the prince
your son!
WARWICK. What good is this to England and himself!
WESTMORELAND. Base, fearful, and despairing Henry!
CLIFFORD. How hast thou injured both thyself and us!
WESTMORELAND. I cannot stay to hear these articles. 180
NORTHUMBERLAND. Nor I.
CLIFFORD. Come, cousin, let us tell the queen these
news.
WESTMORELAND. Farewell, faint-hearted and
degenerate king,
In whose cold blood no spark of honour bides.
NORTHUMBERLAND. Be thou a prey unto the house of
York,
And die in bands for this unmanly deed!
CLIFFORD. In dreadful war mayst thou be overcome,
Or live in peace abandoned and despised!

Northumberland, Clifford, and
Westmoreland depart

WARWICK. Turn this way, Henry, and regard them
not.
EXETER. They seek revenge and therefore will not
yield. 190
KING HENRY. Ah, Exeter!
WARWICK. Why should you sigh, my lord?
KING HENRY. Not for myself, Lord Warwick, but my
son,
Whom I unnaturally shall disinherit.

But be it as it may: I here entail   *To York*
The crown to thee and to thine heirs for ever;
Conditionally, that here thou take an oath
To cease this civil war; and, whilst I live,
To honour me as thy king and sovereign;
And neither by treason nor hostility
To seek to put me down and reign thyself.   200
YORK. This oath I willingly take and will perform.
WARWICK. Long live King Henry! Plantagenet,
embrace him.
KING HENRY. And long live thou and these thy forward
sons!
YORK. Now York and Lancaster are reconciled.
EXETER. Accursed be he that seeks to make them foes!
        Sennet; here they come down
YORK. Farewell, my gracious lord; I'll to my castle.
WARWICK. And I'll keep London with my soldiers.
NORFOLK. And I to Norfolk with my followers.
MONTAGUE. And I unto the sea from whence I came.
        York departs with his sons,
        Warwick, Norfolk, Montague,
        their soldiers, and attendants
KING HENRY. And I with grief and sorrow to the
court.   210

Enter Queen Margaret and the Prince of Wales

EXETER. Here comes the queen, whose looks bewray
her anger:
I'll steal away.
KING HENRY.   Exeter, so will I.
QUEEN MARGARET. Nay, go not from me, I will follow
thee.
KING HENRY. Be patient, gentle queen, and I will stay.
QUEEN MARGARET. Who can be patient in such
extremes?
Ah, wretched man! would I had died a maid,
And never seen thee, never borne thee son,
Seeing thou hast proved so unnatural a father!
Hath he deserved to lose his birthright thus?
Hadst thou but loved him half so well as I,   220
Or felt that pain which I did for him once,
Or nourished him as I did with my blood,
Thou wouldst have left thy dearest heart-blood
there,
Rather than have made that savage duke thine heir
And disinherited thine only son.
PRINCE. Father, you cannot disinherit me:
If you be king, why should not I succeed?
KING HENRY. Pardon me, Margaret; pardon me, sweet
son:
The Earl of Warwick and the duke enforced me.
QUEEN MARGARET. Enforced thee! art thou king, and
wilt be forced?   230
I shame to hear thee speak. Ah, timorous wretch!
Thou hast undone thyself, thy son and me;
And given unto the house of York such head
As thou shalt reign but by their sufferance.
To entail him and his heirs unto the crown,
What is it, but to make thy sepulchre,
And creep into it far before thy time?
Warwick is chancellor and the lord of Calais;
Stern Falconbridge commands the Narrow Seas;
The duke is made Protector of the realm;   240
And yet shalt thou be safe? such safety finds
The trembling lamb environèd with wolves,
Had I been there, which am a silly woman,
The soldiers should have tossed me on their pikes

Before I would have granted to that act.
But thou preferr'st thy life before thine honour:
And seeing thou dost, I here divorce myself
Both from thy table, Henry, and thy bed,
Until that act of parliament be repealed
Whereby my son is disinherited.   250
The northern lords that have forsworn thy colours
Will follow mine, if once they see them spread;
And spread they shall be, to thy foul disgrace
And utter ruin of the house of York.
Thus do I leave thee. Come, son, let's away;
Our army is ready; come, we'll after them.
KING HENRY. Stay, gentle Margaret, and hear
me speak.
QUEEN MARGARET. Thou hast spoke too much already;
get thee gone.
KING HENRY. Gentle son Edward, thou wilt stay
with me?
QUEEN MARGARET. Ay, to be murdered by his enemies.   260
PRINCE. When I return with victory from the field,
I'll see your grace: till then I'll follow her.
QUEEN MARGARET. Come, son, away; we may not
linger thus.   *They go*
KING HENRY. Poor queen! how love to me and to her
son   270
Hath made her break out into terms of rage!
Revenged may she be on that hateful duke,
Whose haughty spirit, wingèd with desire,
Will cost my crown, and like an empty eagle
Tire on the flesh of me and of my son!
The loss of those three lords torments my heart:
I'll write unto them and entreat them fair.
Come, cousin, you shall be the messenger.
EXETER. And I, I hope, shall reconcile them all.
        Flourish; they go

Scene 2: *A plain before Sandal Castle near Wakefield*

Enter Richard, Edward, and Montague

RICHARD. Brother, though I be youngest, give me
leave.
EDWARD. No, I can better play the orator.
MONTAGUE. But I have reasons strong and forcible.

Enter the Duke of York

YORK. Why, how now, sons and brother! at a strife?
What is your quarrel? how began it first?
EDWARD. No quarrel, but a slight contention.
YORK. About what?
RICHARD. About that which concerns your grace
and us;
The crown of England, father, which is yours.
YORK. Mine, boy? not till King Henry be dead.   10
RICHARD. Your right depends not on his life or death.
EDWARD. Now you are heir, therefore enjoy it now:
By giving the house of Lancaster leave to breathe,
It will outrun you, father, in the end.
YORK. I took an oath that he should quietly reign.
EDWARD. But for a kingdom any oath may be broken:
I would break a thousand oaths to reign one year.
RICHARD. No; God forbid your grace should be
forsworn.
YORK. I shall be, if I claim by open war.
RICHARD. I'll prove the contrary, if you'll hear me
speak.   20
YORK. Thou canst not, son; it is impossible.

RICHARD. An oath is of no moment, being not took
  Before a true and lawful magistrate,
  That hath authority over him that swears:
  Henry had none, but did usurp the place;
  Then, seeing 'twas he that made you to depose,
  Your oath, my lord, is vain and frivolous.
  Therefore, to arms! And, father, do but think
  How sweet a thing it is to wear a crown;
  Within whose circuit is Elysium   30
  And all that poets feign of bliss and joy.
  Why do we linger thus? I cannot rest
  Until the white rose that I wear be dyed
  Even in the lukewarm blood of Henry's heart.
YORK. Richard, enough; I will be king, or die.
  Brother, thou shalt to London presently,
  And whet on Warwick to this enterprise.
  Thou, Richard, shalt to the Duke of Norfolk,
  And tell him privily of our intent.
  You, Edward, shall unto my Lord Cobham,   40
  With whom the Kentishmen will willingly rise:
  In them I trust; for they are soldiers,
  Witty, courteous, liberal, full of spirit.
  While you are thus employed, what resteth more,
  But that I seek occasion how to rise,
  And yet the king not privy to my drift,
  Nor any of the house of Lancaster?

Enter a Messenger

  But, stay, what news? Why com'st thou in such
    post?
MESSENGER. The queen with all the northern earls and
    lords   50
  Intend here to besiege you in your castle:
  She is hard by with twenty thousand men;
  And therefore fortify your hold, my lord.
YORK. Ay, with my sword. What! think'st thou that
    we fear them?
  Edward and Richard, you shall stay with me;
  My brother Montague shall post to London:
  Let noble Warwick, Cobham, and the rest,
  Whom we have left protectors of the king,
  With powerful policy strengthen themselves,
  And trust not simple Henry nor his oaths.   60
MONTAGUE. Brother, I go; I'll win them, fear it not:
  And thus most humbly I do take my leave.
                                            He goes

Enter Sir John Mortimer and Sir Hugh Mortimer

YORK. Sir John and Sir Hugh Mortimer, mine uncles,
  You are come to Sandal in a happy hour;
  The army of the queen mean to besiege us.
SIR JOHN. She shall not need, we'll meet her in
    the field.
YORK. What! with five thousand men?
RICHARD. Ay, with five hundred, father, for a need:
  A woman's general; what should we fear?
                              A march afar off 70
EDWARD. I hear their drums: let's set our men in order,
  And issue forth and bid them battle straight.
YORK. Five men to twenty! though the odds be great,
  I doubt not, uncle, of our victory.
  Many a battle have I won in France,
  When as the enemy hath been ten to one:
  Why should I not now have the like success?
                                          They go

Scene 3

Alarum. Enter Rutland and his Tutor

RUTLAND. Ah, whither shall I fly to 'scape their hands?
  Ah, tutor, look where bloody Clifford comes!

Enter Clifford and soldiers

CLIFFORD. Chaplain, away! thy priesthood saves thy
    life.
  As for the brat of this accursèd duke,
  Whose father slew my father, he shall die.
TUTOR. And I, my lord, will bear him company.
CLIFFORD. Soldiers, away with him!
TUTOR. Ah, Clifford, murder not this innocent child,
  Less thou be hated both of God and man!
                   He is dragged off by soldiers 10
CLIFFORD. How now! is he dead already? or is it fear
  That makes him close his eyes? I'll open them.
RUTLAND. So looks the pent-up lion o'er the wretch
  That trembles under his devouring paws;
  And so he walks, insulting o'er his prey,
  And so he comes, to rend his limbs asunder.
  Ah, gentle Clifford, kill me with thy sword,
  And not with such a cruel threat'ning look.
  Sweet Clifford, hear me speak before I die.
  I am too mean a subject for thy wrath: 20
  Be thou revenged on men, and let me live.
CLIFFORD. In vain thou speak'st, poor boy; my
    father's blood
  Hath stopped the passage where thy words should
    enter.
RUTLAND. Then let my father's blood open it again:
  He is a man, and, Clifford, cope with him.
CLIFFORD. Had I thy brethren here, their lives and thine
  Were not revenge sufficient for me;
  No, if I digged up thy forefathers' graves
  And hung their rotten coffins up in chains,
  It could not slake mine ire, nor ease my heart.   30
  The sight of any of the house of York
  Is as a fury to torment my soul;
  And till I root out their accursèd line
  And leave not one alive, I live in hell.
  Therefore—   *Lifting his hand*
RUTLAND. O, let me pray before I take my death!
  To thee I pray; sweet Clifford, pity me!
CLIFFORD. Such pity as my rapier's point affords.
RUTLAND. I never did thee harm: why wilt thou slay
    me?
CLIFFORD. Thy father hath.
RUTLAND.   But 'twas ere I was born. 40
  Thou hast one son; for his sake pity me,
  Lest in revenge thereof, sith God is just,
  He be as miserably slain as I.
  Ah, let me live in prison all my days;
  And when I give occasion of offence,
  Then let me die, for now thou hast no cause.
CLIFFORD. No cause!
  Thy father slew my father; therefore, die.
                                        Stabs him
RUTLAND. Di faciant laudis summa sit ista tuae!
                                            Dies
CLIFFORD. Plantagenet! I come, Plantagenet!   50
  And this thy son's blood cleaving to my blade
  Shall rust upon my weapon, till thy blood,
  Congealed with his, do make me wipe off both.
                                        He goes

Scene 4: *Another part of the field*

Alarum. Enter Richard, Duke of York

YORK. The army of the queen hath got the field:
My uncles both are slain in rescuing me;
And all my followers to the eager foe
Turn back and fly, like ships before the wind
Or lambs pursued by hunger-starvéd wolves.
My sons, God knows what hath bechancéd them:
But this I know, they have demeaned themselves
Like men born to renown by life or death.
Three times did Richard make a lane to me,
And thrice cried 'Courage, father! fight it out!'   10
And full as oft came Edward to my side,
With purple falchion, painted to the hilt
In blood of those that had encountered him:
And when the hardiest warriors did retire,
Richard cried, 'Charge! and give no foot of
     ground!'
And cried, 'A crown, or else a glorious tomb!
A sceptre, or an earthly sepulchre!'
With this, we charged again: but, out, alas!
We budged again; as I have seen a swan
With bootless labour swim against the tide   20
And spend her strength with over-matching waves.
               A short alarum heard
Ah, hark! the fatal followers do pursue;
And I am faint, and cannot fly their fury:
And were I strong, I would not shun their fury:
The sands are numbered that make up my life;
Here must I stay, and here my life must end.

*Enter the Queen, Clifford, Northumberland, the young
Prince, and soldiers*

Come, bloody Clifford, rough Northumberland,
I dare your quenchless fury to more rage:
I am your butt, and I abide your shot.
NORTHUMBERLAND. Yield to our mercy, proud
     Plantagenet.   30
CLIFFORD. Ay, to such mercy as his ruthless arm,
With downright payment, showed unto my father.
Now Phaëton hath tumbled from his car,
And made an evening at the noontide prick.
YORK. My ashes, as the phoenix, may bring forth
A bird that will revenge upon you all:
And in that hope I throw mine eyes to heaven,
Scorning whate'er you can afflict me with.
Why come you not? what! multitudes, and fear?
CLIFFORD. So cowards fight when they can fly no
     further;   40
So doves do peck the falcon's piercing talons;
So desperate thieves, all hopeless of their lives,
Breathe out invectives 'gainst the officers.
YORK. O Clifford, but bethink thee once again,
And in thy thought o'er-run my former time;
And, if thou canst for blushing, view this face,
And bite thy tongue, that slanders him with
     cowardice
Whose frown hath made thee faint and fly ere this!
CLIFFORD. I will not bandy with thee word for word,
but buckler with thee these blows, twice two for one.   50
QUEEN MARGARET. Hold, valiant Clifford! for a
     thousand causes
I would prolong awhile the traitor's life.
Wrath makes him deaf: speak thou,
     Northumberland.

NORTHUMBERLAND. Hold, Clifford! do not honour
     him so much
To prick thy finger, though to wound his heart:
What valour were it, when a cur doth grin,
For one to thrust his hand between his teeth,
When he might spurn him with his foot away?
It is war's prize to take all vantages;
And ten to one is no impeach of valour.   60
         They lay hands on York, who
                 struggles
CLIFFORD. Ay, ay, so strives the woodcock with the
     gin.
NORTHUMBERLAND. So doth the cony struggle in the
     net.
YORK. So triumph thieves upon their conquered
     booty;
So true men yield, with robbers so o'er-matched.
NORTHUMBERLAND. What would your grace have
     done unto him now?
QUEEN MARGARET. Brave warriors, Clifford and
     Northumberland,
Come, make him stand upon this molehill here
That raught at mountains with outstretchéd arms,
Yet parted but the shadow with his hand.
What! was it you that would be England's king?   70
Was't you that revelled in our parliament,
And made a preachment of your high descent?
Where are your mess of sons to back you now?
The wanton Edward, and the lusty George?
And where's that valiant crook-back prodigy,
Dicky your boy, that with his grumbling voice
Was wont to cheer his dad in mutinies?
Or, with the rest, where is your darling, Rutland?
Look, York, I stained this napkin with the blood
That valiant Clifford, with his rapier's point,   80
Made issue from the bosom of the boy;
And if thine eyes can water for his death,
I give thee this to dry thy cheeks withal.
Alas, poor York! but that I hate thee deadly,
I should lament thy miserable state.
I prithee, grieve, to make me merry, York.
What! hath thy fiery heart so parched thine entrails
That not a tear can fall for Rutland's death?
Why art thou patient, man? thou shouldst be mad;
And I, to make thee mad, do mock thee thus.   90
Stamp, rave, and fret, that I may sing and dance.
Thou wouldst be fee'd, I see, to make me sport:
York cannot speak, unless he wear a crown.
A crown for York! and, lords, bow low to him:
Hold you his hands, whilst I do set it on.
            Putting a paper crown
                on his head
Ay, marry, sir, now looks he like a king!
Ay, this is he that took King Henry's chair;
And this is he was his adopted heir.
But how is it that great Plantagenet
Is crowned so soon, and broke his solemn oath?   100
As I bethink me, you should not be king
Till our King Henry had shook hands with death.
And will you pale your head in Henry's glory,
And rob his temples of the diadem,
Now in his life, against your holy oath?
O, 'tis a fault too too unpardonable!
Off with the crown; and, with the crown, his head;
And, whilst we breathe, take time to do him dead.
CLIFFORD. That is my office, for my father's sake.

QUEEN MARGARET. Nay, stay; let's hear the orisons he makes.

YORK. She-wolf of France, but worse than wolves of France,
Whose tongue more poisons than the adder's tooth!
How ill-beseeming is it in thy sex
To triumph, like an Amazonian trull,
Upon their woes whom fortune captivates!
But that thy face is, vizard-like, unchanging,
Made impudent with use of evil deeds,
I would assay, proud queen, to make thee blush.
To tell thee whence thou cam'st, of whom derived,
Were shame enough to shame thee, wert thou not shameless.
Thy father bears the type of King of Naples,
Of both the Sicils and Jerusalem,
Yet not so wealthy as an English yeoman.
Hath that poor monarch taught thee to insult?
It needs not, nor it boots thee not, proud queen,
Unless the adage must be verified,
That beggars mounted run their horse to death.
'Tis beauty that doth oft make women proud;
But, God he knows, thy share thereof is small:
'Tis virtue that doth make them most admired;
The contrary doth make thee wondered at:
'Tis government that makes them seem divine;
The want thereof makes thee abominable;
Thou art as opposite to every good
As the Antipodes are unto us,
Or as the south to the Septentrion.
O tigress' heart wrapped in a woman's hide!
How couldst thou drain the life-blood of the child,
To bid the father wipe his eyes withal,
And yet be seen to bear a woman's face?
Women are soft, mild, pitiful and flexible;
Thou stern, obdurate, flinty, rough, remorseless.
Bid'st thou me rage? why, now thou hast thy will:
Wouldst have me weep? Why, now thou hast thy will:
For raging wind blows up incessant showers,
And when the rage allays, the rain begins.
These tears are my sweet Rutland's obsequies,
And every drop cries vengeance for his death,
'Gainst thee, fell Clifford, and thee, false Frenchwoman.

NORTHUMBERLAND. Beshrew me, but his passion moves me so
That hardly can I check my eyes from tears.

YORK.   That face of his
The hungry cannibals would not have touched,
Would not have stained with blood:
But you are more inhuman, more inexorable,
O, ten times more, than tigers of Hyrcania.
See, ruthless queen, a hapless father's tears:
This cloth thou dip'dst in blood of my sweet boy,
And I with tears do wash the blood away.
Keep thou the napkin, and go boast of this:
And if thou tell'st the heavy story right,
Upon my soul, the hearers will shed tears;
Yea, even my foes will shed fast-falling tears,
And say 'Alas, it was a piteous deed!'
There, take the crown, and, with the crown, my curse;
And in thy need such comfort come to thee
As now I reap at thy too cruel hand!
Hard-hearted Clifford, take me from the world:

My soul to heaven, my blood upon your heads!

NORTHUMBERLAND. Had he been slaughterman to all my kin,
I should not for my life but weep with him,
To see how inly sorrow gripes his soul.

QUEEN MARGARET. What! weeping-ripe, my Lord Northumberland?
Think but upon the wrong he did us all,
And that will quickly dry thy melting tears.

CLIFFORD. Here's for my oath, here's for my father's death.   *Stabbing him*

QUEEN MARGARET. And here's to right our gentle-hearted king.   *Stabbing him*

YORK. Open Thy gate of mercy, gracious God!
My soul flies through these wounds to seek out Thee.   *Dies*

QUEEN MARGARET. Off with his head, and set it on York gates;
So York may overlook the town of York.   *Flourish; they go*

ACT 2

Scene 1: *A plain near Mortimer's Cross in Herefordshire*

A march. Enter Edward, Richard, and their power

EDWARD. I wonder how our princely father 'scaped,
Or whether he be 'scaped away or no
From Clifford's and Northumberland's pursuit:
Had he been ta'en, we should have heard the news;
Had he been slain, we should have heard the news;
Or had he 'scaped, methinks we should have heard
The happy tidings of his good escape.
How fares my brother? why is he so sad?

RICHARD. I cannot joy, until I be resolved
Where our right valiant father is become.
I saw him in the battle range about;
And watched him how he singled Clifford forth.
Methought he bore him in the thickest troop
As doth a lion in a herd of neat;
Or as a bear, encompassed round with dogs,
Who having pinched a few and made them cry,
The rest stand all aloof, and bark at him.
So fared our father with his enemies;
So fled his enemies my warlike father:
Methinks, 'tis prize enough to be his son.
See how the morning opes her golden gates,
And takes her farewell of the glorious sun!
How well resembles it the prime of youth,
Trimmed like a younker prancing to his love!

EDWARD. Dazzle mine eyes, or do I see three suns?

RICHARD. Three glorious suns, each one a perfect sun;
Not separated with the racking clouds,
But severed in a pale clear-shining sky.
See, see! they join, embrace, and seem to kiss,
As if they vowed some league inviolable:
Now are they but one lamp, one light, one sun.
In this the heaven figures some event.

EDWARD. 'Tis wondrous strange, the like yet never heard of.
I think it cites us, brother, to the field,
That we, the sons of brave Plantagenet,
Each one already blazing by our meeds,
Should notwithstanding join our lights together
And over-shine the earth as this the world.
Whate'er it bodes, henceforward will I bear
Upon my target three fair-shining suns.

RICHARD. Nay, bear three daughters: by your leave
   I speak it,
You love the breeder better than the male.

Enter one, blowing a horn

But what art thou, whose heavy looks foretell
Some dreadful story hanging on thy tongue?
MESSENGER. Ah, one that was a woful looker-on
When as the noble Duke of York was slain,
Your princely father and my loving lord!
EDWARD. O, speak no more, for I have heard too
   much.
RICHARD. Say how he died, for I will hear it all.
MESSENGER. Environéd he was with many foes,   50
And stood against them, as the hope of Troy
Against the Greeks that would have entered Troy.
But Hercules himself must yield to odds;
And many strokes, though with a little axe,
Hew down and fell the hardest-timbered oak.
By many hands your father was subdued;
But only slaught'red by the ireful arm
Of unrelenting Clifford and the queen,
Who crowned the gracious duke in high despite,
Laughed in his face; and when with grief he wept,   60
The ruthless queen gave him to dry his cheeks
A napkin steepéd in the harmless blood
Of sweet young Rutland, by rough Clifford slain:
And after many scorns, many foul taunts,
They took his head, and on the gates of York
They set the same; and there it doth remain,
The saddest spectacle that e'er I viewed.
EDWARD. Sweet Duke of York, our prop to lean upon,
Now thou art gone, we have no staff, no stay.
O Clifford, boist'rous Clifford! thou hast slain   70
The flower of Europe for his chivalry;
And treacherously hast thou vanquished him,
For hand to hand he would have vanquished thee.
Now my soul's palace is become a prison:
Ah, would she break from hence, that this my body
Might in the ground be closéd up in rest!
For never henceforth shall I joy again;
Never, O never, shall I see more joy!
RICHARD. I cannot weep; for all my body's moisture
Scarce serves to quench my furnace-burning heart: 80
Nor can my tongue unload my heart's great burden;
For selfsame wind that I should speak withal
Is kindling coals that fires all my breast,
And burns me up with flames that tears would
   quench.
To weep is to make less the depth of grief:
Tears then for babes, blows and revenge for me!
Richard, I bear thy name, I'll venge thy death,
Or die renownéd by attempting it.
EDWARD. His name that valiant duke hath left with
   thee;
His dukedom and his chair with me is left.   90
RICHARD. Nay, if thou be that princely eagle's bird,
Show thy descent by gazing 'gainst the sun:
For chair and dukedom, throne and kingdom say;
Either that is thine, or else thou wert not his.

*March. Enter Warwick, Marquess of Montague, and their
army*

WARWICK. How now, fair lords! What fare? what
   news abroad?

RICHARD. Great Lord of Warwick, if we should
   recompt
Our baleful news, and at each word's deliverance
Stab poniards in our flesh till all were told,
The words would add more anguish than the
   wounds.
O valiant lord, the Duke of York is slain!   100
EDWARD. O Warwick, Warwick! that Plantagenet,
Which held thee dearly as his soul's redemption,
Is by the stern Lord Clifford done to death.
WARWICK. Ten days ago I drowned these news in
   tears;
And now, to add more measure to your woes,
I come to tell you things sith then befall'n.
After the bloody fray at Wakefield fought,
Where your brave father breathed his latest gasp,
Tidings, as swiftly as the posts could run,
Were brought me of your loss and his depart.   110
I, then in London, keeper of the king,
Mustered my soldiers, gathered flocks of friends,
And very well appointed, as I thought,
Marched toward Saint Albans to intercept the
   queen,
Bearing the king in my behalf along;
For by my scouts I was advertiséd
That she was coming with a full intent
To dash our late decree in parliament
Touching King Henry's oath and your succession.
Short tale to make, we at Saint Albans met,   120
Our battles joined, and both sides fiercely fought:
But whether 'twas the coldness of the king,
Who looked full gently on his warlike queen,
That robbed my soldiers of their heated spleen;
Or whether 'twas report of her success;
Or more than common fear of Clifford's rigour,
Who thunders to his captives blood and death,
I cannot judge: but, to conclude with truth,
Their weapons like to lightning came and went;
Our soldiers', like the night-owl's lazy flight,   130
Or like an idle thresher with a flail,
Fell gently down, as if they struck their friends.
I cheered them up with justice of our cause,
With promise of high pay and great rewards:
But all in vain; they had no heart to fight,
And we in them no hope to win the day;
So that we fled; the king unto the queen;
Lord George your brother, Norfolk and myself,
In haste, post-haste, are come to join with you;
For in the marches here we heard you were,   140
Making another head to fight again.
EDWARD. Where is the Duke of Norfolk, gentle
   Warwick?
And when came George from Burgundy to
   England?
WARWICK. Some six miles off the duke is with the
   soldiers;
And for your brother, he was lately sent
From your kind aunt, Duchess of Burgundy,
With aid of soldiers to this needful war.
RICHARD. 'Twas odds, belike, when valiant Warwick
   fled:
Oft have I heard his praises in pursuit,
But ne'er till now his scandal of retire.   150
WARWICK. Nor now my scandal, Richard, dost thou
   hear;
For thou shalt know this strong right hand of mine

Can pluck the diadem from faint Henry's head,
And wring the awful sceptre from his fist,
Were he as famous and as bold in war
As he is famed for mildness, peace, and prayer.

RICHARD. I know it well, Lord Warwick; blame me
    not:
'Tis love I bear thy glories makes me speak.
But in this troublous time what's to be done?
Shall we go throw away our coats of steel,   160
And wrap our bodies in black mourning gowns,
Numb'ring our Ave-Maries with our beads?
Or shall we on the helmets of our foes
Tell our devotion with revengeful arms?
If for the last, say ay, and to it, lords.

WARWICK. Why, therefore Warwick came to seek you
    out,
And therefore comes my brother Montague.
Attend me, lords. The proud insulting queen,
With Clifford and the haught Northumberland,
And of their feather many moe proud birds,   170
Have wrought the easy-melting king like wax.
He swore consent to your succession,
His oath enrollèd in the parliament;
And now to London all the crew are gone,
To frustrate both his oath and what beside
May make against the house of Lancaster.
Their power, I think, is thirty thousand strong:
Now, if the help of Norfolk and myself,
With all the friends that thou, brave Earl of March,
Amongst the loving Welshmen canst procure,   180
Will but amount to five and twenty thousand,
Why, via! to London will we march amain,
And once again bestride our foaming steeds,
And once again cry 'Charge upon our foes!'
But never once again turn back and fly.

RICHARD. Ay, now methinks I hear great Warwick
    speak:
Ne'er may he live to see a sunshine day,
That cries 'Retire,' if Warwick bid him stay.

EDWARD. Lord Warwick, on thy shoulder will I
    lean;
And when thou fail'st—as God forbid the hour!—   190
Must Edward fall, which peril heaven forfend!

WARWICK. No longer Earl of March, but Duke of
    York:
The next degree is England's royal throne;
For King of England shalt thou be proclaimed
In every borough as we pass along;
And he that throws not up his cap for joy
Shall for the fault make forfeit of his head.
King Edward, valiant Richard, Montague,
Stay we no longer, dreaming of renown,
But sound the trumpets, and about our task.   200

RICHARD. Then, Clifford, were thy heart as hard as
    steel,
As thou hast shown it flinty by thy deeds,
I come to pierce it, or to give thee mine.

EDWARD. Then strike up drums: God and Saint
    George for us!

Enter a Messenger

WARWICK. How now! what news?

MESSENGER. The Duke of Norfolk sends you word by
    me,
The queen is coming with a puissant host;
And craves your company for speedy counsel.

WARWICK. Why then it sorts, brave warriors, let's
    away.   *They go*

Scene 2: *Before York*

*Flourish. Enter King Henry, Queen Margaret, the Prince
of Wales, Clifford, and Northumberland, with drum and
trumpets*

QUEEN MARGARET. Welcome, my lord, to this brave
    town of York.
Yonder's the head of that arch-enemy
That sought to be encompassed with your crown:
Doth not the object cheer your heart, my lord?

KING HENRY. Ay, as the rocks cheer them that fear
    their wrack:
To see this sight, it irks my very soul.
Withhold revenge, dear God! 'tis not my fault,
Nor wittingly have I infringed my vow.

CLIFFORD. My gracious liege, this too much lenity
And harmful pity must be laid aside.   10
To whom do lions cast their gentle looks?
Not to the beast that would usurp their den.
Whose hand is that the forest bear doth lick?
Not his that spoils her young before her face.
Who 'scapes the lurking serpent's mortal sting?
Not he that sets his foot upon her back.
The smallest worm will turn being trodden on,
And doves will peck in safeguard of their brood.
Ambitious York did level at thy crown,
Thou smiling while he knit his angry brows: 20
He, but a duke, would have his son a king,
And raise his issue, like a loving sire;
Thou, being a king, blest with a goodly son,
Didst yield consent to disinherit him,
Which argued thee a most unloving father.
Unreasonable creatures feed their young;
And though man's face be fearful to their eyes,
Yet, in protection of their tender ones,
Who hath not seen them, even with those wings
Which sometime they have used with fearful flight,   30
Make war with him that climbed unto their nest,
Offering their own lives in their young's defence?
For shame, my liege, make them your precedent!
Were it not pity that this goodly boy
Should lose his birthright by his father's fault,
And long hereafter say unto his child,
'What my great-grandfather and grandsire got
My careless father fondly gave away'?
Ah, what a shame were this! Look on the boy;
And let his manly face, which promiseth   40
Successful fortune, steel thy melting heart
To hold thine own and leave thine own with him.

KING HENRY. Full well hath Clifford played the orator,
Inferring arguments of mighty force.
But, Clifford, tell me, didst thou never hear
That things ill-got had ever bad success?
And happy always was it for that son
Whose father for his hoarding went to hell?
I'll leave my son my virtuous deeds behind;
And would my father had left me no more!   50
For all the rest is held at such a rate
As brings a thousand-fold more care to keep
Than in possession any jot of pleasure.
Ah, cousin York! would thy best friends did know
How it doth grieve me that thy head is here!

QUEEN MARGARET. My lord, cheer up your spirits: our
  foes are nigh,
And this soft courage makes your followers faint.
You promised knighthood to our forward son:
Unsheathe your sword, and dub him presently.
Edward, kneel down.
KING HENRY. Edward Plantagenet, arise a knight;   60
And learn this lesson, draw thy sword in right.
PRINCE. My gracious father, by your kingly leave,
I'll draw it as apparent to the crown,
And in that quarrel use it to the death.
CLIFFORD. Why, that is spoken like a toward prince.

Enter a Messenger

MESSENGER. Royal commanders, be in readiness:
For with a band of thirty thousand men
Comes Warwick, backing of the Duke of York;
And in the towns, as they do march along,   70
Proclaims him king, and many fly to him:
Darraign your battle, for they are at hand.
CLIFFORD. I would your highness would depart the
  field:
The queen hath best success when you are absent.
QUEEN MARGARET. Ay, good my lord, and leave us to
  our fortune.
KING HENRY. Why, that's my fortune too; therefore I'll
  stay.
NORTHUMBERLAND. Be it with resolution then to fight.
PRINCE. My royal father, cheer these noble lords
And hearten those that fight in your defence:
Unsheathe your sword, good father; cry 'Saint
  George!'   80

*March. Enter Edward, George, Richard, Warwick, Nor-
folk, Montague, and soldiers*

EDWARD. Now, perjured Henry! wilt thou kneel for
  grace,
And set thy diadem upon my head;
Or bide the mortal fortune of the field?
QUEEN MARGARET. Go, rate thy minions, proud
  insulting boy!
Becomes it thee to be thus bold in terms
Before thy sovereign and thy lawful king?
EDWARD. I am his king, and he should bow his knee;
I was adopted heir by his consent:
Since when, his oath is broke; for, as I hear,
You, that are king, though he do wear the crown,   90
Have caused him, by new act of parliament,
To blot out me, and put his own son in.
CLIFFORD. And reason too:
Who should succeed the father but the son?
RICHARD. Are you there, butcher? O, I cannot speak!
CLIFFORD. Ay, crook-back, here I stand to answer thee,
Or any he the proudest of thy sort.
RICHARD. 'Twas you that killed young Rutland, was
  it not?
CLIFFORD. Ay, and old York, and yet not satisfied.
RICHARD. For God's sake, lords, give signal to the
  fight.   100
WARWICK. What say'st thou, Henry, wilt thou
  yield the crown?
QUEEN MARGARET. Why, how now, long-tongued
  Warwick! dare you speak?
When you and I met at Saint Albans last,
Your legs did better service than your hands.

WARWICK. Then 'twas my turn to fly, and now 'tis
  thine.
CLIFFORD. You said so much before, and yet you fled.
WARWICK. 'Twas not your valour, Clifford, drove me
  thence.
NORTHUMBERLAND. No, nor your manhood that durst   60
  make you stay.
RICHARD. Northumberland, I hold thee reverently.
Break off the parley; for scarce I can refrain   110
The execution of my big-swoln heart
Upon that Clifford, that cruel child-killer.
CLIFFORD. I slew thy father, call'st thou him a child?
RICHARD. Ay, like a dastard and a treacherous coward,
As thou didst kill our tender brother Rutland;
But ere sun set I'll make thee curse the deed.
KING HENRY. Have done with words, my lords, and
  hear me speak.
QUEEN MARGARET. Defy them then, or else hold close
  thy lips.
KING HENRY. I prithee, give no limits to my tongue:
I am a king, and privileged to speak.   120
CLIFFORD. My liege, the wound that bred this meeting
  here
Cannot be cured by words; therefore be still.
RICHARD. Then, executioner, unsheathe thy sword:
By him that made us all, I am resolved
That Clifford's manhood lies upon his tongue.
EDWARD. Say, Henry, shall I have my right, or no?
A thousand men have broke their fasts to-day,
That ne'er shall dine unless thou yield the crown.
WARWICK. If thou deny, their blood upon thy head;
For York in justice puts his armour on.   130
PRINCE. If that be right which Warwick says is right,
There is no wrong, but every thing is right.
RICHARD. Whoever got thee, there thy mother stands;
For, well I wot, thou hast thy mother's tongue.
QUEEN MARGARET. But thou art neither like thy sire nor
  dam;
But like a foul mis-shapen stigmatic,
Marked by the destinies to be avoided,
As venom toads, or lizards' dreadful stings.
RICHARD. Iron of Naples hid with English gilt,
Whose father bears the title of a king—   140
As if a channel should be called the sea—
Sham'st thou not, knowing whence thou art
  extraught,
To let thy tongue detect thy base-born heart?
EDWARD. A wisp of straw were worth a thousand
  crowns,
To make this shameless callet know herself.
Helen of Greece was fairer far than thou,
Although thy husband may be Menelaus;
And ne'er was Agamemnon's brother wronged
By that false woman, as this king by thee.
His father revelled in the heart of France,   150
And tamed the king, and made the dauphin stoop;
And had he matched according to his state,
He might have kept that glory to this day;
But when he took a beggar to his bed,
And graced thy poor sire with his bridal-day,
Even then that sunshine brewed a shower for him,
That washed his father's fortunes forth of France,
And heaped sedition on his crown at home.
For what hath broached this tumult but thy pride?
Hadst thou been meek, our title still had slept;   160
And we, in pity of the gentle king,

Had slipped our claim until another age.
GEORGE. But when we saw our sunshine made thy
          spring,
   And that thy summer bred us no increase,
   We set the axe to thy usurping root;
   And though the edge hath something hit ourselves,
   Yet, know thou, since we have begun to strike,
   We'll never leave till we have hewn thee down,
   Or bathed thy growing with our heated bloods.
EDWARD. And, in this resolution, I defy thee;   170
   Not willing any longer conference,
   Since thou deniest the gentle king to speak.
   Sound trumpets! let our bloody colours wave!
   And either victory, or else a grave.
QUEEN MARGARET. Stay, Edward.
EDWARD. No, wrangling woman, we'll no longer
          stay:
   These words will cost ten thousand lives this day.
                                          They go

Scene 3: *A field of battle between Towton and Saxton,*
                    in Yorkshire

Alarum. Excursions. Enter Warwick

WARWICK. Forspent with toil, as runners with a race,
   I lay me down a little while to breathe;
   For strokes received, and many blows repaid,
   Have robbed my strong-knit sinews of their
          strength,
   And spite of spite needs must I rest awhile.

Enter Edward, running

EDWARD. Smile, gentle heaven! or strike, ungentle
          death!
   For this world frowns, and Edward's sun is clouded.
WARWICK. How now, my lord! what hap? what hope
          of good?

Enter George

GEORGE. Our hap is loss, our hope but sad despair;
   Our ranks are broke, and ruin follows us: 10
   What counsel give you? whither shall we fly?
EDWARD. Bootless is flight, they follow us with wings;
   And weak we are and cannot shun pursuit.

Enter Richard

RICHARD. Ah, Warwick, why hast thou withdrawn
          thyself?
   Thy brother's blood the thirsty earth hath drunk,
   Broached with the steely point of Clifford's lance;
   And in the very pangs of death he cried,
   Like to a dismal clangor heard from far,
   'Warwick, revenge! brother, revenge my death!'
   So, underneath the belly of their steeds,   20
   That stained their fetlocks in his smoking blood,
   The noble gentleman gave up the ghost.
WARWICK. Then let the earth be drunken with our
          blood:
   I'll kill my horse, because I will not fly.
   Why stand we like soft-hearted women here,
   Wailing our losses, whiles the foe doth rage;
   And look upon, as if the tragedy
   Were played in jest by counterfeiting actors?
   Here on my knee I vow to God above,
   I'll never pause again, never stand still,   30
   Till either death hath closed these eyes of mine

Or fortune given me measure of revenge.
EDWARD. O Warwick, I do bend my knee with thine;
   And in this vow do chain my soul to thine!
   And, ere my knee rise from the earth's cold face,
   I throw my hands, mine eyes, my heart to thee,
   Thou setter up and plucker down of kings,
   Beseeching thee, if with thy will it stands
   That to my foes this body must be prey,
   Yet that thy brazen gates of heaven may ope,   40
   And give sweet passage to my sinful soul!
   Now, lords, take leave until we meet again,
   Where'er it be, in heaven or in earth.
RICHARD. Brother, give me thy hand; and, gentle
          Warwick,
   Let me embrace thee in my weary arms:
   I, that did never weep, now melt with woe
   That winter should cut off our spring-time so.
WARWICK. Away, away! Once more, sweet lords,
          farewell.
GEORGE. Yet let us all together to our troops,
   And give them leave to fly that will not stay;   50
   And call them pillars that will stand to us;
   And, if we thrive, promise them such rewards
   As victors wear at the Olympian games:
   This may plant courage in their quailing breasts;
   For yet is hope of life and victory.
   Forslow no longer, make we hence amain.
                                          They go

Scene 4

Excursions. Enter Richard and Clifford

RICHARD. Now, Clifford, I have singled thee alone.
   Suppose this arm is for the Duke of York,
   And this for Rutland, both bound to revenge
   Wert thou environed with a brazen wall.
CLIFFORD. Now, Richard, I am with thee here alone.
   This is the hand that stabbed thy father York,
   And this the hand that slew thy brother Rutland,
   And here's the heart that triumphs in their death
   And cheers these hands that slew thy sire and brother
   To execute the like upon thyself;   10
   And so, have at thee!
                          They fight; Warwick comes;
                                          Clifford flies
RICHARD. Nay, Warwick, single out some other chase;
   For I myself will hunt this wolf to death.
                          He pursues; Warwick follows

Scene 5

Alarum. Enter King Henry alone

KING HENRY. This battle fares like to the morning's
          war,
   When dying clouds contend with growing light,
   What time the shepherd, blowing of his nails,
   Can neither call it perfect day nor night.
   Now sways it this way, like a mighty sea
   Forced by the tide to combat with the wind;
   Now sways it that way, like the selfsame sea
   Forced to retire by fury of the wind:
   Sometime the flood prevails, and then the wind;
   Now one the better, then another best;   10
   Both tugging to be victors, breast to breast,
   Yet neither conqueror nor conqueréd:
   So is the equal poise of this fell war.
   Here on this molehill will I sit me down.

To whom God will, there be the victory!
For Margaret my queen, and Clifford too,
Have chid me from the battle; swearing both
They prosper best of all when I am thence.
Would I were dead! if God's good will were so;
For what is in this world but grief and woe?   20
O God! methinks it were a happy life,
To be no better than a homely swain;
To sit upon a hill, as I do now,
To carve out dials quaintly, point by point,
Thereby to see the minutes how they run,
How many make the hour full complete,
How many hours brings about the day,
How many days will finish up the year,
How many years a mortal man may live.
When this is known, then to divide the times: 30
So many hours must I tend my flock,
So many hours must I take my rest,
So many hours must I contemplate,
So many hours must I sport myself,
So many days my ewes have been with young,
So many weeks ere the poor fools will ean,
So many years ere I shall shear the fleece:
So minutes, hours, days, months, and years,
Passed over to the end they were created,
Would bring white hairs unto a quiet grave.   40
Ah, what a life were this! how sweet! how lovely!
Gives not the hawthorn-bush a sweeter shade
To shepherds looking on their silly sheep,
Than doth a rich embroidered canopy
To kings that fear their subjects' treachery?
O, yes, it doth; a thousand-fold it doth.
And to conclude, the shepherd's homely curds,
His cold thin drink out of his leather bottle,
His wonted sleep under a fresh tree's shade,
All which secure and sweetly he enjoys,   50
Is far beyond a prince's delicates,
His viands sparkling in a golden cup,
His body couchèd in a curious bed,
When care, mistrust, and treason waits on him.

*Alarum. Enter a Son that hath killed his father, dragging
in the body*

SON. Ill blows the wind that profits nobody.
  This man, whom hand to hand I slew in fight,
  May be possessèd with some store of crowns;
  And I, that haply take them from him now,
  May yet ere night yield both my life and them
  To some man else, as this dead man doth me....   60
  Who's this? O God! it is my father's face,
  Whom in this conflict I, unwares, have killed.
  O heavy times, begetting such events!
  From London by the king was I pressed forth;
  My father, being the Earl of Warwick's man,
  Came on the part of York, pressed by his master;
  And I, who at his hands received my life,
  Have by my hands of life bereavèd him.
  Pardon me, God, I knew not what I did!
  And pardon, father, for I knew not thee!   70
  My tears shall wipe away these bloody marks;
  And no more words till they have flowed their fill.
KING HENRY. O piteous spectacle! O bloody times!
  Whiles lions war and battle for their dens,
  Poor harmless lambs abide their enmity.
  Weep, wretched man, I'll aid thee tear for tear;
  And let our hearts and eyes, like civil war,

Be blind with tears, and break o'ercharged with
  grief.

*Enter on the other side a Father that hath killed his son,
bringing in the body*

FATHER. Thou that so stoutly hast resisted me,
  Give me thy gold, if thou hast any gold;   80
  For I have bought it with an hundred blows.
  But let me see: is this our foeman's face?
  Ah, no, no, no, it is mine only son!
  Ah, boy, if any life be left in thee,
  Throw up thine eye! see, see what showers arise,
  Blown with the windy tempest of my heart,
  Upon thy wounds, that kill mine eye and heart!
  O, pity, God, this miserable age!
  What stratagems, how fell, how butcherly,
  Erroneous, mutinous and unnatural,   90
  This deadly quarrel daily doth beget!
  O boy, thy father gave thee life too soon,
  And hath bereft thee of thy life too late!
KING HENRY. Woe above woe! grief more than
    common grief!
  O that my death would stay these ruthful deeds!
  O, pity, pity, gentle heaven, pity!
  The red rose and the white are on his face,
  The fatal colours of our striving houses:
  The one his purple blood right well resembles;
  The other his pale cheeks, methinks, presenteth: 100
  Wither one rose, and let the other flourish;
  If you contend, a thousand lives must wither.
SON. How will my mother for a father's death
  Take on with me and ne'er be satisfied!
FATHER. How will my wife for slaughter of my son
  Shed seas of tears and ne'er be satisfied!
KING HENRY. How will the country for these woful
    chances
  Misthink the king and not be satisfied!
SON. Was ever son so rued a father's death?
FATHER. Was ever father so bemoaned his son?   110
KING HENRY. Was ever king so grieved for subject's
    woe?
  Much is your sorrow; mine ten times so much.
SON. I'll bear thee hence, where I may weep my fill.
                              He carries away the body
FATHER. These arms of mine shall be thy
    winding-sheet;
  My heart, sweet boy, shall be thy sepulchre,
  For from my heart thine image ne'er shall go;
  My sighing breast shall be thy funeral bell;
  And so obsequious will thy father be,
  Even for the loss of thee, having no more,
  As Priam was for all his valiant sons.   120
  I'll bear thee hence; and let them fight that will,
  For I have murdered where I should not kill.
                              He carries away the body
KING HENRY. Sad-hearted men, much overgone with
    care,
  Here sits a king more woful than you are.

*Alarums: excursions. Enter the Queen, the Prince, and
Exeter*

PRINCE. Fly, father, fly! for all your friends are fled,
  And Warwick rages like a chafèd bull:
  Away! for death doth hold us in pursuit.
QUEEN MARGARET. Mount you, my lord; towards
    Berwick post amain:

Edward and Richard, like a brace of greyhounds
Having the fearful flying hare in sight,   130
With fiery eyes sparkling for very wrath,
And bloody steel grasped in their ireful hands,
Are at our backs; and therefore hence amain.
EXETER. Away! for vengeance comes along with them:
Nay, stay not to expostulate, make speed;
Or else come after: I'll away before.
KING HENRY. Nay, take me with thee, good sweet
Exeter:
Not that I fear to stay, but love to go
Whither the queen intends. Forward; away!

They go

Scene 6

A loud alarum. Enter Clifford, wounded

CLIFFORD. Here burns my candle out; ay, here it dies,
Which, whiles it lasted, gave King Henry light.
O Lancaster, I fear thy overthrow
More than my body's parting with my soul!
My love and fear glued many friends to thee;
And, now I fall, thy tough commixture melts,
Impairing Henry, strength'ning misproud York.
The common people swarm like summer flies;
And whither fly the gnats but to the sun?
And who shines now but Henry's enemies?   10
O Phoebus, hadst thou never given consent
That Phaëthon should check thy fiery steeds,
Thy burning car never had scorched the earth!
And Henry, hadst thou swayed as kings should do,
Or as thy father and his father did,
Giving no ground unto the house of York,
They never then had sprung like summer flies;
I and ten thousand in this luckless realm
Had left no mourning widows for our death;
And thou this day hadst kept thy chair in peace.   20
For what doth cherish weeds but gentle air?
And what makes robbers bold but too much lenity?
Bootless are plaints, and cureless are my wounds;
No way to fly, nor strength to hold out flight:
The foe is merciless, and will not pity;
For at their hands I have deserved no pity.
The air hath got into my deadly wounds,
And much effuse of blood doth make me faint.
Come, York and Richard, Warwick and the rest;
I stabbed your fathers' bosoms; split my breast.   30

He faints

*Alarum and retreat. Enter Edward, George, Richard,
Montague, Warwick, and soldiers*

EDWARD. Now breathe we, lords: good fortune bids
us pause,
And smooth the frowns of war with peaceful looks.
Some troops pursue the bloody-minded queen,
That led calm Henry, though he were a king,
As doth a sail, filled with a fretting gust,
Command an argosy to stem the waves.
But think you, lords, that Clifford fled with them?
WARWICK. No, 'tis impossible he should escape;
For, though before his face I speak the words,
Your brother Richard marked him for the grave;   40
And wheresoe'er he is, he's surely dead.

Clifford groans, and dies

EDWARD. Whose soul is that which takes her heavy
leave?

RICHARD. A deadly groan, like life and death's
departing.
EDWARD. See who it is: and, now the battle's ended,
If friend or foe, let him be gently used.
RICHARD. Revoke that doom of mercy, for 'tis
Clifford;
Who not contented that he lopped the branch
In hewing Rutland when his leaves put forth,
But set his murdering knife unto the root
From whence that tender spray did sweetly spring, 50
I mean our princely father, Duke of York.
WARWICK. From off the gates of York fetch down
the head,
Your father's head, which Clifford placed there;
Instead whereof let this supply the room:
Measure for measure must be answerèd.
EDWARD. Bring forth that fatal screech-owl to our
house,
That nothing sung but death to us and ours:
Now death shall stop his dismal threat'ning sound
And his ill-boding tongue no more shall speak.
WARWICK. I think his understanding is bereft.   60
Speak, Clifford, dost thou know who speaks to
thee?
Dark cloudy death o'ershades his beams of life,
And he nor sees nor hears us what we say.
RICHARD. O, would he did! and so perhaps he doth:
'Tis but his policy to counterfeit,
Because he would avoid such bitter taunts
Which in the time of death he gave our father.
GEORGE. If so thou think'st, vex him with eager words.
RICHARD. Clifford, ask mercy and obtain no grace.
EDWARD. Clifford, repent in bootless penitence.   70
WARWICK. Clifford, devise excuses for thy faults.
GEORGE. While we devise fell tortures for thy faults.
RICHARD. Thou didst love York, and I am son to
York.
EDWARD. Thou pitied'st Rutland, I will pity thee.
GEORGE. Where's Captain Margaret, to fence
you now?
WARWICK. They mock thee, Clifford: swear as thou
wast wont.
RICHARD. What! not an oath? nay, then the world
goes hard
When Clifford cannot spare his friends an oath.
I know by that he's dead; and, by my soul,
If this right hand would buy two hours' life,   80
That I in all despite might rail at him,
This hand should chop it off, and with the issuing
blood
Stifle the villain whose unstanchèd thirst
York and young Rutland could not satisfy.
WARWICK. Ay, but he's dead: off with the traitor's
head,
And rear it in the place your father's stands.
And now to London with triumphant march,
There to be crownèd England's royal king:
From whence shall Warwick cut the sea to France,
And ask the Lady Bona for thy queen: 90
So shalt thou sinew both these lands together;
And, having France thy friend, thou shalt not dread
The scattered foe that hopes to rise again;
For though they cannot greatly sting to hurt,
Yet look to have them buzz to offend thine ears.
First will I see the coronation;
And then to Brittany I'll cross the sea,

To effect this marriage, so it please my lord.
EDWARD. Even as thou wilt, sweet Warwick, let
　　it be;
　For in thy shoulder do I build my seat,　　　　100
　And never will I undertake the thing
　Wherein thy counsel and consent is wanting.
　Richard, I will create thee Duke of Gloucester,
　And George, of Clarence: Warwick, as ourself,
　Shall do and undo as him pleaseth best.
RICHARD. Let me be Duke of Clarence, George of
　　Gloucester;
　For Gloucester's dukedom is too ominous.
WARWICK. Tut, that's a foolish observation:
　Richard, be Duke of Gloucester. Now to London,
　To see these honours in possession.　　*They go*　110

ACT 3

Scene 1: *A forest in the north of England*

Enter two Keepers, with cross-bows in their hands

1 KEEPER. Under this thick-grown brake we'll shroud
　　ourselves;
　For through this laund anon the deer will come,
　And in this covert will we make our stand,
　Culling the principal of all the deer.
2 KEEPER. I'll stay above the hill, so both may shoot.
1 KEEPER. That cannot be; the noise of thy cross-bow
　Will scare the herd, and so my shoot is lost.
　Here stand we both, and aim we at the best:
　And, for the time shall not seem tedious,
　I'll tell thee what befel me on a day　　　　10
　In this self place where now we mean to stand.
2 KEEPER. Here comes a man, let's stay till he be past.

Enter King Henry, disguised, with a prayer-book

KING HENRY. From Scotland am I stol'n, even of
　　pure love,
　To greet mine own land with my wishful sight.
　No, Harry, Harry, 'tis no land of thine;
　Thy place is filled, thy sceptre wrung from thee,
　Thy balm washed off wherewith thou wast
　　anointed:
　No bending knee will call thee Caesar now,
　No humble suitors press to speak for right,
　No, not a man comes for redress of thee;　　　20
　For how can I help them, and not myself?
1 KEEPER. Ay, here's a deer whose skin's a keeper's fee:
　This is the quondam king; let's seize upon him.
KING HENRY. Let me embrace thee, sour adversity,
　For wise men say it is the wisest course.
2 KEEPER. Why linger we? let us lay hands upon him.
1 KEEPER. Forbear awhile; we'll hear a little more.
KING HENRY. My queen and son are gone to France
　　for aid;
　And, as I hear, the great commanding Warwick
　Is thither gone, to crave the French king's sister　30
　To wife for Edward. If this news be true,
　Poor queen and son, your labour is but lost;
　For Warwick is a subtle orator,
　And Lewis a prince soon won with moving words.
　By this account then Margaret may win him;
　For she's a woman to be pitied much:
　Her sighs will make a battery in his breast;
　Her tears will pierce into a marble heart;
　The tiger will be mild whiles she doth mourn;
　And Nero will be tainted with remorse,　　　　40

To hear and see her plaints, her brinish tears.
　Ay, but she's come to beg, Warwick, to give;
　She, on his left side, craving aid for Henry,
　He, on his right, asking a wife for Edward.
　She weeps, and says her Henry is deposed;
　He smiles, and says his Edward is installed;
　That she, poor wretch, for grief can speak no more;
　Whiles Warwick tells his title, smooths the wrong,
　Inferreth arguments of mighty strength,
　And in conclusion wins the king from her,　　　50
　With promise of his sister, and what else,
　To strengthen and support King Edward's place.
　O Margaret, thus 'twill be; and thou, poor soul,
　Art then forsaken, as thou went'st forlorn!
2 KEEPER. Say, what art thou that talk'st of kings
　　and queens?
KING HENRY. More than I seem, and less than I was
　　born to:
　A man at least, for less I should not be;
　And men may talk of kings, and why not I?
2 KEEPER. Ay, but thou talk'st as if thou wert a king.
KING HENRY. Why, so I am, in mind, and that's
　　enough.　　　　　　　　　　　　　　　　60
2 KEEPER. But, if thou be a king, where is thy crown?
KING HENRY. My crown is in my heart, not on my
　　head;
　Not decked with diamonds and Indian stones,
　Nor to be seen: my crown is called Content:
　A crown it is that seldom kings enjoy.
2 KEEPER. Well, if you be a king crowned with
　　content,
　Your crown content and you must be contented
　To go along with us; for, as we think,
　You are the king King Edward hath deposed;
　And we his subjects sworn in all allegiance　　　70
　Will apprehend you as his enemy.
KING HENRY. But did you never swear, and break an
　　oath?
2 KEEPER. No, never such an oath nor will not now.
KING HENRY. Where did you dwell when I was king
　　of England?
2 KEEPER. Here in this country, where we now remain.
KING HENRY. I was anointed king at nine months old;
　My father and my grandfather were kings,
　And you were sworn true subjects unto me:
　And tell me, then, have you not broke your oaths?
1 KEEPER. No;　　　　　　　　　　　　　　　80
　For we were subjects but while you were king.
KING HENRY. Why, am I dead? do I not breathe a man?
　Ah, simple men, you know not what you swear!
　Look, as I blow this feather from my face,
　And as the air blows it to me again,
　Obeying with my wind when I do blow,
　And yielding to another when it blows,
　Commanded always by the greater gust;
　Such is the lightness of you common men.
　But do not break your oaths; for of that sin　　　90
　My mild entreaty shall not make you guilty.
　Go where you will, the king shall be commanded;
　And be you kings, command, and I'll obey.
1 KEEPER. We are true subjects to the king, King
　　Edward.
KING HENRY. So would you be again to Henry,
　If he were seated as King Edward is.
1 KEEPER. We charge you, in God's name, and the
　　king's,

To go with us unto the officers.
KING HENRY. In God's name, lead; your king's
name be obeyed:
And what God will, that let your king perform;　100
And what he will, I humbly yield unto.

They lead him away

Scene 2: *London. The palace*

Enter King Edward, Gloucester, Clarence, and Lady Grey

KING EDWARD. Brother of Gloucester, at Saint Albans
field
This lady's husband, Sir Richard Grey, was slain,
His lands then seized on by the conqueror:
Her suit is now to repossess those lands;
Which we in justice cannot well deny,
Because in quarrel of the house of York
The worthy gentleman did lose his life.
GLOUCESTER. Your highness shall do well to grant her
suit;
It were dishonour to deny it her.
KING EDWARD. It were no less; but yet I'll make a
pause.　　　　　10
GLOUCESTER [*to Clarence*]. Yea, is it so?
I see the lady hath a thing to grant,
Before the king will grant her humble suit.
CLARENCE [*to Gloucester*]. He knows the game: how
true he keeps the wind!
GLOUCESTER [*to Clarence*]. Silence!
KING EDWARD. Widow, we will consider of your suit;
And come some other time to know our mind.
LADY GREY. Right gracious lord, I cannot brook delay:
May it please your highness to resolve me now,
And what your pleasure is shall satisfy me.　20
GLOUCESTER [*to Clarence*]. Ay, widow? then I'll
warrant you all your lands,
An if what pleases him shall pleasure you.
Fight closer, or, good faith, you'll catch a blow.
CLARENCE [*to Gloucester*]. I fear her not, unless she
chance to fall.
GLOUCESTER [*to Clarence*]. God forbid that! for he'll
take vantages.
KING EDWARD. How many children hast thou, widow?
tell me.
CLARENCE [*to Gloucester*]. I think he means to beg a
child of her.
GLOUCESTER [*to Clarence*]. Nay then, whip me: he'll
rather give her two.
LADY GREY. Three, my most gracious lord.
GLOUCESTER [*to Clarence*]. You shall have four, if you'll
be ruled by him.　　　　　30
KING EDWARD. 'Twere pity they should lose their
father's lands.
LADY GREY. Be pitiful, dread lord, and grant it then,
KING EDWARD. Lords, give us leave: I'll try this
widow's wit.
GLOUCESTER [*to Clarence*]. Ay, good leave have you;
for you will have leave,
Till youth take leave and leave you to the crutch.
*Gloucester and Clarence withdraw
a little*
KING EDWARD. Now tell me, madam, do you love
your children?
LADY GREY. Ay, full as dearly as I love myself.
KING EDWARD. And would you not do much to do
them good?

LADY GREY. To do them good, I would sustain some
harm.
KING EDWARD. Then get your husband's lands, to do
them good.　　　　　40
LADY GREY. Therefore I came unto your majesty.
KING EDWARD. I'll tell you how these lands are to
be got.
LADY GREY. So shall you bind me to your highness'
service.
KING EDWARD. What service wilt thou do me, if I
give them?
LADY GREY. What you command, that rests in me to
do.
KING EDWARD. But you will take exceptions to my
boon.
LADY GREY. No, gracious lord, except I cannot do it.
KING EDWARD. Ay, but thou canst do what I mean
to ask.
LADY GREY. Why, then I will do what your grace
commands.
GLOUCESTER [*to Clarence*]. He plies her hard; and much
rain wears the marble.　　　　　50
CLARENCE [*to Gloucester*]. As red as fire! nay, then
her wax must melt.
LADY GREY. Why stops my lord? shall I not hear my
task?
KING EDWARD. An easy task; 'tis but to love a king.
LADY GREY. That's soon performed, because I am a
subject.
KING EDWARD. Why, then, thy husband's lands I freely
give thee.
LADY GREY. I take my leave with many thousand
thanks.
GLOUCESTER [*to Clarence*]. The match is made; she seals
it with a curtsy.
KING EDWARD. But stay thee, 'tis the fruits of love I
mean.
LADY GREY. The fruits of love I mean, my loving liege.
KING EDWARD. Ay, but, I fear me, in another sense.　60
What love, think'st thou, I sue so much to get?
LADY GREY. My love till death, my humble thanks, my
prayers;
That love which virtue begs and virtue grants.
KING EDWARD. No, by my troth, I did not mean such
love.
LADY GREY. Why, then you mean not as I thought you
did.
KING EDWARD. But now you partly may perceive my
mind.
LADY GREY. My mind will never grant what I perceive
Your highness aims at, if I aim aright.
KING EDWARD. To tell thee plain, I aim to lie with
thee.
LADY GREY. To tell you plain, I had rather lie in
prison.　　　　　70
KING EDWARD. Why, then thou shalt not have thy
husband's lands.
LADY GREY. Why, then mine honesty shall be my
dower;
For by that loss I will not purchase them.
KING EDWARD. Therein thou wrong'st thy children
mightily.
LADY GREY. Herein your highness wrongs both them
and me.
But, mighty lord, this merry inclination
Accords not with the sadness of my suit:

Please you dismiss me, either with 'ay' or 'no'.
KING EDWARD. Ay, if thou wilt say 'ay' to my request;
No, if thou dost say 'no' to my demand.   80
LADY GREY. Then, no, my lord. My suit is at an end.
GLOUCESTER [to Clarence]. The widow likes him not,
she knits her brows.
CLARENCE [to Gloucester]. He is the bluntest wooer in
Christendom.
KING EDWARD [to himself]. Her looks doth argue her
replete with modesty;
Her words doth show her wit incomparable;
All her perfections challenge sovereignty:
One way or other, she is for a king;
And she shall be my love, or else my queen....
[aloud] Say that King Edward take thee for his
queen?
LADY GREY. 'Tis better said than done, my gracious
lord: 90
I am a subject fit to jest withall,
But far unfit to be a sovereign.
KING EDWARD. Sweet widow, by my state I swear to
thee
I speak no more than what my soul intends;
And that is, to enjoy thee for my love.
LADY GREY. And that is more than I will yield
unto:
I know I am too mean to be your queen,
And yet too good to be your concubine.
KING EDWARD. You cavil, widow: I did mean, my
queen.
LADY GREY. 'Twill grieve your grace my sons should
call you father.   100
KING EDWARD. No more than when my daughters call
thee mother.
Thou art a widow, and thou hast some children;
And, by God's mother, I, being but a bachelor,
Have other some: why, 'tis a happy thing
To be the father unto many sons.
Answer no more, for thou shalt be my queen.
GLOUCESTER [to Clarence]. The ghostly father now hath
done his shrift.
CLARENCE [to Gloucester]. When he was made a shriver,
'twas for shift.
KING EDWARD. Brothers, you muse what chat we two
have had.
GLOUCESTER. The widow likes it not, for she looks
very sad.   110
KING EDWARD. You'ld think it strange if I should
marry her.
CLARENCE. To whom, my lord?
KING EDWARD.   Why, Clarence, to myself.
GLOUCESTER. That would be ten days' wonder at the
least.
CLARENCE. That's a day longer than a wonder lasts.
GLOUCESTER. By so much is the wonder in extremes.
KING EDWARD. Well, jest on, brothers: I can tell you
both
Her suit is granted for her husband's lands.

Enter a Nobleman

NOBLEMAN. My gracious lord, Henry your foe is
taken,
And brought your prisoner to your palace gate.
KING EDWARD. See that he be conveyed unto the
Tower: 120
And go we, brothers, to the man that took him,

To question of his apprehension.
Widow, go you along. Lords, use her honourably.
                        All go but Gloucester
GLOUCESTER. Ay, Edward will use women
honourably.
Would he were wasted, marrow, bones and all,
That from his loins no hopeful branch may spring,
To cross me from the golden time I look for!
And yet, between my soul's desire and me—
The lustful Edward's title buried—
Is Clarence, Henry, and his son young Edward,   130
And all the unlooked-for issue of their bodies,
To take their rooms, ere I can place myself:
A cold premeditation for my purpose!
Why then, I do but dream on sovereignty;
Like one that stands upon a promontory,
And spies a far-off shore where he would tread,
Wishing his foot were equal with his eye,
And chides the sea that sunders him from thence,
Saying, he'll lade it dry to have his way:
So do I wish the crown, being so far off;   140
And so I chide the means that keeps me from it;
And so I say, I'll cut the causes off,
Flattering me with impossibilities.
My eye's too quick, my heart o'erweens too much,
Unless my hand and strength could equal them.
Well, say there is no kingdom then for Richard,
What other pleasure can the world afford?
I'll make my heaven in a lady's lap,
And deck my body in gay ornaments,
And witch sweet ladies with my words and looks.   150
O miserable thought! and more unlikely
Than to accomplish twenty golden crowns!
Why, Love forswore me in my mother's womb:
And, for I should not deal in her soft laws,
She did corrupt frail Nature with some bribe,
To shrink mine arm up like a withered shrub;
To make an envious mountain on my back,
Where sits deformity to mock my body;
To shape my legs of an unequal size;
To disproportion me in every part,   160
Like to a chaos, or an unlicked bear-whelp
That carries no impression like the dam.
And am I then a man to be beloved?
O monstrous fault, to harbour such a thought!
Then, since this earth affords no joy to me,
But to command, to check, to o'erbear such
As are of better person than myself,
I'll make my heaven to dream upon the crown,
And, whiles I live, t'account this world but hell,
Until my mis-shaped trunk that bears this head   170
Be round impaléd with a glorious crown.
And yet I know not how to get the crown,
For many lives stand between me and home:
And I—like one lost in a thorny wood,
That rends the thorns and is rent with the thorns,
Seeking a way and straying from the way,
Not knowing how to find the open air,
But toiling desperately to find it out—
Torment myself to catch the English crown:
And from that torment I will free myself,   180
Or hew my way out with a bloody axe.
Why, I can smile, and murder whiles I smile,
And cry 'Content' to that which grieves my heart,
And wet my cheeks with artificial tears,
And frame my face to all occasions.

I'll drown more sailors than the mermaid shall;
I'll slay more gazers than the basilisk;
I'll play the orator as well as Nestor,
Deceive more slily than Ulysses could,
And, like a Sinon, take another Troy. 190
I can add colours to the chameleon,
Change shapes with Proteus for advantages,
And set the murderous Machiavel to school.
Can I do this, and cannot get a crown?
Tut, were it farther off, I'll pluck it down.
He goes

Scene 3: *France. The King's palace*

Flourish. Enter Lewis the French King, his sister Bona, his Admiral, called Bourbon; Prince Edward, Queen Margaret, and the Earl of Oxford. Lewis sits, and rises up again

KING LEWIS. Fair Queen of England, worthy
    Margaret,
Sit down with us: it ill befits thy state
And birth, that thou shouldst stand while Lewis
    doth sit.
QUEEN MARGARET. No, mighty King of France:
    now Margaret
Must strike her sail and learn awhile to serve
Where kings command. I was, I must confess,
Great Albion's queen in former golden days:
But now mischance hath trod my title down,
And with dishonour laid me on the ground;
Where I must take like seat unto my fortune, 10
And to my humble seat conform myself.
KING LEWIS. Why, say, fair queen, whence springs this
    deep despair?
QUEEN MARGARET. From such a cause as fills mine eyes
    with tears
And stops my tongue, while heart is drowned in
    cares.
KING LEWIS. Whate'er it be, be thou still like
    thyself,
And sit thee by our side [*seats her by him*]: yield not
    thy neck
To Fortune's yoke, but let thy dauntless mind
Still ride in triumph over all mischance.
Be plain, Queen Margaret, and tell thy grief;
It shall be eased, if France can yield relief. 20
QUEEN MARGARET. Those gracious words revive my
    drooping thoughts
And give my tongue-tied sorrows leave to speak.
Now, therefore, be it known to noble Lewis,
That Henry, sole possessor of my love,
Is of a king become a banished man,
And forced to live in Scotland a forlorn;
While proud ambitious Edward Duke of York
Usurps the regal title and the seat
Of England's true-anointed lawful king.
This is the cause that I, poor Margaret, 30
With this my son, Prince Edward, Henry's heir,
Am come to crave thy just and lawful aid;
And if thou fail us, all our hope is done:
Scotland hath will to help, but cannot help;
Our people and our peers are both misled,
Our treasure seized, our soldiers put to flight,
And, as thou seest, ourselves in heavy plight.
KING LEWIS. Renownéd queen, with patience calm the
    storm,
While we bethink a means to break it off.

QUEEN MARGARET. The more we stay, the stronger
    grows our foe. 40
KING LEWIS. The more I stay, the more I'll succour
    thee.
QUEEN MARGARET. O, but impatience waiteth on true
    sorrow.
And see where comes the breeder of my sorrow!

Enter Warwick

KING LEWIS. What's he approacheth boldly to our
    presence?
QUEEN MARGARET. Our Earl of Warwick, Edward's
    greatest friend.
KING LEWIS. Welcome, brave Warwick! What brings
    thee to France?   *He descends; she arises*
QUEEN MARGARET [*aside*]. Ay, now begins a second
    storm to rise,
For this is he that moves both wind and tide.
WARWICK. From worthy Edward, king of Albion,
My lord and sovereign, and thy vowéd friend, 50
I come, in kindness and unfeignéd love,
First, to do greetings to thy royal person;
And then to crave a league of amity;
And lastly, to confirm that amity
With nuptial knot, if thou vouchsafe to grant
That virtuous Lady Bona, thy fair sister,
To England's king in lawful marriage.
QUEEN MARGARET [*aside*]. If that go forward, Henry's
    hope is done.
WARWICK [*speaking to Bona*]. And, gracious madam,
    in our king's behalf,
I am commanded, with your leave and favour, 60
Humbly to kiss your hand, and with my tongue
To tell the passion of my sovereign's heart;
Where fame, late ent'ring at his heedful ears,
Hath placed thy beauty's image and thy virtue.
QUEEN MARGARET. King Lewis and Lady Bona, hear
    me speak,
Before you answer Warwick. His demand
Springs not from Edward's well-meant honest love,
But from deceit bred by necessity;
For how can tyrants safely govern home,
Unless abroad they purchase great alliance? 70
To prove him tyrant this reason may suffice,
That Henry liveth still; but were he dead,
Yet here Prince Edward stands, King Henry's son.
Look, therefore, Lewis, that by this league
    and marriage
Thou draw not on thy danger and dishonour;.
For though usurpers sway the rule awhile,
Yet heavens are just, and time suppresseth wrongs.
WARWICK. Injurious Margaret!
PRINCE.   And why not queen?
WARWICK. Because thy father Henry did usurp;
And thou no more art prince than she is queen. 80
OXFORD. Then Warwick disannuls great John of
    Gaunt,
Which did subdue the greatest part of Spain;
And, after John of Gaunt, Henry the Fourth,
Whose wisdom was a mirror to the wisest;
And, after that wise prince, Henry the Fifth,
Who by his prowess conqueréd all France:
From these our Henry lineally descends.
WARWICK. Oxford, how haps it, in this smooth
    discourse,
You told not how Henry the Sixth hath lost

All that which Henry the Fifth had gotten?   90
Methinks these peers of France should smile at that.
But for the rest, you tell a pedigree
Of threescore and two years—a silly time
To make prescription for a kingdom's worth.
OXFORD. Why, Warwick, canst thou speak against
    thy liege,
Whom thou obeyédst thirty and six years,
And not bewray thy treason with a blush?
WARWICK. Can Oxford, that did ever fence
    the right,
Now buckler falsehood with a pedigree?
For shame! leave Henry, and call Edward king.   100
OXFORD. Call him my king by whose injurious doom
My elder brother, the Lord Aubrey Vere,
Was done to death? and more than so, my father,
Even in the downfall of his mellowed years,
When nature brought him to the door of death?
No, Warwick, no; while life upholds this arm,
This arm upholds the house of Lancaster.
WARWICK. And I the house of York.
KING LEWIS. Queen Margaret, Prince Edward, and
    Oxford,
Vouchsafe, at our request, to stand aside,   110
While I use further conference with Warwick.
                        They stand aloof
QUEEN MARGARET. Heavens grant that Warwick's
    words bewitch him not!
KING LEWIS. Now, Warwick, tell me, even upon
    thy conscience,
Is Edward your true king? for I were loath
To link with him that were not lawful chosen.
WARWICK. Thereon I pawn my credit and mine
    honour.
KING LEWIS. But is he gracious in the people's eye?
WARWICK. The more that Henry was unfortunate.
KING LEWIS. Then further, all dissembling set aside,
Tell me for truth the measure of his love   120
Unto our sister Bona.
WARWICK.   Such it seems
As may beseem a monarch like himself.
Myself have often heard him say and swear
That this his love was an eternal plant,
Whereof the root was fixed in virtue's ground,
The leaves and fruit maintained with beauty's sun,
Exempt from envy, but not from disdain,
Unless the Lady Bona quit his pain.
KING LEWIS. Now, sister, let us hear your firm resolve.
BONA. Your grant, or your denial, shall be mine: 130
[*speaks to Warwick*] Yet I confess that often ere
    this day,
When I have heard your king's desert recounted,
Mine ear hath tempted judgment to desire.
KING LEWIS. Then, Warwick, thus: our sister shall be
    Edward's;
And now forthwith shall articles be drawn
Touching the jointure that your king must make,
Which with her dowry shall be counterpoised.
Draw near, Queen Margaret, and be a witness
That Bona shall be wife to the English king.
PRINCE. To Edward, but not to the English king.   140
QUEEN MARGARET. Deceitful Warwick! it was thy
    device
By this alliance to make void my suit:
Before thy coming Lewis was Henry's friend.
KING LEWIS. And still is friend to him and Margaret:

But if your title to the crown be weak,
As may appear by Edward's good success,
Then 'tis but reason that I be released
From giving aid which late I promiséd.
Yet shall you have all kindness at my hand
That your estate requires and mine can yield.   150
WARWICK. Henry now lives in Scotland at his ease,
Where having nothing, nothing can he lose.
And as for you yourself, our quondam queen,
You have a father able to maintain you,
And better 'twere you troubled him than France.
QUEEN MARGARET. Peace, impudent and shameless
    Warwick, peace,
Proud setter up and puller down of kings!
I will not hence, till, with my talk and tears,
Both full of truth, I make King Lewis behold
Thy sly conveyance and thy lord's false love;   160
For both of you are birds of selfsame feather.
                        A horn heard without
KING LEWIS. Warwick, this is some post to us or thee.

Enter the Post

POST [*speaks to Warwick*]. My lord ambassador, these
    letters are for you,
Sent from your brother, Marquess Montague:
[*to Lewis*] These from our king unto your majesty:
[*to Margaret*] And, madam, these for you; from
    whom I know not.   *They all read their letters*
OXFORD. I like it well that our fair queen and mistress
    Smiles at her news, while Warwick frowns at his.
PRINCE. Nay, mark how Lewis stamps, as he were
    nettled:
I hope all's for the best.   170
KING LEWIS. Warwick, what are thy news? and yours,
    fair queen?
QUEEN MARGARET. Mine, such as fill my heart with
    unhoped joys.
WARWICK. Mine, full of sorrow and heart's discontent.
KING LEWIS. What! has your king married the Lady
    Grey?
And now, to soothe your forgery and his,
Sends me a paper to persuade me patience?
Is this th'alliance that he seeks with France?
Dare he presume to scorn us in this manner?
QUEEN MARGARET. I told your majesty as much before:
This proveth Edward's love and Warwick's
    honesty!   180
WARWICK. King Lewis, I here protest, in sight of
    heaven,
And by the hope I have of heavenly bliss,
That I am clear from this misdeed of Edward's,
No more my king, for he dishonours me,
But most himself, if he could see his shame.
Did I forget that by the house of York
My father came untimely to his death?
Did I let pass th'abuse done to my niece?
Did I impale him with the regal crown?
Did I put Henry from his native right?   190
And am I guerdoned at the last with shame?
Shame on himself! for my desert is honour:
And to repair my honour lost for him,
I here renounce him and return to Henry.
My noble queen, let former grudges pass,
And henceforth I am thy true servitor:
I will revenge his wrong to Lady Bona

And replant Henry in his former state.
QUEEN MARGARET. Warwick, these words have turned
    my hate to love;
And I forgive and quite forget old faults,   200
And joy that thou becom'st King Henry's friend.
WARWICK. So much his friend, ay, his unfeignéd
    friend,
That, if King Lewis vouchsafe to furnish us
With some few bands of chosen soldiers,
I'll undertake to land them on our coast
And force the tyrant from his seat by war.
'Tis not his new-made bride shall succour him:
And as for Clarence, as my letters tell me,
He's very likely now to fall from him,
For matching more for wanton lust than honour,   210
Or than for strength and safety of our country.
BONA. Dear brother, how shall Bona be revenged
But by thy help to this distresséd queen?
QUEEN MARGARET. Renownéd prince, how shall poor
    Henry live,
Unless thou rescue him from foul despair?
BONA. My quarrel and this English queen's are one.
WARWICK. And mine, fair Lady Bona, joins with
    yours.
KING LEWIS. And mine with hers, and thine, and
    Margaret's.
Therefore at last I firmly am resolved
You shall have aid.   220
QUEEN MARGARET. Let me give humble thanks for all at
    once.
KING LEWIS. Then, England's messenger, return in
    post,
And tell false Edward, thy supposéd king,
That Lewis of France is sending over masquers
To revel it with him and his new bride:
Thou seest what's passed, go fear thy king withal.
BONA. Tell him, in hope he'll prove a widower
    shortly,
I'll wear the willow garland for his sake.
QUEEN MARGARET. Tell him, my mourning weeds are
    laid aside,
And I am ready to put armour on.   230
WARWICK. Tell him from me that he hath done me
    wrong,
And therefore I'll uncrown him ere't be long.
There's thy reward: be gone.   *The Post goes*
KING LEWIS.   But, Warwick,
Thou and Oxford, with five thousand men,
Shall cross the seas, and bid false Edward battle;
And, as occasion serves, this noble queen
And prince shall follow with a fresh supply.
Yet, ere thou go, but answer me one doubt,
What pledge have we of thy firm loyalty?
WARWICK. This shall assure my constant loyalty,   240
That if our queen and this young prince agree,
I'll join mine eldest daughter and my joy
To him forthwith in holy wedlock bands.
QUEEN MARGARET. Yes, I agree, and thank you for your
    motion.
Son Edward, she is fair and virtuous,
Therefore delay not, give thy hand to Warwick;
And, with thy hand, thy faith irrevocable,
That only Warwick's daughter shall be thine.
PRINCE. Yes, I accept her, for she well deserves it;
And here, to pledge my vow, I give my hand.   250
              He gives his hand to Warwick

KING LEWIS. Why stay we now? These soldiers shall be
    levied,
And thou, Lord Bourbon, our high admiral,
Shalt waft them over with our royal fleet.
I long till Edward fall by war's mischance,
For mocking marriage with a dame of France.
              All go but Warwick
WARWICK. I came from Edward as ambassador,
But I return his sworn and mortal foe:
Matter of marriage was the charge he gave me,
But dreadful war shall answer his demand.
Had he none else to make a stale but me?   260
Then none but I shall turn his jest to sorrow.
I was the chief that raised him to the crown,
And I'll be chief to bring him down again:
Not that I pity Henry's misery,
But seek revenge on Edward's mockery.   *He goes*

ACT 4
Scene 1: *London. The palace*

Enter Gloucester, Clarence, Somerset, and Montague

GLOUCESTER. Now tell me, brother Clarence, what
    think you
Of this new marriage with the Lady Grey?
Hath not our brother made a worthy choice?
CLARENCE. Alas, you know, 'tis far from hence
    to France;
How could he stay till Warwick made return?
SOMERSET. My lords, forbear this talk; here comes the
    king.
GLOUCESTER. And his well-chosen bride.
CLARENCE. I mind to tell him plainly what I think.

*Flourish. Enter King Edward, attended; Lady Grey, as
Queen; Pembroke, Stafford, Hastings, and others. The two
parties come face to face*

KING EDWARD. Now, brother of Clarence, how like
    you our choice,
That you stand pensive, as half malcontent?   10
CLARENCE. As well as Lewis of France, or the Earl
    of Warwick,
Which are so weak of courage and in judgement
That they'll take no offence at our abuse.
KING EDWARD. Suppose they take offence without a
    cause,
They are but Lewis and Warwick: I am Edward,
Your king and Warwick's, and must have my will.
GLOUCESTER. And shall have your will, because our
    king:
Yet hasty marriage seldom proveth well.
KING EDWARD. Yea, brother Richard, are you
    offended too?   20
GLOUCESTER. Not I:
No, God forbid that I should wish them severed
Whom God hath joined together; ay, and 'twere
    pity
To sunder them that yoke so well together.
KING EDWARD. Setting your scorns and your mislike
    aside,
Tell me some reason why the Lady Grey
Should not become my wife and England's queen.
And you too, Somerset and Montague,
Speak freely what you think.
CLARENCE. Then this is mine opinion: that King Lewis

Becomes your enemy, for mocking him   30
About the marriage of the Lady Bona.
GLOUCESTER. And Warwick, doing what you gave in
   charge,
Is now dishonouréd by this new marriage.
KING EDWARD. What if both Lewis and Warwick be
   appeased
By such invention as I can devise?
MONTAGUE. Yet, to have joined with France in such
   alliance
Would more have strengthened this our
   commonwealth
'Gainst foreign storms than any home-bred
   marriage.
HASTINGS. Why, knows not Montague that of itself
England is safe, if true within itself?   40
MONTAGUE. But the safer when 'tis backed with
   France.
HASTINGS. 'Tis better using France than trusting
   France:
Let us be backed with God and with the seas
Which He hath given for fence impregnable,
And with their helps only defend ourselves;
In them and in ourselves our safety lies.
CLARENCE. For this one speech Lord Hastings well
   deserves
To have the heir of the Lord Hungerford.
KING EDWARD. Ay, what of that? it was my will and
   grant;
And for this once my will shall stand for law.   50
GLOUCESTER. And yet methinks your grace hath not
   done well,
To give the heir and daughter of Lord Scales
Unto the brother of your loving bride;
She better would have fitted me or Clarence:
But in your bride you bury brotherhood.
CLARENCE. Or else you would not have bestowed the
   heir
Of the Lord Bonville on your new wife's son,
And leave your brothers to go speed elsewhere.
KING EDWARD. Alas, poor Clarence! is it for a wife
That thou art malcontent? I will provide thee.   60
CLARENCE. In choosing for yourself, you showed your
   judgement,
Which being shallow, you shall give me leave
To play the broker in mine own behalf;
And to that end I shortly mind to leave you.
KING EDWARD. Leave me, or tarry, Edward will be
   king,
And not be tied unto his brother's will.
QUEEN ELIZABETH. My lords, before it pleased his
   majesty
To raise my state to title of a queen,
Do me but right, and you must all confess
That I was not ignoble of descent;   70
And meaner than myself have had like fortune.
But as this title honours me and mine,
So your dislikes, to whom I would be pleasing,
Doth cloud my joys with danger and with sorrow.
KING EDWARD. My love, forbear to fawn upon their
   frowns:
What danger or what sorrow can befall thee,
So long as Edward is thy constant friend,
And their true sovereign, whom they must obey?
Nay, whom they shall obey, and love thee too,
Unless they seek for hatred at my hands;   80

Which if they do, yet will I keep thee safe,
And they shall feel the vengeance of my wrath.
GLOUCESTER [aside]. I hear, yet say not much, but
   think the more.

Enter a Post

KING EDWARD. Now, messenger, what letters or what
   news
From France?
POST. My sovereign liege, no letters; and few words,
But such as I, without your special pardon,
Dare not relate.
KING EDWARD. Go to, we pardon thee: therefore, in
   brief,
Tell me their words as near as thou canst guess them.   90
What answer makes King Lewis unto our letters?
POST. At my depart, these were his very words:
'Go tell false Edward, thy supposéd king,
That Lewis of France is sending over masquers
To revel it with him and his new bride.'
KING EDWARD. Is Lewis so brave? belike he thinks me
   Henry.
But what said Lady Bona to my marriage?
POST. These were her words, uttered with mild
   disdain:
'Tell him, in hope he'll prove a widower shortly,
I'll wear the willow garland for his sake.'   100
KING EDWARD. I blame not her, she could say little
   less;
She had the wrong. But what said Henry's queen?
For I have heard that she was there in place.
POST. 'Tell him,' quoth she, 'my mourning weeds are
   done,
And I am ready to put armour on.'
KING EDWARD. Belike she minds to play the Amazon.
But what said Warwick to these injuries?
POST. He, more incensed against your majesty
Than all the rest, discharged me with these words:
'Tell him from me that he hath done me wrong,   110
And therefore I'll uncrown him ere't be long.'
KING EDWARD. Ha! durst the traitor breathe out so
   proud words?
Well, I will arm me, being thus forewarned:
They shall have wars and pay for their presumption.
But say, is Warwick friends with Margaret?
POST. Ay, gracious sovereign; they are so linked in
   friendship,
That young Prince Edward marries Warwick's
   daughter.
CLARENCE. Belike the elder; Clarence will have the
   younger.
Now, brother king, farewell, and sit you fast,
For I will hence to Warwick's other daughter;   120
That, though I want a kingdom, yet in marriage
I may not prove inferior to yourself.
You that love me and Warwick, follow me.
                                    He goes, followed by Somerset
GLOUCESTER [aside]. Not I:
My thoughts aim at a further matter; I
Stay not for the love of Edward, but the crown.
KING EDWARD. Clarence and Somerset both gone to
   Warwick!
Yet am I armed against the worst can happen;
And haste is needful in this desp'rate case.
Pembroke and Stafford, you in our behalf   130
Go levy men, and make prepare for war;

They are already, or quickly will be, landed:
Myself in person will straight follow you.
Pembroke and Stafford depart
But, ere I go, Hastings and Montague,
Resolve my doubt. You twain, of all the rest,
Are near to Warwick by blood and by alliance:
Tell me if you love Warwick more than me?
If it be so, then both depart to him;
I rather wish you foes than hollow friends:
But if you mind to hold your true obedience,   140
Give me assurance with some friendly vow,
That I may never have you in suspect.
MONTAGUE. So God help Montague as he proves true!
HASTINGS. And Hastings as he favours Edward's cause!
KING EDWARD. Now, brother Richard, will you
    stand by us?
GLOUCESTER. Ay, in despite of all that shall withstand
    you.
KING EDWARD. Why, so! then am I sure of victory.
Now therefore let us hence; and lose no hour,
Till we meet Warwick with his foreign power.
They go

Scene 2: *A plain in Warwickshire*

Enter Warwick and Oxford with French soldiers

WARWICK. Trust me, my lord, all hitherto goes well;
The common people by numbers swarm to us.

Enter Clarence and Somerset

But see where Somerset and Clarence comes!
Speak suddenly, my lords, are we all friends?
CLARENCE. Fear not that, my lord.
WARWICK. Then, gentle Clarence, welcome unto
    Warwick;
And welcome, Somerset: I hold it cowardice
To rest mistrustful where a noble heart
Hath pawned an open hand in sign of love;
Else might I think that Clarence, Edward's brother,   10
Were but a feignéd friend to our proceedings:
But welcome, sweet Clarence; my daughter shall be
    thine.
And now what rests but, in night's coverture,
Thy brother being carelessly encamped,
His soldiers lurking in the towns about,
And but attended by a simple guard,
We may surprise and take him at our pleasure?
Our scouts have found the adventure very easy:
That as Ulysses and stout Diomede
With sleight and manhood stole to Rhesus' tents,   20
And brought from thence the Thracian fatal steeds,
So we, well covered with the night's black mantle,
At unawares may beat down Edward's guard
And seize himself; I say not, slaughter him,
For I intend but only to surprise him.
You that will follow me to this attempt,
Applaud the name of Henry with your leader.
They all cry, Henry!
Why, then, let's on our way in silent sort:
For Warwick and his friends, God and Saint George!
They go

Scene 3: *Edward's camp, near Warwick*

Enter three Watchmen, to guard the King's tent

1 WATCHMAN. Come on, my masters, each man take
    his stand:

The king by this is set him down to sleep.
2 WATCHMAN. What, will he not to bed?
1 WATCHMAN. Why, no; for he hath made a solemn
    vow
Never to lie and take his natural rest
Till Warwick or himself be quite suppressed.
2 WATCHMAN. To-morrow then belike shall be the
    day,
If Warwick be so near as men report.
3 WATCHMAN. But say, I pray, what nobleman is that
That with the king here resteth in his tent?   10
1 WATCHMAN. 'Tis the Lord Hastings, the king's
    chiefest friend.
3 WATCHMAN. O, is it so? But why commands the
    king
That his chief followers lodge in towns about him,
While he himself keeps in the cold field?
2 WATCHMAN. 'Tis the more honour, because more
    dangerous.
3 WATCHMAN. Ay, but give me worship and quietness;
I like it better than a dangerous honour.
If Warwick knew in what estate he stands,
'Tis to be doubted he would waken him.
1 WATCHMAN. Unless our halberds did shut up his
    passage.   20
2 WATCHMAN. Ay, wherefore else guard we his royal
    'tent,
But to defend his person from night-foes?

*Enter Warwick, Clarence, Oxford, Somerset, and French
soldiers, silent all*

WARWICK. This is his tent; and see where stand his
    guard.
Courage, my masters! honour now or never!
But follow me, and Edward shall be ours.
1 WATCHMAN. Who goes there?
2 WATCHMAN. Stay, or thou diest!
*Warwick and the rest cry all, 'Warwick!
Warwick!' and set upon the Guard,
who fly, crying, 'Arm! arm!,'
Warwick and the rest following
them*

*The drum playing and trumpet sounding, re-enter War-
wick, Somerset, and the rest, bringing the King out in his
gown, sitting in a chair. Richard and Hastings escape*

SOMERSET. What are they that fly there?
WARWICK. Richard and Hastings: let them go; here is
The duke.
KING EDWARD.   The duke! Why, Warwick when
    we parted,   30
Thou call'dst me king.
WARWICK.   Ay, but the case is altered:
When you disgraced me in my embassade,
Then I degraded you from being king,
And come now to create you Duke of York.
Alas! how should you govern any kingdom,
That know not how to use ambassadors,
Nor how to be contented with one wife,
Nor how to use your brothers brotherly,
Nor how to study for the people's welfare,
Nor how to shroud yourself from enemies?   40
KING EDWARD. Yea, brother of Clarence, art thou here
    too?
Nay, then I see that Edward needs must down.
Yet, Warwick, in despite of all mischance,

Of thee thyself and all thy complices,
Edward will always bear himself as king:
Though fortune's malice overthrow my state,
My mind exceeds the compass of her wheel.
WARWICK. Then, for his mind, be Edward England's
    king: *Takes off his crown*
But Henry now shall wear the English crown,
And be true king indeed, thou but the shadow.   50
My Lord of Somerset, at my request,
See that forthwith Duke Edward be conveyed
Unto my brother, Archbishop of York.
When I have fought with Pembroke and his fellows,
I'll follow you, and tell what answer
Lewis and the Lady Bona send to him.
Now, for a while farewell, good Duke of York.
KING EDWARD. What fates impose, that men must
    needs abide;
It boots not to resist both wind and tide.
                         They lead him out forcibly
OXFORD. What now remains, my lords, for us to do   60
But march to London with our soldiers?
WARWICK. Ay, that's the first thing that we have to
    do;
To free king Henry from imprisonment
And see him seated in the regal throne.   *They go*

Scene 4: *London. The palace*

Enter Queen Elizabeth and Rivers

RIVERS. Madam, what makes you in this sudden
    change?
QUEEN ELIZABETH. Why, brother Rivers, are you yet
    to learn
What late misfortune is befall'n King Edward?
RIVERS. What! loss of some pitched battle against
    Warwick?
QUEEN ELIZABETH. No, but the loss of his own royal
    person.
RIVERS. Then is my sovereign slain?
QUEEN ELIZABETH. Ay, almost slain, for he is taken
    prisoner,
Either betrayed by falsehood of his guard
Or by his foe surprised at unawares:
And, as I further have to understand,   10
Is new committed to the Bishop of York,
Fell Warwick's brother and by that our foe.
RIVERS. These news I must confess are full of grief;
Yet, gracious madam, bear it as you may:
Warwick may lose, that now hath won the day.
QUEEN ELIZABETH. Till then fair hope must hinder
    life's decay.
And I the rather wean me from despair
For love of Edward's offspring in my womb:
This is it that makes me bridle passion
And bear with mildness my misfortune's cross;   20
Ay, ay, for this I draw in many a tear
And stop the rising of blood-sucking sighs,
Lest with my sighs or tears I blast or drown
King Edward's fruit, true heir to th'English crown.
RIVERS. But, madam, where is Warwick then become?
QUEEN ELIZABETH. I am informéd that he comes
    towards London,
To set the crown once more on Henry's head:
Guess thou the rest; King Edward's friends must
    down.
But, to prevent the tyrant's violence—

For trust not him that hath once broken faith—   30
I'll hence forthwith unto the sanctuary,
To save at least the heir of Edward's right:
There shall I rest secure from force and fraud.
Come, therefore, let us fly while we may fly:
If Warwick take us we are sure to die.   *They go*

Scene 5: *A park in Yorkshire*

Enter Gloucester, Lord Hastings, and Sir William Stanley

GLOUCESTER. Now, my Lord Hastings and Sir
    William Stanley,
Leave off to wonder why I drew you hither,
Into this chiefest thicket of the park.
Thus stands the case: you know our king, my
    brother,
Is prisoner to the bishop here, at whose hands
He hath good usage and great liberty,
And, often but attended with weak guard,
Comes hunting this way to disport himself.
I have advertised him by secret means
That if about this hour he make this way   10
Under the colour of his usual game,
He shall here find his friends with horse and men
To set him free from his captivity.

Enter King Edward and a Huntsman with him

HUNTSMAN. This way, my lord; for this way lies the
    game.
KING EDWARD. Nay, this way, man: see where the
    huntsmen stand.
Now, brother of Gloucester, Lord Hastings, and the
    rest,
Stand you thus close, to steal the bishop's deer?
GLOUCESTER. Brother, the time and case requireth
    haste:
Your horse stands ready at the park-corner.
KING EDWARD. But whither shall we then?
GLOUCESTER.   To Lynn, my lord.   20
KING EDWARD. And ship from thence to Flanders?
GLOUCESTER. Well guessed, believe me; for that was
    my meaning.
KING EDWARD. Stanley, I will requite thy forwardness.
GLOUCESTER. But wherefore stay we? 'tis no time to
    talk.
KING EDWARD. Huntsman, what say'st thou? wilt thou
    go along?
HUNTSMAN. Better do so than tarry and be hanged.
GLOUCESTER. Come then, away; let's ha' no more ado.
KING EDWARD. Bishop, farewell: shield thee from
    Warwick's frown;
And pray that I may repossess the crown.
                                        They go

Scene 6: *London. The Tower*

*Flourish. Enter King Henry the Sixth, Clarence, Warwick,
Somerset, young Henry Richmond, Oxford, Montague,
and Lieutenant of the Tower*

KING HENRY. Master lieutenant, now that God and
    friends
Have shaken Edward from the regal seat,
And turned my captive state to liberty,
My fear to hope, my sorrows unto joys,
At our enlargement what are thy due fees?

LIEUTENANT. Subjects may challenge nothing of their
    sovereigns;
But if an humble prayer may prevail,
I then crave pardon of your majesty.
KING HENRY. For what, lieutenant? for well using me?
Nay, be thou sure I'll well requite thy kindness,   10
For that it made my imprisonment a pleasure;
Ay, such a pleasure as incagéd birds
Conceive when after many moody thoughts
At last by notes of household harmony
They quite forget their loss of liberty.
But, Warwick, after God, thou set'st me free,
And chiefly therefore I thank God and thee;
He was the author, thou the instrument.
Therefore, that I may conquer Fortune's spite
By living low, where Fortune cannot hurt me,   20
And that the people of this blesséd land
May not be punished with my thwarting stars,
Warwick, although my head still wear the crown,
I here resign my government to thee,
For thou art fortunate in all thy deeds.
WARWICK. Your grace hath still been famed for
    virtuous;
And now may seem as wise as virtuous,
By spying and avoiding Fortune's malice,
For few men rightly temper with the stars:
Yet in this one thing let me blame your grace,   30
For choosing me when Clarence is in place.
CLARENCE. No, Warwick, thou art worthy of the
    sway,
To whom the heavens in thy nativity
Adjudged an olive branch and laurel crown,
As likely to be blest in peace and war;
And therefore I yield thee my free consent.
WARWICK. And I choose Clarence only for Protector.
KING HENRY. Warwick and Clarence, give me both
    your hands:
Now join your hands, and with your hands
    your hearts,
That no dissension hinder government: 40
I make you both Protectors of this land,
While I myself will lead a private life,
And in devotion spend my latter days,
To sin's rebuke and my Creator's praise.
WARWICK. What answers Clarence to his sovereign's
    will?
CLARENCE. That he consents, if Warwick yield
    consent;
For on thy fortune I repose myself.
WARWICK. Why, then, though loath, yet must I be
    content:
We'll yoke together, like a double shadow
To Henry's body, and supply his place;   50
I mean, in bearing weight of government,
While he enjoys the honour and his ease.
And, Clarence, now then it is more than needful
Forthwith that Edward be pronounced a traitor,
And all his lands and goods be confiscate.
CLARENCE. What else? and that succession be
    determined.
WARWICK. Ay, therein Clarence shall not want his
    part.
KING HENRY. But, with the first of all your chief
    affairs,
Let me entreat, for I command no more,
That Margaret your queen and my son Edward   60

Be sent for, to return from France with speed;
For, till I see them here, by doubtful fear
My joy of liberty is half eclipsed.
CLARENCE. It shall be done, my sovereign, with all
    speed.
KING HENRY. My Lord of Somerset, what youth is
    that,
Of whom you seem to have so tender care?
SOMERSET. My liege, it is young Henry, earl of
    Richmond.
KING HENRY. Come hither, England's hope. [lays his
    hand on his head] If secret powers
Suggest but truth to my divining thoughts,
This pretty lad will prove our country's bliss.   70
His looks are full of peaceful majesty,
His head by nature framed to wear a crown,
His hand to wield a sceptre, and himself
Likely in time to bless a regal throne.
Make much of him, my lords, for this is he
Must help you more than you are hurt by me.

Enter a Post

WARWICK. What news, my friend?
POST. That Edward is escapéd from your brother,
And fled, as he hears since, to Burgundy.
WARWICK. Unsavoury news! but how made
    he escape?   80
POST. He was conveyed by Richard duke of
    Gloucester
And the Lord Hastings, who attended him
In secret ambush on the forest side
And from the bishop's huntsmen rescued him;
For hunting was his daily exercise.
WARWICK. My brother was too careless of his charge.
But let us hence, my sovereign, to provide
A salve for any sore that may betide.
                All but Somerset, Richmond,
                    and Oxford depart
SOMERSET. My lord, I like not of this flight of
    Edward's;
For doubtless Burgundy will yield him help,   90
And we shall have more wars before't be long.
As Henry's late presaging prophecy
Did glad my heart with hope of this young
    Richmond,
So doth my heart misgive me, in these conflicts
What may befall him, to his harm and ours:
Therefore, Lord Oxford, to prevent the worst,
Forthwith we'll send him hence to Brittany,
Till storms be past of civil enmity.
OXFORD. Ay, for if Edward repossess the crown,
'Tis like that Richmond with the rest shall down.   100
SOMERSET. It shall be so; he shall to Brittany.
Come, therefore, let's about it speedily.   *They go*

Scene 7: *Before York*

*Flourish. Enter King Edward, Gloucester, Hastings, and
soldiers*

KING EDWARD. Now, brother Richard, Lord Hastings,
    and the rest,
Yet thus far Fortune maketh us amends,
And says that once more I shall interchange
My wanéd state for Henry's regal crown.
Well have we passed and now repassed the seas
And brought desiréd help from Burgundy:

What then remains, we being thus arrived
From Ravenspurgh haven before the gates of York,
But that we enter, as into our dukedom?
GLOUCESTER. The gates made fast! Brother, I like not
this;   10
For many men that stumble at the threshold
Are well foretold that danger lurks within.
KING EDWARD. Tush, man, abodements must not now
affright us:
By fair or foul means we must enter in,
For hither will our friends repair to us.
HASTINGS. My liege, I'll knock once more to summon
them.

Enter, on the walls, the Mayor of York and his brethren

MAYOR. My lords, we were forewarnéd of your
coming,
And shut the gates for safety of ourselves;
For now we owe allegiance unto Henry.
KING EDWARD. But, master mayor, if Henry be your
king,   20
Yet Edward at the least is Duke of York.
MAYOR. True, my good lord; I know you for no less.
KING EDWARD. Why, and I challenge nothing but my
dukedom,
As being well content with that alone.
GLOUCESTER [*aside*]. But when the fox hath once got
in his nose,
He'll soon find means to make the body follow.
HASTINGS. Why, master mayor, why stand you in a
doubt?
Open the gates; we are King Henry's friends.
MAYOR. Ay, say you so? the gates shall then be
opened.   *He descends*
GLOUCESTER. A wise stout captain, and soon
persuaded!   30
HASTINGS. The good old man would fain that all were
well,
So 'twere not long of him; but being entered,
I doubt not, I, but we shall soon persuade
Both him and all his brothers unto reason.

Enter the Mayor and two aldermen, below

KING EDWARD. So, master mayor: these gates must
not be shut
But in the night or in the time of war.
What! fear not, man, but yield me up the keys;
                                                                 Takes his keys
For Edward will defend the town and thee,
And all those friends that deign to follow me.

March. Enter Montgomery, with drum and soldiers

GLOUCESTER. Brother, this is Sir John Montgomery, 40
Our trusty friend, unless I be deceived.
KING EDWARD. Welcome, Sir John! But why come
you in arms?
MONTGOMERY. To help King Edward in his time of
storm,
As every loyal subject ought to do.
KING EDWARD. Thanks, good Montgomery; but we
now forget
Our title to the crown and only claim
Our dukedom till God please to send the rest.
MONTGOMERY. Then fare you well, for I will hence
again:
I came to serve a king and not a duke.

Drummer, strike up, and let us march away.   50
                                    The drum begins the march
KING EDWARD. Nay stay, Sir John, awhile, and we'll
debate
By what safe means the crown may be recovered.
MONTGOMERY. What talk you of debating? in few
words,
If you'll not here proclaim yourself our king,
I'll leave you to your fortune and be gone
To keep them back that come to succour you:
Why shall we fight, if you pretend no title?
GLOUCESTER. Why, brother, wherefore stand you on
nice points?
KING EDWARD. When we grow stronger, then we'll
make our claim:
Till then, 'tis wisdom to conceal our meaning.   60
HASTINGS. Away with scrupulous wit! now arms must
rule.
GLOUCESTER. And fearless minds climb soonest unto
crowns.
Brother, we will proclaim you out of hand;
The bruit thereof will bring you many friends.
KING EDWARD. Then be it as you will; for 'tis my
right,
And Henry but usurps the diadem.
MONTGOMERY. Ay, now my sovereign speaketh like
himself;
And now will I be Edward's champion.
HASTINGS. Sound trumpet; Edward shall be here
proclaimed:
Come, fellow-soldier, make thou proclamation.   70
                                                                 Flourish
SOLDIER. Edward the Fourth, by the grace of God,
king of England and France, and lord of Ireland, &c.
MONTGOMERY. And whosoe'er gainsays King
Edward's right,
By this I challenge him to single fight.
                                            Throws down his gauntlet
ALL. Long live Edward the Fourth!
KING EDWARD. Thanks, brave Montgomery; and
thanks unto you all:
If fortune serve me, I'll requite this kindness.
Now, for this night, let's harbour here in York;
And when the morning sun shall raise his car
Above the border of this horizon,   80
We'll forward towards Warwick and his mates;
For well I wot that Henry is no soldier.
Ah, forward Clarence! how evil it beseems thee,
To flatter Henry and forsake thy brother!
Yet, as we may, we'll meet both thee and Warwick.
Come on, brave soldiers: doubt not of the day,
And, that once gotten, doubt not of large pay.
                                                     They enter the city

Scene 8: *London. The Bishop of London's palace*

*Flourish. Enter King Henry, Warwick, Montague,
Clarence, and Oxford*

WARWICK. What counsel, lords? Edward from Belgia,
With hasty Germans and blunt Hollanders,
Hath passed in safety through the Narrow Seas,
And with his troops doth march amain to London;
And many giddy people flock to him.
KING HENRY. Let's levy men, and beat him back again.
CLARENCE. A little fire is quickly trodden out;
Which, being suffered, rivers cannot quench.

WARWICK. In Warwickshire I have true-hearted
  friends,
  Not mutinous in peace, yet bold in war;   10
  Those will I muster up: and thou, son Clarence,
  Shalt stir up in Suffolk, Norfolk and in Kent,
  The knights and gentlemen to come with thee:
  Thou, brother Montague, in Buckingham,
  Northampton and in Leicestershire, shalt find
  Men well inclined to hear what thou command'st:
  And thou, brave Oxford, wondrous well beloved,
  In Oxfordshire shalt muster up thy friends.
  My sovereign, with the loving citizens,
  Like to his island girt in with the ocean,   20
  Or modest Dian circled with her nymphs,
  Shall rest in London till we come to him.
  Fair lords, take leave and stand not to reply.
  Farewell, my sovereign.
KING HENRY. Farewell, my Hector, and my Troy's true
  hope.
CLARENCE. In sign of truth, I kiss your highness' hand.
KING HENRY. Well-minded Clarence, be thou
  fortunate!
MONTAGUE. Comfort, my lord; and so I take my leave.
OXFORD. And thus I seal my truth, and bid adieu.
KING HENRY. Sweet Oxford, and my loving
  Montague,   30
  And all at once, once more a happy farewell.
WARWICK. Farewell, sweet lords: let's meet at
  Coventry.   *They go*

Enter King Henry and Exeter

KING HENRY. Here at the palace will I rest awhile.
  Cousin of Exeter, what thinks your lordship?
  Methinks the power that Edward hath in field
  Should not be able to encounter mine.
EXETER. The doubt is that he will seduce the rest.
KING HENRY. That's not my fear; my meed hath got
  me fame:
  I have not stopped mine ears to their demands,
  Nor posted off their suits with slow delays;   40
  My pity hath been balm to heal their wounds,
  My mildness hath allayed their swelling griefs,
  My mercy dried their water-flowing tears;
  I have not been desirous of their wealth,
  Nor much oppressed them with great subsidies,
  Nor forward of revenge, though they much erred:
  Then why should they love Edward more than me?
  No, Exeter, these graces challenge grace:
  And when the lion fawns upon the lamb,
  The lamb will never cease to follow him.   50
                       Shout without, 'A York! A York!'
EXETER. Hark, hark, my lord! what shouts are these?

Enter King Edward, Gloucester, and soldiers

KING EDWARD. Seize on the shame-faced Henry, bear
  him hence;
  And once again proclaim us king of England.
  You are the fount that makes small brooks to flow;
  Now stops thy spring; my sea shall suck them dry,
  And swell so much the higher by their ebb.
  Hence with him to the Tower; let him not speak.
                                   King Henry is led out
  And, lords, towards Coventry bend we our course,
  Where peremptory Warwick now remains:
  The sun shines hot; and, if we use delay,
  Cold biting winter mars our hoped-for hay.

GLOUCESTER. Away betimes, before his forces join,
  And take the great-grown traitor unawares:
  Brave warriors, march amain towards Coventry.
                                               They go

ACT 5
Scene 1: *Coventry*

*Enter Warwick, the Mayor of Coventry, two Messengers,
and others upon the walls*

WARWICK. Where is the post that came from valiant
  Oxford?
  How far hence is thy lord, mine honest fellow?
1 MESSENGER. By this at Dunsmore, marching
  hitherward.
WARWICK. How far off is our brother Montague?
  Where is the post that came from Montague?
2 MESSENGER. By this at Daintry, with a puissant troop.

Enter Somerville

WARWICK. Say, Somerville, what says my loving son?
  And, by thy guess, how nigh is Clarence now?
SOMERVILLE. At Southam I did leave him with his
  forces,
  And do expect him here some two hours hence.   10
                                             Drum heard
WARWICK. Then Clarence is at hand; I hear his drum.
SOMERVILLE. It is not his, my lord; here Southam lies:
  The drum your honour hears marcheth from
  Warwick.
WARWICK. Who should that be? belike, unlooked-for
  friends.
SOMERVILLE. They are at hand, and you shall quickly
  know.

*March: flourish. Enter King Edward, Gloucester, and
soldiers*

KING EDWARD. Go, trumpet, to the walls, and sound a
  parle.
GLOUCESTER. See how the surly Warwick mans the
  wall!
WARWICK. O unbid spite! is sportful Edward come?
  Where slept our scouts, or how are they seduced,
  That we could hear no news of his repair?   20
KING EDWARD. Now, Warwick, wilt thou ope the city
  gates,
  Speak gentle words and humbly bend thy knee,
  Call Edward king and at his hands beg mercy?
  And he shall pardon thee these outrages.
WARWICK. Nay, rather, wilt thou draw thy forces
  hence,
  Confess who set thee up and plucked thee down,
  Call Warwick patron and be penitent?
  And thou shalt still remain the Duke of York.
GLOUCESTER. I thought, at least, he would have said the
  king;
  Or did he make the jest against his will?   30
WARWICK. Is not a dukedom, sir, a goodly gift?
GLOUCESTER. Ay, by my faith, for a poor earl to give:
  I'll do thee service for so good a gift.
WARWICK. 'Twas I that gave the kingdom to thy
  brother.
KING EDWARD. Why then 'tis mine, if but by
  Warwick's gift.
WARWICK. Thou art no Atlas for so great a weight:
  And, weakling, Warwick takes his gift again;

And Henry is my king, Warwick his subject.
KING EDWARD. But Warwick's king is Edward's
    prisoner:
    And, gallant Warwick, do but answer this: 40
    What is the body when the head is off?
GLOUCESTER. Alas, that Warwick had no more
    forecast,
    But, whiles he thought to steal the single ten,
    The king was slily fingered from the deck!
    You left poor Henry at the Bishop's palace,
    And, ten to one, you'll meet him in the Tower.
KING EDWARD. 'Tis even so, yet you are Warwick still.
GLOUCESTER. Come, Warwick, take the time; kneel
    down, kneel down:
    Nay, when? strike now, or else the iron cools.
WARWICK. I had rather chop this hand off at a blow,   50
    And with the other fling it at thy face,
    Than bear so low a sail, to strike to thee.
KING EDWARD. Sail how thou canst, have wind and
    tide thy friend,
    This hand, fast wound about thy coal-black hair,
    Shall, whiles thy head is warm and new cut off,
    Write in the dust this sentence with thy blood,
    'Wind-changing Warwick now can change no
        more.'
Enter Oxford, with drum and colours

WARWICK. O cheerful colours! see where Oxford
    comes!
OXFORD. Oxford, Oxford, for Lancaster!
                    He and his forces enter the city
GLOUCESTER. The gates are open, let us enter too.   60
KING EDWARD. So other foes may set upon our backs.
    Stand we in good array; for they no doubt
    Will issue out again and bid us battle:
    If not, the city being but of small defence,
    We'll quickly rouse the traitors in the same.
WARWICK. O, welcome, Oxford! for we want thy
    help.
Enter Montague, with drum and colours

MONTAGUE. Montague, Montague, for Lancaster!
                    He and his forces enter the city
GLOUCESTER. Thou and thy brother both shall buy this
    treason
    Even with the dearest blood your bodies bear.
KING EDWARD. The harder matched, the greater
    victory: 70
    My mind presageth happy gain and conquest.
Enter Somerset, with drum and colours

SOMERSET. Somerset, Somerset, for Lancaster!
                    He and his forces enter the city
GLOUCESTER. Two of thy name, both Dukes of
    Somerset,
    Have sold their lives unto the house of York,
    And thou shalt be the third, if this sword hold.
Enter Clarence, with drum and colours

WARWICK. And lo, where George of Clarence sweeps
    along,
    Of force enough to bid his brother battle;
    With whom an upright zeal to right prevails
    More than the nature of a brother's love!
    Come, Clarence, come; thou wilt, if Warwick call.   80
CLARENCE. Father of Warwick, know you what this
    means?   *Taking his red rose out of his hat*

Look here, I throw my infamy at thee:
    I will not ruinate my father's house,
    Who gave his blood to lime the stones together,
    And set up Lancaster. Why, trow'st thou, Warwick,
    That Clarence is so harsh, so blunt, unnatural,
    To bend the fatal instruments of war
    Against his brother and his lawful king?
    Perhaps thou wilt object my holy oath:
    To keep that oath were more impiety   90
    Than Jephthah's, when he sacrificed his daughter.
    I am so sorry for my trespass made
    That, to deserve well at my brother's hands,
    I here proclaim myself thy mortal foe,
    With resolution, wheresoe'er I meet thee—
    As I will meet thee, if thou stir abroad—
    To plague thee for thy foul misleading me.
    And so, proud-hearted Warwick, I defy thee,
    And to my brother turn my blushing cheeks.
    Pardon me, Edward, I will make amends: 100
    And, Richard, do not frown upon my faults,
    For I will henceforth be no more unconstant.
KING EDWARD. Now welcome more, and ten times
    more beloved,
    Than if thou never hadst deserved our hate.
GLOUCESTER. Welcome, good Clarence; this is
    brother-like.
WARWICK. O passing traitor, perjured and unjust!
KING EDWARD. What, Warwick, wilt thou leave the
    town, and fight?
    Or shall we beat the stones about thine ears?
WARWICK. Alas, I am not cooped here for defence!
    I will away towards Barnet presently,   110
    And bid thee battle, Edward, if thou dar'st.
KING EDWARD. Yes, Warwick, Edward dares, and
    leads the way.
    Lords, to the field; Saint George and victory!
                    King Edward and his company
                    march away; Warwick and his
                    company follow

Scene 2: *A field of battle near Barnet*

Alarum and excursions. Enter King Edward, bringing forth
Warwick wounded

KING EDWARD. So, lie thou there: die thou, and die
    our fear;
    For Warwick was a bug that feared us all.
    Now, Montague, sit fast; I seek for thee,
    That Warwick's bones may keep thine company.
                                              He goes
WARWICK. Ah, who is nigh? come to me, friend or
    foe,
    And tell me who is victor, York or Warwick?
    Why ask I that? my mangled body shows,
    My blood, my want of strength, my sick heart
        shows,
    That I must yield my body to the earth;
    And, by my fall, the conquest to my foe.   10
    Thus yields the cedar to the axe's edge,
    Whose arms gave shelter to the princely eagle,
    Under whose shade the ramping lion slept,
    Whose top-branch overpeered Jove's spreading tree
    And kept low shrubs from winter's powerful wind.
    These eyes, that now are dimmed with death's black
        veil,

Have been as piercing as the mid-day sun,
To search the secret treasons of the world:
The wrinkles in my brows, now filled with blood,
Were likened oft to kingly sepulchres;   20
For who lived king, but I could dig his grave?
And who durst smile when Warwick bent his brow?
Lo, now my glory smeared in dust and blood!
My parks, my walks, my manors that I had,
Even now forsake me, and of all my lands
Is nothing left me but my body's length.
Why, what is pomp, rule, reign, but earth and dust?
And, live we how we can, yet die we must.

Enter Oxford and Somerset

SOMERSET. Ah, Warwick, Warwick! wert thou as we
    are,
We might recover all our loss again: 30
The queen from France hath brought a puissant
    power:
Even now we heard the news: ah, couldst thou fly
WARWICK. Why, then I would not fly.
    Ah, Montague,
If thou be there, sweet brother, take my hand,
And with thy lips keep in my soul awhile!
Thou lov'st me not; for, brother, if thou didst,
Thy tears would wash this cold congealéd blood
That glues my lips and will not let me speak.
Come quickly, Montague, or I am dead.
SOMERSET. Ah, Warwick! Montague hath breathed
    his last;   40
And to the latest gasp cried out for Warwick,
And said 'Commend me to my valiant brother.'
And more he would have said, and more he spoke,
Which sounded like a cannon in a vault,
That mought not be distinguished; but at last
I well might hear, delivered with a groan,
'O, farewell, Warwick!'
WARWICK. Sweet rest his soul! Fly, lords, and save
    yourselves;
For Warwick bids you all farewell, to meet in
    heaven.   *Dies*
OXFORD. Away, away, to meet the queen's great
    power!   *Here they bear away his body* 50

Scene 3

*Flourish. Enter King Edward in triumph; with Gloucester,
Clarence, and the rest*

KING EDWARD. Thus far our fortune keeps an upward
    course,
And we are graced with wreaths of victory.
But, in the midst of this bright-shining day,
I spy a black, suspicious, threat'ning cloud,
That will encounter with our glorious sun,
Ere he attain his easeful western bed:
I mean, my lords, those powers that the queen
Hath raised in Gallia have arrived our coast,
And, as we hear, march on to fight with us.
CLARENCE. A little gale will soon disperse that cloud   10
And blow it to the source from whence it came:
Thy very beams will dry those vapours up,
For every cloud engenders not a storm.
GLOUCESTER. The queen is valued thirty thousand
    strong,
And Somerset, with Oxford, fled to her:
If she have time to breathe, be well assured

Her faction will be full as strong as ours.
KING EDWARD. We are advertised by our loving
    friends
That they do hold their course toward Tewkesbury:
We, having now the best at Barnet field,   20
Will thither straight, for willingness rids way;
And, as we march, our strength will be augmented
In every county as we go along.
Strike up the drum; cry 'Courage!' and away.
                                            They go

Scene 4: *Plains near Tewkesbury*

*Flourish. March. Enter Queen Margaret, Prince Edward,
Somerset, Oxford, and soldiers*

QUEEN MARGARET. Great lords, wise men ne'er sit and
    wail their loss,
But cheerly seek how to redress their harms.
What though the mast be now blown overboard,
The cable broke, the holding-anchor lost,
And half our sailors swallowed in the flood?
Yet lives our pilot still. Is't meet that he
Should leave the helm, and like a fearful lad
With tearful eyes add water to the sea,
And give more strength to that which hath too
    much,
Whiles, in his moan, the ship splits on the rock,   10
Which industry and courage might have saved?
Ah, what a shame! ah, what a fault were this!
Say Warwick was our anchor; what of that?
And Montague our topmast; what of him?
Our slaughtered friends the tackles; what of these?
Why, is not Oxford here another anchor?
And Somerset another goodly mast?
The friends of France our shrouds and tacklings?
And, though unskilful, why not Ned and I
For once allowed the skilful pilot's charge?   20
We will not from the helm to sit and weep,
But keep our course, though the rough wind say no,
From shelves and rocks that threaten us with wrack.
As good to chide the waves as speak them fair.
And what is Edward but a ruthless sea?
What Clarence but a quicksand of deceit?
And Richard but a ragged fatal rock?
All these the enemies to our poor bark.
Say you can swim; alas, 'tis but a while!
Tread on the sand; why, there you quickly sink: 30
Bestride the rock; the tide will wash you off,
Or else you famish; that's a threefold death.
This speak I, lords, to let you understand,
If case some one of you would fly from us,
That there's no hoped-for mercy with the brothers
More than with ruthless waves, with sands and
    rocks.
Why, courage then! what cannot be avoided
'Twere childish weakness to lament or fear.
PRINCE. Methinks a woman of this valiant spirit
Should, if a coward heard her speak these words,   40
Infuse his breast with magnanimity,
And make him, naked, foil a man at arms.
I speak not this as doubting any here;
For did I but suspect a fearful man,
He should have leave to go away betimes,
Lest in our need he might infect another
And make him of like spirit to himself.
If any such be here—as God forbid!—

Let him depart before we need his help.

OXFORD. Women and children of so high a courage, 50
And warriors faint! why, 'twere perpetual shame.
O brave young prince! thy famous grandfather
Doth live again in thee: long mayst thou live
To bear his image and renew his glories!

SOMERSET. And he that will not fight for such a hope,
Go home to bed, and like the owl by day,
If he arise, be mocked and wondered at.

QUEEN MARGARET. Thanks, gentle Somerset; sweet
Oxford, thanks.

PRINCE. And take his thanks that yet hath nothing else.

Enter a Messenger

MESSENGER. Prepare you, lords, for Edward is at
hand, 60
Ready to fight; therefore be resolute.

OXFORD. I thought no less: it is his policy
To haste thus fast, to find us unprovided.

SOMERSET. But he's deceived; we are in readiness.

QUEEN MARGARET. This cheers my heart, to see your
forwardness.

OXFORD. Here pitch our battle; hence we will not
budge.

*Flourish and March. Enter King Edward, Gloucester,
Clarence, and soldiers*

KING EDWARD. Brave followers, yonder stands the
thorny wood,
Which, by the heavens' assistance and your strength,
Must by the roots be hewn up yet ere night.
I need not add more fuel to your fire, 70
For well I wot ye blaze to burn them out:
Give signal to the fight, and to it, lords!

QUEEN MARGARET. Lords, knights, and gentlemen,
what I should say
My tears gainsay; for every word I speak,
Ye see, I drink the water of mine eyes.
Therefore, no more but this: Henry, your sovereign,
Is prisoner to the foe; his state usurped,
His realm a slaughter-house, his subjects slain,
His statutes cancelled and his treasure spent;
And yonder is the wolf that makes this spoil. 80
You fight in justice: then, in God's name, lords,
Be valiant, and give signal to the fight.

*Alarum: retreat: excursions: the Lancastrians
are driven from the field*

Scene 5

*Flourish. Enter King Edward, Gloucester, Clarence, and
soldiers; with Queen Margaret, Oxford, and Somerset,
prisoners*

KING EDWARD. Now here a period of tumultuous
broils.
Away with Oxford to Hames Castle straight:
For Somerset, off with his guilty head.
Go, bear them hence; I will not hear them speak.

OXFORD. For my part, I'll not trouble thee with words.

SOMERSET. Nor I, but stoop with patience to my
fortune. *Oxford and Somerset are led away*

QUEEN MARGARET. So part we sadly in this troublous
world,
To meet with joy in sweet Jerusalem.

KING EDWARD. Is proclamation made, that who finds
Edward

Shall have a high reward, and he his life? 10

GLOUCESTER. It is: and lo, where youthful Edward
comes!

KING EDWARD. Bring forth the gallant, let us hear him
speak.

Enter soldiers, with the Prince

What! can so young a thorn begin to prick?
Edward, what satisfaction canst thou make
For bearing arms, for stirring up my subjects,
And all the trouble thou hast turned me to?

PRINCE. Speak like a subject, proud ambitious York!
Suppose that I am now my father's mouth;
Resign thy chair, and where I stand kneel thou,
Whilst I propose the selfsame words to thee, 20
Which, traitor, thou wouldst have me answer to.

QUEEN MARGARET. Ah, that thy father had been so
resolved!

GLOUCESTER. That you might still have worn the
petticoat,
And ne'er have stol'n the breech from Lancaster.

PRINCE. Let Aesop fable in a winter's night;
His currish riddles sorts not with this place.

GLOUCESTER. By heaven, brat, I'll plague ye for that
word.

QUEEN MARGARET. Ay, thou wast born to be a plague
to men.

GLOUCESTER. For God's sake, take away this captive
scold.

PRINCE. Nay, take away this scolding crook-back
rather. 30

KING EDWARD. Peace, wilful boy, or I will charm your
tongue.

CLARENCE. Untutored lad, thou art too malapert.

PRINCE. I know my duty; you are all undutiful:
Lascivious Edward, and thou perjured George,
And thou mis-shapen Dick, I tell ye all
I am your better, traitors as ye are:
And thou usurp'st my father's right and mine.

KING EDWARD. Take that, thou likeness of this railer
here. *Stabs him*

GLOUCESTER. Sprawl'st thou? take that, to end thy
agony. *Stabs him*

CLARENCE. And there's for twitting me with perjury. 40
Stabs him

QUEEN MARGARET. O, kill me too!

GLOUCESTER. Marry, and shall. *Offers to kill her*

KING EDWARD. Hold, Richard, hold; for we have done
too much.

GLOUCESTER. Why should she live, to fill the world
with words?

KING EDWARD. What! doth she swoon? use means for
her recovery.

GLOUCESTER. Clarence, excuse me to the king my
brother;
I'll hence to London on a serious matter:
Ere ye come there, be sure to hear some news.

CLARENCE. What? what?

GLOUCESTER. The Tower, the Tower. *He goes* 50

QUEEN MARGARET. O Ned, sweet Ned! speak to thy
mother, boy!
Canst thou not speak? O traitors! murderers!
They that stabbed Caesar shed no blood at all,
Did not offend, nor were not worthy blame,
If this foul deed were by to equal it:
He was a man; this, in respect, a child:

And men ne'er spend their fury on a child.
What's worse than murderer, that I may name it?
No, no, my heart will burst, an if I speak:
And I will speak, that so my heart may burst.   60
Butchers and villains! bloody cannibals!
How sweet a plant have you untimely cropped!
You have no children, butchers! If you had,
The thought of them would have stirred up
remorse:
But if you ever chance to have a child,
Look in his youth to have him so cut off
As, deathsmen, you have rid this sweet young
prince!

KING EDWARD. Away with her; go, bear her hence
perforce.

QUEEN MARGARET. Nay, never bear me hence, dispatch
me here;
Here sheathe thy sword, I'll pardon thee my death: 70
What! wilt thou not? then, Clarence, do it thou.

CLARENCE. By heaven, I will not do thee so much
ease.

QUEEN MARGARET. Good Clarence, do; sweet
Clarence, do thou do it.

CLARENCE. Didst thou not hear me swear I would not
do it?

QUEEN MARGARET. Ay, but thou usest to forswear
thyself.
'Twas sin before, but now 'tis charity.
What! wilt thou not? Where is that devil's butcher,
Hard-favoured Richard? Richard, where art thou?
Thou art not here: murder is thy alms-deed;
Petitioners for blood thou ne'er put'st back.   80

KING EDWARD. Away, I say; I charge ye, bear
her hence.

QUEEN MARGARET. So come to you and yours, as to this
prince!   *She is led out forcibly*

KING EDWARD. Where's Richard gone?

CLARENCE. To London, all in post; and, as I guess,
To make a bloody supper in the Tower.

KING EDWARD. He's sudden if a thing comes in his
head.
Now march we hence: discharge the common sort
With pay and thanks, and let's away to London,
And see our gentle queen how well she fares:
By this, I hope, she hath a son for me.   *They go* 90

Scene 6: *London. The Tower*

*Enter King Henry, the Lieutenant attending, and
Gloucester.*

GLOUCESTER. Good day, my lord. What! at your book
so hard?

KING HENRY. Ay, my good lord: my lord, I should say
rather;
'Tis sin to flatter; 'good' was little better:
'Good Gloucester' and 'good devil' were alike,
And both preposterous; therefore, not 'good lord.'

GLOUCESTER. Sirrah, leave us to ourselves: we must
confer.   *Lieutenant goes*

KING HENRY. So flies the reckless shepherd from the
wolf;
So first the harmless sheep doth yield his fleece,
And next his throat unto the butcher's knife.
What scene of death hath Roscius now to act?   10

GLOUCESTER. Suspicion always haunts the guilty mind;
The thief doth fear each bush an officer.

KING HENRY. The bird that hath been liméd in a
bush,
With trembling wings misdoubteth every bush;
And I, the hapless male to one sweet bird,
Have now the fatal object in my eye
Where my poor young was limed, was caught and
killed.

GLOUCESTER. Why, what a peevish fool was that of
Crete,
That taught his son the office of a fowl!
And yet, for all his wings, the fool was drowned.   20

KING HENRY. I, Daedalus; my poor boy, Icarus;
Thy father, Minos, that denied our course;
The sun that seared the wings of my sweet boy
Thy brother Edward, and thyself the sea
Whose envious gulf did swallow up his life.
Ah, kill me with thy weapon, not with words!
My breast can better brook thy dagger's point
Than can my ears that tragic history.
But wherefore dost thou come? is't for my life?

GLOUCESTER. Think'st thou I am an executioner?   30

KING HENRY. A persecutor, I am sure, thou art:
If murdering innocents be executing,
Why, then thou art an executioner.

GLOUCESTER. Thy son I killed for his presumption.

KING HENRY. Hadst thou been killed when first thou
didst presume,
Thou hadst not lived to kill a son of mine.
And thus I prophesy, that many a thousand,
Which now mistrust no parcel of my fear,
And many an old man's sigh and many a widow's,
And many an orphan's water-standing eye—   40
Men for their sons, wives for their husbands,
And orphans for their parents' timeless death—
Shall rue the hour that ever thou wast born.
The owl shrieked at thy birth—an evil sign;
The night-crow cried, aboding luckless time;
Dogs howled, and hideous tempest shook down
trees;
The raven rooked her on the chimney's top,
And chattering pies in dismal discords sung.
Thy mother felt more than a mother's pain,
And yet brought forth less than a mother's hope,   50
To wit, an indigested and deforméd lump,
Not like the fruit of such a goodly tree.
Teeth hadst thou in thy head when thou wast born,
To signify thou cam'st to bite the world:
And, if the rest be true which I have heard,
Thou cam'st—

GLOUCESTER. I'll hear no more: die, prophet, in thy
speech: *Stabs him*
For this, amongst the rest, was I ordained.

KING HENRY. Ay, and for much more slaughter after
this.
O, God forgive my sins, and pardon thee!   *Dies* 60

GLOUCESTER. What! will the aspiring blood of
Lancaster
Sink in the ground? I thought it would have
mounted.
See how my sword weeps for the poor king's death!
O, may such purple tears be alway shed
From those that wish the downfall of our house!
If any spark of life be yet remaining,
Down, down to hell; and say I sent thee thither—
                                         Stabs him again
I, that have neither pity, love, nor fear.

Indeed, 'tis true that Henry told me of;
For I have often heard my mother say 70
I came into the world with my legs forward:
Had I not reason, think ye, to make haste,
And seek their ruin that usurped our right?
The midwife wondered and the women cried
'O, Jesus bless us, he is born with teeth!'
And so I was, which plainly signified
That I should snarl and bite and play the dog.
Then, since the heavens have shaped my body so,
Let hell make crooked my mind to answer it.
I have no brother, I am like no brother; 80
And this word 'love,' which greybeards call divine,
Be resident in men like one another
And not in me: I am myself alone.
Clarence, beware; thou keep'st me from the light:
But I will sort a pitchy day for thee;
For I will buzz abroad such prophecies
That Edward shall be fearful of his life,
And then, to purge his fear, I'll be thy death.
King Henry and the prince his son are gone:
Clarence, thy turn is next, and then the rest, 90
Counting myself but bad till I be best.
I'll throw thy body in another room
And triumph, Henry, in thy day of doom.
He drags off the body

Scene 7: London. The palace

*Flourish. Enter King Edward, Queen Elizabeth, Clarence,
Gloucester, Hastings, a nurse with the infant Prince, and
attendants*

KING EDWARD. Once more we sit in England's royal
  throne,
Re-purchased with the blood of enemies.
What valiant foemen, like to autumn's corn,
Have we mowed down in tops of all their pride!
Three Dukes of Somerset, threefold renowned
For hardy and undoubted champions;
Two Cliffords, as the father and the son,
And two Northumberlands; two braver men
Ne'er spurred their coursers at the trumpet's sound;
With them, the two brave bears, Warwick and
  Montague, 10

That in their chains fettered the kingly lion
And made the forest tremble when they roared.
Thus have we swept suspicion from our seat
And made our footstool of security.
Come hither, Bess, and let me kiss my boy.
Young Ned, for thee, thine uncles and myself
Have in our armours watched the winter's night,
Went all afoot in summer's scalding heat,
That thou mightst repossess the crown in peace:
And of our labours thou shalt reap the gain. 20
GLOUCESTER [*aside*]. I'll blast his harvest, if your head
  were laid;
For yet I am not looked on in the world.
This shoulder was ordained so thick to heave;
And heave it shall some weight, or break my back:
Work thou the way—and thou shalt execute.
KING EDWARD. Clarence and Gloucester, love my
  lovely queen;
And kiss your princely nephew, brothers both.
CLARENCE. The duty that I owe unto your majesty
I seal upon the lips of this sweet babe.
KING EDWARD. Thanks, noble Clarence; worthy
  brother, thanks. 30
GLOUCESTER. And, that I love the tree from whence
  thou sprang'st,
Witness the loving kiss I give the fruit.
[*aside*] To say the truth, so Judas kissed his master,
And cried, 'all hail!' when as he meant all harm.
KING EDWARD. Now am I seated as my soul delights,
Having my country's peace and brothers' loves.
CLARENCE. What will your grace have done with
  Margaret?
Reignier, her father, to the king of France
Hath pawned the Sicils and Jerusalem,
And hither have they sent it for her ransom. 40
KING EDWARD. Away with her, and waft her hence to
  France.
And now what rests but that we spend the time
With stately triumphs, mirthful comic shows,
Such as befits the pleasure of the court?
Sound drums and trumpets! farewell sour annoy!
For here, I hope, begins our lasting joy.
Flourish as the King and court depart

Richard III

The scene: London and elsewhere in England

CHARACTERS IN THE PLAY

KING EDWARD *the Fourth*
EDWARD, PRINCE OF WALES, *afterwards*
   King Edward V } *sons to the King*
RICHARD, *Duke of York*
GEORGE, *Duke of Clarence* } *brothers to*
RICHARD, *Duke of Gloucester,* } *King Edward*
   afterwards King Richard III
A young son of Clarence [EDWARD PLANTAGENET]
HENRY, *Earl of Richmond, afterwards King Henry VII*
CARDINAL [*Thomas Bourchier, Archbishop of Canterbury*]
ARCHBISHOP OF YORK [Thomas Rotheram]
BISHOP OF ELY [John Morton]
DUKE OF BUCKINGHAM
DUKE OF NORFOLK
EARL OF SURREY, *his son*
ANTHONY WOODEVILLE, EARL RIVERS, *brother to Elizabeth*
MARQUIS OF DORSET *and* LORD GREY, *sons to Elizabeth*
EARL OF OXFORD
LORD HASTINGS
LORD STANLEY, EARL OF DERBY
LORD LOVEL
SIR THOMAS VAUGHAN

SIR RICHARD RATCLIFFE
SIR WILLIAM CATESBY
SIR JAMES TYRREL
SIR JAMES BLOUNT
SIR WALTER HERBERT
SIR ROBERT BRAKENBURY, *Lieutenant of the Tower*
SIR WILLIAM BRANDON
CHRISTOPHER URSWICK, *a priest*
Another Priest
TRESSEL *and* BERKELEY, *gentlemen attending on the Lady*
   Anne
Lord Mayor of London
Sheriff of Wiltshire
ELIZABETH, *queen to King Edward IV*
MARGARET, *widow of King Henry VI*
DUCHESS OF YORK, *mother to King Edward IV*
LADY ANNE, *widow of Edward Prince of Wales, the son*
   of King Henry VI; afterwards married to Richard
A young daughter of Clarence [MARGARET PLANTAGENET]
Ghosts of those murdered by Richard III, Lords and other
   Attendants; a Pursuivant, Scrivener, Citizens,
   Murderers, Messengers, Soldiers, etc.

Richard III

ACT 1
Scene 1: *London. A street*

Enter Richard, Duke of Gloucester, solus

GLOUCESTER. Now is the winter of our discontent
Made glorious summer by this sun of York;
And all the clouds that loured upon our house
In the deep bosom of the ocean buried.
Now are our brows bound with victorious wreaths;
Our bruiséd arms hung up for monuments;
Our stern alarums changed to merry meetings;
Our dreadful marches to delightful measures.
Grim-visaged war hath smoothed his wrinkléd
    front;
And now, instead of mounting barbéd steeds   10
To fright the souls of fearful adversaries,
He capers nimbly in a lady's chamber
To the lascivious pleasing of a lute.
But I, that am not shaped for sportive tricks,
Nor made to court an amorous looking-glass;
I, that am rudely stamped, and want love's majesty
To strut before a wanton ambling nymph;
I, that am curtailed of this fair proportion,
Cheated of feature by dissembling Nature,
Deformed, unfinished, sent before my time   20
Into this breathing world, scarce half made up,
And that so lamely and unfashionable
That dogs bark at me as I halt by them;
Why, I, in this weak piping time of peace,
Have no delight to pass away the time,
Unless to spy my shadow in the sun
And descant on mine own deformity:
And therefore, since I cannot prove a lover,
To entertain these fair well-spoken days,
I am determinéd to prove a villain   30
And hate the idle pleasures of these days.
Plots have I laid, inductions dangerous,
By drunken prophecies, libels and dreams,
To set my brother Clarence and the king
In deadly hate the one against the other:
And if King Edward be as true and just
As I am subtle, false and treacherous,
This day should Clarence closely be mewed up,
About a prophecy, which says that G
Of Edward's heirs the murderer shall be.   40
Dive, thoughts, down to my soul—here Clarence
    comes.

*Enter Clarence, guarded, and Brakenbury, Lieutenant of
the Tower*

    Brother, good day: what means this arméd guard
That waits upon your grace?
CLARENCE.   His majesty,
Tend'ring my person's safety, hath appointed
This conduct to convey me to the Tower.
GLOUCESTER. Upon what cause?
CLARENCE.   Because my name is George.
GLOUCESTER. Alack, my lord, that fault is none of
    yours;

He should, for that, commit your godfathers:
Belike his majesty hath some intent
That you should be new-christ'ned in the Tower.   50
But what's the matter, Clarence? may I know?
CLARENCE. Yea, Richard, when I know; for I protest
As yet I do not: but, as I can learn,
He hearkens after prophecies and dreams;
And from the cross-row plucks the letter G,
And says a wizard told him that by G
His issue disinherited should be;
And, for my name of George begins with G,
It follows in his thought that I am he.
These, as I learn, and such like toys as these   60
Hath moved his highness to commit me now.
GLOUCESTER. Why, this it is, when men are ruled by
    women:
'Tis not the king that sends you to the Tower;
My Lady Grey his wife, Clarence, 'tis she
That tempers him to this extremity.
Was it not she, and that good man of worship,
Anthony Woodeville, her brother there,
That made him send Lord Hastings to the Tower,
From whence this present day he is delivered?
We are not safe, Clarence, we are not safe.   70
CLARENCE. By heaven, I think there's no man is secure
But the queen's kindred, and night-walking heralds
That trudge betwixt the king and Mistress Shore.
Heard you not what an humble suppliant
Lord Hastings was for his delivery?
GLOUCESTER. Humbly complaining to her deity
Got my Lord Chamberlain his liberty.
I'll tell you what, I think it is our way
If we will keep in favour with the king,
To be her men and wear her livery.   80
The jealous o'erworn widow and herself,
Since that our brother dubbed them gentlewomen,
Are mighty gossips in our monarchy.
BRAKENBURY. Beseech your graces both to pardon
    me;
His majesty hath straitly given in charge
That no man shall have private conference
(Of what degree soever) with his brother.
GLOUCESTER. Even so; an't please your worship,
    Brakenbury,
You may partake of any thing we say:
We speak no treason, man: we say the king   90
Is wise and virtuous, and his noble queen
Well struck in years, fair, and not jealous;
We say that Shore's wife hath a pretty foot,
A cherry lip, a bonny eye, a passing pleasing
    tongue;
And that the queen's kin are made gentle-folks:
How say you, sir? can you deny all this?
BRAKENBURY. With this, my lord, myself have nought
    to do.
GLOUCESTER. Naught to do with Mistress Shore! I
    tell thee fellow,
He that doth naught with her (excepting one)
Were best to do it secretly, alone.   100
BRAKENBURY. What one, my lord?

GLOUCESTER. Her husband, knave: wouldst thou
    betray me?
BRAKENBURY. I do beseech your grace to pardon me:
    Forbear your conference with the noble duke.
CLARENCE. We know thy charge, Brakenbury, and
    will obey.
GLOUCESTER. We are the queen's abjects, and must
    obey.
    Brother, farewell: I will unto the king;
    And whatsoe'er you will employ me in,
    Were it to call King Edward's widow sister,
    I will perform it to enfranchise you.   110
    Meantime, this deep disgrace in brotherhood
    Touches me nearer than you can imagine.
CLARENCE. I know it pleaseth neither of us well.
GLOUCESTER. Well, your imprisonment shall not be
    long;
    I will deliver you, or else lie for you:
    Meantime, have patience.
CLARENCE.   I must perforce. Farewell.
    Clarence, Brakenbury, and the Guard go
GLOUCESTER. Go, tread the path that thou shalt ne'er
    return:
    Simple, plain Clarence, I do love thee so,
    That I will shortly send thy soul to heaven,
    If heaven will take the present at our hands.   120
    But who comes here? the new-deliveréd Hastings?

Enter Lord Hastings

HASTINGS. Good time of day unto my gracious lord!
GLOUCESTER. As much unto my good Lord
    Chamberlain!
    Well are you welcome to the open air.
    How hath your lordship brooked imprisonment?
HASTINGS. With patience, noble lord, as prisoners
    must:
    But I shall live, my lord, to give them thanks
    That were the cause of my imprisonment.
GLOUCESTER. No doubt, no doubt; and so shall
    Clarence too;
    For they that were your enemies are his,   130
    And have prevailed as much on him as you.
HASTINGS. More pity that the eagles should be
    mewed,
    Whiles kites and buzzards prey at liberty.
GLOUCESTER. What news abroad?
HASTINGS. No news so bad abroad as this at home:
    The king is sickly, weak, and melancholy,
    And his physicians fear him mightily.
GLOUCESTER. Now, by Saint John, that news is bad
    indeed.
    O, he hath kept an evil diet long,
    And overmuch consumed his royal person: 140
    'Tis very grievous to be thought upon.
    Where is he, in his bed?
HASTINGS. He is.
GLOUCESTER. Go you before, and I will follow you.
    Hastings departs
    He cannot live, I hope; and must not die
    Till George be packed with post-horse up to
    heaven.
    I'll in, to urge his hatred more to Clarence
    With lies well steeled with weighty arguments;
    And, if I fail not in my deep intent,
    Clarence hath not another day to live: 150
    Which done, God take King Edward to his mercy,

And leave the world for me to bustle in!
For then I'll marry Warwick's youngest daughter.
What though I killed her husband and her father?
The readiest way to make the wench amends
Is to become her husband and her father:
The which will I; not all so much for love
As for another secret close intent
By marrying her which I must reach unto.
But yet I run before my horse to market: 160
Clarence still breathes; Edward still lives and reigns:
When they are gone, then must I count my gains.
                             He goes

Scene 2

*Enter the corpse of Henry the Sixth, with halberds to
guard it; Lady Anne being the mourner attended by
Tressel and Berkeley*

ANNE. Set down, set down your honourable load—
    If honour may be shrouded in a hearse—
    Whilst I awhile obsequiously lament
    Th'untimely fall of virtuous Lancaster.
    Poor key-cold figure of a holy king!
    Pale ashes of the house of Lancaster!
    Thou bloodless remnant of that royal blood!
    Be it lawful that I invocate thy ghost,
    To hear the lamentations of poor Anne,
    Wife to thy Edward, to thy slaught'red son,   10
    Stabbed by the selfsame hand that made these
    wounds!
    Lo, in these windows that let forth thy life
    I pour the helpless balm of my poor eyes.
    O curséd be the hand that made these holes!
    Curséd the blood that let this blood from hence!
    Curséd the heart that had the heart to do it!
    More direful hap betide that hated wretch
    That makes us wretched by the death of thee
    Than I can wish to wolves—to spiders, toads,
    Or any creeping venomed thing that lives!   20
    If ever he have child, abortive be it,
    Prodigious, and untimely brought to light,
    Whose ugly and unnatural aspect
    May fright the hopeful mother at the view;
    And that be heir to his unhappiness!
    If ever he have wife, let her be made
    More miserable by the life of him
    Than I am by my young lord's death and thee!
    Come, now towards Chertsey with your holy load,
    Taken from Paul's to be interréd there;   30
    And still, as you are weary of this weight,
    Rest you, whiles I lament King Henry's corse.

Enter Richard, Duke of Gloucester

GLOUCESTER. Stay, you that bear the corse, and set it
    down.
ANNE. What black magician conjures up this fiend,
    To stop devoted charitable deeds?
GLOUCESTER. Villains, set down the corse; or, by Saint
    Paul,
    I'll make a corse of him that disobeys.
HALBERDIER. My lord, stand back, and let the coffin
    pass.
GLOUCESTER. Unmannered dog! stand thou, when I
    command:
    Advance thy halberd higher than my breast,   40
    Or, by Saint Paul, I'll strike thee to my foot,

And spurn upon thee, beggar, for thy boldness.
ANNE. What, do you tremble? are you all afraid?
  Alas, I blame you not, for you are mortal,
  And mortal eyes cannot endure the devil.
  Avaunt, thou dreadful minister of hell!
  Thou hadst but power over his mortal body,
  His soul thou canst not have; therefore, be gone.
GLOUCESTER. Sweet saint, for charity, be not so curst.
ANNE. Foul devil, for God's sake, hence, and trouble
  us not,   50
  For thou hast made the happy earth thy hell,
  Filled it with cursing cries and deep exclaims.
  If thou delight to view thy heinous deeds,
  Behold this pattern of thy butcheries.
  O, gentlemen, see, see! dead Henry's wounds
  Open their congealed mouths and bleed afresh.
  Blush, blush, thou lump of foul deformity;
  For 'tis thy presence that exhales this blood
  From cold and empty veins, where no blood dwells;
  Thy deeds, inhuman and unnatural,   60
  Provokes this deluge most unnatural.
  O God, which this blood mad'st, revenge his death!
  O earth, which this blood drink'st, revenge his
  death!
  Either, heaven, with lightning strike the murd'rer
  dead,
  Or earth, gape open wide and eat him quick,
  As thou dost swallow up this good king's blood,
  Which his hell-governed arm hath butcheréd!
GLOUCESTER. Lady, you know no rules of charity,
  Which renders good for bad, blessings for curses.
ANNE. Villain, thou know'st no law of God nor man.   70
  No beast so fierce but knows some touch of pity.
GLOUCESTER. But I know none, and therefore am no
  beast.
ANNE. O wonderful, when devils tell the truth!
GLOUCESTER. More wonderful, when angels are so
  angry.
  Vouchsafe, divine perfection of a woman,
  Of these supposéd crimes, to give me leave,
  By circumstance, but to acquit myself.
ANNE. Vouchsafe, diffused infection of a man,
  Of these known evils, but to give me leave,
  By circumstance, to accuse thy curséd self.   80
GLOUCESTER. Fairer than tongue can name thee, let me
  have
  Some patient leisure to excuse myself.
ANNE. Fouler than heart can think thee, thou canst
  make
  No excuse current but to hang thyself.
GLOUCESTER. By such despair, I should accuse myself.
ANNE. And, by despairing, shalt thou stand excused
  For doing worthy vengeance on thyself
  That didst unworthy slaughter upon others.
GLOUCESTER. Say that I slew them not?
ANNE.   Then say they were not slain:
  But dead they are, and, devilish slave, by thee.   90
GLOUCESTER. I did not kill your husband.
ANNE.   Why, then he is alive.
GLOUCESTER. Nay, he is dead; and slain by Edward's
  hands.
ANNE. In thy foul throat thou liest: Queen Margaret
  saw
  Thy murd'rous falchion smoking in his blood;
  The which thou once didst bend against her breast,
  But that thy brothers beat aside the point.

GLOUCESTER. I was provokéd by her sland'rous
  tongue,
  That laid their guilt upon my guiltless shoulders.
ANNE. Thou wast provokéd by thy bloody mind,
  That never dream'st on aught but butcheries: 100
  Didst thou not kill this king?
GLOUCESTER.   I grant ye.
ANNE. Dost grant me, hedgehog? then, God grant me
  too
  Thou mayst be damnéd for that wicked deed!
  O, he was gentle, mild, and virtuous!
GLOUCESTER. The better for the King of heaven, that
  hath him.
ANNE. He is in heaven, where thou shalt never come.
GLOUCESTER. Let him thank me, that holp to send him
  thither;
  For he was fitter for that place than earth.
ANNE. And thou unfit for any place but hell.
GLOUCESTER. Yes, one place else, if you will hear me
  name it.   110
ANNE. Some dungeon.
GLOUCESTER.   Your bed-chamber.
ANNE. Ill rest betide the chamber where thou liest!
GLOUCESTER. So will it, madam, till I lie with you.
ANNE. I hope so.
GLOUCESTER.   I know so. But, gentle Lady Anne,
  To leave this keen encounter of our wits,
  And fall something into a slower method,
  Is not the causer of the timeless deaths
  Of these Plantagenets, Henry and Edward,
  As blameful as the executioner?
ANNE. Thou wast the cause of that accursed effect.   120
GLOUCESTER. Your beauty was the cause of that effect;
  Your beauty, that did haunt me in my sleep
  To undertake the death of all the world,
  So I might live one hour in your sweet bosom.
ANNE. If I thought that, I tell thee, homicide,
  These nails should rend that beauty from my cheeks.
GLOUCESTER. These eyes could not endure that
  beauty's wrack;
  You should not blemish it, if I stood by:
  As all the world is cheeréd by the sun,
  So I by that; it is my day, my life.   130
ANNE. Black night o'ershade thy day, and death thy
  life!
GLOUCESTER. Curse not thyself, fair creature; thou art
  both.
ANNE. I would I were, to be revenged on thee.
GLOUCESTER. It is a quarrel most unnatural,
  To be revenged on him that loveth thee.
ANNE. It is a quarrel just and reasonable,
  To be revenged on him that killed my husband.
GLOUCESTER. He that bereft thee, lady, of thy
  husband,
  Did it to help thee to a better husband.
ANNE. His better doth not breathe upon the earth.   140
GLOUCESTER. He lives that loves thee better than he
  could.
ANNE. Name him.
GLOUCESTER.   Plantagenet.
ANNE.   Why, that was he.
GLOUCESTER. The selfsame name, but one of better
  nature.
ANNE. Where is he?
GLOUCESTER.   Here. [she spits at him] Why
  dost thou spit at me?

ANNE. Would it were mortal poison, for thy sake!
GLOUCESTER. Never came poison from so sweet a
place.
ANNE. Never hung poison on a fouler toad.
Out of my sight! thou dost infect mine eyes.
GLOUCESTER. Thine eyes, sweet lady, have infected
mine.
ANNE. Would they were basilisks to strike thee dead! 150
GLOUCESTER. I would they were, that I might die at
once;
For now they kill me with a living death.
Those eyes of thine from mine have drawn salt
tears,
Shamed their aspects with store of childish drops:
These eyes, which never shed remorseful tear,
No, when my father York and Edward wept,
To hear the piteous moan that Rutland made
When black-faced Clifford shook his sword at him;
Nor when thy warlike father, like a child,
Told the sad story of my father's death,   160
And twenty times made pause to sob and weep
That all the standers-by had wet their cheeks
Like trees bedashed with rain—in that sad time
My manly eyes did scorn an humble tear;
And what these sorrows could not thence exhale
Thy beauty hath, and made them blind with
weeping.
I never sued to friend nor enemy;
My tongue could never learn sweet smoothing
word;
But, now thy beauty is proposed my fee,
My proud heart sues, and prompts my tongue to
speak.   *She looks scornfully at him* 170
Teach not thy lip such scorn, for it was made
For kissing, lady, not for such contempt.
If thy revengeful heart cannot forgive,
Lo, here I lend thee this sharp-pointed sword;
Which if thou please to hide in this true breast,
And let the soul forth that adoreth thee,
I lay it naked to the deadly stroke,
And humbly beg the death upon my knee.
          He lays his breast open: she offers
                 at it with his sword
Nay, do not pause; for I did kill King Henry,
But 'twas thy beauty that provokéd me.   180
Nay, now dispatch; 'twas I that stabbed young
Edward,
But 'twas thy heavenly face that set me on.
                  She falls the sword
Take up the sword again, or take up me.
ANNE. Arise, dissembler: though I wish thy death,
I will not be thy executioner.
GLOUCESTER. Then bid me kill myself, and I will do it.
ANNE. I have already.
GLOUCESTER.   That was in thy rage:
Speak it again, and even with the word
This hand, which, for thy love, did kill thy love,
Shall, for thy love, kill a far truer love;   190
To both their deaths shalt thou be accessary.
ANNE. I would I knew thy heart.
GLOUCESTER. 'Tis figured in my tongue.
ANNE. I fear me both are false.
GLOUCESTER. Then never was man true.
ANNE. Well, well, put up your sword.
GLOUCESTER. Say, then, my peace is made.
ANNE. That shalt thou know hereafter.

GLOUCESTER. But shall I live in hope?
ANNE. All men, I hope, live so.   200
GLOUCESTER. Vouchsafe to wear this ring.
ANNE. To take is not to give.   *She puts on the ring*
GLOUCESTER. Look how my ring encompasseth thy
finger,
Even so thy breast encloseth my poor heart;
Wear both of them, for both of them are thine.
And if thy poor devoted servant may
But beg one favour at thy gracious hand,
Thou dost confirm his happiness for ever.
ANNE. What is it?
GLOUCESTER. That it may please you leave these sad
designs   210
To him that hath most cause to be a mourner,
And presently repair to Crosby House;
Where, after I have solemnly interred
At Chertsey monast'ry this noble king,
And wet his grave with my repentant tears,
I will with all expedient duty see you:
For divers unknown reasons, I beseech you,
Grant me this boon.
ANNE. With all my heart; and much it joys me too,
To see you are become so penitent.   220
Tressel and Berkeley, go along with me.
GLOUCESTER. Bid me farewell.
ANNE.   'Tis more than you deserve;
But since you teach me how to flatter you,
Imagine I have said farewell already.
        She goes, followed by two of the
                     halberds
GLOUCESTER. Sirs, take up the corse.
HALBERDIER.   Towards Chertsey, noble lord?
GLOUCESTER. No, to Whitefriars; there attend my
coming.   *They carry away the corpse*
Was ever woman in this humour wooed?
Was ever woman in this humour won?
I'll have her; but I will not keep her long.
What! I, that killed her husband and his father,   230
To take her in her heart's extremest hate,
With curses in her mouth, tears in her eyes,
The bleeding witness of my hatred by;
Having God, her conscience, and these bars against
me,
And I no friends to back my suit at all,
But the plain devil and dissembling looks,
And yet to win her! all the world to nothing!
Ha!
Hath she forgot already that brave prince,
Edward, her lord, whom I, some three months
since,   240
Stabbed in my angry mood at Tewkesbury?
A sweeter and a lovelier gentleman—
Framed in the prodigality of nature,
Young, valiant, wise, and, no doubt, right royal—
The spacious world cannot again afford:
And will she yet abase her eyes on me,
That cropped the golden prime of this sweet prince,
And made her widow to a woeful bed?
On me, whose all not equals Edward's moiety?
On me, that halts and am misshapen thus?   250
My dukedom to a beggarly denier,
I do mistake my person all this while:
Upon my life, she finds, although I cannot,
Myself to be a marv'llous proper man.
I'll be at charges for a looking-glass,

And entertain a score or two of tailors,
To study fashions to adorn my body:
Since I am crept in favour with myself,
I will maintain it with some little cost.
But first I'll turn yon fellow in his grave;   260
And then return lamenting to my love.
Shine out, fair sun, till I have bought a glass,
That I may see my shadow as I pass.   *He goes*

Scene 3: *London. The palace*

Enter the Queen Mother, Lord Rivers, and Lord Grey

RIVERS. Have patience, madam: there's no doubt his
majesty
Will soon recover his accustomed health.
GREY. In that you brook it ill, it makes him worse:
Therefore, for God's sake, entertain good comfort,
And cheer his grace with quick and merry eyes.
QUEEN ELIZABETH. If he were dead, what would betide
on me?
GREY. No other harm but loss of such a lord.
QUEEN ELIZABETH. The loss of such a lord includes all
harms.
GREY. The heavens have blessed you with a goodly
son,
To be your comforter when he is gone.   10
QUEEN ELIZABETH. Ah, he is young, and his minority
Is put unto the trust of Richard Gloucester,
A man that loves not me, nor none of you.
RIVERS. Is it concluded he shall be Protector?
QUEEN ELIZABETH. It is determined, not concluded yet:
But so it must be, if the king miscarry.

Enter Buckingham and Stanley, Earl of Derby

GREY. Here come the lords of Buckingham and
Derby.
BUCKINGHAM. Good time of day unto your royal
grace!
STANLEY. God make your majesty joyful as you have
been!
QUEEN ELIZABETH. The Countess Richmond, good
my Lord of Derby,
To your good prayer will scarcely say amen.   20
Yet, Derby, notwithstanding she's your wife,
And loves not me, be you, good lord, assured
I hate not you for her proud arrogance.
STANLEY. I do beseech you, either not believe
The envious slanders of her false accusers,
Or if she be accused on true report,
Bear with her weakness, which I think proceeds
From wayward sickness, and no grounded malice.
QUEEN ELIZABETH. Saw you the king to-day, my Lord
of Derby?   30
STANLEY. But now the Duke of Buckingham and I
Are come from visiting his majesty.
QUEEN ELIZABETH. What likelihood of his
amendment, lords?
BUCKINGHAM. Madam, good hope; his grace speaks
cheerfully.
QUEEN ELIZABETH. God grant him health! Did you
confer with him?
BUCKINGHAM. Ay, madam: he desires to make
atonement
Between the Duke of Gloucester and your brothers,
And between them and my Lord Chamberlain;
And sent to warn them to his royal presence.

QUEEN ELIZABETH. Would all were well! but that will
never be: 40
I fear our happiness is at the height.

Enter Gloucester, Hastings, and Derby

GLOUCESTER. They do me wrong, and I will not
endure it.
Who is it that complains unto the king,
That I, forsooth, am stern and love them not?
By holy Paul, they love his grace but lightly
That fill his ears with such dissentious rumours.
Because I cannot flatter and look fair,
Smile in men's faces, smooth, deceive and cog,
Duck with French nods and apish courtesy,
I must be held a rancorous enemy.   50
Cannot a plain man live and think no harm,
But thus his simple truth must be abused
With silken, sly, insinuating Jacks?
GREY. To whom in all this presence speaks your grace?
GLOUCESTER. To thee, that hast nor honesty nor grace.
When have I injured thee? when done thee wrong?
Or thee? or thee? or any of your faction?
A plague upon you all! His royal grace
(Whom God preserve better than you would wish!)
Cannot be quiet scarce a breathing while,   60
But you must trouble him with lewd complaints.
QUEEN ELIZABETH. Brother of Gloucester, you
mistake the matter.
The king, on his own royal disposition
(And not provoked by any suitor else),
Aiming, belike, at your interior hatred,
That in your outward action shows itself
Against my children, brothers, and myself,
Makes him to send, that he may learn the ground
Of your ill-will, and thereby to remove it.
GLOUCESTER. I cannot tell: the world is grown so bad, 70
That wrens make prey where eagles dare not perch:
Since every Jack became a gentleman,
There's many a gentle person made a Jack.
QUEEN ELIZABETH. Come, come, we know your
meaning, brother Gloucester;
You envy my advancement and my friends':
God grant we never may have need of you!
GLOUCESTER. Meantime, God grants that I have need
of you:
Our brother is imprisoned by your means,
Myself disgraced, and the nobility
Held in contempt, while great promotions   80
Are daily given to ennoble those
That scarce some two days since were worth a
noble.
QUEEN ELIZABETH. By Him that raised me to this
careful height
From that contented hap which I enjoyed,
I never did incense his majesty
Against the Duke of Clarence, but have been
An earnest advocate to plead for him.
My lord, you do me shameful injury,
Falsely to draw me in these vile suspects.
GLOUCESTER. You may deny that you were not the
mean   90
Of my Lord Hastings' late imprisonment.
RIVERS. She may, my lord, for—
GLOUCESTER. She may, Lord Rivers! why, who
knows not so?
She may do more, sir, than denying that:

She may help you to many fair preferments
And then deny her aiding hand therein,
And lay those honours on your high desert.
What may she not? She may—ay, marry, may
  she—
RIVERS. What, marry, may she?
GLOUCESTER. What, marry, may she! Marry with a
  king,   100
A bachelor, and a handsome stripling too:
Iwis your grandam had a worser match.
QUEEN ELIZABETH. My Lord of Gloucester, I have too
  long borne
Your blunt upbraidings and your bitter scoffs:
By heaven, I will acquaint his majesty
Of those gross taunts that oft I have endured.
I had rather be a country servant-maid
Than a great queen, with this condition,
To be so baited, scorned, and storméd at.

Enter old Queen Margaret, behind

Small joy have I in being England's queen.   110
QUEEN MARGARET [*aside*]. And less'néd be that small,
  God I beseech him!
Thy honour, state, and seat is due to me.
GLOUCESTER. What! threat you me with telling of the
  king?
Tell him, and spare not: look what I have said
I will avouch't in presence of the king:
I dare adventure to be sent to th'Tower.
'Tis time to speak; my pains are quite forgot.
QUEEN MARGARET [*aside*]. Out, devil! I do remember
  them too well:
Thou kill'dst my husband Henry in the Tower,
And Edward, my poor son, at Tewkesbury.   120
GLOUCESTER. Ere you were queen, ay, or your
  husband king,
I was a pack-horse in his great affairs;
A weeder-out of his proud adversaries,
A liberal rewarder of his friends:
To royalise his blood I spent mine own.
QUEEN MARGARET [*aside*]. Ay, and much better blood
  than his or thine.
GLOUCESTER. In all which time you and your husband
  Grey
Were factious for the house of Lancaster;
And, Rivers, so were you. Was not your husband
In Margaret's battle at Saint Albans slain?   130
Let me put in your minds, if you forget,
What you have been ere this, and what you are;
Withal, what I have been, and what I am.
QUEEN MARGARET [*aside*]. A murd'rous villain, and so
  still thou art.
GLOUCESTER. Poor Clarence did forsake his father,
  Warwick;
Ay, and forswore himself,—which Jesu pardon!—
QUEEN MARGARET [*aside*]. Which God revenge!
GLOUCESTER. To fight on Edward's party for the
  crown;
And for his meed, poor lord, he is mewed up.
I would to God my heart were flint, like Edward's,   140
Or Edward's soft and pitiful, like mine:
I am too childish-foolish for this world.
QUEEN MARGARET [*aside*]. Hie thee to hell for shame
  and leave this world,
Thou cacodemon! there thy kingdom is.
RIVERS. My Lord of Gloucester, in those busy days

Which here you urge to prove us enemies,
We followed then our lord, our sovereign king:
So should we you, if you should be our king.
GLOUCESTER. If I should be! I had rather be a pedlar:
Far be it from my heart, the thought thereof!   150
QUEEN ELIZABETH. As little joy, my lord, as you
  suppose
You should enjoy, were you this country's king,
As little joy you may suppose in me
That I enjoy, being the queen thereof.
QUEEN MARGARET [*aside*]. As little joy enjoys the queen
  thereof;
For I am she, and altogether joyless
I can no longer hold me patient. *Aloud, advancing*
Hear me, you wrangling pirates, that fall out
In sharing that which you have pilled from me!
Which of you trembles not that looks on me?   160
If not that I am queen you bow like subjects,
Yet that, by you deposed, you quake like rebels?
Ah, gentle villain, do not turn away!
GLOUCESTER. Foul wrinkléd witch, what mak'st thou
  in my sight?
QUEEN MARGARET. But repetition of what thou hast
  marred;
That will I make before I let thee go.
GLOUCESTER. Wert thou not banishéd on pain of
  death?
QUEEN MARGARET. I was; but I do find more pain in
  banishment
Than death can yield me here by my abode.
A husband and a son thou ow'st to me;   170
And thou a kingdom; all of you allegiance:
This sorrow that I have, by right is yours,
And all the pleasures you usurp are mine.
GLOUCESTER. The curse my noble father laid on thee,
When thou didst crown his warlike brows with
  paper
And with thy scorns drew'st rivers from his eyes,
And then, to dry them, gav'st the duke a clout
Steeped in the faultless blood of pretty Rutland—
His curses, then from bitterness of soul
Denounced against thee, are all fall'n upon thee;   180
And God, not we, hath plagued thy bloody deed.
QUEEN ELIZABETH. So just is God, to right the
  innocent.
HASTINGS. O, 'twas the foulest deed to slay that babe,
And the most merciless that e'er was heard of!
RIVERS. Tyrants themselves wept when it was
  reported.
DORSET. No man but prophesied revenge for it.
BUCKINGHAM. Northumberland, then present, wept
  to see it.
QUEEN MARGARET. What! were you snarling all before
  I came,
Ready to catch each other by the throat,
And turn you all your hatred now on me?   190
Did York's dread curse prevail so much with heaven
That Henry's death, my lovely Edward's death,
Their kingdom's loss, my woeful banishment,
Should all but answer for that peevish brat?
Can curses pierce the clouds and enter heaven?
Why, then, give way, dull clouds, to my quick
  curses!
Though not by war, by surfeit die your king,
As ours, by murder, to make him a king!
Edward thy son, that now is Prince of Wales,

For Edward our son, that was Prince of Wales,   200
Die in his youth by like untimely violence!
Thyself a queen, for me that was a queen,
Outlive thy glory, like my wretched self!
Long mayst thou live to wail thy children's death;
And see another, as I see thee now,
Decked in thy rights, as thou art stalled in mine!
Long die thy happy days before thy death;
And, after many length'ned hours of grief,
Die neither mother, wife, nor England's queen!
Rivers and Dorset, you were standers by,   210
And so wast thou, Lord Hastings, when my son
Was stabbed with bloody daggers: God I pray him,
That none of you may live his natural age,
But by some unlooked accident cut off!

GLOUCESTER. Have done thy charm, thou hateful
    withered hag!

QUEEN MARGARET. And leave out thee? stay, dog, for
    thou shalt hear me.
If heaven have any grievous plague in store
Exceeding those that I can wish upon thee,
O, let them keep it till thy sins be ripe,
And then hurl down their indignation   220
On thee, the troubler of the poor world's peace!
The worm of conscience still begnaw thy soul!
Thy friends suspect for traitors while thou liv'st,
And take deep traitors for thy dearest friends!
No sleep close up that deadly eye of thine,
Unless it be while some tormenting dream
Affrights thee with a hell of ugly devils!
Thou elvish-marked, abortive, rooting hog!
Thou that wast sealed in thy nativity
The slave of nature and the son of hell!   230
Thou slander of thy heavy mother's womb!
Thou loathéd issue of thy father's loins!
Thou rag of honour! thou detested—

GLOUCESTER. Margaret.

QUEEN MARGARET.   Richard!

GLOUCESTER.   Ha?

QUEEN MARGARET.   I call thee not.

GLOUCESTER. I cry thee mercy then, for I did think
    That thou hadst called me all these bitter names.

QUEEN MARGARET. Why, so I did, but looked for no
    reply.
O, let me make the period to my curse!

GLOUCESTER. 'Tis done by me, and ends in 'Margaret'.

QUEEN ELIZABETH. Thus have you breathed your curse
    against yourself.   240

QUEEN MARGARET. Poor painted queen, vain flourish
    of my fortune!
Why strew'st thou sugar on that bottled spider,
Whose deadly web ensnareth thee about?
Fool, fool! thou whet'st a knife to kill thyself.
The day will come that thou shalt wish for me
To help thee curse this poisonous bunch-backed
    toad.

HASTINGS. False-boding woman, end thy frantic
    curse,
Lest to thy harm thou move our patience.

QUEEN MARGARET. Foul shame upon you! you have all
    moved mine.

RIVERS. Were you well served, you would be taught
    your duty.   250

QUEEN MARGARET. To serve me well, you all should
    do me duty,
Teach me to be your queen, and you my subjects:

O, serve me well, and teach yourselves that duty!

DORSET. Dispute not with her; she is lunatic.

QUEEN MARGARET. Peace, master marquis, you are
    malapert:
Your fire-new stamp of honour is scarce current.
O, that your young nobility could judge
What 'twere to lose it, and be miserable!
They that stand high have many blasts to shake
    them;
And if they fall, they dash themselves to pieces.   260

GLOUCESTER. Good counsel, marry: learn it, learn it,
    marquis.

DORSET. It touches you, my lord, as much as me.

GLOUCESTER. Ay, and much more: but I was born so
    high,
Our aery buildeth in the cedar's top,
And dallies with the wind, and scorns the sun.

QUEEN MARGARET. And turns the sun to shade; alas!
    alas!
Witness my son, now in the shade of death;
Whose bright out-shining beams thy cloudy wrath
Hath in eternal darkness folded up.
Your aery buildeth in our aery's nest.   270
O God, that seest it, do not suffer it;
As it is won with blood, lost be it so!

GLOUCESTER. Peace, peace! for shame, if not for
    charity.

QUEEN MARGARET. Urge neither charity nor shame to
    me:
Uncharitably with me have you dealt,
And shamefully my hopes by you are butchered.
My charity is outrage, life my shame;
And in that shame still live my sorrow's rage!

BUCKINGHAM. Have done, have done.

QUEEN MARGARET. O princely Buckingham, I'll kiss
    thy hand,   280
In sign of league and amity with thee:
Now fair befall thee and thy noble house!
Thy garments are not spotted with our blood,
Nor thou within the compass of my curse.

BUCKINGHAM. Nor no one here; for curses never pass
The lips of those that breathe them in the air.

QUEEN MARGARET. I will not think but they ascend the
    sky,
And there awake God's gentle-sleeping peace.
[aside] O Buckingham, take heed of yonder dog!
Look when he fawns, he bites; and when he bites,   290
His venom tooth will rankle to the death:
Have not to do with him, beware of him;
Sin, death, and hell have set their marks on him,
And all their ministers attend on him.

GLOUCESTER. What doth she say, my Lord of
    Buckingham?

BUCKINGHAM. Nothing that I respect, my gracious
    lord.

QUEEN MARGARET. What, dost thou scorn me for my
    gentle counsel?
And soothe the devil that I warn thee from?
O, but remember this another day,
When he shall split thy very heart with sorrow,   300
And say poor Margaret was a prophetess.
Live each of you the subjects to his hate,
And he to yours, and all of you to God's!
                                        She goes

HASTINGS. My hair doth stand an end to hear her
    curses.

RIVERS. And so doth mine: I muse why she's at liberty.

GLOUCESTER. I cannot blame her: by God's holy mother,
She hath had too much wrong; and I repent
My part thereof that I have done to her.

QUEEN ELIZABETH. I never did her any, to my knowledge.

GLOUCESTER. Yet you have all the vantage of her wrong.
I was too hot to do somebody good,
That is too cold in thinking of it now.
Marry, for Clarence, he is well repaid;
He is franked up to fatting for his pains:
God pardon them that are the cause thereof!

RIVERS. A virtuous and a Christian-like conclusion,
To pray for them that have done scathe to us!

GLOUCESTER. So do I ever—[speaks to himself] being well advised,
For had I cursed now, I had cursed myself.

Enter Catesby

CATESBY. Madam, his majesty doth call for you;   320
And for your grace; and you, my gracious lords.

QUEEN ELIZABETH. Catesby, I come. Lords, will you go with me?

RIVERS. We wait upon your grace.
                     All but Gloucester go

GLOUCESTER. I do the wrong, and first begin to brawl.
The secret mischiefs that I set abroach
I lay unto the grievous charge of others.
Clarence, whom I, indeed, have cast in darkness,
I do beweep to many simple gulls;
Namely to Derby, Hastings, Buckingham;
And tell them 'tis the queen and her allies   330
That stir the king against the duke my brother.
Now, they believe it; and withal whet me
To be revenged on Rivers, Dorset, Grey:
But then I sigh; and, with a piece of Scripture,
Tell them that God bids us do good for evil:
And thus I clothe my naked villany
With odd old ends stol'n forth of Holy Writ;
And seem a saint, when most I play the devil.

Enter two Murderers

But soft! here come my executioners.
How now, my hardy stout resolvéd mates!
Are you now going to dispatch this thing?

I MURDERER. We are, my lord, and come to have the warrant,   340
That we may be admitted where he is.

GLOUCESTER. Well thought upon, I have it here about me.   *Gives the warrant*
When you have done, repair to Crosby Place.
But, sirs, be sudden in the execution,
Withal obdurate, do not hear him plead;
For Clarence is well-spoken, and perhaps
May move your hearts to pity, if you mark him.

I MURDERER. Tut, tut, my lord, we will not stand to prate;   350
Talkers are no good doers: be assured
We go to use our hands and not our tongues.

GLOUCESTER. Your eyes drop millstones, when fools' eyes fall tears.
I like you, lads: about your business straight.
Go, go, dispatch.

I MURDERER.   We will, my noble lord.
                         They go

Scene 4: *London. The Tower*

Enter Clarence and Brakenbury

BRAKENBURY. Why looks your grace so heavily to-day?

CLARENCE. O, I have passed a miserable night,   310
So full of fearful dreams, of ugly sights,
That, as I am a Christian faithful man,
I would not spend another such a night,
Though 'twere to buy a world of happy days,
So full of dismal terror was the time!

BRAKENBURY. What was your dream, my lord? I pray you tell me.

CLARENCE. Methoughts that I had broken from the Tower,
And was embarked to cross to Burgundy,   10
And in my company my brother Gloucester,
Who from my cabin tempted me to walk
Upon the hatches. Thence we looked toward England,
And cited up a thousand heavy times,
During the wars of York and Lancaster
That had befall'n us. As we paced along
Upon the giddy footing of the hatches,
Methought that Gloucester stumbled, and in falling
Struck me, that thought to stay him, overboard,
Into the tumbling billows of the main.   20
O Lord, methought what pain it was to drown!
What dreadful noise of waters in mine ears!
What sights of ugly death within mine eyes!
Methoughts I saw a thousand fearful wracks;
A thousand men that fishes gnawed upon;
Wedges of gold, great ingots, heaps of pearl,
Inestimable stones, unvalued jewels,
All scatt'red in the bottom of the sea.
Some lay in dead men's skulls; and in the holes
Where eyes did once inhabit there were crept,   30
As 'twere in scorn of eyes, reflecting gems,
That wooed the slimy bottom of the deep,
And mocked the dead bones that lay scatt'red by.

BRAKENBURY. Had you such leisure in the time of death
To gaze upon these secrets of the deep?

CLARENCE. Methought I had; and often did I strive
To yield the ghost: but still the envious flood
Stopped in my soul, and would not let it forth
To find the empty, vast, and wand'ring air;
But smothered it within my panting bulk,   40
Who almost burst to belch it in the sea.

BRAKENBURY. Awaked you not in this sore agony?

CLARENCE. No, no, my dream was lengthened after life.
O, then began the tempest to my soul.
I passed, methought, the melancholy flood,
With that sour ferryman which poets write of,
Unto the kingdom of perpetual night.
The first that there did greet my stranger soul,
Was my great father-in-law, renownéd Warwick;
Who spake aloud, 'What scourge for perjury   50
Can this dark monarchy afford false Clarence?'
And so he vanished. Then came wand'ring by
A shadow like an angel, with bright hair
Dabbled in blood, and he shrieked out aloud,

'Clarence is come; false, fleeting, perjured Clarence,
That stabbed me in the field by Tewkesbury:
Seize on him, Furies, take him unto torment!'
With that, methought, a legion of foul fiends
Environed me, and howlèd in mine ears
Such hideous cries that with the very noise   60
I trembling waked, and for a season after
Could not believe but that I was in hell,
Such terrible impression made my dream.
BRAKENBURY. No marvel, lord, though it affrighted
    you;
    I am afraid, methinks, to hear you tell it.
CLARENCE. Ah, Keeper, Keeper, I have done these
    things,
That now give evidence against my soul,
For Edward's sake, and see how he requits me!
O God! if my deep prayers cannot appease thee,
But thou wilt be avenged on my misdeeds,   70
Yet execute thy wrath in me alone;
O, spare my guiltless wife and my poor children!
Keeper, I prithee, sit by me awile,
My soul is heavy, and I fain would sleep.
BRAKENBURY. I will, my lord: God give your grace
    good rest!   *Clarence sleeps*
Sorrow breaks seasons and reposing hours,
Makes the night morning and the noon-tide night.
Princes have but their titles for their glories,
An outward honour for an inward toil;
And for unfelt imaginations   80
They often feel a world of restless cares:
So that between their titles and low name
There's nothing differs but the outward fame.

Enter the two Murderers

1 MURDERER. Ho! who's here?
BRAKENBURY. What wouldst thou, fellow? and how
    cam'st thou hither?
1 MURDERER. I would speak with Clarence, and I came
    hither on my legs.
BRAKENBURY. What, so brief?
2 MURDERER. 'Tis better, sir, than to be tedious.   90
    Let him see our commission, and talk no more.
                        Brakenbury reads it
BRAKENBURY. I am in this commanded to deliver
    The noble Duke of Clarence to your hands.
    I will not reason what is meant hereby,
    Because I will be guiltless from the meaning.
    There lies the duke asleep, and there the keys.
    I'll to the king, and signify to him
    That thus I have resigned to you my charge.
1 MURDERER. You may, sir; 'tis a point of wisdom: fare
    you well.   *Brakenbury goes*   100
2 MURDERER. What, shall I stab him as he sleeps?
1 MURDERER. No; he'll say 'twas done cowardly, when
    he wakes.
2 MURDERER. Why, he shall never wake until the great
    judgement-day.
1 MURDERER. Why, then he'll say we stabbed him
    sleeping.
2 MURDERER. The urging of that word 'judgement'
    hath bred a kind of remorse in me.
1 MURDERER. What, art thou afraid?   110
2 MURDERER. Not to kill him, having a warrant; but
    to be damned for killing him, from the which no
    warrant can defend me.
1 MURDERER. I thought thou hadst been resolute.
2 MURDERER. So I am, to let him live.
1 MURDERER. I'll back to the Duke of Gloucester, and
    tell him so.
2 MURDERER. Nay, I prithee, stay a little: I hope this
    passionate humour of mine will change; it was wont
    to hold me but while one tells twenty.   120
1 MURDERER. How dost thou feel thyself now?
2 MURDERER. Faith, some certain dregs of conscience
    are yet within me.
1 MURDERER. Remember our reward when the deed's
    done.
2 MURDERER. Zounds, he dies: I had forgot the reward.
1 MURDERER. Where's thy conscience now?
2 MURDERER. O, in the Duke of Gloucester's purse.
1 MURDERER. When he opens his purse to give us our
    reward, thy conscience flies out.   130
2 MURDERER. 'Tis no matter, let it go; there's few or
    none will entertain it.
1 MURDERER. What if it come to thee again?
2 MURDERER. I'll not meddle with it: it makes a man
    a coward: a man cannot steal, but it accuseth him;
    a man cannot swear, but it checks him; a man cannot
    lie with his neighbour's wife, but it detects him: 'tis
    a blushing shamefaced spirit that mutinies in a man's
    bosom; it fills a man full of obstacles. It made me
    once restore a purse of gold, that (by chance) I   140
    found; it beggars any man that keeps it: it is turned
    out of towns and cities for a dangerous thing: and
    every man that means to live well endeavours to
    trust to himself and live without it.
1 MURDERER. 'Tis even now at my elbow, persuading
    me not to kill the duke.
2 MURDERER. Take the devil in thy mind, and believe
    him not: he would insinuate with thee but to make
    thee sigh.
1 MURDERER. I am strong-framed, he cannot prevail   150
    with me.
2 MURDERER. Spoke like a tall man that respects thy
    reputation. Come, shall we fall to work?
1 MURDERER. Take him on the costard with the hilts
    of thy sword, and then throw him into the
    malmsey-butt in the next room.
2 MURDERER. O excellent device! and make a sop of
    him.
1 MURDERER. Soft! he wakes.
2 MURDERER. Strike!
1 MURDERER. No, we'll reason with him.   160
CLARENCE. Where art thou, Keeper? give me a cup of
    wine.
2 MURDERER. You shall have wine enough, my lord,
    anon.
CLARENCE. In God's name, what art thou?
1 MURDERER. A man, as you are.
CLARENCE. But not, as I am, royal.
2 MURDERER. Nor you, as we are, loyal.
CLARENCE. Thy voice is thunder, but thy looks are
    humble.
1 MURDERER. My voice is now the king's, my looks
    mine own.
CLARENCE. How darkly and how deadly dost thou
    speak!
    Your eyes do menace me: why look you pale?   170
    Who sent you hither? Wherefore do you come?
2 MURDERER. To, to, to—
CLARENCE. To murder me?
BOTH. Ay, ay.

CLARENCE. You scarcely have the hearts to tell me so,
And therefore cannot have the hearts to do it.
Wherein, my friends, have I offended you?
1 MURDERER. Offended us you have not, but the king.
CLARENCE. I shall be reconciled to him again.
2 MURDERER. Never, my lord; therefore prepare to die. 180
CLARENCE. Are you drawn forth, among a world of men
  To slay the innocent? What is my offence?
  Where is the evidence that doth accuse me?
  What lawful quest have given their verdict up
  Unto the frowning judge? or who pronounced
  The bitter sentence of poor Clarence' death?
  Before I be convict by course of law,
  To threaten me with death is most unlawful.
  I charge you, as you hope to have redemption
  By Christ's dear blood shed for our grievous sins, 190
  That you depart and lay no hands on me:
  The deed you undertake is damnable.
1 MURDERER. What we will do, we do upon command.
2 MURDERER. And he that hath commanded is our king.
CLARENCE. Erroneous vassals! the great King of kings
  Hath in the tables of his law commanded
  That thou shalt do no murder: will you then
  Spurn at his edict, and fulfil a man's?
  Take heed; for he holds vengeance in his hand,
  To hurl upon their heads that break his law. 200
2 MURDERER. And that same vengeance doth he hurl on thee,
  For false forswearing, and for murder too:
  Thou didst receive the sacrament to fight
  In quarrel of the house of Lancaster.
1 MURDERER. And, like a traitor to the name of God,
  Didst break that vow, and with thy treacherous blade
  Unrip'st the bowels of thy sov'reign's son.
2 MURDERER. Whom thou wast sworn to cherish and defend.
1 MURDERER. How canst thou urge God's dreadful law to us,
  When thou hast broke it in such dear degree? 210
CLARENCE. Alas! for whose sake did I that ill deed?
  For Edward, for my brother, for his sake.
  He sends you not to murder me for this;
  For in that sin he is as deep as I.
  If God will be avengéd for the deed,
  O, know you, yet he doth it publicly.
  Take not the quarrel from his powerful arm;
  He needs no indirect or lawless course
  To cut off those that have offended him.
1 MURDERER. Who made thee then a bloody minister, 220
  When gallant-springing brave Plantagenet,
  That princely novice, was struck dead by thee?
CLARENCE. My brother's love, the devil, and my rage.
1 MURDERER. Thy brother's love, our duty, and thy faults,
  Provoke us hither now to slaughter thee.
CLARENCE. If you do love my brother, hate not me;
  I am his brother, and I love him well.
  If you are hired, for meed go back again,
  And I will send you to my brother Gloucester,
  Who shall reward you better for my life 230
  Than Edward will for tidings of my death.
2 MURDERER. You are deceived, your brother Gloucester hates you.
CLARENCE. O, no, he loves me, and he holds me dear:
  Go you to him from me.
1 MURDERER.   Ay, so we will.
CLARENCE. Tell him, when that our princely father York
  Blessed his three sons with his victorious arm,
  And charged us from his soul to love each other,
  He little thought of this divided friendship:
  Bid Gloucester think of this, and he will weep.
1 MURDERER. Ay, millstones, as he lessoned us to weep. 240
CLARENCE. O, do not slander him, for he is kind.
1 MURDERER. As snow in harvest. Come, you deceive yourself:
  'Tis he that sends us to destroy you here.
CLARENCE. It cannot be; for he bewept my fortune,
  And hugged me in his arms, and swore with sobs,
  That he would labour my delivery.
1 MURDERER. Why, so he doth, when he delivers you
  From this earth's thraldom to the joys of heaven.
2 MURDERER. Make peace with God, for you must die, my lord.
CLARENCE. Have you that holy feeling in your souls, 250
  To counsel me to make my peace with God,
  And are you yet to your own souls so blind,
  That you will war with God by murd'ring me?
  O, sirs, consider, they that set you on
  To do this deed will hate you for the deed.
2 MURDERER. What shall we do?
CLARENCE.   Relent, and save your souls.
  Which of you, if you were a prince's son,
  Being pent from liberty, as I am now,
  If two such murderers as yourselves came to you,
  Would not entreat for life? Even so I beg 260
  As you would beg, were you in my distress.
1 MURDERER. Relent! 'tis cowardly and womanish.
CLARENCE. Not to relent is beastly, savage, devilish.
  My friend, [to 2 Murderer] I spy some pity in thy looks;
  O, if thine eye be not a flatterer,
  Come thou on my side, and entreat for me.
  A begging prince what beggar pities not?
2 MURDERER. Look behind you, my lord.
1 MURDERER [stabs him]. Take that, and that: if all this will not do,
  I'll drown you in the malmsey-butt within. 270
                                Drags out the body
2 MURDERER. A bloody deed, and desperately dispatched!
  How fain, like Pilate, would I wash my hands
  Of this most grievous murder!

1 Murderer returns

1 MURDERER. How now! what mean'st thou, that thou help'st me not?
  By heavens, the duke shall know how slack you have been!
2 MURDERER. I would he knew that I had saved his brother!
  Take thou the fee, and tell him what I say,
  For I repent me that the duke is slain.   Goes
1 MURDERER. So do not I: go, coward as thou art.
  Well, I'll go hide the body in some hole, 280
  Till that the duke give order for his burial:
  And when I have my meed, I will away;
  For this will out, and then I must not stay.   Goes

ACT 2
Scene 1: *London. The palace*

Flourish. Enter King Edward sick, borne in a chair, with Queen Elizabeth, Dorset, Rivers, Hastings, Buckingham, Grey, and others.

KING EDWARD. Why, so: now have I done a good
    day's work.
You peers, continue this united league:
I every day expect an embassage
From my Redeemer to redeem me hence;
And more at peace my soul shall part to heaven,
Since I have made my friends at peace on earth.
Hastings and Rivers, take each other's hand;
Dissemble not your hatred, swear your love.

RIVERS. By heaven, my soul is purged from grudging
    hate;
And with my hand I seal my true heart's love.   10

HASTINGS. So thrive I, as I truly swear the like!

KING EDWARD. Take heed you dally not before your
    king;
Lest he that is the supreme King of kings
Confound your hidden falsehood and award
Either of you to be the other's end.

HASTINGS. So prosper I, as I swear perfect love!

RIVERS. And I, as I love Hastings with my heart!

KING EDWARD. Madam, yourself is not exempt from
    this
Nor you, son Dorset; Buckingham, nor you;
You have been factious one against the other.   20
Wife, love Lord Hastings, let him kiss your hand;
And what you do, do it unfeignedly.

QUEEN ELIZABETH. There, Hastings; I will never more
    remember
Our former hatred, so thrive I and mine!

KING EDWARD. Dorset, embrace him; Hastings, love
    lord marquis.

DORSET. This interchange of love, I here protest,
Upon my part shall be inviolable.

HASTINGS. And so swear I.   *They embrace*

KING EDWARD. Now, princely Buckingham, seal thou
    this league
With thy embracements to my wife's allies,   30
And make me happy in your unity.

BUCKINGHAM [*to the Queen*]. Whenever Buckingham
    doth turn his hate
Upon your grace, but with all duteous love
Doth cherish you and yours, God punish me
With hate in those where I expect most love!
When I have most need to employ a friend,
And most assured that he is a friend,
Deep, hollow, treacherous and full of guile,
Be he unto me! this do I beg of God,
When I am cold in love to you or yours.   40
                    They embrace

KING EDWARD. A pleasing cordial, princely
    Buckingham,
Is this thy vow unto my sickly heart.
There wanteth now our brother Gloucester here,
To make the blessed period of this peace.

BUCKINGHAM. And in good time,
Here comes sir Richard Ratcliffe and the duke.

Enter Gloucester and Ratcliffe

GLOUCESTER. Good morrow to my sovereign king
    and queen;

And, princely peers, a happy time of day!

KING EDWARD. Happy indeed, as we have spent the
    day.
Gloucester, we have done deeds of charity,   50
Made peace of enmity, fair love of hate,
Between these swelling wrong-incensèd peers.

GLOUCESTER. A blessèd labour, my most sovereign
    lord.
Among this princely heap, if any here,
By false intelligence, or wrong surmise,
Hold me a foe; if I unwittingly
Have aught committed that is hardly borne
By any in this presence, I desire
To reconcile me to his friendly peace:
'Tis death to me to be at enmity;   60
I hate it, and desire all good men's love.
First, madam, I entreat true peace of you,
Which I will purchase with my duteous service;
Of you, my noble cousin Buckingham,
If ever any grudge were lodged between us;
Of you, and you, Lord Rivers, and Lord Dorset,
Of you, Lord Woodeville and Lord Scales of you,
That all without desert have frowned on me;
Dukes, earls, lords, gentlemen; indeed, of all.
I do not know that Englishman alive   70
With whom my soul is any jot at odds
More than the infant that is born to-night:
I thank my God for my humility.

QUEEN ELIZABETH. A holy day shall this be kept
    hereafter:
I would to God all strifes were well compounded.
My sovereign lord, I do beseech your highness
To take our brother Clarence to your grace.

GLOUCESTER. Why, madam, have I off'red love for
    this,
To be so flouted in this royal presence?
Who knows not that the gentle duke is dead?   80
                    They all start
You do him injury to scorn his corse.

RIVERS. Who knows not he is dead! who knows he is?

QUEEN ELIZABETH. All-seeing heaven, what a world is
    this!

BUCKINGHAM. Look I so pale, Lord Dorset, as the rest?

DORSET. Ay, my good lord, and no man in the
    presence
But his red colour hath forsook his cheeks.

KING EDWARD. Is Clarence dead? the order was
    reversed.

GLOUCESTER. But he, poor man, by your first order
    died,
And that a wingèd Mercury did bear;
Some tardy cripple bare the countermand   90
That came too lag to see him burièd.
God grant that some, less noble and less loyal,
Nearer in bloody thoughts, but not in blood,
Deserve not worse than wretched Clarence did,
And yet go current from suspicion!

Enter Lord Stanley

STANLEY. A boon, my sovereign, for my service done!

KING EDWARD. I prithee, peace: my soul is full of
    sorrow.

STANLEY. I will not rise, unless your highness hear me.

KING EDWARD. Then say at once what is it thou
    requests.

STANLEY. The forfeit, sovereign, of my servant's life;   100

Who slew to-day a riotous gentleman
Lately attendant on the Duke of Norfolk.
KING EDWARD. Have I a tongue to doom my brother's
      death,
And shall that tongue give pardon to a slave?
My brother killed no man—his fault was thought,
And yet his punishment was bitter death.
Who sued to me for him? who, in my wrath,
Kneeled at my feet and bid me be advised?
Who spoke of brotherhood? who spoke of love?
Who told me how the poor soul did forsake   110
The mighty Warwick, and did fight for me?
Who told me, in the field at Tewkesbury
When Oxford had me down, he rescued me
And said 'Dear brother, live, and be a king'?
Who told me, when we both lay in the field
Frozen almost to death, how he did lap me
Even in his garments, and did give himself,
All thin and naked, to the numb cold night?
All this from my remembrance brutish wrath
Sinfully plucked, and not a man of you   120
Had so much grace to put it in my mind.
But when your carters or your waiting-vassals
Have done a drunken slaughter and defaced
The precious image of our dear Redeemer,
You straight are on your knees for pardon, pardon;
And I, unjustly too, must grant it you.
                              Stanley rises
But for my brother not a man would speak,
Nor I, ungracious, speak unto myself
For him, poor soul. The proudest of you all
Have been beholding to him in his life;   130
Yet none of you would once beg for his life.
O God, I fear thy justice will take hold
On me, and you, and mine, and yours, for this!
Come, Hastings, help me to my closet. Ah, poor
      Clarence!
              He is carried out; Hastings, the Queen,
              Rivers, and Dorset in attendance
GLOUCESTER. This is the fruits of rashness. Marked
      you not
How that the guilty kindred of the queen
Looked pale when they did hear of Clarence' death?
O, they did urge it still unto the king!
God will revenge it. Come, lords, will you go
To comfort Edward with our company?   140
BUCKINGHAM. We wait upon your grace.
                              They follow

                         Scene 2

Enter the old Duchess of York, with the two children of
Clarence

BOY. Good grandam, tell us, is our father dead?
DUCHESS. No, boy.
GIRL. Why do you weep so oft, and beat your breast,
      And cry 'O Clarence, my unhappy son!'?
BOY. Why do you look on us, and shake your head,
      And call us orphans, wretches, castaways,
      If that our noble father were alive?
DUCHESS. My pretty cousins, you mistake me both.
      I do lament the sickness of the king,
      As loath to lose him, not your father's death;   10
      It were lost sorrow to wail one that's lost.
BOY. Then you conclude, my grandam, he is dead.
      The king mine uncle is to blame for it:

God will revenge it, whom I will importune
With earnest prayers, all to that effect.
GIRL. And so will I.
DUCHESS. Peace, children, peace! the king doth love
      you well.
Incapable and shallow innocents,
You cannot guess who caused your father's death.
BOY. Grandam, we can; for my good uncle
      Gloucester   20
Told me the king, provoked to it by the queen,
Devised impeachments to imprison him:
And when my uncle told me so, he wept,
And pitied me, and kindly kissed my cheek;
Bade me rely on him as on my father,
And he would love me dearly as a child.
DUCHESS. Ah, that deceit should steal such gentle
      shape,
And with a virtuous vizor hide deep vice!
He is my son, ay, and therein my shame;
Yet from my dugs he drew not this deceit.   30
BOY. Think you my uncle did dissemble, grandam?
DUCHESS. Ay, boy.
BOY. I cannot think it. Hark! what noise is this?

Enter the Queen with her hair about her ears, Rivers
and Dorset after her

QUEEN ELIZABETH. Ah, who shall hinder me to wail
      and weep,
To chide my fortune and torment myself?
I'll join with black despair against my soul,
And to myself become an enemy.
DUCHESS. What means this scene of rude impatience?
QUEEN ELIZABETH. To mark an act of tragic violence.
Edward, my lord, thy son, our king, is dead.   40
Why grow the branches when the root is gone?
Why wither not the leaves that want their sap?
If you will live, lament; if die, be brief,
That our swift-wingéd souls may catch the king's,
Or, like obedient subjects, follow him
To his new kingdom of ne'er-changing night.
DUCHESS. Ah, so much interest have I in thy sorrow
As I had title in thy noble husband!
I have bewept a worthy husband's death,
And lived with looking on his images: 50
But now two mirrors of his princely semblance
Are cracked in pieces by malignant death,
And I for comfort have but one false glass,
That grieves me when I see my shame in him.
Thou art a widow; yet thou art a mother,
And hast the comfort of thy children left:
But death hath snatched my husband from mine
      arms,
And plucked two crutches from my feeble hands,
Clarence and Edward. O, what cause have I,
Thine being but a moiety of my moan,   60
To overgo thy woes and drown thy cries!
BOY. Ah aunt! you wept not for our father's death,
How can we aid you with our kindred tears?
GIRL. Our fatherless distress was left unmoaned;
Your widow-dolour likewise be unwept!
QUEEN ELIZABETH. Give me no help in lamentation;
I am not barren to bring forth complaints:
All springs reduce their currents to mine eyes,
That I, being governed by the watery moon,
May send forth plenteous tears to drown the world! 70
Ah for my husband, for my dear lord Edward!

CHILDREN. Ah for our father, for our dear Lord
 Clarence!
DUCHESS. Alas for both, both mine, Edward and
 Clarence!
QUEEN ELIZABETH. What stay had I but Edward? and
 he's gone.
CHILDREN. What stay had we but Clarence? and he's
 gone.
DUCHESS. What stays had I but they? and they are
 gone.
QUEEN ELIZABETH. Was never widow had so dear a
 loss.
CHILDREN. Were never orphans had so dear a loss.
DUCHESS. Was never mother had so dear a loss.
 Alas, I am the mother of these griefs!   80
 Their woes are parcelled, mine is general.
 She for an Edward weeps, and so do I;
 I for a Clarence weep, so doth not she:
 These babes for Clarence weep, and so do I;
 I for an Edward weep, so do not they:
 Alas, you three on me, threefold distressed,
 Pour all your tears! I am your sorrow's nurse,
 And I will pamper it with lamentation.
DORSET. Comfort, dear mother: God is much
 displeased
 That you take with unthankfulness his doing: 90
 In common worldly things 'tis called ungrateful
 With dull unwillingness to repay a debt
 Which with a bounteous hand was kindly lent;
 Much more to be thus opposite with heaven,
 For it requires the royal debt it lent you.
RIVERS. Madam, bethink you, like a careful mother,
 Of the young prince your son: send straight for
 him;
 Let him be crowned; in him your comfort lives.
 Drown desperate sorrow in dead Edward's grave,
 And plant your joys in living Edward's throne.   100

*Enter Gloucester, Buckingham, Derby, Hastings, and
Ratcliffe*

GLOUCESTER. Sister, have comfort: all of us have cause
 To wail the dimming of our shining star;
 But none can help our harms by wailing them.
 Madam, my mother, I do cry you mercy;
 I did not see your grace [*he kneels*]. Humbly on my
 knee
 I crave your blessing.
DUCHESS. God bless thee, and put meekness in thy
 breast,
 Love, charity, obedience, and true duty!
GLOUCESTER. Amen! [*aside*] and make me die a good
 old man!
 That is the butt-end of a mother's blessing: 110
 I marvel that her grace did leave it out.
BUCKINGHAM. You cloudy princes and heart-
 sorrowing peers,
 That bear this heavy mutual load of moan,
 Now cheer each other in each other's love:
 Though we have spent our harvest of this king,
 We are to reap the harvest of his son.
 The broken rancour of your high-swoln hearts,
 But lately splintered, knit, and joined together,
 Must gently be preserved, cherished, and kept:
 Me seemeth good that, with some little train,   120
 Forthwith from Ludlow the young prince be fet
 Hither to London, to be crowned our king.

RIVERS. Why with some little train, my Lord of
 Buckingham?
BUCKINGHAM. Marry, my lord, lest by a multitude
 The new-healed wound of malice should break out;
 Which would be so much the more dangerous,
 By how much the estate is green and yet
 ungoverned:
 Where every horse bears his commanding rein,
 And may direct his course as please himself,
 As well the fear of harm as harm apparent,   130
 In my opinion, ought to be prevented.
GLOUCESTER. I hope the king made peace with all of us;
 And the compact is firm and true in me.
RIVERS. And so in me; and so, I think, in all.
 Yet, since it is but green, it should be put
 To no apparent likelihood of breach,
 Which haply by much company might be urged:
 Therefore I say with noble Buckingham
 That it is meet so few should fetch the prince.
HASTINGS. And so say I.   140
GLOUCESTER. Then be it so; and go we to determine
 Who they shall be that straight shall post to Ludlow.
 Madam, and you, my sister, will you go
 To give your censures in this business?
QUEEN ELIZABETH. } With all our hearts.
DUCHESS.

             *All go in but Buckingham and
                               Gloucester*
BUCKINGHAM. My lord, whoever journeys to the
 prince,
 For God sake let not us two stay at home:
 For, by the way, I'll sort occasion,
 As index to the story we late talked of,
 To part the queen's proud kindred from the prince.   50
GLOUCESTER. My other self, my counsel's consistory,
 My oracle, my prophet, my dear cousin!
 I, as a child, will go by thy direction.
 Toward Ludlow then, for we'll not stay behind.
                                        They go

                 Scene 3: *London. A Street*

Enter two Citizens, meeting

1 CITIZEN. Good morrow, neighbour, whither away
 so fast?
2 CITIZEN. I promise you, I scarcely know myself:
 Hear you the news abroad?
1 CITIZEN.   Yes, that the king is dead.
2 CITIZEN. Ill news, by'r lady. Seldom comes the
 better.
 I fear, I fear, 'twill prove a giddy world.

Enter another Citizen

3 CITIZEN. Neighbours, God speed!
1 CITIZEN.   Give you good morrow, sir.
3 CITIZEN. Doth the news hold of good King
 Edward's death?
2 CITIZEN. Ay, sir, it is too true, God help the while!
3 CITIZEN. Then, masters, look to see a troublous
 world.
1 CITIZEN. No, no; by God's good grace his son shall
 reign.   10
3 CITIZEN. Woe to that land that's governed by a
 child!
2 CITIZEN. In him there is a hope of government,
 Which, in his nonage, council under him,

And, in his full and ripened years, himself,
No doubt, shall then, and till then, govern well.
1 CITIZEN. So stood the state when Henry the Sixth
    Was crowned in Paris but at nine months old.
3 CITIZEN. Stood the state so? No, no, good friends,
        God wot;
    For then this land was famously enriched
    With politic grave counsel; then the king   20
    Had virtuous uncles to protect his grace.
1 CITIZEN. Why, so hath this, both by his father and
        mother.
3 CITIZEN. Better it were they all came by his father,
    Or by his father there were none at all;
    For emulation who shall now be nearest,
    Will touch us all too near, if God prevent not.
    O, full of danger is the Duke of Gloucester!
    And the queen's sons and brothers haught and
        proud:
    And were they to be ruled, and not to rule,
    This sickly land might solace as before.   30
1 CITIZEN. Come, come, we fear the worst; all will be
        well.
3 CITIZEN. When clouds are seen, wise men put on
        their cloaks;
    When great leaves fall, then winter is at hand;
    When the sun sets, who doth not look for night?
    Untimely storms makes men expect a dearth.
    All may be well; but, if God sort it so,
    'Tis more than we deserve, or I expect.
2 CITIZEN. Truly, the hearts of men are full of fear:
    You cannot reason almost with a man
    That looks not heavily and full of dread.   40
3 CITIZEN. Before the days of change, still is it so:
    By a divine instinct men's minds mistrust
    Ensuing danger; as by proof we see
    The water swell before a boist'rous storm.
    But leave it all to God. Whither away?
2 CITIZEN. Marry, we were sent for to the justices.
3 CITIZEN. And so was I: I'll bear you company.
                                          They go

Scene 4: *London. The palace*

*Enter the Archbishop of York, the young Duke of York,
Queen Elizabeth, and the Duchess of York*

ARCHBISHOP. Last night, I hear, they lay at Stony
        Stratford;
    And at Northampton they do rest to-night:
    To-morrow, or next day, they will be here.
DUCHESS. I long with all my heart to see the prince:
    I hope he is much grown since last I saw him.
QUEEN ELIZABETH. But I hear, no; they say my son of
        York
    Has almost overta'en him in his growth.
YORK. Ay, mother, but I would not have it so.
DUCHESS. Why, my good cousin, it is good to grow.
YORK. Grandam, one night, as we did sit at supper,   10
    My uncle Rivers talked how I did grow
    More than my brother: 'Ay,' quoth my uncle
        Gloucester,
    'Small herbs have grace, ill weeds do grow apace':
    And since, methinks, I would not grow so fast,
    Because sweet flowers are slow and weeds make
        haste.
DUCHESS. Good faith, good faith, the saying did not
        hold

In him that did object the same to thee:
    He was the wretched'st thing when he was young,
    So long a-growing and so leisurely,
    That, if his rule were true, he should be gracious. 20
ARCHBISHOP. And so, no doubt, he is, my gracious
        madam.
DUCHESS. I hope he is, but yet let mothers doubt.
YORK. Now, by my troth, if I had been rememb'red,
    I could have given my uncle's grace a flout,
    To touch his growth nearer than he touched mine.
DUCHESS. How, my young York? I prithee, let me
        hear it.
YORK. Marry, they say my uncle grew so fast
    That he could gnaw a crust at two hours old:
    'Twas full two years ere I could get a tooth.
    Grandam, this would have been a biting jest.   30
DUCHESS. I prithee, pretty York, who told thee this?
YORK. Grandam, his nurse.
DUCHESS. His nurse! why, she was dead ere thou wast
        born.
YORK. If 'twere not she, I cannot tell who told me.
QUEEN ELIZABETH. A parlous boy: go to, you are too
        shrewd.
ARCHBISHOP. Good madam, be not angry with the
        child.
QUEEN ELIZABETH. Pitchers have ears.

Enter a Messenger

ARCHBISHOP. Here comes a messenger. What news?
MESSENGER. Such news, my lord, as grieves me to
        report.
QUEEN ELIZABETH. How doth the prince?
MESSENGER.   Well, madam, and in health. 40
DUCHESS. What is thy news?
MESSENGER.   Lord Rivers and Lord Grey
    Are sent to Pomfret, and with them
    Sir Thomas Vaughan, prisoners.
DUCHESS. Who hath committed them?
MESSENGER.   The mighty dukes,
    Gloucester and Buckingham.
ARCHBISHOP.   For what offence?
MESSENGER. The sum of all I can, I have disclosed;
    Why or for what the nobles were committed
    Is all unknown to me, my gracious lord.
QUEEN ELIZABETH. Ay me, I see the ruin of my house!
    The tiger now hath seized the gentle hind;   50
    Insulting tyranny begins to jet
    Upon the innocent and aweless throne:
    Welcome, destruction, blood, and massacre!
    I see, as in a map, the end of all.
DUCHESS. Accursed and unquiet wrangling days,
    How many of you have mine eyes beheld!
    My husband lost his life to get the crown;
    And often up and down my sons were tossed,
    For me to joy and weep their gain and loss:
    And being seated, and domestic broils   60
    Clean overblown, themselves, the conquerors,
    Make war upon themselves, brother to brother,
    Blood to blood, self to self! Preposterous
    And frantic outrage, end thy damned spleen;
    Or let me die, to look on death no more!
QUEEN ELIZABETH. Come, come, my boy; we will to
        sanctuary.
    Madam, farewell.
DUCHESS.   Stay, I will go with you.
QUEEN ELIZABETH. You have no cause.

ARCHBISHOP.   My gracious lady, go;
And thither bear your treasure and your goods.
For my part, I'll resign unto your grace   70
The seal I keep: and so betide to me
As well I tender you and all of yours!
Go, I'll conduct you to the sanctuary.   *They go*

ACT 3

Scene 1: *London. A street*

The trumpets sound. Enter the young Prince, the Dukes
of Gloucester and Buckingham, the Lord Cardinal, with
Catesby, and others

BUCKINGHAM. Welcome, sweet prince, to London, to
your chamber.
GLOUCESTER. Welcome, dear cousin, my thoughts'
sovereign:
The weary way hath made you melancholy.
PRINCE. No, uncle; but our crosses on the way
Have made it tedious, wearisome, and heavy:
I want more uncles here to welcome me.
GLOUCESTER. Sweet prince, the untainted virtue of
your years
Hath not yet dived into the world's deceit:
Nor more can you distinguish of a man
Than of his outward show, which, God he knows,   10
Seldom or never jumpeth with the heart.
Those uncles which you want were dangerous;
Your grace attended to their sug'red words,
But looked not on the poison of their hearts:
God keep you from them, and from such false
friends!
PRINCE. God keep me from false friends! but they
were none.
GLOUCESTER. My lord, the Mayor of London comes
to greet you.

Enter Lord Mayor, and his train

MAYOR. God bless your grace with health and happy
days!
PRINCE. I thank you, good my lord, and thank you all.
I thought my mother and my brother York   20
Would long ere this have met us on the way:
Fie, what a slug is Hastings, that he comes not
To tell us whether they will come or no!

Enter Lord Hastings

BUCKINGHAM. And, in good time, here comes the
sweating lord.
PRINCE. Welcome, my lord: what, will our mother
come?
HASTINGS. On what occasion God he knows, not I,
The queen your mother and your brother York
Have taken sanctuary: the tender prince
Would fain have come with me to meet your grace,
But by his mother was perforce withheld.   30
BUCKINGHAM. Fie, what an indirect and peevish course
Is this of hers! Lord Cardinal, will your grace
Persuade the queen to send the Duke of York
Unto his princely brother presently?
If she deny, Lord Hastings, go with him,
And from her jealous arms pluck him perforce.
CARDINAL. My Lord of Buckingham, if my weak
oratory

Can from his mother win the Duke of York,
Expect him here; but if she be obdurate
To mild entreaties, God in heaven forbid   40
We should infringe the holy privilege
Of blessed sanctuary! not for all this land
Would I be guilty of so deep a sin.
BUCKINGHAM. You are too senseless-obstinate, my
lord,
Too ceremonious and traditional:
Weigh it but with the grossness of this age,
You break not sanctuary in seizing him.
The benefit thereof is always granted
To those whose dealings have deserved the place
And those who have the wit to claim the place: 50
This prince hath neither claimed it nor deserved it;
Therefore, in mine opinion, cannot have it:
Then, taking him from thence that is not there,
You break no privilege nor charter there.
Oft have I heard of sanctuary men,
But sanctuary children ne'er till now.
CARDINAL. My lord, you shall o'er-rule my mind for
once.
Come on, Lord Hastings, will you go with me?
HASTINGS. I go, my lord.
PRINCE. Good lords, make all the speedy haste you
may.   *Cardinal and Hastings depart* 60
Say, uncle Gloucester, if our brother come,
Where shall we sojourn till our coronation?
GLOUCESTER. Where it seems best unto your royal
self.
If I may counsel you, some day or two
Your highness shall repose you at the Tower:
Then where you please, and shall be thought most
fit
For your best health and recreation.
PRINCE. I do not like the Tower, of any place.
Did Julius Caesar build that place, my lord?
BUCKINGHAM. He did, my gracious lord, begin that
place;   70
Which, since, succeeding ages have re-edified.
PRINCE. Is it upon record, or else reported
Successively from age to age, he built it?
BUCKINGHAM. Upon record, my gracious lord.
PRINCE. But say, my lord, it were not regist'red,
Methinks the truth should live from age to age,
As 'twere retailed to all posterity,
Even to the general all-ending day.
GLOUCESTER [*aside*]. So wise so young, they say, do
ne'er live long.
PRINCE. What say you, uncle?   80
GLOUCESTER. I say, without characters, fame lives
long.
[*aside*] Thus, like the formal Vice, Iniquity,
I moralize two meanings in one word.
PRINCE. That Julius Caesar was a famous man;
With what his valour did enrich his wit,
His wit set down to make his valour live:
Death makes no conquest of this conqueror,
For now he lives in fame, though not in life.
I'll tell you what, my cousin Buckingham—
BUCKINGHAM. What, my gracious lord?   90
PRINCE. An if I live until I be a man,
I'll win our ancient right in France again,
Or die a soldier, as I lived a king.
GLOUCESTER [*aside*]. Short summers lightly have a
forward spring.

Hastings and the Cardinal return with young York

BUCKINGHAM. Now in good time, here comes the Duke of York.

PRINCE. Richard of York! how fares our loving brother?

YORK. Well, my dread lord; so must I call you now.

PRINCE. Ay, brother, to our grief, as it is yours:
Too late he died that might have kept that title,
Which by his death hath lost much majesty.   100

GLOUCESTER. How fares our cousin, noble Lord of York?

YORK. I thank you, gentle uncle. O, my lord,
You said that idle weeds are fast in growth:
The prince my brother hath outgrown me far.

GLOUCESTER. He hath, my lord.

YORK.   And therefore is he idle?

GLOUCESTER. O, my fair cousin, I must not say so.

YORK. Then he is more beholding to you than I.

GLOUCESTER. He may command me as my sovereign;
But you have power in me as in a kinsman.

YORK. I pray you, uncle, give me this dagger.   110

GLOUCESTER. My dagger, little cousin? with all my heart.

PRINCE. A beggar, brother?

YORK. Of my kind uncle, that I know will give't,
Being but a toy, which is no grief to give.

GLOUCESTER. A greater gift than that I'll give my cousin.

YORK. A greater gift? O, that's the sword to it.

GLOUCESTER. Ay, gentle cousin, were it light enough.

YORK. O, then, I see you'll part but with light gifts;
In weightier things you'll say a beggar nay.

GLOUCESTER. It is too heavy for your grace to wear.   120

YORK. I'd weigh it lightly, were it heavier.

GLOUCESTER. What, would you have my weapon, little lord?

YORK. I would, that I might thank you as you call me.

GLOUCESTER. How?

YORK. Little.

PRINCE. My Lord of York will still be cross in talk:
Uncle, your grace knows how to bear with him.

YORK. You mean, to bear me, not to bear with me:
Uncle, my brother mocks both you and me;
Because that I am little, like an ape,   130
He thinks that you should bear me on your shoulders.

BUCKINGHAM [*aside*]. With what a sharp-provided wit he reasons!
To mitigate the scorn he gives his uncle,
He prettily and aptly taunts himself:
So cunning and so young is wonderful.

GLOUCESTER. My lord, will't please you pass along?
Myself and my good cousin Buckingham
Will to your mother, to entreat of her
To meet you at the Tower and welcome you.

YORK. What, will you go unto the Tower, my lord?   140

PRINCE. My Lord Protector needs will have it so.

YORK. I shall not sleep in quiet at the Tower.

GLOUCESTER. Why, what should you fear?

YORK. Marry, my uncle Clarence' angry ghost:
My grandam told me he was murdered there.

PRINCE. I fear no uncles dead.

GLOUCESTER. Nor none that live, I hope.

PRINCE. An if they live, I hope I need not fear.
But come, my lord; so with a heavy heart,

Thinking on them, go I unto the Tower.   150
*A Sennet. Hastings and the Cardinal
accompany the Princes, leaving
Gloucester with Buckingham
and Catesby*

BUCKINGHAM. Think you, my lord, this little prating York
Was not incensèd by his subtle mother
To taunt and scorn you thus opprobriously?

GLOUCESTER. No doubt, no doubt: O, 'tis a parlous boy;
Bold, quick, ingenious, forward, capable:
He is all the mother's, from the top to toe.

BUCKINGHAM. Well, let them rest. Come Catesby, thou art sworn
As deeply to effect what we intend,
As closely to conceal what we impart:
Thou know'st our reasons urged upon the way.   160
What think'st thou? is it not an easy matter
To make Lord William Hastings of our mind,
For the instalment of this noble duke
In the seat royal of this famous isle?

CATESBY. He for his father's sake so loves the prince
That he will not be won to aught against him.

BUCKINGHAM. What think'st thou then of Stanley? will not he?

CATESBY. He will do all in all as Hastings doth.

BUCKINGHAM. Well, then, no more but this: go, gentle Catesby,
And, as it were far off, sound thou Lord Hastings   170
How he doth stand affected to our purpose;
And summon him to-morrow to the Tower,
To sit about the coronation.
If thou dost find him tractable to us,
Encourage him, and tell him all our reasons:
If he be leaden, icy-cold, unwilling,
Be thou so too; and so break off the talk,
And give us notice of his inclination:
For we to-morrow hold divided councils,
Wherein thyself shalt highly be employed.   180

GLOUCESTER. Commend me to Lord William: tell him, Catesby,
His ancient knot of dangerous adversaries
To-morrow are let blood at Pomfret Castle;
And bid my lord, for joy of this good news,
Give Mistress Shore one gentle kiss the more.

BUCKINGHAM. Good Catesby, go, effect this business soundly.

CATESBY. My good lords both, with all the heed I can.

GLOUCESTER. Shall we hear from you, Catesby, ere we sleep?

CATESBY. You shall, my lord.

GLOUCESTER. At Crosby House, there shall you find us both.   *Catesby goes*   190

BUCKINGHAM. My lord, what shall we do, if we perceive
Lord Hastings will not yield to our complots?

GLOUCESTER. Chop off his head—something we will determine.
And look when I am king, claim thou of me
The earldom of Hereford, and all the movables
Whereof the king my brother was possessed.

BUCKINGHAM. I'll claim that promise at your grace's hand.

GLOUCESTER. And look to have it yielded with all kindness.

Come, let us sup betimes, that afterwards
We may digest our complots in some form.   200

They go

Scene 2: *Before Lord Hastings' house*

Enter a Messenger to the door of Hastings

MESSENGER. My lord! my lord!
HASTINGS [*within*]. Who knocks?
MESSENGER. One from the Lord Stanley.
HASTINGS [*within*]. What is't o'clock?
MESSENGER. Upon the stroke of four.

Hastings opens the door

HASTINGS. Cannot my Lord Stanley sleep these
tedious nights?
MESSENGER. So it appears by that I have to say.
First, he commends him to your noble self.
HASTINGS. What then?
MESSENGER. Then certifies your lordship that this night   10
He dreamt the boar had razéd off his helm:
Besides, he says there are two councils kept;
And that may be determined at the one
Which may make you and him to rue at th'other.
Therefore he sends to know your lordship's
pleasure—
If you will presently take horse with him,
And with all speed post with him toward the north,
To shun the danger that his soul divines.
HASTINGS. Go, fellow, go, return unto thy lord;
Bid him not fear the separated councils: 20
His honour and myself are at the one,
And at the other is my good friend Catesby;
Where nothing can proceed that toucheth us
Whereof I shall not have intelligence.
Tell him his fears are shallow, without instance:
And for his dreams, I wonder he's so simple
To trust the mock'ry of unquiet slumbers.
To fly the boar before the boar pursues
Were to incense the boar to follow us
And make pursuit where he did mean no chase.   30
Go, bid thy master rise and come to me;
And we will both together to the Tower,
Where he shall see the boar will use us kindly.
MESSENGER. I'll go, my lord, and tell him what you
say.   *Goes*

Enter Catesby

CATESBY. Many good morrows to my noble lord!
HASTINGS. Good morrow, Catesby, you are early
stirring:
What news, what news, in this our tott'ring state?
CATESBY. It is a reeling world indeed, my lord;
And I believe will never stand upright
Till Richard wear the garland of the realm.   40
HASTINGS. How, wear the garland? dost thou mean
the crown?
CATESBY. Ay, my good lord.
HASTINGS. I'll have this crown of mine cut from my
shoulders
Before I'll see the crown so foul misplaced.
But canst thou guess that he doth aim at it?
CATESBY. Ay, on my life, and hopes to find you
forward
Upon his party for the gain thereof:
And thereupon he sends you this good news,
That this same very day your enemies,

The kindred of the queen, must die at Pomfret.   50
HASTINGS. Indeed, I am no mourner for that news,
Because they have been still my adversaries:
But, that I'll give my voice on Richard's side,
To bar my master's heirs in true descent,
God knows I will not do it, to the death.
CATESBY. God keep your lordship in that gracious
mind!
HASTINGS. But I shall laugh at this a twelve-month
hence,
That they which brought me in my master's hate,
I live to look upon their tragedy.
Well, Catesby, ere a fortnight make me older,   60
I'll send some packing that yet think not on't.
CATESBY. 'Tis a vile thing to die, my gracious lord,
When men are unprepared and look not for it.
HASTINGS. O monstrous, monstrous! and so falls it out
With Rivers, Vaughan, Grey: and so 'twill do
With some men else, that think themselves as safe
As thou and I, who (as thou know'st) are dear
To princely Richard and to Buckingham.
CATESBY. The princes both make high account of
you—
[*aside*] For they account his head upon the Bridge.   70
HASTINGS. I know they do, and I have well deserved it.

Enter Lord Stanley

Come on, come on, where is your boar-spear, man?
Fear you the boar, and go so unprovided?
STANLEY. My lord, good morrow; good morrow,
Catesby:
You may jest on, but, by the holy rood,
I do not like these several councils, I.
HASTINGS. I hold my life as dear as you do yours;
And never in my days, I do protest,
Was it so precious to me as 'tis now:
Think you, but that I know our state secure,   80
I would be so triumphant as I am?
STANLEY. The lords at Pomfret, when they rode from
London,
Were jocund and supposed their states were sure,
And they indeed had no cause to mistrust;
But yet you see how soon the day o'ercast.
This sudden stab of rancour I misdoubt:
Pray God, I say, I prove a needless coward!
What, shall we toward the Tower? the day is spent.
HASTINGS. Come, come, have with you. Wot you
what my lord?
To-day the lords you talked of are beheaded.   90
STANLEY. They, for their truth, might better wear
their heads
Than some that have accused them wear their hats.
But come, my lord, let's away.

Enter a Pursuivant

HASTINGS. Go on before; I'll talk with this good
fellow.   *Stanley and Catesby depart*
How now, sirrah? how goes the world with thee?
PURSUIVANT. The better that your lordship please to
ask.
HASTINGS. I tell thee, man, 'tis better with me now
Than when thou met'st me last where now we
meet:
Then was I going prisoner to the Tower,
By the suggestion of the queen's allies;   100
But now, I tell thee (keep it to thyself)

This day those enemies are put to death,
And I in better state than e'er I was.
PURSUIVANT. God hold it, to your honour's good
content!
HASTINGS. Gramercy, fellow: there, drink that for me.
Throws him his purse
PURSUIVANT. I thank your honour. *Goes*

Enter a Priest

PRIEST. Well met, my lord; I am glad to see your
honour.
HASTINGS. I thank thee, good Sir John, with all my
heart.
I am in your debt for your last exercise;
Come the next Sabbath, and I will content you. 110
He whispers in his ear

Enter Buckingham

BUCKINGHAM. What, talking with a priest, Lord
Chamberlain?
Your friends at Pomfret, they do need the priest:
Your honour hath no shriving work in hand.
HASTINGS. Good faith, and when I met this holy man,
The men you talk of came into my mind.
What, go you toward the Tower?
BUCKINGHAM. I do, my lord; but long I cannot stay
there:
I shall return before your lordship thence.
HASTINGS. Nay, like enough, for I stay dinner there.
BUCKINGHAM [*aside*]. And supper too, although thou
know'st it not. 120
[*aloud*] Come, will you go?
HASTINGS. I'll wait upon your lordship.
They go

Scene 3: *Pomfret Castle*

*Enter Sir Richard Ratcliffe, with halberds, carrying the
nobles Rivers, Grey, and Vaughan to death*

RIVERS. Sir Richard Ratcliffe, let me tell thee this:
To-day shalt thou behold a subject die
For truth, for duty, and for loyalty.
GREY. God bless the prince from all the pack of you!
A knot you are of damnéd blood-suckers.
VAUGHAN. You live that shall cry woe for this
hereafter.
RATCLIFFE. Dispatch; the limit of your lives is out.
RIVERS. O Pomfret, Pomfret! O thou bloody prison,
Fatal and ominous to noble peers!
Within the guilty closure of thy walls 10
Richard the Second here was hacked to death;
And, for more slander to thy dismal seat,
We give to thee our guiltless blood to drink.
GREY. Now Margaret's curse is fall'n upon our heads,
When she exclaimed on Hastings, you, and I,
For standing by when Richard stabbed her son.
RIVERS. Then cursed she Richard, then cursed she
Buckingham,
Then cursed she Hastings. O, remember, God,
To hear her prayer for them, as now for us!
And for my sister and her princely sons, 20
Be satisfied, dear God, with our true blood,
Which, as thou know'st, unjustly must be spilt.
RATCLIFFE. Make haste; the hour of death is expiate.
RIVERS. Come, Grey, come, Vaughan, let us here
embrace:

Farewell, until we meet again in heaven.
They are led away

Scene 4: *The Tower of London*

*Buckingham, Stanley, Hastings, the Bishop of Ely, Rat-
cliffe, Lovel, with others, at a table*

HASTINGS. Now, noble peers, the cause why we are
met
Is to determine of the coronation.
In God's name, speak! when is the royal day?
BUCKINGHAM. Is all things ready for the royal time?
STANLEY. It is, and wants but nomination.
ELY. To-morrow then I judge a happy day.
BUCKINGHAM. Who knows the Lord Protector's mind
herein?
Who is most inward with the noble duke?
ELY. Your grace, we think, should soonest know his
mind.
BUCKINGHAM. We know each other's faces: for our
hearts, 10
He knows no more of mine than I of yours;
Or I of his, my lord, than you of mine.
Lord Hastings, you and he are near in love.
HASTINGS. I thank his grace, I know he loves me well;
But, for his purpose in the coronation,
I have not sounded him, nor he delivered
His gracious pleasure any way therein:
But you, my honourable lords, may name the time;
And in the duke's behalf I'll give my voice,
Which, I presume, he'll take in gentle part. 20

Enter Gloucester

ELY. In happy time, here comes the duke himself.
GLOUCESTER. My noble lords and cousins all, good
morrow.
I have been long a sleeper; but I trust
My absence doth neglect no great design,
Which by my presence might have been concluded.
BUCKINGHAM. Had you not come upon your cue, my
lord,
William Lord Hastings had pronounced your
part—
I mean, your voice for crowning of the king.
GLOUCESTER. Than my Lord Hastings no man might
be bolder;
His lordship knows me well, and loves me well. 30
My lord of Ely, when I was last in Holborn,
I saw good strawberries in your garden there:
I do beseech you send for some of them.
ELY. Marry, and will, my lord, with all my heart.
He goes
GLOUCESTER. Cousin of Buckingham, a word with
you. *Drawing him aside*
Catesby hath sounded Hastings in our business,
And finds the testy gentleman so hot,
That he will lose his head ere give consent
His master's child, as worshipfully he terms it,
Shall lose the royalty of England's throne. 40
BUCKINGHAM. Withdraw yourself a while, I'll go with
you. *They go out*
STANLEY. We have not yet set down this day of
triumph.
To-morrow, in my judgement, is too sudden;
For I myself am not so well provided
As else I would be, were the day prolonged.

The Bishop of Ely returns

ELY. Where is my Lord the Duke of Gloucester?
    I have sent for these strawberries.
HASTINGS. His grace looks cheerfully and smooth this
        morning;
    There's some conceit or other likes him well,
    When that he bids good-morrow with such spirit. 50
    I think there's ne'er a man in Christendom
    Can lesser hide his love or hate than he;
    For by his face straight shall you know his heart.
STANLEY. What of his heart perceive you in his face
    By any likelihood he showed to-day?
HASTINGS. Marry, that with no man here he is
        offended;
    For, were he, he had shown it in his looks.

Gloucester and Buckingham return

GLOUCESTER. I pray you all, tell me what they deserve
    That do conspire my death with devilish plots
    Of damnéd witchcraft, and that have prevailed   60
    Upon my body with their hellish charms?
HASTINGS. The tender love I bear your grace, my lord,
    Makes me most forward in this princely presence
    To doom th'offenders: whosoe'er they be,
    I say, my lord, they have deservéd death.
GLOUCESTER. Then be your eyes the witness of their
        evil.
    Look how I am bewitched; behold, mine arm
    Is like a blasted sapling withered up:
    And this is Edward's wife, that monstrous witch,
    Consorted with that harlot, strumpet Shore,   70
    That by their witchcraft thus have markéd me.
HASTINGS. If they have done this deed, my noble
        lord,—
GLOUCESTER. If! thou protector of this damnéd
        strumpet,
    Talk'st thou to me of 'ifs'? Thou art a traitor:
    Off with his head! Now, by Saint Paul I swear,
    I will not dine until I see the same.
    Lovel and Ratcliffe, look that it be done:
    The rest that love me, rise and follow me.
            All leave but Hastings, Ratcliffe
                                and Lovel
HASTINGS. Woe, woe for England! not a whit for me;
    For I, too fond, might have prevented this.   80
    Stanley did dream the boar did raze our helms,
    And I did scorn it, and disdain to fly:
    Three times to-day my foot-cloth horse did
        stumble,
    And started when he looked upon the Tower,
    As loath to bear me to the slaughter-house.
    O, now I need the priest that spake to me:
    I now repent I told the pursuivant,
    As too triumphing, how mine enemies
    To-day at Pomfret bloodily were butchered,
    And I myself secure in grace and favour.   90
    O Margaret, Margaret, now thy heavy curse
    Is lighted on poor Hastings' wretched head!
RATCLIFFE. Come, come, dispatch; the duke would be
        at dinner:
    Make a short shrift; he longs to see your head.
HASTINGS. O momentary grace of mortal men,
    Which we more hunt for than the grace of God!
    Who builds his hope in air of your good looks
    Lives like a drunken sailor on a mast,
    Ready with every nod to tumble down

Into the fatal bowels of the deep.
LOVEL. Come, come, dispatch; 'tis bootless to exclaim.
HASTINGS. O bloody Richard! miserable England!
    I prophesy the fearfull'st time to thee
    That ever wretched age hath looked upon.
    Come, lead me to the block; bear him my head.
    They smile at me who shortly shall be dead.
                            He is led away

Scene 5: *The Tower-walls*

*Enter Gloucester and Buckingham, in rotten armour,
marvellous ill-favoured*

GLOUCESTER. Come, cousin, canst thou quake, and
        change thy colour,
    Murder thy breath in middle of a word,
    And then again begin, and stop again,
    As if thou wert distraught and mad with terror?
BUCKINGHAM. Tut, I can counterfeit the deep
        tragedian,
    Speak and look back, and pry on every side,
    Tremble and start at wagging of a straw,
    Intending deep suspicion: ghastly looks
    Are at my service, like enforcéd smiles;
    And both are ready in their offices,   10
    At any time, to grace my stratagems.
    But what, is Catesby gone?
GLOUCESTER. He is; and, see, he brings the mayor
        along.

Enter the Mayor and Catesby

BUCKINGHAM. Lord Mayor,—
GLOUCESTER. Look to the drawbridge there!
BUCKINGHAM. Hark! a drum.
GLOUCESTER. Catesby, o'erlook the walls.
BUCKINGHAM. Lord Mayor, the reason we have sent—
GLOUCESTER. Look back, defend thee, here are
        enemies!
BUCKINGHAM. God and our innocence defend and
        guard us!   20
GLOUCESTER. Be patient, they are friends, Ratcliffe
        and Lovel.

Enter Lovel and Ratcliffe, with Hastings' head

LOVEL. Here is the head of that ignoble traitor,
    The dangerous and unsuspected Hastings.
GLOUCESTER. So dear I loved the man, that I must
        weep.
    I took him for the plainest harmless creature
    That breathed upon the earth a Christian;
    Made him my book, wherein my soul recorded
    The history of all her secret thoughts.
    So smooth he daubed his vice with show of virtue
    That, his apparent open guilt omitted,   30
    I mean his conversation with Shore's wife,
    He lived from all attainder of suspects.
BUCKINGHAM. Well, well, he was the covert'st
        shelt'red traitor.
    Would you imagine, or almost believe,
    Were't not that, by great preservation,
    We live to tell it, that the subtle traitor
    This day had plotted, in the council-house
    To murder me and my good Lord of Gloucester?
MAYOR. Had he done so?
GLOUCESTER. What! think you we are Turks or
        infidels?   40

Or that we would, against the form of law,
Proceed thus rashly in the villain's death,
But that the extreme peril of the case,
The peace of England and our persons' safety,
Enforced us to this execution?

MAYOR. Now, fair befall you! he deserved his death:
And your good graces both have well proceeded,
To warn false traitors from the like attempts.

BUCKINGHAM. I never looked for better at his hands,
After he once fell in with Mistress Shore.   50
Yet had we not determined he should die,
Until your lordship came to see his end,
Which now the loving haste of these our friends,
Something against our meanings, have prevented:
Because, my lord, I would have had you hear
The traitor speak and timorously confess
The manner and the purpose of his treasons;
That you might well have signified the same
Unto the citizens, who haply may
Misconster us in him and wail his death.   60

MAYOR. But, my good lord, your grace's words shall
    serve,
As well as I had seen and heard him speak:
And do not doubt, right noble princes both,
But I'll acquaint our duteous citizens
With all your just proceedings in this cause.

GLOUCESTER. And to that end we wished your
    lordship here,
T'avoid the censures of the carping world.

BUCKINGHAM. Which since you come too late of our
    intent,
Yet witness what you hear we did intend:
And so, my good Lord Mayor, we bid farewell.   70
                                       The Mayor goes

GLOUCESTER. Go, after, after, cousin Buckingham.
The mayor towards Guildhall hies him in all post:
There, at your meet'st advantage of the time,
Infer the bastardy of Edward's children:
Tell them how Edward put to death a citizen,
Only for saying he would make his son
Heir to the crown, meaning indeed his house,
Which, by the sign thereof, was terméd so.
Moreover, urge his hateful luxury
And bestial appetite in change of lust;   80
Which stretched unto their servants, daughters,
    wives,
Even where his raging eye or savage heart
Without control listed to make a prey.
Nay, for a need, thus far come near my person:
Tell them, when that my mother went with child
Of that insatiate Edward, noble York
My princely father then had wars in France;
And, by true computation of the time,
Found that the issue was not his begot;
Which well appearéd in his lineaments,   90
Being nothing like the noble duke my father:
Yet touch this sparingly, as 'twere far off,
Because, my lord, you know my mother lives.

BUCKINGHAM. Doubt not, my lord, I'll play the orator
As if the golden fee for which I plead
Were for myself: and so, my lord, adieu.

GLOUCESTER. If you thrive well, bring them to
    Baynard's Castle,
Where you shall find me well accompanied
With reverend fathers and well-learnéd bishops.

BUCKINGHAM. I go, and towards three or four o'clock 100

Look for the news that the Guildhall affords.
                                             Goes

GLOUCESTER. Go, Lovel, with all speed to Doctor
    Shaw;
[To Catesby] Go thou to Friar Penker; bid them both
Meet me within this hour at Baynard's Castle.
                                       They depart
Now will I go to take some privy order
To draw the brats of Clarence out of sight;
And to give notice that no manner person
Have any time recourse unto the princes.
                                          He goes

Scene 6: London. A street

Enter a Scrivener, with a paper in his hand

SCRIVENER. Here is the indictment of the good Lord
    Hastings,
Which in a set hand fairly is engrossed,
That it may be to-day read o'er in Paul's.
And mark how well the sequel hangs together:
Eleven hours I have spent to write it over,
For yesternight by Catesby was it sent me;
The precedent was full as long a-doing:
And yet within these five hours Hastings lived,
Untainted, unexamined, free, at liberty.
Here's a good world the while! Who is so gross, 10
That cannot see this palpable device?
Yet who's so bold, but says he sees it not?
Bad is the world; and all will come to nought,
When such ill dealing must be seen in thought.
                                          He goes

Scene 7: Baynard's Castle

Enter Gloucester and Buckingham at different doors

GLOUCESTER. How now, how now, what say the
    citizens?

BUCKINGHAM. Now, by the holy mother of our Lord,
The citizens are mum, say not a word.

GLOUCESTER. Touched you the bastardy of Edward's
    children?

BUCKINGHAM. I did; with his contract with Lady
    Lucy,
And his contract by deputy in France;
Th'insatiate greediness of his desire,
And his enforcement of the city wives;
His tyranny for trifles; his own bastardy,
As being got, your father then in France,   10
And his resemblance, being not like the duke:
Withal I did infer your lineaments,
Being the right idea of your father,
Both in your form and nobleness of mind;
Laid open all your victories in Scotland,
Your discipline in war, wisdom in peace,
Your bounty, virtue, fair humility;
Indeed left nothing fitting for your purpose
Untouched or slightly handled in discourse:
And when mine oratory drew toward end,   20
I bid them that did love their country's good
Cry 'God save Richard, England's royal king!'

GLOUCESTER. And did they so?

BUCKINGHAM. No, so God help me, they spake not a
    word;
But, like dumb statuas or breathing stones,
Stared each on other, and looked deadly pale.

Which when I saw, I reprehended them,
And asked the Mayor what meant this wilful
  silence:
His answer was, the people were not uséd
To be spoke to but by the Recorder.   30
Then he was urged to tell my tale again:
'Thus saith the duke, thus hath the duke inferred';
But nothing spoke in warrant from himself.
When he had done, some followers of mine own
At lower end of the hall hurled up their caps,
And some ten voices cried 'God save King
  Richard!'
And thus I took the vantage of those few,
'Thanks, gentle citizens and friends'! quoth I,
'This general applause and cheerful shout
Argues your wisdoms and your love to Richard'—   40
And even here brake off and came away.
GLOUCESTER. What tongueless blocks were they!
  would they not speak?
BUCKINGHAM. No, by my troth, my lord.
GLOUCESTER. Will not the Mayor then and his
  brethren come?
BUCKINGHAM. The Mayor is here at hand: intend
  some fear;
Be not you spoke with, but by mighty suit:
And look you get a prayer-book in your hand,
And stand between two churchmen, good my lord;
For on that ground I'll make a holy descant:
And be not easily won to our requests;   50
Play the maid's part, still answer nay, and take it.
GLOUCESTER. I go; and if you plead as well for them
As I can say nay to thee for myself,
No doubt we'll bring it to a happy issue.
BUCKINGHAM. Go, go up to the leads; the Lord
  Mayor knocks.   *Gloucester goes*

The Mayor and Citizens enter

Welcome, my lord: I dance attendance here;
I think the duke will not be spoke withal.

Catesby enters

Catesby, what says your lord to my request?
CATESBY. He doth entreat your grace, my noble lord,
To visit him to-morrow or next day: 60
He is within, with two right reverend fathers,
Divinely bent to meditation;
And in no worldly suits would he be moved,
To draw him from his holy exercise.
BUCKINGHAM. Return, good Catesby, to the gracious
  duke:
Tell him, myself, the Mayor, and Alderman,
In deep designs, in matter of great moment,
No less importing than our general good,
Are come to have some conference with his grace.
CATESBY. I'll signify so much unto him straight.   70
                                   Goes
BUCKINGHAM. Ah, ha, my lord, this prince is not an
  Edward!
He is not lolling on a lewd love-bed,
But on his knees at meditation;
Not dallying with a brace of courtezans,
But meditating with two deep divines;
Not sleeping, to engross his idle body,
But praying, to enrich his watchful soul:
Happy were England, would this virtuous prince
Take on his grace the sovereignty thereof:

But, sure, I fear, we shall not win him to it.   80
MAYOR. Marry, God defend his grace should say us
  nay!
BUCKINGHAM. I fear he will. Here Catesby comes
  again.

Catesby returns

Now, Catesby, what says his grace?
CATESBY. He wonders to what end you have
  assembled
Such troops of citizens to come to him,
His grace not being warned thereof before:
He fears, my lord, you mean no good to him.
BUCKINGHAM. Sorry I am my noble cousin should
Suspect me that I mean no good to him:
By heaven, we come to him in perfit love;   90
And so once more return and tell his grace.
                          Catesby goes again
When holy and devout religious men
Are at their beads, 'tis much to draw them thence,
So sweet is zealous contemplation.

*Gloucester appears aloft, between two Bishops; Catesby
returns*

MAYOR. See, where his grace stands, 'tween two
  clergymen!
BUCKINGHAM. Two props of virtue for a Christian
  prince,
To stay him from the fall of vanity:
And, see, a book of prayer in his hand,
True ornaments to know a holy man.
Famous Plantagenet, most gracious prince,   100
Lend favourable ear to our requests;
And pardon us the interruption
Of thy devotion and right Christian zeal.
GLOUCESTER. My lord, there needs no such apology:
I do beseech your grace to pardon me,
Who, earnest in the service of my God,
Deferred the visitation of my friends.
But, leaving this, what is your grace's pleasure?
BUCKINGHAM. Even that, I hope, which pleaseth God
  above
And all good men of this ungoverned isle.   110
GLOUCESTER. I do suspect I have done some offence
That seems disgracious in the city's eye,
And that you come to reprehend my ignorance.
BUCKINGHAM. You have, my lord: would it might
  please your grace,
On our entreaties, to amend your fault!
GLOUCESTER. Else wherefore breathe I in a Christian
  land?
BUCKINGHAM. Know then, it is your fault that you
  resign
The supreme seat, the throne majestical,
The scept'red office of your ancestors,
Your state of fortune and your due of birth,   120
The lineal glory of your royal house,
To the corruption of a blemished stock:
Whiles, in the mildness of your sleepy thoughts,
Which here we waken to our country's good,
The noble isle doth want her proper limbs;
Her face defaced with scars of infamy,
Her royal stock graffed with ignoble plants,
And almost should'red in the swallowing gulf
Of dark forgetfulness and deep oblivion.
Which to recure, we heartily solicit   130

Your gracious selt to take on you the charge
And kingly government of this your land;
Not as protector, steward, substitute,
Or lowly factor for another's gain;
But as successively, from blood to blood,
Your right of birth, your empery, your own
For this, consorted with the citizens,
Your very worshipful and loving friends,
And by their vehement instigation,
In this just cause come I to move your grace.   140
GLOUCESTER. I cannot tell if to depart in silence
Or bitterly to speak in your reproof
Best fitteth my degree or your condition:
If not to answer, you might haply think
Tongue-tied ambition, not replying, yielded
To bear the golden yoke of sovereignty,
Which fondly you would here impose on me;
If to reprove you for this suit of yours,
So seasoned with your faithful love to me,
Then, on the other side, I checked my friends.   150
Therefore—to speak, and to avoid the first,
And then, in speaking, not to incur the last—
Definitively thus I answer you:
Your love deserves my thanks, but my desert
Unmeritable shuns your high request.
First, if all obstacles were cut away
And that my path were even to the crown,
As the ripe revenue and due of birth,
Yet so much is my poverty of spirit,
So mighty and so many my defects,   160
That I would rather hide me from my greatness,
Being a bark to brook no mighty sea,
Than in my greatness covet to be hid
And in the vapour of my glory smothered.
But, God be thanked, there is no need of me,
And much I need to help you, were there need:
The royal tree hath left us royal fruit,
Which, mellowed by the stealing hours of time,
Will well become the seat of majesty,
And make, no doubt, us happy by his reign.   170
On him I lay that you would lay on me,
The right and fortune of his happy stars,
Which God defend that I should wring from him!
BUCKINGHAM. My lord, this argues conscience in your
grace;
But the respects thereof are nice and trivial,
All circumstances well considered.
You say that Edward is your brother's son:
So say we too, but not by Edward's wife;
For first was he contract to Lady Lucy—
Your mother lives a witness to his vow—   180
And afterward by substitute betrothed
To Bona, sister to the King of France.
These both put off, a poor petitioner,
A care-crazed mother to a many sons,
A beauty-waning and distressèd widow,
Even in the afternoon of her best days,
Made prize and purchase of his wanton eye,
Seduced the pitch and height of his degree
To base declension and loathed bigamy:
By her, in his unlawful bed, he got   190
This Edward, whom our manners call the prince.
More bitterly could I expostulate,
Save that, for reverence to some alive,
I give a sparing limit to my tongue.
Then, good my lord, take to your royal self

This proffered benefit of dignity;
If not to bless us and the land withal,
Yet to draw forth your noble ancestry
From the corruption of abusing times
Unto a lineal true-derivèd course.   200
MAYOR. Do, good my lord, your citizens entreat you.
BUCKINGHAM. Refuse not, mighty lord, this proffered
love.
CATESBY. O, make them joyful, grant their lawful
suit!
GLOUCESTER. Alas, why would you heap this care on
me?
I am unfit for state and majesty:
I do beseech you, take it not amiss;
I cannot nor I will not yield to you.
BUCKINGHAM. If you refuse it—as, in love and zeal,
Loath to depose the child, your brother's son;
As well we know your tenderness of heart   210
And gentle, kind, effeminate remorse,
Which we have noted in you to your kindred,
And egally indeed to all estates—
Yet know, whe'er you accept our suit or no,
Your brother's son shall never reign our king;
But we will plant some other in the throne,
To the disgrace and downfall of your house:
And in this resolution here we leave you.
Come, citizens. Zounds! I'll entreat no more.
GLOUCESTER. O, do not swear, my lord of
Buckingham.   *Buckingham goes; citizens follow*   220
CATESBY. Call him again, sweet prince, accept their
suit:
If you deny them, all the land will rue it.
GLOUCESTER. Will you enforce me to a world of
cares?
Call them again: I am not made of stone,
But penetrable to your kind entreaties,
Albeit against my conscience and my soul.

Buckingham and the rest return

Cousin of Buckingham, and sage grave men,
Since you will buckle fortune on my back,
To bear her burthen, whe'er I will or no,
I must have patience to endure the load: 230
But if black scandal or foul-faced reproach
Attend the sequel of your imposition,
Your mere enforcement shall acquittance me
From all the impure blots and stains thereof;
For God doth know, and you may partly see,
How far I am from the desire of this.
MAYOR. God bless your grace! we see it, and will say it.
GLOUCESTER. In saying so, you shall but say the truth.
BUCKINGHAM. Then I salute you with this royal title:
Long live King Richard, England's worthy king!   240
ALL. Amen.
BUCKINGHAM. To-morrow may it please you to be
crowned?
GLOUCESTER. Even when you please, for you will have
it so.
BUCKINGHAM. To-morrow then we will attend your
grace:
And so most joyfully we take our leave.
GLOUCESTER. Come, let us to our holy work again.
Farewell, my cousin; farewell, gentle friends.
They go

ACT 4

Scene 1: *Before the Tower*

Enter Queen Elizabeth, Duchess of York, and Marquis of Dorset; meeting Anne, Duchess of Gloucester, and Lady Margaret Plantagenet, Clarence's young daughter

DUCHESS. Who meets us here? my niece Plantagenet,
Led in the hand of her kind aunt of Gloucester?
Now, for my life, she's wand'ring to the Tower,
On pure heart's love to greet the tender princes.
Daughter, well met.

ANNE.   God give your graces both
A happy and a joyful time of day!

QUEEN ELIZABETH. As much to you, good sister!
Whither away?

ANNE. No farther than the Tower, and, as I guess,
Upon the like devotion as yourselves,
To gratulate the gentle princes there.   10

QUEEN ELIZABETH. Kind sister, thanks: we'll enter all
together.

Brakenbury comes from the Tower

And, in good time, here the lieutenant comes.
Master Lieutenant, pray you, by your leave,
How doth the prince, and my young son of York?

BRAKENBURY. Right well, dear madam. By your
patience,
I may not suffer you to visit them;
The king hath strictly charged the contrary.

QUEEN ELIZABETH. The king! who's that?

BRAKENBURY. I mean the Lord Protector.

QUEEN ELIZABETH. The Lord protect him from that
kingly title!   20
Hath he set bounds between their love and me?
I am their mother; who shall bar me from them?

DUCHESS. I am their father's mother; I will see them.

ANNE. Their aunt I am in law, in love their mother:
Then bring me to their sights; I'll bear thy blame,
And take thy office from thee, on my peril.

BRAKENBURY. No, madam, no; I may not leave it so;
I am bound by oath, and therefore pardon me.
                                    He goes within

Lord Stanley enters

STANLEY. Let me but meet you, ladies, one hour
hence,
And I'll salute your grace of York as mother,   30
And reverend looker-on, of two fair queens.
[*to Anne*] Come, madam, you must straight to
Westminster,
There to be crownèd Richard's royal queen.

QUEEN ELIZABETH. Ah, cut my lace asunder,
That my pent heart may have some scope to beat,
Or else I swoon with this dead-killing news!

ANNE. Despiteful tidings! O unpleasing news!

DORSET. Be of good cheer: mother, how fares your
grace?

QUEEN ELIZABETH. O Dorset, speak not to me, get thee
gone!
Death and destruction dogs thee at thy heels;   40
Thy mother's name is ominous to children.
If thou wilt outstrip death, go cross the seas,
And live with Richmond, from the reach of hell:
Go, hie thee, hie thee from this slaughter-house,
Lest thou increase the number of the dead;
And make me die the thrall of Margaret's curse,

Nor mother, wife, nor England's counted queen.

STANLEY. Full of wise care is this your counsel,
madam.
[*to Dorset*] Take all the swift advantage of the hours;
You shall have letters from me to my son   50
In your behalf, to meet you on the way:
Be not ta'en tardy by unwise delay.

DUCHESS. O ill-dispersing wind of misery!
O my accursèd womb, the bed of death!
A cockatrice hast thou hatched to the world,
Whose unavoided eye is murderous.

STANLEY. Come, madam, come; I in all haste was sent.

ANNE. And I with all unwillingness will go.
O, would to God that the inclusive verge
Of golden metal that must round my brow   60
Were red-hot steel, to sear me to the brains!
Anointed let me be with deadly venom,
And die ere men can say, 'God save the queen!'

QUEEN ELIZABETH. Go, go, poor soul, I envy not thy
glory:
To feed my humour, wish thyself no harm.

ANNE. No? Why, when he that is my husband now
Came to me, as I followed Henry's corse,
When scarce the blood was well washed from his
hands
Which issued from my other angel husband,
And that dear saint which then I weeping
followed—   70
O, when, I say, I looked on Richard's face,
This was my wish: 'Be thou', quoth I, 'accursed,
For making me, so young, so old a widow!
And, when thou wed'st, let sorrow haunt thy bed;
And be thy wife—if any be so—made
More miserable by the life of thee
Than thou hast made me by my dear lord's death!'
Lo, ere I can repeat this curse again,
Within so small a time, my woman's heart
Grossly grew captive to his honey words   80
And proved the subject of mine own soul's curse,
Which hitherto hath held mine eyes from rest;
For never yet one hour in his bed
Did I enjoy the golden dew of sleep,
But with his timorous dreams was still awaked.
Besides, he hates me for my father Warwick;
And will, no doubt, shortly be rid of me.

QUEEN ELIZABETH. Poor heart, adieu! I pity thy
complaining.

ANNE. No more than with my soul I mourn for yours.

QUEEN ELIZABETH. Farewell, thou woeful welcomer of
glory!   90

ANNE. Adieu, poor soul, that tak'st thy leave of it!

DUCHESS [*to Dorset*]. Go thou to Richmond, and good
fortune guide thee!
[*to Anne*] Go thou to Richard, and good angels tend
thee!
[*to Queen Elizabeth*] Go thou to sanctuary, and good
thoughts possess thee!
I to my grave, where peace and rest lie with me!
Eighty odd years of sorrow have I seen,
And each hour's joy wracked with a week of teen.

QUEEN ELIZABETH. Stay, yet look back with me unto
the Tower.
Pity, you ancient stones, those tender babes
Whom envy hath immured within your walls!   100
Rough cradle for such little pretty ones!
Rude ragged nurse, old sullen playfellow

For tender princes, use my babies well!
So foolish sorrow bids your stones farewell.
They depart

Scene 2: *London. The Palace*

Sennet. Enter Richard, in pomp, crowned; Buckingham,
Catesby, a Page, and others

KING RICHARD. Stand all apart. Cousin of
Buckingham!
BUCKINGHAM. My gracious sovereign!
KING RICHARD. Give me thy hand.

Trumpets sound as he ascends the throne

              Thus high, by thy advice,
And thy assistance, is King Richard seated:
But shall we wear these glories for a day?
Or shall they last, and we rejoice in them?
BUCKINGHAM. Still live they and for ever let them
last!
KING RICHARD. Ah Buckingham, now do I play the
touch,
To try if thou be current gold indeed:
Young Edward lives; think now what I would
speak. 10
BUCKINGHAM. Say on, my loving lord.
KING RICHARD. Why, Buckingham, I say I would be
king.
BUCKINGHAM. Why, so you are, my thrice-renownèd
lord.
KING RICHARD. Ha? am I king? 'tis so—but Edward
lives.
BUCKINGHAM. True, noble prince.
KING RICHARD.   O bitter consequence!
That Edward still should live 'true noble prince'!
Cousin, thou wast not wont to be so dull.
Shall I be plain? I wish the bastards dead,
And I would have it suddenly performed.
What say'st thou now? speak suddenly, be brief. 20
BUCKINGHAM. Your grace may do your pleasure.
KING RICHARD. Tut, tut, thou art all ice, thy kindness
freezes:
Say, have I thy consent that they shall die?
BUCKINGHAM. Give me some little breath, some pause,
dear lord,
Before I positively speak in this:
I will resolve you herein presently.   *He goes*
CATESBY [*aside*]. The king is angry: see, he gnaws his
lip.
KING RICHARD. I will converse with iron-witted fools
And unrespective boys: none are for me
That look into me with considerate eyes: 30
High-reaching Buckingham grows circumspect.
Boy!
PAGE. My lord?
KING RICHARD. Know'st thou not any whom
corrupting gold
Will tempt unto a close exploit of death?
PAGE. I know a discontented gentleman
Whose humble means match not his haughty spirit:
Gold were as good as twenty orators,
And will, no doubt, tempt him to any thing.
KING RICHARD. What is his name?
PAGE.   His name, my lord, is Tyrrel. 40
KING RICHARD. I partly know the man: go, call him
hither, boy.   *Page goes*

The deep-revolving witty Buckingham
No more shall be the neighbour to my counsels.
Hath he so long held out with me untired,
And stops he now for breath? Well, be it so.

Enter Stanley

How now, Lord Stanley!
STANLEY.   Know, my loving lord,
The Marquis Dorset, as I hear, is fled
To Richmond in the parts where he abides.
               Stands apart
KING RICHARD. Come hither, Catesby. Rumour it
abroad
That Anne, my wife, is very grievous sick: 50
I will take order for her keeping close.
Inquire me out some mean poor gentleman,
Whom I will marry straight to Clarence' daughter:
The boy is foolish, and I fear not him.
Look, how thou dream'st! I say again, give out
That Anne, my queen, is sick and like to die.
About it! for it stands me much upon
To stop all hopes whose growth may damage me.
               Catesby goes
I must be married to my brother's daughter,
Or else my kingdom stands on brittle glass ... 60
Murder her brothers, and then marry her!
Uncertain way of gain! But I am in
So far in blood that sin will pluck on sin:
Tear-falling pity dwells not in this eye.

Re-enter Page with Tyrrel

Is thy name Tyrrel?
TYRREL. James Tyrrel, and your most obedient
subject.
KING RICHARD. Art thou, indeed?
TYRREL.   Prove me, my gracious lord.
KING RICHARD. Dar'st thou resolve to kill a friend of
mine?
TYRREL. Please you, I had rather kill two enemies.
KING RICHARD. Why, there thou hast it: two deep
enemies, 70
Foes to my rest and my sweet sleep's disturbers,
Are they that I would have thee deal upon:
Tyrrel, I mean those bastards in the Tower.
TYRREL. Let me have open means to come to them,
And soon I'll rid you from the fear of them.
KING RICHARD. Thou sing'st sweet music. Hark, come
hither, Tyrrel:
Go, by this token: rise, and lend thine ear:
               Whispers
There is no more but so: say it is done,
And I will love thee, and prefer thee for it.
TYRREL. I will dispatch it straight.   *Goes* 80

Buckingham returns

BUCKINGHAM. My lord, I have considered in my mind
The late request that you did sound me in.
KING RICHARD. Well, let that rest. Dorset is fled to
Richmond.
BUCKINGHAM. I hear the news, my lord.
KING RICHARD. Stanley, he is your wife's son: look
unto it.
BUCKINGHAM. My lord, I claim the gift, my due by
promise,
For which your honour and your faith is pawned—
Th'earldom of Hereford and the movables

Which you have promiséd I shall possess.
KING RICHARD. Stanley, look to your wife: if she
    convey   90
Letters to Richmond, you shall answer it.
BUCKINGHAM. What says your highness to my just
    request?
KING RICHARD. I do remember me, Henry the Sixth
Did prophesy that Richmond should be king,
When Richmond was a little peevish boy.
A king! perhaps—
BUCKINGHAM. My lord!
KING RICHARD. How chance the prophet could not at
    that time
Have told me, I being by, that I should kill him?
BUCKINGHAM. My lord, your promise for the
    earldom—   100
KING RICHARD. Richmond! When last I was at Exeter,
The mayor in courtesy showed me the castle,
And called it Rougemont: at which name I
    started,
Because a bard of Ireland told me once
I should not live long after I saw Richmond.
BUCKINGHAM. My lord!
KING RICHARD. Ay, what's o'clock?
BUCKINGHAM. I am thus bold to put your grace in
    mind
Of what you promised me.
KING RICHARD.   Well, but what's o'clock?
BUCKINGHAM. Upon the stroke of ten.
KING RICHARD.   Well, let it strike.   110
BUCKINGHAM. Why let it strike?
KING RICHARD. Because that, like a Jack, thou keep'st
    the stroke
Betwixt thy begging and my meditation.
I am not in the giving vein to-day.
BUCKINGHAM. May it please you to resolve me in my
    suit?
KING RICHARD. Thou troublest me, I am not in the
    vein.   Goes
BUCKINGHAM. And is it thus? repays he my deep
    service
With such contempt? made I him king for this?
O, let me think on Hastings, and be gone
To Brecknock, while my fearful head is on!   120
                                                                             Goes

Scene 3: The same, later

Enter Tyrrel

TYRREL. The tyrannous and bloody act is done,
The most arch deed of piteous massacre
That ever yet this land was guilty of.
Dighton and Forrest, whom I did suborn
To do this piece of ruthless butchery,
Albeit they were fleshed villains, bloody dogs,
Melting with tenderness and mild compassion,
Wept like two children in their death's sad story:
'O, thus,' quoth Dighton, 'lay the gentle babes':
'Thus, thus,' quoth Forrest, 'girdling one another   10
Within their alabaster innocent arms:
Their lips were four red roses on a stalk,
Which in their summer beauty kissed each other.
A book of prayers on their pillow lay;
Which once,' quoth Forrest, 'almost changed my
    mind;
But O! the devil'—there the villain stopped;

Whilst Dighton thus told on: 'We smotheréd
The most replenishéd sweet work of Nature
That from the prime creation e'er she framed.'
Hence all o'er gone with conscience and remorse,   20
They could not speak; and so I left them both,
To bear this tidings to the bloody king.
And here he comes.

Enter King Richard

                              All health, my sovereign lord!
KING RICHARD. Kind Tyrrel, am I happy in thy news?
TYRREL. If to have done the thing you gave in charge
Beget your happiness, be happy then,
For it is done.
KING RICHARD.   But didst thou see them dead?
TYRREL. I did, my lord.
KING RICHARD.   And buried, gentle Tyrrel?
TYRREL. The chaplain of the Tower hath buried them;
But where, to say the truth, I do not know.   30
KING RICHARD. Come to me, Tyrrel, soon at
    after-supper,
When thou shalt tell the process of their death.
Meantime, but think how I may do thee good,
And be inheritor of thy desire.
Farewell till then.
TYRREL.   I humbly take my leave.
                                                                    He goes
KING RICHARD. The son of Clarence have I pent up
    close;
His daughter meanly have I matched in marriage;
The sons of Edward sleep in Abraham's bosom,
And Anne my wife hath bid this world good night.
Now, for I know the Breton Richmond aims   40
At young Elizabeth, my brother's daughter,
And, by that knot, looks proudly on the crown,
To her go I, a jolly thriving wooer.

Enter Ratcliffe

RATCLIFFE. My lord!
KING RICHARD. Good or bad news, that thou com'st
    in so bluntly?
RATCLIFFE. Bad news, my lord: Morton is fled to
    Richmond;
And Buckingham, backed with the hardy
    Welshmen,
Is in the field, and still his power increaseth.
KING RICHARD. Ely with Richmond troubles me more
    near
Than Buckingham and his rash-levied strength.   50
Come, I have learned that fearful commenting
Is leaden servitor to dull delay;
Delay leads impotent and snail-paced beggary:
Then fiery expedition be my wing,
Jove's Mercury, and herald for a king!
Go, muster men: my counsel is my shield;
We must be brief when traitors brave the field.
                                                                    They go

Scene 4: Before the palace

Enter old Queen Margaret

QUEEN MARGARET. So now prosperity begins to
    mellow
And drop into the rotten mouth of death.
Here in these confines slily have I lurked,
To watch the waning of mine enemies.

A dire induction am I witness to,
And will to France, hoping the consequence
Will prove as bitter, black, and tragical.
Withdraw thee, wretched Margaret: who comes
here?

Enter Queen Elizabeth and the Duchess of York

QUEEN ELIZABETH. Ah, my poor princes! ah, my
tender babes!
My unblown flowers, new-appearing sweets!   10
If yet your gentle souls fly in the air
And be not fixed in doom perpetual,
Hover about me with your airy wings
And hear your mother's lamentation!
QUEEN MARGARET [aside]. Hover about her; say, that
right for right
Hath dimmed your infant morn to agèd night.
DUCHESS. So many miseries have crazed my voice,
That my woe-wearied tongue is still and mute.
Edward Plantagenet, why art thou dead?
QUEEN MARGARET [aside]. Plantagenet doth quit
Plantagenet,   20
Edward for Edward pays a dying debt.
QUEEN ELIZABETH. Wilt thou, O God, fly from such
gentle lambs,
And throw them in the entrails of the wolf?
When didst thou sleep when such a deed was done?
QUEEN MARGARET [aside]. When holy Harry died, and
my sweet son.
DUCHESS. Dead life, blind sight, poor mortal living
ghost,
Woe's scene, world's shame, grave's due by life
usurped,
Brief abstract and record of tedious days,
Rest thy unrest on England's lawful earth,
Unlawfully made drunk with innocent blood!   30
                                Sits
QUEEN ELIZABETH. Ah, that thou wouldst as soon
afford a grave
As thou canst yield a melancholy seat!
Then would I hide my bones, not rest them here.
Ah, who hath any cause to mourn but we?
                         Sits down by her
QUEEN MARGARET [advancing]. If ancient sorrow be
most reverend,
Give mine the benefit of seniory,
And let my griefs frown on the upper hand.
If sorrow can admit society,   *Sits down with them*
Tell o'er your woes again by viewing mine:
I had an Edward, till a Richard killed him;   40
I had a Harry, till a Richard killed him:
Thou hadst an Edward, till a Richard killed him;
Thou hadst a Richard, till a Richard killed him.
DUCHESS. I had a Richard too, and thou didst kill
him;
I had a Rutland too, thou holp'st to kill him.
QUEEN MARGARET. Thou hadst a Clarence too, and
Richard killed him.
From forth the kennel of thy womb hath crept
A hell-hound that doth hunt us all to death:
That dog, that had his teeth before his eyes,
To worry lambs and lap their gentle blood;   50
That foul defacer of God's handiwork;
That excellent grand tyrant of the earth,
That reigns in gallèd eyes of weeping souls—

Thy womb let loose, to chase us to our graves.
O upright, just, and true-disposing God,
How do I thank thee, that this carnal cur
Preys on the issue of his mother's body,
And makes her pew-fellow with others' moan!
DUCHESS. O Harry's wife, triumph not in my woes!
God witness with me, I have wept for thine.   60
QUEEN MARGARET. Bear with me; I am hungry for
revenge,
And now I cloy me with beholding it.
They Edward he is dead, that killed my Edward;
Thy other Edward dead, to quit my Edward;
Young York he is but boot, because both they
Matched not the high perfection of my loss:
Thy Clarence he is dead that stabbed my Edward;
And the beholders of this frantic play,
Th'adulterate Hastings, Rivers, Vaughan, Grey,
Untimely smothered in their dusky graves.   70
Richard yet lives, hell's black intelligencer,
Only reserved their factor, to buy souls
And send them thither: but at hand, at hand,
Ensues his piteous and unpitied end:
Earth gapes, hell burns, fiends roar, saints pray,
To have him suddenly conveyed from hence:
Cancel his bond of life, dear God, I plead,
That I may live and say 'The dog is dead!'
QUEEN ELIZABETH. O, thou didst prophesy the time
would come
That I should wish for thee to help me curse   80
That bottled spider, that foul bunch-backed toad!
QUEEN MARGARET. I called thee then vain flourish of
my fortune;
I called thee then poor shadow, painted queen,
The presentation of but what I was;
The flattering index of a direful pageant;
One heaved a-high, to be hurled down below;
A mother only mocked with two fair babes;
A dream of what thou wast, a garish flag,
To be the aim of every dangerous shot;
A sign of dignity, a breath, a bubble;   90
A queen in jest, only to fill the scene.
Where is thy husband now? where be thy brothers?
Where be thy two sons? wherein dost thou joy?
Who sues, and kneels and says, 'God save the
queen'?
Where be the bending peers that flattered thee?
Where be the thronging troops that followèd thee?
Decline all this, and see what now thou art:
For happy wife, a most distressèd widow;
For joyful mother, one that wails the name;
For queen, a very caitiff crowned with care;   100
For one being sued to, one that humbly sues;
For she that scorned at me, now scorned of me;
For she being feared of all, now fearing one;
For she commanding all, obeyed of none.
Thus hath the course of Justice whirled about,
And left thee but a very prey to time;
Having no more but thought of what thou wast,
To torture thee the more, being what thou art.
Thou didst usurp my place, and dost thou not
Usurp the just proportion of my sorrow?   110
Now thy proud neck bears half my burthened yoke;
From which even here I slip my weary head,
And leave the burthen of it all—on thee.
Farewell, York's wife, and queen of sad mischance:
These English woes shall make me smile in France.

QUEEN ELIZABETH. O thou well skilled in curses, stay awhile,
And teach me how to curse mine enemies!
QUEEN MARGARET. Forbear to sleep the nights, and fast the days;
Compare dead happiness with living woe;
Think that thy babes were sweeter than they were, 120
And he that slew them fouler than he is:
Bett'ring thy loss makes the bad causer worse:
Revolving this will teach thee how to curse.
QUEEN ELIZABETH. My words are dull; O, quicken them with thine!
QUEEN MARGARET. Thy woes will make them sharp and pierce like mine.   *She goes*
DUCHESS. Why should calamity be full of words?
QUEEN ELIZABETH. Windy attorneys to their client woes,
Airy succeeders of intestate joys,
Poor breathing orators of miseries!
Let them have scope: though what they will impart 130
Help nothing else, yet do they ease the heart.
DUCHESS. If so, then be not tongue-tied: go with me,
And in the breath of bitter words let's smother
My damnèd son, that thy two sweet sons smothered.
The trumpet sounds: be copious in exclaims.

Enter King Richard and his train, marching with drums and trumpets

KING RICHARD. Who intercepts me in my expedition?
DUCHESS. O, she that might have intercepted thee,
By strangling thee in her accursèd womb,
From all the slaughters, wretch, that thou hast done!
QUEEN ELIZABETH. Hid'st thou that forehead with a golden crown,   140
Where should be branded, if that right were right,
The slaughter of the prince that owed that crown,
And the dire death of my poor sons and brothers?
Tell me, thou villain slave, where are my children?
DUCHESS. Thou toad, thou toad, where is thy brother Clarence?
And little Ned Plantagenet, his son?
QUEEN ELIZABETH. Where is the gentle Rivers, Vaughan, Grey?
DUCHESS. Where is kind Hastings?
KING RICHARD. A flourish, trumpets! strike alarum, drums!
Let not the heavens hear these tell-tale women 150
Rail on the Lord's anointed: strike, I say!
                            Flourish. Alarums
Either be patient, and entreat me fair,
Or with the clamorous report of war
Thus will I drown your exclamations.
DUCHESS. Art thou my son?
KING RICHARD. Ay, I thank God, my father, and yourself.
DUCHESS. Then patiently hear my impatience.
KING RICHARD. Madam, I have a touch of your condition,
That cannot brook the accent of reproof.
DUCHESS. O, let me speak!
KING RICHARD.   Do then; but I'll not hear. 160
DUCHESS. I will be mild and gentle in my words.
KING RICHARD. And brief, good mother, for I am in haste.

DUCHESS. Art thou so hasty? I have stayed for thee,
God knows, in torment and in agony.
KING RICHARD. And came I not at last to comfort you?
DUCHESS. No, by the holy rood, thou know'st it well,
Thou cam'st on earth to make the earth my hell.
A grievous burthen was thy birth to me;
Tetchy and wayward was thy infancy;
Thy school-days frightful, desp'rate, wild, and furious;   170
Thy prime of manhood daring, bold, and venturous;
Thy age confirmed, proud, subtle, sly and bloody,
More mild but yet more harmful—kind in hatred.
What comfortable hour canst thou name,
That ever graced me with thy company?
KING RICHARD. Faith, none, but Humphrey Hour, that called your grace
To breakfast once forth of my company.
If I be so disgracious in your eye,
Let me march on, and not offend you, madam.
Strike up the drum.
DUCHESS.   I prithee, hear me speak. 180
KING RICHARD. You speak too bitterly.
DUCHESS.   Hear me a word;
For I shall never speak to thee again.
KING RICHARD. So.
DUCHESS. Either thou wilt die, by God's just ordinance,
Ere from this war thou turn a conqueror,
Or I with grief and extreme age shall perish
And never more behold thy face again.
Therefore take with thee my most grievous curse,
Which, in the day of battle, tire thee more
Than all the complete armour that thou wear'st! 190
My prayers on the adverse party fight;
And there the little souls of Edward's children
Whisper the spirits of thine enemies
And promise them success and victory.
Bloody thou art, bloody will be thy end;
Shame serves thy life and doth thy death attend.
                            She goes
QUEEN ELIZABETH. Though far more cause, yet much less spirit to curse
Abides in me; I say amen to her.
KING RICHARD. Stay, madam; I must talk a word with you.
QUEEN ELIZABETH. I have no moe sons of the royal blood   200
For thee to slaughter: for my daughters, Richard,
They shall be praying nuns, not weeping queens;
And therefore level not to hit their lives.
KING RICHARD. You have a daughter called Elizabeth,
Virtuous and fair, royal and gracious.
QUEEN ELIZABETH. And must she die for this? O, let her live,
And I'll corrupt her manners, stain her beauty,
Slander myself as false to Edward's bed,
Throw over her the veil of infamy:
So she may live unscarred of bleeding slaughter, 210
I will confess she was not Edward's daughter.
KING RICHARD. Wrong not her birth, she is a royal princess.
QUEEN ELIZABETH. To save her life, I'll say she is not so.
KING RICHARD. Her life is safest only in her birth.
QUEEN ELIZABETH. And only in that safety died her brothers.

KING RICHARD. No, at their births good stars were
  opposite.
QUEEN ELIZABETH. No, to their lives ill friends were
  contrary.
KING RICHARD. All unavoided is the doom of destiny.
QUEEN ELIZABETH. True, when avoided grace makes
  destiny:
  My babes were destined to a fairer death,   220
  If grace had blessed thee with a fairer life.
KING RICHARD. You speak as if that I had slain my
  cousins!
QUEEN ELIZABETH. Cousins indeed, and by their uncle
  cozened
  Of comfort, kingdom, kindred, freedom, life.
  Whose hand soever lanced their tender hearts,
  Thy head, all indirectly, gave direction:
  No doubt the murd'rous knife was dull and blunt
  Till it was whetted on thy stone-hard heart
  To revel in the entrails of my lambs.
  But that still use of grief makes wild grief tame,   230
  My tongue should to thy ears not name my boys
  Till that my nails were anchored in thine eyes;
  And I, in such a desp'rate bay of death,
  Like a poor bark, of sails and tackling reft,
  Rush all to pieces on thy rocky bosom.
KING RICHARD. Madam, so thrive I in my enterprise
  And dangerous success of bloody wars,
  As I intend more good to you and yours
  Than ever you or yours by me were harmed!
QUEEN ELIZABETH. What good is covered with the face
  of heaven,   240
  To be discovered, that can do me good?
KING RICHARD. Th'advancement of your children,
  gentle lady.
QUEEN ELIZABETH. Up to some scaffold, there to lose
  their heads?
KING RICHARD. Unto the dignity and height of
  fortune,
  The high imperial type of this earth's glory.
QUEEN ELIZABETH. Flatter my sorrow with report of it;
  Tell me what state, what dignity, what honour,
  Canst thou demise to any child of mine?
KING RICHARD. Even all I have; ay, and myself and all,
  Will I withal endow a child of thine;   250
  So in the Lethe of thy angry soul
  Thou drown the sad remembrance of those wrongs
  Which thou supposest I have done to thee.
QUEEN ELIZABETH. Be brief, lest that the process of thy
  kindness
  Last longer telling than thy kindness' date.
KING RICHARD. Then know, that from my soul I love
  thy daughter.
QUEEN ELIZABETH. My daughter's mother thinks it
  with her soul.
KING RICHARD. What do you think?
QUEEN ELIZABETH. That thou dost love my daughter
  from thy soul:
  So from thy soul's love didst thou love her
  brothers;   260
  And from my heart's love I do thank thee for it.
KING RICHARD. Be not so hasty to confound my
  meaning:
  I mean that with my soul I love thy daughter,
  And do intend to make her Queen of England.
QUEEN ELIZABETH. Well then, who dost thou mean
  shall be her king?

KING RICHARD. Even he that makes her queen: who
  else should be?
QUEEN ELIZABETH. What, thou?
KING RICHARD. Even so: how think you of it?
QUEEN ELIZABETH. How canst thou woo her?
KING RICHARD.   That would I learn of you,
  As one being best acquainted with her humour.   270
QUEEN ELIZABETH. And wilt thou learn of me?
KING RICHARD.   With all my heart.
QUEEN ELIZABETH. Send to her, by the man that slew
  her brothers,
  A pair of bleeding hearts; thereon engrave
  'Edward' and 'York'; then haply will she weep:
  Therefore present to her—as sometimes Margaret
  Did to thy father, steeped in Rutland's blood—
  A handkerchief; which, say to her, did drain
  The purple sap from her sweet brother's body,
  And bid her wipe her weeping eyes withal.
  If this inducement move her not to love,   280
  Send her a letter of thy noble deeds;
  Tell her thou mad'st away her uncle Clarence,
  Her uncle Rivers; ay—and for her sake—
  Mad'st quick conveyance with her good aunt Anne.
KING RICHARD. You mock me, madam; this is not the
  way
To win your daughter.
QUEEN ELIZABETH.   There is no other way;
  Unless thou couldst put on some other shape,
  And not be Richard that hath done all this.
KING RICHARD. Say that I did all this for love of her.
QUEEN ELIZABETH. Nay, then indeed she cannot choose
  but hate thee,   290
  Having bought love with such a bloody spoil.
KING RICHARD. Look what is done cannot be now
  amended:
  Men shall deal unadvisedly sometimes,
  Which after-hours gives leisure to repent.
  If I did take the kingdom from your sons,
  To make amends I'll give it to your daughter.
  If I have killed the issue of your womb,
  To quicken your increase I will beget
  Mine issue of your blood upon your daughter:
  A grandam's name is little less in love   300
  Than is the doting title of a mother;
  They are as children but one step below,
  Even of your mettle, of your very blood,
  Of all one pain, save for a night of groans
  Endured of her, for whom you bid like sorrow.
  Your children were vexation to your youth,
  But mine shall be a comfort to your age.
  The loss you have is but a son being king,
  And by that loss your daughter is made queen.
  I cannot make you what amends I would,   310
  Therefore accept such kindness as I can.
  Dorset your son, that with a fearful soul
  Leads discontented steps in foreign soil,
  This fair alliance quickly shall call home
  To high promotions and great dignity:
  The king, that calls your beauteous daughter wife,
  Familiarly shall call thy Dorset brother;
  Again shall you be mother to a king,
  And all the ruins of distressful times
  Repaired with double riches of content.   320
  What! we have many goodly days to see:
  The liquid drops of tears that you have shed
  Shall come again, transformed to orient pearl,

Advantaging their loan with interest
Of ten times double gain of happiness.
Go, then, my mother, to thy daughter go;
Make bold her bashful years with your experience;
Prepare her ears to hear a wooer's tale;
Put in her tender heart th'aspiring flame
Of golden sovereignty; acquaint the princess   330
With the sweet silent hours of marriage joys:
And when this arm of mine hath chastiséd
The petty rebel, dull-brained Buckingham,
Bound with triumphant garlands will I come
And lead thy daughter to a conqueror's bed;
To whom I will retail my conquest won,
And she shall be sole victoress, Caesar's Caesar.

QUEEN ELIZABETH. What were I best to say? her
    father's brother
Would be her lord? or shall I say her uncle?
Or he that slew her brothers and her uncles?   340
Under what title shall I woo for thee,
That God, the law, my honour, and her love,
Can make seem pleasing to her tender years?

KING RICHARD. Infer fair England's peace by this
    alliance.

QUEEN ELIZABETH. Which she shall purchase with still-
    lasting war.

KING RICHARD. Tell her the king, that may command,
    entreats.

QUEEN ELIZABETH. That at her hands which the king's
    King forbids.

KING RICHARD. Say she shall be a high and mighty
    queen.

QUEEN ELIZABETH. To vail the title, as her mother doth.

KING RICHARD. Say I will love her everlastingly.   350

QUEEN ELIZABETH. But how long shall that title 'ever'
    last?

KING RICHARD. Sweetly in force unto her fair life's
    end.

QUEEN ELIZABETH. But how long fairly shall her sweet
    life last?

KING RICHARD. As long as heaven and nature
    lengthens it.

QUEEN ELIZABETH. As long as hell and Richard likes of
    it.

KING RICHARD. Say, I, her sovereign, am her subject
    love.

QUEEN ELIZABETH. But she, your subject, loathes such
    sovereignty.

KING RICHARD. Be eloquent in my behalf to her.

QUEEN ELIZABETH. An honest tale speeds best being
    plainly told.

KING RICHARD. Then plainly to her tell my loving tale.   360

QUEEN ELIZABETH. Plain and not honest is too harsh a
    style.

KING RICHARD. Your reasons are too shallow and too
    quick.

QUEEN ELIZABETH. O no, my reasons are too deep and
    dead;
Too deep and dead, poor infants, in their graves.

KING RICHARD. Harp not on that string, madam; that
    is past.

QUEEN ELIZABETH. Harp on it still shall I till
    heart-strings break.

KING RICHARD. Now, by my George, my garter, and
    my crown—

QUEEN ELIZABETH. Profaned, dishonoured, and the
    third usurped.

KING RICHARD. I swear—

QUEEN ELIZABETH.   By nothing; for this is no oath:
Thy George, profaned, hath lost his lordly honour;   370
Thy garter, blemished, pawned his knightly virtue;
Thy crown, usurped, disgraced his kingly glory.
If something thou wouldst swear to be believed,
Swear then by something that thou hast not
    wronged.

KING RICHARD. Then, by my self—

QUEEN ELIZABETH.   Thy self is self-misused.

KING RICHARD. Now, by the world—

QUEEN ELIZABETH.   'Tis full of thy foul wrongs.

KING RICHARD. My father's death—

QUEEN ELIZABETH.   Thy life hath it dishonoured.

KING RICHARD. Why then, by God—

QUEEN ELIZABETH.   God's wrong is most of all.
If thou didst fear to break an oath with Him,
The unity the king my husband made   380
Thou hadst not broken, nor my brothers died:
If thou hadst feared to break an oath by Him,
Th'imperial metal, circling now thy head,
Had graced the tender temples of my child,
And both the princes had been breathing here,
Which now, two tender bedfellows for dust,
Thy broken faith hath made the prey for worms.
What canst thou swear by now?

KING RICHARD.   The time to come.

QUEEN ELIZABETH. That thou hast wrongéd in the time
    o'erpast;
For I myself have many tears to wash   390
Hereafter time, for time past wronged by thee.
The children live whose fathers thou hast
    slaughtered,
Ungoverned youth, to wail it in their age;
The parents live whose children thou hast
    butchered,
Old barren plants, to wail it with their age.
Swear not by time to come; for that thou hast
Misused ere used, by times ill-used o'erpast.

KING RICHARD. As I intend to prosper and repent,
So thrive I in my dangerous affairs
Of hostile arms! myself myself confound!   400
Heaven and fortune bar me happy hours!
Day, yield me not thy light; nor, night, thy rest!
Be opposite, all planets of good luck,
To my proceeding!—if, with dear heart's love,
Immaculate devotion, holy thoughts,
I tender not thy beauteous princely daughter!
In her consists my happiness and thine;
Without her, follows to myself and thee,
Herself, the land, and many a Christian soul,
Death, desolation, ruin, and decay: 410
It cannot be avoided but by this;
It will not be avoided but by this.
Therefore, dear mother—I must call you so—
Be the attorney of my love to her;
Plead what I will be, not what I have been—
Not my deserts, but what I will deserve;
Urge the necessity and state of times,
And be not peevish-fond in great designs.

QUEEN ELIZABETH. Shall I be tempted of the devil thus?

KING RICHARD. Ay, if the devil tempt you to do good.   420

QUEEN ELIZABETH. Shall I forget myself to be myself?

KING RICHARD. Ay, if yourself's remembrance wrong
    yourself.

QUEEN ELIZABETH. Yet thou didst kill my children.

KING RICHARD. But in your daughter's womb I bury them:
Where in that nest of spicery they will breed
Selves of themselves, to your recomforture.
QUEEN ELIZABETH. Shall I go win my daughter to thy will?
KING RICHARD. And be a happy mother by the deed.
QUEEN ELIZABETH. I go. Write to me very shortly,
And you shall understand from me her mind. 430
KING RICHARD. Bear her my true love's kiss [*kissing her*]; and so, farewell. *She goes*
Relenting fool, and shallow-changing woman!

Enter Ratcliffe; Catesby following

How now! what news?
RATCLIFFE. Most mighty sovereign, on the western coast
Rideth a puissant navy; to our shores
Throng many doubtful hollow-hearted friends,
Unarmed, and unresolved to beat them back:
'Tis thought that Richmond is their admiral;
And there they hull, expecting but the aid
Of Buckingham to welcome them ashore. 440
KING RICHARD. Some light-foot friend post to the Duke of Norfolk:
Ratcliffe, thyself—or Catesby; where is he?
CATESBY. Here, my good lord.
KING RICHARD. Catesby, fly to the duke.
CATESBY. I will, my lord, with all convenient haste.
KING RICHARD. Ratcliffe, come hither! post to Salisbury:
When thou comest thither—[*to Catesby*] Dull unmindful villain,
Why stay'st thou here, and go'st not to the duke?
CATESBY. First, mighty liege, tell me your highness' pleasure,
What from your grace I shall deliver to him.
KING RICHARD. O, true, good Catesby: bid him levy straight 450
The greatest strength and power that he can make,
And meet me suddenly at Salisbury.
CATESBY. I go. *He goes*
RATCLIFFE. What may it please you, shall I do at Salisbury?
KING RICHARD. Why, what wouldst thou do there before I go?
RATCLIFFE. Your highness told me I should post before.
KING RICHARD. My mind is changed.

Enter Lord Stanley

Stanley, what news with you?
STANLEY. None good, my liege, to please you with the hearing;
Nor none so bad, but well may be reported.
KING RICHARD. Hoyday, a riddle! neither good nor bad! 460
What need'st thou run so many miles about,
When thou mayest tell thy tale the nearest way?
Once more, what news?
STANLEY. Richmond is on the seas.
KING RICHARD. There let him sink, and be the seas on him!
White-livered runagate, what doth he there?
STANLEY. I know not, mighty sovereign, but by guess.
KING RICHARD. Well, as you guess?

STANLEY. Stirred up by Dorset, Buckingham, and Morton,
He makes for England, here to claim the crown.
KING RICHARD. Is the chair empty? is the sword unswayed? 470
Is the king dead? the empire unpossessed?
What heir of York is there alive but we?
And who is England's king but great York's heir?
Then, tell me, what makes he upon the seas?
STANLEY. Unless for that, my liege, I cannot guess.
KING RICHARD. Unless for that he comes to be your liege,
You cannot guess wherefore the Welshman comes.
Thou wilt revolt and fly to him, I fear.
STANLEY. No, my good lord; therefore mistrust me not.
KING RICHARD. Where is thy power then to beat him back? 480
Where be thy tenants and thy followers?
Are they not now upon the western shore,
Safe-conducting the rebels from their ships?
STANLEY. No, my good lord, my friends are in the north.
KING RICHARD. Cold friends to me: what do they in the north,
When they should serve their sovereign in the west?
STANLEY. They have not been commanded, mighty king:
Pleaseth your majesty to give me leave,
I'll muster up my friends, and meet your grace
Where and what time your majesty shall please. 490
KING RICHARD. Ay, ay, thou wouldst be gone to join with Richmond:
But I'll not trust thee.
STANLEY. Most mighty sovereign,
You have no cause to hold my friendship doubtful:
I never was nor never will be false.
KING RICHARD. Go then, and muster men; but, leave behind
Your son, George Stanley: look your heart be firm,
Or else his head's assurance is but frail.
STANLEY. So deal with him as I prove true to you.
Goes

Enter a Messenger

MESSENGER. My gracious sovereign, now in Devonshire,
As I by friends am well advértiséd, 500
Sir Edward Courtney, and the haughty prelate,
Bishop of Exeter, his elder brother,
With many moe confederates, are in arms.

Enter another Messenger

2 MESSENGER. In Kent, my liege, the Guildfords are in arms;
And every hour more competitors
Flock to the rebels and their power grows strong.

Enter another Messenger

3 MESSENGER. My lord, the army of great Buckingham—
KING RICHARD. Out on you, owls! nothing but songs of death? *He strikes him*
There, take thou that, till thou bring better news.
3 MESSENGER. The news I have to tell your majesty 510
Is that, by sudden floods and fall of waters,

Buckingham's army is dispersed and scattered;
And he himself wand'red away alone,
No man knows whither.

KING RICHARD.   I cry thee mercy:
There is my purse to cure that blow of thine.
Hath any well-advicéd friend proclaimed
Reward to him that brings the traitor in?

3 MESSENGER. Such proclamation hath been made, my
lord.

Enter another Messenger

4 MESSENGER. Sir Thomas Lovel and Lord Marquis
Dorset,
'Tis said, my liege, in Yorkshire are in arms.   520
But this good comfort bring I to your highness,
The Breton navy is dispersed by tempest:
Richmond, in Dorsetshire, sent out a boat
Unto the shore, to ask those on the banks
If they were his assistants, yea or no;
Who answered him, they came from Buckingham
Upon his party: he, mistrusting them,
Hoised sail and made his course again for Brittany.

KING RICHARD. March on, march on, since we are up
in arms;
If not to fight with foreign enemies,   530
Yet to beat down these rebels here at home.

Catesby returns

CATESBY. My liege, the Duke of Buckingham is taken;
That is the best news: that the Earl of Richmond
Is with a mighty power landed at Milford
Is colder tidings, yet they must be told.

KING RICHARD. Away towards Salisbury! While we
reason here,
A royal battle might be won and lost:
Some one take order Buckingham be brought
To Salisbury; the rest march on with me.

                        A flourish as they go

Scene 5: *Lord Stanley's house*

Enter Lord Stanley and Sir Christopher Urswick, a priest

STANLEY. Sir Christopher, tell Richmond this from
me:
That in the sty of the most deadly boar
My son George Stanley is franked up in hold:
If I revolt, off goes young George's head:
The fear of that holds off my present aid.
So, get thee gone; commend me to thy lord.
Withal say that the queen hath heartily consented
He should espouse Elizabeth her daughter.
But, tell me, where is princely Richmond now?

CHRISTOPHER. At Pembroke, or at Ha'rford-west, in
Wales.   10

STANLEY. What men of name resort to him?

CHRISTOPHER. Sir Walter Herbert, a renownéd
soldier;
Sir Gilbert Talbot, Sir William Stanley,
Oxford, redoubted Pembroke, Sir James Blunt,
And Rice ap Thomas, with a valiant crew,
And many other of great name and worth:
And towards London do they bend their power,
If by the way they be not fought withal.

STANLEY. Well, hie thee to thy lord; I kiss his hand:
My letter will resolve him of my mind.   20
Farewell.   *They go*

ACT 5

Scene 1: *Salisbury. An open place*

*Enter a Sheriff with halberds, leading Buckingham to
execution*

BUCKINGHAM. Will not King Richard let me speak
with him?

SHERIFF. No, my good lord; therefore be patient.

BUCKINGHAM. Hastings, and Edward's children, Grey
and Rivers,
Holy King Henry, and thy fair son Edward,
Vaughan, and all that have miscarriéd
By underhand corrupted foul injustice,
If that your moody discontented souls
Do through the clouds behold this present hour,
Even for revenge mock my destruction!
This is All-Souls' day, fellow, is it not?   10

SHERIFF. It is, my lord.

BUCKINGHAM. Why, then All-Souls' day is my body's
doomsday.
This is the day which in King Edward's time
I wished might fall on me when I was found
False to his children and his wife's allies;
This is the day wherein I wished to fall
By the false faith of him whom most I trusted;
This, this All-Souls' day to my fearful soul
Is the determined respite of my wrongs:
That high All-Seer which I dallied with   20
Hath turned my feignéd prayer on my head,
And given in earnest what I begged in jest.
Thus doth He force the swords of wicked men
To turn their own points in their masters' bosoms:
Thus Margaret's curse falls heavy on my neck;
'When he,' quoth she, 'shall split thy heart with
sorrow,
Remember Margaret was a prophetess.'
Come, lead me, officers, to the block of shame;
Wrong hath but wrong, and blame the due of
blame.
                                They go

Scene 2: *The camp near Tamworth*

*Enter Richmond, Oxford, Blunt, Herbert, and others,
with drum and colours*

RICHMOND. Fellows in arms, and my most loving
friends,
Bruised underneath the yoke of tyranny,
Thus far into the bowels of the land
Have we marched on without impediment;
And here receive we from our father Stanley
Lines of fair comfort and encouragement.
The wretched, bloody, and usurping boar,
That spoils your summer fields and fruitful vines,
Swills your warm blood like wash, and makes his
trough
In your embowelled bosoms—this foul swine   10
Is now even in the centre of this isle,
Near to the town of Leicester, as we learn.
From Tamworth thither is but one day's march.
In God's name, cheerly on, courageous friends,
To reap the harvest of perpetual peace
By this one bloody trial of sharp war.

OXFORD. Every man's conscience is a thousand men,
To fight against this guilty homicide.

HERBERT. I doubt not but his friends will turn to us.

BLUNT. He hath no friends but what are friends for
　fear,
Which in his dearest need will fly from him.　　　　20
RICHMOND. All for our vantage. Then, in God's
　name, march:
True hope is swift, and flies with swallow's wings;
Kings it makes gods, and meaner creatures kings.
　　　　　　　　　　　　　　　　　　　They go

Scene 3: *Bosworth Field*

*Enter King Richard in arms with Norfolk, the Earl of
Surrey, and others*

KING RICHARD. Here pitch our tent, even here in
　Bosworth field.
My Lord of Surrey, why look you so sad?
SURREY. My heart is ten times lighter than my looks.
KING RICHARD. My Lord of Norfolk,—
NORFOLK. 　　　　　　　Here, most gracious liege.
KING RICHARD. Norfolk, we must have knocks, ha?
　must we not?
NORFOLK. We must both give and take, my loving
　lord.
KING RICHARD. Up with my tent! Here will I lie
　to-night—
But where to-morrow? Well, all's one for that.
Who hath descried the number of the traitors?
NORFOLK. Six or seven thousand is their utmost
　power.　　　　　　　　　　　　　　　　　　10
KING RICHARD. Why, our battalia trebles that account:
Besides, the king's name is a tower of strength,
Which they upon the adverse faction want.
Up with the tent! Come, noble gentlemen,
Let us survey the vantage of the ground.
Call for some men of sound direction:
Let's lack no discipline, make no delay;
For, lords, to-morrow is a busy day.
　　　　　　　　　*They depart while soldiers pitch
　　　　　　　　　　　　　　　　the royal tent*

*Enter, on the other side of the field, Richmond, Sir
William Brandon, Oxford, and others. Soldiers pitch
Richmond's tent*

RICHMOND. The weary sun hath made a golden set,
And by the bright tract of his fiery car
Gives token of a goodly day to-morrow.　　　　　20
Sir William Brandon, you shall bear my standard.
Give me some ink and paper in my tent:
I'll draw the form and model of our battle,
Limit each leader to his several charge,
And part in just proportion our small power.
My Lord of Oxford, you, Sir William Brandon,
And you, Sir Walter Herbert, stay with me.
The Earl of Pembroke keeps his regiment:
Good Captain Blunt, bear my good-night to him,　30
And by the second hour in the morning
Desire the earl to see me in my tent:
Yet one thing more, good captain, do for me—
Where is Lord Stanley quartered, do you know?
BLUNT. Unless I have mista'en his colours much,
Which well I am assured I have not done,
His regiment lies half a mile at least
South from the mighty power of the king.
RICHMOND. If without peril it be possible,
Sweet Blunt, make some good means to speak with
　him,　　　　　　　　　　　　　　　　　40

And give him from me this most needful note.
BLUNT. Upon my life, my lord, I'll undertake it;
And so, God give you quiet rest to-night!
RICHMOND. Good night, good Captain Blunt. Come,
　gentlemen,
Let us consult upon to-morrow's business:
In to my tent! the dew is raw and cold.
　　　　　　　　　They withdraw into the tent

*Enter, to his tent, King Richard, Norfolk, Ratcliffe,
Catesby, and others*

KING RICHARD. What is't o'clock?
CATESBY. 　　　　　It's supper-time, my lord;
　It's nine o'clock.
KING RICHARD. 　　　　　I will not sup to-night.
Give me some ink and paper.
What, is my beaver easier than it was?　　　　　50
And all my armour laid into my tent?
CATESBY. It is, my liege; and all things are in readiness.
KING RICHARD. Good Norfolk, hie thee to thy charge;
Use careful watch, choose trusty sentinels.
NORFOLK. I go, my lord.
KING RICHARD. Stir with the lark to-morrow, gentle
　Norfolk.
NORFOLK. I warrant you, my lord. 　　　*He goes*
KING RICHARD. Catesby!
CATESBY. My lord?
KING RICHARD. 　　　Send out a pursuivant-at-arms
To Stanley's regiment; bid him bring his power　60
Before sunrising, lest his son George fall
Into the blind cave of eternal night.　*Catesby goes*
Fill me a bowl of wine. Give me a watch.
Saddle white Surrey for the field to-morrow.
Look that my staves be sound, and not too heavy.
Ratcliffe!
RATCLIFFE. My lord!
KING RICHARD. Saw'st thou the melancholy Lord
　Northumberland?
RATCLIFFE. Thomas the Earl of Surrey and himself,
Much about cock-shut time, from troop to troop　70
Went through the army, cheering up the soldiers.
KING RICHARD. So, I am satisfied. A bowl of wine:
I have not that alacrity of spirit
Nor cheer of mind that I was wont to have.
Set it down. Is ink and paper ready?
RATCLIFFE. It is, my lord.
KING RICHARD. 　　　　Bid my guard watch. Leave me.
Ratcliffe, about the mid of night come to my tent
And help to arm me. Leave me, I say.
　　　　　　　　　*Ratcliffe goes; Richard withdraws
　　　　　　　　　　　　　　　　into his tent*
*Enter Stanley to Richmond in his tent, Lords and others
attending*

STANLEY. Fortune and victory sit on thy helm!
RICHMOND. All comfort that the dark night can afford　80
Be to thy person, noble father-in-law!
Tell me, how fares our loving mother?
STANLEY. I, by attorney, bless thee from thy mother,
Who prays continually for Richmond's good:
So much for that. The silent hours steal on,
And flaky darkness breaks within the east.
In brief, for so the season bids us be,
Prepare thy battle early in the morning,
And put thy fortune to th'arbitrement
Of bloody strokes and mortal-staring war.　　　90
I, as I may—that which I would I cannot—

With best advantage will deceive the time,
And aid thee in this doubtful shock of arms:
But on thy side I may not be too forward,
Lest, being seen, thy brother, tender George,
Be executed in his father's sight.
Farewell: the leisure and the fearful time
Cuts off the ceremonious vows of love
And ample interchange of sweet discourse
Which so long sund'red friends should dwell upon. 100
God give us leisure for these rites of love!
Once more, adieu: be valiant, and speed well!
RICHMOND. Good lords, conduct him to his regiment:
I'll strive with troubled thoughts to take a nap,
Lest leaden slumber peise me down to-morrow,
When I should mount with wings of victory:
Once more, good night, kind lords and gentlemen.
                              They leave: Richmond kneels
O Thou, whose captain I account myself,
Look on my forces with a gracious eye;
Put in their hands thy bruising irons of wrath,   110
That they may crush down with a heavy fall
Th'usurping helmets of our adversaries!
Make us thy ministers of chastisement,
That we may praise thee in the victory!
To thee I do commend my watchful soul,
Ere I let fall the windows of mine eyes:
Sleeping and waking, O, defend me still!   *Sleeps*

*The Ghost of Prince Edward, son to Henry the Sixth,
appears between the tents*

GHOST [*to Richard*]. Let me sit heavy on thy soul
    to-morrow!
Think how thou stab'st me in my prime of youth
At Tewkesbury: despair therefore, and die!   120
[*to Richmond*] Be cheerful, Richmond; for the
    wrongèd souls
Of butchered princes fight in thy behalf:
King Henry's issue, Richmond, comforts thee.
                                          Vanishes

The Ghost of Henry the Sixth appears

GHOST [*to Richard*]. When I was mortal, my anointed
    body
By thee was punchèd full of deadly holes:
Think on the Tower and me: despair, and die!
Harry the Sixth bids thee despair and die!
[*to Richmond*] Virtuous and holy, be thou
    conqueror!
Harry, that prophesied thou shouldst be king,
Doth comfort thee in thy sleep: live and flourish! 130
                                          Vanishes

The Ghost of Clarence appears

GHOST [*to Richard*]. Let me sit heavy on thy soul
    to-morrow!
I that was washed to death with fulsome wine,
Poor Clarence, by thy guile betrayed to death.
To-morrow in the battle think on me,
And fall thy edgeless sword: despair, and die!
[*to Richmond*] Thou offspring of the house of
    Lancaster,
The wrongèd heirs of York do pray for thee:
Good angels guard thy battle! live, and flourish!
                                          Vanishes

The Ghosts of Rivers, Grey, and Vaughan appear

GHOST OF RIVERS [*to Richard*]. Let me sit heavy on thy
    soul to-morrow,
Rivers, that died at Pomfret! Despair, and die!   140
GHOST OF GREY [*to Richard*]. Think upon Grey, and let
    thy soul despair!
GHOST OF VAUGHAN [*to Richard*]. Think upon
    Vaughan, and, with guilty fear,
Let fall thy lance: despair, and die!
[*All to Richmond*] Awake, and think our wrongs in
    Richard's bosom
Will conquer him! awake, and win the day!
                                          They vanish

The Ghost of Lord Hastings appears

GHOST [*to Richard*]. Bloody and guilty, guiltily
    awake,
And in a bloody battle end thy days!
Think on Lord Hastings: despair, and die!
[*to Richmond*] Quiet untroubled soul, awake, awake!
Arm, fight, and conquer, for fair England's sake! 150
                                          Vanishes

The Ghosts of the two young Princes appear

GHOSTS [*to Richard*]. Dream on thy cousins smotherèd
    in the Tower:
Let us be lead within thy bosom, Richard,
And weigh thee down to ruin, shame, and death!
Thy nephews' souls bid thee despair and die!
[*to Richmond*] Sleep, Richmond, sleep in peace, and
    wake in joy;
Good angels guard thee from the boar's annoy!
Live, and beget a happy race of kings!
Edward's unhappy sons to bid thee flourish.
                                          They vanish

The Ghost of Anne his wife appears

GHOST [*to Richard*]. Richard, thy wife, that wretched
    Anne thy wife,
That never slept a quiet hour with thee,   160
Now fills thy sleep with perturbations:
To-morrow in the battle think on me,
And fall thy edgeless sword: despair, and die!
[*to Richmond*] Thou quiet soul, sleep thou a quiet
    sleep:
Dream of success and happy victory!
Thy adversary's wife doth pray for thee.
                                          Vanishes

The Ghost of Buckingham appears

GHOST [*to Richard*]. The first was I that helped thee
    to the crown;
The last was I that felt thy tyranny:
O, in the battle think on Buckingham,
And die in terror of thy guiltiness!   170
Dream on, dream on, of bloody deeds and death:
Fainting, despair; despairing, yield thy breath!
[*to Richmond*] I died for hope ere I could lend thee
    aid:
But cheer thy heart, and be thou not dismayed:
God and good angels fight on Richmond's side;
And Richard falls in height of all his pride.
                                          Vanishes

King Richard starts out of his dream

KING RICHARD. Give me another horse! bind up my
    wounds!

Have mercy, Jesu!—Soft, I did but dream.
O coward conscience, how dost thou afflict me!
The lights burn blue. It is now dead midnight. 180
Cold fearful drops stand on my trembling flesh.
What do I fear? myself? there's none else by.
Richard loves Richard; that is, I am I.
Is there a murderer here? No—yes, I am:
Then fly. What, from myself? Great reason why—
Lest I revenge. Myself upon myself?
Alack, I love myself. For any good
That I myself have done unto myself?
O, no! Alas, I rather hate myself
For hateful deeds committed by myself! 190
I am a villain: yet I lie, I am not.
Fool, of thyself speak well: fool, do not flatter.
My conscience hath a thousand several tongues,
And every tongue brings in a several tale,
And every tale condemns me for a villain.
Perjury, perjury, in the high'st degree;
Murder, stern murder, in the dir'st degree;
All several sins, all used in each degree,
Throng to the bar, crying all 'Guilty! guilty!'.
I shall despair. There is no creature loves me; 200
And if I die, no soul will pity me:
Nay, wherefore should they, since that I myself
Find in myself no pity to myself?
Methought the souls of all that I had murdered
Came to my tent, and every one did threat
To-morrow's vengeance on the head of Richard.

Ratcliffe comes to the tent

RATCLIFFE. My lord!
KING RICHARD. Zounds! who is there?
RATCLIFFE. My lord; 'tis I. The early village cock
  Hath twice done salutation to the morn; 210
  Your friends are up, and buckle on their armour.
KING RICHARD. O Ratcliffe, I have dreamed a fearful
  dream!
  What thinkest thou, will all our friends prove true?
RATCLIFFE. No doubt, my lord.
KING RICHARD.   Ratcliffe, I fear, I fear—
RATCLIFFE. Nay, good my lord, be not afraid of
  shadows.
KING RICHARD. By the apostle Paul, shadows to-night
  Have struck more terror to the soul of Richard
  Than can the substance of ten thousand soldiers
  Arméd in proof, and led by shallow Richmond.
  'Tis not yet near day. Come, go with me; 220
  Under our tents I'll play the eaves-dropper,
  To hear if any mean to shrink from me.
                               They go

Enter the Lords to Richmond, sitting in his tent

LORDS. Good morrow, Richmond!
RICHMOND. Cry mercy, lords and watchful
  gentlemen,
  That you have ta'en a tardy sluggard here!
LORDS. How have you slept, my lord?
RICHMOND. The sweetest sleep and fairest-boding
  dreams
  That ever ent'red in a drowsy head
  Have I since your departure had, my lords.
  Methought their souls whose bodies Richard
  murdered
230 Came to my tent and cried on victory:
  I promise you my soul is very jocund

In the remembrance of so fair a dream.
How far into the morning is it, lords?
LORDS. Upon the stroke of four.
RICHMOND. Why, then 'tis time to arm and give
  direction.

His oration to his soldiers, who gather about the tent

More than I have said, loving countrymen,
The leisure and enforcement of the time
Forbids to swell upon: yet remember this,
God and our good cause fight upon our side; 240
The prayers of holy saints and wrongéd souls,
Like high-reared bulwarks, stand before our faces.
Richard except, those whom we fight against
Had rather have us win than him they follow:
For what is he they follow? truly, gentlemen,
A bloody tyrant and a homicide;
One raised in blood, and one in blood established;
One that made means to come by what he hath,
And slaughtered those that were the means to help
  him;
A base foul stone, made precious by the foil 250
Of England's chair, where he is falsely set;
One that hath ever been God's enemy.
Then, if you fight against God's enemy,
God will in justice ward you as his soldiers;
If you do sweat to put a tyrant down,
You sleep in peace, the tyrant being slain;
If you do fight against your country's foes,
Your country's fat shall pay your pains the hire;
If you do fight in safeguard of your wives,
Your wives shall welcome home the conquerors; 260
If you do free your children from the sword,
Your children's children quits it in your age.
Then, in the name of God and all these rights,
Advance your standards, draw your willing swords.
For me, the ransom of my bold attempt
Shall be this cold corpse on the earth's cold face;
But if I thrive, the gain of my attempt
The least of you shall share his part thereof.
Sound drums and trumpets bold and cheerfully;
God and Saint George! Richmond and victory! 270
                               They go

King Richard returns with Ratcliffe

KING RICHARD. What said Northumberland as
  touching Richmond?
RATCLIFFE. That he was never trainéd up in arms.
KING RICHARD. He said the truth: and what said
  Surrey then?
RATCLIFFE. He smiled and said 'The better for our
  purpose.'
KING RICHARD. He was in the right; and so indeed it
  is.   *Clock strikes*
  Tell the clock there. Give me a calendar.
  Who saw the sun to-day?
RATCLIFFE.   Not I, my lord.
KING RICHARD. Then he disdains to shine; for by the
  book
  He should have braved the east an hour ago:
  A black day will it be to somebody. 280
  Ratcliffe!
RATCLIFFE. My lord?
KING RICHARD.   The sun will not be seen to-day;
  The sky doth frown and lour upon our army.
  I would these dewy tears were from the ground.

Not shine to-day! Why, what is that to me.
More than to Richmond? for the selfsame heaven
That frowns on me looks sadly upon him.

Norfolk enters

NORFOLK. Arm, arm, my lord; the foe vaunts in the
field.
KING RICHARD. Come, bustle, bustle. Caparison my
horse.
Call up Lord Stanley, bid him bring his power: 290
I will lead forth my soldiers to the plain,
And thus my battle shall be orderéd:
My foreward shall be drawn out all in length,
Consisting equally of horse and foot;
Our archers shall be placéd in the midst:
John Duke of Norfolk, Thomas Earl of Surrey,
Shall have the leading of this foot and horse.
They thus directed, we will follow
In the main battle, whose puissance on either side
Shall be well wingéd with our chiefest horse.   300
This, and Saint George to boot! What think'st thou,
Norfolk?
NORFOLK. A good direction, warlike sovereign.
This found I on my tent this morning.
                              He shows him a paper
KING RICHARD [*reads*]. 'Jockey of Norfolk, be not too
bold,
For Dickon thy master is bought and sold.'
A thing devised by the enemy.
Go, gentlemen, every man unto his charge:
Let not our babbling dreams affright our souls:
Conscience is but a word that cowards use,
Devised at first to keep the strong in awe: 310
Our strong arms be our conscience, swords our law.
March on, join bravely, let us to it pell-mell;
If not to heaven, then hand in hand to hell.

His oration to his army

What shall I say more than I have inferred?
Remember whom you are to cope withal—
A sort of vagabonds, rascals, and runaways,
A scum of Bretons, and base lackey peasants,
Whom their o'er-cloyéd country vomits forth
To desperate ventures and assured destruction.
You sleeping safe, they bring to you unrest;   320
You having lands, and blest with beauteous wives,
They would distrain the one, distain the other.
And who doth lead them but a paltry fellow,
Long kept in Bretagne at our mother's cost?
A milksop, one that never in his life
Felt so much cold as over shoes in snow?
Let's whip these stragglers o'er the seas again,
Lash hence these overweening rags of France,
These famished beggars, weary of their lives,
Who, but for dreaming on this fond exploit,   330
For want of means, poor rats, had hanged
themselves.
If we be conquered, let men conquer us,
And not these bastard Bretons, whom our fathers
Have in their own land beaten, bobbed, and
thumped,
And in record left them the heirs of shame.
Shall these enjoy our lands? lie with our wives?
Ravish our daughters? [*drum afar off*] Hark! I hear
their drum.
Fight, gentlemen of England! fight, bold yeomen!

Draw, archers, draw your arrows to the head!
Spur your proud horses hard, and ride in blood   340
Amaze the welkin with your broken staves!

Enter a Messenger

What says Lord Stanley? will he bring his power?
MESSENGER. My lord, he doth deny to come.
KING RICHARD. Off with his son George's head!
NORFOLK. My lord, the enemy is past the marsh:
After the battle let George Stanley die.
KING RICHARD. A thousand hearts are great within my
bosom:
Advance our standards, set upon our foes;
Our ancient word of courage, fair Saint George,
Inspire us with the spleen of fiery dragons!   350
Upon them! Victory sits on our helms.   *They go*

Scene 4

*Alarum: excursions. Re-enter Norfolk; and forces fighting;
to him Catesby*

CATESBY. Rescue, my Lord of Norfolk, rescue, rescue!
The king enacts more wonders than a man,
Daring and opposite to every danger:
His horse is slain, and all on foot he fights,
Seeking for Richmond in the throat of death.
Rescue, fair lord, or else the day is lost!

Alarums. Enter Richard

KING RICHARD. A horse! a horse! my kingdom for a
horse!
CATESBY. Withdraw, my lord; I'll help you to a horse.
KING RICHARD. Slave, I have set my life upon a cast,
And I will stand the hazard of the die.   10
I think there be six Richmonds in the field;
Five have I slain to-day instead of him.
A horse! a horse! my kingdom for a horse!
                                        They go

Scene 5

*Alarum. Enter Richard with Richmond; they fight; Richard
is slain. A retreat is sounded; then with a flourish re-enter
Richmond, and Stanley bearing the crown, with divers other
lords*

RICHMOND. God and your arms be praised, victorious
friends!
The day is ours; the bloody dog is dead.
STANLEY. Courageous Richmond, well hast thou
acquit thee.
Lo, here, this long usurpéd royalty
From the dead temples of this bloody wretch
Have I plucked off, to grace thy brows withal:
Wear it, enjoy it, and make much of it.
RICHMOND. Great God of heaven, say Amen to all!
But, tell me, is thy young George Stanley living?
STANLEY. He is, my lord, and safe in Leicester town; 10
Whither, if it please you, we may now withdraw us.
RICHMOND. What men of name are slain on either
side?
STANLEY. John Duke of Norfolk, Walter Lord Ferrers,
Sir Robert Brakenbury, and Sir William Brandon.
RICHMOND. Inter their bodies as becomes their births:
Proclaim a pardon to the soldiers fled
That in submission will return to us:
And then, as we have ta'en the sacrament,

We will unite the white rose and the red.
Smile heaven upon this fair conjunction,   20
That long have frowned upon their enmity!
What traitor hears me, and says not Amen?
England hath long been mad, and scarred herself;
The brother blindly shed the brother's blood,
The father rashly slaughtered his own son,
The son, compelled, been butcher to the sire:
All that divided York and Lancaster
Divided in their dire division,
O, now let Richmond and Elizabeth,
The true succeeders of each royal house,   30
By God's fair ordinance conjoin together!

And let their heirs, God if his will be so,
Enrich the time to come with smooth-faced peace,
With smiling plenty and fair prosperous days!
Abate the edge of traitors, gracious Lord,
That would reduce these bloody days again,
And make poor England weep in streams of blood!
Let them not live to taste this land's increase
That would with treason wound this fair land's
    peace!
Now civil wounds are stopped, Peace lives again: 40
That she may long live here, God say Amen!

They go

King Henry the Eighth

The scene: London, Westminster, Kimbolton

CHARACTERS IN THE PLAY

KING HENRY *the Eighth*
CARDINAL WOLSEY
CARDINAL CAMPEIUS
CAPUCIUS, *Ambassador from the Emperor Charles V*
CRANMER, *Archbishop of Canterbury*
DUKE OF NORFOLK
DUKE OF BUCKINGHAM
DUKE OF SUFFOLK
EARL OF SURREY
Lord Chamberlain
Lord Chancellor
GARDINER, *Bishop of Winchester*
Bishop of Lincoln
LORD ABERGAVENNY
LORD SANDS
SIR HENRY GUILDFORD
SIR THOMAS LOVELL
SIR ANTHONY DENNY
SIR NICHOLAS VAUX

Secretaries to Wolsey
CROMWELL, *Servant to Wolsey*
GRIFFITH, *Gentleman-usher to Queen Katharine*
Three Gentlemen
DOCTOR BUTTS, *Physician to the King*
Garter King-at-Arms
Surveyor to the Duke of Buckingham
BRANDON, *and a Sergeant-at-Arms*
Door-keeper of the Council-chamber
Page to Gardiner. A Crier
Porter and his Man at the gate of the Palace
QUEEN KATHARINE, *wife to King Henry, afterwards divorced*
ANNE BULLEN, *her Maid of Honour, afterwards Queen*
An old Lady, friend to Anne Bullen
PATIENCE, *woman to Queen Katharine*
Several Lords and Ladies in the Dumb Shows, Women attending upon the Queen, Scribes, Officers, Guards, and other Attendants, Spirits

King Henry the Eighth

THE PROLOGUE

I come no more to make you laugh; things now
That bear a weighty and a serious brow,
Sad, high, and working, full of state and woe,
Such noble scenes as draw the eye to flow,
We now present. Those that can pity, here
May, if they think it well, let fall a tear:
The subject will deserve it. Such as give
Their money out of hope they may believe
May here find truth too. Those that come to see
Only a show or two, and so agree   10
The play may pass, if they be still and willing,
I'll undertake may see away their shilling
Richly in two short hours. Only they
That come to hear a merry bawdy play,
A noise of targets, or to see a fellow
In a long motley coat guarded with yellow,
Will be deceived; for, gentle hearers, know,
To rank our chosen truth with such a show
As fool and fight is, beside forfeiting
Our own brains and the opinion that we bring   20
To make that only true we now intend,
Will leave us never an understanding friend.
Therefore, for goodness' sake, and as you are known
The first and happiest hearers of the town,
Be sad, as we would make ye. Think ye see
The very persons of our noble story
As they were living; think you see them great,
And followed with the general throng and sweat
Of thousand friends; then, in a moment, see
How soon this mightiness meets misery.   30
And if you can be merry then, I'll say
A man may weep upon his wedding-day.

ACT 1
Scene 1: *London. The palace*

*Enter the Duke of Norfolk at one door; at the other the
Duke of Buckingham and the Lord Abergavenny*

BUCKINGHAM. Good morrow, and well met. How
  have ye done
Since last we saw in France?
NORFOLK.   I thank your grace,
  Healthful, and ever since a fresh admirer
  Of what I saw there.
BUCKINGHAM.   An untimely ague
  Stayed me a prisoner in my chamber when
  Those suns of glory, those two lights of men,
  Met in the vale of Andren.
NORFOLK.   'Twixt Guynes and Arde;
  I was then present, saw them salute on horseback;
  Beheld them, when they lighted, how they clung
  In their embracement, as they grew together;
  Which had they, what four throned ones could   10
    have weighed
  Such a compounded one?
BUCKINGHAM.   All the whole time
  I was my chamber's prisoner.

NORFOLK.   Then you lost
  The view of earthly glory; men might say,
  Till this time pomp was single, but now married
  To one above itself. Each following day
  Became the next day's master, till the last
  Made former wonders its. To-day the French,
  All clinquant, all in gold, like heathen gods,
  Shone down the English; and to-morrow they   20
  Made Britain India: every man that stood
  Showed like a mine. Their dwarfish pages were
  As cherubins, all gilt; the madams too,
  Not used to toil, did almost sweat to bear
  The pride upon them, that their very labour
  Was to them as a painting. Now this masque
  Was cried incomparable; and th'ensuing night
  Made it a fool and beggar. The two kings,
  Equal in lustre, were now best, now worst,
  As presence did present them: him in eye   30
  Still him in praise; and being present both,
  'Twas said they saw but one, and no discerner
  Durst wag his tongue in censure. When these suns—
  For so they phrase 'em—by their heralds challenged
  The noble spirits to arms, they did perform
  Beyond thought's compass, that former fabulous
    story,
  Being now seen possible enough, got credit,
  That Bevis was believed.
BUCKINGHAM.   O, you go far.
NORFOLK. As I belong to worship, and affect
  In honour honesty, the tract of every thing   40
  Would by a good discourser lose some life
  Which action's self was tongue to. All was royal;
  To the disposing of it nought rebell'd;
  Order gave each thing view; the office did
  Distinctly his full function.
BUCKINGHAM.   Who did guide,
  I mean, who set the body and the limbs
  Of this great sport together, as you guess?
NORFOLK. One, certes, that promises no element
  In such a business.
BUCKINGHAM.   I pray you, who, my lord?
NORFOLK. All this was ord'red by the good discretion   50
  Of the right reverend Cardinal of York.
BUCKINGHAM. The devil speed him! no man's pie is
    freed
  From his ambitious finger. What had he
  To do in these fierce vanities? I wonder
  That such a keech can with his very bulk
  Take up the rays o'th'beneficial sun,
  And keep it from the earth.
NORFOLK.   Surely, sir,
  There's in him stuff that puts him to these ends;
  For, being not propped by ancestry, whose grace
  Chalks successors their way, nor called upon   60
  For high feats done to th'crown, neither allied
  To eminent assistants, but spider-like,
  Out of his self-drawing web, 'a gives us note,
  The force of his own merit makes his way—
  A gift that heaven gives for him, which buys
  A place next to the king.

ABERGAVENNY.   I cannot tell
What heaven hath given him; let some graver eye
Pierce into that; but I can see his pride
Peep through each part of him. Whence has he that?
If not from hell, the devil is a niggard,   70
Or has given all before, and he begins
A new hell in himself.
BUCKINGHAM.   Why the devil,
Upon this French going out, took he upon him,
Without the privity o'th'king, t'appoint
Who should attend on him? He makes up the file
Of all the gentry; for the most part such
To whom as great a charge as little honour
He meant to lay upon; and his own letter,
The honourable board of council out,
Must fetch him in he papers.
ABERGAVENNY.   I do know   80
Kinsmen of mine, three at the least, that have
By this so sickened their estates that never
They shall abound as formerly.
BUCKINGHAM.   O, many
Have broke their backs with laying manors on 'em
For this great journey. What did this vanity
But minister communication of
A most poor issue?
NORFOLK.   Grievingly I think,
The peace between the French and us not values
The cost that did conclude it.
BUCKINGHAM.   Every man,
After the hideous storm that followed, was   90
A thing inspired, and, not consulting, broke
Into a general prophecy: that this tempest,
Dashing the garment of this peace, aboded
The sudden breach on't.
NORFOLK.   Which is budded out;
For France hath flawed the league, and hath attached
Our merchants' goods at Bordeaux.
ABERGAVENNY.   Is it therefore
Th'ambassador is silenced?
NORFOLK.   Marry, is't.
ABERGAVENNY. A proper title of a peace, and
          purchased
At a superfluous rate!
BUCKINGHAM.   Why, all this business
Our reverend cardinal carried.
NORFOLK.   Like it your grace,   100
The state takes notice of the private difference
Betwixt you and the cardinal. I advise you—
And take it from a heart that wishes towards you
Honour and plenteous safety—that you read
The cardinal's malice and his potency
Together; to consider further that
What his high hatred would effect wants not
A minister in his power. You know his nature,
That he's revengeful, and I know his sword
Hath a sharp edge; it's long and 't may be said   110
It reaches far, and where 'twill not extend,
Thither he darts it. Bosom up my counsel,
You'll find it wholesome. Lo, where comes that
          rock
That I advise your shunning.

*Enter Cardinal Wolsey, the purse borne before him, certain
of the Guard, and two Secretaries with papers. The
Cardinal in his passage fixeth his eye on Buckingham,
and Buckingham on him, both full of disdain*

WOLSEY. The Duke of Buckingham's surveyor, ha?
Where's his examination?
FIRST SECRETARY.   Here, so please you.
WOLSEY. Is he in person ready?
FIRST SECRETARY.   Ay, please your grace.
WOLSEY. Well, we shall then know more; and
          Buckingham
Shall lessen this big look.   *Wolsey and his Train go*
BUCKINGHAM. This butcher's cur is venom-mouthed,
          and I   120
Have not the power to muzzle him; therefore best
Not wake him in his slumber. A beggar's book
Outworths a noble's blood.
NORFOLK.   What, are you chafed?
Ask God for temperance; that's th'appliance only
Which your disease requires.
BUCKINGHAM.   I read in's looks
Matter against me, and his eye reviled
Me as his abject object. At this instant
He bores me with some trick. He's gone to th'king;
I'll follow and outstare him.
NORFOLK.   Stay, my lord,
And let your reason with your choler question   130
What 'tis you go about. To climb steep hills
Requires slow pace at first. Anger is like
A full hot horse, who being allowed his way,
Self-mettle tires him. Not a man in England
Can advise me like you; be to yourself
As you would to your friend.
BUCKINGHAM.   I'll to the king,
And from a mouth of honour quite cry down
This Ipswich fellow's insolence, or proclaim
There's difference in no persons.
NORFOLK.   Be advised;
Heat not a furnace for your foe so hot   140
That it do singe yourself. We may outrun
By violent swiftness that which we run at,
And lose by over-running. Know you not
The fire that mounts the liquor till't run o'er
In seeming to augment it wastes it? Be advised.
I say again there is no English soul
More stronger to direct you than yourself,
If with the sap of reason you would quench,
Or but allay, the fire of passion.
BUCKINGHAM.   Sir,
I am thankful to you, and I'll go along   150
By your prescription; but this top-proud fellow—
Whom from the flow of gall I name not, but
From sincere motions—by intelligence
And proofs as clear as founts in July when
We see each grain of gravel, I do know
To be corrupt and treasonous.
NORFOLK.   Say not 'treasonous'.
BUCKINGHAM. To th'king I'll say 't; and make my
          vouch as strong
As shore of rock. Attend. This holy fox,
Or wolf, or both—for he is equal ravenous
As he is subtle, and as prone to mischief   160
As able to perform't, his mind and place
Infecting one another, yea, reciprocally—
Only to show his pomp as well in France
As here at home, suggests the king our master
To this last costly treaty, th'interview,
That swallowed so much treasure, and like a glass
Did break i'th'wrenching.
NORFOLK.   Faith, and so it did.

BUCKINGHAM. Pray give me favour, sir. This cunning
  cardinal
The articles o'th'combination drew
As himself pleased; and they were ratified
As he cried 'Thus let be', to as much end
As give a crutch to th'dead. But our count-cardinal
Has done this, and 'tis well; for worthy Wolsey,
Who cannot err, he did it. Now this follows—
Which, as I take it, is a kind of puppy
To th'old dam, treason—Charles the emperor,
Under pretence to see the queen his aunt—
For 'twas indeed his colour, but he came
To whisper Wolsey—here makes visitation;
His fears were that the interview betwixt
England and France might through their amity
Breed him some prejudice; for from this league
Peeped harms that menaced him: he privily
Deals with our cardinal; and, as I trow—
Which I do well, for I am sure the emperor
Paid ere he promised; whereby his suit was granted
Ere it was asked—but when the way was made
And paved with gold, the emperor thus desired,
That he would please to alter the king's course
And break the foresaid peace. Let the king know,
As soon he shall by me, that thus the cardinal
Does buy and sell his honour as he pleases,
And for his own advantage.
NORFOLK.   I am sorry
To hear this of him, and could wish he were
Something mistaken in't.
BUCKINGHAM.   No, not a syllable:
I do pronounce him in that very shape
He shall appear in proof.

*Enter Brandon, a Sergeant at arms before him, and two
or three of the Guard*

BRANDON. Your office, sergeant: execute it.
SERGEANT.   Sir,
My lord the Duke of Buckingham, and Earl
Of Hereford, Stafford, and Northampton, I
Arrest thee of high treason, in the name
Of our most sovereign king.
BUCKINGHAM.   Lo you, my lord,
The net has fall'n upon me! I shall perish
Under device and practice.
BRANDON.   I am sorry
To see you ta'en from liberty, to look on
The business present; 'tis his highness' pleasure
You shall to the Tower.
BUCKINGHAM.   It will help me nothing
To plead mine innocence; for that dye is on me
Which makes my whit'st part black. The will of
  heaven
Be done in this and all things! I obey.
O my Lord Aberga'ny, fare you well!
BRANDON. Nay, he must bear you company.
  [*To Abergavenny*] The king
Is pleased you shall to th'Tower, till you know
How he determines further.
ABERGAVENNY.   As the duke said,
The will of heaven be done, and the king's pleasure
By me obeyed!
BRANDON.   Here is a warrant from
The king t'attach Lord Montacute, and the bodies
Of the duke's confessor, John de la Car,
One Gilbert Parke, his chancellor—

BUCKINGHAM.   So, so;
These are the limbs o'th'plot; no more, I hope.
BRANDON. A monk o'th'Chartreux.
BUCKINGHAM.   O, Nicholas Hopkins?
BRANDON.   He.
BUCKINGHAM. My surveyor is false; the o'er-great
  cardinal
Hath showed him gold; my life is spanned already.
I am the shadow of poor Buckingham,
Whose figure even this instant cloud puts on,
By darkening my clear sun. My lord, farewell.
                              They go

Scene 2: *The same. The council-chamber*

*Cornets. Enter King Henry, leaning on the Cardinal's
shoulder; the Nobles, and Sir Thomas Lovell: the Cardinal
places himself under the King's feet on his right side*

KING. My life itself, and the best heart of it,
Thanks you for this great care; I stood i'th'level
Of a full-charged confederacy, and give thanks
To you that choked it. Let be called before us
That gentleman of Buckingham's; in person
I'll hear him his confessions justify;
And point by point the treasons of his master
He shall again relate.

*A noise within, crying 'Room for the Queen!' Enter Queen
Katharine, ushered by the Duke of Norfolk, and the Duke
of Suffolk: she kneels. The King riseth from his state, takes
her up, kisses and placeth her by him.*

Q. KATHARINE. Nay, we must longer kneel: I am a
  suitor.
KING. Arise, and take place by us. Half your suit
Never name to us: you have half our power.
The other moiety ere you ask is given;
Repeat your will and take it.
Q. KATHARINE.   Thank your majesty.
That you would love yourself, and in that love
Not unconsidered leave your honour nor
The dignity of your office, is the point
Of my petition.
KING.   Lady mine, proceed.
Q. KATHARINE. I am solicited, not by a few,
And those of true condition, that your subjects
Are in great grievance: there have been commissions
Sent down among 'em, which hath flawed the heart
Of all their loyalties; wherein although,
My good lord cardinal, they vent reproaches
Most bitterly on you as putter-on
Of these exactions, yet the king our master—
Whose honour heaven shield from soil!—even he
  escapes not
Language unmannerly; yea, such which breaks
The sides of loyalty, and almost appears
In loud rebellion.
NORFOLK.   Not almost appears—
It doth appear; for, upon these taxations,
The clothiers all, not able to maintain
The many to them 'longing, have put off
The spinsters, carders, fullers, weavers, who,
Unfit for other life, compelled by hunger
And lack of other means, in desperate manner
Daring th'event to th'teeth, are all in uproar,
And danger serves among them.
KING.   Taxation?

Wherein? and what taxation? My lord cardinal,
You that are blamed for it alike with us,
Know you of this taxation?
WOLSEY.   Please you, sir,   40
I know but of a single part in aught
Pertains to th'state, and front but in that file
Where others tell steps with me.
Q. KATHARINE.   No, my lord?
You know no more than others? But you frame
Things that are known alike, which are not
    wholesome
To those which would not know them, and yet
    must
Perforce be their acquaintance. These exactions,
Whereof my sovereign would have note, they are
Most pestilent to th'hearing; and to bear 'em
The back is sacrifice to th'load. They say   50
They are devised by you, or else you suffer
Too hard an exclamation.
KING.   Still exaction!
The nature of it? in what kind, let's know,
Is this exaction?
Q. KATHARINE.   I am much too venturous
In tempting of your patience, but am bold'ned
Under your promised pardon. The subject's grief
Comes through commissions, which compels from
    each
The sixth part of his substance, to be levied
Without delay; and the pretence for this
Is named your wars in France. This makes bold
    mouths;   60
Tongues spit their duties out, and cold hearts freeze
Allegiance in them; their curses now
Live where their prayers did; and it's come to pass,
This tractable obedience is a slave
To each incensed will. I would your highness
Would give it quick consideration, for
There is no primer business.
KING.   By my life,
This is against our pleasure.
WOLSEY.   And for me,
I have no further gone in this than by
A single voice, and that not passed me but   70
By learned approbation of the judges. If I am
Traduced by ignorant tongues, which neither know
My faculties nor person, yet will be
The chronicles of my doing, let me say
'Tis but the fate of place, and the rough brake
That virtue must go through. We must not stint
Our necessary actions in the fear
To cope malicious censurers, which ever,
As ravenous fishes, do a vessel follow
That is new-trimmed, but benefit no further   80
Than vainly longing. What we oft do best,
By sick interpreters, once weak ones, is
Not ours or not allowed; what worst, as oft,
Hitting a grosser quality, is cried up
For our best act. If we shall stand still,
In fear our motion will be mocked or carped at,
We should take root here where we sit,
Or sit state-statues only.
KING.   Things done well,
And with a care, exempt themselves from fear;
Things done without example, in their issue   90
Are to be feared. Have you a precedent
Of this commission? I believe, not any.

We must not rend our subjects from our laws,
And stick them in our will. Sixth part of each?
A trembling contribution! Why, we take
From every tree lop, bark, and part o'th'timber,
And though we leave it with a root, thus hacked,
The air will drink the sap. To every county
Where this is questioned send our letters with
Free pardon to each man that has denied   100
The force of this commission. Pray look to't;
I put it to your care.
WOLSEY.   [To the Secretary] A word with you.
Let there be letters writ to every shire
Of the king's grace and pardon. The grievéd
    commons
Hardly conceive of me—let it be noised
That through our intercession this revokement
And pardon comes. I shall anon advise you
Further in the proceeding.   Secretary goes

Enter Surveyor

Q. KATHARINE. I am sorry that the Duke of
    Buckingham
Is run in your displeasure.
KING.   It grieves many.   110
The gentleman is learned and a most rare speaker;
To nature none more bound; his training such
That he may furnish and instruct great teachers,
And never seek for aid out of himself. Yet see,
When these so noble benefits shall prove
Not well disposed, the mind growing once corrupt,
They turn to vicious forms, ten times more ugly
Than ever they were fair. This man so complete,
Who was enrolled 'mongst wonders, and when we,
Almost with ravished listening, could not find   120
His hour of speech a minute—he, my lady,
Hath into monstrous habits put the graces
That once were his, and is become as black
As if besmeared in hell. Sit by us; you shall hear—
This was his gentleman in trust—of him
Things to strike honour sad. Bid him recount
The fore-recited practices, whereof
We cannot feel too little, hear too much.
WOLSEY. Stand forth, and with bold spirit relate what
    you,
Most like a careful subject, have collected   130
Out of the Duke of Buckingham.
KING.   Speak freely.
SURVEYOR. First, it was usual with him—every day
It would infect his speech—that if the king
Should without issue die, he'll carry it so
To make the sceptre his. These very words
I've heard him utter to his son-in-law,
Lord Aberga'ny, to whom by oath he menaced
Revenge upon the cardinal.
WOLSEY.   Please your highness, note
His dangerous conception in this point.
Not friended by his wish, to your high person   140
His will is most malignant, and it stretches
Beyond you to your friends.
Q. KATHARINE.   My learned lord cardinal,
Deliver all with charity.
KING.   Speak on.
How grounded he his title to the crown
Upon our fail? to this point hast thou heard him
At any time speak aught?
SURVEYOR.   He was brought to this

By a vain prophecy of Nicholas Henton.
KING. What was that Henton?
SURVEYOR. Sir, a Chartreux friar,
His confessor, who fed him every minute
With words of sovereignty.
KING. How know'st thou this? 150
SURVEYOR. Not long before your highness sped to
France,
The duke being at the Rose, within the parish
Saint Lawrence Poultney, did of me demand
What was the speech among the Londoners
Concerning the French journey. I replied
Men feared the French would prove perfidious,
To the king's danger. Presently the duke
Said 'twas the fear indeed and that he doubted
'Twould prove the verity of certain words
Spoke by a holy monk 'that oft', says he, 160
'Hath sent to me, wishing me to permit
John de la Car, my chaplain, a choice hour
To hear from him a matter of some moment
Whom after under the confession's seal
He solemnly had sworn that what he spoke
My chaplain to no creature living but
To me should utter, with demure confidence
This pausingly ensued: 'Neither the king nor's heirs,
Tell you the duke, shall prosper; bid him strive
To win the love o'th'commonalty; the duke 170
Shall govern England'.
Q. KATHARINE. If I know you well,
You were the duke's surveyor, and lost your office
On the complaint o'th'tenants; take good heed
You charge not in your spleen a noble person
And spoil your nobler soul; I say, take heed;
Yes, heartily beseech you.
KING. Let him on.
Go forward.
SURVEYOR. On my soul, I'll speak but truth.
I told my lord the duke, by th'devil's illusions
The monk might be deceived, and that 'twas
dangerous
To ruminate on this so far, until 180
It forged him some design, which, being believed,
It was much like to do. He answered 'Tush,
It can do me no damage'; adding further,
That, had the king in his last sickness failed,
The cardinal's and Sir Thomas Lovell's heads
Should have gone off.
KING. Ha! what, so rank? Ah, ha!
There's mischief in this man. Canst thou say further?
SURVEYOR. I can, my liege.
KING. Proceed.
SURVEYOR. Being at Greenwich,
After your highness had reproved the duke
About Sir William Bulmer—
KING. I remember 190
Of such a time: being my sworn servant,
The duke retained him his. But on; what hence?
SURVEYOR. 'If' quoth he 'I for this had been
committed,
As to the Tower I thought, I would have played
The part my father meant to act upon
The usurper Richard; who, being at Salisbury,
Made suit to come in's presence; which if granted,
As he made semblance of his duty, would
Have put his knife into him'.
KING. A giant traitor!

WOLSEY. Now, madam, may his highness live in
freedom, 200
And this man out of prison?
Q. KATHARINE. God mend all!
KING. There's something more would out of thee;
what say'st?
SURVEYOR. After 'the duke his father', with the 'knife',
He stretched him, and with one hand on his dagger,
Another spread on's breast, mounting his eyes,
He did discharge a horrible oath, whose tenour
Was, were he evil used, he would outgo
His father by as much as a performance
Does an irresolute purpose.
KING. There's his period,
To sheathe his knife in us. He is attached; 210
Call him to present trial. If he may
Find mercy in the law, 'tis his; if none,
Let him not seek't of us. By day and night!
He's traitor to th'height. They go

Scene 3: The palace

Enter Lord Chamberlain and Lord Sands

CHAMBERLAIN. Is't possible the spells of France should
juggle
Men into such strange mysteries?
SANDS. New customs,
Though they be never so ridiculous,
Nay, let 'em be unmanly, yet are followed.
CHAMBERLAIN. As far as I see, all the good our
English
Have got by the late voyage is but merely
A fit or two o'th'face; but they are shrewd ones;
For when they hold 'em, you would swear directly
Their very noses had been counsellors
To Pepin or Clotharius, they keep state so. 10
SANDS. They have all new legs, and lame ones; one
would take it,
That never saw 'em pace before, the spavin
Or springhalt reigned among 'em.
CHAMBERLAIN. Death! my lord,
Their clothes are after such a pagan cut to't,
That, sure, they've worn out Christendom.

Enter Sir Thomas Lovell

How now?
What news, Sir Thomas Lovell?
LOVELL. Faith, my lord,
I hear of none but the new proclamation
That's clapped upon the court gate.
CHAMBERLAIN. What is't for?
LOVELL. The reformation of our travelled gallants
That fill the court with quarrels, talk, and tailors. 20
CHAMBERLAIN. I'm glad 'tis there; now I would pray
our monsieurs
To think an English courtier may be wise,
And never see the Louvre.
LOVELL. They must either,
For so run the conditions, leave those remnants
Of fool and feather that they got in France,
With all their honourable points of ignorance
Pertaining thereunto, as fights and fireworks,
Abusing better men than they can be
Out of a foreign wisdom, renouncing clean
The faith they have in tennis and tall stockings, 30
Short blist'red breeches, and those types of travel,

And understand again like honest men,
Or pack to their old playfellows; there, I take it,
They may, cum privilegio, 'oui' away
The lag-end of their lewdness, and be laughed at.
SANDS. 'Tis time to give 'em physic, their diseases
Are grown so catching.
CHAMBERLAIN.   What a loss our ladies
Will have of these trim vanities!
LOVELL.   Ay, marry,
There will be woe indeed, lords: the sly whoresons
Have got a speeding trick to lay down ladies.   40
A French song and a fiddle has no fellow.
SANDS. The devil fiddle 'em! I am glad they are going,
For, sure, there's no converting of 'em. Now
An honest country lord, as I am, beaten
A long time out of play, may bring his plain-song,
And have an hour of hearing; and, by'r lady,
Held current music too.
CHAMBERLAIN.   Well said, Lord Sands;
Your colt's tooth is not cast yet?
SANDS.   No, my lord;
Nor shall not, while I have a stump.
CHAMBERLAIN.   Sir Thomas,
Whither were you a-going?
LOVELL.   To the cardinal's;   50
Your lordship is a guest too.
CHAMBERLAIN.   O, 'tis true;
This night he makes a supper, and a great one,
To many lords and ladies; there will be
The beauty of this kingdom, I'll assure you.
LOVELL. That churchman bears a bounteous mind
indeed,
A hand as fruitful as the land that feeds us;
His dews fall everywhere.
CHAMBERLAIN.   No doubt he's noble;
He had a black mouth that said other of him.
SANDS. He may, my lord; has wherewithal. In him
Sparing would show a worse sin than ill doctrine: 60
Men of his way should be most liberal,
They are set here for examples.
CHAMBERLAIN.   True, they are so;
But few now give so great ones. My barge stays;
Your lordship shall along. Come, good Sir Thomas,
We shall be late else; which I would not be,
For I was spoke to, with Sir Henry Guildford
This night to be comptrollers.
SANDS.   I am your lordship's.   *They go*

Scene 4: *A Hall in York Place*

*Hautboys. A small table under a state for the Cardinal,
a longer table for the guests. Then enter Anne Bullen and
divers other Ladies and Gentlemen as guests, at one door;
at another door, enter Sir Henry Guildford*

GUILDFORD. Ladies, a general welcome from his grace
Salutes ye all; this night he dedicates
To fair content and you. None here, he hopes,
In all this noble bevy, has brought with her
One care abroad; he would have all as merry
As, first, good company, good wine, good
welcome,
Can make good people.

*Enter Lord Chamberlain, Lord Sands, and Sir Thomas
Lovell*

                    O, my lord, you're tardy;

The very thought of this fair company
Clapped wings to me.
CHAMBERLAIN. You are young, Sir Harry Guildford.
SANDS. Sir Thomas Lovell, had the cardinal   10
But half my lay thoughts in him, some of these
Should find a running banquet, ere they rested,
I think would better please 'em; by my life,
They are a sweet society of fair ones.
LOVELL. O, that your lordship were but now confessor
To one or two of these!
SANDS.   I would I were;
They should find easy penance.
LOVELL.   Faith, how easy?
SANDS. As easy as a down bed would afford it.
CHAMBERLAIN. Sweet ladies, will it please you sit?
Sir Harry,
Place you that side; I'll take the charge of this.   20
His grace is entering. Nay, you must not freeze.
Two women placed together makes cold weather.
My Lord Sands, you are one will keep em' waking:
Pray, sit between these ladies.
SANDS.   By my faith,
And thank your lordship. By your leave, sweet
ladies.
If I chance to talk a little wild, forgive me;
I had it from my father.
ANNE.   Was he mad, sir?
SANDS. O, very mad, exceeding mad, in love too;
But he would bite none; just as I do now,
He would kiss you twenty with a breath.
                                        Kisses her
CHAMBERLAIN.   Well said, my lord. 30
So, now you're fairly seated. Gentlemen,
The penance lies on you, if these fair ladies
Pass away frowning.
SANDS.   For my little cure,
Let me alone.

Hautboys. Enter Cardinal Wolsey, and takes his state

WOLSEY. You're welcome, my fair guests. That noble
lady
Or gentleman that is not freely merry,
Is not my friend. This, to confirm my welcome;
And to you all, good health.   *Drinks*
SANDS.   Your grace is noble;
Let me have such a bowl may hold my thanks,
And save me so much talking.
WOLSEY.   My Lord Sands,   40
I am beholding to you; cheer your neighbours.
Ladies, you are not merry; gentlemen,
Whose fault is this?
SANDS.   The red wine first must rise
In their fair cheeks, my lord; then we shall have 'em
Talk us to silence.
ANNE.   You are a merry gamester,
My Lord Sands.
SANDS.   Yes, if I make my play.
Here's to your ladyship; and pledge it, madam,
For 'tis to such a thing—
ANNE.   You cannot show me.
SANDS. I told your grace they would talk anon.
                    Drum and trumpet: chambers discharged
WOLSEY.   What's that?
CHAMBERLAIN. Look out there, some of ye.
WOLSEY.   What warlike voice, 50
And to what end, is this? Nay, ladies, fear not;

By all the laws of war you're privileged.

Enter a Servant

CHAMBERLAIN. How now, what is't?
SERVANT.   A noble troop of strangers,
For so they seem. They've left their barge, and
    landed;
And hither make, as great ambassadors
From foreign princes.
WOLSEY.   Good lord chamberlain,
Go, give 'em welcome: you can speak the French
    tongue;
And pray receive 'em nobly and conduct 'em
Into our presence, where this heaven of beauty
Shall shine at full upon them. Some attend him.   60
                Chamberlain goes out, attended.
                All rise, and tables removed
You have now a broken banquet, but we'll mend it.
A good digestion to you all; and once more
I shower a welcome on ye: welcome all.

*Hautboys. Enter King and others, as masquers, habited like
shepherds, ushered by the Lord Chamberlain. They pass
directly before the Cardinal, and gracefully salute him*

A noble company! what are their pleasures?
CHAMBERLAIN. Because they speak no English, thus
    they prayed
To tell your grace, that, having heard by fame
Of this so noble and so fair assembly
This night to meet here, they could do no less,
Out of the great respect they bear to beauty,
But leave their flocks, and, under your fair conduct,   70
Crave leave to view these ladies and entreat
An hour of revels with 'em.
WOLSEY.   Say, lord chamberlain,
They have done my poor house grace; for which I
    pay 'em
A thousand thanks and pray 'em take their pleasures.
                *They choose. The King chooses
                                    Anne Bullen*
KING. The fairest hand I ever touched! O beauty,
Till now I never knew thee!   *Music. Dance*
WOLSEY. My lord!
CHAMBERLAIN.   Your grace?
WOLSEY.   Pray, tell 'em thus much from me:
There should be one amongst 'em by his person,
More worthy this place than myself; to whom,
If I but knew him, with my love and duty   80
I would surrender it.
CHAMBERLAIN.   I will, my lord.
                Whispers the Masquers
WOLSEY. What say they?
CHAMBERLAIN.   Such a one, they all confess,
There is indeed; which they would have your grace
Find out, and he will take it.
WOLSEY.   Let me see then.
By all your good leaves, gentlemen; here I'll make
My royal choice.
KING [*unmasking*]. Ye have found him, cardinal.
You hold a fair assembly; you do well, lord.
You are a churchman, or, I'll tell you, cardinal,
I should judge now unhappily.
WOLSEY.   I am glad
Your grace is grown so pleasant.
KING.   My lord chamberlain,   90
Prithee come hither: what fair lady's that?

CHAMBERLAIN. An't please your grace, Sir Thomas
    Bullen's daughter,
The Viscount Rochford, one of her highness'
    women.
KING. By heaven, she is a dainty one. Sweetheart,
I were unmannerly to take you out
And not to kiss you. A health, gentlemen!
Let it go round.
WOLSEY. Sir Thomas Lovell, is the banquet ready
I'th'privy chamber?
LOVELL.   Yes, my lord.
WOLSEY.   Your grace,
I fear, with dancing is a little heated.   100
KING. I fear, too much.
WOLSEY.   There's fresher air, my lord,
In the next chamber.
KING. Lead in your ladies, every one. Sweet
    partner,
I must not yet forsake you. Let's be merry,
Good my lord cardinal: I have half a dozen healths
To drink to these fair ladies, and a measure
To lead 'em once again; and then let's dream
Who's best in favour. Let the music knock it.
                They go, to the sound of trumpets

                        ACT 2
                Scene 1: *Westminster. A street*

Enter two Gentlemen, meeting

1 GENTLEMAN. Whither away so fast?
2 GENTLEMAN.   O, God save ye!
Even to the Hall, to hear what shall become
Of the great Duke of Buckingham.
1 GENTLEMAN.   I'll save you
That labour, sir. All's now done but the ceremony
Of bringing back the prisoner.
2 GENTLEMAN.   Were you there?
1 GENTLEMAN. Yes, indeed was I.
2 GENTLEMAN.   Pray speak what has happened.
1 GENTLEMAN. You may guess quickly what.
2 GENTLEMAN.   Is he found guilty?
1 GENTLEMAN. Yes, truly is he, and condemned upon't.
2 GENTLEMAN. I am sorry for't.
1 GENTLEMAN.   So are a number more.
2 GENTLEMAN. But, pray, how passed it?   10
1 GENTLEMAN. I'll tell you in a little. The great duke
Came to the bar; where to his accusations
He pleaded still not guilty, and allegéd
Many sharp reasons to defeat the law.
The king's attorney on the contrary
Urged on the examinations, proofs, confessions
Of divers witnesses; which the duke desired
To him brought viva voce to his face;
At which appeared against him his surveyor,
Sir Gilbert Parke his chancellor, and John Car,   20
Confessor to him, with that devil monk,
Hopkins, that made this mischief.
2 GENTLEMAN.   That was he
That fed him with his prophecies?
1 GENTLEMAN.   The same.
All these accused him strongly, which he fain
Would have flung from him; but indeed he could
    not;
And so his peers upon this evidence
Have found him guilty of high treason. Much

He spoke, and learnedly, for life; but all
Was either pitied in him or forgotten.
2 GENTLEMAN. After all this, how did he bear himself?   30
1 GENTLEMAN. When he was brought again to th'bar,
      to hear
His knell rung out, his judgement, he was stirred
With such an agony he sweat extremely,
And something spoke in choler, ill and hasty;
But he fell to himself again, and sweetly
In all the rest showed a most noble patience.
2 GENTLEMAN. I do not think he fears death.
1 GENTLEMAN.   Sure, he does not;
He never was so womanish; the cause
He may a little grieve at.
2 GENTLEMAN.   Certainly
The cardinal is the end of this.
1 GENTLEMAN.   'Tis likely,   40
By all conjectures: first, Kildare's attainder,
Then deputy of Ireland, who removed,
Earl Surrey was sent thither, and in haste too,
Lest he should help his father.
2 GENTLEMAN.   That trick of state
Was a deep envious one.
1 GENTLEMAN.   At his return
No doubt he will requite it. This is noted,
And generally, whoever the king favours,
The cardinal instantly will find employment,
And far enough from court too.
2 GENTLEMAN.   All the commons
Hate him perniciously, and, o' my conscience,   50
Wish him ten fathom deep. This duke as much
They love and dote on; call him bounteous
      Buckingham,
The mirror of all courtesy—

*Enter Buckingham from his arraignment, tipstaves before
him, the axe with the edge towards him, halberds on each
side, accompanied with Sir Thomas Lovell, Sir Nicholas
Vaux, Sir Walter Sands, and common people, etc.*

1 GENTLEMAN.   Stay there, sir,
And see the noble ruined man you speak of.
2 GENTLEMAN. Let's stand close, and behold him.
BUCKINGHAM.   All good people,
You that thus far have come to pity me,
Hear what I say, and then go home and lose me.
I have this day received a traitor's judgement,
And by that name must die; yet, heaven bear
      witness,
And if I have a conscience, let it sink me   60
Even as the axe falls, if I be not faithful!
The law I bear no malice for my death:
'T has done, upon the premises, but justice.
But those that sought it I could wish more
      Christians:
Be what they will, I heartily forgive 'em;
Yet let 'em look they glory not in mischief,
Nor build their evils on the graves of great men;
For then my guiltless blood must cry against 'em.
For further life in this world I ne'er hope,
Nor will I sue, although the king have mercies   70
More than I dare make faults. You few that loved
      me
And dare be bold to weep for Buckingham,
His noble friends and fellows, whom to leave
Is only bitter to him, only dying,
Go with me like good angels to my end;

And as the long divorce of steel falls on me,
Make of your prayers one sweet sacrifice,
And lift my soul to heaven. Lead on, o' God's name.
LOVELL. I do beseech your grace, for charity,
If ever any malice in your heart   80
Were hid against me, now to forgive me frankly.
BUCKINGHAM. Sir Thomas Lovell, I as free forgive you
As I would be forgiven: I forgive all.
There cannot be those numberless offences
'Gainst me that I cannot take peace with. No black
      envy
Shall mark my grave. Commend me to his grace;
And if he speak of Buckingham, pray tell him
You met him half in heaven: my vows and prayers
Yet are the king's, and, till my soul forsake,
Shall cry for blessings on him. May he live   90
Longer than I have time to tell his years;
Ever beloved and loving may his rule be;
And when old time shall lead him to his end,
Goodness and he fill up one monument!
LOVELL. To the water side I must conduct your grace;
Then give my charge up to Sir Nicholas Vaux,
Who undertakes you to your end.
VAUX.   Prepare there;
The duke is coming; see the barge be ready,
And fit it with such furniture as suits
The greatness of his person.
BUCKINGHAM.   Nay, Sir Nicholas,   100
Let it alone; my state now will but mock me.
When I came hither, I was lord high constable
And Duke of Buckingham; now, poor Edward
      Bohun.
Yet I am richer than my base accusers
That never knew what truth meant; I now seal it;
And with that blood will make 'em one day groan
      for't.
My noble father, Henry of Buckingham,
Who first raised head against usurping Richard,
Flying for succour to his servant Banister,
Being distressed, was by that wretch betrayed,   110
And without trial fell; God's peace be with him!
Henry the Seventh succeeding, truly pitying
My father's loss, like a most royal prince,
Restored me to my honours, and out of ruins
Made my name once more noble. Now his son,
Henry the Eighth, life, honour, name and all
That made me happy, at one stroke has taken
For ever from the world. I had my trial,
And must needs say a noble one; which makes me
A little happier than my wretched father;   120
Yet thus far we are one in fortunes: both
Fell by our servants, by those men we loved most—
A most unnatural and faithless service!
Heaven has an end in all. Yet, you that hear me,
This from a dying man receive as certain:
Where you are liberal of your loves and counsels
Be sure you be not loose; for those you make friends
And give your hearts to, when they once perceive
The least rub in your fortunes, fall away
Like water from ye, never found again   130
But where they mean to sink ye. All good people,
Pray for me! I must now forsake ye; the last hour
Of my long weary life is come upon me.
Farewell;
And when you would say something that is sad,
Speak how I fell. I have done; and God forgive me!

Duke and Train·go

1 GENTLEMAN. O, this is full of pity! Sir, it calls,
I fear, too many curses on their heads
That were the authors.
2 GENTLEMAN.   If the duke be guiltless,
'Tis full of woe; yet I can give you inkling   140
Of an ensuing evil, if it fall,
Greater than this.
1 GENTLEMAN.   Good angels keep it from us!
What may it be? You do not doubt my faith, sir?
2 GENTLEMAN. This secret is so weighty, 'twill require
A strong faith to conceal it.
1 GENTLEMAN.   Let me have it;
I do not talk much.
2 GENTLEMAN.   I am confident;
You shall, sir. Did you not of late days hear
A buzzing of a separation
Between the king and Katharine?
1 GENTLEMAN.   Yes, but it held not;
For when the king once heard it, out of anger   150
He sent command to the lord mayor straight
To stop the rumour and allay those tongues
That durst disperse it.
2 GENTLEMAN.   But that slander, sir,
Is found a truth now; for it grows again
Fresher than e'er it was, and held for certain
The king will venture at it. Either the cardinal
Or some about him near have, out of malice
To the good queen, possessed him with a scruple
That will undo her. To confirm this too,
Cardinal Campeius is arrived, and lately;   160
As all think, for this business.
1 GENTLEMAN.   'Tis the cardinal;
And merely to revenge him on the emperor
For not bestowing on him at his asking
The archbishopric of Toledo, this is purposed.
2 GENTLEMAN. I think you have hit the mark; but is't
not cruel
That she should feel the smart of this? The cardinal
Will have his will, and she must fall.
1 GENTLEMAN.   'Tis woeful.
We are too open here to argue this;
Let's think in private more.   *They go*

Scene 2: *The palace*

Enter Lord Chamberlain, reading this letter

CHAMBERLAIN. 'My lord, the horses your lordship sent
for, with all the care I had, I saw well chosen, ridden,
and furnished. They were young and handsome,
and of the best breed in the north. When they were
ready to set out for London, a man of my lord
cardinal's, by commission and main power, took
'em from me, with this reason: his master would be
served before a subject, if not before the king; which
stopped our mouths, sir.'

I fear he will indeed. Well, let him have them.   10
He will have all, I think.

*Enter to the Lord Chamberlain, the Dukes of Norfolk and
Suffolk*

NORFOLK. Well met, my lord chamberlain.
CHAMBERLAIN. Good day to both your graces.
SUFFOLK. How is the king employed?
CHAMBERLAIN.   I left him private,
Full of sad thoughts and troubles.
NORFOLK.   What's the cause?
CHAMBERLAIN. It seems the marriage with his brother's
wife
Has crept too near his conscience.
SUFFOLK [*aside*].   No, his conscience
Has crept too near another lady.
NORFOLK.   'Tis so;
This is the cardinal's doing; the king-cardinal,
That blind priest, like the eldest son of fortune,   20
Turns what he list. The king will know him one day.
SUFFOLK. Pray God he do! he'll never know himself
else.
NORFOLK. How holily he works in all his business,
And with what zeal! for, now he has cracked the
league
Between us and the emperor, the queen's great
nephew,
He dives into the king's soul, and there scatters
Dangers, doubts, wringing of the conscience,
Fears and despairs; and all these for his marriage.
And out of all these to restore the king,
He counsels a divorce, a loss of her   30
That like a jewel has hung twenty years
About his neck, yet never lost her lustre;
Of her that loves him with that excellence
That angels love good men with, even of her
That, when the greatest stroke of fortune falls,
Will bless the king; and is not this course pious?
CHAMBERLAIN. Heaven keep me from such counsel!
'Tis most true
These news are everywhere; every tongue speaks
'em,
And every true heart weeps for't. All that dare
Look into these affairs see this main end,   40
The French king's sister. Heaven will one day open
The king's eyes, that so long have slept upon
This bold bad man.
SUFFOLK.   And free us from his slavery.
NORFOLK. We had need pray,
And heartily, for our deliverance;
Or this imperious man will work us all
From princes into pages. All men's honours
Lie like one lump before him, to be fashioned
Into what pitch he please.
SUFFOLK.   For me, my lords,
I love him not, nor fear him—there's my creed;   50
As I am made without him, so I'll stand,
If the king please; his curses and his blessings
Touch me alike; they're breath I not believe in.
I knew him, and I know him; so I leave him
To him that made him proud, the pope.
NORFOLK.   Let's in;
And with some other business put the king
From these sad thoughts that work too much
upon him:
My lord, you'll bear us company?
CHAMBERLAIN.   Excuse me,
The king has sent me otherwhere; besides,
You'll find a most unfit time to disturb him.   60
Health to your lordships.
NORFOLK.   Thanks, my good lord chamberlain.
*Lord Chamberlain goes; the King draws
the curtain and sits reading pensively*
SUFFOLK. How sad he looks; sure, he is much afflicted.

KING. Who's there, ha?

NORFOLK.   Pray God he be not angry.

KING. Who's there, I say? How dare you thrust
    yourselves
Into my private meditations?
Who am I, ha?

NORFOLK. A gracious king that pardons all offences
Malice ne'er meant. Our breach of duty this way
Is business of estate, in which we come
To know your royal pleasure.

KING.   Ye are too bold.   70
Go to; I'll make ye know your times of business.
Is this an hour for temporal affairs, ha?

Enter Wolsey and Campeius, with a commission

Who's there? my good lord cardinal? O my Wolsey,
The quiet of my wounded conscience,
Thou art a cure fit for a king. [*to Campeius*]
    You're welcome,
Most learnéd reverend sir, into our kingdom:
Use us and it. [*to Wolsey*] My good lord, have
    great care
I be not found a talker.

WOLSEY.   Sir, you cannot.
I would your grace would give us but an hour
Of private conference.

KING [*to Norfolk and Suffolk*]. We are busy; go.   80

NORFOLK [*aside to Suffolk*]. This priest has no pride in
    him.

SUFFOLK [*aside to Norfolk*].   Not to speak of.
I would not be so sick though for his place.
But this cannot continue.

NORFOLK [*aside to Suffolk*]. If it do,
I'll venture one have-at-him.

SUFFOLK [*aside to Norfolk*].   I another.
                              Norfolk and Suffolk go

WOLSEY. Your grace has given a precedent of wisdom
Above all princes, in committing freely
Your scruple to the voice of Christendom.
Who can be angry now? what envy reach you?
The Spaniard, tied by blood and favour to her,
Must now confess, if they have any goodness,   90
The trial just and noble. All the clerks,
I mean the learnéd ones, in Christian kingdoms
Have their free voices. Rome, the nurse of
    judgement,
Invited by your noble self, hath sent
One general tongue unto us, this good man,
This just and learnéd priest, Cardinal Campeius,
Whom once more I present unto your highness.

KING. And once more in mine arms I bid him
    welcome,
And thank the holy conclave for their loves.
They have sent me such a man I would have
    wished for.   100

CAMPEIUS. Your grace must needs deserve all
    strangers' loves,
You are so noble. To your highness' hand
I tender my commission; by whose virtue,
The court of Rome commanding, you, my lord
Cardinal of York, are joined with me their servant
In the unpartial judging of this business.

KING. Two equal men. The queen shall be
    acquainted
Forthwith for what you come. Where's Gardiner?

WOLSEY. I know your majesty has always loved her

So dear in heart not to deny her that   110
A woman of less place might ask by law:
Scholars allowed freely to argue for her.

KING. Ay, and the best she shall have; and my favour
To him that does best—God forbid else. Cardinal,
Prithee call Gardiner to me, my new secretary;
I find him a fit fellow.

Enter Gardiner. Wolsey meets him at the door

WOLSEY [*aside*]. Give me your hand: much joy and
    favour to you;
You are the king's now.

GARDINER [*aside*].   But to be commanded
For ever by your grace, whose hand has raised me.

KING. Come hither, Gardiner.   120
                          *Walks apart and whispers with
                                            Gardiner*

CAMPEIUS. My Lord of York, was not one Doctor Pace
In this man's place before him?

WOLSEY.   Yes, he was.

CAMPEIUS. Was he not held a learnéd man?

WOLSEY.   Yes, surely.

CAMPEIUS. Believe me, there's an ill opinion spread
    then,
Even of yourself, lord cardinal.

WOLSEY.   How? of me?

CAMPEIUS. They will not stick to say you envied him,
And fearing he would rise, he was so virtuous,
Kept him a foreign man still; which so grieved him
That he ran mad and died.

WOLSEY.   Heaven's peace be with him!
That's Christian care enough; for living murmurers   130
There's places of rebuke. He was a fool;
For he would needs be virtuous. That good fellow,
If I command him, follows my appointment;
I will have none so near else. Learn this, brother,
We live not to be griped by meaner persons.

KING [*returning*]. Deliver this with modesty to
    th'queen.   *Gardiner goes*
The most convenient place that I can think of
For such receipt of learning is Blackfriars;
There ye shall meet about this weighty business.
My Wolsey, see it furnished. O, my lord,   140
Would it not grieve an able man to leave
So sweet a bedfellow? But, conscience, conscience!
O, 'tis a tender place, and I must leave her.
                                            They go

Scene 3: *The Queen's apartments*

Enter Anne Bullen and an old Lady

ANNE. Not for that neither; here's the pang that
    pinches:
His highness having lived so long with her, and she
So good a lady that no tongue could ever
Pronounce dishonour of her—by my life,
She never knew harm-doing—O, now, after
So many courses of the sun enthronéd,
Still growing in a majesty and pomp, the which
To leave a thousand-fold more bitter than
'Tis sweet at first t'acquire—after this process,
To give her the avaunt, it is a pity   10
Would move a monster.

OLD LADY.   Hearts of most hard temper
Melt and lament for her.

ANNE.   O, God's will! much better
She ne'er had known pomp; though't be temporal,

Yet, if that quarrel, fortune, do divorce
It from the bearer, 'tis a sufferance panging
As soul and body's severing.
OLD LADY.   Alas, poor lady!
She's a stranger now again.
ANNE.   So much the more
Must pity drop upon her. Verily,
I swear, 'tis better to be lowly born
And range with humble livers in content   20
Than to be perked up in a glistering grief
And wear a golden sorrow.
OLD LADY.   Our content
Is our best having.
ANNE.   By my troth and maidenhead,
I would not be a queen.
OLD LADY.   Beshrew me, I would,
And venture maidenhead for't; and so would you,
For all this spice of your hypocrisy.
You that have so fair parts of woman on you,
Have too a woman's heart, which ever yet
Affected eminence, wealth, sovereignty;
Which, to say sooth, are blessings; and which gifts, 30
Saving your mincing, the capacity
Of your soft cheveril conscience would receive,
If you might please to stretch it.
ANNE.   Nay, good troth.
OLD LADY. Yes, troth and troth; you would not be a
   queen?
ANNE. No, not for all the riches under heaven.
OLD LADY. 'Tis strange: a threepence bowed would
   hire me,
Old as I am, to queen it. But, I pray you,
What think you of a duchess? have you limbs
To bear that load of title?
ANNE.   .   No, in truth.
OLD LADY. Then you are weakly made. Pluck off a
   little;   40
I would not be a young count in your way,
For more than blushing comes to. If your back
Cannot vouchsafe this burden, 'tis too weak
Ever to get a boy.
ANNE.   How you do talk!
I swear again, I would not be a queen
For all the world.
OLD LADY.   In faith, for little England
You'ld venture an emballing. I myself
Would for Caernarvonshire, although there 'longed
No more to th'crown but that. Lo, who comes here?

Enter Lord Chamberlain

CHAMBERLAIN. Good morrow, ladies. What were't
   worth to know   50
The secret of your conference?
ANNE.   My good lord,
Not your demand; it values not your asking.
Our mistress' sorrows we were pitying.
CHAMBERLAIN. It was a gentle business, and becoming
The action of good women; there is hope
All will be well.
ANNE.   Now, I pray God, amen!
CHAMBERLAIN. You bear a gentle mind, and heavenly
   blessings
Follow such creatures. That you may, fair lady,
Perceive I speak sincerely, and high note's
Ta'en of your many virtues, the king's majesty   60
Commends his good opinion of you, and

Does purpose honour to you no less flowing
Than Marchioness of Pembroke; to which title
A thousand pound a year, annual support,
Out of his grace he adds.
ANNE.   I do not know
What kind of my obedience I should tender;
More than my all is nothing; nor my prayers
Are not words duly hallowed, nor my wishes
More worth than empty vanities; yet prayers and
   wishes
Are all I can return. Beseech your lordship,   70
Vouchsafe to speak my thanks and my obedience,
As from a blushing handmaid, to his highness;
Whose health and royalty I pray for.
CHAMBERLAIN.   Lady,
I shall not fail t'approve the fair conceit
The king hath of you. [*aside*] I have perused her well;
Beauty and honour in her are so mingled
That they have caught the king; and who knows
   yet
But from this lady may proceed a gem
To lighten all this isle? [*aloud*] I'll to the king,
And say I spoke with you.
ANNE.   My honoured lord.   80
                        Lord Chamberlain goes
OLD LADY. Why, this it is: see, see!
I have been begging sixteen years in court,
Am yet a courtier beggarly, nor could
Come pat betwixt too early and too late
For any suit of pounds; and you, O fate!
A very fresh fish here—fie, fie, fie upon
This compelled fortune!—have your mouth filled
   up
Before you open it.
ANNE.   This is strange to me.
OLD LADY. How tastes it? is it bitter? forty pence, no.
There was a lady once—'tis an old story—   90
That would not be a queen, that would she not,
For all the mud in Egypt; have you heard it?
ANNE. Come, you are pleasant.
OLD LADY.   With your theme, I could
O'ermount the lark. The Marchioness of
   Pembroke?
A thousand pounds a year for pure respect?
No other obligation? By my life,
That promises moe thousands: honour's train
Is longer than his foreskirt. By this time
I know your back will bear a duchess. Say,
Are you not stronger than you were?
ANNE.   Good lady,   100
Make yourself mirth with your particular fancy,
And leave me out on't. Would I had no being,
If this salute my blood a jot; it faints me,
To think what follows.
The queen is comfortless, and we forgetful
In our long absence: pray, do not deliver
What here you've heard to her.
OLD LADY.   What do you think me? *They go*

Scene 4: A hall in Blackfriars

*Trumpets, sennet and cornets. Enter two Vergers, with short
silver wands; next them, two Scribes, in the habit of doctors;
after them, the [Arch]bishop of Canterbury alone; after him,
the Bishops of Lincoln, Ely, Rochester, and Saint Asaph;
next them, with some small distance, follows a Gentleman
bearing the purse, with the great seal, and a cardinal's hat;*

*then two Priests, bearing each a silver cross; then a Gentle-
man Usher bareheaded, accompanied with a Sergeant at
arms bearing a silver mace; then two Gentlemen bearing two
great silver pillars; after them, side by side, the two
Cardinals; two Noblemen with the sword and mace. The
King takes place under the cloth of state; the two Cardinals
sit under him as judges. The Queen takes place some
distance from the King. The Bishops place themselves on
each side the court, in manner of a consistory; below them,
the Scribes. The Lords sit next the Bishops. The rest of the
Attendants stand in convenient order about the stage*

WOLSEY. Whilst our commission from Rome is read,
Let silence be commanded.
KING. What's the need?
It hath already publicly been read,
And on all sides th'authority allowed;
You may then spare that time.
WOLSEY. Be't so. Proceed.
SCRIBE. Say 'Henry King of England, come into the
court'.
CRIER. Henry King of England, &c.
KING. Here.
SCRIBE. Say 'Katharine Queen of England, come into 10
the court'.
CRIER. Katharine Queen of England, &c.

*The Queen makes no answer, rises
out of her chair, goes about the
court, comes to the King, and
kneels at his feet; then speaks*

Q. KATHARINE. Sir, I desire you do me right and
justice,
And to bestow your pity on me; for
I am a most poor woman and a stranger,
Born out of your dominions; having here
No judge indifferent, nor no more assurance
Of equal friendship and proceeding. Alas, sir,
In what have I offended you? what cause
Hath my behaviour given to your displeasure 20
That thus you should proceed to put me off
And take your good grace from me? Heaven
witness,
I have been to you a true and humble wife,
At all times to your will conformable,
Ever in fear to kindle your dislike,
Yea, subject to your countenance, glad or sorry
As I saw it inclined. When was the hour
I ever contradicted your desire,
Or made it not mine too? Or which of your friends
Have I not strove to love, although I knew 30
He were mine enemy? what friend of mine
That had to him derived your anger did I
Continue in my liking? nay, gave notice
He was from thence discharged? Sir, call to mind
That I have been your wife in this obedience
Upward of twenty years, and have been blest
With many children by you. If, in the course
And process of this time, you can report,
And prove it too, against mine honour aught,
My bond to wedlock or my love and duty, 40
Against your sacred person, in God's name,
Turn me away, and let the foul'st contempt
Shut door upon me, and so give me up
To the sharp'st kind of justice. Please you, sir,
The king, your father, was reputed for
A prince most prudent, of an excellent

And unmatched wit and judgement; Ferdinand,
My father, king of Spain, was reckoned one
The wisest prince that there had reigned by many
A year before. It is not to be questioned 50
That they had gathered a wise council to them
Of every realm that did debate this business,
Who deemed our marriage lawful. Wherefore I
humbly
Beseech you, sir, to spare me, till I may
Be by my friends in Spain advised, whose counsel
I will implore. If not, i'th'name of God,
Your pleasure be fulfilled!
WOLSEY. You have here, lady,
And of your choice, these reverend fathers, men
Of singular integrity and learning,
Yea, the elect o'th'land, who are assembled 60
To plead your cause. It shall be therefore bootless
That longer you desire the court, as well
For your own quiet, as to rectify
What is unsettled in the king.
CAMPEIUS. His grace
Hath spoken well and justly; therefore, madam,
It's fit this royal session do proceed,
And that without delay their arguments
Be now produced and heard.
Q. KATHARINE. Lord cardinal,
To you I speak.
WOLSEY. Your pleasure, madam?
Q. KATHARINE. Sir,
I am about to weep; but, thinking that 70
We are a queen, or long have dreamed so, certain
The daughter of a king, my drops of tears
I'll turn to sparks of fire.
WOLSEY. Be patient yet.
Q. KATHARINE. I will, when you are humble;
nay, before,
Or God will punish me. I do believe,
Induced by potent circumstances, that
You are mine enemy, and make my challenge
You shall not be my judge; for it is you
Have blown this coal betwixt my lord and me—
Which God's dew quench! Therefore I say again, 80
I utterly abhor, yea, from my soul
Refuse you for my judge, whom, yet once more,
I hold my most malicious foe and think not
At all a friend to truth.
WOLSEY. I do profess
You speak not like yourself, who ever yet
Have stood to charity and displayed the effects
Of disposition gentle and of wisdom
O'ertopping woman's power. Madam, you do
me wrong:
I have no spleen against you, nor injustice
For you or any; how far I have proceeded, 90
Or how far further shall, is warranted
By a commission from the consistory,
Yea, the whole consistory of Rome. You charge me
That I have blown this coal. I do deny it;
The king is present; if it be known to him
That I gainsay my deed, how may he wound,
And worthily, my falsehood! yea, as much
As you have done my truth. If he know
That I am free of your report, he knows
I am not of your wrong. Therefore in him 100
It lies to cure me, and the cure is to
Remove these thoughts from you; the which before
His highness shall speak in, I do beseech

You, gracious madam, to unthink your speaking
And to say so no more.
Q. KATHARINE.   My lord, my lord,
I am a simple woman, much too weak
T'oppose your cunning. You're meek and
    humble-mouthed;
You sign your place and calling, in full seeming,
With meekness and humility; but your heart
Is crammed with arrogancy, spleen, and pride.   110
You have, by fortune and his highness' favours,
Gone slightly o'er low steps, and now are mounted
Where powers are your retainers, and your words,
Domestics to you, serve your will as't please
Yourself pronounce their office. I must tell you,
You tender more your person's honour than
Your high profession spiritual; that again
I do refuse you for my judge, and here,
Before you all, appeal unto the pope,
To bring my whole cause 'fore his holiness,   120
And to be judged by him.
                    She curtsies to the King, and offers
                                        to depart
CAMPEIUS.   The queen is obstinate,
Stubborn to justice, apt to accuse it and
Disdainful to be tried by't; 'tis not well.
She's going away.
KING. Call her again.
CRIER. Katharine Queen of England, come into the
    court.
GENTLEMAN USHER. Madam, you are called back.
Q. KATHARINE. What need you note it? pray you keep
    your way;
When you are called, return. Now the Lord help!
They vex me past my patience. Pray you pass on: 130
I will not tarry; no, nor ever more
Upon this business my appearance make
In any of their courts.
                    Queen and her Attendants go
KING.   Go thy ways, Kate;
That man i'th'world who shall report he has
A better wife, let him in nought be trusted,
For speaking false in that. Thou art, alone—
If thy rare qualities, sweet gentleness,
Thy meekness saint-like, wife-like government,
Obeying in commanding, and thy parts
Sovereign and pious else, could speak thee out—   140
The queen of earthly queens. She's noble born,
And like her true nobility she has
Carried herself towards me.
WOLSEY.   Most gracious sir,
In humblest manner I require your highness,
That it shall please you to declare in hearing
Of all these ears—for where I am robbed and bound,
There must I be unloosed, although not there
At once and fully satisfied—whether ever I
Did broach this business to your highness, or
Laid any scruple in your way which might   150
Induce you to the question on't, or ever
Have to you, but with thanks to God for such
A royal lady, spake one the least word that might
Be to the prejudice of her present state,
Or touch of her good person?
KING.   My lord cardinal,
I do excuse you; yea, upon mine honour,
I free you from't. You are not to be taught
That you have many enemies that know not
Why they are so, but, like to village curs,

Bark when their fellows do. By some of these   160
The queen is put in anger. You're excused.
But will you be more justified? you ever
Have wished the sleeping of this business, never
    desired
It to be stirred, but oft have hind'red, oft,
The passages made toward it. On my honour
I speak my good lord cardinal to this point,
And thus far clear him. Now, what moved me to't,
I will be bold with time and your attention.
Then mark the inducement. Thus it came; give heed
    to't:
My conscience first received a tenderness,   170
Scruple, and prick, on certain speeches uttered
By th'Bishop of Bayonne, then French ambassador,
Who had been hither sent on the debating
A marriage 'twixt the Duke of Orleans and
Our daughter Mary. I'th'progress of this business,
Ere a determinate resolution, he,
I mean the bishop, did require a respite,
Wherein he might the king his lord advertise
Whether our daughter were legitimate,
Respecting this our marriage with the dowager,   180
Sometimes our brother's wife. This respite shook
The bosom of my conscience, entered me,
Yea, with a spitting power, and made to tremble
The region of my breast; which forced such way
That many mazed considerings did throng
And pressed in with this caution. First, methought
I stood not in the smile of heaven, who had
Commanded nature that my lady's womb,
If it conceived a male child by me, should
Do no more offices of life to't than   190
The grave does to the dead; for her male issue
Or died where they were made, or shortly after
This world had aired them. Hence I took a thought
This was a judgement on me, that my kingdom,
Well worthy the best heir o'th'world, should not
Be gladded in't by me. Then follows that
I weighed the danger which my realms stood in
By this my issue's fail, and that gave to me
Many a groaning throe. Thus hulling in
The wild sea of my conscience, I did steer   200
Toward this remedy whereupon we are
Now present here together; that's to say,
I meant to rectify my conscience, which
I then did feel full sick, and yet not well,
By all the reverend fathers of the land
And doctors learned. First I began in private
With you, my Lord of Lincoln; you remember
How under my oppression I did reek,
When I first moved you.
LINCOLN.   Very well, my liege.
KING. I have spoke long; be pleased yourself to say   210
How far you satisfied me.
LINCOLN.   So please your highness,
The question did at first so stagger me,
Bearing a state of mighty moment in't
And consequence of dread, that I committed
The daring'st counsel which I had to doubt,
And did entreat your highness to this course
Which you are running here.
KING.   I then moved you,
My Lord of Canterbury, and got your leave
To make this present summons. Unsolicited
I left no reverend person in this court,   220
But by particular consent proceeded

Under your hands and seals; therefore, go on,
For no dislike i'th'world against the person
Of the good queen, but the sharp thorny points
Of my allegéd reasons, drives this forward:
Prove but our marriage lawful, by my life
And kingly dignity, we are contented
To wear our mortal state to come with her,
Katharine our queen, before the primest creature
That's paragoned o'th'world.
CAMPEIUS.   So please your highness, 230
The queen being absent, 'tis a needful fitness
That we adjourn this court till further day;
Meanwhile must be an earnest motion
Made to the queen to call back her appeal
She intends unto his holiness.
KING [aside].   I may perceive
These cardinals trifle with me. I abhor
This dilatory sloth and tricks of Rome.
My learned and well-belovéd servant, Cranmer,
Prithee return; with thy approach, I know,
My comfort comes along. [aloud] Break up the
court;   240
I say, set on.   They go out in manner as they entered

ACT 3
Scene 1: London. The Queen's apartments

Enter Queen and her Women, as at work

Q. KATHARINE. Take thy lute, wench; my soul grows
sad with troubles;
Sing and disperse 'em, if thou canst; leave working.

Song
Orpheus with his lute made trees,
And the mountain tops that freeze,
    Bow themselves when he did sing.
To his music plants and flowers
Ever sprung, as sun and showers
    There had made a lasting spring.

Every thing that heard him play,
Even the billows of the sea,   10
    Hung their heads, and then lay by.
In sweet music is such art,
Killing care and grief of heart
    Fall asleep, or hearing die.

Enter a Gentleman

Q. KATHARINE. How now?
GENTLEMAN. An't please your grace, the two great
cardinals
Wait in the presence.
Q. KATHARINE.   Would they speak with me?
GENTLEMAN. They willed me say so, madam.
Q. KATHARINE.   Pray their graces
To come near. What can be their business
With me, a poor weak woman, fall'n from favour? 20
I do not like their coming. Now I think on't,
They should be good men, their affairs as righteous;
But all hoods make not monks.

Enter the two Cardinals, Wolsey and Campeius, ushered in
by the Gentleman

WOLSEY.   Peace to your highness!
Q. KATHARINE. Your graces find me here part of a
housewife—

I would be all—against the worst may happen.
What are your pleasures with me, reverend lords?
WOLSEY. May it please you, noble madam, to
withdraw
Into your private chamber, we shall give you
The full cause of our coming.
Q. KATHARINE.   Speak it here;
There's nothing I have done yet, o' my conscience, 30
Deserves a corner. Would all other women
Could speak this with as free a soul as I do!
My lords, I care not—so much I am happy
Above a number—if my actions
Were tried by every tongue, every eye saw 'em,
Envy and base opinion set against 'em,
I know my life so even. If your business
Seek me out, and that way I am wife in,
Out with it boldly: truth loves open dealing.
WOLSEY. Tanta est erga te mentis integritas, regina 40
serenissima—
Q. KATHARINE. O, good my lord, no Latin;
I am not such a truant since my coming,
As not to know the language I have lived in;
A strange tongue makes my cause more strange,
suspicious;
Pray speak in English; here are some will thank you,
If you speak truth, for their poor mistress' sake;
Believe me, she has had much wrong. Lord cardinal,
The willing'st sin I ever yet committed
May be absolved in English.
WOLSEY.   Noble lady,   50
I am sorry my integrity should breed,
And service to his majesty and you,
So deep suspicion, where all faith was meant.
We come not by the way of accusation,
To taint that honour every good tongue blesses,
Nor to betray you any way to sorrow—
You have too much, good lady—but to know
How you stand minded in the weighty difference
Between the king and you, and to deliver,
Like free and honest men, our just opinions   60
And comforts to your cause.
CAMPEIUS.   Most honoured madam,
My Lord of York, out of his noble nature,
Zeal and obedience he still bore your grace,
Forgetting, like a good man, your late censure
Both of his truth and him, which was too far,
Offers, as I do, in a sign of peace,
His service and his counsel.
Q. KATHARINE [aside].   To betray me.
[aloud] My lords, I thank you both for your good
wills;
Ye speak like honest men—pray God ye prove so!—
But how to make ye suddenly an answer,   70
In such a point of weight, so near mine honour,
More near my life, I fear, with my weak wit,
And to such men of gravity and learning,
In truth I know not. I was set at work
Among my maids, full little, God knows, looking
Either for such men or such business.
For her sake that I have been—for I feel
The last fit of my greatness—good your graces,
Let me have time and counsel for my cause.
Alas, I am a woman, friendless, hopeless!   80
WOLSEY. Madam, you wrong the king's love with
these fears;
Your hopes and friends are infinite.

Q. KATHARINE.　　　　　　　　　　　In England
But little for my profit; can you think, lords,
That any Englishman dare give me counsel?
Or be a known friend, 'gainst his highness'
　　pleasure—
Though he be grown so desperate to be honest—
And live a subject? Nay, forsooth, my friends,
They that must weigh out my afflictions,
They that my trust must grow to, live not here;
They are, as all my other comforts, far hence　　90
In mine own country, lords.
CAMPEIUS.　　　　　　　　　　I would your grace
Would leave your griefs, and take my counsel.
Q. KATHARINE.　　　　　　　　　　　How, sir?
CAMPEIUS. Put your main cause into the king's
　　protection;
He's loving and most gracious. 'Twill be much
Both for your honour better and your cause;
For if the trial of the law o'ertake ye,
You'll part away disgraced.
WOLSEY.　　　　　　　　He tells you rightly.
Q. KATHARINE. Ye tell me what ye wish for both,
　　my ruin.
Is this your Christian counsel? out upon ye!
Heaven is above all yet; there sits a judge　　100
That no king can corrupt.
CAMPEIUS.　　　　　　　Your rage mistakes us.
Q. KATHARINE. The more shame for ye; holy men I
　　thought ye,
Upon my soul, two reverend cardinal virtues;
But cardinal sins and hollow hearts I fear ye.
Mend 'em, for shame, my lords. Is this your
　　comfort?
The cordial that ye bring a wretched lady,
A woman lost among ye, laughed at, scorned?
I will not wish ye half my miseries:
I have more charity. But say I warned ye;
Take heed, for heaven's sake, take heed, lest at once　110
The burden of my sorrows fall upon ye.
WOLSEY. Madam, this is a mere distraction;
You turn the good we offer into envy.
Q. KATHARINE. Ye turn me into nothing. Woe upon
　　ye,
And all such false professors! would you have me—
If you have any justice, any pity,
If ye be any thing but churchmen's habits—
Put my sick cause into his hands that hates me?
Alas, has banished me his bed already,
His love, too long ago! I am old, my lords,　　120
And all the fellowship I hold now with him
Is only my obedience. What can happen
To me above this wretchedness? all your studies
Make me a curse like this.
CAMPEIUS.　　　　　　　Your fears are worse.
Q. KATHARINE. Have I lived thus long—let me speak
　　myself,
Since virtue finds no friends—a wife, a true one?
A woman, I dare say without vain-glory,
Never yet branded with suspicion?
Have I with all my full affections
Still met the king? loved him next heaven? obeyed
　　him?　　130
Been, out of fondness, superstitious to him?
Almost forgot my prayers to content him?
And am I thus rewarded? 'tis not well, lords.
Bring me a constant woman to her husband,

One that ne'er dreamed a joy beyond his pleasure,
And to that woman, when she has done most,
Yet will I add an honour—a great patience.
WOLSEY. Madam, you wander from the good we
　　aim at.
Q. KATHARINE. My lord, I dare not make myself so
　　guilty
To give up willingly that noble title　　140
Your master wed me to; nothing but death
Shall e'er divorce my dignities.
WOLSEY.　　　　　　　　　Pray hear me.
Q. KATHARINE. Would I had never trod this English
　　earth,
Or felt the flatteries that grow upon it!
Ye have angels' faces, but heaven knows your hearts.
What will become of me now, wretched lady!
I am the most unhappy woman living.
Alas, poor wenches, where are now your fortunes?
Shipwrecked upon a kingdom, where no pity,
No friends, no hope; no kindred weep for me;　　150
Almost no grave allowed me. Like the lily,
That once was mistress of the field, and flourished,
I'll hang my head and perish.
WOLSEY.　　　　　　　　If your grace
Could but be brought to know our ends are honest,
You'ld feel more comfort. Why should we, good
　　lady,
Upon what cause, wrong you? alas, our places,
The way of our profession is against it;
We are to cure such sorrows, not to sow 'em.
For goodness' sake, consider what you do;
How you may hurt yourself, ay, utterly　　160
Grow from the king's acquaintance, by this carriage.
The hearts of princes kiss obedience,
So much they love it; but to stubborn spirits
They swell, and grow as terrible as storms.
I know you have a gentle, noble temper,
A soul as even as a calm. Pray think us
Those we profess, peace-makers, friends and
　　servants.
CAMPEIUS. Madam, you'll find it so. You wrong your
　　virtues
With these weak women's fears. A noble spirit,
As yours was put into you, ever casts　　170
Such doubts, as false coin, from it. The king loves
　　you;
Beware you lose it not. For us, if you please
To trust us in your business, we are ready
To use our utmost studies in your service.
Q. KATHARINE. Do what ye will, my lords; and pray
　　forgive me;
If I have used myself unmannerly,
You know I am a woman, lacking wit
To make a seemly answer to such persons.
Pray do my service to his majesty;
He has my heart yet, and shall have my prayers　　180
While I shall have my life. Come, reverend fathers,
Bestow your counsels on me; she now begs
That little thought, when she set footing here,
She should have bought her dignities so dear.
　　　　　　　　　　　　　　　　　　They go

Scene 2: *Ante-chamber to the King's apartment*

*Enter the Duke of Norfolk, Duke of Suffolk, Lord Surrey,
and Lord Chamberlain*

NORFOLK. If you will now unite in your complaints
And force them with a constancy, the cardinal
Cannot stand under them. If you omit
The offer of this time, I cannot promise
But that you shall sustain moe new disgraces,
With these you bear already.
SURREY.   I am joyful
To meet the least occasion that may give me
Remembrance of my father-in-law, the duke,
To be revenged on him.
SUFFOLK.   Which of the peers
Have uncontemned gone by him, or at least   10
Strangely neglected? when did he regard
The stamp of nobleness in any person
Out of himself?
CHAMBERLAIN.   My lords, you speak your pleasures.
What he deserves of you and me I know;
What we can do to him, though now the time
Gives way to us, I much fear. If you cannot
Bar his access to th'king, never attempt
Any thing on him; for he hath a witchcraft
Over the king in's tongue.
NORFOLK.   O, fear him not;
His spell in that is out; the king hath found   20
Matter against him that for ever mars
The honey of his language. No, he's settled,
Not to come off, in his displeasure.
SURREY.   Sir,
I should be glad to hear such news as this
Once every hour.
NORFOLK.   Believe it, this is true.
In the divorce his contrary proceedings
Are all unfolded; wherein he appears
As I would wish mine enemy.
SURREY.   How came
His practices to light?
SUFFOLK.   Most strangely.
SURREY.   O, how, how?
SUFFOLK. The cardinal's letters to the pope miscarried, 30
And came to th'eye o'th'king; wherein was read
How that the cardinal did entreat his holiness
To stay the judgement o'th'divorce; for if
It did take place, 'I do' quoth he 'perceive
My king is tangled in affection to
A creature of the queen's, Lady Anne Bullen'.
SURREY. Has the king this?
SUFFOLK.   Believe it.
SURREY.   Will this work?
CHAMBERLAIN. The king in this perceives him how he
  coasts
And hedges his own way. But in this point
All his tricks founder and he brings his physic   40
After his patient's death: the king already
Hath married the fair lady.
SURREY.   Would he had!
SUFFOLK. May you be happy in your wish, my lord!
For, I profess, you have it.
SURREY.   Now, all my joy
Trace the conjunction!
SUFFOLK.   My amen to't!
NORFOLK.   All men's!
SUFFOLK. There's order given for her coronation;
Marry, this is yet but young, and may be left
To some ears unrecounted. But my lords,
She is a gallant creature and complete
In mind and feature. I persuade me, from her   50

Will fall some blessing to this land, which shall
In it be memorized.
SURREY.   But will the king
Digest this letter of the cardinal's?
The Lord forbid!
NORFOLK.   Marry, amen!
SUFFOLK.   No, no;
There be moe wasps that buzz about his nose
Will make this sting the sooner. Cardinal Campeius
Is stol'n away to Rome; hath ta'en no leave;
Has left the cause o'th'king unhandled, and
Is posted as the agent of our cardinal
To second all his plot. I do assure you   60
The king cried 'Ha!' at this.
CHAMBERLAIN.   Now God incense him,
And let him cry 'Ha!' louder!
NORFOLK.   But, my lord,
When returns Cranmer?
SUFFOLK. He is returned in his opinions, which
Have satisfied the king for his divorce,
Together with all famous colleges
Almost in Christendom. Shortly, I believe,
His second marriage shall be published, and
Her coronation. Katharine no more
Shall be called queen, but princess dowager   70
And widow to Prince Arthur.
NORFOLK.   This same Cranmer's
A worthy fellow, and hath ta'en much pain
In the king's business.
SUFFOLK.   He has; and we shall see him
For it an archbishop.
NORFOLK.   So I hear.
SUFFOLK.   'Tis so.
The cardinal!

Enter Wolsey and Cromwell

NORFOLK.   Observe, observe, he's moody.
WOLSEY. The packet, Cromwell,
Gave't you the king?
CROMWELL.   To his own hand, in's bedchamber.
WOLSEY. Looked he o'th'inside of the paper?
CROMWELL.   Presently
He did unseal them, and the first he viewed,
He did it with a serious mind; a heed   80
Was in his countenance. You he bade
Attend him here this morning.
WOLSEY.   Is he ready
To come abroad?
CROMWELL.   I think by this he is.
WOLSEY. Leave me awhile.   *Cromwell goes*
[aside] It shall be to the Duchess of Alençon,
The French king's sister; he shall marry her.
Anne Bullen? No; I'll no Anne Bullens for him;
There's more in't than fair visage. Bullen?
No, we'll no Bullens. Speedily I wish
To hear from Rome. The Marchioness of
  Pembroke?   90
NORFOLK. He's discontented.
SUFFOLK.   May be he hears the king
Does whet his anger to him.
SURREY.   Sharp enough,
Lord, for thy justice!
WOLSEY [aside]. The late queen's gentlewoman, a
  knight's daughter,
To be her mistress' mistress? the queen's queen?
This candle burns not clear; 'tis I must snuff it,

Then out it goes. What though I know her
  virtuous
And well deserving? yet I know her for
A spleeny Lutheran, and not wholesome to
Our cause that she should lie i'th'bosom of   100
Our hard-ruled king. Again, there is sprung up
An heretic, an arch one, Cranmer, one
Hath crawled into the favour of the king,
And is his oracle.
NORFOLK.   He is vexed at something.

Enter King, reading of a schedule, and Lovell

SURREY. I would 'twere something that would fret
  the string,
The master-cord on's heart!
SUFFOLK.   The king, the king!
KING. What piles of wealth hath he accumulated
To his own portion! and what expense by th'hour
Seems to flow from him! How, i'th'name of thrift,
Does he rake this together? Now, my lords,   110
Saw you the cardinal?
NORFOLK.   My lord, we have
Stood here observing him. Some strange
  commotion
Is in his brain: he bites his lip, and starts;
Stops on a sudden, looks upon the ground,
Then lays his finger on his temple; straight
Springs out into fast gait; then stops again,
Strikes his breast hard, and anon he casts
His eye against the moon. In most strange postures
We have seen him set himself.
KING.   It may well be
There is a mutiny in's mind. This morning   120
Papers of state he sent me to peruse,
As I required; and wot you what I found
There, on my conscience, put unwittingly?
Forsooth, an inventory, thus importing:
The several parcels of his plate, his treasure,
Rich stuffs, and ornaments of household, which
I find at such proud rate that it outspeaks
Possession of a subject.
NORFOLK.   It's heaven's will;
Some spirit put this paper in the packet
To bless your eye withal.
KING.   If we did think   130
His contemplation were above the earth,
And fixed on spiritual object, he should still
Dwell in his musings; but I am afraid
His thinkings are below the moon, not worth
His serious considering.

*King takes his seat; whispers Lovell, who goes to the
Cardinal*

WOLSEY.   Heaven forgive me!
Ever God bless your highness!
KING.   Good my lord,
You are full of heavenly stuff, and bear the
  inventory
Of your best graces in your mind; the which
You were now running o'er. You have scarce time
To steal from spiritual leisure a brief span   140
To keep your earthly audit; sure, in that
I deem you an ill husband, and am glad
To have you therein my companion.
WOLSEY.   Sir,
For holy offices I have a time; a time

To think upon the part of business which
I bear i'th'state; and Nature does require
Her times of preservation, which perforce
I, her frail son, amongst my brethren mortal,
Must give my tendance to.
KING.   You have said well.
WOLSEY. And ever may your highness yoke together,   150
As I will lend you cause, my doing well
With my well saying!
KING.   'Tis well said again;
And 'tis a kind of good deed to say well;
And yet words are no deeds. My father loved you,
He said he did, and with his deed did crown
His word upon you. Since I had my office
I have kept you next my heart; have not alone
Employed you where high profits might come
  home,
But pared my present havings, to bestow
My bounties upon you.
WOLSEY [*aside*].   What should this mean?   160
SURREY [*aside*]. The Lord increase this business!
KING.   Have I not made you
The prime man of the state? I pray you tell me
If what I now pronounce you have found true;
And, if you may confess it, say withal,
If you are bound to us or no. What say you?
WOLSEY. My sovereign, I confess your royal graces,
Showered on me daily, have been more than could
My studied purposes requite; which went
Beyond all man's endeavours. My endeavours
Have ever come too short of my desires,   170
Yet filed with my abilities; mine own ends
Have been mine so that evermore they pointed
To th'good of your most sacred person and
The profit of the state. For your great graces
Heaped upon me, poor undeserver, I
Can nothing render but allegiant thanks,
My prayers to heaven for you, my loyalty,
Which ever has and ever shall be growing
Till death, that winter, kill it.
KING.   Fairly answered;
A loyal and obedient subject is   180
Therein illustrated; the honour of it
Does pay the act of it; as, i'th'contrary,
The foulness is the punishment. I presume
That, as my hand has opened bounty to you,
My heart dropped love, my power rained
  honour, more
On you than any, so your hand and heart,
Your brain and every function of your power,
Should, notwithstanding that your bond of duty,
As 'twere in love's particular, be more
To me, your friend, than any.
WOLSEY.   I do profess   190
That for your highness' good I ever laboured
More than mine own; that am, have, and will be—
Though all the world should crack their duty to
  you,
And throw it from their soul; though perils did
Abound, as thick as thought could make 'em, and
Appear in forms more horrid—yet my duty,
As doth a rock against the chiding flood,
Should the approach of this wild river break,
And stand unshaken yours.
KING.   'Tis nobly spoken.
Take notice, lords, he has a loyal breast,   200

For you have seen him open't. [*giving him papers*]
  Read o'er this;
And after, this; and then to breakfast with
What appetite you have.
                  King departs, frowning upon the
                  Cardinal: the nobles throng after
                  him, smiling and whispering
WOLSEY.   What should this mean?
What sudden anger's this? how have I reaped it?
He parted frowning from me, as if ruin
Leaped from his eyes. So looks the chaféd lion
Upon the daring huntsman that has galled him;
Then makes him nothing. I must read this paper;
I fear, the story of his anger. 'Tis so;
This paper has undone me. 'Tis the account   210
Of all that world of wealth I have drawn together
For mine own ends; indeed, to gain the popedom,
And fee my friends in Rome. O negligence,
Fit for a fool to fall by! what cross devil
Made me put this main secret in the packet
I sent the king? Is there no way to cure this?
No new device to beat this from his brains?
I know 'twill stir him strongly; yet I know
A way, if it take right, in spite of fortune
Will bring me off again. What's this? 'To th'Pope'? 220
The letter, as I live, with all the business
I writ to's holiness. Nay then, farewell!
I have touched the highest point of all my greatness,
And, from that full meridian of my glory,
I haste now to my setting. I shall fall
Like a bright exhalation in the evening,
And no man see me more.

Enter to Wolsey the Dukes of Norfolk and Suffolk, the
Earl of Surrey, and the Lord Chamberlain

NORFOLK. Hear the king's pleasure, cardinal, who
    commands you
To render up the great seal presently
Into our hands, and to confine yourself   230
To Asher house, my Lord of Winchester's,
Till you hear further from his highness.
WOLSEY.   Stay:
Where's your commission, lords? words cannot
    carry
Authority so weighty.
SUFFOLK.   Who dare cross 'em,
Bearing the king's will from his mouth expressly?
WOLSEY. Till I find more than will or words to do it—
I mean your malice—know, officious lords,
I dare, and must deny it. Now I feel
Of what coarse metal ye are moulded—envy;
How eagerly ye follow my disgraces,   240
As if it fed ye; and how sleek and wanton
Ye appear in every thing may bring my ruin!
Follow your envious courses, men of malice;
You have Christian warrant for 'em, and no doubt
In time will find their fit rewards. That seal
You ask with such a violence, the king,
Mine and your master, with his own hand gave me;
Bade me enjoy it, with the place and honours,
During my life; and, to confirm his goodness,
Tied it by letters-patents. Now, who'll take it?   250
SURREY. The king, that give it.
WOLSEY.   It must be himself, then.
SURREY. Thou art a proud traitor, priest.
WOLSEY.   Proud lord, thou liest.

Within these forty hours Surrey durst better
Have burnt that tongue than said so.
SURREY.   Thy ambition,
Thou scarlet sin, robbed this bewailing land
Of noble Buckingham, my father-in-law.
The heads of all thy brother cardinals,
With thee and all thy best parts bound together,
Weighed not a hair of his. Plague of your policy!
You sent me deputy for Ireland;   260
Far from his succour, from the king, from all
That might have mercy on the fault thou gavest him;
Whilst your great goodness, out of holy pity,
Absolved him with an axe.
WOLSEY.   This, and all else
This talking lord can lay upon my credit,
I answer, is most false. The duke by law
Found his deserts. How innocent I was
From any private malice in his end,
His noble jury and foul cause can witness.
If I loved many words, lord, I should tell you   270
You have as little honesty as honour,
That in the way of loyalty and truth
Toward the king, my ever royal master,
Dare mate a sounder man than Surrey can be,
And all that love his follies.
SURREY.   By my soul,
Your long coat, priest, protects you; thou shouldst
    feel
My sword i'th'life-blood of thee else. My lords,
Can ye endure to hear this arrogance?
And from this fellow? If we live thus tamely,
To be thus jaded by a piece of scarlet,   280
Farewell nobility; let his grace go forward,
And dare us with his cap like larks.
WOLSEY.   All goodness
Is poison to thy stomach.
SURREY.   Yes, that goodness
Of gleaning all the land's wealth into one,
Into your own hands, cardinal, by extortion;
The goodness of your intercepted packets
You writ to th'pope against the king: your
    goodness,
Since you provoke me, shall be most notorious.
My Lord of Norfolk, as you are truly noble,
As you respect the common good, the state   290
Of our despised nobility, our issues,
Who, if he live, will scarce be gentlemen,
Produce the grand sum of his sins, the articles
Collected from his life. I'll startle you
Worse than the sacring bell, when the brown wench
Lay kissing in your arms, lord cardinal.
WOLSEY. How much, methinks, I could despise this
    man,
But that I am bound in charity against it!
NORFOLK. Those articles, my lord, are in the
    king's hand;
But, thus much, they are foul ones.
WOLSEY.   So much fairer   300
And spotless shall mine innocence arise,
When the king knows my truth.
SURREY.   This cannot save you.
I thank my memory I yet remember
Some of these articles, and out they shall.
Now, if you can blush and cry 'guilty', cardinal,
You'll show a little honesty.
WOLSEY.   Speak on, sir;

I dare your worst objections; if I blush,
It is to see a nobleman want manners.
SURREY. I had rather want those than my head.
    Have at you!
First that, without the king's assent or knowledge, 310
You wrought to be a legate; by which power
You maimed the jurisdiction of all bishops.
NORFOLK. Then that in all you writ to Rome, or else
To foreign princes, 'Ego et Rex meus'
Was still inscribed; in which you brought the king
To be your servant.
SUFFOLK.   Then, that without the knowledge
Either of king or council, when you went
Ambassador to the emperor, you made bold
To carry into Flanders the great seal.
SURREY. Item, you sent a large commission   320
To Gregory de Cassado, to conclude,
Without the king's will or the state's allowance,
A league between his highness and Ferrara.
SUFFOLK. That out of mere ambition you have caused
Your holy hat to be stamped on the king's coin.
SURREY. Then that you have sent innumerable
    substance—
By what means got, I leave to your own
    conscience—
To furnish Rome and to prepare the ways
You have for dignities, to the mere undoing
Of all the kingdom. Many more there are;   330
Which, since they are of you and odious,
I will not taint my mouth with.
CHAMBERLAIN.   O my lord!
Press not a falling man too far; 'tis virtue.
His faults lie open to the laws; let them,
Not you, correct him. My heart weeps to see him
So little of his great self.
SURREY.   I forgive him.
SUFFOLK. Lord cardinal, the king's further pleasure is—
Because all those things you have done of late,
By your power legatine, within this kingdom,
Fall into th'compass of a præmunire—   340
That therefore such a writ be sued against you:
To forfeit all your goods, lands, tenements,
Chattels, and whatsoever, and to be
Out of the king's protection. This is my charge.
NORFOLK. And so we'll leave you to your meditations
How to live better. For your stubborn answer
About the giving back the great seal to us,
The king shall know it, and, no doubt, shall thank
    you.
So fare you well, my little good lord cardinal.
                        All but Wolsey go
WOLSEY. So farewell to the little good you bear me. 350
Farewell! a long farewell to all my greatness!
This is the state of man: to-day he puts forth
The tender leaves of hopes; to-morrow blossoms,
And bears his blushing honours thick upon him;
The third day comes a frost, a killing frost,
And, when he thinks, good easy man, full surely
His greatness is a-ripening, nips his root,
And then he falls, as I do. I have ventured,
Like little wanton boys that swim on bladders,
This many summers in a sea of glory,   360
But far beyond my depth; my high-blown pride
At length broke under me and now has left me,
Weary and old with service, to the mercy
Of a rude stream that must for ever hide me.

Vain pomp and glory of this world, I hate ye:
I feel my heart new opened. O, how wretched
Is that poor man that hangs on princes' favours!
There is, betwixt that smile we would aspire to,
That sweet aspect of princes, and their ruin,
More pangs and fears than wars or women have; 370
And when he falls, he falls like Lucifer,
Never to hope again.

Enter Cromwell, standing amazed
                        Why, how now, Cromwell?
CROMWELL. I have no power to speak, sir.
WOLSEY.   What, amazed
At my misfortunes? can thy spirit wonder
A great man should decline? Nay, an you weep,
I am fall'n indeed.
CROMWELL.   How does your grace?
WOLSEY.   Why, well;
Never so truly happy, my good Cromwell.
I know myself now; and I feel within me
A peace above all earthly dignities,
A still and quiet conscience. The king has cured me, 380
I humbly thank his grace; and from these shoulders,
These ruined pillars, out of pity, taken
A load would sink a navy—too much honour.
O, 'tis a burden, Cromwell, 'tis a burden
Too heavy for a man that hopes for heaven!
CROMWELL. I am glad your grace has made that right
    use of it.
WOLSEY. I hope I have. I am able now, methinks,
Out of a fortitude of soul I feel,
To endure more miseries and greater far
Than my weak-hearted enemies dare offer.   390
What news abroad?
CROMWELL.   The heaviest and the worst
Is your displeasure with the king.
WOLSEY.   God bless him!
CROMWELL. The next is, that Sir Thomas More is
    chosen
Lord chancellor in your place.
WOLSEY.   That's somewhat sudden.
But he's a learnèd man. May he continue
Long in his highness' favour, and do justice
For truth's sake and his conscience; that his bones,
When he has run his course and sleeps in blessings,
May have a tomb of orphans' tears wept on him!
What more?
CROMWELL. That Cranmer is returned with welcome, 400
Installed lord archbishop of Canterbury.
WOLSEY. That's news indeed.
CROMWELL.   Last, that the Lady Anne,
Whom the king hath in secrecy long married,
This day was viewed in open as his queen,
Going to chapel; and the voice is now
Only about her coronation.
WOLSEY. There was the weight that pulled me
    down. O Cromwell,
The king has gone beyond me. All my glories
In that one woman I have lost for ever.
No sun shall ever usher forth mine honours,   410
Or gild again the noble troops that waited
Upon my smiles. Go get thee from me, Cromwell;
I am a poor fall'n man, unworthy now
To be thy lord and master. Seek the king—
That sun I pray may never set—I have told him
What and how true thou art; he will advance thee;

Some little memory of me will stir him—
I know his noble nature—not to let
Thy hopeful service perish too. Good Cromwell,
Neglect him not; make use now, and provide   420
For thine own future safety.
CROMWELL.   O my lord,
Must I then leave you? must I needs forego
So good, so noble and so true a master?
Bear witness, all that have not hearts of iron,
With what a sorrow Cromwell leaves his lord.
The king shall have my service, but my prayers
For ever and for ever shall be yours.
WOLSEY. Cromwell, I did not think to shed a tear'
In all my miseries; but thou hast forced me,
Out of thy honest truth, to play the woman.   430
Let's dry our eyes; and thus far hear me, Cromwell;
And when I am forgotten, as I shall be,
And sleep in dull cold marble, where no mention
Of me more must be heard of, say I taught thee,
Say, Wolsey, that once trod the ways of glory,
And sounded all the depths and shoals of honour,
Found thee a way, out of his wreck, to rise in—
A sure and safe one, though thy master missed it.
Mark but my fall and that that ruined me.
Cromwell, I charge thee, fling away ambition: 440
By that sin fell the angels; how can man then,
The image of his Maker, hope to win by it?
Love thyself last; cherish those hearts that hate thee;
Corruption wins not more than honesty.
Still in thy right hand carry gentle peace
To silence envious tongues. Be just, and fear not;
Let all the ends thou aim'st at be thy country's,
Thy God's, and truth's; then if thou fall'st,
  O Cromwell,
Thou fall'st a blessed martyr. Serve the king;
And prithee, lead me in: 450
There take an inventory of all I have
To the last penny; 'tis the king's. My robe,
And my integrity to heaven, is all
I dare now call mine own. O Cromwell, Cromwell,
Had I but served my God with half the zeal
I served my king, he would not in mine age
Have left me naked to mine enemies.
CROMWELL. Good sir, have patience.
WOLSEY.   So I have. Farewell
The hopes of court! my hopes in heaven do dwell.
                                        They go

ACT 4

Scene 1: A street in Westminster

Enter two Gentlemen, meeting one another

1 GENTLEMAN. You're well met once again.
2 GENTLEMAN.   So are you.
1 GENTLEMAN. You come to take your stand here,
  and behold
The Lady Anne pass from her coronation?
2 GENTLEMAN. 'Tis all my business. At our last
  encounter
The Duke of Buckingham came from his trial.
1 GENTLEMAN. 'Tis very true. But that time offered
  sorrow;
This, general joy.
2 GENTLEMAN.   'Tis well. The citizens,
I am sure, have shown at full their royal minds—

As, let 'em have their rights, they are ever forward—
In celebration of this day with shows,   10
Pageants, and sights of honour.
1 GENTLEMAN.   Never greater,
Nor, I'll assure you, better taken, sir.
2 GENTLEMAN. May I be bold to ask what that
  contains,
That paper in your hand?
1 GENTLEMAN.   Yes, 'tis the list
Of those that claim their offices this day
By custom of the coronation.
The Duke of Suffolk is the first, and claims
To be high steward; next, the Duke of Norfolk,
He to be earl marshal; you may read the rest.
2 GENTLEMAN. I thank you, sir; had I not known
  those customs,   20
I should have been beholding to your paper.
But, I beseech you, what's become of Katharine,
The princess dowager? how goes her business?
1 GENTLEMAN. That I can tell you too. The
  Archbishop
Of Canterbury, accompanied with other
Learnéd and reverend fathers of his order,
Held a late court at Dunstable, six miles off
From Ampthill, where the princess lay; to which
She was often cited by them, but appeared not;
And, to be short, for not appearance and   30
The king's late scruple, by the main assent
Of all these learnéd men she was divorced,
And the late marriage made of none effect;
Since which she was removed to Kimbolton,
Where she remains now sick.
2 GENTLEMAN.   Alas, good lady!
                                        Trumpets
The trumpets sound: stand close, the queen is
  coming.   Hautboys

THE ORDER OF THE CORONATION

1. *A lively flourish of trumpets.*
2. *Then two judges.*
3. *Lord Chancellor, with purse and mace before him.*
4. *Choristers, singing.*   Music.
5. *Mayor of London, bearing the mace. Then Garter,
   in his coat of arms, and on his head he wore a gilt
   copper crown.*
6. *Marquess Dorset, bearing a sceptre of gold, on his head
   a demicoronal of gold. With him, the Earl of Surrey,
   bearing the rod of silver with the dove, crowned with
   an earl's coronet. Collars of SS.*
7. *Duke of Suffolk, in his robe of estate, his coronet
   on his head, bearing a long white wand, as High
   Steward. With him, the Duke of Norfolk, with the
   rod of marshalship, a coronet on his head. Collars
   of SS.*
8. *A canopy borne by four of the Cinque-ports; under it,
   the Queen in her robe, in her hair, richly adorned with
   pearl, crowned. On each side her, the Bishops of London
   and Winchester.*
9. *The old Duchess of Norfolk, in a coronal of gold,
   wrought with flowers, bearing the Queen's train*
10. *Certain Ladies or Countesses, with plain circlets of
   gold without flowers*

*As they pass over the stage in order and state, the two
Gentlemen comment upon them*

2 GENTLEMAN. A royal train, believe me. These I
    know.
    Who's that that bears the sceptre?
1 GENTLEMAN.   Marquess Dorset;
    And that the Earl of Surrey, with the rod.
2 GENTLEMAN. A bold brave gentleman. That should
    be   40
    The Duke of Suffolk?
1 GENTLEMAN.   'Tis the same: high steward.
2 GENTLEMAN. And that my Lord of Norfolk?
1 GENTLEMAN.   Yes.
2 GENTLEMAN [looking on the Queen]. Heaven bless thee!
    Thou hast the sweetest face I ever looked on.
    Sir, as I have a soul, she is an angel;
    Our king has all the Indies in his arms,
    And more and richer, when he strains that lady;
    I cannot blame his conscience.
1 GENTLEMAN.   They that bear
    The cloth of honour over her, are four barons
    Of the Cinque-ports.
2 GENTLEMAN. Those men are happy; and so are all
    are near her.   50
    I take it, she that carries up the train
    Is that old noble lady, Duchess of Norfolk.
1 GENTLEMAN. It is, and all the rest are countesses.
2 GENTLEMAN. Their coronets say so. These are stars
    indeed.
1 GENTLEMAN. And sometimes falling ones.
2 GENTLEMAN.   No more of that.
        The last of the procession leaves; and
        then a great flourish of trumpets sounds

Enter a third Gentleman

1 GENTLEMAN. God save you, sir! where have you been
    broiling?
3 GENTLEMAN. Among the crowd i'th'abbey; where a
    finger
    Could not be wedged in more: I am stifled
    With the mere rankness of their joy.
2 GENTLEMAN.   You saw
    The ceremony?
3 GENTLEMAN.   That I did.
1 GENTLEMAN.   How was it?   60
3 GENTLEMAN. Well worth the seeing.
2 GENTLEMAN.   Good sir, speak it to us.
3 GENTLEMAN. As well as I am able. The rich stream
    Of lords and ladies, having brought the queen
    To a prepared place in the choir, fell off
    A distance from her; while her grace sat down
    To rest awhile, some half an hour or so,
    In a rich chair of state, opposing freely
    The beauty of her person to the people.
    Believe me, sir, she is the goodliest woman
    That every lay by man; which when the people   70
    Had the full view of, such a noise arose
    As the shrouds make at sea in a stiff tempest,
    As loud and to as many tunes; hats, cloaks,—
    Doublets, I think—flew up, and had their faces
    Been loose, this day they had been lost. Such joy
    I never saw before. Great-bellied women,
    That had not half a week to go, like rams
    In the old time of war, would shake the press,
    And make 'em reel before 'em. No man living
    Could say 'This is my wife' there, all were woven   80
    So strangely in one piece.
2 GENTLEMAN.   But what followed?

3 GENTLEMAN. At length her grace rose, and with
    modest paces
    Came to the altar, where she kneeled, and saintlike
    Cast her fair eyes to heaven and prayed devoutly;
    Then rose again and bowed her to the people;
    When by the Archbishop of Canterbury
    She had all the royal makings of a queen,
    As holy oil, Edward Confessor's crown,
    The rod, and bird of peace, and all such emblems
    Laid nobly on her; which performed, the choir,   90
    With all the choicest music of the kingdom,
    Together sung 'Te Deum'. So she parted,
    And with the same full state paced back again
    To York place, where the feast is held.
1 GENTLEMAN.   Sir,
    You must no more call it York place: that's past;
    For since the cardinal fell that title's lost:
    'Tis now the king's, and called Whitehall.
3 GENTLEMAN.   I know it;
    But 'tis so lately altered that the old name
    Is fresh about me.
2 GENTLEMAN.   What two reverend bishops
    Were those that went on each side of the queen?   100
3 GENTLEMAN. Stokesly and Gardiner: the one of
    Winchester,
    Newly preferred from the king's secretary,
    The other, London.
2 GENTLEMAN.   He of Winchester
    Is held no great good lover of the archbishop's,
    The virtuous Cranmer.
3 GENTLEMAN.   All the land knows that:
    However, yet there is no great breach; when it
    comes,
    Cranmer will find a friend will not shrink from him.
2 GENTLEMAN. Who may that be, I pray you?
3 GENTLEMAN.   Thomas Cromwell,
    A man in much esteem with th'king, and truly
    A worthy friend. The king has made him master   110
    O'th'jewel house,
    And one, already, of the privy council.
2 GENTLEMAN. He will deserve more.
3 GENTLEMAN.   Yes, without all doubt.
    Come, gentlemen, ye shall go my way,
    Which is to th'court, and there ye shall be my guests;
    Something I can command. As I walk thither,
    I'll tell ye more.
BOTH.   You may command us, sir.
                                            They go

Scene 2: Kimbolton

Enter Katharine, Dowager, sick; led between Griffith, her
Gentleman Usher, and Patience, her woman

GRIFFITH. How does your grace?
KATHARINE.   O Griffith, sick to death.
    My legs like loaden branches bow to th'earth,
    Willing to leave their burden. Reach a chair.
    So—now, methinks, I feel a little ease.
    Didst thou not tell me, Griffith, as thou led'st me,
    That the great child of honour, Cardinal Wolsey,
    Was dead?
GRIFFITH. Yes, madam; but I think your grace,
    Out of the pain you suffered, gave no ear to't.
KATHARINE. Prithee, good Griffith, tell me how he
    died.

If well, he stepped before me happily   10
For my example.
GRIFFITH.   Well, the voice goes, madam;
For after the stout Earl Northumberland
Arrested him at York, and brought him forward,
As a man sorely tainted, to his answer,
He fell sick suddenly, and grew so ill
He could not sit his mule.
KATHARINE.   Alas, poor man!
GRIFFITH. At last, with easy roads, he came to Leicester,
Lodged in the abbey; where the reverend abbot,
With all his covent, honourably received him;
To whom he gave these words, 'O father abbot,   20
An old man, broken with the storms of state,
Is come to lay his weary bones among ye;
Give him a little earth for charity'.
So went to bed; where eagerly his sickness
Pursued him still; and three nights after this,
About the hour of eight, which he himself
Foretold should be his last, full of repentance,
Continual meditations, tears and sorrows,
He gave his honours to the world again,
His blessèd part to heaven, and slept in peace.   30
KATHARINE. So may he rest; his faults lie gently on
him!
Yet thus far, Griffith, give me leave to speak him,
And yet with charity. He was a man
Of an unbounded stomach, ever ranking
Himself with princes; one that by suggestion
Tied all the kingdom: simony was fair play;
His own opinion was his law. I'th'presence
He would say untruths, and be ever double
Both in his words and meaning. He was never,
But where he meant to ruin, pitiful.   40
His promises were, as he then was, mighty;
But his performance, as he is now, nothing.
Of his own body he was ill, and gave
The clergy ill example.
GRIFFITH.   Noble madam,
Men's evil manners live in brass; their virtues
We write in water. May it please your highness
To hear me speak his good now?
KATHARINE.   Yes, good Griffith;
I were malicious else.
GRIFFITH.   This Cardinal,
Though from an humble stock, undoubtedly
Was fashioned to much honour from his cradle.   50
He was a scholar, and a ripe and good one;
Exceeding wise, fair-spoken and persuading;
Lofty and sour to them that loved him not,
But to those men that sought him, sweet as summer.
And though he were unsatisfied in getting,
Which was a sin, yet in bestowing, madam,
He was most princely: ever witness for him
Those twins of learning that he raised in you,
Ipswich and Oxford! one of which fell with him,
Unwilling to outlive the good that did it;   60
The other, though unfinished, yet so famous,
So excellent in art, and still so rising,
That Christendom shall ever speak his virtue.
His overthrow heaped happiness upon him;
For then, and not till then, he felt himself,
And found the blessedness of being little.
And, to add greater honours to his age
Than man could give him, he died fearing God.
KATHARINE. After my death I wish no other herald,

No other speaker of my living actions,   70
To keep mine honour from corruption,
But such an honest chronicler as Griffith.
Whom I most hated living, thou hast made me,
With thy religious truth and modesty,
Now in his ashes honour: peace be with him!
Patience, be near me still, and set me lower:
I have not long to trouble thee. Good Griffith,
Cause the musicians play me that sad note
I named my knell, whilst I sit meditating
On that celestial harmony I go to.   80
                              Sad and solemn music
GRIFFITH. She is asleep. Good wench, let's sit down
quiet,
For fear we wake her. Softly, gentle Patience.

THE VISION.

*Enter, solemnly tripping one after another, six personages,
clad in white robes, wearing on their heads garlands of bays,
and golden vizards on their faces; branches of bays or palm
in their hands. They first congee unto her, then dance; and,
at certain changes, the first two hold a spare garland over
her head; at which the other four make reverent curtsies; then
the two that held the garland deliver the same to the other
next two, who observe the same order in their changes, and
holding the garland over her head; which done, they deliver
the same garland to the last two, who likewise observe the
same order; at which, as it were by inspiration, she makes
in her sleep signs of rejoicing, and holdeth up her hands to
heaven; and so in their dancing vanish, carrying the garland
with them. The music continues*

KATHARINE. Spirits of peace, where are ye? are ye
all gone,
And leave me here in wretchedness behind ye?
GRIFFITH. Madam, we are here.
KATHARINE.   It is not you I call for
Saw ye none enter since I slept?
GRIFFITH.   None, madam.
KATHARINE. No? Saw you not even now a blessèd
troop
Invite me to a banquet, whose bright faces
Cast thousand beams upon me, like the sun?
They promised me eternal happiness,   90
And brought me garlands, Griffith, which I feel
I am not worthy yet to wear: I shall, assuredly.
GRIFFITH. I am most joyful, madam, such good dreams
Possess your fancy.
KATHARINE.   Bid the music leave;
They are harsh and heavy to me.   *Music ceases*
PATIENCE.   Do you note
How much her grace is altered on the sudden?
How long her face is drawn? how pale she looks,
And of an earthy cold? Mark her eyes.
GRIFFITH. She is going, wench. Pray, pray.
PATIENCE.   Heaven comfort her!

Enter a Messenger

MESSENGER. An't like your grace—
KATHARINE.   You are a saucy fellow;   100
Deserve we no more reverence?
GRIFFITH.   You are to blame,
Knowing she will not lose her wonted greatness,
To use so rude behaviour. Go to, kneel.
MESSENGER. I humbly do entreat your highness'
pardon;
My haste made me unmannerly. There is staying

A gentleman, sent from the king, to see you.
KATHARINE. Admit him entrance, Griffith: but this
    fellow
Let me ne'er see again.   *Messenger goes*

Griffith ushers in Capucius

                         If my sight fail not,
You should be lord ambassador from the emperor,
My royal nephew, and your name Capucius.   110
CAPUCIUS. Madam, the same. Your servant.
KATHARINE.   O, my lord,
The times and titles now are altered strangely
With me since first you knew me. But I pray you,
What is your pleasure with me?
CAPUCIUS.   Noble lady,
First, mine own service to your grace; the next,
The king's request that I would visit you,
Who grieves much for your weakness, and by me
Sends you his princely commendations,
And heartily entreats you take good comfort.
KATHARINE. O my good lord, that comfort comes
    too late;   120
'Tis like a pardon after execution.
That gentle physic, given in time, had cured me;
But now I am past all comforts here but prayers.
How does his highness?
CAPUCIUS.   Madam, in good health.
KATHARINE. So may he ever do! and ever flourish,
When I shall dwell with worms, and my poor name
Banished the kingdom! Patience, is that letter
I caused you write yet sent away?
PATIENCE.   No, madam.
                         Giving it to Katharine
KATHARINE. Sir, I most humbly pray you to deliver
This to my lord the king.
CAPUCIUS.   Most willing, madam.   130
KATHARINE. In which I have commended to his
    goodness
The model of our chaste loves, his young
    daughter—
The dews of heaven fall thick in blessings on her!—
Beseeching him to give her virtuous breeding—
She is young, and of a noble modest nature;
I hope she will deserve well—and a little
To love her for her mother's sake that loved him
Heaven knows how dearly. My next poor petition
Is that his noble grace would have some pity
Upon my wretched women that so long   140
Have followed both my fortunes faithfully;
Of which there is not one, I dare avow—
And now I should not lie—but will deserve,
For virtue and true beauty of the soul,
For honesty and decent carriage,
A right good husband, let him be a noble;
And, sure, those men are happy that shall have 'em.
The last is, for my men; they are the poorest,
But poverty could never draw 'em from me;
That they may have their wages duly paid 'em, 150
And something over to remember me by.
If heaven had pleased to have given me longer life
And able means, we had not parted thus.
These are the whole contents; and, good my lord,
By that you love the dearest in this world,
As you wish Christian peace to souls departed,
Stand these poor people's friend, and urge the king
To do me this last right.

CAPUCIUS.   By heaven, I will,
Or let me lose the fashion of a man!
KATHARINE. I thank you, honest lord. Remember me 160
In all humility unto his highness;
Say his long trouble now is passing
Out of this world. Tell him in death I blessed him,
For so I will. Mine eyes grow dim. Farewell,
My lord. Griffith, farewell. Nay, Patience,
You must not leave me yet. I must to bed;
Call in more women. When I am dead, good
    wench,
Let me be used with honour; strew me over
With maiden flowers, that all the world may know
I was a chaste wife to my grave. Embalm me,   170
Then lay me forth; although unqueened, yet like
A queen and daughter to a king, inter me.
I can no more.   *They go out, leading Katharine*

ACT 5
Scene 1: *London. A gallery in the palace*

*Enter Gardiner, Bishop of Winchester, a Page with a torch
before him, met by Sir Thomas Lovell*

GARDINER. It's one o'clock, boy, is't not?
BOY.   It hath struck.
GARDINER. These should be hours for necessities,
Not for delights; times to repair our nature
With comforting repose, and not for us
To waste these times. Good hour of night,
    Sir Thomas!
Whither so late?
LOVELL.   Came you from the king, my lord?
GARDINER. I did, Sir Thomas, and left him at primero
With the Duke of Suffolk.
LOVELL.   I must to him too,
Before he go to bed. I'll take my leave.
GARDINER. Not yet, Sir Thomas Lovell. What's the
    matter?   10
It seems you are in haste; an if there be
No great offence belongs to't, give your friend
Some touch of your late business. Affairs that walk,
As they say spirits do, at midnight, have
In them a wilder nature than the business
That seeks dispatch by day.
LOVELL.   My lord, I love you;
And durst commend a secret to your ear
Much weightier than this work. The queen's in
    labour,
They say, in great extremity, and feared
She'll with the labour end.
GARDINER.   The fruit she goes with 20
I pray for heartily, that it may find
Good time, and live; but for the stock, Sir Thomas,
I wish it grubbed up now.
LOVELL.   Methinks I could
Cry the amen; and yet my conscience says
She's a good creature, and, sweet lady, does
Deserve our better wishes.
GARDINER.   But, sir, sir,
Hear me, Sir Thomas, you're a gentleman
Of mine own way; I know you wise, religious;
And, let me tell you, it will ne'er be well,
'Twill not, Sir Thomas Lovell, take't of me,   30
Till Cranmer, Cromwell, her two hands, and she,
Sleep in their graves.
LOVELL.   Now, sir, you speak of two

The most remarked i'th'kingdom. As for
  Cromwell,
Beside that of the jewel house, is made master
O'th'rolls, and the king's secretary; further, sir,
Stands in the gap and trade of moe preferments,
With which the time will load him. Th'archbishop
Is the king's hand and tongue, and who dare speak
One syllable against him?
GARDINER.   Yes, yes, Sir Thomas,
There are that dare; and I myself have ventured   40
To speak my mind of him; and indeed this day,
Sir, I may tell it you, I think I have
Insensed the lords o'th'council that he is—
For, so I know he is, they know he is—
A most arch heretic, a pestilence
That does infect the land; with which they moved
Have broken with the king, who hath so far
Given ear to our complaint, of his great grace
And princely care foreseeing those fell mischiefs
Our reasons laid before him, hath commanded   50
To-morrow morning to the council board
He be converted. He's a rank weed,
  Sir Thomas,
And we must root him out. From your affairs
I hinder you too long. Good night, Sir Thomas.
                      Gardiner and Page go
LOVELL. Many good nights, my lord; I rest your
  servant.

Enter King and Suffolk

KING. Charles, I will play no more to-night;
My mind's not on't; you are too hard for me.
SUFFOLK. Sir, I did never win of you before.
KING. But little, Charles,
Nor shall not, when my fancy's on my play.   60
Now, Lovell, from the queen what is the news?
LOVELL. I could not personally deliver to her
What you commanded me, but by her woman
I sent your message; who returned her thanks
In the great'st humbleness, and desired your
  highness
Most heartily to pray for her.
KING.   What say'st thou, ha?
To pray for her? what, is she crying out?
LOVELL. So said her woman, and that her sufferance
  made
Almost each pang a death.
KING.   Alas, good lady!
SUFFOLK. God safely quit her of her burden, and   70
With gentle travail, to the gladding of
Your highness with an heir!
KING.   'Tis midnight, Charles;
Prithee, to bed; and in thy prayers remember
Th'estate of my poor queen. Leave me alone;
For I must think of that which company
Would not be friendly to.
SUFFOLK.   I wish your highness
A quiet night, and my good mistress will
Remember in my prayers.
KING.   Charles, good night.   *Suffolk goes*

Enter Sir Anthony Denny

Well, sir, what follows?
DENNY. Sir, I have brought my lord the archbishop, 80
As you commanded me.
KING.   Ha? Canterbury?

DENNY. Ay, my good lord.
KING.   'Tis true: where is he, Denny?
DENNY. He attends your highness' pleasure.
KING.   Bring him to us.   *Denny goes*
LOVELL [*aside*]. This is about that which the bishop
  spake;
I am happily come hither.

Enter Cranmer and Denny

KING. Avoid the gallery. [*Lovell seems to stay*] Ha? I
  have said. Be gone.
What!   *Lovell and Denny go*
CRANMER [*aside*]. I am fearful. Wherefore frowns he
  thus?
'Tis his aspect of terror. All's not well.
KING. How now, my lord? you do desire to know
Wherefore I sent for you.
CRANMER [*kneeling*].   It is my duty   90
T'attend your highness' pleasure.
KING.   Pray you, arise,
My good and gracious Lord of Canterbury.
Come, you and I must walk a turn together;
I have news to tell you; come, come, give me your
  hand.
Ah, my good lord, I grieve at what I speak,
And am right sorry to repeat what follows.
I have, and most unwillingly, of late
Heard many grievous, I do say, my lord,
Grievous complaints of you; which, being
  considered,
Have moved us and our council, that you shall   100
This morning come before us; where I know
You cannot with such freedom purge yourself
But that, till further trial in those charges
Which will require your answer, you must take
Your patience to you and be well contented
To make your house our Tower; you a brother of
  us,
It fits we thus proceed, or else no witness
Would come against you.
CRANMER [*kneeling*]. I humbly thank your highness,
And am right glad to catch this good occasion
Most throughly to be winnowèd, where my chaff 110
And corn shall fly asunder; for I know
There's none stands under more calumnious tongues
Than I myself, poor man.
KING.   Stand up, good Canterbury;
Thy truth and thy integrity is rooted
In us, thy friend. Give me thy hand, stand up;
Prithee, let's walk. Now, by my holidame,
What manner of man are you? My lord, I looked
You would have given me your petition, that
I should have ta'en some pains to bring together
Yourself and your accusers, and to have heard you, 120
Without indurance further.
CRANMER.   Most dread liege,
The good I stand on is my truth and honesty;
If they shall fail, I with mine enemies
Will triumph o'er my person; which I weigh not,
Being of those virtues vacant. I fear nothing
What can be said against me.
KING.   Know you not
How your state stands i'th'world, with the whole
  world?
Your enemies are many, and not small; their
  practices

Must bear the same proportion; and not ever
The justice and the truth o'th'question carries   130
The due o'th'verdict with it; at what ease
Might corrupt minds procure knaves as corrupt
To swear against you? Such things have been done.
You are potently opposed, and with a malice
Of as great size. Ween you of better luck,
I mean, in perjured witness, than your master,
Whose minister you are, whiles here he lived
Upon this naughty earth? Go to, go to;
You take a precipice for no leap of danger,
And woo your own destruction.

CRANMER.   God and your majesty   140
Protect mine innocence, or I fall into
The trap is laid for me!

KING.   Be of good cheer;
They shall no more prevail than we give way to.
Keep comfort to you, and this morning see
You do appear before them. If they shall chance,
In charging you with matters, to commit you,
The best persuasions to the contrary
Fail not to use, and with what vehemency
The occasion shall instruct you. If entreaties
Will render you no remedy, this ring   150
Deliver them, and your appeal to us
There make before them. Look, the good man
weeps!
He's honest, on mine honour. God's blest mother,
I swear he is true-hearted, and a soul
None better in my kingdom. Get you gone,
And do as I have bid you. [*Cranmer goes*] He
has strangled
His language in his tears.

Enter Old Lady; Lovell following

GENTLEMAN [*within*]. Come back: what mean you?
OLD LADY. I'll not come back; the tidings that I bring
Will make my boldness manners. Now, good angels
Fly o'er thy royal head, and shade thy person   160
Under their blessed wings!

KING.   Now by thy looks
I guess thy message. Is the queen delivered?
Say 'ay', and of a boy.

OLD LADY.   Ay, ay, my liege,
And of a lovely boy: the God of heaven
Both now and ever bless her! 'tis a girl
Promises boys hereafter. Sir, your queen
Desires your visitation, and to be
Acquainted with this stranger; 'tis as like you
As cherry is to cherry.

KING.   Lovell!
LOVELL.   Sir?
KING. Give her an hundred marks. I'll to the queen.   170
                                Goes
OLD LADY. An hundred marks? By this light, I'll ha'
more.
An ordinary groom is for such payment.
I will have more, or scold it out of him.
Said I for this, the girl was like to him? I'll
Have more, or else unsay't; and now, while 'tis hot,
I'll put it to the issue.   *They go*

Scene 2: Before the council-chamber

Enter Cranmer, Archbishop of Canterbury

CRANMER. I hope I am not too late; and yet the
gentleman

That was sent to me from the council prayed me
To make great haste. All fast? what means this? Ho!
Who waits there? [*The keeper comes forth*] Sure, you
know me?
KEEPER.   Yes, my lord;
But yet I cannot help you.
CRANMER. Why?
KEEPER. Your grace must wait till you be called for.

Enter Doctor Butts

CRANMER.   So.
BUTTS [*aside*]. This is a piece of malice. I am glad
I came this way so happily. The king
Shall understand it presently.   *Goes*
CRANMER [*aside*].   'Tis Butts,   10
The king's physician; as he passed along,
How earnestly he cast his eyes upon me!
Pray heaven he sound not my disgrace! For certain,
This is of purpose laid by some that hate me—
God turn their hearts! I never sought their malice—
To quench mine honour; they would shame to
make me
Wait else at door, a fellow-councillor,
'Mong boys, grooms and lackeys. But their
pleasures
Must be fulfilled, and I attend with patience.

Enter the King and Butts at a window above

BUTTS. I'll show your grace the strangest sight—
KING.   What's that, Butts?   20
BUTTS. I think your highness saw this many a day.
KING. Body o' me, where is it?
BUTTS.   There, my lord:
The high promotion of his grace of Canterbury,
Who holds his state at door 'mongst pursuivants,
Pages and footboys.
KING.   Ha? 'tis he, indeed.
Is this the honour they do one another?
'Tis well there's one above 'em yet; I had thought
They had parted so much honesty among 'em,
At least good manners, as not thus to suffer
A man of his place and so near our favour   30
To dance attendance on their lordships' pleasures,
And at the door too, like a post with packets.
By holy Mary, Butts, there's knavery.
Let 'em alone, and draw the curtain close;
We shall hear more anon.
            They withdraw behind the curtain;
                   Cranmer waits without

*Scene 3: The Council-chamber, with a chair of state and
beneath it a table with chairs and stools*

*Enter Lord Chancellor, places himself at the upper end of the
table on the left hand; a seat being left void above him, as
for Canterbury's seat; Duke of Suffolk, Duke of Norfolk,
Surrey, Lord Chamberlain, Gardiner, seat themselves in
order on each side. Cromwell at lower end, as secretary.
Keeper at the door*

CHANCELLOR. Speak to the business, master secretary;
Why are we met in council?
CROMWELL.   Please your honours,
The chief cause concerns his grace of Canterbury.
GARDINER. Has he had knowledge of it?
CROMWELL.   Yes.
NORFOLK.   Who waits there?
KEEPER. Without, my noble lords?

GARDINER.   Yes.
KEEPER.   My lord archbishop;
And has done half an hour, to know your pleasures.
CHANCELLOR. Let him come in.
KEEPER.   Your grace may enter now.

Cranmer enters and approaches the council-table

CHANCELLOR. My good lord archbishop, I'm very
    sorry
To sit here at this present and behold
That chair stand empty; but we are all men,   10
In our own natures frail and capable
Of our flesh; few are angels; out of which frailty
And want of wisdom, you, that best should teach us,
Have misdemeaned yourself, and not a little,
Toward the king first, then his laws, in filling
The whole realm, by your teaching and your
    chaplains'—
For so we are informed—with new opinions,
Divers and dangerous; which are heresies,
And, not reformed, may prove pernicious.
GARDINER. Which reformation must be sudden too,   20
My noble lords; for those that tame wild horses
Pace 'em not in their hands to make 'em gentle,
But stop their mouths with stubborn bits and
    spur 'em
Till they obey the manage. If we suffer,
Out of our easiness and childish pity
To one man's honour, this contagious sickness,
Farewell all physic; and what follows then?
Commotions, uproars, with a general taint
Of the whole state; as of late days our neighbours,
The upper Germany, can dearly witness,   30
Yet freshly pitied in our memories.
CRANMER. My good lords, hitherto, in all the progress
Both of my life and office, I have laboured,
And with no little study, that my teaching
And the strong course of my authority
Might go one way, and safely; and the end
Was ever to do well; nor is there living,
I speak it with a single heart, my lords,
A man that more detests, more stirs against,
Both in his private conscience and his place,   40
Defacers of a public peace, than I do.
Pray heaven, the king may never find a heart
With less allegiance in it! Men that make
Envy and crookéd malice nourishment
Dare bite the best. I do beseech your lordships,
That, in this case of justice, my accusers,
Be what they will, may stand forth face to face,
And freely urge against me.
SUFFOLK.   Nay, my lord,
That cannot be; you are a councillor,
And, by that virtue, no man dare accuse you.   50
GARDINER. My lord, because we have business of
    more moment,
We will be short with you. 'Tis his highness'
    pleasure,
And our consent, for better trial of you,
From hence you be committed to the Tower;
Where, being but a private man again,
You shall know many dare accuse you boldly,
More than, I fear, you are provided for.
CRANMER. Ah, my good Lord of Winchester, I thank
    you;
You are always my good friend; if your will pass,

I shall both find your lordship judge and juror,   60
You are so merciful. I see your end;
'Tis my undoing. Love and meekness, lord,
Become a churchman better than ambition;
Win straying souls with modesty again,
Cast none away. That I shall clear myself,
Lay all the weight ye can upon my patience,
I make as little doubt as you do conscience
In doing daily wrongs. I could say more,
But reverence to your calling makes me modest.
GARDINER. My lord, my lord, you are a sectary,   70
That's the plain truth; your painted gloss discovers,
To men that understand you, words and
    weakness.
CROMWELL. My Lord of Winchester, you are a little,
By your good favour, too sharp; men so noble,
However faulty, yet should find respect
For what they have been; 'tis a cruelty
To load a falling man.
GARDINER.   Good master secretary,
I cry your honour mercy; you may, worst
Of all this table, say so.
CROMWELL.   Why, my lord?
GARDINER. Do not I know you for a favourer   80
Of this new sect? ye are not sound.
CROMWELL.   Not sound?
GARDINER. Not sound, I say.
CROMWELL.   Would you were half so honest!
Men's prayers then would seek you, not their fears.
GARDINER. I shall remember this bold language.
CROMWELL.   Do.
Remember your bold life too.
CHANCELLOR.   This is too much;
Forbear, for shame, my lords.
GARDINER.   I have done.
CROMWELL.   And I.
CHANCELLOR. Then thus for you, my lord: it stands
    agreed,
I take it, by all voices, that forthwith
You be conveyed to th'Tower a prisoner;
There to remain till the king's further pleasure   90
Be known unto us. Are you all agreed, lords?
ALL. We are.
CRANMER.   Is there no other way of mercy,
But I must needs to th'Tower, my lords?
GARDINER.   What other
Would you expect? you are strangely troublesome.
Let some o'th'guard be ready there.

Enter the Guard

CRANMER.   For me?
Must I go like a traitor thither?
GARDINER.   Receive him,
And see him safe i'th'Tower.
CRANMER.   Stay, good my lords,
I have a little yet to say. Look there, my lords;
By virtue of that ring, I take my cause
Out of the gripes of cruel men, and give it   100
To a most noble judge, the king my master.
CHAMBERLAIN. This is the king's ring.
SURREY.   'Tis no counterfeit.
SUFFOLK. 'Tis the right ring, by heaven. I told ye all,
When we first put this dangerous stone a-rolling,
'Twould fall upon ourselves.
NORFOLK.   Do you think, my lords,
The king will suffer but the little finger

Of this man to be vexed?
CHAMBERLAIN.   'Tis now too certain;
How much more is his life in value with him?
Would I were fairly out on't!
CROMWELL.   My mind gave me,
In seeking tales and informations   110
Against this man, whose honesty the devil
And his disciples only envy at,
Ye blew the fire that burns ye; now have at ye!

Enter King, frowning on them; takes his seat

GARDINER. Dread sovereign, how much are we bound
    to heaven
In daily thanks, that gave us such a prince,
Not only good and wise, but most religious;
One that in all obedience makes the church
The chief aim of his honour, and, to strengthen
That holy duty, out of dear respect,
His royal self in judgement comes to hear   120
The cause betwixt her and this great offender.
KING. You were ever good at sudden commendations,
Bishop of Winchester. But know, I come not
To hear such flattery now, and in my presence
They are too thin and bare to hide offences.
To me you cannot reach you play the spaniel,
And think with wagging of your tongue to win me;
But, whatsoe'er thou takest me for, I'm sure
Thou hast a cruel nature and a bloody.
[*to Cranmer*] Good man, sit down. Now let me see
    the proudest,   130
He that dares most, but wag his finger at thee.
By all that's holy, he had better starve
Than but once think this place becomes thee not.
SURREY. May it please your grace—
KING.   No, sir, it does not please me.
I had thought I had had men of some understanding
And wisdom of my council; but I find none.
Was it discretion, lords, to let this man,
This good man—few of you deserve that title—
This honest man, wait like a lousy footboy
At chamber door? and one as great as you are?   140
Why, what a shame was this! Did my commission
Bid ye so far forget yourselves? I gave ye
Power as he was a councillor to try him,
Not as a groom. There's some of ye, I see,
More out of malice than integrity,
Would try him to the utmost, had ye mean;
Which ye shall never have while I live.
CHANCELLOR.   Thus far,
My most dread sovereign, may it like your grace
To let my tongue excuse all. What was purposed
Concerning his imprisonment, was rather,   150
If there be faith in men, meant for his trial
And fair purgation to the world, than malice,
I'm sure, in me.
KING.   Well, well, my lords, respect him;
Take him and use him well; he's worthy of it.
I will say thus much for him, if a prince
May be beholding to a subject, I
Am for his love and service so to him.
Make me no more ado, but all embrace him:
Be friends, for shame, my lords. My Lord of
    Canterbury,
I have a suit which you must not deny me: 160
That is, a fair young maid that yet wants baptism;
You must be godfather, and answer for her.

CRANMER. The greatest monarch now alive may glory
In such an honour; how may I deserve it,
That am a poor and humble subject to you?
KING. Come, come, my lord, you'ld spare your
spoons. You shall have two noble partners with you:
the old Duchess of Norfolk, and Lady Marquess
Dorset. Will these please you?
Once more, my Lord of Winchester, I charge you,   170
Embrace and love this man.
GARDINER.   With a true heart
And brother-love I do it.
CRANMER.   And let heaven
Witness how dear I hold this confirmation.
KING. Good man, those joyful tears show thy true
    heart.
The common voice, I see, is verified
Of thee, which says thus: 'Do my Lord of
    Canterbury
A shrewd turn, and he is your friend for ever'.
Come, lords, we trifle time away; I long
To have this young one made a Christian.
As I have made ye one, lords, one remain;   180
So I grow stronger, you more honour gain.

                    They go

Scene 4: *The palace yard*

Noise and tumult outside. Enter Porter and his Man

PORTER. You'll leave your noise anon, ye rascals; do
you take the court for Parish garden? ye rude slaves,
leave your gaping.
[*A voice from without*] Good master porter, I belong
to th'larder.
PORTER. Belong to th'gallows, and be hanged, ye
rogue! Is this a place to roar in? Fetch me a dozen
crab-tree staves, and strong ones: these are but
switches to 'em. I'll scratch your heads. You must be
seeing christenings? do you look for ale and cakes   10
here, you rude rascals?
MAN. Pray, sir, be patient; 'tis as much impossible—
Unless we sweep 'em from the door with cannons—
To scatter 'em, as 'tis to make 'em sleep
On May-day morning, which will never be:
We may as well push against Paul's as stir 'em.
PORTER. How got they in, and be hanged?
MAN. Alas, I know not: how gets the tide in?
As much as one sound cudgel of four foot—
You see the poor remainder—could distribute,   20
I made no spare, sir.
PORTER.   You did nothing, sir.
MAN. I am not Samson, nor Sir Guy, nor Colbrand,
To mow 'em down before me; but if I spared any
That had a head to hit, either young or old,
He or she, cuckold or cuckold-maker,
Let me ne'er hope to see a chine again;
And that I would not for a cow, God save her!
[*Another voice from without*] Do you hear, master
    porter?
PORTER. I shall be with you presently, good master
puppy. Keep the door close, sirrah.   30
MAN. What would you have me do?
PORTER. What should you do, but knock 'em down by
th'dozens? Is this Moorfields to muster in? or have
we some strange Indian with the great tool come
to court, the women so besiege us? Bless me, what a
fry of fornication is at door! On my Christian

conscience, this one christening will beget a
thousand; here will be father, godfather, and all
together.

MAN. The spoons will be the bigger, sir. There is a 40
fellow somewhat near the door, he should be a
brazier by his face, for, o' my conscience, twenty of
the dog-days now reign in's nose; all that stand
about him are under the line, they need no other
penance; that fire-drake did I hit three times on the
head, and three times was his nose discharged against
me; he stands there, like a mortarpiece, to blow us.
There was a haberdasher's wife of small wit near
him, that railed upon me till her pinked porringer
fell off her head, for kindling such a combustion in 50
the state. I missed the meteor once, and hit that
woman, who cried out 'Clubs!' when I might see
from far some forty truncheoners draw to her succour, which were the hope o'th'Strand, where she
was quartered. They fell on; I made good my place;
at length they came to th'broomstaff with me; I
defied 'em still; when suddenly a file of boys behind
'em, loose shot, delivered such a shower of pebbles,
that I was fain to draw mine honour in and let 'em
win the work; the devil was amongst 'em, I think, 60
surely.

PORTER. These are the youths that thunder at a playhouse and fight for bitten apples; that no audience,
but the tribulation of Tower-hill, or the limbs of
Limehouse, their dear brothers, are able to endure.
I have some of 'em in Limbo Patrum, and there they
are like to dance these three days; besides the running
banquet of two beadles that is to come.

Enter Lord Chamberlain

CHAMBERLAIN. Mercy o' me, what a multitude are
here!
They grow still too; from all parts they are coming, 70
As if we kept a fair here. Where are these porters,
These lazy knaves? You've made a fine hand,
fellows.
There's a trim rabble let in: are all these
Your faithful friends o'th'suburbs? We shall have
Great store of room, no doubt, left for the ladies,
When they pass back from the christening.

PORTER.   An't please your honour,
We are but men; and what so many may do,
Not being torn a-pieces, we have done:
An army cannot rule 'em.

CHAMBERLAIN.   As I live,
If the king blame me for't, I'll lay ye all   80
By the heels, and suddenly; and on your heads
Clap round fines for neglect. You're lazy knaves;
And here ye lie baiting of bombards when
Ye should do service. Hark! the trumpets sound;
They're come already from the christening;
Go, break among the press, and find a way out
To let the troop pass fairly, or I'll find
A Marshalsea shall hold ye play these two months.

PORTER. Make way there for the princess.

MAN.   You great fellow,
Stand close up, or I'll make your head ache.   90

PORTER. You i'th'camlet, get up o'th'rail;
I'll peck you o'er the pales else.

                                          They go

Scene 5

*Enter Trumpets, sounding; then two Aldermen, Lord
Mayor, Garter, Cranmer, Duke of Norfolk with his
marshal's staff, Duke of Suffolk, two Noblemen bearing
great standing-bowls for the christening-gifts; then four
Noblemen bearing a canopy, under which the Duchess of
Norfolk, godmother, bearing the child richly habited in a
mantle, etc., train borne by a Lady; then follows the
Marchioness Dorset, the other godmother, and Ladies. The
troop pass once about the stage, and Garter speaks*

GARTER. Heaven, from thy endless goodness, send
prosperous life, long, and ever happy, to the high
and mighty princess of England, Elizabeth!

Flourish. Enter King and Guard

CRANMER [*kneeling*]. And to your royal grace, and the
good queen,
My noble partners and myself thus pray:
All comfort, joy, in this most gracious lady
Heaven ever laid up to make parents happy
May hourly fall upon ye!

KING.   Thank you, good lord archbishop.
What is her name?

CRANMER.   Elizabeth.

KING.   Stand up, lord.
       The King kisses the child
With this kiss take my blessing: God protect thee! 10
Into whose hand I give thy life.

CRANMER.   Amen.

KING. My noble gossips, you've been too prodigal;
I thank ye heartily; so shall this lady,
When she has so much English.

CRANMER.   Let me speak, sir,
For heaven now bids me; and the words I utter
Let none think flattery, for they'll find 'em truth.
This royal infant—heaven still move about her!—
Though in her cradle, yet now promises
Upon this land a thousand thousand blessings,
Which time shall bring to ripeness. She shall be— 20
But few now living can behold that goodness—
A pattern to all princes living with her
And all that shall succeed. Saba was never
More covetous of wisdom and fair virtue
Than this pure soul shall be. All princely graces
That mould up such a mighty piece as this is,
With all the virtues that attend the good,
Shall still be doubled on her. Truth shall nurse her,
Holy and heavenly thoughts still counsel her;
She shall be loved and feared. Her own shall
bless her; .   30
Her foes shake like a field of beaten corn,
And hang their heads with sorrow. Good grows
with her;
In her days every man shall eat in safety
Under his own vine what he plants, and sing
The merry songs of peace to all his neighbours.
God shall be truly known, and those about her
From her shall read the perfect ways of honour,
And by those claim their greatness, not by blood.
Nor shall this peace sleep with her; but as when
The bird of wonder dies, the maiden phoenix,   40
Her ashes new create another heir
As great in admiration as herself,
So shall she leave her blessedness to one—

When heaven shall call her from this cloud of
 darkness—
Who from the sacred ashes of her honour
Shall star-like rise, as great in fame as she was,
And so stand fixed. Peace, plenty, love, truth, terror,
That were the servants to this chosen infant,
Shall then be his, and like a vine grow to him;
Wherever the bright sun of heaven shall shine,   50
His honour and the greatness of his name
Shall be, and make new nations; he shall flourish,
And like a mountain cedar reach his branches
To all the plains about him; our children's children
Shall see this, and bless heaven.
KING.   Thou speakest wonders.
CRANMER. She shall be, to the happiness of England,
An agéd princess; many days shall see her,
And yet no day without a deed to crown it.
Would I had known no more! but she must die—
She must, the saints must have her—yet a virgin,   60
A most unspotted lily shall she pass
To th'ground, and all the world shall mourn her.
KING. O lord archbishop,
Thou hast made me now a man; never before
This happy child did I get anything.
This oracle of comfort has so pleased me
That when I am in heaven I shall desire

To see what this child does, and praise my Maker.
I thank ye all. To you, my good lord mayor,
And your good brethren, I am much beholding;   70
I have received much honour by your presence,
And ye shall find me thankful. Lead the way, lords;
Ye must all see the queen, and she must thank ye;
She will be sick else. This day, no man think
Has business at his house; for all shall stay:
This little one shall make it holiday.   *They go*

THE EPILOGUE

'Tis ten to one this play can never please
All that are here. Some come to take their ease,
And sleep an act or two; but those, we fear,
We've frighted with our trumpets; so, 'tis clear,
They'll say 'tis naught; others, to hear the city
Abused extremely, and to cry 'That's witty!'
Which we have not done neither; that, I fear,
All the expected good we're like to hear
For this play at this time, is only in
The merciful construction of good women;   10
For such a one we showed 'em. If they smile,
And say 'twill do, I know, within a while
All the best men are ours; for 'tis ill hap
If they hold when their ladies bid 'em clap.

Troilus and Cressida

The scene: Troy, and the Greek camp

CHARACTERS IN THE PLAY

PRIAM, *king of Troy*
HECTOR
TROILUS
PARIS } *his sons*
DEIPHOBUS
HELENUS
MARGARELON, *a bastard son of Priam*
ÆNEAS
ANTENOR } *Trojan commanders*
CALCHAS, *a Trojan Priest, taking part with the Greeks*
PANDARUS, *uncle to Cressida*
AGAMEMNON, *the Greek general*
MENELAUS, *his brother*
ACHILLES
AJAX
ULYSSES
NESTOR } *Greek commanders*
DIOMEDES
PATROCLUS

THERSITES, *a deformed and scurrilous Greek*
ALEXANDER, *servant to Cressida*
Servant to Troilus
Servant to Paris
Servant to Diomedes
The Prologue
HELEN, *wife to Menelaus*
ANDROMACHE, *wife to Hector*
CASSANDRA, *daughter to Priam; a prophetess*
CRESSIDA, *daughter to Calchas*
Trojan and Greek Soldiers, and Attendants

Troilus and Cressida

PROLOGUE

PROLOGUE. In Troy there lies the scene. From isles
  of Greece
The princes orgulous, their high blood chafed,
Have to the port of Athens sent their ships,
Fraught with the ministers and instruments
Of cruel war; sixty and nine, that wore
Their crownets regal, from th'Athenian bay
Put forth toward Phrygia, and their vow is made
To ransack Troy, within whose strong immures
The ravished Helen, Menelaus' queen,
With wanton Paris sleeps—and that's the quarrel.   10
To Tenedos they come,
And the deep-drawing barks to there disgorge
Their warlike fraughtage; now on Dardan plains
The fresh and yet unbruiséd Greeks do pitch
Their brave pavilions: Priam's six-gated city,
Dardan, and Timbria, Helias, Chetas, Troien,
And Antenorides, with massy staples
And corresponsive and fulfilling bolts,
Sperr up the sons of Troy.
Now expectation, tickling skittish spirits   20
On one and other side, Trojan and Greek,
Sets all on hazard—and hither am I come
A Prologue armed, but not in confidence
Of author's pen or actor's voice, but suited
In like condition as our argument,
To tell you, fair beholders, that our play
Leaps o'er the vaunt and firstlings of those broils,
Beginning in the middle; starting thence away
To what may be digested in a play.
Like or find fault; do as your pleasures are: 30
Now good or bad, 'tis but the chance of war.
                               Goes

ACT 1
Scene 1: *Troy. Before Priam's palace*

Enter Pandarus and Troilus in armour

TROILUS. Call here my varlet; I'll unarm again:
Why should I war without the walls of Troy
That find such cruel battle here within?
Each Trojan that is master of his heart,
Let him to field; Troilus, alas, hath none!
PANDARUS. Will this gear ne'er be mended?
TROILUS. The Greeks are strong, and skilful to
  their strength,
Fierce to their skill, and to their fierceness valiant,
But I am weaker than a woman's tear,
Tamer than sleep, fonder than ignorance,   10
Less valiant than the virgin in the night,
And skilless as unpractised infancy.
PANDARUS. Well, I have told you enough of this; for
my part, I'll not meddle nor make no farther. He
that will have a cake out of the wheat must tarry
the grinding.
TROILUS. Have I not tarried?
PANDARUS. Ay, the grinding; but you must tarry the
bolting.

TROILUS. Have I not tarried?   20
PANDARUS. Ay, the bolting; but you must tarry the
leavening.
TROILUS. Still have I tarried.
PANDARUS. Ay, to the leavening; but there's yet in the
word hereafter, the kneading, the making of the
cake, the heating of the oven, and the baking; nay,
you must stay the cooling too, or you may chance
to burn your lips.
TROILUS. Patience herself, what goddess e'er she be,
Doth lesser blench at sufferance than I do;   30
At Priam's royal table do I sit,
And when fair Cressid comes into my thoughts—
So, traitor! 'When she comes!'—When is she
  thence?
PANDARUS. Well, she looked yesternight fairer than
ever I saw her look, or any woman else.
TROILUS. I was about to tell thee—when my heart,
As wedgéd with a sigh, would rive in twain,
Lest Hector or my father should perceive me,
I have, as when the sun doth light a storm,
Buried this sigh in wrinkle of a smile: 40
But sorrow that is couched in seeming gladness
Is like that mirth fate turns to sudden sadness.
PANDARUS. An her hair were not somewhat darker
than Helen's—well, go to—there were no more
comparison between the women. But, for my part,
she is my kinswoman; I would not, as they term it,
praise her, but I would somebody had heard her
talk yesterday, as I did. I will not dispraise your
sister Cassandra's wit, but—
TROILUS. O Pandarus! I tell thee, Pandarus—   50
When I do tell thee there my hopes lie drowned,
Reply not in how many fathoms deep
They lie indrenched. I tell thee I am mad
In Cressid's love. Thou answer'st she is fair;
Pour'st in the open ulcer of my heart
Her eyes, her hair, her cheek, her gait, her voice;
Handlest in thy discourse—O, that her hand,
In whose comparison all whites are ink
Writing their own reproach, to whose soft seizure
The cygnet's down is harsh, and spirit of sense   60
Hard as the palm of ploughman! this thou tell'st me,
As true thou tell'st me, when I say I love her;
But saying thus, instead of oil and balm,
Thou lay'st in every gash that love hath given me
The knife that made it.
PANDARUS. I speak no more than truth.
TROILUS. Thou dost not speak so much.
PANDARUS. Faith, I'll not meddle in 't. Let her be as
she is. If she be fair, 'tis the better for her; an she
be not, she has the mends in her own hands.   70
TROILUS. Good Pandarus, how now, Pandarus!
PANDARUS. I have had my labour for my travail:
ill thought on of her, and ill thought on of you;
gone between and between, but small thanks for my
labour.
TROILUS. What, art thou angry, Pandarus? what,
  with me?
PANDARUS. Because she's kin to me, therefore she's not

so fair as Helen; an she were not kin to me, she would be as fair o' Friday as Helen is o' Sunday. But what care I? I care not an she were a blackamoor; 80 'tis all one to me.

TROILUS. Say I she is not fair?

PANDARUS. I do not care whether you do or no. She's a fool to stay behind her father. Let her to the Greeks, and so I'll tell her the next time I see her. For my part, I'll meddle nor make no more i'th' matter.

TROILUS. Pandarus—

PANDARUS. Not I.

TROILUS. Sweet Pandarus— 90

PANDARUS. Pray you, speak no more to me: I will leave all as I found it, and there an end.

Goes; alarum

TROILUS. Peace, you ungracious clamours! peace, rude sounds!
Fools on both sides! Helen must needs be fair,
When with your blood you daily paint her thus.
I cannot fight upon this argument;
It is too starved a subject for my sword.
But Pandarus—O gods, how do you plague me!
I cannot come to Cressid but by Pandar,
And he's as tetchy to be wooed to woo 100
As she is stubborn-chaste against all suit.
Tell me, Apollo, for thy Daphne's love,
What Cressid is, what Pandar, and what we?
Her bed is India; there she lies, a pearl;
Between our Ilium and where she resides
Let it be called the wild and wandering flood;
Ourself the merchant, and this sailing Pandar,
Out doubtful hope, our convoy and our bark.

Alarum. Enter Æneas

ÆNEAS. How now, Prince Troilus! Wherefore not afield?

TROILUS. Because not there; this woman's answer sorts,
For womanish it is to be from thence. 110
What news, Æneas, from the field today?

ÆNEAS. That Paris is returnéd home, and hurt.

TROILUS. By whom, Æneas?

ÆNEAS. Troilus, by Menelaus.

TROILUS. Let Paris bleed: 'tis but a scar to scorn;
Paris is gored with Menelaus' horn. *Alarum*

ÆNEAS. Hark what good sport is out of town today!

TROILUS. Better at home, if 'would I might' were 'may'.
But to the sport abroad: are you bound thither?

ÆNEAS. In all swift haste.

TROILUS. Come, go we then together. 120

They go

Scene 2: *The same. A street*

Enter Cressida and Alexander, her man

CRESSIDA. Who were those went by?

ALEXANDER. Queen Hecuba and Helen.

CRESSIDA. And whither go they?

ALEXANDER. Up to the eastern tower,
Whose height commands as subject all the vale,
To see the battle. Hector, whose patience
Is as a virtue fixed, today was moved:
He chid Andromache and struck his armourer;
And, like as there were husbandry in war,

Before the sun rose he was harnessed light,
And to the field goes he; where every flower
Did, as a prophet, weep what it foresaw 10
In Hector's wrath.

CRESSIDA. What was his cause of anger?

ALEXANDER. The noise goes this: there is among the Greeks
A lord of Trojan blood, nephew to Hector;
They call him Ajax.

CRESSIDA. Good; and what of him?

ALEXANDER. They say he is a very man per se,
And stands alone.

CRESSIDA. So do all men, unless they are drunk, sick, or have no legs.

ALEXANDER. This man, lady, hath robbed many beasts of their particular additions: he is as valiant as the 20 lion, churlish as the bear, slow as the elephant—a man into whom nature hath so crowded humours that his valour is crushed into folly, his folly forced with discretion. There is no man hath a virtue that he hath not a glimpse of, nor any man an attaint but he carries some stain of it; he is melancholy without cause and merry against the hair; he hath the joints of everything, but everything so out of joint that he is a gouty Briareus, many hands and no use, or a purblind Argus, all eyes and no sight. 30

CRESSIDA. But how should this man, that makes me smile, make Hector angry?

ALEXANDER. They say he yesterday coped Hector in the battle and struck him down, the disdain and shame whereof hath ever since kept Hector fasting and waking.

CRESSIDA. Who comes here?

ALEXANDER. Madam, your uncle Pandarus.

Enter Pandarus

CRESSIDA. Hector's a gallant man.

ALEXANDER. As may be in the world, lady. 40

PANDARUS. What's that? what's that?

CRESSIDA. Good morrow, uncle Pandarus.

PANDARUS. Good morrow, cousin Cressid. What do you talk of? Good morrow, Alexander. How do you, cousin? When were you at Ilium?

CRESSIDA. This morning, uncle.

PANDARUS. What were you talking of when I came? Was Hector armed and gone ere you came to Ilium? Helen was not up, was she?

CRESSIDA. Hector was gone; but Helen was not up. 50

PANDARUS. E'en so: Hector was stirring early.

CRESSIDA. That were we talking of, and of his anger.

PANDARUS. Was he angry?

CRESSIDA. So he says here.

PANDARUS. True, he was so; I know the cause too; he'll lay about him today, I can tell them that. And there's Troilus will not come far behind him; let them take heed of Troilus, I can tell them that too.

CRESSIDA. What, is he angry too?

PANDARUS. Who, Troilus? Troilus is the better man 60 of the two.

CRESSIDA. O Jupiter! there's no comparison.

PANDARUS. What, not between Troilus and Hector? Do you know a man if you see him?

CRESSIDA. Ay, if I ever saw him before and knew him.

PANDARUS. Well, I say Troilus is Troilus.

CRESSIDA. Then you say as I say; for I am sure he is not Hector.

PANDARUS. No, nor Hector is not Troilus in some degrees. 70

CRESSIDA. 'Tis just to each of them; he is himself.

PANDARUS. Himself! Alas, poor Troilus! I would he were—

CRESSIDA. So he is.

PANDARUS. Condition I had gone barefoot to India.

CRESSIDA. He is not Hector.

PANDARUS. Himself! no, he's not himself. Would 'a were himself! Well, the gods are above; time must friend or end. Well, Troilus, well, I would my heart were in her body! No, Hector is not a better 80 man than Troilus.

CRESSIDA. Excuse me.

PANDARUS. He is elder.

CRESSIDA. Pardon me, pardon me.

PANDARUS. Th'other's not come to't. You shall tell me another tale when th'other's come to't. Hector shall not have his wit this year.

CRESSIDA. He shall not need it, if he have his own.

PANDARUS. Nor his qualities.

CRESSIDA. No matter. 90

PANDARUS. Nor his beauty.

CRESSIDA. 'Twould not become him; his own's better.

PANDARUS. You have no judgement, niece. Helen herself swore th'other day that Troilus for a brown favour, for so 'tis, I must confess—not brown neither—

CRESSIDA. No, but brown.

PANDARUS. Faith, to say the truth, brown and not brown.

CRESSIDA. To say the truth, true and not true. 100

PANDARUS. She praised his complexion above Paris.

CRESSIDA. Why, Paris hath colour enough.

PANDARUS. So he has.

CRESSIDA. Then Troilus should have too much: if she praised him above, his complexion is higher than his; he having colour enough, and the other higher, is too flaming a praise for a good complexion. I had as lief Helen's golden tongue had commended Troilus for a copper nose.

PANDARUS. I swear to you, I think Helen loves him 110 better than Paris.

CRESSIDA. Then she's a merry Greek indeed.

PANDARUS. Nay, I am sure she does. She came to him th'other day into the compassed window—and, you know, he has not past three or four hairs on his chin—

CRESSIDA. Indeed, a tapster's arithmetic may soon bring his particulars therein to a total.

PANDARUS. Why, he is very young; and yet will he within three pound lift as much as his brother 120 Hector.

CRESSIDA. Is he so young a man and so old a lifter?

PANDARUS. But to prove to you that Helen loves him: she came and puts me her white hand to his cloven chin—

CRESSIDA. Juno have mercy! how came it cloven?

PANDARUS. Why, you know, 'tis dimpled. I think his smiling becomes him better than any man in all Phrygia.

CRESSIDA. O, he smiles valiantly. 130

PANDARUS. Does he not?

CRESSIDA. O yes, an 'twere a cloud in autumn.

PANDARUS. Why, go to, then! But to prove to you that Helen loves Troilus—

CRESSIDA. Troilus will stand to the proof, if you'll prove it so.

PANDARUS. Troilus! Why, he esteems her no more than I esteem an addle egg.

CRESSIDA. If you love an addle egg as well as you love an idle head, you would eat chickens i'th'shell. 140

PANDARUS. I cannot choose but laugh to think how she tickled his chin; indeed, she has a marvellous white hand, I must needs confess—

CRESSIDA. Without the rack.

PANDARUS. And she takes upon her to spy a white hair on his chin.

CRESSIDA. Alas, poor chin! many a wart is richer.

PANDARUS. But there was such laughing! Queen Hecuba laughed, that her eyes ran o'er.

CRESSIDA. With millstones. 150

PANDARUS. And Cassandra laughed.

CRESSIDA. But there was a more temperate fire under the pot of her eyes. Did her eyes run o'er too?

PANDARUS. And Hector laughed.

CRESSIDA. At what was all this laughing?

PANDARUS. Marry, at the white hair that Helen spied on Troilus' chin.

CRESSIDA. An't had been a green hair, I should have laughed too.

PANDARUS. They laughed not so much at the hair as at 160 his pretty answer.

CRESSIDA. What was his answer?

PANDARUS. Quoth she, 'Here's but two and fifty hairs on your chin, and one of them is white'.

CRESSIDA. This is her question.

PANDARUS. That's true; make no question of that. 'Two and fifty hairs', quoth he, 'and one white; that white hair is my father, and all the rest are his sons.' 'Jupiter!' quoth she, 'which of these hairs is Paris my husband?' 'The forked one,' quoth he; 'pluck't out, 170 and give it him.' But there was such laughing, and Helen so blushed, and Paris so chafed, and all the rest so laughed, that it passed!

CRESSIDA. So let it now; for it has been a great while going by.

PANDARUS. Well, cousin, I told you a thing yesterday; think on't.

CRESSIDA. So I do.

PANDARUS. I'll be sworn 'tis true; he will weep you an 'twere a man born in April. 180

CRESSIDA. And I'll spring up in his tears an 'twere a nettle against May. *Retreat sounded*

PANDARUS. Hark! they are coming from the field. Shall we stand up here and see them as they pass toward Ilion? Good niece, do, sweet niece Cressida.

CRESSIDA. At your pleasure.

PANDARUS. Here, here, here's an excellent place; here we may see most bravely. I'll tell you them all by their names as they pass by. But mark Troilus above the rest. 190

CRESSIDA. Speak not so loud.

Æneas passes

PANDARUS. That's Æneas. Is not that a brave man? He's one of the flowers of Troy, I can tell you. But mark Troilus; you shall see Troilus anon.

Antenor passes

CRESSIDA. Who's that?

PANDARUS. That's Antenor. He has a shrewd wit, I can

tell you, and he's a man good enough: he's one o'th' soundest judgements in Troy whosoever, and a proper man of person. When comes Troilus? I'll show you Troilus anon. If he see me, you shall see him nod at me.

CRESSIDA. Will he give you the nod?

PANDARUS. You shall see.

CRESSIDA. If he do, the rich shall have more.

Hector passes

PANDARUS. That's Hector, that, that, look you, that; there's a fellow! Go thy way, Hector! There's a brave man, niece. O brave Hector! Look how he looks! There's a countenance! Is't not a brave man?

CRESSIDA. O, a brave man!

PANDARUS. Is 'a not? It does a man's heart good. Look you what hacks are on his helmet! Look you yonder, do you see? look you there: there's no jesting; there's laying on, take't off who will, as they say; there be hacks!

CRESSIDA. Be those with swords?

PANDARUS. Swords! anything, he cares not; an the devil come to him, it's all one. By God's lid, it does one's heart good. Yonder comes Paris, yonder comes Paris.

Paris passes

Look ye yonder, niece; is't not a gallant man too, is't not? Why, this is brave now. Who said he came home hurt today? He's not hurt. Why, this will do Helen's heart good now, ha! Would I could see Troilus now! You shall see Troilus anon.

Helenus passes

CRESSIDA. Who's that?

PANDARUS. That's Helenus. I marvel where Troilus is. That's Helenus. I think he went not forth today. That's Helenus.

CRESSIDA. Can Helenus fight, uncle?

PANDARUS. Helenus! no—yes, he'll fight indifferent well. I marvel where Troilus is. Hark! do you not hear the people cry 'Troilus'? Helenus is a priest.

CRESSIDA. What sneaking fellow comes yonder?

Troilus passes

PANDARUS. Where? yonder? that's Deiphobus. 'Tis Troilus! there's a man, niece! Hem! Brave Troilus! the prince of chivalry!

CRESSIDA. Peace, for shame, peace!

PANDARUS. Mark him; note him. O brave Troilus! Look well upon him, niece; look you how his sword is bloodied, and his helm more hacked than Hector's, and how he looks, and how he goes! O admirable youth! he ne'er saw three and twenty. Go thy way, Troilus, go thy way! Had I a sister were a grace, or a daughter a goddess, he should take his choice. O admirable man! Paris? Paris is dirt to him; and, I warrant, Helen, to change, would give an eye to boot.

Common Soldiers pass

CRESSIDA. Here come more.

PANDARUS. Asses, fools, dolts! chaff and bran, chaff and bran! porridge after meat! I could live and die i' th' eyes of Troilus. Ne'er look, ne'er look; the eagles are gone: crows and daws, crows and daws! I had

rather be such a man as Troilus than Agamemnon and all Greece.

CRESSIDA. There is among the Greeks Achilles, a better man than Troilus.

PANDARUS. Achilles! a drayman, a porter, a very camel.

CRESSIDA. Well, well.

PANDARUS. Well, well! Why, have you any discretion? have you any eyes? do you know what a man is? Is not birth, beauty, good shape, discourse, manhood, learning, gentleness, virtue, youth, liberality, and such like, the spice and salt that season a man?

CRESSIDA. Ay, a minced man; and then to be baked with no date in the pie, for then the man's date is out.

PANDARUS. You are such another woman, a man knows not at what ward you lie.

CRESSIDA. Upon my back, to defend my belly; upon my wit, to defend my wiles; upon my secrecy, to defend mine honesty; my mask, to defend my beauty; and you, to defend all these: and at all these wards I lie, at a thousand watches.

PANDARUS. Say one of your watches.

CRESSIDA. Nay, I'll watch you for that; and that's one of the chiefest of them too: if I cannot ward what I would not have hit, I can watch you for telling how I took the blow; unless it swell past hiding, and then it's past watching.

PANDARUS. You are such another!

Enter Troilus' Boy

BOY. Sir, my lord would instantly speak with you.

PANDARUS. Where?

BOY. At your own house; there he unarms him.

PANDARUS. Good boy, tell him I come.   *Boy goes* I doubt he be hurt. Fare ye well, good niece.

CRESSIDA. Adieu, uncle.

PANDARUS. I'll be with you, niece, by and by.

CRESSIDA. To bring, uncle?

PANDARUS. Ay, a token from Troilus.

CRESSIDA. By the same token, you are a bawd.

Pandarus goes

Words, vows, gifts, tears, and love's full sacrifice,
He offers in another's enterprise;
But more in Troilus thousandfold I see
Than in the glass of Pandar's praise may be.
Yet hold I off: women are angels, wooing;
Things won are done—joy's soul lies in the doing.
That she beloved knows nought that knows not this:
Men prize the thing ungained more than it is.
That she was never yet that ever knew
Love got so sweet as when desire did sue.
Therefore this maxim out of love I teach:
'Achievement is command; ungained, beseech.'
Then though my heart's content firm love doth
    bear,
Nothing of that shall from mine eyes appear.

They go

Scene 3: *The Greek Camp. Before Agamemnon's tent*

Sennet. Enter Agamemnon, Nestor, Ulysses, Menelaus, with others

AGAMEMNON. Princes,
What grief hath set this jaundice on your cheeks?
The ample proposition that hope makes

In all designs begun on earth below
Fails in the promised largeness: checks
  and disasters
Grow in the veins of actions highest reared,
As knots, by the conflux of meeting sap,
Infect the sound pine and divert his grain
Tortive and errant from his course of growth
Nor, princes, is it matter new to us   10
That we come short of our suppose so far
That after seven years' siege yet Troy walls stand;
Sith every action that hath gone before
Whereof we have record, trial did draw
Bias and thwart, not answering the aim
And that unbodied figure of the thought
That gave't surmiséd shape. Why then, you princes,
Do you with cheeks abashed behold our works,
And call them shames, which are indeed nought else
But the protractive trials of great Jove   20
To find persistive constancy in men?
The fineness of which metal is not found
In fortune's love: for then the bold and coward,
The wise and fool, the artist and unread,
The hard and soft, seem all affined and kin;
But, in the wind and tempest of her frown,
Distinction with a broad and powerful fan,
Puffing at all, winnows the light away,
And what hath mass or matter, by itself
Lies rich in virtue and unmingléd.   30
NESTOR. With due observance of thy godlike seat,
Great Agamemnon, Nestor shall apply
Thy latest words. In the reproof of chance
Lies the true proof of men: the sea being smooth,
How many shallow bauble boats dare sail
Upon her patient breast, making their way
With those of nobler bulk!
But let the ruffian Boreas once enrage
The gentle Thetis, and anon behold
The strong-ribbed bark through liquid mountains
  cut,   40
Bounding between the two moist elements
Like Perseus' horse; where's then the saucy boat
Whose weak untimbered sides but even now
Co-rivalled greatness?—either to harbour fled,
Or made a toast for Neptune. Even so
Doth valour's show and valour's worth divide
In storms of fortune: for in her ray and brightness
The herd hath more annoyance by the breese
Than by the tiger; but when the splitting wind
Makes flexible the knees of knotted oaks   50
And flies flee under shade, why then the thing
  of courage,
As roused with rage, with rage doth sympathize,
And with an accent tuned in selfsame key
Retorts to chiding fortune.
ULYSSES.   Agamemnon,
Thou great commander, nerve and bone of Greece,
Heart of our numbers, soul and only spirit,
In whom the tempers and the minds of all
Should be shut up, hear what Ulysses speaks.
Besides th'applause and approbation
The which, [to Agamemnon] most mighty for thy
  place and sway,   60
[to Nestor] And thou most reverend for thy
  stretched-out life,
I give to both your speeches, which were such
As, Agamemnon, all the hands of Greece

Should hold up high in brass, and such again
As, venerable Nestor, hatched in silver,
Should with a bond of air, strong as the axletree
On which heaven rides, knit all the Greekish ears
To his experienced tongue—yet let it please both,
Thou great, and wise, to hear Ulysses speak.
AGAMEMNON. Speak, Prince of Ithaca; and be't of
  less expect   70
That matter needless, of importless burden,
Divide thy lips than we are confident,
When rank Thersites opes his mastic jaws,
We shall hear music, wit and oracle.
ULYSSES. Troy, yet upon his basis, had been down,
And the great Hector's sword had lacked a master,
But for these instances:
The specialty of rule hath been neglected;
And look how many Grecian tents do stand
Hollow upon this plain, so many hollow factions.   80
When that the general is not like the hive
To whom the foragers shall all repair,
What honey is expected? Degree being vizarded,
Th'unworthiest shows as fairly in the mask.
The heavens themselves, the planets, and this centre,
Observe degree, priority, and place,
Insisture, course, proportion, season, form,
Office, and custom, in all line of order;
And therefore is the glorious planet Sol
In noble eminence enthroned and sphered   90
Amidst the other; whose medicinable eye
Corrects the influence of evil planets,
And posts, like the commandment of a king,
Sans check to good and bad. But when the planets
In evil mixture to disorder wander,
What plagues and what portents, what mutiny,
What raging of the sea, shaking of earth,
Commotion in the winds, frights, changes, horrors,
Divert and crack, rend and deracinate
The unity and married calm of states   100
Quite from their fixure! O, when degree is shaked,
Which is the ladder of all high designs,
The enterprise is sick! How could communities,
Degrees in schools, and brotherhoods in cities,
Peaceful commerce from dividable shores,
The primogenitive and due of birth,
Prerogative of age, crowns, sceptres, laurels,
But by degree, stand in authentic place?
Take but degree away, untune that string,
And hark what discord follows! each thing meets   110
In mere oppugnancy: the bounded waters
Should lift their bosoms higher than the shores,
And make a sop of all this solid globe;
Strength should be lord of imbecility,
And the rude son should strike his father dead;
Force should be right; or rather, right and wrong,
Between whose endless jar justice resides,
Should lose their names, and so should justice too.
Then everything includes itself in power,
Power into will, will into appetite;   120
And appetite, an universal wolf,
So doubly seconded with will and power,
Must make perforce an universal prey,
And last eat up himself. Great Agamemnon,
This chaos, when degree is suffocate,
Follows the choking.
And this neglection of degree it is
That by a pace goes backward, with a purpose

It hath to climb. The general's disdained
By him one step below, he by the next,   130
That next by him beneath; so every step,
Exampled by the first pace that is sick
Of his superior, grows to an envious fever
Of pale and bloodless emulation—
And 'tis this fever that keeps Troy on foot,
Not her own sinews: to end a tale of length,
Troy in our weakness stands, not in her strength.
NESTOR. Most wisely hath Ulysses here discovered
The fever whereof all our power is sick.
AGAMEMNON. The nature of the sickness found,
   Ulysses,   140
What is the remedy?
ULYSSES. The great Achilles, whom opinion crowns
The sinew and the forehand of our host,
Having his ear full of his airy fame,
Grows dainty of his worth, and in his tent
Lies mocking our designs. With him, Patroclus,
Upon a lazy bed, the livelong day
Breaks scurril jests,
And with ridiculous and awkward action,
Which, slanderer, he imitation calls,
He pageants us. Sometime, great Agamemnon,   150
Thy topless deputation he puts on,
And, like a strutting player whose conceit
Lies in his hamstring, and doth think it rich
To hear the wooden dialogue and sound
'Twixt his stretched footing and the scaffoldage,
Such to-be-pitied and o'er-wrested seeming
He acts thy greatness in; and, when he speaks,
'Tis like a chime a-mending; with terms unsquared,
Which, from the tongue of roaring Typhon
   dropped,
Would seem hyperboles. At this fusty stuff,   160
The large Achilles, on his pressed bed lolling,
From his deep chest laughs out a loud applause,
Cries 'Excellent! 'tis Agamemnon right!
Now play me Nestor: hem, and stroke thy beard,
As be being dressed to some oration.'
That's done—as near as the extremest ends
Of parallels, as like as Vulcan and his wife.
Yet god Achilles still cries 'Excellent!
'Tis Nestor right! Now play him me, Patroclus,   170
Arming to answer in a night alarm.'
And then, forsooth, the faint defects of age
Must be the scene of mirth: to cough and spit,
And, with a palsy fumbling on his gorget,
Shake in and out the rivet. And at this sport
Sir Valour dies; cries 'O, enough, Patroclus,
Or give me ribs of steel! I shall split all
In pleasure of my spleen!' And in this fashion,
All our abilities, gifts, natures, shapes,
Severals and generals of grace exact,   180
Achievements, plots, orders, preventions,
Excitements to the field or speech for truce,
Success or loss, what is or is not, serves
As stuff for these two to make paradoxes.
NESTOR. And in the imitation of these twain,
Who, as Ulysses says, opinion crowns
With an imperial voice, many are infect.
Ajax is grown self-willed and bears his head
In such a rein, in full as proud a place
As broad Achilles; keeps his tent like him;   190
Makes factious feasts; rails on our state of war
Bold as an oracle; and sets Thersites,

A slave whose gall coins slanders like a mint,
To match us in comparisons with dirt,
To weaken and discredit our exposure,
How rank soever rounded in with danger.
ULYSSES. They tax our policy and call it cowardice,
Count wisdom as no member of the war,
Forestall prescience, and esteem no act
But that of hand; the still and mental parts   200
That do contrive how many hands shall strike
When fitness calls them on, and know by measure
Of their observant toil the enemy's weight—
Why, this hath not a finger's dignity:
They call this bed-work, mappery, closet-war;
So that the ram that batters down the wall,
For the great swing and rudeness of his poise,
They place before his hand that made the engine
Or those that with the fineness of their souls
By reason guide his execution.   210
NESTOR. Let this be granted, and Achilles' horse
Makes many Thetis' sons.   *Tucket*
AGAMEMNON. What trumpet? look, Menelaus.
MENELAUS. From Troy.

Enter Æneas

AGAMEMNON. What would you 'fore our tent?
ÆNEAS. Is this great Agamemnon's tent, I pray you?
AGAMEMNON. Even this.
ÆNEAS. May one that is a herald and a prince
Do a fair message to his kingly eyes?
AGAMEMNON. With surety stronger than Achilles'
   arms   220
'Fore all the Greekish heads, which with one voice
Call Agamemnon head and general.
ÆNEAS. Fair leave and large security. How may
A stranger to those most imperial looks
Know them from eyes of other mortals?
AGAMEMNON.   How?
ÆNEAS. Ay:
I ask, that I might waken reverence,
And bid the cheek be ready with a blush
Modest as morning when she coldly eyes
The youthful Phoebus.   230
Which is that god in office, guiding men?
Which is the high and mighty Agamemnon?
AGAMEMNON. This Trojan scorns us, or the men
   of Troy
Are ceremonious courtiers.
ÆNEAS. Courtiers as free, as debonair, unarmed,
As bending angels: that's their fame in peace.
But when they would seem soldiers, they have galls,
Good arms, strong joints, true swords, and—
   Jove's accord—
Nothing so full of heart. But peace, Æneas,
Peace, Trojan; lay thy finger on thy lips!   240
The worthiness of praise distains his worth,
If that the praised himself bring the praise forth:
But what the repining enemy commends,
That breath fame blows; that praise, sole
   pure, transcends.
AGAMEMNON. Sir you of Troy, call you
   yourself Æneas?
ÆNEAS. Ay, Greek, that is my name.
AGAMEMNON. What's your affair, I pray you?
ÆNEAS. Sir, pardon: 'tis for Agamemnon's ears.   190
AGAMEMNON. He hears nought privately that comes
   from Troy.

ÆNEAS. Nor I from Troy come not to whisper him;   250
  I bring a trumpet to awake his ear,
  To set his sense on the attentive bent,
  And then to speak.
AGAMEMNON.   Speak frankly as the wind;
  It is not Agamemnon's sleeping hour.
  That thou shalt know, Trojan, he is awake,
  He tells thee so himself.
ÆNEAS.   Trumpet, blow loud,
  Send thy brass voice through all these lazy tents;
  And every Greek of mettle, let him know,
  What Troy means fairly shall be spoke aloud.

                         Trumpet sounds

  We have, great Agamemnon, here in Troy   260
  A prince called Hector—Priam is his father—
  Who in this dull and long-continued truce
  Is resty grown. He bade me take a trumpet,
  And to this purpose speak: kings, princes, lords!
  If there be one among the fair'st of Greece,
  That holds his honour higher than his ease,
  That seeks his praise more than he fears his peril,
  That knows his valour and knows not his fear,
  That loves his mistress more than in confession
  With truant vows to her own lips he loves,   270
  And dare avow her beauty and her worth
  In other arms than hers—to him this challenge!
  Hector, in view of Trojans and of Greeks,
  Shall make it good, or do his best to do it,
  He hath a lady, wiser, fairer, truer,
  Than ever Greek did couple in his arms;
  And will tomorrow with his trumpet call
  Midway between your tents and walls of Troy,
  To rouse a Grecian that is true in love.
  If any come, Hector shall honour him;   280
  If none, he'll say in Troy when he retires,
  The Grecian dames are sunburnt and not worth
  The splinter of a lance. Even so much.
AGAMEMNON. This shall be told our lovers, Lord
    Æneas.
  If none of them have soul in such a kind,
  We left them all at home. But we are soldiers;
  And may that soldier a mere recreant prove,
  That means not, hath not, or is not in love!
  If then one is, or hath, or means to be,
  That one meets Hector; if none else, I am he.   290
NESTOR. Tell him of Nestor, one that was a man
  When Hector's grandsire sucked. He is old now;
  But if there be not in our Grecian host
  One noble man that hath one spark of fire,
  To answer for his love, tell him from me
  I'll hide my silver beard in a gold beaver
  And in my vantbrace put this withered brawn,
  And, meeting him, will tell him that my lady
  Was fairer than his grandam and as chaste
  As may be in the world: his youth in flood,
  I'll prove this truth with my three drops of blood.   300
ÆNEAS. Now heavens forfend such scarcity of youth!
ULYSSES. Amen.
AGAMEMNON. Fair Lord Æneas, let me touch
    your hand;
  To our pavilion shall I lead you first.
  Achilles shall have word of this intent;
  So shall each lord of Greece, from tent to tent.
  Yourself shall feast with us before you go,
  And find the welcome of a noble foe.

          They go; Ulysses detains Nestor

ULYSSES. Nestor!   310
NESTOR. What says Ulysses?
ULYSSES. I have a young conception in my brain;
  Be you my time to bring it to some shape.
NESTOR. What is't?
ULYSSES. This 'tis:
  Blunt wedges rive hard knots; the seeded pride
  That hath to this maturity blown up
  In rank Achilles must or now be cropped,
  Or, shedding, breed a nursery of like evil
  To overbulk us all.
NESTOR.   Well, and how?   320
ULYSSES. This challenge that the gallant Hector sends,
  However it is spread in general name,
  Relates in purpose only to Achilles.
NESTOR. True: the purpose is perspicuous
    as substance,
  Whose grossness little characters sum up;
  And, in the publication, make no strain
  But that Achilles, were his brain as barren
  As banks of Libya—though, Apollo knows,
  'Tis dry enough—will, with great speed of
    judgement,
  Ay, with celerity, find Hector's purpose   330
  Pointing on him.
ULYSSES. And wake him to the answer, think you?
NESTOR. Why, 'tis most meet. Who may you
    else oppose
  That can from Hector bring his honour off,
  If not Achilles? Though't be a sportful combat,
  Yet in this trial much opinion dwells:
  For here the Trojans taste our dear'st repute
  With their fin'st palate—and trust to me, Ulysses,
  Our imputation shall be oddly poised
  In this wild action; for the success,   340
  Although particular, shall give a scantling
  Of good or bad unto the general;
  And in such indexes, although small pricks
  To their subsequent volumes, there is seen
  The baby figure of the giant mass
  Of things to come at large. It is supposed
  He that meets Hector issues from our choice;
  And choice, being mutual act of all our souls,
  Makes merit her election, and doth boil,
  As 'twere from forth us all, a man distilled   350
  Out of our virtues; who miscarrying,
  What heart receives from hence a conquering part,
  To steel a strong opinion to themselves?
  Which entertained, limbs are his instruments,
  E'en no less working than are swords and bows
  Directive by the limbs.
ULYSSES. Give pardon to my speech: therefore 'tis meet
  Achilles meet not Hector. Let us, like merchants,
  First show foul wares, and think perchance they'll
    sell.
  If not, the lustre of the better shall exceed   360
  By showing the worse first. Do not consent
  That ever Hector and Achilles meet;
  For both our honour and our shame in this
  Are dogged with two strange followers.
NESTOR. I see them not with my old eyes: what
    are they?
ULYSSES. What glory our Achilles shares
    from Hector,
  Were he not proud, we all should share with him.
  But he already is too insolent;

And we were better parch in Afric sun
Than in the pride and salt scorn of his eyes,   370
Should he scape Hector fair: if he were foiled,
Why, then we did our main opinion crush
In taint of our best man. No, make a lottery,
And by device let blockish Ajax draw
The sort to fight with Hector; 'mong ourselves
Give him allowance as the better man;
For that will physic the great Myrmidon,
Who broils in loud applause, and make him fall
His crest that prouder than blue Iris bends.
If the dull brainless Ajax come safe off,   380
We'll dress him up in voices; if he fail,
Yet go we under our opinion still
That we have better men. But, hit or miss,
Our project's life this shape of sense assumes—
Ajax employed plucks down Achilles' plumes.

NESTOR. Ulysses,
Now I begin to relish thy advice,
And I will give a taste thereof forthwith
To Agamemnon. Go we to him straight.
Two curs shall tame each other: pride alone   390
Must tarre the mastiffs on, as 'twere their bone.

They go

ACT 2

Scene 1: *The Greek camp*

Enter Ajax and Thersites

AJAX. Thersites!

THERSITES. Agamemnon—how if he had boils, full, all over, generally?

AJAX. Thersites!

THERSITES. And those boils did run? Say so: did not the general run then? were not that a botchy core?

AJAX. Dog!

THERSITES. Then would come some matter from him; I see none now.

AJAX. Thou bitch-wolf's son, canst thou not hear?   10
Feel, then. *Strikes him*

THERSITES. The plague of Greece upon thee, thou mongrel beef-witted lord!

AJAX. Speak then, thou vinewed'st leaven, speak! I will beat thee into handsomeness!

THERSITES. I shall sooner rail thee into wit and holiness; but I think thy horse will sooner con an oration than thou learn a prayer without book. Thou canst strike, canst thou? A red murrain o' thy jade's tricks!

AJAX. Toadstool, learn me the proclamation.   20

THERSITES. Dost thou think I have no sense, thou strikest me thus?

AJAX. The proclamation!

THERSITES. Thou art proclaimed a fool, I think.

AJAX. Do not, porpentine, do not; my fingers itch.

THERSITES. I would thou didst itch from head to foot and I had the scratching of thee; I would make thee the loathsomest scab in Greece. When thou art forth in the incursions, thou strikest as slow as another.

AJAX. I say, the proclamation!   30

THERSITES. Thou grumblest and railest every hour on Achilles, and thou art as full of envy at his greatness as Cerberus is at Proserpina's beauty, ay, that thou barkest at him.

AJAX. Mistress Thersites!

THERSITES. Thou shouldst strike him.

AJAX. Cobloaf!

THERSITES. He would pun thee into shivers with his fist, as a sailor breaks a biscuit.

AJAX. You whoreson cur! *Strikes him* 40

THERSITES. Do, do, thou stool for a witch! ay, do, do, thou sodden-witted lord! Thou hast no more brain in thy head than I have in mine elbows; an assinego may tutor thee. Thou scurvy-valiant ass! thou art here but to thrash Trojans; and thou art bought and sold among those of any wit, like a barbarian slave. If thou use to beat me, I will begin at thy heel and tell what thou art by inches, thou thing of no bowels, thou!

AJAX. You dog!   50

THERSITES. You scurvy lord!

AJAX. You cur! *Strikes him*

THERSITES. Mars his idiot! do, rudeness; do, camel, do, do.

Enter Achilles and Patroclus

ACHILLES. Why, how now, Ajax! Wherefore do you thus? How now, Thersites! What's the matter, man?

THERSITES. You see him there, do you?

ACHILLES. Ay; what's the matter?

THERSITES. Nay, look upon him.

ACHILLES. So I do; what's the matter?   60

THERSITES. Nay, but regard him well.

ACHILLES. 'Well!'—why, so I do.

THERSITES. But yet you look not well upon him: for whosoever you take him to be, he is Ajax.

ACHILLES. I know that, fool.

THERSITES. Ay, but that fool knows not himself.

AJAX. Therefore I beat thee.

THERSITES. Lo, lo, lo, lo, what modicums of wit he utters! His evasions have ears thus long. I have bobbed his brain more than he has beat my bones. 70
I will buy nine sparrows for a penny, and his pia mater is not worth the ninth part of a sparrow. This lord, Achilles—Ajax, who wears his wit in his belly and his guts in his head—I'll tell you what I say of him.

ACHILLES. What?

THERSITES. I say this Ajax— *Ajax offers to strike him*

ACHILLES. Nay, good Ajax.

THERSITES. Has not so much wit—

ACHILLES. Nay, I must hold you.   80

THERSITES. As will stop the eye of Helen's needle, for whom he comes to fight.

ACHILLES. Peace, fool!

THERSITES. I would have peace and quietness, but the fool will not—he there; that he; look you there!

AJAX. O thou damned cur! I shall—

ACHILLES. Will you set your wit to a fool's?

THERSITES. No, I warrant you; for the fool's will shame it.

PATROCLUS. Good words, Thersites.   90

ACHILLES. What's the quarrel?

AJAX. I bade the vile owl go learn me the tenour of the proclamation, and he rails upon me.

THERSITES. I serve thee not.

AJAX. Well, go to, go to.

THERSITES. I serve here voluntary.

ACHILLES. Your last service was sufferance, 'twas not voluntary. No man is beaten voluntary. Ajax was here the voluntary, and you as under an impress.

THERSITES. E'en so; a great deal of your wit too lies in 100 your sinews, or else there be liars. Hector shall have a great catch an 'a knock out either of your brains: 'a were as good crack a fusty nut with no kernel.

ACHILLES. What, with me too, Thersites?

THERSITES. There's Ulysses and old Nestor, whose wit was mouldy ere your grandsires had nails on their toes, yoke you like draught-oxen, and make you plough up the wars.

ACHILLES. What? what?

THERSITES. Yes, good sooth: to, Achilles! to, Ajax, to! 110

AJAX. I shall cut out your tongue.

THERSITES. 'Tis no matter; I shall speak as much wit as thou afterwards.

PATROCLUS. No more words, Thersites; peace!

THERSITES. I will hold my peace when Achilles' brach bids me, shall I?

ACHILLES. There's for you, Patroclus.

THERSITES. I will see you hanged, like clotpolls, ere I come any more to your tents. I will keep where there is wit stirring, and leave the faction of fools. 120

Goes

PATROCLUS. A good riddance.

ACHILLES. Marry, this, sir, is proclaimed through all our host:
That Hector, by the fifth hour of the sun,
Will with a trumpet 'twixt our tents and Troy
Tomorrow morning call some knight to arms
That hath a stomach, and such a one that dare
Maintain—I know not what; 'tis trash. Farewell.

AJAX. Farewell. Who shall answer him?

ACHILLES. I know not. 'Tis put to lottery; otherwise
He knew his man. 130

AJAX. O, meaning you. I'll go learn more of it.

They go

Scene 2: *Troy. Priam's palace*

Enter Priam, Hector, Troilus, Paris, and Helenus

PRIAM. After so many hours, lives, speeches spent,
Thus once again says Nestor from the Greeks:
'Deliver Helen, and all damage else—
As honour, loss of time, travail, expense,
Wounds, friends, and what else dear that
is consumed
In hot digestion of this cormorant war—
Shall be struck off.' Hector, what say you to't?

HECTOR. Though no man lesser fears the Greeks
than I
As far as toucheth my particular,
Yet dread Priam, 10
There is no lady of more softer bowels,
More spongy to suck in the sense of fear,
More ready to cry out 'Who knows what follows?'
Than Hector is. The wound of peace is surety,
Surety secure; but modest doubt is called
The beacon of the wise, the tent that searches
To th'bottom of the worst. Let Helen go.
Since the first sword was drawn about this question,
Every tithe-soul 'mongst many thousand dismes
Hath been as dear as Helen—I mean, of ours. 20
If we have lost so many tenths of ours
To guard a thing not ours, nor worth to us—
Had it our name—the value of one ten,
What merit's in that reason which denies
The yielding of her up?

TROILUS.   Fie, fie, my brother!

Weigh you the worth and honour of a king
So great as our dread father in a scale
Of common ounces? Will you with counters sum
The past-proportion of his infinite,
And buckle in a waist most fathomless 30
With spans and inches so diminutive
As fears and reasons? Fie, for godly shame!

HELENUS. No marvel though you bite so sharp
at reasons,
You are so empty of them. Shall not our father
Bear the great sway of his affairs with reasons,
Because your speech hath none that tells him so?

TROILUS. You are for dreams and slumbers,
brother priest.
You fur your gloves with reasons. Here are
your reasons:
You know an enemy intends you harm;
You know a sword employed is perilous, 40
And reason flies the object of all harm;
Who marvels then, when Helenus beholds
A Grecian and his sword, if he do set
The very wings of reason to his heels
And fly, like chidden Mercury from Jove
Or like a star disorbed? Nay, if we talk of reason,
Let's shut our gates and sleep. Manhood
and honour
Should have hare hearts, would they but fat
their thoughts
With this crammed reason; reason and respect
Make livers pale and lustihood deject. 50

HECTOR. Brother, she is not worth what she doth cost
The keeping.

TROILUS.   What's aught, but as 'tis valued?

HECTOR. But value dwells not in particular will:
It holds his estimate and dignity
As well wherein 'tis precious of itself
As in the prizer. 'Tis mad idolatry
To make the service greater than the god;
And the will dotes that is attributive
To what infectiously itself affects,
Without some image of th'affected merit. 60

TROILUS. I take today a wife, and my election
Is led on in the conduct of my will;
My will enkindled by mine eyes and ears—
Two traded pilots 'twixt the dangerous shores
Of will and judgement—how may I avoid,
Although my will distaste what it elected,
The wife I chose? There can be no evasion
To blench from this and to stand firm by honour.
We turn not back the silks upon the merchant
When we have soiled them; nor the remainder
viands 70
We do not throw in unrespective sieve
Because we now are full. It was thought meet
Paris should do some vengeance on the Greeks;
Your breath of full consent bellied his sails;
The seas and winds, old wranglers, took a truce,
And did him service; he touched the ports desired;
And for an old aunt whom the Greeks held captive
He brought a Grecian queen, whose youth
and freshness
Wrinkles Apollo's and makes pale the morning.
Why keep we her?—the Grecians keep our aunt; 80
Is she worth keeping?—why, she is a pearl
Whose price hath launched above a thousand ships
And turned crowned kings to merchants.

If you'll avouch 'twas wisdom Paris went—
As you must needs, for you all cried 'Go, go';
If you'll confess he brought home worthy prize—
As you must needs, for you all clapped your hands
And cried 'Inestimable!'; why do you now
The issue of your proper wisdoms rate,
And do a deed that Fortune never did,   90
Beggar the estimation which you prized
Richer than sea and land? O, theft most base,
That we have stolen what we do fear to keep!
But thieves unworthy of a thing so stolen,
That in their country did them that disgrace
We fear to warrant in our native place!
CASSANDRA [within]. Cry, Trojans, cry!
PRIAM.   What noise, what shriek is this?
TROILUS. 'Tis our mad sister, I do know her voice.
CASSANDRA [within]. Cry, Trojans!
HECTOR. It is Cassandra.   100

Enter Cassandra, raving, with her hair about her ears

CASSANDRA. Cry, Trojans, cry! lend me ten
         thousand eyes,
And I will fill them with prophetic tears.
HECTOR. Peace, sister, peace!
CASSANDRA. Virgins and boys, mid-age and
         wrinkled eld,
Soft infancy, that nothing canst but cry,
Add to my clamours! Let us pay betimes
A moiety of that mass of moan to come.
Cry, Trojans, cry! Practise your eyes with tears!
Troy must not be, nor goodly Ilion stand;
Our firebrand brother, Paris, burns us all.   110
Cry, Trojans, cry! a Helen and a woe:
Cry, cry! Troy burns, or else let Helen go.   *Goes*
HECTOR. Now youthful Troilus, do not these
         high strains
Of divination in our sister work
Some touches of remorse, or is your blood
So madly hot that no discourse of reason,
Nor fear of bad success in a bad cause,
Can qualify the same?
TROILUS.   Why, brother Hector,
We may not think the justness of each act
Such and no other than event doth form it,   120
Nor once deject the courage of our minds
Because Cassandra's mad. Her brainsick raptures
Cannot distaste the goodness of a quarrel
Which hath our several honours all engaged
To make it gracious. For my private part,
I am no more touched than all Priam's sons;
And Jove forbid there should be done amongst us
Such things as might offend the weakest spleen
To fight for and maintain!
PARIS. Else might the world convince of levity   130
As well my undertakings as your counsels;
But I attest the gods, your full consent
Gave wings to my propension and cut off
All fears attending on so dire a project.
For what, alas, can these my single arms?
What propugnation is in one man's valour
To stand the push and enmity of those
This quarrel would excite? Yet, I protest,
Were I alone to pass the difficulties
And had as ample power as I have will,   140
Paris should ne'er retract what he hath done,
Nor faint in the pursuit.

PRIAM.   Paris, you speak
Like one besotted on your sweet delights;
You have the honey still, but these the gall:
So to be valiant is no praise at all.
PARIS. Sir, I propose not merely to myself
The pleasures such a beauty brings with it,
But I would have the soil of her fair rape
Wiped off in honourable keeping her.
What treason were it to the ransacked queen,   150
Disgrace to your great worths, and shame to me.
Now to deliver her possession up
On terms of base compulsion! Can it be
That so degenerate a strain as this
Should once set footing in your generous bosoms?
There's not the meanest spirit on our party
Without a heart to dare or sword to draw
When Helen is defended; nor none so noble
Whose life were ill bestowed or death unfamed
Where Helen is the subject. Then, I say,   160
Well may we fight for her whom we know well
The world's large spaces cannot parallel.
HECTOR. Paris and Troilus, you have both said well,
And on the cause and question now in hand
Have glozed—but superficially; not much
Unlike young men, whom Aristotle thought
Unfit to hear moral philosophy.
The reasons you allege do more conduce
To the hot passion of distempered blood
Than to make up a free determination   170
'Twixt right and wrong: for pleasure and revenge
Have ears more deaf than adders to the voice
Of any true decision. Nature craves
All dues be rendered to their owners: now,
What nearer debt in all humanity
Than wife is to the husband? If this law
Of nature be corrupted through affection,
And that great minds, of partial indulgence
To their benumbéd wills, resist the same,
There is a law in each well-ordered nation   180
To curb those raging appetites that are
Most disobedient and refractory.
If Helen then be wife to Sparta's king,
And it is known she is, these moral laws
Of nature and of nations speak aloud
To have her back returned. Thus to persist
In doing wrong extenuates not wrong,
But makes it much more heavy. Hector's opinion
Is this in way of truth. Yet, ne'ertheless,
My sprightly brethren, I propend to you   190
In resolution to keep Helen still;
For 'tis a cause that hath no mean dependence
Upon our joint and several dignities.
TROILUS. Why, there you touched the life of
         our design:
Were it not glory that we more affected
Than the performance of our heaving spleens,
I would not wish a drop of Trojan blood
Spent more in her defence. But, worthy Hector,
She is a theme of honour and renown,
A spur to valiant and magnanimous deeds,   200
Whose present courage may beat down our foes,
And fame in time to come canonize us;
For I presume brave Hector would not lose
So rich advantage of a promised glory
As smiles upon the forehead of this action
For the wide world's revenue.

HECTOR.   I am yours,
You valiant offspring of great Priamus.
I have a roisting challenge sent amongst
The dull and factious nobles of the Greeks
Will strike amazement to their drowsy spirits.   210
I was advertised their great general slept,
Whilst emulation in the army crept:
This, I presume, will wake him.   *They go*

Scene 3: *The Greek camp. Before the tent of Achilles*

Enter Thersites, solus

THERSITES. How now, Thersites! What, lost in the
labyrinth of thy fury! Shall the elephant Ajax carry
it thus? He beats me, and I rail at him. O worthy
satisfaction! Would it were otherwise: that I could
beat him, whilst he railed at me. 'Sfoot, I'll learn to
conjure and raise devils but I'll see some issue of my
spiteful execrations. Then there's Achilles—a rare
enginer. If Troy be not taken till these two undermine it, the walls will stand till they fall of themselves. O thou great thunder-darter of Olympus,   10
forget that thou art Jove, the king of gods, and,
Mercury, lose all the serpentine craft of thy cadu-
ceus, if ye take not that little little less than little wit
from them that they have! which short-armed
ignorance itself knows is so abundant scarce, it will
not in circumvention deliver a fly from a spider
without drawing their massy irons and cutting the
web. After this, the vengeance on the whole camp!
or, rather, the Neapolitan bone-ache? for that,
methinks, is the curse dependent on those that war   20
for a placket. I have said my prayers; and devil Envy
say 'Amen'. What ho! my Lord Achilles!

PATROCLUS [*within*]. Who's there? Thersites? Good
Thersites, come in and rail.

THERSITES. If I could a' remembered a gilt counterfeit,
thou wouldst not have slipped out of my contemplation; but it is no matter—thyself upon thyself!
The common curse of mankind, folly and ignorance, be thine in great revenue! Heaven bless thee
from a tutor, and discipline come not near thee!   30
Let thy blood be thy direction till thy death! Then
if she that lays thee out says thou art a fair corpse,
I'll be sworn and sworn upon't she never shrouded
any but lazars. Amen.

Enter Patroclus

Where's Achilles?

PATROCLUS. What, art thou devout? Wast thou in
prayer?

THERSITES. Ay; the heavens hear me!

PATROCLUS. Amen.

ACHILLES [*within*]. Who's there?   40

PATROCLUS. Thersites, my lord.

Enter Achilles

ACHILLES. Where, where? O where? Art thou come?
Why, my cheese, my digestion, why hast thou not
served thyself in to my table so many meals? Come,
what's Agamemnon?

THERSITES. Thy commander, Achilles; then tell me,
Patroclus, what's Achilles?

PATROCLUS. Thy lord, Thersites; then tell me, I pray
thee, what's thyself?

THERSITES. Thy knower, Patroclus; then tell me,   50
Patroclus, what art thou?

PATROCLUS. Thou mayst tell that knowest.

ACHILLES. O tell, tell.

THERSITES. I'll decline the whole question. Agamemnon commands Achilles; Achilles is my lord; I am
Patroclus' knower, and Patroclus is a fool.

PATROCLUS. You rascal!

THERSITES. Peace, fool! I have not done.

ACHILLES. He is a privileged man. Proceed, Thersites.

THERSITES. Agamemnon is a fool; Achilles is a fool;   60
Thersites is a fool, and, as aforesaid, Patroclus is a
fool.

ACHILLES. Derive this; come.

THERSITES. Agamemnon is a fool to offer to command
Achilles; Achilles is a fool to be commanded of
Agamemnon; Thersites is a fool to serve such a
fool; and Patroclus is a fool positive.

PATROCLUS. Why am I a fool?

THERSITES. Make that demand of the Creator. It
suffices me thou art. Look you, who comes here?   70

ACHILLES. Patroclus, I'll speak with nobody. Come in
with me, Thersites.   *Enters his tent*

THERSITES. Here is such patchery, such juggling and
such knavery! All the argument is a whore and a
cuckold—a good quarrel to draw emulous factions
and bleed to death upon. Now, the dry serpigo on
the subject, and war and lechery confound all!
                                       Enters the tent

Enter Agamemnon, Ulysses, Nestor, Diomedes, and Ajax

AGAMEMNON. Where is Achilles?

PATROCLUS. Within his tent; but ill-disposed, my lord.

AGAMEMNON. Let it be known to him that we are here.   80
We sent our messengers, and we lay by
Our appertainments, visiting of him.
Let him be told so, lest perchance he think
We dare not move the question of our place,
Or know not what we are.

PATROCLUS.   I shall say so to him.   *Goes in*

ULYSSES. We saw him at the opening of his tent:
He is not sick.

AJAX. Yes, lion-sick, sick of proud heart. You may
call it melancholy, if you will favour the man; but,
by my head, 'tis pride. But why, why? Let him show   90
us the cause. A word, my lord.
                          Takes Agamemnon aside

NESTOR. What moves Ajax thus to bay at him?

ULYSSES. Achilles hath inveigled his fool from him.

NESTOR. Who, Thersites?

ULYSSES. He.

NESTOR. Then will Ajax lack matter, if he have lost
his argument.

ULYSSES. No, you see, he is his argument that has his
argument—Achilles.

NESTOR. All the better: their fraction is more our wish   100
than their faction. But it was a strong composure
a fool could disunite!

ULYSSES. The amity that wisdom knits not, folly may
easily untie.

Re-enter Patroclus

Here comes Patroclus.

NESTOR. No Achilles with him.

ULYSSES. The elephant hath joints, but none for

courtesy: his legs are legs for necessity, not for
flexure.
PATROCLUS. Achilles bids me say he is much sorry 110
If anything more than your sport and pleasure
Did move your greatness and this noble state
To call upon him; he hopes it is no other
But for your health and your digestion's sake,
An after-dinner's breath.
AGAMEMNON.   Hear you, Patroclus:
We are too well acquainted with these answers;
But his evasion, winged thus swift with scorn,
Cannot outfly our apprehensions.
Much attribute he hath, and much the reason
Why we ascribe it to him; yet all his virtues, 120
Not virtuously on his own part beheld,
Do in our eyes begin to lose their gloss,
Yea, like fair fruit in an unwholesome dish,
Are like to rot untasted. Go and tell him
We come to speak with him; and you shall not sin
If you do say we think him over-proud
And under-honest, in self-assumption greater
Than in the note of judgement; and worthier
   than himself
Here tend the savage strangeness he puts on,
Disguise the holy strength of their command, 130
And underwrite in an observing kind
His humorous predominance; yea, watch
His pettish lunes, his ebbs and flows, as if
The passage and whole carriage of this action
Rode on his tide. Go tell him this, and add
That if he overhold his price so much
We'll none of him but let him, like an engine
Not portable, lie under this report:
'Bring action hither; this cannot go to war:
A stirring dwarf we do allowance give 140
Before a sleeping giant.' Tell him so.
PATROCLUS. I shall; and bring his answer presently.
                                         Enters the tent
AGAMEMNON. In second voice we'll not be satisfied;
We come to speak with him. Ulysses, enter you.
                                         Ulysses follows
AJAX. What is he more than another?
AGAMEMNON. No more than what he thinks he is.
AJAX. Is he so much? Do you not think he thinks
himself a better man than I am?
AGAMEMNON. No question.
AJAX. Will you subscribe his thought and say he is? 150
AGAMEMNON. No, noble Ajax; you are as strong, as
valiant, as wise, no less noble, much more gentle,
and altogether more tractable.
AJAX. Why should a man be proud? How doth pride
grow? I know not what pride is.
AGAMEMNON. Your mind is the clearer, Ajax, and your
virtues the fairer. He that is proud eats up himself:
pride is his own glass, his own trumpet, his own
chronicle; and whatever praises itself but in the deed,
devours the deed in the praise. 160
AJAX. I do hate a proud man as I do hate the
engendering of toads.
NESTOR. And yet he loves himself: is it not strange?

Re-enter Ulysses

ULYSSES. Achilles will not to the field tomorrow.
AGAMEMNON. What's his excuse?
ULYSSES.   He doth rely on none,
But carries on the stream of his dispose

Without observance or respect of any,
In will peculiar and in self-admission.
AGAMEMNON. Why will he not, upon our fair request, 170
Untent his person and share th'air with us?
ULYSSES. Things small as nothing, for request's
   sake only,
He makes important; possessed he is with greatness,
And speaks not to himself but with a pride
That quarrels at self-breath: imagined worth
Holds in his blood such swollen and hot discourse
That 'twixt his mental and his active parts
Kingdomed Achilles in commotion rages
And batters down himself. What should I say?
He is so plaguey proud that the death-tokens of it
Cry 'No recovery'.
AGAMEMNON.   Let Ajax go to him. 180
Dear lord, go you and greet him in his tent.
'Tis said he holds you well, and will be led,
At your request, a little from himself.
ULYSSES. O Agamemnon, let it not be so!
We'll consecrate the steps that Ajax makes
When they go from Achilles. Shall the proud lord
That bastes his arrogance with his own seam
And never suffers matter of the world
Enter his thoughts, save such as doth revolve
And ruminate himself, shall he be worshipped 190
Of that we hold an idol more than he?
No, this thrice-worthy and right valiant lord
Must not so stale his palm, nobly acquired,
Nor, by my will, assubjugate his merit—
As amply titled as Achilles is—
By going to Achilles:
That were to enlard his fat-already pride,
And add more coals to Cancer when he burns
With entertaining great Hyperion.
This lord go to him! Jupiter forbid, 200
And say in thunder 'Achilles go to him'.
NESTOR [*aside*]. O, this is well; he rubs the vein of him.
DIOMEDES [*aside*]. And how his silence drinks up
   this applause!
AJAX. If I go to him, with my arméd fist
I'll pash him o'er the face.
AGAMEMNON. O, no, you shall not go.
AJAX. An 'a be proud with me, I'll feeze his pride:
Let me go to him.
ULYSSES. Not for the worth that hangs upon
   our quarrel.
AJAX. A paltry, insolent fellow! 210
NESTOR [*aside*]. How he describes himself!
AJAX. Can he not be sociable?
ULYSSES [*aside*]. The raven chides blackness.
AJAX. I'll let his humour's blood.
AGAMEMNON [*aside*]. He will be the physician that
should be the patient.
AJAX. An all men were o' my mind—
ULYSSES [*aside*]. Wit would be out of fashion.
AJAX. 'A should not bear it so; 'a should eat swords
first. Shall pride carry it? 220
NESTOR [*aside*]. An 'twould, you'ld carry half.
ULYSSES [*aside*]. 'A would have ten shares.
AJAX. I'll knead him, I'll make him supple.
NESTOR [*aside*]. He's not yet through warm. Force him
with praises: pour in, pour in; his ambition is dry.
ULYSSES [*to Agamemnon*]. My lord, you feed too much
on this dislike.
NESTOR. Our noble general, do not do so.

DIOMEDES. You must prepare to fight
    without Achilles.
ULYSSES. Why, 'tis this naming of him does him harm.
    Here is a man—but 'tis before his face: 230
    I will be silent.
NESTOR.   Wherefore should you so?
    He is not emulous, as Achilles is.
ULYSSES. Know the whole world, he is as valiant.
AJAX. A whoreson dog, that shall palter thus
    with us!
    Would he were a Trojan!
NESTOR. What a vice were it in Ajax now—
ULYSESS. If he were proud—
DIOMEDES. Or covetous of praise—
ULYSSES. Ay, or surly borne—
DIOMEDES. Or strange, or self-affected!   240
ULYSSES. Thank the heavens, lord, thou art of
    sweet composure;
    Praise him that got thee, she that gave thee suck;
    Famed be thy tutor, and thy parts of nature
    Thrice-famed beyond, beyond all erudition:
    But he that disciplined thine arms to fight,
    Let Mars divide eternity in twain,
    And give him half; and, for thy vigour,
    Bull-bearing Milo his addition yield
    To sinewy Ajax. I will not praise thy wisdom,
    Which, like a bourn, a pale, a shore, confines   250
    Thy spacious and dilated parts. Here's Nestor,
    Instructed by the antiquary times;
    He must, he is, he cannot but be wise:
    But pardon, father Nestor, were your days
    As green as Ajax', and your brain so tempered,
    You should not have the eminence of him,
    But be as Ajax.
AJAX.   Shall I call you father?
NESTOR. Ay, my good son.
DIOMEDES.   Be ruled by him, Lord Ajax.
ULYSSES. There is no tarrying here: the
    hart Achilles
    Keeps thicket. Please it our great general   260
    To call together all his state of war:
    Fresh kings are come to Troy; tomorrow
    We must with all our main of power stand fast;
    And here's a lord, come knights from east to west,
    And cull their flower, Ajax shall cope the best.
AGAMEMNON. Go we to council. Let Achilles sleep:
    Light boats sail swift, though greater hulks draw
    deep.   *They go*

ACT 3
Scene 1: *Troy. Priam's palace*

Enter Pandarus and a Servant

PANDARUS. Friend, you, pray you, a word: do you not
    follow the young Lord Paris?
SERVANT. Ay sir, when he goes before me.
PANDARUS. You depend upon him, I mean?
SERVANT. Sir, I do depend upon the Lord.
PANDARUS. You depend upon a noble gentleman;
    I must needs praise him.
SERVANT. The Lord be praised!
PANDARUS. You know me, do you not?
SERVANT. Faith, sir, superficially.   10
PANDARUS. Friend, know me better: I am the Lord
    Pandarus.

SERVANT. I hope I shall know your honour better.
PANDARUS. I do desire it.
SERVANT. You are in the state of grace.
PANDARUS. Grace! not so, friend: honour and lordship
    are my titles. [*music within*] What music is this?
SERVANT. I do but partly know, sir: it is music in
    parts.
PANDARUS. Know you the musicians?   20
SERVANT. Wholly, sir.
PANDARUS. Who play they to?
SERVANT. To the hearers, sir.
PANDARUS. At whose pleasure, friend?
SERVANT. At mine, sir, and theirs that love music.
PANDARUS. Command, I mean, friend.
SERVANT. Who shall I command, sir?
PANDARUS. Friend, we understand not one another:
    I am too courtly, and thou art too cunning. At
    whose request do these men play?   30
SERVANT. That's to't, indeed, sir: marry, sir, at the
    request of Paris my lord, who is there in person;
    with him, the mortal Venus, the heart-blood of
    beauty, love's indivisible soul.
PANDARUS. Who, my cousin Cressida?
SERVANT. No, sir, Helen. Could you not find out that
    by her attributes?
PANDARUS. It should seem, fellow, that thou hast not
    seen the Lady Cressida. I come to speak with Paris
    from the Prince Troilus; I will make a complimental   40
    assault upon him, for my business seethes.
SERVANT. Sodden business! There's a stewed phrase
    indeed!

Enter Paris and Helen, attended

PANDARUS. Fair be to you, my lord, and to all this fair
    company! Fair desires, in all fair measure, fairly
    guide them! Especially to you, fair queen, fair
    thoughts be your fair pillow!
HELEN. Dear lord, you are full of fair words.
PANDARUS. You speak your fair pleasure, sweet queen.
    Fair prince, here is good broken music.   50
PARIS. You have broke it, cousin; and, by my life,
    you shall make it whole again: you shall piece it out
    with a piece of your performance. Nell, he is full of
    harmony.
PANDARUS. Truly, lady, no.
HELEN. O, sir—
PANDARUS. Rude, in sooth; in good sooth, very rude.
PARIS. Well said, my lord! well, you say so in fits.
PANDARUS. I have business to my lord, dear queen.
    My lord, will you vouchsafe me a word?   60
HELEN. Nay, this shall not hedge us out; we'll hear
    you sing, certainly.
PANDARUS. Well, sweet queen, you are pleasant with
    me.—But, marry, thus, my lord: my dear lord, and
    most esteemed friend, your brother Troilus—
HELEN. My Lord Pandarus; honey-sweet lord—
PANDARUS. Go to, sweet queen, go to—commends
    himself most affectionately to you—
HELEN. You shall not bob us out of our melody. If
    you do, our melancholy upon your head!   70
PANDARUS. Sweet queen, sweet queen; that's a sweet
    queen, i'faith.
HELEN. And to make a sweet lady sad is a sour offence.
PANDARUS. Nay, that shall not serve your turn; that
    shall it not, in truth, la. Nay, I care not for such
    words; no, no.—And, my lord, he desires you, that

if the king call for him at supper you will make his
excuse.

HELEN. My Lord Pandarus—

PANDARUS. What says my sweet queen, my very very 80
sweet queen?

PARIS. What exploit's in hand? where sups he tonight?

HELEN. Nay, but, my lord—

PANDARUS. What says my sweet queen?—My cousin
will fall out with you. You must not know where
he sups.

PARIS. I'll lay my life, with my disposer Cressida.

PANDARUS. No, no, no such matter; you are wide:
come, your disposer is sick.

PARIS. Well, I'll make's excuse.   90

PANDARUS. Ay, good my lord. Why should you say
Cressida? no, your poor disposer's sick.

PARIS. I spy.

PANDARUS. You spy! What do you spy? Come, give
me an instrument. Now, sweet queen.

HELEN. Why, this is kindly done.

PANDARUS. My niece is horribly in love with a thing
you have, sweet queen.

HELEN. She shall have it, my lord, if it be not my
lord Paris.   100

PANDARUS. He! no, she'll none of him; they two are
twain.

HELEN. Falling in, after falling out, may make them
three.

PANDARUS. Come, come, I'll hear no more of this.
I'll sing you a song now.

HELEN. Ay, ay, prithee now. By my troth, sweet lord,
thou hast a fine forehead.

PANDARUS. Ay, you may, you may.

HELEN. Let thy song be love; this love will undo us all. 110
O Cupid, Cupid, Cupid!

PANDARUS. Love! ay, that it shall, i'faith.

PARIS. Ay, good now, love, love, nothing but love.

PANDARUS. In good troth, it begins so.   *Sings*

Love, love, nothing but love, still love, still more!
    For, O, Love's bow
    Shoots buck and doe;
    The shaft confounds
    Not that it wounds,
But tickles still the sore.   120
These lovers cry Oh, oh, they die!
    Yet that which seems the wound to kill,
Doth turn oh! oh! to ha! ha! he!
    So dying love lives still.
Oh! oh! a while, but ha! ha! ha!
Oh! oh! groans out for ha! ha! ha!

Heigh-ho!

HELEN. In love, i'faith, to the very tip of the nose.

PARIS. He eats nothing but doves, love, and that
breeds hot blood, and hot blood begets hot 130
thoughts, and hot thoughts beget hot deeds, and hot
deeds is love.

PANDARUS. Is this the generation of love?—hot blood,
hot thoughts, and hot deeds? Why, they are vipers.
Is love a generation of vipers? Sweet lord, who's
afield today?

PARIS. Hector, Deiphobus, Helenus, Antenor, and all
the gallantry of Troy. I would fain have armed
today, but my Nell would not have it so. How
chance my brother Troilus went not?   140

HELEN. He hangs the lip at something; you know all,
Lord Pandarus.

PANDARUS. Not I, honey-sweet queen. I long to hear
how they sped today.—You'll remember your
brother's excuse?

PARIS. To a hair.

PANDARUS. Farewell, sweet queen.

HELEN. Commend me to your niece.

PANDARUS. I will, sweet queen.   *Goes*
                            Retreat sounded

PARIS. They're come from th'field: let us to
   Priam's hall,   150
To greet the warriors. Sweet Helen, I must woo you
To help unarm our Hector. His stubborn buckles,
With these your white enchanting fingers touched,
Shall more obey than to the edge of steel
Or force of Greekish sinews. You shall do more
Than all the island kings—disarm great Hector.

HELEN. 'Twill make us proud to be his
   servant, Paris;
Yea, what he shall receive of us in duty
Gives us more palm in beauty than we have,
Yea, overshines ourself.   160

PARIS. Sweet, above thought I love thee.   *They go*

Scene 2: *The same. Pandarus' orchard*

Enter Pandarus and Troilus' Boy, meeting

PANDARUS. How now! Where's thy master? At my
cousin Cressida's?

BOY. No, sir; he stays for you to conduct him thither.

PANDARUS. O, here he comes.

Enter Troilus

How now, how now!

TROILUS. Sirrah, walk off.   *Boy goes*

PANDARUS. Have you seen my cousin?

TROILUS. No, Pandarus; I stalk about her door,
Like a strange soul upon the Stygian banks
Staying for waftage. O, be thou my Charon,   10
And give me swift transportance to those fields
Where I may wallow in the lily beds
Proposed for the deserver! O gentle Pandar,
From Cupid's shoulder pluck his painted wings,
And fly with me to Cressid!

PANDARUS. Walk here i'th'orchard; I'll bring her
straight.   *Goes*

TROILUS. I am giddy: expectation whirls me round.
Th'imaginary relish is so sweet
That it enchants my sense. What will it be   20
When that the watery palate tastes indeed
Love's thrice repurèd nectar?—death, I fear me,
Swooning distraction, or some joy too fine,
Too subtle-potent, tuned too sharp in sweetness.
For the capacity of my ruder powers;
I fear it much, and I do fear besides
That I shall lose distinction in my joys,
As doth a battle, when they charge on heaps
The enemy flying.

Re-enter Pandarus

PANDARUS. She's making her ready; she'll come 30
straight. You must be witty now: she does so blush,
and fetches her wind so short as if she were frayed
with a sprite. I'll fetch her. It is the prettiest villain;
she fetches her breath as short as a new-ta'en
sparrow.   *Goes*

TROILUS. Even such a passion doth embrace my bosom:
My heart beats thicker than a feverous pulse;
And all my powers do their bestowing lose,
Like vassalage at unawares encountering
The eye of majesty. 40

Re-enter Pandarus and Cressida

PANDARUS. Come, come, what need you blush? Shame's a baby. Here she is now. Swear the oaths now to her that you have sworn to me. What, are you gone again? You must be watched ere you be made tame, must you? Come your ways, come your ways; an you draw backward, we'll put you i'th' fills. Why do you not speak to her? Come, draw this curtain, and let's see your picture. Alas the day, how loath you are to offend daylight! An 'twere dark, you'ld close sooner. So, so; rub on, and 50 kiss the mistress. How now! a kiss in fee-farm!— build there, carpenter; the air is sweet. Nay, you shall fight your hearts out ere I part you—the falcon as the tercel, for all the ducks i'th'river. Go to, go to.

TROILUS. You have bereft me of all words, lady.

PANDARUS. Words pay no debts, give her deeds; but she'll bereave you o'th'deeds too, if she call your activity in question. What, billing again? Here's 'In witness whereof the parties interchangeably'— Come in, come in; I'll go get a fire. *Goes* 60

CRESSIDA. Will you walk in, my lord?

TROILUS. O Cressida, how often have I wished me thus!

CRESSIDA. Wished, my lord?—The gods grant—O, my lord!

TROILUS. What should they grant? What makes this pretty abruption? What too curious dreg espies my sweet lady in the fountain of our love?

CRESSIDA. More dregs than water, if my fears have eyes. 70

TROILUS. Fears make devils of cherubins; they never see truly.

CRESSIDA. Blind fear, that seeing reason leads, finds safer footing than blind reason stumbling without fear: to fear the worst oft cures the worse.

TROILUS. O, let my lady apprehend no fear: in all Cupid's pageant there is presented no monster.

CRESSIDA. Nor nothing monstrous neither?

TROILUS. Nothing but our undertakings, when we vow to weep seas, live in fire, eat rocks, tame tigers; 80 thinking it harder for our mistress to devise imposition enough than for us to undergo any difficulty imposed. This is the monstruosity in love, lady— that the will is infinite and the execution confined; that the desire is boundless and the act a slave to limit.

CRESSIDA. They say all lovers swear more performance than they are able, and yet reserve an ability that they never perform; vowing more than the perfection of ten, and discharging less than the tenth part 90 of one. They that have the voice of lions and the act of hares, are they not monsters?

TROILUS. Are there such? Such are not we. Praise us as we are tasted, allow us as we prove. Our head shall go bare till merit crown it: no perfection in reversion shall have a praise in present. We will not name desert before his birth; and, being born, his addition shall be humble. Few words to fair

faith: Troilus shall be such to Cressid as what envy can say worst shall be a mock for his truth; and 100 what truth can speak truest, not truer than Troilus.

CRESSIDA. Will you walk in, my lord?

Re-enter Pandarus

PANDARUS. What, blushing still? Have you not done talking yet?

CRESSIDA. Well, uncle, what folly I commit, I dedicate to you.

PANDARUS. I thank you for that: if my lord get a boy of you, you'll give him me. Be true to my lord; if he flinch, chide me for it.

TROILUS. You know now your hostages: your uncle's 110 word and my firm faith.

PANDARUS. Nay, I'll give my word for her too. Our kindred, though they be long ere they are wooed, they are constant being won. They are burs, I can tell you; they'll stick where they are thrown.

CRESSIDA. Boldness comes to me now and brings me heart:
Prince Troilus, I have loved you night and day
For many weary months.

TROILUS. Why was my Cressid then so hard to win?

CRESSIDA. Hard to seem won; but I was won,
my lord, 120
With the first glance that ever—pardon me;
If I confess much, you will play the tyrant.
I love you now; but not, till now, so much
But I might master it. In faith, I lie!
My thoughts were like unbridled children, grown
Too headstrong for their mother. See, we fools!
Why have I blabbed? Who shall be true to us,
When we are so unsecret to ourselves?
But, though I loved you well, I wooed you not;
And yet, good faith, I wished myself a man, 130
Or that we women had men's privilege
Of speaking first. Sweet, bid me hold my tongue;
For in this rapture I shall surely speak
The thing I shall repent. See, see, your silence,
Cunning in dumbness, from my weakness draws
My very soul of counsel! Stop my mouth.

TROILUS. And shall, albeit sweet music issues thence.
Kisses her

PANDARUS. Pretty, i'faith.

CRESSIDA. My lord, I do beseech you, pardon me:
'Twas not my purpose thus to beg a kiss: 140
I am ashamed. O heavens! what have I done?
For this time will I take my leave, my lord.

TROILUS. Your leave, sweet Cressid?

PANDARUS. Leave! An you take leave till tomorrow morning—

CRESSIDA. Pray you, content you.

TROILUS. What offends you, lady?

CRESSIDA. Sir, mine own company.

TROILUS. You cannot shun yourself.

CRESSIDA. Let me go and try. 150
I have a kind of self resides with you,
But an unkind self that itself will leave
To be another's fool. I would be gone.
Where is my wit? I know not what I speak.

TROILUS. Well know they what they speak that speak so wisely.

CRESSIDA. Perchance, my lord, I show more craft than love,
And fell so roundly to a large confession

To angle for your thoughts; but you are wise,
Or else you love not: for to be wise and love
Exceeds man's might; that dwells with gods above. 160
TROILUS. O that I thought it could be in a woman—
As, if it can, I will presume in you—
To feed for aye her lamp and flame of love;
To keep her constancy in plight and youth,
Outliving beauties outward, with a mind
That doth renew swifter than blood decays!
Or that persuasion could but thus convince me
That my integrity and truth to you
Might be affronted with the match and weight
Of such a winnowed purity in one— 170
How were I then uplifted! But, alas,
I am as true as truth's simplicity,
And simpler than the infancy of truth!
CRESSIDA. In that I'll war with you.
TROILUS.   O virtuous fight,
When right with right wars who shall be most right!
True swains in love shall in the world to come
Approve their truths by Troilus. When their
  rhymes,
Full of protest, of oath, and big compare,
Want similes, truth tired with iteration—
'As true as steel, as plantage to the moon, 180
As sun to day, as turtle to her mate,
As iron to adamant, as earth to th'centre'—
Yet, after all comparisons of truth,
As truth's authentic author to be cited,
'As true as Troilus' shall crown up the verse
And sanctify the numbers.
CRESSIDA.   Prophet may you be!
If I be false, or swerve a hair from truth,
When time is old and hath forgot itself,
When waterdrops have worn the stones of Troy,
And blind oblivion swallowed cities up, 190
And mighty states characterless are grated
To dusty nothing, yet let memory,
From false to false, among false maids in love,
Upbraid my falsehood! When they've said 'as false
As air, as water, wind or sandy earth,
As fox to lamb, or wolf to heifer's calf,
Pard to the hind, or stepdame to her son',
Yea let them say, to stick the heart of falsehood,
'As false as Cressid'.
PANDARUS. Go to, a bargain made. Seal it, seal it. 200
I'll be the witness. Here I hold your hand; here my
cousin's. If ever you prove false one to another,
since I have taken such pains to bring you together,
let all pitiful goers-between be called to the world's
end after my name—call them all Pandars: let all
constant men be Troiluses, all false women Cressids,
and all brokers-between Pandars! Say 'amen'.
TROILUS. Amen.
CRESSIDA. Amen.
PANDARUS. Amen. Whereupon I will show you a 210
chamber with a bed; which bed, because it shall not
speak of your pretty encounters, press it to death.
Away!   *They go*
And Cupid grant all tongue-tied maidens here
Bed, chamber, pandar, to provide this gear! *Goes*

Scene 3: *The Greek camp*

*Flourish. Enter Agamemnon, Ulysses, Diomedes, Nestor,
Ajax, Menelaus, and Calchas*

CALCHAS. Now, princes, for the service I have done,
Th'advantage of the time prompts me aloud
To call for recompense. Appear it to your minds
That, through the sight I bear in things to come,
I have abandoned Troy, left my possession,
Incurred a traitor's name, exposed myself,
From certain and possessed conveniences,
To doubtful fortunes; sequestering from me all
That time, acquaintance, custom and condition
Made tame and most familiar to my nature; 10
And here, to do you service, am become
As new into the world, strange, unacquainted.
I do beseech you, as in way of taste,
To give me now a little benefit
Out of those many registered in promise,
Which, you say, live to come in my behalf.
AGAMEMNON. What wouldst thou of us, Trojan?
  Make demand.
CALCHAS. You have a Trojan prisoner
  called Antenor,
Yesterday took; Troy holds him very dear.
Oft have you—often have you thanks therefore— 20
Desired my Cressid in right great exchange,
Whom Troy hath still denied; but this Antenor
I know is such a wrest in their affairs,
That their negotiations all must slack,
Wanting his manage; and they will almost
Give us a prince of blood, a son of Priam,
In change of him. Let him be sent, great princes,
And he shall buy my daughter; and her presence
Shall quite strike off all service I have done
In most accepted pain.
AGAMEMNON.   Let Diomed bear him, 30
And bring us Cressid hither; Calchas shall have
What he requests of us. Good Diomed,
Furnish you fairly for this interchange;
Withal, bring word if Hector will tomorrow
Be answered in his challenge: Ajax is ready.
DIOMEDES. This shall I undertake, and 'tis a burden
Which I am proud to bear.
                       Diomedes and Calchas go

Enter Achilles and Patroclus, before their tent

ULYSSES. Achilles stands i'th'entrance of his tent:
Please it our general pass strangely by him,
As if he were forgot; and, princes all, 40
Lay negligent and loose regard upon him.
I will come last. 'Tis like he'll question me
Why such unplausive eyes are bent on him.
If so, I have derision medicinable
To use between your strangeness and his pride,
Which his own will shall have desire to drink.
It may do good: pride hath no other glass
To show itself but pride; for supple knees
Feed arrogance and are the proud man's fees.
AGAMEMNON. We'll execute your purpose and put on 50
A form of strangeness as we pass along;
So do each lord, and either greet him not
Or else disdainfully, which shall shake him more
Than if not looked on. I will lead the way.
                                          They go
ACHILLES. What, comes the general to speak with me?
You know my mind: I'll fight no more 'gainst Troy.
AGAMEMNON. What says Achilles? Would he aught
  with us?
NESTOR. Would you, my lord, aught with the general?

ACHILLES. No.

NESTOR. Nothing, my lord. 60

AGAMEMNON. The better. *Agamemnon and Nestor go*

ACHILLES. Good day, good day.

MENELAUS. How do you? how do you? *Goes*

ACHILLES. What, does the cuckold scorn me?

AJAX. How now, Patroclus!

ACHILLES. Good morrow, Ajax.

AJAX. Ha?

ACHILLES. Good morrow.

AJAX. Ay, and good next day too. *Goes*

ACHILLES. What mean these fellows? Know they
  not Achilles? 70

PATROCLUS. They pass by strangely. They were used
  to bend,
To send their smiles before them to Achilles,
To come as humbly as they use to creep
To holy altars.

ACHILLES.   What, am I poor of late?
'Tis certain, greatness, once fallen out with fortune,
Must fall out with men too. What the declined is
He shall as soon read in the eyes of others
As feel in his own fall; for men, like butterflies,
Show not their mealy wings but to the summer,
And not a man, for being simply man, 80
Hath any honour but honour for those honours
That are without him—as place, riches, and favour,
Prizes of accident as oft as merit;
Which, when they fall, as being slippery standers,
The love that leaned on them as slippery too,
Doth one pluck down another and together
Die in the fall. But 'tis not so with me:
Fortune and I are friends; I do enjoy
At ample point all that I did possess,
Save these men's looks; who do, methinks, find out 90
Something not worth in me such rich beholding
As they have often given. Here is Ulysses;
I'll interrupt his reading.
How now, Ulysses!

ULYSSES.   Now, great Thetis' son!

ACHILLES. What are you reading?

ULYSSES.   A strange fellow here
Writes me that man, how dearly ever parted,
How much in having, or without or in,
Cannot make boast to have that which he hath,
Nor feels not what he owes, but by reflection;
As when his virtues, shining upon others, 100
Heat them and they retort that heat again
To the first giver.

ACHILLES.   This is not strange, Ulysses.
The beauty that is borne here in the face
The bearer knows not, but commends itself
To others' eyes; nor doth the eye itself,
That most pure spirit of sense, behold itself,
Not going from itself; but eye to eye opposed
Salutes each other with each other's form:
For speculation turns not to itself
Till it hath travelled and is mirrored there 110
Where it may see itself. This is not strange at all.

ULYSSES. I do not strain at the position—
It is familiar—but at the author's drift;
Who in his circumstance expressly proves
That no man is the lord of anything,
Though in and of him there be much consisting,
Till he communicate his parts to others;
Nor doth he of himself know them for aught

Till he behold them forméd in th'applause
Where they're extended; who, like an
  arch, reverberate 120
The voice again; or, like a gate of steel
Fronting the sun, receives and renders back
His figure and his heat. I was much rapt in this,
And apprehended here immediately
The unknown Ajax.
Heavens! what a man is there! a very horse,
That has he knows not what. Nature, what things
  there are
Most abject in regard and dear in use!
What things again most dear in the esteem
And poor in worth! Now shall we see tomorrow— 130
An act that very chance doth throw upon him—
Ajax renowned. O heavens, what some men do,
While some men leave to do!
How some men creep in skittish Fortune's hall,
While others play the idiots in her eyes!
How one man eats into another's pride,
While pride is fasting in his wantonness!
To see these Grecian lords!—why, even already
They clap the lubber Ajax on the shoulder,
As if his foot were on brave Hector's breast 140
And great Troy shrinking.

ACHILLES. I do believe it; for they passed by me
As misers do by beggars, neither gave to me
Good word nor look. What, are my deeds forgot?

ULYSSES. Time hath, my lord, a wallet at his back
Wherein he puts alms for oblivion,
A great-sized monster of ingratitude.
Those scraps are good deeds past, which are
  devoured
As fast as they are made, forgot as soon
As done. Perseverance, dear my lord, 150
Keeps honour bright: to have done, is to hang
Quite out of fashion, like a rusty mail
In monumental mockery. Take the instant way;
For honour travels in a strait so narrow
Where one but goes abreast. Keep then the path;
For emulation hath a thousand sons
That one by one pursue. If you give way,
Or hedge aside from the direct forthright,
Like to an entered tide they all rush by
And leave you hindmost; 160
Or, like a gallant horse fallen in first rank,
Lie there for pavement to the abject rear,
O'er-run and trampled on. Then what they do
  in present,
Though less than yours in past, must o'ertop yours;
For Time is like a fashionable host
That slightly shakes his parting guest by th'hand
And, with his arms outstretched as he would fly,
Grasps in the comer: welcome ever smiles,
And farewell goes out sighing. O, let not virtue seek
Remuneration for the thing it was; 170
For beauty, wit,
High birth, vigour of bone, desert in service,
Love, friendship, charity, are subject all
To envious and calumniating Time.
One touch of nature makes the whole world kin,
That all with one consent praise new-born gawds,
Though they are made and moulded of things past,
And give to dust that is a little gilt
More laud than gilt o'er-dusted.
The present eye praises the present object: 180

Then marvel not, thou great and complete man,
That all the Greeks begin to worship Ajax;
Since things in motion sooner catch the eye
Than what not stirs. The cry went once on thee,
And still it might, and yet it may again,
If thou wouldst not entomb thyself alive
And case thy reputation in thy tent,
Whose glorious deeds but in these fields of late
Made emulous missions 'mongst the gods
   themselves,
And drave great Mars to faction.
ACHILLES.   Of this my privacy 190
  I have strong reasons.
ULYSSES.   But 'gainst your privacy
  The reasons are more potent and heroical.
  'Tis known, Achilles, that you are in love
  With one of Priam's daughters.
ACHILLES.   Ha! known?
ULYSSES. Is that a wonder?
  The providence that's in a watchful state
  Knows almost every grain of Pluto's gold,
  Finds bottom in th'uncomprehensive deeps,
  Keeps place with thought and almost like the gods
  Does thoughts unveil in their dumb cradles. 200
  There is a mystery, with whom relation
  Durst never meddle, in the soul of state,
  Which hath an operation more divine
  Than breath or pen give expressure to.
  All the commerce that you have had with Troy
  As perfectly is ours as yours, my lord;
  And better would it fit Achilles much
  To throw down Hector than Polyxena.
  But it must grieve young Pyrrhus now at home,
  When fame shall in our islands sound her trump, 210
  And all the Greekish girls shall tripping sing
  'Great Hector's sister did Achilles win,
  But our great Ajax bravely beat down him'.
  Farewell, my lord. I as your lover speak:
  The fool slides o'er the ice that you should break.
                            Goes
PATROCLUS. To this effect, Achilles, have I
  moved you.
  A woman impudent and mannish grown
  Is not more loathed than an effeminate man
  In time of action. I stand condemned for this:
  They think my little stomach to the war 220
  And your great love to me restrains you thus.
  Sweet, rouse yourself, and the weak wanton Cupid
  Shall from your neck unloose his amorous fold
  And, like a dew-drop from the lion's mane,
  Be shook to air.
ACHILLES.   Shall Ajax fight with Hector?
PATROCLUS. Ay, and perhaps receive much honour
  by him.
ACHILLES. I see my reputation is at stake;
  My fame is shrewdly gored.
PATROCLUS.   O, then, beware:
  Those wounds heal ill that men do give themselves:
  Omission to do what is necessary 230
  Seals a commission to a blank of danger;
  And danger, like an ague, subtly taints
  Even then when we sit idly in the sun.
ACHILLES. Go call Thersites hither, sweet Patroclus;
  I'll send the fool to Ajax and desire him
  T'invite the Trojan lords after the combat
  To see us here unarmed. I have a woman's longing,

An appetite that I am sick withal,
To see great Hector in his weeds of peace,
To talk with him, and to behold his visage, 240
Even to my full of view.

Enter Thersites

                    A labour saved!
THERSITES. A wonder!
ACHILLES. What?
THERSITES. Ajax goes up and down the field, asking
  for himself.
ACHILLES. How so?
THERSITES. He must fight singly tomorrow with
  Hector, and is so prophetically proud of an heroical
  cudgelling that he raves in saying nothing.
ACHILLES. How can that be? 250
THERSITES. Why, 'a stalks up and down like a peacock—a stride and a stand; ruminates like an hostess
  that hath no arithmetic but her brain to set down her
  reckoning; bites his lip with a politic regard, as who
  should say 'There were wit in this head, an 'twould
  out'—and so there is; but it lies as coldly in him as
  fire in a flint, which will not show without knocking. The man's undone for ever, for if Hector break
  not his neck i'th' combat, he'll break't himself in
  vainglory. He knows not me. I said 'Good morrow, 260
  Ajax', and he replies 'Thanks, Agamemnon'. What
  think you of this man, that takes me for the general?
  He's grown a very landfish, languageless, a monster.
  A plague of opinion!—a man may wear it on both
  sides, like a leather jerkin.
ACHILLES. Thou must be my ambassador to him,
  Thersites.
THERSITES. Who, I? Why, he'll answer nobody. He
  professes not answering. Speaking is for beggars; he
  wears his tongue in's arms. I will put on his presence. 270
  Let Patroclus make demands to me, you shall see the
  pageant of Ajax.
ACHILLES. To him, Patroclus. Tell him I humbly
  desire the valiant Ajax to invite the most valorous
  Hector to come unarmed to my tent, and to procure
  safe-conduct for his person of the magnanimous
  and most illustrious six-or-seven-times honoured
  captain-general of the Grecian army, Agamemnon,
  et cetera. Do this.
PATROCLUS. Jove bless great Ajax! 280
THERSITES. Hum!
PATROCLUS. I come from the worthy Achilles—
THERSITES. Ha!
PATROCLUS. Who most humbly desires you to invite
  Hector to his tent—
THERSITES. Hum!
PATROCLUS. And to procure safe-conduct from
  Agamemnon.
THERSITES. Agamemnon?
PATROCLUS. Ay, my lord. 290
THERSITES. Ha!
PATROCLUS. What say you to't?
THERSITES. God bu'y you, with all my heart.
PATROCLUS. Your answer, sir.
THERSITES. If tomorrow be a fair day, by eleven
  o'clock it will go one way or other. Howsoever, he
  shall pay for me ere he has me.
PATROCLUS. Your answer, sir.
THERSITES. Fare you well, with all my heart.
ACHILLES. Why, but he is not in this tune, is he? 300

THERSITES. No, but he's out o' tune thus. What music will be in him when Hector has knocked out his brains, I know not; but, I am sure, none, unless the fiddler Apollo gets his sinews to make catlings on.

ACHILLES. Come, thou shalt bear a letter to him straight.

THERSITES. Let me carry another to his horse; for that's the more capable creature.

ACHILLES. My mind is troubled like a fountain stirred, And I myself see not the bottom of it. 310

Achilles and Patroclus go in

THERSITES. Would the fountain of your mind were clear again, that I might water an ass at it! I had rather be a tick in a sheep than such a valiant ingorance. *Goes*

ACT 4
Scene 1: *Troy. A street*

Enter, at one side, Æneas, and Servant with a torch; at the other, Paris, Deiphobus, Antenor, Diomedes, and others, with torches

PARIS. See, ho! who is that there?

DEIPHOBUS. It is the Lord Æneas.

ÆNEAS. Is the prince there in person?
Had I so good occasion to lie long
As you, Prince Paris, nothing but heavenly business
Should rob my bed-mate of my company.

DIOMEDES. That's my mind too. Good morrow,
Lord Æneas.

PARIS. A valiant Greek, Æneas—take his hand—
Witness the process of your speech, wherein
You told you Diomed, a whole week by days, 10
Did haunt you in the field.

ÆNEAS. Health to you, valiant sir,
During all question of the gentle truce;
But when I meet you armed, as black defiance
As heart can think or courage execute.

DIOMEDES. The one and other Diomed embraces
Our bloods are now in calm; and so long, health!
But when contention and occasion meet,
By Jove, I'll play the hunter for thy life
With all my force, pursuit, and policy. 20

ÆNEAS. And thou shalt hunt a lion, that will fly
With his face backward. In humane gentleness,
Welcome to Troy! now, by Anchises' life,
Welcome indeed! By Venus' hand I swear
No man alive can love in such a sort
The thing he means to kill more excellently.

DIOMEDES. We sympathise. Jove, let Æneas live,
If to my sword his fate be not the glory,
A thousand complete courses of the sun!
But, in mine emulous honour, let him die 30
With every joint a wound, and that tomorrow.

ÆNEAS. We know each other well.

DIOMEDES. We do; and long to know each other
worse.

PARIS. This is the most despiteful-gentle greeting,
The noblest-hateful love, that e'er I heard of.
What business, lord, so early?

ÆNEAS. I was sent for to the king; but why,
I know not.

PARIS. His purpose meets you: 'twas to bring this
Greek
To Calchas' house, and there to render him,

For the enfreed Antenor, the fair Cressid. 40
Let's have your company, or, if you please,
Haste there before us. I constantly do think—
Or rather, call my thought a certain knowledge—
My brother Troilus lodges there tonight;
Rouse him and give him note of our approach,
With the whole quality wherefore; I fear
We shall be much unwelcome.

ÆNEAS. That I assure you,
Troilus had rather Troy were borne to Greece
Than Cressid borne from Troy.

PARIS. There is no help;
The bitter disposition of the time 50
Will have it so. On, lord; we'll follow you.

ÆNEAS. Good morrow all. *Goes, with Servant*

PARIS. And tell me, noble Diomed, faith, tell me true,
Even in the soul of sound good-fellowship,
Who, in your thoughts, merits fair Helen most,
Myself or Menelaus?

DIOMEDES. Both alike:
He merits well to have her that doth seek her,
Not making any scruple of her soilure,
With such a hell of pain and world of charge;
And you as well to keep her that defend her, 60
Not palating the taste of her dishonour,
With such a costly loss of wealth and friends,
He, like a puling cuckold, would drink up
The lees and dregs of a flat taméd piece;
You, like a lecher, out of whorish loins
Are pleased to breed out your inheritors.
Both merits poised, each weighs nor less nor more;
But he as he, the heavier for a whore.

PARIS. You are too bitter to your countrywoman.

DIOMEDES. She's bitter to her country. Hear me, Paris: 70
For every false drop in her bawdy veins
A Grecian's life hath sunk; for every scruple
Of her contaminated carrion weight
A Trojan hath been slain; since she could speak,
She hath not given so many good words breath
As for her Greeks and Trojans suffered death.

PARIS. Fair Diomed, you do as chapmen do,
Dispraise the thing that you desire to buy;
But we in silence hold this virtue well,
We'll but commend what we intend to sell. 80
Here lies our way. *They go*

Scene 2: *The same. The court of Pandarus' house*

Enter Troilus and Cressida

TROILUS. Dear, trouble not yourself; the morn is cold.

CRESSIDA. Then, sweet my lord, I'll call mine
uncle down;
He shall unbolt the gates.

TROILUS. Trouble him not;
To bed, to bed! sleep lull those pretty eyes,
And give as soft attachment to thy senses
As infants empty of all thought!

CRESSIDA. Good morrow, then.

TROILUS. I prithee now, to bed!

CRESSIDA. Are you aweary of me?

TROILUS. O Cressida! but that the busy day,
Waked by the lark, hath roused the ribald crows,
And dreaming night will hide our joys no longer, 10
I would not from thee.

CRESSIDA. Night hath been too brief.

TROILUS. Beshrew the witch! with venomous wights
    she stays
  As tediously as hell, but flies the grasps of love
  With wings more momentary-swift than thought.
  You will catch cold, and curse me.

CRESSIDA.   Prithee, tarry.
  You men will never tarry.
  O foolish Cressid! I might have still held off,
  And then you would have tarried. Hark! there's
  one up.

PANDARUS [within]. What's all the doors open here?

TROILUS. It is your uncle.   20

CRESSIDA. A pestilence on him! now will he
  be mocking;
  I shall have such a life!

Enter Pandarus

PANDARUS. How now, how now! how go maiden-
  heads? Here, you maid! where's my cousin Cressid?

CRESSIDA. Go hang yourself, you naughty
  mocking uncle!
  You bring me to do—and then you flout me too.

PANDARUS. To do what? to do what? let her say what!
  What have I brought you to do?

CRESSIDA. Come, come, beshrew your heart! you'll
  ne'er be good,
  Nor suffer others.   30

PANDARUS. Ha, ha! Alas, poor wretch! a poor
  capocchia! Has't not slept tonight? Would he not,
  a naughty man, let it sleep? A bugbear take him!

CRESSIDA. Did not I tell you? Would he were
  knocked i'th' head!   *Knocking*
  Who's that at door? Good uncle, go and see.
  My lord, come you again into my chamber.
  You smile and mock me, as if I meant naughtily.

TROILUS. Ha, ha!

CRESSIDA. Come, you're deceived, I think of no
  such thing.   *Knocking*
  How earnestly they knock! Pray you, come in;   40
  I would not for half Troy have you seen here.

            Troilus and Cressida go

PANDARUS. Who's there? what's the matter? will you
  beat down the door? How now! what's the matter?

Enter Æneas

ÆNEAS. Good morrow, lord, good morrow.

PANDARUS. Who's there? my Lord Æneas! By my
  troth, I knew you not. What news with you so
  early?

ÆNEAS. Is not prince Troilus here?

PANDARUS. Here! what should he do here?

ÆNEAS. Come, he is here, my lord. Do not deny him; 50
  It doth import him much to speak with me.

PANDARUS. Is he here, say you? 'Tis more than I know,
  I'll be sworn; for my own part, I came in late. What
  should he do here?

ÆNEAS. Ho! nay, then; come, come, you'll do him
  wrong ere you're ware; you'll be so true to him,
  to be false to him. Do not you know of him, but
  yet go fetch him hither; go.

Re-enter Troilus

TROILUS. How now! what's the matter?

ÆNEAS. My lord, I scarce have leisure to salute you,   60
  My matter is so rash: there is at hand
  Paris your brother and Deiphobus,

The Grecian Diomed, and our Antenor
Delivered to us; and for him forthwith,
Ere the first sacrifice, within this hour,
We must give up to Diomedes' hand
The Lady Cressida.

TROILUS.   Is it so concluded?

ÆNEAS. By Priam and the general state of Troy.
  They are at hand and ready to effect it.

TROILUS. How my achievements mock me!   70
  I will go meet them; and, my Lord Æneas,
  We met by chance: you did not find me here.

ÆNEAS. Good, good, my lord; the secrets of
  neighbour Pandar
  Have not more gift in taciturnity.

           Troilus and Æneas go

PANDARUS. Is't possible? no sooner got but lost? The
  devil take Antenor! The young prince will go mad.
  A plague upon Antenor! I would they had broke's
  neck!

Re-enter Cressida

CRESSIDA. How now! what's the matter? who was
  here?   80

PANDARUS. Ah, ah!

CRESSIDA. Why sigh you so profoundly? Where's my
  lord? Gone? Tell me, sweet uncle, what's the matter?

PANDARUS. Would I were as deep under the earth as
  I am above!

CRESSIDA. O the gods! What's the matter?

PANDARUS. Prithee, get thee in. Would thou hadst
  ne'er been born! I knew thou wouldst be his death.
  O, poor gentleman! A plague upon Antenor!

CRESSIDA. Good uncle, I beseech you, on my knees 90
  I beseech you, what's the matter?

PANDARUS. Thou must be gone, wench, thou must be
  gone; thou art changed for Antenor; thou must to
  thy father, and be gone from Troilus: 'twill be his
  death; 'twill be his bane; he cannot bear it.

CRESSIDA. O you immortal gods! I will not go.

PANDARUS. Thou must.

CRESSIDA. I will not, uncle. I have forgot my father;
  I know no touch of consanguinity;
  No kin, no love, no blood, no soul so near me   100
  As the sweet Troilus. O you gods divine!
  Make Cressid's name the very crown of falsehood,
  If ever she leave Troilus! Time, force, and death,
  Do to this body what extremes you can;
  But the strong base and building of my love
  Is as the very centre of the earth,
  Drawing all things to it. I'll go in and weep

PANDARUS. Do, do.

CRESSIDA. Tear my bright hair and scratch my
  praisèd cheeks,
  Crack my clear voice with sobs and break my heart 110
  With sounding Troilus. I will not go from Troy.

            They go

Scene 3: *The same. A street before Pandarus' house*

*Enter Paris, Troilus, followed by Æneas, Deiphobus,
Antenor, and Diomedes*

PARIS. It is great morning, and the hour prefixed
  For her delivery to this valiant Greek
  Comes fast upon us. Good my brother Troilus,
  Tell you the lady what she is to do
  And haste her to the purpose.

TROILUS.   Walk into her house;
I'll bring her to the Grecian presently;
And to his hand when I deliver her,
Think it an altar, and thy brother Troilus
A priest, there offering to it his own heart.   *Goes*
PARIS. I know what 'tis to love,   10
And would, as I shall pity, I could help!
Please you walk in, my lords.   *They go*

       Scene 4: *The same. Pandarus' house*

Enter Pandarus and Cressida

PANDARUS. Be moderate, be moderate.
CRESSIDA. Why tell you me of moderation?
The grief is fine, full, perfect, that I taste,
And violenteth in a sense as strong
As that which causeth it. How can I moderate it?
If I could temporise with my affection,
Or brew it to a weak and colder palate,
The like allayment could I give my grief.
My love admits no qualifying dross;
No more my grief, in such a precious loss.   10

Enter Troilus

PANDARUS. Here, here, here he comes. Ah sweet
ducks!
CRESSIDA. O Troilus! Troilus!   *Embracing him*
PANDARUS. What a pair of spectacles is here! Let me
embrace too. 'O heart,' as the goodly saying is,
     O heart, O heavy heart,
     Why sigh'st thou without breaking?
where he answers again,
     Because thou canst not ease thy smart
     By friendship nor by speaking.   20
There was never a truer rhyme. Let us cast away
nothing, for we may live to have need of such a
verse. We see it, we see it. How now, lambs!
TROILUS. Cressid, I love thee in so strained a purity,
That the blest gods, as angry with my fancy,
More bright in zeal than the devotion which
Cold lips blow to their deities, take thee from me.
CRESSIDA. Have the gods envy?
PANDARUS. Ay, ay, ay, ay; 'tis too plain a case.
CRESSIDA. And is it true that I must go from Troy?   30
TROILUS. A hateful truth.
CRESSIDA.   What, and from Troilus too?
TROILUS. From Troy and Troilus.
CRESSIDA.   Is it possible?
TROILUS. And suddenly; where injury of chance
Puts back leave-taking, jostles roughly by
All time of pause, rudely beguiles our lips
Of all rejoindure, forcibly prevents
Our locked embraces, strangles our dear vows
Even in the birth of our own labouring breath.
We two, that with so many thousand sighs
Did buy each other, must poorly sell ourselves   40
With the rude brevity and discharge of one.
Injurious Time now with a robber's haste
Crams his rich thievery up, he knows not how:
As many farewells as be stars in heaven,
With distinct breath and consigned kisses to them,
He fumbles up into a loose adieu,
And scants us with a single famished kiss,
Distasted with the salt of broken tears.
ÆNEAS [*within*]. My lord, is the lady ready?
TROILUS. Hark! you are called. Some say the Genius so   50

Cries 'Come!' to him that instantly must die.
Bid them have patience; she shall come anon.
PANDARUS. Where are my tears? Rain, to lay this
wind, or my heart will be blown up by th'root!
                              Goes
CRESSIDA. I must then to the Grecians?
TROILUS.   No remedy.
CRESSIDA. A woeful Cressid 'mongst the merry
Greeks!
When shall we see again?
TROILUS. Hear me, my love: be thou but true
of heart—
CRESSIDA. I true! how now! what wicked deem
is this?
TROILUS. Nay, we must use expostulation kindly,   60
For it is parting from us.
I speak not 'be thou true', as fearing thee,
For I will throw my glove to Death himself
That there's no maculation in thy heart;
But 'be thou true' say I, to fashion in
My sequent protestation: be thou true,
And I will see thee.
CRESSIDA. O, you shall be exposed, my lord, to
dangers
As infinite as imminent! But I'll be true.
TROILUS. And I'll grow friend with danger. Wear
this sleeve.   70
CRESSIDA. And you this glove. When shall I see you?
TROILUS. I will corrupt the Grecian sentinels,
To give thee nightly visitation.
But yet, be true.
CRESSIDA.   O heavens! 'Be true' again!
TROILUS. Hear why I speak it, love:
The Grecian youths are full of quality;
Their loving well composed with gifts of nature,
And flowing e'er with arts and exercise.
How novelties may move and parts with person—
Alas, a kind of godly jealousy,   80
Which, I beseech you, call a virtuous sin—
Makes me afeard.
CRESSIDA.   O heavens! you love me not.
TROILUS. Die I a villain then!
In this I do not call your faith in question
So mainly as my merit: I cannot sing,
Nor heel the high lavolt, nor sweeten talk,
Nor play at subtle games—fair virtues all,
To which the Grecians are most prompt and
pregnant;
But I can tell that in each grace of these
There lurks a still and dumb-discoursive devil   90
That tempts most cunningly. But be not tempted.
CRESSIDA. Do you think I will?
TROILUS. No;
But something may be done that we will not,
And sometimes we are devils to ourselves,
When we will tempt the frailty of our powers,
Presuming on their changeful potency.
ÆNEAS [*within*]. Nay, good my lord!
TROILUS.   Come, kiss; and let us part.
PARIS [*within*]. Brother Troilus!
TROILUS.   Good brother, come
you hither;
And bring Æneas and the Grecian with you.   100
CRESSIDA. My lord, will you be true?
TROILUS. Who, I? alas, it is my vice, my fault!
Whiles others fish with craft for great opinion,

I with great truth catch mere simplicity;
Whilst some with cunning gild their copper crowns,
With truth and plainness I do wear mine bare.
Fear not my truth: the moral of my wit
Is 'plain and true'; there's all the reach of it.

Enter Æneas, Paris, Antenor, Deiphobus, and Diomedes

Welcome, Sir Diomed! Here is the lady
Which for Antenor we deliver you.   110
At the port, lord, I'll give her to thy hand,
And by the way possess thee what she is.
Entreat her fair; and, by my soul, fair Greek,
If e'er thou stand at mercy of my sword,
Name Cressid, and thy life shall be as safe
As Priam is in Ilion.
DIOMEDES.   Fair Lady Cressid,
So please you, save the thanks this prince expects.
The lustre in your eye, heaven in your cheek,
Pleads your fair usage; and to Diomed
You shall be mistress, and command him wholly.   120
TROILUS. Grecian, thou dost not use me courteously,
To shame the zeal of my petition to thee
In praising her. I tell thee, lord of Greece,
She is as far high-soaring o'er thy praises
As thou unworthy to be called her servant.
I charge thee use her well, even for my charge;
For, by the dreadful Pluto, if thou dost not,
Though the great bulk Achilles be thy guard,
I'll cut thy throat.
DIOMEDES.   O, be not moved, Prince Troilus.
Let me be privileged by my place and message   130
To be a speaker free. When I am hence,
I'll answer to my lust; and know you, lord,
I'll nothing do on charge: to her own worth
She shall be prized; but that you say 'Be't so',
I'll speak it in my spirit and honour 'No!'
TROILUS. Come, to the port. I'll tell thee, Diomed,
This brave shall oft make thee to hide thy head.
Lady, give me your hand; and, as we walk,
To our own selves bend we our needful talk.
                Troilus, Cressida, and Diomedes go;
                              trumpet sounds
PARIS. Hark! Hector's trumpet.
ÆNEAS.   How have we spent
    this morning!   140
The prince must think me tardy and remiss,
That swore to ride before him to the field.
PARIS. 'Tis Troilus' fault; come, come, to field
    with him.
DEIPHOBUS. Let us make ready straight.
ÆNEAS. Yea, with a bridegroom's fresh alacrity,
Let us address to tend on Hector's heels.
The glory of our Troy doth this day lie
On his fair worth and single chivalry.   *They go*

Scene 5: *The Greek camp. Lists set out*

*Enter Ajax, armed; Agamemnon, Achilles, Patroclus,
Menelaus, Ulysses, Nestor, and others*

AGAMEMNON. Here art thou in appointment fresh
    and fair,
Anticipating time with starting courage.
Give with thy trumpet a loud note to Troy,
Thou dreadful Ajax, that the appalled air
May pierce the head of the great combatant
And hale him hither.

AJAX.   Thou trumpet, there's my purse.
Now crack thy lungs, and split thy brazen pipe;
Blow, villain, till thy spheréd bias cheek
Outswell the choller of puffed Aquilon.
Come, stretch thy chest, and let thy eyes spout
    blood;   10
Thou blow'st for Hector.   *Trumpet sounds*
ULYSSES. No trumpet answers.
ACHILLES.   'Tis but early days.
AGAMEMNON. Is not yon Diomed, with
    Calchas' daughter?
ULYSSES. 'Tis he, I ken the manner of his gait:
He rises on the toe; that spirit of his
In aspiration lifts him from the earth.

Enter Diomedes, with Cressida

AGAMEMNON. Is this the Lady Cressid?
DIOMEDES.   Even she.
AGAMEMNON. Most dearly welcome to the Greeks,
    sweet lady.   *Kisses her*
NESTOR. Our general doth salute you with a kiss.
ULYSSES. Yet is the kindness but particular;   20
'Twere better she were kissed in general.
NESTOR. And very courtly counsel. I'll begin.
So much for Nestor.   *Kisses her*
ACHILLES. I'll take that winter from your lips, fair lady.
Achilles bids you welcome.   *Kisses her*
MENELAUS. I had good argument for kissing once.
PATROCLUS. But that's no argument for kissing now;
For thus popped Paris in his hardiment,
And parted thus you and your argument.
                                          Kisses her
ULYSSES. O deadly gall, and theme of all our scorns! 30
For which we lose our heads to gild his horns.
PATROCLUS. The first was Menelaus' kiss; this, mine—
Patroclus kisses you.   *Kisses her again*
MENELAUS.   O, this is trim!
PATROCLUS. Paris and I kiss evermore for him.
MENELAUS. I'll have my kiss, sir. Lady, by your leave.
CRESSIDA. In kissing, do you render or receive?
MENELAUS. Both take and give.
CRESSIDA.   I'll make my match
    to live,
The kiss you take is better than you give;
Therefore no kiss.
MENELAUS. I'll give you boot, I'll give you three
    for one.   40
CRESSIDA. You're an odd man; give even, or
    give none.
MENELAUS. An odd man, lady! every man is odd.
CRESSIDA. No, Paris is not; for you know 'tis true
That you are odd, and he is even with you.
MENELAUS. You fillip me o'th' head.
CRESSIDA.   No, I'll be sworn.
ULYSSES. It were no match, your nail against his horn.
May I, sweet lady, beg a kiss of you?
CRESSIDA. You may.
ULYSSES.   I do desire it.
CRESSIDA.   Why, beg too.
ULYSSES. Why then, for Venus' sake, give me a kiss
When Helen is a maid again, and his.   50
CRESSIDA. I am your debtor; claim it when 'tis due.
ULYSSES. Never's my day, and then a kiss of you.
DIOMEDES. Lady, a word; I'll bring you to
    your father.   *Goes, with Cressida*
NESTOR. A woman of quick sense.

ULYSSES. Fie, fie upon her!
There's language in her eye, her cheek, her lip,
Nay, her foot speaks; her wanton spirits look out
At every joint and motive of her body.
O, these encounterers, so glib of tongue,
That give accosting welcome ere it comes,
And wide unclasp the tables of their thoughts 60
To every tickling reader!—set them down
For sluttish spoils of opportunity
And daughters of the game. *Trumpet within*
ALL. The Trojans' trumpet.
AGAMEMNON. Yonder comes the troop.

Flourish. Enter Hector, armed; Æneas, Troilus, and other Trojans, with Attendants

ÆNEAS. Hail, all the state of Greece! What shall be done
To him that victory commands? Or do you purpose
A victor shall be known? Will you the knights
Shall to the edge of all extremity
Pursue each other, or shall they be divided
By any voice or order of the field? 70
Hector bade ask.
AGAMEMNON. Which way would Hector have it?
ÆNEAS. He cares not; he'll obey conditions.
AGAMEMNON. 'Tis done like Hector.
ACHILLES. But securely done,
A little proudly, and great deal misprizing
The knight opposed.
ÆNEAS. If not Achilles, sir.
What is your name?
ACHILLES. If not Achilles, nothing.
ÆNEAS. Therefore Achilles. But whate'er, know this:
In the extremity of great and little,
Valour and pride excel themselves in Hector;
The one almost as infinite as all, 80
The other blank as nothing. Weigh him well,
And that which looks like pride is courtesy.
This Ajax is half made of Hector's blood;
In love whereof, half Hector stays at home;
Half heart, half hand, half Hector comes to seek
This blended knight, half Trojan and half Greek.
ACHILLES. A maiden battle then? O, I perceive you.

Re-enter Diomedes

AGAMEMNON. Here is Sir Diomed. Go, gentle knight,
Stand by our Ajax. As you and Lord Æneas
Consent upon the order of their fight, 90
So be it; either to the uttermost,
Or else a breath. The combatants being kin
Half stints their strife before their strokes begin.
Ajax and Hector enter the lists
ULYSSES. They are opposed already.
AGAMEMNON. What Trojan is that same that looks
so heavy?
ULYSSES. The youngest son of Priam, a true knight;
Not yet mature, yet matchless-firm of word;
Speaking in deeds and deedless in his tongue;
Not soon provoked nor, being provoked, soon
calmed;
His heart and hand both open and both free; 100
For what he has he gives, what thinks he shows;
Yet gives he not till judgement guide his bounty,
Nor dignifies an impair thought with breath;
Manly as Hector, but more dangerous;
For Hector in his blaze of wrath subscribes
To tender objects, but he in heat of action

Is more vindicative than jealous love;
They call him Troilus, and on him erect
A second hope, as fairly built as Hector:
Thus says Æneas, one that knows the youth 110
Even to his inches, and with private soul
Did in great Ilion thus translate him to me.
Alarum; Hector and Ajax fight
AGAMEMNON. They are in action.
NESTOR. Now, Ajax, hold thine own!
TROILUS. Hector, thou sleep'st;
Awake thee!
AGAMEMNON. His blows are well disposed.
There, Ajax! *Trumpets cease*
DIOMEDES. You must no more.
ÆNEAS. Princes, enough, so please you.
AJAX. I am not warm yet; let us fight again.
DIOMEDES. As Hector pleases.
HECTOR. Why, then will I no more: 120
Thou art, great lord, my father's sister's son,
A cousin-german to great Priam's seed;
The obligation of our blood forbids
A gory emulation 'twixt us twain.
Were thy commixtion Greek and Trojan so,
That thou couldst say 'This hand is Grecian all,
And this is Trojan; the sinews of this leg
All Greek, and this all Troy; my mother's blood
Runs on the dexter cheek, and this sinister
Bounds in my father's', by Jove multipotent,
Thou shouldst not bear from me a Greekish member 130
Wherein my sword had not impressure made
Of our rank feud; but the just gods gainsay
That any drop thou borrow'dst from thy mother,
My sacred aunt, should by my mortal sword
Be drainéd! Let me embrace thee, Ajax.
By him that thunders, thou hast lusty arms;
Hector would have them fall upon him thus.
Cousin, all honour to thee!
AJAX. I thank thee, Hector.
Thou art too gentle and too free a man.
I came to kill thee, cousin, and bear hence 140
A great addition earnéd in thy death.
HECTOR. Not Neoptolemus so mirable,
On whose bright crest Fame with her loud'st oyez
Cries 'This is he', could promise to himself
A thought of added honour torn from Hector.
ÆNEAS. There is expectance here from both
the sides
What further you will do.
HECTOR. We'll answer it:
The issue is embracement; Ajax, farewell.
AJAX. If I might in entreaties find success,
As seld I have the chance, I would desire 150
My famous cousin to our Grecian tents.
DIOMEDES. 'Tis Agamemnon's wish; and great
Achilles
Doth long to see unarmed the valiant Hector.
HECTOR. Æneas, call my brother Troilus to me,
And signify this loving interview
To the expecters of our Trojan part;
Desire them home. Give me thy hand, my cousin;
I will go eat with thee, and see your knights.
AJAX. Great Agamemnon comes to meet us here.
HECTOR. The worthiest of them tell me name
by name; 160
But for Achilles, my own searching eyes
Shall find him by his large and portly size.

AGAMEMNON. Worthy of arms! as welcome as to one
    That would be rid of such an enemy—
    But that's no welcome; understand more clear,
    What's past and what's to come is strewed with
        husks
    And formless ruin of oblivion;
    But in this extant moment, faith and troth,
    Strained purely from all hollow bias-drawing,
    Bids thee, with most divine integrity,   170
    From heart of very heart, great Hector, welcome.
HECTOR. I thank thee, most imperious Agamemnon.
AGAMEMNON [to Troilus]. My well-famed lord of
    Troy, no less to you.
MENELAUS. Let me confirm my princely brother's
        greeting;
    You brace of warlike brothers, welcome hither.
HECTOR. Who must we answer?
ÆNEAS.   The noble Menelaus.
HECTOR. O, you, my lord! by Mars his gauntlet,
        thanks!
    Mock not that I affect th'untraded oath;
    Your quondam wife swears still by Venus' glove.
    She's well, but bade me not commend her to you.   180
MENELAUS. Name her not now, sir; she's a deadly
        theme.
HECTOR. O, pardon; I offend.
NESTOR. I have, thou gallant Trojan, seen thee oft,
    Labouring for destiny, make cruel way
    Through ranks of Greekish youth; and I have
        seen thee,
    As hot as Perseus, spur thy Phrygian steed,
    And seen thee scorning forfeits and subduements
    When thou hast hung thy advancèd sword i'th'air,
    Not letting it decline on the declined,
    That I have said to some my standers-by   190
    'Lo, Jupiter is yonder, dealing life!'
    And I have seen thee pause and take thy breath
    When that a ring of Greeks have hemmed thee in,
    Like an Olympian wrestling. This have I seen,
    But this thy countenance, still locked in steel,
    I never saw till now. I knew thy grandsire,
    And once fought with him. He was a soldier good;
    But, by great Mars the captain of us all,
    Never like thee. O, let an old man embrace thee;
    And, worthy warrior, welcome to our tents.   200
ÆNEAS. 'Tis the old Nestor.
HECTOR. Let me embrace thee, good old chronicle,
    That hast so long walked hand in hand with time;
    Most reverend Nestor, I am glad to clasp thee.
NESTOR. I would my arms could match thee in
        contention,
    As they contend with thee in courtesy.
HECTOR. I would they could.
NESTOR. Ha!
    By this white beard, I'd fight with thee tomorrow.
    Well, welcome, welcome! I have seen the time.   210
ULYSSES. I wonder now how yonder city stands
    When we have here her base and pillar by us.
HECTOR. I know your favour, Lord Ulysses, well.
    Ah, sir, there's many a Greek and Trojan dead,
    Since first I saw yourself and Diomed
    In Ilion, on your Greekish embassy.
ULYSSES. Sir, I foretold you then what would ensue.
    My prophecy is but half his journey yet;
    For yonder walls, that pertly front your town,
    Yon towers, whose wanton tops do buss the clouds,   220

    Must kiss their own feet.
HECTOR.   I must not believe you.
    There they stand yet; and modestly I think
    The fall of every Phrygian stone will cost
    A drop of Grecian blood. The end crowns all;
    And that old common arbitrator, Time,
    Will one day end it.
ULYSSES.   So to him we leave it.
    Most gentle and most valiant Hector, welcome.
    After the general, I beseech you next
    To feast with me and see me at my tent.
ACHILLES. I shall forestall thee, Lord Ulysses, thou!   230
    Now Hector, I have fed mine eyes on thee;
    I have with exact view perused thee, Hector,
    And quoted joint by joint.
HECTOR.   Is this Achilles?
ACHILLES. I am Achilles.
HECTOR. Stand fair, I pray thee; let me look on thee.
ACHILLES. Behold thy fill.
HECTOR.   Nay, I have done already.
ACHILLES. Thou art too brief. I will the second time,
    As I would buy thee, view thee limb by limb.
HECTOR. O, like a book of sport thou'lt read me o'er;
    But there's more in me than thou understand'st.   240
    Why dost thou so oppress me with thine eye?
ACHILLES. Tell me, you heavens, in which part of
        his body
    Shall I destroy him?—whether there, or there, or
        there?—
    That I may give the local wound a name,
    And make distinct the very breach whereout
    Hector's great spirit flew. Answer me, heavens!
HECTOR. It would discredit the blest gods, proud man,
    To answer such a question. Stand again;
    Think'st thou to catch my life so pleasantly
    As to prenominate in nice conjecture   250
    Where thou wilt hit me dead?
ACHILLES.   I tell thee yea.
HECTOR. Wert thou an oracle to tell me so,
    I'd not believe thee. Henceforth guard thee well;
    For I'll not kill thee there, nor there, nor there;
    But, by the forge that stithied Mars his helm,
    I'll kill thee everywhere, yea, o'er and o'er.
    You wisest Grecians, pardon me this brag:
    His insolence draws folly from my lips;
    But I'll endeavour deeds to match these words,
    Or may I never—
AJAX.   Do not chafe thee, cousin;   260
    And you, Achilles, let these threats alone
    Till accident or purpose bring you to't.
    You may have every day enough of Hector,
    If you have stomach. The general state, I fear,
    Can scarce entreat you to be odd with him.
HECTOR. I pray you, let us see you in the field;
    We have had pelting wars since you refused
    The Grecians' cause.
ACHILLES.   Dost thou entreat me, Hector?
    Tomorrow do I meet thee, fell as death;
    Tonight all friends.
HECTOR.   Thy hand upon that match.   270
AGAMEMNON. First, all you peers of Greece, go to
        my tent;
    There in the full convive we. Afterwards,
    As Hector's leisure and your bounties shall
    Concur together, severally entreat him.
    Beat loud the taborins, let the trumpets blow,

That this great soldier may his welcome know.
    Flourish; all go but Troilus and Ulysses
TROILUS. My Lord Ulysses, tell me, I beseech you,
In what place of the field doth Calchas keep?
ULYSSES. At Menelaus' tent, most princely Troilus.
There Diomed doth feast with him tonight;   280
Who neither looks upon the heaven nor earth,
But gives all gaze and bent of amorous view
On the fair Cressid.
TROILUS. Shall I, sweet lord, be bound to you
   so much,
After we part from Agamemnon's tent,
To bring me thither?
ULYSSES.   You shall command me, sir.
As gentle tell me, of what honour was
This Cressida in Troy? Had she no lover there
That wails her absence?
TROILUS. O, sir, to such as boasting show their scars, 290
A mock is due. Will you walk on, my lord?
She was beloved, she loved; she is, and doth;
But still sweet love is food for fortune's tooth.
           · *They go*

ACT 5
Scene 1: *The same. Before Achilles' tent*

Enter Achilles and Patroclus

ACHILLES. I'll heat his blood with Greekish wine
   tonight,
Which with my scimitar I'll cool tomorrow.
Patroclus, let us feast him to the height.
PATROCLUS. Here comes Thersites.

Enter Thersites

ACHILLES.   How now, thou core of envy!
Thou crusty botch of nature, what's the news?
THERSITES. Why, thou picture of what thou seemest,
   and idol of idiot-worshippers, here's a letter for thee.
ACHILLES. From whence, fragment?
THERSITES. Why, thou full dish of fool, from Troy.
PATROCLUS. Who keeps the tent now?   10
THERSITES. The surgeon's box, or the patient's wound.
PATROCLUS. Well said, adversity! and what need these
   tricks!
THERSITES. Prithee, be silent, boy; I profit not by thy
   talk; thou art thought to be Achilles' male varlet.
PATROCLUS. Male varlet, you rogue! what's that?
THERSITES. Why, his masculine whore. Now, the
   rotten diseases of the south, the guts-griping,
   ruptures, catarrhs, loads o' gravel i'th'back, lethar-
   gics, cold palsies, raw eyes, dirt-rotten livers, wheez- 20
   ing lungs, bladders full of impostume, sciaticas,
   limekilns i'th'palm, incurable bone-ache, and the
   rivelled fee-simple of the tetter, take and take again
   such preposterous discoveries!
PATROCLUS. Why, thou damnable box of envy, thou;
   what mean'st thou to curse thus?
THERSITES. Do I curse thee?
PATROCLUS. Why, no, you ruinous butt; you whoreson indistinguishable cur, no.
THERSITES. No! Why art thou then exasperate, thou 30
   idle immaterial skein of sleave-silk, thou green
   sarsenet flap for a sore eye, thou tassel of a prodigal's
   purse, thou? Ah, how the poor world is pestered
   with such waterflies, diminutives of nature!

PATROCLUS. Out, gall!
THERSITES. Finch-egg!
ACHILLES. My sweet Patroclus, I am thwarted quite
From my great purpose in tomorrow's battle.
Here is a letter from Queen Hecuba,
A token from her daughter, my fair love,   40
Both taxing me and gaging me to keep
An oath that I have sworn. I will not break it:
Fall Greeks; fail fame; honour or go or stay;
My major vow lies here; this I'll obey.
Come, come, Thersites, help to trim my tent;
This night in banqueting must all be spent.
Away Patroclus!   *Achilles and Patroclus go in*
THERSITES. With too much blood and too little brain,
   these two may run mad; but if with too much brain
   and too little blood they do, I'll be a curer of 50
   madmen. Here's Agamemnon, an honest fellow
   enough and one that loves quails, but he has not so
   much brain as earwax; and the goodly transformation of Jupiter there, his brother, the bull, the
   primitive statue and oblique memorial of cuckolds,
   a thrifty shoeing-horn in a chain, hanging at his
   brother's leg—to what form but that he is, should
   wit larded with malice and malice forced with wit
   turn him to? To an ass, were nothing: he is both ass
   and ox; to an ox, were nothing: he is both ox and 60
   ass. To be a dog, a mule, a cat, a fitchew, a toad,
   a lizard, an owl, a puttock, or a herring without a
   roe, I would not care; but to be Menelaus, I would
   conspire against destiny! Ask me not what I would
   be, if I were not Thersites; for I care not to be the
   louse of a lazar, so I were not Menelaus. Hoy-day!
   spirits and fires!

*Enter Hector, Troilus, Ajax, Agamemnon, Ulysses,
Nestor, Menelaus, and Diomedes, with lights*

AGAMEMNON. We go wrong, we go wrong.
AJAX.   No, yonder 'tis;
   There, where we see the lights.
HECTOR.   I trouble you.
AJAX. No, not a whit.

Re-enter Achilles

ULYSSES.   Here comes himself to guide you. 70
ACHILLES. Welcome, brave Hector; welcome,
   princes all.
AGAMEMNON. So now, fair Prince of Troy, I bid
   good night.
Ajax commands the guard to tend on you.
HECTOR. Thanks and good night to the Greeks'
   general.
MENELAUS. Good night, my lord.
HECTOR.   Good night, sweet Lord Menelaus.
THERSITES. Sweet draught: sweet, quoth 'a! sweet sink,
   sweet sewer.
ACHILLES. Good night and welcome, both at once,
   to those
   That go or tarry.
AGAMEMNON. Good night.   80
                 Agamemnon and Menelaus go
ACHILLES. Old Nestor tarries; and you too, Diomed,
   Keep Hector company an hour or two.
DIOMEDES. I cannot, lord; I have important business,
The tide whereof is now. Good night, great Hector.
HECTOR. Give me your hand.

ULYSSES [aside to Troilus]. Follow his torch; he goes
    to Calchas' tent.
I'll keep you company.
TROILUS.   Sweet sir, you honour me.
HECTOR. And so, good night.

*Diomedes goes; Ulysses and
Troilus following*

ACHILLES. Come, come, enter my tent.

Achilles, Hector, Ajax and Nestor go in

THERSITES. That same Diomed's a false-hearted rogue, 90
a most unjust knave; I will no more trust him when
he leers than I will a serpent when he hisses; he
will spend his mouth and promise, like Babbler the
hound; but when he performs, astronomers foretell
it; it is prodigious, there will come some change;
the sun borrows of the moon when Diomed keeps
his word. I will rather leave to see Hector than not
to dog him. They say he keeps a Trojan drab and
uses the traitor Calchas' tent; I'll after. Nothing but
lechery! all incontinent varlets!   *Goes* 100

Scene 2: *The same. Before Calchas' tent*

Enter Diomedes

DIOMEDES. What, are you up here, ho? speak.
CALCHAS [*within*]. Who calls?
DIOMEDES. Diomed. Calchas, I think. Where's your
    daughter?
CALCHAS [*within*]. She comes to you.

*Enter Troilus and Ulysses, at a distance; after them
Thersites*

ULYSSES. Stand where the torch may not discover us.

Enter Cressida

TROILUS. Cressid comes forth to him.
DIOMEDES.   How now, my charge!
CRESSIDA. Now, my sweet guardian! Hark, a word
    with you.   *Whispers*
TROILUS. Yea, so familiar!
ULYSSES. She will sing any man at first sight.   10
THERSITES. And any man may sing her, if he can take
    her clef; she's noted.
DIOMEDES. Will you remember?
CRESSIDA. Remember? Yes.
DIOMEDES. Nay, but do then;
    And let your mind be coupled with your words.
TROILUS. What should she remember?
ULYSSES. List.
CRESSIDA. Sweet honey Greek, tempt me no more
    to folly.
THERSITES. Roguery!   20
DIOMEDES. Nay, then—
CRESSIDA. I'll tell you what—
DIOMEDES. Foh, foh! come, tell a pin; you are
    forsworn.
CRESSIDA. In faith, I cannot. What would you have
    me do?
THERSITES. A juggling trick—to be secretly open.
DIOMEDES. What did you swear you would bestow
    on me?
CRESSIDA. I prithee, do not hold me to mine oath;
    Bid me do anything but that, sweet Greek.
DIOMEDES. Good night.
TROILUS. Hold, patience!   30
ULYSSES. How now, Trojan!

CRESSIDA. Diomed—
DIOMEDES. No no, good night; I'll be your fool
    no more.
TROILUS. Thy better must.
CRESSIDA. Hark, one work in your ear.
TROILUS. O plague and madness!
ULYSSES. You are moved, prince; let us depart,
    I pray you,
Lest your displeasure should enlarge itself
To wrathful terms. This place is dangerous;
The time right deadly; I beseech you, go.   40
TROILUS. Behold, I pray you!
ULYSSES.   Nay, good my lord. go off;
You flow to great distraction; come, my lord.
TROILUS. I pray thee, stay.
ULYSSES.   You have not patience; come.
TROILUS. I pray you, stay; by hell and all hell's
    torments,
I will not speak a word.
DIOMEDES.   And so, good night.
CRESSIDA. Nay, but you part in anger.
TROILUS.   Doth that grieve thee?
    O withered truth!
ULYSSES.   Why, how now, lord!
TROILUS.   By Jove,
    I will be patient.
CRESSIDA.   Guardian! Why, Greek!
DIOMEDES. Foh, foh! adieu; you palter.
CRESSIDA. In faith, I do not; come hither once again. 50
ULYSSES. You shake, my lord, at something; will
    you go?
You will break out.
TROILUS   She strokes his cheek!
ULYSSES.   Come, come.
TROILUS. Nay, stay; by Jove, I will not speak a word:
    There is between my will and all offences
    A guard of patience. Stay a little while.
THERSITES. How the devil luxury, with his fat rump
    and potato-finger, tickles these together! Fry,
    lechery, fry!
DIOMEDES. But will you then?
CRESSIDA. In faith, I will, la; never trust me else.   60
DIOMEDES. Give me some token for the surety of it.
CRESSIDA. I'll fetch you one.   *Goes*
ULYSSES. You have sworn patience.
TROILUS.   Fear me not, sweet lord;
    I will not be myself, nor have cognition
    Of what I feel. I am all patience.

Re-enter Cressida

THERSITES. Now the pledge; now, now, now!
CRESSIDA. Here, Diomed, keep this sleeve.
TROILUS. O beauty! where is thy faith?
ULYSSES.   My lord—
TROILUS. I will be patient; outwardly I will.
CRESSIDA. You look upon that sleeve; behold it well. 70
    He loved me—O false wench!—Give't me again.
DIOMEDES. Whose was't?
CRESSIDA. It is no matter, now I have't again.
    I will not meet with you tomorrow night.
    I prithee, Diomed, visit me no more.
THERSITES. Now she sharpens; well said, whetstone!
DIOMEDES. I shall have it.
CRESSIDA.   What, this?
DIOMEDES.   Ay, that.
CRESSIDA. O, all you gods! O pretty, pretty pledge!

Thy master now lies thinking in his bed
Of thee and me, and sighs, and takes my glove, 80
And gives memorial dainty kisses to it,
As I kiss thee. Nay, do not snatch it from me;
He that takes that doth take my heart withal.
DIOMEDES. I had your heart before; this follows it.
TROILUS. I did swear patience.
CRESSIDA. You shall not have it, Diomed; faith, you
shall not;
I'll give you something else.
DIOMEDES. I will have this. Whose was it?
CRESSIDA. It is no matter.
DIOMEDES. Come, tell me whose it was.
CRESSIDA. 'Twas one's that loved me better than
you will. 90
But now you have it, take it.
DIOMEDES. Whose was it?
CRESSIDA. By all Diana's waiting-women yond,
And by herself, I will not tell you whose.
DIOMEDES. Tomorrow will I wear it on my helm,
And grieve his spirit that dares not challenge it.
TROILUS. Wert thou the devil, and wor'st it on thy
horn,
It should be challenged.
CRESSIDA. Well, well, 'tis done, 'tis past—and yet it
is not;
I will not keep my word.
DIOMEDES. Why then, farewell;
Thou never shalt mock Diomed again. 100
CRESSIDA. You shall not go; one cannot speak a word,
But it straight starts you.
DIOMEDES. I do not like this fooling.
TROILUS. Nor I, by Pluto; but that that likes not you
Pleases me best.
DIOMEDES. What, shall I come? the hour?
CRESSIDA. Ay, come. O Jove! do come; I shall be
plagued.
DIOMEDES. Farewell till then.
CRESSIDA. Good night; I prithee, come.
Diomedes goes
Troilus, farewell! One eye yet looks on thee,
But with my heart the other eye doth see.
Ah, poor our sex! this fault in us I find,
The error of our eye directs our mind; 110
What error leads must err—O, then conclude
Minds swayed by eyes are full of turpitude. *Goes*
THERSITES. A proof of strength she could not publish
more,
Unless she said 'My mind is now turned whore'.
ULYSSES. All's done, my lord.
TROILUS. It is.
ULYSSES. Why stay we then?
TROILUS. To make a recordation to my soul
Of every syllable that here was spoke.
But if I tell how these two did co-act,
Shall I not lie in publishing a truth?
Sith yet there is a credence in my heart,
An esperance so obstinately strong, 120
That doth invert th'attest of eyes and tears;
And if those organs had deceptious functions,
Created only to calumniate,
Was Cressid here?
ULYSSES. I cannot conjure, Trojan.
TROILUS. She was not, sure.
ULYSSES. Most sure she was.
TROILUS. Why, my negation hath no taste of madness.

ULYSSES. Nor mine, my lord; Cressid was here but
now.
TROILUS. Let it not be believed for womanhood!
Think we had mothers. Do not give advantage 130
To stubborn critics, apt without a theme
For depravation, to square the general sex
By Cressid's rule; rather think this not Cressid.
ULYSSES. What hath she done, prince, that can soil
our mothers?
TROILUS. Nothing at all, unless that this were she.
THERSITES. Will 'a swagger himself out on's own eyes?
TROILUS. This she? No; this is Diomed's Cressida.
If beauty have a soul, this is not she;
If souls guide vows, if vows be sanctimonies,
If sanctimony be the gods' delight, 140
If there be rule in unity itself,
This is not she. O madness of discourse,
That cause sets up with and against itself!
Bifold authority! where reason can revolt
Without perdition, and loss assume all reason
Without revolt. This is, and is not, Cressid!
Within my soul there doth conduce a fight
Of this strange nature, that a thing inseparate
Divides more wider than the sky and earth;
And yet the spacious breadth of this division 150
Admits no orifex for a point as subtle
As Ariachne's broken woof to enter.
Instance, O instance! strong as Pluto's gates:
Cressid is mine, tied with the bonds of heaven.
Instance, O instance! strong as heaven itself:
The bonds of heaven are slipped, dissolved and
loosed,
And with another knot, five-finger-tied,
The fractions of her faith, orts of her love,
The fragments, scraps, the bits and greasy relics
Of her o'ereaten faith are given to Diomed. 160
ULYSSES. May worthy Troilus be but half attached
With that which here his passion doth express?
TROILUS. Ay, Greek; and that shall be divulgèd well
In characters as red as Mars his heart
Inflamed with Venus. Never did young man fancy
With so eternal and so fixed a soul.
Hark, Greek: as much as I do Cressid love,
So much by weight hate I her Diomed.
That sleeve is mine that he'll bear on his helm.
Were it a casque composed by Vulcan's skill, 170
My sword should bite it. Not the dreadful spout
Which shipmen do the hurricano call,
Constringed in mass by the almighty sun,
Shall dizzy with more clamour Neptune's ear
In his descent, than shall my prompted sword
Falling on Diomed.
THERSITES. He'll tickle it for his concupy.
TROILUS. O Cressid! O false Cressid! false, false, false!
Let all untruths stand by thy stainèd name,
And they'll seem glorious.
ULYSSES. O, contain yourself; 180
Your passion draws ears hither.

Enter Æneas

ÆNEAS. I have been seeking you this hour, my lord.
Hector by this is arming him in Troy;
Ajax your guard stays to conduct you home.
TROILUS. Have with you, prince. My courteous
lord, adieu.
Farewell, revolted fair! and, Diomed,

Stand fast, and wear a castle on thy head!
ULYSSES. I'll bring you to the gates.
TROILUS. Accept distracted thanks.
                    Troilus, Æneas, and Ulysses go
THERSITES. Would I could meet that rogue Diomed! I   190
would croak like a raven; I would bode, I would
bode. Patroclus will give me anything for the
intelligence of this whore; the parrot will not do
more for an almond than he for a commodious
drab. Lechery, lechery! Still wars and lechery!
Nothing else holds fashion. A burning devil take
them!   *Goes*

        Scene 3: *Troy. Before Priam's palace*

Enter Hector and Andromache

ANDROMACHE. When was my lord so much urgently
    tempered,
To stop his ears against admonishment?
Unarm, unarm, and do not fight today.
HECTOR. You train me to offend you; get you in.
By all the everlasting gods, I'll go!
ANDROMACHE. My dreams will sure prove ominous
    to the day.
HECTOR. No more, I say.

Enter Cassandra

CASSANDRA.   Where is my brother Hector?
ANDROMACHE. Here, sister; armed, and bloody in
    intent.
Consort with me in loud and dear petition;
Pursue we him on knees; for I have dreamed   10
Of bloody turbulence, and this whole night
Hath nothing been but shapes and forms of
    slaughter.
CASSANDRA. O, 'tis true.
HECTOR.   Ho! bid my trumpet sound!
CASSANDRA. No notes of sally, for the heavens,
    sweet brother.
HECTOR. Be gone, I say. The gods have heard me
    swear.
CASSANDRA. The gods are deaf to hot and peevish
    vows:
They are polluted offerings, more abhorred
Than spotted livers in the sacrifice.
ANDROMACHE. O, be persuaded! Do not count it holy
To hurt by being just; it is as lawful,   20
For we would give much, to use violent thefts
And rob in the behalf of charity.
CASSANDRA. It is the purpose that makes strong the
    vow;
But vows to every purpose must not hold.
Unarm, sweet Hector.
HECTOR.   Hold you still, I say;
Mine honour keeps the weather of my fate.
Life every man holds dear; but the dear man
Holds honour far more precious-dear than life.

Enter Troilus

How now, young man! Mean'st thou to fight
    today?
ANDROMACHE. Cassandra, call my father to persuade.   30
                              Cassandra goes
HECTOR. No, faith, young Troilus; doff thy harness,
    youth;
I am today i'th'vein of chivalry.

Let grow thy sinews till their knots be strong,
And tempt not yet the brushes of the war.
Unarm thee, go; and doubt thou not, brave boy,
I'll stand today for thee and me and Troy.
TROILUS. Brother, you have a vice of mercy in you,   190
Which better fits a lion than a man.
HECTOR. What vice is that? Good Troilus, chide me
    for it.
TROILUS. When many times the captive Grecian falls, 40
Even in the fan and wind of your fair sword,
You bid them rise and live.
HECTOR. O, 'tis fair play.
TROILUS.   Fool's play, by heaven, Hector.
HECTOR. How now! How now!
TROILUS.   For th'love of all the gods,
Let's leave the hermit pity with our mother;
And when we have our armours buckled on,
The venomed vengeance ride upon our swords,
Spur them to ruthful work, rein them from ruth!
HECTOR. Fie, savage, fie!
TROILUS.   Hector, then 'tis wars.
HECTOR. Troilus, I would not have you fight today.   50
TROILUS. Who should withhold me?
Not fate, obedience, nor the hand of Mars
Beckoning with fiery truncheon my retire;
Not Priamus and Hecuba on knees,
Their eyes o'ergallèd with recourse of tears;
Nor you, my brother, with your true sword drawn,
Opposed to hinder me, should stop my way,
But by my ruin.

Re-enter Cassandra, with Priam

CASSANDRA. Lay hold upon him, Priam, hold him fast;
He is thy crutch; now if thou lose thy stay,   60
Thou on him leaning, and all Troy on thee,
Fall all together.
PRIAM.   Come, Hector, come, go back.
Thy wife hath dreamed; thy mother hath had
    visions;
Cassandra doth foresee; and I myself
Am like a prophet suddenly enrapt,
To tell thee that this day is ominous;
Therefore, come back.
HECTOR.   Æneas is afield;
And I do stand engaged to many Greeks,
Even in the faith of valour, to appear
This morning to them.
PRIAM.   Ay, but thou shalt not go.   70
HECTOR. I must not break my faith.
You know me dutiful; therefore, dear sir,
Let me not shame respect, but give me leave
To take that course by your consent and voice
Which you do here forbid me, royal Priam.
CASSANDRA. O Priam, yield not to him!
ANDROMACHE.   Do not, dear father.
HECTOR. Andromache, I am offended with you;
Upon the love you bear me, get you in.   *She goes*
TROILUS. This foolish, dreaming, superstitious girl
Makes all these bodements.
CASSANDRA.   O, farewell, dear Hector! 80
Look how thou diest! look how thy eye turns pale!
Look how thy wounds do bleed at many vents!
Hark how Troy roars! how Hecuba cries out!
How poor Andromache shrills her dolours forth!
Behold, distraction, frenzy, and amazement,
Like witless antics, one another meet,

And all cry 'Hector! Hector's dead! O Hector!'
TROILUS. Away! away!
CASSANDRA. Farewell—yet soft! Hector, I take
　my leave;
Thou dost thyself and all our Troy deceive.　*Goes* 90
HECTOR. You are amazed, my liege, at her exclaims.
Go in and cheer the town; we'll forth and fight,
Do deeds worth praise and tell you them at night.
PRIAM. Farewell. The gods with safety stand about
　thee!　　　　　　　*Priam and Hector go severally;*
　　　　　　　　　　　　　　　　alarum
TROILUS. They are at it, hark! Proud Diomed, believe,
I come to lose my arm, or win my sleeve.

Enter Pandarus

PANDARUS. Do you hear, my lord? do you hear?
TROILUS. What now?
PANDARUS. Here's a letter from yon poor girl.
TROILUS. Let me read.　　　　　　　　　　　　100
PANDARUS. A whoreson tisick, a whoreson rascally
tisick so troubles me, and the foolish fortune of this
girl; and what one thing, what another, that I shall
leave you one o'these days. And I have a rheum in
mine eyes too, and such an ache in my bones that,
unless a man were cursed, I cannot tell what to think
on't. What says she there?
TROILUS. Words, words, mere words; no matter
　from the heart;
Th'effect doth operate another way.
　　　　　　　　　　　Tearing the letter
Go, wind, to wind! there turn and change together. 110
My love with words and errors still she feeds,
But edifies another with her deeds.
　　　　　　　　　　They go severally

Scene 4: *The field between Troy and the Greek camp*

Alarums. Excursions. Enter Thersites

THERSITES. Now they are clapper-clawing one another; I'll go look on. That dissembling abominable
varlet, Diomed, has got that same scurvy doting
foolish young knave's sleeve of Troy there in his
helm. I would fain see them meet; that that same
young Trojan ass, that loves the whore there, might
send that Greekish whore-masterly villain with the
sleeve back to the dissembling luxurious drab of a
sleeveless errand. O't'other side, the policy of those
crafty-swearing rascals, that stale old mouse-eaten 10
dry cheese, Nestor, and that same dog-fox, Ulysses,
is proved not worth a blackberry. They set me up
in policy that mongrel cur, Ajax, against that dog of
as bad a kind, Achilles; and now is the cur Ajax
prouder than the cur Achilles, and will not arm
today; whereupon the Grecians begin to proclaim
barbarism, and policy grows into an ill opinion.
Soft! here comes sleeve, and t'other.

Enter Diomedes, Troilus following

TROILUS. Fly not; for shouldst thou take the river Styx,
I would swim after.
DIOMEDES.　　　　　　　Thou dost miscall retire; 20
I do not fly; but advantageous care
Withdrew me from the odds of multitude.
Have at thee!
THERSITES. Hold thy whore, Grecian! Now for thy
whore, Trojan! Now the sleeve, now the sleeve!
　　　　　Troilus and Diomedes go off fighting

Enter Hector

HECTOR. What art thou, Greek? Art thou for
　Hector's match?
Art thou of blood and honour?
THERSITES. No, no; I am a rascal; a scurvy railing
knave; a very filthy rogue.
HECTOR. I do believe thee. Live　　　　*Goes* 30
THERSITES. God-a-mercy, that thou wilt believe me;
but a plague break thy neck for frighting me! What's
become of the wenching rogues! I think they have
swallowed one another. I would laugh at that
miracle; yet in a sort lechery eats itself. I'll seek
them.　　　　　　　　　　　　　　　*Goes*

Scene 5: *Another part of the field*

Enter Diomedes and Servant

DIOMEDES. Go, go, my servant, take thou Troilus'
　horse;
Present the fair steed to my lady Cressid.
Fellow, commend my service to her beauty;
Tell her I have chastised the amorous Trojan,
And am her knight by proof.
SERVANT.　　　　　　　I go, my lord.　*Goes*

Enter Agamemnon

AGAMEMNON. Renew, renew! The fierce Polydamas
Hath beat down Menon; bastard Margarelon
Hath Doreus prisoner,
And stands colossus-wise, waving his beam,
Upon the pashèd corpses of the kings　　　　10
Epistrophus and Cedius; Polyxenes is slain;
Amphimachus and Thoas deadly hurt;
Patroclus ta'en or slain; and Palamedes
Sore hurt and bruised; the dreadful sagittary
Appals our numbers; haste we, Diomed,
To reinforcement, or we perish all.　　　*Goes*

Enter Nestor and other Greeks

NESTOR. Go, bear Patroclus' body to Achilles,
And bid the snail-paced Ajax arm for shame.
　　　　　　　　　　　　　　　　Some go
There is a thousand Hectors in the field:
Now here he fights on Galathe his horse,　　20
And there lacks work; anon he's there afoot,
And there they fly or die, like scalèd sculls
Before the belching whale; then is he yonder,
And there the strawy Greeks, ripe for his edge,
Fall down before him, like a mower's swath;
Here, there and everywhere he leaves and takes,
Dexterity so obeying appetite
That what he will he does, and does so much
That proof is called impossibility.

Enter Ulysses

ULYSSES. O, courage, courage, princes! great Achilles 30
Is arming, weeping, cursing, vowing vengeance;
Patroclus' wounds have roused his drowsy blood,
Together with his mangled Myrmidons,
That noseless, handless, hacked and chipped, come
　to him,
Crying on Hector. Ajax hath lost a friend,
And foams at mouth, and he is armed and at it,
Roaring for Troilus; who hath done today
Mad and fantastic execution,

Engaging and redeeming of himself
With such a careless force and forceless care   40
As if that luck, in very spite of cunning,
Bade him win all.

Enter Ajax

AJAX. Troilus! thou coward Troilus!   *Goes*
DIOMEDES.   Ay, there, there.   *Follows*
NESTOR. So, so, we draw together.

Enter Achilles

ACHILLES.   Where is this Hector?
Come, come, thou boy-queller, show me thy face;
Know what it is to meet Achilles angry;
Hector! where's Hector? I will none but Hector.
                                        They go

Scene 6: *Another part of the field*

Enter Ajax

AJAX. Troilus, thou coward Troilus, show thy head!

Enter Diomedes

DIOMEDES. Troilus, I say! where's Troilus?
AJAX.   What wouldst thou?
DIOMEDES. I would correct him.
AJAX. Were I the general, thou shouldst have my
    office
Ere that correction. Troilus, I say! what, Troilus!

Enter Troilus

TROILUS. O traitor Diomed! Turn thy false face,
    thou traitor,
And pay the life thou ow'st me for my horse.
DIOMEDES. Ha! art thou there?
AJAX. I'll fight with him alone; stand, Diomed.
DIOMEDES. He is my prize; I will not look upon.   10
TROILUS. Come both you cogging Greeks; have at
    you both!   *They go, fighting*

Enter Hector

HECTOR. Yea, Troilus? O, well fought, my youngest
    brother!

Enter Achilles

ACHILLES. Now do I see thee; ha! have at thee,
    Hector!   *They fight*
HECTOR. Pause, if thou wilt.
ACHILLES. I do disdain thy courtesy, proud Trojan.
Be happy that my arms are out of use;
My rest and negligence befriends thee now,
But thou anon shalt hear of me again;
Till when, go seek thy fortune.   *Goes*
HECTOR.   Fare thee well.
I would have been much more a fresher man,   20
Had I expected thee.

Re-enter Troilus

                    How now, my brother!
TROILUS. Ajax hath ta'en Æneas. Shall it be?
No, by the flame of yonder glorious heaven,
He shall not carry him; I'll be ta'en too,
Or bring him off. Fate, hear me what I say!
I reck not though thou end my life today.   *Goes*

Enter one in sumptuous armour

HECTOR. Stand, stand, thou Greek; thou art a
    goodly mark.
No! wilt thou not? I like thy armour well;
I'll frush it and unlock the rivets all,
But I'll be master of it. [*the Greek goes*] Wilt
    thou not, beast, abide?   30
Why then, fly on; I'll hunt thee for thy hide.
                                    Goes after

Scene 7: *Another part of the field*

Enter Achilles, with Myrmidons

ACHILLES. Come here about me, you my Myrmidons;
Mark what I say. Attend me where I wheel;
Strike not a stroke, but keep yourselves in breath,
And when I have the bloody Hector found
Empale him with your weapons round about;
In fellest manner execute your arms.
Follow me, sirs, and my proceedings eye;
It is decreed Hector the great must die.   *They go*

Enter Menelaus and Paris, fighting; then Thersites

THERSITES. The cuckold and the cuckold-maker are at
it. Now, bull! now, dog! 'Loo, Paris, 'loo! now, my   10
double-horned Spartan! 'loo, Paris, 'loo! The bull
has the game. Ware horns, ho!
                        Paris and Menelaus go

Enter Margarelon

MARGARELON. Turn, slave, and fight.
THERSITES. What art thou?
MARGARELON. A bastard son of Priam's.
THERSITES. I am a bastard too; I love bastards. I am
a bastard begot, bastard instructed, bastard in mind,
bastard in valour, in everything illegitimate. One
bear will not bite another, and wherefore should
one bastard? Take heed; the quarrel's most ominous   20
to us; if the son of a whore fight for a whore, he
tempts judgement. Farewell, bastard.   *Goes*
MARGARELON. The devil take thee, coward!   *Goes*

Scene 8: *Another part of the field*

Enter Hector

HECTOR. Most putrefiéd core, so fair without,
Thy goodly armour thus hath cost thy life.
Now is my day's work done. I'll take good breath.
Rest, sword; thou hast thy fill of blood and death.
                                    Disarms

Enter Achilles and Myrmidons

ACHILLES. Look, Hector, how the sun begins to set,
How ugly night comes breathing at his heels;
Even with the vail and darking of the sun,
To close the day up, Hector's life is done.
HECTOR. I am unarmed; forego this vantage, Greek.
ACHILLES. Strike, fellows, strike; this is the man
    I seek.   *Hector falls*   10
So, Ilion, fall thou next! now, Troy, sink down!
Here lies thy heart, thy sinews, and thy bone.
On, Myrmidons, and cry you all amain
'Achilles hath the mighty Hector slain'.
                            Retreat sounded
Hark! a retire upon our Grecian part.
MYRMIDON. The Trojan trumpets sound the like,
    my lord.

ACHILLES. The dragon wing of night o'erspreads
  the earth,
And stickler-like the armies separates.
My half-supped sword that frankly would have fed,
Pleased with this dainty bait, thus goes to bed.   20
                          Sheathes his sword
Come, tie his body to my horse's tail;
Along the field I will the Trojan trail.
                          They go; retreat sounded

Scene 9: *Another part of the field*

*Enter Agamemnon, Ajax, Menelaus, Nestor, Diomedes,
and the rest, marching. Shouts within*

AGAMEMNON. Hark! hark! what shout is that?
NESTOR. Peace, drums!
SOLDIERS [*within*]. Achilles! Achilles! Hector's slain!
  Achilles!
DIOMEDES. The bruit is Hector's slain, and by
  Achilles.
AJAX. If it be so, yet bragless let it be;
  Great Hector was as good a man as he.
AGAMEMNON. March patiently along. Let one be sent
  To pray Achilles see us at our tent.
  If in his death gods have us befriended,
  Great Troy is ours, and our sharp wars are ended. 10
                          They march off

Scene 10: *Another part of the field*

Enter Æneas, Paris, Antenor, and Deiphobus

ÆNEAS. Stand, ho! yet are we masters of the field.
  Never go home; here starve we out the night.

Enter Troilus

TROILUS. Hector is slain.
ALL.   Hector! The gods forbid!
TROILUS. He's dead; and at the murderer's horse's tail
  In beastly sort dragged through the shameful field.
  Frown on, you heavens, effect your rage with speed!
  Sit, gods, upon your thrones, and smite at Troy!
  I say, at once let your brief plagues be mercy,
  And linger not our sure destructions on!
ÆNEAS. My lord, you do discomfort all the host. 10
TROILUS. You understand me not that tell me so;
  I dare not speak of flight, of fear, of death,
  But dare all imminence that gods and men

Address their dangers in. Hector is gone:
Who shall tell Priam so, or Hecuba?
Let him that will a screech-owl aye be called:
Go in to Troy and say there 'Hector's dead',
There is a word will Priam turn to stone,
Make wells and Niobes of the maids and wives,
Cold statues of the youth, and, in a word,   20
Scare Troy out of itself. But march away.
Hector is dead; there is no more to say.
Stay yet. You vile abominable tents,
Thus proudly pight upon our Phrygian plains
Let Titan rise as early as he dare,
I'll through and through you! and thou great-
  sized coward,
No space of earth shall sunder our two hates;
I'll haunt thee like a wicked conscience still,
That mouldeth goblins swift as frenzy's thoughts.
Strike a free march to Troy! with comfort go: 30
Hope of revenge shall hide our inward woe.
                          Æneas and Trojans go

Enter Pandarus

PANDARUS. But hear you, hear you!
TROILUS. Hence, broker-lackey! ignomy and shame
  Pursue thy life, and live aye with thy name! *Goes*
PANDARUS. A goodly medicine for my aching bones!
  O world! world! world! thus is the poor agent
  despised! O traders and bawds, how earnestly are
  you set a-work, and how ill requited! Why should
  our endeavour be so desired and the performance
  so loathed? What verse for it? what instance for it? 40
  Let me see:
      Full merrily the humble-bee doth sing
      Till he hath lost his honey and his sting;
      And being once subdued in arméd tail,
      Sweet honey and sweet notes together fail.
  Good traders in the flesh, set this in your painted
    cloths:
  As many as be here of Pandar's hall,
  Your eyes, half out, weep out at Pandar's fall;
  Or if you cannot weep, yet give some groans,
  Though not for me, yet for your aching bones. 50
  Brethren and sisters of the hold-door trade,
  Some two months hence my will shall here be made.
  It should be now, but that my fear is this,
  Some galléd goose of Winchester would hiss.
  Till then I'll sweat and seek about for eases,
  And at that time bequeath you my diseases. *Goes*

Coriolanus

The scene: Rome and the neighbourhood; Corioli
and the neighbourhood; Antium

CHARACTERS IN THE PLAY

CAIUS MARCIUS, *afterwards* CAIUS MARCIUS CORIOLANUS
TITUS LARTIUS,
COMINIUS, } *generals against the Volscians*
MENENIUS AGRIPPA, *friend to Coriolanus*
SICINIUS VELUTUS,
JUNIUS BRUTUS, } *Tribunes of the people*
YOUNG MARCIUS, *son to Coriolanus*
A Roman Herald
NICANOR, *a Roman*
TULLUS AUFIDIUS, *general of the Volscians*
Lieutenant to Aufidius
Conspirators with Aufidius

ADRIAN, *a Volscian*
A Citizen of Antium
Two Volscian Guards
VOLUMNIA, *mother to Coriolanus*
VIRGILIA, *wife to Coriolanus*
VALERIA, *friend to Virgilia*
Gentlewoman attending on Virgilia
Usher attending on Valeria
Roman and Volscian Senators, Patricians, Ædiles,
   Lictors, Soldiers, Citizens, Messengers, Servants to
   Aufidius, and other Attendants

Coriolanus

ACT 1
Scene 1: *Rome. A street*

Enter a company of mutinous Citizens, with staves, clubs, and other weapons

1 CITIZEN. Before we proceed any further, hear me speak.

ALL. Speak, speak.

1 CITIZEN. You are all resolved rather to die than to famish?

ALL. Resolved, resolved.

1 CITIZEN. First, you know Caius Marcius is chief enemy to the people.

ALL. We know't, we know't.

1 CITIZEN. Let us kill him, and we'll have corn at our own price. Is't a verdict?   10

ALL. No more talking on't; let it be done. Away, away!

2 CITIZEN. One word, good citizens.

1 CITIZEN. We are accounted poor citizens, the patricians good. What authority surfeits on would relieve us. If they would yield us but the superfluity while it were wholesome, we might guess they relieved us humanely; but they think we are too dear: the leanness that afflicts us, the object of our   20 misery, is as an inventory to particularize their abundance; our sufferance is a gain to them. Let us revenge this with our pikes ere we become rakes; for the gods know I speak this in hunger for bread, not in thirst for revenge.

2 CITIZEN. Would you proceed especially against Caius Marcius?

1 CITIZEN. Against him first: he's a very dog to the commonalty.

2 CITIZEN. Consider you what services he has done for   30 his country?

1 CITIZEN. Very well, and could be content to give him good report for't, but that he pays himself with being proud.

2 CITIZEN. Nay, but speak not maliciously.

1 CITIZEN. I say unto you, what he hath done famously he did it to that end; though soft-conscienced men can be content to say it was for his country, he did it partly to please his mother and to be proud, which he is, even to the altitude of his virtue.   40

2 CITIZEN. What he cannot help in his nature you account a vice in him. You must in no way say he is covetous.

1 CITIZEN. If I must not, I need not be barren of accusations; he hath faults (with surplus) to tire in repetition. [*shouts*]. What shouts are these? The other side o' the city is risen: why stay we prating here? To th' Capitol!

ALL. Come, come.

1 CITIZEN. Soft! who comes here?   50

Enter Menenius Agrippa

2 CITIZEN. Worthy Menenius Agrippa, one that hath always loved the people.

1 CITIZEN. He's one honest enough; would all the rest were so!

MENENIUS. What work's, my countrymen, in hand? Where go you
With bats and clubs? The matter? Speak, I pray you.

1 CITIZEN. Our business is not unknown to th' Senate; they have had inkling this fortnight what we intend to do, which now we'll show 'em in deeds. They say poor suitors have strong breaths: they shall know we have strong arms too.   60

MENENIUS. Why, masters, my good friends, mine honest neighbours,
Will you undo yourselves?

1 CITIZEN. We cannot, sir; we are undone already.

MENENIUS. I tell you, friends, most charitable care
Have the patricians of you. For your wants,
Your suffering in this dearth, you may as well
Strike at the heaven with your staves as lift them
Against the Roman state, whose course will on
The way it takes; cracking ten thousand curbs   70
Of more strong link asunder than can ever
Appear in your impediment. For the dearth,
The gods, not the patricians, make it, and
Your knees to them (not arms) must help. Alack,
You are transported by calamity
Thither where more attends you; and you slander
The helms o' th' state, who care for you like fathers,
When you curse them as enemies.

1 CITIZEN. Care for us! True, indeed! They ne'er cared for us yet. Suffer us to famish, and their storehouses   80 crammed with grain; make edicts for usury, to support usurers; repeal daily any wholesome act established against the rich, and provide more piercing statutes daily to chain up and restrain the poor. If the wars eat us not up, they will; and there's all the love they bear us.

MENENIUS. Either you must
Confess yourselves wondrous malicious,
Or be accused of folly. I shall tell you
A pretty tale: it may be you have heard it;   90
But, since it serves my purpose, I will venture
To stale't a little more.

1 CITIZEN. Well, I'll hear it, sir: yet you must not think to fob off our disgrace with a tale: but, an't please you, deliver.

MENENIUS. There was a time when all the body's members
Rebelled against the Belly; thus accused it:
That only like a gulf it did remain
I' th' midst o' th' body, idle and unactive,
Still cupboarding the viand, never bearing   100
Like labour with the rest; where th' other instruments
Did see and hear, devise, instruct, walk, feel,
And, mutually participate, did minister
Unto the appetite and affection common
Of the whole body. The Belly answered—

1 CITIZEN. Well, sir, what answer made the Belly?

MENENIUS. Sir, I shall tell you. With a kind of smile,
Which ne'er came from the lungs, but even thus—

For, look you, I may make the Belly smile
As well as speak—it tauntingly replied
To th' discontented members, the mutinous parts
That envied his receipt; even so most fitly
As you malign our senators for that
They are not such as you.
1 CITIZEN.   Your Belly's answer—What?
The kingly crownèd head, the vigilant eye,
The counsellor heart, the arm our soldier,
Our steed the leg, the tongue our trumpeter,
With other muniments and petty helps
In this our fabric, if that they—
MENENIUS.   What then?
'Fore me, this fellow speaks! what then? what then? 120
1 CITIZEN. Should by the cormorant Belly be
restrained,
Who is the sink o' th' body,—
MENENIUS.   Well, what then?
1 CITIZEN. The former agents, if they did complain,
What could the Belly answer?
MENENIUS.   I will tell you;
If you'll bestow a small (of what you have little)
Patience awhile, you'st hear the belly's answer.
1 CITIZEN. You're long about it.
MENENIUS.   Note me this, good friend;
Your most grave Belly was deliberate,
Not rash like his accusers, and thus answered:
'True it is, my incorporate friends,' quoth he,   130
'That I receive the general food at first,
Which you do live upon; and fit it is,
Because I am the storehouse and the shop
Of the whole body. But, if you do remember,
I send it through the rivers of your blood,
Even to the court, the heart, to th'seat o' th' brain;
And, through the cranks and offices of man,
The strongest nerves and small inferior veins
From me receive their natural competency
Whereby they live: and though that all at once,   140
You, my good friends'—this says the Belly, mark
me—
1 CITIZEN. Ay, sir; well, well.
MENENIUS.   'Though all at once cannot
See what I do deliver out to each,
Yet I can make my audit up, that all
From me do back receive the flour of all,
And leave me but the bran.' What say you to't?
1 CITIZEN. It was an answer. How apply you this?
MENENIUS. The senators of Rome are this good Belly,
And you the mutinous members: for examine
Their counsels and their cares, digest things rightly 150
Touching the weal o'th' common, you shall find
No public benefit which you receive
But it proceeds or comes from them to you,
And no way from yourselves. What do you think,
You, the great toe of this assembly?
1 CITIZEN. I the great toe! why the great toe?
MENENIUS. For that, being one o'th' lowest, basest,
poorest,
Of this most wise rebellion, thou goest foremost.
Thou rascal, that art worst in blood to run,
Lead'st first to win some vantage.   160
But make you ready your stiff bats and clubs:
Rome and her rats are at the point of battle;
The one side must have bale.

Enter Caius Marcius

                              Hail, noble Marcius!
MARCIUS. Thanks. What's the matter, you dissentious 110
rogues
That, rubbing the poor itch of your opinion,
Make yourselves scabs?
1 CITIZEN.   We have ever your good word.
MARCIUS. He that will give good words to thee will
flatter
Beneath abhorring. What would you have, you
curs,
That like nor peace nor war? the one affrights you,
The other makes you proud. He that trusts to you, 170
Where he should find you lions, finds you hares;
Where foxes, geese: you are no surer, no,
Than is the coal of fire upon the ice,
Or hailstone in the sun. Your virtue is
To make him worthy whose offence subdues him
And curse that justice did it. Who deserves greatness
Deserves your hate. And your affections are
A sick man's appetite, who desires most that
Which would increase his evil. He that depends
Upon your favours swims with fins of lead   180
And hews down oaks with rushes. Hang ye! Trust
ye?
With every minute you do change a mind,
And call him noble that was now your hate,
Him vile that was your garland. What's the matter
That in these several places of the city
You cry against the noble Senate, who
(Under the gods) keep you in awe, which else
Would feed on one another? What's their seeking?
MENENIUS. For corn at their own rates, whereof they
say
The city is well stored.
MARCIUS.   Hang 'em! They say!   190
They'll sit by th'fire, and presume to know
What's done i'th' Capitol: who's like to rise,
Who thrives and who declines; side factions and
give out
Conjectural marriages, making parties strong,
And feebling such as stand not in their liking
Below their cobbled shoes. They say there's grain
enough!
Would the nobility lay aside their ruth,
And let me use my sword, I'd make a quarry
With thousands of these quartered slaves, as high
As I could pick my lance.   200
MENENIUS. Nay, these are all most thoroughly
persuaded;
For though abundantly they lack discretion,
Yet are they passing cowardly. But, I beseech you,
What says the other troop?
MARCIUS.   They are dissolved: hang 'em!
They said they were an-hungry; sighed forth
proverbs—
That hunger broke stone walls, that dogs must eat,
That meat was made for mouths, that the gods sent
not
Corn for the rich men only: with these shreds
They vented their complainings; which being
answered,
And a petition granted them—a strange one,   210
To break the heart of generosity
And make bold power look pale—they threw their
caps
As they would hang them on the horns o'th' moon,

Shouting their emulation.

MENENIUS. What is granted them?

MARCIUS. Five tribunes to defend their vulgar
wisdoms,
Of their own choice. One's Junius Brutus, one
Sicinius Velutus, and—I know not. 'Sdeath!
The rabble should have first unroofed the city,
Ere so prevailed with me: it will in time
Win upon power and throw forth greater themes 220
For insurrection's arguing.

MENENIUS. This is strange.

MARCIUS. Go, get you home, you fragments!

Enter a Messenger, hastily

MESSENGER. Where's Caius Marcius?

MARCIUS. Here: what's the matter?

MESSENGER. The news is, sir, the Volsces are in arms.

MARCIUS. I am glad on 't: then we shall ha' means to
vent
Our musty superfluity. See, our best elders.

*Enter Cominius, Titus Lartius, and other Senators;
Junius Brutus and Sicinius Velutus*

I SENATOR. Marcius, 'tis true that you have lately told
us;
The Volsces are in arms.

MARCIUS. They have a leader,
Tullus Aufidius, that will put you to 't.
I sin in envying his nobility;
And were I anything but what I am, 230
I would wish me only he.

COMINIUS. You have fought together.

MARCIUS. Were half to half the world by th' ears, and
he
Upon my party, I'd revolt, to make
Only my wars with him. He is a lion
That I am proud to hunt.

I SENATOR. Then, worthy Marcius,
Attend upon Cominius to these wars.

COMINIUS. It is your former promise.

MARCIUS. Sir, it is,
And I am constant. Titus Lartius, thou
Shalt see me once more strike at Tullus' face. 240
What, art thou stiff? stand'st out?

TITUS. No, Caius Marcius;
I'll lean upon one crutch and fight with t'other
Ere stay behind this business.

MENENIUS. O, true-bred!

I SENATOR. Your company to th' Capitol; where
I know
Our greatest friends attend us.

TITUS [*to Cominius*]. Lead you on.
[*to Marcius*] Follow Cominius; we must follow you;
Right worthy you priority.

COMINIUS. Noble Marcius!

I SENATOR [*to the citizens*]. Hence to your homes; be
gone!

MARCIUS. Nay, let them follow.
The Volsces have much corn; take these rats thither
To gnaw their garners [*citizens steal away*];
Worshipful mutineers, 250
Your valour puts well forth. Pray, follow.
All go but Sicinius and Brutus

SICINIUS. Was ever man so proud as is this Marcius?

BRUTUS. He has no equal.

SICINIUS. When we were chosen tribunes for the
people—

BRUTUS. Marked you his lip and eyes?

SICINIUS. Nay, but his taunts.

BRUTUS. Being moved, he will not spare to gird the
gods.

SICINIUS. Bemock the modest moon.

BRUTUS. The present wars devour him! He is grown
Too proud to be so valiant.

SICINIUS. Such a nature,
Tickled with good success, disdains the shadow 260
Which he treads on at noon. But I do wonder
His insolence can brook to be commanded
Under Cominius.

BRUTUS. Fame, at the which he aims,
In whom already he's well graced, can not
Better be held, nor more attained, than by
A place below the first: for what miscarries
Shall be the general's fault, though he perform
To th' utmost of a man; and giddy censure
Will then cry out of Marcius 'O, if he
Had borne the business!'

SICINIUS. Besides, if things go well, 270
Opinion, that so sticks on Marcius, shall
Of his demerits rob Cominius.

BRUTUS. Come:
Half all Cominius' honours are to Marcius,
Though Marcius earned them not; and all his faults
To Marcius shall be honours, though indeed
In aught he merit not.

SICINIUS. Let's hence, and hear
How the dispatch is made; and in what fashion,
More than his singularity, he goes
Upon this present action.

BRUTUS. Let's along. *They go*

Scene 2: *Corioli. The Senate-House*

Enter Tullus Aufidius, with Senators of Corioli

I SENATOR. So, your opinion is, Aufidius,
That they of Rome are ent'red in our counsels,
And know how we proceed.

AUFIDIUS. Is it not yours?
What ever hath been thought on in this state
That could be brought to bodily act ere Rome
Had circumvention? 'Tis not four days gone
Since I heard thence: these are the words: I think
I have the letter here: yes, here it is:
[*reads*] 'They have pressed a power, but it is not
known
Whether for east or west. The dearth is great; 10
The people mutinous: and it is rumoured,
Cominius, Marcius your old enemy
(Who is of Rome worse hated than of you),
And Titus Lartius, a most valiant Roman,
These three lead on this preparation
Whither 'tis bent: most likely 'tis for you:
Consider of it.'

I SENATOR. Our army's in the field:
We never yet made doubt but Rome was ready
To answer us.

AUFIDIUS. Nor did you think it folly
To keep your great pretences veiled till when 20
They needs must show themselves; which in the
hatching,
It seemed, appeared to Rome. By the discovery

We shall be short'ned in our aim, which was
To take in many towns ere almost Rome
Should know we were afoot.
2 SENATOR.   Noble Aufidius,
Take your commission; hie you to your bands:
Let us alone to guard Corioli.
If they set down before 's, for the remove
Bring up your army; but I think you'll find
They've not prepared for us.
AUFIDIUS.   O, doubt not that;   30
I speak from certainties. Nay, more,
Some parcels of their power are forth already,
And only hitherward. I leave your honours.
If we and Caius Marcius chance to meet,
'Tis sworn between us we shall ever strike
Till one can do no more.
ALL.   The gods assist you!
AUFIDIUS. And keep your honours safe!
1 SENATOR.   Farewell.
2 SENATOR.   Farewell.
ALL. Farewell.   *They go*

Scene 3: *Rome. A room in Marcius' house*

*Enter Volumnia and Virgilia, mother and wife to Marcius:
they set them down on two low stools, and sew*

VOLUMNIA. I pray you, daughter, sing, or express
yourself in a more comfortable sort: if my son were
my husband, I should freelier rejoice in that absence
wherein he won honour than in the embracements
of his bed where he would show most love. When
yet he was but tender-bodied, and the only son of
my womb; when youth with comeliness plucked all
gaze his way; when, for a day of kings' entreaties,
a mother should not sell him an hour from her
beholding; I, considering how honour would be-   10
come such a person—that it was no better than
picture-like to hang by th'wall, if renown made it
not stir—was pleased to let him seek danger where
he was like to find fame. To a cruel war I sent
him, from whence he returned his brows bound
with oak. I tell thee, daughter, I sprang not more in
joy at first hearing he was a man-child than now in
first seeing he had proved himself a man.
VIRGILIA. But had he died in the business, madam,
how then?   20
VOLUMNIA. Then his good report should have been
my son; I therein would have found issue. Hear me
profess sincerely: had I a dozen sons, each in my love
alike, and none less dear than thine and my good
Marcius, I had rather had eleven die nobly for their
country than one voluptuously surfeit out of action.

Enter a Gentlewoman

GENTLEWOMAN. Madam, the Lady Valeria is come to
visit you.
VIRGILIA. Beseech you give me leave to retire myself.
VOLUMNIA. Indeed, you shall not.   30
Methinks I hear hither your husband's drum;
See him pluck Aufidius down by th' hair;
As children from a bear, the Volsces shunning him.
Methinks I see him stamp thus, and call thus:
'Come on, you cowards! you were got in fear,
Though you were born in Rome.' His bloody brow
With his mailed hand then wiping, forth he goes,
Like to a harvest-man that's tasked to mow
Or all or lose his hire.

VIRGILIA. His bloody brow? O Jupiter, no blood!   40
VOLUMNIA. Away, you fool! It more becomes a man
Than gilt his trophy. The breasts of Hecuba,
When she did suckle Hector, looked not lovelier
Than Hector's forehead when it spit forth blood
At Grecian sword, contemning. Tell Valeria
We are fit to bid her welcome.
                                    Gentlewoman goes
VIRGILIA. Heavens bless my lord from fell Aufidius!
VOLUMNIA. He'll beat Aufidius' head below his knee,
And tread upon his neck.

Re-enter Gentlewoman with Valeria and her Usher

VALERIA. My ladies both, good day to you.   50
VOLUMNIA. Sweet madam!
VIRGILIA. I am glad to see your ladyship.
VALERIA. How do you both? you are manifest house-
keepers. What are you sewing here? A fine spot, in
good faith. How does your little son?
VIRGILIA. I thank your ladyship; well, good madam.
VOLUMNIA. He had rather see the swords and hear a
drum than look upon his schoolmaster.
VALERIA. O' my word, the father's son: I'll swear 'tis
a very pretty boy. O' my troth, I looked upon him 60
o' Wednesday half an hour together: has such a confirmed countenance! I saw him run after a gilded
butterfly; and when he caught it, he let it go again;
and after it again; and over and over he comes, and
up again; catched it again: or whether his fall
enraged him, or how 'twas, he did so set his teeth,
and tear it; O, I warrant, how he mammocked it!
VOLUMNIA. One on's father's moods.
VALERIA. Indeed, la, 'tis a noble child.
VIRGILIA. A crack, madam.   70
VALERIA. Come, lay aside your stitchery; I must have
you play the idle huswife with me this afternoon.
VIRGILIA. No, good madam; I will not out of doors.
VALERIA. Not out of doors!
VOLUMNIA. She shall, she shall.
VIRGILIA. Indeed, no, by your patience; I'll not over
the threshold till my lord return from the wars.
VALERIA. Fie, you confine yourself most unreasonably;
come, you must go visit the good lady that lies in.
VIRGILIA. I will wish her speedy strength, and visit her 80
with my prayers; but I cannot go thither.
VOLUMNIA. Why I pray you?
VIRGILIA. 'Tis not to save labour, nor that I want love.
VALERIA. You would be another Penelope; yet, they
say, all the yarn she spun in Ulysses' absence did but
fill Ithaca full of moths. Come; I would your
cambric were sensible as your finger, that you might
leave pricking it for pity. Come, you shall go with
us.
VIRGILIA. No, good madam, pardon me; indeed, I will 90
not forth.
VALERIA. In truth, la, go with me, and I'll tell you
excellent news of your husband.
VIRGILIA. O, good madam, there can be none yet.
VALERIA. Verily, I do not jest with you; there came
news from him last night.
VIRGILIA. Indeed, madam?
VALERIA. In earnest, it's true; I heard a senator speak
it. Thus it is: the Volsces have an army forth; against
whom Cominius the general is gone, with one part 100
of our Roman power: your lord and Titus Lartius
are set down before their city Corioli; they nothing

doubt prevailing, and to make it brief wars. This is
true, on mine honour; and so, I pray, go with us.
VIRGILIA. Give me excuse, good madam; I will obey
you in every thing hereafter.
VOLUMNIA. Let her alone, lady; as she is now, she will
but disease our better mirth.
VALERIA. In troth, I think she would. Fare you well,
then. Come, good sweet lady. Prithee, Virgilia, turn 110
they solemness out o' door, and go along with us.
VIRGILIA. No, at a word, madam; indeed, I must not.
I wish you much mirth.
VALERIA. Well then, farewell. *They go*

Scene 4: *Before the gates of Corioli*

*Enter Marcius, Titus Lartius, Captains and Soldiers,
with drum, trumpet, and colours. To them a Messenger*

MARCIUS. Yonder comes news: a wager they have
met.
LARTIUS. My horse to yours, no.
MARCIUS. 'Tis done.
LARTIUS. Agreed.
MARCIUS. Say, has our general met the enemy?
MESSENGER. They lie in view, but have not spoke as
yet.
LARTIUS. So, the good horse is mine.
MARCIUS. I'll buy him of you.
LARTIUS. No, I'll nor sell nor give him: lend you him
I will
For half a hundred years. [*to the trumpeter*] Summon
the town.
MARCIUS. How far off lie these armies?
MESSENGER. Within this mile and half.
MARCIUS. Then shall we hear their 'larum, and they
ours.
Now, Mars, I prithee, make us quick in work, 10
That we with smoking swords may march from
hence
To help our fielded friends! Come, blow thy blast.

*They sound a parley. Enter two Senators with others, on
the walls*

Tullus Aufidius, is he within your walls?
1 SENATOR. No, nor a man that fears you less than he;
That's lesser than a little. [*drum afar off*] Hark, our
drums
Are bringing forth our youth. We'll break our walls
Rather than they shall pound us up: our gates,
Which yet seem shut, we have but pinned with
rushes;
They'll open of themselves. [*alarum far off*] Hark
you, far off!
There is Aufidius. List what work he makes 20
Amongst your cloven army.
MARCIUS. O, they are at it!
LARTIUS. Their noise be our instruction. Ladders, ho!

The gates open and the Volsces enter

MARCIUS. They fear us not, but issue forth their city.
Now put your shields before your hearts, and fight
With hearts more proof than shields. Advance,
brave Titus.
They do disdain us much beyond our thoughts,
Which makes me sweat with wrath. Come on, my
fellows.
He that retires, I'll take him for a Volsce,

And he shall feel mine edge.

*Alarum. The Romans are beat back to their trenches.
Enter Marcius, cursing*

MARCIUS. All the contagion of the south light on you, 30
You shames of Rome! you herd of—Boils and
plagues
Plaster you o'er, that you may be abhorred
Farther than seen, and one infect another
Against the wind a mile! You souls of geese
That bear the shapes of men, how have you run
From slaves that apes would beat! Pluto and hell!
All hurt behind! backs red, and faces pale
With flight and agued fear! Mend and charge home,
Or, by the fires of heaven, I'll leave the foe,
And make my wars on you. Look to't. Come on; 40
If you'll stand fast, we'll beat them to their wives,
As they us to our trenches.

*Another alarum. The Volsces fly, and Marcius follows
them to the gates*

So, now the gates are ope: now prove good seconds:
'Tis for the followers Fortune widens them,
Not for the fliers. Mark me, and do the like.
Enters the gates
1 SOLDIER. Fool-hardiness; not I.
2 SOLDIER. Nor I. *Marcius is shut in*
1 SOLDIER. See, they have shut him in.
ALL. To th' pot, I warrant him.
Alarum continues

Enter Titus Lartius

LARTIUS. What is become of Marcius?
ALL. Slain, sir, doubtless.
1 SOLDIER. Following the fliers at the very heels, 50
With them he enters; who, upon the sudden,
Clapped to their gates. He is himself alone,
To answer all the city.
LARTIUS. O noble fellow!
Who sensibly outdares his senseless sword,
And when it bows stand'st up! Thou art lost,
Marcius!
A carbuncle entire, as big as thou art,
Were not so rich a jewel. Thou wast a soldier
Even to Cato's wish, not fierce and terrible
Only in strokes; but with thy grim looks and
The thunder-like percussion of thy sounds 60
Thou mad'st thine enemies shake, as if the world
Were feverous and did tremble.

*The gates re-open, and Marcius, bleeding, assaulted by
the enemy is seen within*

1 SOLDIER. Look, sir.
LARTIUS. O, 'tis Marcius!
Let's fetch him off, or make remain alike.
They fight, and all enter the city

Scene 5

Certain Romans, with spoils come running from the city

1 ROMAN. This will I carry to Rome.
2 ROMAN. And I this.
3 ROMAN. A murrain on't! I took this for silver.
Sounds of the distant battle still heard

Enter Marcius and Titus Lartius with a trumpeter

MARCIUS. See here these movers that do prize their
  honours
At a cracked drachma! Cushions, leaden spoons,
Irons of a doit, doublets that hangmen would
Bury with those that wore them, these base slaves,
Ere yet the fight be done, pack up. Down with
  them!
And hark, what noise the general makes! To him!
There is the man of my soul's hate, Aufidius,   10
Piercing our Romans: then, valiant Titus, take
Convenient numbers to make good the city;
Whilst I, with those that have the spirit, will haste
To help Cominius.

LARTIUS.   Worthy sir, thou bleed'st;
Thy exercise hath been too violent
For a second course of fight.

MARCIUS.   Sir, praise me not;
My work hath yet not warmed me. Fare you well:
The blood I drop is rather physical
Than dangerous to me. To Aufidius thus
I will appear, and fight.

LARTIUS.   Now the fair goddess, Fortune, 20
Fall deep in love with thee; and her great charms
Misguide thy opposers' swords! Bold gentleman,
Prosperity be thy page!

MARCIUS.   Thy friend no less
Than those she placeth highest! So farewell.

LARTIUS. Thou worthiest Marcius!   *Marcius goes*
Go, sound thy trumpet in the market-place;
Call thither all the officers o'th' town,
Where they shall know our mind. Away!

                                   They go

Scene 6: Near the Roman camp

Enter Cominius, as it were in retire, with soldiers

COMINIUS. Breathe you, my friends: well fought; we
  are come off
Like Romans, neither foolish in our stands
Nor cowardly in retire. Believe me, sirs,
We shall be charged again. Whiles we have struck,
By interims and conveying gusts we have heard
The charges of our friends. The Roman gods,
Lead their successes as we wish our own,
That both our powers, with smiling fronts
  encount'ring,
May give you thankful sacrifice!

Enter a Messenger

                           Thy news?

MESSENGER. The citizens of Corioli have issued, 10
And given to Lartius and to Marcius battle:
I saw our party to their trenches driven,
And then I came away.

COMINIUS.   Though thou speak'st truth,
Methinks thou speak'st not well. How long is't
  since?

MESSENGER. Above an hour, my lord.

COMINIUS. 'Tis not a mile; briefly we heard their
  drums.
How couldst thou in a mile confound an hour,
And bring thy news so late?

MESSENGER.   Spies of the Volsces
Held me in chase, that I was forced to wheel
Three or four miles about; else had I, sir, 20
Half an hour since brought my report.

Marcius approaches

COMINIUS.   Who's yonder
That does appear as he were flayed? O gods!
He has the stamp of Marcius, and I have
Before-time seen him thus.

MARCIUS.   Come I too late?

COMINIUS. The shepherd knows not thunder from a
  tabor
More than I know the sound of Marcius' tongue
From every meaner man.

MARCIUS.   Come I too late?

COMINIUS. Ay, if you come not in the blood of others,
But mantled in your own.

MARCIUS.   O, let me clip ye
In arms as sound as when I wooed; in heart   30
As merry as when our nuptial day was done,
And tapers burned to bedward!

COMINIUS.   Flower of warriors!—
How is't with Titus Lartius?

MARCIUS. As with a man busied about decrees:
Condemning some to death and some to exile;
Ransoming him or pitying, threat'ning th' other;
Holding Corioli in the name of Rome,
Even like a fawning greyhound in the leash,
To let him slip at will.

COMINIUS.   Where is that slave
Which told me they had beat you to your trenches? 40
Where is he? call him hither.

MARCIUS.   Let him alone;
He did inform the truth. But for our gentlemen,
The common file—a plague! tribunes for them!—
The mouse ne'er shunned the cat as they did budge
From rascals worse than they.

COMINIUS.   But how prevailed you?

MARCIUS. Will the time serve to tell? I do not think.
Where is the enemy? Are you lords o' th' field?
If not, why cease you till you are so?

COMINIUS.   Marcius,
We have at disadvantage fought and did
Retire to win our purpose.   50

MARCIUS. How lies their battle? know you on which
  side
They have placed their men of trust?

COMINIUS.   As I guess, Marcius,
Their bands i' th' vaward are the Antiates,
Of their best trust; o'er them Aufidius,
Their very heart of hope.

MARCIUS.   I do beseech you,
By all the battles wherein we have fought,
By th' blood we have shed together, by th' vows
We have made to endure friends, that you directly
Set me against Aufidius and his Antiates;
And that you not delay the present, but,   60
Filling the air with swords advanced and darts,
We prove this very hour.

COMINIUS.   Though I could wish
You were conducted to a gentle bath,
And balms applied to you, yet dare I never
Deny your asking: take your choice of those
That best can aid your action.

MARCIUS.   Those are they
That most are willing. If any such be here—
As it were sin to doubt—that love this painting
Wherein you see me smeared; if any fear
Lesser his person than an ill report;   70

If any think brave death outweighs bad life,
And that his country's dearer than himself;
Let him alone, or so many so minded,
Wave thus, to express his disposition,
And follow Marcius.

*They all shout, and wave their
swords; take him up in their
arms, and cast up their caps*

O me, alone! Make you a sword of me?
If these shows be not outward, which of you
But is four Volsces? none of you but is
Able to bear against the great Aufidius
A shield as hard as his. A certain number,   80
Though thanks to all, must I select from all: the rest
Shall bear the business in some other fight,
As cause will be obeyed. Please you to march;
And I shall quickly draw out my command,
Which men are best inclined.

COMINIUS.   March on, my fellows:
Make good this ostentation, and you shall
Divide in all with us.   *They go*

Scene 7: *Before the gates of Corioli*

*Titus Lartius, having set a guard upon Corioli, going
with drum and trumpet toward Cominius and Caius
Marcius, enters with a Lieutenant, other Soldiers, and a
Scout*

LARTIUS. So, let the ports be guarded: keep your
      duties
As I have set them down. If I do send, dispatch
Those centuries to our aid; the rest will serve
For a short holding. If we lose the field,
We cannot keep the town.

LIEUTENANT.   Fear not our care, sir.

LARTIUS. Hence, and shut your gates upon 's.
Our guider, come; to th' Roman camp conduct us.
                                          They go

Scene 8: *Near the Roman camp*

*Alarum as in battle. Enter Marcius and Aufidius, from
opposite sides*

MARCIUS. I'll fight with none but thee, for I do hate
      thee
Worse than a promise-breaker.

AUFIDIUS.   We hate alike:
Not Afric owns a serpent I abhor
More than thy fame and envy. Fix thy foot.

MARCIUS. Let the first budger die the other's slave,
And the gods doom him after!

AUFIDIUS.   If I fly, Marcius,
Holloa me like a hare.

MARCIUS.   Within these three hours, Tullus,
Alone I fought in your Corioli walls,
And made what work I pleased. 'Tis not my blood
Wherein thou seest me masked. For thy revenge   10
Wrench up thy power to th' highest.

AUFIDIUS.   Wert thou the Hector
That was the whip of your bragged progeny,
Thou shouldst not scape me here.

*Here they fight, and certain Volsces come in the aid of
Aufidius*

Officious, and not valiant, you have shamed me
In your condemnèd seconds.

Marcius fights till they be driven away breathless

Scene 9

*Flourish. Alarum. A retreat is sounded. Enter, from one
side, Cominius with the Romans; from the other side,
Marcius, with his arm in a scarf*

COMINIUS. If I should tell thee o'er this thy day's work,
Thou't not believe thy deeds: but I'll report it
Where senators shall mingle tears with smiles;
Where great patricians shall attend, and shrug,
I' th' end admire; where ladies shall be frighted,
And, gladly quaked, hear more; where the dull
      tribunes,
That with the fusty plebeians hate thine honours,
Shall say against their hearts 'We thank the gods
Our Rome hath such a soldier.'
Yet cam'st thou to a morsel of this feast,   10
Having fully dined before.

Enter Titus Lartius, with his power, from the pursuit

LARTIUS.   O general,
Here is the steed, we the caparison!
Hadst thou beheld—

MARCIUS.   Pray now, no more: my mother,
Who has a charter to extol her blood,
When she does praise me grieves me. I have done
As you have done—that's what I can: induced
As you have been—that's for my country:
He that has but effected his good will
Hath overta'en mine act.

COMINIUS.   You shall not be
The grave of your deserving; Rome must know   20
The value of her own: 'twere a concealment
Worse than a theft, no less than a traducement,
To hide your doings; and to silence that
Which, to the spire and top of praises vouched,
Would seem but modest: therefore, I beseech you,
In sign of what you are, not to reward
What you have done, before our army hear me.

MARCIUS. I have some wounds upon me, and they
      smart
To hear themselves rememb'red.

COMINIUS.   Should they not,
Well might they fester 'gainst ingratitude,   30
And tent themselves with death. Of all the horses—
Whereof we have ta'en good, and good store—of
      all
The treasure in this field achieved and city,
We render you the tenth; to be ta'en forth
Before the common distribution at
Your only choice.

MARCIUS.   I thank you, general;
But cannot make my heart consent to take
A bribe to pay my sword: I do refuse it,
And stand upon my common part with those
That have upheld the doing.   40

*A long flourish. They all cry Marcius!
Marcius! cast up their caps and lances:
Cominius and Lartius stand bare*

MARCIUS. May these same instruments which you
      profane
Never sound more! When drums and trumpets shall
I' th' field prove flatterers, let courts and cities be
Made all of false-faced soothing!
When steel grows soft as the parasite's silk,
Let him be made a coverture for th' wars!
No more, I say! For that I have not washed

My nose that bled, or foiled some debile wretch,
Which without note here's many else have done,
You shout me forth   50
In acclamations hyperbolical;
As if I loved my little should be dieted
In praises sauced with lies.
COMINIUS.   Too modest are you;
More cruel to your good report than grateful
To us that give you truly. By your patience,
If 'gainst yourself you be incensed, we'll put you
(Like one that means his proper harm) in manacles,
Then reason safely with you. Therefore, be it
     known,
As to us, to all the world, that Caius Marcius
Wears this war's garland: in token of the which,   60
My noble steed, known to the camp, I give him,
With all his trim belonging; and from this time,
For what he did before Corioli, call him,
With all th' applause and clamour of the host,
CAIUS MARCIUS CORIOLANUS.
Bear th' addition nobly ever!
               Flourish; trumpets sound, and drums
ALL. Caius Marcius Coriolanus!
CORIOLANUS. I will go wash;
And when my face is fair, you shall perceive
Whether I blush, or no. Howbeit, I thank you: 70
I mean to stride your steed, and at all times
To undercrest your good addition
To th' fairness of my power.
COMINIUS.   So, to our tent;
Where, ere we do repose us, we will write
To Rome of our success. You, Titus Lartius,
Must to Corioli back: send us to Rome
The best, with whom we may articulate
For their own good and ours.
LARTIUS.   I shall, my lord.
CORIOLANUS. The gods begin to mock me. I, that now
Refused most princely gifts, am bound to beg   80
Of my lord general.
COMINIUS.   Take't; 'tis yours. What is't?
CORIOLANUS. I sometime lay here in Corioli
And at a poor man's house; he used me kindly.
He cried to me; I saw him prisoner;
But then Aufidius was within my view,
And wrath o'erwhelmed my pity. I request you
To give my poor host freedom.
COMINIUS.   O, well begged!
Were he the butcher of my son, he should
Be free as is the wind. Deliver him, Titus.
LARTIUS. Marcius, his name?
CORIOLANUS.   By Jupiter, forgot!   90
I am weary; yea, my memory is tired.
Have we no wine here?
COMINIUS.   Go we to our tent:
The blood upon your visage dries; 'tis time
It should be looked to: come.   *They go*

Scene 10: *The camp of the Volsces*

*A flourish. Cornets. Enter Tullus Aufidius bloody, with
two or three soldiers*

AUFIDIUS. The town is ta'en!
I SOLDIER. 'Twill be delivered back on good
     condition.
AUFIDIUS. Condition!
I would I were a Roman; for I cannot,

Being a Volsce, be that I am. Condition!
What good condition can a treaty find
I' th' part that is at mercy? Five times, Marcius,
I have fought with thee; so often hast thou beat me;
And wouldst do so, I think, should we encounter
As often as we eat. By th' elements,   10
If e'er again I meet him beard to beard,
He's mine or I am his. Mine emulation
Hath not that honour in't it had; for where
I thought to crush him in an equal force,
True sword to sword, I'll potch at him some way,
Or wrath or craft may get him.
I SOLDIER.   He's the devil.
AUFIDIUS. Bolder, though not so subtle. My valour's
     poisoned
With only suff'ring stain by him; for him
Shall fly out of itself. Nor sleep nor sanctuary,
Being naked, sick, nor fane nor Capitol,   20
The prayers of priests nor times of sacrifice,
Embarquements all of fury, shall lift up
Their rotten privilege and custom 'gainst
My hate to Marcius. Where I find him, were it
At home, upon my brother's guard, even there,
Against the hospitable canon, would I
Wash my fierce hand in's heart. Go you to th' city;
Learn how 'tis held, and what they are that must
Be hostages for Rome.
I SOLDIER.   Will not you go?
AUFIDIUS. I am attended at the cypress grove: I pray
     you—   30
'Tis south the city mills—bring me word thither
How the world goes, that to the pace of it
I may spur on my journey.
I SOLDIER.   I shall, sir.   *They go*

ACT 2
Scene 1: *Rome. A public place*

*Enter Menenius, with the two Tribunes of the people,
Sicinius, and Brutus*

MENENIUS. The augurer tells me we shall have news
     to-night.
BRUTUS. Good or bad?
MENENIUS. Not according to the prayer of the people,
     for they love not Marcius.
SICINIUS. Nature teaches beasts to know their friends.
MENENIUS. Pray you, who does the wolf love?
SICINIUS. The lamb.
MENENIUS. Ay, to devour him, as the hungry plebeians
     would the noble Marcius.   10
BRUTUS. He's a lamb indeed, that baas like a bear.
MENENIUS. He's a bear indeed, that lives like a lamb.
     You two are old men: tell me one thing that I shall
     ask you.
BOTH. Well, sir.
MENENIUS. In what enormity is Marcius poor in, that
     you two have not in abundance?
BRUTUS. He's poor in no one fault, but stored with all.
SICINIUS. Especially in pride.
BRUTUS. And topping all others in boasting.   20
MENENIUS. This is strange now. Do you two know
     how you are censured here in the city—I mean of
     us o'th' right-hand file? do you?
BOTH. Why, how are we censured?

MENENIUS. Because you talk of pride now—will you not be angry?

BOTH. Well, well, sir, well.

MENENIUS. Why, 'tis no great matter; for a very little thief of occasion will rob you of a great deal of patience. Give your dispositions the reins, and be 30 angry at your pleasures; at the least, if you take it as a pleasure to you in being so. You blame Marcius for being proud?

BRUTUS. We do it not alone, sir.

MENENIUS. I know you can do very little alone; for your helps are many, or else your actions would grow wondrous single: your abilities are too infantlike for doing much alone. You talk of pride. O that you could turn your eyes toward the napes of your necks, and make but an interior survey of your good 40 selves! O that you could!

BOTH. What then, sir?

MENENIUS. Why, then you should discover a brace of unmeriting, proud, violent, testy magistrates (alias fools) as any in Rome.

SICINIUS. Menenius, you are known well enough too.

MENENIUS. I am known to be a humorous patrician, and one that loves a cup of hot wine with not a drop of allaying Tiber in't; said to be something imperfect in favouring the first complaint, hasty and tinder- 50 like upon too trivial motion; one that converses more with the buttock of the night than with the forehead of the morning. What I think I utter, and spend my malice in my breath. Meeting two such wealsmen as you are—I cannot call you Lycurguses —if the drink you give me touch my palate adversely, I make a crooked face at it. I cannot say your worships have delivered the matter well, when I find the ass in compound with the major part of your syllables; and though I must be content to bear 60 with those that say you are reverend grave men, yet they lie deadly that tell you you have good faces. If you see this in the map of my microcosm, follows it that I am known well enough too? what harm can your bisson conspectuities glean out of this character, if I be known well enough too?

BRUTUS. Come, sir, come, we know you well enough.

MENENIUS. You know neither me, yourselves, nor any thing. You are ambitious for poor knaves' caps and legs: you wear out a good wholesome forenoon in 70 hearing a cause between an orange-wife and a faucet-seller, and then rejourn the controversy of three-pence to a second day of audience. When you are hearing a matter between party and party, if you chance to be pinched with the colic, you make faces like mummers, set up the bloody flag against all patience, and, in roaring for a chamber-pot, dismiss the controversy bleeding, the more entangled by your hearing. All the peace you make in their cause is calling both the parties knaves. You are a pair of 80 strange ones.

BRUTUS. Come, come, you are well understood to be a perfecter giber for the table than a necessary bencher in the Capitol.

MENENIUS. Our very priests must become mockers, if they shall encounter such ridiculous subjects as you are. When you speak best unto the purpose, it is not worth the wagging of your beards; and your beards deserve not so honourable a grave as to stuff a botcher's cushion or to be entombed in an ass's pack- 90

saddle. Yet you must be saying Marcius is proud; who, in a cheap estimation, is worth all your predecessors since Deucalion; though peradventure some of the best of 'em were hereditary hangmen. God-den to your worships: more of your conversation would infect my brain, being the herdsmen of the beastly plebeians. I will be bold to take my leave of you.   *Brutus and Sicinius stand aside*

Enter Volumnia, Virgilia, and Valeria

How now, my as fair as noble ladies—and the moon, were she earthly, no nobler—whither do you 100 follow your eyes so fast?

VOLUMNIA. Honourable Menenius, my boy Marcius approaches; for the love of Juno, let's go.

MENENIUS. Ha? Marcius coming home!

VOLUMNIA. Ay, worthy Menenius; and with most prosperous approbation.

MENENIUS. Take my cap, Jupiter, and I thank thee. Hoo! Marcius coming home!

VIRGILIA. }
VALERIA. }   Nay, 'tis true.

VOLUMNIA. Look, here's a letter from him: the state 110 hath another, his wife another; and, I think, there's one at home for you.

MENENIUS. I will make my very house reel to-night. A letter for me?

VIRGILIA. Yes, certain, there's a letter for you; I saw 't.

MENENIUS. A letter for me! it gives me an estate of seven years' health; in which time I will make a lip at the physician: the most sovereign prescription in Galen is but empiricutic, and, to this preservative, of no better report than a horse-drench. Is he not 120 wounded? he was wont to come home wounded.

VIRGILIA. O, no, no, no.

VOLUMNIA. O, he is wounded; I thank the gods for't.

MENENIUS. So do I too, if it be not too much. Brings a' victory in his pocket, the wounds become him.

VOLUMNIA. On's brows, Menenius. He comes the third time home with the oaken garland.

MENENIUS. Has he disciplined Aufidius soundly?

VOLUMNIA. Titus Lartius writes they fought together, but Aufidius got off. 130

MENENIUS. And 'twas time for him too, I'll warrant him that: an he had stayed by him, I would not have been so fidiused for all the chests in Corioli, and the gold that's in them. Is the Senate possessed of this?

VOLUMNIA. Good ladies, let's go. Yes, yes, yes: the Senate has letters from the General, wherein he gives my son the whole name of the war: he hath in this action outdone his former deeds doubly.

VALERIA. In troth, there's wondrous things spoke of 140 him.

MENENIUS. Wondrous! ay, I warrant you, and not without his true purchasing.

VIRGILIA. The gods grant them true!

VOLUMNIA. True! pooh-pooh!

MENENIUS. True! I'll be sworn they are true. Where is he wounded?—[*observing the tribunes*] God save your good worships! Marcius is coming home: he has more cause to be proud.—Where is he wounded? 150

VOLUMNIA. I' th' shoulder and i' th' left arm: there will be large cicatrices to show the people, when he

shall stand for his place. He received in the repulse
of Tarquin seven hurts i' th' body.
MENENIUS. One i' th' neck, and two i' th' thigh—
there's nine that I know.
VOLUMNIA. He had before this last expedition twenty-
five wounds upon him.
MENENIUS. Now it's twenty-seven: every gash was an
enemy's grave. [*A shout and flourish*] Hark! the 160
trumpets.
VOLUMNIA. These are the ushers of Marcius. Before
him he carries noise, and behind him he leaves tears:
Death, that dark spirit, in's nervy arm doth lie,
Which, being advanced, declines, and then men die.

*A sennet. Trumpets sound. Enter Cominius the general
and Titus Lartius; between them, Coriolanus, crowned
with an oaken garland; with Captains and Soldiers, and
a Herald*

HERALD. Know, Rome, that all alone Marcius did
fight
Within Corioli gates, where he hath won,
With fame, a name to Caius Marcius; these
In honour follows Coriolanus.
Welcome to Rome, renownéd Coriolanus! 170
Flourish
ALL. Welcome to Rome, renownéd Coriolanus!
CORIOLANUS. No more of this, it does offend my heart;
Pray now, no more.
COMINIUS. Look, sir, your mother!
CORIOLANUS. O, *Kneels*
You have, I know, petitioned all the gods
For my prosperity!
VOLUMNIA. Nay, my good soldier, up;
My gentle Marcius, worthy Caius, and
By deed-achieving honour newly named—
What is it?—Coriolanus must I call thee?—
But, O, thy wife!
CORIOLANUS. My gracious silence, hail!
Wouldst thou have laughed had I come coffined
home, 180
That weep'st to see me triumph? Ah, my dear,
Such eyes the widows in Corioli wear,
And mothers that lack sons.
MENENIUS. Now, the gods crown thee!
CORIOLANUS. And live you yet? [*sees Valeria*] O my
sweet lady, pardon.
VOLUMNIA. I know not where to turn: O, welcome
home!
And welcome, General: and you're welcome all.
MENENIUS. A hundred thousand welcomes. I could
weep
And I could laugh, I am light and heavy. Welcome!
A curse begnaw the very root on's heart
That is not glad to see thee! You are three 190
That Rome should dote on: yet, by the faith of
men,
We have some old crab-trees here at home that will
not
Be grafted to your relish. Yet welcome, warriors:
We call a nettle but a nettle, and
The faults of fools but folly.
COMINIUS. Ever right.
CORIOLANUS. Menenius, ever, ever.
HERALD. Give way there, and go on.
CORIOLANUS [*to wife and mother*]. Your hand, and
yours!

Ere in our own house I do shade my head,
The good patricians must be visited; 200
From whom I have received not only greetings,
But with them change of honours.
VOLUMNIA. I have lived
To see inherited my very wishes
And the buildings of my fancy: only
There's one thing wanting, which I doubt not but
Our Rome will cast upon thee.
CORIOLANUS. Know, good mother,
I had rather be their servant in my way
Than away with them in theirs.
COMINIUS. On, to the Capitol!
*Flourish; cornets. Exeunt in state, as before.
Brutus and Sicinius come forward*
BRUTUS. All tongues speak of him, and the bleared
sights
Are spectacled to see him. Your prattling nurse 210
Into a rapture lets her baby cry
While she chats him: the kitchen malkin pins
Her richest lockram 'bout her reechy neck,
Clamb'ring the walls to eye him: stalls, bulks,
windows,
Are smothered up, leads filled and ridges horsed
With variable complexions, all agreeing
In earnestness to see him: seld-shown flamens
Do press among the popular throngs, and puff
To win a vulgar station: our veiled dames
Commit the war of white and damask in 220
Their nicely-guarded cheeks to th' wanton spoil
Of Phœbus' burning kisses: such a pother,
As if that whatsoever god who leads him
Were slily crept into his human powers,
And gave him graceful posture.
SICINIUS. On the sudden,
I warrant him consul.
BRUTUS. Then our office may
During his power go sleep.
SICINIUS. He cannot temp'rately transport his honours
From where he should begin and end, but will
Lose those he hath won.
BRUTUS. In that there's comfort.
SICINIUS. Doubt not 230
The commoners, for whom we stand, but they
Upon their ancient malice will forget
With the least cause these his new honours; which
That he will give make I as little question
As he is proud to do't.
BRUTUS. I heard him swear,
Were he to stand for consul, never would he
Appear i' th' market-place, nor on him put
The napless vesture of humility;
Nor, showing, as the manner is, his wounds
To th' people, beg their stinking breaths.
SICINUS. 'Tis right. 240
BRUTUS. It was his word. O, he would miss it rather
Than carry it but by the suit of the gentry to him
And the desire of the nobles.
SICINIUS. I wish no better
Than have him hold that purpose and to put it
In execution.
BRUTUS. 'Tis most like he will.
SICINIUS. It shall be to him then as our good wills:
A sure destruction.
BRUTUS. So it must fall out
To him or our authorities. For an end,

We must suggest the people in what hatred
He still hath held them; that to's power he would   240
Have made them mules, silenced their pleaders and
Dispropertied their freedoms; holding them,
In human action and capacity,
Of no more soul nor fitness for the world
Than camels in the war, who have their provand
Only for bearing burthens, and sore blows
For sinking under them.
SICINIUS.   This, as you say, suggested
At some time when his soaring insolence
Shall touch the people—which time shall not want,
If he be put upon't, and that's as easy   250
As to set dogs on sheep—will be the fire
To kindle their dry stubble; and their blaze
Shall darken him for ever.

Enter a Messenger

BRUTUS.   What's the matter?
MESSENGER. You are sent for to the Capitol. 'Tis
    thought
    That Marcius shall be consul.
I have seen the dumb men throng to see him and
The blind to hear him speak; matrons flung gloves,
Ladies and maids their scarfs and handkerchers,
Upon him as he passed; the nobles bended,
As to Jove's statue, and the commons made   260
A shower and thunder with their caps and shouts.
I never saw the like.
BRUTUS.   Let's to the Capitol,
And carry with us ears and eyes for th' time,
But hearts for the event.
SICINIUS.   Have with you.
                                        They go

Scene 2: *Rome. The Senate House at the Capitol*

Enter two Officers, to lay cushions

1 OFFICER. Come, come, they are almost here. How
    many stand for consulships?
2 OFFICER. Three, they say: but 'tis thought of every
    one Coriolanus will carry it.
1 OFFICER. That's a brave fellow; but he's vengeance
    proud, and loves not the common people.
2 OFFICER. Faith, there hath been many great men that
    have flattered the people, who ne'er loved them; and
    there be many that they have loved, they know not
    wherefore: so that, if they love they know not why,   10
    they hate upon no better a ground. Therefore, for
    Coriolanus neither to care whether they love or hate
    him manifests the true knowledge he has in their
    disposition; and out of his noble carelessness lets
    them plainly see't.
1 OFFICER. If he did not care whether he had their love
    or no, he waved indifferently 'twixt doing them
    neither good nor harm. But he seeks their hate with
    greater devotion than they can render it him, and
    leaves nothing undone that may fully discover him   20
    their opposite. Now, to seem to affect the malice
    and displeasure of the people is as bad as that which
    he dislikes, to flatter them for their love.
2 OFFICER. He hath deserved worthily of his country;
    and his ascent is not by such easy degrees as those
    who, having been supple and courteous to the
    people, bonneted, without any further deed to have
    them at all, into their estimation and report. But he

hath so planted his honours in their eyes and his
actions in their hearts that for their tongues to be   30
silent and not confess so much were a kind of
ingrateful injury; to report otherwise were a malice
that, giving itself the lie, would pluck reproof and
rebuke from every ear that heard it.
1 OFFICER. No more of him; he's a worthy man. Make
    way, they are coming.

*A sennet. Enter the Patricians and the Tribunes of the
People, Lictors before them; Coriolanus, Menenius,
Cominius the Consul. Siginius and Brutus take their
places by themselves*

MENENIUS. Having determined of the Volsces, and
    To send for Titus Lartius, it remains,
    As the main point of this our after-meeting,
    To gratify his noble service that   40
    Hath thus stood for his country: therefore, please
        you
    Most reverend and grave elders, to desire
    The present consul, and last general
    In our well-found successes, to report
    A little of that worthy work performed
    By Caius Marcius Coriolanus; whom
    We met here both to thank and to remember
    With honours like himself.
1 SENATOR.   Speak, good Cominius:
    Leave nothing out for length, and make us think
    Rather our state's defective for requital   50
    Than we to stretch it out. [*to the Tribunes*] Masters
        o' th' people,
    We do request your kindest ears; and, after,
    Your loving motion toward the common body,
    To yield what passes here.
SICINIUS.   We are convented
    Upon a pleasing treaty, and have hearts
    Inclinable to honour and advance
    The theme of our assembly.
BRUTUS.   Which the rather
    We shall be blessed to do, if he remember
    A kinder value of the people than
    He hath hereto prized them at.
MENENIUS.   That's off, that's off;   60
    I would you rather had been silent. Please you
    To hear Cominius speak?
BRUTUS.   Most willingly:
    But yet my caution was more pertinent
    Than the rebuke you give it.
MENENIUS.   He loves your people;
    But tie him not to be their bedfellow.
    Worthy Cominius, speak.
            Coriolanus rises and offers to go away
                          Nay, keep your place.
1 SENATOR. Sit, Coriolanus; never shame to hear
    What you have nobly done.
CORIOLANUS.   Your Honours' pardon:
    I had rather have my wounds to heal again
    Than hear say how I got them.
BRUTUS.   Sir, I hope   70
    My words disbenched you not.
CORIOLANUS.   No, sir: yet oft,
    When blows have made me stay, I fled from words.
    You soothed not, therefore hurt not: but your
        people,
    I love them as they weigh—
MENENIUS.   Pray now, sit down.

CORIOLANUS. I had rather have one scratch my head i'
    th' sun
When the alarum were struck than idly sit
To hear my nothings monstered.   *He goes*
MENENIUS.   Masters of the people,
Your multiplying spawn how can he flatter—
That's thousand to one good one—when you now
    see
He had rather venture all his limbs for honour   80
Than one on's ears to hear it? Proceed, Cominius.
COMINIUS. I shall lack voice: the deeds of Coriolanus
Should not be uttered feebly. It is held
That valour is the chiefest virtue and
Most dignifies the haver: if it be,
The man I speak of cannot in the world
Be singly counterpoised. At sixteen years,
When Tarquin made a head for Rome, he fought
Beyond the mark of others: our then dictator,
Whom with all praise I point at, saw him fight,   90
When with his Amazonian chin he drove
The bristled lips before him: he bestrid
An o'erpressed Roman, and i' th' consul's view
Slew three opposers: Tarquin's self he met,
And struck him on his knee: in that day's feats,
When he might act the woman in the scene,
He proved best man i' th' field, and for his meed
Was brow-bound with the oak. His pupil age
Man-ent'red thus, he waxéd like a sea;
And, in the brunt of seventeen battles since,   100
He lurched all swords of the garland. For this
    last,
Before and in Corioli, let me say,
I cannot speak him home. He stopped the fliers,
And by his rare example made the coward
Turn terror into sport: as weeds before
A vessel under sail, so men obeyed,
And fell below his stem. His sword, death's stamp,
Where it did mark, it took; from face to foot
He was a thing of blood, whose every motion
Was timed with dying cries. Alone he ent'red   110
The mortal gate of th' city, which he painted
With shunless destiny; aidless came off,
And with a sudden re-enforcement struck
Corioli like a planet. Now all's his,
When by and by the din of war 'gan pierce
His ready sense, then straight his doubled spirit
Re-quickened what in flesh was fatigate,
And to the battle came he; where he did
Run reeking o'er the lives of men, as if
'Twere a perpetual spoil: and till we called   120
Both field and city ours, he never stood
To ease his breast with panting.
MENENIUS.   Worthy man!
1 SENATOR. He cannot but with measure fit the
    honours
Which we devise him.
COMINIUS.   Our spoils he kicked at,
And looked upon things precious as they were
The common muck of the world: he covets less
Than misery itself would give, rewards
His deeds with doing them, and is content
To spend the time to end it.
MENENIUS.   He's right noble:
Let him be called for.
1 SENATOR.   Call Coriolanus.
OFFICER. He doth appear.   130

Coriolanus returns

MENENIUS. The Senate, Coriolanus, are well pleased
To make thee consul.
CORIOLANUS.   I do owe them still
My life and services.
MENENIUS.   It then remains
That you do speak to the people.
CORIOLANUS.   I do beseech you
Let me o'erleap that custom, for I cannot
Put on the gown, stand naked, and entreat them,
For my wounds' sake, to give their suffrage: please
    you
That I may pass this doing.
SICINIUS.   Sir, the people
Must have their voices; neither will they bate   140
One jot of ceremony.
MENENIUS.   Put them not to't.
Pray you, go fit you to the custom, and
Take to you, as your predecessors have,
Your honour with your form.
CORIOLANUS.   It is a part
That I shall blush in acting, and might well
Be taken from the people.
BRUTUS.   Mark you that.
CORIOLANUS. To brag unto them, 'Thus I did, and
    thus!'
Show them th' unaching scars which I should hide,
As if I had received them for the hire
Of their breath only!
MENENIUS.   Do not stand upon't.   150
[*aloud*] We recommend to you, tribunes of the
    people,
Our purpose to them: and to our noble consul
Wish we all joy and honour.
SENATORS. To Coriolanus come all joy and honour!
          *Flourish of cornets; all leave the Senate
                  House but Sicinius and Brutus*
BRUTUS. You see how he intends to use the people.
SICINIUS. May they perceive's intent! He will require
    them,
As if he did contemn what he requested
Should be in them to give.
BRUTUS.   Come, we'll inform them
Of our proceedings here. On th' market-place,
I know, they do attend us.   *They follow* 160

Scene 3: *Rome. The Forum*

Enter seven or eight Citizens

1 CITIZEN. Once, if he do require our voices, we ought
    not to deny him.
2 CITIZEN. We may, sir, if we will.
3 CITIZEN. We have power in ourselves to do it, but it
    is a power that we have no power to do: for if he
    show us his wounds and tell us his deeds, we are to
    put our tongues into those wounds and speak for
    them; so, if he tell us his noble deeds, we must also
    tell him our noble acceptance of them. Ingratitude
    is monstrous: and for the multitude to be ingrateful, 10
    were to make a monster of the multitude; of the
    which we being members, should bring ourselves to
    be monstrous members.
1 CITIZEN. And to make us no better thought of, a
    little help will serve; for once we stood up about the

corn, he himself stuck not to call us the many-headed multitude.

3 CITIZEN. We have been called so of many; not that our heads are some brown, some black, some abram, some bald, but that our wits are so diversely 20 coloured: and truly I think, if all our wits were to issue out of one skull, they would fly east, west, north, south, and their consent of one direct way should be at once to all the points o' th' compass.

2 CITIZEN. Think you so? Which way do you judge my wit would fly?

3 CITIZEN. Nay, your wit will not so soon out as another man's will; 'tis strongly wedged up in a blockhead; but if it were at liberty, 'twould, sure, southward. 30

2 CITIZEN. Why that way?

3 CITIZEN. To lose itself in a fog; where being three parts melted away with rotten dews, the fourth would return for conscience sake, to help to get thee a wife.

2 CITIZEN. You are never without your tricks: you may, you may.

3 CITIZEN. Are you all resolved to give your voices? But that's no matter, the greater part carries it. I say, if he would incline to the people, there was 40 never a worthier man.

Enter Coriolanus in a gown of humility, with Menenius

Here he comes, and in the gown of humility: mark his behaviour. We are not to stay all together, but to come by him where he stands, by ones, by twos, and by threes. He's to make his requests by particulars; wherein every one of us has a single honour, in giving him our own voices with our own tongues: therefore follow me, and I'll direct you how you shall go by him.

ALL. Content, content. *They go* 50

MENENIUS. O sir, you are not right: have you not known
The worthiest men have done 't?

CORIOLANUS. What must I say?—
'I pray, sir'—Plague upon't! I cannot bring
My tongue to such a pace. 'Look, sir, my wounds!
I got them in my country's service, when
Some certain of your brethren roared and ran
From th' noise of our own drums.'

MENENIUS. O me, the gods!
You must not speak of that: you must desire them
To think upon you.

CORIOLANUS. Think upon me! hang 'em!
I would they would forget me, like the virtues 60
Which our divines lose by 'em.

MENENIUS. You'll mar all.
I'll leave you. Pray you, speak to 'em, I pray you,
In wholesome manner. *He goes*

Re-enter Second and Third Citizens

CORIOLANUS. Bid them wash their faces,
And keep their teeth clean. So, here comes a brace.
You know the cause, sir, of my standing here.

3 CITIZEN. We do, sir; tell us what hath brought you to 't.

CORIOLANUS. Mine own desert.

2 CITIZEN. Your own desert?

CORIOLANUS. Ay, not mine own desire. 70

3 CITIZEN. How not your own desire?

CORIOLANUS. No, sir, 'twas never my desire yet to trouble the poor with begging.

3 CITIZEN. You must think, if we give you any thing, we hope to gain by you.

CORIOLANUS. Well then, I pray, your price o' th' consulship?

3 CITIZEN. The price is, to ask it kindly.

CORIOLANUS. Kindly, sir, I pray let me ha't: I have wounds to show you, which shall be yours in 80 private. [*to the Second Citizen*] Your good voice, sir; what say you?

2 CITIZEN. You shall ha' it, worthy sir.

CORIOLANUS. A match, sir. There's in all two worthy voices begged. I have your alms: adieu.

3 CITIZEN. But this is something odd.

2 CITIZEN. An 'twere to give again—but 'tis no matter. *They go*

Enter two other Citizens

CORIOLANUS. Pray you now, if it may stand with the tune of your voices that I may be consul, I have 90 here the customary gown.

4 CITIZEN. You have deserved nobly of your country, and you have not deserved nobly.

CORIOLANUS. Your enigma?

4 CITIZEN. You have been a scourge to her enemies, you have been a rod to her friends. You have not indeed loved the common people.

CORIOLANUS. You should account me the more virtuous, that I have not been common in my love. I will, sir, flatter my sworn brother, the people, to 100 earn a dearer estimation of them; 'tis a condition they account gentle: and since the wisdom of their choice is rather to have my hat than my heart, I will practise the insinuating nod, and be off to them most counterfeitly; that is, sir, I will counterfeit the bewitchment of some popular man, and give it bountiful to the desirers. Therefore, beseech you I may be consul.

5 CITIZEN. We hope to find you our friend; and therefore give you our voices heartily. 110

4 CITIZEN. You have received many wounds for your country.

CORIOLANUS. I will not seal your knowledge with showing them. I will make much of your voices and so trouble you no farther.

BOTH CITIZENS. The gods give you joy, sir, heartily! *They go*

CORIOLANUS. Most sweet voices!
Better it is to die, better to starve,
Than crave the hire which first we do deserve.
Why in this woolvish toge should I stand here, 120
To beg of Hob and Dick that do appear
Their needless vouches? Custom calls me to't.
What custom wills, in all things should we do't,
The dust on antique time would lie unswept,
And mountainous error be too highly heaped
For truth to o'erpeer. Rather than fool it so,
Let the high office and the honour go
To one that would do thus. I am half through:
The one part suffered, the other will I do.

Enter three Citizens more

Here come moe voices. 130
Your voices! For your voices I have fought;
Watched for your voices; for your voices bear

Of wounds two dozen odd; battles thrice six
I have seen, and heard of; for your voices have
Done many things, some less, some more. Your
    voices!
Indeed, I would be consul.
5 CITIZEN. He has done nobly, and cannot go without
any honest man's voice.
6 CITIZEN. Therefore let him be consul: the gods give
him joy, and make him good friend to the people!   140
ALL. Amen, amen. God save thee, noble consul!
                                                      They go
CORIOLANUS. Worthy voices!

Enter Menenius, with Brutus and Sicinius

MENENIUS. You have stood your limitation; and the
    tribunes
Endue you with the people's voice. Remains
That in th' official marks invested you
Anon do meet the Senate.
CORIOLANUS.   Is this done?
SICINIUS. The custom of request you have discharged:
The people do admit you, and are summoned
To meet anon upon your approbation.
CORIOLANUS. Where? at the Senate House?
SICINIUS.   There, Coriolanus.   150
CORIOLANUS. May I change these garments?
SICINIUS.   You may, sir.
CORIOLANUS. That I'll straight do, and, knowing
    myself again,
Repair to th' Senate House.
MENENIUS. I'll keep you company. Will you along?
BRUTUS. We stay here for the people.
SICINIUS.   Fare you well.
                    Coriolanus and Menenius depart
He has it now; and, by his looks, methinks
'Tis warm at's heart.
BRUTUS.   With a proud heart he wore
His humble weeds. Will you dismiss the people?

Citizens return

SICINIUS. How now, my masters! have you chose this
    man?
1 CITIZEN. He has our voices, sir.   160
BRUTUS. We pray the gods he may deserve your loves.
2 CITIZEN. Amen, sir: to my poor unworthy notice,
He mocked us when he begged our voices.
3 CITIZEN.   Certainly;
He flouted us downright.
1 CITIZEN. No, 'tis his kind of speech—he did not
mock us.
2 CITIZEN. Not one amongst us, save yourself, but says
He used us scornfully: he should have showed us
His marks of merit, wounds received for's country.
SICINIUS. Why, so he did, I am sure.   170
ALL. No, no; no man saw 'em.
3 CITIZEN. He said he had wounds which he could
show in private;
And with his hat, thus waving it in scorn,
'I would be consul,' says he: 'agèd custom,
But by your voices, will not so permit me;
Your voices therefore.' When we granted that,
Here was 'I thank you for your voices. Thank you,
Your most sweet voices. Now you have left your
    voices,
I have no further with you.' Was not this mockery?
SICINIUS. Why either were you ignorant to see't,   180

Or, seeing it, of such childish friendliness
To yield your voices?
BRUTUS.   Could you not have told him—
As you were lessoned—when he had no power,
But was a petty servant to the state,
He was your enemy, ever spake against
Your liberties and the charters that you bear
I' th' body of the weal: and now, arriving
A place of potency and sway o' th' state,
If he should still malignantly remain
Fast foe to th' plebeii, your voices might   190
Be curses to yourselves? You should have said
That as his worthy deeds did claim no less
Than what he stood for, so his gracious nature
Would think upon you for your voices, and
Translate his malice towards you into love,
Standing your friendly lord.
SICINIUS.   Thus to have said,
As you were fore-advised, had touched his spirit
And tried his inclination; from him plucked
Either his gracious promise, which you might,
As cause had called you up, have held him to;   200
Or else it would have galled his surly nature,
Which easily endures not article
Tying him to aught: so, putting him to rage,
You should have ta'en th' advantage of his choler.
And passed him unelected.
BRUTUS.   Did you perceive
He did solicit you in free contempt
When he did need your loves; and do you think
That his contempt shall not be bruising to you
When he hath power to crush? Why, had your
    bodies
No heat among you? or had you tongues to cry   210
Against the rectorship of judgement?
SICINIUS.   Have you
Ere now denied the asker, and now again,
Of him that did not ask but mock, bestow
Your sued-for tongues?
3 CITIZEN. He's not confirmed; we may deny him yet.
2 CITIZEN. And will deny him:
I'll have five hundred voices of that sound.
1 CITIZEN. I twice five hundred; and their friends to
piece 'em.
BRUTUS. Get you hence instantly, and tell those
    friends   220
They have chose a consul that will from them take
Their liberties, make them of no more voice
Than dogs that are as often beat for barking
As therefore kept to do so.
SICINIUS.   Let them assemble;
And, on a safer judgement, all revoke
Your ignorant election. Enforce his pride
And his old hate unto you: besides, forget not
With what contempt he wore the humble weed,
How in his suit he scorned you: but your loves,
Thinking upon his services, took from you   230
Th' apprehension of his present portance,
Which, gibingly, ungravely, he did fashion
After the inveterate hate he bears you.
BRUTUS.   Lay
A fault on us, your tribunes, that we laboured,
No impediment between, but that you must
Cast your election on him.
SICINIUS.   Say you chose him
More after our commandment than as guided

By your own true affections; and that your minds,
Pre-occupied with what you rather must do
Than what you should, made you against the grain   240
To voice him consul. Lay the fault on us.

BRUTUS. Ay, spare us not. Say we read lectures to you,
How youngly he began to serve his country,
How long continued; and what stock he springs of,
The noble house o' th' Marcians, from whence
   came
That Ancus Marcius, Numa's daughter's son,
Who after great Hostilius here was king;
Of the same house Publius and Quintus were,
That our best water brought by conduits hither;
[And Censorinus that was so surnamed]   250
And nobly naméd so, twice being censor,
Was his great ancestor.

SICINIUS.   One thus descended,
That hath beside well in his person wrought
To be set high in place, we did commend
To your remembrances: but you have found,
Scaling his present bearing with his past,
That he's your fixéd enemy, and revoke
Your sudden approbation.

BRUTUS.   Say you ne'er had done't—
Harp on that still—but by our putting on:
And presently, when you have drawn your   260
   number,
Repair to th' Capitol.

CITIZENS.   We will so: almost all
Repent in their election.   *They go*

BRUTUS.   Let them go on;
This mutiny were better put in hazard
Than stay, past doubt, for greater:
If, as his nature is, he fall in rage
With their refusal, both observe and answer
The vantage of his anger.

SICINIUS.   To th' Capitol, come:
We will be there before the stream o' th' people;
And this shall seem, as partly 'tis, their own,
Which we have goaded onward.   *They go* 270

ACT 3

Scene 1: *Rome. A street*

*Cornets. Enter Coriolanus, Menenius, all the Gentry,
Cominius, Titus Lartius, and other Senators*

CORIOLANUS. Tullus Aufidius then had made new
   head?

LARTIUS. He had, my lord; and that it was which
   caused
Our swifter composition.

CORIOLANUS. So then the Volsces stand but as at first;
Ready, when time shall prompt them, to make
   road
Upon's again.

COMINIUS.   They are worn, Lord Consul, so
That we shall hardly in our ages see
Their banners wave again.

CORIOLANUS.   Saw you Aufidius?

LARTIUS. On safeguard he came to me; and did curse
Against the Volsces, for they had so vilely   10
Yielded the town: he is retired to Antium.

CORIOLANUS. Spoke he of me?

LARTIUS.   He did, my lord.

CORIOLANUS.   How? what?

LARTIUS. How often he had met you, sword to
   sword;
That of all things upon the earth he hated
Your person most; that he would pawn his fortunes
To hopeless restitution, so he might
Be called your vanquisher.

CORIOLANUS.   At Antium lives he?

LARTIUS. At Antium.

CORIOLANUS. I wish I had a cause to seek him there,
To oppose his hatred fully. Welcome home.   20

Enter Sicinius and Brutus

Behold, these are the tribunes of the people,
The tongues o' th' common mouth. I do despise
   them;
For they do prank them in authority,
Against all noble sufferance.

SICINIUS.   Pass no further.

CORIOLANUS. Ha? what is that?

BRUTUS. It will be dangerous to go on—no further.

CORIOLANUS. What makes this change?

MENENIUS. The matter?

COMINIUS. Hath he not passed the noble and the
   common?

BRUTUS. Cominius, no.

CORIOLANUS.   Have I had children's voices? 30

1 SENATOR. Tribunes, give way; he shall to th'
   market-place.

BRUTUS. The people are incensed against him.

SICINIUS.   Stop,
Or all will fall in broil.

CORIOLANUS.   Are these your herd?
Must these have voices, that can yield them now,
And straight disclaim their tongues? What are your
   offices?
You being their mouths, why rule you not their
   teeth?
Have you not set them on?

MENENIUS.   Be calm, be calm.

CORIOLANUS. It is a purposed thing, and grows by
   plot,   270
To curb the will of the nobility;
Suffer't, and live with such as cannot rule,   40
Nor ever will be ruled.

BRUTUS.   Call't not a plot:
The people cry you mocked them; and of late,
When corn was given them gratis, you repined,
Scandaled the suppliants for the people, called them
Time-pleasers, flatterers, foes to nobleness.

CORIOLANUS. Why, this was known before.

BRUTUS.   Not to them all.

CORIOLANUS. Have you informed them sithence?

BRUTUS.   How! I inform them!

CORIOLANUS. You are like to do such business.

BRUTUS.   Not unlike
Each way to better yours.

CORIOLANUS. Why then should I be consul? By yond
   clouds,
Let me deserve so ill as you, and make me   50
Your fellow tribune.

SICINIUS.   You show too much of that
For which the people stir: if you will pass
To where you are bound, you must inquire your
   way,
Which you are out of, with a gentler spirit,
Or never be so noble as a consul,

Nor yoke with him for tribune.
MENENIUS.   Let's be calm.
COMINIUS. The people are abused; set on. This
    palt'ring
    Becomes not Rome; nor has Coriolanus
    Deserved this so dishonoured rub, laid falsely   60
    I' th' plain way of his merit.
CORIOLANUS.   Tell me of corn!
    This was my speech, and I will speak't again—
MENENIUS. Not now, not now.
I SENATOR.   Not in this heat, sir, now.
CORIOLANUS. Now, as I live, I will.
    My nobler friends, I crave their pardons. For
    The mutable, rank-scented meiny, let them
    Regard me as I do not flatter, and
    Therein behold themselves. I say again,
    In soothing them, we nourish 'gainst our Senate
    The cockle of rebellion, insolence, sedition,   70
    Which we ourselves have ploughed for, sowed, and
        scattered,
    By mingling them with us, the honoured number;
    Who lack not virtue, no, nor power, but that
    Which they have given to beggars.
MENENIUS.   Well, no more.
I SENATOR. No more words, we beseech you.
CORIOLANUS.   How! no more!
    As for my country I have shed my blood,
    Not fearing outward force, so shall my lungs
    Coin words till their decay against those measles,
    Which we disdain should tetter us, yet sought
    The very way to catch them.
BRUTUS.   You speak o' th' people, 80
    As if you were a god, to punish; not
    A man of their infirmity.
SICINIUS.   'Twere well
    We let the people know't.
MENENIUS.   What, what? his choler?
CORIOLANUS. Choler!
    Were I as patient as the midnight sleep,
    By Jove, 'twould be my mind!
SICINIUS.   It is a mind
    That shall remain a poison where it is,
    Not poison any further.
CORIOLANUS.   Shall remain!
    Hear you this Triton of the minnows? mark you
    His absolute 'shall'?
COMINIUS.   'Twas from the canon.
CORIOLANUS.   'Shall'! 90
    O good but most unwise patricians! Why,
    You grave but reckless senators, have you thus
    Given Hydra here to choose an officer,
    That with his peremptory 'shall,' being but
    The horn and noise o' th' monster's, wants not
        spirit
    To say he'll turn your current in a ditch,
    And make your channel his? If he have power,
    Then vail your ignorance; if none, awake
    Your dangerous lenity. If you are learned,
    Be not as common fools; if you are not,   100
    Let them have cushions by you. You are plebeians,
    If they be senators; and they no less,
    When, both your voices blended, the great'st taste
    Most palates theirs. They choose their magistrate;
    And such a one as he, who puts his 'shall,'
    His popular 'shall', against a graver bench
    Than ever frowned in Greece. By Jove himself,

It makes the consuls base! and my soul aches
To know, when two authorities are up,
Neither supreme, how soon confusion   110
May enter 'twixt the gap of both and take
The one by th' other.
COMINIUS.   Well, on to th' market-place.
CORIOLANUS. Whoever gave that counsel to give forth
    The corn o' th' storehouse gratis, as 'twas used
    Sometime in Greece—
MENENIUS.   Well, well, no more of that.
CORIOLANUS. Though there the people had more
        absolute power,
    I say they nourished disobedience, fed
    The ruin of the state.
BRUTUS.   Why shall the people give
    One that speaks thus their voice?
CORIOLANUS.   I'll give my reasons,
    More worthier than their voices. They know the
        corn   120
    Was not our recompense, resting well assured
    They ne'er did service for't. Being pressed to th'
        war,
    Even when the navel of the state was touched,
    They would not thread the gates; this kind of
        service
    Did not deserve corn gratis. Being i' th' war,
    Their mutinies and revolts, wherein they showed
    Most valour, spoke not for them. Th' accusation
    Which they have often made against the Senate,
    All cause unborn, could never be the native
    Of our so frank donation. Well, what then?   130
    How shall this bosom multiplied digest
    The Senate's courtesy? Let deeds express
    What's like to be their words: 'We did request it;
    We are the greater poll, and in true fear
    They gave us our demands.' Thus we debase
    The nature of our seats, and make the rabble
    Call our cares fears; which will in time
    Break ope the locks o' th' Senate and bring in
    The crows to peck the eagles.
MENENIUS.   Come, enough.
BRUTUS. Enough, with over measure.
CORIOLANUS.   No, take more. 140
    What may be sworn by, both divine and human,
    Seal what I end withal! This double worship,
    Where one part does disdain with cause, the other
    Insult without all reason; where gentry, title,
        wisdom,
    Cannot conclude but by the yea and no
    Of general ignorance—it must omit
    Real necessities, and give way the while
    To unstable slightness. Purpose so barred, it follows
    Nothing is done to purpose. Therefore, beseech
        you—
    You that will be less fearful than discreet;   150
    That love the fundamental part of state
    More than you doubt the change on 't; that prefer
    A noble life before a long, and wish
    To jump a body with a dangerous physic
    That's sure of death without it—at once pluck out
    The multitudinous tongue; let them not lick
    The sweet which is their poison. Your dishonour
    Mangles true judgement, and bereaves the state
    Of that integrity which should become't;
    Not having the power to do the good it would,   160
    For th' ill which doth control 't.

BRUTUS.   Has said enough.
SICINIUS. Has spoken like a traitor and shall answer
　As traitors do.
CORIOLANUS. Thou wretch, despite o'erwhelm thee!
　What should the people do with these bald tribunes,
　On whom depending, their obedience fails
　To th' greater bench? In a rebellion,
　When what's not meet, but what must be, was law,
　Then were they chosen: in a better hour
　Let what is meet be said it must be meet,
　And throw their power i' th' dust.   170
BRUTUS. Manifest treason!
SICINIUS.   This a consul? No.
BRUTUS. The ædiles, ho!

Enter an Ædile

　　　　　　　　　　　Let him be apprehended.
SICINIUS. Go, call the people: [*Ædile goes*] in whose
　name myself
　Attach thee as a traitorous innovator,
　A foe to th' public weal. Obey, I charge thee,
　And follow to thine answer.
CORIOLANUS.   Hence, old goat!
SENATORS, & c. We'll surety him.
COMINIUS.   Agéd sir, hands off.
CORIOLANUS. Hence, rotten thing! or I shall shake thy
　bones
　Out of thy garments.
SICINIUS.   Help, ye citizens!

Enter a rabble of Plebeians with the Ædiles

MENENIUS. On both sides more respect.   180
SICINIUS. Here's he that would take from you all your
　power.
BRUTUS. Seize him, ædiles!
CITIZENS. Down with him! down with him!
2 SENATOR. Weapons, weapons, weapons!
　　　　　　　　They all bustle about Coriolanus
CRIES. 'Tribunes!' 'Patricians!' 'Citizens!' 'What, ho!'
　'Sicinius!' 'Brutus!' 'Coriolanus!' 'Citizens!'
　'Peace, peace, peace!' 'Stay! hold! peace!'
MENENIUS. What is about to be? I am out of breath.
　Confusion's near. I cannot speak. You, tribunes
　To th' people! Coriolanus, patience!   190
　Speak, good Sicinius.
SICINIUS.   Hear me, people; peace!
CITIZENS. Let's hear our tribune: peace!—Speak,
　speak, speak.
SICINIUS. You are at point to lose your liberties:
　Marcius would have all from you; Marcius,
　Whom late you have named for consul.
MENENIUS.   Fie, fie, fie!
　This is the way to kindle, not to quench.
1 SENATOR. To unbuild the city, and to lay all flat.
SICINIUS. What is the city but the people?
CITIZENS.   True,
　The people are the city.
BRUTUS. By the consent of all, we were established   200
　The people's magistrates.
CITIZENS.   You so remain.
MENENIUS. And so are like to do.
COMINIUS. That is the way to lay the city flat,
　To bring the roof to the foundation,
　And bury all which yet distinctly ranges,
　In heaps and piles of ruin.
SICINIUS.   This deserves death.

BRUTUS. Or let us stand to our authority,
　Or let us lose it. We do here pronounce,
　Upon the part o' th' people, in whose power
　We were elected theirs, Marcius is worthy   210
　Of present death.
SICINIUS.   Therefore lay hold of him;
　Bear him to th' rock Tarpeian, and from thence
　Into destruction cast him.
BRUTUS.   Ædiles, seize him!
CITIZENS. Yield, Marcius, yield!
MENENIUS.   Hear me one word;
　Beseech you, tribunes, hear me but a word.
ÆDILES. Peace, peace!
MENENIUS. [*to Brutus*]. Be that you seem, truly your
　country's friend,
　And temp'rately proceed to what you would
　Thus violently redress.
BRUTUS.   Sir, those cold ways,
　That seem like prudent helps, are very poisonous   220
　Where the disease is violent. Lay hands upon him,
　And bear him to the rock.
CORIOLANUS [*draws his sword*]. No, I'll die here.
　There's some among you have beheld me fighting:
　Come, try upon yourselves what you have seen me.
MENENIUS. Down with that sword! Tribunes,
　withdraw awhile.
BRUTUS. Lay hands upon him.
MENENIUS.   Help Marcius, help,
　You that be noble; help him, young and old!
CITIZENS. Down with him, down with him!

*In this mutiny, the Tribunes, the Ædiles, and the people,
are beat in*

MENENIUS. Go, get you to your house; be gone, away!
　All will be naught else.
2 SENATOR.   Get you gone.
CORIOLANUS.   Stand fast;   230
　We have as many friends as enemies.
MENENIUS. Shall it be put to that?
1 SENATOR.   The gods forbid!
　I prithee, noble friend, home to thy house;
　Leave us to cure this cause.
MENENIUS.   For 'tis a sore upon us
　You cannot tent yourself: be gone, beseech you.
COMINIUS. Come, sir, along with us.
CORIOLANUS. I would they were barbarians, as they
　are,
　Though in Rome littered; not Romans, as they are
　not,
　Though calved i' th' porch o' th' Capitol.
MENENIUS.   Be gone.
　Put not your worthy rage into your tongue: 240
　One time will owe another.
CORIOLANUS.   On fair ground
　I could beat forty of them.
MENENIUS.   I could myself
　Take up a brace o' th' best of them; yea, the two
　tribunes.
COMINIUS. But now 'tis odds beyond arithmetic;
　And manhood is called foolery when it stands
　Against a falling fabric. Will you hence
　Before the tag return? whose rage doth rend
　Like interrupted waters, and o'erbear
　What they are used to bear.
MENENIUS.   Pray you, be gone.
　I'll try whether my old wit be in request   250

With those that have but little: this must be patched
With cloth of any colour.
COMINIUS [to Coriolanus].   Nay, come away
                    Coriolanus and Cominius depart
I PATRICIAN. This man has marred his fortune.
MENENIUS. His nature is too noble for the world:
He would not flatter Neptune for his trident,
Or Jove for's power to thunder. His heart's his
    mouth:
What his breast forges, that his tongue must vent;
And, being angry, does forget that ever
He heard the name of death.
                    Noise of the people returning
Here's goodly work!
2 PATRICIAN.   I would they were a-bed!   260
MENENIUS. I would they were in Tiber! What the
    vengeance,
Could he not speak 'em fair?

Enter Brutus and Sicinius, with the rabble again

SICINIUS.   Where is this viper
That would depopulate the city and
Be every man himself?
MENENIUS.   You worthy tribunes—
SICINIUS. He shall be thrown down the Tarpeian rock
With rigorous hands: he hath resisted law,
And therefore law shall scorn him further trial
Than the severity of the public power,
Which he so sets at nought.
I CITIZEN.   He shall well know
The noble tribunes are the people's mouths,   270
And we their hands.
ALL THE CITIZENS. He shall, sure on't.
MENENIUS.   Sir, sir—
SICINIUS. Peace!
MENENIUS. Do not cry havoc, where you should but
    hunt
With modest warrant.
SICINIUS.   Sir, how comes't that you
Have holp to make this rescue?
MENENIUS.   Hear me speak:
As I do know the consul's worthiness,
So can I name his faults.
SICINIUS.   Consul! what consul?
MENENIUS. The consul Coriolanus.
BRUTUS.   He consul!
ALL THE CITIZENS. No, no, no, no, no.
MENENIUS. If, by the tribunes' leave, and yours, good
    people,   280
I may be heard, I would crave a word or two;
The which shall turn you to no further harm
Than so much loss of time.
SICINIUS.   Speak briefly then;
For we are peremptory to dispatch
This viperous traitor: to eject him hence
Were but our danger, and to keep him here
Our certain death: therefore it is decreed
He dies to-night.
MENENIUS.   Now the good gods forbid
That our renownéd Rome, whose gratitude
Towards her deservéd children is enrolled   290
In Jove's own book, like an unnatural dam
Should now eat up her own!
SICINIUS. He's a disease that must be cut away.
MENENIUS. O, he's a limb that has but a disease;
Mortal, to cut it off; to cure it, easy.

What has he done to Rome that's worthy death?
Killing our enemies, the blood he hath lost—
Which I dare vouch is more than that he hath
By many an ounce—he dropped it for his country;
And what is left, to lose it by his country   300
Were to us all that do't and suffer it
A brand to th' end o' th' world.
SICINIUS.   This is clean kam.
BRUTUS. Merely awry: when he did love his country,
It honoured him.
SICINIUS.   The service of the foot
Being once gangrened, is not then respected
For what before it was.
BRUTUS.   We'll hear no more.
Pursue him to his house and pluck him thence,
Lest his infection, being of catching nature,
Spread further.
MENENIUS.   One word more, one word!
This tiger-footed rage, when it shall find   310
The harm of unscanned swiftness, will, too late,
Tie leaden pounds to's heels. Proceed by process;
Lest parties—as he is beloved—break out,
And sack great Rome with Romans.
BRUTUS.   If it were so—
SICINIUS. What do ye talk?
Have we not had a taste of his obedience?
Our aediles smote? ourselves resisted? Come!
MENENIUS. Consider this: he has been bred i' th' wars
Since a' could draw a sword, and is ill schooled
In bolted language; meal and bran together   320
He throws without distinction. Give me leave,
I'll go to him, and undertake to bring him
Where he shall answer, by a lawful form,
In peace, to his utmost peril.
I SENATOR.   Noble tribunes,
It is the human way: the other course
Will prove too bloody; and the end of it
Unknown to the beginning.
SICINIUS.   Noble Menenius,
Be you then as the people's officer.
Masters, lay down your weapons.
BRUTUS.   Go not home.
SICINIUS. Meet on the market-place. We'll attend you
    there: 330
Where, if you bring not Marcius, we'll proceed
In our first way.
MENENIUS.   I'll bring him to you.
[to the Senators] Let me desire your company: he
    must come,
Or what is worst will follow.
SENATORS.   Pray you, let's to him.
                    They go

Scene 2: Rome. The house of Coriolanus

Enter Coriolanus with Nobles

CORIOLANUS. Let them pull all about mine ears;
    present me
Death on the wheel or at wild horses' heels;
Or pile ten hills on the Tarpeian rock,
That the precipitation might down stretch
Below the beam of sight; yet will I still
Be thus to them.
A NOBLE.   You do the nobler.
CORIOLANUS. I muse my mother
Does not approve me further, who was wont

To call them woollen vassals, things created
To buy and sell with groats; to show bare heads 10
In congregations, to yawn, be still and wonder,
When one but of my ordinance stood up
To speak of peace or war.

Enter Volumnia

                     I talk of you:
Why did you wish me milder? would you have me
False to my nature? Rather say I play
The man I am.
VOLUMNIA.   O, sir, sir, sir,
I would have had you put your power well on,
Before you had worn it out.
CORIOLANUS.   Let go.
VOLUMNIA. You might have been enough the man
   you are,
With striving less to be so: lesser had been 20
The thwartings of your dispositions, if
You had not showed them how ye were
   disposed
Ere they lacked power to cross you.
CORIOLANUS.   Let them hang.
VOLUMNIA. Ay, and burn too.

Enter Menenius with the Senators

MENENIUS. Come, come, you have been too rough,
   something too rough;
You must return and mend it.
SENATOR.   There's no remedy,
Unless, by not so doing, our good city
Cleave in the midst and perish.
VOLUMNIA.   Pray be counselled:
I have a heart as little apt as yours,
But yet a brain that leads my use of anger 30
To better vantage.
MENENIUS.   Well said, noble woman!
Before he should thus stoop to th' herd—but that
The violent fit o' th' time craves it as physic
For the whole state—I would put mine armour on,
Which I can scarcely bear.
CORIOLANUS.   What must I do?
MENENIUS. Return to th' tribunes.
CORIOLANUS.   Well, what then? what then?
MENENIUS. Repent what you have spoke.
CORIOLANUS. For them! I cannot do it to the gods;
Must I then do't to them?
VOLUMNIA.   You are too absolute;
Though therein you can never be too noble 40
But when extremities speak. I have heard you say,
Honour and policy, like unsevered friends,
I' th' war do grow together: grant that, and tell me
In peace what each of them by th' other lose
That they combine not there.
CORIOLANUS.   Tush, tush!
MENENIUS.   A good demand.
VOLUMNIA. If it be honour in your wars to seem
The same you are not, which for your best ends
You adopt your policy, how is it less or worse
That it shall hold companionship in peace
With honour as in war; since that to both 50
It stands in like request?
CORIOLANUS.   Why force you this?
VOLUMNIA. Because that now it lies you on to speak
To th' people, not by your own instruction,
Nor by th' matter which your heart prompts you,

But with such words that are but roted in
Your tongue, though but bastards and syllables
Of no allowance to your bosom's truth.
Now, this no more dishonours you at all
Than to take in a town with gentle words,
Which else would put you to your fortune and 60
The hazard of much blood.
I would dissemble with my nature, where
My fortunes and my friends at stake required
I should do so in honour. I am in this,
Your wife, your son, these senators, the nobles;
And you will rather show our general louts
How you can frown than spend a fawn upon 'em
For the inheritance of their loves and safeguard
Of what that want might ruin.
MENENIUS.   Noble lady!
Come, go with us; speak fair: you may salve so, 70
Not what is dangerous present, but the loss
Of what is past.
VOLUMNIA.   I prithee now, my son,
Go to them with this bonnet in thy hand;
And thus far having stretched it, here be with them,
Thy knee bussing the stones—[*curtseys*] for in such
   business
Action is eloquence, and the eyes of th' ignorant
More learnèd than the ears. Waving thy head,
With often thus correcting thy stout heart
(Now humble as the ripest mulberry
That will not hold the handling), say to them, 80
Thou art their soldier, and being bred in broils
Hast not the soft way which, thou dost confess,
Were fit for thee to use, as they to claim,
In asking their good loves; but thou wilt frame
Thyself, forsooth, hereafter theirs, so far
As thou hast power and person.
MENENIUS.   This but done,
Even as she speaks, why, their hearts were yours;
For they have pardons, being asked, as free
As words to little purpose.
VOLUMNIA.   Prithee now,
Go, and be ruled: although I know thou hadst
   rather 90
Follow thine enemy in a fiery gulf
Than flatter him in a bower.

Enter Cominius

                 Here is Cominius.
COMINIUS. I have been i' th' market-place; and, sir,
   'tis fit
You make strong party, or defend yourself
By calmness or by absence: all's in anger.
MENENIUS. Only fair speech.
COMINIUS.   I think 'twill serve, if he
Can thereto frame his spirit.
VOLUMNIA.   He must, and will.
Prithee now, say you will, and go about it.
CORIOLANUS. Must I go show them my unbarbèd
   sconce?
With my base tongue give to my noble heart 100
A lie that it must bear? Well, I will do't:
Yet, were there but this single plot to lose,
This mould of Marcius, they to dust should grind it,
And throw't against the wind. To th' market-place!
You have put me now to such a part which never
I shall discharge to th' life.
COMINIUS.   Come, come, we'll prompt you.

VOLUMNIA. I prithee now, sweet son, as thou hast said
My praises made thee first a soldier, so,
To have my praise for this, perform a part
Thou hast not done before.
CORIOLANUS.   Well, I must do't.   110
Away, my disposition, and possess me
Some harlot's spirit! My throat of war be turned,
Which choiréd with my drum, into a pipe
Small as an eunuch or the virgin voice
That babies lulls asleep! The smiles of knaves
Tent in my cheeks, and schoolboys' tears take up
The glasses of my sight! A beggar's tongue
Make motion through my lips, and my armed
  knees,
Who bowed but in my stirrup, bend like his
That hath received an alms! I will not do't;   120
Lest I surcease to honour mine own truth,
And by my body's action teach my mind
A most inherent baseness.
VOLUMNIA.   At thy choice then.
To beg of thee, it is my more dishonour
Than thou of them. Come all to ruin: let
Thy mother rather feel thy pride than fear
Thy dangerous stoutness, for I mock at death
With as big heart as thou. Do as thou list.
Thy valiantness was mine, thou suck'dst it from me,
But owe thy pride thyself.
CORIOLANUS.   Pray, be content: 130
Mother, I am going to the market-place;
Chide me no more. I'll mountebank their loves,
Cog their hearts from them, and come home
  beloved
Of all the trades in Rome. Look, I am going:
Commend me to my wife. I'll return consul;
Or never trust to what my tongue can do
I' th' way of flattery further.
VOLUMNIA.   Do your will.
                                        She goes
COMINIUS. Away! the tribunes do attend you. Arm
  yourself
To answer mildly; for they are prepared
With accusations, as I hear, more strong   140
Than are upon you yet.
CORIOLANUS. The word is 'mildly.' Pray you, let us
  go.
Let them accuse me by invention, I
Will answer in mine honour.
MENENIUS.   Ay, but mildly.
CORIOLANUS. Well, mildly be it then—mildly.
                                        They go

                Scene 3: *Rome. The Forum*

Enter Sicinius and Brutus

BRUTUS. In this point charge him home, that he
  affects
Tyrannical power. If he evade us there,
Enforce him with his envy to the people,
And that the spoil got on the Antiates
Was ne'er distributed.

Enter an Ædile

                        What, will he come?
ÆDILE. He's coming.
BRUTUS.   How accompanied?

ÆDILE. With old Menenius and those senators
That always favoured him.
SICINIUS.   Have you a catalogue
Of all the voices that we have procured,
Set down by th' poll?
ÆDILE.   I have; 'tis ready.   10
SICINIUS. Have you collected them by tribes?
ÆDILE.   I have.
SICINIUS. Assemble presently the people hither:
And when they hear me say 'It shall be so
I' th' right and strength o' th' commons,' be it
  either
For death, for fine, or banishment, then let them,
If I say 'Fine', cry 'Fine!' if 'Death', cry 'Death!'
Insisting on the old prerogative
And power i' th' truth o' th' cause.
ÆDILE.   I shall inform them.
BRUTUS. And when such time they have begun to cry,
Let them not cease, but with a din confused   20
Enforce the present execution
Of what we chance to sentence.
ÆDILE.   Very well.
SICINIUS. Make them be strong, and ready for this
  hint,
When we shall hap to give't them.
BRUTUS.   Go about it.   *The Ædile goes*
Put him to choler straight. He hath been used
Ever to conquer and to have his worth
Of contradiction: being once chafed, he cannot
Be reined again to temperance; then he speaks
What's in his heart; and that is there which looks
With us to break his neck.
SICINIUS.   Well, here he comes.   30

*Enter Coriolanus, Menenius, and Cominius, with
Senators and Patricians*

MENENIUS. Calmly, I do beseech you.
CORIOLANUS. Ay, as an ostler, that for th' poorest
  piece
Will bear the knave by th' volume. [*aloud*] Th'
  honoured gods
Keep Rome in safety, and the chairs of justice
Supplied with worthy men! plant love among 's!
Throng our large temples with the shows of peace,
And not our streets with war!
I SENATOR.   Amen, amen.
MENENIUS. A noble wish.

Enter the Ædile, with the Plebeians

SICINIUS. Draw near, ye people.
ÆDILE. List to your tribunes. Audience! peace, I say!   40
CORIOLANUS. First, hear me speak.
BOTH TRIBUNES.   Well, say. Peace, ho!
CORIOLANUS. Shall I be charged no further than this
  present?
Must all determine here?
SICINIUS.   I do demand,
If you submit you to the people's voices,
Allow their officers, and are content
To suffer lawful censure for such faults
As shall be proved upon you?
CORIOLANUS.   I am content.
MENENIUS. Lo, citizens, he says he is content.
The warlike service he has done, consider; think
Upon the wounds his body bears, which show   50
Like graves i' th' holy churchyard.

CORIOLANUS.   Scratches with briers,
    Scars to move laughter only.
MENENIUS.   Consider further,
    That when he speaks not like a citizen,
    You find him like a soldier: do not take
    His rougher accents for malicious sounds,
    But, as I say, such as become a soldier
    Rather than envy you.
COMINIUS.   Well, well, no more.
CORIOLANUS. What is the matter
    That, being passed for consul with full voice,
    I am so dishonoured that the very hour   60
    You take it off again?
SICINIUS.   Answer to us.
CORIOLANUS. Say, then: 'tis true, I ought so.
SICINIUS. We charge you, that you have contrived to
    take
    From Rome all seasoned office, and to wind
    Yourself into a power tyrannical;
    For which you are a traitor to the people.
CORIOLANUS. How! traitor!
MENENIUS.   Nay, temperately! your promise.
CORIOLANUS. The fires i' th' lowest hell fold in the
    people!
    Call me their traitor! Thou injurious tribune!
    Within thine eyes sat twenty thousand deaths,   70
    In thy hands clutched as many millions, in
    Thy lying tongue both numbers, I would say
    'Thou liest' unto thee with a voice as free
    As I do pray the gods.
SICINIUS.   Mark you this, people?
CITIZENS. To th' rock, to th' rock with him!
SICINIUS.   Peace!
    We need not put new matter to his charge.
    What you have seen him do and heard him speak,
    Beating your officers, cursing yourselves,
    Opposing laws with strokes, and here defying
    Those whose great power must try him—even this, 80
    So criminal and in such capital kind,
    Deserves th' extremest death.
BRUTUS.   But since he hath
    Served well for Rome—
CORIOLANUS.   What do you prate of service?
BRUTUS. I talk of that that know it.
CORIOLANUS. You!
MENENIUS. Is this the promise that you made your
    mother?
COMINIUS. Know, I pray you—
CORIOLANUS.   I'll know no further.
    Let them pronounce the steep Tarpeian death,
    Vagabond exile, flaying, pent to linger
    But with a grain a day, I would not buy   90
    Their mercy at the price of one fair word,
    Nor check my courage for what they can give,
    To have't with saying 'Good morrow.'
SICINIUS.   For that he has
    (As much as in him lies) from time to time
    Envied against the people, seeking means
    To pluck away their power, as now at last
    Given hostile strokes, and that not in the presence
    Of dreaded justice, but on the ministers
    That do distribute it—in the name o' th' people,
    And in the power of us the tribunes, we,   100
    Even from this instant, banish him our city,
    In peril of precipitation
    From off the rock Tarpeian, never more

To enter our Rome gates. I' th' people's name,
    I say it shall be so.
CITIZENS. It shall be so, it shall be so! Let him away!
    He's banished, and it shall be so.
COMINIUS. Hear me, my masters and my common
    friends—
SICINIUS. He's sentenced; no more hearing.
COMINIUS.   Let me speak.
    I have been consul, and can show for Rome   110
    Her enemies' marks upon me. I do love
    My country's good with a respect more tender,
    More holy and profound, than mine own life,
    My dear wife's estimate, her womb's increase
    And treasure of my loins; then if I would
    Speak that—
SICINIUS.   We know your drift. Speak what?
BRUTUS. There's no more to be said, but he is
    banished
    As enemy to the people and his country.
    It shall be so.
CITIZENS.   It shall be so, it shall be so.
CORIOLANUS. You common cry of curs! whose breath
    I hate   120
    As reek o' th' rotten fens, whose loves I prize
    As the dead carcasses of unburied men
    That do corrupt my air—I banish you.
    And here remain with your uncertainty!
    Let every feeble rumour shake your hearts!
    Your enemies, with nodding of their plumes,
    Fan you into despair! Have the power still
    To banish your defenders, till at length
    Your ignorance—which finds not till it feels,
    Making but reservation of yourselves,   130
    Still your own foes—deliver you as most
    Abated captives to some nation
    That won you without blows! Despising
    For you the city, thus I turn my back:
    There is a world elsewhere.
            He goes, followed by Cominius,
            Menenius, Senators and Patricians
ÆDILE. The people's enemy is gone, is gone!
CITIZENS. Our enemy is banished! he is gone!
    Hoo—oo!   *They all shout, and throw up*
                        their caps
SICINIUS. Go see him out at gates, and follow him,
    As he hath followed you, with all despite;
    Give him deserved vexation. Let a guard   140
    Attend us through the city.
CITIZENS. Come, come, let's see him out at gates;
    come!
    The gods preserve our noble tribunes! Come.
                        They go

ACT 4

Scene 1: *Rome. Before a gate of the city*

Enter Coriolanus, Volumnia, Virgilia, Menenius,
Cominius, with the young Nobility of Rome

CORIOLANUS. Come, leave your tears; a brief farewell!
    The beast
    With many heads butts me away. Nay, mother,
    Where is your ancient courage? you were used
    To say extremity was the trier of spirits;
    That common chances common men could bear;
    That when the sea was calm all boats alike

Showed mastership in floating; fortune's blows,
When most struck home, being gentle wounded,
  craves
A noble cunning. You were used to load me
With precepts that would make invincible   10
The heart that conned them.
VIRGILIA. O heavens! O heavens!
CORIOLANUS.   Nay, I prithee, woman—
VOLUMNIA. Now the red pestilence strike all trades in
  Rome,
And occupations perish!
CORIOLANUS.   What, what, what!
I shall be loved when I am lacked. Nay, mother,
Resume that spirit when you were wont to say,
If you had been the wife of Hercules,
Six of his labours you'ld have done, and saved
Your husband so much sweat. Cominius,
Droop not; adieu. Farewell, my wife, my mother: 20
I'll do well yet. Thou old and true Menenius,
Thy tears are salter than a younger man's,
And venomous to thine eyes. My sometime
  general,
I have seen thee stern, and thou hast oft beheld
Heart-hard'ning spectacles; tell these sad women
'Tis fond to wail inevitable strokes,
As 'tis to laugh at 'em. Mother, you wot well
My hazards still have been your solace: and
Believe't not lightly—though I go alone,
Like to a lonely dragon that his fen   30
Makes feared and talked of more than seen—your
  son
Will or exceed the common or be caught
With cautelous baits and practice.
VOLUMNIA.   My first son,
Whither wilt thou go? Take good Cominius.
With thee awhile: determine on some course
More than a wild exposure to each chance
That starts i' th' way before thee.
VIRGILIA.   O the gods!
COMINIUS. I'll follow thee a month, devise with thee
Where thou shalt rest, that thou mayst hear of us
And we of thee: so, if the time thrust forth   40
A cause for thy repeal, we shall not send
O'er the vast world to seek a single man,
And lose advantage, which doth ever cool
I' th' absence of the needer.
CORIOLANUS.   Fare ye well:
Thou hast years upon thee; and thou art too full
Of the wars' surfeits to go rove with one
That's yet unbruised: bring me but out at gate.
Come, my sweet wife, my dearest mother, and
My friends of noble touch; when I am forth,
Bid me farewell, and smile. I pray you, come.   50
While I remain above the ground you shall
Hear from me still, and never of me aught
But what is like me formerly.
MENENIUS.   That's worthily
As any ear can hear. Come, let's not weep.
If I could shake off but one seven years
From these old arms and legs, by the good gods,
I'ld with thee every foot.
CORIOLANUS.   Give me thy hand.
Come.   *They go*

Scene 2: *Rome. A street near the gate*

*Enter the two Tribunes, Sicinius and Brutus, with the
Ædile*

SICINIUS. Bid them all home; he's gone, and we'll no
  further.
The nobility are vexed, whom we see have sided
In his behalf.
BRUTUS.   Now we have shown our power,
Let us seem humbler after it is done
Than when it was a-doing.
SICINIUS.   Bid them home:
Say their great enemy is gone, and they
Stand in their ancient strength.
BRUTUS.   Dismiss them home.
                            The Ædile goes
Here comes his mother.

Enter Volumnia, Virgilia, and Menenius

SICINIUS.   Let's not meet her.
BRUTUS.   Why?
SICINIUS. They say she's mad.
BRUTUS. They have ta'en note of us: keep on your
  way.   10
VOLUMNIA. O, you're well met: th' hoarded plague o'
  th' gods
Requite your love!
MENENIUS.   Peace, peace, be not so loud.
VOLUMNIA. If that I could for weeping, you should
  hear—
Nay, and you shall hear some. [*to Brutus*] Will you
  be gone?
VIRGILIA [*to Sicinius*]. You shall stay too. I would I had
  the power
To say so to my husband,
SICINIUS.   Are you mankind?
VOLUMNIA. Ay, fool; is that a shame? Note but this,
  fool.
Was not a man my father? Hadst thou foxship
To banish him that struck more blows for Rome
Than thou hast spoken words?
SICINIUS.   O blessed heavens! 20
VOLUMNIA. Moe noble blows than ever thou wise
  words;
And for Rome's good. I'll tell thee what—yet go!
Nay, but thou shalt stay too. I would my son
Were in Arabia, and thy tribe before him,
His good sword in his hand.
SICINIUS.   What then?
VIRGILIA.   What then!
He'ld make an end of thy posterity.
VOLUMNIA. Bastards and all.
Good man, the wounds that he does bear for
  Rome!
MENENIUS. Come, come, peace.
SICINIUS. I would he had continued to his country 30
As he began, and not unknit himself
The noble knot he made.
BRUTUS.   I would he had.
VOLUMNIA. 'I would he had!' 'Twas you incensed the
  rabble;
Cats, that can judge as fitly of his worth
As I can of those mysteries which heaven
Will not have earth to know.
BRUTUS.   Pray, let's go.
VOLUMNIA. Now, pray, sir, get you gone;

You have done a brave deed. Ere you go, hear this:
As far as doth the Capitol exceed
The meanest house in Rome, so far my son— 40
This lady's husband here, this, do you see?
Whom you have banished—does exceed you all.

BRUTUS. Well, well, we'll leave you.

SICINIUS.   Why stay we to be baited
With one that wants her wits?

VOLUMNIA.   Take my prayers with you.
                                   Tribunes go
I would the gods had nothing else to do
But to confirm my curses! Could I meet 'em
But once a day, it would unclog my heart
Of what lies heavy to't.

MENENIUS.   You have told them home,
And by my troth you have cause. You'll sup with
     me?

VOLUMNIA. Anger's my meat; I sup upon myself, 50
And so shall starve with feeding. Come, let's go:
Leave this faint puling, and lament as I do,
In anger, Juno-like. Come, come, come.
                     Volumnia and Virgilia depart

MENENIUS. Fie, fie, fie!   *He follows*

Scene 3: *A highway between Rome and Antium*

Enter a Roman and a Volsce, meeting

ROMAN. I know you well, sir, and you know me: your
name, I think, is Adrian.

VOLSCE. It is so, sir: truly, I have forgot you.

ROMAN. I am a Roman; and my services are, as you
are, against 'em. Know you me yet?

VOLSCE. Nicanor? no.

ROMAN. The same, sir.

VOLSCE. You had more beard when I last saw you; but
your favour is well approved by your tongue.
What's the news in Rome? I have a note from the 10
Volscian state to find you out there: you have well
saved me a day's journey.

ROMAN. There hath been in Rome strange insurrec-
tions; the people against the senators, patricians, and
nobles.

VOLSCE. Hath been! is it ended then? Our state thinks
not so: they are in a most warlike preparation, and
hope to come upon them in the heat of their
division.

ROMAN. The main blaze of it is past, but a small thing 20
would make it flame again; for the nobles receive so
to heart the banishment of that worthy Coriolanus,
that they are in a ripe aptness to take all power from
the people and to pluck from them their tribunes
for ever. This lies glowing, I can tell you, and is
almost mature for the violent breaking out.

VOLSCE. Coriolanus banished!

ROMAN. Banished, sir.

VOLSCE. You will be welcome with this intelligence,
Nicanor.   30

ROMAN. The day serves well for them now. I have
heard it said the fittest time to corrupt a man's wife
is when she's fall'n out with her husband. Your
noble Tullus Aufidius will appear well in these wars,
his great opposer, Coriolanus, being now in no
request of his country.

VOLSCE. He cannot choose. I am most fortunate thus
accidentally to encounter you: you have ended my
business, and I will merrily accompany you home.

ROMAN. I shall, between this and supper, tell you most 40
strange things from Rome; all tending to the good
of their adversaries. Have you an army ready, say
you?

VOLSCE. A most royal one; the centurions and their
charges, distinctly billeted, already in th' entertainment, and to be on foot at an hour's warning.

ROMAN. I am joyful to hear of their readiness, and am
the man, I think, that shall set them in present action.
So, sir, heartily well met, and most glad of your
company.   50

VOLSCE. You take my part from me, sir; I have the
most cause to be glad of yours.

ROMAN. Well, let us go together.   *They go*

Scene 4: *Antium. Before Aufidius's house*

Enter Coriolanus in mean apparel, disguised and muffled

CORIOLANUS. A goodly city is this Antium. City,
'Tis I that made thy widows: many an heir
Of these fair edifices 'fore my wars
Have I heard groan and drop. Then know me not,
Lest that thy wives with spits and boys with stones
In puny battle slay me.

Enter a Citizen
                                   Save you, sir.

CITIZEN. And you.

CORIOLANUS.   Direct me, if it be your will,
Where great Aufidius lies. Is he in Antium?

CITIZEN. He is, and feasts the nobles of the state
At his house this night.

CORIOLANUS.   Which is his house, beseech you? 10

CITIZEN. This here before you.

CORIOLANUS.   Thank you, sir: farewell.
                                   Citizen goes
O world, thy slippery turns! Friends now fast
     sworn,
Whose double bosoms seem to wear one heart,
Whose hours, whose bed, whose meal and exercise
Are still together, who twin, as 'twere, in love
Unseparable, shall within this hour,
On a dissension of a doit, break out
To bitterest enmity: so fellest foes,
Whose passions and whose plots have broke their
     sleep
To take the one the other, by some chance, 20
Some trick not worth an egg, shall grow dear
     friends
And interjoin their issues. So with me:
My birth-place hate I, and my love's upon
This enemy town. I'll enter: if he slay me,
He does fair justice; if he give me way,
I'll do his country service.   *He enters the house*

Scene 5: *Antium. A hall in Aufidius's house*

Music plays. Enter a Servingman

1 SERVINGMAN. Wine, wine, wine! What service is
there!
I think our fellows are asleep.   *Goes*

Enter another Servingman from the chamber

2 SERVINGMAN. Where's Cotus? my master calls for
him. Cotus!   *Returns*

Enter Coriolanus from without

CORIOLANUS. A goodly house. The feast smells well,
  but I
Appear not like a guest.

Re-enter 1 Servingman

1 SERVINGMAN. What would you have, friend? whence
are you? Here's no place for you: pray go to the
door!   *Goes*
CORIOLANUS. I have deserved no better entertainment,
In being Coriolanus.   10

Re-enter 2 Servingman

2 SERVINGMAN. Whence are you, sir? Has the porter
his eyes in his head that he gives entrance to such
companions? Pray get you out.
CORIOLANUS. Away!
2 SERVINGMAN. 'Away!' Get you away.
CORIOLANUS. Now thou'rt troublesome.
2 SERVINGMAN. Are you so brave? I'll have you talked
with anon.

Enter 3 Servingman with 1 Servingman

3 SERVINGMAN. What fellow's this?
1 SERVINGMAN. A strange one as ever I looked on!   20
I cannot get him out o' th' house. Prithee call my
master to him.
3 SERVINGMAN. What have you to do here, fellow?
Pray you avoid the house.
CORIOLANUS. Let me but stand; I will not hurt your
hearth.
3 SERVINGMAN. What are you?
CORIOLANUS. A gentleman.
3 SERVINGMAN. A marv'llous poor one.
CORIOLANUS. True, so I am.   30
3 SERVINGMAN. Pray you, poor gentleman, take up
some other station; here's no place for you. Pray you
avoid. Come.
CORIOLANUS. Follow your function, go and batten on
cold bits.   *Pushes him away from him*
3 SERVINGMAN. What, you will not? Prithee, tell my
master what a strange guest he has here.
2 SERVINGMAN. And I shall.   *Goes*
3 SERVINGMAN. Where dwell'st thou?
CORIOLANUS. Under the canopy.   40
3 SERVINGMAN. Under the canopy!
CORIOLANUS. Ay.
3 SERVINGMAN. Where's that?
CORIOLANUS. I' th' city of kites and crows.
3 SERVINGMAN. I' th' city of kites and crows! What
an ass it is! then thou dwell'st with daws too?
CORIOLANUS. No, I serve not thy master.
3 SERVINGMAN. How, sir! do you meddle with my
master?
CORIOLANUS. Ay; 'tis an honester service than to   50
meddle with thy mistress. Thou prat'st, and prat'st;
serve with thy trencher. Hence!
                                   Beats him from the room

Enter Aufidius with 2 Servingman

AUFIDIUS. Where is this fellow?
2 SERVINGMAN. Here, sir. I'ld have beaten him like a
dog, but for disturbing the lords within.   *Returns*
AUFIDIUS. Whence com'st thou? What wouldst thou?
  Thy name?
Why speak'st not? Speak, man. What's thy name?
CORIOLANUS [*unmuffling*].   If, Tullus,

Not yet thou know'st me, and, seeing me, dost not
Think me for the man I am, necessity
Commands me name myself.
AUFIDIUS.   What is thy name?   60
CORIOLANUS. A name unmusical to the Volscians' ears,
And harsh in sound to thine.
AUFIDIUS.   Say, what's thy name?
Thou hast a grim appearance, and thy face
Bears a command in't; though thy tackle's torn,
Thou show'st a noble vessel. What's thy name?
CORIOLANUS. Prepare thy brow to frown—know'st
  thou me yet?
AUFIDIUS. I know thee not. Thy name!
CORIOLANUS. My name is Caius Marcius, who hath
  done
To thee particularly, and to all the Volsces,
Great hurt and mischief; thereto witness may   70
My surname, Coriolanus. The painful service,
The extreme dangers, and the drops of blood
Shed for my thankless country, are requited
But with that surname—a good memory
And witness of the malice and displeasure
Which thou shouldst bear me. Only that name
  remains:
The cruelty and envy of the people,
Permitted by our dastard nobles, who
Have all forsook me, hath devoured the rest;
And suffered me by th' voice of slaves to be   80
Whooped out of Rome. Now, this extremity
Hath brought me to thy hearth: not out of hope—
Mistake me not—to save my life; for if
I had feared death, of all the men i' th' world
I would have 'voided thee; but in mere spite,
To be full quit of those my banishers,
Stand I before thee here. Then if thou hast
A heart of wreak in thee, that wilt revenge
Thine own particular wrongs and stop those maims
Of shame seen through thy country, speed thee
  straight   90
And make my misery serve thy turn. So use it
That my revengeful services may prove
As benefits to thee; for I will fight
Against my cank'red country with the spleen
Of all the under fiends. But if so be
Thou dar'st not this and that to prove more fortunes
Thou'rt tired, then, in a word, I also am
Longer to live most weary, and present
My throat to thee and to thy ancient malice;
Which not to cut would show thee but a fool,   100
Since I have ever followed thee with hate,
Drawn tuns of blood out of thy country's breast,
And cannot live but to thy shame, unless
It be to do thee service.
AUFIDIUS.   O Marcius, Marcius!
Each word thou hast spoke hath weeded from my
  heart
A root of ancient envy. If Jupiter
Should from yond cloud speak divine things,
And say 'Tis true', I'ld not believe them more
Than thee, all noble Marcius. Let me twine
Mine arms about that body, where against   110
My grainéd ash an hundred times hath broke
And scarred the moon with splinters: here I clip
The anvil of my sword, and do contest
As hotly and as nobly with thy love
As ever in ambitious strength I did

Contend against thy valour. Know thou first,
I loved the maid I married; never man
Sighed truer breath; but that I see thee here,
Thou noble thing, more dances my rapt heart
Than when I first my wedded mistress saw 120
Bestride my threshold. Why, thou Mars, I tell thee,
We have a power on foot, and I had purpose
Once more to hew thy target from thy brawn,
Or lose mine arm for't. Thou hast beat me out
Twelve several times, and I have nightly since
Dreamt of encounters 'twixt thyself and me;
We have been down together in my sleep,
Unbuckling helms, fisting each other's throat;
And waked half dead with nothing. Worthy
      Marcius,
Had we no quarrel else to Rome but that 130
Thou art thence banished, we would muster all
From twelve to seventy, and pouring war
Into the bowels of ungrateful Rome,
Like a bold flood o'erbear't. O, come, go in,
And take our friendly senators by th' hands,
Who now are here, taking their leaves of me
Who am prepared against your territories,
Though not for Rome itself.
CORIOLANUS.   You bless me, gods!
AUFIDIUS. Therefore, most absolute sir, if thou wilt
      have
The leading of thine own revenges, take 140
Th' one half of my commission, and set down—
As best thou art experienced, since thou know'st
Thy country's strength and weakness—thine own
      ways,
Whether to knock against the gates of Rome,
Or rudely visit them in parts remote
To fright them ere destroy. But come in:
Let me commend thee first to those that shall
Say yea to thy desires. A thousand welcomes!
And more a friend than e'er an enemy;
Yet, Marcius, that was much. Your hand: most
      welcome!   *Coriolanus and Aufidius go* 150

Enter two of the Servingmen

1 SERVINGMAN. Here's a strange alteration!
2 SERVINGMAN. By my hand, I had thought to have
strucken him with a cudgel; and yet my mind gave
me his clothes made a false report of him.
1 SERVINGMAN. What an arm he has! he turned me
about with his finger and his thumb, as one would
set up a top.
2 SERVINGMAN. Nay, I knew by his face that there
was something in him; he had, sir, a kind of face,
methought—I cannot tell how to term it. 160
1 SERVINGMAN. He had so, looking as it were—Would
I were hanged, but I thought there was more in him
than I could think.
2 SERVINGMAN. So did I, I'll be sworn: he is simply
the rarest man i' th' world.
1 SERVINGMAN. I think he is; but a greater soldier than
he, you wot one.
2 SERVINGMAN. Who, my master?
1 SERVINGMAN. Nay, it's no matter for that.
2 SERVINGMAN. Worth six on him. 170
1 SERVINGMAN. Nay, not so neither: but I take him to
be the greater soldier.
2 SERVINGMAN. Faith, look you, one cannot tell how to

say that: for the defence of a town our general is
excellent.
1 SERVINGMAN. Ay, and for an assault too.

Enter the third Servingman

3 SERVINGMAN. O slaves, I can tell you news—news,
you rascals!
1, 2 SERVINGMEN. What, what, what? Let's partake.
3 SERVINGMAN. I would not be a Roman, of all nations; 180
I had as lief be a condemned man.
1, 2 SERVINGMEN. Wherefore? wherefore?
3 SERVINGMAN. Why, here's he that was wont to
thwack our general—Caius Marcius.
1 SERVINGMAN. Why do you say 'thwack our general'?
3 SERVINGMAN. I do not say 'thwack our general', but
he was always good enough for him.
2 SERVINGMAN. Come, we are fellows and friends. He
was ever too hard for him; I have heard him say so
himself. 190
1 SERVINGMAN. He was too hard for him directly. To
say the troth on't, before Corioli he scotched him
and notched him like a carbonado.
2 SERVINGMAN. An he had been cannibally given, he
might have broiled and eaten him too.
1 SERVINGMAN. But more of thy news?
3 SERVINGMAN. Why, he is so made on here within as
if he were son and heir to Mars; set at upper end
o' th' table; no question asked him by any of the
senators but they stand bald before him. Our general 200
himself makes a mistress of him; sanctifies himself
with's hand, and turns up the white o' th' eye to his
discourse. But the bottom of the news is, our general
is cut i' th' middle and but one half of what he was
yesterday, for the other has half by the entreaty and
grant of the whole table. He'll go, he says, and sowl
the porter of Rome gates by th' ears; he will mow
all down before him, and leave his passage polled.
2 SERVINGMAN. And he's as like to do't as any man I can
imagine. 210
3 SERVINGMAN. Do't! he will do't; for look you, sir, he
has as many friends as enemies; which friends, sir,
as it were, durst not—look you, sir—show themselves, as we term it, his friends whilst he's in
dejectitude.
1 SERVINGMAN. Dejectitude! what's that?
3 SERVINGMAN. But when they shall see, sir, his crest
up again and the man in blood, they will out of their
burrows, like conies after rain, and revel all with
him. 220
1 SERVINGMAN. But when goes this forward?
3 SERVINGMAN. To-morrow, to-day, presently. You
shall have the drum struck up this afternoon; 'tis as
it were a parcel of their feast, and to be executed
ere they wipe their lips.
2 SERVINGMAN. Why, then we shall have a stirring
world again. This peace is nothing but to rust iron,
increase tailors, and breed ballad-makers.
1 SERVINGMAN. Let me have war, say I; it exceeds peace
as far as day does night; it's sprightly, waking, 230
audible, and full of vent. Peace is a very apoplexy,
lethargy; mulled, deaf, sleepy, insensible; a getter of
more bastard children than war's a destroyer of men.
2 SERVINGMAN. 'Tis so: and as war in some sort may be
said to be a ravisher, so it cannot be denied but peace
is a great maker of cuckolds.

1 SERVINGMAN. Ay, and it makes men hate one another.
3 SERVINGMAN. Reason: because they then less need one another. The wars for my money. I hope to see 240 Romans as cheap as Volscians. They are rising, they are rising.
1, 2 SERVINGMEN. In, in, in, in! *They go*

Scene 6: *Rome. A public place*

Enter the two Tribunes, Sicinius and Brutus

SICINIUS. We hear not of him, neither need we fear him.
His remedies are tame. The present peace
And quietness of tne people, which before
Were in wild hurry, here do make his friends
Blush that the world goes well; who rather had,
Though they themselves did suffer by't, behold
Dissentious numbers pest'ring streets than see
Our tradesmen singing in their shops, and going
About their functions friendly.
BRUTUS. We stood to't in good time.

Enter Menenius

                        Is this Menenius? 10
SICINIUS. 'Tis he, 'tis he. O, he is grown most kind
Of late. Hail, sir!
MENENIUS.   Hail to you both!
SICINIUS. Your Coriolanus is not much missed
But with his friends. The commonwealth doth stand,
And so would do, were he more angry at it.
MENENIUS. All's well; and might have been much better, if
He could have temporized.
SICINIUS.   Where is he, hear you?
MENENIUS. Nay, I hear nothing: his mother and his wife
Hear nothing from him.

Enter three or four Citizens

CITIZENS. The gods preserve you both!
SICINIUS.   God-den, our neighbours. 20
BRUTUS. God-den to you all, god-den to you all.
1 CITIZEN. Ourselves, our wives, and children, on our knees,
Are bound to pray for you both.
SICINIUS.   Live, and thrive!
BRUTUS. Farewell, kind neighbours: we wished Coriolanus
Had loved you as we did.
CITIZENS.   Now the gods keep you!
BOTH TRIBUNES. Farewell, farewell. *Citizens pass on*
SICINIUS. This is a happier and more comely time
Than when these fellows ran about the streets
Crying confusion.
BRUTUS.   Caius Marcius was
A worthy officer i' th' war, but insolent,   30
O'ercome with pride, ambitious past all thinking,
Self-loving—
SICINIUS.   And affecting one sole throne,
Without assistance.
MENENIUS.   I think not so.
SICINIUS. We should by this, to all our lamentation,
If he had gone forth consul, found it so.

BRUTUS. The gods have well prevented it, and Rome
Sits safe and still without him.

Enter an Ædile

ÆDILE.   Worthy tribunes,
There is a slave, whom we have put in prison,
Reports the Volsces with two several powers
Are ent'red in the Roman territories,   40
And with the deepest malice of the war
Destroy what lies before 'em.
MENENIUS.   'Tis Aufidius,
Who, hearing of our Marcius' banishment,
Thrusts forth his horns again into the world,
Which were inshelled when Marcius stood for Rome,
And durst not once peep out.
SICINIUS.   Come, what talk you
Of Marcius?
BRUTUS. Go see this rumourer whipped. It cannot be
The Volsces dare break with us.
MENENIUS.   Cannot be!
We have record that very well it can;   50
And three examples of the like hath been
Within my age. But reason with the fellow,
Before you punish him, where he heard this,
Lest you shall chance to whip your information
And beat the messenger who bids beware
Of what is to be dreaded.
SICINIUS.   Tell not me:
I know this cannot be.
BRUTUS.   Not possible.

Enter a Messenger

MESSENGER. The nobles in great earnestness are going
All to the Senate House: some news is come
That turns their countenances.
SICINIUS.   'Tis this slave—   60
Go whip him 'fore the people's eyes—his raising,
Nothing but his report.
MESSENGER.   Yes, worthy sir,
The slave's report is seconded; and more,
More fearful, is delivered.
SICINIUS.   What more fearful?
MESSENGER. It is spoke freely out of many mouths—
How probable I do not know—that Marcius,
Joined with Aufidius, leads a power 'gainst Rome,
And vows revenge as spacious as between
The young'st and oldest thing.
SICINIUS.   This is most likely!
BRUTUS. Raised only that the weaker sort may wish 70
Good Marcius home again.
SICINIUS.   The very trick on't.
MENENIUS. This is unlikely:
He and Aufidius can no more atone
Than violent'st contrarieties.

Enter a second Messenger

2 MESSENGER. You are sent for to the Senate.
A fearful army, led by Caius Marcius
Associated with Aufidius, rages
Upon our territories, and have already
O'erborne their way, consumed with fire, and took
What lay before them.   80

Enter Cominius

COMINIUS. O, you have made good work!

MENENIUS.   What news? what news?
COMINIUS. You have holp to ravish your own
    daughters and
To melt the city leads upon your pates,
To see your wives dishonoured to your noses—
MENENIUS. What's the news? what's the news?
COMINIUS. Your temples burnèd in their cement, and
Your franchises, whereon you stood, confined
Into an auger's bore.
MENENIUS.   Pray now, your news?—
You have made fair work, I fear me.—Pray, your
    news?—
If Marcius should be joined wi' th' Volscians—
COMINIUS.   If! 90
He is their god; he leads them like a thing
Made by some other deity than Nature,
That shapes man better; and they follow him
Against us brats with no less confidence
Than boys pursuing summer butterflies,
Or butchers killing flies.
MENENIUS.   You have made good work,
You and your apron-men; you that stood so much
Upon the voice of occupation and
The breath of garlic-eaters!
COMINIUS.   He will shake
Your Rome about your ears.
MENENIUS.   As Hercules   100
Did shake down mellow fruit. You have made
    fair work!
BRUTUS. But is this true, sir?
COMINIUS.   Ay; and you'll look pale
Before you find it other. All the regions
Do smilingly revolt, and who resist
Are mocked for valiant ignorance,
And perish constant fools. Who is't can blame him?
Your enemies and his find something in him.
MENENIUS. We are all undone, unless
The noble man have mercy.
COMINIUS.   Who shall ask it?
The tribunes cannot do't for shame; the people 110
Deserve such pity of him as the wolf
Does of the shepherds; for his best friends, if they
Should say 'Be good to Rome,' they charged him
    even
As those should do that had deserved his hate,
And therein showed like enemies.
MENENIUS.   'Tis true:
If he were putting to my house the brand
That should consume it, I have not the face
To say 'Beseech you, cease.' You have made fair
    hands,
You and your crafts! you have crafted fair!
COMINIUS.   You have brought
A trembling upon Rome, such as was never   120
S' incapable of help.
BOTH TRIBUNES.   Say not we brought it.
MENENIUS. How! Was't we? We loved him, but, like
    beasts
And cowardly nobles, gave way unto your clusters,
Who did hoot him out o' th' city.
COMINIUS.   But I fear
They'll roar him in again. Tullus Aufidius,
The second name of men, obeys his points
As if he were his officer. Desperation
Is all the policy, strength, and defence,
That Rome can make against them.

Enter a troop of Citizens

MENENIUS.   Here come the clusters.
And is Aufidius with him? You are they   130
That made the air unwholesome when you cast
Your stinking greasy caps in hooting at
Coriolanus' exile. Now he's coming,
And not a hair upon a soldier's head
Which will not prove a whip; as many coxcombs
As you threw caps up will he tumble down,
And pay you for your voices. 'Tis no matter;
If he could burn us all into one coal,
We have deserved it.
CITIZENS. Faith, we hear fearful news.
1 CITIZEN.   For mine own part, 140
When I said banish him, I said 'twas pity.
2 CITIZEN. And so did I.
3 CITIZEN. And so did I; and, to say the truth, so did
very many of us. That we did, we did for the best;
and though we willingly consented to his banish-
ment, yet it was against our will.
COMINIUS. You're goodly things, you voices!
MENENIUS.   You have made
Good work, you and your cry! Shall's to the
    Capitol?
COMINIUS. O, ay, what else?
                         Cominius and Menenius go
SICINIUS. Go masters, get you home; be not dismayed; 150
These are a side that would be glad to have
This true which they so seem to fear. Go home,
And show no sign of fear.
1 CITIZEN. The gods be good to us! Come, masters,
let's home. I ever said we were i'th' wrong when
we banished him.
2 CITIZEN. So did we all. But come, let's home.
                                          Citizens go
BRUTUS. I do not like this news.
SICINIUS. Nor I.
BRUTUS. Let's to the Capitol. Would half my wealth 160
Would buy this for a lie!
SICINIUS.   Pray, let us go.
                                             They go

Scene 7: *A camp at a small distance from Rome*

Enter Aufidius with his Lieutenant

AUFIDIUS. Do they still fly to th' Roman?
LIEUTENANT. I do not know what witchcraft's in him,
    but
Your soldiers use him as the grace 'fore meat,
Their talk at table and their thanks at end;
And you are dark'ned in this action sir,
Even by your own.
AUFIDIUS.   I cannot help it now,
Unless by using means I lame the foot
Of our design. He bears himself more proudlier,
Even to my person, than I thought he would
When first I did embrace him; yet his nature   10
In that's no changeling, and I must excuse
What cannot be amended.
LIEUTENANT.   Yet I wish, sir—
I mean for your particular—you had not
Joined in commission with him, but either
Had borne the action of yourself, or else
To him had left it solely.
AUFIDIUS. I understand thee well; and be thou sure,

When he shall come to his account, he knows not
What I can urge against him. Although it seems,
And so he thinks, and is no less apparent   20
To th' vulgar eye, that he bears all things fairly
And shows good husbandry for the Volscian state,
Fights dragon-like, and does achieve as soon
As draw his sword; yet he hath left undone
That which shall break his neck or hazard mine,
Whene'er we come to our account.
LIEUTENANT. Sir, I beseech you, think you he'll carry
    Rome?
AUFIDIUS. All places yield to him ere he sits down,
    And the nobility of Rome are his;
    The senators and patricians love him too.   30
    The tribunes are no soldiers, and their people
    Will be as rash in the repeal, as hasty
    To expel him thence. I think he'll be to Rome
    As is the osprey to the fish, who takes it
    By sovereignty of nature. First he was
    A noble servant to them, but he could not
    Carry his honours even. Whether 'twas pride,
    Which out of daily fortune ever taints
    The happy man; whether defect of judgement,
    To fail in the disposing of those chances   40
    Which he was lord of; or whether nature,
    Not to be other than one thing, not moving
    From th' casque to th' cushion, but commanding
        peace
    Even with the same austerity and garb
    As he controlled the war; but one of these—
    As he hath spices of them all—not all,
    For I dare so far free him—made him feared,
    So hated, and so banished: but he has a merit
    To choke it in the utt'rance. So our virtues
    Lie in th' interpretation of the time;   50
    And power, unto itself most commendable,
    Hath not a tomb so evident as a chair
    T' extol what it hath done.
    One fire drives out one fire; one nail, one nail;
    Rights by rights falter, strengths by strengths do
        fail.
    Come, let's away. When, Caius, Rome is thine,
    Thou art poor'st of all; then shortly art thou mine.
                                        They go

ACT 5
Scene 1: *Rome. A public place*

*Enter Menenius, Cominius, Sicinius, Brutus, the two
Tribunes, with others*

MENENIUS. No, I'll not go: you hear what he hath said
    Which was sometime his general, who loved him
    In a most dear particular. He called me father;
    But what o' that? Go you that banished him,
    A mile before his tent fall down, and knee
    The way into his mercy. Nay, if he coyed
    To hear Cominius speak, I'll keep at home.
COMINIUS. He would not seem to know me.
MENENIUS.   Do you hear?
COMINIUS. Yet one time he did call me by my name.
    I urged our old acquaintance, and the drops   10
    That we have bled together. 'Coriolanus'
    He would not answer to; forbad all names;
    He was a kind of nothing, titleless,
    Till he had forged himself a name i' th' fire

Of burning Rome.
MENENIUS.   Why, so! You have made good work!
    A pair of tribunes that have wrecked fair Rome
    To make coals cheap—a noble memory!
COMINIUS. I minded him how royal 'twas to pardon
    When it was less expected; he replied,
    It was a bare petition of a state   20
    To one whom they had punished.
MENENIUS.   Very well.
    Could he say less?
COMINIUS. I offered to awaken his regard
    For 's private friends: his answer to me was,
    He could not stay to pick them in a pile
    Of noisome musty chaff. He said 'twas folly,
    For one poor grain or two, to leave unburnt
    And still to nose th' offence.
MENENIUS.   For one poor grain or two!
    I am one of those; his mother, wife, his child,
    And this brave fellow too, we are the grains: 30
    You are the musty chaff, and you are smelt
    Above the moon. We must be burnt for you.
SICINIUS. Nay, pray, be patient: if you refuse your aid
    In this so never-needed help, yet do not
    Upbraid's with our distress. But, sure, if you
    Would be your country's pleader, your good
        tongue,
    More than the instant army we can make,
    Might stop our countryman.
MENENIUS.   No, I'll not meddle.
SICINIUS. Pray you, go to him.
MENENIUS.   What should I do?
BRUTUS. Only make trial what your love can do   40
    For Rome, towards Marcius.
MENENIUS.   Well, and say that Marcius
    Return me, as Cominius is returned,
    Unheard—what then?
    But as a discontented friend, grief-shot
    With his unkindness? Say 't be so?
SICINIUS.   Yet your good will
    Must have that thanks from Rome after the
        measure
    As you intended well.
MENENIUS.   I'll undertake 't:
    I think he'll hear me. Yet to bite his lip
    And hum at good Cominius much unhearts me.
    He was not taken well; he had not dined: 50
    The veins unfilled, our blood is cold, and then
    We pout upon the morning, are unapt
    To give or to forgive; but when we have stuffed
    These pipes and these conveyances of our blood
    With wine and feeding, we have supper souls
    Than in our priest-like fasts: therefore I'll watch him
    Till he be dieted to my request,
    And then I'll set upon him.
BRUTUS. You know the very road into his kindness,
    And cannot lose your way.
MENENIUS.   Good faith, I'll prove him,   60
    Speed how it will. I shall ere long have knowledge
    Of my success.   *Goes*
COMINIUS.   He'll never hear him.
SICINIUS.   Not?
COMINIUS. I tell you he does sit in gold, his eye
    Red as 'twould burn Rome, and his injury
    The gaoler to his pity. I kneeled before him;
    'Twas very faintly he said 'Rise;' dismissed me
    Thus with his speechless hand. What he would do

He sent in writing after me; what he would not,
Bound with an oath to yield to his conditions:
So that all hope is vain,   70
Unless his noble mother, and his wife—
Who, as I hear, mean to solicit him
For mercy to his country. Therefore, let's hence,
And with our fair entreaties haste them on.
                    They go

Scene 2: *Entrance of the Volscian camp before Rome*

Enter Menenius to the Watch on Guard

1 WATCH. Stay. Whence are you?
2 WATCH.   Stand, and go back.
MENENIUS. You guard like men, 'tis well; but, by your
    leave,
I am an officer of state, and come
To speak with Coriolanus.
1 WATCH.   From whence?
MENENIUS.   From Rome.
1 WATCH. You may not pass, you must return: our
    general
Will no more hear from thence.
2 WATCH. You'll see your Rome embraced with fire,
    before
You'll speak with Coriolanus.
MENENIUS.   Good my friends,
If you have heard your general talk of Rome
And of his friends there, it is lots to blanks   10
My name hath touched your ears: it is Menenius.
1 WATCH. Be it so; go back. The virtue of your name
Is not here passable.
MENENIUS.   I tell thee, fellow,
Thy general is my lover. I have been
The book of his good acts whence men have read
His fame unparalleled—haply amplified;
For I have ever varnishéd my friends
(Of whom he's chief) with all the size that verity
Would without lapsing suffer: nay, sometimes,
Like to a bowl upon a subtle ground,   20
I have tumbled past the throw, and in his praise
Have almost stamped the leasing: therefore, fellow,
    I must have leave to pass.
1 WATCH. Faith, sir, if you had told as many lies in his
behalf as you have uttered words in your own, you
should not pass here; no, though it were as virtuous
to lie as to live chastely. Therefore go back.
MENENIUS. Prithee, fellow, remember my name is
Menenius, always factionary on the party of your
general.   30
2 WATCH. Howsoever you have been his liar, as you
say you have, I am one that, telling true under him,
must say you cannot pass. Therefore go back.
MENENIUS. Has he dined, canst thou tell? For I would
not speak with him till after dinner.
1 WATCH. You are a Roman, are you?
MENENIUS. I am, as thy general is.
1 WATCH. Then you should hate Rome, as he does.
Can you, when you have pushed out your gates the
very defender of them, and in a violent popular   40
ignorance given your enemy your shield, think to
front his revenges with the easy groans of old
women, the virginal palms of your daughters, or
with the palsied intercession of such a decayed
dotant as you seem to be? Can you think to blow
out the intended fire your city is ready to flame in,

with such weak breath as this? No, you are deceived;
therefore, back to Rome, and prepare for your
execution. You are condemned; our general has
sworn you out of reprieve and pardon.   50
MENENIUS. Sirrah, if thy captain knew I were here, he
would use me with estimation.
2 WATCH. Come, my captain knows you not.
MENENIUS. I mean, thy general.
1 WATCH. My general cares not for you. Back, I say;
go, lest I let forth your half-pint of blood. Back—
that's the utmost of your having. Back.
MENENIUS. Nay, but, fellow, fellow—

Enter Coriolanus with Aufidius

CORIOLANUS. What's the matter?
MENENIUS. Now, you companion, I'll say an errand   60
for you; you shall know now that I am in estimation;
you shall perceive that a Jack guardant cannot office
me from my son Coriolanus. Guess but by me entertainment with him if thou stand'st not i' th' state of
hanging, or of some death more long in spectator-
ship and crueller in suffering; behold now presently,
and swoon for what's to come upon thee. [*to
Coriolanus*] The glorious gods sit in hourly synod
about thy particular prosperity, and love thee no
worse than thy old father Menenius does! O my   70
son, my son! thou art preparing fire for us; look
thee, here's water to quench it. I was hardly moved
to come to thee; but being assured none but myself
could move thee, I have been blown out of your
gates with sighs; and conjure thee to pardon Rome
and thy petitionary countrymen. The good gods
assuage thy wrath, and turn the dregs of it upon
this varlet here; this, who, like a block, hath denied
my access to thee.
CORIOLANUS. Away!   80
MENENIUS. How! away!
CORIOLANUS. Wife, mother, child, I know not. My
    affairs
Are servanted to others. Though I owe
My revenge properly, my remission lies
In Volscian breasts. That we have been familiar,
Ingrate forgetfulness shall poison rather
Than pity note how much. Therefore be gone.
Mine ears against your suits are stronger than
Your gates against my force. Yet, for I loved thee,
Take this along; I writ it for thy sake,   90
And would have sent it. [*gives him a letter*] Another
    word, Menenius,
I will not hear thee speak. This man, Aufidius,
Was my beloved in Rome: yet thou behold'st.
AUFIDIUS. You keep a constant temper.
                Coriolanus and Aufidius go
1 WATCH. Now, sir, is your name Menenius?
2 WATCH. 'Tis a spell, you see, of much power. You
know the way home again.
1 WATCH. Do you hear how we are shent for keeping
your greatness back?
2 WATCH. What cause, do you think, I have to swoon? 100
MENENIUS. I neither care for th' world nor your
general: for such things as you, I can scarce think
there's any, you're so slight. He that hath a will to
die by himself fears it not from another. Let your
general do his worst. For you, be that you are, long;
and your misery increase with your age! I say to you,
as I was said to, Away!   *Goes*

1 WATCH. A noble fellow, I warrant him.
2 WATCH. The worthy fellow is our general: he's the
rock, the oak not to be wind-shaken. *They go* 110

Scene 3: *The tent of Coriolanus*

Enter Coriolanus with Aufidius and others

CORIOLANUS. We will before the walls of Rome
to-morrow
Set down our host. My partner in this action,
You must report to th' Volscian lords how plainly
I have borne this business.
AUFIDIUS. Only their ends
You have respected; stopped your ears against
The general suit of Rome; never admitted
A private whisper—no, not with such friends
That thought them sure of you.
CORIOLANUS. This last old man,
Whom with a cracked heart I have sent to Rome,
Loved me above the measure of a father, 10
Nay, godded me indeed. Their latest refuge
Was to send him; for whose old love I have—
Though I showed sourly to him—once more
offered
The first conditions, which they did refuse
And cannot now accept; to grace him only
That thought he could do more, a very little
I have yielded to. Fresh embassies and suits,
Nor from the state nor private friends, hereafter
Will I lend ear to. [*shouting heard*] Ha! what shout
is this?
Shall I be tempted to infringe my vow 20
In the same time 'tis made? I will not.

*Enter, in mourning habits, Virgilia, Volumnia, Valeria,
young Marcius, with Attendants*

[*Aside*] My wife comes foremost; then the
honoured mould
Wherein this trunk was framed, and in her hand
The grandchild to her blood. But out, affection!
All bond and privilege of nature, break!
Let it be virtuous to be obstinate.
What is that curtsy worth? or those doves' eyes,
Which can make gods forsworn? I melt, and am not
Of stronger earth than others. My mother bows;
As if Olympus to a molehill should 30
In supplication nod: and my young boy
Hath an aspect of intercession which
Great Nature cries 'Deny not.' Let the Volsces
Plough Rome, and harrow Italy: I'll never
Be such a gosling to obey instinct, but stand
As if a man were author of himself
And knew no other kin.
VIRGILIA. My lord and husband!
CORIOLANUS. These eyes are not the same I wore in
Rome.
VIRGILIA. The sorrow that delivers us thus changed
Makes you think so.
CORIOLANUS. Like a dull actor now 40
I have forgot my part and I am out,
Even to a full disgrace. Best of my flesh,
Forgive my tyranny; but do not say,
For that, 'Forgive our Romans.' O, a kiss
Long as my exile, sweet as my revenge!
Now, by the jealous queen of heaven, that kiss
I carried from thee, dear, and my true lip

Hath virgined it e'er since. You gods! I prate,
And the most noble mother of the world
Leave unsaluted. Sink, my knee, i' th' earth; 50
Kneels
Of thy deep duty more impression show
Than that of common sons.
VOLUMNIA. O, stand up blest!
Whilst with no softer cushion than the flint
I kneel before thee, and unproperly
Show duty, as mistaken all this while
Between the child and parent. *Kneels*
CORIOLANUS. What's this?
Your knees to me? to your corrected son?
Raises her
Then let the pebbles on the hungry beach
Fillip the stars; then let the mutinous winds
Strike the proud cedars 'gainst the fiery sun, 60
Murd'ring impossibility, to make.
What cannot be, slight work.
VOLUMNIA. Thou art my warrior;
I holp to frame thee. Do you know this lady?
CORIOLANUS. The noble sister of Publicola,
The moon of Rome, chaste as the icicle
That's curdied by the frost from purest snow
And hangs on Dian's temple—dear Valeria!
VOLUMNIA [*showing young Marcius*]. This is a poor
epitome of yours,
Which by th' interpretation of full time
May show like all yourself.
CORIOLANUS. The god of soldiers, 70
With the consent of supreme Jove, inform
Thy thoughts with nobleness, that thou mayst
prove
To shame unvulnerable, and stick i' th' wars
Like a great sea-mark, standing every flaw,
And saving those that eye thee!
VOLUMNIA. Your knee, sirrah.
CORIOLANUS. That's my brave boy!
VOLUMNIA. Even he, your wife, this lady, and myself
Are suitors to you.
CORIOLANUS. I beseech you, peace!
Or, if you'ld ask, remember this before:
The thing I have forsworn to grant may never 80
Be held by you denials. Do not bid me
Dismiss my soldiers, or capitulate
Again with Rome's mechanics. Tell me not
Wherein I seem unnatural; desire not
T' allay my rages and revenges with
Your colder reasons.
VOLUMNIA. O, no more, no more!
You have said you will not grant us any thing;
For we have nothing else to ask but that
Which you deny already. Yet we will ask,
That, if you fail in our request, the blame 90
May hang upon your hardness: therefore hear us.
CORIOLANUS. Aufidius, and you Volsces, mark; for
we'll
Hear nought from Rome in private. [*sits*]
Your request?
VOLUMNIA. Should we be silent and not speak, our
raiment
And state of bodies would bewray what life
We have led since thy exile. Think with thyself
How more unfortunate than all living women
Are we come hither; since that thy sight, which
should

Make our eyes flow with joy, hearts dance with
    comforts,
Constrains them weep and shake with fear and
    sorrow,   100
Making the mother, wife, and child, to see
The son, the husband, and the father, tearing
His country's bowels out. And to poor we
Thine enmity's most capital: thou barr'st us
Our prayers to the gods, which is a comfort
That all but we enjoy. For how can we,
Alas, how can we for our country pray,
Whereto we are bound, together with thy victory,
Whereto we are bound? Alack, or we must lose
The country, our dear nurse, or else thy person,   110
Our comfort in the country. We must find
An evident calamity, though we had
Our wish, which side should win; for either thou
Must as a foreign recreant be led
With manacles thorough our streets, or else
Triumphantly tread on thy country's ruin,
And bear the palm for having bravely shed
Thy wife and children's blood. For myself, son,
I purpose not to wait on fortune till
These wars determine: if I can not persuade thee   120
Rather to show a noble grace to both parts
Than seek the end of one, thou shalt no sooner
March to assault thy country than to tread—
Trust to't, thou shalt not—on thy mother's womb,
That brought thee to this world.
VIRGILIA.   Ay, and mine,
That brought you forth this boy, to keep your name
Living to time.
BOY.   A' shall not tread on me;
I'll run away till I am bigger, but then I'll fight.
CORIOLANUS. Not of a woman's tenderness to be,
Requires nor child nor woman's face to see.   130
I have sat too long.   *Rising*
VOLUMNIA.   Nay, go not from us thus.
If it were so that our request did tend
To save the Romans, thereby to destroy
The Volsces whom you serve, you might
    condemn us,
As poisonous of your honour: no; our suit
Is, that you reconcile them: while the Volsces
May say 'This mercy we have showed,' the
    Romans,
'This we received;' and each in either side
Give the all-hail to thee, and cry 'Be blest
For making up this peace!' Thou know'st, great son, 140
The end of war's uncertain; but this certain,
That, if thou conquer Rome, the benefit
Which thou shalt thereby reap is such a name
Whose repetition will be dogged with curses;
Whose chronicle thus writ: 'The man was noble,
But with his last attempt he wiped it out,
Destroyed his country, and his name remains
To th' ensuing age abhorred.' Speak to me, son:
Thou hast affected the fine strains of honour,
To imitate the graces of the gods;   150
To tear with thunder the wide cheeks o' th' air,
And yet to charge thy sulphur with a bolt
That should but rive an oak. Why dost not speak?
Think'st thou it honourable for a noble man
Still to remember wrongs? Daughter, speak you:
He cares not for your weeping. Speak thou, boy:
Perhaps thy childishness will move him more

Than can our reasons. There's no man in the world
More bound to 's mother, yet here he lets me prate
Like one i' th' stocks. Thou hast never in thy life 160
Showed thy dear mother any courtesy,
When she, poor hen, fond of no second brood,
Has clucked thee to the wars, and safely home
Loaden with honour. Say my request's unjust,
And spurn me back; but if it be not so,
Thou art not honest, and the gods will plague thee,
That thou restrain'st from me the duty which
To a mother's part belongs. He turns away:
Down, ladies; let us shame him with our knees.
To his surname Coriolanus 'longs more pride   170
Than pity to our prayers. Down: an end;
This is the last: so we will home to Rome,
And die among our neighbours. Nay, behold's!
This boy, that cannot tell what he would have,
But kneels and holds up hands for fellowship,
Does reason our petition with more strength
Than thou hast to deny 't. Come, let us go:
This fellow had a Volscian to his mother;
His wife is in Corioli, and his child
Like him by chance. Yet give us our dispatch.   180
I am hushed until our city be a-fire,
And then I'll speak a little.
CORIOLANUS [*Holds her by the hand, silent*].
                                 O mother, mother!
What have you done? Behold, the heavens do ope,
The gods look down, and this unnatural scene
They laugh at. O my mother, mother! O!
You have won a happy victory to Rome;
But, for your son—believe it, O, believe it—
Most dangerously you have with him prevailed,
If not most mortal to him. But let it come.
Aufidius, though I cannot make true wars,   190
I'll frame convenient peace. Now, good Aufidius,
Were you in my stead, would you have heard
A mother less? or granted less, Aufidius?
AUFIDIUS. I was moved withal.
CORIOLANUS.   I dare be sworn you were!
And, sir, it is no little thing to make
Mine eyes to sweat compassion. But, good sir,
What peace you'll make, advise me: for my part,
I'll not to Rome, I'll back with you; and pray you
Stand to me in this cause. O mother! wife!
                         Speaks with them apart
AUFIDIUS [*aside*]. I am glad thou hast set thy mercy
    and thy honour   200
At difference in thee. Out of that I'll work
Myself a former fortune.
CORIOLANUS [*coming forward with Volumnia and
    Virgilia*].   Ay, by and by;
But we will drink together; and you shall bear
A better witness back than words, which we
On like conditions will have counter-sealed.
Come, enter with us. Ladies, you deserve
To have a temple built you. All the swords
In Italy, and her confederate arms,
Could not have made this peace.   *They go*

Scene 4: *Rome. A street near the gate*

Enter Menenius and Sicinius

MENENIUS. See you yond coign o' th' Capitol, yond
cornerstone?

SICINIUS. Why, what of that?

MENENIUS. If it be possible for you to displace it with your little finger, there is some hope the ladies of Rome, especially his mother, may prevail with him. But I say there is no hope in't: our throats are sentenced, and stay upon execution.

SICINIUS. Is't possible that so short a time can alter the condition of a man? 10

MENENIUS. There is differency between a grub and a butterfly; yet your butterfly was a grub. This Marcius is grown from man to dragon: he has wings; he's more than a creeping thing.

SICINIUS. He loved his mother dearly.

MENENIUS. So did he me: and he no more remembers his mother now than an eight-year-old horse. The tartness of his face sours ripe grapes; when he walks, he moves like an engine and the ground shrinks before his treading. He is able to pierce a corslet 20 with his eye, talks like a knell, and his hum is a battery. He sits in his state as a thing made for Alexander. What he bids be done is finished with his bidding. He wants nothing of a god but eternity and a heaven to throne in.

SICINIUS. Yes, mercy, if you report him truly.

MENENIUS. I paint him in the character. Mark what mercy his mother shall bring from him: there is no more mercy in him than there is milk in a male tiger; that shall our poor city find. And all this is 30 'long of you.

SICINIUS. The gods be good unto us!

MENENIUS. No, in such a case the gods will not be good unto us. When we banished him, we respected not them; and, he returning to break our necks, they respect not us.

Enter a Messenger

MESSENGER. Sir, if you'ld save your life, fly to your house:
The plebeians have got your fellow-tribune,
And hale him up and down; all swearing if
The Roman ladies bring not comfort home 40
They'll give him death by inches.

Enter another Messenger

SICINIUS.   What's the news?

2 MESSENGER. Good news, good news! The ladies have prevailed,
The Volscians are dislodged, and Marcius gone.
A merrier day did never yet greet Rome,
No, not th' expulsion of the Tarquins.

SICINIUS.   Friend,
Art thou certain this is true? Is't most certain?

2 MESSENGER. As certain as I know the sun is fire.
Where have you lurked, that you make doubt of it?
Ne'er through an arch so hurried the blown tide,
As the recomforted through the gates. Why, hark you! 50

Trumpets, hautboys, drums, beat, all together

The trumpets, sackbuts, psalteries, and fifes,
Tabors and cymbals, and the shouting Romans,
Make the sun dance. [*a shout*] Hark you!

MENENIUS.   This is good news.
I will go meet the ladies. This Volumnia
Is worth of consuls, senators, patricians,
A city full; of tribunes such as you,

A sea and land full. You have prayed well to-day:
This morning for ten thousand of your throats
I'ld not have given a doit. [*shouts, trumpets, etc. heard louder*] Hark, how they joy!

SICINIUS. First, the gods bless you for your tidings; next, 60
Accept my thankfulness.

2 MESSENGER.   Sir, we have all
Great cause to give great thanks.

SICINIUS.   They are near the city!

2 MESSENGER. Almost at point to enter.

SICINIUS.   We will meet them,
And help the joy.   *They go towards the gate*

Scene 5

Enter in procession the Ladies with a great press of Senators, Patricians and People

1 SENATOR. Behold our patroness, the life of Rome!
Call all your tribes together, praise the gods,
And make triumphant fires; strew flowers before them.
Unshout the noise that banished Marcius,
Repeal him with the welcome of his mother;
Cry 'Welcome, ladies, welcome!'

ALL.   Welcome, ladies,
Welcome!

                              *They pass on; a flourish with
                                     drums and trumpets*

Scene 6: *Corioli. A public place*

Enter Tullus Aufidius, with Attendants

AUFIDIUS. Go tell the lords o' th' city I am here:
Deliver them this paper: having read it,
Bid them repair to th' market-place, where I,
Even in theirs and in the commons' ears,
Will vouch the truth of it. Him I accuse
The city ports by this hath entered, and
Intends t' appear before the people, hoping
To purge himself with words. Dispatch.
                                   Attendants go

Enter three or four Conspirators of Aufidius' faction

Most welcome!

1 CONSPIRATOR. How it is with our general?

AUFIDIUS.   Even so
As with a man by his own alms empoisoned, 10
And with his charity slain.

2 CONSPIRATOR.   Most noble sir,
If you do hold the same intent wherein
You wished us parties, we'll deliver you
Of your great danger.

AUFIDIUS.   Sir, I cannot tell;
We must proceed as we do find the people.

3 CONSPIRATOR. The people will remain uncertain whilst
'Twixt you there's difference; but the fall of either
Makes the survivor heir of all.

AUFIDIUS.   I know it,
And my pretext to strike at him admits
A good construction. I raised him, and I pawned 20
Mine honour for his truth; who being so heightened,
He watered his new plants with dews of flattery,
Seducing so my friends; and, to this end,
He bowed his nature, never known before

But to be rough, unswayable, and free.

3 CONSPIRATOR. Sir, his stoutness
When he did stand for consul, which he lost
By lack of stooping—

AUFIDIUS. That I would have spoke of.
Being banished for't, he came unto my hearth;
Presented to my knife his throat: I took him, 30
Made him joint-servant with me; gave him way
In all his own desires; nay, let him choose
Out of my files, his projects to accomplish,
My best and freshest men; served his designments
In mine own person; holp to reap the fame
Which he did end all his; and took some pride
To do myself this wrong: till at the last
I seemed his follower, not partner; and
He waged me with his countenance, as if
I had been mercenary.

1 CONSPIRATOR. So he did, my lord: 40
The army marvelled at it; and, in the last,
When he had carried Rome and that we looked
For no less spoil than glory—

AUFIDIUS. There was it;
For which my sinews shall be stretched upon him.
At a few drops of women's rheum, which are
As cheap as lies, he sold the blood and labour
Of our great action: therefore shall he die,
And I'll renew me in his fall. But hark!

Drums and trumpets sound, with great shouts of the people

1 CONSPIRATOR. Your native town you entered like a post,
And had no welcomes home; but he returns, 50
Splitting the air with noise.

1 CONSPIRATOR. And patient fools,
Whose children he hath slain, their base throats tear
With giving him glory.

3 CONSPIRATOR. Therefore, at your vantage,
Ere he express himself or move the people
With what he would say, let him feel your sword,
Which we will second. When he lies along,
After your way his tale pronounced shall bury
His reasons with his body.

AUFIDIUS. Say no more:
Here come the lords.

Enter the Lords of the city

LORDS. You are most welcome home.

AUFIDIUS. I have not deserved it. 60
But, worthy lords, have you with heed perused
What I have written to you?

LORDS. We have.

1 LORD. And grieve to hear 't.
What faults he made before the last, I think
Might have found easy fines; but there to end
Where he was to begin, and give away
The benefit of our levies, answering us
With our own charge, making a treaty where
There was a yielding—this admits no excuse.

AUFIDIUS. He approaches: you shall hear him.

Enter Coriolanus, marching with drum and colours; the commoners being with him

CORIOLANUS. Hail, lords! I am returned your soldier; 70
No more infected with my country's love
Than when I parted hence, but still subsisting
Under your great command. You are to know

That prosperously I have attempted, and
With bloody passage led your wars even to
The gates of Rome. Our spoils we have brought
home
Doth more than counterpoise a full third part
The charges of the action. We have made peace
With no less honour to the Antiates
Than shame to th' Romans; and we here deliver, 80
Subscribed by th' consuls and patricians,
Together with the seal o' th' senate, what
We have compounded on.

AUFIDIUS. Read it not, noble lords;
But tell the traitor in the highest degree
He hath abused your powers.

CORIOLANUS. Traitor! how now!

AUFIDIUS. Ay, traitor, Marcius!

CORIOLANUS. Marcius!

AUFIDIUS. Ay, Marcius, Caius Marcius! Dost thou
think
I'll grace thee with that robbery, thy stol'n name
Coriolanus, in Corioli?
You lords and heads o' th' state, perfidiously 90
He has betrayed your business and given up,
For certain drops of salt, your city Rome,
I say 'your city', to his wife and mother;
Breaking his oath and resolution, like
A twist of rotten silk; never admitting
Counsel o' th' war; but at his nurse's tears
He whined and roared away your victory;
That pages blushed at him and men of heart
Looked wond'ring each at other.

CORIOLANUS. Hear'st thou, Mars?

AUFIDIUS. Name not the god, thou boy of tears!

CORIOLANUS. Ha! 100

AUFIDIUS. No more.

CORIOLANUS. Measureless liar, thou hast made my
heart
Too great for what contains it. 'Boy!' O slave!
Pardon me, lords, 'tis the first time that ever
I was forced to scold. Your judgements, my grave
lords,
Must give this cur the lie: and his own notion—
Who wears my stripes impressed upon him; that
Must bear my beating to his grave—shall join
To thrust the lie unto him.

1 LORD. Peace, both, and hear me speak. 110

CORIOLANUS. Cut me to pieces, Volsces; men and lads,
Stain all your edges on me. 'Boy'! False hound!
If you have writ your annals true, 'tis there,
That, like an eagle in a dove-cote, I
Fluttered your Volscians in Corioli.
Alone I did it. 'Boy!'

AUFIDIUS. Why, noble lords,
Will you be put in mind of his blind fortune,
Which was your shame, by this unholy braggart,
'Fore your own eyes and ears?

THE CONSPIRATORS. Let him die for't.

THE PEOPLE. 'Tear him to pieces.' 'Do it presently.' 120
'He killed my son.' 'My daughter.' 'He killed my
cousin Marcus.' 'He killed my father.'

2 LORD. Peace, ho! no outrage! peace!
The man is noble, and his fame folds in
This orb o' th' earth. His last offences to us
Shall have judicious hearing. Stand, Aufidius,
And trouble not the peace.

CORIOLANUS. O that I had him,

With six Aufidiuses or more—his tribe,
To use my lawful sword!
AUFIDIUS.   Insolent villain!
THE CONSPIRATORS. Kill, kill, kill, kill, kill him!

The Conspirators draw, and kill Coriolanus: Aufidius
stands on his body

LORDS.   Hold, hold, hold, hold! 130
AUFIDIUS. My noble masters, hear me speak.
1 LORD.   O Tullus!
2 LORD. Thou has done a deed whereat valour will
    weep.
3 LORD. Tread not upon him. Masters all, be quiet;
    Put up your swords.
AUFIDIUS. My lords, when you shall know—as in this
    rage
    Provoked by him, you cannot—the great danger
    Which this man's life did owe you, you'll rejoice
    That he is thus cut off. Please it your honours
    To call me to your senate, I'll deliver

Myself your loyal servant, or endure   140
Your heaviest censure.
1 LORD.   Bear from hence his body,
And mourn you for him. Let him be regarded
As the most noble corse that ever herald
Did follow to his urn.
2 LORD.   His own impatience
Takes from Aufidius a great part of blame.
Let's make the best of it.
AUFIDIUS.   My rage is gone,
And I am struck with sorrow. Take him up:
Help, three o' th' chiefest soldiers; I'll be one.
Beat thou the drum, that it speak mournfully:
Trail your steel pikes. Though in this city he   150
Hath widowed and unchilded many a one,
Which to this hour bewail the injury,
Yet he shall have a noble memory.
Assist.
                    Exeunt bearing away the body of Coriolanus;
                                   a dead march sounded

Titus Andronicus

The scene: Rome, and the country near by

CHARACTERS IN THE PLAY

SATURNINUS, *son to the late Emperor of Rome, afterwards
Emperor*
BASSIANUS, *brother to Saturninus*
TITUS ANDRONICUS, *a noble Roman*
MARCUS ANDRONICUS, *tribune of the people, and brother
to Titus*
LUCIUS
QUINTUS
MARTIUS } *sons to Titus Andronicus*
MUTIUS
Young LUCIUS, *a boy, son to Lucius*
PUBLIUS, *son to Marcus Andronicus*

ÆMILIUS, *a noble Roman*
ALARBUS
DEMETRIUS } *sons to Tamora*
CHIRON
AARON, *a Moor, beloved by Tamora*
*A Captain, Tribune, Messenger, and Clown; Romans
and Goths*
TAMORA, *Queen of the Goths*
LAVINIA, *daughter to Titus Andronicus*
Nurse, and a blackamoor Child
*Kinsmen of Titus, Senators, Tribunes, Officers, Soldiers,
and Attendants*

Titus Andronicus

ACT 1

Scene 1: *Rome, before the Capitol, beside which there stands the monument of the Andronici. Through a window opening on to the balcony of an upper chamber in the Capitol may be seen the Senate in session. Drums and trumpets are heard*

Saturninus and his followers march into the square on one side; Bassianus and his followers on the other

SATURNINUS. Noble patricians, patrons of my right,
  Defend the justice of my cause with arms;
  And, countrymen, my loving followers,
  Plead my successive title with your swords:
  I am his first-born son, that was the last
  That ware the imperial diadem of Rome;
  Then let my father's honours live in me,
  Nor wrong mine age with this indignity.
BASSIANUS. Romans, friends, followers, favourers of
    my right,
  If ever Bassianus, Cæsar's son,   10
  Were gracious in the eyes of royal Rome,
  Keep then this passage to the Capitol,
  And suffer not dishonour to approach
  The imperial seat, to virtue consecrate,
  To justice, continence, and nobility:
  But let desert in pure election shine,
  And, Romans, fight for freedom in your choice.

Marcus Andronicus comes forward on to the balcony bearing a crown in his hands

MARCUS. Princes, that strive by factions and by friends
  Ambitiously for rule and empery,
  Know that the people of Rome, for whom we stand 20
  A special party, have by common voice,
  In election for the Roman empery,
  Chosen Andronicus, surnaméd Pius
  For many good and great deserts to Rome.
  A noble man, a braver warrior,
  Lives not this day within the city walls.
  He by the senate is accited home
  From weary wars against the barbarous Goths;
  That with his sons, a terror to our foes,
  Hath yoked a nation strong, trained up in arms.   30
  Ten years are spent since first he undertook
  This cause of Rome, and chastiséd with arms
  Our enemies' pride: five times he hath returned
  Bleeding to Rome, bearing his valiant sons
  In coffins from the field [and as this day
  To the monument of the Andronici
  Done sacrifice of expiation,
  And slain the noblest prisoner of the Goths.]
  And now at last, laden with honour's spoils,
  Returns the good Andronicus to Rome,   40
  Renownéd Titus, flourishing in arms.
  Let us entreat, by honour of his name,
  Whom worthily you would have now succeed,
  And in the Capitol and senate's right,
  Whom you pretend to honour and adore,
  That you withdraw you and abate your strength,
  Dismiss your followers, and, as suitors should,
  Plead your deserts in peace and humbleness.
SATURNINUS. How fair the tribune speaks to calm my
    thoughts!
BASSIANUS. Marcus Andronicus, so I do affy   50
  In thy uprightness and integrity,
  And so I love and honour thee and thine,
  Thy nobler brother Titus and his sons,
  And her to whom my thoughts are humbled all,
  Gracious Lavinia, Rome's rich ornament,
  That I will here dismiss my loving friends;
  And to my fortune's and the people's favour
  Commit my cause in balance to be weighed.
                          His followers disperse
SATURNINUS. Friends, that have been thus forward in
    my right,
  I thank you all, and here dismiss you all,   60
  And to the love and favour of my country
  Commit myself, my person, and the cause.
                          His followers disperse
  Rome, be as just and gracious unto me,
  As I am confident and kind to thee.
  Open the gates and let me in.
BASSIANUS. Tribunes, and me, a poor competitor.
                  They go up into the Senate-house

Enter a Captain

CAPTAIN. Romans, make way! the good Andronicus,
  Patron of virtue, Rome's best champion,
  Successful in the battles that he fights,
  With honour and with fortune is returned,   70
  From where he circumscribéd with his sword,
  And brought to yoke, the enemies of Rome.

A sound of drums and trumpets. Then enter in procession Mutius and Martius, two soldiers bearing a coffin covered with black, Quintus and Lucius, and Titus Andronicus, followed by his prisoners Tamora Queen of the Goths, her sons Alarbus, Chiron, and Demetrius, Aaron the Moor, and others. The soldiers set down the coffin, and Titus speaks

TITUS. Hail, Rome, victorious in thy mourning
    weeds!
  Lo, as the bark that hath discharged his fraught
  Returns with precious lading to the bay
  From whence at first she weighed her anchorage,
  Cometh Andronicus, bound with laurel boughs,
  To re-salute his country with his tears,
  Tears of true joy for his return to Rome.
  Thou great defender of this Capitol,   80
  Stand gracious to the rites that we intend!
  Romans, of five and twenty valiant sons,
  Half of the number that King Priam had,
  Behold the poor remains, alive and dead!
  These that survive let Rome reward with love;
  These that I bring unto their latest home,
  With burial amongst their ancestors.
  Here Goths have given me leave to sheathe my
    sword,
  Titus, unkind and careless of thine own,
  Why suffer'st thou thy sons, unburied yet,   90
  To hover on the dreadful shore of Styx?

Make way to lay them by their bretheren.
They open the tomb
There greet in silence, as the dead are wont,
And sleep in peace, slain in your country's wars!
O sacred receptacle of my joys,
Sweet cell of virtue and nobility,
How many sons hast thou of mine in store,
That thou wilt never render to me more!
LUCIUS. Give us the proudest prisoner of the Goths,
That we may hew his limbs, and on a pile   100
'Ad manes fratrum' sacrifice his flesh,
Before this earthy prison of their bones,
That so the shadows be not unappeased,
Nor we disturbed with prodigies on earth.
TITUS. I give him you, the noblest that survives,
The eldest son of this distressèd queen.
TAMORA. Stay, Roman brethren! Gracious conqueror,
Victorious Titus, rue the tears I shed,
A mother's tears in passion for her son:
And if thy sons were ever dear to thee,   110
O, think my son to be as dear to them!
Sufficeth not that we are brought to Rome,
To beautify thy triumphs and return,
Captive to thee and to thy Roman yoke;
But must my sons be slaughtered in the streets,
For valiant doings in their country's cause?
O, if to fight for king and commonweal
Were piety in thine, it is in these:
Andronicus, stain not thy tomb with blood.
Wilt thou draw near the nature of the gods?   120
Draw near them then in being merciful:
Sweet mercy is nobility's true badge;
Thrice-noble Titus, spare my first-born son.
TITUS. Patient yourself, madam, and pardon me.
These are their brethren, whom your Goths beheld
Alive and dead, and for their brethren slain
Religiously they ask a sacrifice:
To this your son is marked, and die he must,
T' appease their groaning shadows that are gone.
LUCIUS. Away with him! and make a fire straight,   130
And with our swords, upon a pile of wood,
Let's hew his limbs till they be clean consumed.
The sons of Titus bring out Alarbus
TAMORA. O cruel, irreligious piety!
CHIRON. Was never Scythia half so barbarous.
DEMETRIUS. Oppose not Scythia to ambitious Rome.
Alarbus goes to rest, and we survive
To tremble under Titus' threat'ning look.
Then, madam, stand resolved, but hope withal
The self-same gods that armed the Queen of Troy
With opportunity of sharp revenge   140
Upon the Thracian tyrant in her tent
May favour Tamora, the Queen of Goths,
(When Goths were Goths and Tamora was queen)
To quit the bloody wrongs upon her foes.

Enter the sons of Andronicus again, with their swords bloody

LUCIUS. See, lord and father, how we have performed
Our Roman rites! Alarbus' limbs are lopped,
And entrails feed the sacrificing fire,
Whose smoke like incense doth perfume the sky.
Remaineth naught but to inter our brethren,
And with loud 'larums welcome them to Rome.   150
TITUS. Let it be so, and let Andronicus
Make this his latest farewell to their souls.

*Trumpets sounded and the coffin
laid in the tomb*
In peace and honour rest you here, my sons,
Rome's readiest champions, repose you here in rest,
Secure from worldly chances and mishaps!
Here lurks no treason, here no envy swells,
Here grow no damnèd drugs, here are no storms,
No noise, but silence and eternal sleep:

Enter Lavinia

In peace and honour rest you here, my sons!
LAVINIA. In peace and honour live Lord Titus long,   160
My noble lord and father, live in fame!
Lo, at this tomb my tributary tears
I render for my brethren's obsequies,
And at thy feet I kneel, with tears of joy
Shed on this earth for thy return to Rome.
O, bless me here with thy victorious hand,
Whose fortunes Rome's best citizens applaud.
TITUS. Kind Rome, that hast thus lovingly reserved
The cordial of mine age to glad my heart!
Lavinia, live, outlive thy father's days,   170
And fame's eternal date, for virtue's praise!

Enter above Marcus Andronicus, Saturninus, Bassianus, and others

MARCUS. Long live Lord Titus, my belovèd brother,
Gracious triumpher in the eyes of Rome!
TITUS. Thanks, gentle tribune, noble brother Marcus.
MARCUS. And welcome, nephews, from successful wars,
You that survive, and you that sleep in fame!
Fair lords, your fortunes are alike in all,
That in your country's service drew your swords,
But safer triumph is this funeral pomp,
That hath aspired to Solon's happiness,   180
And triumphs over chance in honour's bed.
Titus Andronicus, the people of Rome,
Whose friend in justice thou hast ever been,
Send thee by me, their tribune and their trust,
This palliament of white and spotless hue,
And name thee in election for the empire
With these our late-deceasèd emperor's sons:
Be 'candidatus' then, and put it on,
And help to set a head on headless Rome.
TITUS. A better head her glorious body fits   190
Than his that shakes for age and feebleness:
What should I don this robe and trouble you?
Be chosen with proclamations to-day,
To-morrow yield up rule, resign my life,
And set abroad new business for you all?
Rome, I have been thy soldier forty years,
And led my country's strength successfully,
And buried one and twenty valiant sons,
Knighted in field, slain manfully in arms,
In right and service of their noble country: 200
Give me a staff of honour for mine age,
But not a sceptre to control the world.
Upright he held it, lords, that held it last.
MARCUS. Titus, thou shalt obtain and ask the empery.
SATURNINUS. Proud and ambitious tribune, canst thou tell?
TITUS. Patience, Prince Saturninus.
SATURNINUS.   Romans, do me right.
Patricians, draw your swords and sheathe them not
Till Saturninus be Rome's emperor:

Andronicus, would thou were shipped to hell,
Rather than rob me of the people's hearts.   210
LUCIUS. Proud Saturnine, interrupter of the good
That noble-minded Titus means to thee!
TITUS. Content thee, prince, I will restore to thee
The people's hearts, and wean them from
themselves.
BASSIANUS. Andronicus, I do not flatter thee,
But honour thee, and will do till I die;
My faction if thou strengthen with thy friends,
I will most thankful be, and thanks to men
Of noble minds is honourable meed.
TITUS. People of Rome, and people's tribunes here,   220
I ask your voices and your suffrages.
Will ye bestow them friendly on Andronicus?
TRIBUNE. To gratify the good Andronicus,
And gratulate his safe return to Rome,
The people will accept whom he admits.
TITUS. Tribunes, I thank you, and this suit I make,
That you create our emperor's eldest son,
Lord Saturnine; whose virtues will I hope
Reflect on Rome as Titan's rays on earth,
And ripen justice in this commonweal: 230
Then if you will elect by my advice,
Crown him, and say, 'Long live our emperor!'
MARCUS. With voices and applause of every sort,
Patricians and plebians, we create
Lord Saturninus Rome's great emperor,
And say 'Long live our Emperor Saturnine!'
                                 A long flourish till they come down
SATURNINUS. Titus Andronicus, for thy favours done
To us in our election this day,
I give thee thanks in part of thy deserts,
And will with deeds requite thy gentleness: 240
And for an onset, Titus, to advance
Thy name and honourable family,
Lavinia will I make my emperess,
Rome's royal mistress, mistress of my heart,
And in the sacred Pantheon her espouse:
Tell me, Andronicus, doth this motion please thee?
TITUS. It doth, my worthy lord, and in this match
I hold me highly honoured of your grace,
And here in sight of Rome to Saturnine,
King and commander of our commonweal,   250
The wide world's emperor, do I consecrate
My sword, my chariot, and my prisoners,
Presents well worthy Rome's imperious lord:
Receive them then, the tribute that I owe,
Mine honour's ensigns humbled at thy feet.
SATURNINUS. Thanks, noble Titus, father of my life!
How proud I am of thee and of thy gifts
Rome shall record, and when I do forget
The least of these unspeakable deserts,
Romans, forget your fealty to me.   260
TITUS [*to Tamora*]. Now, madam, are you prisoner to
an emperor,
To him that, for your honour and your state,
Will use you nobly and your followers.
SATURNINUS. A goodly lady, trust me! Of the hue
That I would choose, were I to choose anew.
[*aloud*] Clear up, fair queen, that cloudy
countenance.
Though chance of war hath wrought this change
of cheer,
Thou com'st not to be made a scorn in Rome.
Princely shall be thy usage every way.

Rest on my word, and let not discontent   270
Daunt all your hopes. Madam, he comforts you
Can make you greater than the Queen of Goths.
Lavinia, you are not displeased with this?
LAVINIA. Not I, my lord, sith true nobility
Warrants these words in princely courtesy.
SATURNINUS. Thanks, sweet Lavinia. Romans, let us
go.
Ransomless here we set our prisoners free.
Proclaim our honours, lords, with trump and drum.
                       Flourish. Saturninus courts Tamora
                                                        in dumb show
BASSIANUS [*seizing Lavinia*]. Lord Titus, by your leave,
this maid is mine.
TITUS. How, sir! are you in earnest then, my lord?   280
BASSIANUS. Ay, noble Titus, and resolved withal
To do myself this reason and this right.
MARCUS. 'Suum cuique' is our Roman justice.
This prince in justice seizeth but his own.
LUCIUS. And that he will, and shall, if Lucius live.
TITUS. Traitors, avaunt! Where is the
emperor's guard?
Treason, my lord! Lavinia is surprised!
SATURNINUS. Surprised! by whom?
BASSIANUS.   By him that justly may
Bear his betrothed from all the world away.
MUTIUS. Brothers, help to convey her hence away,   290
And with my sword I'll keep this door safe.

*Marcus, Bassianus and the brothers Lucius, Quintus, and
Martius leave with Lavinia*

TITUS. Follow, my lord, and I'll soon bring her back.

*Saturninus, Tamora, and her sons go up into the Capitol
with Aaron*

MUTIUS. My lord, you pass not here.
TITUS.   What, villain boy!
Barr'st me my way in Rome?   *They fight*
MUTIUS [*falling*].   Help, Lucius, help!

Lucius returns

LUCIUS. My lord, you are unjust; and more than so,
In wrongful quarrel you have slain your son.
TITUS. Nor thou, nor he, are any sons of mine:
My sons would never so dishonour me.
Traitor, restore Lavinia to the emperor.
LUCIUS. Dead if you will, but not to be his wife,   300
That is another's lawful promised love.   *He goes*

*Enter aloft the Emperor with Tamora and her two sons and
Aaron the Moor*

SATURNINUS. No, Titus, no, the emperor needs her
not,
Not her, nor thee, nor any of thy stock:
I'll trust by leisure him that mocks me once,
Thee never, nor thy traitorous haughty sons,
Confederates all thus to dishonour me.
Was none in Rome to make a stale
But Saturnine? Full well, Andronicus,
Agree the deeds with that proud brag of thine,
That saidst, I begged the empire at thy hands.   310
TITUS. O monstrous! what reproachful words are
these?
SATURNINUS. But go thy ways, go, give that changing
piece
To him that flourished for her with his sword:

A valiant son-in-law thou shalt enjoy,
One fit to bandy with thy lawless sons,
To ruffle in the commonwealth of Rome.
TITUS. These words are razors to my wounded heart.
SATURNINUS. And therefore, lovely Tamora, Queen of
    Goths,
That like the stately Phœbe 'mongst her nymphs
Dost overshine the gallant'st dames of Rome,   320
If thou be pleased with this my sudden choice,
Behold, I choose thee, Tamora, for my bride,
And will create thee emperess of Rome.
Speak, Queen of Goths, dost thou applaud my
    choice?
And here I swear by all the Roman Gods,
Sith priest and holy water are so near,
And tapers burn so bright, and every thing
In readiness for Hymenæus stand,
I will not re-salute the streets of Rome,
Or climb my palace, till from forth this place   330
I lead espoused my bride along with me.
TAMORA. And here in sight of heaven to Rome I
    swear,
If Saturnine advance the Queen of Goths,
She will a handmaid be to his desires,
A loving nurse, a mother to his youth.
SATURNINUS. Ascend, fair queen, Pantheon. Lords,
    accompany
Your noble emperor and his lovely bride,
Sent by the heavens for Prince Saturnine,
Whose wisdom hath her fortune conquered.
There shall we consummate our spousal rites.   340
                 They go within
TITUS. I am not bid to wait upon this bride.
Titus, when wert thou wont to walk alone,
Dishonoured thus and challengéd of wrongs?

Re-enter Marcus, Lucius, Quintus, and Martius

MARTIUS. O Titus, see, O, see, what thou hast done!
In a bad quarrel slain a virtuous son.
TITUS. No, foolish tribune, no; no son of mine,
Nor thou, nor these, confederates in the deed
That hath dishonoured all our family,
Unworthy brother, and unworthy sons!
LUCIUS. But let us give him burial as becomes;   350
Give Mutius burial with our bretheren.
TITUS. Traitors, away! he rests not in this tomb:
This monument five hundred years hath stood,
Which I have sumptuously re-edified:
Here none but soldiers and Rome's servitors
Repose in fame; none basely slain in brawls.
Bury him where you can, he comes not here.
MARCUS. My lord, this is impiety in you.
My nephew Mutius' deeds do plead for him,
He must be buried with his bretheren.   360
QUINTUS, MARTIUS. And shall, or him we will
    accompany.
TITUS. And shall? what villain was it spake that word?
QUINTUS. He that would vouch it in any place but
    here.
TITUS. What, would you bury him in my despite?
MARCUS. No, noble Titus, but entreat of thee
To pardon Mutius and to bury him.
TITUS. Marcus, even thou hast struck upon my crest,
And with these boys mine honour thou hast
    wounded.
My foes I do repute you every one,

So trouble me no more, but get you gone.   370
MARTIUS. He is not with himself, let us withdraw.
QUINTUS. Not I, till Mutius' bones be buried.
             The brother and the sons kneel
MARCUS. Brother, for in that name doth nature
    plead,—
QUINTUS. Father, and in that name doth nature
    speak,—
TITUS. Speak thou no more, if all the rest will speed.
MARCUS. Renownéd Titus, more than half my soul
LUCIUS. Dear father, soul and substance of us all—
MARCUS. Suffer thy brother Marcus to inter
His noble nephew here in virtue's nest,
That died in honour and Lavinia's cause.   380
Thou art a Roman, be not barbarous:
The Greeks upon advice did bury Ajax
That slew himself; and wise Laertes' son
Did graciously plead for his funerals:
Let not young Mutius then, that was thy joy,
Be barred his entrance here.
TITUS.   Rise, Marcus, rise.
The dismal'st day is this that e'er I saw,
To be dishonoured by my sons in Rome!
Well, bury him, and bury me the next.

They put him in the tomb

LUCIUS. There lie thy bones, sweet Mutius, with thy
    friends,   390
Till we with trophies do adorn thy tomb.

They all kneel and say

ALL. No man shed tears for noble Mutius,
He lives in fame that died in virtue's cause.
MARCUS. My lord, to step out of these dreary dumps,
How comes it that the subtle Queen of Goths
Is of a sudden thus advanced in Rome?
TITUS. I know not, Marcus, but I know it is,
(Whether by device or no, the heavens can tell.)
Is she not then beholding to the man
That brought her for this high good turn so far?   400
Yes, and will nobly him remunerate.

*Re-enter, from one side, Saturninus attended, Tamora,
Demetrius, Chiron, and Aaron; from the other, Bassianus,
Lavinia, with others*

SATURNINUS. So Bassianus, you have played your
    prize:
God give you joy, sir, of your gallant bride!
BASSIANUS. And you of yours, my lord! I say no more,
Nor wish no less, and so I take my leave.
SATURNINUS. Traitor, if Rome have law, or we have
    power,
Thou and thy faction shall repent this rape.
BASSIANUS. Rape, call you it, my lord, to seize my
    own,
My true-betrothéd love, and now my wife?
But let the laws of Rome determine all,   410
Meanwhile am I possessed of that is mine.
SATURNINUS. 'Tis good, sir; you are very short with us,
But if we live we'll be as sharp with you.
BASSIANUS. My lord, what I have done, as best I may
Answer I must, and shall do with my life.
Only thus much I give your grace to know—
By all the duties that I owe to Rome,
This noble gentleman, Lord Titus here,
Is in opinion and in honour wronged;

That in the rescue of Lavinia
With his own hand did slay his youngest son,
In zeal to you and highly moved to wrath
To be controlled in that he frankly gave.
Receive him then to favour, Saturnine,
That hath expressed himself in all his deeds
A father and a friend to thee and Rome.
TITUS. Prince Bassianus, leave to plead my deeds,
'Tis thou and those that have dishonoured me.
Rome and the righteous heavens be my judge,
How I have loved and honoured Saturnine! 430
TAMORA. My worthy lord, if ever Tamora
Were gracious in those princely eyes of thine,
Then hear me speak indifferently for all;
And at my suit, sweet, pardon what is past.
SATURNINUS. What, madam! be dishonoured openly,
And basely put it up without revenge?
TAMORA. Not so, my lord, the gods of Rome forfend
I should be author to dishonour you!
But on mine honour dare I undertake
For good Lord Titus' innocence in all, 440
Whose fury not dissembled speaks his griefs:
Then at my suit look graciously on him,
Lose not so noble a friend on vain suppose,
Nor with sour looks afflict his gentle heart.
[Aside] My lord, be ruled by me, be won at last,
Dissemble all your griefs and discontents—
You are but newly planted in your throne—
Lest then the people, and patricians too,
Upon a just survey, take Titus' part,
And so supplant you for ingratitude, 450
Which Rome reputes to be a heinous sin.
Yield at entreats: and then let me alone,
I'll find a day to massacre them all,
And raze their faction and their family,
The cruel father and his traitorous sons,
To whom I suéd for my dear son's life;
And make them know what 'tis to let a queen
Kneel in the streets and beg for grace in vain.
[Aloud] Come, come, sweet emperor—come,
Andronicus—
Take up this good old man, and cheer the heart 460
That dies in tempest of thy angry frown.
SATURNINUS. Rise, Titus, rise, my empress hath
prevailed.
TITUS. I thank your majesty, and her, my lord.
These words, these looks, infuse new life in me.
TAMORA. Titus, I am incorporate in Rome,
A Roman now adopted happily,
And must advise the emperor for his good.
This day all quarrels die, Andronicus.
And let it be mine honour, good my lord,
That I have reconciled your friends and you.
For you, Prince Bassianus, I have passed 470
My word and promise to the emperor,
That you will be more mild and tractable.
And fear not, lords, and you, Lavinia;
By my advice, all humbled on your knees,
They kneel
You shall ask pardon of his majesty.
LUCIUS. We do, and vow to heaven, and to his
highness,
That what we did was mildly as we might,
Tend'ring our sister's honour and our own.
MARCUS. That on mine honour here do I protest. 480
SATURNINUS. Away, and talk not, trouble us no more.

TAMORA. Nay, nay, sweet emperor, we must all be 420
friends.
The tribune and his nephews kneel for grace.
I will not be denied. Sweet heart, look back.
SATURNINUS. Marcus, for thy sake, and thy brother's
here,
And at my lovely Tamora's entreats,
I do remit these young men's heinous faults.
Stand up.
Lavinia, though you left me like a churl,
I found a friend, and sure as death I swore 490
I would not part a bachelor from the priest.
Come, if the emperor's court can feast two brides,
You are my guest, Lavinia, and your friends.
This day shall be a love-day, Tamora.
TITUS. To-morrow, an it please your majesty
To hunt the panther and the hart with me,
With horn and hound we'll give your grace
bonjour.
SATURNINUS. Be it so, Titus, and gramercy too.
They go with trumpets blowing.
Aaron remains

ACT 2
Scene 1

AARON. Now climbeth Tamora Olympus' top,
Safe out of fortune's shot, and sits aloft,
Secure of thunder's crack or lightning flash,
Advanced above pale envy's threat'ning reach.
As when the golden sun salutes the morn,
And having gilt the ocean with his beams,
Gallops the zodiac in his glistering coach,
And overlooks the highest-peering hills;
So Tamora.
Upon her wit doth earthly honour wait, 10
And virtue stoops and trembles at her frown.
Then, Aaron, arm thy heart, and fit thy thoughts,
To mount aloft with thy imperial mistress,
And mount her pitch, whom thou in triumph long
Hast prisoner held, fettered in amorous chains,
And faster bound to Aaron's charming eyes,
Than is Prometheus tied to Caucasus.
Away with slavish weeds and servile thoughts!
I will be bright, and shine in pearl and gold,
To wait upon this new-made emperess. 20
To wait, said I? to wanton with this queen,
This goddess, this Semiramis, this nymph,
This siren, that will charm Rome's Saturnine,
And see his shipwreck and his commonweal's.
Holloa! what storm is this? *He steps aside*

Enter Chiron and Demetrius, braving

DEMETRIUS. Chiron, thy years want wit, thy wits want
edge,
And manners, to intrude where I am graced,
And may for aught thou know'st affected be.
CHIRON. Demetrius, thou dost overween in all,
And so in this, to bear me down with braves. 30
'Tis not the difference of a year or two
Makes me less gracious, or thee more fortunate;
I am as able and as fit as thou
To serve, and to deserve my mistress' grace,
And that my sword upon thee shall approve,
And plead my passions for Lavinia's love.

AARON [*aside*]. Clubs, clubs! these lovers will not keep
    the peace.
DEMETRIUS. Why, boy, although our mother,
    unadvised,
Gave you a dancing-rapier by your side,
Are you so desperate grown, to threat your friends? 40
Go to; have your lath glued within your sheath,
Till you know better how to handle it.
CHIRON. Meanwhile, sir, with the little skill I have,
Full well shalt thou perceive how much I dare.
DEMETRIUS. Ay, boy, grow ye so brave? *They draw*
AARON [*comes forward*].   Why, how now, lords!
So near the emperor's palace dare ye draw,
And maintain such a quarrel openly?
Full well I wot the ground of all this grudge.
I would not for a million of gold
The cause were known to them it most concerns, 50
Nor would your noble mother for much more
Be so dishonoured in the court of Rome.
For shame, put up.
DEMETRIUS.   Not I, till I have sheathed
My rapier in his bosom, and withal
Thrust those reproachful speeches down his throat,
That he hath breathed in my dishonour here.
CHIRON. For that I am prepared and full resolved,
Foul-spoken coward, that thund'rest with thy
    tongue
And with thy weapon nothing dar'st perform.
AARON. Away, I say!   60
Now, by the gods that warlike Goths adore,
This petty brabble will undo us all.
Why, lords, and think you not how dangerous
It is to jet upon a prince's right?
What, is Lavinia then become so loose,
Or Bassianus so degenerate,
That for her love such quarrels may be broached
Without controlment, justice, or revenge?
Young lords, beware! an should the empress know
This discord's ground, the music would not please. 70
CHIRON. I care not, I, knew she and all the world:
I love Lavinia more than all the world.
DEMETRIUS. Youngling, learn thou to make some
    meaner choice.
Lavinia is thine elder brother's hope.
AARON. Why, are ye mad? or know ye not, in Rome
How furious and impatient they be,
And cannot brook competitors in love?
I tell you, lords, you do but plot your deaths
By this device.
CHIRON.   Aaron, a thousand deaths
Would I propose to achieve her whom I love. 80
AARON. To achieve her how?
DEMETRIUS.   Why mak'st thou it so strange?
She is a woman, therefore may be wooed;
She is a woman, therefore may be won;
She is Lavinia, therefore must be loved.
What, man! more water glideth by the mill
Than wots the miller of, and easy it is
Of a cut loaf to steal a shive, we know:
Though Bassianus be the emperor's brother,
Better than he have worn Vulcan's badge.
AARON [*aside*]. Ay, and as good as Saturninus may. 90
DEMETRIUS. Then why should he despair that knows
    to court it
With words, fair looks, and liberality?
What, hast thou not full often struck a doe,

And borne her cleanly by the keeper's nose?
AARON. Why then, it seems, some certain snatch or so
Would serve your turns.
CHIRON.   Ay, so the turn were served.
DEMETRIUS. Aaron, thou hast hit it.
AARON.   Would you had hit it too,
Then should not we be tired with this ado.
Why, hark ye, hark ye! and are you such fools
To square for this? would it offend you then   100
That both should speed?
CHIRON.   Faith, not me.
DEMETRIUS. Nor me, so I were one.
AARON. For shame, be friends, and join for that you
    jar.
'Tis policy and stratagem must do
That you affect, and so must you resolve,
That what you cannot as you would achieve,
You must perforce accomplish as you may.
Take this of me, Lucrece was not more chaste
Than this Lavinia, Bassianus' love.
A speedier course than ling'ring languishment   110
Must we pursue, and I have found the path.
My lords, a solemn hunting is in hand,
There will the lovely Roman ladies troop:
The forest walks are wide and spacious,
And many unfrequented plots there are
Fitted by kind for rape and villainy:
Single you thither then this dainty doe,
And strike her home by force, if not by words:
This way, or not at all, stand you in hope.
Come, come, our empress, with her sacred wit   120
To villainy and vengeance consecrate,
Will we acquaint with all that we intend,
And she shall file our engines with advice,
That will not suffer you to square yourselves,
But to your wishes' height advance you both.
The emperor's court is like the House of Fame,
The palace full of tongues, of eyes, and ears:
The woods are ruthless, dreadful, deaf, and dull;
There speak, and strike, brave boys, and take your
    turns,
There serve your lust shadowed from heaven's eye, 130
And revel in Lavinia's treasury.
CHIRON. Thy counsel, lad, smells of no cowardice.
DEMETRIUS. 'Sit fas aut nefas', till I find the stream
To cool this heat, a charm to calm these fits,
'Per Styga, per manes vehor'.   *They go*

Scene 2: *A glade in a forest near Rome*

*Enter Titus Andronicus with his three sons and Marcus,
making a noise with hounds and horns*

TITUS. The hunt is up, the morn is bright and grey,
The fields are fragrant, and the woods are green:
Uncouple here, and let us make a bay,
And wake the emperor and his lovely bride,
And rouse the prince, and ring a hunter's peal,
That all the court may echo with the noise.
Sons, let it be your charge, as it is ours,
To attend the emperor's person carefully:
I have been troubled in my sleep this night,
But dawning day new comfort hath inspired.   10

*Here a cry of hounds, and wind horns in a peal: then enter
Saturninus, Tamora, Bassianus, Lavinia, Chiron, Demetrius, and their attendants*

Many good morrows to your majesty!
Madam, to you as many and as good!
I promiséd your grace a hunter's peal.
SATURNINUS. And you have rung it lustily, my lords,
Somewhat too early for new-married ladies.
BASSIANUS. Lavinia, how say you?
LAVINIA.   I say, no;
I have been broad awake two hours and more.
SATURNINUS. Come on then, horse and chariots let us
have,
And to our sport. [to Tamora] Madam, now shall ye
see
Our Roman hunting.
MARCUS.   I have dogs, my lord,   20
Will rouse the proudest panther in the chase,
And climb the highest promontory top.
TITUS. And I have horse will follow where the game
Makes way and run like swallows o'er the plain.
DEMETRIUS. Chiron, we hunt not, we, with horse nor
hound,
But hope to pluck a dainty doe to ground.
                                        They go

                    Scene 3

Enter Aaron alone, with a bag of gold

AARON. He that had wit would think that I had none,
To bury so much gold under a tree,
And never after to inherit it.
Let him that thinks of me so abjectly
Know that this gold must coin a stratagem,
Which, cunningly effected, will beget
A very excellent piece of villainy:
And so repose, sweet gold, for their unrest,
That have their alms out of the empress' chest.
                                        Hides the gold

Enter Tamora alone to the Moor

TAMORA. My lovely Aaron, wherefore look'st thou
sad,   10
When every thing doth make a gleeful boast?
The birds chaunt melody on every bush,
The snake lies rolléd in the cheerful sun,
The green leaves quiver with the cooling wind,
And make a chequered shadow on the ground:
Under their sweet shade, Aaron, let us sit,
And whilst the babbling echo mocks the hounds,
Replying shrilly to the well-tuned horns,
As if a double hunt were heard at once,
Let us sit down and mark their yellowing noise: 20
And after conflict such as was supposed
The wandering prince and Dido once enjoyed,
When with a happy storm they were surprised,
And curtained with a counsel-keeping cave,
We may, each wreathéd in the other's arms,
(Our pastimes done) possess a golden slumber,
Whiles hounds and horns and sweet melodious birds
Be unto us as is a nurse's song
Of lullaby to bring her babe asleep.
AARON. Madam, though Venus govern your desires,   30
Saturn is dominator over mine:
What signifies my deadly-standing eye,
My silence and my cloudy melancholy,
My fleece of woolly hair that now uncurls
Even as an adder when she doth unroll
To do some fatal execution?

No, madam, these are no venereal signs:
Vengeance is in my heart, death in my hand,
Blood and revenge are hammering in my head.
Hark, Tamora, the empress of my soul,   40
Which never hopes more heaven than rests in thee,
This is the day of doom for Bassianus:
His Philomel must lose her tongue to-day,
Thy sons make pillage of her chastity,
And wash their hands in Bassianus' blood.
Seest thou this letter? take it up, I pray thee,
And give the king this fatal-plotted scroll.
Now question me no more; we are espied;
Here comes a parcel of our hopeful booty,
Which dreads not yet their lives' destruction.   50

Enter Bassianus and Lavinia

TAMORA. Ah, my sweet Moor, sweeter to me than life!
AARON. No more, great empress, Bassianus comes.
Be cross with him, and I'll go fetch thy sons
To back thy quarrels whatsoe'er they be.
                                        He goes
BASSIANUS. Who have we here? Rome's royal
emperess,
Unfurnished of her well-beseeming troop?
Or is it Dian, habited like her,
Who hath abandonéd her holy groves
To see the general hunting in this forest?
TAMORA. Saucy controller of my private steps!   60
Had I the power that some say Dian had,
Thy temples should be planted presently
With horns, as was Actæon's, and the hounds
Should drive upon thy new-transforméd limbs,
Unmannerly intruder as thou art!
LAVINIA. Under your patience, gentle emperess,
'Tis thought you have a goodly gift in horning,
And to be doubted that your Moor and you
Are singled forth to try experiments:
Jove shield your husband from his hounds to-day! 70
'Tis pity they should take him for a stag.
BASSIANUS. Believe me, queen, your swarth
Cimmerian
Doth make your honour of his body's hue,
Spotted, detested, and abominable.
Why are you séquest'réd from all your train,
Dismounted from your snow-white goodly steed,
And wandered hither to an obscure plot,
Accompanied but with a barbarous Moor,
If foul desire had not conducted you?
LAVINIA. And, being intercepted in your sport,   80
Great reason that my noble lord be rated
For sauciness. I pray you, let us hence,
And let her joy her raven-coloured love,
This valley fits the purpose passing well.
BASSIANUS. The king my brother shall have note of
this.
LAVINIA. Ay, for these slips have made him noted long.
Good king, to be so mightily abused!
TAMORA. Why have I patience to endure all this?

Enter Chiron and Demetrius

DEMETRIUS. How now, dear sovereign, and our
gracious mother,
Why doth your highness look so pale and wan?   90
TAMORA. Have I not reason, think you, to look pale?
These two have ticed me hither to this place,
A barren detested vale, you see it is;

The trees, though summer, yet forlorn and lean,
O'ercome with moss and baleful mistletoe:
Here never shines the sun; here nothing breeds,
Unless the nightly owl or fatal raven:
And when they showed me this abhorréd pit,
They told me, here, at dead time of the night
A thousand fiends, a thousand hissing snakes,   100
Ten thousand swelling toads, as many urchins,
Would make such fearful and confuséd cries,
As any mortal body hearing it
Should straight fall mad, or else die suddenly.
No sooner had they told this hellish tale,
But straight they told me they would bind me here
Unto the body of a dismal yew,
And leave me to this miserable death.
And then they called me foul adulteress,
Lascivious Goth, and all the bitterest terms   110
That ever ear did hear to such effect.
And, had you not by wondrous fortune come,
This vengeance on me had they executed:
Revenge it, as you love your mother's life,
Or be ye not henceforth my children called.
DEMETRIUS. This is a witness that I am thy son.
                                        Stabs Bassianus
CHIRON. And this for me, struck home to show my
    strength.   *Stabbing him likewise*
LAVINIA. Ay come, Semiramis, nay, barbarous
    Tamora!
For no name fits thy nature but thy own!
TAMORA. Give me the poniard! you shall know, my
    boys,   120
Your mother's hand shall right your mother's
    wrong.
DEMETRIUS. Stay, madam, here is more belongs to her.
First thrash the corn, then after burn the straw:
This minion stood upon her chastity,
Upon her nuptial vow, her loyalty,
And with that painted hope she braves your
    mightiness:
And shall she carry this unto her grave?
CHIRON. An if she do, I would I were an eunuch.
Drag hence her husband to some secret hole,
And make his dead trunk pillow to our lust.   130
TAMORA. But when ye have the honey ye desire,
Let not this wasp outlive, us both to sting.
CHIRON. I warrant you, madam, we will make that
    sure:
Come, mistress, now perforce we will enjoy
That nice-preservéd honesty of yours.
LAVINIA. O Tamora! thou bear'st a woman's face—
TAMORA. I will not hear her speak, away with her.
LAVINIA. Sweet lords, entreat her hear me but a word.
DEMETRIUS. Listen, fair madam, let it be your glory
To see her tears, but be your heart to them   140
As unrelenting flint to drops of rain.
LAVINIA. When did the tiger's young ones teach the
    dam?
O, do not learn her wrath; she taught it thee.
The milk thou suck'dst from her did turn to marble,
Even at thy teat thou hadst thy tyranny.
Yet every mother breeds not sons alike,
                                            To Chiron
Do thou entreat her show a woman's pity.
CHIRON. What! wouldst thou have me prove myself
    a bastard?
LAVINIA. 'Tis true; the raven doth not hatch a lark:

Yet I have heard—O could I find it now!—   150
The lion, moved with pity, did endure
To have his princely paws pared all away:
Some say that ravens foster forlorn children,
The whilst their own birds famish in their nests:
O, be to me, though thy hard heart say no,
Nothing so kind but something pitiful!
TAMORA. I know not what it means, away with her!
LAVINIA. O, let me teach thee for my father's sake,
That gave thee life when well he might have slain
    thee.
Be not obdurate, open thy deaf ears.   160
TAMORA. Hadst thou in person ne'er offended me,
Even for his sake am I pitiless.
Remember, boys, I poured forth tears in vain
To save your brother from the sacrifice,
But fierce Andronicus would not relent.
Therefore away with her, and use her as you will;
The worse to her, the better loved of me.
LAVINIA. O Tamora, be called a gentle queen,
And with thine own hands kill me in this place!
For 'tis not life that I have begged so long,   170
Poor I was slain when Bassianus died.
TAMORA. What begg'st thou then? fond woman, let
    me go.
LAVINIA. 'Tis present death I beg, and one thing more
That womanhood denies my tongue to tell.
O, keep me from their worse than killing lust,
And tumble me into some loathsome pit,
Where never man's eye may behold my body
Do this, and be a charitable murderer.
TAMORA. So should I rob my sweet sons of their fee.
No, let them satisfy their lust on thee.   180
DEMETRIUS. Away! for thou hast staid us here too long.
LAVINIA. No grace? no womanhood? Ah beastly
    creature!
The blot and enemy to our general name!
Confusion fall——
CHIRON. Nay, then I'll stop your mouth. Bring thou
    her husband.
This is the hole where Aaron bid us hide him.

*Demetrius heaves the corpse into a pit; the two then go off
dragging Lavinia between them*

TAMORA. Farewell, my sons, see that you make her
    sure.
Ne'er let my heart know merry cheer indeed
Till all the Andronici be made away.
Now will I hence to seek my lovely Moor,
And let my spleenful sons this trull deflower.   190
                                            She goes

Enter Aaron with Quintus and Martius

AARON. Come on, my lords, the better foot before!
Straight will I bring you to the loathsome pit
Where I espied the panther fast asleep.
QUINTUS. My sight is very dull, whate'er it bodes.
MARTIUS. And mine, I promise you: were it not for
    shame,
Well could I leave our sport to sleep awhile.
                                        He falls into the pit
QUINTUS. What, art thou fallen? What subtle hole is
    this,
Whose mouth is covered with rude-growing briers,
Upon whose leaves are drops of new-shed blood   200
As fresh as morning dew distilled on flowers?

A very fatal place it seems to me.
Speak, brother, hast thou hurt thee with the fall?
MARTIUS. O, brother, with the dismall'st object hurt
That ever eye with sight made heart lament.
AARON [aside]. Now will I fetch the king to find them
here,
That he thereby may have a likely guess,
How these were they that made away his brother.
                        He goes
MARTIUS. Why dost not comfort me, and help me out
From this unhallowed and blood-stained hole?   210
QUINTUS. I am surprised with an uncouth fear,
A chilling sweat o'er-runs my trembling joints,
My heart suspects more than mine eye can see.
MARTIUS. To prove thou hast a true-divining heart,
Aaron and thou look down into this den,
And see a fearful sight of blood and death.
QUINTUS. Aaron is gone, and my compassionate heart
Will not permit mine eyes once to behold
The thing whereat it trembles by surmise:
O, tell me who it is, for ne'er till now   220
Was I a child to fear I know not what.
MARTIUS. Lord Bassianus lies berayed in blood,
All on a heap, like to a slaughtered lamb,
In this detested, dark, blood-drinking pit.
QUINTUS. If it be dark, how dost thou know 'tis he?
MARTIUS. Upon his bloody finger he doth wear
A precious ring, that lightens all this hole,
Which, like a taper in some monument,
Doth shine upon the dead man's earthy cheeks,
And shows the ragged entrails of this pit: 230
So pale did shine the moon on Pyramus,
When he by night lay bathed in maiden blood.
O brother, help me with thy fainting hand—
If fear hath made thee faint, as me it hath—
Out of this fell devouring receptacle,
As hateful as Cocytus' misty mouth.
QUINTUS. Reach me thy hand, that I may help thee
out;
Or, wanting strength to do thee so much good,
I may be plucked into the swallowing womb
Of this deep pit, poor Bassianus' grave.   240
I have no strength to pluck thee to the brink.
MARTIUS. Nor I no strength to climb without thy help.
QUINTUS. Thy hand once more, I will not loose again,
Till thou art here aloft or I below:
Thou canst not come to me, I come to thee.
                        He falls in

Enter the Emperor and Aaron the Moor

SATURNINUS. Along with me! I'll see what hole is here,
And what he is that now is leaped into it.
Say, who art thou, that lately didst descend
Into this gaping hollow of the earth?
MARTIUS. The unhappy sons of old Andronicus,   250
Brought hither in a most unlucky hour,
To find thy brother Bassianus dead.
SATURNINUS. My brother dead! I know thou dost but
jest:
He and his lady both are at the lodge,
Upon the north side of this pleasant chase;
'Tis not an hour since I left them there.
MARTIUS. We know not where you left them all alive,
But, out alas! here have we found him dead.

Enter Tamora, Andronicus, and Lucius

TAMORA. Where is my lord the king?
SATURNINUS. Here, Tamora, though griped with
killing grief.   260
TAMORA. Where is thy brother, Bassianus?
SATURNINUS. Now to the bottom dost thou search my
wound;
Poor Bassianus here lies murdered.
TAMORA. Then all too late I bring this fatal writ,
The complot of this timeless tragedy;
And wonder greatly that man's face can fold
In pleasing smiles such murderous tyranny.
          She giveth Saturnine a letter
SATURNINUS [reads]. 'An if we miss to meet him
handsomely—
Sweet huntsman, Bassianus 'tis we mean—
Do thou so much as dig the grave for him.   270
Thou know'st our meaning. Look for thy reward
Among the nettles at the elder tree,
Which overshades the mouth of that same pit
Where we decreed to bury Bassianus.
Do this and purchase us thy lasting friends.'
O, Tamora! was ever heard the like?
This is the pit, and this the elder-tree.
Look, sirs, if you can find the huntsman out
That should have murdered Bassianus here.
AARON. My gracious lord, here is the bag of gold.   280
SATURNINUS [to Titus]. Two of thy whelps, fell curs
of bloody kind,
Have here bereft my brother of his life.
Sirs, drag them from the pit unto the prison,
There let them bide until we have devised
Some never-heard-of torturing pain for them.
TAMORA. What, are they in this pit? O wondrous
thing!
How easily murder is discovered!
TITUS. High emperor, upon my feeble knee
I beg this boon, with tears not lightly shed,
That this fell fault of my accursed sons,   290
Accursed, if the fault be proved in them—
SATURNINUS. If it be proved! you see, it is apparent.
Who found this letter? Tamora, was it you?
TAMORA. Andronicus himself did take it up.
TITUS. I did, my lord, yet let me be their bail,
For by my father's reverend tomb I vow
They shall be ready at your highness' will,
To answer their suspicion with their lives.
SATURNINUS. Thou shalt not bail them, see thou follow
me.
Some bring the murdered body, some the
murderers,   300
Let them not speak a word, the guilt is plain,
For by my soul were there worse end than death,
That end upon them should be executed.
TAMORA. Andronicus, I will entreat the king,
Fear not thy sons, they shall do well enough.
TITUS. Come, Lucius, come, stay not to talk with
them.   *They go*

Scene 4

*Enter the Empress' sons with Lavinia, her hands cut off,
and her tongue cut out, and ravished*

DEMETRIUS. So, now go tell, an if thy tongue can
speak,
Who 'twas that cut thy tongue and ravished thee.

CHIRON. Write down thy mind, bewray thy meaning
   so,
  And, if thy stumps will let thee, play the scribe.
DEMETRIUS. See, how with signs and tokens she can
  scrowl.
CHIRON. Go home, call for sweet water, wash thy
  hands.
DEMETRIUS. She hath no tongue to call nor hands to
  wash,
  And so let's leave her to her silent walks.
CHIRON. An 'twere my cause, I should go hang myself.
DEMETRIUS. If thou hadst hands to help thee knit the
  cord.   *They go* 10

Enter Marcus from hunting

MARCUS. Who is this? my niece, that flies away so fast!
  Cousin, a word, where is your husband?
  If I do dream, would all my wealth would wake me!
  If I do wake, some planet strike me down,
  That I may slumber an eternal sleep!
  Speak, gentle niece, what stern ungentle hands
  Hath lopped and hewed and made thy body bare
  Of her two branches? those sweet ornaments,
  Whose circling shadows kings have sought to sleep
   in,
  And might not gain so great a happiness   20
  As half thy love? Why dost not speak to me?
  Alas, a crimson river of warm blood,
  Like to a bubbling fountain stirred with wind,
  Doth rise and fall between thy roséd lips,
  Coming and going with thy honey breath.
  But, sure, some Tereus hath deflowered thee,
  And, lest thou shouldst detect him, cut thy tongue.
  Ah, now thou turn'st away thy face for shame!
  And, notwithstanding all this loss of blood,
  As from a conduit with three issuing spouts,   30
  Yet do thy cheeks look red as Titan's face
  Blushing to be encountered with a cloud.
  Shall I speak for thee? shall I say 'tis so?
  O, that I knew thy heart, and knew the beast,
  That I might rail at him to ease my mind!
  Sorrow concealéd, like an oven stopped,
  Doth burn the heart to cinders where it is.
  Fair Philomel, why she but lost her tongue,
  And in a tedious sampler sewed her mind:
  But lovely niece, that mean is cut from thee;   40
  A craftier Tereus, cousin, hast thou met,
  And he hath cut those pretty fingers off,
  That could have better sewed than Philomel.
  O, had the monster seen those lily hands
  Tremble like aspen leaves upon a lute,
  And make the silken strings delight to kiss them,
  He would not then have touched them for his life!
  Or, had he heard the heavenly harmony
  Which that sweet tongue hath made,
  He would have dropped his knife, and fell asleep   50
  As Cerberus at the Thracian poet's feet.
  Come, let us go and make thy father blind,
  For such a sight will blind a father's eye.
  One hour's storm will drown the fragrant meads,
  What will whole months of tears thy father's eyes?
  Do not draw back, for we will mourn with thee:
  O, could our mourning ease thy misery!
                           They go

ACT 3
Scene 1

*Enter the Judges and Senators with Titus' two sons bound,
passing on to the palace of execution, and Titus going before,
pleading*

TITUS. Hear me, grave fathers! noble tribunes, stay!
  For pity of mine age, whose youth was spent
  In dangerous wars, whilst you securely slept;
  For all my blood in Rome's great quarrel shed,
  For all the frosty nights that I have watched,
  And for these bitter tears, which now you see
  Filling the agéd wrinkles in my cheeks,
  Be pitiful to my condemnéd sons,
  Whose souls are not corrupted as 'tis thought.
  For two and twenty sons I never wept,   10
  Because they died in honour's lofty bed;

Andronicus lieth down and the Judges pass by him

  For these, tribunes, in the dust I write
  My heart's deep languor and my soul's sad tears:
  Let my tears stanch the earth's dry appetite;
  My sons' sweet blood will make it shame and blush.
  O earth, I will befriend thee more with rain,
  That shall distil from these two ancient urns,
  Than youthful April shall with all his showers:
  In summer's drought I'll drop upon thee still,
  In winter with warm tears I'll melt the snow,   20
  And keep eternal spring-time on thy face,
  So thou refuse to drink my dear sons' blood.

Enter Lucius, with his weapon drawn

  O reverend tribunes! O gentle agéd men!
  Unbind my sons, reverse the doom of death,
  And let me say, that never wept before,
  My tears are now prevailing orators.
LUCIUS. O noble father, you lament in vain,
  The tribunes hear you not, no man is by,
  And you recount your sorrows to a stone.
TITUS. Ah, Lucius, for thy brothers let me plead.   30
  Grave tribunes, once more I entreat of you.
LUCIUS. My gracious lord, no tribune hears you speak.
TITUS. Why, 'tis no matter, man, if they did hear
  They would not mark me, if they did mark
  They would not pity me, yet plead I must,
  And bootless unto them ...
  Therefore I tell my sorrows to the stones,
  Who though they cannot answer my distress,
  Yet in some sort they are better than the tribunes,
  For that they will not intercept my tale: 40
  When I do weep, they humbly at my feet
  Receive my tears, and seem to weep with me;
  And were they but attiréd in grave weeds,
  Rome could afford no tribunes like to these.
  A stone is soft as wax, tribunes more hard than
   stones:
  A stone is silent and offendeth not,
  And tribunes with their tongues doom men to
   death.   *Rises*
  But wherefore stand'st thou with thy weapon
   drawn?
LUCIUS. To rescue my two brothers from their death:
  For which attempt the judges have pronounced   50
  My everlasting doom of banishment.
TITUS. O happy man! they have befriended thee:
  Why foolish Lucius, dost thou not perceive

That Rome is but a wilderness of tigers?
Tigers must prey, and Rome affords no prey
But me and mine. How happy art thou then,
From these devourers to be banishéd!
But who comes with our brother Marcus here?

Enter Marcus with Lavinia

MARCUS. Titus, prepare thy agéd eyes to weep,
Or if not so, thy noble heart to break: 60
I bring consuming sorrow to thine age.
TITUS. Will it consume me? let me see it then.
MARCUS. This was thy daughter.
TITUS.   Why, Marcus, so she is.
LUCIUS. Ah me! this object kills me!
TITUS. Faint-hearted boy, arise, and look upon her.
Speak, Lavinia, what accurséd hand
Hath made thee handless in thy father's sight?
What fool hath added water to the sea,
Or brought a faggot to bright-burning Troy?
My grief was at the height before thou cam'st,   70
And now like Nilus it disdaineth bounds.
Give me a sword, I'll chop off my hands too,
For they have fought for Rome, and all in vain;
And they have nursed this woe, in feeding life;
In bootless prayer have they been held up,
And they have served me to effectless use.
Now all the service I require of them
Is, that the one will help to cut the other.
'Tis well, Lavinia, that thou hast no hands,
For hands to do Rome service is but vain.   80
LUCIUS. Speak, gentle sister, who hath martyred thee?
MARCUS. O, that delightful engine of her thoughts,
That blabbed them with such pleasing eloquence,
Is torn from forth that pretty hollow cage,
Where like a sweet melodious bird it sung
Sweet varied notes, enchanting every ear!
LUCIUS. O, say thou for her, who hath done this
deed?
MARCUS. O, thus I found her, straying in the park,
Seeking to hide herself, as doth the deer
That hath received some unrecuring wound.   90
TITUS. It was my dear, and he that wounded her
Hath hurt me more than had he killed me dead:
For now I stand as one upon a rock,
Environed with a wilderness of sea,
Who marks the waxing tide grow wave by wave,
Expecting ever when some envious surge
Will in his brinish bowels swallow him.
This way to death my wretched sons are gone,
Here stands my other son, a banished man,
And here my brother weeping at my woes: 100
But that which gives my soul the greatest
Is dear Lavinia, dearer than my soul.
Had I but seen thy picture in this plight,
It would have madded me: what shall I do
Now I behold thy lively body so?
Thou hast no hands to wipe away thy tears,
Nor tongue to tell me who hath martyred thee:
Thy husband he is dead, and for his death
Thy brothers are condemned, and dead by this.
Look, Marcus! ah, son Lucius, look on her!   110
When I did name her brothers, then fresh tears
Stood on her cheeks, as doth the honey-dew
Upon a gathered lily almost withered.
MARCUS. Perchance she weeps because they killed her
husband,

Perchance because she knows them innocent.
TITUS. If they did kill thy husband, then be
joyful,
Because the law hath ta'en revenge on them.
No, no, they would not do so foul a deed,
Witness the sorrow that their sister makes.
Gentle Lavinia, let me kiss thy lips,   120
Or make some sign how I may do thee ease:
Shall thy good uncle, and thy brother Lucius,
And thou, and I, sit round about some fountain,
Looking all downwards, to behold our cheeks
How they are stained, like meadows yet not dry
With miry slime left on them by a flood?
And in the fountain shall we gaze so long
Till the fresh taste be taken from that clearness,
And made a brine-pit with our bitter tears?
Or shall we cut away our hands, like thine?   130
Or shall we bite our tongues, and in dumb shows
Pass the remainder of our hateful days?
What shall we do? let us, that have our tongues,
Plot some device of further misery,
To make us wondered at in time to come.
LUCIUS. Sweet father, cease your tears, for at your grief
See how my wretched sister sobs and weeps.
MARCUS. Patience, dear niece. Good Titus, dry thine
eyes.
TITUS. Ah, Marcus, Marcus! brother, well I wot
Thy napkin cannot drink a tear of mine,   140
For thou, poor man, hast drowned it with thine
own.
LUCIUS. Ah, my Lavinia, I will wipe thy cheeks.
TITUS. Mark, Marcus, mark! I understand her signs:
Had she a tongue to speak, now would she say
That to her brother which I said to thee:
His napkin, with his true tears all bewet,
Can do no service on her sorrowful cheeks.
O, what a sympathy of woe is this!
As far from help as Limbo is from bliss!

Enter Aaron the Moor alone

AARON. Titus Andronicus, my lord the emperor   150
Sends thee this word, that, if thou love thy sons,
Let Marcus, Lucius, or thyself, old Titus,
Or any one of you, chop off your hand,
And send it to the king: he for the same
Will send thee hither both thy sons alive,
And that shall be the ransom for their fault.
TITUS. O, gracious emperor! O, gentle Aaron!
Did ever raven sing so like a lark,
That gives sweet tidings of the sun's uprise?
With all my heart, I'll send the emperor   160
My hand;
Good Aaron, wilt thou help to chop it off?
LUCIUS. Stay, father! for that noble hand of thine,
That hath thrown down so many enemies,
Shall not be sent: my hand will serve the turn.
My youth can better spare my blood than you,
And therefore mine shall save my brothers' lives.
MARCUS. Which of your hands hath not defended
Rome,
And reared aloft the bloody battle-axe,
Writing destruction on the enemy's castle?   170
O, none of both but are of high desert:
My hand hath been but idle, let it serve
To ransom my two nephews from their death,
Then have I kept it to a worthy end.

AARON. Nay, come, agree whose hand shall go along,
For fear they die before their pardon come.
MARCUS. My hand shall go.
LUCIUS. By heaven, it shall not go.
TITUS. Sirs, strive no more; such withered herbs
    as these
Are meet for plucking up, and therefore mine.
LUCIUS. Sweet father, if I shall be thought thy son,   180
Let me redeem my brothers both from death.
MARCUS. And, for our father's sake and mother's care,
Now let me show a brother's love to thee.
TITUS. Agree between you, I will spare my hand.
LUCIUS. Then I'll go fetch an axe.
MARCUS. But I will use the axe.

Lucius and Marcus go

TITUS. Come hither, Aaron. I'll deceive them both;
Lend me thy hand, and I will give thee mine.
AARON. If that be called deceit, I will be honest,
And never whilst I live deceive men so: 190
But I'll deceive you in another sort,
And that you'll say, ere half an hour pass.

He cuts off Titus' hand

Enter Lucius and Marcus again

TITUS. Now stay your strife, what shall be is
    dispatched.
Good Aaron, give his majesty my hand,
Tell him it was a hand that warded him
From thousand dangers, bid him bury it—
More hath it merited, that let it have:
As for my sons, say I account of them
As jewels purchased at an easy price,
And yet dear too because I bought mine own.   200
AARON. I go, Andronicus, and for thy hand
Look by and by to have thy sons with thee.
[*Aside*] Their heads, I mean. O, how this villainy
Doth fat me with the very thoughts of it!
Let fools do good, and fair men call for grace,
Aaron will have his soul black like his face.

He goes

TITUS. O, here I lift this one hand up to heaven,
And bow this feeble ruin to the earth.
If any power pities wretched tears,
To that I call! [*to Lavinia*] What, wouldst thou
    kneel with me?   210
Do then, dear heart, for heaven shall hear our
    prayers,
Or with our sighs we'll breathe the welkin dim,
And stain the sun with fog, as sometime clouds
When they do hug him in their melting bosoms.
MARCUS. O brother, speak with possibility,
And do not break into these deep extremes.
TITUS. Is not my sorrow deep, having no bottom?
Then be my passions bottomless with them.
MARCUS. But yet let reason govern thy lament.
TITUS. If there were reason for these miseries,   220
Then into limits could I bind my woes:
When heaven doth weep, doth not the earth
    o'erflow?
If the winds rage, doth not the sea wax mad,
Threat'ning the welkin with his big-swoln face?
And wilt thou have a reason for this coil?
I am the sea; hark, how her sighs doth blow!
She is the weeping welkin, I the earth:
Then must my sea be movéd with her sighs,
Then must my earth with her continual tears

Become a deluge, overflowed and drowned: 230
For why? my bowels cannot hide her woes,
But like a drunkard must I vomit them.
Then give me leave, for losers will have leave
To ease their stomachs with their bitter tongues.

Enter a Messenger, with two heads and a hand

MESSENGER. Worthy Andronicus, ill art thou repaid
For that good hand thou sent'st the emperor:
Here are the heads of thy two noble sons,
And here's thy hand in scorn to thee sent back,
Thy griefs their sports, thy resolution mocked:
That woe is me to think upon thy woes,   240
More than remembrance of my father's death.

He goes

MARCUS. Now let hot Ætna cool in Sicily,
And be my heart an ever-burning hell!
These miseries are more than may be borne!
To weep with them that weep doth ease some deal,
But sorrow flouted at is double death.
LUCIUS. Ah, that this sight should make so deep a
    wound,
And yet detested life not shrink thereat!
That ever death should let life bear his name,
Where life hath no more interest but to breathe!   250

Lavinia kisses Titus

MARCUS. Alas, poor heart, that kiss is comfortless
As frozen water to a starvéd snake.
TITUS. When will this fearful slumber have an end?
MARCUS. Now, farewell, flattery, die Andronicus,
Thou dost not slumber, see thy two sons' heads,
Thy warlike hand, thy mangled daughter here,
Thy other banished son with this dear sight
Struck pale and bloodless, and thy brother, I,
Even like a stony image cold and numb.
Ah! now no more will I control thy griefs: 260
Rend off thy silver hair, thy other hand
Gnawing with thy teeth, and be this dismal sight
The closing up of our most wretched eyes:
Now is a time to storm, why art thou still?
TITUS. Ha, ha, ha!
MARCUS. Why dost thou laugh? it fits not with this
    hour.
TITUS. Why, I have not another tear to shed;
Besides, this sorrow is an enemy,
And would usurp upon my wat'ry eyes,
And make them blind with tributary tears;   270
Then which way shall I find Revenge's Cave?
For these two heads do seem to speak to me,
And threat me I shall never come to bliss
Till all these mischiefs be returned again,
Even in their throats that hath committed them.
Come, let me see what task I have to do.
You heavy people, circle me about,
That I may turn me to each one of you,
And swear unto my soul to right your wrongs.
The vow is made. Come, brother, take a head;   280
And in this hand the other will I bear.
And Lavinia, thou shalt be employed in this;
Bear thou my hand, sweet wench, between thy
    teeth:
As for thee, boy, go, get thee from my sight.
Thou art an exile, and thou must not stay.
Hie to the Goths, and raise an army there,
And, if ye love me, as I think you do,
Let's kiss and part, for we have much to do.

Titus departs with Marcus and Lavinia

LUCIUS. Farewell, Andronicus, my noble father,
The woefull'st man that ever lived in Rome!　290
Farewell, proud Rome! till Lucius come again,
He leaves his pledges dearer than his life:
Farewell, Lavinia, my noble sister,
O, would thou wert as thou tofore hast been!
But now nor Lucius nor Lavinia lives
But in oblivion and hateful griefs.
If Lucius live, he will requite your wrongs,
And make proud Saturnine and his emperess
Beg at the gates, like Tarquin and his queen.
Now will I to the Goths and raise a power,　300
To be revenged on Rome and Saturnine.
He goes

Scene 2: *A room in Titus' house. A banquet set out*

Enter Titus, Marcus, Lavinia, and young Lucius

TITUS. So, so, now sit, and look you eat no more
Than will preserve just so much strength in us
As will revenge these bitter woes of ours.
Marcus, unknit that sorrow-wreathen knot:
Thy niece and I, poor creatures, want our hands,
And cannot passionate our tenfold grief
With folded arms. This poor right hand of mine
Is left to tyrannize upon my breast;
Who, when my heart all mad with misery
Beats in this hollow prison of my flesh,　10
Then thus I thump it down.
[*To Lavinia*] Thou map of woe, that thus dost talk
    in signs,
When thy poor heart beats with outrageous beating,
Thou canst not strike it thus to make it still.
Wound it with sighing, girl, kill it with groans;
Or get some little knife between thy teeth,
And just against thy heart make thou a hole,
That all the tears that thy poor eyes let fall
May run into that sink, and soaking in
Drown the lamenting fool in sea-salt tears.　20
MARCUS. Fie, brother, fie! teach her not thus to lay
Such violent hands upon her tender life.
TITUS. How now! has sorrow made thee dote already?
Why, Marcus, no man should be mad but I.
What violent hands can she lay on her life!
Ah, wherefore dost thou urge the name of hands,
To bid Æneas tell the tale twice o'er,
How Troy was burnt and he made miserable?
O, handle not the theme, to talk of hands,
Lest we remember still that we have none.　30
Fie, fie, how frantically I square my talk,
As if we should forget we had no hands,
If Marcus did not name the word of hands!
Come, let's fall to; and, gentle girl, eat this.
Here is no drink? Hark, Marcus, what she says—
I can interpret all her martyred signs—
She says she drinks no other drink but tears,
Brewed with her sorrows, meshed upon her cheeks.
Speechless complainer, I will learn thy thought;
In thy dumb action will I be as perfect　40
As begging hermits in their holy prayers:
Thou shalt not sigh, nor hold thy stumps to heaven,
Nor wink, nor nod, nor kneel, nor make a sign,
But I of these will wrest an alphabet,
And by still practice learn to know thy meaning.
BOY. Good grandsire, leave these bitter deep laments.

Make my aunt merry with some pleasing tale.
MARCUS. Alas, the tender boy, in passion moved,
Doth weep to see his grandsire's heaviness.
TITUS. Peace, tender sapling, thou art made of tears,　50
And tears will quickly melt thy life away.
Marcus strikes the dish with a knife
What dost thou strike at, Marcus, with thy knife?
MARCUS. At that that I have killed, my lord,—a fly.
TITUS. Out on thee, murderer! thou kill'st my heart;
Mine eyes are cloyed with view of tyranny:
A deed of death done on the innocent
Becomes not Titus' brother: get thee gone;
I see thou art not for my company.
MARCUS. Alas, my lord, I have but killed a fly.
TITUS. 'But!' How, if that fly had a father and mother?　60
How would he hang his slender gilded wings,
And buzz lamenting doings in the air!
Poor harmless fly,
That, with his pretty buzzing melody,
Came here to make us merry! and thou hast killed
    him.
MARCUS. Pardon me, sir; it was a black ill-favoured fly,
Like to the empress' Moor. Therefore I killed him.
TITUS. O, O, O,
Then pardon me for reprehending thee,
For thou hast done a charitable deed.　70
Give me thy knife, I will insult on him,
Flattering myself, as if it were the Moor,
Come hither purposely to poison me.
There's for thyself, and that's for Tamora.
Ah, sirrah!
Yet I think we are not brought so low,
But that between us we can kill a fly
That comes in likeness of a coal-black Moor.
MARCUS. Alas, poor man! grief has so wrought on him,
He takes false shadows for true substances.　80
TITUS. Come, take away. Lavinia, go with me:
I'll to thy closet, and go read with thee
Sad stories chancèd in the times of old.
Come, boy, and go with me: thy sight is young,
And thou shalt read when mine begins to dazzle.
They go

ACT 4

Scene 1: *Before Titus' house*

*Enter Lucius' son and Lavinia running after him; and the
boy flies from her with his books under his arm. Then enter
Titus and Marcus*

BOY. Help, grandsire, help! my aunt Lavinia
Follows me everywhere, I know not why.
Good uncle Marcus, see how swift she comes.
Alas, sweet aunt, I know not what you mean.
MARCUS. Stand by me, Lucius, do not fear thine aunt.
TITUS. She loves thee, boy, too well to do thee harm.
BOY. Ay, when my father was in Rome she did.
MARCUS. What means my niece Lavinia by these signs?
TITUS. Fear her not, Lucius. Somewhat doth she mean.
See, Lucius, see, how much she makes of thee:　10
Somewhither would she have thee go with her.
Ah, boy, Cornelia never with more care
Read to her sons than she hath read to thee
Sweet poetry and Tully's Orator.
Canst thou not guess wherefore she plies thee thus?

BOY. My lord, I know not, I, nor can I guess,
Unless some fit or frenzy do possess her:
For I have heard my grandsire say full oft,
Extremity of griefs would make men mad;
And I have read that Hecuba of Troy   20
Ran mad for sorrow. That made me to fear,
Although, my lord, I know my noble aunt
Loves me as dear as e'er my mother did,
And would not, but in fury, fright my youth:
Which made me down to throw my books and fly,
Causeless perhaps. But pardon me, sweet aunt:
And, madam, if my uncle Marcus go,
I will most willingly attend your ladyship.
MARCUS. Lucius, I will.
          *Lavinia with her stumps turns over
          the books which Lucius has let fall*
TITUS. How now, Lavinia? Marcus, what means this?   30
Some book there is that she desires to see:
Which is it, girl, of these? Open them, boy.
But thou art deeper read, and better skilled:
Come, and take choice of all my library,
And so beguile thy sorrow, till the heavens
Reveal the damned contriver of this deed.
Why lifts she up her arms in sequence thus?
MARCUS. I think she means that there were more than
   one
Confederate in the fact. Ay, more there was;
Or else to heaven she heaves them for revenge.   40
TITUS. Lucius, what book is that she tosseth so?
BOY. Grandsire, 'tis Ovid's Metamorphoses;
My mother gave it me.
MARCUS.   For love of her that's gone,
Perhaps she culled it from among the rest.
TITUS. Soft! so busily she turns the leaves!
Help her!
What would she find? Lavinia, shall I read?
This is the tragic tale of Philomel,
And treats of Tereus' treason and his rape;
And rape, I fear, was root of thy annoy.   50
MARCUS. See, brother, see, note how she quotes the
   leaves.
TITUS. Lavinia, wert thou thus surprised, sweet girl,
Ravished and wronged, as Philomela was,
Forced in the ruthless, vast, and gloomy woods?
See, see!
Ay, such a place there is, where we did hunt,—
O, had we never, never hunted there!—
Patterned by that the poet here describes,
By nature made for murders and for rapes.
MARCUS. O, why should nature build so foul a den,   60
Unless the gods delight in tragedies?
TITUS. Give signs, sweet girl, for here are none but
   friends,
What Roman lord it was durst do the deed:
Or slunk not Saturnine, as Tarquin erst,
That left the camp to sin in Lucrece' bed?
MARCUS. Sit down, sweet niece: brother, sit down by
   me.
Apollo, Pallas, Jove, or Mercury,
Inspire me, that I may this treason find!
My lord, look here: look here, Lavinia:
          *He writes his name with his
          staff, and guides it with
          feet and mouth.*
This sandy plot is plain; guide, if thou canst,   70
This after me. I have writ my name

Without the help of any hand at all.
Cursed be that heart that forced us to this shift!
Write thou, good niece, and here display at last
What God will have discovered for revenge:
Heaven guide thy pen to print thy sorrows plain,
That we may know the traitors and the truth!
          *She takes the staff in her mouth,
          and guides it with her stumps
          and writes*
TITUS. O, do ye read, my lord, what she hath writ?
'Stuprum. Chiron. Demetrius.'
MARCUS. What, what! the lustful sons of Tamora   80
Performers of this heinous, bloody deed?
TITUS. Magni Dominator poli,
Tam lentus audis scelera? tam lentus vides?
MARCUS. O, calm thee, gentle lord! although I know
There is enough written upon this earth
To stir a mutiny in the mildest thoughts,
And arm the minds of infants to exclaims.
My lord, kneel down with me; Lavinia, kneel;
And kneel, sweet boy, the Roman Hector's hope;
And swear with me, as, with the woful fere   90
And father of that chaste dishonoured dame,
Lord Junius Brutus sware for Lucrece' rape,
That we will prosecute by good advice
Mortal revenge upon these traitorous Goths,
And see their blood, or die with this reproach.
TITUS. 'Tis sure enough, an you knew how,
But if you hurt these bear-whelps, then beware:
The dam will wake; and if she wind ye once,
She's with the lion deeply still in league,
And lulls him whilst she playeth on her back,   100
And when he sleeps will she do what she list.
You are a young huntsman, Marcus, let alone;
And, come, I will go get a leaf of brass,
And with a gad of steel will write these words,
And lay it by: the angry northern wind
Will blow these sands like Sibyl's leaves abroad,
And where's our lesson then? Boy, what say you?
BOY. I say, my lord, that if I were a man,
Their mother's bed-chamber should not be safe
For these base bondmen to the yoke of Rome.   110
MARCUS. Ay, that's my boy! thy father hath full oft
For his ungrateful country done the like.
BOY. And, uncle, so will I, an if I live.
TITUS. Come, go with me into mine armoury:
Lucius, I'll fit thee, and withal my boy
Shall carry from me to the empress' sons
Presents that I intend to send them both:
Come, come; thou'lt do my message, wilt thou not?
BOY. Ay, with my dagger in their bosoms, grandsire.
TITUS. No, boy, not so; I'll teach thee another course.   120
Lavinia, come. Marcus, look to my house.
Lucius and I'll go brave it at the court;
Ah, marry, will we, sir; and we'll be waited on.
          *He goes; Lavinia and young Lucius
          follow*
MARCUS. O heavens, can you hear a good man groan,
And not relent, or not compassion him?
Marcus, attend him in his ecstasy,
That hath more scars of sorrow in his heart,
Than foe-men's marks upon his battered shield,
But yet so just that he will not revenge.
Revenge the heavens for old Andronicus!   130
          He goes

Scene 2: *A room in the palace*

*Enter Aaron, Chiron, and Demetrius, at one door: at
another door, young Lucius and another, with a bundle of
weapons and verses writ upon them*

CHIRON. Demetrius, here's the son of Lucius,
  He hath some message to deliver us.
AARON. Ay, some mad message from his mad
  grandfather.
BOY. My lords, with all the humbleness I may,
  I greet your honours from Andronicus.
  [*Aside*] And pray the Roman gods confound you
  both.
DEMETRIUS. Gramercy, lovely Lucius, what's the
  news?
BOY [*aside*]. That you are both deciphered, that's the
  news,
  For villains marked with rape. [*aloud*] May it
  please you,
  My grandsire, well-advised, hath sent by me   10
  The goodliest weapons of his armoury
  To gratify your honourable youth,
  The hope of Rome; for so he bade me say;
  And so I do, and with his gifts present
  Your lordships, that whenever you have need,
  You may be arméd and appointed well.
  And so I leave you both ... [*aside*] like bloody
  villains.   *He goes*
DEMETRIUS. What's here? a scroll, and written round
  about?
  Let's see:
  'Integer vitæ, scelerisque purus,   20
  Non eget Mauri jaculis, nec arcu.'
CHIRON. O, 'tis a verse in Horace; I know it well:
  I read it in the grammar long ago.
AARON. Ay, just; a verse in Horace; right, you have it.
  [*Aside*] Now, what a thing it is to be an ass!
  Here's no sound jest! the old man hath found their
  guilt,
  And sends them weapons wrapped about with lines
  That wound, beyond their feeling, to the quick.
  But were our witty empress well afoot,
  She would applaud Andronicus' conceit.   30
  But let her rest in her unrest awhile.
  [*Aloud*] And now, young lords, was't not a happy
  star
  Led us to Rome, strangers, and more than so,
  Captives, to be advancéd to this height?
  It did me good, before the palace gate
  To brave the tribune in his brother's hearing.
DEMETRIUS. But me more good, to see so great a lord
  Basely insinuate and send us gifts.
AARON. Had he not reason, lord Demetrius?
  Did you not use his daughter very friendly?   40
DEMETRIUS. I would we had a thousand Roman dames
  At such a bay, by turn to serve our lust.
CHIRON. A charitable wish and full of love.
AARON. Here lacks but your mother for to say amen.
CHIRON. And that would she for twenty thousand
  more.
DEMETRIUS. Come, let us go, and pray to all the gods
  For our belovéd mother in her pains.
AARON [*aside*]. Pray to the devils, the gods have given
  us over.   *Trumpets sound*
DEMETRIUS. Why do the emperor's trumpets flourish
  thus?

CHIRON. Belike, for joy the emperor hath a son.   50
DEMETRIUS. Soft! who comes here?

Enter Nurse with a blackamoor child

NURSE.   Good morrow, lords.
  O, tell me, did you see Aaron the Moor?
AARON. Well, more or less, or ne'er a whit at all,
  Here Aaron is; and what with Aaron now?
NURSE. O gentle Aaron, we are all undone!
  Now help, or woe betide thee evermore!
AARON. Why, what a caterwauling dost thou keep?
  What dost thou wrap and fumble in thy arms?
NURSE. O, that which I would hide from heaven's eye,
  Our empress' shame and stately Rome's disgrace!   60
  She is delivered, lords, she is delivered.
AARON. To whom?
NURSE.   I mean, she is brought a-bed.
AARON. Well, God give her good rest! What hath he
  sent her?
NURSE. A devil.
AARON.   Why, then she is the devil's dam;
  A joyful issue.
NURSE. A joyless, dismal, black, and sorrowful issue!
  Here is the babe, as loathsome as a toad
  Amongst the fair-faced breeders of our clime.
  The empress sends it thee, thy stamp, thy seal,
  And bids thee christen it with thy dagger's point.   70
AARON. Zounds, ye whore! is black so base a hue?
  Sweet blowse, you are a beauteous blossom, sure.
DEMETRIUS. Villain, what hast thou done?
AARON. That which thou canst not undo.
CHIRON. Thou hast undone our mother.
AARON. Villain, I have done thy mother.
DEMETRIUS. And therein, hellish dog, thou hast
  undone her.
  Woe to her chance, and damned her loathéd choice!
  Accursed the offspring of so foul a fiend!
CHIRON. It shall not live.   80
AARON. It shall not die.
NURSE. Aaron, it must; the mother wills it so.
AARON. What, must it, nurse? then let no man but I
  Do execution on my flesh and blood.
DEMETRIUS. I'll broach the tadpole on my rapier's
  point:
  Nurse, give it me; my sword shall soon dispatch it.
AARON. Sooner this sword shall plough thy bowels up.
              Takes the child from the nurse, and draws
  Stay, murderous villains! will you kill your brother?
  Now, by the burning tapers of the sky,
  That shone so brightly when this boy was got,   90
  He dies upon my scimitar's sharp point
  That touches this my first-born son and heir!
  I tell you, younglings, not Enceladus,
  With all his threat'ning band of Typhon's brood,
  Nor great Alcides, nor the god of war,
  Shall seize this prey out of his father's hands.
  What, what, ye sanguine, shallow-hearted boys!
  Ye white-limed walls! ye alehouse painted signs!
  Coal-black is better than another hue,
  In that it scorns to bear another hue;   100
  For all the water in the ocean
  Can never turn the swan's black legs to white,
  Although she lave them hourly in the flood.
  Tell the empress from me, I am of age
  To keep mine own, excuse it how she can.
DEMETRIUS. Wilt thou betray thy noble mistress thus?

AARON. My mistress is my mistress, this my self,
  The vigour and the picture of my youth:
  This before all the world do I prefer;
  This maugre all the world will I keep safe,   110
  Or some of you shall smoke for it in Rome.
DEMETRIUS. By this our mother is for ever shamed.
CHIRON. Rome will despise her for this foul escape.
NURSE. The emperor in his rage will doom her death.
CHIRON. I blush to think upon this ignomy.
AARON. Why, there's the privilege your beauty bears:
  Fie, treacherous hue! that will betray with blushing
  The close enacts and counsels of thy heart!
  Here's a young lad framed of another leer:
  Look, how the black slave smiles upon the father,   120
  As who should say, 'Old lad, I am thine own'.
  He is your brother, lords, sensibly fed
  Of that self blood that first gave life to you,
  And from that womb where you imprisoned were
  He is enfranchisèd and come to light:
  Nay, he's your brother by the surer side,
  Although my seal be stampèd in his face.
NURSE. Aaron, what shall I say unto the empress?
DEMETRIUS. Advise thee, Aaron, what is to be done,
  And we will all subscribe to thy advice: 130
  Save thou the child, so we may all be safe.
AARON. Then sit we down and let us all consult.
  My son and I will have the wind of you:
  Keep there: now talk at pleasure of your safety.
                                          They sit
DEMETRIUS. How many women saw this child of his?
AARON. Why, so, brave lords! when we join in league,
  I am a lamb: but if you brave the Moor,
  The chaféd boar, the mountain lioness,
  The ocean swells not so as Aaron storms.
  But say again, how many saw the child?   140
NURSE. Cornelia the midwife, and myself,
  And no one else but the delivered empress.
AARON. The emperess, the midwife, and yourself:
  Two may keep counsel when the third's away:
  Go to the empress, tell her this I said.
                                          He kills her
  Wheak, wheak!
  So cries a pig preparèd to the spit.
DEMETRIUS. What mean'st thou, Aaron? wherefore
  didst thou this?
AARON. O, lord, sir, 'tis a deed of policy!   150
  Shall she live to betray this guilt of ours?
  A long-tongued babbling gossip? no, lords, no.
  And now be it known to you my full intent.
  Not far one Muly lives, my countryman,
  His wife but yesternight was brought to bed;
  His child is like to her, fair as you are:
  Go pack with him, and give the mother gold,
  And tell them both the circumstance of all,
  And how by this their child shall be advanced,
  And be receivèd for the emperor's heir,
  And substituted in the place of mine,   160
  To calm this tempest whirling in the court;
  And let the emperor dandle him for his own.
  Hark ye, lords; you see I have given her physic,
                                  Points to the body
  And you must needs bestow her funeral;
  The fields are near, and you are gallant grooms.
  This done, see that you take no longer days,
  But send the midwife presently to me.
  The midwife and the nurse well made away,

  Then let the ladies tattle what they please.
CHIRON. Aaron, I see, thou wilt not trust the air   170
  With secrets.
DEMETRIUS.   For this care of Tamora,
  Herself and hers are highly bound to thee.
                                  They bear off the Nurse
AARON. Now to the Goths, as swift as swallow flies,
  There to dispose this treasure in mine arms,
  And secretly to greet the empress' friends.
  Come on, you thick-lipped slave, I'll bear you
  hence;
  For it is you that puts us to our shifts:
  I'll make you feed on berries and on roots,
  And feed on curds and whey, and suck the goat,
  And cabin in a cave, and bring you up   180
  To be a warrior and command a camp.   *He goes*

              Scene 3: *Before the palace in Rome*

*Enter Titus, old Marcus, his son Publius, young Lucius,
and other gentlemen, with bows; and Titus bears arrows
with letters on the ends of them*

TITUS. Come, Marcus, come; kinsmen, this is the way.
  Sir boy, let me see your archery;
  Look ye draw home enough, and 'tis there straight.
  'Terras Astræa reliquit',
  Be you remembered, Marcus: she's gone, she's fled.
  Sirs, take you to your tools. You, cousins, shall
  Go sound the ocean, and cast your nets;
  Haply you may catch her in the sea;
  Yet there's as little justice as at land:
  No, Publius and Sempronius, you must do it;   10
  'Tis you must dig with mattock and with spade,
  And pierce the inmost centre of the earth:
  Then, when you come to Pluto's region,
  I pray you deliver him this petition:
  Tell him, it is for justice and for aid,
  And that it comes from old Andronicus,
  Shaken with sorrows in ungrateful Rome.
  Ah, Rome! Well, well; I made thee miserable
  What time I threw the people's suffrages
  On him that thus doth tyrannize o'er me.   20
  Go, get you gone, and pray be careful all,
  And leave you not a man of war unsearched:
  This wicked emperor may have shipped her hence,
  And, kinsmen, then we may go pipe for justice.
MARCUS. O, Publius, is not this a heavy case,
  To see thy noble uncle thus distract?
PUBLIUS. Therefore, my lord, it highly us concerns
  By day and night t'attend him carefully,
  And feed his humour kindly as we may,
  Till time beget some careful remedy.
MARCUS. Kinsmen, his sorrows are past remedy.   30
  Join with the Goths, and with revengeful war
  Take wreak on Rome for this ingratitude,
  And vengeance on the traitor Saturnine.
TITUS. Publius, how now! how now, my masters!
  What, have you met with her?
PUBLIUS. No, my good lord, but Pluto sends you
  word,
  If you will have revenge from hell, you shall:
  Marry, for Justice, she is so employed,
  He thinks, with Jove in heaven, or somewhere else,   40
  So that perforce you must needs stay a time.
TITUS. He doth me wrong to feed me with delays.
  I'll dive into the burning lake below,

And pull her out of Acheron by the heels.
Marcus, we are but shrubs, no cedars we,
No big-boned men framed of the Cyclops' size;
But metal, Marcus, steel to the very back,
Yet wrung with wrongs more than our backs can
   bear:
And sith there's no justice in earth nor hell,
We will solicit heaven, and move the gods   50
To send down Justice for to wreak our wrongs.
Come, to this gear. You are a good archer, Marcus.
                         He gives them the arrows
'Ad Jovem', that's for you: here, 'Ad Apollinem':
'Ad Martem', that's for myself:
Here, boy, to Pallas: here, to Mercury:
To Saturn, Caius, not to Saturnine:
You were as good to shoot against the wind.
To it, boy! Marcus, loose when I bid.
Of my word, I have written to effect;
There's not a god left unsolicited.   60
MARCUS. Kinsmen, shoot all your shafts into the
     court:
We will afflict the emperor in his pride.
TITUS. Now, masters, draw. [*they shoot*] O, well said,
     Lucius!
Good boy, in Virgo's lap; give it Pallas.
MARCUS. My lord, I aimed a mile beyond the moon;
Your letter is with Jupiter by this.
TITUS. Ha, ha!
Publius, Publius, what hast thou done!
See, see, thou hast shot off one of Taurus' horns.
MARCUS. This was the sport, my lord: when
     Publius shot,   70
The bull being galled, gave Aries such a knock
That down fell both the Ram's horns in the court,
And who should find them but the empress' villain?
She laughed, and told the Moor he should not
     choose
But give them to his master for a present.
TITUS. Why, there it goes! God give his lordship
     joy!

Enter a Clown, with a basket and two pigeons in it

News, news from heaven! Marcus, the post is come.
Sirrah, what tidings? have you any letters?
Shall I have justice? what says Jupiter?
CLOWN. O, the gibbet-maker! he says that he hath   80
taken them down again, for the man must not be
hanged till the next week.
TITUS. But what says Jupiter, I ask thee?
CLOWN. Alas, sir, I know not Jubiter; I never drank
with him in all my life.
TITUS. Why, villain, art not thou the carrier?
CLOWN. Ay, of my pigeons, sir, nothing else.
TITUS. Why, didst thou not come from heaven?
CLOWN. From heaven? alas, sir, I never came there!
God forbid, I should be so bold to press to heaven in   90
my young days. Why, I am going with my pigeons
to the tribunal plebs, to take up a matter of brawl
betwixt my uncle and one of the emperal's men.
MARCUS. Why, sir, that is as fit as can be to serve for
your oration; and let him deliver the pigeons to the
emperor from you.
TITUS. Tell me, can you deliver an oration to the
emperor with a grace?
CLOWN. Nay, truly, sir, I could never say grace in all
my life.   100

TITUS. Sirrah, come hither: make no more ado,
But give your pigeons to the emperor:
By me thou shalt have justice at his hands.
Hold, hold, meanwhile, here's money for thy
   charges.
Give me a pen and ink.
Sirrah, can you with a grace deliver a supplication?
CLOWN. Ay, sir.
TITUS. Then here is a supplication for you. And when
you come to him, at the first approach you must
kneel, then kiss his foot, then deliver up your   110
pigeons, and then look for your reward. I'll be at
hand, sir! See you do it bravely.
CLOWN. I warrant you, sir, let me alone.
TITUS. Sirrah, hast thou a knife? come, let me see it.
Here, Marcus, fold it in the oration,
For thou hast made it like an humble suppliant.
And when thou hast given it to the emperor,
Knock at my door, and tell me what he says.
CLOWN. God be with you, sir; I will.   *He goes*
TITUS. Come, Marcus, let us go. Publius, follow me.   120
                                            They go

                         Scene 4

*Enter Emperor and Empress and her two sons, with lords,
etc. The Emperor brings the arrows in his hand that Titus
shot at him*

SATURNINUS. Why, lords, what wrongs are these!
     Was ever seen
An emperor in Rome thus overborne,
Troubled, confronted thus, and for the extent
Of egal justice used in such contempt?
My lords, you know, as know the mightful gods,
However these disturbers of our peace
Buzz in the people's ears, there naught hath passed
But even with law against the wilful sons
Of old Andronicus. And what an if
His sorrows have so overwhelmed his wits,   10
Shall we be thus afflicted in his wreaks,
His fits, his frenzy, and his bitterness?
And now he writes to heaven for his redress!
See, here's to Jove, and this to Mercury,
This to Apollo, this to the god of war:
Sweet scrolls to fly about the streets of Rome!
What's this but libelling against the senate,
And blazoning our unjustice every where?
A goodly humour, is it not, my lords?
As who would say, in Rome no justice were.   20
But if I live, his feignéd ecstasies
Shall be no shelter to these outrages,
But he and his shall know that justice lives
In Saturninus' health; whom, if she sleep,
He'll so awake, as he in fury shall
Cut off the proud'st conspirator that lives.
TAMORA. My gracious lord, my lovely Saturnine,
Lord of my life, commander of my thoughts,
Calm thee, and bear the faults of Titus' age,
Th'effects of sorrow for his valiant sons,   30
Whose loss hath pierced him deep and scarred his
     heart;
And rather comfort his distresséd plight
Than prosecute the meanest or the best
For these contempts. [*aside*] Why, thus it shall
     become
High-witted Tamora to gloze with all.

But, Titus, I have touched thee to the quick,
Thy life-blood out: if Aaron now be wise,
Then is all safe, the anchor in the port.—

Enter Clown

How now, good fellow? wouldst thou speak with
us?
CLOWN. Yea, forsooth, an your mistress-ship be
emperial. 40
TAMORA. Empress I am, but yonder sits the emperor.
CLOWN. 'Tis he. God and Saint Stephen give you
godden. I have brought you a letter and a couple of
pigeons here. *Saturninus reads the letter*
SATURNINUS. Go, take him away, and hang him
presently.
CLOWN. How much money must I have?
TAMORA. Come, sirrah, you must be hanged.
CLOWN. Hanged! by'r lady, then I have brought up
a neck to a fair end. *Guards lead him away*
SATURNINUS. Despiteful and intolerable wrongs! 50
Shall I endure this monstrous villainy?
I know from whence this same device proceeds.
May this be borne? As if his traitorous sons,
That died by law for murder of our brother,
Have by my means been butchered wrongfully.
Go, drag the villain hither by the hair;
Nor age nor honour shall shape privilege:
For this proud mock I'll be thy slaughterman—
Sly frantic wretch, that holp'st to make me great,
In hope thyself should govern Rome and me. 60

Enter Æmilius, a messenger

What news with thee, Æmilius?
ÆMILIUS. Arm, arm, my lord! Rome never had more
cause.
The Goths have gathered head, and with a power
Of high-resolvéd men, bent to the spoil,
They hither march amain, under condúct
Of Lucius, son to old Andronicus;
Who threats, in course of this revenge, to do
As much as ever Coriolanus did.
SATURNINUS. Is warlike Lucius general of the Goths?
These tidings nip me, and I hang the head 70
As flowers with frost or grass beat down with
storms.
Ay, now begin our sorrows to approach:
'Tis he the common people love so much;
Myself hath often heard them say,
When I have walkéd like a private man,
That Lucius' banishment was wrongfully,
And they have wished that Lucius were their
emperor.
TAMORA. Why should you fear? is not your city
strong?
SATURNINUS. Ay, but the citizens favour Lucius,
And will revolt from me to succour him. 80
TAMORA. King, be thy thoughts imperious, like thy
name.
Is the sun dimmed, that gnats do fly in it?
The eagle suffers little birds to sing,
And is not careful what they mean thereby,
Knowing that with the shadow of his wings
He can at pleasure stint their melody:
Even so mayst thou the giddy men of Rome.
Then cheer thy spirit: for know, thou emperor,
I will enchant the old Andronicus

With words more sweet, and yet more dangerous, 90
Than baits to fish, or honey-stalks to sheep;
Whenas the one is wounded with the bait,
The other rotted with delicious feed.
SATURNINUS. But he will not entreat his son for us.
TAMORA. If Tamora entreat him, then he will:
For I can smooth, and fill his agéd ears
With golden promises, that, were his heart
Almost impregnable, his old ears deaf,
Yet should both ear and heart obey my tongue.
[*To Æmilius*] Go thou before, be our ambassador: 100
Say that the emperor requests a parley
Of warlike Lucius, and appoint the meeting
Even at his father's house, the old Andronicus.
SATURNINUS. Æmilius, do this message honourably,
And if he stand on hostage for his safety,
Bid him demand what pledge will please him best.
ÆMILIUS. Your bidding shall I do effectually.
He goes
TAMORA. Now will I to that old Andronicus,
And temper him with all the art I have,
To pluck proud Lucius from the warlike Goths. 110
And now, sweet emperor, be blithe again,
And bury all thy fear in my devices.
SATURNINUS. Then go successantly, and plead to
him. *They go*

ACT 5

Scene 1: *Plains near Rome*

Enter Lucius, with an army of Goths. Drums and colours

LUCIUS. Approvéd warriors, and my faithful friends,
I have receivéd letters from great Rome,
Which signifies what hate they bear their emperor,
And how desirous of our sight they are.
Therefore, great lords, be as your titles witness
Imperious, and impatient of your wrongs;
And wherein Rome hath done you any scath,
Let him make treble satisfaction.
I GOTH. Brave slip, sprung from the great Andronicus,
Whose name was once our terror, now our comfort, 10
Whose high exploits and honourable deeds
Ingrateful Rome requites with foul contempt,
Be bold in us: we'll follow where thou lead'st,
Like stinging bees in hottest summer's day,
Led by their master to the flow'réd fields,
And be avenged on cursed Tamora.
THE OTHER GOTHS. And as he saith, so say we all
with him.
LUCIUS. I humbly thank him, and I thank you all.
But who comes here, led by a lusty Goth?

Enter a Goth, leading Aaron with his child in his arms

2 GOTH. Renownéd Lucius, from our troops I strayed 20
To gaze upon a ruinous monastery,
And, as I earnestly did fix mine eye
Upon the wasted building, suddenly
I heard a child cry underneath a wall.
I made unto the noise, when soon I heard
The crying babe controlled with this discourse:
'Peace, tawny slave, half me and half thy dam!
Did not thy hue bewray whose brat thou art,
Had nature lent thee but thy mother's look,
Villain, thou mightst have been an emperor: 30
But where the bull and cow are both milk-white,

They never do beget a coal-black calf.
Peace, villain, peace!'—even thus he rates the babe—
'For I must bear thee to a trusty Goth,
Who, when he knows thou art the empress' babe,
Will hold thee dearly for thy mother's sake.'
With this, my weapon drawn, I rushed upon him,
Surprised him suddenly, and brought him hither,
To use as you think needful of the man.

LUCIUS. O worthy Goth, this is the incarnate devil   40
That robbed Andronicus of his good hand.
This is the pearl that pleased your empress' eye,
And here's the base fruit of her burning lust.
Say, wall-eyed slave, whither wouldst thou convey
This growing image of thy fiend-like face?
Why dost not speak? What, deaf? not a word?
A halter, soldiers! hang him on this tree,
And by his side his fruit of bastardy.

AARON. Touch not the boy, he is of royal blood.

LUCIUS. Too like the sire for ever being good.   50
First hang the child, that he may see it sprawl—
A sight to vex the father's soul withal.
Get me a ladder.

*A ladder brought, and Aaron
forced to ascend*

AARON.   Lucius, save the child;
And bear it from me to the emperess.
If thou do this, I'll show thee wondrous things,
That highly may advantage thee to hear:
If thou wilt not, befall what may befall,
I'll speak no more but 'Vengeance rot you all!'

LUCIUS. Say on, and if it please me which thou
speak'st,
Thy child shall live, and I will see it nourished.   60

AARON. And if it please thee! why, assure thee, Lucius,
'Twill vex thy soul to hear what I shall speak;
For I must talk of murders, rapes, and massacres,
Acts of black night, abominable deeds,
Complots of mischief, treason, villainies
Ruthful to hear, yet piteously performed:
And this shall all be buried in my death,
Unless thou swear to me my child shall live.

LUCIUS. Tell on thy mind, I say thy child shall live.

AARON. Swear that he shall, and then I will begin.   70

LUCIUS. Who should I swear by? thou believest no
god:
That granted, how canst thou believe an oath?

AARON. What if I do not? as indeed I do not;
Yet, for I know thou art religious,
And hast a thing within thee callèd conscience,
With twenty popish tricks and ceremonies,
Which I have seen thee careful to observe,
Therefore I urge thy oath; for that I know
An idiot holds his bauble for a god,
And keeps the oath which by that god he swears,   80
To that I'll urge him: therefore thou shalt vow
By that same god, what god soe'er it be,
That thou adorest and hast in reverence,
To save my boy, to nourish and bring him up;
Or else I will discover naught to thee.

LUCIUS. Even by my god I swear to thee I will.

AARON. First know thou, I begot him on the empress.

LUCIUS. O most insatiate and luxurious woman!

AARON. Tut, Lucius, this was but a deed of charity
To that which thou shalt hear of me anon.   90
'Twas her two sons that murdered Bassianus;
They cut thy sister's tongue, and ravished her,

And cut her hands, and trimmed her as thou sawest.

LUCIUS. O detestable villain! call'st thou that
trimming?

AARON. Why, she was washed, and cut, and trimmed!
and 'twas
Trim sport for them which had the doing of it.

LUCIUS. O barbarous, beastly villains, like thyself!

AARON. Indeed, I was their tutor to instruct them.
That codding spirit had they from their mother,
As sure a card as ever won the set;   100
That bloody mind, I think, they learned of me,
As true a dog as ever fought at head.
Well, let my deeds be witness of my worth.
I trained thy brethren to that guileful hole,
Where the dead corpse of Bassianus lay:
I wrote the letter that thy father found,
And hid the gold within that letter mentioned,
Confederate with the queen and her two sons:
And what not done, that thou hast cause to rue,
Wherein I had no stroke of mischief in it?   110
I played the cheater for thy father's hand,
And when I had it drew myself apart,
And almost broke my heart with extreme laughter.
I pried me through the crevice of a wall,
When for his hand he had his two sons' heads;
Beheld his tears and laughed so heartily,
That both mine eyes were rainy like to his:
And when I told the empress of this sport,
She swounded almost at my pleasing tale,
And for my tidings gave me twenty kisses.   120

GOTH. What, canst thou say all this, and never blush?

AARON. Ay, like a black dog, as the saying is.

LUCIUS. Art thou not sorry for these heinous deeds?

AARON. Ay, that I had not done a thousand more.
Even now I curse the day—and yet, I think,
Few come within the compass of my curse—
Wherein I did not some notorious ill:
As kill a man or else devise his death,
Ravish a maid or plot the way to do it,
Accuse some innocent and forswear myself,   130
Set deadly enmity between two friends,
Make poor men's cattle break their necks,
Set fire on barns and hay-stacks in the night,
And bid the owners quench them with their tears.
Oft have I digged up dead men from their graves,
And set them upright at their dear friends' door,
Even when their sorrow almost was forgot,
And on their skins, as on the bark of trees,
Have with my knife carvèd in Roman letters
'Let not your sorrow die, though I am dead.'   140
Tut, I have done a thousand dreadful things
As willingly as one would kill a fly,
And nothing grieves me heartily indeed,
But that I cannot do ten thousand more.

LUCIUS. Bring down the devil, for he must not die
So sweet a death as hanging presently.

AARON. If there be devils, would I were a devil,
To live and burn in everlasting fire,
So I might have your company in hell,
But to torment you with my bitter tongue!   150

LUCIUS. Sirs, stop his mouth, and let him speak no
more.

A Goth comes up

GOTH. My lord, there is a messenger from Rome
Desires to be admitted to your presence.

LUCIUS. Let him come near.

Æmilius is brought forward

Welcome, Æmilius, what's the news from Rome?
ÆMILIUS. Lord Lucius, and you princes of the Goths,
The Roman emperor greets you all by me;
And, for he understands you are in arms,
He craves a parley at your father's house,
Willing you to demand your hostages,   160
And they shall be immediately delivered.
1 GOTH. What says our general?
LUCIUS. Æmilius, let the emperor give his pledges
Unto my father and my uncle Marcus,
And we will come. March away.   *They go*

Scene 2: *Court of Titus' house*

*Enter Tamora and her two sons, disguised as Revenge
attended by Rape and Murder*

TAMORA. Thus, in this strange and sad habiliment,
I will encounter with Andronicus,
And say I am Revenge, sent from below
To join with him and right his heinous wrongs.
Knock at his study, where, they say, he keeps
To ruminate strange plots of dire revenge;
Tell him Revenge is come to join with him,
And work confusion on his enemies.   *They knock*

Titus opens a window above

TITUS. Who doth molest my contemplation?
Is it your trick to make me ope the door,   10
That so my sad decrees may fly away,
And all my study be to no effect?
You are deceived: for what I mean to do
See here in bloody lines I have set down.
And what is written shall be executed.
TAMORA. Titus, I am come to talk with thee.
TITUS. No, not a word. How can I grace my talk,
Wanting a hand to give it action?
Thou hast the odds of me, therefore no more.
TAMORA. If thou didst know me, thou wouldst talk
with me.   20
TITUS. I am not mad, I know thee well enough.
Witness this wretched stump, witness these crimson
lines,
Witness these trenches made by grief and care,
Witness the tiring day and heavy night,
Witness all sorrow, that I know thee well
For our proud empress, mighty Tamora:
Is not thy coming for my other hand?
TAMORA. Know thou, sad man, I am not Tamora;
She is thy enemy, and I thy friend.
I am Revenge, sent from th'infernal kingdom   30
To ease the gnawing vulture of thy mind,
By working wreakful vengeance on thy foes.
Come down and welcome me to this world's light;
Confer with me of murder and of death:
There's not a hollow cave or lurking-place,
No vast obscurity or misty vale,
Where bloody murder or detested rape
Can couch for fear, but I will find them out,
And in their ears tell them my dreadful name,
Revenge, which makes the foul offender quake.   40
TITUS. Art thou Revenge? and art thou sent to me,
To be a torment to mine enemies?
TAMORA. I am, therefore come down and welcome
me.
TITUS. Do me some service ere I come to thee.
Lo, by thy side where Rape and Murder stands;
Now give some surance that thou art Revenge,
Stab them, or tear them on thy chariot wheels;
And then I'll come and be thy waggoner,
And whirl along with thee about the globe.
Provide two proper palfreys, black as jet,   50
To hale thy vengeful waggon swift away,
And find out murderers in their guilty caves:
And when thy car is loaden with their heads,
I will dismount, and by thy waggon-wheel
Trot like a servile footman all day long,
Even from Hyperion's rising in the east,
Until his very downfall in the sea.
And day by day I'll do this heavy task,
So thou destroy Rapine and Murder there.
TAMORA. These are my ministers and come with me. 60
TITUS. Are these thy ministers? what are they called?
TAMORA. Rape and Murder; therefore callèd so,
'Cause they take vengeance of such kind of men.
TITUS. Good Lord, how like the empress' sons they
are!
And you the empress! but we worldly men
Have miserable, mad, mistaking eyes.
O sweet Revenge, now do I come to thee:
And, if one arm's embracement will content thee,
I will embrace thee in it by and by.
                        He shuts the window
TAMORA. This closing with him fits his lunacy.   70
Whate'er I forge to feed his brain-sick humours,
Do you uphold and maintain in your speeches,
For now he firmly takes me for Revenge,
And, being credulous in this mad thought,
I'll make him send for Lucius his son;
And, whilst I at a banquet hold him sure,
I'll find some cunning practice out of hand,
To scatter and disperse the giddy Goths,
Or at the least make them his enemies.
See, here he comes, and I must ply my theme.   80

Titus comes from the house

TITUS. Long have I been forlorn, and all for thee.
Welcome, dread Fury, to my woful house:
Rapine and Murder, you are welcome too:
How like the empress and her sons you are!
Well are you fitted, had you but a Moor:
Could not all hell afford you such a devil?
For well I wot the empress never wags
But in her company there is a Moor;
And, would you represent our queen aright,
It were convenient you had such a devil: 90
But welcome, as you are. What shall we do?
TAMORA. What wouldst thou have us do, Andronicus?
DEMETRIUS. Show me a murderer, I'll deal with him.
CHIRON. Show me a villain that hath done a rape,
And I am sent to be revenged on him.
TAMORA. Show me a thousand that hath done thee
wrong,
And I will be revengèd on them all.
TITUS. Look round about the wicked streets of Rome,
And when thou find'st a man that's like thyself,
Good Murder, stab him; he's a murderer.   100
Go thou with him, and when it is thy hap
To find another that is like to thee,

Good Rapine, stab him; he's a ravisher.
Go thou with them, and in the emperor's court
There is a queen attended by a Moor;
Well shalt thou know her by thine own proportion,
For up and down she doth resemble thee;
I pray thee, do on them some violent death;
They have been violent to me and mine.

TAMORA. Well hast thou lessoned us: this shall we do. 110
But would it please thee, good Andronicus,
To send for Lucius, thy thrice valiant son,
Who leads towards Rome a band of warlike Goths,
And bid him come and banquet at thy house:
When he is here, even at thy solemn feast,
I will bring in the empress and her sons,
The emperor himself, and all thy foes,
And at thy mercy shall they stoop and kneel,
And on them shalt thou ease thy angry heart.
What says Andronicus to this device? 120

TITUS. Marcus, my brother! 'tis sad Titus calls.

Marcus comes forth

Go, gentle Marcus, to thy nephew Lucius;
Thou shalt enquire him out among the Goths:
Bid him repair to me and bring with him
Some of the chiefest princes of the Goths:
Bid him encamp his soldiers where they are:
Tell him the emperor and the empress too
Feast at my house, and he shall feast with them.
This do thou for my love, and so let him,
As he regards his agéd father's life. 130

MARCUS. This will I do, and soon return again.
He goes

TAMORA. Now will I hence about thy business,
And take my ministers along with me.

TITUS. Nay, nay, let Rape and Murder stay with me,
Or else I'll call my brother back again,
And cleave to no revenge but Lucius.

TAMORA [aside]. What say you, boys? will you abide
with him,
Whiles I go tell my lord the emperor
How I have governed our determined jest?
Yield to his humour, smooth and speak him fair, 140
And tarry with him till I turn again.

TITUS [aside]. I knew them all, though they supposed
me mad;
And will o'er-reach them in their own devices,
A pair of curséd hell-hounds and their dam.

DEMETRIUS. Madam, depart at pleasure, leave us here.

TAMORA. Farewell, Andronicus: Revenge now goes
To lay a complot to betray thy foes.

TITUS. I know thou dost; and, sweet Revenge,
farewell. *She goes*

CHIRON. Tell us, old man, how shall we be employed?

TITUS. Tut, I have work enough for you to do. 150
Publius, come hither, Caius, and Valentine!

Publius and others come from the house

PUBLIUS. What is your will?

TITUS. Know you these two?

PUBLIUS. The empress' sons, I take them, Chiron and
Demetrius.

TITUS. Fie, Publius, fie! thou art too much deceived;
The one is Murder, and Rape is the other's name:
And therefore bind them, gentle Publius:
Caius and Valentine, lay hands on them:
Oft have you heard me wish for such an hour, 160

And now I find it: therefore bind them sure;
And stop their mouths, if they begin to cry.
*He goes in
Publius, etc. lay hold on Chiron
and Demetrius*

CHIRON. Villains, forbear! we are the empress' sons.

PUBLIUS. And therefore do we what we are
commanded.
Stop close their mouths, let them not speak a word:
Is he sure bound? look that you bind them fast.

*Enter Titus Andronicus with a knife, and Lavinia with
a basin*

TITUS. Come, come, Lavinia; look, thy foes are
bound.
Sirs, stop their mouths, let them not speak to me,
But let them hear what fearful words I utter.
O villains, Chiron and Demetrius! 170
Here stands the spring whom you have stained with
mud,
This goodly summer with your winter mixed.
You killed her husband, and, for that vile fault
Two of her brothers were condemned to death,
My hand cut off and made a merry jest:
Both her sweet hands, her tongue, and that more
dear
Than hands or tongue, her spotless chastity,
Inhuman traitors, you constrained and forced.
What would you say, if I should let you speak?
Villains, for shame you could not beg for grace. 180
Hark, wretches, how I mean to martyr you.
This one hand yet is left to cut your throats,
Whiles that Lavinia 'tween her stumps doth hold
The basin that receives your guilty blood.
You know your mother means to feast with me,
And calls herself Revenge, and thinks me mad:
Hark, villains, I will grind your bones to dust,
And with your blood and it I'll make a paste,
And of the paste a coffin I will rear,
And make two pasties of your shameful heads, 190
And bid that strumpet, your unhallowed dam,
Like to the earth, swallow her own increase.
This is the feast that I have bid her to,
And this the banquet she shall surfeit on;
For worse than Philomel you used my daughter,
And worse than Progne I will be revenged.
And now prepare your throats. Lavinia, come,
Receive the blood; and when that they are dead,
Let me go grind their bones to powder small,
And with this hateful liquor temper it, 200
And in that paste let their vile heads be baked.
Come, come, be every one officious
To make this banquet, which I wish may prove
More stern and bloody than the Centaurs' feast.
He cuts their throats
So, now bring them in, for I'll play the cook,
And see them ready against their mother comes.
They bear the bodies into the house

Scene 3

*Enter Lucius, Marcus, and the Goths, with Aaron a
prisoner, and the child in the arms of an attendant*

LUCIUS. Uncle Marcus, since 'tis my father's mind
That I repair to Rome, I am content.

1 GOTH. And ours with thine, befall what fortune will.

LUCIUS. Good uncle, take you in this barbarous Moor,
This ravenous tiger, this accursèd devil;
Let him receive no sustenance, fetter him,
Till he be brought unto the empress' face,
For testimony of her foul proceedings:
And see the ambush of our friends be strong;
I fear the emperor means no good to us.   10
AARON. Some devil whisper curses in my ear,
And prompt me, that my tongue may utter forth
The venomous malice of my swelling heart!
LUCIUS. Away, inhuman dog! unhallowed slave!
Sirs, help our uncle to convey him in.
                        Goths lead Aaron in. Trumpets
                                                  sound
The trumpets show the emperor is at hand.

Enter Emperor and Empress, with Tribunes and others

SATURNINUS. What, hath the firmament mo suns than
one?
LUCIUS. What boots it thee to call thyself a sun?
MARCUS. Rome's emperor, and nephew, break the
parle;
These quarrels must be quietly debated.   20
The feast is ready, which the careful Titus
Hath ordained to an honourable end,
For peace, for love, for league, and good to Rome.
Please you, therefore, draw nigh, and take your
places.
SATURNINUS. Marcus, we will.

*Servants bring forth a table. Trumpets sounding, enter
Titus, like a cook, placing the dishes, and Lavinia with a
veil over her face, young Lucius, and others*

TITUS. Welcome, my lord; welcome, dread queen;
Welcome, ye warlike Goths; welcome, Lucius;
And welcome, all: although the cheer be poor,
'Twill fill your stomachs; please you eat of it.
SATURNINUS. Why art thou thus attired, Andronicus? 30
TITUS. Because I would be sure to have all well,
To entertain your highness and your empress.
TAMORA. We are beholding to you, good Andronicus.
TITUS. An if your highness knew my heart, you were.
My lord the emperor, resolve me this:
Was it well done of rash Virginius
To slay his daughter with his own right hand,
Because she was enforced, stained, and deflowered?
SATURNINUS. It was, Andronicus.
TITUS. Your reason, mighty lord!   40
SATURNINUS. Because the girl should not survive her
shame,
And by her presence still renew his sorrows.
TITUS. A reason mighty, strong, and effectual,
A pattern, precedent, and lively warrant,
For me, most wretched, to perform the like.
Die, die, Lavinia, and thy shame with thee,
And with thy shame thy father's sorrow die!
                                      He kills her
SATURNINUS. What hast thou done, unnatural and
unkind?
TITUS. Killed her for whom my tears have made me
blind.
I am as woful as Virginius was,   50
And have a thousand times more cause than he
To do this outrage, and it now is done.
SATURNINUS. What, was she ravished? tell who did the
deed.

TITUS. Will't please you eat? will't please your
highness feed?
TAMORA. Why hast thou slain thine only daughter
thus?
TITUS. Not I; 'twas Chiron and Demetrius:
They ravished her and cut away her tongue;
And they, 'twas they, that did her all this wrong.
SATURNINUS. Go, fetch them hither to us presently.
TITUS. Why, there they are both, bakèd in this pie, 60
Whereof their mother daintily hath fed,
Eating the flesh that she herself hath bred.
'Tis true, 'tis true; witness my knife's sharp point.
                              He stabs the empress
SATURNINUS. Die, frantic wretch, for this accursèd
deed.   *Kills Titus*
LUCIUS. Can the son's eye behold his father bleed?
There's meed for meed, death for a deadly deed.

*He kills Saturninus. A great tumult. Lucius, Marcus, and
others go up into the balcony*

MARCUS. You sad-faced men, people and sons of
Rome,
By uproars severed, as a flight of fowl
Scattered by winds and high tempestuous gusts,
O, let me teach you how to knit again   70
This scattered corn into one mutual sheaf,
These broken limbs again into one body;
Lest Rome herself be bane unto herself,
And she whom mighty kingdoms curt'sy to,
Like a forlorn and desperate castaway,
Do shameful execution on herself.
But if my frosty signs and chaps of age,
Grave witnesses of true experience,
Cannot induce you to attend my words,—
[*to Lucius*] Speak, Rome's dear friend, as erst our
ancestor,   80
When with his solemn tongue he did discourse
To love-sick Dido's sad attending ear
The story of that baleful burning night,
When subtle Greeks surprised King Priam's Troy;
Tell us what Sinon hath bewitched our ears,
Or who hath brought the fatal engine in
That gives our Troy, our Rome, the civil wound.
My heart is not compact of flint nor steel;
Nor can I utter all our bitter grief,
But floods of tears will drown my oratory,   90
And break my utt'rance, even in the time
When it should move ye to attend me most,
And force you to commiseration.
Here's Rome's young captain, let him tell the tale,
While I stand by and weep to hear him speak.
LUCIUS. Then, gracious auditory, be it known to you,
That Chiron and the damned Demetrius
Were they that murderèd our emperor's brother;
And they it were that ravished our sister.
For their fell faults our brothers were beheaded,   100
Our father's tears despised, and basely cozened
Of that true hand that fought Rome's quarrel out
And sent her enemies unto the grave.
Lastly, myself unkindly banishèd,
The gates shut on me, and turned weeping out,
To beg relief among Rome's enemies;
Who drowned their enmity in my true tears,
And oped their arms to embrace me as a friend:
I am the turned-forth, be it known to you,
That have preserved her welfare in my blood,   110

And from her bosom took the enemy's point,
Sheathing the steel in my advent'rous body.
Alas, you know I am no vaunter, I;
My scars can witness, dumb although they are,
That my report is just and full of truth.
But, soft! methinks, I do digress too much,
Citing my worthless praise. O, pardon me,
For when no friends are by, men praise themselves.
MARCUS. Now is my turn to speak. Behold the child:
Points
Of this was Tamora deliveréd,   120
The issue of an irreligious Moor,
Chief architect and plotter of these woes:
The villain is alive in Titus' house,
Damned as he is, to witness this is true.
Now judge what cause had Titus to revenge
These wrongs, unspeakable, past patience,
Or more than any living man could bear.
Now have you heard the truth. What say you,
      Romans?
Have we done aught amiss, show us wherein,
And, from the place where you behold us pleading 130
The poor remainder of Andronici
Will, hand in hand, all headlong hurl ourselves
And on the ragged stones beat forth our souls,
And make a mutual closure of our house.
Speak, Romans, speak, and if you say we shall,
Lo, hand in hand, Lucius and I will fall.
ÆMILIUS. Come, come, thou reverend man of Rome,
And bring our emperor gently in thy hand,
Lucius our emperor; for well I know
The common voice do cry it shall be so.   140
ALL. Lucius, all hail, Rome's royal emperor!
MARCUS [*to soldiers*]. Go, go into old Titus' sorrowful
      house,
And hither hale that misbelieving Moor,
To be adjudged some direful slaught'ring death,
As punishment for his most wicked life.

Lucius, Marcus, and the others descend

ALL. Lucius, all hail, Rome's gracious governor!
LUCIUS. Thanks, gentle Romans: may I govern so,
To heal Rome's harms and wipe away her woe!
But, gentle people, give me aim awhile,
For nature puts me to a heavy task.   150
Stand all aloof; but, uncle, draw you near,
To shed obsequious tears upon this trunk.
                   He kisses the dead Titus
O, take this warm kiss on thy pale cold lips,
These sorrowful drops upon thy blood-stained face,
The last true duties of thy noble son!
MARCUS. Tear for tear and loving kiss for kiss

Thy brother Marcus tenders on thy lips:
O, were the sum of these that I should pay
Countless and infinite, yet would I pay them!
LUCIUS. Come hither, boy; come, come, and learn of
      us   160
To melt in showers: thy grandsire loved thee well:
Many a time he danced thee on his knee,
Sung thee asleep, his loving breast thy pillow;
Many a story hath he told to thee,
And bid thee bear his pretty tales in mind,
And talk of them when he was dead and gone.
MARCUS. How many thousand times hath these poor
      lips,
When they were living, warmed themselves on
      thine!
O, now, sweet boy, give them their latest kiss.
Bid him farewell; commit him to the grave;   170
Do him that kindness, and take leave of him.
BOY. O, grandsire, grandsire! even with all my heart
Would I were dead, so you did live again!—
O Lord, I cannot speak to him for weeping,
My tears will choke me, if I ope my mouth.

Soldiers return with Aaron

ROMAN. You sad Andronici, have done with woes;
Give sentence on this execrable wretch,
That hath been breeder of these dire events.
LUCIUS. Set him breast-deep in earth, and famish him;
There let him stand and rave and cry for food: 180
If any one relieves or pities him,
For the offence he dies. This is our doom.
Some stay, to see him fastened in the earth.
AARON. Ah, why should wrath be mute, and fury
      dumb?
I am no baby, I, that with base prayers
I should repent the evils I have done:
Ten thousand worse than ever yet I did
Would I perform, if I might have my will:
If one good deed in all my life I did,
I do repent it from my very soul.   190
LUCIUS. Some loving friends convey the emperor
      hence,
And give him burial in his father's grave:
My father and Lavinia shall forthwith
Be closéd in our household's monument.
As for that ravenous tiger, Tamora,
No funeral rite, nor man in mourning weed,
No mournful bell shall ring her burial;
But throw her forth to beasts and birds of prey.
Her life was beastly and devoid of pity,
And being dead, let birds on her take pity.   200
                                        They go

Romeo and Juliet

The scene: Verona and Mantua

CHARACTERS IN THE PLAY

ESCALUS, *prince of Verona*
PARIS, *a young nobleman, kinsman to the prince*
MONTAGUE } *heads of two houses at enmity with each*
CAPULET } *other*
An old man, kinsman to Capulet
ROMEO, *son to Montague*
MERCUTIO, *kinsman to the prince, and friend to Romeo*
BENVOLIO, *nephew to Montague, and friend to Romeo*
TYBALT, *nephew to Lady Capulet*
FRIAR LAWRENCE, *a Franciscan*
FRIAR JOHN, *of the same order*
BALTHASAR, *servant to Romeo*
SAMPSON } *servants to Capulet*
GREGORY }

PETER, *servant to Juliet's Nurse*
ABRAHAM, *servant to Montague*
An Apothecary
Three Musicians
Page to Paris, another Page, an Officer
LADY MONTAGUE, *wife to Montague*
LADY CAPULET, *wife to Capulet*
JULIET, *daughter to Capulet*
Nurse to Juliet
Citizens, Kinsfolk of both houses, Guards, Watchmen,
  Servants and Attendants
CHORUS

Romeo and Juliet

THE PROLOGUE

Enter Chorus

CHORUS.
Two households, both alike in dignity,
  In fair Verona, where we lay our scene,
From ancient grudge break to new mutiny,
  Where civil blood makes civil hands unclean.
From forth the fatal loins of these two foes
  A pair of star-crossed lovers take their life
Whose misadventured piteous overthrows
  Doth with their death bury their parents'
  strife.
The fearful passage of their death-marked
  love,   10
  And the continuance of their parents' rage,
Which, but their children's end, nought
  could remove,
  Is now the two hours' traffic of our stage;
The which if you with patient ears attend,
What here shall miss, our toil shall strive to
  mend.

Exit

ACT 1
Scene 1: *Verona. A public place*

Enter Sampson and Gregory of the house of Capulet,
with swords and bucklers

SAMPSON. Gregory, on my word we'll not carry coals.
GREGORY. No, for then we should be colliers.
SAMPSON. I mean, an we be in choler we'll draw.
GREGORY. Ay, while you live draw your neck out of collar.
SAMPSON. I strike quickly, being moved.
GREGORY. But thou art not quickly moved to strike.
SAMPSON. A dog of the house of Montague moves me.
GREGORY. To move is to stir, and to be valiant is to stand: therefore if thou art moved thou runn'st   10 away.
SAMPSON. A dog of that house shall move me to stand: I will take the wall of any man or maid of Montague's.
GREGORY. That shows thee a weak slave, for the weakest goes to the wall.
SAMPSON. 'Tis true, and therefore women, being the weaker vessels, are ever thrust to the wall: therefore I will push Montague's men from the wall, and thrust his maids to the wall.   20
GREGORY. The quarrel is between our masters, and us their men.
SAMPSON. 'Tis all one; I will show myself a tyrant: when I have fought with the men, I will be cruel with the maids: I will cut off their heads.
GREGORY. The heads of the maids?
SAMPSON. Ay, the heads of the maids, or their maidenheads; take it in what sense thou wilt.

GREGORY. They must take it in sense that feel it.
SAMPSON. Me they shall feel while I am able to stand,   30 and 'tis known I am a pretty piece of flesh.
GREGORY. 'Tis well thou art not fish; if thou hadst, thou hadst been poor John. Draw thy tool; here comes two of the house of Montagues.

Enter Abraham and another serving man

SAMPSON. My naked weapon is out: quarrel; I will back thee.
GREGORY. How? Turn thy back and run?
SAMPSON. Fear me not.
GREGORY. No, marry; I fear thee!
SAMPSON. Let us take the law of our sides; let them   40 begin.
GREGORY. I will frown as I pass by, and let them take it as they list.
SAMPSON. Nay, as they dare. I will bite my thumb at them, which is disgrace to them if they bear it.
ABRAHAM. Do you bite your thumb at us, sir?
SAMPSON. I do bite my thumb, sir.
ABRAHAM. Do you bite your thumb at us, sir?
SAMPSON [*aside*]. Is the law of our side if I say ay?
GREGORY [*aside*]. No.   50
SAMPSON. No, sir, I do not bite my thumb at you, sir, but I bite my thumb, sir.
GREGORY. Do you quarrel, sir?
ABRAHAM. Quarrel, sir? No, sir.
SAMPSON. But if you do, sir, I am for you: I serve as good a man as you.
ABRAHAM. No better.
SAMPSON. Well, sir.

Enter Benvolio on one side, Tybalt on the other

GREGORY [*seeing Tybalt*]. Say 'better': here comes one of my master's kinsmen.   60
SAMPSON. Yes, better, sir.
ABRAHAM. You lie.
SAMPSON. Draw, if you be men. Gregory, remember thy washing blow.   *They fight*
BENVOLIO [*intervening from behind*]. Part, fools!
  Put up your swords; you know not what you do.

Tybalt comes up

TYBALT. What, art thou drawn among these heartless hinds?
  Turn thee, Benvolio; look upon thy death.
BENVOLIO. I do but keep the peace: put up thy sword,
  Or manage it to part these men with me.   70
TYBALT. What, drawn, and talk of peace? I hate the word,
  As I hate hell, all Montagues, and thee:
  Have at thee, coward.   *They fight*

Enter three or four Citizens with clubs or partisans, and an Officer

OFFICER. Clubs, bills, and partisans! Strike, beat them down.
  Down with the Capulets, down with the Montagues!

Enter old Capulet in his gown, and his wife

CAPULET. What noise is this? Give me my long
  sword, ho!
LADY CAPULET. A crutch, a crutch! Why call you for
  a sword?
CAPULET. My sword, I say! Old Montague is come,
  And flourishes his blade in spite of me.

Enter old Montague and his wife

MONTAGUE. Thou villain Capulet!—Hold me not, let
  me go.   80
LADY MONTAGUE. Thou shalt not stir one foot to seek
  a foe.

Enter Prince Escalus, with his train

PRINCE. Rebellious subjects, enemies to peace,
  Profaners of this neighbour-stained steel,—
  Will they not hear? What ho! you men, you beasts,
  That quench the fire of your pernicious rage
  With purple fountains issuing from your veins,
  On pain of torture, from those bloody hands
  Throw your mistempered weapons to the
    ground,
  And hear the sentence of your moved prince.
  Three civil brawls, bred of an airy word   90
  By thee, old Capulet, and Montague,
  Have thrice disturbed the quiet of our streets,
  And made Verona's ancient citizens
  Cast by their grave beseeming ornaments
  To wield old partisans, in hands as old,
  Cankered with peace, to part your cankered hate:
  If ever you disturb our streets again,
  Your lives shall pay the forfeit of the peace.
  For this time, all the rest depart away:
  You, Capulet, shall go along with me;   100
  And, Montague, come you this afternoon,
  To know our farther pleasure in this case,
  To old Freetown, our common judgement-place.
  Once more, on pain of death, all men depart.
                All but Montague, Lady Montague,
                     and Benvolio depart
MONTAGUE. Who set this ancient quarrel new
  abroach?
  Speak, nephew, were you by when it began?
BENVOLIO. Here were the servants of your adversary
  And yours, close fighting ere I did approach:
  I drew to part them; in the instant came
  The fiery Tybalt, with his sword prepared,   110
  Which, as he breathed defiance to my ears,
  He swung about his head, and cut the winds,
  Who, nothing hurt withal, hissed him in scorn:
  While we were interchanging thrusts and blows,
  Came more and more, and fought on part and part,
  Till the prince came, who parted either part.
LADY MONTAGUE. O where is Romeo? Saw you him
  today?
  Right glad I am he was not at this fray.
BENVOLIO. Madam, an hour before the worshipped
  sun
  Peered forth the golden window of the east,   120
  A troubled mind drave me to walk abroad,
  Where, underneath the grove of sycamore
  That westward rooteth from this city's side,
  So early walking did I see your son:
  Towards him I made, but he was ware of me,

And stole into the covert of the wood:
I, measuring his affections by my own,
Which then most sought where most might not
  be found,
Being one too many by my weary self,
Pursued my humour, not pursuing his,   130
And gladly shunned who gladly fled from me.
MONTAGUE. Many a morning hath he there been seen,
  With tears augmenting the fresh morning's dew,
  Adding to clouds more clouds with his deep sighs;
  But all so soon as the all-cheering sun
  Should in the farthest east begin to draw
  The shady curtains from Aurora's bed,
  Away from light steals home my heavy son,
  And private in his chamber pens himself,
  Shuts up his windows, locks fair daylight out,   140
  And makes himself an artificial night:
  Black and portentous must this humour prove,
  Unless good counsel may the cause remove.
BENVOLIO. My noble uncle, do you know the cause?
MONTAGUE. I neither know it, nor can learn of him
BENVOLIO. Have you importuned him by any
  means?
MONTAGUE. Both by myself and many other friends:
  But he, his own affections' counsellor,
  Is to himself—I will not say how true—
  But to himself so secret and so close,   150
  So far from sounding and discovery,
  As is the bud bit with an envious worm,
  Ere he can spread his sweet leaves to the air,
  Or dedicate his beauty to the sun.
  Could we but learn from whence his sorrows grow,
  We would as willingly give cure as know.

Enter Romeo

BENVOLIO. See where he comes: so please you,
  step aside;
  I'll know his grievance or be much denied.
MONTAGUE. I would thou wert so happy by thy stay
  To hear true shrift. Come, madam, let's away.   160
                Montague and his wife depart
BENVOLIO. Good morrow, cousin.
ROMEO.   Is the day so young?
BENVOLIO. But new struck nine.
ROMEO.   Ay me, sad hours seem long.
  Was that my father that went hence so fast?
BENVOLIO. It was. What sadness lengthens Romeo's
  hours?
ROMEO. Not having that which, having, makes them
  short.
BENVOLIO. In love?
ROMEO. Out—
BENVOLIO. Of love?
ROMEO. Out of her favour where I am in love.
BENVOLIO. Alas that Love, so gentle in his view,   170
  Should be so tyrannous and rough in proof!
ROMEO. Alas that Love, whose view is muffled still,
  Should without eyes see pathways to his will!
  Where shall we dine?—O me! What fray was here?
  Yet tell me not, for I have heard it all:
  Here's much to do with hate, but more with love:
  Why, then, O brawling love, O loving hate,
  O anything of nothing first create!
  O heavy lightness, serious vanity,
  Misshapen chaos of well-seeming forms,   180

Feather of lead, bright smoke, cold fire, sick health,
Still-waking sleep, that is not what it is!
This love feel I, that feel no love in this.
Dost thou not laugh?
BENVOLIO.   No, coz, I rather weep.
ROMEO. Good heart, at what?
BENVOLIO.   At thy good heart's oppression.
ROMEO. Why, such is love's transgression.
  Griefs of mine own lie heavy in my breast,
  Which thou wilt propagate, to have it pressed
  With more of thine. This love that thou hast shown
  Doth add more grief to too much of mine own.   190
  Love is a smoke made with the fume of sighs:
  Being purged, a fire sparkling in lovers' eyes;
  Being vexed, a sea nourished with lovers' tears.
  What is it else? A madness most discreet,
  A choking gall and a preserving sweet.
  Farewell, my coz.
BENVOLIO.   Soft, I will go along:
  And if you leave me so, you do me wrong.
ROMEO. Tut, I have lost myself, I am not here,
  This is not Romeo, he's some other where.
BENVOLIO. Tell me in sadness, who is that you love?   200
ROMEO. What, shall I groan and tell thee?
BENVOLIO.   Groan? Why no:
  But sadly tell me, who?
ROMEO. Bid a sick man in sadness make his will—
  A word ill urged to one that is so ill.
  In sadness, cousin, I do love a woman.
BENVOLIO. I aimed so near when I supposed you
  loved.
ROMEO. A right good markman! And she's fair I love.
BENVOLIO. A right fair mark, fair coz, is soonest hit.
ROMEO. Well, in that hit you miss. She'll not be hit
  With Cupid's arrow: she hath Dian's wit,   210
  And, in strong proof of chastity well armed,
  From Love's weak childish bow she lives unharmed.
  She will not stay the siege of loving terms,
  Nor bide th'encounter of assailing eyes,
  Nor ope her lap to saint-seducing gold.
  O, she is rich in beauty, only poor
  That, when she dies, with beauty dies her store.
BENVOLIO. Then she hath sworn that she will still live
  chaste?
ROMEO. She hath, and in that sparing makes huge
  waste:
  For beauty, starved with her severity,   220
  Cuts beauty off from all posterity.
  She is too fair, too wise, wisely too fair.
  To merit bliss by making me despair:
  She hath forsworn to love, and in that vow
  Do I live dead, that live to tell it now.
BENVOLIO. Be ruled by me; forget to think of her.
ROMEO. O, teach me how I should forget to think.
BENVOLIO. By giving liberty unto thine eyes;
  Examine other beauties.
ROMEO.   'Tis the way
  To call hers (exquisite) in question more.   230
  These happy masks that kiss fair ladies' brows,
  Being black, puts us in mind they hide the fair.
  He that is strucken blind cannot forget
  The precious treasure of his eyesight lost.
  Show me a mistress that is passing fair:
  What doth her beauty serve but as a note
  Where I may read who passed that passing fair?
  Farewell, thou canst not teach me to forget.

BENVOLIO. I'll pay that doctrine, or else die in debt.
                                        They go

Scene 2: The same

*Enter Capulet, County Paris, and the Clown, servant to
Capulet*

CAPULET. But Montague is bound as well as I,
  In penalty alike; and 'tis not hard, I think,
  For men so old as we to keep the peace.
PARIS. Of honourable reckoning are you both,
  And pity 'tis you lived at odds so long.
  But now, my lord, what say you to my suit?
CAPULET. But saying o'er what I have said before:
  My child is yet a stranger in the world;
  She hath not seen the change of fourteen years:
  Let two more summers wither in their pride   10
  Ere we may think her ripe to be a bride.
PARIS. Younger than she are happy mothers made.
CAPULET. And too soon marred are those so early
  made.
  Earth hath swallowed all my hopes but she;
  She is the hopeful lady of my earth.
  But woo her, gentle Paris, get her heart;
  My will to her consent is but a part:
  And, she agreed, within her scope of choice
  Lies my consent and fair according voice.
  This night I hold an old accustomed feast,   20
  Whereto I have invited many a guest,
  Such as I love; and you among the store,
  One more most welcome, makes my number more.
  At my poor house look to behold this night
  Earth-treading stars that make dark heaven light.
  Such comfort as do lusty young men feel
  When well-apparelled April on the heel
  Of limping winter treads, even such delight
  Among fresh female buds shall you this night
  Inherit at my house: hear all, all see,   30
  And like her most whose merit most shall be:
  Which on more view, of many mine being one
  May stand in number, though in reckoning none.
  Come, go with me. [*to the Clown*] Go, sirrah,
  trudge about
  Through fair Verona; find those persons out
  Whose names are written there, [*giving him a paper*]
  and to them say
  My house and welcome on their pleasure stay.
                            Capulet and Paris go
CLOWN. Find them out whose names are written here!
  It is written that the shoemaker should meddle with   40
  his yard and the tailor with his last, the fisher with
  his pencil and the painter with his nets. But I am sent
  to find those persons whose names are here writ,
  and can never find what names the writing person
  hath here writ. I must to the learned. In good time!

Enter Benvolio and Romeo

BENVOLIO. Tut, man, one fire burns out another's
  burning,
  One pain is lessened by another's anguish;
  Turn giddy, and be holp by backward turning;
  One desperate grief cures with another's languish;
  Take thou some new infection to thy eye,
  And the rank poison of the old will die.   50
ROMEO. Your plantain leaf is excellent for that.
BENVOLIO. For what, I pray thee?

ROMEO. For your broken shin.
BENVOLIO. Why, Romeo, art thou mad?
ROMEO. Not mad, but bound more than a madman is:
Shut up in prison, kept without my food,
Whipped and tormented, and—God-den, good
fellow.
CLOWN. God gi' god-den. I pray, sir, can you read?
ROMEO. Ay, mine own fortune in my misery.
CLOWN. Perhaps you have learned it without book:
but, I pray, can you read anything you see? 60
ROMEO. Ay, if I know the letters and the language.
CLOWN. Ye say honestly: rest you merry.
ROMEO. Stay, fellow; I can read. *He reads the list*
'Signior Martino and his wife and daughters,
County Anselmo and his beauteous sisters,
The lady widow of Vitruvio,
Signior Placentio and his lovely nieces,
Mercutio and his brother Valentine,
Mine uncle Capulet, his wife and daughters,
My fair niece Rosaline and Livia, 70
Signior Valentio and his cousin Tybalt,
Lucio and the lively Helena.'
A fair assembly: whither should they come?
CLOWN. Up.
ROMEO. Whither?
CLOWN. To supper; to our house.
ROMEO. Whose house?
CLOWN. My master's.
ROMEO. Indeed I should have asked thee that before.
CLOWN. Now I'll tell you without asking. My master 80
is the great rich Capulet; and, if you be not of the
house of Montagues, I pray come and crush a cup
of wine. Rest you merry. *Goes*
BENVOLIO. At this same ancient feast of Capulet's
Sups the fair Rosaline whom thou so loves,
With all the admiréd beauties of Verona:
Go thither, and with unattainted eye
Compare her face with some that I shall show,
And I will make thee think thy swan a crow.
ROMEO. When the devout religion of mine eye 90
Maintains such falsehood, then turn tears to fires:
And these who, often drowned, could never die,
Transparent heretics, be burnt for liars.
One fairer than my love! The all-seeing sun
Ne'er saw her match since first the world begun.
BENVOLIO. Tut, you saw her fair, none else being by,
Herself poised with herself in either eye:
But in that crystal scales let there be weighed
Your lady's love against some other maid
That I will show you shining at this feast, 100
And she shall scant show well that now seems best.
ROMEO. I'll go along, no such sight to be shown,
But to rejoice in splendour of mine own. *They go*

Scene 3: *Within Capulet's house*

Enter Capulet's Wife, and Nurse

LADY CAPULET. Nurse, where's my daughter? Call her
forth to me.
NURSE. Now, by my maidenhead at twelve year old,
I bade her come. What, lamb! What, lady-bird!
God forbid! Where's this girl? What, Juliet!

Enter Juliet

JULIET. How now, who calls?
NURSE. Your mother.

JULIET. Madam, I am here. What is your will?
LADY CAPULET. This is the matter. Nurse, give leave
awhile:
We must talk in secret. Nurse, come back again:
I have remembered me; thou's hear our counsel. 10
Thou knowest my daughter's of a pretty age.
NURSE. Faith, I can tell her age unto an hour.
LADY CAPULET. She's not fourteen.
NURSE. I'll lay fourteen of my teeth—
And yet, to my teen be it spoken, I have but four—
She's not fourteen. How long is it now
To Lammas-tide?
LADY CAPULET. A fortnight and odd days.
NURSE. Even or odd, of all days in the year,
Come Lammas-Eve at night shall she be fourteen.
Susan and she—God rest all Christian souls—
Were of an age. Well, Susan is with God; 20
She was too good for me. But, as I said,
On Lammas-Eve at night shall she be fourteen:
That shall she, marry; I remember it well.
'Tis since the earthquake now eleven years,
And she was weaned—I never shall forget it—
Of all the days of the year, upon that day:
For I had then laid wormwood to my dug,
Sitting in the sun under the dove-house wall.
My lord and you were then at Mantua—
Nay, I do bear a brain! But, as I said, 30
When it did taste the wormwood on the nipple
Of my dug, and felt it bitter, pretty fool,
To see it tetchy and fall out with the dug!
'Shake,' quoth the dove-house: 'twas no need, I
trow,
To bid me trudge.
And since that time it is eleven years:
For then she could stand high-lone; nay, by th' rood,
She could have run and waddled all about:
For even the day before, she broke her brow,
And then my husband—God be with his soul, 40
'A was a merry man—took up the child:
'Yea,' quoth he, 'dost thou fall upon thy face?
Thou wilt fall backward when thou hast more wit;
Wilt thou not, Jule?' And, by my holidame,
The pretty wretch left crying, and said 'Ay'.
To see now how a jest shall come about!
I warrant, an I should live a thousand years,
I never should forget it: 'Wilt thou, Jule?'
quoth he;
And, pretty fool, it stinted, and said 'Ay'.
LADY CAPULET. Enough of this; I pray thee hold thy
peace. 50
NURSE. Yes, madam, yet I cannot choose but laugh,
To think it should leave crying, and say 'Ay':
And yet, I warrant, it had upon it brow
A bump as big as a young cockerel's stone,
A perilous knock: and it cried bitterly.
'Yea', quoth my husband, 'fall'st upon thy face?
Thou wilt fall backward when thou comest to age:
Wilt thou not, Jule?' It stinted, and said 'Ay'.
JULIET. And stint thou too, I pray thee, Nurse, say I.
NURSE. Peace, I have done. God mark thee to his
grace! 60
Thou wast the prettiest babe that e'er I nursed:
An I might live to see thee married once,
I have my wish.
LADY CAPULET. Marry, that 'marry' is the very theme
I came to talk of. Tell me, daughter Juliet,

How stands your dispositions to be married?
JULIET. It is an honour that I dream not of.
NURSE. An honour! Were not I thine only nurse,
I would say thou hadst sucked wisdom from thy
teat.
LADY CAPULET. Well, think of marriage now; younger
than you   70
Here in Verona, ladies of esteem,
Are made already mothers. By my count,
I was your mother much upon these years
That you are now a maid. Thus then in brief:
The valiant Paris seeks you for his love.
NURSE. A man, young lady! Lady, such a man
As all the world—Why, he's a man of wax.
LADY CAPULET. Verona's summer hath not such a
flower.
NURSE. Nay, he's a flower; in faith, a very flower.
LADY CAPULET. What say you? Can you love the
gentleman?   80
This night you shall behold him at our feast:
Read o'er the volume of young Paris' face,
And find delight writ there with beauty's pen;
Examine every married lineament,
And see how one another lends content;
And what obscured in this fair volume lies
Find written in the margent of his eyes.
This precious book of love, this unbound lover,
To beautify him, only lacks a cover.
The fish lives in the sea; and 'tis much pride   90
For fair without the fair within to hide.
That book in many's eyes doth share the glory,
That in gold clasps locks in the golden story:
So shall you share all that he doth possess,
By having him making yourself no less.
NURSE. No less! Nay, bigger women grow by men!
LADY CAPULET. Speak briefly, can you like of Paris'
love?
JULIET. I'll look to like, if looking liking move;
But no more deep will I endart mine eye
Than your consent gives strength to make it fly.   100

Enter Servingman

SERVINGMAN. Madam, the guests are come, supper
served up, you called, my young lady asked for, the
nurse cursed in the pantry, and everything in extremity. I must hence to wait; I beseech you follow
straight.
LADY CAPULET. We follow thee. Juliet, the County
stays.
NURSE. Go, girl, seek happy night to happy days.
They go

Scene 4: *Without Capulet's house*

*Enter Romeo, Mercutio, Benvolio, with five or six other
masquers; torch-bearers*

ROMEO. What, shall this speech be spoke for our
excuse?
Or shall we on without apology?
BENVOLIO. The date is out of such prolixity:
We'll have no Cupid hoodwinked with a scarf,
Bearing a Tartar's painted bow of lath,
Scaring the ladies like a crow-keeper:
Nor no without-book prologue, faintly spoke
After the prompter, for our entrance:
But, let them measure us by what they will,

We'll measure them a measure and be gone.   10
ROMEO. Give me a torch: I am not for this ambling;
Being but heavy, I will bear the light.
MERCUTIO. Nay, gentle Romeo, we must have you
dance.
ROMEO. Not I, believe me: you have dancing shoes
With nimble soles; I have a soul of lead
So stakes me to the ground I cannot move.
MERCUTIO. You are a lover: borrow Cupid's wings,
And soar with them above a common bound.
ROMEO. I am too sore enpiercéd with his shaft   20
To soar with his light feathers and so bound;
I cannot bound a pitch above dull woe:
Under love's heavy burden do I sink.
MERCUTIO. And, to sink in it, should you burden
love—
Too great oppression for a tender thing.
ROMEO. Is love a tender thing? It is too rough,
Too rude, too boisterous, and it pricks like thorn.
MERCUTIO. If love be rough with you, be rough with
love;
Prick love for pricking, and you beat love down.
Give me a case to put my visage in:
A visor for a visor! What care I   30
What curious eye doth quote deformities?
Here are the beetle-brows shall blush for me.
                            Putting on a mask
BENVOLIO. Come, knock and enter, and no sooner in
But every man betake him to his legs.
ROMEO. A torch for me; let wantons light of heart
Tickle the senseless rushes with their heels.
For I am proverbed with a grandsire phrase,
I'll be a candle-holder, and look on.
The game was ne'er so fair, and I am done.
MERCUTIO. Tut, dun's the mouse, the constable's own
word: 40
If thou art Dun, we'll draw thee from the mire,
Or save-your-reverence love, wherein thou stickest
Up to the ears. Come, we burn daylight, ho.
ROMEO. Nay, that's not so.
MERCUTIO.   I mean, sir, in delay
We waste our lights in vain, like lights by day.
Take our good meaning, for our judgement sits
Five times in that ere once in our five wits.
ROMEO. And we mean well in going to this masque,
But 'tis no wit to go.
MERCUTIO.   Why, may one ask?
ROMEO. I dreamt a dream tonight.
MERCUTIO.   And so did I.   50
ROMEO. Well, what was yours?
MERCUTIO.   That dreamers often lie.
ROMEO. In bed asleep while they do dream things true.
MERCUTIO. O then I see Queen Mab hath been with
you.
She is the fairies' midwife, and she comes
In shape no bigger than an agate-stone
On the fore-finger of an alderman,
Drawn with a team of little atomi
Over men's noses as they lie asleep.
Her chariot is an empty hazel-nut,
Made by the joiner squirrel or old grub   60
Time out o' mind the fairies' coachmakers:
Her waggon-spokes made of long spinners' legs,
The cover of the wings of grasshoppers,
Her traces of the smallest spider-web,
Her collars of the moonshine's watery beams,

Her ship of cricket's bone, the lash of film;
Her waggoner a small grey-coated gnat,
Not half so big as a round little worm
Pricked from the lazy finger of a maid.
And in this state she gallops night by night 70
Through lovers' brains, and then they dream of
love;
O'er courtiers' knees, that dream on curtsies
straight;
O'er lawyers' fingers who straight dream on fees;
O'er ladies' lips, who straight on kisses dream,
Which oft the angry Mab with blisters plagues
Because their breaths with sweetmeats tainted are
Sometimes she gallops o'er a courtier's nose,
And then dreams he of smelling out a suit:
And sometime comes she with a tithe-pig's tail
Tickling a parson's nose as 'a lies asleep, 80
Then dreams he of another benefice.
Sometimes she driveth o'er a soldier's neck,
And then dreams he of cutting foreign throats,
Of breaches, ambuscadoes, Spanish blades,
Of healths five fathom deep; and then anon
Drums in his ear, at which he starts and wakes,
And being thus frighted swears a prayer or two,
And sleeps again. This is that very Mab
That plats the manes of horses in the night,
And bakes the elf-locks in foul sluttish hairs, 90
Which once untangled much misfortune bodes:
This is the hag, when maids lie on their backs,
That presses them and learns them first to bear,
Making them women of good carriage:
This is she—
ROMEO.   Peace, peace Mercutio, peace!
Thou talkst of nothing.
MERCUTIO.   True, I talk of dreams,
Which are the children of an idle brain,
Begot of nothing but vain fantasy,
Which is as thin of substance as the air, 100
And more inconstant than the wind, who woos
Even now the frozen bosom of the north,
And, being angered, puffs away from thence,
Turning his side to the dew-dropping south.
BENVOLIO. This wind you talk of blows us from
ourselves:
Supper is done, and we shall come too late.
ROMEO. I fear, too early: for my mind misgives
Some consequence, yet hanging in the stars,
Shall bitterly begin his fearful date
With this night's revels, and expire the term
Of a despiséd life closed in my breast,
By some vile forfeit of untimely death.
But He that hath the steerage of my course
Direct my sail! On, lusty gentlemen.
BENVOLIO. Strike, drum.   *They march into the house*

Scene 5: *The hall in Capulet's house; musicians waiting*

Enter the masquers, march round the hall, and stand aside.
Servingmen come forth with napkins

FIRST SERVINGMAN. Where's Potpan, that he helps not
to take away? He shift a trencher! He scrape a
trencher!
SECOND SERVINGMAN. When good manners shall lie all
in one or two men's hands, and they unwashed too,
'tis a foul thing.
FIRST SERVINGMAN. Away with the joined-stools,
remove the court-cupboard, look to the plate—
Good thou, save me a piece of marchpane; and, as
thou loves me, let the porter let in Susan Grindstone 10
and Nell—Antony and Potpan!
THIRD SERVINGMAN. Ay, boy, ready.
FIRST SERVINGMAN. You are looked for and called for,
asked for and sought for, in the great chamber.
FOURTH SERVINGMAN. We cannot be here and there
too. Cheerly, boys; be brisk a while, and the longer
liver take all.   *Servingmen withdraw*

Enter Capulet, and Juliet, with all the guests and
gentlewomen to the masquers

CAPULET. Welcome, gentlemen! Ladies that have their
toes
Unplagued with corns will walk a bout with you.
Ah, my mistresses, which of you all 20
Will now deny to dance? She that makes dainty,
She I'll swear hath corns: am I come near ye now?
Welcome, gentleman! I have seen the day
That I have worn a visor and could tell
A whispering tale in a fair lady's ear,
Such as would please: 'tis gone, 'tis gone, 'tis gone.
You are welcome, gentlemen! Come, musicians,
play.
A hall, a hall! Give room. And foot it, girls.
                    Music plays and they dance
More light, you knaves, and turn the tables up,
And quench the fire—the room is grown too hot. 30
Ah, sirrah, this unlooked-for sport comes well.—
Nay sit, nay sit, good cousin Capulet,
For you and I are past our dancing days.
How long is't now since last yourself and I
Were in a masque?
SECOND CAPULET.   By'r Lady, thirty years.
CAPULET. What, man! 'tis not so much, 'tis not so
much:
'Tis since the nuptial of Lucentio,
Come Pentecost as quickly as it will,
Some five and twenty years, and then we masqued.
SECOND CAPULET. 'Tis more, 'tis more; his son is elder,
sir: 40
His son is thirty.
CAPULET.   Will you tell me that?
His son was but a ward two years ago.
ROMEO [*to a servingman*]. What lady's that which doth
enrich the hand
Of yonder knight?
SERVINGMAN.   I know not, sir. 110
ROMEO. O she doth teach the torches to burn bright!
It seems she hangs upon the cheek of night
As a rich jewel in an Ethiop's ear—
Beauty too rich for use, for earth too dear!
So shows a snowy dove trooping with crows,
As yonder lady o'er her fellows shows. 50
The measure done, I'll watch her place of stand,
And, touching hers, make blesséd my rude hand,
Did my heart love till now? Forswear it, sight!
For I ne'er saw true beauty till this night.
TYBALT. This, by his voice, should be a Montague.
Fetch me my rapier, boy. What dare the slave
Come hither, covered with an antic face,
To fleer and scorn at our solemnity?
Now, by the stock and honour of my kin,
To strike him dead I hold it not a sin. 60

CAPULET. Why, how now, kinsman! wherefore storm
  you so?
TYBALT. Uncle, this is a Montague, our foe:
  A villain that is hither come in spite,
  To scorn at our solemnity this night.
CAPULET. Young Romeo is it?
TYBALT.   'Tis he, that villain Romeo.
CAPULET. Content thee, gentle coz, let him alone,
  'A bears him like a portly gentleman:
  And, to say truth, Verona brags of him
  To be a virtuous and well-governed youth.
  I would not for the wealth of all this town   70
  Here in my house do him disparagement:
  Therefore be patient, take no note of him.
  It is my will, the which if thou respect,
  Show a fair presence and put off these frowns,
  An ill-beseeming semblance for a feast.
TYBALT. It fits when such a villain is a guest:
  I'll not endure him.
CAPULET.   He shall be endured.
  What, goodman boy? I say he shall. Go to,
  Am I the master here, or you? Go to,
  You'll not endure him? God shall mend my soul!   80
  You'll make a mutiny among my guests!
  You will set cock-a-hoop! You'll be the man!
TYBALT. Why, uncle, 'tis a shame.
CAPULET.   Go to, go to,
  You are a saucy boy. Is't so indeed?
  This trick may chance to scathe you, I know what.
  You must contrary me! Marry, 'tis time—
  Well said, my hearts!—You are a princox: go,
  Be quiet, or—More light, more light, for shame!—
  I'll make you quiet.—What, cheerly, my hearts!
TYBALT. Patience perforce with wilful choler meeting   90
  Makes my flesh tremble in their different greeting.
  I will withdraw, but this intrusion shall,
  Now seeming sweet, convert to bitterest gall.
                                          Goes
ROMEO [takes Juliet's hand]. If I profane with my
    unworthiest hand
  This holy shrine, the gentle sin is this:
  My lips, two blushing pilgrims, ready stand
  To smooth that rough touch with a tender kiss.
JULIET. Good pilgrim, you do wrong your hand too
    much,
  Which mannerly devotion shows in this:
  For saints have hands that pilgrims' hands do touch,   100
  And palm to palm is holy palmers' kiss.
ROMEO. Have not saints lips, and holy palmers too?
JULIET. Ay, pilgrim, lips that they must use in
    prayer.
ROMEO. O then, dear saint, let lips do what hands do,
  They pray: grant thou, lest faith turn to despair.
JULIET. Saints do not move, though grant for prayers'
    sake.
ROMEO. Then move not, while my prayer's effect I
    take.
  Thus from my lips by thine my sin is purged.
                                    Kissing her
JULIET. Then have my lips the sin that they have took.
ROMEO. Sin from my lips? O trespass sweetly urged!   110
  Give me my sin again.   *Kissing her*
JULIET.   You kiss by th' book.
NURSE. Madam, your mother craves a word with you.
ROMEO. What is her mother?
NURSE.   Marry, bachelor,

Her mother is the lady of the house,
And a good lady, and a wise and virtuous.
I nursed her daughter that you talked withal.
I tell you, he that can lay hold of her
Shall have the chinks.
ROMEO.   Is she a Capulet?
O dear account! My life is my foe's debt.
BENVOLIO. Away be gone; the sport is at the best.   120
ROMEO. Ay, so I fear; the more is my unrest.
CAPULET. Nay, gentlemen, prepare not to be gone;
  We have a trifling foolish banquet towards.

The masquers excuse themselves, whispering in his ear

Is it e'en so? Why, then, I thank you all:
I thank you, honest gentlemen; good night.
More torches here; come on! then let's to bed.
Ah, sirrah, by my fay, it waxes late:
I'll to my rest.   *All leave but Juliet and Nurse*
JULIET. Come hither, nurse. What is yond gentleman?
NURSE. The son and heir of old Tiberio.   130
JULIET. What's he that now is going out of door?
NURSE. Marry, that I think be young Petruchio.
JULIET. What's he that follows there, that would not
    dance?
NURSE. I know not.
JULIET. Go ask his name.—If he be married,
  My grave is like to be my wedding bed.
NURSE. His name is Romeo, and a Montague,
  The only son of your great enemy.
JULIET. My only love sprung from my only hate!
  Too early seen unknown, and known too late!   140
  Prodigious birth of love it is to me,
  That I must love a loathèd enemy.
NURSE. What's this, what's this?
JULIET.   A rhyme I learned even now
  Of one I danced withal.

One calls within, Juliet

NURSE.   Anon, anon!
  Come, let's away; the strangers all are gone.
                                          They go

ACT 2
Prologue

Enter Chorus

CHORUS.
  Now old desire doth in his deathbed lie,
    And young affection gapes to be his heir;
  That fair for which love groaned for and
      would die,
    With tender Juliet matched, is now not fair.
  Now Romeo is beloved and loves again,
    Alike bewitchèd by the charm of looks,
  But to his foe supposed he must complain,
    And she steal love's sweet bait from
        fearful hooks:
  Being held a foe, he may not have access
    To breathe such vows as lovers use to swear;   10
  And she as much in love, her means much less
    To meet her new belovèd anywhere:
  But passion lends them power, time means,
      to meet,
  Tempering extremities with extreme sweet.
                                          Exit

Scene 1: *Capulet's orchard*

Enter Romeo alone in the lane by the orchard wall

ROMEO. Can I go forward when my heart is here?
Turn back, dull earth, and find thy centre out.

He climbs the wall and leaps into
the orchard

Enter Benvolio with Mercutio in the lane. Romeo listens
behind the wall.

BENVOLIO. Romeo, my cousin Romeo!
MERCUTIO.   He is wise,
And on my life hath stolen him home to bed.
BENVOLIO. He ran this way and leapt this orchard wall.
Call, good Mercutio.
MERCUTIO.   Nay, I'll conjure too.
Romeo, humours, madman, passion, lover!
Appear thou in the likeness of a sigh;
Speak but one rhyme and I am satisfied:
Cry but 'Ay me!', pronounce but 'love' and 'dove'; 10
Speak to my gossip Venus one fair word,
One nickname for her purblind son and heir,
Young Abraham Cupid, he that shot so trim
When King Cophetua loved the beggar maid.
He heareth not, he stirreth not, he moveth not;
The ape is dead, and I must conjure him.
I conjure thee by Rosaline's bright eyes,
By her high forehead and her scarlet lip,
By her fine foot, straight leg, and quivering thigh,
And the demesnes that there adjacent lie,   20
That in thy likeness thou appear to us.
BENVOLIO. An if he hear thee, thou wilt anger him.
MERCUTIO. This cannot anger him. 'Twould anger
him
To raise a spirit in his mistress' circle
Of some strange nature, letting it there stand
Till she had laid it and conjured it down;
That were some spite. My invocation
Is fair and honest; in his mistress' name
I conjure only but to raise up him.
BENVOLIO. Come! He hath hid himself among these
trees   30
To be consorted with the humorous night:
Blind is his love and best befits the dark.
MERCUTIO. If love be blind, love cannot hit the mark.
Now will he sit under a medlar tree,
And wish his mistress were that kind of fruit
As maids call medlars when they laugh alone.
O Romeo, that she were, O that she were
An open-arse and thou a poperin pear!
Romeo, goodnight. I'll to my truckle-bed;
This field-bed is too cold for me to sleep.   40
Come, shall we go?
BENVOLIO.   Go then, for 'tis in vain
To seek him here that means not to be found.

They go

Scene 2

ROMEO. He jests at scars that never felt a wound.

Juliet appears aloft at the window

But soft! What light through yonder window
breaks?
It is the east, and Juliet is the sun.
Arise, fair sun, and kill the envious moon,
Who is already sick and pale with grief
That thou, her maid, art far more fair than she.
Be not her maid, since she is envious.
Her vestal livery is but sick and green,
And none but fools do wear it: cast it off.
It is my lady, O it is my love;   10
O that she knew she were.
She speaks, yet she says nothing. What of that?
Her eye discourses: I will answer it.
I am too bold: 'tis not to me she speaks.
Two of the fairest stars in all the heaven,
Having some business, do entreat her eyes
To twinkle in their spheres till they return.
What if her eyes were there, they in her head?
The brightness of her cheek would shame those stars
As daylight doth a lamp; her eyes in heaven   20
Would through the airy region stream so bright
That birds would sing and think it were not night.
See how she leans her cheek upon her hand!
O that I were a glove upon that hand,
That I might touch that cheek.
JULIET.   Ay me!
ROMEO.   She speaks.
O speak again, bright angel, for thou art
As glorious to this night, being o'er my head,
As is a winged messenger of heaven
Unto the white-upturnéd wondering eyes
Of mortals that fall back to gaze on him   30
When he bestrides the lazy-passing clouds
And sails upon the bosom of the air.
JULIET. O Romeo, Romeo! Wherefore art thou
Romeo?
Deny thy father and refuse thy name:
Or, if thou wilt not, be but sworn my love,
And I'll no longer be a Capulet.
ROMEO [*aside*]. Shall I hear more, or shall I speak at this?
JULIET. 'Tis but thy name that is my enemy.
Thou art thy self, though not a Montague.
O be some other name! What's Montague?   40
It is nor hand, nor foot, nor arm, nor face,
Nor any part belonging to a man.
What's in a name? That which we call a rose
By any other name would smell as sweet.
So Romeo would, were he not Romeo called,
Retain that dear perfection which he owes,
Without that title. Romeo, doff thy name;
And for thy name, which is no part of thee,
Take all myself.
ROMEO.   I take thee at thy word.
Call me but love, and I'll be new baptized;   50
Henceforth I never will be Romeo.
JULIET. What man art thou that, thus bescreened in
night,
So stumblest on my counsel?
ROMEO.   By a name
I know not how to tell thee who I am.
My name, dear saint, is hateful to myself
Because it is an enemy to thee.
Had I it written, I would tear the word.
JULIET. My ears have yet not drunk a hundred words
Of thy tongue's uttering, yet I know the sound.
Art thou not Romeo, and a Montague?   60
ROMEO. Neither, fair maid, if either thee dislike.
JULIET. How camest thou hither, tell me, and
wherefore?
The orchard walls are high and hard to climb,

And the place death, considering who thou art,
If any of my kinsmen find thee here.

ROMEO. With love's light wings did I o'erperch these
    walls;
For stony limits cannot hold love out,
And what love can do, that dares love attempt:
Therefore thy kinsmen are no stop to me.

JULIET. If they do see thee, they will murther thee.   70

ROMEO. Alack, there lies more peril in thine eye
Than twenty of their swords. Look thou but sweet,
And I am proof against their enmity.

JULIET. I would not for the world they saw thee here.

ROMEO. I have night's cloak to hide me from their
    eyes;
And but thou love me, let them find me here:
My life were better ended by their hate
Than death proroguéd, wanting of thy love.

JULIET. By whose direction foundst thou out this
    place?

ROMEO. By love, that first did prompt me to enquire. 80
He lent me counsel, and I lent him eyes.
I am no pilot; yet, wert thou as far
As that vast shore washed with the farthest sea,
I should adventure for such merchandise.

JULIET. Thou knowest the mask of night is on my
    face;
Else would a maiden blush bepaint my cheek,
For that which thou hast heard me speak tonight.
Fain would I dwell on form; fain, fain deny
What I have spoke: but farewell compliment!
Dost thou love me? I know thou wilt say 'Ay',   90
And I will take thy word. Yet, if thou swearst,
Thou mayst prove false. At lovers' perjuries
They say Jove laughs. O gentle Romeo,
If thou dost love, pronounce it faithfully.
Or, if thou think'st I am too quickly won,
I'll frown and be perverse and say thee nay,
So thou wilt woo; but else, not for the world.
In truth, fair Montague, I am too fond,
And therefore thou mayst think my haviour light;
But trust me, gentleman, I'll prove more true   100
Than those that have more cunning to be strange.
I should have been more strange, I must confess,
But that thou overheardst, ere I was ware,
My true-love passion. Therefore pardon me,
And not impute this yielding to light love,
Which the dark night hath so discoveréd.

ROMEO. Lady, by yonder blesséd moon I vow,
That tips with silver all these fruit tree tops—

JULIET. O swear not by the moon, th'inconstant
    moon,
That monthly changes in her circled orb,   110
Lest that thy love prove likewise variable.

ROMEO. What shall I swear by?

JULIET.   Do not swear at all:
Or, if thou wilt, swear by thy gracious self,
Which is the god of my idolatry,
And I'll believe thee.

ROMEO.   If my heart's dear love—

JULIET. Well, do not swear. Although I joy in thee,
I have no joy of this contract tonight:
It is too rash, too unadvised, too sudden,
Too like the lightning, which doth cease to be
Ere one can say 'It lightens'. Sweet, goodnight: 120
This bud of love, by summer's ripening breath,
May prove a beauteous flower when next we meet.

Goodnight, goodnight! As sweet repose and rest
Come to thy heart as that within my breast.

ROMEO. O wilt thou leave me so unsatisfied?

JULIET. What satisfaction canst thou have tonight?

ROMEO. Th'exchange of thy love's faithful vow for
    mine.

JULIET. I gave thee mine before thou didst request it:
And yet I would it were to give again.

ROMEO. Would'st thou withdraw it? For what
    purpose, love?   130

JULIET. But to be frank and give it thee again:
And yet I wish but for the thing I have.
My bounty is as boundless as the sea,
My love as deep: the more I give to thee,
The more I have: for both are infinite.
I hear some noise within. Dear love, adieu—

                        Nurse calls within
Anon, good nurse!—sweet Montague, be true.
Stay but a little; I will come again.   *Juliet goes in*

ROMEO. O blessed, blessed night! I am afeared,
Being in night, all this is but a dream,   140
Too flattering sweet to be substantial.

Juliet reappears at the window

JULIET. Three words, dear Romeo, and good night
    indeed.
If that thy bent of love be honourable,
Thy purpose marriage, send me word tomorrow,
By one that I'll procure to come to thee,
Where and what time thou wilt perform the rite;
And all my fortunes at thy foot I'll lay,
And follow thee my lord throughout the world.

NURSE [*within*]. Madam!

JULIET. I come, anon.—But if thou meanest not well, 150
I do beseech thee—

NURSE [*within*].   Madam!

JULIET.   By and by I come—
To cease thy suit, and leave me to my grief.
Tomorrow will I send.

ROMEO. So thrive my soul—

JULIET.   A thousand times good night!

                            She goes in

ROMEO. A thousand times the worse, to want thy
    light!
Love goes toward love as schoolboys from their
    books,
But love from love, toward school with heavy
    looks.

Juliet returns to the window

JULIET. Hist, Romeo, hist! O for a falconer's voice
To lure this tassel-gentle back again!
Bondage is hoarse and may not speak aloud,   160
Else would I tear the cave where Echo lies,
And make her airy tongue more hoarse than mine
With repetition of my "Romeo!"

ROMEO. It is my soul that calls upon my name.
How silver-sweet sound lovers' tongues by night,
Like softest music to attending ears!

JULIET. Romeo!

ROMEO.   My nièss!

JULIET.   What o'clock tomorrow
Shall I send to thee?

ROMEO.   By the hour of nine.

JULIET. I will not fail. 'Tis twenty year till then.
I have forgot why I did call thee back.   170

ROMEO. Let me stand here till thou remember it.
JULIET. I shall forget, to have thee still stand there,
  Rememb'ring how I love thy company.
ROMEO. And I'll still stay, to have thee still forget,
  Forgetting any other home but this.
JULIET. 'Tis almost morning. I would have thee gone,
  And yet no farther than a wanton's bird,
  That lets it hop a little from her hand,
  Like a poor prisoner in his twisted gyves,
  And with a silk thread plucks it back again,   180
  So loving-jealous of his liberty.
ROMEO. I would I were thy bird.
JULIET.   Sweet, so would I;
  Yet I should kill thee with much cherishing.
  Goodnight, goodnight! Parting is such sweet
    sorrow,
  That I shall say goodnight till it be morrow.
ROMEO. Sleep dwell upon thine eyes, peace in thy
    breast!
  Would I were sleep and peace, so sweet to rest!
                                      She goes in
  Hence will I to my ghostly sire's close cell,
  His help to crave, and my dear hap to tell. *He goes*

Scene 3: *Friar Lawrence's cell*

Enter Friar alone with a basket

FRIAR. The grey-eyed morn smiles on the frowning
    night,
  Check'ring the eastern clouds with streaks of light:
  And darkness flecked like a drunkard reels
  From forth day's pathway, made by Titan's wheels:
  Now ere the sun advance his burning eye,
  The day to cheer and night's dank dew to dry,
  I must upfill this osier cage of ours,
  With baleful weeds and precious-juicéd flowers.
  The earth that's nature's mother is her tomb;
  What is her burying grave, that is her womb;   10
  And from her womb children of divers kind
  We sucking on her natural bosom find:
  Many for many virtues excellent,
  None but for some, and yet all different.
  O mickle is the powerful grace that lies
  In plants, herbs, stones, and their true qualities:
  For nought so vile that on the earth doth live
  But to the earth some special good doth give:
  Nor aught so good but, strained from that fair use,
  Revolts from true birth, stumbling on abuse.   20
  Virtue itself turns vice, being misapplied,
  And vice something by action dignified.

Romeo approaches

  Within the infant rind of this weak flower
  Poison hath residence, and medicine power:
  For this, being smelt, with that part cheers each part;
  Being tasted, stays all senses with the heart.
  Two such opposéd kings encamp them still
  In man as well as herbs—grace and rude will:
  And where the worser is predominant,
  Full soon the canker death eats up that plant.   30
ROMEO. Good morrow, father.
FRIAR.   Benedicite!
  What early tongue so sweet saluteth me?
  Young son, it argues a distempered head,
  So soon to bid goodmorrow to thy bed.
  Care keeps his watch in every old man's eye,

And where care lodges sleep will never lie:
  But where unbruiséd youth with unstuffed brain
  Doth couch his limbs, there golden sleep doth reign.
  Therefore thy earliness doth me assure
  Thou art uprousèd with some distemperature: 40
  Or if not so, then here I hit it right—
  Our Romeo hath not been in bed tonight.
ROMEO. That last is true—the sweeter rest was mine
FRIAR. God pardon sin! Wast thou with Rosaline?
ROMEO. With Rosaline? My ghostly father, no;
  I have forgot that name, and that name's woe.
FRIAR. That's my good son! But where hast thou been
    then?
ROMEO. I'll tell thee ere thou ask it me again.
  I have been feasting with mine enemy,
  Where on a sudden one hath wounded me   50
  That's by me wounded. Both our remedies
  Within thy help and holy physic lies.
  I bear no hatred, blessed man, for lo,
  My intercession likewise steads my foe.
FRIAR. Be plain, good son, and homely in thy drift.
  Riddling confession finds but riddling shrift.
ROMEO. Then plainly know my heart's dear love is set
  On the fair daughter of rich Capulet:
  As mine on hers, so hers is set on mine,
  And all combined save what thou must combine   60
  By holy marriage: when and where and how
  We met, we wooed, and made exchange of vow
  I'll tell thee as we pass; but this I pray,
  That thou consent to marry us today.
FRIAR. Holy Saint Francis, what a change is here!
  Is Rosaline, that thou didst love so dear,
  So soon forsaken? Young men's love then lies
  Not truly in their hearts but in their eyes.
  Jesu Maria, what a deal of brine
  Hath washed thy sallow cheeks for Rosaline!   70
  How much salt water thrown away in waste
  To season love, that of it doth not taste!
  The sun not yet thy sighs from heaven clears,
  Thy old groans ring yet in mine ancient ears;
  Lo, here upon thy cheek the stain doth sit
  Of an old tear that is not washed off yet.
  If e'er thou wast thyself, and these woes thine,
  Thou and these woes were all for Rosaline.
  And art thou changed? Pronounce this sentence,
    then—
  Women may fall, when there's no strength in men.   80
ROMEO. Thou chid'st me oft for loving Rosaline.
FRIAR. For doting, not for loving, pupil mine.
ROMEO. And bad'st me bury love.
FRIAR.   Not in a grave
  To lay one in, another out to have.
ROMEO. I pray thee chide me not. Her I love now
  Doth grace for grace and love for love allow:
  The other did not so.
FRIAR.   O, she knew well
  Thy love did read by rote, that could not spell.
  But come, young waverer, come go with me;
  In one respect I'll thy assistant be: 90
  For this alliance may so happy prove
  To turn your households' rancour to pure love.
ROMEO. O let us hence! I stand on sudden haste.
FRIAR. Wisely and slow. They stumble that run fast.
                                      They go

Scene 4: *A public place*

Enter Benvolio and Mercutio

MERCUTIO. Where the devil should this Romeo be? Came he not home tonight?

BENVOLIO. Not to his father's; I spoke with his man.

MERCUTIO. Why, that same pale hard-hearted wench, that Rosaline, Torments him so, that he will sure run mad.

BENVOLIO. Tybalt, the kinsman to old Capulet, Hath sent a letter to his father's house.

MERCUTIO. A challenge, on my life.

BENVOLIO. Romeo will answer it.

MERCUTIO. Any man that can write may answer a letter. 10

BENVOLIO. Nay, he will answer the letter's master, how he dares being dared.

MERCUTIO. Alas, poor Romeo, he is already dead— stabbed with a white wench's black eye, run through the ear with a love-song, the very pin of his heart cleft with the blind bow-boy's butt-shaft; and is he a man to encounter Tybalt?

BENVOLIO. Why, what is Tybalt?

MERCUTIO. More than Prince of Cats. O, he's the courageous captain of compliments. He fights as 20 you sing pricksong—keeps time, distance, and proportion; he rests his minim rests—one, two, and the third in your bosom. The very butcher of a silk button, a duellist, a duellist, a gentleman of the very first house, of the first and second cause! Ah, the immortal passado, the punto reverso, the hai!

BENVOLIO. The what?

MERCUTIO. The pox of such antic, lisping, affecting fantasticoes, these new tuners of accent! 'By Jesu, a very good blade! a very tall man! a very good 30 whore!' Why, is not this a lamentable thing, grandsire, that we should be thus afflicted with these strange flies, these fashion-mongers, these pardonme's, who stand so much on the new form that they cannot sit at ease on the old bench? O, their bones, their bones!

Enter Romeo

BENVOLIO. Here comes Romeo, here comes Romeo!

MERCUTIO. Without his roe, like a dried herring. O flesh, flesh, how art thou fishified! Now is he for the numbers that Petrarch flowed in. Laura to his lady 40 was a kitchen wench—marry, she had a better love to be-rhyme her!—Dido a dowdy, Cleopatra a gipsy, Helen and Hero hildings and harlots, Thisbe a gray eye or so, but not to the purpose. Signior Romeo, bon jour! There's a French salutation to your French slop. You gave us the counterfeit fairly last night.

ROMEO. Good morrow to you both. What counterfeit did I give you?

MERCUTIO. The slip, sir, the slip. Can you not con- 50 ceive?

ROMEO. Pardon, good Mercutio. My business was great, and in such a case as mine a man may strain courtesy.

MERCUTIO. That's as much as to say, such a case as yours constrains a man to bow in the hams.

ROMEO. Meaning to curtsy?

MERCUTIO. Thou hast most kindly hit it.

ROMEO. A most courteous exposition.

MERCUTIO. Nay, I am the very pink of courtesy. 60

ROMEO. Pink for flower?

MERCUTIO. Right.

ROMEO. Why, then is my pump well flowered.

MERCUTIO. Sure wit! Follow me this jest now till thou hast worn out thy pump, that, when the single sole of it is worn, the jest may remain, after the wearing, solely singular.

ROMEO. O single-soled jest, solely singular for the singleness!

MERCUTIO. Come between us, good Benvolio; my 70 wits faints.

ROMEO. Switch and spurs, switch and spurs; or I'll cry a match.

MERCUTIO. Nay, if our wits run the wild-goose chase, I am done: for thou hast more of the wild goose in one of thy wits than, I am sure, I have in my whole five. Was I with you there for the goose?

ROMEO. Thou wast never with me for anything when thou wast not there for the goose.

MERCUTIO. I will bite thee by the ear for that jest. 80

ROMEO. Nay, good goose, bite not.

MERCUTIO. Thy wit is a very bitter sweeting; it is a most sharp sauce.

ROMEO. And is it not then well served in to a sweet goose?

MERCUTIO. O, here's a wit of cheveril, that stretches from an inch narrow to an ell broad.

ROMEO. I stretch it out for that word 'broad', which, added to the goose, proves thee far and wide a broad goose. 90

MERCUTIO. Why, is not this better now than groaning for love? Now art thou sociable, now art thou Romeo: now art thou what thou art, by art as well as by nature. For this drivelling love is like a great natural that runs lolling up and down to hide his bauble in a hole.

BENVOLIO. Stop there, stop there!

MERCUTIO. Thou desirest me to stop in my tale, against the hair?

BENVOLIO. Thou wouldst else have made thy tale large. 100

MERCUTIO. O, thou art deceived! I would have made it short, for I was come to the whole depth of my tale, and meant indeed to occupy the argument no longer.

Enter the Nurse with her man Peter

ROMEO. Here's goodly gear! A sail, a sail!

MERCUTIO. Two, two! a shirt and a smock.

NURSE. Peter!

PETER. Anon.

NURSE. My fan, Peter.

MERCUTIO. Good Peter, to hide her face; for her fan's 110 the fairer face.

NURSE. God ye good morrow, gentlemen.

MERCUTIO. God ye good-den, fair gentlewoman.

NURSE. Is it good-den?

MERCUTIO. 'Tis no less, I tell ye; for the bawdy hand of the dial is now upon the prick of noon.

NURSE. Out upon you! What a man are you?

ROMEO. One, gentlewoman, that God hath made, himself to mar.

NURSE. By my troth, it is well said. 'For himself to 120

mar,' quoth 'a? Gentlemen, can any of you tell me
where I may find the young Romeo?

ROMEO. I can tell you; but young Romeo will be older
when you have found him than he was when you
sought him. I am the youngest of that name, for
fault of a worse.

NURSE. You say well.

MERCUTIO. Yea, is the worst well? Very well took,
i' faith! Wisely, wisely!

NURSE. If you be he, sir, I desire some confidence with 130
you.

BENVOLIO. She will indite him to some supper.

MERCUTIO. A bawd, a bawd, a bawd! So ho!

ROMEO. What, hast thou found?

MERCUTIO. No hare, sir; unless a hare, sir, in a lenten
pie, that is something stale and hoar ere it be spent.

He walks by them and sings

An old hare hoar
And an old hare hoar
Is very good meat in Lent.
But a hare that is hoar　　　　　140
Is too much for a score
When it hoars ere it be spent.

Romeo, will you come to your father's? We'll to
dinner thither.

ROMEO. I will follow you.

MERCUTIO. Farewell, ancient lady; farewell, [*singing*]
'lady, lady, lady'.　　　　*Mercutio and Benvolio go*

NURSE. I pray you, sir, what saucy merchant was this
that was so full of his ropery?

ROMEO. A gentleman, Nurse, that loves to hear him- 150
self talk, and will speak more in a minute than he
will stand to in a month.

NURSE. And 'a speak anything against me, I'll take
him down and 'a were lustier than he is, and
twenty such Jacks: and if I cannot, I'll find those
that shall. Scurvy knave! I am none of his flirt-gills,
I am none of his skains-mates. [*to Peter*] And thou
must stand by too, and suffer every knave to use
me at his pleasure!

PETER. I saw no man use you at his pleasure. If I had, 160
my weapon should quickly have been out. I warrant
you I dare draw as soon as another man, if I see
occasion in a good quarrel, and the law on my side.

NURSE. Now afore God, I am so vexed that every part
about me quivers. Scurvy knave! Pray you, sir, a
word. And as I told you, my young lady bid me
enquire you out. What she bid me say I will keep
to myself: but first let me tell ye, if ye should lead
her in a fool's paradise, as they say, it were a very
gross kind of behaviour, as they say: for the gentle- 170
woman is young; and therefore, if you should deal
double with her, truly it were an ill thing to be
offered to any gentlewoman, and very weak
dealing.

ROMEO. Nurse, commend me to thy lady and mistress.
I protest unto thee—

NURSE. Good heart! and i' faith I will tell her as much.
Lord, Lord! she will be a joyful woman.

ROMEO. What wilt thou tell her, Nurse? Thou dost not
mark me!　　　　180

NURSE. I will tell her, sir, that you do protest, which,
as I take it, is a gentlemanlike offer.

ROMEO. Bid her devise

Some means to come to shrift this afternoon,
And there she shall at Friar Lawrence' cell
Be shrived and married. Here is for thy pains.

NURSE. No, truly, sir; not a penny.

ROMEO. Go to, I say you shall.

NURSE. This afternoon, sir; well, she shall be there.

ROMEO. And stay, good Nurse, behind the abbey wall. 190
Within this hour my man shall be with thee
And bring thee cords made like a tackled stair,
Which to the high topgallant of my joy
Must be my convoy in the secret night.
Farewell. Be trusty, and I'll quit thy pains.
Farewell. Commend me to thy mistress.

NURSE. Now God in heaven bless thee! Hark you, sir.

ROMEO. What sayst thou, my dear Nurse?

NURSE. Is your man secret? Did you ne'er hear say,
'Two may keep counsel, putting one away'?　　200

ROMEO. I warrant thee my man's as true as steel.

NURSE. Well, sir, my mistress is the sweetest lady.
Lord, Lord! when 'twas a little prating thing—O,
there is a nobleman in town, one Paris, that would
fain lay knife aboard: but she, good soul, had as lief
see a toad, a very toad, as see him. I anger her sometimes, and tell her that Paris is the properer man;
but I'll warrant you, when I say so, she looks as
pale as any clout in the versal world. Doth not
rosemary and Romeo begin both with a letter?　210

ROMEO. Ay, Nurse; what of that? Both with an R.

NURSE. Ah, mocker, that's the dog-name; R is for
the—No; I know it begins with some other letter;
and she hath the prettiest sententious of it, of you
and rosemary, that it would do you good to hear it.

ROMEO. Commend me to thy lady.

NURSE. Ay, a thousand times. [*Romeo goes*] Peter!

PETER. Anon.

NURSE. Before and apace.　　　　*They go*

Scene 5: *Capulet's orchard*

Enter Juliet

JULIET. The clock struck nine when I did send
the Nurse;
In half an hour she promised to return.
Perchance she cannot meet him. That's not so.
O, she is lame! Love's heralds should be thoughts,
Which ten times faster glides than the sun's beams
Driving back shadows over louring hills.
Therefore do nimble-pinioned doves draw Love,
And therefore hath the wind-swift Cupid wings.
Now is the sun upon the highmost hill
Of this day's journey, and from nine till twelve　10
Is three long hours; yet she is not come.
Had she affections and warm youthful blood,
She would be swift in motion as a ball;
My words would bandy her to my sweet love,
And his to me.
But old folks, many feign as they were dead—
Unwieldy, slow, heavy, and pale as lead.

Enter Nurse, with Peter

O God, she comes! O honey Nurse, what news?
Hast thou met with him? Send thy man away.

NURSE. Peter, stay at the gate.　　*Peter withdraws* 20

JULIET. Now good sweet Nurse—O Lord, why
look'st thou sad?
Though news be sad, yet tell them merrily;

If good, thou shamest the music of sweet news
By playing it to me with so sour a face.
NURSE. I am aweary, give me leave a while.
Fie, how my bones ache! What a jaunce have I!
JULIET. I would thou hadst my bones, and I thy
    news:
Nay, come, I pray thee speak; good, good Nurse,
    speak.
NURSE. Jesu, what haste! Can you not stay awhile?
Do you not see that I am out of breath?   30
JULIET. How art thou out of breath when thou hast
    breath
To say to me that thou art out of breath?
The excuse that thou dost make in this delay
Is longer than the tale thou dost excuse.
Is thy news good or bad? Answer to that.
Say either, and I'll stay the circumstance.
Let me be satisfied; is't good or bad?
NURSE. Well, you have made a simple choice; you
    know not how to choose a man. Romeo? No, not
    he. Though his face be better than any man's, yet   40
    his leg excels all men's; and for a hand and a foot
    and a body, though they be not to be talked on,
    yet they are past compare. He is not the flower of
    courtesy, but, I'll warrant him, as gentle as a lamb.
    Go thy ways, wench; serve God. What, have you
    dined at home?
JULIET. No, no. But all this did I know before.
What says he of our marriage, what of that?
NURSE. Lord, how my head aches! what a head have I!
It beats as it would fall in twenty pieces.   50
My back o' t'other side; ah, my back, my back!
Beshrew your heart for sending me about
To catch my death with jauncing up and down.
JULIET. I' faith, I am sorry that thou art not well.
Sweet, sweet, sweet Nurse, tell me, what says my
    love?
NURSE. 'Your love says, like an honest gentleman, and
    a courteous, and a kind, and a handsome, and, I
    warrant, a virtuous—Where is your mother?
JULIET. Where is my mother? Why, she is within.
Where should she be? How oddly thou repliest: 60
'Your love says, like an honest gentleman,
"Where is your mother?"'
NURSE.   O god's Lady dear!
Are you so hot? Marry come up, I trow!
Is this the poultice for my aching bones?
Henceforward do your messages yourself.
JULIET. Here's such a coil! Come, what says Romeo?
NURSE. Have you got leave to go to shrift today?
JULIET. I have.
NURSE. Then hie you hence to Friar Lawrence' cell;
There stays a husband to make you a wife.   70
Now comes the wanton blood up in your cheeks;
They'll be in scarlet straight at any news.
Hie you to church; I must another way,
To fetch a ladder, by the which your love
Must climb a bird's nest soon when it is dark.
I am the drudge, and toil in your delight:
But you shall bear the burden soon at night.
Go; I'll to dinner; hie you to the cell.
JULIET. Hie to high fortune! Honest Nurse, farewell.
                                                They go

Scene 6: *Friar Lawrence's cell*

Enter Friar and Romeo

FRIAR. So smile the heavens upon this holy act
That after-hours with sorrow chide us not.
ROMEO. Amen, amen. But come what sorrow can,
It cannot countervail the exchange of joy
That one short minute gives me in her sight.
Do thou but close our hands with holy words,
Then love-devouring death do what he dare;
It is enough I may but call her mine.
FRIAR. These violent delights have violent ends,
And in their triumph die like fire and powder   10
Which, as they kiss, consume. The sweetest honey
Is loathsome in his own deliciousness,
And in the taste confounds the appetite.
Therefore love moderately; long love doth so:
Too swift arrives as tardy as too slow.
Here comes the lady.

Enter Juliet

                              O, so light a foot
Will ne'er wear out the everlasting flint!
A lover may bestride the gossamers
That idles in the wanton summer air,
And yet not fall; so light is vanity.   20
JULIET. Good even to my ghostly confessor.
FRIAR. Romeo shall thank thee, daughter, for us both.
JULIET. As much to him, else is his thanks too much.
ROMEO. Ah, Juliet, if the measure of thy joy
Be heaped like mine, and that thy skill be more
To blazon it, then sweeten with thy breath
This neighbour air, and let rich music's tongue
Unfold the imagined happiness that both
Receive in either by this dear encounter.
JULIET. Conceit, more rich in matter than in words, 30
Brags of his substance, not of ornament.
They are but beggars that can count their worth;
But my true love is grown to such excess
I cannot sum up sum of half my wealth.
FRIAR. Come, come with me, and we will make short
    work;
For, by your leaves, you shall not stay alone
Till Holy Church incorporate two in one.
                                                They go

ACT 3
Scene 1: *A public place*

Enter Mercutio, Benvolio, and their men

BENVOLIO. I pray thee, good Mercutio, let's retire;
The day is hot, the Capels are abroad:
And if we meet we shall not scape a brawl,
For now, these hot days, is the mad blood stirring.
MERCUTIO. Thou art like one of these fellows that,
    when he enters the confines of a tavern, claps me
    his sword upon the table and says 'God send me no
    need of thee'; and, by the operation of the second
    cup, draws him on the drawer, when indeed there
    is no need.   10
BENVOLIO. Am I like such a fellow?
MERCUTIO. Come, come, thou art as hot a Jack in thy
    mood as any in Italy; and as soon moved to be
    moody, and as soon moody to be moved.
BENVOLIO. And what to?

MERCUTIO. Nay, an there were two such, we should have none shortly, for one would kill the other. Thou? Why, thou wilt quarrel with a man that hath a hair more or a hair less in his beard than thou hast. Thou wilt quarrel with a man for cracking 20 nuts, having no other reason but because thou hast hazel eyes. What eye but such an eye would spy out such a quarrel? Thy head is as full of quarrels as an egg is full of meat, and yet thy head hath been beaten as addle as an egg for quarrelling. Thou hast quarrelled with a man for coughing in the street, because he hath wakened thy dog that hath lain asleep in the sun. Didst thou not fall out with a tailor for wearing his new doublet before Easter? With another for tying his new shoes with old riband? 30 And yet thou wilt tutor me from quarrelling?

BENVOLIO. An I were so apt to quarrel as thou art, any man should buy the fee-simple of my life for an hour and a quarter.

MERCUTIO. The fee-simple? O simple!

Enter Tybalt, and others

BENVOLIO. By my head, here comes the Capulets.

MERCUTIO. By my heel, I care not.

TYBALT. Follow me close, for I will speak to them. Gentlemen, good-den: a word with one of you.

MERCUTIO. And but one word with one of us? Couple 40 it with something; make it a word and a blow.

TYBALT. You shall find me apt enough to that, sir, an you will give me occasion.

MERCUTIO. Could you not take some occasion without giving?

TYBALT. Mercutio, thou consort'st with Romeo—

MERCUTIO. Consort? What, dost thou make us minstrels? An thou make minstrels of us, look to hear nothing but discords. Here's my fiddlestick; here's that shall make you dance. Zounds, consort! 50

BENVOLIO. We talk here in the public haunt of men. Either withdraw unto some private place And reason coldly of your grievances, Or else depart: here all eyes gaze on us.

MERCUTIO. Men's eyes were made to look, and let them gaze. I will not budge for no man's pleasure, I.

Enter Romeo

TYBALT. Well, peace be with you, sir; here comes my man.

MERCUTIO. But I'll be hanged, sir, if he wears your livery. Marry, go before to field, he'll be your follower! Your worship in that sense may call him man. 60

TYBALT. Romeo, the love I bear thee can afford No better term than this: thou art a villain.

ROMEO. Tybalt, the reason that I have to love thee Doth much excuse the appertaining rage To such a greeting. Villain am I none— Therefore farewell; I see thou knowest me not.

TYBALT. Boy, this shall not excuse the injuries That thou hast done me; therefore turn and draw.

ROMEO. I do protest I never injured thee, But love thee better than thou canst devise 70 Till thou shalt know the reason of my love: And so, good Capulet, which name I tender As dearly as mine own, be satisfied.

MERCUTIO. O calm, dishonourable, vile submission!

'Alla stoccata' carries it away. *Draws* Tybalt, you rat-catcher, will you walk?

TYBALT. What wouldst thou have with me?

MERCUTIO. Good King of Cats, nothing but one of your nine lives that I mean to make bold withal and, as you shall use me hereafter, dry-beat the rest of the 80 eight. Will you pluck your sword out of his pilcher by the ears? Make haste, lest mine be about your ears ere it be out.

TYBALT. I am for you. *Draws*

ROMEO. Gentle Mercutio, put thy rapier up.

MERCUTIO. Come, sir, your passado. *They fight*

ROMEO. Draw, Benvolio; beat down their weapons. Gentlemen, for shame forbear this outrage. Tybalt, Mercutio, the prince expressly hath Forbid this bandying in Verona streets. 90 Hold, Tybalt! good Mercutio!

Tybalt under Romeo's arm thrusts Mercutio in and flies

MERCUTIO. I am hurt. A plague o' both your houses! I am sped. Is he gone and hath nothing?

BENVOLIO. What, art thou hurt?

MERCUTIO. Ay, ay, a scratch, a scratch; marry, 'tis enough. Where is my page? Go, villain, fetch a surgeon. *Page goes*

ROMEO. Courage, man; the hurt cannot be much.

MERCUTIO. No, 'tis not so deep as a well, nor so wide as a church door, but 'tis enough, 'twill serve. Ask for me tomorrow and you shall find me a grave man. I am peppered, I warrant, for this world. A 100 plague o' both your houses! Zounds! A dog, a rat, a mouse, a cat, to scratch a man to death! A braggart, a rogue, a villain, that fights by the book of arithmetic! Why the devil came you between us? I was hurt under your arm.

ROMEO. I thought all for the best.

MERCUTIO. Help me into some house, Benvolio, Or I shall faint. A plague o' both your houses! They have made worms' meat of me. I have it, And soundly too. Your houses! 110 *Benvolio helps him away*

ROMEO. This gentleman, the prince's near ally, My very friend, hath got this mortal hurt In my behalf, my reputation stained With Tybalt's slander—Tybalt that an hour Hath been my cousin. O sweet Juliet, Thy beauty hath made me effeminate, And in my temper softened valour's steel!

Benvolio returns

BENVOLIO. O Romeo, Romeo, brave Mercutio's dead. That gallant spirit hath aspired the clouds, Which too untimely here did scorn the earth. 120

ROMEO. This day's black fate on moe days doth depend; This but begins the woe others must end.

Tybalt returns

BENVOLIO. Here comes the furious Tybalt back again.

ROMEO. Again! in triumph, and Mercutio slain! Away to heaven, respective lenity, And fire-eyed fury be my conduct now! Now, Tybalt, take the 'villain' back again

That late thou gavest me, for Mercutio's soul
Is but a little way above our heads,
Staying for thine to keep him company.   130
Either thou or I, or both, must go with him.
TYBALT. Thou wretched boy that didst consort him
     here
Shalt with him hence.
ROMEO.   This shall determine that.
                    They fight, Tybalt falls
BENVOLIO. Romeo, away, be gone!
The citizens are up, and Tybalt slain.
Stand not amazed. The prince will doom thee death
If thou art taken. Hence, be gone, away!
ROMEO. O, I am Fortune's fool.
BENVOLIO.   Why dost thou stay?
                                    Romeo goes

Enter Citizens

A CITIZEN. Which way ran he that killed Mercutio?
Tybalt, that murderer, which way ran he?   140
BENVOLIO. There lies that Tybalt.
A CITIZEN.   Up, sir, go with me:
I charge thee in the prince's name obey.

Enter Prince, old Montague, Capulet, their wives and all

PRINCE. Where are the vile beginners of this fray?
BENVOLIO. O noble Prince, I can discover all
The unlucky manage of this fatal brawl.
There lies the man, slain by young Romeo,
That slew thy kinsman, brave Mercutio.
LADY CAPULET. Tybalt, my cousin, O my
     brother's child!
O prince! O husband! O, the blood is spilled
Of my dear kinsman. Prince, as thou art true,   150
For blood of ours shed blood of Montague.
O cousin, cousin!
PRINCE. Benvolio, who began this bloody fray?
BENVOLIO. Tybalt, here slain, whom Romeo's hand
     did slay.
Romeo, that spoke him fair, bid him bethink
How nice the quarrel was, and urged withal
Your high displeasure. All this—utteréd
With gentle breath, calm look, knees humbly
     bowed—
Could not take truce with the unruly spleen
Of Tybalt deaf to peace, but that he tilts   160
With piercing steel at bold Mercutio's breast,
Who, all as hot, turns deadly point to point,
And, with a martial scorn, with one hand beats
Cold death aside and with the other sends
It back to Tybalt, whose dexterity
Retorts it. Romeo he cries aloud,
'Hold, friends! friends, part!' and, swifter than
     his tongue,
His agile arm beats down their fatal points,
And 'twixt them rushes; underneath whose arm
An envious thrust from Tybalt hit the life   170
Of stout Mercutio, and then Tybalt fled,
But by and by comes back to Romeo
Who had but newly entertained revenge,
And to 't they go like lightning; for, ere I
Could draw to part them, was stout Tybalt slain,
And, as he fell, did Romeo turn and fly:
This is the truth, or let Benvolio die.
LADY CAPULET. He is a kinsman to the Montague;
Affection makes him false, he speaks not true.

Some twenty of them fought in this black strife,   180
And all those twenty could but kill one life.
I beg for justice, which thou, Prince, must give:
Romeo slew Tybalt; Romeo must not live.
PRINCE. Romeo slew him; he slew Mercutio.
Who now the price of his dear blood doth owe?
MONTAGUE. Not Romeo, Prince; he was
     Mercutio's friend;
His fault concludes but what the law should end—
The life of Tybalt.
PRINCE.   And for that offence
Immediately we do exile him hence.
I have an interest in your hearts' proceeding: 190
My blood for your rude brawls doth lie a-bleeding.
But I'll amerce you with so strong a fine
That you shall all repent the loss of mine.
I will be deaf to pleading and excuses;
Nor tears nor prayers shall purchase out abuses.
Therefore use none. Let Romeo hence in haste,
Else, when he is found, that hour is his last.
Bear hence this body, and attend our will.
Mercy but murders, pardoning those that kill.
                                    They go

Scene 2: Capulet's house

Enter Juliet alone

JULIET. Gallop apace, you fiery-footed steeds,
Towards Phoebus' lodging! Such a waggoner
As Phaëton would whip you to the west
And bring in cloudy night immediately.
Spread thy close curtain, love-performing night,
That runaways' eyes may wink, and Romeo
Leap to these arms untalked of and unseen.
Lovers can see to do their amorous rites
By their own beauties; or, if love be blind,
It best agrees with night. Come, civil Night,   10
Thou sober-suited matron all in black,
And learn me how to lose a winning match,
Played for a pair of stainless maidenhoods.
Hood my unmanned blood, bating in my cheeks,
With thy black mantle till strange love, grown bold,
Think true love acted simple modesty.
Come, Night! Come, Romeo! Come, thou day in
     night;
For thou wilt lie upon the wings of night
Whiter than snow upon a raven's back.
Come, gentle Night; come, loving, black-browed
     Night: 20
Give me my Romeo; and, when he shall die,
Take him and cut him out in little stars,
And he will make the face of heaven so fine
That all the world will be in love with night
And pay no worship to the garish sun.
O, I have bought the mansion of a love,
But not possessed it; and though I am sold,
Not yet enjoyed. So tedious is this day
As is the night before some festival
To an impatient child that hath new robes   30
And may not wear them. O, here comes my nurse,

Enter Nurse with cords

And she brings news; and every tongue that speaks
But Romeo's name speaks heavenly eloquence.
Now, Nurse, what news? What hast thou there?
     The cords

That Romeo bid thee fetch?
NURSE.   Ay, ay, the cords.
                     Throws them down
JULIET. Ay me, what news? Why dost thou wring thy
   hands?
NURSE. Ah, weraday! He's dead, he's dead, he's dead!
   We are undone, lady, we are undone.
   Alack the day, he's gone, he's killed, he's dead!
JULIET. Can heaven be so envious?
NURSE.   Romeo can,   40
   Though heaven cannot. O Romeo, Romeo!
   Who ever would have thought it? Romeo!
JULIET. What devil art thou that dost torment me
   thus?
   This torture should be roared in dismal hell.
   Hath Romeo slain himself? Say thou but 'ay',
   And that bare vowel 'I' shall poison more
   Than the death-darting eye of cockatrice.
   I am not I if there be such an 'I',
   Or those eyes shut that makes thee answer 'ay'.
   If he be slain, say 'ay', or, if not, 'no'.   50
   Brief sounds determine of my weal or woe.
NURSE. I saw the wound, I saw it with mine eyes,
   (God save the mark!) here on his manly breast.
   A piteous corse, a bloody piteous corse,
   Pale, pale as ashes, all bedaubed in blood,
   All in gore blood; I swounded at the sight.
JULIET. O break, my heart! Poor bankrout, break at
   once!
   To prison, eyes; ne'er look on liberty.
   Vile earth, to earth resign, end motion here,
   And thou and Romeo press one heavy bier!   60
NURSE. O Tybalt, Tybalt, the best friend I had!
   O courteous Tybalt, honest gentleman,
   That ever I should live to see thee dead!
JULIET. What storm is this that blows so contrary?
   Is Romeo slaught'red? and is Tybalt dead?
   My dearest cousin, and my dearer lord?
   Then, dreadful trumpet, sound the general doom;
   For who is living if those two are gone?
NURSE. Tybalt is gone and Romeo banishéd;
   Romeo that killed him, he is banishéd.   70
JULIET. O God! did Romeo's hand shed Tybalt's
   blood?
NURSE. It did, it did! alas the day, it did!
JULIET. O serpent heart, hid with a flowering face!
   Did ever dragon keep so fair a cave?
   Beautiful tyrant, fiend angelical,
   Dove-feathered raven, wolvish-ravening lamb!
   Despiséd substance of divinest show,
   Just opposite to what thou justly seemst—
   A damnéd saint, an honourable villain!
   O nature, what hadst thou to do in hell   80
   When thou didst bower the spirit of a fiend
   In mortal paradise of such sweet flesh?
   Was ever book containing such vile matter
   So fairly bound? O that deceit should dwell
   In such a gorgeous palace!
NURSE.   There's no trust,
   No faith, no honesty in men; all perjured,
   All forsworn, all naught, all dissemblers.
   Ah, where's my man? Give me sone aqua vitae.
   These griefs, these woes, these sorrows make me old.
   Shame come to Romeo!
JULIET.   Blistered be thy tongue   90
   For such a wish! He was not born to shame.

Upon his brow shame is ashamed to sit:
   For 'tis a throne where honour may be crowned
   Sole monarch of the universal earth.
   O what a beast was I to chide at him!
NURSE. Will you speak well of him that killed your
   cousin?
JULIET. Shall I speak ill of him that is my husband?
   Ah, poor my lord, what tongue shall smooth thy
   name
   When I, thy three-hours wife, have mangled it?
   But wherefore, villain, didst thou kill my cousin? 100
   That villain cousin would have killed my husband.
   Back, foolish tears, back to your native spring!
   Your tributary drops belong to woe
   Which you, mistaking, offer up to joy.
   My husband lives, that Tybalt would have slain,
   And Tybalt's dead that would have slain my
   husband:
   All this is comfort; wherefore weep I then?
   Some word there was, worser than Tybalt's death,
   That murd'red me. I would forget it fain,
   But oh, it presses to my memory   110
   Like damnéd guilty deeds to sinners' minds—
   'Tybalt is dead and Romeo banishéd'.
   That 'banishéd', that one word 'banishéd',
   Hath slain ten thousand Tybalts. Tybalt's death
   Was woe enough if it had ended there:
   Or, if sour woe delights in fellowship
   And needly will be ranked with other griefs,
   Why followed not, when she said 'Tybalt's dead',
   'Thy father', or 'thy mother', nay, or both,
   Which modern lamentation might have moved?   120
   But, with a rearward following Tybalt's death,
   'Romeo is banishéd'! To speak that word
   Is father, mother, Tybalt, Romeo, Juliet,
   All slain, all dead: 'Romeo is banishéd'!
   There is no end, no limit, measure, bound,
   In that word's death; no words can that woe
   sound.
   Where is my father and my mother, Nurse?
NURSE. Weeping and wailing over Tybalt's corse.
   Will you go to them? I will bring you thither.
JULIET. Wash they his wounds with tears? Mine shall
   be spent,   130
   When theirs are dry, for Romeo's banishment.
   Take up those cords. Poor ropes, you are beguiled,
   Both you and I, for Romeo is exiled.
   He made you for a highway to my bed,
   But I, a maid, die maiden-widowéd.
   Come, cords; come, Nurse: I'll to my wedding bed,
   And death, not Romeo, take my maidenhead!
NURSE. Hie to your chamber. I'll find Romeo
   To comfort you: I wot well where he is.
   Hark ye, your Romeo will be here at night: 140
   I'll to him; he is hid at Lawrence' cell.
JULIET. O find him! Give this ring to my true knight
   And bid him come to take his last farewell.
                              They go

                 Scene 3: *Friar Lawrence's cell*

Enter Friar

FRIAR. Romeo, come forth; come forth, thou fearful
   man.
   Affliction is enamoured of thy parts,

And thou art wedded to calamity.

Enter Romeo

ROMEO. Father, what news? What is the prince's
    doom?
    What sorrow craves acquaintance at my hand
    That I yet know not?
FRIAR.   Too familiar
    Is my dear son with such sour company!
    I bring thee tidings of the prince's doom.
ROMEO. What less than doomsday is the prince's
    doom?
FRIAR. A gentler judgement vanished from his lips; 10
    Not body's death, but body's banishment.
ROMEO. Ha, banishment? Be merciful, say 'death':
    For exile hath more terror in his look,
    Much more than death: do not say 'banishment'.
FRIAR. Hence from Verona art thou banishèd.
    Be patient, for the world is broad and wide.
ROMEO. There is no world without Verona walls,
    But purgatory, torture, hell itself:
    Hence banishèd is banished from the world,
    And world's exile is death. Then 'banishèd'   20
    Is death mis-termed. Calling death 'banishèd',
    Thou cut'st my head off with a golden axe,
    And smilest upon the stroke that murders me.
FRIAR. O deadly sin! O rude unthankfulness!
    Thy fault our law calls death, but the kind Prince,
    Taking thy part, hath rushed aside the law,
    And turned that black word 'death' to 'banishment'.
    This is dear mercy, and thou seest it not.
ROMEO. 'Tis torture and not mercy. Heaven is here
    Where Juliet lives, and every cat and dog   30
    And little mouse, every unworthy thing,
    Live here in heaven and may look on her,
    But Romeo may not. More validity,
    More honourable state, more courtship, lives
    In carrion flies than Romeo: they may seize
    On the white wonder of dear Juliet's hand,
    And steal immortal blessing from her lips,
    Who even in pure and vestal modesty
    Still blush, as thinking their own kisses sin;
    This may flies do, when I from this must fly;   40
    And say'st thou yet that exile is not death?
    [But Romeo may not—he is banished.
    Flies may do this, but I from this must fly:
    They are free men, but I am banishèd.]
    Hadst thou no poison mixed, no sharp-ground
        knife,
    No sudden mean of death, though ne'er so mean,
    But 'banishèd' to kill me? 'Banishèd'!
    O friar, the damnèd use that word in hell:
    Howling attends it. How hast thou the heart,
    Being a divine, a ghostly confessor,   50
    A sin-absolver, and my friend professed,
    To mangle me with that word 'banishèd'?
FRIAR. Thou fond mad man, hear me a little speak.
ROMEO. O thou wilt speak again of banishment.
FRIAR. I'll give thee armour to keep off that word—
    Adversity's sweet milk, philosophy,
    To comfort thee though thou art banishèd.
ROMEO. Yet 'banishèd'? Hang up philosophy!
    Unless philosophy can make a Juliet,
    Displant a town, reverse a prince's doom,   60
    It helps not, it prevails not; talk no more.
FRIAR. O then I see that madmen have no ears.

ROMEO. How should they, when that wise men have
    no eyes?
FRIAR. Let me dispute with thee of thy estate.
ROMEO. Thou canst not speak of that thou dost not
    feel.
    Wert thou as young as I, Juliet thy love,
    An hour but married, Tybalt murderèd,
    Doting like me, and like me banishèd,
    Then mightst thou speak, then mightst thou tear
        thy hair,
    And fall upon the ground as I do now,   70
    Taking the measure of an unmade grave.
                                                Knocking without
FRIAR. Arise; one knocks. Good Romeo, hide thyself.
ROMEO. Not I, unless the breath of heartsick groans
    Mist-like infold me from the search of eyes.
                                                Knocking again
FRIAR. Hark, how they knock!—Who's there?—
    Romeo, arisè;
    Thou wilt be taken.—Stay awhile!—Stand up;
                                                Louder knocking
    Run to my study.—By and by!—God's will,
    What simpleness is this?—I come, I come?
                                                Knocking yet again
    Who knocks so hard? Whence come you? What's
    your will?
NURSE [*from without*]. Let me come in and you shall
    know my errand: 80
    I come from Lady Juliet.
FRIAR.   Welcome then.

Enter Nurse

NURSE. O holy friar, O tell me, holy friar,
    Where is my lady's lord? Where's Romeo?
FRIAR. There on the ground, with his own tears made
    drunk.
NURSE. O he is even in my mistress' case,
    Just in her case.
FRIAR.   O woeful sympathy;
    Piteous predicament!
NURSE.   Even so lies she,
    Blubbering and weeping, weeping and blubbering.
    Stand up, stand up! Stand an you be a man;
    For Juliet's sake, for her sake rise and stand: 90
    Why should you fall into so deep an O?
ROMEO [*rising*]. Nurse!
NURSE.   Ah sir, ah sir, death's the end of all.
ROMEO. Spakest thou of Juliet? How is it with her?
    Doth not she think me an old murderer,
    Now I have stained the childhood of our joy
    With blood removed but little from her own?
    Where is she? and how doth she? and what says
    My concealed lady to our cancelled love?
NURSE. O she says nothing, sir, but weeps and weeps,
    And now falls on her bed, and then starts up,   100
    And Tybalt calls, and then on Romeo cries,
    And then down falls again.
ROMEO.   As if that name,
    Shot from the deadly level of a gun,
    Did murder her, as that name's cursèd hand
    Murdered her kinsman. O tell me, friar, tell me,
    In what vile part of this anatomy
    Doth my name lodge? Tell me, that I may sack
    The hateful mansion.
                        *He offers to stab himself, and Nurse
                        snatches the dagger away*

FRIAR.   Hold thy desperate hand!
Art thou a man? Thy form cries out thou art:
Thy tears are womanish, thy wild acts denote   110
The unreasonable fury of a beast.
Unseemly woman in a seeming man,
And ill-beseeming beast in seeming both!
Thou hast amazed me. By my holy order,
I thought thy disposition better tempered.
Hast thou slain Tybalt? Wilt thou slay thyself?
And slay thy lady, that in thy life lives,
By doing damnèd hate upon thyself?
Why rail'st thou on thy birth, the heaven, and
   earth,
Since birth, and heaven, and earth, all three do meet   120
In thee at once, which thou at once wouldst lose?
Fie, fie! thou sham'st thy shape, thy love, thy wit,
Which like a usurer abound'st in all,
And usest none in that true use indeed
Which should bedeck thy shape, thy love, thy wit.
Thy noble shape is but a form of wax,
Digressing from the valour of a man;
Thy dear love sworn but hollow perjury,
Killing that love which thou hast vowed to cherish;
Thy wit, that ornament to shape and love,   130
Misshapen in the conduct of them both,
Like powder in a skilless soldier's flask
Is set afire by thine own ignorance,
And thou dismembered with thine own defence.
What, rouse thee, man! Thy Juliet is alive,
For whose dear sake thou wast but lately dead.
There art thou happy. Tybalt would kill thee,
But thou slewest Tybalt. There art thou happy.
The law that threatened death becomes thy friend,
And turns it to exile. There art thou happy too.   140
A pack of blessings light upon thy back;
Happiness courts thee in her best array;
But, like a misbehaved and sullen wench,
Thou pouts upon thy fortune and thy love.
Take heed, take heed, for such die miserable.
Go get thee to thy love, as was decreed;
Ascend her chamber; hence and comfort her.
But look thou stay not till the watch be set,
For then thou canst not pass to Mantua,
Where thou shalt live till we can find a time   150
To blaze your marriage, reconcile your friends,
Beg pardon of the prince, and call thee back
With twenty hundred thousand times more joy
Than thou wentst forth in lamentation.
Go before, Nurse. Commend me to thy lady,
And bid her hasten all the house to bed,
Which heavy sorrow makes them apt unto.
Romeo is coming.
NURSE. O Lord, I could have stayed here all the night
To hear good counsel; O what learning is!   160
My lord, I'll tell my lady you will come.
ROMEO. Do so, and bid my sweet prepare to chide.

Nurse offers to go in and turns again

NURSE. Here, sir, a ring she bid me give you, sir.
Hie you, make haste, for it grows very late.
                         She goes
ROMEO. How well my comfort is revived by this.
FRIAR. Go hence; goodnight; and here stands all your
   state:
Either be gone before the watch be set,
Or by the break of day disguised from hence.

Sojourn in Mantua. I'll find out your man,
And he shall signify from time to time   170
Every good hap to you that chances here.
Give me thy hand. 'Tis late; farewell, goodnight.
ROMEO. But that a joy past joy calls out on me,
It were a grief so brief to part with thee.
Farewell.   *They go*

Scene 4: *Capulet's house*

Enter old Capulet, his wife, and Paris

CAPULET. Things have fall'n out, sir, so unluckily
That we have had no time to move our daughter.
Look you, she loved her kinsman Tybalt dearly,
And so did I. Well, we were born to die.
'Tis very late; she'll not come down tonight.
I promise you, but for your company,
I would have been abed an hour ago.
PARIS. These times of woe afford no times to woo.
Madam, goodnight; commend me to your
   daughter.
LADY CAPULET. I will, and know her mind early
   tomorrow;   10
Tonight she's mewed up to her heaviness.

Paris offers to go; Capulet calls him again

CAPULET. Sir Paris, I will make a desperate tender
Of my child's love: I think she will be ruled
In all respects by me: nay more, I doubt it not.
Wife, go you to her ere you go to bed;
Acquaint her ear of my son Paris' love,
And bid her, mark you me, on Wednesday next—
But soft, what day is this?
PARIS.   Monday, my lord.
CAPULET. Monday, ha, ha; well, Wednesday is too
   soon;
O' Thursday let it be—O' Thursday, tell her,   20
She shall be married to this noble earl—
Will you be ready? Do you like this haste?
We'll keep no great ado; a friend or two:
For hark you, Tybalt being slain so late,
It may be thought we held him carelessly,
Being our kinsman, if we revel much:
Therefore we'll have some half a dozen friends,
And there an end. But what say you to Thursday?
PARIS. My lord, I would that Thursday were
   tomorrow.
CAPULET. Well, get you gone. O'Thursday be it then.   30
Go you to Juliet ere you go to bed;
Prepare her, wife, against this wedding day.
Farewell, my lord. Light to my chamber, ho!
Afore me, 'tis so very late, that we
May call it early by and by. Goodnight.   *They go*

Scene 5: *Juliet's bedroom: to one side the window above the Orchard; to the other a door*

Romeo and Juliet stand by the window

JULIET. Wilt thou be gone? It is not yet near day.
It was the nightingale, and not the lark,
That pierced the fearful hollow of thine ear.
Nightly she sings on yond pomegranate tree.
Believe me, love, it was the nightingale.
ROMEO. It was the lark, the herald of the morn;
No nightingale. Look, love, what envious streaks
Do lace the severing clouds in yonder east.
Night's candles are burnt out, and jocund day

Stands tiptoe on the misty mountain tops.   10
I must be gone and live, or stay and die.

JULIET. Yond light is not daylight; I know it, I:
It is some meteor that the sun exhaled
To be to thee this night a torchbearer
And light thee on thy way to Mantua.
Therefore stay yet; thou needst not to be gone.

ROMEO. Let me be ta'en, let me be put to
death;
I am content, so thou wilt have it so.
I'll say yon gray is not the morning's eye,
'Tis but the pale reflex of Cynthia's brow;   20
Nor that is not the lark whose notes do beat
The vaulty heaven so high above our heads.
I have more care to stay than will to go:
Come, death, and welcome! Juliet wills it so.
How is't, my soul? Let's talk; it is not day.

JULIET. It is, it is! Hie hence, be gone, away!
It is the lark that sings so out of tune,
Straining harsh discords and unpleasing sharps.
Some say the lark makes sweet division:
This doth not so, for she divideth us.   30
Some say the lark and loathéd toad changed eyes;
O now I would they had changed voices too,
Since arm from arm that voice doth us affray,
Hunting thee hence with hunt's-up to the day.
O now be gone! More light and light it grows.

ROMEO. More light and light, more dark and dark
our woes.

Enter Nurse hastily

NURSE. Madam!

JULIET. Nurse?

NURSE. Your lady mother is coming to your chamber.
The day is broke; be wary, look about.   *She goes*   40

JULIET. Then, window, let day in and let life out.

ROMEO. Farewell, farewell; one kiss, and I'll descend.
      He lowers the ladder and descends

JULIET. Art thou gone so, love, lord, ay husband,
friend?
I must hear from thee every day in the hour,
For in a minute there are many days.
O, by this count I shall be much in years
Ere I again behold my Romeo.

ROMEO [*from the orchard*]. Farewell!
I will omit no opportunity
That may convey my greetings, love, to thee.   50

JULIET. O, think'st thou we shall ever meet again?

ROMEO. I doubt it not; and all these woes shall serve
For sweet discourses in our times to come.

JULIET. O God, I have an ill-divining soul!
Methinks I see thee, now thou art so low,
As one dead in the bottom of a tomb.
Either my eyesight fails or thou look'st pale.

ROMEO. And trust me, love, in my eye so do you.
Dry sorrow drinks our blood. Adieu, adieu!
      He goes

JULIET. O Fortune, Fortune, all men call thee fickle;   60
If thou art fickle, what dost thou with him
That is renowned for faith? Be fickle, Fortune:
For then I hope thou wilt not keep him long,
But send him back.

LADY CAPULET [*without the door*]. Ho, daughter, are
you up?

JULIET. Who is't that calls? It is my lady mother.
Is she not down so late, or up so early?

What unaccustomed cause procures her hither?

Enter Lady Capulet

LADY CAPULET. Why, how now, Juliet?

JULIET.   Madam, I am not well.

LADY CAPULET. Evermore weeping for your cousin's
death?
What, wilt thou wash him from his grave with
tears?   70
An if thou couldst, thou couldst not make him live:
Therefore have done—some grief shows much of
love,
But much of grief shows still some want of wit.

JULIET. Yet let me weep for such a feeling loss.

LADY CAPULET. So shall you feel the loss, but not the
friend
Which you weep for.

JULIET.   Feeling so the loss,
I cannot choose but ever weep the friend.

LADY CAPULET. Well, girl, thou weep'st not so much
for his death,
As that the villain lives which slaughtered him.

JULIET. What villain, madam?

LADY CAPULET.   That same villain Romeo.   80

JULIET [*aside*]. Villain and he be many miles asunder.
[*aloud*] God pardon him; I do, with all my heart:
And yet no man like he doth grieve my heart.

LADY CAPULET. That is because the traitor murderer
lives.

JULIET. Ay, madam, from the reach of these my hands.
Would none but I might venge my cousin's death!

LADY CAPULET. We will have vengeance for it, fear
thou not.
Then weep no more. I'll send to one in Mantua,
Where that same banished runagate doth live,
Shall give him such an unaccustomed dram   90
That he shall soon keep Tybalt company;
And then I hope thou wilt be satisfied.

JULIET. Indeed I never shall be satisfied
With Romeo till I behold him—dead—
Is my poor heart so for a kinsman vexed.
Madam, if you could find out but a man
To bear a poison, I would temper it
That Romeo should upon receipt thereof
Soon sleep in quiet. O how my heart abhors
To hear him named and cannot come to him   100
To wreak the love I bore my cousin
Upon his body that hath slaughtered him.

LADY CAPULET. Find thou the means and I'll find such
a man.
But now I'll tell thee joyful tidings, girl.

JULIET. And joy comes well in such a needy time.
What are they, I beseech your ladyship?

LADY CAPULET. Well, well, thou hast a careful father,
child;
One who, to put thee from thy heaviness,
Hath sorted out a sudden day of joy
That thou expects not, nor I looked not for.   110

JULIET. Madam, in happy time! What day is that?

LADY CAPULET. Marry, my child, early next Thursday
morn
The gallant, young, and noble gentleman,
The County Paris, at Saint Peter's Church
Shall happily make thee there a joyful bride.

JULIET. Now by Saint Peter's Church, and Peter too,

He shall not make me there a joyful bride.
I wonder at this haste, that I must wed
Ere he that should be husband comes to woo.
I pray you tell my lord and father, madam,   120
I will not marry yet; and when I do, I swear
It shall be Romeo, whom you know I hate,
Rather than Paris. These are news indeed!
LADY CAPULET. Here comes your father; tell him so
    yourself,
And see how he will take it at your hands.

Enter Capulet and Nurse

CAPULET. When the sun sets, the air doth drizzle dew;
But for the sunset of my brother's son
It rains downright.
How now, a conduit, girl? What, still in tears?
Evermore showering? In one little body   130
Thou conterfeits a bark, a sea, a wind:
For still thy eyes, which I may call the sea,
Do ebb and flow with tears; the bark thy body is,
Sailing in this salt flood; the winds thy sighs,
Who raging with thy tears, and they with them,
Without a sudden calm will overset
Thy tempest-tosséd body. How now, wife?
Have you delivered to her our decree?
LADY CAPULET. Ay, sir; but she will none, she gives
    you thanks.
I would the fool were married to her grave!   140
CAPULET. Soft, take me with you, take me with you,
    wife.
How? Will she none? Doth she not give us thanks?
Is she not proud? Doth she not count her blest,
Unworthy as she is, that we have wrought
So worthy a gentleman to be her bride?
JULIET. Not proud you have, but thankful that you
    have.
Proud can I never be of what I hate,
But thankful even for hate that is meant love.
CAPULET. How how! how how, chop-logic! what is
    this?
'Proud', and 'I thank you', and 'I thank you not',   150
And yet 'not proud', mistress minion you?
Thank me no thankings nor proud me no prouds,
But fettle your fine joints 'gainst Thursday next
To go with Paris to Saint Peter's Church,
Or I will drag thee on a hurdle thither.
Out, you green-sickness carrion! out, you baggage!
You tallow-face!
LADY CAPULET. Fie, fie! what, are you mad?
JULIET [*kneeling*]. Good father, I beseech you on
    my knees,
Hear me with patience but to speak a word.
CAPULET. Hang thee, young baggage! disobedient
    wretch!   160
I tell thee what; get thee to church o' Thursday,
Or never after look me in the face.
Speak not, reply not, do not answer me!
My fingers itch. Wife, we scarce thought us
    blest
That God had lent us but this only child;
But now I see this one is one too much,
And that we have a curse in having her.
Out on her, hilding!
NURSE.   God in heaven bless her!
You are to blame, my lord, to rate her so.

CAPULET. And why, my Lady Wisdom? Hold your
    tongue,   170
Good Prudence. Smatter with your gossips, go!
NURSE. I speak no treason.
CAPULET.   O Godigoden!
NURSE. May not one speak?
CAPULET.   Peace, you mumbling fool!
Utter your gravity o'er a gossip's bowl,
For here we need it not.
LADY CAPULET.   You are too hot.
CAPULET. God's bread! it makes me mad. Day, night,
    work, play,
Alone, in company, still my care hath been
To have her matched; and having now provided
A gentleman of noble parentage,
Of fair demesnes, youthful and nobly trained,   180
Stuffed, as they say, with honourable parts,
Proportioned as one's thought would wish a man—
And then to have a wretched puling fool,
A whining mammet, in her fortune's tender,
To answer 'I'll not wed, I cannot love;
I am too young, I pray you pardon me'.
But, an you will not wed, I'll pardon you—
Graze where you will; you shall not house with me.
Look to't, think on't; I do not use to jest.
Thursday is near. Lay hand on heart; advise.   190
An you be mine, I'll give you to my friend;
An you be not, hang, beg, starve, die in the streets,
For by my soul I'll ne'er acknowledge thee,
Nor what is mine shall never do thee good:
Trust to 't; bethink you; I'll not be forsworn.
                                He goes
JULIET. Is there no pity sitting in the clouds
That sees into the bottom of my grief?
O sweet my mother, cast me not away!
Delay this marriage for a month, a week;
Or, if you do not, make the bridal bed   200
In that dim monument where Tybalt lies.
LADY CAPULET. Talk not to me, for I'll not speak a
    word;
Do as thou wilt, for I have done with thee.
                                She goes
JULIET. O God!—O nurse, how shall this be
    prevented?
My husband is on earth, my faith in heaven;
How shall that faith return again to earth,
Unless that husband send it me from heaven
By leaving earth? Comfort me, counsel me.
Alack, alack, that heaven should practise stratagems
Upon so soft a subject as myself!   210
What sayst thou? Hast thou not a word of joy?
Some comfort, nurse.
NURSE.   Faith, here it is. Romeo
Is banishéd; and all the world to nothing
That he dares ne'er come back to challenge you;
Or, if he do, it needs must be by stealth.
Then, since the case so stands as now it doth,
I think it best you married with the County.
O, he's a lovely gentleman!
Romeo's a dishclout to him. An eagle, madam,
Hath not so green, so quick, so fair an eye   220
As Paris hath. Beshrew my very heart,
I think you are happy in this second match,
For it excels your first; or, if it did not,
Your first is dead—or 'twere as good he were
As living here and you no use of him.

JULIET. Speakst thou from thy heart?

NURSE. And from my soul too; else beshrew them
  both.

JULIET. Amen!

NURSE. What?

JULIET. Well, thou hast comforted me marvellous
  much.   230
  Go in and tell my lady I am gone,
  Having displeased my father, to Lawrence' cell
  To make confession and to be absolved.

NURSE. Marry, I will; and this is wisely done.
                                  She goes

JULIET. Ancient damnation! O most wicked fiend!
  Is it more sin to wish me thus forsworn,
  Or to dispraise my lord with that same tongue
  Which she hath praised him with above compare
  So many thousand times? Go, counsellor!
  Thou and my bosom henceforth shall be twain.   240
  I'll to the friar to know his remedy.
  If all else fail, myself have power to die.   *She goes*

ACT 4

Scene 1: *Friar Lawrence's cell*

Enter Friar and County Paris

FRIAR. On Thursday, sir? The time is very short.

PARIS. My father Capulet will have it so,
  And I am nothing slow to slack his haste.

FRIAR. You say you do not know the lady's mind?
  Uneven is the course; I like it not.

PARIS. Immoderately she weeps for Tybalt's death,
  And therefore have I little talked of love,
  For Venus smiles not in a house of tears.
  Now, sir, her father counts it dangerous
  That she do give her sorrow so much sway,   10
  And in his wisdom hastes our marriage
  To stop the inundation of her tears,
  Which, too much minded by herself alone,
  May be put from her by society.
  Now do you know the reason of this haste.

FRIAR [*aside*]. I would I knew not why it should be
  slowed—
  Look, sir, here comes the lady toward my cell.

Enter Juliet

PARIS. Happily met, my lady and my wife!

JULIET. That may be, sir, when I may be a wife.

PARIS. That 'may be' must be, love, on Thursday
  next.   20

JULIET. What must be shall be.

FRIAR.   That's a certain text.

PARIS. Come you to make confession to this father?

JULIET. To answer that, I should confess to you.

PARIS. Do not deny to him that you love me.

JULIET. I will confess to you that I love him.

PARIS. So will ye, I am sure, that you love me.

JULIET. If I do so, it will be of more price,
  Being spoke behind your back, than to your face.

PARIS. Poor soul, thy face is much abused with tears.

JULIET. The tears have got small victory by that,   30
  For it was bad enough before their spite.

PARIS. Thou wrong'st it more than tears with that
  report.

JULIET. That is no slander, sir, which is a truth;
  And what I spake, I spake it to my face.

PARIS. Thy face is mine, and thou hast sland'red it.

JULIET. It may be so, for it is not mine own.—
  Are you at leisure, holy father, now,
  Or shall I come to you at evening mass?

FRIAR. My leisure serves me, pensive daughter, now.
  My lord, we must entreat the time alone.   40

PARIS. God shield I should disturb devotion!
  Juliet, on Thursday early will I rouse ye;
  Till then adieu, and keep this holy kiss.   *Goes*

JULIET. O shut the door, and, when thou hast done so,
  Come weep with me—past hope, past cure, past
  help.

FRIAR. O Juliet, I already know thy grief;
  It strains me past the compass of my wits.
  I hear thou must, and nothing may prorogue it,
  On Thursday next be married to this County.

JULIET. Tell me not, friar, that thou hearest of this,   50
  Unless thou tell me how I may prevent it.
  If in thy wisdom thou canst give no help,
  Do thou but call my resolution wise
  And with this knife I'll help it presently.
  God joined my heart and Romeo's, thou our hands;
  And ere this hand, by thee to Romeo's sealed,
  Shall be the label to another deed,
  Or my true heart with treacherous revolt
  Turn to another, this shall slay them both:
  Therefore, out of thy long-experienced time,   60
  Give me some present counsel; or, behold,
  'Twixt my extremes and me this bloody knife
  Shall play the umpire, arbitrating that
  Which the commission of thy years and art
  Could to no issue of true honour bring.
  Be not so long to speak: I long to die
  If what thou speak'st speak not of remedy.

FRIAR. Hold, daughter. I do spy a kind of hope,
  Which craves as desperate an execution
  As that is desperate which we would prevent.   70
  If, rather than to marry County Paris,
  Thou hast the strength of will to slay thyself,
  Then is it likely thou wilt undertake
  A thing like death to chide away this shame,
  That copest with death himself to scape from it;
  And, if thou darest, I'll give thee remedy.

JULIET. O bid me leap, rather than marry Paris,
  From off the battlements of any tower,
  Or walk in thievish ways, or bid me lurk
  Where serpents are; chain me with roaring bears,   80
  Or hide me nightly in a charnel house,
  O'ercovered quite with dead men's rattling bones,
  With reeky shanks and yellow chapless skulls;
  Or bid me go into a new-made grave
  And lay me with a dead man in his shroud—
  Things that, to hear them told, have made me
  tremble—
  And I will do it without fear of doubt,
  To live an unstained wife to my sweet love.

FRIAR. Hold, then. Go home, be merry, give consent
  To marry Paris. Wednesday is tomorrow.   90
  Tomorrow night look that thou lie alone;
  Let not the nurse lie with thee in thy chamber.
  Take thou this vial, being then in bed,
  And this distillèd liquor drink thou off,
  When presently through all thy veins shall run
  A cold and drowsy humour, for no pulse
  Shall keep his native progress, but surcease;
  No warmth, no breath, shall testify thou livest;

The roses in thy lips and cheeks shall fade
To wanny ashes, thy eyes' windows fall 100
Like death when he shuts up the day of life.
Each part, deprived of supple government,
Shall stiff and stark and cold appear like death;
And in this borrowed likeness of shrunk death
Thou shalt continue two and forty hours,
And then awake as from a pleasant sleep.
Now, when the bridegroom in the morning comes
To rouse thee from thy bed, there art thou dead.
Then, as the manner of our country is,
In thy best robes, uncovered on the bier, 110
Thou shalt be borne to that same ancient vault
Where all the kindred of the Capulets lie.
In the meantime, against thou shalt awake,
Shall Romeo by my letters know our drift,
And hither shall he come; and he and I
Will watch thy waking, and that very night
Shall Romeo bear thee hence to Mantua.
And this shall free thee from this present shame,
If no inconstant toy nor womanish fear
Abate thy valour in the acting it. 120
JULIET. Give me, give me! O tell not me of fear!
FRIAR. Hold, get you gone! Be strong and
    prosperous
In this resolve. I'll send a friar with speed
To Mantua with my letters to thy lord.
JULIET. Love give me strength! and strength shall help
    afford.
Farewell, dear father.   *They go*

Scene 2: *Capulet's house*

*Enter Capulet, Lady Capulet, Nurse and two or three
Servingmen*

CAPULET. So many guests invite as here are writ.
                   Servingman goes
[*to another*] Sirrah, go hire me twenty cunning
    cooks.
SERVINGMAN. You shall have none ill, sir; for I'll try
if they can lick their fingers.
CAPULET. How canst thou try them so?
SERVINGMAN. Marry, sir, 'tis an ill cook that cannot
lick his own fingers: therefore he that cannot lick
his fingers goes not with me.
CAPULET. Go, be gone.   *He goes* 10
We shall be much unfurnished for this time.
What, is my daughter gone to Friar Lawrence?
NURSE. Ay, forsooth.
CAPULET. Well, he may chance to do some good on
her.
A peevish self-willed harlotry it is.

Enter Juliet

NURSE. See where she comes from shrift with merry
look.
CAPULET. How now, my headstrong? Where have
you been gadding?
JULIET. Where I have learned me to repent the sin
Of disobedient opposition
To you and your behests, and am enjoined 20
By holy Lawrence to fall prostrate here
To beg your pardon. [*abasing herself*] Pardon, I
    beseech you!
Henceforward I am ever ruled by you.
CAPULET. Send for the County: go tell him of this.

I'll have this knot knit up tomorrow morning.
JULIET. I met the youthful lord at Lawrence' cell
And gave him what becomèd love I might,
Not stepping o'er the bounds of modesty.
CAPULET. Why, I am glad on't; this is well.
    Stand up.
This is as 't should be. Let me see, the County: 30
Ay, marry, go, I say, and fetch him hither.
Now, afore God, this reverend holy friar,
All our whole city is much bound to him.
JULIET. Nurse, will you go with me into my closet
To help me sort such needful ornaments
As you think fit to furnish me tomorrow?
LADY CAPULET. No, not till Thursday; there is
    time enough.
CAPULET. Go, nurse, go with her; we'll to church
    tomorrow.   *Nurse departs with Juliet*
LADY CAPULET. We shall be short in our provision;
'Tis now near night.
CAPULET.   Tush, I will stir about, 40
And all things shall be well, I warrant thee, wife.
Go thou to Juliet; help to deck up her.
I'll not to bed tonight. Let me alone;
I'll play the housewife for this once. What, ho!
They are all forth; well, I will walk myself
To County Paris, to prepare him
Against tomorrow. My heart is wondrous light
Since this same wayward girl is so reclaimed.
                             They go

Scene 3: *Juliet's chamber*

Enter Juliet and Nurse

JULIET. Ay, those attires are best. But, gentle nurse,
I pray thee leave me to myself tonight:
For I have need of many orisons
To move the heavens to smile upon my state,
Which well thou knowest is cross and full of sin.

Enter Lady Capulet

LADY CAPULET. What, are you busy, ho? Need you
    my help?
JULIET. No, madam, we have culled such necessaries
As are behoveful for our state tomorrow.
So please you, let me now be left alone,
And let the nurse this night sit up with you, 10
For I am sure you have your hands full all
In this so sudden business.
LADY CAPULET.   Good night.
Get thee to bed and rest, for thou hast need.
                  She departs with the Nurse
JULIET. Farewell! God knows when we shall meet
    again.
I have a faint cold fear thrills through my veins
That almost freezes up the heat of life.
I'll call them back again to comfort me.
Nurse!—What should she do here?
My dismal scene I needs must act alone.
Come, vial! 20
What if this mixture do not work at all?
Shall I be married then tomorrow morning?
No, no! This shall forbid it. Lie thou there.
                Laying down her knife
What if it be a poison which the friar
Subtly hath minist'red to have me dead,
Lest in this marriage he should be dishonoured

Because he married me before to Romeo?
I fear it is; and yet methinks it should not,
For he hath still been tried a holy man.
How if, when I am laid into the tomb,   30
I wake before the time that Romeo
Come to redeem me? There's a fearful point!
Shall I not then be stifled in the vault,
To whose foul mouth no healthsome air breathes in,
And there die strangled ere my Romeo comes?
Or, if I live, is it not very like
The horrible conceit of death and night,
Together with the terror of the place—
As in a vault, an ancient receptacle
Where for this many hundred years the bones   40
Of all my buried ancestors are packed;
Where bloody Tybalt, yet but green in earth,
Lies festering in his shroud; where, as they say,
At some hours in the night spirits resort—
Alack, alack, is it not like that I,
So early waking—what with loathsome smells,
And shrieks like mandrakes' torn out of the earth,
That living mortals, hearing them, run mad—
O, if I wake, shall I not be distraught,
Environèd with all these hideous fears,   50
And madly play with my forefathers' joints,
And pluck the mangled Tybalt from his shroud,
And, in this rage, with some great kinsman's bone,
As with a club, dash out my desp'rate brains?
O, look! Methinks I see my cousin's ghost
Seeking out Romeo, that did spit his body
Upon a rapier's point. Stay, Tybalt, stay!
Romeo, I come! this do I drink to thee.
    She falls upon her bed within the curtains

Scene 4: *Hall in Capulet's house*

Enter Lady Capulet and Nurse with herbs

LADY CAPULET. Hold, take these keys and fetch more
    spices, nurse.
NURSE. They call for dates and quinces in the pastry.

Enter old Capulet

CAPULET. Come, stir, stir, stir! The second cock hath
    crowed:
    The curfew bell hath rung, 'tis three o'clock.
    Look to the baked meats, good Angelica;
    Spare not for cost.
NURSE.   Go, you cot-quean, go,
    Get you to bed. Faith, you'll be sick tomorrow
    For this night's watching.
CAPULET. No, not a whit. What, I have watched ere
    now
    All night for lesser cause, and ne'er been sick.   10
LADY CAPULET. Ay, you have been a mouse-hunt in
    your time,
    But I will watch you from such watching now.
            She goes out with Nurse
CAPULET. A jealous hood, a jealous hood!

Enter three or four with spits and logs and baskets

                    Now, fellow, what is there?
FIRST SERVINGMAN. Things for the cook, sir; but I
    know not what.
CAPULET. Make haste, make haste. [1 *servingman goes*]
                    Sirrah, fetch drier logs.
    Call Peter; he will show thee where they are.

SECOND SERVINGMAN. I have a head, sir, that will find
    out logs
    And never trouble Peter for the matter.
CAPULET. Mass, and well said; a merry whoreson, ha!
    Thou shalt be loggerhead.   [2 *servingman goes*]
    Good faith, 'tis day!   20
    The County will be here with music straight,
    For so he said he would. [*music*] I hear him near.
    Nurse! Wife! What, ho! What, nurse, I say!

Enter Nurse

    Go waken Juliet; go and trim her up.
    I'll go and chat with Paris. Hie, make haste,
    Make haste! The bridegroom he is come already:
    Make haste, I say.   *They go*

Scene 5: *Juliet's chamber*

Enter Nurse

NURSE. Mistress! what, mistress! Juliet! Fast, I warrant
    her, she.
    Why, lamb! why, lady! Fie, you slug-a-bed!
    Why, love, I say! madam! sweetheart! why, bride!
    What, not a word? You take your pennyworths
    now!
    Sleep for a week; for the next night, I warrant,
    The County Paris hath set up his rest
    That you shall rest but little. God forgive me!
    Marry, and amen! How sound is she asleep!
    I needs must wake her. Madam, madam, madam!
    Ay, let the County take you in your bed;   10
    He'll fright you up, i'faith! Will it not be?
                    Draws back the curtains
    What, dressed, and in your clothes, and down again?
    I must needs wake you. Lady, lady, lady!
    Alas, alas! Help, help! My lady's dead!
    O weraday that ever I was born!
    Some aqua-vitae, ho! My lord! my lady!

Enter Lady Capulet

LADY CAPULET. What noise is here?
NURSE.   O lamentable day!
LADY CAPULET. What is the matter?
NURSE.   Look, look! O heavy day!
LADY CAPULET. O me, O me! My child, my only life!
    Revive, look up, or I will die with thee!   20
    Help, help! Call help.

Enter Capulet

CAPULET. For shame, bring Juliet forth; her lord is
    come.
NURSE. She's dead, deceased: she's dead, alack the day!
LADY CAPULET. Alack the day, she's dead, she's dead,
    she's dead!
CAPULET. Ha, let me see her. Out, alas! She's cold,
    Her blood is settled, and her joints are stiff;
    Life and these lips have long been separated;
    Death lies on her like an untimely frost
    Upon the sweetest flower of all the field.
NURSE. O lamentable day!
LADY CAPULET.   O woeful time!   30
CAPULET. Death, that hath ta'en her hence to make
    me wail,
    Ties up my tongue and will not let me speak.

Enter Friar and the County with Musicians

FRIAR. Come, is the bride ready to go to church?

CAPULET. Ready to go, but never to return.
O son, the night before thy wedding day
Hath Death lain with thy wife. There she lies,
Flower as she was, deflowerèd by him.
Death is my son-in-law, Death is my heir;
My daughter he hath wedded! I will die
And leave him all; life, living, all is Death's.   40

PARIS. Have I thought long to see this morning's face,
And doth it give me such a sight as this?

LADY CAPULET. Accursed, unhappy, wretched, hateful
    day!
Most miserable hour that e'er time saw
In lasting labour of his pilgrimage!
But one, poor one, one poor and loving child,
But one thing to rejoice and solace in,
And cruel Death hath catched it from my sight!

NURSE. O woe! O woeful, woeful, woeful day!
Most lamentable day, most woeful day   50
That ever, ever I did yet behold!
O day, O day, O day, O hateful day!
Never was seen so black a day as this.
O woeful day, O woeful day!

PARIS. Beguiled, divorcèd, wrongèd, spited, slain!
Most detestable Death, by thee beguiled,
By cruel, cruel thee quite overthrown!
O love! O life! Not life, but love in death!

CAPULET. Despisèd, distressèd, hated, martyred, killed!
Uncomfortable time, why cam'st thou now   60
To murder, murder our solemnity?
O child, O child! my soul, and not my child!
Dead art thou. Alack, my child is dead,
And with my child my joys are buriéd!

FRIAR. Peace, ho, for shame! Confusion's cure lives not
In these confusions. Heaven and yourself
Had part in this fair maid; now heaven hath all,
And all the better is it for the maid.
Your part in her you could not keep from death,
But heaven keeps his part in eternal life.   70
The most you sought was her promotion,
For 'twas your heaven she should be advanced;
And weep ye now, seeing she is advanced
Above the clouds as high as heaven itself?
O, in this love you love your child so ill
That you run mad, seeing that she is well.
She's not well married that lives married long,
But she's best married that dies married young.
Dry up your tears and stick your rosemary
On this fair corse, and as the custom is,   80
All in her best array, bear her to church:
For though fond nature bids us all lament,
Yet nature's tears are reason's merriment.

CAPULET. All things that we ordained festival
Turn from their office to black funeral,
Our instruments to melancholy bells,
Our wedding cheer to a sad burial feast;
Our solemn hymns to sullen dirges change,
Our bridal flowers serve for a buried corse,
And all things change them to the contrary.   90

FRIAR. Sir, go you in; and, madam, go with him;
And go, Sir Paris. Everyone prepare
To follow this fair corse unto her grave.
The heavens do lour upon you for some ill;
Move them no more by crossing their high will.
    *All but the Nurse and the Musicians go
    forth, casting rosemary upon her
    and shutting the curtains*

1 MUSICIAN. Faith, we may put up our pipes and be
    gone.

NURSE. Honest good fellows, ah, put up, put up!
For well you know this is a pitiful case.

1 MUSICIAN. Ay, by my troth, the case may be
    amended.   *Nurse goes*

Enter Peter

PETER. Musicians, O musicians, 'Heart's ease', 'Heart's   100
    ease'! O, an you will have me live, play 'Heart's
    ease'.

1 MUSICIAN. Why 'Heart's ease'?

PETER. O musicians, because my heart itself plays 'My
    heart is full of woe'. O play me some merry dump
    to comfort me.

1 MUSICIAN. Not a dump we! 'Tis no time to play now.

PETER. You will not then?

1 MUSICIAN. No.

PETER. I will then give it you soundly.   110

1 MUSICIAN. What will you give us?

PETER. No money, on my faith, but the gleek. I will
    give you the minstrel.

1 MUSICIAN. Then will I give you the serving-creature.

PETER. Then will I lay the serving-creature's dagger on
    your pate. I will carry no crotchets. I'll re you, I'll
    fa you. Do you note me?

1 MUSICIAN. An you re us and fa us, you note us.

2 MUSICIAN. Pray you put up your dagger, and put   120
    out your wit.

PETER. Then have at you with my wit! I will dry-beat
    you with an iron wit, and put up my iron dagger.
    Answer me like men:
    'When griping grief the heart doth wound,
        And doleful dumps the mind oppress,
        Then music with her silver sound—'
    Why 'silver sound'? Why 'music with her silver
    sound'? What say you, Simon Catling?

1 MUSICIAN. Marry, sir, because silver hath a sweet
    sound.   130

PETER. Pretty! What say you, Hugh Rebeck?

2 MUSICIAN. I say 'silver sound', because musicians
    sound for silver.

PETER. Pretty too! What say you, James Soundpost?

3 MUSICIAN. Faith, I know not what to say.

PETER. O, I cry you mercy! You are the singer. I will
    say for you. It is 'music with her silver sound',
    because musicians have no gold for sounding.
    'Then music with her silver sound
        With speedy help doth lend redress.'   140
                                            He goes

1 MUSICIAN. What a pestilent knave is this same!

2 MUSICIAN. Hang him, Jack! Come, we'll in here,
    tarry for the mourners, and stay dinner.
                                            They go

ACT 5
Scene 1: *Mantua. A street*

Enter Romeo

ROMEO. If I may trust the flattering truth of sleep,
My dreams presage some joyful news at hand.
My bosom's lord sits lightly in his throne,
And all this day an unaccustomed spirit
Lifts me above the ground with cheerful thoughts.
I dreamt my lady came and found me dead—

Strange dream that gives a dead man leave to
    think!—
And breathed such life with kisses in my lips
That I revived and was an emperor.
Ah me! how sweet is love itself possessed,   10
When but love's shadows are so rich in joy!

Enter Balthasar, Romeo's man, booted

News from Verona! How now, Balthasar?
Dost thou not bring me letters from the friar?
How doth my lady? Is my father well?
How fares my Juliet? That I ask again,
For nothing can be ill if she be well.
BALTHASAR. Then she is well, and nothing can be ill.
Her body sleeps in Capel's monument,
And her immortal part with angels lives.
I saw her laid low in her kindred's vault,   20
And presently took post to tell it you.
O pardon me for bringing these ill news,
Since you did leave it for my office, sir.
ROMEO. Is it e'en so? Then I defy you, stars!
Thou know'st my lodging. Get me ink and paper,
And hire post-horses; I will hence tonight.
BALTHASAR. I do beseech you, sir, have patience.
Your looks are pale and wild and do import
Some misadventure.
ROMEO.   Tush, thóu art deceived.
Leave me, and do the thing I bid thee do.   30
Hast thou no letters to me from the friar?
BALTHASAR. No, my good lord.
ROMEO.   No matter. Get thee gone,
And hire those horses; I'll be with thee straight.
                                        Balthasar goes
Well, Juliet, I will lie with thee tonight.
Let's see for means. O mischief, thou art swift
To enter in the thoughts of desperate men!
I do remember an apothecary,
And hereabouts 'a dwells, which late I noted
In tatt'red weeds, with overwhelming brows,
Culling of simples. Meagre were his looks;   40
Sharp misery had worn him to the bones:
And in his needy shop a tortoise hung,
An alligator stuffed, and other skins
Of ill-shaped fishes; and about his shelves
A beggarly account of empty boxes,
Green earthen pots, bladders, and musty seeds,
Remnants of packthread, and old cakes of roses
Were thinly scattered, to make up a show.
Noting this penury, to myself I said,
'An if a man did need a poison now,   50
Whose sale is present death in Mantua,
Here lives a caitiff wretch would sell it him'.
O, this same thought did but forerun my need,
And this same needy man must sell it me.
As I remember, this should be the house.
Being holiday, the beggar's shop is shut.
What ho, apothecary!

Enter Apothecary

APOTHECARY.   Who calls so loud?
ROMEO. Come hither, man. I see that thou art poor.
Hold, there is forty ducats; let me have
A dram of poison, such soon-speeding gear   60
As will disperse itself through all the veins
That the life-weary taker may fall dead,
And that the trunk may be discharged of breath

As violently as hasty powder fired
Doth hurry from the fatal cannon's womb.
APOTHECARY. Such mortal drugs I have, but Mantua's
    law
Is death to any he that utters them.
ROMEO. Art thou so bare and full of wretchedness
And fear'st to die? Famine is in thy cheeks,
Need and oppression starveth in thy eyes,   70
Contempt and beggary hangs upon thy back:
The world is not thy friend, nor the world's law;
The world affords no law to make thee rich:
Then be not poor, but break it and take this.
APOTHECARY. My poverty but not my will consents.
ROMEO. I pay thy poverty and not thy will.
APOTHECARY. Put this in any liquid thing you will
And drink it off, and if you had the strength
Of twenty men it would dispatch you straight.
ROMEO. There is thy gold—worse poison to men's   80
    souls,
Doing more murder in this loathsome world,
Than these poor compounds that thou mayst not
    sell.
I sell thee poison; thou hast sold me none.
Farewell; buy food and get thyself in flesh.
                                        Apothecary goes
Come, cordial and not poison, go with me
To Juliet's grave, for there must I use thee.
                                        He passes on

                    Scene 2: *Verona. Friar Lawrence's cell*

Enter Friar John

FRIAR JOHN. Holy Franciscan friar, brother, ho!

Enter Friar Lawrence

FRIAR LAWRENCE. This same should be the voice of
    Friar John.
Welcome from Mantua. What says Romeo?
Or, if his mind be writ, give me his letter.
FRIAR JOHN. Going to find a barefoot brother out,
One of our order, to associate me,
Here in this city visiting the sick,
And finding him, the searchers of the town,
Suspecting that we both were in a house
Where the infectious pestilence did reign,   10
Sealed up the doors, and would not let us forth,
So that my speed to Mantua there was stayed.
FRIAR LAWRENCE. Who bare my letter then to Romeo?
FRIAR JOHN. I could not send it—here it is again—
Nor get a messenger to bring it thee,
So fearful were they of infection.
FRIAR LAWRENCE. Unhappy fortune! By my
    brotherhood,
The letter was not nice, but full of charge,
Of dear import; and the neglecting it
May do much danger. Friar John, go hence,   20
Get me an iron crow and bring it straight
Unto my cell.
FRIAR JOHN. Brother, I'll go and bring it thee. *Goes*
FRIAR LAWRENCE. Now must I to the monument alone.
Within this three hours will fair Juliet wake.
She will beshrew me much that Romeo
Hath had no notice of these accidents;
But I will write again to Mantua,
And keep her at my cell till Romeo come.

Poor living corse, closed in a dead man's tomb!   30
                                          He goes

Scene 3: *Verona. A churchyard; in it the monument of*
                  the Capulets

Enter Paris and his Page, bearing flowers and a torch

PARIS. Give me thy torch, boy. Hence, and stand aloof.
  Yet put it out, for I would not be seen.
  Under yond yew-trees lay thee all along,
  Holding thine ear close to the hollow ground;
  So shall no foot upon the churchyard tread,
  Being loose, unfirm with digging up of graves,
  But thou shalt hear it. Whistle then to me
  As signal that thou hear'st some thing approach.
  Give me those flowers. Do as I bid thee; go.
PAGE [*aside*]. I am almost afraid to stand alone   10
  Here in the churchyard, yet I will adventure.
                                          Retires
PARIS. Sweet flower, with flowers thy bridal bed
    I strew—
  O woe, thy canopy is dust and stones!—
  Which with sweet water nightly I will dew,
  Or, wanting that, with tears distilled by moans.
  The obsequies that I for thee will keep
  Nightly shall be to strew thy grave and weep.
                                    Page whistles
  The boy gives warning something doth approach.
  What cursèd foot wanders this way tonight
  To cross my obsequies and true love's rite?   20
  What, with a torch? Muffle me, night, awhile.
                                          Retires

Enter Romeo and Balthasar, with a torch, a mattock,
and a crow of iron

ROMEO. Give me that mattock and the wrenching
    iron.
  Hold, take this letter. Early in the morning
  See thou deliver it to my lord and father.
  Give me the light. Upon thy life I charge thee,
  Whate'er thou hear'st or seest, stand all aloof
  And do not interrupt me in my course.
  Why I descend into this bed of death
  Is partly to behold my lady's face,
  But chiefly to take thence from her dead finger   30
  A precious ring, a ring that I must use
  In dear employment. Therefore hence, be gone.
  But if thou, jealous, dost return to pry
  In what I farther shall intend to do,
  By heaven, I will tear thee joint by joint
  And strew this hungry churchyard with thy limbs.
  The time and my intents are savage-wild,
  More fierce and more inexorable far
  Than empty tigers or the roaring sea.
BALTHASAR. I will be gone, sir, and not trouble ye.   40
ROMEO. So shalt thou show me friendship. Take thou
    that;
  Live and be prosperous; and farewell, good fellow.
BALTHASAR. [*aside*]. For all this same, I'll hide me
    hereabout.
  His looks I fear, and his intents I doubt.   *Retires*
ROMEO. Thou detestable maw, thou womb of death,
  Gorged with the dearest morsel of the earth,
  Thus I enforce thy rotten jaws to open,
                              Begins to open the tomb
  And in despite I'll cram thee with more food.

PARIS. This is that banished haughty Montague
  That murd'red my love's cousin—with which grief   50
  It is supposèd the fair creature died—
  And here is come to do some villainous shame
  To the dead bodies: I will apprehend him.—
                                    Comes forward
  Stop thy unhallowed toil, vile Montague!
  Can vengeance be pursued further than death?
  Condemnèd villain, I do apprehend thee.
  Obey, and go with me, for thou must die.
ROMEO. I must indeed, and therefore came I hither.
  Good gentle youth, tempt not a desp'rate man.
  Fly hence and leave me. Think upon these gone;   60
  Let them affright thee. I beseech thee, youth,
  Put not another sin upon my head
  By urging me to fury. O be gone!
  By heaven, I love thee better than myself,
  For I come hither armed against myself.
  Stay not, be gone. Live, and hereafter say
  A madman's mercy bid thee run away.
PARIS. I do defy thy conjuration,
  And apprehend thee for a felon here.
ROMEO. Wilt thou provoke me? Then have at
    thee, boy!   *They fight*   70
PAGE. O Lord, they fight! I will go call the watch.
                                          Goes
PARIS. O, I am slain! [*falls*] If thou be merciful,
  Open the tomb, lay me with Juliet.   *Dies*
ROMEO. In faith, I will. Let me peruse this face.
  Mercutio's kinsman, noble County Paris!
  What said my man when my betossèd soul
  Did not attend him as we rode? I think
  He told me Paris should have married Juliet.
  Said he not so? Or did I dream it so?
  Or am I mad, hearing him talk of Juliet,   80
  To think it was so? O give me thy hand,
  One writ with me in sour misfortune's book!
  I'll bury thee in a triumphant grave.
  A grave? O no!—a lanthorn, slaught'red youth:
  For here lies Juliet, and her beauty makes
  This vault a feasting presence full of light.
  Dead, lie thou there, by a dead man interred.
                              Lays Paris within the tomb
  How oft when men are at the point of death
  Have they been merry, which their keepers call
  A light'ning before death! O how may I   90
  Call this a light'ning? O my love, my wife!
  Death, that hath sucked the honey of thy breath,
  Hath had no power yet upon thy beauty.
  Thou art not conquered; beauty's ensign yet
  Is crimson in thy lips and in thy cheeks,
  And death's pale flag is not advancèd there.
  Tybalt, liest thou there in thy bloody sheet?
  O, what more favour can I do to thee
  Than with that hand that cut thy youth in twain
  To sunder his that was thine enemy?   100
  Forgive me, cousin! Ah, dear Juliet,
  Why art thou yet so fair? Shall I believe
  That unsubstantial Death is amorous,
  And that the lean abhorrèd monster keeps
  Thee here in dark to be his paramour?
  For fear of that I still will stay with thee,
  And never from this palace of dim night
  Depart again. Here, here will I remain
  With worms that are thy chambermaids. O, here
  Will I set up my everlasting rest,   110

And shake the yoke of inauspicious stars
From this world-wearied flesh. Eyes, look your last!
Arms, take your last embrace! and lips, O you,
The doors of breath, seal with a righteous kiss
A dateless bargain to engrossing Death!
Come, bitter conduct; come, unsavoury guide!
Thou desperate pilot, now at once run on
The dashing rocks thy seasick weary bark!
Here's to my love! [*drinks*] O true apothecary!
Thy drugs are quick. Thus with a kiss I die.   *Dies* 120

Enter Friar Lawrence with lanthorn, crow, and spade

FRIAR. Saint Francis be my speed! how oft tonight
  Have my old feet stumbled at graves! Who's there?
BALTHASAR. Here's one, a friend, and one that knows
  you well.
FRIAR. Bliss be upon you! Tell me, good my friend,
  What torch is yond that vainly lends his light
  To grubs and eyeless skulls? As I discern,
  It burneth in the Capels' monument.
BALTHASAR. It doth so, holy sir; and there's my master,
  One that you love.
FRIAR.   Who is it?
BALTHASAR.   Romeo.
FRIAR. How long hath he been there?
BALTHASAR.   Full half an hour. 130
FRIAR. Go with me to the vault.
BALTHASAR.   I dare not, sir.
  My master knows not but I am gone hence,
  And fearfully did menace me with death
  If I did stay to look on his intents.
FRIAR. Stay then; I'll go alone. Fear comes upon me.
  O, much I fear some ill unthrifty things.
BALTHASAR. As I did sleep under this yew-tree here,
  I dreamt my master and another fought,
  And that my master slew him.
FRIAR.   Romeo! *Advances*
  Alack, alack, what blood is this which stains   140
  The stony entrance of this sepulchre?
  What mean these masterless and gory swords
  To lie discoloured by this place of peace?
                        Enters the tomb
  Romeo! O, pale! Who else? What, Paris too?
  And steeped in blood? Ah, what an unkind hour
  Is guilty of this lamentable chance!
       The lady stirs.   *Juliet wakes*
JULIET. O comfortable friar, where is my lord?
  I do remember well where I should be,
  And there I am. Where is my Romeo?   150
                       Voices afar off
FRIAR. I hear some noise, lady. Come from that nest
  Of death, contagion, and unnatural sleep.
  A greater power than we can contradict
  Hath thwarted our intents. Come, come away.
  Thy husband in thy bosom there lies dead:
  And Paris too. Come, I'll dispose of thee
  Among a sisterhood of holy nuns.
  Stay not to question, for the watch is coming.
  Come, go, good Juliet; I dare no longer stay.
JULIET. Go, get thee hence, for I will not away.   160
                        He goes
  What's here? A cup, closed in my true love's hand?
  Poison, I see, hath been his timeless end,
  O churl! drunk all, and left no friendly drop
  To help me after? I will kiss thy lips.
  Haply some poison yet doth hang on them

To make me die with a restorative.   *Kisses him*
  Thy lips are warm!

The Page of Paris enters the graveyard with Watch

1 WATCHMAN. Lead, boy. Which way?
JULIET. Yea, noise? Then I'll be brief. O happy dagger,
                  Snatching Romeo's dagger
  This is thy sheath [*stabs herself*]; there rest, and let
  me die.   *Falls on Romeo's body and dies* 170
PAGE. This is the place, there where the torch doth
  burn.
1 WATCHMAN. The ground is bloody. Search about
  the churchyard.
  Go, some of you; whoe'er you find attach.
                   Some Watchmen depart
  Pitiful sight! Here lies the County slain:
  And Juliet bleeding, warm and newly dead,
  Who here hath lain this two days buried.
  Go tell the Prince; run to the Capulets;
  Raise up the Montagues; some others search.
                   Other Watchmen depart
  We see the ground whereon these woes do lie,
  But the true ground of all these piteous woes   180
  We cannot without circumstance descry.

Re-enter some of the Watch, with Balthasar

2 WATCHMAN. Here's Romeo's man; we found him in
  the churchyard.
1 WATCHMAN. Hold him in safety till the Prince come
  hither.

Re-enter another Watchman, with Friar Lawrence

3 WATCHMAN. Here is a friar that trembles, sighs, and
  weeps.
  We took this mattock and this spade from him
  As he was coming from this churchyard's side.
1 WATCHMAN. A great suspicion! Stay the friar too.

Enter the Prince and attendants

PRINCE. What misadventure is so early up,
  That calls our person from our morning rest?

Enter Capulet and his wife

CAPULET. What should it be that is so shrieked abroad? 190
LADY CAPULET. O, the people in the street cry
  'Romeo',
  Some 'Juliet', and some 'Paris', and all run
  With open outcry toward our monument.
PRINCE. What fear is this which startles in our ears?
1 WATCHMAN. Sovereign, here lies the County Paris
  slain;
  And Romeo dead; and Juliet, dead before,
  Warm and new killed.
PRINCE. Search, seek, and know how this foul murder
  comes.
1 WATCHMAN. Here is a friar, and slaughtered
  Romeo's man,
  With instruments upon them fit to open   200
  These dead men's tombs.
CAPULET. O heaven! O wife, look how our daughter
  bleeds!
  This dagger hath mista'en, for, lo, his house
  Is empty on the back of Montague,
  And it mis-sheathed in my daughter's bosom.
LADY CAPULET. O me! this sight of death is as a bell
  That warns my old age to a sepulchre.

Enter Montague

PRINCE. Come Montague; for thou art early up
To see thy son and heir more early down.
MONTAGUE. Alas, my liege, my wife is dead tonight; 210
Grief of my son's exile hath stopped her breath.
What further woe conspires against mine age?
PRINCE. Look and thou shalt see.
MONTAGUE. O thou untaught! what manners is in this,
To press before thy father to a grave?
PRINCE. Seal up the mouth of outrage for a while,
Till we can clear these ambiguities,
And know their spring, their head, their true
    descent;
And then will I be general of your woes,
And lead you even to death. Meantime forbear, 220
And let mischance be slave to patience.
Bring forth the parties of suspicion.

Watchmen bring forward Friar Lawrence and Balthasar

FRIAR. I am the greatest; able to do least,
Yet most suspected, as the time and place
Doth make against me, of this direful murder:
And here I stand both to impeach and purge
Myself condemnèd and myself excused.
PRINCE. Then say at once what thou dost know in this.
FRIAR. I will be brief, for my short date of breath
Is not so long as is a tedious tale. 230
Romeo there dead was husband to that Juliet;
And she, there dead, that Romeo's faithful wife.
I married them; and their stol'n marriage day
Was Tybalt's doomsday, whose untimely death
Banished the new-made bridegroom from this city;
For whom, and not for Tybalt, Juliet pined.
You, to remove that siege of grief from her,
Betrothed and would have married her perforce
To County Paris. Then comes she to me,
And with wild looks bid me devise some mean 240
To rid her from this second marriage,
Or in my cell there would she kill herself.
Then gave I her (so tutored by my art)
A sleeping potion; which so took effect
As I intended, for it wrought on her
The form of death. Meantime I writ to Romeo
That he should hither come as this dire night
To help to take her from her borrowed grave,
Being the time the potion's force should cease.
But he which bore my letter, Friar John, 250
Was stayed by accident, and yesternight
Returned my letter back. Then all alone
At the prefixèd hour of her waking
Came I to take her from her kindred's vault,
Meaning to keep her closely at my cell
Till I conveniently could send to Romeo.
But when I came, some minute ere the time
Of her awakening, here untimely lay

The noble Paris and true Romeo dead.
She wakes; and I entreated her come forth, 260
And bear this work of heaven with patience;
But then a noise did scare me from the tomb,
And she, too desperate, would not go with me,
But, as it seems, did violence on herself.
All this I know; and to the marriage
Her nurse is privy: and if aught in this
Miscarried by my fault, let my old life
Be sacrificed, some hour before his time,
Unto the rigour of severest law.
PRINCE. We still have known thee for a holy man. 270
Where's Romeo's man? What can he say to this?
BALTHASAR. I brought my master news of Juliet's
    death,
And then in post he came from Mantua
To this same place, to this same monument.
This letter he early bid me give his father,
And threat'ned me with death, going in the vault,
If I departed not and left him there.
PRINCE. Give me the letter; I will look on it.
Where is the County's page, that raised the watch?
    Page comes forward
Sirrah, what made your master in this place? 280
PAGE. He came with flowers to strew his lady's grave,
And bid me stand aloof, and so I did.
Anon comes one with light to ope the tomb,
And by and by my master drew on him,
And then I ran away to call the watch.
PRINCE. This letter doth make good the friar's words,
Their course of love, the tidings of her death;
And here he writes that he did buy a poison
Of a poor pothecary, and therewithal
Came to this vault to die, and lie with Juliet. 290
Where be these enemies? Capulet, Montague?
See what a scourge is laid upon your hate,
That heaven finds means to kill your joys with love!
And I, for winking at your discords too,
Have lost a brace of kinsmen. All are punished.
CAPULET. O brother Montague, give me thy hand.
This is my daughter's jointure, for no more
Can I demand.
MONTAGUE.   But I can give thee more;
For I will raise her statue in pure gold,
That, whiles Verona by that name is known, 300
There shall no figure at such rate be set
As that of true and faithful Juliet.
CAPULET. As rich shall Romeo's by his lady's lie—
Poor sacrifices of our enmity!
PRINCE. A glooming peace this morning with it
    brings;
The sun for sorrow will not show his head.
Go hence, to have more talk of these sad things.
Some shall be pardoned, and some punishèd;
For never was a story of more woe
Than this of Juliet and her Romeo.   *They go* 310

The Life of
Timon of Athens

The scene: Athens and neighbourhood

CHARACTERS IN THE PLAY

TIMON, *a noble Athenian*
LUCIUS
LUCULLUS   } *flattering lords*
SEMPRONIUS
VENTIDIUS, *one of Timon's false friends*
ALCIBIADES, *an Athenian captain*
APEMANTUS, *a churlish philosopher*
FLAVIUS, *steward to Timon*
Poet, Painter, Jeweller, and Merchant
An old Athenian
FLAMINIUS
LUCILIUS   } *servants to Timon*
SERVILIUS

CAPHIS
PHILOTUS
TITUS   } *servants to Timon's creditors and to the*
HORTENSIUS   *Lords*
And others
A Page.   A Fool.   Three Strangers
PHRYNIA
TIMANDRA   } *mistresses to Alcibiades*
Cupid and Amazons in the masque
Other Lords, Senators, Officers, Banditti, and Attendants

The Life of Timon of Athens

ACT 1

Scene 1: *Athens. A hall in Timon's house*

Enter Poet, Painter, Jeweller, Merchant, and others, at several doors

POET. Good day, sir.
PAINTER.   I am glad you're well.
POET. I have not seen you long; how goes the world?
PAINTER. It wears, sir, as it grows.
POET.   Ay, that's well known.
  But what particular rarity? what strange,
  Which manifold record not matches? See,
  Magic of bounty, all these spirits thy power
  Hath conjured to attend! I know the merchant.
PAINTER. I know them both; th'other's a jeweller.
MERCHANT. O, 'tis a worthy lord!
JEWELLER.   Nay, that's most fixed.
MERCHANT. A most incomparable man, breathed, as it
  were,   10
  To an untirable and continuate goodness.
  He passes.
JEWELLER. I have a jewel here.
MERCHANT. O, pray, let's see't. For the Lord Timon,
  sir?
JEWELLER. If he will touch the estimate. But for that—
POET [*reciting to himself*]. 'When we for recompense
  have praised the vile,
  It stains the glory in that happy verse
  Which aptly sings the good.'
MERCHANT. 'Tis a good form.
JEWELLER. And rich. Here is a water, look ye.   20
PAINTER. You are rapt, sir, in some work, some
  dedication
  To the great lord.
POET.   A thing slipped idly from me.
  Our poesy is as a gum which oozes
  From whence 'tis nourished. The fire i'th'flint
  Shows not till it be struck: our gentle flame
  Provokes itself, and like the current flies
  Each bound it chafes. What have you there?
PAINTER. A picture, sir. When comes your book forth?
POET. Upon the heels of my presentment, sir.
  Let's see your piece.   30
PAINTER. 'Tis a good piece.
POET. So 'tis; this comes off well and excellent.
PAINTER. Indifferent.
POET.   Admirable. How this grace
  Speaks his own standing! what a mental power
  This eye shoots forth! how big imagination
  Moves in this lip! to th'dumbness of the gesture
  One might interpret.
PAINTER. It is a pretty mocking of the life.
  Here is a touch; is't good?
POET.   I will say of it,
  It tutors nature; artificial strife
  Lives in these touches, livelier than life.   40

Enter certain Senators, and pass by

PAINTER. How this lord is followed!
POET. The senators of Athens—happy man!

PAINTER. Look, moe!
POET. You see this confluence, this great flood of
  visitors:
  I have in this rough work shaped out a man
  Whom this beneath world doth embrace and hug
  With amplest entertainment. My free drift
  Halts not particularly, but moves itself
  In a wide sea of wax; no levelled malice   50
  Infects one comma in the course I hold,
  But flies an eagle flight, bold and forth on,
  Leaving no tract behind.
PAINTER. How shall I understand you?
POET.   I will unbolt to you.
  You see how all conditions, how all minds,
  As well of glib and slipp'ry creatures as
  Of grave and austere quality, tender down
  Their services to Lord Timon. His large fortune,
  Upon his good and gracious nature hanging,
  Subdues and properties to his love and tendance   60
  All sorts of hearts; yea, from the glass-faced flatterer
  To Apemantus, that few things loves better
  Than to abhor himself; even he drops down
  The knee before him, and returns in peace
  Most rich in Timon's nod.
PAINTER.   I saw them speak together.
POET. Sir, I have upon a high and pleasant hill
  Feigned Fortune to be throned. The base
  o'th'mount
  Is ranked with all deserts, all kind of natures,
  That labour on the bosom of this sphere
  To propagate their states; amongst them all   70
  Whose eyes are on this sovereign lady fixed
  One do I personate of Lord Timon's frame,
  Whom Fortune with her ivory hand wafts to her,
  Whose present grace to present slaves and servants
  Translates his rivals.
PAINTER.   'Tis conceived to scope.
  This throne, this Fortune, and this hill, methinks,
  With one man beckoned from the rest below,
  Bowing his head against the steepy mount
  To climb his happiness, would be well expressed
  In our condition.
POET.   Nay, sir, but hear me on.   80
  All those which were his fellows but of late,
  Some better than his value, on the moment
  Follow his strides, his lobbies fill with tendance,
  Rain sacrificial whisperings in his ear,
  Make sacred even his stirrup, and through him
  Drink the free air.
PAINTER.   Ay, marry, what of these?
POET. When Fortune in her shift and change of mood
  Spurns down her late beloved, all his dependants,
  Which laboured after him to the mountain's top
  Even on their knees and hands, let him slip down,   90
  Not one accompanying his declining foot.
PAINTER. 'Tis common:
  A thousand moral paintings I can show,
  That shall demonstrate these quick blows of
  Fortune's
  More pregnantly than words. Yet you do well

To show Lord Timon that mean eyes have seen
The foot above the head.

*Trumpets sound. Enter Lord Timon, addressing himself
courteously to every suitor; a Messenger from Ventidius
talking with him; Lucilius and other servants following*

TIMON.   Imprisoned is he, say you?
MESSENGER. Ay, my good lord; five talents is his debt,
His means most short, his creditors most strait.
Your honourable letter he desires   100
To those have shut him up, which failing
Periods his comfort.
TIMON.   Noble Ventidius! Well.
I am not of that feather to shake off
My friend when he must need me. I do know him
A gentleman that well deserves a help,
Which he shall have. I'll pay the debt and free him.
MESSENGER. Your lordship ever binds him.
TIMON. Commend me to him; I will send his ransom;
And, being enfranchiséd, bid him come to me.
'Tis not enough to help the feeble up,   110
But to support him after. Fare you well.
MESSENGER. All happiness to your honour!   *Goes*

Enter an old Athenian

ATHENIAN. Lord Timon, hear me speak.
TIMON.   Freely, good father.
ATHENIAN. Thou hast a servant named Lucilius.
TIMON. I have so; what of him?
ATHENIAN. Most noble Timon, call the man before
thee.
TIMON. Attends he here, or no? Lucilius!
LUCILIUS. Here, at your lordship's service.
ATHENIAN. This fellow here, Lord Timon, this thy
creature,
By night frequents my house. I am a man   120
That from my first have been inclined to thrift,
And my estate deserves an heir more raised
Than one which holds a trencher.
TIMON.   Well; what further?
ATHENIAN. One only daughter have I, no kin else,
On whom I may confer what I have got.
The maid is fair, o'th'youngest for a bride,
And I have bred her at my dearest cost
In qualities of the best. This man of thine
Attempts her love; I prithee, noble lord,
Join with me to forbid him her resort;   130
Myself have spoke in vain.
TIMON.   The man is honest.
ATHENIAN. Therefore he will be, Timon.
His honesty rewards him in itself;
It must not bear my daughter.
TIMON.   Does she love him?
ATHENIAN. She is young and apt.
Our own precedent passions do instruct us
What levity's in youth.
TIMON [*to Lucilius*].   Love you the maid?
LUCILIUS. Ay, my good lord, and she accepts of it.
ATHENIAN. If in her marriage my consent be missing,
I call the gods to witness, I will choose   140
Mine heir from forth the beggars of the world,
And dispossess her all.
TIMON.   How shall she be endowéd,
If she be mated with an equal husband?
ATHENIAN. Three talents on the present; in future, all.
TIMON. This gentleman of mine hath served me long;

To build his fortune I will strain a little,
For 'tis a bond in men. Give him thy daughter:
What you bestow, in him I'll counterpoise,
And make him weigh with her.
ATHENIAN.   Most noble lord,
Pawn me to this your honour, she is his.   150
TIMON. My hand to thee; mine honour on my
promise.
LUCILIUS. Humbly I thank your lordship; never may
That state or fortune fall into my keeping
Which is not owed to you!
                              Lucilius and Old Athenian go
POET. Vouchsafe my labour, and long live your
lordship!
TIMON. I thank you; you shall hear from me anon.
Go not away. What have you there, my friend?
PAINTER. A piece of painting, which I do beseech
Your lordship to accept.
TIMON.   Painting is welcome.
The painting is almost the natural man;   160
For since dishonour traffics with man's nature,
He is but outside; these pencilled figures are
Even such as they give out. I like your work,
And you shall find I like it; wait attendance
Till you hear further from me.
PAINTER.   The gods preserve ye!
TIMON. Well fare you, gentleman. Give me your
hand;
We must needs dine together. Sir, your jewel
Hath sufferéd under praise.
JEWELLER.   What, my lord, dispraise?
TIMON. A mere satiety of commendations.
If I should pay you for't as 'tis extolled,   170
It would unclew me quite.
JEWELLER.   My lord, 'tis rated
As those which sell would give; but you well know,
Things of like value, differing in the owners,
Are prizéd by their masters. Believe't, dear lord,
You mend the jewel by the wearing it.
TIMON. Well mocked.
MERCHANT. No, my good lord; he speaks the common
tongue
Which all men speak with him.
TIMON. Look who comes here; will you be chid?

Enter Apemantus

JEWELLER. We'll bear, with your lordship.
MERCHANT.   He'll spare none.   180
TIMON. Good morrow to thee, gentle Apemantus.
APEMANTUS. Till I be gentle, stay thou for thy good
morrow;
When thou art Timon's dog, and these knaves
honest.
TIMON. Why dost thou call them knaves? thou
know'st them not.
APEMANTUS. Are they not Athenians?
TIMON. Yes.
APEMANTUS. Then I repent not.
JEWELLER. You know me, Apemantus?
APEMANTUS. Thou know'st I do; I called thee by thy
name.
TIMON. Thou art proud, Apemantus.   190
APEMANTUS. Of nothing so much as that I am not like
Timon.
TIMON. Whither art going?

APEMANTUS. To knock out an honest Athenian's brains.

TIMON. That's a deed thou'lt die for.

APEMANTUS. Right, if doing nothing be death by th'law.

TIMON. How lik'st thou this picture, Apemantus?

APEMANTUS. The best, for the innocence.

TIMON. Wrought he not well that painted it?

APEMANTUS. He wrought better that made the painter; and yet he's but a filthy piece of work. 200

PAINTER. You're a dog.

APEMANTUS. Thy mother's of my generation; what's she, if I be a dog?

TIMON. Wilt dine with me, Apemantus?

APEMANTUS. No; I eat not lords.

TIMON. An thou shouldst, thou'ldst anger ladies.

APEMANTUS. O, they eat lords; so they come by great bellies.

TIMON. That's a lascivious apprehension.

APEMANTUS. So thou apprehend'st it; take it for thy 210 labour.

TIMON. How dost thou like this jewel, Apemantus?

APEMANTUS. Not so well as plain-dealing, which will not cost a man a doit.

TIMON. What dost thou think 'tis worth?

APEMANTUS. Not worth my thinking. How now, poet!

POET. How now, philosopher!

APEMANTUS. Thou liest.

POET. Art not one? 220

APEMANTUS. Yes.

POET. Then I lie not.

APEMANTUS. Art not a poet?

POET. Yes.

APEMANTUS. Then thou liest. Look in thy last work, where thou hast feigned him a worthy fellow.

POET. That's not feigned; he is so.

APEMANTUS. Yes, he is worthy of thee, and to pay thee for thy labour. He that loves to be flattered is worthy o'th'flatterer. Heavens, that I were a lord! 230

TIMON. What wouldst do then, Apemantus?

APEMANTUS. E'en as Apemantus does now: hate a lord with my heart.

TIMON. What, thyself?

APEMANTUS. Ay.

TIMON. Wherefore?

APEMANTUS. That I had no angry wit to be a lord. Art not thou a merchant?

MERCHANT. Ay, Apemantus.

APEMANTUS. Traffic confound thee, if the gods will 240 not!

MERCHANT. If traffic do it, the gods do it.

APEMANTUS. Traffic's thy god, and thy god confound thee!

Trumpet sounds. Enter a Messenger

TIMON. What trumpet's that?

MESSENGER. 'Tis Alcibiades, and some twenty horse, All of companionship.

TIMON. Pray, entertain them; give them guide to us.
Some attendants go
You must needs dine with me. Go not you hence
Till I have thanked you. When dinner's done,
Show me this piece. I am joyful of your sights. 250

Enter Alcibiades, with the rest

Most welcome, sir!

APEMANTUS. So, so, there!
Achës contract and starve your supple joints!
That there should be small love amongst these sweet knaves,
And all this courtesy! The strain of man's bred out
Into baboon and monkey.

ALCIBIADES. Sir, you have saved my longing, and I feed
Most hungerly on your sight.

TIMON. Right welcome, sir!
Ere we depart, we'll share a bounteous time
In different pleasures. Pray you, let us in.
All but Apemantus go

Enter two Lords

1 LORD. What time o' day is't, Apemantus? 260

APEMANTUS. Time to be honest.

1 LORD. That time serves still.

APEMANTUS. The more accursèd thou that still omit'st it.

2 LORD. Thou art going to Lord Timon's feast?

APEMANTUS. Ay, to see meat fill knaves and wine heat fools.

2 LORD. Fare thee well, fare thee well.

APEMANTUS. Thou art a fool to bid me farewell twice.

2 LORD. Why, Apemantus?

APEMANTUS. Shouldst have kept one to thyself, for I mean to give thee none. 270

1 LORD. Hang thyself.

APEMANTUS. No, I will do nothing at thy bidding; make thy requests to thy friend.

2 LORD. Away, unpeaceable dog, or I'll spurn thee hence.

APEMANTUS. I will fly, like a dog, the heels o'th'ass.
Goes

1 LORD. He's opposite to humanity.
Come, shall we in,
And taste Lord Timon's bounty? he outgoes
The very heart of kindness. 280

2 LORD. He pours it out. Plutus, the god of gold,
Is but his steward; no meed, but he repays
Sevenfold above itself; no gift to him
But breeds the giver a return exceeding
All use of quittance.

1 LORD. The noblest mind he carries
That ever governed man.

2 LORD. Long may he live in fortunes! Shall we in?

1 LORD. I'll keep you company. *They go*

Scene 2: *A banqueting-room in Timon's house*

*Hautboys playing loud music. A great banquet served in;
Flavius and others attending; and then enter Lord Timon,
Alcibiades, Lords, Senators, and Ventidius. Then comes,
dropping after all, Apemantus, discontentedly, like himself*

VENTIDIUS. Most honourèd Timon,
It hath pleased the gods to remember my father's age,
And call him to long peace.
He is gone happy, and has left me rich.
Then, as in grateful virtue I am bound
To your free heart, I do return those talents,
Doubled with thanks and service, from whose help
I derived liberty.

TIMON. O, by no means,

Honest Ventidius; you mistake my love;
I gave it freely ever, and there's none   10
Can truly say he gives, if he receives.
If our betters play at that game, we must not dare
To imitate them; faults that are rich are fair.
VENTIDIUS. A noble spirit!
TIMON. Nay, my lords, ceremony was but devised at
first
To set a gloss on faint deeds, hollow welcomes,
Recanting goodness, sorry ere 'tis shown;
But where there is true friendship, there needs none.
Pray, sit; more welcome are ye to my fortunes
Than my fortunes to me.   *They sit* 20
1 LORD. My lord, we always have confessed it.
APEMANTUS. Ho, ho, confessed it? hanged it, have you
not?
TIMON. O, Apemantus, you are welcome.
APEMANTUS.   No;
You shall not make me welcome.
I come to have thee thrust me out of doors.
TIMON. Fie, thou'rt a churl; ye've got a humour there
Does not become a man; 'tis much to blame.
They say, my lords, 'ira furor brevis est'; but yond
man is ever angry. Go, let him have a table by
himself; for he does neither affect company, nor is 30
he fit for't indeed.
APEMANTUS. Let me stay at thine apperil, Timon.
I come to observe, I give thee warning on't.
TIMON. I take no heed of thee; thou'rt an Athenian,
therefore welcome; I myself would have no power
—prithee let my meat make thee silent.
APEMANTUS. I scorn thy meat; 'twould choke me, for
I should ne'er flatter thee. O you gods, what a
number of men eats Timon, and he sees 'em not! It
grieves me to see so many dip their meat in one 40
man's blood; and all the madness is, he cheers them
up too.
I wonder men dare trust themselves with men.
Methinks they should invite them without knives:
Good for their meat, and safer for their lives.
There's much example for't; the fellow that sits next
him, now parts bread with him, pledges the breath
of him in a divided draught, is the readiest man to
kill him:'t has been proved. If I were a huge man, I
should fear to drink at meals,   50
Lest they should spy my windpipe's dangerous
notes.
Great men should drink with harness on their
throats.
TIMON. My lord, in heart; and let the health go round.
2 LORD. Let it flow this way, my good lord.
APEMANTUS. Flow this way? A brave fellow. He keeps
his tides well. Those healths will make thee and thy
state look ill, Timon.
Here's that which is too weak to be a sinner,
Honest water, which ne'er left man i'th'mire.
This and my food are equals; there's no odds.   60
Feasts are too proud to give thanks to the gods.
        APEMANTUS' GRACE
    Immortal gods, I crave no pelf;
    I pray for no man but myself;
    Grant I may never prove so fond
    To trust man on his oath or bond,
    Or a harlot for her weeping,
    Or a dog that seems a-sleeping,
    Or a keeper with my freedom,

Or my friends if I should need 'em.
Amen. So fall to't: 70
Rich men sin, and I eat root.
                          Eats and drinks
Much good dich thy good heart, Apemantus!
TIMON. Captain Alcibiades, your heart's in the field
now.
ALCIBIADES. My heart is ever at your service, my lord.
TIMON. You had rather be at a breakfast of enemies
than a dinner of friends.
ALCIBIADES. So they were bleeding-new, my lord;
there's no meat like 'em; I could wish my best friend
at such a feast.   80
APEMANTUS. Would all those flatterers were thine
enemies, then, that then thou mightst kill 'em—and
bid me to 'em!
1 LORD. Might we but have that happiness, my lord,
that you would once use our hearts, whereby we
might express some part of our zeals, we should
think ourselves for ever perfect.
TIMON. O, no doubt, my good friends, but the gods
themselves have provided that I shall have much
help from you: how had you been my friends else? 90
Why have you that charitable title from thousands,
did not you chiefly belong to my heart? I have told
more of you to myself than you can with modesty
speak in your own behalf; and thus far I confirm
you. O you gods, think I, what need we have any
friends, if we should ne'er have need of 'em? they
were the most needless creatures living, should we
ne'er have use for 'em; and would most resemble
sweet instruments hung up in cases, that keeps their
sounds to themselves. Why, I have often wished 100
myself poorer, that I might come nearer to you. We
are born to do benefits; and what better or properer
can we call our own than the riches of our friends?
O, what a precious comfort 'tis to have so many
like brothers commanding one another's fortunes!
O joy, e'en made away ere't can be born! Mine
eyes cannot hold out water, methinks. To forget
their faults, I drink to you.
APEMANTUS. Thou weep'st to make them drink,
Timon.   110
2 LORD. Joy had the like conception in our eyes,
And at that instant like a babe sprung up.
APEMANTUS. Ho, ho! I laugh to think that babe a
bastard.
3 LORD. I promise you, my lord, you moved me much.
APEMANTUS. Much!   *Tucket heard*
TIMON. What means that trump?

Enter a Servant

                          How now?
SERVANT. Please you, my lord, there are certain ladies
most desirous of admittance.
TIMON. Ladies? what are their wills?
SERVANT. There comes with them a forerunner, my 120
lord, which bears that office to signify their
pleasures.
TIMON. I pray let them be admitted.

Enter Cupid

CUPID. Hail to thee, worthy Timon, and to all
That of his bounties taste! The five best senses
Acknowledge thee their patron, and come freely
To gratulate thy plenteous bosom. Th'ear,

Taste, touch, smell, all pleased from thy table rise;
They only now come but to feast thine eyes.
TIMON. They're welcome all; let 'em have kind
admittance.   130
Music make their welcome!   *Cupid goes*
1 LORD. You see, my lord, how ample you're beloved.

*Music. Re-enter Cupid, with a masque of Ladies as
Amazons, with lutes in their hands, dancing and playing*

APEMANTUS. Hoy-day, what a sweep of vanity comes
this way!
They dance? they are madwomen.
Like madness is the glory of this life
As this pomp shows to a little oil and root.
We make ourselves fools, to disport ourselves,
And spend our flatteries to drink those men
Upon whose age we void it up again
With poisonous spite and envy.   140
Who lives that's not depravéd or depraves?
Who dies that bears not one spurn to their graves
Of their friends' gift?
I should fear those that dance before me now
Would one day stamp upon me. 'T has been done;
Men shut their doors against a setting sun.

*The Lords rise from table, with much adoring of Timon,
and to show their loves, each single out an Amazon, and
all dance, men with women, a lofty strain or two to the
hautboys, and cease*

TIMON. You have done our pleasures much grace, fair
ladies,
Set a fair fashion on our entertainment,
Which was not half so beautiful and kind;
You have added worth unto't and lustre,   150
And entertained me with mine own device.
I am to thank you for't.
1 LADY. My lord, you take us even at the best.
APEMANTUS. Faith, for the worst is filthy, and would
not hold taking, I doubt me.
TIMON. Ladies, there is an idle banquet attends you,
Please you to dispose yourselves.
ALL LADIES. Most thankfully, my lord.
                                Cupid and Ladies go
TIMON. Flavius!
FLAVIUS. My lord?
TIMON.   The little casket bring me hither. 160
FLAVIUS. Yes, my lord. [*aside*] More jewels yet!
There is no crossing him in's humour,
Else I should tell him well, i' faith I should;
When all's spent, he'ld be crossed then, an he could.
'Tis pity bounty had not eyes behind,
That man might ne'er be wretched for his mind.
                                             Goes
1 LORD. Where be our men?
SERVANT. Here, my lord, in readiness.
2 LORD. Our horses!

Re-enter Flavius, with the casket

TIMON. O my friends,   170
I have one word to say to you. Look you, my good
lord,
I must entreat you honour me so much
As to advance this jewel; accept it and wear it,
Kind my lord.
1 LORD. I am so far already in your gifts.
ALL. So are we all.

Enter a Servant

SERVANT. My lord, there are certain nobles of the
senate newly alighted and come to visit you.
TIMON. They are fairly welcome.
FLAVIUS. I beseech your honour, vouchsafe me a word; 180
it does concern you near.
TIMON. Near? why, then, another time I'll hear thee.
I prithee let's be provided to show them enter-
tainment.
FLAVIUS [*aside*]. I scarce know how.

Enter another Servant

2 SERVANT. May it please your honour, Lord Lucius,
Out of his free love, hath presented to you
Four milk-white horses, trapped in silver.
TIMON. I shall accept them fairly. Let the presents
Be worthily entertained.

Enter a third Servant

                             How now? what news? 190
3 SERVANT. Please you, my lord, that honourable
gentleman. Lord Lucullus, entreats your company
to-morrow to hunt with him, and has sent your
honour two brace of greyhounds.
TIMON. I'll hunt with him; and let them be received,
Not without fair reward.
FLAVIUS [*aside*].   What will this come to?
He commands us to provide and give great gifts,
And all out of an empty coffer;
Nor will he know his purse, or yield me this,
To show him what a beggar his heart is,   200
Being of no power to make his wishes good.
His promises fly so beyond his state
That what he speaks is all in debt, he owes
For every word. He is so kind that he now
Pays interest for't; his land's put to their books.
Well, would I were gently put out of office,
Before I were forced out!
Happier is he that has no friend to feed
Than such that do e'en enemies exceed.
I bleed inwardly for my lord.   *Goes* 210
TIMON. You do yourselves much wrong.
You bate too much of your own merits.
Here, my lord, a trifle of our love.
2 LORD. With more than common thanks I will
receive it.
3 LORD. O, he's the very soul of bounty!
TIMON. And now I remember, my lord, you gave
good words the other day of a bay courser I rode
on. 'Tis yours because you liked it.
3 LORD. O, I beseech you pardon me, my lord, in that.
TIMON. You may take my word, my lord; I know no 220
man can justly praise but what he does affect. I
weigh my friend's affection with mine own. I'll tell
you true, I'll call to you.
ALL LORDS. O, none so welcome.
TIMON. I take all and your several visitations
So kind to heart, 'tis not enough to give;
Methinks I could deal kingdoms to my friends,
And ne'er be weary. Alcibiades,
Thou art a soldier, therefore seldom rich.
It comes in charity to thee; for all thy living 230
Is 'mongst the dead, and all the lands thou hast
Lie in a pitched field.
ALCIBIADES. Ay, defiled land, my lord.

1 LORD. We are so virtuously bound—
TIMON. And so am I to you.
2 LORD. So infinitely endeared—
TIMON. All to you. Lights, more lights!
1 LORD. The best of happiness, honour and fortunes,
    Keep with you, Lord Timon!
TIMON. Ready for his friends.
            All leave but Apemantus and Timon
APEMANTUS.   What a coil's here! 240
    Serving of becks and jutting-out of bums!
    I doubt whether their legs be worth the sums
    That are given for 'em. Friendship's full of dregs:
    Methinks false hearts should never have sound legs.
    Thus honest fools lay out their wealth on curtsies.
TIMON. Now, Apemantus, if thou wert not sullen,
    I would be good to thee.
APEMANTUS. No, I'll nothing; for if I should be bribed
    too, there would be none left to rail upon thee, and
    then thou wouldst sin the faster. Thou giv'st so long, 250
    Timon, I fear me thou wilt give away thyself in
    paper shortly. What needs these feasts, pomps and
    vainglories?
TIMON. Nay, an you begin to rail on society once, I
    am sworn not to give regard to you. Farewell, and
    come with better music.   *Goes*
APEMANTUS. So. Thou wilt not hear me now; thou
    shalt not then. I'll lock thy heaven from thee.
    O, that men's ears should be
    To counsel deaf, but not to flattery!   *Goes* 260

ACT 2
Scene 1: *A Senator's house*

Enter a Senator, with papers in his hand

SENATOR. And late five thousand; to Varro and to
    Isidore
He owes nine thousand, besides my former sum,
Which makes it five and twenty. Still in motion
Of raging waste? It cannot hold; it will not.
If I want gold, steal but a beggar's dog
And give it Timon, why, the dog coins gold.
If I would sell my horse and buy twenty moe
Better than he, why, give my horse to Timon,
Ask nothing, give it him, it foals me straight,
And able horses. No porter at his gate,   10
But rather one that smiles, and still invites
All that pass by. It cannot hold; no reason
Can sound his state in safety. Caphis, ho!
Caphis, I say!

Enter Caphis

CAPHIS.   Here, sir; what is your pleasure?
SENATOR. Get on your cloak, and haste you to Lord
    Timon;
Importune him for my moneys; be not ceased
With slight denial; nor then silenced when
'Commend me to your master' and the cap
Plays in the right hand, thus; but tell him
My uses cry to me, I must serve my turn   20
Out of mine own; his days and times are past,
And my reliances on his fracted dates
Have smit my credit. I love and honour him,
But must not break my back to heal his finger.
Immediate are my needs, and my relief
Must not be tossed and turned to me in words,

But find supply immediate. Get you gone;
Put on a most importunate aspect,
A visage of demand; for I do fear,
When every feather sticks in his own wing,   30
Lord Timon will be left a naked gull,
Which flashes now a phoenix. Get you gone.
CAPHIS. I go, sir.
SENATOR.   Take the bonds along with you,
And have the dates in compt.
CAPHIS.   I will, sir.
SENATOR.   Go.
                            They go

Scene 2: *Before Timon's house*

Enter Flavius, with many bills in his hand

FLAVIUS. No care, no stop, so senseless of expense
    That he will neither know how to maintain it,
    Nor cease his flow of riot; takes no account
    How things go from him, nor resumes no care
    Of what is to continue; never mind
    Was to be so unwise to be so kind.
    What shall be done? he will not hear till feel.
    I must be round with him, now he comes from
        hunting.
    Fie, fie, fie, fie!

Enter Caphis, with the Servants of Isidore and Varro

CAPHIS. Good even, Varro. What, you come for
        money?   10
VARRO'S SERVANT. Is't not your business too?
CAPHIS. It is; and yours too, Isidore?
ISIDORE'S SERVANT. It is so.
CAPHIS. Would we were all discharged!
VARRO'S SERVANT. I fear it.
CAPHIS. Here comes the lord.

Enter Timon and his Train, with Alcibiades

TIMON. So soon as dinner's done, we'll forth again,
    My Alcibiades. With me? What is your will?
CAPHIS. My lord, here is a note of certain dues.
TIMON. Dues? Whence are you?
CAPHIS.   Of Athens here, my lord. 20
TIMON. Go to my steward.
CAPHIS. Please it your lordship, he hath put me off
    To the succession of new days this month.
    My master is awaked by great occasion
    To call upon his own, and humbly prays you
    That with your other noble parts you'll suit
    In giving him his right.
TIMON.   Mine honest friend,
    I prithee but repair to me next morning.
CAPHIS. Nay, good my lord—
TIMON.   Contain thyself, good friend.
VARRO'S SERVANT. One Varro's servant, my good 30
    lord—
ISIDORE'S SERVANT. From Isidore; he humbly prays
    your speedy payment.
CAPHIS. If you did know, my lord, my master's
    wants,—
VARRO'S SERVANT. 'Twas due on forfeiture, my lord,
    six weeks and past.
ISIDORE'S SERVANT. Your steward puts me off, my
    lord, and I
    Am sent expressly to your lordship.
TIMON. Give me breath.

I do beseech you, good my lords, keep on;   40
I'll wait upon you instantly.
                    Alcibiades, Lords and others go
            [*to Flavius*] Come hither. Pray you,
How goes the world, that I am thus encount'red
With clamorous demands of broken bonds,
And the detention of long-since-due debts
Against my honour?
FLAVIUS.   Please you, gentlemen,
The time is unagreeable to this business.
Your importunacy cease till after dinner,
That I may make his lordship understand
Wherefore you are not paid.
TIMON. Do so, my friends. See them well entertained. 50
                                         He goes
FLAVIUS. Pray draw near.   *He goes*

Enter Apemantus and Fool

CAPHIS. Stay, stay, here comes the fool with Apeman-
  tus. Let's ha' some sport with 'em.
VARRO'S SERVANT. Hang him, he'll abuse us.
ISIDORE'S SERVANT. A plague upon him, dog!
VARRO'S SERVANT. How dost, fool?
APEMANTUS. Dost dialogue with thy shadow?
VARRO'S SERVANT. I speak not to thee.
APEMANTUS. No, 'tis to thy self [*to the Fool*] Come
  away.
ISIDORE'S SERVANT. There's the fool hangs on your 60
  back already.
APEMANTUS. No, thou stand'st single, thou'rt not on
  him yet.
CAPHIS. Where's the fool now?
APEMANTUS. He last asked the question. Poor rogues,
  and usurers' men, bawds between gold and want!
ALL SERVANTS. What are we, Apemantus?
APEMANTUS. Asses.
ALL SERVANTS. Why?
APEMANTUS. That you ask me what you are, and do 70
  not know yourselves. Speak to 'em, fool.
FOOL. How do you, gentlemen?
ALL SERVANTS. Gramercies, good fool. How does your
  mistress?
FOOL. She's e'en setting on water to scald such chickens
  as you are. Would we could see you at Corinth!
APEMANTUS. Good, gramercy.

Enter Page

FOOL. Look you, here comes my mistress' page.
PAGE [*to the Fool*]. Why, how now, captain? what do
  you in this wise company? How dost thou, 80
  Apemantus?
APEMANTUS. Would I had a rod in my mouth, that I
  might answer thee profitably.
PAGE. Prithee, Apemantus, read me the superscription
  of these letters. I know not which is which.
APEMANTUS. Canst not read?
PAGE. No.
APEMANTUS. There will little learning die then, that
  day thou art hanged. This is to Lord Timon; this
  to Alcibiades. Go, thou wast born a bastard, and 90
  thou'lt die a bawd.
PAGE. Thou wast whelped a dog, and thou shalt famish
  a dog's death. Answer not, I am gone.   *Goes*
APEMANTUS. E'en so thou outrun'st grace. Fool, I will
  go with you to Lord Timon's.
FOOL. Will you leave me there?

APEMANTUS. If Timon stay at home. You three serve
  three usurers?
ALL SERVANTS. Ay; would they served us!
APEMANTUS. So would I—as good a trick as ever hang- 100
  man served thief.
FOOL. Are you three usurers' men?
ALL SERVANTS. Ay, fool.
FOOL. I think no usurer but has a fool to his servant.
  My mistress is one, and I am her fool. When men
  come to borrow of your masters, they approach
  sadly and go away merry; but they enter my
  mistress' house merrily and go away sadly. The
  reason of this?
VARRO'S SERVANT. I could render one.   110
APEMANTUS. Do it then, that we may account thee a
  whoremaster and a knave; which notwithstanding,
  thou shalt be no less esteemed.
VARRO'S SERVANT. What is a whoremaster, fool?
FOOL. A fool in good clothes, and something like thee.
  'Tis a spirit. Sometime 't appears like a lord, sometime like a lawyer, sometime like a philosopher,
  with two stones moe than 's artificial one. He is very
  often like a knight; and generally, in all shapes that
  man goes up and down in, from fourscore to 120
  thirteen, this spirit walks in.
VARRO'S SERVANT. Thou art not altogether a fool.
FOOL. Nor thou altogether a wise man: as much
  foolery as I have, so much wit thou lack'st.
APEMANTUS. That answer might have become Apemantus.
ALL SERVANTS. Aside, aside; here comes Lord Timon.

Re-enter Timon and Flavius

APEMANTUS. Come with me, fool, come.
FOOL. I do not always follow lover, elder brother,
  and woman; sometime the philosopher.   *They go* 130
FLAVIUS. Pray you, walk near: I'll speak with you
  anon.   *Servants withdraw*
TIMON. You make me marvel wherefore ere this time
  Had you not fully laid my state before me,
  That I might so have rated my expense
  As I had leave of means.
FLAVIUS.   You would not hear me.
  At many leisures I proposed—
TIMON.   Go to.
  Perchance some single vantages you took
  When my indisposition put you back,
  And that unaptness made your minister
  Thus to excuse yourself.
FLAVIUS.   O my good lord,   140
  At many times I brought in my accounts,
  Laid them before you; you would throw them off,
  And say you found them in mine honesty.
  When for some trifling present you have bid me
  Return so much, I have shook my head and wept;
  Yea, 'gainst th'authority of manners prayed you
  To hold your hand more close. I did endure
  Not seldom, nor no slight checks, when I have
  Prompted you in the ebb of your estate
  And your great flow of debts. My loved lord— 150
  Though you hear now too late, yet now's a time—
  The greatest of your having lacks a half
  To pay your present debts.
TIMON.   Let all my land be sold.
FLAVIUS. 'Tis all engaged, some forfeited and gone,
  And what remains will hardly stop the mouth

Of present dues. The future comes apace;
What shall defend the interim? and at length
How goes our reck'ning?
TIMON. To Lacedæmon did my land extend.
FLAVIUS. O my good lord, the world is but a word; 160
Were it all yours to give it in a breath,
How quickly were it gone!
TIMON.   You tell me true.
FLAVIUS. If you suspect my husbandry or falsehood,
Call me before th'exactest auditors,
And set me on the proof. So the gods bless me,
When all our offices have been oppressed
With riotous feeders, when our vaults have wept
With drunken spilth of wine, when every room
Hath blazed with lights and brayed with minstrelsy,
I have retired me to a wasteful cock,   170
And set mine eyes at flow.
TIMON.   Prithee no more.
FLAVIUS. Heavens, have I said, the bounty of this lord!
How many prodigal bits have slaves and peasants
This night englutted! Who is not Timon's?
What heart, head, sword, force, means, but is Lord
Timon's?
Great Timon, noble, worthy, royal Timon!
Ah, when the means are gone that buy this praise,
The breath is gone whereof this praise is made.
Feast-won, fast-lost; one cloud of winter showers,
These flies are couched.
TIMON.   Come, sermon me no further. 180
No villainous bounty yet hath passed my heart;
Unwisely, not ignobly, have I given.
Why dost thou weep? Canst thou the conscience
lack
To think I shall lack friends? Secure thy heart;
If I would broach the vessels of my love,
And try the argument of hearts, by borrowing,
Men and men's fortunes could I frankly use
As I can bid thee speak.
FLAVIUS.   Assurance bless your thoughts!
TIMON. And in some sort these wants of mine are
crowned,
That I account them blessings; for by these   190
Shall I try friends:
You shall perceive how you mistake my fortunes;
I am wealthy in my friends.
Within there! Flaminius! Servilius!

Enter Flaminius, Servilius, and another Servant

SERVANTS. My lord, my lord?
TIMON. I will dispatch you severally. You to Lord
Lucius, to Lord Lucullus you—I hunted with his
honour to-day—you to Sempronius, commend me
to their loves; and I am proud, say, that my occasions
have found time to use 'em toward a supply of 200
money. Let the request be fifty talents.
FLAMINIUS. As you have said, my Lord.
FLAVIUS. Lord Lucius and Lucullus? hum!
TIMON. Go you, sir, to the senators,
Of whom, even to the state's best health, I have
Deserved this hearing; bid 'em send o'th'instant
A thousand talents to me.
FLAVIUS.   I have been bold,
For that I knew it the most general way,
To them to use your signet and your name;
But they do shake their heads, and I am here   210
No richer in return.

TIMON.   Is't true? can't be?
FLAVIUS. They answer, in a joint and corporate voice,
That now they are at fall, want treasure, cannot
Do what they would; are sorry—you are
honourable—
But yet they could have wished—they know not—
Something hath been amiss—a noble nature
May catch a wrench—would all were well—'tis
pity;
And so, intending other serious matters,
After distasteful looks, and these hard fractions,
With certain half-caps and cold-moving nods   220
They froze me into silence.
TIMON.   You gods, reward them!
Prithee, man, look cheerly. These old fellows
Have their ingratitude in them hereditary.
Their blood is caked, 'tis cold, it seldom flows;
'Tis lack of kindly warmth they are not kind;
And nature, as it grows again toward earth,
Is fashioned for the journey, dull and heavy.
Go to Ventidius. Prithee, be not sad;
Thou art true and honest; ingeniously I speak,
No blame belongs to thee. Ventidius lately   230
Buried his father, by whose death he's stepped
Into a great estate. When he was poor,
Imprisoned, and in scarcity of friends,
I cleared him with five talents. Greet him from me;
Bid him suppose some good necessity
Touches his friend, which craves to be rememb'red
With those five talents. That had, give't these
fellows
To whom 'tis instant due. Ne'er speak or think
That Timon's fortunes 'mong his friends can sink.
FLAVIUS. I would I could not think it.   240
That thought is bounty's foe;
Being free itself, it thinks all others so.   *They go*

ACT 3

Scene 1: *A room in Lucullus's house*

*Flaminius waiting to speak with Lucullus from his master,
enters a Servant to him*

SERVANT. I have told my lord of you; he is coming
down to you.
FLAMINIUS. I thank you, sir.

Enter Lucullus

SERVANT. Here's my lord.
LUCULLUS [*aside*]. One of Lord Timon's men? a gift, I
warrant. Why, this hits right; I dreamt of a silver
basin and ewer to-night. [*aloud*] Flaminius, honest
Flaminius, you are very respectively welcome, sir.
Fill me some wine. [*Servant goes*] And how does
that honourable, complete, free-hearted gentleman 10
of Athens, thy very bountiful good lord and master?
FLAMINIUS. His health is well, sir.
LUCULLUS. I am right glad that his health is well, sir.
And what hast thou there under thy cloak, pretty
Flaminius?
FLAMINIUS. Faith, nothing but an empty box, sir,
which in my lord's behalf I come to entreat your
honour to supply; who, having great and instant
occasion to use fifty talents, hath sent to your lordship to furnish him, nothing doubting your present 20
assistance therein.

LUCULLUS. La, la, la, la! 'Nothing doubting', says he? Alas, good lord! a noble gentleman 'tis, if he would not keep so good a house. Many a time and often I ha' dined with him, and told him on't, and come again to supper to him of purpose to have him spend less, and yet he would embrace no counsel, take no warning by my coming. Every man has his fault, and honesty is his. I ha' told him on't, but I could ne'er get him from't. 30

Re-enter Servant, with wine

SERVANT. Please your lordship, here is the wine.

LUCULLUS. Flaminius, I have noted thee always wise. Here's to thee.

FLAMINIUS. Your lordship speaks your pleasure.

LUCULLUS. I have observed thee always for a towardly prompt spirit, give thee thy due, and one that knows what belongs to reason; and canst use the time well, if the time use thee well. Good parts in thee. [*to Servant*] Get you gone, sirrah. [*Servant goes*] Draw nearer, honest Flaminius. Thy lord's a bountiful 40 gentleman; but thou art wise, and thou know'st well enough, although thou com'st to me, that this is no time to lend money, especially upon bare friendship without security. Here's three solidares for thee. Good boy, wink at me, and say thou saw'st me not. Fare thee well.

FLAMINIUS. Is't possible the world should so much differ, And we alive that lived? Fly, damnèd baseness, To him that worships thee! *Throwing back the money*

LUCULLUS. Ha! now I see thou art a fool, and fit for 50 thy master. *Goes*

FLAMINIUS. May these add to the number that may scald thee! Let molten coin be thy damnation, Thou disease of a friend, and not himself! Has friendship such a faint and milky heart, It turns in less than two nights? O you gods, I feel my master's passion! this slave, Unto this hour, has my lord's meat in him; Why should it thrive and turn to nutriment, When he is turn'd to poison? 60 O, may diseases only work upon't! And when he's sick to death, let not that part of nature Which my lord paid for be of any power To expel sickness, but prolong his hour! *Goes*

Scene 2: *A public place*

Enter Lucius, with three Strangers

LUCIUS. Who, the Lord Timon? he is my very good friend, and an honourable gentleman.

1 STRANGER. We know him for no less, though we are but strangers to him. But I can tell you one thing, my lord, and which I hear from common rumours: now Lord Timon's happy hours are done and past, and his estate shrinks from him.

LUCIUS. Fie, no, do not believe it; he cannot want for money.

2 STRANGER. But believe you this, my lord, that not 10 long ago one of his men was with the Lord Lucullus to borrow so many talents; nay, urged extremely for't, and showed what necessity belonged to't, and yet was denied.

LUCIUS. How?

2 STRANGER. I tell you, denied, my lord.

LUCIUS. What a strange case was that! now, before the gods, I am ashamed on't. Denied that honourable man? there was very little honour showed in't. For my own part, I must needs confess, I have received 20 some small kindnesses from him, as money, plate, jewels, and such-like trifles, nothing comparing to his; yet, had he mistook him and sent to me, I should ne'er have denied his occasion so many talents.

Enter Servilius

SERVILIUS. See, by good hap, yonder's my lord; I have sweat to see his honour. My honoured lord!

LUCIUS. Servilius? you are kindly met, sir. Fare thee well; commend me to thy honourable virtuous lord, my very exquisite friend.

SERVILIUS. May it please your honour, my lord hath 30 sent—

LUCIUS. Ha! what has he sent? I am so much endeared to that lord; he's ever sending. How shall I thank him, think'st thou? And what has he sent now?

SERVILIUS. Has only sent his present occasion now, my lord; requesting your lordship to supply his instant use with so many talents.

LUCIUS. I know his lordship is but merry with me; He cannot want fifty five hundred talents.

SERVILIUS. But in the mean time he wants less, my lord. 40 If his occasion were not virtuous, I should not urge it half so faithfully.

LUCIUS. Dost thou speak seriously, Servilius?

SERVILIUS. Upon my soul, 'tis true, sir.

LUCIUS. What a wicked beast was I to disfurnish myself against such a good time, when I might ha' shown myself honourable! how unluckily it happ'ned that I should purchase the day before for a little part, and undo a great deal of honour! Servilius, now before the gods, I am not able to 50 do—the more beast, I say—I was sending to use Lord Timon myself, these gentlemen can witness; but I would not, for the wealth of Athens, I had done't now. Commend me bountifully to his good lordship, and I hope his honour will conceive the fairest of me, because I have no power to be kind. And tell him this from me, I count it one of my greatest afflictions, say, that I cannot pleasure such an honourable gentleman. Good Servilius, will you befriend me so far as to use mine own words to him? 60

SERVILIUS. Yes, sir, I shall.

LUCIUS. I'll look you out a good turn, Servilius. *Servilius goes* True, as you said, Timon is shrunk indeed, And he that's once denied will hardly speed. *Goes*

1 STRANGER. Do you observe this, Hostilius?

2 STRANGER. Ay, too well.

1 STRANGER. Why, this is the world's soul; and just of the same piece Is every flatterer's spirit. Who can call him his friend That dips in the same dish? for, in my knowing, Timon has been this lord's father, And kept his credit with his purse; 70 Supported his estate; nay, Timon's money

Has paid his men their wages. He ne'er drinks
But Timon's silver treads upon his lip;
And yet—O, see the monstrousness of man
When he looks out in an ungrateful shape—
He does deny him, in respect of his,
What charitable men afford to beggars.

3 STRANGER. Religion groans at it.

1 STRANGER.   For mine own part,
I never tasted Timon in my life,
Nor came any of his bounties over me,   80
To mark me for his friend. Yet I protest,
For his right noble mind, illustrious virtue,
And honourable carriage,
Had his necessity made use of me,
I would have put my wealth into donation,
And the best half should have returned to him,
So much I love his heart. But I perceive,
Men must learn now with pity to dispense,
For policy sits above conscience.   *They go*

Scene 3: *A room in Sempronius's house*

Enter Sempronius, and a Servant of Timon's

SEMPRONIUS. Must he needs trouble me in't—hum!
    —'bove all others?
    He might have tried Lord Lucius or Lucullus;
    And now Ventidius is wealthy too,
    Whom he redeemed from prison. All these
    Owe their estates unto him.

SERVANT.   My lord,
    They have all been touched and found base metal,
        for
    They have all denied him.

SEMPRONIUS.   How? have they denied him?
    Has Ventidius and Lucullus denied him,
    And does he send to me? Three? hum!
    It shows but little love or judgement in him.   10
    Must I be his last refuge? His friends, like physicians,
    Thrice give him over: must I take th'cure upon me?
    Has much disgraced me in't; I'm angry at him,
    That might have known my place. I see no sense
        for't,
    But his occasions might have wooed me first;
    For, in my conscience, I was the first man
    That e'er receivéd gift from him.
    And does he think so backwardly of me now,
    That I'll requite it last? No;
    So it may prove an argument of laughter   20
    To th'rest, and I 'mongst lords be thought a fool.
    I'd rather than the worth of thrice the sum
    Had sent to me first, but for my mind's sake;
    I'd such a courage to do him good. But now return,
    And with their faint reply this answer join:
    Who bates mine honour shall not know my coin.
                                                Goes

SERVANT. Excellent. Your lordship's a goodly villain.
    The devil knew not what he did when he made man
    politic; he crossed himself by't; and I cannot think
    but in the end the villainies of man will set him clear. 30
    How fairly this lord strives to appear foul! takes
    virtuous copies to be wicked; like those that under
    hot ardent zeal would set whole realms on fire;
    Of such a nature is his politic love.
    This was my lord's best hope; now all are fled,
    Save only the gods. Now his friends are dead,
    Doors that were ne'er acquainted with their wards

Many a bounteous year must be employed
Now to guard sure their master.
And this is all a liberal course allows;   40
Who cannot keep his wealth must keep his house.
                                                Goes

Scene 4: *A hall in Timon's house*

*Enter two Servants of Varro, and the Servant of Lucius,
meeting Titus, Hortensius, and other Servants of Timon's
creditors, waiting his coming out*

1 VARRO'S SERVANT. Well met; good morrow, Titus
    and Hortensius.

TITUS. The like to you, kind Varro.

HORTENSIUS.   Lucius;
    What, do we meet together?

LUCIUS'S SERVANT.   Ay, and I think
    One business does command us all;
    For mine is money.

TITUS.   So is theirs and ours.

Enter Philotus

LUCIUS'S SERVANT. And Sir Philotus too!

PHILOTUS.   Good day at once.

LUCIUS'S SERVANT. Welcome, good brother. What do
    you think the hour?

PHILOTUS. Labouring for nine.

LUCIUS'S SERVANT. So much?

PHILOTUS.   Is not my lord seen yet?

LUCIUS'S SERVANT.   Not yet.

PHILOTUS. I wonder on't; he was wont to shine at
    seven.   10

LUCIUS'S SERVANT. Ay, but the days are waxed shorter
    with him;
    You must consider that a prodigal course
    Is like the sun's, but not, like his, recoverable.
    I fear
    'Tis deepest winter in Lord Timon's purse;
    That is,
    One may reach deep enough and yet find little.

PHILOTUS. I am of your fear for that.

TITUS. I'll show you how t'observe a strange event
    Your lord sends now for money?

HORTENSIUS.   Most true, he does.   20

TITUS. And he wears jewels now of Timon's gift,
    For which I wait for money.

HORTENSIUS. It is against my heart.

LUCIUS'S SERVANT.   Mark, how strange it shows
    Timon in this should pay more than he owes;
    And e'en as if your lord should wear rich jewels
    And send for money for 'em.

HORTENSIUS. I'm weary of this charge, the gods can
        witness;
    I know my lord hath spent of Timon's wealth,
    And now ingratitude makes it worse than stealth.

1 VARRO'S SERVANT. Yes, mine's three thousand
    crowns; what's yours?   30

LUCIUS'S SERVANT. Five thousand mine.

1 VARRO'S SERVANT. 'Tis much deep; and it should
    seem by th'sum
    Your master's confidence was above mine,
    Else, surely, his had equalled.

Enter Flaminius

TITUS. One of Lord Timon's men.

LUCIUS'S SERVANT. Flaminius? Sir, a word. Pray, is my
  lord ready to come forth?
FLAMINIUS. No, indeed he is not.
TITUS. We attend his lordship; pray signify so much.
FLAMINIUS. I need not tell him that; he knows you are 40
  too diligent.   *Goes*

Enter Flavius in a cloak, muffled

LUCIUS'S SERVANT. Ha, is not that his steward muffled
  so?
  He goes away in a cloud. Call him, call him.
TITUS. Do you hear, sir?
2 VARRO'S SERVANT. By your leave, sir.
FLAVIUS. What do ye ask of me, my friend?
TITUS. We wait for certain money here, sir.
FLAVIUS.   Ay,
  If money were as certain as your waiting,
  'Twere sure enough.
  Why then preferred you not your sums and bills, 50
  When your false masters ate of my lord's meat?
  Then they could smile and fawn upon his debts,
  And take down th'interest into their glutt'nous
    maws.
  You do yourselves but wrong to stir me up;
  Let me pass quietly.
  Believe't, my lord and I have made an end;
  I have no more to reckon, he to spend.
LUCIUS'S SERVANT. Ay, but this answer will not serve.
FLAVIUS. If 'twill not serve, 'tis not so base as you,
  For you serve knaves.   *Goes* 60
1 VARRO'S SERVANT. How? what does his cashiered
  worship mutter?
2 VARRO'S SERVANT. No matter what; he's poor, and
  that's revenge enough. Who can speak broader than
  he that has no house to put his head in? such may
  rail against great buildings.

Enter Servilius

TITUS. O, here's Servilius; now we shall know some
  answer.
SERVILIUS. If I might beseech you, gentlemen, to repair
  some other hour, I should derive much from't; for, 70
  take't of my soul, my lord leans wondrously to
  discontent. His comfortable temper has forsook
  him; he's much out of health and keeps his chamber.
LUCIUS'S SERVANT. Many do keep their chambers are
  not sick;
  And if it be so far beyond his health,
  Methinks he should the sooner pay his debts,
  And make a clear way to the gods.
SERVILIUS.   Good gods!
TITUS. We cannot take this for an answer, sir.
FLAMINIUS [*within*]. Servilius, help! My lord, my lord!

Enter Timon, in a rage, Flaminius following

TIMON. What, are my doors opposed against my
  passage?   80
  Have I been ever free, and must my house
  Be my retentive enemy, my gaol?
  The place which I have feasted, does it now,
  Like all mankind, show me an iron heart?
LUCIUS'S SERVANT. Put in now, Titus.
TITUS. My lord, here is my bill.
LUCIUS'S SERVANT. Here's mine.
HORTENSIUS. And mine, my lord.
BOTH VARRO'S SERVANTS. And ours, my lord.

PHILOTUS. All our bills.   90
TIMON. Knock me down with 'em; cleave me to the
  girdle.
LUCIUS'S SERVANT. Alas, my lord—
TIMON. Cut my heart in sums.
TITUS. Mine, fifty talents.
TIMON. Tell out my blood.
LUCIUS'S SERVANT. Five thousand crowns, my lord.
TIMON. Five thousand drops pays that. What yours?
  and yours?
1 VARRO'S SERVANT. My lord—
2 VARRO'S SERVANT. My lord—
TIMON. Tear me, take me, and the gods fall upon you! | 100
                                                         Goes
HORTENSIUS. Faith, I perceive our masters may throw
  their caps at their money; these debts may well be
  called desperate ones, for a madman owes 'em.
                                                     They go

Re-enter Timon and Flavius

TIMON. They have e'en put my breath from me, the
  slaves.
  Creditors? devils!
FLAVIUS. My dear lord—
TIMON. What if it should be so?
FLAVIUS. My lord—
TIMON. I'll have it so. My steward!
FLAVIUS. Here, my lord.   110
TIMON. So fitly! Go, bid all my friends again,
  Lucius, Lucullus, and Sempronius—all.
  I'll once more feast the rascals.
FLAVIUS.   O my lord,
  You only speak from your distracted soul;
  There is not so much left, to furnish out
  A moderate table.
TIMON.   Be it not in thy care;
  Go,
  I charge thee, invite them all: let in the tide
  Of knaves once more; my cook and I'll provide.
                                                     They go

Scene 5: *The Senate-house*

Enter three Senators; Alcibiades, attended, at the door

1 SENATOR. My lord, you have my voice to't; the
  fault's bloody;
  'Tis necessary he should die:
  Nothing emboldens sin so much as mercy.
2 SENATOR. Most true; the law shall bruise him.

Alcibiades is brought forward

ALCIBIADES. Honour, health, and compassion to the
  senate!
1 SENATOR. Now, captain?
ALCIBIADES. I am an humble suitor to your virtues;
  For pity is the virtue of the law,
  And none but tyrants use it cruelly.
  It pleases time and fortune to lie heavy   10
  Upon a friend of mine, who in hot blood
  Hath stepped into the law, which is past depth
  To those that without heed do plunge into't.
  He is a man, setting this fault aside,
  Of comely virtues;
  Nor did he soil the fact with cowardice—
  An honour in him which buys out his fault—
  But with a noble fury and fair spirit,

Seeing his reputation touched to death,
He did oppose his foe;   20
And with such sober and unnoted passion
He did behove his anger, ere 'twas spent,
As if he had but proved an argument.
1 SENATOR. You undergo too strict a paradox,
Striving to make an ugly deed look fair;
Your words have took such pains as if they laboured
To bring manslaughter into form, and set
    quarrelling
Upon the head of valour; which indeed
Is valour misbegot, and came into the world
When sects and factions were newly born.   30
He's truly valiant that can wisely suffer
The worst that man can breathe,
And make his wrongs his outsides,
To wear them like his raiment, carelessly,
And ne'er prefer his injuries to his heart,
To bring it into danger.
If wrongs be evils and enforce us kill,
What folly 'tis to hazard life for ill!
ALCIBIADES. My lord—
1 SENATOR.   You cannot make gross sins look clear:
To revenge is no valour, but to bear.   40
ALCIBIADES. My lords, then, under favour, pardon me
If I speak like a captain.
Why do fond men expose themselves to battle,
And not endure all threats? sleep upon't,
And let the foes quietly cut their throats,
Without repugnancy? If there be
Such valour in the bearing, what make we
Abroad? why then women are more valiant
That stay at home, if bearing carry it,
And the ass more captain than the lion,   50
The felon loaden with irons wiser than the judge,
If wisdom be in suffering. O my lords,
As you are great, be pitifully good.
Who cannot condemn rashness in cold blood?
To kill, I grant, is sin's extremest gust;
But in defence, by Mercy, 'tis most just.
To be in anger is impiety;
But who is man that is not angry?
Weigh but the crime with this.
2 SENATOR. You breathe in vain.
ALCIBIADES.   In vain? His service done 60
At Lacedæmon and Byzantium
Were a sufficient briber for his life.
1 SENATOR. What's that?
ALCIBIADES.   Why, I say, my lords, has done
    fair service,
And slain in fight many of your enemies;
How full of valour did he bear himself
In the last conflict, and made plenteous wounds!
2 SENATOR. He has made too much plenty with 'em.
He's a sworn rioter; he has a sin
That often drowns him and takes his valour
    prisoner.
If there were no foes, that were enough   70
To overcome him. In that beastly fury
He has been known to commit outrages
And cherish factions. 'Tis inferred to us,
His days are foul and his drink dangerous.
1 SEN. He dies.
ALCIBIADES.   Hard fate! he might have died in war.
My lords, if not for any parts in him—
Though his right arm might purchase his own time

And be in debt to none—yet, more to move you,
Take my deserts to his and join 'em both;
And, for I know   80
Your reverend ages love security,
I'll pawn my victories, all my honour to you,
Upon his good returns.
If by this crime he owes the law his life,
Why, let the war receive't in valiant gore,
For law is strict, and war is nothing more.
1 SENATOR. We are for law: he dies; urge it no more,
On height of our displeasure. Friend or brother,
He forfeits his own blood that spills another.
ALCIBIADES. Must it be so? it must not be. My lords, 90
I do beseech you, know me.
2 SENATOR. How?
ALCIBIADES. Call me to your remembrances.
3 SENATOR. What?
ALCIBIADES. I cannot think but your age has forgot
    me;
It could not else be I should prove so base
To sue and be denied such common grace.
My wounds ache at you.
1 SENATOR.   Do you dare our anger?
'Tis in few words, but spacious in effect:
We banish thee for ever.
ALCIBIADES.   Banish me?   100
Banish your dotage, banish usury,
That makes the senate ugly.
1 SENATOR. If, after two days' shine, Athens contain
    thee,
Attend our weightier judgement. And, not to swell
    our spirit,
He shall be executed presently.   Senators go
ALCIBIADES. Now the gods keep you old enough, that
    you may live
Only in bone, that none may look on you!
I'm worse than mad; I have kept back their foes,
While they have told their money and let out
Their coin upon large interest, I myself   110
Rich only in large hurts. All those for this?
Is this the balsam that the usuring senate
Pours into captains' wounds? Banishment!
It comes not ill; I hate not to be banished;
It is a cause worthy my spleen and fury,
That I may strike at Athens. I'll cheer up
My discontented troops, and lay for hearts.
'Tis honour with most lands to be at odds;
Soldiers should brook as little wrongs as gods.
                                         Goes

Scene 6: *A banqueting-room in Timon's house*

Music. Tables set out; Servants attending. Enter divers
Lords, Senators and others, at several doors

1 LORD. The good time of day to you, sir.
2 LORD. I also wish it to you. I think this honourable
lord did but try us this other day.
1 LORD. Upon that were my thoughts tiring when we
encount'red. I hope it is not so low with him as he
made it seem in the trial of his several friends.
2 LORD. It should not be, by the persuasion of his new
feasting.
1 LORD. I should think so. He hath sent me an earnest
inviting, which many my near occasions did urge   10
me to put off; but he hath conjured me beyond
them, and I must needs appear.

2 LORD. In like manner was I in debt to my importunate business, but he would not hear my excuse. I am sorry, when he sent to borrow of me, that my provision was out.

1 LORD. I am sick of that grief too, as I understand how all things go.

2 LORD. Every man here's so. What would he have borrowed of you?   20

1 LORD. A thousand pieces.

2 LORD. A thousand pieces?

1 LORD. What of you?

2 LORD. He sent to me, sir—Here he comes.

Enter Timon and Attendants

TIMON. With all my heart, gentlemen both; and how fare you?

1 LORD. Ever at the best, hearing well of your lordship.

2 LORD. The swallow follows not summer more willing than we your lordship.

TIMON. Nor more willingly leaves winter; such summer birds are men. [*aloud*] Gentlemen, our dinner 30 will not recompense this long stay; feast your ears with the music awhile, if they will fare so harshly o'th'trumpet's sound; we shall to't presently.

1 LORD. I hope it remains not unkindly with your lordship, that I returned you an empty messenger.

TIMON. O, sir, let it not trouble you.

2 LORD. My noble lord,—

TIMON. Ah, my good friend, what cheer?

2 LORD. My most honourable lord, I am e'en sick of 40 shame that when your lordship this other day sent to me I was so unfortunate a beggar.

TIMON. Think not on't, sir.

2 LORD. If you had sent but two hours before—

TIMON. Let it not cumber your better remembrance. [*the banquet brought in*] Come, bring in all together.

2 LORD. All covered dishes.

1 LORD. Royal cheer, I warrant you.

3 LORD. Doubt not that, if money and the season can yield it.   50

1 LORD. How do you? What's the news?

3 LORD. Alcibiades is banished. Hear you of it?

1 AND 2 LORDS. Alcibiades banished?

3 LORD. 'Tis so, be sure of it.

1 LORD. How? how?

2 LORD. I pray you, upon what?

TIMON. My worthy friends, will you draw near?

3 LORD. I'll tell you more anon. Here's a noble feast toward.

2 LORD. This is the old man still.   60

3 LORD. Will't hold? will't hold?

2 LORD. It does; but time will—and so—

3 LORD. I do conceive.

TIMON. Each man to his stool, with that spur as he would to the lip of his mistress; your diet shall be in all places alike. Make not a city feast of it, to let the meat cool ere we can agree upon the first place. Sit, sit. The gods require our thanks.

   You great benefactors, sprinkle our society with thankfulness. For your own gifts, make yourselves 70 praised; but reserve still to give, lest your deities be despised. Lend to each man enough, that one need not lend to another; for, were your godheads to borrow of men, men would forsake the gods. Make the meat be beloved more than the man that gives it. Let no assembly of twenty be without a score of villains. If there sit twelve women at the table, let a dozen of them be—as they are. The rest of your fees, O gods—the senators of Athens, together with the common lag of people—what is amiss in them, 80 you gods, make suitable for destruction. For these my present friends, as they are to me nothing, so in nothing bless them, and to nothing are they welcome.
   Uncover, dogs, and lap.

                         The dishes are uncovered and seen to be
                         full of warm water and stones

SOME SPEAK. What does his lordship mean?

SOME OTHER. I know not.

TIMON. May you a better feast never behold,
   You knot of mouth-friends! smoke and lukewarm water
   Is your perfection. This is Timon's last,   90
   Who, stuck and spangled with your flatteries,
   Washes it off, and sprinkles in your faces
   Your reeking villainy. [*throwing the water in their*
   faces] Live loathed and long,
   Most smiling, smooth, detested parasites,
   Courteous destroyers, affable wolves, meek bears,
   You fools of fortune, trencher-friends, time's flies,
   Cap-and-knee slaves, vapours, and minute-jacks!
   Of man and beast the infinite malady
   Crust you quite o'er! What, dost thou go?
   Soft, take thy physic first; thou too, and thou.   100
   Stay, I will lend thee money, borrow none.

                         Throws the stones at them,
                         and drives them out

   What, all in motion? Henceforth be no feast,
   Whereat a villain's not a welcome guest.
   Burn house! sink Athens! henceforth hated be
   Of Timon man and all humanity!   *Goes*

Re-enter the Lords, Senators, etc.

1 LORD. How now, my lords!

2 LORD. Know you the quality of Lord Timon's fury?

3 LORD. Push! did you see my cap?

4 LORD. I have lost my gown.

1 LORD. He's but a mad lord, and nought but humours 110 sways him. He gave me a jewel th'other day, and now he has beat it out of my hat. Did you see my jewel?

3 LORD. Did you see my cap?

2 LORD. Here 'tis.

4 LORD. Here lies my gown.

1 LORD. Let's make no stay.

2 LORD. Lord Timon's mad.

3 LORD.   I feel't upon my bones.

4 LORD. One day he gives us diamonds, next day stones.   *They go*

ACT 4

Scene 1: *Without the walls of Athens*

Enter Timon

TIMON. Let me look back upon thee. O thou wall
   That girdles in those wolves, dive in the earth,
   And fence not Athens. Matrons, turn incontinent.
   Obedience fail in children. Slaves and fools
   Pluck the grave wrinkled senate from the bench,
   And minister in their steads. To general filths
   Convert o'th'instant, green virginity.
   Do't in your parents' eyes. Bankrupts, hold fast;

Rather than render back, out with your knives,
And cut your trusters' throats. Bound servants, steal: 10
Large-handed robbers your grave masters are,
And pill by law. Maid, to thy master's bed:
Thy mistress is o'th'brothel. Son of sixteen,
Pluck the lined crutch from thy old limping sire,
With it beat out his brains. Piety and fear,
Religion to the gods, peace, justice, truth,
Domestic awe, night-rest, and neighbourhood,
Instruction, manners, mysteries and trades,
Degrees, observances, customs and laws,
Decline to your confounding contraries,   20
And yet confusion live. Plagues incident to men,
Your potent and infectious fevers heap
On Athens, ripe for stroke. Thou cold sciatica,
Cripple our senators, that their limbs may halt
As lamely as their manners. Lust and liberty
Creep in the minds and marrows of our youth,
That 'gainst the stream of virtue they may strive,
And drown themselves in riot. Itches, blains,
Sow all th'Athenian bosoms, and their crop
Be general leprosy! Breath infect breath,   30
That their society, as their friendship, may
Be merely poison! Nothing I'll bear from thee
But nakedness, thou destestable town;
Take thou that too, with multiplying bans.
Timon will to the woods, where he shall find
Th'unkindest beast more kinder than mankind.
The gods confound—hear me, you good gods all—
Th'Athenians both within and out that wall.
And grant, as Timon grows, his hate may grow
To the whole race of mankind, high and low.   40
Amen.   *Goes*

Scene 2: *Athens. Timon's house*

Enter Flavius, with two or three Servants

1 SERVANT. Hear you, master steward, where's our
    master?
    Are we undone? cast off? nothing remaining?
FLAVIUS. Alack, my fellows, what should I say to you?
    Let me be recorded by the righteous gods,
    I am as poor as you.
1 SERVANT.   Such a house broke?
    So noble a master fall'n; all gone, and not
    One friend to take his fortune by the arm,
    And go along with him?
2 SERVANT.   As we do turn our backs
    From our companion thrown into his grave,
    So his familiars to his buried fortunes   10
    Slink all away; leave their false vows with him,
    Like empty purses picked; and his poor self.
    A dedicated beggar to the air,
    With his disease of all-shunned poverty,
    Walks like contempt alone. More of our fellows.

Enter other Servants

FLAVIUS. All broken implements of a ruined house.
3 SERVANT. Yet do our hearts wear Timon's livery,
    That see I by our faces; we are fellows still,
    Serving alike in sorrow. Leaked is our bark,
    And we, poor mates, stand on the dying deck,   20
    Hearing the surges threat; we must all part
    Into this sea of air.
FLAVIUS.   Good fellows all,
    The latest of my wealth I'll share amongst you.

Wherever we shall meet, for Timon's sake
Let's yet be fellows; let's shake our heads, and say,
As 'twere a knell unto our master's fortunes,
'We have seen better days'. Let each take some.
Nay, put out all your hands. Not one word more:
Thus part we rich in sorrow, parting poor.

Servants embrace, and part several ways
O the fierce wretchedness that glory brings us!   30
Who would not wish to be from wealth exempt,
Since riches point to misery and contempt?
Who would be so mocked with glory, or to live
But in a dream of friendship,
To have his pomp and all what state compounds
But only painted, like his varnished friends?
Poor honest lord, brought low by his own heart,
Undone by goodness: strange, unusual blood,
When man's worst sin is, he does too much good.
Who then dares to be half so kind again?   40
For bounty, that makes gods, does still mar men.
My dearest lord, blest to be most accursed,
Rich only to be wretched, thy great fortunes
Are made thy chief afflictions. Alas, kind lord,
He's flung in rage from this ingrateful seat
Of monstrous friends;
Nor has he with him to supply his life,
Or that which can command it.
I'll follow, and inquire him out.
I'll ever serve his mind with my best will;   50
Whilst I have gold, I'll be his steward still.   *Goes*

Scene 3: *Woods and cave, near the sea-shore*

Enter Timon, from the cave

TIMON. O blessed breeding sun, draw from the earth
    Rotten humidity; below thy sister's orb
    Infect the air. Twinned brothers of one womb,
    Whose procreation, residence, and birth,
    Scarce is dividant, touch them with several
        fortunes,
    The greater scorns the lesser. Not nature,
    To whom all sores lay siege, can bear great fortune
    But by contempt of nature.
    Raise me this beggar and deject that lord,
    The senator shall bear contempt hereditary,   10
    The beggar native honour.
    It is the pasture lards the wether's dies,
    The want that makes him lean. Who dares, who
        dares,
    In purity of manhood stand upright,
    And say, 'This man's a flatterer'? If one be,
    So are they all; for every grise of fortune
    Is smoothed by that below. The learnèd pate
    Ducks to the golden fool. All's obliquy;
    There's nothing level in our cursèd natures
    But direct villainy. Therefore be abhorred   20
    All feasts, societies and throngs of men.
    His semblable, yea, himself, Timon disdains;
    Destruction fang mankind. Earth, yield me roots.
                    Digging
    Who seeks for better of thee, sauce his palate
    With thy most operant poison. What is here?
    Gold? yellow, glittering, precious gold?
    No, gods, I am no idle votarist:
    Roots, you clear heavens! thus much of this will
        make

Black white, foul fair, wrong right,
Base noble, old young, coward valiant.   30
Ha, you gods! why this? what this, you gods? Why,
   this
Will lug your priests and servants from your sides,
Pluck stout men's pillows from below their heads.
This yellow slave
Will knit and break religions; bless th'accursed;
Make the hoar leprosy adored; place thieves,
And give them title, knee and approbation
With senators on the bench. This is it
That makes the wappered widow wed again;
She whom the spital-house and ulcerous sores   40
Would cast the gorge at, this embalms and spices
To th'April day again. Come, damnéd earth,
Thou common whore of mankind, that puts odds
Among the rout of nations, I will make thee
Do thy right nature. [*march afar off*] Ha, a drum?
   Thou'rt quick,
But yet I'll bury thee. Thou'lt go, strong thief,
When gouty keepers of thee cannot stand.
Nay, stay thou out for earnest.

                                   Keeping some gold

*Enter Alcibiades, with drum and fife, in warlike manner;
and Phrynia and Timandra*

ALCIBIADES.   What art thou there? speak.
TIMON. A beast, as thou art. The canker gnaw thy
   heart
   For showing me again the eyes of man!   50
ALCIBIADES. What is thy name? Is man so hateful to
   thee,
   That art thyself a man?
TIMON. I am Misanthropos, and hate mankind.
   For thy part, I do wish thou wert a dog,
   That I might love thee something.
ALCIBIADES.   I know thee well;
   But in thy fortunes am unlearned and strange.
TIMON. I know thee too, and more than that I know
   thee
   I not desire to know. Follow thy drum;
   With man's blood paint the ground, gules, gules.
   Religious canons, civil laws are cruel;   60
   Then what should war be? This fell whore of thine
   Hath in her more destruction than thy sword,
   For all her cherubin look.
PHRYNIA.   Thy lips rot off!
TIMON. I will not kiss thee; then the rot returns
   To thine own lips again.
ALCIBIADES. How came the noble Timon to this
   change?
TIMON. As the moon does, by wanting light to give.
   But then renew I could not like the moon;
   There were no suns to borrow of.
ALCIBIADES. Noble Timon, what friendship may I do
   thee?   70
TIMON. None, but to maintain my opinion.
ALCIBIADES. What is it, Timon?
TIMON. Promise me friendship, but perform none. If
   thou wilt not promise, the gods plague thee, for
   thou art a man! If thou dost perform, confound thee,
   for thou art a man!
ALCIBIADES. I have heard in some sort of thy miseries.
TIMON. Thou saw'st them when I had prosperity.
ALCIBIADES. I see them now; then was a blessed time.

TIMON. As thine is now, held with a brace of harlots. 80
TIMANDRA. Is this th'Athenian minion whom the
   world
   Voiced so regardfully?
TIMON.   Art thou Timandra?
TIMANDRA. Yes.
TIMON. Be a whore still; they love not that use
   thee;
   Give them diseases, leaving with thee their lust.
   Make use of thy salt hours. Season the slaves
   For tubs and baths; bring down rose-cheeked youth
   To the tub-fast and the diet.
TIMANDRA.   Hang thee, monster!
ALCIBIADES. Pardon him, sweet Timandra, for his wits
   Are drowned and lost in his calamities.   90
   I have but little gold of late, brave Timon,
   The want whereof doth daily make revolt
   In my penurious band. I have heard, and grieved,
   How curséd Athens, mindless of thy worth,
   Forgetting thy great deeds, when neighbour states,
   But for thy sword and fortune, trod upon them—
TIMON. I prithee beat thy drum and get thee gone.
ALCIBIADES. I am thy friend, and pity thee, dear
   Timon.
TIMON. How dost thou pity him whom thou dost
   trouble?
   I had rather be alone.
ALCIBIADES.   Why, fare thee well;   100
   Here is some gold for thee.
TIMON.   Keep it, I cannot eat it.
ALCIBIADES. When I have laid proud Athens on a
   heap—
TIMON. Warr'st thou 'gainst Athens?
ALCIBIADES.   Ay, Timon, and have cause.
TIMON. The gods confound them all in thy conquest,
   And thee after, when thou hast conquered!
ALCIBIADES. Why me, Timon?
TIMON.   That by killing of villains
   Thou wast born to conquer my country.
   Put up thy gold. Go on, here's gold, go on;
   Be as a planetary plague, when Jove
   Will o'er some high-viced city hang his poison   110
   In the sick air: let not thy sword skip one;
   Pity not honoured age for his white beard;
   He is an usurer. Strike me the counterfeit matron:
   It is her habit only that is honest,
   Herself's a bawd. Let not the virgin's cheek
   Make soft thy trenchant sword; for those milk-paps
   That through the window-bars bore at men's eyes
   Are not within the leaf of pity writ,
   But set them down horrible traitors. Spare not the
   babe
   Whose dimpled smiles from fools exhaust their
   mercy;   120
   Think it a bastard whom the oracle
   Hath doubtfully pronounced thy throat shall cut,
   And mince it sans remorse. Swear against objects;
   Put armour on thine ears and on thine eyes,
   Whose proof nor yells of mothers, maids, nor babes,
   Nor sight of priests in holy vestments bleeding,
   Shall pierce a jot. There's gold to pay thy soldiers;
   Make large confusion; and, thy fury spent,
   Confounded be thyself. Speak not, be gone.
ALCIBIADES. Hast thou gold yet? I'll take the gold thou
   givest me,   130
   Not all thy counsel.

TIMON. Dost thou or dost thou not, heaven's curse
  upon thee!
PHRYNIA AND TIMANDRA. Give us some gold, good
  Timon; hast thou more?
TIMON. Enough to make a whore forswear her trade,
  And to make whores, a bawd. Hold up, you sluts,
  Your aprons mountant; you are not oathable,
  Although, I know, you'll swear, terribly swear,
  Into strong shudders and to heavenly agues,
  Th'immortal gods that hear you. Spare your oaths;
  I'll trust to your conditions. Be whores still;   140
  And he whose pious breath seeks to convert you,
  Be strong in whore, allure him, burn him up;
  Let your close fire predominate his smoke,
  And be no turncoats. Yet may your pains six months
  Be quite contrary: and thatch
  Your poor thin roofs with burdens of the dead—
  Some that were hanged, no matter:
  Wear them, betray with them; whore still;
  Paint till a horse may mire upon your face.
  A pox of wrinkles!
PHRYNIA AND TIMANDRA. Well, more gold. What
  then?   150
  Believe't that we'll do any thing for gold.
TIMON. Consumptions sow
  In hollow bones of man; strike their sharp shins,
  And mar men's spurring. Crack the lawyer's voice,
  That he may never more false title plead,
  Nor sound his quillets shrilly. Hoar the flamen,
  That scolds against the quality of flesh
  And not believes himself. Down with the nose,
  Down with it flat, take the bridge quite away
  Of him that his particular to foresee   160
  Smells from the general weal. Make curled-pate
    ruffians bald;
  And let the unscarred braggarts of the war
  Derive some pain from you. Plague all,
  That your activity may defeat and quell
  The source of all erection. There's more gold.
  Do you damn others, and let this damn you,
  And ditches grave you all!
PHRYNIA AND TIMANDRA. More counsel with more
  money, bounteous Timon.
TIMON. More whore, more mischief first; I have given
  you earnest.
ALCIBIADES. Strike up the drum towards Athens.
  Farewell, Timon;   170
  If I thrive well, I'll visit thee again.
TIMON. If I hope well, I'll never see thee more.
ALCIBIADES. I never did thee harm.
TIMON. Yes, thou spok'st well of me.
ALCIBIADES.   Call'st thou that harm?
TIMON. Men daily find it. Get thee away, and take
  Thy beagles with thee.
ALCIBIADES.   We but offend him. Strike!
                    *Drum beats. Alcibiades, Phrynia,
                                  and Timandra go*
TIMON. That nature, being sick of man's unkindness,
  Should yet be hungry! Common mother, thou,
                                              Digging
  Whose womb unmeasurable and infinite breast
  Teems, and feeds all; whose selfsame mettle,   180
  Whereof thy proud child, arrogant man, is puffed,
  Engenders the black toad and adder blue,
  The gilded newt and eyeless venomed worm,
  With all th'abhorréd births below crisp heaven

Whereon Hyperion's quick'ning fire doth shine;
Yield him, who all thy human sons doth hate,
From forth thy plenteous bosom, one poor root.
Ensear thy fertile and conceptious womb;
Let it no more bring out ingrateful man.
Go great with tigers, dragons, wolves and bears,   190
Teem with new monsters, whom thy upward face
Hath to the marbléd mansion all above
Never presented. O, a root, dear thanks!
Dry up thy marrows, vines and plough-torn leas,
Whereof ingrateful man with liquorish draughts
And morsels unctuous greases his pure mind,
That from it all consideration slips!

Enter Apemantus

  More man? plague, plague!
APEMANTUS. I was directed hither. Men report
  Thou dost affect my manners, and dost use them.   200
TIMON. 'Tis, then, because thou dost not keep a dog,
  Whom I would imitate. Consumption catch thee!
APEMANTUS. This is in thee a nature but infected,
  A poor unmanly melancholy sprung
  From change of fortune. Why this spade? this place?
  This slave-like habit and these looks of care?
  Thy flatterers yet wear silk, drink wine, lie soft,
  Hug their diseased perfumes, and have forgot
  That ever Timon was. Shame not these woods
  By putting on the cunning of a carper.   210
  Be thou a flatterer now, and seek to thrive
  By that which has undone thee; hinge thy knee
  And let his very breath whom thou'lt observe
  Blow off thy cap; praise his most vicious strain
  And call it excellent. Thou wast told thus;
  Thou gav'st thine ears like tapsters that bade
    welcome
  To knaves and all approachers. 'Tis most just
  That thou turn rascal; hadst thou wealth again,
  Rascals should have't. Do not assume my likeness.
TIMON. Were I like thee, I'ld throw away myself.   220
APEMANTUS. Thou hast cast away thyself, being like
    thyself;
  A madman so long, now a fool. What, think'st
  That the bleak air, thy boisterous chamberlain,
  Will put thy shirt on warm? will these mossed trees,
  That have outlived the eagle, page thy heels,
  And skip where thou point'st out? will the cold
    brook,
  Candied with ice, caudle thy morning taste,
  To cure thy o'ernight's surfeit? Call the creatures
  Whose naked natures live in all the spite
  Of wreakful heaven, whose bare unhoused trunks,   230
  To the conflicting elements exposed,
  Answer mere nature; bid them flatter thee;
  O, thou shalt find—
TIMON.   A fool of thee. Depart.
APEMANTUS. I love thee better now than e'er I did.
TIMON. I hate thee worse.
APEMANTUS.   Why?
TIMON.   Thou flatter'st misery.
APEMANTUS. I flatter not, but say thou art a caitiff.
TIMON. Why dost thou seek me out?
APEMANTUS.   To vex thee.
TIMON. Always a villain's office or a fool's.
  Dost please thyself in't?
APEMANTUS.   Ay.
TIMON.   What, a knave too?

APEMANTUS. If thou didst put this sour, cold habit on 240
  To castigate thy pride, 'twere well; but thou
  Dost it enforcedly. Thou'ldst courtier be again,
  Wert thou not beggar. Willing misery
  Outlives incertain pomp, is crowned before;
  The one is filling still, never complete,
  The other at high wish; best state, contentless,
  Hath a distracted and most wretched being,
  Worse than the worst, content.
  Thou shouldst desire to die, being miserable.
TIMON. Not by his breath that is more miserable. 250
  Thou art a slave whom Fortune's tender arm
  With favour never clasped, but bred a dog.
  Hadst thou like us from our first swath proceeded
  The sweet degrees that this brief world affords
  To such as may the passive drugs of it
  Freely command, thou wouldst have plunged
    thyself
  In general riot, melted down thy youth
  In different beds of lust, and never learned
  The icy precepts of respect, but followed
  The sug'red game before thee. But myself, 260
  Who had the world as my confectionary,
  The mouths, the tongues, the eyes and hearts of men
  At duty, more than I could frame employment;
  That numberless upon me stuck, as leaves
  Do on the oak, have with one winter's brush
  Fell from their boughs, and left me open, bare
  For every storm that blows—I to bear this,
  That never knew but better, is some burden.
  Thy nature did commence in sufferance, time
  Hath made thee hard in't. Why shouldst thou hate
    men? 270
  They never flattered thee. What hast thou given?
  If thou wilt curse, thy father, that poor rag,
  Must be thy subject; who in spite put stuff
  To some she-beggar and compounded thee
  Poor rogue hereditary. Hence, be gone.
  If thou hadst not been born the worst of men,
  Thou hadst been a knave and flatterer.
APEMANTUS. Art thou proud yet?
TIMON.   Ay, that I am not thee.
APEMANTUS. I, that I was no prodigal.
TIMON. I, that I am one now. 280
  Were all the wealth I have shut up in thee,
  I'ld give thee leave to hang it. Get thee gone.
  That the whole life of Athens were in this!
  Thus would I eat it.   Eating a root
APEMANTUS.   Here, I will mend thy feast.
                          Offering him another
TIMON. First mend my company; take away thyself.
APEMANTUS. So I shall mend mine own, by th'lack of
  thine.
TIMON. 'Tis not well mended so, it is but botched;
  If not, I would it were.
APEMANTUS. What wouldst thou have to Athens?
TIMON. Thee thither in a whirlwind. If thou wilt, 290
  Tell them there I have gold; look, so I have.
APEMANTUS. Here is no use for gold.
TIMON.   The best and truest;
  For here it sleeps, and does no hiréd harm.
APEMANTUS. Where liest a-nights, Timon?
TIMON. Under that's above me.
  Where feed'st thou a-days, Apemantus?
APEMANTUS. Where my stomach finds meat; or,
  rather, where I eat it.

TIMON. Would poison were obedient, and knew my
  mind! 300
APEMANTUS. Where wouldst thou send it?
TIMON. To sauce thy dishes.
APEMANTUS. The middle of humanity thou never
  knewest, but the extremity of both ends. When
  thou wast in thy gilt and thy perfume, they mocked
  thee for too much curiosity; in thy rags thou
  know'st none, but art despised for the contrary.
  There's a medlar for thee; eat it.
TIMON. On what I hate I feed not.
APEMANTUS. Dost hate a medlar? 310
TIMON. Ay, though it look like thee.
APEMANTUS. An thou'dst hated meddlers sooner, thou
  shouldst have loved thyself better now. What man
  didst thou ever know unthrift that was beloved after
  his means?
TIMON. Who, without those means thou talk'st of,
  didst thou ever know beloved?
APEMANTUS. Myself.
TIMON. I understand thee; thou hadst some means to
  keep a dog. 320
APEMANTUS. What things in the world canst thou
  nearest compare to thy flatterers?
TIMON. Women nearest; but men—men are the things
  themselves. What wouldst thou do with the world,
  Apemantus, if it lay in thy power?
APEMANTUS. Give it the beasts, to be rid of the men.
TIMON. Wouldst thou have thyself fall in the confusion of men, and remain a beast with the beasts?
APEMANTUS. Ay, Timon.
TIMON. A beastly ambition, which the gods grant thee 330
  t'attain to! If thou wert the lion, the fox would
  beguile thee; if thou wert the lamb, the fox would
  eat thee; if thou wert the fox, the lion would suspect
  thee when peradventure thou wert accused by the
  ass; if thou wert the ass, thy dulness would torment
  thee, and still thou livedst but as a breakfast to the
  wolf; if thou wert the wolf, thy greediness would
  afflict thee, and oft thou shouldst hazard thy life for
  thy dinner; wert thou the unicorn, pride and wrath
  would confound thee and make thine own self the 340
  conquest of thy fury; wert thou a bear, thou wouldst
  be killed by the horse; wert thou a horse, thou
  wouldst be seized by the leopard; wert thou a
  leopard, thou wert german to the lion, and the spots
  of thy kindred were jurors on thy life; all thy safety
  were remotion, and thy defence absence. What beast
  couldst thou be that were not subject to a beast? and
  what a beast art thou already, that seest not thy loss
  in transformation!
APEMANTUS. If thou couldst please me with speaking 350
  to me, thou mightst have hit upon it here. The
  commonwealth of Athens is become a forest of
  beasts.
TIMON. How has the ass broke the wall, that thou art
  out of the city?
APEMANTUS. Yonder comes a poet and a painter; the
  plague of company light upon thee! I will fear to
  catch it, and give way. When I know not what else
  to do, I'll see thee again.
TIMON. When there is nothing living but thee, thou 360
  shalt be welcome. I had rather be a beggar's dog than
  Apemantus.
APEMANTUS. Thou art the cap of all the fools alive.
TIMON. Would thou wert clean enough to spit upon!

APEMANTUS. A plague on thee! thou art too bad to curse.

TIMON. All villains that do stand by thee are pure.

APEMANTUS. There is no leprosy but what thou speak'st.

TIMON. If I name thee.   370
I'd beat thee, but I should infect my hands.

APEMANTUS. I would my tongue could rot them off.

TIMON. Away, thou issue of a mangy dog!
Choler does kill me that thou art alive;
I swoon to see thee.

APEMANTUS. Would thou wouldst burst!

TIMON.   Away, thou tedious rogue!
I am sorry I shall lose a stone by thee.
                              Throws a stone at him

APEMANTUS. Beast!

TIMON. Slave!

APEMANTUS. Toad!   380

TIMON. Rogue, rogue, rogue!
I am sick of this false world, and will love nought
But even the mere necessities upon't.
Then, Timon, presently prepare thy grave;
Lie where the light foam of the sea may beat
Thy grave-stone daily; make thine epitaph,
That death in me at others' lives may laugh.
[*To the gold*] O thou sweet king-killer, and dear divorce
'Twixt natural son and sire, thou bright defiler
Of Hymen's purest bed, thou valiant Mars,   390
Thou ever young, fresh, loved, and delicate wooer,
Whose blush doth thaw the consecrated snow
That lies on Dian's lap, thou visible god,
That sold'rest close impossibilities,
And mak'st them kiss; that speak'st with every tongue,
To every purpose! O thou touch of hearts!
Think thy slave man rebels; and by thy virtue
Set them into confounding odds, that beasts
May have the world in empire.

APEMANTUS.   Would 'twere so,
But not till I am dead. I'll say thou'st gold.   400
Thou wilt be thronged to shortly.

TIMON.   Thronged to?

APEMANTUS.   Ay.

TIMON. Thy back, I prithee.

APEMANTUS.   Live, and love thy misery.

TIMON. Long live so, and so die. [*Apemantus goes*] I am quit.
Moe things like men? Eat, Timon, and abhor them.

Enter three Bandits

1 BANDIT. Where should he have this gold? It is some poor fragment, some slender ort of his remainder. The mere want of gold, and the falling-from of his friends, drove him into this melancholy.

2 BANDIT. It is noised he hath a mass of treasure.

3 BANDIT. Let us make the assay upon him; if he care   410
not for't, he will supply us easily; if he covetously reserve it, how shall's get it?

2 BANDIT. True; for he bears it not about him; 'tis hid.

1 BANDIT. Is not this he?

3 BANDIT. Where?

2 BANDIT. 'Tis his description.

3 BANDIT. He? I know him.

BANDITS. Save thee, Timon.

TIMON. Now, thieves?

BANDITS. Soldiers, not thieves.   420

TIMON. Both two, and women's sons.

BANDITS. We are not thieves, but men that much do want.

TIMON. Your greatest want is, you want much of meat.
Why should you want? Behold, the earth hath roots;
Within this mile break forth a hundred springs;
The oaks bear mast, the briers scarlet hips;
The bounteous housewife Nature on each bush
Lays her full mess before you. Want? why want?

1 BANDIT. We cannot live on grass, on berries, water,
As beasts and birds and fishes.   430

TIMON. Nor on the beasts themselves, the birds and fishes;
You must eat men. Yet thanks I must you con
That you are thieves professed, that you work not
In holier shapes; for there is boundless theft
In limited professions. Rascal thieves,
Here's gold. Go, suck the subtle blood o'th'grape,
Till the high fever seethe your blood to froth,
And so 'scape hanging. Trust not the physician;
His antidotes are poison, and he slays
Moe than you rob, takes wealth and lives together.   440
Do villainy, do, since you protest to do't,
Like workmen. I'll example you with thievery:
The sun's a thief, and with his great attraction
Robs the vast sea; the moon's an arrant thief,
And her pale fire she snatches from the sun;
The sea's a thief, whose liquid surge resolves
The moon into salt tears; the earth's a thief,
That feeds and breeds by a composture stol'n
From gen'ral excrement—each thing's a thief.
The laws, your curb and whip, in their rough power   450
Has unchecked theft. Love not yourselves; away,
Rob one another. There's more gold. Cut throats;
All that you meet are thieves; to Athens go,
Break open shops; nothing can you steal,
But thieves do lose it; steal less for this I give you,
And gold confound you howsoe'er. Amen.

3 BANDIT. Has almost charmed me from my profession by persuading me to it.

1 BANDIT. 'Tis in the malice of mankind that he thus advises us, not to have us thrive in our mystery.   460

2 BANDIT. I'll believe him as an enemy, and give other my trade.

1 BANDIT. Let us first see peace in Athens; there is no time so miserable but a man may be true.
                                              Bandits go

Enter Flavius

FLAVIUS. O you gods!
Is yond despised and ruinous man my lord?
Full of decay and failing? O monument
And wonder of good deeds evilly bestowed!
What an alteration of honour has desp'rate want made!
What viler thing upon the earth than friends,   470
Who can bring noblest minds to basest ends!
How rarely does it meet with this time's guise,
When man was wished to love his enemies!
Grant I may ever love, and rather woo
Those that would mischief me than those that do!
Has caught me in his eye;
I will present my honest grief unto him,

And as my lord still serve him with my life.
My dearest master!
TIMON. Away! what art thou?
FLAVIUS.   Have you forgot me, sir? 480
TIMON. Why dost ask that? I have forgot all men.
   Then, if thou grant'st thou'rt a man, I have forgot
   thee.
FLAVIUS. An honest poor servant of yours.
TIMON. Then I know thee not;
   I never had honest man about me, I; all
   I kept were knaves, to serve in meat to villains.
FLAVIUS. The gods are witness,
   Ne'er did poor steward wear a truer grief
   For his undone lord than mine eyes for you.
TIMON. What, dost thou weep? come nearer; then I
   love thee,   490
   Because thou art a woman, and disclaim'st
   Flinty mankind, whose eyes do never give
   But thorough lust and laughter. Pity's sleeping.
   Strange times, that weep with laughing, not with
   weeping!
FLAVIUS. I beg of you to know me, good my lord,
   T'accept my grief, and whilst this poor wealth lasts
   To entertain me as your steward still.
TIMON. Had I a steward
   So true, so just, and now so comfortable?
   It almost turns my dangerous nature mild.   500
   Let me behold thy face. Surely this man
   Was born of woman.
   Forgive my general and exceptless rashness,
   You perpetual-sober gods! I do proclaim
   One honest man—mistake me not, but one;
   No more, I pray—and he's a steward
   How fain would I have hated all mankind,
   And thou redeem'st thyself. But all save thee
   I fell with curses.
   Methinks thou art more honest now than wise; 510
   For, by oppressing and betraying me,
   Thou mightst have sooner got another service;
   For many so arrive at second masters,
   Upon their first lord's neck. But tell me true—
   For I must ever doubt, though ne'er so sure—
   Is not thy kindness subtle-covetous,
   A usuring kindness, as rich men deal gifts,
   Expecting in return twenty for one?
FLAVIUS. No, my most worthy master, in whose
   breast
   Doubt and suspect, alas, are placed too late. 520
   You should have feared false times when you did
   feast:
   Suspect still comes where an estate is least.
   That which I show, heaven knows, is merely love,
   Duty and zeal to your unmatchéd mind,
   Care of your food and living; and believe it,
   My most honoured lord,
   For any benefit that points to me,
   Either in hope or present, I'ld exchange
   For this one wish, that you had power and wealth
   To requite me by making rich yourself.   530
TIMON. Look thee, 'tis so. Thou singly honest man,
   Here, take. The gods, out of my misery,
   Have sent thee treasure. Go, live rich and happy,
   But thus conditioned: thou shalt build from men,
   Hate all, curse all, show charity to none,
   But let the famished flesh slide from the bone
   Ere thou relieve the beggar. Give to dogs

What thou deniest to men. Let prisons swallow 'em,
Debts wither 'em to nothing; be men like blasted
   woods,
And may diseases lick up their false bloods!   540
And so farewell, and thrive.
FLAVIUS. O, let me stay and comfort you, my master.
TIMON. If thou hat'st curses
   Stay not; fly, whilst thou art blest and free;
   Ne'er see thou man, and let me ne'er see thee.
                              They depart severally

ACT 5

Scene 1: *The woods. Before Timon's cave*

Enter Poet and Painter; Timon listens from his cave, unseen

PAINTER. As I took note of the place, it cannot be far
   where he abides.
POET. What's to be thought of him? does the rumour
   hold for true, that he's so full of gold?
PAINTER. Certain. Alcibiades reports it; Phrynia and
   Timandra had gold of him. He likewise enriched
   poor straggling soldiers with great quantity. 'Tis
   said he gave unto his steward a mighty sum.
POET. Then this breaking of his has been but a try for
   his friends.   10
PAINTER. Nothing else. You shall see him a palm in
   Athens again, and flourish with the highest. Therefore 'tis not amiss we tender our loves to him in this
   supposed distress of his; it will show honestly in us,
   and is very likely to load our purposes with what
   they travail for, if it be a just and true report that
   goes of his having.
POET. What have you now to present unto him?
PAINTER. Nothing at this time but my visitation; only
   I will promise him an excellent piece.   20
POET. I must serve him so too, tell him of an intent
   that's coming toward him.
PAINTER. Good as the best. Promising is the very air
   o'th'time; it opens the eyes of expectation. Performance is ever the duller for his act, and but in the
   plainer and simpler kind of people the deed of saying
   is quite out of use. To promise is most courtly and
   fashionable; performance is a kind of will or
   testament which argues a great sickness in his judgement that makes it.   30
TIMON [*aside*]. Excellent workman! thou canst not
   paint a man so bad as is thyself.
POET. I am thinking what I shall say I have provided
   for him. It must be a personating of himself; a satire
   against the softness of prosperity, with a discovery of
   the infinite flatteries that follow youth and
   opulency.
TIMON [*aside*]. Must thou needs stand for a villain in
   thine own work? wilt thou whip thine own faults
   in other men? Do so, I have gold for thee.   40
POET. Nay, let's seek him.
   Then do we sin against our own estate,
   When we may profit meet, and come too late.
PAINTER. True.
   When the day serves, before black-cornered night,
   Find what thou want'st by free and offered light.
   Come.
TIMON [*aside*]. I'll meet you at the turn. What a god's
   gold,
   That he is worshipped in a baser temple

Than where swine feed!   50
'Tis thou that rigg'st the bark and plough'st the
    foam,
Settlest admiréd reverence in a slave.
To thee be worship, and thy saints for aye
Be crowned with plagues, that thee alone obey!
Fit I meet them.   *Coming forward*
POET. Hail, worthy Timon!
PAINTER.   Our late noble master!
TIMON. Have I once lived to see two honest men?
POET. Sir,
Having often of your open bounty tasted,
Hearing you were retired, your friends fall'n off, 60
Whose thankless natures—O abhorréd spirits!—
Not all the whips of heaven are large enough—
What, to you,
Whose star-like nobleness gave life and influence
To their whole being! I am rapt, and cannot cover
The monstrous bulk of this ingratitude
With any size of words.
TIMON. Let it go naked, men may see't the better.
You that are honest, by being what you are,
Make them best seen and known.
PAINTER.   He and myself 70
Have travelled in the great shower of your gifts,
And sweetly felt it.
TIMON.   Ay, you are honest men.
PAINTER. We are hither come to offer you our service.
TIMON. Most honest men. Why, how shall I requite
    you?
Can you eat roots, and drink cold water? no?
BOTH. What we can do, we'll do, to do you service.
TIMON. Ye're honest men: ye've heard that I have
    gold;
I am sure you have. Speak truth; ye're honest men.
PAINTER. So it is said, my noble lord, but therefore
Came not my friend nor I.   80
TIMON. Good honest men. Thou draw'st a counterfeit
Best in all Athens; thou'rt indeed the best;
Thou counterfeit'st most lively.
PAINTER.   So so, my lord.
TIMON. E'en so, sir, as I say. And for thy fiction,
Why, thy verse swells with stuff so fine and smooth
That thou art even natural in thine art.
But for all this, my honest-natured friends,
I must needs say you have a little fault;
Marry, 'tis not monstrous in you, neither wish I
You take much pains to mend.
BOTH.   Beseech your honour 90
To make it known to us.
TIMON.   You'll take it ill.
BOTH. Most thankfully, my lord.
TIMON.   Will you indeed?
BOTH. Doubt it not, worthy lord.
TIMON. There's never a one of you but trusts a knave
That mightily deceives you.
BOTH.   Do we, my lord?
TIMON. Ay, and you hear him cog, see him dissemble,
Know his gross patchery, love him, feed him,
Keep in your bosom; yet remain assured
That he's a made-up villain.
PAINTER. I know none such, my lord.
POET.   Nor I.   100
TIMON. Look you, I love you well; I'll give you gold,
Rid me these villains from your companies.
Hang them or stab them, drown them in a draught,

Confound them by some course, and come to me,
I'll give you gold enough.
BOTH. Name them, my lord, let's know them.
TIMON. You that way, and you this—but two in
    company—
Each man apart, all single and alone,
Yet an arch-villain keeps him company.
If, where thou art, two villains shall not be,   110
Come not near him. If thou wouldst not reside
But where one villain is, then him abandon.
Hence, pack, there's gold; you came for gold, ye
    slaves.
[*to Painter*] You have work for me; there's payment.
    Hence!
[*to Poet*] You are an alchemist, make gold of that.
Out, rascal dogs!   *He beats them out, and retires*
                                            into his cave

Enter Flavius and two Senators

FLAVIUS. It is in vain that you would speak with
    Timon;
For he is set so only to himself
That nothing but himself which looks like man
Is friendly with him.
1 SENATOR.   Bring us to his cave: 120
It is our part and promise to th'Athenians
To speak with Timon.
2 SENATOR.   At all times alike
Men are not still the same; 'twas time and griefs
That framed him thus. Time, with his fairer hand,
Offering the fortunes of his former days,
The former man may make him. Bring us to him,
And chance it as it may.
FLAVIUS.   Here is his cave.
Peace and content be here! Lord Timon, Timon,
Look out, and speak to friends. Th'Athenians
By two of their most reverend senate greet thee.   130
Speak to them, noble Timon.

Timon comes from his cave

TIMON. Thou sun, that comforts, burn! Speak and be
    hanged.
For each true word a blister, and each false
Be as a cantherizing to the root o'th'tongue,
Consuming it with speaking!
1 SENATOR.   Worthy Timon—
TIMON. Of none but such as you, and you of Timon.
1 SENATOR. The senators of Athens greet thee, Timon.
TIMON. I thank them, and would send them back the
    plague,
Could I but catch it for them.
1 SENATOR.   O, forget
What we are sorry for ourselves in thee.   140
The senators with one consent of love
Entreat thee back to Athens, who have thought
On special dignities, which vacant lie
For thy best use and wearing.
2 SENATOR.   They confess
Toward thee forgetfulness too general-gross;
Which now the public body, which doth seldom
Play the recanter, feeling in itself
A lack of Timon's aid, hath sense withal
Of its own fail, restraining aid to Timon;
And send forth us, to make their sorrowéd render, 150
Together with a recompense more fruitful
Than their offence can weigh down by the dram;

Ay, even such heaps and sums of love and wealth
As shall to thee blot out what wrongs were theirs,
And write in thee the figures of their love,
Ever to read them thine.

TIMON.   You witch me in it;
Surprise me to the very brink of tears.
Lend me a fool's heart and a woman's eyes,
And I'll beweep these comforts, worthy senators.

1 SENATOR. Therefore so please thee to return with us, 160
And of our Athens, thine and ours, to take
The captainship, thou shalt be met with thanks,
Allowed with absolute power, and thy good name
Live with authority: so soon we shall drive back
Of Alcibiades th'approaches wild,
Who like a boar too savage doth root up
His country's peace.

2 SENATOR.   And shakes his threat'ning sword
Against the walls of Athens.

1 SENATOR.   Therefore, Timon—

TIMON. Well, sir, I will—therefore I will, sir, thus:
If Alcibiades kill my countrymen,   170
Let Alcibiades know this of Timon,
That Timon cares not. But if he sack fair Athens,
And take our goodly agèd men by th'beards,
Giving our holy virgins to the stain
Of contumelious, beastly, mad-brained war;
Then let him know, and tell him Timon speaks it,
In pity of our agèd and our youth,
I cannot choose but tell him that I care not,
And let him take't at worst; for their knives care not,
While you have throats to answer; for myself,   180
There's not a whittle in th'unruly camp
But I do prize it at my love before
The reverend'st throat in Athens. So I leave you
To the protection of the prosperous gods,
As thieves to keepers.

FLAVIUS.   Stay not, all's in vain.

TIMON. Why, I was writing of my epitaph;
It will be seen to-morrow. My long sickness
Of health and living now begins to mend,
And nothing brings me all things. Go, live still;
Be Alcibiades your plague, you his,   190
And last so long enough!

1 SENATOR.   We speak in vain.

TIMON. But yet I love my country, and am not
One that rejoices in the common wreck,
As common bruit doth put it.

1 SENATOR.   That's well spoke.

TIMON. Commend me to my loving countrymen—

1 SENATOR. These words become your lips as they pass
through them.

2 SENATOR. And enter in our ears like great triumphers
In their applauding gates.

TIMON.   Commend me to them,
And tell them that, to ease them of their griefs,
Their fears of hostile strokes, their achës, losses,   200
Their pangs of love, with other incident throes
That nature's fragile vessel doth sustain
In life's uncertain voyage, I will some kindness do
them;
I'll teach them to prevent wild Alcibiades' wrath.

1 SENATOR. I like this well; he will return again.

TIMON. I have a tree, which grows here in my close,
That mine own use invites me to cut down,
And shortly must I fell it. Tell my friends,
Tell Athens, in the sequence of degree

From high to low throughout, that whoso please 210
To stop affliction, let him take his haste,
Come hither ere my tree hath felt the axe,
And hang himself. I pray you do my greeting.

FLAVIUS. Trouble him no further; thus you still shall
find him.

TIMON. Come not to me again, but say to Athens,
Timon hath made his everlasting mansion
Upon the beachèd verge of the salt flood,
Who once a day with his embossèd froth
The turbulent surge shall cover; thither come,
And let my grave-stone be your oracle.   220
Lips, let four words go by, and language end:
What is amiss, plague and infection mend!
Graves only be men's works, and death their gain!
Sun, hide thy beams; Timon hath done his reign.

Retires to his cave

1 SENATOR. His discontents are unremovably
Coupled to nature.

2 SENATOR. Our hope in him is dead. Let us return,
And strain what other means is left unto us
In our dear peril.

1 SENATOR.   It requires swift foot.

They go

Scene 2: *Before the walls of Athens*

Enter two other Senators, with a Messenger

3 SENATOR. Thou hast painfully discovered; are his
files
As full as thy report?

MESSENGER.   I have spoke the least.
Besides, his expedition promises
Present approach.

4 SENATOR. We stand much hazard if they bring not
Timon.

MESSENGER. I met a courier, one mine ancient friend,
Whom, though in general part we were opposed,
Yet our old love made a particular force,
And made us speak like friends. This man was riding
From Alcibiades to Timon's cave   10
With letters of entreaty, which imported
His fellowship i'th'cause against your city,
In part for his sake moved.

3 SENATOR.   Here come our brothers.

Enter the other Senators from Timon.

1 SENATOR. No talk of Timon, nothing of him expect.
The enemy's drum is heard, and fearful scouring
Doth choke the air with dust: in, and prepare.
Ours is the fall, I fear, our foe's the snare.

They go

Scene 3: *The woods. Timon's cave, and a rude tomb seen*

Enter a Soldier, seeking Timon

SOLDIER. By all description this should be the place.
Who's here? speak, ho! No answer? What is this?
[*reads*] 'Timon is dead, who hath outstretched his
span;
Some beast read this; there does not live a man.'
Dead, sure, and this his grave. What's on this tomb
I cannot read; the character I'll take with wax;
Our captain hath in every figure skill,
An aged interpreter, though young in days;

Before proud Athens he's set down by this,
Whose fall the mark of his ambition is.   *He goes* 10

Scene 4: *Before the walls of Athens*

Trumpets sound. Enter Alcibiades with his powers

ALCIBIADES. Sound to this coward and lascivious town
Our terrible approach.   *Sounds a parley*

The Senators appear upon the walls

Till now you have gone on and filled the time
With all licentious measure, making your wills
The scope of justice. Till now, myself and such
As stepped within the shadow of your power
Have wandered with our traversed arms and
     breathed
Our sufferance vainly; now the time is flush,
When crouching marrow in the bearer strong
Cries of itself 'No more'; now breathless wrong 10
Shall sit and pant in your great chairs of ease,
And pursy insolence shall break his wind
With fear and horrid flight.

1 SENATOR.   Noble and young,
When thy first griefs were but a mere conceit,
Ere thou hadst power or we had cause of fear,
We sent to thee, to give thy rages balm,
To wipe out our ingratitude with loves
Above their quantity.

2 SENATOR.   So did we woo
Transforméd Timon to our city's love
By humble message and by promised means; 20
We were not all unkind, nor all deserve
The common stroke of war.

1 SENATOR.   These walls of ours
Were not erected by their hands from whom
You have received your griefs; nor are they such
That these great towers, trophies, and schools
     should fall
For private faults in them.

2 SENATOR.   Nor are they living
Who were the motives that you first went out;
Shame, that they wanted cunning, in excess
Hath broke their hearts. March, noble lord,
Into our city with thy banners spread; 30
By decimation and a tithéd death,
If thy revenges hunger for that food
Which nature loathes, take thou the destined tenth,
And by the hazard of the spotted die
Let die the spotted.

1 SENATOR.   All have not offended;
For those that were, it is not square to take,
On those that are, revenges; crimes like lands
Are not inherited. Then, dear countryman,
Bring in thy ranks, but leave without thy rage;
Spare thy Athenian cradle and those kin 40
Which, in the bluster of thy wrath, must fall

With those that have offended. Like a shepherd
Approach the fold and cull th'infected forth,
But kill not all together.

2 SENATOR.   What thou wilt,
Thou rather shalt enforce it with thy smile
Than hew to't with thy sword.

1 SENATOR.   Set but thy foot
Against our rampiréd gates, and they shall ope;
So thou wilt send thy gentle heart before,
To say thou'lt enter friendly.

2 SENATOR.   Throw thy glove,
Or any token of thine honour else, 50
That thou wilt use the wars as thy redress
And not as our confusion, all thy powers
Shall make their harbour in our town, till we
Have sealed thy full desire.

ALCIBIADES.   Then there's my glove;
Descend, and open your unchargéd ports;
Those enemies of Timon's, and mine own,
Whom you yourselves shall set out for reproof,
Fall, and no more; and, to atone your fears
With my more noble meaning, not a man
Shall pass his quarter, or offend the stream 60
Of regular justice in your city's bounds,
But shall be rendered to your public laws
At heaviest answer.

BOTH.   'Tis most nobly spoken.

ALCIBIADES. Descend, and keep your words.

          The Senators descend, and open the gates

Enter Soldier

SOLDIER. My noble general, Timon is dead,
Entombed upon the very hem o'th'sea,
And on his grave-stone this insculpture, which
With wax I brought away, whose soft impression
Interprets for my poor ignorance.

ALCIBIADES [*reads*]. 'Here lies a wretched corse, of
     wretched soul bereft; 70
Seek not my name: a plague consume you wicked
     caitiffs left!
Here lie I, Timon, who alive all living men did hate;
Pass by and curse thy fill, but pass, and stay not here
     thy gait.'
These well express in thee thy latter spirits.
Though thou abhorredst in us our human griefs,
Scornedst our brain's flow, and those our droplets
     which
From niggard nature fall, yet rich conceit
Taught thee to make vast Neptune weep for aye
On thy low grave, on faults forgiven. Dead
Is noble Timon, of whose memory 80
Hereafter more. Bring me into your city,
And I will use the olive with my sword,
Make war breed peace, make peace stint war, make
     each
Prescribe to other, as each other's leech.
Let our drums strike.   *They go*

Julius Caesar

The scene: Rome; the neighbourhood of Sardis;
the neighbourhood of Philippi

CHARACTERS IN THE PLAY

JULIUS CÆSAR
OCTAVIUS CÆSAR } *triumvirs after the death of*
MARCUS ANTONIUS *Julius Cæsar*
M. ÆMILIUS LEPIDUS

CICERO
PUBLIUS } *senators*
POPILIUS LENA

MARCUS BRUTUS
CASSIUS
CASCA
TREBONIUS } *conspirators against Julius*
LIGARIUS *Cæsar*
DECIUS BRUTUS
METELLUS CIMBER
CINNA

FLAVIUS *and* MARULLUS, *tribunes*
ARTEMIDORUS of Cnidos, *a teacher of Rhetoric*
A Soothsayer
CINNA, *a poet*

Another poet
LUCILIUS
TITINIUS
MESSALA } *friends to Brutus and Cassius*
YOUNG CATO
VOLUMNIUS
VARRO
CLITUS
CLAUDIUS
STRATO
LUCIUS } *servants to Brutus or his officers*
DARDANIUS
LABEO
FLAVIUS

PINDARUS, *bondman to Cassius*
CALPHURNIA, *wife to Cæsar*
PORTIA, *wife to Brutus*
Senators, Citizens, Officers, Attendants, etc.

Julius Caesar

ACT 1
Scene 1: *Rome. A street*

Flavius, Marullus, and certain commoners

FLAVIUS. Hence! home, you idle creatures, get you
  home:
  Is this a holiday? what! know you not,
  Being mechanical, you ought not walk
  Upon a labouring day without the sign
  Of your profession? Speak, what trade art thou?
1 COMMONER. Why, sir, a carpenter.
MARULLUS. Where is thy leather apron and thy rule?
  What dost thou with thy best apparel on?
  You, sir, what trade are you?
2 COMMONER. Truly, sir, in respect of a fine workman, 10
  I am but as you would say a cobbler.
MARULLUS. But what trade art thou? answer me
  directly.
2 COMMONER. A trade, sir, that I hope I may use with
  a safe conscience, which is indeed, sir, a mender of
  bad soles.
MARULLUS. What trade, thou knave? thou naughty
  knave, what trade?
2 COMMONER. Nay, I beseech you, sir, be not out with
  me: yet if you be out, sir, I can mend you.   20
MARULLUS. What mean'st thou by that? mend me,
  thou saucy fellow!
2 COMMONER. Why, sir, cobble you.
FLAVIUS. Thou art a cobbler, are thou?
2 COMMONER. Truly, sir, all that I live by is with the
  awl: I meddle with no tradesman's matters, nor
  women's matters; but withal I am indeed, sir, a
  surgeon to old shoes; when they are in great danger,
  I recover them. As proper men as ever trod upon
  neat's leather have gone upon my handiwork. 30
FLAVIUS. But wherefore art not in thy shop to-day?
  Why dost thou lead these men about the streets?
2 COMMONER. Truly, sir, to wear out their shoes, to
  get myself into more work. But indeed, sir, we
  make holiday, to see Cæsar and to rejoice in his
  triumph.
MARULLUS. Wherefore rejoice? What conquest brings
  he home?
  What tributaries follow him to Rome,
  To grace in captive bonds his chariot-wheels?
  You blocks, you stones, you worse than senseless
    things!   40
  O you hard hearts, you cruel men of Rome,
  Knew you not Pompey? Many a time and oft
  Have you climbed up to walls and battlements,
  To towers and windows, yea, to chimney-tops,
  Your infants in your arms, and there have sat
  The live-long day with patient expectation
  To see great Pompey pass the streets of Rome:
  And when you saw his chariot but appear,
  Have you not made an universal shout,
  That Tiber trembled underneath her banks 50
  To hear the replication of your sounds
  Made in her concave shores?
  And do you now put on your best attire?
  And do you now cull out a holiday?
  And do you now strew flowers in his way
  That comes in triumph over Pompey's blood?
  Be gone!
  Run to your houses, fall upon your knees,
  Pray to the gods to intermit the plague
  That needs must light on this ingratitude. 60
FLAVIUS. Go, go, good countrymen, and for this fault
  Assemble all the poor men of your sort;
  Draw them to Tiber banks and weep your tears
  Into the channel, till the lowest stream
  Do kiss the most exalted shores of all.
                      The crowd goes
  See, whe'r their basest mettle be not moved;
  They vanish tongue-tied in their guiltiness.
  Go you down that way towards the Capitol;
  This way will I: disrobe the images,
  If you do find them decked with ceremonies. 70
MARULLUS. May we do so?
  You know it is the feast of Lupercal.
FLAVIUS. It is no matter; let no images
  Be hung with Cæsar's trophies. I'll about,
  And drive away the vulgar from the streets:
  So do you too, where you perceive them thick.
  These growing feathers plucked from Cæsar's wing
  Will make him fly an ordinary pitch,
  Who else would soar above the view of men
  And keep us all in servile fearfulness.   *They go*

Scene 2

*Enter Cæsar, Antony, stripped for the course, Calphurnia,
Portia, Decius, Cicero, Brutus, Cassius, Casca, a
Soothsayer, and after them Marullus and Flavius, with a
great crowd following*

CÆSAR. Calphurnia!
CASCA.   Peace, ho! Cæsar speaks.
CÆSAR.   Calphurnia!
CALPHURNIA. Here, my lord.
CÆSAR. Stand you directly in Antonius' way,
  When he doth run his course. Antonius!
ANTONY. Cæsar, my lord?
CÆSAR. Forget not, in your speed, Antonius,
  To touch Calphurnia; for our elders say,
  The barren, touchéd in this holy chase,
  Shake off their sterile curse.
ANTONY.   I shall remember:
  When Cæsar says 'do this,' it is performed. 10
CÆSAR. Set on, and leave no ceremony out.
                               Music
SOOTHSAYER. Cæsar!
CÆSAR. Ha! who calls?
CASCA. Bid every noise be still: peace yet again!
CÆSAR. Who is it in the press that calls on me?
  I hear a tongue, shriller than all the music,
  Cry 'Cæsar.' Speak, Cæsar is turned to hear.
SOOTHSAYER. Beware the ides of March.
CÆSAR.   What man is that?
BRUTUS. A soothsayer bids you beware the ides
  of March.

CÆSAR. Set him before me, let me see his face.   20
CASSIUS. Fellow, come from the throng, look
  upon Cæsar.
CÆSAR. What say'st thou to me now? speak once
  again.
SOOTHSAYER. Beware the ides of March.
CÆSAR. He is a dreamer, let us leave him: pass.
               Sennet; the procession goes
CASSIUS. Will you go see the order of the course?
BRUTUS. Not I.
CASSIUS. I pray you, do.
BRUTUS. I am not gamesome: I do lack some part
  Of that quick spirit that is in Antony.
  Let me not hinder, Cassius, your desires;   30
  I'll leave you.
CASSIUS. Brutus, I do observe you now of late:
  I have not from your eyes that gentleness
  And show of love as I was wont to have:
  You bear too stubborn and too strange a hand
  Over your friend that loves you.
BRUTUS.   Cassius,
  Be not deceived: if I have veiled my look,
  I turn the trouble of my countenance
  Merely upon myself. Vexéd I am
  Of late with passions of some difference,   40
  Conceptions only proper to myself,
  Which give some soil perhaps to my behaviours;
  But let not therefore my good friends be grieved
  (Among which number, Cassius, be you one),
  Nor construe any further my neglect
  Than that poor Brutus with himself at war
  Forgets the shows of love to other men.
CASSIUS. Then, Brutus, I have much mistook your
  passion,
  By means whereof this breast of mine hath buried
  Thoughts of great value, worthy cogitations.   50
  Tell me, good Brutus, can you see your face?
BRUTUS. No, Cassius; for the eye sees not itself
  But by reflection, by some other things.
CASSIUS. 'Tis just,
  And it is very much lamented, Brutus,
  That you have no such mirrors as will turn
  Your hidden worthiness into your eye,
  That you might see your shadow. I have heard
  Where many of the best respect in Rome
  (Except immortal Cæsar), speaking of Brutus,   60
  And groaning underneath this age's yoke,
  Have wished that noble Brutus had his eyes.
BRUTUS. Into what dangers would you lead me,
  Cassius,
  That you would have me seek into myself
  For that which is not in me?
CASSIUS. Therefore, good Brutus, be prepared to hear:
  And since you know you cannot see yourself
  So well as by reflection, I your glass
  Will modestly discover to yourself
  That of yourself which you yet know not of.   70
  And be not jealous on me, gentle Brutus:
  Were I a common laughter, or did use
  To stale with ordinary oaths my love
  To every new protester; if you know
  That I do fawn on men and hug them hard,
  And after scandal them; or if you know
  That I profess myself in banqueting
  To all the rout, then hold me dangerous.
                 Flourish and shout

BRUTUS. What means this shouting? I do fear, the
  people
  Choose Cæsar for their king.
CASSIUS.   Ay, do you fear it?   80
  Then must I think you would not have it so.
BRUTUS. I would not, Cassius, yet I love him well …
  But wherefore do you hold me here so long?
  What is it that you would impart to me?
  If it be aught toward the general good,
  Set honour in one eye and death i'th'other,
  And I will look on both indifferently:
  For let the gods so speed me as I love
  The name of honour more than I fear death.
CASSIUS. I know that virtue to be in you, Brutus,   90
  As well as I do know your outward favour.
  Well, honour is the subject of my story …
  I cannot tell what you and other men
  Think of this life; but, for my single self,
  I had as lief not be as live to be
  In awe of such a thing as I myself.
  I was born free as Cæsar, so were you;
  We both have fed as well, and we can both
  Endure the winter's cold as well as he.
  For once, upon a raw and gusty day,   100
  The troubled Tiber chafing with her shores,
  Cæsar said to me 'Dar'st thou, Cassius, now
  Leap in with me into this angry flood,
  And swim to yonder point?' Upon the word,
  Accoutréd as I was, I plungéd in
  And bade him follow: so indeed he did.
  The torrent roared, and we did buffet it
  With lusty sinews, throwing it aside
  And stemming it with hearts of controversy.
  But ere we could arrive the point proposed,   110
  Cæsar cried 'Help me, Cassius, or I sink!'
  I, as Æneas our great ancestor
  Did from the flames of Troy upon his shoulder
  The old Anchises bear, so from the waves of Tiber
  Did I the tired Cæsar: and this man
  Is now become a god, and Cassius is
  A wretched creature, and must bend his body
  If Cæsar carelessly but nod on him.
  He had a fever when he was in Spain,
  And when the fit was on him, I did mark   120
  How he did shake: 'tis true, this god did shake;
  His coward lips did from their colour fly,
  And that same eye whose bend doth awe the world
  Did lose his lustre: I did hear him groan:
  Ay, and that tongue of his that bade the Romans
  Mark him and write his speeches in their books,
  Alas, it cried, 'Give me some drink, Titinius,'
  As a sick girl … Ye gods! it doth amaze me
  A man of such a feeble temper should
  So get the start of the majestic world,   130
  And bear the palm alone.   *Shout; flourish*
BRUTUS. Another general shout!
  I do believe that these applauses are
  For some new honours that are heaped on Cæsar.
CASSIUS. Why, man, he doth bestride the narrow
  world
  Like a Colossus, and we petty men
  Walk under his huge legs and peep about
  To find ourselves dishonourable graves.
  Men at some time are masters of their fates:
  The fault, dear Brutus, is not in our stars,   140
  But in ourselves, that we are underlings.

Brutus and Cæsar: what should be in that 'Cæsar'?
Why should that name be sounded more than
    yours?
Write them together, yours is as fair a name;
Sound them, it doth become the mouth as well;
Weigh them, it is as heavy; conjure with 'em,
Brutus will start a spirit as soon as Cæsar.
Now, in the names of all the gods at once,
Upon what meat doth this our Cæsar feed,
That he is grown so great? Age, thou art shamed! 150
Rome, thou hast lost the breed of noble bloods!
When went there by an age, since the great flood,
But it was famed with more than with one man?
When could they say, till now, that talked of Rome
That her wide walls encompassed but one man?
Now is it Rome indeed, and room enough,
When there is in it but one only man.
O, you and I have heard our fathers say
There was a Brutus once that would have brooked
Th'eternal devil to keep his state in Rome   160
As easily as a king.
BRUTUS. That you do love me, I am nothing jealous;
What you would work me to, I have some aim:
How I have thought of this and of these times,
I shall recount hereafter; for this present,
I would not (so with love I might entreat you)
Be any further moved. What you have said
I will consider; what you have to say
I will with patience hear, and find a time
Both meet to hear and answer such high things.   170
Till then, my noble friend, chew upon this:
Brutus had rather be a villager
Than to repute himself a son of Rome
Under these hard conditions as this time
Is like to lay upon us.
CASSIUS. I am glad that my weak words
Have struck but thus much show of fire from
    Brutus.

Re-enter Cæsar and his train

BRUTUS. The games are done, and Cæsar is returning.
CASSIUS. As they pass by, pluck Casca by the sleeve,
And he will (after his sour fashion) tell you   180
What hath proceeded worthy note to-day.
BRUTUS. I will do so: but, look you, Cassius
The angry spot doth glow on Cæsar's brow,
And all the rest look like a chidden train:
Calphurnia's cheek is pale, and Cicero
Looks with such ferret and such fiery eyes
As we have seen him in the Capitol,
Being crossed in conference by some senator.
CASSIUS. Casca will tell us what the matter is.
CÆSAR. Antonius!   190
ANTONY. Cæsar?
CÆSAR. Let me have men about me that are fat,
Sleek-headed men, and such as sleep a-nights:
Yond Cassius has a lean and hungry look;
He thinks too much: such men are dangerous.
ANTONY. Fear him not, Cæsar; he's not dangerous;
He is a noble Roman, and well given.
CÆSAR. Would he were fatter! but I fear him not
Yet if my name were liable to fear,
I do not know the man I should avoid   200
So soon as that spare Cassius. He reads much;
He is a great observer, and he looks
Quite through the deeds of men; he loves no plays,

As thou dost, Antony; he hears no music;
Seldom he smiles, and smiles in such a sort
As if he mocked himself and scorned his spirit
That could be moved to smile at any thing.
Such men as he be never at heart's ease
Whiles they behold a greater than themselves,
And therefore are they very dangerous.   210
I rather tell thee what is to be feared
Than what I fear; for always I am Cæsar.
Come on my right hand, for this ear is deaf,
And tell me truly what thou think'st of him.
            Sennet. Cæsar and his train pass on
CASCA. You pulled me by the cloak, would you speak
    with me?
BRUTUS. Ay, Casca, tell us what hath chanced to-day,
That Cæsar looks so sad.
CASCA. Why, you were with him, were you not?
BRUTUS. I should not then ask Casca what had
    chanced.   220
CASCA. Why, there was a crown offered him: and
    being offered him, he put it by with the back of his
    hand, thus: and then the people fell a-shouting.
BRUTUS. What was the second noise for?
CASCA. Why, for that too.
CASSIUS. They shouted thrice: what was the last cry
    for?
CASCA. Why, for that too.
BRUTUS. Was the crown offered him thrice?
CASCA. Ay, marry, was't, and he put it by thrice, every 230
    time gentler than other; and at every putting-by
    mine honest neighbours shouted.
CASSIUS. Who offered him the crown?
CASCA. Why, Antony.
BRUTUS. Tell us the manner of it, gentle Casca.
CASCA. I can as well be hanged as tell the manner of
    it: it was mere foolery, I did not mark it. I saw Mark
    Antony offer him a crown, yet 'twas not a crown
    neither, 'twas one of these coronets: and, as I told
    you, he put it by once: but for all that, to my think- 240
    ing, he would fain have had it. Then he offered it
    to him again; then he put it by again: but, to my
    thinking, he was very loath to lay his fingers off
    it. And then he offered it the third time; he put it
    the third time by: and still as he refused it, the rabble-
    ment hooted and clapped their chopped hands and
    threw up their sweaty night-caps and uttered such a
    deal of stinking breath because Cæsar refused the
    crown, that it had almost choked Cæsar; for he
    swooned and fell down at it: and for mine own part, 250
    I durst not laugh, for fear of opening my lips and
    receiving the bad air.
CASSIUS. But, soft, I pray you: what, did Cæsar swoon?
CASCA. He fell down in the market-place and foamed
    at mouth and was speechless.
BRUTUS. 'Tis very like: he hath the falling-sickness.
CASSIUS. No, Cæsar hath it not; but you, and I,
    And honest Casca, we have the falling-sickness.
CASCA. I know not what you mean by that, but I am
    sure Cæsar fell down. If the tag-rag people did not 260
    clap him and hiss him according as he pleased and
    displeased them, as they use to do the players in the
    theatre, I am no true man.
BRUTUS. What said he when he came unto himself?
CASCA. Marry, before he fell down, when he per-
    ceived the common herd was glad he refused the
    crown, he plucked me ope his doublet and offered

them his throat to cut. An I had been a man of any
occupation, if I would not have taken him at a word,
I would I might go to hell among the rogues. And 270
so he fell. When he came to himself again, he said,
if he had done or said any thing amiss, he desired their
worships to think it was his infirmity. Three or four
wenches, where I stood, cried 'Alas, good soul!' and
forgave him with all their hearts: but there's no heed
to be taken of them; if Cæsar had stabbed their
mothers, they would have done no less.

BRUTUS. And after that, he came, thus sad, away?

CASCA. Ay.

CASSIUS. Did Cicero say any thing? 280

CASCA. Ay, he spoke Greek.

CASSIUS. To what effect?

CASCA. Nay, an I tell you that, I'll ne'er look you i'
th'face again: but those that understood him smiled
at one another and shook their heads; but for mine
own part, it was Greek to me. I could tell you more
news too: Marullus and Flavius, for pulling scarfs
off Cæsar's images, are put to silence. Fare you well.
There was more foolery yet, if I could remember it.

CASSIUS. Will you sup with me to-night, Casca? 290

CASCA. No, I am promised forth.

CASSIUS. Will you dine with me to-morrow?

CASCA. Ay, if I be alive, and your mind hold, and your
dinner worth the eating.

CASSIUS. Good; I will expect you.

CASCA. Do so: farewell, both.   *He goes*

BRUTUS. What a blunt fellow is this grown to be!
He was quick mettle when he went to school.

CASSIUS. So is he now in execution
Of any bold or noble enterprise, 300
However he puts on this tardy form.
This rudeness is a sauce to his good wit,
Which gives men stomach to digest his words
With better appetite.

BRUTUS. And so it is. . . . For this time I will leave you:
To-morrow, if you please to speak with me,
I will come home to you; or, if you will,
Come home to me and I will wait for you.

CASSIUS. I will do so: till then, think of the world.
                                                   Brutus goes
Well, Brutus, thou art noble; yet I see 310
Thy honourable metal may be wrought
From that it is disposed: therefore it is meet
That noble minds keep ever with their likes;
For who so firm that cannot be seduced?
Cæsar doth bear me hard, but he loves Brutus:
If I were Brutus now and he were Cassius,
He should not humour me. I will this night,
In several hands, in at his windows throw,
As if they came from several citizens,
Writings, all tending to the great opinion 320
That Rome holds of his name, wherein obscurely
Cæsar's ambition shall be glancèd at:
And after this let Cæsar seat him sure;
For we will shake him, or worse days endure.
                                                        He goes

Scene 3: *The same*

*Thunder and lightning. Enter, from opposite sides, Casca,
with his sword drawn, and Cicero*

CICERO. Good even, Casca: brought you Cæsar home?
Why are you breathless? and why stare you so?

CASCA. Are not you moved, when all the sway of
      earth
Shapes like a thing unfirm? O Cicero,
I have seen tempests, when the scolding winds
Have rived the knotty oaks, and I have seen
Th'ambitious ocean swell and rage and foam,
To be exalted with the threat'ning clouds;
But never till to-night, never till now,
Did I go through a tempest dropping fire. 10
Either there is a civil strife in heaven,
Or else the world too saucy with the gods
Incenses them to send destruction.

CICERO. Why, saw you anything more wonderful?

CASCA. A common slave—you know him well by
      sight—
Held up his left hand, which did flame and burn
Like twenty torches joined, and yet his hand
Not sensible of fire remained unscorched.
Besides—I ha' not since put up my sword—
Against the Capitol I met a lion, 20
Who glazed upon me and went surly by
Without annoying me: and there were drawn
Upon a heap a hundred ghastly women
Transformèd with their fear, who swore they saw
Men all in fire walk up and down the streets.
And yesterday the bird of night did sit
Even at noon-day upon the market-place,
Hooting and shrieking. When these prodigies
Do so conjointly meet, let not men say
'These are their reasons: they are natural:' 30
For, I believe, they are portentous things
Unto the climate that they point upon.

CICERO. Indeed, it is a strange-disposed time:
But men may construe things, after their fashion,
Clean from the purpose of the things themselves.
Comes Cæsar to the Capitol to-morrow?

CASCA. He doth; for he did bid Antonius
Send word to you he would be there to-morrow.

CICERO. Good night then, Casca: this disturbèd sky
Is not to walk in.

CASCA.   Farewell, Cicero.   *Cicero goes* 40

Cassius enters

CASSIUS. Who's there?

CASCA.   A Roman.

CASSIUS.   Casca, by your voice.

CASCA. Your ear is good. Cassius, what night is this!

CASSIUS. A very pleasing night to honest men.

CASCA. Who ever knew the heavens menace so?

CASSIUS. Those that have known the earth so full of
      faults.
For my part, I have walked about the streets,
Submitting me unto the perilous night,
And thus unbracèd, Casca, as you see,
Have bared my bosom to the thunder-stone;
And when the cross blue lightning seemed to open 50
The breast of heaven, I did present myself
Even in the aim and very flash of it.

CASCA. But wherefore did you so much tempt the
      heavens?
It is the part of men to fear and tremble
When the most mighty gods by tokens send
Such dreadful heralds to astonish us.

CASSIUS. You are dull, Casca, and those sparks of life
That should be in a Roman you do want,
Or else you use not. You look pale and gaze

And put on fear and cast yourself in wonder,   60
To see the strange impatience of the heavens:
But if you would consider the true cause
Why all these fires, why all these gliding ghosts,
Why birds and beasts from quality and kind,
Why old men, fools, and children calculate,
Why all these things change from their ordinance,
Their natures and preforméd faculties,
To monstrous quality, why, you shall find
That heaven hath infused them with these spirits
To make them instruments of fear and warning   70
Unto some monstrous state.
Now could I, Casca, name to thee a man
Most like this dreadful night,
That thunders, lightens, opens graves, and roars
As doth the lion in the Capitol;
A man no mightier than thyself or me
In personal action, yet prodigious grown
And fearful, as these strange eruptions are.
CASCA. 'Tis Cæsar that you mean; is it not, Cassius?
CASSIUS. Let it be who it is: for Romans now   80
Have thews and limbs like to their ancestors;
But, woe the while! our fathers' minds are dead,
And we are governed with our mothers' spirits;
Our yoke and sufferance show us womanish.
CASCA. Indeed they say the senators to-morrow
Mean to establish Cæsar as a king;
And he shall wear his crown by sea and land,
In every place save here in Italy.
CASSIUS. I know where I will wear this dagger then:
Cassius from bondage will deliver Cassius.   90
Therein, ye gods, you make the weak most strong;
Therein, ye gods, you tyrants do defeat.
Nor stony tower, nor walls of beaten brass,
Nor airless dungeon, nor strong links of iron,
Can be retentive to the strength of spirit;
But life, being weary of these worldly bars,
Never lacks power to dismiss itself.
If I know this, know all the world besides,
That part of tyranny that I do bear
I can shake off at pleasure.   *Thunder still*
CASCA.   So can I: 100
So every bondman in his own hand bears
The power to cancel his captivity.
CASSIUS. And why should Cæsar be a tyrant then?
Poor man! I know he would not be a wolf
But that he sees the Romans are but sheep:
He were no lion were not Romans hinds.
Those that with haste will make a mighty fire
Begin it with weak straws: what trash is Rome,
What rubbish and what offal, when it serves
For the base matter to illuminate   110
So vile a thing as Cæsar! But, O grief,
Where hast thou led me? I perhaps speak this
Before a willing bondman; then I know
My answer must be made. But I am armed,
And dangers are to me indifferent.
CASCA. You speak to Casca, and to such a man
That is no fleering tell-tale. Hold, my hand:
Be factious for redress of all these griefs,
And I will set this foot of mine as far
As who goes farthest.
CASSIUS.   There's a bargain made.   120
Now know you, Casca, I have moved already
Some certain of the noblest-minded Romans
To undergo with me an enterprise

Of honourable-dangerous consequence;
And I do know, by this they stay for me
In Pompey's porch: for now, this fearful night,
There is no stir or walking in the streets,
And the complexion of the element
In favour's like the work we have in hand,
Most bloody-fiery and most terrible.   130

Cinna approaches

CASCA. Stand close awhile, for here comes one in haste.
CASSIUS. 'Tis Cinna; I do know him by his gait;
He is a friend. Cinna, where haste you so?
CINNA. To find out you. Who's that? Metellus
Cimber?
CASSIUS. No, it is Casca, one incorporate
To our attempts. Am I not stayed for, Cinna?
CINNA. I am glad on't. What a fearful night is this!
There's two or three of us have seen strange sights.
CASSIUS. Am I not stayed for? tell me.
CINNA.   Yes, you are.
O Cassius, if you could   140
But win the noble Brutus to our party—
CASSIUS. Be you content. Good Cinna, take this paper,
And look you lay it in the prætor's chair,
Where Brutus may but find it; and throw this
In at his window; set this up with wax
Upon old Brutus' statue: all this done,
Repair to Pompey's porch, where you shall find us.
Is Decius Brutus and Trebonius there?
CINNA. All but Metellus Cimber; and he's gone
To seek you at your house. Well, I will hie,   150
And so bestow these papers as you bade me.
CASSIUS. That done, repair to Pompeys' theatre.
                              Cinna goes
Come, Casca, you and I will yet ere day
See Brutus at his house: three parts of him
Is ours already, and the man entire
Upon the next encounter yields him ours.
CASCA. O, he sits high in all the people's hearts;
And that which would appear offence in us
His countenance, like richest alchemy,
Will change to virtue and to worthiness.   160
CASSIUS. Him and his worth and our great need of him
You have right well conceited. Let us go,
For it is after midnight, and ere day
We will awake him and be sure of him.   *They go*

ACT 2
Scene 1: *An orchard beside the house of Brutus*

Enter Brutus

BRUTUS. What, Lucius, ho!
I cannot, by the progress of the stars,
Give guess how near to day. Lucius, I say!
I would it were my fault to sleep so soundly.
When, Lucius, when? awake, I say! what, Lucius!

Lucius appears

LUCIUS. Called you, my lord?
BRUTUS. Get me a taper in my study, Lucius:
When it is lighted, come and call me here.
LUCIUS. I will, my lord.   *Goes in*
BRUTUS. It must be by his death: and, for my part,   10
I know no personal cause to spurn at him,
But for the general—he would be crowned:

How that might change his nature, there's the
question.
It is the bright day that brings forth the adder;
And that craves wary walking ... Crown him!—
that!
And then, I grant, we put a sting in him,
That at his will he may do danger with.
Th'abuse of greatness is when it disjoins
Remorse from power: and, to speak truth of Cæsar,
I have not known when his affections swayed   20
More than his reason. But 'tis a common proof,
That lowliness is young ambition's ladder,
Whereto the climber-upward turns his face;
But when he once attains the upmost round,
He then unto the ladder turns his back,
Looks in the clouds, scorning the base degrees
By which he did ascend: so Cæsar may;
Then, lest he may, prevent. And, since the quarrel
Will bear no colour for the thing he is,
Fashion it thus: that what he is, augmented,   30
Would run to these and these extremities:
And therefore think him as a serpent's egg
Which hatched would as his kind grow
mischievous,
And kill him in the shell.

Lucius returns

LUCIUS. The taper burneth in your colsed, sir.
Searching the window for a flint I found
This paper thus sealed up, and I am sure
It did not lie there when I went to bed.
                              Gives him the letter
BRUTUS. Get you to bed again, it is not day.
Is not to-morrow, boy, the ides of March?   40
LUCIUS. I know not, sir.
BRUTUS. Look in the calendar and bring me word.
LUCIUS. I will, sir.   *Goes in*
BRUTUS. The exhalations whizzing in the air
Gives so much light that I may read by them.
                     Opens the letter and reads
'Brutus, thou sleep'st: awake and see thyself.
Shall Rome, etc. Speak, strike, redress....'
'Brutus, thou sleep'st: awake.'
Such instigations have been often dropped
Where I have took them up.   50
'Shall Rome, etc.' Thus must I piece it out:
Shall Rome stand under one man's awe? What,
Rome?
My ancestors did from the streets of Rome
The Tarquin drive, when he was called a king.
'Speak, strike, redress.' Am I entreated
To speak and strike? O Rome, I make thee promise,
If the redress will follow, thou receivest
Thy full petition at the hand of Brutus!

Lucius returns

LUCIUS. Sir, March is wasted fifteen days. *Knocking*
BRUTUS. 'Tis good. Go to the gate; somebody knocks. 60
                              Lucius obeys
Since Cassius first did whet me against Cæsar
I have not slept.
Between the acting of a dreadful thing
And the first motion all the interim is
Like a phantasma or a hideous dream:
The Genius and the mortal instruments
Are then in council, and the state of man
Like to a little kingdom suffers then
The nature of an insurrection.

Lucius returns

LUCIUS. Sir, 'tis your brother Cassius at the door,   70
Who doth desire to see you.
BRUTUS.   Is he alone?
LUCIUS. No, sir, there are mo with him.
BRUTUS.   Do you know them?
LUCIUS. No, sir, their hats are plucked about their ears,
And half their faces buried in their cloaks,
That by no means I may discover them
By any mark of favour.
BRUTUS.   Let 'em enter. *Lucius goes*
They are the faction. O conspiracy,
Sham'st thou to show thy dang'rous brow by night,
When evils are most free? O, then, by day
Where wilt thou find a cavern dark enough   80
To mask thy monstrous visage? Seek none,
conspiracy;
Hide it in smiles and affability:
For if thou path, thy native semblance on,
Not Erebus itself were dim enough
To hide thee from prevention.

Enter the conspirators, Cassius, Casca, Decius, Cinna,
Metellus, and Trebonius

CASSIUS. I think we are too bold upon your rest:
Good morrow, Brutus, do we trouble you?
BRUTUS. I have been up this hour, awake all night.
Know I these men that come along with you?
CASSIUS. Yes, every man of them; and no man here 90
But honours you; and every one doth wish
You had but that opinion of yourself
Which every noble Roman bears of you.
This is Trebonius.
BRUTUS.   He is welcome hither.
CASSIUS. This, Decius Brutus.
BRUTUS.   He is welcome too.
CASSIUS. This, Casca; this, Cinna; and this, Metellus
Cimber.
BRUTUS. They are all welcome.
What watchful cares do interpose themselves
Betwixt your eyes and night?
CASSIUS. Shall I entreat a word?   *They whisper* 100
DECIUS. Here lies the east: doth not the day break here?
CASCA. No.
CINNA. O, pardon, sir, it doth, and yon grey lines
That fret the clouds are messengers of day.
CASCA. You shall confess that you are both deceived.
Here, as I point my sword, the sun arises;
Which is a great way growing on the south,
Weighing the youthful season of the year.
Some two months hence up higher toward the
north
He first presents his fire, and the high east   110
Stands as the Capitol, directly here.
BRUTUS. Give me your hands all over, one by one.
CASSIUS. And let us swear our resolution.
BRUTUS. No, not an oath: if not the face of men,
The sufferance of our souls, the time's abuse—
If these be motives weak, break off betimes,
And every man hence to his idle bed;
So let high-sighted tyranny range on
Till each man drop by lottery. But if these,
As I am sure they do, bear fire enough   120

To kindle cowards and to steel with valour
The melting spirits of women, then, countrymen,
What need we any spur but our own cause
To prick us to redress? what other bond
Than secret Romans that have spoke the word,
And will not palter? and what other oath
Than honesty to honesty engaged
That this shall be or we will fall for it?
Swear priests and cowards and men cautelous,
Old feeble carrions and such suffering souls   130
That welcome wrongs; unto bad causes swear
Such creatures as men doubt: but do not stain
The even virtue of our enterprise,
Nor th'insuppressive mettle of our spirits,
To think that or our cause or our performance
Did need an oath; when every drop of blood
That every Roman bears, and nobly bears,
Is guilty of a several bastardy
If he do break the smallest particle
Of any promise that hath passed from him.   140
CASSIUS. But what of Cicero? shall we sound him?
I think he will stand very strong with us.
CASCA. Let us not leave him out.
CINNA.   No, by no means.
METELLUS. O, let us have him, for his silver hairs
Will purchase us a good opinion
And buy men's voices to commend our deeds:
It shall be said his judgement ruled our hands;
Our youths and wildness shall no whit appear,
But all be buried in his gravity.
BRUTUS. O, name him not: let us not break with him,   150
For he will never follow anything
That other men begin.
CASSIUS.   Then leave him out.
CASCA. Indeed he is not fit.
DECIUS. Sháll no man else be touched but only Cæsar?
CASSIUS. Decius, well urged: I think it is not meet
Mark Antony, so well beloved of Cæsar,
Should outlive Cæsar: we shall find of him
A shrewd contriver; and you know his means,
If he improve them, may well stretch so far
As to annoy us all: which to prevent,   160
Let Antony and Cæsar fall together.
BRUTUS. Our course will seem too bloody, Caius
Cassius,
To cut the head off and then hack the limbs,
Like wrath in death and envy afterwards;
For Antony is but a limb of Cæsar:
Let us be sacrificers, but not butchers, Caius.
We all stand up against the spirit of Cæsar,
And in the spirit of men there is no blood:
O, that we then could come by Cæsar's spirit,
And not dismember Cæsar! But, alas,   170
Cæsar must bleed for it! And, gentle friends,
Let's kill him boldly, but not wrathfully;
Let's carve him as a dish fit for the gods,
Not hew him as a carcass fit for hounds:
And let our hearts, as subtle masters do,
Stir up their servants to an act of rage
And after seem to chide 'em. This shall make
Our purpose necessary and not envious:
Which so appearing to the common eyes,
We shall be called purgers, not murderers.   180
And for Mark Antony, think not of him;
For he can do no more than Cæsar's arm
When Cæsar's head is off.

CASSIUS.   Yet I fear him,
For in the ingrafted love he bears to Cæsar—
BRUTUS. Alas, good Cassius, do not think of him:
If he love Cæsar, all that he can do
Is to himself, take thought and die for Cæsar:
And that were much he should, for he is given
To sports, to wildness and much company.
TREBONIUS. There is no fear in him; let him not die;   190
For he will live and laugh at this hereafter.
                                        Clock strikes
BRUTUS. Peace! count the clock.
CASSIUS.   The clock hath stricken three.
TREBONIUS. 'Tis time to part.
CASSIUS.   But it is doubtful yet
Whether Cæsar will come forth to-day or no;
For he is superstitious grown of late,
Quite from the main opinion he held once
Of fantasy, of dreams and ceremonies:
It may be these apparent prodigies,
The unaccustomed terror of this night,
And the persuasion of his augurers   200
May hold him from the Capitol to-day.
DECIUS. Never fear that: if he be so resolved,
I can o'ersway him; for he loves to hear
That unicorns may be betrayed with trees
And bears with glasses, elephants with holes,
Lions with toils and men with flatterers:
But when I tell him he hates flatterers,
He says he does, being then most flatteréd.
Let me work;
For I can give his humour the true bent,   210
And I will bring him to the Capitol.
CASSIUS. Nay, we will all of us be there to fetch him.
BRUTUS. By the eighth hour: is that the uttermost?
CINNA. Be that the uttermost, and fail not then.
METELLUS. Caius Ligarius doth bear Cæsar hard,
Who rated him for speaking well of Pompey:
I wonder none of you have thought of him.
BRUTUS. Now, good Metellus, go along by him:
He loves me well, and I have given him reasons;
Send him but hither, and I'll fashion him.   220
CASSIUS. The morning comes upon's: we'll leave you,
Brutus:
And, friends, disperse yourselves: but all remember
What you have said and show yourselves true
Romans.
BRUTUS. Good gentlemen, look fresh and merrily;
Let not our looks put on our purposes;
But bear it as our Roman actors do,
With untired spirits and formal constancy:
And so, good morrow to you every one.
                                All but Brutus depart
Boy! Lucius! Fast asleep! It is no matter;
Enjoy the honey-heavy dew of slumber: 230
Thou hast no figures nor no fantasies,
Which busy care draws in the brains of men;
Therefore thou sleep'st so sound.

Portia enters

PORTIA.   Brutus, my lord!
BRUTUS. Portia, what mean you? wherefore rise
you now?
It is not for your health thus to commit
Your weak condition to the raw cold morning.
PORTIA. Nor for yours neither. You've ungently,
Brutus,

Stole from my bed: and yesternight at supper
You suddenly arose and walked about,
Musing and sighing, with your arms across;   240
And when I asked you what the matter was,
You stared upon me with ungentle looks:
I urged you further; then you scratched your head
And too impatiently stamped with your foot:
Yet I insisted, yet you answered not,
But with an angry wafture of your hand
Gave sign for me to leave you: so I did,
Fearing to strengthen that impatience
Which seemed too much enkindled, and withal
Hoping it was but an effect of humour,   250
Which sometime hath his hour with every man.
It will not let you eat, nor talk, nor sleep,
And, could it work so much upon your shape
As it hath much prevailed on your condition,
I should not know you Brutus. Dear my lord,
Make me acquainted with your cause of grief.
BRUTUS. I am not well in health, and that is all.
PORTIA. Brutus is wise, and, were he not in health,
He would embrace the means to come by it.
BRUTUS. Why, so I do: good Portia, go to bed.   260
PORTIA. Is Brutus sick, and is it physical
To walk unbracéd and suck up the humours
Of the dank morning? What, is Brutus sick,
And will he steal out of his wholesome bed,
To dare the vile contagion of the night
And tempt the rheumy and unpurgéd air
To add unto his sickness? No, my Brutus;
You have some sick offence within your mind,
Which by the right and virtue of my place
I ought to know of: and, upon my knees,   270
I charm you, by my once commended beauty,
By all your vows of love and that great vow
Which did incorporate and make us one,
That you unfold to me, your self, your half,
Why you are heavy—and what men to-night
Have had resort to you; for here have been
Some six or seven, who did hide their faces
Even from darkness.
BRUTUS.   Kneel not, gentle Portia.
PORTIA. I should not need, if you were gentle Brutus.
Within the bond of marriage, tell me, Brutus,   280
Is it excepted I should know no secrets
That appertain to you? Am I your self
But, as it were, in sort or limitation,
To keep with you at meals, comfort your bed,
And talk to you sometimes? Dwell I but in the
    suburbs
Of your good pleasure? If it be no more,
Portia is Brutus' harlot, not his wife.
BRUTUS. You are my true and honourable wife,
As dear to me as are the ruddy drops
That visit my sad heart.   290
PORTIA. If this were true, then should I know this
    secret.
I grant I am a woman, but withal
A woman that Lord Brutus took to wife:
I grant I am a woman, but withal
A woman well reputed, Cato's daughter.
Think you I am no stronger than my sex,
Being so fathered and so husbanded?
Tell me your counsels, I will not disclose 'em;
I have made strong proof of my constancy,
Giving myself a voluntary wound   300

Here in the thigh: can I bear that with patience
And not my husband's secrets?
BRUTUS.   O ye gods,
Render me worthy of this noble wife!   *Knocking*
Hark, hark! one knocks: Portia, go in awhile;
And by and by thy bosom shall partake
The secrets of my heart:
All my engagements I will construe to thee,
All the charactery of my sad brows.
Leave me with haste. [*she goes*] Lucius, who's that
    knocks?

Lucius enters, followed by Ligarius

LUCIUS. Here is a sick man that would speak with you.   310
BRUTUS. Caius Ligarius, that Metellus spake of.
Boy, stand aside. Caius Ligarius! how?
LIGARIUS. Vouchsafe good-morrow from a feeble
    tongue.
BRUTUS. O, what a time have you chose out, brave
    Caius,
To wear a kerchief! Would you were not sick!
LIGARIUS. I am not sick, if Brutus have in hand
Any exploit worthy the name of honour.
BRUTUS. Such an exploit have I in hand, Ligarius,
Had you a healthful ear to hear of it.
LIGARIUS. By all the gods that Romans bow before,   320
I here discard my sickness! Soul of Rome!
Brave son, derived from honourable loins!
Thou, like an exorcist, hast conjured up
My mortifiéd spirit. Now bid me run,
And I will strive with things impossible,
Yea, get the better of them. What's to do?
BRUTUS. A piece of work that will make sick men
    whole.
LIGARIUS. But are not some whole that we must make
    sick?
BRUTUS. That must we also. What it is, my Caius,
I shall unfold to thee, as we are going   330
To whom it must be done.
LIGARIUS.   Set on your foot,
And with a heart new-fired I follow you,
To do I know not what: but it sufficeth
That Brutus leads me on.
BRUTUS.   Follow me then.
                                They go

Scene 2: *Cæsar's house*

*Thunder and lightning. Enter Julius Cæsar, in his
night-gown*

CÆSAR. Nor heaven nor earth have been at peace
    to-night:
Thrice hath Calphurnia in her sleep cried out,
'Help, ho! they murder Cæsar!' Who's within?

A servant appears

SERVANT. My lord?
CÆSAR. Go bid the priests do present sacrifice,
And bring me their opinions of success.
SERVANT. I will, my lord.   *Goes*

Enter Calphurnia

CALPHURNIA. What mean you, Cæsar? think you to
    walk forth?
You shall not stir out of your house to-day.
CÆSAR. Cæsar shall forth: the things that threatened me   10

Ne'er looked but on my back; when they shall see
The face of Cæsar, they are vanishéd.
CALPHURNIA. Cæsar, I never stood on ceremonies,
Yet now they fright me. There is one within,
Besides the things that we have heard and seen,
Recounts most horrid sights seen by the watch.
A lioness hath whelpéd in the streets;
And graves have yawned and yielded up their dead;
Fierce fiery warriors fought upon the clouds,
In ranks and squadrons and right form of war,   20
Which drizzled blood upon the Capitol;
The noise of battle hurtled in the air,
Horses did neigh and dying men did groan,
And ghosts did shriek and squeal about the streets.
O Cæsar! these things are beyond all use,
And I do fear them.
CÆSAR.   What can be avoided
Whose end is purposed by the mighty gods?
Yet Cæsar shall go forth; for these predictions
Are to the world in general as to Cæsar.
CALPHURNIA. When beggars die, there are no
   comets seen;   30
The heavens themselves blaze forth the death of
   princes.
CÆSAR. Cowards die many times before their deaths;
The valiant never taste of death but once.
Of all the wonders that I yet have heard,
It seems to me most strange that men should fear,
Seeing that death, a necessary end,
Will come when it will come.

The servant returns

                              What say the augurers?
SERVANT. They would not have you to stir forth
   to-day.
Plucking the entrails of an offering forth,
They could not find a heart within the beast.   40
CÆSAR. The gods do this in shame of cowardice:
Cæsar should be a beast without a heart
If he should stay at home to-day for fear.
No, Cæsar shall not: Danger knows full well
That Cæsar is more dangerous than he:
We are two lions littered in one day,
And I the elder and more terrible:
And Cæsar shall go forth.
CALPHURNIA.   Alas, my lord,
Your wisdom is consumed in confidence.
Do not go forth to-day: call it my fear   50
That keeps you in the house and not your own.
We'll send Mark Antony to the Senate House,
And he shall say you are not well to-day:
Let me, upon my knee, prevail in this.
CÆSAR. Mark Antony shall say I am not well,
And, for thy humour, I will stay at home.

Enter Decius

Here's Decius Brutus, he shall tell them so.
DECIUS. Cæsar, all hail! good morrow, worthy Cæsar:
I come to fetch you to the Senate House.
CÆSAR. And you are come in very happy time,   60
To bear my greeting to the senators
And tell them that I will not come to-day:
Cannot, is false, and that I dare not, falser:
I will not come to-day: tell them so, Decius.
CALPHURNIA. Say he is sick.
CÆSAR.   Shall Cæsar send a lie?

Have I in conquest stretched mine arm so far,
To be afeard to tell graybeards the truth?
Decius, go tell them Cæsar will not come.
DECIUS. Most mighty Cæsar, let me know some
   cause,
Lest I be laughed at when I tell them so.   70
CÆSAR. The cause is in my will: I will not come;
That is enough to satisfy the senate.
But, for your private satisfaction,
Because I love you, I will let you know.
Calphurnia here, my wife, stays me at home:
She dreamt to-night she saw my statua,
Which like a fountain with an hundred spouts
Did run pure blood, and many lusty Romans
Came smiling and did bathe their hands in it:
And these does she apply for warnings and portents 80
And evils imminent; and on her knee
Hath begged that I will stay at home to-day.
DECIUS. This dream is all amiss interpreted;
It was a vision fair and fortunate:
Your statue spouting blood in many pipes,
In which so many smiling Romans bathed,
Signifies that from you great Rome shall suck
Reviving blood, and that great men shall press
For tinctures, stains, relics, and cognizance.
This by Calphurnia's dream is signified.   90
CÆSAR. And this way have you well expounded it.
DECIUS. I have, when you have heard what I can say:
And know it now: the senate have concluded
To give this day a crown to mighty Cæsar.
If you shall send them word you will not come,
Their minds may change. Besides, it were a mock
Apt to be rendered, for some one to say
'Break up the senate till another time,
When Cæsar's wife shall meet with better dreams.'
If Cæsar hide himself, shall they not whisper   100
'Lo, Cæsar is afraid'?
Pardon me, Cæsar, for my dear dear love
To your proceeding bids me tell you this,
And reason to my love is liable.
CÆSAR. How foolish do your fears seem now,
   Calphurnia!
I am ashaméd I did yield to them.
Give me my robe, for I will go.

Enter Publius, Brutus, Ligarius, Metellus, Casca,
Trebonius, and Cinna

And look where Publius is come to fetch me.
PUBLIUS. Good morrow, Cæsar.
CÆSAR.   Welcome, Publius.
What, Brutus, are you stirred so early too?   110
Good morrow, Casca. Caius Ligarius,
Cæsar was ne'er so much your enemy
As that same ague which hath made you lean.
What is't o'clock?
BRUTUS.   Cæsar, 'tis strucken eight.
CÆSAR. I thank you for your pains and courtesy.

Enter Antony

See! Antony, that revels long a-nights,
Is notwithstanding up. Good morrow, Antony.
ANTONY. So to most noble Cæsar.
CÆSAR [*to Calphurnia*].   Bid them
   prepare within: *She goes*
I am to blame to be thus waited for.
Now, Cinna: now, Metellus: what, Trebonius!   120

I have an hour's talk in store for you;
Remember that you call on me to-day:
Be near me, that I may remember you.
TREBONIUS. Cæsar, I will. [aside] And so near will I be,
That your best friends shall wish I had been further.
CÆSAR. Good friends, go in and taste some wine with
me;
And we like friends will straightway go together.
BRUTUS [aside]. That every like is not the same,
O Cæsar,
The heart of Brutus earns to think upon!   *They go*

Scene 3: *A street near the Capitol, before the house
of Brutus*

Enter Artemidorus, reading a paper

ARTEMIDORUS. 'Cæsar, beware of Brutus; take heed of
Cassius; come not near Casca; have an eye to Cinna;
trust not Trebonius; mark well Metellus Cimber:
Decius Brutus loves thee not: thou hast wronged
Caius Ligarius. There is but one mind in all these
men, and it is bent against Cæsar. If thou beest not
immortal, look about you: security gives way to
conspiracy. The mighty gods defend thee!
Thy lover, ARTEMIDORUS.'
Here will I stand till Cæsar pass along,   10
And as a suitor will I give him this.
My heart laments that virtue cannot live
Out of the teeth of emulation.
If thou read this, O Cæsar, thou mayst live;
If not, the Fates with traitors do contrive.
He stand aside

Scene 4

Portia and Lucius come from the house

PORTIA. I prithee, boy, run to the Senate House;
Stay not to answer me, but get thee gone.
Why dost thou stay?
LUCIUS.   To know my errand, madam.
PORTIUS. I would have had thee there and here again,
Ere I can tell thee what thou shouldst do there.
O constancy, be strong upon my side!
Set a huge mountain 'tween my heart and tongue!
I have a man's mind, but a woman's might.
How hard it is for women to keep counsel!
Art thou here yet?
LUCIUS.   Madam, what should I do?   10
Run to the Capitol, and nothing else?
And so return to you, and nothing else?
PORTIA. Yes, bring me word, boy, if thy lord look
well,
For he went sickly forth: and take good note
What Cæsar doth, what suitors press to him.
Hark, boy! what noise is that?
LUCIUS. I hear none, madam.
PORTIA.   Prithee, listen well:
I heard a bustling rumour like a fray,
And the wind brings it from the Capitol.
LUCIUS. Sooth, madam, I hear nothing.

Enter the Soothsayer

PORTIA.   Come hither, fellow: 20
Which way hast thou been?
SOOTHSAYER.   At mine own house, good lady.
PORTIA. What is't o'clock?

SOOTHSAYER.   About the ninth hour, lady.
PORTIA. Is Cæsar yet gone to the Capitol?
SOOTHSAYER. Madam, not yet: I go to take my stand,
To see him pass on to the Capitol.
PORTIA. Thou hast some suit to Cæsar, hast thou not?
SOOTHSAYER. That I have, lady: if it will please Cæsar
To be so good to Cæsar as to hear me,
I shall beseech him to befriend himself.
PORTIA. Why, know'st thou any harm's intended
towards him?   30
SOOTHSAYER. None that I know will be, much that I
fear may chance.
Good morrow to you. Here the street is narrow:
The throng that follows Cæsar at the heels,
Of senators, of prætors, common suitors,
Will crowd a feeble man almost to death:
I'll get me to a place more void and there
Speak to great Cæsar as he comes along.
He passes on
PORTIA. I must go in.... Ay me, how weak a thing
The heart of woman is! O Brutus,
The heavens speed thee in thine enterprise!   40
Sure, the boy heard me. Brutus hath a suit
That Cæsar will not grant. O, I grow faint.
Run, Lucius, and commend me to my lord;
Say I am merry: come to me again,
And bring me word what he doth say to thee.
Lucius goes forward: she turns home

ACT 3

Scene 1: *Before the Senate House; Senators in session seen
through open doors*

*A crowd of people stand waiting; among them Artemidorus
and the Soothsayer. Flourish. Enter Cæsar, Brutus,
Cassius, Casca, Decius, Metellus, Trebonius, Cinna,
Antony, Lepidus, Popilius, Publius, and others*

CÆSAR [to the Soothsayer]. The ides of March are come.
SOOTHSAYER. Ay, Cæsar; but not gone.
ARTEMIDORUS. Hail, Cæsar! read this schedule.
DECIUS. Trebonius doth desire you to o'er-read,
At your best leisure, this his humble suit.
ARTEMIDORUS. O Cæsar, read mine first; for mine's a
suit
That touches Cæsar nearer: read it, great Cæsar.
CÆSAR. What touches us ourself shall be last served.
ARTEMIDORUS. Delay not, Cæsar, read it instantly.
CÆSAR. What, is the fellow mad?
PUBLIUS.   Sirrah, give place. 10
CASSIUS. What, urge you your petitions in the street?
Come to the Capitol.

Cæsar enters the Senate House, the rest following

POPILIUS. I wish your enterprise to-day may thrive.
CASSIUS. What enterprise, Popilius?
POPILIUS.   Fare you well.
Advances to Cæsar, and they speak together
BRUTUS. What said Popilius Lena?
CASSIUS. He wished to-day our enterprise might
thrive.
I fear our purpose is discoveréd.
BRUTUS. Look, how he makes to Cæsar: mark him.
CASSIUS.   Casca,
Be sudden, for we fear prevention.

Brutus, what shall be done? If this be known,   20
Cassius or Cæsar never shall turn back,
For I will slay myself.
BRUTUS.   Cassius, be constant:
Popilius Lena speaks not of our purposes;
For, look, he smiles, and Cæsar doth not change.
CASSIUS. Trebonius knows his time; for, look you,
   Brutus,
He draws Mark Antony out of the way.
                         Antony and Trebonius depart
DECIUS. Where is Metellus Cimber? Let him go,
And presently prefer his suit to Cæsar.
BRUTUS. He is addressed: press near and second him.
CINNA. Casca, you are the first that rears your hand. 30
CÆSAR. Are we all ready? What is now amiss
That Cæsar and his senate must redress?
METELLUS [*kneels*]. Most high, most mighty, and
   most puissant Cæsar,
Metellus Comber throws before thy seat
An humble heart—
CÆSAR.   I must prevent thee, Cimber.
These couchings and these lowly courtesies
Might fire the blood of ordinary men,
And turn pre-ordinance and first decree
Into the law of children. Be not fond
To think that Cæsar bears such rebel blood   40
That will be thawed from the true quality
With that which melteth fools, I mean, sweet words,
Low-crookéd curtsies and base spaniel-fawning.
Thy brother by decree is banishéd:
If thou dost bend and pray and fawn for him,
I spurn thee like a cur out of my way.
Know, Cæsar doth not wrong, nor without cause
Will he be satisfied.
METELLUS. Is there no voice more worthy than my
   own,
To sound more sweetly in great Cæsar's ear   50
For the repealing of my banished brother?
BRUTUS. I kiss thy hand, but not in flattery, Cæsar;
Desiring thee that Publius Cimber may
Have an immediate freedom of repeal.
CÆSAR. What, Brutus!
CASSIUS.   Pardon, Cæsar; Cæsar, pardon:
As low as to thy foot doth Cassius fall,
To beg enfranchisement for Publius Cimber.
CÆSAR. I could be well moved, if I were as you;
If I could pray to move, prayers would move me:
But I am constant as the northern star,   60
Of whose true-fixed and resting quality
There is no fellow in the firmament.
The skies are painted with unnumbered sparks;
They are all fire and every one doth shine;
But there's but one in all doth hold his place:
So in the world; 'tis furnished well with men,
And men are flesh and blood, and apprehensive;
Yet in the number I do know but one
That unassailable holds on his rank,
Unshaked of motion: and that I am he,   70
Let me a little show it, even in this:
That I was constant Cimber should be banished,
And constant do remain to keep him so.
CINNA. O Cæsar—
CÆSAR.   Hence! wilt thou lift up Olympus?
DECIUS. Great Cæsar—
CÆSAR.   Doth not Brutus bootless kneel?
CASCA. Speak, hands, for me!

                    Strikes him from behind; the conspirators
                                   and Brutus hack at him
CÆSAR. Et tu, Brute? Then fall, Cæsar!   *Dies*
CINNA. Liberty! freedom! Tyranny is dead!
Run hence, proclaim, cry it about the streets.
CASSIUS. Some to the common pulpits, and cry out   80
'Liberty, freedom and enfranchisement!'
BRUTUS. People, and senators, be not affrighted;
Fly not; stand still: ambition's debt is paid.
CASCA. Go to the pulpit, Brutus.
DECIUS. And Cassius too.
BRUTUS. Where's Publius?
CINNA. Here, quite confounded with this mutiny.
METELLUS. Stand fast together, lest some friend of
   Cæsar's
Should chance—
BRUTUS. Talk not of standing. Publius, good cheer;   90
There is no harm intended to your person,
Nor to no Roman else: so tell them, Publius.
CASSIUS. And leave us, Publius, lest that the people
Rushing on us should do your age some mischief.
BRUTUS. Do so: and let no man abide this deed
But we the doers.

Trebonius returns

CASSIUS. Where is Antony?
TREBONIUS.   Fled to his house amazed:
Men, wives and children stare, cry out and run
As it were doomsday.
BRUTUS.   Fates, we will know your pleasures:
That we shall die, we know; 'tis but the time,   100
And drawing days out, that men stand upon.
CASCA. Why, he that cuts off twenty years of life
Cuts off so many years of fearing death.
BRUTUS. Grant that, and then is death a benefit:
So are we Cæsar's friends, that have abridged
His time of fearing death. Stoop, Romans, stoop,
And let us bathe our hands in Cæsar's blood
Up to the elbows, and besmear our swords:
Then walk we forth, even to the market-place,
And waving our red weapons o'er our heads,   110
Let's all cry 'Peace, freedom and liberty!'
CASSIUS. Stoop then, and wash. How many ages
   hence
Shall this our lofty scene be acted over
In states unborn and accents yet unknown!
BRUTUS. How many times shall Cæsar bleed in sport,
That now on Pompey's basis lies along
No worthier than the dust!
CASSIUS.   So oft as that shall be,
So often shall the knot of us be called
The men that gave their country liberty.
DECIUS. What, shall we forth?
CASSIUS.   Ay, every man away: 120
Brutus shall lead, and we will grace his heels
With the most boldest and best hearts of Rome.

A servant enters

BRUTUS. Soft! who comes here? A friend of Antony's.
SERVANT. Thus, Brutus, did my master bid me kneel;
Thus did Mark Antony bid me fall down;
And, being prostrate, thus he bade me say:
Brutus is noble, wise, valiant and honest;
Cæsar was mighty, bold, royal and loving:
Say I love Brutus and I honour him;
Say I feared Cæsar, honoured him and loved him. 130

If Brutus will vouchsafe that Antony
May safely come to him and be resolved
How Cæsar hath deserved to lie in death,
Mark Antony shall not love Cæsar dead
So well as Brutus living, but will follow
The fortunes and affairs of noble Brutus
Thorough the hazards of this untrod state
With all true faith. So says my master Antony.

BRUTUS. Thy master is a wise and valiant Roman;
I never thought him worse. 140
Tell him, so please him come unto this place,
He shall be satisfied; and, by my honour,
Depart untouched.

SERVANT.   I'll fetch him presently.   *Goes*

BRUTUS. I know that we shall have him well to friend.

CASSIUS. I wish we may: but yet have I a mind
That fears him much, and my misgiving still
Falls shrewdly to the purpose.

Enter Antony

BRUTUS. But here comes Antony. Welcome, Mark
Antony.

ANTONY. O mighty Cæsar! dost thou lie so low?
Are all thy conquests, glories, triumphs, spoils, 150
Shrunk to this little measure? Fare thee well.
I know not, gentlemen, what you intend,
Who else must be let blood, who else is rank:
If I myself, there is no hour so fit
As Cæsar's death hour, nor no instrument
Of half that worth as those your swords, made rich
With the most noble blood of all this world.
I do beseech ye, if you bear me hard,
Now, whilst your purpled hands do reek and
smoke,
Fulfil your pleasure. Live a thousand years, 160
I shall not find myself so apt to die:
No place will please me so, no mean of death,
As here by Cæsar, and by you cut off,
The choice and master spirits of this age.

BRUTUS. O Antony, beg not your death of us.
Though now we must appear bloody and cruel,
As, by our hands and this our present act,
You see we do; yet see you but our hands
And this the bleeding business they have done:
Our hearts you see not; they are pitiful; 170
And pity to the general wrong of Rome—
As fire drives our fire, so pity pity—
Hath done this deed on Cæsar. For your part,
To you our swords have leaden points, Mark
Antony:
Our arms in strength of malice, and our hearts
Of brothers' temper, do receive you in
With all kind love, good thoughts and reverence.

CASSIUS. Your voice shall be as strong as any man's
In the disposing of new dignities.

BRUTUS. Only be patient till we have appeased 180
The multitude, beside themselves with fear,
And then we will deliver you the cause
Why I, that did love Cæsar when I struck him,
Have thus proceeded.

ANTONY.   I doubt not of your wisdom.
Let each man render me his bloody hand:
First, Marcus Brutus, will I shake with you;
Next, Caius Cassius, do I take your hand;
Now, Decius Brutus, yours; now yours, Metellus;
Yours, Cinna; and, my valiant Casca, yours;

Though last, not least in love, yours, good
Trebonius. 190
Gentlemen all ... alas, what shall I say?
My credit now stands on such slippery ground,
That one of two bad ways you must conceit me,
Either a coward or a flatterer.
That I did love thee, Cæsar, O, 'tis true:
If then thy spirit look upon us now,
Shall it not grieve thee dearer than thy death,
To see thy Antony making his peace,
Shaking the bloody fingers of thy foes,
Most noble! in the presence of thy corse? 200
Had I as many eyes as thou hast wounds,
Weeping as fast as they stream forth thy blood,
It would become me better than to close
In terms of friendship with thine enemies.
Pardon me, Julius! Here wast thou bayed, brave
hart,
Here didst thou fall, and here thy hunters stand,
Signed in thy spoil and crimsoned in thy lethe.
O world, thou wast the forest to this hart;
And this, indeed, O world, the heart of thee.
How like a deer strucken by many princes 210
Dost thou here lie!

CASSIUS. Mark Antony—

ANTONY.   Pardon me, Caius Cassius:
The enemies of Cæsar shall say this;
Then, in a friend, it is cold modesty.

CASSIUS. I blame you not for praising Cæsar so,
But what compact mean you to have with us?
Will you be pricked in number of our friends,
Or shall we on, and not depend on you?

ANTONY. Therefore I took your hands, but was indeed
Swayed from the point by looking down on Cæsar. 220
Friends am I with you all and love you all,
Upon this hope that you shall give me reasons
Why and wherein Cæsar was dangerous.

BRUTUS. Or else were this a savage spectacle:
Our reasons are so full of good regard
That were you, Antony, the son of Cæsar,
You should be satisfied.

ANTONY.   That's all I seek,
And am moreover suitor that I may
Produce his body to the market-place,
And in the pulpit as becomes a friend 230
Speak in the order of his funeral.

BRUTUS. You shall, Mark Antony.

CASSIUS *[aside]*.   Brutus, a word with you.
You know not what you do: do not consent
That Antony speak in his funeral:
Know you how much the people may be moved
By that which he will utter?

BRUTUS.   By your pardon:
I will myself into the pulpit first,
And show the reason of our Cæsar's death:
What Antony shall speak, I will protest
He speaks by leave and by permission, 240
And that we are contented Cæsar shall
Have all true rites and lawful ceremonies.
It shall advantage more than do us wrong.

CASSIUS. I know not what may fall; I like it not.

BRUTUS. Mark Antony, here, take you Cæsar's body.
You shall not in your funeral speech blame us,
But speak all good you can devise of Cæsar;
And say you do 't by our permission;
Else shall you not have any hand at all

About his funeral. And you shall speak 250
In the same pulpit whereto I am going,
After my speech is ended.
ANTONY. Be it so;
I do desire no more.
BRUTUS. Prepare the body then, and follow us.
They go;
Antony remains
ANTONY. O, pardon me, thou bleeding piece of earth,
That I am meek and gentle with these butchers!
Thou art the ruins of the noblest man
That ever livéd in the tide of times.
Woe to the hands that shed this costly blood!
Over thy wounds now do I prophesy 260
(Which like dumb mouths do ope their ruby lips
To beg the voice and utterance of my tongue),
A curse shall light upon the limbs of men;
Domestic fury and fierce civil strife
Shall cumber all the parts of Italy;
Blood and destruction shall be so in use,
And dreadful objects so familiar,
That mothers shall but smile when they behold
Their infants quartered with the hands of war;
All pity choked with custom of fell deeds: 270
And Cæsar's spirit ranging for revenge,
With Até by his side come hot from hell,
Shall in these confines with a monarch's voice
Cry 'Havoc,' and let slip the dogs of war;
That this foul deed shall smell above the earth
With carrion men, groaning for burial.

Enter a servant

You serve Octavius Cæsar, do you not?
SERVANT. I do, Mark Antony.
ANTONY. Cæsar did write for him to come to Rome.
SERVANT. He did receive his letters and is coming, 280
And bid me say to you by word of mouth—
O Cæsar! *Seeing the body*
ANTONY. Thy heart is big; get thee apart and weep:
Passion I see is catching, for mine eyes,
Seeing those beads of sorrow stand in thine,
Began to water. Is thy master coming?
SERVANT. He lies to-night within seven leagues of
Rome.
ANTONY. Post back with speed, and tell him what hath
chanced:
Here is a mourning Rome, a dangerous Rome,
No Rome of safety for Octavius yet; 290
Hie hence, and tell him so. Yet stay awhile;
Thou shalt not back till I have borne this corse
Into the market-place: there shall I try,
In my oration, how the people take
The cruel issue of these bloody men;
According to the which, thou shalt discourse
To young Octavius of the state of things.
Lend me you hand. *They bear away the body*

Scene 2: The Forum

Enter Brutus and Cassius, and a throng of plebeians

PLEBEIANS. We will be satisfied; let us be satisfied.
BRUTUS. Then follow me, and give me audience,
friends.
Cassius, go you into the other street,
And part the numbers.
Those that will hear me speak, let 'em stay here;

Those that will follow Cassius, go with him;
And public reasons shall be renderéd
Of Cæsar's death.
1 PLEBEIAN. I will hear Brutus speak.
2 PLEBEIAN. I will hear Cassius; and compare their
reasons,
When severally we hear them renderéd. 10
Cassius departs with some of the plebeians.
Brutus goes up into the pulpit
3 PLEBEIAN. The noble Brutus is ascended: silence!
BRUTUS. Be patient till the last.
Romans, countrymen, and lovers! hear me for my
cause, and be silent, that you may hear: believe me
for mine honour, and have respect to mine honour,
that you may believe: censure me in your wisdom,
and awake your senses, that you may the better
judge. If there be any in this assembly, any dear
friend of Cæsar's, to him I say that Brutus' love to
Cæsar was no less than his. If then that friend 20
demand why Brutus rose against Cæsar, this is my
answer: not that I loved Cæsar less, but that I loved
Rome more. Had you rather Cæsar were living, and
die all slaves, than that Cæsar were dead, to live all
free men? As Cæsar loved me, I weep for him; as
he was fortunate, I rejoice at it; as he was valiant,
I honour him; but as he was ambitious, I slew him.
There is tears for his love; joy for his fortune; honour for his valour; and death for his ambition. Who
is here so base that would be a bondman? If any, 30
speak; for him have I offended. Who is here so rude
that would not be a Roman? If any, speak; for him
have I offended. Who is here so vile that will not
love his country? If any, speak; for him have I
offended. I pause for a reply.
ALL. None, Brutus, none.
BRUTUS. Then none have I offended. I have done no
more to Cæsar than you shall do to Brutus. The
question of his death is enrolled in the Capitol; his
glory not extenuated, wherein he was worthy, nor 40
his offences enforced, for which he suffered death.

Antony enters, with bearers carrying Cæsar's body

Here comes his body, mourned by Mark Antony,
who, though he had no hand in his death, shall
receive the benefit of his dying, a place in the
commonwealth; as which of you shall not? With
this I depart—that, as I slew my best lover for the
good of Rome, I have the same dagger for myself,
when it shall please my country to need my death.
ALL. Live, Brutus! live, live!
1 PLEBEIAN. Bring him with triumph home unto his
house. 50
2 PLEBEIAN. Give him a statue with his ancestors.
3 PLEBEIAN. Let him be Cæsar.
4 PLEBEIAN. Cæsar's better parts
Shall be crowned in Brutus.
1 PLEBEIAN. We'll bring him to his house with shouts
and clamours.
BRUTUS. My countrymen—
2 PLEBEIAN. Peace! silence! Brutus speaks.
1 PLEBEIAN. Peace, ho!
BRUTUS. Good countrymen, let me depart alone,
And, for my sake, stay here with Antony:
Do grace to Cæsar's corpse, and grace his speech
Tending to Cæsar's glories, which Mark Antony 60
By our permission is allowed to make.

'I do entreat you, not a man depart,
Save I alone, till Antony have spoke.   *He goes*
1 PLEBEIAN. Stay, ho! and let us hear Mark Antony.
3 PLEBEIAN. Let him go up into the public chair;
We'll hear him. Noble Antony, go up.
ANTONY. For Brutus' sake, I am beholding to you.
                                Goes into the pulpit
4 PLEBEIAN. What does he say of Brutus?
3 PLEBEIAN.   He says, for Brutus' sake,
He finds himself beholding to us all.
4 PLEBEIAN. 'Twere best he speak no harm of Brutus
here.   70
1 PLEBEIAN. This Cæsar was a tyrant.
3 PLEBEIAN.   Nay, that's certain:
We are blest that Rome is rid of him.
2 PLEBEIAN. Peace! let us hear what Antony can say.
ANTONY. You gentle Romans—
ALL.   Peace, ho! let us hear him.
ANTONY. Friends, Romans, countrymen, lend me
    your ears;
I come to bury Cæsar, not to praise him;
The evil that men do lives after them,
The good is oft interréd with their bones,
So let it be with Cæsar.... The noble Brutus
Hath told you Cæsar was ambitious: 80
If it were so, it was a grievous fault,
And grievously hath Cæsar answered it....
Here, under leave of Brutus and the rest,
(For Brutus is an honourable man;
So are they all; all honourable men)
Come I to speak in Cæsar's funeral....
He was my friend, faithful and just to me:
But Brutus says he was ambitious;
And Brutus is an honourable man....
He hath brought many captives home to Rome,   90
Whose ransoms did the general coffers fill:
Did this in Cæsar seem ambitious?
When that the poor have cried, Cæsar hath wept:
Ambition should be made of sterner stuff:
Yet Brutus says he was ambitious;
And Brutus is an honourable man.
You all did see that on the Lupercal
I thrice presented him a kingly crown,
Which he did thrice refuse: was this ambition?
Yet Brutus says he was ambitious;   100
And, sure, he is an honourable man.
I speak not to disprove what Brutus spoke,
But here I am to speak what I do know.
You all did love him once, not without cause:
What cause withholds you then to mourn for him?
O judgement! thou art fled to brutish beasts,
And men have lost their reason.... Bear with me;
My heart is in the coffin there with Cæsar,
And I must pause till it come back to me.
1 PLEBEIAN. Methinks there is much reason in his
sayings.   110
2 PLEBEIAN. If thou consider rightly of the matter,
Cæsar has had great wrong.
3 PLEBEIAN.   Has he, masters?
I fear there will a worse come in his place.
4 PLEBEIAN. Marked ye his words? He would not take
the crown;
Therefore 'tis certain he was not ambitious.
1 PLEBEIAN. If it be found so, some will dear abide it.
2 PLEBEIAN. Poor soul! his eyes are red as fire with
weeping.

3 PLEBEIAN. There's not a nobler man in Rome than
Antony.
4 PLEBEIAN. Now mark him, he begins again to speak.
ANTONY. But yesterday the word of Cæsar might   120
Have stood against the world: now lies he there,
And none so poor to do him reverence.
O masters, if I were disposed to stir
Your hearts and minds to mutiny and rage,
I should do Brutus wrong and Cassius wrong,
Who, you all know, are honourable men:
I will not do them wrong; I rather choose
To wrong the dead, to wrong myself and you,
Than I will wrong such honourable men.
But here's a parchment with the seal of Cæsar;   130
I found it in his closet; 'tis his will:
Let but the commons hear this testament—
Which, pardon me, I do not mean to read—
And they would go and kiss dead Cæsar's wounds,
And dip their napkins in his sacred blood,
Yea, beg a hair of him for memory,
And, dying, mention it within their wills,
Bequeathing it as a rich legacy
Unto their issue.
4 PLEBEIAN. We'll hear the will: read it, Mark Antony. 140
ALL. The will, the will! we will hear Cæsar's will.
ANTONY. Have patience, gentle friends, I must not
read it;
It is not meet you know how Cæsar loved you.
You are not wood, you are not stones, but men;
And, being men, hearing the will of Cæsar,
It will inflame you, it will make you mad:
'Tis good you know not that you are his heirs;
For if you should, O, what would come of it!
4 PLEBEIAN. Read the will; we'll hear it, Antony;
You shall read us the will, Cæsar's will.   150
ANTONY. Will you be patient? will you stay awhile?
I have o'ershot myself to tell you of it:
I fear I wrong the honourable men
Whose daggers have stabbed Cæsar; I do fear it.
4 PLEBEIAN. They were traitors: honourable men!
ALL. The will! the testament!
2 PLEBEIAN. They were villains, murderers: the will!
read the will!
ANTONY. You will compel me then to read the will?
Then make a ring about the corpse of Cæsar,   160
And let me show you him that made the will.
Shall I descend? and will you give me leave?
ALL. Come down.
2 PLEBEIAN. Descend.   *Antony comes down*
3 PLEBEIAN. You shall have leave.
4 PLEBEIAN. A ring; stand round.
1 PLEBEIAN. Stand from the hearse, stand from the
body.
2 PLEBEIAN. Room for Antony, most noble Antony.
ANTONY. Nay, press not so upon me; stand far off.
ALL. Stand back. Room! Bear back.   170
ANTONY. If you have tears, prepare to shed them now.
You all do know this mantle: I remember
The first time ever Cæsar put it on;
'Twas on a summer's evening, in his tent,
That day he overcame the Nervii:
Look, in this place ran Cassius' dagger through:
See what a rent the envious Casca made:
Through this the well-belovéd Brutus stabbed;
And as he plucked his curséd steel away,
Mark how the blood of Cæsar followed it,   180

As rushing out of doors, to be resolved
If Brutus so unkindly knocked, or no:
For Brutus, as you know, was Cæsar's angel:
Judge, O you gods, how dearly Cæsar loved him!
This was the most unkindest cut of all;
For when the noble Cæsar saw him stab,
Ingratitude, more strong than traitors' arms,
Quite vanquished him: then burst his mighty heart;
And, in his mantle muffling up his face,
Even at the base of Pompey's statua   190
(Which all the while ran blood), great Cæsar fell.
O, what a fall was there, my countrymen!
Then I, and you, and all of us fell down,
Whilst bloody Treason flourished over us.
O, now you weep, and I perceive you feel
The dint of pity: these are gracious drops.
Kind souls, what weep you when you but behold
Our Cæsar's vesture wounded? Look you here,
Here is himself, marred, as you see, with traitors.
                                              He lifts the mantle
1 PLEBEIAN. O piteous spectacle!   200
2 PLEBEIAN. O noble Cæsar!
3 PLEBEIAN. O woful day!
4 PLEBEIAN. O traitors, villains!
1 PLEBEIAN. O most bloody sight!
2 PLEBEIAN. We will be revenged.
ALL. Revenge! About! Seek! Burn! Fire! Kill! Slay!
    Let not a traitor live!
ANTONY. Stay, countrymen.
1 PLEBEIAN. Peace there! hear the noble Antony.
2 PLEBEIAN. We'll hear him, we'll follow him, we'll   210
    die with him.
ANTONY. Good friends, sweet friends, let me not stir
    you up
To such a sudden flood of mutiny.
They that have done this deed are honourable.
What private griefs they have, alas, I know not,
That made them do it: they are wise and
    honourable,
And will, no doubt, with reasons answer you.
I come not, friends, to steal away your hearts:
I am no orator, as Brutus is;
But, as you know me all, a plain blunt man,   220
That love my friend; and that they know full well
That gave me public leave to speak of him:
For I have neither wit, nor words, nor worth,
Action, nor utterance, nor the power of speech
To stir men's blood: I only speak right on;
I tell you that which you yourselves do know;
Show you sweet Cæsar's wounds, poor poor dumb
    mouths,
And bid them speak for me: but were I Brutus,
And Brutus Antony, there were an Antony
Would ruffle up your spirits, and put a tongue   230
In every wound of Cæsar, that should move
The stones of Rome to rise and mutiny.
ALL. We'll mutiny.
1 PLEBEIAN. We'll burn the house of Brutus.
3 PLEBEIAN. Away, then! come, seek the conspirators.
ANTONY. Yet hear me, countrymen; yet hear me
    speak.
ALL. Peace, ho! Hear Antony! Most noble Antony!
ANTONY. Why, friends, you go to do you know not
    what:
Wherein hath Cæsar thus deserved your loves?
Alas, you know not; I must tell you then: 240

You have forgot the will I told you of.
ALL. Most true: the will! Let's stay and hear the will.
ANTONY. Here is the will, and under Cæsar's seal.
To every Roman citizen he gives,
To every several man, seventy five drachmas.
2 PLEBEIAN. Most noble Cæsar! we'll revenge his death.
3 PLEBEIAN. O royal Cæsar!
ANTONY. Hear me with patience.
ALL. Peace, ho!
ANTONY. Moreover, he hath left you all his walks,   250
His private arbours and new-planted orchards,
On this side Tiber; he hath left them you,
And to your heirs for ever; common pleasures,
To walk abroad and recreate yourselves.
Here was a Cæsar! when comes such another?
1 PLEBEIAN. Never, never. Come, away, away!
We'll burn his body in the holy place,
And with the brands fire the traitors' houses.
Take up the body.
2 PLEBEIAN. Go fetch fire.   260
3 PLEBEIAN. Pluck down benches.
4 PLEBEIAN. Pluck down forms, windows, anything.
                        They go; the bearers follow with the body
ANTONY. Now let it work. Mischief, thou art afoot,
Take thou what course thou wilt.

Octavius's servant enters

                                          How now, fellow!
SERVANT. Sir, Octavius is already come to Rome.
ANTONY. Where is he?
SERVANT. He and Lepidus are at Cæsar's house.
ANTONY. And thither will I straight to visit him:
He comes upon a wish. Fortune is merry,
And in this mood will give us anything.   270
SERVANT. I heard him say, Brutus and Cassius
Are rid like madmen through the gates of Rome.
ANTONY. Belike they had some notice of the people,
How I had moved them. Bring me to Octavius.
                                              They go

                            Scene 3

Enter Cinna the poet, with plebeians behind him

CINNA. I dreamt to-night that I did feast with Cæsar,
And things unluckily charge my fantasy:
I have no will to wander forth of doors,
Yet something leads me forth.

Plebeians surround him

1 PLEBEIAN. What is your name?
2 PLEBEIAN. Whither are you going?
3 PLEBEIAN. Where do you dwell?
4 PLEBEIAN. Are you a married man or a bachelor?
2 PLEBEIAN. Answer every man directly.
1 PLEBEIAN. Ay, and briefly.   10
4 PLEBEIAN. Ay, and wisely.
3 PLEBEIAN. Ay, and truly, you were best.
CINNA. What is my name? Whither am I going?
Where do I dwell? Am I a married man or a
bachelor? Then, to answer every man directly and
briefly, wisely and truly: wisely I say, I am a
bachelor.
2 PLEBEIAN. That's as much as to say, they are fools
that marry: you'll bear me a bang for that, I fear.
Proceed; directly.   20
CINNA. Directly, I am going to Cæsar's funeral.

1 PLEBEIAN. As a friend or an enemy?
CINNA. As a friend.
2 PLEBEIAN. That matter is answered directly.
4 PLEBEIAN. For your dwelling, briefly.
CINNA. Briefly, I dwell by the Capitol.
3 PLEBEIAN. Your name, sir, truly.
CINNA. Truly, my name is Cinna.
1 PLEBEIAN. Tear him to pieces, he's a conspirator.
CINNA. I am Cinna the poet, I am Cinna the poet.　30
4 PLEBEIAN. Tear him for his bad verses, tear him for
his bad verses.
CINNA. I am not Cinna the conspirator.
4 PLEBEIAN. It is no matter, his name's Cinna; pluck
but his name out of his heart, and turn him going.
3 PLEBEIAN. Tear him, tear him! [*they set upon him*]
Come, brands, ho! fire-brands: to Brutus', to
Cassius', burn all: some to Decius' house, and some
to Casca's; some to Ligarius': away, go!

They go, dragging the body of
Cinna after them

ACT 4

Scene 1: *A room in Antony's house*

Antony, Octavius, and Lepidus, seated at a table

ANTONY. These many then shall die; their names are
pricked.
OCTAVIUS. Your brother too must die; consent you,
Lepidus?
LEPIDUS. I do consent—
OCTAVIUS. 　　　　　　　Prick him down, Antony.
LEPIDUS. Upon condition Publius shall not live,
Who is your sister's son, Mark Antony.
ANTONY. He shall not live; look, with a spot I damn
him.
But, Lepidus, go you to Cæsar's house;
Fetch the will hither, and we shall determine
How to cut off some charge in legacies.
LEPIDUS. What, shall I find you here?　　　　10
OCTAVIUS. Or here, or at the Capitol. *Lepidus goes*
ANTONY. This is a slight unmeritable man,
Meet to be sent on errands: is it fit,
The three-fold world divided, he should stand
One of the three to share it?
OCTAVIUS. 　　　　　So you thought him,
And took his voice who should be pricked to die
In our black sentence and proscription.
ANTONY. Octavius, I have seen more days than you:
And though we lay these honours on this man,
To ease ourselves of divers sland'rous loads,　20
He shall but bear them as the ass bears gold,
To groan and sweat under the business,
Either led or driven, as we point the way;
And having brought our treasure where we will,
Then take we down his load and turn him off,
Like to the empty ass, to shake his ears
And graze in commons.
OCTAVIUS. 　　　　　You may do your will:
But he's a tried and valiant soldier.
ANTONY. So is my horse, Octavius, and for that
I do appoint him store of provender:　　　　30
It is a creature that I teach to fight,
To wind, to stop, to run directly on,
His corporal motion governed by my spirit.
And in some taste is Lepidus but so;

He must be taught, and trained, and bid go forth;
A barren-spirited fellow; one that feeds
On objects, arts, and imitations
Which, out of use and staled by other men,
Begin his fashion: do not talk of him
But as a property. And now, Octavius,　　　40
Listen great things: Brutus and Cassius
Are levying powers: we must straight make head:
Therefore let our alliance be combined,
Our best friends made, our means stretched;
And let us presently go sit in council,
How covert matters may be best disclosed,
And open perils surest answeréd.
OCTAVIUS. Let us do so: for we are at the stake,
And bayed about with many enemies;
And some that smile have in their hearts, I fear,　50
Millions of mischiefs. 　　　　　　　*They go*

Scene 2: *Before Brutus's tent in the camp near Sardis*

*Drum. Enter Lucilius with troops and Pindarus, the
bondman of Cassius. Brutus comes from the tent with
Lucius in attendance*

BRUTUS. Stand, ho!
LUCILIUS. Give the word, ho! and stand!
BRUTUS. What now, Lucilius! is Cassius near?
LUCILIUS. He is at hand, and Pindarus is come
To do you salutation from his master.
BRUTUS. He greets me well. Your master, Pindarus,
In his own change, or by ill officers,
Hath given me some worthy cause to wish
Things done undone: but if he be at hand,
I shall be satisfied.
PINDARUS. 　　　　　I do not doubt　　　　10
But that my noble master will appear
Such as he is, full of regard and honour.
BRUTUS. He is not doubted. A word, Lucilius;
How he received you, let me be resolved.
LUCILIUS. With courtesy and with respect enough,
But not with such familiar instances,
Nor with such free and friendly conference,
As he hath used of old.
BRUTUS. 　　　　　Thou hast described
A hot friend cooling: ever note, Lucilius,
When love begins to sicken and decay,　　　20
It useth an enforcéd ceremony.
There are no tricks in plain and simple faith:
But hollow men, like horses hot at hand,
Make gallant show and promise of their mettle,
But when they should endure the bloody spur,
They fall their crests and like deceitful jades
Sink in the trial. Comes his army on?
LUCILIUS. They mean this night in Sardis to be
quartered;
The greater part, the horse in general,
Are come with Cassius. 　　　　*Drums heard*
BRUTUS. 　　　　　Hark, he is arrived:　30
March gently on to meet him.

Cassius approaches with Titinius and his powers

CASSIUS. Stand, ho!
BRUTUS. Stand, ho! Speak the word along.
1 OFFICER. Stand!
2 OFFICER. Stand!
3 OFFICER. Stand!

CASSIUS. Most noble brother, you have done me
  wrong.
BRUTUS. Judge me, you gods; wrong I mine enemies?
  And, if not so, how should I wrong a brother?
CASSIUS. Brutus, this sober form of yours hides
  wrongs,   40
  And when you do them—
BRUTUS.   Cassius, be content,
  Speak your griefs softly, I do know you well.
  Before the eyes of both our armies here,
  Which should perceive nothing but love from us,
  Let us not wrangle. Bid them move away;
  Then in my tent, Cassius, enlarge your griefs,
  And I will give you audience.
CASSIUS.   Pindarus,
  Bid our commanders lead their charges off
  A little from this ground.
BRUTUS. Lucius, do you the like, and let no man   50
  Come to our tent till we have done our conference.
  Lucilius and Titinius guard our door.

Scene 3

The armies march away; Brutus and Cassius enter the tent;
Lucilius and Titinius stand guard without

CASSIUS. That you have wronged me doth appear in
    this:
  You have condemned and noted Lucius Pella
  For taking bribes here of the Sardians;
  Wherein my letters, praying on his side,
  Because I knew the man, was slighted off.
BRUTUS. You wronged yourself to write in such a case.
CASSIUS. In such a time as this it is not meet
  That every nice offence should bear his comment.
BRUTUS. Let me tell you, Cassius, you yourself
  Are much condemned to have an itching palm,   10
  To sell and mart your offices for gold
  To undeservers.
CASSIUS.   I an itching palm!
  You know that you are Brutus that speaks this,
  Or, by the gods, this speech were else your last.
BRUTUS. The name of Cassius honours this corruption,
  And chastisement doth therefore hide his head.
CASSIUS. Chastisement!
BRUTUS. Remember March, the ides of March
    remember!
  Did not great Julius bleed for justice' sake?
  What villain touched his body, that did stab,   20
  And not for justice? What, shall one of us,
  That struck the foremost man of all this world
  But for supporting robbers, shall we now
  Contaminate our fingers with base bribes,
  And sell the mighty space of our large honours
  For so much trash as may be grasped thus?
  I had rather be a dog, and bay the moon,
  Than such a Roman.
CASSIUS.   Brutus, bay not me,
  I'll not endure it: you forget yourself,
  To hedge me in; I am a soldier, I,   30
  Older in practice, abler than yourself
  To make conditions.
BRUTUS.   Go to; you are not, Cassius.
CASSIUS. I am.
BRUTUS. I say you are not.
CASSIUS. Urge me no more, I shall forget myself;

  Have mind upon your health; tempt me no farther.
BRUTUS. Away, slight man!
CASSIUS. Is't possible?
BRUTUS.   Hear me, for I will speak.
  Must I give way and room to your rash choler?
  Shall I be frighted when a madman stares?   40
CASSIUS. O ye gods, ye gods! must I endure all this?
BRUTUS. All this! ay, more: fret till your proud heart
    break;
  Go show your slaves how choleric you are,
  And make your bondmen tremble. Must I budge?
  Must I observe you? must I stand and crouch
  Under your testy humour? By the gods,
  You shall digest the venom of your spleen,
  Though it do split you; for, from this day forth,
  I'll use you for my mirth, yea, for my laughter,
  When you are waspish.
CASSIUS.   Is it come to this?   50
BRUTUS. You say you are a better soldier:
  Let it appear so; make your vaunting true,
  And it shall please me well: for mine own part,
  I shall be glad to learn of noble men.
CASSIUS. You wrong me every way; you wrong me,
    Brutus;
  I said, an elder soldier, not a better:
  Did I say, better?
BRUTUS.   If you did, I care not.
CASSIUS. When Cæsar lived, he durst not thus have
    moved me.
BRUTUS. Peace, peace! you durst not so have tempted
    him.
CASSIUS. I durst not?   60
BRUTUS. No.
CASSIUS. What, durst not tempt him?
BRUTUS.   For your life you durst not.
CASSIUS. Do not presume too much upon my love,
  I may do that I shall be sorry for.
BRUTUS. You have done that you should be sorry for.
  There is no terror, Cassius, in your threats;
  For I am armed so strong in honesty
  That they pass by me as the idle wind
  Which I respect not. I did send to you
  For certain sums of gold, which you denied me: 70
  For I can raise no money by vile means:
  By heaven, I had rather coin my heart,
  And drop my blood for drachmas, than to wring
  From the hard hands of peasants their vile trash
  By any indirection. I did send
  To you for gold to pay my legions,
  Which you denied me: was that done like Cassius?
  Should I have answered Caius Cassius so?
  When Marcus Brutus grows so covetous,
  To lock such rascal counters from his friends,   80
  Be ready, gods, with all your thunderbolts,
  Dash him to pieces!
CASSIUS.   I denied you not.
BRUTUS. You did.
CASSIUS.   I did not: he was but a fool
  That brought my answer back. Brutus hath rived
    my heart:
  A friend should bear his friend's infirmities,
  But Brutus makes mine greater than they are.
BRUTUS. I do not, till you practise them on me.
CASSIUS. You love me not.
BRUTUS.   I do not like your faults.
CASSIUS. A friendly eye could never see such faults.

BRUTUS. A flatterer's would not, though they do appear 90
As huge as high Olympus.
CASSIUS. Come, Antony, and young Octavius, come,
Revenge yourselves alone on Cassius,
For Cassius is aweary of the world;
Hated by one he loves; braved by his brother;
Checked like a bondman; all his faults observed,
Set in a note-book, learned and conned by rote,
To cast into my teeth. O, I could weep
My spirit from mine eyes! There is my dagger,
And here my naked breast; within, a heart 100
Dearer than Pluto's mine, richer than gold:
If that thou be'st a Roman, take it forth;
I, that denied thee gold, will give my heart:
Strike, as thou didst at Cæsar; for I know,
When thou didst hate him worst, thou lovedst him better
Than ever thou lovedst Cassius.
BRUTUS. Sheathe your dagger:
Be angry when you will, it shall have scope;
Do what you will, dishonour shall be humour.
O Cassius, you are yokéd with a lamb,
That carries anger as the flint bears fire, 110
Who, much enforcéd, shows a hasty spark
And straight is cold again.
CASSIUS. Hath Cassius lived
To be but 'mirth' and 'laughter' to his Brutus,
When grief and blood ill-tempered vexeth him?
BRUTUS. When I spoke that, I was ill-tempered too.
CASSIUS. Do you confess so much? Give me your hand.
BRUTUS. And my heart too.
CASSIUS. O Brutus!
BRUTUS. What's the matter?
CASSIUS. Have not you love enough to bear with me,
When that rash humour which my mother gave me
Makes me forgetful?
BRUTUS. Yes, Cassius, and from henceforth, 120
When you are over-earnest with your Brutus,
He'll think your mother chides, and leave you so.
A VOICE WITHOUT. Let me go in to see the generals;
There is some grudge between 'em; 'tis not meet
They be alone.
LUCILIUS [without]. You shall not come to them.
VOICE WITHOUT. Nothing but death shall stay me.

Enter a poet, followed by Lucilius, Titinius, and Lucius

CASSIUS. How now! what's the matter?
POET. For shame, you generals! what do you mean?
Love and be friends, as two such men should be;
For I have seen more years, I'm sure, than ye. 130
CASSIUS. Ha, ha! how vilely doth this cynic rhyme!
BRUTUS. Get you hence, sirrah; saucy fellow, hence!
CASSIUS. Bear with him, Brutus; 'tis his fashion.
BRUTUS. I'll know his humour when he knows his time:
What should the wars do with these jigging fools?
Companion, hence!
CASSIUS. Away, away, be-gone!
They drive him out
BRUTUS. Lucilius and Titinius, bid the commanders
Prepare to lodge their companies to-night.
CASSIUS. And come yourselves, and bring Messala with you
Immediately to us. *Lucilius and Titinius depart*

BRUTUS. Lucius, a bowl of wine! 140
Lucius goes
CASSIUS. I did not think you could have been so angry.
BRUTUS. O Cassius, I am sick of many griefs.
CASSIUS. Of your philosophy you make no use,
If you give place to accidental evils.
BRUTUS. No man bears sorrow better: Portia is dead.
CASSIUS. Ha! Portia!
BRUTUS. She is dead.
CASSIUS. How scaped I killing when I crossed you so?
O insupportable and touching loss!
Upon what sickness?
BRUTUS. Impatient of my absence, 150
And grief that young Octavius with Mark Antony
Have made themselves so strong: for with her death
That tidings came: with this she fell distract,
And, her attendants absent, swallowed fire.
CASSIUS. And died so?
BRUTUS. Even so.
CASSIUS. O ye immortal gods!

Lucius brings wine and tapers

BRUTUS. Speak no more of her. Give me a bowl of wine.
In this I bury all unkindness, Cassius. *Drinks*
CASSIUS. My heart is thirsty for that noble pledge.
Fill, Lucius, till the wine o'erswell the cup;
I cannot drink too much of Brutus' love. 160
Drinks; Lucius goes

Enter Titinius, with Messala

BRUTUS. Come in, Titinius! Welcome, good Messala.
Now sit we close about this taper here,
And call in question our necessities.
CASSIUS. Portia, art thou gone?
BRUTUS. No more, I pray you.
Messala, I have here receivéd letters,
That young Octavius and Mark Antony
Come down upon us with a mighty power,
Bending their expedition toward Philippi.
MESSALA. Myself have letters of the selfsame tenour.
BRUTUS. With what addition? 170
MESSALA. That by proscription and bills of outlawry
Octavius, Antony, and Lepidus
Have put to death an hundred senators.
BRUTUS. Therein our letters do not well agree;
Mine speak of seventy senators that died
By their proscriptions, Cicero being one.
CASSIUS. Cicero one!
MESSALA. Cicero is dead,
And by that order of proscription.
Had you your letters from your wife, my lord?
BRUTUS. No, Messala. 180
MESSALA. Nor nothing in your letters writ of her?
BRUTUS. Nothing, Messala.
MESSALA. That, methinks, is strange.
BRUTUS. Why ask you? hear you aught of her in yours?
MESSALA. No, my lord.
BRUTUS. Now, as you are a Roman, tell me true.
MESSALA. Then like a Roman bear the truth I tell:
For certain she is dead, and by strange manner.
BRUTUS. Why, farewell, Portia. We must die, Messala:
With meditating that she must die once
I have the patience to endure it now. 190
MESSALA. Even so great men great losses should endure.

CASSIUS. I have as much of this in art as you,
But yet my nature could bear it so.
BRUTUS. Well, to our work alive. What do you think
of marching to Philippi presently?
CASSIUS. I do not think it good.
BRUTUS.   Your reason?
CASSIUS.   This it is:
'Tis better that the enemy seek us:
So shall he waste his means, weary his soldiers,
Doing himself offence; whilst we lying still
Are full of rest, defence and nimbleness.   200
BRUTUS. Good reasons must of force give place to
    better.
The people 'twixt Philippi and this ground
Do stand but in a forced affection,
For they have grudged us contribution:
The enemy, marching along by them,
By them shall make a fuller number up,
Come on refreshed, new-added and encouraged;
From which advantage shall we cut him off
If at Philippi we do face him there,
These people at our back.
CASSIUS.   Hear me, good brother. 210
BRUTUS. Under your pardon. You must note beside
That we have tried the utmost of our friends,
Our legions are brim-full, our cause is ripe:
The enemy increaseth every day;
We, at the height, are ready to decline.
There is a tide in the affairs of men
Which taken at the flood leads on to fortune;
Omitted, all the voyage of their life
Is bound in shallows and in miseries.
On such a full sea are we now afloat,   220
And we must take the current when it serves,
Or lose our ventures.
CASSIUS.   Then, with your will, go on;
We'll along ourselves and meet them at Philippi.
BRUTUS. The deep of night is crept upon our talk,
And nature must obey necessity;
Which we will niggard with a little rest.
There is no more to say?
CASSIUS.   No more. Good night:
Early to-morrow will we rise and hence.
BRUTUS. Lucius! [*Lucius re-enters*] My gown. Farewell,
    good Messala: *Lucius goes*
Good night, Titinius: noble, noble Cassius, 230
Good night, and good repose.
CASSIUS.   O my dear brother!
This was an ill beginning of the night:
Never come such division 'tween our souls!
Let it not, Brutus.
BRUTUS.   Everything is well.
CASSIUS. Good night, my lord.
BRUTUS.   Good night, good brother.
TITINIUS, MESSALA. Good night, Lord Brutus.
BRUTUS.   Farewell, every one.
                          They go

Re-enter Lucius, with the gown

Give me the gown. Where is thy instrument?
LUCIUS. Here in the tent.
BRUTUS.   What, thou speak'st drowsily?
Poor knave, I blame thee not; thou art o'erwatched.
Call Claudius and some other of my men; 240
I'll have them sleep on cushions in my tent.
LUCIUS. Varro and Claudius!

Varro and Claudius enter

VARRO. Calls my lord?
BRUTUS. I pray you, sirs, lie in my tent and sleep;
It may be I shall raise you by and by
On business to my brother Cassius.
VARRO. So please you, we will stand and watch your
    pleasure.
BRUTUS. I will not have it so: lie down, good sirs;
It may be I shall otherwise bethink me.
Look, Lucius, here's the book I sought for so; 250
I put it in the pocket of my gown.
               Varro and Claudius lie down
LUCIUS. I was sure your lordship did not give it me.
BRUTUS. Bear with me, good boy, I am much
    forgetful.
Canst thou hold up thy heavy eyes awhile,
And touch thy instrument a strain or two?
LUCIUS. Ay, my lord, an't please you.
BRUTUS.   It dies, my boy:
I trouble thee too much, but thou art willing.
LUCIUS. It is my duty, sir.
BRUTUS. I should not urge thy duty past thy might;
I know young bloods look for a time of rest. 260
LUCIUS. I have slept, my lord, already.
BRUTUS. It was well done; and thou shalt sleep again;
I will not hold thee long: if I do live,
I will be good to thee.   *Music and a song*
This is a sleepy tune. O murd'rous slumber,
Layest thou thy leaden mace upon my boy,
That plays thee music? Gentle knave, good night;
I will not do thee so much wrong to wake thee:
If thou dost nod, thou break'st thy instrument;
I'll take it from thee; and, good boy, good night. 270
Let me see, let me see; is not the leaf turned down
Where I left reading? Here it is, I think.

Enter the Ghost of Cæsar

How ill this taper burns! Ha! who comes here?
I think it is the weakness of mine eyes
That shapes this monstrous apparition.
It comes upon me. Art thou any thing?
Art thou some god, some angel, or some devil,
That mak'st my blood cold, and my hair to stare?
Speak to me what thou art.
GHOST. Thy evil spirit, Brutus.
BRUTUS.   Why com'st thou? 280
GHOST. To tell thee thou shalt see me at Philippi.
BRUTUS. Well; then I shall see thee again?
GHOST. Ay, at Philippi.
BRUTUS. Why, I will see thee at Philippi then.
               The Ghost disappears
Now I have taken heart thou vanishest.
Ill spirit, I would hold more talk with thee.
Boy, Lucius! Varro! Claudius! Sirs, awake!
Claudius!
LUCIUS. The strings, my lord, are false.
BRUTUS. He thinks he still is at his instrument. 290
Lucius, awake!
LUCIUS. My lord?
BRUTUS. Didst thou dream, Lucius, that thou so criedst
    out?
LUCIUS. My lord, I do not know that I did cry.
BRUTUS. Yes, that thou didst: didst thou see any thing?
LUCIUS. Nothing, my lord.

BRUTUS. Sleep again, Lucius. Sirrah Claudius!
[*to Varro*] Fellow thou, awake!
VARRO. My lord?
CLAUDIUS. My lord?   300
BRUTUS. Why did you so cry out, sirs, in your sleep?
VARRO, CLAUDIUS. Did we, my lord?
BRUTUS.   Ay: saw you any thing?
VARRO. No, my lord, I saw nothing.
CLAUDIUS.   Nor I, my lord.
BRUTUS. Go and commend me to my brother Cassius;
Bid him set on his powers betimes before,
And we will follow.
VARRO, CLAUDIUS.   It shall be done, my lord.
They go

ACT 5
Scene 1: *The plains of Philippi*

Enter Octavius, Antony, and their army

OCTAVIUS. Now, Antony, our hopes are answeréd:
You said the enemy would not come down,
But keep the hills and upper regions;
It proves not so: their battles are at hand;
They mean to warn us at Philippi here,
Answering before we do demand of them.
ANTONY. Tut, I am in their bosoms, and I know
Wherefore they do it: they could be content
To visit other places; and come down
With fearful bravery, thinking by this face   10
To fasten in our thoughts that they have courage;
But 'tis not so.

A messenger comes up

MESSENGER.   Prepare you, generals:
The enemy comes on in gallant show;
Their bloody sign of battle is hung out,
And something to be done immediately.
ANTONY. Octavius, lead your battle softly on,
Upon the left hand of the even field.
OCTAVIUS. Upon the right hand I; keep thou the left.
ANTONY. Why do you cross me in this exigent?
OCTAVIUS. I do not cross you; but I will do so.   20

Drum. Enter Brutus, Cassius, and their army; Lucilius, Titinius, Messala, and others

BRUTUS. They stand, and would have parley.
CASSIUS. Stand fast, Titinius: we must out and talk.
OCTAVIUS. Mark Antony, shall we give sign of battle?
ANTONY. No, Cæsar, we will answer on their charge.
Make forth; the generals would have some words.
OCTAVIUS. Stir not until the signal.
BRUTUS. Words before blows: is it so, countrymen?
OCTAVIUS. Not that we love words better, as you do.
BRUTUS. Good words are better than bad strokes, Octavius.
ANTONY. In your bad strokes, Brutus, you give good words: 30
Witness the hole you made in Cæsar's heart,
Crying 'Long live! hail, Cæsar!'
CASSIUS.   Antony,
The posture of your blows are yet unknown;
But for your words, they rob the Hybla bees,
And leave them honeyless.
ANTONY.   Not stingless too?
BRUTUS. O, yes, and soundless too;
For you have stol'n their buzzing, Antony,

And very wisely threat before you sting.
ANTONY. Villains, you did not so, when your vile daggers
Hacked one another in the sides of Cæsar: 40
You showed your teeth like apes, and fawned like hounds,
And bowed like bondmen, kissing Cæsar's feet;
Whilst damnéd Casca, like a cur, behind
Struck Cæsar on the neck. O you flatterers!
CASSIUS. Flatterers! Now, Brutus, thank yourself:
This tongue had not offended so to-day,
If Cassius might have ruled.
OCTAVIUS. Come, come, the cause: if arguing make us sweat,
The proof of it will turn to redder drops.
Look;   50
I draw my sword against conspirators;
When think you that the sword goes up again?
Never, till Cæsar's three and thirty wounds
Be well avenged, or till another Cæsar
Have added slaughter to the sword of traitors.
BRUTUS. Cæsar, thou canst not die by traitors' hands,
Unless thou bring'st them with thee.
OCTAVIUS.   So I hope;
I was not born to die on Brutus' sword.
BRUTUS. O, if thou wert the noblest of thy strain,
Young man, thou couldst not die more honourable. 60
CASSIUS. A peevish schoolboy, worthless of such honour,
Joined with a masker and a reveller!
ANTONY. Old Cassius still!
OCTAVIUS.   Come, Antony; away!
Defiance, traitors, hurl we in your teeth;
If you dare fight to-day, come to the field:
If not, when you have stomachs.
Octavius, Antony, and their army march away
CASSIUS. Why, now, blow wind, swell billow and swim bark!
The storm is up, and all is on the hazard.
BRUTUS. Ho, Lucilius! hark, a word with you.
LUCILIUS [*standing forth*]. My lord? *They talk apart*
CASSIUS. Messala!
MESSALA. [*standing forth*]. What says my general?
CASSIUS.   Messala, 70
This is my birth-day; as this very day
Was Cassius born. Give me thy hand, Messala:
Be thou my witness that, against my will,
(As Pompey was) am I compelled to set
Upon one battle all our liberties.
You know that I held Epicurus strong,
And his opinion: now I change my mind,
And partly credit things that do presage.
Coming from Sardis, on our former ensign
Two mighty eagles fell, and there they perched, 80
Gorging and feeding from our soldiers' hands;
Who to Philippi here consorted us:
This morning are they fled away and gone,
And in their steads do ravens, crows, and kites
Fly o'er our heads and downward look on us,
As we were sickly prey: their shadows seem
A canopy most fatal, under which
Our army lies, ready to give up the ghost.
MESSALA. Believe not so.
CASSIUS.   I but believe it partly,
For I am fresh of spirit and resolved   90

To meet all perils very constantly.

BRUTUS. Even so, Lucilius.

CASSIUS.   Now, most noble Brutus,
The gods to-day stand friendly, that we may,
Lovers in peace, lead on our days to age!
But, since the affairs of men rest still incertain,
Let's reason with the worst that may befall.
If we do lose this battle, then is this
The very last time we shall speak together:
What are you then determinèd to do?

BRUTUS. Even by the rule of that philosophy   100
By which I did blame Cato for the death
Which he did give himself, I know not how
But I do find it cowardly and vile,
For fear of what might fall, so to prevent
The time of life; arming myself with patience
To stay the providence of some high powers
That govern us below.

CASSIUS.   Then, if we lose this battle,
You are contented to be led in triumph
Thorough the streets of Rome?

BRUTUS. No, Cassius, no! think not, thou noble
     Roman,   110
That ever Brutus will go bound to Rome;
He bears too great a mind. But this same day
Must end that work the ides of March begun;
And whether we shall meet again I know not.   114
Therefore our everlasting farewell take.
For ever, and for ever, farewell, Cassius!
If we do meet again, why, we shall smile;   117
If not, why then this parting was well made.   118

CASSIUS. For ever and for ever farewell, Brutus!
If we do meet again, we'll smile indeed;   120
If not, 'tis true this parting was well made.

BRUTUS. Why then, lead on. O, that a man might
     know
The end of this day's business ere it come!
But it sufficeth that the day will end,
And then the end is known. Come, ho! away!
                                      They go

Scene 2

The noise of battle is heard. Brutus enters with Messala

BRUTUS. Ride, ride, Messala, ride, and give these bills
Unto the legions on the other side:
Let them set on at once; for I perceive
But cold demeanour in Octavius' wing,
And sudden push gives them the overthrow.
Ride, ride, Messala: let them all come down.
                                      They go

Scene 3

Alarums. Enter Cassius and after him Titinius

CASSIUS. O, look, Titinius, look, the villains fly!
Myself have to mine own turned enemy:
This ensign here of mine was turning back;
I slew the coward, and did take it from him.

TITINIUS. O Cassius, Brutus gave the word too early;
Who, having some advantage on Octavius,
Took it too eagerly: his soldiers fell to spoil,
Whilst we by Antony are all enclosed.

Pindarus enters

PINDARUS. Fly further off, my lord, fly further off;

Mark Antony is in your tents, my lord: 10
Fly, therefore, noble Cassius, fly far off.

CASSIUS. This hill is far enough. Look, look, Titinius;
Are those my tents where I perceive the fire?

TITINIUS. They are, my lord.

CASSIUS.   Titinius, if thou lovest me,
Mount thou my horse and hide thy spurs in him,
Till he have brought thee up to yonder troops
And here again; that I may rest assured
Whether yond troops are friend or enemy.

TITINIUS. I will be here again, even with a thought.
                                      He goes

CASSIUS. Go, Pindarus, get higher on that hill;   20
My sight was ever thick; regard Titinius,
And tell me what thou not'st about the field.
                                   Pindarus ascends
This day I breathèd first! time is come round,
And where I did begin, there shall I end;
My life is run his compass. Sirrah, what news?

PINDARUS [*above*]. O my lord!

CASSIUS. What news?

PINDARUS [*above*]. Titinius is enclosèd round about
With horsemen that make to him on the spur;
Yet he spurs on. Now they are almost on him.   30
Now, Titinius! Now some light. O, he lights too.
He's ta'en. [*a shout*] And, hark! they shout for joy.

CASSIUS. Come down, behold no more.
O, coward that I am, to live so long,
To see my best friend ta'en before my face!

Pindarus descends

Come hither, sirrah:
In Parthia did I take thee prisoner;
And then I swore thee, saving of thy life,
That whatsoever I did bid thee do,
Thou shouldst attempt it. Come now, keep thine
     oath!   40
Now be a freeman, and with this good sword
That ran through Cæsar's bowels search this bosom.
Stand not to answer: here, take thou the hilts,
And when my face is covered, as 'tis now,
Guide thou the sword. [*Pindarus thrusts him through*]
     Cæsar, thou art revenged,
Even with the sword that killed thee.   *Dies*

PINDARUS. So, I am free, yet would not so have been,
Durst I have done my will. O Cassius!
Far from this country Pindarus shall run,
Where never Roman shall take note of him.   50
                                      He goes

Titinius returns with Messala

MESSALA. It is but change, Titinius; for Octavius
Is overthrown by noble Brutus' power,
As Cassius' legions are by Antony.

TITINIUS. These tidings will well comfort Cassius.

MESSALA. Where did you leave him?

TITINIUS.   All disconsolate,
With Pindarus his bondman, on this hill.

MESSALA. Is not that he that lies upon the ground?

TITINIUS. He lies not like the living. O my heart!

MESSALA. Is not that he?

TITINIUS.   No, this was he, Messala,
But Cassius is no more. O setting sun,   60
As in thy red rays thou dost sink to night,
So in his red blood Cassius' day is set,
The sun of Rome is set! Our day is gone;

Clouds, dews and dangers come; our deeds are done!
Mistrust of my success hath done this deed.
MESSALA. Mistrust of good success hath done this deed.
O hateful error, melancholy's child,
Why dost thou show to the apt thoughts of men
The things that are not? O error, soon conceived,
Thou never com'st unto a happy birth, 70
But kill'st the mother that engend'red thee!
TITINIUS. What, Pindarus! where art thou, Pindarus?
MESSALA. Seek him, Titinius, whilst I go to meet
The noble Brutus, thrusting this report
Into his ears: I may say 'thrusting' it,
For piercing steel and darts envenoméd
Shall be as welcome to the ears of Brutus
As tiding of this sight.
TITINIUS. Hie you, Messala,
And I will seek for Pindarus the while.
Messala goes
Why didst thou send me forth, brave Cassius? 80
Did I not meet thy friends? and did not they
Put on my brows this wreath of victory,
And bid me give it thee? Didst thou not hear their
shouts?
Alas, thou hast misconstrued everything!
But, hold thee, take this garland on thy brow;
Thy Brutus bid me give it thee, and I
Will do his bidding. Brutus, come apace,
And see how I regarded Caius Cassius.
By your leave, gods: this is a Roman's part:
Come, Cassius' sword, and find Titinius' heart. 90
Kills himself

*The noise of battle dies away; then re-enter Messala, with
Brutus, young Cato, Lucilius, Labeo, Flavius, and others*

BRUTUS. Where, where, Messala, doth his body lie?
MESSALA. Lo, yonder, and Titinius mourning it.
BRUTUS. Titinius' face is upward.
CATO. He is slain.
BRUTUS. O Julius Cæsar, thou art mighty yet!
Thy spirit walks abroad, and turns our swords
In our own proper entrails.
CATO. Brave Titinius!
Look, whe'r he have not crowned dead Cassius!
BRUTUS. Are yet two Romans living such as these?
The last of all the Romans, fare thee well!
It is impossible that ever Rome 100
Should breed thy fellow. Friends, I owe mo tears
To this dead man than you shall see me pay.
I shall find time, Cassius, I shall find time.
Come therefore, and to Thasos send his body:
His funerals shall not be in our camp,
Lest it discomfort us. Lucilius, come,
And come, young Cato: let us to the field.
Labeo and Flavius, set our battles on.
'Tis three o'clock; and, Romans, yet ere night
We shall try fortune in a second fight. 110
They pass on, soldiers bearing off the bodies

Scene 4: *The battle resumes. Presently re-enter Brutus,
Messala, young Cato, Lucilius, and their army, yielding
ground to the opposing force*

BRUTUS. Yet, countrymen! O, yet hold up your heads!
*He charges, followed out by
Messala, and others*
CATO. What bastard doth not? Who will go with me?

I will proclaim my name about the field.
I am the son of Marcus Cato, ho!
A foe to tyrants, and my country's friend;
I am the son of Marcus Cato, ho!
LUCILIUS. And I am Brutus, Marcus Brutus, I;
Brutus, my country's friend; know me for Brutus!
*They charge in turn;
young Cato is slain*
O young and noble Cato, art thou down?
Why, now thou diest as bravely as Titinius, 10
And mayst be honoured, being Cato's son.
1 SOLDIER. Yield, or thou diest.
LUCILIUS. Only I yield to die:
There is so much that thou wilt kill me straight:
Kill Brutus, and be honoured in his death.
1 SOLDIER. We must not: a noble prisoner.
2 SOLDIER. Room, ho! Tell Antony, Brutus is ta'en.
1 SOLDIER. I'll tell the news. Here comes the general.

Enter Antony

Brutus is ta'en, Brutus is ta'en, my lord.
ANTONY. Where is he?
LUCILIUS. Safe, Antony; Brutus is safe enough: 20
I dare assure thee that no enemy
Shall ever take alive the noble Brutus:
The gods defend him from so great a shame!
When you do find him, or alive or dead,
He will be found like Brutus, like himself.
ANTONY. This is not Brutus, friend, but, I assure you,
A prize no less in worth: keep this man safe,
Give him all kindness: I had rather have
Such men my friends than enemies. Go on,
And see whe'r Brutus be alive or dead, 30
And bring us word unto Octavius' tent
How everything is chanced. *They go*

Scene 5

*Enter Brutus, Dardanius, Clitus, Strato,
and Volumnius*

BRUTUS. Come, poor remains of friends, rest on this
rock.
CLITUS. Statilius showed the torch-light, but, my lord,
He came not back: he is or ta'en or slain.
BRUTUS. Sit thee down, Clitus: slaying is the word;
It is a deed in fashion. Hark thee, Clitus. *Whispers*
CLITUS. What, I, my lord? No, not for all the world.
BRUTUS. Peace then, no words.
CLITUS. I'll rather kill myself.
BRUTUS. Hark thee, Dardanius. *Whispers*
DARDANIUS. Shall I do such a deed?
CLITUS. O Dardanius!
DARDANIUS. O Clitus! 10
CLITUS. What ill request did Brutus make to thee?
DARDANIUS. To kill him, Clitus. Look, he meditates.
CLITUS. Now is that noble vessel full of grief,
That it runs over even at his eyes.
BRUTUS. Come hither, good Volumnius; list a word.
VOLUMNIUS. What says my lord?
BRUTUS. Why, this, Volumnius:
The ghost of Cæsar hath appeared to me
Two several times by night: at Sardis once,
And this last night here in Philippi fields:
I know my hour is come.
VOLUMNIUS. Not so, my lord. 20
BRUTUS. Nay, I am sure it is, Volumnius.

Thou seest the world, Volumnius, how it goes;
Our enemies have beat us to the pit:
                    Fighting heard at a distance
It is more worthy to leap in ourselves
Than tarry till they push us. Good Volumnius,
Thou know'st that we two went to school together:
Even for that our love of old, I prithee,
Hold thou my sword-hilts, whilst I run on it.
VOLUMNIUS. That's not an office for a friend my lord.
                              The sound draws near
CLITUS. Fly, fly, my lord, there is no tarrying here.   30
BRUTUS. Farewell to you; and you; and you
    Volumnius.
    Strato, thou hast been all this while asleep;
    Farewell to thee too, Strato. Countrymen,
    My heart doth joy that yet in all my life
    I found no man but he was true to me.
    I shall have glory by this losing day,
    More than Octavius and Mark Antony
    By this vile conquest shall attain unto.
    So, fare you well at once; for Brutus' tongue
    Hath almost ended his life's history: 40
    Night hangs upon mine eyes; my bones would rest,
    That have but laboured to attain this hour.
            Loud alarum and cries of 'Fly, fly, fly!' *heard*
CLITUS. Fly, my lord, fly.
BRUTUS.   Hence! I will follow
                Clitus, Dardanius, and Volumnius go
    I prithee, Strato, stay thou by thy lord:
    Thou art a fellow of a good respect;
    Thy life hath had some smatch of honour in it:
    Hold then my sword, and turn away thy face,
    While I do run upon it. Wilt thou, Strato?
STRATO. Give me your hand first: fare you well, my
    lord.
BRUTUS. Farewell, good Strato. [*runs on his sword*]
    Cæsar, now be still: 50
    I killed not thee with half so good a will.   *Dies*

*Enter the army of Antony, pursuing the remnant of
Brutus' forces, and later sounding the retreat. Then
enter Octavius and Antony, with Messala, Lucilius,
as prisoners*

OCTAVIUS. What man is that?
MESSALA. My master's man. Strato, where is thy
    master?
STRATO. Free from the bondage you are in, Messala:
    The conquerors can but make a fire of him;
    For Brutus only overcame himself,
    And no man else hath honour by his death.
LUCILIUS. So Brutus should be found. I thank thee,
    Brutus,
    That thou hast proved Lucilius' saying true.
OCTAVIUS. All that served Brutus, I will entertain
    them.   60
    Fellow, wilt thou bestow thy time with me?
STRATO. Ay, if Messala will prefer me to you.
OCTAVIUS. Do so, good Messala.
MESSALA. How died my master, Strato?
STRATO. I held the sword, and he did run on it.
MESSALA. Octavius, then take him to follow thee,
    That did the latest service to my master.
ANTONY. This was the noblest Roman of them all:
    All the conspirators save only he
    Did that they did in envy of great Cæsar;   70
    He only, in a general honest thought
    And common good to all, made one of them.
    His life was gentle, and the elements
    So mixed in him that Nature might stand up
    And say to all the world 'This was a man!'
OCTAVIUS. According to his virtue let us use him,
    With all respect and rites of burial.
    Within my tent his bones to-night shall lie,
    Most like a soldier, ordered honourably.
    So call the field to rest, and let's away,   80
    To part the glories of this happy day.
                              They march on

Macbeth

The scene: Scotland and (in 4.3) England

CHARACTERS IN THE PLAY

DUNCAN, *King of Scotland*
MALCOLM ⎫ *his sons*
DONALBAIN ⎭
MACBETH, *at first a general, later King of Scotland*
BANQUO, *a general*
MACDUFF ⎫
LENNOX ⎪
ROSS ⎪
MENTEITH ⎬ *noblemen of Scotland*
ANGUS ⎪
CAITHNESS ⎭
FLEANCE, *son to Banquo*
SIWARD, *Earl of Northumberland, general of the English forces*
YOUNG SIWARD, *his son*
SETON, *armour-bearer to Macbeth*

A Boy, *son to Macduff*
A Captain
A Porter
An Old Man
An English Doctor
A Scotch Doctor
Three Murderers
LADY MACBETH
LADY MACDUFF
A Gentlewoman attending on Lady Macbeth
The Weird Sisters
HECATE
Apparitions
Lords, Gentlemen, Officers, Soldiers, Attendants, and Messengers

Macbeth

ACT 1
Scene 1

Thunder and lightning. Enter three Witches

1 WITCH. When shall we three meet again
In thunder, lightning, or in rain?
2 WITCH. When the hurlyburly's done,
When the battle's lost and won.
3 WITCH. That will be ere the set of sun.
1 WITCH. Where the place?
2 WITCH.   Upon the heath.
3 WITCH. There to meet with Macbeth.
1 WITCH. I come, Graymalkin!
2 WITCH. Paddock calls.
3 WITCH. Anon!   10
ALL. Fair is foul, and foul is fair:
Hover through the fog and filthy air.   *They go*

Scene 2: *A camp*

*Alarum. Enter King Duncan, Malcolm, Donalbain,
Lennox, with attendants, meeting a bleeding Captain*

DUNCAN. What bloody man is that? He can report,
As seemeth by his plight, of the revolt
The newest state.
MALCOLM.   This is the sergeant,
Who like a good and hardy soldier fought
'Gainst my captivity ... Hail, brave friend!
Say to the king the knowledge of the broil
As thou didst leave it.
CAPTAIN.   Doubtful it stood,
As two spent swimmers that do cling together
And choke their art ... The merciless Macdonwald
(Worthy to be a rebel, for to that   10
The multiplying villainies of nature
Do swarm upon him) from the Western Isles
Of kerns and gallowglasses is supplied,
And Fortune, on his damnéd quarrel smiling,
Showed like a rebel's whore: but all's too weak:
For brave Macbeth (well he deserves that name)
Disdaining fortune, with his brandished steel,
Which smoked with bloody execution,
Like Valour's minion carvéd out his passage,
Till he faced the slave;   20
Which ne'er shook hands, nor bade farewell to him,
Till he unseamed him from the nave to th' chops,
And fixed his head upon our battlements.
DUNCAN. O, valiant cousin! worthy gentleman!
CAPTAIN. As whence the sun 'gins his reflection
Shipwracking storms and direful thunders break;
So from that spring whence comfort seemed to
come
Discomfort swells: mark, king of Scotland, mark!
No sooner justice had, with valour armed,
Compelled these skipping kerns to trust their heels, 30
But the Norweyan lord, surveying vantage,
With furbished arms and new supplies of men,
Began a fresh assault.
DUNCAN.   Dismayed not this
Our captains, Macbeth and Banquo?

CAPTAIN.   Yes;
As sparrows, eagles; or the hare, the lion.
If I say sooth, I must report they were
As cannons overcharged with double cracks;
So they
Doubly redoubled strokes upon the foe:
Except they meant to bathe in reeking wounds,   40
Or memorize another Golgotha,
I cannot tell:
But I am faint, my gashes cry for help.
DUNCAN. So well thy words become thee as thy
wounds,
They smack of honour both: Go get him surgeons.
                        Attendants help him thence
Who comes here?

Enter Ross and Angus

MALCOLM.   The worthy thane of Ross.
LENNOX. What a haste looks through his eyes! So
should he look
That seems to speak things strange.
ROSS.   God save the king!
DUNCAN. Whence cam'st thou, worthy thane?
ROSS.   From Fife, great king,
Where the Norweyan banners flout the sky,   50
And fan our people cold.
Norway himself, with terrible numbers,
Assisted by that most disloyal traitor
The thane of Cawdor, began a dismal conflict,
Till that Bellona's bridegroom, lapped in proof,
Confronted him with self-comparisons,
Point against point, rebellious arm 'gainst arm,
Curbing his lavish spirit: and, to conclude,
The victory fell on us.
DUNCAN.   Great happiness!
ROSS. That now   60
Sweno, the Norways' king, craves composition;
Nor would we deign him burial of his men
Till he disburséd, at Saint Colme's Inch,
Ten thousand dollars to our general use.
DUNCAN. No more that thane of Cawdor shall deceive
Our bosom interest: go pronounce his present death,
And with his former title greet Macbeth.
ROSS. I'll see it done.
DUNCAN. What he hath lost, noble Macbeth hath won.
                                          They go

Scene 3: *A barren heath*

Thunder. Enter the three Witches

1 WITCH. Where hast thou been, sister?
2 WITCH. Killing swine.
3 WITCH. Sister, where thou?
1 WITCH. A sailor's wife had chestnuts in her lap,
And munched, and munched, and munched: 'Give
me', quoth I.
'Aroint thee, witch!' the rump-fed ronyon cries.
Her husband's to Aleppo gone, master o'th' Tiger:
But in a sieve I'll thither sail,
And, like a rat without a tail,

I'll do, I'll do, and I'll do. 10
2 WITCH. I'll give thee a wind.
1 WITCH. Th'art kind.
3 WITCH. And I another.
1 WITCH. I myself have all the other,
And the very ports they blow,
All the quarters that they know
I'th' shipman's card.
I will drain him dry as hay:
Sleep shall, neither night nor day
Hang upon his pent-house lid; 20
He shall live a man forbid:
Weary sev'nights nine times nine
Shall he dwindle, peak, and pine:
Though his bark cannot be lost,
Yet it shall be tempest-tost.
Look what I have.
2 WITCH. Show me, show me.
1 WITCH. Here I have a pilot's thumb,
Wrecked as homeward he did come *Drum within*
3 WITCH. A drum, a drum! 30
Macbeth doth come.
ALL. The Weïrd Sisters, hand in hand,
Posters of the sea and land,
Thus do go, about, about,
Thrice to thine, and thrice to mine,
And thrice again, to make up nine.
Peace! the charm's wound up.

Enter Macbeth and Banquo

MACBETH. So foul and fair a day I have not seen.
BANQUO. How far is't called to Forres? What are these,
So withered, and so wild in their attire, 40
That look not like th'inhabitants o'th'earth,
And yet are on't? Live you? or are you aught
That man may question? You seem to understand
me,
By each at once her choppy finger laying
Upon her skinny lips: you should be women,
And yet your beards forbid me to interpret
That you are so.
MACBETH. Speak, if you can: what are you?
1 WITCH. All hail, Macbeth! hail to thee, thane of
Glamis!
2 WITCH. All hail, Macbeth! hail to thee, thane of
Cawdor!
3 WITCH. All hail, Macbeth! that shalt be king
hereafter. 50
BANQUO. Good sir, why do you start, and seem to
fear
Things that do sound so fair? I'th' name of truth,
Are ye fantastical, or that indeed
Which outwardly ye show? My noble partner
You greet with present grace and great prediction
Of noble having and of royal hope,
That he seems rapt withal: to me you speak not.
If you can look into the seeds of time,
And say which grain will grow and which will not,
Speak then to me, who neither beg nor fear 60
Your favours nor your hate.
1 WITCH. Hail!
2 WITCH. Hail!
3 WITCH. Hail!
1 WITCH. Lesser than Macbeth, and greater.
2 WITCH. Not so happy, yet much happier.

3 WITCH. Thou shalt get kings, though thou be none:
So all hail, Macbeth and Banquo!
1 WITCH. Banquo and Macbeth, all hail!
MACBETH. Stay, you imperfect speakers, tell me more: 70
By Sinel's death I know I am thane of Glamis,
But how of Cawdor? the thane of Cawdor lives
A prosperous gentleman; and to be king
Stands not within the prospect of belief,
No more than to be Cawdor. Say from whence
You owe this strange intelligence, or why
Upon this blasted heath you stop our way
With such prophetic greeting. Speak, I charge you.
They disappear
BANQUO. The earth hath bubbles, as the water has,
And these are of them: whither are they vanished? 80
MACBETH. Into the air; and what seemed corporal,
melted,
As breath into the wind. Would they had stayed!
BANQUO. Were such things here as we do speak about?
Or have we eaten on the insane root
That takes the reason prisoner?
MACBETH. Your children shall be kings.
BANQUO. You shall be king.
MACBETH. And thane of Cawdor too: went it not so?
BANQUO. To th'selfsame tune and words. Who's here?

Enter Ross and Angus

ROSS. The king hath happily received, Macbeth,
The news of thy success: and when he reads 90
Thy personal venture in the rebels' fight,
His wonders and his praises do contend
Which should be thine or his: silenced with that,
In viewing o'er the rest o'th' self-same day,
He finds thee in the stout Norweyan ranks,
Nothing afeard of what thyself didst make
Strange images of death. As thick as hail
Came post with post, and every one did bear
Thy praises in his kingdom's great defence,
And poured them down before him.
ANGUS. We are sent 100
To give thee from our royal master thanks,
Only to herald thee into his sight,
Not pay thee.
ROSS. And for an earnest of a greater honour,
He bade me, from him, call thee thane of Cawdor:
In which addition, hail, most worthy thane,
For it is thine.
BANQUO. What, can the devil speak true?
MACBETH. The thane of Cawdor lives: why do you
dress me
In borrowed robes?
ANGUS. Who was the thane lives yet,
But under heavy judgment bears that life 110
Which he deserves to lose. Whether he was
combined
With those of Norway, or did line the rebel
With hidden help and vantage, or that with both
He laboured in his country's wreck, I know not;
But treasons capital, confessed, and proved,
Have overthrown him.
MACBETH. [*aside*]. Glamis, and thane of
Cawdor:
The greatest is behind.—[*aloud*] Thanks for your
pains—
[*aside to Banquo*] Do you not hope your children shall
be kings,

When those that gave the thane of Cawdor to me
Promised no less to them?

BANQUO.   That, trusted home,   120
Might yet enkindle you unto the crown,
Besides the thane of Cawdor. But 'tis strange:
And oftentimes, to win us to our harm,
The instruments of darkness tell us truths,
Win us with honest trifles, to betray's
In deepest consequence.
Cousins, a word, I pray you.

MACBETH [aside].   Two truths are told,
As happy prologues to the swelling act
Of the imperial theme. [aloud] I thank you, gentle-
men.
[aside] This supernatural soliciting   130
Cannot be ill; cannot be good. If ill,
Why hath it given me earnest of success,
Commencing in a truth? I am thane of Cawdor.
If good, why do I yield to that suggestion
Whose horrid image doth unfix my hair,
And make my seated heart knock at my ribs,
Against the use of nature? Present fears
Are less than horrible imaginings:
My thought, whose murder yet is but fantastical,
Shales so my single state of man that function   140
Is smothered in surmise, and nothing is
But what is not.

BANQUO.   Look how our partner's rapt.

MACBETH [aside]. If chance will have me king, why,
     chance may crown me,
Without my stir.

BANQUO.   New honours come upon him,
Like our strange garments, cleave not to their mould
But with the aid of use.

MACBETH [aside].   Come what come may,
Time and the hour runs through the roughest day.

BANQUO. Worthy Macbeth, we stay upon your
     leisure.

MACBETH. Give me your favour: my dull brain was
     wrought
With things forgotten. Kind gentlemen, your pains   150
Are registered where every day I turn
The leaf to read them.... Let us toward the king.
                             Aside to Banquo
Think upon what hath chanced; and at more time,
The interim having weighed it, let us speak
Our free hearts each to other.

BANQUO.   Very gladly.

MACBETH. Till then, enough.... Come, friends.
                                  They go

Scene 4: *Forres. The Palace*

Flourish. Enter King Duncan, Malcolm, Donalbain,
Lennox, and Attendants

DUNCAN. Is execution done on Cawdor? Are not
     Those in commission yet returned?

MALCOLM.   My liege,
They are not yet come back. But I have spoke
With one that saw him die: who did report
That very frankly he confessed his treasons,
Implored your highness' pardon, and set forth
A deep repentance: nothing in his life
Became him like the leaving it; he died
As one that had been studied in his death,
To throw away the dearest thing he owed   10

As 'twere a careless trifle.

DUNCAN.   There's no art
To find the mind's construction in the face:
He was a gentleman on whom I built
An absolute trust.

Enter Macbeth, Banquo, Ross, and Angus

                   O worthiest cousin!
The sin of my ingratitude even now
Was heavy on me. Thou art so far before,
That swiftest wing of recompense is slow
To overtake thee. Would thou hadst less deserved,
That the proportion both of thanks and payment
Might have been mine! only I have left to say,   20
More is thy due than more than all can pay.

MACBETH. The service and the loyalty I owe,
In doing it, pays itself. Your highness' part
Is to receive our duties: and our duties
Are to your throne and state children and servants;
Which do but what they should, by doing every
     thing
Safe toward your love and honour.

DUNCAN.   Welcome hither:
I have begun to plant thee, and will labour
To make thee full of growing. Noble Banquo,
That hast no less deserved, nor must be known   30
No less to have done so: let me infold thee,
And hold thee to my heart.

BANQUO.   There if I grow,
The harvest is your own.

DUNCAN.   My plenteous joys,
Wanton in fulness, seek to hide themselves
In drops of sorrow.... Sons, kinsmen, thanes,
And you whose places are the nearest, know,
We will establish our estate upon
Our eldest, Malcolm, whom we name hereafter
The Prince of Cumberland: which honour must
Not unaccompanied invest him only,   40
But signs of nobleness, like stars, shall shine
On all deservers.... From hence to Inverness,
And bind us further to you.

MACBETH. The rest is labour, which is not used for
     you:
I'll be myself the harbinger, and make joyful
The hearing of my wife with your approach;
So humbly take my leave.

DUNCAN.   My worthy Cawdor!

MACBETH. The Prince of Cumberland! that is a step
On which I must fall down, or else o'er-leap,
For in my way it lies. Stars, hide your fires!   50
Let not light see my black and deep desires:
The eye wink at the hand; yet let that be
Which the eye fears, when it is done, to see.
                               He goes

DUNCAN. True, worthy Banquo; he is full so valiant,
And in his commendations I am fed;
It is a banquet to me. Let's after him,
Whose care is gone before to bid us welcome:
It is a peerless kinsman.   Flourish. They go

Scene 5: *Inverness. Macbeth's castle*

Enter Macbeth's wife alone, with a letter

LADY M. [reads] 'They met me in the day of success;
and I have learned by the perfect'st report, they have
more in them than mortal knowledge. When I

burned in desire to question them further, they
made themselves air, into which they vanished.
Whiles I stood rapt in the wonder of it, came
missives from the king, who all-hailed me, 'Thane
of Cawdor', by which title, before, these Weïrd
Sisters saluted me, and referred me to the coming
on of time, with 'Hail, king that shalt be!' This
have I thought good to deliver thee (my dearest
partner of greatness) that thou mightst not lose the
dues of rejoicing, by being ignorant of what great-
ness is promised thee. Lay it to thy heart, and fare-
well.'
Glamis thou art, and Cawdor, and shalt be
What thou art promised: yet do I fear thy nature,
It is too full o'th' milk of human kindness
To catch the nearest way: thou wouldst be great,
Art not without ambition, but without
The illness should attend it: what thou wouldst
highly,
That wouldst thou holily; wouldst not play false,
And yet wouldst wrongly win: thou'ldst have, great
Glamis,
That which cries 'Thus thou must do', if thou
have it,
And that which rather thou dost fear to do
Than wishest should be undone. Hie thee hither,
That I may pour my spirits in thine ear,
And chastise with the valour of my tongue
All that impedes thee from the golden round,
Which fate and metaphysical aid doth seem
To have thee crowned withal.

An attendant enters

What is your tidings?
ATTENDANT. The king comes here to-night.
LADY M. Thou'rt mad to say it!
Is not thy master with him? who, were't so,
Would have informed for preparation.
ATTENDANT. So please you, it is true: our thane is
coming:
One of my fellows had the speed of him;
Who, almost dead for breath, had scarcely more
Than would make up his message.
LADY M. Give him tending,
He brings great news. [*attendant goes*] The raven
himself is hoarse
That croaks the fatal entrance of Duncan
Under my battlements.... Come, you spirits
That tend on mortal thoughts, unsex me here,
And fill me, from the crown to the toe, top-full
Of direst cruelty! make thick my blood,
Stop up th'access and passage to remorse,
That no compunctious visitings of nature
Shake my fell purpose, nor keep peace between
Th'effect and it! Come to my woman's breasts,
And take my milk for gall, you murd'ring ministers,
Wherever in your sightless substances
You wait on nature's mischief! Come, thick night,
And pall thee in the dunnest smoke of hell,
That my keen knife see not the wound it makes,
Nor heaven peep through the blanket of the dark,
To cry 'Hold, hold!'

Enter Macbeth

Great Glamis! worthy Cawdor!
Greater than both, by the all-hail hereafter!

Thy letters have transported me beyond
This ignorant present, and I feel now
The future in the instant.
MACBETH. My dearest love,
Duncan comes here to-night.
LADY M. And when goes hence?
MACBETH. To-morrow, as he purposes.
LADY M. O, never
Shall sun that morrow see!
Your face, my thane, is as a book, where men
May read strange matters. To beguile the time,
Look like the time, bear welcome in your eye,
Your hand, your tongue: look like th'innocent
flower,
But be the serpent under't. He that's coming
Must be provided for: and you shall put
This night's great business into my dispatch,
Which shall to all our nights and days to come
Give solely sovereign sway and masterdom.
MACBETH. We will speak further.
LADY M. Only look up clear:
To alter favour ever is to fear:
Leave all the rest to me. *They go*

Scene 6

Hautboys. Enter King Duncan, Malcolm, Donalbain,
Banquo, Lennox, Macduff, Ross, Angus, and attendants

DUNCAN. This castle hath a pleasant seat; the air
Nimbly and sweetly recommends itself
Unto our gentle senses.
BANQUO. This guest of summer,
The temple-haunting martlet, does approve,
By his loved mansionry, that the heaven's breath
Smells wooingly here: no jutty, frieze,
Buttress, nor coign of vantage, but this bird
Hath made his pendent bed and procreant cradle:
Where they most breed and haunt, I have observed
The air is delicate.

Enter Lady Macbeth

DUNCAN. See, see! our honoured hostess!
The love that follows us sometime is our trouble,
Which still we thank as love. Herein I teach you
How you shall bid God 'ield us for your pains,
And thank us for your trouble.
LADY M. All our service
In every point twice done, and then done double,
Were poor and single business to contend
Against those honours deep and broad, wherewith
Your majesty loads our house: for those of old,
And the late dignities heaped up to them,
We rest your hermits.
DUNCAN. Where's the thane of Cawdor?
We coursed him at the heels, and had a purpose
To be his purveyor: but he rides well,
And his great love (sharp as his spur) hath holp him
To his home before us. Fair and noble hostess,
We are your guest to-night.
LADY M. Your servants ever
Have theirs, themselves, and what is theirs, in
compt,
To make their audit at your highness' pleasure,
Still to return your own.
DUNCAN. Give me your hand:
Conduct me to mine host; we love him highly,

And shall continue our graces towards him.   30
By your leave, hostess.   *They go*

Scene 7: *A court in Macbeth's castle*

Hautboys. Torches. Enter a sewer directing divers servants who pass with dishes and service across the court. Then enter Macbeth.

MACBETH. If it were done, when 'tis done, then 'twere
        well
It were done quickly: if th'assassination
Could trammel up the consequence, and catch,
With his surcease, success; that but this blow
Might be the be-all and the end-all.... here,
But here, upon this bank and shoal of time,
We'ld jump the life to come. But in these cases
We still have judgement here—that we but teach
Bloody instructions, which being taught return
To plague th'inventor: this even-handed justice   10
Commends th'ingredience of our poisoned chalice
To our own lips. He's here in double trust:
First, as I am his kinsman and his subject,
Strong both against the deed; then, as his host,
Who should against his murderer shut the door,
Not bear the knife myself. Besides, this Duncan
Hath borne his faculties so meek, hath been
So clear in his great office, that his virtues
Will plead like angels, trumpet-tongued, against
The deep damnation of his taking-off: 20
And pity, like a naked new-born babe,
Striding the blast, or Heaven's cherubin, horsed
Upon the sightless couriers of the air,
Shall blow the horrid deed in every eye,
That tears shall drown the wind. I have no spur
To prick the sides of my intent, but only
Vaulting ambition, which o'erleaps itself,
And falls on th'other—

Enter Lady Macbeth

                    How now, what news?
LADY M. He has almost supped: why have you left
        the chamber?
MACBETH. Hath he asked for me?
LADY M.   Know you not he has?   30
MACBETH. We will proceed no further in this business:
He hath honoured me of late, and I have bought
Golden opinions from all sorts of people,
Which would be worn now in their newest gloss,
Not cast aside so soon.
LADY M.   Was the hope drunk
Wherein you dressed yourself? hath it slept since?
And wakes it now, to look so green and pale
At what it did so freely? From this time
Such I account thy love. Art thou afeard
To be the same in thine own act and valour   40
As thou art in desire? Wouldst thou have that
Which thou esteem'st the ornament of life,
And live a coward in thine own esteem,
Letting 'I dare not' wait upon 'I would',
Like the poor cat i'th'adage?
MACBETH.   Prithee, peace:
I dare do all that may become a man;
Who dares do more, is none.
LADY M.   What beast was't then
That made you break this enterprise to me?
When you durst do it, then you were a man;

And, to be more than what you were, you would   50
Be so much more the man. Nor time nor place
Did then adhere, and yet you would make both:
They have made themselves, and that their fitness
        now
Does unmake you. I have given suck, and know
How tender 'tis to love the babe that milks me—
I would, while it was smiling in my face,
Have plucked my nipple from his boneless gums,
And dashed the brains out, had I so sworn as you
Have done to this.
MACBETH.   If we should fail?
LADY M.   We fail?
But screw your courage to the sticking place,   60
And we'll not fail. When Duncan is asleep
(Whereto the rather shall his day's hard journey
Soundly invite him) his two chamberlains
Will I with wine and wassail so convince,
That memory, the warder of the brain,
Shall be a fume, and the receipt of reason
A limbec only: when in swinish sleep
Their drenchéd natures lie as in a death,
What cannot you and I perform upon
Th'unguarded Duncan? what not put upon   70
His spongy officers, who shall bear the guilt
Of our great quell?
MACBETH.   Bring forth men-children only!
For thy undaunted mettle should compose
Nothing but males. Will it not be received,
When we have marked with blood those sleepy two
Of his own chamber, and used their very daggers,
That they have done't?
LADY M.   Who dares receive it other,
As we shall make our griefs and clamour roar
Upon his death?
MACBETH.   I am settled, and bend up
Each corporal agent to this terrible feat.   80
Away, and mock the time with fairest show:
False face must hide what the false heart doth know.
                                    They go

ACT 2

Scene 1: *The same*

Enter Banquo, and Fleance with a torch before him

BANQUO. How goes the night, boy?
FLEANCE. The moon is down; I have not heard the
        clock.
BANQUO. And she goes down at twelve.
FLEANCE.   I take't, 'tis later, sir.
BANQUO. Hold, take my sword.... There's husbandry
        in heaven,
Their candles are all out....
                    Unclasps his belt with its dagger
                    Take thee that too.
A heavy summons lies like lead upon me,
And yet I would not sleep. Merciful powers,
Restrain in me the curséd thoughts that nature
Gives way to in repose! Give me my sword,

Enter Macbeth, and a servant with a torch

Who's there?   10
MACBETH. A friend.
BANQUO. What, sir, not yet at rest? The king's a-bed.
He hath been in unusual pleasure, and
Sent forth great largess to your offices.

This diamond he greets your wife withal,
By the name of most kind hostess; and shut up
In measureless content.
MACBETH.　　　　　　　　Being unprepared.
Our will became the servant to defect,
Which else should free have wrought.
BANQUO.　　　　　　　　　　　　　All's well.
I dreamt last night of the three Wierd Sisters:　　20
To you they have showed some truth.
MACBETH.　　　　　　　　　　I think not of them:
Yet, when we can entreat an hour to serve,
We would spend it in some words upon that
　　business,
If you would grant the time.
BANQUO.　　　　　　　　　At your kind'st leisure.
MACBETH. If you shall cleave to my consent, when 'tis,
It shall make honour for you.
BANQUO.　　　　　　　　　　　　So I lose none
In seeking to augment it, but still keep
My bosom franchised and allegiance clear,
I shall be counselled.
MACBETH.　　　　　　　　Good repose the while!
BANQUO. Thanks, sir: the like to you!　　　　30
　　　　　　　　　　　　Banquo and Fleance go
MACBETH. Go bid thy mistress, when my drink is
　　ready,
She strike upon the bell. Get thee to bed.
　　　　　　　　　　　　The servant goes
Is this a dagger which I see before me,
The handle toward my hand? Come, let me clutch
　　there:
I have thee not, and yet I see thee still.
Art thou not, fatal vision, sensible
To feeling as to sight? or art thou but
A dagger of the mind, a false creation,
Proceeding from the heat-oppresséd brain?
I see thee yet, in form as palpable　　　　　40
As this which now I draw.
Thou marshall'st me the way that I way going,
And such an instrument I was to use!
Mine eyes are made the fools o'th'other senses,
Or else worth all the rest: I see thee still;
And on thy blade and dudgeon gouts of blood,
Which was not so before. There's no such thing:
It is the bloody business which informs
Thus to mine eyes.... Now o'er the one half-world
Nature seems dead, and wicked dreams abuse　　50
The curtained sleep; Witchcraft celebrates
Pale Hecate's off'ring; and withered Murder,
Alarumed by his sentinel, the wolf,
Whose howl's his watch, thus with his stealthy pace,
With Tarquin's ravishing strides, towards his design
Moves like a ghost. Thou sure and firm-set earth,
Hear not my steps, which way they walk, for fear
Thy very stones prate of my whereabout,
And take the present horror from the time,
Which now suits with it. Whiles I threat, he lives:　60
Words to the heat of deeds too cold breath gives.
　　　　　　　　　　　　A bell rings
I go, and it is done: the bell invites me.
Hear it not, Duncan, for it is a knell
That summons thee to heaven, or to hell.
　　　　　　　　　　　　He goes

Scene 2

Lady Macbeth enters

LADY M. That which hath made them drunk hath
　　made me bold:
What hath quenched them hath given me fire. Hark!
　　Peace:
It was the owl that shrieked, the fatal bellman,
Which gives the stern'st good-night. He is about it:
The doors are open; and the surfeited grooms
Do mock their charge with snores: I have drugged
　　their possets.
That death and nature do contend about them,
Whether they live or die.
MACBETH [*within*].　　　　　Who's there? what, ho!
LADY M. Alack! I am afraid they have awaked,
And 'tis not done: th'attempt and not the deed　　10
Confounds us. Hark! I laid their daggers ready,
He could not miss 'em. Had he not resembled
My father as he slept, I had done't.

Macbeth enters
　　　　　　　　　　　　　　　My husband!
MACBETH. I have done the deed.... Didst thou not
　　hear a noise?
LADY M. I heard the owl scream, and the crickets cry.
Did not you speak?
MACBETH.　　　　　　　　　　　When?
LADY M.　　　　　　　　　　　Now.
MACBETH.　　　　　　　　　As I descended?
LADY M. Ay.
MACBETH. Hark!
Who lies i'th' second chamber?
LADY M.　　　　　　　　　　Donalbain.
MACBETH. This is a sorry sight.　　　　　　20
　　　　　　　　Stretching forth his right hand
LADY M. A foolish thought, to say a sorry sight.
MACBETH. There's one did laugh in's sleep, and one
　　cried 'Murder!'
That they did wake each other: I stood and heard
　　them:
But they did say their prayers, and addressed them
Again to sleep.
LADY M.　　　　　There are two lodged together.
MACBETH. One cried 'God bless us!' and 'Amen' the
　　other,
As they had seen me with these hangman's hands:
List'ning their fear, I could not say 'Amen',
When they did say 'God bless us'.
LADY M. Consider it not so deeply.　　　　　30
MACBETH. But wherefore could not I pronounce
　　'Amen'?
I had most need of blessing, and 'Amen'
Stuck in my throat.
LADY M.　　　　　These deeds must not be thought
After these ways; so, it will make us mad.
MACBETH. Methought I heard a voice cry 'Sleep no
　　more!
Macbeth does murder sleep'—the innocent sleep,
Sleep that knits up the ravelled sleave of care,
The death of each day's life, sore labour's bath,
Balm of hurt minds, great Nature's second course,
Chief nourisher in life's feast,—
LADY M.　　　　　　　　　　What do you mean?　40
MACBETH. Still it cried 'Sleep no more!' to all the
　　house:
'Glamis hath murdered sleep, and therefore Cawdor

Shall sleep no more: Macbeth shall sleep no more!'

LADY M. Who was it that thus cried? Why, worthy thane,
You do unbend your noble strength, to think
So brainsickly of things. Go get some water,
And wash this filthy witness from your hand.
Why did you bring these daggers from the place?
They must lie there: go carry them, and smear
The sleepy grooms with blood.

MACBETH.   I'll go no more: 50
I am afraid to think what I have done;
Look on't again I dare not.

LADY M.   Infirm of purpose!
Give me the daggers: the sleeping and the dead
Are but as pictures: 'tis the eye of childhood
That fears a painted devil. If he do bleed,
I'll gild the faces of the grooms withal,
For it must seem their guilt.
              She goes up. A knocking heard.

MACBETH.   Whence is that knocking?
How is't with me, when every noise appals me?
What hands are here? ha! they pluck out mine eyes!
Will all great Neptune's ocean wash this blood   60
Clean from my hand? No; this my hand will rather
The multitudinous seas incarnadine,
Making the green—one red.

Lady Macbeth returns

LADY M. My hands are of your colour; but I shame
To wear a heart so white. [*knocking*] I hear a
     knocking
At the south entry: retire we to our chamber:
A little water clears us of this deed:
How easy is it then! Your constancy
Hath left you unattended. [*knocking*] Hark! more
     knocking.
Get on your nightgown, lest occasion call us   70
And show us to be watchers: be not lost
So poorly in your thoughts.

MACBETH. To know my deed, 'twere best not know
     myself.   *Knocking*
Wake Duncan with thy knocking! I would thou
     couldst!   *They go*

Scene 3

*The knocking grows louder; a drunken Porter enters
the court*

PORTER. Here's a knocking indeed! If a man were
porter of hell-gate, he should have old turning the
key.[*knocking*] Knock, knock, knock! Who's there,
i'th' name of Beelzebub? Here's a farmer, that
hanged himself on th'expectation of plenty: come
in, time-server; have napkins enow about you, here
you'll sweat for't. [*knocking*] Knock, knock! Who's
there, in th'other devil's name? Faith, here's an
equivocator, that could swear in both the scales
against either scale, who committed treason enough   10
for God's sake, yet could not equivocate to heaven:
O, come in, equivocator. [*knocking*] Knock, knock,
knock! Who's there? Faith, here's an English tailor
come hither, for stealing out of a French hose: come
in, tailor, here you may roast your goose. [*knocking*]
Knock, knock! never at quiet! What are you? But
this place is too cold for hell. I'll devil-porter it no
further: I had thought to have let in some of all

professions, that go the primrose way to th'everlasting bonfire. [*knocking*] Anon, anon! I pray you,   20
remember the porter.   *Opens the gate*

Enter Macduff and Lennox

MACDUFF. Was it so late, friend, ere you went to bed,
That you do lie so late?

PORTER. Faith, sir, we were carousing till the second
cock: and drink, sir, is a great provoker of three
things.

MACDUFF. What three things does drink especially
provoke?

PORTER. Marry, sir, nose-painting, sleep, and urine.
Lechery, sir, it provokes and unprovokes: it pro-   30
vokes the desire, but it takes away the performance.
Therefore, much drink may be said to be an
equivocator with lechery: it makes him, and it mars
him; it sets him on, and it takes him off; it persuades
him, and disheartens him; makes him stand to, and
not stand to: in conclusion, equivocates him in a
sleep, and giving him the lie, leaves him.

MACDUFF. I believe drink gave thee the lie last night.

PORTER. That it did, sir, i'the very throat on me: but
I requited him for his lie, and, I think, being too   40
strong for him, though he took up my legs sometime, yet I made a shift to cast him.

MACDUFF. Is thy master stirring?

Macbeth returns

Our knocking has awaked him; here he comes.

LENNOX. Good-morrow, noble sir.

MACBETH.   Good-morrow, both.

MACDUFF. Is the king stirring, worthy thane?

MACBETH.   Not yet.

MACDUFF. He did command me to call timely on him;
I have almost slipped the hour.

MACBETH.   I'll bring you to him.

MACDUFF. I know this is a joyful trouble to you;
But yet 'tis one.   50

MACBETH. The labour we delight in physics pain.
This is the door.

MACDUFF.   I'll make so bold to call,
For 'tis my limited service.   *He goes in*

LENNOX. Goes the king hence to-day?

MACBETH. He does: he did appoint so.

LENNOX. The night has been unruly: where we lay,
Our chimneys were blown down, and, as they say,
Lamentings heard i'th'air, strange screams of death,
And prophesying with accents terrible
Of dire combustion and confused events   60
New hatched to th' woeful time. The obscure bird
Clamoured the livelong night: some say, the earth
Was feverous and did shake.

MACBETH.   'Twas a rough night.

LENNOX. My young remembrance cannot parallel
A fellow to it.

Macduff returns

MACDUFF. O horror! horror! horror! Tongue, nor
     heart,
Cannot conceive nor name thee!

MACBETH, LENNOX.   What's the matter?

MACDUFF. Confusion now hath made his masterpiece!
Most sacrilegious murder hath broke ope
The Lord's anointed temple, and stole thence   70
The life o'th' building.

MACBETH. What is't you say? the life?
LENNOX. Mean you his majesty?
MACDUFF. Approach the chamber, and destroy your
sight
With a new Gorgon: do not bid me speak;
See, and then speak yourselves.
                                        Macbeth and Lennox go
                                        Awake! awake!
Ring the alarum bell! Murder and treason!
Banquo and Donalbain! Malcolm, awake!
Shake off this downy sleep, death's counterfeit,
And look on death itself! up, up, and see
The great doom's image! Malcolm! Banquo!   80
As from your graves rise up, and walk like sprites,
To countenance this horror!   *Bell rings*

Enter Lady Macbeth

LADY M.   What's the business,
That such a hideous trumpet calls to parley
The sleepers of the house? speak, speak!
MACDUFF.   O, gentle lady,
'Tis not for you to hear what I can speak:
The repetition, in a woman's ear,
Would murder as it fell.

Enter Banquo

                                O Banquo! Banquo!
Our royal master's murdered!
LADY M.   Woe, alas!
What, in our house?
BANQUO.   Too cruel, any where.
Dear Duff, I prithee, contradict thyself,   90
And say it is not so.

Macbeth and Lennox return

MACBETH. Had I but died an hour before this chance,
I had lived a blessèd time; for from this instant
There's nothing serious in mortality:
All is but toys: renown and grace is dead,
The wine of life is drawn, and the mere lees
Is left this vault to brag of.

Enter Malcolm and Donalbain

DONALBAIN. What is amiss?
MACBETH.   You are, and do not know't:
The spring, the head, the fountain of your blood
Is stopped—the very source of it is stopped.   100
MACDUFF. Your royal father's murdered.
MALCOLM.   O, by whom?
LENNOX. Those of his chamber, as it seemed, had
done't:
Their hands and faces were all badged with blood,
So were their daggers, which unwiped we found
Upon their pillows:
They stared and were distracted, no man's life
Was to be trusted with them.
MACBETH. O, yet I do repent me of my fury,
That I did kill them.
MACDUFF.   Wherefore did you so?
MACBETH. Who can be wise, amazed, temp'rate and
furious,   110
Loyal and neutral, in a moment? no man:
Th'expedition of my violent love
Outrun the pauser, reason. Here lay Duncan,
His silver skin laced with his golden blood,
And his gashed stabs looked like a breach in nature

For ruin's wasteful entrance: there, the murderers,
Steeped in the colours of their trade, their daggers
Unmannerly breeched with gore: who could
refrain,
That had a heart to love, and in that heart
Courage to make's love known?
LADY M.   Help me hence, ho! 120
MACDUFF. Look to the lady.
MALCOLM [*aside*].   Why do we hold our tongues,
That most may claim this argument for ours?
DONALBAIN [*aside*]. What should be spoken here, where
our fate,
Hid in an auger-hole, may rush and seize us?
Let's away.
Our tears are not yet brewed.
MALCOLM [*aside*].   Nor our strong sorrow
Upon the foot of motion.   *Enter waiting-women*
BANQUO.   Look to the lady . . .
                                        They lead her out
And when we have our naked frailties hid,
That suffer in exposure, let us meet,
And question this most bloody piece of work,   130
To know it further. Fears and scruples shake us:
In the great hand of God I stand, and thence
Against the undivulged pretence I fight
Of treasonous malice.
MACDUFF.   And so do I.
ALL.   So all.
MACBETH. Let's briefly put on manly readiness,
And meet i'th'hall together.
ALL.   Well contented.
                                All go but Malcolm and Donalbain
MALCOLM. What will you do? Let's not consort with
them:
To show an unfelt sorrow is an office
Which the false man does easy. I'll to England.
DONALBAIN. To Ireland, I: our separated fortune   140
Shall keep us both the safer: where we are
There's daggers in men's smiles: the near in blood,
The nearer bloody.
MALCOLM.   This murderous shaft that's shot
Hath not yet lighted, and our safest way
Is to avoid the aim. Therefore to horse,
And let us not be dainty of leave-taking,
But shift away: there's warrant in that theft
Which steals itself when there's no mercy left.
                                        They go

Scene 4: Before Macbeth's castle

Enter Ross with an Old Man

OLD MAN. Threescore and ten I can remember well,
Within the volume of which time I have seen
Hours dreadful and things strange; but this sore
night
Hath trifled former knowings.
ROSS.   Ha, good father,
Thou seest the heavens, as troubled with man's act,
Threatens his bloody stage: by th' clock 'tis day,
And yet dark night strangles the travelling lamp:
Is't night's predominance, or the day's shame,
That darkness does the face of earth entomb,
When living light should kiss it?
OLD MAN.   'Tis unnatural,   10
Even like the deed that's done. On Tuesday last
A falcon towering in her pride of place

Was by a mousing owl hawked at and killed.
ROSS. And Duncan's horses—a thing most strange and
  certain—
  Beauteous and swift, the minions of their race,
  Turned wild in nature, broke their stalls, flung out,
  Contending 'gainst obedience, as they would make
  War with mankind.
OLD MAN.   'Tis said they eat each other.
ROSS. They did so, to th'amazement of mine eyes,
  That looked upon't.

Macduff enters

                          Here comes the good Macduff. 20
  How goes the world, sir, now?
MACDUFF.   Why, see you not?
ROSS. Is't known who did this more than bloody deed?
MACDUFF. Those that Macbeth hath slain.
ROSS.   Alas, the day!
  What good could they pretend?
MACDUFF.   They were suborned.
  Malcolm and Donalbain, the king's two sons,
  Are stol'n away and fled, which puts upon them
  Suspicion of the deed.
ROSS.   'Gainst nature still!
  Thriftless ambition, that wilt ravin up
  Thine own life's means! Then 'tis most like
  The sovereignty will fall upon Macbeth.   30
MACDUFF. He is already named, and gone to Scone
  To be invested.
ROSS.   Where is Duncan's body?
MACDUFF. Carried to Colme kill,
  The sacred storehouse of his predecessors,
  And guardian of their bones.
ROSS.   Will you to Scone?
MACDUFF. No cousin, I'll to Fife.
                          Well, I will thither.
MACDUFF. Well, may you see things well done there;
  adieu!
  Lest our old robes sit easier than our new!
ROSS. Farewell, father.
OLD MAN. God's benison go with you, and with those 40
  That would make good of bad and friends of foes!
                                              They go

ACT 3
Scene 1: *The palace at Forres*

Banquo enters

BANQUO. Thou hast it now, King, Cawdor, Glamis,
  all,
  As the weïrd women promised, and I fear
  Thou play'dst most foully for't: yet it was said
  It should not stand in thy posterity,
  But that myself should be the root and father
  Of many kings. If there come truth from them—
  As upon thee, Macbeth, their speeches shine—
  Why, by the verities on thee made good,
  May they not be my oracles as well,
  And set me up in hope? But hush, no more.   10

*Sennet sounded. Enter Macbeth, as King, Lady Macbeth,
as Queen, Lennox, Ross, Lords, and attendants*

MACBETH. Here's our chief guest.
LADY M.   If he had been forgotten,
  It had been as a gap in our great feast,
  And all-thing unbecoming.

MACBETH. To-night we hold a solemn supper, sir,
  And I'll request your presence.
BANQUO   Let your highness
  Command upon me, to the which my duties
  Are with a most indissoluble tie
  For ever knit.
MACBETH. Ride you this afternoon?
BANQUO.   Ay, my good lord.
MACBETH. We should have else desired your good
  advice   20
  (Which still hath been both grave and prosperous)
  In this day's council; but we'll take to-morrow.
  Is't far you ride?
BANQUO. As far, my lord, as will fill up the time
  'Twixt this and supper. Go not my horse the better,
  I must become a borrower of the night
  For a dark hour or twain.
MACBETH.   Fail not our feast.
BANQUO. My lord, I will not.
MACBETH. We hear our bloody cousins are bestowed
  In England and in Ireland, not confessing   30
  Their cruel parricide, filling their hearers
  With strange invention: but of that to-morrow,
  When therewithal we shall have cause of state
  Craving us jointly. Hie you to horse: adieu,
  Till you return at night. Goes Fleance with you?
BANQUO. Ay, my good lord: our time does call upon's.
MACBETH. I wish your horses swift and sure of foot;
  And so I do commend you to their backs.
  Farewell.   *Banquo goes*
  Let every man be master of his time   40
  Till seven at night; to make society
  The sweeter welcome, we will keep ourself
  Till supper-time alone: while then, God be with
  you!
                    All depart but Macbeth and a servant
  Sirrah, a word with you: attend those men
  Our pleasure?
ATTENDANT. They are, my lord, without the palace
  gate.
MACBETH. Bring them before us.   *The servant goes*
                          To be thus is nothing,
  But to be safely thus: our fears in Banquo
  Stick deep, and in his royalty of nature
  Reigns that which would be feared. 'Tis much he
  dares,   50
  And, to that dauntless temper of his mind,
  He hath a wisdom that doth guide his valour
  To act in safety. There is none but he
  Whose being I do fear: and under him
  My Genius is rebuked, as it is said
  Mark Antony's was by Cæsar. He chid the Sisters,
  When first they put the name of king upon me,
  And bade them speak to him; then prophet-like
  They hailed him father to a line of kings:
  Upon my head they placed a fruitless crown,   60
  And put a barren sceptre in my gripe,
  Thence to be wrenched with an unlineal hand,
  No son of mine succeeding. If't be so,
  For Banquo's issue have I filed my mind,
  For them the gracious Duncan have I murdered,
  Put rancours in the vessel of my peace
  Only for them, and mine eternal jewel
  Given to the common enemy of man,
  To make them kings, the seed of Banquo kings!
  Rather than so, come Fate into the list,   70

And champion me to th'utterance. Who's there?

The servant returns with two murderers

Now go to the door, and stay there till we call.
                     Servant goes
Was it not yesterday we spoke together?
1 MURDERER. It was, so please your highness.
MACBETH.   Well then, now
Have you considered of my speeches? Know
That it was he in the times past which held you
So under fortune, which you thought had been
Our innocent self: this I made good to you
In our last conference; passed in probation with you,
How you were borne in hand, how crossed, the
     instruments,   80
Who wrought with them, and all things else that
     might
To half a soul and to a notion crazed
Say 'Thus did Banquo'.
1 MURDERER.   You made it known to us.
MACBETH. I did so; and went further, which is now
Our point of second meeting. Do you find
Your patience so predominant in your nature,
That you can let this go? Are you so gospelled,
To pray for this good man, and for his issue,
Whose heavy hand hath bowed you to the grave
And beggared yours for ever?
1 MURDERER.   We are men, my liege.   90
MACBETH. Ay, in the catalogue ye go for men,
As hounds and greyhounds, mongrels, spaniels, curs,
Shoughs, water-rugs, and demi-wolves, are clept
All by the name of dogs: the valued file
Distinguishes the swift, the slow, the subtle,
The housekeeper, the hunter, every one
According to the gift which bounteous nature
Hath in him closed, whereby he does receive
Particular addition, from the bill
That writes them all alike: and so of men.   100
Now, if you have a station in the file,
Not i'th' worst rank of manhood, say't,
And I will put that business in your bosoms,
Whose execution takes your enemy off,
Grapples you to the heart and love of us,
Who wear our health but sickly in his life,
Which in his death were perfect.
2 MURDERER.   I am one, my liege,
Whom the vile blows and buffets of the world
Hath so incensed that I am reckless what
I do to spite the world.
1 MURDERER.   And I another   110
So weary with disasters, tugged with fortune,
That I would set my life on any chance,
To mend it, or be rid on't.
MACBETH.   Both of you
Know Banquo war your enemy.
BOTH MURDERERS.   True, my lord.
MACBETH. So is he mine: and in such bloody distance,
That every minute of his being thrusts
Against my near'st of life: and though I could
With barefaced power sweep him from my sight,
And bid my will avouch it, yet I must not,
For certain friends that are both his and mine,   120
Whose loves I may not drop, but wail his fall
Who I myself struck down: and thence it is
That I to your assistance do make love,
Masking the business from the common eye,

For sundry weighty reasons.
2 MURDERER.   We shall, my lord,
Perform what you command us.
1 MURDERER.   Though our lives—
MACBETH. Your spirits shine through you. Within this
     hour at most
I will advise you where to plant yourselves,
Acquaint you with the perfect spy o'th' time,
The moment on't, for't must be done to-night,   130
And something from the palace; always thought
That I require a clearness: and with him
To leave no rubs nor botches in the work—
Fleance his son, that keeps him company,
Whose absence is no less material to me
Than is his father's, must embrace the fate
Of that dark hour. Resolve yourselves apart;
I'll come to you anon.
BOTH MURDERERS.   We are resolved, my lord.
MACBETH. I'll call upon you straight; abide within.
                         They go
It is concluded: Banquo, thy soul's flight,   140
If it find heaven, must find it out to-night.
                 He leaves by another door

Scene 2

Lady Macbeth enters with a servant

LADY M. Is Banquo gone from court?
SERVANT. Ay, madam, but returns again to-night.
LADY M. Say to the king, I would attend his leisure
For a few words.
SERVANT.   Madam, I will.   *He goes*
LADY M.   Nought's had, all's spent,
Where our desire is got without content:
'Tis safer to be that which we destroy
Than by destruction dwell in doubtful joy.

Macbeth enters

How now, my lord! why do you keep alone,
Of sorriest fancies your companions making,
Using those thought which should indeed have died   10
With them they think on? Things without all
     remedy
Should be without regard: what's done, is done.
MACBETH. We have scorched the snake, not killed it:
She'll close and be herself, whilst our poor malice
Remains in danger of her former tooth.
But let the frame of things disjoint, both the worlds
     suffer,
Ere we will eat our meal in fear, and sleep
In the affliction of these terrible dreams
That shake us nightly: better be with the dead,
Whom we, to gain our peace, have sent to peace,   20
Than on the torture of the mind to lie
In restless ecstasy. Duncan is in his grave;
After life's fitful fever he sleeps well;
Treason has done his worst: nor steel, nor poison,
Malice domestic, foreign levy, nothing,
Can touch him further.
LADY M.   Come on;
Gentle my lord, sleek o'er your rugged looks,
Be bright and jovial among your guests to-night.
MACBETH. So shall I, love, and so I pray be you:
Let your remembrance apply to Banquo;   30
Present him eminence, both with eye and tongue:
Unsafe the while, that we

Must lave our honours in these flattering streams,
And make our faces vizards to our hearts,
Disguising what they are.
LADY M.   You must leave this.
MACBETH. O, full of scorpions is my mind, dear
    wife!
Thou know'st that Banquo and his Fleance lives.
LADY M. But in them nature's copy's not eterne.
MACBETH. There's comfort yet, they are assailable,
Then be thou jocund: ere the bat hath flown   40
His cloistered flight, ere to black Hecate's summons
The shard-borne beetle with his drowsy hums
Hath rung night's yawning peal, there shall be done
A deed of dreadful note.
LADY M.   What's to be done?
MACBETH. Be innocent of the knowledge, dearest
    chuck,
Till thou applaud the deed ... Come, seeling night,
Scarf up the tender eye of pitiful day,
And with thy bloody and invisible hand
Cancel and tear to pieces that great bond
Which keeps me paled! Light thickens, and the crow   50
Makes wing to th' rooky wood:
Good things of day begin to droop and drowse,
Whiles night's black agents to their preys do rouse.
Thou marvell'st at my words: but hold thee still;
Things bad begun make strong themselves by ill:
So, prithee, go with me.   They go

Scene 3: *The royal park, some way from the palace.*

The two murderers enter, with a third

1 MURDERER. But who did bid thee join with us?
3 MURDERER.   Macbeth.
2 MURDERER. He needs not our mistrust, since he
    delivers
Our offices and what we have to do,
To the direction just.
1 MURDERER.   Then stand with us.
The west yet glimmers with some streaks of day:
Now spurs the lated traveller apace
To gain the timely inn, and near approaches
The subject of our watch.
3 MURDERER.   Hark! I hear horses.
BANQUO [*at a distance*]. Give us a light there, ho!
2 MURDERER.   Then 'tis he; the rest
That are within the note of expectation   10
Already are i'th' court.
1 MURDERER.   His horses go about.
3 MURDERER. Almost a mile: but he does usually—
So all men do—from hence to th' palace gate
Make it their walk.

Enter Banquo and Fleance with a torch

2 MURDERER.   A light, a light!
3 MURDERER.   'Tis he.
1 MURDERER. Stand to't.
BANQUO. It will be rain to-night.
1 MURDERER.   Let it come down.
                            They set upon Banquo
BANQUO. O, treachery! Fly, good Fleance, fly, fly, fly!
Thou mayst revenge. O slave!
                        He dies; Fleance escapes
3 MURDERER. Who did strike out the light?
1 MURDERER.   Was't not the way?
3 MURDERER. There's but one down; the son is fled.

2 MURDERER.   We have lost   20
Best half of our affair.
1 MURDERER. Well, let's away, and say how much is
    done.   *They go*

Scene 4: *The hall of the palace.*

*A banquet prepared. Enter Macbeth, Lady Macbeth, Ross,
Lennox, lords, and attendants*

MACBETH. You know your own degrees, sit down at
    first
And last, the hearty welcome.
LORDS.   Thanks to your majesty.
MACBETH. Ourself will mingle with society,
And play the humble host:
Our hostess keeps her state, but in best time
We will require her welcome.
LADY M. Pronounce it for me, sir, to all our friends,
For my heart speaks they are welcome.

1 Murderer appears at the door

MACBETH. See, they encounter thee with their hearts'
    thanks.
Both sides are even: here I'll sit i'th' midst.   10
Be large in mirth, anon we'll drink a measure
The table round.
[*turns to the door*] There's blood upon thy face.
MURDERER. 'Tis Banquo's then.
MACBETH. 'Tis better thee without than he within.
Is he dispatched?
MURDERER. My lord, his throat is cut, that I did for
    him.
MACBETH. Thou art the best o'th' cut-throats! Yet
    he's good
That did the like for Fleance: if thou didst it,
Thou art the nonpareil.
MURDERER.   Most royal sir,
Fleance is 'scaped.   20
MACBETH. Then comes my fit again: I had else been
    perfect;
Whole as the marble, founded as the rock,
As broad and general as the casing air:
But now I am cabined, cribbed, confined, bound in
To saucy doubts and fears. But Banquo's safe?
MURDERER. Ay, my good lord: safe in a ditch he bides,
With twenty trenchèd gashes on his head;
The least a death to nature.
MACBETH.   Thanks for that:
There the grown serpent lies; the worm that's fled
Hath nature that in time will venom breed,   30
No teeth for th' present. Get thee gone; to-morrow
We'll hear ourselves again.   *Murderer goes*
LADY M.   My royal lord,
You do not give the cheer. The feast is sold
That is not often vouched, while 'tis a-making,
'Tis given with welcome: to feed were best at home;
From thence the sauce to meat is ceremony;
Meeting were bare without it.

The Ghost of Banquo appears, and sits in Macbeth's place

MACBETH.   Sweet remembrancer!
Now good digestion wait on appetite,
And health on both!
LENNOX.   May't please your highness sit?
MACBETH. Here had we now our country's honour
    roofed,   40

Were the gracéd person of our Banquo present;
Who may I rather challenge for unkindness
Than pity for mischance!
ROSS.   His absence, sir,
Lays blame upon his promise. Please't your highness
To grace us with your royal company?
MACBETH. The table's full.
LENNOX.   Here is a place reserved, sir.
MACBETH. Where?
LENNOX. Here, my good lord.... What is't that moves
your highness?
MACBETH. Which of you have done this?
LORDS.   What, my good lord?
MACBETH. Thou canst not say I did it: never shake   50
Thy gory locks at me.
ROSS. Gentlemen, rise, his highness is not well.
LADY M. Sit, worthy friends: my lord is often thus,
And hath been from his youth: pray you, keep seat,
The fit is momentary, upon a thought
He will again be well: if much you note him,
You shall offend him and extend his passion:
Feed, and regard him not. [aside] Are you a man?
MACBETH. Ay, and a bold one, that dare look on that
Which might appal the devil.
LADY M.   O proper stuff!   60
This is the very painting of your fear:
This is the air-drawn dagger which, you said,
Led you to Duncan. O, these flaws and starts
(Imposter to true fear) would well become
A woman's story at a winter's fire,
Authorized by her grandam.... Shame itself!
Why do you make such faces? When all's done,
You look but on a stool.
MACBETH. Prithee, see there! behold! look! lo! how say
you?
Why what care I? If thou canst nod, speak too.   70
If charnel-houses and our graves must send
Those that we bury back, our monuments
Shall be the maws of kites.   The Ghost vanishes
LADY M.   What! quite unmanned in folly?
MACBETH. If I stand here, I saw him.
LADY M.   Fie, for shame!
MACBETH. Blood hath been shed ere now, i'th'olden
time,
Ere humane statute purged the gentle weal;
Ay, and since too, murders have been performed
Too terrible for the ear: the time has been,
That, when the brains were out, the man would die,
And there an end: but now they rise again,   80
With twenty mortal murders on their crowns,
And push us from our stools.... This is more strange
Than such a murder is.
LADY M.   My worthy lord,
Your noble friends do lack you.
MACBETH.   I do forget ...
Do not muse at me, my most worthy friends;
I have a strange infirmity, which is nothing
To those that know me. Come, love and health
to all;
Then I'll sit down. Give me some wine, fill full.
                         The Ghost reappears
I drink to th' general joy o'th' whole table,
And to our dear friend Banquo, whom we miss;   90
Would he were here! to all, and him we thirst,
And all to all!
LORDS.   Our duties, and the pledge.

MACBETH. Avaunt! and quit my sight! let the earth
hide thee!
Thy bones are marrowless, thy blood is cold;
Thou hast no speculation in those eyes
Which thou dost glare with!
LADY M.   Think of this, good peers,
But as a thing of custom: 'tis no other;
Only it spoils the pleasure of the time.
MACBETH. What man dare, I dare:
Approach thou like the ruggéd Russian bear,   100
The armed rhinoceros, or th'Hyrcan tiger,
Take any shape but that, and my firm nerves
Shall never tremble: or be alive again,
And dare me to the desert with thy sword;
If trembling I inhabit then, protest me
The baby of a girl. Hence, horrible shadow!
Unreal mock'ry, hence!   The Ghost vanishes
                              Why, so; being gone,
I am a man again. Pray you, sit still.
LADY M. You have displaced the mirth, broke the good
meeting,
With most admired disorder.
MACBETH.   Can such things be,   110
And overcome us like a summer's cloud,
Without our special wonder? You make me strange
Even to the disposition that I owe,
When now I think you can behold such sights,
And keep the natural ruby of your cheeks,
When mine is blanched with fear.
ROSS.   What sights, my lord?
LADY M. I pray you, speak not; he grows worse and
worse;
Question enrages him: at once, good night.
Stand not upon the order of your going,
But go at once.
LENNOX.   Good night, and better health   120
Attend his majesty!
LADY M.   A kind good night to all!
                                   They leave
MACBETH. It will have blood; they say, blood will have
blood:
Stones have been known to move and trees to speak;
Augures and understood relations have
By maggot-pies and choughs and rooks brought
forth
The secret'st man of blood.... What is the night?
LADY M. Almost at odds with morning, which is
which
MACBETH. How say'st thou, that Macduff denies his
person
At our great bidding?
LADY M.   Did you send to him, sir?
MACBETH. I hear it by the way; but I will send: 130
There's not a one of them but in his house
I keep a servant fee'd.... I will to-morrow
(And betimes I will) to the Weïrd Sisters:
More shall they speak; for now I am bent to know,
By the worst means, and worst. For mine own good
All causes shall give way: I am in blood
Stepped in so far that, should I wade no more,
Returning were as tedious as go o'er:
Strange things I have in head that will to hand,
Which must be acted ere they may be scanned.   140
LADY M. You lack the season of all natures, sleep.
MACBETH. Come, we'll to sleep. My strange and
self-abuse

Is the initiate fear that wants hard use:
We are yet but young in deed. *They go*

Scene 5: *A heath*

Thunder. Enter the three Witches, meeting Hecate

1 WITCH. Why, how now, Hecat, you look angerly.
HECATE. Have I not reason, beldams as you are,
Saucy and overbold? How did you dare
To trade and traffic with Macbeth
In riddles and affairs of death;
And I, the mistress of your charms,
The close contriver of all harms,
Was never called to bear my part,
Or show the glory of our art?
And, which is worse, all you have done   10
Hath been but for a wayward son,
Spiteful and wrathful, who (as others do)
Loves for his own ends, not for you.
But make amends now: get you gone,
And at the pit of Acheron
Meet me i'th' morning: thither he
Will come to know his destiny.
Your vessels and your spells provide,
Your charms and every thing beside.
I am for th'air; this night I'll spend   20
Unto a dismal and a fatal end.
Great business must be wrought ere noon:
Upon the corner of the moon
There hangs a vap'rous drop profound;
I'll catch it ere it come to ground:
And that distilled by magic sleights
Shall raise such artificial sprites
As by the strength of their illusion
Shall draw him on to his confusion.
He shall spurn fate, scorn death, and bear   30
His hopes 'bove wisdom, grace, and fear:
And you all know security
Is mortals' chiefest enemy.

Music and a song: 'Come away, come away' etc.

Hark, I am called: my little spirit, see,
Sits in a foggy cloud, and stays for me. *She goes*
1 WITCH. Come, let's make haste; she'll soon be back
again. *They vanish*

Scene 6: *A castle in Scotland*

Enter Lennox and another Lord

LENNOX. My former speeches have but hit your
thoughts,
Which can interpret farther: only I say
Things have been strangely borne. The gracious
Duncan
Was pitied of Macbeth: marry, he was dead:
And the right valiant Banquo walked too late—
Whom you may say (if't please you) Fleance killed,
For Fleance fled: men must not walk too late.
Who cannot want the thought, how monstrous
It was for Malcolm and for Donalbain
To kill their gracious father? damnéd fact!   10
How it did grieve Macbeth! did he not straight,
In pious rage, the two delinquents tear,
That were the slaves of drink and thralls of sleep?
Was not that nobly done? Ay, and wisely too;
For 'twould have angered any heart alive

To hear the men deny't. So that, I say,
He has borne all things well: and I do think
That, had he Duncan's sons under his key
(As, an't please heaven, he shall not) they should find
What 'twere to kill a father; so should Fleance.   20
But, peace! for from broad words, and 'cause he
failed
His presence at the tyrant's feast, I hear,
Macduff lives in disgrace. Sir, can you tell
Where he bestows himself?
LORD.   The son of Duncan
(From whom this tyrant holds the due of birth)
Lives in the English court, and is received
Of the most pious Edward with such grace
That the malevolence of fortune nothing
Takes from his high respect. Thither Macduff
Is gone to pray the holy king, upon his aid   30
To wake Northumberland and warlike
Siward,
That by the help of these (with Him above
To ratify the work) we may again
Give to our tables meat, sleep to our nights;
Free from our feasts and banquets bloody knives;
Do faithful homage and receive free honours:
All which we pine for now. And this report
Hath so exasperate the king that he
Prepares for some attempt of war.
LENNOX.   Sent he to Macduff?
LORD. He did: and with an absolute 'Sir, not I',   40
The cloudy messenger turns me his back,
And hums, as who should say, 'You'll rue the time
That clogs me with this answer'.
LENNOX.   And that well might
Advise him to a caution, t'hold what distance
His wisdom can provide. Some holy angel
Fly to the court of England and unfold
His message ere he come, that a swift blessing
May soon return to this our suffering country
Under a hand accursed!
LORD.   I'll send my prayers with him.
They go

ACT 4

Scene 1: *A cavern and in the midst a boiling cauldron*

Thunder. Enter the Weird Sisters

1 WITCH. Thrice the brinded cat hath mewed.
2 WITCH. Thrice and once the hedge-pig whined.
3 WITCH. Harpier cries:—'Tis time, 'tis time.
1 WITCH. Round about the cauldron go:
In the poisoned entrails throw.
Toad, that under cold stone
Days and nights has thirty-one
Sweltered venom sleeping got,
Boil thou first i'th' charméd pot!
ALL. Double, double toil and trouble;   10
Fire burn and cauldron bubble.
2 WITCH. Fillet of a fenny snake,
In the cauldron boil and bake:
Eye of newt and toe of frog,
Wool of bat and tongue of dog,
Adder's fork and blind-worm's sting,
Lizard's leg and howlet's wing,
For a charm of powerful trouble,
Like a hell-broth boil and bubble.

ALL. Double, double toil and trouble;
  Fire burn and cauldron bubble.
3 WITCH. Scale of dragon, tooth of wolf,
  Witch's mummy, maw and gulf
  Of the ravined salt-sea shark,
  Root of hemlock digged i'th' dark,
  Liver of blaspheming Jew,
  Gall of goat and slips of yew
  Slivered in the moon's eclipse,
  Nose of Turk and Tartar's lips,
  Finger of birth-strangled babe
  Ditch-delivered by a drab,   30
  Make the gruel thick and slab:
  Add thereto a tiger's chaudron,
  For th'ingredience of our cauldron.
ALL. Double, double toil and trouble;
  Fire burn and cauldron bubble.
2 WITCH. Cool it with a baboon's blood,
  Then the charm is firm and good.

Enter Hecate and the other three Witches.

HECATE. O, well done! I commend your pains,
  And every one shall share i'th' gains:
  And now about the cauldron sing,   40
  Like elves and fairies in a ring,
  Enchanting all that you put in.

Music and a song: Black spirits, etc. Hecate goes

2 WITCH. By the pricking of my thumbs,
  Something wicked this way comes:
  Open, locks,
  Whoever knocks!

Macbeth enters

MACBETH. How now, you secret, black, and midnight
    hags!
  What is't you do?
ALL.   A deed without a name.
MACBETH. I conjure you, by that which you profess   50
  (Howe'er you come to know it) answer me:
  Though you untie the winds and let them fight
  Against the churches; though the yesty waves
  Confound and swallow navigation up;
  Though bladed corn be lodged and trees blown
    down;
  Though castles topple on their warders' heads;
  Though palaces and pyramids do slope
  Their heads to their foundations; though the
    treasure
  Of Nature's germens tumble all together,
  Even till destruction sicken; answer me   60
  To what I ask you.
1 WITCH.   Speak.
2 WITCH.   Demand.
3 WITCH.   We'll answer.
1 WITCH. Say if th'hadst rather hear it from our
    mouths,
  Or from our masters.
MACBETH.   Call 'em, let me see 'em!
1 WITCH. Pour in sow's blood, that hath eaten
  Her nine farrow; grease that's sweaten
  From the murderer's gibbet throw
  Into the flame.
ALL.   Come, high or low;
  Thyself and office deftly show.

Thunder. First Apparition, an armed head

20 MACBETH. Tell me, thou unknown power—
1 WITCH.   He knows thy thought:
  Hear his speech, but say thou nought.   70
1 APPARITION. Macbeth! Macbeth! Macbeth! beware
    Macduff.
  Beware the thane of Fife. Dismiss me. Enough.
                       Descends
MACBETH. Whate'er thou art, for thy good caution
  thanks;
  Thou hast harped my fear aright. But one word
  more—
1 WITCH. He will not be commanded: here's another,
  More potent than the first.

Thunder. Second Apparition, a bloody child

2 APPARITION. Macbeth! Macbeth! Macbeth!
MACBETH. Had I three ears, I'd hear thee.
2 APPARITION. Be bloody, bold, and resolute: laugh to
  scorn
  The power of man; for none of woman born   80
  Shall harm Macbeth.   *Descends*
MACBETH. Then live, Macduff: what need I fear of
  thee?
  But yet I'll make assurance double sure,
  And take a bond of fate: thou shalt not live,
  That I may tell pale-hearted fear it lies,
  And sleep in spite of thunder.

*Thunder. Third Apparition, a child crowned, with a tree
in his hand*

                       What is this,
  That rises like the issue of a king,
  And wears upon his baby-brow the round
  And top of sovereignty?
ALL.   Listen, but speak not to't.
3 APPARITION. Be lion-mettled, proud, and take no
  care   90
  Who chafes, who frets, or where conspirers are:
  Macbeth shall never vanquished be until
  Great Birnam wood to high Dunsinane hill
  Shall come against him.   *Descends*
MACBETH.   That will never be;
  Who can impress the forest, bid the tree
  Unfix his earth-bound root? Sweet bodements!
  good.
  Rebellious dead, rise never, till the wood
  Of Birnam rise, and our high-placed Macbeth
  Shall live the lease of nature, pay his breath
  To time and mortal custom. Yet my heart   100
  Throbs to know one thing; tell me, if your art
  Can tell so much: shall Banquo's issue ever
  Reign in this kingdom?
ALL.   Seek to know no more.
MACBETH. I will be satisfied: deny me this,
  And an eternal curse fall on you! Let me know....

Hautboys

  Why sinks that cauldron? and what noise is this?
1 WITCH. Show!
2 WITCH. Show!
3 WITCH. Show!
ALL. Show his eyes, and grieve his heart;   110
  Come like shadows, so depart.

*A show of eight kings, the last with a glass in his hand;
Banquo's Ghost following*

MACBETH. Thou art too like the spirit of Banquo:
down!
Thy crown does sear mine eye-balls. And thy hair,
Thou other gold-bound brow, is like the first.
A third is like the former. Filthy hags!
Why do you show me this?—A fourth? Start, eyes!
What, will the line stretch out to th' crack of doom?
Another yet? A seventh? I'll see no more:
And yet the eighth appears, who bears a glass
Which shows me many more; and some I see   120
That two-fold balls and treble sceptres carry.
Horrible sight! ... Now I see 'tis true,
For the blood-boltered Banquo smiles upon me,
And points at them for his. What, is this so?
1 WITCH. Ay, sir, all this is so. But why
Stands Macbeth thus amazedly?
Come, sisters, cheer we up his sprites,
And show the best of our delights.
I'll charm the air to give a sound,
While you perform your antic round: 130
That this great king may kindly say
Our duties did his welcome pay.

Music. The Witches dance, and vanish

MACBETH. Where are they? Gone? Let this pernicious
hour
Stand aye accursèd in the calendar
Come in, without there!

Enter Lennox

LENNOX.   What's your grace's will?
MACBETH. Saw you the Weïrd Sisters?
LENNOX.   No, my lord.
MACBETH. Came they not by you?
LENNOX.   No indeed, my lord.
MACBETH. Infected be the air whereon they ride,
And damned all those that trust them! I did hear
The galloping of horse. Who was't came by?   140
LENNOX. 'Tis two or three, my lord, that bring you
word
Macduff is fled to England.
MACBETH.   Fled to England!
LENNOX. Ay, my good lord.
MACBETH [aside]. Time, thou anticipat'st my dread
exploits:
The flighty purpose never is o'ertook
Unless the deed go with it. From this moment
The very firstlings of my heart shall be
The firstlings of my hand. And even now
To crown my thoughts with acts, be it thought and
done:
The castle of Macduff I will surprise,   150
Seize upon Fife, give to th'edge o'th' sword
His wife, his babes, and all unfortunate souls
That trace him in his line. No boasting like a fool;
This deed I'll do before this purpose cool.
But no more sights! [aloud] Where are these
gentlemen?
Come, bring me where they are.   *They go*

Scene 2: *Fife. Macduff's castle*

Enter Macduff's Wife, her Son, and Ross

L. MACDUFF. What had he done, to make him fly the
land?

ROSS. You must have patience, madam.
L. MACDUFF.   He had none:
His flight was madness: when our actions do not,
Our fears do make us traitors.
ROSS.   You know not
Whether it was his wisdom or his fear.
L. MACDUFF. Wisdom! to leave his wife, to leave his
babes,
His mansion and his titles, in a place
From whence himself does fly? He loves us not;
He wants the natural touch: for the poor wren,
The most diminutive of birds, will fight,   10
Her young ones in her nest, against the owl.
All is the fear and nothing is the love;
As little is the wisdom, where the flight
So runs against all reason.
ROSS.   My dearest coz,
I pray you, school yourself. But, for your husband,
He is noble, wise, judicious, and best knows
The fits o'th' season. I dare not speak much further,
But cruel are the times, when we are traitors
And do not know ourselves; when we hold rumour
From what we fear, yet know not what we fear,   20
But float upon a wild and violent sea,
Each way and none. I take my leave of you:
Shall not be long but I'll be here again:
Things at the worst will cease, or else climb upward
To what they were before. My pretty cousin,
Blessing upon you!
L. MACDUFF. Fathered he is, and yet he's fatherless.
ROSS. I am so much a fool, should I stay longer
It would be my disgrace and your discomfort.
I take my leave at once.   *He goes*
L. MACDUFF.   Sirrah, your father's dead,   30
And what will you do now? How will you live?
SON. As birds do, mother.
L. MACDUFF.   What, with worms and flies?
SON. With what I get, I mean, and so do they.
L. MACDUFF. Poor bird! thou'ldst never fear the net
nor lime,
The pitfall nor the gin.
SON. Why should I, mother? Poor birds they are not
set for.
My father is not dead, for all your saying.
L. MACDUFF. Yes, he is dead: how wilt thou do for a
father?
SON. Nay, how will you do for a husband?
L. MACDUFF. Why, I can buy me twenty at any market.   40
SON. Then you'll buy 'em to sell again.
L. MACDUFF. Thou speak'st with all thy wit, and yet
i'faith
With wit enough for thee.
SON. Was my father a traitor, mother?
L. MACDUFF. Ay, that he was.
SON. What is a traitor?
L. MACDUFF. Why, one that swears and lies.
SON. And be all traitors that do so?
L. MACDUFF. Every one that does so is a traitor, and
must be hanged.
SON. And must they all be hanged that swear and lie?   50
L. MACDUFF. Every one.
SON. Who must hang them?
L. MACDUFF. Why, the honest men.
SON. Then the liars and swearers are fools; for there
are liars and swearers enow to beat the honest men
and hang up them.

L. MACDUFF. Now God help thee, poor monkey! But
    how wilt thou do for a father?
SON. If he were dead, you'ld weep for him: if you
    would not, it were a good sign that I should quickly   60
    have a new father.
L. MACDUFF. Poor prattler, how thou talk'st!

Enter a Messenger

MESSENGER. Bless you, fair dame! I am not to you
    known,
Though in your state of honour I am perfect.
I doubt some danger does approach you nearly.
If you will take a homely man's advice,
Be not found here; hence, with your little ones.
To fright you thus, methinks I am too savage;
To do worse to you were fell cruelty,
Which is too nigh your person. Heaven preserve
    you!   70
I dare abide no longer.   *He goes*
L. MACDUFF.   Whither should I fly?
I have done no harm. But I remember now
I am in this earthly world; where to do harm
Is often laudable, to do good sometime
Accounted dangerous folly: why then, alas,
Do I put up that womanly defence,
To say I have done no harm?

Enter Murderers

                    What are these faces?
MURDERER. Where is your husband?
L. MACDUFF. I hope in no place so unsanctified
Where such as thou mayst find him.
MURDERER.   He's a traitor.   80
SON. Thou liest, thou shag-haired villain.
MURDERER.   What, you egg!   *Stabs him*
Young fry of treachery!
SON.   He has killed me, mother:
Run away, I pray you.   *Dies*
        *Lady Macduff goes, crying murder
        and pursued by the Murderers*

Scene 3: *England. Before the palace of King Edward the
        Confessor*

Enter Malcolm and Macduff

MALCOLM. Let us seek out some desolate shade, and
    there
Weep our sad bosoms empty.
MACDUFF.   Let us rather
Hold fast the mortal sword, and like good men
Bestride our down-fall'n birthdom: each new morn
New widows howl, new orphans cry, new sorrows
Strike heaven on the face, that it resounds
As if it felt with Scotland and yelled out
Like syllable of dolour.
MALCOLM.   What I believe, I'll wail;
What know, believe; and what I can redress,
As I shall find the time to friend, I will.   10
What you have spoke, it may be so perchance.
This tyrant, whose sole name blisters our tongues,
Was once thought honest: you have loved him well;
He hath not touched you yet. I am young, but
    something
You may deserve of him through me; and wisdom
To offer up a weak, poor, innocent lamb,
T'appease an angry god.
MACDUFF. I am not treacherous.

MALCOLM.   But Macbeth is.
A good and virtuous nature may recoil
In an imperial charge. But I shall crave your pardon;   20
That which you are, my thoughts cannot transpose:
Angels are bright still, though the brightest fell:
Though all things foul would wear the brows of
    grace,
Yet grace must still look so.
MACDUFF.   I have lost my hopes.
MALCOLM. Perchance even there where I did find my
    doubts.
Why in that rawness left you wife and child,
Those precious motives, those strong knots of love,
Without leave-taking? I pray you,
Let not my jealousies be your dishonours,
But mine own safeties: you may be rightly just,   30
Whatever I shall think.
MACDUFF.   Bleed, bleed, poor country!
Great tyranny, lay thou thy basis sure,
For goodness dares not check thee: wear thou thy
    wrongs,
The title is affeered! Fare thee well, lord:
I would not be the villain that thou think'st
For the whole space that's in the tyrant's grasp,
And the rich East to boot.
MALCOLM.   Be not offended:
I speak not as in absolute fear of you:
I think our country sinks beneath the yoke,
It weeps, it bleeds, and each new day a gash   40
Is added to her wounds. I think withal
There would be hands uplifted in my right;
And here from gracious England have I offer
Of goodly thousands. But for all this,
When I shall tread upon the tyrant's head,
Or wear it on my sword, yet my poor country
Shall have more vices than it had before,
More suffer and more sundry ways than ever,
By him that shall succeed.
MACDUFF.   What should he be?
MALCOLM. It is myself I mean: in whom I know   50
All the particulars of vice so grafted
That, when they shall be opened, black Macbeth
Will seem as pure as snow, and the poor state
Esteem him as a lamb, being compared
With my confineless harms.
MACDUFF.   Not in the legions
Of horrid hell can come a devil more damned
In evils to top Macbeth.
MALCOLM.   I grant him bloody,
Luxurious, avaricious, false, deceitful,
Sudden, malicious, smacking of every sin
That has a name: but there's no bottom, none,   60
In my voluptuousness: your wives, your daughters,
Your matrons and your maids, could not fill up
The cistern of my lust, and my desire
All continent impediments would o'erbear
That did oppose my will. Better Macbeth,
Than such an one to reign.
MACDUFF.   Boundless intemperance
In nature is a tyranny; it hath been
Th'untimely emptying of the happy throne,
And fall of many kings. But fear not yet
To take upon you what is yours: you may   70
Convey your pleasures in a spacious plenty,
And yet seem cold, the time you may so hoodwink:
We have willing dames enough; there cannot be

That vulture in you, to devour so many
As will to greatness dedicate themselves,
Finding it so inclined.
MALCOLM.   With this there grows
In my most ill-composed affection such
A stanchless avarice that, were I king,
I should cut off the nobles for their lands,
Desire his jewels and this other's house,
And my more-having would be as a sauce
To make me hunger more, that I should forge
Quarrels unjust against the good and loyal,
Destroying them for wealth.
MACDUFF.   This avarice
Sticks deeper; grows with more pernicious root
Than summer-seeming lust: and it hath been
The sword of our slain kings: yet do not fear;
Scotland hath foisons to fill up your will
Of your mere own. All these are portable,
With other graces weighed.
MALCOLM. But I have none. The king-becoming
    graces,
As justice, verity, temp'rance, stableness,
Bounty, perseverance, mercy, lowliness,
Devotion, patience, courage, fortitude,
I have no relish of them, but abound
In the division of each several crime,
Acting it many ways. Nay, had I power, I should
Pour the sweet milk of concord into hell,
Uproot the universal peace, confound
All unity on earth.
MACDUFF.   O Scotland! Scotland!
MALCOLM. If such a one be fit to govern, speak:
I am as I have spoken.
MACDUFF.   Fit to govern!
No, not to live. O nation miserable!
With an untitled tyrant bloody-sceptred,
When shalt thou see thy wholesome days again,
Since that the truest issue of thy throne
By his own interdiction stands accurst,
And does blaspheme his breed? Thy royal father
Was a most sainted king; the queen that bore thee
Oft'ner upon her knees than on her feet,
Died every day she lived. Fare thee well!
These evils thou repeat'st upon thyself
Hath banished me from Scotland. O my breast,
Thy hope ends here!
MALCOLM.   Macduff, this noble passion,
Child of integrity, hath from my soul
Wiped the black scruples, reconciled my thoughts
To thy good truth and honour. Devilish Macbeth
By many of these trains hath sought to win me
Into his power; and modest wisdom plucks me
From over-credulous haste: but God above
Deal between thee and me! for even now
I put myself to thy direction, and
Unspeak mine own detraction; here abjure
The taints and blames I laid upon myself,
For strangers to my nature. I am yet
Unknown to woman, never was forsworn,
Scarcely have coveted what was mine own,
At no time broke my faith, would not betray
The devil to his fellow, and delight
No less in truth than life: my first false speaking
Was this upon myself: what I am truly
Is thine and my poor country's to command:
Whither indeed, before thy here-approach,

Old Siward, with ten thousand warlike men,
Already at a point, was setting forth:
Now we'll together, and the chance of goodness
Be like our warranted quarrel! Why are you silent?
MACDUFF. Such welcome and unwelcome things at
    once
'Tis hard to reconcile.

A Doctor enters

MALCOLM. Well, more anon. Comes the king forth,
    I pray you?
DOCTOR. Ay, sir: there are a crew of wretched souls
That stay his cure: their malady convinces
The great assay of art; but at his touch,
Such sanctity hath heaven given his hand,
They presently amend.
MALCOLM.   I thank you, doctor.   *The Doctor goes*
MACDUFF. What's the disease he means?
MALCOLM.   'Tis called the evil:
A most miraculous work in this good king,
Which often, since my here-remain in England,
I have seen him do. How he solicits heaven,
Himself best knows: but strangely-visited people,
All swoln and ulcerous, pitiful to the eye,
The mere despair of surgery, he cures,
Hanging a golden stamp about their necks,
Put on with holy prayers: and 'tis spoken,
To the succeeding royalty he leaves
The healing benediction. With this strange virtue
He hath a heavenly gift of prophecy,
And sundry blessings hang about his throne
That speak him full of grace.

Ross approaches

MACDUFF.   See who comes here.
MALCOLM. My countryman; but yet I know him not.
MACDUFF. My ever gentle cousin, welcome hither.
MALCOLM. I know him now: good God, betimes
    remove
The means that makes us strangers!
ROSS.   Sir, amen.
MACDUFF. Stands Scotland where it did?
ROSS.   Alas, poor country,
Almost afraid to know itself! It cannot
Be called our mother, but our grave; where nothing,
But who knows nothing, is once seen to smile;
Where sighs and groans and shrieks that rend the
    air,
Are made, not marked; where violent sorrow seems
A modern ecstasy: the dead man's knell
Is there scarce asked for who, and good men's lives
Expire before the flowers in their caps,
Dying or ere they sicken.
MACDUFF.   O, relation
Too nice, and yet too true!
MALCOLM.   What's the newest grief?
ROSS. That of an hour's age doth hiss the speaker;
Each minute teems a new one.
MACDUFF.   How does my wife?
ROSS. Why, well.
MACDUFF.   And all my children?
ROSS.   Well too.
MACDUFF. The tyrant has not battered at their peace?
ROSS. No, they were well at peace, when I did leave
    'em.

MACDUFF. Be not a niggard of your speech: how
    goes't?   180
ROSS. When I came hither to transport the tidings
    Which I have heavily borne, there ran a rumour
    Of many worthy fellows that were out;
    Which to my belief witnessed the rather,
    For that I saw the tyrant's power a-foot.
    Now is the time of help: your eye in Scotland
    Would create soldiers, make our women fight,
    To doff their dire distresses.
MALCOLM.   Be't their comfort
    We are coming thither: gracious England hath
    Lent us good Siward and ten thousand men;   190
    An older and a better soldier none
    That Christendom gives out.
ROSS.   Would I could answer
    This comfort with the like! But I have words,
    That would be howled out in the desert air,
    Where hearing should not latch them.
MACDUFF.   What concern they?
    The general cause? or is it a fee-grief
    Due to some single breast?
ROSS.   No mind that's honest
    But in it shares some woe, though the main part
    Pertains to you alone.
MACDUFF.   If it be mine,
    Keep it not from me, quickly let me have it.   200
ROSS. Let not your ears despise my tongue for ever,
    Which shall possess them with the heaviest sound
    That ever yet they heard.
MACDUFF.   Humh! I guess at it.
ROSS. Your castle is surprised; your wife and babes
    Savagely slaughtered: to relate the manner,
    Were, on the quarry of these murdered deer,
    To add the death of you.
MALCOLM.   Merciful heaven!
    What, man! ne'er pull your hat upon your brows;
    Give sorrow words: the grief that does not speak
    Whispers the o'er-fraught heart and bids it break.   210
MACDUFF. My children too?
ROSS.   Wife, children, servants, all
    That could be found.
MACDUFF.   And I must be from thence!
    My wife killed too?
ROSS.   I have said.
MALCOLM.   Be comforted:
    Let's make us med'cines of our great revenge,
    To cure this deadly grief.
MACDUFF. He has no children. All my pretty ones?
    Did you say all? O, hell-kite! All?
    What, all my pretty chickens and their dam
    At one fell swoop?
MALCOLM. Dispute it like a man.
MACDUFF.   I shall do so;   220
    But I must also feel it as a man:
    I cannot but remember such things were,
    That were most precious to me. Did heaven look on,
    And would not take their part? Sinful Macduff,
    They were all struck for thee! naught that I am,
    Not for their own demerits, but for mine,
    Fell slaughter on their souls: heaven rest them now!
MALCOLM. Be this the whetstone of your sword:
    let grief
    Convert to anger; blunt not the heart, enrage it.
MACDUFF. O, I could play the woman with mine eyes,   230
    And braggart with my tongue! But, gentle heavens,

    Cut short all intermission; front to front
    Bring thou this fiend of Scotland and myself;
    Within my sword's length set him; if he 'scape,
    Heaven forgive him too!
MALCOLM.   This tune goes manly.
    Come, go we to the king, our power is ready,
    Our lack is nothing but our leave. Macbeth
    Is ripe for shaking, and the Powers above
    Put on their instruments. Receive what cheer you
    may;
    The night is long that never finds the day.   240
                                They go

ACT 5

Scene 1: *Dunsinane. A room in the castle*

Enter a Doctor of Physic, and a Waiting Gentlewoman

DOCTOR. I have two nights watched with you, but can
    perceive no truth in your report. When was it she
    last walked?
GENTLEWOMAN. Since his majesty went into the field,
    I have seen her rise from her bed, throw her night-
    gown upon her, unlock her closet, take forth paper,
    fold it, write upon't, read it, afterwards seal it, and
    again return to bed; yet all this while in a most fast
    sleep.
DOCTOR. A great perturbation in nature, to receive at   10
    once the benefit of sleep and do the effects of
    watching! In this slumbry agitation, besedes her
    walking and other actual performances, what, at any
    time, have you heard her say?
GENTLEWOMAN. That, sir, which I will not report after
    her.
DOCTOR. You may to me, and 'tis most meet you
    should.
GENTLEWOMAN. Neither to you nor any one, having
    no witness to confirm my speech.   20

Enter Lady Macbeth, with a taper

    Lo you, here she comes! This is her very guise, and
    upon my life fast asleep. Observe her, stand close.
DOCTOR. How came she by that light?
GENTLEWOMAN. Why, it stood by her: she has light by
    her continually, 'tis her command.
DOCTOR. You see, her eyes are open.
GENTLEWOMAN. Ay, but their sense are shut.
DOCTOR. What is it she does now? Look, how she
    rubs her hands.
GENTLEWOMAN. It is an accustomed action with her, to   30
    seem thus washing her hands: I have known her
    continue in this a quarter of an hour.
LADY. M. Yet here's a spot.
DOCTOR. Hark, she speaks! I will set down what comes
    from her, to satisfy my remembrance the more
    strongly.
LADY M. Out, damnéd spot! out, I say! One: two:
    why, then 'tis time to do't. Hell is murky! Fie, my
    lord, fie! a soldier, and afeard? What need we fear
    who knows it, when none can call our power to   40
    accompt? Yet who would have thought the old man
    to have had so much blood in him?
DOCTOR. Do you mark that?
LADY M. The Thane of Fife had a wife; where is she
    now? What, will these hands ne'er be clean? No
    more o'that, my lord, no more o'that: you mar all
    with this starting.

DOCTOR. Go to, go to; you have known what you should not.

GENTLEWOMAN. She has spoke what she should not, I 50 am sure of that: heaven knows what she has known.

LADY M. Here's the smell of the blood still: all the perfumes of Arabia will not sweeten this little hand. Oh! oh! oh!

DOCTOR. What a sigh is there! The heart is sorely charged.

GENTLEWOMAN. I would not have such a heart in my bosom, for the dignity of the whole body.

DOCTOR. Well, well, well,—

GENTLEWOMAN. Pray God it be, sir. 60

DOCTOR. This disease is beyond my practice: yet I have known those which have walked in their sleep who have died holily in their beds.

LADY M. Wash your hands, put on your night-gown, look not so pale: I tell you yet again, Banquo's buried; he cannot come out on's grave.

DOCTOR. Even so?

LADY M. To bed, to bed: there's knocking at the gate: come, come, come, come, give me your hand: what's done, cannot be undone: to bed, to bed, to 70 bed.   *She goes*

DOCTOR. Will she go now to bed?

GENTLEWOMAN. Directly.

DOCTOR. Foul whisp'rings are abroad: unnatural deeds Do breed unnatural troubles: infected minds To their deaf pillows will discharge their secrets: More needs she the divine than the physician: God, God forgive us all! Look after her, Remove from her the means of all annoyance, And still keep eyes upon her. So, good night: 80 My mind she has mated and amazed my sight: I think, but dare not speak.

GENTLEWOMAN.   Good night, good doctor.   *They go*

Scene 2: *The country near Dunsinane. Drum and Colours*

Enter Menteith, Caithness, Angus, Lennox, Soldiers

MENTEITH. The English power is near, led on by Malcolm, His uncle Siward and the good Macduff. Revenges burn in them: for their dear causes Would to the bleeding and the grim alarm Excite the mortified man.

ANGUS.   Near Birnam wood Shall we well meet them, that way are they coming.

CAITHNESS. Who knows if Donalbain be with his brother?

LENNOX. For certain, sir, he is not: I have a file Of all the gentry: there is Siward's son, And many unrough youths, that even now 10 Protest their first of manhood.

MENTEITH.   What does the tyrant?

CAITHNESS. Great Dunsinane he strongly fortifies: Some say he's mad; others, that lesser hate him, Do call it valiant fury: but, for certain, He cannot buckle his distempered cause Within the belt of rule.

ANGUS.   Now does he feel His secret murders sticking on his hands; Now minutely revolts upbraid his faith-breach; Those he commands move only in command, Nothing in love: now does he feel his title 20

Hang loose about him, like a giant's robe Upon a dwarfish thief.

MENTEITH.   Who then shall blame His pestered senses to recoil and start, When all that is within him does condemn Itself for being there?

CAITHNESS.   Well, march we on, To give obedience where 'tis truly owed: Meet we the med'cine of the sickly weal, And with him pour we, in our country's purge, Each drop of us.

LENNOX.   Or so much as it needs To dew the sovereign flower and drown the weeds. 30 Make we our march towards Birnam.   *Exeunt, marching*

Scene 3: *Dunsinane. A court in the castle*

Enter Macbeth, Doctor, and Attendants

MACBETH. Bring me no more reports, let them fly all: Till Birnam wood remove to Dunsinane I cannot taint with fear. What's the boy Malcolm? Was he not born of woman? The spirits that know All mortal consequences have pronounced me thus: 'Fear not, Macbeth, no man that's born of a woman Shall e'er have power upon thee'. Then fly, false thanes, And mingle with the English epicures: The mind I sway by and the heart I bear Shall never sag with doubt nor shake with fear. 10

A servant enters

The devil damn thee black, thou cream-faced loon! Where got'st thou that goose look?

SERVANT. There is ten thousand—

MACBETH.   Geese, villain?

SERVANT.   Soldiers, sir.

MACBETH. Go prick thy face and over-red thy fear, Thou lily-livered boy. What soldiers, patch? Death of thy soul! those linen cheeks of thine Are counsellors to fear. What soldiers, whey-face?

SERVANT. The English force, so please you.

MACBETH. Take thy face hence.   *Servant goes* Seton!—I am sick at heart, When I behold—Seton, I say!—This push 20 Will cheer me ever, or disseat me now. I have lived long enough: my way of life Is fall'n into the sere, the yellow leaf, And that which should accompany old age, As honour, love, obedience, troops of friends, I must not look to have; but, in their stead, Curses, not loud but deep, mouth-honour, breath Which the poor heart would fain deny and dare not. Seton!

Seton enters

SETON. What's your gracious pleasure?

MACBETH.   What news more? 30

SETON. All is confirmed, my lord, which was reported.

MACBETH. I'll fight, till from my bones my flesh be hacked. Give me my armour.

SETON.   'Tis not needed yet.

MACBETH. I'll put it on. Send out moe horses, skirr the country round,

Hang those that talk of fear. Give me mine
  armour....   *Seton goes*
How does your patient, doctor?
DOCTOR.   Not so sick, my lord,
  As she is troubled with thick-coming fancies,
  That keep her from her rest.
MACBETH.   Cure her of that:
  Canst thou not minister to a mind diseased,   40
  Pluck from the memory a rooted sorrow,
  Raze out the written troubles of the brain,
  And with some sweet oblivious antidote
  Cleanse the stuffed bosom of that perilous stuff
  Which weighs upon the heart?
DOCTOR.   Therein the patient
  Must minister to himself.
MACBETH. Throw physic to the dogs, I'll none of it.
  Come, put mine armour on; give me my staff;
  Seton, send out; doctor, the thanes fly from me;
  Come, sir, dispatch.—If thou couldst, doctor, cast 50
  The water of my land, find her disease,
  And purge it to a sound and pristine health,
  I would applaud thee to the very echo,
  That should applaud again.—Pull't off, I say.—
  What rhubarb, senna, or what purgative drug,
  Would scour these English hence? Hear'st thou of
  them?
DOCTOR. Ay, my good lord; your royal preparation
  Makes us hear something.
MACBETH.   Bring it after me.
  I will not be afraid of death and bane
  Till Birnam forest come to Dunsinane.   *He goes* 60
DOCTOR. Were I from Dunsinane away and clear,
  Profit again should hardly draw me here.
                                        He goes

Scene 4: *Country near Birnam. Drum and Colours*

*Enter Malcolm, Siward, Macduff, Siward's Son, Menteith,
Caithness, Angus, Lennox, Ross, and Soldiers, marching*

MALCOLM. Cousins, I hope, the days are near at hand
  That chambers will be safe.
MENTEITH.   We doubt it nothing.
SIWARD. What wood is this before us?
MENTEITH.   The wood of Birnam.
MALCOLM. Let every soldier hew him down a bough,
  And bear't before him: thereby shall we shadow
  The number of our host, and make discovery
  Err in report of us.
SOLDIER.   It shall be done.
SIWARD. We learn no other but the confident tyrant
  Keeps still in Dunsinane, and will endure
  Our setting down before't.
MALCOLM.   'Tis his main hope: 10
  For where there is advantage to be gone,
  Both more and less have given him the revolt,
  And none serve with him but constrainèd things
  Whose hearts are absent too.
MACDUFF.   Let our just censures
  Attend the true event, and put we on
  Industrious soldiership.
SIWARD.   The time approaches,
  That will with due decision make us know
  What we shall say we have and what we owe.
  Thoughts speculative their unsure hopes relate,
  But certain issue strokes must arbitrate: 20

Towards which advance the war.
                                Exeunt, marching

Scene 5: *Dunsinane. The court of the castle as before*

Enter Macbeth, Seton, and Soldiers with Drum and Colours

MACBETH. Hang out our banners on the outward
  walls;
  The cry is still 'They come': our castle's strength
  Will laugh a siege to scorn: here let them lie
  Till famine and the ague eat them up:
  Were they not forced with those that should be ours,
  We might have met them dareful, beard to beard,
  And beat them backward home.
                      A cry within of women
                      What is that noise?
SETON. It is the cry of women, my good lord.   *Goes*
MACBETH. I have almost forgot the taste of fears:
  The time has been, my senses would have cooled 10
  To hear a night-shriek, and my fell of hair
  Would at a dismal treatise rouse and stir
  As life were in't: I have supped full with horrors;
  Direness, familiar to my slaughterous thoughts,
  Cannot once start me.
Seton returns
                      Wherefore was that cry?
SETON. The queen, my lord, is dead.
MACBETH. She should have died hereafter;
  There would have been a time for such a word.
  To-morrow, and to-morrow, and to-morrow,
  Creeps in this petty pace from day to day,   20
  To the last syllable of recorded time;
  And all our yesterdays have lighted fools
  The way to dusty death. Out, out, brief candle!
  Life's but a walking shadow, a poor player
  That struts and frets his hour upon the stage,
  And then is heard no more: it is a tale
  Told by an idiot, full of sound and fury,
  Signifying nothing.
Enter a messenger
  Thou com'st to use thy tongue; thy story quickly.
MESSENGER. Gracious my lord,   30
  I should report that which I say I saw,
  But know not how to do't.
MACBETH.   Well, say, sir.
MESSENGER. As I did stand my watch upon the hill,
  I looked toward Birnam, and anon methought
  The wood began to move.
MACBETH.   . Liar and slave!
MESSENGER. Let me endure your wrath, if't be not so:
  Within this three mile may you see it coming.
  I say, a moving grove.
MACBETH.   If thou speak'st false,
  Upon the next tree shalt thou hang alive,
  Till famine cling thee: if thy speech be sooth,   40
  I care not if thou dost for me as much.
  I pall in resolution, and begin
  To doubt th'equivocation of the fiend
  That lies like truth: 'Fear not, till Birnam wood
  Do come to Dunsinane'; and now a wood
  Comes toward Dunsinane. Arm, arm, and out!
  If this which he avouches does appear,
  There is nor flying hence nor tarrying here.
  I 'gin to be aweary of the sun,
  And wish th'estate o'th' world were now undone. 50

Ring the alarum bell! Blow, wind! come, wrack!
At least we'll die with harness on our back.
They go

Scene 6: *Dunsinane. Before the castle gate. Drum
and Colours*

*Enter Malcolm, Siward, Macduff, and their army,
with boughs*

MALCOLM. Now near enough: your leavy screens
throw down,
And show like those you are. You, worthy uncle,
Shall with my cousin your right noble son
Lead our first battle: worthy Macduff and we
Shall take upon's what else remains to do,
According to our order.
SIWARD.   Fare you well.
Do we but find the tyrant's power to-night,
Let us be beaten, if we cannot fight.
MACDUFF. Make all our trumpets speak; give them all
breath,
Those clamorous harbingers of blood and death.   10

They go forward, their trumpets sounding

Scene 7

Enter Macbeth

MACBETH. They have tied me to a stake; I cannot fly,
But bear-like I must fight the course. What's he
That was not born of woman? Such a one
Am I to fear, or none.

Young Siward comes up

YOUNG SIWARD. What is thy name?
MACBETH.   Thou'lt be afraid to hear it.
YOUNG SIWARD. No; though thou call'st thyself a
hotter name
Than any is in hell.
MACBETH.   My name's Macbeth.
YOUNG SIWARD. The devil himself could not
pronounce a title
More hateful to mine ear.
MACBETH.   No, nor more fearful.
YOUNG SIWARD. Thou liest, abhorréd tyrant, with my
sword   10
I'll prove the lie thou speak'st.
              They fight, and young Siward is slain
MACBETH.   Thou wast born of woman.
But swords I smile at, weapons laugh to scorn,
Brandished by man that's of a woman born.

He passes on. Macduff comes up

MACDUFF. That way the noise is. Tyrant, show thy
face!
If thou beest slain and with no stroke of mine,
My wife and children's ghosts will haunt me still.
I cannot strike at wretched kerns, whose arms
Are hired to bear their staves; either thou, Macbeth,
Or else my sword with an unbattered edge
I sheathe again undeeded. There thou shouldst be;   20
By this great clatter, one of greatest note
Seems bruited. Let me find him, fortune!
And more I beg not. *He follows Macbeth. Alarums*

Malcolm and old Siward come up

SIWARD. This way, my lord; the castle's gently
rendered:
The tyrant's people on both sides do fight,
The noble thanes do bravely in the war,
The day almost itself professes yours,
And little is to do.
MALCOLM.   We have met with foes
That strike beside us.
SIWARD.   Enter, sir, the castle
They go. Alarum

Scene 8

Macbeth returns

MACBETH. Why should I play the Roman fool, and die
On mine own sword? whiles I see lives, the gashes
Do·better upon them.

Macduff returns, following him

MACDUFF.   Turn, hell hound, turn.
MACBETH. Fall men else I have avoided thee:
But get thee back, my soul is too much charged
With blood of thine already.
MACDUFF.   I have no words:
My voice is my sword, thou bloodier villain
Than terms can give thee out! *They fight. Alarum*
MACBETH.   Thou losest labour.
As easy mayst thou the intrenchant air
With thy keen sword impress as make me bleed: 10
Let fall thy blade on vulnerable crests,
I bear a charméd life, which must not yield
To one of woman born.
MACDUFF.   Despair thy charm,
And let the angel whom thou still hast served
Tell thee, Macduff was from his mother's womb
Untimely ripped.
MACBETH. Accurséd be that tongue that tells me so,
For it hath cowed my better part of man!
And be these juggling fiends no more believed,
That palter with us in a double sense,   20
That keep the word of promise to our ear,
And break it to our hope. I'll not fight with thee.
MACDUFF. Then yield thee, coward,
And live to be the show and gaze o'th' time.
We'll have thee, as our rarer monsters are,
Painted upon a pole, and underwrit,
'Here may you see the tyrant'.
MACBETH.   I will not yield,
To kiss the ground before young Malcolm's feet,
And to be baited with the rabble's curse.
Though Birnam wood be come to Dunsinane,   30
And thou opposed, being of no woman born,
Yet I will try the last. Before my body
I throw my warlike shield: lay on, Macduff,
And damned be him that first cries 'Hold, enough'.
              They fight until Macbeth is slain

Scene 9: *Within the castle*

*Retreat and flourish. Enter, with Drum and Colours,
Malcolm, Siward, Ross, Thanes and Soldiers*

MALCOLM. I would the friends we miss were safe
arrived.
SIWARD. Some must go off: and yet, by these I see,
So great a day as this is cheaply bought.
MALCOLM. Macduff is missing, and your noble son.

ROSS. Your son, my lord, has paid a soldier's debt:
He only lived but till he was a man,
The which no sooner had his prowess confirmed
In the unshrinking station where he fought,
But like a man he died.
SIWARD.   Then he is dead?
ROSS. Ay, and brought off the field: your cause of
    sorrow
Must not be measured by his worth, for then
It hath no end.
SIWARD.   Had he his hurts before?
ROSS. Ay, on the front.
SIWARD.   Why then, God's soldier be he!
Had I as many sons as I have hairs,
I would not wish them to a fairer death:
And so his knell is knolled.
MALCOLM.   He's worth more sorrow,
And that I'll spend for him.
SIWARD.   He's worth no more.
They say he parted well and paid his score:
And so God be with him! Here comes newer
comfort.

Enter Macduff, with Macbeth's head

MACDUFF. Hail, king! for so thou art. Behold, where
    stands
Th'usurper's cursèd head: the time is free:
I see thee compassed with thy kingdom's pearl,
That speak my salutation in their minds;
Whose voices I desire aloud with mine:
Hail, king of Scotland!
ALL.   Hail, King of Scotland!   *Flourish*
MALCOLM. We shall not spend a large expense of time
Before we reckon with your several loves,
And make us even with you. My thanes and
    kinsmen,
Henceforth be earls, the first that ever Scotland
In such an honour named. What's more to do,
Which would be planted newly with the time,
As calling home our exiled friends abroad
That fled the snares of watchful tyranny,
Producing forth the cruel ministers
Of this dead butcher and his fiend-like queen,
Who, as 'tis thought, by self and violent hands
Took off her life; this, and what needful else
That calls upon us, by the grace of Grace
We will perform in measure, time, and place:
So thanks to all at once, and to each one,
Whom we invite to see us crowned at Scone.
                   Flourish. They go

The Tragedy of
Hamlet,
Prince of Denmark

The scene: Denmark

CHARACTERS IN THE PLAY

CLAUDIUS, *King of Denmark*
HAMLET, *Prince of Denmark, son to the late, and nephew
  to the present king*
POLONIUS, *Principal Secretary of State*
HORATIO, *friend to Hamlet*
LAERTES, *son to Polonius*
VALTEMAND ⎱ *ambassadors to Norway*
CORNELIUS ⎰
ROSENCRANTZ ⎱ *formerly fellow-students with Hamlet*
GUILDENSTERN ⎰
OSRIC, *a fantastic fop*
A gentleman
A Doctor of Divinity

MARCELLUS ⎱
BARNARDO ⎰ *Gentlemen of the Guard*
FRANCISCO
REYNALDO, *servant to Polonius*
Four or five Players
Two grave-diggers
FORTINBRAS, *Prince of Norway*
A Norwegian Captain
English Ambassadors
GERTRUDE, *Queen of Denmark, mother to Hamlet*
OPHELIA, *daughter to Polonius*
*Lords, Ladies, Soldiers, Sailors, Messenger, and
  Attendants*
The GHOST *of Hamlet's father*

The Tragedy of Hamlet, Prince of Denmark

ACT 1

Scene 1: *The castle at Elsinore. A narrow platform upon the battlements*

Francisco, a sentinel. Enter Barnardo, another sentinel

BARNARDO. Who's there?

FRANCISCO. Nay, answer me. Stand and unfold yourself.

BARNARDO. Long live the king!

FRANCISCO. Barnardo?

BARNARDO. He.

FRANCISCO. You come most carefully upon your hour.

BARNARDO. 'Tis now struck twelve, get thee to bed, Francisco.

FRANCISCO. For this relief much thanks, 'tis bitter cold,
And I am sick at heart.

BARNARDO. Have you had quiet guard?

FRANCISCO.   Not a mouse stirring. 10

BARNARDO. Well, good night:
If you do meet Horatio and Marcellus,
The rivals of my watch, bid them make haste.

Horatio and Marcellus enter

FRANCISCO. I think I hear them. Stand ho, who is there?

HORATIO. Friends to this ground.

MARCELLUS.   And liegemen to the Dane.

FRANCISCO. Give you good night.

MARCELLUS.   O, farewell honest soldier,
Who hath relieved you?

FRANCISCO.   Barnardo hath my place;
Give you good night.   *Francisco goes*

MARCELLUS.   Holla, Barnado!

BARNARDO.   Say,
What, is Horatio there?

HORATIO.   A piece of him.

BARNARDO. Welcome Horatio, welcome good Marcellus. 20

HORATIO. What, has this thing appeared again to-night?

BARNARDO. I have seen nothing.

MARCELLUS. Horatio says 'tis but our fantasy,
And will not let belief take hold of him
Touching this dreaded sight twice seen of us,
Therefore I have entreated him along
With us to watch the minutes of this night,
That if again this apparition come,
He may approve our eyes and speak to it.

HORATIO. Tush, tush, 'twill not appear.

BARNARDO.   Sit down awhile, 30
And let us once again assail your ears,
That are so fortified against our story,
What we have two nights seen.

HORATIO.   Well, sit we down,
And let us hear Barnardo speak of this.

BARNARDO. Last night of all,
When yon same star that's westward from the pole
Had made his course t'illume that part of heaven
Where now it burns, Marcellus and myself,
The bell then beating one——

A Ghost appears

MARCELLUS. Peace, break thee off, look where it comes again! 40

BARNARDO. In the same figure like the king that's dead.

MARCELLUS. Thou art a scholar, speak to it, Horatio.

BARNARDO. Looks a' not like the king? mark it, Horatio.

HORATIO. Most like, it harrows me with fear and wonder.

BARNARDO. It would be spoke to.

MARCELLUS.   Question it, Horatio.

HORATIO. What art thou that usurp'st this time of night,
Together with that fair and warlike form
In which the majesty of buried Denmark
Did sometimes march? by heaven I charge thee speak.

MARCELLUS. It is offended.

BARNARDO.   See, it stalks away. 50

HORATIO. Stay, speak, speak, I charge thee speak.
                  The Ghost vanishes

MARCELLUS. 'Tis gone and will not answer.

BARNARDO. How now Horatio, you tremble and look pale,
Is not this something more than fantasy?
What think you on't?

HORATIO. Before my God, I might not this believe
Without the sensible and true avouch
Of mine own eyes.

MARCELLUS.   Is it not like the king?

HORATIO. As thou art to thyself.
Such was the very armour he had on, 60
When he the ambitious Norway combated,
So frowned he once, when in an angry parle
He smote the sledded Polacks on the ice.
'Tis strange.

MARCELLUS. Thus twice before, and jump at this dead hour,
With martial stalk hath he gone by our watch.

HORATIO. In what particular thought to work I know not,
But in the gross and scope of mine opinion,
This bodes some strange eruption to our state.

MARCELLUS. Good now sit down, and tell me he that knows, 70
Why this same strict and most observant watch
So nightly toils the subject of the land,
And why such daily cast of brazen cannon
And foreign mart for implements of war,
Why such impress of shipwrights, whose sore task
Does not divide the Sunday from the week,
What might be toward that this sweaty haste
Doth make the night joint-labourer with the day,
Who is't that can inform me?

HORATIO.   That can I,
At least the whisper goes so; our last king, 80
Whose image even but now appeared to us,
Was as you know by Fortinbras of Norway,

Thereto pricked on by a most emulate pride,
Dared to the combat; in which our valiant Hamlet
(For so this side of our known world esteeméd him)
Did slay this Fortinbras, who by a sealed compact,
Well ratified by law and heraldy,
Did forfeit (with his life) all those his lands
Which he stood seized of, to the conqueror,
Against the which a moiety competent   90
Was gagéd by our king, which had returned
To the inheritance of Fortinbras,
Had he been vanquished; as by the same co-mart,
And carriage of the article designed,
His fell to Hamlet; now sir, young Fortinbras,
Of unimprovéd mettle hot and full,
Hath in the skirts of Norway here and there
Sharked up a list of lawless resolutes
For food and diet to some enterprise
That hath a stomach in't, which is no other,   100
As it doth well appear unto our state,
But to recover of us by strong hand
And terms compulsatory, those foresaid lands
So by his father lost; and this, I take it,
Is the main motive of our preparations,
The source of this our watch, and the chief head
Of this post-haste and romage in the land.
BARNARDO. I think it be no other but e'en so;
Well may it sort that this portentous figure
Comes arméd through our watch so like the king   110
That was and is the question of these wars.
HORATIO. A mote it is to trouble the mind's eye:
In the most high and palmy state of Rome,
A little ere the mightiest Julius fell,
The graves stood tenantless, and the sheeted dead
Did squeak and gibber in the Roman streets,
And even the like precurse of fierce events,
As harbingers preceding still the fates
And prologue to the omen coming on,
Have heaven and earth together demonstrated   120
Unto our climatures and countrymen,
As stars with trains of fire and dews of blood,
Disasters in the sun; and the moist star,
Upon whose influence Neptune's empire stands,
Was sick almost to doomsday with eclipse.

The Ghost reappears

But soft, behold, lo where it comes again!
I'll cross it though it blast me ...
                              He spreads his arms
                              Stay, illusion!
If thou hast any sound or use of voice,
Speak to me.
If there be any good thing to be done   130
That may to thee do ease, and grace to me,
Speak to me.
If thou art privy to thy country's fate
Which happily foreknowing may avoid,
O, speak!
Or if thou hast uphoarded in thy life
Extorted treasure in the womb of earth,
For which they say you spirits oft walk in death,
                              A cock crows
Speak of it—stay and speak—stop it, Marcellus!
MARCELLUS. Shall I strike at it with my partisan?   140
HORATIO. Do if it will not stand.
BARNARDO.   'Tis here!
HORATIO.   'Tis here!

MARCELLUS. 'Tis gone!   *The Ghost vanishes*
We do it wrong being so majestical
To offer it the show of violence,
For it is as the air, invulnerable,
And our vain blows malicious mockery.
BARNARDO. It was about to speak when the cock crew.
HORATIO. And then it started like a guilty thing,
Upon a fearful summons; I have heard
The cock that is the trumpet to the morn   150
Doth with his lofty and shrill-sounding throat
Awake the god of day, and at his warning
Whether in sea or fire, in earth or air,
Th'extravagant and erring spirit hies
To his confine, and of the truth herein
This present object made probation.
MARCELLUS. It faded on the crowing of the cock.
Some say that ever 'gainst that season comes
Wherein our Saviour's birth is celebrated
This bird of dawning singeth all night long,   160
And then they say no spirit dare stir abroad,
The nights are wholesome, then no planets strike,
No fairy takes, nor witch hath power to charm,
So hallowed, and so gracious is that time.
HORATIO. So have I heard and do in part believe it.
But look, the morn in russet mantle clad
Walks o'er the dew of yon high eastward hill.
Break we our watch up and by my advice
Let us impart what we have seen to-night
Unto young Hamlet, for upon my life   170
This spirit dumb to us, will speak to him:
Do you consent we shall acquaint him with it,
As needful in our loves, fitting our duty?
MARCELLUS. Let's do't, I pray, and I this morning
    know
Where we shall find him most convenient.
                                        They go

Scene 2: *The Council Chamber in the castle*

*A flourish of trumpets. Enter Claudius King of Denmark,
Gertrude the Queen, Councillors, Polonius and his son
Laertes, Valtemand and Cornelius; and last of all Prince
Hamlet*

KING. Though yet of Hamlet our dear brother's death
The memory be green, and that it us befitted
To bear our hearts in grief, and our whole kingdom
To be contracted in one brow of woe,
Yet so far hath discretion fought with nature,
That we with wisest sorrow think on him
Together with remembrance of ourselves:
Therefore our sometime sister, now our queen,
Th'imperial jointress to this warlike state,
Have we as 'twere with a defeated joy,   10
With an auspicious, and a dropping eye,
With mirth in funeral, and with dirge in marriage,
In equal scale weighing delight and dole,
Taken to wife: nor have we herein barred
Your better wisdoms, which have freely gone
With this affair along—for all, our thanks.
Now follows that you know, young Fortinbras,
Holding a weak supposal of our worth,
Or thinking by our late dear brother's death
Our state to be disjoint and out of frame,   20
Colleaguéd with this dream of his advantage,
He hath not failed to pester us with message
Importing the surrender of those lands
Lost by his father, with all bands of law,

To our most valiant brother—so much for him:
Now for ourself, and for this time of meeting,
Thus much the business is. We have here writ
To Norway, uncle of young Fortinbras—
Who impotent and bed-rid scarcely hears
Of this his nephew's purpose—to suppress 30
His further gait herein, in that the levies,
The lists, and full proportions, are all made
Out of his subject. And we here dispatch
You good Cornelius, and you Valtemand,
For bearers of this greeting to old Norway,
Giving to you no further personal power
To business with the king, more than the scope
Of these delated articles allow:
Farewell, and let your haste commend your duty.
CORNELIUS, VALTEMAND. In that, and all things, will we
    show our duty. 40
KING. We doubt it nothing, heartily farewell.
                    Valtemand and Cornelius depart
And now, Laertes, what's the news with you?
You told us of some suit, what is't, Laertes?
You cannot speak of reason to the Dane,
And lose your voice; what wouldst thou beg,
    Laertes,
That shall not be my offer, not thy asking?
The head is not more native to the heart,
The hand more instrumental to the mouth,
Than is the throne of Denmark to thy father.
What wouldst thou have, Laertes?
LAERTES.   My dread lord, 50
Your leave and favour to return to France,
From whence though willingly I came to Denmark,
To show my duty in your coronation;
Yet now I must confess, that duty done,
My thoughts and wishes bend again toward France,
And bow them to your gracious leave and pardon.
KING. Have you your father's leave? what says
    Polonius?
POLONIUS. He hath, my lord, wrung from me my
    slow leave
By laboursome petition, and at last
Upon his will I sealed my hard consent. 60
I do beseech you give him leave to go.
KING. Take thy fair hour, Laertes, time be thine,
And thy best graces spend it at thy will . . .
But now my cousin Hamlet, and my son—
HAMLET [*aside*]. A little more than kin, and less than
    kind.
KING. How is it that the clouds still hang on you?
HAMLET. Not so, my lord, I am too much in the 'son.'
QUEEN. Good Hamlet, cast thy nighted colour off,
And let thine eye look like a friend on Denmark,
Do not for ever with thy vailéd lids 70
Seek for thy noble father in the dust,
Thou know'st 'tis common, all that lives must die,
Passing through nature to eternity.
HAMLET. Ay, madam, it is common.
QUEEN.   If it be,
Why seems it so particular with thee?
HAMLET. Seems, madam! nay it is, I know not 'seems.'
'Tis not alone my inky cloak, good mother,
Nor customary suits of solemn black,
Nor windy suspiration of forced breath,
No, nor the fruitful river in the eye, 80
Nor the dejected haviour of the visage,
Together with all forms, modes, shapes of grief,

That can denote me truly. These indeed seem,
For they are actions that a man might play,
But I have that within which passes show,
These but the trappings and the suits of woe.
KING. 'Tis sweet and commendable in your nature,
    Hamlet,
To give these mourning duties to your father,
But you must know your father lost a father,
That father lost, lost his, and the survivor bound 90
In filial obligation for some term
To do obsequious sorrow. But to persever
In obstinate condolement is a course
Of impious stubbornness, 'tis unmanly grief,
It shows a will most incorrect to heaven,
A heart unfortified, a mind impatient,
An understanding simple and unschooled.
For what we know must be and is as common
As any the most vulgar thing to sense,
Why should we in our peevish opposition 100
Take it to heart? fie, 'tis a fault to heaven,
A fault against the dead, a fault to nature,
To reason most absurd, whose common theme
Is death of fathers, and who still hath cried,
From the first corse till he that died to-day,
'This must be so' . . . We pray you throw to earth
This unprevailing woe, and think of us
As of a father, for let the world take note
You are the most immediate to our throne,
And with no less nobility of love 110
Than that which dearest father bears his son,
Do I impart toward you . . . For your intent
In going back to school in Wittenberg,
It is most retrograde to our desire,
And we beseech you, bend you to remain
Here in the cheer and comfort of our eye,
Our chiefest courtier, cousin, and our son.
QUEEN. Let not thy mother lose her prayers, Hamlet,
I pray thee stay with us, go not to Wittenberg.
HAMLET. I shall in all my best obey you, madam. 120
KING. Why, 'tis a loving and a fair reply,
Be as ourself in Denmark. Madam, come.
This gentle and unforced accord of Hamlet
Sits smiling to my heart, in grace whereof,
No jocund health that Denmark drinks to-day,
But the great cannon to the clouds shall tell,
And the king's rouse the heaven shall bruit again,
Re-speaking earthly thunder; come away.
                    Flourish. Exeunt all but Hamlet
HAMLET. O, that this too too sullied flesh would melt,
Thaw and resolve itself into a dew, 130
Or that the Everlasting had not fixed
His canon 'gainst self-slaughter. O God, God,
How weary, stale, flat, and unprofitable
Seem to me all the uses of this world!
Fie on't, ah fie, 'tis an unweeded garden
That grows to seed, things rank and gross in nature
Possess it merely. That it should come to this,
But two months dead, nay not so much, not two,
So excellent a king, that was to this
Hyperion to a satyr, so loving to my mother, 140
That he might not beteem the winds of heaven
Visit her face too roughly—heaven and earth
Must I remember? why, she would hang on him
As if increase of appetite had grown
By what it fed on, and yet within a month,
Let me not think on't . . . frailty thy name is woman!

A little month or ere those shoes were old
With which she followed my poor father's body
Like Niobe all tears, why she, even she—
O God, a beast that wants discourse of reason 150
Would have mourned longer—married with my
uncle,
My father's brother, but no more like my father
Than I to Hercules, within a month,
Ere yet the salt of most unrighteous tears
Had left the flushing in her gallèd eyes
She married. O most wicked speed ... to post
With such dexterity to incestuous sheets!
It is not, nor it cannot come to good,
But break my heart, for I must hold my tongue.

Horatio, Marcellus and Barnardo enter

HORATIO. Hail to your lordship!
HAMLET.   I am glad to see you well; 160
Horatio—or I do forget my self!
HORATIO. The same, my lord, and your poor servant
ever.
HAMLET. Sir, my good friend, I'll change that name
with you.
And what make you from Wittenberg, Horatio?
Marcellus.
MARCELLUS. My good lord!
HAMLET. I am very glad to see you—good even, sir.
                              To Barnardo
But what in faith make you from Wittenberg?
HORATIO. A truant disposition, good my lord.
HAMLET. I would not hear your enemy say so, 170
Nor shall you do mine ear that violence
To make it truster of your own report
Against yourself. I know you are no truant,
But what is your affair in Elsinore?
We'll teach you to drink deep ere you depart.
HORATIO. My lord, I came to see your father's funeral.
HAMLET. I prithee thee do not mock me
fellow-student;
I think it was to see my mother's wedding.
HORATIO. Indeed, my lord, it followed hard upon.
HAMLET. Thrift, thrift, Horatio, the funeral baked
meats 180
Did coldly furnish forth the marriage tables.
Would I had met my dearest foe in heaven
Or ever I had seen that day, Horatio—
My father, methinks I see my father.
HORATIO. Where, my lord?
HAMLET.   In my mind's eye, Horatio.
HORATIO. I saw him once, a' was a goodly king—
HAMLET. A' was a man, take him for all in all,
I shall not look upon his like again.
HORATIO. My lord, I think I saw him yesternight.
HAMLET. Saw? who? 190
HORATIO. My lord, the king your father.
HAMLET.   The king my father!
HORATIO. Season your admiration for a while
With an attent ear till I may deliver
Upon the witness of these gentlemen
This marvel to you.
HAMLET.   For God's love let me hear!
HORATIO. Two nights together had these gentlemen,
Marcellus and Barnardo, on their watch
In the dead waste and middle of the night,
Been thus encountered. A figure like your father
Armèd at point exactly, cap-a-pe, 200

Appears before them, and with solemn march,
Goes slow and stately by them; thrice he walked
By their oppressed and fear-surprisèd eyes
Within his truncheon's length, whilst they distilled
Almost to jelly with the act of fear,
Stand dumb and speak not to him; this to me
In dreadful secrecy impart they did,
And I with them the third night kept the watch,
Where, as they had delivered, both in time,
Form of the thing, each word made true and good, 210
The apparition comes: I knew your father,
These hands are not more like.
HAMLET.   But where was this?
MARCELLUS. My lord, upon the platform where we
watch.
HAMLET. Did you not speak to it?
HORATIO.   My lord, I did,
But answer made it none, yet once methought
It lifted up it head, and did address
Itself to motion like as it would speak:
But even then the morning cock crew loud,
And at the sound it shrunk in haste away
And vanished from our sight.
HAMLET.   'Tis very strange. 220
HORATIO. As I do live my honoured lord 'tis true,
And we did think it writ down in our duty
To let you know of it.
HAMLET. Indeed, indeed, sirs, but this troubles me.
Hold you the watch to-night?
ALL.   We do, my lord.
HAMLET. Armed, say you?
ALL. Armed, my lord.
HAMLET. From top to toe?
ALL.   My lord, from head to foot.
HAMLET. Then saw you not his face.
HORATIO. O yes, my lord, he wore his beaver up. 230
HAMLET. What, looked he frowningly?
HORATIO. A countenance more in sorrow than in
anger.
HAMLET. Pale, or red?
HORATIO. Nay, very pale.
HAMLET.   And fixed his eyes upon you?
HORATIO. Most constantly.
HAMLET.   I would I had been there.
HORATIO. It would have much amazed you.
HAMLET. Very like, very like, stayed it long?
HORATIO. While one with moderate haste might tell a
hundred.
MARCELLUS, BARNARDO. Longer, longer.
HORATIO. Not when I saw't.
HAMLET.   His beard was grizzled, no? 240
HORATIO. It was as I have seen it in his life,
A sable silvered.
HAMLET.   I will watch to-night,
Perchance 'twill walk again.
HORATIO.   I war'nt it will.
HAMLET. If it assume my noble father's person,
I'll speak to it though hell itself should gape
And bid me hold my peace; I pray you all
If you have hitherto concealed this sight
Let it be tenable in your silence still,
And whatsomever else shall hap to-night,
Give it an understanding but no tongue. 250
I will requite your loves, so fare you well:
Upon the platform 'twixt eleven and twelve
I'll visit you.

ALL.   Our duty to your honour.

HAMLET. Your loves, as mine to you. Farewell.
They depart
My father's spirit (in arms!) all is not well,
I doubt some foul play, would the night were come,
Till then sit still my soul, foul deeds will rise,
Though all the earth o'erwhelm them, to men's
eyes.   *He goes*

Scene 3: *A room in the house of Polonius*

Enter Laertes and Ophelia his sister

LAERTES. My necessaries are embarked, farewell,
And sister, as the winds give benefit
And convoy is assistant, do not sleep,
But let me hear from you.

OPHELIA.   Do you doubt that?

LAERTES. For Hamlet, and the trifling of his favour,
Hold it a fashion, and a toy in blood,
A violet in the youth of primy nature,
Forward, not permanent, sweet, not lasting,
The perfume and suppliance of a minute,
No more.

OPHELIA.   No more but so?

LAERTES.   Think it no more.   10
For nature crescent does not grow alone
In thews and bulk, but as this temple waxes
The inward service of the mind and soul
Grows wide withal. Perhaps he loves you now,
And now no soil nor cautel doth besmirch
The virtue of his will. But you must fear,
His greatness weighed, his will is not his own,
For he himself is subject to his birth.
He may not, as unvalued persons do,
Carve for himself, for on his choice depends   20
The sanity and health of this whole state,
And therefore must his choice be circumscribed
Unto the voice and yielding of that body
Whereof he is the head. Then if he says he loves you,
It fits your wisdom so far to believe it
As he in his particular act and place
May give his saying deed, which is no further
Than the main voice of Denmark goes withal.
Then weigh what loss your honour may sustain
If with too credent ear you list his songs,   30
Or lose your heart, or your chaste treasure open
To his unmast'red importunity.
Fear it Ophelia, fear it my dear sister,
And keep you in the rear of your affection,
Out of the shot and danger of desire.
"The chariest maid is prodigal enough
"If she unmask her beauty to the moon."
"Virtue itself 'scapes not calumnious strokes."
"The canker galls the infants of the spring
"Too oft before their buttons be disclosed,   40
"And in the morn and liquid dew of youth
"Contagious blastments are most imminent."
Be wary then—best safety lies in fear,
Youth to itself rebels, though none else near.

OPHELIA. I shall the effect of this good lesson keep
As watchman to my heart. But good my brother
Do not, as some ungracious pastors do,
Show me the steep and thorny way to heaven,
Whiles like a puffed and reckless libertine
Himself the primrose path of dalliance treads,   50
And recks not his own rede.

Polonius enters

LAERTES.   O fear me not,
I stay too long—but here my father comes.
A double blessing is a double grace,
Occasion smiles upon a second leave.

POLONIUS. Yet here Laertes? aboard, aboard for
shame!
The wind sits in the shoulder of your sail,
And you are stayed for. There—my blessing with
thee,   *He lays his hand on Laertes' head*
And these few precepts in thy memory
Look thou character. Give thy thoughts no tongue,
Nor any unproportioned thought his act.   60
Be thou familiar, but by no means vulgar,
Those friends thou hast, and their adoption tried,
Grapple them unto thy soul with hoops of steel,
But do not dull thy palm with entertainment
Of each new-hatched unfledged courage. Beware
Of entrance to a quarrel, but being in,
Bear't that th'opposèd may beware of thee.
Give every man thy ear, but few thy voice,
Take each man's censure, but reserve thy
judgement.
Costly thy habit as thy purse can buy,   70
But not expressed in fancy; rich not gaudy.
For the apparel oft proclaims the man,
And they in France of the best rank and station,
Or of a most select and generous, chief in that:
Neither a borrower nor a lender be,
For loan oft loses both itself and friend,
And borrowing dulls the edge of husbandry;
This above all, to thine own self be true
And it must follow as the night the day
Thou canst not then be false to any man ...   80
Farewell—my blessing season this in thee.

LAERTES. Most humbly do I take my leave, my lord.

POLONIUS. The time invites you, go, your servants
tend.

LAERTES. Farewell, Ophelia, and remember well
What I have said to you.

OPHELIA.   'Tis in my memory locked,
And you yourself shall keep the key of it.

LAERTES. Farewell.   *He goes*

POLONIUS. What is't, Ophelia, he hath said to you?

OPHELIA. So please you, something touching the Lord
Hamlet.

POLONIUS. Marry, well bethought.   90
'Tis told me he hath very oft of late
Given private time to you, and you yourself
Have of your audience been most free and
bounteous.
If it be so—as so 'tis put on me,
And that in way of caution—I must tell you,
You do not understand yourself so clearly
As it behoves my daughter and your honour.
What is between you? give me up the truth.

OPHELIA. He hath, my lord, of late made many tenders
Of his affection to me.   100

POLONIUS. Affection, pooh! you speak like a green girl
Unsifted in such perilous circumstance.
Do you believe his tenders as you call them?

OPHELIA. I do not know, my lord, what I should
think.

POLONIUS. Marry, I will teach you—think yourself a
baby

That you have ta'en these tenders for true pay
Which are not sterling. Tender yourself more
    dearly,
Or (not to crack the wind of the poor phrase,
Running it thus) you'll tender me a fool.
OPHELIA. My lord, he hath importuned me with love 110
In honourable fashion.
POLONIUS. Ay, fashion you may call it, go to, go to.
OPHELIA. And hath given countenance to his speech,
    my lord,
With almost all the holy vows of heaven.
POLONIUS. Ay, springes to catch woodcocks. I do
    know
When the blood burns, how prodigal the soul
Lends the tongue vows. These blazes daughter,
Giving more light than heat, extinct in both,
Even in their promise, as it is a-making,
You must not take for fire. From this time   120
Be something scanter of your maiden presence,
Set your entreatments at a higher rate
Than a command to parle; for Lord Hamlet,
Believe so much in him that he is young,
And with a larger tether may he walk
Than may be given you: in few Ophelia,
Do not believe his vows, for they are brokers
Not of that dye which their investments show,
But mere implorators of unholy suits,
Breathing like sanctified and pious bonds   130
The better to beguile ... This is for all,
I would not in plain terms from this time forth
Have you so slander any moment leisure
As to give words or talk with the Lord Hamlet.
Look to't I charge you, come your ways.
OPHELIA. I shall obey, my lord.   *They go*

Scene 4: *The platform on the battlements*

Enter Hamlet, Horatio and Marcellus

HAMLET. The air bites shrewdly, it is very cold.
HORATIO. It is a nipping and an eager air.
HAMLET. What hour now?
HORATIO.   I think it lacks of twelve.
MARCELLUS. No, it is struck.
HORATIO. Indeed? I heard it not—it then draws near
    the season,
Wherein the spirit held his wont to walk.
         A flourish of trumpets, and ordnance shot off
What does this mean, my lord?
HAMLET. The king doth wake to-night and takes his
    rouse,
Keeps wassail and the swagg'ring upspring reels:
And as he drains his draughts of Rhenish down,   10
The kettle-drum and trumpet thus bray out
The triumph of his pledge.
HORATIO.   Is it a custom?
HAMLET. Ay marry is't,
But to my mind, though I am native here
And to the manner born, it is a custom
More honoured in the breach than the observance.
This heavy-headed revel east and west
Makes us traduced and taxed of other nations.
They clepe us drunkards, and with swinish phrase
Soil our addition, and indeed it takes   20
From our achievements, though performed at
    height,
The pith and marrow of our attribute.

So, oft it chances in particular men,
That for some vicious mole of nature in them,
As in their birth, wherein they are not guilty
(Since nature cannot choose his origin),
By the o'ergrowth of some complexion,
Oft breaking down the pales and forts of reason,
Or by some habit, that too much o'er-leavens
The form of plausive manners—that these men,   30
Carrying I say the stamp of one defect,
Being nature's livery, or fortune's star,
His virtues else be they as pure as grace,
As infinite as man may undergo,
Shall in the general censure take corruption
From that particular fault: the dram of evil
Doth all the noble substance of a doubt,
To his own scandal.

The Ghost appears

HORATIO.   Look, my lord, it comes!
HAMLET. Angels and ministers of grace defend us!
Be thou a spirit of health, or goblin damned,   40
Bring with thee airs from heaven, or blasts from
    hell,
Be thy intents wicked, or charitable,
Thou com'st in such a questionable shape,
That I will speak to thee. I'll call thee Hamlet,
King, father, royal Dane. O, answer me!
Let me not burst in ignorance, but tell
Why thy canonized bones hearséd in death
Have burst their cerements? why the sepulchre,
Wherein we saw thee quietly inurned,
Hath oped his ponderous and marble jaws   50
To cast thee up again? what may this mean
That thou, dead corse, again in complete steel
Revisits thus the glimpses of the moon,
Making night hideous, and we fools of nature
So horridly to shake our disposition
With thoughts beyond the reaches of our souls?
Say why is this? wherefore? what should we do?
                                   The Ghost beckons
HORATIO. It beckons you to go away with it,
As if it some impartment did desire
To you alone.
MARCELLUS.   Look with what courteous action 60
It waves you to a more removéd ground,
But do not go with it.
HORATIO.   No, by no means.
HAMLET. It will not speak, then I will follow it.
HORATIO. Do not my lord.
HAMLET.   Why, what should be the fear?
I do not set my life at a pin's fee,
And for my soul, what can it do to that
Being a thing immortal as itself;
It waves me forth again, I'll follow it.
HORATIO. What if it tempt you toward the flood, my
    lord,
Or to the dreadful summit of the cliff   70
That beetles o'er his base into the sea,
And there assume some other horrible form,
Which might deprive your sovereignty of reason,
And draw you into madness? think of it—
The very place puts toys of desperation,
Without more motive, into every brain
That looks so many fathoms to the sea
And hears it roar beneath.

HAMLET.   It waves me still.
  Go on, I'll follow thee.
MARCELLUS. You shall not go, my lord.
HAMLET.   Hold off your hands. 80
HORATIO. Be ruled, you shall not go.
HAMLET.   My fate cries out,
  And makes each petty artere in this body
  As hardy as the Nemean lion's nerve;
  Still am I called, unhand me gentlemen,
  By heaven I'll make a ghost of him that lets me!
  I say, away! go on, I'll follow thee.
                    The Ghost goes, Hamlet following
HORATIO. He waxes desperate with imagination.
MARCELLUS. Let's follow, 'tis not fit thus to obey him.
HORATIO. Have after—to what issue will this come?
MARCELLUS. Something is rotten in the state of
  Denmark.   90
HORATIO. Heaven will direct it.
MARCELLUS.   Nay, let's follow him.
                                      They follow

           Scene 5: *At the foot of the castle wall*

Enter the Ghost, and Hamlet after

HAMLET. Whither wilt thou lead me? speak, I'll go no
  further.
GHOST. Mark me.
HAMLET.   I will.
GHOST.   My hour is almost come,
  When I to sulph'rous and tormenting flames
  Must render up myself.
HAMLET.   Alas poor ghost!
GHOST. Pity me not, but lend thy serious hearing
  To what I shall unfold.
HAMLET.   Speak, I am bound to hear.
GHOST. So art thou to revenge, when thou shalt hear.
HAMLET. What?
GHOST. I am thy father's spirit,
  Doomed for a certain term to walk the night,   10
  And for the day confined to fast in fires,
  Till the foul crimes done in my days of nature
  Are burnt and purged away: but that I am forbid
  To tell the secrets of my prison-house,
  I could a tale unfold whose lightest word
  Would harrow up thy soul, freeze thy young blood,
  Make thy two eyes like stars start from their spheres,
  Thy knotted and combinéd locks to part,
  And each particular hair to stand an end,
  Like quills upon the fretful porpentine.   20
  But this eternal blazon must not be
  To ears of flesh and blood. List, list, O list!
  If thou didst ever thy dear father love——
HAMLET. O God!
GHOST. Revenge his foul and most unnatural murder.
HAMLET. Murder!
GHOST. Murder most foul, as in the best it is,
  But this most foul, strange and unnatural.
HAMLET. Haste me to know't, that I with wings as
  swift
  As meditation or the thoughts of love,   30
  May sweep to my revenge.
GHOST.   I find thee apt,
  And duller shouldst thou be than the fat weed
  That rots itself in ease on Lethe wharf,
  Wouldst thou not stir in this; now Hamlet hear,
  'Tis given out, that sleeping in my orchard,

A serpent stung me, so the whole ear of Denmark
Is by a forgéd process of my death
Rankly abused: but know, thou noble youth,
The serpent that did sting thy father's life
Now wears his crown.
HAMLET.   O, my prophetic soul! 40
  My uncle?
GHOST. Ay, that incestuous, that adulterate beast,
  With witchcraft of his wit, with traitorous gifts,
  O wicked wit and gifts, that have the power
  So to seduce; won to his shameful lust
  The will of my most seeming-virtuous queen;
  O Hamlet, what a falling-off was there!
  From me whose love was of that dignity,
  That it went hand in hand even with the vow
  I made to her in marriage, and to decline   50
  Upon a wretch whose natural gifts were poor
  To those of mine;
  But virtue, as it never will be moved,
  Though lewdness court it in a shape of heaven,
  So lust, though to a radiant angel linked,
  Will sate itself in a celestial bed
  And prey on garbage.
  But soft, methinks I scent the morning air,
  Brief let me be; sleeping within my orchard,
  My custom always of the afternoon,   60
  Upon my secure hour thy uncle stole
  With juice of cursed hebona in a vial,
  And in the porches of my ears did pour
  The leperous distilment, whose effect
  Holds such an enmity with blood of man,
  That swift as quicksilver it courses through
  The natural gates and alleys of the body,
  And with a sudden vigour it doth posset
  And curd, like eager droppings into milk,
  The thin and wholesome blood; so did it mine,   70
  And a most instant tetter barked about
  Most lazar-like with vile and loathsome crust
  All my smooth body....
  Thus was I sleeping by a brother's hand,
  Of life, of crown, of queen at once dispatched,
  Cut even in the blossoms of my sin,
  Unhouseled, disappointed, unaneled,
  No reck'ning made, but sent to my account
  With all my imperfections on my head.
  O, horrible! O, horrible! most horrible!   80
  If thou hast nature in thee bear it not,
  Let not the royal bed of Denmark be
  A couch for luxury and damnéd incest....
  But howsomever thou pursues this act,
  Taint not thy mind, nor let thy soul contrive
  Against thy mother aught—leave her to heaven,
  And to those thorns that in her bosom lodge
  To prick and sting her. Fare thee well at once,
  The glow-worm shows the matin to be near,
  And 'gins to pale his uneffectual fire.   90
  Adieu, adieu, adieu, remember me.
                                The Ghost vanishes
HAMLET. O all you host of heaven! O earth! what else?
  And shall I couple hell? O fie! Hold, hold, my heart,
  And you, my sinews, grow not instant old,
  But bear me stiffly up ... Remember thee?
  Ay thou poor ghost whiles memory holds a seat
  In this distracted globe. Remember thee?
  Yea, from the table of my memory
  I'll wipe away all trivial fond records,

All saws of books, all forms, all pressures past   100
That youth and observation copied there,
And thy commandment all alone shall live
Within the book and volume of my brain,
Unmixed with baser matter—yes by heaven!
O most pernicious woman!
O villain, villain, smiling, damnéd villain!
My tables, meet it is I set it down   *He writes*
That one may smile, and smile, and be a villain,
At least I am sure it may be so in Denmark ...
So, uncle, there you are. Now, to my Word,   110
It is 'Adieu, adieu, remember me.'...
I have sworn't.

Enter Horatio and Marcellus

HORATIO. My lord, my lord!
MARCELLUS.   Lord Hamlet!
HORATIO.   Heaven secure him!
HAMLET. So be it!
MARCELLUS. Illo, ho, ho, my lord!
HAMLET. Hillo, ho, ho, boy! come, bird, come.
MARCELLUS. How is't, my noble lord?
HORATIO.   What news, my lord?
HAMLET. O, wonderful!
HORATIO.   Good my lord, tell it.
HAMLET. No, you will reveal it.
HORATIO. Not I, my lord, by heaven.
MARCELLUS.   Nor I, my lord.   120
HAMLET. How say you then, would heart of man once
   think it?
   But you'll be secret?
HORATIO, MARCELLUS.   Ay, by heaven, my lord.
HAMLET. There's ne'er a villain dwelling in all
   Denmark
   But he's an arrant knave.
HORATIO. There needs no ghost, my lord, come from
   the grave,
   To tell us this.
HAMLET.   Why right, you are in the right,
   And so without more circumstance at all
   I hold it fit that we shake hands and part,
   You, as your business and desire shall point you,
   For every man hath business and desire   130
   Such as it is, and for my own poor part,
   Look you, I will go pray.
HORATIO. These are but wild and whirling words, my
   lord.
HAMLET. I am sorry they offend you, heartily,
   Yes, faith, heartily.
HORATIO.   There's no offence, my lord.
HAMLET. Yes, by Saint Patrick, but there is, Horatio,
   And much offence too—touching this vision here,
   It is an honest ghost that let me tell you—
   For your desire to know what is between us,
   O'ermaster't as you may. And now, good friends,   140
   As you are friends, scholars, and soldiers,
   Give me one poor request.
HORATIO. What is't, my lord? we will.
HAMLET. Never make known what you have seen
   to-night.
BOTH. My lord, we will not.
HAMLET.   Nay, but swear't.
HORATIO.   In faith,
   My lord, not I.
MARCELLUS.   Nor I, my lord, in faith.
HAMLET. Upon my sword.

MARCELLUS.   We have sworn, my lord, already.
HAMLET. Indeed, upon my sword, indeed.
GHOST [*beneath*]. Swear.
HAMLET. Ha, ha, boy! say'st thou so? art thou there,
   truepenny?   150
   Come on, you hear this fellow in the cellarage,
   Consent to swear.
HORATIO.   Propose the oath, my lord.
HAMLET. Never to speak of this that you have seen,
   Swear by my sword.
GHOST [*beneath*]. Swear.
HAMLET. Hic et ubique? then we'll shift our ground:
   Come hither gentlemen,
   And lay your hands again upon my sword.
   Swear by my sword,
   Never to speak of this that you have heard.   160
GHOST [*beneath*]. Swear by his sword.
HAMLET. Well said, old mole! canst work i'th'earth so
   fast?
   A worthy pioner! Once more remove, good
   friends.
HORATIO. O day and night, but this is wondrous
   strange!
HAMLET. And therefore as a stranger give it welcome.
   There are more things in heaven and earth, Horatio,
   Than are dreamt of in your philosophy.
   But come—
   Here as before, never, so help you mercy
   (How strange or odd some'er I bear myself,   170
   As I perchance hereafter shall think meet
   To put an antic disposition on)
   That you at such times seeing me, never shall
   With arms encumbered thus, or this head-shake,
   Or by pronouncing of some doubtful phrase,
   As 'Well, well, we know,' or 'We could an if we
   would,'
   Or 'If we list to speak,' or 'There be an if they
   might,'
   Or such ambiguous giving out, to note
   That you know aught of me—this do swear,
   So grace and mercy at your most need help you!   180
GHOST [*beneath*]. Swear.
HAMLET. Rest, rest, perturbéd spirit! [*they swear*] So,
   gentlemen,
   With all my love I do commend me to you,
   And what so poor a man as Hamlet is
   May do t'express his love and friending to you
   God willing shall not lack. Let us go in together,
   And still your fingers on your lips I pray.
   The time is out of joint, O cursèd spite,
   That ever I was born to set it right!
   Nay come, let's go together.   *They go*   190

ACT 2

Scene 1: *A room in the house of Polonius*

Polonius and Reynaldo

POLONIUS. Give him this money, and these notes,
   Reynaldo,
REYNALDO. I will, my lord.
POLONIUS. You shall do marvellous wisely, good
   Reynaldo,
   Before you visit him, to make inquire
   Of his behaviour.
REYNALDO.   My lord, I did intend it.

POLONIUS. Marry, well said, very well said; look you sir,
Inquire me first what Danskers are in Paris,
And how, and who, what means, and where they keep,
What company, at what expense, and finding
By this encompassment and drift of question   10
That they do know my son, come you more nearer
Than your particular demands will touch it,
Take you as 'twere some distant knowledge of him,
As thus, 'I know his father, and his friends,
And in part him'—do you mark this, Reynaldo?
REYNALDO. Ay, very well, my lord.
POLONIUS. 'And in part him, but,' you may say, 'not well,
But if't be he I mean, he's very wild,
Addicted so and so.' And there put on him
What forgeries you please, marry none so rank   20
As may dishonour him, take heed of that,
But sir such wanton, wild, and usual slips,
As are companions noted and most known
To youth and liberty.
REYNALDO.   As gaming, my lord.
POLONIUS. Ay, or drinking, fencing, swearing, quarrelling,
Drabbing—you may go so far.
REYNALDO. My lord, that would dishonour him.
POLONIUS. Faith no, as you may season it in the charge.
You must not put another scandal on him,
That he is open to incontinency,   30
That's not my meaning, but breathe his faults so quaintly
That they may seem the taints of liberty,
The flash and outbreak of a fiery mind,
A savageness in unreclaiméd blood,
Of general assault.
REYNALDO.   But, my good lord——
POLONIUS. Wherefore should you do this?
REYNALDO.   Ay my lord,
I would know that.
POLONIUS.   Marry sir, here's my drift,
And I believe it is a fetch of warrant,
You laying these slight sullies on my son,
As 'twere a thing a little soiled i'th' working,   40
Mark you, your party in converse, him you would sound,
Having ever seen in the prenominate crimes
The youth you breathe of guilty, be assured
He closes with you in this consequence,
'Good sir,' or so, or 'friend,' or 'gentleman,'
According to the phrase, or the addition
Of man and country.
REYNALDO.   Very good, my lord.
POLONIUS. And then sir, does a' this, a' does, what was I about to say?
By the mass I was about to say something.
Where did I leave?
REYNALDO.   At 'closes in the consequence,'   50
At 'friend, or so, and gentleman.'
POLONIUS. At 'closes in the consequence.' ay marry—
He closes thus, 'I know the gentleman,
I saw him yesterday, or th'other day,
Or then, or then, with such or such, and as you say,
There was a' gaming, there o'ertook in's rouse,
There falling out at tennis,' or perchance,

'I saw him enter such a house of sale,'
Videlicet, a brothel, or so forth. See you now,
Your bait of falsehood takes this carp of truth,   60
And thus do we of wisdom, and of reach,
With windlasses, and with assays of bias,
By indirections find directions out,
So by my former lecture and advice
Shall you my son; you have me, have you not?
REYNALDO. My lord, I have.
POLONIUS.   God bye ye, fare ye well.
REYNALDO. Good, my lord.
POLONIUS. Observe his inclination in yourself.
REYNALDO. I shall, my lord.
POLONIUS. And let him ply his music.
REYNALDO.   Well, my lord.   *He goes*   70
POLONIUS. Farewell.

Ophelia enters

                    How now Ophelia, what's the matter?
OPHELIA. O my lord, my lord, I have been so affrighted!
POLONIUS. With what, i'th'name of God?
OPHELIA. My lord, as I was sewing in my closet,
Lord Hamlet with his doublet all unbraced,
No hat upon his head, his stockings fouled,
Ungart'red, and down-gyvéd to his ankle,
Pale as his shirt, his knees knocking each other,
And with a look so piteous in purport
As if he had been looséd out of hell   80
To speak of horrors—he comes before me.
POLONIUS. Mad for thy love?
OPHELIA.   My lord, I do not know,
But truly I do fear it.
POLONIUS.   What said he?
OPHELIA. He took me by the wrist, and held me hard,
Then goes he to the length of all his arm,
And with his other hand thus o'er his brow,
He falls to such perusal of my face
As a' would draw it. Long stayed he so,
At last, a little shaking of mine arm,
And thrice his head thus waving up and down,   90
He raised a sigh so piteous and profound
As it did seem to shatter all his bulk,
And end his being; that done, he lets me go,
And with his head over his shoulder turned
He seemed to find his way without his eyes,
For out adoors he went without their helps,
And to the last bended their light on me.
POLONIUS. Come, go with me. I will go seek the king.
This is the very ecstasy of love,
Whose violent property fordoes itself,   100
And leads the will to desperate undertakings,
As oft as any passion under heaven
That does afflict our natures: I am sorry—
What, have you given him any hard words of late?
OPHELIA. No, my good lord, but as you did command
I did repel his letters, and denied
His access to me.
POLONIUS.   That hath made him mad.
I am sorry that with better heed and judgement
I had not quoted him. I feared he did but trifle
And meant to wreck thee, but beshrew my jealousy: 110
By heaven it is as proper to our age
To cast beyond ourselves in our opinions,
As it is common for the younger sort
To lack discretion; come, go we to the king.

This must be known, which, being kept close,
  might move
More grief to hide, than hate to utter love.
Come.   *They go*

Scene 2: An audience chamber in the castle

*A flourish of trumpets. The King and Queen enter followed
by Rosencrantz, Guildenstern and attendants*

KING. Welcome, dear Rosencrantz and Guildenstern!
Moreover that we much did long to see you,
The need we have to use you did provoke
Our hasty sending. Something have you heard
Of Hamlet's transformation—so call it,
Sith nor th'exterior nor the inward man
Resembles that it was. What it should be,
More than his father's death, that thus hath put him
So much from th'understanding of himself,
I cannot dream of: I entreat you both,   10
That being of so young days brought up with him,
And sith so neighboured to his youth and haviour,
That you vouchsafe your rest here in our court
Some little time, so by your companies
To draw him on to pleasures, and to gather
So much as from occasion you may glean
Whether aught to us unknown afflicts him thus,
That opened lies within our remedy.
QUEEN. Good gentlemen, he hath much talked of you,
And sure I am two men there are not living   20
To whom he more adheres. If it will please you
To show us so much gentry and good will
As to expend your time with us awhile,
For the supply and profit of our hope,
Your visitation shall receive such thanks
As fits a king's remembrance.
ROSENCRANTZ.   Both your majesties
Might by the sovereign power you have of us,
Put your dread pleasures more into command
Than to entreaty.
GUILDENSTERN.   But we both obey,
And here give up ourselves in the full bent,   30
To lay our service freely at your feet
To be commanded.
KING. Thanks Rosencrantz, and gentle Guildenstern.
QUEEN. Thanks Guildenstern, and gentle Rosencrantz,
And I beseech you instantly to visit
My too much changéd son. Go some of you
And bring these gentlemen where Hamlet is.
GUILDENSTERN. Heavens make our presence and our
  practices
Pleasant and helpful to him!
QUEEN.   Ay, amen!
        Rosencrantz and Guildenstern depart

Polonius enters

POLONIUS. The ambassadors from Norway, my good
  lord,   40
Are joyfully returned.
KING. Thou still hast been the father of good news.
POLONIUS. Have I, my lord? Assure you, my good
  liege,
I hold my duty as I hold my soul,
Both to my God and to my gracious king;
And I do think, or else this brain of mine
Hunts not the trail of policy so sure
As it hath used to do, that I have found

The very cause of Hamlet's lunacy.
KING. O speak of that, that do I long to hear.   50
POLONIUS. Give first admittance to th'ambassadors.
My news shall be the fruit to that great feast.
KING. Thyself do grace to them, and bring them in.
                          Polonius goes
He tells me, my dear Gertrude, he hath found
The head and source of all your son's distemper.
QUEEN. I doubt it is no other but the main,
His father's death and our o'erhasty marriage.
KING. Well, we shall sift him.

Polonius returns with Valtemand and Cornelius

                       Welcome, my good friends!
Say Valtemand, what from our brother Norway?
VALTEMAND. Most fair return of greetings and desires; 60
Upon our first, he sent out to suppress
His nephew's levies, which to him appeared
To be a preparation 'gainst the Polack,
But better looked into, he truly found
It was against your highness, whereat grieved
That so his sickness, age and impotence
Was falsely borne in hand, sends out arrests
On Fortinbras, which he in brief obeys,
Receives rebuke from Norway, and in fine,
Makes vow before his uncle never more   70
To give th'assay of arms against your majesty:
Whereon old Norway, overcome with joy,
Gives him threescore thousand crowns in annual
  fee,
And his commission to employ those soldiers,
So levied, as before, against the Polack,
With an entreaty, herein further shown,
That it might please you to give quiet pass
Through your dominions for this enterprise,
On such regards of safety and allowance
As therein are set down.   *He proffers a paper*
KING.   It likes us well,   80
And at our more considered time, we'll read,
Answer, and think upon this business:
Meantime, we thank you for your well-took
  labour.
Go to your rest, at night we'll feast together.
Most welcome home!
        Valtemand and Cornelius depart
POLONIUS.   This business is well ended....
My liege and madam, to expostulate
What majesty should be, what duty is,
Why day is day, night night, and time is time,
Were nothing but to waste night, day and time.
Therefore since brevity is the soul of wit,   90
And tediousness the limbs and outward flourishes,
I will be brief—your noble son is mad:
Mad call I it, for to define true madness,
What is't but to be nothing else but mad?
But let that go.
QUEEN.   More matter, with less art.
POLONIUS. Madam, I swear I use no art at all.
That he is mad 'tis true, 'tis true 'tis pity,
And pity 'tis 'tis true—a foolish figure,
But farewell it, for I will use no art.
Mad let us grant him then, and now remains   100
That we find out the cause of this effect,
Or rather say, the cause of this defect,
For this effect defective comes by cause:
Thus it remains, and the remainder thus.

Perpend.
I have a daughter, have while she is mine,
Who in her duty and obedience, mark,
Hath given me this, now gather and surmise.
[*he reads*] 'To the celestial, and my soul's idol, the
most beautified Ophelia,'— 110
That's an ill phrase, a vile phrase, 'beautified' is a vile
phrase, but you shall hear. Thus: *He reads*
'In her excellent white bosom, these, etc.'—
QUEEN. Came this from Hamlet to her?
POLONIUS. Good madam stay awhile, I will be
faithful—   *He reads*
          'Doubt thou the stars are fire,
            Doubt that the sun doth move,
          Doubt truth to be a liar,
            But never doubt I love.
O dear Ophelia, I am ill at these numbers, I have 120
not art to reckon my groans, but that I love thee
best, O most best, believe it. Adieu.
        Thine evermore, most dear lady, whilst
          this machine is to him, HAMLET.'
This in obedience hath my daughter shown me,
And more above hath his solicitings,
As they fell out by time, by means, and place,
All given to mine ear.
KING.   But how hath she
Received his love?
POLONIUS.   What do you think of me?
KING. As of a man faithful and honourable.   130
POLONIUS. I would fain prove so. But what might you
think
When I had seen this hot love on the wing,
As I perceived it (I must tell you that)
Before my daughter told me, what might you,
Or my dear majesty your queen here think,
If I had played the desk or table-book,
Or given my heart a working mute and dumb,
Or looked upon this love with idle sight,
What might you think? no, I went round to work,
And my young mistress thus I did bespeak—   140
'Lord Hamlet is a prince out of thy star,
This must not be': and then I prescripts gave her
That she should lock herself from his resort,
Admit no messengers, receive no tokens.
Which done, she took the fruits of my advice:
And he repelléd, a short tale to make,
Fell into a sadness, then into a fast,
Thence to a watch, thence into a weakness,
Thence to a lightness, and by this declension,
Into the madness wherein now he raves,   150
And all we mourn for.
KING.   Do you think 'tis this?
QUEEN. It may be, very like.
POLONIUS. Hath there been such a time, I would fain
know that,
That I have positively said ''Tis so,'
When it proved otherwise?
KING.   Not that I know.
POLONIUS. Take this from this, if this be otherwise;
          He points to his head and shoulder
If circumstances lead me, I will find
Where truth is hid, though it were hid indeed
Within the Centre.

*Hamlet, reading a book, enters at the back; he pauses a
moment, unobserved*

KING.   How may we try it further?
POLONIUS. You know sometimes he walks four hours
together   150
Here in the lobby.
QUEEN.   So he does, indeed.
POLONIUS. At such a time I'll loose my daughter to
him.
Be you and I behind an arras then,
Mark the encounter, if he love her not,
And be not from his reason fall'n thereon,
Let me be no assistant for a state,
But keep a farm and carters.
KING.   We will try it.

Hamlet comes forward, his eyes on the book

QUEEN. But look where sadly the poor wretch comes
reading.
POLONIUS. Away, I do beseech you both away,
I'll board him presently, O give me leave.   170
                        The King and Queen go
How does my good Lord Hamlet?
HAMLET. Well, God-a-mercy.
POLONIUS. Do you know me, my lord?
HAMLET. Excellent well, you are a fishmonger.
POLONIUS. Not I, my lord.
HAMLET. Then I would you were so honest a man.
POLONIUS. Honest, my lord?
HAMLET. Ay sir, to be honest as this world goes, is to
be one man picked out of ten thousand.
POLONIUS. That's very true, my lord.   180
HAMLET. For if the sun breed maggots in a dead dog,
being a good kissing carrion.... have you a
daughter?
POLONIUS. I have, my lord.
HAMLET. Let her not walk i'th'sun. Conception is a
blessing, but as your daughter may conceive, friend
look to't.
POLONIUS [*aside*]. How say you by that? still harping
on my daughter, yet he knew me not at first, a' said
I was a fishmonger. A' is far gone, far gone, and 190
truly in my youth I suffered much extremity for
love, very near this.... I'll speak to him again....
What do you read, my lord?
HAMLET. Words, words, words.
POLONIUS. What is the matter, my lord?
HAMLET. Between who?
POLONIUS. I mean the matter that you read, my lord.
HAMLET. Slanders, sir; for the satirical rogue says here
that old men have grey beards, that their faces are
wrinkled, their eyes purging thick amber and plum- 200
tree gum, and that they have a plentiful lack of wit,
together with most weak hams—all which, sir,
though I most powerfully and potently believe, yet
I hold it not honesty to have it thus set down, for
yourself, sir, shall grow old as I am ... if like a crab
you could go backward.
POLONIUS [*aside*]. Though this be madness, yet there is
method in't.
Will you walk out of the air, my lord?
HAMLET. Into my grave.   210
POLONIUS [*aside*]. Indeed, that's out of the air; how
pregnant sometimes his replies are! a happiness that
often madness hits on, which reason and sanity could
not so prosperously be delivered of. I will leave him,
and suddenly contrive the means of meeting
between him and my daughter.

My honourable lord, I will most humbly take my
leave of you.

HAMLET. You cannot, sir, take from me any thing that
I will more willingly part withal: except my life, 220
except my life, except my life.

POLONIUS. Fare you well, my lord.

HAMLET. These tedious old fools!

Rosencrantz and Guildenstern enter

POLONIUS. You go to seek the Lord Hamlet, there he
is.

ROSENCRANTZ [*to Polonius*]. God save you, sir!
Polonius goes

GUILDENSTERN. My honoured lord!

ROSENCRANTZ. My most dear lord!

HAMLET. My excellent good friends! How dost thou,
Guildenstern?
Ah, Rosencrantz! Good lads, how do you both? 230

ROSENCRANTZ. As the indifferent children of the earth.

GUILDENSTERN. Happy, in that we are not over-happy,
On Fortune's cap we are not the very button.

HAMLET. Nor the soles of her shoe?

ROSENCRANTZ. Neither, my lord.

HAMLET. Then you live about her waist, or in the
middle of her favours?

GUILDENSTERN. Faith, her privates we.

HAMLET. In the secret parts of fortune? O most true,
she is a strumpet. What's the news? 240

ROSENCRANTZ. None, my lord, but that the world's
grown honest.

HAMLET. Then is doomsday near. But your news is not
true. Let me question more in particular: what have
you, my good friends, deserved at the hands of
Fortune, that she sends you to prison hither?

GUILDENSTERN. Prison, my lord!

HAMLET. Denmark's a prison.

ROSENCRANTZ. Then is the world one.

HAMLET. A goodly one, in which there are many con- 250
fines, wards and dungeons; Denmark being one
o'th'worst.

ROSENCRANTZ. We think not so, my lord.

HAMLET. Why, then 'tis none to you; for there is
nothing either good or bad, but thinking makes it
so: to me it is a prison.

ROSENCRANTZ. Why, then your ambition makes it
one: 'tis too narrow for your mind.

HAMLET. O God! I could be bounded in a nut-shell,
and count myself a king of infinite space; were it 260
not that I have bad dreams.

GUILDENSTERN. Which dreams, indeed, are ambition:
for the very substance of the ambitious is merely the
shadow of a dream.

HAMLET. A dream itself is but a shadow.

ROSENCRANTZ. Truly, and I hold ambition of so airy
and light a quality, that it is but a shadow's shadow.

HAMLET. Then are our beggars bodies, and our monarchs and outstretched heroes the beggars' shadows
... Shall we to th' court? for, by my fay, I cannot 270
reason.

ROSENCRANTZ, GUILDENSTERN. We'll wait upon you.

HAMLET. No such matter: I will not sort you with the
rest of my servants; for to speak to you like an
honest man, I am most dreadfully attended.... But,
in the beaten way of friendship, what make you at
Elsinore?

ROSENCRANTZ. To visit you, my lord, no other occasion.

HAMLET. Beggar that I am, I am even poor in thanks, 280
but I thank you—and sure, dear friends, my thanks
are too dear a halfpenny: were you not sent for? is
it your own inclining? is it a free visitation? come,
come, deal justly with me, come, come, nay speak.

GUILDENSTERN. What should we say, my lord?

HAMLET. Why, any thing but to th'purpose ... You
were sent for, and there is a kind of confession in
your looks, which your modesties have not craft
enough to colour—I know the good king and queer
have sent for you. 290

ROSENCRANTZ. To what end, my lord?

HAMLET. That you must teach me: but let me conjure
you, by the rights of our fellowship, by the consonancy of our youth, by the obligation of our ever-
preserved love, and by what more dear a better
proposer can charge you withal, be even and direct
with me whether you were sent for or no?

ROSENCRANTZ [*aside to Guildenstern*]. What say you?

HAMLET [*aside*]. Nay then, I have an eye of you!
[*aloud*] If you love me, hold not off. 300

GUILDENSTERN. My lord, we were sent for.

HAMLET. I will tell you why, so shall my anticipation
prevent your discovery, and your secrecy to the
king and queen moult no feather. I have of late, but
wherefore I know not, lost all my mirth, forgone all
custom of exercises: and indeed it goes so heavily
with my disposition, that this goodly frame the
earth, seems to me a sterile promontory, this most
excellent canopy the air, look you, this brave
o'erhanging firmament, this majestical roof fretted 310
with golden fire, why it appeareth nothing to me
but a foul and pestilent congregation of vapours....
What a piece of work is a man, how noble in
reason, how infinite in faculties, in form and
moving, how express and admirable in action, how
like an angel in apprehension, how like a god: the
beauty of the world; the paragon of animals; and yet
to me, what is this quintessence of dust? man delights
not me, no, nor woman neither, though by your
smiling you seem to say so. 320

ROSENCRANTZ. My lord, there was no such stuff in my
thoughts.

HAMLET. Why did ye laugh then, when I said 'man
delights not me'?

ROSENCRANTZ. To think, my lord, if you delight not
in man, what lenten entertainment the players shall
receive from you. We coted them on the way, and
hither are they coming to offer you service.

HAMLET. He that plays the King shall be welcome, his
majesty shall have tribute on me, the adventurous 330
Knight shall use his foil and target, the Lover shall
not sigh gratis, the Humorous Man shall end his part
in peace, the Clown shall make those laugh whose
lungs are tickle o'th'sere, and the Lady shall say her
mind freely ... or the blank verse shall halt for't.
What players are they?

ROSENCRANTZ. Even those you were wont to take such
delight in, the tragedians of the city.

HAMLET. How chances it they travel? their residence
both in reputation and profit was better both ways. 340

ROSENCRANTZ. I think their inhibition comes by the
means of the late innovation.

HAMLET. Do they hold the same estimation they did

when I was in the city; are they so followed?

ROSENCRANTZ. No, indeed, are they not.

HAMLET. How comes it? do they grow rusty?

ROSENCRANTZ. Nay, their endeavour keeps in the wonted pace; but there is, sir, an aery of children, little eyases, that cry out on the top of question, and are most tyrannically clapped for't: these are now the fashion, and so berattle the common stages (so they call them) that many wearing rapiers are afraid of goose-quills, and dare scarce come thither. 350

HAMLET. What, are they children? who maintains 'em? how are they escoted? Will they pursue the quality no longer than they can sing? will they not say afterwards if they should grow themselves to common players (as it is like most will if their means are not better) their writers do them wrong, to make them exclaim against their own succession? 360

ROSENCRANTZ. Faith, there has been much to-do on both sides: and the nation holds it no sin to tarre them to controversy. There was, for a while, no money bid for argument, unless the Poet and the Player went to cuffs in the question.

HAMLET. Is't possible?

GUILDENSTERN. O, there has been much throwing about of brains.

HAMLET. Do the boys carry it away?

ROSENCRANTZ. Ay, that they do my lord, Hercules and his load too. 370

HAMLET. It is not very strange, for my uncle is king of Denmark, and those that would make mows at him while my father lived, give twenty, forty, fifty, a hundred ducats apiece for his picture in little. 'Sblood, there is something in this more than natural, if philosophy could find it out.

A flourish of trumpets heard

GUILDENSTERN. There are the players.

HAMLET. Gentlemen, you are welcome to Elsinore [*he bows*]. Your hands? come then, th'appurtenance of welcome is fashion and ceremony; let me comply with you in this garb ... lest my extent to the players, which I tell you must show fairly outwards, should more appear like entertainment than yours ... You are welcome: but my uncle-father, and aunt-mother, are deceived. 380

GUILDENSTERN. In what, my dear lord?

HAMLET. I am but mad north-north-west; when the wind is southerly, I know a hawk from a handsaw.

Polonius enters

POLONIUS. Well be with you, gentlemen! 390

HAMLET [*aside*]. Hark you Guildenstern, and you too, at each ear a hearer—that great baby you see there is not yet out of his swaddling-clouts.

ROSENCRANTZ. Happily he is the second time come to them, for they say an old man is twice a child.

HAMLET. I will prophesy, he comes to tell me of the players, mark it.
[*raises his voice*] You say right sir, a Monday morning, 'twas then indeed.

POLONIUS. My lord, I have news to tell you. 400

HAMLET. My lord, I have news to tell you ... When Roscius was an actor in Rome—

POLONIUS. The actors are come hither, my lord.

HAMLET. Buz, buz!

POLONIUS. Upon my honour—

HAMLET. 'Then came each actor on his ass'—

POLONIUS. The best actors in the world, either for tragedy, comedy, history, pastoral, pastoral-comical, historical-pastoral, tragical-historical, tra-gical-comical-historical-pastoral, scene individable, or poem unlimited. Seneca cannot be too heavy nor Plautus too light for the law of writ and the liberty, these are the only men. 410

HAMLET. O Jephthah, judge of Israel, what a treasure hadst thou!

POLONIUS. What a treasure had he, my lord?

HAMLET. Why
'One fair daughter, and no more,
    The which he lovéd passing well.'

POLONIUS [*aside*]. Still on my daughter. 420

HAMLET. Am I not i'th' right, old Jephthah?

POLONIUS. If you call me Jephthah, my lord, I have a daughter that I love passing well.

HAMLET. Nay, that follows not.

POLONIUS. What follows then, my lord?

HAMLET. Why,
            'As by lot, God wot,'
and then you know
            'It came to pass, as most like it was ...'
the first row of the pious chanson will show you more, for look where my abridgement comes. 430

Enter four or five Players

You are welcome masters, welcome all—I am glad to see thee well—Welcome, good friends—O, my old friend! why, thy face is valanced since I saw thee last, com'st thou to beard me in Denmark?—What, my young lady and mistress! by'r lady, your lady-ship is nearer to heaven than when I saw you last by the altitude of a chopine. Pray God your voice, like a piece of uncurrent gold, be not cracked within the ring ... Masters, you are all welcome. We'll e'en to't like French falconers, fly at any thing we see, we'll have a speech straight. Come give us a taste of your quality, come a passionate speech. 440

1 PLAYER. What speech, my good lord?

HAMLET. I heard thee speak me a speech once, but it was never acted, or if it was, not above once, for the play I remember pleased not the million, 'twas caviary to the general, but it was—as I received it, and others, whose judgements in such matters cried in the top of mine—an excellent play, well digested in the scenes, set down with as much modesty as cunning.... I remember one said there were no sallets in the lines, to make the matter savoury, nor no matter in the phrase that might indict the author of affection, but called it an honest method, as wholesome as sweet, and by very much more hand-some than fine: one speech in't I chiefly loved, 'twas Æneas' tale to Dido, and thereabout of it especially where he speaks of Priam's slaughter. If it live in your memory begin at this line, let me see, let me see— 450, 460
    'The rugged Pyrrhus, like th'Hyrcanian beast'—
'tis not so, it begins with Pyrrhus—
'The rugged Pyrrhus, he whose sable arms,
Black as his purpose, did the night resemble
When he lay couchéd in th'ominous horse,
Hath now this dread and black complexion smeared
With heraldy more dismal: head to foot

Now is he total gules, horridly tricked
With blood of fathers, mothers, daughters, sons, 470
Baked and impasted with the parching streets,
That lend a tyrannous and a damnéd light
To their lord's murder. Roasted in wrath and fire,
And thus o'er-sizéd with coagulate gore,
With eyes like carbuncles, the hellish Pyrrhus
Old grandsire Priam seeks' . . .
So proceed you.

POLONIUS. Fore God, my lord, well spoken, with
good accent and good discretion.

1 PLAYER.   'Anon he finds him 480
Striking too short at Greeks, his antique sword,
Rebellious to his arm, lies where it falls,
Repugnant to command; unequal matched,
Pyrrhus at Priam drives, in rage strikes wide,
But with the whiff and wind of his fell sword
Th'unnerved father falls: then senseless Ilium,
Seeming to feel this blow, with flaming top
Stoops to his base; and with a hideous crash
Takes prisoner Pyrrhus' ear. For lo! his sword,
Which was declining on the milky head   490
Of reverend Priam, seemed i'th'air to stick,
So as a painted tyrant Pyrrhus stood,
And like a neutral to his will and matter,
Did nothing:
But as we often see, against some storm,
A silence in the heavens, the rack stand still,
The bold winds speechless, and the orb below
As hush as death, anon the dreadful thunder
Doth rend the region, so after Pyrrhus' pause,
A rouséd vengeance sets him new awork,   500
And never did the Cyclops' hammers fall
On Mars's armour, forged for proof eterne,
With less remorse than Pyrrhus' bleeding sword
Now falls on Priam.
Out, out, thou strumpet Fortune! All you gods,
In general synod take away her power,
Break all the spokes and fellies from her wheel,
And bowl the round nave down the hill of heaven
As low as to the fiends.'

POLONIUS. This is too long.   510

HAMLET. It shall to the barber's with your beard;
prithee say on—he's for a jig, or a tale of bawdry, or
he sleeps—say on, come to Hecuba.

1 PLAYER. 'But who, ah woe! had seen the mobled
queen—'

HAMLET. 'The mobled queen'?

POLONIUS. That's good, 'mobled queen' is good.

1 PLAYER. 'Run barefoot up and down, threat'ning
the flames
With bisson rheum, a clout upon that head
Where late the diadem stood, and for a robe,
About her lank and all o'er-teeméd loins,   520
A blanket in the alarm of fear caught up—
Who this had seen, with tongue in venom steeped,
'Gainst Fortune's state would treason have
pronounced;
But if the gods themselves did see her then,
When she saw Pyrrhus make malicious sport
In mincing with his sword her husband's limbs,
The instant burst of clamour that she made,
Unless things mortal move them not at all,
Would have made milch the burning eyes of
heaven, .
And passion in the gods.'   530

POLONIUS. Look whe'r he has not turned his colour,
and has tears in's eyes—prithee no more.

HAMLET. 'Tis well, I'll have thee speak out the rest of
this soon. Good my lord, will you see the players
well bestowed; do you hear, let them be well used,
for they are the abstracts and brief chronicles of the
time; after your death you were better have a bad
epitaph than their ill report while you live.

POLONIUS. My lord, I will use them according to their
desert.   540

HAMLET. God's bodkin, man, much better! use every
man after his desert, and who shall 'scape whipping?
Use them after your own honour and dignity—the
less they deserve the more merit is in your bounty.
Take them in.

POLONIUS. Come, sirs.

HAMLET. Follow him, friends, we'll hear a play to-
morrow; [he stops the First Player] dost thou hear me,
old friend, can you play The Murder of Gonzago?

1 PLAYER. Ay, my lord.   550

HAMLET. We'll ha't to-morrow night. You could for a
need study a speech of some dozen or sixteen lines,
which I would set down and insert in't, could you
not?

1 PLAYER. Ay, my lord.
                      Polonius and the Players go out

HAMLET. Very well. Follow that lord, and look you
mock him not.   *First Player goes*
[*to Rosencrantz and Guildenstern*] My good friends,
I'll leave you till night. You are welcome to
Elsinore.   560

ROSENCRANTZ. Good my lord.   *They go*

HAMLET. Ay, so, God bye to you! now I am alone.
O, what a rogue and peasant slave am I!
Is it not monstrous that this player here,
But in a fiction, in a dream of passion,
Could force his soul so to his own conceit
That from her working all his visage wanned,
Tears in his eyes, distraction in his aspect,
A broken voice, and his whole function suiting
With forms to his conceit; and all for nothing! 570
For Hecuba!
What's Hecuba to him, or he to Hecuba,
That he should weep for her? what would he do,
Had he the motive and the cue for passion
That I have? he would drown the stage with tears,
And cleave the general ear with horrid speech,
Make mad the guilty and appal the free,
Confound the ignorant, and amaze indeed
The very faculties of eyes and ears; yet I,
A dull and muddy-mettled rascal, peak   580
Like John-a-dreams, unpregnant of my cause,
And can say nothing; no, not for a king,
Upon whose property and most dear life
A damned defeat was made: am I a coward?
Who calls me villain, breaks my pate across,
Plucks off my beard and blows it in my face,
Tweaks me by the nose, gives me the lie i'th'throat
As deep as to the lungs? who does me this?
Ha, 'swounds, I should take it: for it cannot be
But I am pigeon-livered, and lack gall   590
To make oppression bitter, or ere this
I should ha' fatted all the region kites
With this slave's offal. Bloody, bawdy villain!
Remorseless, treacherous, lecherous, kindless
villain!

O, vengeance!
Why, what an ass am I. This is most brave,
That I, the son of a dear father murdered,
Prompted to my revenge by heaven and hell,
Must like a whore unpack my heart with words,
And fall a-cursing like a very drab;   600
A stallion! fie upon't! foh!
About, my brains; hum, I have heard
That guilty creatures sitting at a play
Have by the very cunning of the scene
Been struck so to the soul, that presently
They have proclaimed their malefactions:
For murder, though it have no tongue, will speak
With most miraculous organ: I'll have these players
Play something like the murder of my father
Before mine uncle, I'll observe his looks,   610
I'll tent him to the quick, if a' do blench
I know my course.... The spirit that I have seen
May be a devil, and the devil hath power
T'assume a pleasing shape, yea, and perhaps
Out of my weakness and my melancholy,
As he is very potent with such spirits,
Abuses me to damn me; I'll have grounds
More relative than this—the play's the thing
Wherein I'll catch the conscience of the king.
                                                    He goes

ACT 3
Scene 1: *The lobby of the audience chamber*

*The King and the Queen enter with Polonius, Rosencrantz,
and Guildenstern; Ophelia follows a little behind*

KING. And can you by no drift of conference
     Get from him why he puts on this confusion,
     Grating so harshly all his days of quiet
     With turbulent and dangerous lunacy?
ROSENCRANTZ. He does confess he feels himself
     distracted,
     But from what cause a' will by no means speak.
GUILDENSTERN. Nor do we find him forward to be
     sounded,
     But with a crafty madness keeps aloof
     When we would bring him on to some confession
     Of his true state.
QUEEN.   Did he receive you well?   10
ROSENCRANTZ. Most like a gentleman.
GUILDENSTERN. But with much forcing of his
     disposition.
ROSENCRANTZ. Niggard of question, but of our
     demands
     Most free in his reply.
QUEEN.   Did you assay him
     To any pastime?
ROSENCRANTZ. Madam, it so fell out that certain
     players
     We o'er-raught on the way. Of these we told him,
     And there did seem in him a kind of joy
     To hear of it: they are here about the court,
     And as I think, they have already order   20
     This night to play before him.
POLONIUS.   'Tis most true,
     And he beseeched me to entreat your majesties
     To hear and see the matter.
KING. With all my heart, and it doth much content me
     To hear him so inclined.

Good gentlemen, give him a further edge,
And drive his purpose into these delights.
ROSENCRANTZ. We shall, my lord.
                           Rosencrantz and Guildenstern go
KING.   Sweet Gertrude, leave us too,
     For we have closely sent for Hamlet hither,
     That he, as 'twere by accident, may here   30
     Affront Ophelia;
     Her father and myself, lawful espials,
     Will so bestow ourselves, that seeing unseen,
     We may of their encounter frankly judge,
     And gather by him as he is behaved,
     If't be th'affliction of his love or no
     That thus he suffers for.
QUEEN.   I shall obey you—
     And for your part, Ophelia, I do wish
     That your good beauties be the happy cause
     Of Hamlet's wildness, so shall I hope your virtues 40
     Will bring him to his wonted way again,
     To both your honours.
OPHELIA.   Madam, I wish it may.
                                         The Queen goes
POLONIUS. Ophelia, walk you here. Gracious, so please
     you,
     We will bestow ourselves ... Read on this book,
     That show of such an exercise may colour
     Your loneliness; we are oft to blame in this,
     'Tis too much proved, that with devotion's visage
     And pious action we do sugar o'er
     The devil himself.
KING [*aside*].   O, 'tis too true,
     How smart a lash that speech doth give my
     conscience.   50
     The harlot's cheek, beautied with plast'ring art,
     Is not more ugly to the thing that helps it,
     Than is my deed to my most painted word:
     O heavy burden!
POLONIUS. I hear him coming, let's withdraw, my
     lord.   *They do so*

Hamlet enters

HAMLET. To be, or not to be, that is the question,
     Whether 'tis nobler in the mind to suffer
     The slings and arrows of outrageous fortune,
     Or to take arms against a sea of troubles,
     And by opposing, end them. To die, to sleep—   60
     No more, and by a sleep to say we end
     The heart-ache, and the thousand natural shocks
     That flesh is heir to; 'tis a consummation
     Devoutly to be wished to die to sleep!
     To sleep, perchance to dream, ay there's the rub,
     For in that sleep of death what dreams may come
     When we have shuffled off this mortal coil
     Must give us pause—there's the respect
     That makes calamity of so long life:
     For who would bear the whips and scorns of time, 70
     Th'oppressor's wrong, the proud man's contumely,
     The pangs of disprized love, the law's delay,
     The insolence of office, and the spurns
     That patient merit of th'unworthy takes,
     When he himself might his quietus make
     With a bare bodkin; who would fardels bear,
     To grunt and sweat under a weary life,
     But that the dread of something after death,
     The undiscovered country, from whose bourn
     No traveller returns, puzzles the will,   80

And makes us rather bear those ills we have,
Than fly to others that we know not of?
Thus conscience does make cowards of us all,
And thus the native hue of resolution
Is sicklied o'er with the pale cast of thought,
And enterprises of great pitch and moment
With this regard their currents turn awry,
And lose the name of action.... Soft you now,
The fair Ophelia—Nymph, in thy orisons
Be all my sins remembered.

OPHELIA.   Good my lord,   90
How does your honour for this many a day?

HAMLET. I humbly thank you, well, well, well.

OPHELIA. My lord, I have remembrances of yours,
That I have longed long to re-deliver.
I pray you now receive them.

HAMLET.   No, not I,
I never gave you aught.

OPHELIA. My honoured lord, you know right well
    you did,
And with them words of so sweet breath composed
As made the things more rich. Their perfume lost,
Take these again, for to the noble mind   100
Rich gifts wax poor when givers prove unkind.
There, my lord.

HAMLET.   Ha, ha! are you honest?

OPHELIA. My lord?

HAMLET. Are you fair?

OPHELIA. What means your lordship?

HAMLET. That if you be honest and fair, your honesty
should admit no discourse to your beauty.

OPHELIA. Could beauty, my lord, have better commerce than with honesty?

HAMLET. Ay truly, for the power of beauty will sooner   110
transform honesty from what it is to a bawd, than
the force of honesty can translate beauty into his
likeness. This was sometime a paradox, but now the
time gives it proof. I did love you once.

OPHELIA. Indeed, my lord, you made me believe so.

HAMLET. You should not have believed me, for virtue
cannot so inoculate our old stock, but we shall relish
of it—I loved you not.

OPHELIA. I was the more deceived.

HAMLET. Get thee to a nunnery, why wouldst thou be   120
a breeder of sinners? I am myself indifferent honest,
but yet I could accuse me of such things, that it
were better my mother had not borne me: I am very
proud, revengeful, ambitious, with more offences at
my beck, than I have thoughts to put them in,
imagination to give them shape, or time to act them
in: what should such fellows as I do crawling
between earth and heaven? we are arrant knaves all,
believe none of us—go thy ways to a nunnery....
Where's your father?   130

OPHELIA. At home, my lord.

HAMLET. Let the doors be shut upon him, that he may
play the fool no where but in's own house. Farewell.

OPHELIA. O help him, you sweet heavens!

HAMLET. If thou dost marry, I'll give thee this plague
for thy dowry—be thou as chaste as ice, as pure as
snow, thou shalt not escape calumny; get thee to a
nunnery, go, farewell.... Or if thou wilt needs
marry, marry a fool, for wise men know well
enough what monsters you make of them: to a   140
nunnery, go, and quickly too, farewell.

OPHELIA. O heavenly powers, restore him!

HAMLET. I have heard of your paintings too, well
enough. God hath given you one face and you make
yourselves another, you jig, you amble, and you
lisp, you nickname God's creatures, and make your
wantonness your ignorance; go to, I'll no more on't,
it hath made me mad. I say we will have no mo
marriage—those that are married already, all but
one, shall live, the rest shall keep as they are: to a   150
nunnery, go.   *He departs*

OPHELIA. O, what a noble mind is here o'erthrown!
The courtier's, soldier's, scholar's, eye, tongue,
    sword,
Th'expectancy and rose of the fair state,
The glass of fashion, and the mould of form,
Th'observed of all observers, quite quite down,
And I of ladies most deject and wretched,
That sucked the honey of his music vows,
Now see that noble and most sovereign reason
Like sweet bells jangled, out of tune and harsh,   160
That unmatched form and feature of blown youth,
Blasted with ecstasy! O, woe is me!
T'have seen what I have seen, see what I see!
                                        She prays

The King and Polonius come forward

KING. Love! his affections do not that way tend,
Nor what he spake, though it lacked form a little,
Was not like madness—there's something in his
    soul,
O'er which his melancholy sits on brood,
And I do doubt the hatch and the disclose
Will be some danger; which for to prevent,
I have in quick determination   170
Thus set it down: he shall with speed to England,
For the demand of our neglected tribute.
Haply the seas, and countries different,
With variable objects, shall expel
This something-settled matter in his heart,
Whereon his brains still beating puts him thus
From fashion of himself. What think you on't?
                              Ophelia comes forward

POLONIUS. It shall do well. But yet do I believe
The origin and commencement of his grief
Sprung from neglected love ... How now,
    Ophelia?   180
You need not tell us what Lord Hamlet said,
We heard it all ... My lord, do as you please,
But if you hold it fit, after the play,
Let his queen-mother all alone entreat him
To show his grief, let her be round with him,
And I'll be placed (so please you) in the ear
Of all their conference. If she find him not,
To England send him; or confine him where
Your wisdom best shall think.

KING.   It shall be so,
Madness in great ones must not unwatched go.   190
                                        They depart

Scene 2: *The hall of the castle*

Enter Hamlet, and three of the Players

HAMLET. Speak the speech I pray you as I pronounced
it to you, trippingly on the tongue, but if you mouth
it as many of your players do, I had as lief the
town-crier spoke my lines. Nor do not saw the air
too much with your hand thus, but use all gently, for

in the very torrent, tempest, and as I may say whirlwind of your passion, you must acquire and beget a
temperance that may give it smoothness. O, it
offends me to the soul, to hear a robustious periwig-
pated fellow tear a passion to tatters, to very rags, 10
to split the ears of the groundlings, who for the most
part are capable of nothing but inexplicable dumb-
shows and noise: I would have such a fellow
whipped for o'erdoing Termagant, it out-herods
Herod, pray you avoid it.

1 PLAYER. I warrant your honour.

HAMLET. Be not too tame neither, but let your own
discretion be your tutor, suit the action to the word,
the word to the action, with this special observance,
that you o'erstep not the modesty of nature: for any 20
thing so o'erdone is from the purpose of playing,
whose end both at the first, and now, was and is,
to hold as 'twere the mirror up to nature, to show
virtue her own feature, scorn her own image, and
the very age and body of the time his form and
pressure ... Now this overdone, or come tardy off,
though it make the unskilful laugh, cannot but make
the judicious grieve, the censure of the which one
must in your allowance o'erweigh a whole theatre
of others. O there be players that I have seen play— 30
and heard others praise, and that highly—not to
speak it profanely, that neither having th'accent of
Christians, nor the gait of Christian, pagan, nor
man, have so strutted and bellowed, that I have
thought some of nature's journeymen had made
men, and not made them well, they imitated
humanity so abominably.

1 PLAYER. I hope we have reformed that indifferently
with us, sir.

HAMLET. O reform it altogether, and let those that play 40
your clowns speak no more than is set down for
them, for there be of them that will themselves
laugh, to set on some quantity of barren spectators
to laugh too, though in the mean time some
necessary question of the play be then to be considered. That's villanous, and shows a most pitiful
ambition in the fool that uses it ... Go, make you
ready.   *The Players go*

Polonius enters with Rosencrantz and Guildenstern

How now, my lord? will the king hear this piece of
work?

POLONIUS. And the queen too, and that presently.   50

HAMLET. Bid the players make haste.
                                               Polonius departs
Will you two help to hasten them?

ROSENCRANTZ. Ay, my lord.
                    Rosencrantz and Guildenstern follow Polonius
HAMLET. What, ho! Horatio!

Horatio comes in

HORATIO. Here, sweet lord, at your service.

HAMLET. Horatio, thou art e'en as just a man
As e'er my conversation coped withal.

HORATIO. O, my dear lord,—

HAMLET.   Nay, do not think I flatter,
For what advancement may I hope from thee,
That no revenue hast but thy good spirits   60
To feed and clothe thee? why should the poor be
flattered,
No, let the candied tongue lick absurd pomp,

And crook the pregnant hinges of the knee
Where thrift may follow fawning ... Dost thou
hear?
Since my dear soul was mistress of her choice,
And could of men distinguish her election,
Sh'hath sealed thee for herself, for thou hast been
As one in suff'ring all that suffers nothing,
A man that Fortune's buffets and rewards
Hast ta'en with equal thanks; and blest are those 70
Whose blood and judgement are so well co-medled,
That they are not a pipe for Fortune's finger
To sound what stop she please: give me that man
That is not passion's slave, and I will wear him
In my heart's core, ay in my heart of heart,
As I do thee. Something too much of this—
There is a play to-night before the king,
One scene of it comes near the circumstance
Which I have told thee of my father's death.
I prithee when thou seest that act afoot,   80
Even with the very comment of thy soul
Observe my uncle—if his occulted guilt
Do not itself unkennel in one speech,
It is a damnéd ghost that we have seen,
And my imaginations are as foul
As Vulcan's stithy; give him heedful note,
For I mine eyes will rivet to his face,
And after we will both our judgements join
In censure of his seeming.

HORATIO.   Well, my lord,
If a' steal aught the whilst this play is playing, 90
And 'scape detecting, I will pay the theft.
                         Trumpets and kettle-drums heard
HAMLET. They are coming to the play. I must be idle.
Get you a place.

*The King and Queen enter, followed by Polonius, Ophelia,
Rosencrantz, Guildenstern, and other courtiers*

KING. How fares our cousin Hamlet?

HAMLET. Excellent i'faith, of the chameleon's dish, I
eat the air, promise-crammed—you cannot feed
capons so.

KING. I have nothing with this answer, Hamlet. These
words are not mine.

HAMLET. No, nor mine now. [*to Polonius*] My lord, 100
you played once i'th'university, you say?

POLONIUS. That did I, my lord, and was accounted a
good actor.

HAMLET. What did you enact?

POLONIUS. I did enact Julius Cæsar. I was killed i'th'
Capitol, Brutus killed me.

HAMLET. It was a brute part of him to kill so capital a
calf there. Be the players ready?

ROSENCRANTZ. Ay, my lord, they stay upon your
patience.   110

QUEEN. Come hither, my dear Hamlet, sit by me.

HAMLET. No, good mother, here's metal more attractive.

POLONIUS [*to the King*]. O ho! do you mark that?

HAMLET. Lady, shall I lie in your lap?

OPHELIA. No, my lord.

HAMLET. I mean, my head upon your lap?

OPHELIA. Ay, my lord.   *He lies at her feet*

HAMLET. Do you think I meant country matters?

OPHELIA. I think nothing, my lord.   120

HAMLET. That's a fair thought to lie between maids'
legs.

OPHELIA. What is, my lord?

HAMLET. Nothing.

OPHELIA. You are merry, my lord.

HAMLET. Who, I?

OPHELIA. Ay, my lord.

HAMLET. O God, your only jig-maker. What should a man do but be merry, for look you how cheerfully my mother looks, and my father died within's two 130 hours.

OPHELIA. Nay, 'tis twice two months, my lord.

HAMLET. So long? nay then let the devil wear black, for I'll have a suit of sables; O heavens, die two months ago, and not forgotten yet? then there's hope a great man's memory may outlive his life half a year, but by'r lady a' must build churches then, or else shall a' suffer not thinking on, with the hobby-horse, whose epitaph is 'For O! for O! the hobby-horse is forgot.'   140

The trumpets sound, and a Dumb-Show follows

The Dumb-Show

Enter a King and a Queen, very lovingly, the Queen embracing him and he her, she kneels and makes show of protestation unto him, he takes her up and declines his head upon her neck, he lies him down upon a bank of flowers, she seeing him asleep leaves him: anon comes in another man, takes off his crown, kisses it, and pours poison in the sleeper's ears and leaves him: the Queen returns, finds the King dead, and makes passionate action: the poisoner with some three or four mutes comes in again, seeming to condole with her: the dead body is carried away: the poisoner wooes the Queen with gifts, she seems harsh awhile, but in the end accepts his love   *They go*

OPHELIA. What means this, my lord?

HAMLET. Marry, this is miching mallecho, it means mischief.

OPHELIA. Belike this show imports the argument of the play.

Enter a player

HAMLET. We shall know by this fellow. The players cannot keep counsel, they'll tell all.

OPHELIA. Will a' tell us what this show meant?

HAMLET. Ay, or any show that you will show him— be not you ashamed to show, he'll not shame to tell 150 you what it means.

OPHELIA. You are naught, you are naught, I'll mark the play.

PLAYER.   For us and for our tragedy,
            Here stooping to your clemency,
            We beg your hearing patiently.   *Exit*

HAMLET. Is this a prologue, or the posy of a ring?

OPHELIA. 'Tis brief, my lord.

HAMLET. As woman's love.

Enter two Players, a King and a Queen

PLAYER KING. Full thirty times hath Phœbus' cart gone round   160
   Neptune's salt wash, and Tellus' orbéd ground,
   And thirty dozen moons with borrowed sheen
   About the world have times twelve thirties been,
   Since love our hearts and Hymen did our hands
   Unite commutual in most sacred bands.

PLAYER QUEEN. So many journeys may the sun and moon

   Make us again count o'er ere love be done!
   But woe is me, you are so sick of late,
   So far from cheer, and from your former state,
   That I distrust you. Yet though I distrust,   170
   Discomfort you, my lord, it nothing must.
   For women fear too much, even as they love,
   And women's fear and love hold quantity,
   In neither aught, or in extremity.
   Now what my love is proof hath made you know,
   And as my love is sized, my fear is so.
   Where love is great, the littlest doubts are fear,
   Where little fears grow great, great love grows there.

PLAYER KING. Faith, I must leave thee, love, and shortly too.
   My operant powers their functions leave to do,   180
   And thou shalt live in this fair world behind,
   Honoured, beloved, and haply one as kind
   For husband shalt thou—

PLAYER QUEEN.   O, confound the rest!
   Such love must needs be treason in my breast,
   In second husband let me be accurst,
   None wed the second, but who killed the first.

HAMLET. That's wormwood, wormwood.

PLAYER QUEEN. The instances that second marriage move
   Are base respects of thrift, but none of love.
   A second time I kill my husband dead,   190
   When second husband kisses me in bed.

PLAYER KING. I do believe you think what now you speak,
   But what we do determine, oft we break.
   Purpose is but the slave to memory,
   Of violent birth but poor validity,
   Which now like fruit unripe sticks on the tree,
   But fall unshaken when they mellow be.
   Most necessary 'tis that we forget
   To pay ourselves what to ourselves is debt.
   What to ourselves in passion we propose,   200
   The passion ending, doth the purpose lose,
   The violence of either grief or joy
   Their own enactures with themselves destroy,
   Where joy most revels, grief doth most lament,
   Grief joys, joy grieves, on slender accident.
   This world is not for aye, nor 'tis not strange
   That even our loves should with our fortunes change:
   For 'tis a question left us yet to prove,
   Whether love lead fortune, or else fortune love.
   The great man down, you mark his favourite flies, 210
   The poor advanced makes friends of enemies,
   And hitherto doth love on fortune tend,
   For who not needs shall never lack a friend,
   And who in want a hollow friend doth try,
   Directly seasons him his enemy.
   But orderly to end where I begun,
   Our wills and fates do so contrary run,
   That our devices still are overthrown,
   Our thoughts are ours, their ends none of our own—
   So think thou wilt no second husband wed,   220
   But die thy thoughts when thy first lord is dead.

PLAYER QUEEN. Nor earth to me give food nor heaven light,
   Sport and repose lock from me day and night,
   To desperation turn my trust and hope,

An anchor's cheere in prison be my scope,
Each opposite that blanks the face of joy
Meet what I would have well and it destroy,
Both here and hence pursue me lasting strife,
If once a widow, ever I be wife!
HAMLET. If she should break it now!   230
PLAYER KING. 'Tis deeply sworn. Sweet leave me here
    awhile,
My spirits grow dull, and fain I would beguile
The tedious day with sleep.   *He sleeps*
PLAYER QUEEN.   Sleep rock thy brain,
And never come mischance between us twain!
                          Exit
HAMLET. Madam, how like you this play?
QUEEN. The lady doth protest too much methinks.
HAMLET. O, but she'll keep her word.
KING. Have you heard the argument? is there no
    offence in't?
HAMLET. No, no, they do but jest, poison in jest, no   240
    offence i'th'world.
KING. What do you call the play?
HAMLET. The Mouse-trap. Marry, how?—tropically.
    This play is the image of a murder done in Vienna.
    Gonzago is the duke's name, his wife Baptista, you
    shall see anon, 'tis a knavish piece of work, but what
    of that? your majesty, and we that have free souls,
    it touches us not—let the galled jade wince, our
    withers are unwrung....

Enter First Player for Lucianus

    This is one Lucianus, nephew to the king.   250
OPHELIA. You are as good as a chorus, my lord.
HAMLET. I could interpret between you and your love,
    if I could see the puppets dallying.
OPHELIA. You are keen, my lord, you are keen.
HAMLET. It would cost you a groaning to take off mine
    edge.
OPHELIA. Still better and worse.
HAMLET. So you mis-take your husbands.... Begin,
    murderer. Pox! leave thy damnable faces and begin!
    Come——'the croaking raven doth bellow for   260
    revenge.'
LUCIANUS. Thoughts black, hands apt, drugs fit, and
    time agreeing,
Confederate season, else no creature seeing,
Thou mixture rank, of midnight weeds collected,
With Hecate's ban thrice blasted, thrice infected,
Thy natural magic and dire property
On wholesome life usurps immediately.
              Pours the poison in his ears
HAMLET. A' poisons him i'th'garden for's estate, his
    name's Gonzago, the story is extant, and written in
    very choice Italian, you shall see anon how the   270
    murderer gets the love of Gonzago's wife.
OPHELIA. The king rises.
HAMLET. What, frighted with false fire!
QUEEN. How fares my lord?
POLONIUS. Give o'er the play.
KING. Give me some light—away!   *He goes*
POLONIUS. Lights, lights, lights!
        All but Hamlet and Horatio depart
HAMLET.
Why, let the stricken deer go weep,
   The hart ungalléd play,
For some must watch while some must sleep,   280
   Thus runs the world away.

Would not this, sir, and a forest of feathers, if the
rest of my fortunes turn Turk with me, with two
Provincial roses on my razed shoes, get me a fellow-
ship in a cry of players, sir?
HORATIO. Half a share.
HAMLET. A whole one, I.
    For thou dost know, O Damon dear,
       This realm dismantled was
    Of Jove himself, and now reigns here   290
       A very, very—peacock.
HORATIO. You might have rhymed.
HAMLET. O good Horatio, I'll take the ghost's word
    for a thousand pound.... Didst perceive?
HORATIO. Very well, my lord.
HAMLET. Upon the talk of the poisoning?
HORATIO. I did very well note him.

Rosencrantz and Guildenstern return

HAMLET. Ah, ha! Come, some music! come, the
    recorders!
    For if the king like not the comedy,   300
       Why then, belike,—he likes it not, perdy.
Come, some music!
GUILDENSTERN. Good my lord, vouchsafe me a word
    with you.
HAMLET. Sir, a whole history.
GUILDENSTERN. The king, sir,—
HAMLET. Ay, sir, what of him?
GUILDENSTERN. Is in his retirement marvellous dis-
    tempered.
HAMLET. With drink, sir?   310
GUILDENSTERN. No, my lord, rather with choler.
HAMLET. Your wisdom should show itself more richer
    to signify this to the doctor. For, for me to put him
    to his purgation, would perhaps plunge him into
    more choler.
GUILDENSTERN. Good my lord, put your discourse into
    some frame, and start not so wildly from my affair.
HAMLET. I am tame, sir—pronounce.
GUILDENSTERN. The queen your mother, in most great
    affliction of spirit, hath sent me to you.   320
HAMLET. You are welcome.
GUILDENSTERN. Nay, good my lord, this courtesy is
    not of the right breed. If it shall please you to make
    me a wholesome answer, I will do your mother's
    commandment. If not, your pardon and my return
    shall be the end of my business.
HAMLET. Sir, I cannot.
ROSENCRANTZ. What, my lord?
HAMLET. Make you a wholesome answer—my wit's
    diseased. But, sir, such answer as I can make, you   330
    shall command, or rather as you say, my mother.
    Therefore no more, but to the matter—my mother,
    you say—
ROSENCRANTZ. Then thus she says, your behaviour
    hath struck her into amazement and admiration.
HAMLET. O wonderful son that can so stonish a
    mother! but is there no sequel at the heels of this
    mother's admiration? impart.
ROSENCRANTZ. She desires to speak with you in her
    closet ere you go to bed.   340
HAMLET. We shall obey, were she ten times our
    mother. Have you any further trade with us?
ROSENCRANTZ. My lord, you once did love me.
HAMLET. And do still, by these pickers and stealers.
ROSENCRANTZ. Good my lord, what is your cause of

distemper? you do surely bar the door upon your
own liberty, if you deny your griefs to your friend.
HAMLET. Sir, I lack advancement.
ROSENCRANTZ. How can that be, when you have the
voice of the king himself for your succession in   350
Denmark?
HAMLET. Ay, sir, but 'While the grass grows'—the
proverb is something musty.

Players bring in recorders

O, the recorders, let me see one. To withdraw with
you, why do you go about to recover the wind of
me, as if you would drive me into a toil?
GUILDENSTERN. O, my lord, if my duty be too bold,
my love is too unmannerly.
HAMLET. I do not well understand that—will you play
upon this pipe?   360
GUILDENSTERN. My lord, I cannot.
HAMLET. I pray you.
GUILDENSTERN. Believe me, I cannot.
HAMLET. I do beseech you.'
GUILDENSTERN. I know no touch of it, my lord.
HAMLET. It is as easy as lying; govern these ventages
with your fingers and thumb, give it breath with
your mouth, and it will discourse most eloquent
music—look you, these are the stops.
GUILDENSTERN. But these cannot I command to any   370
utt'rance of harmony, I have not the skill.
HAMLET. Why, look you now, how unworthy a thing
you make of me! you would play upon me, you
would seem to know my stops, you would pluck
out the heart of my mystery, you would sound me
from my lowest note to the top of my compass—
and there is much music, excellent voice, in this little
organ, yet cannot you make it speak. 'Sblood, do
you think I am easier to be played on than a pipe?
call me what instrument you will, though you can   380
fret me, you cannot play upon me.

Polonius enters

God bless you, sir!
POLONIUS. My lord, the queen would speak with you,
and presently.
HAMLET. Do you see yonder cloud that's almost in
shape of a camel?
POLONIUS. By th'mass and 'tis, like a camel indeed.
HAMLET. Methinks it is like a weasel.
POLONIUS. It is backed like a weasel.
HAMLET. Or, like a whale?   390
POLONIUS. Very like a whale.
HAMLET. Then I will come to my mother by and by.
[*aside*] They fool me to the top of my bent—
I will come by and by.
POLONIUS. I will say so.
                Polonius, Rosencrantz and Guildenstern depart
HAMLET. 'By and by' is easily said.
Leave me, friends.   *The rest go*
'Tis now the very witching time of night,
When churchyards yawn, and hell itself breathes out
Contagion to this world: now could I drink hot
blood,   400
And do such bitter business as the day
Would quake to look on: soft, now to my mother—
O heart, lose not thy nature, let not ever
The soul of Nero enter this firm bosom,
Let me be cruel not unnatural.

I will speak daggers to her, but use none.
My tongue and soul in this be hypocrites,
How in my words somever she be shent,
To give them seals never, my soul, consent!
                                        He goes

Scene 3: *The lobby; the audience chamber without*

Enter the King, Rosencrantz and Guildenstern

KING. I like him not, nor stands it safe with us
To let his madness range. Therefore prepare you,
I your commission will forthwith dispatch,
And he to England shall along with you.
The terms of our estate may not endure
Hazard so near's as doth hourly grow
Out of his brows.
GUILDENSTERN.   We will ourselves provide.
Most holy and religious fear it is
To keep those many many bodies safe
That live and feed upon your majesty.   10
ROSENCRANTZ. The single and peculiar life is bound
With all the strength and armour of the mind
To keep itself from noyance, but much more
That spirit upon whose weal depends and rests
The lives of many. The cess of majesty
Dies not alone; but like a gulf doth draw
What's near it with it. O, 'tis a massy wheel
Fixed on the summit of the highest mount,
To whose huge spokes ten thousand lesser things
Are mortised and adjoined, which when it falls,   20
Each small annexment, petty consequence,
Attends the boist'rous ruin. Never alone
Did the king sigh, but with a general groan.
KING. Arm you, I pray you, to this speedy voyage,
For we will fetters put about this fear,
Which now goes too free-footed.
ROSENCRANTZ.   We will haste us.
                                        They go

Polonius enters

POLONIUS. My lord, he's going to his mother's
closet—
Behind the arras I'll convey myself
To hear the process—I'll warrant she'll tax him
home,
And as you said, and wisely was it said,   30
'Tis meet that some more audience than a mother,
Since nature makes them partial, should o'erhear
The speech of vantage; fare you well, my liege,
I'll call upon you ere you go to bed,
And tell you what I know.
KING.   Thanks, dear my lord....
                                        Polonius goes
O, my offence is rank, it smells to heaven,
It hath the primal eldest curse upon't,
A brother's murder! Pray can I not,
Though inclination be as sharp as will.
My stronger guilt defeats my strong intent,   40
And like a man to double business bound,
I stand in pause where I shall first begin,
And both neglect. What if this cursèd hand
Were thicker than itself with brother's blood,
Is there not rain enough in the sweet heavens
To wash it white as snow? whereto serves mercy
But to confront the visage of offence?
And what's in prayer but this two-fold force,

To be forestallèd ere we come to fall,
Or pardoned being down? then I'll look up.... 50
My fault is past, but O, what form of prayer
Can serve my turn? 'Forgive me my foul murder'?
That cannot be since I am still possessed
Of those effects for which I did the murder;
My crown, mine own ambition, and my queen;
May one be pardoned and retain th'offence?
In the corrupted currents of this world
Offence's gilded hand may shove by justice,
And oft 'tis seen the wicked prize itself
Buys out the law. But 'tis not so above, 60
There is no shuffling, there the action lies
In his true nature, and we ourselves compelled
Even to the teeth and forehead of our faults
To give in evidence. What then? what rests?
Try what repentance can—what can it not?
Yet what can it, when one can not repent?
O wretched state! O bosom black as death!
O limèd soul, that struggling to be free,
Art more engaged; help, angels! Make assay,
Bow stubborn knees, and heart, with strings of steel, 70
Be soft as sinews of the new-born babe—
All may be well. *He kneels*

Hamlet enters

HAMLET. Now might I do it pat, now a'is a-praying—
And now I'll do't, and so a' goes to heaven,
And so am I revenged. That would be scanned:
A villain kills my father, and for that
I his sole son do this same villain send
To heaven....
Why, this is bait and salary, not revenge.
A' took my father grossly, full of bread, 80
With all his crimes broad blown, as flush as May,
And how his audit stands who knows save heaven?
But in our circumstance and course of thought,
'Tis heavy with him: and am I then revenged
To take him in the purging of his soul,
When he is fit and seasoned for his passage?
No.
Up, sword, and know thou a more horrid hent,
When he is drunk asleep, or in his rage,
Or in th'incestuous pleasure of his bed, 90
At game, a-swearing, or about some act
That has no relish of salvation in't,
Then trip him that his heels may kick at heaven,
And that his soul may be as damned and black
As hell whereto it goes; my mother stays,
This physic but prolongs thy sickly days.
He passes on
KING [*rises*]. My words fly up, my thoughts remain
below.
Words without thoughts never to heaven go.
He goes

Scene 4: *The Queen's closet*

Enter the Queen and Polonius

POLONIUS. A' will come straight. Look you lay home
to him,
Tell him his pranks have been too broad to bear
with,
And that your grace hath screened and stood
between
Much heat and him. I'll silence me even here—

Pray you be round with him.
HAMLET [*without*]. Mother, mother, mother!
QUEEN. I'll war'nt you,
Fear me not. Withdraw, I hear him coming.
Polonius hides behind the arras

Hamlet enters

HAMLET. Now, mother, what's the matter?
QUEEN. Hamlet, thou hast thy father much offended.
HAMLET. Mother, you have my father much offended. 10
QUEEN. Come, come, you answer with an idle tongue.
HAMLET. Go, go, you question with a wicked tongue.
QUEEN. Why, how now, Hamlet?
HAMLET. What's the matter now?
QUEEN. Have you forgot me?
HAMLET. No, by the rood not so,
You are the queen, your husband's brother's wife,
And would it were not so, you are my mother.
QUEEN. Nay then, I'll set those to you that can speak.
HAMLET. Come, come, and sit you down, you shall
not budge,
You go not till I set you up a glass
Where you may see the inmost part of you. 20
QUEEN. What wilt thou do? thou wilt not murder me?
Help, help, ho!
POLONIUS [*behind the arras*]. What, ho! help, help, help!
HAMLET [*draws*]. How now! a rat? dead, for a ducat,
dead. *He makes a pass through the arras*
POLONIUS [*falls*]. O, I am slain!
QUEEN. O me, what hast thou done?
HAMLET. Nay, I know no..
Is it the king?
He lifts up the arras and discovers Polonius, dead
QUEEN. O what a rash and bloody deed is this!
HAMLET. A bloody deed—almost as bad, good
mother,
As kill a king, and marry with his brother.
QUEEN. As kill a king!
HAMLET. Ay, lady, it was my word.... 30
[*to Polonius*] Thou wretched, rash, intruding fool,
farewell!
I took thee for thy better, take thy fortune,
Thou find'st to be too busy is some danger.
Leave wringing of your hands, peace, sit you down,
And let me wring your heart, for so I shall
If it be made of penetrable stuff,
If damnèd custom have not brassed it so,
That it be proof and bulwark against sense.
QUEEN. What have I done, that thou dar'st wag thy
tongue
In noise so rude against me?
HAMLET. Such an act 40
That blurs the grace and blush of modesty,
Calls virtue hypocrite, takes off the rose
From the fair forehead of an innocent love
And sets a blister there, makes marriage vows
As false as dicers' oaths, O such a deed
As from the body of contraction plucks
The very soul, and sweet religion makes
A rhapsody of words; heaven's face does glow,
And this solidity and compound mass
With heated visage, as against the doom, 50
Is thought-sick at the act.
QUEEN. Ay me, what act,
That roars so loud, and thunders in the index?
HAMLET. Look here, upon this picture, and on this,

The counterfeit presentment of two brothers.
See what a grace was seated on this brow—
Hyperion's curls, the front of Jove himself,
An eye like Mars to threaten and command,
A station like the herald Mercury,
New-lighted on a heaven-kissing hill,
A combination and a form indeed,   60
Where every god did seem to set his seal
To give the world assurance of a man.
This was your husband—Look you now what
    follows.
Here is your husband, like a mildewed ear,
Blasting his wholesome brother. Have you eyes?
Could you on this fair mountain leave to feed,
And batten on this moor? ha! have you eyes?
You cannot call it love, for at your age
The hey-day in the blood is tame, it's humble,
And waits upon the judgement, and what
    judgement   70
Would step from this to this? Sense sure you have
Else could you not have motion, but sure that sense
Is apoplexed, for madness would not err,
Nor sense to ecstasy was ne'er so thralled,
But it reserved some quantity of choice
To serve in such a difference. What devil was't
That thus hath cozened you at hoodman-blind?
Eyes without feeling, feeling without sight,
Ears without hands or eyes, smelling sans all,
Or but a sickly part of one true sense   80
Could not so mope: O shame, where is thy blush?
Rebellious hell,
If thou canst mutine in a matron's bones,
To flaming youth let virtue be as wax
And melt in her own fire. Proclaim no shame
When the compulsive ardour gives the charge,
Since frost itself as actively doth burn,
And reason pandars will.
QUEEN.   O Hamlet, speak no more.
Thou turn'st my eyes into my very soul,
And there I see such black and grainéd spots   90
As will not leave their tinct.
HAMLET.   Nay, but to live
In the rank sweat of an enseaméd bed
Stewed in corruption, honeying, and making love
Over the nasty sty—
QUEEN.   O speak to me no more,
These words like daggers enter in mine ears,
No more, sweet Hamlet.
HAMLET.   A murderer and a villain,
A slave that is not twentieth part the tithe
Of your precedent lord, a vice of kings,
A cutpurse of the empire and the rule,
That from a shelf the precious diadem stole   100
And put it in his pocket—
QUEEN.   No more.
HAMLET. A king of shreds and patches—

Enter the Ghost in his night-gown

Save me and hover o'er me with your wings,
You heavenly guards!—What would your gracious
    figure?
QUEEN. Alas, he's mad.
HAMLET. Do you not come your tardy son to chide,
That lapsed in time and passion lets go by
Th'important acting of your dread command?
O, say!

GHOST. Do not forget! this visitation   110
Is but to whet thy almost blunted purpose—
But look, amazement on thy mother sits,
O step between her and her fighting soul,
Conceit in weakest bodies strongest works,
Speak to her, Hamlet.
HAMLET.   How is it with you, lady?
QUEEN. Alas, how is't with you,
That you do bend your eye on vacancy,
And with th'incorporal air do hold discourse?
Forth at your eyes your spirits wildly peep,
And as the sleeping soldiers in th'alarm,   120
Your bedded hairs like life in excrements
Start up and stand an end. O gentle son,
Upon the heat and flame of thy distemper
Sprinkle cool patience. Whereon do you look?
HAMLET. On him! on him! Look you, how pale he
    glares!
His form and cause conjoined, preaching to stones,
Would make them capable. Do not look upon me,
Lest with this piteous action you convert
My stern effects, then what I have to do
Will want true colour, tears perchance for blood. 130
QUEEN. To whom do you speak this?
HAMLET.   Do you see nothing there?
QUEEN. Nothing at all, yet all that is I see.
HAMLET. Nor did you nothing hear?
QUEEN.   No, nothing but ourselves.
HAMLET. Why, look you there! look how it steals
    away!
My father in his habit as he lived,
Look where he goes, even now, out at the portal.
                                        The Ghost vanishes
QUEEN. This is the very coinage of your brain!
This bodiless creation ecstasy
Is very cunning in.
HAMLET.   Ecstasy!
My pulse as yours doth temperately keep time,   140
And makes as healthful music—it is not madness
That I have uttered, bring me to the test
And I the matter will re-word, which madness
Would gambol from. Mother, for love of grace,
Lay not that flattering unction to your soul,
That not your trespass but my madness speaks,
It will but skin and film the ulcerous place,
Whiles rank corruption mining all within
Infects unseen. Confess yourself to heaven,
Repent what's past, avoid what is to come,   150
And do not spread the compost on the weeds
To make them ranker. Forgive me this my virtue,
For in the fatness of these pursy times
Virtue itself of vice must pardon beg,
Yea curb and woo for leave to do him good.
QUEEN. O Hamlet, thou hast cleft my heart in twain.
HAMLET. O throw away the worser part of it,
And live the purer with the other half.
Good night, but go not to my uncle's bed,
Assume a virtue if you have it not.   160
That monster custom, who all sense doth eat
Of habits evil, is angel yet in this,
That to the use of actions fair and good
He likewise gives a frock or livery
That aptly is put on. Refrain to-night,
And that shall lend a kind of easiness
To the next abstinence, the next more easy:
For use almost can change the stamp of nature,

And either ... the devil, or throw him out,
With wondrous potency: once more, good night, 170
And when you are desirous to be blessed,
I'll blessing beg of you. For this same lord,
Pointing to Polonius
I do repent; but heaven hath pleased it so,
To punish me with this, and this with me,
That I must be their scourge and minister.
I will bestow him and will answer well
The death I gave him; so, again, good night.
I must be cruel only to be kind.
This bad begins, and worse remains behind....
One word more, good lady.
QUEEN. What shall I do? 180
HAMLET. Not this by no means that I bid you do—
Let the bloat king tempt you again to bed,
Pinch wanton on your cheek, call you his mouse,
And let him for a pair of reechy kisses,
Or paddling in your neck with his damned fingers,
Make you to ravel all this matter out
That I essentially am not in madness,
But mad in craft. 'Twere good you let him know,
For who that's but a queen, fair, sober, wise,
Would from a paddock, from a bat, a gib, 190
Such dear concernings hide? who would do so?
No, in despite of sense and secrecy,
Unpeg the basket on the house's top,
Let the birds fly, and like the famous ape,
To try conclusions in the basket creep,
And break your own neck down.
QUEEN. Be thou assured, if words be made of breath,
And breath of life, I have no life to breathe
What thou hast said to me.
HAMLET. I must to England, you know that?
QUEEN. Alack, 200
I had forgot, 'tis so concluded on.
HAMLET. There's letters sealed, and my two
 school-fellows,
Whom I will trust as I will adders fanged,
They bear the mandate—they must sweep my way
And marshal me to knavery: let it work,
For 'tis the sport to have the enginer
Hoist with his own petar, and't shall go hard
But I will delve one yard below their mines,
And blow them at the moon: O, 'tis most sweet
When in one line two crafts directly meet. 210
This man shall set me packing,
I'll lug the guts into the neighbour room;
Mother, good night indeed. This counsellor
Is now most still, most secret, and most grave,
Who was in life a foolish prating knave....
Come, sir, to draw toward an end with you....
Good night, mother.
He drags the body from the room

ACT 4
Scene 1

The King enters with Rosencrantz and Guildenstern

KING. There's matter in these sighs, these profound
 heaves,
You must translate, 'tis fit we understand them.
Where is your son?
QUEEN. Bestow this place on us a little while....
Rosencrantz and Guildenstern depart

Ah, mine own lord, what have I seen to-night!
KING. What, Gertrude? how does Hamlet?
QUEEN. Mad as the sea and wind when both contend
Which is the mightier—in his lawless fit,
Behind the arras hearing something stir,
Whips out his rapier, cries 'A rat, a rat!' 10
And in this brainish apprehension kills
The unseen good old man.
KING. O heavy deed!
It had been so with us had we been there.
His liberty is full of threats to all,
To you yourself, to us, to every one.
Alas, how shall this bloody deed be answered?
It will be laid to us, whose providence
Should have kept short, restrained, and out of haunt
This mad young man; but so much was our love,
We would not understand what was most fit, 20
But like the owner of a foul disease,
To keep it from divulging, let it feed
Even on the pith of life: where is he gone?
QUEEN. To draw apart the body he hath killed,
O'er whom his very madness, like some ore
Among a mineral of metals base,
Shows itself pure—a' weeps for what is done.
KING. O, Gertrude, come away!
The sun no sooner shall the mountains touch,
But we will ship him hence, and this vile deed 30
We must with all our majesty and skill
Both countenance and excuse. Ho! Guildenstern!

Rosencrantz and Guildenstern return

Friends both, go join you with some further aid—
Hamlet in madness hath Polonius slain,
And from his mother's closet hath he dragged
 him—
Go, seek him out, speak fair, and bring the body
Into the chapel; I pray you, haste in this.
They go
Come, Gertrude, we'll call up our wisest friends,
And let them know both what we mean to do
And what's untimely done: [so haply slander,] 40
Whose whisper o'er the world's diameter,
As level as the cannon to his blank,
Transports his poisoned shot, may miss our name,
And hit the woundless air. O, come away!
My soul is full of discord and dismay. *They go*

Scene 2: *Another room of the castle*

Hamlet enters

HAMLET. Safely stowed.
CALLING WITHOUT. Hamlet! Lord Hamlet!
HAMLET. But soft, what noise, who calls on Hamlet?
O, here they come!

Rosencrantz and Guildenstern enter

ROSENCRANTZ. What have you done, my lord, with
 the dead body?
HAMLET. Compounded it with dust whereto 'tis kin.
ROSENCRANTZ. Tell us where 'tis that we may take it
 thence,
And bear it to the chapel.
HAMLET. Do not believe it.
ROSENCRANTZ. Believe what? 10
HAMLET. That I can keep your counsel and not mine

own. Besides, to be demanded of a sponge, what replication should be made by the son of a king?

ROSENCRANTZ. Take you me for a sponge, my lord?

HAMLET. Ay, sir, that soaks up the king's countenance, his rewards, his authorities. But such officers do the king best service in the end, he keeps them like an apple in the corner of his jaw, first mouthed to be last swallowed—when he needs what you have gleaned, it is but squeezing you, and, sponge, you 20 shall be dry again.

ROSENCRANTZ. I understand you not, my lord.

HAMLET. I am glad of it—a knavish speech sleeps in a foolish ear.

ROSENCRANTZ. My lord, you must tell us where the body is, and go with us to the king.

HAMLET. The body is with the king, but the king is not with the body. The king is a thing——

GUILDENSTERN. A thing, my lord!

HAMLET. Of nothing, bring me to him. Hide fox, and 30 all after. *He goes; they pursue*

Scene 3: *The hall of the castle, as before*

Enter the King with two or three councillors of state

KING. I have sent to seek him, and to find the body.
How dangerous is it that this man goes loose!
Yet must not we put the strong law on him,
He's loved of the distracted multitude,
Who like not in their judgement but their eyes,
And where 'tis so, th'offender's scourge is weighed
But never the offence: to bear all smooth and even,
This sudden sending him away must seem
Deliberate pause. Diseases desperate grown
By desperate appliance are relieved, 10
Or not at all.

Rosencrantz, Guildenstern and others enter

How now! what hath befallen?

ROSENCRANTZ. Where the dead body is bestowed, my lord,
We cannot get from him.

KING. But where is he?

ROSENCRANTZ. Without, my lord, guarded, to know your pleasure.

KING. Bring him before us.

ROSENCRANTZ. Ho! bring in the lord.

Hamlet enters guarded by soldiers

KING. Now, Hamlet, where's Polonius?

HAMLET. At supper.

KING. At supper? where?

HAMLET. Not where he eats, but where a' is eaten—a certain convocation of politic worms are e'en at 20 him: your worm is your only emperor for diet, we fat all creatures else to fat us, and we fat ourselves for maggots. Your fat king and your lean beggar is but variable service, two dishes, but to one table—that's the end.

KING. Alas, alas!

HAMLET. A man may fish with the worm that hath eat of a king, and eat of the fish that hath fed of that worm.

KING. What dost thou mean by this? 30

HAMLET. Nothing, but to show you how a king may go a progress through the guts of a beggar.

KING. Where is Polonius?

HAMLET. In heaven—send thither to see, if your messenger find him not there, seek him i'th'other place yourself. But if indeed you find him not within this month, you shall nose him as you go up the stairs into the lobby.

KING [*to attendants*]. Go seek him there.

HAMLET. A' will stay till you come. *They depart* 40

KING. Hamlet, this deed, for thine especial safety,
Which we do tender, as we dearly grieve
For that which thou hast done, must send thee hence
With fiery quickness. Therefore prepare thyself,
The bark is ready, and the wind at help,
Th'associates tend, and every thing is bent
For England.

HAMLET. For England.

KING. Ay. Hamlet.

HAMLET. Good.

KING. So is it if thou knew'st our purposes.

HAMLET. I see a cherub that sees them. But, come, for England! Farewell, dear mother. 50

KING. Thy loving father, Hamlet.

HAMLET. My mother—father and mother is man and wife, man and wife is one flesh, and so my mother: come, for England! *They go*

KING [*to Rosencrantz and Guildenstern*]. Follow him at foot, tempt him with speed aboard,
Delay it not, I'll have him hence to-night.
Away! for every thing is sealed and done
That else leans on th'affair—pray you, make haste. . . .

All depart save the King

And, England, if my love thou hold'st at aught—
As my great power thereof may give thee sense, 60
Since yet thy cicatrice looks raw and red
After the Danish sword, and thy free awe
Pays homage to us—thou mayst not coldly set
Our sovereign process, which imports at full
By letters congruing to that effect,
The present death of Hamlet. Do it, England,
For like the hectic in my blood he rages,
And thou must cure me; till I know 'tis done,
Howe'er my haps, my joys were ne'er begun.

He goes

Scene 4: *A plain near to a port in Denmark*

Prince Fortinbras, with his army on the march

FORTINBRAS. Go, captain, from me greet the Danish king,
Tell him that by his license Fortinbras
Craves the conveyance of a promised march
Over his kingdom. You know the rendezvous.
If that his majesty would aught with us,
We shall express our duty in his eye,
And let him know so.

CAPTAIN. I will do't, my lord.

FORTINBRAS [*to the troops*]. Go softly on.

Fortinbras and the army go

The Captain meets Hamlet, Rosencrantz, Guildenstern and the guard

HAMLET. Good sir, whose powers are these?

CAPTAIN. They are of Norway, sir. 10

HAMLET. How purposed, sir, I pray you?

CAPTAIN. Against some part of Poland.

HAMLET. Who commands them, sir?

CAPTAIN. The nephew to old Norway, Fortinbras.
HAMLET. Goes it against the main of Poland, sir,
Or for some frontier?
CAPTAIN. Truly to speak, and with no addition,
We go to gain a little patch of ground
That hath in it no profit but the name.
To pay five ducats, five, I would not farm it;   20
Nor will it yield to Norway or the Pole
A ranker rate should it be sold in fee.
HAMLET. Why, then the Polack never will defend it.
CAPTAIN. Yes, 'tis already garrisoned.
HAMLET. Two thousand souls and twenty thousand
ducats
Will not debate the question of this straw!
This is th'imposthume of much wealth and peace,
That inward breaks, and shows no cause without
Why the man dies.... I humbly thank you, sir.
CAPTAIN. God bye you, sir.   *He goes*
ROSENCRANTZ.   Will't please you go, my lord?   30
HAMLET. I'll be with you straight, go a little before....
Rosencrantz, Guildenstern and the rest pass on
How all occasions do inform against me,
And spur my dull revenge! What is a man,
If his chief good and market of his time
Be but to sleep and feed? a beast, no more:
Sure he that made us with such large discourse,
Looking before and after, gave us not
That capability and god-like reason
To fust in us unused. Now, whether it be
Bestial oblivion, or some craven scruple   40
Of thinking too precisely on th'event—
A thought which quartered hath but one part
wisdom,
And ever three parts coward—I do not know
Why yet I live to say 'This thing's to do,'
Sith I have cause, and will, and strength, and means,
To do't ... Examples gross as earth exhort me.
Witness this army of such mass and charge,
Led by a delicate and tender prince,
Whose spirit with divine ambition puffed
Makes mouths at the invisible event,   50
Exposing what is mortal and unsure
To all that fortune, death and danger dare,
Even for an egg-shell.... Rightly to be great
Is not to stir without great argument,
But greatly to find quarrel in a straw
When honour's at the stake. How stand I then,
That have a father killed, a mother stained,
Excitements of my reason and my blood,
And let all sleep? while to my shame I see
The imminent death of twenty thousand men,   60
That for a fantasy and trick of fame
Go to their graves like beds, fight for a plot
Whereon the numbers cannot try the cause,
Which is not tomb enough and continent
To hide the slain? O, from this time forth,
My thoughts be bloody, or be nothing worth!
                                        He follows on

Scene 5: *A room in the castle of Elsinore.*

The Queen with her ladies, Horatio and a gentleman

QUEEN. I will not speak with her.
GENTLEMAN. She is importunate, indeed distract,
Her mood will needs be pitied.
QUEEN.   What would she have?
GENTLEMAN. She speaks much of her father, says she
hears
There's tricks i'th'world, and hems, and beats her
heart,
Spurns enviously at straws, speaks things in doubt
That carry but half sense. Her speech is nothing,
Yet the unshapéd use of it doth move
The hearers to collection—they aim at it,
And botch the words up fit to their own thoughts,   10
Which as her winks and nods and gestures yield
them,
Indeed would make one think there might be
thought,
Though nothing sure, yet much unhappily.
HORATIO. 'Twere good she were spoken with, for she
may strew
Dangerous conjectures in ill-breeding minds.
QUEEN. Let her come in.   *The gentleman goes out*
[*aside*] "To my sick soul, as sin's true nature is,
Each toy seems prologue to some great amiss,
So full of artless jealousy is guilt,
It spills itself, in fearing to be spilt."   20

*The gentleman returns with Ophelia, distracted, a lute in
her hands and her hair about her shoulders*

OPHELIA. Where is the beauteous majesty of
Denmark?
QUEEN. How now, Ophelia?
OPHELIA [*sings*]
        How should I your true love know
            From another one?
        By his cockle hat and staff,
            And his sandal shoon.
QUEEN. Alas, sweet lady, what imports this song?
OPHELIA. Say you? nay, pray you mark.
    [*sings*]   He is dead and gone, lady,
            He is dead and gone,   30
        At his head a grass-green turf,
            At his heels a stone.
    O, ho!
QUEEN.   Nay, but Ophelia—
OPHELIA.   Pray you mark.
    [*sings*] White his shroud as the mountain snow—

The King enters

QUEEN. Alas, look here, my lord.
OPHELIA [*sings*].
        Larded all with sweet flowers,
        Which bewept to the grave did not go,
            With true-love showers.
KING. How do you, pretty lady?
OPHELIA. Well, God dild you! they say the owl was a   40
baker's daughter. Lord, we know what we are, but
know not what we may be.... God be at your
table!
KING. Conceit upon her father.
OPHELIA. Pray you let's have no words of this, but
when they ask you what it means, say you this....
    [*sings*] To-morrow is Saint Valentine's day,
            All in the morning betime,
        And I a maid at your window
            To be your Valentine.   50
        Then up he rose, and donned his clo'es,
            And dupped the chamber door,
        Let in the maid, that out a maid
            Never departed more.

KING. Pretty Ophelia!

OPHELIA. Indeed, la, without an oath, I'll make an
end on't—
[*sings*] By Gis and by Saint Charity,
   Alack and fie for shame!
  Young men will do't, if they come to't, 60
  By Cock, they are to blame.
  Quoth she, Before you tumbled me,
  You promised me to wed.
(He answers.)
  So would I ha' done, by yonder sun,
  An thou hadst not come to my bed.

KING. How long hath she been thus?

OPHELIA. I hope all will be well. We must be patient,
but I cannot choose but weep to think they would
lay him i'th'cold ground. My brother shall know of 70
it, and so I thank you for your good counsel. Come,
my coach! Good night, ladies, good night. Sweet
ladies, good night, good night.   *She goes*

KING. Follow her close, give her good watch, I pray
you.   *Horatio and the gentleman follow her*
O, this is the poison of deep grief, it springs
All from her father's death—and now behold!
O Gertrude, Gertrude,
When sorrows come, they come not single spies,
But in battalions: first her father slain,
Next your son gone, and he most violent author 80
Of his own just remove, the people muddied,
Thick and unwholesome in their thoughts and
 whispers
For good Polonius' death—and we have done but
 greenly,
In hugger-mugger to inter him—poor Ophelia
Divided from herself and her fair judgement,
Without the which we are pictures or mere beasts,
Last, and as much containing as all these,
Her brother is in secret come from France,
Feeds on his wonder, keeps himself in clouds,
And wants not buzzers to infect his ear 90
With pestilent speeches of his father's death,
Wherein necessity, of matter beggared,
Will nothing stick our person to arraign
In ear and ear: O my dear Gertrude, this
Like to a murdering-piece in many places
Gives me superfluous death! *A tumult without*

QUEEN.   Alack! what noise is this?

KING [*calls*]. Attend!   *An attendant enters*
Where are my Switzers? let them guard the door.
What is the matter?

ATTENDANT.   Save yourself, my lord!
The ocean, overpeering of his list, 100
Eats not the flats with more impiteous haste
Than young Laertes in a riotous head
O'erbears your officers: the rabble call him lord,
And as the world were now but to begin,
Antiquity forgot, custom not known,
The ratifiers and props of every word,
They cry 'Choose we, Laertes shall be king!'
Caps, hands, and tongues applaud it to the clouds,
'Laertes shall be king, Laertes king!'
      The shouts grow louder

QUEEN. How cheerfully on the false trail they cry! 110
O, this is counter, you false Danish dogs!

KING. The doors are broke.

Enter Laertes, armed, with Danes following

LAERTES. Where is this king? Sirs, stand you all
 without.

DANES. No, let's come in.

LAERTES.   I pray you, give me leave.

DANES. We will, we will.
     They retire without the door

LAERTES. I thank you, keep the door. O thou vile king,
Give me my father.

QUEEN.   Calmly, good Laertes.

LAERTES. That drop of blood that's calm proclaims me
 bastard,
Cries cuckold to my father, brands the harlot,
Even here, between the chaste unsmirchéd brows 120
Of my true mother.

KING.   What is the cause, Laertes,
That thy rebellion looks so giant-like?
Let him go Gertrude, do not fear our person,
There's such divinity doth hedge a king,
That treason can but peep to what it would,
Acts little of his will. Tell me, Laertes,
Why thou art thus incensed—let him go,
 Gertrude—
Speak, man.

LAERTES. Where is my father?

KING.   Dead.

QUEEN.   But not by him.

KING. Let him demand his fill. 130

LAERTES. How came he dead? I'll not be juggled with
To hell allegiance, vows to the blackest devil,
Conscience and grace to the profoundest pit!
I dare damnation. To this point I stand,
That both the worlds I give to negligence,
Let come what comes, only I'll be revenged
Most throughly for my father.

KING.   Who shall stay you?

LAERTES. My will, not all the world's:
And for my means, I'll husband them so well,
They shall go far with little.

KING.   Good Laertes, 140
If you desire to know the certainty
Of your dear father, is't writ in your revenge,
That, sweepstake, you will draw both friend and
 foe,
Winner and loser?

LAERTES. None but his enemies.

KING.   Will you know them then?

LAERTES. To his good friends thus wide I'll ope my
 arms,
And like the kind life-rend'ring pelican,
Repast them with my blood.

KING.   Why, now you speak
Like a good child and a true gentleman.
That I am guiltless of your father's death, 150
And am most sensibly in grief for it,
It shall as level to your judgement 'pear,
As day does to your eye.

SHOUTING WITHOUT. Let her come in.

LAERTES. How now! what noise is that?

Ophelia re-enters

O heat, dry up my brains, tears seven times salt,
Burn out the sense and virtue of mine eye!
By heaven, thy madness shall be paid with weight,
Till our scale turn the beam. O rose of May,
Dear maid, kind sister, sweet Ophelia!
O heavens, is't possible a young maid's wits 160

Should be as mortal as an old man's life?
Nature is fine in love, and where 'tis fine,
It sends some precious instance of itself
After the thing it loves.

OPHELIA [*sings*].
　　They bore him barefaced on the bier,
　　Hey non nonny, nonny, hey nonny,
　　And in his grave rained many a tear—
Fare you well, my dove!

LAERTES. Hadst thou thy wits, and didst persuade
　revenge,
It could not move thus.   170

OPHELIA. You must sing, 'Adown adown,' an you call
him adown-a. O, how the wheel becomes it! It is
the false steward that stole his master's daughter.

LAERTES. This nothing's more than matter.

OPHELIA [*to Laertes*]. There's rosemary, that's for remembrance—pray you, love, remember—and
there is pansies, that's for thoughts.

LAERTES. A document in madness, thoughts and remembrance fitted.

OPHELIA [*to the King*]. There's fennel for you, and   180
columbines. [*to the Queen*] There's rue for you, and
here's some for me, we may call it herb of grace
o'Sundays—O, you must wear your rue with a
difference. There's a daisy. I would give you some
violets, but they withered all, when my father
died—they say a' made a good end——
[*sings*]　For bonny sweet Robin is all my joy—

LAERTES. Thought and affliction, passion, hell itself,
She turns to favour and to prettiness.

OPHELIA [*sings*].
　　And will a' not come again?   190
　　And will a' not come again?
　　　No, no, he is dead,
　　　Go to thy death-bed,
　　He never will come again.

　　His beard was as white as snow,
　　All flaxen was his poll,
　　　He is gone, he is gone,
　　　And we cast away moan,
　　God ha' mercy on his soul!—
And of all Christian souls I pray God. God bye you.   200
　　　　　　　　　　　　　　　　　　She goes

LAERTES. Do you see this, O God?

KING. Laertes, I must commune with your grief,
Or you deny me right. Go but apart,
Make choice of whom your wisest friends you will,
And they shall hear and judge 'twixt you and me.
If by direct or by collateral hand
They find us touched, we will our kingdom give,
Our crown, our life, and all that we call ours,
To you in satisfaction; but if not,
Be you content to lend your patience to us,   210
And we shall jointly labour with your soul
To give it due content.

LAERTES.　　　　　　　　Let this be so.
His means of death, his obscure funeral,
No trophy, sword, nor hatchment o'er his bones,
No noble rite, nor formal ostentation,
Cry to be heard as 'twere from heaven to earth,
That I must call't in question.

KING.　　　　　　　　So you shall,
And where th'offence is let the great axe fall.
I pray you, go with me.　　　　　　　*They go*

Scene 6

Horatio and others enter

HORATIO. What are they that would speak with me?

GENTLEMAN. Seafaring men, sir. They say they have
letters for you.

HORATIO. Let them come in.　*An attendant goes out*
[*aside*] I do not know from what part of the world
I should be greeted, if not from Lord Hamlet.

The attendant brings in sailors

1 SAILOR. God bless you, sir.

HORATIO. Let him bless thee too.

1 SAILOR. A' shall, sir, an't please him. There's a letter
for you, sir, it came from th'ambassador that was   10
bound for England, if your name be Horatio, as I
am let to know it is.

HORATIO [*turns aside and reads*]. 'Horatio, when thou
shalt have overlooked this, give these fellows some
means to the king, they have letters for him . . . Ere
we were two days old at sea, a pirate of very warlike appointment gave us chase. Finding ourselves
too slow of sail, we put on a compelled valour, and
in the grapple I boarded them. On the instant they
got clear of our ship, so I alone became their   20
prisoner. They have dealt with me like thieves of
mercy, but they knew what they did. I am to do a
good turn for them. Let the king have the letters I
have sent, and repair thou to me with as much speed
as thou wouldest fly death. I have words to speak
in thine ear will make thee dumb, yet are they much
too light for the bore of the matter. These good
fellows will bring thee where I am. Rosencrantz
and Guildenstern hold their course for England—of
them I have much to tell thee. Farewell.   30
　　　　　He that thou knowest thine, HAMLET.'
Come, I will give you way for these your letters,
And do't the speedier that you may direct me
To him from whom you brought them.
　　　　　　　　　　　　　　　　　　They go

Scene 7

The King and Laertes return

KING. Now must your conscience my acquittance seal,
And you must put me in your heart for friend,
Sith you have heard and with a knowing ear
That he which hath your noble father slain
Pursued my life.

LAERTES.　　　　　It well appears: but tell me,
Why you proceeded not against these feats,
So crimeful and so capital in nature,
As by your safety, greatness, wisdom, all things else,
You mainly were stirred up.

KING.　　　　　　　　O, for two special reasons,
Which may to you perhaps seem much unsinewed,   10
But yet to me they're strong. The queen his mother
Lives almost by his looks, and for myself,
My virtue or my plague, be it either which,
She is so conjunctive to my life and soul,
That as the star moves not but in his sphere
I could not but by her. The other motive,
Why to a public count I might not go,
Is the great love the general gender bear him,
Who dipping all his faults in their affection,
Would like the spring that turneth wood to stone,   20

Convert his gyves to graces, so that my arrows,
Too slightly timbered for so loud a wind,
Would have reverted to my bow again,
And not where I had aimed them.
LAERTES. And so have I a noble father lost,
A sister driven into desperate terms,
Whose worth, if praises may go back again,
Stood challenger on mount of all the age
For her perfections. But my revenge will come.
KING. Break not your sleeps for that, you must not
    think   30
That we are made of stuff so flat and dull,
That we can let our beard be shook with danger
And think it pastime. You shortly shall hear more.
I loved your father, and we love ourself,
And that I hope will teach you to imagine—

Enter a Messenger with letters

How now! what news?
MESSENGER.   Letters, my lord, from Hamlet.
These to your majesty, these to the queen.
KING. From Hamlet! who brought them?
MESSENGER. Sailors, my lord, they say, I saw them not.
They were given me by Claudio, he received them 40
Of him that brought them.
KING.   Leave us. Laertes, you shall hear them ...
Leave us.   *The Messenger goes*
[reads] 'High and mighty, you shall know I am set
naked on your kingdom. To-morrow shall I beg
leave to see your kingly eyes, when I shall, first
asking your pardon thereunto, recount the occasion
of my sudden and more strange return. HAMLET.'
What should this mean? are all the rest come back?
Or is it some abuse, and no such thing?
LAERTES. Know you the hand?
KING.   'Tis Hamlet's character.... 'Naked'— 50
And in a postscript here he says 'alone.'
Can you devise me?
LAERTES. I am lost in it, my lord, but let him come!
It warms the very sickness in my heart
That I shall live and tell him to his teeth
'Thus diddest thou.'
KING.   If it be so, Laertes,—
As how should it be so? how otherwise?—
Will you be ruled by me?
LAERTES.   Ay, my lord,
So you will not o'errule me to a peace.
KING. To thine own peace. If he be now returned, 60
As checking at his voyage, and that he means
No more to undertake it, I will work him
To an exploit, now ripe in my device,
Under the which he shall not choose but fall:
And for his death no wind of blame shall breathe,
But even his mother shall uncharge the practice,
And call it accident.
LAERTES.   My lord, I will be ruled,
The rather if you could devise it so
That I might be the organ.
KING.   It falls right.
You have been talked of since your travel much, 70
And that in Hamlet's hearing, for a quality
Wherein they say you shine. Your sum of parts
Did not together pluck such envy from him,
As did that one, and that in my regard
Of the unworthiest siege.
LAERTES.   What part is that, my lord?

KING. A very riband in the cap of youth,
Yet needful too, for youth no less becomes
The light and careless livery that it wears,
Than settled age his sables and his weeds
Importing health and graveness; two months since, 80
Here was a gentleman of Normandy—
I have seen myself, and served against, the French,
And they can well on horseback—but this gallant
Had witchcraft in't, he grew unto his seat,
And to such wondrous doing brought his horse,
As had he been incorpsed and demi-natured
With the brave beast. So far he topped my thought,
That I in forgery of shapes and tricks
Come short of what he did.
LAERTES.   A Norman, was't?
KING. A Norman.   90
LAERTES. Upon my life, Lamord.
KING.   The very same.
LAERTES. I know him well, he is the brooch indeed
And gem of all the nation.
KING. He made confession of you,
And gave you such a masterly report
For art and exercise in your defence,
And for your rapier most especial,
That he cried out 'twould be a sight indeed
If one could match you; the scrimers of their nation
He swore had neither motion, guard, nor eye, 100
If you opposed them; sir, this report of his
Did Hamlet so envenom with his envy,
That he could nothing do but wish and beg
Your sudden coming o'er to play with him.
Now, out of this—
LAERTES.   What out of this, my lord?
KING. Laertes, was your father dear to you?
Or are you like the painting of a sorrow,
A face without a heart?
LAERTES.   Why ask you this?
KING. Not that I think you did not love your father,
But that I know love is begun by time, 110
And that I see in passages of proof
Time qualifies the spark and fire of it.
There lives within the very flame of love
A kind of wick or snuff that will abate it,
And nothing is at a like goodness still,
For goodness, growing to a plurisy,
Dies in his own too-much. That we would do
We should do when we would: for this 'would'
    changes,
And hath abatements and delays as many
As there are tongues, are hands, are accidents, 120
And then this 'should' is like a spendthrift sigh,
That hurts by easing; but to the quick o'th'ulcer—
Hamlet comes back, what would you undertake
To show yourself your father's son in deed
More than in words?
LAERTES.   To cut his throat i'th'church.
KING. No place indeed should murder sanctuarize,
Revenge should have no bounds: but, good Laertes,
Will you do this, keep close within your chamber.
Hamlet returned shall know you are come home.
We'll put on those shall praise your excellence, 130
And set a double varnish on the fame
The Frenchman gave you, bring you in fine
    together,
And wager on your heads; he being remiss,
Most generous, and free from all contriving,

Will not peruse the foils, so that with ease,
Or with a little shuffling, you may choose
A sword unbated, and in a pass of practice
Requite him for your father.
LAERTES.   I will do't,
And, for the purpose, I'll anoint my sword.
I bought an unction of a mountebank,   140
So mortal, that but dip a knife in it,
Where it draws blood, no cataplasm so rare,
Collected from all simples that have virtue
Under the moon, can save the thing from death
That is but scratched withal. I'll touch my point
With this contagion, that if I gall him slightly,
It may be death.
KING.   Let's further think of this,
Weigh what convenience both of time and means
May fit us to our shape. If this should fail,
And that our drift look through our bad
    performance,   150
'Twere better not assayed. Therefore this project
Should have a back or second that might hold,
If this did blast in proof; soft, let me see,
We'll make a solemn wager on your cunnings—
I ha't!
When in your motion you are hot and dry,
As make your bouts more violent to that end,
And that he calls for drink, I'll have preferred him
A chalice for the nonce, whereon but sipping,
If he by chance escape your venomed stuck,   160
Our purpose may hold there ... But stay, what
    noise?

The Queen enters

QUEEN. One woe doth tread upon another's heel,
So fast they follow; your sister's drowned, Laertes.
LAERTES. Drowned! O, where?
QUEEN. There is a willow grows askant the brook,
That shows his hoar leaves in the glassy stream,
Therewith fantastic garlands did she make
Of crow-flowers, nettles, daisies, and long purples
That liberal shepherds give a grosser name,
But our cold maids do dead men's fingers call them.   170
There on the pendent boughs her crownet weeds
Clamb'ring to hang, an envious sliver broke,
When down her weedy trophies and herself
Fell in the weeping brook. Her clothes spread wide,
And mermaid-like awhile they bore her up,
Which time she chanted snatches of old lauds,
As one incapable of her own distress,
Or like a creature native and indued
Unto that element. But long it could not be
Till that her garments, heavy with their drink,   180
Pulled the poor wretch from her melodious lay
To muddy death.
LAERTES.   Alas then, she is drowned?
QUEEN. Drowned, drowned.
LAERTES. Too much of water hast thou, poor Ophelia,
And therefore I forbid my tears; but yet
It is our trick, nature her custom holds,
Let shame say what it will—when these are gone,
The woman will be out ... Adieu, my lord!
I have a speech o' fire that fain would blaze,
But that this folly douts it.   *He goes*
KING.   Let's follow, Gertrude.   190
How much I had to do to calm his rage!

Now fear I this will give it start again,
Therefore let's follow.   *They follow*

ACT 5
Scene 1: *A graveyard*

Enter two clowns (a sexton and his mate) with spades and mattocks

1 CLOWN. Is she to be buried in Christian burial when she wilfully seeks her own salvation?
2 CLOWN. I tell thee she is, therefore make her grave straight. The crowner hath sat on her, and finds it Christian burial.
1 CLOWN. How can that be, unless she drowned herself in her own defence?
2 CLOWN. Why, 'tis found so.
1 CLOWN. It must be 'se offendendo,' it cannot be else. For here lies the point, if I drown myself wittingly, 10 it argues an act, and an act hath three branches, it is to act, to do, and to perform—argal, she drowned herself wittingly.
2 CLOWN. Nay, but hear you, goodman delver.
1 CLOWN. Give me leave. Here lies the water—good. Here stands the man—good. If the man go to this water and drown himself, it is, will he nill he, he goes, mark you that. But if the water come to him, and drown him, he drowns not himself—argal, he that is not guilty of his own death, shortens not his 20 own life.
2 CLOWN. But is this law?
1 CLOWN. Ay, marry is't, crowner's quest law.
2 CLOWN. Will you ha' the truth an't? if this had not been a gentlewoman, she should have been buried out a Christian burial.
1 CLOWN. Why, there thou say'st, and the more pity that great folk should have countenance in this world to drown or hang themselves more than their even-Christen ... Come, my spade! there is no 30 ancient gentlemen but gardeners, ditchers and grave-makers—they hold up Adam's profession.
2 CLOWN. Was he a gentleman?
1 CLOWN. A' was the first that ever bore arms.
2 CLOWN. Why, he had none.
1 CLOWN. What, art a heathen? how dost thou understand the Scripture? the Scripture says Adam digged; could he dig without arms? I'll put another question to thee. If thou answerest me not to the purpose, confess thyself—   40
2 CLOWN. Go to.
1 CLOWN. What is he that builds stronger than either the mason, the shipwright, or the carpenter?
2 CLOWN. The gallows-maker, for that frame outlives a thousand tenants.
1 CLOWN. I like thy wit well in good faith, the gallows does well—but how does it well? it does well to those that do ill. Now thou dost ill to say the gallows is built stronger than the church—argal, the gallows may do well to thee. To't again, come.   50
2 CLOWN. 'Who builds stronger than a mason, a ship-wright, or a carpenter?'
1 CLOWN. Ay, tell me that, and unyoke.
2 CLOWN. Marry, now I can tell.
1 CLOWN. To't.
2 CLOWN. Mass, I cannot tell.
1 CLOWN. Cudgel thy brains no more about it, for

your dull ass will not mend his pace with beating.
And when you are asked this question next, say 'a
grave-maker.' The houses he makes lasts till dooms- 60
day. Go, get thee to Yaughan, and fetch me a stoup
of liquor.   *Second Clown goes*

Hamlet and Horatio are seen entering the graveyard

First Clown digs and sings

   In youth when I did love, did love,
      Methought it was very sweet,
   To contract o' the time for a my behove,
      O, methought there a was nothing a meet.

HAMLET. Has this fellow no feeling of his business that
a' sings in grave-making?
HORATIO. Custom hath made it in him a property of
easiness.   70
HAMLET. 'Tis e'en so, the hand of little employment
hath the daintier sense.
I CLOWN [*sings*].
      But age with his stealing steps
         Hath clawed me in his clutch,
      And hath shipped me intil the land,
         As if I had never been such.
                        He throws up a skull
HAMLET. That skull had a tongue in it, and could sing
once! how the knave jowls it to the ground, as if
'twere Cain's jaw-bone, that did the first murder!
This might be the pate of a politician, which this ass 80
now o'er-reaches; one that would circumvent God,
might it not?
HORATIO. It might, my lord.
HAMLET. Or of a courtier, which could say 'Good
morrow, sweet lord! how dost thou, good lord?'
This might be my lord such-a-one, that praised my
lord such-a-one's horse, when a' meant to beg it,
might it not?
HORATIO. It might, my lord.
HAMLET. Why, e'en so, and now my Lady Worm's, 90
chopless and knocked about the mazzard with a
sexton's spade; here's fine revolution an we had the
trick to see't! did these bones cost no more the
breeding, but to play at loggats with them? mine
ache to think on't.
I CLOWN [*sings*].
      A pick-axe, and a spade, a spade,
         For and a shrouding sheet,
      O, a pit of clay for to be made
         For such a guest is meet.
                        He throws up a second skull
HAMLET. There's another. Why may not that be the 100
skull of a lawyer? Where be his quiddities now, his
quillities, his cases, his tenures, and his tricks? why
does he suffer this rude knave now to knock him
about the sconce with a dirty shovel, and will not
tell him of his action of battery? Hum! this fellow
might be in's time a great buyer of land, with his
statutes, his recognizances, his fines, his double
vouchers, his recoveries: is this the fine of his fines,
and the recovery of his recoveries, to have his fine
pate full of fine dirt? will his vouchers vouch him no 110
more of his purchases, and double ones too, than the
length and breadth of a pair of indentures? the very
conveyances of his lands will scarcely lie in this box,
and must th'inheritor himself have no more, ha?
HORATIO. Not a jot more, my lord.

HAMLET. Is not parchment made of sheep-skins?
HORATIO. Ay, my lord, and of calves'-skins too.
HAMLET. They are sheep and calves which seek out
assurance in that. I will speak to this fellow.... [*they
go forward*] Whose grave's this, sirrah?   120
I CLOWN. Mine, sir—
[*sings*]   O, a pit of clay for to be made
               For such a guest is meet.
HAMLET. I think it be thine, indeed, for thou liest in't.
I CLOWN. You lie out on't sir, and therefore 'tis not
yours; for my part I do not lie in't, and yet it is
mine.
HAMLET. Thou dost lie in't, to be in't and say it is thine.
'Tis for the dead, not for the quick—therefore thou
liest.   130
I CLOWN. 'Tis a quick lie, sir, 'twill away again from
me to you.
HAMLET. What man dost thou dig it for?
I CLOWN. For no man, sir.
HAMLET. What woman then?
I CLOWN. For none neither.
HAMLET. Who is to be buried in't?
I CLOWN. One that was a woman, sir, but rest her
soul she's dead.
HAMLET. How absolute the knave is! we must speak 140
by the card or equivocation will undo us. By the
Lord, Horatio, this three years I have took note of it,
the age is grown so picked, that the toe of the
peasant comes so near the heel of the courtier he galls
his kibe.... How long hast thou been grave-maker?
I CLOWN. Of all the days i'th'year I came to't that
day that our last king Hamlet overcame Fortinbras.
HAMLET. How long is that since?
I CLOWN. Cannot you tell that? every fool can tell
that. It was that very day that young Hamlet was 150
born: he that is mad and sent into England.
HAMLET. Ay, marry, why was he sent into England?
I CLOWN. Why, because a' was mad: a' shall recover
his wits there, or if a' do not, 'tis no great matter
there.
HAMLET. Why?
I CLOWN. 'Twill not be seen in him there, there the
men are as mad as he.
HAMLET. How came he mad?
I CLOWN. Very strangely, they say.   160
HAMLET. How strangely?
I CLOWN. Faith, e'en with losing his wits.
HAMLET. Upon what ground?
I CLOWN. Why, here in Denmark: I have been sexton
here man and boy thirty years.
HAMLET. How long will a man lie i'th'earth ere he rot?
I CLOWN. Faith, if a' be not rotten before a' die, as we
have many pocky corses now-a-days that will scarce
hold the laying in, a' will last you some eight year,
or nine year. A tanner will last you nine year.   170
HAMLET. Why he more than another?
I CLOWN. Why sir, his hide is so tanned with his trade,
that a' will keep out water a great while; and your
water is a sore decayer of your whoreson dead body.
Here's a skull now: this skull hath lien you i'th'earth
three-and-twenty years.
HAMLET. Whose was it?
I CLOWN. A whoreson mad fellow's it was, whose do
you think it was?
HAMLET. Nay, I know not.   180
I CLOWN. A pestilence on him for a mad rogue! a'

poured a flagon of Rhenish on my head once; this same skull, sir, was, sir, Yorick's skull, the king's jester.

HAMLET. This?

1 CLOWN. E'en that.

HAMLET. Let me see. [*he takes the skull*] Alas, poor Yorick! I knew him, Horatio—a fellow of infinite jest, of most excellent fancy. He hath borne me on his back a thousand times, and now how abhorred 190 in my imagination it is! my gorge rises at it.... Here hung those lips that I have kissed I know not how oft. Where be your gibes now? your gambols, your songs, your flashes of merriment, that were wont to set the table on a roar? not one now to mock your own grinning? quite chopfallen? Now get you to my lady's chamber, and tell her, let her paint an inch thick, to this favour she must come. Make her laugh at that.... Prithee, Horatio, tell me one thing.

HORATIO. What's that, my lord. 200

HAMLET. Dost thou think Alexander looked o' this fashion i'th'earth?

HORATIO. E'en so.

HAMLET. And smelt so? pah! *He sets down the skull*

HORATIO. E'en so, my lord.

HAMLET. To what base uses we may return, Horatio! Why may not imagination trace the noble dust of Alexander, till a' find it stopping a bung-hole?

HORATIO. 'Twere to consider too curiously, to consider so. 210

HAMLET. No, faith, not a jot, but to follow him thither with modesty enough, and likelihood to lead it; as thus—Alexander died, Alexander was buried, Alexander returneth to dust, the dust is earth, of earth we make loam, and why of that loam whereto he was converted might they not stop a beer-barrel? Imperious Cæsar, dead and turned to clay, Might stop a hole to keep the wind away. O, that that earth, which kept the world in awe, Should patch a wall t'expel the winter's flaw! 220 But soft, but soft, awhile—here comes the king, The queen, the courtiers.

A procession enters the graveyard: the corpse of Ophelia, with Laertes, the King, the Queen, courtiers and a Doctor of Divinity following

Who is this they follow?
And with such maiméd rites? This doth betoken
The corse they follow did with desp'rate hand
Fordo 'it own life. 'Twas of some estate.
Couch we awhile, and mark. *They retire*

LAERTES. What ceremony else?

HAMLET. That is Laertes,
A very noble youth—mark.

LAERTES. What ceremony else?

DOCTOR. Her obsequies have been as far enlarged 230
As we have warranty. Her death was doubtful,
And but that great command o'ersways the order,
She should in ground unsanctified have lodged
Till the last trumpet: for charitable prayers,
Shards, flints and pebbles should be thrown on her:
Yet here she is allowed her virgin crants,
Her maiden strewments, and the bringing home
Of bell and burial.

LAERTES. Must there no more be done?

DOCTOR. No more be done!
We should profane the service of the dead 240

To sing sage requiem and such rest to her
As to peace-parted souls.

LAERTES. Lay her i'th'earth,
And from her fair and unpolluted flesh
May violets spring! I tell thee, churlish priest,
A minist'ring angel shall my sister be,
When thou liest howling.

HAMLET. What, the fair Ophelia!

QUEEN [*scattering flowers*]. Sweets to the sweet.
Farewell!
I hoped thou shouldst have been my Hamlet's wife:
I thought thy bride-bed to have decked, sweet maid,
And not have strewed thy grave.

LAERTES. O, treble woe 250
Fall ten times treble on that curséd head
Whose wicked deed thy most ingenious sense
Deprived thee of! Hold off the earth awhile,
Till I have caught her once more in mine arms;
Leaps in the grave
Now pile your dust upon the quick and dead,
Till of this flat a mountain you have made
T'o'ertop old Pelion, or the skyish head
Of blue Olympus.

HAMLET [*comes forward*]. What is he whose grief
Bears such an emphasis? whose phrase of sorrow
Conjures the wand'ring stars, and makes them stand 260
Like wonder-wounded hearers? This is I,
Hamlet the Dane. *Leaps in after Laertes*

LAERTES [*grappling with him*]. The devil take thy soul

HAMLET. Thou pray'st not well.
I prithee take thy fingers from my throat,
For though I am not splenitive and rash,
Yet have I in me something dangerous,
Which let thy wiseness fear; hold off thy hand.

KING. Pluck them asunder.

QUEEN. Hamlet, Hamlet!

ALL. Gentlemen!

HORATIO. Good my lord, be quiet.
Attendants part them, and they come up out of the grave

HAMLET. Why, I will fight with him upon this theme 270
Until my eyelids will no longer wag.

QUEEN. O my son, what theme?

HAMLET. I loved Ophelia, forty thousand brothers
Could not with all their quantity of love
Make up my sum.... What wilt thou do for her?

KING. O, he is mad, Laertes.

QUEEN. For love of God, forbear him.

HAMLET. 'Swounds, show me what thou't do:
Woo't weep? woo't fight? woo't fast? woo't tear
thyself?
Woo't drink up eisel? eat a crocodile? 280
I'll do't. Dost thou come here to whine?
To outface me with leaping in her grave?
Be buried quick with her, and so will I.
And if thou prate of mountains, let them throw
Millions of acres on us, till our ground,
Singeing his pate against the burning zone,
Make Ossa like a wart! nay, an thou'lt mouth,
I'll rant as well as thou.

QUEEN. This is mere madness,
And thus awhile the fit will work on him.
Anon as patient as the female dove 290
When that her golden couplets are disclosed
His silence will sit drooping.

HAMLET. Hear you, sir,

What is the reason that you use me thus?
I loved you ever, but it is no matter,
Let Hercules himself do what he may,
The cat will mew, and dog will have his day.

He goes

KING. I pray thee, good Horatio, wait upon him. . . .

Horatio follows

[*to Laertes*] Strengthen your patience in our last
    night's speech,
We'll put the matter to the present push. . . .
Good Gertrude, set some watch over your son.   300
This grave shall have a living monument.
An hour of quiet shortly shall we see,
Till then, in patience our proceeding be.

They go

Scene 2: *The hall of the castle*

Hamlet and Horatio enter

HAMLET. So much for this, sir, now shall you see the
    other—
    You do remember all the circumstance?
HORATIO. Remember it, my lord!
HAMLET. Sir, in my heart there was a kind of fighting
    That would not let me sleep—methought I lay
    Worse than the mutines in the bilboes. Rashly,
    And praised be rashness for it. . . . let us know
    Our indiscretion sometime serves us well,
    When our deep plots do pall, and that should learn
    us
    There's a divinity that shapes our ends,   10
    Rough-hew them how we will—
HORATIO.   That is most certain.
HAMLET. Up from my cabin,
    My sea-gown scarfed about me, in the dark
    Groped I to find out them, had my desire,
    Fingered their packet, and in fine withdrew
    To mine own room again, making so bold,
    My fears forgetting manners, to unseal
    Their grand commission; where I found, Horatio—
    Ah, royal knavery!—an exact command,
    Larded with many several sorts of reasons,   20
    Importing Denmark's health and England's too,
    With, ho! such bugs and goblins in my life,
    That on the supervise, no leisure bated,
    No, not to stay the grinding of the axe,
    My head should be struck off.
HORATIO.   Is't possible?
HAMLET. Here's the commission, read it at more
    leisure.
    But wilt thou hear now how I did proceed?
HORATIO. I beseech you.
HAMLET. Being thus be-netted round with villanies—
    Or I could make a prologue to my brains   30
    They had begun the play. I sat me down,
    Devised a new commission, wrote it fair—
    I once did hold it, as our statists do,
    A baseness to write fair, and laboured much
    How to forget that learning, but, sir, now
    It did me yeoman's service. Wilt thou know
    Th'effect of what I wrote?
HORATIO.   Ay, good my lord.
HAMLET. An earnest conjuration from the king,
    As England was his faithful tributary,
    As love between them like the palm might flourish,   40
    As peace should still her wheaten garland wear

And stand a comma 'tween their amities,
And many such like 'as'es' of great charge,
That on the view and knowing of these contents,
Without debatement further, more or less,
He should those bearers put to sudden death,
Not shriving-time allowed.
HORATIO.   How was this sealed?
HAMLET. Why, even in that was heaven ordinant,
    I had my father's signet in my purse,
    Which was the model of that Danish seal,   50
    Folded the writ up in the form of th'other,
    Subscribed it, gave't th'impression, placed it safely,
    The changeling never known: now, the next day
    Was our sea-fight, and what to this was sequent
    Thou knowest already.
HORATIO. So Guildenstern and Rosencrantz go to't.
HAMLET. Why, man, they did make love to this
    employment,
    They are not near my conscience, their defeat
    Does by their own insinuation grow.
    'Tis dangerous when the baser nature comes   60
    Between the pass and fell incensèd points
    Of mighty opposites.
HORATIO.   Why, what a king is this!
HAMLET. Does it not, think thee, stand me now
    upon—
    He that hath killed my king, and whored my
    mother,
    Popped in between th'election and my hopes,
    Thrown out his angle for my proper life,
    And with such cozenage—is't not perfect conscience
    To quit him with this arm? and is't not to be
    damned,
    To let this canker of our nature come
    In further evil?   70
HORATIO. It must be shortly known to him from
    England
    What is the issue of the business there.
HAMLET. It will be short, the interim is mine,
    And a man's life's no more than to say 'One' . . .
    But I am very sorry, good Horatio,
    That to Laertes I forgot myself;
    For by the image of my cause I see
    The portraiture of his; I'll court his favours:
    But sure the bravery of his grief did put me
    Into a towering passion.
HORATIO.   Peace, who comes here?   80

Enter Osric, a courtier

OSRIC. Your lordship is right welcome back to
    Denmark.
HAMLET. I humbly thank you, sir. . . . Dost know this
    water-fly?
HORATIO. No, my good lord.
HAMLET. Thy state is the more gracious, for 'tis a vice
    to know him. He hath much land, and fertile: let a
    beast be lord of beasts, and his crib shall stand at the
    king's mess. 'Tis a chough, but, as I say, spacious in
    the possession of dirt.   90
OSRIC. Sweet lord, if your lordship were at leisure, I
    should impart a thing to you from his majesty.
HAMLET. I will receive it, sir, with all diligence of spirit.
    Put your bonnet to his right use, 'tis for the head.
OSRIC. I thank your lordship, it is very hot.
HAMLET. No, believe me, 'tis very cold, the wind is
    northerly.

OSRIC. It is indifferent cold, my lord, indeed.

HAMLET. But yet, methinks, it is very sultry and hot for my complexion. 100

OSRIC. Exceedingly, my lord, it is very sultry—as 'twere—I cannot tell how ... But, my lord, his majesty bade me signify to you that a' has laid a great wager on your head. Sir, this is the matter,—

HAMLET [moves him to put on his hat]. I beseech you remember—

OSRIC. Nay, good my lord, for mine ease, in good faith. Sir, here is newly come to court Laertes—believe me, an absolute gentleman, full of most excellent differences, of very soft society, and great 110 showing: indeed, to speak sellingly of him, he is the card or calendar of gentry; for you shall find in him the continent of what parts a gentleman would see.

HAMLET. Sir, his definement suffers no perdition in you, though I know to divide him inventorially would dizzy th'arithmetic of memory, and yet but yaw neither in respect of his quick sail, but in the verity of extolment I take him to be a soul of great article, and his infusion of such dearth and rareness, as to make true diction of him, his semblable is his 120 mirror, and who else would trace him?—his umbrage, nothing more.

OSRIC. Your lordship speaks most infallibly of him.

HAMLET. The concernancy, sir? why do we wrap the gentleman in our more rawer breath?

OSRIC. Sir?

HORATIO. Is't not possible to understand in another tongue? You will to't, sir, really.

HAMLET. What imports the nomination of this gentleman? 130

OSRIC. Of Laertes?

HORATIO. His purse is empty already, all's golden words are spent.

HAMLET. Of him, sir.

OSRIC. I know you are not ignorant—

HAMLET. I would you did, sir, yet in faith if you did, it would not much approve me. Well, sir?

OSRIC. You are not ignorant of what excellence Laertes is—

HAMLET. I dare not confess that, lest I should compare 140 with him in excellence, but to know a man well were to know himself.

OSRIC. I mean, sir, for his weapon, but in the imputation laid on him by them in his meed, he's unfellowed.

HAMLET. What's his weapon?

OSRIC. Rapier and dagger.

HAMLET. That's two of his weapons—but, well.

OSRIC. The king, sir, hath wagered with him six Barbary horses, against the which he has impawned, 150 as I take it, six French rapiers and poniards, with their assigns, as girdle, hangers, and so. Three of the carriages in faith are very dear to fancy, very responsive to the hilts, most delicate carriages, and of very liberal conceit.

HAMLET. What call you the carriages?

HORATIO. I knew you must be edified by the margent ere you had done.

OSRIC. The carriages, sir, are the hangers.

HAMLET. The phrase would be more germane to the 160 matter, if we could carry a cannon by our sides—I would it might be hangers till then. But on! six Barbary horses against six French swords, their

assigns, and three liberal-conceited carriages—that's the French bet against the Danish. Why is this all 'impawned' as you call it?

OSRIC. The king, sir, hath laid, sir, that in a dozen passes between yourself and him he shall not exceed you three hits. He hath laid on twelve for nine. And it would come to immediate trial, if your lordship 170 would vouchsafe the answer.

HAMLET. How if I answer 'no'?

OSRIC. I mean, my lord, the opposition of your person in trial.

HAMLET. Sir, I will walk here in the hall, if it please his majesty. It is the breathing time of day with me. Let the foils be brought, the gentleman willing, and the king hold his purpose, I will win for him an I can, if not I will gain nothing but my shame and the odd hits. 180

OSRIC. Shall I re-deliver you e'en so?

HAMLET. To this effect, sir,—after what flourish your nature will.

OSRIC. I commend my duty to your lordship.

HAMLET. Yours, yours.   *Osric goes*
He does well to commend it himself, there are no tongues else for's turn.

HORATIO. This lapwing runs away with the shell on his head.

HAMLET. A' did comply, sir, with his dug before a' 190 sucked it. Thus has he—and many more of the same bevy that I know the drossy age dotes on—only got the tune of the time and, out of an habit of encounter, a kind of yeasty collection, which carries them through and through the most profound and winnowed opinions, and do but blow them to their trial, the bubbles are out.

A lord enters

LORD. My lord, his majesty commended him to you by young Osric, who brings back to him that you attend him in the hall. He sends to know if your 200 pleasure hold to play with Laertes, or that you will take longer time.

HAMLET. I am constant to my purposes, they follow the king's pleasure. If his fitness speaks, mine is ready; now or whensoever, provided I be so able as now.

LORD. The king, and queen, and all are coming down.

HAMLET. In happy time.

LORD. The queen desires you to use some gentle entertainment to Laertes before you fall to play. 210

HAMLET. She well instructs me.   *The lord departs*

HORATIO. You will lose this wager, my lord.

HAMLET. I do not think so. Since he went into France, I have been in continual practice. I shall win at the odds; but thou wouldst not think how ill all's here about my heart—but it is no matter.

HORATIO. Nay, good my lord—

HAMLET. It is but foolery, but it is such a kind of gain-giving as would perhaps trouble a woman.

HORATIO. If your mind dislike any thing, obey it. I will 220 forestall their repair hither, and say you are not fit.

HAMLET. Not a whit, we defy augury. There is special providence in the fall of a sparrow. If it be now, 'tis not to come—if it be not to come, it will be now—if it be not now, yet it will come—the readiness is all. Since no man, of aught he leaves, knows what is't to leave betimes, let be.

Attendants enter to set benches and carry in cushions for the spectators; next follow trumpeters and drummers with kettle-drums, the King, the Queen and all the court, Osric and another lord, as judges, bearing foils and daggers which are placed upon a table near the wall, and last of all Laertes dressed for the fence

KING. Come, Hamlet, come and take this hand from
      me.
                              *He puts the hand of Laertes into
                                        the hand of Hamlet*
HAMLET. Give me your pardon, sir. I have done you
      wrong,
      But pardon't, as you are a gentleman.   230
      This presence knows, and you must needs have
      heard,
      How I am punished with a sore distraction.
      What I have done
      That might your nature, honour and exception
      Roughly awake, I here proclaim was madness.
      Was't Hamlet wronged Laertes? never Hamlet.
      If Hamlet from himself be ta'en away,
      And when he's not himself does wrong Laertes,
      Then Hamlet does it not, Hamlet denies it.
      Who does it then? his madness. If't be so,   240
      Hamlet is of the faction that is wronged,
      His madness is poor Hamlet's enemy.
      Sir, in this audience,
      Let my disclaiming from a purposed evil
      Free me so far in your most generous thoughts,
      That I have shot my arrow o'er the house,
      And hurt my brother.
LAERTES.   I am satisfied in nature,
      Whose motive in this case should stir me most
      To my revenge, but in my terms of honour
      I stand aloof, and will no reconcilement,   250
      Till by some elder masters of known honour
      I have a voice and precedent of peace,
      To keep my name ungored: but till that time,
      I do receive your offered love like love,
      And will not wrong it.
HAMLET.   I embrace it freely,
      And will this brother's wager frankly play....
      Give us the foils, come on.
LAERTES.   Come. one for me.
HAMLET. I'll be your foil, Laertes. In mine ignorance
      Your skill shall like a star i'th'darkest night
      Stick fiery off indeed.
LAERTES.   You mock me, sir.   260
HAMLET. No, by this hand.
KING. Give them the foils, young Osric. Cousin
      Hamlet,
      You know the wager?
HAMLET.   Very well, my lord.
      Your grace has laid the odds o'th'weaker side.
KING. I do not fear it, I have seen you both—
      But since he is bettered, we have therefore odds.
LAERTES. This is too heavy: let me see another.
HAMLET. This likes me well. These foils have all a
      length?
OSRIC. Ay, my good lord.

*Hamlet makes ready; servants bear in flagons of wine with
cups*

KING. Set me the stoups of wine upon that table.   270
      If Hamlet give the first or second hit,

Or quit in answer of the third exchange,
Let all the battlements their ordnance fire.
The king shall drink to Hamlet's better breath,
And in the cup an union shall he throw,
Richer than that which four successive kings
In Denmark's crown have worn: give me the cups,
And let the kettle to the trumpet speak,
The trumpet to the cannoneer without,
The cannons to the heavens, the heaven to earth,   280
'Now the king drinks to Hamlet.' Come, begin,
And you, the judges, bear a wary eye.

Trumpets sound; Hamlet and Laertes take their stations

HAMLET. Come on, sir.
LAERTES.   Come, my lord.

They play

HAMLET.   One!
LAERTES.   No.
HAMLET.   Judgement?
OSRIC. A hit, a very palpable hit.
                    *The kettle-drum sounds, the trumpets blow,
                           and a cannon-shot is heard without*
LAERTES.   Well, again.
KING. Stay, give me drink. Hamlet, this pearl is thine.
      Here's to thy health! Give him the cup.
HAMLET. I'll play this bout first, set it by a while.
      Come. [*they play again*] Another hit! What say you?
LAERTES. A touch, a touch, I do confess't.
KING. Our son shall win.
QUEEN.   He's fat, and scant of breath.   290
      Here, Hamlet, take my napkin, rub thy brows.
      The queen carouses to thy fortune, Hamlet.
HAMLET. Good madam!
KING.   Gertrude, do not drink.
QUEEN. I will, my lord, I pray you pardon me.
KING [*aside*]. It is the poisoned cup, it is too late!
HAMLET. I dare not drink yet, madam—by and by.
QUEEN. Come, let me wipe thy face.
LAERTES. My lord, I'll hit him now.
KING.   I do not think't.
LAERTES. And yet 'tis almost 'gainst my conscience.
HAMLET. Come, for the third, Laertes. You do but
      dally,   300
      I pray you pass with your best violence.
      I am afeard you make a wanton of me.
LAERTES. Say you so? come on.

They play the third bout

OSRIC. Nothing neither way.
LAERTES. Have at you now!
                         *He wounds Hamlet slightly; in
                            scuffling they change rapiers*
KING.   Part them, they are incensed.
HAMLET. Nay, come again.   *The Queen falls*
OSRIC.   Look to the queen there, ho!
                         Hamlet wounds Laertes deeply
HORATIO. They bleed on both sides!—how is it, my
      lord?   *Laertes falls*
OSRIC. How is't, Laertes?
LAERTES. Why, as a woodcock to my own springe,
      Osric!
      I am justly killed with mine own treachery.   310
HAMLET. How does the queen?
KING.   She swoons to see them bleed.

QUEEN. No, no, the drink, the drink—O my dear
    Hamlet—
    The drink, the drink! I am poisoned!   *She dies*
HAMLET. O villainy! ho! let the door be locked—
    Treachery! seek it out.
LAERTES. It is here, Hamlet. Hamlet, thou art slain,
    No medicine in the world can do thee good,
    In thee there is not half an hour of life,
    The treacherous instrument is in thy hand,
    Unbated and envenomed. The foul practice   320
    Hath turned itself on me, lo, here I lie,
    Never to rise again—thy mother's poisoned—
    I can no more—the king, the king's to blame.
HAMLET. The point envenomed too!—
    Then, venom, to thy work.   *He stabs the King*
ALL. Treason! treason!
KING. O, yet defend me, friends, I am but hurt.
HAMLET. Here, thou incestuous, murderous, damnéd
    Dane,
    Drink off this potion. Is thy union here?
    Follow my mother.   *The King dies*
LAERTES.   He is justly served,   330
    It is a poison tempered by himself.
    Exchange forgiveness with me, noble Hamlet,
    Mine and my father's death come not upon thee,
    Nor thine on me!   *He dies*
HAMLET. Heaven make thee free of it! I follow thee . . .
                  He falls
    I am dead, Horatio. Wretched queen, adieu!
    You that look pale and tremble at this chance,
    That are but mutes or audience to this act,
    Had I but time, as this fell sergeant, Death,
    Is strict in his arrest, O, I could tell you—   340
    But let it be; Horatio, I am dead,
    Thou livest, report me and my cause aright
    To the unsatisfied.
HORATIO.   Never believe it;
    I am more an antique Roman than a Dane—
    Here's yet some liquor left.
HAMLET.   As thou'rt a man,
    Give me the cup, let go, by heaven I'll ha't!
    O God, Horatio, what a wounded name,
    Things standing thus unknown, shall live behind
    me!
    If thou didst ever hold me in thy heart,
    Absent thee from felicity awhile,   350
    And in this harsh world draw thy breath in pain,
    To tell my story . . .
        The tread of soldiers marching heard afar off,
                  and later a shot; Osric goes out
    What warlike noise is this?
OSRIC [*returning*]. Young Fortinbras, with conquest
    come from Poland,
    To th'ambassadors of England gives
    This warlike volley.
HAMLET.   O, I die, Horatio,
    The potent poison quite o'er-crows my spirit,
    I cannot live to hear the news from England,
    But I do prophesy th'election lights
    On Fortinbras, he has my dying voice.

So tell him, with th'occurrents more and less   360
    Which have solicited—the rest is silence.   *He dies*
HORATIO. Now cracks a noble heart. Good night,
    sweet prince;
    And flights of angels sing thee to thy rest!
    Why does the drum come hither?

Prince Fortinbras, the English ambassadors, and others enter

FORTINBRAS. Where is this sight?
HORATIO.   What is it you would see?
    If aught of woe or wonder cease your search.
FORTINBRAS. This quarry cries on havoc. O proud
    death,
    What feast is toward in thine eternal cell,
    That thou so many princes at a shot
    So bloodily hast struck?
I AMBASSADOR.   The sight is dismal,   370
    And our affairs from England come too late.
    The ears are senseless that should give us hearing,
    To tell him his commandment is fulfilled,
    That Rosencrantz and Guildenstern are dead.
    Where should we have our thanks?
HORATIO.   Not from his mouth,
    Had it th'ability of life to thank you;
    He never gave commandment for their death;
    But since, so jump upon this bloody question,
    You from the Polack wars, and you from England,
    Are here arrived, give order that these bodies   380
    High on a stage be placéd to the view,
    And let me speak to th'yet unknowing world
    How these things came about; so shall you hear
    Of carnal, bloody and unnatural acts,
    Of accidental judgements, casual slaughters,
    Of deaths put on by cunning and forced cause,
    And, in this upshot, purposes mistook
    Fall'n on th'inventors' heads: all this can I
    Truly deliver.
FORTINBRAS.   Let us haste to hear it,
    And call the noblest to the audience.   390
    For me, with sorrow I embrace my fortune.
    I have some rights of memory in this kingdom,
    Which now to claim my vantage doth invite me.
HORATIO. Of that I shall have also cause to speak,
    And from his mouth whose voice will draw on
    more.
    But let this same be presently performed,
    Even while men's minds are wild, lest more
    mischance
    On plots and errors happen.
FORTINBRAS.   Let four captains
    Bear Hamlet like a soldier to the stage,
    For he was likely, had he been put on,   400
    To have proved most royal; and for his passage,
    The soldiers' music and the rite of war
    Speak loudly for him:
    Take up the bodies—such a sight as this
    Becomes the field, but here shows much amiss.
    Go, bid the soldiers shoot.

*The soldiers bear away the bodies, the while a dead march
is heard; after the which a peal of ordnance is shot off*

King Lear

The scene: Britain

CHARACTERS IN THE PLAY

LEAR, *king of Britain*
KING OF FRANCE
DUKE OF BURGUNDY
DUKE OF CORNWALL, *husband to Regan*
DUKE OF ALBANY, *husband to Goneril*
EARL OF KENT
EARL OF GLOUCESTER
EDGAR, *son to Gloucester*
EDMUND, *bastard son to Gloucester*
CURAN, *a courtier*

OSWALD, *steward to Goneril*
OLD MAN, *tenant to Gloucester*
DOCTOR
FOOL
GONERIL
REGAN   } *daughters to Lear*
CORDELIA
*Gentleman, Herald, Captains, Knights of Lear's train,
   Messengers, Soldiers, Attendants, Servants*

King Lear

Enter Kent, Gloucester, and Edmund

KENT. I thought the king had more affected the Duke of Albany than Cornwall.

GLOUCESTER. It did always seem so to us; but now, in the division of the kingdom, it appears not which of the dukes he values most, for equalities are so weighed that curiosity in neither can make choice of either's moiety.

KENT. Is not this your son, my lord?

GLOUCESTER. His breeding, sir, hath been at my charge. I have so often blushed to acknowledge him 10 that now I am brazed to 't.

KENT. I cannot conceive you.

GLOUCESTER. Sir, this young fellow's mother could; whereupon she grew round-wombed, and had indeed, sir, a son for her cradle ere she had a husband for her bed. Do you smell a fault?

KENT. I cannot wish the fault undone, the issue of it being so proper.

GLOUCESTER. But I have a son, sir, by order of law, some year elder than this, who yet is no dearer in 20 my account. Though this knave came something saucily to the world before he was sent for, yet was his mother fair; there was good sport at his making, and the whoreson must be acknowledged. Do you know this noble gentleman, Edmund?

EDMUND. No, my lord.

GLOUCESTER. My lord of Kent. Remember him hereafter as my honourable friend.

EDMUND. My services to your lordship.

KENT. I must love you, and sue to know you better. 30

EDMUND. Sir, I shall study deserving.

GLOUCESTER. He hath been out nine years, and away he shall again. [*a sennet sounded*] The king is coming.

Enter one bearing a coronet. Enter King Lear, Cornwall, Albany, Goneril, Regan, Cordelia, and attendants

LEAR. Attend the lords of France and Burgundy, Gloucester.

GLOUCESTER. I shall, my liege.
                        He goes out, attended by Edmund

LEAR. Meantime we shall express our darker purpose.
Give me the map there. Know that we have divided
In three our kingdom; and 'tis our fast intent
To shake all cares and business from our age,
Conferring them on younger strengths while we 40
Unburdened crawl toward death. Our son of
    Cornwall,
And you, our no less loving son of Albany,
We have this hour a constant will to publish
Our daughters' several dowers, that future strife
May be prevented now. The princes, France and
    Burgundy,
Great rivals in our youngest daughter's love,
Long in our court have made their amorous sojourn,
And here are to be answered. Tell me, my daughters
(Since now we will divest us both of rule,

Interest of territory, cares of state), 50
Which of you shall we say doth love us most,
That we our largest bounty may extend
Where nature doth with merit challenge. Goneril,
Our eldest-born, speak first.

GONERIL. Sir, I love you more than word can wield the
    matter;
Dearer than eyesight, space and liberty;
Beyond what can be valued rich or rare;
No less than life with grace, health, beauty, honour;
As much as child e'er loved, or father found:
A love that makes breath poor, and speech unable. 60
Beyond all manner of "so much" I love you.

CORDELIA [*aside*]. What shall Cordelia speak? Love,
    and be silent.

LEAR. Of all these bounds, even from this line to this,
With shadowy forests and with champaigns riched,
With plenteous rivers and wide-skirted meads,
We make thee lady. To thine and Albany's issues
Be this perpetual. What says our second daughter,
Our dearest Regan, wife of Cornwall?

REGAN. I am made of that self metal as my sister,
And prize me at her worth. In my true heart 70
I find she names my very deed of love:
Only she comes too short, that I profess
Myself an enemy to all other joys
Which the most precious spirit of sense possesses,
And find I am alone felicitate
In your dear Highness' love.

CORDELIA [*aside*].   Then poor Cordelia!
And yet not so, since I am sure my love's
More ponderous than my tongue.

LEAR. To thee and thine, hereditary ever,
Remain this ample third of our fair kingdom, 80
No less in space, validity, and pleasure
Than that conferred on Goneril. Now, our joy,
Although our last and least, to whose young love
The vines of France and milk of Burgundy
Strive to be interessed, what can you say to draw
A third more opulent than your sisters? Speak.

CORDELIA. Nothing, my lord.

LEAR. Nothing?

CORDELIA. Nothing.

LEAR. Nothing will come of nothing; speak again. 90

CORDELIA. Unhappy that I am, I cannot heave
My heart into my mouth. I love your Majesty
According to my bond, no more nor less.

LEAR. How, how, Cordelia? Mend your speech a little,
Lest you may mar your fortunes.

CORDELIA.   Good my lord,
You have begot me, bred me, loved me. I
Return those duties back as are right fit,
Obey you, love you, and most honour you.
Why have my sisters husbands, if they say
They love you all? Haply, when I shall wed, 100
That lord whose hand must take my plight shall
    carry
Half my love with him, half my care and duty.
Sure I shall never marry like my sisters,
To love my father all.

LEAR. But goes thy heart with this?
CORDELIA.   Ay, my good lord.
LEAR. So young, and so untender?
CORDELIA. So young, my lord, and true.
LEAR. Let it be so; thy truth then be thy dower!
For, by the sacred radiance of the sun,
The mysteries of Hecate and the night,   110
By all the operation of the orbs
From whom we do exist and cease to be,
Here I disclaim all my paternal care,
Propinquity and property of blood,
And as a stranger to my heart and me
Hold thee from this for ever. The barbarous
      Scythian,
Or he that makes his generation messes
To gorge his appetite, shall to my bosom
Be as well neighboured, pitied, and relieved,
As thou my sometime daughter.
KENT.   Good my liege— 120
LEAR. Peace, Kent!
Come not between the dragon and his wrath.
I loved her most, and thought to set my rest
On her kind nursery. [to Cordelia] Hence, and avoid
      my sight!—
So be my grave my peace as here I give
Her father's heart from her. Call France! Who stirs?
Call Burgundy! Cornwall and Albany,
With my two daughters' dowers digest the third;
Let pride, which she calls plainness, marry her.
I do invest you jointly with my power,   130
Pre-eminence, and all the large effects
That troop with majesty. Ourself, by monthly
      course,
With reservation of an hundred knights
By you to be sustained, shall our abode
Make with you by due turn. Only we shall retain
The name and all th' addition to a king: the sway,
Revenue, execution of the rest,
Belovèd sons, be yours; which to confirm,
This coronet part between you.
KENT.   Royal Lear,
Whom I have ever honoured as my king,   140
Loved as my father, as my master followed,
As my great patron thought on in my prayers—
LEAR. The bow is bent and drawn; make from the
      shaft.
KENT. Let it fall rather, though the fork invade
The region of my heart! Be Kent unmannerly
When Lear is mad. What wouldst thou do, old man?
Think'st thou that duty shall have dread to speak
When power to flattery bows? To plainness
      honour's bound
When majesty stoops to folly. Reserve thy state,
And in thy best consideration check   150
This hideous rashness. Answer my life my
      judgement,
Thy youngest daughter does not love thee least,
Nor are those empty-hearted whose low sounds
Reverb no hollowness.
LEAR.   Kent, on thy life, no more!
KENT. My life I never held but as a pawn
To wage against thine enemies; ne'er feared to lose
      it,
Thy safety being motive.
LEAR.   Out of my sight!
KENT. See better, Lear, and let me still remain

The true blank of thine eye.
LEAR. Now by Apollo—
KENT.   Now by Apollo, king, 160
Thou swear'st thy gods in vain.
LEAR.   O vassal! miscreant!
                              Laying his hand on his sword
ALBANY.   }
CORNWALL. } Dear sir, forbear!
KENT. Kill thy physician, and the fee bestow
Upon the foul disease. Revoke thy gift,
Or, whilst I can vent clamour from my throat,
I'll tell thee thou dost evil.
LEAR.   Hear me, recreant,
On thine allegiance, hear me!
That thou hast sought to make us break our vow—
Which we durst never yet—and with strained pride
To come betwixt our sentence and our power— 170
Which nor our nature nor our place can bear,—
Our potency made good, take thy reward.
Five days we do allot thee for provision
To shield thee from disasters of the world,
And on the sixth to turn thy hated back
Upon our kingdom. If, on the tenth day following,
Thy banished trunk be found in our dominions,
The moment is thy death. Away! By Jupiter,
This shall not be revoked.
KENT. Fare thee well, king; sith thus thou wilt appear, 180
Freedom lives hence and banishment is here.
[to Cordelia] The gods to their dear shelter take thee,
      maid,
That justly think'st and hast most rightly said.
[to Goneril and Regan] And your large speeches may
      your deeds approve,
That good effects may spring from words of love.
Thus Kent, O princes, bids you all adieu;
He'll shape his old course in a country new.
                              He goes

*Flourish. Re-enter Gloucester, with France, Burgundy, and
Attendants*

GLOUCESTER. Here's France and Burgundy, my noble
      lord.
LEAR. My lord of Burgundy,
We first address toward you, who with this king 190
Hath rivalled for our daughter. What in the least
Will you require in present dower with her,
Or cease your quest of love?
BURGUNDY.   Most royal majesty,
I crave no more than hath your highness offered—
Nor will you tender less?
LEAR.   Right noble Burgundy,
When she was dear to us, we did hold her so;
But now her price is fall'n. Sir, there she stands.
If aught within that little seeming-substance,
Or all of it, with our displeasure pieced,
And nothing more, may fitly like your grace, 200
She's there, and she is yours.
BURGUNDY.   I know no answer.
LEAR. Will you, with those infirmities she owes,
Unfriended, new adopted to our hate,
Dowered with our curse and strangered with our
      oath,
Take her or leave her?
BURGUNDY.   Pardon me, royal sir.
Election makes not up on such conditions.

LEAR. Then leave her, sir; for, by the power that made
      me,
   I tell you all her wealth. [to France] For you, great
      king,
   I would not from your love make such a stray
   To match you where I hate; therefore beseech you 210
   T' avert your liking a more worthier way
   Than on a wretch whom Nature is ashamed
   Almost t' acknowledge hers.
FRANCE.   This is most strange,
   That she whom even but now was your best object,
   The argument of your praise, balm of your age,
   The best, the dearest, should in this trice of time
   Commit a thing so monstrous to dismantle
   So many folds of favour. Sure her offence
   Must be of such unnatural degree
   That monsters it, or your-vouched affection   220
   Fall into taint; which to believe of her
   Must be a faith that reason without miracle
   Should never plant in me.
CORDELIA.   I yet beseech your majesty—
   If for I want that glib and oily art
   To speak and purpose not, since what I well intend,
   I'll do 't before I speak—that you make known
   It is no vicious blot, murder or foulness,
   No unchaste action or dishonoured step,
   That hath deprived me of your grace and favour;
   But even for want of that for which I am richer— 230
   A still-soliciting eye, and such a tongue
   That I am glad I have not, though not to have it
   Hath lost me in your liking.
LEAR.   Better thou
   Hadst not been born than not t' have pleased me
      better.
FRANCE. Is it but this—a tardiness in nature
   Which often leaves the history unspoke
   That it intends? My lord of Burgundy,
   What say you to the lady? Love's not love
   When it is mingled with regards that stands
   Aloof from th' entire point. Will you have her?   240
   She is herself a dowry.
BURGUNDY.   Royal king,
   Give but that portion which yourself proposed,
   And here I take Cordelia by the hand,
   Duchess of Burgundy.
LEAR. Nothing. I have sworn; I am firm.
BURGUNDY. I am sorry then you have so lost a father
   That you must lose a husband.
CORDELIA.   Peace be with Burgundy!
   Since that respect and fortunes are his love,
   I shall not be his wife.
FRANCE. Fairest Cordelia, that art most rich, being
      poor;   250
   Most choice, forsaken; and most loved, despised;
   Thee and thy virtues here I seize upon.
   Be it lawful I take up what's cast away.
   Gods, gods! 'Tis strange that from their cold'st
      neglect
   My love should kindle to inflamed respect.
   Thy dowerless daughter, king, thrown to my
      chance,
   Is queen of us, of ours, and our fair France.
   Not all the dukes of wat'rish Burgundy
   Can buy this unprized precious maid of me.
   Bid them farewell, Cordelia, though unkind;   260
   Thou losest here, a better where to find.

LEAR. Thou hast her, France; let her be thine, for we
   Have no such daughter, nor shall ever see
   That face of hers again. Therefore be gone
   Without our grace, our love, our benison.
   Come, noble Burgundy.

                  Flourish. Lear, Burgundy, Cornwall,
                     Albany, Gloucester, and
                           attendants depart
FRANCE.   Bid farewell to your sisters.
CORDELIA. The jewels of our father, with washed eyes
   Cordelia leaves you, I know you what you are,
   And like a sister am most loath to call
   Your faults as they are named. Love well our father; 270
   To your professèd bosoms I commit him:
   But yet, alas, stood I within his grace,
   I would prefer him to a better place.
   So farewell to you both.
REGAN. Prescribe not us our duty.
GONERIL.   Let your study
   Be to content your lord, who hath received you
   At Fortune's alms. You have obedience scanted,
   And well are worth the want that you have wanted.
CORDELIA. Time shall unfold what plighted cunning
      hides,
   Who covert faults at last with shame derides.   280
   Well may you prosper.
FRANCE.   Come, my fair Cordelia.
                                 He leads her away
GONERIL. Sister, it is not little I have to say of what
   most nearly appertains to us both. I think our father
   will hence tonight.
REGAN. That's most certain, and with you; next month
   with us.
GONERIL. You see how full of changes his age is. The
   observation we have made of it hath not been little.
   He always loved our sister most, and with what poor
   judgement he hath now cast her off appears too 290
   grossly.
REGAN. 'Tis the infirmity of his age; yet he hath ever
   but slenderly known himself.
GONERIL. The best and soundest of his time hath been
   but rash; then must we look from his age to receive,
   not alone the imperfections of long-engraffed condition, but therewithal the unruly waywardness that
   infirm and choleric years bring with them.
REGAN. Such unconstant starts are we like to have from
   him as this of Kent's banishment.   300
GONERIL. There is further compliment of leave-taking
   between France and him. Pray you let us hit together. If our father carry authority with such disposition as he bears, this last surrender of his will but
   offend us.
REGAN. We shall further think of it.
GONERIL. We must do something, and i' th' heat.
                                           They go

Scene 2: *The Earl of Gloucester's castle*

Enter Edmund, with a letter

EDMUND. Thou, Nature, art my goddess; to thy law
   My services are bound. Wherefore should I
   Stand in the plague of custom, and permit
   The curiosity of nations to deprive me,
   For that I am some twelve or fourteen moonshines
   Lag of a brother? Why bastard? wherefore base?
   When my dimensions are as well compact,

My mind as generous, and my shape as true,
As honest madam's issue? Why brand they us
With base? with baseness? bastardy? base, base?   10
Who, in the lusty stealth of Nature, take
More composition and fierce quality
Than doth, within a dull, stale, tiréd bed,
Go to th' creating a whole tribe of fops
Got 'tween a sleep and wake? Well then,
Legitimate Edgar, I must have your land.
Our father's love is to the bastard Edmund
As to th' legitimate. Fine word, 'legitimate'!
Well, my legitimate, if this letter speed,
And my invention thrive, Edmund the base   20
Shall top th' legitimate. I grow, I prosper.
Now, gods, stand up for bastards!

Enter Gloucester

GLOUCESTER. Kent banished thus? and France in choler
    parted?
And the king gone to-night? Prescribed his power?
Confined to exhibition? All this done
Upon the gad?—Edmund, how now? What news?
EDMUND. So please your lordship, none.
                    Putting the letter in his pocket
GLOUCESTER. Why so earnestly seek you to put up that
    letter?
EDMUND. I know no news, my lord.   30
GLOUCESTER. What paper were you reading?
EDMUND. Nothing, my lord.
GLOUCESTER. No? What needed then that terrible dis-
    patch of it into your pocket? The quality of nothing
    hath not such need to hide itself. Let's see. Come,
    if it be nothing, I shall not need spectacles.
EDMUND. I beseech you, sir, pardon me. It is a letter
    from my brother that I have not all o'er-read; and
    for so much as I have perused, I find it not fit for
    your o'erlooking.   40
GLOUCESTER. Give me the letter, sir.
EDMUND. I shall offend either to detain or give it. The
    contents, as in part I understand them, are to blame.
GLOUCESTER. Let's see, let's see.
EDMUND. I hope, for my brother's justification, he
    wrote this but as an essay or taste of my virtue.
GLOUCESTER [*reads*]. 'This policy and reverence of age
    makes the world bitter to the best of our times, keeps
    our fortunes from us till our oldness cannot relish
    them. I begin to find an idle and fond bondage in   50
    the oppression of aged tyranny, who sways, not as it
    hath power, but as it is suffered. Come to me, that
    of this I may speak more. If our father would sleep
    till I waked him, you should enjoy half his revenue
    for ever, and live the beloved of your brother.
                                                    Edgar.'
Hum! Conspiracy? 'Sleep till I waked him, you
should enjoy half his revenue.' My son Edgar! Had
he a hand to write this? A heart and brain to breed
it in? When came you to this? Who brought it?   60
EDMUND. It was not brought me, my lord: there's the
    cunning of it. I found it thrown in at the casement
    of my closet.
GLOUCESTER. You know the character to be your
    brother's?
EDMUND. If the matter were good, my lord, I durst
    swear it were his; but, in respect of that, I would fain
    think it were not.
GLOUCESTER. It is his.

EDMUND. It is his hand, my lord; but I hope his heart   70
    is not in the contents.
GLOUCESTER. Has he never before sounded you in this
    business?
EDMUND. Never, my lord. But I have heard him oft
    maintain it to be fit that, sons at perfect age, and
    fathers declined, the father should be as ward to the
    son, and the son manage his revenue.
GLOUCESTER. O villain, villain! His very opinion in
    the letter! Abhorred villain! Unnatural, detested,
    brutish villain! Worse than brutish! Go, sirrah, seek   80
    him. I'll apprehend him. Abominable villain! Where
    is he?
EDMUND. I do not well know, my lord. If it shall please
    you to suspend your indignation against my brother
    till you can derive from him better testimony of his
    intent, you should run a certain course; where, if you
    violently proceed against him, mistaking his pur-
    pose, it would make a great gap in your own
    honour, and shake in pieces the heart of his obedi-
    ence. I dare pawn down my life for him that he hath   90
    writ this to feel my affection to your honour, and
    to no other pretence of danger.
GLOUCESTER. Think you so?
EDMUND. If your honour judge it meet, I will place
    you where you shall hear us confer of this and by
    an auricular assurance have your satisfaction, and
    that without any further delay than this very
    evening.
GLOUCESTER. He cannot be such a monster!
EDMUND. Nor is not, sure.   100
GLOUCESTER. To his father, that so tenderly and
    entirely loves him! Heaven and earth! Edmund, seek
    him out; wind me into him, I pray you; frame the
    business after your own wisdom. I would unstate
    myself to be in a due resolution.
EDMUND. I will seek him, sir, presently; convey the
    business as I shall find means, and acquaint you
    withal.
GLOUCESTER. These late eclipses in the sun and moon
    portend no good to us. Though the wisdom of   110
    nature can reason it thus and thus, yet nature finds
    itself scourged by the sequent effects. Love cools,
    friendship falls off, brothers divide. In cities, mutin-
    ies; in countries, discord; in palaces, treason; and the
    bond cracked 'twixt son and father. This villain of
    mine comes under the prediction; there's son against
    father: the king falls from bias of nature; there's
    father against child. We have seen the best of our
    time. Machinations, hollowness, treachery, and all
    ruinous disorders follow us disquietly to our graves.   120
    Find out this villain, Edmund; it shall lose thee
    nothing; do it carefully. And the noble and true-
    hearted Kent banished; his offence, honesty! 'Tis
    strange.   *He goes*
EDMUND. This is the excellent foppery of the world
    that when we are sick in fortune, often the surfeits
    of our own behaviour, we make guilty of our
    disasters the sun, the moon and stars; as if we were
    villains on necessity, fools by heavenly compulsion,
    knaves, thieves, and treachers by spherical pre-   130
    dominance, drunkards, liars, and adulterers by an
    enforced obedience of planetary influence, and all
    that we are evil in by a divine thrusting on. An
    admirable evasion of whoremaster man, to lay his
    goatish disposition to the charge of a star! My father

compounded with my mother under the Dragon's
tail, and my nativity was under Ursa Major, so that
it follows I am rough and lecherous. Fut, I should
have been that I am, had the maidenliest star in the
firmament twinkled on my bastardizing. Edgar— 140

Enter Edgar

Pat! he comes, like the catastrophe of the old
comedy. My cue is villainous melancholy, with a
sigh like Tom o' Bedlam—O these eclipses do portend these divisions. [*humming sadly*] Fa, sol, la, me.
EDGAR. How now, brother Edmund? What serious
contemplation are you in?
EDMUND. I am thinking, brother, of a prediction I read
this other day, what should follow these eclipses.
EDGAR. Do you busy yourself with that?
EDMUND. I promise you, the effects he writes of 150
succeed unhappily, as of unnaturalness between the
child and the parent, death, dearth, dissolutions of
ancient amities, divisions in state, menaces and male-
dictions against king and nobles, needless diffi-
dences, banishment of friends, dissipation of cohorts,
nuptial breaches, and I know not what.
EDGAR. How long have you been a sectary astronomical?
EDMUND. When saw you my father last?
EDGAR. The night gone by. 160
EDMUND. Spake you with him?
EDGAR. Ay, two hours together.
EDMUND. Parted you in good terms? Found you no
displeasure in him, by word nor countenance?
EDGAR. None at all.
EDMUND. Bethink yourself wherein you may have
offended him; and at my entreaty forbear his
presence until some little time hath qualified the heat
of his displeasure, which at this instant so rageth in
him that with the mischief of your person it would 170
scarcely allay.
EDGAR. Some villain hath done me wrong.
EDMUND. That's my fear. I pray you have a continent
forbearance till the speed of his rage goes slower;
and, as I say, retire with me to my lodging, from
whence I will fitly bring you to hear my lord speak.
Pray ye, go; there's my key. If you do stir abroad, go
armed.
EDGAR. Armed, brother?
EDMUND. Brother, I advise you to the best. I am no 180
honest man if there be any good meaning toward
you. I have told you what I have seen and heard—
but faintly, nothing like the image and horror of it.
Pray you, away!
EDGAR. Shall I hear from you anon?
EDMUND. I do serve you in this business. *Edgar goes*
A credulous father! and a brother noble
Whose nature is so far from doing harms
That he suspects none; on whose foolish honesty
My practices ride easy! I see the business. 190
Let me, if not by birth, have lands by wit;
All with me's meet that I can fashion fit. *He goes*

Scene 3: *The Duke of Albany's palace*

Enter Goneril and Oswald, her steward

GONERIL. Did my father strike my gentleman for
chiding of his fool?
OSWALD. Ay, madam.

GONERIL. By day and night he wrongs me. Every hour
He flashes into one gross crime or other
That sets us all at odds. I'll not endure it.
His knights grow riotous, and himself upbraids us
On every trifle. When he returns from hunting
I will not speak with him: say I am sick.
If you come slack of former services, 10
You shall do well; the fault of it I'll answer.
Horns heard
OSWALD. He's coming, madam; I hear him.
GONERIL. Put on what weary negligence you please,
You and your fellows; I'd have it come to question.
If he distaste it, let him to my sister,
Whose mind and mine I know in that are one,
Not to be overruled. Idle old man,
That still would manage those authorities
That he hath given away! Now, by my life,
Old fools are babes again, and must be used 20
With checks as flatteries, when they are seen abused.
Remember what I have said.
OSWALD. Well, madam.
GONERIL. And let his knights have colder looks among
you;
What grows of it, no matter. Advise your fellows
so.
I would breed from hence occasions, and I shall,
That I may speak. I'll write straight to my sister
To hold my very course. Prepare for dinner.
They go

Scene 4: *A hall in the same*

Enter Kent disguised

KENT. If but as well I other accents borrow,
That can my speech diffuse, my good intent
May carry through itself to that full issue
For which I razed my likeness. Now, banished Kent,
If thou canst serve where thou dost stand
condemned,
So may it come thy master whom thou lov'st
Shall find thee full of labours.

*Horns heard. Lear enters from hunting, with Knights and
Attendants*

LEAR. Let me not stay a jot for dinner; go get it ready.
Attendant goes out
How now! what art thou?
KENT. A man, sir. 10
LEAR. What dost thou profess? What would'st thou
with us?
KENT. I do profess to be no less than I seem, to serve
him truly that will put me in trust, to love him that
is honest, to converse with him that is wise and says
little, to fear judgement, to fight when I cannot
choose, and to eat no fish.
LEAR. What art thou?
KENT. A very honest-hearted fellow, and as poor as the
king. 20
LEAR. If thou be'st as poor for a subject as he's for a
king, thou art poor enough. What would'st thou?
KENT. Service.
LEAR. Who would'st thou serve?
KENT. You.
LEAR. Dost thou know me, fellow?
KENT. No, sir; but you have that in your countenance
which I would fain call master.

LEAR. What's that?

KENT. Authority. 30

LEAR. What services canst thou do?

KENT. I can keep honest counsel, ride, run, mar a curious tale in telling it, and deliver a plain message bluntly; that which ordinary men are fit for I am qualified in, and best of me is diligence.

LEAR. How old art thou?

KENT. Not so young, sir, to love a woman for singing, nor so old to dote on her for anything. I have years on my back forty-eight.

LEAR. Follow me; thou shalt serve me. If I like thee 40 no worse after dinner I will not part from thee yet. Dinner, ho! dinner! Where's my knave? my fool? Go you and call my fool hither. *Attendant goes out*

Enter Oswald

You! you, sirrah! Where's my daughter?

OSWALD. So please you— *Goes out*

LEAR. What says the fellow there? Call the clotpoll back! [*Knight goes out*] Where's my fool? Ho! I think the world's asleep. [*Knight returns*] How now? Where's that mongrel?

KNIGHT. He says, my lord, your daughter is not well. 50

LEAR. Why came not the slave back to me when I called him?

KNIGHT. Sir, he answered me in the roundest manner he would not.

LEAR. He would not?

KNIGHT. My lord, I know not what the matter is, but to my judgement your highness is not entertained with that ceremonious affection as you were wont. There's a great abatement of kindness appears as well in the general dependants as in the duke 60 himself also and your daughter.

LEAR. Ha! say'st thou so?

KNIGHT. I beseech you pardon me, my lord, if I be mistaken, for my duty cannot be silent when I think your highness wronged.

LEAR. Thou but rememb'rest me of mine own conception. I have perceived a most faint neglect of late, which I have rather blamed as mine own jealous curiosity than as a very pretence and purpose of unkindness; I will look further into't. But where's my 70 fool? I have not seen him this two days.

KNIGHT. Since my young lady's going into France, sir, the fool hath much pined away.

LEAR. No more of that; I have noted it well. Go you and tell my daughter I would speak with her. [*Attendant goes out*] Go you, call hither my fool. [*Second attendant goes out*]

Oswald returns

O you sir, you, come you hither, sir. Who am I, sir?

OSWALD. My lady's father.

LEAR. 'My lady's father', my lord's knave? You whoreson dog, you slave, you cur! 80

OSWALD. I am none of these, my lord; I beseech your pardon.

LEAR. Do you bandy looks with me, you rascal?
Strikes him

OSWALD. I'll not be strucken, my lord.

KENT. Nor tripped neither, you base football player.
Tripping up his heels

LEAR. I thank thee, fellow. Thou serv'st me, and I'll love thee.

KENT. Come, sir, arise, away! I'll teach you differences. Away, away! If you will measure your lubber's length again, tarry; but away! Go to; have you 90 wisdom? [*Oswald goes*] So.

LEAR. Now, my friendly knave, I thank thee. There's earnest of thy service. [*giving money*]

Enter Fool

FOOL. Let me hire him too. Here's my coxcomb.
Offers Kent his cap

LEAR. How now, my pretty knave? How dost thou?

FOOL. Sirrah, you were best take my coxcomb.

KENT. Why, fool?

FOOL. Why? For taking one's part that's out of favour. Nay, an thou canst not smile as the wind sits, thou'lt catch cold shortly. There, take my coxcomb! Why, 100 this fellow has banished two on's daughters, and did the third a blessing against his will. If thou follow him thou must needs wear my coxcomb. How now, nuncle? Would I had two coxcombs and two daughters!

LEAR. Why, my boy?

FOOL. If I gave them all my living, I'ld keep my coxcombs myself. There's mine; beg another of thy daughters.

LEAR. Take heed, sirrah—the whip. 110

FOOL. Truth's a dog must to kennel; he must be whipped out, when the Lady's brach may stand by th' fire and stink.

LEAR. A pestilent gall to me!

FOOL. Sirrah, I'll teach thee a speech.

LEAR. Do.

FOOL. Mark it, nuncle!
Have more than thou showest,
Speak less than thou knowest,
Lend less than thou owest, 120
Ride more than thou goest,
Learn more than thou trowest,
Set less than thou throwest;
Leave thy drink and thy whore,
And keep in-a-door,
And thou shalt have more
Than two tens to a score.

KENT. This is nothing, fool.

FOOL. Then 'tis like the breath of an unfeed lawyer— you gave me nothing for't. Can you make no use of 130 nothing, nuncle?

LEAR. Why, no, boy; nothing can be made out of nothing.

FOOL [*to Kent*]. Prithee tell him, so much the rent of his land comes to. He will not believe a fool.

LEAR. A bitter fool!

FOOL. Dost thou know the difference, my boy, between a bitter fool and a sweet one?

LEAR. No, lad; teach me.

FOOL. That lord that counselled thee 140
To give away thy land,
Come place him here by me—
Do thou for him stand.
The sweet and bitter fool
Will presently appear:
The one in motley here,
The other found out—there!

LEAR. Dost thou call me fool, boy?

FOOL. All thy other titles thou hast given away; that thou wast born with. 150

KENT. This is not altogether fool, my lord.

FOOL. No, faith, lords and great men·will not let me; if I had a monopoly out, they would have part on't: and ladies too, they will not let me have all the fool to myself; they'll be snatching. Nuncle, give me an egg, and I'll give thee two crowns.

LEAR. What two crowns shall they be?

FOOL. Why, after I have cut the egg i'th'middle and eat up the meat, the two crowns of the egg. When thou clovest thy crown i'th'middle and gav'st away 160 both parts, thou bor'st thine ass on thy back o'er the dirt. Thou hadst little wit in thy bald crown when thou gav'st thy golden one away. If I speak like myself in this, let him be whipped that first finds it so.

[singing] Fools had ne'er less grace in a year;
    For wise men are grown foppish,
And know not how their wits to wear,
    Their manners are so apish.

LEAR. When were you wont to be so full of songs, 170 sirrah?

FOOL. I have used it, nuncle, e'er since thou mad'st thy daughters thy mothers— for when thou gav'st them the rod and putt'st down thine own breeches,
[singing] Then they for sudden joy did weep,
    And I for sorrow sung,
That such a king should play bo-peep,
    And go the fools among.
Prithee, nuncle, keep a schoolmaster that can teach thy fool to lie: I would fain learn to lie. 180

LEAR. An you lie, sirrah, we'll have you whipped.

FOOL. I marvel what kin thou and thy daughters are: they'll have me whipped for speaking true, thou'lt have me whipped for lying; and sometimes I am whipped for holding my peace. I had rather be any kind o' thing than a fool: and yet I would not be thee, nuncle; thou hast pared thy wit o' both sides and left nothing i'th' middle. Here comes one o' the parings.

Enter Goneril

LEAR. How now, daughter? What makes that front- 190 let on? You are too much of late i'th'frown.

FOOL. Thou wast a pretty fellow when thou hadst no need to care for her frowning; now thou art an O without a figure. I am better than thou art now; I am a fool, thou art nothing. [to Goneril] Yes, forsooth, I will hold my tongue; so your face bids me, though you say nothing.
    Mum, mum:
He that keeps nor crust nor crumb,
    Weary of all, shall want some. 200
[pointing to Lear] That's a shelled peascod.

GONERIL. Not only, sir, this your all-licensed fool, But other of your insolent retinue Do hourly carp and quarrel, breaking forth In rank and not-to-be-enduréd riots. I had thought, by making this well known unto you, To have found a safe redress; but now grow fearful, By what yourself too late have spoke and done, That you protect this course, and put it on By your allowance; which if you should, the fault 210 Would not scape censure, nor the redresses sleep Which, in the tender of a wholesome weal, Might in their working do you that offence, Which else were shame, that then necessity Will call discreet proceeding.

FOOL.   For you know, nuncle,
The hedge-sparrow fed the cuckoo so long
That it had it head bit off by it young.
So out went the candle, and we were left darkling.

LEAR. Are you our daughter? 220

GONERIL. I would you would make use of your good wisdom (Whereof I know you are fraught) and put away These dispositions which of late transport you From what you rightly are.

FOOL. May not an ass know when the cart draws the horse? Whoop, Jug! I love thee.

LEAR. Does any here know me? This is not Lear. Does Lear walk thus, speak thus? Where are his eyes? Either his notion weakens, his discernings Are lethargied—Ha! Waking? 'Tis not so? 230 Who is it that can tell me who I am?

FOOL. Lear's shadow!

LEAR. I would learn that; for by the marks Of sovereignty, knowledge, and reason, I should be false persuaded I had daughters.

FOOL. Which they will make an obedient father.

LEAR. Your name, fair gentlewoman?

GONERIL. This admiration, sir, is much o' th' savour Of other your new pranks. I do beseech you To understand my purposes aright. 240 As you are old and reverend, should be wise. Here do you keep a hundred knights and squires— Men so disordered, so debauched and bold, That this our court, infected with their manners, Shows like a riotous inn. Epicurism and lust Makes it more like a tavern or a brothel Than a graced palace. The shame itself doth speak For instant remedy. Be then desired, By her that else will take the thing she begs, A little to disquantity your train; 250 And the remainders, that shall still depend, To be such men as may besort your age, Which know themselves and you.

LEAR.   Darkness and devils! Saddle my horses; call my train together! Degenerate bastard, I'll not trouble thee; Yet have I left a daughter.

GONERIL. You strike my people, and your disordered rabble Make servants of their betters.

Enter Albany

LEAR. Woe that too late repents!—O, are you come? Is it your will? Speak, sir!—Prepare my horses. 260 Ingratitude, thou marble-hearted fiend, More hideous when thou show'st thee in a child Than the sea-monster!

ALBANY.   Pray, sir, be patient.

LEAR [to Goneril]. Detested kite, thou liest! My train are men of choice and rarest parts, That all particulars of duty know, And in the most exact regard support The worships of their name. O most small fault, How ugly didst thou in Cordelia show, Which, like an engine, wrenched my frame of nature 270 From the fixed place, drew from my heart all love, And added to the gall. O Lear, Lear, Lear!

Beat at this gate that let thy folly in
                                              Striking his head
And thy dear judgement out! Go, go, my people.
                                              Knights and Kent go
ALBANY. My lord, I am guiltless, as I am ignorant
    Of what hath moved you.
LEAR.   It may be so, my lord.
    Hear, Nature; hear, dear goddess; hear!
    Suspend thy purpose, if thou didst intend
    To make this creature fruitful.
    Into her womb convey sterility;   280
    Dry up in her the organs of increase;
    And from her derogate body never spring
    A babe to honour her! If she must teem,
    Create her child of spleen, that it may live
    And be a thwart disnatured torment to her.
    Let it stamp wrinkles in her brow of youth.
    With cadent tears fret channels in her cheeks,
    Turn all her mother's pains and benefits
    To laughter and contempt, that she may feel
    How sharper than a serpent's tooth it is   290
    To have a thankless child! Away, away!   *He goes*
ALBANY. Now, gods that we adore, whereof comes
    this?
GONERIL. Never afflict yourself to know more of it,
    But let his disposition have that scope
    As dotage gives it.

Lear returns

LEAR. What, fifty of my followers at a clap?
    Within a fortnight?
ALBANY.   What's the matter, sir?
LEAR. I'll tell thee. [*to Goneril*] Life and death!
    I am ashamed
    That thou hast power to shake my manhood thus;
    That these hot tears, which break from me perforce, 300
    Should make thee worth them. Blasts and fogs upon
    thee!
    Th'untented woundings of a father's curse
    Pierce every sense about thee! Old fond eyes,
    Beweep this cause again, I'll pluck ye out,
    And cast you, with the waters that you loose,
    To temper clay. Yea, is't come to this?
    Ha! Let it be so. I have another daughter,
    Who I am sure is kind and comfortable.
    When she shall hear this of thee, with her nails
    She'll flay thy wolvish visage. Thou shalt find   310
    That I'll resume the shape which thou dost think
    I have cast off for ever.   *He goes*
GONERIL.   Do you mark that?
ALBANY. I cannot be so partial, Goneril,
    To the great love I bear you—
GONERIL. Pray you, content. What, Oswald, ho!
    [*to the Fool*] You, sir, more knave than fool, after
    your master!
FOOL. Nuncle Lear, nuncle Lear! Tarry; take the fool
    with thee.
          A fox, when one has caught her,
          And such a daughter,   320
          Should sure to the slaughter,
          If my cap would buy a halter.
          So the fool follows after.   *He goes*
GONERIL. This man hath had good counsel! A hundred
    knights!
    'Tis politic and safe to let him keep

At point a hundred knights; yes, that on every
    dream,
    Each buzz, each fancy, each complaint, dislike,
    He may enguard his dotage with their powers,
    And hold our lives in mercy. Oswald, I say!
ALBANY. Well, you may fear too far.
GONERIL.   Safer than trust too far.   330
    Let me still take away the harms I fear,
    Not fear still to be taken. I know his heart.
    What hath uttered I have writ my sister.
    If she sustain him and his hundred knights,
    When I have showed th'unfitness—

Enter Oswald

                                     How now, Oswald?
    What, have you writ that letter to my sister?
OSWALD. Ay, madam.
GONERIL. Take you some company, and away to
    horse!
    Inform her full of my particular fear,
    And thereto add such reasons of your own   340
    As may compact it more. Get you gone,
    And hasten your return. [*Oswald goes*] No, no, my
    lord,
    This milky gentleness and course of yours
    Though I condemn not, yet, under pardon,
    You are much more attaxed for want of wisdom
    Than praised for harmful mildness.
ALBANY. How far your eyes may pierce I cannot tell:
    Striving to better, oft we mar what's well.
GONERIL. Nay, then—
ALBANY. Well, well; th'event.   *They go* 350

Scene 5: Court before the same

Enter Lear, Kent, and Fool

LEAR. Go you before to Cornwall with these letters.
    Acquaint my daughter no further with anything
    you know than comes from her demand out of the
    letter. If your diligence be not speedy, I shall be there
    afore you.
KENT. I will not sleep, my lord, till I have delivered
    your letter.   *He goes*
FOOL. If a man's brains were in's heels, were't not in
    danger of kibes?
LEAR. Ay, boy.   10
FOOL. Then I prithee be merry; thy wit shall not go
    slip-shod.
LEAR. Ha, ha, ha!
FOOL. Shalt see thy other daughter will use thee
    kindly; for, though she's as like this as a crab's like
    an apple, yet I can tell what I can tell.
LEAR. What canst tell, boy?
FOOL. She will taste as like this as a crab does to a
    crab. Thou canst tell why one's nose stands
    i'th'middle on's face?   20
LEAR. No.
FOOL. Why, to keep one's eyes of either side's nose,
    that what a man cannot smell out, he may spy into.
LEAR. I did her wrong.
FOOL. Canst tell how an oyster makes his shell?
LEAR. No.
FOOL. Nor I neither; but I can tell why a snail has a
    house.
LEAR. Why?

FOOL. Why, to put's head in; not to give it away to his 30
daughters, and leave his horns without a case.

LEAR. I will forget my nature. So kind a father! Be my
horses ready?

FOOL. Thy asses are gone about 'em. The reason why
the seven stars are no moe than seven is a pretty
reason.

LEAR. Because they are not eight.

FOOL. Yes, indeed; thou would'st make a good fool.

LEAR. To take't again perforce! Monster Ingratitude!

FOOL. If thou wert my fool, nuncle, I'd have thee 40
beaten for being old before thy time.

LEAR. How's that?

FOOL. Thou should'st not have been old till thou hadst
been wise.

LEAR. O, let me not be mad, not mad, sweet heaven!
Keep me in temper; I would not be mad!'

Enter Gentleman

How now! Are the horses ready?

GENTLEMAN. Ready, my lord.

LEAR. Come, boy.

FOOL. She that's a maid now, and laughs at my
departure, 50
Shall not be a maid long, unless things be cut shorter.
They go

ACT 2
Scene 1: *The castle of the Earl of Gloucester*

Enter Edmund and Curan, meeting

EDMUND. Save thee, Curan.

CURAN. And you, sir. I have been with your father,
and given him notice that the Duke of Cornwall
and Regan his Duchess will be here with him this
night.

EDMUND. How comes that?

CURAN. Nay, I know not. You have heard of the news
abroad, I mean the whispered ones, for they are yet
but ear-bussing arguments?

EDMUND. Not I. Pray you, what are they? 10

CURAN. Have you heard of no likely wars toward
'twixt the Dukes of Cornwall and Albany?

EDMUND. Not a word.

CURAN. You may do, then, in time. Fare you well, sir.
He goes

EDMUND. The Duke be here tonight? The better! best!
This weaves itself perforce into my business.
My father hath set guard to take my brother;
And I have one thing, of a queasy question,
Which I must act. Briefness and fortune, work!
Brother, a word! Descend! Brother, I say! 20

Enter Edgar

My father watches: O sir, fly this place!
Intelligence is given where you are hid.
You have now the good advantage of the night.
Have you not spoken 'gainst the Duke of Cornwall?
He's coming hither, now i'th'night, i'th' haste,
And Regan with him. Have you nothing said
Upon his party 'gainst the Duke of Albany?
Advise yourself.

EDGAR.   I am sure on't, not a word.

EDMUND. I hear my father coming. Pardon me,
In cunning I must draw my sword upon you. 30

Draw, seem to defend yourself; now quit you
well.—
Yield! Come before my father. Light, ho! Here!—
Fly, brother.—Torches, torches!   *Edgar goes*
So; farewell.
Some blood drawn on me would beget opinion
Of my more fierce endeavour. [*Wounds his arm*]
I have seen drunkards
Do more than this in sport—Father, father!
Stop, stop! No help?

Enter Gloucester, and servants with torches

GLOUCESTER.   Now, Edmund, where's the villain?

EDMUND. Here stood he in the dark, his sharp sword
out,
Mumbling of wicked charms, conjuring the moon
To stand auspicious mistress.

GLOUCESTER.   But where is he? 40

EDMUND. Look, sir, I bleed.

GLOUCESTER.   Where is the villain, Edmund?

EDMUND. Fled this way, sir, when by no means he
could—

GLOUCESTER. Pursue him, ho! Go after. [*Some servants
go*] By no means what?

EDMUND. Persuade me to the murder of your lordship.
But that I told him the revenging gods
'Gainst parricides did all the thunder bend,
Spoke with how manifold and strong a bond
The child was bound to th'father—sir, in fine,
Seeing how loathly opposite I stood
To his unnatural purpose, in fell motion 50
With his preparéd sword he charges home
My unprovided body, latched mine arm;
And when he saw my best alarumed spirits,
Bold in the quarrel's right, roused to th'encounter,
Or whether gasted by the noise I made,
Full suddenly he fled.

GLOUCESTER.   Let him fly far:
Not in this land shall he remain uncaught;
And found—dispatch. The noble Duke my master,
My worthy arch and patron, comes tonight.
By his authority I will proclaim it, 60
That he which finds him shall deserve our thanks,
Bringing the murderous coward to the stake;
He that conceals him, death.

EDMUND. When I dissuaded him from his intent,
And found him pight to do it, with curst speech
I threatened to discover him. He replied,
'Thou unpossessing bastard, dost thou think,
If I would stand against thee, would the reposal
Of any trust, virtue, or worth in thee
Make thy words faithed? No. What I should deny, 70
(As this I would—ay, though thou didst produce
My very character) I'd turn it all
To thy suggestion, plot, and damnéd practice;
And thou must make a dullard of the world,
If they not thought the profits of my death
Were very pregnant and potential spurs
To make thee seek it.'

GLOUCESTER.   O strange and fastened villain!
Would he deny his letter, said he? I never got him.
A tucket heard
Hark, the Duke's trumpets! I know not why he
comes.
All ports I'll bar; the villain shall not scape; 80
The Duke must grant me that. Besides, his picture

I will send far and near, that all the kingdom
May have due note of him; and of my land,
Loyal and natural boy, I'll work the means
To make thee capable.

Enter Cornwall, Regan, and attendants

CORNWALL. How now, my noble friend? Since I came
hither,
Which I can call but now, I have heard strange news.
REGAN. If it be true, all vengeance comes too short
Which can pursue th'offender. How dost, my lord?
GLOUCESTER. O madam, my old heart is cracked, it's
cracked.   90
REGAN. What! Did my father's godson seek your life?
He whom my father named, your Edgar?
GLOUCESTER. O lady, lady, shame would have it hid!
REGAN. Was he not companion with the riotous
knights
That tended upon my father?
GLOUCESTER. I know not, madam. 'Tis too bad, too
bad!
EDMUND. Yes, madam; he was of that consort.
REGAN. No marvel, then, though he were ill affected.
'Tis they have put him on the old man's death,
To have th'expense and waste of his revenues.   100
I have this present evening from my sister
Been well informed of them, and with such cautions
That, if they come to sojourn at my house,
I'll not be there.
CORNWALL.   Nor I, assure thee, Regan.
Edmund, I hear that you have shown your father
A childlike office.
EDMUND.   It was my duty, sir.
GLOUCESTER. He did bewray his practice; and received
This hurt you see, striving to apprehend him.
CORNWALL. Is he pursued?
GLOUCESTER.   Ay, my good lord.
CORNWALL. If he be taken, he shall never more   110
Be feared of doing harm. Make your own purpose,
How in my strength you please. For you, Edmund,
Whose virtue and obedience doth this instant
So much commend itself, you shall be ours.
Natures of such deep trust we shall much need;
You we first seize on.
EDMUND.   I shall serve you, sir,
Truly, however else.
GLOUCESTER.   For him I thank your Grace.
CORNWALL. You know not why we came to visit you?
REGAN. Thus out of season, threading dark-eyed night:
Occasions, noble Gloucester, of some prize,   120
Wherein we must have use of your advice.
Our father he hath writ, so hath our sister,
Of differences, which I best thought it fit
To answer from our home. The several messengers
From hence attend dispatch. Our good old friend,
Lay comforts to your bosom, and bestow
Your needful counsel to our businesses,
Which craves the instant use.
GLOUCESTER.   I serve you, madam.
Your Graces are right welcome. *Flourish. They go*

Scene 2: Before Gloucester's castle

Enter Kent and Oswald, meeting

OSWALD. Good dawning to thee, friend. Art of this
house?

KENT. Ay.
OSWALD. Where may we set our horses?
KENT. I'th'mire.
OSWALD. Prithee, if thou lov'st me, tell me.
KENT. I love thee not.
OSWALD. Why then, I care not for thee.
KENT. If I had thee in Lipsbury Pinfold, I would
make thee care for me.
OSWALD. Why dost thou use me thus? I know thee
not.   10
KENT. Fellow I know thee.
OSWALD. What dost thou know me for?
KENT. A knave, a rascal, an eater of broken meats;
a base, proud, shallow, beggarly, three-suited,
hundred-pound, filthy worsted-stocking knave; a
lily-livered, action-taking, whoreson, glass-gazing,
super-serviceable, finical rogue; one-trunk-inherit-
ing slave; one that wouldst be a bawd in way of good
service, and art nothing but the composition of a
knave, beggar, coward, pandar, and the son and heir   20
of a mongrel bitch: one whom I will beat into
clamorous whining if thou deni'st the least syllable
of thy addition.
OSWALD. Why, what a monstrous fellow art thou,
thus to rail on one that is neither known of thee nor
knows thee!
KENT. What a brazen-faced varlet art thou, to deny
thou knowest me! Is it two days since I tripped up
thy heels and beat thee before the king? Draw, you
rogue; for, though it be night, yet the moon shines.   30
I'll make a sop o' th' moonshine of you, you whoreson cullionly barber-monger. Draw!
                                                    Drawing his sword
OSWALD. Away! I have nothing to do with thee.
KENT. Draw, you rascal! You come with letters against
the king, and take Vanity the puppet's part against
the royalty of her father. Draw, you rogue, or I'll so
carbonado your shanks! Draw, you rascal! Come
your ways!
OSWALD. Help, ho! murder! help!
KENT. Strike, you slave! Stand, rogue! Stand, you neat   40
slave! Strike!   *Beating him*
OSWALD. Help, ho! murder, murder!

Enter Edmund, with his rapier drawn

EDMUND. How now? What's the matter? Part!
KENT. With you, goodman boy, if you please! Come,
I'll flesh ye; come on, young master!

Enter Cornwall, Regan, Gloucester and servants

GLOUCESTER. Weapons? Arms? What is the matter
here?
CORNWALL. Keep peace, upon your lives!
He dies that strikes again. What is the matter?
REGAN. The messengers from our sister and the king!   50
CORNWALL. What is your difference? Speak.
OSWALD. I am scarce in breath, my lord.
KENT. No marvel, you have so bestirred your valour.
You cowardly rascal, Nature disclaims in thee; a
tailor made thee.
CORNWALL. Thou art a strange fellow; a tailor make
a man?
KENT. A tailor, sir. A stone-cutter or a painter could
not have made him so ill, though they had been but
two years o'th'trade.   60
CORNWALL. Speak yet, how grew your quarrel?

OSWALD. This ancient ruffian, sir, whose life I have
  spared
  At suit of his grey beard—
KENT. Thou whoreson zed, thou unnecessary letter!
  My lord, if you will give me leave, I will tread this
  unbolted villain into mortar and daub the wall of a
  jakes with him. Spare my grey beard, you wagtail?
CORNWALL. Peace, sirrah!
  You beastly knave, know you no reverence?
KENT. Yes, sir; but anger hath a privilege.   70
CORNWALL. Why art thou angry?
KENT. That such a slave as this should wear a sword,
  Who wears no honesty. Such smiling rogues as
    these,
  Like rats, oft bite the holy cords atwain
  Which are too intrince t'unloose: smooth every
    passion
  That in the natures of their lords rebel,
  Bring oil to fire, snow to the colder moods;
  Renege, affirm, and turn their halcyon beaks
  With every gale and vary of their masters,
  Knowing nought (like dogs) but following.   80
  A plague upon your epileptic visage!
  Smile you my speeches, as I were a Fool?
  Goose, if I had you upon Sarum Plain,
  I'd drive ye cackling home to Camelot.
CORNWALL. What, art thou mad, old fellow?
GLOUCESTER. How fell you out? Say that.
KENT. No contraries hold more antipathy
  Than I and such a knave.
CORNWALL. Why dost thou call him knave? What is
  his fault?
KENT. His countenance likes me not.   90
CORNWALL. No more perchance does mine, nor his,
  nor hers.
KENT. Sirs, 'tis my occupation to be plain:
  I have seen better faces in my time
  Than stands on any shoulder that I see
  Before me at this instant.
CORNWALL.   This is some fellow,
  Who, having been praised for bluntness, doth affect
  A saucy roughness, and constrains the garb
  Quite from his nature. He cannot flatter, he!
  An honest mind and plain, he must speak truth!
  An they will take it, so; if not, he's plain.   100
  These kind of knaves I know which in this plainness
  Harbour more craft and more corrupter ends
  Than twenty silly-ducking observants
  That stretch their duties nicely.
KENT. Sir, in good faith, in sincere verity,
  Under th'allowance of your great aspect,
  Whose influence, like the wreath of radiant fire
  On flick'ring Phoebus' front—
CORNWALL.   What mean'st by this?
KENT. To go out of my dialect, which you
  discommend so much.
  I know, sir, I am no flatterer. He that beguiled you 110
  in a plain accent was a plain knave, which for my
  part I will not be, though I should win "your
  Displeasure" to entreat me to 't.
CORNWALL. What was th'offence you gave him?
OSWALD. I never gave him any.
  It pleased the king his master very late
  To strike at me upon his misconstruction,
  When he, compact, and flattering his displeasure,
  Tripped me behind: being down, insulted, railed,

And put upon him such a deal of man   120
  That worthied him, got praises of the king
  For him attempting who was self-subdued,
  And, in the fleshment of this dread exploit,
  Drew on me here again.
KENT.   None of these rogues and cowards
  But Ajax is their fool.
CORNWALL.   Fetch forth the stocks!
  You stubborn ancient knave, you reverend
    braggart,
  We'll teach you!
KENT.   Sir, I am too old to learn.
  Call not your stocks for me; I serve the king,
  On whose employment I was sent to you.
  You shall do small respect, show too bold malice 130
  Against the grace and person of my master,
  Stocking his messenger.
CORNWALL.   Fetch forth the stocks!
  As I have life and honour, there shall he sit till noon.
REGAN. Till noon? Till night, my lord, and all night
  too.
KENT. Why, madam, if I were your father's dog,
  You should not use me so.
REGAN.   Sir, being his knave, I will.
CORNWALL. This is a fellow of the self-same colour
  Our sister speaks of. Come, bring away the stocks.
                        Stocks brought out
GLOUCESTER. Let me beseech your Grace not to do so.
  His fault is much, and the good king his master 140
  Will check him for't. Your purposed low correction
  Is such as basest and contemnéd'st wretches
  For pilf'rings and most common trespasses
  Are punished with. The king must take it ill
  That he, so slightly valued in his messenger,
  Should have him thus restrained.
CORNWALL.   I'll answer that.
REGAN. My sister may receive it much more worse
  To have her gentleman abused, assaulted,
  For following her affairs. Put in his legs.
                     Kent is put in the stocks
  [*to Cornwall*] Come my lord, away.   150
                           All go in
             except Gloucester and Kent
GLOUCESTER. I am sorry for thee, friend; 'tis the duke's
  pleasure,
  Whose disposition, all the world well knows,
  Will not be rubbed nor stopped. I'll entreat for thee.
KENT. Pray do not, sir. I have watched, and travelled
  hard.
  Some time I shall sleep out, the rest I'll whistle.
  A good man's fortune may grow out at heels.
  Give you good morrow!
GLOUCESTER. The duke's to blame in this; 'twill be ill
  taken.   *He goes*
KENT. Good king, that must approve the common
  saw,
  Thou out of heaven's benediction com'st   160
  To the warm sun!
  Approach, thou beacon to this under globe,
  That by thy comfortable beams I may
  Peruse this letter. Nothing almost sees miracles
  But misery. I know 'tis from Cordelia,
  Who hath most fortunately been informed
  Of my obscuréd course and shall find time....
  From this enormous state, seeking to give
  Losses their remedies. All weary and o'erwatched,

Take vantage, heavy eyes, not to behold   170
This shameful lodging.
Fortune, good night; smile once more; turn thy
    wheel.   *Sleeps*

Scene 3: *The open country*

Enter Edgar

EDGAR. I heard myself proclaimed,
And by the happy hollow of a tree
Escaped the hunt. No port is free, no place
That guard and most unusual vigilance
Does not attend my taking. Whiles I may scape
I will preserve myself; and am bethought
To take the basest and most poorest shape
That ever penury in contempt of man
Brought near to beast. My face I'll grime with filth,
Blanket my loins, elf all my hairs in knots,   10
And with presented nakedness outface
The winds and persecutions of the sky.
The country gives me proof and precedent
Of Bedlam beggars who, with roaring voices,
Strike in their numbed and mortified bare arms
Pins, wooden pricks, nails, sprigs of rosemary;
And with this horrible object, from low farms,
Poor pelting villages, sheep-cotes, and mills,
Sometimes with lunatic bans, sometime with
    prayers,
Enforce their charity. 'Poor Turlygod, poor Tom!'   20
That's something yet! Edgar I nothing am.   *He goes*

Scene 4: *Before Gloucester's castle. Kent in the stocks*

Enter Lear, Fool and Gentleman

LEAR. 'Tis strange that they should so depart from
    home,
And not send back my messenger.
GENTLEMAN.   As I learned,
The night before there was no purpose in them
Of this remove.
KENT.   Hail to thee, noble master!
LEAR. Ha!
Mak'st thou this shame thy pastime?
KENT.   No, my lord.
FOOL. Ha, ha! He wears cruel garters. Horses are tied
by the heads, dogs and bears by th' neck, monkies
by th' loins, and men by th' legs. When a man's
over-lusty at legs, then he wears wooden nether-   10
stocks.
LEAR. What's he that hath so much thy place mistook
To set thee here?
KENT.   It is both he and she,
Your son and daughter.
LEAR. No.
KENT. Yes.
LEAR. No, I say.
KENT. I say yea.
LEAR. No, no, they would not.
KENT. Yes, yes, they have.   20
LEAR. By Jupiter, I swear no!
KENT. By Juno, I swear ay!
LEAR.   They durst not do 't,
They could not, would not do 't; 'tis worse than
    murder
To do upon respect such violent outrage.
Resolve me with all modest haste which way

Thou mightst deserve or they impose this usage,
Coming from us.
KENT.   My lord, when at their home
I did commend your Highness' letters to them,
Ere I was risen from the place that showed
My duty kneeling, came there a reeking post,   30
Stewed in his haste, half breathless, panting forth
From Goneril his mistress salutations;
Delivered letters, spite of intermission,
Which presently they read: on whose contents
They summoned up their meiny, straight took
    horse,
Commanded me to follow and attend
The leisure of their answer, gave me cold looks:
And meeting here the other messenger,
Whose welcome I perceived had poisoned mine—
Being the very fellow which of late   40
Displayed so saucily against your Highness—
Having more man than wit about me, drew.
He raised the house with loud and coward cries.
Your son and daughter found this trespass worth
The shame which here it suffers.
FOOL. Winter's not gone yet if the wild geese fly that
    way.
        Fathers that wear rags
            Do make their children blind,
        But fathers that bear bags
            Shall see their children kind.   50
        Fortune, that arrant whore,
            Ne'er turns the key to th' poor.
But for all this thou shalt have as many dolours
from thy daughters as thou canst tell in a year.
LEAR. O, how this mother swells up toward my
    heart!
Hysterica passio! Down, thou climbing sorrow;
Thy element's below. Where is this daughter?
KENT. With the earl, sir, here within.
LEAR.   Follow me not; stay here.
                                                    He goes in
GENTLEMAN. Made you no more offence but what you
    speak of?   60
KENT. None.
How chance the king comes with so small a
    number?
FOOL. An thou hadst been set i'th'stocks for that
question, thou'dst well deserved it.
KENT. Why, fool?
FOOL. We'll set thee to school to an ant, to teach thee
there's no labouring i'th'winter. All that follow
their noses are led by their eyes but blind men, and
there's not a nose among twenty but can smell him   70
that's stinking. Let go thy hold when a great wheel
runs down a hill, lest it break thy neck with following; but the great one that goes upward, let him
draw thee after. When a wise man gives thee better
counsel, give me mine again. I would ha' none but
knaves use it, since a fool gives it.
        That sir which serves and seeks for gain
            And follows but for form,
        Will pack when it begins to rain
            And leave thee in the storm.   80
        But I will tarry; the Fool will stay
            And let the wise man fly.
        The knave turns fool that runs away;
            The Fool no knave, perdy.
KENT. Where learned you this, fool?

FOOL. Not i'th'stocks, fool!

Re-enter Lear, with Gloucester

LEAR. Deny to speak with me? They are sick, they are
weary,
They have travelled all the night? Mere fetches; ay,
The images of revolt and flying off.
Fetch me a better answer.

GLOUCESTER.   My dear lord,   90
You know the fiery quality of the duke,
How unremovable and fixed he is
In his own course.

LEAR.   Vengeance! plague! death! confusion!
Fiery? What quality? Why, Gloucester, Gloucester,
I'ld speak with the Duke of Cornwall and his wife.

GLOUCESTER. Well, my good lord, I have informed
them so.

LEAR. Informed them? Dost thou understand me,
man?

GLOUCESTER. Ay, my good lord.

LEAR. The king would speak with Cornwall; the dear
father
Would with his daughter speak, commands her
service.   100
Are they informed of this? My breath and blood!
Fiery? the fiery duke? Tell the hot duke that—
No, but not yet; may be he is not well:
Infirmity doth still neglect all office
Whereto our health is bound. We are not ourselves
When nature, being oppressed, commands the mind
To suffer with the body. I'll forbear,
And am fall'n out with my more headier will
To take the indisposed and sickly fit
For the sound man. [*looking on Kent*] Death on my
state! Wherefore   110
Should he sit here? This act persuades me
That this remotion of the duke and her
Is practice only. Give me my servant forth.
Go tell the duke and 's wife I'ld speak with them
Now, presently; bid them come forth and hear me,
Or at their chamber door I'll beat the drum
Till it cry sleep to death.

GLOUCESTER. I would have all well betwixt you.
                                                  Goes

LEAR. O me, my heart! My rising heart! But down!

FOOL. Cry to it, nuncle, as the cockney did to the eels 120
when she put 'em i' th' paste alive. She knapped 'em
o'th' coxcombs with a stick and cried 'Down,
wantons, down!' 'Twas her brother that, in pure
kindness to his horse, buttered his hay.

Re-enter Gloucester, with Cornwall, Regan, and servants

LEAR. Good morrow to you both.

CORNWALL.   Hail to your Grace!
                              Kent here set at liberty

REGAN. I am glad to see your Highness.

LEAR. Regan, I think you are. I know what reason
I have to think so; if thou shouldst not be glad,
I would divorce me from thy mother's tomb,
Sepulchring an adultress. [*to Kent*] O, are you free? 130
Some other time for that.—Beloved Regan,
Thy sister's naught. O Regan, she hath tied
Sharp-toothed unkindness, like a vulture, here.
                              Points to his heart
I can scarce speak to thee; thou'lt not believe
With how depraved a quality—O Regan!

REGAN. I pray you, sir, take patience. I have hope
You less know how to value her desert
Than she to scant her duty.

LEAR.   Say? How is that?

REGAN. I cannot think my sister in the least
Would fail her obligation. If, sir, perchance   140
She have restrained the riots of your followers,
'Tis on such ground, and to such wholesome end,
As clears her from all blame.

LEAR. My curses on her!

REGAN.   O sir, you are old;
Nature in you stands on the very verge
Of his confine. You should be ruled and led
By some discretion that discerns your state
Better than you yourself. Therefore I pray you
That to our sister you do make return;
Say you have wronged her.

LEAR.   Ask her forgiveness?   150
Do you but mark how this becomes the house!
'Dear daughter, I confess that I am old: *Kneeling*
Age is unnecessary; on my knees I beg
That you'll vouchsafe me raiment, bed, and food!'

REGAN. Good sir, no more; these are unsightly tricks.
Return you to my sister.

LEAR [*rising*].   Never, Regan!
She hath abated me of half my train,
Looked black upon me, struck me with her tongue
Most serpent-like upon the very heart.
All the stored vengeances of heaven fall   160
On her ingrateful top. Strike her young bones,
You taking airs, with lameness!

CORNWALL.   Fie, sir, fie!

LEAR. You nimble lightnings, dart your blinding
flames
Into her scornful eyes! Infect her beauty,
You fen-sucked fogs, drawn by the pow'rful sun
To fall and blister her!

REGAN.   O the blest gods!
So will you wish on me when the rash mood—

LEAR. No, Regan, thou shalt never have my curse.
Thy tender-hefted nature shall not give
Thee o'er to harshness. Her eyes are fierce; but thine 170
Do comfort and not burn. 'Tis not in thee
To grudge my pleasures, to cut off my train,
To bandy hasty words, to scant my sizes,
And in conclusion to oppose the bolt
Against my coming in. Thou better know'st
The offices of nature, bond of childhood,
Effects of courtesy, dues of gratitude:
Thy half o' th' kingdom hast thou not forgot,
Wherein I thee endowed.

REGAN.   Good sir, to th' purpose.

LEAR. Who put my man i' th' stocks?   *Tucket heard*

CORNWALL.   What trumpet's that? 180

REGAN. I know't—my sister's. This approves her
letter,
That she would soon be here.

Enter Oswald

                                    Is your lady come?

LEAR. This is a slave, whose easy-borrowed pride
Dwells in the sickly grace of her he follows.
Out, varlet, from my sight!

CORNWALL.   What means your Grace?

LEAR. Who stocked my servant? Regan, I have good
hope

Thou didst not know on't.

Enter Goneril

                    Who comes here? O heavens,
If you do love old men, if your sweet sway
Allow obedience, if you yourselves are old,
Make it your cause; send down and take my part! 190
[*to Goneril*] Art not ashamed to look upon this
    beard?
O Regan! will you take her by the hand?
GONERIL. Why not by th' hand, sir? How have I
    offended?
All's not offence that indiscretion finds
And dotage terms so.
LEAR.   O sides, you are too tough!
Will you yet hold? How came my man i' th' stocks?
CORNWALL. I set him there, sir; but his own disorders
Deserved much less advancement.
LEAR.   You? Did you?
REGAN. I pray you, father, being weak, seem so.
If, till the expiration of your month, 200
You will return and sojourn with my sister,
Dismissing half your train, come then to me.
I am now from home, and out of that provision
Which shall be needful for your entertainment.
LEAR. Return to her? and fifty men dismissed?
No, rather I abjure all roofs, and choose
To wage against the enmity o'th'air,
To be a comrade with the wolf and owl—
Necessity's sharp pinch! Return with her?
Why, the hot-blooded France, that dowerless took 210
Our youngest born, I could as well be brought
To knee his throne and, squire-like, pension beg
To keep base life afoot. Return with her?
Persuade me rather to be slave and sumpter
To this detested groom.   *Looking at Oswald*
GONERIL.   At your choice, sir.
LEAR. I prithee, daughter, do not make me mad.
I will not trouble thee, my child; farewell;
We'll no more meet, no more see one another.
But yet thou art my flesh, my blood, my daughter—
Or rather a disease that's in my flesh, 220
Which I must needs call mine. Thou art a boil,
A plague-sore, or embossèd carbuncle
In my corrupted blood. But I'll not chide thee:
Let shame come when it will, I do not call it;
I do not bid the thunder-bearer shoot,
Nor tell tales of thee to high-judging Jove.
Mend when thou canst; be better at thy leisure:
I can be patient; I can stay with Regan,
I and my hundred knights.
REGAN.   Not altogether so.
I looked not for you yet, nor am provided 230
For your fit welcome. Give ear, sir, to my sister;
For those that mingle reason with your passion
Must be content to think you old, and so—
But she knows what she does.
LEAR.   Is this well spoken?
REGAN. I dare avouch it, sir. What! fifty followers?
Is it not well? What should you need of more?
Yea, or so many, sith that both charge and danger
Speak 'gainst so great a number? How in one
    house
Should many people, under two commands,
Hold amity? 'Tis hard, almost impossible. 240

GONERIL. Why might not you, my lord, receive
    attendance
From those that she calls servants, or from mine?
REGAN. Why not, my lord? If then they chanced to
    slack ye,
We could control them. If you will come to me
(For now I spy a danger), I entreat you
To bring but five and twenty: to no more
Will I give place or notice.
LEAR. I gave you all—
REGAN.   And in good time you gave it.
LEAR. Made you my guardians, my depositaries,
But kept a reservation to be followed 250
With such a number. What! must I come to you
With five and twenty? Regan, said you so?
REGAN. And speak 't again, my lord; no more with
    me.
LEAR. Those wicked creatures yet do look
    well-favoured
When others are more wicked; not being the worst
Stands in some rank of praise. [*to Goneril*] I'll go with
    thee.
Thy fifty yet doth double five and twenty,
And thou art twice her love.
GONERIL.   Hear me, my lord.
What need you five and twenty, ten, or five,
To follow in a house where twice so many 260
Have a command to tend you?
REGAN.   What need one?
LEAR. O reason not the need! Our basest beggars
Are in the poorest things superfluous.
Allow not nature more than nature needs,
Man's life is cheap as beast's. Thou art a lady;
If only to go warm were gorgeous,
Why, nature need not what thou gorgeous wear'st,
Which scarcely keeps thee warm. But for true
    need—
You heavens, give me patience—patience I need!
You see me here, you gods, a poor old man, 270
As full of grief as age, wretched in both.
If it be you that stirs these daughters' hearts
Against their father, fool me not so much
To bear it tamely; touch me with noble anger,
And let not women's weapons, water drops,
Stain my man's cheeks. No, you unnatural hags,
I will have such revenges on you both
That all the world shall—I will do such things—
What they are yet I know not, but they shall be
The terrors of the earth! You think I'll weep; 280
No, I'll not weep:
I have full cause of weeping, [*storm heard approaching*]
    but this heart
Shall break into a hundred thousand flaws
Or ere I'll weep. O Fool, I shall go mad!
               He goes, the Fool, Gloucester,
                     and Kent following
CORNWALL. Let us withdraw; 'twill be a storm.
REGAN. This house is little: the old man and's people
Cannot be well bestowed.
GONERIL. 'Tis his own blame; hath put himself from
    rest,
And must needs taste his folly.
REGAN. For his particular, I'll receive him gladly, 290
But not one follower.
GONERIL.   So am I purposed.
Where is my lord of Gloucester?

CORNWALL. Followed the old man forth. [*Gloucester re-enters*] He is returned.
GLOUCESTER. The king is in high rage.
CORNWALL. Whither is he going?
GLOUCESTER. He calls to horse, but will I know not whither.
CORNWALL. 'Tis best to give him way; he leads himself.
GONERIL. My lord, entreat him by no means to stay.
GLOUCESTER. Alack, the night comes on, and the bleak winds
Do sorely ruffle. For many miles about
There's scarce a bush.
REGAN.   O sir, to wilful men   300
The injuries that they themselves procure
Must be their schoolmasters. Shut up your doors;
He is attended with a desperate train,
And what they may incense him to, being apt
To have his ear abused, wisdom bids fear.
CORNWALL. Shut up your doors, my lord; 'tis a wild night:
My Regan counsels well. Come out o' th' storm.
                                                They go in

ACT 3
Scene 1: *A heath*

A storm with thunder and lightning. Enter Kent and a Gentleman meeting

KENT. Who's there besides foul weather?
GENTLEMAN. One minded like the weather, most unquietly.
KENT. I know you. Where's the King?
GENTLEMAN. Contending with the fretful elements;
Bids the wind blow the earth into the sea,
Or swell the curlèd waters 'bove the main,
That things might change or cease; tears his white hair,
Which the impetuous blasts with eyeless rage
Catch in their fury and make nothing of;
Strives in his little world of man to out-storm   10
The to-and-fro-conflicting wind and rain.
This night, wherein the cub-drawn bear would couch,
The lion and the belly-pinchèd wolf
Keep their fur dry, unbonneted he runs,
And bids what will take all.
KENT.   But who is with him?
GENTLEMAN. None but the Fool, who labours to outjest
His heart-struck injuries.
KENT.   Sir, I do know you,
And dare upon the warrant of my note
Commend a dear thing to you. There is division,   20
Although as yet the face of it is covered
With mutual cunning, 'twixt Albany and Cornwall,
Who have—as who have not, that their great stars
Throned and set high?—servants, who seem no less,
Which are to France the spies and speculations
Intelligent of our state. What hath been seen,
Either in snuffs and packings of the Dukes,
Or the hard rein which both of them hath borne
Against the old kind King; or something deeper
Whereof perchance these are but furnishings....
But true it is from France there comes a power   30

Into this scattered kingdom, who already,
Wise in our negligence, have secret feet
In some of our best ports and are at point
To show their open banner. Now to you:
If on my credit you dare build so far
To make your speed to Dover, you shall find
Some that will thank you, making just report
Of how unnatural and bemadding sorrow
The King hath cause to plain.
I am a gentleman of blood and breeding,   40
And from some knowledge and assurance offer
This office to you.
GENTLEMAN. I will talk further with you.
KENT.   No, do not.
For confirmation that I am much more
Than my out-wall, open this purse and take
What it contains. If you shall see Cordelia
(As fear not but you shall), show her this ring,
And she will tell you who your fellow is
That yet you do not know. Fie on this storm!
I will go seek the King.   50
GENTLEMAN. Give me your hand. Have you no more to say?
KENT. Few words, but, to effect, more than all yet—
That when we have found the King (in which your pain
That way, I'll this) he that first lights on him
Holla the other.   *They go their separate ways*

Scene 2: *Another part of the heath*

Storm still. Enter Lear with Fool

LEAR. Blow, winds, and crack your cheeks! rage! blow!
You cataracts and hurricanoes, spout
Till you have drenched our steeples, drowned the cocks!
You sulph'rous and thought-executing fires,
Vaunt-couriers of oak-cleaving thunderbolts,
Singe my white head! And thou, all-shaking thunder,
Strike flat the thick rotundity o'th'world,
Crack Nature's moulds, all germens spill at once
That make ingrateful man!
FOOL. O nuncle, court holy water in a dry house is   10
better than this rain-water out o' door. Good
nuncle, in; ask thy daughters blessing! Here's a night
pities neither wise men nor fools.
LEAR. Rumble thy bellyful! Spit, fire! spout, rain!
Nor rain, wind, thunder, fire are my daughters.
I tax not you, you elements, with unkindness:
I never gave you kingdom, called you children;
You owe me no subscription. Then let fall
Your horrible pleasure. Here I stand your slave,
A poor, infirm, weak, and despised old man: 20
But yet I call you servile ministers,
That will with two pernicious daughters join
Your high-engendered battles 'gainst a head
So old and white as this. O, ho! 'tis foul!
FOOL. He that has a house to put's head in has a good head-piece.
          The codpiece that will house
          Before the head has any,
          The head and he shall louse:
          So beggars marry many.   30
          The man that makes his toe

What he his heart should make
Shall of a corn cry woe,
And turn his sleep to wake.
For there was never yet fair woman but she made
mouths in a glass.

Enter Kent

LEAR. No, I will be the pattern of all patience;
I will say nothing.
KENT. Who's there?
FOOL. Marry, here's grace and a codpiece; that's a wise 40
man and a fool.
KENT. Alas, sir, are you here? Things that love night
Love not such nights as these. The wrathful skies
Gallow the very wanderers of the dark
And make them keep their caves. Since I was man,
Such sheets of fire, such bursts of horrid thunder,
Such groans of roaring wind and rain, I never
Remember to have heard. Man's nature cannot
carry
Th'affliction nor the fear.
LEAR.   Let the great gods,
That keep this dreadful pudder o'er our heads,   50
Find out their enemies now. Tremble, thou wretch
That hast within thee undivulgéd crimes
Unwhipped of justice. Hide thee, thou bloody hand,
Thou perjured, and thou simular of virtue
That art incestuous. Caitiff, to pieces shake,
That under covert and convenient seeming
Hast practised on man's life. Close pent-up guilts,
Rive your concealing continents, and cry
These dreadful summoners grace. I am a man
More sinned against than sinning.
KENT.   Alack, bare-headed? 60
Gracious my lord, hard by here is a hovel;
Some friendship will it lend you 'gainst the tempest:
Repose you there, while I to this hard house
(More harder than the stones whereof 'tis raised,
Which even but now, demanding after you,
Denied me to come in) return, and force
Their scanted courtesy.
LEAR.   My wits begin to turn.
Come on, my boy. How dost, my boy? Art cold?
I am cold myself. Where is this straw, my fellow?
The art of our necessities is strange,   70
And can make vile things precious. Come, your
hovel.
Poor fool and knave, I have one part in my heart
That's sorry yet for thee.
FOOL [*sings*].
He that has and a little tiny wit—
With heigh-ho, the wind and the rain—
Must make content with his fortunes fit,
Though the rain it raineth every day.
LEAR. True, boy. Come, bring us to this hovel.
Lear and Kent go
FOOL. This is a brave night to cool a courtesan! I'll
speak a prophecy ere I go: 80
When priests are more in word than matter;
When brewers mar their malt with water;
When nobles are their tailors' tutors;
No heretics burned, but wenches' suitors;
Then shall the realm of Albion
Come to great confusion.
When every case in law is right;
No squire in debt nor no poor knight;

When slanders do not live in tongues,
Nor cutpurses come not to throngs;   90
When usurers tell their gold i'th'field,
And bawds and whores do churches build;
Then comes the time, who lives to see 't,
That going shall be used with feet.

This prophecy Merlin shall make, for I live before
his time.   *Goes*

Scene 3: *Gloucester's castle*

Enter Gloucester and Edmund, with lights

GLOUCESTER. Alack, alack, Edmund, I like not this unnatural dealing. When I desired their leave that I
might pity him, they took from me the use of mine
own house, charged me on pain of perpetual displeasure neither to speak of him, entreat for him, or
any way sustain him.
EDMUND. Most savage and unnatural!
GLOUCESTER. Go to; say you nothing. There is
division between the Dukes, and a worse matter
than that. I have received a letter this night—'tis 10
dangerous to be spoken—I have locked the letter in
my closet. These injuries the King now bears will
be revenged home. There is part of a power already
footed; we must incline to the King. I will look him
and privily relieve him; go you and maintain talk
with the Duke, that my charity be not of him perceived; if he ask for me, I am ill and gone to bed. If
I die for it (as no less is threat'ned me), the King, my
old master, must be relieved. There is strange things
toward, Edmund; pray you be careful.   *He goes* 20
EDMUND. This courtesy, forbid thee, shall the Duke
Instantly know, and of that letter too.
This seems a fair deserving, and must draw me
That which my father loses—no less than all.
The younger rises when the old doth fall.

He goes

Scene 4: *The heath. Before a hovel Storm still*

Enter Lear, Kent, and Fool

KENT. Here is the place, my lord; good my lord, enter:
The tyranny of the open night 's too rough
For nature to endure.
LEAR.   Let me alone.
KENT. Good my lord, enter here.
LEAR.   Wilt break my heart?
KENT. I had rather break mine own. Good my lord,
enter.
LEAR. Thou think'st 'tis much that this contentious
storm
Invades us to the skin: so 'tis to thee;
But where the greater malady is fixed,
The lesser is scarce felt. Thou'dst shun a bear;
But if thy flight lay toward the roaring sea,   10
Thou'dst meet the bear i'th'mouth. When the
mind's free,
The body's delicate; this tempest in my mind
Doth from my senses take all feeling else
Save what beats there—filial ingratitude!
Is it not as this mouth should tear this hand
For lifting food to 't? But I will punish home!
No, I will weep no more. In such a night
To shut me out? Pour on; I will endure.

In such a night as this? O Regan, Goneril!
Your old kind father whose frank heart gave all!   20
O, that way madness lies; let me shun that!
No more of that.

KENT.   Good my lord, enter here.

LEAR. Prithee go in thyself, seek thine own ease;
This tempest will not give me leave to ponder
On things would hurt me more. But I'll go in.
[*to the Fool*] In, boy, go first. You houseless
    poverty—
Nay, get thee in; I'll pray, and then I'll sleep—
                      Fool goes in
Poor naked wretches, whereso'er you are,
That bide the pelting of this pitiless storm,
How shall your houseless heads and unfed sides,   30
Your looped and windowed raggedness, defend you
From seasons such as these? O, I have ta'en
Too little care of this! Take physic, pomp;
Expose thyself to feel what wretches feel,
That thou mayst shake the superflux to them
And show the heavens more just.

EDGAR [*within*]. Fathom and half, fathom and half!
Poor Tom!   *The Fool runs out from the hovel*

FOOL. Come not in here, nuncle, here's a spirit.
Help me, help me!   40

KENT. Give me thy hand. Who's there?

FOOL. A spirit, a spirit! He says his name's poor Tom.

KENT. What art thou that dost grumble there
    i'th'straw?
Come forth?

Enter Edgar, disguised as a madman, from the hovel

EDGAR. Away! The foul fiend follows me!
Through the sharp hawthorn blow the cold winds.
Humh! Go to thy bed and warm thee.

LEAR. Didst thou give all to thy daughters? And art
thou come to this?

EDGAR. Who gives anything to poor Tom? whom the   50
foul fiend hath led through fire and through flame,
through ford and whirlpool, o'er bog and quagmire; that hath laid knives under his pillow, and
halters in his pew; set ratsbane by his porridge; made
him proud of heart, to ride on a bay trotting horse
over four-inched bridges, to course his own shadow
for a traitor. Bless thy five wits! Tom's a-cold. O,
do de, do de, do de. Bless thee from whirlwinds,
star-blasting, and taking! Do poor Tom some
charity, whom the foul fiend vexes. There could I   60
have him now—and there—and there again—and
there!   *Storm still*

LEAR. What, has his daughters brought him to this
    pass?
Couldst thou save nothing? Wouldst thou give 'em
    all?

FOOL. Nay, he reserved a blanket; else we had been all
shamed.

LEAR. Now all the plagues that in the pendulous air
Hang fated o'er men's faults light on thy daughters!

KENT. He hath no daughters, sir.

LEAR. Death, traitor! Nothing could have subdued
    nature   70
To such a lowness but his unkind daughters.
Is it the fashion that discarded fathers
Should have thus little mercy on their flesh?
Judicious punishment! 'Twas this flesh begot
Those pelican daughters.

EDGAR. Pillicock sat on Pillicock Hill.
    Alow! alow, loo, loo!

FOOL. This cold night will turn us all to fools and
madmen.

EDGAR. Take heed o'th'foul fiend. Obey thy parents,   80
keep thy word justly, swear not, commit not with
man's sworn spouse, set not thy sweet heart on
proud array. Tom's a-cold.

LEAR. What hast thou been?

EDGAR. A servingman! proud in heart and mind; that
curled my hair, wore gloves in my cap; served the
lust of my mistress' heart, and did the act of darkness
with her; swore as many oaths as I spake words, and
broke them in the sweet face of heaven; one that
slept in the contriving of lust, and waked to do it.   90
Wine loved I deeply, dice dearly; and in woman
out-paramoured the Turk. False of heart, light of
ear, bloody of hand; hog in sloth, fox in stealth, wolf
in greediness, dog in madness, lion in prey. Let not
the creaking of shoes nor the rustling of silks betray
thy poor heart to woman. Keep thy foot out of
brothels, thy hand out of plackets, thy pen from
lenders' books, and defy the foul fiend.
Still through the hawthorn blows the cold wind,
Says suum, mun, hey nonny nonny.   100
Dolphin my boy, boy!—sessa! let him trot by.
                              Storm still

LEAR. Thou wert better in a grave than to answer
with thy uncovered body this extremity of the skies.
Is man no more than this? Consider him well. Thou
ow'st the worm no silk, the beast no hide, the sheep
no wool, the cat no perfume. Ha! Here's three on's
are sophisticated: thou art the thing itself. Unaccom-
modated man is no more but such a poor, bare,
forked animal as thou art. Off, off, you lendings!
Come, unbutton here!   *Strives to tear off his clothes*   110

FOOL. Prithee, nuncle, be contented; 'tis a naughty
night to swim in!

Sees Gloucester approaching with a torch

Now a little fire in a wild field were like an old
lecher's heart—a small spark, all the rest on's body
cold. Look, here comes a walking fire.

EDGAR. This is the foul Flibbertigibbet. He begins at
curfew, and walks till first cock. He gives the web
and the pin, squinies the eye, and makes the harelip;
mildews the white wheat, and hurts the poor
creature of earth.   120
    S'Withold footed thrice the 'old:
He met the Nightmare and her nine fold;
    Bid her alight
    And her troth plight—
And aroint thee, witch, aroint thee!

KENT. How fares your grace?

LEAR. What's he?

KENT. Who's there? What is't you seek?

GLOUCESTER. What are you there? Your names?

EDGAR. Poor Tom, that eats the swimming frog, the   130
toad, the tadpole, the wall-newt and the water; that
in the fury of his heart, when the foul fiend rages,
eats cow-dung for sallets, swallows the old rat and
the ditch-dog, drinks the green mantle of the standing pool; who is whipped from tithing to tithing,
and stock-punished and imprisoned; who hath had
three suits to his back, six shirts to his body,

Horse to ride, and weapon to wear;
But mice and rats and such small deer
Have been Tom's food for seven long year.   140
Beware my follower. Peace, Smulkin; peace, thou
    fiend!
GLOUCESTER. What, hath your Grace no better
    company?
EDGAR. The Prince of Darkness is a gentleman!
    Modo he's called, and Mahu.
GLOUCESTER. Our flesh and blood, my lord, is grown
    so vile,
    That it doth hate what gets it.
EDGAR. Poor Tom's a-cold.
GLOUCESTER. Go in with me; my duty cannot suffer
    T' obey in all your daughters' hard commands.   150
    Though their injunction be to bar my doors
    And let this tyrannous night take hold upon you,
    Yet have I ventured to come seek you out
    And bring you where both fire and food is ready.
LEAR. First let me talk with this philosopher.
    What is the cause of thunder?
KENT. Good my lord, take his offer; go into th' house.
LEAR. I'll talk a word with this same learned
    Theban.
    What is your study?
EDGAR. How to prevent the fiend and to kill vermin.   160
LEAR. Let me ask you one word in private.
KENT. Importune him once more to go, my lord;
    His wits begin t' unsettle.
GLOUCESTER.   Canst thou blame him?
                                          Storm still
    His daughters seek his death. Ah, that good Kent!
    He said it would be thus, poor banished man!
    Thou sayest the King grows mad; I'll tell thee,
        friend,
    I am almost mad myself. I had a son,
    Now outlawed from my blood: he sought my life
    But lately, very late: I loved him, friend,
    No father his son dearer: true to tell thee,   170
    The grief hath crazed my wits. What a night's this!
    I do beseech your Grace—
LEAR.   O, cry you mercy, sir.
    Noble philosopher, your company.
EDGAR. Tom's a-cold.
GLOUCESTER. In, fellow, there, into th' hovel; keep
    thee warm.
LEAR. Come, let's in all.
KENT.   This way, my lord.
LEAR.   With him!
    I will keep still with my philosopher.
KENT. Good my lord, soothe him; let him take the
    fellow.
GLOUCESTER. Take him you on.
KENT. Sirrah, come on; go along with us.   180
LEAR. Come, good Athenian.
GLOUCESTER. No words, no words; hush!
EDGAR. Childe Roland to the dark tower came.
    His word was still 'Fie, foh, and fum.
    I smell the blood of a British man.'   *They go*

Scene 5: *Gloucester's castle*

Enter Cornwall and Edmund

CORNWALL. I will have my revenge ere I depart his
    house.
EDMUND. How, my lord, I may be censured, that

nature thus gives way to loyalty, something fears me
    to think of.
CORNWALL. I now perceive it was not altogether your
    brother's evil disposition made him seek his death;
    but a provoking merit, set awork by a reproveable
    badness in himself.
EDMUND. How malicious is my fortune, that I must   10
    repent to be just! This is the letter he spoke of, which
    approves him an intelligent party to the advantages
    of France. O heavens! that this treason were not—or
    not I the detector!
CORNWALL. Go with me to the Duchess.
EDMUND. If the matter of this paper be certain, you
    have mighty business in hand.
CORNWALL. True or false, it hath made thee Earl of
    Gloucester. Seek out where thy father is, that he may
    be ready for our apprehension.   20
EDMUND [*aside*]. If I find him comforting the King, it
    will stuff his suspicion more fully. [*to Cornwall*] I
    will persever in my course of loyalty, though the
    conflict be sore between that and my blood.
CORNWALL. I will lay trust upon thee; and thou shalt
    find a dearer father in my love.   *They leave*

Scene 6: *A room in a farmhouse adjoining Gloucester's
                          castle*

Enter Gloucester and Kent

GLOUCESTER. Here is better than the open air; take it
    thankfully. I will piece out the comfort with what
    addition I can: I will not be long from you.
KENT. All the power of his wits have given way to his
    impatience. The gods reward your kindness!
                                    Gloucester goes out

Enter Lear, Edgar, and Fool

EDGAR. Frateretto calls me, and tells me Nero is an
    angler in the lake of darkness. Pray, innocent, and
    beware the foul fiend.
FOOL. Prithee, nuncle, tell me whether a madman be a
    gentleman or a yeoman.   10
LEAR. A king, a king!
FOOL. No, he's a yeoman that has a gentleman to his
    son; for he's a mad yeoman that sees his son a gentle-
    man before him.
LEAR. To have a thousand with red burning spits
    Come hizzing in upon 'em!
EDGAR. The foul fiend bites my back.
FOOL. He's mad that trusts in the tameness of a wolf,
    a horse's health, a boy's love, or a whore's oath.
LEAR. It shall be done; I will arraign them straight. 20
    [*to Edgar*] Come sit thou here, most learned justicer;
    [*to the Fool*] Thou sapient sir, sit here. Now, you
    she-foxes—
EDGAR. Look where he stands and glares! Want'st thou
    eyes at trial, madam? [*sings*]
                Come o'er the burn, Bessy, to me.
FOOL [*sings*]   Her boat hath a leak,
                And she must not speak
        Why she dares not come over to thee.
EDGAR. The foul fiend haunts poor Tom in the voice
    of a nightingale. Hoppedance cries in Tom's belly   30
    for two white herring. Croak not, black angel; I
    have no food for thee.
KENT. How do you, sir? Stand you not so amazed.
    Will you lie down and rest upon the cushions?

LEAR. I'll see their trial first. Bring in their evidence.
　　[to Edgar] Thou robéd man of justice, take thy
　　　　place;
　　[to the Fool] And thou, his yokefellow of equity,
　　Bench by his side. [to Kent] You are
　　　　o'th'commission;
　　Sit you too.
EDGAR. Let us deal justly. 　　　　　　　　　　　40
　　Sleepest or wakest thou, jolly shepherd?
　　　　Thy sheep be in the corn;
　　And for one blast of thy minikin mouth
　　　　Thy sheep shall take no harm.
　　Purr the cat is gray.
LEAR. Arraign her first; 'tis Goneril. I here take my
　　oath before this honourable assembly, she kicked the
　　poor king, her father.
FOOL. Come hither, mistress; is your name Goneril?
LEAR. She cannot deny it. 　　　　　　　　　　50
FOOL. Cry you mercy, I took you for a jointed-stool.
LEAR. And here's another, whose warped looks
　　proclaim
　　What stone her heart is made on. Stop her there!
　　Arms, arms, sword, fire! Corruption in the place!
　　False justicer, why hast thou let her scape?
EDGAR. Bless thy five wits!
KENT. O pity! Sir, where is the patience now
　　That you so oft have boasted to retain?
EDGAR. My tears begin to take his part so much
　　They mar my counterfeiting. 　　　　　　　60
LEAR. The little dogs and all,
　　Tray, Blanche, and Sweetheart; see, they bark at me.
EDGAR. Tom will throw his head at them. Avaunt,
　　you curs!
　　　Be thy mouth or black or white,
　　　Tooth that poisons if it bite;
　　　Mastiff, greyhound, mongrel grim,
　　　Hound or spaniel, brach or lym,
　　　Or bobtail tyke or trundle-tail,
　　　Tom will make him weep and wail; 　　　　70
　　　For, with throwing thus my head,
　　　Dogs leaped the hatch, and all are fled.
　　Do, de, de, de. Sessa! Come, march to wakes and
　　fairs and market towns. Poor Tom, thy horn is dry.
LEAR. Then let them anatomize Regan; see what
　　breeds about her heart. Is there any cause in nature
　　that make these hard hearts? [to Edgar] You, sir, I
　　entertain for one of my hundred; only I do not like
　　the fashion of your garments. You will say they are
　　Persian; but let them be changed. 　　　　80
KENT. Now, good my lord, lie here and rest awhile.
LEAR. Make no noise, make no noise; draw the cur-
　　tains. So, so; we'll go to supper i'th'morning.
FOOL. And I'll go to bed at noon.

Enter Gloucester

GLOUCESTER. Come hither, friend. Where is the King
　　my master?
KENT. Here, sir: but trouble him not; his wits are
　　gone.
GLOUCESTER. Good friend, I prithee take him in thy
　　arms.
　　I have o'erheard a plot of death upon him.
　　There is a litter ready; lay him in't,
　　And drive toward Dover, friend, where thou shalt
　　　meet 　　　　　　　　　　　　　　　90
　　Both welcome and protection. Take up thy master;

If thou should'st dally half an hour, his life,
With thine, and all that offer to defend him,
Stand in assuréd loss. Take up, take up,
And follow me, that will to some provision
Give thee quick conduct.
KENT. 　　　　　　　　Oppresséd nature sleeps.
This rest might yet have balmed thy broken sinews,
Which, if convenience will not allow,
Stand in hard cure. [to the Fool] Come, help to
　　bear thy master;
Thou must not stay behind.
GLOUCESTER. 　　　　　　Come, come, away! 　100
　　　　　　　Gloucester, Kent, and the Fool
　　　　　　　　leave, carrying Lear
EDGAR. When we our betters see bearing our woes,
We scarcely think our miseries our foes.
Who alone suffers, suffers most i'th'mind,
Leaving free things and happy shows behind.
But then the mind much sufferance doth o'erskip
When grief hath mates, and bearing fellowship.
How light and portable my pain seems now,
When that which makes me bend makes the King
　　bow.
He childed as I fathered! Tom, away!
Mark the high noises, and thyself bewray 　　110
When false opinion, whose wrong thoughts
　　defile thee,
In thy just proof repeals and reconciles thee.
What will hap more tonight, safe scape the King!
Lurk, lurk. 　　　　　　　　　　　　*He goes*

*

Scene 7: *Gloucester's castle*

Enter Cornwall, Regan, Goneril, Edmund and Servants

CORNWALL [to Goneril]. Post speedily to my lord your
　　husband; show him this letter: the army of France is
　　landed. Seek out the traitor Gloucester.
REGAN. Hang him instantly.
GONERIL. Pluck out his eyes.
CORNWALL. Leave him to my displeasure. Edmund,
　　keep you our sister company. The revenges we are
　　bound to take upon your traitorous father are not fit
　　for your beholding. Advise the Duke, where you are
　　going, to a most festinate preparation: we are bound 　10
　　to the like. Our posts shall be swift and intelligent
　　betwixt us. Farewell, dear sister; farewell, my Lord
　　of Gloucester.

Enter Oswald

　　How now? Where's the King?
OSWALD. My Lord of Gloucester hath conveyed him
　　hence.
　　Some five or six and thirty of his knights,
　　Hot questrists after him, met him at gate,
　　Who, with some other of the lord's dependants,
　　Are gone with him toward Dover, where they
　　　boast
　　To have well-arméd friends.
CORNWALL. 　　　　　　Get horses for your mistress. 　20
GONERIL. Farewell, sweet lord, and sister.
CORNWALL. Edmund, farewell.
　　　　　　　　Goneril, Edmund, and Oswald go
　　Go seek the traitor Gloucester;
　　Pinion him like a thief, bring him before us.
　　　　　　　　　　　　　　　　Servants go

Though well we may not pass upon his life
Without the form of justice, yet our power
Shall do a court'sy to our wrath, which men
May blame, but not control.

Re-enter Servants, with Gloucester prisoner

Who's there? The traitor?
REGAN. Ingrateful fox! 'tis he.
CORNWALL. Bind fast his corky arms.
GLOUCESTER. What means your Graces? Good my
friends, consider 30
You are my guests. Do me no foul play, friends.
CORNWALL. Bind him, I say. *Servants bind him*
REGAN. Hard, hard. O filthy traitor!
GLOUCESTER. Unmerciful lady as you are, I'm none.
CORNWALL. To this chair bind him. *They do so*
Villain, thou shalt find—
Regan plucks his beard
GLOUCESTER. By the kind gods, 'tis most ignobly done
To pluck me by the beard.
REGAN. So white, and such a traitor?
GLOUCESTER. Naughty lady,
These hairs which thou dost ravish from my chin
Will quicken and accuse thee. I am your host:
With robbers' hands my hospitable favours 40
You should not ruffle thus. What will you do?
CORNWALL. Come, sir. What letters had you late
from France?
REGAN. Be simple-answered, for we know the truth.
CORNWALL. And what confederacy have you with
the traitors
Late footed in the kingdom?
REGAN. To whose hands
You have sent the lunatic king ... Speak.
GLOUCESTER. I have a letter, guessingly set down,
Which came from one that's of a neutral heart,
And not from one opposed.
CORNWALL. Cunning.
REGAN. And false.
CORNWALL. Where hast thou sent the King?
GLOUCESTER. To Dover. 50
REGAN. Wherefore to Dover? Wast thou not charged
at peril—
CORNWALL. Wherefore to Dover? Let him answer
that.
GLOUCESTER. I am tied to th' stake, and I must stand
the course.
REGAN. Wherefore to Dover?
GLOUCESTER. Because I would not see thy cruel nails
Pluck out his poor old eyes, nor thy fierce sister
In his anointed flesh rash boarish fangs.
The sea, with such a storm as his loved head
In hell-black night endured, would have buoyed up,
And quenched the stelléd fires; 60
Yet, poor old heart, he holp the heavens to rain.
If wolves had at thy gate howled that dearn time,
Thou should'st have said 'Good porter, turn the
key'.
All cruels else subscribe: but I shall see
The wingéd Vengeance overtake such children.
CORNWALL. See 't shalt thou never. Fellows, hold the
chair.
Upon these eyes of thine I'll set my foot.
GLOUCESTER. He that will think to live till he be old,
Give me some help.... O cruel! O you gods!
REGAN. One side will mock another. Th'other too! 70

CORNWALL. If you see vengeance—
I SERVANT. Hold your hand, my lord!
I have served you ever since I was a child,
But better service have I never done you
Than now to bid you hold.
REGAN. How, now, you dog?
I SERVANT. If you did wear a beard upon your chin,
I'd shake it on this quarrel.
REGAN. What do you mean?
CORNWALL. My villain? *He unsheathes his sword*
I SERVANT [*drawing his weapon*]. Nay, then, come on,
and take the chance of anger.
REGAN [*to another Servant*]. Give me thy sword. A
peasant stand up thus?
*She takes a sword and
runs at him behind*
I SERVANT. O, I am slain! My lord, you have one
eye left 80
To see some mischief on him. O! *He dies*
CORNWALL. Lest it see more, prevent it. Out, vile jelly!
Where is thy lustre now?
GLOUCESTER. All dark and comfortless! Where's my
son Edmund?
Edmund, enkindle all the sparks of nature
To quit this horrid act.
REGAN. Out, treacherous villain!
Thou call'st on him that hates thee. It was he
That made the overture of thy treasons to us,
Who is too good to pity thee.
GLOUCESTER. O, my follies! Then Edgar was abused. 90
Kind gods, forgive me that, and prosper him!
REGAN. Go thrust him out at gates, and let him smell
His way to Dover. *They lead him out*
How is 't, my lord? How look you?
CORNWALL. I have received a hurt. Follow me, lady.
Turn out that eyeless villain. Throw this slave
Upon the dunghill. Regan, I bleed apace.
Untimely comes this hurt. Give me your arm.
He goes in, supported by Regan
2 SERVANT. I'll never care what wickedness I do,
If this man come to good.
3 SERVANT. If she live long,
And in the end meet the old course of death, 100
Women will all turn monsters.
2 SERVANT. Let's follow the old earl, and get the
bedlam
To lead him where he would; his roguish madness
Allows itself to anything.
3 SERVANT. Go thou; I'll fetch some flax and whites
of eggs
To apply to his bleeding face. Now heaven help
him! *They go*

ACT 4
Scene 1: *The heath*

Enter Edgar

EDGAR. Yet better thus, and known to be contemned,
Than still contemned and flattered. To be worst,
The lowest and most dejected thing of Fortune,
Stands still in esperance, lives not in fear.
The lamentable change is from the best;
The worst returns to laughter. Welcome, then,
Thou unsubstantial air that I embrace:

The wretch that thou hast blown unto the worst
Owes nothing to thy blasts.

Enter Gloucester, led by an old man

                         But who comes here?
My father, poorly eyed! World, world, O world! 10
But that thy strange mutations make us hate thee,
Life would not yield to age.
OLD MAN.   O my good lord,
I have been your tenant, and your father's tenant,
These fourscore years.
GLOUCESTER. Away, get thee away! Good friend, be
    gone:
Thy comforts can do me no good at all;
Thee they may hurt.
OLD MAN.   You cannot see your way.
GLOUCESTER. I have no way, and therefore want no
    eyes;
I stumbled when I saw. Full oft 'tis seen
Our means secure us, and our mere defects   20
Prove our commodities. O dear son Edgar,
The food of thy abuséd father's wrath!
Might I but live to see thee in my touch,
I'd say I had eyes again.
OLD MAN.   How now? Who's there?
EDGAR [*aside*]. O gods! Who is't can say 'I am at the
    worst'?
I am worse than e'er I was.
OLD MAN.   'Tis poor mad Tom.
EDGAR [*aside*]. And worse I may be yet: the worst is not
So long as we can say 'This is the worst'.
OLD MAN. Fellow, where goest?
GLOUCESTER.   Is it a beggar-man?
OLD MAN. Madman, and beggar too.   30
GLOUCESTER. He has some reason, else he could not
    beg.
I' th' last night's storm I such a fellow saw,
Which made me think a man a worm. My son
Came then into my mind, and yet my mind
Was then scarce friends with him: I have heard
    more since.
As flies to wanton boys are we to th' gods;
They kill us for their sport.
EDGAR [*aside*].   How should this be?
Bad is the trade that must play fool to sorrow,
Ang'ring itself and others.—Bless thee, master!
GLOUCESTER. Is that the naked fellow?
OLD MAN.   Ay, my lord. 40
GLOUCESTER. Then prithee get thee away. If, for my
    sake,
Thou wilt o'ertake us hence a mile or twain
I' th' way toward Dover, do it for ancient love;
And bring some covering for this naked soul
Which I'll entreat to lead me.
OLD MAN.   Alack, sir, he is mad!
GLOUCESTER. 'Tis the time's plague when madmen
    lead the blind.
Do as I bid thee; or rather do thy pleasure:
Above the rest, be gone.
OLD MAN. I'll bring him the best 'parel that I have,
Come on't what will.   *He goes*
GLOUCESTER.   Sirrah, naked fellow!   50
EDGAR. Poor Tom's a-cold. [*aside*] I cannot daub it
    further.
GLOUCESTER. Come hither, fellow.

EDGAR [*aside*]. And yet I must. Bless thy sweet eyes,
    they bleed!
GLOUCESTER. Know'st thou the way to Dover?
EDGAR. Both stile and gate, horseway and footpath.
Poor Tom hath been scared out of his good wits.
Bless thee, good man's son, from the foul fiend! Five
fiends have been in poor Tom at once: as Obidicut,
of lust; Hobbididence, prince of darkness; Mahu, of
stealing; Modo, of murder; Flibbertigibbet, of 60
mocking and mowing, who since possesses
chambermaids and waiting-women. So, bless thee,
master!
GLOUCESTER. Here, take this purse, thou whom the
    heavens' plagues
Have humbled to all strokes: that I am wretched
Makes thee the happier; Heavens, deal so still!
Let the superfluous and lust-dieted man,
That slaves your ordinance, that will not see
Because he does not feel, feel your power quickly;
So distribution should undo excess,   70
And each man have enough. Dost thou know
    Dover?
EDGAR. Ay, master.
GLOUCESTER. There is a cliff, whose high and bending
    head
Looks fearfully in the confinéd deep.
Bring me but to the very brim of it,
And I'll repair the misery thou dost bear
With something rich about me. From that place
I shall no leading need.
EDGAR.   Give me thy arm;
Poor Tom shall lead thee.   *They go*

        Scene 2: *Before the Duke of Albany's palace*

Enter Goneril and Edmund

GONERIL. Welcome, my lord. I marvel our mild
    husband
Not met us on the way.

Enter Oswald

                   Now, where's your master?
OSWALD. Madam, within; but never man so changed.
I told him of the army that was landed;
He smiled at it: I told him you were coming;
His answer was, 'The worse'. Of Gloucester's
    treachery
And of the loyal service of his son
When I informed him, then he called me sot
And told me I had turned the wrong side out.
What most he should dislike seems pleasant to him; 10
What like, offensive.
GONERIL [*to Edmund*]. Then shall you go no further.
It is the cowish terror of his spirit,
That dares not undertake; he'll not feel wrongs
Which tie him to an answer. Our wishes on the
    way
May prove effects. Back, Edmund, to my brother;
Hasten his musters and conduct his powers:
I must change arms at home and give the distaff
Into my husband's hands. This trusty servant
Shall pass between us: ere long you are like to hear
(If you dare venture in your own behalf)   20
A mistress's command. Wear this [*giving a favour*].
    Spare speech;
Decline your head: this kiss, if it durst speak,

Would stretch thy spirits up into the air.
Conceive, and fare thee well.

EDMUND. Yours in the ranks of death!

GONERIL.   My most dear Gloucester!
                                                     Edmund goes

O, the difference of man and man!
To thee a woman's services are due;
A fool usurps my bed.

OSWALD.   Madam, here comes my lord.
                                                     He goes

Enter Albany

GONERIL. I have been worth the whistling.

ALBANY.   O Goneril,
You are not worth the dust which the rude wind 30
Blows in your face! I fear your disposition.
That nature which contemns it origin
Cannot be bordered certain in itself.
She that herself will sliver and disbranch
From her material sap, perforce must wither
And come to deadly use.

GONERIL. No more! The text is foolish.

ALBANY. Wisdom and goodness to the vile seem vile;
Filths savour but themselves. What have you done?
Tigers, not daughters, what have you performed? 40
A father, and a gracious agèd man,
Whose reverence even the head-lugged bear would
   lick,
Most barbarous, most degenerate, have you
   madded.
Could my good brother suffer you to do it?
A man, a prince, by him so benefited!
If that the heavens do not their visible spirits
Send quickly down to tame these vile offences,
It will come
Humanity must perforce prey on itself
Like monsters of the deep.

GONERIL.   Milk-livered man! 50
That bear'st a cheek for blows, a head for wrongs;
Who hast not in thy brows an eye discerning
Thine honour from thy suffering; that not know'st
Fools do those villains pity who are punished
Ere they have done their mischief. Where's thy
   drum?
France spreads his banners in our noiseless land,
With plumèd helm thy state begins to threat,
Whilst thou, a moral fool, sits still and cries
'Alack, why does he so?'

ALBANY.   See thyself, devil!
Proper deformity shows not in the fiend   60
So horrid as in woman.

GONERIL.   O vain fool!

ALBANY. Thou changèd and self-covered thing, for
   shame
Bemonster not thy feature! Were't my fitness
To let these hands obey my blood,
They are apt enough to dislocate and tear
Thy flesh and bones: howe'er thou art a fiend,
A woman's shape doth shield thee.

GONERIL. Marry, your manhood! mew!

Enter a Messenger

ALBANY. What news?

MESSENGER. O, my good lord, the Duke of Cornwall's
   dead,   70
Slain by his servant, going to put out

The other eye of Gloucester.

ALBANY.   Gloucester's eyes!

MESSENGER. A servant that he bred, thrilled with
   remorse,
Opposed against the act, bending his sword
To his great master; who, thereat enraged,
Flew on him, and amongst them felled him dead;
But not without that harmful stroke which since
Hath plucked him after.

ALBANY.   This shows you are above,
You justicers, that these our nether crimes
So speedily can venge! But, O poor Gloucester!   80
Lost he his other eye!

MESSENGER.   Both, both, my lord.
This letter, madam, craves a speedy answer;
'Tis from your sister.   *Presents a letter*

GONERIL [*aside*].   One way I like this well;
But being widow, and my Gloucester with her,
May all the building in my fancy pluck
Upon my hateful life. Another way
The news is not so tart.—I'll read, and answer.
                                                     She goes out

ALBANY. Where was his son when they did take his
   eyes?

MESSENGER. Come with my lady hither.

ALBANY.   He is not here.

MESSENGER. No, my good lord; I met him back again. 90

ALBANY. Knows he the wickedness?

MESSENGER. Ay, my good lord; 'twas he informed
   against him,
And quit the house on purpose, that their
   punishment
Might have the freer course.

ALBANY.   Gloucester, I live
To thank thee for the love thou show'dst the
   King,
And to revenge thine eyes. Come hither, friend;
Tell me what more thou know'st.   *They go*

Scene 3: *The French camp near Dover*

Enter Kent and a Gentleman

KENT. Why the King of France is so suddenly gone
back know you no reason?

GENTLEMAN. Something he left imperfect in the state,
which since his coming forth is thought of, which
imports to the kingdom so much fear and danger
that his personal return was most required and
necessary.

KENT. Who hath he left behind him general?

GENTLEMAN. The Marshal of France, Monsieur La Far.

KENT. Did your letters pierce the queen to any   10
demonstration of grief?

GENTLEMAN. Ay, sir; she took them, read them in my
   presence,
And now and then an ample tear trilled down
Her delicate cheek. It seemed she was a queen
Over her passion, who, most rebel-like,
Sought to be king o'er her.

KENT.   O, then it moved her.

GENTLEMAN. Not to a rage; patience and sorrow strove
Who should express her goodliest. You have seen
Sunshine and rain at once; her smiles and tears
Were like, a better way: those happy smilets   20
That played on her ripe lip seemed not to know
What guests were in her eyes, which parted thence

As pearls from diamonds dropped. In brief,
Sorrow would be a rarity most beloved
If all could so become it.
KENT.   Made she no verbal question?
GENTLEMAN. Faith, once or twice she heaved the name
    of 'father'
pantingly forth, as if it pressed her heart;
Cried 'Sisters, sisters! Shame of ladies! Sisters!
Kent! father! sisters! What, i'th'storm? i'th'night?
Let pity not believe it!' There she shook   30
The holy water from her heavenly eyes
That clamour moistened; then away she started
To deal with grief alone.
KENT.   It is the stars,
The stars above us, govern our conditions;
Else one self mate and make could not beget
Such different issues. You spoke not with her since?
GENTLEMAN. No.
KENT. Was this before the King returned?
GENTLEMAN.   No, since
KENT. Well, sir, the poor distressèd Lear's i'th'town,
Who sometime, in his better tune, remembers   40
What we are come about, and by no means
Will yield to see his daughter.
GENTLEMAN.   Why, good sir?
KENT. A sovereign shame so elbows him: his own
    unkindness,
That stripped her from his benediction, turned her
To foreign casualties, gave her dear rights
To his dog-hearted daughters—these things sting
His mind so venomously that burning shame
Detains him from Cordelia.
GENTLEMAN.   Alack, poor gentleman!
KENT. Of Albany's and Cornwall's powers you heard
    not?
GENTLEMAN. 'Tis so, they are afoot.   50
KENT. Well, sir, I'll bring you to our master Lear
And leave you to attend him. Some dear cause
Will in concealment wrap me up awhile;
When I am known aright, you shall not grieve
Lending me this acquaintance. I pray you go
Along with me.   *They go*

Scene 4: *The same*

*Enter, with drum and colours, Cordelia, Doctor, and
Soldiers*

CORDELIA. Alack, 'tis he! Why, he was met even now
As mad as the vexed sea, singing aloud,
Crowned with rank fumiter and furrow-weeds,
With hardocks, hemlock, nettles, cuckoo-flowers,
Darnel, and all the idle weeds that grow
In our sustaining corn. A century send forth;
Search every acre in the high-grown field,
And bring him to our eye. [*an Officer goes*] What
    can man's wisdom
In the restoring his bereavèd sense?
He that helps him take all my outward worth.   10
DOCTOR. There is means, madam.
Our foster-nurse of nature is repose,
The which he lacks. That to provoke in him
Are many simples operative, whose power
Will close the eye of anguish.
CORDELIA.   All blest secrets,
All you unpublished virtues of the earth,
Spring with my tears! Be aidant and remediate

In the good man's distress!—Seek, seek for him,
Lest his ungoverned rage dissolve the life
That wants the means to lead it.

Enter Messenger

MESSENGER.   News, madam!   20
The British powers are marching hitherward.
CORDELIA. 'Tis known before; our preparation stands
In expectation of them. O dear father,
It is thy business that I go about!
Therefore great France
My mourning and importuned tears hath pitied.
No blown ambition doth our arms incite,
But love, dear love, and our agèd father's right.
Soon may I hear and see him!   *They go*

Scene 5: *Gloucester's castle*

Enter Regan and Oswald

REGAN. But are my brother's powers set forth?
OSWALD.   Ay, madam.
REGAN. Himself in person there?
OSWALD.   Madam, with much ado.
Your sister is the better soldier.
REGAN. Lord Edmund spake not with your lord at
    home?
OSWALD. No, madam.
REGAN. What might import my sister's letter to him?
OSWALD. I know not, lady.
REGAN. Faith, he is posted hence on serious matter.
It was great ignorance, Gloucester's eyes being out,
To let him live: where he arrives he moves   10
All hearts against us. Edmund, I think, is gone,
In pity of his misery, to dispatch
His nighted life; moreover, to descry
The strength o'th'enemy.
OSWALD. I must needs after him, madam, with my
    letter.
REGAN. Our troops set forth tomorrow. Stay with us;
The ways are dangerous.
OSWALD.   I may not, madam;
My lady charged my duty in this business.
REGAN. Why should she write to Edmund? Might
    not you
Transport her purposes by word? Belike,   20
Some things, I know not what. I'll love thee
    much—
Let me unseal the letter.
OSWALD.   Madam, I had rather—
REGAN. I know your lady does not love her husband;
I am sure of that: and at her late being here
She gave strange oeillades and most speaking looks
To noble Edmund. I know you are of her bosom.
OSWALD. I, madam!
REGAN. I speak in understanding: you are: I know't;
Therefore I do advise you take this note.
My lord is dead; Edmund and I have talked,   30
And more convenient is he for my hand
Than for your lady's. You may gather more.
If you do find him, pray you give him this;
And when your mistress hears thus much from you,
I pray desire her call her wisdom to her.
So fare you well.
If you do chance to hear of that blind traitor,
Preferment falls on him that cuts him off.

OSWALD. Would I could meet him, madam! I should show
What party I do follow.
REGAN.　　　　　　　　　Fare thee well.　*They go* 40

Scene 6: *The Country near Dover*

Enter Gloucester, and Edgar dressed like a peasant

GLOUCESTER. When shall I come to th' top of that same hill?
EDGAR. You do climb up it now; look how we labour.
GLOUCESTER. Methinks the ground is even.
EDGAR.　　　　　　　　　　Horrible steep.
Hark, do you hear the sea?
GLOUCESTER.　　　　　　　No, truly.
EDGAR. Why, then your other senses grow imperfect
By your eyes' anguish.
GLOUCESTER.　　　　　So may it be indeed.
Methinks thy voice is altered, and thou speak'st
In better phrase and matter than thou didst.
EDGAR. You're much deceived: in nothing am I changed
But in my garments.
GLOUCESTER.　　　　　Methinks you're better spoken. 10
EDGAR. Come on, sir, here's the place: stand still; how fearful
And dizzy 'tis to cast one's eyes so low!
The crows and choughs that wing the midway air
Show scarce so gross as beetles. Half way down
Hangs one that gathers samphire—dreadful trade!
Methinks he seems no bigger than his head.
The fishermen that walk upon the beach
Appear like mice: and yond tall anchoring bark
Diminished to her cock; her cock a buoy
Almost too small for sight. The murmuring surge, 20
That on th'unnumb'réd idle pebble chafes,
Cannot be heard so high. I'll look no more,
Lest my brain turn, and the deficient sight
Topple down headlong.
GLOUCESTER.　　　　　Set me where you stand.
EDGAR. Give me your hand. You are now within a foot
Of th'extreme verge. For all beneath the moon
Would I not leap upright.
GLOUCESTER.　　　　　Let go my hand.
Here, friend, 's another purse, in it a jewel
Well worth a poor man's taking. Fairies and gods
Prosper it with thee! Go thou further off: 30
Bid me farewell, and let me hear thee going.
EDGAR. Now fare ye well, good sir.
GLOUCESTER.　　　　　With all my heart!
EDGAR. Why I do trifle thus with his despair
Is done to cure it.
GLOUCESTER.　　　　　O you mighty gods! *He kneels*
This world I do renounce, and in your sights
Shake patiently my great affliction off.
If I could bear it longer, and not fall
To quarrel with your great opposeless wills,
My snuff and loathéd part of nature should
Burn itself out. If Edgar live, O bless him! 40
Now, fellow, fare thee well.
EDGAR.　　　　　　　　Gone, sir; farewell!
Gloucester falls forward, and swoons
[*aside*] And yet I know not how conceit may rob
The treasury of life when life itself

Yields to the theft. Had he been where he thought,
By this had thought been past. [*aloud*] Alive, or dead?
Ho, you sir! friend! hear you, sir! Speak!
[*aside*] Thus might he pass indeed: yet he revives.
[*aloud*] What are you, sir?
GLOUCESTER.　　　　　Away, and let me die.
EDGAR. Hadst thou been aught but gossamer, feathers, air,
(So many fathom down precipitáting), 50
Thou'dst shivered like an egg: but thou dost breathe,
Hast heavy substance, bleed'st not, speak'st, art sound.
Ten masts at each make not the altitude
Which thou hast perpendicularly fell:
Thy life's a miracle. Speak yet again.
GLOUCESTER. But have I fall'n, or no?
EDGAR. From the dread summit of this chalky bourn.
Look up a-height; the shrill-gorged lark so far
Cannot be seen, or heard. Do but look up.
GLOUCESTER. Alack, I have no eyes. 60
Is wretchedness deprived that benefit
To end itself by death? 'Twas yet some comfort
When misery could beguile the tyrant's rage
And frustrate his proud will.
EDGAR.　　　　　　　　Give me your arm.
Up; so. How is't? Feel you your legs? You stand.
GLOUCESTER. Too well, too well.
EDGAR.　　　　　　This is above all strangeness.
Upon the crown o'th'cliff what thing was that
Which parted from you?
GLOUCESTER.　　　　　A poor unfortunate beggar.
EDGAR. As I stood here below methought his eyes
Were two full moons; he had a thousand noses, 70
Horns whelked and waved like the enridgéd sea.
It was some fiend. Therefore, thou happy father,
Think that the clearest gods, who make them honours
Of men's impossibilities, have preserved thee.
GLOUCESTER. I do remember now. Henceforth I'll bear
Affliction till it do cry out itself
'Enough, enough,' and die. That thing you speak of,
I took it for a man. Often 'twould say
'The fiend, the fiend',—he led me to that place.
EDGAR. Bear free and patient thoughts.

Enter Lear, crowned with wild flowers and nettles

　　　　　　　　　　But who comes here? 80
The safer sense will ne'er accommodate
His master thus.
LEAR. No, they cannot touch me for coining; I am the king himself.
EDGAR. O thou side-piercing sight!
LEAR. Nature's above art in that respect. There's your press-money. That fellow handles his bow like a crow-keeper: draw me a clothier's yard. Look, look, a mouse! Peace, peace; this piece of toasted cheese will do't. There's my gauntlet; I'll prove it on a 90 giant. Bring up the brown bills. O, well flown, bird! i'th'clout, i'th'clout: hewgh! Give the word.
EDGAR. Sweet marjoram.
LEAR. Pass.
GLOUCESTER. I know that voice.
LEAR. Ha! Goneril with a white beard? They flattered me like a dog, and told me I had the white hairs in my beard ere the black ones were there. To say 'ay'

and 'no' to everything that I said! 'Ay,' and 'no' too,
was no good divinity. When the rain came to wet 100
me once and the wind to make me chatter, when
the thunder would not peace at my bidding, there I
found 'em, there I smelt 'em out! Go to, they are not
men o' their words: they told me I was everything;
'tis a lie— I am not ague-proof.
GLOUCESTER. The trick of that voice I do well
remember:
Is't not the king?
LEAR.   Ay, every inch a king!
When I do stare, see how the subject quakes.
I pardon that man's life. What was thy cause?
Adultery?   110
Thou shalt not die. Die for adultery? No!
The wren goes to 't, and the small gilded fly
Does lecher in my sight.
Let copulation thrive: for Gloucester's bastard son
Was kinder to his father than my daughters
Got 'tween the lawful sheets.
To 't, luxury, pell-mell! for I lack soldiers.
Behold yond simp'ring dame
Whose face between her forks presages snow,
That minces virtue and does shake the head   120
To hear of pleasure's name;
The fitchew nor the soiléd horse goes to 't
With a more riotous appetite.
Down from the waist they are centaurs,
Though women all above.
But to the girdle do the gods inherit,
Beneath is all the fiend's.
There's hell, there's darkness, there is the sulphurous
pit;
Burning, scalding, stench, consumption: fie, fie, fie,
pah, pah!
Give me an ounce of civet; good apothecary,   130
sweeten my imagination: there's money for thee.
GLOUCESTER. O, let me kiss that hand!
LEAR. Let me wipe it first; it smells of mortality.
GLOUCESTER. O ruined piece of Nature! This great
world
Shall so wear out to naught. Dost thou know me?
LEAR. I remember thine eyes well enough. Dost thou
squiny at me?
No, do thy worst, blind Cupid; I'll not love.
Read thou this challenge; mark but the penning of
it.
GLOUCESTER. Were all thy letters suns, I could not
see.
EDGAR [aside]. I would not take this from report. It is, 140
And my heart breaks at it.
LEAR. Read.
GLOUCESTER. What! With the case of eyes?
LEAR. O ho, are you there with me? No eyes in your
head, nor no money in your purse? Your eyes are
in a heavy case, your purse in a light; yet you see
how this world goes.
GLOUCESTER. I see it feelingly.
LEAR. What! Art mad? A man may see how this world
goes with no eyes. Look with thine ears: see how 150
yond justice rails upon yond simple thief. Hark in
thine ear: change places and, handy-dandy, which is
the justice, which is the thief? Thou hast seen a
farmer's dog bark at a beggar?
GLOUCESTER. Ay, sir.
LEAR. And the creature run from the cur? there thou

mightst behold the great image of authority—a
dog's obeyed in office.
Thou rascal beadle, hold thy bloody hand!
Why dost thou lash that whore? Strip thy own back; 160
Thou hotly lusts to use her in that kind
For which thou whipp'st her. The usurer hangs the
cozener.
Through tattered clothes great vices do appear;
Robes and furred gowns hide all. Plate sin with
gold,
And the strong lance of justice hurtless breaks:
Arm it in rags, a pigmy's straw does pierce it.
None does offend, none, I say none. I'll able 'em;
Take that of me, my friend, who have the power
To seal th'accuser's lips. Get thee glass eyes
And, like a scurvy politician, seem   170
To see the things thou dost not. Now, now, now,
now!
Pull off my boots; harder, harder! So.
EDGAR. O, matter and impertinency mixed!
Reason in madness!
LEAR. If thou wilt weep my fortunes, take my eyes.
I know thee well enough; thy name is Gloucester.
Thou must be patient. We came crying hither;
Thou know'st the first time that we smell the air
We wawl and cry. I will preach to thee: mark!
GLOUCESTER. Alack, alack the day!   180
LEAR. When we are born, we cry that we are come
To this great stage of fools. This' a good block!
                                        Taking off the crown
It were a delicate stratagem to shoe
A troop of horse with felt: I'll put't in proof,
And when I have stol'n upon these son-in-laws,
Then kill, kill, kill, kill, kill, kill!

Enter a Gentleman with attendants

GENTLEMAN. O, here he is: lay hand upon him. Sir,
Your most dear daughter—
LEAR. No rescue? What, a prisoner? I am even
The natural fool of Fortune. Use me well;   190
You shall have ransom. Let me have surgeons;
I am cut to th'brains.
GENTLEMAN.   You shall have anything.
LEAR. No seconds? All myself?
Why, this would make a man a man of salt,
To use his eyes for garden water-pots,
Ay, and laying autumn's dust. I will die bravely,
Like a smug bridegroom. What! I will be jovial.
Come, come, I am a king, masters, know you that?
GENTLEMAN. You are a royal one, and we obey you.
LEAR. Then there's life in't. Come, an you get it you 200
shall get it by running. Sa, sa, sa, sa.
                                        He runs away; attendants follow
GENTLEMAN. A sight most pitiful in the meanest
wretch,
Past speaking of in a king! Thou hast one daughter
Who redeems nature from the general curse
Which twain have brought her to.
EDGAR. Hail, gentle sir!
GENTLEMAN.   Sir, speed you. What's your will?
EDGAR. Do you hear aught, sir, of a battle toward?
GENTLEMAN. Most sure, and vulgar: every one hears
that,
Which can distinguish sound.
EDGAR.   But, by your favour,
How near's the other army?   210

GENTLEMAN. Near, and on speedy foot: the main descry
Stands on the hourly thought.
EDGAR.   I thank you, sir:
that's all.
GENTLEMAN. Though that the queen on special cause is here,
Her army is moved on.
EDGAR.   I thank you, sir.
Gentleman goes
GLOUCESTER. You ever-gentle gods, take my breath from me;
Let not my worser spirit tempt me again
To die before you please!
EDGAR.   Well pray you, father.
GLOUCESTER. Now, good sir, what are you?
EDGAR. A most poor man, made tame to Fortune's blows,
Who, by the art of known and feeling sorrows,   220
Am pregnant to good pity. Give me your hand;
I'll lead you to some biding.
GLOUCESTER.   Hearty thanks:
The bounty and the benison of Heaven
To boot, and boot!

Enter Oswald

OSWALD.   A proclaimed prize! Most happy!
That eyeless head of thine was first framed flesh
To raise my fortunes. Thou old unhappy traitor,
Briefly thyself remember; the sword is out
That must destroy thee.
GLOUCESTER.   Now let thy friendly hand
Put strength enough to't.   *Edgar interposes*
OSWALD.   Wherefore, bold peasant,
Dar'st thou support a published traitor? Hence,   230
Lest that th'infection of his fortune take
Like hold on thee. Let go his arm.
EDGAR. Chill not let go, zir, without vurther cagion.
OSWALD. Let go, slave, or thou di'st.
EDGAR. Good gentleman, go your gate, and let poor
voke pass. An 'chud ha' bin zwaggered out of my
life, 'twould not ha' bin zo long as 'tis by a vortnight.
Nay, come not near th'old man; keep out, che vor'
ye, or Ice try whither your costard or my ballow be
the harder. Chill be plain with you.   240
OSWALD. Out, dunghill!   *They fight*
EDGAR. Chill pick your teeth, zir. Come; no matter
vor your foins.   *Oswald falls*
OSWALD. Slave, thou hast slain me. Villain, take my purse:
If ever thou wilt thrive, bury my body,
And give the letters which thou find'st about me
To Edmund, Earl of Gloucester; seek him out
Upon the British party. O, untimely death! Death!
He dies
EDGAR. I know thee well—a serviceable villain,
As duteous to the vices of thy mistress   250
As badness would desire.
GLOUCESTER.   What, is he dead?
EDGAR. Sit you down, father; rest you.
Let's see these pockets; the letters that he speaks of
May be my friends. He's dead; I am only sorry
He had no other deathsman. Let us see.
Leave, gentle wax; and, manners, blame us not:
To know our enemies' minds we rip their hearts;
Their papers is more lawful.   *Reads the letter*

'Let our reciprocal vows be rememb'red. You have
many opportunities to cut him off: if your will want   260
not, time and place will be fruitfully offered. There
is nothing done if he return the conqueror: then am
I the prisoner, and his bed my gaol; from the loathed
warmth whereof deliver me, and supply the place
for your labour.
     Your (wife, so I would say) affectionate servant,
                                             Goneril.'
O indistinguished space of woman's will!
A plot upon her virtuous husband's life,
And the exchange my brother! Here in the sands   270
Thee I'll rake up, thou post unsanctified
Of murderous lechers; and in the mature time
With this ungracious paper strike the sight
Of the death-practised Duke. For him 'tis well
That of thy death and business I can tell.
GLOUCESTER. The King is mad; how stiff is my vile sense
That I stand up and have ingenious feeling
Of my huge sorrows! Better I were distract:
So should my thoughts be severed from my griefs,
And woes by wrong imaginations lose   280
The knowledge of themselves.   *Drum afar off*
EDGAR.   Give me your hand:
Far off methinks I hear the beaten drum.
Come, father, I'll bestow you with a friend.
They go

Scene 7: *A tent in the French camp*

Enter Cordelia, Kent, Doctor and Gentleman

CORDELIA. O thou good Kent, how shall I live and work
To match thy goodness? My life will be too short,
And every measure fail me.
KENT. To be acknowledged, madam, is o'er-paid.
All my reports go with the modest truth;
Nor more, nor clipped, but so.
CORDELIA.   Be better suited:
These weeds are memories of those worser hours;
I prithee put them off.
KENT.   Pardon, dear madam;
Yet to be known shortens my made intent.
My boon I make it that you know me not   10
Till time, and I, think meet.
CORDELIA. Then be't so, my good lord. [*to the Doctor*]
How does the King?
DOCTOR. Madam, sleeps still.
CORDELIA. O you kind gods,
Cure this great breach in his abusèd nature!
Th'untuned and jarring senses, O, wind up
Of this child-changèd father!
DOCTOR.   So please your Majesty
That we may wake the King? He hath slept long.
CORDELIA. Be goverened by your knowledge, and proceed
I'th'sway of your own will. Is he arrayed?   20
GENTLEMAN. Ay, madam: in the heaviness of sleep
We put fresh garments on him.
DOCTOR. Be by, good madam, when we do awake him;
I doubt not of his temperance.
CORDELIA.   Very well.

Enter Lear asleep in a chair carried by servants. Soft music

DOCTOR. Please you draw near. Louder the music
    there!
CORDELIA. O my dear father, restoration hang
    Thy medicine on my lips, and let this kiss
    Repair those violent harms that my two sisters
    Have in thy reverence made!
KENT.   Kind and dear princess!
CORDELIA. Had you not been their father, these white
    flakes   30
    Did challenge pity of them. Was this a face
    To be opposed against the warring winds?
    To stand against the deep dread-bolted thunder
    In the most terrible and nimble stroke
    Of quick cross lightning? To watch—poor perdu!—
    With this thin helm? Mine enemy's dog,
    Though he had bit me, should have stood that night
    Against my fire; and wast thou fain, poor father,
    To hovel thee with swine and rogues forlorn,
    In short and musty straw? Alack, alack!   40
    'Tis wonder that thy life and wits at once
    Had not concluded all. He wakes; speak to him.
DOCTOR. Madam, do you; 'tis fittest.
CORDELIA. How does my royal lord? How fares your
    Majesty?
LEAR. You do me wrong to take me out o'th'grave:
    Thou art a soul in bliss; but I am bound
    Upon a wheel of fire, that mine own tears
    Do scald like molten lead.
CORDELIA.   Sir, do you know me?
LEAR. You are a spirit, I know; when did you die?
CORDELIA. Still, still, far wide!   50
DOCTOR. He's scarce awake; let him alone awhile.
LEAR. Where have I been? Where am I? Fair daylight?
    I am mightily abused; I should e'en die with pity
    To see another thus. I know not what to say.
    I will not swear these are my hands: let's see;
    I feel this pin prick. Would I were assured
    Of my condition!
CORDELIA.   O, look upon me, sir,
    And hold your hand in benediction o'er me;
    No, sir, you must not kneel.
LEAR.   Pray do not mock me;
    I am a very foolish fond old man,   60
    Fourscore and upward, not an hour more nor less;
    And, to deal plainly,
    I fear I am not in my perfect mind.
    Methinks I should know you, and know this man,
    Yet I am doubtful: for I am mainly ignorant
    What place this is; and all the skill I have
    Remembers not these garments, nor I know not
    Where I did lodge last night. Do not laugh at me,
    For (as I am a man) I think this lady
    To be my child Cordelia.
CORDELIA.   And so I am: I am!   70
LEAR. Be your tears wet? Yes, faith: I pray weep not.
    If you have poison for me, I will drink it:
    I know you do not love me, for your sisters
    Have (as I do remember) done me wrong;
    You have some causes; they have not.
CORDELIA.   No cause, no cause.
LEAR. Am I in France?
KENT.   In your own kingdom, sir.
LEAR. Do not abuse me.
DOCTOR. Be comforted, good madam: the great rage,
    You see, is killed in him; and yet it is danger
    To make him even o'er the time he has lost.   80

    Desire him to go in; trouble him no more
    Till further settling.
CORDELIA. Will't please your Highness walk?
LEAR. You must bear with me. Pray you now, forget
    and forgive; I am old and foolish.
                     All go but Kent and the Gentleman
GENTLEMAN. Holds it true, sir, that the Duke of Corn-
    wall was so slain?
KENT. Most certain, sir.
GENTLEMAN. Who is conductor of his people?
KENT. As 'tis said, the bastard son of Gloucester.   90
GENTLEMAN. They say Edgar, his banished son, is with
    the Earl of Kent in Germany.
KENT. Report is changeable. 'Tis time to look about;
    the powers of the kingdom approach apace.
GENTLEMAN. The arbitrement is like to be bloody.
    Fare you well, sir.   *Goes*
KENT. My point and period will be throughly
    wrought,
    Or well or ill, as this day's battle's fought.   *Goes*

ACT 5
Scene 1: *The British camp near Dover*

*Enter, with drum and colours, Edmund, Regan, officers,
and soldiers*

EDMUND. Know of the Duke if his last purpose hold,
    Or whether, since, he is advised by aught
    To change the course; he's full of alteration
    And self-reproving; bring his constant pleasure.
                  To an officer, who goes out
REGAN. Our sister's man is certainly miscarried.
EDMUND. 'Tis to be doubted, madam.
REGAN.   Now, sweet lord,
    You know the goodness I intend upon you.
    Tell me—but truly—but then speak the truth—
    Do you not love my sister?
EDMUND.   In honoured love.
REGAN. But have you never found my brother's way   10
    To the forfended place?
EDMUND.   That thought abuses you.
REGAN. I am doubtful that you have been conjunct
    And bosomed with her, as far as we call hers.
EDMUND. No, by mine honour, madam.
REGAN. I never shall endure her: dear my lord,
    Be not familiar with her.
EDMUND.   Fear me not.
    She and the Duke her husband!

Enter, with drum and colours, Albany, Goneril, soldiers

GONERIL [*aside*]. I had rather lose the battle than that
    sister
    Should loosen him and me.
ALBANY. Our very loving sister, well be-met.   20
    Sir, this I hear: the King is come to his daughter,
    With others whom the rigour of our state
    Forced to cry out. Where I could not be honest,
    I never yet was valiant: for this business,
    It touches us as France invades our land,
    Not bolds the King, with others whom, I fear,
    Most just and heavy causes make oppose.
EDMUND. Sir, you speak nobly.
REGAN.   Why is this reasoned?
GONERIL. Combine together 'gainst the enemy;
    For these domestic and particular broils   30

Are not the question here.
ALBANY.   Let's then determine
With th'ancient of war on our proceeding.
EDMUND. I shall attend you presently at your tent.
REGAN. Sister, you'll go with us?
GONERIL. No.
REGAN. 'Tis most convenient; pray go with us.
GONERIL [aside]. O ho, I know the riddle.—I will go.

As they are going out, enter Edgar disguised

EDGAR. If e'er your Grace had speech with man so
     poor,
Hear me one word.
ALBANY.   I'll overtake you.
                          All but Albany and Edgar depart
                                                    Speak.
EDGAR. Before you fight the battle, ope this letter.   40
If you have victory, let the trumpet sound
For him that brought it: wretched though I seem,
I can produce a champion that will prove
What is avouchéd there. If you miscarry,
Your business of the world hath so an end,
And machination ceases. Fortune love you!
ALBANY. Stay till I have read the letter.
EDGAR.   I was forbid it.
When time shall serve, let but the herald cry,
And I'll appear again.
ALBANY.   Why, fare thee well;
I will o'erlook thy paper.   *Edgar goes* 50

Edmund returns

EDMUND. The enemy's in view; draw up your powers.
Here is the guess of their true strength and forces,
By diligent discovery; [*hands a paper*] but your haste
Is now urged on you.
ALBANY.   We will greet the time.
                                                    He goes
EDMUND. To both these sisters have I sworn my
     love;
Each jealous of the other, as the stung
Are of the adder. Which of them shall I take?
Both? One? Or neither? Neither can be enjoyed
If both remain alive: to take the widow
Exasperates, makes mad her sister Goneril;   60
And hardly shall I carry out my side,
Her husband being alive. Now then, we'll use
His countenance for the battle, which being done,
Let her who would be rid of him devise
His speedy taking off. As for the mercy
Which he intends to Lear and to Cordelia,
The battle done, and they within our power,
Shall never see his pardon: for my state
Stands on me to defend, not to debate.   *He goes*

Scene 2: *A field between the two camps*

*Alarum. Enter the French army, Cordelia leading Lear by
the hand, and pass by. Enter Edgar and Gloucester*

EDGAR. Here, father, take the shadow of this tree
For your good host. Pray that the right may thrive..
If ever I return to you again,
I'll bring you comfort.
GLOUCESTER.   Grace go with you, sir!
                                                    Edgar goes

*Alarum heard from the battlefield hard by, and later a
retreat. Enter Edgar*

EDGAR. Away, old man; give me thy hand, away!
King Lear hath lost, he and his daughter ta'en.
Give me thy hand; come on!
GLOUCESTER. No further, sir; a man may rot even here.
EDGAR. What, in ill thoughts again? men must endure
Their going hence, even as their coming hither;   10
Ripeness is all. Come on.
GLOUCESTER.   And that's true too.
                                                    They go

Scene 3: *The British camp near Dover*
*Enter in conquest with drum and colours, Edmund; Lear and
Cordelia as prisoners; soldiers, Captain*

EDMUND. Some officers take them away: good guard,
Until their greater pleasures first be known
That are to censure them.
CORDELIA.   We are not the first
Who with best meaning have incurred the worst.
For thee, oppresséd King, I am cast down;
Myself could else out-frown false Fortune's frown.
Shall we not see these daughters and these sisters?
LEAR. No, no, no, no! Come, let's away to prison:
We two alone will sing like birds i'th'cage;
When thou dost ask me blessing, I'll kneel down 10
And ask of thee forgiveness. So we'll live,
And pray, and sing, and tell old tales, and laugh
At gilded butterflies, and hear poor rogues
Talk of court news; and we'll talk with them too—
Who loses and who wins, who's in, who's out—
And take upon 's the mystery of things,
As if we were God's spies; and we'll wear out,
In a walled prison, packs and sects of great ones
That ebb and flow by th'moon.
EDMUND.   Take them away.
LEAR. Upon such sacrifices, my Cordelia,   20
The gods themselves throw incense. Have I caught
     thee?
He that parts us shall bring a brand from heaven
And fire us hence like foxes. Wipe thine eyes;
The good-years shall devour them, flesh and fell,
Ere they shall make us weep! We'll see 'em starved
     first.
Come.   *Lear and Cordelia are led away
                                  under guard*
EDMUND. Come hither, captain; hark.
Take thou this note; [*giving a paper*] go follow them
     to prison.
One step I have advanced thee; if thou dost
As this instructs thee, thou dost make thy way   30
To noble fortunes. Know thou this, that men
Are as the time is: to be tender-minded
Does not become a sword: thy great employment
Will not bear question; either say thou'lt do't,
Or thrive by other means.
CAPTAIN.   I'll do't, my lord.
EDMUND. About it; and write happy when thou'st
     done.
Mark,—I say instantly; and carry it so
As I have set it down.
CAPTAIN. I cannot draw a cart, nor eat dried oats;
If it be man's work I'll do't.   *He goes* 40

Flourish. Enter Albany, Goneril, Regan, Soldiers

ALBANY. Sir, you have showed today your valiant
     strain,
And Fortune led you well. You have the captives

Who were the opposites of this day's strife:
I do require them of you, so to use them
As we shall find their merits and our safety
May equally determine.

EDMUND.   Sir, I thought it fit
To send the old and miserable King
To some retention and appointed guard;
Whose age had charms in it, whose title more,
To pluck the common bosom on his side   50
And turn our impressed lances in our eyes
Which do command them. With him I sent the
   Queen,
My reason all the same; and they are ready
Tomorrow, or at further space, t'appear
Where you shall hold your session. At this time
We sweat and bleed: the friend hath lost his friend;
And the best quarrels, in the heat, are cursed
By those that feel their sharpness.
The question of Cordelia and her father
Requires a fitter place.

ALBANY.   Sir, by your patience,   60
I hold you but a subject of this war,
Not as a brother.

REGAN.   That's as we list to grace him.
Methinks our pleasure might have been demanded
Ere you had spoke so far. He led our powers,
Bore the commission of my place and person
The which immediacy may well stand up
And call itself your brother.

GONERIL.   Not so hot!
In his own grace he doth exalt himself
More than in your addition.

REGAN.   In my rights
By me invested, he compeers the best.   70

ALBANY. That were the most if he should husband you.

REGAN. Jesters do oft prove prophets.

GONERIL.   Holla, holla!
That eye that told you so looked but asquint.

REGAN. Lady, I am not well, else I should answer
From a full-flowing stomach. General,
Take thou my soldiers, prisoners, patrimony:
Dispose of them, of me; the walls are thine.
Witness the world that I create thee here
My lord and master.

GONERIL.   Mean you to enjoy him?

ALBANY. The let-alone lies not in your good will.   80

EDMUND. Nore in thine, lord.

ALBANY.   Half-blooded fellow, yes.

REGAN [to Edmund]. Let the drum strike; and prove my
   title thine.

ALBANY. Stay yet; hear reason. Edmund, I arrest thee
On capital treason, and, in thy attaint,
                              Pointing to Goneril
This gilded serpent. For your claim, fair sister,
I bar it in the interest of my wife;
'Tis she is sub-contracted to this lord,
And I, her husband, contradict your banns.
If you will marry, make your loves to me;
My lady is bespoke.

GONERIL.   An interlude!   90

ALBANY. Thou art armed, Gloucester: let the trumpet
   sound;
If none appear to prove upon thy person
Thy heinous, manifest, and many treasons,
There is my pledge! [throwing down a glove] I'll make
   it on thy heart,

Ere I taste bread, thou art in nothing less
Than I have here proclaimed thee.

REGAN.   Sick, O sick!

GONERIL [aside]. If not, I'll ne'er trust medicine.

EDMUND. There's my exchange! [throwing down a
   glove] What in the world he is
That names me traitor, villain-like he lies.
Call by the trumpet; he that dares approach,   100
On him, on you—who not?—I will maintain
My truth and honour firmly.

ALBANY. A herald, ho!

EDMUND.   A herald, ho, a herald!

ALBANY. Trust to thy single virtue; for thy soldiers,
All levied in my name, have in my name
Took their discharge.

REGAN.   My sickness grows upon me.

ALBANY. She is not well; convey her to my tent.
                              Regan is led away

Enter a Herald

Come hither, herald—Let the trumpet sound—
And read out this.   A trumpet sounds

HERALD [reads]. If any man of quality or degree within 110
   the lists of the army will maintain upon Edmund,
   supposed Earl of Gloucester, that he is a manifold
   traitor, let him appear by the third sound of the
   trumpet. He is bold in his defence.   First trumpet
Again!   Second trumpet
Again!   Third trumpet

An answering trumpet heard. Enter Edgar, in armour

ALBANY. Ask him his purposes—why he appears
Upon this call o'th'trumpet.

HERALD.   What are you?
Your name, your quality, and why you answer
This present summons?

EDGAR.   Know my name is lost;   120
By treason's tooth bare-gnawn and canker-bit;
Yet am I noble as the adversary
I come to cope.

ALBANY.   Which is that adversary?

EDGAR. What's he that speaks for Edmund, Earl of
   Gloucester?

EDMUND. Himself: what say'st thou to him?

EDGAR.   Draw thy sword,
That, if my speech offend a noble heart,
Thy arm may do thee justice; here is mine:
Behold, it is the privilege of mine honours,
My oath, and my profession. I protest,
Maugre thy strength, place, youth, and eminence,   130
Despite thy victor-sword and fire-new fortune,
Thy valour and thy heart, thou art a traitor,
False to thy gods, thy brother, and thy father,
Conspirant 'gainst this high illustrious prince,
And, from th'extremest upward of thy head
To the descent and dust below thy foot,
A most toad-spotted traitor. Say thou no,
This sword, this arm, and my best spirits are bent
To prove upon thy heart, whereto I speak,
Thou liest.

EDMUND.   In wisdom I should ask thy name;   140
But since thy outside looks so fair and warlike,
And that thy tongue some say of breeding breathes,
What safe and nicely I might well delay

By rule of knighthood, I disdain and spurn.
Back do I toss these treasons to thy head,
With the hell-hated lie o'erwhelm thy heart,
Which, for they yet glance by and scarcely bruise,
This sword of mine shall give them instant way
Where they shall rest for ever. Trumpets, speak!
     Alarums. They fight. Edmund falls
ALBANY. Save him, save him!
GONERIL.   This is practice, Gloucester: 150
By th' law of war thou wast not bound to answer
An unknown opposite: thou art not vanquished,
But cozened and beguiled.
ALBANY.   Shut your mouth, dame,
Or with this paper shall I stop it.—Hold, sir.—
Thou worse than any name, read thine own evil.
No tearing, lady! I perceive you know it.
GONERIL. Say if I do—the laws are mine, not thine;
Who can arraign me for't?
ALBANY.   Most monstrous! O!
Know'st thou this paper?
GONERIL.   Ask me not what I know. *Goes*
ALBANY. Go after her: she's desperate; govern her. 160
          Officer goes
EDMUND. What you have charged me with, that have
 I done,
And more, much more; the time will bring it out:
'Tis past, and so am I. But what are thou
That hast this fortune on me? If thou'rt noble,
I do forgive thee.
EDGAR.   Let's exchange charity.
I am no less in blood than thou art, Edmund;
If more, the more thou'st wronged me.
My name is Edgar, and thy father's son.
The gods are just, and of our pleasant vices
Make instruments to plague us: 170
The dark and vicious place where thee he got
Cost him his eyes.
EDMUND.   Thou'st spoken right, 'tis true.
The wheel is come full circle; I am here.
ALBANY [*to Edgar*]. Methought thy very gait did
 prophesy
A royal nobleness: I must embrace thee;
Let sorrow split my heart if ever I
Did hate thee or thy father.
EDGAR.   Worthy prince, I know't.
ALBANY. Where have you hid yourself?
How have you known the miseries of your father?
EDGAR. By nursing them, my lord. List a brief tale; 180
And when 'tis told, O that my heart would burst!
The bloody proclamation to escape
That followed me so near (O, our life's sweetness!
That we the pain of death would hourly die,
Rather than die at once!) taught me to shift
Into a madman's rags, t'assume a semblance
That very dogs disdained: and in this habit
Met I my father with his bleeding rings,
Their precious stones new lost; became his guide,
Led him, begged for him, saved him from despair; 190
Never (O fault!) revealed myself unto him
Until some half hour past, when I was armed.
Not sure, though hoping, of this good success,
I asked his blessing, and from first to last
Told him our pilgrimage. But his flawed heart
(Alack, too weak the conflict to support)
'Twixt two extremes of passion, joy and grief,
Burst smilingly.

EDMUND.   This speech of yours hath moved me,
And shall perchance do good: but speak you on;
You look as you had something more to say. 200
ALBANY. If there be more, more woeful, hold it in;
For I am almost ready to dissolve,
Hearing of this.
EDGAR.   This would have seemed a period
To such as love not sorrow; but another,
To amplify too much, would make much more,
And top extremity. Whilst I
Was big in clamour, came there in a man,
Who, having seen me in my worst estate,
Shunned my abhorred society; but then, finding
Who 'twas that so endured, with his strong arms 210
He fastened on my neck and bellowed out
As he'd burst heaven: threw him on my father;
Told the most piteous tale of Lear and him
That ever ear received, which in recounting
His grief grew puissant and the strings of life
Began to crack: twice then the trumpets sounded,
And there I left him tranced.
ALBANY.   But who was this?
EDGAR. Kent, sir, the banished Kent, who in disguise
Followed his enemy king and did him service
Improper for a slave.   220

Enter a Gentleman, with a bloody knife

GENTLEMAN. Help, help! O help!
EDGAR.   What kind of help?
ALBANY.   Speak, man!
EDGAR. What means this bloody knife?
GENTLEMAN.   'Tis hot, it smokes;
It came even from the heart of—O, she's dead!
ALBANY. Who dead? Speak, man!
GENTLEMAN. Your lady, sir, your lady: and her sister
By her is poisoned; she confesses it.
EDMUND. I was contracted to them both; all three
Now marry in an instant.
EDGAR.   Here comes Kent.

Enter Kent

ALBANY. Produce the bodies, be they alive or dead;
         Gentleman goes
This judgement of the heavens, that makes us
 tremble,   230
Touches us not with pity. [*notices Kent*] O, is this he?
The time will not allow the compliment
Which very manners urges.
KENT.   I am come
To bid my king and master aye good night.
Is he not here?
ALBANY.   Great thing of us forgot!
Speak, Edmund; where's the king? and where's
 Cordelia?
     The bodies of Goneril and Regan
          are brought in
See'st thou this object, Kent?
KENT. Alack, why thus?
EDMUND.   Yet Edmund was beloved:
The one the other poisoned for my sake,
And after slew herself.   240
ALBANY. Even so. Cover their faces.
EDMUND. I pant for life. Some good I mean to do,
Despite of mine own nature. Quickly send
(Be brief in it) to th' castle, for my writ
Is on the life of Lear and on Cordelia.

Nay, send in time!
ALBANY.   Run, run, O run!
EDGAR. To who, my lord?—[to Edmund] Who has the
  office? Send
  Thy token of reprieve.
EDMUND. Well thought on. Take my sword,
  Give it to the captain.
ALBANY.   Haste thee, for thy life!   250
                              Edgar hurries forth
EDMUND. He hath commission from thy wife and me
  To hang Cordelia in the prison and
  To lay the blame upon her own despair,
  That she fordid herself.
ALBANY. The gods defend her!
  Bear him hence awhile.   *Edmund is borne off*

*Enter Lear with Cordelia in his arms, Edgar, Captain, and
others following*

LEAR. Howl, howl, howl! O, you are men of stones!
  Had I your tongues and eyes, I'd use them so
  That heaven's vault should crack! She's gone for
    ever.
  I know when one is dead, and when one lives;   260
  She's dead as earth. Lend me a looking-glass;
  If that her breath will mist or stain the stone,
  Why, then she lives.
KENT.   Is this the promised end?
EDGAR. Or image of that horror.
ALBANY.   Fall and cease!
LEAR. This feather stirs—she lives! If it be so,
  It is a chance which does redeem all sorrows
  That ever I have felt.
KENT [*kneeling*].   O my good master!
LEAR. Prithee away!
EDGAR.   'Tis noble Kent, your friend.
LEAR. A plague upon you, murderers, traitors all!
  I might have saved her; now she's gone for ever!   270
  Cordelia, Cordelia, stay a little!—Ha?
  What is't thou say'st?—Her voice was ever soft,
  Gentle and low, an excellent thing in woman—
  I killed the slave that was a-hanging thee.
OFFICER. 'Tis true, my lords, he did.
LEAR.   Did I not, fellow?
  I have seen the day, with my good biting falchion
  I would have made them skip: I am old now,
  And these same crosses spoil me. Who are you?
  Mine eyes are not o' th' best; I'll tell you straight.
KENT. If Fortune brag of two she loved and hated,   280
  One of them we behold.
LEAR. This is a dull sight. Are you not Kent?
KENT.   The same:
  Your servant Kent. Where is your servant Caius?
LEAR. He's a good fellow, I can tell you that;
  He'll strike, and quickly too. He's dead and rotten.

KENT. No, my good lord; I am the very man—
LEAR. I'll see that straight.
KENT. That from your first of difference and decay
  Have followed your sad steps—
LEAR.   You are welcome hither.
KENT. Nor no man else. All's cheerless, dark, and
  deadly.   290
  Your eldest daughters have fordone themselves,
  And desperately are dead.
LEAR.   Ay, so I think.
ALBANY. He knows not what he says, and vain is it
  That we present us to him.
EDGAR.   Very bootless.

Enter Captain

CAPTAIN. Edmund is dead, my lord.
ALBANY.   That's but a trifle here.
  You lords and noble friends, know our intent:
  What comfort to this great decay may come
  Shall be applied. For us, we will resign,
  During the life of this old majesty,
  To him our absolute power; [to Edgar and Kent] to
    you your rights,   300
  With boot and such addition as your honours
  Have more than merited. All friends shall taste
  The wages of their virtue, and all foes
  The cup of their deservings. O see, see!
LEAR. And my poor fool is hanged! No, no, no life!
  Why should a dog, a horse, a rat have life,
  And thou no breath at all? Thou'lt come no more,
  Never, never, never, never, never!
  Pray you, undo this button. Thank you, sir.
  Do you see this? Look on her! Look—her lips!   310
  Look there, look there!
EDGAR.   He faints! My lord my lord!
KENT. Break, heart! I prithee break.
EDGAR.   Look up, my lord.
KENT. Vex not his ghost: O, let him pass; he hates him,
  That would upon the rack of this tough world
  Stretch him out longer.   *Lear dies*
EDGAR.   He is gone indeed.
KENT. The wonder is he hath endured so long;
  He but usurped his life.
ALBANY. Bear them from hence. Our present business
  Is general woe. [to Kent and Edgar] Friends of my
    soul, you twain
  Rule in this realm, and the gored state sustain.   320
KENT. I have a journey, sir, shortly to go:
  My master calls me; I must not say no.
EDGAR. The weight of this sad time we must obey;
  Speak what we feel, not what we ought to say.
  The oldest hath borne most: we that are young
  Shall never see so much, nor live so long.
                              *The bodies are borne out, all
                              follow with a dead march*

Othello

The scene: Venice; Cyprus

CHARACTERS IN THE PLAY

DUKE OF VENICE
BRABANTIO, *a senator, father to Desdemona*
Other Senators
GRATIANO, *brother to Brabantio*
LODOVICO, *kinsman to Brabantio*
OTHELLO, *a noble Moor in the service of the Venetian state*
CASSIO, *his lieutenant*
IAGO, his ancient

RODERIGO, *a Venetian gentleman*
MONTANO, *Othello's predecessor as governor of Cyprus*
Clown, servant to Othello
DESDEMONA, *daughter to Brabantio and wife to Othello*
EMILIA, *wife to Iago*
BIANCA, *mistress to Cassio*
Sailor, Messenger, Herald, Officers, Gentlemen, Musicians, and Attendants

Othello

ACT 1
Scene 1: *Venice. A street*

Enter Roderigo and Iago

RODERIGO. Tush, never tell me; I take it much
  unkindly
  That thou, Iago, who hast had my purse
  As if the strings were thine, shouldst know of this.
IAGO. 'Sblood, but you'll not hear me.
  If ever I did dream of such a matter,
  Abhor me.
RODERIGO. Thou told'st me thou didst hold him in thy
  hate.
IAGO. Despise me if I do not. Three great ones of the
  city,
  In personal suit to make me his lieutenant,
  Off-capped to him; and, by the faith of man,   10
  I know my price: I am worth no worse a place.
  But he, as loving his own pride and purposes,
  Evades them with a bombast circumstance
  Horribly stuffed with epithets of war;
  And, in conclusion,
  Nonsuits my mediators: for, 'Certes,' says he,
  'I have already chose my officer.'
  And what was he?
  Forsooth, a great arithmetician,
  One Michael Cassio, a Florentine,   20
  A fellow almost damned in a fair wife,
  That never set a squadron in the field,
  Nor the division of a battle knows
  More than a spinster—unless the bookish theoric,
  Wherein the togéd consuls can propose
  As masterly as he; mere prattle without practice
  Is all his soldiership. But he, sir, had th'election;
  And I, of whom his eyes had seen the proof
  At Rhodes, at Cyprus, and on other grounds
  Christian and heathen, must be be-lee'd and calmed 30
  By debitor-and-creditor: this counter-caster,
  He, in good time, must his lieutenant be,
  And I—God bless the mark!—his Moorship's
  ancient.
RODERIGO. By heaven, I rather would have been his
  hangman.
IAGO. Why, there's no remedy: 'tis the curse of service;
  Preferment goes by letter and affection,
  And not by old gradation, where each second
  Stood heir to th'first. Now, sir, be judge yourself
  Whether I in any just term am affined
  To love the Moor.
RODERIGO.   I would not follow him then. 40
IAGO. O, sir, content you.
  I follow him to serve my turn upon him.
  We cannot all be masters, nor all masters
  Cannot be truly followed. You shall mark
  Many a duteous and knee-crooking knave
  That, doting on his own obsequious bondage,
  Wears out his time, much like his master's ass,
  For nought but provender, and, when he's old,
  cashiered.
  Whip me such honest knaves. Others there are

Who, trimmed in forms and visages of duty, 50
Keep yet their hearts attending on themselves;
And, throwing but shows of service on their lords,
Do well thrive by them; and, when they've lined
  their coats,
Do themselves homage. These fellows have some
  soul,
And such a one do I profess myself:
For, sir,
It is as sure as you are Roderigo,
Were I the Moor, I would not be Iago;
In following him, I follow but myself;
Heaven is my judge, not I for love and duty, 60
But seeming so, for my peculiar end;
For when my outward action doth demonstrate
The native act and figure of my heart
In compliment extern, 'tis not long after
But I will wear my heart upon my sleeve
For daws to peck at—I am not what I am.
RODERIGO. What a full fortune does the thick-lips owe,
  If he can carry't thus!
IAGO.   Call up her father,
  Rouse him, make after him, poison his delight,
  Proclaim him in the streets, incense her kinsmen, 70
  And, though he in a fertile climate dwell,
  Plague him with flies; though that his joy be joy,
  Yet throw such changes of vexation on't
  As it may lose some colour.
RODERIGO. Here is her father's house; I'll call aloud.
IAGO. Do; with like timorous accent and dire yell
  As when, by night and negligence, the fire
  Is spied in populous cities.
RODERIGO. What, ho, Brabantio! Signior Brabantio,
  ho!
IAGO. Awake! what, ho, Brabantio! thieves! thieves!
  thieves! 80
  Look to your house, your daughter, and your bags!
  Thieves! thieves!

Brabantio appears above, at a window

BRABANTIO. What is the reason of this terrible
  summons?
  What is the matter there?
RODERIGO. Signior, is all your family within?
IAGO. Are your doors locked?
BRABANTIO.   Why, wherefore ask you this?
IAGO. 'Zounds, sir, you're robbed; for shame, put on
  your gown;
  Your heart is burst; you have lost half your soul;
  Even now, now, very now, an old black ram
  Is tupping your white ewe. Arise, arise; 90
  Awake the snorting citizens with the bell,
  Or else the devil will make a grandsire of you.
  Arise, I say.
BRABANTIO.   What, have you lost your wits?
RODERIGO. Most reverend signior, do you know my
  voice?
BRABANTIO. Not I; what are you?
RODERIGO. My name is Roderigo.
BRABANTIO.   The worser welcome:

I have charged thee not to haunt about my doors;
In honest plainness thou hast heard me say
My daughter is not for thee; and now, in madness,
Being full of supper and distempering draughts,　　100
Upon malicious knavery dost thou come
To start my quiet.
RODERIGO. Sir, sir, sir—
BRABANTIO.　　　　　　　But thou must needs be sure
My spirit and my place have in them power
To make this bitter to thee.
RODERIGO.　　　　　　　　　Patience, good sir.
BRABANTIO. What tell'st thou me of robbing? This is
　　Venice:
My house is not a grange.
RODERIGO.　　　　　　　　Most grave Brabantio,
In simple and pure soul I come to you.
IAGO. 'Zounds, sir, you are one of those that will not
serve God, if the devil bid you. Because we come to　110
do you service and you think we are ruffians, you'll
have your daughter covered with a Barbary horse;
you'll have your nephews neigh to you; you'll have
coursers for cousins, and jennets for germans.
BRABANTIO. What profane wretch art thou?
IAGO. I am one, sir, that comes to tell you your
daughter and the Moor are now making the beast
with two backs.
BRABANTIO. Thou art a villain.
IAGO.　　　　　　　　　You are a senator.
BRABANTIO. This thou shalt answer; I know thee,
　　Roderigo.　　　　　　　　　　　　　　　　120
RODERIGO. Sir, I will answer anything. But I beseech
　　you,
If't be your pleasure and most wise consent,
As partly I find it is, that your fair daughter,
At this odd-even and dull watch o' th'night,
Transported with no worse nor better guard
But with a knave of common hire, a gondolier,
To the gross clasps of a lascivious Moor—
If this be known to you, and your allowance,
We then have done you bold and saucy wrong;
But if you know not this, my manners tell me　　130
We have your wrong rebuke. Do not believe
That, from the sense of all civility,
I thus would play and trifle with your reverence.
Your daughter, if you have not given her leave,
I say again, hath made a gross revolt,
Tying her duty, beauty, wit, and fortunes
In an extravagant and wheeling stranger
Of here and everywhere. Straight satisfy yourself.
If she be in her chamber or your house,
Let loose on me the justice of the state　　140
For thus deluding you.
BRABANTIO.　　　　　　　Strike on the tinder, ho!
Give me a taper! call up all my people!
This accident is not unlike my dream;
Belief of it oppresses me already.
Light, I say! light!　　　　　　　　　　He goes in
IAGO.　　　　　　　Farewell, for I must leave you:
It seems not meet nor wholesome to my place
To be produced—as, if I stay, I shall—
Against the Moor; for I do know the state,
However this may gall him with some check,
Cannot with safety cast him; for he's embarked　150
With such loud reason to the Cyprus wars,
Which even now stand in act, that, for their souls,
Another of his fathom they have none

To lead their business: in which regard,
Though I do hate him as I do hell-pains,
Yet, for necessity of present life,
I must show out a flag and sign of love,
Which is indeed but sign. That you shall surely find
　　him,
Lead to the Sagittary the raisèd search,
And there will I be with him. So farewell.　　160
　　　　　　　　　　　　　　　　　He goes

Enter, below, Brabantio, and Servants with torches

BRABANTIO. It is too true an evil: gone she is;
And what's to come of my despisèd time
Is nought but bitterness. Now, Roderigo,
Where didst thou see her? O unhappy girl!
With the Moor, say'st thou? Who would be a
　　father!
How didst thou know 'twas she? O, she deceives me
Past thought! What said she to you? Get more
　　tapers.
Raise all my kindred. Are they married, think you?
RODERIGO. Truly, I think they are.
BRABANTIO. O heaven! How got she out? O treason
　　of the blood!　　　　　　　　　　　　　　170
Fathers, from hence trust not your daughters' minds
By what you see them act! Is there not charms
By which the property of youth and maidhood
May be abused? Have you not read, Roderigo,
Of some such thing?
RODERIGO.　　　　　　　Yes, sir, I have indeed.
BRABANTIO. Call up my brother. O, that you had had
　　her!
Some one way, some another. Do you know
Where we may apprehend her and the Moor?
RODERIGO. I think I can discover him, if you please
To get good guard and go along with me.　　180
BRABANTIO. Pray you, lead on. At every house I'll call;
I may command at most. Get weapons, ho!
And raise some special officers of night.
On, good Roderigo; I'll deserve your pains.
　　　　　　　　　　　　　　　　　They go

Scene 2: *Another street*

Enter Othello, Iago, and Attendants with torches

IAGO. Though in the trade of war I have slain men,
Yet do I hold it very stuff o'th'conscience
To do no contrived murder. I lack iniquity
Sometimes to do me service. Nine or ten times
I had thought t'have jerked him here under the ribs.
OTHELLO. 'Tis better as it is.
IAGO.　　　　　　　Nay, but he prated,
And spoke such scurvy and provoking terms
Against your honour
That, with the little godliness I have,
I did full hard forbear him. But I pray, sir,　　10
Are you fast married? For be sure of this,
That the magnifico is much beloved,
And hath in his effect a voice potential
As double as the duke's. He will divorce you,
Or put upon you what restraint and grievance
The law, with all his might to enforce it on,
Will give him cable.
OTHELLO.　　　　　　　Let him do his spite;
My services which I have done the signiory
Shall out-tongue his complaints. 'Tis yet to know—

Which, when I know that boasting is an honour, 20
I shall promulgate—I fetch my life and being
From men of royal siege; and my demerits
May speak unbonneted to as proud a fortune
As this that I have reached. For know, Iago,
But that I love the gentle Desdemona,
I would not my unhoused free condition
Put into circumscription and confine
For the sea's worth. But look what lights come
    yond!
IAGO. Those are the raised father and his friends.
    You were best go in.
OTHELLO.   Not I; I must be found. 30
    My parts, my title, and my perfect soul,
    Shall manifest me rightly. Is it they?
IAGO. By Janus, I think no.

Enter Cassio, and certain Officers with torches

OTHELLO. The servants of the duke, and my lieutenant!
    The goodness of the night upon you, friends!
    What is the news?
CASSIO.   The duke does greet you, general,
    And he requires your haste-post-haste appearance
    Even on the instant.
OTHELLO.   What is the matter, think you?
CASSIO. Something from Cyprus, as I may divine.
    It is a business of some heat: the galleys 40
    Have sent a dozen sequent messengers
    This very night at one another's heels;
    And many of the consuls, raised and met,
    Are at the duke's already. You have been hotly
    called for;
    When, being not at your lodging to be found,
    The senate hath sent about three several quests
    To search you out.
OTHELLO.   'Tis well I am found by you.
    I will but spend a word here in the house,
    And go with you.   *He goes in*
CASSIO.   Ancient, what makes he here?
IAGO. Faith, he tonight hath boarded a land carack; 50
    If it prove lawful prize, he's made for ever.
CASSIO. I do not understand.
IAGO.   He's married.
CASSIO.   To who?

Re-enter Othello

IAGO. Marry, to—Come, captain, will you go?
OTHELLO.   Have with you.
CASSIO. Here comes another troop to seek for you.
IAGO. It is Brabantio. General, be advised;
    He comes to bad intent.

*Enter Brabantio, Roderigo, and Officers with torches and
weapons*

OTHELLO.   Holla! stand there!
RODERIGO. Signior, it is the Moor.
                    Down with him, thief!
                    They draw on both sides
IAGO. You, Roderigo! come sir, I am for you.
OTHELLO. Keep up your bright swords, for the dew
    will rust them.
    Good signior, you shall more command with years 60
    Than with your weapons.
BRABANTIO. O thou foul thief, where hast thou stowed
    my daughter?
    Damned as thou art, thou hast enchanted her:

For I'll refer me to all things of sense,
If she in chains of magic were not bound,
Whether a maid so tender, fair, and happy,
So opposite to marriage that she shunned
The wealthy curléd darlings of our nation,
Would ever have, t'incur a general mock,
Run from her guardage to the sooty bosom 70
Of such a thing as thou—to fear, not to delight.
Judge me the world, if 'tis not gross in sense
That thou hast practised on her with foul charms,
Abused her delicate youth with drugs or minerals
That weaken motion: I'll have't disputed on;
'Tis probable and palpable to thinking.
I therefore apprehend and do attach thee
For an abuser of the world, a practiser
Of arts inhibited and out of warrant.
Lay hold upon him. If he do resist, 80
Subdue him at his peril.
OTHELLO.   Hold your hands,
    Both you of my inclining and the rest:
    Were it my cue to fight, I should have known it
    Without a prompter. Where will you that I go
    To answer this your charge?
BRABANTIO.   To prison, till fit time
    Of law and course of direct session
    Call thee to answer.
OTHELLO.   What if I do obey?
    How may the duke be therewith satisfied,
    Whose messengers are here about my side,
    Upon some present business of the state 90
    To bring me to him?
1 OFFICER.   'Tis true, most worthy signior;
    The duke's in council, and your noble self,
    I am sure, is sent for.
BRABANTIO.   How! the duke in council!
    In this time of the night! Bring him away.
    Mine's not an idle cause: the duke himself,
    Or any of my brothers of the state,
    Cannot but feel this wrong as 'twere their own;
    For if such actions may have passage free,
    Bond-slaves and pagans shall our statesmen be.
                                    They go

Scene 3: A council-chamber

The Duke and Senators sitting at a table; Officers attending

DUKE. There is no composition in these news
    That gives them credit.
1 SENATOR.   Indeed they are disproportioned:
    My letters say a hundred and seven galleys.
DUKE. And mine, a hundred and forty.
2 SENATOR.   And mine, two hundred;
    But though they jump not on a just account—
    As in these cases where the aim reports
    'Tis oft with difference—yet do they all confirm
    A Turkish fleet, and bearing up to Cyprus.
DUKE. Nay, it is possible enough to judgement;
    I do not so secure me in the error, 10
    But the main article I do approve
    In fearful sense.
SAILOR [*without*]. What, ho! what, ho! what, ho!
1 OFFICER. A messenger from the galleys.

Enter Sailor

DUKE.   Now, what's the business?
SAILOR. The Turkish preparation makes for Rhodes;

So was I bid report here to the state
By Signior Angelo.
DUKE. How say you by this change?
1 SENATOR.   This cannot be,
By no assay of reason; 'tis a pageant
To keep us in false gaze. When we consider
Th'importance of Cyprus to the Turk,   20
And let ourselves again but understand
That, as it more concerns the Turk than Rhodes,
So may he with more facile question bear it,
For that it stands not in such warlike brace,
But altogether lacks th'abilities
That Rhodes is dressed in—if we make thought of
   this,
We must not think the Turk is so unskilful
To leave that latest which concerns him first,
Neglecting an attempt of ease and gain
To wake and wage a danger profitless.   30
DUKE. Nay, in all confidence, he's not for Rhodes.
1 OFFICER. Here is more news.

Enter a Messenger

MESSENGER. The Ottomites, reverend and gracious,
Steering with due course toward the isle of Rhodes,
Have there injointed with an after fleet.
1 SENATOR. Ay, so I thought. How many, as you
guess?
MESSENGER. Of thirty sail; and now they do re-stem
Their backward course, bearing with frank
   appearance
Their purposes toward Cyprus. Signior Montano,
Your trusty and most valiant servitor,   40
With his free duty recommends you thus,
And prays you to relieve him.
DUKE. 'Tis certain then for Cyprus.
Marcus Luccicos, is not he in town?
1 SENATOR. He's now in Florence.
DUKE. Write from us to him; post-post-haste dispatch.
1 SENATOR. Here comes Brabantio and the valiant
Moor.

Enter Brabantio, Othello, Iago, Roderigo, and Officers

DUKE. Valiant Othello, we must straight employ you
Against the general enemy Ottoman.
   [*to Brabantio*] I did not see you; welcome, gentle
   signior;   50
We lacked your counsel and your help tonight.
BRABANTIO. So did I yours. Good your grace, pardon
me:
Neither my place nor aught I heard of business
Hath raised me from my bed, nor doth the general
   care
Take hold on me; for my particular grief
Is of so flood-gate and o'erbearing nature
That it engluts and swallows other sorrows,
And yet is still itself.
DUKE.   Why, what's the matter?
BRABANTIO. My daughter! O, my daughter!
ALL.   Dead?
BRABANTIO.   Ay, to me:
She is abused, stolen from me and corrupted   60
By spells and medicines bought of mountebanks;
For nature so preposterously to err,
Being not deficient, blind, or lame of sense,
Sans witchcraft could not.
DUKE. Whoe'er he be that in this foul proceeding

Hath thus beguiled your daughter of herself,
And you of her, the bloody book of law
You shall yourself read in the bitter letter
After your own sense, yea, though our proper son
Stood in your action.
BRABANTIO.   Humbly I thank your grace. 70
Here is the man: this Moor, whom now, it seems,
Your special mandate for the state affairs
Hath hither brought.
ALL.   We are very sorry for't.
DUKE [*to Othello*]. What in your own part can you say
   to this?
BRABANTIO. Nothing, but this is so.
OTHELLO. Most potent, grave, and reverend signiors,
My very noble and approved good masters,
That I have ta'en away this old man's daughter,
It is most true; true, I have married her:
The very head and front of my offending   80
Hath this extent, no more. Rude am I in my speech,
And little blest with the soft phrase of peace:
For since these arms of mine had seven years' pith
Till now some nine moons wasted, they have used
Their dearest action in the tented field;
And little of this great world can I speak
More than pertains to feats of broil and battle;
And therefore little shall I grace my cause
In speaking for myself. Yet, by your patience,
I will a round unvarnished tale deliver   90
Of my whole course of love: what drugs, what
   charms,
What conjuration, and what mighty magic—
For such proceedings I am charged withal—
I won his daughter.
BRABANTIO.   A maiden never bold;
Of spirit so still and quiet that her motion
Blushed at herself; and she—in spite of nature,
Of years, of country, credit, everything—
To fall in love with what she feared to look on!
It is a judgement maimed and most imperfect
That will confess perfection so could err   100
Against all rules of nature, and must be driven
To find out practices of cunning hell
Why this should be. I therefore vouch again
That with some mixtures powerful o'er the blood,
Or with some dram conjured to this effect,
He wrought upon her.
DUKE.   To vouch this is no proof,
Without more wider and more overt test
Than these thin habits and poor likelihoods
Of modern seeming do prefer against him.
1 SENATOR. But, Othello, speak: 110
Did you by indirect and forcéd courses
Subdue and poison this young maid's affections?
Or came it by request and such fair question
As soul to soul affordeth?
OTHELLO.   I beseech you,
Send for the lady to the Sagittary,
And let her speak of me before her father;
If you do find me foul in her report,
The trust, the office I do hold of you,
Not only take away, but let your sentence
Even fall upon my life.
DUKE.   Fetch Desdemona hither.   120
OTHELLO. Ancient, conduct them; you best know the
   place.   *Iago departs with attendants*
And till she come, as truly as to heaven

I do confess the vices of my blood,
So justly to your grave ears I'll present
How I did thrive in this fair lady's love,
And she in mine.
DUKE. Say it, Othello.
OTHELLO. Her father loved me, oft invited me,
Still questioned me the story of my life
From year to year—the battles, sieges, fortunes,   130
That I have passed.
I ran it through, even from my boyish days
To th'very moment that he bade me tell it:
Wherein I spake of most disastrous chances,
Of moving accidents by flood and field,
Of hair-breadth scapes i'th'imminent deadly breach,
Of being taken by the insolent foe,
And sold to slavery; of my redemption thence,
And portance in my travels' history:
Wherein of antres vast and deserts idle,   140
Rough quarries, rocks, and hills whose heads touch
      heaven,
It was my hint to speak—such was the process;
And of the Cannibals that each other eat,
The Anthropophagi, and men whose heads
Do grow beneath their shoulders. This to hear
Would Desdemona seriously incline;
But still the house affairs would draw her thence,
Which ever as she could with haste dispatch
She'ld come again, and with a greedy ear
Devour up my discourse; which I observing,   150
Took once a pliant hour, and found good means
To draw from her a prayer of earnest heart
That I would all my pilgrimage dilate,
Whereof by parcels she had something heard,
But not intentively. I did consent,
And often did beguile her of her tears
When I did speak of some distressful stroke
That my youth suffered. My story being done,
She gave me for my pains a world of sighs:
She swore, in faith 'twas strange, 'twas passing
      strange;   160
'Twas pitiful, 'twas wondrous pitiful;
She wished she had not heard it, yet she wished
That heaven had made her such a man; she
      thanked me,
And bade me, if I had a friend that loved her,
I should but teach him how to tell my story,
And that would woo her. Upon this hint I spake;
She loved me for the dangers I had passed,
And I loved her that she did pity them.
This only is the witchcraft I have used.
Here comes the lady; let her witness it.   170

Enter Desdemona, Iago, and Attendants

DUKE. I think this tale would win my daughter too.
Good Brabantio,
Take up this mangled matter at the best:
Men do their broken weapons rather use
Than their bare hands.
BRABANTIO.   I pray you, hear her speak.
If she confess that she was half the wooer,
Destruction on my head, if my bad blame
Light on the man! Come hither, gentle mistress:
Do you perceive in all this company
Where most you owe obedience?
DESDEMONA.   My noble father,   180
I do perceive here a divided duty.

To you I am bound for life and education;
My life and education both do learn me
How to respect you. You are the lord of duty;
I am hitherto your daughter. But here's my
      husband;
And so much duty as my mother showed
To you, preferring you before her father,
So much I challenge that I may profess
Due to the Moor my lord.
BRABANTIO.   God bu'y! I've done.
Please it your grace, on to the state affairs.   190
I had rather to adopt a child than get it.
Come hither, Moor:
I here do give thee that with all my heart,
Which, but thou hast already, with all my heart
I would keep from thee. For your sake, jewel,
I am glad at soul I have no other child;
For thy escape would teach me tyranny,
To hang clogs on them. I have done, my Lord.
DUKE. Let me speak like yourself, and lay a sentence
Which, as a grise or step, may help these lovers   200
Into your favour.
When remedies are past, the griefs are ended
By seeing the worst, which late on hopes depended.
To mourn a mischief that is past and gone
Is the next way to draw new mischief on.
What cannot be preserved when Fortune takes,
Patience her injury a mockery makes.
The robbed that smiles steals something from the
      thief;
He robs himself that spends a bootless grief.
BRABANTIO. So let the Turk of Cyprus us beguile,   210
We lose it not so long as we can smile.
He bears the sentence well that nothing bears
But the free comfort which from thence he hears;
But he bears both the sentence and the sorrow
That to pay grief must of poor patience borrow.
These sentences, to sugar or to gall,
Being strong on both sides, are equivocal.
But words are words: I never yet did hear
That the bruised heart was piecèd through the ear.
I humbly beseech you, proceed to th'affairs of state. 220
DUKE. The Turk with a most mighty preparation
makes for Cyprus. Othello, the fortitude of the place
is best known to you; and though we have there a
substitute of most allowed sufficiency, yet opinion,
a sovereign mistress of effects, throws a more safer
voice on you: you must therefore be content to
slubber the gloss of your new fortunes with this
more stubborn and boisterous expedition.
OTHELLO. The tyrant Custom, most grave senators,
Hath made the flinty and steel couch of war   230
My thrice-driven bed of down. I do agnize
A natural and prompt alacrity
I find in hardness; and do undertake
These present wars against the Ottomites.
Most humbly therefore bending to your state,
I crave fit disposition for my wife,
Due reference of place and exhibition,
With such accommodation and besort
As levels with her breeding.
DUKE.   Why, if you please,
Be't at her father's.
BRABANTIO.   I'll not have it so.   240
OTHELLO. Nor I.
DESDEMONA.   Nor I; I would not there reside,

To put my father in impatient thoughts
By being in his eye. Most gracious duke,
To my unfolding lend your prosperous ear,
And let me find a charter in your voice
T'assist my simpleness.

DUKE. What would you, Desdemona?

DESDEMONA. That I did love the Moor to live with
  him,
My downright violence and scorn of fortunes
May trumpet to the world. My heart's subdued   250
Even to the very quality of my lord.
I saw Othello's visage in his mind,
And to his honours and his valiant parts
Did I my soul and fortunes consecrate.
So that, dear lords, if I be left behind,
A moth of peace, and he go to the war,
The rights for why I love him are bereft me,
And I a heavy interim shall support
By his dear absence. Let me go with him.

OTHELLO. Let her have your voice.   260
Vouch with me, heaven, I therefore beg it not
To please the palate of my appetite;
Nor to comply with heat and young affects
In my distinct and proper satisfaction;
But to be free and bounteous to her mind.
And heaven defend your good souls that you think
I will your serious and great business scant
For she is with me. No, when light-winged toys
Of feathered Cupid seel with wanton dullness
My speculative and officed instruments,   270
That my disports corrupt and taint my business,
Let housewives make a skillet of my helm,
And all indign and base adversities
Make head against my estimation!

DUKE. Be it as you shall privately determine,
Either for her stay or going; th'affair cries haste,
And speed must answer it.

I SENATOR. You must away tonight.

OTHELLO.   With all my heart.

DUKE. At nine i'th'morning here we'll meet again.
Othello, leave some officer behind,   280
And he shall our commission bring to you;
With such things else of quality and respect
As doth import you.

OTHELLO.   So please your grace, my ancient:
A man he is of honesty and trust;
To his conveyance I assign my wife,
With what else needful your good grace shall think
To be sent after me.

DUKE.   Let it be so.
Good night to everyone. [to Brabantio] And,
  noble signior,
If virtue no delighted beauty lack,
Your son-in-law is far more fair than black.   290

I SENATOR. Adieu, brave Moor; use Desdemona well.

BRABANTIO. Look to her, Moor, if thou hast eyes to
  see:
She has deceived her father, and may thee.

OTHELLO. My life upon her faith!

             Duke, Senators, Officers, etc.
                                depart
                Honest Iago,
My Desdemona must I leave to thee;
I prithee, let thy wife attend on her,
And bring them after in the best advantage.
Come, Desdemona, I have but an hour

Of love, of worldly matter and direction,
To spend with thee: we must obey the time.   300
           Othello and Desdemona go out

RODERIGO. Iago!

IAGO. What say'st thou, noble heart?

RODERIGO. What will I do, think'st thou?

IAGO. Why, go to bed and sleep.

RODERIGO. I will incontinently drown myself.

IAGO. If thou dost, I shall never love thee after. Why,
thou silly gentleman!

RODERIGO. It is silliness to live when to live is torment;
and then have we a prescription to die when death
is our physician.   310

IAGO. O villanous! I have looked upon the world for
four times seven years; and since I could distinguish
betwixt a benefit and an injury, I never found a man
that knew how to love himself. Ere I would say I
would drown myself for the love of a guinea-hen, I
would change my humanity with a baboon.

RODERIGO. What should I do? I confess it is my shame
to be so fond, but it is not in my virtue to amend it.

IAGO. Virtue! a fig! 'tis in ourselves that we are thus
or thus. Our bodies are gardens, to the which our   320
wills are gardeners; so that if we will plant nettles
or sow lettuce, set hyssop and weed up tine, supply
it with one gender of herbs or distract it with many,
either to have it sterile with idleness or manured
with industry—why, the power and corrigible
authority of this lies in our wills. If the beam of our
lives had not one scale of reason to poise another
of sensuality, the blood and baseness of our natures
would conduct us to most preposterous conclusions.
But we have reason to cool our raging motions, our   330
carnal stings, our unbitted lusts; whereof I take this,
that you call love, to be a set or scion.

RODERIGO. It cannot be.

IAGO. It is merely a lust of the blood and a permission
of the will. Come, be a man. Drown thyself! Drown
cats and blind puppies. I have professed me thy
friend, and I confess me knit to thy deserving with
cables of perdurable toughness. I could never better
stead thee than now. Put money in thy purse;
follow thou these wars; defeat thy favour with an   340
usurped beard. I say, put money in thy purse. It
cannot be that Desdemona should long continue her
love to the Moor—put money in thy purse—nor he
his to her: it was a violent commencement, and thou
shalt see an answerable sequestration—put but
money in thy purse. These Moors are changeable in
their wills—fill thy purse with money. The food
that to him now is as luscious as locusts, shall be
to him shortly as bitter as coloquintida. She must
change for youth: when she is sated with his body,   350
she will find the error of her choice. Therefore put
money in thy purse. If thou wilt needs damn thyself,
do it a more delicate way than drowning. Make all
the money thou canst. If sanctimony and a frail vow
betwixt an erring barbarian and a supersubtle
Venetian be not too hard for my wits and all the
tribe of hell, thou shalt enjoy her; therefore make
money. A pox of drowning thyself! 'Tis clean out of
the way. Seek thou rather to be hanged in compassing thy joy than to be drowned and go without   360
her.

RODERIGO. Wilt thou be fast to my hopes, if I depend
on the issue?

IAGO. Thou art sure of me. Go, make money. I have
told thee often, and I re-tell thee again and again,
I hate the Moor. My cause is hearted; thine hath no
less reason. Let us be conjunctive in our revenge
against him. If thou canst cuckold him, thou dost
thyself a pleasure, me a sport. There are many events
in the womb of time, which will be delivered. 370
Traverse! go; provide thy money. We will have
more of this tomorrow. Adieu.
RODERIGO. Where shall we meet i'th'morning?
IAGO. At my lodging.
RODERIGO. I'll be with thee betimes.
IAGO. Go to; farewell. Do you hear, Roderigo?
RODERIGO. What say you?
IAGO. No more of drowning, do you hear?
RODERIGO. I am changed.
IAGO. Go to; farewell. Put money enough in your 380
purse.
RODERIGO. I'll sell all my land. *Goes*
IAGO. Thus do I ever make my fool my purse;
For I mine own gained knowledge should profane
If I would time expend with such a snipe
But for my sport and profit. I hate the Moor;
And it is thought abroad that 'twixt my sheets
He's done my office. I know not if't be true;
Yet I, for mere suspicion in that kind,
Will do as if for surety. He holds me well; 390
The better shall my purpose work on him.
Cassio's a proper man: let me see now;
To get his place, and to plume up my will
In double knavery. How? How? Let's see:
After some time to abuse Othello's ear
That he is too familiar with his wife;
He hath a person and a smooth dispose
To be suspected—framed to make women false.
The Moor is of a free and open nature
That thinks men honest that but seem to be so, 400
And will as tenderly be led by th'nose
As asses are.
I have't. It is engendered. Hell and night
Must bring this monstrous birth to the world's light.
Goes

ACT 2
Scene 1: *A sea-port in Cyprus. An open place near
the quay*

Enter Montano and two Gentlemen

MONTANO. What from the cape can you discern at sea?
1 GENTLEMAN. Nothing at all: it is a high-wrought
flood;
I cannot 'twixt the heaven and the main
Descry a sail.
MONTANO. Methinks the wind hath spoke aloud at
land;
A fuller blast ne'er shook our battlements.
If it hath ruffianed so upon the sea,
What ribs of oak, when mountains melt on them,
Can hold the mortise? What shall we hear of this?
2 GENTLEMAN. A segregation of the Turkish fleet: 10
For do but stand upon the foaming shore,
The chidden billow seems to pelt the clouds;
The wind-shaked surge, with high and monstrous
mane,
Seems to cast water on the burning Bear,
And quench the guards of th'ever-fixéd pole.

I never did like molestation view
On the enchaféd flood.
MONTANO. If that the Turkish fleet
Be not ensheltered and embayed, they are drowned;
It is impossible they bear it out.

Enter a third Gentleman

3 GENTLEMAN. News, lads! our wars are done: 20
The desperate tempest hath so banged the Turks
That their designment halts. A noble ship of Venice
Hath seen a grievous wreck and sufferance
On most part of their fleet.
MONTANO. How! is this true?
3 GENTLEMAN. The ship is here put in,
A Veronesa; Michael Cassio,
Lieutenant to the warlike Moor Othello,
Is come on shore; the Moor himself at sea,
And is in full commission here for Cyprus.
MONTANO. I am glad on't; 'tis a worthy governor. 30
3 GENTLEMAN. But this same Cassio, though he speak
of comfort
Touching the Turkish loss, yet he looks sadly,
And prays the Moor be safe; for they were parted
With foul and violent tempest.
MONTANO. Pray heaven he be;
For I have served him, and the man commands
Like a full soldier. Let's to the sea-side, ho!
As well to see the vessel that's come in
As to throw out our eyes for brave Othello,
Even till we make the main and th'aerial blue
An indistinct regard.
3 GENTLEMAN. Come, let's do so; 40
For every minute is expectancy
Of more arrivance.

Enter Cassio

CASSIO. Thanks you, the valiant of this warlike isle,
That so approve the Moor! O, let the heavens
Give him defence against the elements,
For I have lost him on a dangerous sea.
MONTANO. Is he well shipped?
CASSIO. His bark is stoutly timbered, and his pilot
Of very expert and approved allowance;
Therefore my hopes, not forfeited to death, 50
Stand in bold cure.
[*a cry heard*]: 'A sail, a sail, a sail!'

Enter a fourth Gentleman

CASSIO. What noise?
4 GENTLEMAN. The town is empty; on the brow
o'th'sea
Stand ranks of people, and they cry 'A sail!'
CASSIO. My hopes do shape him for the Governor.
Guns heard
2 GENTLEMAN. They do discharge their shot of
courtesy:
Our friends at least.
CASSIO. I pray you, sir, go forth,
And give us truth who 'tis that is arrived.
2 GENTLEMAN. I shall. *Goes*
MONTANO. But, good lieutenant, is your general
wived? 60
CASSIO. Most fortunately: he hath achieved a maid
That paragons description and wild fame;
One that excels the quirks of blazoning pens,
And in th'essential vesture of creation
Does tire the ingener.

Re-enter second Gentleman

       How now! who has put in?
2 GENTLEMAN. 'Tis one Iago, ancient to the general.
CASSIO. He's had most favourable and happy speed:
 Tempests themselves, high seas, and howling winds,
 The guttered rocks, and congregated sands,
 Traitors insteeped to clog the guiltless keel,   70
 As having sense of beauty, do omit
 Their mortal natures, letting go safely by
 The divine Desdemona.
MONTANO.   What is she?
CASSIO. She that I spake of, our great captain's captain,
 Left in the conduct of the bold Iago;
 Whose footing here anticipates our thoughts
 A se'nnight's speed. Great Jove, Othello guard,
 'And swell his sail with thine own powerful breath,
 That he may bless this bay with his tall ship,
 Make love's quick pants in Desdemona's arms, 80
 Give renewed fire to our extincted spirits,
 And bring all Cyprus comfort.

Enter Desdemona, Emilia, Iago, Roderigo, and Attendants

       O, behold,
 The riches of the ship is come on shore!
 You men of Cyprus, let her have your knees.
 Hail to thee, lady! and the grace of heaven,
 Before, behind thee, and on every hand,
 Enwheel thee round!
DESDEMONA.   I thank you, valiant Cassio.
 What tidings can you tell me of my lord?
CASSIO. He is not yet arrived; nor know I aught
 But that he's well and will be shortly here.   90
DESDEMONA. O, but I fear—How lost you company?
CASSIO. The great contention of the sea and skies
 Parted our fellowship. But, hark! a sail!
   [*a cry heard*], 'A sail, a sail!', [*and then guns*]
2 GENTLEMAN. They give their greeting to the citadel:
 This likewise is a friend.
CASSIO.   See for the news.
         Gentleman goes
 Good ancient, you are welcome. [*to Emilia*]
  Welcome, mistress.
 Let it not gall your patience, good Iago,
 That I extend my manners; 'tis my breeding
 That gives me this bold show of courtesy.
         Kisses her
IAGO. Sir, would she give you so much of her lips 100
 As of her tongue she oft bestows on me,
 You'ld have enough.
DESDEMONA. Alas, she has no speech.
IAGO.   In faith, too much;
 I find it still when I have list to sleep.
 Marry, before your ladyship, I grant,
 She puts her tongue a little in her heart
 And chides with thinking.
EMILIA. You have little cause to say so.
IAGO. Come on, come on; you are pictures out of
 doors, bells in your parlours, wild-cats in your 110
 kitchens; saints in your injuries, devils being
 offended; players in your housewifery, and hussies
 in your beds.
DESDEMONA. O, fie upon thee, slanderer!
IAGO. Nay, it is true, or else I am a Turk:
 You rise to play, and go to bed to work.

EMILIA. You shall not write my praise.
IAGO.   No, let me not.
DESDEMONA. What wouldst thou write of me, if thou
 shouldst praise me?
IAGO. O gentle lady, do not put me to't;
 For I am nothing if not critical.   120
DESDEMONA. Come on, assay—There's one gone to
 the harbour?
IAGO. Ay, madam.
DESDEMONA [*aside*]. I am not merry; but I do beguile
 The thing I am by seeming otherwise.
 [*aloud*] Come, how wouldst thou praise me?
IAGO. I am about it; but indeed my invention comes
 from my pate as birdlime does from frieze—it
 plucks out brains and all. But my muse labours, and
 thus she is delivered.
  If she be fair and wise, fairness and wit,
  The one's for use, the other useth it.
DESDEMONA. Well praised! How if she be black and
 witty?
IAGO. If she be black, and thereto have a wit, 130
  She'll find a white that shall her blackness hit.
DESDEMONA. Worse and worse.
EMILIA. How if fair and foolish?
IAGO. She never yet was foolish that was fair;
  For even her folly helped her to an heir.
DESDEMONA. These are old fond paradoxes to make
 fools laugh i'th'alehouse. What miserable praise hast 140
 thou for her that's foul and foolish?
IAGO. There's none so foul, and foolish thereunto,
  But does foul pranks which fair and wise
   ones do.
DESDEMONA. O heavy ignorance! thou praisest the
 worst best. But what praise couldst thou bestow on
 a deserving woman indeed—one that in the
 authority of her merit did justly put on the vouch
 of very malice itself?
IAGO. She that was ever fair, and never proud,
  Had tongue at will, and yet was never loud, 150
  Never lacked gold, and yet went never gay,
  Fled from her wish, and yet said 'Now
   I may';
  She that, being angered, her revenge
   being nigh,
  Bade her wrong stay, and her displeasure fly;
  She that in wisdom never was so frail
  To change the cod's head for the
   salmon's tail;
  She that could think, and ne'er disclose
   her mind,
  See suitors following, and not look behind;
  She was a wight, if ever such wight were—
DESDEMONA. To do what?   160
IAGO. To suckle fools and chronicle small beer.
DESDEMONA. O most lame and impotent conclusion!
 Do not learn of him, Emilia, though he be thy
 husband. How say you, Cassio? Is he not a most
 profane and liberal counsellor?
CASSIO. He speaks home, madam. You may relish him
 more in the soldier than in the scholar.
IAGO [*aside*]. He takes her by the palm. Ay, well said,
 whisper. With as little a web as this will I ensnare as
 great a fly as Cassio. Ay, smile upon her, do; I will 170
 gyve thee in thine own courtship. You say true:
 'tis so, indeed. If such tricks as these strip you out
 of your lieutenantry, it had been better you had not

kissed your three fingers so oft, which now again you are most apt to play the sir in. Very good; well kissed! an excellent courtesy! 'tis so, indeed, Yet again your fingers to your lips? Would they were clyster-pipes for your sake! *Trumpets within* [*aloud*] The Moor! I know his trumpet.

CASSIO. 'Tis truly so.

DESDEMONA. Let's meet him and receive him.

CASSIO. Lo where he comes! 180

Enter Othello and Attendants

OTHELLO. O my fair warrior!

DESDEMONA. My dear Othello!

OTHELLO. It gives me wonder great as my content
To see you here before me. O my soul's joy!
If after every tempest come such calms,
May the winds blow till they have wakened death!
And let the labouring bark climb hills of seas
Olympus-high and duck again as low
As hell's from heaven! If it were now to die,
'Twere now to be most happy; for I fear,
My soul hath her content so absolute 190
That not another comfort like to this
Succeeds in unknown fate.

DESDEMONA. The heavens forbid
But that our loves and comforts should increase,
Even as our days do grow!

OTHELLO. Amen to that, sweet powers!
I cannot speak enough of this content:
It stops me here; it is too much of joy.
And this, and this, the greatest discords be

They kiss

That e'er our hearts shall make!

IAGO [*aside*]. O, you are well tuned now! But I'll set
down the pegs that make this music, as honest as 200
I am.

OTHELLO. Come, let's to the castle.
News, friends: our wars are done; the Turks are
drowned.
How does my old acquaintance of this isle?
Honey, you shall be well desired in Cyprus;
I have found great love amongst them. O my sweet,
I prattle out of fashion, and I dote
In mine own comfort. I prithee, good Iago,
Go to the bay, and disembark my coffers;
Bring thou the master to the citadel; 210
He is a good one, and his worthiness
Does challenge much respect. Come, Desdemona,
Once more well met at Cyprus.

All but Iago and Roderigo depart

IAGO. Do thou meet me presently at the harbour.
Come hither. If thou be'st valiant—as they say base
men being in love have then a nobility in their
natures more than is native to them—list me. The
lieutenant tonight watches on the court of guard.
First, I must tell thee this: Desdemona is directly
in love with him. 220

RODERIGO. With him! why, 'tis not possible.

IAGO. Lay thy finger thus, and let thy soul be instructed. Mark me with what violence she first loved
the Moor but for bragging and telling her fantastical
lies. And will she love him still for prating?—let not
thy discreet heart think it. Her eye must be fed; and
what delight shall she have to look on the devil?
When the blood is made dull with the act of sport,
there should be—again to inflame it and to give

satiety a fresh appetite—loveliness in favour, 230
sympathy in years, manners, and beauties; all which
the Moor is defective in. Now, for want of these
required conveniencies, her delicate tenderness will
find itself abused, begin to heave the gorge, disrelish
and abhor the Moor. Very nature will instruct her
in it and compel her to some second choice.
Now, sir, this granted—as it is a most pregnant and
unforced position—who stands so eminent in the
degree of this fortune as Cassio does?—a knave very
voluble; no further conscionable than in putting on 240
the mere form of civil and humane seeming, for the
better compassing of his salt and most hidden loose
affection. Why, none; why, none—a slipper and
subtle knave; a finder-out of occasions; that has an
eye can stamp and counterfeit advantages, though
true advantage never present itself; a devilish knave!
Besides, the knave is handsome, young, and hath all
those requisites in him that folly and green minds
look after; a pestilent complete knave; and the
woman hath found him already. 250

RODERIGO. I cannot believe that in her; she's full of
most blest condition.

IAGO. Blest fig's-end! The wine she drinks is made of
grapes. If she had been blest, she would never have
loved the Moor. Blest pudding! Didst thou not see
her paddle with the palm of his hand? Didst not
mark that?

RODERIGO. Yes, that I did; but that was but courtesy.

IAGO. Lechery, by this hand; an index and obscure
prologue to the history of lust and foul thoughts. 260
They met so near with their lips that their breaths
embraced together—villanous thoughts, Roderigo!
When these mutualities so marshal the way, hard at
hand comes the master and main exercise, th'incorporate conclusion. Pish! But, sir, be you ruled
by me. I have brought you from Venice. Watch you
tonight; for the command, I'll lay't upon you.
Cassio knows you not; I'll not be far from you. Do
you find some occasion to anger Cassio, either by
speaking too loud or tainting his discipline, or from 270
what other course you please which the time shall
more favourably minister.

RODERIGO. Well.

IAGO. Sir, he's rash and very sudden in choler, and
haply may strike at you—provoke him that he may;
for even out of that will I cause these of Cyprus
to mutiny, whose qualification shall come into no
true taste again but by the displanting of Cassio.
So shall you have a shorter journey to your desires
by the means I shall then have to prefer them, and 280
the impediment most profitably removed, without
the which there were no expectation of our
prosperity.

RODERIGO. I will do this, if you can bring it to any
opportunity.

IAGO. I warrant thee. Meet me by and by at the
citadel. I must fetch his necessaries ashore. Farewell.

RODERIGO. Adieu. *Goes*

IAGO. That Cassio loves her, I do well believe't;
That she loves him, 'tis apt and of great credit. 290
The Moor, howbeit that I endure him not,
Is of a constant, loving, noble nature;
And I dare think he'll prove to Desdemona
A most dear husband. Now, I do love her too,
Not out of absolute lust—though peradventure

I stand accountant for as great a sin—
But partly led to diet my revenge
For that I do suspect the lusty Moor
Hath leaped into my seat, the thought whereof
Doth like a poisonous mineral gnaw my inwards;   300
And nothing can or shall content my soul
Till I am evened with him, wife for wife;
Or failing so, yet that I put the Moor
At least into a jealousy so strong
That judgement cannot cure. Which thing to do,
If this poor trash of Venice, whom I leash
For his quick hunting, stand the putting on,
I'll have our Michael Cassio on the hip,
Abuse him to the Moor in the rank garb—
For I fear Cassio with my night-cap too—   310
Make the Moor thank me, love me, and reward me,
For making him egregiously an ass,
And practising upon his peace and quiet
Even to madness. 'Tis here, but yet confused;
Knavery's plain face is never seen till used.   *Goes*

Scene 2: *A street*

Enter a Herald with a proclamation; people following

HERALD. It is Othello's pleasure, our noble and valiant
general, that, upon certain tidings now arrived importing the mere perdition of the Turkish fleet,
every man put himself into triumph; some to dance,
some to make bonfires, each man to what sport and
revels his addiction leads him: for, besides these
beneficial news, it is the celebration of his nuptial.
So much was his pleasure should be proclaimed.
All offices are open, and there is full liberty of feasting from this present hour of five till the bell have   10
told eleven. Heaven bless the isle of Cyprus and our
noble general Othello!   *He moves on*

Scene 3: *A hall in the citadel*

Enter Othello, Desdemona, Cassio, and Attendants

OTHELLO. Good Michael, look you to the guard
tonight.
Let's teach ourselves that honourable stop,
Not to outsport discretion.
CASSIO. Iago hath direction what to do;
But notwithstanding with my personal eye
Will I look to't.
OTHELLO.   Iago is most honest.
Michael, good night; tomorrow with your earliest
Let me have speech with you. Come, my dear love,
The purchase made, the fruits are to ensue;
That profit's yet to come 'tween me and you.   10
Good night.
Othello, Desdemona, and
Attendants depart

Enter Iago

CASSIO. Welcome, Iago; we must to the watch.
IAGO. Not this hour, lieutenant; 'tis not yet ten
o'clock. Our general cast us thus early for the love
of his Desdemona; who let us not therefore blame:
he hath not yet made wanton the night with her, and
she is sport for Jove.
CASSIO. She's a most exquisite lady.
IAGO. And, I'll warrant her, full of game.
CASSIO. Indeed she's a most fresh and delicate creature.   20

IAGO. What an eye she has! methinks it sounds a parley
to provocation.
CASSIO. An inviting eye; and yet methinks right
modest.
IAGO. And when she speaks, is it not an alarum to love?
CASSIO. She is indeed perfection.
IAGO. Well, happiness to their sheets! Come, lieutenant, I have a stoup of wine; and here without
are a brace of Cyprus gallants that would fain have
a measure to the health of black Othello.   30
CASSIO. Not tonight, good Iago; I have very poor and
unhappy brains for drinking. I could well wish
courtesy would invent some other custom of entertainment.
IAGO. O, they are our friends—but one cup; I'll drink
for you.
CASSIO. I have drunk but one cup tonight, and that
was craftily qualified too, and behold what innova-
tion it makes here. I am unfortunate in the infirmity
and dare not task my weakness with any more.   40
IAGO. What, man! 'Tis a night of revels; the gallants
desire it.
CASSIO. Where are they?
IAGO. Here at the door; I pray you, call them in.
CASSIO. I'll do't; but it dislikes me.   *Goes*
IAGO. If I can fasten but one cup upon him,
With that which he hath drunk tonight already,
He'll be as full of quarrel and offence
As my young mistress' dog. Now my sick fool
Roderigo,
Whom love hath turned almost the wrong side out,   50
To Desdemona hath tonight caroused
Potations pottle-deep; and he's to watch.
Three else of Cyprus, noble swelling spirits,
That hold their honours in a wary distance,
The very elements of this warlike isle,
Have I tonight flustered with flowing cups;
And they watch too. Now, 'mongst this flock of
drunkards,
Am I to put our Cassio in some action
That may offend the isle. But here they come;
If consequence do but approve my dream,   60
My boat sails freely, both with wind and stream.

Re-enter Cassio; with him Montano and Gentlemen;
Servants following with wine

CASSIO. 'Fore God, they have given me a rouse
already.
MONTANO. Good faith, a little one; not past a pint, as
I am a soldier.
IAGO. Some wine, ho!
[*sings*] And let me the canakin clink, clink;
And let me the canakin clink;
A soldier's a man;
O, man's life's but a span;   70
Why, then, let a soldier drink.
Some wine, boys!
CASSIO. 'Fore God, an excellent song.
IAGO. I learned it in England, where indeed they are
most potent in potting; your Dane, your German,
and your swag-bellied Hollander—Drink, ho!—are
nothing to your English.
CASSIO. Is your Englishman so exquisite in his
drinking?
IAGO. Why, he drinks you with facility your Dane   80
dead drunk; he sweats not to overthrow your

Almain; he gives your Hollander a vomit ere the next pottle can be filled.

CASSIO. To the health of our general!

MONTANO. I am for it, lieutenant, and I'll do you justice.

IAGO. O sweet England!

[sings] King Stephen was and-a worthy peer,
    His breeches cost him but a crown;
    He held them sixpence all too dear,   90
      With that he called the tailor lown.

    He was a wight of high renown,
      And thou art but of low degree;
    'Tis pride that pulls the country down;
      Then take thy auld cloak about thee.

Some wine, ho!

CASSIO. Why, this is a more exquisite song than the other.

IAGO. Will you hear't again?

CASSIO. No; for I hold him to be unworthy of his place   100
that does those things. Well, God's above all; and
there be souls must be saved, and there be souls must
not be saved.

IAGO. It's true, good lieutenant.

CASSIO. For mine own part—no offence to the
general, nor any man of quality—I hope to be saved.

IAGO. And so do I too, lieutenant.

CASSIO. Ay, but, by your leave, not before me; the
lieutenant is to be saved before the ancient. Let's
have no more of this; let's to our affairs. God forgive   110
us our sins! Gentlemen, let's look to our business.
Do not think, gentlemen, I am drunk: this is my
ancient; this is my right hand, and this is my left
hand. I am not drunk now: I can stand well enough,
and I speak well enough.

ALL. Excellent well.

CASSIO. Why, very well then; you must not think then
that I am drunk.   *Goes out*

MONTANO. To th'platform, masters; come, let's set the
watch.   120

IAGO. You see this fellow that is gone before;
He is a soldier fit to stand by Caesar
And give direction; and do but see his vice—
'Tis to his virtue a just equinox,
The one as long as th'other. 'Tis pity of him.
I fear the trust Othello puts him in,
On some odd time of his infirmity,
Will shake this island.   But is he often thus?

IAGO. 'Tis evermore the prologue to his sleep:
He'll watch the horologe a double set,   130
If drink rock not his cradle.

MONTANO.   It were well
The general were put in mind of it.
Perhaps he sees it not, or his good nature
Prizes the virtue that appears in Cassio,
And looks not on his evil: is not this true?

Enter Roderigo

IAGO [aside]. How, now, Roderigo!
I pray you, after the lieutenant; go.   *Roderigo goes*

MONTANO. And 'tis great pity that the noble Moor
Should hazard such a place as his own second
With one of an ingraft infirmity: 140
It were an honest action to say
So to the Moor.

IAGO.   Not I, for this fair island:
I do love Cassio well, and would do much
To cure him of this evil.[a cry within], 'Help! Help!'
                    But hark! what noise?

Re-enter Cassio, pursuing Roderigo

CASSIO. 'Zounds, you rogue, you rascal!

MONTANO. What's the matter, lieutenant?

CASSIO. A knave teach me my duty! I'll beat the knave
Into a twiggen bottle.

RODERIGO.   Beat me!

CASSIO.   Dost prate, rogue?
                  Striking Roderigo

MONTANO. Nay, good lieutenant; pray sir, hold your hand.

CASSIO. Let go, sir, or I'll knock you o'er the mazard.   150

MONTANO. Come, come, you're drunk.

CASSIO. Drunk!   *They fight*

IAGO [aside]. Away, I say; go out and cry a mutiny.
                  Roderigo goes
[aloud] Nay, good lieutenant! God's will, gentlemen!
Help, ho!—lieutenant—sir—Montano—sir—
Help, masters!—Here's a goodly watch indeed!
                    A bell rings
Who's that that rings the bell?—Diablo, ho!
The town will rise. God's will, lieutenant, hold;
You will be shamed for ever.

Re-enter Othello and Attendants

OTHELLO. What is the matter here?

MONTANO.   'Zounds, I bleed still.   160
I am hurt to th'death. He dies.
                Assailing Cassio again

OTHELLO.   Hold, for your lives!

IAGO. Hold, ho! Lieutenant—sir—Montano—
    gentlemen—
Have you forgot all sense of place and duty?
The general speaks to you; hold, hold, for shame!

OTHELLO. Why, how now, ho! from whence ariseth
    this?
Are we turned Turks, and to ourselves do that
Which heaven hath forbid the Ottomites?
For Christian shame, put by this barbarous brawl.
He that stirs next to carve for his own rage
Holds his soul light; he dies upon his motion.   170
Silence that dreadful bell; it frights the isle
From her propriety. What is the matter, masters?
Honest Iago, that look'st dead with grieving,
Speak who began this; on thy love, I charge thee.

IAGO. I do not know. Friends all but now, even now,
In quarter and in terms like bride and groom
Divesting them for bed; and then, but now,
As if some planet had unwitted men,
Swords out, and tilting one at other's breast,
In opposition bloody. I cannot speak   180
Any beginning to this peevish odds;
And would in action glorious I had lost
Those legs that brought me to a part of it!

OTHELLO. How comes it, Michael, you are thus
    forgot?

CASSIO. I pray you, pardon me; I cannot speak.

OTHELLO. Worthy Montano, you were wont be civil;
The gravity and stillness of your youth
The world hath noted, and your name is great
In mouths of wisest censure: what's the matter
That you unlace your reputation thus,   190

And spend your rich opinion for the name
Of a night-brawler? give me answer to it.
MONTANO. Worthy Othello, I am hurt to danger;
Your officer, Iago, can inform you—
While I spare speech, which something now offends
    me—
Of all that I do know; nor know I aught
By me that's said or done amiss this night—
Unless self-charity be sometimes a vice,
And to defend ourselves it be a sin
When violence assails us.
OTHELLO.   Now, by heaven,   200
My blood begins my safer guides to rule,
And passion, having my best judgement collied,
Assays to lead the way. If I once stir,
Or do but lift this arm, the best of you
Shall sink in my rebuke. Give me to know
How this foul rout began, who set it on,
And he that is approved in this offence,
Though he had twinned with me, both at a birth,
Shall lose me. What! in a town of war,
Yet wild, the people's hearts brimful of fear,   210
To manage private and domestic quarrel,
In night, and on the court and guard of safety!
'Tis monstrous. Iago, who began't?
MONTANO. If partially affined, or leagued in office,
Thou dost deliver more or less than truth,
Thou art no soldier.
IAGO.   Touch me not so near;
I had rather have this tongue cut from my mouth
Than it should do offence to Michael Cassio;
Yet, I persuade myself, to speak the truth
Shall nothing wrong him. This it is, general.   220
Montano and myself being in speech,
There comes a fellow crying out for help,
And Cassio following with determined sword
To execute upon him. Sir, this gentleman
Steps in to Cassio and entreats his pause;
Myself the crying fellow did pursue,
Lest by his clamour—as it so fell out—
The town might fall in fright; he, swift of foot,
Outran my purpose; and I returned the rather
For that I heard the clink and fall of swords,   230
And Cassio high in oath; which till tonight
I ne'er might say before. When I came back—
For this was brief—I found them close together
At blow and thrust; even as again they were
When you yourself did part them.
More of this matter can I not report;
But men are men; the best sometimes forget.
Though Cassio did some little wrong to him,
As men in rage strike those that wish them best,
Yet surely Cassio, I believe, received   240
From him that fled some strange indignity,
Which patiencē could not pass.
OTHELLO.   I know, Iago,
Thy honesty and love doth mince this matter,
Making it light to Cassio. Cassio, I love thee;
But never more be officer of mine.

Re-enter Desdemona, attended

Look if my gentle love be not raised up!
I'll make thee an example.
DESDEMONA.   What's the matter?
OTHELLO. All's well, dear sweeting; come away to
    bed.

Sir, for your hurts, myself will be your surgeon.
                              They lead Montano away
Iago, look with care about the town,   250
And silence those whom this vile brawl distracted.
Come, Desdemona: 'tis the soldiers' life
To have their balmy slumbers waked with strife.
                              All but Iago and Cassio depart
IAGO. What, are you hurt, lieutenant?
CASSIO. Ay, past all surgery.
IAGO. Marry, heaven forbid!
CASSIO. Reputation, reputation, reputation! O, I have
lost my reputation! I have lost the immortal part of
myself, and what remains is bestial. My reputation,
Iago, my reputation!   260
IAGO. As I am an honest man, I thought you had
received some bodily wound; there is more sense in
that than in reputation. Reputation is an idle and
most false imposition; oft got without merit and lost
without deserving. You have lost no reputation at
all, unless you repute yourself such a loser. What,
man! there are ways to recover the general again.
You are but now cast in his mood, a punishment
more in policy than in malice; even so as one would
beat his offenceless dog to affright an imperious lion.   270
Sue to him again, and he's yours.
CASSIO. I will rather sue to be despised than to deceive
so good a commander with so light, so drunken,
and so indiscreet an officer. Drunk! and speak
parrot! and squabble! swagger! swear! and discourse
fustian with one's own shadow! O thou invisible
spirit of wine, if thou hast no name to be known
by, let us call thee devil!
IAGO. What was he that you followed with your
sword? What had he done to you?   280
CASSIO. I know not.
IAGO. Is't possible?
CASSIO. I remember a mass of things, but nothing
distinctly; a quarrel, but nothing wherefore. O, that
men should put an enemy in their mouths to steal
away their brains! that we should, with joy,
pleasance, revel and applause, transform ourselves
into beasts!
IAGO. Why, but you are now well enough. How
came you thus recovered?   290
CASSIO. It hath pleased the devil drunkenness to give
place to the devil wrath: one unperfectness shows
me another, to make me frankly despise myself.
IAGO. Come, you are too severe a moraller. As the
time, the place, and the condition of this country
stands, I could heartily wish this had not befallen;
but since it is as it is, mend it for your own good.
CASSIO. I will ask him for my place again; he shall tell
me I am a drunkard! Had I as many mouths as
Hydra, such an answer would stop them all. To be   300
now a sensible man, by and by a fool, and presently
a beast! O strange! Every inordinate cup is unblest,
and the ingredience is a devil.
IAGO. Come, come, wine is a good familiar creature,
if it be well used; exclaim no more against it. And,
good lieutenant, I think you think I love you.
CASSIO. I have well approved it, sir. I drunk!
IAGO. You or any man living may be drunk at a time.
I'll tell you what you shall do. Our general's wife is
now the general: I may say so in this respect, for that   310
he hath devoted and given up himself to the con-
templation, mark and denotement of her parts and

graces. Confess yourself freely to her; importune her help to put you in your place again. She is of so free, so kind, so apt, so blessed a disposition, she holds it a vice in her goodness not to do more than she is requested. This broken joint between you and her husband entreat her to splinter; and, my fortunes against any lay worth naming, this crack of your love shall grow stronger than it was before. 320

CASSIO. You advise me well.

IAGO. I protest, in the sincerity of love and honest kindness.

CASSIO. I think it freely; and betimes in the morning I will beseech the virtuous Desdemona to undertake for me. I am desperate of my fortunes if they check me here.

IAGO. You are in the right. Good night, lieutenant; I must to the watch.

CASSIO. Good night, honest Iago. *Goes* 330

IAGO. And what's he then that says I play the villain, When this advice I give is free and honest, Probal to thinking, and indeed the course To win the Moor again? For 'tis most easy Th'inclining Desdemona to subdue In any honest suit. She's framed as fruitful As the free elements. And then for her To win the Moor, were't to renounce his baptism, All seals and symbols of redeemèd sin, His soul is so enfettered to her love 340 That she may make, unmake, do what she list, Even as her appetite shall play the god With his weak function. How am I then a villain To counsel Cassio to this parallel course, Directly to his good? Divinity of hell! When devils will the blackest sins put on, They do suggest at first with heavenly shows, As I do now; for while this honest fool Plies Desdemona to repair his fortunes, And she for him pleads strongly to the Moor, 350 I'll pour this pestilence into his ear, That she repeals him for her body's lust; And by how much she strives to do him good, She shall undo her credit with the Moor. So will I turn her virtue into pitch, And out of her own goodness make the net That shall enmesh them all.

Enter Roderigo

How now, Roderigo!

RODERIGO. I do follow here in the chase, not like a hound that hunts, but one that fills up the cry. My money is almost spent; I have been tonight exceed- 360 ingly well cudgelled; and I think the issue will be, I shall have so much experience for my pains; and so, with no money at all and a little more wit, return again to Venice.

IAGO. How poor are they that have not patience! What wound did ever heal but by degrees? Thou know'st we work by wit and not by witchcraft, And wit depends on dilatory time. Does't not go well? Cassio hath beaten thee, And thou by that small hurt hast cashiered Cassio. 370 Though other things grow fair against the sun, Yet fruits that blossom first will first be ripe. Content thyself awhile. By th'mass, 'tis morning; Pleasure and action make the hours seem short.

Retire thee; go where thou art billeted. Away, I say; thou shalt know more hereafter. Nay, get thee gone. *Roderigo goes* Two things are to be done: My wife must move for Cassio to her mistress— I'll set her on— Myself the while to draw the Moor apart, 380 And bring him jump when he may Cassio find Soliciting his wife. Ay, that's the way; Dull not device by coldness and delay. *Goes*

ACT 3
Scene 1: *The citadel. Outside Othello's lodging*

Enter Cassio and some Musicians

CASSIO. Masters, play here; I will content your pains; Something that's brief; and bid 'Good morrow, general'. *Music*

Enter Clown

CLOWN. Why, masters, have your instruments been in Naples, that they speak i'th'nose thus?

1 MUSICIAN. How, sir, how?

CLOWN. Are these, I pray you, wind instruments?

1 MUSICIAN. Ay, marry, are they, sir.

CLOWN. O, thereby hangs a tail.

1 MUSICIAN. Whereby hangs a tale, sir?

CLOWN. Marry, sir, by many a wind instrument that 10 I know. But, masters, here's money for you; and the general so likes your music, that he desires you, for love's sake, to make no more noise with it.

1 MUSICIAN. Well, sir, we will not.

CLOWN. If you have any music that may not be heard, to't again; but, as they say, to hear music the general does not greatly care.

1 MUSICIAN. We have none such, sir.

CLOWN. Then put up your pipes in your bag, for I'll away. Go; vanish into air; away! *Musicians go* 20

CASSIO. Dost thou hear, my honest friend?

CLOWN. No, I hear not your honest friend; I hear you.

CASSIO. Prithee, keep up thy quillets. There's a poor piece of gold for thee: if the gentlewoman that attends the general's wife be stirring, tell her there's one Cassio entreats her a little favour of speech. Wilt thou do this?

CLOWN. She is stirring, sir; if she will stir hither, I shall seem to notify unto her.

CASSIO. Do, good my friend. *Clown goes*

Enter Iago

In happy time, Iago. 30

IAGO. You have not been abed then?

CASSIO. Why, no; the day had broke before we parted. I have made bold, Iago, To send in to your wife: my suit to her Is that she will to virtuous Desdemona Procure me some access.

IAGO. I'll send her to you presently; And I'll devise a mean to draw the Moor Out of the way, that your converse and business May be more free.

CASSIO. I humbly thank you for't. [*Iago goes*] I never knew 40 A Florentine more kind and honest.

Enter Emilia

EMILIA. Good morrow, good lieutenant: I am sorry
For your displeasure; but all will sure be well.
The general and his wife are talking of it,
And she speaks for you stoutly. The Moor replies
That he you hurt is of great fame in Cyprus
And great affinity, and that in wholesome wisdom
He might not but refuse you; but he protests he
  loves you,
And needs no other suitor but his liking
To take the safest occasion by the front   50
To bring you in again.
CASSIO.   Yet, I beseech you,
If you think fit, or that it may be done,
Give me advantage of some brief discourse
With Desdemon alone.
EMILIA.   Pray you, come in;
I will bestow you where you shall have time
To speak your bosom freely.
CASSIO   I am much bound to you. *They go*

Scene 2: *A room in the citadel*

Enter Othello, Iago, and Gentlemen

OTHELLO. These letters give, Iago, to the pilot,
And by him do my duties to the senate.
That done, I will be walking on the works;
Repair there to me.
IAGO.   Well, my good lord, I'll do't. *Goes*
OTHELLO. This fortification, gentlemen, shall we see't?
GENTLEMEN. We'll wait upon your lordship. *They go*

Scene 3: *Before the citadel*

Enter Desdemona, Cassio, and Emilia

DESDEMONA. Be thou assured, good Cassio, I will do
All my abilities in thy behalf.
EMILIA. Good madam, do; I warrant it grieves my
  husband
As if the case were his.
DESDEMONA. O, that's an honest fellow. Do not doubt,
  Cassio,
But I will have my lord and you again
As friendly as you were.
CASSIO.   Bounteous madam,
Whatever shall become of Michael Cassio,
He's never anything but your true servant.
DESDEMONA. I know't; I thank you. You do love my
  lord;   10
You have known him long; and be you well assured
He shall in strangeness stand no farther off
Than in a politic distance.
CASSIO.   Ay, but, lady,
That policy may either last so long,
Or feed upon such nice and waterish diet,
Or breed itself so out of circumstance,
That, I being absent, and my place supplied,
My general will forget my love and service.
DESDEMONA. Do not doubt that: before Emilia here
I give thee warrant of thy place. Assure thee,   20
If I do vow a friendship, I'll perform it
To the last article. My lord shall never rest:
I'll watch him tame, and talk him out of patience;
His bed shall seem a school, his board a shrift;
I'll intermingle everything he does
With Cassio's suit. Therefore be merry, Cassio;
For thy solicitor shall rather die

Than give thy cause away.

Enter Othello and Iago, at a distance

EMILIA. Madam, here comes my lord.
CASSIO. Madam, I'll take my leave.   30
DESDEMONA. Why, stay, and hear me speak.
CASSIO. Madam, not now: I am very ill at ease,
Unfit for mine own purposes.
DESDEMONA. Well, do your discretion.   *Cassio goes*
IAGO. Ha! I like not that.
OTHELLO. What dost thou say?
IAGO. Nothing, my lord; or if—I know not what.
OTHELLO. Was not that Cassio parted from my wife?
IAGO. Cassio, my lord! No, sure, I cannot think it,
That he would steal away so guilty-like,   40
Seeing you coming.
OTHELLO.   I do believe 'twas he.
DESDEMONA. How now, my lord!
I have been talking with a suitor here,
A man that languishes in your displeasure.
OTHELLO. Who is't you mean?
DESDEMONA. Why, your lieutenant, Cassio. Good
  my lord,
If I have any grace or power to move you,
His present reconciliation take;
For if he be not one that truly loves you,
That errs in ignorance and not in cunning,   50
I have no judgement in an honest face.
I prithee, call him back.
OTHELLO.   Went he hence now?
DESDEMONA. Ay, sooth; so humbled,
That he hath left part of his grief with me
To suffer with him. Good love, call him back.
OTHELLO. Not now, sweet Desdemon; some other
  time.
DESDEMONA. But shall't be shortly?
OTHELLO.   The sooner, sweet, for you.
DESDEMONA. Shall't be tonight at supper?
OTHELLO.   No, not tonight.
DESDEMONA. Tomorrow dinner then?
OTHELLO.   I shall not dine at home:
I meet the captains at the citadel.   60
DESDEMONA. Why then, tomorrow night; or Tuesday
  morn;
On Tuesday noon, or night; On Wednesday morn.
I prithee, name the time; but let it not
Exceed three days. In faith, he's penitent;
And yet his trespass, in our common reason—
Save that, they say, the wars must make example
Out of their best—is not almost a fault
T'incur a private check. When shall he come?
Tell me, Othello. I wonder in my soul
What you would ask me that I should deny,   70
Or stand so mammering on. What! Michael Cassio,
That came a-wooing with you, and so many a time,
When I have spoke of you dispraisingly,
Hath ta'en your part—to have so much to do
To bring him in! Trust me, I could do much—
OTHELLO. Prithee, no more. Let him come when he
  will;
I will deny thee nothing.
DESDEMONA.   Why, this is not a boon;
'Tis as I should entreat you wear your gloves,
Or feed on nourishing dishes, or keep you warm,
Or sue to you to do peculiar profit   80
To your own person. Nay, when I have a suit

Wherein I mean to touch your love indeed,
It shall be full of poise and difficult weight,
And fearful to be granted.
OTHELLO.   I will deny thee nothing.
Whereon, I do beseech thee, grant me this,
To leave me but a little to myself.
DESDEMONA. Shall I deny you? no; farewell, my lord.
OTHELLO. Farewell, my Desdemona, I'll come
straight.
DESDEMONA. Emilia, come. Be as your fancies teach
you;
Whate'er you be, I am obedient.   90
                Desdemona and Emilia go
OTHELLO. Excellent wretch! Perdition catch my soul
But I do love thee; and when I love thee not
Chaos is come again.
IAGO.   My noble lord—
OTHELLO. What dost thou say, Iago?
IAGO.   Did Michael Cassio,
When you wooed my lady, know of your love?
OTHELLO. He did, from first to last. Why dost thou
ask?
IAGO. But for a satisfaction of my thought;
No further harm.
OTHELLO.   Why of thy thought, Iago?
IAGO. I did not think he had been acquainted with her.
OTHELLO. O, yes, and went between us very oft.   100
IAGO. Indeed!
OTHELLO. Indeed? ay, indeed. Discern'st thou aught
in that?
Is he not honest?
IAGO. Honest, my lord?
OTHELLO. Honest? ay, honest.
IAGO. My lord, for aught I know.
OTHELLO. What dost thou think?
IAGO. Think, my lord?
OTHELLO. Think, my lord! Alas, thou echo'st me,
As if there were some monster in thy thought   110
Too hideous to be shown. Thou dost mean some-
thing:
I heard thee say even now, thou likedst not that,
When Cassio left my wife. What didst not like?
And when I told thee he was of my counsel
In my whole course of wooing, thou criedst
'Indeed!'
And didst contract and purse thy brow together,
As if thou then hadst shut up in thy brain
Some horrible conceit. If thou dost love me,
Show me thy thought.
IAGO. My lord, you know I love you.
OTHELLO.   I think thou dost;   120
And for I know thou'rt full of love, and honest,
And weigh'st thy words before thou giv'st them
breath,
Therefore these stops of thine fright me the more:
For such things in a false disloyal knave
Are tricks of custom; but in a man that's just
They're close dilations, working from the heart
That passion cannot rule.
IAGO.   For Michael Cassio,
I dare be sworn I think that he is honest.
OTHELLO. I think so too.
IAGO.   Men should be what they seem;
Or those that be not, would they might seem none!   130
OTHELLO. Certain, men should be what they seem.
IAGO. Why then, I think Cassio's an honest man.

OTHELLO. Nay, yet there's more in this.
I prithee, speak to me as to thy thinkings,
As thou dost ruminate, and give thy worst of
thoughts
The worst of words.
IAGO.   Good my lord, pardon me:
Though I am bound to every act of duty,
I am not bound to that all slaves are free to.
Utter my thoughts! Why, say they are vile and
false—
As where's that palace whereinto foul things   140
Sometimes intrude not? who has a breast so pure,
But some uncleanly apprehensions
Keep leets and law-days, and in session sit
With meditations lawful?
OTHELLO. Thou dost conspire against thy friend, Iago,
If thou but think'st him wronged and mak'st his ear
A stranger to thy thoughts.
IAGO.   I do beseech you—
Though I perchance am vicious in my guess,
As, I confess, it is my nature's plague
To spy into abuses, and oft my jealousy   150
Shapes faults that are not—that your wisdom then,
From one that so imperfectly conceits,
Would take no notice, nor build yourself a trouble
Out of his scattering and unsure observance.
It were not for your quiet nor your good,
Nor for my manhood, honesty, or wisdom,
To let you know my thoughts.
OTHELLO.   What dost thou mean?
IAGO. Good name in man and woman, dear my lord,
Is the immediate jewel of their souls:
Who steals my purse steals trash—'tis something,
nothing;   160
'Twas mine, 'tis his, and has been slave to thousands;
But he that filches from me my good name
Robs me of that which not enriches him
And makes me poor indeed.
OTHELLO.   I'll know thy thoughts!
IAGO. You cannot, if my heart were in your hand;
Nor shall not, while 'tis in my custody.
OTHELLO. Ha!
IAGO.   O, beware, my lord, of jealousy;
It is the green-eyed monster, which doth mock
The meat it feeds on: that cuckold lives in bliss
Who, certain of his fate, loves not his wronger;   170
But, O, what damnéd minutes tells he o'er
Who dotes, yet doubts, suspects, yet fondly loves!
OTHELLO. O misery!
IAGO. Poor and content is rich, and rich enough;
But riches fineless is as poor as winter
To him that ever fears he shall be poor.
Good heaven the souls of all my tribe defend
From jealousy!
OTHELLO.   Why, why is this?
Think'st thou I'ld make a life of jealousy,
To follow still the changes of the moon   180
With fresh suspicions? No; to be once in doubt
Is once resolved. Exchange me for a goat,
When I shall turn the business of my soul
To such exsufflicate and blown surmise
Matching thy inference. 'Tis not to make me
jealous
To say my wife is fair, loves company,
Is free of speech, sings, plays and dances well;
Where virtue is, these are more virtuous;

Nor from mine own weak merits will I draw
The smallest fear or doubt of her revolt;
For she had eyes and chose me. No, Iago:
I'll see before I doubt; when I doubt, prove;
And on the proof, there is no more but this,
Away at once with love or jealousy!
IAGO. I am glad of it; for now I shall have reason
To show the love and duty that I bear you
With franker spirit. Therefore, as I am bound,
Receive it from me. I speak not yet of proof.
Look to your wife; observe her well with Cassio;
Wear your eye thus not jealous nor secure:
I would not have your free and noble nature
Out of self-bounty be abused. Look to't:
I know our country disposition well;
In Venice they do let heaven see the pranks
They dare not show their husbands; their best
    conscience
Is not to leave't undone, but keep't unknown.
OTHELLO. Dost thou say so?
IAGO. She did deceive her father, marrying you;
And when she seemed to shake and fear your looks,
She loved them most.
OTHELLO.   And so she did.
IAGO.   Why then,
She that so young could give out such a
    seeming,
To seel her father's eyes up close as oak,
He thought 'twas witchcraft—but I am much to
    blame;
I humbly do beseech you of your pardon
For too much loving you.
OTHELLO.   I am bound to thee for ever.
IAGO. I see this hath a little dashed your spirits.
OTHELLO. Not a jot, not a jot.
IAGO.   In faith, I fear it has.
I hope you will consider what is spoke
Comes from my love. But I do see you're moved.
I am to pray you not to strain my speech
To grosser issues nor to larger reach
Than to suspicion.
OTHELLO. I will not.
IAGO.   Should you do so, my lord,
My speech should fall into such vile success
As my thought aimed not at. Cassio's my worthy
    friend—
My lord, I see you're moved.
OTHELLO.   No, not much moved:
I do not think but Desdemona's honest.
IAGO. Long live she so! and long live you to think so!
OTHELLO. And yet, how nature erring from itself—
IAGO. Ay, there's the point: as—to be bold with you—
Not to affect many proposéd matches
Of her own clime, complexion, and degree,
Whereto we see in all things nature tends—
Foh! one may smell, in such, a will most rank,
Foul disproportion, thoughts unnatural.
But pardon me: I do not in position
Distinctly speak of her; though I may fear
Her will, recoiling to her better judgement,
May fall to match you with her country forms,
And happily repent.
OTHELLO.   Farewell, farewell.
If more thou dost perceive, let me know more;
Set on thy wife to observe. Leave me, Iago.
IAGO [going]. My lord, I take my leave.

OTHELLO. Why did I marry? This honest creature
    doubtless
Sees and knows more, much more, than he unfolds.
IAGO [returning]. My lord, I would I might entreat
    your honour
To scan this thing no further. Leave it to time:
Although 'tis fit that Cassio have his place—
For sure he fills it up with great ability—
Yet if you please to hold him off awhile,
You shall by that perceive him and his means;
Note if your lady strain his entertainment
With any strong or vehement importunity—
Much will be seen in that. In the mean time,
Let me be thought too busy in my fears—
As worthy cause I have to fear I am—
And hold her free, I do beseech your honour.
OTHELLO. Fear not my government.
IAGO. I once more take my leave.   Goes
OTHELLO. This fellow's of exceeding honesty,
And knows all qualities, with a learnéd spirit,
Of human dealings. If I do prove her haggard,
Though that her jesses were my dear heart-strings,
I'ld whistle her off and let her down the wind
To prey at fortune. Haply, for I am black
And have not those soft parts of conversation
That chamberers have, or for I am declined
Into the vale of years—yet that's not much—
She's gone; I am abused, and my relief
Must be to loathe her. O curse of marriage,
That we can call these delicate creatures ours,
And not their appetites! I had rather be a toad,
And live upon the vapour of a dungeon,
Than keep a corner in the thing I love
For others' uses. Yet, 'tis the plague of great ones;
Prerogatived are they less than the base;
'Tis destiny unshunnable, like death:
Even then this forkéd plague is fated to us
When we do quicken. Look where she comes:

Re-enter Desdemona and Emilia

If she be false, O, then heaven mocks itself!
I'll not believe't.
DESDEMONA.   How now, my dear Othello!
Your dinner, and the generous islanders
By you invited, do attend your presence.
OTHELLO. I am to blame.
DESDEMONA.   Why do you speak so faintly?
Are you not well?
OTHELLO. I have a pain upon my forehead here.
DESDEMONA. Faith, that's with watching; 'twill away
    again:
Let me but bind it hard, within this hour
It will be well.
OTHELLO.   Your napkin is too little;
          *He puts the handkerchief from
                    him; and she drops it*
Let it alone. Come, I'll go in with you.
DESDEMONA. I am very sorry that you are not well.
                              Othello and Desdemona go
EMILIA. I am glad I've found this napkin:
This was her first remembrance from the Moor;
My wayward husband hath a hundred times
Wooed me to steal it; but she so loves the token,
For he conjured her she should ever keep it,
That she reserves it evermore about her
To kiss and talk to. I'll have the work ta'en out,

And give't Iago. What he will do with it
Heaven knows, not I: 300
I nothing but to please his fantasy.

Re-enter Iago

IAGO. How now! What do you here alone?
EMILIA. Do not you chide; I have a thing for you.
IAGO. A thing for me? it is a common thing—
EMILIA. Ha!
IAGO. To have a foolish wife.
EMILIA. O, is that all? What will you give me now
  For that same handkerchief?
IAGO.   What handkerchief?
EMILIA. What handkerchief!
  Why, that the Moor first gave to Desdemona;   310
  That which so often you did bid me steal.
IAGO. Hast stole it from her?
EMILIA. No, faith; she let it drop by negligence,
  And, to th'advantage, I being here took't up.
  Look, here it is.
IAGO.   A good wench; give it me.
EMILIA. What will you do with't, that you've been so
    earnest
  To have me filch it?
IAGO [*snatching it*].   Why, what's that to you?
EMILIA. If't be not for some purpose of import,
  Give't me again. Poor lady, she'll run mad
  When she shall lack it.   320
IAGO. Be not acknown on't; I have use for it.
  Go, leave me.   *Emilia goes*
  I will in Cassio's lodging lose this napkin,
  And let him find it. Trifles light as air
  Are to the jealous confirmations strong
  As proofs of Holy Writ: this may do something.
  The Moor already changes with my poison:
  Dangerous conceits are in their natures poisons
  Which at the first are scarce found to distaste
  But, with a little act upon the blood,   330
  Burn like the mines of sulphur.

Re-enter Othello

                                    I did say so:
  Look where he comes! Not poppy, nor
    mandragora,
  Nor all the drowsy syrups of the world,
  Shall ever medicine thee to that sweet sleep
  Which thou owedst yesterday.
OTHELLO.   Ha! Ha! false to me?
IAGO. Why, how now, general! no more of that.
OTHELLO. Avaunt! be gone! thou hast set me on the
    rack:
  I swear 'tis better to be much abused
  Than but to know't a little.
IAGO.   How now, my lord!
OTHELLO. What sense had I of her stolen hours of lust? 340
  I saw't not, thought it not, it harmed not me:
  I slept the next night well, fed well, was merry;
  I found not Cassio's kisses on her lips.
  He that is robbed, not wanting what is stolen,
  Let him not know't, and he's not robbed at all.
IAGO. I am sorry to hear this.
OTHELLO. I had been happy, if the general camp,
  Pioneers and all, had tasted her sweet body,
  So I had nothing known. O, now for ever
  Farewell the tranquil mind! farewell content!   350
  Farewell the pluméd troops, and the big wars

That make ambition virtue—O, farewell!
Farewell the neighing steed and the shrill trump,
The spirit-stirring drum, th'ear-piercing fife,
The royal banner, and all quality,
Pride, pomp, and circumstance, of glorious war!
And, O you mortal engines, whose rude throats
Th'immortal Jove's dread clamours counterfeit,
Farewell! Othello's occupation's gone!
IAGO. Is't possible, my lord?   360
OTHELLO. Villain, be sure thou prove my love a
    whore;
  Be sure of it; give me the ocular proof;
                                Takes him by the throat
  Or, by the worth of mine eternal soul,
  Thou hadst been better have been born a dog
  Than answer my waked wrath!
IAGO.   Is't come to this?
OTHELLO. Make me to see't; or, at the least, so prove it,
  That the probation bear no hinge nor loop
  To hang a doubt on; or woe upon thy life!
IAGO. My noble lord—
OTHELLO. If thou dost slander her and torture me,   370
  Never pray more; abandon all remorse;
  On horror's head horrors accumulate;
  Do deeds to make heaven weep, all earth amazed;
  For nothing canst thou to damnation add
  Greater than that.
IAGO.   O grace! O heaven forgive me!
  Are you a man? have you a soul, or sense?
  God bu'y you; take mine office. O wretched fool,
  That liv'st to make thine honesty a vice!
  O monstrous world! Take note, take note, O world,
  To be direct and honest is not safe.   380
  I thank you for this profit, and from hence
  I'll love no friend sith love breeds such offence.
OTHELLO. Nay, stay; thou shouldst be honest.
IAGO. I should be wise; for honesty's a fool,
  And loses that it works for.
OTHELLO.   By the world,
  I think my wife be honest, and think she is not;
  I think that thou art just, and think thou art not;
  I'll have some proof. Her name, that was as fresh
  As Dian's visage, is now begrimed and black
  As mine own face. If there be cords, or knives,   390
  Poison, or fire, or suffocating streams,
  I'll not endure it. Would I were satisfied!
IAGO. I see, sir, you are eaten up with passion:
  I do repent me that I put it to you.
  You would be satisfied?
OTHELLO.   Would! nay, and will.
IAGO. And may; but how? how satisfied, my lord?
  Would you, the supervisor, grossly gape on—
  Behold her topped?
OTHELLO.   Death and damnation! O!
IAGO. It were a tedious difficulty, I think,
  To bring them to that prospect: damn them then, 400
  If ever mortal eyes do see them bolster
  More than their own! What then? how then?
  What shall I say? Where's satisfaction?
  It is impossible you should see this,
  Were they as prime as goats, as hot as monkeys,
  As salt as wolves in pride, and fools as gross
  As ignorance made drunk. But yet, I say,
  If imputation and strong circumstance,
  Which lead directly to the door of truth,
  Will give you satisfaction, you might have't.   410

OTHELLO. Give me a living reason she's disloyal.
IAGO. I do not like the office;
But sith I am entered in this cause so far,
Pricked to't by foolish honesty and love,
I will go on. I lay with Cassio lately,
And being troubled with a raging tooth,
I could not sleep.
There are a kind of men so loose of soul,
That in their sleeps will mutter their affairs:
One of this kind is Cassio.   420
In sleep I heard him say 'Sweet Desdemona,
Let us be wary, let us hide our loves';
And then, sir, would he gripe and wring my hand,
Cry 'O sweet creature!' and then kiss me hard,
As if he plucked up kisses by the roots,
That grew upon my lips; then laid his leg
Over my thigh, and sighed, and kissed, and then
Cried 'Cursèd fate that gave thee to the Moor!'
OTHELLO. O monstrous! monstrous!
IAGO.   Nay, this was but his dream.
OTHELLO. But this denoted a foregone conclusion: 430
'Tis a shrewd doubt, though it be but a dream.
IAGO. And this may help to thicken other proofs
That do demonstrate thinly.
OTHELLO.   I'll tear her all to pieces.
IAGO. Nay, but be wise: yet we see nothing done;
She may be honest yet. Tell me but this:
Have you not sometimes seen a handkerchief
Spotted with strawberries in your wife's hand?
OTHELLO. I gave her such a one; 'twas my first gift.
IAGO. I know not that; but such a handkerchief—
I am sure it was your wife's—did I today   440
See Cassio wipe his beard with.
OTHELLO.   If it be that—
IAGO. If it be that, or any that was hers,
It speaks against her with the other proofs.
OTHELLO. O, that the slave had forty thousand lives!
One is too poor, too weak for my revenge.
Now do I see 'tis true. Look: here, Iago,
All my fond love thus do I blow to heaven—
'Tis gone.
Arise, black vengeance, from thy hollow cell!
Yield up, O love, thy crown and hearted throne   450
To tyrannous hate! Swell, bosom, with thy fraught,
For 'tis of aspics' tongues!
IAGO.   Yet be content.
OTHELLO. O, blood, blood, blood!
IAGO. Patience, I say; your mind perhaps may change.
OTHELLO. Never, Iago: like to the Pontic sea,
Whose icy current and compulsive course
Ne'er feels retiring ebb, but keeps due on
To the Propontic and the Hellespont;
Even so my bloody thoughts, with violent pace,
Shall ne'er look back, ne'er ebb to humble love,   460
Till that a capable and wide revenge
Swallow them up. Now, by yond marble heaven,
In the due reverence of a sacred vow   *Kneels*
I here engage my words.
IAGO.   Do not rise yet.   *Kneels*
Witness you ever-burning lights above,
You elements that clip us round about,
Witness that here Iago doth give up
The execution of his wit, hands, heart,
To wronged Othello's service! Let him command,
And to obey shall be without remorse,   470
What bloody business ever.   *They rise*

OTHELLO.   I greet thy love,
Not with vain thanks, but with acceptance
bounteous,
And will upon the instant put thee to't:
Within these three days let me hear thee say
That Cassio's not alive.
IAGO.   My friend is dead;
'Tis done at your request. But let her live.
OTHELLO. Damn her, lewd minx! O, damn her!
damn her!
Come, go with me apart; I will withdraw,
To furnish me with some swift means of death
For the fair devil. Now art thou my lieutenant.   480
IAGO. I am your own for ever.   *They go*

Scene 4: *The same*

Enter Desdemona, Emilia, and Clown

DESDEMONA. Do you know, sirrah, where Lieutenant
Cassio lies?
CLOWN. I dare not say he lies anywhere.
DESDEMONA. Why, man?
CLOWN. He's a soldier; and for one to say a soldier
lies, is stabbing.
DESDEMONA. Go to: where lodges he?
CLOWN. To tell you where he lodges, is to tell you
where I lie.
DESDEMONA. Can anything be made of this?   10
CLOWN. I know not where he lodges; and for me to
devise a lodging, and say he lies here or he lies there,
were to lie in mine own throat.
DESDEMONA. Can you inquire him out, and be edified
by report?
CLOWN. I will catechize the world for him: that is,
make questions and by them answer.
DESDEMONA. Seek him; bid him come hither. Tell him
I have moved my lord on his behalf, and hope all
will be well.   20
CLOWN. To do this is within the compass of man's wit,
and therefore I will attempt the doing it.   *Goes*
DESDEMONA. Where should I lose that handkerchief,
Emilia?
EMILIA. I know not, madam.
DESDEMONA. Believe me, I had rather lose my purse
Full of crusadoes; and but my noble Moor
Is true of mind and made of no such baseness
As jealous creatures are, it were enough
To put him to ill thinking.
EMILIA.   Is he not jealous?
DESDEMONA. Who, he! I think the sun where he was
born   30
Drew all such humours from him.
EMILIA.   Look where he comes!
DESDEMONA. I will not leave him now till Cassio
Be called to him.

Enter Othello

                                    How is't with you, my lord?
OTHELLO. Well, my good lady.[*aside*] O, hardness to
dissemble!
How do you, Desdemona?
DESDEMONA.   Well, my good lord.
OTHELLO. Give me your hand: this hand is moist, my
lady.
DESDEMONA. It yet hath felt no age nor known no
sorrow.

OTHELLO. This argues fruitfulness and liberal heart:
Hot, hot, and moist. This hand of yours requires
A sequester from liberty, fasting and prayer,   40
Much castigation, exercise devout;
For there's a young and sweating devil here
That commonly rebels. 'Tis a good hand,
A frank one.
DESDEMONA.   You may, indeed, say so;
For 'twas that hand that gave away my heart.
OTHELLO. A liberal hand: the hearts of old gave hands;
But our new heraldry is hands, not hearts.
DESDEMONA. I cannot speak of this. Come now, your
promise.
OTHELLO. What promise, chuck?
DESDEMONA. I have sent to bid Cassio come speak with
you.   50
OTHELLO. I have a salt and sorry rheum offends me;
Lend my thy handkerchief.
DESDEMONA. Here, my lord.
OTHELLO. That which I gave you.
DESDEMONA. I have it not about me.
OTHELLO. Not?
DESDEMONA. No, indeed, my lord.
OTHELLO. That's a fault. That handkerchief
Did an Egyptian to my mother give;
She was a charmer, and could almost read   60
The thoughts of people: she told her, while she
    kept it
'Twould make her amiable and subdue my father
Entirely to her love; but if she lost it
Or made a gift of it, my father's eye
Should hold her loathéd and his spirits should hunt
After new fancies. She dying gave it me,
And bid me, when my fate would have me wive,
To give it her. I did so; and take heed on't:
Make it a darling like your precious eye;
To lose't or give't away were such perdition   70
As nothing else could match.
DESDEMONA.   Is't possible?
OTHELLO. 'Tis true. There's magic in the web of it:
A sibyl, that had numbered in the world
The sun to course two hundred compasses,
In her prophetic fury sewed the work;
The worms were hallowed that did breed the silk;
And it was dyed in mummy which the skilful
Conserved of maidens' hearts.
DESDEMONA.   Indeed! is't true?
OTHELLO. Most veritable; therefore look to't well.
DESDEMONA. Then would to God that I had never
seen't!   80
OTHELLO. Ha! wherefore?
DESDEMONA. Why do you speak so startingly and rash?
OTHELLO. Is't lost? is't gone? speak, is it out o'th'way?
DESDEMONA. Heaven bless us!
OTHELLO. Say you?
DESDEMONA. It is not lost; but what an if it were?
OTHELLO. How!
DESDEMONA. I say it is not lost.
OTHELLO. Fetch't; let me see't.
DESDEMONA. Why, so I can, sir, but I will not now.   90
This is a trick to put me from my suit:
Pray you, let Cassio be received again.
OTHELLO. Fetch me the handkerchief: my mind
    misgives.
DESDEMONA. Come, come;
You'll never meet a more sufficient man.

OTHELLO. The handkerchief!
DESDEMONA.   I pray, talk me of Cassio.
OTHELLO. The handkerchief!
DESDEMONA.   A man that all his time
Hath founded his good fortunes on your love,
Shared dangers with you—
OTHELLO. The handkerchief!   100
DESDEMONA. In sooth, you are to blame.
OTHELLO. Away!   He goes
EMILIA. Is not this man jealous?
DESDEMONA. I ne'er saw this before.
Sure there's some wonder in this handkerchief:
I am most unhappy in the loss of it.
EMILIA. 'Tis not a year or two shows us a man:
They are all but stomachs and we all but food;
They eat us hungerly, and when they are full
They belch us. Look you, Cassio and my husband. 110

Enter Cassio and Iago

IAGO. There is no other way: 'tis she must do't;
And, lo, the happiness! go and importune her.
DESDEMONA. How now, good Cassio! what's the news
with you?
CASSIO. Madam, my former suit: I do beseech you
That, by your virtuous means, I may again
Exist and be a member of his love
Whom I with all the office of my heart
Entirely honour. I would not be delayed:
If my offence be of such mortal kind
That nor my service past nor present sorrow,   120
Nor purposed merit in futurity,
Can ransom me into his love again,
But to know so must be my benefit;
So shall I clothe me in a forced content
And shut myself up in some other course
To fortune's alms.
DESDEMONA.   Alas, thrice-gentle Cassio!
My advocation is not now in tune;
My lord is not my lord, nor should I know him
Were he in favour as in humour altered.
So help me every spirit sanctified,   130
As I have spoken for you all my best
And stood within the blank of his displeasure
For my free speech! You must awhile be patient:
What I can do I will; and more I will
Than for myself I dare—let that suffice you.
IAGO. Is my lord angry?
EMILIA.   He went hence but now,
And certainly in strange unquietness.
IAGO. Can he be angry? I have seen the cannon
When it hath blown his ranks into the air
And, like the devil, from his very arm   140
Puffed his own brother; and is he angry?
Something of moment then: I will go meet him;
There's matter in't indeed if he be angry.
DESDEMONA. I prithee, do so.   *Iago goes*
              Something sure of state,
Either from Venice, or some unhatched practice
Made demonstrable here in Cyprus to him,
Hath puddled his clear spirit; and in such cases
Men's natures wrangle with inferior things,
Though great ones are their object. 'Tis even so;
For let our finger ache, and it indues   150
Our other healthful members to a sense
Of pain. Nay, we must think men are not gods,
Nor of them look for such observancy

As fits the bridal. Beshrew me much, Emilia,
I was, unhandsome warrior as I am,
Arraigning his unkindness with my soul;
But now I find I had suborned the witness,
And he's indicted falsely.
EMILIA. Pray heaven it be state matters, as you think,
And no conception nor no jealous toy   160
Concerning you.
DESDEMONA. Alas the day, I never gave him cause!
EMILIA. But jealous souls will not be answered so;
They are not ever jealous for the cause,
But jealous for they're jealous: 'tis a monster
Begot upon itself, born on itself.
DESDEMONA. Heaven keep that monster from
Othello's mind!
EMILIA. Lady, amen.
DESDEMONA. I will go seek him. Cassio, walk
hereabout:
If I do find him fit, I'll move your suit,   170
And seek to effect it to my uttermost.
CASSIO. I humbly thank your ladyship.
Desdemona and Emilia depart

Enter Bianca

BIANCA. 'Save you, friend Cassio!
CASSIO.   What make you from home?
How is it with you, my most fair Bianca?
In faith, sweet love, I was coming to your house.
BIANCA. And I was going to your lodging, Cassio.
What, keep a week away? seven days and nights?
Eight score eight hours? and lovers' absent hours,
More tedious than the dial eight score times?
O weary reckoning!
CASSIO.   Pardon me, Bianca: 180
I have this while with leaden thoughts been pressed;
But I shall in a more continuate time
Strike off this score of absence. Sweet Bianca,
Giving Desdemona's handkerchief
Take me this work out.
BIANCA.   O Cassio, whence came this?
This is some token from a newer friend:
To the felt absence now I feel a cause;
Is't come to this? Well, well.
CASSIO.   Go to, woman!
Throw your vile guesses in the devil's teeth,
From whence you have them. You are jealous now
That this is from some mistress, some remembrance: 190
No, by my faith, Bianca.
BIANCA.   Why, whose is it?
CASSIO. I know not neither. I found it in my
chamber.
I like the work well. Ere it be demanded—
As like enough it will—I'ld have it copied:
Take it, and do't; and leave me for this time.
BIANCA. Leave you! wherefore?
CASSIO. I do attend here on the general;
And think it no addition, nor my wish,
To have him see me womaned.
BIANCA.   Why, I pray you?
CASSIO. Not that I love you not.
BIANCA.   But that you do not love me.   200
I pray you, bring me on the way a little;
And say if I shall see you soon at night.
CASSIO. 'Tis but a little way that I can bring you,
For I attend here; but I'll see you soon.

BIANCA. 'Tis very good; I must be circumstanced.
They go

ACT 4

Scene 1: *The same*

Enter Othello and Iago

IAGO. Will you think so?
OTHELLO.   Think so, Iago!
IAGO.   What,
To kiss in private?
OTHELLO.   An unauthorised kiss.
IAGO. Or to be naked with her friend in bed
An hour or more, not meaning any harm?
OTHELLO. Naked in bed, Iago, and not mean harm!
It is hypocrisy against the devil:
They that mean virtuously and yet do so,
The devil their virtue tempts and they tempt
heaven.
IAGO. So they do nothing, 'tis a venial slip:
But if I give my wife a handkerchief—   10
OTHELLO. What then?
IAGO. Why, then, 'tis hers, my lord; and being hers,
She may, I think, bestow't on any man.
OTHELLO. She is protectress of her honour too:
May she give that?
IAGO. Her honour is an essence that's not seen;
They have it very oft that have it not:
But for the handkerchief—
OTHELLO. By heaven, I would most gladly have
forgot it.
Thou said'st—O, it comes o'er my memory,   20
As doth the raven o'er the infected house,
Boding to all—he had my handkerchief.
IAGO. Ay, what of that?
OTHELLO.   That's not so good now.
IAGO.   What
If I had said I had seen him do you wrong?
Or heard him say—as knaves be such abroad,
Who having, by their own importunate suit,
Or voluntary dotage of some mistress,
Convinced or supplied them, cannot choose
But they must blab—
OTHELLO.   Hath he said anything?
IAGO. He hath, my lord; but, be you well assured,   30
No more than he'll unswear.
OTHELLO.   What hath he said?
IAGO. Faith, that he did—I know not what he did.
OTHELLO. What? what?
IAGO. Lie—
OTHELLO. With her?
IAGO.   With her, on her; what you will.
OTHELLO. Lie with her! lie on her!—We say lie on her,
when they belie her.—Lie with her! 'Zounds, that's
fulsome! Handkerchief—confessions—handker-
chief! To confess and be hanged for his labour; first,
to be hanged; and then to confess. I tremble at it.
Nature would not invest herself in such shadowing   40
passion without some instruction. It is not words
that shakes me thus. Pish! Noses, ears, and lips. Is't
possible?—Confess?—Handkerchief?—O devil!
Falls in a trance

IAGO. Work on,
My medicine, work! Thus credulous fools are
caught;

And many worthy and chaste dames even thus,
All guiltless, meet reproach. What, ho! my lord!
My lord, I say! Othello!

Enter Cassio

                   How now, Cassio!
CASSIO. What's the matter?
IAGO. My lord is fallen into an epilepsy.   50
  This is his second fit; he had one yesterday.
CASSIO. Rub him about the temples.
IAGO.   No, forbear;
  The lethargy must have his quiet course;
  If not, he foams at mouth, and by and by
  Breaks out to savage madness. Look, he stirs.
  Do you withdraw yourself a little while.
  He will recover straight; when he is gone,
  I would on great occasion speak with you.
                            Cassio goes
  How is it, general? have you not hurt your head?
OTHELLO. Dost thou mock me?
IAGO.   I mock you! no, by heaven. 60
  Would you would bear your fortune like a man!
OTHELLO. A hornéd man's a monster and a beast.
IAGO. There's many a beast then in a populous city,
  And many a civil monster.
OTHELLO. Did he confess it?
IAGO.   Good sir, be a man:
  Think every bearded fellow that's but yoked
  May draw with you. There's millions now alive
  That nightly lie in those unproper beds
  Which they dare swear peculiar; your case is better.
  O, 'tis the spite of hell, the fiend's arch-mock, 70
  To lip a wanton in a secure couch,
  And to suppose her chaste! No, let me know;
  And knowing what I am, know what shall be.
OTHELLO. O, thou art wise; 'tis certain.
IAGO.   Stand you awhile apart;
  Confine yourself but in a patient list.
  Whilst you were here o'erwhelméd with your
     grief—
  A passion most unsuiting such a man—
  Cassio came hither; I shifted him away,
  And laid good scuse upon your ecstasy;
  Bade him anon return and speak with me; 80
  The which he promised. Do but encave yourself,
  And mark the fleers, the gibes, and notable scorns,
  That dwell in every region of his face;
  For I will make him tell the tale anew,
  Where, how, how oft, how long ago and when
  He hath and is again to cope your wife.
  I say, but mark his gestures. Marry, patience;
  Or I shall say you're all in all a spleen,
  And nothing of a man.
OTHELLO.   Dost thou hear, Iago?
  I will be found most cunning in my patience; 90
  But—dost thou hear?—most bloody.
IAGO.   That's not amiss;
  But yet keep time in all. Will you withdraw?
                          Othello retires
  Now will I question Cassio of Bianca,
  A hussy that by selling her desires
  Buys herself bread and clothes: it is a creature
  That dotes on Cassio; as 'tis the strumpet's plague
  To beguile many and be beguiled by one.
  He, when he hears of her, cannot refrain
  From the excess of laughter. Here he comes.

Re-enter Cassio

  As he shall smile, Othello shall go mad;   100
  And his unbookish jealousy must construe
  Poor Cassio's smiles, gestures, and light behaviours,
  Quite in the wrong. How do you now, lieutenant?
CASSIO. The worser that you give me the addition
  Whose want even kills me.
IAGO. Ply Desdemona well, and you are sure on't.
  Now, if this suit lay in Bianca's power,
  How quickly should you speed!
CASSIO.   Alas, poor caitiff!
OTHELLO. Look how he laughs already!
IAGO. I never knew a woman love man so.   110
CASSIO. Alas, poor rogue! I think, in faith, she loves
  me.
OTHELLO. Now he denies it faintly, and laughs it out.
IAGO. Do you hear, Cassio?
OTHELLO. Now he importunes him to tell it o'er.
  Go to; well said, well said.
IAGO. She gives it out that you shall marry her.
  Do you intend it?
CASSIO, Ha, ha, ha!
OTHELLO. Do you triumph, Roman? do you triumph?
CASSIO. I marry her! what, a customer! I prithee, bear 120
  some charity to my wit; do not think it so unwhole-
  some. Ha, ha, ha!
OTHELLO. So, so, so, so; they laugh that win.
IAGO. Faith, the cry goes that you marry her.
CASSIO. Prithee, say true.
IAGO. I am a very villain else.
OTHELLO. Have you scored me? Well.
CASSIO. This is the monkey's own giving out: she is
  persuaded I will marry her, out of her own love and
  flattery, not out of my promise.   130
OTHELLO. Iago beckons me; now he begins the story.
CASSIO. She was here even now; she haunts me in
  every place. I was the other day talking on the sea-
  bank with certain Venetians; and thither comes the
  bauble, and, by this hand, falls me thus about my
  neck—
OTHELLO. Crying 'O dear Cassio!' as it were: his
  gesture imports it.
CASSIO. So hangs, and lolls, and weeps upon me; so
  shakes, and pulls me: ha, ha, ha!   140
OTHELLO. Now he tells how she plucked him to my
  chamber. O, I see that nose of yours, but not that
  dog I shall throw it to.
CASSIO. Well, I must leave her company.
IAGO. Before me! look where she comes!
CASSIO. 'Tis such another fitchew! marry, a perfumed
  one.

Enter Bianca

  What do you mean by this haunting of me?
BIANCA. Let the devil and his dam haunt you! What
  did you mean by that same handkerchief you gave 150
  me even now? I was a fine fool to take it. I must
  take out the work? A likely piece of work that you
  should find it in your chamber and not know who
  left it there! This is some minx's token, and I must
  take out the work? There; give it your hobby-horse.
  Wheresoever you had it, I'll take out no work on't.
CASSIO. How now, my sweet Bianca! how now! how
  now!
OTHELLO. By heaven, that should be my handkerchief!

BIANCA. An you'll come to supper tonight, you may; an you will not, come when you are next prepared for.   *Goes* [160]
IAGO. After her, after her.
CASSIO. Faith, I must; she'll rail in the street else.
IAGO. Will you sup there?
CASSIO. Faith, I intend so.
IAGO. Well, I may chance to see you; for I would very fain speak with you.
CASSIO. Prithee, come; will you?
IAGO. Go to; say no more.   *Cassio goes* [170]
OTHELLO [comes forward]. How shall I murder him, Iago?
IAGO. Did you perceive how he laughed at his vice?
OTHELLO. O Iago!
IAGO. And did you see the handkerchief?
OTHELLO. Was that mine?
IAGO. Yours, by this hand—and to see how he prizes the foolish woman your wife! She gave it him, and he hath given it his whore.
OTHELLO. I would have him nine years a-killing. A fine woman! a fair woman! a sweet woman! [180]
IAGO. Nay, you must forget that.
OTHELLO. Ay, let her rot, and perish, and be damned tonight; for she shall not live. No, my heart is turned to stone: I strike it, and it hurts my hand. O, the world hath not a sweeter creature: she might lie by an emperor's side and command him tasks.
IAGO. Nay, that's not your way.
OTHELLO. Hang her! I do but say what she is: so delicate with her needle, an admirable musician— O, she will sing the savageness out of a bear—of so high and plenteous wit and invention— [190]
IAGO. She's the worse for all this.
OTHELLO. O, a thousand, thousand times—and then, of so gentle a condition!
IAGO. Ay, too gentle.
OTHELLO. Nay, that's certain; but yet the pity of it, Iago! O Iago, the pity of it, Iago!
IAGO. If you be so fond over her iniquity, give her patent to offend; for, if it touch not you, it comes near nobody. [200]
OTHELLO. I will chop her into messes—cuckold me!
IAGO. O, 'tis foul in her.
OTHELLO. With mine officer!
IAGO. That's fouler.
OTHELLO. Get me some poison, Iago—this night. I'll not expostulate with her, lest her body and beauty unprovide my mind again—this night, Iago.
IAGO. Do it not with poison: strangle her in her bed, even the bed she hath contaminated. [210]
OTHELLO. Good, good: the justice of it pleases; very good.
IAGO. And for Cassio, let me be his undertaker: you shall hear more by midnight.
OTHELLO. Excellent good. [a trumpet sounds] What trumpet is that same?
IAGO. I warrant, something from Venice.

Enter Lodovico, Desdemona, and Attendants

                                        'Tis Lodovico!
This comes from the Duke; and see, your wife is with him.
LODOVICO. God save you, worthy general!

OTHELLO.   With all my heart, sir.
LODOVICO. The Duke and senators of Venice greet you.   *Gives him a letter*
OTHELLO. I kiss the instrument of their pleasures. [220]
                                        Opens and reads
DESDEMONA. And what's the news, good cousin Lodovico?
IAGO. I am very glad to see you, signior; Welcome to Cyprus.
LODOVICO. I thank you. How does Lieutenant Cassio?
IAGO. Lives, sir.
DESDEMONA. Cousin, there's fallen between him and my lord
An unkind breach; but you shall make all well.
OTHELLO. Are you sure of that?
DESDEMONA. My lord?
OTHELLO [reads]. 'This fail you not to do, as you will—' [230]
LODOVICO. He did not call; he's busy in the paper. Is there division 'twixt my lord and Cassio?
DESDEMONA. A most unhappy one; I would do much T'atone them, for the love I bear to Cassio.
OTHELLO. Fire and brimstone!
DESDEMONA. My lord?
OTHELLO. Are you wise?
DESDEMONA. What, is he angry?
LODOVICO.   May be the letter moved him; For, as I think, they do command him home, Deputing Cassio in his government. [240]
DESDEMONA. By my troth, I am glad on't.
OTHELLO.   Indeed!
DESDEMONA.   My lord?
OTHELLO. I am glad to see you mad.
DESDEMONA.   Why, sweet Othello!
OTHELLO. Devil!   *Striking her*
DESDEMONA. I have not deserved this.
LODOVICO. My lord, this would not be believed in Venice,
Though I should swear I saw't. 'Tis very much. Make her amends; she weeps.
OTHELLO.   O devil, devil! [200]
If that the earth could teem with woman's tears, Each drop she falls would prove a crocodile. Out of my sight!
DESDEMONA.   I will not stay to offend you.   *Going* [250]
LODOVICO. Truly, an obedient lady.
I do beseech your lordship, call her back.
OTHELLO. Mistress!
DESDEMONA. My lord?
OTHELLO. What would you with her, sir?
LODOVICO.   Who, I, my lord? [210]
OTHELLO. Ay; you did wish that I would make her turn.
Sir, she can turn and turn, and yet go on And turn again; and she can weep, sir, weep; And she's obedient, as you say, obedient, Very obedient. Proceed you in your tears.— [260]
Concerning this, sir,—O well-painted passion!— I am commanded home.—Get you away; I'll send for you anon.—Sir, I obey the mandate, And will return to Venice.—Hence, avaunt!—
                                        Desdemona goes
Cassio shall have my place. And, sir, tonight, I do entreat that we may sup together. You are welcome, sir, to Cyprus.—Goats and monkeys!   *He goes*

LODOVICO. Is this the noble Moor whom our full
    senate
  Call all in all sufficient? Is this the nature
  Whom passion could not shake? whose solid virtue 270
  The shot of accident nor dart of chance
  Could neither graze nor pierce?
IAGO.   He is much changed.
LODOVICO. Are his wits safe? is he not light of brain?
IAGO. He's that he is. I may not breathe my censure
  What he might be; if what he might he is not,
  I would to heaven he were!
LODOVICO.   What, strike his wife!
IAGO. Faith, that was not so well; yet would I knew
  That stroke would prove the worst!
LODOVICO.   Is it his use?
  Or did the letters work upon his blood,
  And new-create this fault?
IAGO.   Alas, alas! 280
  It is not honesty in me to speak
  What I have seen and known. You shall observe
    him,
  And his own courses will denote him so
  That I may save my speech; do but go after,
  And mark how he continues.
LODOVICO. I am sorry that I am deceived in him.
                                    They go

            Scene 2: *A room in the citadel*

Enter Othello and Emilia

OTHELLO. You have seen nothing, then?
EMILIA. Nor ever heard, nor ever did suspect.
OTHELLO. Yes, you have seen Cassio and she together.
EMILIA. But then I saw no harm, and then I heard
  Each syllable that breath made up between them.
OTHELLO. What, did they never whisper?
EMILIA.   Never, my lord.
OTHELLO. Nor send you out o'th'way?
EMILIA. Never.
OTHELLO. To fetch her fan, her gloves, her mask, nor
    nothing?
EMILIA. Never, my lord. 10
OTHELLO. That's strange.
EMILIA. I durst, my lord, to wager she is honest,
  Lay down my soul at stake. If you think other,
  Remove your thought: it doth abuse your bosom.
  If any wretch have put this in your head,
  Let heaven requite it with the serpent's curse!
  For if she be not honest, chaste, and true,
  There's no man happy: the purest of their wives
  Is foul as slander.
OTHELLO.   Bid her come hither; go. *Emilia goes*
  She says enough; yet she's a simple bawd 20
  That cannot say as much. This is a subtle whore,
  A closet lock and key of villanous secrets;
  And yet she'll kneel and pray; I have seen her do't.

Enter Desdemona with Emilia

DESDEMONA. My lord, what is your will?
OTHELLO.   Pray, chuck, come hither.
DESDEMONA. What is your pleasure?
OTHELLO.   Let me see your eyes;
  Look in my face.
DESDEMONA.   What horrible fancy's this?
OTHELLO [*to Emilia*]. Some of your function, mistress:
  Leave procreants alone and shut the door;
  Cough, or cry hem, if anybody come—

Your mystery, your mystery; nay, dispatch. 30
                            Emilia goes out
DESDEMONA. Upon my knees, what doth your speech
    import?
  I understand a fury in your words,
  But not the words.
OTHELLO. Why, what art thou?
DESDEMONA.   Your wife, my lord; your true and loyal
    wife.
OTHELLO. Come, swear it, damn thyself;
  Lest, being like one of heaven, the devils themselves
  Should fear to seize thee. Therefore be double-
    damned:
  Swear thou art honest.
DESDEMONA.   Heaven doth truly know it.
OTHELLO. Heaven truly knows that thou art false as
    hell. 40
DESDEMONA. To whom, my lord? with whom? how
    am I false?
OTHELLO. Ah, Desdemon! Away! away! away!
DESDEMONA. Alas the heavy day! Why do you weep?
  Am I the motive of these tears, my lord?
  If haply you my father do suspect
  An instrument of this your calling back,
  Lay not your blame on me; if you have lost him,
  Why, I have lost him too.
OTHELLO.   Had it pleased heaven
  To try me with affliction; had they rained
  All kind of sores and shames on my bare head, 50
  Steeped me in poverty to the very lips,
  Given to captivity me and my utmost hopes,
  I should have found in some place of my soul
  A drop of patience; but, alas, to make me
  A fixed figure for the time of scorn
  To point his slow unmoving finger at!
  Yet could I bear that too; well, very well;
  But there, where I have garnered up my heart,
  Where either I must live or bear no life,
  The fountain from the which my current runs, 60
  Or else dries up—to be discarded thence!
  Or keep it as a cistern for foul toads
  To knot and gender in! Turn thy complexion there,
  Patience, thou young and rose-lipped cherubin,
  Ay, there, look grim as hell!
DESDEMONA. I hope my noble lord esteems me honest.
OTHELLO. O, ay; as summer flies are in the shambles,
  That quicken even with blowing. O thou weed,
  Who art so lovely fair and smell'st so sweet
  That the sense aches at thee, would thou hadst ne'er
  been born! 70
DESDEMONA. Alas, what ignorant sin have I
    committed?
OTHELLO. Was this fair paper, this most goodly book,
  Made to write 'whore' upon? What committed!
  Committed! O thou public commoner!
  I should make very forges of my cheeks,
  That would to cinders burn up modesty,
  Did I but speak thy deeds. What committed!
  Heaven stops the nose at it, and the moon winks;
  The bawdy wind, that kisses all it meets,
  Is hushed within the hollow mine of earth, 80
  And will not hear it. What committed!
  Impudent strumpet!
DESDEMONA.   By heaven, you do me wrong.
OTHELLO. Are not you a strumpet?
DESDEMONA.   No, as I am a Christian.

If to preserve this vessel for my lord
From any other foul unlawful touch
Be not to be a strumpet, I am none.
OTHELLO. What, not a whore?
DESDEMONA.   No, as I shall be saved.
OTHELLO. Is't possible?
DESDEMONA. O, heaven forgive us!
OTHELLO.   I cry you mercy then:
I took you for that cunning whore of Venice   90
That married with Othello. [*raising his voice*] You,
mistress,
That have the office opposite to Saint Peter,
And keep the gate of hell!

Re-enter Emilia

                        You, you, ay, you!
We've done our course; there's money for your
pains:
I pray you, turn the key, and keep our counsel.
                                                Goes
EMILIA. Alas, what does this gentleman conceive?
How do you, madam? how do you, my good lady?
DESDEMONA. Faith, half asleep.
EMILIA. Good madam, what's the matter with my
lord?
DESDEMONA. With who?   100
EMILIA. Why, with my lord, madam.
DESDEMONA. Who is thy lord?
EMILIA.   He that is yours, sweet lady.
DESDEMONA. I have none: do not talk to me, Emilia;
I cannot weep, nor answers have I none
But what should go by water. Prithee, tonight
Lay on my bed my wedding sheets—remember;
And call thy husband hither.
EMILIA.   Here's a change indeed!   *Goes*
DESDEMONA. 'Tis meet I should be used so, very meet.
How have I been behaved, that he might stick
The small'st opinion on my least misuse?   110

Re-enter Emilia with Iago

IAGO. What is your pleasure, madam? How is't with
you?
DESDEMONA. I cannot tell. Those that do teach young
babes
Do it with gentle means and easy tasks:
He might have chid me so; for, in good faith,
I am a child to chiding.
IAGO.   What's the matter, lady?
EMILIA. Alas, Iago, my lord hath so bewhored her.
Thrown such despite and heavy terms upon her,
As true heart cannot bear.
DESDEMONA. Am I that name, Iago?
IAGO.   What name, fair lady?
DESDEMONA. Such as she said my lord did say I was.   120
EMILIA. He called her whore: a beggar in his drink
Could not have laid such terms upon his callet.
IAGO. Why did he so?
DESDEMONA. I do not know; I am sure I am none
such.
IAGO. Do not weep, do not weep. Alas the day!
EMILIA. Hath she forsook so many noble matches,
Her father, and her country, and her friends,
To be called whore? Would it not make one weep?
DESDEMONA. It is my wretched fortune.
IAGO.   Beshrew him for't!
How comes this trick upon him!

DESDEMONA.   Nay, heaven doth know.   130
EMILIA. I will be hanged, if some eternal villain,
Some busy and insinuating rogue,
Some cogging, cozening slave, to get some office,
Have not devised this slander; I'll be hanged else.
IAGO. Fie, there is no such man; it is impossible.
DESDEMONA. If any such there be, heaven pardon him!
EMILIA. A halter pardon him! and hell gnaw his bones!
Why should he call her whore? who keeps her
company?
What place? what time? what form? what
likelihood?
The Moor's abused by some most villanous knave,   140
Some base notorious knave, some scurvy fellow.
O heaven, that such companions thou'ldst unfold,
And put in every honest hand a whip
To lash the rascals naked through the world
Even from the east to th'west!
IAGO.   Speak within door.
EMILIA. O, fie upon them! Some such squire he was
That turned your wit the seamy side without,
And made you to suspect me with the Moor.
IAGO. You are a fool; go to.
DESDEMONA.   Alas, Iago,
What shall I do to win my lord again?   150
Good friend, go to him; for, by this light of heaven,
I know not how I lost him. Here I kneel:
If e'er my will did trespass 'gainst his love
Either in discourse of thought or actual deed,
Or that mine eyes, mine ears, or any sense,
Delighted them in any other form,
Or that I do not yet, and ever did,
And ever will, though he do shake me off
To beggarly divorcement, love him dearly,
Comfort forswear me! Unkindness may do much;   160
And his unkindness may defeat my life,
But never taint my love. I cannot say 'whore':
It does abhor me now I speak the word;
To do the act that might the addition earn
Not the world's mass of vanity could make me.
IAGO. I pray you, be content; 'tis but his humour:
The business of the state does him offence,
And he does chide with you.
DESDEMONA.   If 'twere no other!
IAGO. 'Tis but so, I warrant.   *Trumpets sound*
Hark how these instruments summon to supper!   170
The messengers of Venice stay the meat:
Go in, and weep not; all things shall be well.
                        Desdemona and Emilia go

Enter Roderigo

How now, Roderigo!
RODERIGO. I do not find that thou deal'st justly with
me.
IAGO. What in the contrary?
RODERIGO. Every day thou daff'st me with some
device, Iago; and rather, as it seems to me now,
keep'st from me all conveniency than suppliest me
with the least advantage of hope. I will indeed no   180
longer endure it; nor am I yet persuaded to put up
in peace what already I have foolishly suffered.
IAGO. Will you hear me, Roderigo?
RODERIGO. Faith, I have heard too much; for your
words and performances are no kin together.
IAGO. You charge me most unjustly.
RODERIGO. With nought but truth. I have wasted

myself out of my means. The jewels you have had from me to deliver to Desdemona would half have corrupted a votarist. You have told me she hath received them and returned me expectations and comforts of sudden respect and acquaintance; but I find none. 190

IAGO. Well; go to; very well.

RODERIGO. Very well! go to! I cannot go to, man; nor 'tis not very well. By this hand, I think 'tis very scurvy, and begin to find myself fopped in it.

IAGO. Very well.

RODERIGO. I tell you 'tis not very well. I will make myself known to Desdemona. If she will return me my jewels, I will give over my suit and repent my unlawful solicitation; if not, assure yourself I will seek satisfaction of you. 200

IAGO. You have said now.

RODERIGO. Ay, and said nothing but what I protest intendment of doing.

IAGO. Why, now I see there's mettle in thee; and even from this instant do build on thee a better opinion than ever before. Give me thy hand, Roderigo: thou hast taken against me a most just exception; but yet, I protest, I have dealt most directly in thy affair. 210

RODERIGO. It hath not appeared.

IAGO. I grant indeed it hath not appeared, and your suspicion is not without wit and judgement. But, Roderigo, if thou hast that in thee indeed, which I have greater reason to believe now than ever—I mean purpose, courage, and valour—this night show it: if thou the next night following enjoy not Desdemona, take me from this world with treachery and devise engines for my life. 220

RODERIGO. Well, what is it? is it within reason and compass?

IAGO. Sir, there is especial commission come from Venice to depute Cassio in Othello's place.

RODERIGO. Is that true? why, then, Othello and Desdemona return again to Venice.

IAGO. O, no; he goes into Mauritania, and takes away with him the fair Desdemona, unless his abode be lingered here by some accident: wherein none can be so determinate as the removing of Cassio. 230

RODERIGO. How do you mean removing of him?

IAGO. Why, by making him uncapable of Othello's place; knocking out his brains.

RODERIGO. And that you would have me do?

IAGO. Ay, if you dare do yourself a profit and a right. He sups tonight with a harlotry, and thither will I go to him: he knows not yet of his honourable fortune. If you will watch his going thence, which I will fashion to fall out between twelve and one, you may take him at your pleasure. I will be near 240 to second your attempt, and he shall fall between us. Come, stand not amazed at it, but go along with me; I will show you such a necessity in his death that you shall think yourself bound to put it on him. It is now high supper-time, and the night grows to waste. About it.

RODERIGO. I will hear further reason for this.

IAGO. And you shall be satisfied. *They go*

Scene 3: *Another room in the citadel*

Enter Othello, Lodovico, Desdemona, Emilia, and Attendants

LODOVICO. I do beseech you, sir, trouble yourself no further.

OTHELLO. O, pardon me; 'twill do me good to walk.

LODOVICO. Madam, good night; I humbly thank your ladyship.

DESDEMONA. Your honour is most welcome.

OTHELLO. Will you walk, sir? O, Desdemona!

DESDEMONA. My lord?

OTHELLO. Get you to bed on th'instant; I will be returned forthwith. Dismiss your attendant there: look't be done. 10

DESDEMONA. I will, my lord.

Othello, Lodovico, and Attendants go

EMILIA. How goes it now? he looks gentler than he did.

DESDEMONA. He says he will return incontinent: He hath commanded me to go to bed, And bade me to dismiss you.

EMILIA. Dismiss me!

DESDEMONA. It was his bidding; therefore, good Emilia, Give me my nightly wearing, and adieu: We must not now displease him.

EMILIA. I would you had never seen him!

DESDEMONA. So would not I: my love doth so approve him, 20 That even his stubbornness, his checks, his frowns— Prithee, unpin me—have grace and favour in them.

EMILIA. I have laid those sheets you bade me on the bed.

DESDEMONA. All's one. Good faith, how foolish are our minds! If I do die before thee, prithee, shroud me In one of those same sheets.

EMILIA. Come, come, you talk.

DESDEMONA. My mother had a maid called Barbara. She was in love; and he she loved proved mad And did forsake her. She had a song of 'willow'— An old thing 'twas, but it expressed her fortune, 30 And she died singing it. That song tonight Will not go from my mind. I have much to do But to go hang my head all at one side And sing it like poor Barbara. Prithee, dispatch.

EMILIA. Shall I go fetch your night-gown?

DESDEMONA. No, unpin me here. This Lodovico is a proper man.

EMILIA. A very handsome man.

DESDEMONA. He speaks well.

EMILIA. I know a lady in Venice would have walked barefoot to Palestine for a touch of his nether lip. 40

DESDEMONA [*sings*].
The poor soul sat sighing by a sycamore tree,
    Sing all a green willow;
Her hand on her bosom, her head on her knee,
    Sing willow, willow, willow:
The fresh streams ran by her, and murmured her moans;
    Sing willow, willow, willow;
Her salt tears fell from her, and softened the stones—
Lay by these—
    Sing willow, willow, willow;
Prithee, hie thee; he'll come anon— 50
    Sing all a green willow must be my garland.
Let nobody blame him; his scorn I approve—
Nay, that's not next. Hark! who is't that knocks?

EMILIA. It's the wind.
DESDEMONA [sings]
  I called my love false love; but what said he then?
    Sing willow, willow, willow;
  If I court moe women, you'll couch with moe
    men.
So, get thee gone; good night. Mine eyes do itch;
Does that bode weeping?
EMILIA.   'Tis neither here nor there.
DESDEMONA. I have heard it said so. O, these men,
  these men!   60
Dost thou in conscience think—tell me, Emilia—
That there be women do abuse their husbands
In such gross kind?
EMILIA.   There be some such, no question.
DESDEMONA. Wouldst thou do such a deed for all the
  world?
EMILIA. Why, would not you?
DESDEMONA.   No, by this heavenly light!
EMILIA. Nor I neither by this heavenly light: I might
  do't as well i'th'dark.
DESDEMONA. Wouldst thou do such a deed for all the
  world?
EMILIA. The world's a huge thing: it is a great prize 70
  for a small vice.
DESDEMONA. In troth, I think thou wouldst not.
EMILIA. In troth, I think I should; and undo't when
  I had done't. Marry, I would not do such a thing for
  a joint-ring, nor for measures of lawn, nor for
  gowns, petticoats, nor caps, nor any petty exhibition. But for all the whole world—ud's pity, who
  would not make her husband a cuckold to make him
  a monarch? I should venture purgatory for't.
DESDEMONA. Beshrew me, if I would do such a wrong 80
  for the whole world.
EMILIA. Why, the wrong is but a wrong i'th'world;
  and having the world for your labour, 'tis a wrong
  in your own world, and you might quickly make
  it right.
DESDEMONA. I do not think there is any such woman.
EMILIA. Yes, a dozen; and as many to th'vantage as
  would store the world they played for.
But I do think it is their husbands' faults
If wives do fall. Say that they slack their duties   90
And pour our treasures into foreign laps,
Or else break out in peevish jealousies,
Throwing restraint upon us; or say they strike us,
Or scant our former having in despite—
Why, we have galls, and though we have some
  grace,
Yet have we some revenge. Let husbands know
Their wives have sense like them: they see, and
  smell,
And have their palates both for sweet and sour,
As husbands have. What is it that they do
When they change us for others? Is it sport?   100
I think it is. And doth affection breed it?
I think it doth. Is't frailty that thus errs?
It is so too. And have not we affections,
Desires for sport, and frailty, as men have?
Then let them use us well: else let them know,
The ills we do, their ills instruct us so.
DESDEMONA. Good night, good night.   Emilia goes
                Heaven me such uses send,
Not to pick bad from bad, but by bad mend!   Goes

ACT 5
Scene 1: A street

Enter Iago and Roderigo

IAGO. Here, stand behind this bulk; straight will he
  come.
Wear thy good rapier bare, and put it home;
Quick, quick; fear nothing; I'll be at thy elbow.
It makes us, or it mars us; think on that,
And fix most firm thy resolution.
RODERIGO. Be near at hand; I may miscarry in't.
IAGO. Here, at thy hand. Be bold, and take thy stand.
                                Retires
RODERIGO. I have no great devotion to the deed;
And yet he hath given me satisfying reasons.
'Tis but a man gone. Forth, my sword: he dies.   10
IAGO. I have rubbed this young quat almost to the
  sense,
And he grows angry. Now, whether he kill Cassio,
Or Cassio him, or each do kill the other,
Every way makes my gain: live Roderigo,
He calls me to a restitution large
Of gold and jewels that I bobbed from him,
As gifts to Desdemona—
It must not be; if Cassio do remain,
He hath a daily beauty in his life
That makes me ugly; and besides, the Moor   20
May unfold me to him—there stand I in much peril.
No, he must die. Be't so. I hear him coming.

Enter Cassio

RODERIGO. I know his gait; 'tis he. Villain, thou diest!
                     Makes a pass at Cassio
CASSIO. That thrust had been mine enemy indeed,
But that my coat is better than thou think'st.
I will make proof of thine.
              Draws, and wounds Roderigo
RODERIGO.   O, I am slain!
           Iago from behind strikes at Cassio's
                legs, and hurries off
CASSIO. I am maimed for ever. Help, ho! murder!
  murder!   *Falls*

Enter Othello

OTHELLO. The voice of Cassio: Iago keeps his word.
RODERIGO. O, villain that I am!
OTHELLO.   It is even so.
CASSIO. O, help, ho! light! a surgeon!   30
OTHELLO. 'Tis he. O brave Iago, honest and just,
That hast such noble sense of thy friend's wrong!
Thou teachest me: minion, your dear lies dead,
And your unblest fate hies. Strumpet, I come!
Forth of my heart, those charms, thine eyes, are
  blotted;
Thy bed lust-stained shall with lust's blood be
  spotted.   *He goes*

Enter Lodovico and Gratiano

CASSIO. What, ho! no watch? no passage?
  murder! murder!
GRATIANO. 'Tis some mischance; the voice is very
  direful.
CASSIO. O, help!
LODOVICO. Hark!   40
RODERIGO. O wretched villain!
LODOVICO. Two or three groan. It is a heavy night;
  These may be counterfeits: let's think't unsafe

To come in to the cry without more help.

They stand aside

RODERIGO. Nobody come? then shall I bleed to death.
LODOVICO. Hark!

Re-enter Iago, with a light

GRATIANO. Here's one comes in his shirt, with light
  and weapons.
IAGO. Who's there? whose noise is this that cries on
  murder?
LODOVICO. We do not know.
IAGO.   Did not you hear a cry?
CASSIO. Here, here! for heaven's sake, help me!
IAGO.   What's the matter? 50
GRATIANO. This is Othello's ancient, as I take it.
LODOVICO. The same indeed; a very valiant fellow.
IAGO. What are you here that cry so grievously?
CASSIO. Iago? O, I am spoiled, undone by villains!
  Give me some help.
IAGO. O me, lieutenant! what villains have done this?
CASSIO. I think that one of them is hereabout,
  And cannot make away.
IAGO.   O treacherous villains!
  What are you there? [*spies Lodovico and Gratiano*].
  Come in and give some help.
RODERIGO. O, help me here!   60
CASSIO. That's one of them.
IAGO.   O murderous slave! O villain!

Stabs Roderigo

RODERIGO. O damned Iago! O inhuman dog!
IAGO. Kill men i'th'dark! Where be these bloody
  thieves?
  How silent is this town! Ho! murder! murder!

Lodovico and Gratiano come forward

What may you be? are you of good or evil?
LODOVICO. As you shall prove us, praise us.
IAGO. Signior Lodovico?
LODOVICO. He, sir.
IAGO. I cry you mercy. Here's Cassio hurt by villains.
GRATIANO. Cassio!   70
IAGO. How is't, brother?
CASSIO. My leg is cut in two.
IAGO.   Marry, heaven forbid!
  Light, gentlemen: I'll bind it with my shirt.

Enter Bianca

BIANCA. What is the matter, ho? who is't that cried?
IAGO. Who is't that cried!
BIANCA. O my dear Cassio! my sweet Cassio! O
  Cassio, Cassio, Cassio!
IAGO. O notable strumpet! Cassio, may you suspect
  Who they should be that have thus mangled you?
CASSIO. No.   80
GRATIANO. I am sorry to find you thus: I have been
  to seek you.
IAGO. Lend me a garter. So. O, for a chair,
  To bear him easily hence!
BIANCA. Alas, he faints! O Cassio, Cassio, Cassio!
IAGO. Gentlemen all, I do suspect this trash
  To be a party in this injury.
  Patience awhile, good Cassio. Come, come;
  Lend me a light. Know we this face or no?
  Alas, my friend and my dear countryman
  Roderigo? No—yes, sure; 'tis Roderigo.   90
GRATIANO. What, of Venice?
IAGO. Even he, sir. Did you know him?

GRATIANO.   Know him! ay.
IAGO. Signior Gratiano? I cry your gentle pardon:
  These bloody accidents must excuse my manners,
  That so neglected you.
GRATIANO.   I am glad to see you.
IAGO. How do you, Cassio? O, a chair, a chair!
GRATIANO. Roderigo!
IAGO. He, he, 'tis he. [*a chair brought*] O, that's well
  said; the chair.
  Some good man bear him carefully from hence; 100
  I'll fetch the general's surgeon. [*to Bianca*] For you,
  mistress,
  Save you your labour. He that lies slain here, Cassio,
  Was my dear friend: what malice was between you?
CASSIO. None in the world; nor do I know the man.
IAGO [*to Bianca*]. What, look you pale? O, bear him
  out o'th'air.

*Cassio is borne in, and the
body of Roderigo removed*

Stay you, good gentlemen. Look you pale, mistress?
Do you perceive the gastness of her eye?
Nay, if you stare, we shall hear more anon.
Behold her well; I pray you, look upon her:
Do you see, gentlemen? nay, guiltiness will speak,
Though tongues were out of use.   110

Enter Emilia

EMILIA. 'Las, what's the matter? what's the matter,
  husband?
IAGO. Cassio hath here been set on in the dark
  By Roderigo, and fellows that are scaped:
  He's almost slain, and Roderigo dead.
EMILIA. Alas, good gentleman! alas, good Cassio!
IAGO. This is the fruits of whoring. Prithee, Emilia,
  Go know of Cassio where he supped tonight.
  What, do you shake at that?
BIANCA. He supped at my house; but I therefore shake
  not.
IAGO. O, did he so? I charge you, go with me.   120
EMILIA. O, fie upon thee, strumpet!
BIANCA. I am no strumpet; but of life as honest
  As you that thus abuse me.
EMILIA.   As I! foh! fie upon thee!
IAGO. Kind gentlemen, let's see poor Cassio dressed.
  Come, mistress, you must tell's another tale.
  Emilia, run you to the citadel,
  And tell my lord and lady what hath happed.
  Will you go on afore? [*aside*] This is the night
  That either makes me or fordoes me quite.   *They go*

Scene 2: *A chamber in the citadel; Desdemona asleep
in her bed*

Enter Othello with a light; he locks the door

OTHELLO. It is the cause, it is the cause, my soul.
  Let me not name it to you, you chaste stars!
  It is the cause. Yet I'll not shed her blood,
  Nor scar that whiter skin of hers than snow
  And smooth as monumental alabaster—
  Yet she must die, else she'll betray more men.
  Put out the light, and then put out the light:
  If I quench thee, thou flaming minister,
  I can again thy former light restore
  Should I repent me; but once put out thy light, 10
  Thou cunning'st pattern of excelling nature,

I know not where is that Promethean heat
That can thy light relume. *Sets down the taper*
                    When I have plucked the rose,
I cannot give it vital growth again,
It needs must wither: I'll smell it on the tree.
                                        Kisses her
O balmy breath, that dost almost persuade
Justice to break her sword! One more, one more.
Be thus when thou art dead, and I will kill thee,
And love thee after. One more, and that's the last.
So sweet was ne'er so fatal. I must weep,   20
But they are cruel tears; this sorrow's heavenly:
It strikes where it doth love. She wakes.
DESDEMONA. Who's there? Othello?
OTHELLO. Ay, Desdemona.
DESDEMONA. Will you come to bed, my lord?
OTHELLO. Have you prayed tonight, Desdemona?
DESDEMONA.   Ay, my lord.
OTHELLO. If you bethink yourself of any crime
    Unreconciled as yet to heaven and grace,
    Solicit for it straight.
DESDEMONA. Alack, my lord, what may you mean by
    that?   30
OTHELLO. Well, do it, and be brief; I will walk by:
    I would not kill thy unprepared spirit;
    No—heaven forfend!—I would not kill thy soul.
DESDEMONA. Talk you of killing?
OTHELLO. Ay, I do.
DESDEMONA. Then heaven have mercy on me!
OTHELLO. Amen, with all my heart!
DESDEMONA. If you say so, I hope you will not kill me.
OTHELLO. Hum!
DESDEMONA. And yet I fear you; for you're fatal then   40
    When your eyes roll so. Why I should fear I know
    not,
    Since guiltiness I know not; but yet I feel I fear.
OTHELLO. Think on thy sins.
DESDEMONA.   They are loves I bear to you.
OTHELLO. Ay, and for that thou diest.
DESDEMONA. That death's unnatural that kills for
    loving.
    Alas, why gnaw you so your nether lip?
    Some bloody passion shakes your very frame:
    These are portents; but yet I hope, I hope,
    They do not point on me.
OTHELLO.   Peace, and be still!
DESDEMONA. I will so. What's the matter?   50
OTHELLO. That handkerchief which I so loved and
    gave thee,
    Thou gav'st to Cassio.
DESDEMONA.   No, by my life and soul!
    Send for the man, and ask him.
OTHELLO.   Sweet soul, take heed,
    Take heed of perjury: thou art on thy death-bed.
DESDEMONA. Ay, but not yet to die.
OTHELLO.   Yes, presently:
    Therefore confess thee freely of thy sin;
    For to deny each article with oath
    Cannot remove nor choke the strong conception
    That I do groan withal. Thou art to die.
DESDEMONA. O Lord have mercy on me!
OTHELLO.   I say, amen.   60
DESDEMONA. And have you mercy too! I never did
    Offend you in my life; never loved Cassio
    But with such general warranty of heaven
    As I might love. I never gave him token.

OTHELLO. By heaven, I saw my handkerchief in's
    hand.
    O perjured woman! thou dost stone my heart,
    And mak'st me call what I intend to do
    A murder, which I thought a sacrifice.
    I saw the handkerchief.
DESDEMONA.   He found it then;
    I never gave it him. Send for him hither: 70
    Let him confess a truth.
OTHELLO.   He hath confessed.
DESDEMONA. What, my lord?
OTHELLO. That he hath used thee.
DESDEMONA.   How? unlawfully?
OTHELLO. Ay.
DESDEMONA. He will not say so.
OTHELLO.   No, his mouth is stopped;
    Honest Iago hath ta'en order for't.
DESDEMONA. O, my fear interprets! what, is he dead?
OTHELLO. Had all his hairs been lives, my great
    revenge
    Had stomach for them all.
DESDEMONA. Alas, he is betrayed, and I undone!   80
OTHELLO. Out, strumpet! weep'st thou for him to my
    face?
DESDEMONA. O, banish me, my lord, but kill me not!
OTHELLO. Down, strumpet!
DESDEMONA. Kill me tomorrow; let me live tonight!
OTHELLO. Nay, if you strive—
DESDEMONA. But half an hour!
OTHELLO.   Being done, there is no pause.
DESDEMONA. But while I say one prayer!
OTHELLO.   It is too late.   *He smothers her*
EMILIA [*at the door without*]. My lord, my lord!
    what, ho! my lord, my lord!
OTHELLO. What noise is this?—Not dead? not yet quite
    dead?
    I that am cruel am yet merciful;   90
    I would not have thee linger in thy pain.
    So, so.
EMILIA [*without*].   What, ho! my lord, my lord!
OTHELLO.   Who's there?
EMILIA [*without*]. O, good my lord, I'ld speak a word
    with you!
OTHELLO. Yes: 'tis Emilia.—By and by.—She's dead.
    'Tis like she comes to speak of Cassio's death;
    The noise was high. Ha! no more moving?
    Still as the grave. Shall she come in? were't good?
    I think she stirs again. No. What's best to do?
    If she come in, she'll sure speak to my wife—
    My wife! my wife! what wife? I have no wife.   100
    O, insupportable! O heavy hour!
    Methinks it should be now a huge eclipse
    Of sun and moon, and that th'affrighted globe
    Should yawn at alteration.
EMILIA [*without*].   I do beseech
    That I may speak with you. O, good my lord!
OTHELLO. I had forgot thee: O, come in, Emilia.
    Soft; by and by. Let me the curtains draw.
    Where art thou?   *Unlocks the door*

Enter Emilia

                    What's the matter with thee now?
EMILIA. O, my good lord, yonder's foul murder done!
OTHELLO. What, now?   110
EMILIA. But now, my lord.
OTHELLO. It is the very error of the moon;

She comes more nearer earth than she was wont
And makes men mad.
EMILIA. Cassio, my lord, hath killed a young Venetian
Called Roderigo.
OTHELLO.   Roderigo killed!
And Cassio killed!
EMILIA.   No, Cassio is not killed.
OTHELLO. Not Cassio killed! then murder's out of
  tune,
And sweet revenge grows harsh.
DESDEMONA. O, falsely, falsely murdered!
EMILIA.   .   Alas, what cry is that? 120
OTHELLO. That! what?
EMILIA. Out, and alas! that was my lady's voice.
                          She draws back the curtain
Help! help, ho! help! O lady, speak again!
Sweet Desdemona! O sweet mistress, speak!
DESDEMONA. A guiltless death I die.
EMILIA. O, who hath done this deed?
DESDEMONA. Nobody: I myself. Farewell;
Commend me to my kind lord: O, farewell!   *Dies*
OTHELLO. Why, how should she be murdered?
EMILIA.   Alas, who knows?
OTHELLO. You heard her say herself, it was not I. 130
EMILIA. She said so: I must needs report the truth.
OTHELLO. She's like a liar gone to burning hell:
'Twas I that killed her.
EMILIA.   O, the more angel she,
And you the blacker devil!
OTHELLO. She turned to folly, and she was a whore.
EMILIA. Thou dost belie her, and thou art a devil.
OTHELLO. She was false as water.
EMILIA.   Thou art rash as fire to say
That she was false: O, she was heavenly true!
OTHELLO. Cassio did top her: ask thy husband else;
O, I were damned beneath all depth in hell 140
But that I did proceed upon just grounds
To this extremity. Thy husband knew it all.
EMILIA. My husband!
OTHELLO. Thy husband.
EMILIA. That she was false to wedlock?
OTHELLO. Ay, with Cassio. Nay, had she been true,
If heaven would make me such another world
Of one entire and perfect chrysolite,
I'ld not have sold her for it.
EMILIA. My husband!
OTHELLO.   Ay, 'twas he that told me on her first; 150
An honest man he is, and hates the slime
That sticks on filthy deeds.
EMILIA.   My husband!
OTHELLO. What needs this iterance, woman? I say thy
  husband.
EMILIA. O mistress, villany hath made mocks with
  love!
My husband say that she was false!
OTHELLO.   He, woman:
I say thy husband; dost understand the word?
My friend, thy husband, honest, honest Iago.
EMILIA. If he say so, may his pernicious soul
Rot half a grain a day! He lies to th'heart.
She was too fond of her most filthy bargain. 160
OTHELLO. Ha!
EMILIA. Do thy worst:
This deed of thine is no more worthy heaven
Than thou wast worthy her.
OTHELLO.   Peace, you were best.

EMILIA. Thou hast not half that power to do me harm
As I have to be hurt. O gull! O dolt!
As ignorant as dirt! thou hast done a deed—
I care not for thy sword; I'll make thee known,
Though I lost twenty lives. Help! help, ho! help!
The Moor hath killed my mistress! Murder! murder! 170

Enter Montano, Gratiano, Iago, and others

MONTANO. What is the matter? How now, general!
EMILIA. O, are you come, Iago? You have done well,
That men must lay their murders on your neck.
GRATIANO. What is the matter?
EMILIA. Disprove this villain, if thou be'st a man:
He says thou told'st him that his wife was false.
I know thou didst not, thou'rt not such a villain.
Speak, for my heart is full.
IAGO. I told him what I thought, and told no more
Than what he found himself was apt and true. 180
EMILIA. But did you ever tell him she was false?
IAGO. I did.
EMILIA. You told a lie, an odious, damnéd lie;
Upon my soul, a lie, a wicked lie!
She false with Cassio! Did you say with Cassio?
IAGO. With Cassio, mistress. Go to, charm your
  tongue.
EMILIA. I will not charm my tongue; I am bound to
  speak:
My mistress here lies murdered in her bed—
ALL. O heavens forfend!
EMILIA. And your reports have set the murder on. 190
OTHELLO. Nay, stare not, masters: it is true indeed.
GRATIANO. 'Tis a strange truth.
MONTANO. O monstrous act!
EMILIA.   Villany, villany, villany!
I think upon't; I think—I smell't: O villany!
I thought so then; I'll kill myself for grief:
O villany, villany!
IAGO. What, are you mad? I charge you, get you
  home.
EMILIA. Good gentlemen, let me have leave to speak:
'Tis proper I obey him, but not now.
Perchance, Iago, I will ne'er go home.   200
OTHELLO. O! O! O!   *Falls on the bed*
EMILIA.   Nay, lay thee down and roar;
For thou hast killed the sweetest innocent
That e'er did lift up eye.
OTHELLO [*rising*].   O, she was foul!
I scarce did know you, uncle. There lies your niece,
Whose breath indeed these hands have newly
  stopped.
I know this act shows horrible and grim.
GRATIANO. Poor Desdemon! I am glad thy father's
  dead.
Thy match was mortal to him, and pure grief
Shore his old thread in twain. Did he live now,
This sight would make him do a desperate turn, 210
Yea, curse his better angel from his side,
And fall to reprobance.
OTHELLO. 'Tis pitiful; but yet Iago knows
That she with Cassio hath the act of shame
A thousand times committed. Cassio confessed it;
And she did gratify his amorous works
With that recognizance and pledge of love
Which I first gave her—I saw it in his hand:
It was a handkerchief, an antique token
My father gave my mother.   220

EMILIA. O God! O heavenly God!

IAGO. 'Zounds! hold your peace.

EMILIA.   'Twill out, 'twill out. I peace!
No, I will speak as liberal as the north;
Let heaven and men and devils, let them all,
All, all, cry shame against me, yet I'll speak.

IAGO. Be wise, and get you home.

EMILIA.   I will not.

Iago offers to stab her

GRATIANO.   Fie!
Your sword upon a woman!

EMILIA. O thou dull Moor! that handkerchief thou
    speak'st of
I found by fortune, and did give my husband;
For often with a solemn earnestness,   230
More than indeed belonged to such a trifle,
He begged of me to steal it.

IAGO.   Villanous whore!

EMILIA. She give it Cassio! no, alas, I found it,
And I did give't my husband.

IAGO.   Filth, thou liest!

EMILIA. By heaven, I do not, I do not, gentlemen.
O murderous coxcomb! what should such a fool
Do with so good a wife?

OTHELLO.   Are there no stones in heaven
But what serve for the thunder? Precious villain!

*He runs at Iago, but Montano
disarms him; in the confusion,
Iago stabs Emilia from behind
and escapes*

GRATIANO. The woman falls; sure, he hath killed his
    wife.

EMILIA. Ay, ay. O, lay me by my mistress' side.   240

GRATIANO. He's gone, but his wife's killed.

MONTANO. 'Tis a notorious villain. Take you this
    weapon,
Which I have here recovered from the Moor.
Come, guard the door without; let him not pass,
But kill him rather. I'll after that same villain,
For 'tis a damnéd slave.

*All but Othello and Emilia
depart*

OTHELLO.   I am not valiant neither,
But every puny whipster gets my sword.
But why should honour outlive honesty?
Let it go all.

EMILIA.   What did thy song bode, lady?
Hark, canst thou hear me? I will play the swan,   250
And die in music. [*singing*] Willow, willow, willow.
Moor, she was chaste; she loved thee, cruel Moor;
So come my soul to bliss, as I speak true;
So speaking as I think, alas, I die.   *Dies*

OTHELLO. I have another weapon in this chamber:
It was a sword of Spain, the ice brook's temper—
O, here it is. Uncle, I must come forth.

GRATIANO [*at the door*]. If thou attempt it, it will cost
    thee dear:
Thou hast no weapon, and perforce must suffer.

OTHELLO. Look in upon me then, and speak with me,   260
Or, naked as I am, I will assault thee.

Re-enter Gratiano

GRATIANO. What is the matter?

OTHELLO.   Behold, I have a weapon:
A better never did itself sustain
Upon a soldier's thigh. I have seen the day

That with this little arm and this good sword
I have made my way through more impediments
Than twenty times your stop—but, O vain boast!
Who can control his fate?—'tis not so now.
Be not afraid, though you do see me weaponed:
Here is my journey's end, here is my butt   270
And very sea-mark of my utmost sail.
Do you go back dismayed? 'tis a lost fear:
Man but a rush against Othello's breast,
And he retires. Where should Othello go?
Now, [*he turns to the bed*] how dost thou look now?
    O ill-starred wench!
Pale as thy smock! When we shall meet at compt,
This look of thine will hurl my soul from heaven,
And fiends will snatch at it. Cold, cold, my girl!
Even like thy chastity.
O curséd, curséd slave! Whip me, ye devils,   280
From the possession of this heavenly sight!
Blow me about in winds! roast me in sulphur!
Wash me in steep-down gulfs of liquid fire!
O Desdemon! dead Desdemon! dead! O! O!

*Enter Lodovico, Montano, Cassio carried in a chair, and
Officers with Iago, prisoner*

LODOVICO. Where is this rash and most unfortunate
    man?

OTHELLO. That's he that was Othello: here I am.

LODOVICO. Where is that viper? Bring the villain
    forth.

OTHELLO. I look down towards his feet: but that's a
    fable;
If that thou be'st a devil, I cannot kill thee.

Wounds Iago

LODOVICO. Wrench his sword from him.

IAGO.   I bleed, sir, but not killed.   290

OTHELLO. I am not sorry neither: I'ld have thee live;
For, in my sense, 'tis happiness to die.

LODOVICO. O thou Othello, that wert once so good,
Fallen in the practice of a damnéd slave
What shall be said to thee?

OTHELLO.   Why, anything:
An honourable murderer, if you will;
For nought did I in hate, but all in honour.

LODOVICO. This wretch hath part confessed his
    villany.
Did you and he consent in Cassio's death?

OTHELLO. Ay.   300

CASSIO. Dear general, I never gave you cause.

OTHELLO. I do believe it, and I ask your pardon.
Will you, I pray, demand that demi-devil
Why he hath thus ensnared my soul and body?

IAGO. Demand me nothing: what you know, you
    know;
From this time forth I never will speak word.

LODOVICO. What, not to pray?

GRATIANO.   Torments will ope your lips.

OTHELLO. Well, thou dost best.

LODOVICO. Sir, you shall understand what hath
    befallen,
Which, as I think, you know not. Here is a letter,   310
Found in the pocket of the slain Roderigo,
And here another: the one of them imports
The death of Cassio to be undertook
By Roderigo.

OTHELLO. O villain!

CASSIO.   Most heathenish and most gross!

LODOVICO. Now here's another discontented paper,
Found in his pocket too: and this, it seems,
Roderigo meant t'have sent this damnéd villain;
But that, belike, Iago in the nick
Came in and satisfied him.
OTHELLO.   O the pernicious caitiff! 320
How came you, Cassio, by that handkerchief
That was my wife's?
CASSIO.   I found it in my chamber:
And he himself confessed but even now
That there he dropped it for a special purpose
Which wrought to his desire.
OTHELLO.   O fool! fool! fool!
CASSIO. There is besides, in Roderigo's letter,
How he upbraids Iago that he made him
Brave me upon the watch; whereon it came
That I was cast; and even but now he spake—
After long seeming dead—Iago hurt him, 330
Iago set him on.
LODOVICO. You must forsake this room, and go with
us;
Your power and your command is taken off,
And Cassio rules in Cyprus. For this slave,
If there be any cunning cruelty
That can torment him much and hold him long,
It shall be his. You shall close prisoner rest,
Till that the nature of your fault be known
To the Venetian state. Come, bring away.
OTHELLO. Soft you; a word or two before you go. 340
I have done the state some service, and they know't.
No more of that. I pray you, in your letters,
When you shall these unlucky deeds relate,
Speak of me as I am; nothing extenuate,
Nor set down aught in malice. Then must you
speak

Of one that loved not wisely but too well;
Of one not easily jealous but, being wrought,
Perplexed in the extreme; of one whose hand,
Like the base Indian, threw a pearl away
Richer than all his tribe; of one whose subdued eyes, 350
Albeit unuséd to the melting mood,
Drop tears as fast as the Arabian trees
Their medicinable gum—Set you down this;
And say besides, that in Aleppo once,
Where a malignant and a turbaned Turk
Beat a Venetian and traduced the state,
I took by th'throat the circumciséd dog
And smote him—thus.   *He stabs himself*
LODOVICO. O bloody period!
GRATIANO.   All that's spoke is marred.
OTHELLO. I kissed thee ere I killed thee: no way but
this, 360
Killing myself, to die upon a kiss.
                            Falls on the bed, and dies
CASSIO. This did I fear, but thought he had no weapon;
For he was great of heart.
LODOVICO [*to Iago*].   O Spartan dog,
More fell than anguish, hunger, or the sea!
Look on the tragic loading of this bed—
This is thy work. The object poisons sight;
Let it be hid. [*they draw the curtains*] Gratiano,
keep the house,
And seize upon the fortunes of the Moor,
For they succeed on you. To you, lord governor,
Remains the censure of this hellish villain, 370
The time, the place, the torture: O, enforce it!
Myself will straight aboard, and to the state
This heavy act with heavy heart relate.   *They go*

Antony and Cleopatra

The scene: the Roman Empire

CHARACTERS IN THE PLAY

ANTONY
OCTAVIUS CÆSAR } *triumvirs*
LEPIDUS
SEXTUS POMPEIUS
DOMITIUS ENOBARBUS
VENTIDIUS
EROS
SCARUS } *friends to Antony*
DERCETUS
DEMETRIUS
PHILO
MÆCENAS
AGRIPPA
DOLABELLA
PROCULEIUS } *friends to Cæsar*
THIDIAS
GALLUS

MENAS
MENECRATES } *friends to Sextus Pompeius*
VARRIUS
TAURUS, *lieutenant-general to Cæsar*
CANIDIUS, *lieutenant-general to Antony*
SILIUS, *an officer in Ventidius' army*
A Schoolmaster, *ambassador from Antony to Cæsar*
ALEXAS
MARDIAN, *a eunuch*
SELEUCUS } *attendants on Cleopatra*
DIOMEDES
A Soothsayer
A Clown
CLEOPATRA, *queen of Egypt*
OCTAVIA, *sister to Cæsar, and wife to Antony*
CHARMIAN
IRAS } *attendants on Cleopatra*
Officers, soldiers, messengers, and other attendants

Anthony and Cleopatra

ACT 1

Scene 1: *Alexandria. A room in Cleopatra's palace*

Enter Demetrius and Philo

PHILO. Nay, but this dotage of our general's
O'erflows the measure: those his goodly eyes,
That o'er the files and musters of the war
Have glowed like plated Mars—now bend, now
   turn,
The office and devotion of their view
Upon a tawny front: his captain's heart,
Which in the scuffles of great fights hath burst
The buckles on his breast, reneges all temper,
And is become the bellows and the fan
To cool a gipsy's lust.

*Flourish. Enter Antony, Cleopatra, her ladies, the train,
with eunuchs fanning her*

               Look where they come: 10
Take but good note, and you shall see in him
The triple pillar of the world transformed
Into a strumpet's fool. Behold and see.
CLEOPATRA. If it be love indeed, tell me how much.
ANTONY. There's beggary in the love that can
   be reckoned.
CLEOPATRA. I'll set a bourn how far to be beloved.
ANTONY. Then must thou needs find out new heaven,
   new earth.

Enter an Attendant

ATTENDANT. News, my good lord, from Rome.
ANTONY.   Grates me! the sum.
CLEOPATRA. Nay, hear them, Antony:
Fulvia perchance is angry; or, who knows   20
If the scarce-bearded Cæsar have not sent
His powerful mandate to you, 'Do this, or this;
Take in that kingdom, and enfranchise that;
Perform't, or else we damn thee.'
ANTONY.   How, my love?
CLEOPATRA. Perchance? nay, and most like:
You must not stay here longer, your dismission
Is come from Cæsar; therefore hear it, Antony.
Where's Fulvia's process? Cæsar's I would say? both?
Call in the messengers. As I am Egypt's queen,
Thou blushest, Antony, and that blood of thine   30
Is Cæsar's homager: else so thy cheek pays shame
When shrill-tongued Fulvia scolds. The messengers!
ANTONY. Let Rome in Tiber melt, and the wide arch
Of the ranged empire fall! Here is my space.
Kingdoms are clay: our dungy earth alike
Feeds beast as man: the nobleness of life
Is to do thus; when such a mutual pair   *Embracing*
And such a twain can do't, in which I bind,
On pain of punishment, the world to weet
We stand up peerless.
CLEOPATRA.   Excellent falsehood!   40
Why did he marry Fulvia, and not love her?
I'll seem the fool I am not; Antony
Will be himself.
ANTONY.   But stirred by Cleopatra.

Now, for the love of Love and her soft hours,
Let's not confound the time with conference harsh:
There's not a minute of our lives should stretch
Without some pleasure new. What sport to-night?
CLEOPATRA. Hear the ambassadors.
ANTONY.   Fie, wrangling queen!
Whom every thing becomes, to chide, to laugh,
To weep; whose every passion fully strives   50
To make itself, in thee, fair and admired!
No messenger but thine, and all alone
To-night we'll wander through the streets and note
The qualities of people. Come, my queen;
Last night you did desire it. [*to the Attendant*] Speak
   not to us.

          *Antony and Cleopatra depart
              with their train*

DEMETRIUS. Is Cæsar with Antonius prized so slight?
PHILO. Sir, sometimes, when he is not Antony,
He comes too short of that great property
Which still should go with Antony.
DEMETRIUS.   I am full sorry
That he approves the common liar, who   60
Thus speaks of him at Rome: but I will hope
Of better deeds to-morrow. Rest you happy!

                    They go

Scene 2: *The same*

*Enter Enobarbus, three other Romans, a Soothsayer, Cleo-
patra's attendants Charmian, Iras, Mardian the Eunuch,
and Alexas*

CHARMIAN. Lord Alexas, sweet Alexas, most any thing
Alexas, almost most absolute Alexas, where's the
soothsayer that you praised so to th'queen? O, that
I knew this husband, which, you say, must charge
his horns with garlands!
ALEXAS. Soothsayer!
SOOTHSAYER. Your will?
CHARMIAN. Is this the man? Is't you, sir, that know
things?
SOOTHSAYER. In Nature's infinite book of secrecy
A little I can read.
ALEXAS.   Show him your hand.   10
ENOBARBUS [*to a servant*]. Bring in the banquet
quickly; wine enough
Cleopatra's health to drink.
CHARMIAN. Good sir, give me good fortune.
SOOTHSAYER. I make not, but foresee.
CHARMIAN. Pray then, foresee me one.
SOOTHSAYER. You shall be yet far fairer than you are.
CHARMIAN. He means in flesh.
IRAS. No, you shall paint when you are old.
CHARMIAN. Wrinkles forbid!
ALEXAS. Vex not his prescience, be attentive.   20
CHARMIAN. Hush!
SOOTHSAYER. You shall be more beloving than be-
loved.
CHARMIAN. I had rather heat my liver with drinking.
ALEXAS. Nay, hear him.
CHARMIAN. Good now, some excellent fortune! Let

me be married to three kings in a forenoon, and
widow them all: let me have a child at fifty, to
whom Herod of Jewry may do homage: find me to
marry me with Octavius Cæsar, and companion me 30
with my mistress.

SOOTHSAYER. You shall outlive the lady whom you
serve.

CHARMIAN. O excellent! I love long life better than
figs.

SOOTHSAYER. You have seen and proved a fairer
former fortune
Than that which is to approach.

CHARMIAN. Then belike my children shall have no
names: prithee, how many boys and wenches must
I have? 40

SOOTHSAYER. If every of your wishes had a womb,
And fertile every wish, a million.

CHARMIAN. Out, fool! I forgive thee for a witch.

ALEXAS. You think none but your sheets are privy to
your wishes.

CHARMIAN. Nay, come, tell Iras hers.

ALEXAS. We'll know all our fortunes.

ENOBARBUS. Mine and most of our fortunes to-night
shall be—drunk to bed.

IRAS. There's a palm presages chastity, if nothing else. 50

CHARMIAN. E'en as the o'erflowing Nilus presageth
famine.

IRAS. Go, you wild bedfellow, you cannot soothsay.

CHARMIAN. Nay, if an oily palm be not a fruitful
prognostication, I cannot scratch mine ear. Prithee,
tell her but a worky-day fortune.

SOOTHSAYER. Your fortunes are alike.

IRAS. But how, but how? give me particulars.

SOOTHSAYER. I have said.

IRAS. Am I not an inch of fortune better than she? 60

CHARMIAN. Well, if you were but an inch of fortune
better than I . . . where would you choose it?

IRAS. Not in my husband's nose.

CHARMIAN. Our worser thoughts heavens mend!
Alexas—come, his fortune, his fortune! O, let him
marry a woman that cannot go, sweet Isis, I beseech
thee! and let her die too, and give him a worse! and
let worse follow worse, till the worst of all follow
him laughing to his grave, fifty-fold a cuckold!
Good Isis, hear me this prayer, though thou deny 70
me a matter of more weight; good Isis, I beseech
thee!

IRAS. Amen, dear goddess, hear that prayer of thy
people! For, as it is a heart-breaking to see a handsome man loose-witted, so it is a deadly sorrow to
behold a foul knave uncuckolded: therefore, dear
Isis, keep decorum, and fortune him accordingly!

CHARMIAN. Amen.

ALEXAS. Lo, now, if it lay in their hands to make me
a cuckold, they would make themselves whores but 80
they'ld do't!

ENOBARBUS. Hush! here comes Antony.

Enter Cleopatra

CHARMIAN.   Not he, the queen.

CLEOPATRA. Saw you my lord?

ENOBARBUS. No, lady.

CLEOPATRA. Was he not here?

CHARMIAN. No, madam.

CLEOPATRA. He was disposed to mirth, but on the
sudden

A Roman thought hath struck him. Enobarbus!

ENOBARBUS. Madam?

CLEOPATRA. Seek him, and bring him hither.   *He goes*
Where's Alexas? 90

ALEXAS. Here, at your service. My lord approaches.

Enter Antony with a Messenger and Attendants

CLEOPATRA. We will not look upon him: go with us.
                         They leave

MESSENGER. Fulvia thy wife first came into the field.

ANTONY. Against my brother Lucius?

MESSENGER. Ay:
But soon that war had end, and the time's state
Made friends of them, jointing their force 'gainst
Cæsar,
Whose better issue in the war from Italy
Upon the first encounter drave them.

ANTONY.   Well, what worst?

MESSENGER. The nature of bad news infects the teller. 100

ANTONY. When it concerns the fool or coward. On!
Things that are past are done. With me, 'tis thus—
Who tells me true, though in his tale lie death,
I hear him as he flattered.

MESSENGER.   Labienus—
This is stiff news—hath with his Parthian force
Extended Asia from Euphrates,
His conquering banner shook from Syria
To Lydia and to Ionia,
Whilst—

ANTONY. Antony, thou wouldst say—

MESSENGER.   O, my lord!

ANTONY. Speak to me home, mince not the general
tongue, 110
Name Cleopatra as she is called in Rome;
Rail thou in Fulvia's phrase, and taunt my faults
With such full license as both truth and malice
Have power to utter. O, then we bring forth weeds
When our quick minds lie still, and our ills told us
Is as our earing. Fare thee well awhile.

MESSENGER. At your noble pleasure.   *He goes*

ANTONY. From Sicyon, ho, the news! Speak there!

1 ATTENDANT. The man from Sicyon, is there such
an one?

2 ATTENDANT. He stays upon your will.

ANTONY.   Let him appear. 120
These strong Egyptian fetters I must break,
Or lose myself in dotage.

Enter another Messenger, with a letter

                What are you?

2 MESSENGER. Fulvia thy wife is dead.

ANTONY.   Where died she?

2 MESSENGER. In Sicyon:
Her length of sickness, with what else more serious
Importeth thee to know, this bears.   *Gives a letter*

ANTONY.   Forbear me.
         Messenger and Attendants withdraw
There's a great spirit gone! Thus did I desire it:
What our contempts doth often hurl from us,
We wish it ours again; the present pleasure,
By revolution lowering, does become 130
The opposite of itself: she's good, being gone;
The hand could pluck her back that shoved her on.
I must from this enchanting queen break off:
Ten thousand harms, more than the ills I know,
My idleness doth hatch. Ho, now! Enobarbus!

Enobarbus returns

ENOBARBUS. What's your pleasure, sir?

ANTONY. I must with haste from hence.

ENOBARBUS. Why then we kill all our women. We see
how mortal an unkindness is to them; if they suffer
our departure death's the word.   140

ANTONY. I must be gone.

ENOBARBUS. Under a compelling occasion let women
die. It were pity to cast them away for nothing,
though between them and a great cause they should
be esteemed nothing. Cleopatra, catching but the
least noise of this, dies instantly; I have seen her die
twenty times upon far poorer moment: I do think
there is mettle in death, which commits some loving
act upon her, she hath such a celerity in dying.

ANTONY. She is cunning past man's thought.   150

ENOBARBUS. Alack, sir, no; her passions are made of
nothing but the finest part of pure love. We cannot
call her winds and waters sighs and tears; they are
greater storms and tempests than almanacs can
report. This cannot be cunning in her; if it be, she
makes a shower of rain as well as Jove.

ANTONY. Would I had never seen her!

ENOBARBUS. O, sir, you had then left unseen a wonderful piece of work, which not to have been blest
withal would have discredited your travel.   160

ANTONY. Fulvia is dead.

ENOBARBUS. Sir?

ANTONY. Fulvia is dead.

ENOBARBUS. Fulvia!

ANTONY. Dead.

ENOBARBUS. Why, sir, give the gods a thankful sacrifice. When it pleaseth their deities to take the wife
of a man from him, it shows to man the tailors of
the earth; comforting therein, that when old robes
are worn out there are members to make new. If   170
there were no more women but Fulvia, then had
you indeed a cut, and the case to be lamented: this
grief is crowned with consolation; your old smock
brings forth a new petticoat: and indeed the tears
live in an onion that should water this sorrow.

ANTONY. The business she hath broached in the state
Cannot endure my absence.

ENOBARBUS. And the business you have broached here
cannot be without you; especially that of Cleopatra's, which wholly depends on your abode.   180

ANTONY. No more light answers. Let our officers
Have notice what we purpose. I shall break
The cause of our expedience to the queen,
And get her leave to part. For not alone
The death of Fulvia, with more urgent touches,
Do strongly speak to us, but the letters too
Of many our contriving friends in Rome
Petition us at home: Sextus Pompeius
Hath given the dare to Cæsar and commands
The empire of the sea: our slippery people,   190
Whose love is never linked to the deserver
Till his deserts are past, begin to throw
Pompey the Great and all his dignities
Upon his son; who, high in name and power,
Higher than both in blood and life, stands up
For the main soldier: whose quality, going on,
The sides o'th'world may danger. Much is breeding,
Which, like the courser's hair, hath yet but life
And not a serpent's poison. Say, our pleasure,

To such whose place is under us, requires   200
Our quick remove from hence.

ENOBARBUS. I shall do't.   *They go*

Scene 3

Enter Cleopatra, Charmian, Iras, and Alexas

CLEOPATRA. Where is he?

CHARMIAN.   I did not see him since.

CLEOPATRA. See where he is, who's with him, what
he does:
I did not send you: if you find him sad,
Say I am dancing; if in mirth, report
That I am sudden sick. Quick, and return.
                               Alexas goes

CHARMIAN. Madam, methinks, if you did love him
dearly,
You do not hold the method to enforce
The like from him.

CLEOPATRA.   What should I do, I do not?

CHARMIAN. In each thing give him way, cross him
in nothing.

CLEOPATRA. Thou teachest like a fool: the way to
lose him.   10

CHARMIAN. Tempt him not so too far; iwis, forbear:
In time we hate that which we often fear.

Antony enters

But here comes Antony.

CLEOPATRA.   I am sick and sullen.

ANTONY. I am sorry to give breathing to my
purpose—

CLEOPATRA. Help me away, dear Charmian, I shall fall.
It cannot be thus long, the sides of nature
Will not sustain it.

ANTONY.   Now, my dearest queen—

CLEOPATRA. Pray you, stand farther from me.

ANTONY.   What's the matter?

CLEOPATRA. I know, by that same eye, there's some
good news.
What, says the married woman you may go?   20
Would she had never given you leave to come!
Let her not say 'tis I that keep you here.
I have no power upon you; hers you are.

ANTONY. The gods best know—

CLEOPATRA.   O, never was there queen
So mightily betrayed! yet at the first
I saw the treasons planted.

ANTONY.   Cleopatra—

CLEOPATRA. Why should I think you can be mine
and true
(Though you in swearing shake the thronéd gods),
Who have been false to Fulvia! Riotous madness,
To be entangled with those mouth-made vows,   30
Which break themselves in swearing!

ANTONY.   Most sweet queen—

CLEOPATRA. Nay, pray you, seek no colour for
your going,
But bid farewell, and go: when you sued staying,
Then was the time for words: no going then;
Eternity was in our lips and eyes,
Bliss in our brows' bent; none our parts so poor
But was a race of heaven: they are so still,
Or thou, the greatest soldier of the world,
Art turned the greatest liar.

ANTONY.   How now, lady!

CLEOPATRA. I would I had thy inches; thou
  shouldst know
  There were a heart in Egypt.
ANTONY.   Hear me, queen:
  The strong necessity of time commands
  Our services awhile; but my full heart
  Remains in use with you. Our Italy
  Shines o'er with civil swords: Sextus Pompeius
  Makes his approaches to the port of Rome:
  Equality of two domestic powers
  Breed scrupulous faction: the hated, grown to
    strength,
  Are newly grown to love: the condemned Pompey,
  Rich in his father's honour, creeps apace   50
  Into the hearts of such as have not thrived
  Upon the present state, whose numbers threaten;
  And quietness grown sick of rest would purge
  By any desperate change. My more particular,
  And that which most with you should safe my
    going,
  Is Fulvia's death.
CLEOPATRA. Though age from folly could not give
  me freedom,
  It does from childishness: can Fulvia die?
ANTONY. She's dead, my queen.
  Look here, and at thy sovereign leisure read   60
  The garboils she awaked: at the last, best,
  See when and where she died.
CLEOPATRA.   O most false love!
  Where be the sacred vials thou shouldst fill
  With sorrowful water? Now I see, I see,
  In Fulvia's death, how mine received shall be.
ANTONY. Quarrel no more, but be prepared to know
  The purposes I bear; which are, or cease,
  As you shall give th'advice. By the fire
  That quickens Nilus' slime, I go from hence
  Thy soldier, servant, making peace or war   70
  As thou affects.
CLEOPATRA.   Cut my lace, Charmian, come;
  But let it be—I am quickly ill, and well—
  So Antony loves.
ANTONY.   My precious queen, forbear;
  And give true evidence to his love, which stands
  An honourable trial.
CLEOPATRA.   So Fulvia told me.
  I prithee, turn aside and weep for her,
  Then bid adieu to me, and say the tears
  Belong to Egypt: good now, play one scene
  Of excellent dissembling, and let it look
  Like perfect honour.
ANTONY.   You'll heat my blood: no more.   80
CLEOPATRA. You can do better yet; but this is meetly.
ANTONY. Now, by my sword
CLEOPATRA.   And target. Still he mends;
  But this is not the best. Look, prithee, Charmian,
  How this Herculean Roman does become
  The carriage of his chafe.
ANTONY. I'll leave you, lady.
CLEOPATRA.   Courteous lord, one word.
  Sir, you and I must part, but that's not it:
  Sir, you and I have loved, but there's not it;
  That you know well: something it is I would:
  O, my oblivion is a very Antony,   90
  And I am all forgotten.
ANTONY.   But that your royalty
  Holds idleness your subject, I should take you

For idleness itself.
CLEOPATRA.   'Tis sweating labour
  To bear such idleness so near the heart
  As Cleopatra this. But, sir, forgive me,
  Since my becomings kill me when they do not
  Eye well to you. Your honour calls you hence;
  Therefore be deaf to my unpitied folly,
  And all the gods go with you! Upon your sword
  Sit laurel victory! and smooth success   100
  Be strewed before your feet!
ANTONY.   Let us go. Come;
  Our separation so abides and flies,
  That thou, residing here, goes yet with me,
  And I, hence fleeing, here remain with thee.
  Away!   *They go*

Scene 4: *Rome. Cæsar's house*

Enter Octavius Cæsar, reading a letter, Lepidus, and their
train

CÆSAR. You may see, Lepidus, and henceforth know,
  It is not Cæsar's natural vice to hate
  Our great competitor. From Alexandria
  This is the news: he fishes, drinks and wastes
  The lamps of night in revel: is not more manlike
  Than Cleopatra, nor the queen of Ptolemy
  More womanly than he: hardly gave audience, or
  Vouchsafed to think he had partners: you shall find
    there
  A man who is the abstract of all faults
  That all men follow.
LEPIDUS.   I must not think there are   10
  Evils enow to darken all his goodness:
  His faults in him seem as the spots of heaven,
  More fiery by night's blackness, hereditary
  Rather than purchased, what he cannot change
  Than what he chooses.
CÆSAR. You are too indulgent. Let's grant it is not
  Amiss to tumble on the bed of Ptolemy,
  To give a kingdom for a mirth, to sit
  And keep the turn of tippling with a slave,
  To reel the streets at noon and stand the buffet   20
  With knaves that smell of sweat: say this
    becomes him—
  As his composure must be rare indeed
  Whom these things cannot blemish—yet must
    Antony
  No way excuse his foils, when we do bear
  So great weight in his lightness. If he filled
  His vacancy with his voluptuousness,
  Full surfeits and the dryness of his bones
  Call on him for't: but to confound such time
  That drums him from his sport and speaks as loud
  As his own state and ours—'tis to be chid   30
  As we rate boys, who, being mature in knowledge,
  Pawn their experience to their present pleasure,
  And so rebel to judgement.

Enter a Messenger

LEPIDUS.   Here's more news.
MESSENGER. Thy biddings have been done, and
  every hour,
  Most noble Cæsar, shalt thou have report
  How 'tis abroad. Pompey is strong at sea,
  And it appears he is beloved of those
  That only have feared Cæsar: to the fleets

The discontents repair, and men's reports
Give him much wronged.
CÆSAR.   I should have known no less: 40
It hath been taught us from the primal state,
That he which is was wished until he were;
And the ebbed man, ne'er loved till ne'er worth
love,
Comes deared by being lacked. This common body,
Like to a vagabond flag upon the stream,
Goes to and back, lackeying the varying tide,
To rot itself with motion.
MESSENGER.   Cæsar, I bring thee word,
Menecrates and Menas, famous pirates,
Make the sea serve them, which they ear and wound
With keels of every kind: many hot inroads 50
They make in Italy; the borders maritime
Lack blood to think on't, and flush youth revolt:
No vessel can peep forth, but 'tis as soon
Taken as seen; for Pompey's name strikes more
Than could his war resisted.
CÆSAR.   Antony,
Leave thy lascivious wassails. When thou once
Wast beaten from Modena, where thou slew'st
Hirtius and Pansa, consuls, at thy heel
Did famine follow, whom thou fought'st against
(Though daintily brought up) with patience more 60
Than savages could suffer: thou didst drink
The stale of horses and the gilded puddle
Which beasts would cough at: thy palate then did
deign
The roughest berry on the rudest hedge;
Yea, like the stag, when snow the pasture sheets,
The barks of trees thou browsed. On the Alps
It is reported thou didst eat strange flesh,
Which some did die to look on: and all this—
It wounds thine honour that I speak it now—
Was borne so like a soldier that thy cheek 70
So much as lanked not.
LEPIDUS.   'Tis pity of him.
CÆSAR. Let his shames quickly
Drive him to Rome. 'Tis time we twain
Did show ourselves i'th'field, and to that end
Assemble we immediate council. Pompey
Thrives in our idleness.
LEPIDUS.   To-morrow, Cæsar,
I shall be furnished to inform you rightly
Both what by sea and land I can be able
To front this present time.
CÆSAR.   Till which encounter,
It is my business too. Farewell. 80
LEPIDUS. Farewell, my lord: what you shall know
meantime
Of stirs abroad, I shall beseech you, sir,
To let me be partaker.
CÆSAR.   Doubt not, sir;
I knew it for my bond.   *They go*

Scene 5: *Alexandria. Cleopatra's palace*

Enter Cleopatra, Charmian, Iras, and Mardian

CLEOPATRA. Charmian!
CHARMIAN. Madam?
CLEOPATRA. Ha, ha!
Give me to drink mandragora.
CHARMIAN.   Why, madam?

CLEOPATRA. That I might sleep out this great tap of
time
My Antony is away.
CHARMIAN.   You think of him too much.
CLEOPATRA. O, 'tis treason!
CHARMIAN.   Madam, I trust not so.
CLEOPATRA. Thou, eunuch Mardian!
MARDIAN.   What's your highness' pleasure?
CLEOPATRA. Not now to hear thee sing; I take
no pleasure
In aught an eunuch has: 'tis well for thee, 10
That, being unseminared, thy freer thoughts
May not fly forth of Egypt. Hast thou affections?
MARDIAN. Yes, gracious madam.
CLEOPATRA. Indeed?
MARDIAN. Not in deed, madam, for I can do nothing
But what indeed is honest to be done:
Yet have I fierce affections, and think
What Venus did with Mars.
CLEOPATRA.   O Charmian,
Where think'st thou he is now? Stands he, or sits
he?
Or does he walk? or is he on his horse? 20
O happy horse, to bear the weight of Antony!
Do bravely, horse! for wot'st thou whom thou
mov'st?
The demi-Atlas of this earth, the arm
And burgonet of men. He's speaking now,
Or murmuring 'Where's my serpent of old Nile?'
For so he calls me: now I feed myself
With most delicious poison. Think on me,
That am with Phœbus' amorous pinches black
And wrinkled deep in time? Broad-fronted Cæsar,
When thou wast here above the ground, I was 30
A morsel for a monarch: and great Pompey
Would stand and make his eyes grow in my brow;
There would he anchor his aspéct and die
With looking on his life.

Enter Alexas from Antony

ALEXAS.   Sovereign of Egypt, hail!
CLEOPATRA. How much unlike art thou Mark Antony!
Yet, coming from him, that great med'cine hath
With his tinct gilded thee.
How goes it with my brave Mark Antony?
ALEXAS. Last thing he did, dear queen,
He kissed—the last of many doubled kisses— 40
This orient pearl. His speech sticks in my heart.
CLEOPATRA. Mine ear must pluck in thence.
ALEXAS.   'Good friend,' quoth he,
'Say, the firm Roman to great Egypt sends
This treasure of an oyster; at whose foot,
To mend the petty present, I will piece
Her opulent throne with kingdoms; all the east,
Say thou, shall call her mistress.' So he nodded,
And soberly did mount an arm-gaunt steed,
Who neighed so high, that what I would have spoke
Was beastly dumbed by him.
CLEOPATRA.   What was he, sad or merry? 50
ALEXAS. Like to the time o'th'year between the
extremes
Of hot and cold, he was nor sad nor merry.
CLEOPATRA. O well divided disposition! Note him,
Note him, good Charmian, 'tis the man; but note
him:
He was not sad, for he would shine on those

That make their looks by his; he was not merry,
Which seemed to tell them his remembrance lay
In Egypt with his joy; but between both.
O heavenly mingle! Be'st thou sad or merry,
The violence of either thee becomes,   60
So does it no man else. Met'st thou my posts?
ALEXAS. Ay, madam, twenty several messengers:
  Why do you send so thick?
CLEOPATRA.   Who's born that day
When I forget to send to Antony,
Shall die a beggar. Ink and paper, Charmian.
Welcome, my good Alexas. Did I, Charmian,
Ever love Cæsar so?
CHARMIAN.   O that brave Cæsar!
CLEOPATRA. Be choked with such another emphasis!
  Say, the brave Antony.
CHARMIAN.   The valiant Cæsar!
CLEOPATRA. By Isis, I will give thee bloody teeth,   70
  If thou with Cæsar paragon again
  My man of men.
CHARMIAN.   By your most gracious pardon,
  I sing but after you.
CLEOPATRA.   My salad days,
When I was green in judgement, cold in blood,
To say as I said then. But come, away,
Get me ink and paper.
He shall have every day a several greeting,
Or I'll unpeople Egypt.   *They go*

ACT 2

Scene 1: *Messina. Pompey's house*

Enter Pompey, Menecrates, and Menas, in warlike manner

POMPEY. If the great gods be just, they shall assist
  The deeds of justest men.
MENAS.   Know, worthy Pompey,
  That what they do delay, they not deny.
POMPEY. Whiles we are suitors to their throne, decays
  The thing we sue for.
MENAS.   We, ignorant of ourselves,
  Beg often our own harms, which the wise powers
  Deny us for our good; so find we profit
  By losing of our prayers.
POMPEY.   I shall do well:
  The people love me, and the sea is mine;
  My powers are crescent, and my auguring hope   10
  Says it will come to th'full. Mark Antony
  In Egypt sits at dinner, and will make
  No wars without doors: Cæsar gets money where
  He loses hearts: Lepidus flatters both,
  Of both is flattered, but he neither loves,
  Not either cares for him.
MENAS.   Cæsar and Lepidus.
  Are in the field: a mighty strength they carry.
POMPEY. Where have you this? 'tis false.
MENAS.   From Silvius, sir.
POMPEY. He dreams: I know they are in Rome
    together,
  Looking for Antony. But all the charms of love,   20
  Salt Cleopatra, soften thy waned lip!
  Let witchcraft join with beauty, lust with both!
  Tie up the libertine in a field of feasts,
  Keep his brain fuming; Epicurean cooks
  Sharpen with cloyless sauce his appetite;

That sleep and feeding may prorogue his honour
Even till a Lethe'd dulness—

Enter Varrius

                    How now, Varrius!
VARRIUS. This is most certain that I shall deliver:
  Mark Antony is every hour in Rome
  Expected: since he went from Egypt 'tis   30
  A space for farther travel.
POMPEY.   I could have given less matter
  A better ear. Menas, I did not think
  This amorous surfeiter would have donned his helm
  For such a petty war: his soldiership
  Is twice the other twain: but let us rear
  The higher our opinion, that our stirring
  Can from the lap of Egypt's widow pluck
  The ne'er-lust-wearied Antony.
MENAS.   I cannot hope
  Cæsar and Antony shall well greet together:
  His wife that's dead did trespasses to Cæsar;   40
  His brother warred upon him, although I think
  Not moved by Antony.
POMPEY.   I know not, Menas,
  How lesser enmities may give way to greater.
  Were't not that we stand up against them all,
  'Twere pregnant they should square between
    themselves;
  For they have entertainéd cause enough
  To draw their swords: but how the fear of us
  May cement their divisions and bind up
  The petty difference, we yet not know.
  Be't as our gods will have't! It only stands   50
  Our lives upon to use our strongest hands.
  Come, Menas.   *They go*

Scene 2: *Rome. The house of Lepidus*

Enter Enobarbus and Lepidus

LEPIDUS. Good Enobarbus, 'tis a worthy deed,
  And shall become you well, to entreat your captain
  To soft and gentle speech.
ENOBARBUS.   I shall entreat him
  To answer like himself: if Cæsar move him,
  Let Antony look over Cæsar's head,
  And speak as loud as Mars. By Jupiter,
  Were I wearer of Antonio's beard,
  I would not shave't to-day.
LEPIDUS.   'Tis not a time
  For private stomaching.
ENOBARBUS.   Every time
  Serves for the matter that is then born in't.   10
LEPIDUS. But small to greater matters must give way.
ENOBARBUS. Not if the small come first.
LEPIDUS.   Your speech is passion:
  But, pray you, stir no embers up. Here comes
  The noble Antony.

Antony and Ventidius enter

ENOBARBUS.   And yonder, Cæsar.

Cæsar, Mæcenas, and Agrippa enter

ANTONY. If we compose well here, to Parthia:
  Hark, Ventidius.
CÆSAR.   I do not know,
  Mæcenas; ask Agrippa.
LEPIDUS.   Noble friends,

That which combined us was most great, and
let not
A leaner action rend us. What's amiss,
May it be gently heard: when we debate 20
Our trivial difference loud, we do commit
Murder in healing wounds: then, noble partners,
The rather for I earnestly beseech,
Touch you the sourest points with sweetest terms,
Nor curstness grow to th'matter.
ANTONY.   'Tis spoken well.
Were we before our armies and to fight,
I should do thus.   *Flourish*
CÆSAR. Welcome to Rome.
ANTONY.   Thank you.
CÆSAR.   Sit.
ANTONY.   Sit, sir.
CÆSAR.   Nay, then.
ANTONY. I learn, you take things ill which are not so;
Or being, concern you not.
CÆSAR.   I must be laughed at, 30
If, or for nothing or a little, I
Should say myself offended, and with you
Chiefly i'th'world; more laughed at, that I should
Once name you derogately, when to sound your
name
It not concerned me.
ANTONY.   My being in Egypt, Cæsar,
What was't to you?
CÆSAR. No more than my residing here at Rome
Might be to you in Egypt: yet, if you there
Did practise on my state, your being in Egypt
Might be my question.
ANTONY.   How intend you, practised? 40
CÆSAR. You may be pleased to catch at mine intent
By what did here befall me. Your wife and brother
Made wars upon me, and their contestation
Was then for you, you were the word of war.
ANTONY. You do mistake your business; my brother
never
Did urge me in his act; I did inquire it,
And have my learning from some true reports
That drew their swords with you. Did he not rather
Discredit my authority with yours,
And make the wars alike against my stomach,
Having alike your cause? Of this my letters 50
Before did satisfy you. If you'll patch a quarrel,
As matter whole you have to make it with,
It must not be with this.
CÆSAR.   You praise yourself.
By laying defects of judgement to me, but
You patched up your excuses.
ANTONY.   Not so, not so;
I know you could not lack, I am certain on't,
Very necessity of this thought, that I,
Your partner in the cause 'gainst which he fought,
Could not with grateful eyes attend those wars 60
Which fronted mine own peace. As for my wife,
I would you had her spirit in such another:
The third o'th'world is yours, which with a snaffle
You may pace easy, but not such a wife—
ENOBARBUS. Would we had all such wives, that the
men might go to wars with the women!
ANTONY. —So much incurable; her garboils, Cæsar,
Made out of her impatience (which not wanted
Shrewdness of policy too), I grieving grant
Did you too much disquiet: for that you must 70

But say, I could not help it.
CÆSAR.   I wrote to you.
When rioting in Alexandria you
Did pocket up my letters, and with taunts
Did gibe my missive out of audience.
ANTONY.   Sir,
He fell upon me, ere admitted, then:
Three kings I had newly feasted and did want
Of what I was i'th'morning: but next day
I told him of myself, which was as much
As to have asked him pardon. Let this fellow
Be nothing of our strife; if we contend, 80
Out of our question wipe him.
CÆSAR.   You have broken
The article of your oath, which you shall never
Have tongue to charge me with.
LEPIDUS.   Soft, Cæsar!
ANTONY. No, Lepidus, let him speak:
The honour is sacred which he talks on now,
Supposing that I lacked it. But on, Cæsar;
The article of my oath—
CÆSAR. To lend me arms and aid when I required
them;
The which you both denied.
ANTONY.   Neglected rather,
And then when poisoned hours had bound me up 90
From mine own knowledge. As nearly as I may,
I'll play the penitent to you: but mine honesty
Shall not make poor my greatness, nor my power
Work without it. Truth is that Fulvia,
To have me out of Egypt, made wars here;
For which myself, the ignorant motive, do
So far ask pardon as befits mine honour
To stoop in such a case.
LEPIDUS.   'Tis noble spoken.
MÆCENAS. If it might please you, to enforce no further
The griefs between ye: to forget them quite 100
Were to remember that the present need
Speaks to atone you.
LEPIDUS.   Worthily spoken, Mæcenas.
ENOBARBUS. Or, if you borrow one another's love for
the instant, you may, when you hear no more
words of Pompey, return it again: you shall have
time to wrangle in when you have nothing else to do.
ANTONY. Thou art a soldier only: speak no more.
ENOBARBUS. That truth should be silent I had
almost forgot.
ANTONY. You wrong this presence; therefore speak
no more.
ENOBARBUS. Go to, then; your considerate stone. 110
CÆSAR. I do not much dislike the matter, but
The manner of his speech; for't cannot be
We shall remain in friendship, our conditions
So differing in their acts. Yet, if I knew
What hoop should hold us staunch from edge
to edge
O'th'world, I would pursue it.
AGRIPPA.   Give me leave, Cæsar.
CÆSAR. Speak, Agrippa.
AGRIPPA. Thou hast a sister by the mother's side,
Admired Octavia: great Mark Antony
Is now a widower.
CÆSAR.   Say not so, Agrippa: 120
If Cleopatra heard you, your reproof
Were well deserved of rashness.
ANTONY. I am not married, Cæsar: let me hear

Agrippa further speak.

AGRIPPA. To hold you in perpetual amity,
To make you brothers, and to knit your hearts
With an unslipping knot, take Antony
Octavia to his wife; whose beauty claims
No worse a husband than the best of men;
Whose virtue and whose general graces speak   130
That which none else can utter. By this marriage
All little jealousies which now seem great,
And all great fears which now import their dangers,
Would then be nothing: truths would be tales,
Where now half tales be truths: her love to both
Would each to other and all loves to both
Draw after her. Pardon what I have spoke,
For 'tis a studied, not a present thought,
By duty ruminated.

ANTONY.   Will Cæsar speak?

CÆSAR. Not till he hears how Antony is touched   140
With what is spoken already.

ANTONY.   What power is in Agrippa,
If I would say, 'Agrippa, be it so,'
To make this good?

CÆSAR.   The power of Cæsar, and
His power unto Octavia.

ANTONY.   May I never
(To this good purpose, that so fairly shows)
Dream of impediment! Let me have thy hand:
Further this act of grace; and from this hour
The heart of brothers govern in our loves
And sway our great designs!

CÆSAR.   There's my hand.
A sister I bequeath you, whom no brother   150
Did ever love so dearly: let her live
To join our kingdoms and our hearts—and never
Fly off our loves again!

LEPIDUS.   Happily, amen!

ANTONY. I did not think to draw my sword
'gainst Pompey;
For he hath laid strange courtesies and great
Of late upon me. I must thank him only,
Lest my remembrance suffer ill report;
At heel of that, defy him.

LEPIDUS.   Time calls upon's:
Of us must Pompey presently be sought,
Or else he seeks out us.

ANTONY.   Where lies he?   160

CÆSAR. About the Mount Misenum.

ANTONY.   What is his strength
By land?

CÆSAR.   Great and increasing: but by sea
He is an absolute master.

ANTONY.   So is the fame.
Would we had spoke together! Haste we for it:
Yet, ere we put ourselves in arms, dispatch we
The business we have talked of.

CÆSAR.   With most gladness;
And do invite you to my sister's view,
Whither straight I'll lead you.

ANTONY.   Let us, Lepidus,
Not lack your company.

LEPIDUS.   Noble Antony,
Not sickness should detain me.   170

Flourish. Cæsar, Antony, and
Lepidus go out together

MÆCENAS. Welcome from Egypt, sir.

ENOBARBUS. Half the heart of Cæsar, worthy Mæcenas! My honourable friend, Agrippa!

AGRIPPA. Good Enobarbus!

MÆCENAS. We have cause to be glad that matters are
so well digested. You stayed well by't in Egypt.

ENOBARBUS. Ay, sir; we did sleep day out of countenance, and made the night light with drinking.

MÆCENAS. Eight wild-boars roasted whole at a breakfast, and but twelve persons there; is this true?   180

ENOBARBUS. This was but as a fly by an eagle: we had
much more monstrous matter of feast, which
worthily deserved noting.

MÆCENAS. She's a most triumphant lady, if report be
square to her.

ENOBARBUS. When she first met Mark Antony, she
pursed up his heart, upon the river of Cydnus.

AGRIPPA. There she appeared indeed; or my reporter
devised well for her.

ENOBARBUS. I will tell you.   190
The barge she sat in, like a burnisht throne
Burned on the water: the poop was beaten gold;
Purple the sails, and so perfumed that
The winds were love-sick with them; the oars
were silver,
Which to the tune of flutes kept stroke and made
The water which they beat to follow faster,
As amorous of their strokes. For her own person,
It beggared all description, she did lie
In her pavilion, cloth-of-gold, of tissue,
O'er-picturing that Venus where we see   200
The fancy outwork nature: on each side her
Stood pretty dimpled boys, like smiling Cupids,
With divers-coloured fans, whose wind did seem
To glow the delicate cheeks which they did cool,
And what they undid did.

AGRIPPA.   O, rare for Antony!

ENOBARBUS. Her gentlewomen, like the Nereides,
So many mermaids, tended her i'th'eyes,
And made their bends adornings: at the helm
A seeming mermaid steers: the silken tackle
Swell with the touches of those flower-soft hands,   210
That yarely frame the office. From the barge
A strange invisible perfume hits the sense
Of the adjacent wharfs. The city cast
Her people out upon her; and Antony,
Enthroned i'th'market-place, did sit alone,
Whistling to th'air; which, but for vacancy,
Had gone to gaze on Cleopatra too,
And made a gap in nature.

AGRIPPA.   Rare Egyptian!

ENOBARBUS. Upon her landing, Antony sent to her,
Invited her to supper: she replied,   220
It should be better he became her guest;
Which she entreated: our courteous Antony,
Whom ne'er the word of 'No' woman heard speak,
Being barbered ten times o'er, goes to the feast,
And, for his ordinary, pays his heart
For what his eyes eat only.

AGRIPPA.   Royal wench!
She made great Cæsar lay his sword to bed:
He ploughed her, and she cropped.

ENOBARBUS.   I saw her once
Hop forty paces through the public street;
And having lost her breath, she spoke, and panted,   230
That she did make defect perfection,
And, breathless, power breathe forth.

MÆCENAS. Now Antony must leave her utterly.

ENOBARBUS. Never; he will not:
Age cannot wither her, nor custom stale
Her infinite variety: other women cloy
The appetites they feed, but she makes hungry
Where most she satisfies: for vilest things
Become themselves in her, that the holy priests
Bless her when she is riggish.   240
MÆCENAS. If beauty, wisdom, modesty, can settle
The heart of Antony, Octavia is
A blessed lottery to him.
AGRIPPA.   Let us go.
Good Enobarbus, make yourself my guest
Whilst you abide here.
ENOBARBUS.   Humbly, sir, I thank you.
                          They go

Scene 3: *The same. Cæsar's house*

Enter Antony, Cæsar, and Octavia between them

ANTONY. The world and my great office will
     sometimes
Divide me from your bosom.
OCTAVIA.   All which time
Before the gods my knee shall bow in prayers
To them for you.
ANTONY.   Good night, sir. My Octavia,
Read not my blemishes in the world's report:
I have not kept my square, but that to come
Shall all be done by th'rule. Good night, dear lady.
OCTAVIA. Good night, sir.
CÆSAR. Good night.   *He leads his sister away*

Enter Soothsayer

ANTONY. Now, sirrah; you do wish yourself in Egypt? 10
SOOTHSAYER. Would I had never come from thence,
nor you hither!
ANTONY. If you can, you reason?
SOOTHSAYER. I see it in my motion, have it not in my
tongue: but yet hie you to Egypt again.
ANTONY. Say to me, whose fortunes shall rise higher,
Cæsar's or mine?
SOOTHSAYER. Cæsar's.
Therefore, O Antony, stay not by his side.
Thy demon, that thy spirit which keeps thee, is   20
Noble, courageous, high, unmatchable,
Where Cæsar's is not. But near him thy angel
Becomes a fear; as being o'erpowered. Therefore
Make space enough between you.
ANTONY.   Speak this no more.
SOOTHSAYER. To none but thee: no more but when
to thee.
If thou dost play with him at any game,
Thou art sure to lose; and, of that natural luck,
He beats thee 'gainst the odds: thy lustre thickens,
When he shines by: I say again, thy spirit
Is all afraid to govern thee near him,   30
But he away, 'tis noble.
ANTONY.   Get thee gone:
Say to Ventidius I would speak with him.
He shall to Parthia. [*Soothsayer goes*] Be it art or hap,
He hath spoken true: the very dicé obey him,
And in our sports my better cunning faints
Under his chance: if we draw lots, he speeds;
His cocks do win the battle still of mine
When it is all to nought, and his quails ever
Beat mine, inhooped, at odds. I will to Egypt: 40

And though I make this marriage for my peace,
I'th'East my pleasure lies.

Enter Ventidius
                O, come, Ventidius,
You must to Parthia: your commission's ready;
Follow me, and receive't.   *They go*

Scene 4: *The same. A street*

Enter Lepidus, Mæcenas, and Agrippa

LEPIDUS. Trouble yourselves no further: pray you,
hasten
Your generals after.
AGRIPPA.   Sir, Mark Antony
Will e'en but kiss Octavia, and we'll follow.
LEPIDUS. Till I shall see you in your soldier's dress,
Which will become you both, farewell.
MÆCENAS.   We shall,
As I conceive the journey, be at th'Mount
Before you, Lepidus.
LEPIDUS.   Your way is shorter;
My purposes do draw me much about:
You'll win two days upon me.
MÆCENAS. }
AGRIPPA.   }   Sir, good success!
LEPIDUS. Farewell.   *They go* 10

Scene 5: *Alexandria. Cleopatra's palace*

Enter Cleopatra, Charmian, Iras, and Alexas

CLEOPATRA. Give me some music; music, moody food
Of us that trade in love.
ALL.   The music, ho!

Enter Mardian the Eunuch

CLEOPATRA. Let it alone, let's to billiards: come,
Charmian.
CHARMIAN. My arm is sore; best play with Mardian.
CLEOPATRA. As well a woman with an eunuch played
As with a woman. Come, you'll play with me, sir?
MARDIAN. As well as I can, madam.
CLEOPATRA. And when good will is showed, though't
come too short,
The actor may plead pardon. I'll none now,
Give me mine angle, we'll to th'river: there,   10
My music playing far off, I will betray
Tawny-finned fishes; my bended hook shall pierce
Their slimy jaws, and as I draw them up,
I'll think them every one an Antony,
And say 'Ah, ha! you're caught.'
CHARMIAN.   'Twas merry when
You wagered on your angling; when your diver
Did hang a salt-fish on his hook, which he
With fervency drew up.
CLEOPATRA.   That time—O times!—
I laughed him out of patience; and that night
I laughed him into patience; and next morn,   20
Ere the ninth hour, I drunk him to his bed;
Then put my tires and mantles on him, whilst
I wore his sword Philippan.

Enter a Messenger
                O, from Italy!
Rain thou thy fruitful tidings in mine ears,
That long time have been barren.
MESSENGER.   Madam, madam,—

CLEOPATRA. Antonio's dead! If thou say so, villain,
Thou kill'st thy mistress: but well and free,
If thou so yield him, there is gold, and here
My bluest veins to kiss: a hand that kings
Have lipped, and trembled kissing.   30
MESSENGER. First, madam, he is well.
CLEOPATRA.   Why, there's more gold.
But, sirrah, mark, we use
To say the dead are well: bring it to that,
The gold I give thee well I melt and pour
Down thy ill-uttering throat.
MESSENGER. Good madam, hear me.
CLEOPATRA.   Well, go to, I will;
But there's no goodness in thy face. If Antony
Be free and healthful—so tart a favour
To trumpet such good tidings! If not well,
Thou shouldst come like a Fury crowned with
    snakes,   40
Not like a formal man.
MESSENGER.   Will't please you hear me?
CLEOPATRA. I have a mind to strike thee ere thou
    speak'st:
Yet, if thou say Antony lives, is well,
Or friends with Cæsar, or not captive to him,
I'll set thee in a shower of gold, and hail
Rich pearls upon thee.
MESSENGER.   Madam, he's well.
CLEOPATRA.   Well said.
MESSENGER. And friends with Cæsar.
CLEOPATRA.   Thou'rt an honest man.
MESSENGER. Cæsar and he are greater friends than
    ever.
CLEOPATRA. Make thee a fortune from me.
MESSENGER.   But yet, madam,—
CLEOPATRA. I do not like 'But yet,' it does allay   50
The good precedence; fie upon 'But yet'?
'But yet' is as a gaoler to bring forth
Some monstrous malefactor. Prithee, friend,
Pour out the pack of matter to mine ear,
The good and bad together: he's friends with
    Cæsar,
In state of health, thou say'st, and thou say'st, free.
MESSENGER. Free, madam! no; I made no such report:
He's bound unto Octavia.
CLEOPATRA.   For what good turn?
MESSENGER. For the best turn i'th'bed.
CLEOPATRA.   I am pale, Charmian.
MESSENGER. Madam, he's married to Octavia.   60
CLEOPATRA. The most infectious pestilence upon thee!
                                   Strikes him down
MESSENGER. Good madam, patience.
CLEOPATRA.   What say you?
    [*strikes him again*] Hence,
Horrible villain! or I'll spurn thine eyes
Like balls before me; I'll unhair thy head,
                        She hales him up and down
Thou shalt be whipped with wire, and stewed in
    brine,
Smarting in ling'ring pickle.
MESSENGER.   Gracious madam,
I that do bring the news made not the match.
CLEOPATRA. Say 'tis not so, a province I will give thee,
And make thy fortunes proud: the blow thou hadst
Shall make thy peace for moving me to rage,   70
And I will boot thee with what gift beside
Thy modesty can beg.

MESSENGER.   He's married, madam.
CLEOPATRA. Rogue, thou hast lived too long.
                                   Draws a knife
MESSENGER.   Nay, then I'll run.
What mean you, madam? I have made no fault.
                                            Goes
CHARMIAN. Good madam, keep yourself within
    yourself.
The man is innocent.
CLEOPATRA. Some innocents 'scape not the
    thunderbolt.
Melt Egypt into Nile! and kindly creatures
Turn all to serpents! Call the slave again:
Though I am mad, I will not bite him. Call!   80
CHARMIAN. He is afeard to come.
CLEOPATRA.   I will not hurt him.
                                   Charmian goes
These hands do lack nobility, that they strike
A meaner than myself; since I myself
Have given myself the cause.

Charmian returns with the Messenger

                        Come hither, sir.
Though it be honest, it is never good
To bring bad news: give to a gracious message
An host of tongues, but let ill tidings tell
Themselves when they be felt.
MESSENGER.   I have done my duty.
CLEOPATRA. Is he married?
I cannot hate thee worser than I do,   90
If thou again say 'Yes.'
MESSENGER.   He's married, madam.
CLEOPATRA. The gods confound thee! dost thou hold
    there still?
MESSENGER. Should I lie, madam?
CLEOPATRA.   O, I would thou didst,
So half my Egypt were submerged and made
A cistern for scaled snakes! Go, get thee hence:
Hadst thou Narcissus in thy face, to me
Thou wouldst appear most ugly. He is married?
MESSENGER. I crave your highness' pardon.
CLEOPATRA.   He is married?
MESSENGER. Take no offence that I would not offend
    you:
To punish me for what you make me do   100
Seems much unequal: he's married to Octavia.
CLEOPATRA. O, that his fault should make a knave
    of thee,
Thou art not what thou'rt sure of! Get thee hence:
The merchandise which thou hast brought from
    Rome
Are all too dear for me: lie they upon thy hand,
And be undone by 'em!   *He goes*
CHARMIAN.   Good your highness, patience.
CLEOPATRA. In praising Antony, I have dispraised
    Cæsar.
CHARMIAN. Many times, madam.
CLEOPATRA.   I am paid for't now.
Lead me from hence;
I faint, O Iras, Charmian: 'tis no matter.   110
Go to the fellow, good Alexas; bid him
Report the feature of Octavia: her years,
Her inclination, let him not leave out
The colour of her hair. Bring me word quickly.
                                   Alexas goes
Let him for ever go! let him not—Charmian—

Though he be painted one way like a Gorgon,
The other way's a Mars. [*to Mardian*] Bid you Alexas
Bring me word how tall she is. Pity me, Charmian,
But do not speak to me. Lead me to my chamber.
They go

Scene 6: *Near Misenum; the sea in the distance*

*Flourish. Enter Pompey and Menas from one side, with
drum and trumpet: at another, Cæsar, Antony, Lepidus,
Enobarbus, Mæcenas, Agrippa, with soldiers marching*

POMPEY. Your hostages I have, so have you mine;
And we shall talk before we fight.
CÆSAR.   Most meet
That first we come to words; and therefore have we
Our written purposes before us sent;
Which, if thou hast considered, let us know
If 'twill tie up thy discontented sword
And carry back to Sicily much tall youth
That else must perish here.
POMPEY.   To you all three,
The senators alone of this great world,
Chief factors for the gods: I do not know   10
Wherefore my father should have revengers want,
Having a son and friends, since Julius Cæsar,
Who at Philippi the good Brutus ghosted,
There saw you labouring for him. What was't
That moved pale Cassius to conspire, and what
Made the all-honoured honest Roman, Brutus,
With the armed rest, courtiers of beauteous
    freedom,
To drench the Capitol, but that they would
Have one man but a man? And that is it
Hath made me rig my navy, at whose burthen   20
The angered ocean foams; with which I meant
To scourge th'ingratitude that despiteful Rome
Cast on my noble father.
CÆSAR.   Take your time.
ANTONY. Thou canst not fear us, Pompey with thy
    sails;
We'll speak with thee at sea: at land, thou know'st
How much we do o'ercount thee.
POMPEY.   At land indeed
Thou dost o'ercount me of my father's house:
But since the cuckoo builds not for himself,
Remain in't as thou mayst.
LEPIDUS.   Be pleased to tell us—
For this is from the present—how you take   30
The offers we have sent you.
CÆSAR.   There's the point.
ANTONY. Which do not be entreated to, but weigh
What it is worth embraced.
CÆSAR.   And what may follow,
To try a larger fortune.
POMPEY.   You have made me offer
Of Sicily, Sardinia; and I must
Rid all the sea of pirates; then, to send
Measures of wheat to Rome; this 'greed upon,
To part with unhacked edges and bear back
Our targes undinted.
CÆSAR. ⎫
ANTONY. ⎬   That's our offer.
LEPIDUS. ⎭
POMPEY.   Know then,
I came before you here a man prepared   40
To take this offer: but Mark Antony

Put me to some impatience: though I lose
The praise of it by telling, you must know,
When Cæsar and your brother were at blows,
Your mother came to Sicily and did find
Her welcome friendly.
ANTONY.   I have heard it, Pompey,
And am well studied for a liberal thanks
Which I do owe you.
POMPEY.   Let me have your hand:
I did not think, sir, to have met you here.
ANTONY. The beds i'th'east are soft; and thanks to you, 50
That called me timelier than my purpose hither;
For I have gained by't.
CÆSAR.   Since I saw you last.
There's a change upon you.
POMPEY.   Well, I know not
What counts harsh Fortune casts upon my face,
But in my bosom shall she never come,
To make my heart her vassal.
LEPIDUS.   Well met here.
POMPEY. I hope so, Lepidus. Thus we are agreed:
I crave our composition may be written
And sealed between us.
CÆSAR.   That's the next to do.
POMPEY. We'll feast each other ere we part, and let's 60
Draw lots who shall begin.
ANTONY.   That will I, Pompey.
POMPEY. No, Antony, take the lot:
But, first or last, your fine Egyptian cookery
Shall have the fame. I have heard that Julius Cæsar—
Grew fat with feasting there.
ANTONY.   You have heard much.
POMPEY. I have fair meanings, sir.
ANTONY.   And fair words to them.
POMPEY. Then so much have I heard:
And I have heard, Apollodorus carried—
ENOBARBUS. No more of that: he did so.
POMPEY.   What, I pray you?
ENOBARBUS. A certain queen to Cæsar in a mattress. 70
POMPEY. I know thee now, how far'st thou, soldier?
ENOBARBUS.   Well,
And well am like to do, for I perceive
Four feasts are toward.
POMPEY.   Let me shake thy hand.
I never hated thee: I have seen thee fight,
When I have envied thy behaviour.
ENOBARBUS.   Sir,
I never loved you much, but I ha'praised ye
When you have well deserved ten times as much
As I have said you did.
POMPEY.   Enjoy thy plainness,
It nothing ill becomes thee.
Aboard my galley I invite you all: 80
Will you lead, lords?
CÆSAR.   ⎫
ANTONY. ⎬   Show's the way, sir.
LEPIDUS. ⎭
POMPEY.   Come.
*They go; Menas and
Enobarbus remain*

MENAS [*aside*]. Thy father, Pompey, would ne'er have
    made this treaty. [*to Enobarbus*] You and I have
    known, sir.
ENOBARBUS. At sea, I think.
MENAS. We have, sir.
ENOBARBUS. You have done well by water.

MENAS. And you by land.

ENOBARBUS. I will praise any man that will praise me; though it cannot be denied what I have done by 90 land.

MENAS. Nor what I have done by water.

ENOBARBUS. Yes, something you can deny for your own safety: you have been a great thief by sea.

MENAS. And you by land.

ENOBARBUS. There I deny my land service. But give me your hand, Menas: if our eyes had authority, here they might take two thieves kissing.

MENAS. All men's faces are true, whatsome'er their hands are. 100

ENOBARBUS. But there is never a fair woman has a true face.

MENAS. No slander, they steal hearts.

ENOBARBUS. We came hither to fight with you.

MENAS. For my part, I am sorry it is turned to a drinking. Pompey doth this day laugh away his fortune.

ENOBARBUS. If he do, sure he cannot weep't back again.

MENAS. You've said, sir. We looked not for Mark 110 Antony here: pray you, is he married to Cleopatra?

ENOBARBUS. Cæsar's sister is called Octavia.

MENAS. True, sir; she was the wife of Caius Marcellus.

ENOBARBUS. But she is now the wife of Marcus Antonius.

MENAS. Pray ye, sir?

ENOBARBUS. 'Tis true.

MENAS. Then is Cæsar and he for ever knit together.

ENOBARBUS. If I were bound to divine of this unity, I would not prophesy so. 120

MENAS. I think the policy of that purpose made more in the marriage than the love of the parties.

ENOBARBUS. I think so too. But you shall find, the band that seems to tie their friendship together will be the very strangler of their amity: Octavia is of a holy, cold, and still conversation.

MENAS. Who would not have his wife so?

ENOBARBUS. Not he that himself is not so; which is Mark Antony. He will to his Egyptian dish again: then shall the sighs of Octavia blow the fire up in 130 Cæsar, and, as I said before, that which is the strength of their amity shall prove the immediate author of their variance. Antony will use his affection where it is: he married but his occasion here.

MENAS. And thus it may. Come, sir, will you aboard? I have a health for you.

ENOBARBUS. I shall take it, sir: we have used our throats in Egypt.

MENAS. Come, let's away.   *They follow the others*

Scene 7: *The deck of Pompey's galley, off Misenum*

Music plays. Enter two or three Servants, with a banquet

1 SERVANT. Here they'll be, man. Some o'their plants are ill-rooted already; the least wind i'th'world will blow them down.

2 SERVANT. Lepidus is high-coloured.

1 SERVANT. They have made him drink alms-drink.

2 SERVANT. As they pinch one another by the disposition, he cries out 'No more'; reconciles them to his entreaty and himself to th'drink.

1 SERVANT. But it raises the greater war between him and his discretion. 10

2 SERVANT. Why, this it is to have a name in great men's fellowship: I had as lief have a reed that will do me no service as a partisan I could not heave.

1 SERVANT. To be called into a huge sphere, and not to be seen to move in't, are the holes where eyes should be, which pitifully disaster the cheeks.

A sennet sounded. Cæsar, Antony, Pompey, Lepidus, Agrippa, Mæcenas, Enobarbus, Menas, with other captains, come up on deck; Pompey assists Lepidus.

ANTONY [*to Cæsar*]. Thus do they, sir; they take the flow o'th'Nile

By certain scales i'th'pyramid; they know,

By th'height, the lowness, or the means, if dearth

Or foison follow: the higher Nilus swells, 20

The more it promises: as it ebbs, the seedsman

Upon the slime and ooze scatters his grain,

And't shortly comes to harvest.

LEPIDUS. You've strange serpents there?

ANTONY. Ay, Lepidus.

LEPIDUS. Your serpent of Egypt is bred now of your mud by the operation of your sun: so is your crocodile.

ANTONY. They are so.

POMPEY. Sit—and some wine! A health to Lepidus! 30

LEPIDUS. I am not so well as I should be, but I'll ne'er out.

ENOBARBUS. Not till you have slept; I fear me you'll be in till then.

LEPIDUS. Nay, certainly, I have heard the Ptolemies' pyramises are very goodly things; without contradiction, I have heard that.

MENAS [*aside*]. Pompey, a word. 120

POMPEY [*aside*].   Say in mine ear, what is't?

MENAS [*whispers in's ear*]. Forsake thy seat, I do beseech thee, captain,

And hear me speak a word.

POMPEY [*aside*].   Forbear me till anon.— 40

[*calls*] This wine for Lepidus!

LEPIDUS. What manner o'thing is your crocodile?

ANTONY. It is shaped, sir, like itself, and it is as broad as it hath breadth: it is just so high as it is, and moves with it own organs: it lives by that which nourisheth it, and the elements once out of it, it transmigrates.

LEPIDUS. What colour is it of?

ANTONY. Of it own colour too.

LEPIDUS. 'Tis a strange serpent. 50

ANTONY. 'Tis so, and the tears of it are wet.

CÆSAR. Will this description satisfy him?

ANTONY. With the health that Pompey gives him, else he is a very epicure.   *Menas whispers again*

POMPEY [*aside*]. Go hang, sir, hang! Tell me of that? away! Do as I bid you. [*aloud*] Where's this cup I called for?

MENAS [*aside*]. If for the sake of merit thou wilt hear me,

Rise from thy stool.

POMPEY [*aside*]. I think thou'rt mad. The matter? 60

                        Rises, and walks aside

MENAS. I have ever held my cap off to thy fortunes.

POMPEY. Thou hast served me with much faith. What's else to say?

Be jolly, lords.

ANTONY.   These quick-sands, Lepidus,

Keep off them, for you sink.

MENAS. Wilt thou be lord of all the world?
POMPEY.   What say'st thou?
MENAS. Wilt thou be lord of the whole world?
    That's twice.
POMPEY. How should that be?
MENAS.   But entertain it,
    And, though thou think me poor, I am the man
    Will give thee all the world.
POMPEY.   Hast thou drunk well?
MENAS. No, Pompey, I have kept me from the cup. 70
    Thou art, if thou dar'st be, the earthly Jove:
    Whate'er the ocean pales, or sky inclips,
    Is thine, if thou wilt ha't.
POMPEY.   Show me which way.
MENAS. These three world-sharers, these competitors,
    Are in thy vessel: let me cut the cable;
    And, when we are put off, fall to their throats:
    All then is thine.
POMPEY.   Ah, this thou shouldst have done,
    And not have spoke on't! In me 'tis villany;
    In thee't had been good service. Thou must know,
    'Tis not my profit that does lead mine honour; 80
    Mine honour, it. Repent that e'er thy tongue
    Hath so betrayed thine act: being done unknown,
    I should have found it afterwards well done,
    But must condemn it now. Desist, and drink.
MENAS [to himself]. For this
    I'll never follow thy palled fortunes more.
    Who seeks, and will not take when once 'tis offered,
    Shall never find it more.
POMPEY.   This health to Lepidus!
ANTONY. Bear him ashore. I'll pledge it for him,
    Pompey.
ENOBARBUS. Here's to thee, Menas!
MENAS.   Enobarbus, welcome! 90
POMPEY. Fill till the cup be hid.
ENOBARBUS. There's a strong fellow, Menas.
        Pointing to the attendant who carries off Lepidus
MENAS. Why?
ENOBARBUS. A' bears the third part of the world, man;
    see'st not?
MENAS. The third part then is drunk: would it were all,
    That it might go on wheels!
ENOBARBUS. Drink thou; increase the reels.
MENAS. Come.
POMPEY. This is not yet an Alexandrian feast.
ANTONY. It ripens towards it. Strike the vessels, ho! 100
    Here's to Cæsar!
CÆSAR.   I could well forbear't.
    It's monstrous labour, when I wash my brain
    And it grows fouler.
ANTONY.   Be a child o'th'time.
CÆSAR. Possess it, I'll make answer:
    But I had rather fast from all, four days,
    Than drink so much in one.
ENOBARBUS [to Antony].   Ha, my brave emperor!
    Shall we dance now the Egyptian Bacchanals,
    And celebrate our drink?
POMPEY.   Let's ha't, good soldier.
ANTONY. Come, let's all take hands,
    Till that the conquering wine hath steeped our sense 110
    In soft and delicate Lethe.
ENOBARBUS.   All take hands.
    Make battery to our ears with the loud music:
    The while I'll place you: then the boy shall sing;
    The holding every man shall bear as loud

As his strong sides can volley.
        Music plays. Enobarbus places
                        them hand in hand

    Come, thou monarch of the vine,
    Plumpy Bacchus with pink eyne!
    In thy fats our cares be drowned,
    With thy grapes our hairs be crowned.
    Cup us, till the world go round,   120
    Cups us, till the world go round!
CÆSAR. What would you more? Pompey, good night.
    Good brother,
    Let me request you off: our graver business
    Frowns at this levity. Gentle lords, let's part;
    You see we have burnt our cheeks: strong Enobarb
    Is weaker than the wine; and mine own tongue
    Splits what it speaks: the wild disguise hath almost
    Anticked us all. What needs more words?
    Good night.
    Good Antony, your hand.
POMPEY.   I'll try you on the shore.
ANTONY. And shall, sir: give's your hand.
POMPEY.   O Antony,   130
    You have my father's house—But, what? we are
    friends.
    Come down into the boat.   They go down
ENOBARBUS.   Take heed you fall not.
                    Enobarbus and Menas remain
    Menas, I'll not on shore.
MENAS.   No, to my cabin.
    These drums! these trumpets, flutes! what!
    Let Neptune hear we bid a loud farewell
    To these great fellows: sound and be hanged, sound
    out!
            Musicians sound a flourish, with drums
ENOBARBUS. Hoo! says a'. There's my cap.
MENAS. Hoo! Noble captain, come.   They go below

ACT 3
Scene 1: A plain in Syria

Enter Ventidius as it were in triumph, the dead body of
Pacorus borne before him; with Silius, and other Romans,
officers, and soldiers

VENTIDIUS. Now, darting Parthia, art thou struck,
    and now
    Pleased fortune does of Marcus Crassus' death
    Make me revenger. Bear the king's son's body
    Before our army. Thy Pacorus, Orodes,
    Pays this for Marcus Crassus.
SILIUS.   Noble Ventidius,
    Whilst yet with Parthian blood thy sword is warm,
    The fugitive Parthians follow; spur through Media,
    Mesopotamia, and the shelters whither
    The routed fly: so thy grand captain Antony
    Shall set thee on triumphant chariots and   10
    Put garlands on thy head.
VENTIDIUS.   O Silius, Silius,
    I have done enough: a lower place, note well,
    May make too great an act; for learn this, Silius,
    Better to leave undone than by our deed
    Acquire too high a fame when him we serve's away.
    Cæsar and Antony have ever won
    More in their officer than person: Sossius,

One of my place in Syria, his lieutenant,
For quick accumulation of renown,
Which he achieved by th'minute, lost his favour.   20
Who does i'th'wars more than his captain can
Becomes his captain's captain: and ambition,
The soldier's virtue, rather makes choice of loss
Than gain which darkens him.
I could do more to do Antonius good
But 'twould offend him, and in his offence
Should my performance perish.
SILIUS.   Thou hast, Ventidius, that
Without the which a soldier and his sword
Grants scarce distinction. Thou wilt write to
Antony?
VENTIDIUS. I'll humbly signify what in his name,   30
That magical word of war, we have effected;
How, with his banners and his well-paid ranks,
The ne'er-yet-beaten horse of Parthia
We have jaded out o'th'field.
SILIUS.   Where is he now?
VENTIDIUS. He purposeth to Athens: whither, with
what haste
The weight we must convey with's will permit,
We shall appear before him. On, there; pass along!
                                   They go forward

Scene 2: *Rome. An antechamber in Cæsar's house*

Enter Agrippa at one door, Enobarbus at another

AGRIPPA. What, are the brothers parted?
ENOBARBUS. They have dispatched with Pompey; he
is gone;
The other three are sealing. Octavia weeps
To part from Rome; Cæsar is sad, and Lepidus
Since Pompey's feast, as Menas says, is troubled
With the greensickness.
AGRIPPA.   'Tis a noble Lepidus.
ENOBARBUS. A very fine one: O, how he loves Cæsar!
AGRIPPA. Nay, but how dearly he adores Mark
Antony!
ENOBARBUS. Cæsar? Why, he's the Jupiter of men.
AGRIPPA. What's Antony? The god of Jupiter.
ENOBARBUS. Spake you of Cæsar? How! the nonpareil!   10
AGRIPPA. O Antony! O thou Arabian bird!
ENOBARBUS. Would you praise Cæsar, say 'Cæsar': go
no further.
AGRIPPA. Indeed, he plied them both with excellent
praises.
ENOBARBUS. But he loves Cæsar best; yet he loves
Antony:
Hoo! hearts, tongues, figures, scribes, bards, poets,
cannot
Think, speak, cast, write, sing, number—hoo!—
His love to Antony. But as for Cæsar,
Kneel down, kneel down, and wonder.
AGRIPPA.   Both he loves.
ENOBARBUS. They are his shards, and he their beetle.
   [*trumpet within*] So!   20
This is to horse. Adieu, noble Agrippa.
AGRIPPA. Good fortune, worthy soldier, and farewell.

Enter Cæsar, Antony, Lepidus, and Octavia

ANTONY. No further, sir.
CÆSAR. You take from me a great part of myself;
Use me well in't. Sister, prove such a wife
As my thoughts make thee, and as my farthest band

Shall pass on thy approof. Most noble Antony,
Let not the piece of virtue which is set
Betwixt us as the cement of our love,
To keep it builded, be the ram to batter   30
The fortress of it; for better might we
Have loved without this means, if on both parts
This be not cherished.
ANTONY.   Make me not offended.
In your distrust.
CÆSAR.   I have said.
ANTONY.   You shall not find,
Though you be therein curious, the least cause
For what you seem to fear: so, the gods keep you,
And makes the hearts of Romans serve your ends!
We will here part.
CÆSAR. Farewell, my dearest sister, fare thee well:
The elements be kind to thee, and make   40
Thy spirits all of comfort! fare thee well.
OCTAVIA. My noble brother!
ANTONY. The April's in her eyes: it is love's spring,
And these the showers to bring it on. Be cheerful.
OCTAVIA. Sir, look well to my husband's house, and—
CÆSAR.   What,
Octavia?
OCTAVIA.   I'll tell you in your ear.
ANTONY. Her tongue will not obey her heart, nor can
Her heart inform her tongue—the swan's down-
feather,
That stands upon the swell at full of tide
And neither way inclines.   50
ENOBARBUS [*aside to Agrippa*]. Will Cæsar weep?
AGRIPPA [*aside*].   He has a cloud in's face.
ENOBARBUS [*aside*]. He were the worse for that, were
he a horse;
So is he, being a man.
AGRIPPA [*aside*].   Why, Enobarbus,
When Antony found Julius Cæsar dead,
He cried almost to roaring; and he wept
When at Philippi he found Brutus slain.
ENOBARBUS. That year indeed he was troubled with
a rheum;
What willingly he did confound he wailed,
Believe't, till I wept too.
CÆSAR.   No, sweet Octavia,
You shall hear from me still; the time shall not   60
Out-go my thinking on you.
ANTONY.   Come, sir come;
I'll wrestle with you in my strength of love:
Look, here I have you; thus I let you go,
And give you to the gods.
CÆSAR.   Adieu; be happy!
LEPIDUS. Let all the number of the stars give light
To thy fair way!
CÆSAR.   Farewell, farewell!   *Kisses Octavia*
ANTONY.   Farewell!
                                   Trumpets sound; they go

Scene 3: *Alexandria. Cleopatra's palace*

Enter Cleopatra, Charmian, Iras, and Alexas

CLEOPATRA. Where is the fellow?
ALEXAS.   Half afeard to come.
CLEOPATRA. Go to, go to.

Enter the Messenger as before

                                   Come hither, sir.

ALEXAS. Good majesty,
Herod of Jewry dare not look upon you
But when you are well pleased.
CLEOPATRA. That Herod's head
I'll have: but how, when Antony is gone
Through whom I might command it? Come thou
near.
MESSENGER. Most gracious majesty,—
CLEOPATRA. Didst thou behold
Octavia?
MESSENGER. Ay, dread queen.
CLEOPATRA. Where?
MESSENGER. Madam, in Rome.
I looked her in the face, and saw her led
Between her brother and Mark Antony. 10
CLEOPATRA. Is she as tall as me?
MESSENGER. She is not, madam.
CLEOPATRA. Didst hear her speak? is she shrill-tongued
or low?
MESSENGER. Madam, I heard her speak; she is
low-voiced.
CLEOPATRA. That's not so good: he cannot like her
long.
CHARMIAN. Like her! O Isis! 'tis impossible.
CLEOPATRA. I think so, Charmian: dull of tongue
and dwarfish.
What majesty is in her gait? Remember,
If e'er thou look'dst on majesty.
MESSENGER. She creeps:
Her motion and her station are as one;
She shows a body rather than a life,
A statue than a breather. 20
CLEOPATRA. Is this certain?
MESSENGER. Or I have no observance.
CHARMIAN. Three in Egypt
Cannot make better note.
CLEOPATRA. He's very knowing;
I do perceive't: there's nothing in her yet:
The fellow has good judgement.
CHARMIAN. Excellent.
CLEOPATRA. Guess at her years, I prithee.
MESSENGER. Madam,
She was a widow—
CLEOPATRA. Widow! Charmian, hark.
MESSENGER. And I do think she's thirty.
CLEOPATRA. Bear'st thou her face in mind? is't long
or round?
MESSENGER. Round, even to faultiness. 30
CLEOPATRA. For the most part, too, they are foolish
that are so.
Her hair, what colour?
MESSENGER. Brown, madam: and her forehead
As low as she would wish it.
CLEOPATRA. There's gold for thee.
Thou must not take my former sharpness ill:
I will employ thee back again; I find thee
Most fit for business: go make thee ready;
Our letters are prepared. He goes
CHARMIAN. A proper man.
CLEOPATRA. Indeed, he is so: I repent me much
That so I harried him. Why, methinks, by him,
This creature's no such thing.
CHARMIAN. Nothing, madam. 40
CLEOPATRA. The man hath seen some majesty, and
should know.
CHARMIAN. Hath he seen majesty? Isis else defend,

And serving you so long!
CLEOPATRA. I have one thing more to ask him yet,
good Charmian:
But 'tis no matter, thou shalt bring him to me
Where I will write. All may be well enough.
CHARMIAN. I warrant you, madam. They go

Scene 4: *Athens. A Room in Antony's house*

Enter Antony and Octavia

ANTONY. Nay, nay, Octavia, not only that,
That were excusable, that and thousands more
Of semblable import, but he hath waged
New wars 'gainst Pompey, made his will and read it
To public ear,
Spoke scantly of me, when perforce he could not
But pay me terms of honour, cold and sickly
He vented them, most narrow measure lent me,
When the best hint was given him he not took't,
Or did it from his teeth.
OCTAVIA. O my good lord, 10
Believe not all, or if you must believe,
Stomach not all. A more unhappy lady,
If this division chance, ne'er stood between,
Praying for both parts:
The good gods will mock me presently,
When I shall pray, 'O, bless my lord and husband!'
Undo that prayer, by crying out as loud,
'O, bless my brother!' Husband win, win brother,
Prays, and destroys the prayer—no midway
'Twixt these extremes at all.
ANTONY. Gentle Octavia, 20
Let your best love draw to that point which seeks
Best to preserve it: if I lose mine honour,
I lose myself: better I were not yours
Than yours so branchless. But, as you requested,
Yourself shall go between's: the mean time, lady,
I'll raise the preparation of a war
Shall stain your brother: make your soonest haste;
So your desires are yours.
OCTAVIA. Thanks to my lord.
The Jove of Power make me most weak, most weak,
Your reconciler! Wars 'twixt you twain would be 30
As if the world should cleave, and that slain men
Should solder up the rift.
ANTONY. When it appears to you where this begins,
Turn your displeasure that way; for our faults
Can never be so equal, that your love
Can equally move with them. Provide your going;
Choose your own company, and command what
cost
Your heart has mind to. They go

Scene 5: *The same. Another room*

Enter Enobarbus and Eros, meeting

ENOBARBUS. How now, friend Eros!
EROS. There's strange news come, sir.
ENOBARBUS. What, man?
EROS. Cæsar and Lepidus have made wars upon
Pompey.
ENOBARBUS. This is old: what is the success?
EROS. Cæsar having made use of him in the wars
'gainst Pompey presently denied him rivality,
would not let him partake in the glory of the
action, and not resting here accuses him of letters 10

he had formerly wrote to Pompey; upon his own
appeal, seizes him: so the poor third is up, till death
enlarge his confine.

ENOBARBUS. Then, world, thou hast a pair of chaps,
  no more;
And throw between them all the food thou hast,
They'll grind the one the other. Where's Antony?

EROS. He's walking in the garden—thus, and spurns
The rush that lies before him, cries 'Fool Lepidus!'
And threats the throat of that his officer
That murdered Pompey.

ENOBARBUS.   Our great navy's rigged.   20

EROS. For Italy and Cæsar. More, Domitius;
My lord desires you presently: my news
I might have told hereafter.

ENOBARBUS.   'Twill be naught:
But let it be. Bring me to Antony.

EROS. Come, sir.   *They go*

Scene 6: *Rome. Cæsar's house*

Enter Cæsar, Agrippa, and Mæcenas

CÆSAR. Contemning Rome, he has done all this,
  and more,
In Alexandria: here's the manner of't:
I'th'market-place, on a tribunal silvered
Cleopatra and himself in chairs of gold
Were publicly enthroned: at the feet sat
Cæsarion, whom they call my father's son,
And all the unlawful issue that their lust
Since then hath made between them. Unto her
He gave the stablishment of Egypt; made her
Of lower Syria, Cyprus, Lydia,   10
Absolute queen.

MÆCENAS.   This in the public eye?

CÆSAR. I'th'common show-place, where they
  exercise.
His sons he there proclaimed the kings of kings:
Great Media, Parthia and Armenia,
He gave to Alexander; to Ptolemy he assigned
Syria, Cilicia and Phœnicia: she
In th'habiliments of the goddess Isis
That day appeared, and oft before gave audience,
As 'tis reported, so.

MÆCENAS.   Let Rome be thus
Informed.

AGRIPPA. Who, queasy with his insolence   20
Already, will their good thoughts call from him.

CÆSAR. The people know it, and have now received
His accusations.

AGRIPPA.   Who does he accuse?

CÆSAR. Cæsar, and that having in Sicily
Sextus Pompeius spoiled we had not rated him
His part o'th'isle: then does he say, he lent me
Some shipping unrestored: lastly, he frets
That Lepidus of the triumvirate
Should be deposed; and, being, that we detain
All his revenue.

AGRIPPA.   Sir, this should be answered.   30

CÆSAR. 'Tis done already, and the messenger gone.
I have told him, Lepidus was grown too cruel,
That he his high authority abused
And did deserve his change: for what I have
  conquered,
I grant him part; but then, in his Armenia
And other of his conquered kingdoms, I

Demand the like.

MÆCENAS.   He'll never yield to that.

CÆSAR. Nor must not then be yielded to in this.

Enter Octavia, with her train

OCTAVIA. Hail, Cæsar, and my lord! hail, most dear
  Cæsar!

CÆSAR. That ever I should call thee castaway!   40

OCTAVIA. You have not called me so, nor have you
cause.

CÆSAR. Why have you stol'n upon us thus? You
  come not
Like Cæsar's sister: the wife of Antony
Should have an army for an usher, and
The neighs of horse to tell of her approach
Long ere she did appear; the trees by th'way
Should have borne men, and expectation fainted,
Longing for what it had not; nay, the dust
Should have ascended to the roof of heaven,
Raised by your populous troops: but you are come   50
A market-maid to Rome, and have prevented
The ostentation of our love, which, left unshown,
Is often left unloved: we should have met you
By sea and land, supplying every stage
With an augmented greeting.

OCTAVIA.   Good my lord,
To come thus was I not constrained, but did it
On my free will. My lord, Mark Antony,
Hearing that you prepared for war, acquainted
My grievèd ear withal; whereon, I begged
His pardon for return.

CÆSAR.   Which soon he granted,   60
Being an abstract 'tween his lust and him.

OCTAVIA. Do not say so, my lord.

CÆSAR.   I have eyes upon him,
And his affairs come to me on the wind.
Where is he now?

OCTAVIA.   My lord, in Athens.

CÆSAR. No, my most wrongèd sister, Cleopatra
Hath nodded him to her. He hath given his empire
Up to a whore, who now are levying
The kings o'th'earth for war: he hath assembled
Bocchus the king of Libya, Archelaus
Of Cappadocia, Philadelphos king   70
Of Paphlagonia, the Thracian king Adallas,
King Manchus of Arabia, King of Pont,
Herod of Jewry, Mithridates king
Of Comagene, Polemon and Amyntas
The kings of Mede and Lycaonia,
With a more larger list of sceptres.

OCTAVIA.   Ay me, most wretched,
That have my heart parted betwixt two friends
That do afflict each other!

CÆSAR.   Welcome hither:
Your letters did withhold our breaking forth,
Till we perceived both how you were wrong led   80
And we in negligent danger. Cheer your heart:
Be you not troubled with the time, which drives
O'er your content these strong necessities,
But let determined things to destiny
Hold unbewailed their way. Welcome to Rome;
Nothing more dear to me. You are abused
Beyond the mark of thought: and the high gods,
To do you justice, make his ministers
Of us and those that love you. Best of comfort,
And ever welcome to us.

AGRIPPA.   Welcome, lady.   90
MÆCENAS. Welcome, dear madam.
  Each heart in Rome does love and pity you:
  Only th'adulterous Antony, most large
  In his abominations, turns you off;
  And gives his potent regiment to a trull,
  That noises it against us.
OCTAVIA.   Is it so, sir?
CÆSAR. Most certain. Sister, welcome: pray you,
  Be ever known to patience: my dear'st sister!
                              He leads her out

              Scene 7: *Actium*

Enter Cleopatra and Enobarbus

CLEOPATRA. I will be even with thee, doubt it not.
ENOBARBUS. But why, why, why?
CLEOPATRA. Thou hast forspoke my being in these
    wars,
  And say'st it is not fit.
ENOBARBUS.   Well, is it, is it?
CLEOPATRA. Is't not denounced against us? Why
    should not we
  Be there in person?
ENOBARBUS [*aside*]. Well, I could reply:
  If we should serve with horse and mares together,
  The horse were merely lost; the mares would bear
  A soldier and his horse.
CLEOPATRA.   What is't you say?
ENOBARBUS. Your presence needs must puzzle
    Antony;   10
  Take from his heart, take from his brain, from's
    time,
  What should not then be spared. He is already
  Traduced for levity, and 'tis said in Rome
  That Photinus, an eunuch, and your maids
  Manage this war.
CLEOPATRA.   Sink Rome, and their tongues rot
  That speak against us! A charge we bear i'th'war,
  And, as the president of my kingdom, will
  Appear there for a man. Speak not against it,
  I will not stay behind.
ENOBARBUS.   Nay, I have done.
  Here comes the emperor.

Enter Antony and Canidius

ANTONY.   Is it not strange, Canidius, 20
  That from Tarentum and Brundusium
  He could so quickly cut the Ionian sea,
  And take in Toryne? You have heard on't, sweet?
CLEOPATRA. Celerity is never more admired
  Than by the negligent.
ANTONY.   A good rebuke,
  Which might have well becomed the best of men,
  To taunt at slackness. Canidius, we
  Will fight with him by sea.
CLEOPATRA.   By sea! what else?
CANIDIUS. Why will my lord do so?
ANTONY.   For that he dares us to't.
ENOBARBUS. So hath my lord dared him to single fight. 30
CANIDIUS. Ay, and to wage this battle at Pharsalia,
  Where Cæsar fought with Pompey: but these offers,
  Which serve not for his vantage, he shakes off,
  And so should you.
ENOBARBUS.   Your ships are not well manned,
  Your mariners are muleters, reapers, people

Ingrossed by swift impress; in Cæsar's fleet
  Are those that often have 'gainst Pompey fought:
  Their ships are yare, yours heavy: no disgrace
  Shall fall you for refusing him at sea,
  Being prepared for land.
ANTONY.   By sea, by sea.   40
ENOBARBUS. Most worthy sir, you therein throw away
  The absolute soldiership you have by land,
  Distract your army, which doth most consist
  Of war-marked footmen, leave unexecuted
  Your own renownéd knowledge, quite forgo
  The way which promises assurance, and
  Give up yourself merely to chance and hazard
  From firm security.
ANTONY.   I'll fight at sea.
CLEOPATRA. I have sixty sails, Cæsar none better.
ANTONY. Our overplus of shipping will we burn;   50
  And, with the rest full-manned, from th'head of
    Actium
  Beat th'approaching Cæsar. But if we fail,
  We then can do't at land.

Enter a Messenger

                              Thy business?
MESSENGER. The news is true, my lord; he is descried;
  Cæsar has taken Toryne.
ANTONY. Can he be there? in person 'tis impossible;
  Strange that his power should be. Canidius,
  Our nineteen legions thou shalt hold by land,
  And our twelve thousand horse. We'll to our ship:
  Away, my Thetis!

Enter a Soldier

                    How now, worthy soldier?   60
SOLDIER. O noble emperor, do not fight by sea;
  Trust not to rotten planks. Do you misdoubt
  This sword and these my wounds? Let th'Egyptians
  And the Phœnicians go a-ducking: we
  Have used to conquer standing on the earth
  And fighting foot to foot.
ANTONY.   Well, well, away!
                  He goes with Cleopatra,
                      Enobarbus following
SOLDIER. By Hercules, I think I am i'th'right.
CANIDIUS. Soldier, thou art: but his whole action
    grows
  Not in the power on't: so our leader's led,
  And we are women's men.
SOLDIER.   You keep by land   70
  The legions and the horse whole, do you not?
CANIDIUS. Marcus Octavius, Marcus Justeius,
  Publicola and Cælius, are for sea:
  But we keep whole by land. This speed of Cæsar's
  Carries beyond belief.
SOLDIER.   While he was yet in Rome,
  His power went out in such distractions as
  Beguiled all spies.
CANIDIUS.   Who's his lieutenant, hear you?
SOLDIER. They say, one Taurus.
CANIDIUS.   Well I know the man.

Enter a Messenger

MESSENGER. The emperor calls Canidius.
CANIDIUS. With news the time's in labour, and
    throes forth   80
  Each minute some.   *They go*

Scene 8

Enter Cæsar, and Taurus, with his army, marching

CÆSAR. Taurus!

TAURUS. My lord?

CÆSAR. Strike not by land, keep whole, provoke
    not battle
    Till we have done at sea. Do not exceed
    The prescript of this scroll: our fortune lies
    Upon this jump.   *They go*

Scene 9

Enter Antony and Enobarbus

ANTONY. Set we our squadrons on yond side o'th'hill,
    In eye of Cæsar's battle; from which place
    We may the number of the ships behold,
    And so proceed accordingly.   *They go*

Scene 10

*Canidius marcheth with his land army one way and
Taurus, the lieutenant of Cæsar, the other way. After
their going in, is heard the noise of a sea-fight.*

Alarum. Enter Enobarbus

ENOBARBUS. Naught, naught, all naught! I can behold
    no longer:
    Th'Antoniad, the Egyptian admiral,
    With all their sixty, fly and turn the rudder:
    To see't mine eyes are blasted.

Enter Scarus

SCARUS.   Gods and goddesses,
    All the whole synod of them!

ENOBARBUS.   What's thy passion?

SCARUS. The greater cantle of the world is lost
    With very ignorance. We have kissed away
    Kingdoms and provinces.

ENOBARBUS.   How appears the fight?

SCARUS. On our side like the tokened pestilence,
    Where death is sure. Yon ribald-rid nag of Egypt— 10
    Whom leprosy o'ertake!—i'th'midst o'th'fight,
    When vantage like a pair of twins appeared,
    Both as the same, or rather ours the elder—
    The breese upon her, like a cow in June!—
    Hoists sails and flies.

ENOBARBUS. That I beheld:
    Mine eyes did sicken at the sight, and could not
    Endure a further view.

SCARUS.   She once being luffed,
    The noble ruin of her magic, Antony,
    Claps on his sea-wing, and (like a doting mallard), 20
    Leaving the fight in height, flies after her:
    I never saw an action of such shame;
    Experience, manhood, honour, ne'er before
    Did violate so itself.

ENOBARBUS.   Alack, alack!

Enter Canidius

CANIDIUS. Our fortune on the sea is out of breath,
    And sinks most lamentably. Had our general
    Been what he knew himself, it had gone well:
    O, he has given example for our flight
    Most grossly by his own!

ENOBARBUS.   Ay, are you thereabouts?
    Why then good night indeed.   30

CANIDIUS. Toward Peloponnesus are they fled.

SCARUS. 'Tis easy to't; and there I will attend
    What further comes.

CANIDIUS.   To Cæsar will I render
    My legions and my horse: six kings already
    Show me the way of yielding.

ENOBARBUS.   I'll yet follow
    The wounded chance of Antony, though my reason
    Sits in the wind against me.   *They go*

Scene 11: *Alexandria. Cleopatra's palace*

Enter Antony with Attendants

ANTONY. Hark! the land bids me tread no more
    upon't—
    It is ashamed to bear me. Friends, come hither:
    I am so lated in the world that I
    Have lost my way for ever. I have a ship
    Laden with gold, take that, divide it; fly,
    And make your peace with Cæsar.

ALL.   Fly! not we.

ANTONY. I have fled myself, and have instructed
    cowards
    To run and show their shoulders. Friends, be gone;
    I have myself resolved upon a course
    Which has no need of you. Be gone.   10
    My treasure's in the harbour, take it. O,
    I followed that I blush to look upon:
    My very hairs do mutiny, for the white
    Reprove the brown for rashness, and they them
    For fear and doting. Friends, be gone: you shall
    Have letters from me to some friends that will
    Sweep your way for you. Pray you, look not sad,
    Nor make replies of loathness: take the hint
    Which my despair proclaims; let that be left
    Which leaves itself: to the sea-side straightway: 20
    I will possess you of that ship and treasure.
    Leave me, I pray, a little: pray you now,
    Nay, do so; for indeed I have lost command,
    Therefore I pray you: I'll see you by and by.
                               Sits down

Enter Cleopatra led by Charmian and Eros; Iras following

EROS. Nay, gentle madam, to him, comfort him.

IRAS. Do, most dear queen.

CHARMIAN. Do! why, what else?

CLEOPATRA. Let me sit down. O Juno!

ANTONY. No, no, no, no, no.

EROS. See you here, sir?   30

ANTONY. O fie, fie, fie!

CHARMIAN. Madam!

IRAS. Madam, O good empress!

EROS. Sir, sir!

ANTONY. Yes, my lord, yes; he at Philippi kept
    His sword e'en like a dancer; while I struck
    The lean and wrinkled Cassius; and 'twas I
    That the mad Brutus ended: he alone
    Dealt on lieutenantry and no practice had
    In the brave squares of war: yet now: no matter. 40

CLEOPATRA. Ah! stand by.

EROS. The queen, my lord, the queen.

IRAS. Go to him, madam, speak to him,
    He is unqualified with very shame.

CLEOPATRA. Well then, sustain me: O!

EROS. Most noble sir, arise, the queen approaches:
    Her head's declined, and death will seize her, but
    Your comfort makes the rescue.

ANTONY. I have offended reputation,
A most unnoble swerving.

EROS.   Sir, the queen.

ANTONY. O, whither hast thou led me, Egypt? See,
How I convey my shame out of thine eyes
By looking back what I have left behind
Stroyed in dishonour.

CLEOPATRA.   O my lord, my lord
Forgive my fearful sails! I little thought
You would have followed.

ANTONY.   Egypt, thou knew'st too well
My heart was to thy rudder tied by th'strings,
And thou shouldst tow me after: o'er my spirit
Thy full supremacy thou knew'st, and that
Thy beck might from the bidding of the gods
Command me.

CLEOPATRA.   O, my pardon!

ANTONY.   Now I must
To the young man send humble treaties, dodge
And palter in the shifts of lowness; who
With half the bulk o'th'world played as I pleased,
Making and marring fortunes. You did know
How much you were my conqueror, and that
My sword, made weak by my affection, would
Obey it on all cause.

CLEOPATRA.   Pardon, pardon!

ANTONY. Fall not a tear, I say; one of them rates
All that is won and lost: give me a kiss;
Even this repays me.
We sent our schoolmaster; is a' come back?
Love, I am full of lead.
Some wine, within there, and our viands!
    Fortune knows
We scorn her most when most she offers blows.
                                        They go in

Scene 12: *Egypt. Cæsar's camp*

Enter Cæsar, Agrippa, Dolabella, Thidias, with others

CÆSAR. Let him appear that's come from Antony.
Know you him?

DOLABELLA.   Cæsar, 'tis his schoolmaster—
An argument that he is plucked, when hither
He sends so poor a pinion of his wing,
Which had superfluous kings for messengers
Not many moons gone by.

Enter a Schoolmaster, as ambassador from Antony

CÆSAR.   Approach, and speak.

SCHOOLMASTER. Such as I am, I come from Antony:
I was of late as petty to his ends
As is the morn-dew on the myrtle-leaf
To his grand sea.

CÆSAR.   Be't so: declare thine office.

SCHOOLMASTER. Lord of his fortunes he salutes thee,
    and
Requires to live in Egypt, which not granted,
He lessens his requests, and to thee sues
To let him breathe between the heavens and earth,
A private man in Athens: this for him.
Next, Cleopatra does confess thy greatness,
Submits her to thy might, and of thee craves
The circle of the Ptolemies for her heirs,
Now hazarded to thy grace.

CÆSAR.   For Antony,
I have no ears to his request. The queen

Of audience nor desire shall fail, so she
From Egypt drive her all-disgracéd friend,
Or take his life there: this if she perform,
She shall not sue unheard. So to them both.

SCHOOLMASTER. Fortune pursue thee.

CÆSAR.   Bring him through the bands.
                                        The Schoolmaster goes
[*to Thidias*] To try thy eloquence, now 'tis time:
    dispatch;
From Antony win Cleopatra: promise,
And in our name, what she requires; add more,
As thine invention offers. Women are not
In their best fortunes strong, but want will perjure
The ne'er-touched vestal. Try thy cunning, Thidias;
Make thine own edict for thy pains, which we
Will answer as a law.

THIDIAS.   Cæsar, I go.

CÆSAR. Observe how Antony becomes his flaw,
And what thou think'st his very action speaks
In every power that moves.

THIDIAS.   Cæsar, I shall.   *They go*

Scene 13: *Alexandria. Cleopatra's palace*

Enter Cleopatra, Enobarbus, Charmian, and Iras

CLEOPATRA. What shall we do, Enobarbus?

ENOBARBUS.   Think, and die.

CLEOPATRA. Is Antony or we in fault for this?

ENOBARBUS. Antony only, that would make his will
Lord of his reason. What though you fled
From that great face of war, whose several ranges
Frighted each other, why should he follow?
The itch of his affection should not then
Have nicked his captainship at such a point,
When half to half the world opposed, he being
The meréd question: 'twas a shame no less
Than was his loss, to course your flying flags
And leave his navy gazing.

CLEOPATRA.   Prithee, peace.

Enter Antony, with the Schoolmaster

ANTONY. Is that his answer?

SCHOOLMASTER. Ay, my lord.

ANTONY. The queen shall then have courtesy, so she
Will yield us up.

SCHOOLMASTER.   He says so.

ANTONY.   Let her know't.
To the boy Cæsar send this grizzled head,
And he will fill thy wishes to the brim
With principalities.

CLEOPATRA.   That head, my lord?

ANTONY. To him again! tell him he wears the rose
Of youth upon him; from which the world should
    note
Something particular: his coin, ships, legions,
May be a coward's, whose ministers would prevail
Under the service of a child as soon
As i'th'command of Cæsar. I dare him therefore
To lay his gay comparisons apart
And answer me declined, sword against sword,
Ourselves alone: I'll write it: follow me.
                                He goes, attended by the Schoolmaster

ENOBARBUS [*aside*]. Yes, like enough, high battled
    Cæsar will
Unstate his happiness and be staged to th'show
Against a sworder! I see men's judgements are

A parcel of their fortunes, and things outward
Do draw the inward quality after them,
To suffer all alike. That he should dream,
Knowing all measures, the full Cæsar will
Answer his emptiness! Cæsar, thou hast subdued
His judgement too.

Enter a Servant

SERVANT.   A messenger from Cæsar.
CLEOPATRA. What, no more ceremony? See, my
      women,
Against the blown rose may they stop their nose
That kneeled unto the buds. Admit him, sir.   40
                              The Servant goes
ENOBARBUS [*aside*]. Mine honesty and I begin to
      square.
The loyalty well held to fools does make
Our faith mere folly: yet he that can endure
To follow with allegiance a fall'n lord
Does conquer him that did his master conquer,
And earns a place i'th'story.

Enter Thidias

CLEOPATRA.   Cæsar's will?
THIDIAS. Hear it apart.
CLEOPATRA.   None but friends: say boldly.
THIDIAS. So, haply, are they friends to Antony.
ENOBARBUS. He needs as many, sir, as Cæsar has,
Or needs not us. If Cæsar please, our master   50
Will leap to be his friend: for us, you know,
Whose he is we are, and that is Cæsar's.
THIDIAS.   So.
Thus then, thou most renowned, Cæsar entreats
Not to consider in what case thou stand'st
Further than he is Cæsar.
CLEOPATRA.   Go on: right royal.
THIDIAS. He knows that you embraced not Antony
As you did love, but as you feared him.
CLEOPATRA.   O!
THIDIAS. The scars upon your honour therefore he
Does pity as constrainèd blemishes,
Not as deserved.
CLEOPATRA.   He is a god and knows   60
What is most right: mine honour was not yielded,
But conquered merely.
ENOBARBUS [*aside*].   To be sure of that,
I will ask Antony. Sir, sir, thou art so leaky
That we must leave thee to thy sinking, for
Thy dearest quit thee.   *He goes out*
THIDIAS.   Shall I say to Cæsar
What you require of him? for he partly begs
To be desired to give. It much would please him,
That of his fortunes you should make a staff
To lean upon. But it would warm his spirits,
To hear from me you had left Antony,   70
And put yourself under his shroud,
The universal landlord.
CLEOPATRA.   What's your name?
THIDIAS. My name is Thidias.
CLEOPATRA.   Most kind messenger,
Say to great Cæsar this: in deputation
I kiss his conqu'ring hand: tell him, I am prompt
To lay my crown at's feet, and there to kneel:
Tell him, from his all-obeying breath I hear
The doom of Egypt.
THIDIAS.   'Tis your noblest course.
Wisdom and fortune combating together,

If that the former dare but what it can,   80
No chance may shake it. Give me grace to lay
My duty on your hand.
CLEOPATRA.   Your Cæsar's father oft
(When he hath mused of taking kingdoms in)
Bestowed his lips on that unworthy place,
As it rained kisses.

Re-enter Antony and Enobarbus

ANTONY.   Favours, by Jove that thunders!
What art thou, fellow?
THIDIAS.   One that but performs
The bidding of the fullest man and worthiest
To have command obeyed.
ENOBARBUS [*aside*].   You will be whipped.
ANTONY [*shouts*]. Approach, there! [*to Cleopatra*] Ah,
      you kite! [*pause*] Now, gods and devils!
Authority melts from me. Of late when I cried 'Ho!'   90
Like boys unto a muss, kings would start forth,
And cry 'Your will?'

Enter Attendants in haste

                              Have you no ears?
I am Antony yet. Take hence this Jack, and whip
      him.
ENOBARBUS. 'Tis better playing with a lion's whelp
Than with an old one dying.
ANTONY.   Moon and stars!
Whip him! Were't twenty of the greatest tributaries
That do acknowledge Cæsar, should I find them
So saucy with the hand of she here—what's her name
Since she was Cleopatra? Whip him, fellows,
Till like a boy you see him cringe his face,   100
And whine aloud for mercy. Take him hence.
THIDIAS. Mark Antony—
ANTONY.   Tug him away: being whipped,
Bring him again. This Jack of Cæsar's shall
Bear us an errand to him,
                    Attendants take Thidias out
You were half blasted ere I knew you ... Ha!
Have I my pillow left unpressed in Rome,
Forborne the getting of a lawful race,
And by a gem of women, to be abused
By one that looks on feeders?
CLEOPATRA.   Good my lord—   110
ANTONY. You have been a boggler ever:
But when we in our viciousness grow hard—
O misery on't!—the wise gods seel our eyes,
In our own filth drop our clear judgements, make us
Adore our errors, laugh at's while we strut
To our confusion.
CLEOPATRA.   O, is't come to this?
ANTONY. I found you as a morsel cold upon
Dead Cæsar's trencher; nay, you were a fragment
Of Gnæus Pompey's; besides what hotter hours,
Unregistered in vulgar fame, you have
Luxuriously picked out: for I am sure,   120
Though you can guess what temperance should be,
You know not what it is.
CLEOPATRA.   Wherefore is this?
ANTONY. To let a fellow that will take rewards
And say 'God quit you!' be familiar with
My playfellow, your hand, this kingly seal
And plighter of high hearts! O, that I were
Upon the hill of Basan, to outroar
The hornèd herd! for I have savage cause;
And to proclaim it civilly, were like

A haltered neck which does the hangman thank
For being yare about him.

Re-enter Attendants with Thidias

                                    Is he whipped?
1 ATTENDANT. Soundly, my lord.
ANTONY.   Cried he? and begged a' pardon?
1 ATTENDANT. He did ask favour.
ANTONY. If that thy father live, let him repent
Thou wast not made his daughter; and be thou sorry
To follow Cæsar in his triumph, since
Thou hast been whipped for following him:
    henceforth
The white hand of a lady fever thee,
Shake thou to look on't. Get thee back to Cæsar,
Tell him thy entertainment: look thou say   140
He makes me angry with him. For he seems
Proud and disdainful, harping on what I am,
Not what he knew I was. He makes me angry,
And at this time most easy 'tis to do't:
When my good stars that were my former guides
Have empty left their orbs and shot their fires
Into th'abysm of hell. If he mislike
My speech and what is done, tell him he has
Hipparchus, my enfranchéd bondman, whom
He may at pleasure whip, or hang, or torture,   150
As he shall like, to quit me. Urge it thou:
Hence with thy stripes, be gone!   *Thidias goes*
CLEOPATRA. Have you done yet?
ANTONY.   Alack, our terrene moon
Is now eclipsed, and it portends alone
The fall of Antony.
CLEOPATRA.   I must stay his time.
ANTONY. To flatter Cæsar, would you mingle eyes
With one that ties his points?
CLEOPATRA.   Not know me yet?
ANTONY. Cold-hearted toward me?
CLEOPATRA.   Ah, dear, if I be so,
From my cold heart let heaven engender hail,
And poison it in the course, and the first stone   160
Drop in my neck: as it determines, so
Dissolve my life! the next Cæsarion smite!
Till by degrees the memory of my womb,
Together with my brave Egyptians all,
By the discandying of this pelleted storm
Lie graveless, till the flies and gnats of Nile
Have buried them for prey!
ANTONY.   I am satisfied.
Cæsar sets down in Alexandria, where
I will oppose his fate. Our force by land
Hath nobly held, our severed navy too   170
Have knit again, and fleet, threat'ning most sea-like.
Where hast thou been, my heart? Dost thou hear,
    lady?
If from the field I shall return once more
To kiss these lips, I will appear in blood;
I and my sword will earn our chronicle.
There's hope in't yet.
CLEOPATRA. That's my brave lord!
ANTONY. I will be treble-sinewed, hearted, breathed,
And fight maliciously: for when mine hours
Were nice and lucky, men did ransom lives   180
Of me for jests; but now I'll set my teeth,
And send to darkness all that stop me. Come,
Let's have one other gaudy night: call to me
All my sad captains; fill our bowls once more:

Let's mock the midnight bell.
CLEOPATRA.   It is my birth-day,   130
I had thought t'have held it poor. But since my lord
Is Antony again, I will be Cleopatra.
ANTONY. We will yet do well.
CLEOPATRA. Call all his noble captains to my lord.
ANTONY. Do so, we'll speak to them, and to-night
    I'll force   190
The wine peep through their scars. Come on,
    my queen;
There's sap in't yet. The next time I do fight
I'll make death love me; for I will contend
Even with his pestilent scythe.   *They go*
ENOBARBUS. Now he'll outstare the lightning. To
    be furious
Is to be frighted out of fear, and in that mood
The dove will peck the estridge; and I see still
A diminution in our captain's brain
Restores his heart: when valour preys on reason,
It eats the sword it fights with. I will seek   200
Some way to leave him.   *He follows*

ACT 4
Scene 1: *Before Alexandria*

Enter Cæsar, Agrippa, and Mæcenas, with his army;   150
Cæsar reading a letter

CÆSAR. He calls me boy, and chides as he had power
To beat me out of Egypt; my messenger
He hath whipped with rods; dares me to personal
    combat,
Cæsar to Antony. Let the old ruffian know
I have many other ways to die; meantime
Laugh at his challenge.
MÆCENAS.   Cæsar must think,
When one so great begins to rage, he's hunted
Even to falling. Give him no breath, but now
Make boot of his distraction. Never anger
Make good guard for itself.
CÆSAR.   Let our best heads   10
Know that to-morrow the last of many battles
We mean to fight. Within our files there are,
Of those that served Mark Antony but late,
Enough to fetch him in. See it done:
And feast the army; we have store to do't,
And they have earned the waste. Poor Antony!
                                    They go

Scene 2: *Alexandria. Cleopatra's palace*

Enter Antony, Cleopatra, Enobarbus, Charmian, Iras,
Alexas, with others

ANTONY. He will not fight with me, Domitius?
ENOBARBUS.   No.
ANTONY. Why should he not?
ENOBARBUS. He thinks, being twenty times of better
    fortune,
He is twenty men to one.
ANTONY.   To-morrow, soldier,
By sea and land I'll fight: or I will live,
Or bathe my dying honour in the blood
Shall make it live again. Woo't thou fight well?   180
ENOBARBUS. I'll strike, and cry 'Take all.'
ANTONY.   Well said. Come on:
Call forth my household servants: let's to-night
Be bounteous at our meal.

Enter three or four Servitors

                            Give me thy hand,   10
Thou has been rightly honest, so hast thou,
Thou, and thou, and thou: you have served me well,
And kings have been your fellows.
CLEOPATRA.   What means this?
ENOBARBUS. 'Tis one of those odd tricks which
  sorrow shoots
Out of the mind.
ANTONY.   And thou art honest too.
I wish I could be made so many men,
And all of you clapped up together in
An Antony, that I might do you service
So good as you have done.
ALL.   The gods forbid!
ANTONY. Well, my good fellows, wait on me
  to-night: 20
Scant not my cups, and make as much of me
As when mine empire was your fellow too
And suffered my command.
CLEOPATRA.   What does he mean?
ENOBARBUS. To make his followers weep.
ANTONY.   Tend me to-night;
May be it is the period of your duty;
Haply you shall not see me more, or if,
A mangled shadow. Perchance to-morrow
You'll serve another master. I look on you
As one that takes his leave. Mine honest friends,
I turn you not away; but, like a master   30
Married to your good service, stay till death:
Tend me to-night two hours, I ask no more,
And the gods yield you for't!
ENOBARBUS.   What mean you, sir,
To give them this discomfort? Look, they weep,
And I, an ass, am onion-eyed: for shame,
Transform us not to women.
ANTONY.   Ho, ho, ho!
Now the witch take me, if I meant it thus!
Grace grow where those drops fall! My hearty
  friends,
You take me in too dolorous a sense;
For I spake to you for your comfort, did desire you   40
To burn this night with torches: know, my hearts,
I hope well of to-morrow, and will lead you
Where rather I'll expect victorious life
Than death and honour. Let's to supper, come,
And drown consideration.   *They go*

Scene 3: *The same. A platform before the palace*

Enter a company of Soldiers

1 SOLDIER. Brother, good night: to-morrow is the day.
2 SOLDIER. It will determine one way: fare you well.
  Heard you of nothing strange about the streets?
1 SOLDIER. Nothing: what news?
2 SOLDIER. Belike 'tis but a rumour. Good night to
  you.
1 SOLDIER. Well, sir, good night.

They meet other Soldiers

2 SOLDIER. Soldiers, have careful watch.
3 SOLDIER. And you. Good night, good night.

They place themselves in every corner of the platform

4 SOLDIER. Here we: and if to-morrow

Our navy thrive, I have an absolute hope   10
Our landmen will stand up.
3 SOLDIER.   'Tis a brave army,
And full of purpose
                 Strange music is heard below
4 SOLDIER.   Peace! what noise?
1 SOLDIER.   List, list!
2 SOLDIER. Hark!
1 SOLDIER.   Music i'th'air.
3 SOLDIER.   Under the earth.
4 SOLDIER. It signs well, does it not?
3 SOLDIER.   No.
1 SOLDIER.   Peace, I say!
What should this mean?
2 SOLDIER. 'Tis the god Hercules, whom Antony
  loved,
Now leaves him.
1 SOLDIER.   Walk, let's see if other watchmen
Do hear what we do.
2 SOLDIER.   How now, masters!
ALL [*speaking together*].   How now!
How now! Do you hear this?
1 SOLDIER.   Ay, is't not strange?
3 SOLDIER. Do you hear, masters? do you hear?   20
1 SOLDIER. Follow the noise so far as we have quarter;
Let's see how it will give off.
ALL.   Content. 'Tis strange.
                        They move off

Scene 4: *Cleopatra's palace*

*Enter Antony and Cleopatra, Charmian and others
attending*

ANTONY. Eros! mine armour, Eros!
CLEOPATRA.   Sleep a little.
ANTONY. No, my chuck. Eros, come; mine armour,
  Eros!

Enter Eros with armour

Come, good fellow, put thine iron on.
If fortune be not ours to-day, it is
Because we brave her: come.
CLEOPATRA.   Nay, I'll help too.
What's this for?
ANTONY.   Ah, let be, let be! thou art
The armourer of my heart: false, false: this, this.
CLEOPATRA. Sooth, la, I'll help: thus it must be.
ANTONY.   Well, well,
We shall thrive now. Seest thou, my good fellow?
Go put on thy defences.
EROS.   Briefly, sir.   10
CLEOPATRA. Is not this buckled well?
ANTONY.   Rarely, rarely:
He that unbuckles this, till we do please
To daff't for our repose, shall hear a storm.
Thou fumblest, Eros; and my queen's a squire
More tight at this than thou: dispatch. O love,
That thou couldst see my wars to-day, and knew'st
The royal occupation! thou shouldst see
A workman in't.

Enter an armed Soldier

            Good morrow to thee, welcome,
Thou look'st like him that knows a warlike charge:
To business that we love we rise betime,   20
And to go to't with delight.
SOLDIER.   A thousand, sir.

Early though't be, have on their riveted trim,
And at the port expect you.

Shout. Trumpets flourish

Enter Captains and Soldiers

CAPTAIN. The morn is fair. Good morrow, general.
ALL. Good morrow, general.
ANTONY.   'Tis well blown, lads:
This morning, like the spirit of a youth
That means to be of note, begins betimes.
So, so; come, give me that: this way—well said!
Fare thee well, dame; whate'er becomes of me,
This is a soldier's kiss: rebukeable   30
And worthy shameful check it were, to stand
On more mechanic compliment. I'll leave thee
Now like a man of steel. You that will fight,
Follow me close; I'll bring you to't. Adieu.

*They go, leaving Cleopatra and
Charmian behind*

CHARMIAN. Please you, retire to your chamber?
CLEOPATRA.   Lead me.
He goes forth gallantly. That he and Cæsar might
Determine this great war in single fight!
Then Antony—but now—Well, on.   *They go*

Scene 5: *Before Alexandria*

*Trumpets sound. Enter Antony and Eros; a Soldier meeting
them*

SOLDIER. The gods make this a happy day to Antony!
ANTONY. Would thou and those thy scars had once
     prevailed
To make me fight at land!
SOLDIER.   Hadst thou done so,
The kings that have revolted and the soldier
That has this morning left thee would have still
Followed thy heels.
ANTONY.   Who's gone this morning?
SOLDIER.   Who!
One ever near thee: call for Enobarbus,
He shall not hear thee, or from Cæsar's camp
Say 'I am none of thine.'
ANTONY.   What sayest thou?
SOLDIER.   Sir,
He is with Cæsar.
EROS.   Sir, his chests and treasure   10
He has not with him.
ANTONY.   Is he gone?
SOLDIER.   Most certain.
ANTONY. Go, Eros, send his treasure after; do it;
Detain no jot, I charge thee: write to him—
I will subscribe—gentle adieus and greetings;
Say that I wish he never find more cause
To change a master. O, my fortunes have
Corrupted honest men! Dispatch. Enobarbus!

They go

Scene 6

Flourish. Enter Cæsar with Agrippa, Enobarbus, and others

CÆSAR. Go forth, Agrippa, and begin the fight:
Our will is Antony be took alive;
Make it so known.
AGRILLA. Cæsar, I shall.   *Goes*
CÆSAR. The time of universal peace is near:

Prove this a prosp'rous day, the three-nooked world
Shall bear the olive freely.

Enter a Messenger

MESSENGER.   Antony
Is come into the field.
CÆSAR.   Go charge Agrippa
Plant those that have revolted in the vant,
That Antony may seem to spend his fury   10
Upon himself.   *All but Enobarbus go*
ENOBARBUS. Alexas did revolt, and went to Jewry on
Affairs of Antony; there did dissuade
Great Herod to incline himself to Cæsar
And leave his master Antony: for this pains
Cæsar hath hanged him. Canidius and the rest
That fell away have entertainment, but
No honourable trust. I have done ill,
Of which I do accuse myself so sorely
That I will joy no more.

Enter a Soldier of Cæsar's

SOLDIER.   Enobarbus, Antony   20
Hath after thee sent all thy treasure, with
His bounty overplus. The messenger
Came on my guard, and at thy tent is now
Unloading of his mules.
ENOBARBUS.   I give it you.
SOLDIER. Mock not, Enobarbus,
I tell you true: 't were best you safed the bringer
Out of the host; I must attend mine office,
Or would have done't myself. Your emperor
Continues still a Jove.   *He goes*
ENOBARBUS. I am alone the villain of the earth,   30
And feel I am so most. O Antony,
Thou mine of bounty, how wouldst thou have paid
My better service, when my turpitude
Thou dost so crown with gold! This blows my
     heart:
If swift thought break it not, a swifter mean
Shall outstrike thought: but thought will do't, I feel.
I fight against thee! No, I will go seek
Some ditch wherein to die; the foul'st best fits
My latter part of life.   *He goes*

Scene 7

Alarum. Drums and trumpets. Enter Agrippa and others

AGRIPPA. Retire, we have engaged ourselves too far:
Cæsar himself has work, and our oppression
Exceeds what we expected.   *They go*

Alarums. Enter Antony, and Scarus wounded

SCARUS. O my brave emperor, this is fought indeed!
Had we done so at first, we had droven them home
With clouts about their heads.
ANTONY.   Thou bleed'st apace.
SCARUS. I had a wound here that was like a 't',
But now 'tis made an 'h'.   *Retreat sounded afar off*
ANTONY.   They do retire.
SCARUS. We'll beat 'em into bench-holes. I have yet
Room for six scotches more   10

Enter Eros

EROS. They are beaten, sir, and our advantage serves
For a fair victory.

SCARUS.   Let us score their backs
And snatch 'em up, as we take hares, behind:
'Tis sport to maul a runner.
ANTONY.   I will reward thee
Once for thy sprightly comfort, and ten-fold
For thy good valour. Come thee on.
SCARUS.   I'll half after.
                              They go forward

Scene 8

Alarum. Antony returns with Scarus and his army, march-
ing as from victory, with drums and trumpets

ANTONY. We have beat him to his camp: run one
       before,
And let the queen know of our gests. To-morrow,
Before the sun shall see's, we'll spill the blood
That has to-day escaped. I thank you all,
For doughty-handed are you, and have fought
Not as you served the cause, but as't had been
Each man's like mine; you have shown all Hectors.
Enter the city, clip your wives, your friends,
Tell them your feats, whilst they with joyful tears
Wash the congealment from your wounds and kiss 10
The honoured gashes whole.

Enter Cleopatra, attended

                [*to Scarus*] Give me thy hand;
To this great Fairy I'll commend thy acts,
Make her thanks bless thee. O thou day o'th'world,
Chain mine armed neck; leap thou, attire and all,
Through proof of harness to my heart, and there
Ride on the pants triumphing!
CLEOPATRA.   Lord of lords!
O infinite virtue, comest thou smiling from
The world's great snare uncaught?
ANTONY.   My nightingale,
We have beat them to their beds. What, girl!
       though grey
Do something mingle with our younger brown,
       yet ha'we   20
A brain that nourishes our nerves and can
Get goal for goal of youth. Behold this man;
Commend unto his lips thy favouring hand:
Kiss it, my warrior: he hath fought to-day
As if a god in hate of mankind had
Destroyed in such a shape.
CLEOPATRA.   I'll give thee, friend,
An armour all of gold; it was a king's.
ANTONY. He has deserved it, were it carbuncled
Like holy Phœbus' ear. Give me thy hand.
Through Alexandria make a jolly march,   30
Bear our hacked targets like the men that owe them.
Had our great palace the capacity
To camp this host, we all would sup together.
And drink carouses to the next day's fate,
Which promises royal peril. Trumpeters,
With brazen din blast you the city's ear;
Make mingle with our rattling tabourines;
That heaven and earth may strike their sounds
       together,
Applauding our approach.   *They go*

Scene 9

Enter a centurion and his company; Enobarbus follows

CENT. If we be not relieved within this hour,
We must return to th'court of guard: the night
Is shiny, and they say we shall embattle
By th'second hour i'th'morn.
1 WATCH.   This last day was
A shrewd one to's.
ENOBARBUS.   O, bear me witness, night,—
2 WATCH. What man is this?
1 WATCH.   Stand close, and list him.
                              They go aside
ENOBARBUS. Be witness to me, O thou blessed moon.
When men revolted shall upon record
Bear hateful memory, poor Enobarbus did
Before thy face repent!
CENT.   Enobarbus!
2 WATCH.   Peace!   10
Hark further.
ENOBARBUS. O sovereign mistress of true melancholy,
The poisonous damp of night disponge upon me,
That life, a very rebel to my will,
May hang no longer on me: throw my heart
Against the flint and hardness of my fault;
Which, being dried with grief, will break to
       powder,
And finish all foul thoughts. O Antony,
Nobler than my revolt is infamous,
Forgive me in thine own particular,   20
But let the world rank me in register
A master-leaver and a fugitive:
O Antony! O Antony!   *Dies*
1 WATCH.   Let's speak to him.
CENT. Let's hear him, for the things he speaks
May concern Cæsar.
2 WATCH.   Let's do so. But he sleeps.
CENT. Swoons rather; for so bad a prayer as his
Was never yet for sleep.
1 WATCH.   Go we to him.
2 WATCH. Awake, sir, awake, speak to us.
1 WATCH.   Hear you, sir?
CENT. The hand of death hath raught him.
                              Drums afar off
Hark! the drums demurely wake the sleepers. 30
Let's bear him to th'court of guard: he is of note.
Our hour is fully out.
2 WATCH. Come on, then; he may recover yet.
                              They carry off the body

Scene 10

Enter Antony and Scarus, with their army

ANTONY. Their preparation is to-day by sea,
We please them not by land.
SCARUS.   For both, my lord.
ANTONY. I would they'ld fight i'th'fire or i'th'air;
We'ld fight there too. But this it is, our foot
Upon the hills adjoining to the city
Shall stay with us—Order for sea is given;
They have put forth the haven—
Where their appointment we may best discover,
And look on their endeavour.   *They go forward*

Scene 11

Enter Cæsar and his army

CÆSAR. But being charged, we will be still by land,
Which as I take't we shall, for his best force
Is forth to man his galleys. To the vales,

And hold our best advantage.

They march off

Scene 12: *Hills adjoining to Alexandria*

Enter Antony and Scarus

ANTONY. Yet they are not joined: where yond pine
  does stand,
  I shall discover all: I'll bring thee word
  Straight, how 'tis like to go.   *He goes up*

Alarum afar off, as at a sea-fight

SCARUS.   Swallows have built
  In Cleopatra's sails their nests: the augurers
  Say they know not, they cannot tell; look grimly
  And dare not speak their knowledge. Antony
  Is valiant, and dejected, and by starts
  His fretted fortunes give him hope, and fear,
  Of what he has, and has not.

Antony returns

ANTONY.   All is lost!
  This foul Egyptian hath betrayéd me: 10
  My fleet hath yielded to the foe, and yonder
  They cast their caps up and carouse together
  Like friends long lost. Triple-turned whore! 'tis thou
  Hast sold me to this novice, and my heart
  Makes only wars on thee. Bid them all fly!
  For when I am revenged upon my charm,
  I have done all. Bid them all fly, begone!

                   Scarus goes
  O sun, thy uprise shall I see no more:
  Fortune and Antony part here, even here
  Do we shake hands! All come to this? The hearts   20
  That spanieled me at heels, to whom I gave
  Their wishes, do discandy, melt their sweets
  On blossoming Cæsar; and this pine is barked,
  That overtopped them all. Betrayed I am.
  O this false soul of Egypt! this grave charm—
  Whose eye becked forth my wars and called them
    home,
  Whose bosom was my crownet, my chief end—
  Like a right gispy hath at fast and loose
  Beguiled me to the very heart of loss.
  What, Eros, Eros!

Enter Cleopatra

           Ah, thou spell! Avaunt!   30
CLEOPATRA. Why is my lord enraged against his love?
ANTONY. Vanish, or I shall give thee thy deserving,
  And blemish Cæsar's triumph. Let him take thee,
  And hoist thee up to the shouting plebeians:
  Follow his chariot, like the greatest spot
  Of all thy sex: most monster-like, be shown
  For poor'st diminutives, for dolts, and let
  Patient Octavia plough thy visage up
  With her preparéd nails.   *She goes*
             'Tis well thou'rt gone,
  If it be well to live; but better 'twere   40
  Thou fell'st into my fury, for one death
  Might have prevented many. Eros, ho!
  The shirt of Nessus is upon me: teach me,
  Alcides, thou mine ancestor, thy rage:
  Let me lodge Lichas on the horns o'th'moon,
  And with those hands that grasped the heaviest club
  Subdue my worthiest self ... The witch shall die.

To the young Roman boy she hath sold me, and
  I fall
  Under this plot: she dies for't. Eros, ho!
                    He goes

Scene 13: *Alexandria. Cleopatra's palace*

Enter Cleopatra, Charmian, Iras, Mardian

CLEOPATRA. Help me, my women! O, he's more mad
  Than Telamon for his shield; the boar of Thessaly
  Was never so embossed.
CHARMIAN.   To th'monument!
  There lock yourself, and send him word you are
  dead.
  The soul and body rive not more in parting
  Than greatness going off.
CLEOPATRA.   To th'monument!
  Mardian, go tell him I have slain myself;
  Say that the last I spoke was 'Antony,'
  And word it, prithee, piteously. Hence, Mardian,
  And bring me how he takes my death. To
  th'monument!   10
                   They go

Scene 14

Enter Antony and Eros

ANTONY. Eros, thou yet behold'st me?
EROS.   Ay, noble lord.
ANTONY. Sometimes we see a cloud that's dragonish,
  A vapour sometimes like a bear or lion,
  A towered citadel, a pendent rock,
  A forkéd mountain, or blue promontory
  With trees upon't, that nod unto the world
  And mock our eyes with air: thou hast seen these
  signs;
  They are black Vesper's pageants.
EROS.   Ay, my lord.
ANTONY. That which is now a horse, even with a
  thought
  The rack dislimns, and makes it indistinct   10
  As water is in water.
EROS.   It does, my lord.
ANTONY. My good knave Eros, now thy captain is
  Even such a body: here I am Antony,
  Yet cannot hold this visible shape, my knave.
  I made these wars for Egypt, and the queen—
  Whose heart I thought I had, for she had mine,
  Which, whilst it was mine, had annexed unto't
  A million moe, now lost—she, Eros, has
  Packed cards with Cæsar, and false-played my glory
  Unto an enemy's triumph.   20
  Nay, weep not, gentle Eros, there is left us
  Ourselves to end ourselves.

Enter Mardian

            O, thy vile lady!
  She has robbed me of my sword.
MARDIAN.   No, Antony,
  My mistress loved thee and her fortunes mingled
  With thine entirely.
ANTONY.   Hence, saucy eunuch, peace!
  She hath betrayed me, and shall die the death.
MARDIAN. Death of one person can be paid but once,
  And that she has discharged. What thou wouldst do
  Is done unto thy hand: the last she spake

Was 'Antony! most noble Antony!'
Then in the midst a tearing groan did break
The name of Antony; it was divided
Between her heart and lips: she rendered life,
Thy name so buried in her.
ANTONY.   Dead then?
MARDIAN.   Dead.
ANTONY. Unarm, Eros, the long day's task is done,
And we must sleep. [to Mardian] That thou depart'st
    hence safe,
Does pay thy labour richly; go. [Mardian goes] Off,
    pluck off!
The seven-fold shield of Ajax cannot keep
This battery from my heart. O, cleave, my sides!
Heart, once be stronger than thy continent,   40
Crack thy frail case! Apace, Eros, apace!
No more a soldier: bruiséd pieces, go;
You have been nobly borne. From me awhile.
                                        Eros goes
I will o'ertake thee, Cleopatra, and
Weep for my pardon. So it must be, for now
All length is torture: since the torch is out,
Lie down and stray no farther: now all labour
Mars what it does; yea, very force entangles
Itself with strength: seal then, and all is done.
Eros!—I come, my queen. Eros!—Stay for me.   50
Where souls do couch on flowers, we'll hand
    in hand,
And with our sprightly port make the ghosts gaze:
Dido and her Aeneas shall want troops,
And all the haunt be ours. Come, Eros, Eros!

Eros returns

EROS. What would my lord?
ANTONY.   Since Cleopatra died
I have lived in such dishonour that the gods
Detest my baseness. I, that with my sword
Quartered the world, and o'er green Neptune's back
With ships made cities, condemn myself to lack
The courage of a woman—less noble mind   60
Than she which by her death our Cæsar tells
'I am conqueror of myself.' Thou art sworn, Eros,
That, when the exigent should come (which now
Is come indeed) when I should see behind me
Th'inevitable prosecution of
Disgrace and horror, that, on my command,
Thou then wouldst kill me. Do't, the time is come:
Thou strik'st not me, 'tis Cæsar thou defeat'st.
Put colour in thy cheek.
EROS.   The gods withhold me!
Shall I do that which all the Parthian darts,   70
Though enemy, lost aim and could not?
ANTONY.   Eros,
Wouldst thou be windowed in great Rome, and see
Thy master thus with pleached arms, bending down
His corrigible neck, his face subdued
To penetrative shame; whilst the wheeled seat
Of fortunate Cæsar, drawn before him, branded
His baseness that ensued?
EROS.   I would not see't.
ANTONY. Come, then; for with a wound I must
    be cured.
Draw that thy honest sword, which thou hast worn
Most useful for thy country.
EROS.   O, sir, pardon me!   80

ANTONY. When I did make thee free, swor'st thou
    not then
To do this when I bade thee? Do it at once;
Or thy precedent services are all
But accidents unpurposed. Draw, and come.
EROS. Turn from me then that noble countenance,
Wherein the worship of the whole world lies.
ANTONY [turns]. Lo thee!
EROS. My sword is drawn.
ANTONY.   Then let it do at once
The thing why thou hast drawn it.
EROS.   My dear master,
My captain, and my emperor, let me say,   90
Before I strike this bloody stroke, farewell.
ANTONY. 'Tis said, man—and farewell.
EROS. Farewell, great chief. Shall I strike now?
ANTONY.   Now, Eros.
EROS. Why, there then: thus I do escape the sorrow
Of Antony's death.   *Kills himself*
ANTONY.   Thrice-nobler than myself!
Thou teachest me, O valiant Eros, what
I should and thou couldst not. My queen and Eros
Have by their brave instruction got upon me
A nobleness in record: but I will be
A bridegroom in my death, and run into't   100
As to a lover's bed. Come then; and, Eros,
Thy master dies thy scholar: to do thus
                        Falling on his sword
I learned of thee. How! not dead? not dead?
The guard, ho! O, dispatch me!

Enter Dercetus and Guard

1 GUARD.   What's the noise?
ANTONY. I have done my work ill, friends: O, make
    an end
Of what I have begun.
2 GUARD.   The star is fall'n.
1 GUARD. And time is at his period.
ALL.   Alas, and woe!
ANTONY. Let him that loves me strike me dead.
1 GUARD.   Not I.
2 GUARD. Nor I.
3 GUARD. Nor any one.   *They fly* 110
DERCETUS. Thy death and fortunes bid thy followers
    fly.
This sword but shown to Cæsar, with this tidings,
Shall enter me with him.

Diomedes enters

DIOMEDES. Where's Antony?
DERCETUS.   There, Diomed, there.
DIOMEDES.   Lives he?
Wilt thou not answer, man?   *Dercetus goes*
ANTONY. Art thou there, Diomed? Draw thy sword,
    and give me
Sufficing strokes for death.
DIOMEDES.   Most absolute lord,
My mistress Cleopatra sent me to thee.
ANTONY. When did she send thee?
DIOMEDES.   Now, my lord.
ANTONY.   Where is she?
DIOMEDES. Locked in her monument. She had a
    prophesying fear   120
Of what hath come to pass: for when she saw—
Which never shall be found—you did suspect
She had disposed with Cæsar, and that your rage

Would not be purged, she sent you word she
was dead;
But, fearing since how it might work, hath sent
Me to proclaim the truth, and I am come,
I dread, too late.
ANTONY. Too late, good Diomed: call my guard,
I prithee.
DIOMEDES. What, ho, the emperor's guard! The guard,
what, ho!
Come, your lord calls.   130

Enter four or five of the Guard of Antony

ANTONY. Bear me, good friends, where Cleopatra
bides,
'Tis the last service that I shall command you.
1 GUARD. Woe, woe are we, sir, you may not live
to wear
All your true followers out.
ALL.   Most heavy day!
ANTONY. Nay, good my fellows, do not please sharp
fate
To grace it with your sorrows: bid that welcome
Which comes to punish us, and we punish it
Seeming to bear it lightly. Take me up.
I have led you oft, carry me now, good friends,
And have my thanks for all.   140
                    They bear him away on his shield

Scene 15: *Alexandria. Cleopatra's monument*

Cleopatra, Charmian, Iras and maids come out upon the roof

CLEOPATRA. O Charmian, I will never go from hence.
CHARMIAN. Be comforted, dear madam.
CLEOPATRA.   No, I will not:
All strange and terrible events are welcome,
But comforts we despise; our size of sorrow,
Proportioned to our cause, must be as great
As that which makes it.

Enter Diomedes below

                    How now! is he dead?
DIOMEDES. His death's upon him, but not dead.
Look out o'th'other side your monument;
His guard have brought him thither.

Enter Antony, borne by the Guard

CLEOPATRA.   O sun,
Burn the great sphere thou mov'st in! darkling stand   10
The varying shore o'th'world. O Antony,
Antony, Antony! Help, Charmian, help, Iras, help;
Help, friends below, let's draw him hither.
ANTONY.   Peace!
Not Cæsar's valour hath o'erthrown Antony,
But Antony's hath triumphed on itself.
CLEOPATRA. So it should be, that none but Anthony
Should conquer Antony, but woe 'tis so!
ANTONY. I am dying, Egypt, dying; only
I here importune death awhile, until
Of many thousand kisses the poor last   20
I lay upon thy lips.
CLEOPATRA.   I dare not, dear,
Dear my lord, pardon: I dare not open,
Lest I be taken. Not th'imperious show
Of the full-fortuned Cæsar ever shall
Be brooched with me, if knife, drugs, serpents, have
Edge, string, or operation. I am safe:

Your wife Octavia, with her modest eyes
And still conclusion, shall acquire no honour
Demurring upon me. But come, come, Antony—
Help me, my women—we must draw thee up;   30
Assist, good friends.
ANTONY.   O, quick, or I am gone.
CLEOPATRA. Here's sport indeed! How heavy weighs
my lord!
Our strength is all gone into heaviness;
That makes the weight. Had I great Juno's power,
The strong-winged Mercury should fetch thee up
And set thee by Jove's side. Yet come a little—
Wishers were ever fools—O, come, come, come;
                    They heave Antony aloft to Cleopatra
And welcome, welcome! Die when thou hast lived,
Quicken with kissing: had my lips that power,
Thus would I wear them out.
ALL.   Ah, heavy sight.   40
ANTONY. I am dying, Egypt, dying.
Give me some wine, and let me speak a little.
CLEOPATRA. No, let me speak, and let me rail so high,
That the false huswife Fortune break her wheel,
Provoked by my offence.
ANTONY.   One word, sweet queen.
Of Cæsar seek your honour, with your safety. O!
CLEOPATRA. They do not go together.
ANTONY.   Gentle, hear me:
None about Cæsar trust but Proculeius.
CLEOPATRA. My resolution and my hands I'll trust;
None about Cæsar.   50
ANTONY. The miserable change now at my end
Lament nor sorrow at: but please your thoughts
In feeding them with those my former fortunes
Wherein I lived ... the greatest prince o'th'world,
The noblest ... and do now not basely die,
Not cowardly put off my helmet to
My countryman ... a Roman by a Roman
Valiantly vanquished. Now my spirit is going,
I can no more.
CLEOPATRA.   Noblest of men, woo't die?
Hast thou no care of me? shall I abide   60
In this dull world, which in thy absence is
No better than a sty? O, see, my women ...
                                        Antony dies
The crown o'th'earth doth melt. My lord!
O, withered is the garland of the war,
The soldier's pole is fall'n: young boys and girls
Are level now with men: the odds is gone,
And there is nothing left remarkable
Beneath the visiting moon.
CHARMIAN.   O, quietness, lady!
                                        Cleopatra faints
IRAS. She's dead too, our sovereign.
CHARMIAN.   Lady!
IRAS.   Madam!
CHARMIAN. O madam, madam, madam!   70
IRAS. Royal Egypt, Empress!
CHARMIAN. Peace, peace, Iras!
CLEOPATRA. No more but e'en a woman, and
commanded
By such poor passion as the maid that milks
And does the meanest chares. It were for me
To throw my sceptre at the injurious gods,
To tell them that this world did equal theirs
Till they had stol'n our jewel. All's but naught;
Patience is sottish, and impatience does

Become a dog that's mad: then is it sin
To rush into the secret house of death,
Ere death dare come to us? How do you, women?
What, what! good cheer! Why, how now,
    Charmian!
My noble girls! Ah, women, women, look,
Our lamp is spent, it's out! Good sirs, take heart:
We'll bury him; and then, what's brave, what's
    noble,
Let's do it after the high Roman fashion,
And make death proud to take us. Come, away.
This case of that huge spirit now is cold:
Ah, women, women! Come, we have no friend 90
But resolution and the briefest end.
    They go, bearing off Antony's body

ACT 5
Scene 1: *Alexandria. Cæsar's camp*

Enter Cæsar, with Agrippa, Dolabella, Mæcenas, Gallus, Proculeius, and his council of war

CÆSAR. Go to him, Dolabella, bid him yield;
Being so frustrate, tell him he mocks
The pauses that he makes.
DOLABELLA.   Cæsar, I shall. *He goes*

Enter Dercetus, with the sword of Antony

CÆSAR. Wherefore is that? and what art thou that
    darest
    Appear thus to us?
DERCETUS.   I am called Dercetus.
Mark Antony I served, who best was worthy
Best to be served: whilst he stood up and spoke,
He was my master, and I wore my life
To spend upon his haters. If thou please
To take me to thee, as I was to him 10
I'll be to Cæsar; if thou pleasest not,
I yield thee up my life.
CÆSAR.   What is't thou say'st?
DERCETUS. I say, O Cæsar, Antony is dead.
CÆSAR. The breaking of so great a thing should make
A greater crack: the round world
Should have shook lions into civil streets,
And citizens to their dens. The death of Antony
Is not a single doom; in that name lay
A moiety of the world.
DERCETUS.   He is dead, Cæsar,
Not by a public minister of justice, 20
Nor by a hiréd knife; but that self hand
Which writ his honour in the acts it did,
Hath, with the courage which the heart did lend it,
Splitted the heart. This is his sword;
I robbed his wound of it; behold it stained
With his most noble blood.
CÆSAR.   Look you sad, friends?
The gods rebuke me, but it is tidings
To wash the eyes of kings.
AGRIPPA.   And strange it is
That nature must compel us to lament
Our most persisted deeds.
MÆCENAS.   His taints and honours 30
Waged equal with him.
AGRIPPA.   A rarer spirit never
Did steer humanity: but you, gods, will give us
Some faults to make us men. Cæsar is touched.

MÆCENAS. When such a spacious mirror's set before 80
    him,
He needs must see himself.
CÆSAR.   O Antony!
I have followed thee to this. But we do lance
Diseases in our bodies: I must perforce
Have shown to thee such a declining day,
Or look on thine; we could not stall together
In the whole world. But yet let me lament 40
With tears as sovereign as the blood of hearts,
That thou, my brother, my competitor
In top of all design, my mate in empire
Friend and companion in the front of war,
The arm of mine own body, and the heart
Where mine his thoughts did kindle, that our stars
Unreconciliable should divide
Our equalness to this. Hear me, good friends—

Enter an Egyptian

But I will tell you at some meeter season.
The business of this man looks out of him; 50
We'll hear him what he says. Whence are you?
EGYPTIAN. A poor Egyptian, yet the queen my
    mistress,
Confined in all she has, her monument,
Of thy intents desires instruction,
That she preparédly may frame herself
To th'way she's forced to.
CÆSAR.   Bid her have good heart:
She soon shall know of us, by some of ours,
How honourable and how kindly we
Determine for her; for Cæsar cannot live
To be ungentle.
EGYPTIAN.   So the gods preserve thee! 60
                                    He departs
CÆSAR. Come hither, Proculeius. Go and say,
We purpose her no shame: give her what comforts
The quality of her passion shall require;
Lest in her greatness by some mortal stroke
She do defeat us. For her life in Rome
Would be eternal in our triumph: go,
And with your speediest bring us to what she says
And how you find of her.
PROCULEIUS.   Cæsar, I shall. *He goes*
CÆSAR. Gallus, go you along. (*Gallus also goes*]
    Where's Dolabella,
To second Proculeius?
ALL.   Dolabella! 70
CÆSAR. Let him alone; for I remember now
How he's employed: he shall in time be ready.
Go with me to my tent, where you shall see
How hardly I was drawn into this war,
How calm and gentle I proceeded still
In all my writings. Go with me, and see
What I can show in this.   *They go*

Scene 2: *Alexandria. The monument*

Enter Cleopatra, Charmian, Iras and Mardian seen within through the bars of the gate

CLEOPATRA. My desolation does begin to make
A better life. 'Tis paltry to be Cæsar;
Not being Fortune, he's but Fortune's knave,
A minister of her will: and it is great
To do that thing that ends all other deeds;
Which shackles accidents and bolts up change;

Which sleeps, and never palates more the dung,
The beggar's nurse and Cæsar's.

Enter Proculeius. As he speaks with Cleopatra through the
bars, Gallus and soldiers enter, unseen by those within,
mount to the top with ladders, and go down into the
monument

PROCULEIUS. Cæsar sends greeting to the Queen of
  Egypt,
  And bids thee study on what fair demands   10
  Thou mean'st to have him grant thee.
CLEOPATRA.   What's thy name?
PROCULEIUS. My name is Proculeius.
CLEOPATRA.   Antony
  Did tell me of you, bade me trust you, but
  I do not greatly care to be deceived,
  That have no use for trusting. If your master
  Would have a queen his beggar, you must tell him,
  That majesty, to keep decorum, must
  No less beg than a kingdom: if he please
  To give me conquered Egypt for my son,
  He gives me so much of mine own as I   20
  Will kneel to him with thanks.
PROCULEIUS.   Be of good cheer;
  You're fall'n into a princely hand, fear nothing.
  Make your full reference freely to my lord,
  Who is so full of grace that it flows over
  On all that need. Let me report to him
  Your sweet dependence, and you shall find
  A conqueror that will pray in aid for kindness,
  Where he for grace is kneeled to.
CLEOPATRA.   Pray you, tell him
  I am his fortune's vassal, and I send him
  The greatness he has got. I hourly learn   30
  A doctrine of obedience, and would gladly
  Look him i'th'face.
PROCULEIUS. This I'll report, dear lady.
  Have comfort, for I know your plight is pitied
  Of him that caused it.

The doors are suddenly flung open, showing Gallus and
soldiers standing behind Cleopatra and her women

GALLUS. You see how easily she may be surprised.
  Guard her till Cæsar come.   *He goes*
IRAS. Royal queen!
CHARMIAN. O Cleopatra! thou art taken, queen!
CLEOPATRA. Quick, quick, good hands.
                     Drawing a dagger
PROCULEIUS.   Hold, worthy lady, hold:
                 Seizes and disarms her
  Do not yourself such wrong, who are in this   40
  Relieved, but not betrayed.
CLEOPATRA.   What, of death too,
  That rids our dogs of languish?
PROCULEIUS.   Cleopatra,
  Do not abuse my master's bounty by
  Th'undoing of yourself: let the world see
  His nobleness well acted, which your death
  Will never let come forth.
CLEOPATRA.   Where art thou, death?
  Come hither, come! come, come, and take a queen
  Worth many babes and beggars!
PROCULEIUS.   O, temperance, lady!
CLEOPATRA. Sir, I will eat no meat, I'll not drink, sir—
  If idle talk will once be necessary—   50
  I'll not sleep neither. This mortal house I'll ruin,

Do Cæsar what he can. Know, sir, that I
Will not wait pinioned at your master's court,
Nor once be chastised with the sober eye
Of dull Octavia. Shall they hoist me up
And show me to the shouting varletry
Of censuring Rome? Rather a ditch in Egypt
Be gentle grave unto me! rather on Nilus' mud
Lay me stark nak'd, and let the water-flies
Blow me into abhorring! rather make   60
My country's high pyramides my gibbet,
And hang me up in chains!
PROCULEIUS.   You do extend
  These thoughts of horror further than you shall
  Find cause in Cæsar.

Enter Dolabella

DOLABELLA.   Proculeius,
  What thou hast done thy master Cæsar knows,
  And he hath sent for thee: for the queen,
  I'll take her to my guard.
PROCULEIUS.   So, Dolabella,
  It shall content me best: be gentle to her.
  [*to Cleopatra*] To Cæsar I will speak what you
    shall please,
  If you'll employ me to him.
CLEOPATRA.   Say, I would die.   70
                    Proculeius goes
DOLABELLA. Most noble Empress, you have heard
  of me?
CLEOPATRA. I cannot tell.
DOLABELLA.   Assuredly you know me.
CLEOPATRA. No matter, sir, what I have heard or
  known.
  You laugh when boys or women tell their dreams;
  Is't not your trick?
DOLABELLA.   I understand not, madam.
CLEOPATRA. I dreamed there was an Emperor Antony.
  O, such another sleep, that I might see
  But such another man!
DOLABELLA.   If it might please ye—
CLEOPATRA. His face was as the heavens, and therein
  stuck
  A sun and moon, which kept their course and
  lighted   80
  The little O, the earth.
DOLABELLA.   Most sovereign creature—
CLEOPATRA. His legs bestrid the ocean, his reared arm
  Crested the world: his voice was propertied
  As all the tunéd spheres, and that to friends;
  But when he meant to quail and shake the orb,
  He was as rattling thunder. For his bounty,
  There was no winter in't; an autumn 'twas
  That grew the more by reaping: his delights
  Were dolphin-like, they showed his back above
  The element they lived in: in his livery   90
  Walked crowns and crownets; realms and islands
  were
  As plates dropped from his pocket.
DOLABELLA.   Cleopatra—
CLEOPATRA. Think you there was, or might be, such
  a man
  As this I dreamed of?
DOLABELLA.   Gentle madam, no.
CLEOPATRA. You lie, up to the hearing of the gods.
  But if there be, or ever were, one such,
  It's past the size of dreaming: nature wants stuff

To vie strange forms with Fancy, yet 'timagine
An Antony were Nature's piece 'gainst Fancy,
Condemning shadows quite.
DOLABELLA.   Hear me, good madam. 100
Your loss is as yourself, great; and you bear it
As answering to the weight: would I might never
O'ertake pursued success, but I do feel,
By the rebound of yours, a grief that smites
My very heart at root.
CLEOPATRA.   I thank you, sir.
Know you what Cæsar means to do with me?
DOLABELLA. I am loath to tell you what I would
  you knew.
CLEOPATRA. Nay, pray you, sir,—
DOLABELLA.   Though he be honourable,—
CLEOPATRA. He'll lead me then in triumph?
DOLABELLA. Madam, he will, I know't.   Flourish
[Shouting heard]   Make way there! Cæsar! 110

Enter Cæsar, Gallus, Proculeius, Mæcenas, and others of
his train

CÆSAR. Which is the Queen of Egypt?
DOLABELLA. It is the Emperor, madam.
                                        Cleopatra kneels
CÆSAR. Arise, you shall not kneel:
  I pray you, rise, rise, Egypt.
CLEOPATRA.   Sir, the gods
Will have it thus; my master and my lord
I must obey.
CÆSAR.   Take to you no hard thoughts:
The record of what injuries you did us,
Though written in our flesh, we shall remember
As things but done by chance.
CLEOPATRA.   Sole sir o'th'world,
I cannot project mine own cause so well   120
To make it clear, but do confess I have
Been laden with like frailties which before
Have often shamed our sex.
CÆSAR.   Cleopatra, know,
We will extenuate rather than enforce:
If you apply yourself to our intents,
Which towards you are most gentle, you shall find
A benefit in this change; but if you seek
To lay on me a cruelty by taking
Antony's course, you shall bereave yourself
Of my good purposes and put your children   130
To that destruction which I'll guard them from
If thereon you rely. I'll take my leave.
CLEOPATRA. And may, through all the world: 'tis
  yours; and we,
Your scrutcheons and your signs of conquest, shall
Hang in what place you please. Here, my good lord.
                              She proffers a paper
CÆSAR. You shall advise me in all for Cleopatra.
CLEOPATRA. This is the brief of money, plate and
  jewels,
I am possessed of: 'tis exactly valued,
Not petty things admitted. Where's Seleucus?

Seleucus comes forward

SELEUCUS. Here, madam.
CLEOPATRA. This is my treasurer. Let him speak,   140
  my lord,
Upon his peril, that I have reserved
To myself nothing. Speak the truth, Seleucus.
SELEUCUS. Madam,

I had rather seal my lips than to my peril
Speak that which is not.
CLEOPATRA.   What have I kept back?
SELEUCUS. Enough to purchase what you have
  made known.
CÆSAR. Nay, blush not, Cleopatra, I approve
Your wisdom in the deed.
CLEOPATRA.   See, Cæsar! O, behold,
How pomp is followed! mine will now be yours,   150
And, should we shift estates, yours would be mine.
The ingratitude of this Seleucus does
Even make me wild. O slave, of no more trust
Than love that's hired! What, goest thou back?
  thou shalt
Go back, I warrant thee; but I'll catch thine eyes,
Though they had wings: slave, soulless villain, dog!
O rarely base!
CÆSAR.   Good queen, let us entreat you.
CLEOPATRA. O Cæsar, what a wounding shame is this,
That thou, vouchsafing here to visit me,
Doing the honour of thy lordliness   160
To one so meek, that mine own servant should
Parcel the sum of my disgraces by
Addition of his envy! Say, good Cæsar,
That I some lady trifles have reserved,
Immoment toys, things of such dignity
As we greet modern friends withal; and say,
Some nobler token I have kept apart
For Livia and Octavia, to induce
Their mediation; must I be unfolded
With one that I have bred? The gods! it smites me 170
Beneath the fall I have. [to Seleucus] Prithee, go
  hence;
Or I shall show the cinders of my spirits
Through th'ashes of my chance: wert thou a man,
Thou wouldst have mercy on me.
CÆSAR.   Forbear Seleucus
                                    Seleucus goes
CLEOPATRA. Be it known, that we, the greatest, are
  misthought
For things that others do, and when we fall,
We answer others' merits in our name,
Are therefore to be pitied.
CÆSAR.   Cleopatra,
Not what you have reserved, nor what
  acknowledged,
Put we i'th'roll of conquest: still be't yours,   180
Bestow it at your pleasure, and believe
Cæsar's no merchant, to make price with you
Of things that merchants sold. Therefore be
  cheered;
Make not your thoughts your prisons: no, dear
  queen;
For we intend so to dispose you as
Yourself shall give us counsel. Feed, and sleep:
Our care and pity is so much upon you
That we remain your friend; and so, adieu.
CLEOPATRA. My master, and my lord!
CÆSAR.   Not so. Adieu.
                      Flourish. Cæsar and his train depart
CLEOPATRA. He words me, girls, he words me, that
  I should not   190
Be noble to myself: but, hark thee, Charmian.
                                            Whispers
IRAS. Finish, good lady, the bright day is done,
And we are for the dark.

CLEOPATRA.   Hie thee again,
I have spoke already, and it is provided,
Go put it to the haste.
CHARMIAN.   Madam, I will.

Re-enter Dolabella

DOLABELLA. Where's the queen?
CHARMIAN [*going*].   Behold, sir.
CLEOPATRA.   Dolabella?
DOLABELLA. Madam, as thereto sworn by your
   command
(Which my love makes religion to obey),
I tell you this: Cæsar through Syria
Intends his journey, and within three days   200
You with your children will he send before.
Make your best use of this: I have performed
Your pleasure and my promise.
CLEOPATRA.   Dolabella.
I shall remain your debtor.
DOLABELLA.   I your servant.
Adieu, good queen; I must attend on Cæsar.
CLEOPATRA. Farewell, and thanks.   *He goes*
          Now, Iras, what think'st thou?
Thou, an Egyptian puppet, shalt be shown
In Rome, as well as I: mechanic slaves
With greasy aprons, rules and hammers, shall
Uplift us to the view: in their thick breaths,   210
Rank of gross diet, shall we be enclouded
And forced to drink their vapour.
IRAS.   The gods forbid!
CLEOPATRA. Nay, 'tis most certain, Iras: saucy lictors
Will catch at us like strumpets, and scald rhymers
Ballad us out o'tune: the quick comedians
Extemporally will stage us and present
Our Alexandrian revels; Antony
Shall be brought drunken forth, and I shall see
Some squeaking Cleopatra boy my greatness
I'th'posture of a whore.
IRAS.   O the good gods!   220
CLEOPATRA. Nay, that's certain.
IRAS. I'll never see't! for I am sure my nails
Are stronger than mine eyes.
CLEOPATRA.   Why, that's the way
To fool their preparations, and to conquer
Their most absurd intents.

Charmian returns

                Now, Charmian!
Show me, my women, like a queen: go fetch
My best attires. I am again for Cydnus,
To meet Mark Antony. Sirrah Iras, go.
Now, noble Charmian, we'll dispatch indeed,
And when thou hast done this chare I'll give thee
   leave   230
To play till doomsday. Bring our crown and all.
         Iras goes. Loud voices heard
Wherefore's this noise?

Enter a Guardsman

GUARDSMAN.   Here is a rural fellow
That will not be denied your highness' presence.
He brings you figs.
CLEOPATRA. Let him come in.   *Guardsman goes*
          What poor an instrument
May do a noble deed! he brings me liberty.
My resolution's placed, and I have nothing

Of woman in me: now from head to foot
I am marble-constant; now the fleeting moon
No planet is of mine.

Guardsman returns with Clown, bringing in a basket

GUARDSMAN.   This is the man.   240
CLEOPATRA. Avoid, and leave him.   *He goes*
Hast thou the pretty worm of Nilus there,
That kills and pains not?
CLOWN. Truly, I have him: but I would not be the
party that should desire you to touch him, for his
biting is immortal; those that do die of it do seldom
or never recover.
CLEOPATRA. Remember'st thou any that have died
on't?
CLOWN. Very many, men and women too. I heard of   250
one of them no longer than yesterday—a very
honest woman, but something given to lie, as a
woman should not do but in the way of honesty—
how she died of the biting of it, what pain she
felt. Truly, she makes a very good report
o'th'worm; but he that will believe all that they say,
shall never be saved by half that they do: but this
is most falliable, the worm's an odd worm.
CLEOPATRA. Get thee hence; farewell.
CLOWN. I wish you all joy of the worm.   260
          Setting down the basket
CLEOPATRA. Farewell.
CLOWN. You must think this, look you, that the worm
will do his kind.
CLEOPATRA. Ay, ay; farewell.
CLOWN. Look you, the worm is not to be trusted
but in the keeping of wise people: for indeed there
is no goodness in the worm.
CLEOPATRA. Take thou no care, it shall be heeded.
CLOWN. Very good: give it nothing, I pray you, for it
is not worth the feeding.   270
CLEOPATRA. Will it eat me?
CLOWN. You must not think I am so simple but I
know the devil himself will not eat a woman: I
know that a woman is a dish for the gods, if the
devil dress her not. But, truly, these same whoreson
devils do the gods great harm in their women; for in
every ten that they make, the devils mar five.
CLEOPATRA. Well, get thee gone; farewell.
CLOWN. Yes, forsooth: I wish you joy o'th'worm.
                       Goes

Re-enter Iras with a robe, crown, etc.

CLEOPATRA. Give me my robe, put on my crown, I
have   280
Immortal longings in me. Now no more
The juice of Egypt's grape shall moist this lip.
Yare, yare, good Iras; quick. Methinks I hear
Antony call; I see him rouse himself
To praise my noble act; I hear him mock
The luck of Cæsar, which the gods give men
To excuse their after wrath. Husband, I come:
Now to that name my courage prove my title!
I am fire and air; my other elements
I give to baser life. So, have you done?   290
Come then and take the last warmth of my lips.
Farewell, kind Charmian, Iras, long farewell.
        Kisses them. Iras falls and dies
Have I the aspic in my lips? Dost fall?
If thou and nature can so gently part,

The stroke of death is as a lover's pinch,
Which hurts, and is desired. Dost thou lie still?
If thus thou vanishest, thou tell'st the world
It is not worth leave-taking.
CHARMIAN. Dissolve, thick cloud, and rain, that I
    may say
The gods themselves do weep!
CLEOPATRA.   This proves me base: 300
If she first meet the curlèd Antony,
He'll make demand of her, and spend that kiss
Which is my heaven to have. Come, thou mortal
    wretch,
        To an asp, which she applies to her breast
With thy sharp teeth this knot intrinsicate
Of life at once untie: poor venomous fool,
Be angry, and dispatch. O, couldst thou speak,
That I might hear thee call great Cæsar ass,
Unpolicied!
CHARMIAN. O eastern star!
CLEOPATRA.   Peace, peace!
Dost thou not see my baby at my breast,
That sucks the nurse asleep?
CHARMIAN.   O, break! O, break! 310
CLEOPATRA. As sweet as balm, as soft as air, as gentle—
O Antony!—Nay, I will take thee too:
        Applying another asp to her arm
What should I stay—   *Dies*
CHARMIAN. In this wild world? So, fare thee well!
Now boast thee, death, in thy possession lies
A lass unparalleled. Downy windows, close;
And golden Phœbus never be beheld
Of eyes again so royal! Your crown's awry,
I'll mend it, and then play—

Enter the Guard, rustling in

I GUARD. Where's the queen?
CHARMIAN.   Speak softly, wake her not. 320
I GUARD. Cæsar hath sent—
CHARMIAN   Too slow a messenger.
               Applies an asp
O, come apace, dispatch, I partly feel thee.
I GUARD. Approach, ho! All's not well: Cæsar's
    beguiled.
2 GUARD. There's Dolabella sent from Cæsar; call him.
I GUARD. What work is here! Charmian, is this
    well done?
CHARMIAN. It is well done, and fitting for a princess
Descended of so many royal kings.
Ah, soldier!   *Charmian dies*

Re-enter Dolabella

DOLABELLA. How goes it here?
2 GUARD.   All dead.
DOLABELLA.   Cæsar, thy thoughts
Touch their effects in this: thyself art coming   330
To see performed the dreaded act which thou
So sought'st to hinder.
[*shouts heard*] A way there, a way for Cæsar!

Enter Cæsar and all his train, marching

DOLABELLA. O sir, you are too sure an augurer;
That you did fear is done.
CÆSAR.   Bravest at the last,
She levelled at our purposes, and being royal
Took her own way. The manner of their deaths?
I do not see them bleed.
DOLABELLA.   Who was last with them?
I GUARD. A simple countryman, that brought her figs:
This was his basket.
CÆSAR.   Poisoned then.
I GUARD.   O Cæsar,   340
This Charmian lived but now, she stood and spake:
I found her trimming up the diadem
On her dead mistress; tremblingly she stood,
And on the sudden dropped.
CÆSAR.   O noble weakness!
If they had swallowed poison, 'twould appear
By external swelling: but she looks like sleep,
As she would catch another Antony
In her strong toil of grace.
DOLABELLA.   Here, on her breast,
There is a vent of blood, and something blown.
The like is on her arm.   350
I GUARD. This is an aspic's trail, and these fig-leaves
Have slime upon them, such as th'aspic leaves
Upon the caves of Nile.
CÆSAR.   Most probable
That so she died; for her physician tells me
She hath pursued conclusions infinite
Of easy ways to die. Take up her bed,
And bear her women from the monument.
She shall be buried by her Antony.
No grave upon the earth shall clip in it
A pair so famous. High events as these   360
Strike those that make them; and their story is
No less in pity than his glory which
Brought them to be lamented. Our army shall
In solemn show attend this funeral,
And then to Rome. Come, Dolabella, see
High order in this great solemnity.
      They go; the soldiers bearing off the dead bodies

Cymbeline

The scene: Britain and Rome

CHARACTERS IN THE PLAY

CYMBELINE, *king of Britain*
CLOTEN, *son to the Queen by a former husband*
POSTHUMUS LEONATUS, *a gentleman, husband to Imogen*
BELARIUS, *a banished lord, disguised under the name of*
  Morgan

GUIDERIUS }
ARVIRAGUS } *sons to Cymbeline, disguised under the names*
  of Polydore and Cadwal, supposed sons to
  Morgan

PHILARIO, *friend to Posthumus* }
JACHIMO, *friend to Philario* } *Italians*
CAIUS LUCIUS, *general of the Roman forces*
PISANIO, *servant to Posthumus*
CORNELIUS, *a physician*

A Roman Captain
Two British Captains
A Frenchman, friend to Philario
Two Lords of Cymbeline's court
Two Gentlemen of the same
Two Gaolers
QUEEN, *wife to Cymbeline*
IMOGEN, *daughter to Cymbeline by a former queen*
HELEN, *a lady attending on Imogen*
Lords, Ladies, Roman Senators, Tribunes, a Soothsayer,
  a Dutchman, a Spaniard, Musicians, Officers,
  Captains, Soldiers, Messengers, and other Attendants,
  Apparitions

Cymbeline

ACT 1

Scene 1: *Britain. The garden of Cymbeline's palace*

Enter two Gentlemen

1 GENTLEMAN. You do not meet a man but frowns.
  Our bloods
No more obey the heavens than our courtiers
Still seem as does the king.
2 GENTLEMAN.   But what's the matter?
1 GENTLEMAN. His daughter, and the heir of's
  kingdom, whom
He purposed to his wife's sole son—a widow
That late he married—hath referred herself
Unto a poor but worthy gentleman. She's wedded;
Her husband banished; she imprisoned. All
Is outward sorrow, though I think the king
Be touched at very heart.
2 GENTLEMAN.   None but the king?   10
1 GENTLEMAN. He that hath lost her too. So is the
  queen,
That most desired the match. But not a courtier,
Although they wear their faces to the bent
Of the king's looks, hath a heart that is not
Glad of the thing they scowl at.
2 GENTLEMAN.   And why so?
1 GENTLEMAN. He that hath missed the princess is a
  thing
Too bad for bad report; and he that hath her—
I mean, that married her, alack, good man!
And therefore banished—is a creature such
As, to seek through the regions of the earth   20
For one his like, there would be something failing
In him that should compare. I do not think
So fair an outward and such stuff within
Endows a man but he.
2 GENTLEMAN.   You speak him far.
1 GENTLEMAN. I do extend him, sir, within himself,
Crush him together, rather than unfold
His measure duly.
2 GENTLEMAN.   What's his name and birth?
1 GENTLEMAN. I cannot delve him to the root. His
  father
Was called Sicilius, who did join his honour
Against the Romans with Cassibelan,   30
But had his titles by Tenantius, whom
He served with glory and admired success,
So gained the sur-addition Leonatus;
And had, besides this gentleman in question,
Two other sons, who in the wars o'th'time
Died with their swords in hand; for which their
  father,
Then old and fond of issue, took such sorrow
That he quit being; and his gentle lady,
Big of this gentleman, our theme, deceased
As he was born. The king he takes the babe   40
To his protection, calls him Posthumus Leonatus,
Breeds him and makes him of his bed-chamber,
Puts to him all the learnings that his time
Could make the receiver of, which he took
As we do air, fast as 'twas minist'red,

And in's spring became a harvest; lived in court—
Which rare it is to do—most praised, most loved;
A sample to the youngest, to th'more mature
A glass that feated them, and to the graver
A child that guided dotards. To his mistress,   50
For whom he now is banished, her own price
Proclaims how she esteemed him; and his virtue
By her election may be truly read,
What kind of man he is.
2 GENTLEMAN.   I honour him
Even out of your report. But pray you tell me,
Is she sole child to th'king?
1 GENTLEMAN.   His only child.
He had two sons—if this be worth your hearing,
Mark it—the eldest of them at three years old,
I'th'swathing clothes the other, from their nursery
Were stol'n, and to this hour no guess in knowledge   60
Which way they went.
2 GENTLEMAN.   How long is this ago?
1 GENTLEMAN. Some twenty years.
2 GENTLEMAN. That a king's children should be so
  conveyed,
So slackly guarded, and the search so slow
That could not trace them!
1 GENTLEMAN.   Howsoe'er 'tis strange,
Or that the negligence may well be laughed at,
Yet is it true, sir.
2 GENTLEMAN.   I do well believe you.
1 GENTLEMAN. We must forbear. Here comes the
  gentleman,
The queen and princess.   *They go*

Enter the Queen, Posthumus and Imogen

QUEEN. No, be assured you shall not find me,
  daughter,   70
After the slander of most stepmothers,
Evil-eyed unto you. You're my prisoner, but
Your gaoler shall deliver you the keys
That lock up your restraint. For you, Posthumus,
So soon as I can win th'offended king,
I will be known your advocate. Marry, yet
The fire of rage is in him, and 'twere good
You leaned unto his sentence with what patience
Your wisdom may inform you.
POSTHUMUS.   Please your highness,
I will from hence to-day.
QUEEN.   You know the peril.   80
I'll fetch a turn about the garden, pitying
The pangs of barred affections, though the king
Hath charged you should not speak together.
                                        She goes
IMOGEN.   O
Dissembling courtesy! How fine this tyrant
Can tickle where she wounds! My dearest husband,
I something fear my father's wrath, but nothing—
Always reserved my holy duty—what
His rage can do on me. You must be gone,
And I shall here abide the hourly shot
Of angry eyes, not comforted to live,   90
But that there is this jewel in the world

That I may see again.

POSTHUMUS.   My queen, my mistress:
O lady, weep no more, lest I give cause
To be suspected of more tenderness
Than doth become a man. I will remain
The loyal'st husband that did e'er plight troth.
My residence in Rome at one Philario's,
Who to my father was a friend, to me
Known but by letter; thither write, my queen,
And with mine eyes I'll drink the words you send,   100
Though ink be made of gall.

Re-enter Queen

QUEEN.   Be brief, I pray you.
If the king come, I shall incur I know not
How much of his displeasure. [*aside*] Yet I'll move
      him
To walk this way. I never do him wrong
But he does buy my injuries, to be friends;
Pays dear for my offences.   *She goes*
POSTHUMUS.   Should we be taking leave
As long a term as yet we have to live,
The loathness to depart would grow. Adieu!
IMOGEN. Nay, stay a little.
Were you but riding forth to air yourself,   110
Such parting were too petty. Look here, love:
This diamond was my mother's; take it, heart;
But keep it till you woo another wife,
When Imogen is dead.
POSTHUMUS.   How, how? another?
You gentle gods, give me but this I have,
And cere up my embracements from a next
With bonds of death. [*putting on the ring.*] Remain,
      remain thou here
While sense can keep it on. And, sweetest, fairest,
As I my poor self did exchange for you
To your so infinite loss, so in our trifles   120
I still win of you. For my sake wear this;
It is a manacle of love; I'll place it
Upon this fairest prisoner.
                    Putting a bracelet on her arm
IMOGEN.   O the gods!
When shall we see again?

Enter Cymbeline and Lords

POSTHUMUS.   Alack, the king!
CYMBELINE. Thou basest thing, avoid hence, from my
      sight!
If after this command thou fraught the court
With thy unworthiness, thou diest. Away!
Thou'rt poison to my blood.
POSTHUMUS.   The gods protect you,
And bless the good remainders of the court.
I am gone.   *He goes*
IMOGEN.   There cannot be a pinch in death   130
More sharp than this is.
CYMBELINE.   O disloyal thing,
That shouldst repair my youth, thou heap'st
A year's age on me.
IMOGEN.   I beseech you, sir,
Harm not yourself with your vexation.
I am senseless of your wrath; a touch more rare
Subdues all pangs, all fears.
CYMBELINE.   Past grace? obedience?
IMOGEN. Past hope, and in despair; that way past grace.

CYMBELINE. That mightst have had the sole son of my
      queen!
IMOGEN. O blessèd, that I might not; I chose an eagle,
And did avoid a puttock.   140
CYMBELINE. Thou took'st a beggar, wouldst have
      made my throne
A seat for baseness.
IMOGEN.   No, I rather added
A lustre to it.
CYMBELINE. O thou vile one!
IMOGEN.   Sir,
It is your fault that I have loved Posthumus:
You bred him as my playfellow, and he is
A man worth any woman; overbuys me
Almost the sum he pays.
CYMBELINE.   What, art thou mad?
IMOGEN. Almost, sir. Heaven restore me! Would I
      were
A neat-herd's daughter, and my Leonatus
Our neighbour shepherd's son!

Re-enter Queen

CYMBELINE.   Thou foolish thing!   150
[*to the Queen*] They were again together; you have
      done
Not after our command. Away with her,
And pen her up.
QUEEN.   Beseech your patience. Peace,
Dear lady daughter, peace! Sweet sovereign,
Leave us to ourselves, and make yourself some
      comfort
Out of your best advice.
CYMBELINE.   Nay, let her languish
A drop of blood a day; and, being aged,
Die of this folly.   *Cymbeline and lords go*

Enter Pisanio

QUEEN.   Fie, you must give way.
Here is your servant. How now, sir? What news?
PISANIO. My lord your son drew on my master.
QUEEN.   Ha?   160
No harm, I trust, is done?
PISANIO.   There might have been,
But that my master rather played than fought,
And had no help of anger; they were parted
By gentlemen at hand.
QUEEN.   I am very glad on't.
IMOGEN. Your son's my father's friend; he takes his
      part
To draw upon an exile. O brave sir!
I would they were in Afric both together;
Myself by with a needle, that I might prick
The goer-back. Why came you from your master?
PISANIO. On his command. He would not suffer me   170
To bring him to the haven; left these notes
Of what commands I should be subject to
When't pleased you to employ me.
QUEEN.   This hath been
Your faithful servant. I dare lay mine honour
He will remain so.
PISANIO.   I humbly thank your highness.
QUEEN. Pray walk awhile.
IMOGEN. About some half-hour hence, pray you speak
      with me.
You shall at least go see my lord aboard.
For this time leave me.   *They go*

Scene 2: *The same. A public place*

Enter Cloten and two Lords

1 LORD. Sir, I would advise you to shift a shirt; the
    violence of action hath made you reek as a sacrifice.
    Where air comes out, air comes in; there's none
    'abroad so wholesome as that you vent.
CLOTEN. If my shirt were bloody, then to shift it.
    Have I hurt him?
2 LORD. No, faith; not so much as his patience.
1 LORD. Hurt him? his body's a passable carcass, if he
    be not hurt. It is a throughfare for steel, if it be not
    hurt.   10
2 LORD. His steel was in debt; it went o'th'backside
    the town.
CLOTEN. The villain would not stand me.
2 LORD. No, but he fled forward still, toward your
    face.
1 LORD. Stand you? You have land enough of your
    own; but he added to your having, gave you some
    ground.
2 LORD. As many inches as you have oceans. Puppies!
CLOTEN. I would they had not come between us.   20
2 LORD. So would I, till you had measured how long
    a fool you were upon the ground.
CLOTEN. And that she should love this fellow, and
    refuse me!
2 LORD. If it be a sin to make a true election, she is
    damned.
1 LORD. Sir, as I told you always, her beauty and her
    brain go not together. She's a good sign, but I have
    seen small reflection of her wit.
2 LORD. She shines not upon fools, lest the reflection 30
    should hurt her.
CLOTEN. Come, I'll to my chamber. Would there had
    been some hurt done!
2 LORD. I wish not so; unless it had been the fall of
    an ass, which is no great hurt.
CLOTEN. You'll go with us?
1 LORD. I'll attend your lordship.
CLOTEN. Nay, come, let's go together.
2 LORD. Well, my lord.   *They go*

Scene 3: *A room in Cymbeline's palace*

Enter Imogen and Pisanio

IMOGEN. I would thou grew'st unto the shores
        o'th'haven,
    And questionedst every sail; if he should write
    And I not have it, 'twere a paper lost
    As offered mercy is. What was the last
    That he spake to thee?
PISANIO.   It was his queen, his queen!
IMOGEN. Then waved his handkerchief?
PISANIO.   And kissed it, madam.
IMOGEN. Senseless linen, happier therein than I!
    And that was all?
PISANIO.   No, madam; for so long
    As he could make me with this eye or ear
    Distinguish him from the others, he did keep   10
    The deck, with glove, or hat, or handkerchief,
    Still waving, as the fits and stirs of's mind
    Could best express how slow his soul sailed on,
    How swift his ship.
IMOGEN.   Thou shouldst have made him
    As little as a crow, or less, ere left

To after-eye him.
PISANIO.   Madam, so I did.
IMOGEN. I would have broke mine eye-strings,
        cracked them but
    To look upon him, till the diminution
    Of space had pointed him sharp as my needle;
    Nay, followed him till he had melted from   20
    The smallness of a gnat to air; and then
    Have turned mine eye, and wept. But, good
        Pisanio,
    When shall we hear from him?
PISANIO.   Be assured, madam,
    With his next vantage.
IMOGEN. I did not take my leave of him, but had
    Most pretty things to say. Ere I could tell him
    How I would think on him at certain hours
    Such thoughts and such; or I could make him swear
    The shes of Italy should not betray
    Mine interest and his honour; or have charged him, 30
    At the sixth hour of morn, at noon, at midnight,
    T'encounter me with orisons, for then
    I am in heaven for him; or ere I could
    Give him that parting kiss which I had set
    Betwixt two charming words, comes in my father,
    And like the tyrannous breathing of the north
    Shakes all our buds from growing.

Enter a Lady

LADY.   The queen, madam,
    Desires your highness' company.
IMOGEN. Those things I bid you do, get them
        dispatched.
    I will attend the queen.
PISANIO.   Madam, I shall.   *They go* 40

Scene 4: *Rome. Philario's house*

*Enter Philario, Jachimo, a Frenchman, a Dutchman, and
a Spaniard*

JACHIMO. Believe it, sir, I have seen him in Britain;
    he was then of a crescent note, expected to prove so
    worthy as since he hath been allowed the name of.
    But I could then have looked on him without the
    help of admiration, though the catalogue of his
    endowments had been tabled by his side, and I to
    peruse him by items.
PHILARIO. You speak of him when he was less furn-
    ished than now he is with that which makes him
    both without and within.   10
FRENCHMAN. I have seen him in France; we had very
    many there could behold the sun with as firm eyes as
    he.
JACHIMO. This matter of marrying his king's daugh-
    ter, wherein he must be weighed rather by her value
    than his own, words him, I doubt not, a great deal
    from the matter.
FRENCHMAN. And then his banishment.
JACHIMO. Ay, and the approbation of those that weep
    this lamentable divorce under her colours are   20
    wonderfully to extend him, be it but to fortify her
    judgement, which else an easy battery might lay flat,
    for taking a beggar without less quality. But how
    comes it he is to sojourn with you? how creeps
    acquaintance?
PHILARIO. His father and I were soldiers together, to

whom I have been often bound for no less than my life.

Enter Posthumus

Here comes the Briton. Let him be so entertained amongst you as suits with gentlemen of your know- 30
ing to a stranger of his quality. I beseech you all be better known to this gentleman, whom I commend to you as a noble friend of mine. How worthy he is I will leave to appear hereafter, rather than story him in his own hearing.

FRENCHMAN. Sir, we have known together in Orleans.

POSTHUMUS. Since when I have been debtor to you for courtesies which I will be ever to pay and yet pay still.

FRENCHMAN. Sir, you o'er-rate my poor kindness; I 40
was glad I did atone my countryman and you; it had been pity you should have been put together, with so mortal a purpose as then each bore, upon importance of so slight and trivial a nature.

POSTHUMUS. By your pardon, sir, I was then a young traveller; rather shunned to go even with what I heard than in my every action to be guided by others' experiences; but upon my mended judgement—if I offend not to say it is mended—my quarrel was not altogether slight. 50

FRENCHMAN. Faith, yes, to be put to the arbitrement of swords, and by such two that would by all likelihood have confounded one the other, or have fall'n both.

JACHIMO. Can we with manners ask what was the difference?

FRENCHMAN. Safely, I think; 'twas a contention in public, which may without contradiction suffer the report. It was much like an argument that fell out last night, where each of us fell in praise of our 60
country mistresses; this gentleman at that time vouching—and upon warrant of bloody affirmation —his to be more fair, virtuous, wise, chaste, con-
stant, qualified, and less attemptable than any the rarest of our ladies in France.

JACHIMO. That lady is not now living; or this gentleman's opinion, by this, worn out.

POSTHUMUS. She holds her virtue still, and I my mind.

JACHIMO. You must not so far prefer her 'fore ours of Italy. 70

POSTHUMUS. Being so far provoked as I was in France, I would abate her nothing, though I profess myself her adorer, not her friend.

JACHIMO. As fair and as good—a kind of hand-in-
hand comparison—had been something too fair and too good for any lady in Britain. If she went before others I have seen, as that diamond of yours out-
lustres many I have beheld, I could not but believe she excelled many; but I have not seen the most precious diamond that is, nor you the lady. 80

POSTHUMUS. I praised her as I rated her: so do I my stone.

JACHIMO. What do you esteem it at?

POSTHUMUS. More than the world enjoys.

JACHIMO. Either your unparagoned mistress is dead, or she's outprized by a trifle.

POSTHUMUS. You are mistaken: the one may be sold or given, or if there were wealth enough for the purchase, or merit for the gift; the other is not a thing for sale, and only the gift of the gods. 90

JACHIMO. Which the gods have given you?

POSTHUMUS. Which by their graces I will keep.

JACHIMO. You may wear her in title yours; but you know strange fowl light upon neighbouring ponds. Your ring may be stol'n too, so your brace of unprizable estimations, the one is but frail and the other casual; a cunning thief, or a that way accomplished courtier, would hazard the winning both of first and last.

POSTHUMUS. Your Italy contains none so accom- 100
plished a courtier to convince the honour of my mistress, if in the holding or loss of that you term her frail. I do nothing doubt you have store of thieves; notwithstanding, I fear not my ring.

PHILARIO. Let us leave here, gentlemen.

POSTHUMUS. Sir, with all my heart. This worthy signior, I thank him, makes no stranger of me; we are familiar at first.

JACHIMO. With five times so much conversation, I should get ground of your fair mistress; make her go 110
back even to the yielding, had I admittance, and opportunity to friend.

POSTHUMUS. No, no.

JACHIMO. I dare thereupon pawn the moiety of my estate to your ring, which in my opinion o'ervalues it something. But I make my wager rather against your confidence than her reputation; and to bar your offence herein too, I durst attempt it against any lady in the world.

POSTHUMUS. You are a great deal abused in too bold a 120
persuasion, and I doubt not you sustain what you're worthy of by your attempt.

JACHIMO. What's that?

POSTHUMUS. A repulse; though your attempt, as you call it, deserve more—a punishment too.

PHILARIO. Gentlemen, enough of this. It came in too suddenly; let it die as it was born, and I pray you be better acquainted.

JACHIMO. Would I had put my estate and my neighbour's on th'approbation of what I have spoke— 130

POSTHUMUS. What lady would you choose to assail?

JACHIMO. Yours, whom in constancy you think stands so safe. I will lay you ten thousand ducats to your ring that, commend me to the court where your lady is, with no more advantage than the opportunity of a second conference, and I will bring from thence that honour of hers which you imagine so reserved.

POSTHUMUS. I will wage against your gold, gold to it. My ring I hold dear as my finger; 'tis part of it. 140

JACHIMO. You are a friend, and therein the wiser. If you buy lady's flesh at a million a dram, you cannot preserve it from tainting; but I see you have some religion in you, that you fear.

POSTHUMUS. This is but a custom in your tongue; you bear a graver purpose, I hope.

JACHIMO. I am the master of my speeches, and would undergo what's spoken, I swear.

POSTHUMUS. Will you? I shall but lend my diamond till your return. Let there be covenants drawn 150
between's. My mistress exceeds in goodness the hugeness of your unworthy thinking. I dare you to this match: here's my ring.

PHILARIO. I will have it no lay.

JACHIMO. By the gods, it is one. If I bring you no sufficient testimony that I have enjoyed the dearest

bodily part of your mistress, my ten thousand ducats
are yours; so is your diamond too. If I come off, and
leave her in such honour as you have trust in, she
your jewel, this your jewel, and my gold are yours 160
—provided I have your commendation for my
more free entertainment.

POSTHUMUS. I embrace these conditions; let us have
articles betwixt us. Only, thus far you shall answer:
if you make your voyage upon her, and give me
directly to understand you have prevailed, I am no
further your enemy; she is not worth our debate. If
she remain unseduced, you not making it appear
otherwise, for your ill opinion and th'assault you
have made to her chastity, you shall answer me with 170
your sword.

JACHIMO. Your hand—a covenant. We will have these
things set down by lawful counsel, and straight
away for Britain, lest the bargain should catch cold
and starve. I will fetch my gold, and have our two
wagers recorded.

POSTHUMUS. Agreed. *Posthumus and Jachimo go*

FRENCHMAN. Will this hold, think you?

PHILARIO. Signior Jachimo will not from it. Pray let
us follow 'em. *They go* 180

Scene 5: *Britain. A room in Cymbeline's palace*

Enter Queen, Ladies, and Cornelius

QUEEN. Whiles yet the dew's on ground, gather those
flowers;
Make haste. Who has the note of them?

1 LADY. I, madam.

QUEEN. Dispatch. *Ladies go*
Now, master doctor, have you brought those drugs?

CORNELIUS. Pleaseth your highness, ay. Here they are,
madam. *Presenting a small box*
But I beseech your grace, without offence—
My conscience bids me ask—wherefore you have
Commanded of me these most poisonous
compounds,
Which are the movers of a languishing death,
But though slow, deadly.

QUEEN. I wonder, doctor, 10
Thou ask'st me such a question. Have I not been
Thy pupil long? Hast thou not learned me how
To make perfumes? distil? preserve? yea, so
That our great king himself doth woo me oft
For my confections? Having thus far proceeded—
Unless thou think'st me devilish—is't not meet
That I did amplify my judgement in
Other conclusions? I will try the forces
Of these thy compounds on such creatures as
We count not worth the hanging—but none
human— 20
To try the vigour of them and apply
Allayments to their act, and by them gather
Their several virtues and effects.

CORNELIUS. Your highness
Shall from this practice but make hard your heart;
Besides, the seeing these effects will be
Both noisome and infectious.

QUEEN. O, content thee.

Enter Pisanio

[aside] Here comes a flattering rascal; upon him
Will I first work. He's factor for his master,

And enemy to my son. [aloud] How now, Pisanio?
Doctor, your service for this time is ended; 30
Take your own way.

CORNELIUS [aside]. I do suspect you, madam;
But you shall do no harm.

QUEEN [to Pisanio]. Hark thee, a word.

CORNELIUS [aside]. I do not like her. She doth think she
has
Strange ling'ring poisons. I do know her spirit,
And will not trust one of her malice with
A drug of such damned nature. Those she has
Will stupefy and dull the sense awhile,
Which first perchance she'll prove on cats and dogs,
Then afterward up higher; but there is
No danger in what show of death it makes, 40
More than the locking up the spirits a time,
To be more fresh, reviving. She is fooled
With a most false effect; and I the truer
So to be false with her.

QUEEN. No further service, doctor,
Until I send for thee.

CORNELIUS. I humbly take my leave.
Goes

QUEEN. Weeps she still, say'st thou? Dost thou think
in time
She will not quench, and let instructions enter
Where folly now possesses? Do thou work.
When thou shalt bring me word she loves my son,
I'll tell thee on the instant thou art then 50
As great as is thy master; greater, for
His fortunes all lie speechless, and his name
Is at last gasp. Return he cannot, nor
Continue where he is. To shift his being
Is to exchange one misery with another,
And every day that comes comes to decay
A day's work in him. What shalt thou expect
To be depender on a thing that leans,
Who cannot be new built, nor has no friends
So much as but to prop him? [*the Queen drops the box:
Pisanio takes it up*] Thou tak'st up 60
Thou know'st not what; but take it for thy labour:
It is a thing I made, which hath the king
Five times redeemed from death. I do not know
What is more cordial. Nay, I prithee take it;
It is an earnest of a further good
That I mean to thee. Tell thy mistress how
The case stands with her; do't as from thyself.
Think what a chance thou changest on; but think
Thou hast thy mistress still; to boot, my son,
Who shall take notice of thee. I'll move the king 70
To any shape of thy preferment, such
As thou'lt desire; and then myself, I chiefly,
That set thee on to this desert, am bound
To load thy merit richly. Call my women.
Think on my words. *Pisanio goes*
A sly and constant knave;
Not to be shaked; the agent for his master,
And the remembrancer of her to hold
The hand-fast to her lord. I have given him that
Which, if he take, shall quite unpeople her
Of liegers for her sweet; and which she after, 80
Except she bend her humour, shall be assured
To taste of too.

Re-enter Pisanio with Ladies

So, so; well done, well done.

The violets, cowslips, and the primroses,
Bear to my closet. Fare thee well, Pisanio;
Think on my words.   *Queen and ladies go*
PISANIO.   And shall do.
But when to my good lord I prove untrue,
I'll choke myself—there's all I'll do for you.
                           Goes

Scene 6: The same. Another room in the palace

Enter Imogen alone

IMOGEN. A father cruel and a step-dame false,
A foolish suitor to a wedded lady
That hath her husband banished. O, that husband,
My supreme crown of grief, and those repeated
Vexations of it! Had I been thief-stol'n,
As my two brothers, happy; but most miserable
Is the desire that's glorious. Blest be those,
How mean soe'er, that have their honest wills,
Which seasons comfort. Who may this be? Fie!

Enter Pisanio and Jachimo

PISANIO. Madam, a noble gentleman of Rome,   10
Comes from my lord with letters.
JACHIMO.   Change you, madam?
The worthy Leonatus is in safety,
And greets your highness dearly.   *Presents a letter*
IMOGEN.   Thanks, good sir;
You're kindly welcome.
JACHIMO. All of her that is out of door most rich!
If she be furnished with a mind so rare,
She is alone th'Arabian bird, and I
Have lost the wager. Boldness be my friend;
Arm me audacity from head to foot;
Or, like the Parthian, I shall flying fight;   20
Rather, directly fly.
IMOGEN [*reads*]. 'He is one of the noblest note, to
whose kindnesses I am most infinitely tied. Reflect
upon him accordingly, as you value your trust—
                       LEONATUS.'
So far I read aloud.
But even the very middle of my heart
Is warmed by th'rest, and takes it thankfully.
You are as welcome, worthy sir, as I
Have words to bid you, and shall find it so
In all that I can do.
JACHIMO.   Thanks, fairest lady.   30
What, are men mad? Hath nature given them eyes
To see this vaulted arch and the rich crop
Of sea and land, which can distinguish 'twixt
The fiery orbs above and the twinned stones
Upon the numbered beach, and can we not
Partition make with spectacles so precious
'Twixt fair and foul?
IMOGEN.   What makes your admiration?
JACHIMO. It cannot be i'th'eye—for apes and
     monkeys,
'Twixt two such shes, would chatter this way and
Contemn with mows the other; nor
     i'th'judgement—   40
For idiots in this case of favour would
Be wisely definite; nor i'th'appetite—
Sluttery, to such neat excellence opposed,
Should make desire vomit emptiness,
Not so allured to feed.
IMOGEN. What is the matter, trow?

JACHIMO.   The cloyéd will,
That satiate yet unsatisfied desire, that tub
Both filled and running, ravening first the lamb,
Longs after for the garbage.
IMOGEN.   What, dear sir,
Thus raps you? Are you well?
JACHIMO.   Thanks, madam, well.   50
[*to Pisanio*] Beseech you sir,
Desire my man's abode where I did leave him:
He's strange and peevish.
PISANIO.   I was going, sir,
To give him welcome.   *Goes*
IMOGEN. Continues well my lord? His health, beseech
     you?
JACHIMO. Well, madam.
IMOGEN. Is he disposed to mirth? I hope he is.
JACHIMO. Exceeding pleasant; none a stranger there
So merry and so gamesome: he is called
The Briton reveller.
IMOGEN.   When he was here   60
He did incline to sadness, and oft-times
Not knowing why.
JACHIMO.   I never saw him sad.
There is a Frenchman his companion, one
An eminent monsieur, that, it seems, much loves
A Gallian girl at home. He furnaces
The thick sighs from him; whiles the jolly Briton—
Your lord, I mean—laughs from's free lungs, cries,
     'O,
Can my sides hold, to think that man, who knows
By history, report, or his own proof,
What woman is, yea, what she cannot choose   70
But must be, will's free hours languish for
Assuréd bondage?'
IMOGEN.   Will my lord say so?
JACHIMO. Ay, madam; with his eyes in flood with
     laughter.
It is a recreation to be by
And hear him mock the Frenchman. But heavens
     know
Some men are much to blame.
IMOGEN.   Not he, I hope.
JACHIMO. Not he; but yet heaven's bounty towards
     him might
Be used more thankfully. In himself 'tis much;
In you, which I account his, beyond all talents.
Whilst I am bound to wonder, I am bound   80
To pity too.
IMOGEN.   What do you pity, sir?
JACHIMO. Two creatures heartily.
IMOGEN.   Am I one, sir?
You look on me: what wreck discern you in me
Deserves your pity?
JACHIMO.   Lamentable! What,
To hide me from the radiant sun, and solace
I'th'dungeon by a snuff?
IMOGEN.   I pray you, sir,
Deliver with more openness your answers
To my demands. Why do you pity me?
JACHIMO. That others do,
I was about to say, enjoy your——But   90
It is an office of the gods to venge it,
Not mine to speak on't.
IMOGEN.   You seem to know
Something of me, or what concerns me; pray you
Since doubting things go ill often hurts more

Than to be sure they do; for certainties
Either are past remedies, or, timely knowing,
The remedy then born—discover to me
What both you spur and stop.

JACHIMO.   Had I this cheek
To bathe my lips upon; this hand, whose touch,
Whose every touch, would force the feeler's soul   100
To th'oath of loyalty; this object, which
Takes prisoner the wild motion of mine eye,
Fixing it only here; should I, damned then,
Slaver with lips as common as the stairs
That mount the Capitol; join gripes with hands
Made hard with hourly falsehood—falsehood as
With labour; then by-peeping in an eye
Base and illustrous as the smoky light
That's fed with stinking tallow—it were fit
That all the plagues of hell should at one time   110
Encounter such revolt.

IMOGEN.   My lord, I fear,
Has forgot Britain.

JACHIMO.   And himself. Not I
Inclined to this intelligence pronounce
The beggary of his change, but 'tis your graces
That from my mutest conscience to my tongue
Charms this report out.

IMOGEN.   Let me hear no more.

JACHIMO. O dearest soul, your cause doth strike my
    heart
With pity that doth make me sick. A lady
So fair, and fastened to an empery
Would make the great'st king double, to be
    partnered   120
With tomboys hired with that self exhibition
Which your own coffers yield; with diseased
    ventures
That play with all infirmities for gold
Which rottenness can lend nature; such boiled stuff
As well might poison poison. Be revenged,
Or she that bore you was no queen, and you
Recoil from your great stock.

IMOGEN.   Revenged?
How should I be revenged? If this be true—   130
As I have such a heart that both mine ears
Must not in haste abuse—if it be true,
How should I be revenged?

JACHIMO.   Should he make me
Live like Diana's priest betwixt cold sheets,
Whiles he is vaulting variable ramps,
In your despite, upon your purse—revenge it.
I dedicate myself to your sweet pleasure,
More noble than that runagate to your bed,
And will continue fast to your affection,
Still close as sure.

IMOGEN.   What ho, Pisanio!

JACHIMO. Let me my service tender on your lips.

IMOGEN. Away, I do condemn mine ears that have   140
So long attended thee. If thou wert honourable,
Thou wouldst have told this tale for virtue, not
For such an end thou seek'st, as base as strange.
Thou wrong'st a gentleman who is as far
From thy report as thou from honour, and
Solicits here a lady that disdains
Thee and the devil alike. What ho, Pisanio!
The king my father shall be made acquainted
Of thy assault. If he shall think it fit
A saucy stranger in his court to mart   150

As in a Romish stew, and to expound
His beastly mind to us, he hath a court
He little cares for and a daughter who
He not respects at all. What ho, Pisanio!

JACHIMO. O happy Leonatus! I may say,
The credit that thy lady hath of thee
Deserves thy trust, and thy most perfect goodness
Her assured credit. Blessèd live you long,
A lady to the worthiest sir that ever
Country called his; and you his mistress, only   160
For the most worthiest fit. Give me your pardon.
I have spoke this to know if your affiance
Were deeply rooted, and shall make your lord
That which he is new o'er; and he is one
The truest mannered, such a holy witch
That he enchants societies into him;
Half all men's hearts are his.

IMOGEN.   You make amends.

JACHIMO. He sits 'mongst men like a descended god;
He hath a kind of honour sets him off,
More than a mortal seeming. Be not angry,   170
Most mighty princess, that I have adventured
To try your taking of a false report, which hath
Honoured with confirmation your great judgement
In the election of a sir so rare,
Which you know cannot err. The love I bear him
Made me to fan you thus, but the gods made you,
Unlike all others, chaffless. Pray your pardon.

IMOGEN. All's well, sir: take my power i'th'court for
    yours.

JACHIMO. My humble thanks. I had almost forgot
T'entreat your grace but in a small request,   180
And yet of moment too, for it concerns
Your lord; myself and other noble friends
Are partners in the business.

IMOGEN.   Pray what is't?

JACHIMO. Some dozen Romans of us, and your lord—
The best feather of our wing—have mingled sums
To buy a present for the emperor;
Which I, the factor for the rest, have done
In France. 'Tis plate of rare device, and jewels
Of rich and exquisite form, their values great;
And I am something curious, being strange,   190
To have them in safe stowage. May it please you
To take them in protection?

IMOGEN.   Willingly;
And pawn mine honour for their safety; since
My lord hath interest in them, I will keep them
In my bedchamber.

JACHIMO.   They are in a trunk,
Attended by my men. I will make bold
To send them to you, only for this night;
I must aboard to-morrow.

IMOGEN.   O, no, no.

JACHIMO. Yes, I beseech; or I shall short my word
By length'ning my return. From Gallia   200
I crossed the seas on purpose and on promise
To see your grace.

IMOGEN.   I thank you for your pains;
But not away to-morrow!

JACHIMO.   O, I must, madam.
Therefore I shall beseech you, if you please
To greet your lord with writing, do't to-night.
I have outstood my time, which is material
To th'tender of our present.

IMOGEN.   I will write.

Send your trunk to me; it shall safe be kept
And truly yielded you. You're very welcome.
They go

ACT 2
Scene 1: *Britain. Before Cymbeline's palace*

Enter Cloten and two Lords

CLOTEN. Was there ever man had such luck? when I
kissed the jack upon an upcast, to be hit away! I
had a hundred pound on't; and then a whoreson
jackanapes must take me up for swearing, as if I
borrowed mine oaths of him, and might not spend
them at my pleasure.

1 LORD. What got he by that? You have broke his pate
with your bowl.

2 LORD [*aside*]. If his wit had been like him that broke
it, it would have run all out. 10

CLOTEN. When a gentleman is disposed to swear, it is
not for any standers-by to curtail his oaths, ha?

2 LORD. No, my lord; [*aside*] nor crop the ears of them.

CLOTEN. Whoreson dog! I give him satisfaction?
Would he had been one of my rank!

2 LORD [*aside*]. To have smelt like a fool.

CLOTEN. I am not vexed more at any thing in th'earth.
A pox on't! I had rather not be so noble as I am; they
dare not fight with me, because of the queen my
mother. Every jack-slave hath his bellyful of fight- 20
ing, and I must go up and down like a cock that
nobody can match.

2 LORD [*aside*]. You are cock and capon too; and you
crow cock with your comb on.

CLOTEN. Sayest thou?

2 LORD. It is not fit your lordship should undertake
every companion that you give offence to.

CLOTEN. No, I know that; but it is fit I should commit
offence to my inferiors.

2 LORD. Ay, it is fit for your lordship only. 30

CLOTEN. Why, so I say.

1 LORD. Did you hear of a stranger that's come to
court to-night?

CLOTEN. A stranger, and I not know on't?

2 LORD [*aside*]. He's a strange fellow himself, and
knows it not.

1 LORD. There's an Italian come, and, 'tis thought, one
of Leonatus' friends.

CLOTEN. Leonatus? a banished rascal; and he's another,
whatsoever he be. Who told you of this stranger? 40

1 LORD. One of your lordship's pages.

CLOTEN. Is it fit I went to look upon him? is there no
derogation in't?

2 LORD. You cannot derogate, my lord.

CLOTEN. Not easily, I think.

2 LORD [*aside*]. You are a fool granted; therefore your
issues, being foolish, do not derogate.

CLOTEN. Come, I'll go see this Italian. What I have
lost to-day at bowls I'll win to-night of him. Come,
go. 50

2 LORD. I'll attend your lordship.
Cloten and 1 Lord go
That such a crafty devil as is his mother
Should yield the world this ass! a woman that
Bears all down with her brain; and this her son
Cannot take two from twenty, for his heart,
And leave eighteen. Alas, poor princess,

Thou divine Imogen, what thou endur'st,
Betwixt a father by thy step-dame governed,
A mother hourly coining plots, a wooer
More hateful than the foul expulsion is 60
Of thy dear husband, than that horrid act
Of the divorce he'ld make. The heavens hold firm
The walls of thy dear honour; keep unshaked
That temple, thy fair mind, that thou mayst stand
T'enjoy thy banished lord and this great land!
Goes

Scene 2: *Imogen's bedchamber in Cymbeline's palace: a trunk in one corner of it*

Imogen in bed, reading; a Lady attending

IMOGEN. Who's there? my woman Helen?

LADY.　　　　　　　　　Please you, madam.

IMOGEN. What hour is it?

LADY.　　　　　　　　Almost midnight, madam.

IMOGEN. I have read three hours then. Mine eyes are
weak;
Fold down the leaf where I have left; to bed.
Take not away the taper, leave it burning;
And if thou canst awake by four o'th'clock,
I prithee call me. Sleep hath seized me wholly.
Lady goes
To your protection I commend me, gods.
From fairies and the tempters of the night
Guard me, beseech ye. 10
Sleeps. Jachimo comes from the trunk

JACHIMO. The crickets sing, and man's o'er-laboured
sense
Repairs itself by rest. Our Tarquin thus
Did softly press the rushes ere he wakened
The chastity he wounded. Cytherea,
How bravely thou becomest thy bed! fresh lily,
And whiter than the sheets! That I might touch,
But kiss, one kiss! Rubies unparagoned,
How dearly they do't! 'Tis her breathing that
Perfumes the chamber thus. The flame o'th'taper
Bows toward her and would under-peep her lids 20
To see th'enclosèd lights, now canopied
Under these windows, white and azure-laced
With blue of heaven's own tinct. But my design—
To note the chamber. I will write all down:
Such and such pictures; there the window; such
Th'adornment of her bed; the arras, figures,
Why, such and such; and the contents o'th'story.
Ah, but some natural notes about her body
Above ten thousand meaner movables
Would testify, t'enrich mine inventory. 30
O sleep, thou ape of death, lie dull upon her,
And be her sense but as a monument,
Thus in a chapel lying. Come off, come off;
Taking off her bracelet
As slippery as the Gordian knot was hard.
'Tis mine; and this will witness outwardly,
As strongly as the conscience does within,
To th'madding of her lord. On her left breast
A mole cinque-spotted, like the crimson drops
I'th'bottom of a cowslip. Here's a voucher,
Stronger than ever law could make; this secret 40
Will force him think I have picked the lock and ta'en
The treasure of her honour. No more. To what end?
Why should I write this down that's riveted,
Screwed to my memory? She hath been reading late

The tale of Tereus; here the leaf's turned down
Where Philomel gave up. I have enough;
To th'trunk again, and shut the spring of it.
Swift, swift, you dragons of the night, that dawning
May bare the raven's eye! I lodge in fear;
Though this a heavenly angel, hell is here.   50
                                                Clock strikes
One, two, three. Time, time!
                                                Goes into the trunk

Scene 3: *An ante-chamber adjoining Imogen's apartments*

Enter Cloten and Lords

1 LORD. Your lordship is the most patient man in loss,
the most coldest that ever turned up ace.
CLOTEN. It would make any man cold to lose.
1 LORD. But not every man patient after the noble
temper of your lordship. You are most hot and
furious when you win.
CLOTEN. Winning will put any man into courage. If I
could get this foolish Imogen, I should have gold
enough. It's almost morning, is't not?
1 LORD. Day, my lord.   10
CLOTEN. I would this music would come. I am advised
to give her music o' mornings; they say it will
penetrate.

Enter Musicians

Come on, tune. If you can penetrate her with your
fingering, so; we'll try with tongue too. If none will
do, let her remain; but I'll never give o'er. First, a
very excellent good-conceited thing; after, a
wonderful sweet air, with admirable rich words to
it; and then let her consider.

                              SONG
Hark, hark, the lark at heaven's gate sings,   20
     And Phoebus 'gins arise,
His steeds to water at those springs
     On chaliced flowers that lies;
And winking Mary-buds begin
     To ope their golden eyes;
With every thing that pretty is,
     My lady sweet, arise;
          Arise, arise!

CLOTEN. So, get you gone. If this penetrate, I will
consider your music the better; if it do not, it is a   30
vice in her ears, which horse-hairs and calf's-guts,
nor the voice of unpaved eunuch to boot, can never
amend.   *Musicians go*

Enter Cymbeline and Queen

2 LORD. Here comes the king.
CLOTEN. I am glad I was up so late, for that's the
reason I was up so early. He cannot choose but take
this service I have done fatherly. Good morrow to
your majesty and to my gracious mother.
CYMBELINE. Attend you here the door of our stern
daughter? Will she not forth?   40
CLOTEN. I have assailed her with musics, but she
vouchsafes no notice.
CYMBELINE. The exile of her minion is too new;
She hath not yet forgot him. Some more time
Must wear the print of his remembrance out,
And then she's yours.
QUEEN.   You are most bound to th'king,

Who lets go by no vantages that may
Prefer you to his daughter. Frame yourself
To orderly solicits, and be friended
With aptness of the season; make denials   50
Increase your services; so seem as if
You were inspired to do those duties which
You tender to her; that you in all obey her,
Save when command to your dismission tends,
And therein you are senseless.
CLOTEN.   Senseless? not so.

Enter a Messenger

MESSENGER. So like you, sir, ambassadors from Rome;
The one is Caius Lucius.
CYMBELINE.   A worthy fellow,
Albeit he comes on angry purpose now;
But that's no fault of his. We must receive him
According to the honour of his sender;   60
And towards himself, his goodness forespent on us,
We must extend our notice. Our dear son,
When you have given good morning to your
     mistress,
Attend the queen and us; we shall have need
T'employ you towards this Roman. Come, our
     queen.   *All but Cloten go*
CLOTEN. If she be up, I'll speak with her; if not,
Let her lie still and dream. By your leave, ho!
                                                Knocks
I know her women are about her; what
If I do line one of their hands? 'Tis gold
Which buys admittance—oft it doth—yea, and
     makes   70
Diana's rangers false themselves, yield up
Their deer to th'stand o'th'stealer; and 'tis gold
Which makes the true man killed and saves the thief;
Nay, sometime hangs both thief and true man.
     What
Can it not do and undo? I will make
One of her women lawyer to me, for
I yet not understand the case myself.
By your leave.   *Knocks*

Enter a Lady

LADY. Who's there that knocks?
CLOTEN.   A gentleman.
LADY.   No more?
CLOTEN. Yes, and a gentlewoman's son.
LADY.   That's more   80
Than some whose tailors are as dear as yours
Can justly boast of. What's your lordship's pleasure?
CLOTEN. Your lady's person; is she ready?
LADY.   Ay,
To keep her chamber.
CLOTEN.   There is gold for you;
Sell me your good report.
LADY. How, my good name? or to report of you
What I shall think is good? The princess.
                                                Lady goes

Enter Imogen

CLOTEN. Good morrow, fairest sister. Your sweet
hand.
IMOGEN. Good morrow, sir. You lay out too much
     pains
For purchasing but trouble. The thanks I give   90
Is telling you that I am poor of thanks,

And scarce can spare them.
CLOTEN.   Still I swear I love you.
IMOGEN. If you but said so, 'twere as deep with me.
  If you swear still, your recompense is still
  That I regard it not.
CLOTEN.   This is no answer.
IMOGEN. But that you shall not say I yield being silent,
  I would not speak. I pray you, spare me. Faith,
  I shall unfold equal discourtesy
  To your best kindness; one of your great knowing
  Should learn, being taught, forbearance.   100
CLOTEN. To leave you in your madness, 'twere my sin.
  I will not.
IMOGEN. Fools are not mad folks.
CLOTEN.   Do you call me fool?
IMOGEN. As I am mad, I do.
  If you'll be patient, I'll no more be mad;
  That cures us both. I am much sorry, sir,
  You put me to forget a lady's manners
  By being so verbal; and learn now for all
  That I, which know my heart, do here pronounce
  By th'very truth of it, I care not for you,   110
  And am so near the lack of charity
  To accuse myself I hate you; which I had rather
  You felt than make't my boast.
CLOTEN.   You sin against
  Obedience, which you owe your father. For
  The contract you pretend with that base wretch,
  One bred of alms and fostered with cold dishes,
  With scraps o'th'court, it is no contract, none.
  And though it be allowed in meaner parties—
  Yet who than he more mean?—to knit their souls,
  On whom there is no more dependency   120
  But brats and beggary, in self-figured knot;
  Yet you are curbed from that enlargement by
  The consequence o'th'crown, and must not foil
  The precious note of it with a base slave,
  A hilding for a livery, a squire's cloth,
  A pantler—not so eminent.
IMOGEN.   Profane fellow,
  Wert thou the son of Jupiter, and no more
  But what thou art besides, thou wert too base
  To be his groom; thou wert dignified enough,
  Even to the point of envy, if 'twere made   130
  Comparative for your virtues, to be styled
  The under-hangman of his kingdom, and hated
  For being preferred so well.
CLOTEN.   The south fog rot him!
IMOGEN. He never can meet more mischance than
    come
  To be but named of thee. His meanest garment
  That ever hath but clipped his body is dearer
  In my respect than all the hairs above thee,
  Were they all made such men. How now, Pisanio!

Enter Pisanio

CLOTEN. 'His garment'! Now the devil—
IMOGEN. To Dorothy my woman hie thee presently.   140
CLOTEN. 'His garment'!
IMOGEN.   I am sprited with a fool,
  Frighted, and ang'red worse. Go bid my woman
  Search for a jewel that too casually
  Hath left mine arm. It was thy master's. 'Shrew me
  If I would lose it for a revenue
  Of any king's in Europe! I do think
  I saw't this morning; confident I am

Last night 'twas on mine arm; I kissed it.
  I hope it be not gone to tell my lord
  That I kiss aught but he.
PISANIO.   'Twill not be lost.   150
IMOGEN. I hope so; go and search.   *Pisanio goes*
CLOTEN.   You have abused me.
  'His meanest garment'!
IMOGEN.   Ay, I said so, sir.
  If you will make't an action, call witness to't.
CLOTEN. I will inform your father.
IMOGEN.   Your mother too.
  She's my good lady, and will conceive, I hope,
  But the worst of me. So I leave you, sir,
  To th'worse of discontent.   *Goes*
CLOTEN.   I'll be revenged.
  'His meanest garment'! Well.   *Goes*

Scene 4: *Rome. Philario's house*

Enter Posthumus and Philario

POSTHUMUS. Fear it not, sir; I would I were so sure
  To win the king as I am bold her honour
  Will remain hers.
PHILARIO.   What means do you make to him?
POSTHUMUS. Not any; but abide the change of time,
  Quake in the present winter's state, and wish
  That warmer days would come. In these fear'd
    hopes,
  I barely gratify your love; they failing,
  I must die much your debtor.
PHILARIO. Your very goodness and your company
  O'erpays all I can do. By this, your king   10
  Hath heard of great Augustus. Caius Lucius
  Will do's commission throughly. And I think
  He'll grant the tribute, send th'arrearages,
  Or look upon our Romans, whose remembrance
  Is yet fresh in their grief.
POSTHUMUS.   I do believe,
  Statist though I am none, nor like to be,
  That this will prove a war; and you shall hear
  The legions now in Gallia sooner landed
  In our not-fearing Britain than have tidings
  Of any penny tribute paid. Our countrymen   20
  Are men more ordered than when Julius Caesar
  Smiled at their lack of skill, but found their courage
  Worthy his frowning at. Their discipline,
  Now mingled with their courage, will make known
  To their approvers they are people such
  That mend upon the world.

Enter Jachimo

PHILARIO.   See, Jachimo!
POSTHUMUS. The swiftest harts have posted you by
    land,
  And winds of all the corners kissed your sails,
  To make your vessel nimble.
PHILARIO.   Welcome, sir.
POSTHUMUS. I hope the briefness of your answer made   30
  The speediness of your return.
JACHIMO.   Your lady
  Is one the fairest that I have looked upon—
POSTHUMUS. And therewithal the best, or let her
    beauty
  Look through a casement to allure false hearts,
  And be false with them.
JACHIMO.   Here are letters for you.

POSTHUMUS. Their tenour good, I trust.
JACHIMO. 'Tis very like.
PHILARIO. Was Caius Lucius in the Briton court
When you were there?
JACHIMO. He was expected then,
But not approached.
POSTHUMUS. All is well yet.
Sparkles this stone as it was wont, or is't not 40
Too dull for your good wearing?
JACHIMO. If I have lost it,
I should have lost the worth of it in gold.
I'll make a journey twice as far t'enjoy
A second night of such sweet shortness which
Was mine in Britain; for the ring is won.
POSTHUMUS. The stone's too hard to come by.
JACHIMO. Not a whit,
Your lady being so easy.
POSTHUMUS. Make not, sir,
Your loss your sport. I hope you know that we
Must not continue friends.
JACHIMO. Good sir, we must,
If you keep covenant. Had I not brought 50
The knowledge of your mistress home, I grant
We were to question farther; but I now
Profess myself the winner of her honour,
Together with your ring; and not the wronger
Of her or you, having proceeded but
By both your wills.
POSTHUMUS. If you can make't apparent
That you have tasted her in bed, my hand
And ring is yours. If not, the foul opinion
You had of her pure honour gains or loses
Your sword or mine, or masterless leaves both 60
To who shall find them.
JACHIMO. Sir, my circumstances,
Being so near the truth as I will make them,
Must first induce you to believe; whose strength
I will confirm with oath; which I doubt not
You'll give me leave to spare, when you shall find
You need it not.
POSTHUMUS. Proceed.
JACHIMO. First, her bedchamber—
Where I confess I slept not, but profess
Had that was well worth watching—it was hanged
With tapestry of silk and silver; the story
Proud Cleopatra when she met her Roman, 70
And Cydnus swelled above the banks, or for
The press of boats or pride; a piece of work
So bravely done, so rich, that it did strive
In workmanship and value; which I wondered
Could be so rarely and exactly wrought,
Since the true life was out on't.
POSTHUMUS. This is true;
And this you might have heard of here, by me
Or by some other.
JACHIMO. More particulars
Must justify my knowledge.
POSTHUMUS. So they must,
Or do your honour injury.
JACHIMO. The chimney 80
Is south the chamber, and the chimney-piece
Chaste Dian bathing. Never saw I figures
So likely to report themselves; the cutter
Was as another nature; dumb, outwent her,
Motion and breath left out.
POSTHUMUS. This is a thing

Which you might from relation likewise reap,
Being, as it is, much spoke of.
JACHIMO. The roof o'th'chamber
With golden cherubins is fretted; her andirons—
I had forgot them—were two winking Cupids
Of silver, each on one foot standing, nicely 90
Depending on their brands.
POSTHUMUS. This is her honour!
Let it be granted you have seen all this—and praise
Be given to your remembrance—the description
Of what is in her chamber nothing saves
The wager you have laid.
JACHIMO. Then, if you can
Showing the bracelet
Be pale, I beg but leave to air this jewel. See!
And now 'tis up again; it must be married
To that your diamond; I'll keep them.
POSTHUMUS. Jove!
Once more let me behold it. Is it that
Which I left with her?
JACHIMO. Sir, I thank her, that. 100
She stripped it from her arm; I see her yet;
Her pretty action did outsell her gift,
And yet enriched it too. She gave it me
And said she prized it once.
POSTHUMUS. May be she plucked it off
To send it me.
JACHIMO. She writes so to you, doth she?
POSTHUMUS. O, no, no, no, 'tis true! Here, take this
too; *Gives the ring*
It is a basilisk unto mine eye,
Kills me to look on't. Let there be no honour
Where there is beauty; truth where semblance; love
Where there's another man. The vows of women 110
Of no more bondage be to where they are made
Than they are to their virtues, which is nothing.
O, above measure false!
PHILARIO. Have patience, sir,
And take your ring again; 'tis not yet won.
It may be probable she lost it, or
Who knows if one her women, being corrupted,
Hath stol'n it from her?
POSTHUMUS. Very true;
And so I hope he came by't. Back my ring;
Render to me some corporal sign about her
More evident than this; for this was stol'n. 120
JACHIMO. By Jupiter, I had it from her arm.
POSTHUMUS. Hark you, he swears; by Jupiter he
swears.
'Tis true, nay, keep the ring, 'tis true. I am sure
She would not lose it. Her attendants are
All sworn and honourable. They induced to steal it?
And by a stranger? No, he hath enjoyed her.
The cognizance of her incontinency
Is this. She hath bought the name of whore thus
dearly.
There, take thy hire; and all the fiends of hell
Divide themselves between you!
PHILARIO. Sir, be patient; 130
This is not strong enough to be believed
Of one persuaded well of.
POSTHUMUS. Never talk on't;
She hath been colted by him.
JACHIMO. If you seek
For further satisfying, under her breast—
Worthy the pressing—lies a mole, right proud

Of that most delicate lodging. By my life,
I kissed it, and it gave me present hunger
To feed again, though full. You do remember
This stain upon her?

POSTHUMUS.　　　　　Ay, and it doth confirm
Another stain, as big as hell can hold,　　　　140
Were there no more but it.

JACHIMO.　　　　　　Will you hear more?

POSTHUMUS. Spare your arithmetic; never count the
turns.
Once, and a million!

JACHIMO.　　　　　I'll be sworn.

POSTHUMUS.　　　　　No swearing.
If you will swear you have not done't, you lie;
And I will kill thee if thou dost deny
Thou'st made me cuckold.

JACHIMO.　　　　　I'll deny nothing.

POSTHUMUS. O that I had her here to tear her
limb-meal!
I will go there and do't i'th'court, before
Her father. I'll do something.　　　　*Goes*

PHILARIO.　　　　　Quite besides
The government of patience! You have won.　　　150
Let's follow him and pervert the present wrath
He hath against himself.

JACHIMO.　　　　　With all my heart.
　　　　　　　　　　　　　They go

Scene 5

Re-enter Posthumus

POSTHUMUS. Is there no way for men to be, but
women
Must be half-workers? We are all bastards,
And that most venerable man which I
Did call my father was I know not where
When I was stamped. Some coiner with his tools
Made me a counterfeit; yet my mother seemed
The Dian of that time; so doth my wife
The nonpareil of this. O, vengeance, vengeance!
Me of my lawful pleasure she restrained,
And prayed me oft forbearance; did it with　　　10
A pudency so rosy, the sweet view on't
Might well have warmed old Saturn; that I thought
her
As chaste as unsunned snow. O, all the devils!
This yellow Jachimo in an hour—was't not?—
Or less—at first? Perchance he spoke not, but
Like a full-acorned boar, a German one,
Cried 'O!' and mounted; found no opposition
But what he looked for should oppose and she
Should from encounter guard. Could I find out
The woman's part in me—for there's no motion　　20
That tends to vice in man but I affirm
It is the woman's part; be it lying, note it,
The woman's; flattering, hers; deceiving, hers;
Lust and rank thoughts, hers, hers; revenges, hers;
Ambitions, covetings, change of prides, disdain,
Nice longing, slanders, mutability,
All faults that man may name, nay, that hell knows,
Why, hers, in part or all, but rather all;
For even to vice
They are not constant, but are changing still　　30
One vice but of a minute old for one
Not half so old as that. I'll write against them,
Detest them, curse them; yet 'tis greater skill

In a true hate, to pray they have their will:
The very devils cannot plague them better.
　　　　　　　　　　　　　Goes

ACT 3

Scene 1: *Britain. A hall in Cymbeline's palace*

*Enter in state, Cymbeline, Queen, Cloten, and Lords at
one door, and at another, Caius Lucius and attendants*

CYMBELINE. Now say, what would Augustus Cæsar
with us?

LUCIUS. When Julius Cæsar, whose remembrance yet
Lives in men's eyes, and will to ears and tongues
Be theme and hearing ever, was in this Britain,
And conquered it, Cassibelan, thine uncle,
Famous in Cæsar's praises no whit less
Than in his feats deserving it, for him
And his succession granted Rome a tribute,
Yearly three thousand pounds, which by thee lately
Is left untendered.

QUEEN.　　　　　And, to kill the marvel,　　10
Shall be so ever.

CLOTEN.　　　　　There be many Cæsars
Ere such another Julius. Britain's a world
By itself, and we will nothing pay
For wearing our own noses.

QUEEN.　　　　　　That opportunity
Which then they had to take from's, to resume
We have again. Remember, sir, my liege,
The kings your ancestors, together with
The natural bravery of your isle, which stands
As Neptune's park, ribbed and paled in
With rocks unscalable and roaring waters,　　20
With sands that will not bear your enemies' boats,
But suck them up to th'topmast. A kind of conquest
Cæsar made here, but made not here his brag
Of 'Came, and saw, and overcame'. With shame—
The first that ever touched him—he was carried
From off our coast, twice beaten; and his shipping,
Poor ignorant baubles, on our terrible seas,
Like egg-shells moved upon their surges, cracked
As easily 'gainst our rocks; for joy whereof
The famed Cassibelan, who was once at point—　　30
O giglot fortune!—to master Cæsar's sword,
Made Lud's town with rejoicing fires bright,
And Britons strut with courage.

CLOTEN. Come, there's no more tribute to be paid.
Our kingdom is stronger than it was at that time;
and, as I said, there is no moe such Cæsars. Other
of them may have crooked noses, but to owe such
straight arms, none.

CYMBELINE. Son, let your mother end.

CLOTEN. We have yet many among us can gripe as　　40
hard as Cassibelan. I do not say I am one; but I have
a hand. Why tribute? why should we pay tribute?
If Cæsar can hide the sun from us with a blanket,
or put the moon in his pocket, we will pay him
tribute for light; else, sir, no more tribute, pray you
now.

CYMBELINE. You must know,
Till the injurious Romans did extort
This tribute from us, we were free. Cæsar's
ambition,
Which swelled so much that it did almost stretch　　50
The sides o'th'world, against all colour here

Did put the yoke upon's; which to shake off
Becomes a warlike people, whom we reckon
Ourselves to be. We do say then to Cæsar,
Our ancestor was that Mulmutius which
Ordained our laws, whose use the sword of Cæsar
Hath too much mangled; whose repair and franchise
Shall, by the power we hold, be our good deed,
Though Rome be therefore angry. Mulmutius
    made our laws,
Who was the first of Britain which did put   60
His brows within a golden crown, and called
Himself a king.
LUCIUS.   I am sorry, Cymbeline,
That I am to pronounce Augustus Cæsar—
Cæsar, that hath moe kings his servants than
Thyself domestic officers—thine enemy
Receive it from me, then: war and confusion
In Cæsar's name pronounce I 'gainst thee. Look
For fury not to be resisted. Thus defied,
I thank thee for myself.
CYMBELINE.   Thou art welcome, Caius.
Thy Cæsar knighted me; my youth I spent   70
Much under him; of him I gathered honour;
Which he to seek of me again, perforce,
Behoves me keep at utterance. I am perfect
That the Pannonians and Dalmatians for
Their liberties are now in arms, a precedent
Which not to read would show the Britons cold;
So Cæsar shall not find them.
LUCIUS.   Let proof speak.
CLOTEN. His majesty bids you welcome. Make pas-
time with us a day or two, or longer. If you seek us
afterwards in other terms, you shall find us in our   80
salt-water girdle. If you beat us out of it, it is yours,
if you fall in the adventure, our crows shall fare the
better for you; and there's an end.
LUCIUS. So, sir.
CYMBELINE. I know your master's pleasure, and he
    mine.
All the remain is 'Welcome'.   *They go*

Scene 2

Enter Pisanio, reading of a letter

PISANIO. How? of adultery? Wherefore write you not
What monster's her accuser? Leonatus,
O master, what a strange infection
Is fall'n into thy ear! What false Italian,
As poisonous tongued as handed, hath prevailed
On thy too ready hearing? Disloyal? No.
She's punished for her truth, and undergoes,
More goddess-like than wife-like, such assaults
As would take in some virtue. O my master,
Thy mind to her is now as low as were   10
Thy fortunes. How? that I should murder her?
Upon the love and truth and vows which I
Have made to thy command? I, her? her blood?
If it be so to do good service, never
Let me be counted serviceable. How look I,
That I should seem to lack humanity
So much as this fact comes to? [*reading*] 'Do't. The
    letter
That I have sent her, by her own command
Shall give thee opportunity.' O damned paper,
Black as the ink that's on thee! Senseless bauble,   20
Art thou a fedary for this act, and look'st

So virgin-like without? Lo, here she comes.

Enter Imogen

I am ignorant in what I am commanded.
IMOGEN. How now, Pisanio!
PISANIO. Madam, here is a letter from my lord.
IMOGEN. Who, thy lord? that is my lord Leonatus?
O, learned indeed were that astronomer
That knew the stars as I his characters;
He'ld lay the future open. You good gods,
Let what is here contained relish of love,   30
Of my lord's health, of his content—yet not
That we two are asunder; let that grieve him.
Some griefs are medicinable; that is one of them,
For it doth physic love—of his content
All but in that. Good wax, thy leave. Blest be
You bees that make these locks of counsel! Lovers
And men in dangerous bonds pray not alike;
Though forfeiters you cast in prison, yet
You clasp young Cupid's tables. Good news, gods!
[*reads*] 'Justice, and your father's wrath, should he   40
take me in his dominion, could not be so cruel to me,
as you, O the dearest of creatures, would even renew
me with your eyes. Take notice that I am in
Cambria, at Milford Haven. What your own love
will out of this advise you, follow. So he wishes you
all happiness, that remains loyal to his vow, and your
increasing in love   LEONATUS POSTHUMUS.'
O, for a horse with wings! Hear'st thou, Pisanio?
He is at Milford Haven. Read, and tell me
How far 'tis thither. If one of mean affairs   50
May plod it in a week, why may not I
Glide thither in a day? Then, true Pisanio,
Who long'st like me to see thy lord, who long'st—
O let me bate—but not like me—yet long'st,
But in a fainter kind—O, not like me,
For mine's beyond beyond; say, and speak thick—
Love's counsellor should fill the bores of hearing,
To th'smothering of the sense—how far it is
To this same blessèd Milford. And by th'way
Tell me how Wales was made so happy as   60
T'inherit such a haven. But first of all,
How we may steal from hence; and for the gap
That we shall make in time from our hence-going
And our return, to excuse—but first, how get hence.
Why should excuse be born or ere begot?
We'll talk of that hereafter. Prithee speak,
How many score of miles may we well ride
'Twixt hour and hour?
PISANIO.   One score 'twixt sun and sun,
Madam, 's enough for you, and too much too.
IMOGEN. Why, one that rode to's execution, man,   70
Could never go so slow. I have heard of riding
    wagers
Where horses have been nimbler than the sands
That run i'th'clock's behalf. But this is fool'ry.
Go bid my woman feign a sickness, say
She'll home to her father; and provide me presently
A riding-suit, no costlier than would fit
A franklin's housewife.
PISANIO.   Madam, you're best consider.
IMOGEN. I see before me, man. Nor here, nor here,
Nor what ensues, but have a fog in them,
That I cannot look through. Away, I prithee;   80
Do as I bid thee. There's no more to say;
Accessible is none but Milford way.   *They go*

Scene 3: *Wales: a mountainous country with a cave*

Enter Belarius, Guiderius, and Arviragus

BELARIUS. A goodly day not to keep house with such
  Whose roof's as low as ours. Stoop, boys; this gate
  Instructs you how t'adore the heavens, and bows
    you
  To a morning's holy office. The gates of monarchs
  Are arched so high that giants may jet through
  And keep their impious turbans on, without
  Good morrow to the sun. Hail, thou fair heaven!
  We house i'th'rock, yet use thee not so hardly
  As prouder livers do.
GUIDERIUS.   Hail, heaven!
ARVIRAGUS.   Hail, heaven!
BELARIUS. Now for our mountain sport. Up to yond
    hill,   10
  Your legs are young; I'll tread these flats. Consider,
  When you above perceive me like a crow,
  That it is place which lessens and sets off;
  And you may then revolve what tales I have told
    you
  Of courts, of princes, of the tricks in war;
  This service is not service, so being done,
  But being so allowed. To apprehend thus
  Draws us a profit from all things we see;
  And often to our comfort shall we find
  The sharded beetle in a safer hold   20
  Than is the full-winged eagle. O, this life
  Is nobler than attending for a check,
  Richer than doing nothing for a bauble,
  Prouder than rustling in unpaid-for silk;
  Such gain the cap of him that makes them fine,
  Yet keeps his book uncrossed. No life to ours.
GUIDERIUS. Out of your proof you speak; we, poor
    unfledged,
  Have never winged from view o'th'nest, nor know
    not
  What air's from home. Haply this life is best,
  If quiet life be best; sweeter to you   30
  That have a sharper known; well corresponding
  With your stiff age; but unto us it is
  A cell of ignorance, travelling abed,
  A prison, or a debtor that not dares
  To stride a limit.
ARVIRAGUS.   What should we speak of
  When we are old as you? when we shall hear
  The rain and wind beat dark December, how
  In this our pinching cave shall we discourse
  The freezing hours away? We have seen nothing;
  We are beastly-subtle as the fox for prey,   40
  Like warlike as the wolf for what we eat;
  Our valour is to chase what flies; our cage
  We make a choir, as doth the prisoned bird,
  And sing our bondage freely.
BELARIUS.   How you speak!
  Did you but know the city's usuries,
  And felt them knowingly; the art o'th'court,
  As hard to leave as keep, whose top to climb
  Is certain falling, or so slipp'ry that
  The fear's as bad as falling; the toil o'th'war,
  A pain that only seems to seek out danger   50
  I'th'name of fame and honour, which dies
    i'th'search
  And hath as oft a sland'rous epitaph
  As record of fair act; nay, many times,

Doth ill deserve by doing well; what's worse,
  Must curtsy at the censure. O, boys, this story
  The world may read in me; my body's marked
  With Roman swords, and my report was once
  First with the best of note. Cymbeline loved me;
  And when a soldier was the theme, my name
  Was not far off. Then was I as a tree   60
  Whose boughs did bend with fruit; but in one night
  A storm, or robbery, call it what you will,
  Shook down my mellow hangings, nay, my leaves,
  And left me bare to weather.
GUIDERIUS.   Uncertain favour!
BELARIUS. My fault being nothing, as I have told you
    oft,
  But that two villains, whose false oaths prevailed
  Before my perfect honour, swore to Cymbeline
  I was confederate with the Romans. So
  Followed my banishment, and this twenty years
  This rock and these demesnes have been my world,   70
  Where I have lived at honest freedom, paid
  More pious debts to heaven than in all
  The fore-end of my time. But up to th'mountains!
  This is not hunters' language. He that strikes
  The venison first shall be the lord o'th'feast;
  To him the other two shall minister;
  And we will fear no poison, which attends
  In place of greater state. I'll meet you in the valleys.
                              Guiderius and Arviragus go
  How hard it is to hide the sparks of nature!
  These boys know little they are sons to th'king,   80
  Nor Cymbeline dreams that they are alive.
  They think they are mine; and though trained up
    thus meanly,
  I'th'cave wherein they bow, their thoughts do hit
  The roofs of palaces, and nature prompts them
  In simple and low things to prince it much
  Beyond the trick of others. This Polydore,
  The heir of Cymbeline and Britain, who
  The king his father called Guiderius—Jove!
  When on my three-foot stool I sit and tell
  The warlike feats I have done, his spirits fly out 90
  Into my story; say 'Thus mine enemy fell,
  And thus I set my foot on's neck', even then
  The princely blood flows in his cheek, he sweats,
  Strains his young nerves, and puts himself in posture
  That acts my words. The younger brother, Cadwal,
  Once Arviragus, in as like a figure
  Strikes life into my speech and shows much more
  His own conceiving. Hark, the game is roused!
  O Cymbeline, heaven and my conscience knows
  Thou didst unjustly banish me; whereon,   100
  At three and two years old, I stole these babes,
  Thinking to bar thee of succession as
  Thou reft'st me of my lands. Euriphile,
  Thou wast their nurse; they took thee for their
    mother,
  And every day do honour to her grave.
  Myself, Belarius, that am Morgan called,
  They take for natural father. The game is up.
                                                Goes

Scene 4: *Country near Milford Haven*

Enter Pisanio and Imogen

IMOGEN. Thou told'st me, when we came from horse,
    the place

Was near at hand. Ne'er longed my mother so
To see me first as I have now. Pisanio, man,
Where is Posthumus? What is in thy mind,
That makes thee stare thus? Wherefore breaks that
    sigh
From th'inward of thee? One but painted thus
Would be interpreted a thing perplexed
Beyond self-explication. Put thyself
Into a haviour of less fear, ere wildness
Vanquish my staider senses. What's the matter?   10
Why tender'st thou that paper to me with
A look untender? If't be summer news,
Smile to't before; if winterly, thou need'st
But keep that countenance still. My husband's hand?
That drug-damned Italy hath out-craftied him,
And he's at some hard point. Speak, man; thy
    tongue
May take off some extremity, which to read
Would be even mortal to me.
PISANIO.   Please you read,
And you shall find me, wretched man, a thing
The most disdained of fortune.   20
IMOGEN [reads]. 'Thy mistress, Pisanio, hath played the
strumpet in my bed; the testimonies whereof lie
bleeding in me. I speak not out of weak surmises, but
from proof as strong as my grief and as certain as I
expect my revenge. That part thou, Pisanio, must
act for me, if thy faith be not tainted with the breach
of hers. Let thine own hands take away her life; I
shall give thee opportunity at Milford Haven. She
hath my letter for the purpose; where, if thou fear
to strike, and to make me certain it is done, thou   30
art the pandar to her dishonour, and equally to me
disloyal.'
PISANIO. What shall I need to draw my sword? the
    paper
Hath cut her throat already. No, 'tis slander,
Whose edge is sharper than the sword, whose
    tongue
Outvenoms all the worms of Nile, whose breath
Rides on the posting winds and doth belie
All corners of the world. Kings, queens, and states,
Maids, matrons, nay, the secrets of the grave
This viperous slander enters. What cheer, madam?   40
IMOGEN. False to his bed? What is it to be false?
To lie in watch there, and to think on him?
To weep 'twixt clock and clock? if sleep charge
    nature,
To break it with a fearful dream of him,
And cry myself awake? that's false to's bed, is it?
PISANIO. Alas, good lady!
IMOGEN. I false? Thy conscience witness. Jachimo,
Thou didst accuse him of incontinency;
Thou then look'dst like a villain; now, methinks,
Thy favour's good enough. Some jay of Italy,   50
Whose mother was her painting, hath betrayed him.
Poor I am stale, a garment out of fashion;
And, for I am richer than to hang by th'walls,
I must be ripped. To pieces with me! O,
Men's vows are women's traitors! All good
    seeming,
By thy revolt, O husband, shall be thought
Put on for villainy; not born where't grows,
But worn a bait for ladies.
PISANIO.   Good madam, hear me.
IMOGEN. True honest men being heard like false Æneas

Were in his time thought false; and Sinon's weeping 60
Did scandal many a holy tear, took pity
From most true wretchedness. So thou, Posthumus,
Wilt lay the leaven on all proper men;
Goodly and gallant shall be false and perjured
From thy great fail. Come, fellow, be thou honest;
Do thou thy master's bidding. When thou see'st
    him,
A little witness my obedience. Look,
I draw the sword myself; take it, and hit
The innocent mansion of my love, my heart.
Fear not; 'tis empty of all things but grief;   70
Thy master is not there, who was indeed
The riches of it. Do his bidding; strike.
Thou mayst be valiant in a better cause,
But now thou seem'st a coward.
PISANIO.   Hence, vile instrument!
Thou shalt not damn my hand.
IMOGEN.   Why, I must die;
And if I do not by thy hand, thou art
No servant of thy master's. Against self-slaughter
There is a prohibition so divine
That cravens my weak hand. Come, here's my
    heart:
Something's afore't. Soft, soft! we'll no defence;   80
Obedient as the scabbard. What is here?
The scriptures of the loyal Leonatus,
All turned to heresy? Away, away,
Corrupters of my faith! you shall no more
Be stomachers to my heart. Thus may poor fools
Believe false teachers; though those that are betrayed
Do feel the treason sharply, yet the traitor
Stands in worse case of woe. And thou, Posthumus,
That didst set up
My disobedience 'gainst the king my father,   90
And make me put into contempt the suits
Of princely fellows, shalt hereafter find
It is no act of common passage, but
A strain of rareness; and I grieve myself
To think, when thou shalt be disedged by her
That now thou tirest on, how thy memory
Will then be panged by me. Prithee, dispatch;
The lamb entreats the butcher. Where's thy knife?
Thou art too slow to do thy master's bidding
When I desire it too.
PISANIO.   O gracious lady,   100
Since I received command to do this business
I have not slept one wink.
IMOGEN.   Do't, and to bed then.
PISANIO. I'll wake mine eye-balls out first.
IMOGEN.   Wherefore then
Didst undertake it? Why hast thou abused
So many miles with a pretence? this place?
Mine action, and thine own? our horses' labour?
The time inviting thee? the perturbed court,
For my being absent? whereunto I never
Purpose return. Why hast thou gone so far,
To be unbent when thou hast ta'en thy stand,   110
Th'elected deer before thee?
PISANIO.   But to win time
To lose so bad employment; in the which
I have considered of a course. Good lady,
Hear me with patience.
IMOGEN.   Talk thy tongue weary; speak.
I have heard I am a strumpet, and mine ear,
Therein false struck, can take no greater wound,

Nor tent to bottom that. But speak.

PISANIO. Then, madam,
I thought you would not back again.

IMOGEN. Most like,
Bringing me here to kill me.

PISANIO. Not so, neither;
But if I were as wise as honest, then 120
My purpose would prove well. It cannot be
But that my master is abused. Some villain,
Ay, and singular in his art, hath done you both
This curséd injury.

IMOGEN. Some Roman courtezan.

PISANIO. No, on my life.
I'll give but notice you are dead, and send him
Some bloody sign of it; for 'tis commanded
I should do so. You shall be missed at court,
And that will well confirm it.

IMOGEN. Why, good fellow,
What shall I do the while? where bide? how live? 130
Or in my life what comfort, when I am
Dead to my husband?

PISANIO. If you'll back to th'court—

IMOGEN. No court, no father, nor no more ado
With that harsh, feeble, noble, simple nothing,
That Cloten, whose love-suit hath been to me
As fearful as a siege.

PISANIO. If not at court,
Then not in Britain must you bide.

IMOGEN. Where then?
Hath Britain all the sun that shines? Day, night,
Are they not but in Britain? I'th'world's volume
Our Britain seems as of it, but not in't; 140
In a great pool a swan's nest. Prithee think
There's livers out of Britain.

PISANIO. I am most glad
You think of other place. Th'ambassador,
Lucius the Roman, comes to Milford Haven
To-morrow. Now if you could wear a mind
Dark as your fortune is, and but disguise
That which t'appear itself must not yet be
But by self-danger, you should tread a course
Pretty and full of view; yea, haply, near
The residence of Posthumus; so nigh, at least, 150
That though his actions were not visible, yet
Report should render him hourly to your ear
As truly as he moves.

IMOGEN. O, for such means,
Though peril to my modesty, not death on't,
I would adventure.

PISANIO. Well then, here's the point:
You must forget to be a woman; change
Command into obedience; fear and niceness—
The handmaids of all women, or, more truly,
Woman it pretty self—into a waggish courage,
Ready in gibes, quick-answered, saucy and 160
As quarrelous as the weasel. Nay, you must
Forget that rarest treasure of your cheek,
Exposing it—but, O, the harder heart!
Alack, no remedy!—to the greedy touch
Of common-kissing Titan, and forget
Your laboursome and dainty trims, wherein
You made great Juno angry.

IMOGEN. Nay, be brief.
I see into thy end, and am almost
A man already.

PISANIO. First, make yourself but like one.

Forethinking this, I have already fit— 170
'Tis in my cloak-bag—doublet, hat, hose, all
That answer to them. Would you, in their serving,
And with what imitation you can borrow
From youth of such a season, 'fore noble Lucius
Present yourself, desire his service, tell him
Wherein you're happy—which will make him
know
If that his head have ear in music—, doubtless
With joy he will embrace you; for he's honourable,
And, doubling that, most holy, Your means
abroad—
You have me, rich; and I will never fail 180
Beginning nor supplyment.

IMOGEN. Thou art all the comfort
The gods will diet me with. Prithee away;
There's more to be considered; but we'll even
All that good time will give us. This attempt
I am soldier to, and will abide it with
A prince's courage. Away, I prithee.

PISANIO. Well, madam, we must take a short farewell,
Lest, being missed, I be suspected of
Your carriage from the court. My noble mistress,
Here is a box—I had it from the queen— 190
What's in't is precious; if you are sick at sea,
Or stomach-qualmed at land, a dram of this
Will drive away distemper. To some shade,
And fit you to your manhood; may the gods
Direct you to the best!

IMOGEN. Amen. I thank thee.
They go in opposite directions

Scene 5: *A room in Cymbeline's palace*

Enter Cymbeline, Queen, Cloten, Lucius, and Lords

CYMBELINE. Thus far, and so farewell.

LUCIUS. Thanks, royal sir.
My emperor hath wrote I must from hence;
And am right sorry that I must report ye
My master's enemy.

CYMBELINE. Our subjects, sir,
Will not endure his yoke; and for ourself
To show less sovereignty than they, must needs
Appear unkinglike.

LUCIUS. So, sir. I desire of you
A conduct over land to Milford Haven.
Madam, all joy befall your grace, and you.

CYMBELINE. My lords, you are appointed for that
office; 10
The due of honour in no point omit.
So farewell, noble Lucius.

LUCIUS. Your hand, my lord.

CLOTEN. Receive it friendly; but from this time forth
I wear it as your enemy.

LUCIUS. Sir, the event
Is yet to name the winner. Fare you well.

CYMBELINE. Leave not the worthy Lucius, good my
lords,
Till he hath crossed the Severn. Happiness!
Lucius and lords go

QUEEN. He goes hence frowning; but it honours us
That we have given him cause.

CLOTEN. 'Tis all the better;
Your valiant Britons have their wishes in it. 20

CYMBELINE. Lucius hath wrote already to the emperor
How it goes here. It fits us therefore ripely

Our chariots and our horsemen be in readiness.
The powers that he already hath in Gallia
Will soon be drawn to head, from whence he moves
His war for Britain.
QUEEN.   'Tis not sleepy business,
But must be looked to speedily and strongly.
CYMBELINE. Our expectation that it would be thus
Hath made us forward. But, my gentle queen,
Where is our daughter? She hath not appeared   30
Before the Roman, nor to us hath tendered
The duty of the day. She looks us like
A thing more made of malice than of duty;
We have noted it. Call her before us, for
We have been too slight in sufferance.
                                        An attendant goes
QUEEN.   Royal sir,
Since the exile of Posthumus, most retired
Hath her life been; the cure whereof, my lord,
'Tis time must do. Beseech your majesty,
Forbear sharp speeches to her. She's a lady
So tender of rebukes that words are strokes,   40
And strokes death to her.

Re-enter Attendant

CYMBELINE.   Where is she, sir? How
Can her contempt be answered?
ATTENDANT.   Please you, sir,
Her chambers are all locked, and there's no answer
That will be given to th'loud'st of noise we make.
QUEEN. My lord, when last I went to visit her,
She prayed me to excuse her keeping close;
Whereto constrained by her infirmity
She should that duty leave unpaid to you,
Which daily she was bound to proffer. This
She wished me to make known; but our great court 50
Made me to blame in memory.
CYMBELINE.   Her doors locked?
Not seen of late? Grant, heavens, that which I fear
Prove false!   *Goes*
QUEEN. Son, I say, follow the king.
CLOTEN. That man of hers, Pisanio, her old servant,
I have not seen these two days.
QUEEN.   Go, look after.
                                        Cloten goes
Pisanio, thou that stand'st so for Posthumus!
He hath a drug of mine. I pray his absence
Proceed by swallowing that; for he believes
It is a thing most precious. But for her,   60
Where is she gone? Haply despair hath seized her;
Or, winged with fervour of her love, she's flown
To her desired Posthumus. Gone she is
To death or to dishonour, and my end
Can make good use of either. She being down,
I have the placing of the British crown.

Re-enter Cloten

How now, my son?
CLOTEN.   'Tis certain she is fled.
Go in and cheer the king; he rages, none
Dare come about him.
QUEEN.   All the better. May
This night forestall him of the coming day!   70
                                        Goes
CLOTEN. I love and hate her. For she's fair and royal,
And that she hath all courtly parts more exquisite
Than lady, ladies, woman—from every one

The best she hath, and she, of all compounded,
Outsells them all—I love her therefore; but
Disdaining me and throwing favours on
The low Posthumus slanders so her judgement
That what's else rare is choked; and in that point
I will conclude to hate her, nay, indeed,
To be revenged upon her. For when fools   80
Shall—

Enter Pisanio

                Who is here? What, are you packing, sirrah?
Come hither. Ah, you precious pandar! Villain,
Where is thy lady? In a word, or else
Thou art straightway with the fiends.
PISANIO.   O, good my lord!
CLOTEN. Where is thy lady? or, by Jupiter,
I will not ask again. Close villain,
I'll have this secret from thy heart, or rip
Thy heart to find it. Is she with Posthumus?
From whose so many weights of baseness cannot
A dram of worth be drawn.
PISANIO.   Alas, my lord,   90
How can she be with him? When was she missed?
He is in Rome.
CLOTEN.   Where is she, sir? Come nearer.
No farther halting; satisfy me home
What is become of her.
PISANIO. O, my all-worthy lord!
CLOTEN.   All-worthy villain,
Discover where thy mistress is at once,
At the next word; no more of 'worthy lord'!
Speak, or thy silence on the instant is
Thy condemnation and thy death.
PISANIO.   Then, sir,
This paper is the history of my knowledge   100
Touching her flight.   *Presenting a letter*
CLOTEN.   Let's see't. I will pursue her
Even to Augustus' throne.
PISANIO [*aside*].   Or this or perish.
She's far enough, and what he learns by this
May prove his travel, not her danger.
CLOTEN.   Hum!
PISANIO [*aside*]. I'll write to my lord she's dead. O
    Imogen,
Safe mayst thou wander, safe return again!
CLOTEN. Sirrah, is this letter true?
PISANIO. Sir, as I think.
CLOTEN. It is Posthumus' hand; I know't. Sirrah, if   110
thou wouldst not be a villain, but do me true service,
undergo those employments wherein I should have
cause to use thee with a serious industry—that is,
what villainy soe'er I bid thee do, to perform it
directly and truly—I would think thee an honest
man; thou shouldst neither want my means for thy
relief, nor my voice for thy preferment.
PISANIO. Well, my good lord.
CLOTEN. Wilt thou serve me? for since patiently and
constantly thou hast stuck to the bare fortune of that 120
beggar Posthumus, thou canst not in the course of
gratitude but be a diligent follower of mine. Wilt
thou serve me?
PISANIO. Sir, I will.
CLOTEN. Give me thy hand; here's my purse. Hast any
of thy late master's garments in thy possession?
PISANIO. I have, my lord, at my lodging the same suit
he wore when he took leave of my lady and mistress.

CLOTEN. The first service thou dost me, fetch that suit hither. Let it be thy first service; go.

PISANIO. I shall, my lord. *Goes* 130

CLOTEN. Meet thee at Milford Haven! I forgot to ask him one thing; I'll remember't anon. Even there, thou villain Posthumus, will I kill thee. I would these garments were come. She said upon a time—the bitterness of it I now belch from my heart—that she held the very garment of Posthumus in more respect than my noble and natural person, together with the adornment of my qualities. With that suit upon my back will I ravish her; first kill him, and in her eyes; there shall she see my valour, which will then be a 140 torment to her contempt. He on the ground, my speech of insultment ended on his dead body, and when my lust hath dined—which, as I say, to vex her I will execute in the clothes that she so praised— to the court I'll knock her back, foot her home again. She hath despised me rejoicingly, and I'll be merry in my revenge.

Re-enter Pisanio, with the clothes

Be those the garments?

PISANIO. Ay, my noble lord.

CLOTEN. How long is't since she went to Milford 150 Haven?

PISANIO. She can scarce be there yet.

CLOTEN. Bring this apparel to my chamber; that is the second thing that I have commanded thee. The third is that thou wilt be a voluntary mute to my design. Be but duteous and true, preferment shall tender itself to thee. My revenge is now at Milford; would I had wings to follow it! Come, and be true. *Goes*

PISANIO. Thou bid'st me to my loss; for, true to thee Were to prove false, which I will never be 160 To him that is most true. To Milford go, And find not her whom thou pursuest. Flow, flow, You heavenly blessings, on her. This fool's speed Be crossed with slowness; labour be his meed. *Goes*

Scene 6: *Wales: before the cave of Belarius*

Enter Imogen alone, in boy's clothes

IMOGEN. I see a man's life is a tedious one. I have tired myself, and for two nights together Have made the ground my bed. I should be sick, But that my resolution helps me. Milford, When from the mountain-top Pisanio showed thee, Thou wast within a ken. O Jove, I think Foundations fly the wretched: such, I mean, Where they should be relieved. Two beggars told me I could not miss my way. Will poor folks lie, That have afflictions on them, knowing 'tis 10 A punishment or trial? Yes; no wonder, When rich ones scarce tell true. To lapse in fulness Is sorer than to lie for need; and falsehood Is worse in kings than beggars. My dear lord, Thou art one o'th'false ones. Now I think on thee My hunger's gone; but even before, I was At point to sink for food. But what is this? Here is a path to't; 'tis some savage hold. I were best not call; I dare not call; yet famine, Ere clean it o'erthrow nature, makes it valiant. 20

Plenty and peace breeds cowards; hardness ever Of hardiness is mother. Ho! who's here? If any thing that's civil, speak; if savage, Take or lend. Ho! no answer? then I'll enter. Best draw my sword; and if mine enemy But fear the sword like me, he'll scarcely look on't. Such a foe, good heavens! *Goes into the cave*

Enter Belarius, Guiderius, and Arviragus

BELARIUS. You, Polydore, have proved best woodman and Are master of the feast. Cadwal and I Will play the cook and servant; 'tis our match. 30 The sweat of industry would dry and die But for the end it works to. Come, our stomachs Will make what's homely savoury; weariness Can snore upon the flint, when resty sloth Finds the down pillow hard. Now peace be here, Poor house, that keep'st thyself.

GUIDERIUS. I am throughly weary.

ARVIRAGUS. I am weak with toil, yet strong in appetite.

GUIDERIUS. There is cold meat i'th'cave; we'll browse on that Whilst what we have killed be cooked.

BELARIUS [*looking into the cave*]. Stay, come not in. But that it eats our victuals, I should think 40 Here were a fairy.

GUIDERIUS. What's the matter, sir?

BELARIUS. By Jupiter, an angel; or, if not, An earthly paragon. Behold divineness No elder than a boy.

Imogen comes from the cave

IMOGEN. Good masters, harm me not. Before I entered here I called, and thought To have begged or bought what I have took. Good troth, I have stol'n nought; nor would not though I had found Gold strewed i'th'floor. Here's money for my meat. I would have left it on the board so soon 50 As I had made my meal, and parted With prayers for the provider.

GUIDERIUS. Money, youth?

ARVIRAGUS. All gold and silver rather turn to dirt, As 'tis no better reckoned but of those Who worship dirty gods.

IMOGEN. I see you're angry. Know, if you kill me for my fault, I should Have died had I not made it.

BELARIUS. Whither bound?

IMOGEN. To Milford Haven.

BELARIUS. What's your name?

IMOGEN. Fidele, sir. I have a kinsman who 60 Is bound for Italy; he embarked at Milford; To whom being going, almost spent with hunger, I am fall'n in this offence.

BELARIUS. Prithee, fair youth, Think us no churls, nor measure our good minds By this rude place we live in. Well encountered. 'Tis almost night; you shall have better cheer Ere you depart, and thanks to stay and eat it. Boys, bid him welcome.

GUIDERIUS. Were you a woman, youth, I should woo hard but be your groom in honesty;

I bid for you as I'ld buy.
ARVIRAGUS.   I'll make't my comfort 70
He is a man, I'll love him as my brother:
And such a welcome as I'ld give to him
After long absence, such is yours. Most welcome.
Be sprightly, for you fall 'mongst friends.
IMOGEN.   'Mongst friends?
—If brothers. [aside] Would it had been so that they
Had been my father's sons! then had my prize
Been less, and so more equal ballasting
To thee, Posthumus.
BELARIUS.   He wrings at some distress.
GUIDERIUS. Would I could free't!
ARVIRAGUS.   Or· I; whate'er it be,
What pain it cost, what danger! Gods!
BELARIUS.   Hark, boys. 80
                                            Whispering

IMOGEN. Great men
That had a court no bigger than this cave,
That did attend themselves, and had the virtue
Which their own conscience sealed them, laying by
That nothing-gift of differing multitudes,
Could not outpeer these twain. Pardon me, gods,
I'ld change my sex to be companion with them,
Since Leonatus' false.
BELARIUS.   It shall be so.
Boys, we'll go dress our hunt. Fair youth, come in;
Discourse is heavy, fasting; when we have supped, 90
We'll mannerly demand thee of thy story,
So far as thou wilt speak it.
GUIDERIUS.   Pray draw near.
ARVIRAGUS. The night to th'owl and morn to th'lark
   less welcome.
IMOGEN.· Thanks, sir.
ARVIRAGUS. I pray draw near.   *They go*

Scene 7: *Rome. A public place*

Enter two Roman Senators and Tribunes

1 SENATOR. This is the tenour of the emperor's writ:
That since the common men are now in action
'Gainst the Pannonians and Dalmatians,
And that the legions now in Gallia are
Full weak to undertake our wars against
The fall'n-off Britons, that we do incite
The gentry to this business. He creates
Lucius proconsul; and to you the tribunes,
For this immediate levy, he commends
His absolute commission. Long live Cæsar! 10
1 TRIBUNE. Is Lucius general of the forces?
2 SENATOR.   Ay.
1 TRIBUNE. Remaining now in Gallia?
1 SENATOR.   With those legions
Which I have spoke of, whereunto your levy
Must be supplyant. The words of your commission
Will tie you to the numbers and the time
Of their dispatch.
1 TRIBUNE.   We will discharge our duty.
                                            They go

ACT 4
Scene 1: *Wales: near the cave of Belarius*

Enter Cloten alone

CLOTEN. I am near to th'place where they should meet,

if Pisanio have mapped it truly. How fit his garments serve me! Why should his mistress, who was
made by him that made the tailor, not be fit too? the
rather—saving reverence of the word—for 'tis said a
woman's fitness comes by fits. Therein I must play
the workman. I dare speak it to myself, for it is not
vain-glory for a man and his glass to confer in his
own chamber; I mean, the lines of my body are as
well drawn as his; no less young, more strong, not 10
beneath him in fortunes, beyond him in the advantage of the time, above him in birth, alike conversant in general services, and more remarkable in
single oppositions; yet this imperceiverant thing
loves him in my despite. What mortality is! Posthumus, thy head, which now is growing upon thy
shoulders, shall within this hour be off; thy mistress
enforced; thy garments·cut to pieces before her face;
and all this done, spurn her home to her father, who
may haply be a little angry for my so rough usage; 20
but my mother, having power of his testiness, shall
turn all into my commendations. My horse is tied
up safe; out, sword, and to a sore purpose! Fortune
put them into my hand. This is the very description
of their meeting-place;· and the fellow dares not
deceive me.   *Goes*

Scene 2: *Before the cave of Belarius*

Enter Belarius, Guiderius, Arviragus, and Imogen from the cave

BELARIUS [*to Imogen*]. You are not well. Remain here
   in the cave;
We'll come to you after hunting.
ARVIRAGUS [*to Imogen*].   Brother, stay here.
Are we not brothers?
IMOGEN.   So man and man should be;
But clay and clay differs in dignity,
Whose dust is both alike. I am very sick.
GUIDERIUS. Go you to hunting; I'll abide with him.
IMOGEN. So sick I am not, yet I am not well;
But not so citizen a wanton as
To seem to die ere sick. So please you, leave me;
Stick to your journal course: the breach of custom 10
Is breach of all. I am ill, but your being by me
Cannot amend me. Society is no comfort
To one not sociable. I am not very sick,
Since I can reason of it. Pray you trust me here:
I'll rob none but myself; and let me die,
Stealing so poorly.
GUIDERIUS.   I love thee, I have spoke it,
How much the quantity, the weight as much,
As I do love my father.
BELARIUS.   What? how, how?
ARVIRAGUS. If it be sin to say so, sir, I yoke me
In my good brother's fault. I know not why   20
I love this youth, and I have heard you say,
Love's reason's without reason. The bier at door,
And a demand who is't shall die, I'ld say
'My father, not this youth'.
BELARIUS [*aside*].   O noble strain!
O worthiness of nature, breed of greatness!
"Cowards father cowards and base things sire base;
Nature hath meal and bran, contempt and grace."
I'm not their father; yet who this should be
Doth miracle itself, loved before me.

[*to Guiderius and Arviragus*] 'Tis the ninth hour
o'th'morn.

ARVIRAGUS.   Brother, farewell.   30

IMOGEN. I wish ye sport.

ARVIRAGUS.   You health. [*to Belarius*] So
please you, sir.

IMOGEN [*aside*]. These are kind creatures. Gods, what
lies I have heard!
Our courtiers say all's savage but at court.
Experience, O, thou disprovest report!
Th'imperious seas breeds monsters; for the dish
Poor tributary rivers as sweet fish.
I am sick still, heart-sick. Pisanio,
I'll now taste of thy drug.   *Swallows some*

GUIDERIUS.   I could not stir him.
He said he was gentle, but unfortunate;
Dishonestly afflicted, but yet honest.   40

ARVIRAGUS. Thus did he answer me; yet said hereafter
I might know more.

BELARIUS.   To th'field, to th'field.
We'll leave you for this time; go in and rest.

ARVIRAGUS. We'll not be long away.

BELARIUS.   Pray be not sick,
For you must be our housewife.

IMOGEN.   Well or ill,
I am bound to you.

BELARIUS.   And shalt be ever.
                    Imogen goes into the cave
This youth, howe'er distress'd, appears he hath had
Good ancestors.

ARVIRAGUS.   How angel-like he sings!

GUIDERIUS. But his neat cookery! he cut our roots in
characters;
And sauced our broths, as Juno had been sick,   50
And he her dieter.

ARVIRAGUS.   Nobly he yokes
A smiling with a sigh, as if the sigh
Was that it was for not being such a smile;
The smile mocking the sigh that it would fly
From so divine a temple to commix
With winds that sailors rail at.

GUIDERIUS.   I do note
That grief and patience, rooted in him both,
Mingle their spurs together.

ARVIRAGUS.   Grow patience,
And let the stinking elder, grief, untwine
His perishing root with the increasing vine.   60

BELARIUS. It is great morning. Come away. Who's
there?

Enter Cloten

CLOTEN. I cannot find those runagates; that villain
Hath mocked me. I am faint.

BELARIUS.   'Those runagates'?
Means he not us? I partly know him; 'tis
Cloten, the son o'th'queen. I fear some ambush.
I saw him not these many years, and yet
I know 'tis he. We are held as outlaws. Hence!

GUIDERIUS. He is but one; you and my brother search
What companies are near; pray you, away;
Let me alone with him. *Belarius and Arviragus go*

CLOTEN.   Soft, what are you   70
That fly me thus? some villain mountaineers?
I have heard of such. What slave art thou?

GUIDERIUS.   A thing
More slavish did I ne'er than answering .

A slave without a knock.

CLOTEN.   Thou art a robber,
A law-breaker, a villain. Yield thee, thief.

GUIDERIUS. To who? to thee? What art thou? Have
not I
An arm as big as thine, a heart as big?
Thy words, I grant, are bigger; for I wear not
My dagger in my mouth. Say what thou art,
Why I should yield to thee.

CLOTEN.   Thou villain base,   80
Know'st me not by my clothes?

GUIDERIUS.   No, nor thy tailor, rascal,
Who is thy grandfather. He made those clothes,
Which, as it seems, make thee.

CLOTEN.   Thou precious varlet,
My tailor made them not.

GUIDERIUS.   Hence then, and thank
The man that gave them thee. Thou art some fool;
I am loath to beat thee.

CLOTEN.   Thou injurious thief,
Hear but my name, and tremble.

GUIDERIUS.   What's thy name?

CLOTEN. Cloten, thou villain.

GUIDERIUS. Cloten, thou double villain, be thy name,
I cannot tremble at it: were it Toad, or Adder,
Spider,   90
'Twould move me sooner.

CLOTEN.   To thy further fear,
Nay, to thy mere confusion, thou shalt know
I am son to th'queen.

GUIDERIUS.   I am sorry for't; not seeming
So worthy as thy birth.

CLOTEN.   Art not afeard?

GUIDERIUS. Those that I reverence, those I fear, the
wise.
At fools I laugh, not fear them.

CLOTEN.   Die the death.
When I have slain thee with my proper hand,
I'll follow those that even now fled hence,
And on the gates of Lud's town set your heads.
Yield, rustic mountaineer.   *They go out fighting* 100

Re-enter Belarius and Arviragus

BELARIUS. No company's abroad?

ARVIRAGUS. None in the world; you did mistake him,
sure.

BELARIUS. I cannot tell; long is it since I saw him,
But time hath nothing blurred those lines of favour
Which then he wore; the snatches in his voice,
And burst of speaking, were as his; I am absolute
'Twas very Cloten.

ARVIRAGUS.   In this place we left them;
I wish my brother make good time with him,
You say he is so fell.

BELARIUS.   Being scarce made up,
I mean to man, he had not apprehension   110
Of roaring terrors: for defect of judgement
Is oft the cease of fear.

Re-enter Guiderius with Cloten's head

                    But see, thy brother.

GUIDERIUS. This Cloten was a fool, an empty purse;
There was no money in't. Not Hercules
Could have knocked out his brains, for he had none.
Yet I not doing this, the fool had borne
My head as I do his.

BELARIUS.   What hast thou done?
GUIDERIUS. I am perfect what: cut off one Cloten's
   head,
   Son to the queen, after his own report,
   Who called me traitor, mountaineer, and swore   120
   With his own single hand he'ld take us in,
   Displace our heads where—thank the gods—they
      grow,
   And set them on Lud's town.
BELARIUS.   We are all undone.
GUIDERIUS. Why, worthy father, what have we to lose
   But that he swore to take, our lives? The law
   Protects not us; then why should we be tender
   To let ah arrogant piece of flesh threat us,
   Play judge and executioner all himself,
   For we do fear the law? What company
   Discover you abroad?
BELARIUS.   No single soul   130
   Can we set eye on; but in all safe reason
   He must have some attendants. Though his humour
   Was nothing but mutation, ay, and that
   From one bad thing to worse, not frenzy, not
   Absolute madness could so far have raved,
   To bring him here alone. Although perhaps
   It may be heard at court that such as we
   Cave here, hunt here, are outlaws, and in time
   May make some stronger head, the which he
      hearing—
   As it is like him—might break out, and swear   140
   He'ld fetch us in; yet is't not probable
   To come alone, either he so undertaking,
   Or they so suffering. Then on good ground we fear,
   If we do fear this body hath a tail
   More perilous than the head.
ARVIRAGUS.   Let ordinance
   Come as the gods foresay it; howsoe'er,
   My brother hath done well.
BELARIUS.   I had no mind
   To hunt this day. The boy Fidele's sickness
   Did make my way long forth.
GUIDERIUS.   With his own sword,
   Which he did wave against my throat, I have ta'en   150
   His head from him. I'll throw't into the creek
   Behind our rock, and let it to the sea,
   And tell the fishes he's the queen's son, Cloten.
   That's all I reck.   Goes
BELARIUS.   I fear 'twill be revenged.
   Would, Polydore, thou hadst not done't, though
      valour
   Becomes thee well enough.
ARVIRAGUS.   Would I had done't,
   So the revenge alone pursued me. Polydore,
   I love thee brotherly, but envy much
   Thou hast robbed me of this deed. I would revenges
   That possible strength might meet would seek us
      through   160
   And put us to our answer.
BELARIUS.   Well, 'tis done.
   We'll hunt no more to-day, nor seek for danger
   'Where there's no profit. I prithee to our rock;
   You and Fidele play the cooks; I'll stay
   Till hasty Polydore return, and bring him
   To dinner presently.
ARVIRAGUS.   Poor sick Fidele,
   I'll willingly to him. To gain his colour
   I'ld let a parish of such Clotens blood,
   And praise myself for charity.   Goes
BELARIUS.   O thou goddess,
   Thou divine Nature, how thyself thou blazon'st   170
   In these two princely boys! They are as gentle
   As zephyrs blowing below the violet,
   Not wagging his sweet head; and yet as rough,
   Their royal blood enchafed, as the rud'st wind
   That by the top doth take the mountain pine
   And make him stoop to th'vale. 'Tis wonder
   That an invisible instinct should frame them
   To royalty unlearned, honour untaught,
   Civility not seen from other, valour
   That wildly grows in them, but yields a crop   180
   As if it had been sowed. Yet still it's strange
   What Cloten's being here to us portends,
   Or what his death will bring us.

Re-enter Guiderius

GUIDERIUS.   Where's my brother?
   I have sent Cloten's clotpoll down the stream,
   In embassy to his mother; his body's hostage
   For his return.   *Solemn music*
BELARIUS.   My ingenious instrument!
   Hark, Polydore, it sounds. But what occasion
   Hath Cadwal now to give it motion? Hark!
GUIDERIUS. Is he at home?
BELARIUS.   He went hence even now.
GUIDERIUS. What does he mean? Since death of my
   dear'st mother   190
   It did not speak before. All solemn things
   Should answer solemn accidents. The matter?
   Triumphs for nothing and lamenting toys
   Is jollity for apes and grief for boys.
   Is Cadwal mad?

*Re-enter Arviragus with Imogen, dead, bearing her in his
arms*

BELARIUS.   Look, here he comes,
   And brings the dire occasion in his arms
   Of what we blame him for.
ARVIRAGUS.   The bird is dead
   That we have made so much on. I had rather
   Have skipped from sixteen years of age to sixty,
   To have turned my leaping time into a crutch,   200
   Than have seen this.
GUIDERIUS.   O sweetest, fairest lilly!
   My brother wears thee not the one half so well
   As when thou grew'st thyself.
BELARIUS.   O melancholy!
   Who ever yet could sound thy bottom? find
   The ooze, to show what coast thy sluggish crare
   Might easiliest harbour in? Thou blessed thing,
   Jove knows what man thou mightst have made;
      but I,
   Thou diedst, a most rare boy, of melancholy.
   How found you him?
ARVIRAGUS.   Stark, as you see;
   Thus smiling, as some fly had tickled slumber,   210
   Not as death's dart being laughed at; his right cheek
   Reposing on a cushion.
GUIDERIUS.   Where?
ARVIRAGUS.   O'th'floor,
   His arms thus leagued; I thought he slept, and put
   My clouted brogues from off my feet, whose
      rudeness
   Answered my steps too loud.

GUIDERIUS.   Why, he but sleeps.
  If he be gone, he'll make his grave a bed;
  With female fairies will his tomb be haunted,
  And worms will not come to thee.
ARVIRAGUS.   With fairest flowers,
  Whilst summer lasts, and I live here, Fidele,
  I'll sweeten thy sad grave. Thou shalt not lack   220
  The flower that's like thy face, pale primrose, nor
  The azured harebell, like thy veins; no, nor
  The leaf of eglantine, whom not to slander,
  Out-sweet'ned not thy breath. The ruddock would
  With charitable bill—O bill sore shaming
  Those rich-left heirs that let their fathers lie
  Without a monument!—bring thee all this;
  Yea, and furred moss besides, when flowers are
    none,
  To winter-ground thy corse.
GUIDERIUS.   Prithee have done,
  And do not play in wench-like words with that   230
  Which is so serious. Let us bury him,
  And not protract with admiration what
  Is now due debt. To th'grave.
ARVIRAGUS.   Say, where shall's lay him?
GUIDERIUS. By good Euriphile, our mother.
ARVIRAGUS.   Be't so;
  And let us, Polydore, though now our voices
  Have got the mannish crack, sing him to th'ground,
  As once our mother; use like note and words,
  Save that 'Euriphile' must be 'Fidele'.
GUIDERIUS. Cadwal,
  I cannot sing. I'll weep, and word it with thee;   240
  For notes of sorrow out of tune are worse
  Than priests and fanes that lie.
ARVIRAGUS.   We'll speak it then.
BELARIUS. Great griefs, I see, medicine the less; for
    Cloten
  Is quite forgot. He was a queen's son, boys;
  And though he came our enemy, remember
  He was paid for that; though mean and mighty
    rotting
  Together have one dust, yet reverence,
  That angel of the world, doth make distinction
  Of place 'tween high and low. Our foe was princely,
  And though you took his life as being our foe,   250
  Yet bury him as a prince.
GUIDERIUS.   Pray you fetch him hither.
  Thersites' body is as good as Ajax'
  When neither are alive.
ARVIRAGUS.   If you'll go fetch him,
  We'll say our song the whilst. Brother, begin.
                              Belarius goes
GUIDERIUS. Nay, Cadwal, we must lay his head to
    th'east;
  My father hath a reason for it.
ARVIRAGUS.   'Tis true.
GUIDERIUS. Come on then and remove him.
ARVIRAGUS.   So. Begin.

                      SONG
GUIDERIUS.
  Fear no more the heat o'th'sun,
    Nor the furious winter's rages;
  Thou thy worldly task hast done,   260
    Home art gone and ta'en thy wages.
  Golden lads and girls all must,
  As chimney-sweepers, come to dust.

ARVIRAGUS.
    Fear no more the frown o'th'great;
      Thou art past the tyrant's stroke;
    Care no more to clothe and eat;
      To thee the reed is as the oak.
    The sceptre, learning, physic, must
    All follow this and come to dust.

GUIDERIUS. Fear no more the lightning flash,   270
ARVIRAGUS.   Nor th'all-dreaded thunder-stone;
GUIDERIUS. Fear not slander, censure rash;
ARVIRAGUS.   Thou hast finished joy and moan.
BOTH.   All lovers young, all lovers must
    Consign to thee and come to dust.

GUIDERIUS. No exorciser harm thee!
ARVIRAGUS. Nor no witchcraft charm thee!
GUIDERIUS. Ghost unlaid forbear thee!
ARVIRAGUS. Nothing ill come near thee!
BOTH.   Quiet consummation have;   280
    And renownèd be thy grave!

Re-enter Belarius with the body of Cloten

GUIDERIUS. We have done our obsequies. Come, lay
    him down.
BELARIUS. Here's a few flowers, but 'bout midnight
    more:
  The herbs that have on them cold dew o'th'night
  Are strewings fitt'st for graves. Upon their faces.
  You were as flowers, now wither'd; even so
  These herblets shall, which we upon you strew.
  Come on, away; apart upon our knees.
  The ground that gave them first has them again.   290
  Their pleasures here are past, so is their pain.
              Belarius, Guiderius and Arviragus go
IMOGEN [*awaking*]. Yes, sir, to Milford Haven; which
    is the way?—
  I thank you. By yond bush? Pray, how far thither?
  'Ods pittikins, can it be six mile yet?
  I have gone all night. Faith, I'll lie down and sleep.
  But, soft, no bedfellow! O gods and goddesses!
              Seeing the body of Cloten
  These flowers are like the pleasures of the world;
  This bloody man, the care on't, I hope I dream;
  For so I thought I was a cave-keeper,
  And cook to honest creatures. But 'tis not so;
  'Twas but a bolt of nothing, shot at nothing,   300
  Which the brain makes of fumes. Our very eyes
  Are sometimes like our judgements, blind. Good
    faith,
  I tremble still with fear; but if there be
  Yet left in heaven as small a drop of pity
  As a wren's eye, feared gods, a part of it!
  The dream's here still; even when I wake, it is
  Without me, as within me; not imagined, felt.
  A headless man? The garments of Posthumus?
  I know the shape of's leg; this is his hand;
  His foot Mercurial; his Martial thigh;   310
  The brawns of Hercules; but his Jovial face—
  Murder in heaven? How? 'Tis gone. Pisanio,
  All curses madded Hecuba gave the Greeks,
  And mine to boot, be darted on thee! Thou,
  Conspired with that irregulous devil, Cloten,
  Hath here cut off my lord. To write and read
  Be henceforth treacherous! Damned Pisanio
  Hath with his forgèd letters—damned Pisanio—
  From this most bravest vessel of the world

Struck the main-top. O Posthumus, alas,   320
Where is thy head? where's that? Ay me! where's
    that?
Pisanio might have killed thee at the heart,
And left this head on. How should this be? Pisanio?
'Tis he and Cloten; malice and lucre in them
Have laid this woe here. O, 'tis pregnant, pregnant!
The drug he gave me, which he said was precious
And cordial to me, have I not found it
Murd'rous to th'senses? That confirms it home.
This is Pisanio's deed, and Cloten's. O!
Give colour to my pale cheek with thy blood,   330
That we the horrider may seem to those
Which chance to find us. O, my lord, my lord!
                                        Falls on the body

Enter Lucius, a Captain and other Officers, and a Sooth-
sayer

CAPTAIN. To them the legions garrisoned in Gallia
After your will have crossed the sea, attending
You here at Milford Haven with your ships.
They are here in readiness.
LUCIUS.   But what from Rome?
CAPTAIN. The senate hath stirred up the confiners
And gentlemen of Italy, most willing spirits
That promise noble service; and they come
Under the conduct of bold Jachimo,   340
Siena's brother.
LUCIUS.   When expect you them?
CAPTAIN. With the next benefit o'th'wind.
LUCIUS.   This forwardness
Makes our hopes fair. Command our present
    numbers
Be mustered; bid the captains look to't. Now, sir,
What have you dreamed of late of this war's
    purpose?
SOOTHSAYER. Last night the very gods showed me a
    vision—
I fast and prayed for their intelligence—thus:
I saw Jove's bird, the Roman eagle, winged
From the spongy south to this part of the west,
There vanished in the sunbeams; which portends,   350
Unless my sins abuse my divination,
Success to th'Roman host.
LUCIUS.   Dream often so,
And never false. Soft, ho, what trunk is here
Without his top? The ruin speaks that sometime
It was a worthy building. How? a page?
Or dead or sleeping on him? But dead rather;
For nature doth abhor to make his bed
With the defunct, or sleep upon the dead.
Let's see the boy's face.
CAPTAIN.   He's alive, my lord.
LUCIUS. He'll then instruct us of this body. Young
    one,   360
Inform us of thy fortunes, for it seems
They crave to be demanded. Who is this
Thou makest thy bloody pillow? Or who was he
That, otherwise than noble nature did,
Hath altered that good picture? What's thy interest
In this sad wreck? How came't? Who is't?
What art thou?
IMOGEN.   I am nothing; or if not,
Nothing to be were better. This was my master,
A very valiant Briton and a good,
That here by mountaineers lies slain. Alas,   370

There is no more such masters. I may wander
From east to occident; cry out for service;
Try many, all good; serve truly; never
Find such another master.
LUCIUS.   'Lack, good youth,
Thou mov'st no less with thy complaining than
Thy master in bleeding. Say his name, good friend.
IMOGEN. Richard du Champ. [*aside*] If I do lie, and do
No harm by it, though the gods hear, I hope
They'll pardon it. [*to Lucius*] Say you, sir?
LUCIUS. Thy name?   380
IMOGEN. Fidele, sir.
LUCIUS. Thou dost approve thyself the very same:
Thy name fits well thy faith, thy faith thy name.
Wilt take thy chance with me? I will not say
Thou shalt be so well mastered, but be sure,
No less beloved. The Roman emperor's letters
Sent by a consul to me should not sooner
Than thine own worth prefer thee. Go with me.
IMOGEN. I'll follow, sir. But first, an't please the gods,
I'll hide my master from the flies, as deep   390
As these poor pickaxes can dig; and when
With wild wood-leaves and weeds I ha' strewed his
    grave
And on it said a century of prayers,
Such as I can, twice o'er, I'll weep and sigh,
And leaving so his service, follow you,
So please you entertain me.
LUCIUS.   Ay, good youth,
And rather father thee than master thee.
My friends,
The boy hath taught us manly duties; let us
Find out the prettiest daisied plot we can,   400
And make him with our pikes and partisans
A grave. Come, arm him. Boy, he is preferred
By thee to us, and he shall be interred
As soldiers can. Be cheerful; wipe thine eyes.
Some falls are means the happier to arise.
                                              They go

Scene 3: *A room in Cymbeline's palace*

Enter Cymbeline, Lords, Pisanio, and attendants

CYMBELINE. Again; and bring me word how 'tis with
    her.   *An attendant goes*
A fever with the absence of her son;
A madness, of which her life's in danger. Heavens,
How deeply you at once do touch me! Imogen,
The great part of my comfort, gone; my queen
Upon a desperate bed, and in a time
When fearful wars point at me; her son gone,
So needful for this present. It strikes me past
The hope of comfort. But for thee, fellow,
Who needs must know of her departure and   10
Dost seem so ignorant, we'll enforce it from thee
By a sharp torture.
PISANIO.   Sir, my life is yours;
I humbly set it at your will; but for my mistress,
I know nothing where she remains, why gone,
Nor when she purposes return. Beseech your
    highness,
Hold me your loyal servant.
I LORD.   Good my liege,
The day that she was missing he was here;
I dare be bound he's true and shall perform
All parts of his subjection loyally. For Cloten,

There wants no diligence in seeking him,   20
And will no doubt be found.
CYMBELINE.   The time is troublesome.
[*to Pisanio*] We'll slip you for a season, but our
  jealousy
Does yet depend.
1 LORD.   So please your majesty,
The Roman legions, all from Gallia drawn,
Are landed on your coast, with a supply
Of Roman gentlemen by the senate sent.
CYMBELINE. Now for the counsel of my son and queen!
I am amazed with matter.
1 LORD.   Good my liege,
Your preparation can affront no less
Than what you hear of. Come more, for more
  you're ready.   30
The want is but to put those powers in motion
That long to move.
CYMBELINE.   I thank you. Let's withdraw,
And meet the time as it seeks us. We fear not
What can from Italy annoy us, but
We grieve at chances here. Away!
                   All but Pisanio go
PISANIO. I heard no letter from my master since
I wrote him Imogen was slain. 'Tis strange.
Nor hear I from my mistress, who did promise
To yield me often tidings. Neither know I
What is betid to Cloten, but remain   40
Perplexed in all. The heavens still must work.
Wherein I am false I am honest; not true, to be true.
These present wars shall find I love my country,
Even to the note o'th'king, or I'll fall in them.
All other doubts, by time let them be cleared:
Fortune brings in some boats that are not steered.
                         Goes

Scene 4: *Wales: Before the cave of Belarius*

Enter Belarius, Guiderius, and Arviragus

GUIDERIUS. The noise is round about us.
BELARIUS.   Let us from it.
ARVIRAGUS. What pleasure, sir, find we in life, to
  lock it
From action and adventure?
GUIDERIUS.   Nay, what hope
Have we in hiding us? This way the Romans
Must or for Britons slay us or receive us
For barbarous and unnatural revolts
During their use, and slay us after.
BELARIUS.   Sons,
We'll higher to the mountains; there secure us.
To the king's party there's no going. Newness
Of Cloten's death—we being not known, not
  mustered   10
Among the bands—may drive us to a render
Where we have lived, and so extort from's that
Which we have done, whose answer would be death
Drawn on with torture.
GUIDERIUS.   This is, sir, a doubt
In such a time nothing becoming you,
Nor satisfying us.
ARVIRAGUS.   It is not likely
That when they hear the Roman horses neigh,
Behold their quartered fires, have both their eyes
And ears so cloyed importantly as now,
That they will waste their time upon our note,   20

To know from whence we are.
BELARIUS.   O, I am known
Of many in the army. Many years,
Though Cloten then but young, you see, not wore
  him
From my remembrance. And besides, the king
Hath not deserved my service nor your loves,
Who find in my exile the want of breeding,
The certainty of this hard life; aye hopeless
To have the courtesy your cradle promised,
But to be still hot summer's tanlings and
The shrinking slaves of winter.
GUIDERIUS.   Than be so   30
Better to cease to be. Pray, sir, to th'army.
I and my brother are not known; yourself
So out of thought, and thereto so o'ergrown,
Cannot be questioned.
ARVIRAGUS.   By this sun that shines
I'll thither. What thing is't that I never
Did see man die, scarce ever looked on blood,
But that of coward hares, hot goats, and venison,
Never bestrid a horse, save one that had
A rider like myself, who ne'er wore rowel
Nor iron on his heel! I am ashamed   40
To look upon the holy sun, to have
The benefit of his blest beams, remaining
So long a poor unknown.
GUIDERIUS.   By heavens, I'll go;
If you will bless me sir, and give me leave,
I'll take the better care; but if you will not,
The hazard therefore due fall on me by
The hands of Romans!
ARVIRAGUS.   So say I; amen.
BELARIUS. No reason I, since of your lives you set
So slight a valuation, should reserve
My cracked one to more care. Have with you, boys!   50
If in your country wars you chance to die,
That is my bed too, lads, and there I'll lie.
Lead, lead. [*aside*] The time seems long; their blood
  thinks scorn
Till it fly out and show them princes born.
                        They go

ACT 5

Scene 1: *Britain. The Roman camp*

Enter Posthumus alone, with a bloody handkerchief

POSTHUMUS. Yea, bloody cloth, I'll keep thee; for I
  wished
Thou shouldst be coloured thus. You married ones,
If each of you should take this course, how many
Must murder wives much better than themselves
For wrying but a little! O Pisanio,
Every good servant does not all commands;
No bond but to do just ones. Gods, if you
Should have ta'en vengeance on my faults, I never
Had lived to put on this; so had you saved
The noble Imogen to repent, and struck   10
Me, wretch, more worth your vengeance. But
  alack,
You snatch some hence for little faults; that's love,
To have them fall no more; you some permit
To second ills with ills, each elder worse,
And make them dread it, to the doers' thrift.
But Imogen is your own; do your best wills,

And make me blest to obey. I am brought hither
Among th'Italian gentry, and to fight
Against my lady's kingdom. 'Tis enough
That, Britain, I have killed thy mistress; peace,   20
I'll give no wound to thee. Therefore, good heavens,
Hear patiently my purpose. I'll disrobe me
Of these Italian weeds, and suit myself
As does a Briton peasant. So I'll fight
Against the part I come with; so I'll die
For thee, O Imogen, even for whom my life
Is every breath a death; and thus, unknown,
Pitied nor hated, to the face of peril
Myself I'll dedicate. Let me make men know
More valour in me than my habits show.   30
Gods, put the strength o'th'Leonati in me.
To shame the guise o'th'world, I will begin
The fashion—less without and more within.

                                                      Goes

Scene 2: *Field of battle between the British and Roman
                                camps*

*Enter from one side, Lucius, Jachimo, and the Roman
Army; from the other side, the British Army; Leonatus
Posthumus following, like a poor soldier. They march over
and go out. Then enter again, in skirmish, Jachimo and
Posthumus: he vanquisheth and disarmeth Jachimo, and then
leaves him*

JACHIMO. The heaviness and guilt within my bosom
    Takes off my manhood. I have belied a lady,
    The princess of this country, and the air on't
    Revengingly enfeebles me; or could this carl,
    A very drudge of nature's, have subdued me
    In my profession? Knighthoods and honours borne
    As I wear mine are titles but of scorn.
    If that thy gentry, Britain, go before
    This lout as he exceeds our lords, the odds
    Is that we scarce are men and you are gods.   10

                                                      Goes

*The battle continues; the Britons fly; Cymbeline is taken:
then enter, to his rescue, Belarius, Guiderius and Arviragus*

BELARIUS. Stand, stand, we have the advantage of the
                                ground;
    The lane is guarded; nothing routs us but
    The villainy of our fears.
GUIDERIUS   }
AND ARVIRAGUS.   }   Stand, stand, and fight.

*Re-enter Posthumus, and seconds the Britons: they rescue
Cymbeline and go out. Then re-enter Lucius, Jachimo, with
Imogen*

LUCIUS. Away, boy, from the troops, and save thyself;
    For friends kill friends, and the disorder's such
    As war were hoodwinked.
JACHIMO.   'Tis their fresh supplies.
LUCIUS. It is a day turned strangely; or betimes
    Let's reinforce, or fly.   *They go*

Scene 3: *Another part of the field*

Enter Posthumus and a British Lord

LORD. Cam'st thou from where they made the stand?
POSTHUMUS.   I did;
    Though you, it seems, come from the fliers?
LORD.   I did.

POSTHUMUS. No blame be to you, sir; for all was lost,
    But that the heavens fought. The king himself
    Of his wings destitute, the army broken,
    And but the backs of Britons seen, all flying
    Through a strait lane; the enemy full-hearted,
    Lolling the tongue with slaught'ring, having work
    More plentiful than tools to do't, struck down
    Some mortally, some slightly touched, some falling   10
    Merely through fear, that the strait pass was
                                dammed
    With dead men hurt behind, and cowards living
    To die with length'ned shame.
LORD.   Where was this lane?
POSTHUMUS. Close by the battle, ditched, and walled
                                with turf;
    Which gave advantage to an ancient soldier,
    An honest one, I warrant, who deserved
    So long a breeding as his white beard came to,
    In doing this for's country. Athwart the lane
    He, with two striplings—lads more like to run
    The country base than to commit such slaughter;   20
    With faces fit for masks, or rather fairer
    Than those for preservation cased, or shame—
    Made good the passage; cried to those that fled,
    'Our Britain's harts die flying, not our men:
    To darkness fleet souls that fly backwards. Stand,
    Or we are Romans, and will give you that
    Like beasts which you shun beastly, and may save
    But to look back in frown. Stand, stand'. These
                                three,
    Three thousand confident, in act as many—
    For three performers are the file when all   30
    The rest do nothing—with this word 'Stand, stand',
    Accommodated by the place, more charming
    With their own nobleness, which could have turned
    A distaff to a lance, gilded pale looks;
    Part shame, part spirit renewed, that some, turned
                                coward
    But by example—O, a sin in war,
    Damned in the first beginners!—'gan to look
    The way that they did and to grin like lions
    Upon the pikes o'th'hunters. Then began
    A stop i'th'chaser, a retire; anon   40
    A rout, confusion thick; forthwith they fly
    Chickens, the way which they stooped eagles;
                                slaves,
    The strides they victors made; and now our
                                cowards,
    Like fragments in hard voyages, became
    The life o'th'need. Having found the back-door
                                open
    Of the unguarded hearts, heavens, how they
                                wound!
    Some slain before, some dying, some their friends
    O'er-borne i'th'former wave, ten chased by one,
    Are now each one the slaughterman of twenty.
    Those that would die or ere resist are grown   50
    The mortal bugs o'th'field.
LORD.   This was strange chance:
    A narrow lane, an old man, and two boys.
POSTHUMUS. Nay, do not wonder at it; you are made
    Rather to wonder at the things you hear
    Than to work any. Will you rhyme upon't,
    And vent if for a mock'ry? Here is one:
    'Two boys, an old man—twice a boy—a lane,
    Preserved the Britons, was the Romans' bane.'

LORD. Nay, be not angry, sir.
POSTHUMUS.   'Lack, to what end?
  Who dares not stand his foe, I'll be his friend;   60
  For if he'll do as he is made to do,
  I know he'll quickly fly my friendship too.
  You have put me into rhyme.
LORD.   Farewell; you're angry.
                                Goes
POSTHUMUS. Still going? This is a lord! O noble
  misery,
  To be i'th'field, and ask 'what news?' of me!
  To-day how many would have given their honours
  To have saved their carcasses! took heel to do't,
  And yet died too! I, in mine own woe charmed,
  Could not find death where I did hear him groan,
  Nor feel him where he struck. Being an ugly
  monster,   70
  'Tis strange he hides him in fresh cups, soft beds,
  Sweet words; or hath moe ministers than we
  That draw his knives i'th'war. Well, I will find him;
  For being now a favourer to the Briton,
  No more a Briton, I have resumed again
  The part I came in. Fight I will no more,
  But yield me to the veriest hind that shall
  Once touch my shoulder. Great the slaughter is
  Here made by th'Roman; great the answer be
  Britons must take. For me, my ransom's death;   80
  On either side I come to spend my breath,
  Which neither here I'll keep nor bear again,
  But end it by some means for Imogen.

Enter two British Captains and Soldiers

1 CAPTAIN. Great Jupiter be praised, Lucius is taken.
  'Tis thought the old man and his sons were angels.
2 CAPTAIN. There was a fourth man, in a silly habit,
  That gave th'affront with them.
1 CAPTAIN.   So 'tis reported;
  But none of 'em can be found. Stand, who's there?
POSTHUMUS. A Roman,
  Who had not now been drooping here if seconds 90
  Had answered him.
2 CAPTAIN.   Lay hands on him; a dog!
  A leg of Rome shall not return to tell
  What crows have pecked them here. He brags his
  service
  As if he were of note: bring him to th'king.

*Enter Cymbeline, Belarius, Guiderius, Arviragus, Pisanio,
and Roman Captives. The Captains present Posthumus to
Cymbeline, who delivers him over to a Gaoler: then all go*

Scene 4: *A British prison*

Enter Posthumus and two Gaolers

1 GAOLER. You shall not now be stol'n, you have locks
  upon you;
  So graze as you find pasture.
2 GAOLER.   Ay, or a stomach.
                        The gaolers go
POSTHUMUS. Most welcome, bondage, for thou art a
  way,
  I think, to liberty. Yet am I better
  Than one that's sick o'th'gout, since he had rather
  Groan so in perpetuity than be cured
  By th'sure physician, death, who is the key

T'unbar these locks. My conscience, thou art
  fettered
More than my shanks and wrists. You good gods,
  give me
The penitent instrument to pick that bolt,   10
Then, free for ever. Is't enough I am sorry?
So children temporal fathers do appease;
Gods are more full of mercy. Must I repent,
I cannot do it better than in gyves,
Desired more than constrained. To satisfy,
If of my freedom 'tis the main part, take
No stricter render of me than my all.
I know you are more clement than vile men,
Who of their broken debtors take a third,
A sixth, a tenth, letting them thrive again   20
On their abatement; that's not my desire.
For Imogen's dear life take mine; and though
'Tis not so dear, yet 'tis a life; you coined it.
'Tween man and man they weigh not every stamp;
Though light, take pieces for the figure's sake;
You rather mine, being yours. And so, great
  powers,
If you will take this audit, take this life,
And cancel these cold bonds. O Imogen,
I'll speak to thee in silence.   *Sleeps*

*Solemn music. Enter, as in an apparition, Sicilius Leonatus,
father to Posthumus, an old man, attired like a warrior;
leading in his hand an ancient matron, his wife and mother
to Posthumus, with music before them. Then, after other
music, follow the two young Leonati, brothers to Posthumus,
with wounds as they died in the wars. They circle
Posthumus round as he lies sleeping*

SICILIUS.   No more, thou thunder-master, show   30
        Thy spite on mortal flies.
    With Mars fall out, with Juno chide,
        That thy adulteries
            Rates and revenges.
    Hath my poor boy done aught but well,
        Whose face I never saw?
    I died whilst in the womb he stayed
        Attending nature's law;
    Whose father then—as men report
        Thou orphans' father art—   40
    Thou shouldst have been, and shielded
        him
        From this earth-vexing smart.
MOTHER.   Lucina lent not me her aid,
        But took me in my throes,
    That from me was Posthumus ripped,
        Came crying 'mongst his foes,
        A thing of pity.
SICILIUS.   Great nature like his ancestry
        Moulded the stuff so fair
    That he deserved the praise o'th'world,   50
        As great Sicilius' heir.
1 BROTHER. When once he was mature for man,
        In Britain where was he
    That could stand up his parallel,
        Or fruitful object be
    In eye of Imogen, that best
        Could deem his dignity?
MOTHER.   With marriage wherefore was he
        mocked,
        To be exiled, and thrown
    From Leonati seat, and cast   60

From her his dearest one,
    Sweet Imogen?
SICILIUS. Why did you suffer Jachimo,
    Slight thing of Italy,
    To taint his nobler heart and brain
    With needless jealousy,
        And to become the geck and scorn
    O'th'other's villainy?
2 BROTHER. For this from stiller seats we came,
    Our parents and us twain, 70
    That striking in our country's cause
    Fell bravely and were slain,
    Our fealty and Tenantius' right
    With honour to maintain.
1 BROTHER. Like hardiment Posthumus hath
    To Cymbeline performed.
    Then, Jupiter, thou king of gods,
    Why hast thou thus adjourned
    The graces for his merits due,
    Being all to dolours turned? 80
SICILIUS. Thy crystal window ope; look out;
    No longer exercise
    Upon a valiant race thy harsh
    And potent injuries.
MOTHER. Since, Jupiter, our son is good,
    Take off his miseries.
SICILIUS. Peep through thy marble mansion; help;
    Or we poor ghosts will cry
    To th'shining synod of the rest
    Against thy deity. 90
BOTH BROTHERS. Help, Jupiter, or we appeal,
    And from thy justice fly.

*Jupiter descends in thunder and lightning, sitting upon an
eagle; he throws a thunderbolt. The ghosts fall on their
knees*

JUPITER. No more, you petty spirits of region low,
    Offend our hearing; hush! How dare you
        ghosts
    Accuse the thunderer, whose bolt, you know,
    Sky-planted, batters all rebelling coasts?
    Poor shadows of Elysium, hence, and rest
    Upon your never-withering banks
        of flowers.
    Be not with mortal accidents oppressed;
    No care of yours it is; you know 'tis ours. 100
    Whom best I love I cross; to make my gift,
    The more delayed, delighted. Be content;
    Your low-laid son our godhead will uplift;
    His comforts thrive, his trials well are
        spent.
    Our Jovial star reigned at his birth, and in
    Our temple was he married. Rise,
        and fade.
    He shall be lord of lady Imogen,
    And happier much by his affliction made.
    This tablet lay upon his breast, wherein
    Our pleasure his full fortune doth confine; 110
    And so away; no farther with your din
    Express impatience, lest you stir up mine.
    Mount, eagle, to my palace crystalline.
                         Ascends
SICILIUS. He came in thunder; his celestial breath
  Was sulphurous to smell; the holy eagle
  Stooped, as to foot us. His ascension is
  More sweet than our blest fields. His royal bird

  Prunes the immortal wing and cloys his beak,
  As when his god is pleased.
ALL.   Thanks, Jupiter.
SICILIUS. The marble pavement closes, he is entered 120
  His radiant roof. Away, and, to be blest,
  Let us with care perform his great behest.
                   The ghosts vanish
POSTHUMUS [*waking*]. Sleep, thou hast been a
    grandsire, and begot
A father to me; and thou hast created
A mother and two brothers. But, O scorn,
Gone! they went hence so soon as they were born;
And so I am awake. Poor wretches that depend
On greatness' favour dream as I have done;
Wake, and find nothing. But, alas, I swerve;
Many dream not to find, neither deserve, 130
And yet are steeped in favours; so am I,
That have this golden chance, and know not why.
What fairies haunt this ground? A book? O rare one,
Be not, as is our fangled world, a garment
Nobler than that it covers. Let thy effects
So follow to be most unlike our courtiers,
As good as promise.   *Reads*
   'When as a lion's whelp shall, to himself un-
known, without seeking find, and be embraced by
a piece of tender air, and when from a stately cedar 140
shall be lopped branches which, being dead many
years, shall after revive, be jointed to the old stock,
and freshly grow; then shall Posthumus end his
miseries, Britain be fortunate and flourish in peace
and plenty.'
'Tis still a dream; or else such stuff as madmen
Tongue, and brain not; either both, or nothing,
Or senseless speaking, or a speaking such
As sense cannot untie. Be what it is,
The action of my life is like it, which 150
I'll keep, if but for sympathy.

Re-enter Gaolers

1 GAOLER. Come, sir, are you ready for death?
POSTHUMUS. Over-roasted rather; ready long ago.
1 GAOLER. Hanging is the word, sir; if you be ready
for that you are well cooked.
POSTHUMUS. So, if I prove a good repast to the spectators, the dish pays the shot.
1 GAOLER. A heavy reckoning for you, sir. But the
comfort is, you shall be called to no more payments,
fear no more tavern bills, which are as often the 160
sadness of parting, as the procuring of mirth. You
come in faint for want of meat, depart reeling with
too much drink; sorry that you have paid too much,
and sorry that you are paid too much; purse and
brain both empty: the brain the heavier for being
too light, the purse too light, being drawn of
heaviness. Of this contradiction you shall now be
quit. O, the charity of a penny cord! it sums up
thousands in a trice; you have no true debitor-and-
creditor but it; of what's past, is, and to come, the 170
discharge; your neck, sir, is pen, book, and counters;
so the acquittance follows.
POSTHUMUS. I am merrier to die than thou art to live.
1 GAOLER. Indeed, sir, he that sleeps feels not the
toothache; but a man that were to sleep your sleep,
and a hangman to help him to bed, I think he
would change places with his officer; for look you,
sir, you know not which way you shall go.

POSTHUMUS. Yes indeed do I, fellow.

1 GAOLER. Your death has eyes in's head then; I have not seen him so pictured. You must either be directed by some that take upon them to know, or take upon yourself that which I am sure you do not know, or jump the after-inquiry on your own peril; and how you shall speed in your journey's end, I think you'll never return to tell on. 180

POSTHUMUS. I tell thee, fellow, there are none want eyes to direct them the way I am going, but such as wink and will not use them.

1 GAOLER. What an infinite mock is this, that a man should have the best use of eyes to see the way of blindness! I am sure hanging's the way of winking. 190

Enter a Messenger

MESSENGER. Knock off his manacles; bring your prisoner to the king.

POSTHUMUS. Thou bringest good news, I am called to be made free.

1 GAOLER. I'll be hanged then.

POSTHUMUS. Thou shalt be then freer than a gaoler; no bolts for the dead.   *All but 1 Gaoler go*

1 GAOLER. Unless a man would marry a gallows and beget young gibbets, I never saw one so prone. Yet, on my conscience there are verier knaves desire to live, for all he be a Roman; and there be some of them too that die against their wills; so should I, if I were one. I would we were all of one mind, and one mind good. O, there were desolation of gaolers and gallowses! I speak against my present profit, but my wish hath a preferment in't.   *Goes* 200

Scene 5: *Cymbeline's tent*

Enter Cymbeline, Belarius, Guiderius, Arviragus, Pisanio, Lords, Officers, and Attendants

CYMBELINE. Stand by my side, you whom the gods have made
Preservers of my throne. Woe is my heart
That the poor soldier that so richly fought,
Whose rags shamed gilded arms, whose naked breast
Stepped before targes of proof, cannot be found.
He shall be happy that can find him, if
Our grace can make him so.

BELARIUS.   I never saw
Such noble fury in so poor a thing;
Such precious deeds in one that promised nought
But beggary and poor looks.

CYMBELINE.   No tidings of him? 10

PISANIO. He hath been searched among the dead and living,
But no trace of him.

CYMBELINE.   To my grief, I am
The heir of his reward; [*to Belarius, Guiderius, and Arviragus*] which I will add
To you, the liver, heart, and brain of Britain,
By whom I grant she lives. 'Tis now the time
To ask of whence you are. Report it.

BELARIUS.   Sir,
In Cambria are we born, and gentlemen;
Further to boast were neither true nor modest,
Unless I add, we are honest.

CYMBELINE.   Bow your knees.
Arise my knights o'th'battle; I create you
Companions to our person, and will fit you
With dignities becoming your estates. 20

Enter Cornelius and Ladies

There's business in these faces. Why so sadly
Greet you our victory? you look like Romans,
And not o'th'court of Britain

CORNELIUS.   Hail, great king!
To sour your happiness, I must report
The queen is dead.

CYMBELINE.   Who worse than a physician
Would this report become? But I consider,
By medicine life may be prolonged, yet death
Will seize the doctor too. How ended she? 30

CORNELIUS. With horror, madly dying, like her life,
Which, being cruel to the world, concluded
Most cruel to herself. What she confessed
I will report, so please you; these her women
Can trip me if I err, who with wet cheeks
Were present when she finished.

CYMBELINE.   Prithee say.

CORNELIUS. First, she confessed she never loved you; only
Affected greatness got by you, not you;
Married your royalty, was wife to your place;
Abhorred your person.

CYMBELINE.   She alone knew this; 40
And but she spoke it dying, I would not
Believe her lips in opening it. Proceed.

CORNELIUS. Your daughter whom she bore in hand to love
With such integrity, she did confess
Was as a scorpion to her sight; whose life,
But that her flight prevented it, she had
Ta'en off by poison.

CYMBELINE.   O most delicate fiend!
Who is't can read a woman? Is there more?

CORNELIUS. More, sir, and worse. She did confess she had
For you a mortal mineral, which, being took, 50
Should by the minute feed on life, and, ling'ring,
By inches waste you. In which time she purposed,
By watching, weeping, tendance, kissing, to
O'ercome you with her show; and in time,
When she had fitted you with her craft, to work
Her son into th'adoption of the crown;
But failing of her end by his strange absence,
Grew shameless-desperate; opened, in despite
Of heaven and men, her purposes; repented
The evils she hatched were not effected; so 60
Despairing died.

CYMBELINE.   Heard you all this, her women?

LADIES. We did, so please your highness.

CYMBELINE.   Mine eyes
Were not in fault, for she was beautiful;
Mine ears that heard her flattery, nor my heart
That thought her like her seeming. It had been vicious
To have mistrusted her; yet, O my daughter,
That it was folly in me thou mayst say,
And prove it in thy feeling. Heaven mend all!

Enter Lucius, Jachimo, the Soothsayer, and other Roman Prisoners, guarded; Posthumus behind, and Imogen

Thou com'st not, Caius, now for tribute; that
The Britons have razed out, though with the loss   70
Of many a bold one; whose kinsmen have made suit
That their good souls may be appeased with
    slaughter
Of you their captives, which ourself have granted;
So think of your estate.
LUCIUS.   Consider, sir, the chance of war; the day
Was yours by accident; had it gone with us,
We should not, when the blood was cool, have
    threatened
Our prisoners with the sword. But since the gods
Will have it thus, that nothing but our lives
May be called ransom, let it come. Sufficeth   80
A Roman with a Roman's heart can suffer.
Augustus lives to think on't; and so much
For my peculiar care. This one thing only
I will entreat: my boy, a Briton born,
Let him be ransomed. Never master had
A page so kind, so duteous, diligent,
So tender over his occasions, true,
So feat, so nurse-like; let his virtue join
With my request, which I'll make bold your
    highness
Cannot deny; he hath done no Briton harm   90
Though he have served a Roman. Save him, sir,
And spare no blood beside.
CYMBELINE.   I have surely seen him.
His favour is familiar to me. Boy,
Thou hast looked thyself into my grace,
And art mine own. I know not why, wherefore,
To say, 'Live, boy'. Ne'er thank thy master; live;
And ask of Cymbeline what boon thou wilt,
Fitting my bounty and thy state, I'll give it;
Yea, though thou do demand a prisoner,
The noblest ta'en.
IMOGEN.   I humbly thank your highness.   100
LUCIUS.   I do not bid thee beg my life, good lad,
And yet I know thou wilt.
IMOGEN.   No, no; alack,
There's other work in hand. I see a thing
Bitter to me as death; your life, good master,
Must shuffle for itself.
LUCIUS.   The boy disdains me,
He leaves me, scorns me. Briefly die their joys
That place them on the truth of girls and boys.
Why stands he so perplexed?
CYMBELINE.   What wouldst thou, boy?
I love thee more and more; think more and more
What's best to ask. Know'st him thou look'st on?
    speak,   110
Wilt have him live? Is he thy kin? thy friend?
IMOGEN.   He is a Roman, no more kin to me
Than I to your highness; who, being born your
    vassal,
Am something nearer.
CYMBELINE.   Wherefore ey'st him so?
IMOGEN.   I'll tell you, sir, in private, if you please
To give me hearing.
CYMBELINE.   Ay, with all my heart,
And lend my best attention. What's thy name?
IMOGEN.   Fidele, sir.
CYMBELINE.   Thou'rt my good youth, my page;
I'll be thy master. Walk with me; speak freely.
                        Cymbeline and Imogen walk
                                            aside

BELARIUS.   Is not this boy revived from death?
ARVIRAGUS.   One sand another   120
Not more resembles—that sweet rosy lad
Who died, and was Fidele. What think you?
GUIDERIUS.   The same dead thing alive.
BELARIUS.   Peace, peace, see further; he eyes us not;
    forbear;
Creatures may be alike; were't he, I am sure
He would have spoke to us.
GUIDERIUS.   But we saw him dead.
BELARIUS.   Be silent; let's see further.
PISANIO [aside].   It is my mistress.
Since she is living, let the time run on
To good or bad.
                        Cymbeline and Imogen come
                                            forward
CYMBELINE.   Come, stand thou by our side;
Make thy demand aloud. [to Jachimo] Sir, step you
    forth;   130
Give answer to this boy, and do it freely,
Or, by our greatness and the grace of it,
Which is our honour, bitter torture shall
Winnow the truth from falsehood. On, speak to
    him.
IMOGEN.   My boon is that this gentleman may render
Of whom he had this ring.
POSTHUMUS [aside].   What's that to him?
CYMBELINE.   That diamond upon your finger, say
How came it yours?
JACHIMO.   Thou'lt torture me to leave unspoken that
Which, to be spoke, would torture thee.
CYMBELINE.   How? me?   140
JACHIMO.   I am glad to be constrained to utter that
Torments me to conceal. By villainy
I got this ring; 'twas Leonatus' jewel,
Whom thou didst banish; and—which more may
    grieve thee,
As it doth me—a nobler sir ne'er lived
'Twixt sky and ground. Wilt thou hear more, my
    lord?
CYMBELINE.   All that belongs to this.
JACHIMO.   That paragon, thy daughter,
For whom my heart drops blood, and my false
    spirits
Quail to remember—Give me leave; I faint.
CYMBELINE.   My daughter? what of her? Renew thy
    strength;   150
I had rather thou shouldst live while nature will
Than die ere I hear more. Strive, man, and speak.
JACHIMO.   Upon a time—unhappy was the clock
That struck the hour!—it was in Rome—accursed
The mansion where!—'twas at a feast—O, would
Our viands had been poisoned, or at least
Those which I heaved to head!—the good
    Posthumus—
What should I say? he was too good to be
Where ill men were, and was the best of all
Amongst the rar'st of good ones—sitting sadly,   160
Hearing us praise our loves of Italy
For beauty that made barren the swelled boast
Of him that best could speak; for feature, laming
The shrine of Venus or straight-pight Minerva,
Postures beyond brief Nature; for condition,
A shop of all the qualities that man
Loves woman for; besides that hook of wiving,
Fairness which strikes the eye—

CYMBELINE. I stand on fire.
Come to the matter.
JACHIMO. All too soon I shall,
Unless thou wouldst grieve quickly. This
Posthumus,
Most like a noble lord in love and one
That had a royal lover, took his hint,
And not dispraising whom we praised—therein
He was as calm as virtue—he began
His mistress' picture; which by his tongue being
made,
And then a mind put in't, either our brags
Were cracked of kitchen-trulls, or his description
Proved us unspeaking sots.
CYMBELINE. Nay, nay, to th'purpose.
JACHIMO. Your daughter's chastity—there it begins.
He spake of her as Dian had hot dreams 180
And she alone were cold; whereat I, wretch,
Made scruple of his praise, and wagered with him
Pieces of gold 'gainst this which then he wore
Upon his honoured finger, to attain
In suit the place of's bed and win this ring
By hers and mine adultery. He, true knight,
No lesser of her honour confident
Than I did truly find her, stakes this ring;
And would so, had it been a carbuncle
Of Phœbus' wheel; and might so safely, had it 190
Been all the worth of's car. Away to Britain
Post I in this design. Well may you, sir,
Remember me at court; where I was taught
Of your chaste daughter the wide difference
'Twixt amorous and villainous. Being thus
quenched
Of hope, not longing, mine Italian brain
'Gan in your duller Britain operate
Most vilely; for my vantage, excellent.
And, to be brief, my practice so prevailed,
That I returned with simular proof enough 200
To make the noble Leonatus mad,
By wounding his belief in her renown
With tokens thus and thus; averring notes
Of chamber-hanging, pictures, this her bracelet—
O cunning, how I got it!—nay, some marks
Of secret on her person, that he could not
But think her bond of chastity quite cracked,
I having ta'en the forfeit. Whereupon—
Methinks I see him now—
POSTHUMUS [advancing]. Ay, so thou dost,
Italian fiend! Ay me, most credulous fool, 210
Egregious murderer, thief, any thing
That's due to all the villains past, in being,
To come! O, give me cord, or knife, or poison,
Some upright justicer! Thou, king, send out
For torturers ingenious: it is I
That all th'abhorréd things o'th'earth amend
By being worse than they. I am Posthumus,
That killed thy daughter; villain-like, I lie;
That caused a lesser villain than myself,
A sacrilegious thief, to do't. The temple 220
Of virtue was she; yea, and she herself.
Spit, and throw stones, cast mire upon me, set
The dogs o'th'street to bay me. Every villain
Be called Posthumus Leonatus, and
Be 'villain' less than 'twas! O Imogen!
My queen, my life, my wife! O Imogen,
Imogen, Imogen!

IMOGEN. Peace, my lord; hear, hear.
POSTHUMUS. Shall's have a play of this? Thou scornful
page,
There lie thy part. Strikes her: she falls
PISANIO. O gentlemen, help! 170
Mine and your mistress! O my lord Posthumus, 230
You ne'er killed Imogen till now. Help, help!
Mine honoured lady!
CYMBELINE. Does the world go round?
POSTHUMUS. How comes these staggers on me?
PISANIO. Wake, my mistress!
CYMBELINE. If this be so, the gods do mean to strike me
To death with mortal joy.
PISANIO. How fares my mistress?
IMOGEN. O, get thee from my sight;
Thou gavest me poison. Dangerous fellow, hence!
Breathe not where princes are.
CYMBELINE. The tune of Imogen.
PISANIO. Lady,
The gods throw stones of sulphur on me, if 240
That box I gave you was not thought by me
A precious thing; I had it from the queen.
CYMBELINE. New matter still.
IMOGEN. It poisoned me.
CORNELIUS. O gods!
I left out one thing which the queen confessed,
Which must approve thee honest: 'If Pisanio
Have' said she 'given his mistress that confection
Which I gave him for a cordial, she is served
As I would serve a rat.'
CYMBELINE. What's this, Cornelius?
CORNELIUS. The queen, sir, very oft importuned me
To temper poisons for her, still pretending 250
The satisfaction of her knowledge only
In killing creatures vile, as cats and dogs,
Of no esteem. I, dreading that her purpose
Was of more danger, did compound for her
A certain stuff which being ta'en would cease
The present power of life, but in short time
All offices of nature should again
Do their due functions. Have you ta'en of it?
IMOGEN. Most like I did, for I was dead.
BELARIUS. My boys,
There was our error.
GUIDERIUS. This is, sure, Fidele. 260
IMOGEN. Why did you throw your wedded lady from
you?
Think that you are upon a lock, and now
Throw me again. Embracing him
POSTHUMUS. Hang there like fruit, my soul,
Till the tree die!
CYMBELINE. How now, my flesh? my child?
What, mak'st thou me a dullard in this act?
Wilt thou not speak to me?
IMOGEN [kneeling]. Your blessing, sir.
BELARIUS [to Guiderius and Arviragus]. Though you did
love this youth, I blame ye not;
You had a motive for't.
CYMBELINE. My tears that fall
Prove holy water on thee! Imogen,
Thy mother's dead.
IMOGEN. I am sorry for't, my lord. 270
CYMBELINE. O, she was naught; and long of her it was
That we meet here so strangely; but her son
Is gone, we know not how or where.
PISANIO. My lord,

Now fear is from me, I'll speak troth. Lord Cloten,
Upon my lady's missing, came to me
With his sword drawn, foamed at the mouth, and
swore,
If I discovered not which way she was gone,
It was my instant death. By accident,
I had a feignéd letter of my master's
Then in my pocket, which directed him   280
To seek her on the mountains near to Milford;
Where, in a frenzy, in my master's garments,
Which he enforced from me, away he posts
With unchaste purpose, and with oath to violate
My lady's honour. What became of him
I further know not.
GUIDERIUS.   Let me end the story:
I slew him there.
CYMBELINE.   Marry, the gods forfend!
I would not thy good deeds should from my lips
Pluck a hard sentence. Prithee, valiant youth,
Deny't again.
GUIDERIUS.   I have spoke it, and I did it.   290
CYMBELINE. He was a prince.
GUIDERIUS. A most incivil one. The wrongs he did me
Were nothing prince-like; for he did provoke me
With language that would make me spurn the sea,
If it could so roar to me. I cut off's head,
And am right glad he is not standing here
To tell this tale of mine.
CYMBELINE.   I am sorrow for thee.
By thine own tongue thou art condemned, and must
Endure our law. Thou'rt dead.
IMOGEN.   That headless man
I thought had been my lord.
CYMBELINE.   Bind the offender,   300
And take him from our presence.
BELARIUS.   Stay, sir king.
This man is better than the man he slew,
As well descended as thyself, and hath
More of thee merited than a band of Clotens
Had ever scar for. [to the guard] Let his arms alone;
They were not born for bondage.
CYMBELINE.   Why, old soldier:
Wilt thou undo the worth thou art unpaid for,
By tasting of our wrath? How of descent
As good as we?
ARVIRAGUS.   In that he spake too far.
CYMBELINE. And thou shalt die for't.
BELARIUS.   We will die all three   310
But I will prove that two on's are as good
As I have given out him. My sons, I must
For mine own part unfold a dangerous speech,
Though haply well for you.
ARVIRAGUS.   Your danger's ours.
GUIDERIUS. And our good his.
BELARIUS.   Have at it then; by leave,
Thou hadst, great king, a subject who
Was called Belarius.
CYMBELINE.   What of him? he is
A banished traitor.
BELARIUS.   He it is that hath
Assumed this age; indeed a banished man,
I know not how a traitor.
CYMBELINE.   Take him hence;   320
The whole world shall not save him.
BELARIUS.   Not too hot;
First pay me for the nursing of thy sons,

And let it be confiscate all, so soon
As I have received it.
CYMBELINE.   Nursing of my sons?
BELARIUS. I am too blunt and saucy: here's my knee.
Ere I arise I will prefer my sons,
Then spare not the old father. Mighty sir,
These two young gentlemen that call me father,
And think they are my sons, are none of mine;
They are the issue of your loins, my liege,   330
And blood of your begetting.
CYMBELINE.   How? my issue?
BELARIUS. So sure as you your father's. I, old Morgan,
Am that Belarius whom you sometime banished.
Your pleasure was my mere offence, my
punishment
Itself, and all my treason; that I suffered
Was all the harm I did. These gentle princes—
For such and so they are—these twenty years
Have I trained up; those arts they have as I
Could put into them. My breeding was, sir, as
Your highness knows. Their nurse, Euriphile,   340
Whom for the theft I wedded, stole these children
Upon my banishment; I moved her to't,
Having received the punishment before
For that which I did then. Beaten for loyalty
Excited me to treason. Their dear loss,
The more of you 'twas felt, the more it shaped
Unto my end of stealing them. But gracious sir,
Here are your sons again, and I must lose
Two of the sweet'st companions in the world.
The benediction of these covering heavens   350
Fall on their heads like dew! for they are worthy
To inlay heaven with stars.
CYMBELINE.   Thou weep'st, and speak'st.
The service that you three have done is more
Unlike than this thou tell'st. I lost my children;
If these be they, I know not how to wish
A pair of worthier sons.
BELARIUS.   Be pleased awhile.
This gentleman, whom I call Polydore,
Most worthy prince, as yours, is true Guiderius;
This gentleman, my Cadwal, Arviragus,
Your younger princely son; he, sir, was lapped   360
In a most curious mantle, wrought by th'hand
Of his queen mother, which for more probation
I can with ease produce.
CYMBELINE.   Guiderius had
Upon his neck a mole, a sanguine star;
It was a mark of wonder.
BELARIUS.   This is he,
Who hath upon him still that natural stamp.
It was wise nature's end in the donation,
To be his evidence now.
CYMBELINE.   O, what am I?
A mother to the birth of three? Ne'er mother
Rejoiced deliverance more. Blest pray you be,   370
That, after this strange starting from your orbs,
You may reign in them now! O Imogen,
Thou hast lost by this a kingdom.
IMOGEN.   No, my lord;
I have got two worlds by't. O my gentle brothers,
Have we thus met? O, never say hereafter
But I am truest speaker: you called me brother,
When I was but your sister; I you brothers,
When ye were so indeed.
CYMBELINE.   Did you e'er meet?

ARVIRAGUS. Ay, my good lord.

GUIDERIUS.   And at first meeting loved,
Continued so until we thought he died.   380

CORNELIUS. By the queen's dram she swallowed.

CYMBELINE.   O rare instinct!
When shall I hear all through? This fierce
   abridgement
Hath to it circumstantial branches which
Distinction should be rich in. Where? how lived
   you?
And when came you to serve our Roman captive?
How parted with your brothers? how first met
   them?
Why fled you from the court? and whither? These,
And your three motives to the battle, with
I know not how much more, should be demanded,
And all the other by-dependences,   390
From chance to chance; but nor the time nor place
Will serve our long inter'gatories. See
Posthumus anchors upon Imogen;
And she, like harmless lightning, throws her eye
On him, her brothers, me, her master, hitting
Each object with a joy; the counterchange
Is severally in all. Let's quit this ground,
And smoke the temple with our sacrifices.
[to Belarius] Thou art my brother; so we'll hold thee
   ever.

IMOGEN. You are my father too, and did relieve me   400
To see this gracious season.

CYMBELINE.   All o'erjoyed,
Save these in bonds; let them be joyful too,
For they shall taste our comfort.

IMOGEN.   My good master,
I will yet do you service.

LUCIUS.   Happy be you!

CYMBELINE. The forlorn soldier that so nobly fought,
He would have well becomed this place and graced
The thankings of a king.

POSTHUMUS.   I am, sir,
The soldier that did company these three
In poor beseeming; 'twas a fitment for
The purpose I then followed. That I was he,   410
Speak, Jachimo. I had you down, and might
Have made you finish.

JACHIMO [kneeling].   I am down again;
But now my heavy conscience sinks my knee,
As then your force did. Take that life, beseech you,
Which I so often owe; but your ring first,
And here the bracelet of the truest princess
That ever swore her faith.

POSTHUMUS.   Kneel not to me.
The power that I have on you is to spare you;
The malice towards you to forgive you. Live,
And deal with others better.

CYMBELINE.   Nobly doomed!   420
We'll learn our freeness of a son-in-law;
Pardon's the word to all.

ARVIRAGUS.   You holp us, sir,
As you did mean indeed to be our brother;
Joyed are we that you are.

POSTHUMUS. Your servant, princes. Good my lord of
   Rome,
Call forth your soothsayer. As I slept, methought
Great Jupiter, upon his eagle backed,
Appeared to me, with other spritely shows

Of mine own kindred. When I waked, I found
This label on my bosom; whose containing   430
Is so from sense in hardness that I can
Make no collection of it. Let him show
His skill in the construction.

LUCIUS.   Philarmonus!

SOOTHSAYER. Here, my good lord.

LUCIUS.   Read, and declare the meaning.

SOOTHSAYER [reads]. 'When as a lion's whelp shall, to
himself unknown, without seeking find, and be
embraced by a piece of tender air; and when from a
stately cedar shall be lopped branches which, being
dead many years, shall after revive, be jointed to the
old stock, and freshly grow; then shall Posthumus   440
end his miseries, Britain be fortunate and flourish in
peace and plenty.'
Thou, Leonatus, art the lion's whelp;
The fit and apt construction of thy name,
Being Leo-natus, doth import so much.
[to Cymbeline] The piece of tender air, thy virtuous
   daughter,
Which we call 'mollis aer'; and 'mollis aer'
We term it 'mulier'; [to Posthumus] which 'mulier'
   I divine
Is this most constant wife; who even now,
Answering the letter of the oracle,   450
Unknown to you, unsought, were clipped about
With this most tender air.

CYMBELINE.   This hath some seeming.

SOOTHSAYER. The lofty cedar, royal Cymbeline,
Personates thee; and thy lopped branches point
Thy two sons forth, who, by Belarius stol'n,
For many years thought dead, are now revived,
To the majestic cedar joined, whose issue
Promises Britain peace and plenty.

CYMBELINE.   Well;
My peace we will begin. And, Caius Lucius,
Although the victor, we submit to Cæsar   460
And to the Roman empire, promising
To pay our wonted tribute, from the which
We were dissuaded by our wicked queen,
Whom heavens in justice both on her and hers
Have laid most heavy hand.

SOOTHSAYER. The fingers of the powers above do tune
The harmony of this peace. The vision,
Which I made known to Lucius ere the stroke
Of this yet scarce-cold battle, at this instant
Is full accomplished; for the Roman eagle,   470
From south to west on wing soaring aloft,
Lessened herself, and in the beams o'th'sun
So vanished; which foreshowed our princely eagle,
Th'imperial Cæsar, should again unite
His favour with the radiant Cymbeline,
Which shines here in the west.

CYMBELINE.   Laud we the gods,
And let our crookéd smokes climb to their nostrils
From our blest altars. Publish we this peace
To all our subjects. Set we forward; let
A Roman and a British ensign wave   480
Friendly together; so through Lud's town march,
And in the temple of great Jupiter
Our peace we'll ratify; seal it with feasts.
Set on there. Never was a war did cease,
Ere bloody hands were washed, with such a peace.

They go

Pericles, Prince of Tyre

The scene: dispersedly in various countries

CHARACTERS IN THE PLAY

ANTIOCHUS, *King of Antioch*
PERICLES, *Prince of Tyre*
HELICANUS }
ESCANES } *two lords of Tyre*
SIMONIDES, *King of Pentapolis*
CLEON, *Governor of Tharsus*
LYSIMACHUS, *Governor of Mytilene*
CERIMON, *a lord of Ephesus*
THALIARD, *a lord of Antioch*
PHILEMON, *servant to Cerimon*
LEONINE, *servant to Dionyza*
Marshal

A Pandar
BOULT, *his servant*
The daughter of Antiochus
DIONYZA, *wife to Cleon*
THAISA, *daughter to Simonides*
MARINA, *daughter to Pericles and Thaisa*
LYCHORIDA, *nurse to Marina*
A Bawd
Lords, Knights, Gentlemen, Sailors, Pirates, Fishermen,
  and Messengers
DIANA
GOWER, *as Chorus*

Pericles, Prince of Tyre

ACT 1

Prologue: *Before the palace of Antioch, with heads displayed above the entrance*

Enter Gower, as Chorus

GOWER. To sing a song that old was sung,
From ashes ancient Gower is come,
Assuming man's infirmities,
To glad your ear and please your eyes.
It hath been sung at festivals,
On ember-eves and holy ales;
And lords and ladies in their lives
Have read it for restoratives;
The purchase is to make men glorious;
Et bonum quo antiquius, eo melius. 10
If you, born in these latter times
When wit's more ripe, accept my rhymes,
And that to hear an old man sing
May to your wishes pleasure bring,
I life would wish, and that I might
Waste it for you like taper-light.
This Antioch, then; Antiochus the great
Built up this city for his chiefest seat,
The fairest in all Syria;
I tell you what mine authors say: 20
This king unto him took a fere,
Who died and left a female heir,
So buxom, blithe and full of face
As heaven had lent her all his grace;
With whom the father liking took,
And her to incest did provoke.
Bad child, worse father, to entice his own
To evil should be done by none.
But custom what they did begin
Made with long use account no sin. 30
The beauty of this sinful dame
Made many princes thither frame,
To seek her as a bed-fellow,
In marriage-pleasures play-fellow;
Which to prevent he made a law,
To keep her still and men in awe,
That whoso asked her for his wife,
His riddle told not, lost his life.
So for her many a wight did die,
As yon grim looks do testify. 40
What now ensues, to the judgement of your eye
I give my cause, who best can justify. *He goes*

Scene 1

Enter Antiochus, Prince Pericles and followers

ANTIOCHUS. Young Prince of Tyre, you have at large received
The danger of the task you undertake.
PERICLES. I have, Antiochus, and, with a soul
Embold'ned with the glory of her praise,
Think death no hazard in this enterprise.
ANTIOCHUS. Bring in our daughter, clothéd like a bride,

For the embracements even of Jove himself;
At whose conception, till Lucina reigned,
Nature this dowry gave: to glad her presence,
The senate-house of planets all did sit, 10
To knit in her their best perfections.

Music. Enter Antiochus' Daughter

PERICLES. See where she comes, apparelled like the spring,
Graces her subjects, and her thoughts the king
Of every virtue gives renown to men!
Her face the book of praises, where is read
Nothing but curious pleasures, as from thence
Sorrow were ever razed, and testy wrath
Could never be her mild companion.
You gods that made me man and sway in love,
That have inflamed desire in my breast 20
To taste the fruit of yon celestial tree
Or die in the adventure, be my helps,
As I am son and servant to your will,
To compass such a boundless happiness!
ANTIOCHUS. Prince Pericles—
PERICLES. That would be son to great Antiochus.
ANTIOCHUS. Before thee stands this fair Hesperides,
With golden fruit, but dangerous to be touched;
For death-like dragons here affright thee hard.
Her face, like heaven, enticeth thee to view 30
Her countless glory, which desert must gain;
And which without desert because thine eye
Presumes to reach, all the whole heap must die.
Yon sometimes famous princes, like thyself,
Drawn by report, advent'rous by desire,
Tell thee, with speechless tongues and semblance pale,
That without covering save yon field of stars,
Here they stand martyrs, slain in Cupid's wars;
And with dead cheeks advise thee to desist
For going on death's net, whom none resist. 40
PERICLES. Antiochus, I thank thee, who hath taught
My frail mortality to know itself,
And by those fearful objects to prepare
This body, like to them, to what I must;
For death remembered should be like a mirror,
Who tells us life's but breath, to trust it error.
I'll make my will then, and, as sick men do,
Who know the world, see heaven, but feeling woe
Gripe not at earthly joys as erst they did,
So I bequeath a happy peace to you 50
And all good men, as every prince should do;
My riches to the earth from whence they came;
But my unspotted fire of love to you.
To the princess
Thus ready for the way of life or death,
I wait the sharpest blow, Antiochus.
ANTIOCHUS. Scorning advice, read the conclusion then:
Which read and not expounded, 'tis decreed,
As these before thee thou thyself shalt bleed.
DAUGHTER. Of all 'sayed yet, mayst thou prove prosperous!

Of all 'sayed yet, I wish thee happiness!
PERICLES. Like a bold champion I assume the lists,
Nor ask advice of any other thought
But faithfulness and courage.

He reads the riddle

    'I am no viper, yet I feed
    On mother's flesh that did me breed.
    I sought a husband, in which labour
    I found that kindness from a father.
    He's father, son, and husband mild;
    I mother, wife, and yet his child.
    How this may be, and yet in two,   70
    As you will live, resolve it you.'
[aside] Sharp physic is the last: but, O you powers
That gives heaven countless eyes to view men's acts,
Why cloud they not their sights perpetually,
If this be true, which makes me pale to read it?
Fair glass of light, I loved you, and could still,
Were not this glorious casket stored with ill.
But I must tell you, now my thoughts revolt;
For he's no man on whom perfections wait
That, knowing sin within, will touch the gate.   80
You are a fair viol and your sense the strings,
Who, fingered to make man his lawful music,
Would draw heaven down and all the gods to
    hearken,
But being played upon before your time,
Hell only danceth at so harsh a chime.
Good sooth, I care not for you.
ANTIOCHUS. Prince Pericles, touch not, upon thy life,
For that's an article within our law,
As dangerous as the rest. Your time's expired:
Either expound now or receive your sentence.   90
PERICLES. Great king,
Few love to hear the sins they love to act;
'Twould braid yourself too near for me to tell it.
Who has a book of all that monarchs do,
He's more secure to keep it shut than shown;
For vice repeated is like the wand'ring wind,
Blows dust in others' eyes, to spread itself;
And yet the end of all is bought thus dear,
The breath is gone, and the sore eyes see clear
To stop the air would hurt them. The blind mole
    casts   100
Copped hills towards heaven, to tell the earth is
    thronged
By man's oppression; and the poor worm doth die
    for't.
Kings are earth's gods; in vice their law's their will;
And if Jove stray, who dares say Jove doth ill?
It is enough you know; and it is fit,
What being more known grows worse, to smother
    it.
All love the womb that their first being bred,
Then give my tongue like leave to love my head.
ANTIOCHUS [aside]. Heaven, that I had thy head! He has
    found the meaning
But I will gloze with him. [aloud] Young prince of
    Tyre,   110
Though by the tenour of our strict edict,
Your exposition misinterpreting,
We might proceed to cancel of your days;
Yet hope, succeeding from so fair a tree
As your fair self, doth tune us otherwise.
Forty days longer we do respite you;

If by which time our secret be undone,   60
This mercy shows we'll joy in such a son;
And until then your entertain shall be
As doth befit our honour and your worth.   120
                            All but Pericles go
PERICLES. How courtesy would seem to cover sin,
When what is done is like an hypocrite,
The which is good in nothing but in sight!
If it be true that I interpret false,
Then were it certain you were not so bad
As with foul incest to abuse your soul;
Where now you're both a father and a son,
By your uncomely claspings with your child,
Which pleasures fits a husband, not a father;
And she an eater of her mother's flesh,   130
By the defiling of her parents' bed;
And both like serpents are, who though they feed
On sweetest flowers, yet they poison breed.
Antioch, farewell! for wisdom sees, those men
Blush not in actions blacker than the night,
Will shun no course to keep them from the light.
One sin, I know, another doth provoke;
Murder's as near to lust as flame to smoke.
Poison and treason are the hands of sin,
Ay, and the targets, to put off the shame.   140
Then, lest my life be cropped to keep you clear,
By flight I'll shun the danger which I fear.   *He goes*

Re-enter Antiochus

ANTIOCHUS. He hath found the meaning,
For which we mean to have his head.
He must not live to trumpet forth my infamy,
Nor tell the world Antiochus doth sin
In such a loathéd manner;
And therefore instantly this prince must die;
For by his fall my honour must keep high.
Who attends us there?   150

Enter Thaliard

THALIARD. Doth your highness call?
ANTIOCHUS. Thaliard, you are of our chamber,
    Thaliard,
And our mind partakes her private actions
To your secrecy; and for your faithfulness
We will advance you, Thaliard.
Behold, here's poison, and here's gold;
We hate the prince of Tyre, and thou must kill him:
It fits thee not to ask the reason why;
Because we bid it. Say, is it done?
THALIARD. My lord, 'tis done.
ANTIOCHUS.   Enough.   160

Enter a Messenger

Let your breath cool yourself, telling your haste.
MESSENGER. My lord, prince Pericles is fled.   *He goes*
ANTIOCHUS. As thou wilt live, fly after; and like an
arrow shot from a well experienced archer hits the
mark his eye doth level at, so thou never return
unless thou say 'Prince Pericles is dead.'
THALIARD. My lord, if I can get him within my pistol's
length, I'll make him sure enough: so, farewell to
your highness.
ANTIOCHUS. Thaliard, adieu! [Thaliard goes] Till
    Pericles be dead,   170
My heart can lend no succour to my head.
                                     He goes

Scene 2: *Tyre. A room in the palace*

Enter Pericles

PERICLES [*to lords without*]. Let none disturb us. Why
  should this change of thoughts.
  The sad companion, dull-eyed melancholy,
  Be my so used a guest as not an hour
  In the day's glorious walk, or peaceful night,
  The tomb where grief should sleep, can breed me
    quiet?
  Here pleasures court mine eyes, and mine eyes
    shun them,
  And danger, which I feared, is at Antioch,
  Whose arm seems far too short to hit me here;
  Yet neither pleasure's art can joy my spirits,
  Nor yet the other's distance comfort me.   10
  Then it is thus: the passions of the mind,
  That have their first conception by misdread,
  Have after-nourishment and life by care;
  And what was first but fear what might be done,
  Grows elder now and cares it be not done.
  And so with me: the great Antiochus,
  'Gainst whom I am too little to contend,
  Since he's so great can make his will his act,
  Will think me speaking, though I swear to silence;
  Nor boots it me to say I honour him,   20
  If he suspect I may dishonour him.
  And what may make him blush in being known,
  He'll stop the course by which it might be known;
  With hostile forces he'll o'erspread the land,
  And with th'ostent of war will look so huge,
  Amazement shall drive courage from the state,
  Our men be vanquished ere they do resist,
  And subjects punished that ne'er thought offence:
  Which care of them, not pity of myself,
  Who am no more but as the tops of trees   30
  Which fence the roots they grow by and defend
    them,
  Makes both my body pine and soul to languish,
  And punish that before that he would punish.

Enter Helicanus, with other Lords

FIRST LORD. Joy and all comfort in your sacred breast!
SECOND LORD. And keep your mind, till you return to
  us,
  Peaceful and comfortable!
HELICANUS. Peace, peace, and give experience tongue.
  They do abuse the king that flatter him:
  For flattery is the bellows blows up sin;
  The thing the which is flattered, but a spark,   40
  To which that blast gives heat and stronger glowing;
  Whereas reproof, obedient and in order,
  Fits kings, as they are men, for they may err.
  When Signior Soothe here does proclaim a peace,
  He flatters you, makes war upon your life.
  Prince, pardon me, or strike me, if you please;
                              Kneeling
  I cannot be much lower than my knees.
PERICLES. All leave us else; but let your cares o'erlook
  What shipping and what lading's in our haven,
  And then return to us. [*the lords go*] Helicanus, thou   50
  Hast movéd us: what seest thou in our looks?
HELICANUS. An angry brow, dread lord.
PERICLES. If there be such a dart in princes' frowns,
  How durst thy tongue move anger to our face?
HELICANUS. How dares the plants look up to heaven,

From whence they have their nourishment?
PERICLES. Thou knowest I have power to take thy life
  from thee.
HELICANUS. I have ground the axe myself;
  Do but you strike the blow.
PERICLES. Rise, prithee, rise; sit down; thou art no
  flatterer;   60
  I thank thee for't; and heaven forbid
  That kings should let their ears hear their faults hid!
  Fit counsellor and servant for a prince,
  Who by thy wisdom makes a prince thy servant,
  What wouldst thou have me do?
HELICANUS.   To bear with patience
  Such griefs as you do lay upon yourself.
PERICLES. Thou speak'st like a physician, Helicanus,
  That ministers a potion unto me
  That thou wouldst tremble to receive thyself.
  Attend me then: I went to Antioch,   70
  Where as thou know'st against the face of death
  I sought the purchase of a glorious beauty,
  From whence an issue I might propagate,
  Are arms to princes and bring joys to subjects.
  Her face was to mine eye beyond all wonder;
  The rest—hark in thine ear—as black as incest;
  Which by my knowledge found, the sinful father
  Seemed not to strike, but smooth; but thou know'st
    this,
  'Tis time to fear when tyrants seems to kiss.
  Which fear so grew in me, I hither fled,   80
  Under the covering of a careful night,
  Who seemed my good protector; and, being here,
  Bethought me what was past, what might succeed.
  I knew him tyrannous; and tyrants' fears
  Decrease not, but grow faster than the years;
  And should he doubt, as 'tis no doubt he doth,
  That I should open to the list'ning air
  How many worthy princes' bloods were shed,
  To keep his bed of blackness un-laid-ope,
  To lop that doubt, he'll fill this land with arms,   90
  And make pretence of wrong that I have done him;
  When all, for mine, if I may call offence,
  Must feel war's blow, who spares not innocence:
  Which love to all, of which thyself art one,
  Who now reprovedst me for't,—
HELICANUS.   Alas, sir!
PERICLES. Drew sleep out of mine eyes, blood from my
  cheeks,
  Musings into my mind, with thousand doubts
  How I might stop this tempest ere it came;
  And finding little comfort to relieve them,
  I thought it princely charity to grieve them.   100
HELICANUS. Well, my lord, since you have given me
  leave to speak,
  Freely will I speak. Antiochus you fear,
  And justly, too, I think you fear the tyrant
  Who either by public war or private treason
  Will take away your life.
  Therefore, my lord, go travel for a while,
  Till that his rage and anger be forgot,
  Or till the Destinies do cut his thread of life.
  Your rule direct to any; if to me,
  Day serves not light more faithful than I'll be.   110
PERICLES. I do not doubt thy faith;
  But should he wrong my liberties in my absence?
HELICANUS. We'll mingle our bloods together in the
  earth,

From whence we had our being and our birth.
PERICLES. Tyre, I now look from thee then, and to Tharsus
Intend my travel, where I'll hear from thee;
And by whose letters I'll dispose myself.
The care I had and have of subjects' good
On thee I lay, whose wisdom's strength can bear it.
I'll take thy word for faith, not ask thine oath: 120
Who shuns not to break one will crack them both.
But in our orbs we'll live so round and safe,
That time of both this truth shall ne'er convince,
Thou show'dst a subject's shine, I a true prince'.

They go

Scene 3: *Tyre. An ante-chamber in the palace*

Enter Thaliard solus

THALIARD. So, this is Tyre, and this the court. Here must I kill King Pericles; and if I do it not, I am sure to be hanged at home: 'tis dangerous. Well, I perceive he was a wise fellow and had good discretion, that, being bid to ask what he would of the king, desired he might know none of his secrets: now do I see he had some reason for't; for if a king bid a man be a villain, he's bound by the indenture of his oath to be one. Husht! here comes the lords of Tyre.

Enter Helicanus, Escanes, with other Lords

HELICANUS. You shall not need, my fellow peers of Tyre,   10
Further to question of your king's departure.
His sealed commission left in trust with me
Does speak sufficiently he's gone to travel.
THALIARD [*aside*]. How? the king gone?
HELICANUS. If further yet you will be satisfied,
Why, as it were unlicensed of your loves,
He would depart, I'll give some light unto you.
Being at Antioch—
THALIARD [*aside*].   What from Antioch?
HELICANUS. Royal Antiochus—on what cause I know not—
Took some displeasure at him; at least he judged so;   20
And doubting lest that he had erred or sinned,
To show his sorrow, he'ld correct himself;
So puts himself unto the shipman's toil,
With whom each minute threatens life or death.
THALIARD [*aside*]. Well, I perceive I shall not be hanged now, although I would;
But since he's gone, the king's ears it must please;
He scaped the land, to perish at the seas.
I'll present myself. Peace to the lords of Tyre!
HELICANUS. Lord Thaliard from Antiochus is welcome.
THALIARD. From him I come   30
With message unto princely Pericles;
But since my landing I have understood
Your lord has betook himself to unknown travels,
My message must return from whence it came.
HELICANUS. We have no reason to desire it,
Commended to our master, not to us;
Yet, ere you shall depart, this we desire,
As friends to Antioch, we may feast in Tyre.

They go

Scene 4: *Tharsus. A room in the Governor's house*

Enter Cleon the Governor of Tharsus, with his wife Dionyza and others

CLEON. My Dionyza, shall we rest us here,
And by relating tales of others' griefs,
See if 'twill teach us to forget our own?
DIONYZA. That were to blow at fire in hope to quench it;
For who digs hills because they do aspire
Throws down one mountain to cast up a higher.
O my distresséd lord, even such our griefs are;
Here they are but felt, and seen with mischief's eyes,
But like to groves, being topped, they higher rise.
CLEON. O Dionyza,   10
Who wanteth food, and will not say he wants it,
Or can conceal his hunger till he famish?
Our tongues and sorrows to sound deep
Our woes into the air; our eyes to weep,
Till tongues fetch breath that may proclaim them louder;
That, if heaven slumber while their creatures want,
They may awake their helps to comfort them.
I'll then discourse our woes, felt several years,
And wanting breath to speak help me with tears.
DIONYZA. I'll do my best, sir.   20
CLEON. This Tharsus, o'er which I have the government,
A city on whom plenty held full hand,
For riches strewed herself even in her streets;
Whose towers bore heads so high they kissed the clouds,
And strangers ne'er beheld but wond'red at;
Whose men and dames so jetted and adorned,
Like one another's glass to trim them by;
Their tables were stored full, to glad the sight,
And not so much to feed on as delight;
All poverty was scorned, and pride so great,   30
The name of help grew odious to repeat.
DIONYZA. O, 'tis too true.
CLEON. But see what heaven can do by this our change:
Those mouths, who but of late earth, sea and air
Were all too little to content and please,
Although they gave their creatures in abundance,
As houses are defiled for want of use,
They are now starved for want of exercise;
Those palates who, not yet two summers younger,
Must have inventions to delight the taste,   40
Would now be glad of bread, and beg for it;
Those mothers who, to nuzzle up their babes,
Thought nought too curious, are ready now
To eat those little darlings whom they loved.
So sharp are hunger's teeth, that man and wife
Draw lots who first shall die to lengthen life;
Here stands a lord, and there a lady weeping;
Here many sink, yet those which see them fall
Have scarce strength left to give them burial.
Is not this true?   50
DIONYZA. Our cheeks and hollow eyes do witness it.
CLEON. O, let those cities that of plenty's cup
And her prosperities so largely taste,
With their superfluous riots, hear these tears!
The misery of Tharsus may be theirs.

LORD. Where's the lord governor?
CLEON. Here.
  Speak out thy sorrows which thou bring'st in haste,
  For comfort is too far for us to expect.
LORD. We have descried, upon our neighbouring
    shore, 60
  A portly sail of ships make hitherward.
CLEON. I thought all as much.
  One sorrow never comes but brings an heir,
  That may succeed as his inheritor;
  And so in ours: some neighbouring nation,
  Taking advantage of our misery,
  Hath stuffed the hollow vessels with their power,
  To beat us down, the which are down already,
  And make a conquest of unhappy men,
  Whereas no glory's got to overcome. 70
LORD. That's the least fear; for, by the semblance
  Of their white flags displayed, they bring us peace,
  And come to us as favourers, not as foes.
CLEON. Thou speak'st like him's untutored to repeat:
  Who makes the fairest show means most deceit.
  But bring they what they will, what need we fear?
  On ground's the lowest, and we are half way there.
  Go tell their general we attend him here,
  To know for what he comes and whence he comes
  And what he craves. 80
LORD. I go, my lord. *He goes*
CLEON. Welcome is peace, if he on peace consist;
  If wars, we are unable to resist.

Enter Pericles with Attendants

PERICLES. Lord governor, for so we hear you are,
  Let not our ships and number of our men
  Be like a beacon fired t'amaze your eyes.
  We have heard your miseries as far as Tyre,
  And seen the desolation of your streets;
  Nor come we to add sorrow to your tears,
  But to relieve them of their heavy load; 90
  And these our ships, you happily may think
  Are like the Trojan horse was stuffed within
  With bloody veins expecting overthrow,
  Are stored with corn to make your needy bread,
  And give them life whom hunger starved half dead.
ALL. The gods of Greece protect you!
  And we'll pray for you.
PERICLES. Arise, I pray you, rise;
  We do not look for reverence, but for love
  And harbourage for ourself, our ships and men.
CLEON. The which when any shall not gratify, 100
  Or pay you with unthankfulness in thought,
  Be it our wives, our children, or ourselves,
  The curse of heaven and men succeed their evils!
  Till when,—the which I hope shall ne'er be seen—
  Your grace is welcome to our town and us.
PERICLES. Which welcome we'll accept; feast here
    awhile,
  Until our stars that frown lend us a smile.
        They go

ACT 2
Prologue

Enter Gower

GOWER. Here have you seen a mighty king
  His child, I wis, to incest bring;
  A better prince and benign lord
  Prove awful both in deed and word.
  Be quiet then as men should be,
  Till he hath passed necessity.
  I'll show you those in trouble's reign
  Losing a mite, a mountain gain.
  The good in conversation,
  To whom I give my benison, 10
  Is still at Tharsus, where each man
  Thinks all is writ he spoken can;
  And, to remember what he does,
  Build his statue to make him glorious.
  But tidings to the contrary
  Are brought your eyes; what need speak I?

Dumb Show

*Enter, at one door, Pericles, talking with Cleon; all the
train with them. Enter, at another door, a Gentleman, with
a letter to Pericles; Pericles shows the letter to Cleon,
Pericles gives the Messenger a reward, and knights him.
Exit Pericles at one door, and Cleon at another*

  Good Helicane, that stayed at home,
  Not to eat honey like a drone
  From others' labours; for though he strive
  To killen bad, keep good alive; 20
  And to fulfil his prince' desire,
  Sends word of all that haps in Tyre:
  How Thaliard came full bent with sin
  And had intent to murder him;
  And that in Tharsus was not best
  Longer for him to make his rest.
  He, doing so, put forth to seas,
  Where when men been, there's seldom ease;
  For now the wind begins to blow;
  Thunder above and deeps below 30
  Makes such unquiet that the ship
  Should house him safe is wrecked and split;
  And he, good prince, having all lost,
  By waves from coast to coast is tossed.
  All perishen of man, of pelf,
  Ne aught escapened but himself;
  Till fortune, tired with doing bad,
  Threw him ashore, to give him glad.
  And here he comes. What shall be next,
  Pardon old Gower,—this 'longs the text. *He goes* 40

Scene 1: *Pentapolis. An open place by the sea-side*

Enter Pericles, wet

PERICLES. Yet cease your ire, you angry stars of heaven!
  Wind, rain, and thunder, remember, earthly man
  Is but a substance that must yield to you;
  And I, as fits my nature, do obey you.
  Alas, the seas hath cast me on the rocks,
  Washed me from shore to shore, and left me breath
  Nothing to think on but ensuing death.
  Let it suffice the greatness of your powers
  To have bereft a prince of all his fortunes;
  And having thrown him from your wat'ry grave, 10
  Here to have death in peace is all he'll crave.

Enter three Fishermen

1 FISHERMAN. What, ho, Pilch!
2 FISHERMAN. Ha, come and bring away the nets!
1 FISHERMAN. What, Patchbreech, I say!

3 FISHERMAN. What say you, master?

1 FISHERMAN. Look how thou stirrest now! come away, or I'll fetch thee with a wanion.

3 FISHERMAN. Faith, master, I am thinking of the poor men that were cast away before us even now.

1 FISHERMAN. Alas, poor souls, it grieved my heart to hear what pitiful cries they made to us to help them, when, well-a-day, we could scarce help ourselves. 20

3 FISHERMAN. Nay, master, said not I as much when I saw the porpoise, how he bounced and tumbled? they say they're half fish, half flesh: a plague on them, they ne'er come but I look to be washed. Master, I marvel how the fishes live in the sea.

1 FISHERMAN. Why, as men do a-land: the great ones eat up the little ones. I can compare our rich misers to nothing so fitly as to a whale; a' plays and tumbles, 30 driving the poor fry before him, and at last devours them all at a mouthful: such whales have I heard on a'th'land, who never leave gaping till they ha' swallowed the whole parish, church, steeple, bells, and all.

PERICLES [aside]. A pretty moral.

3 FISHERMAN. But, master, if I had been the sexton, I would have been that day in the belfry.

2 FISHERMAN. Why, man?

3 FISHERMAN. Because he should have swallowed me 40 too; and when I had been in his belly, I would have kept such a jangling of the bells, that he should never have left till he cast bells, steeple, church, and parish, up again. But if the good King Simonides were of my mind,—

PERICLES [aside]. Simonides?

3 FISHERMAN. We would purge the land of these drones, that rob the bee of her honey.

PERICLES [aside]. How from the finny subject of the sea These fishers tell the infirmities of men; 50 And from their wat'ry empire recollect All that may men approve or men detect! Peace be at your labour, honest fishermen.

2 FISHERMAN. Honest! good fellow, what's that? If it be a day fits you, search out of the calendar, and nobody look after it.

PERICLES. May see the sea hath cast upon your coast—

2 FISHERMAN. What a drunken knave was the sea to cast thee in our way!

PERICLES. A man whom both the waters and the wind, 60 In that vast tennis-court, hath made the ball For them to play upon, entreats you pity him; He asks of you, that never used to beg.

1 FISHERMAN. No, friend, cannot you beg? Here's them in our country of Greece gets more with begging than we can do with working.

2 FISHERMAN. Canst thou catch any fishes then?

PERICLES. I never practised it.

2 FISHERMAN. Nay, then thou wilt starve, sure; for here's nothing to be got now-a-days, unless thou 70 canst fish for't.

PERICLES. What I have been I have forgot to know; But what I am, want teaches me to think on: A man thronged up with cold; my veins are chill, And have no more of life than may suffice To give my tongue that heat to ask your help; Which if you shall refuse, when I am dead, For that I am a man, pray you see me buried.

1 FISHERMAN. Die quoth-a? Now gods forbid't, an I have a gown here; come, put it on; keep thee warm. 80

Now, afore me, a handsome fellow! Come, thou shalt go home, and we'll have flesh for holidays, fish for fasting-days, and moreo'er puddings and flapjacks, and thou shalt be welcome.

PERICLES. I thank you, sir.

2 FISHERMAN. Hark you, my friend; you said you could not beg.

PERICLES. I did but crave.

2 FISHERMAN. But crave? Then I'll turn craver too, and so I shall 'scape whipping. 90

PERICLES. Why, are your beggars whipped then?

2 FISHERMAN. O, not all, my friend, not all; for if all your beggars were whipped, I would wish no better office than to be beadle. But, master, I'll go draw up the net.   *He goes with 3 Fisherman*

PERICLES [aside]. How well this honest mirth becomes their labour!

1 FISHERMAN. Hark you, sir, do you know where ye are?

PERICLES. Not well. 100

1 FISHERMAN. Why, I'll tell you: this is called Pentapolis, and our king the good Simonides.

PERICLES. The good Simonides, do you call him?

1 FISHERMAN. Ay, sir; and he deserves so to be called for his peaceable reign and good government.

PERICLES. He is a happy king, since he gains from his subjects the name of good by his government. How far is his court distant from this shore?

1 FISHERMAN. Marry, sir, half a day's journey; and I'll tell you, he hath a fair daughter, and to-morrow 110 is her birthday; and there are princes and knights come from all parts of the world to joust and tourney for her love.

PERICLES. Were my fortunes equal to my desires, I could wish to make one there.

1 FISHERMAN. O, sir, things must be as they may; and what a man cannot get, he may lawfully deal for his wife's soul.

Enter the two Fishermen, drawing up a net

2 FISHERMAN. Help, master, help! here's a fish hangs in the net, like a poor man's right in the law; 'twill 120 hardly come out. Ha! bots on't, 'tis come at last, and 'tis turned to a rusty armour.

PERICLES. An armour, friends! I pray you, let me see it.
    Thanks, Fortune, yet, that after all thy crosses
    Thou givest me somewhat to repair myself;
    And though it was mine own, part of my heritage,
    Which my dead father did bequeath to me,
    With this strict charge, even as he left his life,
    'Keep it, my Pericles; it hath been a shield
    'Twixt me and death:'—and pointed to this brace— 130
    'For that it saved me, keep it; in like necessity—
    The which the gods protect thee from!—may
        defend thee.'
    It kept where I kept, I so dearly loved it;
    Till the rough seas, that spares not any man,
    Took it in rage, though calmed have given't again:
    I thank thee for't: my shipwreck now's no ill,
    Since I have here my father gave in his will.

1 FISHERMAN. What mean you, sir?

PERICLES. To beg of you, kind friends, this coat of worth,
    For it was sometime target to a king; 140
    I know it by this mark, He loved me dearly,

And for his sake I wish the having of it;
And that you'ld guide me to your sovereign's court,
Where with it I may appear a gentleman;
And if that ever my low fortunes better,
I'll pay your bounties; till then rest your debtor.

1 FISHERMAN. Why, wilt thou tourney for the lady?

PERICLES. I'll show the virtue I have borne in arms.

1 FISHERMAN. Why, d'ye take it, and the gods give
thee good on't!   150

2 FISHERMAN. Ay, but hark you, my friend; 'twas we
that made up this garment through the rough seams
of the waters: there are certain condolements, certain vails. I hope, sir, if you thrive, you'll remember
from whence you had it.

PERICLES. Believe't, I will.
By your furtherance I am clothed in steel;
And spite of all the rapture of the sea
This jewel holds his building on my arm.
Unto thy value I will mount myself   160
Upon a courser, whose delightful steps
Shall make the gazer joy to see him tread.
Only, my friends, I yet am unprovided
Of a pair of bases.

2 FISHERMAN. We'll sure provide: thou shalt have my
best gown to make thee a pair; and I'll bring thee
to the court myself.

PERICLES. Then honour be but equal to my will,
This day I'll rise, or else add ill to ill.   *They go*

Scene 2: *The same. A public way or platform leading to
the lists. A pavilion by the side of it for the reception of
the King, Princess, Lords, etc.*

Enter Simonides, Thaisa, Lords, and Attendants

SIMONIDES. Are the knights ready to begin the
triumph?

1 LORD. They are, my liege,
And stay your coming to present themselves.

SIMONIDES. Return them, we are ready; and our
daughter,
In honour of whose birth these triumphs are,
Sits here, like Beauty's child, whom Nature gat
For men to see and seeing wonder at.
                                            A Lord goes

THAISA. It pleaseth you, my royal father, to express
My commendations great, whose merit's less.

SIMONIDES. It's fit it should be so; for princes are   10
A model which heaven makes like to itself:
As jewels lose their glory if neglected,
So princes their renowns if not respected.
'Tis now your honour, daughter, to entertain
The labour of each knight in his device.

THAISA. Which, to preserve mine honour, I'll
perform.
                    *The first Knight passes by, and
                    his Squire presents his shield to
                    the Princess*

SIMONIDES. Who is the first that doth prefer himself?

THAISA. A knight of Sparta, my renownéd father;
And the device he bears upon his shield
Is a black Ethiop reaching at the sun;   20
The word, 'Lux tua vit mihi.'

SIMONIDES. He loves you well that holds his life of you.
                    The second Knight passes
Who is the second that presents himself?

THAISA. A prince of Macedon, my royal father;

And the device he bears upon his shield
Is an arméd knight that's conquered by a lady;
The motto thus, in Spanish, 'Piu per dolcera que per
força.'   *The third Knight passes*

SIMONIDES. And who the third?

THAISA.   The third of Antioch:
And his device, a wreath of chivalry;
The word, 'Me pompae provexit apex.'   30
                          The fourth Knight passes

SIMONIDES. What is the fourth?

THAISA. A burning torch that's turnéd upside down;
The word, 'Qui me alit, me extinguit.'

SIMONIDES. Which shows that beauty hath his power
at will,
Which can as well inflame as it can kill.
                          The fifth Knight passes

THAISA. The fifth, an hand environéd with clouds,
Holding out gold that's by the touchstone tried;
The motto thus, 'Sic spectanda fides.'
                          The sixth Knight, Pericles, passes

SIMONIDES. And what's
The sixth and last, the which the knight himself   40
With such a graceful courtesy delivered?

THAISA. He seems to be a stranger; but his present is
A withered branch, that's only green at top;
The motto, 'In hac spe vivo.'

SIMONIDES. A pretty moral;
From the dejected state wherein he is,
He hopes by you his fortunes yet may flourish.

1 LORD. He had need mean better than his outward
show
Can any way speak in his just commend;
For by his rusty outside he appears   50
To have practised more the whipstock than the
lance.

2 LORD. He well may be a stranger, for he comes
To an honoured triumph strangely furnishéd.

3 LORD. And on set purpose let his armour rust
Until this day, to scour it in the dust.

SIMONIDES. Opinion's but a fool, that makes us scan
The outward habit by the inward man.
But stay, the knights are coming; we will withdraw
Into the gallery.   *They go*

Great shouts heard from the lists, and cries of 'The
mean knight'

Scene 3: *The same. A hall of state: a banquet prepared*

*Enter Simonides, Thaisa, Lords, Knights, and Attendants,
from tilting*

SIMONIDES. Knights,
To say you're welcome were superfluous.
To place upon the volume of your deeds,
As in a title-page, your worth in arms,
Were more than you expect, or more than's fit,
Since every worth in show commends itself.
Prepare for mirth, for mirth becomes a feast.
You are princes and my guests.

THAISA. But you, my knight and guest;
To whom this wreath of victory I give,   10
And crown you king of this day's happiness.

PERICLES. 'Tis more by fortune, lady, than my merit.

SIMONIDES. Call it by what you will, the day is yours;
And here, I hope, is none that envies it.
In framing artists, art hath thus decreed,

To make some good, but others to exceed;
And you are her laboured scholar. Come, queen
o'th'feast—
For, daughter, so you are— here take your place:
Marshal the rest as they deserve their grace.
KNIGHTS. We are honoured much by good Simonides.   20
SIMONIDES. Your presence glads our days: honour we
love;
For who hates honour hates the gods above.
MARSHAL. Sir, yonder is your place.
PERICLES.   Some other is more fit.
I KNIGHT. Contend not, sir; for we are gentlemen
Have neither in our hearts nor outward eyes
Envied the great nor shall the low despise.
PERICLES. You are right courteous knights.
SIMONIDES.   Sit, sir, sit.
[aside] By Jove, I wonder, that is king of thoughts,
These cates resist me, he not thought upon.
THAISA [aside]. By Juno, that is queen of marriage,   30
All viands that I eat do seem unsavoury,
Wishing him my meat.—Sure he's a gallant
gentleman.
SIMONIDES. He's but a country gentleman; has done no
more
Than other knights have done; has broken a staff
Or so; so let it pass.
THAISA [aside]. To me he seems like diamond to glass.
PERICLES [aside]. Yon king's to me like to my father's
picture,
Which tells me in that glory once he was;
Had princes sit, like stars, about his throne,
And he the sun, for them to reverence;   40
None that beheld him but, like lesser lights,
Did vail their crowns to his supremacy;
Where now his son's a glow-worm in the night,
The which hath fire in darkness, none in light:
Whereby I see that Time's the king of men;
He's both their parent, and he is their grave,
And gives them what he will, not what they crave.
SIMONIDES. What, are you merry, knights?
KNIGHTS. Who can be other in this royal presence?
SIMONIDES. Here, with a cup that's stored unto the
brim,—   50
As you do love, fill to your mistress' lips,—
We drink this health to you.
KNIGHTS.   We thank your grace.
SIMONIDES. Yet pause awhile:
Yon knight doth sit too melancholy,
As if the entertainment in our court
Had not a show might countervail his worth.
Note it not you, Thaisa?
THAISA. What is't to me, my father?
SIMONIDES. O, attend, my daughter:
Princes, in this, should live like gods above,   60
Who freely give to every one that come
To honour them;
And princes not doing so are like to gnats,
Which make a sound, but killed are wond'red at.
Therefore to make his entrance more sweet,
Here, say we drink this standing-bowl of wine to
him.
THAISA. Alas, my father, it befits not me
Unto a stranger knight to be so bold:
He may my proffer take for an offence,
Since men take women's gifts for impudence.   70
SIMONIDES. How?

Do as I bid you, or you'll move me else.
THAISA [aside]. Now, by the gods, he could not please
me better.
SIMONIDES. And furthermore tell him, we desire to
know of him,
Of whence he is, his name and parentage.
THAISA. The king my father, sir, has drunk to you.
PERICLES. I thank him.
THAISA. Wishing it so much blood unto your life.
PERICLES. I thank both him and you, and pledge him
freely.
THAISA. And further he desires to know of you   80
Of whence you are, your name and parentage.
PERICLES. A gentleman of Tyre; my name, Pericles;
My education been in arts and arms;
Who, looking for adventures in the world,
Was by the rough seas reft of ships and men,
And after shipwreck driven upon this shore.
THAISA. He thanks your grace; names himself Pericles,
A gentleman of Tyre,
Who only by misfortune of the seas
Bereft of ships and men, cast on this shore.   90
SIMONIDES. Now, by the gods, I pity his misfortune,
And will awake him from his melancholy.
Come, gentlemen, we sit too long on trifles,
And waste the time, which looks for other revels.
Even in your armours, as you are addressed,
Will well become a soldier's dance.
I will not have excuse with saying this:
Loud music is too harsh for ladies' heads,
Since they love men in arms as well as beds.

The Knights dance

So, this was well asked, 'twas so well performed.   100
Come, sir, here's a lady that wants breathing too;
And I have heard, you knights of Tyre
Are excellent in making ladies trip,
And that their measures are as excellent.
PERICLES. In those that practise them they are, my
lord.
SIMONIDES. O, that's as much as you would be denied
Of your fair courtesy.

The knights and Ladies dance

                              Unclasp, unclasp:
Thanks, gentlemen, to all; all have done well,
[to Pericles] But you the best. Pages and lights
conduct
These knights unto their several lodgings! Yours, sir,   110
We have given order should be next our own.
PERICLES. I am at your grace's pleasure.
SIMONIDES. Princes, it is too late to talk of love,
And that's the mark I know you level at.
Therefore each one betake him to his rest;
To-morrow all for speeding do their best.
                                        They go

Scene 4: *Tyre. A room in the Governor's house*

Enter Helicanus and Escanes

HELICANUS. No, Escanes, know this of me,
Antiochus from incest lived not free;
For which,
The most high gods not minding longer to
Withhold the vengeance that they had in store,
Due to this heinous capital offence,

Even in the height and pride of all his glory,
When he was seated in a chariot
Of an inestimable value, and
His daughter with him, a fire from heaven came, 10
And shrivelled up their bodies, even to loathing;
For they so stunk,
That all those eyes adored them ere their fall
Scorn now their hand should give them burial.
ESCANES. 'Twas very strange.
HELICANUS. And yet but justice; for though this king
    were great,
His greatness was no guard to bar heaven's shaft,
But sin had his reward.
ESCANES. 'Tis very true.

Enter two or three Lords

1 LORD. See, not a man in private conference
    Or council has respect with him but he. 20
2 LORD. It shall no longer grieve without reproof.
3 LORD. And cursed be he that will not second it.
1 LORD. Follow me then. Lord Helicane, a word.
HELICANUS. With me? and welcome; happy day, my
    lords.
1 LORD. Know that our griefs are risen to the top,
    And now at length they overflow their banks.
HELICANUS. Your griefs! for what? wrong not the
    prince you love.
1 LORD. Wrong not yourself, then, noble Helicane;
    But if the prince do live, let us salute him,
    Or know what ground's made happy by his breath. 30
    If in the world he live, we'll seek him out;
    If in his grave he rest, we'll find him there;
    And be resolved he lives to govern us,
    Or dead, gives cause to mourn his funeral,
    And leaves us to our free election.
2 LORD. Whose death's indeed the strongest in our
    censure;
    And knowing this: kingdoms without a head,
    Like goodly buildings left without a roof
    Soon fall to ruin, your noble self,
    That best know how to rule and how to reign, 40
    We thus submit unto—our sovereign.
ALL. Live, noble Helicane!
HELICANUS. For Honour's cause, forbear your
    suffrages.
    If that you love Prince Pericles, forbear.
    Take I your wish, I leap into the seas,
    Where's hourly trouble for a minute's ease.
    A twelvemonth longer, let me entreat you
    To forbear the absence of your king;
    If in which time expired he not return,
    I shall with agéd patience bear your yoke. 50
    But if I cannot win you to this love,
    Go search like nobles, like noble subjects,
    And in your search spend your adventurous worth;
    Whom if you find and win unto return,
    You shall like diamonds sit about his crown.
1 LORD. To wisdom he's a fool that will not yield;
    And since Lord Helicane enjoineth us,
    We with our travels will endeavour it.
HELICANUS. Then you love us, we you, and we'll
    clasp hands:
    When peers thus knit, a kingdom ever stands. 60
                                        They go

Scene 5: Pentapolis. A room in the palace

*Enter the King, Simonides, reading of a letter, at one door:
the Knights meet him*

1 KNIGHT. Good morrow to the good Simonides.
SIMONIDES. Knights, from my daughter this I let you
    know,
    That for this twelvemonth she'll not undertake
    A married life.
    Her reason to herself is only known,
    Which from her by no means can I get.
2 KNIGHT. May we not have access to her, my lord?
SIMONIDES. Faith, by no means; she hath so strictly
    Tied her to her chamber, that 'tis impossible.
    One twelve moons more she'll wear Diana's livery; 10
    This by the eye of Cynthia hath she vowed,
    And on her virgin honour will not break it.
3 KNIGHT. Loath to bid farewell, we take our leaves.
                                    The Knights go
SIMONIDES. So,
    They are well dispatched; now to my daughter's
    letter:
    She tells me here, she'll wed the stranger knight,
    Or never more to view nor day nor light.
    'Tis well, mistress; your choice agrees with mine;
    I like that well; nay, how absolute she's in't,
    Not minding whether I dislike or no! 20
    Well, I do commend her choice;
    And will no longer have it be delayed.
    Soft, here he comes: I must dissemble it.

Enter Pericles

PERICLES. All fortune to the good Simonides!
SIMONIDES. To you as much: sir, I am beholding to
    you
    For your sweet music this last night. I do
    Protest my ears were never better fed
    With such delightful pleasing harmony.
PERICLES. It is your grace's pleasure to commend;
    Not my desert.
SIMONIDES.   Sir, you are music's master. 30
PERICLES. The worst of all her scholars, my good lord.
SIMONIDES. Let me ask you one thing:
    What do you think of my daughter, sir?
PERICLES. A most virtuous princess.
SIMONIDES. And she is fair too, is she not?
PERICLES. As a fair day in summer, wondrous fair.
SIMONIDES. Sir, my daughter thinks very well of you;
    Ay, so well, that you must be her master,
    And she will be your scholar: therefore look to it.
PERICLES. I am unworthy for her schoolmaster. 40
SIMONIDES. She thinks not so; peruse this writing else.
PERICLES [*aside*]. What's here?
    A letter, that she loves the knight of Tyre!
    'Tis the king's subtlety to have my life.
    [*aloud*] O, seek not to entrap me, gracious lord,
    A stranger and distresséd gentleman,
    That never aimed so high to love your daughter,
    But bent all offices to honour her.
SIMONIDES. Thou hast bewitched my daughter, and
    thou art
    A villain.
PERICLES.   By the gods, I have not. 50
    Never did thought of mine levy offence;
    Nor never did my actions yet commence
    A deed might gain her love or your displeasure.

SIMONIDES. Traitor, thou liest.
PERICLES. Traitor!
SIMONIDES. Ay, traitor.
PERICLES. Even in his throat—unless it be the king—
That calls me traitor, I return the lie.
SIMONIDES [aside]. Now, by the gods, I do applaud his
courage.
PERICLES. My actions are as noble as my thoughts,
That never relished of a base descent.
I came unto your court for honour's cause,   60
And not to be a rebel to your state;
And he that otherwise accounts of me,
This sword shall prove he's honour's enemy.
SIMONIDES. No?
Here comes my daughter, she can witness it.

Enter Thaisa

PERICLES. Then, as you are as virtuous as fair,
Resolve your angry father, if my tongue
Did e'er solicit, or my hand subscribe
To any syllable that made love to you.
THAISA. Why, sir, say if you had, who takes offence   70
At that would make me glad?
SIMONIDES. Yea, mistress, are you so peremptory?
[aside] I am glad on't with all my heart.—
I'll tame you; I'll bring you in subjection.
Will you, not having my consent,
Bestow your love and your affections
Upon a stranger? [aside] who, for aught I know,
May be, nor can I think the contrary,
As great in blood as I myself.
Therefore hear you, mistress; either frame   80
Your will to mine—and you, sir, hear you,
Either be ruled by me, or I will make you—
Man and wife.
Nay, come, your hands and lips must seal it too;
And being joined, I'll thus your hopes destroy;
And for a further grief,—God give you joy!
What, are you both pleased?
THAISA. Yes, if you love me, sir.
PERICLES. Even as my life my blood that fosters it.
SIMONIDES. What, are you both agreed?
BOTH. Yes, if't please your majesty.   90
SIMONIDES. It pleaseth me so well, that I will see you
wed;
And then, with what haste you can, get you to bed.
They go

ACT 3
Prologue

Enter Gower

GOWER. Now sleep y-slackéd hath the rout;
No din but snores the house about,
Made louder by the o'er-fed breast
Of this most pompous marriage-feast.
The cat, with eyne of burning coal,
Now couches 'fore the mouse's hole;
And crickets at the oven's mouth
Sing the blither for their drouth.
Hymen hath brought the bride to bed,
Where by the loss of maidenhead   10
A babe is moulded. Be attent,
And time that is so briefly spent
With your fine fancies quaintly eche.
What's dark in show I'll plain with speech.

Dumb Show

*Enter Pericles and Simonides at one door, with attendants;
a Messenger meets them, kneels, and gives Pericles a letter;
Pericles shows it Simonides; the Lords kneel to him. Then
enter Thaisa with child, with Lychorida, a nurse; the
King shows her the letter; she rejoices; she and Pericles take
leave of her father, and depart with Lychorida and their
attendants. Then Simonides and the rest go*

By many a dern and painful perch
Of Pericles the careful search,
By the four opposing coigns
Which the world together joins,
Is made with all due diligence
That horse and sail and high expense   20
Can stead the quest. At last from Tyre,
Fame answering the most strange inquire,
To th'court of King Simonides
Are letters brought, the tenour these:
Antiochus and his daughter dead,
The men of Tyrus on the head
Of Helicanus would set on
The crown of Tyre, but he will none.
The mutiny he there hastes t'appease;
Says to 'em, if King Pericles   30
Come not home in twice six moons,
He, obedient to their dooms,
Will take the crown. The sum of this,
Brought hither to Pentapolis,
Y-ravishéd the regions round,
And every one with claps can sound,
'Our heir-apparent is a king!
Who dreamed, who thought of such a thing?'
Brief, he must hence depart to Tyre.
His queen with child makes her desire—   40
Which who shall cross?—along to go.
Omit we all their dole and woe.
Lychorida, her nurse, she takes,
And so to sea; their vessel shakes
On Neptune's billow; half the flood
Hath their keel cut; but fortune's mood
Varies again; the grisléd north
Disgorges such a tempest forth,
That, as a duck for life that dives,
So up and down the poor ship drives.   50
The lady shrieks and well-a-near
Does fall in travail with her fear;
And what ensues in this fell storm
Shall for itself itself perform.
I nill relate, action may
Conveniently the rest convey;
Which might not what by me is told.
In your imagination hold
This stage the ship, upon whose deck
The sea-tossed Pericles appears to speak. *He goes* 60

Scene 1

Enter Pericles, a-shipboard

PERICLES. The god of this great vast, rebuke these
surges,
Which wash both heaven and hell; and thou that
hast
Upon the winds command, bind them in brass,

Having called them from the deep! O, still
Thy deaf'ning dreadful thunders; gently quench
Thy nimble sulphurous flashes! O, how, Lychorida,
How does my queen? Thou stormest venomously;
Wilt thou spit all thyself? The seaman's whistle
Is as a whisper in the ears of death,
Unheard. Lychorida!—Lucina, O   10
Divinest patroness and midwife gentle
To those that cry by night, convey thy deity
Aboard our dancing boat; make swift the pangs
Of my queen's travails! Now, Lychorida!

Enter Lychorida, with an Infant

LYCHORIDA. Here is a thing too young for such a place,
Who, if it had conceit, would die, as I
Am like to do; take in your arms this piece
Of your dead queen.
PERICLES.   How? how, Lychorida?
LYCHORIDA. Patience, good sir; do not assist the storm.   20
Here's all that is left living of your queen,
A little daughter: for the sake of it,
Be manly, and take comfort.
PERICLES.   O you gods!
Why do you make us love your goodly gifts,
And snatch them straight away? We here below
Recall not what we give, and therein may
Use honour with you.
LYCHORIDA.   Patience, good sir,
Even for this charge.
PERICLES.   Now, mild may be thy life!
For a more blusterous birth had never babe;
Quiet and gentle thy conditions! for
Thou art the rudeliest welcome to this world   30
That e'er was princess' child. Happy what follows!
Thou hast as chiding a nativity
As fire, air, water, earth and heaven can make,
To herald thee from the womb.
Even at the first thy loss is more than can
Thy portage quit, with all thou canst find here.
Now, the good gods throw their best eyes upon't!

Enter two Sailors

1 SAILOR. What courage, sir? God save you!
PERICLES. Courage enough: I do not fear the flaw;
It hath done to me the worst. Yet, for the love   40
Of this poor infant, this fresh-new seafarer,
I would it would be quiet.
1 SAILOR. Slack the bolins there! Thou wilt not, wilt
thou? Blow, and split thyself.
2 SAILOR. But sea-room, an the brine and cloudy
billow kiss the moon, I care not.
1 SAILOR. Sir, your queen must overboard; the sea
works high, the wind is loud, and will not lie till the
ship be cleared of the dead.
PERICLES. That's your superstition.   50
1 SAILOR. Pardon us, sir; with us at sea it hath been
still observed; and we are strong in custom. Therefore briefly yield her; for she must overboard
straight.
PERICLES. As you think meet. Most wretched queen!
LYCHORIDA. Here she lies, sir.
PERICLES. A terrible childbed hast thou had, my dear;
No light, no fire: th'unfriendly elements
Forgot thee utterly; nor have I time
To give thee hallowed to thy grave, but straight   60
Must cast thee, scarcely coffined, in the ooze;

Where, for a monument upon thy bones,
And e'er-remaining lamps, the belching whale   3.2
And humming water must o'erwhelm thy corpse,
Lying with simple shells. O Lychorida,
Bid Nestor bring me spices, ink and paper,
My casket and my jewels; and bid Nicander
Bring me the satin coffer; lay the babe
Upon the pillow; hie thee, whiles I say
A priestly farewell to her; suddenly, woman.   70
                 Lychorida goes
2 SAILOR. Sir, we have a chest beneath the hatches,
Caulked and bituméd ready.
PERICLES. I thank thee. Mariner, say what coast is this?
2 SAILOR. We are near Tharsus.
PERICLES. Thither, gentle mariner,
Alter thy course from Tyre. When canst thou reach
it?
2 SAILOR. By break of day, if the wind cease.
PERICLES. O, make for Tharsus!
There will I visit Cleon, for the babe
Cannot hold out to Tyrus; there I'll leave it   80
At careful nursing. Go thy ways, good mariner:
I'll bring the body presently.   *They go*

Scene 2: *Ephesus. A room in Cerimon's house*

*Enter Lord Cerimon with a Servant, and persons who have
been shipwrecked*

CERIMON. Philemon, ho!

Enter Philemon

PHILEMON. Doth my lord call?
CERIMON. Get fire and meat for these poor men:
'T'as been a turbulent and stormy night.
SERVANT. I have been in many; but such a night as this,
Till now, I ne'er enduréd.
CERIMON. Your master will be dead ere you return;
There's nothing can be minist'red to nature
That can recover him. Give this to the pothecary,
And tell me how it works.   *All but Cerimon go*

Enter two Gentlemen

1 GENTLEMAN.   Good morrow.   .10
2 GENTLEMAN. Good morrow to your lordship.
CERIMON.   Gentlemen,
Why do you stir so early?
1 GENTLEMAN. Sir,
Our lodgings, standing bleak upon the sea,
Shook as the earth did quake;
The very principals did seem to rend
And all to topple; pure surprise and fear
Made me to quit the house.
2 GENTLEMAN. That is the cause we trouble you so
early;
'Tis not our husbandry.
CERIMON.   O, you say well.   20
1 GENTLEMAN. But I much marvel that your lordship,
having
Rich tire about you, should at these early hours
Shake off the golden slumber of repose.
'Tis most strange,
Nature should be so conversant with pain,
Being thereto not compelled.
CERIMON.   I held it ever,
Virtue and cunning were endowments greater
Than nobleness and riches: careless heirs

May the two latter darken and expend,
But immortality attends the former,   30
Making a man a god. 'Tis known, I ever
Have studied physic, though which secret art,
By turning o'er authorities, I have,
Together with my practice, made familiar
To me and to my aid the blest infusions
That dwells in vegetives, in metals, stones;
And I can speak of the disturbances
That nature works, and of her cures; which doth
    give me
A more content in course of true delight
Than to be thirsty after tottering honour,   40
Or tie my treasure up in silken bags,
To please the fool and death.
2 GENTLEMAN. Your honour has through Ephesus
    poured forth
Your charity, and hundreds call themselves
Your creatures, who by you have been restored;
And not your knowledge, your personal pain, but
    even
Your purse, still open, hath built Lord Cerimon
Such strong renown as time shall never [raze].

Enter two or three with a chest

1 SERVANT. So; lift there.
CERIMON. What's that?   50
1 SERVANT. Sir,
Even now did the sea toss up on our shore
This chest: 'tis of some wreck.
CERIMON. Set't down, let's look upon't.
2 GENTLEMAN. 'Tis like a coffin, sir.
CERIMON.   Whate'er it be,
'Tis wondrous heavy. Wrench it open straight.
If the sea's stomach be o'ercharged with gold,
'Tis a good constraint of fortune it belches upon us.
2 GENTLEMAN. 'Tis so, my lord.
CERIMON. How close 'tis caulked and bitumed! Did 60
    the sea cast it up?
1 SERVANT. I never saw so huge a billow, sir, as tossed
    it up on shore.
CERIMON. Wrench it open: soft! it smells most sweetly
    in my sense.
2 GENTLEMAN. A delicate odour.
CERIMON. As ever hit my nostril. So, up with it.
O you most potent gods! what's here? a corse!
2 GENTLEMAN. Most strange!
CERIMON. Shrouded in cloth of state; balmed and en- 70
    treasured with full bags of spices! A passport too!
Apollo, perfect me in the characters!
                          Reads from a scroll
'Here I give to understand,
If e'er this coffin drives a-land,
I, King Pericles, have lost
This queen, worth all our mundane cost.
Who finds her, give her burying;
She was the daughter of a king.
Besides this treasure for a fee,
The gods requite his charity!'   80
If thou livest, Pericles, thou hast a heart
That even cracks for woe! This chanced to-night.
2 GENTLEMAN. Most likely, sir.
CERIMON.   Nay, certainly to-night;
For look how fresh she looks! They were too rough
That threw her in the sea. Make a fire within.
Fetch hither all my boxes in my closet.

Death may usurp on nature many hours,
And yet the fire of life kindle again
The o'erpressed spirits. I heard of an Egyptian
That had nine hours lien dead,   90
Who was by good appliance recoveréd.

Enter one with napkins and fire

Well said, well said; the fire and cloths.
The still and woful music that we have,
Cause it to sound, beseech you.
The vial once more; how thou stirr'st, thou block!
The music there! I pray you, give her air.
Gentlemen,
This queen will live; nature awakes; a warmth
Breathes out of her; she hath not been entranced
Above five hours; see how she 'gins to blow   100
Into life's flower again!
1 GENTLEMAN.   The heavens,
Through you, increase our wonder, and set up
Your fame for ever.
CERIMON.   She is alive; behold,
Her eyelids, cases to those heavenly jewels
Which Pericles hath lost, begin to part
Their fringes of bright gold; the diamonds
Of a most praiséd water doth appear
To make the world twice rich. Live,
And make us weep to hear your fate, fair creature,
Rare as you seem to be.   *She moves*
THAISA.   O dear Diana,   110
Where am I? Where's my lord? What world is this?
2 GENTLEMAN. Is not this strange?
1 GENTLEMAN. Most rare.
CERIMON. Hush, my gentle neighbours!
Lend me your hands; to the next chamber bear her.
Get linen: now this matter must be looked to,
For her relapse is mortal. Come, come;
And Æsculapius guide us!   *They carry her away*

Scene 3: *Tharsus. A room in the Governor's house*

*Enter Pericles, Cleon, Dionyza, and Lychorida with
Marina in her arms*

PERICLES. Most honoured Cleon, I must needs be gone;
My twelve months are expired, and Tyrus stands
In a litigious peace. You, and your lady,
Take from my heart all thankfulness! The gods
Make up the rest upon you!
CLEON.   Your shafts of fortune,
Though they hurt you mortally, yet glance
Full woundingly on us.
DIONYZA.   O your sweet queen!
That the strict fates had pleased you had brought
    her hither,
To have blessed mine eyes with her!
PERICLES.   We cannot but obey
The powers above us. Could I rage and roar   10
As doth the sea she lies in, yet the end
Must be as 'tis. My gentle babe Marina,
Whom, for she was born at sea, I have named so,
    here
I charge your charity withal, leaving her
The infant of your care; beseeching you
To give her princely training, that she may
Be mannered as she is born.
CLEON.   Fear not, my lord, but think
Your grace, that fed my country with your corn,

For which the people's prayers still fall upon you,
Must in your child be thought on. If neglection 20
Should therein make me vile, the common body,
By you relieved, would force me to my duty.
But if to that my nature need a spur,
The gods revenge it upon me and mine,
To the end of generation!

PERICLES.   I believe you;
Your honour and your goodness teach me to't,
Without your vows. Till she be married, madam,
By bright Diana, whom we honour all,
Unscissored shall this hair of mine remain,
Though I show ill in't. So I take my leave. 30
Good madam, make me blessèd in your care
In bringing up my child.

DIONYZA.   I have one myself,
Who shall not be more dear to my respect
Than yours, my lord.

PERICLES.   Madam, my thanks and prayers.

CLEON. We'll bring your grace e'en to the edge
o'th'shore,
Then give you up to the masked Neptune and
The gentlest winds of heaven.

PERICLES.   I will embrace
Your offer. Come, dearest madam. O, no tears,
Lychorida, no tears;
Look to your little mistress, on whose grace 40
You may depend hereafter. Come, my lord.
                                                    They go

Scene 4: *Ephesus. A room in Cerimon's house*

Enter Cerimon and Thaisa

CERIMON. Madam, this letter, and some certain jewels,
Lay with you in your coffer; which are at your
command.
Know you the character?

THAISA.   It is my lord's.
That I was shipped at sea, I well remember,
Even on my eaning time; but whether there
Delivered, by the holy gods,
I cannot rightly say. But since King Pericles,
My wedded lord, I ne'er shall see again,
A vestal livery will I take me to,
And never more have joy. 10

CERIMON. Madam, if this you purpose as ye speak,
Diana's temple is not distant far,
Where you may abide till your date expire.
Moreover, if you please, a niece of mine
Shall there attend you.

THAISA. My recompense is thanks, that's all;
Yet my good will is great, though the gift small.
                                                    They go

ACT 4
Prologue

Enter Gower

GOWER. Imagine Pericles arrived at Tyre,
Welcomed and settlèd to his own desire.
His woeful queen we leave at Ephesus,
Unto Diana there 's a votaress.
Now to Marina bend your mind,
Whom our fast-growing scene must find
At Tharsus, and by Cleon trained
In music's letters; who hath gained

Of education all the grace,
Which makes her both the heart and place 10
Of general wonder. But, alack,
That monster envy, oft the wrack
Of earnéd praise, Marina's life
Seeks to take off by treason's knife,
And in this kind:—our Cleon hath
One daughter, and a full grown wench,
Even ripe for marriage rite; this maid
Hight Philoten; and it is said
For certain in our story, she
Would ever with Marina be; 20
Be't when she weaved the sleided silk
With fingers long, small, white as milk;
Or when she would with sharp néele wound
The cambric, which she made more sound
By hurting it; or when to th'lute
She sung, and made the night-bird mute,
That still records with moan; or when
She would with rich and constant pen
Vail to her mistress Dian; still
This Philoten contends in skill 30
With absolute Marina: so
With dove of Paphos might the crow
Vie feathers white. Marina gets
All praises, which are paid as debts,
And not as given. This so darks
In Philoten all graceful marks,
That Cleon's wife, with envy rare
A present murderer does prepare
For good Marina, that her daughter
Might stand peerless by this slaughter. 40
The sooner her vile thoughts to stead,
Lychorida, our nurse, is dead;
And cursèd Dionyza hath
The pregnant instrument of wrath
Prest for this blow. The unborn event
I do commend to your content;
Only I carried wingèd time
Post on the lame feet of my rhyme;
Which never could I so convey,
Unless your thoughts went on my way. 50
Dionyza does appear,
With Leonine, a murderer.   *He goes*

Scene 1: *Tharsus. An open place near the sea-shore*

Enter Dionyza with Leonine

DIONYZA. Thy oath remember; thou hast sworn to
do't.
'Tis but a blow, which never shall be known.
Thou canst not do a thing in the world so soon,
To yield thee so much profit. Let not conscience,
Which is but cold, in flaming, thy love bosom,
Inflame too nicely; nor let pity, which
Even women have cast off, melt thee, but be
A soldier to thy purpose.

LEONINE. I will do't; but yet she is a goodly creature.

DIONYZA. The fitter then the gods should have her. 10
Here she comes weeping for her only mistress'
death.
Thou art resolved?

LEONINE. I am resolved.

Enter Marina, with a basket of flowers

MARINA. No, I will rob Tellus of her weed,
To strew thy green with flowers; the yellows, blues,
The purple violets, and marigolds,
Shall, as a carpet, hang upon thy grave,
While summer-days doth last. Ay me! poor maid,
Born in a tempest when my mother died,
This world to me is as a lasting storm, 20
Whirring me from my friends.
DIONYZA. How now, Marina! why do you keep
alone?
How chance my daughter is not with you?
Do not consume your blood with sorrowing:
Have you a nurse of me! Lord, how your favour's
Changéd with this unprofitable woe!
Come, give me your flowers, ere the sea mar it.
Walk with Leonine; the air is quick there,
And it pierces and sharpens the stomach.
Come, Leonine, take her by the arm, walk with her. 30
MARINA. No, I pray you; I'll not bereave you of your
servant.
DIONYZA. Come, come;
I love the king your father and yourself
With more than foreign heart. We every day
Expect him here: when he shall come, and find
Our paragon to all reports thus blasted,
He will repent the breadth of his great voyage;
Blame both my lord and me, that we have taken
No care to your best courses. Go, I pray you, 40
Walk, and be cheerful once again; resume
That excellent complexion, which did steal
The eyes of young and old. Care not for me;
I can go home alone.
MARINA. Well, I will go;
But yet I have no desire to it.
DIONYZA. Come, come, I know 'tis good for you.
Walk half an hour, Leonine, at the least.
Remember what I have said.
LEONINE. I warrant you, madam.
DIONYZA. I'll leave you, my sweet lady, for a while.
Pray, walk softly, do not heat your blood. 50
What! I must have care of you.
MARINA. My thanks, sweet madam.
Dionyza goes
Is this wind westerly that blows?
LEONINE. South-west.
MARINA. When I was born, the wind was north.
LEONINE. Was't so?
MARINA. My father, as nurse said, did never fear,
But cried 'Good seamen!' to the sailors, galling
His kingly hands, haling ropes;
And, clasping to the mast, endured a sea
That almost burst the deck.
LEONINE. When was this?
MARINA. When I was born. 60
Never was waves nor wind more violent;
And from the ladder-tackle washes off
A canvas-climber. 'Ha!' says one, 'wolt out?'
And with a dropping industry they skip
From stem to stern; the boatswain whistles, and
The master calls and trebles their confusion.
LEONINE. Come, say your prayers.
MARINA. What mean you?
LEONINE. If you require a little space for prayer,
I grant it. Pray; but be not tedious, 70
For the gods are quick of ear, and I am sworn
To do my work with haste.

MARINA. Why will you kill me?
LEONINE. To satisfy my lady.
MARINA. Why would she have me killed?
Now, as I can remember, by my troth,
I never did her hurt in all my life.
I never spake bad word, nor did ill turn
To any living creature; believe me, la,
I never killed a mouse, nor hurt a fly,
Nor trod upon a worm against my will, 80
But I wept for't. How have I offended,
Wherein my death might yield her any profit,
Or my life imply her any danger?
LEONINE. My commission
Is not to reason of the deed, but do't.
MARINA. You will not do't for all the world, I hope.
You are well-favoured, and your looks foreshow
You have a gentle heart. I saw you lately,
When you caught hurt in parting two that fought.
Good sooth, it showed well in you. Do so now. 90
Your lady seeks my life; come you between.
And save poor me, the weaker.
LEONINE. I am sworn,
And will dispatch. *He seizes her*

Enter Pirates

1 PIRATE. Hold, villain! *Leonine runs away*
2 PIRATE. A prize! a prize!
3 PIRATE. Half-part, mates, half-part. Come let's
have her aboard suddenly. *They carry off Marina*

Re-enter Leonine

LEONINE. These roguing thieves serve the great pirate
Valdes;
And they have seized Marina. Let her go;
There's no hope she will return. I'll swear she's dead, 100
And thrown into the sea. But I'll see further.
Perhaps they will but please themselves upon her,
Not carry her abroad. If she remain,
Whom they have ravished must by me be slain.
He goes

Scene 2: *Mytilene. A room in a brothel*

Enter Pandar, Bawd, and Boult

PANDAR. Boult!
BOULT. Sir?
PANDAR. Search the market narrowly; Mytilene is full
of gallants. We lost too much money this mart by
being too wenchless.
BAWD. We were never so much out of creatures. We
have but poor three, and they can do no more than
they can do; and with continual action are even as
good as rotten.
PANDAR. Therefore let's have fresh ones, whate'er we 10
pay for them. If there be not a conscience to be used
in every trade, we shall never prosper.
BAWD. Thou sayest true: 'tis not our bringing up of
poor bastards—as, I think, I have brought up some
eleven—
BOULT. Ay, to eleven; and brought them down again.
But shall I search the market?
BAWD. What else, man? The stuff we have, a strong
wind will blow it to pieces, they are so pitifully
sodden. 20
PANDAR. Thou sayest true; they're too unwholesome,

o' conscience. The poor Transylvanian is dead, that
lay with the little baggage.

BOULT. Ay, she quickly pooped him; she made him
roast-meat for worms. But I'll go search the market.

He goes

PANDAR. Three or four thousand chequins were as
pretty a proportion to live quietly, and so give over.

BAWD. Why to give over, I pray you? is it a shame
to get when we are old?

PANDAR. O, our credit comes not in like the com-   30
modity, nor the commodity wages not with the
danger: therefore, if in our youths we could pick up
some pretty estate, 'twere not amiss to keep our door
hatched. Besides, the sore terms we stand upon
with the gods will be strong with us for giving o'er.

BAWD. Come, other sorts offend as well as we.

PANDAR. As well as we? ay, and better too; we offend
worse. Neither is our profession any trade; it's no
calling. But here comes Boult.

Re-enter Boult, with the Pirates and Marina

BOULT. Come your ways, my masters; you say she's a   40
virgin?

I PIRATE. O, sir, we doubt it not.

BOULT. Master, I have gone through for this piece you
see. If you like her, so; if not, I have lost my earnest.

BAWD. Boult, has she any qualities?

BOULT. She has a good face, speaks well, and has
excellent good clothes; there's no farther necessity of
qualities can make her be refused.

BAWD. What's her price, Boult?

BOULT. It cannot be bated one doit of a thousand   50
pieces.

PANDAR. Well, follow me, my masters, you shall have
your money presently. Wife, take her in; instruct
her what she has to do, that she may not be raw in
her entertainment.   *Pandar and Pirates go*

BAWD. Boult, take you the marks of her, the colour
of her hair, complexion, height, her age, with
warrant of her virginity; and cry 'He that will give
most shall have her first.' Such a maidenhead were
no cheap thing, if men were as they have been. Get   60
this done as I command you.

BOULT. Performance shall follow.   *He goes*

MARINA. Alack that Leonine was so slack, so slow!
He should have struck, not spoke; or that these
pirates,
Not enough barbarous, had not o'erboard
Thrown me to seek my mother!

BAWD. Why lament you, pretty one?

MARINA. That I am pretty.

BAWD. Come, the gods have done their part in you.

MARINA. I accuse them not.   70

BAWD. You are light into my hands, where you are
like to live.

MARINA. The more my fault,
To 'scape his hands where I was like to die.

BAWD. Ay, and you shall live in pleasure.

MARINA. No.

BAWD. Yes, indeed shall you, and taste gentlemen of
all fashions. You shall fare well; you shall have the
difference of all complexions. What do you stop
your ears?   80

MARINA. Are you a woman?

BAWD. What would you have me be, an I be not a
woman?

MARINA. An honest woman, or not a woman.

BAWD. Marry, whip the gosling: I think I shall have   4.2
something to do with you. Come, you're a young
foolish sapling, and must be bowed as I would have
you.

MARINA. The gods defend me!

BAWD. If it please the gods to defend you by men,   90
then men must comfort you, men must feed you,
men stir you up. Boult's returned.

Re-enter Boult

Now, sir, hast thou cried her through the market?

BOULT. I have cried her almost to the number of her
hairs; I have drawn her picture with my voice.

BAWD. And I prithee tell me, how dost thou find the
inclination of the people, especially of the younger
sort?

BOULT. Faith, they listened to me as they would have
hearkened to their father's testament. There was a   100
Spaniard's mouth wat'red, and he went to bed to her
very description.

BAWD. We shall have him here to-morrow with his
best ruff on.

BOULT. To-night, to-night. But, mistress, do you
know the French knight that cowers i'the hams?

BAWD. Who, Monsieur Veroles?

BOULT. Ay, he: he offered to cut a caper at the proclamation; but he made a groan at it, and swore he
would see her to-morrow.   110

BAWD. Well, well; as for him, he brought his disease
hither: here he does but repair it. I know he will
come in our shadow, to scatter his crowns in the sun.

BOULT. Well, if we had of every nation a traveller, we
should lodge them with this sign.

BAWD. Pray you, come hither awhile. You have
fortunes coming upon you. Mark me: you must
seem to do that fearfully which you commit
willingly, despise profit where you have most gain.
To weep that you live as ye do makes pity in   120
your lovers: seldom but that pity begets you a good
opinion, and that opinion a mere profit.

MARINA. I understand you not.

BOULT. O, take her home, mistress, take her home;
these blushes of hers must be quenched with some
present practice.

BAWD. Thou sayest true, i'faith, so they must; for
your bride goes to that with shame which is her way
to go with warrant.

BOULT. Faith, some do, and some do not. But,   130
mistress, if I have bargained for the joint—

BAWD. Thou mayest cut a morsel off the spit.

BOULT. I may so?

BAWD. Who should deny it? Come, young one,
I like the manner of your garments well.

BOULT. Ay, by my faith, they shall not be changed
yet.

BAWD. Boult, spend thou that in the town; report
what a sojourner we have; you'll lose nothing by
custom. When nature framed this piece, she meant   140
thee a good turn; therefore say what a paragon she is,
and thou hast the harvest out of thine own report.

BOULT. I warrant you, mistress, thunder shall not so
awake the beds of eels as my giving out her beauty
stir up the lewdly inclined. I'll bring home some
to-night.

BAWD. Come your ways; follow me.

MARINA. If fires be hot, knives sharp, or waters deep,
Untied I still my virgin knot will keep.
Diana, aid my purpose!   150
BAWD. What have we to do with Diana? Pray you,
will you go with us?   *They go*

Scene 3: *Tharsus. A room in the Governor's house*

Enter Cleon and Dionyza

DIONYZA. Why are you foolish? Can it be undone?
CLEON. O Dionyza, such a piece of slaughter
The sun and moon ne'er looked upon!
DIONYZA. I think you'll turn a child again.
CLEON. Were I chief lord of all this spacious world,
I'ld give it to undo the deed. A lady,
Much less in blood than virtue, yet a princess
To equal any single crown o'th'earth
I'th'justice of compare! O villain Leonine!
Whom thou hast pois'ned too.   10
If thou hadst drunk to him, 't had been a kindness
Becoming well thy fact. What canst thou say
When noble Pericles shall demand his child?
DIONYZA. That she is dead. Nurses are not the fates.
To foster is not ever to preserve.
She died at night; I'll say so. Who can cross it?
Unless you play the pious innocent,
And for an honest attribute cry out
'She died by foul play.'
CLEON.   O, go to. Well, well.
Of all the faults beneath the heavens, the gods   20
Do like this worst.
DIONYZA.   Be one of those that thinks
The petty wrens of Tharsus will fly hence
And open this to Pericles. I do shame
To think of what a noble strain you are
And of how coward a spirit.
CLEON.   To such proceeding
Who ever but his approbation added,
Though not his prime consent, he did not flow
From honourable sources.
DIONYZA.   Be it so, then.
Yet none does know, but you, how she came dead,
Nor none can know, Leonine being gone.   30
She did distain my child, and stood between
Her and her fortunes; none would look on her,
But cast their gazes on Marina's face;
Whilst ours was blurted at, and held a malkin,
Not worth the time of day. It pierced me thorough;
And though you call my course unnatural,
You not your child well loving, yet I find
It greets me as an enterprise of kindness
Performed to your sole daughter.
CLEON.   Heavens forgive it!
DIONYZA. And as for Pericles, what should he say?   40
We wept after her hearse, and yet we mourn.
Her monument
Is almost finished, and her epitaphs
In glitt'ring golden characters express
A general praise to her, and care in us
At whose expense 'tis done.
CLEON.   Thou art like the harpy,
Which, to betray, dost, with thine angel's face,
Seize with thine eagle's talents.
DIONYZA. Ye're like one that superstitiously
Do swear to th'gods that winter kills the flies;   50
But yet I know you'll do as I advise.   *They go*

Scene 4

Enter Gower, before the monument of Marina at Tharsus

GOWER. Thus time we waste, and longest leagues
make short;
Sail seas in cockles, have and wish but for't;
Making, to take imagination,
From bourn to bourn, region to region.
By you being pardoned, we commit no crime
To use one language in each several clime
Where our scene seems to live. I do beseech you
To learn of me, who stand i'th'gaps to teach you
The stages of our story. Pericles
Is now again thwarting the wayward seas,   10
Attended on by many a lord and knight,
To see his daughter, all his life's delight.
Old Helicanus goes along. Behind
Is left to govern it, you bear in mind,
Old Escanes, whom Helicanus late
Advanced in time to great and high estate.
Well-sailing ships and bounteous winds have
brought
This king to Tharsus—think his pilot thought;
So with his steerage shall your thoughts go on—
To fetch his daughter home, who first is gone.   20
Like motes and shadows see them move awhile;
Your ears unto your eyes I'll reconcile.

Dumb Show

*Enter Pericles at one door, with all his train; Cleon and
Dionyza at the other. Cleon shows Pericles the tomb;
whereat Pericles makes lamentation, puts on sackcloth, and
in a mighty passion departs. Then Cleon, Dionyza, and the
rest go also*

See how belief may suffer by foul show!
This borrowed passion stands for true-owed woe;
And Pericles, in sorrow all devoured,
With sighs shot through and biggest tears
o'ershowered,
Leaves Tharsus and again embarks. He swears
Never to wash his face, nor cut his hairs.
He puts on sackcloth, and to sea. He bears
A tempest, which his mortal vessel tears,   30
And yet he rides it out. Now please you wit
The epitaph is for Marina writ
By wicked Dionyza.
       Reads the inscription on Marina's monument
'The fairest, sweet'st and best, lies here,
Who withered in her spring of year.
She was of Tyrus the king's daughter,
On whom foul death hath made this slaughter;
Marina was she called; and at her birth,
Thetis, being proud, swallowed some part
o'th'earth.
Therefore the earth, fearing to be o'erflowed,   40
Hath Thetis' birth-child on the heavens bestowed;
Wherefore she does, and swears she'll never stint,
Make raging battery upon shores of flint.'

No visor does become black villainy
So well as soft and tender flattery.
Let Pericles believe his daughter's dead,
And bear his courses to be ordered
By Lady Fortune; while our scene must play
His daughter's woe and heavy well-a-day
In her unholy service. Patience, then,   50
And think you now are all in Mytilen.   *He goes*

Scene 5: *Mytilene. A street before the brothel*

Enter two Gentlemen from the brothel

1 GENTLEMAN. Did you ever hear the like?

2 GENTLEMAN. No, nor never shall do in such a place as this, she being once gone.

1 GENTLEMAN. But to have divinity preached there! did you ever dream of such a thing?

2 GENTLEMAN. No, no. Come, I am for no more bawdy-houses; shall's go hear the vestals sing?

1 GENTLEMAN. I'll do any thing now that is virtuous; but I am out of the road of rutting for ever.

They go

Scene 6: *The same. A room in the brothel*

Enter Pandar, Bawd, and Boult

PANDAR. Well, I had rather than twice the worth of her she had ne'er come here.

BAWD. Fie, fie upon her! she's able to freeze the god Priapus, and undo a whole generation. We must either get her ravished or be rid of her. When she should do for clients her fitment and do me the kindness of our profession, she has me her quirks, her reasons, her master-reasons, her prayers, her knees; that she would make a puritan of the devil, if he should cheapen a kiss of her.

BOULT. Faith, I must ravish her, or she'll disfurnish us of all our cavalleria and make our swearers priests. 10

PANDAR. Now, the pox upon her green-sickness for me!

BAWD. Faith, there's no way to be rid on't but by the way to the pox. Here comes the Lord Lysimachus disguised.

BOULT. We should have both lord and lown, if the peevish baggage would but give way to customers.

Enter Lysimachus

LYSIMACHUS. How now! How a dozen of virginities? 20

BAWD. Now, the gods to-bless your honour!

BOULT. I am glad to see your honour in good health.

LYSIMACHUS. You may so; 'tis the better for you that your resorters stand upon sound legs. How now, wholesome iniquity, have you that a man may deal withal, and defy the surgeon?

BAWD. We have here one, sir, if she would—but there never came her like in Mytilene.

LYSIMACHUS. If she'ld do the deed of darkness, thou wouldst say. 30

BAWD. Your honour knows what 'tis to say well enough.

LYSIMACHUS. Well, call forth, call forth.

BOULT. For flesh and blood, sir, white and red, you shall see a rose; and she were a rose indeed, if she had but—

LYSIMACHUS. What, prithee?

BOULT. O, sir, I can be modest.

LYSIMACHUS. That dignifies the renown of a bawd, no less than it gives a good report to a number to be 40 chaste.   *Boult goes*

BAWD. Here comes that which grows to the stalk; never plucked yet, I can assure you.

Re-enter Boult with Marina

Is she not a fair creature?

LYSIMACHUS. Faith, she would serve after a long 4.6 voyage at sea. Well, there's for you: leave us.

BAWD. I beseech your honour, give me leave a word, and I'll have done presently.

LYSIMACHUS. I beseech you, do.

BAWD [*to Marina*]. First, I would have you note, this 50 is an honourable man.

MARINA. I desire to find him so, that I may worthily note him.

BAWD. Next, he's the governor of this country, and a man whom I am bound to.

MARINA. If he govern the country, you are bound to him indeed; but how honourable he is in that, I know not.

BAWD. Pray you, without any more virginal fencing, will you use him kindly? He will line your apron 60 with gold.

MARINA. What he will do graciously, I will thankfully receive.

LYSIMACHUS. Ha' you done?

BAWD. My lord, she's not paced yet; you must take some pains to work her to your manage. Come, we will leave his honour and her together. Go thy ways.

Bawd, Pandar, and Boult depart

LYSIMACHUS. Now, pretty one, how long have you been at this trade?

MARINA. What trade, sir? 70

LYSIMACHUS. Why, I cannot name't but I shall offend.

MARINA. I cannot be offended with my trade. Please you to name it.

LYSIMACHUS. How long have you been of this profession?

MARINA. E'er since I can remember.

LYSIMACHUS. Did you go to't so young? Were you a gamester at five or at seven?

MARINA. Earlier too, sir, if now I be one.

LYSIMACHUS. Why, the house you dwell in proclaims 80 you to be a creature of sale.

MARINA. Do you know this house to be a place of such resort, and will come into't? I hear say you're of honourable parts and are the governor of this place.

LYSIMACHUS. Why, hath your principal made known unto you who I am?

MARINA. Who is my principal?

LYSIMACHUS. Why, your herb-woman; she that sets seeds and roots of shame and iniquity. O, you have 90 heard something of my power, and so stand aloof for more serious wooing. But I protest to thee, pretty one, my authority shall not see thee, or else look friendly upon thee. Come, bring me to some private place. Come, come.

MARINA. If you were born to honour, show it now; If put upon you, make the judgement good That thought you worthy of it.

LYSIMACHUS. How's this? How's this? Some more; be sage.

MARINA.   For me
That am a maid, though most ungentle fortune 100
Have placed me in this sty, where, since I came,
Diseases have been sold dearer than physic—
That the gods
Would set me free from this unhallowed place,
Though they did change me to the meanest bird
That flies i'th'purer air!

LYSIMACHUS. I did not think thou couldst have spoke
  so well;
  Ne'er dreamed thou couldst.
  Had I brought hither a corrupted mind,
  Thy speech had altered it. Hold, here's gold for 110
  thee:
  Persever in that clear way thou goest,
  And the gods strengthen thee!
MARINA.   The good gods preserve you!
LYSIMACHUS. For me, be you thoughten
  That I came with no ill intent; for to me
  The very doors and windows savour vilely.
  Fare thee well. Thou art a piece of virtue, and
  I doubt not but thy training hath been noble.
  Hold, here's more gold for thee.
  A curse upon him, die he like a thief,
  That robs thee of thy goodness! If thou dost 120
  Hear from me, it shall be for thy good.

Re-enter Boult

BOULT. I beseech your honour, one piece for me.
LYSIMACHUS. Avaunt, thou damned door-keeper!
  Your house, but for this virgin that doth prop it,
  Would sink, and overwhelm you. Away! *He goes*
BOULT. How's this? We must take another course
  with you. If your peevish chastity, which is not
  worth a breakfast in the cheapest country under the
  cope, shall undo a whole household, let me be
  gelded like a spaniel. Come your ways. 130
MARINA. Whither would you have me?
BOULT. I must have your maidenhead taken off, or the
  common hangman shall execute it. Come your
  ways. We'll have no more gentlemen driven away.
  Come your ways, I say.

Re-enter Bawd and Pandar

BAWD. How now! what's the matter?
BOULT. Worse and worse, mistress; she has here
  spoken holy words to the Lord Lysimachus.
BAWD. O abominable!
BOULT. She makes our profession as it were to stink 140
  afore the face of the gods.
BAWD. Marry, hang her up for ever!
BOULT. The nobleman would have dealt with her like
  a nobleman, and she sent him away as cold as a
  snowball, saying his prayers too.
BAWD. Boult, take her away; use her at thy pleasure.
  Crack the glass of her virginity, and make the rest
  malleable.
BOULT. An if she were a thornier piece of ground than
  she is, she shall be ploughed. 150
MARINA. Hark, hark, you gods!
BAWD. She conjures: away with her! Would she had
  never come within my doors! Marry, hang you!
  She's born to undo us. Will you not go the way of
  womenkind? Marry, come up, my dish of chastity
  with rosemary and bays! *The Bawd and Pandar go*
BOULT. Come, mistress; come your ways with me.
MARINA. Whither wilt thou have me?
BOULT. To take from you the jewel you hold so dear.
MARINA. Prithee, tell me one thing first. 160
BOULT. Come now, your one thing.
MARINA. What canst thou wish thine enemy to be?
BOULT. Why, I could wish him to be my master, or
  rather, my mistress.
MARINA. Neither of these are so bad as thou art,

Since they do better thee in their command.
  Thou hold'st a place, for which the pained'st fiend
  Of hell would not in reputation change.
  Thou art the damnéd door-keeper to every
  Coistrel that comes inquiring for his Tib; 170
  To the choleric fisting of every rogue
  Thy ear is liable; thy food is such
  As hath been belched on by infected lungs.
BOULT. What would you have me do? go to the wars,
  would you? where a man may serve seven years for
  the loss of a leg, and have not money enough in the
  end to buy him a wooden one?
MARINA. Do any thing
  But this thou doest. Empty old receptacles,
  Or common shores, of filth; 180
  Serve by indenture to the common hangman.
  Any of these ways are yet better than this;
  For what thou professest, a baboon, could he speak,
  Would own a name too dear. That the gods
  Would safely deliver me from this place!
  Here, here's gold for thee.
  If that thy master would gain by me,
  Proclaim that I can sing, weave, sew, and dance,
  With other virtues, which I'll keep from boast;
  And I will undertake all these to teach. 190
  I doubt not but this populous city will
  Yield many scholars.
BOULT. But can you teach all this you speak of?
MARINA. Prove that I cannot, take me home again,
  And prostitute me to the basest groom
  That doth frequent your house.
BOULT. Well, I will see what I can do for thee; if I
  can place thee, I will.
MARINA. But amongst honest women.
BOULT. Faith, my acquaintance lies little amongst 200
  them. But since my master and mistress hath bought
  you, there's no going but by their consent; therefore
  I will make them acquainted with your purpose, and
  I doubt not but I shall find them tractable enough.
  Come, I'll do for thee what I can; come your ways.
                              They go

ACT 5
Prologue

Enter Gower

GOWER. Marina thus the brothel 'scapes, and chances
  Into an honest house, our story says.
  She sings like one immortal, and she dances
  As goddess-like to her admiréd lays;
  Deep clerks she dumbs, and with her neele composes
  Nature's own shape, of bud, bird, branch, or berry,
  That even her art sisters the natural roses;
  Her inkle, silk, twin with the rubied cherry;
  That pupils lacks she none of noble race,
  Who pour their bounty on her, and her gain 10
  She gives the curséd bawd. Here we her place;
  And to her father turn our thoughts again,
  Where we left him on the sea. We there him lost;
  Whence, driven before the winds, he is arrived
  Here where his daughter dwells; and on this coast
  Suppose him now at anchor; the city strived
  God Neptune's annual feast to keep; from whence
  Lysimachus our Tyrian ship espies,
  His banners sable, trimmed with rich expense;
  And to him in his barge with fervour hies. 20

In your supposing once more put your sight;
Of heavy Pericles, think this his bark;
Where what is done in action, more, if might,
Shall be discovered, please you sit and hark.

He goes

Scene 1: *On board Pericle's ship, off Mytilene. A pavilion on deck, with a curtain before it; Pericles within, reclining on a couch. A barge lies beside the Tyrian vessel*

Enter two Sailors, one belonging to the Tyrian vessel, the other to the barge; to them Helicanus

TYRIAN SAILOR [*to the Sailor of Mytilene*]. Where is
  Lord Helicanus? he can resolve you.
  O, here he is.
  Sir, there is a barge put off from Mytilene,
  And in it is Lysimachus the governor,
  Who craves to come aboard. What is your will?
HELICANUS. That he have his. Call up some gentlemen.
TYRIAN SAILOR. Ho, gentlemen! my lord calls.

Enter two or three Gentlemen

1 GENTLEMAN. Doth your lordship call?
HELICANUS. Gentlemen, there is some of worth would
  come aboard;
  I pray, greet him fairly.   10

*The Gentlemen and the two Sailors
descend, and go on board the barge*

Enter from thence, Lysimachus, and Lords; with the Gentlemen and the two Sailors

TYRIAN SAILOR. Sir,
  This is the man that can, in aught you would,
  Resolve you.
LYSIMACHUS. Hail, reverend sir! the gods preserve you!
HELICANUS. And you, sir, to outlive the age I am,
  And die as I would do.
LYSIMACHUS.   You wish me well.
· Being on shore, honouring of Neptune's triumphs,
  Seeing this goodly vessel ride before us,
  I made to it, to know of whence you are.
HELICANUS. First, what is your place?   20
LYSIMACHUS. I am the governor of this place you
  lie before.
HELICANUS. Sir,
  Our vessel is of Tyre, in it the king;
  A man who for this three months hath not spoken
  To any one, nor taken sustenance
  But to prorogue his grief.
LYSIMACHUS. Upon what ground is his
  distemperature?
HELICANUS. 'Twould be too tedious to repeat;
  But the main grief springs from the loss
  Of a belovéd daughter and a wife.   30
LYSIMACHUS. May we not see him?
HELICANUS. You may;
  But bootless is your sight; he will not speak
  To any.
LYSIMACHUS. Yet let me obtain my wish.
HELICANUS. Behold him. [*Pericles discovered*] This was
  a goodly person,
  Till the disaster that, one mortal night,
  Drove him to this.
LYSIMACHUS. Sir king, all hail! the gods preserve you!
  Hail, royal sir! .

HELICANUS. It is in vain; he will not speak to you.   40
1 LORD. Sir,
  We have a maid in Mytilene, I durst wager,
  Would win some words of him.
LYSIMACHUS.   'Tis well bethought.
  She, questionless, with her sweet harmony
  And other chosen attractions, would allure,
  And make a batt'ry through his deafened ports,
  Which now are midway stopped.
  She is all happy as the fairest of all,
  And with her fellow maids is now upon
  The leafy shelter that abuts against   50
  The island's side.   *Whispers a Lord, who goes off
                             in the barge of Lysimachus*
HELICANUS. Sure, all effectless; yet nothing we'll omit
  That bears recovery's name. But, since your
  kindness
  We have stretched thus far, let us beseech you
  That for our gold we may provision have,
  Wherein we are not destitute for want,
  But weary for the staleness.
LYSIMACHUS.   O, sir, a courtesy
  Which if we should deny, the most just gods
  For every graff would send a caterpillar,
  And so inflict our province. Yet once more   60
  Let me entreat to know at large the cause
  Of your king's sorrow.
HELICANUS. Sit, sir, I will recount it to you.
  But see, I am prevented.

The Lord returns in the barge with Marina and one of her attendants

LYSIMACHUS. O, here's the lady that I sent for.
  Welcome, fair one!—It's not a goodly presence?
HELICANUS. She's a gallant lady.
LYSIMACHUS. She's such a one, that, were I well assured
  Came of a gentle kind and noble stock,
  I'ld wish no better choice, and think me rarely wed. 70
  Fair one, all goodness that consists in beauty,
  Expect even here, where is a kingly patient,
  If that thy prosperous and artificial feat
  Can draw him but to answer thee in aught,
  Thy sacred physic shall receive such pay
  As thy desires can wish.
MARINA.   Sir, I will use
  My utmost skill in his recovery, provided
  That none but I and my companion maid
  Be suffered to come near him.
LYSIMACHUS.   Come, let us leave her;
  And the gods make her prosperous!   80

They withdraw; Marina sings

LYSIMACHUS. Marked he your music?
MARINA.   No, nor looked on us.
LYSIMACHUS. See, she will speak to him.
MARINA. Hail, sir! my lord, lend ear.
PERICLES. Hum, ha!   *Roughly repulses her*
MARINA. I am a maid,
  My lord, that ne'er before invited eyes,
  But have been gazed on like a comet; she speaks,
  My lord, that, may be, hath endured a grief
  Might equal yours, if both were justly weighed.
  Though wayward fortune did malign my state,   90
  My derivation was from ancestors
  Who stood equivalent with mighty kings;
  But time hath rooted out my parentage,

And to the world and awkward casualties
Bound me in servitude. [*aside*] I will desist;
But there is something glows upon my cheek,
And whispers in mine ear 'Go not till he speak.'
PERICLES. My fortunes—parentage—good
    parentage—
To equal mine— was it not thus? what say you?
MARINA. I said, my lord, if you did know my
    parentage, 100
You would not do me violence.
PERICLES. I do think so. Pray you, turn your eyes upon
    me.
You're like something that—What
    countrywoman?
Here of these shores?
MARINA.   No, nor of any shores;
Yet I was mortally brought forth, and am
No other than I appear.
PERICLES. I am great with woe, and shall deliver
    weeping.
My dearest wife was like this maid,
And such a one my daughter might have been:
My queen's square brows; her stature to an inch; 110
As wand-like straight, as silver-voiced;
Her eyes as jewel-like and cased as richly;
In pace another Juno;
Who starves the ears she feeds, and makes them
    hungry,
The more she gives them speech. Where do you
    live?
MARINA. Where I am but a stranger: from the deck
You may discern the place.
PERICLES.   Where were you bred?
And how achieved you these endowments, which
You make more rich to owe?
MARINA. If I 120
Should tell my history, it would seem like lies
Disdained in the reporting.
PERICLES.   Prithee, speak.
Falseness cannot come from thee; for thou look'st
Modest as Justice, and thou seem'st a palace
For the crowned Truth to dwell in. I will believe
    thee,
And make my senses credit thy relation
To points that seem impossible; for thou look'st
Like one I loved indeed. What were thy friends?
Didst thou not say, when I did push thee back—
Which was when I perceived thee—that thou cam'st 130
From good descending?
MARINA.   So indeed I did.
PERICLES. Report thy parentage. I think thou said'st
Thou hadst been tossed from wrong to injury,
And that thou thoughts' thy griefs might equal
    mine,
If both were opened.
MARINA.   Some such thing I said,
And said no more but what my thoughts
Did warrant me was likely.
PERICLES.   Tell thy story;
If thine considered prove the thousandth part
Of my endurance, thou art a man, and I
Have suffered like a girl; yet thou dost look 140
Like Patience gazing on kings' graves and smiling
Extremity out of act. What were thy friends?
How lost thou them? Thy name, my most kind
    virgin?

Recount, I do beseech thee: come, sit by me.
MARINA. My name is Marina.
PERICLES.   O, I am mocked,
And thou by some incensèd god sent hither
To make the world laugh at me.
MARINA.   Patience, good sir,
Or here I'll cease.
PERICLES.   Nay, I'll be patient.
Thou little know'st how thou dost startle me,
To call thyself Marina.
MARINA.   The name 150
Was given me by one that had some power,
My father, and a king.
PERICLES.   How, a king's daughter?
And called Marina?
MARINA.   You said you would believe me;
But, not to be a troubler of your peace,
I will end here.
PERICLES.   But are you flesh and blood?
Have you a working pulse, and are no fairy?
Motion as well? Speak on. Where were you born?
And wherefore called Marina?
MARINA.   Called Marina
For I was born at sea.
PERICLES.   At sea! what mother?
MARINA. My mother was the daughter of a king; 160
Who died the minute I was born,
As my good nurse Lychorida hath oft
Delivered weeping.
PERICLES.   O, stop there a little!—
This is the rarest dream that e'er dulled sleep
Did mock sad fools withal: this cannot be
My daughter—buried!—Well, where were you
    bred?
I'll hear you more, to th'bottom of your story,
And never interrupt you.
MARINA. You scorn; believe me, 'twere best I did give
    o'er.
PERICLES. I will believe you by the syllable 170
Of what you shall deliver. Yet, give me leave:
How came you in these parts? where were you bred?
MARINA. The king my father did in Tharsus leave me;
Till cruel Cleon, with his wicked wife,
Did seek to murder me;
And having wooed a villain to attempt it,
Who having drawn to do't,
A crew of pirates came and recued me;
Brought me to Mytilene. But, good sir,
Whither will you have me? Why do you weep? It
    may be, 180
You think me an impostor: no, good faith;
I am the daughter to King Pericles,
If good King Pericles be.
PERICLES. Ho, Helicanus!
HELICANUS. Calls my lord?
PERICLES. Thou art a grave and noble counsellor,
Most wise in general. Tell me, if thou canst,
What this maid is, or what is like to be,
That thus hath made me weep?
HELICANUS.   I know not;
But here's the regent, sir, of Mytilene 190
Speaks nobly of her.
LYSIMACHUS.   She never would tell
Her parentage; being demanded that,
She would sit still and weep.
PERICLES. O Helicanus, strike me, honoured sir;

Give me a gash, put me to present pain;
Lest this great sea of joys rushing upon me
O'erbear the shores of my mortality,
And drown me with their sweetness. O, come
   hither,
Thou that beget'st him that did thee beget;
Thou that wast born at sea, buried at Tharsus,   200
And found at sea again! O Helicanus,
Down on thy knees; thank the holy gods as loud
As thunder threatens us: this is Marina.
What was thy mother's name? tell me but that,
For truth can never be confirmed enough,
Though doubts did ever sleep.

MARINA. First, sir, I pray,
What is your title?

PERICLES. I am Pericles of Tyre: but tell me now
My drowned queen's name, as in the rest you said   210
Thou hast been godlike perfect, the heir of
   kingdoms,
And another life to Pericles thy father.

MARINA. Is it no more to be your daughter than
To say my mother's name was Thaisa?
Thaisa was my mother, who did end
The minute I began.

PERICLES. Now, blessing on thee! rise; thou art my
   child.
Give me fresh garments, mine own Helicanus.
She is not dead at Tharsus, as she should have been,
By savage Cleon; she shall tell thee all;
When thou shalt kneel, and justify in knowledge
She is thy very princess. Who is this?

HELICANUS. Sir, 'tis the governor of Mytilene,
Who, hearing of your melancholy state,
Did come to see you.

PERICLES. I embrace you.
Give me my robes. I am wild in my beholding.
O heavens bless my girl! But, hark, what music?
Tell Helicanus, my Marina, tell him
O'er, point by point, for yet he seems to doubt,   230
How sure you are my daughter. But, what music?

HELICANUS. My lord, I hear none.

PERICLES. None?
The music of the spheres! List, my Marina.

LYSIMACHUS. It is not good to cross him; give him
   way.

PERICLES. Rarest sounds! Do ye not hear?

LYSIMACHUS. Music, my lord?

PERICLES. I hear most heavenly music.
It nips me unto list'ning, and thick slumber
Hangs upon mine eyes: let me rest.   *He sleeps*

LYSIMACHUS. A pillow for his head: so leave him all.   240
Well, my companion friends,
If this but answer to my just belief,
I'll well remember you.   *All but Pericles go*

Diana appears to Pericles in a vision

DIANA. My temple stands in Ephesus: hie thee thither,
And do upon mine altar sacrifice.
There, when my maiden priests are met together,
Before the people all,
Reveal how thou at sea didst lose thy wife.
To mourn thy crosses, with thy daughter's, call,
And give them repetition to the life.   250
Perform my bidding, or thou livest in woe;
Do't, and be happy; by my silver bow!
Awake, and tell thy dream.   *Disappears*

PERICLES. Celestial Dian, goddess argentine,
I will obey thee. Helicanus!

Re-enter Helicanus, Lysimachus, and Marina

HELICANUS.   Sir?

PERICLES. My purpose was for Tharsus, there to strike
The inhospitable Cleon; but I am
For other service first: toward Ephesus
Turn our blown sails; eftsoons I'll tell thee why.
[*to Lysimachus*] Shall we refresh us, sir, upon your
   shore,   260
And give you gold for such provision
As our intents will need?

LYSIMACHUS. Sir,
With all my heart; and, when you come ashore,
I have another suit.

PERICLES.   You shall prevail,
Were it to woo my daughter; for it seems
You have been noble towards her.

LYSIMACHUS.   Sir, lend me your arm.

PERICLES. Come, my Marina.   *They go*

Scene 2: *The temple of Diana at Ephesus; Thaisa standing
near the altar, as high priestess; a number of Virgins on each
side; Cerimon and other Inhabitants of Ephesus attending*

Enter Gower

GOWER. Now our sands are almost run;
More a little, and then dumb.
This, my last boon, give me,
For such kindness must relieve me,
That you aptly will suppose
What pageantry, what feats, what shows,
What minstrelsy and pretty din,
The regent made in Mytilin,
To greet the king. So he thrived,   10
That he is promised to be wived
To fair Marina; but in no wise
Till he had done his sacrifice,
As dian bade: whereto being bound,
The interim, pray you, all confound.
In feathered briefness sails are filled,
And wishes fall out as they're willed.
At Ephesus, the temple see,
Our king and all his company.
That he can hither come so soon,
Is by your fancies' thankful doom.   *He goes* 20

Scene 3

*Enter Pericles, with his train; Lysimachus, Helicanus, and
Marina*

PERICLES. Hail, Dian! to perform thy just command,
I here confess myself the king of Tyre;
Who, frighted from my country, did wed
At Pentapolis the fair Thaisa.
At sea in childbed died she, but brought forth
A maid-child called Marina; who, O goddess,
Wears yet thy silver livery. She at Tharsus
Was nursed with Cleon; who at fourteen years
He sought to murder; but her better stars
Brought her to Mytilene; 'gainst whose shore   10
Riding, her fortunes brought the maid aboard us,
Where, by her own most clear remembrance, she
Made known herself my daughter.

THAISA.   Voice and favour!
You are, you are—O royal Pericles!—   *Faints*
PERICLES. What means the nun? she dies! help,
  gentlemen!
CERIMON. Noble sir,
  If you have told Diana's altar true,
  This is your wife.
PERICLES.   Reverend appearer, no;
  I threw her overboard with these very arms.
CERIMON. Upon this coast, I warrant you.
PERICLES.   'Tis most certain.   20
CERIMON. Look to the lady. O, she's but overjoyed.
  Early one blustering morn this lady was
  Thrown upon this shore. I oped the coffin,
  Found there rich jewels; recovered her, and placed
    her
  Here in Diana's temple.
PERICLES.   May we see them?
CERIMON. Great sir, they shall be brought you to my
    house,
  Whither I invite you. Look, Thaisa is
  Recovered.
THAISA. O, let me look!
  If he be none of mine, my sanctity   30
  Will to my sense bend no licentious ear,
  But curb it, spite of seeing. O, my lord,
  Are you not Pericles? Like him you spake,
  Like him you are. Did you not name a tempest,
  A birth, and death?
PERICLES.   The voice of dead Thaisa!
THAISA. That Thaisa am I,
  Supposéd dead and drowned.
PERICLES. Immortal Dian!
THAISA.   Now I know you better.
  When we with tears parted Pentapolis,
  The king my father gave you such a ring.   40
                                        Shows a ring
PERICLES. This, this: no more, you gods! your present
    kindness
  Makes my past miseries sports. You shall do well,
  That on the touching of her lips I may
  Melt, and no more be seen. O, come, be buried
  A second time within these arms.
MARINA.   My heart
  Leaps to be gone into my mother's bosom.
                                        Kneels to Thaisa
PERICLES. Look who kneels here, flesh of thy flesh,
    Thaisa;
  Thy burden at the sea, and called Marina
  For she was yielded there.
THAISA.   Blest, and mine own!
HELICANUS. Hail, madam, and my queen!
THAISA.   I know you not.   50
PERICLES. You have heard me say, when I did fly
    from Tyre,
  I left behind an ancient substitute.
  Can you remember what I called the man?
  I have named him oft.
THAISA.   'Twas Helicanus, then.

PERICLES. Still confirmation.
  Embrace him, dear Thaisa; this is he.
  Now do I long to hear how you were found;
  How possibly preserved; and who to thank,
  Besides the gods, for this great miracle.
THAISA. Lord Cerimon, my lord; this man,   60
  Through whom the gods have shown their power;
    that can
  From first to last resolve you.
PERICLES.   Reverend sir,
  The gods can have no mortal officer
  More like a god than you. Will you deliver
  How this dead queen re-lives?
CERIMON.   I will, my lord.
  Beseech you first, go with me to my house,
  Where shall be shown you all was found with her;
  How she came placed here in the temple;
  No needful thing omitted.
PERICLES.   Pure Dian,
  I bless thee for thy vision, and will offer   70
  Nightly oblations to thee. Thaisa,
  This prince, the fair betrothéd of your daughter,
  Shall marry her at Pentapolis. And now,
  This ornament
  Makes me look dismal will I clip to form;
  And what this fourteen years no razor touched,
  To grace thy marriage-day, I'll beautify.
THAISA. Lord Cerimon hath letters of good credit;
  Sir, my father's dead.
PER. Heavens make a star of him! Yet there, my
    queen,   80
  We'll celebrate their nuptials, and ourselves
  Will in that kingdom spend our following days.
  Our son and daughter shall in Tyrus reign.
  Lord Cerimon, we do our longing stay
  To hear the rest untold: sir, lead's the way.
                                        They go

Enter Gower

GOWER. In Antiochus and his daughter you have heard
  Of monstrous lust the due and just reward.
  In Pericles, his queen and daughter, seen,
  Although assailed with fortune fierce and keen,
  Virtue preserved from fell destruction's blast,   90
  Led on by heaven and crowned with joy at last.
  In Helicanus may you well descry
  A figure of truth, of faith, of loyalty.
  In reverend Cerimon there well appears
  The worth that learnéd charity aye wears.
  For wicked Cleon and his wife, when fame
  Had spread their curséd deed to th'honoured name
  Of Pericles, to rage the city turn,
  That him and his they in his palace burn;
  The gods for murder seeméd so content   100
  To punish, although not done, but meant.
  So, on your patience evermore attending,
  New joy wait on you! Here our play has ending.
                                        He goes

The Poems

Venus and Andonis

Vilia miretur vulgus; mihi flavus Apollo
Pocula Castalia plena ministret aqua

TO THE

RIGHT HONOURABLE
HENRY WRIOTHESLEY,
EARL OF SOUTHAMPTON, AND BARON
OF TITCHFIELD

Right Honourable,
I know not how I shall offend in dedicating my unpolished lines to your lordship, nor how the world will censure me for choosing so strong a prop to support so weak a burden: only, if your honour seem but pleased, I account my self highly praised, and vow to take advantage of all idle hours, till I have honoured you with some graver labour. But if the first heir of my invention prove deformed, I shall be sorry it had so noble a godfather, and never after ear so barren a land, for fear it yield me still so bad a harvest. I leave it to your honourable survey, and your honour to your heart's content; which I wish may always answer your own wish, and the world's hopeful expectations.

Your honour's in all duty,
William Shakespeare

Even as the sun with purple-coloured face
Had ta'en his last leave of the weeping morn,
Rose-cheeked Adonis hied him to the chase;
Hunting he loved, but love he laughed to scorn;
  Sick-thoughted Venus makes amain unto him,   5
  And like a bold-faced suitor 'gins to woo him.

'Thrice fairer than myself,' thus she began,
'The field's chief flower, sweet above compare,
Stain to all nymphs, more lovely than a man,
More white and red than doves or roses are;   10
  Nature that made thee with herself at strife
  Saith that the world hath ending with thy life.

'Vouchsafe, thou wonder, to alight thy steed,
And rein his proud head to the saddle-bow;
If thou wilt deign this favour, for thy meed   15
A thousand honey secrets shalt thou know.
  Here come and sit, where never serpent hisses,
  And being set, I'll smother thee with kisses;

'And yet not cloy thy lips with loathed saiety,
But rather famish them amid their plenty,   20
Making them red and pale with fresh variety;
Ten kisses short as one, one long as twenty.
  A summer's day will seem an hour but short,
  Being wasted in such time-beguiling sport.'

With this she seizeth on his sweating palm,   25
The precedent of pith and livelihood,
And, trembling in her passion, calls it balm,
Earth's sovereign salve to do a goddess good.
  Being so enraged, desire doth lend her force
  Courageously to pluck him from his horse.   30

Over one arm the lusty courser's rein,
Under her other was the tender boy,
Who blushed and pouted in a dull disdain,
With leaden appetite, unapt to toy;
  She red and hot as coals of glowing fire,   35
  He red for shame, but frosty in desire.

The studded bridle on a ragged bough
Nimbly she fastens—O, how quick is love!
The steed is stallèd up, and even now
To tie the rider she begins to prove.   40
  Backward she pushed him, as she would be thrust,
  And governed him in strength, though not in lust.

So soon was she along as he was down,
Each leaning on their elbows and their hips;
Now doth she stroke his cheek, now doth he frown, 45
And 'gins to chide, but soon she stops his lips,
  And kissing speaks, with lustful language broken,
  'If thou wilt chide, thy lips shall never open.'

He burns with bashful shame; she with her tears
Doth quench the maiden burning of his cheeks;   50
Then with her windy sighs and golden hairs
To fan and blow them dry again she seeks.
  He saith she is immodest, blames her miss;
  What follows more she murders with a kiss.

Even as an empty eagle, sharp by fast,   55
Tires with her beak on feathers, flesh and bone,
Shaking her wings, devouring all in haste,
Till either gorge be stuffed or prey be gone;
  Even so she kissed his brow, his cheek, his chin,
  And where she ends she doth anew begin.   60

Forced to content, but never to obey,
Panting he lies and breatheth in her face;
She feedeth on the steam as on a prey,
And calls it heavenly moisture, air of grace,
    Wishing her cheeks were gardens full of flowers, 65
    So they were dewed with such distilling showers.

Look how a bird lies tangled in a net,
So fast'ned in her arms Adonis lies;
Pure shame and awed resistance made him fret,
Which bred more beauty in his angry eyes. 70
    Rain added to a river that is rank
    Perforce will force it overflow the bank.

Still she entreats, and prettily entreats,
For to a pretty ear she tunes her tale;
Still is he sullen, still he lours and frets, 75
'Twixt crimson shame and anger ashy-pale;
    Being red, she loves him best, and being white,
    Her best is bettered with a more delight.

Look how he can, she cannot choose but love;
And by her fair immortal hand she swears 80
From his soft bosom never to remove
Till he take truce with her contending tears,
    Which long have rained, making her cheeks all wet;
    And one sweet kiss shall pay this countless debt.

Upon this promise did he raise his chin, 85
Like a dive-dapper peering through a wave,
Who, being looked on, ducks as quickly in;
So offers he to give what she did crave;
    But when her lips were ready for his pay,
    He winks, and turns his lips another way. 90

Never did passenger in summer's heat
More thirst for drink than she for this good turn.
Her help she sees, but help she cannot get;
She bathes in water, yet her fire must burn.
    'O, pity,' 'gan she cry. 'flint-hearted boy! 95
    'Tis but a kiss I beg; why art thou coy?

'I have been wooed, as I entreat thee now,
Even by the stern and direful god of war,
Whose sinewy neck in battle ne'er did bow,
Who conquers where he comes in every jar; 100
    Yet hath he been my captive and my slave,
    And begged for that which thou unasked shalt have.

'Over my altars hath he hung his lance,
His batt'red shield, his uncontrollèd crest,
And for my sake hath learned to sport and dance, 105
To toy, to wanton, dally, smile and jest,
    Scorning his churlish drum and ensign red,
    Making my arms his field, his tent my bed.

'Thus he that overruled I overswayèd,
Leading him prisoner in a red-rose chain; 110
Strong-tempered steel his stronger strength obeyèd,
Yet was he servile to my coy disdain.
    O, be not proud, nor brag not of thy might,
    For mast'ring her that foiled the god of fight!

'Touch but my lips with those fair lips of thine— 115
Though mine be not so fair, yet are they red—
The kiss shall be thine own as well as mine.
What see'st thou in the ground? hold up thy head;
    Look in mine eyeballs, there thy beauty lies;
    Then why not lips on lips, since eyes in eyes? 120

'Art thou ashamed to kiss? then wink again,
And I will wink; so shall the day seem night.
Love keeps his revels where there are but twain;
Be bold to play, our sport is not in sight.
    These blue-veined violets whereon we lean 125
    Never can blab, nor know not what we mean.

'The tender spring upon thy tempting lip
Shews thee unripe; yet mayst thou well be tasted;
Make use of time, let not advantage slip;
Beauty within itself should not be wasted. 130
    Fair flowers that are not gath'red in their prime
    Rot and consume themselves in little time.

'Were I hard-favoured, foul, or wrinkled-old,
Ill-nurtured, crooked, churlish, harsh in voice,
O'erworn, despisèd, rheumatic and cold, 135
Thick-sighted, barren, lean, and lacking juice,
    Then mightst thou pause, for then I were not for
      thee;
    But having no defects, why dost abhor me?

'Thou canst not see one wrinkle in my brow;
Mine eyes are grey and bright and quick in turning; 140
My beauty as the spring doth yearly grow,
My flesh is soft and plump, my marrow burning;
    My smooth moist hand, were it with thy hand felt,
    Would in thy palm dissolve, or seem to melt.

'Bid me discourse, I will enchant thine ear, 145
Or, like a fairy, trip upon the green,
Or, like a nymph, with long dishevellèd hair,
Dance on the sands, and yet no footing seen.
    Love is a spirit all compact of fire,
    Not gross to sink, but light, and will aspire. 150

'Witness this primrose bank whereon I lie;
These forceless flowers like sturdy trees support me;
Two strengthless doves will draw me through the sky
From morn till night, even where I list to sport me.
    Is love so light, sweet boy, and may it be 155
    That thou should think it heavy unto thee?

'Is thine own heart to thine own face affected?
Can thy right hand seize love upon thy left?
Then woo thyself, be of thyself rejected,
Steal thine own freedom, and complain on theft. 160
    Narcissus so himself himself forsook,
    And died to kiss his shadow in the brook.

'Torches are made to light, jewels to wear,
Dainties to taste, fresh beauty for the use,
Herbs for their smell, and sappy plants to bear; 165
Things growing to themselves are growth's abuse.
    Seeds spring from seeds and beauty breedeth beauty;
    Thou wast begot; to get it is thy duty.

'Upon the earth's increase why shouldst thou feed,
Unless the earth with thy increase be fed? 170
By law of nature thou art bound to breed,
That thine may live when thou thyself art dead;
　And so in spite of death thou dost survive,
　In that thy likeness still is left alive.'

By this, the love-sick queen began to sweat, 175
For where they lay the shadow had forsook them,
And Titan, tirèd in the mid-day heat,
With burning eyè did hotly overlook them,
　Wishing Adonis had his team to guide,
　So he were like him, and by Venus' side. 180

And now Adonis, with a lazy sprite,
And with a heavy, dark, disliking eye,
His louring brows o'erwhelming his fair sight,
Like misty vapours when they blot the sky,
　Souring his cheeks, cries 'Fie, no more of love! 185
　The sun doth burn my face; I must remove.'

'Ay me,' quoth Venus, 'young, and so unkind!
What bare excuses mak'st thou to be gone!
I'll sigh celestial breath, whose gentle wind 190
Shall cool the heat of this descending sun;
　I'll make a shadow for thee of my hairs;
　If they burn too, I'll quench them with my tears.

'The sun that shines from heaven shines but warm,
And lo, I lie between that sun and thee; 195
The heat I have from thence doth little harm;
Thine eye darts forth the fire that burneth me;
　And were I not immortal, life were done
　Between this heavenly and earthly sun.

'Art thou obdurate, flinty, hard as steel? 200
Nay, more than flint, for stone at rain relenteth.
Art thou a woman's son, and canst not feel
What 'tis to love, how want of love tormenteth?
　O, had thy mother borne so hard a mind,
　She had not brought forth thee, but died unkind. 205

'What am I that thou shouldst contemn me this?
Or what great danger dwells upon my suit?
What were thy lips the worse for one poor kiss?
Speak, fair; but speak fair words, or else be mute.
　Give me one kiss, I'll give it thee again, 210
　And one for int'rest, if thou wilt have twain.

'Fie, lifeless picture, cold and senseless stone,
Well painted idol, image dull and dead,
Statue contenting but the eye alone,
Thing like a man, but of no woman bred! 215
　Thou art no man, though of a man's complexion,
　For men will kiss even by their own direction.'

This said, impatience chokes her pleading tongue,
And swelling passion doth provoke a pause;
Red cheeks and fiery eyes blaze forth her wrong; 220
Being judge in love, she cannot right her cause;
　And now she weeps, and now she fain would speak,
　And now her sobs do her intendments break.

Sometimes she shakes her head, and then his hand,
Now gazeth she on him, now on the ground; 225
Sometime her arms infold him like a band;
She would, he will not in her arms be bound;
　And when from thence he struggles to be gone,
　She locks her lily fingers one in one.

'Fondling,' she saith, 'since I have hemmed thee here 230
Within the circuit of this ivory pale,
I'll be a park, and thou shalt be my deer;
Feed where thou wilt, on mountain or in dale;
　Graze on my lips, and if those hills be dry,
　Stray lower, where the pleasant fountains lie. 235

'Within this limit is relief enough,
Sweet bottom-grass and high delightful plain,
Round rising hillocks, brakes obscure and rough,
To shelter thee from tempest and from rain:
　Then be my deer, since I am such a park; 240
　No dog shall rouse thee, though a thousand bark.'

At this Adonis smiles as in disdain,
That in each cheek appears a pretty dimple.
Love made those hollows, if himself were slain,
He might be buried in a tomb so simple; 245
　Foreknowing well, if there he came to lie,
　Why, there Love lived, and there he could not die.

These lovely caves, these round enchanting pits,
Opened their mouths to swallow Venus' liking.
Being mad before, how doth she now for wits? 250
Struck dead at first, what needs a second striking?
　Poor queen of love, in thine own law forlorn,
　To love a cheek that smiles at thee in scorn!

Now which way shall she turn? what shall she say?
Her words are done, her woes the more increasing; 255
The time is spent, her object will away,
And from her twining arms doth urge releasing.
　'Pity,' she cries, 'some favour, some remorse!'
　Away he springs, and hasteth to his horse.

But lo, from forth a copse that neighbours by, 260
A breeding jennet, lusty, young and proud,
Adonis' trampling courser doth espy,
And forth she rushes, snorts and neighs aloud.
　The strong-necked steed, being tied unto a tree,
　Breaketh his rein and to her straight goes he. 265

Imperiously he leaps, he neighs, he bounds,
And now his woven girths he breaks asunder;
The bearing earth with his hard hoof he wounds,
Whose hollow womb resounds like heaven's thunder;
　The iron bit he crusheth 'tween his teeth, 270
　Controlling what he was controllèd with.

His ears up-pricked; his braided hanging mane
Upon his compassed crest now stand on end;
His nostrils drink the air, and forth again,
As from a furnace, vapours doth he send; 275
　His eye, which scornfully glisters like fire,
　Shows his hot courage and his high desire.

Sometime he trots, as if he told the steps,
With gentle majesty and modest pride;
Anon he rears upright, curvets and leaps,   280
As who should say 'Lo, thus my strength is tried,
    And this I do to captivate the eye
    Of the fair breeder that is standing by.'

What recketh he his rider's angry stir,
His flattering 'Holla' or his 'Stand, I say'?   285
What cares he now for curb or pricking spur?
For rich caparisons or trappings gay?
    He sees his love, and nothing else he sees,
    For nothing else with his proud sight agrees.

Look when a painter would surpass the life   290
In limning out a well-proportionéd steed,
His art with nature's workmanship at strife,
As if the dead the living should exceed;
    So did this horse excel a common one
    In shape, in courage, colour, pace and bone.   295

Round-hoofed, short-jointed, fetlocks shag and long,
Broad breast, full eye, small head and nostril wide,
High crest, short ears, straight legs and passing strong,
Thin mane, thick tail, broad buttock, tender hide;
    Look what a horse should have he did not lack,   300
    Save a proud rider on so proud a back.

Sometime he scuds far off, and there he stares;
Anon he starts at stirring of a feather;
To bid the wind a base he now prepares,
And whe'er he run or fly they know not whether;   305
    For through his mane and tail the high wind sings,
    Fanning the hairs, who wave like feath'red wings.

He looks upon his love and neighs unto her;
She answers him as if she knew his mind;
Being proud, as females are, to see him woo her,   310
She puts on outward strangeness, seems unkind,
    Spurns at his love and scorns the heat he feels,
    Beating his kind embracements with her heels.

Then, like a melancholy malcontent,
He vails his tail, that, like a falling plume,   315
Cool shadow to his melting buttock lent;
He stamps, and bites the poor flies in his fume.
    His love, perceiving how he was enraged,
    Grew kinder, and his fury was assuaged.

His testy master goeth about to take him,   320
When, lo, the unbacked breeder, full of fear,
Jealous of catching, swiftly doth forsake him,
With her the horse, and left Adonis there.
    As they were mad, unto the wood they hie them,
    Out-stripping crows that strive to over-fly them. 325

All swoln with chafing, down Adonis sits,
Banning his boist'rous and unruly beast;
And now the happy season once more fits
That love-sick Love by pleading may be blest;
    For lovers say the heart hath treble wrong   330
    When it is barred the aidance of the tongue.

An oven that is stopped, or river stayed,
Burneth more hotly, swelleth with more rage;
So of concealéd sorrow may be said,
Free vent of words love's fire doth assuage;   335
    But when the heart's attorney once is mute,
    The client breaks, as desperate in his suit.

He sees her coming, and begins to glow,
Even as a dying coal revives with wind,
And with his bonnet hides his angry brow,   340
Looks on the dull earth with disturbéd mind,
    Taking no notice that she is so nigh,
    For all askance he holds her in his eye.

O, what a sight it was, wistly to view
How she came stealing to the wayward boy!   345
To note the fighting conflict of her hue,
How white and red each other did destroy!
    But now her cheek was pale, and by and by
    It flashed forth fire, as lightning from the sky.

Now was she just before him as he sat,   350
And like a lowly lover down she kneels;
With one fair hand she heaveth up his hat,
Her other tender hand his fair cheek feels;
    His tend'rer cheek receives her soft hand's print
    As apt as new-fall'n snow takes any dint.   355

O, what a war of looks was then between them,
Her eyes petitioners to his eyes suing!
His eyes saw her eyes as they had not seen them;
Her eyes wooed still, his eyes disdained the wooing;
    And all this dumb play had his acts made plain   360
    With tears which chorus-like her eyes did rain.

Full gently now she takes him by the hand,
A lily prisoned in a gaol of snow,
Or ivory in an alabaster band;
So white a friend engirts so white a foe: 365
    This beauteous combat, wilful and unwilling,
    Showed like two silver doves that sit a-billing.

Once more the engine of her thoughts began:
'O fairest mover on this mortal round,
Would thou wert as I am, and I a man,   370
My heart all whole as thine, thy heart my wound;
    For one sweet look thy help I would assure thee,
    Though nothing but my body's bane would cure
        thee.'

'Give me my hand,' saith he; 'why dost thou feel it?'
'Give me my heart,' saith she, 'and thou shalt have it; 375
O, give it me, lest thy hard heart do steel it,
And being steeled, soft sighs can never grave it;
    Then love's deep groans I never shall regard,
    Because Adonis' heart hath made mine hard.'

'For shame,' he cries, 'let go, and let me go;   380
My day's delight is past, my horse is gone,
And 'tis your fault I am bereft him so.
I pray you hence, and leave me here alone;
    For all my mind, my thought, my busy care,
    Is how to get my palfrey from the mare.'   385

Thus she replies: 'Thy palfrey, as he should,
Welcomes the warm approach of sweet desire.
Affection is a coal that must be cooled;
Else, suffered, it will set the heart on fire.
   The sea hath bounds, but deep desire hath none,   390
   Therefore no marvel though thy horse be gone.

'How like a jade he stood tied to the tree,
Servilely mastered with a leathern rein!
But when he saw his love, his youth's fair fee,
He held such petty bondage in disdain,   395
   Throwing the base thong from his bending crest,
   Enfranchising his mouth, his back, his breast.

'Who sees his true-love in her naked bed,
Teaching the sheets a whiter hue than white,
But, when his glutton eye so full hath fed,   400
His other agents aim at like delight?
   Who is so faint that dares not be so bold
   To touch the fire, the weather being cold?

'Let me excuse thy courser, gentle boy;
And learn of him, I heartily beseech thee,   405
To take advantage on presented joy;
Though I were dumb, yet his proceedings teach thee.
   O, learn to love; the lesson is but plain,
   And once made perfect, never lost again.'

'I know not love,' quoth he, 'nor will not know it,   410
Unless it be a boar, and then I chase it.
'Tis much to borrow, and I will not owe it.
My love to love is love but to disgrace it;
   For I have heard it is a life in death,
   That laughs, and weeps, and all but with a breath.   415

'Who wears a garment shapeless and unfinished?
Who plucks the bud before one leaf put forth?
If springing things be any jot diminished,
They wither in their prime, prove nothing worth.
   The colt that's backed and burdened being young   420
   Loseth his pride, and never waxeth strong.

'You hurt my hand with wringing; let us part,
And leave this idle theme, this bootless chat;
Remove your siege from my unyielding heart;
To love's alarms it will not ope the gate.   425
   Dismiss your vows, your feignéd tears, your flatt'ry;
   For where a heart is hard they make no batt'ry.'

'What, canst thou talk?' quoth she, 'hast thou a tongue?
O, would thou hadst not, or I had no hearing!
Thy mermaid's voice hath done me double wrong;   430
I had my load before, now pressed with bearing:
   Melodious discord, heavenly tune harsh sounding,
   Ears' deep-sweet music, and heart's deep-sore
      wounding.

'Had I no eyes but ears, my ears would love
That inward beauty and invisible;   435
Or were I deaf, thy outward parts would move
Each part in me that were but sensible.
   Though neither eyes nor ears, to hear nor see,
   Yet should I be in love by touching thee.

'Say that the sense of feeling were bereft me,   440
And that I could not see, nor hear, nor touch,
And nothing but the very smell were left me,
Yet would my love to thee be still as much;
   For from the stillitory of thy face excelling
   Comes breath perfumed, that breedeth love by   445
      smelling.

'But O, what banquet wert thou to the taste,
Being nurse and feeder of the other four!
Would they not wish the feast might ever last,
And bid Suspicion double-lock the door,
   Lest Jealousy, that sour unwelcome guest,   450
   Should by his stealing in disturb the feast?'

Once more the ruby-coloured portal opened,
Which to his speech did honey passage yield;
Like a red morn, that ever yet betokened
Wrack to the seaman, tempest to the field,   455
   Sorrow to shepherds, woe unto the birds,
   Gusts and foul flaws to herdmen and to herds.

This ill presage advisedly she marketh.
Even as the wind is hushed before it raineth,
Or as the wolf doth grin before he barketh,   460
Or as the berry breaks before it staineth,
   Or like the deadly bullet of a gun,
   His meaning struck her ere his words begun.

And at his look she flatly falleth down,
For looks kill love, and love by looks reviveth;   465
A smile recures the wounding of a frown.
But blesséd bankrupt that by loss so thriveth!
   The silly boy, believing she is dead,
   Claps her pale cheek, till clapping makes it red;

And all amazed brake off his late intent,   470
For sharply he did think to reprehend her,
Which cunning love did wittily prevent.
Fair fall the wit that can so well defend her!
   For on the grass she lies as she were slain,
   Till his breath breatheth life in her again.   475

He wrings her nose, he strikes her on the cheeks,
He bends her fingers, holds her pulses hard,
He chafes her lips, a thousand ways he seeks
To mend the hurt that his unkindness marred;
   He kisses her; and she, by her good will,   480
   Will never rise, so he will kiss her still.

The night of sorrow now is turned to day:
Her two blue windows faintly she upheaveth,
Like the fair sun, when in his fresh array
He cheers the morn, and all the earth relieveth;   485
   And as the bright sun glorifies the sky,
   So is her face illumined with her eye;

Whose beams upon his hairless face are fixed,
As if from thence they borrowéd all their shine.
Were never four such lamps together mixed,   490
Had not his clouded with his brow's repine;
   But hers, which through the crystal tears gave light,
   Shone like the moon in water seen by night.

'O, where am I?' quoth she; 'in earth or heaven,
Or in the ocean drenched, or in the fire? 495
What hour is this? or morn or weary even?
Do I delight to die, or life desire?
  But now I lived, and life was death's annoy;
  But now I died, and death was lively joy.

'O, thou didst kill me: kill me once again. 500
Thy eyes' shrewd tutor, that hard heart of thine,
Hath taught them scornful tricks, and such disdain
That they have murd'red this poor heart of mine;
  And these mine eyes, true leaders to their queen,
  But for thy piteous lips no more had seen. 505

'Long may they kiss each other, for this cure!
O, never let their crimson liveries wear!
And as they last, their verdure still endure
To drive infection from the dangerous year!
  That the star-gazers, having writ on death, 510
  May say, the plague is banished by thy breath.

'Pure lips, sweet seals in my soft lips imprinted,
What bargains may I make, still to be sealing?
To sell myself I can be well contented,
So thou wilt buy, and pay, and use good dealing; 515
  Which purchase if thou make, for fear of slips
  Set thy seal manual on my wax-red lips.

'A thousand kisses buys my heart from me;
And pay them at thy leisure, one by one.
What is ten hundred touches unto thee? 520
Are they not quickly told and quickly gone?
  Say for non-payment that the debt should double,
  Is twenty hundred kisses such a trouble?'

'Fair queen,' quoth he, 'if any love you owe me,
Measure my strangeness with my unripe years; 525
Before I know myself, seek not to know me;
No fisher but the ungrown fry forbears.
  The mellow plum doth fall, the green sticks fast,
  Or being early plucked is sour to taste.

'Look, the world's comforter, with weary gait, 530
His day's hot task hath ended in the west;
The owl, night's herald, shrieks 'tis very late;
The sheep are gone to fold, birds to their nest;
  And coal-black clouds that shadow heaven's light
  Do summon us to part, and bid good night. 535

'Now let me say "Good night", and so say you;
If you will say so, you shall have a kiss.'
'Good night', quoth she; and, ere he says 'Adieu',
The honey fee of parting tend'red is:
  Her arms do lend his neck a sweet embrace; 540
  Incorporate then they seem; face grows to face.

Till breathless he disjoined, and backward drew
The heavenly moisture, that sweet coral mouth,
Whose precious taste her thirsty lips well knew,
Whereon they surfeit, yet complain on drouth. 545
  He with her plenty pressed, she faint with dearth,
  Their lips together glued, fall to the earth.

Now quick desire hath caught the yielding prey,
And glutton-like she feeds, yet never filleth;
Her lips are conquerors, his lips obey, 550
Paying what ransom the insulter willeth;
  Whose vulture thought doth pitch the price so high
  That she will draw his lips' rich treasure dry.

And having felt the sweetness of the spoil,
With blindfold fury she begins to forage; 555
Her face doth reek and smoke, her blood doth boil,
And careless lust stirs up a desperate courage,
  Planting oblivion, beating reason back,
  Forgetting shame's pure blush and honour's wrack.

Hot, faint and weary, with her hard embracing, 560
Like a wild bird being tamed with too much handling,
Or as the fleet-foot roe that's tired with chasing,
Or like the froward infant stilled with dandling,
  He now obeys and now no more resisteth,
  While she takes all she can, not all she listeth. 565

What wax so frozen but dissolves with temp'ring,
And yields at last to every light impression?
Things out of hope are compass'd oft with vent'ring,
Chiefly in love, whose leave exceeds commission:
  Affection faints not like a pale-face coward, 570
  But then woos best when most his choice is froward.

When he did frown, O, had she then gave over,
Such nectar from his lips she had not sucked.
Foul words and frowns must not repel a lover;
What though the rose have prickles, yet 'tis plucked. 575
  Were beauty under twenty locks kept fast,
  Yet love breaks through, and picks them all at last.

For pity now she can no more detain him;
The poor fool prays her that he may depart;
She is resolved no longer to restrain him; 580
Bids him farewell, and look well to her heart,
  The which by Cupid's bow she doth protest
  He carries thence incagéd in his breast.

'Sweet boy,' she says, 'this night I'll waste in sorrow,
For my sick heart commands mine eyes to watch. 585
Tell me, love's master, shall we meet to-morrow?
Say, shall we? shall we? wilt thou make the match?'
  He tells her, no; to-morrow he intends
  To hunt the boar with certain of his friends.

'The boar!' quoth she: whereat a sudden pale, 590
Like lawn being spread upon the blushing rose,
Usurps her cheek; she trembles at his tale,
And on his neck her yoking arms she throws.
  She sinketh down, still hanging by his neck,
  He on her belly falls, she on her back. 595

Now is she in the very lists of love,
Her champion mounted for the hot encounter.
All is imaginary she doth prove;
He will not manage her, although he mount her;
  That worse than Tantalus' is her annoy, 600
  To clip Elysium and to lack her joy.

Even so poor birds, deceived with painted grapes,
Do surfeit by the eye and pine the maw;
Even so she languisheth in her mishaps
As those poor birds that helpless berries saw.   605
  The warm effects which she in him finds missing
  She seeks to kindly with continual kissing.

But all in vain, good queen, it will not be.
She hath assayed as much as may be proved;
Her pleading hath deserved a greater fee;   610
She's Love, she loves, and yet she is not loved.
  'Fie, fie,' he says, 'you crush me; let me go;
  You have no reason to withhold me so.'

'Thou hadst been gone,' quoth she, 'sweet boy, ere this,
But that thou told'st me thou wouldst hunt the boar. 615
O, be advised: thou know'st not what it is
With javelin's point a churlish swine to gore,
  Whose tushes never sheathed he whetteth still,
  Like to a mortal butcher bent to kill.

'On his bow-back he hath a battle set   620
Of bristly pikes that ever threat his foes;
His eyes like glow-worms shine when he doth fret;
His snout digs sepulchres where'er he goes;
  Being moved, he strikes whate'er is in his way,
  And whom he strikes his crookéd tushes slay.   625

'His brawny sides, with hairy bristles arméd,
Are better proof than thy spear's point can enter;
His short thick neck cannot be easily harméd;
Being ireful, on the lion he will venter:
  The thorny brambles and embracing bushes,   630
  As fearful of him, part; through whom he rushes.

'Alas, he nought esteems that face of thine,
To which Love's eyes pays tributary gazes,
Nor thy soft hands, sweet lips and crystal eyne,
Whose full perfection all the world amazes;   635
  But having thee at vantage—wondrous dread!—
  Would root these beauties as he roots the mead.

'O, let him keep his loathsome cabin still;
Beauty hath nought to do with such foul fiends.
Come not within his danger by thy will;   640
They that thrive well take counsel of their friends.
  When thou didst name the boar, not to dissemble,
  I feared thy fortune, and my joints did tremble.

'Didst thou not mark my face? was it not white?
Saws't thou not signs of fear lurk in mine eye?   645
Grew I not faint? and fell I not downright?
Within my bosom, whereon thou dost lie,
  My boding heart pants, beats, and takes no rest,
  But, like an earthquake, shakes thee on my breast.

'For where Love reigns, disturbing Jealousy   650
Doth call himself Affection's sentinel;
Gives false alarms, suggesteth mutiny,
And in a peaceful hour doth cry "Kill, kill!"
  Distemp'ring gentle Love in his desire,
  As air and water do abate the fire.   655

'This sour informer, this bate-breeding spy,
This canker that eats up Love's tender spring,
This carry-tale, dissentious Jealousy,
That sometime true news, sometime false doth bring,
  Knocks at my heart, and whispers in mine ear   660
  That if I love thee I thy death should fear;

'And more than so, presenteth to mine eye
The picture of an angry chafing boar
Under whose sharp fangs on his back doth lie
An image like thyself, all stained with gore;   665
  Whose blood upon the fresh flowers being shed
  Doth make them droop with grief and hang the
    head.

'What should I do, seeing thee so indeed,
That tremble at th'imagination?
The thought of it doth make my faint heart bleed,   670
And fear doth teach it divination:
  I prophesy thy death, my living sorrow,
  If thou encounter with the boar to-morrow.

'But if thou needs wilt hunt, be ruled by me;
Uncouple at the timorous flying hare,   675
Or at the fox which lives by subtlety,
Or at the roe which no encounter dare.
  Pursue these fearful creatures o'er the downs,
  And on thy well-breathed horse keep with thy
    hounds.

'And when thou hast on foot the purblind hare,   680
Mark the poor wretch, to overshoot his troubles,
How he outruns the wind, and with what care
He cranks and crosses with a thousand doubles.
  The many musits through the which he goes
  Are like a labyrinth to amaze his foes.   685

'Sometime he runs among a flock of sheep,
To make the cunning hounds mistake their smell,
And sometime where earth-delving conies keep,
To stop the loud pursuers in their yell;
  And sometime sorteth with a herd of deer.   690
  Danger deviseth shifts; wit waits on fear.

'For there his smell with others being mingled,
The hot scent-snuffing hounds are driven to doubt,
Ceasing their clamorous cry till they have singled
With much ado the cold fault cleanly out.   695
  Then do they spend their mouths; Echo replies,
  As if another chase were in the skies.

'By this, poor Wat, far off upon a hill,
Stands on his hinder legs with list'ning ear,
To hearken if his foes pursue him still;   700
Anon their loud alarums he doth hear;
  And now his grief may be compared well
  To one sore sick that hears the passing-bell.

'Then shalt thou see the dew-bedabbled wretch
Turn, and return, indenting with the way;   705
Each envious brier his weary legs do scratch,
Each shadow makes him stop, each murmur stay;
  For misery is trodden on by many,
  And being low never relieved by any.

'Lie quietly and hear a little more;   710
Nay, do not struggle, for thou shalt not rise.
To make thee hate the hunting of the boar,
Unlike myself thou hear'st me moralize,
　　Applying this to that, and so to so;
　　For love can comment upon every woe.   715

'Where did I leave?' 'No matter where,' quoth he;
'Leave me, and then the story aptly ends.
The night is spent.' 'Why, what of that?' quoth she.
'I am', quoth he, 'expected of my friends;
　　And now 'tis dark, and going I shall fall.'   720
　　'In night', quoth she, 'desire sees best of all.

'But if thou fall, O, then imagine this,
The earth, in love with thee, thy footing trips,
And all is but to rob thee of a kiss.
Rich preys make true men thieves; so do thy lips   725
　　Make modest Dian cloudy and forlorn,
　　Lest she should steal a kiss, and die forsworn.

'Now of this dark night I perceive the reason:
Cynthia for shame obscures her silver shine,
Till forging Nature be condemned of treason,   730
For stealing moulds from heaven that were divine,
　　Wherein she framed thee, in high heaven's despite,
　　To shame the sun by day and her by night.

'And therefore hath she bribed the Destinies
To cross the curious workmanship of Nature,   735
To mingle beauty with infirmities
And pure perfection with impure defeature,
　　Making it subject to the tyranny
　　Of mad mischances and much misery;

'As burning fevers, agues pale and faint,   740
Life-poisoning pestilence and frenzies wood,
The marrow-eating sickness whose attaint
Disorder breeds by heating of the blood,
　　Surfeits, imposthumes, grief and damned despair,
　　Swear Nature's death for framing thee so fair.   745

'And not the least of all these maladies
But in one minute's fight brings beauty under.
Both favour, savour, hue and qualities,
Whereat th'impartial gazer late did wonder,
　　Are on the sudden wasted, thawed and done,   750
　　As mountain snow melts with the midday sun.

'Therefore, despite of fruitless chastity,
Love-lacking vestals and self-loving nuns,
That on the earth would breed a scarcity
And barren dearth of daughters and of sons,   755
　　Be prodigal: the lamp that burns by night
　　Dries up his oil to lend the world his light.

'What is thy body but a swallowing grave,
Seeming to bury that posterity
Which by the rights of time thou needs must have, 760
If thou destroy them not in dark obscurity?
　　If so, the world will hold thee in disdain,
　　Sith in thy pride so fair a hope is slain.

'So in thyself thyself art made away;
A mischief worse than civil home-bred strife,   765
Or theirs whose desperate hands themselves do slay,
Or butcher sire that reaves his son of life.
　　Foul cank'ring rust the hidden treasure frets,
　　But gold that's put to use more gold begets.'

'Nay, then,' quoth Adon, 'you will fall again   770
Into your idle over-handled theme;
The kiss I gave you is bestowed in vain,
And all in vain you strive against the stream;
　　For, by this black-faced night, desire's foul nurse,
　　Your treatise makes me like you worse and worse. 775

'If love have lent you twenty thousand tongues,
And every tongue more moving than your own,
Bewitching like the wanton mermaid's songs,
Yet from mine ear the tempting tune is blown;
　　For know, my heart stands armed in mine ear,   780
　　And will not let a false sound enter there,

'Lest the deceiving harmony should run
Into the quiet closure of my breast;
And then my little heart were quite undone,
In his bedchamber to be barred of rest.   785
　　No, lady, no; my heart longs not to groan,
　　But soundly sleeps, while now it sleeps alone.

'What have you urged that I cannot reprove?
The path is smooth that leadeth on to danger;
I hate not love, but your device in love   790
That lends embracements unto every stranger.
　　You do it for increase: O strange excuse,
　　When reason is the bawd to lust's abuse!

'Call it not love, for Love to heaven is fled
Since sweating Lust on earth usurped his name;   795
Under whose simple semblance he hath fed
Upon fresh beauty, blotting it with blame;
　　Which the hot tyrant stains and soon bereaves,
　　As caterpillars do the tender leaves.

'Love comforteth like sunshine after rain,   800
But Lust's effect is tempest after sun;
Love's gentle spring doth always fresh remain,
Lust's winter comes ere summer half be done;
　　Love surfeits not, Lust like a glutton dies;
　　Love is all truth, Lust full of forgéd lies.   805

'More I could tell, but more I dare not say;
The text is old, the orator too green.
Therefore, in sadness, now I will away;
My face is full of shame, my heart of teen:
　　Mine ears that to your wanton talk attended   810
　　Do burn themselves for having so offended.'

With this, he breaketh from the sweet embrace
Of those fair arms which bound him to her breast,
And homeward through the dark lawnd runs apace;
Leaves Love upon her back deeply distressed.   815
　　Look how a bright star shooteth from the sky,
　　So glides he in the night from Venus' eye;

Which after him she darts, as one on shore
Gazing upon a late-embarkéd friend,
Till the wild waves will have him seen no more,   320
Whose ridges with the meeting clouds contend;
    So did the merciless and pitchy night
    Fold in the object that did feed her sight.

Whereat amazed as one that unaware
Hath dropped a precious jewel in the flood,   825
Or 'stonished as night-wand'rers often are,
Their light blown out in some mistrustful wood;
    Even so confounded in the dark she lay,
    Having lost the fair discovery of her way.

And now she beats her heart, whereat it groans,   830
That all the neighbour caves, as seeming troubled,
Make verbal repetition of her moans;
Passion on passion deeply is redoubled:
    'Ay me!' she cries, and twenty times, 'Woe, woe!'
    And twenty echoes twenty times cry so.   835

She, marking them, begins a wailing note,
And sings extemporally a woeful ditty;
How love makes young men thrall, and old men dote;
How love is wise in folly, foolish witty:
    Her heavy anthem still concludes in woe,   840
    And still the choir of echoes answer so.

Her song was tedious, and outwore the night,
For lovers' hours are long, though seeming short;
If pleased themselves, others, they think, delight
In such-like circumstance, with such-like sport.   845
    Their copious stories, oftentimes begun,
    End without audience, and are never done.

For who hath she to spend the night withal
But idle sounds resembling parasites,
Like shrill-tongued tapsters answering every call,   850
Soothing the humour of fantastic wits?
    She says ' 'Tis so'; they answer all ' 'Tis so';
    And would say after her, if she said 'No'.

Lo, here the gentle lark, weary of rest,
From his moist cabinet mounts up on high,   855
And wakes the morning, from whose silver breast
The sun ariseth in his majesty;
    Who doth the world so gloriously behold
    That cedar-tops and hills seem burnished gold.

Venus salutes him with this fair good-morrow: 860
'O thou clear god, and patron of all light,
From whom each lamp and shining star doth borrow
The beauteous influence that makes him bright,
    There lives a son that sucked an earthly mother
    May lend thee light, as thou dost lend to other.' 865

This said, she hasteth to a myrtle grove,
Musing the morning is so much o'erworn,
And yet she hears no tidings of her love;
She hearkens for his hounds and for his horn.
    Anon she hears them chant it lustily,   870
    And all in haste she coasteth to the cry.

And as she runs, the bushes in the way
Some catch her by the neck, some kiss her face,
Some twind about her thigh to make her stay;
She wildly breaketh from their strict embrace,   875
    Like a milch doe, whose swelling dugs do ache,
    Hasting to feed her fawn hid in some brake.

By this she hears the hounds are at a bay;
Whereat she starts, like one that spies an adder
Wreathed up in fatal folds just in his way,   880
The fear whereof doth make him shake and shudder;
    Even so the timorous yelping of the hounds
    Appals her senses and her spirit confounds.

For now she knows it is no gentle chase,
But the blunt boar, rough bear, or lion proud,   885
Because the cry remaineth in one place,
Where fearfully the dogs exclaim aloud.
    Finding their enemy to be so curst,
    They all strain court'sy who shall cope him first.

This dismal cry rings sadly in her ear,   890
Through which it enters to surprise her heart;
Who, overcome by doubt and bloodless fear,
With cold-pale weakness numbs each feeling part;
    Like soldiers, when their captain once doth yield,
    They basely fly and dare not stay the field.   895

Thus stands she in a trembling ecstasy;
Till, cheering up her senses all dismayed,
She tells them 'tis a causeless fantasy,
And childish error, that they are afraid;
    Bids them leave quaking, bids them fear no more; 900
    And with that word she spied the hunted boar,

Whose frothy mouth, bepainted all with red,
Like milk and blood being mingled both together,
A second fear through all her sinews spread,
Which madly hurries her she knows not whither: 905
    This way she runs, and now she will no further,
    But back retires to rate the boar for murther.

A thousand spleens bear her a thousand ways;
She treads the path that she untreads again;
Her more than haste is mated with delays,   910
Like the proceedings of a drunken brain,
    Full of respects, yet nought at all respecting,
    In hand with all things, nought at all effecting.

Here kennelled in a brake she finds a hound,
And asks the weary caitiff for his master;   915
And there another licking of his wound,
'Gainst venomed sores the only sovereign plaster;
    And here she meets another sadly scowling,
    To whom she speaks, and he replies with howling.

When he hath ceased his ill-resounding noise,   920
Another flap-mouthed mourner, black and grim,
Against the welkin volleys out his voice;
Another and another answer him,
    Clapping their proud tails to the ground below,
    Shaking their scratched ears, bleeding as they go. 925

Look how the world's poor people are amazéd
At apparitions, signs and prodigies,
Whereon with fearful eyes they long have gazéd,
Infusing them with dreadful prophecies;
    So she at these sad signs draws up her breath,   930
    And, sighing it again, exclaims on Death.

'Hard-favoured tyrant, ugly, meagre, lean,
Hateful divorce of love'—thus chides she Death—
'Grim-grinning ghost, earth's worm, what dost thou
    mean
To stifle beauty and to steal his breath   935
    Who when he lived, his breath and beauty set
    Gloss on the rose, smell to the violet?

'If he be dead—O no, it cannot be,
Seeing his beauty, thou shouldst strike at it—
O yes, it may; thou hast no eyes to see,   940
But hatefully at random dost thou hit.
    Thy mark is feeble age; but thy false dart
    Mistakes that aim, and cleaves an infant's heart.

'Hadst thou but bid beware, then he had spoke,
And, hearing him, thy power had lost his power.   945
The Destinies will curse thee for this stroke;
They bid thee crop a weed, thou pluck'st a flower.
    Love's golden arrow at him should have fled,
    And not Death's ebon dart, to strike him dead.

'Dost thou drink tears, that thou provokest such
    weeping?   950
What may a heavy groan advantage thee?
Why hast thou cast into eternal sleeping
Those eyes that taught all other eyes to see?
    Now Nature cares not for thy mortal vigour,
    Since her best work is ruined with thy rigour.'   955

Here overcome as one full of despair,
She vailed her eyelids, who, like sluices, stopped
The crystal tide that from her two cheeks fair
In the sweet channel of her bosom dropped;
    But through the flood-gates breaks the silver rain,   960
    And with his strong course opens them again.

O, how her eyes and tears did lend and borrow!
Her eye seen in the tears, tears in her eye;
Both crystals, where they viewed each other's sorrow,
Sorrow that friendly sighs sought still to dry;   965
    But like a stormy day, now wind, now rain,
    Sighs dry her cheeks, tears make them wet again.

Variable passions throng her constant woe,
As striving who should best become her grief;
All entertained, each passion labours so   970
That every present sorrow seemeth chief,
    But none is best. Then join they all together,
    Like many clouds consulting for foul weather.

By this, far off she hears some huntsman holla;
A nurse's song ne'er pleased her babe so well.   975
The dire imagination she did follow
This sound of hope doth labour to expel;
    For now reviving joy bids her rejoice,
    And flatters her it is Adonis' voice.

Whereat her tears began to turn their tide,   980
Being prisoned in her eye like pearls in glass;
Yet sometimes falls an orient drop beside,
Which her cheek melts, as scorning it should pass
    To wash the foul face of the sluttish ground,
    Who is but drunken when she seemeth drowned.   985

O hard-believing love, how strange it seems
Not to believe, and yet too credulous!
Thy weal and woe are both of them extremes;
Despair, and hope makes thee ridiculous:
    The one doth flatter thee in thoughts unlikely,   990
    In likely thoughts the other kills thee quickly.

Now she unweaves the web that she hath wrought;
Adonis lives, and Death is not to blame;
It was not she that called him all to nought.
Now she adds honours to his hateful name;   995
    She clepes him king of graves, and grave for kings,
    Imperious supreme of all mortal things.

'No, no,' quoth she, 'sweet Death, I did but jest;
Yet pardon me, I felt a kind of fear
When as I met the boar, that bloody beast,   1000
Which knows no pity, but is still severe.
    Then, gentle shadow—truth I must confess—
    I railed on thee, fearing my love's decease.

''Tis not my fault: the boar provoked my tongue;
Be wreaked on him, invisible commander;   1005
'Tis he, foul creature, that hath done thee wrong;
I did but act, he's author of thy slander.
    Grief hath two tongues, and never woman yet
    Could rule them both without ten women's wit.'

Thus, hoping that Adonis is alive,   1010
Her rash suspect she doth extenuate;
And that his beauty may the better thrive,
With Death she humbly doth insinuate;
    Tells him of trophies, statues, tombs, and stories
    His victories, his triumphs and his glories.   1015

'O Jove,' quoth she, 'how much a fool was I
To be of such a weak and silly mind
To wail his death who lives and must not die
Till mutual overthrow of mortal kind!
    For he being dead, with him is Beauty slain,   1020
    And, Beauty dead, black Chaos comes again.

'Fie, fie, fond love, thou art as full of fear
As one with treasure laden, hemmed with thieves;
Trifles unwitnesséd with eye or ear
Thy coward heart with false bethinking grieves.'   1025
    Even at this word she hears a merry horn,
    Whereat she leaps that was but late forlorn.

As falcons to the lure, away she flies;
The grass stoops not, she treads on it so light;
And in her haste unfortunately spies   1030
The foul boar's conquest on her fair delight;
    Which seen, her eyes, as murd'red with the view,
    Like stars ashamed of day, themselves withdrew;

Or as the snail, whose tender horns being hit,
Shrinks backward in his shelly cave with pain,   1035
And there all smoth'red up in shade doth sit,
Long after fearing to creep forth again;
    So at his bloody view her eyes are fled
    Into the deep-dark cabins of her head;

Where they resign their office and their light   1040
To the disposing of her troubled brain;
Who bids them still consort with ugly night,
And never wound the heart with looks again;
    Who, like a king perplexéd in his throne,
    By their suggestion gives a deadly groan,   1045

Whereat each tributary subject quakes;
As when the wind, imprisoned in the ground,
Struggling for passage, earth's foundation shakes,
Which with cold terror doth men's minds confound.
    This mutiny each part doth so surprise,   1050
    That from their dark beds once more leap her eyes;

And being opened, threw unwilling light
Upon the wide wound that the boar had trenched
In his soft flank; whose wonted lily white
With purple tears that his wound wept was drenched: 1055
    No flower was nigh, no grass, herb, leaf or weed,
    But stole his blood.and seemed with him to bleed.

This solemn sympathy poor Venus noteth;
Over one shoulder doth she hang her head;
Dumbly she passions, franticly she doteth;   1060
She thinks he could not die, he is not dead.
    Her voice is stopped, her joints forget to bow;
    Her eyes are mad that they have wept till now.

Upon his hurt she looks so steadfastly
That her sight dazzling makes the wound seem three;   1065
And then she reprehends her mangling eye
That makes more gashes where no breach should be:
    His face seems twain, each several limb is doubled;
    For oft the eye mistakes, the brain being troubled.

'My tongue cannot express my grief for one,   1070
And yet,' quoth she, 'behold two Adons dead!
My sighs are blown away, my salt tears gone,
Mine eyes are turned to fire, my heart to lead;
    Heavy heart's lead, melt at mine eyes' red fire!
    So shall I die by drops of hot desire.   1075

'Alas, poor world, what treasure hast thou lost!
What face remains alive that's worth the viewing?
Whose tongue is music now? what canst thou boast
Of things long since, or any thing ensuing?
    The flowers are sweet, their colours fresh and trim; 1080
    But true sweet beauty lived and died with him.

'Bonnet nor veil henceforth no creature wear;
Nor sun nor wind will ever strive to kiss you.
Having no fair to lose, you need not fear;
The sun doth scorn you, and the wind doth hiss you.   1085
    But when Adonis lived, sun and sharp air
    Lurked like two thieves to rob him of his fair;

'And therefore would he put his bonnet on,
Under whose brim the gaudy sun would peep;
The wind would blow it off, and, being gone,   1090
Play with his locks. Then would Adonis weep;
    And straight, in pity of his tender years,
    They both would strive who first should dry his
      tears.

'To see his face the lion walked along
Behind some hedge, because he would not fear him;   1095
To recreate himself when he hath sung,
The tiger would be tame and gently hear him;
    If he had spoke, the wolf would leave his prey,
    And never fright the silly lamb that day.

'When he beheld his shadow in the brook,   1100
The fishes spread on it their golden gills;
When he was by, the birds such pleasure took
That some would sing, some other in their bills
    Would bring him mulberries and ripe-red cherries;
    He fed them with his sight, they him with berries. 1105

'But this foul, grim, and urchin-snouted boar,
Whose downward eye still looketh for a grave,
Ne'er saw the beauteous livery that he wore;
Witness the entertainment that he gave.
    If he did see his face, why then I know   1110
    He thought to kiss him, and hath killed him so.

''Tis true, 'tis true; thus was Adonis slain:
He ran upon the boar with his sharp spear,
Who did not whet his teeth at him again,
But by a kiss thought to persuade him there;   1115
    And nuzzling in his flank, the loving swine
    Sheathed unaware the tusk in his soft groin.

'Had I been toothed like him, I must confess,
With kissing him I should have killed him first;
But he is dead, and never did he bless   1120
My youth with his; the more am I accurst.'
    With this, she falleth in the place she stood,
    And stains her face with his congealéd blood.

She looks upon his lips, and they are pale;
She takes him by the hand, and that is cold;   1125
She whispers in his ears a heavy tale,
As if they heard the woeful words she told;
    She lifts the coffer-lids that close his eyes,
    Where, lo, two lamps, burnt out, in darkness lies;

Two glasses, where herself herself beheld   1130
A thousand times, and now no more, reflect;
Their virtue lost wherein they late excelled,
And every beauty robbed of his effect.
    'Wonder of time,' quoth she, 'this is my spite,
    That, thou being dead, the day should yet be light. 1135

'Since thou art dead, lo, here I prophesy
Sorrow on love hereafter shall attend;
It shall be waited on with jealousy,
Find sweet beginning but unsavoury end;
    Ne'er settled equally, but high or low,   1140
    That all love's pleasure shall not match his woe.

'It shall be fickle, false and full of fraud;
Bud, and be blasted, in a breathing while;
The bottom poison, and the top o'erstrawed
With sweets that shall the truest sight beguile;   1145
  The strongest body shall it make most weak,
  Strike the wise dumb, and teach the fool to speak.

'It shall be sparing, and too full of riot,
Teaching decrepit age to tread the measures;
The staring ruffian shall it keep in quiet,   1150
Pluck down the rich, enrich the poor with treasures;
  It shall be raging-mad, and silly-mild,
  Make the young old, the old become a child.

'It shall suspect where is no cause of fear;
It shall not fear where it should most mistrust;   1155
It shall be merciful and too severe,
And most deceiving when it seems most just;
  Perverse it shall be where it shows most toward,
  Put fear to valour, courage to the coward.

'It shall be cause of war and dire events,   1160
And set dissension 'twixt the son and sire;
Subject and servile to all discontents,
As dry combustious matter is to fire.
  Sith in his prime death doth my love destroy,
  They that love best their loves shall not enjoy.'   1165

By this the boy that by her side lay killed
Was melted like a vapour from her sight,
And in his blood that on the ground lay spilled
A purple flower sprung up, chequ'red with white,
  Resembling well his pale cheeks, and the blood   1170
  Which in round drops upon their whiteness stood.

She bows her head the new-sprung flower to smell,
Comparing it to her Adonis' breath;
And says within her bosom it shall dwell,
Since he himself is reft from her by death;   1175
  She crops the stalk, and in the breach appears
  Green-dropping sap, which she compares to tears.

'Poor flower,' quoth she, 'this was thy father's guise—
Sweet issue of a more sweet-smelling sire—
For every little grief to wet his eyes.   1180
To grow unto himself was his desire,
  And so 'tis thine; but know, it is as good
  To wither in my breast as in his blood.

'Here was thy father's bed, here in my breast;
Thou art the next of blood, and 'tis thy right.   1185
Lo, in this hollow cradle take thy rest;
My throbbing heart shall rock thee day and night;
  There shall not be one minute in an hour
  Wherein I will not kiss my sweet love's flower.'

Thus weary of the world, away she hies,   1190
And yokes her silver doves, by whose swift aid
Their mistress, mounted, through the empty skies
In her light chariot quickly is conveyed,
  Holding their course to Paphos, where their queen
  Means to immure herself and not be seen.   1195

The Rape of Lucrece

TO THE
RIGHT HONOURABLE
HENRY WRIOTHESLEY,
EARL OF SOUTHAMPTON, AND BARON
OF TITCHFIELD

The love I dedicate to your lordship is without end: whereof this pamphlet, without beginning is but a superfluous moiety. The warrant I have of your honourable disposition, not the worth of my untutored lines, make it assured of acceptance. What I have done is yours; what I have to do is yours; being part in all I have, devoted yours. Were my worth greater, my duty would show greater; meantime, as it is, it is bound to your lordship, to whom I wish long life still lengthened with all happiness.

Your lordship's in all duty,
William Shakespeare

THE ARGUMENT

Lucius Tarquinius, for his excessive pride surnamed Superbus, after he had caused his own father-in-law Servius Tullius to be cruelly murdered, and, contrary to the Roman laws and customs, not requiring or staying for the people's suffrages, had possessed himself of the kingdom, went accompanied with his sons and other noblemen of Rome, to besiege Ardea. During which siege the principal men of the army meeting one evening at the tent of Sextus Tarquinius, the king's son, in their discourses after supper every one commended the virtues of his own wife; among whom Collatinus extolled the incomparable chastity of his wife Lucretia. In that pleasant humour they all posted to Rome; and intending, by their secret and sudden arrival, to make trial of that which every one had before avouched, only Collatinus finds his wife, though it were late in the night, spinning amongst her maids: the other ladies were all found dancing and revelling, or in several disports. Whereupon the noblemen yielded Collatinus the victory, and his wife the fame. At that time Sextus Tarquinius being inflamed with Lucrece' beauty, yet smothering his passions for the present, departed with the rest back to the camp; from whence he shortly after privily withdrew himself, and was, according to his estate, royally entertained and lodged by Lucrece at Collatium. The same night he treacherously stealeth into her chamber, violently ravished her, and early in the morning speedeth away. Lucrece, in this lamentable plight, hastily dispatcheth messengers, one to Rome for her father, another to the camp for Collatine. They came, the one accompanied with Junius Brutus, the other with Publius Valerius; and finding Lucrece attired in mourning habit, demanded the cause of her sorrow. She, first taking an oath of them for her revenge, revealed the actor and whole manner of his dealing, and withal suddenly stabbed herself. Which done, with one consent they all vowed to root out the whole hated family of the Tarquins; and bearing the dead body to Rome, Brutus acquainted the people with the doer and manner of the vile deed, with a bitter invective against the tyranny of the king: wherewith the people were so moved, that with one consent and a general acclamation the Tarquins were all exiled, and the state government changed from kings to consuls.

From the besiegéd Ardea all in post,
Borne by the trustless wings of false desire,
Lust-breathéd Tarquin leaves the Roman host,
And to Collatium bears the lightless fire
Which, in pale embers hid, lurks to aspire   5
   And girdle with embracing flames the waist
   Of Collatine's fair love, Lucrece the chaste.

Haply that name of chaste unhapp'ly set
This bateless edge on his keen appetite;
When Collatine unwisely did not let   10
To praise the clear unmatchéd red and white
Which triumphed in that sky of his delight,
   Where mortal stars, as bright as heaven's beauties,
   With pure aspects did him peculiar duties.

For he the night before, in Tarquin's tent,   15
Unlocked the treasure of his happy state;
What priceless wealth the heavens had him lent
In the possession of his beauteous mate;
Reck'ning his fortune at such high-proud rate
   That kings might be espoused to more fame,   20
   But king nor peer to such a peerless dame.

O happiness enjoyed but of a few!
And, if possessed, as soon decayed and done
As is the morning silver-melting dew
Against the golden splendour of the sun!   25
An expired date, cancelled ere well begun:
   Honour and beauty, in the owner's arms,
   Are weakly fortressed from a world of harms.

Beauty itself doth of itself persuade
The eyes of men without an orator;   30
What needeth then apology be made,
To set forth that which is so singular?
Or why is Collatine the publisher
   Of that rich jewel he should keep unknown
   From thievish ears, because it is his own?   35

Perchance his boast of Lucrece' sov'reignty
Suggested this proud issue of a king;
For by our ears our hearts oft tainted be.
Perchance that envy of so rich a thing,
Braving compare, disdainfully did sting   40
   His high-pitched thoughts, that meaner men should
     vaunt
   That golden hap which their superiors want.

But some untimely thought did instigate
His all too timeless speed, if none of those.
His honour, his affairs, his friends, his state,   45
Neglected all, with swift intent he goes
To quench the coal which in his liver glows.
   O rash-false heat, wrapped in repentant cold,
   Thy hasty spring still blasts, and ne'er grows old!

When at Collatium this false lord arrivéd,   50
Well was he welcomed by the Roman dame,
Within whose face beauty and virtue strivéd
Which of them both should underprop her fame:
When virtue bragged, beauty would blush for shame;
   When beauty boasted blushes, in despite   55
   Virtue would stain that o'er with silver white.

But beauty, in that white entituléd,
From Venus' doves doth challenge that fair field;
Then virtue claims from beauty beauty's red,
Which virtue gave the golden age to gild   60
Their silver cheeks, and called it then their shield;
   Teaching them thus to use it in the fight,
   When shame assailed, the red should fence the white.

This heraldry in Lucrece' face was seen,
Argued by beauty's red and virtue's white;   65
Of either's colour was the other queen,
Proving from world's minority their right;
Yet their ambition makes them still to fight,
   The sovereignty of either being so great
   That oft they interchange each other's seat.   70

This silent war of lilies and of roses
Which Tarquin viewed in her fair face's field,
In their pure ranks his traitor eye encloses;
Where, lest between them both it should be killed,
The coward captive vanquishéd doth yield   75
   To those two armies that would let him go
   Rather than triumph in so false a foe.

Now thinks he that her husband's shallow tongue,
The niggard prodigal that praised her so,
In that high task hath done her beauty wrong,   80
Which far exceeds his barren skill to show;
Therefore that praise which Collatine doth owe
   Enchanted Tarquin answers with surmise,
   In silent wonder of still-gazing eyes.

This earthly saint, adored by this devil,   85
Little suspecteth the false worshipper;
"For unstained thoughts do seldom dream on evil;
"Birds never limed no secret bushes fear.
So guiltless she securely gives good cheer
   And reverend welcome to her princely guest,   90
   Whose inward ill no outward harm expressed;

For that he coloured with his high estate,
Hiding base sin in pleats of majesty;
That nothing in him seemed inordinate,
Save sometime too much wonder of his eye,   95
Which, having all, all could not satisfy;
   But, poorly rich, so wanteth in his store
   That cloyed with much he pineth still for more.

But she, that never coped with stranger eyes,
Could pick no meaning from their parling looks,   100
Nor read the subtle-shining secrecies
Writ in the glassy margents of such books.
She touched no unknown baits, nor feared no hooks;
   Nor could she moralize his wanton sight,
   More than his eyes were opened to the light.   105

He stories to her ears her husband's fame,
Won in the fields of fruitful Italy;
And decks with praises Collatine's high name,
Made glorious by his manly chivalry
With bruiséd arms and wreaths of victory.   110
   Her joy with heaved-up hand she doth express,
   And wordless so greets heaven for his success.

Far from the purpose of his coming thither,
He makes excuses for his being there.
No cloudy show of stormy blust'ring weather 115
Doth yet in his fair welkin once appear;
Till sable Night, mother of dread and fear,
    Upon the world dim darkness doth display,
    And in her vaulty prison stows the day.

For then is Tarquin brought unto his bed, 120
Intending weariness with heavy sprite;
For after supper long he questionéd
With modest Lucrece, and wore out the night.
Now leaden slumber with life's strength doth fight;
    And every one to rest himself betakes, 125
    Save thieves and cares and troubled minds that
      wakes.

As one of which doth Tarquin lie revolving
The sundry dangers of his will's obtaining;
Yet ever to obtain his will resolving,
Though weak-built hopes persuade him to abstaining; 130
Despair to gain doth traffic oft for gaining,
    And when great treasure is the meed proposéd,
    Though death be adjunct, there's no death supposéd.

Those that much covet are with gain so fond
That what they have not, that which they possess, 135
They scatter and unloose it from their bond,
And so, by hoping more, they have but less;
Or, gaining more, the profit of excess
    Is but to surfeit, and such griefs sustain
    That they prove bankrupt in this poor-rich gain. 140

The aim of all is but to nurse the life
With honour, wealth and ease, in waning age;
And in this aim there is such thwarting strife
That one for all or all for one we gage:
As life for honour in fell battle's rage; 145
    Honour for wealth; and oft that wealth doth cost
    The death of all, and all together lost.

So that in vent'ring ill we leave to be
The things we are for that which we expect;
And this ambitious foul infirmity, 150
In having much, torments us with defect
Of that we have; so then we do neglect
    The thing we have, and, all for want of wit,
    Make something nothing by augmenting it.

Such hazard now must doting Tarquin make, 155
Pawning his honour to obtain his lust;
And for himself himself he must forsake:
Then where is truth, if there be no self-trust?
When shall he think to find a stranger just
    When he himself himself confounds, betrays 160
    To sland'rous tongues and wretched hateful days?

Now stole upon the time the dead of night,
When heavy sleep had closed up mortal eyes;
No comfortable star did lend his light,
No noise but owls' and wolves' death-boding cries; 165
Now serves the season that they may surprise
    The silly lambs. Pure thoughts are dead and still,
    While lust and murder wakes to stain and kill.

And now this lustful lord, leaped from his bed,
Throwing his mantle rudely o'er his arm, 170
Is madly tossed between desire and dread;
Th'one sweetly flatters, th'other feareth harm;
But honest fear, bewitched with lust's foul charm,
    Doth too too oft betake him to retire,
    Beaten away by brain-sick rude desire. 175

His falchion on a flint he softly smiteth,
That from the cold stone sparks of fire do fly,
Whereat a waxen torch forthwith he lighteth,
Which must be lode-star to his lustful eye;
And to the flame thus speaks advisedly: 180
    'As from this cold flint I enforced this fire,
    So Lucrece must I force to my desire.'

Here pale with fear he doth premeditate
The dangers of his loathsome enterprise,
And in his inward mind he doth debate 185
What following sorrow may on this arise;
Then, looking scornfully, he doth despise
    His naked armour of still-slaughteréd lust,
    And justly thus controls his thoughts unjust:

'Fair torch, burn out thy light, and lend it not 190
To darken her whose light excelleth thine;
And die, unhallowéd thoughts, before you blot
With your uncleanness that which is divine;
Offer pure incense to so pure a shrine;
    Let fair humanity abhor the deed 195
    That spots and stains love's modest snow-white
      weed.

'O shame to knighthood and to shining arms!
O foul dishonour to my household's grave!
O impious act, including all foul harms!
A martial man to be soft fancy's slave! 200
True valour still a true respect should have;
    Then my digression is so vile, so base,
    That it will live engraven in my face.

'Yea, though I die, the scandal will survive,
And be an eye-sore in my golden coat; 205
Some loathsome dash the herald will contrive,
To cipher me how fondly I did dote;
That my posterity, shamed with the note,
    Shall curse my bones, and hold it for no sin
    To wish that I their father had not been. 210

'What win I, if I gain the thing I seek?
A dream, a breath, a froth of fleeting joy.
Who buys a minute's mirth to wail a week?
Or sells eternity to get a toy?
For one sweet grape who will the vine destroy? 215
    Or what fond beggar, but to touch the crown,
    Would with the sceptre straight be strucken down?

'If Collatinus dream of my intent,
Will he not wake, and in a desp'rate rage
Post hither, this vile purpose to prevent?— 220
This siege that hath engirt his marriage,
This blur to youth, this sorrow to the sage,
    This dying virtue, this surviving shame,
    Whose crime will bear an ever-during blame.

'O what excuse can my invention make,   225
When thou shalt charge me with so black a deed?
Will not my tongue be mute, my frail joints shake,
Mine eyes forego their light, my false heart bleed?
The guilt being great, the fear doth still exceed;
    And extreme fear can neither fight nor fly,   230
    But coward-like with trembling terror die.

'Had Collatinus killed my son or sire,
Or lain in ambush to betray my life,
Or were he not my dear friend, this desire
Might have excuse to work upon his wife,   235
As in revenge or quittal of such strife;
    But as he is my kinsman, my dear friend,
    The shame and fault finds no excuse nor end.

'Shameful it is—ay, if the fact be known;
Hateful it is—there is no hate in loving;   240
I'll beg her love—but she is not her own;
The worst is but denial and reproving.
My will is strong, past reason's weak removing.—
    Who fears a sentence or an old man's saw
    Shall by a painted cloth be kept in awe.'   245

Thus graceless holds he disputation
'Tween frozen conscience and hot-burning will,
And with good thoughts makes dispensation,
Urging the worser sense for vantage still;
Which in a moment doth confound and kill   250
    All pure effects, and doth so far proceed
    That what is vile shows like a virtuous deed.

Quoth he, 'She took me kindly by the hand,
And gazed for tidings in my eager eyes,
Fearing some hard news from the warlike band   255
Where her belovéd Collatinus lies.
O how her fear did make her colour rise!
    First red as roses that on lawn we lay,
    Then white as lawn, the roses took away.

'And how her hand, in my hand being locked,   260
Forced it to tremble with her loyal fear!
Which struck her sad, and then it faster rocked
Until her husband's welfare she did hear;
Whereat she smiléd with so sweet a cheer
    That had Narcissus seen her as she stood   265
    Self-love had never drowned him in the flood.

'Why hunt I then for colour or excuses?
All orators are dumb when beauty pleadeth;
Poor wretches have remorse in poor abuses;
Love thrives not in the heart that shadows dreadeth; 270
Affection is my captain, and he leadeth;
    And when his gaudy banner is displayed,
    The coward fights and will not be dismayed.

'Then childish fear avaunt! debating die!
Respect and reason wait on wrinkled age!   275
My heart shall never countermand mine eye;
Sad pause and deep regard beseems the sage;
My part is youth, and beats these from the stage:
    Desire my pilot is, beauty my prize;
    Then who fears sinking where such treasure lies?' 280

As corn o'ergrown by weeds, so heedful fear
Is almost choked by unresisted lust.
Away he steals with open list'ning ear,
Full of foul hope and full of fond mistrust;
Both which, as servitors to the unjust,   285
    So cross him with their opposite persuasion
    That now he vows a league and now invasion.

Within his thought her heavenly image sits,
And in the selfsame seat sits Collatine.
That eye which looks on her confounds his wits;   290
That eye which him beholds, as more divine,
Unto a view so false will not incline;
    But with a pure appeal seeks to the heart,
    Which once corrupted takes the worser part;

And therein heartens up his servile powers,   295
Who, flatt'red by their leader's jocund show,
Stuff up his lust, as minutes fill up hours;
And as their captain, so their pride doth grow,
Paying more slavish tribute than they owe.
    By reprobate desire thus madly led,   300
    The Roman lord marcheth to Lucrece' bed.

The locks between her chamber and his will,
Each one by him enforced, retires his ward;
But, as they open, they all rate his ill,
Which drives the creeping thief to some regard.   305
The threshold grates the door to have him heard;
    Night-wand'ring weasels shriek to see him there;
    They fright him, yet he still pursues his fear.

As each unwilling portal yields him way,
Through little vents and crannies of the place   310
The wind wars with his torch to make him stay,
And blows the smoke of it into his face,
Extinguishing his conduct in this case;
    But his hot heart, which fond desire doth scorch,
    Puffs forth another wind that fires the torch;   315

And being lighted, by the light he spies
Lucretia's glove, wherein her needle sticks;
He takes it from the rushes where it lies,
And griping it, the needle his finger pricks,
As who should say 'This glove to wanton tricks   320
    Is not inured. Return again in haste;
    Thou see'st our mistress' ornaments are chaste.'

But all these poor forbiddings could not stay him;
He in the worst sense consters their denial:
The doors, the wind, the glove, that did delay him, 325
He takes for accidental things of trial;
Or as those bars which stop the hourly dial,
    Who with a ling'ring stay his course doth let,
    Till every minute pays the hour his debt.

'So, so,' quoth he, 'these lets attend the time,   330
Like little frosts that sometime threat the spring,
To add a more rejoicing to the prime,
And give the sneapéd birds more cause to sing.
Pain pays the income of each precious thing;
    Huge rocks, high winds, strong pirates, shelves and
        sands   335
    The merchant fears, ere rich at home he lands.'

Now is he come unto the chamber door
That shuts him from the heaven of his thought,
Which with a yielding latch, and with no more,
Hath barred him from the blessèd thing he sought.   340
So from himself impiety hath wrought,
    That for his prey to pray he doth begin,
    As if the heavens should countenance his sin.

But in the midst of his unfruitful prayer,
Having solicited th'eternal power   345
That his foul thoughts might compass his fair fair,
And they would stand auspicious to the hour,
Even there he starts; quoth he 'I must deflower:
    The powers to whom I pray abhor this fact;
    How can they then assist me in the act?   350

'Then Love and Fortune be my gods, my guide!
My will is backed with resolution.
Thoughts are but dreams till their effects be tried;
The blackest sin is cleared with absolution;
Against love's fire fear's frost hath dissolution.   355
    The eye of heaven is out, and misty night
    Covers the shame that follows sweet delight.'

This said, his guilty hand plucked up the latch,
And with his knee the door he opens wide.
The dove sleeps fast that this night-owl will catch. 360
Thus treason works ere traitors be espied.
Who sees the lurking serpent steps aside;
    But she, sound sleeping, fearing no such thing,
    Lies at the mercy of his mortal sting.

Into the chamber wickedly he stalks   365
And gazeth on her yet unstainèd bed.
The curtains being close, about he walks,
Rolling his greedy eyeballs in his head.
By their high treason is his heart misled,
    Which gives the watch-word to his hand full soon 370
    To draw the cloud that hides the silver moon.

Look as the fair and fiery-pointed sun,
Rushing from forth a cloud, bereaves our sight;
Even so, the curtain drawn, his eyes begun
To wink, being blinded with a greater light;   375
Whether it is that she reflects so bright
    That dazzleth them, or else some shame supposèd,
    But blind they are, and keep themselves enclosèd.

O, had they in that darksome prison died!
Then had they seen the period of their ill;   380
Then Collatine again, by Lucrece' side,
In his clear bed might have reposèd still;
But they must ope, this blessèd league to kill;
    And holy-thoughted Lucrece to their sight
    Must sell her joy, her life, her world's delight. 385

Her lily hand her rosy cheek lies under,
Coz'ning the pillow of a lawful kiss;
Who, therefore angry, seems to part in sunder,
Swelling on either side to want his bliss;
Between whose hills her head entombèd is;   390
    Where, like a virtuous monument, she lies,
    To be admired of lewd unhallowèd eyes.

Without the bed her other fair hand was,
On the green coverlet; whose perfect white
Showed like an April daisy on the grass,   395
With pearly sweat resembling dew of night.
Her eyes, like marigolds, had sheathed their light,
    And canopied in darkness sweetly lay,
    Till they might open to adorn the day.

Her hair, like golden threads, played with her breath— 400
O modest wantons! wanton modesty!—
Showing life's triumph in the map of death,
And death's dim look in life's mortality:
Each in her sleep themselves so beautify:
    As if between them twain there were no strife,   405
    But that life lived in death and death in life.

Her breasts, like ivory globes circled with blue,
A pair of maiden worlds unconquerèd,
Save of their lord no bearing yoke they knew,
And him by oath they truly honourèd.   410
These worlds in Tarquin new ambition bred,
    Who like a foul usurper went about
    From this fair throne to heave the owner out.

What could he see but mightily he noted?
What did he note but strongly he desirèd?   415
What he beheld, on that he firmly doted,
And in his will his wilful eye he tirèd.
With more than admiration he admirèd
    Her azure veins, her alabaster skin,
    Her coral lips, her snow-white dimpled chin.   420

As the grim lion fawneth o'er his prey,
Sharp hunger by the conquest satisfied,
So o'er this sleeping soul doth Tarquin stay,
His rage of lust by gazing qualified;
Slacked, not suppressed; for standing by her side,   425
    His eye, which late this mutiny restrains,
    Unto a greater uproar tempts his veins;

And they, like straggling slaves for pillage fighting,
Obdurate vassals fell exploits effecting,
In bloody death and ravishment delighting,   430
Nor children's tears nor mothers' groans respecting,
Swell in their pride, the onset still expecting.
    Anon his beating heart, alarum striking,
    Gives the hot charge, and bids them do their liking.

His drumming heart cheers up his burning eye,   435
His eye commends the leading to his hand;
His hand, as proud of such a dignity,
Smoking with pride, marched on to make his stand
On her bare breast, the heart of all her land;
    Whose ranks of blue veins as his hand did scale, 440
    Left their round turrets destitute and pale.

They, must'ring to the quiet cabinet
Where their dear governess and lady lies,
Do tell her she is dreadfully beset,
And fright her with confusion of their cries.   445
She, much amazed, breaks ope her locked-up eyes,
    Who, peeping forth this tumult to behold,
    Are by his flaming torch dimmed and controlled.

Imagine her as one in dead of night
From forth dull sleep by dreadful fancy waking,   450
That thinks she hath beheld some ghastly sprite,
Whose grim aspect sets every joint a-shaking;
What terror 'tis! but she, in worser taking,
  From sleep disturbéd, heedfully doth view
  The sight which makes supposéd terror true.   455

Wrapped and confounded in a thousand fears,
Like to a new-killed bird she trembling lies;
She dares not look; yet, winking, there appears
Quick-shifting antics, ugly in her eyes.
"Such shadows are the weak brain's forgeries,   460
  Who, angry that the eyes fly from their lights,
  In darkness daunts them with more dreadful sights.

His hand that yet remains upon her breast—
Rude ram, to batter such an ivory wall!—
May feel her heart, poor citizen, distressed,   465
Wounding itself to death, rise up and fall,
Beating her bulk, that his hand shakes withal.
  This moves in him more rage and lesser pity,
  To make the breach and enter this sweet city.

First like a trumpet doth his tongue begin   470
To sound a parley to his heartless foe,
Who o'er the white sheet peers her whiter chin,
The reason of this rash alarm to know,
Which he by dumb demeanour seeks to show;
  But she with vehement prayers urgeth still   475
  Under what colour he commits this ill.

Thus he replies: 'The colour in thy face,
That even for anger makes the lily pale
And the red rose blush at her own disgrace,
Shall plead for me and tell my loving tale.   480
Under that colour am I come to scale
  Thy never-conqueréd fort. The fault is thine,
  For those thine eyes betray thee unto mine.

'Thus I forestall thee, if thou mean to chide:
Thy beauty hath ensnared thee to this night,   485
Where thou with patience must my will abide,
My will that marks thee for my earth's delight,
Which I to conquer sought with all my might;
  But as reproof and reason beat it dead,
  By thy bright beauty was it newly bred.   490

'I see what crosses my attempt will bring;
I know what thorns the growing rose defends;
I think the honey guarded with a sting,
All this beforehand counsel comprehends.
But will is deaf and hears no heedful friends;   495
  Only he hath an eye to gaze on beauty,
  And dotes on what he looks, 'gainst law or duty.

'I have debated, even in my soul,
What wrong, what shame, what sorrow I shall breed;
But nothing can affection's course control,   500
Or stop the headlong fury of his speed.
I know repentant tears ensue the deed,
  Reproach, disdain and deadly enmity;
  Yet strive I to embrace mine infamy.'

This said, he shakes aloft his Roman blade,   505
Which, like a falcon tow'ring in the skies,
Coucheth the fowl below with his wings' shade,
Whose crooked beak threats if he mount he dies.
So under his insulting falchion lies
  Harmless Lucretia, marking what he tells   510
  With trembling fear, as fowl hear falcons' bells.

'Lucrece,' quoth he, 'this night I must enjoy thee.
If thou deny, then force must work my way,
For in thy bed I purpose to destroy thee;
That done, some worthless slave of thine I'll slay, 515
To kill thine honour with thy life's decay;
  And in thy dead arms do I mean to place him,
  Swearing I slew him, seeing thee embrace him.

'So thy surviving husband shall remain
The scornful mark of every open eye;   520
Thy kinsmen hang their heads at this disdain,
Thy issue blurred with nameless bastardy;
And thou, the author of their obloquy,
  Shalt have thy trespass cited up in rhymes
  And sung by children in succeeding times.   525

'But if thou yield, I rest thy secret friend:
The fault unknown is as a thought unacted;
"A little harm done to a great good end
For lawful policy remains enacted.
"The poisonous simple sometime is compacted   530
  In a pure compound; being so applied,
  His venom in effect is purified.

'Then, for thy husband and thy children's sake,
Tender my suit; bequeath not to their lot
The shame that from them no device can take,   535
The blemish that will never be forgot;
Worse than a slavish wipe or birth-hour's blot;
  For marks descried in men's nativity
  Are nature's faults, not their own infamy.'

Here with a cockatrice' dead-killing eye   540
He rouseth up himself, and makes a pause;
While she, the picture of pure piety,
Like a white hind under the gripe's sharp claws,
Pleads in a wilderness where are no laws
  To the rough beast that knows no gentle right,   545
  Nor aught obeys but his foul appetite.

But when a black-faced cloud the world doth threat,
In his dim mist th'aspiring mountains hiding,
From earth's dark womb some gentle gust doth get,
Which blows these pitchy vapours from their biding, 550
Hind'ring their present fall by this dividing;
  So his unhalloweéd haste her words delays,
  And moody Pluto winks while Orpheus plays.

Yet, foul night-waking cat, he doth but dally,
While in his hold-fast foot the weak mouse panteth; 555
Her sad behaviour feeds his vulture folly,
A swallowing gulf that even in plenty wanteth;
His ear her prayers admits, but his heart granteth
  No penetrable entrance to her plaining.
  "Tears harden lust, though marble wear with
     raining.   560

Her pity-pleading eyes are sadly fixéd
In the remorseless wrinkles of his face;
Her modest eloquence with sighs is mixéd,
Which to her oratory adds more grace.
She puts the period often from his place, 565
  And midst the sentence so her accent breaks
  That twice she doth begin ere once she speaks.

She conjures him by high almighty Jove,
By knighthood, gentry, and sweet friendship's oath,
By her untimely tears, her husband's love, 570
By holy human law and common troth,
By heaven and earth, and all the power of both,
  That to his borrowéd bed he make retire,
  And stoop to honour, not to foul desire.

Quoth she: 'Reward not hospitality 575
With such black payment as thou hast pretended;
Mud not the fountain that gave drink to thee;
Mar not the thing that cannot be amended;
End thy ill aim before thy shoot be ended.
  He is no woodman that doth bend his bow 580
  To strike a poor unseasonable doe.

'My husband is thy friend—for his sake spare me;
Thyself art mighty—for thine own sake leave me;
Myself a weakling—do not then ensnare me;
Thou look'st not like deceit—do not deceive me. 585
My sighs like whirlwinds labour hence to heave thee.
  If ever man were moved with woman's moans,
  Be movéd with my tears, my sighs, my groans;

'All which together, like a troubled ocean,
Beat at thy rocky and wrack-threat'ning heart, 590
To soften it with their continual motion;
For stones dissolved to water do convert.
O, if no harder than a stone thou art,
  Melt at my tears, and be compassionate!
  Soft pity enters at an iron gate. 595

'In Tarquin's likeness I did entertain thee;
Hast thou put on his shape to do him shame?
To all the host of heaven I complain me
Thou wrong'st his honour, wound'st his princely
    name.
Thou art not what thou seem'st; and if the same, 600
  Thou seem'st not what thou art, a god, a king;
  For kings, like gods should govern every thing.

'How will thy shame be seeded in thine age,
When thus thy vices bud before thy spring?
If in thy hope thou dar'st do such outrage, 605
What dar'st thou not when once thou art a king?
O, be rememb'red, no outrageous thing
  From vassal actors can be wiped away;
  Then kings' misdeeds cannot be hid in clay.

'This deed will make thee only loved for fear, 610
But happy monarchs still are feared for love;
With foul offenders thou perforce must bear,
When they in thee the like offences prove.
If but for fear of this, thy will remove;
  For princes are the glass, the school, the book, 615
  Where subjects' eyes do learn, do read, do look.

'And wilt thou be the school where Lust shall learn?
Must he in thee read lectures of such shame?
Wilt thou be glass wherein it shall discern
Authority for sin, warrant for blame, 620
To privilege dishonour in thy name?
  Thou back'st reproach against long-living laud,
  And mak'st fair reputation but a bawd.

'Hast thou command? by him that gave it thee,
From a pure heart command thy rebel will; 625
Draw not thy sword to guard iniquity,
For it was lent thee all that brood to kill.
Thy princely office how canst thou fulfil,
  When patterned by thy fault foul sin may say
  He learned to sin, and thou didst teach the way? 630

'Think but how vile a spectacle it were
To view thy present trespass in another.
Men's faults do seldom to themselves appear;
Their own transgressions partially they smother;
This guilt would seem death-worthy in thy brother. 635
  O, how are they wrapped in with infamies
  That from their own misdeeds askance their eyes!

'To thee, to thee, my heaved-up hands, appeal,
Not to seducing lust, thy rash relier;
I sue for exiled majesty's repeal; 640
Let him return, and flatt'ring thoughts retire.
His true respect will prison false desire,
  And wipe the dim mist from thy doting eyne,
  That thou shalt see thy state and pity mine.'

'Have done,' quoth he, 'my uncontrolléd tide 645
Turns not, but swells the higher by this let.
Small lights are soon blown out, huge fires abide,
And with the wind in greater fury fret.
The petty streams that pay a daily debt
  To their salt sovereign, with their fresh falls' haste 650
  Add to his flow, but alter not his taste.'

'Thou art', quoth she, 'a sea, a sovereign king;
And, lo, there falls into thy boundless flood
Black lust, dishonour, shame, misgoverning,
Who seek to stain the ocean of thy blood; 655
If all these petty ills shall change thy good;
  Thy sea within a puddle's womb is hearséd,
  And not the puddle in thy sea disperséd.

'So shall these slaves be king, and thou their slave;
Thou nobly base, they basely dignified; 660
Thou their fair life, and they thy fouler grave;
Thou loathéd in their shame, they in thy pride.
The lesser thing should not the greater hide;
  The cedar stoops not to the base shrub's foot,
  But low shrubs wither at the cedar's root. 665

'So let thy thoughts, low vassals to thy state'—
'No more,' quoth he; 'by heaven, I will not hear thee.
Yield to my love; if not, enforcéd hate,
Instead of love's coy touch, shall rudely tear thee;
That done, despitefully I mean to bear thee 670
  Unto the base bed of some rescal groom,
  To be thy partner in this shameful doom.'

This said, he sets his foot upon the light,
For light and lust are deadly enemies;
Shame folded up in blind concealing night,   675
When most unseen, then most doth tyrannize.
The wolf hath seized his prey, the poor lamb cries,
    Till with her own white fleece her voice controlled
    Entombs her outcry in her lips' sweet fold;

For with the nightly linen that she wears   680
He pens her piteous clamours in her head,
Cooling his hot face in the chastest tears
That ever modest eyes with sorrow shed.
O, that prone lust should stain so pure a bed!
    The spots whereof could weeping purify,   685
    Her tears should drop on them perpetually.

But she hath lost a dearer thing than life,
And he hath won what he would lose again.
This forcéd league doth force a further strife;
This momentary joy breeds months of pain;   690
This hot desire converts to cold disdain;
    Pure Chastity is rifled of her store,
    And Lust, the thief, far poorer than before.

Look as the full-fed hound or gorgéd hawk,
Unapt for tender smell or speedy flight,   695
Make slow pursuit, or altogether balk
The prey wherein by nature they delight,
So surfeit-taking Tarquin fares this night:
    His taste delicious, in digestion souring,
    Devours his will, that lived by foul devouring.   700

O, deeper sin than bottomless conceit
Can comprehend in still imagination!
Drunken Desire must vomit his receipt,
Ere he can see his own abomination.
While Lust is in his pride, no exclamation   705
    Can curb his heat or rein his rash desire,
    Till, like a jade, Self-will himself doth tire.

And then with lank and lean discoloured cheek,
With heavy eye, knit brow, and strengthless pace,
Feeble Desire, all recreant, poor and meek,   710
Like to a bankrupt beggar wails his case:
The flesh being proud, Desire doth fight with Grace,
    For there it revels, and when that decays
    The guilty rebel for remission prays.

So fares it with this faultful lord of Rome,   715
Who this accomplishment so hotly chaséd;
For now against himself he sounds this doom,
That through the length of times he stands disgracéd;
Besides, his soul's fair temple is defacéd,
    To whose weak ruins muster troops of cares,   720
    To ask the spotted princess how she fares.

She says her subjects with foul insurrection
Have battered down her consecrated wall,
And by their mortal fault brought in subjection
Her immortality, and made her thrall   725
To living death and pain perpetual;
    Which in her prescience she controlléd still,
    But her foresight could not forestall their will.

Ev'n in this thought through the dark night he stealeth,
A captive victor that hath lost in gain;   730
Bearing away the wound that nothing healeth,
The scar that will, despite of cure, remain;
Leaving his spoil perplexed in greater pain.
    She bears the load of lust he left behind,
    And he the burden of a guilty mind.   735

He like a thievish dog creeps sadly thence;
She like a wearied lamb lies panting there;
He scowls, and hates himself for his offence;
She, desperate, with her nails her flesh doth tear;
He faintly flies, sweating with guilty fear;   740
    She stays, exclaiming on the direful night;
    He runs, and chides his vanished, loathed delight.

He thence departs a heavy convertite;
She there remains a hopeless castaway;
He in his speed looks for the morning light;   745
She prays she never may behold the day.
'For day', quoth she, 'night's scapes doth open lay,
    And my true eyes have never practised how
    To cloak offences with a cunning brow.

'They think not but that every eye can see   750
The same disgrace which they themselves behold;
And therefore would they still in darkness be,
To have their unseen sin remain untold;
For they their guilt with weeping will unfold,
    And grave, like water that doth eat in steel,   755
    Upon my cheeks what helpless shame I feel.'

Here she exclaims against repose and rest,
And bids her eyes hereafter still be blind.
She wakes her heart by beating on her breast,
And bids it leap from thence, where it may find   760
Some purer chest to close so pure a mind.
    Frantic with grief thus breathes she forth her spite
    Against the unseen secrecy of night:

'O comfort-killing Night, image of hell!
Dim register and notary of shame!   765
Black stage for tragedies and murders fell!
Vast sin-concealing chaos! nurse of blame!
Blind muffled bawd! dark harbour for defame!
    Grim cave of death! whisp'ring conspirator
    With close-tongued treason and the ravisher!   770

'O hateful, vaporous and foggy Night!
Since thou art guilty of my cureless crime,
Muster thy mists to meet the eastern light,
Make war against proportioned course of time;
Or if thou wilt permit the sun to climb   775
    His wonted height, yet ere he go to bed,
    Knit poisonous clouds about his golden head.

'With rotten damps ravish the morning air;
Let their exhaled unwholesome breaths make sick
The life of purity, the supreme fair,   780
Ere he arrive his weary noon-tide prick;
And let thy musty vapours march so thick
    That in their smoky ranks his smoth'red light
    May set at noon and make perpetual night.

'Were Tarquin Night, as he is but Night's child,   785
The silver-shining queen he would distain;
Her twinkling handmaids too, by him defiled,
Through Night's black bosom should not peep again;
So should I have co-partners in my pain;
   And fellowship in woe doth woe assuage,   790
   As palmers' chat makes short their pilgrimage.

'Where now I have no one to blush with me,
To cross their arms and hang their heads with mine,
To mask their brows and hide their infamy;
But I alone alone must sit and pine,   795
Seasoning the earth with show'rs of silver brine,
   Mingling my talk with tears, my grief with groans,
   Poor wasting monuments of lasting moans.

'O Night, thou furnace of foul-reeking smoke,
Let not the jealous Day behold that face   800
Which underneath thy black all-hiding cloak
Immodestly lies martyred with disgrace!
Keep still possession of thy gloomy place,
   That all the faults which in thy reign are made
   May likewise be sepulchred in thy shade!   805

'Make me not object to the tell-tale Day.
The light will show, charactered in my brow,
The story of sweet chastity's decay,
The impious breach of holy wedlock vow;
Yea, the illiterate, that know not how   810
   To cipher what is writ in learnéd books,
   Will quote my loathsome trespass in my looks.

'The nurse, to still her child, will tell my story,
And fright her crying babe with Tarquin's name;
The orator, to deck his oratory,   815
Will couple my reproach to Tarquin's shame;
Feast-finding minstrels, tuning my defame,
   Will tie the hearers to attend each line,
   How Tarquin wrongéd me, I Collatine.

'Let my good name, that senseless reputation,   820
For Collatine's dear love be kept unspotted;
If that be made a theme for disputation,
The branches of another root are rotted,
And undeserved reproach to him allotted
   That is as clear from this attaint of mine   825
   As I ere this was pure to Collatine.

'O unseen shame! invisible disgrace!
O unfelt sore! crest-wounding, private scar!
Reproach is stamped in Collatinus' face,
And Tarquin's eye may read the mot afar,   830
"How he in peace is wounded, not in war.
   "Alas, how many bear such shameful blows,
   Which not themselves, but he that gives them
     knows!

'If, Collatine, thine honour lay in me,
From me by strong assault it is bereft.   835
My honey lost, and I, a drone-like bee,
Have no perfection of my summer left,
But robbed and ransacked by injurious theft.
   In thy weak hive a wand'ring wasp hath crept,
   And sucked the honey which thy chaste bee kept.   840

'Yet am I guilty of thy honour's wrack;
Yet for thy honour did I entertain him;
Coming from thee, I could not put him back,
For it had been dishonour to disdain him;
Besides, of weariness he did complain him,   845
   And talked of virtue: O unlooked-for evil,
   When virtue is profaned in such a devil!

'Why should the worm intrude the maiden bud?
Or hateful cuckoos hatch in sparrows' nests?
Or toads infect fair founts with venom mud?   850
Or tyrant folly lurk in gentle breasts?
Or kings be breakers of their own behests?
   "But no perfection is so absolute
   That some impurity doth not pollute.

'The agéd man that coffers up his gold   855
Is plagued with cramps and gouts and painful fits,
And scarce hath eyes his treasure to behold,
But like still-pining Tantalus he sits,
And useless barns the harvest of his wits,
   Having no other pleasure of his gain   860
   But torment that it cannot cure his pain.

'So then he hath it when he cannot use it,
And leaves it to be mast'red by his young;
Who in their pride do presently abuse it.
Their father was too weak, and they too strong,   865
To hold their curséd-blesséd fortune long.
   "The sweets we wish for turn to loathéd sours
   "Even in the moment that we call them ours.

'Unruly blasts wait on the tender spring;
Unwholesome weeds take root with precious flowers: 870
The adder hisses where the sweet birds sing;
What virtue breeds iniquity devours.
We have no good that we can say is ours
   But ill-annexéd Opportunity
   Or kills his life or else his quality.   875

'O Opportunity, thy guilt is great!
'Tis thou that execut'st the traitor's treason;
Thou sets the wolf where he the lamb may get;
Whoever plots the sin, thou point'st the season;
'Tis thou that spurn'st at right, at law, at reason,   880
   And in thy shady cell, where none may spy him,
   Sits Sin, to seize the souls that wander by him.

'Thou mak'st the vestal violate her oath;
Thou blow'st the fire when temperance is thawed;
Thou smother'st honesty, thou murd'rest troth;   885
Thou foul abettor! thou notorious bawd!
Thou plantest scandal and displacest laud.
   Thou ravisher, thou traitor, thou false thief,
   Thy honey turns to gall, thy joy to grief!

'Thy secret pleasure turns to open shame,   890
Thy private feasting to a public fast,
Thy smoothing titles to a ragged name,
Thy sugared tongue to bitter wormwood taste;
Thy violent vanities can never last.
   How comes it then, vile Opportunity,   895
   Being so bad, such numbers seek for thee?

'When wilt thou be the humble suppliant's friend,
And bring him where his suit may be obtainéd?
When wilt thou sort an hour great strifes to end?
Or free that soul which wretchedness hath chainéd?   900
Give physic to the sick, ease to the painéd?
  The poor, lame, blind, halt, creep, cry out for thee;
  But they ne'er meet with Opportunity.

'The patient dies while the physician sleeps;
The orphan pines while the oppressor feeds;   905
Justice is feasting while the widow weeps;
Advice is sporting while infection breeds;
Thou grant'st no time for charitable deeds;
  Wrath, envy, treason, rape, and murder's rages,
  Thy heinous hours wait on them as their pages.   910

'When Truth and Virtue have to do with thee,
A thousand crosses keep them from thy aid;
They buy thy help, but Sin ne'er gives a fee;
He gratis comes, and thou art well appaid
As well to hear as grant what he hath said.   915
  My Collatine would else have come to me
  When Tarquin did, but he was stayed by thee.

'Guilty thou art of murder and of theft,
Guilty of perjury and subornation,
Guilty of treason, forgery and shift,   920
Guilty of incest, that abomination;
An accessary by thine inclination
  To all sins past and all that are to come,
  From the creation to the general doom.

'Misshapen Time, copesmate of ugly Night,   925
Swift subtle post, carrier of grisly care,
Eater of youth, false slave to false delight,
Base watch of woes, sin's pack-horse, virtue's snare;
Thou nursest all and murd'rest all that are.
  O, hear me then, injurious, shifting Time!   930
  Be guilty of my death, since of my crime.

'Why hath thy servant Opportunity
Betrayed the hours thou gavest me to repose,
Cancelled my fortunes and enchainéd me
To endless date of never-ending woes?   935
Time's office is to fine the hate of foes,
  To eat up errors by opinion bred,
  Not spend the dowry of a lawful bed.

'Time's glory is to calm contending kings,
To unmask falsehood and bring truth to light,   940
To stamp the seal of time in agéd things,
To wake the morn and sentinel the night,
To wrong the wronger till he render right,
  To ruinate proud buildings with thy hours
  And smear with dust their glitt'ring golden towers;   945

'To fill with worm-holes stately monuments,
To feed oblivion with decay of things,
To blot old books and alter their contents,
To pluck the quills from ancient ravens' wings,
To dry the old oak's sap and cherish springs,   950
  To spoil antiquities of hammered steel
  And turn the giddy round of Fortune's wheel;

'To show the beldam daughters of her daughter,
To make the child a man, the man a child,
To slay the tiger that doth live by slaughter,   955
To tame the unicorn and lion wild,
To mock the subtle in themselves beguiled,
  To cheer the ploughman with increased crops,
  And waste huge stones with little water-drops.

'Why work'st thou mischief in thy pilgrimage,   960
Unless thou couldst return to make amends?
One poor retiring minute in an age
Would purchase thee a thousand thousand friends,
Lending him wit that to bad debtors lends.
  O, this dread night, wouldst thou one hour come
    back,   965
  I could prevent this storm and shun thy wrack!

'Thou ceaseless lackey to eternity,
With some mischance cross Tarquin in his flight;
Devise extremes beyond extremity,
To make him curse this curséd crimeful night;   970
Let ghastly shadows his lewd eyes affright,
  And the dire thought of his committed evil
  Shape every bush a hideous shapeless devil.

'Disturb his hours of rest with restless trances,
Afflict him in his bed with bedrid groans;   975
Let there bechance him pitiful mischances,
To make him moan, but pity not his moans.
Stone him with hard'ned hearts, harder than stones;
  And let mild women to him lose their mildness,
  Wilder to him than tigers in their wildness.   980

'Let him have time to tear his curléd hair,
Let him have time against himself to rave,
Let him have time of time's help to despair,
Let him have time to live a loathéd slave,
Let him have time a beggar's orts to crave,   985
  And time to see one that by alms doth live
  Disdain to him disdainéd scraps to give.

'Let him have time to see his friends his foes,
And merry fools to mock at him resort;
Let him have time to mark how slow time goes   990
In time of sorrow, and how swift and short
His time of folly and his time of sport;
  And ever let his unrecalling crime
  Have time to wail th'abusing of his time.

'O Time, thou tutor both to good and bad,   995
Teach me to curse him that thou taught'st this ill!
At his own shadow let the thief run mad,
Himself himself seek every hour to kill!
Such wretched hands such wretched blood should spill;
  For who so base would such an office have   1000
  As sland'rous deathsman to so base a slave?

'The baser is he, coming from a king,
To shame his hope with deeds degenerate.
The mightier man, the mightier is the thing
That makes him honoured or begets him hate;   1005
For greatest scandal waits on greatest state.
  The moon being clouded presently is missed,
  But little stars may hide them when they list.

'The crow may bathe his coal-black wings in mire
And unperceived fly with the filth away;   1010
But if the like the snow-white swan desire,
The stain upon his silver down will stay.
Poor grooms are sightless night, kings glorious day.
  Gnats are unnoted wheresoe'er they fly,
  But eagles gazed upon with every eye.   1015

'Out, idle words, servants to shallow fools!
Unprofitable sounds, weak arbitrators!
Busy yourselves in skill-contending schools;
Debate where leisure serves with dull debaters;
To trembling clients be you mediators.   1020
  For me, I force not argument a straw,
  Since that my case is past the help of law.

'In vain I rail at Opportunity,
At Time, at Tarquin, and uncheerful Night;
In vain I cavil with mine infamy,   1025
In vain I spurn at my confirmed despite:
This helpless smoke of words doth me no right.
  The remedy indeed to do me good
  Is to let forth my foul-defiléd blood.

'Poor hand, why quiver'st thou at this decree?   1030
Honour thyself to rid me of this shame;
For if I die, my honour lives in thee,
But if I live, thou livest in my defame.
Since thou couldst not defend thy loyal dame
  And wast afeard to scratch her wicked foe,   1035
  Kill both thyself and her for yielding so.'

This said, from her betumbled couch she starteth,
To find some desp'rate instrument of death.
But this no slaughterhouse no tool imparteth
To make more vent for passage of her breath,   1040
Which, thronging through her lips, so vanisheth
  As smoke from Etna that in air consumes,
  Or that which from dischargéd cannon fumes.

'In vain,' quoth she, 'I live, and seek in vain
Some happy mean to end a hapless life.   1045
I feared by Tarquin's falchion to be slain,
Yet for the selfsame purpose seek a knife;
But when I feared I was a loyal wife:
  So am I now—O no, that cannot be;
  Of that true type hath Tarquin rifled me.   1050

'O, that is gone for which I sought to live,
And therefore now I need not fear to die.
To clear this spot by death, at least I give
A badge of fame to slander's livery,
A dying life to living infamy.   1055
  Poor helpless help, the treasure stol'n away,
  To burn the guiltless casket where it lay!

'Well, well, dear Collatine, thou shalt not know
The stainéd taste of violated troth;
I will not wrong thy true affection so,   1060
To flatter thee with an infringéd oath;
This bastard graff shall never come to growth:
  He shall not boast who did thy stock pollute
  That thou art doting father of his fruit.

'Nor shall he smile at thee in secret thought,   1065
Nor laugh with his companions at thy state;
But thou shalt know thy int'rest was not bought
Basely with gold, but stol'n from forth thy gate.
For me, I am the mistress of my fate,
  And with my trespass never will dispense,   1070
  Till life to death acquit my forced offence.

'I will not poison thee with my attaint,
Nor fold my fault in cleanly-coined excuses;
My sable ground of sin I will not paint
To hide the truth of this false night's abuses.   1075
My tongue shall utter all; mine eyes, like sluices,
  As from a mountain-spring that feeds a dale,
  Shall gush pure streams to purge my impure tale.'

By this, lamenting Philomel had ended
The well-tuned warble of her nightly sorrow,   1080
And solemn night with slow sad gait descended
To ugly hell; when lo, the blushing morrow
Lends light to all fair eyes that light will borrow;
  But cloudy Lucrece shames herself to see,
  And therefore still in night would cloist'red be.   1085

Revealing day through every cranny spies,
And seems to point her out where she sits weeping;
To whom she sobbing speaks: 'O eye of eyes,
Why pry'st thou through my window? leave thy
    peeping;
Mock with thy tickling beams eyes that are sleeping;   1090
  Brand not my forehead with thy piercing light,
  For day hath nought to do what's done by night.'

Thus cavils she with every thing she sees.
True grief is fond and testy as a child,
Who wayward once, his mood with nought agrees.   1095
Old woes, not infant sorrows, bear them mild;
Continuance tames the one; the other wild,
  Like an unpractised swimmer plunging still
  With too much labour drowns for want of skill.

So she, deep-drenchéd in a sea of care,   1100
Holds disputation with each thing she views,
And to herself all sorrow doth compare;
No object but her passion's strength renews,
And as one shifts, another straight ensues.
  Sometime her grief is dumb and hath no words;   1105
  Sometime 'tis mad and too much talk affords.

The little birds that tune their morning's joy
Make her moans mad with their sweet melody;
"For mirth doth search the bottom of annoy;
"Sad souls are slain in merry company;   1110
"Grief best is pleased with grief's society
  True sorrow then is feelingly suffíced
  When with like semblance it is sympathized.

"'Tis double death to drown in ken of shore;
"He ten times pines that pines beholding food;   1115
"To see the salve doth make the wound ache more;
"Great grief grieves most at that would do it good;
"Deep woes roll forward like a gentle flood,
  Who, being stopped, the bounding banks o'erflows;
  Grief dallied with nor law nor limit knows.   1120

'You mocking birds,' quoth she, 'your tunes entomb
Within your hollow-swelling featheréd breasts,
And in my hearing be you mute and dumb.
My restless discord loves no stops nor rests;
"A woeful hostess brooks not merry guests. 1125
  Relish your nimble notes to pleasing ears;
  "Distress likes dumps when time is kept with
    tears.

'Come, Philomel, that sing'st of ravishment,
Make thy sad grove in my dishevelled hair.
As the dank earth weeps at thy languishment, 1130
So I at each sad strain will strain a tear,
And with deep groans the diapason bear;
  For burden-wise I'll hum on Tarquin still,
  While thou on Tereus descants better skill.

'And whiles against a thorn thou bear'st thy part 1135
To keep thy sharp woes waking, wretched I,
To imitate thee well, against my heart
Will fix a sharp knife to affright mine eye;
Who, if it wink, shall thereon fall and die.
  These means, as frets upon an instrument, 1140
  Shall tune our heart-strings to true languishment.

'And for, poor bird, thou sing'st not in the day,
As shaming any eye should thee behold,
Some dark deep desert, seated from the way,
That knows not parching heat nor freezing cold, 1145
Will we find out; and there we will unfold
  To creatures stern sad tunes, to change their kinds.
  Since men prove beasts, let beasts bear gentle minds.'

As the poor frighted deer, that stands at gaze,
Wildly determining which way to fly, 1150
Or one encompassed with a winding maze
That cannot tread the way out readily;
So with herself is she in mutiny,
  To live or die which of the twain were better,
  When life is shamed and death reproach's debtor. 1155

'To kill myself,' quoth she, 'alack, what were it,
But with my body my poor soul's pollution?
They that lose half with greater patience bear it
Than they whose whole is swallowed in confusion.
That mother tries a merciless conclusion 1160
  Who, having two sweet babes, when death takes
    one,
  Will slay the other and be nurse to none.

'My body or my soul, which was the dearer,
When the one pure, the other made divine?
Whose love of either to myself was nearer, 1165
When both were kept for heaven and Collatine?
Ay me! the bark pilled from the lofty pine,
  His leaves will wither and his sap decay;
  So must my soul, her bark being pilled away.

'Her house is sacked, her quiet interrupted, 1170
Her mansion battered by the enemy;
Her sacred temple spotted, spoiled, corrupted,
Grossly engirt with daring infamy;
Then let it not be called impiety
  If in this blemished fort I make some hole 1175
  Through which I may convey this troubled soul.

'Yet die I will not till my Collatine
Have heard the cause of my untimely death,
That he may vow, in that sad hour of mine,
Revenge on him that made me stop my breath. 1180
My stainéd blood to Tarquin I'll bequeath,
  Which by him tainted shall for him be spent,
  And as his due writ in my testament.

'My honour I'll bequeath unto the knife
That wounds my body so dishonouréd. 1185
'Tis honour to deprive dishonoured life;
The one will live, the other being dead.
So of shame's ashes shall my fame be bred;
  For in my death I murder shameful scorn.
  My shame so dead, mine honour is new born. 1190

'Dear lord of that dear jewel I have lost,
What legacy shall I bequeath to thee?
My resolution, love, shall be thy boast,
By whose example thou revenged mayst be.
How Tarquin must be used, read it in me: 1195
  Myself, thy friend, will kill myself, thy foe,
  And, for my sake, serve thou false Tarquin so.

'This brief abridgement of my will I make:
My soul and body to the skies and ground;
My resolution, husband, do thou take; 1200
Mine honour be the knife's that makes my wound;
My shame be his that did my fame confound;
  And all my fame that lives disburséd be
  To those that live and think no shame of me.

'Thou, Collatine, shalt oversee this will; 1205
How was I overseen that thou shalt see it!
My blood shall wash the slander of mine ill;
My life's foul deed, my life's fair end shall free it.
Faint not, faint heart, but stoutly say "So be it".
  Yield to my hand; my hand shall conquer thee; 1210
  Thou dead, both die and both shall victors be.'

This plot of death when sadly she had laid,
And wiped the brinish pearl from her bright eyes,
With untuned tongue she hoarsely calls her maid,
Whose swift obedience to her mistress hies; 1215
  "For fleet-winged duty with thought's feathers flies.
  Poor Lucrece' cheeks unto her maid seem so
  As winter meads when sun doth melt their snow.

Her mistress she doth give demure good-morrow
With soft slow tongue, true mark of modesty, 1220
And sorts a sad look to her lady's sorrow,
For why her face wore sorrow's livery,
But durst not ask of her audaciously
  Why her two suns were cloud-eclipséd so,
  Nor why her fair cheeks over-washed with woe. 1225

But as the earth doth weep, the sun being set,
Each flower moist'ned like a melting eye,
Even so the maid with swelling drops 'gan wet
Her circled eyne, enforced by sympathy
Of those fair suns set in her mistress' sky, 1230
  Who in a salt-waved ocean quench their light,
  Which makes the maid weep like the dewy night.

A pretty while these pretty creatures stand,
Like ivory conduits coral cisterns filling.
One justly weeps; the other takes in hand   1235
No cause but company of her drops spilling:
Their gentle sex to weep are often willing,
    Grieving themselves to guess at others' smarts,
    And then they drown their eyes or break their
        hearts.

For men have marble, women waxen, minds,   1240
And therefore are they formed as marble will;
The weak oppressed, th'impression of strange kinds
Is formed in them by force, by fraud, or skill.
Then call them not the authors of their ill,
    No more than wax shall be accounted evil   1245
Wherein is stamped the semblance of a devil.

Their smoothness, like a goodly champaign plain,
Lays open all the little worms that creep;
In men, as in a rough-grown grove, remain
Cave-keeping evils that obscurely sleep.   1250
Through crystal walls each little mote will peep.
    Though men can cover crimes with bold stern
        looks,
    Poor women's faces are their own faults' books.

No man inveigh against the witheréd flower,
But chide rough winter that the flower hath killed. 1255
Not that devoured, but that which doth devour,
Is worthy blame. O, let it not be hild
Poor women's faults that they are so fulfilled
    With men's abuses: those proud lords to blame
    Make weak-made women tenants to their shame. 1260

The precedent whereof in Lucrece view,
Assailed by night with circumstances strong
Of present death, and shame that might ensue
By that her death, to do her husband wrong.
Such danger to resistance did belong,   1265
    That dying fear through all her body spread;
    And who cannot abuse a body dead?

By this, mild patience bid fair Lucrece speak
To the poor counterfeit of her complaining.
'My girl,' quoth she, 'on what occasion break   1270
Those tears from thee that down thy cheeks are
    raining?
If thou dost weep for grief of my sustaining,
    Know, gentle wench, it small avails my mood;
    If tears could help, mine own would do me good.

'But tell me, girl, when went'—and there she stayed 1275
Till after a deep groan—'Tarquin from hence?'
'Madam, ere I was up,' replied the maid,
'The more to blame my sluggard negligence.
Yet with the fault I thus far can dispense:
    Myself was stirring ere the break of day,   1280
    And ere I rose was Tarquin gone away.

'But, lady, if your maid may be so bold,
She would request to know your heaviness.'
'O, peace!' quoth Lucrece: 'if it should be told,
The repetition cannot make it less,   1285
For more it is than I can well express;
    And that deep torture may be called a hell
    When more is felt than one hath power to tell.

'Go, get me hither paper, ink and pen;
Yet save that labour, for I have them here.   1290
What should I say? One of my husband's men
Bid thou be ready by and by to bear
A letter to my lord, my love, my dear.
    Bid him with speed prepare to carry it;
    The cause craves haste and it will soon be writ.' 1295

Her maid is gone, and she prepares to write,
First hovering o'er the paper with her quill.
Conceit and grief an eager combat fight;
What wit sets down is blotted straight with will;
This is too curious-good, this blunt and ill: 1300
    Much like a press of people at a door,
    Throng her inventions, which shall go before.

At last she thus begins: 'Thou worthy lord
Of that unworthy wife that greeteth thee,
Health to thy person! next vouchsafe t'afford—   1305
If ever, love, thy Lucrece thou wilt see—
Some present speed to come and visit me.
    So I commend me, from our house in grief;
    My woes are tedious, though my words are brief.'

Here folds she up the tenor of her woe,   1310
Her certain sorrow writ uncertainly.
By this short schedule Collatine may know
Her grief, but not her grief's true quality;
She dares not thereof make discovery,
    Lest he should hold it her own gross abuse,   1315
    Ere she with blood had stained her stained excuse.

Besides, the life and feeling of her passion
She hoards, to spend when he is by to hear her,
When sighs and groans and tears may grace the fashion
Of her disgrace, the better so to clear her   1320
From that suspicion which the world might bear her.
    To shun this blot, she would not blot the letter
    With words, till action might become them better.

To see sad sights moves more than hear them told;
For then the eye interprets to the ear   1325
The heavy motion that it doth behold,
When every part a part of woe doth bear.
'Tis but a part of sorrow that we hear:
    Deep sounds make lesser noise than shallow fords,
    And sorrow ebbs, being blown with wind of words. 1330

Her letter now is sealed and on it writ
'At Ardea to my lord with more than haste.'
The post attends, and she delivers it,
Charging the sour-faced groom to hie as fast
As lagging fowls before the northern blast.   1335
    Speed more than speed but dull and slow she deems:
    Extremity still urgeth such extremes.

The homely villain curtsies to her low,
And blushing on her, with a steadfast eye
Receives the scroll without or yea or no,   1340
And forth with bashful innocence doth hie.
But they whose guilt within their bosoms lie
    Imagine every eye beholds their blame;
    For Lucrece thought he blushed to see her shame:

When, silly groom, God wot, it was defect   1345
Of spirit, life and bold audacity.
Such harmless creatures have a true respect
To talk in deeds, while others saucily
Promise more speed but do it leisurely.
  Even so this pattern of the worn-out age   1350
  Pawned honest looks, but laid no words to gage.

His kindled duty kindled her mistrust,
That two red fires in both their faces blazéd;
She thought he blushed, as knowing Tarquin's lust,
And blushing with him, wistly on him gazéd;   1355
Her earnest eye did make him more amazed;
  The more she saw the blood his cheeks replenish,
  The more she thought he spied in her some blemish.

But long she thinks till he return again,
And yet the duteous vassal scarce is gone.   1360
The weary time she cannot entertain,
For now 'tis stale to sigh, to weep and groan;
So woe hath wearied woe, moan tiréd moan,
  That she her plaints a little while doth stay,
  Pausing for means to mourn some newer way.   1365

At last she calls to mind where hangs a piece
Of skilful painting, made for Priam's Troy,
Before the which is drawn the power of Greece,
For Helen's rape the city to destroy,
Threat'ning cloud-kissing Ilion with annoy;   1370
  Which the conceited painter drew so proud
  As heaven, it seemed, to kiss the turrets bowed.

A thousand lamentable objects there,
In scorn of nature, art gave lifeless life:
Many a dry drop seemed a weeping tear,   1375
Shed for the slaught'red husband by the wife;
The red blood reeked, to show the painter's strife;
  And dying eyes gleamed forth their ashy lights,
  Like dying coals burnt out in tedious nights.

There might you see the labouring pioneer   1380
Begrimed with sweat and smeared all with dust;
And from the towers of Troy there would appear
The very eyes of men through loop-holes thrust,
Gazing upon the Greeks with little lust.
  Such sweet observance in this work was had   1385
  That one might see those far-off eyes look sad.

In great commanders grace and majesty
You might behold, triumphing in their faces;
In youth, quick bearing and dexterity;
And here and there the painter interlaces   1390
Pale cowards marching on with trembling paces,
  Which heartless peasants did so well resemble
  That one would swear he saw them quake
    and tremble.

In Ajax and Ulysses, O what art
Of physiognomy might one behold!   1395
The face of either ciphered either's heart;
Their face their manners most expressly told:
In Ajax' eyes blunt rage and rigour rolled;
  But the mild glance that sly Ulysses lent
  Showed deep regard and smiling government.   1400

There pleading might you see grave Nestor stand,
As 'twere encouraging the Greeks to fight,
Making such sober action with his hand
That it beguiled attention, charmed the sight.
In speech, it seemed, his beard all silver white   1405
  Wagged up and down, and from his lips did fly
  Thin winding breath which purled up to the sky.

About him were a press of gaping faces,
Which seemed to swallow up his sound advice,
All jointly list'ning, but with several graces,   1410
As if some mermaid did their ears entice,
Some high, some low, the painter was so nice;
  The scalps of many, almost hid behind,
  To jump up higher seemed, to mock the mind.

Here one man's hand leaned on another's head,   1415
His nose being shadowéd by his neighbour's ear;
Here one being thronged bears back, all boll'n and red;
Another smothered seems to pelt and swear;
And in their rage such signs of rage they bear
  As, but for loss of Nestor's golden words,   1420
  It seemed they would debate with angry swords.

For much imaginary work was there;
Conceit deceitful, so compact, so kind,
That for Achilles' image stood his spear
Griped in an arméd hand; himself behind   1425
Was left unseen, save to the eye of mind:
  A hand, a foot, a face, a leg, a head,
  Stood for the whole to be imaginéd.

And from the walls of strong-besiegéd Troy
When their brave hope, bold Hector, marched to field,   1430
Stood many Trojan mothers sharing joy
To see their youthful sons bright weapons wield;
And to their hope they such odd action yield
  That through their light joy seeméd to appear,
  Like bright things stained, a kind of heavy fear.   1435

And from the strand of Dardan where they fought
To Simois' reedy banks the red blood ran,
Whose waves to imitate the battle sought
With swelling ridges; and their ranks began
To break upon the galléd shore, and than   1440
  Retire again, till meeting greater ranks
  They join and shoot their foam at Simois' banks.

To this well-painted piece is Lucrece come,
To find a face where all distress is stelled.
Many she sees where cares have carvéd some,   1445
But none where all distress and dolour dwelled,
Till she despairing Hecuba beheld,
  Staring on Priam's wounds with her old eyes,
  Which bleeding under Pyrrhus' proud foot lies.

In her the painter had anatomized   1450
Time's ruin, beauty's wrack, and grim care's reign;
Her cheeks with chaps and wrinkles were disguised;
Of what she was no semblance did remain;
Her blue blood changed to black in every vein,
  Wanting the spring that those shrunk pipes had fed,   1455
  Showed life imprisoned in a body dead.

On this sad shadow Lucrece spends her eyes,
And shapes her sorrow to the beldam's woes,
Who nothing wants to answer her but cries,
And bitter words to ban her cruel foes: 1460
The painter was no god to lend her those;
    And therefore Lucrece swears he did her wrong,
    To give her so much grief and not a tongue.

'Poor instrument', quoth she, 'without a sound,
I'll tune thy woes with my lamenting tongue,   1465
And drop sweet balm in Priam's painted wound,
And rail on Pyrrhus that hath done him wrong,
And with my tears quench Troy that burns so long,
    And with my knife scratch out the angry eyes
    Of all the Greeks that are thine enemies.   1470

'Show me the strumpet that began this stir,
That with my nails her beauty I may tear.
Thy heat of lust, fond Paris, did incur
This load of wrath that burning Troy doth bear.
Thy eye kindled the fire that burneth here;   1475
    And here in Troy, for trespass of thine eye,
    The sire, the son, the dame and daughter die.

'Why should the private pleasure of some one
Become the public plague of many moe?
Let sin, alone committed, light alone   1480
Upon his head that hath transgressèd so;
Let guiltless souls be freed from guilty woe.
    For one's offence why should so many fall,
    To plague a private sin in general?

'Lo, here weeps Hecuba, here Priam dies,   1485
Here manly Hector faints, here Troilus swounds,
Here friend by friend in bloody channel lies,
And friend to friend gives unadvisèd wounds,
And one man's lust these many lives confounds.
    Had doting Priam checked his son's desire,   1490
    Troy had been bright with fame and not with fire.'

Here feelingly she weeps Troy's painted woes;
For sorrow, like a heavy-hanging bell
Once set on ringing, with his own weight goes;
Then little strength rings out the dolefull knell;   1495
So Lucrece, set a-work, sad tales doth tell
    To pencilled pensiveness and coloured sorrow;
    She lends them words, and she their looks
        doth borrow.

She throws her eyes about the painting round,
And who she finds forlorn she doth lament.   1500
At last she sees a wretched image bound
That piteous looks to Phrygian shepherds lent;
His face, though full of cares, yet showed content;
    Onward to Troy with the blunt swains he goes,
    So mild that Patience seemed to scorn his woes.   1505

In him the painter laboured with his skill
To hide deceit and give the harmless show
An humble gait, calm looks, eyes wailing still,
A brow unbent that seemed to welcome woe;
Cheeks neither red nor pale, but mingled so   1510
    That blushing red no guilty instance gave,
    Nor ashy pale the fear that false hearts have.

But, like a constant and confirmèd devil,
He entertained a show so seeming just,
And therein so ensconced his secret evil,   1515
That jealousy itself could not mistrust
False creeping craft and perjury should thrust
    Into so bright a day such black-faced storms,
    Or blot with hell-born sin such saint-like forms.

The well-skilled workman this mild image drew   1520
For perjured Sinon, whose enchanting story
The credulous old Priam after slew;
Whose words, like wildfire, burnt the shining glory
Of rich-built Ilion, that the skies were sorry,
    And little stars shot from their fixèd places,   1525
    When their glass fell wherein they viewed their
        faces.

This picture she advisedly perused,
And chid the painter for his wondrous skill,
Saying, some shape in Sinon's was abused;
So fair a form lodged not a mind so ill: 1530
And still on him she gazed, and gazing still
    Such signs of truth in his plain face she spied
    That she concludes the picture was belied.

'It cannot be', quoth she, 'that so much guile'—
She would have said 'can lurk in such a look';   1535
But Tarquin's shape came in her mind the while,
And from her tongue 'can lurk' from 'cannot' took;
'It cannot be' she in that sense forsook,
    And turned it thus, 'It cannot be, I find,
    But such a face should bear a wicked mind;   1540

'For even as subtle Sinon here is painted,
So sober-sad, so weary and so mild,
As if with grief or travail he had fainted,
To me came Tarquin armèd to beguild
With outward honesty, but yet defiled   1545
    With inward vice. As Priam him did cherish,
    So did I Tarquin; so my Troy did perish.

'Look, look, how list'ning Priam wets his eyes,
To see those borrowèd tears that Sinon sheds.
Priam, why art thou old and yet not wise?   1550
For every tear he falls a Trojan bleeds;
His eye drops fire, no water thence proceeds;
    Those round clear pearls of his that move thy pity
    Are balls of quenchless fire to burn thy city.

'Such devils steal effects from lightless hell;   1555
For Sinon in his fire doth quake with cold,
And in that cold hot-burning fire doth dwell;
These contraries such unity do hold
Only to flatter fools and make them bold;
    So Priam's trust false Sinon's tears doth flatter 1560
    That he finds means to burn his Troy with water.'

Here, all enraged, such passion her assails,
That patience is quite beaten from her breast.
She tears the senseless Sinon with her nails,
Comparing him to that unhappy guest   1565
Whose deed hath made herself herself detest.
    At last she smilingly with this gives o'er:
    'Fool, fool!' quoth she, 'his wounds will not be sore.'

Thus ebbs and flows the current of her sorrow,
And time doth weary time with her complaining.   1570
She looks for night, and then she longs for morrow,
And both she thinks too long with her remaining.
Short time seems long in sorrow's sharp sustaining;
 Though woe be heavy, yet it seldom sleeps,
 And they that watch see time how slow it creeps.   1575

Which all this time hath overslipped her thought
That she with painted images hath spent,
Being from the feeling of her own grief brought
By deep surmise of others' detriment,
Losing her woes in shows of discontent.   1580
 It easeth some, though none it ever curéd,
 To think their dolour others have enduréd.

But now the mindful messenger come back
Brings home his lord and other company;
Who finds his Lucrece clad in mourning black,   1585
And round about her tear-distainéd eye
Blue circles streamed, like rainbows in the sky.
 These water-galls in her dim element
 Foretell new storms to those already spent.

Which when her sad-beholding husband saw,   1590
Amazedly in her sad face he stares:
Her eyes, though sod in tears, looked red and raw,
Her lively colour killed with deadly cares.
He hath no power to ask her how she fares;
 Both stood, like old acquaintance in a trance,   1595
 Met far from home, wond'ring each other's chance.

At last he takes her by the bloodless hand,
And thus begins: 'What uncouth ill event
Hath thee befall'n, that thou dost trembling stand?
Sweet love, what spite hath thy fair colour spent?   1600
Why art thou thus attired in discontent?
 Unmask, dear dear, this moody heaviness,
 And tell thy grief, that we may give redress.'

Three times with sighs she gives her sorrow fire
Ere once she can discharge one word of woe;   1605
At length addressed to answer his desire,
She modestly prepares to let them know
Her honour is ta'en prisoner by the foe;
 While Collatine and his consorted lords
 With sad attention long to hear her words.   1610

And now this pale swan in her wat'ry nest
Begins the sad dirge of her certain ending.
'Few words,' quoth she, 'shall fit the trespass best,
Where no excuse can give the fault amending:
In me moe woes than words are now depending;   1615
 And my laments would be drawn out too long,
 To tell them all with one poor tiréd tongue.

'Then be this all the task it hath to say:
Dear husband, in the interest of thy bed
A stranger came, and on that pillow lay   1620
Where thou wast wont to rest thy weary head;
And what wrong else may be imagined
 By foul enforcement might be done to me,
 From that, alas, thy Lucrece is not free.

'For in the dreadful dead of dark midnight,   1625
With shining falchion in my chamber came
A creeping creature with a flaming light,
And softly cried "Awake, thou Roman dame,
And entertain my love; else lasting shame
 On thee and thine this night I will inflict,   1630
 If thou my love's desire do contradict.

' "For some hard-favoured groom of thine," quoth he,
"Unless thou yoke thy liking to my will,
I'll murder straight, and then I'll slaughter thee,
And swear I found you where you did fulfil   1635
The loathsome act of lust, and so did kill
 The lechers in their deed: this act will be
 My fame, and thy perpetual infamy."

'With this, I did begin to start and cry,
And then against my heart he set his sword,   1640
Swearing, unless I took all patiently,
I should not live to speak another word;
So should my shame still rest upon record,
 And never be forgot in mighty Rome
 Th'adulterate death of Lucrece and her groom.   1645

'Mine enemy was strong, my poor self weak,
And far the weaker with so strong a fear.
My bloody judge forbade my tongue to speak;
No rightful plea might plead for justice there.
His scarlet lust came evidence to swear   1650
 That my poor beauty had purloined his eyes,
 And when the judge is robbed, the prisoner dies.

'O, teach me how to make mine own excuse!
Or, at the least, this refuge let me find:
Though my gross blood be stained with this abuse,   1655
Immaculate and spotless is my mind;
That was not forced; that never was inclined
 To accessary yieldings, but still pure
 Doth in her poisoned closet yet endure.'

Lo, here, the hopeless merchant of this loss,   1660
With head declined, and voice damned up with woe,
With sad-set eyes and wreathéd arms across,
From lips new waxen pale begins to blow
The grief away that stops his answer so;
 But, wretched as he is, he strives in vain;   1665
 What he breathes out his breath drinks up again.

As through an arch the violent roaring tide
Outruns the eye that doth behold his haste,
Yet in the eddy boundeth in his pride
Back to the strait that forced him on so fast,   1670
In rage sent out, recalled in rage, being past;
 Even so his sighs, his sorrows, make a saw,
 To push grief on and back the same grief draw.

Which speechless woe of his poor she attendeth
And his untimely frenzy thus awaketh: 1675
'Dear lord, thy sorrow to my sorrow lendeth
Another power; no flood by raining slaketh.
My woe too sensible thy passion maketh
 More feeling-painful. Let it then suffice
 To drown one woe, one pair of weeping eyes.   1680

'And for my sake, when I might charm thee so,
For she that was thy Lucrece, now attend me:
Be suddenly revengéd on my foe,
Thine, mine, his own; suppose thou dost defend me
From what is past. The help that thou shalt lend me 1685
  Comes all too late, yet let the traitor die;
  "For sparing justice feeds iniquity.

'But ere I name him, you fair lords', quoth she,
Speaking to those that came with Collatine,
'Shall plight your honourable faiths to me,   1690
With swift pursuit to venge this wrong of mine;
For 'tis a meritorious fair design
  To chase injustice with revengeful arms:
  Knights, by their oaths, should right poor
    ladies' harms.'

At this request, with noble disposition   1695
Each present lord began to promise aid,
As bound in knighthood to her imposition,
Longing to hear the hateful foe bewrayed.
But she, that yet her sad task hath not said,
  The protestation stops. 'O, speak,' quoth she,   1700
  'How may this forcéd stain be wiped from me?

'What is the quality of my offence,
Being constrained with dreadful circumstance?
May my pure mind with the foul act dispense,
My low-declinéd honour to advance?   1705
May any terms acquit me from this chance?
  The poisonéd fountain clears itself again;
  And why not I from this compelléd stain?'

With this, they all at once began to say,
Her body's stain her mind untainted clears;   1710
While with a joyless smile she turns away
The face, that map which deep impression bears
Of hard misfortune, carved in it with tears.
  'No, no,' quoth she, 'no dame hereafter living
  By my excuse shall claim excuse's giving.'   1715

Here with a sigh, as if her heart would break,
She throws forth Tarquin's name: 'He, he,' she says,
But more than 'he' her poor tongue could not speak;
Till after many accents and delays,
Untimely breathings, sick and short assays,   1720
  She utters this: 'He, he, fair lords, 'tis he,
  That guides this hand to give this wound to me.'

Even here she sheathéd in her harmless breast
A harmful knife, that thence her soul unsheathéd:
That blow did bail it from the deep unrest   1725
Of that polluted prison where it breathéd.
Her contrite sighs unto the clouds bequeathéd
  Her wingéd sprite and through her wounds doth fly
  Life's lasting date from cancelled destiny.

Stone-still, astonished with this deadly deed,   1730
Stood Collatine and all his lordly crew;
Till Lucrece' father, that beholds her bleed,
Himself on her self-slaught'red body threw;
And from the purple fountain Brutus drew
  The murd'rous knife, and, as it left the place,   1735
  Her blood, in poor revenge, held it in chase;

And bubbling from her breast, it·doth divide
In two slow rivers, that the crimson blood
Circles her body in on every side,
Who like a late-sacked island vastly stood   1740
Bare and unpeopled in this fearful flood.
  Some of her blood still pure and red remained,
  And some looked black, and that false
    Tarquin stained.

About the mourning and congealéd face
Of that black blood a wat'ry rigol goes,   1745
Which seems to weep upon the tainted place;
And ever since, as pitying Lucrece' woes,
Corrupted blood some watery token shows;
  And blood untainted still doth red abide,
  Blushing at that which is so putrified.   1750

'Daughter, dear daughter,' old Lucretius cries,
'That life was mine which thou hast here deprivéd.
If in the child the father's image lies,
Where shall I live now Lucrece is unlivéd?
Thou wast not to this end from me derivéd.   1755
  If children predecease progenitors,
  We are their offspring, and they none of ours.

'Poor broken glass, I often did behold
In thy sweet semblance my old age new born;
But now that fair fresh mirror, dim and old,   1760
Shows me a bare-boned death by time outworn;
O, from thy cheeks my image thou hast torn,
  And shivered all the beauty of my glass,
  That I no more can see what once I was.

'O time, cease thou thy course and last no longer,   1765
If they surcease to be that should survive.
Shall rotten death make conquest of the stronger,
And leave the falt'ring feeble souls alive?
The old bees die, the young possess their hive.
  Then live, sweet Lucrece, live again, and see   1770
  Thy father die, and not thy father thee.'

By this, starts Collatine as from a dream,
And bids Lucretius give his sorrow place;
And then in key-cold Lucrece' bleeding stream
He falls, and bathes the pale fear in his face,   1775
And counterfeits to die with her a space;
  Till manly shame bids him possess his breath,
  And live to be revengéd on her death.

The deep vexation of his inward soul
Hath served a dumb arrest upon his tongue;   1780
Who, mad that sorrow should his use control
Or keep him from heart-easing words so long,
Begins to talk; but through his lips do throng
  Weak words, so thick come in his poor heart's aid
  That no man could distinguish what he said.   1785

Yet sometime 'Tarquin' was pronouncéd plain,
But through his teeth, as if the name he tore.
This windy tempest, till it blow up rain,
Held back his sorrow's tide, to make it more;
At last it rains, and busy winds give o'er,   1790
  Then son and father weep with equal strife
  Who should weep most, for daughter or for
    wife.

The one doth call her his, the other his,
Yet neither may possess the claim they lay.
The father says 'She's mine'. 'O, mine she is,'   1795
Replies her husband: 'do not take away
My sorrow's interest; let no mourner say
    He weeps for her, for she was only mine,
    And only must be wailed by Collatine.'

'O,' quoth Lucretius, 'I did give that life   1800
Which she too early and too late hath spilled.'
'Woe, woe,' quoth Collatine, 'she was my wife;
I owed her, and 'tis mine that she hath killed.'
'My daughter' and 'my wife' with clamours filled
    The dispersed air, who, holding Lucrece' life,   1805
    Answered their cries, 'my daughter' and 'my
        wife'.

Brutus, who plucked the knife from Lucrece' side,
Seeing such emulation in their woe,
Began to clothe his wit in state and pride,
Burying in Lucrece' wound his folly's show.   1810
He with the Romans was esteeméd so
    As silly jeering idiots are with kings,
    For sportive words and utt'ring foolish things.

But now he throws that shallow habit by
Wherein deep policy did him disguise,   1815
And armed his long-hid wits advisedly
To check the tears in Collatinus' eyes.
'Thou wrongéd lord of Rome,' quoth he, 'arise;
    Let my unsounded self, supposed a fool,
    Now set thy long-experienced wit to school.   1820

'Why, Collatine, is woe the cure for woe?
Do wounds help wounds, or grief help grievous
        deeds?
Is it revenge to give thyself a blow
For his foul act by whom thy fair wife bleeds?
Such childish humour from weak minds proceeds.   1825
    Thy wretched wife mistook the matter so
    To slay herself, that should have slain her foe.

'Courageous Roman, do not steep thy heart
In such relenting dew of lamentations,
But kneel with me and help to bear thy part   1830
To rouse our Roman gods with invocations
That they will suffer these abominations,
    Since Rome herself in them doth stand disgracéd,
    By our strong arms from forth her fair streets
        chaséd.

'Now by the Capitol that we adore,   1835
And by this chaste blood so unjustly stainéd,
By heaven's fair sun that breeds the fat earth's store,
By all our country rights in Rome maintainéd,
And by chaste Lucrece' soul that late complainéd
    Her wrongs to us, and by this bloody knife,   1840
    We will revenge the death of this true wife.'

This said, he struck his hand upon his breast,
And kissed the fatal knife to end his vow,
And to his protestation urged the rest,
Who, wond'ring at him, did his words allow;   1845
Then jointly to the ground their knees they bow,
    And that deep vow which Brutus made before
    He doth again repeat, and that they swore.

When they had sworn to this adv:séd doom,
They did conclude to bear dead Lucrece thence,   1850
To show her bleeding body thorough Rome,
And so to publish Tarquin's foul offence;
Which being done with speedy diligence,
    The Romans plausible did give consent
    To Tarquin's everlasting banishment.   1855

The Passionate Pilgrim

1

When my love swears that she is made of truth,
I do believe her, though I know she lies,
That she might think me some untutored youth,
Unskilful in the world's false forgeries.
Thus vainly thinking that she thinks me young,   5
Although I know my years be past the best,
I smiling credit her false-speaking tongue,
Outfacing faults in love with love's ill rest.
But wherefore says my love that she is young?
And wherefore say not I that I am old?   10
O, love's best habit's in a soothing tongue,
And age in love loves not to have years told.
   Therefore I'll lie with love, and love with me,
   Since that our faults in love thus smothered be.

2

Two loves I have, of comfort and despair,
That like two spirits do suggest me still;
My better angle is a man right fair,
My worser spirit a woman coloured ill.
To win me soon to hell, my female evil   5
Tempteth my better angel from my side,
And would corrupt my saint to be a devil,
Wooing his purity with her fair pride.
And whether that my angle be turned fiend,
Suspect I may, yet not directly tell;   10
For being both to me, both to each friend,
I guess one angel in another's hell.
   The truth I shall not know, but live in doubt,
   Till my bad angel fire my good one out.

3

Did not the heavenly rhetoric of thine eye,
'Gainst whom the world could not hold argument,
Persuade my heart to this false perjury?
Vows for thee broke deserve not punishment.
A woman I forswore; but I will prove,   5
Thou being a goddess, I forswore not thee:
My vow was earthly, thou a heavenly love;
Thy grace being gained cures all disgrace in me.
My vow was breath, and breath a vapour is;
Then, thou fair sun, that on this earth doth shine,   10
Exhal'st this vapour vow; in thee it is:
If broken, then it is no fault of mine.
   If by me broke, what fool is not so wise
   To break an oath, to win a paradise?

4

Sweet Cytherea, sitting by a brook
With young Adonis, lovely, fresh and green,
Did court the lad with many a lovely look,
Such looks as none could look but beauty's queen.
She told him stories to delight his ear;   5
She showed him favours to allure his eye;
To win his heart, she touched him here and there;
Touches so soft still conquer chastity.

But whether unripe years did want conceit,
Or he refused to take her figuréd proffer,   10
The tender nibbler would not touch the bait,
But smile and jest at every gentle offer:
   Then fell she on her back, fair queen, and toward:
   He rose and ran away; ah, fool too froward.

5

If love make me forsworn, how shall I swear to love?
O never faith could hold, if not to beauty vowéd:
Though to myself forsworn, to thee I'll constant
   prove;
Those thoughts, to me like oaks, to thee like
   osiers bowéd.
Study his bias leaves, and makes his book thine eyes,   5
Where all those pleasures live that art can comprehend.
If knowledge be the mark, to know thee shall suffice;
Well learnéd is that tongue that well can thee
   commend:
All ignorant that soul that sees thee without wonder;
Which is to me some praise, that I thy parts admire.   10
Thine eye Jove's lightning seems, thy voice his
   dreadful thunder,
Which, not to anger bent, is music and sweet fire.
   Celestial as thou art, O do not love that wrong,
   To sing heaven's praise with such an earthly tongue.

6

Scarce had the sun dried up the dewy morn,
And scarce the herd gone to the hedge for shade,
When Cytherea, all in love forlorn,
A longing tarriance for Adonis made
Under an osier growing by a brook,   5
A brook where Adon used to cool his spleen.
Hot was the day; she hotter that did look
For his approach, that often there had been.
Anon he comes, and throws his mantle by,
And stood stark naked on the brook's green brim: 10
The sun looked on the world with glorious eye,
Yet not so wistly as this queen on him.
   He, spying her, bounced in whereas he stood;
   'O Jove,' quoth she, 'why was not I a flood!'

7

Fair is my love, but not so fair as fickle;
Mild as a dove, but neither true nor trusty;
Brighter than glass, and yet, as glass is, brittle;
Softer than wax, and yet as iron rusty;
   A lily pale, with damask dye to grace her;   5
   None fairer, nor none falser to deface her.

Her lips to mine how often hath she joinéd,
Between each kiss her oaths of true love swearing!
How many tales to please me hath she coinéd,
Dreading my love, the loss thereof still fearing!   10
   Yet in the midst of all her pure protestings
   Her faith, her oaths, her tears, and all were jestings.

She burned with love, as straw with fire flameth;
She burned out love, as soon as straw out-burneth;
She framed the love, and yet she foiled the framing; 15
She bade love last, and yet she fell a-turning.
    Was this a lover, or a lecher whether?
    Bad in the best, though excellent in neither.

8

If music and sweet poetry agree,
As they must needs, the sister and the brother,
Then must the love be great 'twixt thee and me,
Because thou lov'st the one and I the other.
Dowland to thee is dear, whose heavenly touch 5
Upon the lute doth ravish human sense;
Spenser to me, whose deep conceit is such
As passing all conceit needs no defence.
Thou lov'st to hear the sweet melodious sound
That Phoebus' lute, the queen of music, makes; 10
And I in deep delight am chiefly drowned
When as himself to singing he betakes.
    One god is god of both, as poets feign;
    One knight loves both, and both in thee remain.

9

Fair was the morn, when the fair queen of love,
. . . .
Paler for sorrow than her milk-white dove,
For Adon's sake, a youngster proud and wild,
Her stand she takes upon a steep-up hill,
Anon Adonis comes with horn and hounds; 5
She, silly queen, with more than love's good will,
Forbade the boy he should not pass those grounds.
'Once', quoth she, 'did I see a fair sweet youth
Here in these brakes deep-wounded with a boar, 10
Deep in the thigh, a spectacle of ruth!
See, in my thigh,' quoth she, 'here was the sore.'
    She showed hers; he saw more wounds than one,
    And blushing fled, and left her all alone.

10

Sweet rose, fair flower, untimely plucked, soon vaded,
Plucked in the bud and vaded in the spring!
Bright orient pearl, alack, too timely shaded!
Fair creature, killed too soon by death's sharp sting!
Like a green plum that hangs upon a tree, 5
And falls through wind before the fall should be.

I weep for thee and yet no cause I have;
For why thou left'st me nothing in thy will.
And yet thou left'st me more than I did crave,
For why I craved nothing of thee still: 10
    O yes, dear friend, I pardon crave of thee,
    Thy discontent thou didst bequeath to me.

11

Venus with young Adonis sitting by her
Under a myrtle shade began to woo him;
She told the youngling how god Mars did try her,
And as he fell to her, so fell she to him.
'Even thus', quoth she, 'the warlike god embraced me', 5
And then she clipped Adonis in her arms;
'Even thus', quoth she, 'the warlike god unlaced me',
As if the boy should use like loving charms;
'Even thus', quoth she, 'he seized on my lips',

And with her lips on his did act the seizure;
And as she fetchéd breath, away he skips,
And would not take her meaning nor her pleasure.
    Ah, that I had my lady at this bay,
    To kiss and clip me till I run away!

12

Crabbéd age and youth cannot live together:
Youth is full of pleasance, age is full of care;
Youth like summer morn, age like winter weather;
Youth like summer brave, age like winter bare.
Youth is full of sport, age's breath is short; 5
    Youth is nimble, age is lame.
Youth is hot and bold, age is weak and cold;
    Youth is wild and age is tame.
Age, I do abhor thee; youth, I do adore thee;
    O, my love, my love is young! 10
Age, I do defy thee. O, sweet shepherd, hie thee,
    For methinks thou stay too long.

13

Beauty is but a vain and doubtful good,
A shining gloss that vadeth suddenly,
A flower that dies when first it 'gins to bud,
A brittle glass that's broken presently;
    A doubtful good, a gloss, a glass, a flower, 5
    Lost, vaded, broken, dead within an hour.

And as goods lost are seld or never found,
As vaded gloss no rubbing will refresh,
As flowers dead lie witheréd on the ground,
As broken glass no cement can redress: 10
    So beauty blemished once, for ever lost,
    In spite of physic, painting, pain and cost.

14

Good night, good rest: ah, neither be my share;
She bade good night that kept my rest away;
And daffed me to a cabin hanged with care,
To descant on the doubts of my decay.
    'Farewell,' quoth she, 'and come again to-morrow'; 5
    Fare well I could not, for I supped with sorrow.

Yet at my parting sweetly did she smile,
In scorn or friendship nill I conster whether;
'T may be, she joyed to jest at my exile,
'T may be, again to make me wander thither: 10
    'Wander', a word for shadows like myself,
    As take the pain, but cannot pluck the pelf.

Lord, how mine eyes throw gazes to the east!
My heart doth charge the watch; the morning rise
Doth cite each moving sense from idle rest, 15
Not daring trust the office of mine eyes,
    While Philomela sings, I sit and mark,
    And wish her lays were tunéd like the lark.

For she doth welcome daylight with her ditty,
And drives away dark dreaming night:
The night so packed, I post unto my pretty; 20
Heart hath his hope and eyes their wishéd sight;
    Sorrow changed to solace and solace mixed
      with sorrow;
    For why, she sighed, and bade me come to-morrow.

Were I with her, the night would post too soon, 25
But now are minutes added to the hours;
To spite me now, each minute seems a moon;
Yet not for me, shine sun to succour flowers!
  Pack night, peep day; good day, of night now
    borrow;
  Short night, to-night, and length thyself
    to-morrow. 30

15

It was a lording's daughter, the fairest one of three,
That likéd of her master as well as well might be,
Till looking on an Englishman, the fairest that eye
  could see,
  Her fancy fell a-turning.
Long was the combat doubtful that love with love
  did fight, 5
To leave the master loveless, or kill the gallant knight;
To put in practice either, alas, it was a spite
  Unto the silly damsel!
But one must be refuséd; more mickle was the pain
That nothing could be uséd to turn them both to gain, 10
For of the two the trusty knight was wounded
  with disdain:
  Alas, she could not help it!
Thus art with arms contending was victor of the day,
Which by a gift of learning did bear the maid away:
Then, lullaby, the learnéd man hath got the lady gay; 15
  For now my song is ended.

16

On a day, alack the day!
Love, whose month was ever May,
Spied a blossom passing fair,
Playing in the wanton air.
Through the velvet leaves the wind 5
All unseen 'gan passage find,
That the lover, sick to death,
Wished himself the heaven's breath,
'Air', quoth he, 'thy cheeks may blow;
Air, would I might triumph so! 10
But, alas! my hand hath sworn
Ne'er to pluck thee from thy thorn;
Vow, alack! for youth unmeet,
Youth, so apt to pluck a sweet.
Thou for whom Jove would swear 15
Juno but an Ethiope were;
And deny himself for Jove,
Turning mortal for thy love.'

17

My flocks feed not, my ewes breed not,
My rams speed not, all is amiss;
Love is dying, faith's defying,
Heart's denying, causer of this.
All my merry jigs are quite forgot, 5
All my lady's love is lost, God wot;
Where her faith was firmly fixed in love,
There a nay is placed without remove.
  One silly cross wrought all my loss;
  O frowning Fortune, curséd fickle dame! 10
  For now I see inconstancy
  More in women than in men remain.

In black mourn I, all fears scorn I,
Love hath forlorn me, living in thrall:
Heart is bleeding, all help needing, 15
O cruel speeding, fraughted with gall.
My shepherd's pipe can sound no deal;
My wether's bell rings doleful knell;
My curtal dog that wont to have played,
Plays not at all, but seems afraid; 20
  My sighs so deep procures to weep,
  In howling wise, to see my doleful plight.
  How sighs resound through heartless ground,
  Like a thousand vanquished men in bloody fight!

Clear wells spring not, sweet birds sing not, 25
Green plants bring not forth their dye;
Herds stand weeping, flocks all sleeping,
Nymphs back peeping fearfully.
All our pleasure known to us poor swains,
All our merry meetings on the plains, 30
All our evening sport from us is fled,
All our love is lost, for Love is dead.
  Farewell, sweet lass, thy like ne'er was
  For a sweet content, the cause of all my moan:
  Poor Corydon must live alone; 35
  Other help for him I see that there is none.

18

When as thine eye hath chose the dame,
And stalled the deer that thou shouldst strike,
Let reason rule things worthy blame,
As well as fancy, partial might;
  Take counsel of some wiser head, 5
  Neither too young nor yet unwed.

And when thou com'st thy tale to tell,
Smooth not thy tongue with filéd talk,
Lest she some subtle practice smell—
A cripple soon can find a halt— 10
  But plainly say thou lov'st her well,
  And set thy person forth to sell.

And to her will frame all thy ways;
Spare not to spend, and chiefly there
Where thy desert may merit praise, 15
By ringing in thy lady's ear:
  The strongest castle, tower and town,
  The golden bullet beats it down.

Serve always with assuréd trust,
And in thy suit be humble true; 20
Unless thy lady prove unjust,
Press never thou to choose anew:
  When time shall serve, be thou not slack
  To proffer, though she put thee back.

What though her frowning brows be bent, 25
Her cloudy looks will calm ere night,
And then too late she will repent
That thus dissembled her delight;
  And twice desire, ere it be day,
  That which with scorn she put away. 30

What though she strive to try her strength,
And ban and brawl, and say thee nay,
Her feeble force will yield at length,

When craft hath taught her thus to say:
  'Had women been so strong as men,   35
  In faith, you had not had it then,'

The wiles and guiles that women work,
Dissembled with an outward show,
The tricks and toys that in them lurk,
The cock that treads them shall not know.   40
  Have you not heard it said full oft,
  A woman's nay doth stand for nought?

Think women still to strive with men,
To sin and never for to saint:
There is no heaven, by holy then,   45
When time with age shall them attaint.
  Were kisses all the joys in bed,
  One woman would another wed.

But, soft, enough, too much I fear,
Lest that my mistress hear my song;   50
She will not stick to round me on th'ear,
To teach my tongue to be so long,
  Yet will she blush, here be it said,
  To hear her secrets so bewrayed.

19

Live with me, and be my love,
And we will all the pleasures prove
That hills and valleys, dales and fields,
And all the craggy mountains yield.

There will we sit upon the rocks,   5
And see the shepherds feed their flocks,
By shallow rivers, by whose falls
Melodious birds sing madrigals.

There will I make thee a bed of roses,
With a thousand fragrant posies,   10
A cap of flowers, and a kirtle
Embroider'd all with leaves of myrtle.

A belt of straw and ivy buds,
With coral clasps and amber studs;
And if these pleasures may thee move,   15
Then live with me and be my love.

LOVE'S ANSWER

If that the world and love were young,
And truth in every shepherd's tongue,
These pretty pleasures might me move
To live with thee and be thy love.   20

20

As it fell upon a day
In the merry month of May,
Sitting in a pleasant shade
Which a grove of myrtles made,
Beasts did leap and birds did sing,   5
Trees did grow and plants did spring;
Every thing did banish moan,
Save the nightingale alone:
She, poor bird, as all forlorn,
Leaned her breast up-till a thorn,   10
And there sung the dolefull'st ditty,
That to hear it was great pity:
'Fie, fie, fie', now would she cry;
'Tereu, Tereu!' by and by;
That to hear her so complain,   15
Scarce I could from tears refrain;
For her griefs so lively shown
Made me think upon mine own.
Ah, thought I, thou mourn'st in vain!
None takes pity on thy pain: 20
Senseless trees they cannot hear thee;
Ruthless beasts they will not cheer thee:
King Pandion he is dead;
All thy friends are lapped in lead;
All thy fellow birds do sing,   25
Careless of thy sorrowing.
Whilst as fickle Fortune smiled,
Thou and I were both beguiled.
  Every one that flatters thee
Is no friend in misery.   30
Words are easy, like the wind;
Faithful friends are hard to find:
Every man will be thy friend
Whilst thou hast wherewith to spend;
But if store of crowns be scant,   35
No man will supply thy want.
If that one be prodigal,
Bountiful they will him call,
And with such-like flattering,
'Pity but he were a king';   40
If he be addict to vice,
Quickly him they will entice;
If to women he be bent,
They have at commandment.
But if Fortune once do frown,   45
Then farewell his great renown;
They that fawned on him before
Use his company no more.
He that is thy friend indeed,
He will help thee in thy need: 50
If thou sorrow, he will weep;
If thou wake, he cannot sleep;
Thus of every grief in heart
He with thee doth bear a part.
These are certain signs to know   55
Faithful friend from flatt'ring foe.

The Phoenix and the Turtle

Let the bird of loudest lay,
On the sole Arabian tree,
Herald sad and trumpet be,
To whose sound chaste wings obey.

But thou shrieking harbinger, 5
Foul precurrer of the fiend,
Augur of the fever's end,
To this troop come thou not near!

From this session interdict
Every fowl of tyrant wing, 10
Save the eagle, feath'red king:
Keep the obsequy so strict.

Let the priest in surplice white,
That defunctive music can,
Be the death-divining swan, 15
Lest the requiem lack his right.

And thou treble-dated crow,
That thy sable gender mak'st
With the breath thou giv'st and tak'st,
'Mongst our mourners shalt thou go. 20

Here the anthem doth commence:
Love and constancy is dead;
Phoenix and the turtle fled
In a mutual flame from hence.

So they loved, as love in twain 25
Had the essence but in one;
Two distincts, division none:
Number there in love was slain.

Hearts remote, yet not asunder;
Distance, and no space was seen 30
'Twixt this turtle and his queen:
But in them it were a wonder.

So between them love did shine,
That the turtle saw his right
Flaming in the phoenix' sight; 35
Either was the other's mine.

Property was thus appalléd,
That the self was not the same;
Single nature's double name
Neither two nor one was calléd. 40

Reason, in itself confounded,
Saw division grow together,
To themselves yet either neither,
Simple were so well compounded;

That it cried, How true a twain 45
Seemeth this concordant one!
Love hath reason, reason none,
If what parts can so remain.

Whereupon it made this threne
To the phoenix and the dove, 50
Co-supremes and stars of love,
As chorus to their tragic scene.

THRENOS

Beauty, truth, and rarity,
Grace in all simplicity, 55
Here enclosed, in cinders lie.

Death is now the phoenix' nest;
And the turtle's loyal breast
To eternity doth rest.

Leaving no posterity,
'Twas not their infirmity, 60
It was married chastity.

Truth may seem, but cannot be;
Beauty brag, but 'tis not she;
Truth and beauty buried be.

To this urn let those repair 65
That are either true or fair;
For these dead birds sigh a prayer.

A Lover's Complaint

From off a hill whose concave womb reworded
A plaintful story from a sist'ring vale,
My spirits t'attend this double voice accorded,
And down I laid to list the sad-tuned tale,
Ere long espied a fickle maid full pale,   5
Tearing of papers, breaking rings atwain,
Storming her world with sorrow's wind and rain.

Upon her head a platted hive of straw,
Which fortified her visage from the sun,
Whereon the thought might think sometime it saw   10
The carcase of a beauty spent and done.
Time had not scythéd all that youth begun,
Nor youth all quit, but spite of heaven's fell rage
Some beauty peeped through lattice of seared age.

Oft did she heave her napkin to her eyne,   15
Which on it had conceited characters,
Laund'ring the silken figures in the brine
That seasonéd woe had pelleted in tears,
And often reading what contents it bears;
As often shrieking undistinguished woe,   20
In clamours of all size, both high and low.

Sometimes her levelled eyes their carriage ride,
As they did batt'ry to the spheres intend;
Sometime diverted their poor balls are tied
To th'orbéd earth; sometimes they do extend   25
Their view right on; anon their gazes lend
To every place at once, and nowhere fixed,
The mind and sight distractedly commixed.

Her hair, nor loose nor tied in formal plat,
Proclaimed in her a careless hand of pride;   30
For some, untucked, descended her sheaved hat,
Hanging her pale and pinéd cheek beside;
Some in her threaden fillet still did bide,
And, true to bondage, would not break from
      thence,
Though slackly braided in loose negligence.   35

A thousand favours from a maund she drew
Of amber, crystal, and of beaded jet,
Which one by one she in a river threw,
Upon whose weeping margent she was set;
Like usury applying wet to wet,   40
Or monarchs' hands that lets not bounty fall
Where want cries some, but where excess begs all.

Of folded schedules had she many a one,
Which she perused, sighed, tore, and gave the flood;
Cracked many a ring of posied gold and bone,   45
Bidding them find their sepulchres in mud;
Found yet moe letters sadly penned in blood,
With sleided silk feat and affectedly
Enswathed and sealed to curious secrecy.

These often bathed she in her fluxive eyes,   50
And often kissed, and often 'gan to tear;
Cried, 'O false blood, thou register of lies,
What unapprovéd witness dost thou bear!
Ink would have seemed more black and damnéd here!
This said, in top of rage the lines she rents,   55
Big discontents so breaking their contents.

A reverend man that grazed his cattle nigh,
Sometime a blusterer that the ruffle knew
Of court, of city, and had let go by
The swiftest hours observéd as they flew,   60
Towards this afflicted fancy fastly drew;
And, privileged by age, desires to know
In brief the grounds and motives of her woe.

So slides he down upon his grainéd bat,
And comely distant sits he by her side;   65
When he again desires her, being sat,
Her grievance with his hearing to divide.
If that from him there may be aught applied
Which may her suffering ecstasy assuage,
'Tis promised in the charity of age.   70

'Father,' she says, 'though in me you behold
The injury of many a blasting hour,
Let it not tell your judgement I am old:
Not age, but sorrow, over me hath power.
I might as yet have been a spreading flower,   75
Fresh to myself, if I had self-applied
Love to myself, and to no love beside.

'But woe is me! too early I attended
A youthful suit—it was to gain my grace—
O, one by nature's outwards so commended   80
That maidens' eyes stuck over all his face.
Love lacked a dwelling and made him her place;
And when in his fair parts she did abide,
She was new lodged and newly deified.

'His browny locks did hang in crookéd curls;   85
And every light occasion of the wind
Upon his lips their silken parcels hurls.
What's sweet to do, to do will aptly find:
Each eye that saw him did enchant the mind;
For on his visage was in little drawn   90
What largeness thinks in Paradise was sawn.

'Small show of man was yet upon his chin;
His phoenix down began but to appear,
Like unshorn velvet, on that termless skin,
Whose bare out-bragged the web it seemed to wear;   95
Yet showed his visage by that cost more dear;
And nice affections wavering stood in doubt
If best were as it was, or best without.

'His qualities were beauteous as his form,
For maiden-tongued he was, and thereof free;   100
Yet if men moved him, was he such a storm
As oft 'twixt May and April is to see,
When winds breathe sweet, unruly though they be.
His rudeness so with his authorized youth
Did livery falseness in a pride of truth.   105

'Well could he ride, and often men would say,
"That horse his mettle from his rider takes:
Proud of subjection, noble by the sway,
What rounds, what bounds, what course, what stop
    he makes!"
And controversy hence a question takes,   110
Whether the horse by him became his deed,
Or he his manage by th'well-doing steed.

'But quickly on this side the verdict went:
His real habitude gave life and grace
To appertainings and to ornament,   115
Accomplished in himself, not in his case,
All aids, themselves made fairer by their place,
Came for additions; yet their purposed trim
Pierced not his grace, but were all graced by him.

'So on the tip of his subduing tongue   120
All kind of arguments and question deep,
All replication prompt, and reason strong,
For his advantage still did wake and sleep.
To make the weeper laugh, the laugher weep,
He had the dialect and different skill,   125
Catching all passions in his craft of will,

'That he did in the general bosom reign
Of young, of old, and sexes both enchanted,
To dwell with him in thoughts, or to remain
In personal duty, following where he haunted.   130
Consents bewitched, ere he desire, have granted,
And dialogued for him what he would say,
Asked their own wills, and made their wills obey.

'Many there were that did his picture get,
To serve their eyes, and in it put their mind;   135
Like fools that in th'imagination set
The goodly objects which abroad they find
Of lands and mansions, theirs in thought assigned;
And labouring in moe pleasures to bestow them
Than the true gouty landlord which doth owe them. 140

'So many have, that never touched his hand,
Sweetly supposed them mistress of his heart.
My woeful self, that did in freedom stand,
And was my own fee-simple, not in part,
What with his art in youth, and youth in art,   145
Threw my affections in his charmed power
Reserved the stalk and gave him all my flower.

'Yet did I not, as some my equals did,
Demand of him, nor being desirèd yielded;
Finding myself in honour so forbid,   150
With safest distance I mine honour shielded.
Experience for me many bulwarks builded
Of proofs new-bleeding, which remained the foil
Of this false jewel, and his amorous spoil.

'But ah, who ever shunned by precedent   155
The destined ill she must herself assay?
Or forced examples, 'gainst her own content,
To put the by-past perils in her way?
Counsel may stop awhile what will not stay;
For when we rage, advice is often seen   160
By blunting us to make our wills more keen.

'Nor gives it satisfaction to our blood
That we must curb it upon others' proof,
To be forbod the sweets that seems so good
For fear of harms that preach in our behoof.   165
O appetite, from judgement stand aloof!
The one a palate hath that needs will taste,
Though Reason weep, and cry it is thy last.

'For further I could say this man's untrue,
And knew the patterns of his foul beguiling;   170
Heard where his plants in others' orchards grew;
Saw how deceits were gilded in his smiling;
Knew vows were ever brokers to defiling;
Thought characters and words merely but art,
And bastards of his foul adulterate heart.   175

'And long upon these terms I held my city,
Till thus he 'gan besiege me: "Gentle maid,
Have of my suffering youth some feeling pity,
And be not of my holy vows afraid.
That's to ye sworn to none was ever said;   180
For feasts of love I have been called unto,
Till now did ne'er invite nor never woo.

'"All my offences that abroad you see
Are errors of the blood, none of the mind;
Love made them not; with acture they may be,   185
Where neither party is nor true nor kind.
They sought their shame that so their shame did find;
And so much less of shame in me remains
By how much of me their reproach contains.

'"Among the many that mine eyes have seen,   190
Not one whose flame my heart so much as warmèd,
Or my affection put to th'smallest teen,
Or any of my leisures ever charmèd.
Harm have I done to them, but ne'er was harmèd;
Kept hearts in liveries, but mine own was free,   195
And reigned commanding in his monarchy.

'"Look here what tributes wounded fancies sent me,
Of palèd pearls and rubies red as blood;
Figuring that they their passions likewise lent me
Of grief and blushes, aptly understood   200
In bloodless white and the encrimsoned mood—
Effects of terror and dear modesty,
Encamped in hearts, but fighting outwardly.

'"And, lo, behold these talents of their hair,
With twisted metal amorously empleached,   205
I have receiv'd from many a several fair,
Their kind acceptance weepingly beseeched,
With the annexions of fair gems enriched,
And deep-brained sonnets that did amplify
Each stone's dear nature, worth, and quality.   210

' "The diamond? why, 'twas beautiful and hard,
Whereto his invised properties did tend;
The deep-green em'rald, in whose fresh regard
Weak sights their sickly radiance do amend;
The heaven-hued sapphire and the opal blend   215
With objects manifold; each several stone,
With wit well blazoned, smiled, or made some moan.

' "Lo, all these trophies of affections hot,
Of pensived and subdued desires the tender,
Nature hath charged me that I hoard them not,   220
But yield them up where I myself must render—
That is, to you, my origin and ender;
For these, of force, must your oblations be,
Since I their altar, you enpatron me.

' "O then advance of yours that phraseless hand   225
Whose white weighs down the airy scale of praise;
Take all these similes to your own command,
Hallowéd with sighs that burning lungs did raise;
What me your minister for you obeys
Works under you; and to your audit comes   230
Their distract parcels in combinéd sums.

' "Lo, this device was sent me from a nun,
Or sister sanctified, of holiest note,
Which late her noble suit in court did shun,
Whose rarest havings made the blossoms dote;   235
For she was sought by spirits of richest coat,
But kept cold distance, and did thence remove
To spend her living in eternal love.

' "But, O my sweet, what labour is't to leave
The thing we have not, mast'ring what not strives,   240
Playing the place which did no form receive,
Playing patient sports in unconstrainéd gyves!
She that her fame so to herself contrives,
The scars of battle scapeth by the flight,
And makes her absence valiant, not her might.   245

' "O pardon me in that my boast is true!
The accident which brought me to her eye
Upon the moment did her force subdue,
And now she would the cagéd cloister fly.
Religious love put out religion's eye.   250
Not to be tempted, would she be immuréd,
And now to tempt all liberty procuréd.

' "How mighty then you are, O hear me tell!
The broken bosoms that to me belong
Have emptied all their fountains in my well,   255
And mine I pour your ocean all among.
I strong o'er them, and you o'er me being strong,
Must for your victory us all congest,
As compound love to physic your cold breast.

' "My parts had pow'r to charm a sacred nun,   260
Who, disciplined, ay, dieted in grace,
Believed her eyes when they t'assail begun,
All vows and consecrations giving place,
O most potential love, vow, bond, nor space,
In thee hath neither sting, knot, nor confine,   265
For thou art all, and all things else are thine.

' "When thou impressest, what are precepts worth
Of stale example? When thou wilt inflame,
How coldly those impediments stand forth,
Of wealth, of filial fear, law, kindred, fame!   270

Love's arms are peace, 'gainst rule, 'gainst sense,
  'gainst shame.
And sweetens, in the suff'ring pangs it bears,
The aloes of all forces, shocks and fears.

' "Now all these hearts that do on mine depend,
Feeling it break, with bleeding groans they pine,   275
And supplicant their sighs to your extend,
To leave the batt'ry that you make 'gainst mine,
Lending soft audience to my sweet design,
And credent soul to that strong-bonded oath,
That shall prefer and undertake my troth."   280

'This said, his wat'ry eyes he did dismount,
Whose sights till then were levelled on my face;
Each cheek a river running from a fount
With brinish current downward flowed apace.
O, how the channel to the stream gave grace!   285
Who glazed with crystal gate the glowing roses
That flame through water which their hue encloses.

'O father, what a hell of witchcraft lies
In the small orb of one particular tear!
But with the inundation of the eyes   290
What rocky heart to water will not wear?
What breast so cold that is not warméd here?
O cleft effect! cold modesty, hot wrath,
Both fire from hence and chill extincture hath.

'For lo, his passion, but an art of craft,   295
Even there resolved my reason into tears;
There my white stole of chastity I daffed,
Shook off my sober guards and civil fears;
Appear to him as he to me appears,
All melting; though our drops this diff'rence bore: 300
His poisoned me, and mine did him restore.

'In him a plenitude of subtle matter,
Applied to cautels, all strange forms receives,
Of burning blushes or of weeping water,
Or swooning paleness; and he takes and leaves,   305
In either's aptness, as it best deceives,
To blush at speeches rank, to weep at woes,
Or to turn white and swoon at tragic shows;

'That not a heart which in his level came
Could scape the hail of his all-hurting aim,   310
Showing fair nature is both kind and tame;
And, veiled in them, did win whom he would maim.
Against the thing he sought he would exclaim;
When he most burned in heart-wished luxury,
He preached pure maid and praised cold chastity.   315

'Thus merely with the garment of a Grace
The naked and concealéd fiend he covered,
That th'unexperient gave the tempter place,
Which, like a cherubin, above them hovered.
Who, young and simple, would not be so lovered?   320
Ay me, I fell, and yet do question make
What I should do again for such a sake.

'O, that infected moisture of his eye,
O, that false fire which in his cheek so glowéd,
O, that forced thunder from his heart did fly,   325
O, that sad breath his spongy lungs bestowéd,
O, all that borrowéd motion, seeming owéd,
Would yet again betray the fore-betrayed,
And new pervert a reconciléd maid.'

The Sonnets

TO. THE. ONLIE. BEGETTER. OF.
THESE. INSUING. SONNETS.
MR. W. H. ALL. HAPPINESSE.
AND. THAT. ETERNITIE.
PROMISED.
BY.
OUR. EVER-LIVING. POET.
WISHETH.
THE. WELL-WISHING.
ADVENTURER. IN.
SETTING.
FORTH.

T.T.

The Sonnets

1

From fairest creatures we desire increase,
That thereby beauty's rose might never die,
But as the riper should by time decease,
His tender heir might bear his memory:
But thou contracted to thine own bright eyes,
Feed'st thy light's flame with self-substantial fuel,
Making a famine where abundance lies,
Thy self thy foe, to thy sweet self too cruel:
Thou that art now the world's fresh ornament,
And only herald to the gaudy spring,
Within thine own bud buriest thy content,
And tender churl mak'st waste in niggarding:
 Pity the world, or else this glutton be,
 To eat the world's due, by the grave and thee.

2

When forty winters shall besiege thy brow,
And dig deep trenches in thy beauty's field,
Thy youth's proud livery so gazed on now,
Will be a tattered weed of small worth held:
Then being asked, where all thy beauty lies,
Where all the treasure of thy lusty days;
To say within thine own deep sunken eyes,
Were an all-eating shame, and thriftless praise.
How much more praise deserved thy beauty's use,
If thou couldst answer 'This fair child of mine
Shall sum my count, and make my old excuse'
Proving his beauty by succession thine.
 This were to be new made when thou art old,
 And see thy blood warm when thou feel'st it cold.

3

Look in thy glass and tell the face thou viewest,
Now is the time that face should form another,
Whose fresh repair if now thou not renewest,
Thou dost beguile the world, unbless some mother.
For where is she so fair whose uneared womb
Disdains the tillage of thy husbandry?
Or who is he so fond will be the tomb,
Of his self-love to stop posterity?
Thou art thy mother's glass and she in thee
Calls back the lovely April of her prime,
So thou through windows of thine age shalt see,
Despite of wrinkles this thy golden time.
 But if thou live remembered not to be,
 Die single and thine image dies with thee.

4

Unthrifty loveliness why dost thou spend,
Upon thy self thy beauty's legacy?
Nature's bequest gives nothing but doth lend,
And being frank she lends to those are free:
Then beauteous niggard why dost thou abuse,
The bounteous largess given thee to give?
Profitless usurer why dost thou use
So great a sum of sums yet canst not live?
For having traffic with thy self alone,
Thou of thy self thy sweet self dost deceive,
Then how when nature calls thee to be gone,
What acceptable audit canst thou leave?
 Thy unused beauty must be tombed with thee,
 Which uséd lives th' executor to be.

5

Those hours that with gentle work did frame
The lovely gaze where every eye doth dwell
Will play the tyrants to the very same,
And that unfair which fairly doth excel:
For never-resting time leads summer on
To hideous winter and confounds him there,
Sap checked with frost and lusty leaves quite gone,
Beauty o'er-snowed and bareness every where:
Then were not summer's distillation left
A liquid prisoner pent in walls of glass,
Beauty's effect with beauty were bereft,
Nor it nor no remembrance what it was.
 But flowers distilled though they with winter meet,
 Leese but their show, their substance still lives sweet.

6

Then let not winter's raggéd hand deface,
In thee thy summer ere thou be distilled:
Make sweet some vial; treasure thou some place,
With beauty's treasure ere it be self-killed:
That use is not forbidden usury,
Which happies those that pay the willing loan;
That's for thy self to breed another thee,
Or ten times happier be it ten for one,
Ten times thy self were happier than thou art,
If ten of thine ten times refigured thee:
Then what could death do if thou shouldst depart,
Leaving thee living in posterity?
 Be not self-willed for thou art much too fair,
 To be death's conquest and make worms thine heir.

7

Lo in the orient when the gracious light
Lifts up his burning head, each under eye
Doth homage to his new-appearing sight,
Serving with looks his sacred majesty,
And having climbed the steep-up heavenly hill,   5
Resembling strong youth in his middle age,
Yet mortal looks adore his beauty still,
Attending on his golden pilgrimage:
But when from highmost pitch with weary car,
Like feeble age he reeleth from the day,   10
The eyes (fore duteous) now converted are
From his low tract and look another way:
  So thou, thy self out-going in thy noon:
  Unlooked on diest unless thou get a son.

8

Music to hear, why hear'st thou music sadly?
Sweets with sweets war not, joy.delights in joy:
Why lov'st thou that which thou receiv'st not gladly,
Or else receiv'st with pleasure thine annoy?
If the true concord of well-tunéd sounds,   5
By unions married do offend thine ear,
They do but sweetly chide thee, who confounds
In singleness the parts that thou shouldst bear:
Mark how one string sweet husband to another,
Strikes each in each by mutual ordering;   10
Resembling sire, and child, and happy mother,
Who all in one, one pleasing note do sing:
  Whose speechless song being many, seeming one,
  Sings this to thee, 'Thou single wilt prove none'.

9

Is it for fear to wet a widow's eye,
That thou consum'st thy self in single life?
Ah, if thou issueless shalt hap to die,
The world will wail thee like a makeless wife,
The world will be thy widow and still weep,   5
That thou no form of thee hast left behind,
When every private widow well may keep,
By children's eyes, her husband's shape in mind:
Look what an unthrift in the world doth spend
Shifts but his place, for still the world enjoys it;   10
But beauty's waste hath in the world an end,
And kept unused the user so destroys it:
  No love toward others in that bosom sits
  That on himself such murd'rous shame commits.

10

For shame deny that thou bear'st love to any
Who for thy self art so unprovident.
Grant if thou wilt, thou art beloved of many,
But that thou none lov'st is most evident:
For thou art so possessed with murd'rous hate,   5
That 'gainst thy self thou stick'st not to conspire,
Seeking that beauteous roof to ruinate
Which to repair should be thy chief desire:
O change thy thought, that I may change my mind,
Shall hate be fairer lodged than gentle love?   10
Be as thy presence is gracious and kind,
Or to thy self at least kind-hearted prove,
  Make thee another self for love of me,
  That beauty still may live in thine or thee.

11

As fast as thou shalt wane so fast thou grow'st,
In one of thine, from that which thou departest,
And that fresh blood which youngly thou bestow'st,
Thou mayst call thine, when thou from youth
    convertest,
Herein lives wisdom, beauty, and increase,   5
Without this folly, age, and cold decay,
If all were minded so, the times should cease,
And threescore year would make the world away:
Let those whom nature hath not made for store,
Harsh, featureless, and rude, barrenly perish: 10
Look whom she best endowed, she gave thee more;
Which bounteous gift thou shouldst in bounty cherish:
  She carved thee for her seal, and meant thereby,
  Thou shouldst print more, not let that copy die.

12

When I do count the clock that tells the time,
And see the brave day sunk in hideous night,
When I behold the violet past prime,
And sable curls all silvered o'er with white:
When lofty trees I see barren of leaves,   5
Which erst from heat did canopy the herd
And summer's green all girded up in sheaves
Borne on the bier with white and bristly beard:
Then of thy beauty do I question make
That thou among the wastes of time must go,   10
Since sweets and beauties do themselves forsake,
And die as fast as they see others grow,
  And nothing 'gainst Time's scythe can make defence
  Save breed to brave him, when he takes thee hence.

13

O that you were your self, but love you are
No longer yours, than you your self here live,
Against this coming end you should prepare,
And your sweet semblance to some other give.
So should that beauty which you hold in lease   5
Find no determination, then you were
Your self again after your self's decease,
When your sweet issue your sweet form should bear.
Who lets so fair a house fall to decay,
Which husbandry in honour might uphold,   10
Against the stormy gusts of winter's day
And barren rage of death's eternal cold?
  O none but unthrifts, dear my love you know,
  You had a father, let your son say so.

14

Not from the stars do I my judgement pluck,
And yet methinks I have astronomy,
But not to tell of good, or evil luck,
Of plagues, of dearths, or seasons' quality,
Nor can I fortune to brief minutes tell;   5
Pointing to each his thunder, rain and wind,
Or say with princes if it shall go well
By oft predict that I in heaven find.
But from thine eyes my knowledge I derive,
And constant stars in them I read such art   10
As truth and beauty shall together thrive
If from thy self, to store thou wouldst convert:
  Or else of thee this I prognosticate,
  Thy end is truth's and beauty's doom and date.

15

When I consider every thing that grows
Holds in perfection but a little moment.
That this huge stage presenteth nought but shows
Whereon the stars in secret influence comment.
When I perceive that men as plants increase,   5
Cheered and checked even by the self-same sky:
Vaunt in their youthful sap, at height decrease,
And wear their brave state out of memory.
Then the conceit of this inconstant stay,
Sets you most rich in youth before my sight,   10
Where wasteful time debateth with decay
To change your day of youth to sullied night,
    And all in war with Time for love of you,
    As he takes from you, I engraft you new.

16

But wherefore do not you a mightier way
Make war upon this bloody tyrant Time?
And fortify your self in your decay
With means more blessed than my barren rhyme?
Now stand you on the top of happy hours,   5
And many maiden gardens yet unset,
With virtuous wish would bear you living flowers,
Much liker than your painted counterfeit:
So should the lines of life that life repair
Which this (Time's pencil) or my pupil pen   10
Neither in inward worth nor outward fair
Can make you live your self in eyes of men.
    To give away your self, keeps your self still,
    And you must live drawn by your own sweet skill.

17

Who will believe my verse in time to come
If it were filled with your most high deserts?
Though yet heaven knows it is but as a tomb
Which hides your life, and shows not half your parts:
If I could write the beauty of your eyes,   5
And in fresh numbers number all your graces,
The age to come would say this poet lies,
Such heavenly touches ne'er touched earthly faces.
So should my papers (yellowed with their age)
Be scorned, like old men of less truth than tongue,   10
And your true rights be termed a poet's rage,
And stretchéd metre of an antique song,
    But were some child of yours alive that time,
    You should live twice in it, and in my rhyme.

18

Shall I compare thee to a summer's day?
Thou art more lovely and more temperate:
Rough winds do shake the darling buds of May,
And summer's lease hath all too short a date:
Sometime too hot the eye of heaven shines,   5
And often is his gold complexion dimmed,
And every fair from fair sometime declines,
By chance, or nature's changing course untrimmed:
But thy eternal summer shall not fade,
Nor lose possession of that fair thou ow'st,   10
Nor shall death brag thou wand'rest in his shade,
When in eternal lines to time thou grow'st,
    So long as men can breathe or eyes can see,
    So long lives this, and this gives life to thee.

19

Devouring Time blunt thou the lion's paws,
And make the earth devour her own sweet brood,
Pluck the keen teeth from the fierce tiger's jaws,
And burn the long-lived phœnix in her blood,
Make glad and sorry seasons as thou fleet'st,   5
And do whate'er thou wilt swift-footed Time
To the wide world and all her fading sweets:
But I forbid thee one most heinous crime,
O carve not with thy hours my love's fair brow,
Nor draw no lines there with thine antique pen,   10
Him in thy course untainted do allow,
For beauty's pattern to succeeding men.
    Yet do thy worst old Time: despite thy wrong,
    My love shall in my verse ever live young.

20

A woman's face with nature's own hand painted,
Hast thou the master mistress of my passion,
A woman's gentle heart but not acquainted
With shifting change as is false women's fashion,
An eye more bright than theirs, less false in rolling: 5
Gilding the object whereupon it gazeth,
A man in hue all hues in his controlling,
Which steals men's eyes and women's souls amazeth.
And for a woman wert thou first created,
Till nature as she wrought thee fell a-doting,   10
And by addition me of thee defeated,
By adding one thing to my purpose nothing.
    But since she pricked thee out for women's pleasure,
    Mine be thy love and thy love's use their treasure.

21

So is it not with me as with that muse,
Stirred by a painted beauty to his verse,
Who heaven it self for ornament doth use,
And every fair with his fair doth rehearse,
Making a couplement of proud compare   5
With sun and moon, with earth and sea's rich gems:
With April's first-born flowers and all things rare,
That heaven's air in this huge rondure hems.
O let me true in love but truly write,
And then believe me, my love is as fair,   10
As any mother's child, though not so bright
As those gold candles fixed in heaven's air:
    Let them say more that like of hearsay well,
    I will not praise that purpose not to sell.

22

My glass shall not persuade me I am old,
So long as youth and thou are of one date,
But when in thee time's furrows I behold,
Then look I death my days should expiate.
For all that beauty that doth cover thee,   5
Is but the seemly raiment of my heart,
Which in thy breast doth live, as thine in me,
How can I then be elder than thou art?
O therefore love be of thyself so wary,
As I not for my self, but for thee will,   10
Bearing thy heart which I will keep so chary
As tender nurse her babe from faring ill.
    Presume not on thy heart when mine is slain,
    Thou gav'st me thine not to give back again.

23

As an unperfect actor on the stage,
Who with his fear is put beside his part,
Or some fierce thing replete with too much rage,
Whose strength's abundance weakens his own heart;
So I for fear of trust, forget to say, 5
The perfect ceremony of love's rite,
And in mine own love's strength seem to decay,
O'ercharged with burthen of mine own love's might:
O let my looks be then the eloquence,
And dumb presagers of my speaking breast, 10
Who plead for love, and look for recompense,
More than that tongue that more hath more expressed.
   O learn to read what silent love hath writ,
   To hear with eyes belongs to love's fine wit.

24

Mine eye hath played the painter and hath stelled,
Thy beauty's form in table of my heart,
My body is the frame wherein 'tis held,
And perspective it is best painter's art.
For through the painter must you see his skill, 5
To find where your true image pictured lies,
Which in my bosom's shop is hanging still,
That hath his windows glazéd with thine eyes:
Now see what good turns eyes for eyes have done,
Mine eyes have drawn thy shape, and thine for me 10
Are windows to my breast, where-through the sun
Delights to peep, to gaze therein on thee;
   Yet eyes this cunning want to grace their art,
   They draw but what they see, know not the heart.

25

Let those who are in favour with their stars,
Of public honour and proud titles boast,
Whilst I whom fortune of such triumph bars
Unlooked for joy in that I honour most;
Great princes' favourites their fair leaves spread, 5
But as the marigold at the sun's eye,
And in themselves their pride lies buriéd,
For at a frown they in their glory die.
The painful warrior famouséd for fight,
After a thousand victories once foiled, 10
Is from the book of honour razéd quite,
And all the rest forgot for which he toiled:
   Then happy I that love and am beloved
   Where I may not remove nor be removed.

26

Lord of my love, to whom in vassalage
Thy merit hath my duty strongly knit;
To thee I send this written embassage
To witness duty, not to show my wit.
Duty so great, which wit so poor as mine 5
May make seem bare, in wanting words to show it;
But that I hope some good conceit of thine
In thy soul's thought (all naked) will bestow it:
Till whatsoever star that guides my moving,
Points on me graciously with fair aspect, 10
And puts apparel on my tattered loving,
To show me worthy of thy sweet respect,
   Then may I dare to boast how I do love thee,
   Till then, not show my head where thou mayst
     prove me.

27

Weary with toil, I haste me to my bed,
The dear respose for limbs with travel tired,
But then begins a journey in my head
To work my mind, when body's work's expired.
For then my thoughts (from far where I abide) 5
Intend a zealous pilgrimage to thee,
And keep my drooping eyelids open wide,
Looking on darkness which the blind do see.
Save that my soul's imaginary sight
Presents thy shadow to my sightless view, 10
Which like a jewel (hung in ghastly night)
Makes black night beauteous, and her old face new.
   Lo thus by day my limbs, by night my mind,
   For thee, and for my self, no quiet find.

28

How can I then return in happy plight
That am debarred the benefit of rest?
When day's oppression is not eased by night,
But day by night and night by day oppressed.
And each (though enemies to either's reign) 5
Do in consent shake hands to torture me,
The one by toil, the other to complain
How far I toil, still farther off from thee.
I tell the day to please him thou art bright,
And dost him grace when clouds do blot the heaven: 10
So flatter I the swart-complexioned night,
When sparkling stars twire not thou gild'st the even.
   But day doth daily draw my sorrows longer,
   And night doth nightly make grief's length seem
     stronger

29

When in disgrace with Fortune and men's eyes,
I all alone beweep my outcast state,
And trouble deaf heaven with my bootless cries,
And look upon my self and curse my fate,
Wishing me like to one more rich in hope, 5
Featured like him, like him with friends possessed,
Desiring this man's art, and that man's scope,
With what I most enjoy contented least,
Yet in these thoughts my self almost despising,
Haply I think on thee, and then my state, 10
(Like to the lark at break of day arising
From sullen earth) sings hymns at heaven's gate,
   For thy sweet love remembered such wealth brings,
   That then I scorn to change my state with kings.

30

When to the sessions of sweet silent thought,
I summon up remembrance of things past,
I sigh the lack of many a thing I sought,
And with old woes new wail my dear time's waste:
Then can I drown an eye (unused to flow) 5
For precious friends hid in death's dateless night,
And weep afresh love's long since cancelled woe,
And moan th' expense of many a vanished sight.
Then can I grieve at grievances foregone,
And heavily from woe to woe tell o'er 10
The sad account of fore-bemoanéd moan,
Which I new pay as if not paid before.
   But if the while I think on thee (dear friend)
   All losses are restored, and sorrows end.

31

Thy bosom is endearéd with all hearts,
Which I by lacking have supposéd dead,
And there reigns love and all love's loving parts,
And all those friends which I thought buriéd.
How many a holy and obsequious tear   5
Hath dear religious love stol'n from mine eye,
As interest of the dead, which now appear,
But things removed that hidden in thee lie.
Thou art the grave where buried love doth live,
Hung with the trophies of my lovers gone,   10
Who all their parts of me to thee did give,
That due of many, now is thine alone.
    Their images I loved, I view in thee,
    And thou (all they) hast all the all of me.

32

If thou survive my well-contented day,
When that churl death my bones with dust shall cover
And shalt by fortune once more re-survey
These poor rude lines of thy deceaséd lover:
Compare them with the bett'ring of the time,   5
And though they be outstripped by every pen,
Reserve them for my love, not for their rhyme,
Exceeded by the height of happier men.
O then vouchsafe me but this loving thought,
'Had my friend's Muse grown with this growing age, 10
A dearer birth than this his love had brought
To march in ranks of better equipage:
    But since he died and poets better prove,
    Theirs for their style I'll read, his for his love'.

33

Full many a glorious morning have I seen,
Flatter the mountain tops with sovereign eye,
Kissing with golden face the meadows green;
Gilding pale streams with heavenly alchemy:
Anon permit the basest clouds to ride,   5
With ugly rack on his celestial face,
And from the forlorn world his visage hide
Stealing unseen to west with this disgrace:
Even so my sun one early morn did shine,
With all triumphant splendour on my brow,   10
But out alack, he was but one hour mine,
The region cloud hath masked him from me now.
    Yet him for this, my love no whit disdaineth,
    Suns of the world may stain, when heaven's
        sun staineth.

34

Why didst thou promise such a beauteous day,
And make me travel forth without my cloak,
To let base clouds o'ertake me in my way,
Hiding thy brav'ry in their rotten smoke?
'Tis not enough that through the cloud thou break, 5
To dry the rain on my storm-beaten face,
For no man well of such a salve can speak,
That heals the wound, and cures not the disgrace:
Nor can thy shame give physic to my grief,
Though thou repent, yet I have still the loss,   10
Th' offender's sorrow lends but weak relief
To him that bears the strong offence's cross.
    Ah but those tears are pearl which thy love sheds,
    And they are rich, and ransom all ill deeds.

35

No more be grieved at that which thou hast done,
Roses have thorns, and silver fountains mud,
Clouds and eclipses stain both moon and sun,
And loathsome canker lives in sweetest bud.
All men make faults, and even I in this,   5
Authorizing thy trespass with compare,
My self corrupting salving thy amiss,
Excusing thy sins more than thy sins are:
For to thy sensual fault I bring in sense,
Thy adverse party is thy advocate,   10
And 'gainst my self a lawful plea commence:
Such civil war is in my love and hate,
    That I an accessary needs must be,
    To that sweet thief which sourly robs from me.

36

Let me confess that we two must be twain,
Although our undivided loves are one:
So shall those blots that do with me remain,
Without thy help, by me be borne alone.
In our two loves there is but one respect,   5
Though in our lives a separable spite,
Which though it alter not love's sole effect,
Yet doth it steal sweet hours from love's delight.
I may not evermore acknowledge thee,
Lest my bewailéd guilt should do thee shame,   10
Nor thou with public kindness honour me,
Unless thou take that honour from thy name:
    But do not so, I love thee in such sort,
    As thou being mine, mine is thy good report.

37

As a decrepit father takes delight,
To see his active child do deeds of youth,
So I, made lame by Fortune's dearest spite
Take all my comfort of thy worth and truth.
For whether beauty, birth, or wealth, or wit,   5
Or any of these all, or all, or more
Entitled in thy parts, do crownéd sit,
I make my love engrafted to this store:
So then I am not lame, poor, nor despised,
Whilst that this shadow doth such substance give, 10
That I in thy abundance am sufficed,
And by a part of all thy glory live:
    Look what is best, that best I wish in thee,
    This wish I have, then ten times happy me.

38

How can my muse want subject to invent
While thou dost breathe that pour'st into my verse,
Thine own sweet argument, too excellent,
For every vulgar paper to rehearse?
O give thy self the thanks if aught in me,   5
Worthy perusal stand against thy sight,
For who's so dumb that cannot write to thee,
When thou thy self dost give invention light?
Be thou the tenth Muse, ten times more in worth
Than those old nine which rhymers invocate,   10
And he that calls on thee, let him bring forth
Eternal numbers to outlive long date.
    If my slight muse do please these curious days,
    The pain be mine, but thine shall be the praise.

39

O how thy worth with manners may I sing,
When thou art all the better part of me?
What can mine own praise to mine own self bring:
And what is't but mine own when I praise thee? 5
Even for this, let us divided live,
And our dear love lose name of single one,
That by this separation I may give:
That due to thee which thou deserv'st alone:
O absence what a torment wouldst thou prove,
Were it not thy sour leisure gave sweet leave, 10
To entertain the time with thoughts of love,
Which time and thoughts so sweetly doth deceive.
  And that thou teachest how to make one twain,
  By praising him here who doth hence remain.

40

Take all my loves, my love, yea take them all,
What hast thou then more than thou hadst before?
No love, my love, that thou mayst true love call,
All mine was thine, before thou hadst this more:
Then if for my love, thou my love receivest, 5
I cannot blame thee, for my love thou usest,
But yet be blamed, if thou thy self deceivest
By wilful taste of what thy self refusest.
I do forgive thy robbery gentle thief
Although thou steal thee all my poverty: 10
And yet love knows it is a greater grief
To bear love's wrong, than hate's known injury.
  Lascivious grace, in whom all ill well shows,
  Kill me with spites yet we must not be foes.

41

Those pretty wrongs that liberty commits,
When I am sometime absent from thy heart,
Thy beauty, and thy years full well befits,
For still temptation follows where thou art.
Gentle thou art, and therefore to be won, 5
Beauteous thou art, therefore to be assailed.
And when a woman woos, what woman's son,
Will sourly leave her till he have prevailed?
Ay me, but yet thou mightst my seat forbear,
And chide thy beauty, and thy straying youth, 10
Who lead thee in their riot even there
Where thou art forced to break a twofold truth:
  Hers by thy beauty tempting her to thee,
  Thine by thy beauty being false to me.

42

That thou hast her it is not all my grief,
And yet it may be said I loved her dearly,
That she hath thee is of my wailing chief,
A loss in love that touches me more nearly.
Loving offenders thus I will excuse ye, 5
Thou dost love her, because thou know'st I love her,
And for my sake even so doth she abuse me,
Suff'ring my friend for my sake to approve her.
If I lose thee, my loss is my love's gain,
And losing her, my friend hath found that loss, 10
Both find each other, and I lose both twain,
And both for my sake lay on me this cross,
  But here's the joy, my friend and I are one,
  Sweet flattery, then she loves but me alone.

43

When most I wink then do mine eyes best see,
For all the day they view things unrespected,
But when I sleep, in dreams they look on thee,
And darkly bright, are bright in dark directed.
Then thou whose shadow shadows doth make bright, 5
How would thy shadow's form, form happy show,
To the clear day with thy much clearer light,
When to unseeing eyes thy shade shines so!
How would (I say) mine eyes be blessèd made,
By looking on thee in the living day, 10
When in dead night thy fair imperfect shade,
Through heavy sleep on sightless eyes doth stay!
  All days are nights to see till I see thee,
  And nights bright days when dreams do show thee me.

44

If the dull substance of my flesh were thought,
Injurious distance should not stop my way,
For then despite of space I would be brought,
From limits far remote, where thou dost stay,
No matter then although my foot did stand 5
Upon the farthest earth removed from thee,
For nimble thought can jump both sea and land,
As soon as think the place where he would be.
But ah, thought kills me that I am not thought
To leap large lengths of miles when thou art gone, 10
But that so much of earth and water wrought,
I must attend, time's leisure with my moan.
  Receiving nought by elements so slow,
  But heavy tears, badges of either's woe.

45

The other two, slight air, and purging fire,
Are both with thee, wherever I abide,
The first my thought, the other my desire,
These present-absent with swift motion slide.
For when these quicker elements are gone 5
In tender embassy of love to thee,
My life being made of four, with two alone,
Sinks down to death, oppressed with melancholy.
Until life's composition be recured,
By those swift messengers returned from thee, 10
Who even but now come back again assured,
Of thy fair health, recounting it to me.
  This told, I joy, but then no longer glad,
  I send them back again and straight grow sad.

46

Mine eye and heart are at a mortal war,
How to divide the conquest of thy sight,
Mine eye, my heart thy picture's sight would bar,
My heart, mine eye the freedom of that right,
My heart doth plead that thou in him dost lie, 5
(A closet never pierced with crystal eyes)
But the defendant doth that plea deny,
And says in him thy fair appearance lies.
To side this title is impanellèd
A quest of thoughts, all tenants to the heart, 10
And by their verdict is determinèd
The clear eye's moiety, and the dear heart's part.
  As thus, mine eye's due is thy outward part,
  And my heart's right, thy inward love of heart.

47

Betwixt mine eye and heart a league is took,
And each doth good turns now unto the other,
When that mine eye is famished for a look,
Or heart in love with sighs himself doth smother;
With my love's picture then my eye doth feast, 5
And to the painted banquet bids my heart:
Another time mine eye is my heart's guest,
And in his thoughts of love doth share a part.
So either by thy picture or my love,
Thy self away, art present still with me, 10
For thou not farther than my thoughts canst move,
And I am still with them, and they with thee.
  Or if they sleep, thy picture in my sight
  Awakes my heart, to heart's and eye's delight.

48

How careful was I when I took my way,
Each trifle under truest bars to thrust,
That to my use it might unuséd stay
From hands of falsehood, in sure wards of trust!
But thou, to whom my jewels trifles are, 5
Most worthy comfort, now my greatest grief,
Thou best of dearest, and mine only care,
Art left the prey of every vulgar thief.
Thee have I not locked up in any chest,
Save where thou art not, though I feel thou art, 10
Within the gentle closure of my breast,
From whence at pleasure thou mayst come and part,
  And even thence thou wilt be stol'n I fear,
  For truth proves thievish for a prize so dear.

49

Against that time (if ever that time come)
When I shall see thee frown on my defects,
When as thy love hath cast his utmost sum,
Called to that audit by advised respects,
Against that time when thou shalt strangely pass, 5
And scarcely greet me with that sun thine eye,
When love converted from the thing it was
Shall reasons find of settled gravity;
Against that time do I ensconce me here
Within the knowledge of mine own desert, 10
And this my hand, against my self uprear,
To guard the lawful reasons on thy part,
  To leave poor me, thou hast the strength of laws,
  Since why to love, I can allege no cause.

50

How heavy do I journey on the way,
When what I seek (my weary travel's end)
Doth teach that ease and that repose to say
'Thus far the miles are measured from thy friend.'
The beast that bears me, tiréd with my woe, 5
Plods dully on, to bear that weight in me,
As if by some instinct the wretch did know
His rider loved not speed being made from thee:
The bloody spur cannot provoke him on,
That sometimes anger thrusts into his hide, 10
Which heavily he answers with a groan,
More sharp to me than spurring to his side,
  For that same groan doth put this in my mind,
  My grief lies onward and my joy behind.

51

Thus can my love excuse the slow offence,
Of my dull bearer, when from thee I speed,
From where thou art, why should I haste me thence?
Till I return of posting is no need.
O what excuse will my poor beast then find, 5
When swift extremity can seem but slow?
Then should I spur though mounted on the wind,
In wingéd speed no motion shall I know,
Then can no horse with my desire keep pace,
Therefore desire (of perfect'st love being made) 10
Shall neigh (no dull flesh) in his fiery race,
But love, for love, thus shall excuse my jade,
  Since from thee going, he went wilful-slow,
  Towards thee I'll run, and give him leave to go.

52

So am I as the rich whose blesséd key,
Can bring him to his sweet up-lockéd treasure,
The which he will not every hour survey,
For blunting the fine point of seldom pleasure.
Therefore are feasts so solemn and so rare, 5
Since seldom coming in that long year set,
Like stones of worth they thinly placed are,
Or captain jewels in the carcanet.
So is the time that keeps you as my chest,
Or as the wardrobe which the robe doth hide, 10
To make some special instant special-blest,
By new unfolding his imprisoned pride.
  Blesséd are you whose worthiness gives scope,
  Being had to triumph, being lacked to hope.

53

What is your substance, whereof are you made,
That millions of strange shadows on you tend?
Since every one, hath every one, one shade,
And you but one, can every shadow lend:
Describe Adonis and the counterfeit, 5
Is poorly imitated after you,
On Helen's cheek all art of beauty set,
And you in Grecian tires are painted new:
Speak of the spring, and foison of the year,
The one doth shadow of your beauty show, 10
The other as your bounty doth appear,
And you in every blesséd shape we know.
  In all external grace you have some part,
  But you like none, none you for constant heart.

54

O how much more doth beauty beauteous seem,
By that sweet ornament which truth doth give!
The rose looks fair, but fairer we it deem
For that sweet odour, which doth in it live:
The canker blooms have full as deep a dye, 5
As the perfuméd tincture of the roses,
Hang on such thorns, and play as wantonly,
When summer's breath their maskéd buds discloses:
But for their virtue only is their show,
They live unwooed, and unrespected fade, 10
Die to themselves. Sweet roses do not so,
Of their sweet deaths, are sweetest odours made:
  And so of you, beauteous and lovely youth,
  When that shall vade, by verse distills your truth.

55

Not marble, nor the gilded monuments
Of princes shall outlive this powerful rhyme,
But you shall shine more bright in these contents
Than unswept stone, besmeared with sluttish time.
When wasteful war shall statues overturn,   5
And broils root out the work of masonry,
Nor Mars his sword, nor war's quick fire shall burn:
The living record of your memory.
'Gainst death, and all-oblivious enmity
Shall you pace forth, your praise shall still find room,   10
Even in the eyes of all posterity
That wear this world out to the ending doom.
　　So till the judgment that your self arise,
　　You live in this, and dwell in lovers' eyes.

56

Sweet love renew thy force, be it not said
Thy edge should blunter be than appetite,
Which but to-day by feeding is allayed,
To-morrow sharpened in his former might.
So love be thou, although to-day thou fill   5
Thy hungry eyes, even till they wink with fulness,
To-morrow see again, and do not kill
The spirit of love, with a perpetual dulness:
Let this sad interim like the ocean be
Which parts the shore, where two contracted new,   10
Come daily to the banks, that when they see:
Return of love, more blest may be the view.
　　Or call it winter, which being full of care,
　　Makes summer's welcome, thrice more wished,
　　　　more rare.

57

Being your slave what should I do but tend,
Upon the hours, and times of your desire?
I have no precious time at all to spend;
Nor services to do till you require.
Nor dare I chide the world-without-end hour,   5
Whilst I (my sovereign) watch the clock for you,
Nor think the bitterness of absence sour,
When you have bid your servant once adieu.
Nor dare I question with my jealous thought,
Where you may be, or your affairs suppose,   10
But like a sad slave stay and think of nought
Save where you are, how happy you make those.
　　So true a fool is love, that in your will,
　　(Though you do any thing) he thinks no ill.

58

That god forbid, that made me first your slave,
I should in thought control your times of pleasure,
Or at your hand th' account of hours to crave,
Being your vassal bound to stay your leisure.
O let me suffer (being at your beck)   5
Th' imprisoned absence of your liberty,
And patience tame to sufferance bide each check,
Without accusing you of injury.
Be where you list, your charter is so strong,
That you your self may privilege your time   10
To what you will, to you it doth belong,
Your self to pardon of self-doing crime.
　　I am to wait, though waiting so be hell,
　　Not blame your pleasure be it ill or well.

59

If there be nothing new, but that which is,
Hath been before, how are our brains beguiled,
Which labouring for invention bear amiss
The second burthen of a former child!
O that record could with a backward look,   5
Even of five hundred courses of the sun,
Show me your image in some antique book,
Since mind at first in character was done.
That I might see what the old world could say,
To this composéd wonder of your frame,   10
Whether we are mended, or whether better they,
Or whether revolution be the same.
　　O sure I am the wits of former days,
　　To subjects worse have given admiring praise.

60

Like as the waves make towards the pebbled shore,
So do our minutes hasten to their end,
Each changing place with that which goes before,
In sequent toil all forwards do contend.
Nativity once in the main of light,   5
Crawls to maturity, wherewith being crowned,
Crookéd eclipses 'gainst his glory fight,
And Time that gave, doth now his gift confound.
Time doth transfix the flourish set on youth,
And delves the parallels in beauty's brow,   10
Feeds on the rarities of nature's truth,
And nothing stands but for his scythe to mow.
　　And yet to times in hope, my verse shall stand
　　Praising thy worth, despite his cruel hand.

61

Is it thy will, thy image should keep open
My heavy eyelids to the weary night?
Dost thou desire my slumbers should be broken,
While shadows like to thee do mock my sight?
Is it thy spirit that thou send'st from thee   5
So far from home into my deeds to pry,
To find out shames and idle hours in me,
The scope and tenure of thy jealousy?
O no, thy love though much, is not so great,
It is my love that keeps mine eye awake,   10
Mine own true love that doth my rest defeat,
To play the watchman ever for thy sake.
　　For thee watch I, whilst thou dost wake elsewhere,
　　From me far off, with others all too near.

62

Sin of self-love possesseth all mine eye,
And all my soul, and all my every part;
And for this sin there is no remedy,
It is so grounded inward in my heart.
Methinks no face so gracious is as mine,   5
No shape so true, no truth of such account,
And for my self mine own worth do define,
As I all other in all worths surmount.
But when my glass shows me my self indeed
Beated and chopt with tanned antiquity,   10
Mine own self-love quite contrary I read:
Self, so self-loving were iniquity.
　　'Tis thee (my self) that for my self I praise,
　　Painting my age with beauty of thy days.

63

Against my love shall be as I am now
With Time's injurious hand crushed and o'erworn,
When hours have drained his blood and filled his brow
With lines and wrinkles, when his youthful morn
Hath travelled on to age's steepy night,   5
And all those beauties whereof now he's king
Are vanishing, or vanished out of sight,
Stealing away the treasure of his spring:
For such a time do I now fortify
Against confounding age's cruel knife,   10
That he shall never cut from memory
My sweet love's beauty, though my lover's life.
　His beauty shall in these black lines be seen,
　And they shall live, and he in them still green.

64

When I have seen by Time's fell hand defaced
The rich-proud cost of outworn buried age,
When sometime lofty towers I see down-rased,
And brass eternal slave to mortal rage.
When I have seen the hungry ocean gain   5
Advantage on the kingdom of the shore,
And the firm soil win of the watery main,
Increasing store with loss, and loss with store,
When I have seen such interchange of state,
Or state it self confounded, to decay,   10
Ruin hath taught me thus to ruminate
That Time will come and take my love away.
　This thought is as a death which cannot choose
　But weep to have, that which it fears to lose.

65

Since brass, nor stone, nor earth, nor boundless sea,
But sad mortality o'ersways their power,
How with this rage shall beauty hold a plea,
Whose action is no stronger than a flower?
O how shall summer's honey breath hold out,   5
Against the wrackful siege of batt'ring days,
When rocks impregnable are not so stout,
Nor gates of steel so strong but time decays?
O fearful meditation, where alack,
Shall Time's best jewel from Time's chest lie hid?   10
Or what strong hand can hold his swift foot back,
Or who his spoil of beauty can forbid?
　O none, unless this miracle have might,
　That in black ink my love may still shine bright.

66

Tired with all these for restful death I cry,
As to behold desert a beggar born,
And needy nothing trimmed in jollity,
And purest faith unhappily forsworn,
And gilded honour shamefully misplaced,   5
And maiden virtue rudely strumpeted,
And right perfection wrongfully disgraced,
And strength by limping sway disabled,
And art made tongue-tied by authority,
And folly (doctor-like) controlling skill,   10
And simple truth miscalled simplicity,
And captive good attending captain ill.
　Tired with all these, from these would I be gone,
　Save that to die, I leave my love alone.

67

Ah wherefore with infection should he live,
And with his presence grace impiety,
That sin by him advantage should achieve,
And lace it self with his society?
Why should false painting imitate his cheek,   5
And steal dead seeming of his living hue?
Why should poor beauty indirectly seek,
Roses of shadow, since his rose is true?
Why should he live, now nature bankrupt is,
Beggared of blood to blush through lively veins,   10
For she hath no exchequer now but his,
And proud of many, lives upon his gains?
　O him she stores, to show what wealth she had,
　In days long since, before these last so bad.

68

Thus is his cheek the map of days outworn,
When beauty lived and died as flowers do now,
Before these bastard signs of fair were born,
Or durst inhabit on a living brow:
Before the golden tresses of the dead,   5
The right of sepulchres, were shorn away,
To live a second life on second head,
Ere beauty's dead fleece made another gay:
In him those holy antique hours are seen,
Without all ornament, it self and true,   10
Making no summer of another's green,
Robbing no old to dress his beauty new,
　And him as for a map doth Nature store,
　To show false Art what beauty was of yore.

69

Those parts of thee that the world's eye doth view,
Want nothing that the thought of hearts can mend:
All tongues (the voice of souls) give thee that due,
Uttering bare truth, even so as foes commend.
Thy outward thus with outward praise is crowned,   5
But those same tongues that give thee so thine own,
In other accents do this praise confound
By seeing farther than the eye hath shown.
They look into the beauty of thy mind,
And that in guess they measure by thy deeds,   10
Then churls their thoughts (although their eyes
　　were kind)
To thy fair flower add the rank smell of weeds:
　But why thy odour matcheth not thy show,
　The soil is this, that thou dost common grow.

70

That thou art blamed shall not be thy defect,
For slander's mark was ever yet the fair,
The ornament of beauty is suspect,
A crow that flies in heaven's sweetest air.
So thou be good, slander doth but approve,   5
Thy worth the greater being wooed of time,
For canker vice the sweetest buds doth love,
And thou present'st a pure unstained prime.
Thou hast passed by the ambush of young days,
Either not assailed, or victor being charged,   10
Yet this thy praise cannot be so thy praise,
To tie up envy, evermore enlarged,
　If some suspect of ill masked not thy show,
　Then thou alone kingdoms of hearts shouldst owe.

71

No longer mourn for me when I am dead,
Than you shall hear the surly sullen bell
Give warning to the world that I am fled
From this vile world with vilest worms to dwell:
Nay if you read this line, remember not,   5
The hand that writ it, for I love you so,
That I in your sweet thoughts would be forgot,
If thinking on me then should make you woe.
O if (I say) you look upon this verse,
When I (perhaps) compounded am with clay,   10
Do not so much as my poor name rehearse;
But let your love even with my life decay.
　Lest the wise world should look into your moan,
　And mock you with me after I am gone.

72

O lest the world should task you to recite,
What merit lived in me that you should love
After my death (dear love) forget me quite,
For you in me can nothing worthy prove.
Unless you would devise some virtuous lie,   5
To do more for me than mine own desert,
And hang more praise upon deceasèd I,
Than niggard truth would willingly impart:
O lest your true love may seem false in this,
That you for love speak well of me untrue,   10
My name be buried where my body is,
And live no more to shame nor me, nor you.
　For I am shamed by that which I bring forth,
　And so should you, to love things nothing worth.

73

That time of year thou mayst in me behold,
When yellow leaves, or none, or few do hang
Upon those boughs which shake against the cold,
Bare ruined choirs, where late the sweet birds sang.
In me thou seest the twilight of such day,   5
As after sunset fadeth in the west,
Which by and by black night doth take away,
Death's second self that seals up all in rest.
In me thou seest the glowing of such fire,
That on the ashes of his youth doth lie,   10
As the death-bed, whereon it must expire,
Consumed with that which it was nourished by.
　This thou perceiv'st, which makes thy love more
　　strong,
　To love that well, which thou must leave ere long.

74

But be contented when that fell arrest,
Without all bail shall carry me away,
My life hath in this line some interest,
Which for memorial still with thee shall stay.
When thou reviewest this, thou dost review,   5
The very part was consecrate to thee,
The earth can have but earth, which is his due,
My spirit is thine the better part of me,
So then thou hast but lost the dregs of life,
The prey of worms, my body being dead,   10
The coward conquest of a wretch's knife,
Too base of thee to be rememberèd,
　The worth of that, is that which it contains,
　And that is this, and this with thee remains.

75

So are you to my thoughts as food to life,
Or as sweet-seasoned showers are to the ground;
And for the peace of you I hold such strife
As 'twixt a miser and his wealth is found.
Now proud as an enjoyer, and anon   5
Doubting the filching age will steal his treasure,
Now counting best to be with you alone,
Then bettered that the world may see my pleasure,
Sometime all full with feasting on your sight,
And by and by clean starvèd for a look,   10
Possessing or pursuing no delight
Save what is had, or must from you be took.
　Thus do I pine and surfeit day by day,
　Or gluttoning on all, or all away.

76

Why is my verse so barren of new pride?
So far from variation or quick change?
Why with the time do I not glance aside
To new-found methods, and to compounds strange?
Why write I still all one, ever the same,   5
And keep invention in a noted weed,
That every word doth almost tell my name,
Showing their birth, and where they did proceed?
O know sweet love I always write of you,
And you and love are still my argument: 10
So all my best is dressing old words new,
Spending again what is already spent:
　For as the sun is daily new and old,
　So is my love still telling what is told.

77

Thy glass will show thee how thy beauties wear,
Thy dial how thy precious minutes waste,
These vacant leaves thy mind's imprint will bear,
And of this book, this learning mayst thou taste.
The wrinkles which thy glass will truly show,   5
Of mouthèd graves will give thee memory,
Thou by thy dial's shady stealth mayst know,
Time's thievish progress to eternity.
Look what thy memory cannot contain,
Commit to these waste blanks, and thou shalt find 10
Those children nursed, delivered from thy brain,
To take a new acquaintance of thy mind.
　These offices, so oft as thou wilt look,
　Shall profit thee, and much enrich thy book.

78

So oft have I invoked thee for my muse,
And found such fair assistance in my verse,
As every alien pen hath got my use,
And under thee their poesy disperse.
Thine eyes, that taught the dumb on high to sing, 5
And heavy ignorance aloft to fly,
Have added feathers to the learnèd's wing,
And given grace a double majesty.
Yet be most proud of that which I compile,
Whose influence is thine, and born of thee,   10
In others' works thou dost but mend the style,
And arts with thy sweet graces gracèd be.
　But thou art all my art, and dost advance
　As high as learning, my rude ignorance.

79

Whilst I alone did call upon thy aid,
My verse alone had all thy gentle grace,
But now my gracious numbers are decayed,
And my sick muse doth give an other place.
I grant (sweet love) thy lovely argument   5
Deserves the travail of a worthier pen,
Yet what of thee thy poet doth invent,
He robs thee of, and pays it thee again,
He lends thee virtue, and he stole that word,
From thy behaviour, beauty doth he give   10
And found it in thy cheek: he can afford
No praise to thee, but what in thee doth live.
    Then thank him not for that which he doth say,
    Since what he owes thee, thou thy self dost pay.

80

O how I faint when I of you do write,
Knowing a better spirit doth use your name,
And in the praise thereof spends all his might,
To make me tongue-tied speaking of your fame.
But since your worth (wide as the ocean is)   5
The humble as the proudest sail doth bear,
My saucy bark (inferior far to his)
On your broad main doth wilfully appear.
Your shallowest help will hold me up afloat,
Whilst he upon your soundless deep doth ride,   10
Or (being wrecked) I am a worthless boat,
He of tall building, and of goodly pride.
    Then if he thrive and I be cast away,
    The worst was this, my love was my decay.

81

Or I shall live your epitaph to make,
Or you survive when I in earth am rotten,
From hence your memory death cannot take,
Although in me each part will be forgotten.
Your name from hence immortal life shall have,   5
Though I (once gone) to all the world must die,
The earth can yield me but a common grave,
When you entombéd in men's eyes shall lie,
Your monument shall be my gentle verse,
Which eyes not yet created shall o'er-read,   10
And tongues to be, your being shall rehearse,
When all the breathers of this world are dead,
    You still shall live (such virtue hath my pen)
    Where breath most breathes, even in the mouths
        of men.

82

I grant thou wert not married to my muse,
And therefore mayst without attaint o'erlook
The dedicated words which writers use
Of their fair subject, blessing every book.
Thou art as fair in knowledge as in hue,   5
Finding thy worth a limit past my praise,
And therefore art enforced to seek anew,
Some fresher stamp of the time-bettering days.
And do so love, yet when they have devised,
What strainéd touches rhetoric can lend,   10
Thou truly fair, wert truly sympathized,
In true plain words, by thy true-telling friend.
    And their gross painting might be better used,
    Where cheeks need blood, in thee it is abused.

83

I never saw that you did painting need,
And therefore to your fair no painting set,
I found (or thought I found) you did exceed,
That barren tender of a poet's debt:
And therefore have I slept in your report,   5
That you your self being extant well might show,
How far a modern quill doth come too short,
Speaking of worth, what worth in you doth grow.
This silence for my sin you did impute,
Which shall be most my glory being dumb,   10
For I impair not beauty being mute,
When others would give life, and bring a tomb.
    There lives more life in one of your fair eyes,
    Than both your poets can in praise devise.

84

Who is it that says most, which can say more,
Than this rich praise, that you alone, are you?
In whose confine immuréd is the store,
Which should example where your equal grew.
Lean penury within that pen doth dwell,   5
That to his subject lends not some small glory,
But he that writes of you, if he can tell,
That you are you, so dignifies his story.
Let him but copy what in you is writ,
Not making worse what nature made so clear,   10
And such a counterpart shall fame his wit,
Making his style admiréd every where.
    You to your beauteous blessings add a curse,
    Being fond on praise, which makes your praises
        worse.

85

My tongue-tied muse in manners holds her still,
While comments of your praise richly compiled,
Reserve their character with golden quill,
And precious phrase by all the Muses filed.
I think good thoughts, whilst other write good words,   5
And like unlettered clerk still cry Amen,
To every hymn that able spirit affords,
In polished form of well refinéd pen.
Hearing you praised, I say 'tis so, 'tis true,
And to the most of praise add something more,   10
But that is in my thought, whose love to you
(Though words come hindmost) holds his rank before,
    Then others, for the breath of words respect,
    Me for my dumb thoughts, speaking in effect.

86

Was it the proud full sail of his great verse,
Bound for the prize of (all too precious) you,
That did my ripe thoughts in my brain inhearse,
Making their tomb the womb wherein they grew?
Was it his spirit, by spirits taught to write,   5
Above a mortal pitch, that struck me dead?
No, neither he, nor his compeers by night
Giving him aid, my verse astonishéd.
He nor that affable familiar ghost
Which nightly gulls him with intelligence,   10
As victors of my silence cannot boast,
I was not sick of any fear from thence.
    But when your countenance filled up his line,
    Then lacked I matter, that enfeebled mine.

87

Farewell! thou art too dear for my possessing,
And like enough thou know'st thy estimate,
The charter of thy worth gives thee releasing:
My bonds in thee are all determinate.
For how do I hold thee but by thy granting,   5
And for that riches where is my deserving?
The cause of this fair gift in me is wanting,
And so my patent back again is swerving.
Thy self thou gav'st, thy own worth then not
    knowing,
Or me to whom thou gav'st it, else mistaking,   10
So thy great gift upon misprision growing,
Comes home again, on better judgment making.
    Thus have I had thee as a dream doth flatter,
    In sleep a king, but waking no such matter.

88

When thou shalt be disposed to set me light,
And place my merit in the eye of scorn,
Upon thy side, against my self I'll fight,
And prove thee virtuous, though thou art forsworn:
With mine own weakness being best acquainted,   5
Upon thy part I can set down a story
Of faults concealed, wherein I am attainted:
That thou in losing me, shalt win much glory:
And I by this will be a gainer too,
For bending all my loving thoughts on thee,   10
The injuries that to my self I do,
Doing thee vantage, double-vantage me.
    Such is my love, to thee I so belong,
    That for thy right, my self will bear all wrong.

89

Say that thou didst forsake me for some fault,
And I will comment upon that offence,
Speak of my lameness, and I straight will halt:
Against thy reasons making no defence.
Thou canst not (love) disgrace me half so ill,   5
To set a form upon desiréd change,
As I'll my self disgrace, knowing thy will,
I will acquaintance strangle and look strange:
Be absent from thy walks and in my tongue,
Thy sweet belovéd name no more shall dwell,   10
Lest I (too much profane) should do it wrong:
And haply of our old acquaintance tell.
    For thee, against my self I'll vow debate,
    For I must ne'er love him whom thou dost hate.

90

Then hate me when thou wilt, if ever, now,
Now while the world is bent my deeds to cross,
Join with the spite of fortune, make me bow,
And do not drop in for an after-loss:
Ah do not, when my heart hath 'scaped this sorrow, 5
Come in the rearward of a conquered woe,
Give not a windy night a rainy morrow,
To linger out a purposed overthrow.
If thou wilt leave me, do not leave me last,
When other petty griefs have done their spite,   10
But in the onset come, so shall I taste
At first the very worst of fortune's might.
    And other strains of woe, which now seem woe,
    Compared with loss of thee, will not seem so.

91

Some glory in their birth, some in their skill,
Some in their wealth, some in their body's force,
Some in their garments though new-fangled ill:
Some in their hawks and hounds, some in their horse.
And every humour hath his adjunct pleasure,   5
Wherein it finds a joy above the rest,
But these particulars are not my measure,
All these I better in one general best.
Thy love is better than high birth to me,
Richer than wealth, prouder than garments' costs,   10
Of more delight than hawks and horses be:
And having thee, of all men's pride I boast.
    Wretched in this alone, that thou mayst take,
    All this away, and me most wretched make.

92

But do thy worst to steal thy self away,
For term of life thou art assuréd mine,
And life no longer than thy love will stay,
For it depends upon that love of thine.
Then need I not to fear the worst of wrongs,   5
When in the least of them my life hath end,
I see, a better state to me belongs
Than that, which on thy humour doth depend.
Thou canst not vex me with inconstant mind,
Since that my life on thy revolt doth lie,   10
O what a happy title do I find,
Happy to have thy love, happy to die!
    But what's so blesséd-fair that fears no blot?
    Thou mayst be false, and yet I know it not.

93

So shall I live, supposing thou art true,
Like a deceivéd husband, so love's face,
May still seem love to me, though altered new:
Thy looks with me, thy heart in other place.
For there can live no hatred in thine eye,   5
Therefore in that I cannot know thy change,
In many's looks, the false heart's history
Is writ in moods and frowns and wrinkles strange.
But heaven in thy creation did decree,
That in thy face sweet love should ever dwell,   10
Whate'er thy thoughts, or thy heart's workings be,
Thy looks should nothing thence, but sweetness tell.
    How like Eve's apple doth thy beauty grow,
    If thy sweet virtue answer not thy show.

94

They that have power to hurt, and will do none,
That do not do the thing, they most do show,
Who moving others, are themselves as stone,
Unmovéd, cold, and to temptation slow:
They rightly do inherit heaven's graces,   5
And husband nature's riches from expense,
They are the lords and owners of their faces,
Others, but stewards of their excellence:
The summer's flower is to the summer sweet,
Though to it self, it only live and die,   10
But if that flower with base infection meet,
The basest weed outbraves his dignity:
    For sweetest things turn sourest by their deeds,
    Lilies that fester, smell far worse than weeds.

95

How sweet and lovely dost thou make the shame,
Which like a canker in the fragrant rose,
Doth spot the beauty of thy budding name!
O in what sweets dost thou thy sins enclose!
That tongue that tells the story of thy days,   5
(Making lascivious comments on thy sport)
Cannot dispraise, but in a kind of praise,
Naming thy name, blesses an ill report.
O what a mansion have those vices got,
Which for their habitation chose out thee,   10
Where beauty's veil doth cover every blot,
And all things turns to fair, that eyes can see!
    Take heed (dear heart) of this large privilege,
    The hardest knife ill-used doth lose his edge.

96

Some say thy fault is youth, some wantonness,
Some say thy grace is youth and gentle sport,
Both grace and faults are loved of more and less:
Thou mak'st faults graces, that to thee resort:
As on the finger of a thronéd queen,   5
The basest jewel will be well esteemed:
So are those errors that in thee are seen,
To truths translated, and for true things deemed.
How many lambs might the stern wolf betray,
If like a lamb he could his looks translate!   10
How many gazers mightst thou lead away,
If thou wouldst use the strength of all thy state!
    But do not so, I love thee in such sort,
    As thou being mine, mine is thy good report.

97

How like a winter hath my absence been
From thee, the pleasure of the fleeting year!
What freezings have I felt, what dark days seen!
What old December's bareness everywhere!
And yet this time removed was summer's time,   5
The teeming autumn big with rich increase,
Bearing the wanton burden of the prime,
Like widowed wombs after their lords' decease:
Yet this abundant issue seemed to me
But hope of orphans, and unfathered fruit,   10
For summer and his pleasures wait on thee,
And thou away, the very birds are mute.
    Or if they sing, 'tis with so dull a cheer,
    That leaves look pale, dreading the winter's near.

98

From you have I been absent in the spring,
When proud-pied April (dressed in all his trim)
Hath put a spirit of youth in every thing:
That heavy Saturn laughed and leaped with him.
Yet nor the lays of birds, nor the sweet smell   5
Of different flowers in odour and in hue,
Could make me any summer's story tell:
Or from their proud lap pluck them where they grew:
Nor did I wonder at the lily's white,
Nor praise the deep vermilion in the rose,   10
They were but sweet, but figures of delight:
Drawn after you, you pattern of all those.
    Yet seemed it winter still, and you away,
    As with your shadow I with these did play.

99

The forward violet thus did I chide,
Sweet thief, whence didst thou steal thy sweet that
        smells,
If not from my love's breath? The purple pride
Which on thy soft cheek for complexion dwells,
In my love's veins thou hast too grossly dyed.   5
The lily I condemnéd for thy hand,
And buds of marjoram had stol'n thy hair,
The roses fearfully on thorns did stand,
One blushing shame, another white despair:
A third nor red, nor white, had stol'n of both,   10
And to his robbery had annexed thy breath,
But for his theft in pride of all his growth
A vengeful canker eat him up to death.
    More flowers I noted, yet I none could see,
    But sweet, or colour it had stol'n from thee.

100

Where art thou Muse that thou forget'st so long,
To speak of that which gives thee all thy might?
Spend'st thou thy fury on some worthless song,
Darkening thy power to lend base subjects light?
Return forgetful Muse, and straight redeem,   5
In gentle numbers time so idly spent,
Sing to the ear that doth thy lays esteem,
And gives thy pen both skill and argument.
Rise resty Muse, my love's sweet face survey,
If time have any wrinkle graven there,   10
If any, be a satire to decay,
And make time's spoils despiséd everywhere.
    Give my love fame faster than Time wastes life,
    So thou prevent'st his scythe, and crookéd knife.

101

O truant Muse what shall be thy amends,
For thy neglect of truth in beauty dyed?
Both truth and beauty on my love depends:
So dost thou too, and therein dignified:
Make answer Muse, wilt thou not haply say,   5
'Truth needs no colour with his colour fixed,
Beauty no pencil, beauty's truth to lay:
But best is best, if never intermixed'?
Because he needs no praise, wilt thou be dumb?
Excuse not silence so, for't lies in thee,   10
To make him much outlive a gilded tomb:
And to be praised of ages yet to be.
    Then do thy office Muse, I teach thee how,
    To make him seem long hence, as he shows now.

102

My love is strengthened though more weak in
        seeming,
I love not less, though less the show appear,
That love is merchandized, whose rich esteeming,
The owner's tongue doth publish every where.
Our love was new, and then but in the spring,   5
When I was wont to greet it with my lays,
As Philomel in summer's front doth sing,
And stops her pipe in growth of riper days:
Not that the summer is less pleasant now
Than when her mournful hymns did hush the night,   10
But that wild music burthens every bough,
And sweets grown common lose their dear delight.
    Therefore like her, I sometime hold my tongue:
    Because I would not dull you with my song.

103

Alack what poverty my muse brings forth,
That having such a scope to show her pride,
The argument all bare is of more worth
Than when it hath my added praise beside.
O blame me not if I no more can write!   5
Look in your glass and there appears a face,
That over-goes my blunt invention quite,
Dulling my lines, and doing me disgrace.
Were it not sinful then striving to mend,
To mar the subject that before was well?   10
For to no other pass my verses tend,
Than of your graces and your gifts to tell.
    And more, much more than in my verse can sit,
    Your own glass shows you, when you look in it.

104

To me fair friend you never can be old,
For as you were when first your eye I eyed,
Such seems your beauty still: three winters cold,
Have from the forests shook three summers' pride,
Three beauteous springs to yellow autumn turned,   5
In process of the seasons have I seen,
Three April perfumes in three hot Junes burned,
Since first I saw you fresh which yet are green.
Ah yet doth beauty like a dial hand,
Steal from his figure, and no pace perceived,   10
So your sweet hue, which methinks still doth stand
Hath motion, and mine eye may be deceived.
    For fear of which, hear this thou age unbred,
    Ere you were born was beauty's summer dead.

105

Let not my love be called idolatry,
Nor my belovéd as an idol show,
Since all alike my songs and praises be
To one, of one, still such, and ever so.
Kind is my love to-day, to-morrow kind,   5
Still constant in a wondrous excellence,
Therefore my verse to constancy confined,
One thing expressing, leaves out difference.
Fair, kind, and true, is all my argument,
Fair, kind, and true, varying to other words,   10
And in this change is my invention spent,
Three themes in one, which wondrous scope affords.
    Fair, kind, and true, have often lived alone.
    Which three till now, never kept seat in one.

106

When in the chronicle of wasted time,
I see descriptions of the fairest wights,
And beauty making beautiful old rhyme,
In praise of ladies dead, and lovely knights,
Then in the blazon of sweet beauty's best,   5
Of hand, of foot, of lip, of eye, of brow,
I see their antique pen would have expressed,
Even such a beauty as you master now.
So all their praises are but prophecies
Of this our time, all you prefiguring,   10
And for they looked but with divining eyes,
They had not skill enough your worth to sing:
    For we which now behold these present days,
    Have eyes to wonder, but lack tongues to praise.

107

Not mine own fears, nor the prophetic soul,
Of the wide world, dreaming on things to come,
Can yet the lease of my true love control,
Supposed as forfeit to a confined doom.
The mortal moon hath her eclipse endured,   5
And the sad augurs mock their own presage,
Incertainties now crown themselves assured,
And peace proclaims olives of endless age.
Now with the drops of this most balmy time,
My love looks fresh, and death to me subscribes,   10
Since spite of him I'll live in this poor rhyme,
While he insults o'er dull and speechless tribes.
    And thou in this shalt find thy monument,
    When tyrants' crests and tombs of brass are spent.

108

What's in the brain that ink may character,
Which hath not figured to thee my true spirit,
What's new to speak, what now to register,
That may express my love, or thy dear merit?
Nothing sweet boy, but yet like prayers divine,   5
I must each day say o'er the very same,
Counting no old thing old, thou mine, I thine,
Even as when first I hallowed thy fair name.
So that eternal love in love's fresh case,
Weighs not the dust and injury of age,   10
Nor gives to necessary wrinkles place,
But makes antiquity for aye his page,
    Finding the first conceit of love there bred,
    Where time and outward form would show it dead.

109

O never say that I was false of heart,
Though absence seemed my flame to qualify,
As easy might I from my self depart,
As from my soul which in thy breast doth lie:
That is my home of love, if I have ranged,   5
Like him that travels I return again,
Just to the time, not with the time exchanged,
So that my self bring water for my stain,
Never believe though in my nature reigned,
All frailties that besiege all kinds of blood,   10
That it could so preposterously be stained,
To leave for nothing all thy sum of good:
    For nothing this wide universe I call,
    Save thou my rose, in it thou art my all.

110

Alas 'tis true, I have gone here and there,
And made my self a motley to the view,
Gored mine own thoughts, sold cheap what is most
     dear,
Made old offences of affections new.
Most true it is, that I have looked on truth   5
Askance and strangely: but by all above,
These blenches gave my heart another youth,
And worse essays proved thee my best of love.
Now all is done, have what shall have no end,
Mine appetite I never more will grind   10
On newer proof, to try an older friend,
A god in love, to whom I am confined.
    Then give me welcome, next my heaven the best,
    Even to thy pure and most most loving breast.

111

O for my sake do you with Fortune chide,
The guilty goddess of my harmful deeds,
That did not better for my life provide,
Than public means which public manners breeds.
Thence comes it that my name receives a brand,   5
And almost thence my nature is subdued
To what it works in, like the dyer's hand:
Pity me then, and wish I were renewed,
Whilst like a willing patient I will drink,
Potions of eisel 'gainst my strong infection,   10
No bitterness that I will bitter think,
Nor double penance to correct correction.
  Pity me then dear friend, and I assure ye,
  Even that your pity is enough to cure me.

112

Your love and pity doth th' impression fill,
Which vulgar scandal stamped upon my brow,
For what care I who calls me well or ill,
So you o'er-green my bad, my good allow?
You are my all the world, and I must strive,   5
To know my shames and praises from your tongue,
None else to me, nor I to none alive,
That my steeled sense or changes right or wrong.
In so profound abysm I throw all care
Of others' voices, that my adder's sense,   10
To critic and to flatterer stoppéd are:
Mark how with my neglect I do dispense.
  You are so strongly in my purpose bred,
  That all the world besides methinks are dead.

113

Since I left you, mine eye is in my mind,
And that which governs me to go about,
Doth part his function, and is partly blind,
Seems seeing, but effectually is out:
For it no form delivers to the heart   5
Of bird, of flower, or shape which it doth latch,
Of his quick objects hath the mind no part,
Nor his own vision holds what it doth catch:
For if it see the rud'st or gentlest sight,
The most sweet favour or deformed'st creature,   10
The mountain, or the sea, the day, or night:
The crow, or dove, it shapes them to your feature.
  Incapable of more, replete with you,
  My most true mind thus maketh mine untrue.

114

Or whether doth my mind being crowned with you
Drink up the monarch's plague this flattery?
Or whether shall I say mine eye saith true,
And that your love taught it this alchemy?
To make of monsters, and things indigest,   5
Such cherubins as your sweet self resemble,
Creating every bad a perfect best
As fast as objects to his beams assemble:
O 'tis the first, 'tis flattery in my seeing,
And my great mind most kingly drinks it up,   10
Mine eye well knows what with his gust is 'greeing,
And to his palate doth prepare the cup.
  If it be poisoned, 'tis the lesser sin,
  That mine eye loves it and doth first begin.

115

Those lines that I before have writ do lie,
Even those that said I could not love you dearer,
Yet then my judgment knew no reason why,
My most full flame should afterwards burn clearer,
But reckoning time, whose millioned accidents   5
Creep in 'twixt vows, and change decrees of kings,
Tan sacred beauty, blunt the sharp'st intents,
Divert strong minds to the course of alt'ring things:
Alas why fearing of time's tyranny,
Might I not then say 'Now I love you best,'   10
When I was certain o'er incertainty,
Crowning the present, doubting of the rest?
  Love is a babe, then might I not say so
  To give full growth to that which still doth grow.

116

Let me not to the marriage of true minds
Admit impediments, love is not love
Which alters when it alteration finds,
Or bends with the remover to remove.
O no, it is an ever-fixéd mark   5
That looks on tempests and is never shaken;
It is the star to every wand'ring bark,
Whose worth's unknown, although his height be
      taken.
Love's not Time's fool, though rosy lips and cheeks
Within his bending sickle's compass come,   10
Love alters not with his brief hours and weeks,
But bears it out even to the edge of doom:
  If this be error and upon me proved,
  I never writ, nor no man ever loved.

117

Accuse me thus, that I have scanted all,
Wherein I should your great deserts repay,
Forgot upon your dearest love to call,
Whereto all bonds do tie me day by day,
That I have frequent been with unknown minds,   5
And given to time your own dear-purchased right,
That I have hoisted sail to all the winds
Which should transport me farthest from your sight.
Book both my wilfulness and errors down,
And on just proof surmise, accumulate,   10
Bring me within the level of your frown,
But shoot not at me in your wakened hate:
  Since my appeal says I did strive to prove
  The constancy and virtue of your love.

118

Like as to make our appetite more keen
With eager compounds we our palate urge,
As to prevent our maladies unseen,
We sicken to shun sickness when we purge.
Even so being full of your ne'er-cloying sweetness,   5
To bitter sauces did I frame my feeding;
And sick of welfare found a kind of meetness,
To be diseased ere that there was true needing.
Thus policy in love t' anticipate
The ills that were not, grew to faults assured,   10
And brought to medicine a healthful state
Which rank of goodness would by ill be cured.
  But thence I learn and find the lesson true,
  Drugs poison him that so fell sick of you.

119

What potions have I drunk of Siren tears
Distilled from limbecks foul as hell within,
Applying fears to hopes, and hopes to fears,
Still losing when I saw my self to win!
What wretched errors hath my heart committed,   5
Whilst it hath thought it self so blesséd never!
How have mine eyes out of their spheres been fitted
In the distraction of this madding fever!
O benefit of ill, now I find true
That better is, by evil still made better.   10
And ruined love when it is built anew
Grows fairer than at first, more strong, far greater.
    So I return rebuked to my content,
    And gain by ills thrice more than I have spent.

120

That you were once unkind befriends me now,
And for that sorrow, which I then did feel,
Needs must I under my transgression bow,
Unless my nerves were brass or hammered steel.
For if you were by my unkindness shaken   5
As I by yours, y'have passed a hell of time,
And I a tyrant have no leisure taken
To weigh how once I suffered in your crime.
O that our night of woe might have remembered
My deepest sense, how hard true sorrow hits,   10
And soon to you, as you to me then tendered
The humble salve, which wounded bosoms fits!
    But that your trespass now becomes a fee,
    Mine ransoms yours, and yours must ransom me.

121

'Tis better to be vile than vile esteemed,
When not to be, receives reproach of being,
And the just pleasure lost, which is so deemed,
Not by our feeling, but by others' seeing.
For why should others' false adulterate eyes   5
Give salutation to my sportive blood?
Or on my frailties why are frailer spies,
Which in their wills count bad what I think good?
No, I am that I am, and they that level
At my abuses, reckon up their own,   10
I may be straight though they themselves be bevel;
By their rank thoughts, my deeds must not be shown
    Unless this general evil they maintain,
    All men are bad and in their badness reign.

122

Thy gift, thy tables, are within my brain
Full charactered with lasting memory,
Which shall above that idle rank remain
Beyond all date even to eternity.
Or at the least, so long as brain and heart   5
Have faculty by nature to subsist,
Till each to razed oblivion yield his part
Of thee, thy record never can be missed:
That poor retention could not so much hold,
Nor need I tallies thy dear love to score,   10
Therefore to give them from me was I bold,
To trust those tables that receive thee more:
    To keep an adjunct to remember thee
    Were to import forgetfulness in me.

123

No! Time, thou shalt not boast that I do change,
Thy pyramids built up with newer might
To me are nothing novel, nothing strange,
They are but dressings of a former sight:
Our dates are brief, and therefore we admire,   5
What thou dost foist upon us that is old,
And rather make them born to our desire,
Than think that we before have heard them told:
Thy registers and thee I both defy,
Not wond'ring at the present, nor the past,   10
For thy records, and what we see doth lie,
Made more or less by thy continual haste:
    This I do vow and this shall ever be,
    I will be true despite thy scythe and thee.

124

If my dear love were but the child of state,
It might for Fortune's bastard be unfathered,
As subject to time's love or to time's hate,
Weeds among weeds, or flowers with flowers
    gathered.
No it was builded far from accident,   5
It suffers not in smiling pomp, nor falls
Under the blow of thralléd discontent,
Whereto th' inviting time our fashion calls:
It fears not policy that heretic,
Which works on leases of short-numbered hours,   10
But all alone stands hugely politic,
That it nor grows with heat, nor drowns with showers.
    To this I witness call the fools of time,
    Which die for goodness, who have lived for crime.

125

Were't aught to me I bore the canopy,
With my extern the outward honouring,
Or laid great bases for eternity,
Which proves more short than waste or ruining?
Have I not seen dwellers on form and favour   5
Lose all, and more by paying too much rent
For compound sweet; forgoing simple savour,
Pitiful thrivers in their gazing spent?
No, let me be obsequious in thy heart,
And take thou my oblation, poor but free,   10
Which is not mixed with seconds, knows no art,
But mutual render, only me for thee.
    Hence, thou suborned informer, a true soul
    When most impeached, stands least in thy control.

126

O thou my lovely boy who in thy power,
Dost hold Time's fickle glass his fickle hour:
Who hast by waning grown, and therein show'st,
Thy lovers withering, as thy sweet self grow'st.
If Nature (sovereign mistress over wrack)   5
As thou goest onwards still will pluck thee back,
She keeps thee to this purpose, that her skill
May time disgrace, and wretched minutes kill.
Yet fear her O thou minion of her pleasure,
She may detain, but not still keep her treasure!   10
    Her audit (though delayed) answered must be,
    And her quietus is to render thee.

127

In the old age black was not counted fair,
Or if it were it bore not beauty's name:
But now is black beauty's successive heir,
And beauty slandered with a bastard shame,
For since each hand hath put on nature's power,   5
Fairing the foul with art's false borrowed face,
Sweet beauty hath no name no holy bower,
But is profaned, if not lives in disgrace.
Therefore my mistress' eyes are raven black,
Her eyes so suited, and they mourners seem,   10
At such who not born fair no beauty lack,
Slandering creation with a false esteem,
    Yet so they mourn becoming of their woe,
    That every tongue says beauty should look so.

128

How oft when thou, my music, music play'st,
Upon that blesséd wood whose motion sounds
With thy sweet fingers when thou gently sway'st
The wiry concord that mine ear confounds,
Do I envy those jacks that nimble leap,   5
To kiss the tender inward of thy hand,
Whilst my poor lips which should that harvest reap,
At the wood's boldness by thee blushing stand.
To be so tickled they would change their state
And situation with those dancing chips,   10
O'er whom thy fingers walk with gentle gait,
Making dead wood more blest than living lips,
    Since saucy jacks so happy are in this,
    Give them thy fingers, me thy lips to kiss.

129

Th' expense of spirit in a waste of shame
Is lust in action, and till action, lust
Is perjured, murd'rous, bloody full of blame,
Savage, extreme, rude, cruel, not to trust,
Enjoyed no sooner but despised straight,   5
Past reason hunted, and no sooner had
Past reason hated as a swallowed bait,
On purpose laid to make the taker mad.
Mad in pursuit and in possession so,
Had, having, and in quest, to have extreme,   10
A bliss in proof and proved, a very woe,
Before a joy proposed behind a dream.
    All this the world well knows yet none knows well,
    To shun the heaven that leads men to this hell.

130

My mistress' eyes are nothing like the sun,
Coral is far more red, than her lips red,
If snow be white, why then her breasts are dun:
If hairs be wires, black wires grow on her head:
I have seen roses damasked, red and white,   5
But no such roses see I in her cheeks,
And in some perfumes is there more delight,
Than in the breath that from my mistress reeks.
I love to hear her speak, yet well I know,
That music hath a far more pleasing sound: 10
I grant I never saw a goddess go,
My mistress when she walks treads on the ground.
    And yet by heaven I think my love as rare,
    As any she belied with false compare.

131

Thou art as tyrannous, so as thou art,
As those whose beauties proudly make them cruel;
For well thou know'st to my dear doting heart
Thou art the fairest and most precious jewel.
Yet in good faith some say that thee behold,   5
Thy face hath not the power to make love groan;
To say they err, I dare not be so bold,
Although I swear it to my self alone.
And to be sure that is not false I swear,
A thousand groans but thinking on thy face,   10
One on another's neck do witness bear
Thy black is fairest in my judgment's place.
    In nothing art thou black save in thy deeds,
    And thence this slander as I think proceeds.

132

Thine eyes I love, and they as pitying me,
Knowing thy heart torment me with disdain,
Have put on black, and loving mourners be,
Looking with pretty ruth upon my pain.
And truly not the morning sun of heaven   5
Better becomes the grey cheeks of the east,
Nor that full star that ushers in the even
Doth half that glory to the sober west
As those two mourning eyes become thy face:
O let it then as well beseem thy heart   10
To mourn for me since mourning doth thee grace,
And suit thy pity like in every part.
    Then will I swear beauty herself is black,
    And all they foul that thy complexion lack.

133

Beshrew that heart that makes my heart to groan
For that deep wound it gives my friend and me;
Is't not enough to torture me alone,
But slave to slavery my sweet'st friend must be?
Me from my self thy cruel eye hath taken,   5
And my next self thou harder hast engrossed,
Of him, my self, and thee I am forsaken,
A torment thrice three-fold thus to be crossed:
Prison my heart in thy steel bosom's ward,
But then my friend's heart let my poor heart bail,   10
Whoe'er keeps me, let my heart be his guard,
Thou canst not then use rigour in my gaol.
    And yet thou wilt, for I being pent in thee,
    Perforce am thine and all that is in me.

134

So now I have confessed that he is thine,
And I my self am mortgaged to thy will,
My self I'll forfeit, so that other mine,
Thou wilt restore to be my comfort still:
But thou wilt not, nor he will not be free,   5
For thou art covetous, and he is kind,
He learned but surety-like to write for me,
Under that bond that him as fast doth bind.
The statute of thy beauty thou wilt take,
Thou usurer that put'st forth all to use,   10
And sue a friend, came debtor for my sake,
So him I lose through my unkind abuse.
    Him have I lost, thou hast both him and me,
    He pays the whole, and yet am I not free.

135

Whoever hath her wish, thou hast thy will,
And 'Will' to boot, and 'Will' in over-plus,
More than enough am I that vex thee still,
To thy sweet will making addition thus.
Wilt thou whose will is large and spacious, 5
Not once vouchsafe to hide my will in thine?
Shall will in others seem right gracious,
And in my will no fair acceptance shine?
The sea all water, yet receives rain still,
And in abundance addeth to his store, 10
So thou being rich in will add to thy will
One will of mine to make thy large will more.
  Let no unkind, no fair beseechers kill,
  Think all but one, and me in that one 'Will.'

136

If thy soul check thee that I come so near,
Swear to thy blind soul that I was thy 'Will',
And will thy soul knows is admitted there,
Thus far for love, my love-suit sweet fulfil.
'Will', will fulfil the treasure of thy love, 5
Ay, fill it full with wills, and my will one,
In things of great receipt with ease we prove,
Among a number one is reckoned none.
Then in the number let me pass untold,
Though in thy store's account I one must be, 10
For nothing hold me, so it please thee hold,
That nothing me, a something sweet to thee.
  Make but my name thy love, and love that still,
  And then thou lov'st me for my name is Will.

137

Thou blind fool Love, what dost thou to mine eyes,
That they behold and see not what they see?
They know what beauty is, see where it lies,
Yet what the best is, take the worst to be.
If eyes corrupt by over-partial looks, 5
Be anchored in the bay where all men ride,
Why of eyes' falsehood hast thou forgèd hooks,
Whereto the judgment of my heart is tied?
Why should my heart think that a several plot,
Which my heart knows the wide world's common
    place? 10
Or mine eyes seeing this, say this is not
To put fair truth upon so foul a face?
  In things right true my heart and eyes have erred,
  And to this false plague are they now transferred.

138

When my love swears that she is made of truth,
I do believe her though I know she lies,
That she might think me some untutored youth,
Unlearnèd in the world's false subtleties.
Thus vainly thinking that she thinks me young, 5
Although she knows my days are past the best,
Simply I credit her false-speaking tongue,
On both sides thus is simple truth suppressed:
But wherefore says she not she is unjust?
And wherefore say not I that I am old? 10
O love's best habit is in seeming trust,
And age in love, loves not to have years told.
  Therefore I lie with her, and she with me,
  And in our faults by lies we flattered be.

139

O call not me to justify the wrong,
That thy unkindness lays upon my heart,
Wound me not with thine eye but with thy tongue,
Use power with power, and slay me not by art,
Tell me thou lov'st elsewhere; but in my sight, 5
Dear heart forbear to glance thine eye aside,
What need'st thou wound with cunning when thy
    might
Is more than my o'erpressed defence can bide?
Let me excuse thee, ah my love well knows,
Her pretty looks have been mine enemies, 10
And therefore from my face she turns my foes,
That they elsewhere might dart their injuries:
  Yet do not so, but since I am near slain,
  Kill me outright with looks, and rid my pain.

140

Be wise as thou art cruel, do not press
My tongue-tied patience with too much disdain:
Lest sorrow lend me words and words express,
The manner of my pity-wanting pain.
If I might teach thee wit better it were, 5
Though not to love, yet love to tell me so,
As testy sick men when their deaths be near,
No news but health from their physicians know.
For if I should despair I should grow mad,
And in my madness might speak ill of thee, 10
Now this ill-wresting world is grown so bad,
Mad slanderers by mad ears believèd be.
  That I may not be so, nor thou belied,
  Bear thine eyes straight, though thy proud heart go
    wide.

141

In faith I do not love thee with mine eyes,
For they in thee a thousand errors note,
But 'tis my heart that loves what they despise,
Who in despite of view is pleased to dote.
Nor are mine ears with thy tongue's tune delighted, 5
Nor tender feeling to base touches prone,
Nor taste, nor smell, desire to be invited
To any sensual feast with thee alone:
But my five wits, nor my five senses can
Dissuade one foolish heart from serving thee, 10
Who leaves unswayed the likeness of a man,
Thy proud heart's slave and vassal wretch to be:
  Only my plague thus far I count my gain,
  That she that makes me sin, awards me pain.

142

Love is my sin, and thy dear virtue hate,
Hate of my sin, grounded on sinful loving,
O but with mine, compare thou thine own state,
And thou shalt find it merits not reproving,
Or if it do, not from those lips of thine, 5
That have profaned their scarlet ornaments,
And sealed false bonds of love as oft as mine,
Robbed others' beds' revenues of their rents.
Be it lawful I love thee as thou lov'st those,
Whom thine eyes woo as mine importune thee, 10
Root pity in thy heart that when it grows,
Thy pity may deserve to pitied be.
  If thou dost seek to have what thou dost hide,
  By self-example mayst thou be denied.

143

Lo as a careful huswife runs to catch,
One of her feathered creatures broke away,
Sets down her babe and makes all swift dispatch
In pursuit of the thing she would have stay:
Whilst her neglected child holds her in chase,   5
Cries to catch her whose busy care is bent,
To follow that which flies before her face:
Not prizing her poor infant's discontent;
So run'st thou after that which flies from thee,
Whilst I thy babe chase thee afar behind,   10
But if thou catch thy hope turn back to me:
And play the mother's part, kiss me, be kind.
    So will I pray that thou mayst have thy Will,
    If thou turn back and my loud crying still.

144

Two loves I have of comfort and despair,
Which like two spirits do suggest me still,
The better angel is a man right fair:
The worser spirit a woman coloured ill.
To win me soon to hell my female evil,   5
Tempteth my better angel from my side,
And would corrupt my saint to be a devil:
Wooing his purity with her foul pride.
And whether that my angel be turned fiend,
Suspect I may, yet not directly tell,   10
But being both from me both to each friend,
I guess one angel in another's hell.
    Yet this shall I ne'er know but live in doubt,
    Till my bad angel fire my good one out.

145

Those lips that Love's own hand did make,
Breathed forth the sound that said 'I hate',
To me that languished for her sake:
But when she saw my woeful state,
Straight in her heart did mercy come,   5
Chiding that tongue that ever sweet,
Was used in giving gentle doom:
And taught it thus anew to greet:
'I hate' she altered with an end,
That followed it as gentle day,   10
Doth follow night who like a fiend
From heaven to hell is flown away.
    'I hate', from hate away she threw,
    And saved my life saying 'not you'.

146

Poor soul the centre of my sinful earth,
My sinful earth these rebel powers array,
Why dost thou pine within and suffer dearth
Painting thy outward walls so costly gay?
Why so large cost having so short a lease,   5
Dost thou upon thy fading mansion spend?
Shall worms inheritors of this excess
Eat up thy charge? is this thy body's end?
Then soul live thou upon thy servant's loss,
And let that pine to aggravate thy store;   10
Buy terms divine in selling hours of dross;
Within be fed, without be rich no more,
    So shall thou feed on death, that feeds on men,
    And death once dead, there's no more dying then.

147

My love is as a fever longing still,
For that which longer nurseth the disease,
Feeding on that which doth preserve the ill,
Th' uncertain sickly appetite to please:
My reason the physician to my love,   5
Angry that his prescriptions are not kept
Hath left me, and I desperate now approve,
Desire is death, which physic did except.
Past cure I am, now reason is past care,
And frantic-mad with evermore unrest,   10
My thoughts and my discourse as mad men's are,
At random from the truth vainly expressed.
    For I have sworn thee fair, and thought thee bright,
    Who art as black as hell, as dark as night.

148

O me! what eyes hath love put in my head,
Which have no correspondence with true sight,
Or if they have, where is my judgment fled,
That censures falsely what they see aright?
If that be fair whereon my false eyes dote,   5
What means the world to say it is not so?
If it be not, then love doth well denote,
Love's eye is not so true as all men's: no,
How can it? O how can love's eye be true,
That is so vexed with watching and with tears?   10
No marvel then though I mistake my view,
The sun it self sees not, till heaven clears.
    O cunning love, with tears thou keep'st me blind,
    Lest eyes well-seeing thy foul faults should find.

149

Canst thou O cruel, say I love thee not,
When I against my self with thee partake?
Do I not think on thee when I forgot
Am of my self, all-tyrant, for thy sake?
Who hateth thee that I do call my friend,   5
On whom frown'st thou that I do fawn upon,
Nay if thou lour'st on me do I not spend
Revenge upon my self with present moan?
What merit do I in my self respect,
That is so proud thy service to despise,   10
When all my best doth worship thy defect,
Commanded by the motion of thine eyes?
    But love hate on for now I know thy mind,
    Those that can see thou lov'st, and I am blind.

150

O from what power hast thou this powerful might,
With insufficiency my heart to sway,
To make me give the lie to my true sight,
And swear that brightness doth not grace the day?
Whence hast thou this becoming of things ill,   5
That in the very refuse of thy deeds,
There is such strength and warrantise of skill,
That in my mind thy worst all best exceeds?
Who taught thee how to make me love thee more,
The more I hear and see just cause of hate?   10
O though I love what others do abhor,
With others thou shouldst not abhor my state.
    If thy unworthiness raised love in me,
    More worthy I to be beloved of thee.

151

Love is too young to know what conscience is,
Yet who knows not conscience is born of love?
Then gentle cheater urge not my amiss,
Lest guilty of my faults thy sweet self prove.
For thou betraying me, I do betray   5
My nobler part to my gross body's treason,
My soul doth tell my body that he may,
Triumph in love, flesh stays no farther reason,
But rising at thy name doth point out thee,
As his triumphant prize, proud of this pride,   10
He is contented thy poor drudge to be,
To stand in thy affairs, fall by thy side.
  No want of conscience hold it that I call,
  Her love, for whose dear love I rise and fall.

152

In loving thee thou know'st I am forsworn,
But thou art twice forsworn to me love swearing,
In act thy bed-vow broke and new faith torn,
In vowing new hate after new love bearing:
But why of two oaths' breach do I accuse thee,   5
When I break twenty? I am perjured most,
For all my vows are oaths but to misuse thee:
And all my honest faith in thee is lost.
For I have sworn deep oaths of thy deep kindness:
Oaths of thy love, thy truth, thy constancy,   10
And to enlighten thee gave eyes to blindness,
Or made them swear against the thing they see.
  For I have sworn thee fair: more perjured I,
  To swear against the truth so foul a lie.

153

Cupid laid by his brand and fell asleep,
A maid of Dian's this advantage found,
And his love-kindling fire did quickly steep
In a cold valley-fountain of that ground:
Which borrowed from this holy fire of Love,   5
A dateless lively heat still to endure,
And grew a seeting bath which yet men prove,
Against strange maladies a sovereign cure:
But at my mistress' eye Love's brand new-fired,
The boy for trial needs would touch my breast,   10
I sick withal the help of bath desired,
And thither hied a sad distempered guest.
  But found no cure, the bath for my help lies,
  Where Cupid got new fire; my mistress' eyes.

154

The little Love-god lying once asleep,
Laid by his side his heart-inflaming brand,
Whilst many nymphs that vowed chaste life to keep,
Came tripping by, but in her maiden hand,
The fairest votary took up that fire,   5
Which many legions of true hearts had warmed,
And so the general of hot desire,
Was sleeping by a virgin hand disarmed.
This brand she quenchéd in a cool well by,
Which from Love's fire took heat perpetual,   10
Growing a bath and healthful remedy,
For men diseased, but I my mistress' thrall,
  Came there for cure and this by that I prove,
  Love's fire heats water, water cools not love.

Glossary

ABATE, omit, except, blunt

ABATEMENT, depreciation, reduction

ABHOMINABLE, a frequent 16th–17th cent. spelling, inhuman

ABIDE, sojourn, for a while only

ABILITY, strength

ABLE, suitable, appropriate

ABLE (for), a match for

ABODE, (i) delay; (ii) presage

ABORTIVE, unnatural, at once untimely and monstrous

ABRIDGEMENT, (i) a short or shortened play for an evening's entertainment at court; (ii) that which cut's one short

ABROACH, on foot

ABROGATE SCURRILITY, cut out indecency

ABRUPTION, breaking off (in speech)

ABSEY BOOK, a primer, ABC book

ABSTRACT, (i) epitome; (ii) abridgement (of distance), a short cut

ABSYRTUS, brother of Medea, murdered and cut into pieces by her to delay her father's pursuit on her flight from Colchos to Jason

ABUSE, (i) deceive; (ii) misuse, maltreat

ABY, pay the penalty for

ACADEME, a philosophical school or association of students

ACCIDENT, incident

ACCITE, summon

ACCOMMODATIONS, comforts, conveniences

ACCOMPT (beyond), unprecedented

AGCORD, concord, harmony

ACCORDINGLY, in proportion

ACCOST, nautical term (to coast) then coming into fashion, meaning greet politely

ACE, throw of one at dice

ACHERON, one of the rivers of Hades

ACHILLES' SPEAR, Telephus, Priam's son-in-law, wounded by Achilles, was cured by rust scraped from the spear

ACQUITTANCE, written acknowledgement of debt

ACROSS, expression from the tilt yard implying a jest or sally has missed its mark

ACT, activity, the life of action

ACTAEON, was transformed into a stag with horns and pursued by his own hounds—the classical prototype of the Elizabethan cuckold

AD UNGUEM, Lat. at the fingers' ends

ADAMANT, fabulous rock or stone to which were ascribed properties of the diamond and of the loadstone or magnet

ADDITION, title, style of address

ADDRESS, ready, equip, prepare

ADHERE, cohere

ADMIRAL, flagship

ADMIRATION, wonder, marvel; notes of —, notes of exclamation

ADONIS' GARDENS, orig. beds of plants surrounding images of Adonis, their rapid withering being the usual point of the allusion

ADOPTIOUS, assumed, adopted (a coinage of Shakespeare's)

ADVANCE, (i) raise, lift up; (ii) reveal

ADVENTURE, accident, chance

ADVERTISE, (i) instruct, inform; (ii) warn

ADVICE, prudence, forethought; 'upon more —', 'on further consideration'

ADVISE, consider, reflect, take care

AEACIDES, descendants of Aeacus, e.g. Ajax

AEDILE, the Tribunes were allowed two aediles to arrest and execute and to carry out other civil duties

AERY, (i) nest of a bird of prey; (ii) a brood of young eagles

AESCULAPIUS, god of medicine, son of Apollo

AESOP, the reputed fabulist, said to have been a hunch-backed Phygian slave

AFFECT, (sb) passion, desire; (vb) resort to

AFFECTED, (i) in love; (ii) attacked by disease

AFFECTION, disposition, inclination

AFFRAY, startle

AFFRONT, confront

AFFY, betroth

AFTER-SUPPER, rather a dessert at the end of supper than a rere- or second supper late at night

AGAIN, in consequence

AGAINST THE HAIR, against the grain, derived from stroking an animal the wrong way

AGAMEMNON, chief leader of the Greeks against Troy

AGATE, very diminutive person, in allusion to small figures, cut in agate, used as seals

AGENOR, father of Europa

AGGRAVATE, exaggerate; '— his style', give him a new title.

AGLET-BABY, small figure forming tag of a point or lace

AGNIZE, acknowledge

AGONY, agony of death, death throes

AGOOD, in good earnest

A-HOLD, A-HAULED, hauled right into the wind so as to reset canvas

AIM, 'aim better at me', think better of me

AIM AT, guess at, hint at

AJAX, son of Telamon, who in a fit of madness at Ulysses being awarded the arms of Achilles, slew a flock of sheep, thinking them his enemies

ALARUM, trumpet call to arms

ALBION, Britain

ALCIDES, name of Hercules as grandson of Alcaeus

ALE, 'go to the ale with a Christian', a reference to Church-ale, a parish festival

ALECTO, one of the Furies

ALL-AMORT, sick to death, dejected

ALLA NOSTRA CASA BEN VENUTO, welcome to our house

ALLHALLOWMASS, All Saints' Day, November 1st

ALLICHOLY, melancholy

ALLOTTERY, assignment of a share

ALLOW, prove, approve, permit by authority

ALLUSION, jest, allegory, riddle

ALLY, kinsman

ALMAIN, German

ALMS, an act of charity

ALMS-BASKET, in which broken meats from the tables of the wealthy were collected for distribution among the poor

ALONE, peerless, unique

ALTERING, changing physical processes for the bad (by disease) or for the good (by medicine)

ALTHAEA, wife of king of Calydon. Informed by the Fates at the birth of her son Meleager that he would die when a brand on the fire was consumed, she snatched it from the hearth, later to burn it after Meleager slew his brothers

AMAIN, at full speed

AMAIMON, a mighty devil

AMAZE, confuse, bewilder

AMBLE, a favourite Elizabethan pace

AMES-ACE, i.e. ambs-ace, the lowest possible throw at dice, the double ace

ANATOMIZE, (i) dissect (surg.); (ii) lay open minutely, expose

ANATOMY, (i) skeleton; (ii) a corpse for dissection

ANCHISES, father of Aeneas, who carried him from burning Troy

ANCIENT, ensign, standard-bearer

ANCIENTRY, antique style, old people

ANCUS MARCIUS, legendary fourth king of Rome

AN-END, perpetually

ANGEL, gold coin, value c. 50p, another name for the noble

ANGLE, hook

ANSWER, (i) discharge a debt; (ii) reply to a charge, hence charge

ANSWER (sb), return hit in fencing

ANTHEM, song of grief or mourning

ANTHROPOPHAGINIAN, man-eater

ANTIATES, people of Antium, in Latium, chief city of the Volsces

ANTIC, (i) buffoon, clown, fool; (ii) pageant, masque; (adj.) quaint, grotesque, fantastic

APE-BEARER, one who carries a monkey about for exhibition, a strolling buffoon

APPARENT, obvious, evident, open

APPEACH, turn informer, accuse

APPEAL (sb), impeachment of treason which the accuser is prepared to prove by combat

APPELLANT (sb and adj.) challenger, accusing

APPENDIX, jocularly, one who follows behind

APPERTAINMENT, prerogative

APPLE-JOHN, ripened about St John's Day (midsummer) and eaten two years later when shrivelled and wrinkled

APPLIANCES, medical applications

APPOINT, ordain, devote (a person or thing)

APPOINTMENT, (i) engagement, business; (ii) equipment

APPREHEND, seize a point

APPREHENSION, quickness of wit

APPROBATION, credit, proof

APPROOF, confirmed reputation

APPROPRIATION, special attribute

APPROVE, (i) test, try; (ii) confirm, prove

APPURTENANCE, adjunct

APRICOCK, obs. form of 'apricot'.

AQUA-VITAE, ardent spirits

AQUILON, the north or north-north-east wind

ARABIAN BIRD, the phoenix, q.v.

ARAISE, raise from the dead

ARBITREMENT, scrutiny

ARGAL, a perversion of 'ergo'

ARGIER, old form of Algiers

ARGOSY, 'merchant vessel of largest size and burden' (OED)

ARGUMENT, (i) theme of conversation, of contention, esp. for jest or scorn; (ii) proof, evidence

ARGUS, of the hundred eyes, set by Juno as guard over Io, to prevent Jupiter making love to her

ARION, the Greek musician who, threatened with death on board ship, threw himself into the sea, and was saved by a dolphin who had heard his lute-playing

ARMADO, a fleet of warships

ARMIGERO, an armiger, an esquire

ARMIPOTENT, mighty in arms

ARMS CROSSED, hold down sorrow

ARRAS, tapestry wall-hanging

ARREST, seize as security

ART, learning, science, magic, the skill or power learning bestows

ARTERIES ('the nimble spirits in the'), refers to old medical notion that arteries were the channel, not only of blood, but also of the vital 'spirits'

ARTHUR'S SHOW, 'The Ancient Order of Prince Arthur and his knightly Armory' gave an annual exhibition of archery at Mile End

ARTIFICIAL, skilled in art, q.v.

ARTIST, man of skill or learning, a physician

ASCANIUS, son of Aeneas

ASHER HOUSE, a residence of the Bishop of Winchester near Hampton Court. Asher is now Esher

ASKANCE, scornful, sidelong glance

ASPECT, (i) a glance; (ii) the favourable or unfavourable influence of a planet according to the old astrologers; (iii) appearance

ASPERSION, dew, shower

ASSAY, (i) attempt; (ii) learn by experience

ASSINEGO, young ass, fool

ASSUME, (i) take to oneself formally the insignia of office or symbol of vocation (OED); (ii) put or take on garb, aspect or character. Term in demonology for devils disguising themselves as some dead person

ASSURED, betrothed

ASTRAEA, goddess of Justice, who lived among men in the Golden Age and thereafter deserted earth for heaven

ASTRINGER, austringer, falconer, keeper of goshawks

ATE, goddess of mischief and bloodshed; 'more Ates'—more instigation

ATOMIES, motes, specks of dust in a sunbeam

ATONE, unite, reconcile

ATTACHED, seized, arrested

ATTAINDER, (i) 'in — of', condemned to; (ii) dishonouring stain

ATTENTIVE, observant

ATTORNEY (vb), perform at second hand

ATTORNEYED, employed as attorney or agent

ATTORNEY-GENERAL, legal representative acting under a general power of attorney

AUGURER, augur, member of Roman priestly college whose duty was to study auguries

AURORA, goddess of the dawn

AURORA'S HARBINGER, Venus Phosphor, the morning star

AUSTERELY, with self-restraint

AUTHENTIC, (i) of established credit; (ii) legally qualified or authorised

AVAIL, be profitable, of use

AVES, acclamations

AVOID, depart, quit

AWFUL, commanding respect

BACKARE!, stand back!

BACK-FRIEND, lit. a pretended or false friend

BACK-TRICK, uncertain, perhaps a caper backwards in dancing, a reverse in the galliard

BADGE, hallmark, lit. the mark worn by retainers

BAFFLE, (i) subject to public disgrace or infamy; (ii) dupe, hoodwink

BAILIFF, 'officer of justice under a sheriff who executes writs and processes, distrains and arrests; warrant officer, poursuivant or catchpole' (OED)

BAILLEZ, bring

BALDRIC, belt or girdle, usually leather, richly ornamented, used to support sword or bugle

BALK, omit, neglect

BALK LOGIC, chop logic

BALM, annoint with fragrant liquid

BALSAMUM, balm

BANBURY CHEESE, a very thin cheese

BAND, (i) bond, for debt; (ii) a leash to tie up a dog

BANDETTO, earliest Eng. form of bandit

BANDY, to strike ball to and fro at tennis; to give and take recriminations

BANKROUT, bankrupt

BANNER, properly 'banderole', fringed silk flag on a trumpet

BANQUET, dessert of fruit and wine served some time after supper

BAR IN LAW, plea which effectually prevents an action or claim

BARBARISM, ignorance

BARBARY COCK-PIGEON, fancy variety of pigeon

BARBASON, a prince of devils

BARBED, of a horse, armed with a barb, a protective covering for flanks and breast

BARE, shave

BARFUL, full of difficulties

BARGAIN (sell a), make a fool of

BARGULUS, a pirate who fought against Philip of Macedon

BARK ON TREE (sure as), the union of bark and tree was commonly taken as symbol of married state

BARM, yeast

BARN, bairn, child

BARNACLE, kind of wild goose

BARREN, dull-witted

BARTHOLOMEW BOAR-PIG, young porker fattened for sale at Bartholomew Fair on 24th August

BASE, boys' game, in which a player who leaves his base is chased and if caught is made prisoner

BASES, two-part embroidered mantle worn by knights on horse-back

BASIMECU, contemptuous term for Frenchman, from Fr. 'baisez mon cul'

BASKET-HILT, lit. a hilt of steel plates curved like a basket, but often an epithet for a poor swordsman

BASS-VIOL, violoncello

BASTA, enough

BASTARD, (i) brown or white sweet Spanish wine; (ii) the product of the artificial crossing of two different stocks

BASTED ON, tacked or sewn on loosely

BASTINADO, beating or cudgelling, esp. on the soles of the feet

BATE, (i) deduct; (ii) blunt; (iii) except; (iv) depress, reduce in weight; (v) flutter the wings impatiently

BAT-FOWLING, (i) killing birds by holding a lantern close to their roost and knocking down the victims as they blunder against the light; (ii) gulling a simpleton

BATLER, wooden club for beating clothes in wash

BATTLE, army, large armed force

BAUBLE, a fool's stick, ending in a fool's head

BAUBLING, trifling, toylike

BAWCOCK, fine fellow, colloquial term of endearment, from Fr. 'beau coq'

BAY, chorus of barking hounds in conflict with an animal, hence the animal's last stand

BAYNARD'S CASTLE, on the N. bank of the Thames, close to present Blackfriar's Br., once the house of Richard, Duke of York

BEAD, (i) a minute object; (ii) a prayer

BEADLE, parish constable, authorised to whip petty offenders

BEADSMAN, one who tells beads or prays for another

BEAGLE, lit. a small hound, also used contemptuously of a woman

BEAK, prow

BEAR, (i) carry off, win; (ii) 'bear a hand', treat in a certain way; (iii) 'bear hard', bear ill will to; (iv) 'bear it', conduct oneself; (v) 'bear with you', endure; (vi) 'bear in hand', delude or abuse with false pretences

BEAR'ARD, bear-herd, bear-ward

BEAR-BAITING, one of the most popular Eng. sports of the time, the bear was tied by a long chain to a stake in a ring and set upon by mastiffs

BEAR-HERD, one who leads a bear about the country for exhibition

BEARING-CLOTH, christening robe

BEAT, flap the wings

BEAVER, helmet, face-guard or visor of helmet

BEDLAM, corr. of Bethlehem Hospital for the insane, hence also a lunatic

BED-SWERVER, one unfaithful in marriage

BEETLE, (sb) heavy hammer or mallet; (vb) overhang

BEFORE ME, (i) in my presence; (ii) upon my soul

BEG, petition the court of wards for the custody of a minor, heiress, or idiot, as feudal superior

BELDAM, grandam

BELLMAN, watchman who called the hours

BELL-WETHER, ram with a bell at its neck to lead the flock

BE-METE, measure

BEMOIL, befoul

BEN VENUTO, welcome

BENCH, raise to official dignity

BENCHER, member of Roman senate, a senator

BENEDICITE, 'Bless you', exclamation of surprise, or salutation

BENT, lit. the extent to which a bow may be bent, hence the limit of capacity or endurance

BERGOMASK, dance of clowns or rustics, from Bergamo, Venice

BERMOOTHES, the Bermudas. On 29th July 1609 the *Sea Adventure*, carrying colonists to Virginia, was wrecked on the Bermudas

BESHREW, mischief take

BESONIAN, lit. raw, needy recruit, hence beggar or rascal

BESTOW, confer as a gift; '— oneself', acquit oneself, bear oneself

BESTRAUGHT, distracted, out of one's mind

BETEEM, grant, vouchsafe, pour

BETIME, betide

BETWEEN THIS AND HIS HEAD, a common phrase of the time

BEVIS, Saxon knight, of Southampton, hero of early Eng. metrical romance *Sir B. of Hampton*

BEVY, technical term for covey of quail or lapwing

BIAS, natural tendency or leaning, from the lead in one side of a bowl which makes it turn

BIBLE BABBLE, idle prating

BIDDY, fowl, chicken

BIDE UPON, dwell upon, insist upon

BIGGEN, or biggin, nightcap

BILBO, finely tempered sword of Bilbao manufacture

BILBOE, kind of stocks used on board ship

BILL, (i) long wooden-handled weapon, with blade or axe-shaped head; (ii) advertisement

BILLETS, logs of wood for fuel

BILLS (set up), posted up advertisements, i.e. issued a general challenge

BIRDBOLT, blunt, wooden-headed heavy arrow, used for shooting small birds from a short distance

BITUME, make watertight with bitumen

BLACK MONDAY, Easter Monday

BLANK, the white spot in the centre of the target

BLAZON, description, lit. interpretation of armorial bearings

BLENCH, swerve, start aside

BLENT, blended, mingled

BLOCK, (i) mould for a hat, hence fashion, style; (ii) blockhead, simpleton; (iii) stump for chopping

BLOOD (in), in full vigour, a hunting phrase

BLOODS, gallant fellows

BLOODY, blood-thirsty

BLOW (vb), (i) blow upon, puff out; (ii) make to blossom, i.e. blush

BLUE-CAPS, blue-bonnets, a term of contempt for the Scots

BLUE-EYED, (i) with blue-eyelids, a sign of pregnancy; (ii) with dark circles around the eye from excessive weeping or sleeplessness

BLUNT, (i) rude, unceremonious; (ii) not to be sharpened

BOAR OF THESSALY, sent by Artemis to ravage Calydon, brought to bay and slain by Meleager and Atalanta

BOARD, (i) accost, address; (ii) board a ship

BOB, lit. (i) trick deception; (ii) sharp rap or blow with fist, combining the two meanings a taunt or bitter jest

BODGES, clumsy phrases

BODKIN, long jewelled pin, with engraved or modelled top, for ladies' hair

BOGGLE, shy like a startled horse, take alarm

BOHEMIAN TARTAR, *v.* Hungarian

BOIL, seethe

BOILED-BRAINS, hot-headed youth

BOLD (be), be assured

BOLD-BEATING, prob. misprint for 'bowl-beating', i.e. pot-thumping

BOLIN, early form of 'bowline', a rope from the weather side of square sail to the bow

BOLT, (sb) sieve, strainer; (vb) sift

BOMBARD, large leather vessel containing liquor

BOMBAST, cotton-wool for padding or stuffing

BONA ROBA, high class courtesan, fr. It. 'Buona roba', good stuff

BONA TERRA, MALA GENS, Lat. a good land, a bad people

BOND, (i) signed contract; (ii) fetter

BONNY, often had sense of fine size, big

BOOK (without), from memory, by heart

BOOKS (in your), in favour with you

BOOR, husbandman, peasant

BOOT, (i) 'Grace to boot', Heaven help me; (ii) recompense

BOOT-HOSE, overstocking which covers the leg like a jackboot

BOOTS, 'Give me not the boots', don't make game of me

BOREAS, the north wind

BOSOM, desires or intimate thoughts

BOTCH UP, put together or stitch together clumsily

BOTCHER, repairing tailor; bungling workman

BOTS, horse disease caused by worms

BOTTLE, bundle of hay or straw, the feed prescribed for a horse by Elizabethan horse-keepers

BOTTOM, (i) core of the skein upon which wool was wound; (ii) dell, valley

BOUGHT AND SOLD, in modern slang 'sold'

BOUND, indentured under contract of service

BOUNDS (of feed), limits within which one had rights of pasturage, prob. in respect of common land

BOURN, boundary, landmark, stream

BOUT, round, turn

BOW, yoke for oxen

BOWHAND, *v.* wide

BOY, term of abuse or contempt

BOY (to her), a hunting cry

BRABBLE, brawl

BRACH, bitch

BRAID, of doubtful meaning and origin, possibly loose, lascivious

BRAINFORD, Brentford

BRANCHED, figured

BRAVELY, (i) with a light heart; (ii) at a high rate or value

BRAWL, the most ancient type of figure dancing

BREACH (of the sea), lit. where the waves break, the surf

BREAK, break faith, disband

BREAK A COMPARISON, metaphor from 'breaking a lance' at tilting

BREAK UP, (i) open a letter (break the wax); (ii) cut up, dismember (fowl or deer)

BREAK WITH, reveal, divulge

BREAKING GULF, the waves

BREAK-NECK, downfall, destruction

BREAST, voice for singing

BREATH, speech, utterance

BREATHE, take exercise

BREATHED, in training, with a good wind

BREATHER, living being, creature

BRED OUT, exhausted, degenerated

BREECHING SCHOLAR, schoolboy liable to be whipped

BRIAREUS, in Gr. mythology a monster with a hundred arms

BRIBED-DUCK, stolen deer

BRIEF, (i) list, summary; (ii) legal document

BROACH, let blood, lit. 'tap'

BROCK, badger, stinker

BROKE, act as procurer

BROKE CROSS, it was dishonourable for a tilter to have his lance broken cross-wise instead of length-wise against an opponent's shield

BROKEN, gap-toothed

BROKER, pander, go-between

BROOCH, ornament, often worn in the hat

BROW, (i) countenance; (ii) 'strike at the brow':— strike at the brow antler, i.e. aim for the lowest part of the stag's horn, the right mark for the archer

BROWN BILL, painted brown halberd, used by watchmen

BROWNIST, lit. follower of Robt. Browne, a founder of Independency, hence an extreme type of puritan

BRUISE, crush

BRUIT, noise, report

BUBUKLE, pimple, a confusion of 'bubo' abscess and 'carbuncle'

BUCK, (i) male deer, stag; (ii) dirty linen to be steeped in alkaline lye as the first process in buck-washing or bleaching

BUCKLE IN, encompass, limit

BUCKLERS (give the), yield, admit defeat

BUCKLERSBURY, London street for grocers and apothecaries, whose shops were full of herbs in 'simple time'

BUDGET, leather wallet or pouch

BUFF, stout leather, made of ox-hide, oiled, with a characteristic fuzzy surface and a dull whitish-yellow colour, used for the attire of sergeants, bum-bailiffs and soldiers

BUG, bogey, bugbear

BUGLE, ornamental tube-shaped bead-work, a black, glass bead

BULLY, (sb) gallant (a term of endearment)

BUM-BAILY, petty sheriff's officer who could arrest for theft

BUNCH OF GRAPES, the name of a room in an ale-house

BUR, (i) prickly seed-vessel; (ii) anything that produced a choking sensation in the throat

BURDEN, part for the bass singer

BURGONET, a kind of helmet

BURN DAYLIGHT, waste time

BURNING ZONE, the belt between the tropics of Cancer and Capricorn in the celestial sphere

BURST, smash

BURTHEN, accompaniment to a song, bass part, refrain

BUSH, lit. 'a branch or bunch of ivy', perhaps as a plant sacred to Bacchus, hung up as a vintner's sign, and hence the tavern sign

BUTCHERY, slaughterhouse, shambles

BUTTERY-BAR, ledge at the door of the buttery, hatch on which to rest tankards, etc.

BUTT-SHAFT, an unbarbed arrow used at the butts

BUZZ, (i) buzz of a bee; (ii) rumour, scandal

BUZZARD, inferior kind of hawk, unteachable by falconer, hence a type of stupidity; moth, cockchafer

BY ABOUT, concerning

BY'R LAKIN, vulgar form of 'By our Lady'

CABALLERO, Sp. gallant, good fellow

CABBAGE, cabbagehead, hence fool

CACODEMON, evil spirit

CADDIS, worsted yarn; '— ribbon', worsted tape from which garters were made

CADE, barrel of six score herrings

CADWALLADER, last British king, killed A.D. 635

CAELUM, Lat. sky

CAGE OF RUSHES, a 'cage' was a lock-up for petty male-factors, a cage of rushes would be a flimsy prison

CAITIFF, basely wretched

CAKE OF ROSES, or rose-cake, preparation of rose petals in the form of a cake and used as perfume

CALENDAR, register

CALF, dolt, ass

CALIVER, light musket

CALLET, a scold

CAMBRIA, Wales

CAMBYSES, son of Cyrus, King of Persia

CAMOMILE, creeping plant often covering paths of Elizabethan gardens

CANARY, (sb) (i) lively Spanish dance; (ii) sweet wine from the Canaries; (vb) to move the feet as in the canary

CANDIDATUS, candidate for office in Rome, lit. one clothed in white

CANDIED, frozen

CANDLE-CASE, receptacle for candle ends

CANDLE-HOLDER, an attendant who lighted others in a ceremony at night

CANDLE-MINE, tallow magazine

CANDLE-WASTER, book-worm, who burns the midnight oil

CANKER, the dog-rose

CANKER-BLOSSOM, a worm that cankers a blossom

CANKERED, (i) of weapons, rusted, corroded through disuse; (ii) of persons, malignant

CANTLE, segment of a sphere

CANTON, variant of 'canzon', a song

CANZONET, a short song

CAPABLE, (i) impressionable, intelligent; (ii) of marriageable age

CAPARISON, lit. ornamental trappings of a horse, hence outfit

CAPER, lit. a goat's leap, as a dancing movement it consisted of beating the feet in the air

CAPILET, a name for a horse

CAPITOL, temple of Jupiter on Capitoline Hill

CAPOCCHIA, It. simpleton

CAPON, (i) lit. a castrated cock, often signified a dull fool; (ii) a billet-doux

CAPRICCIO, it. caprice

CAPTIOUS, (i) fallacious, deceptive; (ii) receptive

CARACT, or 'charact', a mark, sign or symbol

CARBONADOED, stashed or stored, like a piece of meat for broiling

CARBUNCLE, red precious stone

CARCANET, 'ornamental collar or necklace, usually of gold or studded with jewels' (OED)

CARCASS OF A BUTT, a leaky old tub of a vessel

CARD OF TEN, card with ten pips

CARDECUE, Fr. 'quart d'écu', a silver coin worth about 7½p

CARD-MAKER, a card was an instrument with iron teeth for combing out wool fibres by hand

CARDUUS BENEDICTUS, the blessed thistle, a popular medicinal remedy of the time

CAREER, gallop or charge in the lists of a tournament; 'passed the —', ran away

CAREFUL, full of care

CARET, Lat. it is missing

CARL, churl

CAROL, orig. a ring dance with a song, hence any kind of song sung at festival times

CARP, (i) fresh-water, pond-bred fish; (ii) talkative person

CARPET, tapestry used for window-seats, bed-valances, etc.

CARPET-MONGER, CARPET-KNIGHT, contemptuous terms for one whose prowess belongs rather to the boudoir than the battle-field

CARRACK, galleon, lit. heavy-armed merchantman

CARRIAGE, (i) behaviour, line of action; (ii) demeanour

CARRION, putrefying, like a skeleton from which the flesh has rotted away

CARRY, (i) conquer, gain the prize; (ii) manage, carry out; '— coals', submit tamely to insult

CART, 'to cart with', bawds and harlots were punished by public exposure and whipping in a cart drawn through the streets

CARVE, (i) show great courtesy and affability; (ii) make advances by signalling in a peculiar way with the fingers—'a digitary ogle'

CASE, (sb) (i) cause, suit; (ii) condition; (iii) technical term for skin of fox or other vermin, mask; (vb) skin, strip (term in venery)

CASHIER, (i) discard; (ii) cheat, rob

CASSIBELAN, uncle of Cymbeline, the Latin Cassivelaunus, leader of resistance in Britain to Caesar's second invasion

CASSOCK, long loose cloak worn by musketeers and others in 16th and 17th cent.

CAST, (i) cast-off, discarded; (ii) put into a state or category of

CATAIAN, cheat, lit. an inhabitant of Cathay

CAT-A-MOUNTAIN, CAT O'MOUNTAIN, wild cat

CATAPLASM, plaster, poultice

CATASTROPHE, lit. the denouement of a play, hence a conclusion of any kind, the tail end

CATE, dainty, delicacy

CATER-COUSIN, 'scarce —', hardly on speaking terms

CATERPILLAR, rapacious person, extortioner

CATO, the elder, 234–149 B.C., famous after the 3rd Punic War for his 'delenda est Carthago'

CAUDLE, warm drink of thin gruel and wine, sweetened and spiced, for sick persons, especially women in childbirth

CAUSE, (i) 'first and second cause', reasons according to the laws of the duello for accepting or refusing a challenge; the laws of the duello in general; (ii) sickness, disease

CAUTEL, deceit, craft

CAVALERY, Cavaliero, form of address meaning 'gallant, gentleman'

CAVETO, Lat. caution (imp. of 'caveo', beware)

CENSER, a perforated fumigator

CENSORINUS, MARTIUS C., of the family of Coriolanus, but not his ancestor, censor c. 265 B.C.

CENSURE, judge, estimate (but not necessarily unfavourably)

CENTRE, lit. the centre of the earth, in Ptolemaic astronomy the centre of the universe, and so, figuratively, man's soul

CENTURY, a division of the Roman army, orig. a hundred men, commanded by a centurion

CERECLOTH, winding sheet

CESSE, archaic form of 'cease'

CHAFE, (i) irritate, vex; (ii) excite, heat

CHALLENGE, lay claim to, demand as a right

CHAM (the great), emperor of China (Cham:—Khan)

CHAMBERLAIN, male servant for bedchambers

CHAMPIAN, variant of 'champaign'

CHAMPION, (sb) one who fights for a cause in single combat; (vb) oppose in a 'wager of battle'

CHANCE, opportunity, possibility of good or bad fortune

CHANTRY, private chapel endowed for maintenance of one or more priests to sing daily mass for the souls of the departed

CHAPELESS, without the chape, the metal plate of the scabbard covering the point of the sword

CHAPMEN, merchants

CHARACTER, (sb) hidden meaning; (vb) engrave

CHARACTERY, symbolical writing

CHARGE, (sb) burden, load, hence importance, value; (ii) load, as the cannon with shot; load with arguments

CHARGEFUL, expensive

CHARINESS, scrupulous integrity

CHARLES' (orig. Charlemagne's) WAIN, the Great Bear constellation

CHARNECO, type of port wine named after village near Lisbon

CHASE, (sb) hunted animal, quarry; (vb) harass

CHEAPEN, make a bid for

CHEAT, (i) something stolen, theft; (ii) a thievish trick

CHEATER, escheator, an official of the Exchequer and because of opportunity for fraud, fig. a sharper

CHECK, a hawking term

CHEER, countenance, face; cheerly—blithely

CHEESE, the Welshman's love of cheese was a popular subject of jest at this time

CHEQUIN (It. zecchino), gold coin of Italy and Turkey worth about 35–50p

CHEERY-PIT, children's game of throwing cherry stones into a small pit or hole

CHEVERIL, lit. of kid leather, and therefore easily stretched, hence pliable, elastic

CHEWET, jackdaw, chatterbox

CHIDING, brawling or angry noise, esp. of hounds

CHILDE, title, in ballads and romances, of youth of noble birth, lit. one not yet knighted

CHILDING, breeding, fruitful, pregnant

CHIRRAH! Hail!

CHOICE, special value, estimation

CHOIR (vb), make music

CHOLLER, jowl

CHOPFT, chapped

CHOPINE, cork-soled shoe worn in Italy and Spain

CHORUS, Presenter or Prologue, to make plain the action

CHOUGH, jackdaw, chattern

CHISTENDOM, christian name

CHRISTOM CHILD, corr. of 'chrisom child', one who, dying within a month of birth, was buried in its chrisom cloth or christening robe

CHRYSOLITE, name of various golden-coloured gems

CHUCK, (i) familiar name of endearment applied to close relatives and dear friends; (ii) chicken

CICATRICE, lit. the scar of a wound, hence a scar-like mark

CIMMERIAN, 'black man', from Cimmerians in Homer, on whose land the sun never shone

CINQUE-PACE, a galliard of five steps

CIRCUMSTANCE, (i) evidence, argument; (ii) condition; (iii) circumlocution

CITE WITNESS, legal term, to call witnesses

CITTERN-HEAD, referring to the grotesquely carved head of the cittern, a common, wire-stringed instrument

CIVET, musk-smelling perfume, from the secretions of the civet cat, much used by gentry at that time

CIVIL, (i) grave, solemn; (ii) civilised, refined; (iii) becoming, seemly

CLACK-DISH, or clap-dish, lidded wooden dish, carried and clacked by beggars

CLAMMER, or clamber, tech. term of bell-ringing, to increase the strokes preparatory to stopping altogether, hence to stop from noise, to silence

CLAP, strike hands in token of a bargain

CLAP INTO, enter upon anything with alacrity and briskness, strike up

CLAP O' TH' SHOULDER, arrest

CLAPPER-CLAW (vb), maul, thrash

CLAP UP, fix up hastily, concoct hurriedly

CLAW, (vb) (i) scratch; (ii) tickle, fawn upon, flatter

CLEAN-TIMBERED, well built

CLEAR, (adj.) serene, innocent; (vb) purify, acquit, free from guilt

CLEAVE, (i) split or hit (the pin in the centre of the target); (ii) grasp

CLEFT, two-fold

CLEPE, call, name

CLERESTORY, orig. the upper part of the nave, with windows clear of the roof of the aisle, hence any large window high in the wall

CLERKLY, (i) like a scholar; (ii) smartly

CLEW, ball of thread or yarn

CLIMATE, (sb) clime, region; (vb) reside

CLINQUANT, glittering with gold or silver

CLIPT, (i) abbreviated; (ii) embraced

CLODPOLE, numskull, thickhead

CLOG, encumberance

CLOSE, (adj.) secluded, secret; (adv.) still!

CLOSE-STOOL, commode

CLOTHARIUS, prob. Clotaire, son of Clovis, early Merovingian king

CLOUD, (i) mask, veil; (ii) sully, defame

CLOUT, the mark in archery

CLUBS!, cry to summon aid to stop a brawl

CLYSTER-PIPE, tube for injecting an enema

COARSELY, meanly, slightingly

COCKATRICE, fabulous reptile, also called a basilisk, half-cock, half-serpent, supposed to be able to kill by its breath or look

COCKLE, darnel, tares

COCKLE-HAT, hat with cockle or scallop shell, as a sign of the wearer having been at the shrine of St James of Compostella in Spain

COCKNEY, spoilt child, pampered darling

COCK'S PASSION, corr. of oath 'God's Passion'

COCYTUS, one of the rivers of Hades

CODLING, immature or half-grown apple

CODPIECE, part of male hose or breeches made indelicately conspicuous in Shakespeare's time

CODS, (i) pods; (ii) testicles

COFFER, lit. strong box, hence a person's wealth

COG, cheat, at dice play

COGNIZANCE, term in heraldry for device or emblem worn by retainers, generally a distinctive badge

COIL, tumult, fuss, bother

COLDBRAND, a Danish giant defeated by Guy of Warwick

COLD, without power to move or influence (OED)

COLD SCENT, weak or faint scent in hunting

COLDLY, calmly, coolly

COLLIED, begrimed, murky

COLLOP, lit. a cut off the joint of meat, hence 'a chip off the old block'

COLLUSION, 'trick or ambiguity in words or reasoning' (OED)

COLOQUINTIDA, colocynth or bitter apple, which furnished an intensely bitter purgative

COLOSSUS, gigantic statue of Apollo which bestrode the harbour at Rhodes

COLOUR, pretext

COLOURING, (i) dyeing; (ii) giving a specious appearance

COLOURABLE COLOURS, plausible pretexts

COLOURS (fear no), fear no foe, have no fear

COLT, (i) a young horse; (ii) a lascivious male; (iii) a young or inexperienced person

COMBINATE, betrothed, affianced

COMBINED, tied, bound

COME AWAY, come here, come along

COME NEAR, begin to understand

COME OFF, pay up

COMEDIAN, stage player

COMES OFF WELL, turns out well

COME UPON, attack

COMFECT, 'Count Comfect', Count Sugar-plum

COMFORTABLE, of good comfort, cheerful, lending moral or spiritual support

COMFORTING, in legal sense abetting, countenancing

COMING-IN, (sb) allowance

COMMENDATIONS, rememberances

COMMODITY, (i) advantages, privileges; (ii) goods. The sale of commodities ('brown paper and old ginger', i.e. worthless rubbish) was a fictitious device adopted by usurers to circumvent the law and bleed their victims

COMMON ('make a common of'), make free of, take liberties with

COMMONER, prostitute

COMPACT, (sb) plot, conspiracy; (adj.) composed, made up of

COMPANION, fellow (contemptuous)

COMPASS, get possession of

COMPASSED, cut so as to fall in a circle

COMPETENT, legally admissible

COMPETITOR, partner, confederate

COMPLEMENT, formal civility; 'compliment' is a French word not anglicised before the end of the 17th cent.

COMPLETE, fully equipped, accomplished, consummate

COMPLEXION, (i) colour of skin, appearance; (ii) temperament, nature. Old medical theory said the complexion or composition of a man's body was made up of four humours or fluids, and if the proportion was disturbed disease would follow

COMPOSITION, the sum agreed upon

COMPROMISE, come to terms, settle differences

COMPT, reckoning

COMPTIBLE, lit. countable, liable to give account, and so liable to answer to, sensitive to

CON, commit to memory, learn one's part as actor

CON THANKS, offer thanks, acknowledge gratitude

CONCAVE, hollow

CONCEIT, (sb) (i) understanding, wit; (ii) imagination, fancy; (iii) ingenious or witty notion; (vb) form notions, entertain ideas

CONCEIVE, understand

CONCERN, engage the attention, affect with care, cause trouble

CONCOLINEL, meaning obscure, prob. title or opening word of a song

CONCUPY, concupiscence

CONDIGN, well-merited, worthy

CONDITION, character, characteristic; 'best conditioned':—best tempered

CONDOLE, grieve, lament

CONDUCT, (sb) (i) leadership, command; (ii) escort, safe conduct

CONDUIT, fountain

CONFEDERACY, conspiracy

CONFERENCE, conversation, talk (less formal and more general than its modern meaning)

CONFINES (sb) region, territory

CONFIRMED, unmoved, resolute

CONFOUND, ruin, destroy

CONFUTE, (i) render futile; (ii) silence in argument

CONGEE WITH, take leave of

CONGRUENT, fitting, agreeable

CONJECTURE, suspicion, evil surmise

CONJURER, lit. one who deals with devils or spirits

CONSIDER, remunerate, 'tip'

CONSISTORY, meeting of college of cardinals

CONSONANCY, consistency

CONSONANT, nonentity (a consonant being unable to stand alone like a vowel)

CONSORT, company, generally of musicians

CONSTABLE, LORD HIGH, principal officer in royal households of France and England

CONSTANT, resolute, self-possessed, (of a colour) uniform; 'constant question':—formally conducted discussion

CONSTELLATION, the configuration of 'stars' (planets) as supposed to have influence on men esp. at birth, hence disposition or character as determined by 'one's stars'

CONSTER, old form of 'construe'

CONSTRINGE, compress

CONTAGIOUS, catchy, catching (like a disease)

CONTAIN, retain, keep in one's possession or under one's control

CONTEMPTIBLE, scornful, contemptuous

CONTINENT, total sum; 'continents', the banks which should contain them

CONTINENT CANNON, variously explained as the law enjoining continence and the law contained in the edict

CONTINUE, contain, be continent

CONTINUER, horse with a good wind and staying power

CONTRIVE, spend or pass the time

CONTRIVER, schemer, plotter

CON TUTTO IL CUORE BEN TROVATO, with all my heart well met

CONVENTED, summoned

CONVERTITE, convert to a religious faith or way of life

CONVEYANCE, sleight of hand, dexterity

CONVEYED HIMSELF, passed himself off

CONVOY, means of transport, conveyance

CONY-CATCH (vb) cheat, swindle; cony (rabbit) was the dupe

COOLING CARD, 'apparently a term of some unknown game applied figuratively or punningly to anything that "cools" a person's passion or enthusiasm' (OED)

COPATAIN HAT, sugar-loaf hat

COPE, (i) strike, encounter; (ii) buy, barter, give in exchange for; (iii) debate with

COPHETUA, African king, known only in the ballad King Cophetua and the Beggarmaid

COPPER, ? false coin, perhaps referring to the newly introduced copper farthings

COPULATIVE, orig. a grammatical term, but also 'one about to be or desirous of being married'

COPY (of our conference), agenda, subject matter

CORAGIO!, Courage!

CORAM, quorum; Justices of Quorum or Coram sat on the bench at County Sessions

CORANTO, a lively dance

CORDELION, Coeur de Lion

CORDIAL, restoring, reviving

CORIN and Phillida, traditional names of lovers in pastoral poetry

CORINTH, Gr. town notorious in ancient times for its prostitutes; 'Corinthian', a gay dog

COMORANT, glutinous

CORNER-CAP, a symbol of authority to Elizabethans; three- or four-cornered cap worn by divines and members of the universities

CORNET, company of cavalry, from its standard, a horn-shaped pennon

CORNUTO, horned cuckold

COROLLARY, supernumerary

CORPORALL, champion. 'Corporal of the field' was 'a superior officer of the army in the 16th and 17th cent., who acted as assistant ... to the sergeant-major' (OED); there were four to each regiment

COST, extravagance, display

COSTARD, head (lit. a large apple)

COT-QUEAN, man who meddled with matters properly a house-wife's concern

COTSALL, the Cotswolds, a favourite resort for coursing matches

COUCH (lance), lower in order to attack

COUNSEL, resolution; 'in —', in private

COUNT OF, reckon with, attend to

COUNTENANCE, confidence of mien, hypocrisy, worldly credit

COUNTER, (sb) token coin used for arithmetical calculations; (adv.) opposite (to the trail taken by the game). The Counter was also a debtors' prison

COUNTERCHECK, rebuke or rebuff in retaliation

COUNTER-GATE, gate of the debtors' prison, notorious for its smell

COUNTERMAIDS (the passage of), forbids entry

COUNTERPOINT, counterpane

COUNTY, count, earl

COUPLE A GORGE, Fr. 'couper la gorge', cut the throat

COUPLEMENT, couple

COURSES, two small sails attached to the lower yards of a ship

COUSIN, any collateral relative more distant than brother or sister; 'cousin-german', first cousin

COUT, colt

COVENT, old form of 'Convent' (cf. Covent Garden)

COVER, (i) lay the cloth; (ii) cover the head

COVERED GOBLET, an empty goblet. Goblets were usually fitted with ornamental covers removed when in use

COVERT'ST, most secret

COWL-STAFF, stout pole passed through the handles of a cowl (lit. water-tub) so that it could be hoisted by two men

COX MY PASSION!, variant of 'Cock's passion' q.v.

COXCOMB, fool's cap

COY (vb), pat, caress

COYSTRILL, base fellow, originally a groom

COZ, cousin, used of any close relationship

COZEN, cheat; 'cozenage', fraud, imposture

COZIER, cobbler

CRAB, (i) crab apple; (ii) cross-grained

CRACK, (sb) (i) flaw, defect; (ii) pert boy; (vb) boast, make explosive sound

CRACK-HEMP, gallows bird

CRAMPS, rheumatic pains esp. of old people

CRANTS, garland, usually of white paper, hung in church on occasion of young girl's funeral

CRAVEN, a cock that 'cried creak' or acknowledged defeat

CRAZED, unsound, flawed

CREDIBLE, trustworthy

CREEK, winding narrow passage

CRESSET, iron basket on a pole, in which pitched rope, etc. was burnt for illumination

CREST, (i) helmet; (ii) ridge of neck of horse

CRISP, rippled; 'crisped', closely, stiffly curled

CRISPIN CRISPIAN, 25th October. SS Crispinus and Crispianus (brothers) were martyred at Soissons c. A.D. 287

CRITIC, fault-finder, jeerer

CRONE, withered old woman

CROSS, (i) thwart; (ii) sign with the cross in blessing; (iii) coin, with cross stamped on it

CROSS-GARTERED, wearing the garters above and below the knee so as to be crossed at the back

CROTCHET, (i) note in music; (ii) silly notion

CROW, 'pluck a crow together', proverb, to settle accounts, to pick a bone together

CROWFLOWER, buttercup

CROWN IMPERIAL, the cultivated fritillary

CROWNER, coroner

CROWNET, coronet

CRUPPER, leather strap which passes in a loop from the saddle round the horse's tail to keep the saddle from slipping

CRY, a pack of hounds

CRY AIM, applaud (archery term)

CRY OUT ON, denounce

CUCKOO-BUDS, unexplained; marsh marigold, buttercup and cowslip have all been suggested

CUCULLUS NON FACIT MONACHUM, a hood does not make a monk

CUE, v. part

CULL, choose, select

CULLION, base fellow, lit. testicle

CULVERIN, small cannon

CUM PRIVILEGIO AD IMPRIMENDUM SOLUM, with the privilege of sole printing

CURFEW BELL, orig. bell rung in evening to indicate 'domestic fires out' (Fr. 'couvre feu') but also a bell rung at three or four in the morning

CURIOUS, (i) particular; (ii) requiring care and attention

CURIOUS-KNOTTED, quaintly designed or laid out

CURSITORY, wandering, cursory

CURST, ill-tempered, shrewish, vicious

CURTAL, horse with its tail cut short

CURTAL-DOG, dog with a docked tail of no service in the chase

CURTLE-AXE, heavy sword for cutting or slashing

CURTSY, (i) bow (of any kind); (ii) a trifle

CURVET, manège term for a special type of horse leap

CUSHES, armour for the thighs

CUSTALORUM, a contraction of 'custos rotulorum', the keeper of the rolls

CUSTARD-COFFIN, custard pie

CUSTOM, trade

CUSTOMER, common woman, prostitute

CUT, lit. cart-horse, hence a term of abuse

CUT AND LONG TAIL, horses or dogs of all sorts

CUTS, ornamental slashes in a garment

CYCLOPS, race of one-eyed giants in Homer

CYDNUS, river in Cilicia on which Anthony first saw Cleopatra

CYNTHIA, the moon personified as a goddess

CYPRESS, (i) cypress tree; (ii) piece of black lawn used as kerchief as sign of mourning

CYMBELINE, name only derived from Cimobellinus, king of most of Britain c. 12 B.C. to c. A.D. 43

CYTHEREA, Venus, the name derived from Cythera in Cypress, one of the chief places of her worship

DAEDALUS, v. Icarus

DALLY WITH, linger lovingly over

DAFF, put off, thrust aside

DAMASK, the colour of the damask-rose, i.e. blush-colour

DAMON, a faithful friend (referring to the classical story of Damon and Pythias)

DANCE BAREFOOT, the elder unmarried sister was supposed to dance bare-foot at the wedding of a younger, hence 'to remain unmarried'

DANCING-HORSE, a well-known performing horse

DAPHNE, a nymph, who, fleeing from Apollo's importunities, was changed into a laurel at her own wish

DARDAN, Trojan

DÀRKLING, in the dark

DARNEL, could be tares or the common poppy

DARRAIGN, dispose in battle array

DATCHET-MEAD, between Windsor Little Park and the Thames

DANGER (within his), in his power, at his mercy

DAUBERY, false show

DAY-BED, sofa, prob. introduced towards the end of the 16th cent. and regarded by old-fashioned folk as luxurious if not wicked

DAZZLING, becoming dim or dazzled

DEAD, DEADLY, pale, death-like, mortal

DEALER, 'plain dealer' is one devoid of wit or conceit

DEAR, grievous, dire, sore

DEAREST, best

DEATH'S FACE, a skull; 'death-tokens', plague spots

DEBATE, contention

DEBILE, weak

DEBONAIR, gentle, meek

DEBOSHED, old form of 'debauched'

DECEIVABLE, deceptive

DECK, pack of cards; 'above deck', above board; poop deck in the stern of a vessel

DECK (vb), adorn, as with jewels

DECLINE, incline

DEEP-VOW (Master), a lover

DEFAULT (in the), at a need

DEFEATURE, disfigurement

DEFY, reject, disdain, disown

DELIVER, declare, make known, discover

DELIVERANCE, manner of speech, speech

DEMI-CANON, large gun with 6½ inch bore

DENAY, variant of 'deny'

DENIER, very small French coin

DENUNCIATION, formal announcement

DEPART WITHAL, part with, surrender

DEPOSE, examine on oath

DERACINATE, root up

DERIVE, inherit, bring down upon

DESCANT, (sb) variations; (vb) (i) warble; (ii) comment at length

DESPITE ('in the despite of'), in contempt of

DESTINIES, the Fates, Clotho, Lachesis and Atropos, who spin and weave the thread of life

DETERMINATE, intended, determined upon

DETESTED, abjured, renounced by oath

DEUCALION, the Noah of classical mythology, son of Prometheus

DEUCE-ACE, low throw at dice, two and one

DEVICE, a play or masque written for private presentation, an invention, ingenuity

DEWLAP, pendulous fold of skin on throat

DEXTER, heraldic term, right

DEY, woman, dairy woman

DIAL, may refer to watch, pocket sun-dial or mariner's compass

DIANA, goddess of the moon and chastity

DIAPASON, a bass in direct concord in octaves with the air

DIBBLE, tool for making holes for planting seeds

DICK, fellow, a term of contempt

DICKON, familiar form of Dick, Richard

DICTYNNA, a recondite name for the moon

DIDO, queen of Carthage, who slew herself when deserted by Aeneas

DIET, (sb) board and lodging, regimen; (vb) pay off after a day's work

DIFACIANT LAUDIS SUMMA SIT ISTA TUAE! The gods grant this may be the height of thy glory

DIFFERENCE, 'alteration or addition to a coat of arms to distinguish a junior member or branch of a family' (NED)

DIFFUSED, generally interpreted as 'disorderly' but could mean 'dispersed'

DIGEST, assimilate, amalgamate

DIGNITY, (i) worth; (ii) grandeur

DIGRESS, transgress, deviate

DILATED, extended

DILDO, lit. the phallus, a word often found in ballad refrains

DILEMMA, alternative course of action, difficulty to be faced

DILUCULO SURGERE SALUBERRIMUM EST, to get up early at dawn is most healthy

DIMENSION, bodily parts, proportions

DIOMEDE, one of the Greek leaders at Troy, who with Odysseus entered the Trojan camp and stole the horses of the King of Thrace

DIRECTION-GIVER, one who directs the archer's aim

DIS, Pluto, god of the underworld

DISABLE, disparage, belittle

DISBENCH, cause to leave seat, usually of Inns of Court membership

DISCANDY, melt, liquify

DISCARD, dismiss, discharge

DISCASE, undress

DISCHARGE, (sb) performance, a theatrical term; (vb) to pay (a debt), get rid of

DISCIPLINE, instruction

DISCOMFORTABLE, destroying comfort or happiness

DISCONTENTING, displeasing

DISCOURSE, reason, thought

DISCOVER, reveal by drawing aside a curtain

DISCOVERY, (i) disclosure; (ii) exploration

DISCRETION, discrimination

DISGRACIOUS, displeasing, out of favour

DISHONEST, (i) discreditable; (ii) immodest, unchaste

DISLIKEN, disguise

DISME, dime, tenth part, tithe

DISMOUNT, remove something from that on which it is mounted, e.g. a cannon from its carriage or a gem from its setting

DISPARK, convert to other purposes land where game is preserved

DISPOSED, in a jocund mood, inclined to mirth

DISPUTABLE, disputatious

DISPUTE, reason about, discuss

DISSOLVE, (i) break faith or troth, discharge; (ii) melt

DISTANCE, v. fencing

DISTEMPER, render unhealthy

DISTEMPERATURE, climatic inclemency or unwholesomeness. The word 'temperature' at this time comprised all atmospheric conditions

DISTINCTLY, separately

DISTRACTED, torn asunder, divided

DITTY, 'the words of a song as distinguished from its music or tune' (NED)

DIVERTED BLOOD. Technical medical language: old doctors claimed to be able to 'divert' the course of the humours or the blood by medicinal means

DIVINITY, divination

DIZY, could be 'dicey', given to dice, but 'dizy' was a common form of 'dizzy', giddy or foolish

DOCTRINE, science, knowledge

DOG ('to be a dog at'), to be expert

DOG-APE, a dog-faced baboon

DOG-DAYS, hottest period of the year, 13th July to 15th August, when Sirius, the Dog-star, rises nearly at the same time as the sun

DOIT, small Dutch coin, half an English farthing

DOLE, portion sparingly doled out

DOLLAR, the German thaler

DOLPHIN, (i) the Dauphin; (ii) sea mammal

DOMINEER, swagger, feast uproariously

DOMINICAL, the red letter denoting Sundays in the old almanacs

DOTAGE, doting, infatuation

DOTER, fond lover

DOUBLET-AND-HOSE, the male attire of the time

DOUBLE-TONGUE (i) deceitful tongue; (ii) alluding to the leathern tongue on the inside of a mask, held in the mouth to keep it in place

DOUBTFUL, dreadful

DOUGH ('my cake is dough'), I have failed

DOWAGER, widow with a dowage or jointure charged upon an estate

DOWER, one who gives a dowry to a bride

DOWLAS, coarse linen

DOWLE, a filament of a feather

DOWSABEL, Eng. form of 'Dulcibella' 'applied generically to a sweetheart' (OED)

DOXY, a beggar's mistress

DRAB, harlot

DRACHMA, Gr. silver coin, worth about 3½p

DRAFF, hog's wash

DRAM, 1/16th oz avoir. 1/8th oz fluid, hence a very small quantity

DRAUGHT, cesspool, sewer

DRAW DRY-FOOT, track game by mere scent of the footprint

DRAWN IN, taken in, cheated

DRESSINGS, ceremonial attire

DRIBBLING DART, an arrow falling feebly and so unable to pierce a corselet

DRIFT, plot, intention

DRIVE, drift

DROLLERY, puppet-show, comic picture

DROP FORTH, bring forth

DROP-HEIR, an heir who is gradually pining away

DRUM, drummer

DRUM (John or Tom), 'Tom Drum's entertainment': —a rough reception; many references in Elizabethan literature, probably to a tale now lost

DRUMBLE, loiter, be sluggish

DRY, (i) dull, stupid; (ii) thirsty; (iii) mean; (iv) lacking in amorousness

DRY BASTE, DRY BEAT, beat severely

DRY BRAIN. In the physiology of the day a dry brain accompanied slowness of apprehension

DRY HAND, a sign of old age; a moist hand was a supposed sign of lasciviousness

DUCAT, Spanish gold coin

DUELLO, the art of duelling; its code and practice

DULL, blunt

DUMB-SHOW, silent performance of part of a play to explain briefly events between the acts and to foreshadow what is to follow

DUMP, plaintive melody or song

DURANCE, (i) imprisonment; (ii) a stout kind of cloth, probably buff q.v.

DUTCH DISH, the German (Dutch) fondness for greasy cooking was apparently known at that time

DUTY, curtsy, due, reward

EAGLE-SIGHTED, able to gaze upon the sun

EANLING, newly born lamb

EAR (vb), plough

EARNEST, money paid as an instalment

EARNEST-GAPING, eagerly gazing, longing intensely

ECHE (vb), add to, lengthen

EDWARD SHOVEL-BOARDS, old broad shillings of Edward VI, worn smooth by age and use, and so convenient for the game of shovel-board or shove-groat

EFFIGY, likeness, portrait

EFTEST, possibly a misprint for 'estest':—pleasantest

EGALL, equal

EGLANTINE, the sweet briar

EGRESS AND REGRESS, legal term meaning right of entry esp. into harbours and waterways

EIGHT AND SIX, alternate lines of eight and six syllables, a common ballad metre

EISEL, vinegar

ELD, antiquity, old age

ELDER-GUN, popgun

ELEMENT (i) sky, firmament; (ii) sphere of life or comprehension.

ELEMENTS (the four), air, earth, fire and water, out of which, according to the old philosophy, everything, including man, was composed

ELEVEN AND TWENTY LONG, just the right length

ELL, 1¼ yards

ELVISH-MARKED, marked by malign fairies at birth

ELYSIUM, place of abode after death of those favoured by the gods

EMBLAZE, proclaim as a heraldic device

EMBOSS, drive a hunted animal to extremity; -ed, (i) swollen, tumid; (ii) played out, dead beat

EMBOWEL, disembowel

EMPALE, hem in

EMPERY, absolute dominion, territory under an absolute ruler

EMPIRIC, quack

EMPLOYMENT, business

EMULATION, ambition, jealous rivalry

ENCELADUS, one of the Titans who warred against the Olympian gods

ENCHANTINGLY, as under the influence of a charm

ENCOUNTER, external behaviour

ENDING ANTHEM, requiem

ENDS (old), tags, quotations

ENEW, lit. 'in eau', drive the quarry into covert or water

ENFORCED, violated

ENGAGE, pledge

ENGLUTTED, swallowed up

ENGROSS, buy up wholesale, monopolise.

ENJOINED (penitents), persons upon whom penance has been imposed by their spiritual adviser

ENRAGED, mad

ENSCONCE, conceal. lit. shelter within a fortification

ENTER, entry, theatrical term

ENTERTAIN, (i) engage in battle; (ii) treat, take into one's service

ENTERTAINMENT, reception, service

ENTRANCE, entrance fee

ENVIOUS, spiteful, hateful

EPHESIAN, boon companion

EPICURISM, 'conformity to the supposed principles of Epicurus' (OED), hence sensuality or gluttony

EPITHETON, descriptive term, orig. form of 'epithet'

EQUINOCTIAL, prob. means the celestial equator

EQUIPAGE, usually camp-followers' pickings or stolen goods, but 'in equipage':— step by step, therefore in instalments

ERCLES, Hercules

EREBUS, the classical hell

EREWHILE, a little while back

ERINGOES, candied roots of sea-holly, considered provocative

ERNE, grieve

ESCAPES OF WIT. OED explains as 'sallies' but Shakespeare seems to mean the little falsehoods a witty person allows himself in conversation

ETHIOPEAN, could refer to 'Ethiop's martial', a metallic compound known to the old chemists

ESTATE, (vb) bestow as an estate upon; (sb) class, rank; 'on all estates', on all sorts of person

ESTEEM, (i) value of a property; (ii) reputation of a man

ET BONUM QUO ANTIQUIUS EO MELIUS, the more ancient a good thing is the better

EVEN, (adj.) plain, easy, impartial; (vb) accomplish, carry out; tally, balance

EVENTS ('to his events'), to the issue of his affair

EVERLASTING, 'material used in 16th and 17th cent. for the dress of sergeants and catchpoles, app. identical with durance' (OED)

EVITATE, avoid

EXAMINE, test, question closely

EXCEPT, (i) find fault with; (ii) leave out of account

EXCREMENT, any outgrowth of the body, e.g. hair

EXERCISE, (i) religious observance, sermon; (ii) (in pl.) athletic field sports, military exercises

EXHALE, draw forth

EXHIBITION, maintenance allowance

EXORCIST, strictly one who expels spirits, but commonly used at the time as one who conjures or summons up spirits

EXPEDIENT, expeditious, prompt

EXPLICATION, explanation

EXPRESSURE, expression

EXTEMPORAL, extempore, without thought or trouble

EXTENT, seizure of lands in execution of a writ, sequestration

EXTORT, torture

EXTRACT, distil, extract quintessence

EXTREME, hyperbole

EYAS-MUSKET, young male sparrow-hawk; the musket was the smallest of the breed but a good hawk

EYE, spot of colour; 'be in eye', be within range

EYE-GLASS, the crystalline lens of the eye

EYNE, old plural of 'eyes'

FABLE, falsehood

FACE, (i) trim with braid or other material; (ii) bully; 'face it with a card of two', put a bold face on it

FACILITY, fluency

FACING, (i) trimming; (ii) browbeating

FACINOROUS, infamous, abominably wicked

FACT, crime

FACTION, dissension, factious quarrel

FACTOR, commercial agent

FADGE, (i) fit, be suitable; (ii) turn out, succeed

FADING, 'the refrain of a popular song of indecent character' (OED)

FAIR, fine; 'fair-faced', a specious deceiver; 'Fair fall!', good luck to!

FAIRING, lit. a present bought at a fair, hence any complimentary gift

FAITOR, rogue

FALCHION, single-edged sword

FALCON, female hawk

FALL, (sb) decline, decadence; (vb) let fall

FALLOW, brownish-yellow

FALSE GALLOP, a canter

FALSELY, treacherously

FALSING, deceiving, defrauding

FAMILIAR, (i) familiar spirit; (ii) intimate friend

FANATICAL, frantic, extravagant

FANCY, (sb) (i) love, affectation; (ii) imagination, fantasy; (iii) inclination, baseless supposition; (vb) fall in love

FANCY-MONGER, one who deals in love

FANE, temple

FANG, (sb) grip; (vb) seize

FANTASY, extravagant fancy, imagination

FARBOROUGH, mispronunciation of 'Tharborough', third borough, a petty constable

FARCE (vb), stuff, cram full, metaphorically pad out with pompous phrases

FARDEL, bundle

FARM (vb), lease the right of taxing to the highest bidder for a fixed cash payment

FARRE, old comparative of 'fair'

FARTHINGALE, hooped skirt, extending behind but not in front of the body

FASHIONS, the farcy, or farcin, a horse disease resembling glanders

FAST AND LOOSE, old cheating game, esp. with gypsies

FAST MY WIFE, 'handfasting' or betrothal, which was considered valid without religious ceremony

FAT, (i) gross, nauseating; (ii) slow-witted, dull

FATED, fateful, controlling man's destiny

FATHER (vb), (i) beget; (ii) act like a father;

FAULT, check caused by failure of scent

FAUSTE, PRECOR, etc., 'I pray thee, Faustus ...', opening words of Mantuan's first eclogue

FAVOUR (sb), (i) leave, leniency; (ii) face, countenance; (iii) lit. good will, so something given or worn as mark of affection or goodwill

FEAR, (sb) doubt; (vb) frighten, be afraid of

FEATFULLY, gracefully

FEATURE, limb, shape, part of the body

FEDARY, accomplice, confederate

FEE'D, employed

FEEDER, shepherd, servant

FEEDING, lit. feeding ground for sheep, hence landed property

FEEL (his meaning), perceive, sense

FEELINGLY, to the purpose, exactly

FEE-SIMPLE, in absolute possession

FEEZE, lit. frighten off, hence to flog. Pot-house term often meaning 'settle the hash of'

FELL, (adj.) angry, cruel; (sb) hide of an animal with wool or hair

FENCING TERMS. Distance: regulation interval between fencers; foin, veney, stoccado (stock) and punto: different kinds of hit or thrust; reverse; punto reverso, or back-handed thrust; montant, or montanto: upright blow

FESTINATELY, quickly

FETCH IN, take in, cheat

FETCH OFF, do for, kill

FIA, mispronunciation of 'via' *q.v.*

FICO, Italian for fig

FIELD, (i) 'surface of an escutcheon' (OED); (ii) field of battle, battle

FIERCE, ardent, excessive

FIGHTS, canvas screens to conceal men on shipboard before going into action

FIGURES, (i) astrological figures; (ii) waxen figures for purposes of enchantment; (iii) phantasms

FILE, lit. 'row of persons' used by Shakespeare for any collection of individuals. (i) roll, list; (ii) rank, line of soldiers; (iii) file for letters

FILED, polished

FILL-HORSE, cart-horse; the 'fills' were the shafts

FIND, (i) find out; (ii) unmask

FINE, (adj.) subtle; (vb) (i) bring to an end; (ii) punish

FINE AND RECOVERY, a legal procedure by which entailed property might be converted into fee-simple

FINGER, play upon a stringed instrument

FIRE-DRAKE, man with a fiery nose

FIRE-NEW, brand new

FIREWORK, pyrotechnical display, very popular at this time

FIRST AND SECOND CAUSE, technical excuses to escape a duel

FISH-WHOLE, thoroughly sound and healthy

FISNAMY, old form of 'physiognomy', face

FISTULA, long sinuous pipe-like ulcer with a narrow orifice

FIT, (adj.) apt, to the point; (vb) supply

FITCHEW, polecat

FIVES, vives, or avives, a swelling of the parotid glands in horses

FIXTURE, poise, tread

FIXURE, stability

FLAMEN, ancient Roman priest, devoted to the service of a particular god

FLAP-DRAGON, a burning raisin or plum floating alight in liquor and swallowed by topers

FLASK, a soldier's powderhorn

FLAT-LONG, with the flat of the sword

FLATNESS, completeness

FLATTER UP, pamper, coddle

FLATTERY, charm, palliation

FLAUNTS, ostentatious finery

FLAW, (i) sudden squall of wind; (ii) flakes or sparks of fire

FLAX-WENCH, female flax worker, type of coarse woman

FLEDGE, obs. form of 'fledged'

FLEER, grin

FLEET, (sbs) prison of the Star Chamber and Chancery Courts; (vb) while away the time

FLESH, (i) sate, gratify; (ii) inure to bloodshed

FLEWS, the large chops of a deep-mouthed hound

FLIGHT, (i) carrying power; (ii) special light arrows for long distance target-shooting

FLORENTIUS, Sir Florent, character in Gower's *Confessio Amantis*

FLOTE, fleet, also interpreted as 'the sea'

FLOURISH, varnish, embellishment

FLOUT, jeer, mock

FLOW, melt, stream down

FLOWER-DE-LUCE, fleur de lys, iris

FLUX, (i) continuous stream; (ii) discharge from the body

FLYING AT THE BROOK, hawking for water-fowl

FOH, exclamation of disgust

FOIN, fencing term

FOISON, plenty

FOLLOW, attend upon, wait

FOND, eager, glad, foolish

FOOL, Shakespeare often uses 'fool' as a term of endearment

FOOTBOY, boy attendant

FOOTCLOTH, richly ornamented covering for a horse

FOOTING, (i) foothold; (ii) establishment

FOOTMAN, foot soldier

FOPPERY, dupery, deceit, folly

FOR THE LORD'S SAKE, the cry of prisoners, through the grate, beseeching passers-by to place alms or food in the basket hung outside the window, esp. associated with Ludgate gaol

FORCE, (i) enforce; (ii) attach importance to

FORCED, far-fetched, strained

FORDONE, tired out

FORE-PAST, already passed, previous

FORFEITS IN A BARBER'S SHOP, teeth, which after extraction were hung up on a lute string in the barber's shops of the day. Barbers were also dentists

FORFEITURE, penalty for non-payment on required date

FORGERY, invention (not in a bad sense)

FORKED HEADS. Arrows were of two sorts, one with the points looking backwards and called the broad-headed or swallow-tail, the other with the points stretching forward and called the fork-headed or barbed

FORM, (i) order, orderly performance; (ii) excellence, proficiency

FORMAL, (i) normal, sane; (ii) punctilious, ceremonious

FORSAKE, refuse, abandon

FORTED, fortified

FORTHRIGHTS AND MEANDERS, paths straight and winding

FORTUNA DE LA GUERRA, the fortune of war

FOUL, (i) ugly, unpleasant; (ii) dirty; (iii) evil, vile

FOUNDERED, gone lame

FRAME, the action of framing, creation

FRAMPOLD, crusty, disagreeable

FRANCISCO, a Frenchman

FRANK, liberal, generous, free

FRANKLIN, yeoman

FRAUGHT, FRAUGHTAGE, cargo

FREE, (i) untainted by disease, free from care; (ii) unattached to a lover; (iii) generous; (iv) innocent; (v) gracious, willing

FREESTONE-COLOURED, with the dirty white or grey colour of limestone

FRENCH CROWN, (i) the 'écu', a French gold coin; (ii) the baldness caused by the 'French disease', i.e. syphilis

FRESH, hungry or thirsty

FRESHES, FRESHETS, streams of fresh water

FRET, (i) chequer; (ii) wear, fray; (iii) of merchandise, to deteriorate through moth, decay, etc.

FRETS, rings of gut or bars of wood to regulate the fingering on a lute

FRIEND, (i) sweetheart; (ii) relative, ancestor

FRIENDSHIP, favour, friendly aid

FRIEZE, a coarse cloth with a nap

FRIPPERY, old clothes shop

FRONT, (i) forehead; (ii) opening period

FROTH AND LIME, give short measure by frothing the ale too much, and mitigating the sourness of ale or wine by doctoring with lime

FRUSH, smash, batter

FULSOME, rank

FUME, 'noxious vapour supposed formerly to rise to the brain from the stomach' chiefly as the result of intoxication (OED)

FURNISH, equip

FURNITURE, outfit, trappings

FURRED GOWN. Most contemporary descriptions of usurers refer to 'fox fur' and 'budge' (lambskin)

FURRED PACK, bundle, borne on pedlar's back and covered with skin with hair outward

FUSTIAN, coarse cloth of cotton or flax, hence worthless, rubbishy

GABERDINE, cloak, long coat, worn loose or girdled, with long sleeves

GAGE, pledge, bind with formal promise

GALEN, Claudius Galenus (A.D. 131–?200), celebrated Greek physician whose medical writings remained authoritative in Europe for more than a thousand years

GALL, (i) a raw or sore place; (ii) bile, bitterness of spirit

GALLIA, GALLIAN, France, French

GALLIARD, quick, lively dance in triple time

GALLIASS, heavy, low-built vessel, larger than a galley

GALLIMAUFRY, medley, promiscuity

GALLOWAY, nag, small Scottish horse

GALLOWGLASS, heavy-armed Irish foot-soldier

GALLOWS, gallows-bird, one fit for hanging

GAMESTER, (i) athlete, gambler, adventurer; (ii) merry frolicsome person; (iii) lewd person, male or female

GAMUT, the musical scale or its lowest note

GAPING PIG, pig's head, mouth open, prepared for the table

GARBOIL, disturbance, brawl

GARGANTUA, Rabelais' voracious giant, with a mouth so large he swallowed five pilgrims with their staves in a salad

GARNISH, outfit, garment

GARTER, Garter King at Arms, the chief herald

GASKINS, short for galligaskins, wide hose

GAUD, toy, trinket

GAUDY, festive

GEAR, (i) dress; (ii) purpose, business

GELDED, mutilated, depreciated in value (of landed property)

GEMINY, pair

GENERALLY, completely

GENERATION, offspring

GENEROUS, noble, highborn

GENIUS, tutelary spirit, guardian spirit

GENTILITY, politeness, good manners

GENTLE, lit. well-born, hence gracious, kind

GEORGE, jewel, on which is a figure of St George, pendant to a collar, which is part of the insignia of the Garter

GERMAN, closely akin

GERMAN CLOCK, 'one of elaborate construction, often containing automatic figures of persons or animals' (OED)

GEST, the stage of a royal progress or journey, hence the time allotted for such a stage or halt

GESTURE, bearing, manner

GIB, cat

GIDDILY, lightly, carelessly

GIG, a whipping top

GIGLOTS, a lewd woman

GILDED, flushed, made drunken

GILLYVOR, clove-scented pink

GILT, 'a gilt nutmeg', i.e. 'endored' or glazed with the yoke of an egg, used for spicing ale or wine, a common lover's gift at that time

GIMMALED, 'consisting of two similar parts hinged together' (OED)

GIMMOR, joint or hinge in clockwork

GING, old form of 'gang'

GIRD, biting remark

GIRDLE (turn his), so as to bring his dagger, generally worn behind the right hip, round to his right hand

GIVE, consider, set down as

GIVE AIM, act as direction giver, q.v.

GIVE HORNS, make a husband a cuckold

GLANCE, cast reflection on, allude to

GLANDERS, a contagious horse disease

GLASS, hourglass

GLEAN, glean corn, cut off stragglers in battle

GLIB, geld, castrate

GLIMPSE, flash, transient brightness

GLOZE, (sb) pretence, disguise; (vb) make glosses, comment

GNAT, an insignificant creature that flutters about a light

GO ABOUT TO, intend to

GO TO!, Come! Come!

GO TO THE WORLD, get married

GO UNDER, go under the name of, appear to be

GOD BUY YOU, the Elizabethan half-way house between 'God be with you' and the modern 'good-bye'

GOD-DIG-YOU-DEN, God give you good even

GOD 'ILD YOU, God yield you (when 'yield':—reward, repay)

GOD'S A GOOD MAN, proverb, 'the world is as God made it, and all is for the best'

GOD'S BLESSING ON YOUR BEARD!, may you have sense more fitting a grey beard!

GOGS-WOUNS, by God's wounds, a common oath

GOLDEN LETTER, v. dominical

GOLGOTHA, graveyard, charnel-house

GOOD, well to do

GOOD DEED, indeed, in sooth

GOOD EVEN AND TWENTY, good day and plenty of them, even being any time after noon

GOOD-DEN, God give you good even

GOOD-JER (or 'Good-year'), not explained, possibly 'What the good-year':—'What the devil'

GOOD WORD, kindness

GOODLY, gracious, benign

GOOSE, tailor's smoothing iron

GOOSE OF WINCHESTER, one affected by VD, known as Winchester goose. The Southwark stews were formerly under the control of the Bishop of Winchester

GORDIAN KNOT, tied by Gordian, king of Phrygia, cut by Alexander the Great

GORDOBUC, mythical British king, hero of Sackville and Norton's *Gordobuc*

GOSLING, greenhorn, inexperienced person

GOSSIP, lit. sponsor to a child, so friend (esp. female) invited to attend a birth or act as god-parent, hence 'talkative person'

GOTTEN IN DRINK, cowards were credited with this origin

GOT-'UDGE-ME, God judge me

GOURD AND FULLAM, species of false dice

GOVERN, GOVERNMENT, 'regulate an instrument by means of its stops'

GRACE, (i) sense of duty; (ii) grace of God, i.e. redemption; (iii) favour; (iv) that which wins favour, reputation; (v) that which adorns

GRAFF, archaic variant of graft

GRAIN (in grain), indelible, ineradicable, short for 'dyed in grain':—fast dyed

GRAINED, furrowed, lined

GRANGE, lonely country house

GRASS (long for grass), long for freedom

GRATED, worried, pestered

GRAVEL, story

GRAVEL-BLIND, a jocular link between 'sand-blind' (partially blind) and 'stone-blind'

GRAVELLED, perplexed, non-plussed

GRAYMALKIN, or Grimalkin (lit. little grey Mall or Mary), common name for a cat

GREASILY, indecently, smuttily

GREAT CHAMBER, large reception room, a new feature in wealthy houses of the time

GREEK (sb) (i) cunning or wily person, cheat, sharper; (ii) a merry fellow, buffoon

GREEN GOOSE, a young goose, lit. one hatched in the autumn, green-fed in spring and sold in May

GREEN SICKNESS, a type of anaemia affecting young women

GREEN-SLEEVES (the tune of), an amorous ballad tune, associated somehow with harlotry

GRIFFIN, fabulous monster with the head of an eagle and body of a lion

GRISE, a step

GRISLY, terrible to behold

GRIZZLE, a sprinkling of grey hairs

GROAT, fourpenny piece

GROSS, obvious, palpable; 'by gross', wholesale

GROUND, basis, fundamental principle; lowest note

GROUNDLING, spectator who paid a penny to stand on the floor of the playhouse, hence an uncritical or unrefined auditor

GROW, accrue

GROW TO A POINT, come to the point

GROW UPON, (i) increase, grow up, so as to become more troublesome; (ii) take liberties with, presume upon

GUARDS, (i) ornamental borders, trimming or facings; (ii) two stars of Lesser Bear constellation pointing to Pole Star

GUIDON, standard, used by generals or kings

GUILED, treacherous, endowed with guile

GULES, heraldic name for red

GULL, trick

GUNSTONE, cannon ball

GURNET, gurnard, marine fish

GUST, taste, catch the flavour of

GUY OF WARWICK, famed in romance as the slayer of the Danish giant, Colbrand

HA?, eh?

HACK, appears to mean 'take to the road as a highwayman', or, of a female, 'to become a harlot', but NED gives 'to ride on the road, as distinguished from cross-country or military riding'

HACKNEY, (i) a horse kept for hire; (ii) a prostitute

HADE LAND, unploughed strip between two portions of field used as boundary or means of access

HAGGARD, hawk which has moulted at least once before being caught and is therefore much more difficult to train; a wild hawk

HALBERD, 15th and 16th cent. weapon, combination of spear and battleaxe

HALYCON, bird supposed by the ancients to charm the waves to a calm, while breeding in a nest floating on the sea about the time of the winter solstice; 'halcyon days' were fourteen days of calm at this season

HALF ('your half'), your wife

HALF-BLOODED, of good family by virtue of one parent only

HALF-CAN, larger than the 'pot', which it had put out of fashion among topers

HALF-CHECKED BIT, one with the bridle attached half way up the cheek, giving inadequate leverage

HALF-CHEEK, profile

HALFPENNY PURSE, minuted purse, halfpennies being tiny silver coins at that time

HAMMER OF (vb), deliberate earnestly, turn over in one's mind

HAND (vb), deal with, handle

HAND (at any), in any case

HAND-FAST, under arrest

HANDS (at two), at close quarters in conflict

HANDS (man of one's hands), man of vigour and courage

HANDY-DANDY, child's game where an object is passed from hand to hand behind one's back whilst another guesses as to which hand it is in

HANGMAN, fit for the hangman, rascal

HANNIBAL, blunder, common at the time, for 'cannibal'

HAPPILY, haply

HAPPY MAN BE HIS DOLE, prov.:—may his dole (i.e. lot) be that of a happy man

HARBINGER, orig. one who provides or procures lodgings, hence forerunner, esp. of royal household

HARD, with an uneasy pace

HARD-FAVOURED, ugly

HAREBELL, wild hyacinth

HARE-FINDER, one 'whose business is to find or espy a hare in form' before coursing (NED), hence a very mild sort of huntsman

HARLOT, orig. vagabond, rascal (of either sex), generally used in reference to fornication; (adj.), lewd

HATCH (sit down at the), keep silence

HATCHES, movable planks forming a deck

HAUD CREDO, Lat. I do not believe it

HAUNTED, frequented

HAUTBOY, oboe

HAVE WITH YOU!, Here's for you!

HAVE WITH YOU, let's go together

HAVING, property, possession

HAVIOUR, appearance

HAVOC, merciless slaughter; 'cry havoc':—cry 'no quarter'

HAWK, (i) mattock or pick-axe; (ii) falcon

HAWK FOR THE BUSH, short-winged hawk for quarry such as pheasant, rabbit, etc. in woodland country

HAWKING, keen as a hawk's

HAY, 'country dance having a winding or serpentine motion, or being of the nature of a reel' (OED)

HEADBOROUGH, 'parish officer identical in function with petty constable' (NED)

HEADED, come to a head, like a boil

HEADSTALL, part of the bridle which surrounds the horse's head

HEAR, do you hear?, listen

HEARKEN, lie in wait

HEARSED, coffined

HEART-BURNED, suffering from heart-burn

HEART OF ELDER, of pith, as contrasted with 'heart of oak'

HEAVENS (for the), in heaven's name

HEAVY, stupid with grief

HEBONA, an imaginary poison, associated with henbane

HIC ET UBIQUE, here and everywhere

HECATE (the triple), the goddess was Diana on earth, Phoebe in the heavens and Hecate in the underworld, guardian of all witches

HECTOR, Trojan hero of the Iliad, regarded by Elizabethans as the type of blustering braggart

HECUBA, Hector's mother, wife of Priam, king of Troy

HEDGE-PRIEST, unlearned priest in minor orders

HEED, that which one heeds or attends to

HEEL (on the), at the end

HEELS ('light o' love with your heels'), light-heeled, i.e. unchaste, loose

HEFT, heaving, retching

HELEN, (i) in classical mythology the most beautiful woman of her time, wife of Menelaus, carried off to Troy by Paris, whence arose the Trojan wars; (ii) St Helena, mother of Constantine, reputed to have discovered the true cross buried on Calvary, led there by a vision

HELL, a debtors' prison; the name was originally given to part of the law courts at Westminster, used as a prison for the King's debtors

HELLESPONT, the Dardanelles

HELP, cure

HEMPEN HOME-SPUN, 'home-spun cloth made of hemp, hence one clad in such cloth, one of rustic or coarse manners' (OED)

HEMPSEED, tiny boy destined for the gallows

HEN, a chicken-hearted person

HENCHMAN, 'a squire or page to a prince or great man, who walked or rode beside him' (OED)

HENT, take possession of

HERALDRY, rank, precedence

HERB OF GRACE, or herb-grace, the old name for rue

HERCULES, Lat. name for Greek mythological hero Heracles, famed for supernormal strength

HERMES, Mercury, who invented the pipe, and with it lulled to sleep Argus of the hundred eyes

HERO, in classical mythology, a priestess of Aphrodite at Sestos on the European side of the Hellespont, loved by Leander, who swam to her at night from Abydos on the opposite shore; when he was drowned she threw herself into the waters

HEROD OF JEWRY, a type of outrageous audacity

HEY-HO, 'utterance apparently of nautical origin and marking the rhythm of movement in heaving and hauling; often used in the burdens of songs, with various emotional expression according to the intonation' (NED)

HICK AND HACK, copulate

HID-FOX, the child who hides in the Elizabethan game of hide-and-seek

HIGH AND LOW, false dice, loaded so as to cast high and low numbers at will

HIGH-CROSS, the cross in the centre of the town

HIGH-DAY, old form of 'hey-day', holiday

HIGH-PROOF, capable of enduring the severest tests

HIGH STEWARD, LORD, official in charge of coronation ceremony or presiding at a peer's trial

HIGH-STOMACHED, haughty

HIGHT, is called

HILDING, jade, baggage, good-for-nothing

HIND, (i) stag; (ii) peasant; (iii) farm servant

HINT, occasion

HIP (to have upon), a wrestling metaphor

HIPPED, lame in the hip

HIREN, Irene, mistress of Sultan Mahomet II, and later beheaded by him

HOB, NOB, variant of 'hab, nab':—'have it, have it not', i.e. come what may

HOBBY-HORSE, (i) figure in a morris dance 'formed by a man inside a frame with the head and tail of a horse, and with trappings reaching to the ground and hiding the actor, who prance and cavorted about' (Sh. Eng.) 'The hobby-horse is forgot' is generally supposed to be a quotation from some ballad satirizing Puritan opposition to morris-dancing; (ii) a prostitute

HOBOY, oboe

HOBGOBLIN, 'Hob' was a variant of Robert or Robin, hence 'Hobgoblin' was equivalent to Robin Goodfellow

HODGE-PUDDING, a large sausage of boar's or hog's meat, still a dainty in the west of England

HOLD, OR CUT BOWSTRINGS, archer's expression, not yet satisfactorily explained; possibly 'come rain, hail or shine' or 'keep your promises or give up the play'

HOLD IT UP, HOLD OUT, keep it up, persist

HOLDING, consistency, coherence

HOLE MADE IN ONE'S COAT, proverbial, hole in one's reputation; 'find a hole', catch one out

HOLIDAME (by my), by my Holy Dame, i.e. Our Lady

HOLLAND, fine linen fabric, first made in Holland

HOLLOW ('thy bones are hollow'), a supposed result of venereal disease

HOLY BREAD, 'the (ordinary unleavened) bread blessed after the Eucharist, and distributed to those who had not communicated' (NED)

HOLY-ROOD DAY, 14th September

HOLY-THISTLE, v. Carduus Benedictus

HOME (adv.), completely, effectively, back again to its right place

HOMELY, rude, uncomely

HONEST, chaste

HONEYDEW, 'sweet sticky substance formed on stems of leaves and plants' (OED)

HONEY-STALKS, stalks of clover flowers

HONORIFICABILITUDINITATIBUS, a jest of the medieval schools, supposed to be the longest word known; the nominative is a real word meaning 'the state of being loaded with honours'

HOODMAN, the blind man in 'hoodman-blind' or 'blind-man's-buff'

HOODWINK, cover up, a hawking term

HOOKING, 'hookers' were a species of rogue who 'carried with them a staff of five or six feet long, in which ... a little hole ... an iron hook, and with the same they will pluck ... quickly anything' through windows left open at night

HOOP, shout with astonishment

HORN-BOOK, a spelling primer, 'framed in wood, and covered with a thin plate of transparent horn'

HORN-MAD, mad with rage like a bull

HORNPIPE, a wind instrument, said to have been so called from bell and mouthpiece being made of horn

HORSE (vb), set one thing upon another, suggesting a jogging motion, and perhaps also the sense of 'covering' (the mare by the stallion)

HOST (vb), lodge, put up

HOSTILIUS, legendary third king of Rome

HOT BACKS, HOT-BACKED, lustful

HOT-HOUSE, a bathing house with hot baths

HOUSE-KEEPING, hospitality

HOVEL-POST, post used in the making of a stack of corn

HOW?, Well, what about it?

HOW NOW, exclamation of surprise, greeting, or simulated anger

HOX, hamstring

HOY, small vessel for short coastal jorneys

HULL (vb), drift with sails furled

HUMBLE, kind, civil

HUMILITY, humanity

HUMOROUS, moody, fanciful

HUMOUR, (sb) disposition, inclination, caprice; (vb) adapt oneself

HUNDRED MERRY TALES, a coarse jest book published in 1526

HUNGARIAN, in reference to discarded and cashiered soldiers from Hungary

HUNTER, dog for hunting

HURLY, tumult

HURRICANO, waterspout

HURTLING, noise of an encounter, collision or battle

HUSBAND, (sb) housekeeper; (vb) manage economically

HUSBANDRY, administration of the household

HUSHT, variant of 'hush', 'whist', etc., not a word

HYBLA, town in Sicily, famous for its honey

HYDRA, mythical nine-headed beast, slain by Hercules

HYEN, hyena

HYMENAEUS, Hymen, god of marriage, hence the wedding ceremony

HYPERION, god of the sun, the sun

HYRCANIA, land south of Caspian Sea, proverbial for wildness and savagery; 'Hyrcanian beast', the tiger

HYSSOP, aromatic herb, formerly much used in medicine

ICARUS, Daedalus made wings for himself and his son, Icarus, to fly from the labyrinth of Crete. He escaped, but Icarus flew too high, the sun melted the wax in his wings and he fell to the sea

IDEA, mental image

IDES, 13th or 15th day of the month (15th in March) in the Roman calendar

IDLE, foolish, cracked, delirious

I'FECKS, in faith

IGNOMY, old form of 'ignominy'

ILL, (i) savage, (ii) miserable

ILL-FAVOUREDLY, in an ugly fashion

ILLUSTRATE, illustrious

IMAGE, representative

IMBRUE, lit. 'stain with blood', hence pierce so as to cause blood

IMITARI, Lat. to copy

IMMEDIATELY, exactly, precisely

IMMODEST, excessive, immoderate

IMP, (sb) lit. sapling, scion (without any connection with evil), hence, youngster; (vb) falconry term, to engraft feathers in the wing of a bird to restore or improve flight, hence, enlarge

IMPARTIAL, taking no part, indifferent

IMPATIENT, angry

IMPAWN, give as a hostage

IMPEACH, (sb) accusation, charge; (vb) discredit, cast imputation upon, call in question

IMPETTICOAT (vb), pocket, in reference to fool's long coat

IMPORTANCE, import

IMPORTANT, urgent, importunate, not to be withstood

IMPOSE, IMPOSITION, injunction

IMPOSTUME, abscess

IMPRESE, for It. 'impresa', heraldic device imposed on a shield, with an attached motto

IMPRESSURE, impression

IMPUGN, dispute validity of a statement or line of action

IN, involved

IN CAPITE, held directly from the Crown

INCARNADINE, lit. make the colour of flesh, turn blood-red

INCENSE, instigate

INCIDENCY, incident

INCISION, (i) blood-letting; (ii) engrafting

INCLINING, partiality, favouritism

INCONSIDERATE, thoughtless, brainless

INCONTINENT, (i) straightway; (ii) unchaste

INCONY, delicious, rare, pretty

INDIFFERENT, (adj.) (i) impartial; (ii) ordinary, usual, correct; (adv.) tolerably, fairly

INCREASE, crops, vegetable products

INDIRECT, wrong, unjust

INDUCEMENT, instigation, influence

INFAMONIZE, defame

INFLUENCE, i.e. of a star in the astrological sense

INFORMAL, foolish, crazy

INFUSED WITH, inspired with

INGENEROUS, dastardly

INHERIT, possess, own

INHIBITED, forbidden

INJURIOUS, insulting

INKLE, a kind of linen tape

INLAND, belonging to the districts near the capital as opposed to the remote wilder parts

INLY, intimate, heartfelt

INN (vb), gather in grain, Harvest

INNOCENT, imbecile

INQUISITIVE, seeking to know or to find

INSANIA, madness

INSCULPED, engraved

INSINUATE, ingratiate oneself with, wheedle, insert

INSISTURE, steady continuance

INSTALMENT, seat in which a Knight of the Garter was installed

INSTANCE, illustration, example, argument

INSULT, triumph in an insolent fashion

INTEEMABLE, incapable of being emptied, inexhaustible

INTELLIGENCING, playing the spy

INTELLIGISNE, DOMINE?, do you understand, sir?

INTEND, pretend, offer

INTENDMENT, intention, project

INTENT, destination

INTER'GATORY, legal expression:—a question formally put or to be put to an accused person or witness

INTERIM, something done during an interval, respite

INTERLUDE, short play, generally for performance in a great banqueting hall

INTERMISSION, rest during work

INTERPRET, expound the meaning of a puppet show

INTIMATION, generally glossed as 'suggestion', but probably means 'interruption'

INTOLERABLE, excessive

INVENTION, artistic or literary faculty

INVITIS NUBIBUS, despite the clouds

INWARD, secret, privy, intimate

IRIS, goddess who appeared as the rainbow, the rainbow

IRK, distress, pain

ISIS, Egyptian goddess representing the moon and the female productive forces of nature

ITHACA, Aegean island, home of Ulysses

IWIS, certainly

JACK, (i) knave; (ii) serving man; (iii) leather drinking vessel; (iv) Jack o' Lantern or Will o' the Wisp

JACK-A-LENT, dressed-up puppet for boys to throw at in Lent

JACK-AN-APES, lit. monkey, but also 'satyr', a kind of ape

JADE, (sb) vicious, or ill-conditioned mare or woman; (vb) fool, play tricks with

JANGLING, altercation, wrangling

JANUS, Roman god with two faces

JAR, tick of the clock

JAYS, symbolical of loose women

JEALOUSY, suspicion, anxiety

JENNET, small Spanish horse

JEPHTHAH, a Judge of Israel who sacrificed his daughter in fulfilment of a foolish vow

JERKS OF INVENTION, sallies of wit

JERUSALEM CHAMBER, at West front of Westminster Abbey, now used as Chapter House

JESSES, narrow strips of soft leather, silk or other material, fastened to the legs of a trained hawk and connected to the falconer's wrist

JEST, masque, pageant

JET, strut, like a turkey

JEW, probably a playful diminutive of 'juvenal'

JEW'S EYE, proverbial expression for something valued lightly

JIG, (sb) (i) rapid lively dance time; (ii) farce or entertainment of singing and dancing performed after a play

JILL, (i) servant maid; (ii) gill, metal drinking vessel holding ¼ pint

JOAN, a generic term for a country witch

JOCKEY, familiar form of Jack, John

JOINED STOOL, JOINT-STOOL, wooden stool, fitted by a joiner as opposed to one of cruder make

JOLLITY, 'pleasure, enjoyment, esp. sexual' (OED)

JOLLY, arrogant, overbearing

JOWL (vb), to dash or knock (two heads) together

JUGGLER, deceiver, trickster

JUMP, agree, coincide, tally

JUNO, wife of Jupiter, queen of the gods

JUST, just so, exactly so, cf. 'quite' today

JUSTIFY, prove, confirm

JUVENAL, a young fellow, from 'juvenile'

KECKSY, hemlock or cow parsnip

KEECH, lump of animal fat

KEEL, to cool a hot or boiling liquid by adding something cold

KEEP, inhabit, keep to

KEEPER, guardian angel

KENDAL GREEN, coarse green cloth worn only by labourers

KENNEL, gutter, channel

KERN, Irish foot soldier

KERSEY, stout coarse English cloth

KIBE, ulcerated chilblain on the heel

KICKSHAW, (Fr. quelquechose), orig. a fancy dish in cookery, a 'something French', hence a trifle, a gewgaw

KICKY-WICKY, jocular or ludicrous term for a wife, which suggests a humerous formation after the pattern of 'kicksy-whinsy', a whim or erratic fancy

KILL, subdue

KILL-HOLE, or kiln-hole, a small building or hovel containing a surface for drying grain, etc. or making malt

KILL THE HEART, utterly discourage

KIND, (sb) (i) sex; (ii) nature, character; (adj.) natural

KINDLY (adj. and adv.), natural (as belonging to a father), fittingly, by all means

KINDLE, give birth to, esp. hares, rabbits

KINDNESS, natural instinct

KISSING-COMFITS, perfumed sugar-plums, used by women to sweeten the breath

KITCHENED, entertained in the kitchen

KITE, falcon

KNACK, (i) sweetmeat, pastry; (ii) trifle, trinket; (iii) deceitful or crafty contrivance

KNAP, bite with a crackling sound

KNOT, band, company

KNOT-GRASS, well known weed, 'polygonum aviculare', an infusion of which was supposed to stunt the growth

KNOWINGLY, with knowledge to justify one's opinion

LABEL, lit. to add to a document a 'label' or strip of parchment with supplementary matter, hence to add a codicil

LACEDAEMON, Sparta

LACED-MUTTON, cant term for a courtesan; 'laced' possibly refers to a slashed bodice, with a pun on 'lace':—to make incisions in the breast of a bird before cooking

LADY-SMOCK, generally interpreted as cuckoo-flower, which however, is pale lilac, not 'silver-white'; we suggest 'stitchwort', the whitest of all spring flowers

LADY WALLED ABOUT WITH DIAMONDS, piece of jewellery much affected at the time, in the form of brooch or pendant; the figure might be an allegorical nude or a portrait

LA FIN COURONNE LES OEUVRES, the end crowns the works

LAM-DAMN, thrash to death

LAMPASS, a disease in which the roof of the horse's mouth swells and prevents mastication

LAND-SERVICE, (i) military service; (ii) a meal

LANDS (narrow), possibly the strips into which the fields were divided under the old agricultural system

LANTHORN, (i) lighthouse, or windowed turret on the roof of a hall; (ii) a lantern

LAPLAND SORCERERS, Lapps and Finns were said to have a reputation for sorcery

LAPSE, (sb) fall, ruin; (vb) apprehend, arrest

LAPWING, peewit, plover

LARGE, broad, loose, liberal, copious

LAROON, thief

LATCH, moisten

LATTEN, tin

LAUGHTER, a sitting of eggs

LAUND, glade

LAUS DEO, BONE, INTELLIGO, God be praised, my good friend, understand

LAVOLT, lavolta, 'a lively dance for two, consisting a good deal in high and active bounds' (OED)

LAY, exorcise or calm (a disturbed spirit)

LEAD APES IN HELL, the fate of old maids, since they could not lead children into heaven

LEADEN SWORD, imitation sword, stage property

LEAGUER, camp

LEASING, lying

LEAVE, oart with, lose

LEAVE OFF, give up as incurable

LEAVENED AND PREPARED CHOICE, 'a choice not hasty but considerate'

LECTURE, lesson

LEDA'S DAUGHTER, Helen of Troy

LEER, (i) face, complexion; (ii) ogle

LEET, a court held by the Lord of the Manor

LEGE, DOMINE, Lat. read, sir

LEIGER, resident ambassador

LEMON STUCK WITH CLOVES, for spicing ale

LENTEN, meagre, feeble; 'Lenten pie', properly pie containing no meat, and so fit for consumption in Lent

L'ENVOY, short stanza at the end of a poem, often defining its points, e.g. as in the Sonnets

LET, permit to remain, leave behind

LET ME ALONE, rely on me to

LETHE, river of Hades; 'lethe'd', oblivious

LETTERS-PATENT, an open letter from a Sovereign conferring some right, privilege or title

LEVEL, LEVEL AT, aim, guess at

LEWD, vile, worthless

LIBBARD, properly a leopard, but 'libbard' and 'lion' were synonymous terms in respect of the royal coat of arms

LIBERAL, loose in talk, gross, too free

LIBERTY, unrestrained action, licence

LICENCE, liberty of action (not licentiousness)

LICHAS, servant of Hercules who unwittingly brought him the Nessus shirt

LICTOR, Roman functionary who walked before the magistrates carrying the *fasces*

LIE, lodge, sojourn

LIE BY, (i) dwell near; (ii) take a mistress

LIE DROWNING THE WASHING OF TEN TIDES, i.e. worse than the fate of captured pirates, who were fastened to the shore, near Wapping Old Stairs, at low water mark, until three tides has passed over them

LIEGER, resident ambassador

LIEU, 'in lieu of', as a payment for, in acknowledgement of

LIFE IS A SHUTTLE, *cf.* Job, vii, 6 'my days are swifter than a weaver's shuttle'

LIGHT, (i) wanton, loose; (ii) slightly built, active, nimble

LIGHT O' LOVE, the tune, but not the words, of this dance song has survived

LIKELY, comely

LIKENESS, seeming, hypocrisy

LIMBEC, alembic, distilling vessel

LIMBER, limp, flabby

LIMBO PATRUM, Lat. 'limbus patrum', the place between heaven and hell where the righteous who died before Christ waited

LIME, to catch with bird-lime (a glutinous substance smeared on twigs to take small birds)

LIMIT, allotted time, prescribed period

LINE, (i) delineate, sketch; (ii) line, as a dog a bitch; (iii) the equator

LING (old), salted ling, commonly eaten in Lent

LINK, torch, the material of burnt torches, used for blacking

LINSEY-WOOLSEY, lit. coarse material, part wool, part flax. Hence neither one thing or the other, a medley, nonsense

LINSTOCK, staff to hold the gunner's lighted match

LION THAT HOLDS HIS POLL-AXE, traditional representation of Alexander's arms

LIQUOR, grease, oil

LIST, LISTS, selvage of cloth, border-edge, hence limits, bounds

LITTLE (in), in miniature

LIVE (of a vessel in a storm), escape destruction, remain afloat

LIVELIHOOD, animation

LIVELY, lifelike

LIVER, formerly considered the seat of the passions

LIVERY, dress, distinctive garb worn by retainers of a great lord

LIVING (sb), property, landed estate

LOACH, small fresh water pike

LOB, clown, lout, lubber

LOCKRAM, loosely woven hempen fabric

LODE-STAR, the star which shows the 'lode' or way and upon which the sailor's gaze and hopes are fixed

LOFTY, sublime, (or possibly) haughty

LOGGATS, a game rather like ninepins

LONG OF, along of, owing to

LONG PURPLE, early purple orchis, *orchis mascula*

'LONGING, belonging

LONGLY, for a long while

LOOSE, (adj.) random, not serious; (sb) 'at his very loose':—at the very last moment; (vb) turn loose (for breeding)

LOOSE OF QUESTION (in the), in the freedom of conversation

LORD HAVE MERCY UPON US, slogan written on the door of a plague-ridden house

LORD'S TOKENS, marks or spots which appeared on the patient at the last stage of the plague

LOSE, orig.:—to ruin, hence to ruin in estimation

LOSS, perdition, destruction

LOUD, windy, stormy

LOUSY, contemptible, of no importance

LOVE, appraise, set a value on

LOVE-IN-IDLENESS, (i) the heartsease, the pansy; (ii) love without serious intention

LOVE-SPRINGS, 'springs', the first tender shoots of a plant or tree

LOVES (of all), a phrase of strong entreaty

LOWER CHAIR. 'Every house had formerly ... what was called a 'low chair', designed for the ease of sick people, and, occasionally, occupied by lazy ones' (Steevens)

LOW-SPIRITED, base

LOZEL, or losel, good-for-nothing

LUBBER, over-grown, loutish fellow

LUCE, (i) pike (fresh-water); (ii) cod, hake (salt-water)

LUCIFER, properly the Morning Star, then the Devil

LUCINA, name given to Juno (she who brings light) as presiding over childbirth

LUD'S TOWN, London, from Lud, legendary British king and Cymbeline's grandfather in legends

LUGGAGE, military baggage, camp followers' pickings

LUMPISH, low-spirited

LUNES, tantrums, fits of lunacy

LUPERCAL, the Lupercalia, ancient fertility festival in honour of Pan

LURCH, pilfer

LURE, leather frame, decked with feathers and garnished with pieces of meat, which the falconer carried in his hand

LUSTY, gay, bright

LUTE, stringed instrument associated with love and serenades

LUXURY, lust, lasciviousness

LYM, bloodhound

MACE, spice consisting of the dried outer covering of the nutmeg

MACULATION, stain of impurity

MADONNA, mistress, my lady

MAGGOT-PIE, magpie

MAGNIFICENT, vainglorious, arrogant

MAGNIFICO, Venetian grandee

MAID, the young of skate or other fish

MAIL, wallet, budget

MAIL UP (a hawk), wrap her up in a cloth so that she cannot stir or struggle

MAIN-COURSE, mainsail

MAINTAIN, defend

MAKE (the door), shut, close, bar

MAKE (up), piece together, make good

MAKING, build, make, personal appearance

MALAPERT, impudent

MALIGNANCY, baleful or virulent character. The term is both medical and astrological

MALKIN, untidy female esp. servant, slut

MALLECHO, from Sp. 'malhecho', misdeed, iniquity

MALMSEY, a strong sweet wine

MALT-HORSE, a clumsy kind of horse used by malsters, a heavy stupid person

MALT-WORM, drunkard, lit. malt-weevil

MOMMET, doll, puppet; orig. 'mawmet' (Mahomet)

MAMMOCK, tear into fragments

MAN (a hawk), to accustom the bird to the presence of man, to tame

MANAGE, control, wield, a short gallop at full speed in a riding school

MANAKAN, or manikin, an artist's lay figure

MANDRAKE, poisonous plant, fabled to shriek when uprooted

MANKIND, infuriated, mad

MANNER (taken with the), more properly 'taken with the mainour', i.e. in the act

MANNERS, (i) polite behaviour; (ii) the older sense of moral character

MANTLE, of liquids, to become covered with a coating or scum

MANTUAN, i.e. Battista Spagnuoli of Mantua (d. 1576), whose *Eclogues* became a school text-book throughout Europe

MANUAL SEAL, authorised warrant

MANU CITA, with swift hand

MAP, epitome, embodiment

MARCH-CHICK, precocious youngster

MARGENT, margin of a page, the commentary or illuminated border in such a margin

MARK, (i) two nobles or about 65p, a sum of money, not a coin; (ii) target, butt, anything at which aim is taken; (iii) 'God bless the mark', exclamatory phrase by way of apology for some horrible, disgusting or profane mention

MARKET (ended the), an allusion to the proverb 'three women and a goose make a market'

MARL, clay

MARRY, orig. the name of the Virgin Mary, then indeed, to be sure

MARRY TRAP, Dr Johnson interpreted it as 'an exclamation of insult, when a man was caught in his own stratagem'

MARS, Roman god of war

MARSHAL, officer in a palace or nobleman's house charged with the arrangement of ceremonies and presentation of guests

MARSHALSEA, debtors' prison in Southwark

MART, traffic

MARTLEMAS, referring to the slaughter of beasts, etc. on St Martin's Day (11th November) for salting and winter consumption

MARTLET, house-martin

MASQUING, stuff, cheap material fit only for masques or amateur theatricals

MATCH (sb), bargain

MATED, amazed, confounded

MATERIAL, (i) stocked with notions; (ii) gross, carnal

MATTER, topics for discussion or conversation

MAUGRE, in spite of

MAUND, woven basket with handles

MAZES (in the green) labyrinths marked out on the grass and kept fresh by the tread of boys' feet

MEACOCK, tame timid, milksop

MEALED, spotted stained, moled

MEAN, (adj.) moderate, mild; (sb) (i) tenor part; (ii) opportunity; (iii) sum of money; (vb) (i) moan, lament for the dead; (ii) lodge a formal complaint

MEASURE, a stately dance, moderation

MEASURABLE, meet, competent

MECHANICAL (sb), artisan, mechanic

MEDAL, metal disc, bearing a figure or inscription and used as a charm or trinket

MEDDLE WITH, mingle with, engage in conflict

MEDEA, v. Absyrtus

MEDLAR, eaten when decayed to a soft pulpy state

MEET, keep an appointment; 'be meet with', be quits with

MEHERCLE!, By Hercules!

MEINY, body of retainers

MEND, (i) make amends; (ii) improve, grow more perfect

MENELAUS, Helen's husband, brother of Agamemnon

MERCATANTE, It. merchant

MERCURY, in Latin mythology the messenger of the gods, whose feet were shod with winged sandals

MERE, complete, absolute; 'upon his mere request', solely because he asked me

MERELY, as a matter of fact, nothing but

MERIT, (i) payment for service done; (ii) (theol.) works

MEROPS' SON. Phaeton was the son of Phoebus and Clymene, wife of Merops

MESS, lit. a party of four seated at the same table and feeding from the same dish; dish

METE AT, aim at

METEOR, was any aerial phenomenon, e.g. the aurora borealis

METHEGLINS, Welsh mead, spiced with honey

METHOD, conduct

METTLE, courage, disposition, vital energy

MEW, cage up, a falconry term. Lit. mew was the cage where the hawk was kept during moulting or mewing

MEWL, mew like a cat

MIDDLE EARTH (man of), mortal

MIGHT, 'takes it in might, not merit', values it for the effort expended rather than the skill shown

MILL SIXPENCE, newly-introduced machine-made coin with hard edges to replace the crudely hammered coins

MILO, or Milon, famous athlete of Crotona of 6th cent. B.C., said to have carried a bull on his shoulders

MIMIC, buffoon, burlesque player, contemptuous term for actors in general

MINIME, by no means

MINIMUS, a creature of the smallest size

MINOS, mythical king of Crete, creator of the labyrinth

MINOTAUR, monster, half man, half bull, kept in the labyrinth of Minos

MINSTRELSY, domestic or court entertainers, not necessarily musicians

MI PERDONATO, pardon me

MISANTHROPOS, Gr. man-hater

MISCARRY, come to harm

MISCONSTER, misjudge

MISPRISION, (i) misapprehension; (ii) mistake of identity

MISPRIZE, despise, mistake, fail to appreciate

MISSGRAFFED, ill-grafted together, badly matched

MISSINGLY, with a sense of loss or distress

MISTAKEN, MISTOOK, taken to the wrong person, miscarried

MISUSE, abuse, revile, misrepresent

MO, MOE, more in number

MOCKED, (i) deceived; (ii) ridiculed

MODEL, the technical term for an architect's or a builder's plan

MODERN, commonplace, trite

MODESTY, self-restraint, moderation

MOIETY, share, portion; lit. half

MOME, blockhead, dolt

MOMENTANY, very common alternative to 'momentary' at this time

MONARCHO, a mad, but harmless Italian, suffering from megalomania, who haunted Elizabeth's court some time before 1580

MONGING, trafficking

MONMOUTH CAP, round, brimless, high-crowned hat worn by sailors and soldiers

MONTANT, v. fencing

MONTH'S MIND, a strong inclination (orig. a mass said a month after the death of a person)

MONUMENT, portent

MOONISH, changeable, fickle

MOONSHINE IN THE WATER, appearance without reality, foolishness

MOPING, bewildered

MORAL, secret meaning

MORALISE, interpret, expound, esp. moral sentiments

MORISCO, Morris dancer

MORRIS DANCE, rustic dance, sometimes associated with May or Whitsun games, in which Robin Hood and Maid Marian figured

MORRIS-PIKE, a formidable kind of pike, said to be of Moorish origin

MORTAL, (i) subject to death; (ii) mortally foolish

MORTAL-BREATHING, i.e. like a mortal, breathing (and yet like a saint)

MORTIFIED, dead to the pressures of the world, a theological expression

MORTIFYING, death–causing. Sighs and groans were supposed to drain the blood

MORT O' TH' DEER, hunting call at the death of the deer

MOSE IN THE CHINE, suffer from glanders

MOTH, mote

MOTION, (i) puppet-show; 'this sensible warm motion', the body, conceived as a puppet; 'a motion generative', a puppet of the masculine gender; (ii) 'we in your motion turn, and you may move us' refers to the motions of the heavenly spheres in the old astronomy, i.e. woman is a planet, set in the sphere, man; (iii) inward prompting or impulse, emotion

MOTLEY. There were two sorts of fool: the motley fool and the fool in the yellow petticoat, the former being the superior intellectually, the latter being the 'natural' or idiot

MOUNTANTO, montanto, v. fencing

MOUNTEBANK (vb), win, like a quack at a fair, by tricking simpletons

MOUNTED, set up in position

MOUSE, a playful term of endearment

MUCH UPON THIS, 'TIS,:—That's about the size of it

MULMUTIUS, king of Britain, hero of a lost play of 1599

MUMBUDGET, probably derived from some children's game

MUMMY, (i) a pulpy substance or mass; (ii) a common drug, orig. made from Egyptian mummies

MURDERING PIECE, small cannon loaded with shrapnel

MURRION, a cattle disease, usu. spelt 'murrain'

MUSCADEL, sweet wine, commonly drunk by bridal party at conclusion of wedding

MUSE, marvel at

MUSSEL-SHELL, empty fool

MUTTON AND PORRIDGE, i.e. mutton-broth, with perhaps a side-glance at 'mutton' a loose woman

MUTTON ON FRIDAYS, 'mutton', a courtesan

MUTUAL, common to more than two

MYRMIDONS, Thessalian warriors brought to Troy by Achilles

MYSTERY, craft, trade

NAIL, (i) cloth measure of 2¼ in; (ii) 'blow one's nail', wait patiently while one has nothing to do, not 'warm one's hands' as generally interpreted

NAMELESS, inexpressible

NAPKIN, handkerchief

NARCISSUS, the youth who fell in love with his own reflection and killed himself in despair

NATIVE, nature

NATURAL, (i) idiot; (ii) not unnatural; 'natural philosopher', scientist, esp. physicist

NATURE, (i) natural affection between relatives; (ii) natural order of things; (iii) goddess, personifying the forces that create the phenomena of the material world; (iv) human nature, human race; (v) character, disposition; (vi) bodily constitution, vital functions

NAUGHT, (i) worthless, useless; (ii) 'be naught', keep quiet, make yourself scarce

NAUGHTY, wicked, worthless, good-for-naught

NAYWARD, denial

NAY-WORD, pass-word, watch-word, proverb

NEAF, fist

NEAPOLITAN BONEACHE,:—syphilis, supposed to have originated in Naples

NEAR-LEGGED BEFORE, standing with fore-legs close together and back legs wide apart

NEAT'S TONGUE, cured or dried ox-tongue

NEB, break

NEELE, needle

NEEZE, variant of sneeze

NEMEAN LION, fierce lion killed by Hercules

NEMESIS, 'goddess of retribution or vengeance, hence one who avenges or punishes' (OED)

NEPTUNE, god of the sea, hence the sea

NEREIDES, sea nymphs, daughters of Nereus

NERVES, sinews

NESSUS, the centaur whose poisoned shirt caused Hercules such agony

NESTOR, aged counsellor of the Greeks before Troy, hence the type of old age

NEW-FANGLED, carried away by novelty, giddy-pated

NEW MADE (man), man regenerate

NICE, modest, fastidious, refined

NICELY, ingeniously

NICK (out of all), beyond all computations

NICKNAME (vb) call by incorrect or improper name

NICK'S HIM LIKE A FOOL, 'Fools, undoubtedly, were shaved and nicked in a particular manner'

NIESS, or nyas, a young hawk in the aerie

NIGHT-CROW, 'bird supposed to croak or cry at night and to be of evil omen, probably an owl or night-jar' (OED)

NIGHT-GOWN, generally silk or satin faced with fur and fulfilling the purpose of a dressing-gown. Night-gowns proper were not introduced until mid-16th cent.

NIGHT-RULE, revels

NINE-MEN'S MORRIS, or Merels, a game for two players or parties, each of whom had the same number of pebbles, discs, pegs or pins. It was known as Nine Men's, Fivepenny or Three Men's Morris according to the number of men used. Not unlike hopscotch

NINE WORTHIES, traditionally Hector, Alexander, Julius Caesar, Joshua, David, Judas Maccabeus, Arthur, Charlemagne and Guy of Warwick or Godfrey of Bouillon. The list varies, but elsewhere Hercules and Pompey are not included

NINNY, 'pied ninny', referring to the jester's motley

NIOBE, in Greek mythology, the daughter of Tantalus who wept unceasingly for her children, slain by the gods, and was turned into a pillar of stone which continued to weep

NIT, lit. the egg of a louse, hence a very small insect or fly

NOBLE, a gold coin worth about 35p

NODDY, simpleton; (adj.) foolish

NOLL, noddle, head, jocular or contemptuous

NON-COME, taken by some as a nonsensical abbreviation of 'non compos', but perhaps intended as a substitute for 'non-plus'

NONSUIT, legal term, bring about the voluntary withdrawal of the plaintiff

NOOK-SHOTTEN, highly indented

NO POINT, a phrase from the French:—not at all

NORTH POLE, the pole star, symbol of constant determination

NOTE, (i) of music; (ii) stigma, mark of disgrace; 'out of my note', not in my list

NOTORIOUS, disgraceful, shameful

NO-VERBS, usually interpreted as 'words which do not exist', but possibly:—naywords, q.v.

NOVI HOMINEM TANQUAM TE, I know the man as well as I know you (from Lyly's *Grammar*)

NOVUM, a dice game, properly 'novem quinque', from its two main throws of nine and five

NUMA, legendary second king of Rome

NUMBERS RATIFIED, metrically correct verse

NUNNERY, a cant word for a house of ill fame

NURSE, housekeeper

NUTHOOK, catchpole, constable. 'Nutcrackers' was likewise a cant term for the pillory

NYM (vb), steal, filch

O, (plural OES), a small circle or spot, spangle

O LORD, SIR, a common exclamation:—surely

OAK, oak leaves, actually the symbolic prize of a soldier, who had rescued another captured in battle, but also 'garland', an emblem of victory

OBLIGED FAITH, faith bound by contract

OBSCENELY, occasionally used deliberately as if connected with 'seen' and meaning 'openly, so as to be seen'

OBSEQUIOUS, zealous, dutiful

OBSERVANCE, respectful attention

OBSERVATION, observance

OBSTRUCTION, cessation of the vital functions, stoppage

OCCASION, events as they fall out, 'an opportunity of attacking, fault-finding, giving or taking offence' (OED)

ODDS, superiority, advantage

ODE, ditty, applied to lyrical verse in general at this time

OD'S LIFELINGS, perversion of oath 'God's life'

OD'S NOUNS, perversion of 'God's wounds'

OEILLADES, sheep's eyes, amorous glances

O'ER-LOOKED, i.e. with the evil eye

O'ERPARTED, having too difficult a part, or too many parts to play

O'ER-RAUGHT, over-reached, cheated

O'ERSHOT, wide of the mark

O'ERWEEN, to be arrogant or presumptuous

OFFENCE, displeasure, annoyance

OFFICER, sheriff's officer, catchpole

OLD, (i) coll.—plentiful, great; (ii) of long practice and experience, also (slang) clever, knowing; (iii) stale, worn out

OLIVER AND ROLAND, two chief knights of Charlemagne, commonly pitted against each other for martial exploits, hence the types of ideal knighthood

OLYMPUS, home of the gods in Greek mythology; type of high mountain

OMIT, disregard

OMNE BENE, Lat. all is well

ONCE, (i) ''tis once', once for all, in short; (ii) ever, at any time

OPEN, give tongue, like a hound

OPINION, self-conceit, reputation

OPPOSITE, (sb) opponent; (adj.) contradictory, obstructive, hostile

OPPUGNANCY, conflict

ORANGE-TAWNY, deep or dark yellow

ORBS UPON THE GREEN, fairy rings

ORCHARD, garden

ORDINARY, either 'commonplace', 'vulgar' or belonging to an ordinary (eating house)

ORGAN, feature, any part of the body

ORGULOUS, proud

ORIENT PEARL, a pearl from the Indian seas, more beautiful than those found in European mussels, hence a brilliant or precious pearl, esp. lustrous or shining

ORPHEUS, mythical lyre-player, son of the Muse, Calliope

ORTS, left-over scraps of food

OSIER, made of willow twigs

OSTENT, show, display

OTHERGATES, in other fashion

OTTOMITES, Ottoman Turks

OUNCE, lynx

OUPH, elf, lit. 'elf's child, changeling'

OUSEL, blackbird

OUT, out of pocket; 'out o' th' way', beside the point, gone astray

OUTSWEAR, footwear

OVERFLOWN, overwhelmed (as by a flood)

OVERPEER, tower over

OVER-SHOES, OVER-BOOTS, phrases expressing reckless continuance in a course already begun

OVER-TOPPING, v. trash

OVERTURE, declaration

OVERWATCH, sit up late at night

OVER-WEATHERED, worn by exposure to the weather

OWE (adj. and vb), own

OX, 'to make an ox of one', to make one out a fool

OYES, i.e. 'oyez', the crier's call

PACK, plot, conspiracy, gang of rascals; 'packed with', in conspiracy with

PADDOCK, toad

PAGEANT, movable scaffold on which open-air scenes were enacted or tableaux displayed in the miracle plays and civic shows

PAIN, (i) labour, toil, trouble; (ii) penalty

PAINFUL, pains-taking

PAINTED, feigning, specious, fictitious

PAINTED CLOTH, cloth or canvas, used as wall hangings or room partitions and painted in oil. The Worthies (q.v.) was a favourite subject

PAIR OF SHEARS, 'there went but a pair of shears between us', we are all of a piece

PAIR OF STAIRS, flight of stairs ('pair':—set)

PALABRAS, probably meaning 'pocas plabras' ('few words'), a Sp. phrase current at the time

PALFREY, saddle horse for ordinary riding

PALTER, play fast and loose

PANCAKE, fritter, flapjack

PANNONIANS, inhabitants of present-day Hungary

PANTALOON, orig. stock figure of It. comic stage, representing Venice; a dotard, old fool

PANTHEON, temple to all the gods, erected in Rome, 27 B.C.

PANTLER, servant in charge of the pantry

PARAGON (vb), compare as equals

PARCEL, (sb) constituent, part, lot, set; (vb) commercial term, enumerate by items

PARCEL-BAWD, partly a bawd (and partly a tapster)

PARIS-BALL, tennis ball

PARISH GARDEN, Paris Garden, a bear garden on Bankside, near the Globe Theatre

PARITOR, officer of the bishop's court who carries out citations

PARK, 'over park, over pale':—over enclosed private property, 'park' being an enclosure for game, and 'pale' any fenced piece of ground

PALMER, 'pilgrim returned from the Holy Land, in sign of which he carried a palm branch or leaf, often simply a pilgrim' (OED)

PARLE, negotiation or conference under truce

PARLOUS, syncopate form of 'perilous'

PART, (i) a player's 'part' comprised all his speeches written out on strips of paper. It included cues, the final words of speeches preceding his own and serving as signals to come in'; (ii) allotted portion, lot in life; (iii) wealth, rank; (iv) office duty, function

PART (vb), depart

PARTHIANS, warlike people to the S.E. of the Caspian Sea, famed for shooting arrows behind them when taking flight, hence Parthian shot

PART-COATED, in motley

PARTICULAR (sb), individual, personal concern

PARTISAN, (i) party adherent; (ii) long-shafted spear with broad head

PARTITION, (i) wall; (ii) section of learned book

PARTLET (Dame), used as the proper name of the hen in 'Reynard the Fox'

PASH, dial. word for 'head'

PASS, accomplish, execute, enact, settle (business)

PASS UPON, impose upon, make a fool of

PASSADO, from Sp. passada:—forward thrust with the sword, advancing the foot at the same time

PASSAGE, act, course, procedure

PASSANT, (i) excellently; (ii) heraldic term, of a beast, walking and looking to the dexter side with one forepaw raised

PASSES, tricks, devices

PASSION, (sb) bodily disorder, suffering, any powerful feeling either of mirth or sorrow; (vb) to be affected with deep feeling, grieve (obs)

PAT (adv.), just right

PATCH, fool, derived from fool's garb

PATEN, the small dish used with the chalice in the celebration of Holy Communion

PATENT, privilege

PATHETICAL, moving

PAUCA PALLABRIS (Palabras), PAUCA VERBA, few words, almost:—not a word

PAVED BED, probably refers to the method of burial in prison

PAVED FOUNTAIN, clear fountain with pebbly bottom

PAVILION, tent for a champion at a tournament

PAWN, stake, wager

PAX. For the kiss of peace given at mass in the early church there was substituted in the 13th cent. the practice of passing a tablet, called a 'pax', depicting the crucifixion, to the communicants to kiss

PAY, beat, punish, give an opponent his deserts; 'pay home', fully repay

PEACH, impeach, bring to trial

PEAKING, sneaking, prying

PEAL, a salvo of ordinance

PEARLS, cataracts

PEAT, spoiled child

PECK, a round vessel used as a peck measure

PEDANT, schoolmaster (without any necessary implication of contempt)

PEDASCULE, a word coined from 'pedant'

PEER, to be seen peeping through

PEEVISH, senseless, silly, morose

PEISE, the weights used in winding a clock

PELION, lofty range of mountains in Thessaly

PELL-MELL, lit. 'confusedly, without keeping ranks', and so headlong, recklessly

PELTING, paltry, petty

PENCIL, paint brush for a lady's toilet

PENELOPE, wife of Ulysses

PENNYWORTH, lit. a bargain; 'fit ... with a pennyworth', take revenge upon him

PENSIONERS, the gentlemen pensioners or royal bodyguard

PENTECOST, Whitsuntide

PEPIN (King), first of Carlovingian kings, father of Charlemagne, d. A.D. 768

PERDURABLY, everlastingly

PERDY, verily indeed (lit. by God par dieu)

PEREGRINATE, foreign fashioned. This 'singular and choice' epithet may be intended to suggest the astrological term 'peregrine' used of a planet out of its appropriate position in the Zodiac.

PERFECT, certain, assured

PERGE, Lat. proceed

PERIOD, goal

PERJURE, perjurer. Perjurers were punished at this time by being publicly exhibited with a paper on head or breast setting forth their guilt

PERPEND, ponder, consider, attend to

PERSPECTIVE, some kind of stereoscope

PERT, lively, sprightly

PETAR, petard, mortar, small engine of war to blow up walls, etc.

PETITION (that prays well for peace), the authorised form of grace concluded with 'God save our Queen and Realm and send us peace in Christ'

PETTITOES, trotters

PETRACH, 14th cent. It. poet who wrote famous love sonnets

PHAETHON, the type of youthful presumption. Son of Helios, drove the sun's chariot for a day but lost control and was struck down by a thunderbolt from Jupiter

PHANTASIME, fantastic being

PHARAMOND, semi-mythical Frankish ruler of the early 5th cent.

PHEAZAR, vizier

PHIBBUS, Phoebus, the sun god

PHILEMON. Ovid tells the story of Jupiter and Mercury visiting the old couple Baucis and Philemon in their cottage, the roof whereof was thatched

PHILIP AND JACOB, the festival of SS Philip and James, 1st May

PHILLIDA, v. Corin

PHILOMEL, Athenian maid, outraged by her brother-in-law, cut out her own tongue

PHILOMELE, classical name for the nightingale

PHILOSOPHER, person learned in any science, including demonology. 'Philosopher's Stone', the goal of alchemy, which would turn all metals to gold and give immortality to those who drank it

PHOEBUS, the sun god in Greek mythology

PHOENIX, fabulous Arabian bird which was reborn out of its own ashes

PHRYGIA, of Phrygia, the part of Asia Minor in which Troy was situated

PHRYGIAN TURK, v. Hungarian

PIA MATER, brain, lit. a membrane enclosing it

PICKED, fastidious

PICKT-HATCH, 'your manor of Pickthatch', a disreputable quarter of London

PIECE, work of art

PIECE UP, make up

PIKE, a detachable spike for thrusting at the enemy in the centre of the buckler

PILCH, outer garment of skin or leather

PILE, the downy nap on velvet or other fabrics (cf. three-pile); 'piled':—pilled or peeled, i.e. hairless, bald; 'piled for a French velvet' refers to the baldness consequent upon the 'French disease' (cf. French crown)

PILLICOCK, term of endearment for young boy

PIN, (sb) 'peg, nail or stud fixed in the centre of a target; (vb) 'pins the wenches on his sleeve', flaunts their dependence on him

PIN AND WEB, disease of the eye, probably characterised by a spot or excrescence like a pin's head and a film covering the general surface

PINCH, to reduce to straits (in argument), to put in a tight place

PINFOLD, pound for stray cattle

PINNACE, (i) light vessel, often in attendance on a larger one; (ii) go-between, bawd

PIONED AND TWILLED, 'pioned':—probably dug and sloped like a glacis, and 'twilled':—platted like a hurdle

PIONEER, soldier armed with spade or pick-axe to dig trenches, etc., the lowest of the camp

PIRE, peer, examine closely

PISSING-CONDUIT, popular name of a conduit or fountain at the west end of Cheapside

PITCH, lit. height, so excellence of any kind

PITCH A TOIL, set a snare

PITTANCE, scanty meal; orig. a sum of money left to a religious house to provide additional allowance of food, wine, etc. at a festival or anniversary

PLACE (sb), official position; 'place where':—fit place, right spot; 'take place', take effect, succeed, find acceptance

PLACES, texts, extracts, short passages from books, topics or subjects of discourse

PLACKET, petticoat, or a slit in the same

PLAIN-SONG. Term orig. applied to simple ecclesiastical chants, usually in a minor key. Apt to a metaphor drawn from the cuckoo's monotonous song in a minor third

PLANCHED, made of board or planks

PLANETARY, astrological notion, caused by the influence of a planet

PLANT, set up, furnish, esp. in connection with new colonies

PLANTAIN. The application of a plantain leaf as the popular remedy for bruises and wounds is constantly referred to in Elizabethan literature

PLANTATION, colonisation

PLASH, pool

PLAUSIVE, pleasing, gracious, popular

PLAY THE MEN, pipe all hands

PLEA, that which is claimed

PLEACHED, fenced, bordered, or over-arched with intertwisted boughs and twigs

PLEAD A NEW STATE, v. state

PLEASANT, jocular, facetious merry

PLEASE-MAN, ? officious parasite

PLUMMET, (i) a woollen fabric; (ii) plummet-line, for fathoming

PLUTO, god of Hades

PLUTUS, god of gold, and therefore of alchemists

POCKET UP, conceal (political slang)

POINT, (sb) (i) summit; (ii) matters in discussion; (iii) lace attaching hose to doublet; (iv) 'stand upon points', bother about trifles; 'point-devise' (adj.) extremely precise, perfectly correct; (vb) direct; 'point upon', astrological term, direct a malign influence on

POKING STICK, or putting stick, of iron, steel or brass, heated and used for starched ruffs

POLE, probably the long staff used by thieves on the Border

POLITIC, cunning, scheming, intrigue

POLL, the number of soldiers in the muster

POLL-CLIFT, pruned

POMANDER, scent ball hung about the neck

POMEWATER, large juicy kind of apple, popular in the 16th cent. but now forgotten

POMGARNET, pomegranate

POMPEY'S PORCH, portico of the theatre built by Pompey in 55 B.C.

POMPION, pumpkin, 'often applied in contempt to a big man' (OED)

PONTIC SEA, the Black Sea

POOR-JOHN, salted hake

POPERIN PEAR, variety of pear from Poperinghe in Flanders

POPINJAY, parrot, chattering overdressed coxcomb

PORPENTINE, porcupine

PORT, gate, grand or expensive style of living

POSITION, arrangement, disposition

POSSESSED, (i) informed, instructed; (ii) possessed by the devil

POSSET, 'drink composed of hot milk curdled with ale, wine, etc., formerly used as delicacy or remedy' (OED)

POST, (sb) stock, courier, messenger; (vb) ride as quickly as possible

POSY, a short motto, originally a line of verse inscribed on a knife as a heraldic motto

POTATOES, i.e. the 'batata' or sweet potato, considered provocative

POTTLE, two quarts

POUNCET-BOX, small perfume box with perforated lid

POWDERED, salted, pickled

PRACTICE, plot, conspiracy

PRAEMUNIRE, statute limiting the power of the Pope in England

PRAETOR, Roman magistrate, subordinate to consul, elected annually

PRAISE, appraise, i.e. sip; 'praise in departing', proverbial expression:—wait till the end before praising

PRANK, adorn, not in any disparaging sense

PRAT, PRATS, buttocks

PREACHMENT, 'obtrusive or wearisome discourse' (OED)

PREAMBULATE, go on before

PRECEPTIAL, composed of precepts

PRECINCT, a place under someone's control or rule

PRECISE, puritanical; 'precisian', puritan

PRE-CONTRACT, formal betrothal, which in Shakespeare's day was considered a legally valid marriage without religious ceremony (cf. Fast my wife)

PREDOMINATE. An astrological term: a predominant star was one in the ascendant, i.e. in that degree of the Zodiac which at any given moment is just rising above the horizon

PREFER, recommend, select for consideration

PREGNANT, resourceful, teeming with devices

PREMISES, stipulations

PREPARATIONS, accomplishments

PREPOSTEROUS, highly improper, perverse

PRESENT, represent; act or perform a part

PRESENTATION, semblance

PRESENTLY, at once, immediately

PRESS TO DEATH, reference to 'peine fort et dure', a torture laying heavy weights upon the victim's chest until he confessed

PRESS-MONEY, initial payment given to a man on his being 'pressed' into military service

PREST, ready

PRESTER JOHN. Fabulous Christian king of vast wealth and power who was supposed to live in Asia. In the 16th cent. the name was applied to the King of Abyssinia, whose title 'Prestigian' was easily deflected and altered to Prester John.

PRETENCE, intention, design

PRETTY AND, pretty (adv.), quite, very

PREVENT, forestall, anticipate

PREYFUL, killing much prey

PRIAPUS, classical god of fertility

PRICK, spot in the centre of the target, pin

PRICKET, a buck in its second year

PRIME, (i) springtime; (ii) the choisest quality of youth

PRIMERO, a popular card game

PRINCIPALITY, a spiritual being of high rank

PRISCIAN, late Latin grammarian fl. A.D. 525

PRIVATE (sb), privacy

PRIVILEGE, protection, lit. right of immunity

PRIZE, match contest; 'prizer', prize fighter

PRIZE (vb), reckon

PROCESS, story

PROCLAMATION, open declaration. 'Give him a better proclamation':—Show him to be a better man than you have declared

PRODITOR, traitor

PROFACE, formula of welcome in eating or drinking

PROFIT, progress in learning

PROGNE, sister of Philomel (q.v.) in revenge for whose violation she killed her son and fed her husband the flesh

PROLIXIOUS, superfluous, tedious

PROLONG, postpone

PROMETHEAN FIRE, fire of heaven, such as Prometheus stole (Greek mythology)

PROOF, trial, experiment; 'to the proof', so armed as to be invulnerable

PROPER, (i) own, peculiar to, belonging distinctively to; (ii) handsome, goodly

PROPERTY, (sb) particular quality; (vb) (i) make a tool of, use for one's own ends; (ii) take possession of; (iii) treat like a theatrical property

PROPONTIC SEA, Sea of Marmora

PROPOSE, converse, discuss, usually interpreted as 'purpose'

PROPORTION, (i) metrical form; (ii) portion, dowry

PROPRIETY, individuality, personal identity

PROTESTATION, solemn declaration

PROTEUS, the 'old man of the sea', who escaped by assuming a variety of shapes

PROUD, hot-blooded, lascivious, sensually excited

PRUNE, dress up, trim

PSALTERY, ancient and medieval stringed instrument

PUCELLE, maid; the French title adopted for Joan of Arc

PUDDINGS, guts of an animal, sausages and entrails stuffed with meat (cf. hodge-pudding)

PUKE, vomit

PUKE-STOCKINGS, cheap stockings of dyed cloth

PULPIT, platform, Rostra (erected for orations in the Roman Forum)

PUMPION, pumpkin

PUNK, harlot

PUNTO, v. fencing

PUNY, lit. junior, hence young and inexperienced

PUR, the name of the knave in the card game 'post and pair'

PURCHASE (after so many years'), the price of land reckoned in terms of its annual rent or return; 'purchased', acquired (legal term)

PURE (adv.), purely, entirely

PURGATION, (i) laxative; (ii) cleansing from guilt or suspicion

PURLIEU, a piece of land on the fringe of a forest

PURPLE-IN-GRAIN, fast-dyed purple or scarlet

PURSENT, present, represent

PUSH, pish!

PUSH-PIN, 'a child's game in which each player pushes or fillips his pin with the object of crossing that of another player' (OED)

PUT DOWN, (i) take down, snub, make a fool of; (ii) make incapable with drink; 'put off', baffle, repulse; 'put on', lay on (as a blow), pass off, force something upon one

PUTTER-OUT OF FIVE TO ONE, one who gambles on the risks of travel

PUTTING ON, incitement, pressing forward

PUTTOCK, kite, basest of hawk kind

PYRAMUS, lover of Thisbe

PYRRHUS, son of Achilles, instrumental in the capture of Troy

PYTHAGORAS, Greek philosopher who preached the doctrine of the transmigration of souls

QUAIL, slacken, become feeble

QUAINT, (i) ingenious, knowing; (ii) dainty

QUALIFIED, possessed of qualities

QUALIFY, abate, soften, moderate

QUALITY, (i) rank, business, social position; (ii) trait, human characteristic

QUALM, sudden feeling of faintness or sickness

QUANTITY, fragment

QUATCH-BUTTOCK, probably 'quatch':—quat, i.e. fat

QUEAN, hussy

QUEASY, squeamish

QUELL, destroy, kill

QUERN, hand-mill for grinding corn

QUESTANT, a Shakespearian coinage from 'quest' = (of hunting dogs) to search for game

QUESTION, discussion, debate, conversation; 'in question', of doubtful quality

QUEST, 'run with these false and most contrarious quests', a hunting metaphor, a quest being the cry of the hound upon the scent

QUICK, keen, vigorous (of the appetite)

QUICK RECREATION, lively sport

QUILL, pipe, reference to the shrill note of the wren

QUILLET, subtlety, verbal nicety

QUINTAIN, wooden figure at which to tilt

QUINTESSENCE, the 'fifth essence' of ancient and medieval philosophers supposed to be latent in all things, its extraction being one of the great objects of alchemy

QUIP, retort, sarcastic remark

QUIRK, quibbling argument, conceit, caprice. Orig. probably a 'sudden flourish or twist in writing or drawing'

QUIT, (i) absolve, acquit; (ii) pay one back; (iii) requite with reward

QUITTANCE, discharge from debt, receipt

QUOIT, tight-fitting cap

QUOTE, (i) refer to by citing page or chapter of book; (ii) observe, note; 'quoted', well-known, notorious

QUOTIDIAN, continuous fever or ague

RACE, herd, stud

RACK, strain, exaggerate, examine under torture, tear to pieces

RAG, worthless creature, a farthing

RAMPALLIAN, riotous strumpet

RAMPING, fierce, fr. heraldic term 'rampant'

RANGE, (i) fly wide — of a falcon; (ii) prove inconstant — of a woman

RANKLE, cause festering wound, breed corruption

RANKNESS, luxuriousness of growth

RAPIER, long, pointed sword for thrusting

RASCAL, RABBLE, often used collectively for the young inferior deer of a herd, but also in the sense of a deer who would neither fight nor run

RATE, (sb) style, mode of living; (vb) value

RATIONAL HIND, intelligent rustic

RATTLES, bladders with dried peas or beans inside

RAUGHT, reached

RAVIN DOWN, gulp down

RAWLY LEFT, unprovided for

RAYED, soiled, befouled

RAZE, erase, blot out; 'razure', obliteration

REASON, talk, hold conversation

REAVE, rob by force

REBATE, make dull, blunt

REBATO, stiff collar, in use c. 1590–1650

REBEL (vb), lust

RECEIVING, understanding, perception

RECHEAT, the sound for calling hounds together

RECKONING, keeping accounts

RECOLLECTED, lit. collected together, hence studied, far-fetched

RECOMFORTURE, consolation

RECORD, (sb) recollection; (vb) sing, warble

RECORDATION, reminder

RECORDER, vertical flute with whistle mouthpiece, its tone being soft and mournful

RECOUNTMENT, recital, relation

RECOVER, get hold of, obtain

RECREANT (sb and adj.), one who yields in combat, hence cowardly, craven

RECTOR, ruler, governor

RED DOMINICAL, v. Dominical

REDTIME TE CAPTUM QUAM QUEAS MINIMO, free yourself from captivity at the lowest ransom you may

RED-LATTICE, of the ale-house, red lattice windows being commonly found in ale-houses

RED-PLAGUE, bubonic plague

REECHY, smoky, dirty

REED-VOICE, a reedy or squeaking voice

REEK, rise like vapour; the word did not become offensive until the 19th cent.

REFELLED, repelled, refused to admit my plea

REGISTER, catalogue

REGREETS, salutations

REHEARSE, mention, formally recite

RELICS, mementoes, souvenirs, 'the sights'

RELISH, (sb) taste, trace, hint; (vb) make pleasant to the palate

REMAINDER, interest in an estate coming into effect on the death of the legatee

REMEMBRANCER, legal term, one employed to remember

REMONSTRANCE, usually explained as demonstration, manifestation

REMORSE, pity, compassion

REMOVE, departure from one place to another

RENDER, report, represent, describe

REPEAL, recall from exile

REPORT, legal term:—formal account of a case argued and determined in court

REPROVE, disprove

RERE-MOUSE, bat

RESERVE (vb), keep for oneself

RESIDENCE, continuance in a course of action

RESOLVE, set the mind at rest

RESPECT, reputation, regard; 'in my respect', as far as I am concerned; 'without respect', without reference to other things

RESPECTIVE, careful, regardful

RESPICE FINEM, a common jest, respect your end

REST (to set up one's), to be resolved, determined. Derived from primero, a card game, in which 'the rest' was the reserved stakes; originally meant to risk one's all, hence do one's utmost

RESTRAIN, forbid, prohibit, draw tight

RETENTION, medical term, the body's power to retain its proper contents, hence metaphorically stability or consistency

RETROGRADE (star), one apparently 'moving contrary to the order of the signs of the Zodiac or from East to West' (OED)

REVEL, take part in a noisy festivity, make one of a party of masquers

REVERBERATE (adj.), reverberating

REVERSE, *v.* fencing

REVERSION, 'the return of an estate to the donor or grantor or his heirs after the expiration of the grant' (OED); expectation

REVERTED, revolted

REVOLT, sudden revulsion of mind or feeling, generally in reference to passion

REVOLVE, consider

RHENISH, white Rhein wine such as hock or Moselle

RHEUM, catarrh; 'rheumatic diseases', diseases affecting the 'rheum' including catarrhs and colds of all kinds

RHODOPE, (Rhodopsis), Greek courtesan, reputed builder of the third pyramid

RIALTO, the Exchange in Venice

RIB, enclose

RID, destroy, discharge

RIDDLE-LIKE, mysteriously

RIGHT, straight; 'the right', the real, genuine

RIGOL, ring, circle

RINGLET, circular dance, fairy ring

RING-CARRIER, go-between

RINGWOOD, popular Elizabethan name for a hound

RIPE, ready, prepared

ROAD, roadstead

ROARERS, roisterers

RONYON, a term of abuse, scabby, mangy

ROOD, the Cross on which Christ was crucified

ROPE'S END, (i) commonly used as an instrument of punishment; (ii) a halter or hangman's noose

ROSCIUS, famous Roman comedian (d. 62 B.C.), supposed by Elizabethans to have been a tragic actor

ROSE, The Red Rose, the Duke of Buckingham's Manor, from 1561 became Merchant Taylor's School

ROSEMARY, used at both weddings and funerals as a symbol of remembrance

ROTE (by rote), from memory

ROTH, obs. spelling of 'ruth', calamity, grief

ROUGH, violent

ROUND (adj.), (i) spherical; (ii) severe, plain-spoken; 'roundly', outspokenly

ROUND, ROUNDEL, (i) simplest form of country dance in which the dancers from a circle; (ii) a roundabout course

ROYAL, coin worth about 50p

ROYNISH, scurvy, base

RUB, 'The Rub is any object or impediment which diverts the bowl from its course. It is a feature that lends itself to punning and metaphorical application (Sh. Eng.)

RUB THE ELBOW, to express pleasurable satisfaction

RUDDOCK, robin red-breast

RUDESBY, boisterous, unmannerly fellow

RUFF, or ruffle, 'the loose turned-over portion or flap of a top-boot' (OED)

RUIN, refuse, rubbish

RULE, conduct, behaviour

RUN, (i) flee in battle; (ii) make water

RUNAGATE, (i) deserter; (ii) runaway, vagabond

RUSSET, red, or sometimes grey

RUTH, pity

SACK, general name for white Spanish or Canary wines; 'burnt sack', a hot drink of sack and sugar

SACKBUT, brass trumpet, with slide like a trombone

SACKERSON, a famous bear at Paris Garden in Shakespeare's day

SADNESS, seriousness, soberness

SAFFRON, orange-red colouring matter used in confectionery, liqueurs, etc.

SAGGITARY, centaur

ST NICHOLAS, the patron saint of scholars

SALE-WORK, ready-made goods

SALT RHEUM, a running cold

SALVE, (i) ointment; (ii) salutation

SALVED, lit. anointed, hence palliated, softened

SANCTUARY, church or other sacred place where, by law, immunity from arrest was secured

SAND-BLIND, partially blind

SANDED, sandy-coloured

SATIS QUOD SUFFICIT, enough is as good as a feast

SATURN, planet and god, though of as cold, sluggish and gloomy

SAUCE THEM, make it hot for them

SAUCY, wanton, lascivious, presumptuous

SAVE YOUR REVERENCE, *v.* Sir Reverence

SAW, discourse

SAY, cloth resembling serge

SCAB, a scurvy fellow

SCALED, weighed in the balance, tested

SCALL, i.e. 'scald', scabby

SCAMBLING, roistering, contentious

SCAMELS, ? seamels, i.e. gulls

SCANDALLED, infamous

SCANT (vb), limit, restrict, cut short

SCAPE, escapade, breach of chastity

SCARFED, decked with streamers

SCATHE, harm

SCHOOL, university

SCHOOL OF NIGHT, if text not corrupt probably denotes a coterie of the day to which Raleigh, Harriot and Chapman belonged, dabbling in astronomy and unorthodox religious opinion

SCIATICA, supposedly a symptom of venereal disease

SCIENCE, profound knowledge

SCONCE, (i) a head; (ii) small fort; (iii) a protective screen

SCOPE, (i) room to move in; (ii) license; (iii) liberty

SCORE, (i) to keep count by notches or marks on stick or pot; (ii) obtain drink or goods on credit

SCOTCH JIG, lively round dance for a large number of people

SCOUT, lie in wait

SCRUBBED, undersized, insignificant

SCRUPLE, (i) apothecary's weight (20 grains), a minute portion; (ii) doubt, objection

SCUT, short tail of hare or deer

SEA-COAL, coal brought by sea from Newcastle, as opposed to charcoal

SEALED (in approbation), stamped with the official seal guaranteeing authenticity i.e. hall-marked

SEAL UP, make up one's mind

SEARCH, probe a wound, as with a surgeon's knife

SEASON, (i) mix something with food to make it more palatable, hence temper, alleviate; (ii) preserve by salting, embalm

SEASON (sb), occasion, opportunity; 'of the season', in the rutting season

SEA-WATER GREEN, colour associated with courtesy

SECRET, remedy or prescription known to doctors only

SECTARY ASTRONOMICAL, student of astronomy

SECTS, classes, ranks

SECURITY, legal security, e.g. signing a bond for a friend

SEEDNESS, the sowing of seed

SEEMING, hypocrisy

SEESE, Welsh pronunciation of 'cheese' q.v.

SEIZE UPON, take possession of

SEMBLATIVE, resembling, a Shakespearian coinage

SEMIRAMIS, mythical Assyrian queen, wife of Ninus, proverbial for her sexual licence

SENNET, trumpet or cornet fanfare for ceremonial entries and exits

SENSE, (i) desire; (ii) perception; (iii) reason; 'in all sense', on every account; 'sense of sense', the apprehension of the senses

SENSIBLY, with emotion

SENTENCES, saws, aphorisms, maxims

SENTENTIOUS, full of pithy sayings

SEQUESTERD, excommunicated, cut off from one's fellows

SERE, dry, dull, withered

SERGEANT, an officer whose duty it is to summon persons to appear before a court. 'Sergeant of the Band', is, strictly speaking, the commander of a company of soldiers

SERPIGO, general term for creeping or spreading skin disease

SERVANT, one devoted to the service of a lady, who was not pledged by accepting it

SERVE ONE'S TURN, (i) be of service to; (ii) satisfy sexually

SERVER, attendant at meal 'who superintended the arrangement of the table, seating and tasting and serving of the dishes' (OED)

SERVICE, (i) military service; (ii) food served up at table

SERVITOR, attendant

SESSA!, meaning doubtful, possibly an exclamation of encouragement, formerly a cry of triumph at a hit in fencing

SET (vb), set to music, put down; 'set against', oppose; 'set down', lay siege; 'set forth', (i) extol; (ii) carve up at table; 'set the world on wheels', let things go slide, enjoy oneself

SET (adj.), deliberate, not spontaneous

SETEBOS, mentioned in Eden's History of Travel (1577) as a deity or devil of the Patagonians

SHADOWED, shaded, umbrated (heraldic term)

SHAFT OR BOLT ON'T (make a), proverbial:—do one thing or another. A shaft was an arrow for the long-bow, a bolt a shorter one for the cross-bow; if the wood was too short for the one it would do for the other

SHAKE UP, rate soundly, abuse violently

SHARP, famished

SHEARMAN, one who cuts the superfluous nap in cloth-making

SHEEP-BITING, shifty, sneaking

SHEER-ALE, meaning doubtful, either thin or small ale, or undiluted ale

SHELVY, made of shelves or sandbanks

SHENT, rated, scolded

SHERIFF'S POST, Posts painted in two colours were formerly set up at the side of the door of a mayor, sheriff or other magistrate as a sign of office

SHIFT OUT OF, change out of (one suit of clothes for another)

SHIP-TIRE, head-dress, shaped like a ship, or having a ship-like ornament

SHOG, move off (slang)

SHOP, the organ of generation

SHORE, limit

SHORT KNIFE AND A THRONG, the cut-purse's requisites

SHOT, tavern reckoning

SHOTTEN (of a herring), one that has shed its roe, hence emaciated, good-for-nothing

SHOULDER-CLAPPER, an officer who arrests an offender

SHOULDER-SHOTTEN, with a dislocated shoulder

SHOVEL-BOARDS, v. Edward Shovel-boards

SHREWISHLY, sharply, ill-temperedly

SHREWD, (i) shrewish, sharp, keen-witted; (ii) mischievous, malicious; 'a shrewd turn', a nasty trick

SHRIEVE, old form of sheriff

SHRIFT, hearing of confession and giving of absolution thereafter

SHRINE, image of a saint or god

SHRIVE, 'shrive you a thousand idle pranks', I will call you to confession and make you tell your tricks; 'shriver', father confessor

SHROW, variant of shrew

SHUFFLE OFF, get rid of or evade something in a perfunctory manner

SHY, reserved

SYBIL, generic name of ancient Italian prophetesses, e.g. Sibylla, the Sybil of Cumae, to whom Apollo granted that her years should be as many of the grains in a handful of sand

SICILS, 'the Sicils', Naples and Sicily

SICLES, old form of shekels

SIDES, thighs, loins

SIEGE, seat, stool, excrement

SIGHT (in), conspicuously

SIGN, token, badge or device for identification

SIGNIFICANT, token

SIGNORY, domain, estate; 'signories', states of Northern Italy

SILLY, helpless, innocent

SIMPLE, poor, wretched, pitiful

SIMPLES, ingredients in medicine, not necessarily herbs, but later identified with that sense

SIMPLICITY, folly, silliness, harmlessness

SINCE, 'since night', a night ago

SINEWS, nerves

SINGLE, (i) poor, weak; (ii) unbroken

SINGLE BOND, meaning doubtful, either (i) an unconditional bond, or (ii) a bond without the names of the sureties attached

SINGLED, separated

SINISTER, (i) discourteous; (ii) heraldic term, left

SINK-A-PACE, or cinque -pace, a galliard of five steps

SINON, Greek warrior who induced the Trojans to allow into Troy the wooden horse

SIR, title prefixed to Christian names of persons, esp. priests or ministers, who had not graduated. The plural could be used of either sex

SIR REVERENCE, a corruption of 'save-reverence', an apology for mentioning an unpleasant fact; often used as euphemism for dung

SIRRAH, form of address to inferiors, esp. servants

SISTERING, neighbouring

SIT AT, live at

SKILL, knowledge, science

SKIN BETWEEN HIS BROWS. The phrase is always used with emphasising force after 'as honest as', 'as true as', etc. Possibly takes its origin from the practice of branding criminals between their brows

SKIPPER, light-brained, skipping fellow

SLEIDED, divided into filaments

SLICE, generally taken as referring to Banbury cheese (q.v.) but may be the hawking term for mute

'SLIGHT, an oath, God's light

SLIPS (in the), on the leash

SLIPS OF PROLIXITY, lapses into tediousness

SLOPS, wide, loose breeches, trunk hose

SLOW, heavy

SLUBBER, perform in a slovenly manner

SMACK, savour of, be strongly suggestive of

SMALL, the part of the leg below the calf

SMOCK, women's undergarment, shift, chemise

SMOKE, (sb), exhalation, so metaphorically verbiage, idle words; (vb) smell out, suspect

SMOTHER, the dense smoke of a flameless fire

SMUG, trim, neat

SNATCH, quibble, captious comment

SNEAPING, nipping

SNECK UP (or snick up), go and be hanged

SNIP, a snatch

SNIPT-TAFFETA, slashed silk

SNUFF (in), (i) in need of snuffing; (ii) in a rage; 'take in snuff', take offence

SOB, rest given to a horse to recover its wind

SOD, past part. of 'seethe' = boil to a decoction

SOFTLY-SPRIGHTED, a polite way of saying he was a coward

SO-HO, view halloo in hare-coursing

SOJOURN TO, travel to

SOLA!, hallo!

SOLACE, provide amusement

SOLEMN, ceremonial

SOLON, statesman of Athens (c. 640–558 B.C.), famous for his new constitution for Athens

SONNET, used loosely for any short poem of an amatory character

SONTIES, saints, dim. of 'sont', old form of 'saint'

SOON AT, betimes, near (of time)

SOPHISTER, cunning, cavilling disputer

SOPHY, Shah of Persia

SORE, severe, harsh

SORE, SOREL, bucks in respectively their fourth, third, year

SORT, (sb) (i) rank; (ii) set, crew; (iii) manner, method; 'in sort', in company, assembled together; (vb) (i) associate with; (ii) select; (iii) ordain, dispose

SOT, fool, drunkard

SOW, scatter, sprinkle

SPAN-COUNTER, a boys' game with counters or coins

SPAVIN, swelling of joint in horses

SPECIALTY, 'special contract, obligation or bond, expressed in an instrument under seal' (OED)

SPECTACLES, organs of vision

SPED, finished, done for

SPELL BACKWARD, misrepresent, distort

SPERR, fasten with bar or bolt, secure

SPHERE, one of the 'concentric transparent hollow globes imagined by the old astronomers as revolving round the earth and respectively carrying with them the several heavenly bodies' (OED)

SPIRITS, 'the nimble spirits in the arteries', v. arteries; 'faculties of perception' (OED)

SPITAL, lazar-house, a low class of hospital esp. for the leprous and the syphilitic

SPLAY, geld, castrate

SPLEEN, outburst, sudden access of passion, sport; the spleen was the seat of laughter as well as of anger

SPLIT (to make all), i.e. with agony or laughter

SPOILED, undone, ruined

SPOON-MEAT, lit. food prepared for infants, so dainties, delicacies

SPOTTED, wicked, morally stained

SPRAG, mispronunciation of 'sprack', brisk, alert

SPRIGHTFULLY, with great spirit

SPRING, beginning

SPRINGHALT, affection of hind legs of horse, causing muscles to contract spasmodically

SPRUCE, dandified, affected

SPUR, ask questions

SQUAND'RING, stray, straggling, lavishly distributed

SQUARE, (sb) (i) carpenter's set square; (ii) quarrel; (vb) frame or adjust something according to some standard or principle; also possibly 'strut, swagger'; 'squarer', a contentious or quarrelsome person

SQUASH, the unripe pod of a pea

STAFF, stave, verse, stanza

STAGGERS, a disease in horses accompanied by giddiness

STAIRS (keep below), remain a servant

STALE, (i) decoy, lure; (ii) dupe, laughing stock, lover or mistress whose devotion is turned into ridicule for the amusement of a rival; (iii) urine of cattle; (iv) harlot, common fellow

STALK, STALKING-HORSE, alludes to fowling with a stalking-horse, i.e. an old horse or ox, or an imitation of same, behind which the fowler lurks

STALL, keep, a metaphor from the stable

STALLION, ? dial. variant of 'staniel', a kestrel hawk, useless for falconry

STAND (a special), a sheltered position or covert for shooting at game

STAND TO, fall to; 'stand upon', concern

STANDARD, (i) standard-bearer; (ii) conduit

STANZE, STANZO, old and new forms of 'stanza'

STAPLE, the fibre of wool from which the yarn is spun

STAR-CHAMBER MATTER, the King's Council, sitting in the Star Chamber, exercised jurisdiction with regard to such offences as riots, slanders and libels, or even criticisms of magistrates. In 1590 a deer-stealing case was before it

STAR-CROSSED, thwarted by adverse influence of the planets

STARE, SWAGGER, behave in overbearing manner

STARKLY, stiffly, rigidly

STARRED, astrologically fated

STARS, a person's fortune or destiny viewed as determined by the stars

START, alarm, startle, swerve aside like a horse

STATE, (i) pose, deportment; (ii) dignity; (iii) property, estate; (iv) order, civil discipline; 'plead a new state', a term of rhetoric, with 'state':—the point in question or debate between contending parties

STATUTE-CAPS, prentice caps, woollen caps, decreed by the City of London to be worn by apprentices

STAY THANKSGIVING, wait for the grace at the end

STEAD UP, take another person's place

STEEP UP, precipitous, perpendicular

STEW, brothel; 'stewed prunes', a common term for prostitutes, from the 'stews'

STICK, fix, pin (like an ornament)

STICKLER-LIKE, like an umpire

STIGMATICAL, crooked, deformed

STILL, always, for ever

STILL SWINE EATS ALL THE DRAFF, prov.—the quiet sow eats all the hog's wash or refuse

STING, carnal impulse, sexual appetite

STOCCADO, v. fencing

STOCK, stocking, dowry

STOCK-FISH, dried cod, beaten before boiling

STOMACH, (i) courage; (ii) appetite

STOMACHER, ornamented chest garment worn by women

STONE-BOW, crossbow from which small stones or pellets were shot in fowling

STONES, testicles

STOOP, in falconry, fly to the lure

STOP, (i) obstruction, hindrance; (ii) pause, sudden check of a horse in the career; (iii) a fret on a lute; 'stopped', stuffed, deaf

STORY, dupe, laughing stock

STOUP, lit. a measure for liquor (2 quarts), hence a vessel for wine

STOVER, coarse grass

STRAIGHT, at once

STRAIN, (i) disposition, tendency; (ii) painful feeling

STRANGE, distant, unfriendly, severe

STRAPPADO, torture by disjointing the limbs

STRATAGEM, deed of violence

STRAY, cause to stray or wander

STREAK, smear

STRICTURE, strictness, severity of life

STRIFE, endeavour

STRIKE, astrological term; planets 'in opposition' were supposed to blast or strike objects beneath them. Cf. modern 'moon-struck'

STROSSERS, trousers

STUCK, (adj.) fastened; (sb) thrust, lunge, in fencing

STUDY, meditate, ponder

STYGIAN, of the Styx, the river of Hades across which the dead were ferried by Charon

SUBMISSION, confession

SUBORNATION, procuring or inciting one to crime

SUBSCRIBE FOR, undertake on behalf of

SUBSTANTIAL, 'your reason was not substantial why' i.e. your reason does not prove why

SUCCEEDING, consequences

SUCCESSION UPON, the line of heirs is never extinct

SUCK OUR BREATH, connected with old folk lore idea that the breath of man was his soul

SUDDENLY, immediately

SUE LIVERY, institute a suit for delivery or surrender of lands in the hands of the feudal suzerain until the heir could prove he was of age

SUFFERANCE, distress

SUFFICIENT, substantial, well-to-do

SUFFICIENCY, qualifications, ability

SUGGEST, prompt, tempt

SUIT, wooing, courtship; 'in all suits', in all respects; 'out of all suit', surpassingly; 'suited', (i) in accord; (ii) clothed in several suits

SUITOR, possibly:—shooter

SULLENS, morbid state of sullenness

SULPHUROUS, of lighting

SULTAN SOLYMAN, Solyman the Magnificent, Sultan of Turkey 1490–1566

SUN, 'get the sun of', get on the sunward side of an enemy so the sun shines in his eyes

SUN-BURNT. Elizabethan ladies were very careful to keep the sun from their complexions

SUN-EXPELLING MASK, much worn by ladies of quality when riding

SUP, provide supper for

SUPERSCRIPT, superscription, address

SUPPLANT, root out, pull out

SUPPLY, furnish with an occupant, fill

SUPPORTANCE, assistance; 'for the supportance of':—for the sake of

SUPPOSES, suppositions

SURECARD, winning card, hence a person bound to succeed

SUR-REINED, over-ridden, lit. over-reined

SUSTAINING GARMENTS, their clothes keep them afloat

SUTLER, one who sells supplies to the army, a camp-follower, not an officer

SUUM CUIQUE, to each his own

SWABBER, a sailor who had to see the ship was kept neat and clean

SWASHING, swaggering, dashing

SWAY, (i) control, in the astrological sense; (ii) determine opinion, influence judgement

SWAYED IN THE BACK, with a sunken back-bone

SWEAR OUT, forswear, abjure

SWEAT, 'a febrile disease characterised by profuse sweating, of which highly and rapidly fatal epidemics occurred in the 15th and 16th cents'

SWEET AND TWENTY, very sweet. The words 'and twenty' are used as an intensive

SWEET MOUTH, 'she has a sweet mouth', she is wanton, lecherous

SWINGE, (i) beat; (ii) have sexual intercourse

SWITZERS, Swiss mercenaries

SYLLA, Elizabethan spelling for L. Cornelius Sulla, Roman dictator

SYMPATHIZED, affected all alike

TABLE, (i) tablet for memoranda; (ii) in palmistry, the quadrangular space formed by the four principle lines on the palm of the hand; (iii) a board or flat surface on which a picture was painted, hence the picture itself; (iv) back-gammon board; 'table-book', note-book

TABOR, small drum, used generally with a pipe, traditional instruments of stage clown

TABOURINE, military drum

TACKLINGS, rigging

TAFFETA, thin silken stuff of lustrous appearance from which masks and vizards were made

TAILOR, the cry on a sudden fall backwards, with reference to the tailor's squatting position

TAKE, bewitch; 'take a button-hole lower', help undress, take down a peg; 'take off', relieve on of; 'take up', scold, reconcile

TALE, talk, remark

TALK APACE, chatter

TALENT, orig. a weight in Greece and Rome, then the value of this in gold or silver

TALL, sturdy

TALLENT, common 16th cent. form of 'talon'

TALLY, wooden stick marked with notches, to record a score, q.v.

TAMED, broached (like a flask)

TANG, clang, utter like a bell

TANTALUS, in Greek mythology, punished in Hades for his sin by having his thirst and hunger tormented by water receding when he is about to drink and fruit always eluding his grasp, hence tantalize

TARPEIAN ROCK, on the Capitoline Hill in Rome, from which traitors were hurled to their death

TARQUIN, Tarquinius Superbus, the younger of the two kings of this name, the violator of Lucrece in Shakespeare's poem

TARRE ON, incite

TARRIANCE, waiting

TARTAR-LIMBO, WORSE THAN HELL. Limbo:—hell, though also:—prison. 'Tartar' is a common abbreviation for Tartarus, hell

TASK (vb), impose a task upon, give a lesson to

TASTE, make trial of, hence (i) make use of; (ii) test

TAWDRY LACE, woman's silk lace or neck-tie, named after St Audrey (St Etheldreda)

TAWNY, dark-skinned, tanned

TAX, (sb) censure, blame; (vb) (i) task, make demands on; (ii) accuse; (iii) traduce, censure

TAXATION, satire, censure; lit. assessment of dues, hence imposition

TEAR A CAT, play the part of roistering hero

TEEN, sorrow, trouble

TELAMON, Ajax, son of Telamon, classical type of madman

TELL, count

TELLUS, the earth

TEMPER, concoct, compound, mix

TEMPERANCE, temperature. A puritan name

TEMPLE, not uncommonly used for church in 16th and 17th cents

TEMPORIZE WITH THE HOURS, put off the evil day

TEMPORARY, temporal

TENDER, have regard for, value

TENEMENT, land or real property held of another by any tenure

TENNIS BALLS, in Shakespeare's day made of white leather stuffed with hair

TENT, bed tester or canopy

TERCEL, male falcon

TERMAGENT, imaginary Muslim deity of turbulent character in the old morality plays

TERMINATIONS, definitions, expressions of opinion

TERMS, 'in terms of', in respect of

TESTER, sixpence; 'testerned', tipped with sixpence

TESTRIL, diminutive of 'tester'

TETTER, skin eruption

TEXT, to write in capitals, or in a text-hand, one of the more elaborate and formal scripts

THERSITES, scurrilous, deformed and ugly Greek warrior at the siege of Troy

THETIS, sea nymph, daughter of Nereus and mother of Achilles

THICK-PLEACHED, v. pleached

THIN-BELLY DOUBLET, doublet with unpadded lower part

THIRDBOROUGH, petty constable

THISBE, in classical mythology, maiden loved by Pyramus, a youth of Babylon

THISNE, or thissen, in this manner. Dialect word of north and midlands

THRASONICAL, boastful. Thraso is the braggart in Terence

THREE-PILE, the most expensive kind of velvet

THRIFT, (i) thriving, success; (ii) gain profit

THRILLING, piercing (with cold)

THROW, 'at this throw', on this occasion

THROW UPON, bestow

THRUM, tufted end of weaver's warp; 'thrummed hat', made of weavers' thrums, or possibly fringed with them to conceal the face

THUMP, imitation of the noise of a cannon

THUNDERSTONE, thunderbolt

TICKLE, (adj.) insecure, ticklish; (vb) (i) 'tickle' trout; (ii) flatter; (iii) ironical for punish or beat

TICK-TACK, a kind of backgammon

TIGHT, water-tight, sound; 'tightly', safely

TILLVALLY!, nonsense, fiddlesticks

TILTH, (i) tillage; (ii) fallow field

TIMBERED, v. clean-timbered

TIME, (i) favourable, propitious moment; (ii) with reference to the time of music; (iii) time of life, age; 'in good time', indeed!, forsooth!, well and good, just at the right moment; 'to the time', to eternity, for ever; 'timeless', untimely

TIME-PLEASER, time-server

TIMON, i.e. scorner of the world, esp. of women

TIPSTAFF, TIPSTAVES, officers whose staffs were tipped with silver and who took prisoners into custody; bailiffs

TIRED, (i) incorrigibly lazy; (ii) lit. 'attired', hence harnessed

TIRE ON, tear at, feed ravenously. Falconry term

TIRE-VALIANT, some kind of fanciful head-dress

TISICK, phthisic, consumptive

TITAN, Hyperion, the sun god, the sun

TITLE, what one is worth, lit. that to which one has a title

TOAZE, lit. count out (wool, etc.), hence elicit by close examination

TOIL, snare, net

TOLL, to get rid of, lit. to enter for sale on the toll book of a market

TONGS, rude musical instrument played with a key like the triangle

TOOTH, appetite

TOOTHPICKER. Tooth-picks, introduced from abroad, were much in request at the time

TOP, 'take the present time by the top', i.e. by the forelock

TOPGALLANT, platform for third section of mast above the deck

TOUCH, (i) sexual contact; (ii) hit or stroke in fencing; (iii) note, strain, lit. the fingering of a musical instrument; (iv) trait; (v) feeling, emotion of a subtle kind

TOUCH, TOUCHSTONE, hard basaltic stone upon which metal to be assayed was rubbed

TOUSE, tear

TOWER, falconry term to soar

TOY (sb), trifle

TRAIN, entice, lure

TRANSECT, prob. misprint of 'traject'

TRANSLATED, transformed

TRANSLATION OF, commentary upon

TRASH FOR OVER-TOPPING, a hunting phrase; 'trash':—check a hound by fastening a weight to its neck; 'over-topping':—out-stripping

TREATISE, story, discourse

TREBLE, make thrice as great

TREBLE HAUTBOY, smallest Elizabethan reed instrument

TRENCHER-KNIGHT, one who serves ladies at table

TRENCHER-MAN, glutton

TREY, throw of three at dice

TREY-TRIP, dice game probably depending on the throw of a three

TRIBUTARY, captive prince or chief who will pay tribute

TRICK, (i) device; (ii) particular habit, custom; (iii) characteristic expression of face or voice

TRICKSY, clever, full of devices

TRIFLE, trick of magic

TRIGON, astrological term: triple combination of hot and dry zodiacal signs, Aries, Leo and Saggitarius

TRIM, pretty, fine (generally ironical)

TRIP, trip in wrestling

TRIPLE, one of three, third

TRIPLEX, triple time in music

TRIUMPH, public festivity

TROLL-MY-DAMES, or Troll-madam, game for ladies, not unlike bagatelle

TROT, contemptuous epithet for an old woman

TROW, wonder

TROYAN, good fellow, boon companion

TRUCKLE-BED, small couch on castors

TRUE, honest

TRUNK SLEEVE, large wide sleeve

TRUST, conviction, belief

TRY WITH MAIN-COURSE, bring the ship close into the wind, with only the mainsail set

TUB. A reference to the treatment of venereal disease 'by a course of suffumigation with cinnabar in a meat-pickling vat' (Sh. Eng.)

TUCK, rapier

TUCKET, a flourish on a trumpet

TULLY, Cicero, Roman statesman and orator

TUMBLERS' HOOP, hoop garnished with ribbons, with which the tumbler did his tricks, and which he wore across his body

TUN-DISH, funnel

TUNE, humour, mood, temper

TUNEABLE, musical

TURK, (i) the Sultan of Turkey; (ii) the infidel

TURN, (i) be inconstant; (ii) shape or fashion a work of art, poem, tune or compliment

TURNED SPIT, the turn-spit was the lowest menial in the kitchen

TURN INTO, bring into

TURTLES, turtle-doves, proverbial for fidelity

TWICE-SOD SIMPLICITY, quintessence of stupidity

TWILLED, pioned

TWO AND THIRTY, A PIP OUT, not quite up to the mark. A jesting allusion, common at the time, to the card game 'one-and-thirty'

TWO OF THE FIRST, in heraldry, the first is the colour first mentioned in blazoning a coat of arms

TYPHON, mythical monster with tremendous voice, father of the Titans

TYRANNY, cruelty

UMBER, brown earth used as pigment

UNBANDED, without a hat band

UNBATED, unabated

UNBREATHED, unexercised; 'breathed':—in good wind

UNCASE, undress

UNCHARY (adv.), thriftlessly, carelessly

UNCIVIL, (i) disorderly, barbarous; (ii) impolite, discourteous

UNCONFIRMED, inexperienced

UNCOPE, unmuzzle

UNDERGO, take upon oneself

UNDERHAND, quiet, unobtrusive

UNDERTAKER, (i) one who takes up a challenge for another; (ii) contractor

UNDO, untie, release

UNEVEN, crooked

UNEXPRESSIVE, not to be expressed

UNFOLD, disclose, reveal

UNFOLDING STAR, the morning star

UNFURNISHED, unprovided with its fellow

UNGARTERED, the conventional sign of a love-lorn swain

UNHANDLED, not broken into

UNHATCHED, without dint or stain, i.e. never used in combat

UNKENNEL, unearth; kennel = fox's hole

UNMANNED, falconry term, unused to the presence of a man

UNPINKED. To pink leather was to ornament it by scalloping and punching out a pattern

UNPITIED, pitiless

UNPRIZABLE, of small account

UNQUESTIONABLE, taciturn, averse to conversation

UNRAKED, not banked up with ashes to keep the fire in all night

UNSEEMING, not seeming willingly

UNSHRUBBED, bare of bush or tree

UNSHUNNED, unshunnable, inevitable

UNSKILFULLY, without discernment

UNSTAUNCHED, not able to contain water

UNTAPIS, come out of cover or hiding

UNTOWARD, unmannerly

UNTREAD, retrace

UNTRUSSING, untying the points, unbuttoning

UNUM CITA, take one example

UNWEIGHING, thoughtless

UP AND DOWN, exactly, for all the world

UPSHOOT, archery term, the best shot up to any point in a contest

UPSHOT, the final shot in archery, and so the conclusion of the sport

UP-STARING, standing on end

UPSURPING, false

URCHINS, hedgehogs, or fiends in that form; 'urchin-shows', apparitions of urchins. The hedgehog was recognised as an emblem of the devil in Shakespeare's day

URINAL, physician's glass for testing the patient's water

URSA MAJOR, the Great Bear constellation

USE, interest, profit, benefit

USURP, ASSUME, supplant, misappropriate

UTIS (or utas), high jinks, lit. the octave of a festival

UTTER, (i) speak; (ii) offer for sale

UTTERANCE (to the), à l'outrance, to the last extremity

VAGRAM, a confusion of 'fragrant' and 'vagrant'

VAIL, (i) lower (nautical); (ii) do homage

VAILS, leavings of a feast

VAIN, false, silly

VALANCE, drapery hanging around frame of bedstead

VALENTINE, true-love token

VALIDITY, value, strength

VANTAGE, opportunity

VANTBRACE, defensive armour for forearm

VARA, (dial.) very

VARLETRY, mob, rabble

VARNISH, lend freshness to

VASSAL, abject creature

VAST OF NIGHT, the desolate hours of night when nature sleeps

VASTIDITY, immensity

VAWARD, vanward, forepart

VENDIBLE, 'a maid not vendible', an old maid past marriageable age, lit. past her market

VENETIA, VENETIA, CHI NON TI VEDE, NON TI PRETIA, a tag of Italian phrase found in several Elizabethan books:—Venice, Venice, who seeketh thee not, praiseth thee not

VENEW, VENEY, a thrust at fencing q.v.

VENGEANCE, mischief, harm

VENT (vb), lit. discharge, evacuate, hence utter; 'make vent of', talk of

VENTRICLE, of the brain, in medieval nomenclature the first and second were the seats of imagination and reason, and the third of memory

VENTURE, commercial speculation

VERDURE, freshness, vigour

VESTAL, priestess of Vesta in Rome, vowed to chastity

VEX, afflict, torment

VIA, adverb of encouragement, much used by commanders, and riders to their horses

VICE, comic character of the old moralities

VIDEO ET GAUDEO, I see and rejoice

VIDESNE QUIS VENIT, Do you see who comes

VIE, (i) to increase in number by addition or repetition; (ii) to hazard a sum at cards on the strength of one's hand

VILLAIN, slave, bondman, and ordinarily a rascal

VILLIAGO (fr. It. vigliacco, coward), vile or contemptible person

VIOL-DE-GAMBOYS, violoncello, bass viol

VIRGINALLING, lightly fingering, as if playing on the virginal

VIR SAPIT QUI PAUCA LOQUITUR, from Lyly's Grammar, That man is wise who speaketh few things or words

VIRTUE, essence; 'virtuous', of efficacious or powerful properties

VISITATION, affliction

VISITED, plague-stricken

VISITOR, one taking food

VISOR (or vizard), a mask

VIZAMENTS, advisements

VLOUTING-STOG, flouting-stock:—laughing-stock

VOICE, rumour, report

VOIDING LOBBY. Corridor or passage in which suppliants waited in hopes of admission to a lord's or a monarch's presence chamber

VOLABLE, quick

VOLQUESSEN, ancient country of the Velocasses, whose capital was Rouen

VOUCHER AND DOUBLE VOUCHER. Legal devices for recovery or converting estate entail into fee simple involving fictitious actions and the summoning (vouching) of men of straw to warrant titles which all parties wish invalidated, and which become invalidated by the vouchees defaulting

VULCAN, armourer of the gods, husband of Venus, cuckolded by Mars

VULGAR, public, common, well-known

WAFTAGE, passage by boat

WAINROPE, cart rope

WAIST, midship

WALLON, the part of the Netherlands bordering on France, its inhabitants Walloons

WAIT, attend upon

WAKE, a village feast

WANTON, rank-growing, out of hand

WARD, (i) generally explained as cell; (ii) bolts, lock, properly part of a lock; (iii) guard, 'come from thy ward':—come, off thy guard'

WARDER, staff or truncheon used to give signal for commencement or cessation of hostilities

WARDEN-PIE, a pie made of Warden pears or apples, called after the Cistercian Abbey at Warden, Bedfordshire

WARE, aware, cautious

WARE, BED OF, large bed 11 ft square, at Ware

WARP, cause to shrink or corrugate, go astray, deviate; 'warped':—crooked

WARRANTY, authorisation

WARRENER, rabbit-keeper

WASH, the barber's wash

WASHED AND SCOURED, knocked down and beaten

WASSAIL, revelry, carouse; 'wassail candle', a large candle to last the night of festivity

WATCH, keep a hawk awake

WATCHED, caught in the act

WATER-STANDING, perpetually filled with tears

WATERS FOR ALL, ready for anything

WAX, increase

WEAR, (sb) fashion; (vb) (i) be in the fashion; (ii) make weary

WEATHERCOCK, referring to a page's fantastic attire, a weathercock often having a pennon attached to it

WEEDS, dress, clothes

WEEK, 'in by the week':—trapped, caught. Lit. meaning unknown

WEEPING-RIPE, ready to weep

WEIGH, (i) be the same weight as; (ii) value at a certain rate

WELKIN, heaven

WELL-A-DAY!, Alas!

WELL-ADVISED, in one's right mind

WELL-DERIVED, well-born, well-descended

WELL-DIVULGED, well-received, of good report

WELL-ENTERED, thoroughly initiated, well trained

WELL-FAVOURED, gracious, beloved

WELL-FOUND, of tried merit

WELL-LIKING, in good condition, plump

WELL-SEEN, well taught

WELL TO LIVE, in capital health

WESTWARD-HO!, cry of Thames watermen leaving London, for Westminster

WEZAND, wind-pipe

WHALE BONE, WHITE AS, proverbial phrase, often found in early English poetry

WHAT TIME O' DAY?, when may that be?

WHELK, a pimple

WHEN? CAN YOU TELL?, a scornful expression to parry an impertinent question or request, similar in meaning to 'What next?'

WHIFFLER, officer who clears the way for a procession by flourishing a sword or a javelin

WHIRLS, metaphor from Fortune's wheel

WHILE-ERE, a while since

WHIRLIGIG, spinning contrivance, probably not a top but a cage upon a pivot for the punishment of thieves

WHITE, the white area at the centre of the target around the pin

WHITELY, pale

WHITING, bleaching

WHITSTERS, bleachers

WHOLE, solid

WIDE O' THE BOW HAND, wide of the mark. Lit. wide on the left or bowhand side of the target

WIDOW, to settle an estate (widowhood) upon a widow

WILDERNESS, wildness

WILL, intention, lust; 'by my will', intentionally

WILLOW, WILLOW GARLAND, the symbol of forlorn love

WIMPLED, muffled, blind-folded

WIND ABOUT, metaphor from stalking game—beat about the bush

WINDGALLS, disease of the fetlock in horses

WINDY SIDE, to the windward, so as to be able to escape easily

WINK, close the eyes, sleep, glimpse

WISH, commend

WIT-OLD (i) feeble witted; (ii) quibble on 'wittol', a contented cuckold

WOMAN OF THE WORLD, a married woman

WONT, is wont

WOOD, mad

WOODBINE, probably an error for 'bindweed'

WOODCOCK, the easiest bird to catch in a snare, hence a type of stupidity, a fool

WOODMAN, woman hunter

WOOLLEN (in the), between the blankets, without sheets

WOOLWARD, with woollen clothing next the skin

WORD, a pithy sentence; 'at a word', in short

WORKING, operation, effect, endeavour

WORLD (go to), get married

WORM, used as an expression of pity, esp. for those in love

WORT, sweet unfermented beer

WORTH, standing, authority, personal qualities; 'her worth, worth yours':—her personal qualities are worthy of your standing

WORTHY, excellence

WOT, pres. indic. of 'to wit', i.e. to know

WRACK, old form of 'wreck'

WRATH, wrathful; 'wrath of love', violent passion, ecstacy of love

WREATH (of chivalry), heraldic term, a chaplet of two different colours wound round each other and placed on top of a knight's helm

WREST, tuning key for certain wire-stringed instruments

WRING, writhe

WRITE, attain to: (i) 'to write man':—to reach man's estate; (ii) 'writ as little beard':—attained to as little beard

WRITE AGAINST, denounce

YARD, membrum virile

YARE, quick, ready, easily manageable (of a ship)

YCLIPED, called (deliberately archaic)

YEA AND NO (by), a puritan expletive

YEARS, 'in years', into wrinkles

YELLOWS, jaundice, generally of horses, but being a disease of the liver, formerly supposed to be the seat of the passions, also used for jealousy in man

YERK (of a horse), lash out with the heels, kick

YET, this word clearly had some comic significance, now lost

YOKE, couple; 'yoke-fellow', fellow worker

YOUNG, strong

YOUNGER, the younger son of the parable of the Prodigal Son, Luke xv, 12

YOUNG-EYES, with sight ever-young

YOUTH IN A BASKET, proverbial:—fortunate lover

ZANY, stage buffoon who initiated the tricks of the principal clown or fool

ZEALOUS, fervent

ZENITH, i.e. the height of my fortunes; an astrological term

ZEPHYR, mild, gentle breeze, the west wind

ZOUNDS, an oath, 'God's wounds'

ABBREVIATIONS

NED—The New English Dictionary

OED—Oxford English Dictionary

Sh. Eng.—Shakespeare's England